P9-CEO-220

The Sporting News

BASEBALL REGISTER

1998 EDITION

Editors/Baseball Register
MARK BONAVITA
SEAN STEWART

Contributing Editor/Baseball Register
JOHN DUXBURY

The Sporting News

Efrem Zimbalist III, President and Chief Executive Officer, Times Mirror Magazines; **James H. Nuckols,** President, The Sporting News; **Francis X. Farrell,** Senior Vice President, Publisher; **John D. Rawlings,** Senior Vice President, Editorial Director; **John Kastberg,** Vice President, General Manager; **Kathy Kinkeade,** Vice President, Operations; **Steve Meyerhoff,** Executive Editor; **Mike Huguenin,** Assistant Managing Editor; **Joe Hoppel,** Senior Editor; **Craig Carter,** Statistical Editor; **Ron Smith,** Associate Editor; **Brendan Roberts,** Assistant Editor; **Marilyn Kasal,** Production Director; **Terry Shea,** Database Analyst; **Michael Bruner,** Prepress Director; **Michael Behrens and Christen Webster,** Macintosh Production Artists; **Daniel Wetmore,** Editorial Assistant.

A Times Mirror Company

Major league statistics compiled by STATS, Inc., Skokie, Ill.

Minor league statistics compiled by Howe Sportsdata International Inc., Boston.

ISBN: 0-89204-593-0

10 9 8 7 6 5 4 3 2 1

CONTENTS

EXPLANATION OF FOOTNOTES AND ABBREVIATIONS

Note for statistical comparisons: Player strikes forced the cancellation of games in the 1972 season (10 days missed), the 1981 season (50 days missed), the 1994 season (52 days missed) and the 1995 season (18 games missed).

Positions are listed in descending order of games played; because of limited space, pinch-hitter and pinch-runner are listed in the regular-season section only if a player did not play a defensive position.

* Led league. For fielding statistics, the player led the league at the position shown.

• Tied for league lead. For fielding statistics, the player tied for the league lead at the position shown.

† Led league, but number indicated is total figure for two or more positions. Actual league-leading figure for a position is mentioned in "Statistical Notes" section.

‡ Tied for league lead, but number indicated is total figure for two or more positions. Actual league-tying figure for a position is mentioned in "Statistical Notes" section.

§ Led or tied for league lead, but total figure is divided between two different teams. Actual league-leading or league-tying figure is mentioned in "Statistical Notes" section.

■ Indicates a player's movement from one major league organization to another major league organization or to an independent minor league organization.

... Statistic unavailable, inapplicable, unofficial or mathematically impossible to calculate.

— Manager statistic inapplicable.

LEAGUES: A.A., Am. Assoc.—American Association. A.L.—American. App., Appal.—Appalachian. Ar., Ariz.—Arizona. Cal., Calif.—California. Car., Caro.—Carolina. CRL—Cocoa Rookie. DSL—Dominican Summer. East.—Eastern. Evan.—Evangeline. Fla. St., Florida St., FSL—Florida State. GCL—Gulf Coast. GSL—Gulf States. In.-Am.—Inter-American. Int'l.—International. J.P., Jap. Pac., Jp. Pac.—Japan Pacific. Jp. Cen., Jp. Cn.—Japan Central. Mex.—Mexican. Mex. Cen.—Mexican Center. Mid., Midw.—Midwest. Miss.-O.V.—Mississippi-Ohio Valley. N.C. St.—North Carolina State. N.L.—National. North.—Northern. N'west—Northwest. NYP, NY-Penn—New York-Pennsylvania. Pac. Coast, PCL—Pacific Coast. Pio.—Pioneer. S. Atl., SAL—South Atlantic. Soph.—Sophomore. Sou., South.—Southern. Taiw.—Taiwan. Tex.—Texas. W. Car., W. Caro.—Western Carolinas.

TEAMS: Aguas.—Aguascalientes. Alb./Colon.—Albany/Colonie. Ariz.—Arizona. Belling.—Bellingham. Birm.—Birmingham. Brevard Co.—Brevard County. Cant./Akr.—Canton/Akron. Ced. Rap.—Cedar Rapids. Cent. Ore.—Central Oregon. Central Vall.—Central Valley. Char., Charl.—Charleston. Chatt.—Chattanooga. Chiba Lot.—Chiba Lotte. Ciu. Juarez—Ciudad Juarez. Colo. Spr., Colo. Springs—Colorado Springs. Dall./Fort W.—Dallas/Fort Worth. Day. Beach.—Daytona Beach. Dm., Dom.—Dominican. Dom. B. Jays—Dominican Blue Jays. Elizabeth.—Elizabethton. Estadio Quis.—Estadio Quisqueya. Eve.—Everett. Fort Lauder.—Fort Lauderdale. Fukuoka—Fukuoka Daiei. GC—Gulf Coast. GC Astros-Or.—Gulf Coast Astros-Orange. GC Royals-Bl.—Gulf Coast Royals-Blue. GC Whi. Sox—Gulf Coast White Sox. Grays Har.—Grays Harbor. Greens.—Greensboro. Greenw.—Greenwood. Guana.—Guanajuato. H.P.-Thomas.—High Point-Thomasville. Hunting.—Huntington. Jacksonv.—Jacksonville. Johns. City—Johnson City. Kane Co.—Kane County. Lake Charl.—Lake Charles. Matt.—Mattoon. M.C., Mex. City—Mexico City. Med. Hat—Medicine Hat. Monc.—Monclova. Niag. F., Niag. Falls—Niagara Falls. Okla. City—Oklahoma City. Pan. City—Panama City. Phoe.—Phoenix. Pomp. Beach—Pompano Beach. Pres. Lions—President Lions. Prin. Will., Prin. William—Prince William. Ral./Dur.—Raleigh/Durham. Rancho Cuca.—Rancho Cucamonga. Rocky Mount.—Rocky Mountain. Salt.—Saltillo. San. Dom., San. Domingo—Santo Domingo. San Bern.—San Bernardino. San Fran.—San Francisco. Schen.—Schenectady. Scran./W.B.—Scranton/Wilkes-Barre. S.C.—South Carolina. S.F. de Mac.—San Francisco de Macoris. San Luis Pot.—San Luis Potosi. S. Oregon—Southern Oregon. Spartan.—Spartanburg. St. Cath., St. Cathar.—St. Catharines. St. Peters.—St. Petersburg. States.—Statesville. Stock.—Stockton. T.-C.—Tri-Cities. Vanc.—Vancouver. Vent. Co.—Ventura County. W. Mich.—West Michigan. Win.-Salem, Winst.-Salem—Winston-Salem. Wis. Rap., Wis. Rapids—Wisconsin Rapids. W.P. Beach—West Palm Beach. W.Va.—West Virginia. Yuc.—Yucatan.

STATISTICS: A—assists. AB—at-bats. Avg.—average. BB—bases on balls. CG—complete games. E—errors. ER—earned runs. ERA—earned-run average. G—games. GIDP—grounded into double plays. GS—games started. H—hits. HR—home runs. IP—innings pitched. L—losses. Pct.—winning percentage. PO—putouts. Pos.—position. R—runs. RBI—runs batted in. SB—stolen bases. ShO—shutouts. SO—strikeouts. Sv.—saves. W—wins. 2B—doubles. 3B—triples.

PLAYERS

A

ABBOTT, JEFF   OF   WHITE SOX

PERSONAL: Born August 17, 1972, in Atlanta. ... 6-2/190. ... Bats right, throws left. ... Full name: Jeffrey William Abbott.
HIGH SCHOOL: Dunwoody (Ga.).
COLLEGE: Kentucky.
TRANSACTIONS/CAREER NOTES: Selected by Chicago White Sox organization in 32nd round of free-agent draft (June 3, 1993); did not sign. ... Selected by White Sox organization in fourth round of free-agent draft (June 2, 1994).

								BATTING							FIELDING		
Year Team (League)	Pos.	G	AB	R	H	2B	3B	HR	RBI	Avg.	BB	SO	SB	PO	A	E	Avg.
1994— Sarasota (Gulf Coast).	OF	4	15	4	7	1	0	1	3	.467	4	0	2	4	0	0	1.000
— Hickory (S. Atl.)	OF	63	224	47	88	16	6	6	48	.393	38	33	2	106	0	2	.981
1995— Prince William (Car.) ..	OF	70	264	41	92	16	0	4	47	.348	26	25	7	88	3	4	.958
— Birmingham (Sou.).....	OF	55	197	25	63	11	1	3	28	.320	19	20	1	55	1	2	.966
1996— Nashville (A.A.)	OF	113	440	64	143	27	1	14	60	.325	32	50	12	186	5	2	.990
1997— Nashville (A.A.)	OF	118	465	*88	152	35	3	11	63	.327	41	52	12	237	6	0	*1.000
— Chicago (A.L.)	OF-DH	19	38	8	10	1	0	1	2	.263	0	6	0	15	0	0	1.000
Major league totals (1 year)		19	38	8	10	1	0	1	2	.263	0	6	0	15	0	0	1.000

ABBOTT, KURT   IF   ATHLETICS

PERSONAL: Born June 2, 1969, in Zanesville, Ohio. ... 6-0/190. ... Bats right, throws right. ... Full name: Kurt Thomas Abbott.
HIGH SCHOOL: Dixie Hollins (St. Petersburg, Fla.).
JUNIOR COLLEGE: St. Petersburg (Fla.) Junior College.
TRANSACTIONS/CAREER NOTES: Selected by Oakland Athletics organization in 15th round of free-agent draft (June 5, 1989). ... On Modesto disabled list (May 26-June 6, 1991). ... Traded by A's to Florida Marlins for OF Kerwin Moore (December 20, 1993). ... On Florida disabled list (April 19-May 6, 1995); included rehabilitation assignment to Charlotte (April 30-May 6). ... On Florida disabled list (May 6-21, 1996); included rehabilitation assignment to Charlotte (May 16-20). ... Traded by Marlins to A's for P Eric Ludwick (December 19, 1997).
STATISTICAL NOTES: Led Arizona League shortstops with .922 fielding percentage in 1989. ... Led Southern League shortstops with 87 double plays in 1992. ... Career major league grand slams: 3.
MISCELLANEOUS: Holds Florida Marlins all-time record for most triples (19).

								BATTING							FIELDING		
Year Team (League)	Pos.	G	AB	R	H	2B	3B	HR	RBI	Avg.	BB	SO	SB	PO	A	E	Avg.
1989— Arizona A's (Ariz.).......	SS-2B-3B	36	155	27	42	5	3	0	25	.271	8	40	0	59	90	10	†.937
— S. Oregon (N'west).....	SS	10	2	1	0	0	0	1	.100	0	3	1	6	7	1	.929
1990— Madison (Midwest)	SS-2B-3B	104	362	38	84	18	0	0	28	.232	47	74	21	180	268	40	.918
1991— Modesto (California) ..	SS	58	216	36	55	8	2	3	25	.255	29	55	6	78	130	9	.959
— Huntsville (Southern).	SS	53	182	18	46	6	1	0	11	.253	17	39	6	89	164	13	.951
1992— Huntsville (Southern).	SS	124	452	64	115	14	5	9	52	.254	31	75	16	196	342	29	*.949
— Tacoma (PCL)	SS	11	39	2	6	1	0	0	1	.154	4	9	1	21	32	4	.930
1993— Tacoma (PCL)	SS	123	480	75	153	36	11	12	79	.319	33	123	19	*210	367	30	.951
— Oakland (A.L.)	OF-SS-2B	20	61	11	15	1	0	3	9	.246	3	20	2	36	13	2	.961
1994— Florida (N.L.)■..........	SS	101	345	41	86	17	3	9	33	.249	16	98	3	162	260	15	.966
1995— Charlotte (Int'l).........	SS	5	18	3	5	0	0	1	3	.278	1	3	1	5	15	2	.909
— Florida (N.L.)	SS	120	420	60	107	18	7	17	60	.255	36	110	4	149	290	19	.959
1996— Florida (N.L.)	SS-3B-2B	109	320	37	81	18	7	8	33	.253	22	99	3	123	205	12	.965
— Charlotte (Int'l).........	SS-2B-3B	18	69	20	26	10	1	5	11	.377	7	18	2	31	60	2	.978
1997— Florida (N.L.) 2-O-S-3-DH		94	252	35	69	18	2	6	30	.274	14	68	3	126	136	8	.970
American League totals (1 year)		20	61	11	15	1	0	3	9	.246	3	20	2	36	13	2	.961
National League totals (4 years)		424	1337	173	343	71	19	40	156	.257	88	375	13	560	891	54	.964
Major league totals (5 years)		444	1398	184	358	72	19	43	165	.256	91	395	15	596	904	56	.964

DIVISION SERIES RECORD

								BATTING							FIELDING		
Year Team (League)	Pos.	G	AB	R	H	2B	3B	HR	RBI	Avg.	BB	SO	SB	PO	A	E	Avg.
1997— Florida (N.L.)	2B-PH	3	8	0	2	0	0	0	0	.250	0	0	0	3	6	0	1.000

CHAMPIONSHIP SERIES RECORD

								BATTING							FIELDING		
Year Team (League)	Pos.	G	AB	R	H	2B	3B	HR	RBI	Avg.	BB	SO	SB	PO	A	E	Avg.
1997— Florida (N.L.)	2B	2	8	0	3	1	0	0	0	.375	0	2	0	4	1	0	1.000

WORLD SERIES RECORD

NOTES: Member of World Series championship team (1997).

								BATTING							FIELDING		
Year Team (League)	Pos.	G	AB	R	H	2B	3B	HR	RBI	Avg.	BB	SO	SB	PO	A	E	Avg.
1997— Florida (N.L.)	DH-PH	3	3	0	0	0	0	0	0	.000	0	1	0	0	0	0	...

ABBOTT, PAUL   P

PERSONAL: Born September 15, 1967, in Van Nuys, Calif. ... 6-3/194. ... Throws right, bats right. ... Full name: Paul David Abbott.
HIGH SCHOOL: Sunny Hills (Fullerton, Calif.).
TRANSACTIONS/CAREER NOTES: Selected by Minnesota Twins organization in third round of free-agent draft (June 3, 1985). ... On Minnesota disabled list (March 28-June 5 and August 14-September 1, 1992). ... Released by Twins (March 2, 1993). ... Signed by Charlotte, Cleveland Indians organization (March 27, 1993). ... On Charlotte disabled list (April 8-May 6, 1993). ... Granted free agency (October 15, 1993). ... Signed by Omaha, Kansas City Royals organization (November 21, 1993). ... On disabled list (March 18-May 25 and June 16-30,

1994). ... Released by Omaha (June 30, 1994). ... Signed by Iowa, Chicago Cubs organization (March 17, 1995). ... Granted free agency (October 16, 1995). ... Signed by San Diego Padres organization (November 29, 1995). ... Granted free agency (October 15, 1996). ... Signed by Seattle Mariners organization (January 10, 1997). ... On Tacoma disabled list (May 23-July 14, 1997). ... Granted free agency (October 15, 1997).

STATISTICAL NOTES: Pitched 3-0 no-hit victory against Palm Springs (June 26, 1988, seven innings).

Year Team (League)	W	L	Pct.	ERA	G	GS	CG	ShO	Sv.	IP	H	R	ER	BB	SO
1985— Elizabethton (Appal.)	1	5	.167	6.94	10	10	1	0	0	35	33	32	27	32	34
1986— Kenosha (Midwest)	6	10	.375	4.50	25	15	1	0	0	98	102	62	49	73	73
1987— Kenosha (Midwest)	13	6	.684	3.65	26	25	1	0	0	145 1/3	102	76	59	103	138
1988— Visalia (California)	11	9	.550	4.18	28	•28	4	2	0	172 1/3	141	95	80	*143	*205
1989— Orlando (South.)	9	3	.750	4.37	17	17	1	0	0	90 2/3	71	48	44	48	102
1990— Portland (PCL)	5	14	.263	4.56	23	23	4	1	0	128 1/3	110	75	65	82	129
— Minnesota (A.L.)	0	5	.000	5.97	7	7	0	0	0	34 2/3	37	24	23	28	25
1991— Portland (PCL)	2	3	.400	3.89	8	8	1	1	0	44	36	19	19	28	40
— Minnesota (A.L.)	3	1	.750	4.75	15	3	0	0	0	47 1/3	38	27	25	36	43
1992— Portland (PCL)	4	1	.800	2.33	7	7	0	0	0	46 1/3	30	13	12	31	46
— Minnesota (A.L.)	0	0	...	3.27	6	0	0	0	0	11	12	4	4	5	13
1993— Cant./Akr. (Eastern)■	4	5	.444	4.06	13	12	1	0	0	75 1/3	72	34	34	28	86
— Cleveland (A.L.)	0	1	.000	6.38	5	5	0	0	0	18 1/3	19	15	13	11	7
— Charlotte (Int'l)	0	1	.000	6.63	4	4	0	0	0	19	25	16	14	7	12
1994— Omaha (Am. Assoc.)■	4	1	.800	4.87	15	10	0	0	0	57 1/3	57	32	31	45	48
1995— Iowa (Am. Assoc.)■	7	7	.500	3.67	46	11	0	0	0	115 1/3	104	50	47	64	*127
1996— Las Vegas (PCL)■	4	2	.667	4.18	28	0	0	0	7	28	27	14	13	12	37
1997— Tacoma (PCL)■	8	4	.667	4.13	17	14	3	0	0	93 2/3	80	48	43	29	117
— Ariz. Mariners (Ariz.)	0	0	...	0.93	3	3	0	0	0	9 2/3	0	2	1	7	13
Major league totals (4 years)	3	7	.300	5.25	33	15	0	0	0	111 1/3	106	70	65	80	88

ABREU, BOB — OF — PHILLIES

PERSONAL: Born March 11, 1974, in Aragua, Venezuela. ... 6-0/160. ... Bats left, throws right. ... Full name: Bob Kelly Abreu. ... Name pronounced a-BREW.
TRANSACTIONS/CAREER NOTES: Signed as non-drafted free agent by Houston Astros organization (August 21, 1990). ... On Houston disabled list (May 25-July 1, 1997); included rehabilitation assignments to Jackson (June 23-26) and New Orleans (June 27-July 1). ... Selected by Tampa Bay Devil Rays in first round (sixth pick overall) of expansion draft (November 18, 1997). ... Traded by Devil Rays to Philadelphia Phillies for SS Kevin Stocker (November 18, 1997).
STATISTICAL NOTES: Led Gulf Coast League outfielders with 11 assists in 1991. ... Led Texas League with .530 slugging percentage in 1994. ... Led Pacific Coast League outfielders with 18 assists in 1995. ... Led Pacific Coast League in caught stealing with 18 in 1996.

Year Team (League)	Pos.	G	AB	R	H	2B	3B	HR	RBI	Avg.	BB	SO	SB	PO	A	E	Avg.
1991— GC Astros (GCL)	OF-SS	56	183	21	55	7	3	0	20	.301	17	27	10	70	†13	5	.943
1992— Asheville (S. Atl.)	OF	135	480	81	140	21	4	8	48	.292	63	79	15	167	15	11	.943
1993— Osceola (Fla. St.)	OF	129	474	62	134	21	17	5	55	.283	51	90	10	179	18	8	.961
1994— Jackson (Texas)	OF	118	400	61	121	25	9	16	73	.303	42	81	12	113	3	4	.967
1995— Tucson (PCL)	OF-2B	114	415	72	126	24	*17	10	75	.304	67	120	16	207	†18	7	.970
1996— Tucson (PCL)	OF	132	484	86	138	14	*16	13	68	.285	83	111	24	202	15	7	.969
— Houston (N.L.)	OF	15	22	1	5	1	0	0	1	.227	2	3	0	6	0	0	1.000
1997— Houston (N.L.)	OF	59	188	22	47	10	2	3	26	.250	21	48	7	84	4	2	.978
— Jackson (Texas)	OF	3	12	2	2	1	0	0	0	.167	1	5	0	1	0	0	1.000
— New Orleans (A.A.)	OF	47	194	25	52	9	4	2	22	.268	21	49	7	99	4	1	.990
Major league totals (2 years)		74	210	23	52	11	2	3	27	.248	23	51	7	90	4	2	.979

DIVISION SERIES RECORD

Year Team (League)	Pos.	G	AB	R	H	2B	3B	HR	RBI	Avg.	BB	SO	SB	PO	A	E	Avg.
1997— Houston (N.L.)	PH	3	3	0	1	0	0	0	0	.333	0	2	1	0	0	0	...

ACEVEDO, JUAN — P — METS

PERSONAL: Born May 5, 1970, in Juarez, Mexico. ... 6-2/218. ... Throws right, bats right. ... Full name: Juan Carlos Acevedo. ... Name pronounced ah-sah-VAY-doh.
HIGH SCHOOL: Dundee-Crown (Carpentersville, Ill.).
JUNIOR COLLEGE: Parkland College (Ill.).
TRANSACTIONS/CAREER NOTES: Selected by Colorado Rockies organization in 14th round of free-agent draft (June 1, 1992). ... Traded by Rockies with P Arnold Gooch to New York Mets for P Bret Saberhagen and a player to be named later (July 31, 1995); Rockies acquired P David Swanson to complete deal (August 4, 1995). ... On New York disabled list (March 26-May 9, 1996); included rehabilitation assignment to Norfolk (April 10-May 9).
HONORS: Named Eastern League Pitcher of the Year (1994).
STATISTICAL NOTES: Tied for Eastern League lead with four balks in 1994. ... Tied for International League lead with four balks in 1997.

Year Team (League)	W	L	Pct.	ERA	G	GS	CG	ShO	Sv.	IP	H	R	ER	BB	SO
1992— Bend (Northwest)	0	0	...	13.50	1	0	0	0	0	2	4	3	3	1	3
— Visalia (California)	3	4	.429	5.43	12	12	1	0	0	64 2/3	75	46	39	33	37
1993— Central Valley (Cal.)	9	8	.529	4.40	27	20	1	0	0	118 2/3	119	68	58	58	107
1994— New Haven (Eastern)	*17	6	.739	*2.37	26	26	5	2	0	174 2/3	142	56	46	38	161
1995— Colorado (N.L.)	4	6	.400	6.44	17	11	0	0	0	65 2/3	82	53	47	20	40
— Colo. Springs (PCL)	1	1	.500	6.14	3	3	0	0	0	14 2/3	18	11	10	7	7
— Norfolk (Int'l)■	0	0	...	0.00	2	2	0	0	0	3	0	0	0	1	2
1996— Norfolk (Int'l)	4	8	.333	5.96	19	19	2	1	0	102 2/3	116	70	68	53	83
1997— Norfolk (Int'l)	6	6	.500	3.86	18	18	1	0	0	116 2/3	111	55	50	34	99
— New York (N.L.)	3	1	.750	3.59	25	2	0	0	0	47 2/3	52	24	19	22	33
Major league totals (2 years)	7	7	.500	5.24	42	13	0	0	0	113 1/3	134	77	66	42	73

ACRE, MARK   P

PERSONAL: Born September 16, 1968, in Concord, Calif. ... 6-8/246. ... Throws right, bats right. ... Full name: Mark Robert Acre.
HIGH SCHOOL: Corning (Calif.) Union.
COLLEGE: New Mexico State.
TRANSACTIONS/CAREER NOTES: Signed as non-drafted free agent by Oakland Athletics organization (August 5, 1991). ... On Modesto disabled list (April 8-23, 1993). ... On disabled list (August 10-September 1, 1995). ... Contract sold by A's to Yakult Swallows of Japan Pacific League (December 4, 1997).

Year Team (League)	W	L	Pct.	ERA	G	GS	CG	ShO	Sv.	IP	H	R	ER	BB	SO
1991— Arizona A's (Arizona)	2	0	1.000	2.70	6	0	0	0	0	10	10	3	3	6	6
1992— Reno (California)	4	4	.500	4.56	35	8	0	0	2	77	67	56	39	50	65
1993— Madison (Midwest)	0	0	...	0.29	28	0	0	0	20	31 1/3	9	1	1	13	41
— Huntsville (Southern)	1	1	.500	2.42	19	0	0	0	10	22 1/3	22	10	6	3	21
1994— Tacoma (PCL)	1	1	.500	1.88	20	0	0	0	6	28 2/3	24	7	6	11	31
— Oakland (A.L.)	5	1	.833	3.41	34	0	0	0	0	34 1/3	24	13	13	23	21
1995— Oakland (A.L.)	1	2	.333	5.71	43	0	0	0	0	52	52	35	33	28	47
1996— Edmonton (PCL)	6	2	.750	2.09	39	0	0	0	8	43	33	11	10	16	50
— Oakland (A.L.)	1	3	.250	6.12	22	0	0	0	2	25	38	17	17	9	18
1997— Oakland (A.L.)	2	0	1.000	5.74	15	0	0	0	0	15 2/3	21	10	10	8	12
— Edmonton (PCL)	3	4	.429	4.15	43	0	0	0	11	47 2/3	48	27	22	20	46
Major league totals (4 years)	**9**	**6**	**.600**	**5.17**	**114**	**0**	**0**	**0**	**2**	**127**	**135**	**75**	**73**	**68**	**98**

ADAMS, TERRY   P   CUBS

PERSONAL: Born March 6, 1973, in Mobile, Ala. ... 6-3/205. ... Throws right, bats right. ... Full name: Terry Wayne Adams.
HIGH SCHOOL: Montgomery (Semmes, Ala.).
TRANSACTIONS/CAREER NOTES: Selected by Chicago Cubs organization in fourth round of free-agent draft (June 3, 1991). ... On disabled list (June 21-September 21, 1993).

Year Team (League)	W	L	Pct.	ERA	G	GS	CG	ShO	Sv.	IP	H	R	ER	BB	SO
1991— Huntington (Appal.)	0	*9	.000	5.77	14	13	0	0	0	57 2/3	67	*56	37	62	52
1992— Peoria (Midwest)	7	12	.368	4.41	25	25	3	1	0	157	144	95	77	86	96
1993— Daytona (Fla. St.)	3	5	.375	4.97	13	13	0	0	0	70 2/3	78	47	39	43	35
1994— Daytona (Fla. St.)	9	10	.474	4.38	39	7	0	0	7	84 1/3	87	47	41	46	64
1995— Orlando (South.)	2	3	.400	1.43	37	0	0	0	19	37 2/3	23	9	6	16	26
— Iowa (Am. Assoc.)	0	0	.000	0.00	7	0	0	0	5	6 1/3	3	0	0	2	10
— Chicago (N.L.)	1	1	.500	6.50	18	0	0	0	1	18	22	15	13	10	15
1996— Chicago (N.L.)	3	6	.333	2.94	69	0	0	0	4	101	84	36	33	49	78
1997— Chicago (N.L.)	2	9	.182	4.62	74	0	0	0	18	74	91	43	38	40	64
Major league totals (3 years)	**6**	**16**	**.273**	**3.92**	**161**	**0**	**0**	**0**	**23**	**193**	**197**	**94**	**84**	**99**	**157**

ADAMS, WILLIE   P   ATHLETICS

PERSONAL: Born October 8, 1972, in Gallup, N.M. ... 6-7/211. ... Throws right, bats right. ... Full name: William Edward Adams.
HIGH SCHOOL: La Serna (Whittier, Calif.).
COLLEGE: Stanford.
TRANSACTIONS/CAREER NOTES: Selected by Detroit Tigers organization in 52nd round of free-agent draft (June 4, 1990); did not sign. ... Selected by Oakland Athletics organization in supplemental round ("sandwich pick" between first and second round, 36th pick overall) of free-agent draft (June 3, 1993); pick received as part of compensation for Toronto Blue Jays signing Type A free-agent P Dave Stewart.

Year Team (League)	W	L	Pct.	ERA	G	GS	CG	ShO	Sv.	IP	H	R	ER	BB	SO
1993— Madison (Midwest)	0	2	.000	3.38	5	5	0	0	0	18 2/3	21	10	7	8	22
1994— Modesto (California)	7	1	.875	3.38	11	5	0	0	2	45 1/3	41	17	17	10	42
— Huntsville (Southern)	4	3	.571	4.30	10	10	0	0	0	60 2/3	58	32	29	23	33
1995— Huntsville (Southern)	6	5	.545	3.01	13	13	0	0	0	80 2/3	75	33	27	17	72
— Edmonton (PCL)	2	5	.286	4.37	11	10	1	0	0	68	73	35	33	15	40
1996— Edmonton (PCL)	10	4	.714	3.78	19	19	3	1	0	112	95	49	47	39	80
— Oakland (A.L.)	3	4	.429	4.01	12	12	1	1	0	76 1/3	76	39	34	23	68
1997— Oakland (A.L.)	3	5	.375	8.18	13	12	0	0	0	58 1/3	73	53	53	32	37
— Edmonton (PCL)	5	4	.556	6.45	13	12	0	0	0	75 1/3	105	57	54	19	58
Major league totals (2 years)	**6**	**9**	**.400**	**5.81**	**25**	**24**	**1**	**1**	**0**	**134 2/3**	**149**	**92**	**87**	**55**	**105**

ADAMSON, JOEL   P   DIAMONDBACKS

PERSONAL: Born July 2, 1971, in Lakewood, Calif. ... 6-4/185. ... Throws left, bats left. ... Full name: Joel Lee Adamson.
HIGH SCHOOL: Artesia (Lakewood, Calif.).
JUNIOR COLLEGE: Cerritos College (Calif.).
TRANSACTIONS/CAREER NOTES: Selected by San Diego Padres organization in 31st round of free-agent draft (June 5, 1989); did not sign. ... Selected by Philadelphia Phillies organization in seventh round of free-agent draft (June 4, 1990). ... On Reading suspended list (June 1-8, 1992). ... Traded by Phillies organization with P Matt Whisenant to Florida Marlins for P Danny Jackson (November 17, 1992). ... On disabled list (August 6-25, 1994 and June 8-July 23, 1995). ... Traded by Marlins to Milwaukee Brewers for a player to be named later (November 25, 1996); Marlins acquired P Ed Collins to complete deal (December 10, 1996). ... Selected by Arizona Diamondbacks in first round (15th pick overall) of expansion draft (November 18, 1997).

Year Team (League)	W	L	Pct.	ERA	G	GS	CG	ShO	Sv.	IP	H	R	ER	BB	SO
1990— Princeton (Appalachian)	2	5	.286	3.88	12	8	1	0	1	48 2/3	56	27	21	12	40
1991— Spartanburg (SAL)	4	4	.500	2.56	14	14	1	1	0	81	72	29	23	22	84
— Clearwater (Fla. St.)	2	1	.667	3.03	5	5	0	0	0	29 2/3	28	12	10	7	20
1992— Clearwater (Fla. St.)	5	6	.455	3.41	15	15	1	1	0	89 2/3	90	35	34	19	52
— Reading (Eastern)	3	6	.333	4.27	10	10	2	0	0	59	68	36	28	13	35

Year Team (League)	W	L	Pct.	ERA	G	GS	CG	ShO	Sv.	IP	H	R	ER	BB	SO
1993— High Desert (Calif.)■	5	5	.500	4.58	22	20	•6	*3	0	129 2/3	160	83	66	30	72
— Edmonton (PCL)	1	2	.333	6.92	5	5	0	0	0	26	39	21	20	13	7
1994— Portland (Eastern)	5	6	.455	4.34	33	11	2	2	7	91 1/3	95	51	44	32	59
1995— Charlotte (Int'l)	8	4	.667	3.29	19	18	2	0	0	115	113	51	42	20	80
1996— Charlotte (Int'l)	6	6	.500	3.78	44	8	0	0	3	97 2/3	108	48	41	28	84
— Florida (N.L.)	0	0	...	7.36	9	0	0	0	0	11	18	9	9	7	7
1997— Tucson (PCL)■	2	1	.667	4.36	6	6	0	0	0	33	38	16	16	8	24
— Milwaukee (A.L.)	5	3	.625	3.54	30	6	0	0	0	76 1/3	78	36	30	19	56
A.L. totals (1 year)	5	3	.625	3.54	30	6	0	0	0	76 1/3	78	36	30	19	56
N.L. totals (1 year)	0	0	...	7.36	9	0	0	0	0	11	18	9	9	7	7
Major league totals (2 years)	5	3	.625	4.02	39	6	0	0	0	87 1/3	96	45	39	26	63

AGUILERA, RICK   P   TWINS

PERSONAL: Born December 31, 1961, in San Gabriel, Calif. ... 6-5/210. ... Throws right, bats right. ... Full name: Richard Warren Aguilera. ... Name pronounced AG-yuh-LAIR-uh.

HIGH SCHOOL: Edgewood (West Covina, Calif.).

COLLEGE: Brigham Young.

TRANSACTIONS/CAREER NOTES: Selected by St. Louis Cardinals organization in 37th round of free-agent draft (June 3, 1980); did not sign. ... Selected by New York Mets organization in third round of free-agent draft (June 6, 1983). ... On New York disabled list (September 3-15, 1985). ... On New York disabled list (May 23-August 24, 1987); included rehabilitation assignment to Tidewater (August 10-24). ... On New York disabled list (April 19-June 19 and July 12-September 7, 1988); included rehabilitation assignments to St. Lucie (June 7-14) and Tidewater (June 15-19). ... Traded by Mets with P David West and three players to be named later to Minnesota Twins for P Frank Viola (July 31, 1989); Portland, Twins organization, acquired P Kevin Tapani and P Tim Drummond (August 1, 1989), and Twins acquired P Jack Savage to complete deal (October 16, 1989). ... Traded by Twins to Boston Red Sox for P Frank Rodriguez and a player to be named later (July 6, 1995); Twins acquired OF J.J. Johnson to complete deal (October 11, 1995). ... Granted free agency (October 31, 1995). ... Signed by Twins (December 11, 1995). ... On Minnesota disabled list (March 24-June 11 and September 7, 1996-remainder of season); included rehabilitation assignment to Fort Myers (May 31-June 11).

MISCELLANEOUS: Holds Minnesota Twins all-time record for most saves (210). ... Made an out in only appearance as pinch-hitter with New York (1989).

Year Team (League)	W	L	Pct.	ERA	G	GS	CG	ShO	Sv.	IP	H	R	ER	BB	SO
1983— Little Falls (NYP)	5	6	.455	3.72	16	15	4	•2	0	104	*109	55	43	26	84
1984— Lynchburg (Caroline)	8	3	.727	2.34	13	13	6	•3	0	88 1/3	72	29	23	28	101
— Jackson (Texas)	4	4	.500	4.57	11	11	2	1	0	67	68	37	34	19	71
1985— Tidewater (Int'l)	6	4	.600	2.51	11	11	2	1	0	79	64	24	22	17	55
— New York (N.L.)	10	7	.588	3.24	21	19	2	0	0	122 1/3	118	49	44	37	74
1986— New York (N.L.)	10	7	.588	3.88	28	20	2	0	0	141 2/3	145	70	61	36	104
1987— New York (N.L.)	11	3	.786	3.60	18	17	1	0	0	115	124	53	46	33	77
— Tidewater (Int'l)	1	1	.500	0.69	3	3	0	0	0	13	8	2	1	1	10
1988— New York (N.L.)	0	4	.000	6.93	11	3	0	0	0	24 2/3	29	20	19	10	16
— St. Lucie (Fla. St.)	0	0	...	1.29	2	2	0	0	0	7	8	1	1	1	5
— Tidewater (Int'l)	0	0	...	1.50	1	1	0	0	0	6	6	1	1	1	4
1989— New York (N.L.)	6	6	.500	2.34	36	0	0	0	7	69 1/3	59	19	18	21	80
— Minnesota (A.L.)■	3	5	.375	3.21	11	11	3	0	0	75 2/3	71	32	27	17	57
1990— Minnesota (A.L.)	5	3	.625	2.76	56	0	0	0	32	65 1/3	55	27	20	19	61
1991— Minnesota (A.L.)	4	5	.444	2.35	63	0	0	0	42	69	44	20	18	30	61
1992— Minnesota (A.L.)	2	6	.250	2.84	64	0	0	0	41	66 2/3	60	28	21	17	52
1993— Minnesota (A.L.)	4	3	.571	3.11	65	0	0	0	34	72 1/3	60	25	25	14	59
1994— Minnesota (A.L.)	1	4	.200	3.63	44	0	0	0	23	44 2/3	57	23	18	10	46
1995— Minnesota (A.L.)	1	1	.500	2.52	22	0	0	0	12	25	20	7	7	6	29
— Boston (A.L.)■	2	2	.500	2.67	30	0	0	0	20	30 1/3	26	9	9	7	23
1996— Fort Myers (Fla. St.)■	2	0	1.000	3.75	2	2	0	0	0	12	13	5	5	1	12
— Minnesota (A.L.)	8	6	.571	5.42	19	19	2	0	0	111 1/3	124	69	67	27	83
1997— Minnesota (A.L.)	5	4	.556	3.82	61	0	0	0	26	68 1/3	65	29	29	22	68
A.L. totals (9 years)	35	39	.473	3.45	435	30	5	0	230	628 2/3	582	269	241	169	539
N.L. totals (5 years)	37	27	.578	3.58	114	59	5	0	7	473	475	211	188	137	351
Major league totals (13 years)	72	66	.522	3.50	549	89	10	0	237	1101 2/3	1057	480	429	306	890

DIVISION SERIES RECORD

Year Team (League)	W	L	Pct.	ERA	G	GS	CG	ShO	Sv.	IP	H	R	ER	BB	SO
1995— Boston (A.L.)	0	0	...	13.50	1	0	0	0	0	2/3	3	1	1	0	1

CHAMPIONSHIP SERIES RECORD

Year Team (League)	W	L	Pct.	ERA	G	GS	CG	ShO	Sv.	IP	H	R	ER	BB	SO
1986— New York (N.L.)	0	0	...	0.00	2	0	0	0	0	5	2	1	0	2	2
1988— New York (N.L.)	0	0	...	1.29	3	0	0	0	0	7	3	1	1	2	4
1991— Minnesota (A.L.)	0	0	...	0.00	3	0	0	0	3	3 1/3	1	0	0	0	3
Champ. series totals (3 years)	0	0	...	0.59	8	0	0	0	3	15 1/3	6	2	1	4	9

WORLD SERIES RECORD

NOTES: Flied out in only appearance as pinch-hitter (1991). ... Member of World Series championship teams (1986 and 1991).

Year Team (League)	W	L	Pct.	ERA	G	GS	CG	ShO	Sv.	IP	H	R	ER	BB	SO
1986— New York (N.L.)	1	0	1.000	12.00	2	0	0	0	0	3	8	4	4	1	4
1991— Minnesota (A.L.)	1	1	.500	1.80	4	0	0	0	2	5	6	1	1	1	3
World Series totals (2 years)	2	1	.667	5.63	6	0	0	0	2	8	14	5	5	2	7

ALL-STAR GAME RECORD

Year League	W	L	Pct.	ERA	GS	CG	ShO	Sv.	IP	H	R	ER	BB	SO
1991— American	0	0	...	0.00	0	0	0	0	1 1/3	2	1	0	0	3
1992— American	0	0	...	13.50	0	0	0	0	2/3	1	1	1	0	0
1993— American	0	0	...	0.00	0	0	0	0	1	2	0	0	0	2
All-Star totals (3 years)	0	0	...	3.00	0	0	0	0	3	5	1	1	0	5

ALBERRO, JOSE   P   YANKEES

PERSONAL: Born June 29, 1969, in San Juan, Puerto Rico. ... 6-2/190. ... Throws right, bats right. ... Full name: Jose E. Alberro.
HIGH SCHOOL: Escuela Superior (Arecibo, Puerto Rico).
TRANSACTIONS/CAREER NOTES: Signed as non-drafted free agent by Texas Rangers organization (June 11, 1991). ... On Oklahoma City disabled list (June 18-August 9, 1993). ... Claimed on waivers by New York Yankees (August 11, 1997).

Year Team (League)	W	L	Pct.	ERA	G	GS	CG	ShO	Sv.	IP	H	R	ER	BB	SO
1991— GC Rangers (GCL)	2	0	1.000	1.48	19	0	0	0	6	30⅓	17	6	5	9	40
— Charlotte (Fla. St.)	0	1	.000	9.53	5	0	0	0	0	5⅔	8	9	6	7	3
1992— Gastonia (S. Atl.)	1	0	1.000	3.48	17	0	0	0	0	20⅔	18	8	8	4	26
— Charlotte (Fla. St.)	1	1	.500	1.20	28	0	0	0	15	45	37	10	6	9	29
1993— Tulsa (Texas)	0	0	...	0.95	17	0	0	0	5	19	11	2	2	8	24
— Oklahoma City (A.A.)	0	0	...	6.88	12	0	0	0	0	17	25	15	13	11	14
1994— Oklahoma City (A.A.)	4	3	.571	4.52	52	0	0	0	11	69⅔	79	40	35	36	50
1995— Texas (A.L.)	0	0	...	7.40	12	0	0	0	0	20⅔	26	18	17	12	10
— Oklahoma City (A.A.)	4	2	.667	3.36	20	10	0	0	0	77⅔	73	34	29	27	55
1996— Oklahoma City (A.A.)	9	9	.500	3.47	29	27	4	2	0	171	154	73	66	57	140
— Texas (A.L.)	0	1	.000	5.79	5	1	0	0	0	9⅓	14	6	6	7	2
1997— Oklahoma City (A.A.)	5	6	.455	4.22	16	16	1	1	0	91⅓	90	48	43	29	59
— Texas (A.L.)	0	3	.000	7.94	10	4	0	0	0	28⅓	37	33	25	17	11
— Columbus (Int'l)■	0	1	.000	3.38	1	1	1	0	0	8	5	4	3	1	6
Major league totals (3 years)	0	4	.000	7.41	27	5	0	0	0	58⅓	77	57	48	36	23

ALDRED, SCOTT   P   DEVIL RAYS

PERSONAL: Born June 12, 1968, in Flint, Mich. ... 6-4/228. ... Throws left, bats left. ... Full name: Scott Phillip Aldred.
HIGH SCHOOL: Hill McCloy (Montrose, Mich.).
TRANSACTIONS/CAREER NOTES: Selected by Detroit Tigers organization in 16th round of free-agent draft (June 2, 1986). ... Selected by Colorado Rockies in first round (15th pick overall) of expansion draft (November 17, 1992). ... Claimed on waivers by Montreal Expos (April 29, 1993). ... On Montreal disabled list (May 15-September 11, 1993). ... Released by Expos (September 11, 1993). ... Missed entire 1994 season with injury. ... Signed by Toledo, Detroit Tigers organization (February 19, 1995). ... Claimed on waivers by Minnesota Twins (May 28, 1996). ... On Salt Lake disabled list (August 7-September 19, 1997). ... Released by Twins following 1997 season. ... Signed by Tampa Bay Devil Rays (December 19, 1997).

Year Team (League)	W	L	Pct.	ERA	G	GS	CG	ShO	Sv.	IP	H	R	ER	BB	SO
1987— Fayetteville (S. Atl.)	4	9	.308	3.60	21	20	0	0	0	110	101	56	44	69	91
1988— Lakeland (Fla. St.)	8	7	.533	3.56	25	25	1	1	0	131⅓	122	61	52	72	102
1989— London (Eastern)	10	6	.625	3.84	20	20	3	1	0	122	98	55	52	59	97
1990— Toledo (Int'l)	6	15	.286	4.90	29	*29	2	0	0	158	145	93	86	81	133
— Detroit (A.L.)	1	2	.333	3.77	4	3	0	0	0	14⅓	13	6	6	10	7
1991— Toledo (Int'l)	8	8	.500	3.92	22	20	2	0	1	135⅓	127	65	59	72	95
— Detroit (A.L.)	2	4	.333	5.18	11	11	1	0	0	57⅓	58	37	33	30	35
1992— Detroit (A.L.)	3	8	.273	6.78	16	13	0	0	0	65	80	51	49	33	34
— Toledo (Int'l)	4	6	.400	5.13	16	13	3	0	0	86	92	57	49	47	81
1993— Colorado (N.L.)■	0	0	...	10.80	5	0	0	0	0	6⅔	10	10	8	9	5
— Montreal (N.L.)■	1	0	1.000	6.75	3	0	0	0	0	5⅓	9	4	4	1	4
1994—								Did not play.							
1995— Lakeland (Fla. St.)■	4	2	.667	3.19	13	7	0	0	2	67⅔	57	25	24	19	64
— Jacksonville (Southern)	1	0	1.000	0.00	2	2	0	0	0	12	9	0	0	1	11
1996— Detroit (A.L.)	0	4	.000	9.35	11	8	0	0	0	43⅓	60	52	45	26	36
— Minnesota (A.L.)■	6	5	.545	5.09	25	17	0	0	0	122	134	73	69	42	75
1997— Minnesota (A.L.)	2	10	.167	7.68	17	15	0	0	0	77⅓	102	66	66	28	33
— Salt Lake (PCL)	3	3	.500	7.03	7	7	0	0	0	39⅔	56	39	31	16	23
A.L. totals (5 years)	14	33	.298	6.36	84	67	1	0	0	379⅓	447	285	268	169	220
N.L. totals (1 year)	1	0	1.000	9.00	8	0	0	0	0	12	19	14	12	10	9
Major league totals (6 years)	15	33	.313	6.44	92	67	1	0	0	391⅓	466	299	280	179	229

ALEXANDER, MANNY   SS/2B   CUBS

PERSONAL: Born March 20, 1971, in San Pedro de Macoris, Dominican Republic. ... 5-10/160. ... Bats right, throws right. ... Full name: Manuel DeJesus Alexander.
TRANSACTIONS/CAREER NOTES: Signed as non-drafted free agent by Baltimore Orioles organization (February 4, 1988). ... On disabled list (April 26-July 23, 1990). ... On Rochester disabled list (May 9-June 9-17, 1993). ... On Baltimore disabled list (March 25-May 2, 1995). ... Traded by Orioles with IF Scott McLain to New York Mets for P Hector Ramirez (March 22, 1997). ... On New York disabled list (June 15-July 10 and July 25-August 11, 1997). ... Traded by Mets to Chicago Cubs (August 14, 1997), as part of deal in which Mets traded OF Lance Johnson and two players to be named later to Cubs for OF Brian McRae, P Mel Rojas and P Turk Wendell (August 8, 1997); Mets traded P Mark Clark to Cubs to complete deal (August 11, 1997).
STATISTICAL NOTES: Led Appalachian League shortstops with 349 total chances in 1989. ... Led Carolina League shortstops with 651 total chances and 93 double plays in 1991.

Year Team (League)	Pos.	G	AB	R	H	2B	3B	HR	RBI	Avg.	BB	SO	SB	PO	A	E	Avg.
1988—						Dominican Summer League statistics unavailable.											
1989— Bluefield (Appal.)	SS	65	*274	49	*85	13	2	2	34	.310	20	49	19	*140	177	*32	.908
1990— Wausau (Midwest)	SS	44	152	16	27	3	1	0	11	.178	12	41	8	66	99	11	.938
1991— Hagerstown (Eastern)	SS	3	9	3	3	1	0	0	2	.333	1	3	0	5	4	0	1.000
— Frederick (Carolina)	SS	134	548	•81	*143	17	3	3	42	.261	44	68	47	*226	*393	32	*.951
1992— Hagerstown (Eastern)	SS	127	499	69	129	23	8	2	41	.259	25	62	43	216	253	36	.929
— Rochester (Int'l)	SS	6	24	3	7	1	0	0	3	.292	1	3	2	12	25	1	.974
— Baltimore (A.L.)	SS	4	5	1	1	0	0	0	0	.200	0	3	0	3	3	0	1.000
1993— Rochester (Int'l)	SS	120	471	55	115	23	8	6	51	.244	22	60	19	184	335	18	*.966
— Baltimore (A.L.)	PR-DH	3	0	1	0	0	0	0	0	...	0	0	0	...	...	...	...

Year	Team (League)	Pos.	G	AB	R	H	2B	3B	HR	RBI	Avg.	BB	SO	SB	PO	A	E	Avg.
								BATTING								FIELDING		
1994—Rochester (Int'l)........	SS-2B	111	426	63	106	23	6	6	39	.249	16	67	30	219	291	33	.939
1995—Baltimore (A.L.).........	2-S-3-DH	94	242	35	57	9	1	3	23	.236	20	30	11	139	170	10	.969
1996—Baltimore (A.L.).........S-2-3-O-DH-P		54	68	6	7	0	0	0	4	.103	3	27	3	26	47	5	.936
1997—New York (N.L.)........	2B-SS-3B	54	149	26	37	9	3	2	15	.248	9	38	11	59	130	4	.979
—St. Lucie (Fla. St.)......	SS	1	4	0	1	0	0	0	0	.250	0	1	0	1	4	0	1.000
—Chicago (N.L.)■........	SS-2B	33	99	11	29	3	1	1	7	.293	8	16	2	38	91	7	.949
American League totals (4 years)		155	315	43	65	9	1	3	27	.206	23	60	14	168	220	15	.963
National League totals (1 year)		87	248	37	66	12	4	3	22	.266	17	54	13	97	221	11	.967
Major league totals (5 years)		242	563	80	131	21	5	6	49	.233	40	114	27	265	441	26	.964

DIVISION SERIES RECORD

Year	Team (League)	Pos.	G	AB	R	H	2B	3B	HR	RBI	Avg.	BB	SO	SB	PO	A	E	Avg.
								BATTING								FIELDING		
1996—Baltimore (A.L.).........	DH-PR	3	0	2	0	0	0	0	0	...	0	0	0	0	0	0	...

RECORD AS PITCHER

Year	Team (League)	W	L	Pct.	ERA	G	GS	CG	ShO	Sv.	IP	H	R	ER	BB	SO
1996—Baltimore (A.L.).................	0	0	...	67.50	1	0	0	0	0	$2/3$	1	5	5	4	0
Major league totals (1 year)........	0	0	...	67.50	1	0	0	0	0	$2/3$	1	5	5	4	0

ALFONSECA, ANTONIO   P   MARLINS

PERSONAL: Born April 16, 1972, in La Romana, Dominican Republic. ... 6-0/235. ... Throws right, bats right.
TRANSACTIONS/CAREER NOTES: Signed as non-drafted free agent by Montreal Expos organization (July 3, 1989). ... Selected by Edmonton, Florida Marlins organization, from Harrisburg, Expos organization in Rule 5 minor league draft (December 13, 1993). ... On disabled list (May 15-June 15, 1995 and July 12-September 3, 1996).

Year	Team (League)	W	L	Pct.	ERA	G	GS	CG	ShO	Sv.	IP	H	R	ER	BB	SO
1990—DSL Expos (DSL)..............	3	5	.375	3.60	13	13	1	0	0	60	60	29	24	32	19
1991—GC Expos (GCL)...............	3	3	.500	3.88	11	10	0	0	0	51	46	33	22	25	38
1992—GC Expos (GCL)..............	3	4	.429	3.68	12	10	1	1	0	66	55	31	27	35	62
1993—Jamestown (NYP).............	2	2	.500	6.15	15	4	0	0	1	$33^2/3$	31	26	23	22	29
1994—Kane County (Midwest)■...	6	5	.545	4.07	32	9	0	0	0	$86^1/3$	78	41	39	21	74
1995—Portland (Eastern)...........	9	3	.750	3.64	19	17	1	0	0	$96^1/3$	81	43	39	42	75
1996—Charlotte (Int'l)..................	4	4	.500	5.53	14	13	0	0	1	$71^2/3$	86	47	44	22	51
1997—Charlotte (Int'l)..................	7	2	.778	4.32	46	0	0	0	7	$58^1/3$	58	34	28	20	45
—Florida (N.L.).....................	1	3	.250	4.91	17	0	0	0	0	$25^2/3$	36	16	14	10	19
Major league totals (1 year).......	1	3	.250	4.91	17	0	0	0	0	$25^2/3$	36	16	14	10	19

WORLD SERIES RECORD

NOTES: Member of World Series championship team (1997).

Year	Team (League)	W	L	Pct.	ERA	G	GS	CG	ShO	Sv.	IP	H	R	ER	BB	SO
1997—Florida (N.L.).....................	0	0	...	0.00	3	0	0	0	0	$6^1/3$	6	0	0	1	5

ALFONZO, EDGARDO   3B   METS

PERSONAL: Born November 8, 1973, in St. Teresa, Venezuela. ... 5-11/187. ... Bats right, throws right. ... Full name: Edgardo Antonio Alfonzo. ... Brother of Roberto Alfonzo, second baseman, New York Mets organization (1993-94).
HIGH SCHOOL: Cecilio Acosto (Venezuela).
TRANSACTIONS/CAREER NOTES: Signed as non-drafted free agent by New York Mets organization (February 19, 1991). ... On disabled list (August 11, 1995-remainder of season).
RECORDS: Shares single-game record for most doubles plays by second baseman—4 (1997).
STATISTICAL NOTES: Led New York-Pennsylvania League shortstops with 389 total chances and 39 double plays in 1992. ... Had 20-game hitting streak (June 10-July 10, 1997). ... Career major league grand slams: 1.

Year	Team (League)	Pos.	G	AB	R	H	2B	3B	HR	RBI	Avg.	BB	SO	SB	PO	A	E	Avg.
								BATTING								FIELDING		
1991—GC Mets (GCL)..........	2B-SS-3B	54	175	29	58	8	4	0	27	.331	34	12	6	99	108	9	.958
1992—St. Lucie (Fla. St.)......	2B	4	5	0	0	0	0	0	0	.000	0	0	0	1	3	0	1.000
—Pittsfield (NYP).........	SS	74	*298	44	*106	13	5	1	44	*.356	18	31	7	*126	*237	*26	.933
1993—St. Lucie (Fla. St.)......	SS	128	494	75	145	18	3	11	86	.294	57	51	26	183	425	29	.954
1994—Binghamton (East.).....	SS-2B-1B	127	498	89	146	34	2	15	75	.293	64	55	14	206	408	27	.958
1995—New York (N.L.).........	3B-2B-SS	101	335	26	93	13	5	4	41	.278	12	37	1	81	171	7	.973
1996—New York (N.L.).........	2B-3B-SS	123	368	36	96	15	2	4	40	.261	25	56	2	146	246	11	.973
1997—New York (N.L.).........	3B-SS-2B	151	518	84	163	27	2	10	72	.315	63	56	11	98	290	12	.970
Major league totals (3 years)		375	1221	146	352	55	9	18	153	.288	100	149	14	325	707	30	.972

ALICEA, LUIS   2B   RANGERS

PERSONAL: Born July 29, 1965, in Santurce, Puerto Rico. ... 5-9/176. ... Bats both, throws right. ... Full name: Luis Rene Alicea. ... Name pronounced AH-la-SAY-uh.
HIGH SCHOOL: Liceo Castro (Rio Piedras, Puerto Rico).
COLLEGE: Florida State.
TRANSACTIONS/CAREER NOTES: Selected by St. Louis Cardinals organization in first round (23rd pick overall) of free-agent draft (June 2, 1986). ... On St. Petersburg disabled list (April 6-June 4, 1990). ... On Louisville disabled list (April 25-May 25, 1991). ... On St. Louis disabled list (June 1-July 6, 1992); included rehabilitation assignment to Louisville (July 2-6). ... Traded by Cardinals to Boston Red Sox for P Nate Minchey and OF Jeff McNeely (December 7, 1994). ... Claimed on waivers by Cardinals (March 19, 1996). ... Granted free agency (October 31, 1996). ... Signed by Anaheim Angels organization (January 20, 1997). ... Granted free agency (October 30, 1997). ... Signed by Texas Rangers (December 9, 1997).

HONORS: Named second baseman on THE SPORTING NEWS college All-America team (1986).
STATISTICAL NOTES: Switch-hit home runs in one game (July 28, 1995). ... Led A.L. second basemen with 699 total chances and 103 double plays in 1995. ... Career major league grand slams: 1.

Year Team (League)	Pos.	G	AB	R	H	2B	3B	HR	RBI	Avg.	BB	SO	SB	PO	A	E	Avg.
1986— Erie (N.Y.-Penn).........	2B	47	163	40	46	6	1	3	18	.282	37	20	27	94	163	12	.955
— Arkansas (Texas)........	2B-SS	25	68	8	16	3	0	0	3	.235	5	11	0	39	63	4	.962
1987— Arkansas (Texas)........	2B	101	337	57	91	14	3	4	47	.270	49	28	13	184	251	11	*.975
— Louisville (A.A.)..........	2B	29	105	18	32	10	2	2	20	.305	9	9	4	69	81	4	.974
1988— Louisville (A.A.).........	2B-SS-OF	49	191	21	53	11	6	1	21	.277	11	21	8	116	165	0	1.000
— St. Louis (N.L.)..........	2B	93	297	20	63	10	4	1	24	.212	25	32	1	206	240	14	.970
1989— Louisville (A.A.)..........	2B	124	412	53	102	20	3	8	48	.248	59	55	13	240	310	16	.972
1990— St. Petersburg (FSL) ..	2B	29	95	14	22	1	4	0	12	.232	20	14	9	20	23	0	1.000
— Arkansas (Texas)........	2B	14	49	11	14	3	1	0	4	.286	7	8	2	24	34	4	.935
— Louisville (A.A.)..........	3B	25	92	10	32	6	3	0	10	.348	5	12	0	14	39	6	.898
1991— Louisville (A.A.)..........	2B	31	112	26	44	6	3	4	16	.393	14	8	5	68	95	5	.970
— St. Louis (N.L.)..........	2B-3B-SS	56	68	5	13	3	0	0	0	.191	8	19	0	19	23	0	1.000
1992— Louisville (A.A.)..........	2B-SS	20	71	11	20	8	0	0	6	.282	16	6	0	44	52	4	.960
— St. Louis (N.L.)..........	2B-SS	85	265	26	65	9	11	2	32	.245	27	40	2	136	233	7	.981
1993— St. Louis (N.L.)..........	2B-OF-3B	115	362	50	101	19	3	3	46	.279	47	54	11	210	281	11	.978
1994— St. Louis (N.L.)..........	2B-OF	88	205	32	57	12	5	5	29	.278	30	38	4	126	149	4	.986
1995— Boston (A.L.)■..........	2B	132	419	64	113	20	6	4	44	.270	63	61	13	254	429	16	.977
1996— St. Louis (N.L.)■	2B	129	380	54	98	26	3	5	42	.258	52	78	11	241	288	*24	.957
1997— Anaheim (A.L.)..........	2B-3B-DH	128	388	59	98	16	7	5	37	.253	69	65	22	223	287	12	.977
American League totals (2 years)		260	807	123	211	36	10	11	81	.261	132	126	35	477	716	28	.977
National League totals (6 years)		566	1577	187	397	79	26	16	173	.252	189	261	29	938	1214	60	.973
Major league totals (8 years)		826	2384	310	608	115	36	27	254	.255	321	387	64	1415	1930	88	.974

DIVISION SERIES RECORD

Year Team (League)	Pos.	G	AB	R	H	2B	3B	HR	RBI	Avg.	BB	SO	SB	PO	A	E	Avg.
1995— Boston (A.L.)..............	2B	3	10	1	6	1	0	1	1	.600	2	2	1	6	11	1	.944
1996— St. Louis (N.L.)...........	2B	3	11	1	2	2	0	0	0	.182	1	4	0	2	5	1	.875
Division series totals (2 years)		6	21	2	8	3	0	1	1	.381	3	6	1	8	16	2	.923

CHAMPIONSHIP SERIES RECORD

Year Team (League)	Pos.	G	AB	R	H	2B	3B	HR	RBI	Avg.	BB	SO	SB	PO	A	E	Avg.
1996— St. Louis (N.L.)...........	2B-PH	5	8	0	0	0	0	0	0	.000	2	1	0	5	7	1	.923

ALLENSWORTH, JERMAINE   OF   PIRATES

PERSONAL: Born January 11, 1972, in Anderson, Ind. ... 6-0/190. ... Bats right, throws right. ... Full name: Jermaine LaMont Allensworth.
HIGH SCHOOL: Madison Heights (Anderson, Ind.).
COLLEGE: Purdue.
TRANSACTIONS/CAREER NOTES: Selected by Pittsburgh Pirates organization in supplemental round ("sandwich pick" between first and second round, 34th pick overall) of free-agent draft (June 3, 1993); pick received as part of compensation for Houston Astros signing Type A free-agent P Doug Drabek. ... On Pittsburgh disabled list (May 16-June 22, 1997); included rehabilitation assignment to Calgary (June 18-22).
STATISTICAL NOTES: Career major league grand slams: 1.

Year Team (League)	Pos.	G	AB	R	H	2B	3B	HR	RBI	Avg.	BB	SO	SB	PO	A	E	Avg.
1993— Welland (NYP)............	OF	67	263	44	81	16	4	1	32	.308	24	38	18	140	2	3	.979
1994— Carolina (Southern)....	OF	118	452	63	109	26	8	1	34	.241	39	79	16	245	5	6	.977
1995— Carolina (Southern)....	OF	56	219	37	59	14	2	1	14	.269	25	34	13	131	3	2	.985
— Calgary (PCL)............	OF	51	190	46	60	13	4	3	11	.316	13	30	13	90	2	1	.989
1996— Calgary (PCL)............	OF	95	352	77	116	23	6	8	43	.330	39	61	25	196	4	6	.971
— Pittsburgh (N.L.)	OF	61	229	32	60	9	3	4	31	.262	23	50	11	139	4	3	.979
1997— Pittsburgh (N.L.)	OF	108	369	55	94	18	2	3	43	.255	44	79	14	189	5	4	.980
— Calgary (PCL)............	OF	5	20	5	8	3	1	0	1	.400	2	4	1	8	0	0	1.000
Major league totals (2 years)		169	598	87	154	27	5	7	74	.258	67	129	25	328	9	7	.980

ALMANZA, ARMANDO   P   CARDINALS

PERSONAL: Born October 26, 1972, in El Paso, Texas. ... 6-3/205. ... Throws left, bats left.
HIGH SCHOOL: Belair (El Paso, Texas).
JUNIOR COLLEGE: New Mexico Junior College.
TRANSACTIONS/CAREER NOTES: Selected by St. Louis Cardinals organization in 21st round of free-agent draft (June 3, 1993). ... On Madison disabled list (April 8-September 7, 1994). ... On Madison reserved list (November 4-December 14, 1994).
STATISTICAL NOTES: Tied for Arizona League lead with 14 wild pitches in 1993.

Year Team (League)	W	L	Pct.	ERA	G	GS	CG	ShO	Sv.	IP	H	R	ER	BB	SO
1993— Ariz. Cardinals (Ariz.)	4	1	.800	3.21	20	4	0	0	0	42	38	19	15	14	56
— Johnson City (App.)	1	1	.500	4.15	3	3	0	0	0	4 1/3	6	2	2	3	4
1994—							Did not play.								
1995— Savannah (S. Atl.)	3	9	.250	3.92	20	20	0	0	0	108	108	62	47	40	72
1996— Peoria (Midwest)...............	8	6	.571	2.76	52	1	0	0	0	62	50	27	19	32	67
1997— Prince William (Caro.)........	2	3	.400	1.67	•58	0	0	0	*36	64 2/3	38	18	12	32	83

ALMANZAR, CARLOS — P — BLUE JAYS

PERSONAL: Born November 6, 1973, in Santiago, Dominican Republic. ... 6-2/165. ... Throws right, bats right. ... Full name: Carlos Manuel Almanzar.

TRANSACTIONS/CAREER NOTES: Signed as non-drafted free agent by Toronto Blue Jays organization (December 10, 1990). ... On Knoxville disabled list (May 27-June 3, 1997).

Year — Team (League)	W	L	Pct.	ERA	G	GS	CG	ShO	Sv.	IP	H	R	ER	BB	SO
1991— Dom. B. Jays (DSL)	3	1	.750	2.83	6	6	1	0	0	35	36	17	11	11	20
1992— Dom. B. Jays (DSL)	10	0	1.000	2.01	13	11	2	1	1	67	45	26	15	31	60
1993— Dom. B. Jays (DSL)	5	2	.714	3.38	16	9	0	0	2	69 1/3	60	35	26	32	59
1994— Medicine Hat (Pio.)	7	4	.636	2.87	14	14	0	0	0	84 2/3	82	38	27	19	77
1995— Knoxville (Southern)	3	12	.200	3.99	35	19	0	0	2	126 1/3	144	77	56	32	93
1996— Knoxville (Southern)	7	8	.467	4.85	54	0	0	0	9	94 2/3	106	58	51	33	105
1997— Knoxville (Southern)	1	1	.500	4.91	21	0	0	0	8	25 2/3	30	14	14	5	25
— Syracuse (Int'l)..................	5	1	.833	1.41	32	0	0	0	3	51	30	9	8	8	47
— Toronto (A.L.)...................	0	1	.000	2.70	4	0	0	0	0	3 1/3	1	1	1	1	4
Major league totals (1 year).......	0	1	.000	2.70	4	0	0	0	0	3 1/3	1	1	1	1	4

ALMANZAR, RICHARD — 2B — TIGERS

PERSONAL: Born April 3, 1976, in San Francisco De Macoris, Dominican Republic. ... 5-10/155. ... Bats right, throws right. ... Full name: Richard Manuel Almanzar.

TRANSACTIONS/CAREER NOTES: Signed as non-drafted free agent by Detroit Tigers organization (May 11, 1993).

STATISTICAL NOTES: Tied for Florida State League lead in caught stealing with 19 in 1996 ... Led Florida State League second basemen with 654 total chances in 1996. ... Led Southern League second basemen with 85 double plays in 1997.

Year — Team (League)	Pos.	G	AB	R	H	2B	3B	HR	RBI	Avg.	BB	SO	SB	PO	A	E	Avg.
1993— Dom. Tigers (DSL)	IF	62	222	46	69	9	1	1	30	.311	32	12	42	102	118	24	.902
1994— Dom. Tigers (DSL)	2B	65	238	72	76	10	3	1	37	.319	59	14	*105	158	163	17	.950
1995— Fayetteville (SAL)	2B	80	308	47	76	12	1	0	16	.247	29	32	39	170	226	12	.971
1996— Lakeland (Fla. St.)	2B	124	471	*81	144	22	2	1	36	.306	49	49	53	*257	378	19	.971
1997— Jacksonville (South.)..	2B	103	387	55	94	20	2	5	35	.243	37	43	20	•237	292	17	.969

ALMONTE, WADY — OF — ORIOLES

PERSONAL: Born April 20, 1975, in Higuey, Dominican Republic. ... 6-0/180. ... Bats right, throws right. ... Full name: Wady Enrique Almonte.

TRANSACTIONS/CAREER NOTES: Signed as non-drafted free agent by Baltimore Orioles organization (January 28, 1993). ... On Frederick disabled list (May 17-June 21, 1996).

Year — Team (League)	Pos.	G	AB	R	H	2B	3B	HR	RBI	Avg.	BB	SO	SB	PO	A	E	Avg.
1993— Dom. Orioles (DSL)....	OF	53	222	53	76	19	0	7	41	.342	22	16	4	92	7	4	.961
1994— GC Orioles (GCL)	OF-3B	42	120	11	24	2	0	2	9	.200	8	22	1	36	25	5	.924
1995— Bluefield (Appal.)........	OF	51	189	37	58	12	1	6	30	.307	9	49	6	52	4	5	.918
1996— Frederick (Carolina)....	OF	85	287	45	82	12	2	12	44	.286	21	59	1	147	17	0	.953
— GC Orioles (GCL).........	OF	1	3	2	1	0	0	0	1	.333	1	0	1	1	0	0	1.000
1997— Bowie (Eastern).........	OF	69	222	25	46	7	2	6	25	.207	27	64	2	94	4	9	.916
— Frederick (Carolina)....	OF	57	202	34	52	13	2	10	36	.257	16	59	4	70	12	4	.953

ALOMAR, ROBERTO — 2B — ORIOLES

PERSONAL: Born February 5, 1968, in Ponce, Puerto Rico. ... 6-0/185. ... Bats both, throws right. ... Full name: Roberto Velazquez Alomar. ... Son of Sandy Alomar Sr., manager, Fort Myers Cubs, Chicago Cubs organization, major league infielder with six teams (1964-78) and coach, San Diego Padres (1986-90); and brother of Sandy Alomar Jr., catcher, Cleveland Indians.

TRANSACTIONS/CAREER NOTES: Signed as non-drafted free agent by San Diego Padres organization (February 16, 1985). ... Traded by Padres with OF Joe Carter to Toronto Blue Jays for 1B Fred McGriff and SS Tony Fernandez (December 5, 1990). ... On suspended list (May 23-24, 1995). ... Granted free agency (October 30, 1995). ... Signed by Baltimore Orioles (December 21, 1995). ... On suspended list (April 1-7, 1997). ... On disabled list (July 30-August 26, 1997).

RECORDS: Holds A.L. career record for most consecutive errorless games by second baseman—104 (June 21, 1994 through July 3, 1995). ... Holds A.L. single-season record for fewest double plays by second baseman (150 or more games)—66 (1992). ... Shares A.L. single-season records for most games with switch-hit home runs—2 (1996); and fewest errors by second baseman (150 or more games)—5 (1992).

HONORS: Won A.L. Gold Glove at second base (1991-96). ... Named second baseman on THE SPORTING NEWS A.L. All-Star team (1992 and 1996). ... Named second baseman on THE SPORTING NEWS A.L. Silver Slugger team (1992 and 1996).

STATISTICAL NOTES: Led South Atlantic League second basemen with 35 errors in 1985. ... Led Texas League shortstops with 167 putouts and 34 errors in 1987. ... Led N.L. with 17 sacrifice hits in 1989. ... Led N.L. second basemen with 17 errors in 1990. ... Switch-hit home runs in one game four times (May 10, 1991; May 3, 1995; July 25 and August 14, 1996). ... Had 22-game hitting streak (May 12-June 8, 1996). ... Hit three home runs in one game (April 26, 1997). ... Career major league grand slams: 3.

Year — Team (League)	Pos.	G	AB	R	H	2B	3B	HR	RBI	Avg.	BB	SO	SB	PO	A	E	Avg.
1985— Char., S.C. (S. Atl.)	2B-SS	*137	*546	89	160	14	3	0	54	.293	61	73	36	298	339	†36	.947
1986— Reno (California)	2B	90	356	53	123	16	4	4	49	*.346	32	38	14	198	265	18	.963
1987— Wichita (Texas)	SS-2B	130	536	88	171	41	4	12	68	.319	49	74	43	†188	309	†36	.932
1988— Las Vegas (PCL)	2B	9	37	5	10	1	0	2	14	.270	1	4	3	22	29	1	.981
— San Diego (N.L.)........	2B	143	545	84	145	24	6	9	41	.266	47	83	24	319	459	16	.980
1989— San Diego (N.L.)	2B	158	623	82	184	27	1	7	56	.295	53	76	42	341	472	*28	.967
1990— San Diego (N.L.)	2B-SS	147	586	80	168	27	5	6	60	.287	48	72	24	316	404	†19	.974

Year Team (League)	Pos.	G	AB	R	H	2B	3B	HR	RBI	Avg.	BB	SO	SB	PO	A	E	Avg.
						BATTING									FIELDING		
1991—Toronto (A.L.)■.......	2B	161	637	88	188	41	11	9	69	.295	57	86	53	333	447	15	.981
1992—Toronto (A.L.)............	2B-DH	152	571	105	177	27	8	8	76	.310	87	52	49	287	378	5	.993
1993—Toronto (A.L.)............	2B	153	589	109	192	35	6	17	93	.326	80	67	55	254	439	14	.980
1994—Toronto (A.L.)............	2B	107	392	78	120	25	4	8	38	.306	51	41	19	176	275	4	.991
1995—Toronto (A.L.)............	2B	130	517	71	155	24	7	13	66	.300	47	45	30	*272	267	4	*.993
1996—Baltimore (A.L.)■.......	2B-DH	153	588	132	193	43	4	22	94	.328	90	65	17	279	445	11	.985
1997—Baltimore (A.L.)..........	2B-DH	112	412	64	137	23	2	14	60	.333	40	43	9	202	301	6	.988
American League totals (7 years)		968	3706	647	1162	218	42	91	496	.314	452	399	232	1803	2552	59	.987
National League totals (3 years)		448	1754	246	497	78	12	22	157	.283	148	231	90	976	1335	63	.973
Major league totals (10 years)		1416	5460	893	1659	296	54	113	653	.304	600	630	322	2779	3887	122	.982

DIVISION SERIES RECORD

Year Team (League)	Pos.	G	AB	R	H	2B	3B	HR	RBI	Avg.	BB	SO	SB	PO	A	E	Avg.
						BATTING									FIELDING		
1996—Baltimore (A.L.)..........	2B	4	17	2	5	0	0	1	4	.294	2	3	0	10	6	0	1.000
1997—Baltimore (A.L.)..........	2B-PH	4	10	1	3	2	0	0	2	.300	1	1	0	3	6	0	1.000
Division series totals (2 years)		8	27	3	8	2	0	1	6	.296	3	4	0	13	12	0	1.000

CHAMPIONSHIP SERIES RECORD

RECORDS: Shares career record for most times grounded into double play—5.

NOTES: Named A.L. Championship Series Most Valuable Player (1992).

Year Team (League)	Pos.	G	AB	R	H	2B	3B	HR	RBI	Avg.	BB	SO	SB	PO	A	E	Avg.
						BATTING									FIELDING		
1991—Toronto (A.L.)............	2B	5	19	3	9	0	0	0	4	.474	2	3	2	14	9	0	1.000
1992—Toronto (A.L.)............	2B	6	26	4	11	1	0	2	4	.423	2	1	5	16	15	0	1.000
1993—Toronto (A.L.)............	2B	6	24	3	7	1	0	0	4	.292	4	3	4	14	19	0	1.000
1996—Baltimore (A.L.)..........	2B	5	23	2	5	2	0	0	1	.217	0	4	0	15	26	2	.953
1997—Baltimore (A.L.)..........	2B	6	22	2	4	0	0	1	2	.182	7	3	0	10	17	2	.931
Championship series totals (5 years)		28	114	14	36	4	0	3	15	.316	15	14	11	69	86	4	.975

WORLD SERIES RECORD

RECORDS: Shares record for most at-bats in one inning—2 (October 20, 1993, eighth inning).

NOTES: Member of World Series championship teams (1992 and 1993).

Year Team (League)	Pos.	G	AB	R	H	2B	3B	HR	RBI	Avg.	BB	SO	SB	PO	A	E	Avg.
						BATTING									FIELDING		
1992—Toronto (A.L.)............	2B	6	24	3	5	1	0	0	0	.208	3	3	3	5	12	0	1.000
1993—Toronto (A.L.)............	2B	6	25	5	12	2	1	0	6	.480	2	3	4	9	21	2	.938
World Series totals (2 years)		12	49	8	17	3	1	0	6	.347	5	6	7	14	33	2	.959

ALL-STAR GAME RECORD

RECORDS: Shares single-game record for most stolen bases—2 (July 14, 1992).

Year League	Pos.	AB	R	H	2B	3B	HR	RBI	Avg.	BB	SO	SB	PO	A	E	Avg.
					BATTING									FIELDING		
1990—National....................	2B	1	0	0	0	0	0	0	.000	0	0	0	1	2	0	1.000
1991—American..................	2B	4	0	0	0	0	0	0	.000	0	0	0	2	5	0	1.000
1992—American..................	2B	3	1	1	0	0	0	0	.333	0	0	2	0	1	0	1.000
1993—American..................	2B	3	1	1	0	0	1	1	.333	0	0	1	0	0	0	...
1994—American..................	2B	3	1	1	0	0	0	0	.333	0	0	1	0	0	0	...
1995—American..................	PR-2B	1	0	0	0	0	0	0	.000	0	0	1	0	0	0	...
1996—American..................	2B	3	0	1	0	0	0	0	.333	0	0	0	3	0	0	1.000
1997—American..................	2B	2	0	0	0	0	0	0	.000	0	0	0	1	5	0	1.000
All-Star Game totals (8 years)		20	3	4	0	0	1	1	.200	0	0	4	4	16	0	1.000

ALOMAR, SANDY　　　　　C　　　　　INDIANS

PERSONAL: Born June 18, 1966, in Salinas, Puerto Rico. ... 6-5/220. ... Bats right, throws right. ... Full name: Santos Velazquez Alomar Jr. ... Son of Sandy Alomar Sr., manager, Fort Myers Cubs, Chicago Cubs organization, major league infielder with six teams (1964-78) and coach, San Diego Padres (1986-90); and brother of Roberto Alomar, second baseman, Baltimore Orioles.

HIGH SCHOOL: Luis Munoz Rivera (Salinas, Puerto Rico).

TRANSACTIONS/CAREER NOTES: Signed as non-drafted free agent by San Diego Padres organization (October 21, 1983). ... Traded by Padres with OF Chris James and 3B Carlos Baerga to Cleveland Indians for OF Joe Carter (December 6, 1989). ... On Cleveland disabled list (May 15-June 17 and July 29, 1991-remainder of season); included rehabilitation assignments to Colorado Springs (June 8-17 and August 9-12). ... On disabled list (May 2-18, 1992). ... On suspended list (July 29-August 2, 1992). ... On Cleveland disabled list (May 1-August 7, 1993); included rehabilitation assignment to Charlotte, S.C. (July 22-August 7). ... On disabled list (April 24-May 11, 1994). ... On Cleveland disabled list (April 19-June 29, 1995); included rehabilitation assignment to Canton/Akron (June 22-29).

RECORDS: Shares major league single-game record for most doubles—4 (1997).

HONORS: Named Minor League co-Player of the Year by The Sporting News (1988). ... Named Pacific Coast League Player of the Year (1988-89). ... Named Minor League Player of the Year by The Sporting News (1989). ... Named A.L. Rookie Player of the Year by The Sporting News (1990). ... Won A.L. Gold Glove at catcher (1990). ... Named A.L. Rookie of the Year by Baseball Writers' Association of America (1990).

STATISTICAL NOTES: Led Northwest League catchers with .985 fielding percentage and 421 putouts in 1984. ... Led Pacific Coast League catchers with 14 errors in 1988. ... Led Pacific Coast League catchers with 573 putouts in 1988 and 702 in 1989. ... Led Pacific Coast League catchers with 633 total chances in 1988 and 761 in 1989. ... Had 30-game hitting streak (May 25-July 6, 1997). ... Career major league grand slams: 1.

MISCELLANEOUS: Batted as switch-hitter (1984-86).

Year Team (League)	Pos.	G	AB	R	H	2B	3B	HR	RBI	Avg.	BB	SO	SB	PO	A	E	Avg.
						BATTING									FIELDING		
1984—Spokane (N'west).......	C-1B	59	219	13	47	5	0	0	21	.215	13	20	3	†465	51	8	†.985
1985—Char., S.C. (S. Atl.).....	C-OF	100	352	38	73	7	0	3	43	.207	31	30	3	779	75	18	.979

Year Team (League)	Pos.	G	AB	R	H	2B	3B	HR	RBI	Avg.	BB	SO	SB	PO	A	E	Avg.
1986—Beaumont (Texas)	C	100	346	36	83	15	1	4	27	.240	15	35	2	505	60	*18	.969
1987—Wichita (Texas)	C	103	375	50	115	19	1	8	65	.307	21	37	1	*606	50	*15	.978
1988—Las Vegas (PCL)	C-OF	93	337	59	100	9	5	16	71	.297	28	35	1	†574	46	†14	.978
—San Diego (N.L.)	PH	1	1	0	0	0	0	0	0	.000	0	1	0	...	...	...	...
1989—Las Vegas (PCL)	C-OF	131	*523	88	160	33	8	13	101	.306	42	58	3	†706	47	12	.984
—San Diego (N.L.)	C	7	19	1	4	1	0	1	6	.211	3	3	0	33	1	0	1.000
1990—Cleveland (A.L.)■......	C	132	445	60	129	26	2	9	66	.290	25	46	4	686	46	*14	.981
1991—Cleveland (A.L.).........	C-DH	51	184	10	40	9	0	0	7	.217	8	24	0	280	19	4	.987
—Colo. Springs (PCL) ...	C	12	35	5	14	2	0	1	10	.400	5	0	0	5	0	1	.833
1992—Cleveland (A.L.).........	C-DH	89	299	22	75	16	0	2	26	.251	13	32	3	477	39	2	.996
1993—Cleveland (A.L.).........	C	64	215	24	58	7	1	6	32	.270	11	28	3	342	25	6	.984
—Charlotte (Int'l)	C	12	44	8	16	5	0	1	8	.364	5	8	0	20	1	0	1.000
1994—Cleveland (A.L.).........	C	80	292	44	84	15	1	14	43	.288	25	31	8	453	41	2	.996
1995—Cant./Akr. (Eastern)	C	6	15	3	6	1	0	0	1	.400	1	1	0	23	0	1	.958
—Cleveland (A.L.).........	C	66	203	32	61	6	0	10	35	.300	7	26	3	364	22	2	.995
1996—Cleveland (A.L.).........	C-1B	127	418	53	110	23	0	11	50	.263	19	42	1	724	48	9	.988
1997—Cleveland (A.L.).........	C-DH	125	451	63	146	37	0	21	83	.324	19	48	0	743	40	*12	.985
American League totals (8 years)		734	2507	308	703	139	4	73	342	.280	127	277	22	4069	280	51	.988
National League totals (2 years)		8	20	1	4	1	0	1	6	.200	3	4	0	33	1	0	1.000
Major league totals (10 years)		742	2527	309	707	140	4	74	348	.280	130	281	22	4102	281	51	.988

DIVISION SERIES RECORD

Year Team (League)	Pos.	G	AB	R	H	2B	3B	HR	RBI	Avg.	BB	SO	SB	PO	A	E	Avg.
1995—Cleveland (A.L.).........	C	3	11	1	2	1	0	0	1	.182	0	1	0	22	1	0	1.000
1996—Cleveland (A.L.).........	C	4	16	0	2	0	0	0	3	.125	0	2	0	40	4	1	.978
1997—Cleveland (A.L.).........	C	5	19	4	6	1	0	2	5	.316	0	2	0	28	1	1	.967
Division series totals (3 years)		12	46	5	10	2	0	2	9	.217	0	5	0	90	6	2	.980

CHAMPIONSHIP SERIES RECORD

Year Team (League)	Pos.	G	AB	R	H	2B	3B	HR	RBI	Avg.	BB	SO	SB	PO	A	E	Avg.
1995—Cleveland (A.L.).........	C	5	15	0	4	1	0	1	1	.267	1	1	0	30	3	1	.971
1997—Cleveland (A.L.).........	C	6	24	3	3	0	0	1	4	.125	1	3	0	49	1	0	1.000
Championship series totals (2 years)		11	39	3	7	1	0	2	5	.179	2	4	0	79	4	1	.988

WORLD SERIES RECORD

Year Team (League)	Pos.	G	AB	R	H	2B	3B	HR	RBI	Avg.	BB	SO	SB	PO	A	E	Avg.
1995—Cleveland (A.L.).........	C	5	15	0	3	2	0	0	1	.200	0	2	0	28	0	0	1.000
1997—Cleveland (A.L.).........	C	7	30	5	11	1	0	2	10	.367	2	3	0	49	3	0	1.000
World Series totals (2 years)		12	45	5	14	3	0	2	11	.311	2	5	0	77	3	0	1.000

NOTES: Named Most Valuable Player (1997).

ALL-STAR GAME RECORD

Year League	Pos.	AB	R	H	2B	3B	HR	RBI	Avg.	BB	SO	SB	PO	A	E	Avg.
1990—American ...	C	3	1	2	0	0	0	0	.667	0	0	0	3	0	0	1.000
1991—American ...	C	2	0	0	0	0	0	0	.000	0	0	0	2	0	0	1.000
1992—American ...	C	3	0	1	0	0	0	0	.333	0	0	0	3	0	0	1.000
1997—American ...	C	1	1	1	0	0	1	2	1.000	0	0	0	4	0	0	1.000
All-Star Game totals (4 years)		9	2	4	0	0	1	2	.444	0	0	0	12	0	0	1.000

ALOU, MOISES — OF — ASTROS

PERSONAL: Born July 3, 1966, in Atlanta. ... 6-3/195. ... Bats right, throws right. ... Full name: Moises Rojas Alou. ... Son of Felipe Alou, manager, Montreal Expos; nephew of Jesus Alou, major league outfielder with four teams (1963-75 and 1978-79); nephew of Matty Alou, major league outfielder with six teams (1960-74); and cousin of Mel Rojas, pitcher, New York Mets. ... Name pronounced moy-SEZZ ah-LOO.

HIGH SCHOOL: C.E.E. (Santo Domingo, Dominican Republic).

COLLEGE: Canada College (Calif.).

TRANSACTIONS/CAREER NOTES: Selected by Pittsburgh Pirates organization in first round (second pick overall) of free-agent draft (January 14, 1986). ... Traded by Pirates organization to Montreal Expos (August 16, 1990), completing deal in which Expos traded P Zane Smith to Pirates for P Scott Ruskin, SS Willie Greene and a player to be named later (August 8, 1990). ... On Montreal disabled list (March 19, 1991-entire season; July 7-27, 1992; September 18, 1993-remainder of season; August 18-September 5, 1995 and September 11, 1995-remainder of season). ... On disabled list (July 8-23, 1996). ... On suspended list (August 23-27, 1996). ... Granted free agency (December 7, 1996). ... Signed by Florida Marlins (December 12, 1996). ... Traded by Marlins to Houston Astros for P Oscar Henriquez, P Manuel Barrios and a player to be named later (November 11, 1997); Marlins acquired P Mark Johnson to complete deal (December 16, 1997).

HONORS: Named outfielder on THE SPORTING NEWS N.L. All-Star team (1994). ... Named outfielder on THE SPORTING NEWS N.L. Silver Slugger team (1994).

STATISTICAL NOTES: Led American Association outfielders with seven double plays in 1990. ... Career major league grand slams: 2.

Year Team (League)	Pos.	G	AB	R	H	2B	3B	HR	RBI	Avg.	BB	SO	SB	PO	A	E	Avg.
1986—Watertown (NYP)	OF	69	254	30	60	9	*8	6	35	.236	22	72	14	134	6	7	.952
1987—Macon (S. Atl.)	OF	4	8	1	1	0	0	0	0	.125	2	4	0	6	0	0	1.000
—Watertown (NYP)	OF	39	117	20	25	6	2	4	8	.214	16	36	6	43	1	2	.957
1988—Augusta (S. Atl.)	OF	105	358	58	112	23	5	7	62	.313	51	84	24	220	10	9	.962
1989—Salem (Carolina)	OF	86	321	50	97	29	2	14	53	.302	35	69	12	166	12	10	.947
—Harrisburg (Eastern) ..	OF	54	205	36	60	5	2	3	19	.293	17	38	8	89	1	2	.978

Year Team (League)	Pos.	G	AB	R	H	2B	3B	HR	RBI	Avg.	BB	SO	SB	PO	A	E	Avg.
1990— Harrisburg (Eastern) ..	OF	36	132	19	39	12	2	3	22	.295	16	21	7	93	2	1	.990
— Buffalo (A.A.).............	OF	75	271	38	74	4	6	5	31	.273	30	43	9	169	10	8	.957
— Pittsburgh (N.L.)........	OF	2	5	0	1	0	0	0	0	.200	0	0	0	3	0	0	1.000
— Indianapolis (A.A.)■ ..	OF	15	55	6	12	1	0	0	6	.218	3	7	4	27	2	0	1.000
— Montreal (N.L.)..........	OF	14	15	4	3	0	1	0	0	.200	0	3	0	6	1	0	1.000
1991—								Did not play.									
1992— Montreal (N.L.).........	OF	115	341	53	96	28	2	9	56	.282	25	46	16	170	6	4	.978
1993— Montreal (N.L.).........	OF	136	482	70	138	29	6	18	85	.286	38	53	17	254	11	4	.985
1994— Montreal (N.L.).........	OF	107	422	81	143	31	5	22	78	.339	42	63	7	201	4	3	.986
1995— Montreal (N.L.).........	OF	93	344	48	94	22	0	14	58	.273	29	56	4	147	5	3	.981
1996— Montreal (N.L.).........	OF	143	540	87	152	28	2	21	96	.281	49	83	9	259	8	3	.989
1997— Florida (N.L.)■..........	OF	150	538	88	157	29	5	23	115	.292	70	85	9	248	4	3	.988
Major league totals (7 years)		760	2687	431	784	167	21	107	488	.292	253	389	62	1288	39	20	.985

DIVISION SERIES RECORD

Year Team (League)	Pos.	G	AB	R	H	2B	3B	HR	RBI	Avg.	BB	SO	SB	PO	A	E	Avg.
1997— Florida (N.L.)..............	OF	3	14	1	3	1	0	0	1	.214	0	3	0	5	0	0	1.000

CHAMPIONSHIP SERIES RECORD

Year Team (League)	Pos.	G	AB	R	H	2B	3B	HR	RBI	Avg.	BB	SO	SB	PO	A	E	Avg.
1997— Florida (N.L.)	OF-PH	5	15	0	1	1	0	0	5	.067	1	3	0	3	0	0	1.000

NOTES: Member of World Series championship team (1997).

WORLD SERIES RECORD

Year Team (League)	Pos.	G	AB	R	H	2B	3B	HR	RBI	Avg.	BB	SO	SB	PO	A	E	Avg.
1997— Florida (N.L.)	OF	7	28	6	9	2	0	3	9	.321	3	6	1	11	0	0	1.000

ALL-STAR GAME RECORD

Year League	Pos.	AB	R	H	2B	3B	HR	RBI	Avg.	BB	SO	SB	PO	A	E	Avg.
1994— National	OF	1	0	1	1	0	0	1	1.000	0	0	0	0	0	...	...
1997— National	OF	2	0	1	0	0	0	0	.500	0	0	0	1	0	0	1.000
All-Star Game totals (2 years)		3	0	2	1	0	0	1	.667	0	0	0	1	0	0	1.000

ALVAREZ, GABE   3B   TIGERS

PERSONAL: Born March 6, 1974, in Navojoa, Sonora, Mexico. ... 6-1/185. ... Bats right, throws right. ... Full name: Gabriel De Jesus Alvarez.
HIGH SCHOOL: Bishop Amat (La Puente, Calif.).
COLLEGE: Southern California.
TRANSACTIONS/CAREER NOTES: Selected by San Diego Padres organization in second round of free-agent draft (June 1, 1995). ... Selected by Arizona Diamondbacks in first round (fifth pick overall) of expansion draft (November 18, 1997). ... Traded by Diamondbacks with IF Joe Randa and P Matt Drews to Detroit Tigers for 3B Travis Fryman (November 18, 1997).
STATISTICAL NOTES: Led Southern League third basemen in errors with 32 in 1997. ... Led Southern League in grounding into double plays with 21 in 1997.

Year Team (League)	Pos.	G	AB	R	H	2B	3B	HR	RBI	Avg.	BB	SO	SB	PO	A	E	Avg.
1995— Rancho Cuca. (Cal.) ...	SS-3B	59	212	41	73	17	2	6	36	.344	29	30	1	52	132	23	.893
— Memphis (Southern)..	2B-SS	2	9	0	5	1	0	0	4	.556	1	1	0	0	6	1	.857
1996— Memphis (Southern)..	3B-SS	104	368	58	91	23	1	8	40	.247	64	87	2	62	161	31	.878
1997— Mobile (Southern)......	3B-SS	114	427	71	128	28	2	14	78	.300	51	64	1	70	209	†33	.894

ALVAREZ, TAVO   P   PIRATES

PERSONAL: Born November 25, 1971, in Obregon, Mexico. ... 6-3/235. ... Throws right, bats right. ... Full name: Cesar Octavo Alvarez. ... Name pronounced TAH-vo.
HIGH SCHOOL: Tucson (Ariz.).
TRANSACTIONS/CAREER NOTES: Selected by Montreal Expos organization in second round of free-agent draft (June 4, 1990); pick received as part of compensation for New York Yankees signing Type A free-agent P Pascual Perez. ... On disabled list (August 30, 1991-remainder of season; June 17-24 and August 1-16, 1993). ... On Ottawa disabled list (April 7, 1994-entire season). ... On Montreal disabled list (May 15-June 1, 1996). ... Granted free agency (October 15, 1997). ... Signed by Pittsburgh Pirates organization (December 18, 1997).

Year Team (League)	W	L	Pct.	ERA	G	GS	CG	ShO	Sv.	IP	H	R	ER	BB	SO
1990— GC Expos (GCL)	5	2	.714	2.60	11	10	0	0	0	52	42	17	15	16	47
1991— Sumter (S. Atl.)	12	10	.545	3.24	25	25	3	1	0	152 2/3	151	68	55	58	158
1992— W.P. Beach (FSL)................	13	4	.765	*1.49	19	19	•7	*4	0	139	124	30	23	24	83
— Harrisburg (Eastern)	4	1	.800	2.85	7	7	2	1	0	47 1/3	48	15	15	9	42
1993— Ottawa (Int'l)	7	10	.412	4.22	25	25	1	0	0	140 2/3	163	80	66	55	77
1994—								Did not play.							
1995— Harrisburg (Eastern)	2	1	.667	2.25	3	3	0	0	0	16	17	8	4	5	14
— Ottawa (Int'l)	2	1	.667	2.49	3	3	0	0	0	21 2/3	17	6	6	5	11
— Montreal (N.L.)	1	5	.167	6.75	8	8	0	0	0	37 1/3	46	30	28	14	17
1996— Ottawa (Int'l)	4	9	.308	4.70	20	20	2	1	0	113	128	66	59	25	86
— Montreal (N.L.)	2	1	.667	3.00	11	5	0	0	0	21	19	10	7	12	9
1997— Ottawa (Int'l)	4	8	.333	4.82	37	13	0	0	0	106 1/3	123	61	57	42	86
**Major league totals (2 years)......	3	6	.333	5.40	19	13	0	0	0	58 1/3	65	40	35	26	26

ALVAREZ, WILSON — P — DEVIL RAYS

PERSONAL: Born March 24, 1970, in Maracaibo, Venezuela. ... 6-1/235. ... Throws left, bats left. ... Full name: Wilson Eduardo Alvarez.
TRANSACTIONS/CAREER NOTES: Signed as non-drafted free agent by Texas Rangers organization (September 23, 1986). ... Traded by Rangers with IF Scott Fletcher and OF Sammy Sosa to Chicago White Sox for OF Harold Baines and IF Fred Manrique (July 29, 1989). ... Traded by White Sox with P Danny Darwin and P Roberto Hernandez to San Francisco Giants for SS Michael Caruso, OF Brian Manning, P Lorenzo Barcelo, P Keith Foulke, P Bobby Howry and P Ken Vining (July 31, 1997). ... Granted free agency (November 1, 1997). ... Signed by Tampa Bay Devil Rays (December 3, 1997).
RECORDS: Shares major league record for most strikeouts in one inning—4 (July 21, 1997, seventh inning).
STATISTICAL NOTES: Tied for Gulf Coast League lead with six home runs allowed in 1987. ... Pitched 7-0 no-hit victory for Chicago against Baltimore (August 11, 1991).

Year—Team (League)	W	L	Pct.	ERA	G	GS	CG	ShO	Sv.	IP	H	R	ER	BB	SO
1987—Gastonia (S. Atl.)	1	5	.167	6.47	8	6	0	0	0	32	39	24	23	23	19
— GC Rangers (GCL)	2	5	.286	5.24	10	10	0	0	0	44 2/3	41	29	26	21	46
1988—Gastonia (S. Atl.)	4	11	.267	2.98	23	23	1	0	0	127	113	63	42	49	134
—Oklahoma City (A.A.)	1	1	.500	3.78	5	3	0	0	0	16 2/3	17	8	7	6	9
1989—Charlotte (Fla. St.)	7	4	.636	2.11	13	13	3	2	0	81	68	29	19	21	51
—Tulsa (Texas)	2	2	.500	2.06	7	7	1	1	0	48	40	14	11	16	29
—Texas (A.L.)	0	1	.000	...	1	1	0	0	0	0	3	3	3	2	0
—Birmingham (Southern)■	2	1	.667	3.03	6	6	0	0	0	35 2/3	32	12	12	16	18
1990—Birmingham (Southern)	5	1	.833	4.27	7	7	1	0	0	46 1/3	44	24	22	25	36
—Vancouver (PCL)	7	7	.500	6.00	17	15	1	0	0	75	91	54	50	51	35
1991—Birmingham (Southern)	10	6	.625	1.83	23	23	3	2	0	152 1/3	109	46	31	74	165
—Chicago (A.L.)	3	2	.600	3.51	10	9	2	1	0	56 1/3	47	26	22	29	32
1992—Chicago (A.L.)	5	3	.625	5.20	34	9	0	0	1	100 1/3	103	64	58	65	66
1993—Chicago (A.L.)	15	8	.652	2.95	31	31	1	1	0	207 2/3	168	78	68	*122	155
—Nashville (A.A.)	0	1	.000	2.84	1	1	0	0	0	6 1/3	7	7	2	2	8
1994—Chicago (A.L.)	12	8	.600	3.45	24	24	2	1	0	161 2/3	147	72	62	62	108
1995—Chicago (A.L.)	8	11	.421	4.32	29	29	3	0	0	175	171	96	84	93	118
1996—Chicago (A.L.)	15	10	.600	4.22	35	35	0	0	0	217 1/3	216	106	102	97	181
1997—Chicago (A.L.)	9	8	.529	3.03	22	22	2	1	0	145 2/3	126	61	49	55	110
—San Francisco (N.L.)■	4	3	.571	4.48	11	11	0	0	0	66 1/3	54	36	33	36	69
A.L. totals (8 years)	67	51	.568	3.79	186	160	10	4	1	1064	981	506	448	525	770
N.L. totals (1 year)	4	3	.571	4.48	11	11	0	0	0	66 1/3	54	36	33	36	69
Major league totals (8 years)	71	54	.568	3.83	197	171	10	4	1	1130 1/3	1035	542	481	561	839

DIVISION SERIES RECORD

Year Team (League)	W	L	Pct.	ERA	G	GS	CG	ShO	Sv.	IP	H	R	ER	BB	SO
1997—San Francisco (N.L.)	0	1	.000	6.00	1	1	0	0	0	6	6	4	4	4	4

CHAMPIONSHIP SERIES RECORD

Year Team (League)	W	L	Pct.	ERA	G	GS	CG	ShO	Sv.	IP	H	R	ER	BB	SO
1993—Chicago (A.L.)	1	0	1.000	1.00	1	1	0	0	0	9	7	1	1	2	6

ALL-STAR GAME RECORD

Year League	W	L	Pct.	ERA	GS	CG	ShO	Sv.	IP	H	R	ER	BB	SO
1994—American	0	0	...	0.00	0	0	0	0	1	0	0	0	0	0

AMARAL, RICH — OF — MARINERS

PERSONAL: Born April 1, 1962, in Visalia, Calif. ... 6-0/175. ... Bats right, throws right. ... Full name: Richard Louis Amaral. ... Name pronounced AM-ar-all.
HIGH SCHOOL: Estancia (Costa Mesa, Calif.).
JUNIOR COLLEGE: Orange Coast College (Calif.).
COLLEGE: UCLA.
TRANSACTIONS/CAREER NOTES: Selected by Chicago Cubs organization in second round of free-agent draft (June 6, 1983). ... Selected by Chicago White Sox organization from Cubs organization in Rule 5 minor league draft (December 6, 1988). ... Granted free agency (October 15, 1990). ... Signed by Seattle Mariners organization (November 25, 1990). ... On Seattle disabled list (May 29-July 17, 1991); included rehabilitation assignment to Calgary (July 11-17). ... On disabled list (August 1-16, 1993).
HONORS: Named second baseman on THE SPORTING NEWS college All-America team (1983).
STATISTICAL NOTES: Tied for New York-Pennsylvania League lead in double plays by second baseman with 39 in 1984. ... Tied for Carolina League lead in errors by second baseman with 25 in 1985. ... Led Pacific Coast League with .433 on-base percentage in 1991.

Year—Team (League)	Pos.	G	AB	R	H	2B	3B	HR	RBI	Avg.	BB	SO	SB	PO	A	E	Avg.
1983—Geneva (NY-Penn)	2B-3B-SS	67	269	63	68	17	3	1	24	.253	45	47	22	135	205	14	.960
1984—Quad Cities (Mid.)	2B-SS	34	119	21	25	1	0	0	7	.210	24	29	12	62	73	6	.957
1985—Win.-Salem (Car.)	2B-3B	124	428	62	116	15	5	3	36	.271	59	68	26	228	318	‡27	.953
1986—Pittsfield (Eastern)	2B	114	355	43	89	12	0	0	24	.251	39	65	25	228	266	14	.972
1987—Pittsfield (Eastern)	2B-1B	104	315	45	80	8	5	0	28	.254	43	50	28	242	274	18	.966
1988—Pittsfield (Eastern)	2-3-1-S-O	122	422	66	117	15	4	4	47	.277	56	53	54	288	262	19	.967
1989—Birmingham (Sou.)■	2B-SS-3B	122	432	*90	123	15	6	4	48	.285	88	66	57	198	256	23	.952
1990—Vancouver (PCL)	S-3-2-0-1	130	462	87	139	*39	5	4	56	.301	88	68	20	154	260	15	.965
1991—Calgary (PCL)■	SS-2B	86	347	79	120	26	2	3	36	*.346	53	37	30	148	284	15	.966
—Seattle (A.L.)	2-3-S-DH-1	14	16	2	1	0	0	0	0	.063	1	5	0	13	16	2	.935
1992—Calgary (PCL)	SS-2B-OF	106	403	79	128	21	8	0	21	.318	67	69	*53	192	329	22	.959
—Seattle (A.L.)	S-3-0-1-2	35	100	9	24	3	0	1	7	.240	5	16	4	33	68	3	.971
1993—Seattle (A.L.)	2-3-S-DH-1	110	373	53	108	24	1	1	44	.290	33	54	19	180	270	10	.978
1994—Seattle (A.L.)	2-O-S-DH-1	77	228	37	60	10	2	4	18	.263	24	28	5	107	118	15	.938
—Calgary (PCL)	2B-OF	13	56	13	18	7	0	0	12	.321	4	6	2	28	35	3	.955
1995—Seattle (A.L.)	OF-DH	90	238	45	67	14	2	2	19	.282	21	33	21	121	6	1	.992
1996—Seattle (A.L.)	O-2-1-DH-3	118	312	69	91	11	3	1	29	.292	47	55	25	195	24	0	1.000
1997—Seattle (A.L.)	O-1-2-DH-3-S	89	190	34	54	5	0	1	21	.284	10	34	12	103	29	3	.978
Major league totals (7 years)		533	1457	249	405	67	8	10	138	.278	141	225	86	752	531	34	.974

DIVISION SERIES RECORD

Year Team (League)	Pos.	G	AB	R	H	2B	3B	HR	RBI	Avg.	BB	SO	SB	PO	A	E	Avg.
1997— Seattle (A.L.)	1B-PH	2	4	2	2	0	0	0	0	.500	0	1	0	7	2	00	1.000

CHAMPIONSHIP SERIES RECORD

Year Team (League)	Pos.	G	AB	R	H	2B	3B	HR	RBI	Avg.	BB	SO	SB	PO	A	E	Avg.
1995— Seattle (A.L.)	PH	2	2	0	0	0	0	0	0	.000	0	1	0	0	0	0	...

AMARO, RUBEN — OF — PHILLIES

PERSONAL: Born February 12, 1965, in Philadelphia. ... 5-10/175. ... Bats both, throws right. ... Son of Ruben Amaro Sr., major league infielder with four teams (1958 and 1960-69).

HIGH SCHOOL: William Penn Charter (Philadelphia).

COLLEGE: Stanford (degree in human biology, 1987).

TRANSACTIONS/CAREER NOTES: Selected by California Angels organization in 11th round of free-agent draft (June 2, 1987). ... Traded by Angels with P Kyle Abbott to Philadelphia Phillies for OF Von Hayes (December 8, 1991). ... On Scranton/Wilkes-Barre disabled list (April 26-May 7, 1993). ... Traded by Phillies to Cleveland Indians for P Heathcliff Slocumb (November 2, 1993). ... On Cleveland disabled list (July 29-September 1, 1995); included rehabilitation assignment to Buffalo (August 13-28). ... Released by Indians (November 9, 1995). ... Signed by Toronto Blue Jays organization (January 24, 1996). ... Released by Blue Jays organization (May 5, 1996). ... Signed by Phillies (May 6, 1996).

STATISTICAL NOTES: Led Northwest League in caught stealing with 11 in 1987. ... Tied for Texas League lead in being hit by pitch with nine in 1990.

Year Team (League)	Pos.	G	AB	R	H	2B	3B	HR	RBI	Avg.	BB	SO	SB	PO	A	E	Avg.
1987— Salem (Northwest)	O-3-1-S-2	71	241	51	68	7	3	3	41	.282	49	28	27	243	53	17	.946
1988— Palm Springs (Cal.)....	2-O-C-S	115	417	96	111	13	3	4	50	.266	105	61	42	258	188	18	.961
— Midland (Texas)..........	2B	13	31	5	4	1	0	0	2	.129	4	5	4	14	30	1	.978
1989— Quad City (Midwest) ..	OF-2B	59	200	50	72	9	4	3	27	.360	45	25	20	94	34	4	.970
— Midland (Texas)..........	OF	29	110	28	42	9	2	3	9	.382	10	19	7	34	2	2	.947
1990— Midland (Texas).........	OF	57	224	50	80	15	6	4	38	.357	29	23	8	97	8	0	1.000
— Edmonton (PCL)	OF-1B	82	318	53	92	15	4	3	32	.289	40	43	32	161	5	2	.988
1991— Edmonton (PCL)	OF-2B-1B	121	472	*95	154	*42	6	3	42	.326	63	48	36	167	23	5	.974
— California (A.L.)	OF-2B-DH	10	23	0	5	1	0	0	2	.217	3	3	0	9	6	1	.938
1992— Philadelphia (N.L.)■ ..	OF	126	374	43	82	15	6	7	34	.219	37	54	11	232	5	2	.992
— Scran./W.B. (Int'l)......	OF	18	68	8	20	4	1	1	10	.294	9	6	2	35	1	0	1.000
1993— Scran./W.B. (Int'l)......	OF-2B	101	412	76	120	30	5	9	37	.291	31	44	25	272	8	5	.982
— Philadelphia (N.L.).....	OF	25	48	7	16	2	2	1	6	.333	6	5	0	25	1	1	.963
1994— Charlotte (Int'l)■........	OF	43	181	39	58	12	4	3	17	.320	15	16	9	84	2	1	.989
— Cleveland (A.L.).........	OF-DH	26	23	5	5	1	0	2	5	.217	2	3	2	10	0	1	.909
1995— Cleveland (A.L.).........	OF-DH	28	60	5	12	3	0	1	7	.200	4	6	1	35	0	0	1.000
— Buffalo (A.A.)............	OF	54	213	42	65	15	3	6	22	.305	18	29	6	102	2	1	.990
1996— Syracuse (Int'l)■........	OF	16	50	8	12	1	0	0	2	.240	10	11	6	23	2	0	1.000
— Philadelphia (N.L.)■ ..	OF-1B	61	117	14	37	10	0	2	15	.316	9	18	0	50	0	0	1.000
— Scran./W.B. (Int'l)......	OF-2B-3B	52	180	28	50	10	3	2	22	.278	14	29	7	110	9	1	.992
1997— Philadelphia (N.L.).....	OF-1B	117	175	18	41	6	1	2	21	.234	21	24	1	79	2	1	.988
American League totals (3 years)		64	106	10	22	5	0	3	14	.208	9	12	3	54	6	2	.968
National League totals (4 years)		329	714	82	176	33	9	12	76	.246	73	101	12	386	8	4	.990
Major league totals (7 years)		393	820	92	198	38	9	15	90	.241	82	113	15	440	14	6	.987

CHAMPIONSHIP SERIES RECORD

Year Team (League)	Pos.	G	AB	R	H	2B	3B	HR	RBI	Avg.	BB	SO	SB	PO	A	E	Avg.
1995— Cleveland (A.L.)..........	PR-DH	3	1	1	0	0	0	0	0	.000	0	0	0	0	0	0	...

WORLD SERIES RECORD

Year Team (League)	Pos.	G	AB	R	H	2B	3B	HR	RBI	Avg.	BB	SO	SB	PO	A	E	Avg.
1995— Cleveland (A.L.)..........	PH-OF	2	2	0	0	0	0	0	0	.000	0	1	0	0	0	0	...

AMBROSE, JOHN — P — WHITE SOX

PERSONAL: Born November 1, 1974, in Evansville, Ind. ... 6-5/180. ... Throws right, bats right.

HIGH SCHOOL: Evansville (Ind.) Memorial.

JUNIOR COLLEGE: John A. Logan College (Ill.).

TRANSACTIONS/CAREER NOTES: Selected by Chicago White Sox organization in second round of free-agent draft (June 3, 1994); choice received from Colorado Rockies as part of compensation for signing Type A free-agent Ellis Burks (April 9-September 6, 1996).

STATISTICAL NOTES: Tied for Carolina League lead with five balks in 1997.

Year Team (League)	W	L	Pct.	ERA	G	GS	CG	ShO	Sv.	IP	H	R	ER	BB	SO
1994— GC White Sox (GCL)	1	2	.333	3.66	11	10	0	0	0	46 2/3	34	21	19	24	43
— Hickory (S. Atl.)	1	1	.500	7.11	3	1	0	0	1	12 2/3	16	11	10	6	7
1995— Hickory (S. Atl.)	4	8	.333	3.95	14	14	0	0	0	73	65	41	32	35	49
— South Bend (Mid.)..............	1	1	.500	5.40	3	3	1	0	0	16 2/3	18	13	10	10	15
1996—							Did not play.								
1997— Win.-Salem (Car.)..............	8	13	.381	5.47	27	27	1	1	0	149 2/3	136	102	*91	*117	137

A

PERSONAL: Born January 18, 1964, in Silver Spring, Md. ... 6-1/190. ... Bats left, throws left. ... Full name: Brady Kevin Anderson.
HIGH SCHOOL: Carlsbad (Calif.).
COLLEGE: UC Irvine.
TRANSACTIONS/CAREER NOTES: Selected by Boston Red Sox organization in 10th round of free-agent draft (June 3, 1985). ... Traded by Red Sox with P Curt Schilling to Baltimore Orioles for P Mike Boddicker (July 29, 1988). ... On Baltimore disabled list (June 8-July 20, 1990); included rehabilitation assignments to Hagerstown (July 5-12) and Frederick (July 13-17). ... On Baltimore disabled list (May 28-June 14, 1991 and June 23-July 8, 1993). ... Granted free agency (October 27, 1997). ... Re-signed by Orioles (December 7, 1997).
RECORDS: Holds major league single-season record for most home runs as leadoff batter—12 (1996).
STATISTICAL NOTES: Led A.L. outfielders with six double plays in 1992. ... Led A.L. in being hit by pitch with 22 in 1996 and 19 in 1997. ... Career major league grand slams: 2.

							BATTING								FIELDING		
Year Team (League)	Pos.	G	AB	R	H	2B	3B	HR	RBI	Avg.	BB	SO	SB	PO	A	E	Avg.
1985—Elmira (N.Y.-Penn)......	OF	71	215	36	55	7	•6	5	21	.256	*67	32	13	119	5	3	.976
1986—Winter Haven (FSL)....	OF	126	417	86	133	19	11	12	87	.319	*107	47	44	280	5	1	*.997
1987—New Britain (Eastern) .	OF	52	170	30	50	4	3	6	35	.294	45	24	7	127	2	2	.985
—Pawtucket (Int'l).........	OF	23	79	18	30	4	0	2	8	.380	16	8	2	48	1	0	1.000
1988—Boston (A.L.).........	OF	41	148	14	34	5	3	0	12	.230	15	35	4	87	3	1	.989
—Pawtucket (Int'l).........	OF	49	167	27	48	6	1	4	19	.287	26	33	8	115	4	2	.983
—Baltimore (A.L.)■......	OF	53	177	17	35	8	1	1	9	.198	8	40	6	156	1	3	.981
1989—Baltimore (A.L.).........	OF-DH	94	266	44	55	12	2	4	16	.207	43	45	16	191	3	3	.985
—Rochester (Int'l).........	OF	21	70	14	14	1	2	1	8	.200	12	13	2	1	0	0	1.000
1990—Baltimore (A.L.).........	OF-DH	89	234	24	54	5	2	3	24	.231	31	46	15	149	3	2	.987
—Hagerstown (Eastern)	OF	9	34	8	13	0	2	1	5	.382	5	5	2	8	1	0	1.000
—Frederick (Carolina)....	OF	2	7	2	3	1	0	0	3	.429	1	1	0	1	0	0	1.000
1991—Baltimore (A.L.).........	OF-DH	113	256	40	59	12	3	2	27	.230	38	44	12	150	3	3	.981
—Rochester (Int'l).........	OF	7	26	5	10	3	0	0	2	.385	7	4	4	19	1	0	1.000
1992—Baltimore (A.L.).........	OF	159	623	100	169	28	10	21	80	.271	98	98	53	382	10	8	.980
1993—Baltimore (A.L.).........	OF-DH	142	560	87	147	36	8	13	66	.263	82	99	24	296	7	2	.993
1994—Baltimore (A.L.).........	OF	111	453	78	119	25	5	12	48	.263	57	75	31	247	4	1	.996
1995—Baltimore (A.L.).........	OF	143	554	108	145	33	10	16	64	.262	87	111	26	268	1	3	.989
1996—Baltimore (A.L.).........	OF-DH	149	579	117	172	37	5	50	110	.297	76	106	21	341	10	3	.992
1997—Baltimore (A.L.).........	OF-DH	151	590	97	170	39	7	18	73	.288	84	105	18	276	2	3	.989
Major league totals (10 years)		1245	4440	726	1159	240	56	140	529	.261	619	804	226	2543	47	32	.988

DIVISION SERIES RECORD

NOTES: Hit home run in first at-bat (October 1, 1996).

							BATTING								FIELDING		
Year Team (League)	Pos.	G	AB	R	H	2B	3B	HR	RBI	Avg.	BB	SO	SB	PO	A	E	Avg.
1996—Baltimore (A.L.).........	OF	4	17	3	5	0	0	2	4	.294	2	3	0	7	0	0	1.000
1997—Baltimore (A.L.).........	OF	4	17	3	6	1	0	1	4	.353	1	4	1	6	0	0	1.000
Division series totals (2 years)		8	34	6	11	1	0	3	8	.324	3	7	1	13	0	0	1.000

CHAMPIONSHIP SERIES RECORD

							BATTING								FIELDING		
Year Team (League)	Pos.	G	AB	R	H	2B	3B	HR	RBI	Avg.	BB	SO	SB	PO	A	E	Avg.
1996—Baltimore (A.L.).........	OF	5	21	5	4	1	0	1	1	.190	3	5	0	8	0	0	1.000
1997—Baltimore (A.L.).........	OF	6	25	5	9	2	0	2	3	.360	4	4	2	13	0	1	.929
Championship series totals (2 years)		11	46	10	13	3	0	3	4	.283	7	9	2	21	0	1	.955

ALL-STAR GAME RECORD

						BATTING							FIELDING		
Year League	Pos.	AB	R	H	2B	3B	HR	RBI	Avg.	BB	SO	SB	PO	A	E	Avg.
1992—American	OF	3	0	0	0	0	0	0	.000	0	0	0	1	0	0	1.000
1996—American	OF	2	0	0	0	0	0	0	.000	0	0	0	0	0	0	...
1997—American	OF	4	0	2	1	0	0	0	.500	0	0	0	1	0	0	1.000
All-Star Game totals (3 years)		9	0	2	1	0	0	0	.222	0	0	0	2	0	0	1.000

PERSONAL: Born April 26, 1972, in Geneva, Ohio. ... 6-1/190. ... Throws left, bats both. ... Full name: Brian James Anderson.
HIGH SCHOOL: Geneva (Ohio).
COLLEGE: Wright State.
TRANSACTIONS/CAREER NOTES: Selected by California Angels organization in first round (third pick overall) of free-agent draft (June 3, 1993). ... On California disabled list (May 7-June 7, 1994); included rehabilitation assignment to Lake Elsinore (May 27-June 7). ... On California disabled list (May 6-June 20, 1995); included rehabilitation assignment to Lake Elsinore (June 4-20). ... Traded by Angels to Cleveland Indians for P Jason Grimsley and P Pep Harris (February 15, 1996). ... On Cleveland disabled list (July 5-August 12, 1997); included rehabilitation assignment to Buffalo (August 3-13). ... Selected by Arizona Diamondbacks in first round (second pick overall) of expansion draft (November 18, 1997).
RECORDS: Shares major league record for most home runs allowed in one inning—4 (September 5, 1995, second inning).
HONORS: Named A.L. Rookie Pitcher of the Year by THE SPORTING NEWS (1994).
STATISTICAL NOTES: Tied for A.L. lead with five balks in 1994 and three in 1995. ... Tied for American Association lead with three balks in 1996.

Year Team (League)	W	L	Pct.	ERA	G	GS	CG	ShO	Sv.	IP	H	R	ER	BB	SO
1993—Midland (Texas).................	0	1	.000	3.38	2	2	0	0	0	10 2/3	16	5	4	0	9
—Vancouver (PCL).................	0	1	.000	12.38	2	2	0	0	0	8	13	12	11	6	2
—California (A.L.).................	0	0	...	3.97	4	1	0	0	0	11 1/3	11	5	5	2	4
1994—California (A.L.).................	7	5	.583	5.22	18	18	0	0	0	101 2/3	120	63	59	27	47
—Lake Elsinore (Calif.).........	0	1	.000	3.00	2	2	0	0	0	12	6	4	4	0	9

Year Team (League)	W	L	Pct.	ERA	G	GS	CG	ShO	Sv.	IP	H	R	ER	BB	SO
1995— California (A.L.)	6	8	.429	5.87	18	17	1	0	0	99 2/3	110	66	65	30	45
— Lake Elsinore (Calif.)	1	1	.500	1.93	3	3	0	0	0	14	10	3	3	1	13
1996— Buffalo (A.A.)■	11	5	.688	3.59	19	19	2	0	0	128	125	57	51	28	85
— Cleveland (A.L.)	3	1	.750	4.91	10	9	0	0	0	51 1/3	58	29	28	14	21
1997— Buffalo (A.A.)	7	1	.875	3.05	15	15	1	1	0	85 2/3	78	33	29	15	60
— Cleveland (A.L.)	4	2	.667	4.69	8	8	0	0	0	48	55	28	25	11	22
Major league totals (5 years)	20	16	.556	5.25	58	53	1	0	0	312	354	191	182	84	139

CHAMPIONSHIP SERIES RECORD

Year Team (League)	W	L	Pct.	ERA	G	GS	CG	ShO	Sv.	IP	H	R	ER	BB	SO
1997— Cleveland (A.L.)	1	0	1.000	1.42	3	0	0	0	0	6 1/3	1	1	1	3	7

WORLD SERIES RECORD

Year Team (League)	W	L	Pct.	ERA	G	GS	CG	ShO	Sv.	IP	H	R	ER	BB	SO
1997— Cleveland (A.L.)	0	0	...	2.45	3	0	0	0	1	3 2/3	2	1	1	0	2

ANDERSON, GARRET — OF — ANGELS

PERSONAL: Born June 30, 1972, in Los Angeles. ... 6-3/190. ... Bats left, throws left. ... Full name: Garret Joseph Anderson.
HIGH SCHOOL: John F. Kennedy (Granada Hills, Calif.), then Palos Verdes Estates (Calif.).
TRANSACTIONS/CAREER NOTES: Selected by California Angels organization in fourth round of free-agent draft (June 4, 1990). ... Angels franchise renamed Anaheim Angels for 1997 season.
HONORS: Named A.L. Rookie Player of the Year by THE SPORTING NEWS (1995).
STATISTICAL NOTES: Collected six hits in one game (September 27, 1996). ... Career major league grand slams: 2.

Year Team (League)	Pos.	G	AB	R	H	2B	3B	HR	RBI	Avg.	BB	SO	SB	PO	A	E	Avg.
1990— Ariz. Angels (Ariz.)	OF	32	127	5	27	2	0	0	14	.213	2	24	3	53	2	2	.965
— Boise (Northwest)	OF	25	83	11	21	3	1	1	8	.253	4	18	0	38	0	2	.950
1991— Quad City (Midwest)	OF	105	392	40	102	22	2	2	42	.260	20	89	5	158	7	10	.943
1992— Palm Springs (Cal.)	OF	81	322	46	104	15	2	1	62	.323	21	61	1	137	4	6	.959
— Midland (Texas)	OF	39	146	16	40	5	0	2	19	.274	9	30	2	62	6	1	.986
1993— Vancouver (PCL)	OF-1B	124	467	57	137	34	4	4	71	.293	31	95	3	198	13	2	.991
1994— Vancouver (PCL)	OF-1B	123	505	75	162	42	6	12	102	.321	28	93	3	196	10	2	.990
— California (A.L.)	OF	5	13	0	5	0	0	0	1	.385	0	2	0	10	0	0	1.000
1995— California (A.L.)	OF-DH	106	374	50	120	19	1	16	69	.321	19	65	6	213	7	5	.978
— Vancouver (PCL)	OF	14	61	9	19	7	0	0	12	.311	5	14	0	22	0	1	.957
1996— California (A.L.)	OF-DH	150	607	79	173	33	2	12	72	.285	27	84	7	316	5	7	.979
1997— Anaheim (A.L.)	OF-DH	154	624	76	189	36	3	8	92	.303	30	70	10	343	14	3	.992
Major league totals (4 years)		415	1618	205	487	88	6	36	234	.301	76	221	23	882	26	15	.984

ANDERSON, JIMMY — P — PIRATES

PERSONAL: Born January 22, 1976, in Portsmouth, Va. ... 6-1/180. ... Throws left, bats left. ... Full name: James Drew Anderson Jr.
HIGH SCHOOL: Western Branch (Chesapeake, Va.).
TRANSACTIONS/CAREER NOTES: Selected by Pittsburgh Pirates organization in ninth round of free-agent draft (June 2, 1994).

Year Team (League)	W	L	Pct.	ERA	G	GS	CG	ShO	Sv.	IP	H	R	ER	BB	SO
1994— GC Pirates (GCL)	5	1	.833	1.60	10	10	0	0	0	56 1/3	35	21	10	27	66
1995— Augusta (S. Atl.)	4	2	.667	1.53	14	14	0	0	0	76 2/3	51	15	13	31	75
— Lynchburg (Caroline)	1	5	.167	4.13	10	9	0	0	0	52 1/3	56	29	24	21	32
1996— Lynchburg (Caroline)	5	3	.625	1.93	11	11	1	1	0	65 1/3	51	25	14	21	56
— Carolina (Southern)	8	5	.615	3.34	17	16	0	0	0	97	92	40	36	44	79
1997— Carolina (Southern)	2	1	.667	1.46	4	4	0	0	0	24 2/3	16	6	4	9	23
— Calgary (PCL)	7	6	.538	5.68	21	21	0	0	0	103	124	78	65	64	71

ANDERSON, MARLON — 2B — PHILLIES

PERSONAL: Born January 6, 1974, in Montgomery, Ala. ... 5-11/190. ... Bats left, throws right. ... Full name: Marlon Ordell Anderson.
HIGH SCHOOL: Prattville (Ala.).
COLLEGE: South Alabama.
TRANSACTIONS/CAREER NOTES: Selected by Philadelphia Phillies organization in second round of free-agent draft (June 1, 1995); choice received from St. Louis Cardinals as part of compensation for Cardinals signing Type-A free agent P Danny Jackson.
STATISTICAL NOTES: Led New York-Pennsylvania League second basemen with 398 total chances and 67 double plays in 1995. ... Led Eastern League with 748 total chances in 1997.

Year Team (League)	Pos.	G	AB	R	H	2B	3B	HR	RBI	Avg.	BB	SO	SB	PO	A	E	Avg.
1995— Batavia (NY-Penn)	2B	74	*312	52	92	13	4	3	40	.295	15	20	22	*153	*231	14	*.965
1996— Clearwater (FSL)	2B	60	257	37	70	10	3	2	22	.272	14	18	26	142	221	16	.958
— Reading (Eastern)	2B	75	314	38	86	14	3	3	28	.274	26	44	17	166	239	18	.957
1997— Reading (Eastern)	2B	137	*553	88	147	18	6	10	62	.266	42	77	27	*323	*396	*29	.961

ANDREWS, SHANE — 3B — EXPOS

PERSONAL: Born August 28, 1971, in Dallas. ... 6-1/215. ... Bats right, throws right. ... Full name: Darrell Shane Andrews.
HIGH SCHOOL: Carlsbad (N.M.) Senior.
TRANSACTIONS/CAREER NOTES: Selected by Montreal Expos organization in first round (11th pick overall) of free-agent draft (June 4, 1990). ... On disabled list (August 3-11, 1993). ... On disabled list (May 1, 1997-remainder of season); included rehabilitation assignments to Ottawa (May 14-18) and West Palm Beach (July 26-August 10).

STATISTICAL NOTES: Led South Atlantic League third basemen with 98 putouts in 1992. ... Led International League third basemen with 436 total chances in 1994. ... Career major league grand slams: 3.

								BATTING							FIELDING		
Year Team (League)	Pos.	G	AB	R	H	2B	3B	HR	RBI	Avg.	BB	SO	SB	PO	A	E	Avg.
1990— GC Expos (GCL)	3B	56	190	31	46	7	1	3	24	.242	29	46	11	42	105	17	.896
1991— Sumter (S. Atl.)	3B	105	356	46	74	16	7	11	49	.208	65	132	5	71	205	29	.905
1992— Albany (S. Atl.)	3B-1B	136	453	76	104	18	1	*25	87	.230	*107	*174	8	†125	212	26	.928
1993— Harrisburg (Eastern) ..	3B-SS	124	442	77	115	29	2	18	70	.260	64	118	10	74	217	23	.927
1994— Ottawa (Int'l)	3B	137	460	79	117	25	2	16	85	.254	80	126	6	84	*320	*32	.927
1995— Montreal (N.L.)..........	3B-1B	84	220	27	47	10	1	8	31	.214	17	68	1	182	97	7	.976
1996— Montreal (N.L.)..........	3B	127	375	43	85	15	2	19	64	.227	35	119	3	64	256	15	.955
1997— Montreal (N.L.)..........	3B	18	64	10	13	3	0	4	9	.203	3	20	0	11	40	6	.895
— Ottawa (Int'l)	3B	3	12	3	3	0	0	1	1	.250	1	0	0	2	4	0	1.000
— W.P. Beach (FSL)........	3B	5	17	2	3	2	0	1	5	.176	2	7	0	2	9	1	.917
Major league totals (3 years)		229	659	80	145	28	3	31	104	.220	55	207	4	257	393	28	.959

ANDUJAR, LUIS — P — BLUE JAYS

PERSONAL: Born November 22, 1972, in Bani, Dominican Republic. ... 6-2/210. ... Throws right, bats right. ... Full name: Luis Sanchez Andujar.
TRANSACTIONS/CAREER NOTES: Signed as non-drafted free agent by Chicago White Sox organization (February 25, 1991). ... On disabled list (July 8-18, 1992). ... On Birmingham disabled list (September 2, 1993-remainder of season; June 10-July 20 and August 9, 1994-remainder of season). ... Traded by White Sox with P Allen Halley to Toronto Blue Jays for P Tony Castillo and IF Domingo Cedeno (August 22, 1996). ... On Toronto disabled list (August 24-September 28, 1997). ... Granted free agency (October 6, 1997). ... Signed by Blue Jays organization (November 11, 1997).
HONORS: Named Southern League Most Outstanding Pitcher (1995).
STATISTICAL NOTES: Pitched 1-0 no-hit victory for Birmingham against Memphis (August 8, 1995).

Year Team (League)	W	L	Pct.	ERA	G	GS	CG	ShO	Sv.	IP	H	R	ER	BB	SO
1991— GC White Sox (GCL)	4	4	.500	2.45	10	10	1	•1	0	62 1/3	60	27	17	10	52
1992— South Bend (Mid.).............	6	5	.545	2.92	32	15	1	1	3	120 1/3	109	49	39	47	91
1993— Sarasota (Florida State).....	6	6	.500	1.99	18	11	2	0	1	86	67	26	19	28	76
— Birmingham (Southern)	5	0	1.000	1.82	6	6	0	0	0	39 2/3	31	9	8	18	48
1994— Birmingham (Southern)	3	7	.300	5.05	15	15	0	0	0	76 2/3	90	50	43	25	64
— GC White Sox (GCL)	1	0	1.000	0.00	2	0	0	0	0	6	3	1	0	1	6
1995— Birmingham (Southern)	14	8	.636	2.85	27	27	2	1	0	167 1/3	147	64	53	44	146
— Chicago (A.L.)	2	1	.667	3.26	5	5	0	0	0	30 1/3	26	12	11	14	9
1996— Nashville (A.A.)	1	4	.200	5.92	8	7	1	0	0	38	50	26	25	8	24
— W. Sox-Cards (GCL)	1	0	1.000	0.00	1	1	0	0	0	6	3	0	0	0	3
— Chicago (A.L.)	0	2	.000	8.22	5	5	0	0	0	23	32	22	21	15	6
— Syracuse (Int'l)■...............	0	0	. . .	2.25	2	2	0	0	0	12	17	7	3	2	10
— Toronto (Int'l)	1	1	.500	5.02	3	2	0	0	0	14 1/3	14	8	8	1	5
1997— Toronto (A.L.)...................	0	6	.000	6.48	17	8	0	0	0	50	76	45	36	21	28
— Syracuse (Int'l)..................	1	6	.143	5.54	13	5	1	0	1	39	37	25	24	14	29
Major league totals (3 years)......	3	10	.231	5.81	30	20	0	0	0	117 2/3	148	87	76	51	48

ANTHONY, ERIC — OF

PERSONAL: Born November 8, 1967, in San Diego. ... 6-2/195. ... Bats left, throws left. ... Full name: Eric Todd Anthony.
HIGH SCHOOL: Sharstown (Houston).
TRANSACTIONS/CAREER NOTES: Selected by Houston Astros organization in 34th round of free-agent draft (June 2, 1986). ... On Houston disabled list (April 10-30, 1990); included rehabilitation assignment to Columbus (April 25-30). ... Traded by Astros to Seattle Mariners for OF Mike Felder and P Mike Hampton (December 10, 1993). ... On disabled list (June 25-July 10, 1994). ... On suspended list (July 10-17, 1994). ... Released by Mariners (December 21, 1994). ... Signed by Cincinnati Reds (April 5, 1995). ... On Cincinnati disabled list (April 17-June 7, July 15-August 14 and August 18-September 2, 1995); included rehabilitation assignments to Indianapolis (June 2-7 and August 11-14). ... On Cincinnati disabled list (March 23-April 14 and June 1-July 2, 1996); included rehabilitation assignments to Indianapolis (April 11-14 and June 28-July 2). ... Contract sold by Reds to Colorado Rockies (July 30, 1996). ... Granted free agency (October 28, 1996). ... Signed by Minnesota Twins organization (December 19, 1996). ... Released by Twins (March 26, 1997). ... Signed by Texas Rangers organization (March 27, 1997). ... On Oklahoma City suspended list (April 14-25, 1997). ... Released by Rangers (April 25, 1997). ... Signed by Los Angeles Dodgers organization (April 28, 1997). ... Granted free agency (October 3, 1997).
HONORS: Named Southern League Most Valuable Player (1989).
STATISTICAL NOTES: Led Gulf Coast League with 110 total bases in 1987. ... Led South Atlantic League with .558 slugging percentage in 1988. ... Led Southern League with .558 slugging percentage in 1989. ... Career major league grand slams: 2.

								BATTING							FIELDING		
Year Team (League)	Pos.	G	AB	R	H	2B	3B	HR	RBI	Avg.	BB	SO	SB	PO	A	E	Avg.
1986— GC Astros (GCL)	OF	13	12	2	3	0	0	0	0	.250	5	5	1	2	1	0	1.000
1987— GC Astros (GCL)	OF	60	216	38	57	11	6	*10	*46	.264	26	58	2	100	•11	5	.957
1988— Asheville (S. Atl.)	OF	115	439	73	120	*36	1	*29	89	.273	40	101	10	152	8	14	.920
1989— Columbus (Southern).	OF	107	403	67	121	16	2	*28	79	.300	35	127	14	178	17	8	.961
— Houston (N.L.)	OF	25	61	7	11	2	0	4	7	.180	9	16	0	34	1	0	1.000
— Tucson (PCL)	OF	12	46	10	10	3	0	3	11	.217	6	11	0	21	0	0	1.000
1990— Houston (N.L.)	OF	84	239	26	46	8	0	10	29	.192	29	78	5	124	5	4	.970
— Columbus (Southern).	OF	4	12	2	2	0	0	1	3	.167	3	4	0	3	0	0	1.000
— Tucson (PCL)	OF	40	161	28	46	10	2	6	26	.286	17	40	8	84	7	4	.958
1991— Tucson (PCL)	OF-1B	79	318	57	107	22	2	9	63	.336	25	58	11	154	9	4	.976
— Houston (N.L.)	OF	39	118	11	18	6	0	1	7	.153	12	41	1	64	5	1	.986
1992— Houston (N.L.)	OF	137	440	45	105	15	1	19	80	.239	38	98	5	173	6	5	.973
1993— Houston (N.L.)	OF	145	486	70	121	19	4	15	66	.249	49	88	3	233	6	3	.988
1994— Seattle (A.L.)■..........	OF-DH	79	262	31	62	14	1	10	30	.237	23	66	6	126	4	2	.985

– 19 –

Year Team (League)	Pos.	G	AB	R	H	2B	3B	HR	RBI	Avg.	BB	SO	SB	PO	A	E	Avg.
1995—Cincinnati (N.L.)■......	OF-1B	47	134	19	36	6	0	5	23	.269	13	30	2	141	12	4	.975
—Indianapolis (A.A.)......	1B-OF	7	24	7	7	0	0	4	8	.292	6	4	2	11	1	1	.923
1996—Indianapolis (A.A.)......	OF	7	21	4	5	1	0	2	7	.238	7	8	0	3	0	1	.750
—Cincinnati (N.L.)........	OF	47	123	22	30	6	0	8	13	.244	22	36	0	35	2	2	.949
—Colorado (N.L.)■	OF	32	62	10	15	2	0	4	9	.242	10	20	0	20	2	0	1.000
1997—Okla. City (A.A.)■......	OF-1B	9	36	3	16	2	0	2	9	.444	2	7	0	18	2	0	1.000
—Albuquerque (PCL)■..	OF-1B	27	105	18	36	6	1	7	27	.343	11	28	2	30	1	1	.969
—Los Angeles (N.L.).....	OF	47	74	8	18	3	2	2	5	.243	12	18	2	26	2	1	.966
American League totals (1 year)		79	262	31	62	14	1	10	30	.237	23	66	6	126	4	2	.985
National League totals (8 years)		603	1737	218	400	67	7	68	239	.230	194	425	18	850	41	20	.978
Major league totals (9 years)		682	1999	249	462	81	8	78	269	.231	217	491	24	976	45	22	.979

CHAMPIONSHIP SERIES RECORD

Year Team (League)	Pos.	G	AB	R	H	2B	3B	HR	RBI	Avg.	BB	SO	SB	PO	A	E	Avg.
1995—Cincinnati (N.L.).........	PH	2	1	0	0	0	0	0	0	.000	1	1	0	0	0	0	...

APPIER, KEVIN — P — ROYALS

PERSONAL: Born December 6, 1967, in Lancaster, Calif. ... 6-2/195. ... Throws right, bats right. ... Full name: Robert Kevin Appier. ... Name pronounced APE-ee-er.
HIGH SCHOOL: Antelope Valley (Lancaster, Calif.).
JUNIOR COLLEGE: Antelope Valley College (Calif.).
COLLEGE: Fresno State.
TRANSACTIONS/CAREER NOTES: Selected by Kansas City Royals organization in first round (ninth pick overall) of free-agent draft (June 2, 1987). ... On disabled list (July 26-August 12, 1995).
RECORDS: Shares major league record for most strikeouts in one inning—4 (September 3, 1996, fourth inning).
HONORS: Named A.L. Rookie Pitcher of the Year by THE SPORTING NEWS (1990).
STATISTICAL NOTES: Pitched 4-0 one-hit, complete-game victory for Kansas City against Detroit (July 7, 1990). ... Pitched 1-0 one-hit, complete-game loss against Texas (July 27, 1993). ... Tied for A.L. lead with 14 wild pitches in 1997.

Year Team (League)	W	L	Pct.	ERA	G	GS	CG	ShO	Sv.	IP	H	R	ER	BB	SO
1987—Eugene (Northwest)	5	2	.714	3.04	15	•15	0	0	0	77	81	43	26	29	72
1988—Baseball City (FSL)............	10	9	.526	2.75	24	24	1	0	0	147 1/3	134	58	45	39	112
—Memphis (Southern)......	2	0	1.000	1.83	3	3	0	0	0	19 2/3	11	5	4	7	18
1989—Omaha (Am. Assoc.)..........	8	8	.500	3.95	22	22	3	2	0	139	141	70	61	42	109
—Kansas City (A.L.)	1	4	.200	9.14	6	5	0	0	0	21 2/3	34	22	22	12	10
1990—Omaha (Am. Assoc.)..........	2	0	1.000	1.50	3	3	0	0	0	18	15	3	3	3	17
—Kansas City (A.L.)	12	8	.600	2.76	32	24	3	3	0	185 2/3	179	67	57	54	127
1991—Kansas City (A.L.)	13	10	.565	3.42	34	31	6	3	0	207 2/3	205	97	79	61	158
1992—Kansas City (A.L.)	15	8	.652	2.46	30	30	3	0	0	208 1/3	167	59	57	68	150
1993—Kansas City (A.L.)	18	8	.692	*2.56	34	34	5	1	0	238 2/3	183	74	68	81	186
1994—Kansas City (A.L.)	7	6	.538	3.83	23	23	1	0	0	155	137	68	66	63	145
1995—Kansas City (A.L.)	15	10	.600	3.89	31	31	4	1	0	201 1/3	163	90	87	80	185
1996—Kansas City (A.L.)	14	11	.560	3.62	32	32	5	1	0	211 1/3	192	87	85	75	207
1997—Kansas City (A.L.)	9	13	.409	3.40	34	34	4	1	0	235 2/3	215	96	89	74	196
Major league totals (9 years)......	104	78	.571	3.30	256	244	31	10	0	1665 1/3	1475	660	610	568	1364

ALL-STAR GAME RECORD

Year League	W	L	Pct.	ERA	GS	CG	ShO	Sv.	IP	H	R	ER	BB	SO
1995—American.........................	0	0	...	0.00	0	0	0	0	2	0	0	0	0	1

ARIAS, ALEX — IF — PHILLIES

PERSONAL: Born November 20, 1967, in New York. ... 6-3/195. ... Bats right, throws right. ... Full name: Alejandro Arias. ... Name pronounced air-REE-ahs.
HIGH SCHOOL: George Washington (New York).
TRANSACTIONS/CAREER NOTES: Selected by Chicago Cubs organization in third round of free-agent draft (June 2, 1987). ... Traded by Cubs with 3B Gary Scott to Florida Marlins for P Greg Hibbard (November 17, 1992). ... On disabled list (June 14-July 2, 1997). ... Released by Marlins (December 12, 1997). ... Signed by Philadelphia Phillies (December 26, 1997).
STATISTICAL NOTES: Led Midwest League shortstops with 655 total chances and 83 double plays in 1989. ... Led Southern League shortstops with 583 total chances and 81 double plays in 1991.

Year Team (League)	Pos.	G	AB	R	H	2B	3B	HR	RBI	Avg.	BB	SO	SB	PO	A	E	Avg.
1987—Wytheville (App.)........	SS-3B	61	233	41	69	7	0	0	24	.296	27	29	16	77	141	16	.932
1988—Char., W.Va. (SAL)......	SS-3B-2B	127	472	57	122	12	1	0	33	.258	54	44	41	184	396	32	.948
1989—Peoria (Midwest)........	SS	*136	506	74	140	10	*11	2	64	.277	49	67	31	*210	*408	37	.944
1990—Charlotte (Southern) ..	SS	119	419	55	103	16	3	4	38	.246	42	53	12	171	284	*42	.915
1991—Charlotte (Southern) ..	SS	134	488	69	134	26	0	4	47	.275	47	42	23	*203	*351	29	*.950
1992—Iowa (Am. Assoc.)......	SS-2B	106	409	52	114	23	3	5	40	.279	44	27	14	183	290	14	.971
—Chicago (N.L.)	SS	32	99	14	29	6	0	0	7	.293	11	13	0	43	74	4	.967
1993—Florida (N.L.)■............	2B-3B-SS	96	249	27	67	5	1	2	20	.269	27	18	1	94	144	6	.975
1994—Florida (N.L.)............	SS-3B	59	113	4	27	5	0	0	15	.239	9	19	0	37	51	2	.978
1995—Florida (N.L.)............	SS-3B-2B	94	216	22	58	9	2	3	26	.269	22	20	1	57	127	9	.953
1996—Florida (N.L.)............	3-S-1-2	100	224	27	62	11	2	3	26	.277	17	28	2	48	127	7	.962
1997—Florida (N.L.)............	3B-SS	74	93	13	23	2	0	1	11	.247	12	12	0	26	38	2	.970
Major league totals (6 years)		455	994	107	266	38	5	9	105	.268	98	110	4	305	561	30	.967

DIVISION SERIES RECORD

					BATTING								FIELDING		
Year Team (League)	Pos.	G	AB	R	H	2B	3B	HR	RBI	Avg.	BB	SO	SB	PO	A	E	Avg.
1997—Florida (N.L.).............	PH	1	1	0	1	0	0	0	1	1.000	0	0	0	0	0	0	...

CHAMPIONSHIP SERIES RECORD

					BATTING								FIELDING		
Year Team (League)	Pos.	G	AB	R	H	2B	3B	HR	RBI	Avg.	BB	SO	SB	PO	A	E	Avg.
1997—Florida (N.L.).............	3B-PH	3	1	0	1	0	0	0	0	1.000	0	0	0	0	0	0	...

WORLD SERIES RECORD

NOTES: Member of World Series championship team (1997).

					BATTING								FIELDING		
Year Team (League)	Pos.	G	AB	R	H	2B	3B	HR	RBI	Avg.	BB	SO	SB	PO	A	E	Avg.
1997—Florida (N.L.).............	3B-PR	2	1	1	0	0	0	0	0	.000	0	0	0	0	0	0	...

ARIAS, GEORGE   3B   PADRES

PERSONAL: Born March 12, 1972, in Tucson, Ariz. ... 5-11/190. ... Bats right, throws right. ... Full name: George Albert Arias.
HIGH SCHOOL: Pueblo (Tucson, Ariz.).
JUNIOR COLLEGE: Pima Community College (Ariz.).
COLLEGE: Arizona.
TRANSACTIONS/CAREER NOTES: Selected by California Angels organization in seventh round of free-agent draft (June 3, 1993). ... Angels franchise renamed Anaheim Angels for 1997 season. ... Traded by Angels to San Diego Padres (August 19, 1997), completing deal in which Padres traded OF Rickey Henderson to Anaheim Angels for P Ryan Hancock, P Stevenson Agosto and a player to be named later (August 13, 1997).
STATISTICAL NOTES: Led California League third basemen with 467 total chances and 27 double plays in 1994. ... Led Pacific Coast League third basemen with 99 putouts in 1997.

					BATTING								FIELDING		
Year Team (League)	Pos.	G	AB	R	H	2B	3B	HR	RBI	Avg.	BB	SO	SB	PO	A	E	Avg.
1993—Cedar Rap. (Midw.)	3B-SS	74	253	31	55	13	3	9	41	.217	31	65	6	59	159	23	.905
1994—Lake Elsinore (Calif.) ..	3B	•134	514	89	144	28	3	23	80	.280	58	111	6	*122	*313	*32	.931
1995—Midland (Texas)..........	3B-SS	134	520	91	145	19	10	30	104	.279	63	119	3	128	300	29	.937
1996—California (A.L.)..........	3B-DH	84	252	19	60	8	1	6	28	.238	16	50	2	50	190	10	.960
—Vancouver (PCL)	3B	59	243	49	82	24	0	9	55	.337	20	38	2	50	135	6	.969
1997—Vancouver (PCL)	3B-SS	105	401	71	112	28	3	11	60	.279	39	51	3	96	213	14	.957
—Anaheim (A.L.)..........	DH-3B	3	6	1	2	0	0	0	1	.333	0	0	0	0	3	0	1.000
—Las Vegas (PCL)■	3B	10	30	4	10	4	1	1	5	.333	3	8	0	§6	15	2	.913
—San Diego (N.L.)	3B	11	22	2	5	1	0	0	2	.227	0	1	0	4	12	1	.941
American League totals (2 years)		87	258	20	62	8	1	6	29	.240	16	50	2	50	193	10	.960
National League totals (1 year)		11	22	2	5	1	0	0	2	.227	0	1	0	4	12	1	.941
Major league totals (2 years)		98	280	22	67	9	1	6	31	.239	16	51	2	54	205	11	.959

AROCHA, RENE   P

PERSONAL: Born February 24, 1966, in Havana, Cuba. ... 6-0/180. ... Throws right, bats right.
HIGH SCHOOL: Regla (Cuba).
TRANSACTIONS/CAREER NOTES: Signed as non-drafted free agent by St. Louis Cardinals organization (November 21, 1991). ... On disabled list (April 21-May 13, 1993 and July 31, 1995-remainder of season). ... Traded by Cardinals to San Francisco Giants (February 12, 1997); completing deal in which Giants traded C Tom Lampkin to Cardinals for a player to be named later or cash (December 19, 1996). ... Released by Giants (August 6, 1997). ... Signed by Columbus, New York Yankees organization (August 15, 1997). ... Granted free agency (October 17, 1997).
HONORS: Named American Association Most Valuable Pitcher (1992).
MISCELLANEOUS: Member of Cuban national baseball team (1986-91). ... Invited to spring training by St. Louis Cardinals (February 3, 1997).

Year Team (League)	W	L	Pct.	ERA	G	GS	CG	ShO	Sv.	IP	H	R	ER	BB	SO
1992—Louisville (A.A.).................	•12	7	.632	2.70	25	25	3	1	0	166²/₃	145	59	50	65	128
1993—St. Louis (N.L.).................	11	8	.579	3.78	32	29	1	0	0	188	197	89	79	31	96
1994—St. Louis (N.L.).................	4	4	.500	4.01	45	7	1	1	11	83	94	42	37	21	62
1995—St. Louis (N.L.).................	3	5	.375	3.99	41	0	0	0	0	49²/₃	55	24	22	18	25
1997—Phoenix (PCL)■...............	7	3	.700	4.76	18	18	1	0	0	111²/₃	121	59	59	27	68
—San Francisco (N.L.)	0	0	...	11.32	6	0	0	0	0	10¹/₃	17	14	13	5	7
—Columbus (Int'l)■..............	1	0	1.000	1.86	4	1	0	0	0	9²/₃	7	2	2	2	10
Major league totals (4 years)......	18	17	.514	4.11	124	36	2	1	11	331	363	169	151	75	190

ARROJO, ROLANDO   P   DEVIL RAYS

PERSONAL: Born July 18, 1968, in Havana, Cuba. ... 6-4/215. ... Bats right, throws right.
TRANSACTIONS/CAREER NOTES: Signed as non-drafted free agent by Tampa Bay Devil Rays organization (April 21, 1997).
MISCELLANEOUS: Member of Cuban national baseball team (1986-96).

Year Team (League)	W	L	Pct.	ERA	G	GS	CG	ShO	Sv.	IP	H	R	ER	BB	SO
1997—St. Petersburg (FSL)	5	6	.455	3.43	16	16	4	1	0	89¹/₃	73	40	34	13	73

ARROYO, BRONSON — P — PIRATES

PERSONAL: Born February 24, 1977, in Key West, Fla. ... 6-5/165. ... Throws right, bats right. ... Full name: Bronson Anthony Arroyo.
HIGH SCHOOL: Hernando (Fla.).
TRANSACTIONS/CAREER NOTES: Selected by Pittsburgh Pirates organization in third round of free-agent draft (June 1, 1995). ... On suspended list (May 29-June 1, 1996).

Year Team (League)	W	L	Pct.	ERA	G	GS	CG	ShO	Sv.	IP	H	R	ER	BB	SO
1995— Bradenton Pirates (GCL)	5	4	.556	4.26	13	9	0	0	0	61 1/3	72	39	29	9	48
1996— Augusta (S. Atl.)................	8	6	.571	3.52	26	26	0	0	0	135 2/3	123	64	53	36	107
1997— Lynchburg (Caroline)	•12	4	.750	3.31	24	24	3	1	0	160 1/3	154	69	59	33	121

ASHBY, ANDY — P — PADRES

PERSONAL: Born July 11, 1967, in Kansas City, Mo. ... 6-5/190. ... Throws right, bats right. ... Full name: Andrew Jason Ashby.
HIGH SCHOOL: Park Hill (Kansas City, Mo.).
COLLEGE: Crowder College (Mo.).
TRANSACTIONS/CAREER NOTES: Signed as non-drafted free agent by Philadelphia Phillies organization (May 4, 1986). ... On Spartanburg disabled list (April 7-July 10, 1988). ... On Spartanburg disabled list (April 6-26, 1989). ... On Philadelphia disabled list (April 27-August 11, 1992); included rehabilitation assignments to Scranton/Wilkes-Barre (July 8-August 2 and August 6-10). ... Selected by Colorado Rockies in first round (25th pick overall) of expansion draft (November 17, 1992). ... Traded by Rockies to San Diego Padres (July 27, 1993), completing deal in which Padres traded P Bruce Hurst and P Greg W. Harris to Rockies for C Brad Ausmus, P Doug Bochtler and a player to be named later (July 26, 1993). ... On disabled list (June 6-22; June 29-July 15; July 27-September 1, 1996; and May 20-June 15, 1997).
RECORDS: Shares major league record by striking out side on nine pitches (June 15, 1991, fourth inning).
MISCELLANEOUS: Had sacrifice hit in only appearance as pinch-hitter (1996). ... Appeared in one game as pinch-runner (1997).

Year Team (League)	W	L	Pct.	ERA	G	GS	CG	ShO	Sv.	IP	H	R	ER	BB	SO
1986— Bend (Northwest)	1	2	.333	4.95	16	6	0	0	2	60	56	40	33	34	45
1987— Spartanburg (SAL)	4	6	.400	5.60	13	13	1	0	0	64 1/3	73	45	40	38	52
— Utica (N.Y.-Penn)..........	3	7	.300	4.05	13	13	0	0	0	60	56	38	27	36	51
1988— Spartanburg (SAL)	1	1	.500	2.70	3	3	0	0	0	16 2/3	13	7	5	7	16
— Batavia (N.Y.-Penn)	3	1	.750	1.61	6	6	2	1	0	44 2/3	25	11	8	16	32
1989— Spartanburg (SAL)	5	9	.357	2.87	17	17	3	1	0	106 2/3	95	48	34	49	100
— Clearwater (Fla. St.)......	1	4	.200	1.24	6	6	2	1	0	43 2/3	28	9	6	21	44
1990— Reading (Eastern)	10	7	.588	3.42	23	23	4	1	0	139 2/3	134	65	53	48	94
1991— Scran./W.B. (Int'l)	11	11	.500	3.46	26	26	•6	•3	0	161 1/3	144	78	62	60	113
— Philadelphia (N.L.)..........	1	5	.167	6.00	8	8	0	0	0	42	41	28	28	19	26
1992— Philadelphia (N.L.)..........	1	3	.250	7.54	10	8	0	0	0	37	42	31	31	21	24
— Scran./W.B. (Int'l)	0	3	.000	3.00	7	7	1	0	0	33	23	13	11	14	18
1993— Colorado (N.L.)■..............	0	4	.000	8.50	20	9	0	0	1	54	89	54	51	32	33
— Colo. Springs (PCL)	4	2	.667	4.10	7	6	1	0	0	41 2/3	45	25	19	12	35
— San Diego (N.L.)■..........	3	6	.333	5.48	12	12	0	0	0	69	79	46	42	24	44
1994— San Diego (N.L.)	6	11	.353	3.40	24	24	4	0	0	164 1/3	145	75	62	43	121
1995— San Diego (N.L.)	12	10	.545	2.94	31	•31	2	2	0	192 2/3	180	79	63	62	150
1996— San Diego (N.L.)	9	5	.643	3.23	24	24	1	0	0	150 2/3	147	60	54	34	85
1997— San Diego (N.L.)	9	11	.450	4.13	30	30	2	0	0	200 2/3	207	108	92	49	144
Major league totals (7 years)	41	55	.427	4.18	159	146	9	2	1	910 1/3	930	481	423	284	627

DIVISION SERIES RECORD

Year Team (League)	W	L	Pct.	ERA	G	GS	CG	ShO	Sv.	IP	H	R	ER	BB	SO
1996— San Diego (N.L.)	0	0	. . .	6.75	1	1	0	0	0	5 1/3	7	4	4	1	5

ASHLEY, BILLY — OF — DODGERS

PERSONAL: Born July 11, 1970, in Taylor, Mich. ... 6-7/235. ... Bats right, throws right. ... Full name: Billy Manual Ashley.
HIGH SCHOOL: Belleville (Mich.).
TRANSACTIONS/CAREER NOTES: Selected by Los Angeles Dodgers organization in third round of free-agent draft (June 1, 1988). ... On disabled list (April 10-May 1, May 19-31 and June 8-July 8, 1991). ... On Albuquerque disabled list (May 1-16, 1994). ... On Los Angeles disabled list (April 21-May 13, 1996); included rehabilitation assignments to Albuquerque (April 30-May 1 and May 7-13).
HONORS: Named Pacific Coast League Most Valuable Player (1994).
STATISTICAL NOTES: Led Texas League with .534 slugging percentage in 1992. ... Led Pacific Coast League with .701 slugging percentage and tied for lead with seven intentional bases on balls received in 1994.

Year Team (League)	Pos.	G	AB	R	H	2B	3B	HR	RBI	Avg.	BB	SO	SB	PO	A	E	Avg.
1988— GC Dodgers (GCL)	OF	9	26	3	4	0	0	0	0	.154	1	9	1	8	2	0	1.000
1989— GC Dodgers (GCL)	OF	48	160	23	38	6	2	1	19	.238	19	42	16	50	3	5	.914
1990— Bakersfield (Calif.)......	OF	99	331	48	72	13	1	9	40	.218	25	135	17	122	3	10	.926
1991— Vero Beach (FSL)	OF	61	206	18	52	11	2	7	42	.252	7	69	9	39	1	0	1.000
1992— San Antonio (Tex.)	OF-1B	101	380	60	106	23	1	*24	66	.279	16	111	13	129	9	3	.979
— Albuquerque (PCL).....	OF	25	95	11	20	7	0	2	10	.211	6	42	1	39	1	2	.952
— Los Angeles (N.L.).....	OF	29	95	6	21	5	0	2	6	.221	5	34	0	34	2	6	.857
1993— Albuquerque (PCL).....	OF	125	482	88	143	31	4	26	*100	.297	35	*143	6	211	7	*11	.952
— Los Angeles (N.L.).....	OF	14	37	0	9	0	0	0	0	.243	2	11	0	11	3	0	1.000
1994— Los Angeles (N.L.).....	OF	2	6	0	2	1	0	0	0	.333	0	2	0	3	0	0	1.000
— Albuquerque (PCL).....	OF	107	388	93	134	19	4	*37	105	.345	53	116	6	119	2	12	.910
1995— Los Angeles (N.L.).....	OF	81	215	17	51	5	0	8	27	.237	25	88	0	102	2	3	.972
1996— Los Angeles (N.L.).....	OF	71	110	18	22	2	1	9	25	.200	21	44	0	38	2	2	.952
— Albuquerque (PCL).....	OF	7	23	6	8	1	0	1	9	.348	7	9	1	11	0	1	.917
1997— Los Angeles (N.L.)	OF	71	131	12	32	7	0	6	19	.244	8	46	0	39	2	4	.911
Major league totals (6 years)		268	594	53	137	20	1	25	77	.231	61	225	0	227	11	15	.941

Year Team (League)	Pos.	G	AB	R	H	2B	3B	HR	RBI	Avg.	BB	SO	SB	PO	A	E	Avg.
1995— Los Angeles (N.L.)	PH	1	0	0	0	0	0	0	0	...	1	0	0	...	...	...	...
1996— Los Angeles (N.L.)	PH	2	2	0	0	0	0	0	0	.000	0	2	0	0	0	0	...
Division series totals (2 years)		3	2	0	0	0	0	0	0	.000	1	2	0	0	0	0	...

ASSENMACHER, PAUL — P — INDIANS

PERSONAL: Born December 10, 1960, in Allen Park, Mich. ... 6-3/210. ... Throws left, bats left. ... Full name: Paul Andre Assenmacher. ... Name pronounced AHSS-en-mahk-ur.
HIGH SCHOOL: Aquinas (Southgate, Mich.).
COLLEGE: Aquinas, Mich. (degree in business administration).
TRANSACTIONS/CAREER NOTES: Signed as non-drafted free agent by Atlanta Braves organization (July 10, 1983). ... On Atlanta disabled list (April 29-May 9, 1987 and August 10-25, 1988). ... Traded by Braves organization to Chicago Cubs for two players to be named later (August 24, 1989); Braves acquired C Kelly Mann and P Pat Gomez to complete deal (September 1, 1989). ... On disabled list (May 19-June 4, 1992). ... Traded by Cubs to New York Yankees as part of a three-way deal in which Yankees sent P John Habyan to Kansas City Royals and Royals sent OF Tuffy Rhodes to Cubs (July 30, 1993). ... Traded by Yankees to Chicago White Sox for P Brian Boehringer (March 21, 1994). ... Granted free agency (October 24, 1994). ... Signed by Cleveland Indians (April 10, 1995). ... Granted free agency (November 3, 1997). ... Re-signed by Indians (November 12, 1997).
RECORDS: Shares major league record for most strikeouts in one inning—4 (August 22, 1989, fifth inning).

Year Team (League)	W	L	Pct.	ERA	G	GS	CG	ShO	Sv.	IP	H	R	ER	BB	SO
1983— GC Braves (GCL)	1	0	1.000	2.21	10	3	1	1	2	36²/₃	35	14	9	4	44
1984— Durham (Carolina).............	6	11	.353	4.28	26	24	3	1	0	147¹/₃	153	78	70	52	147
1985— Durham (Carolina).............	3	2	.600	3.29	14	0	0	0	1	38¹/₃	38	16	14	13	36
— Greenville (Southern)	6	0	1.000	2.56	29	0	0	0	4	52²/₃	47	16	15	11	59
1986— Atlanta (N.L.)	7	3	.700	2.50	61	0	0	0	7	68¹/₃	61	23	19	26	56
1987— Atlanta (N.L.)	1	1	.500	5.10	52	0	0	0	2	54²/₃	58	41	31	24	39
— Richmond (Int'l)	1	2	.333	3.65	4	4	0	0	0	24²/₃	30	11	10	8	21
1988— Atlanta (N.L.)	8	7	.533	3.06	64	0	0	0	5	79¹/₃	72	28	27	32	71
1989— Atlanta (N.L.)	1	3	.250	3.59	49	0	0	0	0	57²/₃	55	26	23	16	64
— Chicago (N.L.)■	2	1	.667	5.21	14	0	0	0	0	19	19	11	11	12	15
1990— Chicago (N.L.)	7	2	.778	2.80	74	1	0	0	10	103	90	33	32	36	95
1991— Chicago (N.L.)	7	8	.467	3.24	75	0	0	0	15	102²/₃	85	41	37	31	117
1992— Chicago (N.L.)	4	4	.500	4.10	70	0	0	0	8	68	72	32	31	26	67
1993— Chicago (N.L.)	2	1	.667	3.49	46	0	0	0	0	38²/₃	44	15	15	13	34
— New York (A.L.)■	2	2	.500	3.12	26	0	0	0	0	17¹/₃	10	6	6	9	11
1994— Chicago (A.L.)■	1	2	.333	3.55	44	0	0	0	1	33	26	13	13	13	29
1995— Cleveland (A.L.)■	6	2	.750	2.82	47	0	0	0	0	38¹/₃	32	13	12	12	40
1996— Cleveland (A.L.)	4	2	.667	3.09	63	0	0	0	1	46²/₃	46	18	16	14	44
1997— Cleveland (A.L.)	5	0	1.000	2.94	75	0	0	0	4	49	43	17	16	15	53
A.L. totals (5 years)	18	8	.692	3.08	255	0	0	0	6	184¹/₃	157	67	63	63	177
N.L. totals (8 years)	39	30	.565	3.44	505	1	0	0	47	591¹/₃	556	250	226	216	558
Major league totals (12 years)....	57	38	.600	3.35	760	1	0	0	53	775²/₃	713	317	289	279	735

RECORDS: Holds career record for most games pitcher—10.

DIVISION SERIES RECORD

Year Team (League)	W	L	Pct.	ERA	G	GS	CG	ShO	Sv.	IP	H	R	ER	BB	SO
1995— Cleveland (A.L.)	0	0	...	0.00	3	0	0	0	0	1²/₃	0	0	0	0	3
1996— Cleveland (A.L.)	1	0	1.000	0.00	3	0	0	0	0	1²/₃	0	0	0	2	2
1997— Cleveland (A.L.)	0	0	...	5.40	4	0	0	0	0	3¹/₃	2	2	2	2	2
Div. series totals (3 years)	1	0	1.000	2.70	10	0	0	0	0	6²/₃	2	2	2	4	7

CHAMPIONSHIP SERIES RECORD

Year Team (League)	W	L	Pct.	ERA	G	GS	CG	ShO	Sv.	IP	H	R	ER	BB	SO
1989— Chicago (N.L.)	0	0	...	13.50	2	0	0	0	0	²/₃	3	1	1	0	0
1995— Cleveland (A.L.)	0	0	...	0.00	3	0	0	0	0	1¹/₃	0	0	0	1	2
1997— Cleveland (A.L.)	1	0	1.000	9.00	5	0	0	0	0	2	5	2	2	1	3
Champ. series totals (3 years)	1	0	1.000	6.75	10	0	0	0	0	4	8	3	3	2	5

WORLD SERIES RECORD

Year Team (League)	W	L	Pct.	ERA	G	GS	CG	ShO	Sv.	IP	H	R	ER	BB	SO
1995— Cleveland (A.L.)	0	0	...	6.75	4	0	0	0	0	1¹/₃	1	2	1	3	3
1997— Cleveland (A.L.)	0	0	...	0.00	5	0	0	0	0	4	5	0	0	0	6
World Series totals (2 years)	0	0	...	1.69	9	0	0	0	0	5¹/₃	6	2	1	3	9

ASTACIO, PEDRO — P — ROCKIES

PERSONAL: Born November 28, 1969, in Hato Mayor, Dominican Republic. ... 6-2/195. ... Throws right, bats right. ... Full name: Pedro Julio Astacio. ... Name pronounced ah-STA-see-oh.
HIGH SCHOOL: Pilar Rondon (Dominican Republic).
TRANSACTIONS/CAREER NOTES: Signed as non-drafted free agent by Los Angeles Dodgers organization (November 21, 1987). ... On Albuquerque disabled list (April 26-May 21, 1992). ... Traded by Dodgers to Colorado Rockies for 2B Eric Young (August 19, 1997).
STATISTICAL NOTES: Led N.L. with nine balks in 1993.

Year Team (League)	W	L	Pct.	ERA	G	GS	CG	ShO	Sv.	IP	H	R	ER	BB	SO
1989— GC Dodgers (GCL)	7	3	.700	3.17	12	12	1	•1	0	76²/₃	77	30	27	12	52
1990— Vero Beach (FSL)	1	5	.167	6.32	8	8	0	0	0	47	54	39	33	23	41
— Yakima (N'west)	2	0	1.000	1.74	3	3	0	0	0	20²/₃	9	8	4	4	22
— Bakersfield (California).......	5	2	.714	2.77	10	7	1	0	0	52	46	22	16	15	34
1991— Vero Beach (FSL)	5	3	.625	1.67	9	9	3	1	0	59¹/₃	44	19	11	8	45
— San Antonio (Tex.)	4	11	.267	4.78	19	19	2	1	0	113	142	67	60	39	62

Year Team (League)	W	L	Pct.	ERA	G	GS	CG	ShO	Sv.	IP	H	R	ER	BB	SO
1992—Albuquerque (PCL)............	6	6	.500	5.47	24	15	1	0	0	98 2/3	115	68	60	44	66
—Los Angeles (N.L.)	5	5	.500	1.98	11	11	4	4	0	82	80	23	18	20	43
1993—Los Angeles (N.L.)	14	9	.609	3.57	31	31	3	2	0	186 1/3	165	80	74	68	122
1994—Los Angeles (N.L.)	6	8	.429	4.29	23	23	3	1	0	149	142	77	71	47	108
1995—Los Angeles (N.L.)	7	8	.467	4.24	48	11	1	1	0	104	103	53	49	29	80
1996—Los Angeles (N.L.)	9	8	.529	3.44	35	32	0	0	0	211 2/3	207	86	81	67	130
1997—Los Angeles (N.L.)	7	9	.438	4.10	26	24	2	1	0	153 2/3	151	75	70	47	115
—Colorado (N.L.)■	5	1	.833	4.25	7	7	0	0	0	48 2/3	49	23	23	14	51
Major league totals (6 years).....	**53**	**48**	**.525**	**3.71**	**181**	**139**	**13**	**9**	**0**	**935 1/3**	**897**	**417**	**386**	**292**	**649**

DIVISION SERIES RECORD

Year Team (League)	W	L	Pct.	ERA	G	GS	CG	ShO	Sv.	IP	H	R	ER	BB	SO
1995—Los Angeles (N.L.)	0	0	...	0.00	3	0	0	0	0	3 1/3	1	0	0	0	5
1996—Los Angeles (N.L.)	0	0	...	0.00	1	0	0	0	0	1 2/3	0	0	0	0	1
Div. series totals (2 years)	**0**	**0**	**...**	**0.00**	**4**	**0**	**0**	**0**	**0**	**5**	**1**	**0**	**0**	**0**	**6**

ATCHLEY, JUSTIN — P — REDS

PERSONAL: Born September 5, 1973, in Sedro Woolley, Wash. ... 6-3/200. ... Throws left, bats left. ... Full name: Justin Scott Atchley.
HIGH SCHOOL: Sedro Woolley (Wash.).
JUNIOR COLLEGE: Walla Walla.
COLLEGE: Texas A&M.
TRANSACTIONS/CAREER NOTES: Selected by San Diego Padres organization in 15th round of free-agent draft (June 3, 1991); did not sign. ... Selected by Atlanta Braves organization in sixth round of free-agent draft (June 1, 1992); did not sign. ... Selected by Cincinnati Reds organization in 12th round of free-agent draft (June 1, 1995).

Year Team (League)	W	L	Pct.	ERA	G	GS	CG	ShO	Sv.	IP	H	R	ER	BB	SO
1995—Billings (Pioneer)................	*10	0	*1.000	3.51	13	13	0	0	0	77	91	33	30	20	65
1996—Char., W.Va. (S. Atl.)	3	3	.500	3.46	17	16	0	0	1	91	98	42	35	23	78
—Win.-Salem (Car.)...............	3	3	.500	5.09	12	12	0	0	0	69	74	48	39	16	50
1997—Chattanooga (Southern)	4	2	.667	4.70	13	13	1	0	0	67	75	45	35	14	48

AURILIA, RICH — SS — GIANTS

PERSONAL: Born September 2, 1971, in Brooklyn, N.Y. ... 6-1/182. ... Bats right, throws right. ... Full name: Richard Aurilia.
HIGH SCHOOL: Xaverian (Brooklyn, N.Y.).
COLLEGE: St. John's.
TRANSACTIONS/CAREER NOTES: Selected by Texas Rangers organization in 24th round of free-agent draft (June 1, 1992). ... On disabled list (April 9-16, 1993). ... Traded by Rangers with IF/OF Desi Wilson to San Francisco Giants organization for P John Burkett (December 22, 1994). ... On San Francisco disabled list (September 24, 1996-remainder of season).
STATISTICAL NOTES: Led Texas League shortstops with 635 total chances and tied for lead with 82 double plays in 1994. ... Career major league grand slams: 1.

Year Team (League)	Pos.	G	AB	R	H	2B	3B	HR	RBI	Avg.	BB	SO	SB	PO	A	E	Avg.
1992—Butte (Pioneer)..........	SS	59	202	37	68	11	3	3	30	.337	42	18	13	78	154	14	*.943
1993—Charlotte (Fla. St.)......	SS	122	440	80	136	16	5	5	56	.309	75	57	15	200	445	24	.964
1994—Tulsa (Texas)	SS	129	458	67	107	18	6	12	57	.234	53	74	10	*237	374	24	*.962
1995—Shreveport (Texas)■..	SS	64	226	29	74	17	1	4	42	.327	27	26	10	122	237	14	.962
—Phoenix (PCL).............	SS	71	258	42	72	12	0	5	34	.279	35	29	2	104	246	9	.975
—San Francisco (N.L.) ..	SS	9	19	4	9	3	0	2	4	.474	1	2	1	8	16	0	1.000
1996—Phoenix (PCL)..........	SS-2B	7	30	9	13	7	0	0	4	.433	2	3	1	10	25	1	.972
—San Francisco (N.L.) ..	SS-2B	105	318	27	76	7	1	3	26	.239	25	52	4	142	246	10	.975
1997—San Francisco (N.L.) ..	SS	46	102	16	28	8	0	5	19	.275	8	15	1	47	91	3	.979
—Phoenix (PCL)..........	SS	8	34	9	10	2	0	1	5	.294	5	4	2	14	22	0	1.000
Major league totals (3 years)		**160**	**439**	**47**	**113**	**18**	**1**	**10**	**49**	**.257**	**34**	**69**	**6**	**197**	**353**	**13**	**.977**

AUSMUS, BRAD — C — ASTROS

PERSONAL: Born April 14, 1969, in New Haven, Conn. ... 5-11/190. ... Bats right, throws right. ... Full name: Bradley David Ausmus.
HIGH SCHOOL: Cheshire (Conn.).
COLLEGE: Dartmouth.
TRANSACTIONS/CAREER NOTES: Selected by New York Yankees organization in 47th round of free-agent draft (June 2, 1987). ... Selected by Colorado Rockies in third round (54th pick overall) of expansion draft (November 17, 1992). ... Traded by Rockies with P Doug Bochtler and a player to be named later to San Diego Padres for P Bruce Hurst and P Greg W. Harris (July 26, 1993); Padres acquired P Andy Ashby to complete deal (July 27, 1993). ... Traded by Padres with SS Andujar Cedeno and P Russ Spear to Detroit Tigers for C John Flaherty and SS Chris Gomez (June 18, 1996). ... On Detroit suspended list (September 4-5, 1996). ... Traded by Tigers with P Jose Lima, P C.J. Nitkowski, P Trever Miller and IF Daryle Ward to Houston Astros for OF Brian L. Hunter, IF Orlando Miller, P Doug Brocail, P Todd Jones and a player to be named later (December 10, 1996).
STATISTICAL NOTES: Led Gulf Coast League catchers with 434 total chances in 1988. ... Led International League catchers with 666 putouts and 738 total chances in 1992. ... Led N.L. catchers with 683 putouts and 749 total chances in 1994. ... Led N.L. catchers with 14 double plays in 1995. ... Tied for N.L. lead in assists by catcher with 63 in 1995. ... Career major league grand slams: 1.

Year Team (League)	Pos.	G	AB	R	H	2B	3B	HR	RBI	Avg.	BB	SO	SB	PO	A	E	Avg.
1988—Oneonta (NYP)..........	C	2	4	0	1	0	0	0	0	.250	0	2	0	0	0	0	...
—Sarasota (Fla. St.)	C	43	133	22	34	2	0	0	15	.256	11	25	5	*378	*47	9	.979
1989—Oneonta (NYP)	C-3B	52	165	29	43	6	0	1	18	.261	22	28	6	401	43	7	.984
1990—Prince William (Car.)..	C	107	364	46	86	12	2	0	27	.236	32	73	2	662	84	5	*.993
1991—Prince William (Car.)..	C	63	230	28	70	14	3	2	30	.304	24	37	17	419	54	5	.990
—Alb./Colon. (Eastern)..	C	67	229	36	61	9	2	1	29	.266	27	36	14	470	56	4	.992

Year Team (League)	Pos.	G	AB	R	H	2B	3B	HR	RBI	Avg.	BB	SO	SB	PO	A	E	Avg.
1992—Alb./Colon. (Eastern)..	C	5	18	0	3	0	1	0	1	.167	2	3	2	30	2	1	.970
—Columbus (Int'l)........	C-OF	111	364	48	88	14	3	2	35	.242	40	56	19	†666	63	9	.988
1993—Colo. Springs (PCL)■	C-OF	76	241	31	65	10	4	2	33	.270	27	41	10	393	57	6	.987
—San Diego (N.L.)■.....	C	49	160	18	41	8	1	5	12	.256	6	28	2	272	34	8	.975
1994—San Diego (N.L.)........	C-1B	101	327	45	82	12	1	7	24	.251	30	63	5	†686	59	7	.991
1995—San Diego (N.L.)........	C-1B	103	328	44	96	16	4	5	34	.293	31	56	16	656	†63	6	.992
1996—San Diego (N.L.)........	C	50	149	16	27	4	0	1	13	.181	13	27	1	300	22	6	.982
—Detroit (A.L.)■........	C	75	226	30	56	12	0	4	22	.248	26	45	3	452	35	4	.992
1997—Houston (N.L.)■........	C	130	425	45	113	25	1	4	44	.266	38	78	14	807	73	7	.992
American League totals (1 year)		75	226	30	56	12	0	4	22	.248	26	45	3	452	35	4	.992
National League totals (5 years)		433	1389	168	359	65	7	22	127	.258	118	252	38	2721	251	34	.989
Major league totals (5 years)		508	1615	198	415	77	7	26	149	.257	144	297	41	3173	286	38	.989

DIVISION SERIES RECORD

Year Team (League)	Pos.	G	AB	R	H	2B	3B	HR	RBI	Avg.	BB	SO	SB	PO	A	E	Avg.
1997—Houston (N.L.)	C	2	5	1	2	1	0	0	2	.400	0	1	0	13	0	0	1.000

AVEN, BRUCE OF INDIANS

PERSONAL: Born March 4, 1972, in Orange, Texas. ... 5-9/180. ... Bats right, throws right. ... Full name: David Bruce Aven.
HIGH SCHOOL: West Orange-Stark (Orange, Texas).
COLLEGE: Lamar.
TRANSACTIONS/CAREER NOTES: Selected by Cleveland Indians organization in 30th round of free-agent draft (June 2, 1994).
STATISTICAL NOTES: Led Eastern League outfielders with 289 total chances in 1996. ... Tied for American Association lead in being hit by pitch with 11 in 1997.

Year Team (League)	Pos.	G	AB	R	H	2B	3B	HR	RBI	Avg.	BB	SO	SB	PO	A	E	Avg.
1994—Watertown (NYP)	OF	61	220	49	73	14	5	5	33	.332	20	45	12	88	6	1	.989
1995—Kinston (Carolina)	OF	130	479	70	125	23	5	23	69	.261	41	109	15	158	11	3	.983
1996—Cant./Akr. (Eastern)	OF	131	481	91	143	31	4	23	79	.297	43	101	22	280	3	6	.979
—Buffalo (A.A.).............	OF	3	9	5	6	0	0	1	2	.667	1	1	0	7	0	0	1.000
1997—Buffalo (A.A.).............	OF	121	432	69	124	27	3	17	77	.287	50	99	10	219	3	2	.991
—Cleveland (A.L.)..........	OF	13	19	4	4	1	0	0	2	.211	1	5	0	15	1	0	1.000
Major league totals (1 year)		13	19	4	4	1	0	0	2	.211	1	5	0	15	1	0	1.000

AVERY, STEVE P RED SOX

PERSONAL: Born April 14, 1970, in Trenton, Mich. ... 6-4/205. ... Throws left, bats left. ... Full name: Steven Thomas Avery. ... Son of Ken Avery, minor league pitcher (1962-63).
HIGH SCHOOL: John F. Kennedy (Taylor, Mich.).
TRANSACTIONS/CAREER NOTES: Selected by Atlanta Braves organization in first round (third pick overall) of free-agent draft (June 1, 1988). ... On Atlanta disabled list (July 13-September 2, 1996); included rehabilitation assignment to Greenville (August 12-18). ... On Boston disabled list (May 4-July 5, 1997); included rehabilitation assignments to Sarasota (June 12-25) and Gulf Coast Red Sox (June 25-July 5). ... Granted free agency (October 31, 1996). ... Signed by Boston Red Sox (January 22, 1997).
HONORS: Named lefthanded pitcher on THE SPORTING NEWS N.L. All-Star team (1993).
MISCELLANEOUS: Received base on balls in only appearance as pinch-hitter and appeared in one game as pinch-runner (1991). ... Appeared in one game as pinch-runner (1997).

Year Team (League)	W	L	Pct.	ERA	G	GS	CG	ShO	Sv.	IP	H	R	ER	BB	SO
1988—Pulaski (Appalachian)........	7	1	.875	1.50	10	10	3	•2	0	66	38	16	11	19	80
1989—Durham (Carolina)............	6	4	.600	1.45	13	13	3	1	0	86²/₃	59	22	14	20	90
—Greenville (Southern)	6	3	.667	2.77	13	13	1	0	0	84¹/₃	68	32	26	34	75
1990—Richmond (Int'l)...............	5	5	.500	3.39	13	13	3	0	0	82¹/₃	85	35	31	21	69
—Atlanta (N.L.).....................	3	11	.214	5.64	21	20	1	1	0	99	121	79	62	45	75
1991—Atlanta (N.L.).....................	18	8	.692	3.38	35	35	3	1	0	210¹/₃	189	89	79	65	137
1992—Atlanta (N.L.).....................	11	11	.500	3.20	35	•35	2	2	0	233²/₃	216	95	83	71	129
1993—Atlanta (N.L.).....................	18	6	.750	2.94	35	35	3	1	0	223¹/₃	216	81	73	43	125
1994—Atlanta (N.L.).....................	8	3	.727	4.04	24	24	1	0	0	151²/₃	127	71	68	55	122
1995—Atlanta (N.L.).....................	7	13	.350	4.67	29	29	3	1	0	173¹/₃	165	92	90	52	141
1996—Atlanta (N.L.).....................	7	10	.412	4.47	24	23	1	0	0	131	146	70	65	40	86
—Greenville (Southern)	0	0	. . .	0.00	1	1	0	0	0	²/₃	0	0	0	0	0
1997—Boston (A.L.)....................	6	7	.462	6.42	22	18	0	0	0	96²/₃	127	76	69	49	51
—Sarasota (Florida State)......	0	0	. . .	0.00	1	1	0	0	0	3	2	0	0	1	3
—GC Red Sox (GCL)	0	0	. . .	1.50	1	1	0	0	0	6	5	3	1	0	8
—Pawtucket (Int'l)................	1	0	1.000	0.00	1	1	0	0	0	5	1	0	0	3	1
A.L. totals (1 year)	6	7	.462	6.42	22	18	0	0	0	96²/₃	127	76	69	49	51
N.L. totals (7 years)	72	62	.537	3.83	203	201	14	6	0	1222¹/₃	1180	577	520	371	815
Major league totals (8 years)......	78	69	.531	4.02	225	219	14	6	0	1319	1307	653	589	420	866

DIVISION SERIES RECORD

Year Team (League)	W	L	Pct.	ERA	G	GS	CG	ShO	Sv.	IP	H	R	ER	BB	SO
1995—Atlanta (N.L.).....................	0	0	. . .	13.50	1	0	0	0	0	²/₃	1	1	1	0	1

CHAMPIONSHIP SERIES RECORD

RECORDS: Holds career record for most consecutive scoreless innings—22¹/₃ (1991-92). ... Holds single-series record for most consecutive scoreless innings—16¹/₃ (1991).
NOTES: Named N.L. Championship Series Most Valuable Player (1991).

Year Team (League)	W	L	Pct.	ERA	G	GS	CG	ShO	Sv.	IP	H	R	ER	BB	SO
1991—Atlanta (N.L.)	2	0	1.000	0.00	2	2	0	0	0	16 1/3	9	0	0	4	17
1992—Atlanta (N.L.)	1	1	.500	9.00	3	2	0	0	0	8	13	8	8	2	3
1993—Atlanta (N.L.)	0	0	...	2.77	2	2	0	0	0	13	9	5	4	6	10
1995—Atlanta (N.L.)	1	0	1.000	0.00	2	1	0	0	0	6	2	0	0	4	6
1996—Atlanta (N.L.)	0	0	...	0.00	2	0	0	0	0	2	2	0	0	1	1
Champ. series totals (5 years)	4	1	.800	2.38	11	7	0	0	0	45 1/3	35	13	12	17	37

WORLD SERIES RECORD

NOTES: Member of World Series championship team (1995).

Year Team (League)	W	L	Pct.	ERA	G	GS	CG	ShO	Sv.	IP	H	R	ER	BB	SO
1991—Atlanta (N.L.)	0	0	...	3.46	2	2	0	0	0	13	10	6	5	1	8
1992—Atlanta (N.L.)	0	1	.000	3.75	2	2	0	0	0	12	11	5	5	3	11
1995—Atlanta (N.L.)	1	0	1.000	1.50	1	1	0	0	0	6	3	1	1	5	3
1996—Atlanta (N.L.)	0	1	.000	13.50	1	0	0	0	0	2/3	1	2	1	4	0
World Series totals (4 years)	1	2	.333	3.41	6	5	0	0	0	31 2/3	25	14	12	13	22

ALL-STAR GAME RECORD

Year League	W	L	Pct.	ERA	GS	CG	ShO	Sv.	IP	H	R	ER	BB	SO
1993—National	0	0	...	0.00	0	0	0	0	1	1	3	0	1	1

AYALA, BOBBY   P   MARINERS

PERSONAL: Born July 8, 1969, in Ventura, Calif. ... 6-3/210. ... Throws right, bats right. ... Full name: Robert Joseph Ayala. ... Name pronounced eye-YAH-luh.
HIGH SCHOOL: Rio Mesa (Oxnard, Calif.).
TRANSACTIONS/CAREER NOTES: Signed as non-drafted free agent by Cincinnati Reds organization (June 27, 1988). ... Traded by Reds with C Dan Wilson to Seattle Mariners for P Erik Hanson and 2B Bret Boone (November 2, 1993). ... On Seattle disabled list (April 23-June 20, 1996); included rehabilitation assignments to Port City (June 6-8) and Tacoma (June 16-20).

Year Team (League)	W	L	Pct.	ERA	G	GS	CG	ShO	Sv.	IP	H	R	ER	BB	SO
1988—GC Reds (GCL)	0	4	.000	3.82	20	0	0	0	3	33	34	23	14	12	24
1989—Greensboro (S. Atl.)	5	8	.385	4.10	22	19	1	0	0	105 1/3	97	73	48	50	70
1990—Cedar Rapids (Midw.)	3	2	.600	3.38	18	7	3	1	1	53 1/3	40	24	20	18	59
—Char., W.Va. (S. Atl.)	6	1	.857	2.43	21	4	2	1	2	74	48	23	20	21	73
1991—Chattanooga (Southern)	3	1	.750	4.67	39	8	1	0	4	90 2/3	79	52	47	58	92
1992—Chattanooga (Southern)	12	6	.667	3.54	27	27	3	3	0	162 2/3	152	75	64	58	154
—Cincinnati (N.L.)	2	1	.667	4.34	5	5	0	0	0	29	33	15	14	13	23
1993—Indianapolis (A.A.)	0	2	.000	5.67	5	5	0	0	0	27	36	19	17	12	19
—Cincinnati (N.L.)	7	10	.412	5.60	43	9	0	0	3	98	106	72	61	45	65
1994—Seattle (A.L.)■	4	3	.571	2.86	46	0	0	0	18	56 2/3	42	25	18	26	76
1995—Seattle (A.L.)	6	5	.545	4.44	63	0	0	0	19	71	73	42	35	30	77
1996—Seattle (A.L.)	6	3	.667	5.88	50	0	0	0	3	67 1/3	65	45	44	25	61
—Port City (Southern)	0	0	...	0.00	2	1	0	0	0	1 2/3	0	0	0	1	2
—Tacoma (PCL)	0	0	...	0.00	1	1	0	0	0	1	0	0	0	1	1
1997—Seattle (A.L.)	10	5	.667	3.82	71	0	0	0	8	96 2/3	91	45	41	41	92
A.L. totals (4 years)	26	16	.619	4.26	230	0	0	0	48	291 2/3	271	157	138	122	306
N.L. totals (2 years)	9	11	.450	5.31	48	14	0	0	3	127	139	87	75	58	88
Major league totals (6 years)	35	27	.565	4.58	278	14	0	0	51	418 2/3	410	244	213	180	394

DIVISION SERIES RECORD

Year Team (League)	W	L	Pct.	ERA	G	GS	CG	ShO	Sv.	IP	H	R	ER	BB	SO
1995—Seattle (A.L.)	0	0	...	54.00	2	0	0	0	0	2/3	6	4	4	1	0
1997—Seattle (A.L.)	0	0	...	40.50	1	0	0	0	0	1 1/3	4	6	6	3	2
Div. series totals (2 years)	0	0	...	45.00	3	0	0	0	0	2	10	10	10	4	2

CHAMPIONSHIP SERIES RECORD

Year Team (League)	W	L	Pct.	ERA	G	GS	CG	ShO	Sv.	IP	H	R	ER	BB	SO
1995—Seattle (A.L.)	0	0	...	2.45	2	0	0	0	0	3 2/3	3	1	1	3	3

AYBAR, MANNY   P   CARDINALS

PERSONAL: Born October 5, 1974, in Bani, Dominican Republic. ... 6-1/165. ... Throws right, bats right. ... Full name: Manuel A. Aybar.
TRANSACTIONS/CAREER NOTES: Signed as non-drafted free agent by St. Louis Cardinals organization (October 21, 1991).

Year Team (League)	W	L	Pct.	ERA	G	GS	CG	ShO	Sv.	IP	H	R	ER	BB	SO
1992—Dom. Cardinals (DSL)	1	0	1.000	0.00	1	0	0	0	0	3	1	0	0	3	1
1993—Dom. Cardinals (DSL)	4	4	.500	3.15	13	11	1	0	0	71 1/3	54	33	25	33	66
1994—Ariz. Cardinals (Ariz.)	6	1	.857	2.12	13	13	1	0	0	72 1/3	69	25	17	9	79
1995—Savannah (S. Atl.)	3	8	.273	3.04	18	18	2	1	0	112 2/3	82	46	38	36	99
—St. Petersburg (FSL)	2	5	.286	3.35	9	9	0	0	0	48 1/3	42	27	18	16	43
1996—Arkansas (Texas)	8	6	.571	3.05	20	20	0	0	0	121	120	53	41	34	83
—Louisville (A.A.)	2	2	.500	3.23	5	5	0	0	0	30 2/3	26	12	11	7	25
1997—Louisville (A.A.)	5	8	.385	3.48	22	22	3	•2	0	137	131	60	53	45	114
—St. Louis (N.L.)	2	4	.333	4.24	12	12	0	0	0	68	66	33	32	29	41
Major league totals (1 year)	2	4	.333	4.24	12	12	0	0	0	68	66	33	32	29	41

RECORD AS POSITION PLAYER

Year Team (League)	Pos.	G	AB	R	H	2B	3B	HR	RBI	Avg.	BB	SO	SB	PO	A	E	Avg.
1992—Dom. Cardinals (DSL)	IF	55	153	18	31	5	0	1	11	.203	10	27	2	53	131	19	.906

BAERGA, CARLOS — 2B — METS

PERSONAL: Born November 4, 1968, in San Juan, Puerto Rico. ... 5-11/200. ... Bats both, throws right. ... Full name: Carlos Obed Ortiz Baerga. ... Name pronounced by-AIR-guh.

HIGH SCHOOL: Barbara Ann Rooshart (Rio Piedra, Puerto Rico).

TRANSACTIONS/CAREER NOTES: Signed as non-drafted free agent by San Diego Padres organization (November 4, 1985). ... Traded by Padres organization with C Sandy Alomar and OF Chris James to Cleveland Indians for OF Joe Carter (December 6, 1989). ... Traded by Indians with IF Alvaro Espinoza to New York Mets for IF Jose Vizcaino and IF Jeff Kent (July 29, 1996).

RECORDS: Holds major league record for switch-hitting home runs in one inning (April 8, 1993, seventh inning). ... Shares major league record for most home runs in one inning—2 (April 8, 1993, seventh inning).

HONORS: Named second baseman on THE SPORTING NEWS A.L. All-Star team (1993 and 1995). ... Named second baseman on THE SPORTING NEWS A.L. Silver Slugger team (1993-94).

STATISTICAL NOTES: Led South Atlantic League second basemen with 29 errors in 1987. ... Led Texas League shortstops with 61 double plays in 1988. ... Led Pacific Coast League third basemen with 380 total chances in 1989. ... Led A.L. second basemen with 138 double plays in 1992. ... Led A.L. second basemen with 894 total chances in 1992 and 809 in 1993. ... Collected six hits in one game (April 11, 1992). ... Switch-hit home runs in one game (April 8, 1993). ... Hit three home runs in one game (June 17, 1993). ... Career major league grand slams: 1.

Year Team (League)	Pos.	G	AB	R	H	2B	3B	HR	RBI	Avg.	BB	SO	SB	PO	A	E	Avg.
1986—Char., S.C. (S. Atl.)	2B-SS	111	378	57	102	14	4	7	41	.270	26	60	6	202	245	27	.943
1987—Char., S.C. (S. Atl.)	2B-SS	134	515	83	157	23	•9	7	50	.305	38	107	26	253	341	†36	.943
1988—Wichita (Texas)	SS-2B	122	444	67	121	28	1	12	65	.273	31	83	4	221	325	33	.943
1989—Las Vegas (PCL)	3B	132	520	63	143	28	2	10	74	.275	30	98	6	*92	256	*32	.916
1990—Cleveland (A.L.)■	3B-SS-2B	108	312	46	81	17	2	7	47	.260	16	57	0	79	164	17	.935
—Colo. Springs (PCL)	3B	12	50	11	19	2	1	1	11	.380	5	4	1	18	31	4	.925
1991—Cleveland (A.L.).........	3B-2B-SS	158	593	80	171	28	2	11	69	.288	48	74	3	217	421	27	.959
1992—Cleveland (A.L.).........	2B-DH	161	657	92	205	32	1	20	105	.312	35	54	10	*400	*475	19	.979
1993—Cleveland (A.L.).........	2B-DH	154	624	105	200	28	6	21	114	.321	34	68	15	*347	*445	17	.979
1994—Cleveland (A.L.).........	2B-DH	103	442	81	139	32	2	19	80	.314	10	45	8	205	335	*15	.973
1995—Cleveland (A.L.).........	2B-DH	135	557	87	175	28	2	15	90	.314	35	31	11	231	*444	19	.973
1996—Cleveland (A.L.).........	2B	100	424	54	113	25	0	10	55	.267	16	25	1	191	308	15	.971
—New York (N.L.)■	1B-3B-2B	26	83	5	16	3	0	2	11	.193	5	2	0	103	12	4	.966
1997—New York (N.L.)..........	2B	133	467	53	131	25	1	9	52	.281	20	54	2	244	371	14	.978
American League totals (7 years)		919	3609	545	1084	190	15	103	560	.300	194	376	48	1670	2592	129	.971
National League totals (2 years)		159	550	58	147	28	1	11	63	.267	25	56	2	347	383	18	.976
Major league totals (8 years)		1078	4159	603	1231	218	16	114	623	.296	219	432	50	2017	2975	147	.971

DIVISION SERIES RECORD

Year Team (League)	Pos.	G	AB	R	H	2B	3B	HR	RBI	Avg.	BB	SO	SB	PO	A	E	Avg.
1995—Cleveland (A.L.).........	2B	3	14	2	4	1	0	0	1	.286	0	1	0	8	5	1	.929

CHAMPIONSHIP SERIES RECORD

Year Team (League)	Pos.	G	AB	R	H	2B	3B	HR	RBI	Avg.	BB	SO	SB	PO	A	E	Avg.
1995—Cleveland (A.L.).........	2B	6	25	3	10	0	0	1	4	.400	2	3	0	12	22		1.000

WORLD SERIES RECORD

Year Team (League)	Pos.	G	AB	R	H	2B	3B	HR	RBI	Avg.	BB	SO	SB	PO	A	E	Avg.
1995—Cleveland (A.L.).........	2B	6	26	1	5	2	0	0	4	.192	1	1	0	15	24	1	.975

ALL-STAR GAME RECORD

Year League	Pos.	AB	R	H	2B	3B	HR	RBI	Avg.	BB	SO	SB	PO	A	E	Avg.
1992—American....................	2B	1	1	1	1	0	0	1	1.000	0	0	0	1	2	0	1.000
1993—American....................	2B	2	1	0	0	0	0	0	.000	0	1	0	0	1	0	1.000
1995—American....................	2B	3	1	3	1	0	0	0	1.000	0	0	0	1	2	0	1.000
All-Star Game totals (3 years)		6	3	4	2	0	0	1	.667	0	1	0	2	5	0	1.000

BAGWELL, JEFF — 1B — ASTROS

PERSONAL: Born May 27, 1968, in Boston. ... 6-0/195. ... Bats right, throws right. ... Full name: Jeffrey Robert Bagwell.

HIGH SCHOOL: Xavier (Middletown, Conn.).

COLLEGE: Hartford.

TRANSACTIONS/CAREER NOTES: Selected by Boston Red Sox organization in fourth round of free-agent draft (June 5, 1989). ... Traded by Red Sox to Houston Astros for P Larry Andersen (August 31, 1990). ... On Houston disabled list (July 31-September 1, 1995); included rehabilitation assignment to Jackson (August 28-September 1).

RECORDS: Shares major league record for most home runs in one inning—2 (June 24, 1994, sixth inning). ... Shares major league single-game record for most doubles—4 (June 14, 1996).

HONORS: Named Eastern League Most Valuable Player (1990). ... Named N.L. Rookie Player of the Year by THE SPORTING NEWS (1991). ... Named N.L. Rookie of the Year by Baseball Writers' Association of America (1991). ... Named Major League Player of the Year by THE SPORTING NEWS (1994). ... Named first baseman on THE SPORTING NEWS N.L. All-Star team (1994, 1996 and 1997). ... Won N.L. Gold Glove at first base (1994). ... Named first baseman on THE SPORTING NEWS N.L. Silver Slugger team (1994 and 1997). ... Named N.L. Most Valuable Player by Baseball Writers' Association of America (1994).

STATISTICAL NOTES: Led Eastern League with 220 total bases and 12 intentional bases on balls received in 1990. ... Led N.L. in being hit by pitch with 13 in 1991. ... Led N.L. with 13 sacrifice flies in 1992. ... Hit three home runs in one game (June 24, 1994). ... Led N.L. with .750 slugging percentage in 1994. ... Led N.L. first basemen with 120 assists in 1994. ... Tied for N.L. lead in errors by first basemen with nine and double plays by first basemen with 94 in 1994.

MISCELLANEOUS: Holds Houston Astros all-time record for highest career batting average (.304).

Year Team (League)	Pos.	G	AB	R	H	2B	3B	HR	RBI	Avg.	BB	SO	SB	PO	A	E	Avg.
1989— GC Red Sox (GCL)	3B-2B	5	19	3	6	1	0	0	3	.316	3	0	0	2	12	2	.875
—Winter Haven (FSL)	3B-2B-1B	64	210	27	65	13	2	2	19	.310	22	25	1	53	109	12	.931
1990— New Britain (Eastern)	3B	136	481	63	*160	•34	7	4	61	.333	73	57	5	93	267	34	.914
1991— Houston (N.L.)■	1B	156	554	79	163	26	4	15	82	.294	75	116	7	1270	106	12	.991
1992— Houston (N.L.)	1B	•162	586	87	160	34	6	18	96	.273	84	97	10	1334	133	7	.995
1993— Houston (N.L.)	1B	142	535	76	171	37	4	20	88	.320	62	73	13	1200	113	9	.993
1994— Houston (N.L.)■	1B-OF	110	400	*104	147	32	2	39	*116	.368	65	65	15	923	†121	‡9	.991
1995— Houston (N.L.)	1B	114	448	88	130	29	0	21	87	.290	79	102	12	1004	*129	7	.994
—Jackson (Texas)	1B	4	12	0	2	0	0	0	0	.167	3	2	0	24	6	0	1.000
1996— Houston (N.L.)	1B	*162	568	111	179	*48	2	31	120	.315	135	114	21	1336	*136	*16	.989
1997— Houston (N.L.)	1B-DH	•162	566	109	162	40	2	43	135	.286	127	122	31	1404	*137	11	.993
Major league totals (7 years)		1008	3657	654	1112	246	20	187	724	.304	627	689	109	8471	875	71	.992

DIVISION SERIES RECORD

Year Team (League)	Pos.	G	AB	R	H	2B	3B	HR	RBI	Avg.	BB	SO	SB	PO	A	E	Avg.
1997— Houston (N.L.)	1B	3	12	0	1	0	0	0	0	.083	1	5	0	17	6	2	.920

ALL-STAR GAME RECORD

Year League	Pos.	AB	R	H	2B	3B	HR	RBI	Avg.	BB	SO	SB	PO	A	E	Avg.
1994— National	PH-1B	4	1	2	0	0	0	0	.500	0	1	0	3	2	0	1.000
1996— National	1B	2	0	0	0	0	0	0	.000	0	1	0	5	0	0	1.000
1997— National	1B	3	0	0	0	0	0	0	.000	0	0	0	8	1	0	1.000
All-Star Game totals (3 years)		9	1	2	0	0	0	0	.222	0	2	0	16	3	0	1.000

BAILES, SCOTT　　　　　　P　　　　　　RANGERS

PERSONAL: Born December 18, 1962, in Chillicothe, Ohio. ... 6-2/171. ... Throws left, bats left. ... Full name: Scott Alan Bailes.
HIGH SCHOOL: Parkview (Springfield, Mo.).
JUNIOR COLLEGE: St. Louis Community College at Meramec.
TRANSACTIONS/CAREER NOTES: Selected by Texas Rangers organization in seventh round of free-agent draft (January 12, 1982). ... Selected by Pittsburgh Pirates organization in secondary phase of free-agent draft (June 7, 1982). ... On disabled list (August 12, 1982-remainder of season). ... Traded by Pirates organization to Cleveland Indians organization (July 3, 1985), completing deal in which Indians traded SS Johnnie LeMaster to Pirates for a player to be named later (May 30, 1985). ... On disabled list (August 13-September 6, 1989). ... Traded by Indians to California Angels for IF Jeff Manto and P Colin Charland (January 9, 1990). ... On disabled list (June 30-July 15, 1991 and April 11-26, 1992). ... Released by Angels (October 15, 1992). ... Signed by Memphis, Kansas City Royals organization (February 26, 1993). ... Released by Memphis (April 3, 1993). ... Signed by Syracuse, Toronto Blue Jays organization (April 25, 1993). ... On voluntarily retired list (June 3, 1993-January 18, 1995). ... Released by Blue Jays (January 18, 1995). ... Signed by Rangers organization (December 16, 1996). ... Granted free agency (November 6, 1997). ... Re-signed by Rangers (December 7, 1997).

Year Team (League)	W	L	Pct.	ERA	G	GS	CG	ShO	Sv.	IP	H	R	ER	BB	SO
1982— Greenwood (S. Atl.)	0	1	.000	7.24	3	1	1	0	0	13²/₃	17	12	11	6	8
1983— Alexandria (Caro.)	5	2	.714	3.36	52	1	0	0	7	75	67	38	28	45	101
1984— Nashua (Eastern)	6	8	.429	3.41	54	1	0	0	3	87	80	43	33	46	61
1985— Nashua (Eastern)	3	3	.500	2.83	30	0	0	0	8	47²/₃	44	22	15	20	42
—Waterbury (Eastern)■	6	3	.667	2.62	13	11	3	1	1	79	78	36	23	23	53
1986— Cleveland (A.L.)	10	10	.500	4.95	62	10	0	0	7	112²/₃	123	70	62	43	60
1987— Cleveland (A.L.)	7	8	.467	4.64	39	17	0	0	6	120¹/₃	145	75	62	47	65
1988— Cleveland (A.L.)	9	14	.391	4.90	37	21	5	2	0	145	149	89	79	46	53
1989— Cleveland (A.L.)	5	9	.357	4.28	34	11	0	0	0	113²/₃	116	57	54	29	47
1990— California (A.L.)■	2	0	1.000	6.37	27	0	0	0	0	35¹/₃	46	30	25	20	16
—Edmonton (PCL)	0	1	.000	6.00	9	3	0	0	0	18	21	13	12	8	12
1991— California (A.L.)	1	2	.333	4.18	42	0	0	0	0	51²/₃	41	26	24	22	41
1992— California (A.L.)	3	1	.750	7.45	32	0	0	0	0	38²/₃	59	34	32	28	25
1993— Syracuse (Int'l)■	0	1	.000	2.21	19	0	0	0	2	20¹/₃	19	10	5	3	22
1997— Oklahoma City (A.A.)■	2	3	.400	3.98	44	0	0	0	4	43	46	22	19	13	37
—Texas (A.L.)	1	0	1.000	2.86	24	0	0	0	0	22	18	9	7	10	14
Major league totals (8 years)	38	44	.463	4.86	297	59	5	2	13	639¹/₃	697	390	345	245	321

BAILEY, CORY　　　　　　P　　　　　　GIANTS

PERSONAL: Born January 24, 1971, in Herrin, Ill. ... 6-1/202. ... Throws right, bats right. ... Full name: Phillip Cory Bailey.
HIGH SCHOOL: Marion (Ill.).
COLLEGE: Southeastern Illinois.
TRANSACTIONS/CAREER NOTES: Selected by Boston Red Sox organization in 15th round of free-agent draft (June 3, 1991). ... Traded by Red Sox with 3B Scott Cooper and a player to be named later to St. Louis Cardinals for P Rheal Cormier and OF Mark Whiten (April 8, 1995). ... Traded by Cardinals to Texas Rangers for P David Chavarria and a player to be named later (December 16, 1996). ... Traded by Rangers to San Francisco Giants for P Chad Hartvigson (July 29, 1997).

Year Team (League)	W	L	Pct.	ERA	G	GS	CG	ShO	Sv.	IP	H	R	ER	BB	SO
1991— GC Red Sox (GCL)	0	0	...	0.00	1	0	0	0	1	2	2	1	0	1	1
—Elmira (N.Y.-Penn)	2	4	.333	1.85	28	0	0	0	*15	39	19	10	8	12	54
1992— Lynchburg (Caroline)	5	7	.417	2.44	49	0	0	0	*23	66¹/₃	43	20	18	30	87
1993— Pawtucket (Int'l)	4	5	.444	2.88	52	0	0	0	20	65²/₃	48	21	21	31	59
—Boston (A.L.)	0	1	.000	3.45	11	0	0	0	0	15²/₃	12	7	6	12	11
1994— Pawtucket (Int'l)	4	3	.571	3.23	53	0	0	0	19	61¹/₃	44	25	22	38	52
—Boston (A.L.)	0	1	.000	12.46	5	0	0	0	0	4¹/₃	10	6	6	3	4
1995— Louisville (A.A.)■	5	3	.625	4.55	55	0	0	0	*25	59¹/₃	51	30	30	30	49
—St. Louis (N.L.)	0	0	...	7.36	3	0	0	0	0	3²/₃	2	3	3	2	5
1996— St. Louis (N.L.)	5	2	.714	3.00	51	0	0	0	0	57	57	21	19	30	38
—Louisville (A.A.)	2	4	.333	5.82	22	0	0	0	1	34	29	22	22	20	27

Year—Team (League)	W	L	Pct.	ERA	G	GS	CG	ShO	Sv.	IP	H	R	ER	BB	SO
1997—Oklahoma City (A.A.)■.......	3	4	.429	3.40	42	0	0	0	15	50 1/3	49	20	19	23	38
—Phoenix (PCL)■................	4	0	1.000	1.56	13	0	0	0	3	17 1/3	16	4	3	6	14
—San Francisco (N.L.)	0	1	.000	8.38	7	0	0	0	0	9 2/3	15	9	9	4	5
A.L. totals (2 years)	0	2	.000	5.40	16	0	0	0	0	20	22	13	12	15	15
N.L. totals (3 years)	5	3	.625	3.97	61	0	0	0	0	70 1/3	74	33	31	36	48
Major league totals (5 years)......	5	5	.500	4.28	77	0	0	0	0	90 1/3	96	46	43	51	63

BAILEY, ROGER   P   ROCKIES

PERSONAL: Born October 3, 1970, in Chattahoochee, Fla. ... 6-1/180. ... Throws right, bats right. ... Full name: Charles Roger Bailey.
HIGH SCHOOL: Chattahoochee (Fla.)
COLLEGE: Florida State.
TRANSACTIONS/CAREER NOTES: Selected by Colorado Rockies organization in third round of free-agent draft (June 1, 1992). ... On Colorado disabled list (April 8-May 1, 1996); included rehabilitation assignment to Colorado Springs (May 1-June 16). ... On disabled list (June 30-July 15, 1997).
MISCELLANEOUS: Shares Colorado Rockies all-time record for most complete games (5) and holds Colorado Rockies all-time record for most shutouts (2). ... Appeared in one game as pinch-runner (1997).

Year—Team (League)	W	L	Pct.	ERA	G	GS	CG	ShO	Sv.	IP	H	R	ER	BB	SO
1992—Bend (Northwest)...............	5	2	.714	2.20	11	11	1	0	0	65 1/3	48	19	16	30	81
1993—Central Valley (Cal.)............	4	7	.364	4.84	22	22	1	1	0	111 2/3	139	78	60	56	84
1994—New Haven (Eastern)..........	9	9	.500	3.23	25	24	1	1	0	159	157	70	57	56	112
1995—Colorado (N.L.)...............	7	6	.538	4.98	39	6	0	0	0	81 1/3	88	49	45	39	33
—Colo. Springs (PCL)	0	0	. . .	2.70	3	3	0	0	0	16 2/3	15	9	5	8	7
1996—Colorado (N.L.)...............	2	3	.400	6.24	24	11	0	0	1	83 2/3	94	64	58	52	45
—Colo. Springs (PCL)	4	4	.500	6.29	9	9	0	0	0	48 2/3	60	34	34	20	27
1997—Colorado (N.L.)...............	9	10	.474	4.29	29	29	5	2	0	191	210	103	91	70	84
Major league totals (3 years)......	18	19	.486	4.90	92	46	5	2	1	356	392	216	194	161	162

BAINES, HAROLD   DH   ORIOLES

PERSONAL: Born March 15, 1959, in St. Michaels, Md. ... 6-2/195. ... Bats left, throws left. ... Full name: Harold Douglas Baines.
HIGH SCHOOL: St. Michaels (Easton, Md.).
TRANSACTIONS/CAREER NOTES: Selected by Chicago White Sox organization in first round (first pick overall) of free-agent draft (June 7, 1977). ... On disabled list (April 7-May 8, 1987). ... Traded by White Sox with IF Fred Manrique to Texas Rangers for SS Scott Fletcher, OF Sammy Sosa and P Wilson Alvarez (July 29, 1989). ... Traded by Rangers to Oakland Athletics for two players to be named later (August 29, 1990); Rangers acquired P Joe Bitker and P Scott Chiamparino to complete deal (September 4, 1990). ... Granted free agency (October 27, 1992); accepted arbitration. ... Traded by A's to Baltimore Orioles for P Bobby Chouinard and P Allen Plaster (January 14, 1993). ... On Baltimore disabled list (May 5-27, 1993); included rehabilitation assignment to Bowie (May 25-27). ... Granted free agency (November 1, 1993). ... Re-signed by Orioles (December 2, 1993). ... Granted free agency (October 20, 1994). ... Re-signed by Orioles (December 23, 1994). ... Granted free agency (November 6, 1995). ... Signed by White Sox (December 11, 1995). ... Granted free agency (November 18, 1996). Re-signed by White Sox (January 10, 1997). ... Re-signed by White Sox (January 10, 1997). ... Traded by White Sox to Orioles for a player to be named later (July 29, 1997); White Sox acquired SS Juan Bautista to complete deal (August 18, 1997). ... Granted free agency (October 29, 1997). ... Re-signed by Orioles (December 19, 1997).
RECORDS: Shares major league single-game record for most plate appearances—12 (May 8, finished May 9, 1984, 25 innings). ... Shares A.L. record for longest errorless game by outfielder—25 innings (May 8, finished May 9, 1984). ... Shares A.L. single-game record for most innings by outfielder—25 (May 8, finished May 9, 1984).
HONORS: Named outfielder on THE SPORTING NEWS A.L. All-Star team (1985). ... Named designated hitter on THE SPORTING NEWS A.L. All-Star team (1988-89). ... Named designated hitter on THE SPORTING NEWS A.L. Silver Slugger team (1989).
STATISTICAL NOTES: Tied for American Association lead in double plays by outfielder with four in 1979. ... Hit three home runs in one game (July 7, 1982; September 17, 1984 and May 7, 1991). ... Led A.L. with 22 game-winning RBIs in 1983. ... Led A.L. with .541 slugging percentage in 1984. ... Career major league grand slams: 12.

Year—Team (League)	Pos.	G	AB	R	H	2B	3B	HR	RBI	Avg.	BB	SO	SB	PO	A	E	Avg.
1977—Appleton (Midwest)....	OF	69	222	37	58	11	2	5	29	.261	36	62	2	94	10	7	.937
1978—Knoxville (Southern) ..	OF-1B	137	502	70	138	16	6	13	72	.275	43	91	3	291	22	13	.960
1979—Iowa (Am. Assoc.)......	OF	125	466	87	139	25	8	22	87	.298	33	80	5	222	•16	11	.956
1980—Chicago (A.L.)	OF-DH	141	491	55	125	23	6	13	49	.255	19	65	2	229	6	9	.963
1981—Chicago (A.L.)	OF-DH	82	280	42	80	11	7	10	41	.286	12	41	6	120	10	2	.985
1982—Chicago (A.L.)	OF	161	608	89	165	29	8	25	105	.271	49	95	10	326	10	7	.980
1983—Chicago (A.L.)	OF	156	596	76	167	33	2	20	99	.280	49	85	7	312	10	9	.973
1984—Chicago (A.L.)	OF	147	569	72	173	28	10	29	94	.304	54	75	1	307	8	6	.981
1985—Chicago (A.L.)	OF-DH	160	640	86	198	29	3	22	113	.309	42	89	1	318	8	2	.994
1986—Chicago (A.L.)	OF-DH	145	570	72	169	29	2	21	88	.296	38	89	2	295	15	5	.984
1987—Chicago (A.L.)	DH-OF	132	505	59	148	26	4	20	93	.293	46	82	0	13	0	0	1.000
1988—Chicago (A.L.)	DH-OF	158	599	55	166	39	1	13	81	.277	67	109	0	14	1	2	.882
1989—Chicago (A.L.)	DH-OF	70	333	55	107	20	1	13	56	.321	60	52	0	52	0	1	.981
—Texas (A.L.)■	DH-OF	46	172	18	49	9	0	3	16	.285	13	27	0	2	0	1	.667
1990—Texas (A.L.)	DH	103	321	41	93	10	1	13	44	.290	47	63	0	. . .	. . .	. . .	. . .
—Oakland (A.L.)■	DH-OF	32	94	11	25	5	0	3	21	.266	20	17	0	5	0	1	.833
1991—Oakland (A.L.)	DH-OF	141	488	76	144	25	1	20	90	.295	72	67	0	11	1	1	.923
1992—Oakland (A.L.)	DH-OF	140	478	58	121	18	0	16	76	.253	59	61	1	27	0	1	.964
1993—Baltimore (A.L.)■	DH	118	416	64	130	22	0	20	78	.313	57	52	0	. . .	. . .	. . .	. . .
—Bowie (Eastern)	DH	2	6	0	0	0	0	0	0	.000	1	1	0	. . .	. . .	. . .	. . .
1994—Baltimore (A.L.)	DH	94	326	44	96	12	1	16	54	.294	30	49	0	. . .	. . .	. . .	. . .
1995—Baltimore (A.L.)	DH	127	385	60	115	19	1	24	63	.299	70	45	0	. . .	. . .	. . .	. . .
1996—Chicago (A.L.)■	DH	143	495	80	154	29	0	22	95	.311	73	62	3	. . .	. . .	. . .	. . .
1997—Chicago (A.L.)	DH-OF	93	318	40	97	18	0	12	52	.305	41	47	0	0	0	0	. . .
—Baltimore (A.L.)■	DH	44	134	15	39	5	0	4	15	.291	14	15	0	0	0	0	. . .
Major league totals (18 years)		2433	8818	1168	2561	439	48	339	1423	.290	932	1287	33	2031	69	47	.978

DIVISION SERIES RECORD

NOTES: Hit home run in first at-bat (October 2, 1997).

Year	Team (League)	Pos.	G	AB	R	H	2B	3B	HR	RBI	Avg.	BB	SO	SB	PO	A	E	Avg.
1997— Baltimore (A.L.)..........		DH-PH	2	5	2	2	0	0	1	1	.400	1	0	0	0	...	...	...

CHAMPIONSHIP SERIES RECORD

Year	Team (League)	Pos.	G	AB	R	H	2B	3B	HR	RBI	Avg.	BB	SO	SB	PO	A	E	Avg.
1983— Chicago (A.L.)		OF	4	16	0	2	0	0	0	0	.125	1	3	0	5	1	0	1.000
1990— Oakland (A.L.)		DH	4	14	2	5	1	0	0	3	.357	2	1	1	...	...	...	...
1992— Oakland (A.L.)		DH	6	25	6	11	2	0	1	4	.440	0	3	0	...	...	...	...
1997— Baltimore (A.L.)..........		DH	6	17	1	6	0	0	1	2	.353	2	1	0	...	...	...	...
Championship series totals (4 years)			20	72	9	24	3	0	2	9	.333	5	8	1	5	1	0	1.000

WORLD SERIES RECORD

Year	Team (League)	Pos.	G	AB	R	H	2B	3B	HR	RBI	Avg.	BB	SO	SB	PO	A	E	Avg.
1990— Oakland (A.L.)		DH-PH	3	7	1	1	0	0	1	2	.143	1	2	0	...	...	...	...

ALL-STAR GAME RECORD

Year	League	Pos.	AB	R	H	2B	3B	HR	RBI	Avg.	BB	SO	SB	PO	A	E	Avg.
1985— American	PH	1	0	1	0	0	0	0	0	1.000	0	0	0	...	...	...	...
1986— American	PH	1	0	0	0	0	0	0	0	.000	0	0	0	...	...	...	...
1987— American	PH	1	0	0	0	0	0	0	0	.000	0	0	0	...	...	...	...
1989— American	DH	3	1	1	0	0	0	1	.333	0	1	0	...	...	...	...
1991— American	PH-DH	1	0	0	0	0	0	1	.000	0	0	0	...	...	...	...
All-Star Game totals (5 years)		7	1	2	0	0	0	2	.286	0	1	0	...	...	...	...

BAKER, JASON   P   EXPOS

PERSONAL: Born November 21, 1974, in Baytown, Texas. ... 6-3/195. ... Throws right, bats right. ... Full name: Jason Ryan Baker.
HIGH SCHOOL: Robert E. Lee (Midland, Texas).
TRANSACTIONS/CAREER NOTES: Selected by Montreal Expos organization in third round of free-agent draft (June 3, 1993). ... On West Palm Beach disabled list (April 30-June 26, 1997).
STATISTICAL NOTES: Tied for Appalachian League lead with 16 hit batsmen and 22 wild pitches in 1996.

Year	Team (League)	W	L	Pct.	ERA	G	GS	CG	ShO	Sv.	IP	H	R	ER	BB	SO
1993— GC Expos (GCL)	1	1	.500	2.25	7	7	0	0	0	32	26	14	8	11	24
1994— Vermont (NYP)..................	6	5	.545	4.82	13	13	0	0	0	61 2/3	55	44	33	40	21
1995— Vermont (NYP)..................	6	5	.545	4.13	14	14	0	0	0	72	59	40	33	47	57
1996— Delmarva (S. Atl.)..............	9	7	.563	2.81	27	27	2	0	0	160 1/3	127	70	50	77	147
1997— W.P. Beach (FSL)..............	3	4	.429	6.00	15	14	1	1	0	72	90	55	48	31	47
— G.C. Expos (GCL)	0	0	...	0.00	2	2	0	0	0	7	4	0	0	3	8

BAKO, PAUL   C   TIGERS

PERSONAL: Born June 20, 1972, in Lafayette, La. ... 6-2/195. ... Bats right, throws left. ... Full name: Gabor Paul Bako.
HIGH SCHOOL: Lafayette (La.).
COLLEGE: Southwestern Louisiana.
TRANSACTIONS/CAREER NOTES: Selected by Cincinnati Reds organization in fifth round of free-agent draft (June 3, 1993). ... Traded by Reds with P Donne Wall to Detroit Tigers for OF Mel Nieves (November 11, 1997).
STATISTICAL NOTES: Tied for Carolina League lead with 15 passed balls in 1995. ... Led Southern League catchers with 791 total chances in 1996. ... Tied for American Association lead in double plays with 10 and passed balls with nine by a catcher in 1997.

Year	Team (League)	Pos.	G	AB	R	H	2B	3B	HR	RBI	Avg.	BB	SO	SB	PO	A	E	Avg.
1993— Billings (Pioneer)........	C-1B	57	194	34	61	11	0	4	30	.314	22	37	5	323	45	6	.984
1994— Win.-Salem (Car.).......	C	90	289	29	59	9	1	3	26	.204	35	81	2	570	73	15	.977
1995— Win.-Salem (Car.).......	C	82	249	29	71	11	2	7	27	.285	42	66	3	478	49	6	.989
1996— Chattanooga (Sou.)....	C	110	360	53	106	27	0	8	48	.294	48	93	1	*694	*84	13	.984
1997— Indianapolis (A.A.)......	C	104	321	34	78	14	1	8	43	.243	34	81	0	622	64	6	.991

BALDWIN, JAMES   P   WHITE SOX

PERSONAL: Born July 15, 1971, in Southern Pines, N.C. ... 6-3/210. ... Throws right, bats right.
HIGH SCHOOL: Pinecrest (Southern Pines, N.C.).
TRANSACTIONS/CAREER NOTES: Selected by Chicago White Sox organization in fourth round of free-agent draft (June 4, 1990). ... On disabled list (August 3-19, 1994).
HONORS: Named A.L. Rookie Pitcher of the Year by THE SPORTING NEWS (1996).
STATISTICAL NOTES: Led American Association with 27 home runs allowed and tied for lead with three balks in 1995.. ... Tied for American Association lead with three balks in 1995. ... Tied for A.L. lead with 14 wild pitches in 1997. ... Tied for A.L. lead with three balks in 1997.

Year	Team (League)	W	L	Pct.	ERA	G	GS	CG	ShO	Sv.	IP	H	R	ER	BB	SO
1990— GC White Sox (GCL)	1	6	.143	4.10	9	7	0	0	0	37 1/3	32	29	17	18	32
1991— GC White Sox (GCL)	3	1	.750	2.12	6	6	0	0	0	34	16	8	8	16	48
— Utica (N.Y.-Penn)............	1	4	.200	5.30	7	7	1	0	0	37 1/3	40	26	22	27	43
1992— South Bend (Mid.)..........	9	5	.643	2.42	21	21	1	1	0	137 2/3	118	53	37	45	137
— Sarasota (Florida State)......	1	2	.333	2.87	6	6	1	0	0	37 2/3	31	13	12	7	39
1993— Birmingham (Southern)	8	5	.615	*2.25	17	17	•4	0	0	120	94	48	30	43	107
— Nashville (A.A.)	5	4	.556	2.61	10	10	1	0	0	69	43	21	20	36	61

Year Team (League)	W	L	Pct.	ERA	G	GS	CG	ShO	Sv.	IP	H	R	ER	BB	SO
1994—Nashville (A.A.)	12	6	.667	3.72	26	26	2	0	0	162	144	75	67	83	*156
1995—Chicago (A.L.)	0	1	.000	12.89	6	4	0	0	0	14²/₃	32	22	21	9	10
—Nashville (A.A.)	5	9	.357	5.85	18	18	0	0	0	95¹/₃	120	76	62	44	89
1996—Nashville (A.A.)	1	1	.500	0.64	2	2	1	0	0	14	5	1	1	4	15
—Chicago (A.L.)	11	6	.647	4.42	28	28	0	0	0	169	168	88	83	57	127
1997—Chicago (A.L.)	12	•15	.444	5.27	32	32	1	0	0	200	205	128	117	83	140
Major league totals (3 years)	23	22	.511	5.18	66	64	1	0	0	383²/₃	405	238	221	149	277

BANKS, BRIAN — OF — BREWERS

B

PERSONAL: Born September 28, 1970, in Mesa, Ariz. ... 6-3/200. ... Bats both, throws right. ... Full name: Brian Glen Banks.
HIGH SCHOOL: Mountain View (Mesa, Ariz.).
COLLEGE: Brigham Young.
TRANSACTIONS/CAREER NOTES: Selected by Milwaukee Brewers organization in second round of free-agent draft (June 3, 1993); pick received as part of compensation for Seattle Mariners signing Type A free-agent P Chris Bosio.
STATISTICAL NOTES: Tied for Midwest League lead in double plays by outfielder with four in 1994. ... Career major league grand slams: 1.

Year Team (League)	Pos.	G	AB	R	H	2B	3B	HR	RBI	Avg.	BB	SO	SB	PO	A	E	Avg.
						BATTING								FIELDING			
1993—Helena (Pioneer)	OF	12	48	8	19	1	1	2	8	.396	11	8	1	25	0	1	.962
—Beloit (Midwest)	OF	38	147	21	36	5	1	4	19	.245	7	34	1	47	2	1	.980
1994—Beloit (Midwest)	OF-1B-3B	65	237	41	71	13	1	9	47	.300	29	40	11	123	5	2	.985
—Stockton (California) ..	OF	67	246	29	58	9	1	4	28	.236	38	46	3	108	5	4	.966
1995—El Paso (Texas)	OF-1B-3B	128	441	81	136	*39	10	12	78	.308	*81	113	9	245	11	10	.962
1996—New Orleans (A.A.)	OF-3B-C	137	487	71	132	29	7	16	64	.271	66	105	17	256	18	8	.972
—Milwaukee (A.L.)	OF-1B	4	7	2	4	2	0	1	2	.571	1	2	0	15	1	0	1.000
1997—Tucson (PCL)	OF-C	98	378	53	112	26	3	10	63	.296	35	83	7	194	13	3	.986
—Milwaukee (A.L.)	O-1-DH-3	28	68	9	14	1	0	1	8	.206	6	17	0	30	7	2	.949
Major league totals (2 years)		32	75	11	18	3	0	2	10	.240	7	19	0	45	8	2	.964

BANKS, WILLIE — P — YANKEES

PERSONAL: Born February 27, 1969, in Jersey City, N.J. ... 6-1/195. ... Throws right, bats right. ... Full name: Willie Anthony Banks.
HIGH SCHOOL: St. Anthony (Jersey City, N.J.).
TRANSACTIONS/CAREER NOTES: Selected by Minnesota Twins organization in first round (third pick overall) of free-agent draft (June 2, 1987). ... Traded by Twins to Chicago Cubs for P Dave Stevens and C Matt Walbeck (November 24, 1993). ... Traded to Los Angeles Dodgers for P Dax Winslett (June 19, 1995). ... Claimed on waivers by Florida Marlins (August 10, 1995). ... Claimed on waivers by Philadelphia Phillies (October 4, 1995). ... Released by Phillies (March 8, 1996). ... Signed by New York Yankees organization (January 3, 1997).
STATISTICAL NOTES: Led Appalachian League with 28 wild pitches and tied for lead with three balks in 1987. ... Pitched 1-0 no-hit victory for Visalia against Palm Springs (May 24, 1989). ... Led California League with 22 wild pitches in 1989. ... Tied for Pacific Coast League lead with 14 wild pitches in 1991. ... Tied for A.L. lead with five balks in 1993.
MISCELLANEOUS: Appeared in two games as pinch-runner and struck out in only appearance as pinch-hitter with Florida (1995).

Year Team (League)	W	L	Pct.	ERA	G	GS	CG	ShO	Sv.	IP	H	R	ER	BB	SO
1987—Elizabethton (Appal.)	1	8	.111	6.99	13	13	0	0	0	65²/₃	73	*71	*51	*62	71
1988—Kenosha (Midwest)	10	10	.500	3.72	24	24	0	0	0	125²/₃	109	73	52	*107	113
1989—Visalia (California)	12	9	.571	2.59	27	27	7	•4	0	174	122	70	50	85	*173
—Orlando (South.)	1	0	1.000	5.14	1	1	0	0	0	7	10	4	4	0	9
1990—Orlando (South.)	7	9	.438	3.93	28	28	1	0	0	162²/₃	161	93	71	98	114
1991—Portland (PCL)	9	8	.529	4.55	25	24	1	1	0	146¹/₃	156	81	74	76	63
—Minnesota (A.L.)	1	1	.500	5.71	5	3	0	0	0	17¹/₃	21	15	11	12	16
1992—Portland (PCL)	6	1	.857	1.92	11	11	2	1	0	75	62	20	16	34	41
—Minnesota (A.L.)	4	4	.500	5.70	16	12	0	0	0	71	80	46	45	37	37
1993—Minnesota (A.L.)	11	12	.478	4.04	31	30	0	0	0	171¹/₃	186	91	77	78	138
1994—Chicago (N.L.)■	8	12	.400	5.40	23	23	1	1	0	138¹/₃	139	88	83	56	91
1995—Chicago (N.L.)	0	1	.000	15.43	10	0	0	0	0	11²/₃	27	23	20	12	9
—Los Angeles (N.L.)■	0	2	.000	4.03	6	6	0	0	0	29	36	21	13	16	23
—Florida (N.L.)■	2	3	.400	4.32	9	9	0	0	0	50	43	27	24	30	30
1997—Columbus (Int'l)■	14	5	.737	4.27	33	24	1	0	3	154	164	87	73	45	130
—New York (A.L.)	3	0	1.000	1.93	5	1	0	0	0	14	9	3	3	6	8
A.L. totals (4 years)	19	17	.528	4.47	57	46	0	0	0	273²/₃	296	155	136	133	199
N.L. totals (2 years)	10	18	.357	5.50	48	38	1	1	0	229	245	159	140	114	153
Major league totals (6 years)	29	35	.453	4.94	105	84	1	1	0	502²/₃	541	314	276	247	352

BARBER, BRIAN — P — ROYALS

PERSONAL: Born March 4, 1973, in Hamilton, Ohio. ... 6-1/175. ... Throws right, bats right. ... Full name: Brian Scott Barber.
HIGH SCHOOL: Dr. Phillips (Orlando).
TRANSACTIONS/CAREER NOTES: Selected by St. Louis Cardinals organization in first round (22nd pick overall) of free-agent draft (June 3, 1991); pick received as part of compensation for New York Mets signing Type B free agent OF Vince Coleman. ... On Louisville disabled list (April 21-May 14, 1994; May 21-June 15 and August 1-September 9, 1996). ... On Louisville suspended list (July 6-8, 1995). ... On St. Louis disabled list (March 23-May 29, 1997); including rehabilitation assignments to Prince William (May 2-7) and Arkansas (May 12-22). ... Granted free agency (December 21, 1997). ... Signed by Kansas City Royals organization (January 5, 1998).

Year Team (League)	W	L	Pct.	ERA	G	GS	CG	ShO	Sv.	IP	H	R	ER	BB	SO
1991—Johnson City (App.)	4	6	.400	5.40	14	13	0	0	0	73¹/₃	62	48	44	38	84
1992—Springfield (Mid.)	3	4	.429	3.73	8	8	0	0	0	50²/₃	39	21	21	24	56
—St. Petersburg (FSL)	5	5	.500	3.26	19	19	1	0	0	113¹/₃	99	51	41	46	102
1993—Arkansas (Texas)	9	8	.529	4.02	24	24	1	0	0	143¹/₃	154	70	64	56	126
—Louisville (A.A.)	0	1	.000	4.76	1	1	0	0	0	5²/₃	4	3	3	4	5

Year—Team (League)	W	L	Pct.	ERA	G	GS	CG	ShO	Sv.	IP	H	R	ER	BB	SO
1994—Louisville (A.A.)	4	7	.364	5.38	19	18	0	0	1	85 1/3	79	58	51	46	95
—Arkansas (Texas)	1	3	.250	3.25	6	6	0	0	0	36	31	15	13	16	54
1995—Louisville (A.A.)	6	5	.545	4.70	20	19	0	0	0	107 1/3	105	67	56	40	94
—St. Louis (N.L.)	2	1	.667	5.22	9	4	0	0	0	29 1/3	31	17	17	16	27
1996—Louisville (A.A.)	0	6	.000	5.62	11	11	1	0	0	49 2/3	49	37	31	26	33
—St. Louis (N.L.)	0	0	...	15.00	1	1	0	0	0	3	4	5	5	6	1
1997—Prince William (Caro.)	1	1	.500	4.09	2	2	0	0	0	11	10	5	5	5	13
—Arkansas (Texas)	0	1	.000	10.47	3	3	0	0	0	16 1/3	28	19	19	5	15
—Louisville (A.A.)	4	8	.333	6.90	18	18	0	0	0	92 2/3	111	80	71	44	74
Major league totals (2 years)	2	1	.667	6.12	10	5	0	0	0	32 1/3	35	22	22	22	28

BARCELO, LORENZO   P   WHITE SOX

PERSONAL: Born August 10, 1977, in San Pedro de Macoris, Dominican Republic. ... 6-4/180. ... Throws right, bats right. ... Full name: Lorenzo A. Barcelo.

TRANSACTIONS/CAREER NOTES: Signed as non-drafted free agent by San Francisco Giants organization (May 23, 1994). ... Traded by Giants with SS Mike Caruso, OF Brian Manning, P Keith Foulke, P Bob Howry and P Ken Vining by Giants to Chicago White Sox for P Wilson Alvarez, P Danny Darwin and P Roberto Hernandez (July 31, 1997).

STATISTICAL NOTES: Led Midwest League with 16 home runs allowed in 1996.

Year—Team (League)	W	L	Pct.	ERA	G	GS	CG	ShO	Sv.	IP	H	R	ER	BB	SO
1995—Bellingham (N'west)	3	2	.600	3.45	12	11	0	0	0	47	43	23	18	19	34
1996—Bellingham (N'west)	12	10	.545	3.54	26	26	1	0	0	152 2/3	138	70	60	46	139
1997—San Jose (California)	5	4	.556	3.94	16	16	1	1	0	89	91	45	39	30	89
—Shreveport (Texas)	2	0	1.000	4.02	5	5	0	0	0	31 1/3	30	19	14	8	20
—Birmingham (Southern)■	2	1	.667	4.86	6	6	0	0	0	33 1/3	36	20	18	9	29

BARKLEY, BRIAN   P   RED SOX

PERSONAL: Born December 8, 1975, in Conroe, Texas. ... 6-2/180. ... Throws left, bats left. ... Full name: Brian Edward Barkley. ... Son of Jeff Barkley, pitcher, Cleveland Indians (1984-85) and grandson of W.S. Barkley, Washington Senators organization.

HIGH SCHOOL: Midway (Hewitt, Texas).

TRANSACTIONS/CAREER NOTES: Selected by Boston Red Sox organization in fifth round of free-agent draft (June 2, 1997).

Year—Team (League)	W	L	Pct.	ERA	G	GS	CG	ShO	Sv.	IP	H	R	ER	BB	SO
1994—GC Red Sox (GCL)	0	1	.000	0.96	4	3	0	0	0	18 2/3	11	7	2	4	14
1995—Sarasota (Florida State)	8	10	.444	3.25	24	24	2	2	0	146 2/3	147	66	53	37	70
1996—Trenton (Eastern)	8	8	.500	5.72	22	21	0	0	0	119 2/3	126	79	76	56	89
1997—Trenton (Eastern)	12	9	.571	4.94	29	•29	4	0	1	178 2/3	*208	*113	*98	*79	121

BARNES, LARRY   1B   ANGELS

PERSONAL: Born July 23, 1974, in Bakersfield, Calif. ... 6-1/195. ... Bats left, throws left. ... Full name: Larry Richard Barnes Jr.

HIGH SCHOOL: Bakersfield (Calif.).

JUNIOR COLLEGE: Bakersfield (Calif.) College.

COLLEGE: Fresno State.

TRANSACTIONS/CAREER NOTES: Selected by Florida Marlins organization in 69th round of free-agent draft (June 3, 1993); did not sign. ... Signed as non-drafted free agent by California Angels organization (June 6, 1995). ... Angels franchise renamed Anaheim Angels for 1997 season.

HONORS: Named Midwest League Most Valuable Player (1996).

STATISTICAL NOTES: Led Arizona League first basemen with 49 double plays in 1995. ... Led Midwest League with 282 total bases and .577 slugging percentage in 1996. ... Tied for Midwest League lead with 80 assists by first baseman in 1996. ... Led California League first basemen with .993 fielding percentage in 1997.

Year—Team (League)	Pos.	G	AB	R	H	2B	3B	HR	RBI	Avg.	BB	SO	SB	PO	A	E	Avg.
1995—Ariz. Angels (Ariz.)	1B	•56	197	•42	61	8	3	3	•37	.310	27	42	12	*494	19	7	.987
1996—Cedar Rap. (Midw.)	1B-OF-C	131	489	84	155	•36	5	*27	*112	.317	58	101	9	1062	‡81	11	.990
1997—Lake Elsinore (Calif.)	1B-OF	115	446	68	128	32	2	13	71	.287	43	84	3	1048	87	8	†.993

BARON, JIM   P   PADRES

PERSONAL: Born February 22, 1974, in Cleveland. ... 6-3/230. ... Throws left, bats left. ... Full name: James Thomas Baron.

HIGH SCHOOL: Humble (Texas).

TRANSACTIONS/CAREER NOTES: Selected by San Diego Padres organization in fifth round of free-agent draft (June 1, 1992). ... Selected by New York Mets organization from Padres organization in Rule 5 major league draft (December 9, 1996). ... Returned by Mets organization to Padres organization (March 31, 1997).

Year—Team (League)	W	L	Pct.	ERA	G	GS	CG	ShO	Sv.	IP	H	R	ER	BB	SO
1992—Ariz. Padres (Ariz.)	2	0	1.000	8.28	14	0	0	0	0	25	24	28	23	25	18
1993—Ariz. Padres (Ariz.)	1	3	.250	4.44	13	8	1	0	1	48 2/3	38	33	24	38	36
1994—Springfield (Mid.)	6	6	.500	6.39	25	23	0	0	0	105 2/3	121	83	75	76	73
1995—Rancho Cucamonga (Cal.)	0	0	...	16.88	3	0	0	0	0	2 2/3	7	8	5	6	3
—Clinton (Midwest)	0	8	.000	6.22	11	9	1	0	0	50 2/3	65	42	35	16	31
—Idaho Falls (Pioneer)	2	3	.400	5.65	27	1	0	0	0	43	51	31	27	19	43
1996—Rancho Cucamonga (Cal.)	6	3	.667	3.00	54	0	0	0	1	87	87	44	29	35	85
1997—Las Vegas (PCL)	0	0	...	11.25	4	0	0	0	0	4	8	5	5	3	3
—Mobile (Southern)	2	4	.333	4.54	19	1	0	0	0	33 2/3	35	21	17	13	30
—Rancho Cucamonga (Cal.)	1	7	.125	3.38	14	14	0	0	0	85 1/3	89	50	32	28	64

BARRETT, MICHAEL   C   EXPOS

PERSONAL: Born October 22, 1976, in Atlanta. ... 6-3/185. ... Bats right, throws right. ... Full name: Michael P. Barrett.
HIGH SCHOOL: Pace Academy (Atlanta).
TRANSACTIONS/CAREER NOTES: Selected by Montreal Expos organization in first round (28th pick overall) of free-agent draft (June 1, 1995).

								BATTING						FIELDING		
Year	Team (League)	Pos.	G	AB	R	H	2B	3B	HR	RBI	Avg.	BB	SO	SB	PO	A	E	Avg.
1995—GC Expos (GCL)	SS-3B	50	183	22	57	13	4	0	19	.311	15	19	7	65	143	25	.893
—Vermont (NYP)	SS	3	10	0	1	0	0	0	1	.100	1	1	0	1	3	0	1.000
1996—Delmarva (S. Atl.)	C-3B	129	474	57	113	29	4	4	62	.238	18	42	5	607	74	15	.978
1997—W.P. Beach (FSL)	C	119	423	52	120	30	0	8	61	.284	36	49	7	629	78	13	.982

BARRIOS, MANUEL   P   MARLINS

B

PERSONAL: Born September 21, 1974, in Cabecea, Panama. ... 6-0/170. ... Throws right, bats right. ... Full name: Manuel Antonio Barrios.
TRANSACTIONS/CAREER NOTES: Signed as non-drafted free agent by Houston Astros organization (March 2, 1993). ... On suspended list (September 4-8, 1996). ... Traded by Astros with P Oscar Henriquez and a player to be named later to Florida Marlins for OF Moises Alou (November 11, 1997).

Year	Team (League)	W	L	Pct.	ERA	G	GS	CG	ShO	Sv.	IP	H	R	ER	BB	SO
1993—Dom. Astros (DSL)	6	1	.857	4.64	13	12	2	0	0	77 2/3	77	57	40	23	59
1994—Quad City (Midwest)	0	6	.000	5.95	43	0	0	0	4	65	73	44	43	23	63
1995—Quad City (Midwest)	1	5	.167	2.25	50	0	0	0	23	52	44	16	13	17	55
1996—Jackson (Texas)	6	4	.600	2.37	60	0	0	0	23	68 1/3	60	29	18	29	69
1997—New Orleans (A.A.)	4	8	.333	3.27	57	0	0	0	0	82 2/3	70	32	30	34	77
—Houston (N.L.)	0	0	...	12.00	2	0	0	0	0	3	6	4	4	3	3
Major league totals (1 year)	0	0	...	12.00	2	0	0	0	0	3	6	4	4	3	3

BARRON, TONY   OF   PHILLIES

PERSONAL: Born August 17, 1966, in Portland. ... 6-0/185. ... Bats right, throws right. ... Full name: Anthony Dirk Barron.
HIGH SCHOOL: Spanaway Lake (Spanaway, Wash.).
JUNIOR COLLEGE: Green River (Auburn, Wash.).
COLLEGE: Willamette (Ore.).
TRANSACTIONS/CAREER NOTES: Selected by Los Angeles Dodgers organization in seventh round of free-agent draft (June 2, 1987). ... Granted free agency (October 15, 1993). ... Signed by Seattle Mariners organization (February 18, 1994). ... Granted free agency (October 15, 1994). ... Signed by Montreal Expos organization (May 15, 1995). ... Granted free agency (October 15, 1996). ... Signed by Philadelphia Phillies organization (November 1, 1996).
STATISTICAL NOTES: Led International League in being hit by pitch with 12 in 1997.

								BATTING						FIELDING		
Year	Team (League)	Pos.	G	AB	R	H	2B	3B	HR	RBI	Avg.	BB	SO	SB	PO	A	E	Avg.
1987—Great Falls (Pio.)	O-3-1-S-C	53	171	33	51	13	2	3	30	.298	13	49	5	57	5	3	.954
1988—Salem (Northwest)	SS-2B	73	261	54	79	6	3	9	38	.303	25	75	36	105	8	5	.958
—Bakersfield (Calif.)	1B-OF	12	20	1	5	2	0	0	4	.250	1	5	0	13	3	0	1.000
1989—Vero Beach (FSL)	OF	105	324	45	79	7	5	4	40	.244	17	90	26	184	14	3	.985
1990—Vero Beach (FSL)	OF	111	344	58	102	21	3	6	60	.297	30	82	42	144	9	3	.981
1991—San Antonio (Tex.)	OF	73	200	35	47	2	2	9	31	.235	28	44	8	110	5	1	.991
1992—San Antonio (Tex.)	OF	28	97	18	39	4	1	7	22	.402	6	22	7	42	1	1	.977
—Albuquerque (PCL)	OF	78	286	40	86	18	2	6	33	.301	17	65	6	155	4	4	.975
1993—Albuquerque (PCL)	OF	107	259	42	75	22	1	8	36	.290	27	59	6	82	5	3	.967
1994—Jacksonville (Sou.)■	OF	108	402	60	119	19	3	18	55	.296	26	85	18	157	11	2	.988
—Calgary (PCL)	OF	2	8	2	2	0	0	2	2	.250	0	0	0	0	0	0	...
1995—Tacoma (PCL)	OF	9	25	4	5	0	0	0	2	.200	2	3	0	11	0	0	1.000
—Harrisburg (East.)■	OF	29	103	20	30	5	0	10	23	.291	10	21	0	37	2	1	.975
—Ottawa (Int'l)	OF	50	147	20	36	10	0	10	22	.245	14	22	0	59	2	0	1.000
1996—Montreal (N.L.)	OF	1	1	0	0	0	0	0	0	.000	0	1	0	0	0	0	...
—Ottawa (Int'l)	OF	105	394	58	126	29	2	14	59	.320	20	74	9	154	7	0	1.000
—Harrisburg (Eastern)	OF-1B	18	67	12	19	3	1	5	12	.284	6	19	1	44	5	1	.980
1997—Scran./W.B. (Int'l)■	OF	92	329	51	108	21	4	18	78	.328	27	64	3	102	3	4	.963
—Philadelphia (N.L.)	OF	57	189	22	54	12	1	4	24	.286	12	38	0	111	3	2	.983
Major league totals (2 years)		58	190	22	54	12	1	4	24	.284	12	39	0	111	3	2	.983

BARRY, JEFF   OF   ROCKIES

PERSONAL: Born September 22, 1968, in Medford, Ore. ... 6-0/200. ... Bats both, throws right. ... Full name: Jeffrey Finis Barry.
HIGH SCHOOL: Medford (Ore.).
COLLEGE: San Diego State.
TRANSACTIONS/CAREER NOTES: Selected by Montreal Expos organization in fourth round of free-agent draft (June 4, 1990). ... On disabled list (September 5-20, 1991). ... Traded by Expos organization to New York Mets organization for P Blaine Beatty (December 9, 1991). ... On St. Lucie disabled list (April 16-September 18, 1992). ... On disabled list (June 2-20, 1994). ... On suspended list (August 14-15, 1994). ... On Binghamton disabled list (August 26-September 5, 1995). ... Traded by Mets to San Diego Padres for P Pedro A. Martinez (December 15, 1995). ... Granted free agency (October 15, 1996). ... Signed by Colorado Rockies organization (January 8, 1997).
STATISTICAL NOTES: Tied for Eastern League lead with nine sacrifice flies in 1995.

Year Team (League)	Pos.	G	AB	R	H	2B	3B	HR	RBI	Avg.	BB	SO	SB	PO	A	E	Avg.
1990—Jamestown (NYP)......	OF	70	263	40	76	18	1	5	38	.289	22	35	20	88	8	5	.950
1991—W.P. Beach (FSL)........	OF	116	437	48	92	16	3	4	31	.211	34	68	20	200	14	7	.968
1992—St. Lucie (Fla. St.)■...	DH	3	9	0	3	2	0	0	1	.333	0	0	0	...	...	...	...
—GC Mets (GCL)..........	DH	8	23	5	4	1	0	0	2	.174	6	2	2	...	...	...	...
1993—St. Lucie (Fla. St.)....	OF	114	420	68	108	17	5	4	50	.257	49	37	17	167	12	1	.994
1994—Binghamton (East.)	OF	110	388	48	118	24	3	9	69	.304	35	62	10	144	6	5	.968
1995—Norfolk (Int'l)	1B	12	41	3	9	2	0	0	6	.220	3	6	0	117	9	2	.984
—Binghamton (East.)	OF-1B	80	290	49	78	17	6	11	53	.269	31	61	4	129	6	0	1.000
—New York (N.L.).........	OF	15	15	2	2	1	0	0	0	.133	1	8	0	2	0	0	1.000
1996—Memphis (Sou.)■.......	3-O-1-2	91	226	29	55	7	0	3	25	.243	29	48	3	90	81	13	.929
—Las Vegas (PCL)........	OF	4	12	1	1	0	0	0	0	.083	3	0	0	12	0	1	.923
1997—New Haven (East.)■....	OF-1B	40	146	21	32	4	0	5	12	.219	4	34	3	122	11	6	.957
—Colo. Springs (PCL) ...	OF	81	273	46	82	13	3	13	70	.300	30	45	5	130	11	0	1.000
Major league totals (1 year)		15	15	2	2	1	0	0	0	.133	1	8	0	2	0	0	1.000

BARTEE, KIMERA — OF — TIGERS

PERSONAL: Born July 21, 1972, in Omaha, Neb. ... 6-0/175. ... Bats both, throws right. ... Full name: Kimera Anotchi Bartee.
HIGH SCHOOL: Central (Omaha, Neb.).
COLLEGE: Creighton.
TRANSACTIONS/CAREER NOTES: Selected by Baltimore Orioles organization in 14th round of free-agent draft (June 3, 1993). ... On Bowie disabled list (June 8-August 8, 1995). ... Traded by Orioles organization to Minnesota Twins organization (September 18, 1995), completing deal in which Orioles acquired P Scott Erickson from Twins for P Scott Klingenbeck and a player to be named later (July 7, 1995). ... Selected by Orioles from Twins organization in Rule 5 major league draft (December 4, 1995). ... Claimed on waivers by Detroit Tigers (March 13, 1996).
STATISTICAL NOTES: Led International League outfielders with 341 total chances in 1997.

Year Team (League)	Pos.	G	AB	R	H	2B	3B	HR	RBI	Avg.	BB	SO	SB	PO	A	E	Avg.
1993—Bluefield (Appal.)........	OF	66	264	59	65	15	2	4	37	.246	44	66	*27	124	5	4	.970
1994—Frederick (Carolina)....	OF	130	514	97	150	22	4	10	57	.292	56	117	44	*304	7	6	.981
1995—GC Orioles (GCL)........	OF	5	21	5	5	0	0	1	3	.238	3	2	1	15	0	0	1.000
—Bowie (Eastern)........	OF	53	218	45	62	9	1	3	19	.284	23	45	22	155	4	6	.964
—Rochester (Int'l)........	OF	15	52	5	8	2	1	0	3	.154	0	16	0	37	2	0	1.000
1996—Detroit (A.L.)■..........	OF-DH	110	217	32	55	6	1	1	14	.253	17	77	20	217	1	2	.991
1997—Toledo (Int'l).............	OF	136	501	67	109	13	7	3	33	.218	52	*154	*33	*336	4	1	.997
—Detroit (A.L.)...........	OF-DH	12	5	4	1	0	0	0	0	.200	2	2	3	3	0	0	1.000
Major league totals (2 years)		122	222	36	56	6	1	1	14	.252	19	79	23	220	1	2	.991

BATCHELOR, RICH — P — INDIANS

PERSONAL: Born April 8, 1967, in Florence, S.C. ... 6-1/195. ... Throws right, bats right. ... Full name: Richard Anthony Batchelor.
HIGH SCHOOL: Hartsville (S.C.).
COLLEGE: South Carolina-Aiken.
TRANSACTIONS/CAREER NOTES: Selected by Chicago White Sox organization in seventh round of free-agent draft (June 1, 1988); did not sign. ... Selected by New York Yankees organization in 38th round of free-agent draft (June 5, 1989); did not sign. ... Signed as non-drafted free agent by Yankees organization (April 17, 1990). ... Traded by Yankees organization to St. Louis Cardinals for P Lee Smith (August 31, 1993). ... On suspended list (May 13-15, 1995). ... On disabled list (August 14-26, 1995). ... Traded by Cardinals with P Danny Jackson and OF Mark Sweeney to San Diego Padres for P Fernando Valenzuela, 3B Scott Livingstone and OF Phil Plantier (June 13, 1997). ... Released by Padres (November 25, 1997). ... Signed by Cleveland Indians (December 5, 1997).

Year Team (League)	W	L	Pct.	ERA	G	GS	CG	ShO	Sv.	IP	H	R	ER	BB	SO
1990—Greensboro (S. Atl.)..........	2	2	.500	1.58	27	0	0	0	8	51 1/3	39	15	9	14	38
1991—Fort Lauderdale (FSL)	4	7	.364	2.76	50	0	0	0	•25	62	55	28	19	22	58
—Alb./Colon. (Eastern)	0	0	...	45.00	1	0	0	0	0	1	5	5	5	1	0
1992—Alb./Colon. (Eastern)	4	5	.444	4.20	58	0	0	0	7	70 2/3	79	40	33	34	45
1993—Alb./Colon. (Eastern)	1	3	.250	0.89	36	0	0	0	19	40 1/3	27	9	4	12	40
—Columbus (Int'l).............	1	1	.500	2.76	15	0	0	0	6	16 1/3	14	5	5	8	17
—St. Louis (N.L.)■..............	0	0	...	8.10	9	0	0	0	0	10	14	12	9	3	4
1994—Louisville (A.A.)................	1	2	.333	3.54	53	0	0	0	0	81 1/3	85	40	32	32	50
1995—Louisville (A.A.)................	5	4	.556	3.28	50	6	0	0	0	85	85	39	31	16	61
1996—Louisville (A.A.)................	5	2	.714	4.12	51	0	0	0	28	54 2/3	59	29	25	19	57
—St. Louis (N.L.).............	2	0	1.000	1.20	11	0	0	0	0	15	9	2	2	1	11
1997—St. Louis (N.L.).............	1	1	.500	4.50	12	0	0	0	0	16	21	12	8	7	8
—Louisville (A.A.).............	0	2	.000	4.50	12	0	0	0	5	14	18	9	7	6	10
—San Diego (N.L.)■	2	0	1.000	7.82	13	0	0	0	0	12 2/3	19	11	11	7	10
—Las Vegas (PCL)	3	0	1.000	6.43	15	0	0	0	0	21	23	15	15	8	19
Major league totals (3 years)......	5	1	.833	5.03	43	0	0	0	0	53 2/3	63	37	30	18	33

BATES, FLETCHER — OF — MARLINS

PERSONAL: Born March 24, 1974, in Wilmington, N.C. ... 6-1/195. ... Bats both, throws right. ... Full name: Fletcher Shannon Bates.
HIGH SCHOOL: New Hanover (Wilmington, N.C.).
TRANSACTIONS/CAREER NOTES: Selected by New York Mets organization in fifth round of free-agent draft (June 3, 1993). ... Traded by Mets with P Scott Comer to Florida Marlins for P Dennis Cook (December 18, 1997).

Year	Team (League)	Pos.	G	AB	R	H	2B	3B	HR	RBI	Avg.	BB	SO	SB	PO	A	E	Avg.
1994—	GC Mets (GCL)..........	OF	52	183	23	39	5	3	5	29	.213	33	49	5	82	2	6	.933
	—St. Lucie (Fla. St.)	OF	7	24	2	6	1	1	1	4	.250	1	5	0	5	0	2	.714
1995—	Pittsfield (NYP)	OF	75	276	52	90	14	9	6	37	.326	41	72	17	119	6	12	.912
	—Binghamton (East.)	OF	2	8	1	0	0	0	0	0	.000	1	6	0	7	0	0	1.000
1996—	Capital City (SAL)......	OF	132	491	84	127	21	*13	15	72	.259	64	162	16	229	11	8	.968
1997—	St. Lucie (Fla. St.)	OF	70	253	49	76	19	11	11	38	.300	33	66	7	100	4	6	.945
	—Binghamton (East.)	OF	68	245	44	63	14	2	12	34	.257	26	71	9	96	7	4	.963

BATES, JASON — 2B/SS — ROCKIES

PERSONAL: Born January 5, 1971, in Downey, Calif. ... 5-10/185. ... Bats both, throws right. ... Full name: Jason Charles Bates.
HIGH SCHOOL: Ezperanza (Anaheim, Calif.).
COLLEGE: Arizona.
TRANSACTIONS/CAREER NOTES: Selected by Colorado Rockies organization in seventh round of free-agent draft (June 1, 1992).
STATISTICAL NOTES: Led Pacific Coast League shortstops with 87 double plays in 1994.

Year	Team (League)	Pos.	G	AB	R	H	2B	3B	HR	RBI	Avg.	BB	SO	SB	PO	A	E	Avg.
1992—	Bend (Northwest).......	SS	70	255	*57	73	10	3	6	31	.286	56	55	18	72	176	17	*.936
1993—	Colo. Springs (PCL) ...	SS-2B	122	449	76	120	21	2	13	62	.267	45	99	9	174	319	29	.944
1994—	Colo. Springs (PCL) ...	SS	125	458	68	131	19	5	10	76	.286	60	57	4	165	411	28	.954
1995—	Colorado (N.L.)	2B-SS-3B	116	322	42	86	17	4	8	46	.267	42	70	3	170	255	5	.988
1996—	Colorado (N.L.)	2B-SS-3B	88	160	19	33	8	1	1	9	.206	23	34	2	66	109	7	.962
1997—	Colorado (N.L.)	2B-SS-3B	62	121	17	29	10	0	3	11	.240	15	27	0	44	68	3	.974
	—Colo. Springs (PCL) ...	SS-2B	35	135	21	32	6	1	3	18	.237	13	36	1	60	95	6	.963
	Major league totals (3 years)		266	603	78	148	35	5	12	66	.245	80	131	5	280	432	15	.979

DIVISION SERIES RECORD

Year	Team (League)	Pos.	G	AB	R	H	2B	3B	HR	RBI	Avg.	BB	SO	SB	PO	A	E	Avg.
1995—	Colorado (N.L.)	3B-PH-2B	4	4	0	1	0	0	0	0	.250	0	0	0	1	3	0	1.000

BATISTA, MIGUEL — P — EXPOS

PERSONAL: Born February 19, 1971, in Santo Domingo, Dominican Republic. ... 6-0/180. ... Throws right, bats right. ... Full name: Miguel Jerez Decartes Batista.
HIGH SCHOOL: Nuevo Horizondes (Dominican Republic).
TRANSACTIONS/CAREER NOTES: Signed as non-drafted free agent by Montreal Expos organization (February 29, 1988). ... Selected by Pittsburgh Pirates organization from Expos organization in Rule 5 major league draft (December 9, 1991). ... Returned to Expos (April 23, 1992). ... On disabled list (April 14-30 and May 7, 1994-remainder of season). ... Released by Expos (November 18, 1994). ... Signed by Florida Marlins organization (December 9, 1994). ... Claimed on waivers by Chicago Cubs (December 17, 1996). ... Traded by Cubs to Expos for OF Henry Rodriguez (December 12, 1997).

Year	Team (League)	W	L	Pct.	ERA	G	GS	CG	ShO	Sv.	IP	H	R	ER	BB	SO
1988—	....															
	Dominican Summer League statistics unavailable.															
1989—	DSL Expos (DSL)	1	7	.125	4.24	13	11	0	0	0	68	56	46	32	50	60
1990—	GC Expos (GCL)	4	3	.571	2.06	9	6	0	0	0	39 1/3	33	16	9	17	21
	—Rockford (Midwest)	0	1	.000	8.76	3	2	0	0	0	12 1/3	16	13	12	5	7
1991—	Rockford (Midwest)	11	5	.688	4.04	23	23	2	1	0	133 2/3	126	74	60	57	90
1992—	Pittsburgh (N.L.)■..........	0	0	....	9.00	1	0	0	0	0	2	4	2	2	3	1
	—W.P. Beach (FSL)■..........	7	7	.500	3.79	24	24	1	0	0	135 1/3	130	69	57	54	92
1993—	Harrisburg (Eastern)	13	5	.722	4.34	26	26	0	0	0	141	139	79	68	86	91
1994—	Harrisburg (Eastern)	0	1	.000	2.38	3	3	0	0	0	11 1/3	8	3	3	9	5
1995—	Charlotte (Int'l)■..........	6	12	.333	4.80	34	18	0	0	0	116 1/3	118	79	62	60	58
1996—	Charlotte (Int'l)...................	4	3	.571	5.38	47	2	0	0	4	77	93	57	46	39	56
	—Florida (N.L.).....................	0	0	....	5.56	9	0	0	0	0	11 1/3	9	8	7	7	6
1997—	Iowa (Am. Assoc.)■..........	9	4	.692	4.20	31	14	2	*2	0	122	117	60	57	38	95
	—Chicago (N.L.)..................	0	5	.000	5.70	11	6	0	0	0	36 1/3	36	24	23	24	27
	Major league totals (3 years)......	0	5	.000	5.80	21	6	0	0	0	49 2/3	49	34	32	34	34

BATISTA, TONY — SS — DIAMONDBACKS

PERSONAL: Born December 9, 1973, in Puerto Plata, Dominican Republic. ... 6-0/195. ... Bats right, throws right. ... Full name: Leocadio Francisco Batista.
TRANSACTIONS/CAREER NOTES: Signed as non-drafted free agent by Oakland Athletics organization (February 8, 1991). ... On Tacoma disabled list (July 29, 1993-remainder of season). ... On Oakland disabled list (August 27-September 12, 1997); included rehabilitation assignment to Edmonton (September 11-12). ... Selected by Arizona Diamondbacks in first round (27th pick overall) of expansion draft (November 18, 1997).
STATISTICAL NOTES: Led California League shortstops with .950 fielding percentage in 1994.

Year	Team (League)	Pos.	G	AB	R	H	2B	3B	HR	RBI	Avg.	BB	SO	SB	PO	A	E	Avg.
1992—	Arizona A's (Ariz.).......	2B-SS-OF	45	167	32	41	6	2	0	22	.246	15	29	1	67	124	8	.960
1993—	Arizona A's (Ariz.).......	3B-2B-SS	24	104	21	34	6	2	2	17	.327	6	14	6	34	54	3	.967
	—Tacoma (PCL)	OF	4	12	1	2	1	0	0	1	.167	1	4	0	6	9	0	1.000
1994—	Modesto (California) ...	SS-2B	119	466	91	131	26	3	17	68	.281	54	108	7	182	372	30	†.949
1995—	Huntsville (Southern) .	SS-2B	120	419	55	107	23	1	16	61	.255	29	98	7	168	371	29	.949
1996—	Edmonton (PCL)	SS	57	205	33	66	17	4	8	40	.322	15	30	2	75	213	8	.973
	—Oakland (A.L.)	2-3-DH-S	74	238	38	71	10	2	6	25	.298	19	49	7	96	191	5	.983
1997—	Oakland (A.L.)	S-3-DH-2	68	188	22	38	10	1	4	18	.202	14	31	2	96	174	6	.971
	—Edmonton (PCL)	SS	33	124	25	39	10	1	3	21	.315	17	18	2	40	78	6	.952
	Major league totals (2 years)		142	426	60	109	20	3	10	43	.256	33	80	9	192	365	13	.977

BAUGHMAN, JUSTIN   IF   ANGELS

PERSONAL: Born August 1, 1974, in Mountain View, Calif. ... 5-11/175. ... Bats right, throws right. ... Full name: Justin Reis Baughman.
HIGH SCHOOL: Bellarmine Prep (San Jose, Calif.).
COLLEGE: Lewis & Clark (Ore.).
TRANSACTIONS/CAREER NOTES: Selected by California Angels organization in fifth round of free-agent draft (June 1, 1995). ... Angels franchise renamed Anaheim Angels for 1997 season.
STATISTICAL NOTES: Led Midwest League with 15 sacrifice hits in 1996. ... Led Midwest League shortstops with 595 total chances in 1996. ... Led California League shortstops with 674 total chances in 1997.

| | | | | | | | BATTING | | | | | | | | | FIELDING | | |
Year Team (League)	Pos.	G	AB	R	H	2B	3B	HR	RBI	Avg.	BB	SO	SB	PO	A	E	Avg.
1995— Boise (Northwest)	SS	58	215	26	50	4	3	1	20	.233	18	38	19	68	157	21	.915
1996— Cedar Rap. (Midw.)	SS	127	464	78	115	17	8	5	48	.248	45	78	•50	*201	360	34	.943
1997— Lake Elsinore (Calif.)	SS	134	478	71	131	14	3	2	48	.274	40	79	*68	*239	*403	32	.953

BAUTISTA, DANNY   OF   BRAVES

PERSONAL: Born May 24, 1972, in Santo Domingo, Dominican Republic. ... 5-11/170. ... Bats right, throws right. ... Full name: Daniel Bautista. ... Stepson of Jesus de la Rosa, outfielder, Houston Astros (1974). ... Name pronounced bough-TEES-tuh.
TRANSACTIONS/CAREER NOTES: Signed as non-drafted free agent by Detroit Tigers organization (June 24, 1989). ... On disabled list (May 24-July 10, 1991). ... On Toledo disabled list (June 8-July 31, 1994). ... Traded by Tigers to Atlanta Braves for OF Anton French (May 31, 1996). ... On Atlanta disabled list (June 28, 1996-remainder of season). ... On Atlanta disabled list (March 23-April 23, 1997); included rehabilition assignment to Richmond (April 18-23).
RECORDS: Shares major league single-game record (nine innings) for most strikeouts—5 (May 28, 1995).

| | | | | | | | BATTING | | | | | | | | | FIELDING | | |
Year Team (League)	Pos.	G	AB	R	H	2B	3B	HR	RBI	Avg.	BB	SO	SB	PO	A	E	Avg.
1989—																	
					Dominican Summer League statistics unavailable.												
1990— Bristol (Appal.)	OF	27	95	9	26	3	0	2	12	.274	8	21	2	43	2	0	1.000
1991— Fayetteville (SAL)	OF	69	234	21	45	6	4	1	30	.192	21	65	7	137	6	4	.973
1992— Fayetteville (SAL)	OF	121	453	59	122	22	0	5	52	.269	29	76	18	210	17	6	.974
1993— London (Eastern)	OF	117	424	55	121	21	1	6	48	.285	32	69	28	256	13	3	.989
— Detroit (A.L.)	OF-DH	17	61	6	19	3	0	1	9	.311	1	10	3	38	2	0	1.000
1994— Detroit (A.L.)	OF-DH	31	99	12	23	4	1	4	15	.232	3	18	1	66	0	0	1.000
— Toledo (Int'l)	OF	27	98	7	25	7	0	2	14	.255	6	23	2	54	1	1	.982
1995— Detroit (A.L.)	OF	89	271	28	55	9	0	7	27	.203	12	68	4	164	3	2	.988
— Toledo (Int'l)	OF	18	58	6	14	3	0	0	4	.241	1	10	1	32	0	2	.943
1996— Detroit (A.L.)	OF-DH	25	64	12	16	2	0	2	8	.250	9	15	1	38	0	1	.974
— Atlanta (N.L.)■	OF	17	20	1	3	0	0	0	1	.150	2	5	0	10	0	0	1.000
1997— Richmond (Int'l)	OF	46	170	28	48	10	3	2	28	.282	19	30	1	104	4	0	1.000
— Atlanta (N.L.)	OF	64	103	14	25	3	2	3	9	.243	5	24	2	59	1	1	.984
American League totals (4 years)		162	495	58	113	18	1	14	59	.228	25	111	9	306	5	3	.990
National League totals (2 years)		81	123	15	28	3	2	3	10	.228	7	29	2	69	1	1	.986
Major league totals (5 years)		243	618	73	141	21	3	17	69	.228	32	140	11	375	6	4	.990

DIVISION SERIES RECORD

| | | | | | | | BATTING | | | | | | | | | FIELDING | | |
Year Team (League)	Pos.	G	AB	R	H	2B	3B	HR	RBI	Avg.	BB	SO	SB	PO	A	E	Avg.
1997— Atlanta (N.L.)	OF	3	3	0	1	0	0	0	2	.333	0	1	0	0	0	0	...

CHAMPIONSHIP SERIES RECORD

| | | | | | | | BATTING | | | | | | | | | FIELDING | | |
Year Team (League)	Pos.	G	AB	R	H	2B	3B	HR	RBI	Avg.	BB	SO	SB	PO	A	E	Avg.
1997— Atlanta (N.L.)	OF	2	4	0	1	0	0	0	0	.250	0	0	0	4	0	0	1.000

BAUTISTA, JOSE   P   CARDINALS

PERSONAL: Born July 25, 1964, in Bani, Dominican Republic. ... 6-2/205. ... Throws right, bats right. ... Full name: Jose Joaquin Bautista. ... Name pronounced bough-TEES-tuh.
HIGH SCHOOL: Bani (Dominican Republic) School.
TRANSACTIONS/CAREER NOTES: Signed as non-drafted free agent by New York Mets organization (April 25, 1981). ... Selected by Baltimore Orioles from Mets organization in Rule 5 major league draft (December 7, 1987). ... On Baltimore disabled list (May 20-June 11, 1989); included rehabilitation assignment to Rochester (May 29-June 11). ... Loaned by Orioles to Miami, independent (April 24-June 1, 1991). ... Loaned by Orioles organization to Oklahoma City (June 1-July 11, 1991). ... Granted free agency (September 23, 1991). ... Signed by Omaha, Kansas City Royals organization (December 20, 1991). ... Granted free agency (October 15, 1992). ... Signed by Chicago Cubs organization (December 17, 1992). ... On suspended list (September 10-13, 1993). ... On disabled list (August 6, 1994-remainder of season). ... Granted free agency (December 23, 1994). ... Signed by San Francisco Giants (April 6, 1995). ... On San Francisco disabled list (September 13, 1996-remainder of season). ... Granted free agency (October 4, 1996). ... Signed by Detroit Tigers organization (January 22, 1997). ... Released by Tigers (March 27, 1997). ... Re-signed by Tigers (April 9, 1997). ... Released by Tigers (July 21, 1997). ... Signed by St. Louis Cardinals organization (August 2, 1997).
STATISTICAL NOTES: Pitched 6-0 no-hit victory against Prince William (May 26, 1985, first game).
MISCELLANEOUS: Appeared in two games as pinch-runner (1993).

Year Team (League)	W	L	Pct.	ERA	G	GS	CG	ShO	Sv.	IP	H	R	ER	BB	SO
1981— Kingsport (Appalachian)	3	6	.333	4.64	13	11	3	2	0	66	84	54	34	17	34
1982— Kingsport (Appalachian)	0	4	.000	8.92	14	4	0	0	5	38 1/3	61	44	38	19	13
1983— GC Mets (GCL)	4	3	.571	2.31	13	13	2	0	0	81 2/3	66	31	21	32	44
1984— Columbia (S. Atl.)	13	4	.765	3.13	19	18	5	3	0	135	121	52	47	35	96
1985— Lynchburg (Caroline)	15	8	.652	2.34	27	25	7	3	1	169	145	49	44	33	109
1986— Jackson (Texas)	0	1	.000	8.31	7	4	0	0	0	21 2/3	36	22	20	8	13
— Lynchburg (Caroline)	8	8	.500	3.94	18	18	5	1	0	118 2/3	120	58	52	24	62

Year Team (League)	W	L	Pct.	ERA	G	GS	CG	ShO	Sv.	IP	H	R	ER	BB	SO
1987— Jackson (Texas)	10	5	.667	3.24	28	25	2	0	0	169 1/3	174	76	61	43	95
1988— Baltimore (A.L.)■.............	6	15	.286	4.30	33	25	3	0	0	171 2/3	171	86	82	45	76
1989— Baltimore (A.L.)	3	4	.429	5.31	15	10	0	0	0	78	84	46	46	15	30
— Rochester (Int'l)	4	4	.500	2.83	15	13	3	1	0	98 2/3	84	41	31	26	47
1990— Baltimore (A.L.)	1	0	1.000	4.05	22	0	0	0	0	26 2/3	28	15	12	7	15
— Rochester (Int'l)	7	8	.467	4.06	27	13	3	0	2	108 2/3	115	51	49	15	50
1991— Baltimore (A.L.)	0	1	.000	16.88	5	0	0	0	0	5 1/3	13	10	10	5	3
— Miami (Florida St.)■	8	2	*.800	2.71	11	11	4	•3	0	76 1/3	63	23	23	11	69
— Oklahoma City (A.A.)■......	0	3	.000	5.29	11	3	0	0	0	32 1/3	38	19	19	6	22
— Rochester (Int'l)■	1	0	1.000	0.59	6	0	0	0	1	15 1/3	8	1	1	3	7
1992— Omaha (Am. Assoc.)■	2	10	.167	4.90	40	7	1	0	2	108 1/3	125	66	59	28	60
— Memphis (Southern)	1	0	1.000	4.50	1	1	0	0	0	6	6	3	3	2	7
1993— Chicago (N.L.)■	10	3	.769	2.82	58	7	1	0	2	111 2/3	105	38	35	27	63
1994— Chicago (N.L.)	4	5	.444	3.89	58	0	0	0	1	69 1/3	75	30	30	17	45
1995— San Francisco (N.L.)■	3	8	.273	6.44	52	6	0	0	0	100 2/3	120	77	72	26	45
1996— Phoenix (PCL)	2	2	.500	4.35	6	6	0	0	0	39 1/3	41	19	19	5	18
— San Francisco (N.L.)	3	4	.429	3.36	37	1	0	0	0	69 2/3	66	32	26	15	28
1997— Detroit (A.L.)	2	2	.500	6.69	21	0	0	0	0	40 1/3	55	32	30	12	19
— Louisville (A.A.)■.............	2	0	1.000	0.00	11	0	0	0	0	17 1/3	3	0	0	2	11
— St. Louis (N.L.)	0	0	. . .	6.57	11	0	0	0	0	12 1/3	15	10	9	2	4
A.L. totals (5 years)	12	22	.353	5.03	96	35	3	0	0	322	351	189	180	84	143
N.L. totals (5 years)	20	20	.500	4.26	216	14	1	0	3	363 2/3	381	187	172	87	185
Major league totals (9 years)	32	42	.432	4.62	312	49	4	0	3	685 2/3	732	376	352	171	328

B

BAUTISTA, JUAN — SS — WHITE SOX

PERSONAL: Born June 24, 1975, in San Pedro de Macoris, Dominican Republic. ... 6-0/165. ... Bats right, throws right. ... Full name: Juan Aquino Bautista. ... Name pronounced bough-TEES-tuh.
TRANSACTIONS/CAREER NOTES: Signed as non-drafted free agent by Baltimore Orioles organization (January 22, 1992). ... On disabled list (April 7-July 14, 1994). ... On Bowie disabled list (April 4-May 4 and May 23-August 18, 1997). ... Traded by Orioles to Chicago White Sox (August 18, 1997), completing deal in which White Sox traded DH Harold Baines to Orioles for a player to be named later (July 29, 1997).
STATISTICAL NOTES: Led Eastern League shortstops with 203 putouts, 354 assists, 29 errors and 586 total chances in 1996.

						BATTING								FIELDING		
Year Team (League)	Pos.	G	AB	R	H	2B	3B	HR	RBI	Avg.	BB	SO	SB	PO	A	E	Avg.
1992— Dom. Orioles (DSL)....	IF	54	176	34	45	7	0	1	16	.256	28	20	4	79	167	35	.875
1993— Albany (S. Atl.)	SS	98	295	24	70	17	2	0	28	.237	14	72	11	124	249	45	.892
1994— GC Orioles (GCL).........	SS	21	65	4	10	2	2	0	3	.154	2	19	3	18	25	4	.915
1995— High Desert (Calif.)......	SS	99	374	54	98	13	4	11	51	.262	18	74	22	154	253	40	.911
— Bowie (Eastern).........	SS	13	38	3	4	2	0	0	0	.105	3	5	1	21	28	5	.907
1996— Bowie (Eastern).........	SS-2B	129	441	35	103	18	3	3	33	.234	21	102	15	†203	†354	†30	.949
1997— Bowie (Eastern)	SS	21	68	9	17	1	0	0	3	.250	5	17	1	25	73	6	.942
— GC Orioles (GCL)........	SS	3	9	3	1	0	0	0	0	.111	1	2	1	2	11	3	.813
— Birmingham (Sou.)■ .	SS	12	46	6	11	3	0	0	4	.239	3	15	0	20	32	5	.912

BEAMON, TREY — OF — TIGERS

PERSONAL: Born February 11, 1974, in Dallas. ... 6-0/192. ... Bats left, throws right. ... Full name: Clifford Beamon.
HIGH SCHOOL: Warren Travis White (Dallas).
TRANSACTIONS/CAREER NOTES: Selected by Pittsburgh Pirates organization in second round of free-agent draft (June 1, 1992). ... Traded by Pirates with OF Angelo Encarnacion to San Diego Padres for OF Mark Smith and P Hal Garrett (March 29, 1997). ... Traded by Padres with P Tim Worrell to Detroit Tigers for P Dan Miceli, P Donne Wall and 3B Ryan Balfe (November 19, 1997).

						BATTING								FIELDING		
Year Team (League)	Pos.	G	AB	R	H	2B	3B	HR	RBI	Avg.	BB	SO	SB	PO	A	E	Avg.
1992— GC Pirates (GCL)........	OF	13	39	9	12	1	0	1	6	.308	4	0	0	25	0	2	.926
— Welland (NYP)..........	OF	19	69	15	20	5	0	3	9	.290	8	9	4	38	1	0	1.000
1993— Augusta (S. Atl.).........	OF	104	373	64	101	18	6	0	45	.271	48	60	19	181	5	6	.969
1994— Carolina (Southern)....	OF	112	434	69	140	18	9	5	47	*.323	33	53	24	170	11	10	.948
1995— Calgary (PCL).............	OF	118	452	74	151	29	5	5	62	.334	39	55	18	201	14	9	.960
1996— Calgary (PCL).............	OF	111	378	62	109	15	3	5	52	.288	55	63	16	161	7	13	.928
— Pittsburgh (N.L.)	OF	24	51	7	11	2	0	0	6	.216	4	6	1	24	0	1	.960
1997— Las Vegas (PCL)■	OF	90	329	64	108	19	4	5	49	.328	48	58	14	111	7	4	.967
— San Diego (N.L.)	OF	43	65	5	18	3	0	0	7	.277	2	17	1	17	3	2	.909
Major league totals (2 years)		67	116	12	29	5	0	0	13	.250	6	23	2	41	3	3	.936

BECK, ROD — P — CUBS

PERSONAL: Born August 3, 1968, in Burbank, Calif. ... 6-1/236. ... Throws right, bats right. ... Full name: Rodney Roy Beck.
HIGH SCHOOL: Grant (Sherman Oaks, Calif.).
TRANSACTIONS/CAREER NOTES: Selected by Oakland Athletics organization in 13th round of free-agent draft (June 2, 1986). ... Traded by A's organization to San Francisco Giants organization for P Charlie Corbell (March 23, 1988). ... On disabled list (April 6-30, 1994). ... Granted free agency (October 27, 1997). ... Signed by Chicago Cubs (January 15, 1998).
MISCELLANEOUS: Holds San Francisco Giants all-time record for most saves (199).

Year Team (League)	W	L	Pct.	ERA	G	GS	CG	ShO	Sv.	IP	H	R	ER	BB	SO
1986— Medford (N'west)	1	3	.250	5.23	13	6	0	0	1	32 2/3	47	25	19	11	21
1987— Medford (N'west)	5	8	.385	5.18	17	12	2	0	0	92	106	74	53	26	69
1988— Clinton (Midwest)■............	12	7	.632	3.00	28	23	5	1	0	177	177	68	59	27	123

Year Team (League)	W	L	Pct.	ERA	G	GS	CG	ShO	Sv.	IP	H	R	ER	BB	SO
1989— San Jose (California).........	11	2	*.846	2.40	13	13	4	0	0	97 1/3	91	29	26	26	88
—Shreveport (Texas).............	7	3	.700	3.55	16	14	4	1	0	99	108	45	39	16	74
1990— Shreveport (Texas).............	10	3	.769	2.23	14	14	2	1	0	93	85	26	23	17	71
—Phoenix (PCL)..................	4	7	.364	4.93	12	12	2	0	0	76 2/3	100	51	42	18	43
1991— Phoenix (PCL)..................	4	3	.571	2.02	23	5	3	0	6	71 1/3	56	18	16	13	35
—San Francisco (N.L.)	1	1	.500	3.78	31	0	0	0	1	52 1/3	53	22	22	13	38
1992— San Francisco (N.L.)	3	3	.500	1.76	65	0	0	0	17	92	62	20	18	15	87
1993— San Francisco (N.L.)	3	1	.750	2.16	76	0	0	0	48	79 1/3	57	20	19	13	86
1994— San Francisco (N.L.)	2	4	.333	2.77	48	0	0	0	28	48 2/3	49	17	15	13	39
1995— San Francisco (N.L.)	5	6	.455	4.45	60	0	0	0	33	58 2/3	60	31	29	21	42
1996— San Francisco (N.L.)	0	9	.000	4.04	63	0	0	0	35	62	56	23	23	10	48
1997— San Francisco (N.L.)	7	4	.636	3.47	73	0	0	0	37	70	67	31	27	8	53
Major league totals (7 years)......	**21**	**28**	**.429**	**2.97**	**416**	**0**	**0**	**0**	**199**	**463**	**404**	**164**	**153**	**93**	**393**

DIVISION SERIES RECORD

Year Team (League)	W	L	Pct.	ERA	G	GS	CG	ShO	Sv.	IP	H	R	ER	BB	SO
1997— San Francisco (N.L.)	0	0	. . .	0.00	1	0	0	0	0	1 1/3	1	0	0	0	1

ALL-STAR GAME RECORD

Year League	W	L	Pct.	ERA	GS	CG	ShO	Sv.	IP	H	R	ER	BB	SO
1993— National	0	0	. . .	9.00	0	0	0	0	1	2	1	1	0	1
1994— National	0	0	. . .	0.00	0	0	0	0	1 2/3	1	0	0	0	1
1997— National................................						Did not play.								
All-Star totals (2 years)	**0**	**0**	**. . .**	**3.38**	**0**	**0**	**0**	**0**	**2 2/3**	**3**	**1**	**1**	**0**	**2**

BECKER, RICH   OF   METS

PERSONAL: Born February 1, 1972, in Aurora, Ill. ... 5-10/192. ... Bats left, throws left. ... Full name: Richard Goodhard Becker.
HIGH SCHOOL: Aurora (Ill.) West.
TRANSACTIONS/CAREER NOTES: Selected by Minnesota Twins organization in third round of free-agent draft (June 4, 1990). ... On Minnesota disabled list (September 13, 1993-remainder of season and April 29-May 17, 1994). ... Traded by Twins to New York Mets for OF Alex Ochoa (December 12, 1997).
STATISTICAL NOTES: Led Appalachian League with .448 on-base percentage in 1990. ... Led Midwest League with 215 total bases in 1991. ... Led California League outfielders with 355 total chances in 1992. ... Led A.L. outfielders in double plays with five in 1995 and nine in 1996. ... Led A.L. outfielders with 412 total chances in 1996.

						BATTING								FIELDING		
Year Team (League)	Pos.	G	AB	R	H	2B	3B	HR	RBI	Avg.	BB	SO	SB	PO	A	E	Avg.
1990— Elizabethton (App.).....	OF	56	194	54	56	5	1	6	24	.289	*53	54	18	87	2	9	.908
1991— Kenosha (Midwest)	OF	130	494	100	132	*38	3	13	53	.267	72	108	19	270	19	11	.963
1992— Visalia (California)......	OF	*136	506	*118	160	37	2	15	82	.316	*114	122	29	*332	17	6	.983
1993— Nashville (Southern) ..	OF	138	516	•93	148	25	7	15	66	.287	94	117	29	303	5	6	.981
—Minnesota (A.L.)	OF	3	7	3	2	2	0	0	0	.286	5	4	1	7	0	1	.875
1994— Minnesota (A.L.)	OF-DH	28	98	12	26	3	0	1	8	.265	13	25	6	87	2	1	.989
—Salt Lake (PCL)	OF	71	282	64	89	21	3	2	38	.316	40	56	7	189	8	3	.985
1995— Salt Lake (PCL)	OF	36	123	26	38	7	0	6	28	.309	26	24	6	108	5	1	.991
—Minnesota (A.L.)	OF	106	392	45	93	15	1	2	33	.237	34	95	8	275	12	4	.986
1996— Minnesota (A.L.)	OF	148	525	92	153	31	4	12	71	.291	68	118	19	*391	18	3	.993
1997— Minnesota (A.L.)	OF	132	443	61	117	22	3	10	45	.264	62	130	17	319	5	5	.985
Major league totals (5 years)		**417**	**1465**	**213**	**391**	**73**	**8**	**25**	**157**	**.267**	**182**	**372**	**51**	**1079**	**37**	**14**	**.988**

BECKETT, ROBBIE   P   ROCKIES

PERSONAL: Born July 16, 1972, in Austin, Texas. ... 6-5/225. ... Throws left, bats right. ... Full name: Robert Joseph Beckett.
HIGH SCHOOL: McCallum (Austin, Texas).
TRANSACTIONS/CAREER NOTES: Selected by San Diego Padres organization in first round (25th pick overall) of free-agent draft (June 4, 1990); pick received as part of compensation for Kansas City Royals signing Type A free-agent P Mark Davis. ... Claimed on waivers by Florida Marlins organization (March 29, 1996). ... Claimed on waivers by Colorado Rockies organization (April 26, 1996).
STATISTICAL NOTES: Led California League with 25 wild pitches in 1993. ... Led Southern League with 19 wild pitches in 1995. ... Pitched 1-0 no-hit loss against Chattanooga (September 2, 1995, second game).

Year Team (League)	W	L	Pct.	ERA	G	GS	CG	ShO	Sv.	IP	H	R	ER	BB	SO
1990— Ariz. Padres (Ariz.)	2	5	.286	4.38	10	10	0	0	0	49 1/3	40	28	24	*45	54
—Riverside (California)	2	1	.667	7.02	3	3	0	0	0	16 2/3	18	13	13	11	11
1991— Charleston, S.C. (S. Atl.)	2	*14	.125	8.23	28	26	1	0	0	109 1/3	115	•111	*100	*117	96
1992— Waterloo (Midw.)	4	10	.286	4.77	24	24	1	1	0	120 2/3	77	88	64	*140	147
1993— Rancho Cucamonga (Cal.) .	2	4	.333	6.02	37	10	0	0	4	83 2/3	75	62	56	93	88
1994— Las Vegas (PCL)	0	1	.000	11.79	23	0	0	0	0	23 2/3	27	36	31	39	30
1995— Memphis (Southern)..........	3	4	.429	4.80	36	8	2	1	0	86 1/3	65	57	46	73	98
1996— Portland (Eastern)■	1	0	1.000	6.23	3	3	0	0	0	13	17	9	9	13	7
—New Haven (Eastern)■...	6	3	.667	4.81	30	4	0	0	0	48 2/3	38	30	26	46	55
—Colo. Springs (PCL)	0	2	.000	2.19	12	0	0	0	1	12 1/3	6	6	3	11	15
—Colorado (N.L.)	0	0	. . .	13.50	5	0	0	0	0	5 1/3	6	8	8	9	6
1997— Colo. Springs (PCL)	1	3	.250	6.79	45	1	0	0	1	54 1/3	61	49	41	47	67
—Colorado (N.L.)	0	0	. . .	5.40	2	0	0	0	0	1 2/3	1	1	1	1	2
Major league totals (2 years)......	**0**	**0**	**. . .**	**11.57**	**7**	**0**	**0**	**0**	**0**	**7**	**7**	**9**	**9**	**10**	**8**

BEECH, MATT   P   PHILLIES

PERSONAL: Born January 20, 1972, in Oakland. ... 6-2/205. ... Throws left, bats left. ... Full name: Lucas Matthew Beech.
HIGH SCHOOL: Tom C. Clark (San Antonio).

COLLEGE: Houston.
TRANSACTIONS/CAREER NOTES: Selected by Philadelphia Phillies organization in seventh round of free-agent draft (June 2, 1994). ... On Philadelphia disabled list (May 9-25, 1997).

Year	Team (League)	W	L	Pct.	ERA	G	GS	CG	ShO	Sv.	IP	H	R	ER	BB	SO
1994—	Spartanburg (SAL)	4	4	.500	2.58	10	10	4	1	0	69²/₃	51	23	20	23	83
	— Batavia (N.Y.-Penn)	2	1	.667	1.93	4	3	0	0	0	18²/₃	9	4	4	12	27
1995—	Clearwater (Fla. St.)	9	4	.692	4.19	15	15	0	0	0	86	87	45	40	30	85
	— Reading (Eastern)	2	4	.333	2.96	14	13	0	0	0	79	67	33	26	33	70
1996—	Reading (Eastern)	11	6	.647	3.17	21	21	0	0	0	133¹/₃	108	57	47	32	132
	— Scran./W.B. (Int'l)	2	0	1.000	2.40	2	2	0	0	0	15	9	6	4	1	14
	— Philadelphia (N.L.)	1	4	.200	6.97	8	8	0	0	0	41¹/₃	49	32	32	11	33
1997—	Clearwater (Fla. St.)	0	0	. . .	0.00	1	1	0	0	0	5²/₃	1	1	0	4	9
	— Scran./W.B. (Int'l)	3	1	.750	5.70	5	5	1	0	0	30	24	20	19	10	38
	— Philadelphia (N.L.)	4	9	.308	5.07	24	24	0	0	0	136²/₃	147	81	77	57	120
Major league totals (2 years)		**5**	**13**	**.278**	**5.51**	**32**	**32**	**0**	**0**	**0**	**178**	**196**	**113**	**109**	**68**	**153**

BELCHER, TIM   P   ROYALS

PERSONAL: Born October 19, 1961, in Sparta, Ohio. ... 6-3/225. ... Throws right, bats right. ... Full name: Timothy Wayne Belcher.
HIGH SCHOOL: Highland (Sparta, Ohio).
COLLEGE: Mt. Vernon (Ohio) Nazarene.
TRANSACTIONS/CAREER NOTES: Selected by Minnesota Twins organization in first round (first pick overall) of free-agent draft (June 6, 1983); did not sign. ... Selected by New York Yankees organization in secondary phase of free-agent draft (January 17, 1984); did not sign. ... Selected by Oakland Athletics organization in player compensation pool draft (February 8, 1984); A's received compensation for Baltimore Orioles signing Type A free-agent P Tom Underwood (February 7, 1984). ... On disabled list (April 10-May 4 and May 5-July 23, 1986). ... Traded by A's organization to Los Angeles Dodgers (September 3, 1987), completing deal in which Dodgers traded P Rick Honeycutt to A's for a player to be named later (August 29, 1987). ... On disabled list (August 17, 1990-remainder of season). ... Traded by Dodgers with P John Wetteland to Cincinnati Reds for OF Eric Davis and P Kip Gross (November 27, 1991). ... Traded by Reds to Chicago White Sox for P Johnny Ruffin & Jeff Pierce (July 31, 1993). ... Granted free agency (October 26, 1993). ... Signed by Detroit Tigers (February 7, 1994). ... Granted free agency (October 20, 1994). ... Signed by Reds organization (May 3, 1995). ... Traded by Reds to Seattle Mariners organization for P Roger Salkeld (May 15, 1995). ... Granted free agency (October 31, 1995). ... Signed by Kansas City Royals (January 31, 1996).
HONORS: Named righthanded pitcher on THE SPORTING NEWS college All-America team (1983). ... Named N.L. Rookie Pitcher of the Year by THE SPORTING NEWS (1988).
STATISTICAL NOTES: Pitched 6-0 one-hit, complete-game victory against Pittsburgh (July 21, 1990). ... Pitched 4-0 one-hit, complete-game victory for Cincinnati against Atlanta (May 26, 1993).

Year	Team (League)	W	L	Pct.	ERA	G	GS	CG	ShO	Sv.	IP	H	R	ER	BB	SO
1984—	Madison (Midwest)	9	4	.692	3.57	16	16	3	1	0	98¹/₃	80	45	39	48	111
	— Alb./Colon. (Eastern)	3	4	.429	3.33	10	10	2	0	0	54	37	30	20	41	40
1985—	Huntsville (Southern)	11	10	.524	4.69	29	26	3	1	0	149²/₃	145	99	78	99	90
1986—	Huntsville (Southern)	2	5	.286	6.57	9	9	0	0	0	37	50	28	27	22	25
1987—	Tacoma (PCL)	9	11	.450	4.42	29	28	2	1	0	163	143	89	80	*133	136
	— Los Angeles (N.L.)■	4	2	.667	2.38	6	5	0	0	0	34	30	11	9	7	23
1988—	Los Angeles (N.L.)	12	6	.667	2.91	36	27	4	1	4	179²/₃	143	65	58	51	152
1989—	Los Angeles (N.L.)	15	12	.556	2.82	39	30	•10	*8	1	230	182	81	72	80	200
1990—	Los Angeles (N.L.)	9	9	.500	4.00	24	24	5	2	0	153	136	76	68	48	102
1991—	Los Angeles (N.L.)	10	9	.526	2.62	33	33	2	1	0	209¹/₃	189	76	61	75	156
1992—	Cincinnati (N.L.)■	15	14	.517	3.91	35	34	2	1	0	227²/₃	201	*104	*99	80	149
1993—	Cincinnati (N.L.)	9	6	.600	4.47	22	22	4	2	0	137	134	72	68	47	101
	— Chicago (A.L.)■	3	5	.375	4.40	12	11	1	1	0	71²/₃	64	36	35	27	34
1994—	Detroit (A.L.)■	7	*15	.318	5.89	25	•25	3	0	0	162	192	*124	106	78	76
1995—	Indianapolis (A.A.)■	0	0	. . .	1.80	2	2	0	0	0	10	6	2	2	1	8
	— Seattle (A.L.)■	10	12	.455	4.52	28	28	1	0	0	179¹/₃	188	101	90	88	96
1996—	Kansas City (A.L.)■	15	11	.577	3.92	35	35	4	1	0	238²/₃	262	117	104	68	113
1997—	Kansas City (A.L.)	13	12	.520	5.02	32	32	3	1	0	213¹/₃	242	128	119	70	113
A.L. totals (5 years)		**48**	**55**	**.466**	**4.72**	**132**	**131**	**12**	**3**	**0**	**865**	**948**	**506**	**454**	**331**	**432**
N.L. totals (7 years)		**74**	**58**	**.561**	**3.34**	**195**	**175**	**27**	**15**	**5**	**1170²/₃**	**1015**	**485**	**435**	**388**	**883**
Major league totals (11 years)		**122**	**113**	**.519**	**3.93**	**327**	**306**	**39**	**18**	**5**	**2035²/₃**	**1963**	**991**	**889**	**719**	**1315**

DIVISION SERIES RECORD

Year	Team (League)	W	L	Pct.	ERA	G	GS	CG	ShO	Sv.	IP	H	R	ER	BB	SO
1995—	Seattle (A.L.)	0	1	.000	6.23	2	0	0	0	0	4¹/₃	4	3	3	5	0

CHAMPIONSHIP SERIES RECORD

Year	Team (League)	W	L	Pct.	ERA	G	GS	CG	ShO	Sv.	IP	H	R	ER	BB	SO
1988—	Los Angeles (N.L.)	2	0	1.000	4.11	2	2	0	0	0	15¹/₃	12	7	7	4	16
1993—	Chicago (A.L.)	1	0	1.000	2.45	1	0	0	0	0	3²/₃	3	1	1	3	1
1995—	Seattle (A.L.)	0	1	.000	6.35	1	1	0	0	0	5²/₃	9	4	4	2	1
Champ. series totals (3 years)		**3**	**1**	**.750**	**4.38**	**4**	**3**	**0**	**0**	**0**	**24²/₃**	**24**	**12**	**12**	**9**	**18**

WORLD SERIES RECORD

NOTES: Member of World Series championship team (1988).

Year	Team (League)	W	L	Pct.	ERA	G	GS	CG	ShO	Sv.	IP	H	R	ER	BB	SO
1988—	Los Angeles (N.L.)	1	0	1.000	6.23	2	2	0	0	0	8²/₃	10	7	6	6	10

BELINDA, STAN   P   REDS

PERSONAL: Born August 6, 1966, in Huntingdon, Pa. ... 6-3/215. ... Throws right, bats right. ... Full name: Stanley Peter Belinda.
HIGH SCHOOL: State College (Pa.) Area.
JUNIOR COLLEGE: Allegany Community College (Md.).

B

TRANSACTIONS/CAREER NOTES: Selected by Pittsburgh Pirates organization in 10th round of free-agent draft (June 2, 1986). ... On Gulf Coast Pirates disabled list (June 21-30, 1986). ... Traded by Pirates to Kansas City Royals for P Jon Lieber and P Dan Miceli (July 31, 1993). ... Granted free agency (December 23, 1994). ... Signed by Boston Red Sox (April 9, 1995). ... On Boston disabled list (April 21-May 6, 1995); included rehabilitation assignment to Sarasota (May 4-5). ... On Boston disabled list (March 19-April 6, May 30-July 26 and August 20, 1996-remainder of season); included rehabilitation assignments to Sarasota (June 6-9) and Pawtucket (July 14-25). ... Granted free agency (October 14, 1996). ... Signed by Cincinnati Reds organization (December 21, 1996).

Year Team (League)	W	L	Pct.	ERA	G	GS	CG	ShO	Sv.	IP	H	R	ER	BB	SO
1986— Watertown (NYP)	0	0	...	3.38	5	0	0	0	2	8	5	3	3	2	5
— GC Pirates (GCL)	3	2	.600	2.66	17	0	0	0	7	20 1/3	23	12	6	2	17
1987— Macon (S. Atl.)	6	4	.600	2.09	50	0	0	0	16	82	59	26	19	27	75
1988— Salem (Carolina)	6	4	.600	2.76	53	0	0	0	14	71 2/3	54	33	22	32	63
1989— Harrisburg (Eastern)	1	4	.200	2.33	32	0	0	0	13	38 2/3	32	13	10	25	33
— Buffalo (A.A.)	2	2	.500	0.95	19	0	0	0	9	28 1/3	13	5	3	13	28
— Pittsburgh (N.L.)	0	1	.000	6.10	8	0	0	0	0	10 1/3	13	8	7	2	10
1990— Buffalo (A.A.)	3	1	.750	1.90	15	0	0	0	5	23 2/3	20	8	5	8	25
— Pittsburgh (N.L.)	3	4	.429	3.55	55	0	0	0	5	58 1/3	48	23	23	29	55
1991— Pittsburgh (N.L.)	7	5	.583	3.45	60	0	0	0	16	78 1/3	50	30	30	35	71
1992— Pittsburgh (N.L.)	6	4	.600	3.15	59	0	0	0	18	71 1/3	58	26	25	29	57
1993— Pittsburgh (N.L.)	3	1	.750	3.61	40	0	0	0	19	42 1/3	35	18	17	11	30
— Kansas City (A.L.)■	1	1	.500	4.28	23	0	0	0	0	27 1/3	30	13	13	6	25
1994— Kansas City (A.L.)	2	2	.500	5.14	37	0	0	0	1	49	47	36	28	24	37
1995— Sarasota (Florida State)■	0	0	...	4.50	1	1	0	0	0	2	2	1	1	0	2
— Boston (A.L.)	8	1	.889	3.10	63	0	0	0	10	69 2/3	51	25	24	28	57
1996— Boston (A.L.)	2	1	.667	6.59	31	0	0	0	2	28 2/3	31	22	21	20	18
— Sarasota (Florida State)	0	1	.000	45.00	1	1	0	0	0	1	6	5	5	1	1
— Pawtucket (Int'l)	1	0	1.000	0.00	6	0	0	0	0	7 2/3	2	2	0	2	7
1997— Cincinnati (N.L.)■	1	5	.167	3.71	84	0	0	0	1	99 1/3	84	42	41	33	114
A.L. totals (4 years)	13	5	.722	4.43	154	0	0	0	13	174 2/3	159	96	86	78	137
N.L. totals (6 years)	20	20	.500	3.58	306	0	0	0	62	360	288	147	143	139	337
Major league totals (9 years)	33	25	.569	3.85	460	0	0	0	75	534 2/3	447	243	229	217	474

DIVISION SERIES RECORD

Year Team (League)	W	L	Pct.	ERA	G	GS	CG	ShO	Sv.	IP	H	R	ER	BB	SO
1995— Boston (A.L.)	0	0	...	0.00	1	0	0	0	0	1/3	0	0	0	0	0

CHAMPIONSHIP SERIES RECORD

Year Team (League)	W	L	Pct.	ERA	G	GS	CG	ShO	Sv.	IP	H	R	ER	BB	SO
1990— Pittsburgh (N.L.)	0	0	...	2.45	3	0	0	0	0	3 2/3	3	1	1	0	4
1991— Pittsburgh (N.L.)	1	0	1.000	0.00	3	0	0	0	0	5	0	0	0	3	4
1992— Pittsburgh (N.L.)	0	0	...	0.00	2	0	0	0	0	1 2/3	2	0	0	1	2
Champ. series totals (3 years)	1	0	1.000	0.87	8	0	0	0	0	10 1/3	5	1	1	4	10

BELL, DAVID   IF   CARDINALS

PERSONAL: Born September 14, 1972, in Cincinnati. ... 5-10/175. ... Bats right, throws right. ... Full name: David Michael Bell. ... Son of Buddy Bell, manager, Detroit Tigers; brother of Mike Bell, third baseman, Arizona Diamondbacks; and grandson of Gus Bell, major league outfielder with four teams (1950-64).

HIGH SCHOOL: Moeller (Cincinnati).

TRANSACTIONS/CAREER NOTES: Selected by Cleveland Indians organization in seventh round of free-agent draft (June 4, 1990). ... Traded by Indians with C Pepe McNeal and P Rick Heiserman to St. Louis Cardinals for P Ken Hill (July 27, 1995). ... On St. Louis disabled list (April 29-June 30, 1997); included rehabilitation assignments to Arkansas (June 10-19) and Louisville (June 20-26).

STATISTICAL NOTES: Led South Atlantic League in grounding into double plays with 22 in 1991. ... Led South Atlantic League third basemen with 389 total chances in 1991. ... Led Eastern League third basemen with 32 double plays in 1993. ... Led International League third basemen with .950 fielding percentage in 1994.

Year Team (League)	Pos.	G	AB	R	H	2B	3B	HR	RBI	Avg.	BB	SO	SB	PO	A	E	Avg.
1990— GC Indians (GCL)	3B	30	111	18	29	5	1	0	13	.261	10	8	1	29	50	7	.919
— Burlington (Appal.)	3B	12	42	4	7	1	1	0	2	.167	2	5	2	8	27	3	.921
1991— Columbus (S. Atl.)	3B	136	491	47	113	24	1	5	63	.230	37	50	3	90	*268	31	.920
1992— Kinston (Carolina)	3B	123	464	52	117	17	2	6	47	.252	54	66	2	83	264	20	.946
1993— Cant./Akr. (Eastern)	3B-2B-SS	129	483	69	141	20	2	9	60	.292	43	54	3	117	283	21	.950
1994— Charlotte (Int'l)	3B-SS-2B	134	481	66	141	17	4	18	88	.293	41	54	2	109	326	20	†.956
1995— Buffalo (A.A.)	3B-SS-2B	70	254	34	69	11	1	8	34	.272	22	37	0	46	172	11	.952
— Cleveland (A.L.)	3B	2	2	0	0	0	0	0	0	.000	0	0	0	0	2	0	1.000
— Louisville (A.A.)■	2B	18	76	9	21	3	1	1	9	.276	2	10	4	39	54	1	.989
— St. Louis (N.L.)	3B-2B	39	144	13	36	7	2	2	19	.250	4	25	1	77	108	7	.964
1996— St. Louis (N.L.)	3B-2B-SS	62	145	12	31	6	0	1	7	.214	10	22	1	45	113	5	.969
— Louisville (A.A.)	2B-3B-SS	42	136	9	24	5	1	0	7	.176	7	15	1	66	114	5	.973
1997— St. Louis (N.L.)	3B-2B-SS	66	142	9	30	7	2	1	12	.211	10	28	1	55	95	8	.949
— Arkansas (Texas)	3B-2B	9	32	3	7	2	0	1	3	.219	2	2	1	3	15	1	.947
— Louisville (A.A.)	2B-3B-SS	6	22	3	5	0	0	1	4	.227	0	6	0	6	10	1	.941
American League totals (1 year)		2	2	0	0	0	0	0	0	.000	0	0	0	0	2	0	1.000
National League totals (3 years)		167	431	34	97	20	4	4	40	.225	24	75	3	177	316	20	.961
Major league totals (3 years)		169	433	34	97	20	4	4	40	.224	24	75	3	177	318	20	.961

BELL, DEREK   OF   ASTROS

PERSONAL: Born December 11, 1968, in Tampa. ... 6-2/215. ... Bats right, throws right. ... Full name: Derek Nathaniel Bell.

HIGH SCHOOL: King (Tampa).

TRANSACTIONS/CAREER NOTES: Selected by Toronto Blue Jays organization in second round of free-agent draft (June 2, 1987). ... On Knoxville disabled list (July 30, 1988-remainder of season; June 13-21 and July 2-12, 1990). ... On Toronto disabled list (April 9-May 8,

1992); included rehabilitation assignment to Dunedin (April 27-May 4). ... Traded by Blue Jays with OF Stoney Briggs to San Diego Padres for OF Darrin Jackson (March 30, 1993). ... On suspended list (July 9-12, 1993 and July 9-17, 1994). ... Traded by Padres with OF Phil Plantier, P Pedro Martinez, P Doug Brocail, IF Craig Shipley and SS Ricky Gutierrez to Houston Astros for 3B Ken Caminiti, OF Steve Finley, SS Andujar Cedeno, 1B Robert Petagine, P Brian Williams and a player to be named later (December 28, 1994); Padres acquired P Sean Fesh to complete deal (May 1, 1995). ... On San Diego disabled list (May 14-June 13, 1997); included rehabilitation assignment to New Orleans (June 6-13).

HONORS: Named International League Most Valuable Player (1991).

STATISTICAL NOTES: Led International League with 243 total bases in 1991. ... Led International League outfielders with seven double plays in 1991.

Year Team (League)	Pos.	G	AB	R	H	2B	3B	HR	RBI	Avg.	BB	SO	SB	PO	A	E	Avg.
1987— St. Catharines (NYP) ..	OF	74	273	46	72	11	3	10	42	.264	18	60	12	126	6	2	.985
1988— Knoxville (Southern) ..	OF	14	52	5	13	3	1	0	4	.250	1	14	2	18	2	2	.909
1989— Knoxville (Southern) ..	OF	136	513	72	124	22	6	16	75	.242	26	92	15	216	12	9	.962
1990— Syracuse (Int'l)	OF	109	402	57	105	13	5	7	56	.261	23	75	21	220	9	5	.979
1991— Syracuse (Int'l)	OF	119	457	*89	*158	22	•12	13	*93	.346	57	69	27	278	*15	*16	.948
— Toronto (A.L.)	OF	18	28	5	4	0	0	0	1	.143	6	5	3	16	0	2	.889
1992— Toronto (A.L.)	OF-DH	61	161	23	39	6	3	2	15	.242	15	34	7	105	4	0	1.000
— Dunedin (Fla. St.)	OF	7	25	7	6	2	0	0	4	.240	4	4	3	13	0	2	.867
1993— San Diego (N.L.)■	OF-3B	150	542	73	142	19	1	21	72	.262	23	122	26	334	37	17	.956
1994— San Diego (N.L.)	OF	108	434	54	135	20	0	14	54	.311	29	88	24	247	3	10	.962
1995— Houston (N.L.)■	OF	112	452	63	151	21	2	8	86	.334	33	71	27	201	10	8	.963
1996— Houston (N.L.)	OF	158	627	84	165	40	3	17	113	.263	40	123	29	283	16	7	.977
1997— Houston (N.L.)	OF-DH	129	493	67	136	29	3	15	71	.276	40	94	15	226	5	8	.967
— New Orleans (A.A.).....	OF	5	13	0	2	0	0	0	1	.154	1	1	1	10	0	0	1.000
American League totals (2 years)		79	189	28	43	6	3	2	16	.228	21	39	10	121	4	2	.984
National League totals (5 years)		657	2548	341	729	129	9	75	396	.286	165	498	121	1291	71	50	.965
Major league totals (7 years)		736	2737	369	772	135	12	77	412	.282	186	537	131	1412	75	52	.966

DIVISION SERIES RECORD

Year Team (League)	Pos.	G	AB	R	H	2B	3B	HR	RBI	Avg.	BB	SO	SB	PO	A	E	Avg.
1997— Houston (N.L.)	OF	3	13	0	0	0	0	0	0	.000	0	3	0	3	0	0	1.000

CHAMPIONSHIP SERIES RECORD

Year Team (League)	Pos.	G	AB	R	H	2B	3B	HR	RBI	Avg.	BB	SO	SB	PO	A	E	Avg.
1992— Toronto (A.L.)	PR-OF	2	0	1	0	0	0	0	0	...	1	0	0	1	0	0	1.000

WORLD SERIES RECORD

NOTES: Member of World Series championship team (1992).

Year Team (League)	Pos.	G	AB	R	H	2B	3B	HR	RBI	Avg.	BB	SO	SB	PO	A	E	Avg.
1992— Toronto (A.L.)	PH	2	1	1	0	0	0	0	0	.000	1	0	0	...	...	...	...

BELL, JAY   SS   DIAMONDBACKS

PERSONAL: Born December 11, 1965, in Eglin AFB, Fla. ... 6-0/185. ... Bats right, throws right. ... Full name: Jay Stuart Bell.

HIGH SCHOOL: Tate (Gonzalez, Fla.).

TRANSACTIONS/CAREER NOTES: Selected by Minnesota Twins organization in first round (eighth pick overall) of free-agent draft (June 4, 1984). ... Traded by Twins with P Curt Wardle, OF Jim Weaver and a player to be named later to Cleveland Indians for P Bert Blyleven (August 1, 1985); Indians organization acquired P Rich Yett to complete deal (September 17, 1985). ... Traded by Indians to Pittsburgh Pirates for SS Felix Fermin (March 25, 1989). ... Traded by Pirates with 1B/3B Jeff King to Kansas City Royals for 3B Joe Randa, P Jeff Granger, P Jeff Martin and P Jeff Wallace (December 13, 1996). ... Granted free agency (November 4, 1997). ... Signed by Arizona Diamondbacks (November 17, 1997).

HONORS: Named shortstop on THE SPORTING NEWS N.L. All-Star team (1993). ... Won N.L. Gold Glove at shortstop (1993). ... Named shortstop on THE SPORTING NEWS N.L. Silver Slugger team (1993).

STATISTICAL NOTES: Led Appalachian League shortstops with 352 total chances and 43 double plays in 1984. ... Led California League shortstops with 84 double plays in 1985. ... Hit home run in first major league at-bat on first pitch (September 29, 1986). ... Led Eastern League shortstops with 613 total chances in 1986. ... Led American Association shortstops with 198 putouts, 322 assists, 30 errors and 550 total chances in 1987. ... Led N.L. with 39 sacrifice hits in 1990 and 30 in 1991. ... Had 22-game hitting streak (August 24-September 17, 1992). ... Led N.L. shortstops with 741 total chances in 1990, 754 in 1991, 816 in 1992, 794 in 1993 and 547 in 1994.. ... Led N.L. shortstops with 94 double plays in 1992. ... Career major league grand slams: 4.

Year Team (League)	Pos.	G	AB	R	H	2B	3B	HR	RBI	Avg.	BB	SO	SB	PO	A	E	Avg.
1984— Elizabethton (App.).....	SS	66	245	43	54	12	1	6	30	.220	42	50	4	*109	*218	25	.929
1985— Visalia (California)	SS	106	376	56	106	16	6	9	59	.282	41	73	10	176	330	53	.905
— Waterbury (Eastern)■	SS	29	114	13	34	11	2	1	14	.298	9	16	3	41	79	6	.952
1986— Waterbury (Eastern)...	SS	138	494	86	137	28	4	7	74	.277	87	65	10	197	*371	*45	.927
— Cleveland (A.L.).........	2B-DH	5	14	3	5	2	0	1	4	.357	2	3	0	1	6	2	.778
1987— Buffalo (A.A.)..............	SS-2B	110	362	71	94	15	4	17	60	.260	70	84	6	†201	†325	†30	.946
— Cleveland (A.L.).........	SS	38	125	14	27	9	1	2	13	.216	8	31	2	67	93	9	.947
1988— Cleveland (A.L.).........	SS-DH	73	211	23	46	5	1	2	21	.218	21	53	4	103	170	10	.965
— Colo. Springs (PCL)..	SS	49	181	35	50	12	2	7	24	.276	26	27	3	87	171	18	.935
1989— Pittsburgh (N.L.)■	SS	78	271	33	70	13	3	2	27	.258	19	47	5	109	197	10	.968
— Buffalo (A.A.)..............	SS-3B	86	298	49	85	15	3	10	54	.285	38	55	12	110	223	16	.954
1990— Pittsburgh (N.L.)	SS	159	583	93	148	28	7	7	52	.254	65	109	10	*260	459	22	.970
1991— Pittsburgh (N.L.)	SS	157	608	96	164	32	8	16	67	.270	52	99	10	239	*491	*24	.968
1992— Pittsburgh (N.L.)	SS	159	632	87	167	36	6	9	55	.264	55	103	7	*268	*526	22	.973

Year Team (League)	Pos.	G	AB	R	H	2B	3B	HR	RBI	Avg.	BB	SO	SB	PO	A	E	Avg.
1993— Pittsburgh (N.L.)	SS	154	604	102	187	32	9	9	51	.310	77	122	16	*256	*527	11	*.986
1994— Pittsburgh (N.L.)	SS	110	424	68	117	35	4	9	45	.276	49	82	2	152	*380	15	.973
1995— Pittsburgh (N.L.)	SS-3B	138	530	79	139	28	4	13	55	.262	55	110	2	206	415	14	.978
1996— Pittsburgh (N.L.)	SS	151	527	65	132	29	3	13	71	.250	54	108	6	215	*478	10	*.986
1997— Kansas City (A.L.)■ ...	SS-3B	153	573	89	167	28	3	21	92	.291	71	101	10	229	450	10	.985
American League totals (4 years)		269	923	129	245	44	5	26	130	.265	102	188	16	400	719	31	.973
National League totals (8 years)		1106	4179	623	1124	233	44	78	423	.269	426	780	58	1705	3473	128	.976
Major league totals (12 years)		1375	5102	752	1369	277	49	104	553	.268	528	968	74	2105	4192	159	.975

CHAMPIONSHIP SERIES RECORD

RECORDS: Shares single-series record for most singles—9 (1991).

Year Team (League)	Pos.	G	AB	R	H	2B	3B	HR	RBI	Avg.	BB	SO	SB	PO	A	E	Avg.
1990— Pittsburgh (N.L.)	SS	6	20	3	5	1	0	1	1	.250	4	3	0	4	22	1	.963
1991— Pittsburgh (N.L.)	SS	7	29	2	12	2	0	1	1	.414	0	10	0	13	19	1	.970
1992— Pittsburgh (N.L.)	SS	7	29	3	5	0	1	1	4	.172	3	4	0	6	8	1	.933
Championship series totals (3 years)		20	78	8	22	5	0	3	6	.282	7	17	0	23	49	1	.960

ALL-STAR GAME RECORD

Year League	Pos.	AB	R	H	2B	3B	HR	RBI	Avg.	BB	SO	SB	PO	A	E	Avg.
1993— National	2B	1	0	0	0	0	0	0	.000	0	0	0	1	1	0	1.000

B

BELL, MIKE   3B   DIAMONDBACKS

PERSONAL: Born December 7, 1974, in Cincinnati. ... 6-2/185. ... Bats right, throws right. ... Full name: Michael J. Bell. ... Son of Buddy Bell, manager, Detroit Tigers; brother of David Bell, infielder, St. Louis Cardinals; and grandson of Gus Bell, major league outfielder with four teams (1950-64).

HIGH SCHOOL: Moeller (Cincinnati).

TRANSACTIONS/CAREER NOTES: Selected by Texas Rangers organization in supplemental round ("sandwich pick" between first and second round, 30th pick overall); pick received as part of compensation for Chicago Cubs signing Type A free-agent Jose Guzman. ... Traded by Rangers to Anaheim Angels for P Matt Perisho (October 31, 1997). ... Selected by Arizona Diamondbacks in second round (55th pick overall) of expansion draft (November 18, 1997).

STATISTICAL NOTES: Led Gulf Coast League with 107 total bases in 1993. ... Led Gulf Coast League third basemen with 144 assists and 191 total chances in 1993. ... Led South Atlantic League third basemen with 51 errors in 1994. ... Led Texas League third basemen with 392 total chances and tied for lead with 28 double plays in 1996.

Year Team (League)	Pos.	G	AB	R	H	2B	3B	HR	RBI	Avg.	BB	SO	SB	PO	A	E	Avg.
1993— GC Rangers (GCL)......	3B-2B	*60	•230	48	*73	13	6	3	34	.317	27	23	9	36	†145	12	.938
1994— Char., S.C. (S. Atl.)......	3B-2B	120	475	58	125	22	6	6	58	.263	47	76	16	96	213	†53	.854
1995— Charlotte (Fla. St.)......	3B	129	470	49	122	20	1	5	52	.260	48	72	9	91	280	*35	.914
1996— Tulsa (Texas)	3B	128	484	62	129	31	3	16	59	.267	42	75	3	*90	*277	25	*.936
1997— Oklahoma City (A.A.)..	2B-3B-1B	93	328	35	77	18	2	5	38	.235	29	78	4	128	190	20	.941
— Tulsa (Texas)	3B	33	123	17	35	11	0	8	23	.285	15	28	0	28	55	9	.902

BELLE, ALBERT   OF   WHITE SOX

PERSONAL: Born August 25, 1966, in Shreveport, La. ... 6-2/225. ... Bats right, throws right. ... Full name: Albert Jojuan Belle. ... Formerly known as Joey Belle.

HIGH SCHOOL: Huntington (Shreveport, La.).

COLLEGE: Louisiana State.

TRANSACTIONS/CAREER NOTES: Selected by Cleveland Indians organization in second round of free-agent draft (June 2, 1987). ... On suspended list (July 12-18, 1991; August 4-8, 1992; June 4-7, 1993; August 1-7, 1994; and June 21-22, 1996). ... Granted free agency (October 28, 1996). ... Signed by Chicago White Sox (November 19, 1996).

RECORDS: Shares major league record for fewest double plays by outfielder (150 or more games)—0 (1996). ... Shares major league recors for most home runs in two consecutive games—5 (September 18 [2] and 19 [3], 1995); and fewest double plays by outfielder (150 or more games)—0 (1997). ... Shares A.L. single-season record for fewest errors by outfielder who led league in errors—9 (1991).

HONORS: Named outfielder on THE SPORTING NEWS A.L. All-Star team (1993-96). ... Named outfielder on THE SPORTING NEWS A.L. Silver Slugger team (1993-96). ... Named Major League Player of the Year by THE SPORTING NEWS (1995).

STATISTICAL NOTES: Hit three home runs in one game (September 4, 1992 and September 19, 1995). ... Led A.L. with 14 sacrifice flies in 1993. ... Led A.L. outfielders with seven double plays in 1993. ... Led A.L. in total bases with 294 in 1994 and 377 in 1995. ... Led A.L. with .690 slugging percentage in 1995. ... Led A.L. in grounding into double plays with 24 in 1995. ... Had 21-game hitting streak (April 27-May 21, 1996). ... Had 27-game hitting streak (May 3-June 1, 1997). ... Led A.L. in grounding into double plays with 26 in 1997. ... Career major league grand slams: 11.

MISCELLANEOUS: Holds Cleveland Indians all-time record for most home runs (242).

Year Team (League)	Pos.	G	AB	R	H	2B	3B	HR	RBI	Avg.	BB	SO	SB	PO	A	E	Avg.
1987— Kinston (Carolina)	OF	10	37	5	12	2	0	3	9	.324	8	16	0	5	0	0	1.000
1988— Kinston (Carolina)	OF	41	153	21	46	16	0	8	39	.301	18	45	2	43	5	5	.906
— Waterloo (Midw.)	OF	9	28	2	7	1	0	1	2	.250	1	9	0	11	1	0	1.000
1989— Cant./Akr. (Eastern)	OF	89	312	48	88	20	0	20	69	.282	32	82	8	136	4	3	.979
— Cleveland (A.L.)..........	OF-DH	62	218	22	49	8	4	7	37	.225	12	55	2	92	3	2	.979
1990— Cleveland (A.L.)..........	DH-OF	9	23	1	4	0	0	1	3	.174	1	6	0	0	0	0	...
— Colo. Springs (PCL) ...	OF	24	96	16	33	3	1	5	19	.344	5	16	4	31	0	2	.939
— Cant./Akr. (Eastern)	OF	9	32	4	8	1	0	0	3	.250	3	7	0	...	...	...	...
1991— Cleveland (A.L.)..........	OF-DH	123	461	60	130	31	2	28	95	.282	25	99	3	170	8	•9	.952
— Colo. Springs (PCL) ...	OF	16	61	9	20	3	2	2	16	.328	2	8	1	19	1	1	.952

Year Team (League)	Pos.	G	AB	R	H	2B	3B	HR	RBI	Avg.	BB	SO	SB	PO	A	E	Avg.
1992— Cleveland (A.L.).........	DH-OF	153	585	81	152	23	1	34	112	.260	52	128	8	94	1	3	.969
1993— Cleveland (A.L.).........	OF-DH	159	594	93	172	36	3	38	*129	.290	76	96	23	338	16	5	.986
1994— Cleveland (A.L.).........	OF-DH	106	412	90	147	35	2	36	101	.357	58	71	9	205	8	6	.973
1995— Cleveland (A.L.).........	OF-DH	143	546	•121	173	•52	1	*50	•126	.317	73	80	5	304	7	6	.981
1996— Cleveland (A.L.).........	OF-DH	158	602	124	187	38	3	48	*148	.311	99	87	11	309	11	10	.970
1997— Chicago (A.L.)■.........	OF-DH	161	634	90	174	45	1	30	116	.274	53	105	4	351	1	10	.972
Major league totals (9 years)		1074	4075	682	1188	268	17	272	867	.292	449	727	65	1863	55	51	.974

DIVISION SERIES RECORD

Year Team (League)	Pos.	G	AB	R	H	2B	3B	HR	RBI	Avg.	BB	SO	SB	PO	A	E	Avg.
1995— Cleveland (A.L.)..........	OF	3	11	3	3	1	0	1	3	.273	4	3	0	7	0	1	.875
1996— Cleveland (A.L.)..........	OF	4	15	2	3	0	0	2	6	.200	4	2	1	11	1	0	1.000
Division series totals (2 years)		7	26	5	6	1	0	3	9	.231	8	5	1	18	1	1	.950

CHAMPIONSHIP SERIES RECORD

Year Team (League)	Pos.	G	AB	R	H	2B	3B	HR	RBI	Avg.	BB	SO	SB	PO	A	E	Avg.
1995— Cleveland (A.L.)..........	OF	5	18	1	4	1	0	1	1	.222	3	5	0	4	0	2	.667

WORLD SERIES RECORD

Year Team (League)	Pos.	G	AB	R	H	2B	3B	HR	RBI	Avg.	BB	SO	SB	PO	A	E	Avg.
1995— Cleveland (A.L.)..........	OF	6	17	4	4	0	0	2	4	.235	7	5	0	10	0	1	.909

ALL-STAR GAME RECORD

Year League	Pos.	AB	R	H	2B	3B	HR	RBI	Avg.	BB	SO	SB	PO	A	E	Avg.
1993— American....................	PH-DH	1	2	1	0	0	0	1	1.000	1	0	0	. . .	. . .	. . .	. . .
1994— American....................	OF	2	0	0	0	0	0	0	.000	0	0	0	1	0	0	1.000
1995— American....................	OF	3	0	0	0	0	0	0	.000	0	1	0	1	0	0	1.000
1996— American....................	OF	4	0	0	0	0	0	0	.000	0	3	0	1	0	0	1.000
1997— American....................							Did not play.									
All-Star Game totals (4 years)		10	2	1	0	0	0	1	.100	1	4	0	3	0	0	1.000

BELLHORN, MARK   3B   ATHLETICS

B

PERSONAL: Born August 23, 1974, in Boston ... 6-0/190. ... Bats both, throws right. ... Full name: Mark Christian Bellhorn.
HIGH SCHOOL: Oviedo (Fla.).
COLLEGE: Auburn.
TRANSACTIONS/CAREER NOTES: Selected by Oakland Athletics organization in second round of free agent draft (June 1, 1995).

Year Team (League)	Pos.	G	AB	R	H	2B	3B	HR	RBI	Avg.	BB	SO	SB	PO	A	E	Avg.
1995— Modesto (California) ..	SS	56	229	35	59	12	0	6	31	.258	27	52	5	94	172	21	.927
1996— Huntsville (Southern) .	IF	131	468	84	117	24	5	10	71	.250	73	124	19	208	344	32	.945
1997— Edmonton (PCL)	2B-SS-3B	70	241	54	79	18	3	11	46	.328	64	59	6	105	187	13	.957
— Oakland (A.L.)............	3-2-DH-S	68	224	33	51	9	1	6	19	.228	32	70	7	72	123	9	.956
Major league totals (1 year)		68	224	33	51	9	1	6	19	.228	32	70	7	72	123	9	.956

BELLIARD, RAFAEL   SS/2B   BRAVES

PERSONAL: Born October 24, 1961, in Pueblo Nuevo, Mao, Dominican Republic. ... 5-6/160. ... Bats right, throws right. ... Full name: Rafael Leonidas Matias Belliard. ... Name pronounced BELL-ee-ard.
TRANSACTIONS/CAREER NOTES: Signed as non-drafted free agent by Pittsburgh Pirates organization (July 10, 1980). ... On Buffalo disabled list (April 19-July 24, 1982). ... On Pittsburgh disabled list (June 28-August 28, 1984; July 28-August 12, 1986; August 27, 1987-remainder of season; and May 19-June 3, 1988). ... Granted free agency (November 5, 1990). ... Signed by Atlanta Braves (December 18, 1990). ... Granted free agency (October 25, 1994). ... Re-signed by Braves (October 28, 1994). ... Granted free agency (October 31, 1996). ... Re-signed by Braves (December 6, 1996). ... Granted free agency (October 29, 1997). ... Re-signed by Braves organization (December 5, 1997).
STATISTICAL NOTES: Led Carolina League with 12 sacrifice hits and tied for lead in caught stealing with 15 in 1981. ... Tied for Eastern League lead in double plays by shortstop with 69 in 1983. ... Led N.L. shortstops with .977 fielding percentage in 1988.

Year Team (League)	Pos.	G	AB	R	H	2B	3B	HR	RBI	Avg.	BB	SO	SB	PO	A	E	Avg.
1980— GC Pirates (GCL)........	SS-2B-3B	12	42	6	9	1	0	0	2	.214	0	3	1	24	39	1	.984
— Shelby (S. Atl.)..........	SS	8	24	1	3	0	0	0	2	.125	1	3	0	10	27	5	.881
1981— Alexandria (Caro.)	SS	127	472	58	102	6	5	0	33	.216	26	92	42	•205	330	29	.949
1982— Buffalo (Eastern)	SS	40	124	14	34	1	1	0	19	.274	8	16	6	56	87	5	.966
— Pittsburgh (N.L.)	SS	9	2	3	1	0	0	0	0	.500	0	0	1	2	2	0	1.000
1983— Lynn (Eastern)	SS-2B	127	431	63	113	13	2	2	37	.262	30	54	12	203	307	26	.951
— Pittsburgh (N.L.)	SS	4	1	1	0	0	0	0	0	.000	0	1	0	1	3	0	1.000
1984— Pittsburgh (N.L.)	SS-2B	20	22	3	5	0	0	0	0	.227	0	1	0	12	13	3	.893
1985— Pittsburgh (N.L.)	SS	17	20	1	4	0	0	0	1	.200	0	5	0	13	23	2	.947
— Hawaii (PCL)	SS-2B	100	341	35	84	12	4	1	18	.246	4	49	9	172	289	6	.989
1986— Pittsburgh (N.L.)	SS-2B	117	309	33	72	5	2	0	31	.233	26	54	12	147	317	12	.975
1987— Pittsburgh (N.L.)	SS-2B	81	203	26	42	4	3	1	15	.207	20	25	5	113	191	6	.981
— Harrisburg (Eastern) ..	SS	37	145	24	49	5	2	0	9	.338	6	16	7	59	115	7	.961
1988— Pittsburgh (N.L.)	SS-2B	122	286	28	61	0	4	0	11	.213	26	47	7	134	261	9	†.978
1989— Pittsburgh (N.L.)	SS-2B-3B	67	154	10	33	4	0	0	8	.214	8	22	5	71	138	3	.986
1990— Pittsburgh (N.L.)	2B-SS-3B	47	54	10	11	3	0	0	6	.204	5	13	1	37	36	2	.973

Year Team (League)	Pos.	G	AB	R	H	2B	3B	HR	RBI	Avg.	BB	SO	SB	PO	A	E	Avg.
								BATTING							FIELDING		
1991—Atlanta (N.L.)■..........	SS	149	353	36	88	9	2	0	27	.249	22	63	3	168	361	18	.967
1992—Atlanta (N.L.)..............	SS-2B	144	285	20	60	6	1	0	14	.211	14	43	0	152	291	14	.969
1993—Atlanta (N.L.)..............	SS-2B	91	79	6	18	5	0	0	6	.228	4	13	0	53	99	1	.993
1994—Atlanta (N.L.)..............	SS-2B	46	120	9	29	7	1	0	9	.242	2	29	0	45	86	1	.992
1995—Atlanta (N.L.)..............	SS-2B	75	180	12	40	2	1	0	7	.222	6	28	2	74	181	1	.996
1996—Atlanta (N.L.)..............	SS-2B	87	142	9	24	7	0	0	3	.169	2	22	3	65	150	5	.977
1997—Atlanta (N.L.)..............	SS-2B	72	71	9	15	3	0	1	3	.211	1	17	0	37	69	1	.991
Major league totals (16 years)		1148	2281	216	503	55	14	2	141	.221	136	383	39	1124	2221	78	.977

DIVISION SERIES RECORD

Year Team (League)	Pos.	G	AB	R	H	2B	3B	HR	RBI	Avg.	BB	SO	SB	PO	A	E	Avg.
								BATTING							FIELDING		
1995—Atlanta (N.L.)..............	SS	4	5	1	0	0	0	0	0	.000	0	1	0	2	5	0	1.000
1996—Atlanta (N.L.)..............	SS	3	0	0	0	0	0	0	0	...	0	0	0	0	0	0	...
Division series totals (2 years)		7	5	1	0	0	0	0	0	.000	0	1	0	2	5	0	1.000

CHAMPIONSHIP SERIES RECORD

Year Team (League)	Pos.	G	AB	R	H	2B	3B	HR	RBI	Avg.	BB	SO	SB	PO	A	E	Avg.
								BATTING							FIELDING		
1990—Pittsburgh (N.L.)........								Did not play.									
1991—Atlanta (N.L.)..............	SS	7	19	0	4	0	0	0	1	.211	3	3	0	9	15	1	.960
1992—Atlanta (N.L.).............	SS-2B-PR	4	2	1	0	0	0	0	0	.000	1	0	0	2	3	0	1.000
1993—Atlanta (N.L.)...........PH-2-PR-S		2	1	1	0	0	0	0	0	.000	0	1	0	0	0	0	...
1995—Atlanta (N.L.)..............	SS	4	11	1	3	0	0	0	0	.273	0	3	0	6	7	1	.929
1996—Atlanta (N.L.).............	2B-SS-PR	4	6	0	4	0	0	0	2	.667	0	0	0	2	5	0	1.000
Championship series totals (5 years)		21	39	3	11	0	0	0	3	.282	4	7	0	19	30	2	.961

WORLD SERIES RECORD

NOTES: Member of World Series championship team (1995).

Year Team (League)	Pos.	G	AB	R	H	2B	3B	HR	RBI	Avg.	BB	SO	SB	PO	A	E	Avg.
								BATTING							FIELDING		
1991—Atlanta (N.L.)..............	SS	7	16	0	6	1	0	0	4	.375	1	2	0	8	21	0	1.000
1992—Atlanta (N.L.)..............	SS-2B	4	4	0	0	0	0	0	0	.000	0	0	0	3	2	0	1.000
1995—Atlanta (N.L.)..............	SS	6	16	0	0	0	0	0	1	.000	0	4	0	3	11	2	.875
1996—Atlanta (N.L.)..............	SS-PR	4	0	0	0	0	0	0	0	...	0	0	0	0	3	0	1.000
World Series totals (4 years)		21	36	0	6	1	0	0	5	.167	1	6	0	14	37	2	.962

BELLIARD, RONNIE — 2B — BREWERS

PERSONAL: Born July 4, 1976, in Bronx, N.Y. ... 5-8/180. ... Bats right, throws right. ... Full name: Ronald Belliard. ... Name pronounced BELL-ee-ard.
HIGH SCHOOL: Central (Miami).
TRANSACTIONS/CAREER NOTES: Selected by Milwaukee Brewers organization in eighth round of free-agent draft (June 2, 1994).
STATISTICAL NOTES: Led Midwest League second basemen with 25 errors in 1995. ... Led Pacific Coast League second basemen with 229 putouts, 358 assists, 24 errors and 611 total chances and tied for league lead with 92 double plays in 1997.

Year Team (League)	Pos.	G	AB	R	H	2B	3B	HR	RBI	Avg.	BB	SO	SB	PO	A	E	Avg.
								BATTING							FIELDING		
1994—Ariz. Brewers (Ariz.) ...	2B-3B-SS	39	143	32	42	7	3	0	27	.294	14	25	7	54	119	12	.935
1995—Beloit (Midwest).........	2B-3B	130	461	76	137	28	5	13	76	.297	36	67	16	221	346	†26	.956
1996—El Paso (Texas)..........	2B	109	416	73	116	20	8	3	57	.279	60	51	26	246	314	16	.972
1997—Tucson (PCL)	2B-SS	118	443	80	125	35	4	4	55	.282	61	69	10	†233	†369	†26	.959

BELTRAN, RIGO — P — CARDINALS

PERSONAL: Born November 13, 1969, in Tijuana, Mexico. ... 5-11/185. ... Throws left, bats left. ... Full name: Rigoberto Beltran.
HIGH SCHOOL: Point Loma (San Diego).
COLLEGE: Wyoming.
TRANSACTIONS/CAREER NOTES: Selected by St. Louis Cardinals organization in 26th round of free-agent draft (June 3, 1991).
STATISTICAL NOTES: Led New York-Pennsylvania League with 12 balks in 1991. ... Led American Association with 18 wild pitches in 1994.

Year Team (League)	W	L	Pct.	ERA	G	GS	CG	ShO	Sv.	IP	H	R	ER	BB	SO
1991—Hamilton (NYP)	5	2	.714	2.63	21	4	0	0	0	48	41	17	14	19	69
1992—Savannah (S. Atl.)	6	1	.857	2.17	13	13	2	1	0	83	38	20	20	40	106
—St. Petersburg (FSL)	0	0	...	0.00	2	2	0	0	0	8	6	0	0	2	3
1993—Arkansas (Texas)........	5	5	.500	3.25	18	16	0	0	0	88²/₃	74	39	32	38	82
1994—Arkansas (Texas)	4	0	1.000	0.64	4	4	1	1	0	28	12	2	2	3	21
—Louisville (A.A.)	11	11	.500	5.07	23	23	1	0	0	138¹/₃	147	82	78	68	87
1995—Louisville (A.A.)	8	9	.471	5.21	24	24	0	0	0	129²/₃	156	81	75	34	92
1996—Louisville (A.A.)	8	6	.571	4.35	38	16	3	1	0	130¹/₃	132	67	63	24	103
1997—Louisville (A.A.)	5	2	.714	2.32	9	8	1	0	0	54¹/₃	45	17	14	21	46
—St. Louis (N.L.)	1	2	.333	3.48	35	4	0	0	1	54¹/₃	47	25	21	17	50
Major league totals (1 year)........	1	2	.333	3.48	35	4	0	0	1	54¹/₃	47	25	21	17	50

BELTRE, ADRIAN — 3B — DODGERS

PERSONAL: Born April 7, 1978, in Santo Domingo, Dominican Republic. ... 5-11/165. ... Bats right, throws right. ... Born April 7, 1978, in Santo Domingo, Dominican Republic... 5-11/165. ... Throws right, bats right. ... Name pronounced bell-TREE.
HIGH SCHOOL: Liceo Maximo Gomez (Santo Domingo, Dominican Republic).

TRANSACTIONS/CAREER NOTES: Signed as non-drafted free agent by Los Angeles Dodgers (July 7, 1994). ... On San Bernardino disabled list (June 25-July 2, 1996).
HONORS: Named Florida State League Most Valuable Player (1997).
STATISTICAL NOTES: Led Florida State League with .561 slugging percentage and 12 intentional bases on balls in 1997. ... Led Florida State League third basemen with 26 double plays in 1997.

														FIELDING		
Year Team (League)	Pos.	G	AB	R	H	2B	3B	HR	RBI	Avg.	BB	SO	SB	PO	A	E	Avg.
1995—Dom. Dodgers (DSL) .	3B	62	218	56	67	15	3	8	40	.307	54	26	2	187	31	19	.920
1996—Savannah (S. Atl.)	3B-2B	68	244	48	75	14	3	16	59	.307	35	46	4	55	143	19	.912
—San Bern. (Calif.).......	3B	63	238	40	62	13	1	10	40	.261	19	44	3	32	110	7	.953
1997—Vero Beach (FSL)	3B-OF	123	435	95	138	24	2	*26	*104	.317	67	66	25	83	231	37	.895

BENARD, MARVIN — OF — GIANTS

B

PERSONAL: Born January 20, 1970, in Bluefields, Nicaragua. ... 5-9/183. ... Bats left, throws left. ... Full name: Marvin Larry Benard.
HIGH SCHOOL: Bell (Bell Gardens, Calif.).
JUNIOR COLLEGE: Los Angeles Harbor College.
COLLEGE: Lewis-Clark State (Idaho).
TRANSACTIONS/CAREER NOTES: Selected by Philadelphia Phillies organization in 20th round of free-agent draft (June 4, 1990); did not sign. ... Selected by San Francisco Giants organization in 50th round of free-agent draft (June 1, 1992). ... On disabled list (April 17-28, 1993).
STATISTICAL NOTES: Tied for Texas League lead in grounding into double plays with 15 in 1994. ... Led Texas League outfielders with five double plays in 1994.

						BATTING								FIELDING		
Year Team (League)	Pos.	G	AB	R	H	2B	3B	HR	RBI	Avg.	BB	SO	SB	PO	A	E	Avg.
1992—Everett (N'west)..........	OF	64	161	31	38	10	2	1	17	.236	24	39	17	90	8	3	.970
1993—Clinton (Midwest).......	OF	112	349	84	105	14	2	5	50	.301	56	66	42	179	10	5	.974
1994—Shreveport (Texas).....	OF	125	454	66	143	32	3	4	48	.315	31	58	24	259	17	*12	.958
1995—Phoenix (PCL)............	OF	111	378	70	115	14	6	6	32	.304	50	66	10	183	5	8	.959
—San Francisco (N.L.) ..	OF	13	34	5	13	2	0	1	4	.382	1	7	1	19	0	0	1.000
1996—Phoenix (PCL)............	OF	4	19	2	7	0	0	0	4	.368	2	2	1	10	0	0	1.000
—San Francisco (N.L.) ..	OF	135	488	89	121	17	4	5	27	.248	59	84	25	309	7	5	.984
1997—San Francisco (N.L.) ..	OF-DH	84	114	13	26	4	0	1	13	.228	13	29	3	27	2	1	.967
—Phoenix (PCL)............	OF	17	60	14	20	5	0	0	5	.333	11	9	4	26	2	1	.966
Major league totals (3 years)		232	636	107	160	23	4	7	44	.252	73	120	29	355	9	6	.984

DIVISION SERIES RECORD

						BATTING								FIELDING		
Year Team (League)	Pos.	G	AB	R	H	2B	3B	HR	RBI	Avg.	BB	SO	SB	PO	A	E	Avg.
1997—San Francisco (N.L.) ..	PH	2	2	0	0	0	0	0	0	.000	0	1	0	0	0	0	...

BENES, ALAN — P — CARDINALS

PERSONAL: Born January 21, 1972, in Evansville, Ind. ... 6-5/215. ... Throws right, bats right. ... Full name: Alan Paul Benes. ... Brother of Andy Benes, pitcher with three major league teams (1989-97); and brother of Adam Benes, pitcher, Cardinals organization. ... Name pronounced BEN-ess.
HIGH SCHOOL: Lake Forest (Ill.).
COLLEGE: Creighton.
TRANSACTIONS/CAREER NOTES: Selected by San Diego Padres organization in 49th round of free-agent draft (June 4, 1990); did not sign. ... Selected by St. Louis Cardinals organization in first round (16th pick overall) of free-agent draft (June 3, 1993). ... On Louisville disabled list (May 3-August 9, 1995 and July 31, 1997-remainder of season).
HONORS: Named N.L. Rookie Pitcher of the Year by THE SPORTING NEWS (1996).

Year Team (League)	W	L	Pct.	ERA	G	GS	CG	ShO	Sv.	IP	H	R	ER	BB	SO
1993—Glens Falls (NYP)...............	0	4	.000	3.65	7	7	0	0	0	37	39	20	15	14	29
1994—Savannah (S. Atl.)	2	0	1.000	1.48	4	4	0	0	0	24 1/3	21	5	4	7	24
—St. Petersburg (FSL)	7	1	.875	1.61	11	11	0	0	0	78 1/3	55	18	14	15	69
—Arkansas (Texas)	7	2	.778	2.98	13	13	1	0	0	87 2/3	58	38	29	26	75
—Louisville (A.A.)..................	1	0	1.000	2.93	2	2	1	0	0	15 1/3	10	5	5	4	16
1995—Louisville (A.A.)..................	4	2	.667	2.41	11	11	2	1	0	56	37	16	15	14	54
—St. Louis (N.L.)..................	1	2	.333	8.44	3	3	0	0	0	16	24	15	15	4	20
1996—St. Louis (N.L.)..................	13	10	.565	4.90	34	32	3	1	0	191	192	120	104	87	131
1997—St. Louis (N.L.)..................	9	9	.500	2.89	23	23	2	0	0	161 2/3	128	60	52	68	160
Major league totals (3 years)......	23	21	.523	4.17	60	58	5	1	0	368 2/3	344	195	171	159	311

CHAMPIONSHIP SERIES RECORD

Year Team (League)	W	L	Pct.	ERA	G	GS	CG	ShO	Sv.	IP	H	R	ER	BB	SO
1996—St. Louis (N.L.)..................	0	1	.000	2.84	2	1	0	0	0	6 1/3	3	2	2	3	5

BENES, ANDY — P

PERSONAL: Born August 20, 1967, in Evansville, Ind. ... 6-6/245. ... Throws right, bats right. ... Full name: Andrew Charles Benes. ... Brother of Alan Benes, pitcher, St. Louis Cardinals; and brother of Adam Benes, pitcher, St. Louis Cardinals organization. ... Name pronounced BEN-ess.
HIGH SCHOOL: Central (Evansville, Ind.).
COLLEGE: Evansville.
TRANSACTIONS/CAREER NOTES: Selected by San Diego Padres organization in first round (first pick overall) of free-agent draft (June 1, 1988). ... On suspended list (September 28, 1993-remainder of season). ... Traded by Padres with a player to be named later to Seattle Mariners for P Ron Villone and OF Marc Newfield (July 31, 1995); Mariners acquired P Greg Keagle to complete deal (September 16, 1995). ... Granted free agency (October 31, 1995). ... Signed by St. Louis Cardinals (December 23, 1995). ... Granted free agency (October 29, 1997). ... On disabled list (March 23-April 28, 1997); included rehabilitation assignments to Prince William (April 11), Louisville (April 16) and Arkansas (April 22).

RECORDS: Holds major league single-season record for fewest hits allowed for leader in most hits allowed—230 (1992).
HONORS: Named N.L. Rookie Pitcher of the Year by THE SPORTING NEWS (1989). ... Named Texas League Pitcher of the Year (1989).
STATISTICAL NOTES: Tied for N.L. lead with five balks in 1990. ... Pitched 7-0 one-hit, complete-game victory against New York (July 3, 1994).
MISCELLANEOUS: Holds San Diego Padres all-time record for most strikeouts (1,036). ... Member of 1988 U.S. Olympic baseball team (1988).

Year Team (League)	W	L	Pct.	ERA	G	GS	CG	ShO	Sv.	IP	H	R	ER	BB	SO
1989—Wichita (Texas)	8	4	.667	2.16	16	16	5	*3	0	108⅓	79	32	26	39	115
—Las Vegas (PCL)	2	1	.667	8.10	5	5	0	0	0	26⅔	41	29	24	12	29
—San Diego (N.L.)	6	3	.667	3.51	10	10	0	0	0	66⅔	51	28	26	31	66
1990—San Diego (N.L.)	10	11	.476	3.60	32	31	2	0	0	192⅓	177	87	77	69	140
1991—San Diego (N.L.)	15	11	.577	3.03	33	33	4	1	0	223	194	76	75	59	167
1992—San Diego (N.L.)	13	14	.481	3.35	34	34	2	2	0	231⅓	*230	90	86	61	169
1993—San Diego (N.L.)	15	15	.500	3.78	34	34	4	2	0	230⅔	200	111	97	86	179
1994—San Diego (N.L.)	6	*14	.300	3.86	25	25	2	2	0	172⅓	155	82	74	51	*189
1995—San Diego (N.L.)	4	7	.364	4.17	19	19	1	1	0	118⅔	121	65	55	45	126
—Seattle (A.L.)■	7	2	.778	5.86	12	12	0	0	0	63	72	42	41	33	45
1996—St. Louis (N.L.)■	18	10	.643	3.83	36	34	3	1	1	230⅓	215	107	98	77	160
1997—St. Louis (N.L.)	10	7	.588	3.10	26	26	0	0	0	177	149	64	61	61	175
—Prince William (Caro.)	0	0	...	0.00	1	1	0	0	0	5	3	1	0	1	9
—Louisville (A.A.)	0	0	...	1.80	1	1	0	0	0	5	3	1	1	1	5
—Arkansas (Texas)	1	0	1.000	1.29	1	1	0	0	0	7*	2	1	1	2	6
A.L. totals (1 year)	7	2	.778	5.86	12	12	0	0	0	63	72	42	41	33	45
N.L. totals (9 years)	97	92	.513	3.56	249	246	18	9	1	1642⅓	1492	710	649	540	1371
Major league totals (9 years)	104	94	.525	3.64	261	258	18	9	1	1705⅓	1564	752	690	573	1416

DIVISION SERIES RECORD

Year Team (League)	W	L	Pct.	ERA	G	GS	CG	ShO	Sv.	IP	H	R	ER	BB	SO
1995—Seattle (A.L.)	0	0	...	5.40	2	2	0	0	0	11⅔	10	7	7	9	8
1996—St. Louis (N.L.)	0	0	...	5.14	1	1	0	0	0	7	6	4	4	1	9
Div. series totals (2 years)	0	0	...	5.30	3	3	0	0	0	18⅔	16	11	11	10	17

CHAMPIONSHIP SERIES RECORD

RECORDS: Shares N.L. single-series record for most hits allowed—19 (1996).

Year Team (League)	W	L	Pct.	ERA	G	GS	CG	ShO	Sv.	IP	H	R	ER	BB	SO
1995—Seattle (A.L.)	0	1	.000	23.14	1	1	0	0	0	2⅓	6	6	6	2	3
1996—St. Louis (N.L.)	0	0	...	5.28	3	2	0	0	0	15⅓	19	9	9	3	9
Champ. series totals (2 years)	0	1	.000	7.64	4	3	0	0	0	17⅔	25	15	15	5	12

ALL-STAR GAME RECORD

Year League	W	L	Pct.	ERA	GS	CG	ShO	Sv.	IP	H	R	ER	BB	SO
1993—National	0	0	...	4.50	0	0	0	0	2	2	1	1	0	2

BENITEZ, ARMANDO   P   ORIOLES

PERSONAL: Born November 3, 1972, in Ramon Santana, Dominican Republic. ... 6-4/225. ... Throws right, bats right.
TRANSACTIONS/CAREER NOTES: Signed as non-drafted free agent by Baltimore Orioles organization (April 1, 1990). ... On Baltimore disabled list (April 20-August 26, 1996); included rehabilitation assignments to Bowie (May 17-19) and Gulf Coast Orioles (August 13-26).

Year Team (League)	W	L	Pct.	ERA	G	GS	CG	ShO	Sv.	IP	H	R	ER	BB	SO
1990—					Dominican Summer League statistics unavailable.										
1991—GC Orioles (GCL)	3	2	.600	2.72	14	3	0	0	0	36⅓	35	16	11	11	33
1992—Bluefield (Appalachian)	1	2	.333	4.31	25	0	0	0	5	31⅓	31	15	15	23	37
1993—Albany (S. Atl.)	5	1	.833	1.52	40	0	0	0	14	53⅓	31	10	9	19	83
—Frederick (Carolina)	3	0	1.000	0.66	12	0	0	0	4	13⅔	7	1	1	4	29
1994—Bowie (Eastern)	8	4	.667	3.14	53	0	0	0	16	71⅔	41	29	25	39	106
—Baltimore (A.L.)	0	0	...	0.90	3	0	0	0	0	10	8	1	1	4	14
1995—Baltimore (A.L.)	1	5	.167	5.66	44	0	0	0	2	47⅔	37	33	30	37	56
—Rochester (Int'l)	2	2	.500	1.25	17	0	0	0	8	21⅔	10	4	3	7	37
1996—Baltimore (A.L.)	1	0	1.000	3.77	18	0	0	0	4	14⅓	7	6	6	6	20
—GC Orioles (GCL)	1	0	1.000	0.00	1	0	0	0	0	2	1	0	0	0	5
—Bowie (Eastern)	0	0	...	4.50	4	4	0	0	0	6	7	3	3	0	8
—Rochester (Int'l)	0	0	...	2.25	2	0	0	0	0	4	3	1	1	1	5
1997—Baltimore (A.L.)	4	5	.444	2.45	71	0	0	0	9	73⅓	49	22	20	43	106
Major league totals (4 years)	6	10	.375	3.53	136	0	0	0	15	145⅓	101	62	57	90	196

DIVISION SERIES RECORD

Year Team (League)	W	L	Pct.	ERA	G	GS	CG	ShO	Sv.	IP	H	R	ER	BB	SO
1996—Baltimore (A.L.)	2	0	1.000	2.25	3	0	0	0	0	4	1	1	1	2	6
1997—Baltimore (A.L.)	0	0	...	3.00	3	0	0	0	0	3	3	1	1	2	4
Div. series totals (2 years)	2	0	1.000	2.57	6	0	0	0	0	7	4	2	2	4	10

CHAMPIONSHIP SERIES RECORD

Year Team (League)	W	L	Pct.	ERA	G	GS	CG	ShO	Sv.	IP	H	R	ER	BB	SO
1996—Baltimore (A.L.)	0	0	...	7.71	3	0	0	0	1	2⅓	3	2	2	4	2
1997—Baltimore (A.L.)	0	2	.000	12.00	4	0	0	0	0	3	3	4	4	4	6
Champ. series totals (2 years)	0	2	.000	10.13	7	0	0	0	1	5⅓	6	6	6	8	8

BENITEZ, YAMIL   OF   DIAMONDBACKS

PERSONAL: Born May 10, 1972, in San Juan, Puerto Rico. ... 6-2/195. ... Bats right, throws right. ... Full name: Yamil Antonio Benitez.
TRANSACTIONS/CAREER NOTES: Signed as non-drafted free agent by Montreal Expos organization (October 26, 1989). ... Traded by Expos to Kansas City Royals for P Melvin Bunch (January 28, 1997). ... Selected by Arizona Diamondbacks in first round (19th pick overall) of expansion draft (November 18, 1997).

Year Team (League)	Pos.	G	AB	R	H	2B	3B	HR	RBI	Avg.	BB	SO	SB	PO	A	E	Avg.
1990— GC Expos (GCL)	OF	22	83	6	19	1	0	1	5	.229	8	18	0	38	2	1	.976
1991— GC Expos (GCL)	OF	54	197	20	47	9	5	5	38	.239	12	55	10	85	2	3	.967
1992— Albany (S. Atl.)	OF	23	79	6	13	3	2	1	6	.165	5	49	0	30	0	1	.968
—Jamestown (NYP)	OF	44	162	24	44	6	6	3	23	.272	14	52	19	61	2	1	.984
1993— Burl. (Midw.)	OF	111	411	70	112	21	5	15	61	.273	29	99	18	167	4	10	.945
1994— Burl. (Eastern)	OF	126	475	58	123	18	4	17	91	.259	36	134	18	252	11	9	.967
1995— Ottawa (Int'l)	OF	127	474	66	123	24	6	18	69	.259	44	128	14	177	10	7	.964
—Montreal (N.L.)	OF	14	39	8	15	2	1	2	7	.385	1	7	0	18	1	1	.950
1996— Ottawa (Int'l)	OF	114	439	56	122	20	2	23	81	.278	28	120	11	197	14	7	.968
—Montreal (N.L.)	OF	11	12	0	2	0	0	0	2	.167	0	4	0	1	0	1	.500
1997— Omaha (A.A.)■	OF	92	329	61	97	14	1	21	71	.295	24	82	12	150	6	6	.963
—Kansas City (A.L.)	OF	53	191	22	51	7	1	8	21	.267	10	49	2	111	0	4	.965
American League totals (1 year)		53	191	22	51	7	1	8	21	.267	10	49	2	111	0	4	.965
National League totals (2 years)		25	51	8	17	2	1	2	9	.333	1	11	0	19	1	2	.909
Major league totals (3 years)		78	242	30	68	9	2	10	30	.281	11	60	2	130	1	6	.956

BENJAMIN, MIKE — SS — RED SOX

PERSONAL: Born November 22, 1965, in Euclid, Ohio. ... 6-0/169. ... Bats right, throws right. ... Full name: Michael Paul Benjamin.
HIGH SCHOOL: Bellflower (Calif.).
JUNIOR COLLEGE: Cerritos College (Calif.).
COLLEGE: Arizona State.
TRANSACTIONS/CAREER NOTES: Selected by Minnesota Twins organization in seventh round of free-agent draft (January 9, 1985); did not sign. ... Selected by San Francisco Giants organization in third round of free-agent draft (June 2, 1987). ... On San Francisco disabled list (March 31-June 5, 1992); included rehabilitation assignment to Phoenix (April 20-May 10). ... On San Francisco disabled list (July 8-August 6, 1993); included rehabilitation assignment to San Jose (August 4-6). ... Traded by Giants to Philadelphia Phillies for P Jeff Juden and OF/1B Tommy Eason (October 6, 1995). ... On Philadelphia disabled list (March 23-April 26, 1996 and July 20, 1996-remainder of season); included rehabilitation assignments to Clearwater (April 8-17) and Scranton/Wilkes-Barre (April 21-26). ... Granted free agency (October 8, 1996). ... Signed by Boston Red Sox organization (January 31, 1997). ... Granted free agency (October 27, 1997). ... Re-signed by Red Sox (November 21, 1997).
RECORDS: Holds modern major league record for most hits in three consecutive games—14 (June 11 [4], 13 [4] and 14 [6], 1995).
STATISTICAL NOTES: Led Pacific Coast League shortstops with 626 total chances in 1990. ... Collected six hits in one game (June 14, 1995).

Year Team (League)	Pos.	G	AB	R	H	2B	3B	HR	RBI	Avg.	BB	SO	SB	PO	A	E	Avg.
1987—Fresno (California)	SS	64	212	25	51	6	4	6	24	.241	24	71	6	89	188	21	.930
1988—Shreveport (Texas)	SS	89	309	48	73	19	5	6	37	.236	22	63	14	134	248	11	.972
—Phoenix (PCL)	SS	37	106	13	18	4	1	0	6	.170	13	32	2	41	74	4	.966
1989—Phoenix (PCL)	SS-2B	113	363	44	94	17	6	3	36	.259	18	82	10	149	332	15	.970
—San Francisco (N.L.)	SS	14	6	6	1	0	0	0	0	.167	0	1	0	4	4	0	1.000
1990—Phoenix (PCL)	SS	118	419	61	105	21	7	5	39	.251	25	89	13	*216	*386	24	.962
—San Francisco (N.L.)	SS	22	56	7	12	3	1	2	3	.214	3	10	1	29	53	1	.988
1991—San Francisco (N.L.)	SS-3B	54	106	12	13	3	0	2	8	.123	7	26	3	64	123	3	.984
—Phoenix (PCL)	SS	64	226	34	46	13	2	6	31	.204	20	67	3	109	252	9	.976
1992—San Francisco (N.L.)	SS-3B	40	75	4	13	2	1	1	3	.173	4	15	1	34	71	1	.991
—Phoenix (PCL)	SS-2B	31	108	15	33	10	2	0	17	.306	3	18	4	51	92	2	.986
1993—San Francisco (N.L.)	SS-2B-3B	63	146	22	29	7	0	4	16	.199	9	23	0	74	133	5	.976
—San Jose (Calif.)	SS-2B	2	8	1	0	0	0	0	0	.000	1	0	0	1	5	0	1.000
1994—San Francisco (N.L.)	SS-2B-3B	38	62	9	16	5	1	1	9	.258	5	16	5	33	70	3	.972
1995—San Francisco (N.L.)	3B-SS-2B	68	186	19	41	6	0	3	12	.220	8	51	11	51	121	4	.977
1996—Clearwater (FSL)■	SS	8	23	3	4	1	0	0	0	.174	3	4	1	9	20	2	.935
—Scran./W.B. (Int'l)	SS	4	13	2	5	2	0	0	4	.385	3	0	0	3	12	0	1.000
—Philadelphia (N.L.)	SS-2B	35	103	13	23	5	1	4	13	.223	12	21	3	38	87	6	.954
1997—Pawtucket (Int'l)■	SS-3B-2B	33	105	12	26	4	1	4	12	.248	8	20	4	46	86	5	.964
—Boston (A.L.)	3-S-2-1-DH-P	49	116	12	27	9	1	0	7	.233	4	27	2	50	81	6	.956
American League totals (1 year)		49	116	12	27	9	1	0	7	.233	4	27	2	50	81	6	.956
National League totals (8 years)		334	740	92	148	31	4	17	64	.200	48	163	24	327	662	23	.977
Major league totals (9 years)		383	856	104	175	40	5	17	71	.204	52	190	26	377	743	29	.975

RECORD AS PITCHER

Year Team (League)	W	L	Pct.	ERA	G	GS	CG	ShO	Sv.	IP	H	R	ER	BB	SO
1997—Boston (A.L.)	0	0	...	0.00	1	0	0	0	0	1	0	0	0	0	0

BENNETT, SHAYNE — P — EXPOS

PERSONAL: Born April 10, 1972, in Adelaide, Australia. ... 6-5/200. ... Throws right, bats right. ... Full name: Shayne Anthony Bennett.
JUNIOR COLLEGE: DuPage (Ill.) Junior College.
TRANSACTIONS/CAREER NOTES: Selected by Boston Red Sox organization in 25th round of free-agent draft (June 2, 1993). ... Traded by Red Sox with P Rheal Cormier and 1B Ryan McGuire to Montreal Expos for SS Wil Cordero and P Bryan Eversgerd (January 10, 1996).

Year Team (League)	W	L	Pct.	ERA	G	GS	CG	ShO	Sv.	IP	H	R	ER	BB	SO
1993—GC Red Sox (GCL)	0	0	...	1.29	2	1	0	0	1	7	2	1	1	1	4
—Fort Lauderdale (FSL)	1	2	.333	1.72	23	0	0	0	6	31 1/3	26	8	6	11	23
1994—Sarasota (Florida State)	1	6	.143	4.47	15	8	0	0	3	48 1/3	46	31	24	27	28
1995—Sarasota (Florida State)	2	5	.286	2.56	52	0	0	0	24	59 2/3	50	23	17	21	69
—Trenton (Eastern)	0	1	.000	5.06	10	0	0	0	3	10 2/3	16	6	6	3	6
1996—Harrisburg (Eastern)■	8	8	.500	2.53	53	0	0	0	12	92 2/3	83	32	26	35	89
1997—Harrisburg (Eastern)	4	2	.667	4.40	23	1	0	0	2	47	47	28	23	20	38
—Ottawa (Int'l)	1	2	.333	1.57	25	0	0	0	14	34 1/3	23	8	6	21	29
—Montreal (N.L.)	0	1	.000	3.18	16	0	0	0	0	22 2/3	21	9	8	9	8
Major league totals (1 year)	0	1	.000	3.18	16	0	0	0	0	22 2/3	21	9	8	9	8

B

BENNETT, TOM | P | ATHLETICS

PERSONAL: Born May 13, 1976, in Oakland. ... 6-4/180. ... Throws right, bats right. ... Full name: Thomas William Bennett.
HIGH SCHOOL: Alameda (Calif.).
JUNIOR COLLEGE: Ohlone College (Calif.).
TRANSACTIONS/CAREER NOTES: Selected by Oakland Athletics organization in eighth round of free-agent draft (June 1, 1995).

Year Team (League)	W	L	Pct.	ERA	G	GS	CG	ShO	Sv.	IP	H	R	ER	BB	SO
1995— Arizona A's (Arizona)	1	1	.500	2.72	11	6	0	0	0	36 1/3	20	16	11	16	46
1996— Arizona A's (Arizona)	0	0	...	1.38	4	4	0	0	0	13	2	2	2	11	12
— West. Mich. (Mid.)	0	1	.000	3.92	6	5	0	0	0	20 2/3	17	11	9	18	17
1997— Modesto (California)	6	9	.400	5.71	25	24	0	0	0	112	118	84	71	73	116

BENSON, KRIS | P | PIRATES

PERSONAL: Born November 7, 1974, in Kennesaw, Ga. ... 6-4/190. ... Throws right, bats right. ... Full name: Kristen James Benson.
HIGH SCHOOL: Spayberry (Marietta, Ga.).
COLLEGE: Clemson.
TRANSACTIONS/CAREER NOTES: Selected by Pittsburgh Pirates organization in first round (first pick overall) of free-agent draft (June 2, 1996).

Year Team (League)	W	L	Pct.	ERA	G	GS	CG	ShO	Sv.	IP	H	R	ER	BB	SO
1997— Rancho Cucamonga (Cal.)	6	3	.667	1.60	14	14	2	1	0	101	74	30	18	31	109
— Mobile (Southern)	6	5	.545	2.56	13	13	1	1	0	88	83	37	25	32	92

BERBLINGER, JEFF | 2B | CARDINALS

PERSONAL: Born November 19, 1970, in Wichita, Kan. ... 6-0/190. ... Bats right, throws right. ... Full name: Jeffrey J. Berblinger.
HIGH SCHOOL: Goddard (Kan.).
COLLEGE: Kansas.
TRANSACTIONS/CAREER NOTES: Selected by St. Louis Cardinals organization in seventh round of free-agent draft (June 3, 1993). ... On disabled list (July 29-September 1, 1995). ... Selected by Detroit Tigers organization from St. Louis Cardinals organization in Rule 5 major league draft (December 9, 1996). ... Traded by Tigers to Los Angeles Dodgers for SS Deivi Cruz and OF Juan Hernaiz (December 9, 1996). ... Returned by Dodgers to Cardinals (March 28, 1997).
STATISTICAL NOTES: Led South Atlantic League in being hit by pitch with 25 in 1994. ... Led South Atlantic League second basemen with 588 total chances in 1994. ... Led American Association second basemen with 258 putouts, 362 assists, 632 total chances and 93 double plays in 1997.

Year Team (League)	Pos.	G	AB	R	H	2B	3B	HR	RBI	Avg.	BB	SO	SB	PO	A	E	Avg.
										BATTING					FIELDING		
1993— Glens Falls (NYP)	2B	38	138	26	43	9	0	2	21	.312	11	14	9	58	82	3	.979
— St. Petersburg (FSL)	2B	19	70	7	13	1	0	0	5	.186	5	10	3	35	65	1	.990
1994— Savannah (S. Atl.)	2B	132	479	86	142	27	7	8	67	.296	52	85	24	237	*335	16	.973
1995— Arkansas (Texas)	2B	87	332	66	106	15	4	5	29	.319	48	40	16	183	270	15	.968
1996— Arkansas (Texas)	2B	134	500	78	144	32	7	11	53	.288	52	66	23	241	310	*28	.952
1997— Louisville (A.A.)	2B-OF	133	513	63	135	19	7	11	58	.263	55	98	24	†258	†362	12	.981
— St. Louis (N.L.)	2B	7	5	1	0	0	0	0	0	.000	0	1	0	4	4	0	1.000
Major league totals (1 year)		7	5	1	0	0	0	0	0	.000	0	1	0	4	4	0	1.000

BERE, JASON | P | WHITE SOX

PERSONAL: Born May 26, 1971, in Cambridge, Mass. ... 6-3/215. ... Throws right, bats right. ... Full name: Jason Phillip Bere. ... Name pronounced burr-AY.
HIGH SCHOOL: Wilmington (Mass.).
JUNIOR COLLEGE: Middlesex Community College (Mass.).
TRANSACTIONS/CAREER NOTES: Selected by Chicago White Sox organization in 36th round of free-agent draft (June 4, 1990). ... On Chicago disabled list (August 5-20, 1995); included rehabilitation assignment to South Bend (August 13-18). ... On Chicago disabled list (April 22-September 3 and September 14, 1996-remainder of season); included rehabilitation assignments to Nashville (May 14-19 and August 27-28), Gulf Coast White Sox (August 5-10), Hickory (August 10-16) and Birmingham (August 16-27). ... On Chicago disabled list (March 31-August 19, 1997), included rehabilitation assignments to Gulf Coast White Sox (July 2-7), Hickory (July 12), Birmingham (July 17-22) and Nashville (July 29-August 14).

Year Team (League)	W	L	Pct.	ERA	G	GS	CG	ShO	Sv.	IP	H	R	ER	BB	SO
1990— GC White Sox (GCL)	0	4	.000	2.37	16	2	0	0	1	38	26	19	10	19	41
1991— South Bend (Mid.)	9	12	.429	2.87	27	27	2	1	0	163	116	66	52	*100	158
1992— Sarasota (Florida State)	7	2	.778	2.41	18	18	1	1	0	116	84	35	31	34	106
— Birmingham (Southern)	4	4	.500	3.00	8	8	4	2	0	54	44	22	18	20	45
— Vancouver (PCL)	0	0	...	0.00	1	0	0	0	0	1	2	0	0	0	2
1993— Nashville (A.A.)	5	1	.833	2.37	8	8	0	0	0	49 1/3	36	19	13	25	52
— Chicago (A.L.)	12	5	.706	3.47	24	24	1	0	0	142 2/3	109	60	55	81	129
1994— Chicago (A.L.)	12	2	*.857	3.81	24	24	0	0	0	141 2/3	119	65	60	80	127
1995— Chicago (A.L.)	8	*15	.348	7.19	27	27	1	0	0	137 2/3	151	120	110	106	110
— Nashville (A.A.)	1	0	1.000	3.38	1	1	0	0	0	5 1/3	6	2	2	2	7
1996— Chicago (A.L.)	0	1	.000	10.26	5	5	0	0	0	16 2/3	26	19	19	18	19
— Nashville (A.A.)	0	0	...	1.42	3	3	0	0	0	12 2/3	9	2	2	4	15
— W. Sox-Cards (GCL)	0	1	.000	6.00	1	1	0	0	0	3	3	2	2	1	3
— Hickory (S. Atl.)	1	0	1.000	0.00	1	1	0	0	0	5	3	0	0	0	5
— Birmingham (Southern)	0	0	...	4.15	1	1	0	0	0	4 1/3	4	2	2	4	5
1997— GC White Sox (GCL)	0	0	...	0.00	2	2	0	0	0	5	2	0	0	0	5
— Hickory (S. Atl.)	0	0	...	6.00	1	1	0	0	0	3	4	2	2	0	2

Year	Team (League)	W	L	Pct.	ERA	G	GS	CG	ShO	Sv.	IP	H	R	ER	BB	SO
	— Birmingham (Southern)	0	1	.000	7.71	2	2	0	0	0	7	8	7	6	2	7
	— Nashville (A.A.)	1	1	.500	5.59	4	4	0	0	0	19 1/3	23	13	12	7	13
	— Chicago (A.L.)	4	2	.667	4.71	6	6	0	0	0	28 2/3	20	15	15	17	21
Major league totals (5 years)......		36	25	.590	4.99	86	86	2	0	0	467 1/3	425	279	259	302	406

CHAMPIONSHIP SERIES RECORD

Year	Team (League)	W	L	Pct.	ERA	G	GS	CG	ShO	Sv.	IP	H	R	ER	BB	SO
1993— Chicago (A.L.)		0	0	...	11.57	1	1	0	0	0	2 1/3	5	3	3	2	3

ALL-STAR GAME RECORD

Year	League	W	L	Pct.	ERA	GS	CG	ShO	Sv.	IP	H	R	ER	BB	SO
1994— American		0	1	.000	...	0	0	0	0	0	2	1	1	0	0

BERGMAN, SEAN   P   ASTROS

B

PERSONAL: Born April 11, 1970, in Joliet, Ill. ... 6-4/225. ... Throws right, bats right. ... Full name: Sean Frederick Bergman.
HIGH SCHOOL: Joliet (Ill.) Catholic Academy.
COLLEGE: Southern Illinois.
TRANSACTIONS/CAREER NOTES: Selected by Detroit Tigers organization in fourth round of free-agent draft (June 3, 1991). ... On Detroit disabled list (June 26-July 17, 1995); included rehabilitation assignment to Toledo (July 10-17). ... Traded by Tigers with P Cade Gaspar and OF Todd Steverson to San Diego Padres for P Richie Lewis, OF Melvin Nieves and C Raul Casanova (March 22, 1996). ... Traded by Padres to Houston Astros for OF James Mouton (January 14, 1998).
MISCELLANEOUS: Fouled out in only appearance as pinch-hitter and appeared in one game as pinch-runner (1996).

Year	Team (League)	W	L	Pct.	ERA	G	GS	CG	ShO	Sv.	IP	H	R	ER	BB	SO
1991— Niagara Falls (NYP)		5	7	.417	4.46	15	15	0	0	0	84 2/3	87	57	42	42	77
1992— Lakeland (Fla. St.)		5	2	.714	2.49	13	13	0	0	0	83	61	28	23	14	67
	— London (Eastern)	4	7	.364	4.28	14	14	1	0	0	88 1/3	85	52	42	45	59
1993— Toledo (Int'l)		8	9	.471	4.38	19	19	3	0	0	117	124	62	57	53	91
	— Detroit (A.L.)	1	4	.200	5.67	9	6	1	0	0	39 2/3	47	29	25	23	19
1994— Toledo (Int'l)		11	8	.579	3.72	25	25	2	0	0	154 2/3	147	77	64	53	145
	— Detroit (A.L.)	2	1	.667	5.60	3	3	0	0	0	17 2/3	22	11	11	7	12
1995— Detroit (A.L.)		7	10	.412	5.12	28	28	1	1	0	135 1/3	169	95	77	67	86
	— Toledo (Int'l)	0	1	.000	6.00	1	1	0	0	0	3	4	2	2	0	4
1996— San Diego (N.L.)■		6	8	.429	4.37	41	14	0	0	0	113 1/3	119	63	55	33	85
1997— San Diego (N.L.)		2	4	.333	6.09	44	9	0	0	0	99	126	72	67	38	74
A.L. totals (3 years)		10	15	.400	5.28	40	37	2	1	0	192 2/3	238	135	113	97	117
N.L. totals (2 years)		8	12	.400	5.17	85	23	0	0	0	212 1/3	245	135	122	71	159
Major league totals (5 years)......		18	27	.400	5.22	125	60	2	1	0	405	483	270	235	168	276

BERKMAN, LANCE   OF   ASTROS

PERSONAL: Born February 10, 1976, in Waco, Texas. ... 6-1/205. ... Bats both, throws left. ... Full name: William Lance Berkman.
HIGH SCHOOL: Canyon (New Braunfels, Texas).
COLLEGE: Rice.
TRANSACTIONS/CAREER NOTES: Selected by Houston Astros organization in first round (16th pick overall) of free-agent draft (June 3, 1997).
HONORS: Named first baseman on THE SPORTING NEWS college All-America first team (1997).

Year	Team (League)	Pos.	G	AB	R	H	2B	3B	HR	RBI	Avg.	BB	SO	SB	PO	A	E	Avg.
							BATTING									FIELDING		
1997— Kissimmee (FSL)........	OF	53	184	31	54	10	0	12	35	.293	37	38	2	70	2	0	1.000

BERROA, GERONIMO   OF/DH

PERSONAL: Born March 18, 1965, in Santo Domingo, Dominican Republic. ... 6-0/210. ... Bats right, throws right. ... Full name: Geronimo Emiliano Berroa. ... Name pronounced her-ON-i-mo bur-OH-uh.
TRANSACTIONS/CAREER NOTES: Signed as non-drafted free agent by Toronto Blue Jays organization (September 4, 1983). ... Selected by Atlanta Braves from Blue Jays organization in Rule 5 major league draft (December 5, 1988). ... Released by Braves (February 1, 1991). ... Signed by Calgary, Seattle Mariners organization (February 27, 1991). ... Contract sold by Mariners organization to Colorado Springs, Cleveland Indians organization (March 28, 1991). ... Granted free agency (October 15, 1991). ... Signed by Nashville, Cincinnati Reds organization (October 31, 1991). ... Released by Reds (November 20, 1992). ... Signed by Florida Marlins (December 9, 1992). ... Granted free agency (October 15, 1993). ... Signed by Oakland Athletics organization (January 20, 1994). ... On disabled list (August 2, 1994-remainder of season). ... Traded by A's to Baltimore Orioles for P Jimmy Haynes and a player to be named later (June 27, 1997); A's acquired P Mark Seaver to complete deal (September 2, 1997). ... Granted free agency (December 21, 1997).
RECORDS: Shares major league single-season record for most games with three home runs—2 (1996).
STATISTICAL NOTES: Led Southern League with 297 total bases in 1987. ... Led International League in being hit by pitch with 10 and tied for lead in sacrifice flies with eight in 1988. ... Led International League in grounding into double plays with 17 in 1990. ... Hit three home runs in one game (May 22 and August 12, 1996). ... Career major league grand slams: 2.

Year	Team (League)	Pos.	G	AB	R	H	2B	3B	HR	RBI	Avg.	BB	SO	SB	PO	A	E	Avg.
							BATTING									FIELDING		
1984— GC Jays (GCL)...........	OF-1B	62	235	31	59	16	1	3	34	.251	12	34	2	104	2	5	.955
1985— Kinston (Carolina)	OF	19	43	4	8	0	0	1	4	.186	4	10	0	13	1	1	.933
	— Medicine Hat (Pio.)	OF	54	201	39	69	*22	2	6	45	.343	18	40	7	58	3	3	.953
	— Florence (S. Atl.)	OF	19	66	7	21	2	0	3	20	.318	6	13	0	24	0	2	.923
1986— Ventura (Calif.)	OF	128	459	76	137	22	5	21	73	.298	38	92	12	194	9	14	.935
	— Knoxville (Southern) ..	OF	1	4	0	0	0	0	0	0	.000	0	1	0	2	0	0	1.000
1987— Knoxville (Southern) ..	OF	134	523	87	150	33	3	36	108	.287	46	104	2	236	6	•15	.942
1988— Syracuse (Int'l)..........	OF	131	470	55	122	•29	1	8	64	.260	38	88	7	243	12	5	.981

Year Team (League)	Pos.	G	AB	R	H	2B	3B	HR	RBI	Avg.	BB	SO	SB	PO	A	E	Avg.
1989—Atlanta (N.L.)■	OF	81	136	7	36	4	0	2	9	.265	7	32	0	67	1	2	.971
1990—Richmond (Int'l)	OF	135	499	56	134	17	2	12	80	.269	34	89	4	200	10	7	.968
—Atlanta (N.L.)	OF	7	4	0	0	0	0	0	0	.000	1	1	0	1	0	0	1.000
1991—Colo. Springs (PCL)■	OF	125	478	81	154	31	7	18	91	.322	35	88	2	151	14	5	.971
1992—Nashville (A.A.)■	OF	112	461	73	151	33	2	22	88	.328	32	69	8	194	16	5	.977
—Cincinnati (N.L.)	OF	13	15	2	4	1	0	0	0	.267	2	1	0	2	1	0	1.000
1993—Edmonton (PCL)■	OF-1B	90	327	64	107	33	4	16	86	.327	36	71	1	210	10	7	.969
—Florida (N.L.)	OF	14	34	3	4	1	0	0	0	.118	2	7	0	9	1	2	.833
1994—Oakland (A.L.)■	DH-OF-1B	96	340	55	104	18	2	13	65	.306	41	62	7	131	5	1	.993
1995—Oakland (A.L.)	DH-OF	141	546	87	152	22	3	22	88	.278	63	98	7	129	5	4	.971
1996—Oakland (A.L.)	DH-OF	153	586	101	170	32	1	36	106	.290	47	122	0	91	6	2	.980
1997—Oakland (A.L.)	OF-DH	73	261	40	81	12	0	16	42	.310	36	58	3	71	1	1	.986
—Baltimore (A.L.)■	DH-OF	83	300	48	78	13	0	10	48	.260	40	62	1	70	1	3	.959
American League totals (4 years)		546	2033	331	585	97	6	97	349	.288	227	402	18	492	18	11	.979
National League totals (4 years)		115	189	12	44	6	0	2	9	.233	12	41	0	79	3	4	.953
Major league totals (8 years)		661	2222	343	629	103	6	99	358	.283	239	443	18	571	21	15	.975

DIVISION SERIES RECORD

Year Team (League)	Pos.	G	AB	R	H	2B	3B	HR	RBI	Avg.	BB	SO	SB	PO	A	E	Avg.
1997—Baltimore (A.L.)	DH-OF	4	13	4	5	1	0	2	2	.385	2	2	0	0	0	0	...

CHAMPIONSHIP SERIES RECORD

Year Team (League)	Pos.	G	AB	R	H	2B	3B	HR	RBI	Avg.	BB	SO	SB	PO	A	E	Avg.
1997—Baltimore (A.L.)	OF-DH	6	21	1	6	2	0	0	3	.286	0	3	0	9	0	0	1.000

BERRY, SEAN — 3B — ASTROS

PERSONAL: Born March 22, 1966, in Santa Monica, Calif. ... 5-11/200. ... Bats right, throws right. ... Full name: Sean Robert Berry.
HIGH SCHOOL: West Torrance (Torrance, Calif.).
COLLEGE: UCLA.
TRANSACTIONS/CAREER NOTES: Selected by Boston Red Sox organization in fourth round of free-agent draft (June 4, 1984); did not sign. ... Selected by Kansas City Royals organization in secondary phase of free-agent draft (January 14, 1986). ... Traded by Royals with P Archie Corbin to Montreal Expos for P Bill Sampen and P Chris Haney (August 29, 1992). ... Traded by Expos to Houston Astros for P Dave Veres and C Raul Chavez (December 20, 1995). ... On Houston disabled list (April 7-22, 1997); including rehabilitation assignment to New Orleans (April 18-22). ... On Houston disabled list (August 23-September 7, 1997). ... Granted free agency (December 21, 1997). ... Re-signed by Astros (January 13, 1998).
STATISTICAL NOTES: Led Northwest League third basemen with 11 double plays in 1986. ... Career major league grand slams: 3.

Year Team (League)	Pos.	G	AB	R	H	2B	3B	HR	RBI	Avg.	BB	SO	SB	PO	A	E	Avg.
1986—Eugene (Northwest)	3B	65	238	53	76	20	2	5	44	.319	44	72	10	*63	96	21	.883
1987—Fort Myers (FSL)	3B	66	205	26	52	7	2	2	30	.254	46	65	5	39	101	23	.859
1988—Baseball City (FSL)	3B-SS-OF	94	304	34	71	6	4	4	30	.234	31	62	24	84	161	28	.897
1989—Baseball City (FSL)	3-0-2-S	116	399	67	106	19	7	4	44	.266	44	68	37	100	199	24	.926
1990—Memphis (Southern)	3B	135	487	73	142	25	4	14	77	.292	44	89	18	79	238	27	.922
—Kansas City (A.L.)	3B	8	23	2	5	1	1	0	4	.217	2	5	0	7	10	1	.944
1991—Omaha (A.A.)	3B-SS-2B	103	368	62	97	21	9	11	54	.264	48	70	8	75	206	20	.934
—Kansas City (A.L.)	3B	31	60	5	8	3	0	0	1	.133	5	23	0	13	52	2	.970
1992—Omaha (A.A.)	3B	122	439	61	126	22	2	21	77	.287	39	87	6	86	239	21	*.939
—Montreal (N.L.)■	3B	24	57	5	19	1	0	1	4	.333	1	11	2	10	19	4	.879
1993—Montreal (N.L.)	3B	122	299	50	78	15	2	14	49	.261	41	70	12	66	153	15	.936
1994—Montreal (N.L.)	3B	103	320	43	89	19	2	11	41	.278	32	50	14	66	147	14	.938
1995—Montreal (N.L.)	3B-1B	103	314	38	100	22	1	14	55	.318	25	53	3	76	165	12	.953
1996—Houston (N.L.)■	3B	132	431	55	121	38	1	17	95	.281	23	58	12	67	194	22	.922
1997—New Orleans (A.A.)	3B	3	9	1	3	0	0	0	0	.333	3	3	0	0	6	0	1.000
—Houston (N.L.)	3B-DH	96	301	37	77	24	1	8	43	.256	25	53	1	47	140	16	.921
American League totals (2 years)		39	83	7	13	4	1	0	5	.157	7	28	0	20	62	3	.965
National League totals (6 years)		580	1722	228	484	119	7	65	287	.281	147	295	44	332	818	83	.933
Major league totals (8 years)		619	1805	235	497	123	8	65	292	.275	154	323	44	352	880	86	.935

DIVISION SERIES RECORD

Year Team (League)	Pos.	G	AB	R	H	2B	3B	HR	RBI	Avg.	BB	SO	SB	PO	A	E	Avg.
1997—Houston (N.L.)	PH	1	1	0	0	0	0	0	0	.000	0	0	0	0	0	0	...

BERRYHILL, DAMON — C — ATHLETICS

PERSONAL: Born December 3, 1963, in South Laguna, Calif. ... 6-0/205. ... Bats both, throws right. ... Full name: Damon Scott Berryhill.
HIGH SCHOOL: Laguna Beach (Calif.).
COLLEGE: Orange Coast College (Calif.).
TRANSACTIONS/CAREER NOTES: Selected by Chicago White Sox organization in 13th round of free-agent draft (January 11, 1983); did not sign. ... Selected by Chicago Cubs organization in first round (fourth pick overall) of free-agent draft (January 17, 1984). ... On Chicago disabled list (June 30-July 15, 1988). ... On Chicago disabled list (March 9-May 1, 1989); included rehabilitation assignment to Iowa (April 24-May 1). ... On Chicago disabled list (August 19-September 29, 1989). ... On Chicago disabled list (April 8-August 15, 1990); included rehabilitation assignments to Peoria (July 16-23) and Iowa (July 24-August 4). ... Traded by Cubs with P Mike Bielecki to Atlanta Braves for P Turk Wendell and P Yorkis Perez (September 29, 1991). ... Granted free agency (December 20, 1993). ... Signed by Pawtucket, Boston Red Sox organization (February 1, 1994). ... Granted free agency (October 31, 1994). ... Signed by Indianapolis, Cincinnati Reds organization

(November 4, 1994). ... On disabled list (July 24-September 1, 1995). ... Released by Reds (February 26, 1996). ... Missed entire 1996 season with injury. ... Signed by San Francisco Giants organization (January 6, 1997). ... On San Francisco disabled list (May 18-June 10, 1997); included rehabilitation assignment to Phoenix (June 5-10). ... On San Francisco disabled list (August 18-September 3, 1997). ... Granted free agency (October 27, 1997). ... Signed by Oakland Athletics (December 22, 1997).

STATISTICAL NOTES: Led Carolina League with 18 passed balls in 1985. ... Led American Association catchers with .990 fielding percentage, 603 putouts, 66 assists, 676 total chances, 11 double plays and 15 passed balls in 1987. ... Career major league grand slams: 1.

MISCELLANEOUS: Batted righthanded only (1984).

Year	Team (League)	Pos.	G	AB	R	H	2B	3B	HR	RBI	Avg.	BB	SO	SB	PO	A	E	Avg.
1984—	Quad Cities (Mid.)	C-1B	62	217	30	60	14	0	0	31	.276	16	44	4	314	31	8	.977
1985—	Win.-Salem (Car.)	C-1B	117	386	31	90	25	1	9	50	.233	32	90	4	625	71	11	.984
1986—	Pittsfield (Eastern)......	C-OF	112	345	33	71	13	1	6	35	.206	37	54	2	449	61	12	.977
1987—	Iowa (Am. Assoc.)	C-1B	121	429	54	123	22	1	18	67	.287	32	58	5	†607	†67	7	†.990
	—Chicago (N.L.)	C	12	28	2	5	1	0	0	1	.179	3	5	0	37	3	4	.909
1988—	Iowa (Am. Assoc.)	C	21	73	11	16	5	1	2	11	.219	7	21	0	117	15	0	1.000
	—Chicago (N.L.)	C	95	309	19	80	19	1	7	38	.259	17	56	1	448	54	9	.982
1989—	Iowa (Am. Assoc.)	C	7	30	4	6	1	0	2	4	.200	1	8	0	40	5	2	.957
	—Chicago (N.L.)	C	91	334	37	86	13	0	5	41	.257	16	54	1	473	41	4	.992
1990—	Peoria (Midwest)........	C	7	26	10	10	2	0	3	8	.385	3	6	0	75	4	1	.988
	—Iowa (Am. Assoc.)	C	22	79	8	17	1	0	3	6	.215	4	18	0	115	13	2	.985
	—Chicago (N.L.)	C	17	53	6	10	4	0	1	9	.189	5	14	0	87	3	2	.978
1991—	Iowa (Am. Assoc.)	C	62	159	13	30	7	0	5	14	.189	11	41	1	211	24	8	.967
	—Iowa (Am. Assoc.)	C	26	97	20	32	4	1	8	24	.330	12	25	0	90	14	2	.981
	—Atlanta (N.L.)■..........	C	1	1	0	0	0	0	0	0	.000	0	1	0	3	0	0	1.000
1992—	Atlanta (N.L.)..............	C	101	307	21	70	16	1	10	43	.228	17	67	0	426	31	1	.998
1993—	Atlanta (N.L.)..............	C	115	335	24	82	18	2	8	43	.245	21	64	0	570	52	6	.990
1994—	Boston (A.L.)■..........	C-DH	82	255	30	67	17	2	6	34	.263	19	59	0	409	29	2	.995
1995—	Cincinnati (N.L.)■......	C-1B	34	82	6	15	3	0	2	11	.183	10	19	0	153	12	2	.988
1996—											Did not play.							
1997—	San Fran. (N.L.)■.......	C-1B	73	167	17	43	8	0	3	23	.257	20	29	0	293	24	3	.991
	—Phoenix (PCL)	C	4	13	0	5	0	0	1	3	.385	2	1	0	14	1	0	1.000
	American League totals (1 year)		82	255	30	67	17	2	6	34	.263	19	59	0	409	29	2	.995
	National League totals (9 years)		601	1775	145	421	89	4	41	223	.237	120	350	3	2701	244	39	.987
	Major league totals (10 years)		683	2030	175	488	106	6	47	257	.240	139	409	3	3110	273	41	.988

DIVISION SERIES RECORD

Year	Team (League)	Pos.	G	AB	R	H	2B	3B	HR	RBI	Avg.	BB	SO	SB	PO	A	E	Avg.
1997—	San Francisco (N.L.) ..	PH	1	1	0	0	0	0	0	0	.000	0	0	0	0	0	...	...

CHAMPIONSHIP SERIES RECORD

Year	Team (League)	Pos.	G	AB	R	H	2B	3B	HR	RBI	Avg.	BB	SO	SB	PO	A	E	Avg.
1992—	Atlanta (N.L.)............	C	7	24	1	4	1	0	0	1	.167	3	2	0	43	5	0	1.000
1993—	Atlanta (N.L.)............	C	6	19	2	4	0	0	1	3	.211	1	5	0	42	0	0	1.000
	Championship series totals (2 years)		13	43	3	8	1	0	1	4	.186	4	7	0	85	5	0	1.000

WORLD SERIES RECORD

Year	Team (League)	Pos.	G	AB	R	H	2B	3B	HR	RBI	Avg.	BB	SO	SB	PO	A	E	Avg.
1992—	Atlanta (N.L.)..............	C	6	22	1	2	0	0	1	3	.091	1	11	0	32	3	0	1.000

BERTOTTI, MIKE   P   WHITE SOX

PERSONAL: Born January 18, 1970, in Jersey City, N.J. ... 6-1/185. ... Throws left, bats left. ... Full name: Michael David Bertotti.
HIGH SCHOOL: Cornwall (N.Y.).
COLLEGE: Iona.
TRANSACTIONS/CAREER NOTES: Selected by Chicago White Sox organization in 31st round of free-agent draft (June 3, 1991).

Year	Team (League)	W	L	Pct.	ERA	G	GS	CG	ShO	Sv.	IP	H	R	ER	BB	SO
1991—	Utica (N.Y.-Penn)..............	3	4	.429	5.79	14	5	0	0	0	37 1/3	38	33	24	36	33
1992—	Utica (N.Y.-Penn).............	2	2	.500	6.21	17	1	0	0	1	33 1/3	36	28	23	31	23
	—South Bend (Mid.)............	0	3	.000	3.72	11	0	0	0	0	19 1/3	12	8	8	22	17
1993—	Hickory (S. Atl.)..............	3	3	.500	2.11	9	9	0	0	0	59 2/3	42	19	14	29	77
	—South Bend (Mid.)............	5	7	.417	3.49	17	16	2	2	0	111	93	51	43	44	108
1994—	Prince William (Caro.)........	7	6	.538	3.53	16	15	2	1	0	104 2/3	90	48	41	43	103
	—Birmingham (Southern)	4	3	.571	2.90	10	10	1	1	0	68 1/3	55	25	22	21	44
1995—	Birmingham (Southern)	2	7	.222	5.00	12	12	1	0	0	63	60	38	35	36	53
	—Nashville (A.A.)	2	3	.400	8.72	7	6	0	0	0	32	41	34	31	17	35
	—Chicago (A.L.)	1	1	.500	12.56	4	4	0	0	0	14 1/3	23	20	20	11	15
1996—	Nashville (A.A.)	5	3	.625	4.37	28	9	1	0	1	82 1/3	80	43	40	42	73
	—Chicago (A.L.)	2	0	1.000	5.14	15	2	0	0	0	28	28	18	16	20	19
1997—	Chicago (A.L.)	0	0	...	7.36	9	0	0	0	0	3 2/3	9	3	3	2	4
	—Nashville (A.A.)	5	9	.357	5.35	21	20	0	0	0	107 2/3	91	70	64	*105	87
	**Major league totals (3 years)......	3	1	.750	7.63	28	6	0	0	0	46	60	41	39	33	38

BERUMEN, ANDRES   P   MARINERS

PERSONAL: Born April 5, 1971, in Tijuana, Mexico. ... 6-2/205. ... Throws right, bats right. ... Name pronounced buh-ROOM-un.
HIGH SCHOOL: Banning (Calif.).

B

TRANSACTIONS/CAREER NOTES: Selected by Kansas City Royals organization in 27th round of free-agent draft (June 5, 1989). ... On Appleton disabled list (July 11-28, 1991). ... Selected by Florida Marlins in second round (45th pick overall) of expansion draft (November 17, 1992). ... Traded by Marlins with P Trevor Hoffman and P Jose Martinez to San Diego Padres for 3B Gary Sheffield and P Rich Rodriguez (June 24, 1993). ... On Wichita disabled list (August 11, 1993-remainder of season). ... On disabled list (May 4-13, 1994). ... On San Diego disabled list (August 11, 1995-remainder of season); included rehabilitation assignment to Rancho Cucamonga (August 18-remainder of season). ... Traded by Padres to Seattle Mariners for P Paul Menhart (June 10, 1997).

STATISTICAL NOTES: Led Pacific Coast League with 17 wild pitches in 1996.

Year — Team (League)	W	L	Pct.	ERA	G	GS	CG	ShO	Sv.	IP	H	R	ER	BB	SO
1989— GC Royals (GCL)	2	4	.333	4.78	12	10	0	0	0	49	57	29	26	17	24
1990— GC Royals (GCL)	0	2	.000	2.38	5	4	0	0	1	22 2/3	24	9	6	8	18
— Baseball City (FSL)	3	5	.375	4.30	9	9	1	1	0	44	30	27	21	28	35
1991— Appleton (Midwest)	2	6	.250	3.51	13	13	0	0	0	56 1/3	55	33	22	26	49
— Baseball City (FSL)	0	5	.000	4.14	7	7	0	0	0	37	34	18	17	18	24
1992— Appleton (Midwest)	5	2	.714	2.65	46	0	0	0	13	57 2/3	50	25	17	23	52
1993— High Desert (Calif.)■	9	2	*.818	3.62	14	13	1	0	0	92	85	45	37	36	74
— Wichita (Texas)■	3	1	.750	5.74	7	7	0	0	0	26 2/3	35	17	17	11	17
1994— Las Vegas (PCL)	4	7	.364	6.54	43	6	0	0	1	75 2/3	93	70	55	57	49
1995— San Diego (N.L.)	2	3	.400	5.68	37	0	0	0	1	44 1/3	37	29	28	36	42
— Las Vegas (PCL)	0	0	...	5.40	3	0	0	0	0	3 1/3	4	2	2	2	3
— Rancho Cucamonga (Cal.)	0	0	...	2.45	4	0	0	0	0	7 1/3	6	2	2	1	11
1996— Las Vegas (PCL)	4	7	.364	6.11	50	0	0	0	1	70 2/3	73	53	48	58	59
— San Diego (N.L.)	0	0	...	5.40	3	0	0	0	0	3 1/3	3	2	2	2	4
1997— Las Vegas (PCL)	2	0	1.000	5.45	18	1	0	0	0	33	49	26	20	16	35
— Tacoma (PCL)■	7	4	.636	4.69	16	15	0	0	0	80 2/3	78	45	42	48	79
Major league totals (2 years)	2	3	.400	5.66	40	0	0	0	1	47 2/3	40	31	30	38	46

BETANCOURT, RAFAEL — P — RED SOX

PERSONAL: Born April 29, 1975, in Cumana, Venezuela. ... 6-2/175. ... Throws right, bats right. ... Full name: Rafael Jose Betancourt.
HIGH SCHOOL: A.J.S. (Cumana, Venezuela).
COLLEGE: Isaac Newton (Pto. La Cruz, Venezuela).
TRANSACTIONS/CAREER NOTES: Signed as non-drafted free agent by Boston Red Sox organization (September 13, 1993).

Year — Team (League)	W	L	Pct.	ERA	G	GS	CG	ShO	Sv.	IP	H	R	ER	BB	SO
1997— Michigan (Midwest)	0	3	.000	1.95	27	0	0	0	11	32 1/3	26	9	7	2	52

RECORD AS POSITION PLAYER

Year — Team (League)	Pos.	G	AB	R	H	2B	3B	HR	RBI	Avg.	BB	SO	SB	PO	A	E	Avg.
1994— GC Red Sox (GCL)	SS-3B	24	63	7	7	0	0	0	3	.111	6	19	1	20	65	9	.904
1995— GC Red Sox (GCL)	2B-3B-SS	51	168	18	43	5	0	0	19	.256	13	31	8	78	114	10	.950
1996— Michigan (Midwest)	SS-2B-3B	62	168	14	28	1	2	3	14	.167	12	39	5	84	125	13	.941

BEVIL, BRIAN — P — ROYALS

PERSONAL: Born September 5, 1971, in Houston. ... 6-4/225. ... Throws right, bats right. ... Full name: Brian Scott Bevil.
HIGH SCHOOL: MacArthur (Houston).
JUNIOR COLLEGE: Angelina College (Texas).
TRANSACTIONS/CAREER NOTES: Selected by Kansas City Royals organization in 30th round of free-agent draft (June 4, 1990). ... On Memphis disabled list (July 24-1993-remainder of season). ... On Wichita temporarily inactive list (April 24-May 9, 1995).

Year — Team (League)	W	L	Pct.	ERA	G	GS	CG	ShO	Sv.	IP	H	R	ER	BB	SO
1991— GC Royals (GCL)	5	3	.625	1.93	13	12	2	0	0	65 1/3	56	20	14	19	70
1992— Appleton (Midwest)	9	7	.563	3.40	26	26	4	•2	0	156	129	67	59	63	168
1993— Wilmington (Caro.)	7	1	.875	2.30	12	12	2	0	0	74 1/3	46	21	19	23	61
— Memphis (Southern)	3	3	.500	4.36	6	6	0	0	0	33	36	17	16	14	26
1994— Memphis (Southern)	5	4	.556	3.51	17	17	0	0	0	100	75	42	39	40	78
1995— Wichita (Texas)	5	7	.417	5.84	15	15	0	0	0	74	85	51	48	35	57
— Omaha (Am. Assoc.)	1	3	.250	9.41	6	6	0	0	0	22	40	31	23	14	10
1996— Wichita (Texas)	9	2	•.818	2.02	13	13	2	0	0	75 2/3	56	22	17	26	74
— Omaha (Am. Assoc.)	7	5	.583	4.12	12	12	0	0	0	67 2/3	62	36	31	19	73
— Kansas City (A.L.)	1	0	1.000	5.73	3	1	0	0	0	11	9	7	7	5	7
1997— Wichita (Texas)	0	0	...	5.63	4	2	0	0	0	8	11	8	5	4	10
— Omaha (Am. Assoc.)	2	1	.667	4.38	26	3	0	0	1	39	34	22	19	22	47
— Kansas City (A.L.)	1	2	.333	6.61	18	0	0	0	1	16 1/3	16	13	12	9	13
Major league totals (2 years)	2	2	.500	6.26	21	1	0	0	1	27 1/3	25	20	19	14	20

BICHETTE, DANTE — OF — ROCKIES

PERSONAL: Born November 18, 1963, in West Palm Beach, Fla. ... 6-3/230. ... Bats right, throws right. ... Full name: Alphonse Dante Bichette. ... Name pronounced bih-SHETT.
HIGH SCHOOL: Jupiter (Fla.).
JUNIOR COLLEGE: Palm Beach Community College (Fla.).
TRANSACTIONS/CAREER NOTES: Selected by California Angels organization in 17th round of free-agent draft (June 4, 1984). ... Traded by Angels to Milwaukee Brewers for DH Dave Parker (March 14, 1991). ... Traded by Brewers to Colorado Rockies for OF Kevin Reimer (November 17, 1992).
HONORS: Named outfielder on THE SPORTING NEWS N.L. All-Star team (1995). ... Named outfielder on THE SPORTING NEWS N.L. Silver Slugger team (1995).
STATISTICAL NOTES: Led A.L. outfielders with seven double plays in 1991. ... Led N.L. outfielders with four double plays in 1994. ... Led N.L. with .620 slugging percentage and 359 total bases in 1995. ... Had 23-game hitting streak (May 22-June 18, 1995). ... Tied for N.L. lead with 10 sacrifice flies in 1996. ... Career major league grand slams: 5.
MISCELLANEOUS: Holds Colorado Rockies all-time records for most runs (464), most hits (882) and most RBIs (571).

Year	Team (League)	Pos.	G	AB	R	H	2B	3B	HR	RBI	Avg.	BB	SO	SB	PO	A	E	Avg.
1984—	Salem (Northwest)	OF-1B-3B	64	250	27	58	9	2	4	30	.232	6	53	6	224	24	11	.958
1985—	Quad Cities (Mid.)	1B-OF-C	137	547	58	145	28	4	11	78	.265	25	89	25	300	21	15	.955
1986—	Palm Springs (Cal.)	OF-3B	68	290	39	79	15	0	10	73	.272	21	53	2	78	68	11	.930
—	Midland (Texas)	OF-3B	62	243	43	69	16	2	12	36	.284	18	50	3	131	30	11	.936
1987—	Edmonton (PCL)	OF-3B	92	360	54	108	20	3	13	50	.300	26	68	3	169	21	9	.955
1988—	Edmonton (PCL)	OF	132	509	64	136	29	•10	14	81	.267	25	78	7	218	*22	*15	.941
—	California (A.L.)	OF	21	46	1	12	2	0	0	8	.261	0	7	0	44	2	1	.979
1989—	California (A.L.)	OF-DH	48	138	13	29	7	0	3	15	.210	6	24	3	95	6	1	.990
—	Edmonton (PCL)	OF	61	226	39	55	11	2	11	40	.243	24	39	4	92	9	1	.990
1990—	California (A.L.)	OF	109	349	40	89	15	1	15	53	.255	16	79	5	183	12	7	.965
1991—	Milwaukee (A.L.)■....	OF-3B	134	445	53	106	18	3	15	59	.238	22	107	14	270	14	7	.976
1992—	Milwaukee (A.L.)	OF-DH	112	387	37	111	27	2	5	41	.287	16	74	18	188	6	2	.990
1993—	Colorado (N.L.)■	OF	141	538	93	167	43	5	21	89	.310	28	99	14	308	14	9	.973
1994—	Colorado (N.L.)	OF	*116	*484	74	147	33	2	27	95	.304	19	70	21	211	10	2	.991
1995—	Colorado (N.L.)	OF	139	579	102	•197	38	2	•40	*128	.340	22	96	13	208	9	3	.986
1996—	Colorado (N.L.)	OF	159	633	114	198	39	3	31	141	.313	45	105	31	255	5	9	.967
1997—	Colorado (N.L.)	OF-DH	151	561	81	173	31	2	26	118	.308	30	90	6	225	4	3	.987
American League totals (5 years)			424	1365	144	347	69	6	38	176	.254	60	291	40	780	40	18	.979
National League totals (5 years)			706	2795	464	882	184	14	145	571	.316	144	460	85	1207	42	26	.980
Major league totals (10 years)			1130	4160	608	1229	253	20	183	747	.295	204	751	125	1987	82	44	.979

DIVISION SERIES RECORD

RECORDS: Shares N.L. career record for most doubles—3.

Year	Team (League)	Pos.	G	AB	R	H	2B	3B	HR	RBI	Avg.	BB	SO	SB	PO	A	E	Avg.
1995—	Colorado (N.L.)	OF	4	17	6	10	3	0	1	3	.588	1	3	0	9	0	0	1.000

ALL-STAR GAME RECORD

Year	League	Pos.	AB	R	H	2B	3B	HR	RBI	Avg.	BB	SO	SB	PO	A	E	Avg.
1994—	National	PH	1	0	1	0	0	0	0	1.000	0	0	0	...	...	...	...
1995—	National	OF	1	0	0	0	0	0	0	.000	0	1	0	2	0	0	1.000
All-Star Game totals (2 years)			2	0	1	0	0	0	0	.500	0	1	0	2	0	0	1.000

BIELECKI, MIKE   P

PERSONAL: Born July 31, 1959, in Baltimore. ... 6-3/200. ... Throws right, bats right. ... Full name: Michael Joseph Bielecki. ... Name pronounced bill-LECK-ee.

HIGH SCHOOL: Dundalk (Baltimore).

JUNIOR COLLEGE: Valencia Community College (Fla.).

COLLEGE: Loyola College (Md.).

TRANSACTIONS/CAREER NOTES: Selected by Kansas City Royals organization in sixth round of free-agent draft (January 9, 1979); did not sign. ... Selected by Pittsburgh Pirates organization in secondary phase of free-agent draft (June 5, 1979). ... Traded by Pirates to Chicago Cubs for P Mike Curtis (March 31, 1988). ... Traded by Cubs with C Damon Berryhill to Atlanta Braves for P Turk Wendell and P Yorkis Perez (September 29, 1991). ... On disabled list (July 29, 1992-remainder of season). ... Granted free agency (October 30, 1992). ... Signed by Cleveland Indians (December 14, 1992). ... Released by Indians (June 19, 1993). ... Signed by Rochester, Baltimore Orioles organization (June 29, 1993). ... Released by Rochester (August 15, 1993). ... Signed by Braves organization (February 10, 1994). ... Granted free agency (October 12, 1994). ... Signed by Vancouver, California Angels organization (April 18, 1995). ... On California disabled list (July 17, 1995-remainder of season); included rehabilitation assignments to Lake Elsinore (August 18-24) and Vancouver (August 24-September 1). ... Granted free agency (November 1, 1995). ... Signed by Richmond, Braves organization (March 31, 1996). ... Granted free agency (October 31, 1996). ... Re-signed by Braves (December 19, 1996). ... On disabled list (August 26, 1997-remainder of season). ... Granted free agency (November 7, 1997).

STATISTICAL NOTES: Tied for Eastern League lead with 24 home runs allowed in 1982.

Year	Team (League)	W	L	Pct.	ERA	G	GS	CG	ShO	Sv.	IP	H	R	ER	BB	SO
1979—	GC Pirates (GCL)	1	4	.200	2.29	9	9	1	0	0	51	48	21	13	21	35
1980—	Shelby (S. Atl.)	3	5	.375	4.55	29	6	1	0	3	99	106	60	50	58	78
1981—	Greenwood (S. Atl.)	12	11	.522	3.42	28	•28	10	2	0	192	172	95	73	82	163
1982—	Buffalo (Eastern)	7	12	.368	4.86	25	25	4	0	0	157 1/3	165	96	•85	75	135
1983—	Lynn (Eastern)	•15	7	.682	3.19	25	25	7	1	0	163 2/3	126	73	58	69	*143
1984—	Hawaii (Pac. Coast)	*19	3	.864	2.97	28	28	9	2	0	187 2/3	162	70	62	88	*162
—	Pittsburgh (N.L.)	0	0	...	0.00	4	0	0	0	0	4 1/3	4	0	0	0	1
1985—	Pittsburgh (N.L.)	2	3	.400	4.53	12	7	0	0	0	45 2/3	45	26	23	31	22
—	Hawaii (Pac. Coast)	8	6	.571	3.83	20	20	2	0	0	129 1/3	117	58	55	56	111
1986—	Pittsburgh (N.L.)	6	11	.353	4.66	31	27	0	0	0	148 2/3	149	87	77	83	83
1987—	Vancouver (PCL)	12	10	.545	3.78	26	26	3	3	0	181	194	89	76	78	140
—	Pittsburgh (N.L.)	2	3	.400	4.73	8	8	2	0	0	45 2/3	43	25	24	12	25
1988—	Chicago (N.L.)■................	2	2	.500	3.35	19	5	0	0	0	48 1/3	55	22	18	16	33
—	Iowa (Am. Assoc.)	3	2	.600	2.63	23	3	1	1	5	54 2/3	34	19	16	20	50
1989—	Chicago (N.L.)	18	7	.720	3.14	33	33	4	3	0	212 1/3	187	82	74	81	147
1990—	Chicago (N.L.)	8	11	.421	4.93	36	29	0	0	1	168	188	101	92	70	103
1991—	Chicago (N.L.)	13	11	.542	4.50	39	25	0	0	0	172	169	91	86	54	72
—	Atlanta (N.L.)■.................	0	0	...	0.00	2	0	0	0	0	1 2/3	2	0	0	2	3
1992—	Atlanta (N.L.)	2	4	.333	2.57	19	14	1	1	0	80 2/3	77	27	23	27	62
1993—	Cleveland (A.L.)	4	5	.444	5.90	13	13	0	0	0	68 2/3	90	47	45	23	38
—	Rochester (Int'l)■.............	5	3	.625	5.03	9	9	0	0	0	48 1/3	56	33	27	16	31
1994—	Atlanta (N.L.)■.................	2	0	1.000	4.00	19	1	0	0	0	27	28	12	12	12	18
1995—	California (A.L.)■.............	4	6	.400	5.97	22	11	0	0	0	75 1/3	80	56	50	31	45
—	Lake Elsinore (Calif.)	0	0	...	4.91	3	2	0	0	0	3 2/3	2	2	2	2	2
—	Vancouver (PCL)	1	0	1.000	0.00	3	1	0	0	0	5	2	3	0	2	4

Year Team (League)	W	L	Pct.	ERA	G	GS	CG	ShO	Sv.	IP	H	R	ER	BB	SO
1996— Atlanta (N.L.)■	4	3	.571	2.63	40	5	0	0	2	75⅓	63	24	22	33	71
1997— Atlanta (N.L.)	3	7	.300	4.08	50	0	0	0	2	57⅓	56	33	26	21	60
A.L. totals (2 years)	8	11	.421	5.94	35	24	0	0	0	144	170	103	95	54	83
N.L. totals (12 years)	62	62	.500	3.95	312	154	7	4	5	1087	1066	530	477	442	700
Major league totals (14 years)	70	73	.490	4.18	347	178	7	4	5	1231	1236	633	572	496	783

DIVISION SERIES RECORD

Year Team (League)	W	L	Pct.	ERA	G	GS	CG	ShO	Sv.	IP	H	R	ER	BB	SO
1996— Atlanta (N.L.)	0	0	...	0.00	1	0	0	0	0	⅔	0	0	0	1	1

CHAMPIONSHIP SERIES RECORD

Year Team (League)	W	L	Pct.	ERA	G	GS	CG	ShO	Sv.	IP	H	R	ER	BB	SO
1989— Chicago (N.L.)	0	1	.000	3.65	2	2	0	0	0	12⅓	7	5	5	6	11
1996— Atlanta (N.L.)	0	0	...	0.00	3	0	0	0	0	3	0	0	0	1	5
Champ. series totals (2 years)	0	1	.000	2.93	5	2	0	0	0	15⅓	7	5	5	7	16

WORLD SERIES RECORD

Year Team (League)	W	L	Pct.	ERA	G	GS	CG	ShO	Sv.	IP	H	R	ER	BB	SO
1996— Atlanta (N.L.)	0	0	...	0.00	2	0	0	0	0	3	0	0	0	3	6

BIESER, STEVEN — OF — PIRATES

PERSONAL: Born August 4, 1967, in Perryville, Mo. ... 5-10/170. ... Bats both, throws right. ... Full name: Steven Ray Bieser.
HIGH SCHOOL: St. Genevieve (Mo.).
JUNIOR COLLEGE: Mineral Area (Mo.).
COLLEGE: Southeast Missouri State.
TRANSACTIONS/CAREER NOTES: Selected by Philadelphia Phillies organization in 32nd round of free-agent draft (June 5, 1989). ... Granted free agency (October 15, 1995). ... Signed by Ottawa, Montreal Expos organization (November 30, 1995). ... Signed by New York Mets organization (November 21, 1996). ... Granted free agency (October 15, 1997). ... Signed by Pittsburgh Pirates organization (December 18, 1997).
STATISTICAL NOTES: Led International League with 23 sacrifice hits in 1996.

Year Team (League)	Pos.	G	AB	R	H	2B	3B	HR	RBI	Avg.	BB	SO	SB	PO	A	E	Avg.
1989— Batavia (NY-Penn)	OF-C	25	75	13	18	3	1	1	13	.240	12	20	2	104	8	2	.982
1990— Batavia (NY-Penn)	OF-3B	54	160	36	37	11	1	0	12	.231	26	28	13	83	7	1	.989
1991— Spartanburg (SAL)	O-C-1-3-S-P	60	168	25	41	6	0	0	13	.244	31	35	17	151	23	3	.983
1992— Clearwater (FSL)	C-OF-2B	73	203	33	58	6	5	0	10	.286	39	28	8	283	39	11	.967
— Reading (Eastern)	OF-C	33	139	20	38	5	4	0	8	.273	6	25	8	106	6	5	.957
1993— Reading (Eastern)	C-OF-P	53	170	21	53	6	3	1	19	.312	15	24	9	199	26	4	.983
— Scran./W.B. (Int'l)	OF-C-1B	26	83	3	21	4	0	0	4	.253	2	14	3	90	3	1	.989
1994— Scran./W.B. (Int'l)	O-C-3-P	93	228	42	61	13	1	0	15	.268	17	40	12	229	18	1	.996
1995— Scran./W.B. (Int'l)	OF-3B	95	245	37	66	12	6	1	33	.269	22	56	14	314	29	10	.972
1996— Ottawa (Int'l)■	O-C-2-P	123	382	63	123	24	4	1	32	.322	35	55	27	337	23	8	.978
1997— New York (N.L.)■	OF-C	47	69	16	17	3	0	0	4	.246	7	20	2	32	2	0	1.000
— Norfolk (Int'l)	O-2-C-3	41	122	6	20	5	0	0	4	.164	9	20	4	41	10	4	.927
Major league totals (1 year)		47	69	16	17	3	0	0	4	.246	7	20	2	32	2	0	1.000

RECORD AS PITCHER

Year Team (League)	W	L	Pct.	ERA	G	GS	CG	ShO	Sv.	IP	H	R	ER	BB	SO
1991— Spartanburg (SAL)	0	0	...	18.00	1	0	0	0	0	1	2	2	2	1	1
1993— Reading (Eastern)	0	0	...	0.00	1	0	0	0	0	1	0	0	0	1	1
1994— Scran./W.B. (Int'l)	0	0	...	0.00	1	0	0	0	0	⅓	0	0	0	0	0
1996— Ottawa (Int'l)■	0	0	...	18.00	1	0	0	0	0	1	3	4	2	3	1

BIGGIO, CRAIG — 2B — ASTROS

PERSONAL: Born December 14, 1965, in Smithtown, N.Y. ... 5-11/180. ... Bats right, throws right. ... Full name: Craig Alan Biggio. ... Name pronounced BEE-jee-oh.
HIGH SCHOOL: Kings Park (N.Y.).
COLLEGE: Seton Hall.
TRANSACTIONS/CAREER NOTES: Selected by Houston Astros organization in first round (22nd pick overall) of free-agent draft (June 2, 1987). ... Granted free agency (October 31, 1995). ... Re-signed by Astros (December 14, 1995).
HONORS: Named catcher on THE SPORTING NEWS college All-America team (1987). ... Named catcher on THE SPORTING NEWS N.L. Silver Slugger team (1989). ... Named second baseman on THE SPORTING NEWS N.L. All-Star team (1994-95 and 1997). ... Won N.L. Gold Glove at second base (1994-97). ... Named second baseman on THE SPORTING NEWS N.L. Silver Slugger team (1994-95 and 1997).
STATISTICAL NOTES: Led N.L. catchers with 889 putouts, 963 total chances and 13 passed balls in 1991. ... Led N.L. in being hit by pitch with 22 in 1995, 27 in 1996 and 34 in 1997. ... Led N.L. second basemen in total chances with 728 in 1995, 811 in 1996 and 863 in 1997. ... Career major league grand slams: 2.

Year Team (League)	Pos.	G	AB	R	H	2B	3B	HR	RBI	Avg.	BB	SO	SB	PO	A	E	Avg.
1987— Asheville (S. Atl.)	C-OF	64	216	59	81	17	2	9	49	.375	39	39	31	378	46	2	.995
1988— Tucson (PCL)	C-OF	77	281	60	90	21	4	3	41	.320	40	39	19	318	33	6	.983
— Houston (N.L.)	C	50	123	14	26	6	1	3	5	.211	7	29	6	292	28	3	.991
1989— Houston (N.L.)	C-OF	134	443	64	114	21	2	13	60	.257	49	64	21	742	56	9	.989
1990— Houston (N.L.)	C-OF	150	555	53	153	24	2	4	42	.276	53	79	25	657	60	13	.982
1991— Houston (N.L.)	C-2B-OF	149	546	79	161	23	4	4	46	.295	53	71	19	†894	73	11	.989
1992— Houston (N.L.)	2B	•162	613	96	170	32	3	6	39	.277	94	95	38	*344	413	12	.984
1993— Houston (N.L.)	2B	155	610	98	175	41	5	21	64	.287	77	93	15	306	*447	14	.982
1994— Houston (N.L.)	2B	114	437	88	139	*44	5	6	56	.318	62	58	*39	*225	*338	7	.988
1995— Houston (N.L.)	2B	141	553	*123	167	30	2	22	77	.302	80	85	33	299	*419	10	.986
1996— Houston (N.L.)	2B	•162	605	113	174	24	4	15	75	.288	75	72	25	*361	*440	10	.988
1997— Houston (N.L.)	2B-DH	•162	619	*146	191	37	8	22	81	.309	84	107	47	*341	*504	18	.979
Major league totals (10 years)		1379	5104	874	1470	282	36	116	545	.288	634	753	268	4461	2778	107	.985

– 54 –

Year Team (League)	Pos.	G	AB	R	H	2B	3B	HR	RBI	Avg.	BB	SO	SB	PO	A	E	Avg.
1997— Houston (N.L.)	2B	3	12	0	1	0	0	0	0	.083	1	0	0	4	8	1	.923

ALL-STAR GAME RECORD

Year League	Pos.	AB	R	H	2B	3B	HR	RBI	Avg.	BB	SO	SB	PO	A	E	Avg.
1991— National	C	1	0	0	0	0	0	0	.000	0	0	0	2	0	1	.667
1992— National	2B	2	0	0	0	0	0	0	.000	0	0	0	0	2	0	1.000
1994— National	2B	1	1	0	0	0	0	0	.000	0	0	0	2	1	0	1.000
1995— National	2B	2	1	1	0	0	1	1	.500	0	0	0	2	1	0	1.000
1996— National	2B	3	0	0	0	0	0	1	.000	0	1	0	1	1	0	1.000
1997— National	2B	3	0	0	0	0	0	0	.000	0	1	0	4	4	0	1.000
All-Star Game totals (6 years)		12	2	1	0	0	1	2	.083	0	2	0	7	9	1	.941

BLAIR, WILLIE   P   DIAMONDBACKS

PERSONAL: Born December 18, 1965, in Paintsville, Ky. ... 6-1/185. ... Throws right, bats right. ... Full name: William Allen Blair.
HIGH SCHOOL: Johnson Central (Paintsville, Ky.).
COLLEGE: Morehead State.
TRANSACTIONS/CAREER NOTES: Selected by Toronto Blue Jays organization in 11th round of free-agent draft (June 2, 1986). ... Traded by Blue Jays to Cleveland Indians for P Alex Sanchez (November 6, 1990). ... Traded by Indians with C Eddie Taubensee to Houston Astros for OF Kenny Lofton and IF Dave Rohde (December 10, 1991). ... Selected by Colorado Rockies in first round (21st pick overall) of expansion draft (November 17, 1992). ... Granted free agency (December 20, 1994). ... Signed by Las Vegas, San Diego Padres organization (April 10, 1995). ... Granted free agency (December 21, 1995). ... Re-signed by Padres (December 27, 1995). ... Traded by Padres with C Brian Johnson to Detroit Tigers for P Joey Eischen and P Cam Smith (December 17, 1996). ... On disabled list (May 5-June 3, 1997); included rehabilitation assignment to West Michigan (May 23-June 3). ... Granted free agency (October 27, 1997). ... Signed by Arizona Diamondbacks (December 6, 1997).
STATISTICAL NOTES: Combined with starter Pat Hentgen and Enrique Burgos in 2-1 no-hit victory for Dunedin against Osceola (May 10, 1988).

Year Team (League)	W	L	Pct.	ERA	G	GS	CG	ShO	Sv.	IP	H	R	ER	BB	SO
1986— St. Catharines (NYP)	5	0	1.000	1.68	21	0	0	0	*12	53 2/3	32	10	10	20	55
1987— Dunedin (Fla. St.)	2	9	.182	4.43	50	0	0	0	13	85 1/3	99	51	42	29	72
1988— Dunedin (Fla. St.)	2	0	1.000	2.70	4	0	0	0	0	6 2/3	5	2	2	4	5
— Knoxville (Southern)	5	5	.500	3.62	34	9	0	0	3	102 *	94	49	41	35	76
1989— Syracuse (Int'l)	5	6	.455	3.97	19	17	3	1	0	106 2/3	94	55	47	38	76
1990— Toronto (A.L.)	3	5	.375	4.06	27	6	0	0	0	68 2/3	66	33	31	28	43
— Syracuse (Int'l)	0	2	.000	4.74	3	3	1	0	0	19	20	13	10	8	6
1991— Colo. Springs (PCL)■	9	6	.600	4.99	26	15	0	0	4	113 2/3	130	74	63	30	57
— Cleveland (A.L.)	2	3	.400	6.75	11	5	0	0	0	36	58	27	27	10	13
1992— Tucson (PCL)■	4	4	.500	2.39	21	2	1	0	2	52 2/3	50	20	14	12	35
— Houston (N.L.)	5	7	.417	4.00	29	8	0	0	0	78 2/3	74	47	35	24	48
1993— Colorado (N.L.)■	6	10	.375	4.75	46	18	1	0	0	146	184	90	77	42	84
1994— Colorado (N.L.)	0	5	.000	5.79	47	1	0	0	3	77 2/3	98	57	50	39	68
1995— San Diego (N.L.)■	7	5	.583	4.34	40	12	0	0	1	114	112	60	55	45	83
1996— San Diego (N.L.)	2	6	.250	4.60	60	0	0	0	1	88	80	52	45	29	67
1997— Detroit (A.L.)■	16	8	.667	4.17	29	27	2	0	0	175	186	85	81	46	90
— West. Mich. (Mid.)	0	0	. . .	0.00	1	1	0	0	0	5	1	0	0	0	7
— Toledo (Int'l)	0	0	. . .	0.00	1	1	0	0	0	7	1	1	0	2	4
A.L. totals (3 years)	21	16	.568	4.47	67	38	2	0	0	279 2/3	310	145	139	84	146
N.L. totals (5 years)	20	33	.377	4.68	222	39	1	0	4	504 1/3	548	306	262	180	350
Major league totals (8 years)	41	49	.456	4.60	289	77	3	0	4	784	858	451	401	264	496

DIVISION SERIES RECORD

Year Team (League)	W	L	Pct.	ERA	G	GS	CG	ShO	Sv.	IP	H	R	ER	BB	SO
1996— San Diego (N.L.)	0	0	. . .	0.00	1	0	0	0	0	2	1	0	0	2	3

BLANCO, HENRY   C   DODGERS

PERSONAL: Born August 29, 1971, in Caracas, Venezuela. ... 5-11/168. ... Bats right, throws right. ... Full name: Henry Ramon Blanco.
HIGH SCHOOL: Antonio Jose de Sucre (Venezuela).
TRANSACTIONS/CAREER NOTES: Signed as non-drafted free agent by Los Angeles Dodgers organization (November 12, 1989). ... On disabled list (June 16-25, 1993).
STATISTICAL NOTES: Led Pioneer League third basemen with .947 fielding percentage and 10 double plays in 1991. ... Led California League third basemen with 345 total chances and 34 double plays in 1992. ... Led Texas League third basemen with .944 fielding percentage, 92 putouts and 270 total chances in 1993. ... Led Texas League catchers with 13 errors and 17 passed balls in 1996. ... Led Pacific Coast League catchers with 64 assists and 11 double plays in 1997.

Year Team (League)	Pos.	G	AB	R	H	2B	3B	HR	RBI	Avg.	BB	SO	SB	PO	A	E	Avg.
1990— GC Dodgers (GCL)	3B	60	178	23	39	8	0	1	19	.219	26	41	7	*48	129	11	.941
1991— Vero Beach (FSL)	3B-SS	5	7	0	1	0	0	0	0	.143	2	0	0	6	4	0	1.000
— Great Falls (Pio.)	3B-1B	62	216	35	55	7	1	5	28	.255	27	39	3	93	99	8	†.960
1992— Bakersfield (Calif.)	3B	124	401	42	94	21	2	5	52	.234	51	91	10	*95	*236	14	*.959
1993— San Antonio (Tex.)	3B-1B-SS	117	374	33	73	19	1	10	42	.195	29	80	3	†150	169	16	†.952
1994— San Antonio (Tex.)	3B-1B-P	*132	405	36	93	23	2	6	38	.230	53	67	6	77	178	21	.924
1995— San Antonio (Tex.)	3B-C	88	302	37	77	18	4	12	48	.255	29	52	1	81	210	11	.964
— Albuquerque (PCL)....	3B-1B-OF	29	97	11	22	4	1	2	13	.227	10	23	0	115	47	2	.988
1996— San Antonio (Tex.)	C-3B	92	307	39	82	14	1	5	40	.267	28	38	2	532	65	13	.979
— Albuquerque (PCL)....	C	2	6	1	1	0	0	0	0	.167	0	3	0	11	1	0	1.000
1997— Albuquerque (PCL)....	C-1B-OF	91	294	38	92	20	1	6	47	.313	37	63	7	607	†68	3	.996
— Los Angeles (N.L.)	1B-3B	3	5	1	2	0	0	1	1	.400	0	1	0	5	0	0	1.000
Major league totals (1 year)		3	5	1	2	0	0	1	1	.400	0	1	0	5	0	0	1.000

RECORD AS PITCHER

Year Team (League)	W	L	Pct.	ERA	G	GS	CG	ShO	Sv.	IP	H	R	ER	BB	SO
1994— San Antonio (Tex.)	0	0	. . .	9.00	1	0	0	0	0	1	3	1	1	0	1

PERSONAL: Born November 8, 1965, in Los Gatos, Calif. ... 6-1/180. ... Bats right, throws right. ... Full name: Jeffrey Michael Blauser. ... Name pronounced BLAU-zer.

HIGH SCHOOL: Placer (Sacramento).

COLLEGE: Sacramento City College.

TRANSACTIONS/CAREER NOTES: Selected by St. Louis Cardinals organization in first round (eighth pick overall) of free-agent draft (January 17, 1984); did not sign. ... Selected by Atlanta Braves organization in secondary phase of free-agent draft (June 4, 1984). ... On disabled list (May 14-30, 1990; May 2-20, 1994 and April 14-May 4 and July 16-September 1, 1996). ... Granted free agency (October 15, 1994). ... Re-signed by Braves (April 12, 1995). ... Granted free agency (November 2, 1997). ... Signed by Chicago Cubs (December 9, 1997).

HONORS: Named shortstop on THE SPORTING NEWS N.L. All-Star team (1997). ... Named shortstop on THE SPORTING NEWS N.L. Silver Slugger team (1997).

STATISTICAL NOTES: Led Carolina League shortstops with 506 total chances in 1986. ... Hit three home runs in one game (July 12, 1992). ... Led N.L. in being hit by pitch with 16 in 1993. ... Career major league grand slams: 4.

Year Team (League)	Pos.	G	AB	R	H	2B	3B	HR	RBI	Avg.	BB	SO	SB	PO	A	E	Avg.
1984—Pulaski (Appalachian).	SS	62	217	41	54	6	1	3	24	.249	38	47	14	61	162	24	.903
1985—Sumter (S. Atl.)	SS	125	422	74	99	19	0	5	49	.235	82	94	36	150	306	35	.929
1986—Durham (Carolina)	SS	123	447	94	128	27	3	13	52	.286	81	92	36	167	*314	25	*.951
1987—Richmond (Int'l)	SS-2B	33	113	11	20	1	0	1	12	.177	11	24	3	56	106	9	.947
—Atlanta (N.L.)	SS	51	165	11	40	6	3	2	15	.242	18	34	7	65	166	9	.963
—Greenville (Southern)	SS	72	265	35	66	13	3	4	32	.249	34	49	5	101	225	8	.976
1988—Richmond (Int'l)	SS	69	271	40	77	19	1	5	23	.284	19	53	6	93	156	15	.943
—Atlanta (N.L.)	2B-SS	18	67	7	16	3	1	2	7	.239	2	11	0	35	59	4	.959
1989—Atlanta (N.L.)	3-2-S-O	142	456	63	123	24	2	12	46	.270	38	101	5	137	254	21	.949
1990—Atlanta (N.L.)	S-2-3-O	115	386	46	104	24	3	8	39	.269	35	70	3	169	288	16	.966
1991—Atlanta (N.L.)	SS-2B-3B	129	352	49	91	14	3	11	54	.259	54	59	5	136	219	17	.954
1992—Atlanta (N.L.)	SS-2B-3B	123	343	61	90	19	3	14	46	.262	46	82	5	119	225	14	.961
1993—Atlanta (N.L.)	SS	161	597	110	182	29	2	15	73	.305	85	109	16	189	426	19	.970
1994—Atlanta (N.L.)	SS	96	380	56	98	21	4	6	45	.258	38	64	1	126	290	13	.970
1995—Atlanta (N.L.)	SS	115	431	60	91	16	2	12	31	.211	57	107	8	151	337	15	.970
1996—Atlanta (N.L.)	SS.	83	265	48	65	14	1	10	35	.245	40	54	6	83	206	23	.926
1997—Atlanta (N.L.)	SS-DH	151	519	90	160	31	4	17	70	.308	70	101	5	204	372	16	.973
Major league totals (11 years)		1184	3961	601	1060	201	28	109	461	.268	483	792	61	1414	2842	167	.962

DIVISION SERIES RECORD

Year Team (League)	Pos.	G	AB	R	H	2B	3B	HR	RBI	Avg.	BB	SO	SB	PO	A	E	Avg.
1995—Atlanta (N.L.)	SS	3	6	0	0	0	0	0	0	.000	1	3	0	5	11	1	.941
1996—Atlanta (N.L.)	SS	3	9	0	1	00	0	0	0	.111	1	3	0	0	7	0	1.000
1997—Atlanta (N.L.)	SS	3	10	2	3	0	0	1	4	.300	2	2	0	2	10	0	1.000
Division series totals (3 years)		9	25	2	4	0	0	1	4	.160	4	8	0	7	28	1	.972

CHAMPIONSHIP SERIES RECORD

RECORDS: Shares single-series record for most times hit by pitch—2 (1996). ... Holds N.L. career record for most runs scored—18. ... Shares N.L. career record for most series with one team—6 (Atlanta, 1991-93 and 1995-97).

Year Team (League)	Pos.	G	AB	R	H	2B	3B	HR	RBI	Avg.	BB	SO	SB	PO	A	E	Avg.
1991—Atlanta (N.L.)	SS-PH	2	2	0	0	0	0	0	0	.000	0	0	0	0	1	1	.500
1992—Atlanta (N.L.)	SS	7	24	3	5	0	1	1	4	.208	3	2	0	7	15	2	.917
1993—Atlanta (N.L.)	SS	6	25	5	7	1	0	2	4	.280	4	7	0	6	14	0	1.000
1995—Atlanta (N.L.)	SS	1	4	0	0	0	0	0	0	.000	1	2	0	4	6	0	1.000
1996—Atlanta (N.L.)	SS	7	17	5	3	0	1	0	2	.176	6	6	0	5	9	1	.933
1997—Atlanta (N.L.)	SS	6	20	5	6	0	0	1	1	.300	3	6	0	6	19	1	.962
Championship series totals (6 years)		29	92	18	21	1	2	4	11	.228	17	23	0	28	64	5	.948

WORLD SERIES RECORD

NOTES: Member of World Series championship team (1995); inactive.

Year Team (League)	Pos.	G	AB	R	H	2B	3B	HR	RBI	Avg.	BB	SO	SB	PO	A	E	Avg.
1991—Atlanta (N.L.)	SS-PH	5	6	0	1	0	0	0	0	.167	1	1	0	3	3	0	1.000
1992—Atlanta (N.L.)	SS	6	24	2	6	0	0	0	0	.250	1	9	2	7	22	0	1.000
1996—Atlanta (N.L.)	SS	6	18	2	3	1	0	0	1	.167	1	4	0	9	15	1	.960
World Series totals (3 years)		17	48	4	10	1	0	0	1	.208	3	14	2	19	40	1	.983

ALL-STAR GAME RECORD

Year League	Pos.	AB	R	H	2B	3B	HR	RBI	Avg.	BB	SO	SB	PO	A	E	Avg.
1993—National	SS	1	0	0	0	0	0	0	.000	0	1	0	1	2	1	.750
1997—National	SS	2	0	1	0	0	0	0	.500	0	0	0	1	1	0	1.000
All-Star Game totals (2 years)		3	0	1	0	0	0	0	.333	0	1	0	2	3	1	.833

PERSONAL: Born July 30, 1971, in Altoona, Pa. ... 6-5/205. ... Throws right, bats right. ... Full name: Ronald Patrick Blazier.

HIGH SCHOOL: Bellwood (Pa.)-Antis.

TRANSACTIONS/CAREER NOTES: Signed as non-drafted free agent by Philadelphia Phillies organization (July 14, 1989).

Year Team (League)	W	L	Pct.	ERA	G	GS	CG	ShO	Sv.	IP	H	R	ER	BB	SO
1990—Princeton (Appalachian)	3	5	.375	4.46	14	13	1	0	0	78 2/3	77	46	39	29	45
1991—Batavia (N.Y.-Penn)	7	5	.583	4.60	24	8	0	0	2	72 1/3	81	40	37	17	77

Year—Team (League)	W	L	Pct.	ERA	G	GS	CG	ShO	Sv.	IP	H	R	ER	BB	SO
1992—Spartanburg (SAL)	•14	7	.667	2.65	30	21	2	0	0	159²/₃	141	55	47	32	149
1993—Clearwater (Fla. St.)	9	8	.529	3.94	27	23	1	0	0	155¹/₃	171	80	68	40	86
1994—Clearwater (Fla. St.)	•13	5	.722	3.38	29	*29	0	0	0	173¹/₃	177	73	65	36	120
1995—Reading (Eastern)	4	5	.444	3.29	56	3	0	0	1	106²/₃	93	44	39	31	102
1996—Scran./W.B. (Int'l)	4	0	1.000	2.57	33	0	0	0	12	42	33	15	12	9	38
—Philadelphia (N.L.)	3	1	.750	5.87	27	0	0	0	0	38¹/₃	49	30	25	10	25
1997—Philadelphia (N.L.)	1	1	.500	5.03	36	0	0	0	0	53²/₃	62	31	30	21	42
—Scran./W.B. (Int'l)	0	3	.000	3.68	11	0	0	0	1	14²/₃	17	9	6	3	10
—Clearwater (Fla. St.)	2	3	.400	2.93	15	0	0	0	3	30²/₃	24	11	10	8	45
Major league totals (2 years)	4	2	.667	5.38	63	0	0	0	0	92	111	61	55	31	67

BLOOD, DARIN — P — GIANTS

PERSONAL: Born August 13, 1974, in Spokane, Wash. ... 6-2/200. ... Throws right, bats right. ... Full name: Darin C. Blood.
HIGH SCHOOL: Central Valley (Veradale, Wash.).
COLLEGE: Gonzaga.
TRANSACTIONS/CAREER NOTES: Selected by San Francisco Giants organization in third round of free-agent draft (June 1, 1995).
HONORS: Named California League Pitcher of the Year (1996).
STATISTICAL NOTES: Led California League with 26 wild pitches in 1996.

Year—Team (League)	W	L	Pct.	ERA	G	GS	CG	ShO	Sv.	IP	H	R	ER	BB	SO
1995—Bellingham (N'west)	6	3	.667	2.54	14	13	0	0	0	74¹/₃	63	26	21	32	78
1996—San Jose (California)	*17	6	.739	*2.65	27	25	2	*2	0	170	140	59	50	71	*193
1997—Shreveport (Texas)	8	10	.444	4.33	27	27	0	0	0	156	152	89	75	*83	90

BLOSSER, GREG — OF — DEVIL RAYS

PERSONAL: Born June 26, 1971, in Bradenton, Fla. ... 6-3/210. ... Bats left, throws left. ... Full name: Gregory Brent Blosser.
HIGH SCHOOL: Sarasota (Fla.).
TRANSACTIONS/CAREER NOTES: Selected by Boston Red Sox organization in first round (16th pick overall) of free-agent draft (June 5, 1989); pick received as part of compensation for San Diego Padres signing Type A free-agent P Bruce Hurst. ... On Pawtucket disabled list (September 4, 1992-remainder of season). ... Granted free agency (October 16, 1995). ... Signed by Rochester, Baltimore Orioles organization (November 1, 1995). ... Signed by Charleston (S.C.), Tampa Bay Devil Rays organization (December 18, 1996). ... On St. Petersburg disabled list (May 18-June 7, 1997). ... Loaned by Devil Rays to Oklahoma City, Texas Rangers organization (June 19, 1997-remainder of season).
STATISTICAL NOTES: Led Eastern League with nine intentional bases on balls received in 1992.

							BATTING								FIELDING		
Year—Team (League)	Pos.	G	AB	R	H	2B	3B	HR	RBI	Avg.	BB	SO	SB	PO	A	E	Avg.
1989—GC Red Sox (GCL)	OF	40	146	17	42	7	3	2	20	.288	25	19	3	54	2	4	.933
—Winter Haven (FSL)	OF	28	94	6	24	1	1	2	14	.255	8	14	1	52	4	4	.933
1990—Lynchburg (Caro.)	OF	119	447	63	126	23	1	*18	62	.282	55	99	5	171	8	14	.927
1991—New Britain (Eastern)	OF	134	452	47	98	21	3	8	46	.217	63	114	9	178	15	•11	.946
1992—New Britain (Eastern)	OF	129	434	59	105	23	4	22	71	.242	64	122	6	189	9	7	.966
—Pawtucket (Int'l)	PH	1	0	1	0	0	0	0	0	...	1	0	0	...	...	...	...
1993—Pawtucket (Int'l)	OF	130	478	66	109	22	2	23	66	.228	58	139	3	199	•13	7	.968
—Boston (A.L.)	OF-DH	17	28	1	2	1	0	0	1	.071	2	7	1	11	1	0	1.000
1994—Boston (A.L.)	OF-DH	5	11	2	1	0	0	0	1	.091	4	4	0	8	0	3	.727
—Pawtucket (Int'l)	OF	97	350	52	91	21	1	17	54	.260	44	97	11	159	•14	9	.951
1995—Pawtucket (Int'l)	OF	17	50	5	10	0	1	4	12	.200	5	13	0	30	1	4	.886
—Trenton (Eastern)	OF	49	179	25	44	13	0	11	34	.246	13	42	3	59	5	0	1.000
1996—Rochester (Int'l)	OF	38	115	11	27	6	1	2	12	.235	12	29	2	15	2	2	.895
1997—St. Peters. (FSL)■	OF	52	189	40	59	9	2	12	32	.312	35	42	7	75	5	2	.976
—Okla. City (A.A.)■	OF-P	54	178	33	54	11	1	12	17	.303	27	46	6	44	2	1	.979
Major league totals (2 years)		22	39	3	3	1	0	0	2	.077	6	11	1	19	1	3	.870

RECORD AS PITCHER

Year—Team (League)	W	L	Pct.	ERA	G	GS	CG	ShO	Sv.	IP	H	R	ER	BB	SO
1997—Oklahoma City (A.A.)■	0	0	...	18.00	1	0	0	0	0	1	4	2	2	0	1

BLOWERS, MIKE — 3B — ATHLETICS

PERSONAL: Born April 24, 1965, in Wurzburg, West Germany. ... 6-2/210. ... Bats right, throws right. ... Full name: Michael Roy Blowers.
HIGH SCHOOL: Bethel (Wash.).
JUNIOR COLLEGE: Tacoma (Wash.) Community College.
COLLEGE: Washington.
TRANSACTIONS/CAREER NOTES: Selected by Seattle Mariners organization in eighth round of free-agent draft (January 17, 1984); did not sign. ... Selected by San Francisco Giants organization in secondary phase of free-agent draft (June 4, 1984); did not sign. ... Selected by Baltimore Orioles organization in secondary phase of free-agent draft (January 9, 1985); did not sign. ... Selected by Montreal Expos organization in 10th round of free-agent draft (June 2, 1986). ... Traded by Expos to New York Yankees (August 31, 1989), completing deal in which Yankees traded P John Candelaria to Expos for a player to be named later (August 29, 1989). ... Traded by Yankees to Mariners for a player to be named later and cash (May 17, 1991); Yankees acquired P Jim Blueberg to complete deal (June 22, 1991). ... Traded by Mariners to Los Angeles Dodgers for 2B Miguel Cairo and 3B Willis Otanez (November 29, 1995). ... On disabled list (July 18, 1996-remainder of season). ... Granted free agency (October 15, 1996). ... Signed by Mariners organization (January 24, 1997). ... Granted free agency (October 28, 1997). ... Signed by Oakland Athletics (December 16, 1997).
RECORDS: Shares major league single-month record for most grand slams—3 (August 1995). ... Shares A.L. single-game record for most errors by third baseman—4 (May 3, 1990).
STATISTICAL NOTES: Led Florida State League third basemen with .944 fielding percentage and 27 double plays in 1987. ... Led Southern League third basemen with 125 putouts and 27 double plays in 1988. ... Led American Association third basemen with .930 fielding percentage in 1989. ... Career major league grand slams: 6.

Year—Team (League)	Pos.	G	AB	R	H	2B	3B	HR	RBI	Avg.	BB	SO	SB	PO	A	E	Avg.
1986—Jamestown (NYP)	SS-3B	32	95	13	24	9	2	1	6	.253	17	18	3	48	73	16	.883
—GC Expos (GCL)	SS	31	115	14	25	3	1	2	17	.217	15	25	2	50	84	15	.899
1987—W.P. Beach (FSL)........	3B-SS-1B	136	491	68	124	30	3	16	71	.253	48	118	4	75	239	18	†.946
1988—Jacksonville (South.)..	3B-SS-2B	137	460	58	115	20	6	15	60	.250	68	114	6	†125	241	34	.915
1989—Indianapolis (A.A.)	3B-SS	131	461	49	123	29	6	14	56	.267	41	109	3	91	214	23	†.930
—New York (A.L.)■......	3B	13	38	2	10	0	0	0	3	.263	3	13	0	9	14	4	.852
1990—New York (A.L.).........	3B-DH	48	144	16	27	4	0	5	21	.188	12	50	1	26	63	10	.899
—Columbus (Int'l)	3B-1B-2B	62	230	30	78	20	6	6	50	.339	29	40	3	64	89	8	.950
1991—New York (A.L.).........	3B	15	35	3	7	0	0	1	1	.200	4	3	0	4	16	3	.870
—Calgary (PCL)■.......	3B-SS-1B	90	329	56	95	20	2	9	59	.289	40	74	3	56	163	19	.920
1992—Calgary (PCL)	3B-1B-OF	83	300	56	95	28	2	9	67	.317	50	64	2	99	87	5	.974
—Seattle (A.L.)	3B-1B	31	73	7	14	3	0	1	2	.192	6	20	0	28	44	1	.986
1993—Seattle (A.L.) 3-DH-0-1-C		127	379	55	106	23	3	15	57	.280	44	98	1	70	225	15	.952
1994—Seattle (A.L.)	3-1-DH-O	85	270	37	78	13	0	9	49	.289	25	60	2	142	109	9	.965
1995—Seattle (A.L.)	3B-1B-OF	134	439	59	113	24	1	23	96	.257	53	128	2	116	174	16	.948
1996—Los Angeles (N.L.)	3B-1B-SS	92	317	31	84	19	2	6	38	.265	37	77	0	76	122	9	.957
1997—Seattle (A.L.)■.......	1-3-O-DH	68	150	22	44	5	0	5	20	.293	21	33	0	271	35	4	.987
American League totals (8 years)		521	1528	201	399	72	4	59	249	.261	168	405	6	666	680	62	.956
National League totals (1 year)		92	317	31	84	19	2	6	38	.265	37	77	0	76	122	9	.957
Major league totals (9 years)		613	1845	232	483	91	6	65	287	.262	205	482	6	742	802	71	.956

DIVISION SERIES RECORD

Year—Team (League)	Pos.	G	AB	R	H	2B	3B	HR	RBI	Avg.	BB	SO	SB	PO	A	E	Avg.
1995—Seattle (A.L.)	3B-1B	5	18	0	3	0	0	0	1	.167	3	7	0	2	6	0	1.000
1997—Seattle (A.L.)	3B	3	5	0	1	0	0	0	0	.200	0	3	0	1	2	0	1.000
Division series totals (2 years)		8	23	0	4	0	0	0	1	.174	3	10	0	3	8	0	1.000

CHAMPIONSHIP SERIES RECORD

NOTES: Hit home run in first at-bat (October 10, 1995).

Year—Team (League)	Pos.	G	AB	R	H	2B	3B	HR	RBI	Avg.	BB	SO	SB	PO	A	E	Avg.
1995—Seattle (A.L.)	3B	6	18	1	4	0	0	1	2	.222	0	4	0	5	9	0	1.000

BLUMA, JAMIE   P   ROYALS

PERSONAL: Born May 18, 1972, in Beaufort, S.C. ... 5-11/195. ... Throws right, bats right. ... Full name: James Andrew Bluma.
HIGH SCHOOL: Owasso (Okla.).
COLLEGE: Wichita State.
TRANSACTIONS/CAREER NOTES: Selected by Kansas City Royals organization in third round of free-agent draft (June 2, 1994). ... On disabled list (March 28, 1997-entire season).

Year—Team (League)	W	L	Pct.	ERA	G	GS	CG	ShO	Sv.	IP	H	R	ER	BB	SO
1994—Eugene (Northwest)	2	1	.667	0.99	26	0	0	0	12	36 1/3	19	5	4	6	35
—Wilmington (Caro.).............	4	0	1.000	0.93	7	0	0	0	2	9 2/3	7	2	1	0	5
1995—Wichita (Texas)................	4	3	.571	3.09	42	0	0	0	22	55 1/3	38	19	19	9	31
—Omaha (Am. Assoc.)...........	0	0	...	3.04	18	0	0	0	4	23 2/3	21	13	8	14	12
1996—Omaha (Am. Assoc.)..........	1	2	.333	3.12	52	0	0	0	25	57 2/3	57	22	20	20	40
—Kansas City (A.L.)	0	0	...	3.60	17	0	0	0	5	20	18	9	8	4	14
1997—Kansas City (A.L.)							Did not play.								
Major league totals (1 year)........	0	0	...	3.60	17	0	0	0	5	20	18	9	8	4	14

BOCACHICA, HIRAM   SS   EXPOS

PERSONAL: Born March 4, 1976, in Ponce, Puerto Rico. ... 5-11/165. ... Bats right, throws right. ... Full name: Hiram Colon Bocachica.
HIGH SCHOOL: Rexville (Bayamon, Puerto Rico).
TRANSACTIONS/CAREER NOTES: Selected by Montreal Expos organization in first round (21st pick overall) of free-agent draft (June 2, 1994). ... On West Palm Beach disabled list (May 16-July 12, 1996). ... On Harrisburg suspended list (June 15-18, 1997). ... On Harrisburg disabled list (June 18-25, 1997).
STATISTICAL NOTES: Led South Atlantic League shortstops with 58 errors in 1995.

Year—Team (League)	Pos.	G	AB	R	H	2B	3B	HR	RBI	Avg.	BB	SO	SB	PO	A	E	Avg.
1994—GC Expos (GCL)	SS	43	168	31	47	9	0	5	16	.280	15	42	11	72	126	*23	.896
1995—Albany (S. Atl.)..........	SS-2B	96	380	65	108	20	10	2	30	.284	52	78	47	165	265	†58	.881
1996—W.P. Beach (FSL).......	SS	71	267	50	90	17	5	2	26	.337	34	47	21	37	88	24	.833
—G.C. Expos (GCL)	DH	9	32	11	8	3	0	0	2	.250	5	3	2	0	0	0	...
1997—Harrisburg (Eastern) ..	SS-2B	119	443	82	123	19	3	11	35	.278	41	98	29	135	186	32	.909

BOCHTLER, DOUG   P   ATHLETICS

PERSONAL: Born July 5, 1970, in West Palm Beach, Fla. ... 6-3/200. ... Throws right, bats right. ... Full name: Douglas Eugene Bochtler. ... Name pronounced BOCK-ler.
HIGH SCHOOL: John I. Leonard (Lake Worth, Fla.).
JUNIOR COLLEGE: Indian River Community College (Fla.).
TRANSACTIONS/CAREER NOTES: Selected by Montreal Expos organization in ninth round of free-agent draft (June 5, 1989). ... On disabled list (June 18-September 6, 1992). ... Selected by Colorado Rockies in second round (32nd pick overall) of expansion draft (November 17,

1992). ... On Colorado Springs disabled list (April 18-26, 1993). ... Traded by Rockies with C Brad Ausmus and a player to be named later to San Diego Padres for P Bruce Hurst and P Greg W. Harris (July 26, 1993); Padres acquired P Andy Ashby to complete deal (July 27, 1993). On disabled list (June 16-24 and August 24, 1994-remainder of season). ... On disabled list (July 2-17, 1997). ... Traded by Padres with IF Jorge Velandia to Oakland Athletics for P Don Wengert and IF David Newhan (November 26, 1997).

Year Team (League)	W	L	Pct.	ERA	G	GS	CG	ShO	Sv.	IP	H	R	ER	BB	SO
1989—GC Expos (GCL)	2	2	.500	3.21	9	9	1	0	0	47²/₃	46	22	17	20	45
1990—Rockford (Midwest)	9	12	.429	3.50	25	25	1	1	0	139	142	82	54	54	109
1991—W.P. Beach (FSL)	•12	9	.571	2.92	26	24	7	2	0	160¹/₃	148	63	52	55	109
1992—Harrisburg (Eastern)	6	5	.545	2.32	13	13	2	1	0	77²/₃	50	25	20	36	89
1993—Colo. Springs (PCL)■	1	4	.200	6.93	12	11	0	0	0	50²/₃	71	41	39	26	38
—Central Valley (Cal.)	3	1	.750	3.40	8	8	0	0	0	47²/₃	40	23	18	28	43
—Las Vegas (PCL)■	0	5	.000	5.22	7	7	1	0	0	39²/₃	52	26	23	11	30
1994—Las Vegas (PCL)	3	7	.300	5.20	22	20	2	1	0	100¹/₃	116	67	58	48	86
1995—Las Vegas (PCL)	2	3	.400	4.25	18	2	0	0	1	36	31	18	17	26	32
—San Diego (N.L.)	4	4	.500	3.57	34	0	0	0	1	45¹/₃	38	18	18	19	45
1996—San Diego (N.L.)	2	4	.333	3.02	63	0	0	0	3	65²/₃	45	25	22	39	68
1997—San Diego (N.L.)	3	6	.333	4.77	54	0	0	0	2	60¹/₃	51	35	32	50	46
Major league totals (3 years)	9	14	.391	3.78	151	0	0	0	6	171¹/₃	134	78	72	108	159

DIVISION SERIES RECORD

Year Team (League)	W	L	Pct.	ERA	G	GS	CG	ShO	Sv.	IP	H	R	ER	BB	SO
1996—San Diego (N.L.)	0	1	.000	27.00	1	0	0	0	0	¹/₃	0	1	1	3	0

BOEHRINGER, BRIAN   P   PADRES

PERSONAL: Born January 8, 1970, in St. Louis. ... 6-2/190. ... Throws right, bats both. ... Full name: Brian Edward Boehringer. ... Name pronounced BO-ring-er.
HIGH SCHOOL: Northwest (House Springs, Mo.).
JUNIOR COLLEGE: St. Louis Community College at Meramec.
COLLEGE: UNLV.
TRANSACTIONS/CAREER NOTES: Selected by Houston Astros organization in 10th round of free-agent draft (June 4, 1990); did not sign. ... Selected by Chicago White Sox organization in fourth round of free-agent draft (June 3, 1991). ... On Utica disabled list (June 29-August 25, 1991). ... On disabled list (June 24-August 25, 1992). ... Traded by White Sox organization to New York Yankees for P Paul Assenmacher (March 21, 1994). ... On New York disabled list (May 27-August 19, 1997); included rehabilitation assignments to Gulf Coast Yankees (August 10-12) and Tampa (August 13-19). ... Selected by Tampa Bay Devil Rays in second round (30th pick overall) of expansion draft (November 18, 1997). ... Traded by Devil Rays with SS Andy Sheets to San Diego Padres for C John Flaherty (November 11, 1997).
STATISTICAL NOTES: Tied for Eastern League lead with four balks in 1994. ... Led International League with 11 hit batsmen in 1996.

Year Team (League)	W	L	Pct.	ERA	G	GS	CG	ShO	Sv.	IP	H	R	ER	BB	SO
1991—GC White Sox (GCL)	1	1	.500	6.57	5	1	0	0	0	12¹/₃	14	9	9	5	10
—Utica (N.Y.-Penn)	1	1	.500	2.37	4	4	0	0	0	19	14	8	5	8	19
1992—South Bend (Mid.)	6	7	.462	4.38	15	15	2	0	0	86¹/₃	87	52	42	40	59
1993—Sarasota (Florida State)	10	4	.714	2.80	18	17	3	0	0	119	103	47	37	51	92
—Birmingham (Southern)	2	1	.667	3.54	7	7	1	0	0	40²/₃	41	20	16	14	29
1994—Alb./Colon. (Eastern)■	10	11	.476	3.62	27	27	5	1	0	171²/₃	165	85	69	57	145
1995—New York (A.L.)	0	3	.000	13.75	7	3	0	0	0	17²/₃	24	27	27	22	10
—Columbus (Int'l)	8	6	.571	2.77	17	17	3	0	0	104	101	39	32	31	58
1996—Columbus (Int'l)	11	7	.611	4.00	25	25	3	1	0	153	155	79	68	56	132
—New York (A.L.)	2	4	.333	5.44	15	3	0	0	0	46¹/₃	46	28	28	21	37
1997—New York (A.L.)	3	2	.600	2.63	34	0	0	0	0	48	39	16	14	32	53
—GC Yankees (GCL)	0	0	. . .	0.00	1	1	0	0	0	2	1	0	0	0	2
—Tampa (Florida State)	0	1	.000	5.00	3	3	0	0	0	9	9	5	5	5	8
Major league totals (3 years)	5	9	.357	5.54	56	6	0	0	0	112	109	71	69	75	100

DIVISION SERIES RECORD

Year Team (League)	W	L	Pct.	ERA	G	GS	CG	ShO	Sv.	IP	H	R	ER	BB	SO
1996—New York (A.L.)	1	0	1.000	6.75	2	0	0	0	0	1¹/₃	3	2	1	2	0
1997—New York (A.L.)	0	0	. . .	0.00	1	0	0	0	0	1²/₃	1	0	0	1	2
Div. series totals (2 years)	1	0	1.000	3.00	3	0	0	0	0	3	4	2	1	3	2

WORLD SERIES RECORD

NOTES: Member of World Series championship team (1996).

Year Team (League)	W	L	Pct.	ERA	G	GS	CG	ShO	Sv.	IP	H	R	ER	BB	SO
1996—New York (A.L.)	0	0	. . .	5.40	2	0	0	0	0	5	5	5	3	0	5

BOGAR, TIM   SS   ASTROS

PERSONAL: Born October 28, 1966, in Indianapolis. ... 6-2/198. ... Bats right, throws right. ... Full name: Tim Paul Bogar.
HIGH SCHOOL: Buffalo Grove (Ill.).
COLLEGE: Eastern Illinois.
TRANSACTIONS/CAREER NOTES: Selected by New York Mets organization in eighth round of free-agent draft (June 2, 1987). ... On disabled list (June 14, 1990-remainder of season). ... On disabled list (August 16-September 1, 1993). ... On New York disabled list (May 6-June 9, 1994); included rehabilitation assignment to Norfolk (June 4-9). ... Traded by Mets to Houston Astros for IF Luis Lopez (March 31, 1997). ... On disabled list (September 5, 1997-remainder of season).
MISCELLANEOUS: Played all nine positions in one game for Tidewater (September 4, 1991).

						BATTING							FIELDING		
Year Team (League)	Pos.	G	AB	R	H	2B	3B	HR	RBI	Avg.	BB	SO	SB	PO	A	E	Avg.
1987—Little Falls (NYP)	SS-2B	58	205	31	48	9	0	0	23	.234	18	39	2	79	194	24	.919
1988—Columbia (S. Atl.)	2B-SS	45	142	19	40	4	2	3	21	.282	22	29	5	89	120	8	.963
—St. Lucie (Fla. St.)	2B-SS-3B	76	236	34	65	7	1	2	30	.275	34	57	9	141	214	19	.949

Year— Team (League)	Pos.	G	AB	R	H	2B	3B	HR	RBI	Avg.	BB	SO	SB	PO	A	E	Avg.
1989— Jackson (Texas)	SS	112	406	44	108	13	5	4	45	.266	41	57	8	185	351	29	.949
1990— Tidewater (Int'l).........	SS	33	117	10	19	2	0	4	4	.162	8	22	1	57	89	10	.936
1991— Williamsport (East.) ...	3-2-1-S	63	243	33	61	12	2	2	25	.251	20	44	13	100	137	8	.967
— Tidewater (Int'l).......S-2-3-C-1-O-P	65	218	23	56	11	0	1	23	.257	20	35	1	111	183	11	.964
1992— Tidewater (Int'l)	2-S-3-P-1	129	481	54	134	32	1	5	38	.279	14	65	7	211	327	15	.973
1993— New York (N.L.)........	SS-3B-2B	78	205	19	50	13	0	3	25	.244	14	29	0	105	217	9	.973
1994— New York (N.L.)........	3-1-S-2-O	50	52	5	8	0	0	2	5	.154	4	11	1	77	38	1	.991
— Norfolk (Int'l)	3B-2B	5	19	0	2	0	0	0	1	.105	1	4	0	5	11	0	1.000
1995— New York (N.L.)........	S-3-1-2-O	78	145	17	42	7	0	1	21	.290	9	25	1	82	100	6	.968
1996— New York (N.L.)........	1-3-S-2	91	89	17	19	4	0	0	6	.213	8	20	1	104	61	1	.994
1997— Houston (N.L.)■.......	SS-3B-1B	97	241	30	60	14	4	4	30	.249	24	42	4	110	229	6	.983
Major league totals (5 years)		394	732	88	179	38	4	10	87	.245	59	127	7	478	645	23	.980

RECORD AS PITCHER

Year— Team (League)	W	L	Pct.	ERA	G	GS	CG	ShO	Sv.	IP	H	R	ER	BB	SO
1991— Tidewater (Int'l)................	0	0	...	27.00	1	0	0	0	0	1/3	0	1	1	0	1
1992— Tidewater (Int'l)................	0	0	...	12.00	3	0	0	0	0	3	4	4	4	3	1

B

BOGGS, WADE   3B   DEVIL RAYS

PERSONAL: Born June 15, 1958, in Omaha, Neb. ... 6-2/197. ... Bats left, throws right. ... Full name: Wade Anthony Boggs.

HIGH SCHOOL: H.B. Plant (Tampa).

JUNIOR COLLEGE: Hillsborough Community College (Fla.).

TRANSACTIONS/CAREER NOTES: Selected by Boston Red Sox organization in seventh round of free-agent draft (June 8, 1976). ... On disabled list (April 20-May 2, 1979). ... Granted free agency (October 26, 1992). ... Signed by New York Yankees (December 15, 1992). ... Granted free agency (November 11, 1995). ... Re-signed by Yankees (December 5, 1995). ... Granted free agency (November 1, 1997). ... Signed by Tampa Bay Devil Rays (December 9, 1997).

RECORDS: Holds A.L. record for most consecutive seasons with 200 or more hits—7 (1983-89). ... Holds A.L. rookie-season record for highest batting average (100 or more games)—.349 (1982). ... Shares major league records for most seasons and most consecutive seasons leading league in intentional bases on balls received—6 (1987-92). ... Shares major league single-season records for most games with at least one hit—135 (1985); and fewest double plays by third baseman (150 or more games)—17 (1988). ... Holds A.L. single-season record for most singles—187 (1985). ... Shares major league single-season record for fewest chances accepted by third baseman (150 or more games)—349 (1990).

HONORS: Named third baseman on THE SPORTING NEWS A.L. All-Star team (1983, 1985-88, 1991 and 1994). ... Named third baseman on THE SPORTING NEWS A.L. Silver Slugger team (1983, 1986-89, 1991 and 1993-94). ... Won A.L. Gold Glove at third base (1994-95).

STATISTICAL NOTES: Led Eastern League third basemen with .953 fielding percentage in 1979. ... Led International League with .3353 batting average in 1981. ... Led A.L with .449 on-base percentage in 1983, .450 in 1985, .453 in 1986, .461 in 1987, .476 in 1988 and .430 in 1989. ... Led A.L. third basemen with 30 double plays in 1984, 37 in 1987, 29 in 1989 and 29 in 1993. ... Had 28-game hitting streak (June 24-July 26, 1985). ... Led A.L. third basemen with 486 total chances in 1985. ... Had 20-game hitting streak (August 29-September 18, 1986). ... Had 25-game hitting streak (May 28-June 24, 1987). ... Led A.L. with 19 intentional bases on balls received in 1987, 1989, 1990 and 1992, with 25 in 1991 and tied for lead with 18 in 1988. ... Led A.L. in grounding into double plays with 23 in 1988. ... Led A.L. third basemen with .981 fielding percentage in 1995. ... Career major league grand slams: 3.

Year— Team (League)	Pos.	G	AB	R	H	2B	3B	HR	RBI	Avg.	BB	SO	SB	PO	A	E	Avg.
1976— Elmira (N.Y.-Penn)......	3B	57	179	29	47	6	0	0	15	.263	29	15	2	36	75	16	.874
1977— Win.-Salem (Car.).......	3B-2B-SS	117	422	67	140	13	1	2	55	.332	65	22	8	145	223	27	.932
1978— Bristol (Eastern)	3-S-2-O	109	354	63	110	14	2	1	32	.311	53	25	1	62	107	7	.960
1979— Bristol (Eastern)	3B-SS-2B	113	406	56	132	17	2	0	41	.325	66	21	11	94	213	15	†.953
1980— Pawtucket (Int'l)........	3B-1B	129	418	51	128	21	0	1	45	.306	64	25	3	108	156	12	.957
1981— Pawtucket (Int'l)........	3B-1B	137	498	67	*167	*41	3	5	60	*.335	89	41	4	359	238	26	.958
1982— Boston (A.L.)...........	1-3-DH-O	104	338	51	118	14	1	5	44	.349	35	21	1	489	168	8	.988
1983— Boston (A.L.)...........	3B	153	582	100	210	44	7	5	74	*.361	92	36	3	118	368	*27	.947
1984— Boston (A.L.)...........	3B-DH	158	625	109	203	31	4	6	55	.325	89	44	3	141	330	•20	.959
1985— Boston (A.L.)...........	3B	161	653	107	*240	42	3	8	78	*.368	96	61	2	134	335	17	.965
1986— Boston (A.L.)...........	3B	149	580	107	207	47	2	8	71	*.357	*105	44	0	*121	267	19	.953
1987— Boston (A.L.)...........	3B-1B-DH	147	551	108	200	40	6	24	89	*.363	105	48	1	112	277	14	.965
1988— Boston (A.L.)...........	3B-DH	155	584	*128	214	*45	6	5	58	*.366	*125	34	2	*122	250	11	.971
1989— Boston (A.L.)...........	3B-DH	156	621	•113	205	*51	7	3	54	.330	107	51	2	*123	264	17	.958
1990— Boston (A.L.)...........	3B-DH	155	619	89	187	44	5	6	63	.302	87	68	0	108	241	20	.946
1991— Boston (A.L.)...........	3B	144	546	93	181	42	2	8	51	.332	89	32	1	89	276	12	.968
1992— Boston (A.L.)...........	3B-DH	143	514	62	133	22	4	7	50	.259	74	31	1	70	229	15	.952
1993— New York (A.L.)■......	3B-DH	143	560	83	169	26	1	2	59	.302	74	49	0	75	*311	12	*.970
1994— New York (A.L.)........	3B-1B	97	366	61	125	19	1	11	55	.342	61	29	2	66	218	10	.966
1995— New York (A.L.)........	3B-1B	126	460	76	149	22	4	5	63	.324	74	50	1	114	198	5	†.984
1996— New York (A.L.)........	3B-DH	132	501	80	156	29	2	2	41	.311	67	32	1	62	201	7	.974
1997— New York (A.L.)........	3B-DH-P	104	353	55	103	23	1	4	28	.292	48	38	0	42	140	4	.978
Major league totals (16 years)		2227	8453	1422	2800	541	56	109	933	.331	1328	668	20	1986	4073	218	.965

DIVISION SERIES RECORD

Year— Team (League)	Pos.	G	AB	R	H	2B	3B	HR	RBI	Avg.	BB	SO	SB	PO	A	E	Avg.
1995— New York (A.L.)........	3B	4	19	4	5	2	0	1	3	.263	3	5	0	4	6	0	1.000
1996— New York (A.L.)........	3B	3	12	0	1	1	0	0	0	.083	0	2	0	2	1	0	1.000
1997— New York (A.L.)........	3B-PH	3	7	1	3	0	0	0	2	.429	0	0	0	0	1	0	1.000
Division series totals (3 years)		10	38	5	9	3	0	1	5	.237	3	7	0	6	10	0	1.000

CHAMPIONSHIP SERIES RECORD

Year— Team (League)	Pos.	G	AB	R	H	2B	3B	HR	RBI	Avg.	BB	SO	SB	PO	A	E	Avg.
1986— Boston (A.L.)..............	3B	7	30	3	7	1	0	2	2	.233	4	1	0	7	13	2	.909
1988— Boston (A.L.)..............	3B	4	13	2	5	0	0	3	3	.385	3	4	0	6	6	0	1.000

Year	Team (League)	Pos.	G	AB	R	H	2B	3B	HR	RBI	Avg.	BB	SO	SB	PO	A	E	Avg.
								BATTING									FIELDING	
1990—Boston (A.L.)	3B	4	16	1	7	1	0	1	1	.438	0	3	0	6	10	0	1.000
1996—New York (A.L.)	3B	3	15	1	2	0	0	0	0	.133	1	3	0	2	11	0	1.000
Championship series totals (4 years)		18	74	7	21	2	1	1	6	.284	8	11	0	21	40	2	.968

WORLD SERIES RECORD

NOTES: Member of World Series championship team (1996).

Year	Team (League)	Pos.	G	AB	R	H	2B	3B	HR	RBI	Avg.	BB	SO	SB	PO	A	E	Avg.
1986—Boston (A.L.)	3B	7	31	3	9	3	0	0	3	.290	4	2	0	4	15	0	1.000
1996—New York (A.L.)	3B-PH	4	11	0	3	1	0	0	2	.273	1	0	0	0	0	0	...
World Series totals (2 years)		11	42	3	12	4	0	0	5	.286	5	2	0	4	15	0	1.000

ALL-STAR GAME RECORD

Year	League	Pos.	AB	R	H	2B	3B	HR	RBI	Avg.	BB	SO	SB	PO	A	E	Avg.
1985—American	3B	0	0	0	0	0	0	0	...	1	0	0	0	0	0	
1986—American	3B	3	0	1	0	0	0	0	.333	1	0	0	0	1	0	1.000
1987—American	3B	3	0	0	0	0	0	0	.000	0	0	0	0	3	0	1.000
1988—American	3B	3	0	1	0	0	0	0	.333	0	0	0	0	1	0	1.000
1989—American	3B	3	1	1	0	0	1	1	.333	0	0	0	1	1	0	1.000
1990—American	3B	2	0	2	0	0	0	0	1.000	1	0	0	0	4	0	1.000
1991—American	3B	2	1	1	0	0	0	0	.500	1	0	0	1	2	0	1.000
1992—American	3B	3	1	1	0	0	0	0	.333	0	1	0	1	0	0	1.000
1993—American	3B	1	0	0	0	0	0	0	.000	1	0	0	1	0	0	1.000
1994—American	3B	3	1	1	0	0	0	0	.333	0	2	0	2	0	0	1.000
1995—American	3B	2	0	1	0	0	0	0	.500	0	0	0	0	1	0	1.000
1996—American	3B	3	0	0	0	0	0	0	.000	0	0	0	1	2	0	1.000
All-Star Game totals (12 years)		28	4	9	0	0	1	1	.321	5	3	0	5	17	0	1.000

RECORD AS PITCHER

Year	Team (League)	W	L	Pct.	ERA	G	GS	CG	ShO	Sv.	IP	H	R	ER	BB	SO
1997—New York (A.L.)	0	0	...	0.00	1	0	0	0	0	1	0	0	0	1	1

BOHANON, BRIAN — P — METS

PERSONAL: Born August 1, 1968, in Denton, Texas. ... 6-3/220. ... Throws left, bats left. ... Full name: Brian Edward Bohanon.
HIGH SCHOOL: North Shore (Houston).
TRANSACTIONS/CAREER NOTES: Selected by Texas Rangers organization in first round (19th pick overall) of free-agent draft (June 2, 1987). ... On disabled list (April 17, 1988-remainder of season). ... On Charlotte disabled list (April 7-May 2, 1989). ... On Texas disabled list (April 7-July 1, 1991); included rehabilitation assignments to Charlotte (June 1-10), Tulsa (June 10-23) and Oklahoma City (June 23-30). ... On Texas disabled list (April 28-May 13, 1992). ... On Texas disabled list (June 9-30, 1993); Included rehabilitation assignment to Oklahoma City (June 21-30). ... Granted free agency (December 23, 1994). ... Signed by Toledo, Detroit Tigers organization (March 6, 1995). ... Released by Tigers (October 13, 1995). ... Signed by Syracuse, Toronto Blue Jays organization (February 20, 1996). ... Granted free agency (October 3, 1996). ... Signed by New York Mets organization (December 18, 1996).
MISCELLANEOUS: Had a single and struck out once in two games as pinch-hitter (1997).

Year	Team (League)	W	L	Pct.	ERA	G	GS	CG	ShO	Sv.	IP	H	R	ER	BB	SO
1987—GC Rangers (GCL)	0	2	.000	4.71	5	4	0	0	0	21	15	13	11	5	21
1988—Charlotte (Fla. St.)	0	1	.000	5.40	2	2	0	0	0	6 2/3	6	4	4	5	9
1989—Charlotte (Fla. St.)	0	3	.000	1.81	11	7	0	0	1	54 2/3	40	16	11	20	33
—Tulsa (Texas)	5	0	1.000	2.20	11	11	1	1	0	73 2/3	59	20	18	27	44
1990—Texas (A.L.)	0	3	.000	6.62	11	6	0	0	0	34	40	30	25	18	15
—Oklahoma City (A.A.)	1	2	.333	3.66	14	4	0	0	1	32	35	16	13	8	22
1991—Charlotte (Fla. St.)	1	0	1.000	3.86	2	2	0	0	0	11 2/3	6	5	5	4	7
—Tulsa (Texas)	0	1	.000	2.31	2	2	0	0	0	11 2/3	9	8	3	11	6
—Oklahoma City (A.A.)	0	4	.000	2.91	7	7	0	0	0	46 1/3	49	19	15	15	37
—Texas (A.L.)	4	3	.571	4.84	11	11	1	0	0	61 1/3	66	35	33	23	34
1992—Oklahoma City (A.A.)	4	2	.667	2.73	9	9	3	0	0	56	53	21	17	15	24
—Texas (A.L.)	1	1	.500	6.31	18	7	0	0	0	45 2/3	57	38	32	25	29
—Tulsa (Texas)	2	1	.667	1.27	6	6	1	0	0	28 1/3	25	7	4	9	25
1993—Texas (A.L.)	4	4	.500	4.76	36	8	0	0	0	92 2/3	107	54	49	46	45
—Oklahoma City (A.A.)	0	1	.000	6.43	2	2	0	0	0	7	7	6	5	3	7
1994—Oklahoma City (A.A.)	5	10	.333	4.12	15	15	2	1	0	98 1/3	106	56	45	33	88
—Texas (A.L.)	2	2	.500	7.23	11	5	0	0	0	37 1/3	51	31	30	8	26
1995—Detroit (A.L.)■	1	1	.500	5.54	52	10	0	0	1	105 2/3	121	68	65	41	63
1996—Toronto (A.L.)■	0	1	.000	7.77	20	0	0	0	1	22	27	19	19	19	17
—Syracuse (Int'l)	4	3	.571	3.86	31	0	0	0	0	58 1/3	56	29	25	17	38
1997—Norfolk (Int'l)■	9	3	.750	2.63	15	14	4	2	0	96	88	37	28	32	84
—New York (N.L.)■	6	4	.600	3.82	19	14	0	0	0	94 1/3	95	49	40	34	66
A.L. totals (7 years)	12	15	.444	5.71	159	47	1	0	2	398 2/3	469	275	253	180	229
N.L. totals (1 year)	6	4	.600	3.82	19	14	0	0	0	94 1/3	95	49	40	34	66
Major league totals (8 years)	18	19	.486	5.35	178	61	1	0	2	493	564	324	293	214	295

BONDS, BARRY — OF — GIANTS

PERSONAL: Born July 24, 1964, in Riverside, Calif. ... 6-2/206. ... Bats left, throws left. ... Full name: Barry Lamar Bonds. ... Son of Bobby Bonds, major league outfielder with eight teams (1968-81), coach, Cleveland Indians (1984-87); and coach, San Francisco Giants (1993-1996).
HIGH SCHOOL: Serra (San Mateo, Calif.).
COLLEGE: Arizona State.

TRANSACTIONS/CAREER NOTES: Selected by San Francisco Giants organization in second round of free-agent draft (June 7, 1982); did not sign. ... Selected by Pittsburgh Pirates organization in first round (sixth pick overall) of free-agent draft (June 3, 1985). ... On disabled list (June 15-July 4, 1992). ... Granted free agency (October 26, 1992). ... Signed by Giants (December 8, 1992).

RECORDS: Shares major league record for most seasons and consecutive seasons leading league in intentional bases on balls received—6 (1992-97). ... Shares major league single-season record for fewest assists by outfielder who led league in assists—14 (1990). ... Holds N.L. career records for most consecutive years leading league in bases on balls—4 (1994-97); and most consecutive seasons leading league in intentional bases on balls received—5 (1992-96). ... Holds N.L. single-season record for most bases on balls—151 (1996). ... Shares major league record for fewest double plays by outfielder (150 or more games)—0 (1997).

HONORS: Named outfielder on THE SPORTING NEWS college All-America team (1985). ... Named Major League Player of the Year by THE SPORTING NEWS (1990). ... Named N.L. Player of the Year by THE SPORTING NEWS (1990-91). ... Named outfielder on THE SPORTING NEWS N.L. All-Star team (1990-94 and 1996-97). ... Won N.L. Gold Glove as outfielder (1990-94 and 1996-97). ... Named outfielder on THE SPORTING NEWS N.L. Silver Slugger team (1990-94, 1996 and 1997). ... Named N.L. Most Valuable Player by Baseball Writers' Association of America (1990 and 1992-93).

STATISTICAL NOTES: Led N.L. with .565 slugging percentage in 1990, .624 in 1992 and .677 in 1993. ... Led N.L. with 32 intentional bases on balls received in 1992, 43 in 1993, 18 in 1994, 22 in 1995, 30 in 1996 and 34 in 1997. ... Led N.L. with .456 on-base percentage in 1992, .458 in 1993 and .431 in 1995. ... Led N.L. with 365 total bases in 1993. ... Hit three home runs in one game (August 2, 1994). ... Career major league grand slams: 7.

Year— Team (League)	Pos.	G	AB	R	H	2B	3B	HR	RBI	Avg.	BB	SO	SB	PO	A	E	Avg.
1985— Prince William (Car.) ..	OF	71	254	49	76	16	4	13	37	.299	37	52	15	202	4	5	.976
1986— Hawaii (PCL)	OF	44	148	30	46	7	2	7	37	.311	33	31	16	109	4	2	.983
—Pittsburgh (N.L.)	OF	113	413	72	92	26	3	16	48	.223	65	102	36	280	9	5	.983
1987— Pittsburgh (N.L.)	OF	150	551	99	144	34	9	25	59	.261	54	88	32	330	15	5	.986
1988— Pittsburgh (N.L.)	OF	144	538	97	152	30	5	24	58	.283	72	82	17	292	5	6	.980
1989— Pittsburgh (N.L.)	OF	159	580	96	144	34	6	19	58	.248	93	93	32	365	14	6	.984
1990— Pittsburgh (N.L.)	OF	151	519	104	156	32	3	33	114	.301	93	83	52	338	•14	6	.983
1991— Pittsburgh (N.L.)	OF	153	510	95	149	28	5	25	116	.292	107	73	43	321	13	3	.991
1992— Pittsburgh (N.L.)	OF	140	473	*109	147	36	5	34	103	.311	*127	69	39	310	4	3	.991
1993— San Fran. (N.L.)■.......	OF	159	539	129	181	38	4	*46	*123	.336	126	79	29	310	7	5	.984
1994— San Francisco (N.L.) ..	OF	112	391	89	122	18	1	37	81	.312	*74	43	29	198	10	3	.986
1995— San Francisco (N.L.) ..	OF	•144	506	109	149	30	7	33	104	.294	*120	83	31	279	12	6	.980
1996— San Francisco (N.L.) ..	OF	158	517	122	159	27	3	42	129	.308	*151	76	40	286	10	6	.980
1997— San Francisco (N.L.) ..	OF	159	532	123	155	26	5	40	101	.291	*145	87	37	289	10	5	.984
Major league totals (12 years)		1742	6069	1244	1750	359	56	374	1094	.288	1227	958	417	3598	123	59	.984

DIVISION SERIES RECORD

Year Team (League)	Pos.	G	AB	R	H	2B	3B	HR	RBI	Avg.	BB	SO	SB	PO	A	E	Avg.
1997— San Francisco (N.L.) ..	OF	3	12	0	3	2	0	0	2	.250	0	3	1	6	0	0	1.000

RECORDS: Shares record for most hits in one inning—2 (October 13, 1992, second inning).

CHAMPIONSHIP SERIES RECORD

Year Team (League)	Pos.	G	AB	R	H	2B	3B	HR	RBI	Avg.	BB	SO	SB	PO	A	E	Avg.
1990— Pittsburgh (N.L.)	OF	6	18	4	3	0	0	0	1	.167	6	5	2	13	0	0	1.000
1991— Pittsburgh (N.L.)	OF	7	27	1	4	1	0	0	0	.148	2	4	3	14	1	1	.938
1992— Pittsburgh (N.L.)	OF	7	23	5	6	1	0	1	2	.261	6	4	1	17	0	0	1.000
Championship series totals (3 years)		20	68	10	13	2	0	1	3	.191	14	13	6	44	1	1	.978

ALL-STAR GAME RECORD

Year League	Pos.	AB	R	H	2B	3B	HR	RBI	Avg.	BB	SO	SB	PO	A	E	Avg.
1990— National	OF	1	0	0	0	0	0	0	.000	1	0	0	2	0	0	1.000
1992— National	OF	3	1	1	1	0	0	0	.333	0	0	0	2	0	0	1.000
1993— National	OF	3	2	2	2	0	0	0	.667	0	0	0	1	0	0	1.000
1994— National	OF	3	0	0	0	0	0	1	.000	0	2	0	1	0	0	1.000
1995— National	OF	3	0	0	0	0	0	0	.000	0	1	0	0	0	0	...
1996— National	OF	3	0	1	0	0	0	0	.333	0	0	0	2	0	0	1.000
1997— National	OF	2	0	0	0	0	0	0	.000	1	1	1	2	0	0	1.000
All-Star Game totals (7 years)		18	3	4	3	0	0	1	.222	2	4	1	10	0	0	1.000

BONES, RICKY — P — TWINS

PERSONAL: Born April 7, 1969, in Salinas, Puerto Rico. ... 6-0/193. ... Throws right, bats right. ... Full name: Ricardo Bones. ... Name pronounced BO-nuss.

HIGH SCHOOL: Guayama (Puerto Rico).

TRANSACTIONS/CAREER NOTES: Signed as non-drafted free agent by San Diego Padres organization (May 13, 1986). ... Traded by Padres with SS Jose Valentin and OF Matt Mieske to Milwaukee Brewers for 3B Gary Sheffield and P Geoff Kellogg (March 27, 1992). ... Traded by Brewers with a player to be named later to New York Yankees as compensation for injured status of OF/IF Pat Listach (August 29, 1996); Yankees acquired IF Gabby Martinez to complete deal (November 5, 1996). ... Granted free agency (October 25, 1996). ... Signed by Cincinnati Reds (December 10, 1996). ... Released by Reds (May 6, 1997). ... Signed by Brewers organization (May 12, 1997). ... Traded by Brewers to Kansas City Royals organization for cash (June 26, 1997). ... Granted free agency (November 5, 1997). ... Signed by Minnesota Twins organization (January 8, 1998).

STATISTICAL NOTES: Led Texas League with 22 home runs allowed in 1989.

MISCELLANEOUS: Appeared in one game as outfielder with no chances (1993). ... Appeared in one game as pinch-runner with Kansas City (1997).

Year Team (League)	W	L	Pct.	ERA	G	GS	CG	ShO	Sv.	IP	H	R	ER	BB	SO
1986— Spokane (N'west)	1	3	.250	5.59	18	9	0	0	0	58	63	44	36	29	46
1987— Charleston, S.C. (S. Atl.)	12	5	.706	3.65	26	26	4	1	0	170 1/3	*183	81	69	45	130
1988— Riverside (California)	15	6	.714	3.64	25	25	5	2	0	175 1/3	162	80	71	64	129
1989— Wichita (Texas)	10	9	.526	5.74	24	24	2	0	0	136 1/3	162	103	87	47	88
1990— Wichita (Texas)	6	4	.600	3.48	21	21	2	1	0	137	138	66	53	45	96
—Las Vegas (PCL)	2	1	.667	3.47	5	5	0	0	0	36 1/3	45	17	14	10	25
1991— Las Vegas (PCL)	8	6	.571	4.22	23	23	1	0	0	136 1/3	155	90	64	43	95
—San Diego (N.L.)	4	6	.400	4.83	11	11	0	0	0	54	57	33	29	18	31

Year— Team (League)	W	L	Pct.	ERA	G	GS	CG	ShO	Sv.	IP	H	R	ER	BB	SO
1992— Milwaukee (A.L.)■	9	10	.474	4.57	31	28	0	0	0	163 1/3	169	90	83	48	65
1993— Milwaukee (A.L.)	11	11	.500	4.86	32	31	3	0	0	203 2/3	222	122	110	63	63
1994— Milwaukee (A.L.)	10	9	.526	3.43	24	24	4	1	0	170 2/3	166	76	65	45	57
1995— Milwaukee (A.L.)	10	12	.455	4.63	32	31	3	0	0	200 1/3	218	108	103	83	77
1996— Milwaukee (A.L.)	7	14	.333	5.83	32	23	0	0	0	145	170	104	94	62	59
— New York (A.L.)■	0	0	...	14.14	4	1	0	0	0	7	14	11	11	6	4
1997— Cincinnati (N.L.)■	0	1	.000	10.19	9	2	0	0	0	17 2/3	31	22	20	11	8
— Tucson (PCL)■	5	0	1.000	2.79	8	7	0	0	0	42	40	18	13	8	22
— Kansas City (A.L.)■	4	7	.364	5.97	21	11	1	0	0	78 1/3	102	59	52	25	36
A.L. totals (6 years)	51	63	.447	4.81	176	149	11	1	0	968 1/3	1061	570	518	332	361
N.L. totals (2 years)	4	7	.364	6.15	20	13	0	0	0	71 2/3	88	55	49	29	39
Major league totals (7 years)	55	70	.440	4.91	196	162	11	1	0	1040	1149	625	567	361	400

ALL-STAR GAME RECORD

Year— League	W	L	Pct.	ERA	GS	CG	ShO	Sv.	IP	H	R	ER	BB	SO
1994— American						Did not play.								

B

BONILLA, BOBBY — 3B — MARLINS

PERSONAL: Born February 23, 1963, in New York. ... 6-4/240. ... Bats both, throws right. ... Full name: Roberto Martin Antonio Bonilla. ... Name pronounced bo-NEE-yah.

HIGH SCHOOL: Lehman (Bronx, N.Y.).

COLLEGE: New York Technical College.

TRANSACTIONS/CAREER NOTES: Signed as non-drafted free agent by Pittsburgh Pirates organization (July 11, 1981). ... On Pittsburgh disabled list (March 25-July 19, 1985). ... Selected by Chicago White Sox from Pirates organization in Rule 5 major league draft (December 10, 1985). ... Traded by White Sox to Pittsburgh Pirates for P Jose DeLeon (July 23, 1986). ... Granted free agency (October 28, 1991). ... Signed by New York Mets (December 2, 1991). ... On suspended list (July 27-28, 1992). ... On disabled list (August 3-19, 1992). ... Traded by Mets with a player to be named later to Baltimore Orioles for OF Alex Ochoa and OF Damon Buford (July 28, 1995); Orioles acquired P Jimmy Williams to complete deal (August 17, 1995). ... Granted free agency (November 18, 1996). ... Signed by Florida Marlins (November 2, 1996).

RECORDS: Holds N.L. career record for most home runs by switch-hitter—222. ... Shares major league record for most doubles in one inning—2 (July 21, 1995, eighth inning). ... Shares A.L. single-season record for most sacrifice flies—17 (1996).

HONORS: Named third baseman on THE SPORTING NEWS N.L. All-Star team (1988). ... Named third baseman on THE SPORTING NEWS N.L. Silver Slugger team (1988). ... Named outfielder on THE SPORTING NEWS N.L. All-Star team (1990-91). ... Named outfielder on THE SPORTING NEWS N.L. Silver Slugger team (1990-91).

STATISTICAL NOTES: Led Eastern League outfielders with 15 errors in 1984. ... Switch-hit home runs in one game six times (July 3, 1987; April 6, 1988; April 23 and June 10, 1993; May 4, 1994; and May 12, 1995). ... Led N.L. third basemen with 489 total chances in 1988. ... Led N.L. third basemen with 35 errors in 1989. ... Led N.L. third basemen with 31 double plays in 1989. ... Led N.L. with 15 sacrifice flies in 1990. ... Had 20-game hitting streak (September 10-October 1, 1995). ... Led A.L. with 17 sacrifice flies in 1996. ... Career major league grand slams: 8.

Year— Team (League)	Pos.	G	AB	R	H	2B	3B	HR	RBI	Avg.	BB	SO	SB	PO	A	E	Avg.
1981— GC Pirates (GCL)	1B-C-3B	22	69	6	15	5	0	0	7	.217	7	17	2	124	23	5	.967
1982— GC Pirates (GCL)	1B	47	167	20	38	3	0	5	26	.228	11	20	2	318	36	*14	.962
1983— Alexandria (Caro.)	OF-1B	•136	504	88	129	19	7	11	59	.256	78	105	28	259	12	15	.948
1984— Nashua (Eastern)	OF-1B	136	484	74	128	19	5	11	71	.264	49	89	15	312	8	†15	.955
1985— Prince William (Car.)	1B-3B	39	130	15	34	4	1	3	11	.262	16	29	1	180	9	2	.990
1986— Chicago (A.L.)■	OF-1B	75	234	27	63	10	2	2	26	.269	33	49	4	361	22	2	.995
— Pittsburgh (N.L.)■	OF-1B-3B	63	192	28	46	6	2	1	17	.240	29	39	4	90	16	3	.972
1987— Pittsburgh (N.L.)	3B-OF-1B	141	466	58	140	33	3	15	77	.300	39	64	3	142	139	16	.946
1988— Pittsburgh (N.L.)	3B	159	584	87	160	32	7	24	100	.274	85	82	3	121	*336	*32	.935
1989— Pittsburgh (N.L.)	3B-1B-OF	•163	616	96	173	37	10	24	86	.281	76	93	8	190	334	†35	.937
1990— Pittsburgh (N.L.)	OF-3B-1B	160	625	112	175	39	7	32	120	.280	45	103	4	315	35	15	.959
1991— Pittsburgh (N.L.)	OF-3B-1B	157	577	102	174	*44	6	18	100	.302	90	67	2	247	144	15	.963
1992— New York (N.L.)■	OF-1B	128	438	62	109	23	0	19	70	.249	66	73	4	277	9	4	.986
1993— New York (N.L.)	OF-3B-1B	139	502	81	133	21	3	34	87	.265	72	96	3	238	112	17	.954
1994— New York (N.L.)	3B	108	403	60	117	24	1	20	67	.290	55	101	1	78	215	*18	.942
1995— New York (N.L.)	3B-OF-1B	80	317	49	103	25	4	18	53	.325	31	48	0	164	80	14	.946
— Baltimore (A.L.)■	3B	61	237	47	79	12	4	10	46	.333	23	31	0	80	48	5	.962
1996— Baltimore (A.L.)	O-DH-1-3	159	595	107	171	27	5	28	116	.287	75	85	1	214	12	6	.974
1997— Florida (N.L.)■	3B-DH-1B	153	562	77	167	39	3	17	96	.297	73	94	6	107	225	22	.938
American League totals (3 years)		295	1066	181	313	49	11	40	188	.294	131	165	5	655	82	13	.983
National League totals (11 years)		1451	5282	812	1497	323	46	222	873	.283	661	860	38	1969	1645	191	.950
Major league totals (12 years)		1746	6348	993	1810	372	57	262	1061	.285	792	1025	43	2624	1727	204	.955

DIVISION SERIES RECORD

Year— Team (League)	Pos.	G	AB	R	H	2B	3B	HR	RBI	Avg.	BB	SO	SB	PO	A	E	Avg.
1996— Baltimore (A.L.)	OF	4	15	4	3	0	0	2	5	.200	4	6	0	9	0	1	.900
1997— Florida (N.L.)	3B	3	12	1	4	0	0	1	3	.333	2	1	0	3	5	0	1.000
Division series totals (2 years)		7	27	5	7	0	0	3	8	.259	6	7	0	12	5	1	.944

CHAMPIONSHIP SERIES RECORD

RECORDS: Shares single-game record for most strikeouts—4 (October 10, 1996).

Year— Team (League)	Pos.	G	AB	R	H	2B	3B	HR	RBI	Avg.	BB	SO	SB	PO	A	E	Avg.
1990— Pittsburgh (N.L.)	OF-3B	6	21	0	4	1	0	0	1	.190	3	1	0	4	5	1	.900
1991— Pittsburgh (N.L.)	OF	7	23	2	7	2	0	0	1	.304	6	2	0	12	1	0	1.000
1996— Baltimore (A.L.)	OF	5	20	1	1	0	0	1	2	.050	1	4	0	11	0	0	1.000
1997— Florida (N.L.)	3B	6	23	3	6	1	0	0	4	.261	1	6	0	5	13	0	1.000
Championship series totals (4 years)		24	87	6	18	4	0	1	8	.207	11	13	0	32	19	1	.981

WORLD SERIES RECORD

NOTES: Member of World Series championship team (1997).

Year Team (League)	Pos.	G	AB	R	H	2B	3B	HR	RBI	Avg.	BB	SO	SB	PO	A	E	Avg.
1997— Florida (N.L.)	3B	7	29	5	6	1	0	1	3	.207	3	5	0	3	20	2	.920

ALL-STAR GAME RECORD

Year League	Pos.	AB	R	H	2B	3B	HR	RBI	Avg.	BB	SO	SB	PO	A	E	Avg.
1988— National	3B	4	0	0	0	0	0	0	.000	0	0	0	0	2	0	1.000
1989— National	PH-DH	2	0	2	0	0	0	0	1.000	0	0	0	...	...	...	...
1990— National	1B	1	0	0	0	0	0	0	.000	0	0	0	1	0	0	1.000
1991— National	DH	4	0	2	0	0	0	1	.500	0	1	0	...	...	...	...
1993— National	OF	1	0	1	0	0	0	1	1.000	0	0	0	2	0	0	1.000
1995— National	3B	1	0	0	0	0	0	0	.000	0	1	0	0	0	0	...
All-Star Game totals (6 years)		13	0	5	0	0	0	1	.385	0	2	0	3	2	0	1.000

BOONE, AARON — 3B — REDS

PERSONAL: Born March 9, 1973, in La Mesa, Calif. ... 6-2/190. ... Throws right, bats right. ... Son of Bob Boone, senior advisor/player personnel, Cincinnati Reds; brother of Bret Boone, second baseman, Cincinnati Reds; grandson of Ray Boone, major league infielder with six teams (1948-60); and nephew of Rodney Boone, minor league catcher/outfielder (1972-75).
HIGH SCHOOL: Villa Park (Calif.).
COLLEGE: Southern California.
TRANSACTIONS/CAREER NOTES: Selected by California Angels organization in 43rd round of free-agent draft (June 3, 1991); did not sign. ... Selected by Cincinnati Reds organization in third round of free-agent draft (June 2, 1994).
STATISTICAL NOTES: Led Pioneer League third basemen with 46 putouts, 156 assists, 220 total chances and 13 double plays in 1994. ... Led Southern League third basemen with 101 putouts, 347 total chances and 28 double plays in 1996. ... Led American Association third basemen with 76 putouts, 241 assists, 336 total chances and 27 double plays in 1997.

Year Team (League)	Pos.	G	AB	R	H	2B	3B	HR	RBI	Avg.	BB	SO	SB	PO	A	E	Avg.
1994— Billings (Pioneer)........	3B-1B	67	256	48	70	15	5	7	55	.273	36	35	6	†60	†158	18	.924
1995— Chattanooga (Sou.)....	3B	23	66	6	15	3	0	0	3	.227	5	12	2	14	28	6	.875
— Win.-Salem (Car.).......	3B	108	395	61	103	19	1	14	50	.261	43	77	11	59	*272	21	*.940
1996— Chattanooga (Sou.)....	3B-SS	136	*548	86	158	*44	7	17	95	.288	38	77	21	†123	257	22	.945
1997— Indianapolis (A.A.)....	3B-SS-2B	131	476	79	138	30	4	22	75	.290	40	81	12	†112	†269	24	.941
— Cincinnati (N.L.)	3B-2B	16	49	5	12	1	0	0	5	.245	2	5	1	11	22	3	.917
Major league totals (1 year)		16	49	5	12	1	0	0	5	.245	2	5	1	11	22	3	.917

BOONE, BRET — 2B — REDS

PERSONAL: Born April 6, 1969, in El Cajon, Calif. ... 5-10/180. ... Bats right, throws right. ... Full name: Bret Robert Boone. ... Son of Bob Boone, senior advisor/player personnel, Cincinnati Reds; brother of Aaron Boone, third baseman, Cincinnati Reds; grandson of Ray Boone, major league infielder with six teams (1948-60); and nephew of Rodney Boone, minor league catcher/outfielder (1972-75).
HIGH SCHOOL: El Dorado (Yorba Linda, Calif.).
COLLEGE: Southern California.
TRANSACTIONS/CAREER NOTES: Selected by Minnesota Twins organization in 28th round of free-agent draft (June 2, 1987); did not sign. ... Selected by Seattle Mariners organization in fifth round of free-agent draft (June 4, 1990). ... Traded by Mariners with P Erik Hanson to Cincinnati Reds for P Bobby Ayala and C Dan Wilson (November 2, 1993). ... On disabled list (April 1-16, 1996).
RECORDS: Holds major league single-season record for highest fielding percentage by second baseman (100 or more games)—.997 (1997).
STATISTICAL NOTES: Tied for Southern League lead in grounding into double plays with 21 in 1991. ... Led Southern League second basemen with 288 putouts in 1991. ... Led Pacific Coast League second basemen with 90 double plays in 1992. ... Led N.L. second basemen with 106 double plays in 1995.

Year Team (League)	Pos.	G	AB	R	H	2B	3B	HR	RBI	Avg.	BB	SO	SB	PO	A	E	Avg.
1990— Peninsula (Caro.)	2B	74	255	42	68	13	2	8	38	.267	47	57	5	154	216	19	.951
1991— Jacksonville (South.)..	2B-3B	•139	475	64	121	18	1	19	75	.255	72	123	9	†300	369	21	.970
1992— Calgary (PCL)	2B-SS	118	439	73	138	26	5	13	73	.314	60	88	17	268	366	10	.984
— Seattle (A.L.)	2B-3B	33	129	15	25	4	0	4	15	.194	4	34	1	72	96	6	.966
1993— Calgary (PCL)	2B	71	274	48	91	18	3	8	56	.332	28	58	3	146	180	8	.976
— Seattle (A.L.)	2B-DH	76	271	31	68	12	2	12	38	.251	17	52	2	140	177	3	.991
1994— Cincinnati (N.L.)■	2B-3B	108	381	59	122	25	2	12	68	.320	24	74	3	191	269	12	.975
1995— Cincinnati (N.L.)	2B	138	513	63	137	34	2	15	68	.267	41	84	5	*311	362	4	*.994
1996— Cincinnati (N.L.)	2B	142	520	56	121	21	3	12	69	.233	31	100	3	315	381	6	*.991
1997— Cincinnati (N.L.)	2B	139	443	40	99	25	1	7	46	.223	45	101	5	271	334	2	*.997
— Indianapolis (A.A.)......	2B	3	7	1	2	1	0	0	1	.286	2	2	1	6	10	0	1.000
American League totals (2 years)		109	400	46	93	16	2	16	53	.233	21	86	3	212	273	9	.982
National League totals (4 years)		527	1857	218	479	105	8	46	251	.258	141	359	16	1088	1346	24	.990
Major league totals (6 years)		636	2257	264	572	121	10	62	304	.253	162	445	19	1300	1619	33	.989

DIVISION SERIES RECORD

Year Team (League)	Pos.	G	AB	R	H	2B	3B	HR	RBI	Avg.	BB	SO	SB	PO	A	E	Avg.
1995— Cincinnati (N.L.)	2B	3	10	4	3	1	0	1	1	.300	1	3	1	7	5	0	1.000

CHAMPIONSHIP SERIES RECORD

Year Team (League)	Pos.	G	AB	R	H	2B	3B	HR	RBI	Avg.	BB	SO	SB	PO	A	E	Avg.
1995— Cincinnati (N.L.)	2B	4	14	1	3	0	0	0	0	.214	1	2	0	9	13	0	1.000

BOOTY, JOSH — 3B — MARLINS

PERSONAL: Born April 29, 1975, in Starkville, Miss. ... 6-3/220. ... Bats right, throws right. ... Full name: Joshua Gibson Booty.
HIGH SCHOOL: Evangel Christian Academy (Shreveport, La.).
COLLEGE: Louisiana State.
TRANSACTIONS/CAREER NOTES: Selected by Florida Marlins organization in first round (fifth pick overall) of free-agent draft (June 2, 1994). ... On Kane County suspended list (May 10-13, 1995). ... On Kane County disabled list (May 17-June 12, 1995).
STATISTICAL NOTES: Led Eastern League third basemen with 361 total chances and 38 double plays in 1997.

							BATTING						FIELDING				
Year	Team (League)	Pos.	G	AB	R	H	2B	3B	HR	RBI	Avg.	BB	SO	SB	PO	A	E	Avg.
1994— GC Marlins (GCL)		IF	10	36	5	8	0	0	1	2	.222	5	8	1	13	32	6	.882
— Elmira (N.Y.-Penn)		SS	4	16	1	4	1	0	0	1	.250	0	4	0	11	8	1	.950
1995— Kane County (Midw.)		3B	31	109	6	11	2	0	1	6	.101	11	45	1	23	71	9	.913
— Elmira (N.Y.-Penn)		3B	74	287	33	63	18	1	6	37	.220	19	85	4	56	173	26	.898
1996— Kane County (Midw.)		3B	128	475	62	98	25	1	21	87	.206	46	*195	2	62	252	28	.918
— Florida (N.L.)		3B	2	2	1	1	0	0	0	0	.500	0	0	0	0	0	0	...
1997— Portland (Eastern)		3B	122	448	42	94	19	2	20	69	.210	27	166	2	*75	*262	24	.934
— Florida (N.L.)		3B	4	5	2	3	0	0	0	1	.600	1	1	0	1	5	1	.857
Major league totals (2 years)			6	7	3	4	0	0	0	1	.571	1	1	0	1	5	1	.857

BORBON, PEDRO — P — BRAVES

PERSONAL: Born November 15, 1967, in Mao, Dominican Republic. ... 6-1/205. ... Throws left, bats left. ... Full name: Pedro Felix Borbon Jr. ... Son of Pedro Borbon, major league pitcher with four teams (1969-80). ... Name pronounced bor-BONE.
HIGH SCHOOL: DeWitt Clinton (Bronx, N.Y.).
JUNIOR COLLEGE: Ranger (Texas) Junior College.
TRANSACTIONS/CAREER NOTES: Selected by Milwaukee Brewers organization in 35th round of free-agent draft (June 3, 1985); did not sign. ... Selected by Los Angeles Dodgers organization in secondary phase of free-agent draft (January 14, 1986); did not sign. ... Signed as non-drafted free agent by Chicago White Sox organization (June 4, 1988). ... Released by White Sox organization (April 1, 1989). ... Signed by Atlanta Braves organization (August 25, 1989). ... On Atlanta disabled list (April 8-26 and August 23, 1996-remainder of season); included rehabilitation assignment to Greenville (April 23-26). ... On disabled list (March 30, 1997-entire season).
STATISTICAL NOTES: Led Gulf Coast League with 14 balks in 1988.

Year	Team (League)	W	L	Pct.	ERA	G	GS	CG	ShO	Sv.	IP	H	R	ER	BB	SO
1988— GC White Sox (GCL)		5	3	.625	2.41	16	11	1	1	1	74²/₃	52	28	20	17	67
1989—							Did not play.									
1990— Burlington (Midw.)■		11	3	.786	1.47	14	14	6	2	0	97²/₃	73	25	16	23	76
— Durham (Carolina) •		4	5	.444	5.43	11	11	0	0	0	61¹/₃	73	40	37	16	37
1991— Durham (Carolina)		4	3	.571	2.27	37	6	1	0	5	91	85	40	23	35	79
— Greenville (Southern)		0	1	.000	2.79	4	4	0	0	0	29	23	12	9	10	22
1992— Greenville (Southern)		8	2	.800	3.06	39	10	0	0	3	94	73	36	32	42	79
— Atlanta (N.L.)		0	1	.000	6.75	2	0	0	0	0	1¹/₃	2	1	1	1	1
1993— Richmond (Int'l)		5	5	.500	4.23	52	0	0	0	1	76²/₃	71	40	36	42	95
— Atlanta (N.L.)		0	0	...	21.60	3	0	0	0	0	1²/₃	3	4	4	3	2
1994— Richmond (Int'l)		3	4	.429	2.79	59	0	0	0	4	80²/₃	66	29	25	41	82
1995— Atlanta (N.L.)		2	2	.500	3.09	41	0	0	0	2	32	29	12	11	17	33
1996— Atlanta (N.L.)		3	0	1.000	2.75	43	0	0	0	1	36	26	12	11	7	31
— Greenville (Southern)		0	0	...	0.00	1	0	0	0	0	1	0	0	0	0	0
1997—							Did not play.									
Major league totals (4 years)		5	3	.625	3.42	89	0	0	0	3	71	60	29	27	28	67

DIVISION SERIES RECORD

Year	Team (League)	W	L	Pct.	ERA	G	GS	CG	ShO	Sv.	IP	H	R	ER	BB	SO
1995— Atlanta (N.L.)		0	0	...	0.00	1	0	0	0	0	1	1	0	0	0	3

WORLD SERIES RECORD

NOTES: Member of World Series championship team (1995).

Year	Team (League)	W	L	Pct.	ERA	G	GS	CG	ShO	Sv.	IP	H	R	ER	BB	SO
1995— Atlanta (N.L.)		0	0	...	0.00	1	0	0	0	1	1	0	0	0	0	2

BORDERS, PAT — C — INDIANS

PERSONAL: Born May 14, 1963, in Columbus, Ohio. ... 6-2/200. ... Bats right, throws right. ... Full name: Patrick Lance Borders. ... Brother of Todd Borders, minor league catcher (1988).
HIGH SCHOOL: Lake Wales (Fla.).
TRANSACTIONS/CAREER NOTES: Selected by Toronto Blue Jays organization in sixth round of free-agent draft (June 7, 1982). ... On Toronto disabled list (July 5-August 19, 1988); included rehabilitation assignment to Syracuse (July 30-August 19). ... Granted free agency (October 21, 1994). ... Signed by Kansas City Royals (April 10, 1995). ... Traded by Royals to Houston Astros for a player to be named later (August 12, 1995); Royals acquired P Rick Huisman to complete deal (August 17, 1995). ... On Houston suspended list (September 8-14, 1995). ... Granted free agency (November 6, 1995). ... Signed by St. Louis Cardinals organization (January 10, 1996). ... Traded by Cardinals to California Angels for P Ben VanRyn (June 15, 1996). ... Traded by Angels to Chicago White Sox for P Robert Ellis (July 27, 1996). ... Granted free agency (November 6, 1996). ... Signed by Cleveland Indians organization (December 13, 1996). ... Granted free agency (November 7, 1997). ... Re-signed by Indians organization (December 17, 1997).
STATISTICAL NOTES: Tied for Southern League lead with 16 passed balls in 1987. ... Led A.L. catchers with 880 total chances in 1992 and 962 in 1993. ... Led A.L. with nine passed balls in 1994. ... Career major league grand slams: 1.

							BATTING						FIELDING				
Year	Team (League)	Pos.	G	AB	R	H	2B	3B	HR	RBI	Avg.	BB	SO	SB	PO	A	E	Avg.
1982— Medicine Hat (Pio.)		3B	61	217	30	66	12	2	5	33	.304	24	52	1	23	96	*25	.826
1983— Florence (S. Atl.)		3B	131	457	62	125	31	4	5	54	.274	46	116	4	70	233	*41	.881

Year Team (League)	Pos.	G	AB	R	H	2B	3B	HR	RBI	Avg.	BB	SO	SB	PO	A	E	Avg.
						BATTING									FIELDING		
1984—Florence (S. Atl.)	1B-3B-OF	131	467	69	129	32	5	12	85	.276	56	109	3	650	77	25	.967
1985—Kinston (Carolina)	1B	127	460	43	120	16	1	10	60	.261	45	116	6	854	42	*20	.978
1986—Florence (S. Atl.)	C-OF	16	40	8	15	7	0	3	9	.375	2	9	0	22	1	0	1.000
—Knoxville (Southern) ..	C-1B	12	34	3	12	1	0	2	5	.353	1	6	0	45	5	3	.943
—Kinston (Carolina)	C-1B-OF	49	174	24	57	10	0	6	26	.328	10	42	0	211	26	7	.971
1987—Dunedin (Fla. St.)	1B	3	11	0	4	0	0	0	1	.364	0	3	0	21	1	0	1.000
—Knoxville (Southern) ..	C-3B	94	349	44	102	14	1	11	51	.292	20	56	2	432	49	12	.976
1988—Toronto (A.L.)	C-DH-2-3	56	154	15	42	6	3	5	21	.273	3	24	0	205	19	7	.970
—Syracuse (Int'l)	C	35	120	11	29	8	0	3	14	.242	16	22	0	202	17	2	.991
1989—Toronto (A.L.)	C-DH	94	241	22	62	11	1	3	29	.257	11	45	2	261	27	6	.980
1990—Toronto (A.L.)	C-DH	125	346	36	99	24	2	15	49	.286	18	57	0	515	46	4	.993
1991—Toronto (A.L.)	C	105	291	22	71	17	0	5	36	.244	11	45	0	505	48	4	.993
1992—Toronto (A.L.)	C	138	480	47	116	26	2	13	53	.242	33	75	1	784	*88	8	.991
1993—Toronto (A.L.)	C	138	488	38	124	30	0	9	55	.254	20	66	2	869	*80	*13	.986
1994—Toronto (A.L.)	C	85	295	24	73	13	1	3	26	.247	15	50	1	583	*60	8	.988
1995—Kansas City (A.L.)■..	C-DH	52	143	14	33	8	1	4	13	.231	7	22	0	182	18	0	1.000
—Houston (N.L.)■	C	11	35	1	4	0	0	0	0	.114	2	7	0	70	5	1	.987
1996—St. Louis (N.L.)■	C-1B	26	69	3	22	3	0	0	4	.319	1	14	0	117	9	3	.977
—California (A.L.)■	C	19	57	6	13	3	0	2	8	.228	3	11	0	111	14	2	.984
—Chicago (A.L.)■	C-DH	31	94	6	26	1	0	3	6	.277	5	18	0	144	16	3	.982
1997—Cleveland (A.L.)■	C	55	159	17	47	7	1	4	15	.296	9	27	0	312	19	0	1.000
American League totals (10 years)		898	2748	247	706	146	11	66	311	.257	135	440	6	4471	435	55	.989
National League totals (2 years)		37	104	4	26	3	0	0	4	.250	3	21	0	187	14	4	.980
Major league totals (10 years)		935	2852	251	732	149	11	66	315	.257	138	461	6	4658	449	59	.989

CHAMPIONSHIP SERIES RECORD

Year Team (League)	Pos.	G	AB	R	H	2B	3B	HR	RBI	Avg.	BB	SO	SB	PO	A	E	Avg.
						BATTING									FIELDING		
1989—Toronto (A.L.)	PH-C	1	1	0	1	0	0	0	1	1.000	0	0	0	1	0	0	1.000
1991—Toronto (A.L.)	C	5	19	0	5	1	0	0	2	.263	0	0	0	38	4	2	.955
1992—Toronto (A.L.)	C	6	22	3	7	0	0	1	3	.318	1	1	0	38	3	1	.976
1993—Toronto (A.L.)	C	6	24	1	6	1	0	0	3	.250	0	6	1	41	4	0	1.000
Championship series totals (4 years)		18	66	4	19	2	0	1	9	.288	1	7	1	118	11	3	.977

WORLD SERIES RECORD

NOTES: Named Most Valuable Player (1992). ... Member of World Series championship teams (1992 and 1993).

Year Team (League)	Pos.	G	AB	R	H	2B	3B	HR	RBI	Avg.	BB	SO	SB	PO	A	E	Avg.
						BATTING									FIELDING		
1992—Toronto (A.L.)	C	6	20	2	9	3	0	1	3	.450	2	1	0	48	5	1	.981
1993—Toronto (A.L.)	C	6	23	2	7	0	0	1	1	.304	2	1	0	50	2	1	.981
World Series totals (2 years)		12	43	4	16	3	0	1	4	.372	4	2	0	98	7	2	.981

BORDICK, MIKE   SS   ORIOLES

PERSONAL: Born July 21, 1965, in Marquette, Mich. ... 5-11/175. ... Bats right, throws right. ... Full name: Michael Todd Bordick.
HIGH SCHOOL: Hampden (Maine.) Academy.
COLLEGE: Maine.
TRANSACTIONS/CAREER NOTES: Signed as non-drafted free agent by Oakland Athletics organization (July 10, 1986). ... On Tacoma disabled list (April 14-May 13, 1991). ... On Oakland disabled list (May 8-27, 1995); included rehabilitation assignment to Modesto (May 23-26). ... Granted free agency (December 7, 1996). ... Signed by Baltimore Orioles (December 13, 1996).
STATISTICAL NOTES: Led Pacific Coast League shortstops with .972 fielding percentage and 82 double plays in 1990. ... Led A.L. shortstops with 280 putouts and tied for lead with 108 double plays in 1993. ... Career major league grand slams: 1.

Year Team (League)	Pos.	G	AB	R	H	2B	3B	HR	RBI	Avg.	BB	SO	SB	PO	A	E	Avg.
						BATTING									FIELDING		
1986—Medford (N'west)	SS	46	187	30	48	3	1	0	19	.257	40	21	6	68	143	18	.921
1987—Modesto (California) ..	SS	133	497	73	133	17	0	3	75	.268	87	92	8	216	305	17	*.968
1988—Huntsville (Southern) .	2B-SS-3B	132	481	48	130	13	2	0	28	.270	87	50	7	260	406	24	.965
1989—Tacoma (PCL)	2B-SS-3B	136	487	55	117	17	1	1	43	.240	58	51	4	261	431	33	.954
1990—Oakland (A.L.)	3B-SS-2B	25	14	0	1	0	0	0	0	.071	1	4	0	9	8	0	1.000
—Tacoma (PCL)	SS-2B	111	348	49	79	16	1	2	30	.227	46	40	3	210	366	16	†.973
1991—Tacoma (PCL)	SS	26	81	15	22	4	1	2	14	.272	17	10	0	35	79	3	.974
—Oakland (A.L.)	SS-2B-3B	90	235	21	56	5	1	0	21	.238	14	37	3	146	213	11	.970
1992—Oakland (A.L.)	2B-SS	154	504	62	151	19	4	3	48	.300	40	59	12	311	449	16	.979
1993—Oakland (A.L.)	SS-2B	159	546	60	136	21	2	3	48	.249	60	58	10	†285	420	13	.982
1994—Oakland (A.L.)	SS-2B	114	391	38	99	18	4	2	37	.253	38	44	7	187	320	14	.973
1995—Oakland (A.L.)	SS-DH	126	428	46	113	13	0	8	44	.264	35	48	11	*245	338	10	.983
—Modesto (California) ..	SS	2	1	0	0	0	0	0	0	.000	0	0	0	2	1	0	1.000
1996—Oakland (A.L.)	SS	155	525	46	126	18	4	5	54	.240	52	59	5	265	*476	16	.979
1997—Baltimore (A.L.)■	SS	153	509	55	120	19	1	7	46	.236	33	66	0	224	424	13	.980
Major league totals (8 years)		976	3152	328	802	113	16	28	298	.254	273	375	48	1672	2648	93	.979

DIVISION SERIES RECORD

Year Team (League)	Pos.	G	AB	R	H	2B	3B	HR	RBI	Avg.	BB	SO	SB	PO	A	E	Avg.
						BATTING									FIELDING		
1997—Baltimore (A.L.)	SS	4	10	4	4	1	0	0	4	.400	4	2	0	4	15	0	1.000

CHAMPIONSHIP SERIES RECORD

Year	Team (League)	Pos.	G	AB	R	H	2B	3B	HR	RBI	Avg.	BB	SO	SB	PO	A	E	Avg.
							BATTING									FIELDING		
1992— Oakland (A.L.)	SS-2B	6	19	1	1	0	0	0	0	.053	1	2	1	15	14	0	1.000
1997— Baltimore (A.L.)	SS	6	19	0	3	1	0	0	2	.158	0	6	0	5	14	0	1.000
Championship series totals (2 years)		12	38	1	4	1	0	0	2	.105	1	8	1	20	28	0	1.000

WORLD SERIES RECORD

Year	Team (League)	Pos.	G	AB	R	H	2B	3B	HR	RBI	Avg.	BB	SO	SB	PO	A	E	Avg.
							BATTING									FIELDING		
1990— Oakland (A.L.)	SS-PR	3	0	0	0	0	0	0	0	...	0	0	0	0	2	0	1.000

BORLAND, TOBY P REDS

PERSONAL: Born May 29, 1969, in Ruston, La. ... 6-6/193. ... Throws right, bats right. ... Full name: Toby Shawn Borland.
HIGH SCHOOL: Quitman (La.).
TRANSACTIONS/CAREER NOTES: Selected by Philadelphia Phillies organization in 27th round of free-agent draft (June 2, 1987). ... On Philadelphia disabled list (June 14-July 8, 1995); included rehabilitation assignment to Scranton/Wilkes-Barre (June 22-July 8). ... Traded by Phillies with P Ricardo Jordan to New York Mets for 1B Rico Brogna (November 27, 1996). ... Traded by Mets to Boston Red Sox for P Rick Trlicek (May 12, 1997). ... Granted free agency (October 15, 1997). ... Signed by Cincinnati Reds organization (November 27, 1997).
STATISTICAL NOTES: Tied for Eastern League lead with three balks in 1991. ... Pitched one inning, combining with starter Craig Holman (two innings), Gregory Brown (two innings) and Ricky Bottalico (two innings) in seven-inning 2-0 no-hit victory for Reading against New Britain (September 4, 1993, first game).

Year	Team (League)	W	L	Pct.	ERA	G	GS	CG	ShO	Sv.	IP	H	R	ER	BB	SO
1988— Martinsville (App.).............	2	3	.400	4.04	34	0	0	0	*12	49	42	26	22	29	43
1989— Spartanburg (SAL)	4	5	.444	2.97	47	0	0	0	9	66²/₃	62	29	22	35	48
1990— Clearwater (Fla. St.)	1	2	.333	2.26	44	0	0	0	5	59²/₃	44	21	15	35	44
— Reading (Eastern)	4	1	.800	1.44	14	0	0	0	0	25	16	6	4	11	26
1991— Reading (Eastern)	8	3	.727	2.70	*59	0	0	0	•24	76²/₃	68	31	23	56	72
1992— Scran./W.B. (Int'l)	0	1	.000	7.24	27	0	0	0	1	27¹/₃	25	23	22	26	25
— Reading (Eastern)	2	4	.333	3.43	32	0	0	0	5	42	39	23	16	32	45
1993— Reading (Eastern)	2	2	.500	2.52	44	0	0	0	13	53²/₃	38	17	15	20	74
— Scran./W.B. (Int'l)	2	4	.333	5.76	26	0	0	0	1	29²/₃	31	20	19	20	26
1994— Scran./W.B. (Int'l)	4	1	.800	1.68	27	1	0	0	4	53²/₃	36	12	10	21	61
— Philadelphia (N.L.).............	1	0	1.000	2.36	24	0	0	0	1	34¹/₃	31	10	9	14	26
1995— Philadelphia (N.L.).............	1	3	.250	3.77	50	0	0	0	6	74	81	37	31	37	59
— Scran./W.B. (Int'l)	0	0	...	0.00	8	0	0	0	1	11¹/₃	5	0	0	6	15
1996— Philadelphia (N.L.).............	7	3	.700	4.07	69	0	0	0	1	90²/₃	83	51	41	43	76
1997— New York (N.L.)■.............	0	1	.000	6.08	13	0	0	0	1	13¹/₃	11	9	9	14	7
— Boston (A.L.)■.............	0	0	...	13.50	3	0	0	0	0	3¹/₃	6	5	5	7	1
— Pawtucket (Int'l)	2	0	1.000	3.99	28	2	0	0	2	47¹/₃	50	22	21	25	46
A.L. totals (1 year)	0	0	...	13.50	3	0	0	0	0	3¹/₃	6	5	5	7	1
N.L. totals (4 years)	9	7	.563	3.81	156	0	0	0	8	212¹/₃	206	107	90	108	168
Major league totals (4 years)	9	7	.563	3.96	159	0	0	0	8	215²/₃	212	112	95	115	169

BOROWSKI, JOE P YANKEES

PERSONAL: Born May 4, 1971, in Bayonne, N.J. ... 6-2/225. ... Throws right, bats right. ... Full name: Joseph Thomas Borowski.
HIGH SCHOOL: Marist (Bayonne, N.J.).
COLLEGE: Rutgers.
TRANSACTIONS/CAREER NOTES: Selected by Chicago White Sox organization in 32nd round of free-agent draft (June 5, 1989). ... Traded by White Sox organization to Baltimore Orioles organization for IF Pete Rose (March 21, 1991). ... Traded by Orioles with P Rachaad Stewart to Atlanta Braves for P Kent Mercker (December 17, 1995). ... Claimed on waivers by New York Yankees (September 15, 1997).

Year	Team (League)	W	L	Pct.	ERA	G	GS	CG	ShO	Sv.	IP	H	R	ER	BB	SO
1990— GC White Sox (GCL)	2	•8	.200	5.58	12	11	0	0	0	61¹/₃	74	*47	*38	25	67
1991— Kane County (Midwest)■...	7	2	.778	2.56	49	0	0	0	13	81	60	26	23	43	76
1992— Frederick (Carolina)...........	5	6	.455	3.70	48	0	0	0	10	80¹/₃	71	40	33	50	85
1993— Frederick (Carolina)...........	1	1	.500	3.61	42	2	0	0	11	62¹/₃	61	30	25	37	70
— Bowie (Eastern).................	3	0	1.000	0.00	9	0	0	0	0	17²/₃	11	0	0	11	17
1994— Bowie (Eastern).................	3	4	.429	1.91	49	0	0	0	14	66	52	14	14	28	73
1995— Rochester (Int'l)	1	3	.250	4.04	28	0	0	0	6	35²/₃	32	16	16	18	32
— Bowie (Eastern).................	2	2	.500	3.92	16	0	0	0	7	20²/₃	16	9	9	7	32
— Baltimore (A.L.).................	0	0	...	1.23	6	0	0	0	0	7¹/₃	5	1	1	4	3
1996— Richmond (Int'l)■.............	1	5	.167	3.71	34	0	0	0	7	53¹/₃	42	25	22	30	40
— Atlanta (N.L.).................	2	4	.333	4.85	22	0	0	0	0	26	33	15	14	13	15
1997— Atlanta (N.L.).................	2	2	.500	3.75	20	0	0	0	0	24	27	11	10	16	6
— Richmond (Int'l)	1	2	.333	3.58	21	0	0	0	2	37²/₃	32	16	15	19	34
— New York (A.L.)■.............	0	1	.000	9.00	1	0	0	0	0	2	2	2	2	4	2
A.L. totals (2 years)	0	1	.000	2.89	7	0	0	0	0	9¹/₃	7	3	3	8	5
N.L. totals (2 years)	4	6	.400	4.32	42	0	0	0	0	50	60	26	24	29	21
Major league totals (3 years)	4	7	.364	4.10	49	0	0	0	0	59¹/₃	67	29	27	37	26

BOSIO, CHRIS P RED SOX

PERSONAL: Born April 3, 1963, in Carmichael, Calif. ... 6-3/225. ... Throws right, bats right. ... Full name: Christopher Louis Bosio. ... Name pronounced BAHZ-ee-o.
HIGH SCHOOL: Cordova (Calif.).
COLLEGE: Sacramento (Calif.) City College.

TRANSACTIONS/CAREER NOTES: Selected by Pittsburgh Pirates organization in 29th round of free-agent draft (June 8, 1981); did not sign. ... Selected by Milwaukee Brewers organization in secondary phase of free-agent draft (January 12, 1982). ... On Milwaukee disabled list (June 29-July 15, 1990); included rehabilitation assignment to Beloit (July 9-15). ... On Milwaukee disabled list (August 2, 1990-remainder of season). ... On disabled list (July 1-16, 1991). ... Granted free agency (October 26, 1992). ... Signed by Seattle Mariners (December 3, 1992). ... On disabled list (April 28-May 28 and June 7-25, 1993). ... On suspended list (June 28-July 3, 1993). ... On disabled list (July 10, 1994-remainder of season). ... On Seattle disabled list (March 26-April 13 and May 22-July 28, 1996); included rehabilitation assignments to Lancaster (April 8-12 and July 19-23), Tacoma (July 11-19) and Everett (July 23-27). ... Granted free agency (November 18, 1996). ... Signed by Boston Red Sox organization (August 12, 1997).

STATISTICAL NOTES: Pitched 7-0 no-hit victory against Boston (April 22, 1993).

MISCELLANEOUS: Appeared in one game as designated hitter but made no plate appearance (1993).

Year Team (League)	W	L	Pct.	ERA	G	GS	CG	ShO	Sv.	IP	H	R	ER	BB	SO
1982— Pikeville (Appal.)	3	2	.600	4.91	13	3	2	1	1	51 1/3	60	31	28	17	53
1983— Beloit (Midwest)	3	10	.231	5.60	17	17	3	0	0	107 2/3	125	82	67	41	71
—Paintsville (Appal.)	2	2	.500	2.84	7	7	2	2	0	44 1/3	30	18	14	18	43
1984— Beloit (Midwest)	*17	6	.739	2.73	26	26	11	2	0	181	159	83	55	56	156
1985— El Paso (Texas)	11	6	.647	3.82	28	25	6	1	2	181 1/3	186	108	77	49	*155
1986— Vancouver (PCL)	7	3	.700	2.28	44	0	0	0	•16	67	47	18	17	13	60
—Milwaukee (A.L.)	0	4	.000	7.01	10	4	0	0	0	34 2/3	41	27	27	13	29
1987— Milwaukee (A.L.)	11	8	.579	5.24	46	19	2	1	2	170	187	102	99	50	150
1988— Milwaukee (A.L.)	7	15	.318	3.36	38	22	9	1	6	182	190	80	68	38	84
—Denver (Am. Assoc.)	1	0	1.000	3.86	2	2	1	0	0	14	13	6	6	4	12
1989— Milwaukee (A.L.)	15	10	.600	2.95	33	33	8	2	0	234 2/3	225	90	77	48	173
1990— Milwaukee (A.L.)	4	9	.308	4.00	20	20	4	1	0	132 2/3	131	67	59	38	76
—Beloit (Midwest)	0	0	...	3.00	1	1	0	0	0	3	4	2	1	1	2
1991— Milwaukee (A.L.)	14	10	.583	3.25	32	32	5	1	0	204 2/3	187	80	74	58	117
1992— Milwaukee (A.L.)	16	6	.727	3.62	33	33	4	2	0	231 1/3	223	100	93	44	120
1993— Seattle (A.L.)■	9	9	.500	3.45	29	24	3	1	1	164 1/3	138	75	63	59	119
1994— Seattle (A.L.)	4	10	.286	4.32	19	19	4	0	0	125	137	72	60	40	67
1995— Seattle (A.L.)	10	8	.556	4.92	31	31	0	0	0	170	211	98	93	69	85
1996— Lancaster (Calif.)	0	0	...	1.13	2	2	0	0	0	8	6	3	1	0	7
—Seattle (A.L.)	4	4	.500	5.93	18	9	0	0	0	60 2/3	72	44	40	24	39
—Everett (Northwest)	0	0	...	2.25	1	1	0	0	0	4	3	1	1	0	8
—Tacoma (PCL)	0	0	...	0.00	2	1	0	0	0	4	2	0	0	0	3
1997— GC Red Sox (GCL)■	0	0	...	0.00	2	2	0	0	0	5	2	0	0	2	4
—Sarasota (Florida State)	0	0	...	1.93	1	1	0	0	0	4 2/3	6	2	1	0	5
Major league totals (11 years)	94	93	.503	3.96	309	246	39	9	9	1710	1742	835	753	481	1059

DIVISION SERIES RECORD

Year Team (League)	W	L	Pct.	ERA	G	GS	CG	ShO	Sv.	IP	H	R	ER	BB	SO
1995— Seattle (A.L.)	0	0	...	10.57	2	2	0	0	0	7 2/3	10	9	9	4	2

CHAMPIONSHIP SERIES RECORD

Year Team (League)	W	L	Pct.	ERA	G	GS	CG	ShO	Sv.	IP	H	R	ER	BB	SO
1995— Seattle (A.L.)	0	1	.000	3.38	1	1	0	0	0	5 1/3	7	3	2	2	3

BOSKIE, SHAWN   P

PERSONAL: Born March 28, 1967, in Hawthorne, Nev. ... 6-3/200. ... Throws right, bats right. ... Full name: Shawn Kealoha Boskie. ... Name pronounced BAH-skee.

HIGH SCHOOL: Reno (Nev.).

JUNIOR COLLEGE: Modesto (Calif.) Junior College.

TRANSACTIONS/CAREER NOTES: Selected by Chicago Cubs organization in first round (10th pick overall) of free-agent draft (January 14, 1986). ... On Chicago disabled list (August 5-September 26, 1990). ... On Chicago disabled list (July 27-September 1, 1992); included rehabilitation assignment to Iowa (August 24-September 1). ... On suspended list (August 31-September 3, 1993). ... Granted free agency (December 20, 1993). ... Re-signed by Cubs (December 22, 1993). ... Traded by Cubs to Philadelphia Phillies for P Kevin Foster (April 12, 1994). ... Traded by Phillies to Seattle Mariners for a player to be named later (July 21, 1994); Phillies acquired 1B Fred McNair to complete deal (September 7, 1994). ... On Seattle disabled list (July 31, 1994-remainder of season). ... Released by Mariners (November 18, 1994). ... Signed by Vancouver, California Angels organization (March 6, 1995). ... On California disabled list (July 6, 1995-remainder of season); included rehabilitation assignments to Lake Elsinore (August 10-24) and Vancouver (August 24-September 21). ... Granted free agency (December 21, 1995). ... Re-signed by Angels organization (January 29, 1996). ... Granted free agency (October 31, 1996). ... Signed by Baltimore Orioles (December 16, 1996). ... On disabled list (August 16-September 1, 1997). ... Granted free agency (October 29, 1997).

STATISTICAL NOTES: Led Appalachian League with 15 wild pitches in 1986. ... Led Carolina League with 17 hit batsmen in 1988. ... Led Southern League with 19 hit batsmen in 1989. ... Tied for A.L. lead with 40 home runs allowed in 1996. ... Tied for A.L. lead with 13 hit batsmen in 1996.

MISCELLANEOUS: Appeared in one game as pinch-runner and made an out in only appearance as pinch-hitter with Chicago (1991). ... Appeared in one game as pinch-runner with Philadelphia (1994). ... Appeared in one game as pinch-runner (1997).

Year Team (League)	W	L	Pct.	ERA	G	GS	CG	ShO	Sv.	IP	H	R	ER	BB	SO
1986— Wytheville (Appal.)	4	4	.500	5.33	14	12	1	0	0	54	42	41	32	57	40
1987— Peoria (Midwest)	9	11	.450	4.35	26	25	1	0	0	149	149	91	72	56	100
1988— Win.-Salem (Car.)	12	7	.632	3.39	27	27	4	2	0	186	176	83	70	89	164
1989— Charlotte (Southern)	11	8	.579	4.38	28	28	5	0	0	181	*196	105	88	84	*164
1990— Iowa (Am. Assoc.)	4	2	.667	3.18	8	8	1	0	0	51	46	22	18	21	51
—Chicago (N.L.)	5	6	.455	3.69	15	15	1	0	0	97 2/3	99	42	40	31	49
1991— Chicago (N.L.)	4	9	.308	5.23	28	20	0	0	0	129	150	78	75	52	62
—Iowa (Am. Assoc.)	2	2	.500	3.57	7	6	2	0	0	45 1/3	43	19	18	11	29
1992— Chicago (N.L.)	5	11	.313	5.01	23	18	0	0	0	91 2/3	96	55	51	36	39
—Iowa (Am. Assoc.)	0	0	...	3.68	2	2	0	0	0	7 1/3	8	4	3	3	3
1993— Chicago (N.L.)	5	3	.625	3.43	39	2	0	0	0	65 2/3	63	30	25	21	39
—Iowa (Am. Assoc.)	6	1	.857	4.27	11	11	1	0	0	71 2/3	70	35	34	21	35
1994— Chicago (N.L.)	0	0	...	0.00	2	0	0	0	0	3 2/3	3	0	0	0	2
—Philadelphia (N.L.)■	4	6	.400	5.23	18	14	1	0	0	84 1/3	85	56	49	29	59
—Seattle (A.L.)■	0	1	.000	6.75	2	1	0	0	0	2 2/3	4	2	2	1	0

Year	Team (League)	W	L	Pct.	ERA	G	GS	CG	ShO	Sv.	IP	H	R	ER	BB	SO
1995—	California (A.L.)■	7	7	.500	5.64	20	20	1	0	0	111²/₃	127	73	70	25	51
	— Lake Elsinore (Calif.)	0	0	...	4.09	3	3	0	0	0	11	15	7	5	4	8
	— Vancouver (PCL)	1	0	1.000	3.00	1	1	0	0	0	6	4	2	2	4	1
1996—	California (A.L.)	12	11	.522	5.32	37	28	1	0	0	189¹/₃	226	126	112	67	133
1997—	Baltimore (A.L.)■	6	6	.500	6.43	28	9	0	0	1	77	95	57	55	26	50
A.L. totals (4 years)		25	25	.500	5.65	87	58	2	0	1	380²/₃	452	258	239	119	234
N.L. totals (5 years)		23	35	.397	4.58	125	69	2	0	0	472	496	261	240	169	250
Major league totals (8 years)		48	60	.444	5.06	212	127	4	0	1	852²/₃	948	519	479	288	484

BOTTALICO, RICKY — P — PHILLIES

B

PERSONAL: Born August 26, 1969, in New Britain, Conn. ... 6-1/208. ... Throws right, bats left. ... Full name: Richard Paul Bottalico. ... Name pronounced ba-TAL-ee-koh.
HIGH SCHOOL: South Catholic (Hartford, Conn.).
COLLEGE: Florida Southern, then Central Connecticut State.
TRANSACTIONS/CAREER NOTES: Signed as non-drafted free agent by Philadelphia Phillies organization (July 21, 1991).
STATISTICAL NOTES: Pitched two innings, combining with starter Craig Holman (two innings), Gregory Brown (two innings) and Toby Borland (one inning) in seven-inning, 2-0 no-hit victory for Reading against New Britain (September 4, 1993, first game).

Year	Team (League)	W	L	Pct.	ERA	G	GS	CG	ShO	Sv.	IP	H	R	ER	BB	SO
1991—	Martinsville (App.)	3	2	.600	4.09	7	6	2	•1	0	33	32	20	15	13	38
	— Spartanburg (SAL)	2	0	1.000	0.00	2	2	0	0	0	15	4	0	0	2	11
1992—	Spartanburg (SAL)	5	10	.333	2.41	42	11	1	0	13	119²/₃	94	41	32	56	118
1993—	Clearwater (Fla. St.)	1	0	1.000	2.75	13	0	0	0	4	19²/₃	19	6	6	5	19
	— Reading (Eastern)	3	3	.500	2.25	49	0	0	0	20	72	63	22	18	26	65
1994—	Scran./W.B. (Int'l)	3	1	.750	8.87	19	0	0	0	3	22¹/₃	32	27	22	22	22
	— Reading (Eastern)	2	2	.500	2.53	38	0	0	0	22	42²/₃	29	13	12	10	51
	— Philadelphia (N.L.)	0	0	...	0.00	3	0	0	0	0	3	3	0	0	1	3
1995—	Philadelphia (N.L.)	5	3	.625	2.46	62	0	0	0	1	87²/₃	50	25	24	42	87
1996—	Philadelphia (N.L.)	4	5	.444	3.19	61	0	0	0	34	67²/₃	47	24	24	23	74
1997—	Philadelphia (N.L.)	2	5	.286	3.65	69	0	0	0	34	74	68	31	30	42	89
Major league totals (4 years)		11	13	.458	3.02	195	0	0	0	69	232¹/₃	168	80	78	108	253

BOTTENFIELD, KENT — P — CARDINALS

PERSONAL: Born November 14, 1968, in Portland, Ore. ... 6-3/245. ... Throws right, bats both. ... Full name: Kent Dennis Bottenfield. ... Twin brother of Keven Bottenfield, minor league catcher/infielder (1986-87).
HIGH SCHOOL: James Madison (Portland, Ore.).
TRANSACTIONS/CAREER NOTES: Selected by Montreal Expos organization in fourth round of free-agent draft (June 2, 1986). ... Traded by Expos to Colorado Rockies for P Butch Henry (July 16, 1993). ... On Colorado disabled list (March 25-May 9, 1994); included rehabilitation assignment to Colorado Springs (April 10-May 9). ... Granted free agency (June 27, 1994). ... Signed by Phoenix, San Francisco Giants organization (June 29, 1994). ... Released by Giants (November 8, 1994). ... Signed by Toledo, Detroit Tigers organization (April 3, 1995). ... Granted free agency (October 16, 1995). ... Signed by Iowa, Chicago Cubs organization (March 9, 1996). ... Granted free agency (December 21, 1997). ... Signed by St. Louis Cardinals (January 8, 1998).

Year	Team (League)	W	L	Pct.	ERA	G	GS	CG	ShO	Sv.	IP	H	R	ER	BB	SO
1986—	GC Expos (GCL)	5	6	.455	3.27	13	13	2	0	0	74¹/₃	73	•42	27	30	41
1987—	Burlington (Midw.)	9	13	.409	4.53	27	27	6	3	0	161	175	98	81	42	103
1988—	W.P. Beach (FSL)	10	8	.556	3.33	27	27	9	4	0	181	165	80	67	47	120
1989—	Jacksonville (Southern)	3	*17	.150	5.26	25	25	1	0	0	138²/₃	137	101	81	73	91
1990—	Jacksonville (Southern)	12	10	.545	3.41	29	28	2	1	0	169	158	72	64	67	121
1991—	Indianapolis (A.A.)	8	15	.348	4.06	29	27	•5	2	0	166¹/₃	155	97	75	61	108
1992—	Indianapolis (A.A.)	•12	8	.600	3.43	25	23	3	1	0	152¹/₃	139	64	58	58	111
	— Montreal (N.L.)	1	2	.333	2.23	10	4	0	0	1	32¹/₃	26	9	8	11	14
1993—	Montreal (N.L.)	2	5	.286	4.12	23	11	0	0	0	83	93	49	38	33	33
	— Colorado (N.L.)■	3	5	.375	6.10	14	14	1	0	0	76²/₃	86	53	52	38	30
1994—	Colo. Springs (PCL)■	1	2	.333	4.94	5	4	1	0	0	31	35	19	17	11	17
	— Colorado (N.L.)	3	1	.750	5.84	15	1	0	0	1	24²/₃	28	16	16	10	15
	— Phoenix (PCL)■	2	1	.667	2.57	8	5	1	1	0	35	30	13	10	11	11
	— San Francisco (N.L.)	0	0	...	10.80	1	0	0	0	0	1²/₃	5	2	2	0	0
1995—	Toledo (Int'l)■	5	11	.313	4.54	27	19	2	1	1	136²/₃	148	80	69	55	68
1996—	Iowa (Am. Assoc.)■	1	2	.333	2.19	28	0	0	0	18	24²/₃	19	9	6	8	14
	— Chicago (N.L.)	3	5	.375	2.63	48	0	0	0	1	61²/₃	59	25	18	19	33
1997—	Chicago (N.L.)	2	3	.400	3.86	64	0	0	0	2	84	82	39	36	35	74
Major league totals (5 years)		14	21	.400	4.20	175	30	1	0	5	364	379	193	170	146	199

BOURNIGAL, RAFAEL — SS — ATHLETICS

PERSONAL: Born May 12, 1966, in Azua, Dominican Republic. ... 5-11/165. ... Bats right, throws right. ... Full name: Rafael Antonio Bournigal.
HIGH SCHOOL: Domax (Dominican Republic).
JUNIOR COLLEGE: Canada College (Calif.).
COLLEGE: Florida State.
TRANSACTIONS/CAREER NOTES: Selected by Texas Rangers organization in 11th round of free-agent draft (January 9, 1985); did not sign. ... Selected by Baltimore Orioles organization in 10th round of free-agent draft (January 14, 1986); did not sign. ... Selected by Los Angeles Dodgers organization in 19th round of free-agent draft (June 2, 1987). ... On Albuquerque temporarily inactive list (April 22-30, 1994). ... Traded by Dodgers organization to Montreal Expos organization for P John Foster (June 9, 1995). ... On Ottawa disabled list (June 26-July 22, 1995). ... Granted free agency (October 16, 1995). ... Signed by Edmonton, Oakland Athletics organization (January 22, 1996). ... On disabled list (July 1-31, 1997); included rehabilitation assignment to Modesto (July 21-31).

STATISTICAL NOTES: Led Northwest League shortstops with .953 fielding percentage in 1988. ... Led Pacific Coast League shortstops with 636 total chances and 97 double plays in 1993.
MISCELLANEOUS: Served as player/coach with Vero Beach (1991).

Year Team (League)	Pos.	G	AB	R	H	2B	3B	HR	RBI	Avg.	BB	SO	SB	PO	A	E	Avg.
1987—Great Falls (Pio.)	2B-SS	30	82	5	12	4	0	0	4	.146	3	7	0	49	47	4	.960
1988—Salem (Northwest)	SS-2B-3B	70	275	54	86	10	1	0	25	.313	38	32	11	76	179	12	†.955
1989—Vero Beach (FSL)	2B-SS	132	484	74	128	11	1	1	37	.264	33	21	18	219	378	15	.975
1990—San Antonio (Tex.)	SS-2B-3B	69	194	20	41	4	2	0	14	.211	8	25	2	99	136	6	.975
1991—Vero Beach (FSL)	SS-3B	20	66	6	16	2	0	0	3	.242	1	3	2	29	56	1	.988
—San Antonio (Tex.)	3B-SS-2B	16	65	6	21	2	0	0	9	.323	2	7	2	28	43	0	1.000
—Albuquerque (PCL).....	SS-2B-3B	66	215	34	63	5	5	0	29	.293	14	13	4	100	188	9	.970
1992—Albuquerque (PCL).....	SS	122	395	47	128	18	1	0	34	.324	22	7	5	*201	369	9	*.984
—Los Angeles (N.L.)	SS	10	20	1	3	1	0	0	0	.150	1	2	0	12	17	1	.967
1993—Albuquerque (PCL).....	SS	134	465	75	129	25	0	4	55	.277	29	18	3	196	*427	13	*.980
—Los Angeles (N.L.)	SS-2B	8	18	0	9	1	0	0	3	.500	0	2	0	5	14	0	1.000
1994—Albuquerque (PCL).....	SS	61	208	29	69	8	0	1	22	.332	9	9	2	66	209	4	.986
—Los Angeles (N.L.)	SS	40	116	2	26	3	1	0	11	.224	9	5	0	56	95	3	.981
1995—Albuquerque (PCL).....	SS	15	31	2	4	1	0	0	1	.129	1	2	0	7	32	2	.951
—Ottawa (Int'l)■	SS-2B-3B	19	54	2	11	4	0	0	6	.204	2	4	0	15	51	1	.985
—Harrisburg (Eastern) ..	SS	29	95	12	21	3	1	0	7	.221	11	8	1	27	64	3	.968
1996—Oakland (A.L.)■	2B-SS	88	252	33	61	14	2	0	18	.242	16	19	4	128	208	2	.994
1997—Oakland (A.L.)	SS-2B	79	222	29	62	9	0	1	20	.279	16	19	2	100	199	6	.980
—Modesto (California) ..	SS	7	21	0	5	1	0	0	2	.238	3	2	1	0	5	7	0	1.000
American League totals (2 years)		167	474	62	123	23	2	1	38	.259	32	38	6	228	407	8	.988
National League totals (3 years)		58	154	3	38	5	1	0	14	.247	10	9	0	73	126	4	.980
Major league totals (5 years)		225	628	65	161	28	3	1	52	.256	42	47	6	301	533	12	.986

BOVEE, MIKE   P   ANGELS

PERSONAL: Born August 21, 1973, in San Diego. ... 5-10/200. ... Throws right, bats right. ... Full name: Michael Craig Bovee.
HIGH SCHOOL: Mira Mesa (San Diego).
TRANSACTIONS/CAREER NOTES: Selected by Kansas City Royals organization in sixth round of free-agent draft (June 3, 1991). ... On disabled list (June 26-July 14, 1993). ... On temporarily inactive list (April 24-May 12, 1995). ... Traded by Royals with P Mark Gubicza to California Angels for DH Chili Davis (October 28, 1996). ... Angels franchise renamed Anaheim Angels for 1997 season.

Year Team (League)	W	L	Pct.	ERA	G	GS	CG	ShO	Sv.	IP	H	R	ER	BB	SO
1991—GC Royals (GCL)	3	1	.750	2.04	11	11	0	0	0	61 2/3	52	19	14	12	*76
1992—Appleton (Midwest)............	9	10	.474	3.56	26	24	1	0	0	149 1/3	143	85	59	41	120
1993—Rockford (Midwest)............	5	9	.357	4.21	20	20	2	0	0	109	118	58	51	30	111
1994—Wilmington (Caro.)...........	13	4	.765	*2.65	28	26	0	0	0	169 2/3	149	58	50	32	154
1995—Wichita (Texas)	8	6	.571	4.18	20	20	1	0	0	114	118	60	53	43	72
1996—Wichita (Texas)	10	11	.476	4.84	27	27	3	2	0	176 2/3	*223	113	95	40	102
1997—Midland (Texas)■............	8	2	.800	4.24	20	13	3	0	0	102	117	53	48	23	61
—Vancouver (PCL)............	4	3	.571	3.44	12	12	1	0	0	89	92	38	34	25	71
—Anaheim (A.L.)	0	0	...	5.40	3	0	0	0	0	3 1/3	3	2	2	1	5
Major league totals (1 year)........	0	0	...	5.40	3	0	0	0	0	3 1/3	3	2	2	1	5

BOWIE, MICAH   P   BRAVES

PERSONAL: Born November 10, 1974, in Humble, Texas. ... 6-4/185. ... Throws left, bats left. ... Full name: Micah Andrew Bowie.
TRANSACTIONS/CAREER NOTES: Signed as non-drafted free agent by Atlanta Braves organization (July 15, 1993). ... On Durham disabled list (July 4, 1996-remainder of season).

Year Team (League)	W	L	Pct.	ERA	G	GS	CG	ShO	Sv.	IP	H	R	ER	BB	SO
1994—GC Braves (GCL)	0	3	.000	3.03	6	5	0	0	0	29 2/3	27	14	10	5	35
—Danville (Appal.)................	3	1	.750	3.58	7	5	0	0	0	32 2/3	28	16	13	13	38
1995—Macon (S. Atl.)	4	1	.800	2.28	5	5	0	0	0	27 2/3	9	8	7	11	36
—Durham (Carolina).............	4	11	.267	3.59	23	23	1	0	0	130 1/3	119	65	52	61	91
1996—Durham (Carolina)............	3	6	.333	3.66	14	13	0	0	0	66 1/3	55	29	27	33	65
1997—Durham (Carolina)............	2	2	.500	3.66	9	6	0	0	0	39 1/3	29	16	16	27	44
—Greenville (Southern)	3	2	.600	3.50	8	7	0	0	0	43 2/3	34	19	17	26	41

BOYD, JASON   P   DIAMONDBACKS

PERSONAL: Born February 23, 1973, in St. Clair, Ill. ... 6-2/165. ... Throws right, bats right. ... Full name: Jason Pernell Boyd.
HIGH SCHOOL: Edwardsville (Ill.).
JUNIOR COLLEGE: John A. Logan College (Ill.).
TRANSACTIONS/CAREER NOTES: Selected by Philadelphia Phillies organization in eighth round of free-agent draft (June 2, 1994). ... Selected by Arizona Diamondbacks in first round (23rd pick overall) of expansion draft (November 18, 1997).

Year Team (League)	W	L	Pct.	ERA	G	GS	CG	ShO	Sv.	IP	H	R	ER	BB	SO
1994—Martinsville (App.)............	3	7	.300	4.17	14	13	1	0	0	69	65	46	32	32	45
1995—Piedmont (S. Atl.)	6	8	.429	3.58	26	24	1	0	0	151	151	77	60	44	129
1996—Clearwater (Fla. St.)	11	8	.579	3.90	26	26	2	0	0	161 2/3	160	75	70	49	120
1997—Reading (Eastern)	10	6	.625	4.82	48	7	0	0	0	115 2/3	113	65	62	64	98

BRAGG, DARREN   OF   RED SOX

PERSONAL: Born September 7, 1969, in Waterbury, Conn. ... 5-9/180. ... Bats left, throws right. ... Full name: Darren W. Bragg.
HIGH SCHOOL: Taft (Watertown, Conn.).
COLLEGE: Georgia Tech.
TRANSACTIONS/CAREER NOTES: Selected by Seattle Mariners organization in 22nd round of free-agent draft (June 30, 1991). ... Traded by Mariners to Boston Red Sox for P Jamie Moyer (July 30, 1996).
STATISTICAL NOTES: Led Carolina League in caught stealing with 19 in 1992. ... Led Pacific Coast League outfielders with 344 total chances and five double plays in 1994. ... Career major league grand slams: 2.

							BATTING								FIELDING		
Year Team (League)	Pos.	G	AB	R	H	2B	3B	HR	RBI	Avg.	BB	SO	SB	PO	A	E	Avg.
1991—Peninsula (Caro.)	OF-2B	69	237	42	53	14	0	3	29	.224	66	72	21	167	9	4	.978
1992—Peninsula (Caro.)	OF	135	428	*83	117	29	5	9	58	.273	*105	76	44	262	11	4	.986
1993—Jacksonville (South.)	OF-P	131	451	74	119	26	3	11	46	.264	81	82	19	306	14	10	.970
1994—Calgary (PCL)	OF	126	500	112	175	33	6	17	85	.350	68	72	28	317	20	7	.980
—Seattle (A.L.)	DH-OF	8	19	4	3	1	0	0	2	.158	2	5	0	1	0	0	1.000
1995—Seattle (A.L.)	OF-DH	52	145	20	34	5	1	3	12	.234	18	37	9	83	7	1	.989
—Tacoma (PCL)	OF	53	212	24	65	13	3	4	31	.307	23	39	10	115	7	4	.968
1996—Seattle (A.L.)	OF	69	195	36	53	12	1	7	25	.272	33	35	8	118	7	1	.992
—Tacoma (PCL)	OF	20	71	17	20	8	0	3	8	.282	14	14	1	32	2	0	1.000
—Boston (A.L.)■	OF	58	222	38	56	14	1	3	22	.252	36	39	6	136	5	2	.986
1997—Boston (A.L.)	OF-3B	153	513	65	132	35	2	9	57	.257	61	102	10	364	11	5	.987
Major league totals (4 years)		340	1094	163	278	67	5	22	118	.254	150	218	33	702	30	9	.988

RECORD AS PITCHER

Year Team (League)	W	L	Pct.	ERA	G	GS	CG	ShO	Sv.	IP	H	R	ER	BB	SO
1993—Jacksonville (Southern)	0	0	...	9.00	1	0	0	0	0	1	3	1	1	0	0

BRANDENBURG, MARK   P   RANGERS

PERSONAL: Born July 14, 1970, in Houston. ... 6-0/180. ... Throws right, bats right. ... Full name: Mark Clay Brandenburg.
HIGH SCHOOL: Humble (Texas).
COLLEGE: Texas Tech.
TRANSACTIONS/CAREER NOTES: Selected by Texas Rangers organization in 26th round of free-agent draft (June 1, 1992). ... On Oklahoma City suspended list (May 29-31, 1995). ... Traded by Rangers with P Kerry Lacy to Boston Red Sox for P Mike Stanton (July 31, 1996). ... On Boston disabled list (March 21-June 2, 1997); including rehabilitation assignment to Sarasota (May 30). ... Traded by Red Sox with P Aaron Sele and C Bill Haselman to Rangers for C Jim Leyritz and OF Damon Buford (November 6, 1997).

Year Team (League)	W	L	Pct.	ERA	G	GS	CG	ShO	Sv.	IP	H	R	ER	BB	SO
1992—Butte (Pioneer)	7	1	.875	4.06	24	1	0	0	2	62	70	32	28	14	78
1993—Charleston, S.C. (S. Atl.)	6	3	.667	1.46	44	0	0	0	4	80	62	23	13	22	67
1994—Charlotte (Fla. St.)	0	2	.000	0.87	25	0	0	0	5	41 1/3	23	5	4	15	44
—Tulsa (Texas)	5	4	.556	1.74	37	0	0	0	8	62	50	17	12	12	63
1995—Oklahoma City (A.A.)	0	5	.000	2.02	35	0	0	0	2	58	52	16	13	15	51
—Texas (A.L.)	0	1	.000	5.93	11	0	0	0	0	27 1/3	36	18	18	7	21
1996—Texas (A.L.)	1	3	.250	3.21	26	0	0	0	0	47 2/3	48	22	17	25	37
—Boston (A.L.)■	4	2	.667	3.81	29	0	0	0	0	28 1/3	28	13	12	8	29
1997—Sarasota (Florida State)	0	0	...	0.00	1	0	0	0	0	3	3	0	0	0	1
—Boston (A.L.)	0	2	.000	5.49	31	0	0	0	0	41	49	25	25	16	34
—Pawtucket (Int'l)	2	1	.667	2.41	9	0	0	0	0	18 2/3	13	6	5	3	23
Major league totals (3 years)	5	8	.385	4.49	97	0	0	0	0	144 1/3	161	78	72	56	121

BRANSON, JEFF   IF   INDIANS

PERSONAL: Born January 26, 1967, in Waynesboro, Miss. ... 6-0/180. ... Bats left, throws right. ... Full name: Jeffery Glenn Branson.
HIGH SCHOOL: Southern Choctaw (Silas, Ala.).
COLLEGE: Livingston (Ala.) University.
TRANSACTIONS/CAREER NOTES: Selected by Cincinnati Reds organization in second round of free-agent draft (June 1, 1988). ... Traded by Reds with P John Smiley to Cleveland Indians for P Danny Graves, P Jim Crowell, P Scott Winchester and IF Damian Jackson (July 31, 1997).
MISCELLANEOUS: Member of 1988 U.S. Olympic baseball team.

							BATTING								FIELDING		
Year Team (League)	Pos.	G	AB	R	H	2B	3B	HR	RBI	Avg.	BB	SO	SB	PO	A	E	Avg.
1989—Cedar Rap. (Midw.)	SS	127	469	70	132	28	1	10	68	.281	41	90	5	172	394	33	.945
1990—Cedar Rap. (Midw.)	SS	62	239	37	60	13	4	6	24	.251	24	44	11	96	152	7	.973
—Chattanooga (Sou.)	2B-SS	63	233	19	49	9	1	2	29	.210	13	48	3	122	151	13	.955
1991—Chattanooga (Sou.)	SS-2B	88	304	35	80	13	3	2	28	.263	31	51	3	126	212	12	.966
—Nashville (A.A.)	SS-2B-OF	43	145	10	35	4	1	0	11	.241	8	31	5	61	93	8	.951
1992—Nashville (A.A.)	S-3-2-0	36	123	18	40	6	3	4	12	.325	9	19	0	59	76	5	.964
—Cincinnati (N.L.)	2B-3B-SS	72	115	12	34	7	1	0	15	.296	5	16	0	46	63	7	.940
1993—Cincinnati (N.L.)	S-2-3-1	125	381	40	92	15	1	3	22	.241	19	73	4	185	260	11	.976
1994—Cincinnati (N.L.)	2-3-S-1	58	109	18	31	4	1	6	16	.284	5	16	0	39	52	1	.989
1995—Cincinnati (N.L.)	3-S-2-1	122	331	43	86	18	2	12	45	.260	44	69	2	84	245	9	.973
1996—Cincinnati (N.L.)	3B-SS-2B	129	311	34	76	16	4	9	37	.244	31	67	2	97	201	14	.955
1997—Indianapolis (A.A.)	SS-3B	15	57	7	12	3	0	1	4	.211	6	10	0	18	32	1	.980
—Cincinnati (N.L.)	3B-2B-SS	65	98	9	15	3	1	1	5	.153	7	23	1	35	56	4	.958
—Cleveland (A.L.)■	2-3-S-DH	29	72	5	19	4	0	2	7	.264	7	17	0	23	60	1	.988
American League totals (1 year)		29	72	5	19	4	0	2	7	.264	7	17	0	23	60	1	.988
National League totals (6 years)		571	1345	156	334	63	10	31	140	.248	111	264	9	486	877	46	.967
Major league totals (6 years)		600	1417	161	353	67	10	33	147	.249	118	281	9	509	937	47	.969

DIVISION SERIES RECORD

Year Team (League)	Pos.	G	AB	R	H	2B	3B	HR	RBI	Avg.	BB	SO	SB	PO	A	E	Avg.
1995— Cincinnati (N.L.)	3B	3	7	0	2	1	0	0	2	.286	2	0	0	1	8	0	1.000

CHAMPIONSHIP SERIES RECORD

Year Team (League)	Pos.	G	AB	R	H	2B	3B	HR	RBI	Avg.	BB	SO	SB	PO	A	E	Avg.
1995— Cincinnati (N.L.)	3B-PH	4	9	2	1	1	0	0	0	.111	0	2	1	1	3	0	1.000
1997— Cleveland (A.L.)	DH	1	2	0	0	0	0	0	0	.000	0	2	0	...	...	...	...
Championship series totals (2 years)		5	11	2	1	1	0	0	0	.091	0	4	1	1	3	0	1.000

WORLD SERIES RECORD

Year Team (League)	Pos.	G	AB	R	H	2B	3B	HR	RBI	Avg.	BB	SO	SB	PO	A	E	Avg.
1997— Cleveland (A.L.)	PH	1	1	0	0	0	0	0	0	.000	0	1	0	...	...	...	...

B

BRANTLEY, JEFF   P   CARDINALS

PERSONAL: Born September 5, 1963, in Florence, Ala. ... 5-10/180. ... Throws right, bats right. ... Full name: Jeffrey Hoke Brantley.
HIGH SCHOOL: W.A. Berry (Florence, Ala.).
COLLEGE: Mississippi State.
TRANSACTIONS/CAREER NOTES: Selected by Montreal Expos organization in 13th round of free-agent draft (June 4, 1984); did not sign. ... Selected by San Francisco Giants organization in sixth round of free-agent draft (June 3, 1985). ... Granted free agency (December 20, 1993). ... Signed by Cincinnati Reds (January 4, 1994). ... Granted free agency (October 17, 1994). ... Re-signed by Reds (October 28, 1994). ... On disabled list (March 19-April 6, 1996). ... On disabled list (March 27-April 15 and May 20, 1997-remainder of season). ... Traded by Reds to St. Louis Cardinals for 1B Dmitri Young (November 10, 1997).
STATISTICAL NOTES: Tied for Pacific Coast League lead with 11 hit batsmen in 1987.
MISCELLANEOUS: Appeared in one game as pinch-runner with San Francisco (1989).

Year Team (League)	W	L	Pct.	ERA	G	GS	CG	ShO	Sv.	IP	H	R	ER	BB	SO
1985— Fresno (California)	8	2	.800	3.33	14	13	3	0	0	94 2/3	83	39	35	37	85
1986— Shreveport (Texas)	8	10	.444	3.48	26	26	•8	3	0	165 2/3	139	78	64	68	125
1987— Shreveport (Texas)	0	1	.000	3.09	2	2	0	0	0	11 2/3	12	7	4	4	7
— Phoenix (PCL)	6	11	.353	4.65	29	28	2	0	0	170 1/3	187	110	88	82	111
1988— Phoenix (PCL)	9	5	.643	4.33	27	19	1	0	0	122 2/3	130	65	59	39	83
— San Francisco (N.L.)	0	1	.000	5.66	9	1	0	0	1	20 2/3	22	13	13	6	11
1989— San Francisco (N.L.)	7	1	.875	4.07	59	1	0	0	0	97 1/3	101	50	44	37	69
— Phoenix (PCL)	1	1	.500	1.26	7	0	0	0	3	14 1/3	6	2	2	6	20
1990— San Francisco (N.L.)	5	3	.625	1.56	55	0	0	0	19	86 2/3	77	18	15	33	61
1991— San Francisco (N.L.)	5	2	.714	2.45	67	0	0	0	15	95 1/3	78	27	26	52	81
1992— San Francisco (N.L.)	7	7	.500	2.95	56	4	0	0	7	91 2/3	67	32	30	45	86
1993— San Francisco (N.L.)	5	6	.455	4.28	53	12	0	0	0	113 2/3	112	60	54	46	76
1994— Cincinnati (N.L.)■...........	6	6	.500	2.48	50	0	0	0	15	65 1/3	46	20	18	28	63
1995— Cincinnati (N.L.)	3	2	.600	2.82	56	0	0	0	28	70 1/3	53	22	22	20	62
1996— Cincinnati (N.L.)	1	2	.333	2.41	66	0	0	0	•44	71	54	21	19	28	76
1997— Cincinnati (N.L.)	1	1	.500	3.86	13	0	0	0	1	11 2/3	9	5	5	7	16
Major league totals (10 years)....	40	31	.563	3.06	484	18	0	0	130	723 2/3	619	268	246	302	601

DIVISION SERIES RECORD

Year Team (League)	W	L	Pct.	ERA	G	GS	CG	ShO	Sv.	IP	H	R	ER	BB	SO
1995— Cincinnati (N.L.)	0	0	...	6.00	3	0	0	0	1	3	5	2	2	0	2

CHAMPIONSHIP SERIES RECORD

Year Team (League)	W	L	Pct.	ERA	G	GS	CG	ShO	Sv.	IP	H	R	ER	BB	SO
1989— San Francisco (N.L.)	0	0	...	0.00	3	0	0	0	0	5	1	0	0	2	3
1995— Cincinnati (N.L.)	0	0	...	0.00	2	0	0	0	0	2 2/3	0	0	0	2	1
Champ. series totals (2 years)	0	0	...	0.00	5	0	0	0	0	7 2/3	1	0	0	4	4

WORLD SERIES RECORD

Year Team (League)	W	L	Pct.	ERA	G	GS	CG	ShO	Sv.	IP	H	R	ER	BB	SO
1989— San Francisco (N.L.)	0	0	...	4.15	3	0	0	0	0	4 1/3	5	2	2	3	1

ALL-STAR GAME RECORD

Year League	W	L	Pct.	ERA	GS	CG	ShO	Sv.	IP	H	R	ER	BB	SO
1990— National	0	1	.000	54.00	0	0	0	0	1/3	2	2	2	0	0

BRANYAN, RUSSELL   3B   INDIANS

PERSONAL: Born December 19, 1975, in Warner Robins, Ga. ... 6-3/195. ... Bats left, throws right.
HIGH SCHOOL: Stratford Academy (Warner Robins, Ga.).
TRANSACTIONS/CAREER NOTES: Selected by Cleveland Indians organization in seventh round of free-agent draft (June 2, 1994).
HONORS: Named Appalachian League Most Valuable Player (1996).
STATISTICAL NOTES: Led Appalachian League with .575 slugging percentage in 1996. ... Led Appalachian League third basemen with 24 double plays in 1996.

Year Team (League)	Pos.	G	AB	R	H	2B	3B	HR	RBI	Avg.	BB	SO	SB	PO	A	E	Avg.
1994— Burlington (Appal.).....	3B	55	171	21	36	10	0	5	13	.211	25	64	4	32	88	21	.851
1995— Columbus (S. Atl.)......	3B	76	277	46	71	8	6	19	55	.256	27	120	1	34	120	26	.856
1996— Columbus (S. Atl.)......	3B	130	482	102	129	20	4	•40	•106	.268	62	166	7	82	256	44	.885
1997— Kinston (Carolina)	3B	83	297	59	86	26	2	27	75	.290	52	94	3	64	118	21	.897
— Akron (Eastern)	3B	41	137	26	32	4	0	12	30	.234	28	56	0	31	98	11	.921

BRAZOBAN, MELVIN — P — PIRATES

PERSONAL: Born January 20, 1977, in Santo Domingo, Dominican Republic. ... 6-3/165. ... Throws right, bats right. ... Full name: Melvin A. Brazoban.
TRANSACTIONS/CAREER NOTES: Signed as non-drafted free agent by Texas Rangers organization (February 4, 1994). ... Selected by Pittsburgh Pirates from Rangers organization in Rule 5 major league draft (December 15, 1997).

Year Team (League)	W	L	Pct.	ERA	G	GS	CG	ShO	Sv.	IP	H	R	ER	BB	SO
1995—Dom. Rangers (DSL)	3	2	.600	5.57	7	7	0	0	0	32⅓	30	25	20	20	27
1996—Dom. Rangers (DSL)	7	5	.583	2.74	16	16	1	0	0	95⅓	74	38	29	34	69
1997—GC Rangers (GCL)	1	3	.250	4.20	14	0	0	0	2	30	28	16	14	14	36

BREDE, BRENT — OF/1B — DIAMONDBACKS

PERSONAL: Born September 13, 1971, in New Baden, Ill. ... 6-4/208. ... Bats left, throws left. ... Full name: Brent David Brede. ... Name pronounced Brady.
HIGH SCHOOL: Wesclin (Trenton, Ill.).
TRANSACTIONS/CAREER NOTES: Selected by Minnesota Twins organization in fifth round of free-agent draft (June 4, 1990). ... Selected by Arizona Diamondbacks in first round (25th pick overall) of expansion draft (November 18, 1997).
STATISTICAL NOTES: Led Appalachian League outfielders with 123 putouts and 1.000 fielding percentage in 1991. ... Tied for Eastern League lead in double plays by outfielder with 10 in 1995. ... Led Pacific Coast League with .446 on-base percentage in 1996.

						BATTING								FIELDING		
Year Team (League)	Pos.	G	AB	R	H	2B	3B	HR	RBI	Avg.	BB	SO	SB	PO	A	E	Avg.
1990—Elizabethton (App.)	OF	46	143	39	35	5	0	0	14	.245	30	30	14	63	3	2	.971
1991—Kenosha (Midwest)	OF	53	156	12	30	3	2	0	10	.192	16	31	4	79	3	1	.988
—Elizabethton (App.)	OF-1B	*68	253	24	61	13	0	3	36	.241	30	48	13	†159	4	0	†1.000
1992—Kenosha (Midwest)	OF-1B-3B	110	363	44	88	15	0	0	29	.242	53	77	10	236	19	7	.973
1993—Fort Myers (FSL)	OF-1B	53	182	27	60	10	1	0	27	.330	32	19	8	83	7	3	.968
1994—Fort Myers (FSL)	OF-1B	116	419	49	110	21	4	2	45	.263	63	60	18	210	10	5	.978
1995—New Britain (Eastern)	OF-1B	134	449	71	123	28	2	3	39	.274	69	82	14	307	19	‡10	.970
1996—Salt Lake (PCL)	OF-1B	132	483	102	168	38	8	11	86	.348	87	87	14	404	24	7	.984
—Minnesota (A.L.)	OF	10	20	2	6	0	1	0	2	.300	1	5	0	12	1	0	1.000
1997—Salt Lake (PCL)	OF-1B	84	328	82	116	27	4	9	76	.354	47	62	4	445	27	7	.985
—Minnesota (A.L.)	OF-1B-DH	61	190	25	52	11	1	3	21	.274	21	38	7	188	9	4	.980
Major league totals (2 years)		71	210	27	58	11	2	3	23	.276	22	43	7	200	10	4	.981

BREWER, BILLY — P — PHILLIES

PERSONAL: Born April 15, 1968, in Fort Worth, Texas. ... 6-1/175. ... Throws left, bats left. ... Full name: William Robert Brewer.
HIGH SCHOOL: Spring Hill (Longview, Texas).
COLLEGE: Dallas Baptist.
TRANSACTIONS/CAREER NOTES: Selected by Cleveland Indians organization in 26th round of free-agent draft (June 5, 1989); did not sign. ... Selected by Montreal Expos organization in 28th round of free-agent draft (June 4, 1990). ... On disabled list (April 12-June 11, 1991). ... Selected by Kansas City Royals from Expos organization in Rule 5 major league draft (December 7, 1992). ... Traded by Royals to Los Angeles Dodgers for SS Jose Offerman (December 17, 1995). ... Traded by Dodgers to New York Yankees for P Mike Judd (June 22, 1996). ... Granted free agency (December 20, 1996). ... Signed by Cincinnati Reds organization (December 21, 1996). ... Released by Reds (March 10, 1997). ... Signed by Oakland Athletics organization (March 18, 1997). ... On Oakland disabled list (April 6-28, 1997); included rehabilitation assignments to Visalia (April 21-24) and Edmonton (April 25-28). ... Granted free agency (May 22, 1997). ... Signed by Philadelphia Phillies organization (May 27, 1997). ... Released by Phillies (October 10, 1997). ... Re-signed by Phillies organization (December 15, 1997).

Year Team (League)	W	L	Pct.	ERA	G	GS	CG	ShO	Sv.	IP	H	R	ER	BB	SO
1990—Jamestown (NYP)	2	2	.500	2.93	11	2	0	0	1	27⅔	23	10	9	13	37
1991—Rockford (Midwest)	3	3	.500	1.98	29	0	0	0	5	41	32	12	9	25	43
1992—W.P. Beach (FSL)	2	2	.500	1.73	28	0	0	0	8	36⅓	27	10	7	14	37
—Harrisburg (Eastern)	2	0	1.000	5.01	20	0	0	0	0	23⅓	25	15	13	18	18
1993—Kansas City (A.L.)■	2	2	.500	3.46	46	0	0	0	0	39	31	16	15	20	28
1994—Kansas City (A.L.)	4	1	.800	2.56	50	0	0	0	3	38⅔	28	11	11	16	25
1995—Kansas City (A.L.)	2	4	.333	5.56	48	0	0	0	0	45⅓	54	28	28	20	31
—Springfield (Mid.)	0	0	...	0.00	1	0	0	0	1	2	2	1	0	1	2
—Omaha (Am. Assoc.)	0	0	...	0.00	6	0	0	0	0	7	1	0	0	7	5
1996—Albuquerque (PCL)	2	2	.500	3.13	31	0	0	0	2	31⅔	28	13	11	22	33
—New York (A.L.)■	1	0	1.000	9.53	4	0	0	0	0	5⅔	7	6	6	8	8
—Columbus (Int'l)	0	2	.000	7.20	13	4	0	0	0	25	27	21	20	19	27
1997—Oakland (A.L.)■	0	0	...	13.50	3	0	0	0	0	2	4	3	3	2	1
—Visalia (California)	0	0	...	0.00	2	2	0	0	0	3	1	1	0	4	5
—Edmonton (PCL)	0	0	...	5.63	7	1	0	0	1	8	8	5	5	6	11
—Scran./W.B. (Int'l)■	2	1	.667	3.00	11	0	0	0	0	9	10	7	3	5	9
—Philadelphia (N.L.)	1	2	.333	3.27	25	0	0	0	0	22	15	8	8	11	16
A.L. totals (5 years)	9	7	.563	4.34	151	0	0	0	3	130⅔	124	64	63	66	93
N.L. totals (1 year)	1	2	.333	3.27	25	0	0	0	0	22	15	8	8	11	16
Major league totals (5 years)	10	9	.526	4.19	176	0	0	0	3	152⅔	139	72	71	77	109

BRITO, TILSON — IF

PERSONAL: Born May 28, 1972, in Santo Domingo, Dominican Republic. ... 6-0/180. ... Bats right, throws right. ... Full name: Tilson Manuel Brito.
TRANSACTIONS/CAREER NOTES: Signed as non-drafted free agent by Toronto Blue Jays organization (January 10, 1990). ... On Syracuse disabled list (May 25-June 9, 1995). ... Claimed on waivers by Oakland Athletics (August 8, 1997). ... On disabled list (August 21-September 12, 1997); included rehabilitation assignments to Modesto (August 28-September 3) and Edmonton (September 3-12). ... Granted free agency (December 21, 1997).
STATISTICAL NOTES: Tied for Florida State League lead in errors by shortstop with 37 in 1993. ... Led Southern League shortstops with 684 total chances and 85 double plays in 1994. ... Led International League shortstops with 32 errors and 72 double plays in 1996.

Year	Team (League)	Pos.	G	AB	R	H	2B	3B	HR	RBI	Avg.	BB	SO	SB	PO	A	E	Avg.
1990—Dom. Dodgers (DSL) .		IF	39	130	31	33	8	2	0	14	.254	13	9	4	...	...	...	...
1991—Dom. Dodgers (DSL) .		IF	70	253	56	85	16	2	4	55	.336	44	19	11	...	...	...	...
1992—GC Jays (GCL)............		3B-2B-SS	54	189	36	58	10	4	3	36	.307	22	22	16	56	127	17	.915
—Knoxville (Southern) ..		SS	7	24	2	5	1	2	0	2	.208	0	9	0	6	19	5	.833
1993—Dunedin (Fla. St.).......		SS-3B-2B	126	465	80	125	21	3	6	44	.269	59	60	27	200	387	‡38	.939
1994—Knoxville (Southern) ..		SS	•139	476	61	127	17	7	5	57	.267	35	68	33	217	*424	43	.937
1995—Syracuse (Int'l)..........		SS-2B	90	327	49	79	16	3	7	32	.242	29	69	17	123	240	18	.953
1996—Toronto (A.L.)...........		2B-SS-DH	26	80	10	19	7	0	1	7	.238	10	18	1	42	60	4	.962
—Syracuse (Int'l)........		SS-3B-2B	108	400	63	111	22	8	10	54	.278	38	65	11	156	290	†32	.933
1997—Toronto (A.L.)...........		2B-3B-SS	49	126	9	28	3	0	0	8	.222	9	28	1	53	92	3	.980
—Oakland (A.L.)■.........		3B-SS-2B	17	46	8	13	2	1	2	6	.283	1	10	0	16	31	2	.959
—Modesto (California) ..		SS	4	9	3	3	1	0	1	3	.333	2	1	0	5	6	2	.846
Major league totals (2 years)			92	252	27	60	12	1	3	21	.238	20	56	2	111	183	9	.970

BROCAIL, DOUG — P — TIGERS

PERSONAL: Born May 16, 1967, in Clearfield, Pa. ... 6-5/235. ... Throws right, bats left. ... Full name: Douglas Keith Brocail.
HIGH SCHOOL: Lamar (Colo.).
JUNIOR COLLEGE: Lamar (Colo.) Community College.
TRANSACTIONS/CAREER NOTES: Selected by San Diego Padres organization in first round (12th pick overall) of free-agent draft (January 14, 1986). ... On Las Vegas disabled list (May 5-12, 1993). ... On San Diego disabled list (April 2-June 28, 1994); included rehabilitation assignments to Wichita (May 26-June 3) and Las Vegas (June 3-23). ... Traded by Padres with OF Phil Plantier, OF Derek Bell, P Pedro Martinez, IF Craig Shipley and SS Ricky Gutierrez to Houston Astros for 3B Ken Caminiti, OF Steve Finley, SS Andujar Cedeno, 1B Robert Petagine, P Brian Williams and a player to be named later (December 28, 1994); Padres acquired P Sean Fesh to complete deal (May 1, 1995). ... On Houston disabled list (May 11-August 15, 1996); included rehabilitation assignments to Jackson (May 27-June 4) and Tucson (July 29-August 15). ... Traded by Astros with OF Brian L. Hunter, IF Orlando Miller, P Todd Jones and a player to be named later to Detroit Tigers for C Brad Ausmus, P Jose Lima, P C.J. Nitkowski, P Trever Miller and IF Daryle Ward (December 10, 1996).
MISCELLANEOUS: Appeared in six games as pinch-runner with San Diego (1993). ... Appeared in two games as pinch-runner with San Diego (1994). ... Appeared in one game as pinch-runner with Houston (1995). ... Appeared in two games as pinch-runner with Houston (1996).

Year	Team (League)	W	L	Pct.	ERA	G	GS	CG	ShO	Sv.	IP	H	R	ER	BB	SO
1986—Spokane (N'west)...............		5	4	.556	3.81	16	•15	0	0	0	85	85	52	36	53	77
1987—Charleston, S.C. (S. Atl.)		2	6	.250	4.09	19	18	0	0	0	92 1/3	94	51	42	28	68
1988—Charleston, S.C. (S. Atl.)		8	6	.571	2.69	22	13	5	0	2	107	107	40	32	25	107
1989—Wichita (Texas)		5	9	.357	5.21	23	22	1	1	0	134 2/3	158	88	78	50	95
1990—Wichita (Texas)		2	2	.500	4.33	12	9	0	0	0	52	53	30	25	24	27
1991—Wichita (Texas)		10	7	.588	3.87	34	16	3	•3	6	146 1/3	147	77	63	43	108
1992—Las Vegas (PCL)		10	10	.500	3.97	29	25	4	0	0	172 1/3	187	82	76	63	103
—San Diego (N.L.)		0	0	...	6.43	3	3	0	0	0	14	17	10	10	5	15
1993—Las Vegas (PCL)		4	2	.667	3.68	10	8	0	0	1	51 1/3	51	26	21	14	32
—San Diego (N.L.)		4	13	.235	4.56	24	24	0	0	0	128 1/3	143	75	65	42	70
1994—Wichita (Texas)		0	0	...	0.00	2	0	0	0	0	4	3	1	0	1	2
—Las Vegas (PCL)		0	0	...	7.11	7	3	0	0	0	12 2/3	21	12	10	2	8
—San Diego (N.L.)		0	0	...	5.82	12	0	0	0	0	17	21	13	11	5	11
1995—Houston (N.L.)■		6	4	.600	4.19	36	7	0	0	0	77 1/3	87	40	36	22	39
—Tucson (PCL)		1	0	1.000	3.86	3	3	0	0	0	16 1/3	18	9	7	4	16
1996—Houston (N.L.)		1	5	.167	4.58	23	4	0	0	0	53	58	31	27	23	34
—Jackson (Texas)		0	0	...	0.00	2	2	0	0	0	4	1	0	0	1	5
—Tucson (PCL)		0	1	.000	7.36	5	1	0	0	0	7 1/3	12	6	6	1	4
1997—Detroit (A.L.)■		3	4	.429	3.23	61	4	0	0	2	78	74	31	28	36	60
A.L. totals (1 year)		3	4	.429	3.23	61	4	0	0	2	78	74	31	28	36	60
N.L. totals (5 years)		11	22	.333	4.63	98	38	0	0	1	289 2/3	326	169	149	97	169
Major league totals (6 years)......		14	26	.350	4.33	159	42	0	0	3	367 2/3	400	200	177	133	229

BROCK, CHRIS — P — BRAVES

PERSONAL: Born February 5, 1970, in Orlando. ... 6-0/175. ... Throws right, bats right. ... Full name: Terrence Christopher Brock.
HIGH SCHOOL: Lyman (Longwood, Fla.).
COLLEGE: Florida State.
TRANSACTIONS/CAREER NOTES: Selected by Atlanta Braves organization in 12th round of free-agent draft (June 1, 1992). ... On disabled list (July 26, 1995-remainder of season).

Year	Team (League)	W	L	Pct.	ERA	G	GS	CG	ShO	Sv.	IP	H	R	ER	BB	SO
1992—Idaho Falls (Pioneer)..........		6	4	.600	2.31	15	15	1	0	0	78	61	27	20	48	72
1993—Macon (S. Atl.)..................		7	5	.583	2.70	14	14	1	0	0	80	61	37	24	33	92
—Durham (Carolina).............		5	2	.714	2.51	12	12	1	0	0	79	63	28	22	35	67
1994—Greenville (Southern)		7	6	.538	3.74	25	23	2	2	0	137 1/3	128	68	57	47	94
1995—Richmond (Int'l)................		2	8	.200	5.40	22	9	0	0	0	60	68	37	36	27	43
1996—Richmond (Int'l)................		10	11	.476	4.67	26	25	3	0	0	150 1/3	137	95	78	61	112
1997—Richmond (Int'l)................		10	6	.625	3.34	20	19	0	0	0	118 2/3	97	50	44	51	83
—Atlanta (N.L.)..................		0	0	...	5.58	7	6	0	0	0	30 2/3	34	23	19	19	16
Major league totals (1 year)........		0	0	...	5.58	7	6	0	0	0	30 2/3	34	23	19	19	16

BROGNA, RICO — 1B — PHILLIES

PERSONAL: Born April 18, 1970, in Turner Falls, Mass. ... 6-2/205. ... Bats left, throws left. ... Full name: Rico Joseph Brogna. ... Name pronounced BRONE-yah.

B

HIGH SCHOOL: Watertown (Conn.).
TRANSACTIONS/CAREER NOTES: Selected by Detroit Tigers organization in first round (26th pick overall) of free-agent draft (June 1, 1988). ... On Toledo disabled list (May 25-June 2, 1991). ... Traded by Tigers to New York Mets for 1B Alan Zinter (March 31, 1994). ... On disabled list (June 20, 1996-remainder of season). ... Traded by Mets to Philadelphia Phillies for P Ricardo Jordan and P Toby Borland (November 27, 1996).
STATISTICAL NOTES: Led Eastern League first basemen with 1,261 total chances and 117 double plays in 1990. ... Career major league grand slams: 2.

							BATTING								FIELDING		
Year Team (League)	Pos.	G	AB	R	H	2B	3B	HR	RBI	Avg.	BB	SO	SB	PO	A	E	Avg.
1988— Bristol (Appal.)	1B-OF	60	209	37	53	11	2	7	33	.254	25	42	3	319	26	6	.983
1989— Lakeland (Fla. St.)	1B	128	459	47	108	20	7	5	51	.235	38	82	2	1098	83	13	.989
1990— London (Eastern)	1B	137	488	70	128	21	3	*21	•77	.262	50	100	1	*1155	*93	13	.990
1991— Toledo (Int'l)	1B	41	132	13	29	6	1	2	13	.220	4	26	2	311	37	5	.986
— London (Eastern)	1B-OF	77	293	40	80	13	1	13	51	.273	25	59	0	368	46	6	.986
1992— Toledo (Int'l)	1B	121	387	45	101	19	4	10	58	.261	31	85	1	896	76	9	.991
— Detroit (A.L.)	1B-DH	9	26	3	5	1	0	1	3	.192	3	5	0	48	6	1	.982
1993— Toledo (Int'l)	1B	129	483	55	132	30	3	11	59	.273	31	94	7	937	97	8	.992
1994— Norfolk (Int'l)■	1B	67	258	33	63	14	5	12	37	.244	15	62	1	583	47	3	.995
— New York (N.L.)	1B	39	131	16	46	11	2	7	20	.351	6	29	1	307	28	1	.997
1995— New York (N.L.)	1B	134	495	72	143	27	2	22	76	.289	39	111	0	1111	93	3	* .998
1996— New York (N.L.)	1B	55	188	18	48	10	1	7	30	.255	19	50	0	440	31	2	.996
1997— Philadelphia (N.L.)■ ..	1B	148	543	68	137	36	1	20	81	.252	33	116	12	1053	119	7	.994
American League totals (1 year)		9	26	3	5	1	0	1	3	.192	3	5	0	48	6	1	.982
National League totals (4 years)		376	1357	174	374	84	6	56	207	.276	97	306	13	2911	271	13	.996
Major league totals (5 years)		385	1383	177	379	85	6	57	210	.274	100	311	13	2959	277	14	.996

BROHAWN, TROY — P — GIANTS

PERSONAL: Born January 14, 1973, in Cambridge, Md. ... 6-1/190. ... Throws left, bats left. ... Full name: Michael Troy Brohawn.
HIGH SCHOOL: South Dorchester (Cambridge, Md.).
COLLEGE: Nebraska.
TRANSACTIONS/CAREER NOTES: Selected by San Francisco Giants organization in fourth round of free-agent draft (June 2, 1994).

Year Team (League)	W	L	Pct.	ERA	G	GS	CG	ShO	Sv.	IP	H	R	ER	BB	SO
1994— San Jose (California)	0	2	.000	7.02	4	4	0	0	0	16²/₃	27	15	13	5	13
1995— San Jose (California)	7	3	.700	1.65	11	10	0	0	0	65¹/₃	45	14	12	20	57
1996— Shreveport (Texas)	9	10	.474	4.60	28	28	0	0	0	156²/₃	163	99	80	49	82
1997— Shreveport (Texas)	13	5	.722	*2.56	26	26	1	•1	0	169	148	57	48	64	98

BROSIUS, SCOTT — 3B — YANKEES

PERSONAL: Born August 15, 1966, in Hillsboro, Ore. ... 6-1/202. ... Bats right, throws right. ... Full name: Scott David Brosius. ... Name pronounced BRO-shus.
HIGH SCHOOL: Rex Putnam (Milwaukie, Ore.).
COLLEGE: Linfield College (Ore.).
TRANSACTIONS/CAREER NOTES: Selected by Oakland Athletics organization in 20th round of free-agent draft (June 2, 1987). ... On Tacoma disabled list (April 17-May 29, 1991). ... On Oakland disabled list (April 18-May 12, 1992); included rehabilitation assignment to Tacoma (May 6-12). ... On Oakland disabled list (July 13-August 3, 1992); included rehabilitation assignment to Tacoma (July 27-August 3). ... On Oakland disabled list (July 28-August 5, 1993). ... On disabled list (June 8-26, 1994). ... On Oakland disabled list (May 5-June 25, 1996); included rehabilitation assignment to Edmonton (June 22-25). ... On Oakland disabled list (August 7-29, 1997); included rehabilitation assignment to Modesto (August 27-29). ... Traded by A's to New York Yankees (November 18, 1997), completing deal in which Yankees traded P Kenny Rogers and cash to A's for a player to be named later (November 7, 1997).
STATISTICAL NOTES: Led Northwest League with seven sacrifice flies in 1987. ... Led Southern League with 274 total bases in 1990. ... Tied for Pacific Coast League lead in double plays by third baseman with 24 in 1992. ... Career major league grand slams: 1.

							BATTING								FIELDING		
Year Team (League)	Pos.	G	AB	R	H	2B	3B	HR	RBI	Avg.	BB	SO	SB	PO	A	E	Avg.
1987— Medford (N'west)	3-S-2-1-P	65	255	34	73	18	1	3	49	.286	26	36	5	123	148	38	.877
1988— Madison (Midwest)	S-3-O-1	132	504	82	153	28	2	9	58	.304	56	67	13	151	305	61	.882
1989— Huntsville (Southern) .	2-3-S-1	128	461	68	125	22	2	7	60	.271	58	62	4	225	316	34	.941
1990— Huntsville (Southern) .	SS-2B-3B	•142	547	94	*162	*39	2	23	88	.296	81	81	12	253	419	41	.942
— Tacoma (PCL)	2B	3	7	2	1	0	1	0	0	.143	1	3	0	3	5	0	1.000
1991— Tacoma (PCL)	3B-SS-2B	65	245	28	70	16	3	8	31	.286	18	29	4	49	168	14	.939
— Oakland (A.L.)	2-0-3-DH	36	68	9	16	5	0	2	4	.235	3	11	3	31	16	0	1.000
1992— Oakland (A.L.)	O-3-1-DH-S	38	87	13	19	2	0	4	13	.218	3	13	3	68	15	1	.988
— Tacoma (PCL)	3B-OF	63	236	29	56	13	0	9	31	.237	23	44	8	50	167	10	.956
1993— Oakland (A.L.)	O-1-3S-DH	70	213	26	53	10	1	6	25	.249	14	37	6	173	29	2	.990
— Tacoma (PCL)	3-0-2-1-S	56	209	38	62	13	2	8	41	.297	21	50	8	101	109	13	.942
1994— Oakland (A.L.)	3B-OF-1B	96	324	31	77	14	1	14	49	.238	24	57	2	82	157	13	.948
1995— Oakland (A.L.)	3-O-1-2-S-DH	123	389	69	102	19	2	17	46	.262	41	67	4	208	121	15	.956
1996— Oakland (A.L.)	3B-1B-OF	114	428	73	130	25	0	22	71	.304	59	85	7	128	234	10	.973
— Edmonton (PCL)	3B	8	8	5	5	1	0	0	0	.625	3	1	0	0	4	2	.667
1997— Oakland (A.L.)	3B-SS-OF	129	479	59	97	20	1	11	41	.203	34	102	9	142	246	10	.975
— Modesto (California) ..	3B	2	3	1	1	0	0	0	1	.333	1	0	0	1	1	1	.667
Major league totals (7 years)		606	1988	280	494	95	5	76	249	.248	178	372	34	832	818	51	.970

RECORD AS PITCHER

Year Team (League)	W	L	Pct.	ERA	G	GS	CG	ShO	Sv.	IP	H	R	ER	BB	SO
1987— Medford (N'west)	0	0	...	0.00	1	0	0	0	0	2	0	0	0	0	1

B

BROW, SCOTT · P · DIAMONDBACKS

PERSONAL: Born March 17, 1969, in Butte, Mont. ... 6-3/200. ... Throws right, bats right. ... Full name: Scott John Brow. ... Name pronounced BRAUH.
HIGH SCHOOL: Hillsboro (Ore.).
COLLEGE: Washington.
TRANSACTIONS/CAREER NOTES: Selected by Toronto Blue Jays organization in seventh round of free-agent draft (June 4, 1990). ... On disabled list (April 20-July 31, 1995). ... Claimed on waivers by Atlanta Braves (September 30, 1996). ... Granted free agency (October 15, 1997). ... Signed by Arizona Diamondbacks organization (December 18, 1997).

Year	Team (League)	W	L	Pct.	ERA	G	GS	CG	ShO	Sv.	IP	H	R	ER	BB	SO
1990—	St. Catharines (NYP)	3	1	.750	2.27	9	7	0	0	0	39 2/3	34	18	10	11	39
1991—	Dunedin (Fla. St.)	3	7	.300	4.78	15	12	0	0	0	69 2/3	73	50	37	28	31
1992—	Dunedin (Fla. St.)	14	2	.875	2.43	25	25	3	1	0	*170 2/3	143	53	46	44	107
1993—	Knoxville (Southern)	1	2	.333	3.32	3	3	1	0	0	19	13	8	7	9	12
	Toronto (A.L.)	1	1	.500	6.00	6	3	0	0	0	18	19	15	12	10	7
	Syracuse (Int'l)	6	8	.429	4.38	20	19	2	0	0	121 1/3	119	63	59	37	64
1994—	Toronto (A.L.)	0	3	.000	5.90	18	0	0	0	2	29	34	27	19	19	15
	Syracuse (Int'l)	5	3	.625	4.31	14	13	1	1	0	79 1/3	77	45	38	38	30
1995—	Syracuse (Int'l)	1	5	.167	9.00	11	5	0	0	0	31	52	39	31	18	14
1996—	Syracuse (Int'l)	5	4	.556	4.93	18	11	0	0	0	76 2/3	84	49	42	26	52
	Toronto (A.L.)	1	0	1.000	5.59	18	1	0	0	0	38 2/3	45	25	24	25	23
1997—	Richmond (Int'l)■	5	9	.357	4.45	61	1	0	0	18	83	89	48	41	35	62
Major league totals (3 years)		2	4	.333	5.78	42	4	0	0	2	85 2/3	98	67	55	54	45

BROWN, ADRIAN · OF · PIRATES

PERSONAL: Born February 7, 1974, in McComb, Miss. ... 6-0/175. ... Bats right, throws right. ... Full name: Adrian Demond Brown.
HIGH SCHOOL: McComb (Miss.).
TRANSACTIONS/CAREER NOTES: Selected by Pittsburgh Pirates organization in 48th round of free-agent draft (June 1, 1992).

Year	Team (League)	Pos.	G	AB	R	H	2B	3B	HR	RBI	Avg.	BB	SO	SB	PO	A	E	Avg.
1992—	GC Pirates (GCL)	OF-1B	39	121	11	31	2	2	0	12	.256	0	12	8	60	4	1	.985
1993—	Lethbridge (Pioneer)	OF	69	282	47	75	12	*9	3	27	.266	17	34	22	119	4	1	*.992
1994—	Augusta (S. Atl.)	OF	79	308	41	80	17	1	1	18	.260	14	38	19	121	6	2	.984
1995—	Lynchburg (Caro.)	OF	54	215	30	52	5	2	1	14	.242	12	20	11	110	6	2	.983
	Augusta (S. Atl.)	OF	76	287	64	86	15	4	4	31	.300	33	23	25	124	8	7	.950
1996—	Lynchburg (Caro.)	OF	52	215	39	69	9	3	4	25	.321	14	24	18	99	4	2	.981
	Carolina (Southern)	OF	84	341	48	101	11	3	3	25	.296	25	40	27	185	5	2	.990
1997—	Carolina (Southern)	OF	37	145	29	44	4	4	2	15	.303	18	12	9	63	2	3	.956
	Pittsburgh (N.L.)	OF	48	147	17	28	6	0	1	10	.190	13	18	8	74	3	1	.987
	Calgary (PCL)	OF	62	248	53	79	10	1	1	19	.319	27	38	20	130	3	1	.993
Major league totals (1 year)			48	147	17	28	6	0	1	10	.190	13	18	8	74	3	1	.987

BROWN, ALVIN · P · DODGERS

PERSONAL: Born September 2, 1970, in Inglewood, Calif. ... 6-1/200. ... Throws right, bats right. ... Full name: Alvin Ray Brown.
HIGH SCHOOL: Crenshaw (Los Angeles).
COLLEGE: Los Angeles City College.
TRANSACTIONS/CAREER NOTES: Selected by Minnesota Twins organization in 12th round of free-agent draft (June 5, 1989). ... Released by Elizabethton, Twins organization (March 27, 1992). ... Signed by Fayetteville, Detroit Tigers organization (August 31, 1992). ... Released by Tigers (March 20, 1996). ... Signed by Yakima, Los Angeles Dodgers organization (April 19, 1996).
STATISTICAL NOTES: Led Appalachian League first basemen with 15 errors in 1991. ... Tied for Appalachian League lead with 14 wild pitches in 1993. ... Led South Atlantic League with 27 wild pitches in 1994.

Year	Team (League)	W	L	Pct.	ERA	G	GS	CG	ShO	Sv.	IP	H	R	ER	BB	SO
1992—						Did not play.											
1993—	Bristol (Appalachian)■	2	2	.500	6.23	15	6	0	0	1	39	27	30	27	47	30
1994—	Lakeland (Fla. St.)	0	0	...	9.00	4	0	0	0	0	7	11	8	7	7	9
	Fayetteville (S. Atl.)	6	7	.462	4.33	33	12	1	1	0	97 2/3	61	60	47	83	109
1995—	Lakeland (Fla. St.)	2	3	.400	4.24	9	9	0	0	0	46 2/3	35	23	22	33	35
1996—	San Bernardino (Calif.)■	2	4	.333	3.80	42	2	0	0	2	68 2/3	43	40	29	62	84
1997—	San Antonio (Tex.)	6	5	.545	3.74	16	16	2	•1	0	96 1/3	83	48	40	33	67
	Albuquerque (PCL)	4	6	.400	6.13	12	11	1	1	0	61 2/3	74	50	42	35	43

RECORD AS POSITION PLAYER

Year	Team (League)	Pos.	G	AB	R	H	2B	3B	HR	RBI	Avg.	BB	SO	SB	PO	A	E	Avg.
1989—	GC Twins (GCL)	C	27	72	2	14	0	0	0	5	.194	9	22	1	102	14	10	.921
1990—	GC Twins (GCL)	C-OF-1B	36	112	18	32	2	3	0	15	.286	12	45	6	110	17	7	.948
1991—	Kenosha (Midwest)	C	5	11	2	0	0	0	0	0	.000	1	6	1	16	2	1	.947
	Elizabethton (App.)	1B-C	57	172	26	35	7	2	1	11	.203	26	65	6	416	29	†18	.961

BROWN, BRANT · 1B · CUBS

PERSONAL: Born June 22, 1971, in Porterville, Calif. ... 6-3/205. ... Bats left, throws left. ... Full name: Brant Michael Brown.
HIGH SCHOOL: Monache (Porterville, Calif.).
COLLEGE: Fresno State.

B

TRANSACTIONS/CAREER NOTES: Selected by Chicago Cubs organization in third round of free-agent draft (June 1, 1992). ... On Daytona disabled list (April 10-25, 1993). ... On Iowa disabled list (July 22-August 11, 1996).

Year Team (League)	Pos.	G	AB	R	H	2B	3B	HR	RBI	Avg.	BB	SO	SB	PO	A	E	Avg.
1992— Peoria (Midwest)	1B	70	248	28	68	14	0	3	27	.274	24	49	3	582	39	6	.990
1993— Daytona (Fla. St.)	1B	75	266	26	91	8	7	3	33	.342	11	38	8	643	55	5	.993
— Orlando (South.)	1B	28	111	17	35	11	3	4	23	.315	6	19	2	237	27	3	.989
1994— Orlando (South.)	1B-OF	127	470	54	127	30	6	5	37	.270	37	86	11	1031	80	12	.989
1995— Orlando (South.)	1B-OF	121	446	67	121	27	4	6	53	.271	39	77	8	931	92	10	.990
1996— Iowa (Am. Assoc.)	1B	94	342	48	104	25	3	10	43	.304	19	65	6	762	66	8	.990
— Chicago (N.L.)	1B	29	69	11	21	1	0	5	9	.304	2	17	3	126	17	0	1.000
1997— Chicago (N.L.)	OF-1B	46	137	15	32	7	1	5	15	.234	7	28	2	121	7	2	.985
— Iowa (Am. Assoc.)	OF-1B	71	256	51	77	19	3	16	51	.301	31	44	6	202	13	4	.982
Major league totals (2 years)		75	206	26	53	8	1	10	24	.257	9	45	5	247	24	2	.993

BROWN, DERMAL — OF — ROYALS

PERSONAL: Born March 27, 1978, in Bronx, N.Y. ... 5-11/210. ... Bats left, throws right. ... Full name: Dermal B. Brown.
HIGH SCHOOL: Marlboro Central (Newburgh, N.Y.).
TRANSACTIONS/CAREER NOTES: Selected by Kansas City Royals organization in first round (14th pick overall) of free-agent draft (June 2, 1996).
HONORS: Named Northwest League Most Valuable Player in 1997.
STATISTICAL NOTES: Led Northwest League with 168 total bases and .564 slugging percentage in 1997.

Year Team (League)	Pos.	G	AB	R	H	2B	3B	HR	RBI	Avg.	BB	SO	SB	PO	A	E	Avg.
1996— GC Royals (GCL)	DH	7	20	1	1	1	0	0	1	.050	0	6	0	...	...	...	...
1997— Spokane (N'west)	DH	75	298	67	97	20	6	13	*73	.326	38	65	17	80	2	7	.921

BROWN, EMIL — OF — PIRATES

PERSONAL: Born December 29, 1974, in Chicago. ... 6-2/195. ... Bats right, throws right. ... Full name: Emil Quincy Brown.
HIGH SCHOOL: Harlan (Chicago).
JUNIOR COLLEGE: Indian River Community College (Fla.).
TRANSACTIONS/CAREER NOTES: Selected by Oakland Athletics organization in sixth round of free-agent draft (June 2, 1994). ... On Modesto disabled list (April 10-July 1, 1996). ... On Modesto suspended list (August 29-September 2, 1996). ... Selected by Pittsburgh Pirates organization from A's organization in Rule 5 major league draft (December 9, 1996).
STATISTICAL NOTES: Led Midwest League outfielders with four double plays in 1995.

Year Team (League)	Pos.	G	AB	R	H	2B	3B	HR	RBI	Avg.	BB	SO	SB	PO	A	E	Avg.
1994— Arizona A's (Ariz.)	OF	32	86	13	19	1	1	3	12	.221	13	12	5	43	3	1	.979
1995— W. Mich. (Mid.)	OF	124	459	63	115	17	3	3	67	.251	52	77	35	165	12	8	.957
1996— Modesto (California)	OF	57	211	50	64	10	1	10	47	.303	32	51	13	97	5	4	.962
— Scottsdale (Ariz.)	OF	4	15	5	4	3	0	0	2	.267	3	2	1	3	1	0	1.000
1997— Pittsburgh (N.L.)■	OF	66	95	16	17	2	1	2	6	.179	10	32	5	53	2	3	.948
Major league totals (1 year)		66	95	16	17	2	1	2	6	.179	10	32	5	53	2	3	.948

BROWN, KEVIN — P — PADRES

PERSONAL: Born March 14, 1965, in McIntyre, Ga. ... 6-4/200. ... Throws right, bats right. ... Full name: James Kevin Brown.
HIGH SCHOOL: Wilkinson County (Irwinton, Ga.).
COLLEGE: Georgia Tech.
TRANSACTIONS/CAREER NOTES: Selected by Texas Rangers organization in first round (fourth pick overall) of free-agent draft (June 2, 1986). ... On disabled list (August 14-29, 1990 and March 27-April 11, 1993). ... Granted free agency (October 15, 1994). ... Signed by Baltimore Orioles (April 9, 1995). ... On disabled list (June 23-July 17, 1995). ... Granted free agency (November 3, 1995). ... Signed by Florida Marlins (December 22, 1995). ... On disabled list (May 13-28, 1996). ... Traded by Marlins to San Diego Padres for P Rafael Medina, P Steve Hoff and 1B Derrek Lee (December 15, 1997).
HONORS: Named righthanded pitcher on THE SPORTING NEWS college All-America team (1986).
STATISTICAL NOTES: Tied for A.L. lead with 13 hit batsmen in 1991. ... Tied for N.L. lead with 16 hit batsmen in 1996. ... Pitched 9-0 no-hit victory against San Francisco (June 10, 1997). ... Pitched 5-1 one-hit, complete-game victory against Los Angeles (July 16, 1997). ... Led N.L. with 14 hit batsmen in 1997.
MISCELLANEOUS: Made an out in only appearance as pinch-hitter (1990). ... Appeared in one game as pinch-runner (1993). ... Appeared in two games as pinch-runner (1996). ... Holds Florida Marlins all-time records for most shutouts (5), most strikeouts (364), most complete games (11) and highest winning percentage (.635).

Year Team (League)	W	L	Pct.	ERA	G	GS	CG	ShO	Sv.	IP	H	R	ER	BB	SO
1986— GC Rangers (GCL)	0	0	...	6.00	3	0	0	0	0	6	7	4	4	2	1
— Tulsa (Texas)	0	0	...	4.50	3	2	0	0	0	10	9	7	5	5	10
— Texas (A.L.)	1	0	1.000	3.60	1	1	0	0	0	5	6	2	2	0	4
1987— Tulsa (Texas)	1	4	.200	7.29	8	8	0	0	0	42	53	36	34	18	26
— Oklahoma City (A.A.)	0	5	.000	10.73	5	5	0	0	0	24 1/3	32	32	29	17	9
— Charlotte (Fla. St.)	0	2	.000	2.72	6	6	1	0	0	36 1/3	33	14	11	17	21
1988— Tulsa (Texas)	12	10	.545	3.51	26	26	5	0	0	174 1/3	174	94	68	61	118
— Texas (A.L.)	1	1	.500	4.24	4	4	1	0	0	23 1/3	33	15	11	8	12
1989— Texas (A.L.)	12	9	.571	3.35	28	28	7	0	0	191	167	81	71	70	104
1990— Texas (A.L.)	12	10	.545	3.60	26	26	6	2	0	180	175	84	72	60	88
1991— Texas (A.L.)	9	12	.429	4.40	33	33	0	0	0	210 2/3	233	116	103	90	96
1992— Texas (A.L.)	•21	11	.656	3.32	35	35	11	1	0	*265 2/3	*262	117	98	76	173

B

Year— Team (League)	W	L	Pct.	ERA	G	GS	CG	ShO	Sv.	IP	H	R	ER	BB	SO
1993— Texas (A.L.)	15	12	.556	3.59	34	34	12	3	0	233	228	105	93	74	142
1994— Texas (A.L.)	7	9	.438	4.82	26	•25	3	0	0	170	*218	109	91	50	123
1995— Baltimore (A.L.)■	10	9	.526	3.60	26	26	3	1	0	172 1/3	155	73	69	48	117
1996— Florida (N.L.)■	17	11	.607	*1.89	32	32	5	*3	0	233	187	60	49	33	159
1997— Florida (N.L.)	16	8	.667	2.69	33	33	6	2	0	237 1/3	214	77	71	66	205
A.L. totals (9 years)	88	73	.547	3.78	213	212	43	7	0	1451	1477	702	610	476	859
N.L. totals (2 years)	33	19	.635	2.30	65	65	11	5	0	470 1/3	401	137	120	99	364
Major league totals (11 years)	121	92	.568	3.42	278	277	54	12	0	1921 1/3	1878	839	730	575	1223

DIVISION SERIES RECORD

Year— Team (League)	W	L	Pct.	ERA	G	GS	CG	ShO	Sv.	IP	H	R	ER	BB	SO
1997— Florida (N.L.)	0	0	...	1.29	1	1	0	0	0	7	4	1	1	0	5

CHAMPIONSHIP SERIES RECORD

RECORDS: Shares single-game record for most hits allowed—11 (Otober 14, 1997).

Year— Team (League)	W	L	Pct.	ERA	G	GS	CG	ShO	Sv.	IP	H	R	ER	BB	SO
1997— Atlanta (N.L.)	2	0	1.000	4.20	2	2	1	0	0	15	16	7	7	5	11

WORLD SERIES RECORD

NOTES: Member of World Series championship team (1997).

Year— Team (League)	W	L	Pct.	ERA	G	GS	CG	ShO	Sv.	IP	H	R	ER	BB	SO
1997— Florida (N.L.)	0	2	.000	8.18	2	2	0	0	0	11	15	10	10	5	6

ALL-STAR GAME RECORD

Year— League	W	L	Pct.	ERA	GS	CG	ShO	Sv.	IP	H	R	ER	BB	SO
1992— American	1	0	1.000	0.00	1	0	0	0	1	0	0	0	0	1
1996— National	0	0	...	0.00	0	0	0	0	1	0	0	0	0	0
1997— National	0	0	...	0.00	0	0	0	0	1	1	0	0	0	0
All-Star totals (3 years)	1	0	1.000	0.00	1	0	0	0	3	1	0	0	0	1

BROWN, KEVIN   C   RANGERS

PERSONAL: Born April 21, 1973, in Valparaiso, Ind. ... 6-2/200. ... Bats right, throws right. ... Full name: Kevin Lee Brown.
HIGH SCHOOL: Pike Central (Petersburg, Ind.).
COLLEGE: Southern Indiana.
TRANSACTIONS/CAREER NOTES: Selected by Texas Rangers organization in second round of free-agent draft (June 2, 1994).
STATISTICAL NOTES: Led American Association catchers with .991 fielding percentage and tied for the league lead in double plays with 10 in 1997.

Year— Team (League)	Pos.	G	AB	R	H	2B	3B	HR	RBI	Avg.	BB	SO	SB	PO	A	E	Avg.
1994— Hudson Valley (NYP)	C	68	233	33	57	*19	1	6	32	.245	23	•86	0	316	34	7	.980
1995— Charlotte (Fla. St.)	C-1B	107	355	48	94	25	1	11	57	.265	50	96	2	535	60	9	.985
— Oklahoma City (A.A.)	C	3	10	1	4	1	0	0	0	.400	2	4	0	6	0	2	.750
1996— Tulsa (Texas)	C-1B	128	460	77	121	27	1	26	86	.263	73	*150	1	594	69	13	.981
— Texas (A.L.)	C-DH	4	4	1	0	0	0	0	1	.000	2	2	0	11	1	0	1.000
1997— Oklahoma City (A.A.)	C-1B	116	403	56	97	18	2	19	50	.241	38	111	2	640	62	5	†.993
— Texas (A.L.)	C	4	5	1	2	0	0	1	1	.400	0	0	0	9	0	1	.900
Major league totals (2 years)		7	9	2	2	0	0	1	2	.222	2	2	0	20	1	1	.955

BROWNSON, MARK   P   ROCKIES

PERSONAL: Born June 17, 1975, in Lake Worth, Fla. ... 6-2/180. ... Throws right, bats left. ... Full name: Mark Phillip Brownson.
HIGH SCHOOL: Wellington (West Palm Beach, Fla.).
JUNIOR COLLEGE: Palm Beach Community College (Fla.).
TRANSACTIONS/CAREER NOTES: Selected by Colorado Rockies organization in 30th round of free-agent draft (June 3, 1993).
STATISTICAL NOTES: Led Eastern league with 14 hit batsmen in 1997.

Year— Team (League)	W	L	Pct.	ERA	G	GS	CG	ShO	Sv.	IP	H	R	ER	BB	SO
1994— Ariz. Rockies (Ariz.)	4	1	.800	1.66	19	4	0	0	3	54 1/3	48	18	10	6	72
1995— Asheville (S. Atl.)	6	7	.462	4.01	23	12	0	0	1	98 2/3	106	52	44	29	94
1996— New Haven (Eastern)	8	13	.381	3.50	37	19	1	0	3	144	141	73	56	43	155
— Salem (Carolina)	2	1	.667	4.02	9	1	0	0	1	15 2/3	16	8	7	10	9
1997— Nashville (Eastern)	10	9	.526	4.19	29	•29	2	0	0	*184 2/3	172	101	86	55	170

BRUMFIELD, JACOB   OF   BLUE JAYS

PERSONAL: Born May 27, 1965, in Bogalusa, La. ... 6-0/186. ... Bats right, throws right. ... Full name: Jacob Donnell Brumfield.
HIGH SCHOOL: Hammond (La.).
TRANSACTIONS/CAREER NOTES: Selected by Chicago Cubs organization in seventh round of free-agent draft (June 6, 1983). ... On disabled list (June 21, 1984-remainder of season). ... Released by Cubs organization (April 9, 1985). ... Signed by Kansas City Royals organization (August 16, 1986). ... Granted free agency (October 15, 1991). ... Signed by Cincinnati Reds organization (November 12, 1991). ... On Nashville disabled list (June 12-July 25, 1992). ... Traded by Reds to Pittsburgh Pirates for OF Danny Clyburn (October 13, 1994). ... On Pittsburgh disabled list (May 19-June 3, 1995); included rehabilitation assignment to Carolina (May 29-June 1). ... Traded by Pittsburgh Pirates to Toronto Blue Jays for 1B D.J. Boston (May 15, 1996). ... On disabled list (March 24-April 16, 1997); included rehabilitation assignment to Dunedin (April 7-16). ... Granted free agency (October 6, 1997). ... Re-signed by Blue Jays organization (January 5, 1998).
STATISTICAL NOTES: Led Florida State League with .429 on-base percentage in 1990. ... Led American Association in caught stealing with 16 in 1991.

Year— Team (League)	Pos.	G	AB	R	H	2B	3B	HR	RBI	Avg.	BB	SO	SB	PO	A	E	Avg.
1983— Pikeville (Appal.)	OF	42	113	17	29	0	1	3	15	.257	25	34	8	34	3	5	.881
1984—							Did not play.										
1985—							Did not play.										

Year	Team (League)	Pos.	G	AB	R	H	2B	3B	HR	RBI	Avg.	BB	SO	SB	PO	A	E	Avg.
									BATTING						FIELDING			
1986—Fort Myers (FSL)■.....		SS	12	41	3	13	3	1	1	5	.317	2	11	0	18	16	8	.810
1987—Fort Myers (FSL)........		OF-3B	114	379	56	93	14	*10	6	34	.245	45	78	43	235	53	19	.938
—Memphis (Southern)..		OF	9	39	7	13	3	2	1	6	.333	3	8	2	35	0	2	.946
1988—Memphis (Southern)..		OF	128	433	70	98	15	5	6	28	.226	52	104	47	239	2	6	.976
1989—Memphis (Southern)..		OF	104	346	43	79	14	2	1	25	.228	53	74	28	217	2	8	.965
1990—Baseball City (FSL).....		OF	109	372	66	125	24	3	0	40	*.336	60	44	47	186	*17	8	.962
—Omaha (A.A.)..............		OF	24	77	10	25	6	1	2	11	.325	7	14	10	45	3	0	1.000
1991—Omaha (A.A.).............		OF	111	397	62	106	14	7	3	43	.267	33	64	*36	227	10	2	.992
1992—Cincinnati (N.L.)■.....		OF	24	30	6	4	0	0	0	2	.133	2	4	6	20	1	0	1.000
—Nashville (A.A.)		OF	56	208	32	59	10	3	5	19	.284	26	35	22	137	4	6	.959
1993—Indianapolis (A.A.).....		OF	33	126	23	41	14	1	4	19	.325	6	14	11	74	4	4	.951
—Cincinnati (N.L.)........		OF-2B	103	272	40	73	17	3	6	23	.268	21	47	20	178	16	7	.965
1994—Cincinnati (N.L.)........		OF	68	122	36	38	10	2	4	11	.311	15	18	6	74	1	1	.987
1995—Pittsburgh (N.L.)■......		OF	116	402	64	109	23	2	4	26	.271	37	71	22	241	8	8	.969
—Carolina (Southern)....		OF	3	12	2	5	0	0	2	2	.417	1	2	0	9	0	0	1.000
1996—Pittsburgh (N.L.)		OF	29	80	11	20	9	0	2	8	.250	5	17	3	34	1	2	.946
—Toronto (A.L.).............		OF-DH	90	308	52	79	19	2	12	52	.256	24	58	12	159	8	3	.982
1997—Dunedin (Fla. St.)		OF	6	25	2	4	0	0	0	2	.160	0	6	1	7	2	1	.900
—Toronto (A.L.).............		OF-DH	58	174	22	36	5	1	2	20	.207	14	31	4	87	6	0	1.000
American League totals (2 years)			148	482	74	115	24	3	14	72	.239	38	89	16	246	14	3	.989
National League totals (5 years)			340	906	157	244	59	7	16	70	.269	80	157	57	547	27	18	.970
Major league totals (6 years)			488	1388	231	359	83	10	30	142	.259	118	246	73	793	41	21	.975

BRUNSON, WILL — P — DODGERS

PERSONAL: Born March 20, 1970, in Irving, Texas. ... 6-6/185. ... Throws left, bats left. ... Full name: William Donald Brunson.
HIGH SCHOOL: DeSoto (Texas).
COLLEGE: Southwest Texas State.
TRANSACTIONS/CAREER NOTES: Selected by Cincinnati Reds organization in 21st round of free-agent draft (June 1, 1992). ... Traded by Reds to Los Angeles Dodgers organization for P Ben VanRyn (December 16, 1994).

Year	Team (League)	W	L	Pct.	ERA	G	GS	CG	ShO	Sv.	IP	H	R	ER	BB	SO
1992—Princeton (Appalachian).....		5	5	.500	3.59	13	13	0	0	0	72²/₃	66	34	29	28	48
1993—Char., W.Va. (S. Atl.)		5	6	.455	3.93	37	15	0	0	0	123²/₃	119	68	54	50	103
1994—Win.-Salem (Car.)		12	7	.632	3.98	30	22	3	0	0	165	161	83	73	58	129
1995—San Bernardino (Calif.)■.....		10	0	1.000	2.05	13	13	0	0	0	83¹/₃	68	24	19	21	70
—San Antonio (Tex.)		4	5	.444	4.95	14	14	0	0	0	80	105	46	44	22	44
1996—San Antonio (Tex.)		3	1	.750	2.14	11	5	0	0	0	42	32	13	10	15	38
—Albuquerque (PCL)		3	4	.429	4.47	9	9	1	0	0	54¹/₃	53	29	27	23	47
1997—Albuquerque (PCL)		1	1	.500	6.49	27	0	0	0	0	26¹/₃	39	19	19	10	25
—San Antonio (Tex.)		5	5	.500	3.47	17	11	2	•1	0	72²/₃	68	30	28	13	71

BRUSKE, JIM — P — DODGERS

PERSONAL: Born October 7, 1964, in East St. Louis, Ill. ... 6-1/185. ... Throws right, bats right. ... Full name: James Scott Bruske.
HIGH SCHOOL: Palmdale (Calif.).
JUNIOR COLLEGE: Antelope Valley (Calif.).
COLLEGE: Loyola Marymount.
TRANSACTIONS/CAREER NOTES: Selected by San Diego Padres organization in seventh round of free-agent draft (January 9, 1985); did not sign. ... Selected by Seattle Mariners organization in third round of secondary phase of free-agent draft (June 3, 1985); did not sign. ... Selected by Cleveland Indians organization in first round (sixth player selected) of secondary phase of free-agent draft (June 2, 1986). ... On Canton-Akron disabled list (May 8-25, 1991). ... On Colorado Springs disabled list (May 7-June 9, 1992). ... Released by Indians organization (June 9, 1992). ... Signed by Houston Astros organization (June 22, 1992). ... On disabled list (May 7-30 and June 9-October 12, 1994). ... Granted free agency (October 15, 1994). ... Signed by Los Angeles Dodgers organization (January 18, 1995). ... On Albuquerque disabled list (May 3-11, 1995). ... Granted free agency (October 16, 1995). ... Re-signed by Dodgers organization (November 12, 1995). ... On Albuquerque disabled list (May 25-June 20, 1996). ... Granted free agency (October 15, 1996). ... On disabled list (August 6-25, 1997). ... Claimed on waivers by Dodgers (October 6, 1997).
MISCELLANEOUS: Struck out in only appearance as pinch-hitter (1997).

Year	Team (League)	W	L	Pct.	ERA	G	GS	CG	ShO	Sv.	IP	H	R	ER	BB	SO
1986—Batavia (N.Y.-Penn)		0	0	. . .	18.00	1	0	0	0	0	1	1	2	2	3	3
1989—Cant./Akr. (Eastern)		0	0	. . .	13.50	2	0	0	0	0	2	3	3	3	2	1
1990—Cant./Akr. (Eastern)		9	3	.750	3.28	32	13	3	2	0	118	118	53	43	42	62
1991—Cant./Akr. (Eastern)		5	2	.714	3.47	17	11	0	0	1	80¹/₃	73	36	31	27	35
—Colo. Springs (PCL)		4	0	1.000	2.45	7	1	0	0	2	25²/₃	19	9	7	8	13
1992—Colo. Springs (PCL)		2	0	1.000	4.58	7	0	0	0	10	17²/₃	24	11	9	6	8
—Jackson (Texas)■		4	3	.571	2.63	13	9	1	0	0	61²/₃	54	23	18	14	48
1993—Jackson (Texas)		9	5	.643	2.31	15	15	1	0	0	97¹/₃	86	34	25	22	83
—Tucson (PCL)		4	2	.667	3.78	12	9	0	0	1	66²/₃	77	36	28	18	42
1994—Tucson (PCL)		3	1	.750	4.15	7	7	0	0	0	39	47	22	18	8	25
1995—Los Angeles (N.L.)■		0	0	. . .	4.50	9	0	0	0	0	10	12	7	5	4	5
—Albuquerque (PCL)		7	5	.583	4.11	43	6	0	0	4	114	128	54	52	41	99
1996—Albuquerque (PCL)		5	2	.714	4.06	36	0	0	0	4	62	63	34	28	21	51
—Los Angeles (N.L.)		0	0	. . .	5.68	11	0	0	0	0	12²/₃	17	8	8	3	12
1997—Las Vegas (PCL)		5	4	.556	4.90	16	9	0	0	0	68	73	41	37	22	67
—San Diego (N.L.)		4	1	.800	3.63	28	0	0	0	0	44²/₃	37	22	18	25	32
Major league totals (3 years)......		4	1	.800	4.14	48	0	0	0	0	67¹/₃	66	37	31	32	49

Year Team (League)	Pos.	G	AB	R	H	2B	3B	HR	RBI	Avg.	BB	SO	SB	PO	A	E	Avg.
1986—Batavia (NY-Penn)......	OF-P	56	181	23	44	2	2	3	14	.243	21	50	7	85	4	5	.947
1987—Kinston (Carolina)......	OF	123	439	62	102	16	3	7	61	.232	65	118	17	188	7	10	.951
1988—Williamsport (East.)...	OF	135	443	49	105	12	3	1	44	.237	45	*138	16	238	11	4	.984
1989—Kinston (Carolina)......	OF	63	217	29	63	12	1	5	36	.290	34	44	13	114	2	2	.983
—Cant./Akr. (Eastern)....	OF-P-SS	51	134	17	32	5	0	1	7	.239	19	28	3	75	4	0	1.000

BRYANT, PAT — OF — RED SOX

PERSONAL: Born October 27, 1972, in Lexington, Ky. ... 5-11/180. ... Bats right, throws right. ... Full name: Patrick Antonio Bryant.
HIGH SCHOOL: Grover Cleveland (Reseda, Calif.).
TRANSACTIONS/CAREER NOTES: Selected by Cleveland Indians organization in second round of free-agent draft (June 4, 1990). ... On disabled list (July 22, 1993-remainder of season). ... On Buffalo disabled list (April 4-14 and August 31, 1996-remainder of season). ... On Canton-Akron disabled list (June 3-July 6, 1996). ... Granted free-agency (October 15, 1996). ... Signed by Boston Red Sox organization (March 30, 1997). ... Released by Red Sox (December 15, 1997). ... Re-signed by Red Sox organization (December 19, 1997).
STATISTICAL NOTES: Led Eastern League outfielders with 318 total chances in 1995.

Year Team (League)	Pos.	G	AB	R	H	2B	3B	HR	RBI	Avg.	BB	SO	SB	PO	A	E	Avg.
1990—Burlington (Appal.)......	OF	17	50	3	5	0	0	1	2	.100	7	23	5	16	1	5	.773
—GC Indians (GCL).......	OF	17	53	3	10	2	0	0	3	.189	8	18	2	25	1	1	.963
1991—Columbus (S. Atl.)......	OF	100	326	51	68	11	0	7	27	.209	49	108	31	130	9	11	.927
1992—Columbus (S. Atl.)......	OF	49	151	36	33	14	2	2	19	.219	30	52	10	69	5	5	.937
—Watertown (NYP)......	OF	63	220	41	58	13	1	7	30	.264	33	61	35	72	7	7	.919
1993—Columbus (S. Atl.)......	OF	121	483	82	127	26	2	16	61	.263	43	117	43	185	11	8	.961
1994—Cant./Akr. (Eastern)...	OF	124	377	61	89	14	2	12	53	.236	48	87	23	236	8	8	.968
1995—Cant./Akr. (Eastern)...	OF	127	421	60	109	22	3	17	59	.259	52	116	16	*302	8	8	.975
1996—Cant./Akr. (Eastern)...	OF	34	109	13	21	2	1	3	17	.193	17	24	8	47	1	1	.980
—Buffalo (A.A.)........	OF	27	64	6	11	1	0	0	0	.172	5	20	0	45	2	1	.979
1997—Trenton (Eastern)■...	OF	104	379	73	109	20	3	19	77	.288	60	76	18	197	6	3	.985
—Pawtucket (Int'l)........	OF	9	34	3	10	2	1	0	4	.294	1	11	2	15	0	2	.882

BUCHANAN, BRIAN — OF — YANKEES

PERSONAL: Born July 21, 1973, in Miami. ... 6-4/220. ... Bats right, throws right. ... Full name: Brian James Buchanan.
HIGH SCHOOL: Fairfax (Va.).
COLLEGE: Virginia.
TRANSACTIONS/CAREER NOTES: Selected by New York Yankees organization in first round (24th pick overall) of free-agent draft (June 2, 1994). ... On disabled list (April 29, 1995 through remainder of season).

Year Team (League)	Pos.	G	AB	R	H	2B	3B	HR	RBI	Avg.	BB	SO	SB	PO	A	E	Avg.
1994—Oneonta (NYP)..........	OF	50	177	28	40	9	2	4	26	.226	24	53	5	87	2	0	1.000
1995—Greensboro (S. Atl.)...	OF	23	96	19	29	3	0	3	12	.302	9	17	7	31	1	1	.970
1996—Tampa (Florida State).	OF	131	526	65	137	22	4	10	58	.260	37	108	23	178	11	6	.969
1997—Norwich (Eastern)......	OF	116	470	75	145	25	2	10	69	.309	32	85	11	192	11	8	.962
—Columbus (Int'l)........	OF	18	61	8	17	1	0	4	7	.279	4	11	2	17	1	1	.947

BUDDIE, MIKE — P — YANKEES

PERSONAL: Born December 12, 1970, in Cleveland. ... 6-3/210. ... Throws right, bats right. ... Full name: Michael J. Buddie.
HIGH SCHOOL: St. Ignatius (Cleveland).
COLLEGE: Wake Forest.
TRANSACTIONS/CAREER NOTES: Selected by New York Yankees organization in fourth round of free-agent draft (June 1, 1992).

Year Team (League)	W	L	Pct.	ERA	G	GS	CG	ShO	Sv.	IP	H	R	ER	BB	SO
1992—Oneonta (N.Y.-Penn).........	1	4	.200	3.88	13	13	1	0	0	67 1/3	69	36	29	34	87
1993—Greensboro (S. Atl.).........	13	10	.565	4.87	27	26	0	0	0	155 1/3	138	104	84	89	143
1994—Tampa (Florida State).........	12	5	.706	4.01	25	24	2	0	0	150 1/3	143	75	67	66	113
1995—Norwich (Eastern)............	10	12	.455	4.81	29	27	2	0	1	149 2/3	155	*102	80	81	106
1996—Norwich (Eastern).............	7	•12	.368	4.45	29	26	4	0	0	159 2/3	176	101	79	71	103
1997—Norwich (Eastern).............	0	0	. . .	0.00	1	0	0	0	0	1	0	0	0	0	3
—Columbus (Int'l)................	6	6	.500	2.64	53	0	0	0	13	75	85	24	22	25	67

BUFORD, DAMON — OF — RED SOX

PERSONAL: Born June 12, 1970, in Baltimore. ... 5-10/170. ... Bats right, throws right. ... Full name: Damon Jackson Buford. ... Son of Don Buford, outfielder, Chicago White Sox and Orioles (1963-72); and brother of Don Buford Jr., minor league infielder (1987-89).
HIGH SCHOOL: Birmingham (Calif.).
COLLEGE: Southern California.
TRANSACTIONS/CAREER NOTES: Selected by Baltimore Orioles organization in 10th round of free-agent draft (June 4, 1990). ... Traded by Orioles with OF Alex Ochoa to New York Mets for 3B/OF Bobby Bonilla and a player to be named later (July 28, 1995); Orioles acquired P Jimmy Williams to complete deal (August 17, 1995). ... Traded by Mets to Texas Rangers for OF Terrell Lowery (January 25, 1996). ... Traded by Rangers with C Jim Leyritz to Boston Red Sox for P Aaron Sele, P Mark Brandenburg and C Bill Haselman (November 6, 1997).
STATISTICAL NOTES: Led Eastern League outfielders with 279 total chances in 1992. ... Led International League outfielders with 347 total chances in 1994. ... Career major league grand slams: 1.

Year	Team (League)	Pos.	G	AB	R	H	2B	3B	HR	RBI	Avg.	BB	SO	SB	PO	A	E	Avg.
1990—	Wausau (Midwest)	OF	41	160	31	48	7	2	1	14	.300	21	32	15	89	2	2	.978
1991—	Frederick (Carolina)....	OF	133	505	71	138	25	6	8	54	.273	51	92	50	293	7	5	.984
1992—	Hagerstown (Eastern)	OF	101	373	53	89	17	3	1	30	.239	42	62	41	*264	13	2	.993
—	Rochester (Int'l)	OF	45	155	29	44	10	2	1	12	.284	14	23	23	100	1	3	.971
1993—	Rochester (Int'l)	OF	27	116	24	33	6	1	1	4	.284	7	16	10	73	3	3	.962
—	Baltimore (A.L.)	OF-DH	53	79	18	18	5	0	2	9	.228	9	19	2	61	2	1	.984
1994—	Baltimore (A.L.)	DH-OF	4	2	2	1	0	0	0	0	.500	0	1	0	0	0	0	...
—	Rochester (Int'l)	OF	111	452	*89	122	21	4	16	66	.270	35	81	31	*339	4	4	.988
1995—	Baltimore (A.L.)	OF	24	32	6	2	0	0	0	2	.063	6	7	3	40	0	0	1.000
—	Rochester (Int'l)	OF	46	188	40	58	12	3	4	18	.309	17	26	17	115	2	2	.983
—	New York (N.L.)■	OF	44	136	24	32	5	0	4	12	.235	19	28	7	67	2	2	.972
1996—	Texas (A.L.)■..............	OF-DH	90	145	30	41	9	0	6	20	.283	15	34	8	93	3	0	1.000
1997—	Texas (A.L.)	OF-DH	122	366	49	82	18	0	8	39	.224	30	83	18	282	7	3	.990
	American League totals (5 years)		293	624	105	144	32	0	16	70	.231	60	144	31	476	12	4	.992
	National League totals (1 year)		44	136	24	32	5	0	4	12	.235	19	28	7	67	2	2	.972
	Major league totals (5 years)		337	760	129	176	37	0	20	82	.232	79	172	38	543	14	6	.989

DIVISION SERIES RECORD

						BATTING								FIELDING			
Year	Team (League)	Pos.	G	AB	R	H	2B	3B	HR	RBI	Avg.	BB	SO	SB	PO	A	E	Avg.
1996—	Texas (A.L.)	PR	2	0	0	0	0	0	0	0	...	0	0	0	0	0	0	...

B

BUHNER, JAY OF MARINERS

PERSONAL: Born August 13, 1964, in Louisville, Ky. ... 6-3/210. ... Bats right, throws right. ... Full name: Jay Campbell Buhner. ... Brother of Shawn Buhner, infielder, Mariners organization. ... Name pronounced BYOO-ner.

HIGH SCHOOL: Clear Creek (League City, Texas).

JUNIOR COLLEGE: McLennan Community College (Texas).

TRANSACTIONS/CAREER NOTES: Selected by Atlanta Braves organization in ninth round of free-agent draft (June 6, 1983); did not sign. ... Selected by Pittsburgh Pirates organization in secondary phase of free-agent draft (January 17, 1984). ... Traded by Pirates organization with IF Dale Berra and P Alfonso Pulido to New York Yankees for OF Steve Kemp, IF Tim Foli and cash (December 20, 1984). ... On disabled list (April 11-July 28, 1986). ... Traded by Yankees with P Rich Balabon and a player to be named later to Seattle Mariners for DH Ken Phelps (July 21, 1988; Mariners acquired P Troy Evers to complete deal (October 12, 1988). ... On Seattle disabled list (June 29-August 19, 1989); included rehabilitation assignment to Calgary (August 16-19). ... On Seattle disabled list (March 31-June 1, 1990); included rehabilitation assignment to Calgary (May 18-June 1). ... On Seattle disabled list (June 17-August 23, 1990). ... Granted free agency (October 28, 1994). ... Re-signed by Mariners (December 21, 1994). ... On disabled list (June 6-22, 1995).

RECORDS: Shares major league records for most strikeouts in two consecutive nine-inning games—8 (August 23-24, 1990); and most strikeouts in three consecutive games—10 (August 23-25, 1990).

HONORS: Won A.L. Gold Glove as outfielder (1996).

STATISTICAL NOTES: Tied for International League lead in double plays by outfielder with six in 1987. ... Hit for the cycle (June 23, 1993). ... Career major league grand slams: 7.

						BATTING								FIELDING			
Year	Team (League)	Pos.	G	AB	R	H	2B	3B	HR	RBI	Avg.	BB	SO	SB	PO	A	E	Avg.
1984—	Watertown (NYP)	OF	65	229	43	74	16	3	9	•58	.323	42	58	3	106	8	1	.991
1985—	Fort Laud. (FSL)■......	OF	117	409	65	121	18	10	11	76	.296	65	76	6	235	12	7	.972
1986—	Fort Lauderdale (FSL)	OF	36	139	24	42	9	1	7	31	.302	15	30	1	84	7	3	.968
1987—	Columbus (Int'l)	OF	134	502	83	140	23	1	*31	85	.279	55	124	4	275	*20	6	.980
—	New York (A.L.)	OF	7	22	0	5	2	0	0	1	.227	1	6	0	11	1	0	1.000
1988—	Columbus (Int'l)	OF	38	129	26	33	5	0	8	18	.256	19	33	1	83	3	1	.989
—	New York (A.L.)..........	OF	25	69	8	13	0	0	3	13	.188	3	25	0	52	2	2	.964
—	Seattle (A.L.)■............	OF	60	192	28	43	13	1	10	25	.224	25	68	1	134	7	1	.993
1989—	Calgary (PCL).............	OF	56	196	43	61	12	1	11	45	.311	44	56	4	97	8	2	.981
—	Seattle (A.L.)	OF	58	204	27	56	15	1	9	33	.275	19	55	1	106	6	4	.966
1990—	Calgary (PCL).............	OF	13	34	6	7	1	0	2	5	.206	7	11	0	14	1	0	1.000
—	Seattle (A.L.)	OF-DH	51	163	16	45	12	0	7	33	.276	17	50	2	55	1	2	.966
1991—	Seattle (A.L.)	OF	137	406	64	99	14	4	27	77	.244	53	117	0	244	15	5	.981
1992—	Seattle (A.L.)	OF	152	543	69	132	16	3	25	79	.243	71	146	0	314	14	2	.994
1993—	Seattle (A.L.)	OF-DH	158	563	91	153	28	3	27	98	.272	100	144	2	263	8	6	.978
1994—	Seattle (A.L.)	OF-DH	101	358	74	100	23	4	21	68	.279	66	63	0	178	11	2	.990
1995—	Seattle (A.L.)	OF-DH	126	470	86	123	23	0	40	121	.262	60	120	0	180	5	2	.989
1996—	Seattle (A.L.)	OF-DH	150	564	107	153	29	0	44	138	.271	84	*159	0	251	9	3	.989
1997—	Seattle (A.L.)	OF-DH	157	540	104	131	18	2	40	109	.243	119	*175	0	295	5	1	*.997
	Major league totals (11 years)		1182	4094	674	1053	193	18	253	795	.257	618	1128	6	2083	84	30	.986

DIVISION SERIES RECORD

						BATTING								FIELDING			
Year	Team (League)	Pos.	G	AB	R	H	2B	3B	HR	RBI	Avg.	BB	SO	SB	PO	A	E	Avg.
1995—	Seattle (A.L.)	OF	5	24	2	11	1	0	1	3	.458	2	4	0	11	1	0	1.000
1997—	Seattle (A.L.)	OF	4	13	2	3	0	0	2	2	.231	3	6	0	5	1	0	1.000
	Division series totals (2 years)		9	37	4	14	1	0	3	5	.378	5	10	0	16	2	0	1.000

CHAMPIONSHIP SERIES RECORD

RECORDS: Shares A.L. single-series record for most home runs—3 (1995); and most strikeouts—8 (1995).

						BATTING								FIELDING			
Year	Team (League)	Pos.	G	AB	R	H	2B	3B	HR	RBI	Avg.	BB	SO	SB	PO	A	E	Avg.
1995—	Seattle (A.L.)	OF	6	23	5	7	2	0	3	5	.304	2	8	0	15	0	1	.938

Year League	Pos.	AB	R	H	2B	3B	HR	RBI	Avg.	BB	SO	SB	PO	A	E	Avg.
1996— American	OF	2	0	0	0	0	0	0	.000	0	0	0	1	0	0	1.000

BULLINGER, JIM — P — WHITE SOX

PERSONAL: Born August 21, 1965, in New Orleans. ... 6-2/185. ... Throws right, bats right. ... Full name: James Eric Bullinger. ... Name pronounced BULL-in-jer.
HIGH SCHOOL: Archbishop Rummel (Metairie, La.).
COLLEGE: New Orleans.
TRANSACTIONS/CAREER NOTES: Selected by Chicago Cubs organization in ninth round of free-agent draft (June 2, 1986). ... On Iowa disabled list (August 5-21, 1993). ... On Chicago disabled list (May 21-June 22, 1995); included rehabilitation assignment to Orlando (June 13-18). ... Granted free agency (December 20, 1996). ... Signed by Montreal Expos (January 16, 1997). ... Granted free agency (October 6, 1997). ... Signed by Chicago White Sox organization (January 9, 1998).
STATISTICAL NOTES: Led Carolina League shortstops with 92 double plays in 1987. ... Hit home run in first major league at-bat (June 8, 1992, first game). ... Pitched 3-1 one-hit, complete-game victory for Chicago against San Francisco (August 30, 1992).
MISCELLANEOUS: Struck out in only appearance as pinch-hitter with Chicago (1995). ... Appeared in one game as pinch-runner (1996).

Year Team (League)	W	L	Pct.	ERA	G	GS	CG	ShO	Sv.	IP	H	R	ER	BB	SO
1989— Charlotte (Southern)	0	0	...	0.00	2	0	0	0	0	3	3	0	0	3	5
1990— Win.-Salem (Car.)	7	6	.538	3.70	14	13	3	0	0	90	81	43	37	46	85
—Charlotte (Southern)	3	4	.429	5.11	9	9	0	0	0	44	42	30	25	18	33
1991— Iowa (Am. Assoc.)	3	4	.429	5.40	8	8	0	0	0	46 2/3	47	32	28	23	30
—Charlotte (Southern)	9	9	.500	3.53	20	20	•8	0	0	142 2/3	132	62	56	61	128
1992— Iowa (Am. Assoc.)	1	2	.333	2.45	20	0	0	0	14	22	17	6	6	12	15
—Chicago (N.L.)	2	8	.200	4.66	39	9	1	0	7	85	72	49	44	54	36
1993— Iowa (Am. Assoc.)	4	6	.400	3.42	49	3	0	0	20	73 2/3	64	29	28	43	74
—Chicago (N.L.)	1	0	1.000	4.32	15	0	0	0	1	16 2/3	18	9	8	9	10
1994— Chicago (N.L.)	6	2	.750	3.60	33	10	1	0	2	100	87	43	40	34	72
1995— Chicago (N.L.)	12	8	.600	4.14	24	24	1	1	0	150	152	80	69	65	93
—Orlando (South.)	0	0	...	0.00	1	1	0	0	0	4	3	0	0	1	2
1996— Chicago (N.L.)	6	10	.375	6.54	37	20	1	1	1	129 1/3	144	101	94	68	90
1997— Montreal (N.L.)■	7	12	.368	5.56	36	25	2	2	0	155 1/3	165	106	96	74	87
Major league totals (6 years)	34	40	.459	4.96	184	88	6	4	11	636 1/3	638	388	351	304	388

RECORD AS POSITION PLAYER

Year Team (League)	Pos.	G	AB	R	H	2B	3B	HR	RBI	Avg.	BB	SO	SB	PO	A	E	Avg.
1986— Geneva (NY-Penn)	SS	*78	248	35	61	•16	1	3	33	.246	*48	50	7	104	207	26	.923
1987— Win.-Salem (Car.)	SS	129	437	58	112	12	3	9	48	.256	50	79	3	210	383	28	.955
1988— Pittsfield (Eastern)	SS	88	242	21	41	6	1	3	33	.169	25	53	1	129	256	21	.948
—Win.-Salem (Car.)	SS	32	104	13	20	4	2	1	11	.192	13	26	4	49	80	11	.921
1989— Charlotte (Southern)	SS-3B	124	320	34	69	13	1	3	28	.216	39	56	3	188	281	26	.947

BURBA, DAVE — P — REDS

PERSONAL: Born July 7, 1966, in Dayton, Ohio. ... 6-4/240. ... Throws right, bats right. ... Full name: David Allen Burba. ... Nephew of Ray Hathaway, pitcher, Brooklyn Dodgers (1945).
HIGH SCHOOL: Kenton Ridge (Springfield, Ohio).
COLLEGE: Ohio State.
TRANSACTIONS/CAREER NOTES: Selected by Seattle Mariners organization in second round of free-agent draft (June 2, 1987). ... Traded by Mariners with P Bill Swift and P Mike Jackson to San Francisco Giants for OF Kevin Mitchell and P Mike Remlinger (December 11, 1991). ... Traded by Giants with OF Darren Lewis and P Mark Portugal to Cincinnati Reds for OF Deion Sanders, P John Roper, P Ricky Pickett, P Scott Service and IF Dave McCarty (July 21, 1995). ... On disabled list (August 7-27, 1997).

Year Team (League)	W	L	Pct.	ERA	G	GS	CG	ShO	Sv.	IP	H	R	ER	BB	SO
1987— Bellingham (N'west)	3	1	.750	1.93	5	5	0	0	0	23 1/3	20	10	5	3	24
—Salinas (Calif.)	1	6	.143	4.61	9	9	0	0	0	54 2/3	53	31	28	29	46
1988— San Bernardino (Calif.)	5	7	.417	2.68	20	20	0	0	0	114	106	41	34	54	102
1989— Williamsport (Eastern)	11	7	.611	3.16	25	25	5	1	0	156 1/3	138	69	55	55	89
1990— Calgary (PCL)	10	6	.625	4.67	31	18	1	0	2	113 2/3	124	64	59	45	47
—Seattle (A.L.)	0	0	...	4.50	6	0	0	0	0	8	8	6	4	2	4
1991— Calgary (PCL)	6	4	.600	3.53	23	9	0	0	4	71 1/3	82	35	28	27	42
—Seattle (A.L.)	2	2	.500	3.68	22	2	0	0	1	36 2/3	34	16	15	14	16
1992— San Francisco (N.L.)■	2	7	.222	4.97	23	11	0	0	0	70 2/3	80	43	39	31	47
—Phoenix (PCL)	5	5	.500	4.72	13	13	0	0	0	74 1/3	86	40	39	24	44
1993— San Francisco (N.L.)	10	3	.769	4.25	54	5	0	0	0	95 1/3	95	49	45	37	88
1994— San Francisco (N.L.)	3	6	.333	4.38	57	0	0	0	0	74	59	39	36	45	84
1995— San Francisco (N.L.)	4	2	.667	4.98	37	0	0	0	0	43 1/3	38	26	24	25	46
—Cincinnati (N.L.)■	6	2	.750	3.27	15	9	1	1	0	63 1/3	52	24	23	26	50
1996— Cincinnati (N.L.)	11	13	.458	3.83	34	33	0	0	0	195	179	96	83	97	148
1997— Cincinnati (N.L.)	11	10	.524	4.73	30	27	2	0	0	160	157	88	84	73	131
A.L. totals (2 years)	2	2	.500	3.83	28	2	0	0	1	44 2/3	42	22	19	16	20
N.L. totals (6 years)	47	43	.522	4.28	250	85	3	1	0	701 1/3	660	365	334	334	594
Major league totals (8 years)	49	45	.521	4.26	278	87	3	1	1	746 1/3	702	387	353	350	614

DIVISION SERIES RECORD

Year Team (League)	W	L	Pct.	ERA	G	GS	CG	ShO	Sv.	IP	H	R	ER	BB	SO
1995— Cincinnati (N.L.)	1	0	1.000	0.00	1	0	0	0	0	1	2	0	0	1	0

CHAMPIONSHIP SERIES RECORD

Year Team (League)	W	L	Pct.	ERA	G	GS	CG	ShO	Sv.	IP	H	R	ER	BB	SO
1995— Cincinnati (N.L.)	0	0	...	0.00	2	0	0	0	0	3 2/3	3	0	0	4	0

BURGER, ROB　　　　　　　P　　　　　　　PHILLIES

PERSONAL: Born March 25, 1976, in Lancaster, Pa. ... 6-1/175. ... Throws right, ... Full name: Robert Paul Burger.
HIGH SCHOOL: Lampeter-Strasburg (Lampeter, Pa.).
TRANSACTIONS/CAREER NOTES: Selected by Philadelphia Phillies organization in 10th round of free-agent draft (June 2, 1994). ... On disabled list (April 6-July 20, 1995).
STATISTICAL NOTES: Pitched 1-0 no-hit victory against Augusta (April 30, 1996).

Year	Team (League)	W	L	Pct.	ERA	G	GS	CG	ShO	Sv.	IP	H	R	ER	BB	SO
1994—	Martinsville (App.)	1	1	.500	5.68	7	5	0	0	0	19	20	13	12	8	30
1995—	Martinsville (App.)	2	4	.333	4.65	9	9	0	0	0	40²/₃	47	25	21	23	54
1996—	Piedmont (S. Atl.)	10	12	.455	3.38	27	26	2	2	0	160	129	74	60	61	171
1997—	Clearwater (Fla. St.)	11	9	.550	3.59	28	27	1	1	0	160²/₃	131	79	64	*93	*154

BURKE, JOHN　　　　　　　P　　　　　　　ROCKIES

PERSONAL: Born February 9, 1970, in Durango, Colo. ... 6-4/215. ... Throws right, bats both. ... Full name: John C. Burke.
HIGH SCHOOL: Cherry Creek (Englewood, Colo.).
COLLEGE: Florida.
TRANSACTIONS/CAREER NOTES: Selected by Baltimore Orioles organization in 34th round of free-agent draft (June 5, 1989); did not sign. ... Selected by Houston Astros organization in first round (sixth pick overall) of free-agent draft (June 3, 1991); did not sign. ... Selected by Colorado Rockies organization in first round (27th pick overall) of free-agent draft (June 1, 1992). ... On Colorado Springs disabled list (April 7-June 22, 1994 and August 8-September 9, 1997). ... On disabled list (July 3-August 1 and August 20, 1995-remainder of season).
MISCELLANEOUS: Received a base on balls and scored once in one game as pinch-hitter and appeared in one game as pinch-runner (1991). ... Appeared in one game as pinch-hitter (1997).

Year	Team (League)	W	L	Pct.	ERA	G	GS	CG	ShO	Sv.	IP	H	R	ER	BB	SO
1992—	Bend (Northwest)	2	0	1.000	2.41	10	10	0	0	0	41	38	13	11	18	32
1993—	Central Valley (Cal.)	7	8	.467	3.18	20	20	2	0	0	119	104	62	42	64	114
—	Colo. Springs (PCL)	3	2	.600	3.14	8	8	0	0	0	48²/₃	44	22	17	23	38
1994—	Colo. Springs (PCL)	0	0	...	19.64	8	0	0	0	0	11	16	25	24	22	6
—	Asheville (S. Atl.)	0	1	.000	1.06	4	4	0	0	0	17	5	3	2	5	16
1995—	Colo. Springs (PCL)	7	1	.875	4.55	19	17	0	0	1	87	79	46	44	48	65
1996—	Colo. Springs (PCL)	2	4	.333	5.94	24	9	0	0	1	63²/₃	75	46	42	28	54
—	Salem (Carolina)	0	0	.000	6.00	3	3	0	0	0	12	10	12	8	9	12
—	Colorado (N.L.)	2	1	.667	7.47	11	0	0	0	0	15²/₃	21	13	13	7	19
1997—	Colorado (N.L.)	2	5	.286	6.56	17	9	0	0	0	59	83	46	43	26	39
—	Colo. Springs (PCL)	1	2	.333	5.82	3	3	0	0	0	17	23	14	11	14	15
Major league totals (2 years)		**4**	**6**	**.400**	**6.75**	**28**	**9**	**0**	**0**	**0**	**74²/₃**	**104**	**59**	**56**	**33**	**58**

BURKETT, JOHN　　　　　　　P　　　　　　　RANGERS

PERSONAL: Born November 28, 1964, in New Brighton, Pa. ... 6-3/215. ... Throws right, bats right. ... Full name: John David Burkett. ... Name pronounced bur-KETT.
HIGH SCHOOL: Beaver (Pa.).
TRANSACTIONS/CAREER NOTES: Selected by San Francisco Giants organization in sixth round of free-agent draft (June 6, 1983). ... Traded by Giants to Texas Rangers for IF Rich Aurilia and OF Desi Wilson (December 22, 1994). ... Granted free agency (April 7, 1995). ... Signed by Florida Marlins (April 9, 1995). ... Traded by Marlins to Texas Rangers for P Ryan Dempster and a player to be named later (August 8, 1996); Marlins acquired P Rick Helling to complete deal (September 3, 1996). ... On disabled list (August 6-31, 1997); included rehabilitation assignment to Oklahoma City (August 26).
STATISTICAL NOTES: Led N.L. 10 hit batsmen in 1991.
MISCELLANEOUS: Had sacrifice hit in only appearance as pinch-hitter (1995).

Year	Team (League)	W	L	Pct.	ERA	G	GS	CG	ShO	Sv.	IP	H	R	ER	BB	SO
1983—	Great Falls (Pio.)	2	6	.250	6.26	13	9	0	0	0	50¹/₃	73	44	35	30	38
1984—	Clinton (Midwest)	7	6	.538	4.33	20	20	2	0	0	126²/₃	128	81	61	38	83
1985—	Fresno (California)	7	4	.636	2.87	20	20	1	1	0	109²/₃	93	43	35	46	72
1986—	Fresno (California)	0	3	.000	5.47	4	4	0	0	0	24²/₃	34	19	15	8	14
—	Shreveport (Texas)	10	6	.625	2.66	22	21	4	2	0	128²/₃	99	46	38	42	73
1987—	Shreveport (Texas)	•14	8	.636	3.34	27	27	6	1	0	*177²/₃	181	75	66	53	126
—	San Francisco (N.L.)	0	0	...	4.50	3	0	0	0	0	6	7	4	3	3	5
1988—	Phoenix (PCL)	5	11	.313	5.21	21	21	0	0	0	114	141	79	66	49	74
—	Shreveport (Texas)	5	1	.833	2.13	7	7	2	1	0	50²/₃	33	15	12	18	34
1989—	Phoenix (PCL)	10	11	.476	5.05	28	•28	2	1	0	167²/₃	197	111	94	59	105
1990—	Phoenix (PCL)	2	1	.667	2.74	3	3	2	1	0	23	18	8	7	3	9
—	San Francisco (N.L.)	14	7	.667	3.79	33	32	2	0	1	204	201	92	86	61	118
1991—	San Francisco (N.L.)	12	11	.522	4.18	36	34	3	1	0	206²/₃	223	103	96	60	131
1992—	San Francisco (N.L.)	13	9	.591	3.84	32	32	3	1	0	231²/₃	194	96	81	45	107
1993—	San Francisco (N.L.)	•22	7	.759	3.65	34	34	2	1	0	231¹/₃	224	100	94	40	145
1994—	San Francisco (N.L.)	6	8	.429	3.62	25	25	0	0	0	159¹/₃	176	72	64	36	85
1995—	Florida (N.L.)■	14	14	.500	4.30	30	30	4	0	0	188¹/₃	208	95	90	57	126
1996—	Florida (N.L.)	6	10	.375	4.32	24	24	1	0	0	154	154	84	74	42	108
—	Texas (A.L.)■	5	2	.714	4.06	10	10	1	1	0	68²/₃	75	33	31	16	47
1997—	Texas (A.L.)	9	12	.429	4.56	30	30	2	0	0	189¹/₃	240	106	96	30	139
—	Oklahoma City (A.A.)	1	0	1.000	3.60	1	1	0	0	0	5	6	2	2	2	3
A.L. totals (2 years)		**14**	**14**	**.500**	**4.43**	**40**	**40**	**3**	**1**	**0**	**258**	**315**	**139**	**127**	**46**	**186**
N.L. totals (8 years)		**87**	**66**	**.569**	**3.95**	**217**	**211**	**15**	**3**	**1**	**1339²/₃**	**1387**	**646**	**588**	**344**	**825**
Major league totals (9 years)		**101**	**80**	**.558**	**4.03**	**257**	**251**	**18**	**4**	**1**	**1597²/₃**	**1702**	**785**	**715**	**390**	**1011**

B

Year	Team (League)	W	L	Pct.	DIVISION SERIES RECORD ERA	G	GS	CG	ShO	Sv.	IP	H	R	ER	BB	SO
1996—	Texas (A.L.)	1	0	1.000	2.00	1	1	1	0	0	9	10	2	2	1	7

Year	League	W	L	Pct.	ALL-STAR GAME RECORD ERA	GS	CG	ShO	Sv.	IP	H	R	ER	BB	SO
1993—	National	0	1	.000	40.50	0	0	0	0	$^2/_3$	4	3	3	0	1

BURKS, ELLIS — OF — ROCKIES

PERSONAL: Born September 11, 1964, in Vicksburg, Miss. ... 6-2/198. ... Bats right, throws right. ... Full name: Ellis Rena Burks.
HIGH SCHOOL: Everman (Texas).
JUNIOR COLLEGE: Ranger (Texas) Junior College.
TRANSACTIONS/CAREER NOTES: Selected by Boston Red Sox organization in first round (20th pick overall) of free-agent draft (January 11, 1983). ... On disabled list (March 26-April 12, 1988). ... On Boston disabled list (June 15-August 1, 1989); included rehabilitation assignment to Pawtucket (July 26-August 1). ... On disabled list (June 25, 1992-remainder of season). ... Granted free agency (December 19, 1992). ... Signed by Chicago White Sox (January 4, 1993). ... Granted free agency (October 27, 1993). ... Signed by Colorado Rockies (November 30, 1993). ... On Colorado disabled list (May 18-July 31, 1994); included rehabilitation assignment to Colorado Springs (July 18-20). ... On Colorado disabled list (April 17-May 5, 1995); included rehabilitation assignment to Colorado Springs (April 25-May 5). ... On disabled list (June 28-July 29, 1997).
RECORDS: Shares major league record for most home runs in one inning—2 (August 27, 1990, fourth inning).
HONORS: Named outfielder on THE SPORTING NEWS A.L. All-Star team (1990). ... Named outfielder on THE SPORTING NEWS A.L. Silver Slugger team (1990). ... Won A.L. Gold Glove as outfielder (1990). ... Named outfielder on THE SPORTING NEWS N.L. All-Star team (1996). ... Named outfielder on THE SPORTING NEWS N.L. Silver Slugger team (1996).
STATISTICAL NOTES: Tied for Florida State League lead in double plays by outfielder with six in 1984. ... Led N.L. with 392 total bases and .639 slugging percentage in 1996. ... Career major league grand slams: 8.

Year	Team (League)	Pos.	G	AB	R	H	2B	3B	BATTING HR	RBI	Avg.	BB	SO	SB	PO	A	FIELDING E	Avg.
1983—Elmira (N.Y.-Penn)......		OF	53	174	30	42	9	0	2	23	.241	17	43	9	89	5	2	.979
1984—Winter Haven (FSL)....		OF	112	375	52	96	15	4	6	43	.256	42	68	29	196	12	5	.977
1985—New Britain (Eastern).		OF	133	476	66	121	25	7	10	61	.254	42	85	17	306	9	8	.975
1986—New Britain (Eastern).		OF	124	462	70	126	20	3	14	55	.273	44	75	31	318	5	5	.985
1987—Pawtucket (Int'l)........		OF	11	40	11	9	3	1	3	6	.225	7	7	1	25	0	0	1.000
—Boston (A.L.)..............		OF-DH	133	558	94	152	30	2	20	59	.272	41	98	27	320	15	4	.988
1988—Boston (A.L.).............		OF-DH	144	540	93	159	37	5	18	92	.294	62	89	25	370	9	9	.977
1989—Boston (A.L.).............		OF-DH	97	399	73	121	19	6	12	61	.303	36	52	21	245	7	6	.977
—Pawtucket (Int'l)........		OF	5	21	4	3	1	0	0	0	.143	2	3	0	16	0	0	1.000
1990—Boston (A.L.).............		OF-DH	152	588	89	174	33	8	21	89	.296	48	82	9	324	7	2	.994
1991—Boston (A.L.).............		OF-DH	130	474	56	119	33	3	14	56	.251	39	81	6	283	2	2	.993
1992—Boston (A.L.).............		OF-DH	66	235	35	60	8	3	8	30	.255	25	48	5	120	3	2	.984
1993—Chicago (A.L.)■......		OF	146	499	75	137	24	4	17	74	.275	60	97	6	313	6	6	.982
1994—Colorado (N.L.)■.......		OF	42	149	33	48	8	3	13	24	.322	16	39	3	79	6	3	.964
—Colo. Springs (PCL)...		OF	2	8	4	4	1	0	1	2	.500	2	1	0	5	0	0	1.000
1995—Colo. Springs (PCL)...		OF	8	29	9	9	2	1	2	6	.310	4	8	0	16	0	0	1.000
—Colorado (N.L.).........		OF	103	278	41	74	10	6	14	49	.266	39	72	7	158	3	5	.970
1996—Colorado (N.L.).........		OF	156	613	*142	211	45	8	40	128	*.344	61	114	32	279	6	5	.983
1997—Colorado (N.L.).........		OF	119	424	91	123	19	2	32	82	.290	47	75	7	207	6	4	.982
American League totals (7 years)			868	3293	515	922	184	31	110	461	.280	311	547	99	1975	49	31	.985
National League totals (4 years)			420	1464	307	456	82	19	99	283	.311	163	300	49	723	17	17	.978
Major league totals (11 years)			1288	4757	822	1378	266	50	209	744	.290	474	847	148	2698	66	48	.983

DIVISION SERIES RECORD

Year	Team (League)	Pos.	G	AB	R	H	2B	3B	BATTING HR	RBI	Avg.	BB	SO	SB	PO	A	FIELDING E	Avg.
1995—Colorado (N.L.)		OF	2	6	1	2	1	0	0	2	.333	0	1	0	4	0	1	.800

CHAMPIONSHIP SERIES RECORD

Year	Team (League)	Pos.	G	AB	R	H	2B	3B	BATTING HR	RBI	Avg.	BB	SO	SB	PO	A	FIELDING E	Avg.
1988—Boston (A.L.).............		OF	4	17	2	4	1	0	0	1	.235	0	3	0	10	0	0	1.000
1990—Boston (A.L.).............		OF	4	15	1	4	2	0	0	0	.267	1	1	0	9	1	0	1.000
1993—Chicago (A.L.)............		OF	6	23	4	7	1	0	1	3	.304	3	5	0	15	0	0	1.000
Championship series totals (3 years)			14	55	7	15	4	0	1	4	.273	4	9	1	34	1	0	1.000

ALL-STAR GAME RECORD

NOTES: Named to A.L. All-Star team for 1990 game; replaced by Brook Jacoby due to injury.

Year	League	Pos.	AB	R	H	2B	3B	BATTING HR	RBI	Avg.	BB	SO	SB	PO	A	FIELDING E	Avg.
1990—	American..................							Selected, did not play—injured.									

BURNITZ, JEROMY — OF — BREWERS

PERSONAL: Born April 15, 1969, in Westminster, Calif. ... 6-0/180. ... Bats left, throws right. ... Full name: Jeromy Neal Burnitz.
HIGH SCHOOL: Conroe (Texas).
COLLEGE: Oklahoma State.
TRANSACTIONS/CAREER NOTES: Selected by Milwaukee Brewers organization in 24th round of free-agent draft (June 2, 1987); did not sign. ... Selected by New York Mets organization in first round (17th pick overall) of free-agent draft (June 4, 1990). ... On disabled list (August 23-September 18, 1992). ... On Norfolk suspended list (August 11-13, 1994). ... Traded by Mets with P Joe Roa to Cleveland Indians for P Paul Byrd, P Jerry DiPoto, P Dave Mlicki and a player to be named later (November 18, 1994); Mets acquired 2B Jesus Azuaje to complete deal (December 6, 1994). ... Traded by Indians to the Milwaukee Brewers for 3B/1B Kevin Seitzer (August 31, 1996).

RECORDS: Shares A.L. record for most home runs by pinch-hitter in consecutive at-bats—2 (August 2 and 3, 1997).
STATISTICAL NOTES: Led New York-Pennsylvania League with .444 on-base percentage and tied for lead with six intentional bases on balls received in 1990. ... Led American Association with .503 slugging percentage in 1995. ... Led American Association with eight intentional bases on balls received in 1995. ... Career major league grand slams: 3.

Year Team (League)	Pos.	G	AB	R	H	2B	3B	HR	RBI	Avg.	BB	SO	SB	PO	A	E	Avg.
1990— Pittsfield (NYP)	OF	51	173	37	52	6	5	6	22	.301	45	39	12	79	2	0	1.000
— St. Lucie (Fla. St.)	OF	11	32	6	5	1	0	0	3	.156	7	12	1	18	1	0	1.000
1991— Williamsport (East.)	OF	135	457	80	103	16	•10	*31	•85	.225	*104	127	31	237	13	•11	.958
1992— Tidewater (Int'l)	OF	121	445	56	108	21	3	8	40	.243	33	84	30	222	11	8	.967
1993— Norfolk (Int'l)	OF	65	255	33	58	15	3	8	44	.227	25	53	10	133	9	1	.993
— New York (N.L.)	OF	86	263	49	64	10	6	13	38	.243	38	66	3	165	6	4	.977
1994— New York (N.L.)	OF	45	143	26	34	4	0	3	15	.238	23	45	1	63	1	2	.970
— Norfolk (Int'l)	OF	85	314	58	75	15	5	14	49	.239	49	82	18	170	13	4	.979
1995— Buffalo (A.A.)	OF	128	443	72	126	26	7	19	*85	.284	50	83	13	241	12	5	.981
— Cleveland (A.L.)	OF-DH	9	7	4	4	1	0	0	0	.571	0	0	0	10	0	0	1.000
1996— Cleveland (A.L.)	OF-DH	71	128	30	36	10	0	7	26	.281	25	31	2	44	0	1	1.000
— Milwaukee (A.L.)■	OF	23	72	8	17	4	0	2	14	.236	8	16	2	38	1	1	.975
1997— Milwaukee (A.L.)	OF	153	494	85	139	37	8	27	85	.281	75	111	20	256	13	7	.975
American League totals (3 years)		256	701	127	196	52	8	36	125	.280	108	158	24	348	14	8	.978
National League totals (2 years)		131	406	75	98	14	6	16	53	.241	61	111	4	228	7	6	.975
Major league totals (5 years)		387	1107	202	294	66	14	52	178	.266	169	269	28	576	21	14	.977

BURROWS, TERRY — P — PIRATES

PERSONAL: Born November 28, 1968, in Lake Charles, La. ... 6-1/185. ... Throws left, bats left. ... Full name: Terry Dale Burrows.
HIGH SCHOOL: Catholic-Point Coupee (New Roads, La.).
COLLEGE: McNeese State.
TRANSACTIONS/CAREER NOTES: Selected by Texas Rangers organization in seventh round of free-agent draft (June 4, 1990). ... On disabled list (April 25-May 2, 1993). ... On Oklahoma City disabled list (August 5-30, 1995). ... Signed by New Orleans, Milwaukee Brewers organization (April 18, 1996). ... Signed by New York Yankees organization (June 25, 1996). ... Granted free agency (October 15, 1996). ... Signed by San Diego Padres organization (December 3, 1997). ... Released by Padres (July 15, 1997). ... Signed by Edmonton, Oakland Athletics organization (July 19, 1997). ... Granted free agency (October 15, 1997). ... Signed by Pittsburgh Pirates organization (December 18, 1997).
STATISTICAL NOTES: Tied for American Association lead with five balks in 1993.

Year Team (League)	W	L	Pct.	ERA	G	GS	CG	ShO	Sv.	IP	H	R	ER	BB	SO
1990— Butte (Pioneer)	3	6	.333	4.02	14	11	1	0	0	62²/₃	56	35	28	35	64
1991— Gastonia (S. Atl.)	12	8	.600	4.45	27	26	0	0	0	147²/₃	107	79	73	78	151
1992— Charlotte (Fla. St.)	4	2	.667	2.03	14	14	0	0	0	80	71	22	18	25	66
— Tulsa (Texas)	6	3	.667	2.13	14	13	1	0	0	76	66	22	18	35	59
— Oklahoma City (A.A.)	1	0	1.000	1.13	1	1	0	0	0	8	3	1	1	5	0
1993— Oklahoma City (A.A.)	7	*15	.318	6.39	27	25	1	0	0	138	171	*107	*98	76	74
1994— Oklahoma City (A.A.)	3	5	.375	4.26	44	5	0	0	1	82¹/₃	75	43	39	37	57
— Texas (A.L.)	0	0	...	9.00	1	0	0	0	0	1	1	1	1	1	0
1995— Texas (A.L.)	2	2	.500	6.45	28	3	0	0	1	44²/₃	60	37	32	19	22
— Oklahoma City (A.A.)	0	1	.000	10.13	5	0	0	0	0	2²/₃	5	4	3	2	4
1996— New Orleans (A.A.)■	3	0	1.000	2.51	18	0	0	0	6	28²/₃	19	9	8	8	17
— Milwaukee (A.L.)	2	0	1.000	2.84	8	0	0	0	0	12²/₃	12	4	4	10	5
— Columbus (Int'l)■	1	0	1.000	5.96	23	0	0	0	0	22²/₃	24	16	15	11	20
1997— Las Vegas (PCL)■	1	5	.167	6.42	31	1	0	0	2	33²/₃	44	24	24	19	26
— San Diego (N.L.)	0	2	.000	10.45	13	0	0	0	0	10¹/₃	12	13	12	8	8
— Edmonton (PCL)■	2	2	.500	5.67	13	0	0	0	0	27	35	18	17	15	24
A.L. totals (3 years)	4	2	.667	5.71	37	3	0	0	1	58¹/₃	73	42	37	30	27
N.L. totals (1 year)	0	2	.000	10.45	13	0	0	0	0	10¹/₃	12	13	12	8	8
Major league totals (4 years)	4	4	.500	6.42	50	3	0	0	1	68²/₃	85	55	49	38	35

BUSBY, MIKE — P — CARDINALS

PERSONAL: Born December 27, 1972, in Lomita, Calif. ... 6-4/210. ... Throws right, bats right. ... Full name: Michael J. Busby.
HIGH SCHOOL: Banning (Wilmington, Calif.).
TRANSACTIONS/CAREER NOTES: Selected by St. Louis Cardinals organization in 14th round of free-agent draft (June 3, 1991). ... On Louisville disabled list (April 17-24, June 16-26, July 3-9, 1996 and April 3-June 10, 1997).

Year Team (League)	W	L	Pct.	ERA	G	GS	CG	ShO	Sv.	IP	H	R	ER	BB	SO
1991— Ariz. Cardinals (Ariz.)	4	3	.571	3.51	11	11	0	0	0	59	67	35	23	29	71
1992— Savannah (S. Atl.)	4	•13	.235	3.67	28	•28	1	0	0	149²/₃	145	96	61	67	84
1993— Savannah (S. Atl.)	12	2	.857	2.44	23	21	1	1	0	143²/₃	116	49	39	31	125
1994— St. Petersburg (FSL)	6	•13	.316	4.45	26	26	1	0	0	151²/₃	166	82	75	49	89
1995— Arkansas (Texas)	7	6	.538	3.29	20	20	1	0	0	134	125	63	49	35	95
— Louisville (A.A.)	2	2	.500	3.29	6	6	1	0	0	38¹/₃	28	18	14	11	26
1996— St. Louis (N.L.)	0	1	.000	18.00	1	1	0	0	0	4	9	13	8	4	4
— Louisville (A.A.)	2	5	.286	6.38	14	14	0	0	0	72	89	57	51	44	53
1997— Louisville (A.A.)	4	8	.333	4.61	15	14	1	0	0	93²/₃	95	49	48	30	65
— St. Louis (N.L.)	0	2	.000	8.79	3	3	0	0	0	14¹/₃	24	14	14	4	6
Major league totals (2 years)	0	3	.000	10.80	4	4	0	0	0	18¹/₃	33	27	22	8	10

BUSH, HOMER — 2B — YANKEES

PERSONAL: Born November 12, 1972, in East St. Louis, Ill. ... 5-10/175. ... Bats right, throws right. ... Full name: Homer Giles Bush.
HIGH SCHOOL: East St. Louis (Ill.).
COLLEGE: Southern Illinois-Edwardsville.

TRANSACTIONS/CAREER NOTES: Selected by San Diego Padres organization in seventh round of free-agent draft (June 3, 1991). ... On Rancho Cucamonga disabled list (April 27-May 4 and May 9-26, 1994). ... On disabled list (May 20, 1996-remainder of season). ... Traded by Padres with rights to P Hideki Irabu, OF Gordon Amerson and player to be named later to New York Yankees for OF Ruben Rivera and $3 million (April 22, 1997); Padres traded OF Vernon Maxwell to Yankees to complete deal (June 9, 1997).

| | | | | | | | | | BATTING | | | | | | FIELDING | | |
Year Team (League)	Pos.	G	AB	R	H	2B	3B	HR	RBI	Avg.	BB	SO	SB	PO	A	E	Avg.
1991— Ariz. Padres (Ariz.)	3B	32	127	16	41	3	2	0	16	.323	4	33	11	25	60	10	.895
1992— Char., S.C. (S. Atl.)	2B	108	367	37	86	10	5	0	18	.234	13	85	14	199	287	*34	.935
1993— Waterloo (Midw.)	2B	130	472	63	*152	19	3	5	51	.322	19	87	39	215	289	38	.930
1994— Rancho Cuca. (Cal.) ...	2B	39	161	37	54	10	3	0	16	.335	9	29	9	69	102	7	.961
— Wichita (Texas)	2B	59	245	35	73	11	4	3	14	.298	10	39	20	101	135	8	.967
1995— Memphis (Southern)..	2B	108	432	53	121	12	5	5	37	.280	15	83	34	235	268	16	.969
1996— Las Vegas (PCL)	2B	32	116	24	42	11	1	2	3	.362	3	33	3	67	88	5	.969
1997— Las Vegas (PCL)	2B	38	155	25	43	10	1	3	14	.277	7	40	5	73	103	4	.978
— Columbus (Int'l)■......	2B	74	275	36	68	10	3	2	26	.247	25	56	12	153	253	9	.978
— New York (A.L.).........	2B-DH	10	11	2	4	0	0	0	3	.364	0	0	0	8	13	2	.913
Major league totals (1 year)		10	11	2	4	0	0	0	3	.364	0	0	0	8	13	2	.913

BUTLER, BRENT   SS   CARDINALS

PERSONAL: Born February 11, 1978, in Laurinburg, N.C. ... 6-0/180. ... Bats right, throws right. ... Full name: Justin B. Butler.
HIGH SCHOOL: Scotland (Laurinburg, N.C.).
TRANSACTIONS/CAREER NOTES: Selected by St. Louis Cardinals organization in third round of free-agent draft (June 2, 1996).

| | | | | | | | | | BATTING | | | | | | FIELDING | | |
Year Team (League)	Pos.	G	AB	R	H	2B	3B	HR	RBI	Avg.	BB	SO	SB	PO	A	E	Avg.
1996— Johnson City (App.) ...	SS	62	248	45	85	21	1	8	50	.343	25	29	8	81	127	12	*.945
1997— Peoria (Midwest)........	SS	129	480	81	147	37	2	15	71	.306	63	69	6	*220	345	35	.942

BUTLER, BRETT   OF

PERSONAL: Born June 15, 1957, in Los Angeles. ... 5-10/161. ... Bats left, throws left. ... Full name: Brett Morgan Butler.
HIGH SCHOOL: Libertyville (Ill.).
TRANSACTIONS/CAREER NOTES: Selected by Atlanta Braves organization in 23rd round of free-agent draft (June 5, 1979). ... Traded by Braves with IF Brook Jacoby to Cleveland Indians (October 21, 1983), completing deal in which Indians traded P Len Barker to Braves for three players to be named later (August 28, 1983); Indians acquired P Rick Behenna as partial completion of deal (September 2, 1983). ... On disabled list (April 11-30, 1987). ... Granted free agency (November 9, 1987). ... Signed by San Francisco Giants (December 1, 1987). ... Granted free agency (December 7, 1990). ... Signed by Los Angeles Dodgers (December 14, 1990). ... Granted free agency (October 21, 1994). ... Signed by New York Mets (April 11, 1995). ... Traded by Mets to Dodgers for OF Dwight Maness and OF Scott Hunter (August 18, 1995). ... Granted free agency (November 7, 1995). ... Re-signed by Dodgers (November 9, 1995). ... On disabled list (May 2-September 6, 1996). ... Granted free agency (November 7, 1996). ... Re-signed by Dodgers (December 4, 1996). ... On disabled list (May 7-June 3, 1997). ... Granted free agency (November 7, 1997).
RECORDS: Shares major league single-season records for fewest double plays by outfielder who led league in double plays—3 (1991); fewest double plays by outfielder (150 or more games)—0 (1990); highest fielding percentage by outfielder (150 or more games)—1.000 (1991 and 1993); and fewest errors by outfielder (150 or more games)—0 (1991 and 1993). ... Holds N.L. record for most consecutive seasons leading league in singles—4 (1990-93). ... Shares N.L. record for most years leading league in singles—4 (1990-93). ... Shares modern N.L. single-game record for most bases on balls received—5 (April 12, 1990).
HONORS: Named International League Most Valuable Player (1981).
STATISTICAL NOTES: Tied for N.L. lead in double plays by outfielder with four in 1983 and three in 1991. ... Led A.L. in caught stealing with 22 in 1984 and 20 in 1985. ... Had 23-game hitting streak (June 15-July 12, 1991). ... Led N.L. in caught stealing with 28 in 1991. ... Tied for N.L. lead in total chances by outfielder with 380 in 1991. ... Led N.L. with 24 sacrifice hits in 1992. ... Tied for N.L. lead with nine triples in 1995. ... Career major league grand slams: 1.

| | | | | | | | | | BATTING | | | | | | FIELDING | | |
Year Team (League)	Pos.	G	AB	R	H	2B	3B	HR	RBI	Avg.	BB	SO	SB	PO	A	E	Avg.
1979— Greenw. (W. Car.)	OF	35	117	26	37	2	4	1	11	.316	24	27	20	45	2	0	1.000
— GC Braves (GCL)	OF	30	111	36	41	7	5	3	20	.369	19	15	5	66	5	0	1.000
1980— Anderson (S. Atl.)	OF	70	255	73	76	12	6	1	26	.298	67	29	44	190	5	1	.995
— Durham (Carolina)	OF	66	224	47	82	15	6	2	39	.366	67	30	36	156	4	3	.982
1981— Richmond (Int'l)........	OF	125	466	*93	156	19	4	3	36	.335	*103	63	44	286	15	3	.990
— Atlanta (N.L.)............	OF	40	126	17	32	2	3	0	4	.254	19	17	9	76	2	1	.987
1982— Atlanta (N.L.)............	OF	89	240	35	52	2	0	0	7	.217	25	35	21	129	2	0	1.000
— Richmond (Int'l)........	OF	41	157	22	57	8	3	1	22	.363	22	19	12	101	2	1	.990
1983— Atlanta (N.L.)............	OF	151	549	84	154	21	*13	5	37	.281	54	56	39	284	13	4	.987
1984— Cleveland (A.L.)■......	OF	159	602	108	162	25	9	3	49	.269	86	62	52	448	13	4	.991
1985— Cleveland (A.L.)........	OF-DH	152	591	106	184	28	14	5	50	.311	63	42	47	437	19	1	*.998
1986— Cleveland (A.L.)........	OF	161	587	92	163	17	*14	4	51	.278	70	65	32	434	9	3	.993
1987— Cleveland (A.L.)........	OF	137	522	91	154	25	8	9	41	.295	91	55	33	393	4	3	.993
1988— San Francisco (N.L.)■	OF	157	568	*109	163	27	9	6	43	.287	97	64	43	395	3	5	.988
1989— San Francisco (N.L.) ..	OF	154	594	100	168	22	4	4	36	.283	59	69	31	407	11	6	.986
1990— San Francisco (N.L.) ..	OF	160	622	108	•192	20	9	3	44	.309	90	62	51	420	4	6	.986
1991— Los Angeles (N.L.)■..	OF	*161	615	*112	182	13	5	2	38	.296	*108	79	38	*372	8	0	*1.000
1992— Los Angeles (N.L.)	OF	157	553	86	171	14	11	3	39	.309	95	67	41	353	9	2	.995
1993— Los Angeles (N.L.)	OF	156	607	80	181	21	10	1	42	.298	86	69	39	369	6	0	*1.000
1994— Los Angeles (N.L.)	OF	111	417	79	131	13	•9	8	33	.314	68	52	27	260	8	2	.993
1995— New York (N.L.)■......	OF	90	367	54	114	13	7	1	25	.311	43	42	21	207	6	1	.995
— Los Angeles (N.L.)■..	OF	39	146	24	40	5	§2	0	13	.274	24	9	11	75	0	1	.987
1996— Los Angeles (N.L.)	OF	34	131	22	35	1	1	0	8	.267	9	22	8	74	1	1	.987
1997— Los Angeles (N.L.)	OF-DH	105	343	52	97	8	3	0	18	.283	42	40	15	116	4	0	1.000
American League totals (4 years)		609	2302	397	663	95	45	21	191	.288	310	224	164	1712	45	12	.993
National League totals (13 years)		1604	5878	962	1712	182	86	33	387	.291	819	683	394	3584	77	29	.992
Major league totals (17 years)		2213	8180	1359	2375	277	131	54	578	.290	1129	907	558	5296	122	41	.992

DIVISION SERIES RECORD

						BATTING								FIELDING		
Year Team (League)	Pos.	G	AB	R	H	2B	3B	HR	RBI	Avg.	BB	SO	SB	PO	A	E	Avg.
1995— Los Angeles (N.L.)	OF	3	15	1	4	0	0	0	1	.267	0	3	0	7	0	0	1.000

CHAMPIONSHIP SERIES RECORD

						BATTING								FIELDING		
Year Team (League)	Pos.	G	AB	R	H	2B	3B	HR	RBI	Avg.	BB	SO	SB	PO	A	E	Avg.
1982— Atlanta (N.L.)	OF-PH	2	1	0	0	0	0	0	0	.000	0	0	0	0	0	0	...
1989— San Francisco (N.L.) ..	OF	5	19	6	4	0	0	0	0	.211	3	3	0	9	0	0	1.000
Championship series totals (2 years)		7	20	6	4	0	0	0	0	.200	3	3	0	9	0	0	1.000

WORLD SERIES RECORD

						BATTING								FIELDING		
Year Team (League)	Pos.	G	AB	R	H	2B	3B	HR	RBI	Avg.	BB	SO	SB	PO	A	E	Avg.
1989— San Francisco (N.L.) ..	OF	4	14	1	4	1	0	0	1	.286	2	1	2	9	0	0	1.000

ALL-STAR GAME RECORD

				BATTING								FIELDING		
Year League	Pos.	AB	R	H	2B	3B	HR	RBI	Avg.	BB	SO	SB	PO	A	E	Avg.
1991— National	PR-OF	1	0	0	0	0	0	0	.000	0	0	0	0	0	0	...

BUTLER, RICH   OF   DEVIL RAYS

PERSONAL: Born May 1, 1973, in Toronto. ... 6-1/190. ... Bats left, throws right. ... Full name: Richard Dwight Butler.
HIGH SCHOOL: East York Collegiate (Toronto).
TRANSACTIONS/CAREER NOTES: Signed as non-drafted free agent by Toronto Blue Jays organization (September 24, 1990). ... On disabled list (April 4-August 17, 1996). ... Selected by Tampa Bay Devil Rays in first round (10th pick overall) of expansion draft (November 18, 1997).
STATISTICAL NOTES: Led International League with 281 total bases in 1997.

						BATTING								FIELDING		
Year Team (League)	Pos.	G	AB	R	H	2B	3B	HR	RBI	Avg.	BB	SO	SB	PO	A	E	Avg.
1991— GC Jays (GCL)............	OF	59	213	30	56	•6	7	0	13	.263	17	45	10	104	2	1	*.991
1992— Myrtle Beach (SAL)	OF	130	441	43	100	14	1	2	43	.227	37	90	11	186	4	8	.960
1993— Knoxville (Southern) ..	OF	6	21	3	2	0	1	0	0	.095	3	5	0	11	0	0	1.000
— Dunedin (Fla. St.)	OF	110	444	68	136	19	8	11	65	.306	48	64	11	157	7	2	.988
1994— Knoxville (Southern) ..	OF	53	192	29	56	7	4	3	22	.292	19	31	7	96	0	3	.970
— Syracuse (Int'l)...........	OF	94	302	34	73	6	2	3	27	.242	22	66	8	219	4	3	.987
1995— Syracuse (Int'l)...........	OF	69	199	20	32	4	2	2	14	.161	9	45	2	101	9	4	.965
— Knoxville (Southern) ..	OF	58	217	27	58	12	3	4	33	.267	25	41	11	106	5	3	.974
1996— Dunedin (Fla. St.)	DH	10	28	1	2	0	0	0	0	.071	5	9	4	...	...	...	...
1997— Syracuse (Int'l)...........	OF	•137	*537	*93	*161	30	9	24	87	.300	60	107	20	236	8	8	.968

BUTLER, ROB   OF   ASTROS

PERSONAL: Born April 10, 1970, in East York, Ont. ... 5-11/185. ... Bats left, throws left. ... Full name: Robert Frank John Butler.
HIGH SCHOOL: East York (Ont.) Collegiate.
TRANSACTIONS/CAREER NOTES: Signed as non-drafted free agent by Toronto Blue Jays organization (September 24, 1990). ... On disabled list (August 7, 1992-remainder of season). ... On Syracuse disabled list (May 12-28, 1993). ... On Toronto disabled list (June 23-September 1, 1993); included rehabilitation assignment to Syracuse (August 13-September 1). ... Traded by Blue Jays to Philadelphia Phillies for a player to be named later (December 5, 1994). ... Granted free agency (October 16, 1995). ... On Philadelphia disabled list (April 30-May 22, 1997); including rehabilitation assignment to Scranton/Wilkes-Barre (May 20-22). ... Released by Phillies following 1997 season. ... Signed by Houston Astros organization (December 22, 1997).
HONORS: Named New York-Pennsylvania League Player of the Year (1991).
STATISTICAL NOTES: Led New York-Pennsylvania League with 152 total bases and five intentional bases on balls received in 1991.

						BATTING								FIELDING		
Year Team (League)	Pos.	G	AB	R	H	2B	3B	HR	RBI	Avg.	BB	SO	SB	PO	A	E	Avg.
1991— St. Catharines (NYP) ..	OF	76	*311	71	*105	16	5	7	45	.338	20	21	33	147	8	3	.981
1992— Dunedin (Fla. St.)	OF	92	391	67	140	13	7	4	41	*.358	22	36	19	186	8	5	.975
1993— Syracuse (Int'l)...........	OF	55	208	30	59	11	2	1	14	.284	15	29	7	93	1	1	.989
— Toronto (A.L.)	OF	17	48	8	13	4	0	0	2	.271	7	12	2	32	0	1	.970
1994— Syracuse (Int'l)...........	OF	25	95	16	25	6	1	1	11	.263	8	12	2	39	2	1	.976
— Toronto (A.L.)	OF-DH	41	74	13	13	0	1	0	5	.176	7	8	0	43	0	1	.977
1995— Scran./W.B. (Int'l).......	OF	92	327	46	98	16	4	3	35	.300	24	39	5	147	4	4	.974
1996— Scran./W.B. (Int'l).......	OF	91	298	39	76	15	8	4	34	.255	20	45	3	130	4	0	1.000
1997— Scran./W.B. (Int'l).......	OF	21	71	8	20	4	0	0	9	.282	1	9	0	23	1	0	1.000
— Philadelphia (N.L.)......	OF	43	89	10	26	9	1	0	13	.292	5	8	1	33	3	0	1.000
American League totals (2 years)		58	122	21	26	4	1	0	7	.213	14	20	2	75	0	2	.974
National League totals (1 year)		43	89	10	26	9	1	0	13	.292	5	8	1	33	3	0	1.000
Major league totals (3 years)		101	211	31	52	13	2	0	20	.246	19	28	3	108	3	2	.982

CHAMPIONSHIP SERIES RECORD

						BATTING								FIELDING		
Year Team (League)	Pos.	G	AB	R	H	2B	3B	HR	RBI	Avg.	BB	SO	SB	PO	A	E	Avg.
1993— Toronto (A.L.)								Did not play.									

WORLD SERIES RECORD

NOTES: Member of World Series championship team (1993).

						BATTING								FIELDING		
Year Team (League)	Pos.	G	AB	R	H	2B	3B	HR	RBI	Avg.	BB	SO	SB	PO	A	E	Avg.
1993— Toronto (A.L.).............	PH	2	2	1	1	0	0	0	0	.500	0	0	0	...	...	...	...

BYRD, PAUL   P   BRAVES

PERSONAL: Born December 3, 1970, in Louisville, Ky. ... 6-1/185. ... Throws right, bats right. ... Full name: Paul Gregory Byrd.
HIGH SCHOOL: St. Xavier (Louisville, Ky.).
COLLEGE: Louisiana State.
TRANSACTIONS/CAREER NOTES: Selected by Cincinnati Reds organization in 13th round of free-agent draft (June 1, 1988); did not sign. ... Selected by Cleveland Indians organization in fourth round of free-agent draft (June 3, 1991). ... On disabled list (August 12, 1992-remainder of season). ... On disabled list (May 23-July 24, 1993). ... Traded by Indians organization with P Dave Mlicki, P Jerry DiPoto and a player to be named later to New York Mets organization for OF Jeromy Burnitz and P Joe Roa (November 18, 1994); Mets acquired 2B Jesus Azuaje to complete deal (December 6, 1994). ... On Norfolk disabled list (June 1-19, 1995). ... On New York disabled list (March 22-June 9, 1996); included rehabilitation assignment to Norfolk (May 27-June 9). ... Traded by Mets with a player to be named later to Atlanta Braves for P Greg McMichael (November 25, 1996); Braves acquired P Andy Zwirchitz to complete deal (May 25, 1997).
STATISTICAL NOTES: Led Carolina League with seven balks in 1991.

Year Team (League)	W	L	Pct.	ERA	G	GS	CG	ShO	Sv.	IP	H	R	ER	BB	SO
1991—Kinston (Carolina)	4	3	.571	3.16	14	11	0	0	0	62 2/3	40	27	22	36	62
1992—Cant./Akr. (Eastern)	14	6	.700	3.01	24	24	4	0	0	152 1/3	122	68	51	75	118
1993—Charlotte (Int'l)	7	4	.636	3.89	14	14	1	1	0	81	80	43	35	30	54
—Cant./Akr. (Eastern)	0	0	...	3.60	2	1	0	0	0	10	7	4	4	3	8
1994—Cant./Akr. (Eastern)	5	9	.357	3.81	21	20	4	1	0	139 1/3	135	70	59	52	106
—Charlotte (Fla. St.)	2	2	.500	3.93	9	4	0	0	1	36 2/3	33	19	16	11	15
1995—Norfolk (Int'l)■	3	5	.375	2.79	22	10	1	0	6	87	71	29	27	21	61
—New York (N.L.)	2	0	1.000	2.05	17	0	0	0	0	22	18	6	5	7	26
1996—New York (N.L.)	1	0	.333	4.24	38	0	0	0	0	46 2/3	48	22	22	21	31
—Norfolk (Int'l)	2	0	1.000	3.52	5	0	0	0	1	7 2/3	4	3	3	4	8
1997—Atlanta (N.L.)■	4	4	.500	5.26	31	4	0	0	0	53	47	34	31	28	37
—Richmond (Int'l)	2	1	.667	3.18	3	3	0	0	0	17	14	6	6	1	14
Major league totals (3 years)	7	6	.538	4.29	86	4	0	0	0	121 2/3	113	62	58	56	94

BYRDAK, TIM   P   ROYALS

PERSONAL: Born October 31, 1973, in Oak Lawn, Ill. ... 5-11/160. ... Throws left, bats left. ... Full name: Timothy Christopher Byrdak.
HIGH SCHOOL: Oak Forest (Ill.).
JUNIOR COLLEGE: South Suburban College (Ill.).
COLLEGE: Rice.
TRANSACTIONS/CAREER NOTES: Selected by Kansas City Royals organization in fifth round of free-agent draft (June 2, 1994). ... On Wichita disabled list (June 27-August 19, 1996). ... On Omaha disabled list (April 3-June 9, 1997).

Year Team (League)	W	L	Pct.	ERA	G	GS	CG	ShO	Sv.	IP	H	R	ER	BB	SO
1994—Eugene (Northwest)	4	5	.444	3.07	15	15	0	0	0	73 1/3	60	33	25	20	77
1995—Wilmington (Caro.)	11	5	.688	2.16	27	26	0	0	0	166 1/3	118	46	40	45	127
1996—Wichita (Texas)	5	7	.417	6.91	15	15	0	0	0	84 2/3	112	73	65	44	47
1997—Wilmington (Caro.)	4	3	.571	3.51	22	2	0	0	3	41	34	17	16	12	47

CABRERA, JOSE   P   ASTROS

PERSONAL: Born March 24, 1972, in Santiago, Dominican Republic. ... 6-0/160. ... Throws right, bats right. ... Full name: Jose Alberto Cabrera.
TRANSACTIONS/CAREER NOTES: Signed as non-drafted free agent by Cleveland Indians organization (October 12, 1990). ... On disabled list (May 11-28, 1993). ... On Buffalo disabled list (April 4-13 and 17-25, 1997). ... Traded by Indians organization to Houston Astros organization for P Al Morman (May 10, 1997).

Year Team (League)	W	L	Pct.	ERA	G	GS	CG	ShO	Sv.	IP	H	R	ER	BB	SO
1991—DSL Indians (DSL)	6	4	.600	3.07	16	12	1	0	0	73 1/3	64	32	25	17	40
1992—Burlington (Appalachian)	•8	3	.727	1.75	13	13	1	0	0	92 1/3	74	27	18	18	79
1993—Columbus (S. Atl.)	11	6	.647	2.67	26	26	1	0	0	155 1/3	122	54	46	53	105
1994—Kinston (Carolina)	4	13	.235	4.44	24	24	0	0	0	133 2/3	134	84	66	43	110
1995—Cant./Akr. (Eastern)	1	1	.500	1.02	4	3	0	0	0	17 2/3	7	2	2	8	19
—Bakersfield (California)	2	2	.500	3.92	7	7	0	0	0	41 1/3	40	25	18	21	52
1996—Cant./Akr. (Eastern)	4	3	.571	5.63	15	7	0	0	0	62 1/3	78	45	39	17	40
1997—Buffalo (A.A.)	3	0	1.000	1.20	5	0	0	0	0	15	8	2	2	7	11
—New Orleans (A.A.)■	2	2	.500	2.54	31	0	0	0	0	46	31	13	13	13	40
—Houston (N.L.)	0	0	...	1.17	12	0	0	0	0	15 1/3	6	2	2	6	18
Major league totals (1 year)	0	0	...	1.17	12	0	0	0	0	15 1/3	6	2	2	6	18

CABRERA, ORLANDO   SS   EXPOS

PERSONAL: Born November 2, 1974, in Cartagena, Columbia. ... 5-9/150. ... Bats right, throws right. ... Full name: Orlando Luis Cabrera. ... Brother of Jolbert Cabrera, infielder, Montreal Expos organization.
TRANSACTIONS/CAREER NOTES: Signed as non-drafted free agent by Montreal Expos organization (June 1, 1993).

Year Team (League)	Pos.	G	AB	R	H	2B	3B	HR	RBI	Avg.	BB	SO	SB	PO	A	E	Avg.
1993—Dom. Expos (DSL)	IF	38	122	24	42	6	1	1	17	.344	18	11	14	86	76	3	.982
1994—GC Expos (GCL)	2B-SS-OF	22	73	13	23	4	1	0	11	.315	5	8	6	22	42	4	.941
1995—Vermont (NYP)	2B-SS	65	248	37	70	12	5	3	33	.282	16	28	15	135	189	17	.950
1996—Delmarva (S. Atl.)	SS-2B	134	512	86	129	28	4	14	65	.252	54	63	51	205	344	27	.953
1997—W.P. Beach (FSL)	SS-2B	69	279	56	77	19	2	5	26	.276	27	33	32	92	162	20	.927
—Harrisburg (Eastern)	SS-2B	35	133	34	41	13	2	5	20	.308	15	18	7	57	83	5	.966
—Ottawa (Int'l)	SS-2B	31	122	17	32	5	2	2	14	.262	7	16	8	45	94	3	.979
—Montreal (N.L.)	SS-2B	16	18	4	4	0	0	0	2	.222	1	3	1	11	15	1	.963
Major league totals (1 year)		16	18	4	4	0	0	0	2	.222	1	3	1	11	15	1	.963

CADARET, GREG

P   **ANGELS**

PERSONAL: Born February 27, 1962, in Detroit. ... 6-3/215. ... Throws left, bats left. ... Full name: Gregory James Cadaret. ... Name pronounced CAD-uh-ray.

HIGH SCHOOL: Central Montacalm (Stanton, Mich.).

COLLEGE: Grand Valley State (Mich.).

TRANSACTIONS/CAREER NOTES: Selected by Oakland Athletics organization in 11th round of free-agent draft (June 6, 1983). ... Traded by A's organization with P Eric Plunk and OF Luis Polonia to New York Yankees for OF Rickey Henderson (June 21, 1989). ... Contract sold by Yankees to Cincinnati Reds (November 6, 1992). ... Released by Reds (July 26, 1993). ... Signed by Kansas City Royals (July 30, 1993). ... Granted free agency (October 25, 1993). ... Signed by Toronto Blue Jays organization (December 21, 1993). ... Released by Blue Jays (June 9, 1994). ... Signed by Detroit Tigers (June 17, 1994). ... Granted free agency (October 21, 1994). ... Signed by Edmonton, A's organization (April 8, 1995). ... Released by A's organization (April 24, 1995). ... Signed by Louisville, St. Louis Cardinals organization (May 2, 1995). ... On Louisville suspended list (May 21-23, 1995). ... Released by Louisville, Cardinals organization (June 6, 1995). ... Signed by Las Vegas, San Diego Padres organization (June 30, 1995). ... Granted free agency (October 16, 1995). ... Signed by Pittsburgh Pirates organization (January 8, 1996). ... Released by Pirates (May 2, 1996). ... Signed by Cleveland Indians organization (May 14, 1996). ... Granted free agency (October 15, 1996). ... Re-signed by Indians organization (January 31, 1997). ... Released by Indians (July 3, 1997). ... Signed by Anaheim Angels organization (July 10, 1997). ... Granted free agency (October 9, 1997). ... Re-signed by Angels organization (December 4, 1997).

Year—Team (League)	W	L	Pct.	ERA	G	GS	CG	ShO	Sv.	IP	H	R	ER	BB	SO
1983— Medford (N'west)	7	3	.700	4.36	12	11	1	1	0	64	73	36	31	36	51
1984— Modesto (California)	13	8	.619	3.05	26	26	6	2	0	171 1/3	162	79	58	82	138
1985— Huntsville (Southern)	3	7	.300	6.12	17	17	0	0	0	82 1/3	96	61	56	57	60
— Modesto (California)	3	9	.250	5.87	12	12	1	1	0	61 1/3	59	50	40	54	43
1986— Huntsville (Southern)	12	5	.706	5.41	28	28	1	0	0	141 1/3	166	106	85	98	113
1987— Huntsville (Southern)	5	2	.714	2.90	24	0	0	0	9	40 1/3	31	16	13	20	48
— Tacoma (PCL)	1	2	.333	3.46	7	0	0	0	0	13	5	6	5	13	12
— Oakland (A.L.)	6	2	.750	4.54	29	0	0	0	0	39 2/3	37	22	20	24	30
1988— Oakland (A.L.)	5	2	.714	2.89	58	0	0	0	3	71 2/3	60	26	23	36	64
1989— Oakland (A.L.)	0	0	...	2.28	26	0	0	0	0	27 2/3	21	9	7	19	14
— New York (A.L.)■	5	5	.500	4.58	20	13	3	1	0	92 1/3	109	53	47	38	66
1990— New York (A.L.)	5	4	.556	4.15	54	6	0	0	3	121 1/3	120	62	56	64	80
1991— New York (A.L.)	8	6	.571	3.62	68	5	0	0	3	121 2/3	110	52	49	59	105
1992— New York (A.L.)	4	8	.333	4.25	46	11	1	1	1	103 2/3	104	53	49	74	73
1993— Cincinnati (N.L.)■	2	1	.667	4.96	34	0	0	0	1	32 2/3	40	19	18	23	23
— Kansas City (A.L.)■	1	1	.500	2.93	13	0	0	0	0	15 1/3	14	5	5	7	2
1994— Toronto (A.L.)■	0	1	.000	5.85	21	0	0	0	0	20	24	15	13	17	15
— Detroit (A.L.)■	1	0	1.000	3.60	17	0	0	0	2	20	17	9	8	16	14
1995— Louisville (A.A.)■	1	0	1.000	3.09	12	0	0	0	0	11 2/3	14	4	4	1	7
— Las Vegas (PCL)■	3	5	.375	5.88	28	4	0	0	0	52	56	40	34	22	52
1996— Calgary (PCL)	0	3	.000	7.30	9	0	0	0	0	12 1/3	20	18	10	12	10
— Buffalo (A.A.)■	1	5	.167	3.66	32	3	0	0	2	64	59	28	26	29	44
1997— Buffalo (A.A.)	2	2	.500	4.86	29	1	0	0	4	50	46	31	27	35	49
— Vancouver (PCL)■	0	1	.000	3.14	9	0	0	0	3	14 1/3	11	5	5	4	16
— Anaheim (A.L.)■	0	0	...	3.29	15	0	0	0	0	13 2/3	11	5	5	8	11
A.L. totals (9 years)	35	29	.547	3.92	367	35	4	2	12	647	627	311	282	362	474
N.L. totals (1 year)	2	1	.667	4.96	34	0	0	0	1	32 2/3	40	19	18	23	23
Major league totals (9 years)	37	30	.552	3.97	401	35	4	2	13	679 2/3	667	330	300	385	497

CHAMPIONSHIP SERIES RECORD

Year—Team (League)	W	L	Pct.	ERA	G	GS	CG	ShO	Sv.	IP	H	R	ER	BB	SO
1988— Oakland (A.L.)	0	0	...	27.00	1	0	0	0	0	1/3	1	1	1	0	0

WORLD SERIES RECORD

Year—Team (League)	W	L	Pct.	ERA	G	GS	CG	ShO	Sv.	IP	H	R	ER	BB	SO
1988— Oakland (A.L.)	0	0	...	0.00	3	0	0	0	0	2	2	0	0	0	3

CAIRO, MIGUEL

2B   **DEVIL RAYS**

PERSONAL: Born May 4, 1974, in Anaco, Venezuela. ... 6-0/192. ... Bats right, throws right. ... Full name: Miguel Jesus Cairo.

TRANSACTIONS/CAREER NOTES: Signed as non-drafted free agent by Los Angeles Dodgers organization (September 20, 1990). ... Traded by Dodgers with 3B Willis Otanez to Seattle Mariners for 3B Mike Blowers (November 29, 1995). ... Traded by Mariners with P Bill Risley to Toronto Blue Jays for P Edwin Hurtado and P Paul Menhart (December 18, 1995). ... Traded by Blue Jays to Chicago Cubs for P Jason Stevenson (November 20, 1996). ... Selected by Tampa Bay Devil Rays in first round (eighth pick overall) of expansion draft (November 18, 1997).

STATISTICAL NOTES: Led California League in caught stealing with 23 in 1994. ... Led International League second basemen with 64 double plays in 1996. ... Led American Association in caught stealing with 15 in 1997.

						BATTING								FIELDING		
Year—Team (League)	Pos.	G	AB	R	H	2B	3B	HR	RBI	Avg.	BB	SO	SB	PO	A	E	Avg.
1991— Dom. Dodgers (DSL)	IF	57	203	16	45	5	1	0	17	.222	0	17	8	...	...	...	...
1992— Vero Beach (FSL)	2B-3B	36	125	7	28	0	0	0	7	.224	11	12	5	69	76	10	.935
— GC Dodgers (GCL)	SS-3B	21	76	10	23	5	2	0	4	.303	2	6	1	26	56	4	.953
1993— Vero Beach (FSL)	2B-SS-3B	90	346	50	109	10	1	1	23	.315	28	22	23	172	244	18	.959
1994— Bakersfield (California)	2B-SS	133	533	76	155	23	4	2	48	.291	34	37	44	268	376	28	.958
1995— San Antonio (Tex.)	2B-SS	107	435	53	121	20	1	1	41	.278	26	31	33	210	316	23	.958
1996— Syracuse (Int'l)■	2B-3B-SS	120	465	71	129	14	4	3	48	.277	26	44	27	193	295	23	.955
— Toronto (A.L.)	2B	9	27	5	6	2	0	0	1	.222	2	9	0	22	18	0	1.000
1997— Iowa (Am. Assoc.)■	2B-SS	135	*569	82	159	35	4	5	46	.279	24	54	*40	248	386	20	.969
— Chicago (N.L.)	2B-SS	16	29	7	7	1	0	0	1	.241	2	3	0	16	18	0	1.000
American League totals (1 year)		9	27	5	6	2	0	0	1	.222	2	9	0	22	18	0	1.000
National League totals (1 year)		16	29	7	7	1	0	0	1	.241	2	3	0	16	18	0	1.000
Major league totals (2 years)		25	56	12	13	3	0	0	2	.232	4	12	0	38	36	0	1.000

CAMERON, MIKE — OF — WHITE SOX

PERSONAL: Born January 8, 1973, in LaGrange, Ga. ... 6-2/190. ... Bats right, throws right. ... Full name: Michael Terrance Cameron.
HIGH SCHOOL: LaGrange (Ga.).
TRANSACTIONS/CAREER NOTES: Selected by Chicago White Sox organization in 18th round of free-agent draft (June 3, 1991).
STATISTICAL NOTES: Tied for Carolina League lead in double plays by outfielder with four in 1994. ... Led Southern League with .600 slugging percentage and tied for lead in caught stealing with 15 in 1996. ... Led Southern League outfielders with 264 total chances in 1996.

Year Team (League)	Pos.	G	AB	R	H	2B	3B	HR	RBI	Avg.	BB	SO	SB	PO	A	E	Avg.
1991— GC Whi. Sox (GCL)	OF	44	136	20	30	3	0	0	11	.221	17	29	13	55	3	3	.951
1992— Utica (N.Y.-Penn).......	OF	26	87	15	24	1	4	2	12	.276	11	26	3	60	3	0	1.000
— South Bend (Mid.)......	OF	35	114	19	26	8	1	1	9	.228	10	37	2	67	0	3	.957
1993— South Bend (Mid.)......	OF	122	411	52	98	14	5	0	30	.238	27	101	19	248	13	4	.985
1994— Prince William (Car.)..	OF	131	468	86	116	15	*17	6	48	.248	60	101	22	275	10	6	.979
1995— Birmingham (Sou.).....	OF	107	350	64	87	20	5	11	60	.249	54	104	21	250	7	4	.985
— Chicago (A.L.)	OF	28	38	4	7	2	0	1	2	.184	3	15	0	33	1	0	1.000
1996— Birmingham (Sou.).....	OF	123	473	*120	142	34	12	28	77	.300	71	117	*39	*249	8	7	.973
— Chicago (A.L.)	OF-DH	11	11	1	1	0	0	0	0	.091	1	3	0	7	0	0	1.000
1997— Nashville (A.A.)	OF	30	120	21	33	7	3	6	17	.275	18	31	4	63	3	1	.985
— Chicago (A.L.)	OF-DH	116	379	63	98	18	3	14	55	.259	55	105	23	334	5	5	.985
Major league totals (3 years)		155	428	68	106	20	3	15	57	.248	59	123	23	374	6	5	.987

CAMINITI, KEN — 3B — PADRES

PERSONAL: Born April 21, 1963, in Hanford, Calif. ... 6-0/200. ... Bats both, throws right. ... Full name: Kenneth Gene Caminiti. ... Name pronounced CAM-uh-NET-ee.
HIGH SCHOOL: Leigh (San Jose, Calif.).
COLLEGE: San Jose State.
TRANSACTIONS/CAREER NOTES: Selected by Houston Astros organization in third round of free-agent draft (June 4, 1984). ... On disabled list (April 19-May 11, 1992). ... Traded by Astros with OF Steve Finley, SS Andujar Cedeno, 1B Robert Petagine, P Brian Williams and a player to be named later to San Diego Padres for OF Phil Plantier, OF Derek Bell, P Pedro Martinez, P Doug Brocail, IF Craig Shipley and SS Ricky Gutierrez (December 28, 1994); Padres acquired P Sean Fesh to complete deal (May 1, 1995). ... On disabled list (May 12-27, 1997).
RECORDS: Holds major league single-season record for most games with switch-hit home runs—3 (1995). ... Holds major league record for most consecutive games with switch-hit home runs—2 (September 16-17, 1995). ... Shares major league single-season record for most runs batted in by switch hitter—130 (1996). ... Holds N.L. single-season record for highest slugging average by switch hitter—.621 (1996), and most games with switch-hit home runs—6 (1996). ... Holds N.L. career record for most games with switch-hit home runs—8. ... Holds N.L. record for most home runs by switch hitter in two consecutive seasons—66 (1995-96).
HONORS: Named third baseman on THE SPORTING NEWS college All-America team (1984). ... Won N.L. Gold Glove at third base (1995-97). ... Named third baseman on THE SPORTING NEWS N.L. All-Star team (1996). ... Named third baseman on THE SPORTING NEWS N.L. Silver Slugger team (1996). ... Named N.L. Most Valuable Player by Baseball Writers' Association of America (1996).
STATISTICAL NOTES: Led Southern League third basemen with 34 double plays in 1986. ... Led Pacific Coast League third basemen with 382 total chances and 25 double plays in 1988. ... Switch-hit home runs in one game eight times (July 3, 1994; September 16, September 17 and September 19, 1995; August 1, August 21, August 28 and September 11, 1996). ... Led N.L. third basemen with 424 total chances and 28 double plays in 1995. ... Tied for N.L. lead with 10 sacrifice flies in 1996. ... Career major league grand slams: 4.

Year Team (League)	Pos.	G	AB	R	H	2B	3B	HR	RBI	Avg.	BB	SO	SB	PO	A	E	Avg.
1985— Osceola (Fla. St.)........	3B	126	468	83	133	26	9	4	73	.284	51	54	14	53	193	20	.925
1986— Columbus (Southern).	3B	137	513	82	154	29	3	12	81	.300	56	79	5	105	*299	33	.924
1987— Columbus (Southern).	3B	95	375	66	122	25	2	15	69	.325	25	58	11	55	205	21	.925
— Houston (N.L.)	3B	63	203	10	50	7	1	3	23	.246	12	44	0	50	98	8	.949
1988— Tucson (PCL)	3B	109	416	54	113	24	7	5	66	.272	29	54	13	*105	*250	27	.929
— Houston (N.L.)	3B	30	83	5	15	2	0	1	7	.181	5	18	0	12	43	3	.948
1989— Houston (N.L.)	3B	161	585	71	149	31	3	10	72	.255	51	93	4	126	335	22	.954
1990— Houston (N.L.)	3B	153	541	52	131	20	2	4	51	.242	48	97	9	118	243	21	.945
1991— Houston (N.L.)	3B	152	574	65	145	30	3	13	80	.253	46	85	4	129	293	23	.948
1992— Houston (N.L.)	3B	135	506	68	149	31	2	13	62	.294	44	68	10	102	210	11	.966
1993— Houston (N.L.)	3B	143	543	75	142	31	0	13	75	.262	49	88	8	123	264	24	.942
1994— Houston (N.L.)	3B	111	406	63	115	28	2	18	75	.283	43	71	4	79	200	9	.969
1995— San Diego (N.L.)■▬....	3B	143	526	74	159	33	0	26	94	.302	69	94	12	102	*295	*27	.936
1996— San Diego (N.L.)	3B	146	546	109	178	37	2	40	130	.326	78	99	11	103	310	20	.954
1997— San Diego (N.L.)	3B	137	486	92	141	28	0	26	90	.290	80	118	11	90	291	24	.941
Major league totals (11 years)		1374	4999	684	1374	278	15	167	759	.275	525	875	73	1034	2582	192	.950

DIVISION SERIES RECORD

RECORDS: Shares single-game record for most home runs—2 (October 5, 1996).

Year Team (League)	Pos.	G	AB	R	H	2B	3B	HR	RBI	Avg.	BB	SO	SB	PO	A	E	Avg.
1996— San Diego (N.L.)	3B	3	10	3	3	0	0	3	3	.300	3	5	0	0	5	3	.625

ALL-STAR GAME RECORD

Year League	Pos.	AB	R	H	2B	3B	HR	RBI	Avg.	BB	SO	SB	PO	A	E	Avg.
1994— National	3B	1	0	0	0	0	0	0	.000	0	0	0	0	0	0	...
1996— National	3B	2	1	1	0	0	1	1	.500	0	1	0	0	0	0	.000
1997— National	3B	2	0	0	0	0	0	0	.000	0	1	0	0	0	1	...
All-Star Game totals (3 years)		5	1	1	0	0	1	1	.200	0	1	0	0	0	1	.000

CANDAELE, CASEY — IF/OF

PERSONAL: Born January 12, 1961, in Lompoc, Calif. ... 5-9/165. ... Bats both, throws right. ... Full name: Casey Todd Candaele. ... Son of Helen St. Aubin, former women's professional baseball player. ... Name pronounced kan-DELL.
HIGH SCHOOL: Lompoc (Calif.).
COLLEGE: Arizona.
TRANSACTIONS/CAREER NOTES: Signed as non-drafted free agent by Montreal Expos organization (August 15, 1982). ... Traded by Expos to Houston Astros for C Mark Bailey (July 23, 1988). ... On disabled list (June 9-July 22, 1989). ... On Houston disabled list (July 17-August 9, 1993); included rehabilitation assignment to Tucson (August 2-9). ... Granted free agency (October 4, 1993). ... Signed by Cincinnati Reds organization (November 24, 1993). ... Granted free agency (October 15, 1994). ... Signed by Los Angeles Dodgers organization (February 1, 1995). ... Released by Dodgers organization (April 26, 1995). ... Signed by Cleveland Indians organization (May 5, 1995). ... Granted free agency (October 16, 1995). ... Re-signed by Indians organization (December 6, 1995). ... Granted free agency (October 15, 1996). ... Re-signed by Indians organization (January 1, 1997). ... Granted free agency (October 15, 1997).
STATISTICAL NOTES: Led Florida State League second basemen with 391 assists, 30 errors and 87 double plays in 1983. ... Led American Association with 11 sacrifice hits in 1986. ... Tied for American Association lead in double plays by second baseman with 68 in 1986. ... Led American Association in grounding into double plays with 21 in 1994.

Year—Team (League)	Pos.	G	AB	R	H	2B	3B	HR	RBI	Avg.	BB	SO	SB	PO	A	E	Avg.
1983—W.P. Beach (FSL)	2-O-3-S	127	*511	77	156	26	9	0	45	.305	51	44	22	271	†403	†32	.955
—Memphis (Southern)..	3B	5	19	4	4	1	0	0	1	.211	1	3	1	2	11	0	1.000
1984—Jacksonville (South.)..	S-O-2-3	132	532	68	145	23	2	2	53	.273	30	35	26	266	352	18	.970
1985—Indianapolis (A.A.)	O-2-S-3	127	390	55	101	13	5	0	35	.259	44	33	13	266	160	6	.986
1986—Indianapolis (A.A.)	2B-OF	119	480	77	145	32	6	2	42	.302	46	29	16	240	319	13	.977
—Montreal (N.L.)	2B-3B	30	104	9	24	4	1	0	6	.231	5	15	3	45	74	2	.983
1987—Montreal (N.L.)	2-O-S-1	138	449	62	122	23	4	1	23	.272	38	28	7	237	176	8	.981
1988—Montreal (N.L.)	2B	36	116	9	20	5	1	0	4	.172	10	11	1	62	102	2	.988
—Indianapolis (A.A.)	SS-2B-OF	60	239	23	63	11	6	2	36	.264	12	20	5	105	161	3	.989
—Tucson (PCL)■	O-2-S-3	17	66	8	17	3	0	0	5	.258	4	6	4	35	29	3	.955
—Houston (N.L.)	2B-OF-3B	21	31	2	5	3	0	0	1	.161	1	6	0	17	24	0	1.000
1989—Tucson (PCL)	O-3-2-S-1	68	206	22	45	6	1	0	17	.218	20	37	6	94	59	5	.968
1990—Tucson (PCL)	2B	7	28	2	6	1	0	0	2	.214	3	2	1	14	24	1	.974
—Houston (N.L.)	O-2-S-3	130	262	30	75	8	6	3	22	.286	31	42	7	147	120	3	.989
1991—Houston (N.L.)	2B-OF-3B	151	461	44	121	20	7	4	50	.262	40	49	9	244	318	10	.983
1992—Houston (N.L.)	S-3-O-2	135	320	19	68	12	1	1	18	.213	24	36	7	130	196	11	.967
1993—Houston (N.L.)	2-O-S-3	75	121	18	29	8	0	1	7	.240	10	14	2	46	40	3	.966
—Tucson (PCL)	OF-SS-2B	6	27	4	8	1	0	0	4	.296	3	2	1	12	10	3	.880
1994—Indianapolis (A.A.)■..	2B-OF	131	511	66	144	31	7	4	52	.282	32	65	8	268	174	3	.993
1995—Albuquerque (PCL)■..	2B-3B	12	27	2	7	0	0	0	2	.259	4	4	0	23	24	2	.959
—Buffalo (A.A.)	2-O-S-3	97	364	50	90	10	7	4	38	.247	22	42	9	172	202	13	.966
1996—Buffalo (A.A.)	2B-OF-SS	94	392	66	122	22	2	6	37	.311	27	35	3	188	175	8	.978
—Cleveland (A.L.)	2B-3R-SS	24	44	8	11	2	0	1	4	.250	1	9	0	22	33	0	1.000
1997—Buffalo (A.A.)	2-3-C-S	79	311	39	71	21	0	7	38	.228	31	43	1	119	203	13	.961
—Cleveland (A.L.)	2B-DH-3B	14	26	5	8	1	0	0	4	.308	1	1	1	10	25	0	1.000
American League totals (2 years)		38	70	13	19	3	0	1	8	.271	2	10	1	32	58	0	1.000
National League totals (7 years)		716	1864	193	464	83	20	10	131	.249	159	201	36	928	1050	39	.981
Major league totals (9 years)		754	1934	206	483	86	20	11	139	.250	161	211	37	960	1108	39	.981

DIVISION SERIES RECORD

Year—Team (League)	Pos.	G	AB	R	H	2B	3B	HR	RBI	Avg.	BB	SO	SB	PO	A	E	Avg.
1996—Cleveland (A.L.)	PH-DH-PR	2	0	1	0	0	0	0	0	...	1	0	0	0	0	0	...

CANDIOTTI, TOM — P — ATHLETICS

PERSONAL: Born August 31, 1957, in Walnut Creek, Calif. ... 6-2/221. ... Throws right, bats right. ... Full name: Thomas Caesar Candiotti. ... Name pronounced KAN-dee-AH-tee.
HIGH SCHOOL: St. Mary's (Calif.).
COLLEGE: St. Mary's, Calif. (degree in business administration, 1979).
TRANSACTIONS/CAREER NOTES: Signed as non-drafted free agent by Victoria, independent (July 17, 1979). ... Released by Victoria (January 4, 1980). ... Signed by Fort Myers, Kansas City Royals organization (January 5, 1980). ... On Jacksonville disabled list (June 7-26, 1980). ... Selected by Vancouver, Milwaukee Brewers organization, from Royals organization in Rule 5 minor league draft (December 9, 1980). ... On Milwaukee disabled list (April 10-May 12, 1981 and April 13, 1982-remainder of season). ... On Vancouver disabled list (May 30-June 15, 1984). ... On Milwaukee disabled list (August 2-September 1, 1984); included rehabilitation assignment to Beloit (August 24-31). ... Granted free agency (October 15, 1985). ... Signed by Cleveland Indians (December 12, 1985). ... On disabled list (August 4-19, 1988; July 2-17, 1989; and May 7-22, 1990). ... Traded by Indians with OF Turner Ward to Toronto Blue Jays for P Denis Boucher, OF Glenallen Hill, OF Mark Whiten and a player to be named later (June 27, 1991); Indians acquired cash instead of player to complete deal (October 15, 1991). ... Granted free agency (November 7, 1991). ... Signed by Los Angeles Dodgers (December 3, 1991). ... On disabled list (August 9-24, 1992). ... Granted free agency (November 3, 1995). ... Re-signed by Dodgers (December 15, 1995). ... On Los Angeles disabled list (July 20-August 13, 1996); included rehabilitation assignment to San Bernardino (August 7-13). ... Granted free agency (October 28, 1997). ... Signed by Oakland Athletics (December 9, 1997).
RECORDS: Shares modern N.L. record for most hit batsmen in nine-inning game—4 (September 13, 1997). ... Shares major league record for most hit batsmen in one inning—3 (September 13, 1997, first inning).
STATISTICAL NOTES: Pitched 2-0 one-hit, complete-game victory against New York (August 3, 1987).

Year—Team (League)	W	L	Pct.	ERA	G	GS	CG	ShO	Sv.	IP	H	R	ER	BB	SO
1979—Victoria (N'west)	5	1	.833	2.44	12	9	3	0	1	70	63	23	19	16	66
1980—Fort Myers (Fla. St.)■	3	2	.600	2.25	7	5	3	0	0	44	32	16	11	9	31
—Jacksonville (Southern)	7	8	.467	2.77	17	17	8	2	0	117	98	45	36	40	93
1981—El Paso (Texas)■	7	6	.538	2.80	21	14	6	1	0	119	137	51	37	27	68
1982—							Did not play.								

C

Year—Team (League)	W	L	Pct.	ERA	G	GS	CG	ShO	Sv.	IP	H	R	ER	BB	SO
1983— El Paso (Texas)	1	0	1.000	2.92	7	0	0	0	2	24²/₃	23	10	8	7	18
— Vancouver (PCL)	6	4	.600	2.81	15	14	5	2	0	99¹/₃	87	35	31	16	61
— Milwaukee (A.L.)	4	4	.500	3.23	10	8	2	1	0	55²/₃	62	21	20	16	21
1984— Vancouver (PCL)	8	4	.667	2.89	15	15	4	0	0	96²/₃	96	36	31	22	53
— Milwaukee (A.L.)	2	2	.500	5.29	8	6	0	0	0	32¹/₃	38	21	19	10	23
— Beloit (Midwest)	0	1	.000	2.70	2	2	0	0	0	10	12	5	3	5	12
1985— El Paso (Texas)	1	0	1.000	2.76	4	4	2	1	0	29¹/₃	29	11	9	7	16
— Vancouver (PCL)	9	13	.409	3.94	24	24	0	0	0	150²/₃	178	83	66	36	97
1986— Cleveland (A.L.)■	16	12	.571	3.57	36	34	*17	3	0	252¹/₃	234	112	100	106	167
1987— Cleveland (A.L.)	7	18	.280	4.78	32	32	7	2	0	201²/₃	193	132	107	93	111
1988— Cleveland (A.L.)	14	8	.636	3.28	31	31	11	1	0	216²/₃	225	86	79	53	137
1989— Cleveland (A.L.)	13	10	.565	3.10	31	31	4	0	0	206	188	80	71	55	124
1990— Cleveland (A.L.)	15	11	.577	3.65	31	29	3	1	0	202	207	92	82	55	128
1991— Cleveland (A.L.)	7	6	.538	2.24	15	15	3	0	0	108¹/₃	88	35	27	28	86
— Toronto (A.L.)■	6	7	.462	2.98	19	19	3	0	0	129²/₃	114	47	43	45	81
1992— Los Angeles (N.L.)■	11	*15	.423	3.00	32	30	6	2	0	203²/₃	177	78	68	63	152
1993— Los Angeles (N.L.)	8	10	.444	3.12	33	32	2	0	0	213²/₃	192	86	74	71	155
1994— Los Angeles (N.L.)	7	7	.500	4.12	23	22	5	0	0	153	149	77	70	54	102
1995— Los Angeles (N.L.)	7	14	.333	3.50	30	30	1	1	0	190¹/₃	187	93	74	58	141
1996— Los Angeles (N.L.)	9	11	.450	4.49	28	27	1	0	0	152¹/₃	172	91	76	43	79
— San Bernardino (Calif.)	0	1	.000	5.00	2	2	0	0	0	9	11	6	5	4	10
1997— Los Angeles (N.L.)	10	7	.588	3.60	41	18	0	0	0	135	128	60	54	40	89
A.L. totals (8 years)	84	78	.519	3.51	213	205	50	8	0	1404²/₃	1349	626	548	461	878
N.L. totals (6 years)	52	64	.448	3.57	187	159	15	3	0	1048	1005	485	416	329	718
Major league totals (14 years)	136	142	.489	3.54	400	364	65	11	0	2452²/₃	2354	1111	964	790	1596

DIVISION SERIES RECORD

Year—Team (League)	W	L	Pct.	ERA	G	GS	CG	ShO	Sv.	IP	H	R	ER	BB	SO
1996— Los Angeles (N.L.)	0	0	...	0.00	1	0	0	0	0	2	0	0	0	0	1

CHAMPIONSHIP SERIES RECORD

Year—Team (League)	W	L	Pct.	ERA	G	GS	CG	ShO	Sv.	IP	H	R	ER	BB	SO
1991— Toronto (A.L.)	0	1	.000	8.22	2	2	0	0	0	7²/₃	17	9	7	2	5

CANGELOSI, JOHN　　　　OF　　　　MARLINS

PERSONAL: Born March 10, 1963, in Brooklyn, N.Y. ... 5-8/160. ... Bats both, throws left. ... Full name: John Anthony Cangelosi. ... Name pronounced KAN-juh-LO-see.

HIGH SCHOOL: Miami Springs (Fla.) Sr.

JUNIOR COLLEGE: Miami-Dade (North) Community College.

TRANSACTIONS/CAREER NOTES: Selected by Chicago White Sox organization in fourth round of free-agent draft (January 12, 1982). ... Loaned by White Sox organization with IF Manny Salinas to Mexico City Reds of Mexican League (March 4-June 1, 1985) as part of deal in which IF Nelson Barrera was purchased by White Sox. ... Traded by White Sox to Pittsburgh Pirates (March 30, 1987), completing deal in which Pirates traded P Jim Winn to White Sox for a player to be named later (March 27, 1987). ... On Pittsburgh disabled list (June 6-27, 1988); included rehabilitation assignment to Buffalo (June 20-27). ... Granted free agency (December 20, 1990). ... Signed by Vancouver, White Sox organization (April 7, 1991). ... Traded by White Sox organization to Milwaukee Brewers for SS Esteban Beltre (May 23, 1991). ... Granted free agency (October 15, 1991). ... Signed by Texas Rangers organization (November 7, 1991). ... Released by Rangers (July 19, 1992). ... Signed by Toledo, Detroit Tigers organization (July 28, 1992). ... Granted free agency (October 15, 1992). ... Re-signed by Toledo, Tigers organization (February 8, 1993). ... On disabled list (April 8-May 4, 1993). ... Granted free agency (October 15, 1993). ... Signed by New York Mets organization (November 17, 1993). ... On suspended list (June 15-18, 1994). ... Released by Mets (July 8, 1994). ... Signed by Tucson, Houston Astros organization (March 23, 1995). ... Granted free agency (November 2, 1995). ... Re-signed by Astros organization (December 7, 1995). ... On suspended list (August 16-19, 1996). ... Granted free agency (November 18, 1996). ... Signed by Florida Marlins (November 26, 1996).

STATISTICAL NOTES: Led Midwest League in caught stealing with 35 in 1983. ... Led International League in caught stealing with 18 in 1993.

Year Team (League)	Pos.	G	AB	R	H	2B	3B	HR	RBI	Avg.	BB	SO	SB	PO	A	E	Avg.
1982— Niagara Falls (NYP)	OF	•76	277	60	80	15	4	5	38	.289	•56	51	45	118	5	4	.969
1983— Appleton (Midwest)	OF	128	439	87	124	12	4	1	48	.282	99	81	*87	262	10	6	.978
1984— Glens Falls (Eastern)	OF	138	464	91	133	17	1	1	38	.287	*101	66	65	310	11	11	.967
1985— M.C. Reds (Mex.)	OF	61	201	46	71	9	4	1	30	.353	50	19	17	127	7	6	.957
— Chicago (A.L.)	OF-DH	5	2	2	0	0	0	0	0	.000	0	1	0	1	0	0	1.000
— Buffalo (A.A.)	OF	78	244	34	58	8	5	1	21	.238	46	32	14	148	9	2	.987
1986— Chicago (A.L.)	OF-DH	137	438	65	103	16	3	2	32	.235	71	61	50	276	7	9	.969
1987— Pittsburgh (N.L.)■	OF	104	182	44	50	8	3	4	18	.275	46	33	21	74	3	3	.963
1988— Pittsburgh (N.L.)	OF-P	75	118	18	30	4	1	0	8	.254	17	16	9	52	0	2	.963
— Buffalo (A.A.)	OF	37	145	23	48	6	0	0	10	.331	19	19	14	89	3	0	1.000
1989— Pittsburgh (N.L.)	OF	112	160	18	35	4	2	0	1	.219	35	20	11	71	1	2	.973
1990— Pittsburgh (N.L.)	OF	58	76	13	15	2	0	0	1	.197	11	12	7	24	0	1	1.000
— Buffalo (A.A.)	OF	24	89	17	31	2	2	0	7	.348	12	8	5	49	0	1	.980
1991— Vancouver (PCL)■	OF	30	102	15	25	1	0	0	10	.245	11	8	9	39	2	3	.932
— Denver (A.A.)■	OF-1B-P	83	303	69	89	8	3	3	25	.294	59	29	26	118	10	3	.977
1992— Texas (A.L.)	OF-DH	73	85	12	16	2	0	1	6	.188	18	16	6	76	4	3	.964
— Toledo (Int'l)■	OF	27	74	9	20	3	0	0	6	.270	7	13	11	48	1	0	1.000
1993— Toledo (Int'l)■	OF-P	113	439	73	128	23	4	6	42	.292	56	59	39	252	5	7	.973
1994— New York (N.L.)■	OF	62	111	14	28	4	0	0	4	.252	19	20	5	64	5	0	1.000
1995— Tucson (PCL)■	OF	30	106	18	39	4	1	0	9	.368	19	11	11	67	2	1	.986
— Houston (N.L.)	OF-P	90	201	46	64	5	2	2	18	.318	48	42	21	92	4	5	.950
1996— Houston (N.L.)	OF	108	262	49	69	11	4	1	12	.263	44	41	17	113	5	3	.975
1997— Florida (N.L.)■	OF-P	103	192	28	47	8	0	1	12	.245	19	33	5	84	1	0	1.000
American League totals (3 years)		215	525	79	119	18	3	3	38	.227	89	78	56	353	11	12	.968
National League totals (8 years)		712	1302	230	338	46	12	8	86	.260	239	217	96	574	19	15	.975
Major league totals (11 years)		927	1827	309	457	64	15	11	124	.250	328	295	152	927	30	27	.973

DIVISION SERIES RECORD

						BATTING									FIELDING		
Year Team (League)	Pos.	G	AB	R	H	2B	3B	HR	RBI	Avg.	BB	SO	SB	PO	A	E	Avg.
1997—Florida (N.L.)	PH	1	1	0	0	0	0	0	0	.000	0	0	0	0	0	0	...

CHAMPIONSHIP SERIES RECORD

						BATTING									FIELDING		
Year Team (League)	Pos.	G	AB	R	H	2B	3B	HR	RBI	Avg.	BB	SO	SB	PO	A	E	Avg.
1997—Florida (N.L.)	PH-OF	3	5	0	1	0	0	0	0	.200	1	0	0	2	0	0	1.000

NOTES: Member of World Series championship team (1997).

WORLD SERIES RECORD

						BATTING									FIELDING		
Year Team (League)	Pos.	G	AB	R	H	2B	3B	HR	RBI	Avg.	BB	SO	SB	PO	A	E	Avg.
1997—Florida (N.L.)	PH	3	3	0	1	0	0	0	0	.333	0	2	0	0	0	0	...

RECORD AS PITCHER

Year Team (League)	W	L	Pct.	ERA	G	GS	CG	ShO	Sv.	IP	H	R	ER	BB	SO
1988—Pittsburgh (N.L.)	0	0	...	0.00	1	0	0	0	0	2	1	0	0	0	0
1991—Denver (Am. Assoc.)■	0	0	...	2.45	2	0	0	0	0	$3\,2/3$	3	1	1	2	1
1993—Toledo (Int'l)	0	0	...	81.00	1	0	0	0	0	$2/3$	7	6	6	1	0
1995—Houston (N.L.)	0	0	...	0.00	1	0	0	0	0	1	0	0	0	1	0
1997—Florida (N.L.)■	0	0	...	0.00	1	0	0	0	0	1	0	0	0	1	0
Major league totals (3 years)	0	0	...	0.00	3	0	0	0	0	4	1	0	0	2	0

CANSECO, JOSE — OF/DH

PERSONAL: Born July 2, 1964, in Havana, Cuba. ... 6-4/240. ... Bats right, throws right. ... Identical twin brother of Ozzie Canseco, outfielder, Oakland Athletics and St. Louis Cardinals (1990 and 1992-93). ... Name pronounced can-SAY-co.

HIGH SCHOOL: Miami Coral Park Senior.

TRANSACTIONS/CAREER NOTES: Selected by Oakland Athletics organization in 15th round of free-agent draft (June 7, 1982). ... On Huntsville disabled list (May 14-June 3, 1985). ... On Oakland disabled list (March 23-July 13, 1989); included rehabilitation assignments to Huntsville (May 6 and June 28-July 13). ... On disabled list (June 8-23, 1990 and July 1-16, 1992). ... Traded by A's to Texas Rangers for OF Ruben Sierra, P Jeff Russell, P Bobby Witt and cash (August 31, 1992). ... On disabled list (June 24, 1993-remainder of season). ... Traded by Rangers to Boston Red Sox for OF Otis Nixon and 3B Luis Ortiz (December 9, 1994). ... On Boston disabled list (May 15-June 20, 1995); included rehabilitation assignment to Pawtucket (June 18-20). ... Granted free agency (October 30, 1995). ... Re-signed by Red Sox (December 6, 1995). ... On Boston disabled list (April 24-May 9 and July 26-September 17, 1996); included rehabilitation assignment to Pawtucket (May 7-9). ... Traded by Red Sox to A's for P John Wasdin and cash (January 27, 1997). ... On disabled list (August 1-20 and August 27, 1997-remainder of season). ... Granted free agency (October 31, 1997).

RECORDS: Shares major league record for most strikeouts in two consecutive games—8 (July 14 [3] and 16 [5], 1997). ... Shares major league single-game record for most strikeouts—5 (July 16, 1997); and most strikeouts in two consecutive games—8 (July 14 [3] and 16 [5], 1997). ... Shares major league single-season record for most consecutive bases on balls received—7 (August 4-5, 1992). ... Shares A.L. single-season record for fewest errors by outfielder who led league in errors—9 (1991).

HONORS: Named Minor League Player of the Year by The Sporting News (1985). ... Named Southern League Most Valuable Player (1985). ... Named A.L. Rookie Player of the Year by The Sporting News (1986). ... Named A.L. Rookie of the Year by Baseball Writers' Association of America (1986). ... Named A.L. Player of the Year by The Sporting News (1988). ... Named outfielder on The Sporting News A.L. All-Star team (1988 and 1990-91). ... Named outfielder on The Sporting News A.L. Silver Slugger team (1988 and 1990-91). ... Named A.L. Most Valuable Player by Baseball Writers' Association of America (1988). ... Named A.L. Comeback Player of the Year by The Sporting News (1994).

STATISTICAL NOTES: Led California League outfielders with eight double plays in 1984. ... Hit three home runs in one game (July 3, 1988 and June 13, 1994). ... Led A.L. with .569 slugging percentage in 1988. ... Led A.L. in grounding into double plays with 20 in 1994. ... Career major league grand slams: 5.

						BATTING									FIELDING		
Year Team (League)	Pos.	G	AB	R	H	2B	3B	HR	RBI	Avg.	BB	SO	SB	PO	A	E	Avg.
1982—Miami (Fla. St.)	3B	6	9	0	1	0	0	0	0	.111	1	3	0	3	1	1	.800
—Idaho Falls (Pio.)	3B-OF	28	57	13	15	3	0	2	7	.263	9	13	3	6	17	3	.885
1983—Madison (Midwest)	OF	34	88	8	14	4	0	3	10	.159	10	36	2	23	2	1	.962
—Medford (N'west)	OF	59	197	34	53	15	2	11	40	.269	30	*78	6	46	5	5	.911
1984—Modesto (California)	OF	116	410	61	113	21	2	15	73	.276	74	127	10	216	17	9	.963
1985—Huntsville (Southern)	OF	58	211	47	67	10	2	25	80	.318	30	55	6	117	9	7	.947
—Tacoma (PCL)	OF	60	233	41	81	16	1	11	47	.348	40	66	5	81	7	2	.978
—Oakland (A.L.)	OF	29	96	16	29	3	0	5	13	.302	4	31	1	56	2	3	.951
1986—Oakland (A.L.)	OF-DH	157	600	85	144	29	1	33	117	.240	65	175	15	319	4	•14	.958
1987—Oakland (A.L.)	OF-DH	159	630	81	162	35	3	31	113	.257	50	157	15	263	12	7	.975
1988—Oakland (A.L.)	OF-DH	158	610	120	187	34	0	*42	*124	.307	78	128	40	304	11	7	.978
1989—Huntsville (Southern)	OF	9	29	2	6	0	0	0	3	.207	5	11	1	9	0	0	1.000
—Oakland (A.L.)	OF-DH	65	227	40	61	9	1	17	57	.269	23	69	6	119	5	3	.976
1990—Oakland (A.L.)	OF-DH	131	481	83	132	14	2	37	101	.274	72	158	19	182	7	1	.995
1991—Oakland (A.L.)	OF-DH	154	572	115	152	32	1	•44	122	.266	78	152	26	245	5	•9	.981
1992—Oakland (A.L.)	OF-DH	97	366	66	90	11	0	22	72	.246	48	104	5	163	5	2	.988
—Texas (A.L.)■	OF-DH	22	73	8	17	4	0	4	15	.233	15	24	1	32	0	1	.970
1993—Texas (A.L.)	OF-DH-P	60	231	30	59	14	1	10	46	.255	16	62	6	94	4	3	.970
1994—Texas (A.L.)	DH	111	429	88	121	19	2	31	90	.282	69	114	15	...	...	...	...
1995—Boston (A.L.)■	DH-OF	102	396	64	121	25	1	24	81	.306	42	93	4	1	0	0	1.000
—Pawtucket (Int'l)	DH	2	6	1	1	0	0	0	1	.167	1	5	0	...	...	...	...
1996—Pawtucket (Int'l)	DH	2	5	0	1	0	0	0	0	.200	0	3	0	...	...	...	...
—Boston (A.L.)	DH-OF	96	360	68	104	22	1	28	82	.289	63	82	3	17	1	0	1.000
1997—Oakland (A.L.)■	DH-OF	108	388	56	91	19	0	23	74	.235	51	122	8	74	2	5	.938
Major league totals (13 years)		1449	5459	920	1470	270	13	351	1107	.269	674	1471	164	1869	58	55	.972

DIVISION SERIES RECORD

						BATTING									FIELDING		
Year Team (League)	Pos.	G	AB	R	H	2B	3B	HR	RBI	Avg.	BB	SO	SB	PO	A	E	Avg.
1995—Boston (A.L.)	DH-OF	3	13	0	0	000	0	0	0	.000	2	2	0	4	0	0	1.000

CHAMPIONSHIP SERIES RECORD

							BATTING								FIELDING		
Year Team (League)	Pos.	G	AB	R	H	2B	3B	HR	RBI	Avg.	BB	SO	SB	PO	A	E	Avg.
1988— Oakland (A.L.)	OF	4	16	4	5	1	0	3	4	.313	1	2	1	6	0	0	1.000
1989— Oakland (A.L.)	OF-PH	5	17	1	5	0	0	1	3	.294	3	7	1	6	1	1	.875
1990— Oakland (A.L.)	OF	4	11	3	2	0	0	0	1	.182	5	5	2	14	0	0	1.000
Championship series totals (3 years)		13	44	8	12	1	0	4	8	.273	9	14	3	26	1	1	.964

WORLD SERIES RECORD

NOTES: Hit home run in first at-bat (October 15, 1988). ... Member of World Series championship team (1989).

							BATTING								FIELDING		
Year Team (League)	Pos.	G	AB	R	H	2B	3B	HR	RBI	Avg.	BB	SO	SB	PO	A	E	Avg.
1988— Oakland (A.L.)	OF	5	19	1	1	0	0	1	5	.053	2	4	1	8	0	0	1.000
1989— Oakland (A.L.)	OF	4	14	5	5	0	0	1	3	.357	4	3	1	6	0	0	1.000
1990— Oakland (A.L.)	OF-PH-DH	4	12	1	1	0	0	1	2	.083	2	3	0	4	0	0	1.000
World Series totals (3 years)		13	45	7	7	0	0	3	10	.156	8	10	2	18	0	0	1.000

ALL-STAR GAME RECORD

						BATTING								FIELDING		
Year League	Pos.	AB	R	H	2B	3B	HR	RBI	Avg.	BB	SO	SB	PO	A	E	Avg.
1986— American....................					Did not play.											
1988— American....................	OF	4	0	0	0	0	0	0	.000	0	1	0	3	0	0	1.000
1989— American....................					Selected, did not play—injured.											
1990— American....................	OF	4	0	0	0	0	0	0	.000	1	1	1	1	0	0	1.000
1992— American....................					Selected, did not play—injured.											
All-Star Game totals (2 years)		8	0	0	0	0	0	0	.000	1	2	1	4	0	0	1.000

RECORD AS PITCHER

Year Team (League)	W	L	Pct.	ERA	G	GS	CG	ShO	Sv.	IP	H	R	ER	BB	SO
1993— Texas (A.L.)	0	0	...	27.00	1	0	0	0	0	1	2	3	3	3	0

CARLSON, DAN   P   DEVIL RAYS

PERSONAL: Born January 26, 1970, in Portland, Ore. ... 6-1/200. ... Throws right, bats right. ... Full name: Dan Scott Carlson.
HIGH SCHOOL: Reynolds (Troutdale, Ore.).
JUNIOR COLLEGE: Mt. Hood Community College (Ore.).
TRANSACTIONS/CAREER NOTES: Selected by San Francisco Giants organization in 33rd round of free-agent draft (June 5, 1989). ... On disabled list (May 14-21, 1995). ... On disabled list (March 31-April 11, 1997); included rehabilitation assignment to Bakersfield (April 5-10). ... Selected by Tampa Bay Devil Rays in first round (28th pick overall) of expansion draft (November 18, 1997).
STATISTICAL NOTES: Tied for Texas League lead with 15 home runs allowed in 1992.

Year Team (League)	W	L	Pct.	ERA	G	GS	CG	ShO	Sv.	IP	H	R	ER	BB	SO
1990— Everett (Northwest)	2	6	.250	5.34	17	11	0	0	0	62 1/3	60	42	37	33	77
1991— Clinton (Midwest)	•16	7	.696	3.08	27	27	5	3	0	181 1/3	149	69	62	76	164
1992— Shreveport (Texas)	*15	9	.625	3.19	27	•27	4	1	0	*186	166	85	66	60	*157
1993— Phoenix (PCL)	5	6	.455	6.56	13	12	0	0	0	70	79	54	51	32	48
— Shreveport (Texas)	7	4	.636	2.24	15	15	2	1	0	100 1/3	86	30	25	26	81
1994— Phoenix (PCL)	*13	6	.684	4.64	31	22	0	0	1	151 1/3	173	80	78	55	117
1995— Phoenix (PCL)	9	5	.643	4.27	23	22	0	0	0	132 2/3	138	67	63	66	93
1996— Phoenix (PCL)	•13	6	.684	3.44	33	15	2	0	1	146 2/3	135	61	56	46	123
— San Francisco (N.L.)	1	0	1.000	2.70	5	0	0	0	0	10	13	6	3	2	4
1997— San Francisco (N.L.)	0	0	...	7.63	6	0	0	0	0	15 1/3	20	14	13	8	14
— Bakersfield (California)	0	0	...	0.00	2	2	0	0	0	6	3	0	0	1	7
— Phoenix (PCL)	13	3	*.813	3.88	29	14	0	0	3	109	102	53	47	36	108
Major league totals (2 years)	1	0	1.000	5.68	11	0	0	0	0	25 1/3	33	20	16	10	18

CARMONA, CESARIN   SS   PADRES

PERSONAL: Born December 20, 1976, in Paya Bani, Dominican Republic. ... 5-10/155. ... Bats both, throws right.
HIGH SCHOOL: Paya Bani (Dominican Republic).
TRANSACTIONS/CAREER NOTES: Signed as non-drafted free agent by San Diego Padres (November 6, 1993).

							BATTING								FIELDING		
Year Team (League)	Pos.	G	AB	R	H	2B	3B	HR	RBI	Avg.	BB	SO	SB	PO	A	E	Avg.
1994— Ariz. Padres (Ariz.)	2B-SS	35	130	19	26	3	4	0	8	.200	18	57	17	48	95	14	.911
— Rancho Cuca. (Cal.) ...	2B	3	2	0	0	0	0	0	0	.000	0	1	0	0	1	0	1.000
1995— Ariz. Padres (Ariz.)	SS	15	51	7	13	2	2	1	4	.255	5	10	3	17	28	7	.865
— Clinton (Midwest)	2B	42	129	13	23	2	1	0	5	.178	15	35	10	50	78	10	.928
1996— Clinton (Midwest)	SS	104	315	38	62	7	2	2	21	.197	44	104	8	90	287	35	.915
1997— Clinton (Midwest)	SS	65	234	33	59	7	2	11	32	.252	14	69	15	90	205	33	.899

CARMONA, RAFAEL   P   MARINERS

PERSONAL: Born October 2, 1972, in Rio Piedras, Puerto Rico. ... 6-2/185. ... Throws right, bats left.
HIGH SCHOOL: Juano Colon (Comerio, Puerto Rico).
JUNIOR COLLEGE: Indian Hills (Iowa).
TRANSACTIONS/CAREER NOTES: Selected by Seattle Mariners organization in 13th round of free-agent draft (June 3, 1993). ... On Tacoma disabled list (April 30-June 8, 1997).

Year Team (League)	W	L	Pct.	ERA	G	GS	CG	ShO	Sv.	IP	H	R	ER	BB	SO
1993— Bellingham (N'west)	2	3	.400	3.79	23	0	0	0	2	35 2/3	33	19	15	14	30
1994— Riverside (California)........	8	2	.800	2.81	50	0	0	0	21	67 1/3	48	22	21	19	63
1995— Port City (Southern)	0	1	.000	1.80	15	0	0	0	4	15	11	5	3	3	17
— Seattle (A.L.)................	2	4	.333	5.66	15	3	0	0	1	47 2/3	55	31	30	34	28
— Tacoma (PCL)	4	3	.571	5.06	8	8	1	1	0	48	52	29	27	19	37
1996— Tacoma (PCL)	0	0	. . .	1.42	4	1	0	0	0	6 1/3	5	1	1	5	9
— Seattle (A.L.)................	8	3	.727	4.28	53	1	0	0	1	90 1/3	95	47	43	55	62
1997— Tacoma (PCL)	2	5	.286	3.79	32	5	0	0	4	59 1/3	52	31	25	35	56
— Seattle (A.L.)................	0	0	. . .	3.18	4	0	0	0	0	5 2/3	3	3	2	2	6
Major league totals (3 years)......	**10**	**7**	**.588**	**4.70**	**72**	**4**	**0**	**0**	**2**	**143 2/3**	**153**	**81**	**75**	**91**	**96**

CARPENTER, CHRIS   P   BLUE JAYS

PERSONAL: Born April 21, 1975, in Exter, N.H. ... 6-5/215. ... Throws right, bats right. ... Full name: Christopher John Carpenter.
HIGH SCHOOL: Trinity (Manchester, N.H.)
TRANSACTIONS/CAREER NOTES: Selected by Toronto Blue Jays organization in first round (15th pick overall) of free-agent draft (June 3, 1993).

Year Team (League)	W	L	Pct.	ERA	G	GS	CG	ShO	Sv.	IP	H	R	ER	BB	SO
1994— Medicine Hat (Pioneer)	6	3	.667	2.76	15	15	0	0	0	84 2/3	76	40	26	39	80
1995— Dunedin (Fla. St.)	3	5	.375	2.17	15	15	0	0	0	99 1/3	83	29	24	50	56
— Knoxville (Southern)	3	7	.300	5.18	12	12	0	0	0	64 1/3	71	47	37	31	53
1996— Knoxville (Southern)	7	9	.438	3.94	28	28	1	0	0	171 1/3	161	94	75	91	150
1997— Syracuse (Int'l).............	4	9	.308	4.50	19	19	3	2	0	120	113	64	60	53	97
— Toronto (A.L.)................	3	7	.300	5.09	14	13	1	1	0	81 1/3	108	55	46	37	55
Major league totals (1 year).......	**3**	**7**	**.300**	**5.09**	**14**	**13**	**1**	**1**	**0**	**81 1/3**	**108**	**55**	**46**	**37**	**55**

CARR, CHUCK   OF

PERSONAL: Born August 10, 1968, in San Bernardino, Calif. ... 5-10/165. ... Bats both, throws right. ... Full name: Charles Lee Glenn Carr Jr.
HIGH SCHOOL: Fontana (Calif.).
TRANSACTIONS/CAREER NOTES: Selected by Cincinnati Reds organization in ninth round of free-agent draft (June 2, 1986). ... Released by Reds organization (March 1987). ... Signed by Bellingham, Seattle Mariners organization (June 15, 1987). ... Traded by Mariners organization to New York Mets organization for P Reggie Dobie (November 18, 1988). ... On Tidewater disabled list (April 10-17 and July 15-August 9, 1991). ... On New York disabled list (August 29-September 13, 1991). ... Traded by Mets to St. Louis Cardinals for P Clyde Keller (December 13, 1991). ... On Louisville disabled list (July 31-August 7, 1992). ... Selected by Florida Marlins in first round (14th pick overall) of expansion draft (November 17, 1992). ... On Florida disabled list (July 1-18, 1993); included rehabilitation assignment to Gulf Coast Marlins (July 11-14). ... On Florida disabled list (May 15-June 11, 1995); included rehabilitation assignments to Charlotte (May 26-30 and June 5-11). ... Traded by Marlins to Milwaukee Brewers for P Juan Gonzalez (December 4, 1995). ... On Milwaukee disabled list (April 22-May 11 and May 31, 1996-remainder of season); included rehabilitation assignment to New Orleans (May 7-11). ... Granted free-agency (May 20, 1997). ... Signed by Houston Astros organization (June 1, 1997). ... Granted free agency (December 21, 1997).
STATISTICAL NOTES: Led N.L. in caught stealing with 22 in 1993. ... Career major league grand slams: 1.
MISCELLANEOUS: Holds Florida Marlins all-time record for most stolen bases (115).

Year Team (League)	Pos.	G	AB	R	H	2B	3B	HR	RBI	Avg.	BB	SO	SB	PO	A	E	Avg.
1986— GC Reds (GCL)...........	2B	44	123	13	21	5	0	0	10	.171	10	27	9	75	100	11	.941
1987— Bellingham (N'west)■	S-O-2-3	44	165	31	40	1	1	1	11	.242	12	38	20	50	58	14	.885
1988— Wausau (Midwest)	OF-SS	82	304	58	91	14	2	6	30	.299	14	49	41	170	17	12	.940
— Vermont (Eastern)......	OF	41	159	26	39	4	2	1	13	.245	8	33	21	105	6	6	.949
1989— Jackson (Texas)■	OF	116	444	45	107	13	1	0	22	.241	27	66	47	280	11	8	.973
1990— Jackson (Texas)	OF	93	361	60	93	19	9	3	24	.258	43	77	48	226	12	8	.967
— Tidewater (Int'l)	OF	20	81	13	21	5	1	0	8	.259	4	12	6	40	3	0	1.000
— New York (N.L.).........	OF	4	2	0	0	0	0	0	0	.000	0	2	1	0	0	0	. . .
1991— Tidewater (Int'l)	OF	64	246	34	48	6	1	1	11	.195	18	37	27	141	8	6	.961
— New York (N.L.).........	OF	12	11	1	2	0	0	0	1	.182	0	2	1	9	0	0	1.000
1992— Arkansas (Texas)■.....	OF	28	111	17	29	5	1	1	6	.261	8	23	8	70	3	1	.986
— Louisville (A.A.)	OF	96	377	68	116	11	9	3	28	.308	31	60	*53	244	9	5	.981
— St. Louis (N.L.)........	OF	22	64	8	14	3	0	0	3	.219	9	6	10	39	1	0	1.000
1993— Florida (N.L.)■........	OF	142	551	75	147	19	2	4	41	.267	49	74	*58	393	7	6	.985
— GC Marlins (GCL)	OF	3	12	4	5	1	0	1	3	.417	0	2	3	9	0	1	.900
1994— Florida (N.L.)	OF	106	433	61	114	19	2	2	30	.263	22	71	32	297	4	6	.980
1995— Florida (N.L.)	OF	105	308	54	70	20	0	2	20	.227	46	49	25	217	8	3	.987
— Charlotte (Int'l)	OF	7	23	5	5	0	1	1	2	.217	2	1	2	9	0	0	1.000
1996— New Orleans (A.A.)■..	OF	4	13	2	5	1	0	0	1	.385	2	1	2	6	2	0	1.000
— Milwaukee (A.L.)	OF	27	106	18	29	6	1	1	11	.274	6	21	5	76	4	0	1.000
1997— Milwaukee (A.L.)	OF	26	46	3	6	3	0	0	0	.130	2	11	1	25	1	0	1.000
— New Orleans (A.A.)......	OF	19	65	8	16	1	0	0	3	.246	8	14	5	35	1	0	1.000
— Houston (N.L.)■........	OF	63	192	34	53	11	2	4	17	.276	15	37	11	111	3	4	.966
American League totals (2 years)		53	152	21	35	9	1	1	11	.230	8	32	6	101	5	0	1.000
National League totals (7 years)		454	1561	233	400	72	6	12	112	.256	141	241	138	1066	23	19	.983
Major league totals (8 years)		507	1713	254	435	81	7	13	123	.254	149	273	144	1167	28	19	.984

DIVISION SERIES RECORD

Year Team (League)	Pos.	G	AB	R	H	2B	3B	HR	RBI	Avg.	BB	SO	SB	PO	A	E	Avg.
1997— Houston (N.L.)	OF	2	4	1	1	0	0	1	1	.250	1	3	0	2	0	0	1.000

C

PERSONAL: Born March 4, 1968, in Edo Anzuategni, Venezuela. ... 6-2/230. ... Throws right, bats right.
TRANSACTIONS/CAREER NOTES: Signed as non-drafted free agent by Toronto Blue Jays organization (January 23, 1990). ... Claimed on waivers by Cincinnati Reds (July 3, 1996). ... Granted free agency (October 15, 1996). ... Signed by Baltimore Orioles organization (November 12, 1996). ... Released by Orioles organization (May 14, 1997). ... Signed by Reds organization (May 17, 1997).

Year Team (League)	W	L	Pct.	ERA	G	GS	CG	ShO	Sv.	IP	H	R	ER	BB	SO
1990— Dom. Dodgers (DSL)	8	2	.800	2.62	15	14	4	0	0	86	88	31	25	28	55
1991— St. Catharines (NYP)	5	2	.714	1.71	15	13	2	•2	0	89 2/3	66	26	17	21	83
1992— Dunedin (Fla. St.)	0	1	.000	4.63	5	4	0	0	0	23 1/3	22	13	12	11	16
—Myrtle Beach (SAL)	11	7	.611	3.14	22	16	1	1	0	100 1/3	86	40	35	36	100
1993— Dunedin (Fla. St.)	6	11	.353	3.45	27	24	1	0	0	140 2/3	136	69	54	59	108
1994— Knoxville (Southern)	13	7	.650	3.89	26	26	1	0	0	164 1/3	158	85	71	59	96
1995— Syracuse (Int'l)	7	7	.500	3.96	21	21	0	0	0	131 2/3	116	72	58	56	81
—Toronto (A.L.)	2	4	.333	7.21	12	7	1	0	0	48 2/3	64	46	39	25	27
1996— Syracuse (Int'l)	4	4	.500	3.58	9	6	1	0	0	37 2/3	37	16	15	12	28
—Toronto (A.L.)	0	1	.000	11.40	11	0	0	0	0	15	23	19	19	12	10
—Indianapolis (A.A.)■	4	0	1.000	0.76	9	6	1	1	1	47 2/3	25	6	4	9	45
—Cincinnati (N.L.)	1	0	1.000	5.87	8	5	0	0	0	23	31	17	15	13	13
1997— Rochester (Int'l)■	4	2	.667	4.44	8	8	1	0	0	46 2/3	45	23	23	16	48
—Indianapolis (A.A.)■	12	5	.706	3.51	19	18	2	0	0	120 2/3	111	50	47	51	105
—Cincinnati (N.L.)	0	1	.000	7.84	2	2	0	0	0	10 1/3	14	9	9	6	5
A.L. totals (2 years)	2	5	.286	8.20	23	7	1	0	0	63 2/3	87	65	58	37	37
N.L. totals (2 years)	1	1	.500	6.48	10	7	0	0	0	33 1/3	45	26	24	19	18
Major league totals (3 years)	3	6	.333	7.61	33	14	1	0	0	97	132	91	82	56	55

C

PERSONAL: Born October 22, 1969, in San Pedro de Macoris, Dominican Republic. ... 6-2/180. ... Throws right, bats right. ... Full name: Hector Pacheco Pipo Carrasco.
HIGH SCHOOL: Liceo Mattias Mella (San Pedro de Macoris, Dominican Republic).
TRANSACTIONS/CAREER NOTES: Signed as non-drafted free agent by New York Mets organization (March 20, 1988). ... Released by Mets organization (January 6, 1992). ... Signed by Houston Astros organization (January 21, 1992). ... Traded by Astros organization with P Brian Griffiths to Florida Marlins organization for P Tom Edens (November 17, 1992). ... Traded by Marlins to Cincinnati Reds (September 10, 1993), completing deal in which Reds traded P Chris Hammond to Marlins for 3B Gary Scott and a player to be named later (March 27, 1993). ... On disabled list (May 12-June 1, 1994). ... Traded by Reds with P Scott Service to Kansas City Royals for OF Jon Nunnally and IF/OF Chris Stynes (July 15, 1997). ... Selected by Arizona Diamondbacks in second round (49th pick overall) of expansion draft (November 18, 1997).

Year Team (League)	W	L	Pct.	ERA	G	GS	CG	ShO	Sv.	IP	H	R	ER	BB	SO
1988— GC Mets (GCL)	0	2	.000	4.17	14	2	0	0	0	36 2/3	37	29	17	13	21
1989— Kingsport (Appalachian)	1	6	.143	5.74	12	10	0	0	0	53 1/3	69	49	34	34	55
1990— Kingsport (Appalachian)	0	0	...	4.05	3	1	0	0	0	6 2/3	8	3	3	1	5
1991— Pittsfield (NYP)	0	1	.000	5.40	12	1	0	0	1	23 1/3	25	17	14	21	20
1992— Asheville (S. Atl.)■	5	5	.500	2.99	49	0	0	0	8	78 1/3	66	30	26	47	67
1993— Kane County (Midwest)■	6	12	.333	4.11	28	*28	0	0	0	149	153	90	68	76	127
1994— Cincinnati (N.L.)■	5	6	.455	2.24	45	0	0	0	6	56 1/3	42	17	14	30	41
1995— Cincinnati (N.L.)	2	7	.222	4.12	64	0	0	0	5	87 1/3	86	45	40	46	64
1996— Cincinnati (N.L.)	4	3	.571	3.75	56	0	0	0	0	74 1/3	58	37	31	45	59
—Indianapolis (A.A.)	0	1	.000	2.14	13	2	0	0	0	21	18	7	5	13	17
1997— Indianapolis (A.A.)	0	0	...	6.23	3	0	0	0	1	4 1/3	5	3	3	3	4
—Cincinnati (N.L.)	1	2	.333	3.68	38	0	0	0	0	51 1/3	51	25	21	25	46
—Kansas City (A.L.)■	1	6	.143	5.45	28	0	0	0	0	34 2/3	29	21	21	16	30
A.L. totals (1 year)	1	6	.143	5.45	28	0	0	0	0	34 2/3	29	21	21	16	30
N.L. totals (4 years)	12	18	.400	3.54	203	0	0	0	11	269 1/3	237	124	106	146	210
Major league totals (4 years)	13	24	.351	3.76	231	0	0	0	11	304	266	145	127	162	240

CHAMPIONSHIP SERIES RECORD

Year Team (League)	W	L	Pct.	ERA	G	GS	CG	ShO	Sv.	IP	H	R	ER	BB	SO
1995— Cincinnati (N.L.)	0	0	...	0.00	1	0	0	0	0	1 1/3	1	0	0	0	3

PERSONAL: Born March 7, 1960, in Oklahoma City. ... 6-3/215. ... Bats right, throws right. ... Full name: Joseph Chris Carter. ... Brother of Fred Carter, minor league outfielder (1985-88); and cousin of Chris Carter, defensive back, New England Patriots.
HIGH SCHOOL: Millwood (Oklahoma City).
COLLEGE: Wichita State.
TRANSACTIONS/CAREER NOTES: Selected by Chicago Cubs organization in first round (second pick overall) of free-agent draft (June 8, 1981). ... On disabled list (April 9-19, 1982). ... Traded by Cubs organization with OF Mel Hall, P Don Schulze and P Darryl Banks to Cleveland Indians for C Ron Hassey, P Rick Sutcliffe and P George Frazier (June 13, 1984). ... On Cleveland disabled list (July 2-17, 1984). ... Traded by Indians to San Diego Padres for C Sandy Alomar, OF Chris James and 3B Carlos Baerga (December 6, 1989). ... Traded by Padres with 2B Roberto Alomar to Toronto Blue Jays for 1B Fred McGriff and SS Tony Fernandez (December 5, 1990). ... Granted free agency (October 30, 1992). ... Re-signed by Blue Jays (December 7, 1992). ... Granted free agency (October 28, 1997). ... Signed by Baltimore Orioles (December 12, 1997).
RECORDS: Shares major league records for most home runs in two consecutive games—5 (July 18 [2] and 19 [3], 1989). ... Shares major league single-season record for most games with three or more home runs—2 (1989). ... Shares major league record for most home runs in one inning—2 (October 3, 1993, second inning). ... Holds A.L. career record for most games with three or more home runs—5.
HONORS: Named outfielder on THE SPORTING NEWS college All-America team (1980-81). ... Named College Player of the Year by THE SPORTING NEWS (1981). ... Named outfielder on THE SPORTING NEWS A.L. All-Star team (1991-92). ... Named outfielder on THE SPORTING NEWS A.L. Silver Slugger team (1991-92).

STATISTICAL NOTES: Led American Association with 265 total bases in 1983. ... Had 21-game hitting streak (May 17-June 8, 1986). ... Hit three home runs in one game five times (August 29, 1986; May 28, 1987; June 24 and July 19, 1989; and August 23, 1993). ... Led A.L. first basemen with 12 errors in 1987. ... Led A.L. in being hit by pitch with 10 in 1991. ... Led A.L. with 13 sacrifice flies in 1992 and 1994. ... Career major league grand slams: 10.

MISCELLANEOUS: Holds Toronto Blue Jays all-time record for most home runs (203).

							BATTING								FIELDING		
Year Team (League)	Pos.	G	AB	R	H	2B	3B	HR	RBI	Avg.	BB	SO	SB	PO	A	E	Avg.
1981—Midland (Texas).........	OF	67	249	42	67	15	3	5	35	.269	8	30	12	100	10	4	.965
1982—Midland (Texas).........	OF	110	427	84	136	22	8	25	98	.319	26	51	15	182	6	5	.974
1983—Iowa (Am. Assoc.)......	OF	124	*522	82	160	27	6	22	83	.307	17	•103	40	204	9	12	.947
—Chicago (N.L.).........	OF	23	51	6	9	1	1	0	1	.176	0	21	1	26	0	0	1.000
1984—Iowa (Am. Assoc.)......	OF	61	248	45	77	12	7	14	67	.310	20	31	11	142	6	2	.987
—Cleveland (A.L.)■......	OF-1B	66	244	32	67	6	1	13	41	.275	11	48	2	169	11	6	.968
1985—Cleveland (A.L.)...O-1-DH-2-3		143	489	64	128	27	0	15	59	.262	25	74	24	311	17	6	.982
1986—Cleveland (A.L.)........	OF-1B	162	663	108	200	36	9	29	*121	.302	32	95	29	800	55	10	.988
1987—Cleveland (A.L.).....	1B-OF-DH	149	588	83	155	27	2	32	106	.264	27	105	31	782	46	†17	.980
1988—Cleveland (A.L.)........	OF	157	621	85	168	36	6	27	98	.271	35	82	27	444	8	7	.985
1989—Cleveland (A.L.).........	OF-1B-DH	•162	•651	84	158	32	4	35	105	.243	39	112	13	443	20	9	.981
1990—San Diego (N.L.)■......	OF-1B	*162	*634	79	147	27	1	24	115	.232	48	93	22	492	16	11	.979
1991—Toronto (A.L.)■.........	OF	•162	638	89	174	42	3	33	108	.273	49	112	20	283	13	8	.974
1992—Toronto (A.L.)........	OF-DH-1B	158	622	97	164	30	7	34	119	.264	36	109	12	284	13	9	.971
1993—Toronto (A.L.)........	OF-DH	155	603	92	153	33	5	33	121	.254	47	113	8	289	7	8	.974
1994—Toronto (A.L.)........	OF-DH	111	435	70	118	25	2	27	103	.271	33	64	11	205	4	2	.991
1995—Toronto (A.L.)........	OF-1B-DH	139	558	70	141	23	0	25	76	.253	37	87	12	316	12	7	.979
1996—Toronto (A.L.)........	OF-1B-DH	157	625	84	158	35	7	30	107	.253	44	106	7	416	23	9	.980
1997—Toronto (A.L.)........	DH-OF-1B	157	612	76	143	30	4	21	102	.234	40	105	8	429	23	4	.991
American League totals (13 years)		1878	7349	1034	1927	382	50	354	1266	.262	455	1212	204	5171	252	102	.982
National League totals (2 years)		185	685	85	156	28	2	24	116	.228	48	114	23	518	16	11	.980
Major league totals (15 years)		2063	8034	1119	2083	410	52	378	1382	.259	503	1326	227	5689	268	113	.981

CHAMPIONSHIP SERIES RECORD

RECORDS: Shares A.L. single-game record for most at-bats—6 (October 11, 1992, 11 innings).

							BATTING								FIELDING		
Year Team (League)	Pos.	G	AB	R	H	2B	3B	HR	RBI	Avg.	BB	SO	SB	PO	A	E	Avg.
1991—Toronto (A.L.).............	OF-DH	5	19	3	5	2	0	1	4	.263	1	5	0	4	1	0	1.000
1992—Toronto (A.L.).............	OF-1B	6	26	2	5	0	0	1	3	.192	2	4	2	16	1	1	.944
1993—Toronto (A.L.).............	OF	6	27	2	7	0	0	0	2	.259	1	5	0	12	1	0	1.000
Championship series totals (3 years)		17	72	7	17	2	0	2	9	.236	4	14	2	32	3	1	.972

WORLD SERIES RECORD

RECORDS: Holds career record for most sacrifice flies—4. ... Holds single-series record for most sacrifice flies—3 (1993).
NOTES: Member of World Series championship teams (1992 and 1993).

							BATTING								FIELDING		
Year Team (League)	Pos.	G	AB	R	H	2B	3B	HR	RBI	Avg.	BB	SO	SB	PO	A	E	Avg.
1992—Toronto (A.L.).............	OF-1B	6	22	2	6	2	0	2	3	.273	3	2	0	27	1	0	1.000
1993—Toronto (A.L.).............	OF	6	25	6	7	1	0	2	8	.280	0	4	0	13	0	2	.867
World Series totals (2 years)		12	47	8	13	3	0	4	11	.277	3	6	0	40	1	2	.953

ALL-STAR GAME RECORD

						BATTING							FIELDING		
Year League	Pos.	AB	R	H	2B	3B	HR	RBI	Avg.	BB	SO	SB	PO	A	E	Avg.
1991—American...................	OF	1	1	1	0	0	0	0	1.000	1	0	0	1	0	0	1.000
1992—American...................	OF	3	1	2	0	0	0	1	.667	0	0	0	1	0	0	1.000
1993—American...................	OF	3	0	1	0	0	0	0	.333	0	1	0	1	0	0	1.000
1994—American...................	OF	3	1	0	0	0	0	0	.000	0	0	0	1	0	0	1.000
1996—American...................	OF	1	0	1	0	0	0	0	1.000	0	0	0	0	0	0	...
All-Star Game totals (5 years)		11	3	5	0	0	0	1	.455	1	1	0	4	0	0	1.000

CARUSO, MIKE   IF   WHITE SOX

PERSONAL: Born May 27, 1977, in Queens, N.Y. ... 6-0/172. ... Bats both, throws right. ... Full name: Michael J. Caruso.
HIGH SCHOOL: Stoneham Douglas (Fort Lauderdale).
TRANSACTIONS/CAREER NOTES: Selected by San Francisco Giants organization in second round of free-agent draft (June 2, 1996). ... Traded by Giants with P Keith Foulke, P Lorenzo Barcelo, P Bobby Howry, P Ken Vining and OF Brian Manning to Chicago White Sox for P Danny Darwin, P Wilson Alvarez and P Roberto Hernandez (July 31, 1997).

							BATTING								FIELDING		
Year Team (League)	Pos.	G	AB	R	H	2B	3B	HR	RBI	Avg.	BB	SO	SB	PO	A	E	Avg.
1996—Bellingham (N'west)...	SS-3B	73	312	48	91	16	1	2	24	.292	16	23	24	107	231	40	.894
1997—San Jose (Calif.)........	SS	108	441	76	147	24	11	2	50	.333	38	19	11	168	300	33	.934
—Win.-Salem (Car.)■....	SS	28	119	12	27	3	2	0	14	.227	4	8	3	44	67	7	.941

CARVER, STEVE   OF   PHILLIES

PERSONAL: Born September 27, 1972, in Houston. ... 6-3/215. ... Bats left, throws right. ... Full name: Steven Grady Carver. ... Nephew of Mark Littell, pitcher with Kansas City Royals and St. Louis Cardinals (1973 and 1975-82).
HIGH SCHOOL: The Bolles School (Jacksonville).
COLLEGE: Stanford (degree in psychology).
TRANSACTIONS/CAREER NOTES: Selected by Boston Red Sox organization in 38th round of free-agent draft (June 3, 1991); did not sign. ... Selected by Philadelphia Phillies organization in fourth round of free-agent draft (June 1, 1995). ... On disabled list (May 5-16 and July 5-August 22, 1997).

Year Team (League)	Pos.	G	AB	R	H	2B	3B	HR	RBI	Avg.	BB	SO	SB	PO	A	E	Avg.
1995— Batavia (NY-Penn)	1B	56	217	35	66	13	2	7	31	.304	17	29	2	451	17	8	.983
1996— Clearwater (FSL)	1B-3B-OF	117	436	59	121	32	0	17	79	.278	52	89	1	670	94	18	.977
1997— Reading (Eastern)	OF	79	282	41	74	11	3	15	43	.262	36	69	2	116	0	7	.943

CASANOVA, RAUL — C — TIGERS

PERSONAL: Born August 23, 1972, in Humacao, Puerto Rico. ... 5-11/200. ... Bats both, throws right.
HIGH SCHOOL: Ponce (Puerto Rico).
TRANSACTIONS/CAREER NOTES: Selected by New York Mets organization in eighth round of free-agent draft (June 4, 1990). ... Traded by Mets organization to San Diego Padres organization (December 7, 1992), completing deal in which Padres traded SS Tony Fernandez to Mets for P Wally Whitehurst, OF D.J. Dozier and a player to be named later (October 26, 1992). ... Traded by Padres with P Richie Lewis and OF Melvin Nieves to Detroit Tigers for P Sean Bergman, P Cade Gaspar and OF Todd Steverson (March 22, 1996). ... On Toledo disabled list (May 3-14, 1996). ... On Detroit disabled list (June 19-August 13, 1996); included rehabilitation assignments to Jacksonville (July 31-August 9) and Toledo (August 9-13).
STATISTICAL NOTES: Switch-hit home runs in one game (June 6, 1996).

Year Team (League)	Pos.	G	AB	R	H	2B	3B	HR	RBI	Avg.	BB	SO	SB	PO	A	E	Avg.
1990— GC Mets (GCL)	C	23	65	4	5	0	0	0	1	.077	4	16	0	141	20	8	.953
1991— GC Mets (GCL)	C	32	111	19	27	4	2	0	9	.243	12	22	3	211	24	5	.979
— Kingsport (Appal.)......	C	5	18	0	1	0	0	0	0	.056	1	10	0	35	4	1	.975
1992— Columbia (S. Atl.)......	C	5	18	2	3	0	0	0	1	.167	1	4	0	29	1	0	1.000
— Kingsport (Appal.)......	C	42	137	25	37	9	1	4	27	.270	26	25	3	286	34	6	.982
1993— Waterloo (Midw.)■ ...	C-3B	76	227	32	58	12	0	6	30	.256	21	46	0	361	50	10	.976
1994— Rancho Cuca. (Cal.) ...	C	123	471	83	*160	27	2	23	120	*.340	43	97	1	593	55	14	.979
1995— Memphis (Southern)..	C	89	306	42	83	18	0	12	44	.271	25	51	4	531	55	*12	.980
1996— Toledo (Int'l)■..........	C	49	161	23	44	11	0	8	28	.273	20	24	0	234	15	2	.992
— Detroit (A.L.)............	C-DH	25	85	6	16	1	0	4	9	.188	6	18	0	123	12	3	.978
— Jacksonville (South.)..	C	8	30	5	10	2	0	4	9	.333	2	7	0	21	1	0	1.000
1997— Toledo (Int'l)	C	12	41	1	8	0	0	1	3	.195	3	8	0	77	8	2	.977
— Detroit (A.L.)............	C-DH	101	304	27	74	10	1	5	24	.243	26	48	1	543	38	9	.985
Major league totals (2 years)		126	389	33	90	11	1	9	33	.231	32	66	1	666	50	12	.984

CASEY, SEAN — 1B — INDIANS

PERSONAL: Born July 2, 1974, in Willingsboro, N.J. ... 6-4/215. ... Bats left, throws right.
COLLEGE: Richmond.
TRANSACTIONS/CAREER NOTES: Selected by Cleveland Indians organization in second round of free-agent draft (June 1, 1995). ... On disabled list (July 23-September 23, 1996). ... On Akron disabled list (April 4-June 8, 1997).
STATISTICAL NOTES: Led Carolina League with .544 slugging percentage in 1996.

Year Team (League)	Pos.	G	AB	R	H	2B	3B	HR	RBI	Avg.	BB	SO	SB	PO	A	E	Avg.
1995— Watertown (NYP)	1B	55	207	26	68	18	0	2	37	.329	18	21	3	510	24	8	.985
1996— Kinston (Carolina)	1B	92	344	62	114	31	3	12	57	*.331	36	47	1	632	15	6	.991
1997— Akron (Eastern)	1B	62	241	38	93	19	1	10	66	.386	23	34	0	405	22	5	.988
— Buffalo (A.A.)...........	1B	20	72	12	26	7	0	5	18	.361	9	11	0	17	1	0	1.000
— Cleveland (A.L.).........	DH-1B	6	10	1	2	0	0	0	1	.200	1	2	0	2	0	0	1.000
Major league totals (1 year)		6	10	1	2	0	0	0	1	.200	1	2	0	2	0	0	1.000

CASIAN, LARRY — P — WHITE SOX

PERSONAL: Born October 28, 1965, in Lynwood, Calif. ... 6-0/175. ... Throws left, bats right. ... Full name: Lawrence Paul Casian. ... Name pronounced CASS-ee-un.
HIGH SCHOOL: Lakewood (Calif.).
COLLEGE: Cal State Fullerton.
TRANSACTIONS/CAREER NOTES: Selected by Minnesota Twins organization in sixth round of free-agent draft (June 2, 1987). ... On Minnesota disabled list (April 14-May 28, 1993); included rehabilitation assignment to Portland (May 14-27). ... Claimed on waivers by Cleveland Indians (July 14, 1994). ... Released by Indians (November 4, 1994). ... Signed by Iowa, Cubs organization (December 12, 1994). ... On Chicago disabled list (June 14-August 1, 1995); included rehabilitation assignment to Iowa (July 13-August 1). ... On Chicago disabled list (April 21-May 6, 1997). ... Claimed on waivers by Kansas City Royals (May 27, 1997). ... Released by Royals (August 25, 1997). ... Signed by Chicago White Sox organization (January 13, 1998).
STATISTICAL NOTES: Pitched two innings, combining with starter David West (six innings) and Greg Johnson (one inning) in 5-0 no-hit victory for Portland against Vancouver (June 7, 1992).

Year Team (League)	W	L	Pct.	ERA	G	GS	CG	ShO	Sv.	IP	H	R	ER	BB	SO
1987— Visalia (California)	10	3	.769	2.51	18	15	2	1	2	97	89	35	27	49	96
1988— Orlando (South.)	9	9	.500	2.95	27	26	4	1	0	174	165	72	57	62	104
— Portland (PCL)	0	1	.000	0.00	1	0	0	0	0	2 2/3	5	3	0	0	2
1989— Portland (PCL)	7	12	.368	4.52	28	27	0	0	0	169 1/3	201	97	85	63	65
1990— Portland (PCL)	9	9	.500	4.48	37	23	1	0	0	156 2/3	171	90	78	59	89
— Minnesota (A.L.)	2	1	.667	3.22	5	3	0	0	0	22 1/3	26	9	8	4	11
1991— Minnesota (A.L.)	0	0	...	7.36	15	0	0	0	0	18 1/3	28	16	15	7	6
— Portland (PCL)	3	2	.600	3.46	34	6	0	0	1	52	51	25	20	16	24
1992— Portland (PCL)	4	0	1.000	2.32	58	0	0	0	11	62	54	16	16	13	43
— Minnesota (A.L.)	1	0	1.000	2.70	6	0	0	0	0	6 2/3	7	2	2	1	2
1993— Minnesota (A.L.)	5	3	.625	3.02	54	0	0	0	1	56 2/3	59	23	19	14	31
— Portland (PCL)	1	0	1.000	0.00	7	0	0	0	2	7 2/3	9	0	0	2	2

Year—Team (League)	W	L	Pct.	ERA	G	GS	CG	ShO	Sv.	IP	H	R	ER	BB	SO
1994—Minnesota (A.L.)	1	3	.250	7.08	33	0	0	0	1	40²/₃	57	34	32	12	18
—Cleveland (A.L.)■	0	2	.000	8.64	7	0	0	0	0	8¹/₃	16	9	8	4	2
1995—Iowa (Am. Assoc.)■	0	0	. . .	2.13	13	0	0	0	1	12²/₃	9	3	3	2	9
—Chicago (N.L.)	1	0	1.000	1.93	42	0	0	0	0	23¹/₃	23	6	5	15	11
1996—Chicago (N.L.)	1	1	.500	1.88	35	0	0	0	0	24	14	5	5	11	15
—Iowa (Am. Assoc.)	3	2	.600	1.71	24	4	0	0	1	47¹/₃	37	13	9	11	32
1997—Chicago (N.L.)	0	1	.000	7.45	12	0	0	0	0	9²/₃	16	9	8	2	7
—Kansas City (A.L.)■	0	2	.000	5.06	32	0	0	0	0	26²/₃	32	15	15	6	16
A.L. totals (6 years)	9	11	.450	4.96	152	3	0	0	2	179²/₃	225	108	99	48	86
N.L. totals (3 years)	2	2	.500	2.84	89	0	0	0	0	57	53	20	18	28	33
Major league totals (8 years)	11	13	.458	4.45	241	3	0	0	2	236²/₃	278	128	117	76	119

CASIMIRO, CARLOS   2B   ORIOLES

PERSONAL: Born November 8, 1976, in San Pedro de Macoris, Dominican Republic. ... 6-0/155. ... Bats right, throws right. ... Full name: Carlos Rafael Casimiro.
TRANSACTIONS/CAREER NOTES: Signed as non-drafted free agent by Baltimore Orioles organization (April 15, 1994).

						BATTING						FIELDING			
Year—Team (League)	Pos.	G	AB	R	H	2B	3B	HR	RBI	Avg.	BB	SO	SB	PO	A	E	Avg.
1994—Dom. Orioles (DSL)	IF	41	157	27	30	6	1	3	22	.191	28	41	14	64	76	19	.881
1995—GC Orioles (GCL)	2B-SS	32	107	14	27	4	2	2	11	.252	10	22	1	48	81	13	.908
1996—Bluefield (Appal.)	2B-3B	62	239	51	66	16	0	10	33	.276	20	52	22	103	131	13	.947
1997—Delmarva (S. Atl.)	2B	122	457	54	111	21	8	9	51	.243	26	108	20	204	287	21	.959

CASTILLA, VINNY   3B   ROCKIES

PERSONAL: Born July 4, 1967, in Oaxaca, Mexico. ... 6-1/200. ... Bats right, throws right. ... Full name: Vinicio Soria Castilla. ... Name pronounced kass-TEE-uh..
HIGH SCHOOL: Instituto Carlos Gracida (Oaxaca, Mexico).
TRANSACTIONS/CAREER NOTES: Signed as non-drafted free agent by Saltillo of Mexican League. ... Contract sold by Saltillo to Atlanta Braves organization (March 19, 1990). ... Selected by Colorado Rockies in second round (40th pick overall) of expansion draft (November 17, 1992). ... On disabled list (May 20-June 4, 1993).
RECORDS: Holds N.L. single-season record for most at-bats without a triple—629 (1996).
HONORS: Named third baseman on THE SPORTING NEWS N.L. All-Star team (1995 and 1997). ... Named third baseman on THE SPORTING NEWS N.L. Silver Slugger team (1995 and 1997).
STATISTICAL NOTES: Led International League shortstops with 550 total chances and 72 double plays in 1992. ... Led N.L. third basemen with 506 total chances and 43 double plays in 1996. ... Had 22-game hitting streak (August 9-September 1, 1997). ... Led N.L. third basemen with 41 double plays in 1997. ... Career major league grand slams: 2.

						BATTING						FIELDING			
Year—Team (League)	Pos.	G	AB	R	H	2B	3B	HR	RBI	Avg.	BB	SO	SB	PO	A	E	Avg.
1987—Saltillo (Mexican)	3B	13	27	0	5	2	0	0	1	.185	0	5	0	10	31	1	.976
1988—Salt.-Monc. (Mex.)■	SS	50	124	22	30	2	2	5	18	.242	8	29	1	53	105	13	.924
1989—Saltillo (Mexican)■	SS-3B	128	462	70	142	25	13	10	58	.307	33	70	11	224	427	34	.950
1990—Sumter (S. Atl.)■	SS	93	339	47	91	15	2	9	53	.268	28	54	2	139	320	23	.952
—Greenville (Southern)	SS	46	170	20	40	5	1	4	16	.235	13	23	4	71	167	7	.971
1991—Greenville (Southern)	SS	66	259	34	70	17	3	7	44	.270	9	35	0	86	221	11	.965
—Richmond (Int'l)	SS	67	240	25	54	7	4	7	36	.225	14	32	1	93	208	12	.962
—Atlanta (N.L.)	SS	12	5	1	1	0	0	0	0	.200	0	2	0	6	6	0	1.000
1992—Richmond (Int'l)	SS	127	449	49	113	29	1	7	44	.252	21	68	1	162	357	*31	.944
—Atlanta (N.L.)	SS-3B	9	16	1	4	1	0	0	1	.250	1	4	0	2	12	1	.933
1993—Colorado (N.L.)■	SS	105	337	36	86	9	7	9	30	.255	13	45	2	141	282	11	.975
1994—Colorado (N.L.)	S-2-3-1	52	130	16	43	11	1	3	18	.331	7	23	2	67	78	2	.986
—Colo. Springs (PCL)	3B-2B-SS	22	78	13	19	6	1	1	11	.244	7	11	0	20	60	3	.964
1995—Colorado (N.L.)	3B-SS	139	527	82	163	34	2	32	90	.309	30	87	2	86	264	15	.959
1996—Colorado (N.L.)	3B	160	629	97	191	34	0	40	113	.304	35	88	7	97	*389	20	.960
1997—Colorado (N.L.)	3B	159	612	94	186	25	2	40	113	.304	44	108	2	112	*323	21	.954
Major league totals (7 years)		636	2256	327	674	114	12	124	365	.299	130	357	15	511	1354	70	.964

DIVISION SERIES RECORD

						BATTING						FIELDING			
Year—Team (League)	Pos.	G	AB	R	H	2B	3B	HR	RBI	Avg.	BB	SO	SB	PO	A	E	Avg.
1995—Colorado (N.L.)	3B	4	15	3	7	1	0	3	6	.467	0	1	0	3	13	1	.941

ALL-STAR GAME RECORD

					BATTING						FIELDING			
Year—League	Pos.	AB	R	H	2B	3B	HR	RBI	Avg.	BB	SO	SB	PO	A	E	Avg.
1995—National	3B	2	0	0	0	0	0	0	.000	0	1	0	0	0	0	. . .

CASTILLO, ALBERTO   C   METS

PERSONAL: Born February 10, 1970, in San Juan de la Maguana, Dominican Republic. ... 6-0/184. ... Bats right, throws right. ... Full name: Alberto Terrero Castillo.
HIGH SCHOOL: Mercedes Maria Mateo (Dominican Republic).
TRANSACTIONS/CAREER NOTES: Signed as non-drafted free agent by New York Mets organization (April 15, 1987). ... On disabled list (July 3, 1992-remainder of season and June 1-July 13, 1994). ... On suspended list (August 27-29, 1994).
STATISTICAL NOTES: Led International League catchers with 827 total chances and nine double plays in 1996.

Year Team (League)	Pos.	G	AB	R	H	2B	3B	HR	RBI	Avg.	BB	SO	SB	PO	A	E	Avg.
1987—Kingsport (Appal.)......	C	7	9	1	1	0	0	0	0	.111	5	3	1	21	4	0	1.000
1988—GC Mets (GCL)......	C	22	68	7	18	4	0	0	10	.265	4	4	2	126	13	1	.993
—Kingsport (Appal.)......	C	24	75	7	22	3	0	1	14	.293	15	14	0	161	18	5	.973
1989—Kingsport (Appal.)......	C-1B	27	74	15	19	4	0	3	12	.257	11	14	2	140	19	1	.994
—Pittsfield (NYP)......	C	34	123	13	29	8	0	1	13	.236	7	26	2	186	26	2	.991
—St. Lucie (Fla. St.)......	...	1	0	0	0	0	0	0	0	...	0	0	0	0	0	0	...
1990—Columbia (S. Atl.)......	C	30	103	8	24	4	3	1	14	.233	10	21	1	187	22	5	.977
—Pittsfield (NYP)......	C-OF-1B	58	187	19	41	8	1	4	24	.219	26	35	3	378	61	9	.980
1991—Columbia (S. Atl.)......	C	90	267	35	74	20	3	3	47	.277	43	44	6	*734	86	15	.982
1992—St. Lucie (Fla. St.)......	C	60	162	11	33	6	0	3	17	.204	16	37	0	317	40	12	.967
1993—St. Lucie (Fla. St.)......	C	105	333	37	86	21	0	5	42	.258	28	46	0	*604	80	12	.983
1994—Binghamton (East.) ...	C-1B	90	315	33	78	14	0	7	42	.248	41	46	1	643	54	6	.991
1995—Norfolk (Int'l)...........	C	69	217	23	58	13	1	4	31	.267	26	32	2	469	44	7	.987
—New York (N.L.)...........	C	13	29	2	3	0	0	0	0	.103	3	9	1	66	9	2	.974
1996—New York (N.L.)...........	C	6	11	1	4	0	0	0	0	.364	0	4	0	23	0	0	1.000
—Norfolk (Int'l)	C	113	341	34	71	12	1	11	39	.208	39	67	2	*747	*72	8	.990
1997—New York (N.L.)...........	C	35	59	3	12	1	0	0	7	.203	9	16	0	142	8	2	.987
—Norfolk (Int'l)	C-OF	34	83	4	18	1	0	1	8	.217	17	16	1	197	16	7	.968
Major league totals (3 years)		54	99	6	19	1	0	0	7	.192	12	29	1	231	17	4	.984

CASTILLO, CARLOS   P   WHITE SOX

PERSONAL: Born April 21, 1975, in Boston. ... 6-2/240. ... Throws right, bats right.
HIGH SCHOOL: Southwest (Miami).
TRANSACTIONS/CAREER NOTES: Selected by Chicago White Sox organization in third round of free-agent draft (June 2, 1994).

Year Team (League)	W	L	Pct.	ERA	G	GS	CG	ShO	Sv.	IP	H	R	ER	BB	SO
1994—GC White Sox (GCL)	4	3	.571	2.59	12	12	0	0	0	59	53	20	17	10	57
—Hickory (S. Atl.)	2	0	1.000	0.00	3	1	0	0	0	12	3	0	0	2	17
1995—Hickory (S. Atl.)	5	6	.455	3.73	14	12	2	0	1	79²/₃	85	42	33	18	67
1996—South Bend (Mid.)	9	9	.500	4.05	20	19	•5	0	0	133¹/₃	131	74	60	29	128
—Prince William (Caro.)........	2	4	.333	3.95	6	6	•4	0	0	43¹/₃	45	22	19	4	30
1997—Chicago (A.L.)..................	2	1	.667	4.48	37	2	0	0	1	66¹/₃	68	35	33	33	43
—Nashville (A.A.)	0	0	...	1.50	4	0	0	0	3	6	4	1	1	0	4
Major league totals (1 year)........	2	1	.667	4.48	37	2	0	0	1	66¹/₃	68	35	33	33	43

CASTILLO, FRANK   P   TIGERS

PERSONAL: Born April 1, 1969, in El Paso, Texas. ... 6-1/200. ... Throws right, bats right. ... Full name: Frank Anthony Castillo.
HIGH SCHOOL: Eastwood (El Paso, Texas).
TRANSACTIONS/CAREER NOTES: Selected by Chicago Cubs organization in sixth round of free-agent draft (June 2, 1987). ... On disabled list (April 1-July 23, 1988). ... On Iowa disabled list (April 12-June 6, 1991). ... On Chicago disabled list (August 11-27, 1991). ... On suspended list (September 20-24, 1993). ... On Chicago disabled list (March 20-May 12, 1994); included rehabilitation assignments to Daytona (April 24), Orlando (April 25-May 2) and Iowa (May 2-10). ... On Iowa disabled list (June 21-July 1, 1994). ... Traded by Cubs to Colorado Rockies for P Matt Pool (July 15, 1997). ... Granted free agency (October 30, 1997). ... Signed by Detroit Tigers (December 11, 1997).
HONORS: Named Appalachian League Player of the Year (1987).
STATISTICAL NOTES: Pitched 4-0 no-hit victory against Huntsville (July 13, 1990, first game). ... Pitched 7-0 one-hit, complete-game victory against St. Louis (September 25, 1995).

Year Team (League)	W	L	Pct.	ERA	G	GS	CG	ShO	Sv.	IP	H	R	ER	BB	SO
1987—Wytheville (Appal.)	*10	1	*.909	2.29	12	12	•5	0	0	90¹/₃	86	31	23	21	83
—Geneva (N.Y.-Penn)	1	0	1.000	0.00	1	1	0	0	0	6	3	1	0	1	6
1988—Peoria (Midwest)	6	1	.857	0.71	9	8	2	2	0	51	25	5	4	10	58
1989—Win.-Salem (Car.)	9	6	.600	2.51	18	18	8	1	0	129¹/₃	118	42	36	24	114
—Charlotte (Southern)	3	4	.429	3.84	10	10	4	0	0	68	73	35	29	12	43
1990—Charlotte (Southern)	6	6	.500	3.88	18	18	4	1	0	111¹/₃	113	54	48	27	112
1991—Iowa (Am. Assoc.)	3	1	.750	2.52	4	4	1	1	0	25	20	7	7	7	20
—Chicago (N.L.)	6	7	.462	4.35	18	18	4	0	0	111²/₃	107	56	54	33	73
1992—Chicago (N.L.)	10	11	.476	3.46	33	33	0	0	0	205¹/₃	179	91	79	63	135
1993—Chicago (N.L.)	5	8	.385	4.84	29	25	2	0	0	141¹/₃	162	83	76	39	84
1994—Daytona (Fla. St.)	0	1	.000	4.50	1	1	0	0	0	4	7	3	2	0	1
—Orlando (South.)	1	0	1.000	1.29	1	1	0	0	0	7	4	2	1	1	2
—Iowa (Am. Assoc.)	4	2	.667	3.27	11	11	0	0	0	66	57	30	24	10	44
—Chicago (N.L.)	2	1	.667	4.30	4	4	0	0	0	23	25	13	11	5	19
1995—Chicago (N.L.)	11	10	.524	3.21	29	29	2	2	0	188	179	75	67	52	135
1996—Chicago (N.L.)	7	•16	.304	5.28	33	33	1	1	0	182¹/₃	209	112	107	46	139
1997—Chicago (N.L.)	6	9	.400	5.42	20	19	0	0	0	98	113	64	59	44	67
—Colorado (N.L.)■	6	3	.667	5.42	14	14	0	0	0	86¹/₃	107	57	52	25	59
Major league totals (7 years)......	53	65	.449	4.39	180	175	10	3	0	1036	1081	551	505	307	711

CASTILLO, LUIS   2B   MARLINS

PERSONAL: Born September 12, 1975, in San Pedro de Macoris, Dominican Republic. ... 5-11/175. ... Bats both, throws right. ... Full name: Luis Antonio Donato Castillo.
HIGH SCHOOL: Colegio San Benito Abad (San Pedro de Macoris, Dominican Republic).
TRANSACTIONS/CAREER NOTES: Signed as non-drafted free agent by Florida Marlins organization (August 19, 1992). ... On disabled list (July 20-September 11, 1995). ... On Florida disabled list (May 7-22, 1997).
STATISTICAL NOTES: Led Gulf Coast League with 12 caught stealing in 1994. ... Led Gulf Coast League second basemen with 142 putouts, 318 total chances, 40 double plays and .972 fielding percentage in 1994. ... Led Eastern League in caught stealing with 28 in 1996. ... Led Eastern League second basemen with 557 total chances and 87 double plays in 1996.

Year Team (League)	Pos.	G	AB	R	H	2B	3B	HR	RBI	Avg.	BB	SO	SB	PO	A	E	Avg.
1993—Dom. Marlins (DSL)...	IF	69	266	48	75	7	1	4	31	.282	36	22	21	151	180	20	.943
1994—GC Marlins (GCL)...	2B-SS	57	216	49	57	8	0	0	16	.264	37	36	31	†144	170	9	†.972
1995—Kane County (Midw.)..	2B	89	340	71	111	4	4	0	23	.326	55	50	41	193	241	17	.962
1996—Portland (Eastern)...	2B	109	420	83	133	15	7	1	35	.317	66	68	*51	217	*326	14	*.975
—Florida (N.L.)...	2B	41	164	26	43	2	1	1	8	.262	14	46	17	99	118	3	.986
1997—Florida (N.L.)...	2B	75	263	27	63	8	1	0	8	.240	27	53	16	129	177	9	.971
—Charlotte (Int'l)...	2B	37	130	25	46	5	0	0	5	.354	16	22	8	66	97	5	.970
Major league totals (2 years)		116	427	53	106	10	1	1	16	.248	41	99	33	228	295	12	.978

CASTILLO, TONY   P   WHITE SOX

PERSONAL: Born March 1, 1963, in Lara, Venezuela. ... 5-10/190. ... Throws left, bats left. ... Full name: Antonio Jose Castillo.

TRANSACTIONS/CAREER NOTES: Signed as non-drafted free agent by Toronto Blue Jays organization (February 16, 1983). ... On disabled list (April 10, 1986-entire season). ... Traded by Blue Jays organization with a player to be named later to Atlanta Braves for P Jim Acker (August 24, 1989); Braves organization acquired C Francisco Cabrera to complete deal (August 24, 1989). ... Traded by Braves with a player to be named later to New York Mets for P Alejandro Pena (August 28, 1991); Mets acquired P Joe Roa to complete deal (August 29, 1991). ... Traded by Mets with OF Mark Carreon to Detroit Tigers for P Paul Gibson and P Randy Marshall (January 22, 1992). ... On disabled list (June 8-August 29, 1992). ... Granted free agency (October 15, 1992). ... Signed by Syracuse, Blue Jays organization (January 11, 1993). ... Traded by Blue Jays with IF Domingo Cedeno to Chicago White Sox for P Luis Andujar and P Allen Halley (August 22, 1996). ... Granted free agency (December 7, 1996). ... Re-signed by White Sox (December 11, 1996). ... On disabled list (May 13-27, 1997).

Year Team (League)	W	L	Pct.	ERA	G	GS	CG	ShO	Sv.	IP	H	R	ER	BB	SO
1983—GC Blue Jays (GCL)...	0	0	...	3.00	1	0	0	0	1	3	3	1	1	0	4
1984—Florence (S. Atl.)...	11	8	.579	3.41	25	24	4	1	0	137 1/3	123	71	52	50	96
1985—Kinston (Carolina)...	11	7	.611	1.90	36	12	0	0	3	127 2/3	111	44	27	48	136
1986— ...							Did not play.								
1987—Dunedin (Fla. St.)...	6	2	.750	3.36	39	0	0	0	6	69 2/3	62	30	26	19	62
1988—Dunedin (Fla. St.)...	4	3	.571	1.48	30	0	0	0	12	42 2/3	31	9	7	10	46
—Knoxville (Southern)...	1	0	1.000	0.00	5	0	0	0	2	8	2	0	0	1	11
—Toronto (A.L.)...	1	0	1.000	3.00	14	0	0	0	0	15	10	5	5	2	14
1989—Toronto (A.L.)...	1	1	.500	6.11	17	0	0	0	1	17 2/3	23	14	12	10	10
—Syracuse (Int'l)...	1	3	.250	2.81	27	0	0	0	5	41 2/3	33	15	13	15	37
—Atlanta (N.L.)■...	0	1	.000	4.82	12	0	0	0	0	9 1/3	8	5	5	4	5
1990—Atlanta (N.L.)...	5	1	.833	4.23	52	3	0	0	1	76 2/3	93	41	36	20	64
—Richmond (Int'l)...	3	1	.750	2.52	5	4	1	1	0	25	14	7	7	6	27
1991—Richmond (Int'l)...	5	6	.455	2.90	23	17	0	0	0	118	89	47	38	32	78
—Atlanta (N.L.)...	1	1	.500	7.27	7	0	0	0	0	8 2/3	13	9	7	5	8
—New York (N.L.)■...	1	0	1.000	1.90	10	3	0	0	0	23 2/3	27	7	5	6	10
1992—Toledo (Int'l)■...	2	3	.400	3.63	12	9	0	0	2	44 2/3	48	23	18	14	24
1993—Syracuse (Int'l)■...	0	0	...	0.00	1	1	0	0	0	6	4	2	0	0	2
—Toronto (A.L.)...	3	2	.600	3.38	51	0	0	0	0	50 2/3	44	19	19	22	28
1994—Toronto (A.L.)...	5	2	.714	2.51	41	0	0	0	1	68	66	22	19	28	43
1995—Toronto (A.L.)...	1	5	.167	3.22	55	0	0	0	13	72 2/3	64	27	26	24	38
1996—Toronto (A.L.)...	2	3	.400	4.23	40	0	0	0	1	72 1/3	72	38	34	20	48
—Chicago (A.L.)■...	3	1	.750	1.59	15	0	0	0	1	22 2/3	23	7	4	4	9
1997—Chicago (A.L.)...	4	4	.500	4.91	64	0	0	0	4	62 1/3	74	48	34	23	42
A.L. totals (7 years)	20	18	.526	3.61	297	0	0	0	21	381 1/3	376	180	153	133	232
N.L. totals (3 years)	7	3	.700	4.03	81	6	0	0	1	118 1/3	141	62	53	35	87
Major league totals (9 years)	27	21	.563	3.71	378	6	0	0	22	499 2/3	517	242	206	168	319

CHAMPIONSHIP SERIES RECORD

Year Team (League)	W	L	Pct.	ERA	G	GS	CG	ShO	Sv.	IP	H	R	ER	BB	SO
1993—Toronto (A.L.)...	0	0	...	0.00	2	0	0	0	0	2	0	0	0	1	1

WORLD SERIES RECORD

NOTES: Member of World Series championship team (1993).

Year Team (League)	W	L	Pct.	ERA	G	GS	CG	ShO	Sv.	IP	H	R	ER	BB	SO
1993—Toronto (A.L.)...	1	0	1.000	8.10	2	0	0	0	0	3 1/3	6	3	3	3	1

CASTRO, JUAN   SS   DODGERS

PERSONAL: Born June 20, 1972, in Los Mochis, Mexico. ... 5-10/163. ... Bats right, throws right.

HIGH SCHOOL: CBTIS 43 (Los Mochis, Mexico).

TRANSACTIONS/CAREER NOTES: Signed as non-drafted free agent by Los Angeles Dodgers organization (June 13, 1991). ... On Los Angeles disabled list (June 5-August 1, 1997).

STATISTICAL NOTES: Tied for Texas League lead in double plays by shortstop with 82 in 1994.

Year Team (League)	Pos.	G	AB	R	H	2B	3B	HR	RBI	Avg.	BB	SO	SB	PO	A	E	Avg.
1991—Great Falls (Pio.)...	SS-2B	60	217	36	60	4	2	1	27	.276	33	31	7	90	155	21	.921
1992—Bakersfield (Calif.)...	SS	113	446	56	116	15	4	4	42	.260	37	64	14	180	309	38	.928
1993—San Antonio (Tex.)...	SS-2B	118	424	55	117	23	8	7	41	.276	30	40	12	169	314	28	.945
1994—San Antonio (Tex.)...	SS	123	445	55	128	25	4	4	44	.288	31	66	4	187	377	29	.951
1995—Albuquerque (PCL)...	SS-2B	104	341	51	91	18	4	3	43	.267	20	42	4	152	344	14	.973
—Los Angeles (N.L.)...	3B-SS	11	4	0	1	0	0	0	0	.250	1	1	0	3	7	0	1.000
1996—Albuquerque (PCL)...	3B-SS-2B	17	56	12	21	4	2	1	8	.375	6	7	1	17	33	2	.962
—Los Angeles (N.L.)...	S-3-2-O	70	132	16	26	5	3	0	5	.197	10	27	1	54	84	3	.979
1997—Albuquerque (PCL)...	SS-2B	27	101	11	31	5	2	2	11	.307	4	20	1	33	83	9	.928
—Los Angeles (N.L.)...	SS-2B-3B	40	75	3	11	3	1	0	4	.147	7	20	0	36	65	1	.990
Major league totals (3 years)		121	211	19	38	8	4	0	9	.180	18	48	1	93	156	4	.984

C

DIVISION SERIES RECORD

Year	Team (League)	Pos.	G	AB	R	H	2B	3B	HR	RBI	Avg.	BB	SO	SB	PO	A	E	Avg.
						BATTING									FIELDING			
1996— Los Angeles (N.L.)		2B	2	5	0	1	1	0	0	1	.200	1	1	0	4	3	0	1.000

CASTRO, NELSON — SS — ANGELS

PERSONAL: Born June 4, 1976, in Monty Cristy, Dominican Republic. ... 5-10/160. ... Bats right, throws both. ... Full name: Nelson D. Castro.
TRANSACTIONS/CAREER NOTES: Signed as non-drafted free agent by California Angels (January 14, 1994). ... Angels franchise renamed Anaheim Angels for 1997 season.
STATISTICAL NOTES: Led Arizona League shortstops with 297 total chances and 32 double plays in 1997. ... Led Northwest League shortstops with 323 total chances in 1997.

Year Team (League)	Pos.	G	AB	R	H	2B	3B	HR	RBI	Avg.	BB	SO	SB	PO	A	E	Avg.
							BATTING								FIELDING		
1994—						Dominican Summer League statistics unavailable.											
1995— Ariz. Angels (Ariz.)	SS	55	190	34	37	1	2	0	22	.195	27	50	15	*106	*173	18	.939
1996— Boise (Northwest)	PH	1	1	0	0	0	0	0	0	.000	0	0	0				...
— Ariz. Angels (Ariz.)	SS	53	222	31	38	4	3	3	14	.171	32	42	25	75	164	14	.945
1997— Boise (Northwest)	SS	69	293	74	86	16	1	7	37	.294	38	53	26	80	218	25	*.923

C

CASTRO, RAMON — C — ASTROS

PERSONAL: Born March 1, 1976, in Vega Baja, Puerto Rico. ... 6-2/225. ... Bats right, throws right.
HIGH SCHOOL: Lino P. Rivera (Vega Baja, Puerto Rico).
TRANSACTIONS/CAREER NOTES: Selected by Houston Astros organization in first round (17th pick overall) of free-agent draft (June 2, 1994).

Year Team (League)	Pos.	G	AB	R	H	2B	3B	HR	RBI	Avg.	BB	SO	SB	PO	A	E	Avg.
							BATTING								FIELDING		
1994— GC Astros (GCL)	C	37	123	17	34	7	0	3	14	.276	17	14	5	210	24	4	.983
1995— Kissimmee (Fla. St.)...	C	36	120	6	25	5	0	0	8	.208	6	21	0	184	18	7	.967
— Auburn (NY-Penn)......	C	63	224	40	67	17	0	9	49	.299	24	27	0	297	46	2	.994
1996— Quad City (Midwest) ..	C	96	314	38	78	15	0	7	43	.248	31	61	2	660	82	10	.987
1997— Kissimmee (Fla. St.)...	C	115	410	53	115	22	1	8	65	.280	53	73	1	630	88	6	*.992

CATALANOTTO, FRANK — 2B — TIGERS

PERSONAL: Born April 27, 1974, in Smithtown, N.Y. ... 6-0/170. ... Bats left, throws right. ... Full name: Frank John Catalanotto.
HIGH SCHOOL: Smithtown East (Smithtown, N.Y.).
TRANSACTIONS/CAREER NOTES: Selected by Detroit Tigers organization in 10th round of free-agent draft (June 1, 1992). ... Selected by Oakland Athletics organization from Tigers organization in Rule 5 major league draft (December 9, 1996). ... Returned to Tigers organization (March 21, 1997).
STATISTICAL NOTES: Led Southern League second basemen with 681 total chances and 95 double plays in 1995. ... Led Southern League second basemen with 689 total chances and 99 double plays in 1996. ... Led International League second basemen with .984 fielding percentage in 1997.

Year Team (League)	Pos.	G	AB	R	H	2B	3B	HR	RBI	Avg.	BB	SO	SB	PO	A	E	Avg.
							BATTING								FIELDING		
1992— Bristol (Appal.)	2B	21	50	6	10	2	0	0	4	.200	8	8	0	8	6	2	.875
1993— Bristol (Appal.)	2B	55	199	37	61	9	5	3	22	.307	15	19	3	96	128	10	.957
1994— Fayetteville (SAL)	2B	119	458	72	149	24	8	3	56	.325	37	54	4	244	304	15	.973
1995— Jacksonville (South.)..	2B	134	491	66	111	19	5	8	44	.226	49	56	13	252	*411	18	*.974
1996— Jacksonville (South.)..	2B	132	497	105	148	34	6	17	67	.298	74	69	15	246	*421	•22	.968
1997— Toledo (Int'l).............	2B-3B-OF	134	500	75	150	32	3	16	68	.300	47	80	12	168	351	18	†.966
— Detroit (A.L.)	2B-DH	13	26	2	8	2	0	0	3	.308	3	7	0	7	9	0	1.000
Major league totals (1 year)		13	26	2	8	2	0	0	3	.308	3	7	0	7	9	0	1.000

CATHER, MIKE — P — BRAVES

PERSONAL: Born December 17, 1970, in San Diego. ... 6-2/195. ... Throws right, bats right. ... Full name: Michael Peter Cather.
HIGH SCHOOL: Folsom (Calif.).
COLLEGE: California.
TRANSACTIONS/CAREER NOTES: Selected by Texas Rangers organization in 41st round of free-agent draft (June 3, 1993). ... Released by Tulsa, Rangers organization (June 14, 1995). ... Signed by Winnipeg Goldeyes, Northern League (July 4, 1995). ... Granted free agency following 1995 season. ... Signed by Atlanta Braves organization (February 9, 1996). ... On disabled list (May 30-June 12, 1996).

Year Team (League)	W	L	Pct.	ERA	G	GS	CG	ShO	Sv.	IP	H	R	ER	BB	SO
1993— GC Rangers (GCL).............	1	1	.500	1.76	25	0	0	0	4	30 2/3	20	7	6	9	30
1994— Charlotte (Fla. St.)	8	6	.571	3.88	44	0	0	0	6	60 1/3	56	33	26	40	53
1995— Tulsa (Texas)	0	2	.000	3.32	18	0	0	0	0	21 2/3	20	11	8	7	15
— Winnipeg (North.)■......	4	2	.667	1.45	45	0	0	0	8	31	18	6	5	12	35
1996— Greenville (Southern)■......	3	4	.429	3.70	53	0	0	0	5	87 2/3	89	42	36	29	61
1997— Greenville (Southern)	5	2	.714	4.34	22	0	0	0	1	37 1/3	37	18	18	7	29
— Richmond (Int'l).................	0	0	...	1.73	13	0	0	0	3	26	17	6	5	9	22
— Atlanta (N.L.)....................	2	4	.333	2.39	35	0	0	0	0	37 2/3	23	12	10	19	29
Major league totals (1 year)........	2	4	.333	2.39	35	0	0	0	0	37 2/3	23	12	10	19	29

Year Team (League)	W	L	Pct.	ERA	G	GS	CG	ShO	Sv.	IP	H	R	ER	BB	SO
1997—Atlanta (N.L.)	0	0	...	0.00	1	0	0	0	0	2	0	0	0	1	2

CHAMPIONSHIP SERIES RECORD

Year Team (League)	W	L	Pct.	ERA	G	GS	CG	ShO	Sv.	IP	H	R	ER	BB	SO
1997—Atlanta (N.L.)	0	0	...	0.00	4	0	0	0	0	2⅔	3	0	0	0	3

CEDENO, DOMINGO   2B/SS   RANGERS

PERSONAL: Born November 4, 1968, in La Romana, Dominican Republic. ... 6-0/170. ... Bats both, throws right.
TRANSACTIONS/CAREER NOTES: Signed as non-drafted free agent by Toronto Blue Jays organization (August 4, 1987). ... On disabled list (April 22-May 28, 1991). ... Traded by Blue Jays with P Tony Castillo to Chicago White Sox for P Luis Andujar and P Allen Halley (August 22, 1996). ... Granted free agency (December 20, 1996). ... Signed by Texas Rangers organization (January 15, 1997). ... On Texas disabled list (April 8-May 15, 1997); included rehabilitation assignment to Tulsa (May 3-15).
STATISTICAL NOTES: Led Florida State League shortstops with 633 total chances and 74 double plays in 1990. ... Led Southern League with 12 sacrifice hits in 1991.

							BATTING							FIELDING		
Year Team (League)	Pos.	G	AB	R	H	2B	3B	HR	RBI	Avg.	BB	SO	SB	PO	A	E	Avg.
1988—						Dominican Summer League statistics unavailable.											
1989—Myrtle Beach (SAL)	SS	9	35	4	7	0	0	0	2	.200	3	12	1	12	20	7	.821
—Dunedin (Fla. St.)	SS	9	28	3	6	0	1	0	1	.214	3	10	0	9	21	1	.968
—Medicine Hat (Pio.)	SS	53	194	28	45	6	4	1	20	.232	23	65	6	100	141	•25	.906
1990—Dunedin (Fla. St.)	SS	124	493	64	109	12	10	7	61	.221	48	127	10	*215	*382	36	.943
1991—Knoxville (Southern)	SS	100	336	39	75	7	6	1	26	.223	29	81	11	140	272	24	.945
1992—Knoxville (Southern)	2B-SS	106	337	31	76	7	7	2	21	.226	18	88	8	189	254	28	.941
—Syracuse (Int'l)	2B-SS	18	57	4	11	4	0	0	5	.193	3	14	0	36	43	0	1.000
1993—Syracuse (Int'l)	SS-2B	103	382	58	104	16	10	2	28	.272	33	67	15	150	242	21	.949
—Toronto (A.L.)	SS-2B	15	46	5	8	0	0	0	7	.174	2	10	1	10	39	1	.980
1994—Toronto (A.L.)	2-S-3-O	47	97	14	19	2	3	0	10	.196	10	31	1	40	64	8	.929
—Syracuse (Int'l)	2B-OF-SS	22	80	11	23	5	1	1	9	.288	8	13	3	42	33	2	.974
1995—Toronto (A.L.)	SS-2B-3B	51	161	18	38	6	1	4	14	.236	10	35	0	85	132	3	.986
1996—Toronto (A.L.)	2B-3B-SS	77	282	44	79	10	2	2	17	.280	15	60	5	127	198	9	.973
—Chicago (A.L.)■	2B-SS-DH	12	19	2	3	2	0	0	3	.158	0	4	1	6	4	1	.909
1997—Texas (A.L.)■	2-S-3-DH	113	365	49	103	19	6	4	36	.282	27	77	3	146	259	17	.960
—Tulsa (Texas)	SS	2	9	0	4	0	1	0	0	.444	0	3	0	3	9	1	.923
—Oklahoma City (A.A.)	2B	6	28	0	10	2	0	0	2	.357	0	6	0	13	20	0	1.000
Major league totals (5 years)		315	970	132	250	39	12	10	87	.258	63	217	11	414	696	39	.966

CEDENO, ROGER   OF   DODGERS

PERSONAL: Born August 16, 1974, in Valencia, Venezuela. ... 6-1/165. ... Bats both, throws right. ... Full name: Roger Leandro Cedeno.
TRANSACTIONS/CAREER NOTES: Signed as non-drafted free agent by Los Angeles Dodgers organization (March 28, 1991). ... On disabled list (June 27-July 14, 1994). ... On Los Angeles disabled list (March 25-April 17 and August 25, 1997-remainder of season); included rehabilitation assignment to Albuquerque (April 17-21).
STATISTICAL NOTES: Tied for Pioneer League lead with three intentional bases on balls received in 1992. ... Led Texas League in caught stealing with 20 in 1993. ... Led Pacific Coast League in caught stealing with 18 in 1995.

							BATTING							FIELDING		
Year Team (League)	Pos.	G	AB	R	H	2B	3B	HR	RBI	Avg.	BB	SO	SB	PO	A	E	Avg.
1991—Dom. Dodgers (DSL)	OF	58	209	25	50	1	1	0	7	.239	0	0	26	...	...	...	...
1992—Great Falls (Pio.)	OF	69	256	60	81	6	5	2	27	.316	51	53	*40	113	6	8	.937
1993—San Antonio (Tex.)	OF	122	465	70	134	12	8	4	30	.288	45	90	28	213	6	9	.961
—Albuquerque (PCL)	OF	6	18	1	4	1	1	0	4	.222	3	3	0	12	0	1	.923
1994—Albuquerque (PCL)	OF	104	383	84	123	18	5	4	49	.321	51	57	30	194	7	8	.962
1995—Albuquerque (PCL)	OF	99	367	67	112	19	9	2	44	.305	53	56	23	189	3	3	.985
—Los Angeles (N.L.)	OF	40	42	4	10	2	0	0	3	.238	3	10	1	43	0	1	.977
1996—Los Angeles (N.L.)	OF	86	211	26	52	11	1	2	18	.246	24	47	5	117	2	2	.983
—Albuquerque (PCL)	OF	33	125	16	28	2	3	1	10	.224	15	22	6	71	2	0	1.000
1997—Los Angeles (N.L.)	OF	80	194	31	53	10	2	3	17	.273	25	44	9	148	1	2	.987
—Albuquerque (PCL)	OF	29	113	21	40	4	4	2	9	.354	22	16	5	53	1	2	.964
Major league totals (3 years)		206	447	61	115	23	3	5	38	.257	52	101	15	308	3	5	.984

CHAMBLEE, JIM   2B/SS   RED SOX

PERSONAL: Born May 6, 1975, in Denton, Texas. ... 6-4/175. ... Bats right, throws right. ... Full name: James N. Chamblee.
HIGH SCHOOL: Odessa (Texas).
JUNIOR COLLEGE: Odessa (Texas) College.
TRANSACTIONS/CAREER NOTES: Selected by Boston Red Sox organization in 12th round of free-agent draft (June 1, 1995).

							BATTING							FIELDING		
Year Team (League)	Pos.	G	AB	R	H	2B	3B	HR	RBI	Avg.	BB	SO	SB	PO	A	E	Avg.
1995—Utica (N.Y.-Penn)	SS	62	200	36	51	9	1	2	16	.255	23	45	9	87	162	30	.892
1996—Michigan (Midwest)	S-O-3-P	100	303	31	66	15	2	1	39	.218	16	75	2	123	263	27	.935
1997—Michigan (Midwest)	2B-SS	133	487	*112	146	29	5	22	73	.300	53	107	18	223	347	27	.955

RECORD AS PITCHER

Year Team (League)	W	L	Pct.	ERA	G	GS	CG	ShO	Sv.	IP	H	R	ER	BB	SO
1996—Michigan (Midwest)	0	0	...	0.00	100	0	0	0	0	⅔	0	0	0	0	0

C

CHARLTON, NORM
P   ORIOLES

PERSONAL: Born January 6, 1963, in Fort Polk, La. ... 6-3/205. ... Throws left, bats both. ... Full name: Norman Wood Charlton III.

HIGH SCHOOL: James Madison (San Antonio).

COLLEGE: Rice (degrees in political science, religion and physical education, 1986).

TRANSACTIONS/CAREER NOTES: Selected by Montreal Expos organization in supplemental round ("sandwich pick" between first and second round, 28th pick overall) of free-agent draft (June 4, 1984); pick received as compensation for San Francisco Giants signing Type B free-agent 2B Manny Trillo. ... Traded by Expos organization with a player to be named later to Cincinnati Reds for IF Wayne Krenchicki (March 31, 1986); Reds acquired 2B Tim Barker to complete deal (April 2, 1986). ... On Cincinnati disabled list (April 6-June 26, 1987); included rehabilitation assignment to Nashville (June 9-26). ... On disabled list (May 26-June 11 and June 17-July 19, 1991). ... On suspended list (September 29 and October 4-6, 1991). ... Traded by Reds to Seattle Mariners for OF Kevin Mitchell (November 17, 1992). ... On suspended list (July 9-16, 1993). ... On disabled list (July 21-August 5 and August 8, 1993-remainder of season). ... Granted free agency (November 18, 1993). ... Signed by Philadelphia Phillies organization (February 3, 1994). ... On disabled list (March 31, 1994-entire season). ... Granted free agency (October 28, 1994). ... Re-signed by Phillies organization (December 22, 1994). ... Released by Phillies (July 10, 1995). ... Signed by Mariners (July 14, 1995). ... Granted free agency (November 7, 1997). ... Signed by Baltimore Orioles organization (December 15, 1997).

STATISTICAL NOTES: Led American Association with 13 wild pitches in 1988.

MISCELLANEOUS: Appeared in one game as pinch-runner (1990). ... Appeared in two games as pinch-runner (1991).

Year Team (League)	W	L	Pct.	ERA	G	GS	CG	ShO	Sv.	IP	H	R	ER	BB	SO
1984—W.P. Beach (FSL)	1	4	.200	4.58	8	8	0	0	0	39 1/3	51	27	20	22	27
1985—W.P. Beach (FSL)	7	10	.412	4.57	24	23	5	2	0	128	135	79	65	79	71
1986—Vermont (Eastern)■	10	6	.625	2.83	22	22	6	1	0	136 2/3	109	55	43	74	96
1987—Nashville (A.A.)	2	8	.200	4.30	18	17	3	1	0	98 1/3	97	57	47	44	74
1988—Nashville (A.A.)	11	10	.524	3.02	27	27	8	1	0	182	149	69	61	56	*161
—Cincinnati (N.L.)	4	5	.444	3.96	10	10	0	0	0	61 1/3	60	27	27	20	39
1989—Cincinnati (N.L.)	8	3	.727	2.93	69	0	0	0	0	95 1/3	67	38	31	40	98
1990—Cincinnati (N.L.)	12	9	.571	2.74	56	16	1	1	2	154 1/3	131	53	47	70	117
1991—Cincinnati (N.L.)	3	5	.375	2.91	39	11	0	0	1	108 1/3	92	37	35	34	77
1992—Cincinnati (N.L.)	4	2	.667	2.99	64	0	0	0	26	81 1/3	79	39	27	26	90
1993—Seattle (A.L.)■	1	3	.250	2.34	34	0	0	0	18	34 2/3	22	12	9	17	48
1994—							Did not play.								
1995—Philadelphia (N.L.)■	2	5	.286	7.36	25	0	0	0	0	22	23	19	18	15	12
—Seattle (A.L.)■	2	1	.667	1.51	30	0	0	0	14	47 2/3	23	12	8	16	58
1996—Seattle (A.L.)	4	7	.364	4.04	70	0	0	0	20	75 2/3	68	37	34	38	73
1997—Seattle (A.L.)	3	8	.273	7.27	71	0	0	0	14	69 1/3	89	59	56	47	55
A.L. totals (4 years)	10	19	.345	4.24	205	0	0	0	66	227 1/3	202	120	107	118	234
N.L. totals (6 years)	33	29	.532	3.19	263	37	1	1	29	522 2/3	452	213	185	205	433
Major league totals (9 years)	43	48	.473	3.50	468	37	1	1	95	750	654	333	292	323	667

DIVISION SERIES RECORD

Year Team (League)	W	L	Pct.	ERA	G	GS	CG	ShO	Sv.	IP	H	R	ER	BB	SO
1995—Seattle (A.L.)	1	0	1.000	2.45	4	0	0	0	1	7 1/3	4	2	2	3	9
1997—Seattle (A.L.)	0	0	...	0.00	2	0	0	0	0	2 1/3	2	0	0	0	1
Div. series totals (2 years)	1	0	1.000	1.86	6	0	0	0	1	9 2/3	6	2	2	3	10

CHAMPIONSHIP SERIES RECORD

Year Team (League)	W	L	Pct.	ERA	G	GS	CG	ShO	Sv.	IP	H	R	ER	BB	SO
1990—Cincinnati (N.L.)	1	1	.500	1.80	4	0	0	0	0	5	4	2	1	3	3
1995—Seattle (A.L.)	1	0	1.000	0.00	3	0	0	0	1	6	1	0	0	1	5
Champ. series totals (2 years)	2	1	.667	0.82	7	0	0	0	1	11	5	2	1	4	8

WORLD SERIES RECORD

NOTES: Member of World Series championship team (1990).

Year Team (League)	W	L	Pct.	ERA	G	GS	CG	ShO	Sv.	IP	H	R	ER	BB	SO
1990—Cincinnati (N.L.)	0	0	...	0.00	1	0	0	0	0	1	1	0	0	0	0

ALL-STAR GAME RECORD

Year League	W	L	Pct.	ERA	GS	CG	ShO	Sv.	IP	H	R	ER	BB	SO
1992—National	0	0	...	0.00	0	0	0	0	1	0	0	0	0	1

CHAVEZ, ERIC
IF   ATHLETICS

PERSONAL: Born December 7, 1977, in Los Angeles. ... 6-1/195. ... Bats left, throws right. ... Full name: Eric Cesar Chavez.

HIGH SCHOOL: Mount Carmel (San Diego).

TRANSACTIONS/CAREER NOTES: Selected by Oakland Athletics in first round (10th pick overall) of free-agent draft (June 2, 1996).

Year Team (League)	Pos.	G	AB	R	H	2B	3B	HR	RBI	Avg.	BB	SO	SB	PO	A	E	Avg.
1996—							Did not play.										
1997—Visalia (California)	3B	134	520	67	141	30	3	18	100	.271	37	91	13	84	268	*32	.917

CHAVEZ, RAUL
C   EXPOS

PERSONAL: Born March 18, 1973, in Valencia, Venezuela. ... 5-11/175. ... Bats right, throws right. ... Full name: Raul Alexander Chavez.

TRANSACTIONS/CAREER NOTES: Signed as non-drafted free agent by Houston Astros organization (January 10, 1990). ... Traded by Astros organization with P Dave Veres to Montreal Expos for 3B Sean Berry (December 20, 1995).

STATISTICAL NOTES: Tied for International League lead in double plays by catcher with nine in 1997.

Year Team (League)	Pos.	G	AB	R	H	2B	3B	HR	RBI	Avg.	BB	SO	SB	PO	A	E	Avg.
1990—GC Astros (GCL)	SS-2B-3B	48	155	23	50	8	1	0	23	.323	7	12	5	67	119	9	.954
1991—Burlington (Midw.)	SS-3B	114	420	54	108	17	0	3	41	.257	25	65	1	144	293	41	.914

Year Team (League)	Pos.	G	AB	R	H	2B	3B	HR	RBI	Avg.	BB	SO	SB	PO	A	E	Avg.
1992—Asheville (S. Atl.)........	C	95	348	37	99	22	1	2	40	.284	16	39	1	456	77	13	.976
1993—Osceola (Fla. St.)........	C	58	197	13	45	5	1	0	16	.228	8	19	1	303	62	5	.986
1994—Jackson (Texas)........	C	89	251	17	55	7	0	1	22	.219	17	41	1	*563	64	9	.986
1995—Tucson (PCL)	C	32	103	14	27	5	0	0	10	.262	8	13	0	203	39	5	.980
—Jackson (Texas)........	C	58	188	16	54	8	0	4	25	.287	8	17	0	316	52	5	.987
1996—Ottawa (Int'l)■.......	C	60	198	15	49	10	0	2	24	.247	11	31	0	363	50	4	.990
—Montreal (N.L.)..........	C	4	5	1	1	0	0	0	0	.200	1	1	1	14	0	1	1.000
1997—Ottawa (Int'l)..........	C	92	310	31	76	17	0	4	46	.245	18	42	1	593	*77	*15	.978
—Montreal (N.L.)..........	C	13	26	0	7	0	0	0	2	.269	0	5	1	47	8	0	1.000
Major league totals (2 years)		17	31	1	8	0	0	0	2	.258	1	6	2	61	8	0	1.000

CHAVEZ, TONY — P — ANGELS

PERSONAL: Born October 22, 1970, in Turlock, Calif. ... 5-10/180. ... Throws right, bats right. ... Full name: Anthony Francisco Chavez.
HIGH SCHOOL: Merced (Calif.).
COLLEGE: San Jose State.
TRANSACTIONS/CAREER NOTES: Selected by California Angels organization in 50th round of free-agent draft (June 1, 1992). ... Angels franchise renamed Anaheim Angels for 1997 season.

Year Team (League)	W	L	Pct.	ERA	G	GS	CG	ShO	Sv.	IP	H	R	ER	BB	SO
1992—Boise (Northwest)	1	1	.500	3.94	14	0	0	0	0	16	22	13	7	4	21
1993—Cedar Rapids (Midw.)	4	5	.444	1.52	44	0	0	0	16	59 1/3	44	17	10	24	87
—Midland (Texas).............	0	0	...	4.15	5	0	0	0	1	8 2/3	11	5	4	4	9
1994—Cedar Rapids (Midw.)	4	3	.571	4.32	39	1	0	0	16	50	48	33	24	28	52
—Lake Elsinore (Calif.)	0	5	.000	10.13	12	0	0	0	1	13 1/3	21	19	15	11	12
1995—Lake Elsinore (Calif.)	4	2	.667	4.23	33	0	0	0	16	44 2/3	51	28	21	19	49
—Midland (Texas).............	0	1	.000	8.00	7	0	0	0	2	9	13	9	8	1	4
—Vancouver (PCL)................	2	0	1.000	1.50	6	0	0	0	1	12	7	4	2	4	8
1996—Lake Elsinore (Calif.)	3	0	1.000	1.98	10	0	0	0	4	13 2/3	8	4	3	3	16
—Midland (Texas).............	2	4	.333	4.21	31	0	0	0	1	72 2/3	81	40	34	24	55
1997—Midland (Texas).............	1	2	.333	4.21	33	1	0	0	0	47	53	23	22	15	35
—Vancouver (PCL)................	4	1	.800	2.54	28	0	0	0	15	28 1/3	21	8	8	6	22
—Anaheim (A.L.)................	0	0	...	0.93	7	0	0	0	0	9 2/3	7	1	1	5	10
Major league totals (1 year).......	0	0	...	0.93	7	0	0	0	0	9 2/3	7	1	1	5	10

CHECO, ROBINSON — P — RED SOX

PERSONAL: Born September 9, 1971, in Santo Domingo, Dominican Republic. ... 6-1/185. ... Throws right, bats right. ... Full name: Robinson Perez Checo. ... Name pronounced CHAY-co.
TRANSACTIONS/CAREER NOTES: Signed as non-drafted free agent by California Angels organization (May 17, 1989). ... Released by Angels (March 5, 1990). ... Played for Hiroshima Toyo Carp organization of Japan Central League (1995 and 1996), including minor league seasons in Japan Western League (1992 and 1993). ... Played in China (1994). ... Rights obtained by Boston Red Sox from Carp (December 4, 1996). ... Signed by Red Sox (December 6, 1996). ... On Boston disabled list (March 21-May 13, 1997); included rehabilitation assignments to Sarasota (May 13-July 3), Pawtucket (July 4-26 and July 29-September 9) and Trenton (July 27-28).

Year Team (League)	W	L	Pct.	ERA	G	GS	CG	ShO	Sv.	IP	H	R	ER	BB	SO
1989—					Dominican Summer League statistics unavailable.										
1995—Hiroshima (Jp. Cn.).............	15	8	.652	2.74	28	17	10	3	...	193 2/3	143	64	59	98	166
1996—Hiroshima (Jp. Cn.).............	4	1	.800	4.80	9	9	3	1	0	50 2/3	52	31	27	24	36
1997—Sarasota (Florida State)■..	1	4	.200	5.30	11	11	0	0	0	56	54	37	33	27	63
—Pawtucket (Int'l)	4	2	.667	3.42	9	9	2	1	0	55 1/3	41	22	21	16	56
—Trenton (Eastern)	1	0	1.000	2.35	1	1	0	0	0	7 2/3	6	3	2	1	9
—Boston (A.L.)................	1	1	.500	3.38	5	2	0	0	0	13 1/3	12	5	5	3	14
Major league totals (1 year).......	1	1	.500	3.38	5	2	0	0	0	13 1/3	12	5	5	3	14

CHEN, BRUCE — P — BRAVES

PERSONAL: Born June 19, 1977, in Panama City, Panama. ... 6-1/150. ... Throws left, bats both. ... Full name: Bruce Kastulo Chen.
TRANSACTIONS/CAREER NOTES: Signed as non-drafted free agent by Atlanta Braves organization (July 1, 1993).

Year Team (League)	W	L	Pct.	ERA	G	GS	CG	ShO	Sv.	IP	H	R	ER	BB	SO
1994—Gulf Coast Braves (GCL)	1	4	.200	3.80	9	7	0	0	1	42 2/3	42	21	18	3	26
1995—Danville (Appal.)	4	4	.500	3.97	14	13	1	0	0	70 1/3	78	42	31	19	56
1996—Eugene (Northwest)	4	1	.800	2.27	11	8	0	0	0	35 2/3	23	13	9	14	55
1997—Macon (S. Atl.).................	12	7	.632	3.51	28	28	1	1	0	146 1/3	120	67	57	44	182

CHRISTENSON, RYAN — OF — ATHLETICS

PERSONAL: Born March 28, 1974, in Redlands, Calif. ... 5-11/175. ... Bats right, throws right. ... Full name: Ryan Alan Christenson.
HIGH SCHOOL: Apple Valley (Calif.).
COLLEGE: Pepperdine.
TRANSACTIONS/CAREER NOTES: Selected by Oakland Athletics organization in 10th round of free-agent draft (June 1, 1995).

Year Team (League)	Pos.	G	AB	R	H	2B	3B	HR	RBI	Avg.	BB	SO	SB	PO	A	E	Avg.
1995—S. Oregon (N'west).....	OF	49	158	14	30	4	1	1	16	.190	22	33	5	84	3	2	.978
1996—S. Oregon (N'west).....	OF	36	136	31	39	11	0	5	21	.287	19	21	8	78	5	4	.954
—W. Mich. (Mid.)	OF-3B	33	122	21	38	2	2	2	18	.311	13	22	2	64	1	3	.956
1997—Visalia (California)	OF	83	308	69	90	18	8	13	54	.292	70	72	20	164	4	3	.982
—Huntsville (Southern) .	OF	29	120	39	44	9	3	2	18	.367	24	23	5	81	1	1	.988
—Edmonton (PCL)	OF	16	49	12	14	2	2	2	5	.286	11	11	2	42	1	0	1.000

CHRISTIANSEN, JASON — P — PIRATES

PERSONAL: Born September 21, 1969, in Omaha, Neb. ... 6-5/230. ... Throws left, bats right. ... Full name: Jason Samuel Christiansen.
HIGH SCHOOL: Elkhorn (Neb.).
JUNIOR COLLEGE: Iowa Western Community College.
COLLEGE: Cameron (Okla.).
TRANSACTIONS/CAREER NOTES: Signed as non-drafted free agent by Pittsburgh Pirates organization (July 5, 1991). ... On Calgary disabled list (August 12-September 5, 1996). ... On Pittsburgh disabled list (March 31-June 19, 1997); included rehabilitation assignment to Carolina (May 23-June 19).

Year Team (League)	W	L	Pct.	ERA	G	GS	CG	ShO	Sv.	IP	H	R	ER	BB	SO
1991— GC Pirates (GCL)	1	0	1.000	0.00	6	0	0	0	1	8	4	0	0	1	8
—Welland (N.Y.-Penn)	0	1	.000	2.53	8	1	0	0	0	21 1/3	15	9	6	12	17
1992—Augusta (S. Atl.)	1	0	1.000	1.80	10	0	0	0	2	20	12	4	4	8	21
—Salem (Carolina)	3	1	.750	3.24	38	0	0	0	2	50	47	20	18	22	59
1993—Salem (Carolina)	1	1	.500	3.15	57	0	0	0	4	71 1/3	48	30	25	24	70
—Carolina (Southern)	0	0	...	0.00	2	0	0	0	0	2 2/3	3	0	0	1	2
1994—Carolina (Southern)	2	1	.667	2.09	28	0	0	0	0	38 2/3	30	10	9	14	43
—Buffalo (A.A.)	3	1	.750	2.41	33	0	0	0	2	33 2/3	19	9	9	16	39
1995—Pittsburgh (N.L.)	1	3	.250	4.15	63	0	0	0	0	56 1/3	49	28	26	34	53
1996—Calgary (PCL)	1	0	1.000	3.27	2	2	0	0	0	11	9	4	4	1	10
—Pittsburgh (N.L.)	3	3	.500	6.70	33	0	0	0	0	44 1/3	56	34	33	19	38
1997—Pittsburgh (N.L.)	3	0	1.000	2.94	39	0	0	0	0	33 2/3	37	11	11	17	37
—Carolina (Southern)	0	1	.000	4.20	8	1	0	0	1	15	17	7	7	5	25
Major league totals (3 years)	7	6	.538	4.69	135	0	0	0	0	134 1/3	142	73	70	70	128

CHRISTOPHERSON, ERIC — C

PERSONAL: Born April 25, 1969, in Long Beach, Calif. ... 6-0/195. ... Bats right, throws right. ... Full name: Eric Spencer Christopherson.
HIGH SCHOOL: Ocean View (Huntington Beach, Calif.).
COLLEGE: San Diego State.
TRANSACTIONS/CAREER NOTES: Selected by San Francisco Giants organization in first round (19th pick overall) of free-agent draft (June 4, 1990); pick received as part of compensation for San Diego Padres signing Type A free-agent P Craig Lefferts. ... On suspended list (July 27-August 31, 1990). ... On Shreveport disabled list (July 29-August 14 and September 1-8, 1992; and April 9-August 3 and September 2-7, 1993). ... Selected by Seattle Mariners from Giants organization in Rule 5 major league draft (December 13, 1993). ... Returned to Giants organization (March 31, 1994). ... On disabled list (July 25-August 7, 1995). ... Granted free agency (October 12, 1995). ... Signed by Houston Astros organization (January 9, 1996). ... Granted free agency (October 15, 1996). ... Re-signed by Astros organization prior to 1997 season. ... Released by New Orleans, Astros organization (April 25, 1997). ... Signed by Tulsa, Texas Rangers organization (June 7, 1997). ... On Tulsa disabled list (August 16-September 27, 1997). ... Granted free agency (October 15, 1997).
STATISTICAL NOTES: Led Midwest League catchers with 840 total chances and tied for lead with eight double plays in 1991.

Year Team (League)	Pos.	G	AB	R	H	2B	3B	HR	RBI	Avg.	BB	SO	SB	PO	A	E	Avg.
1990—Everett (N'west)	C	48	162	20	43	8	1	1	22	.265	31	29	7	299	34	3	*.991
—San Jose (Calif.)	C	7	23	4	4	0	0	0	1	.174	3	6	0	42	1	1	.957
1991—Clinton (Midwest)	C	110	345	45	93	18	0	5	58	.270	68	53	10	*758	73	9	.989
1992—Shreveport (Texas)	C	80	270	36	68	10	1	6	34	.252	37	44	1	604	66	4	.994
1993—Ariz. Giants (Ariz.)	C	8	22	7	9	1	0	0	4	.409	9	1	0	40	4	0	1.000
—Shreveport (Texas)	C	15	46	5	7	2	0	0	2	.152	9	10	1	98	8	2	.981
1994—Shreveport (Texas)	C	88	267	30	67	22	0	6	39	.251	42	55	5	460	46	8	.984
1995—Phoenix (PCL)	C	94	282	21	62	9	1	1	25	.220	35	54	1	*543	44	4	.993
1996—Tucson (PCL)	C	67	223	31	64	15	3	6	36	.287	21	47	2	450	34	5	.990
1997—New Orleans (A.A.)	C-P	9	21	3	4	0	0	0	0	.190	4	7	0	46	2	1	1.000
—Tulsa (Texas)■	C	39	123	26	30	9	0	6	34	.244	25	22	1	237	19	6	.977

RECORD AS PITCHER

Year Team (League)	W	L	Pct.	ERA	G	GS	CG	ShO	Sv.	IP	H	R	ER	BB	SO
1997—New Orleans (A.A.)	0	0	...	0.00	1	0	0	0	0	1	2	0	0	1	1
—Tulsa (Texas)■	0	0	...	0.00	1	0	0	0	0	1	2	0	0	1	1

CIANFROCCO, ARCHI — IF — PADRES

PERSONAL: Born October 6, 1966, in Rome, N.Y. ... 6-5/215. ... Bats right, throws right. ... Full name: Angelo Dominic Cianfrocco. ... Name pronounced AR-kee SEE-un-FROCK-oh.
HIGH SCHOOL: Rome (N.Y.) Free Academy.
JUNIOR COLLEGE: Onondaga Community College (N.Y.).
COLLEGE: Purdue.
TRANSACTIONS/CAREER NOTES: Selected by Pittsburgh Pirates organization in 11th round of free-agent draft (January 14, 1986); did not sign. ... Selected by Pirates organization in secondary phase of free-agent draft (June 2, 1986); did not sign. ... Selected by Montreal Expos organization in fifth round of free-agent draft (June 2, 1987). ... On disabled list (June 27, 1990-remainder of season). ... On Ottawa disabled list (June 3-10, 1993). ... Traded by Expos to San Diego Padres for P Tim Scott (June 23, 1993). ... Released by Padres (November 28, 1994). ... Re-signed by Padres organization (December 1, 1994). ... On disabled list (May 6-21 and July 7-23, 1996).
STATISTICAL NOTES: Led Southern League third basemen with 37 errors in 1989. ... Led Eastern League in being hit by pitch with nine in 1991. ... Led Eastern League first basemen with 95 assists and 110 double plays in 1991. ... Career major league grand slams: 1.

Year Team (League)	Pos.	G	AB	R	H	2B	3B	HR	RBI	Avg.	BB	SO	SB	PO	A	E	Avg.
1987—Jamestown (NYP)	2B-SS-1B	70	251	28	62	8	4	2	27	.247	9	59	2	125	179	22	.933
1988—Rockford (Midwest)	3B	126	455	54	115	34	0	15	65	.253	26	99	6	94	240	29	*.920
1989—Jacksonville (South.)	3B-2B-1B	132	429	46	105	22	7	7	50	.245	37	126	3	99	221	†38	.894

C

Year Team (League)	Pos.	G	AB	R	H	2B	3B	HR	RBI	Avg.	BB	SO	SB	PO	A	E	Avg.
1990— Jacksonville (South.)..	1B-3B-OF	62	196	18	43	10	0	5	29	.219	12	45	0	244	54	7	.977
1991— Harrisburg (Eastern) ..	1B-OF	124	456	71	144	21	•10	9	77	.316	38	112	11	1023	†95	11	.990
1992— Montreal (N.L.)..........	1B-3B-OF	86	232	25	56	5	2	6	30	.241	11	66	3	387	66	8	.983
— Indianapolis (A.A.)......	1B-3B-SS	15	59	12	18	3	0	4	16	.305	5	15	1	62	14	5	.938
1993— Montreal (N.L.)..........	1B	12	17	3	4	1	0	1	1	.235	0	5	0	45	2	0	1.000
— Ottawa (Int'l)	OF-1B-3B	50	188	21	56	14	2	4	27	.298	7	33	4	188	26	3	.986
— San Diego (N.L.)■	3B-1B	84	279	27	68	10	2	11	47	.244	17	64	2	198	95	10	.967
1994— San Diego (N.L.)	3B-1B-SS	59	146	9	32	8	0	4	13	.219	3	39	2	58	67	7	.947
— Las Vegas (PCL)	OF-3B	32	112	11	34	11	1	1	21	.304	12	23	0	43	6	2	.961
1995— Las Vegas (PCL)	1-3-O-C	89	322	51	100	20	2	10	58	.311	16	61	5	412	100	17	.968
— San Diego (N.L.)	1-S-O-2-3	51	118	22	31	7	0	5	31	.263	11	28	0	111	50	3	.982
1996— San Diego (N.L.)	1-3-S-O-2-C	79	192	21	54	13	3	2	32	.281	8	56	1	195	51	3	.988
1997— San Diego (N.L.)	1-3-2-S-O	89	220	25	54	12	0	4	26	.245	25	80	7	262	116	7	.982
Major league totals (6 years)		460	1204	132	299	56	7	33	180	.248	75	338	15	1256	447	38	.978

DIVISION SERIES RECORD

					BATTING									FIELDING			
Year Team (League)	Pos.	G	AB	R	H	2B	3B	HR	RBI	Avg.	BB	SO	SB	PO	A	E	Avg.
1996— San Diego (N.L.)	1B	3	3	1	1	0	0	0	0	.333	0	1	0	8	2	0	1.000

CIRILLO, JEFF — 3B — BREWERS

C

PERSONAL: Born September 23, 1969, in Pasadena, Calif. ... 6-2/188. ... Bats right, throws right. ... Full name: Jeffrey Howard Cirillo.
HIGH SCHOOL: Providence (Burbank, Calif.).
COLLEGE: Southern California.
TRANSACTIONS/CAREER NOTES: Selected by Chicago Cubs organization in 37th round of free-agent draft (June 2, 1987); did not sign. ... Selected by Milwaukee Brewers organization in 11th round of free-agent draft (June 3, 1991). ... On New Orleans disabled list (July 22-August 6, 1993).
STATISTICAL NOTES: Led Pioneer League in grounding into double plays with 11 in 1991. ... Led Pioneer League third basemen with 60 putouts, 104 assists and 179 total chances in 1991. ... Tied for Midwest League lead with six intentional bases on balls received in 1992. ... Led A.L. third basemen with 463 total chances and 29 double plays in 1997. ... Career major league grand slams: 1.

					BATTING									FIELDING			
Year Team (League)	Pos.	G	AB	R	H	2B	3B	HR	RBI	Avg.	BB	SO	SB	PO	A	E	Avg.
1991— Helena (Pioneer)	3B-OF	•70	286	60	100	16	2	10	51	.350	31	28	3	†71	†104	15	.921
1992— Stockton (California) ..	3B	7	27	2	6	1	0	0	5	.222	2	0	1	7	10	0	1.000
— Beloit (Midwest)........	3B-2B	126	444	65	135	27	3	9	71	.304	84	85	21	115	309	26	.942
1993— El Paso (Texas)........	2B-3B	67	249	53	85	16	2	9	41	.341	26	37	2	83	142	9	.962
— New Orleans (A.A.)........	3B-2B-SS	58	215	31	63	13	2	3	32	.293	29	33	2	46	145	5	.974
1994— New Orleans (A.A.)	3B-2B-SS	61	236	45	73	18	2	10	46	.309	28	39	4	67	139	8	.963
— Milwaukee (A.L.)........	3B-2B	39	126	17	30	9	0	3	12	.238	11	16	0	23	60	3	.965
1995— Milwaukee (A.L.)	3-2-1-S	125	328	57	91	19	4	9	39	.277	47	42	7	113	230	15	.958
1996— Milwaukee (A.L.)	3-DH-1-2	158	566	101	184	46	5	15	83	.325	58	69	4	112	242	18	.952
1997— Milwaukee (A.L.)	3B-DH	154	580	74	167	46	2	10	82	.288	60	74	4	•126	*320	17	.963
Major league totals (4 years)		476	1600	249	472	120	11	37	216	.295	176	201	15	374	852	53	.959

ALL-STAR GAME RECORD

				BATTING								FIELDING			
Year League	Pos.	AB	R	H	2B	3B	HR	RBI	Avg.	BB	SO	SB	PO	A	E	Avg.
1997— American	3B	1	0	0	0	0	0	0	.000	0	1	0	0	0	0	...

CLARK, DAVE — OF — ASTROS

PERSONAL: Born September 3, 1962, in Tupelo, Miss. ... 6-2/213. ... Bats left, throws right. ... Full name: David Earl Clark. ... Brother of Louis Clark, wide receiver, Seattle Seahawks (1987-92).
HIGH SCHOOL: Shannon (Miss.).
COLLEGE: Jackson State.
TRANSACTIONS/CAREER NOTES: Selected by Cleveland Indians organization in first round (11th pick overall) of free-agent draft (June 6, 1983). ... Traded by Indians to Chicago Cubs for OF Mitch Webster (November 20, 1989). ... Released by Cubs (April 1, 1991). ... Signed by Omaha, Kansas City Royals organization (April 29, 1991). ... Released by Royals (December 20, 1991). ... Signed by Pittsburgh Pirates organization (January 29, 1992). ... On Buffalo disabled list (May 11-18, 1992). ... On disabled list (July 26-September 11, 1995). ... Traded by Pirates to Los Angeles Dodgers for P Carl South (August 31, 1996). ... Granted free agency (October 28, 1996). ... Signed by Cubs organization (January 29, 1997). ... Granted free agency (October 27, 1997). ... Signed by Houston Astros (November 24, 1997).
HONORS: Named outfielder on THE SPORTING NEWS college All-America team (1983).

					BATTING									FIELDING			
Year Team (League)	Pos.	G	AB	R	H	2B	3B	HR	RBI	Avg.	BB	SO	SB	PO	A	E	Avg.
1983— Waterloo (Midw.)	OF	58	159	20	44	8	1	4	20	.277	19	32	2	37	4	1	.976
1984— Waterloo (Midw.)	OF	110	363	74	112	16	3	15	63	.309	57	68	20	128	10	4	.972
— Buffalo (Eastern)	OF	17	56	12	10	1	0	3	10	.179	9	13	1	23	2	1	.962
1985— Waterbury (Eastern)...	OF	132	463	75	140	24	7	12	64	.302	86	79	27	204	11	11	.951
1986— Maine (Int'l)..............	OF	106	355	56	99	17	2	19	58	.279	52	70	6	150	4	6	.963
— Cleveland (A.L.)........	OF-DH	18	58	10	16	1	0	3	9	.276	7	11	1	26	0	0	1.000
1987— Buffalo (A.A.)..............	OF	108	420	83	143	22	3	30	80	.340	52	62	14	181	*22	6	.971
— Cleveland (A.L.).........	OF-DH	29	87	11	18	5	0	3	12	.207	2	24	1	24	1	0	1.000
1988— Cleveland (A.L.)........	DH-OF	63	156	11	41	4	1	3	18	.263	17	28	0	36	0	2	.947
— Colo. Springs (PCL) ...	OF	47	165	27	49	10	2	4	31	.297	27	37	4	85	6	3	.968
1989— Cleveland (A.L.)........	DH-OF	102	253	21	60	12	0	8	29	.237	30	63	0	27	0	1	.964
1990— Chicago (N.L.)■........	OF	84	171	22	47	4	2	5	20	.275	8	40	7	60	2	0	1.000

Year Team (League)	Pos.	G	AB	R	H	2B	3B	BATTING HR	RBI	Avg.	BB	SO	SB	FIELDING PO	A	E	Avg.
1991— Omaha (A.A.)■	OF-1B	104	359	45	108	24	3	13	64	.301	30	53	6	264	11	4	.986
— Kansas City (A.L.)	OF-DH	11	10	1	2	0	0	0	1	.200	1	1	0	0	0	0	...
1992— Buffalo (A.A.)■	OF-1B	78	253	43	77	17	6	11	55	.304	34	51	6	171	6	6	.967
— Pittsburgh (N.L.)	OF	23	33	3	7	0	0	2	7	.212	6	8	0	10	0	0	1.000
1993— Pittsburgh (N.L.)	OF	110	277	43	75	11	2	11	46	.271	38	58	1	132	3	6	.957
1994— Pittsburgh (N.L.)	OF	86	223	37	66	11	1	10	46	.296	22	48	2	107	5	3	.974
1995— Pittsburgh (N.L.)	OF	77	196	30	55	6	0	4	24	.281	24	38	3	98	1	4	.961
1996— Pittsburgh (N.L.)	OF	92	211	28	58	12	2	8	35	.275	31	51	2	80	3	1	.988
— Los Angeles (N.L.)■ ..	OF	15	15	0	3	0	0	1	1	.200	3	2	0	0	0	0	...
1997— Chicago (N.L.)■	OF-DH	102	143	19	43	8	0	5	32	.301	19	34	1	39	2	2	.953
American League totals (5 years)		223	564	54	137	22	1	17	69	.243	57	127	2	113	1	3	.974
National League totals (7 years)		589	1269	182	354	52	7	45	211	.279	151	279	16	526	16	16	.971
Major league totals (12 years)		812	1833	236	491	74	8	62	280	.268	208	406	18	639	17	19	.972

DIVISION SERIES RECORD

Year Team (League)	Pos.	G	AB	R	H	2B	3B	BATTING HR	RBI	Avg.	BB	SO	SB	FIELDING PO	A	E	Avg.
1996— Los Angeles (N.L.)	PH	2	2	0	0	0	0	0	0	.000	0	2	0	0	0	0	...

CLARK, MARK — P — CUBS

PERSONAL: Born May 12, 1968, in Bath, Ill. ... 6-5/225. ... Throws right, bats right. ... Full name: Mark William Clark.
HIGH SCHOOL: Balyki (Bath, Ill.).
JUNIOR COLLEGE: Lincoln Land Community College (Ill.).
TRANSACTIONS/CAREER NOTES: Selected by St. Louis Cardinals organization in ninth round of free-agent draft (June 1, 1988). ... On Arkansas disabled list (April 12-May 8, 1991). ... Traded by Cardinals with SS Juan Andujar to Cleveland Indians for OF Mark Whiten (March 31, 1993). ... On Cleveland disabled list (July 17-September 9, 1993 and July 21, 1994-remainder of season). ... Traded by Indians to New York Mets for P Reid Cornelius and OF Ryan Thompson (March 31, 1996). ... Traded by Mets to Chicago Cubs (August 11, 1997), as part of deal in which Mets traded OF Lance Johnson and two players to be named later to Cubs for OF Brian McRae, P Mel Rojas and P Turk Wendell (August 8, 1997); Mets traded IF Manny Alexander to Cubs to complete deal (August 14).

Year Team (League)	W	L	Pct.	ERA	G	GS	CG	ShO	Sv.	IP	H	R	ER	BB	SO
1988— Hamilton (NYP)	6	7	.462	3.05	15	15	2	0	0	94 1/3	88	39	32	32	60
1989— Savannah (S. Atl.)	•14	9	.609	2.44	27	27	4	2	0	173 2/3	143	61	47	52	132
1990— St. Petersburg (FSL)	3	2	.600	3.05	10	10	1	1	0	62	63	33	21	14	58
— Arkansas (Texas)	5	11	.313	3.82	19	19	*5	0	0	115 1/3	111	56	49	37	87
1991— Arkansas (Texas)	5	5	.500	4.00	15	15	4	1	0	92 1/3	99	50	41	30	76
— Louisville (A.A.)	3	2	.600	2.98	7	6	1	1	0	45 1/3	43	17	15	15	29
— St. Louis (N.L.)	1	1	.500	4.03	7	2	0	0	0	22 1/3	17	10	10	11	13
1992— Louisville (A.A.)	4	4	.500	2.80	9	9	4	*3	0	61	56	20	19	15	38
— St. Louis (N.L.)	3	10	.231	4.45	20	20	1	1	0	113 1/3	117	59	56	36	44
1993— Cleveland (A.L.)■............	7	5	.583	4.28	26	15	1	0	0	109 1/3	119	55	52	25	57
— Charlotte (Int'l)	1	0	1.000	2.08	2	2	0	0	0	13	9	5	3	2	12
1994— Cleveland (A.L.)	11	3	.786	3.82	20	20	4	1	0	127 1/3	133	61	54	40	60
1995— Cleveland (A.L.)	9	7	.563	5.27	22	21	2	0	0	124 2/3	143	77	73	42	68
— Buffalo (A.A.)	4	0	1.000	3.57	5	5	0	0	0	35 1/3	39	14	14	10	17
1996— New York (N.L.)■	14	11	.560	3.43	32	32	2	0	0	212 1/3	217	98	81	48	142
1997— New York (N.L.)	8	7	.533	4.25	23	22	1	0	0	142	158	74	67	47	72
— Chicago (N.L.)■.............	6	1	.857	2.86	9	9	2	0	0	63	55	22	20	12	51
A.L. totals (3 years)	27	15	.643	4.46	68	56	7	1	0	361 1/3	395	193	179	107	185
N.L. totals (4 years)	32	30	.516	3.81	91	85	6	1	0	553	564	263	234	154	322
Major league totals (7 years)......	59	45	.567	4.07	159	141	13	2	0	914 1/3	959	456	413	261	507

CLARK, TERRY — P — RANGERS

PERSONAL: Born October 10, 1960, in Los Angeles. ... 6-2/195. ... Throws right, bats right. ... Full name: Terry Lee Clark.
HIGH SCHOOL: La Puente (Calif.).
JUNIOR COLLEGE: Mount San Antonio College (Calif.).
TRANSACTIONS/CAREER NOTES: Selected by St. Louis Cardinals organization in 22nd round of free-agent draft (June 5, 1979). ... On disabled list (May 27-August 22, 1984). ... Granted free agency (October 15, 1985). ... Signed by Midland, California Angels organization (February 25, 1986). ... On California disabled list (March 19-May 3, 1989); included rehabilitation assignments to Palm Springs (April 12-20) and Edmonton (April 21-May 1). ... Signed by Angels (October 6, 1989). ... Signed by Tucson, Houston Astros organization (January 26, 1990). ... Granted free agency (October 15, 1991). ... Signed by Colorado Springs, Cleveland Indians organization (January 6, 1992). ... Released by Colorado Springs (July 23, 1992). ... Signed by Rancho Cucamonga, San Diego Padres organization (July 1, 1993). ... Granted free agency (October 15, 1993). ... Signed by Atlanta Braves organization (November 24, 1993). ... Granted free agency (May 16, 1995). ... Signed by Rochester, Baltimore Orioles organization (June 1, 1995). ... Granted free agency (December 21, 1995). ... Signed by Omaha, Kansas City Royals organization (February 19, 1996). ... Released by Royals (July 23, 1996). ... Signed by Astros (July 23, 1996). ... On Houston disabled list (August 8, 1996-remainder of season). ... Granted free agency (October 8, 1996). ... Signed by Indians organization (December 19, 1996). ... Claimed on waivers by Texas Rangers (August 4, 1997). ... Granted free agency (October 27, 1997). ... Re-signed by Rangers organization (December 16, 1997).

Year Team (League)	W	L	Pct.	ERA	G	GS	CG	ShO	Sv.	IP	H	R	ER	BB	SO
1979— Johnson City (App.)	4	2	.667	1.97	•23	0	0	0	*8	32	31	10	7	11	22
1980— Gastonia (S. Atl.)	4	7	.364	3.17	49	0	0	0	0	88	82	34	31	22	50
1981— Gastonia (S. Atl.)	4	5	.444	2.16	*53	0	0	0	0	75	56	23	18	25	66
1982— St. Petersburg (FSL)	10	7	.588	2.55	*58	0	0	0	0	88 1/3	81	32	25	34	61
1983— Arkansas (Texas)	6	6	.500	3.21	52	0	0	0	15	81 1/3	68	31	29	19	63
1984— Louisville (A.A.)	1	3	.250	4.72	18	1	0	0	1	34 1/3	41	19	18	12	24
1985— Arkansas (Texas)	6	5	.545	4.93	42	7	0	0	2	96 2/3	102	64	53	38	67

Year	Team (League)	W	L	Pct.	ERA	G	GS	CG	ShO	Sv.	IP	H	R	ER	BB	SO
1986—	Midland (Texas)■	9	4	.692	3.29	57	2	0	0	4	90 1/3	98	49	33	28	66
1987—	Edmonton (PCL)	8	9	.471	3.84	33	20	5	1	4	154 2/3	140	79	66	56	88
1988—	Edmonton (PCL)	7	6	.538	4.51	16	16	3	0	0	113 2/3	128	62	57	33	59
	California (A.L.)	6	6	.500	5.07	15	15	2	1	0	94	120	54	53	31	39
1989—	Edmonton (PCL)	11	5	.688	3.58	21	20	4	0	0	138 1/3	130	62	55	33	90
	California (A.L.)	0	2	.000	4.91	4	2	0	0	0	11	13	8	6	3	7
1990—	Tucson (PCL)■	11	4	.733	3.54	29	22	3	1	1	155	172	73	61	41	80
	Houston (N.L.)	0	0	...	13.50	1	1	0	0	0	4	9	7	6	3	2
1991—	Tucson (PCL)	•14	7	.667	4.66	26	26	2	0	0	164	•200	104	85	37	97
1992—	Colo. Springs (PCL)■	4	4	.500	3.77	9	9	2	0	0	59 2/3	62	30	25	13	33
1993—	Rancho Cuca. (Cal.)■	0	2	.000	4.66	8	0	0	0	0	9 2/3	7	5	5	4	7
	Wichita (Texas)	3	0	1.000	2.43	19	0	0	0	0	29 2/3	27	10	8	7	30
1994—	Richmond (Int'l)■	5	4	.556	3.02	61	0	0	0	26	83 1/3	72	33	28	27	74
1995—	Atlanta (N.L.)	0	0	...	4.91	3	0	0	0	0	3 2/3	3	2	2	5	2
	Rochester (Int'l)■	1	2	.333	2.70	9	0	0	0	5	10	5	3	3	2	10
	Baltimore (A.L.)	2	5	.286	3.46	38	0	0	0	1	39	40	15	15	15	18
1996—	Kansas City (A.L.)■	1	1	.500	7.79	12	0	0	0	0	17 1/3	28	15	15	7	12
	Omaha (Am. Assoc.)	3	1	.750	2.56	16	2	0	0	2	45 2/3	42	15	13	13	36
	Houston (N.L.)■	0	2	.000	11.37	5	0	0	0	0	6 1/3	16	10	8	2	5
1997—	Buffalo (A.A.)■	7	3	.700	2.85	25	10	•4	1	3	94 2/3	86	34	30	30	63
	Cleveland (A.L.)	0	3	.000	6.15	4	4	0	0	0	26 1/3	29	21	18	13	13
	Texas (A.L.)■	1	4	.200	5.87	9	5	0	0	0	30 2/3	41	20	20	10	11
A.L. totals (5 years)		10	21	.323	5.24	82	26	2	1	1	218 1/3	271	133	127	79	100
N.L. totals (3 years)		0	2	.000	10.29	9	1	0	0	0	14	28	19	16	10	9
Major league totals (6 years)		10	23	.303	5.54	91	27	2	1	1	232 1/3	299	152	143	89	109

C

CLARK, TONY — 1B — TIGERS

PERSONAL: Born June 15, 1972, in Newton, Kan. ... 6-8/250. ... Bats both, throws right. ... Full name: Anthony Christopher Clark.
HIGH SCHOOL: Valhalla (El Cajon, Calif.), then Christian (El Cajon, Calif.).
COLLEGE: Arizona (did not play baseball), then San Diego State.
TRANSACTIONS/CAREER NOTES: Selected by Detroit Tigers organization in first round (second pick overall) of free-agent draft (June 4, 1990). ... On Niagara Falls temporarily inactive list (June 17, 1991-remainder of season and August 17, 1992-remainder of season). ... On disabled list (August 24, 1993-remainder of season).
STATISTICAL NOTES: Switch-hit home runs in one game (April 5, 1997). ... Led A.L. first basemen with 1,533 total chances in 1997. ... Career major league grand slams: 1.

							BATTING								FIELDING		
Year	Team (League)	Pos.	G	AB	R	H	2B	3B	HR	RBI	Avg.	BB	SO	SB	PO	A	E	Avg.
1990—	Bristol (Appal.)	OF	25	73	2	12	2	0	1	8	.164	6	28	0	23	3	0	1.000
1991—							Did not play.											
1992—	Niag. Falls (NYP)	OF	27	85	12	26	9	0	5	17	.306	9	34	1	18	1	0	1.000
1993—	Lakeland (Fla. St.)	OF	36	117	14	31	4	1	1	22	.265	18	32	0	34	0	2	.944
1994—	Trenton (Eastern)	1B	107	394	50	110	25	4	21	86	.279	40	113	0	505	48	•13	.977
	Toledo (Int'l)	1B	25	92	10	24	4	0	2	13	.261	12	25	2	144	12	0	1.000
1995—	Toledo (Int'l)	1B	110	405	50	98	17	2	14	63	.242	52	*129	0	615	51	*13	.981
	Detroit (A.L.)	1B	27	101	10	24	5	1	3	11	.238	8	30	0	253	18	4	.985
1996—	Toledo (Int'l)	1B	55	194	42	58	7	1	14	14	.299	31	58	1	400	28	3	.993
	Detroit (A.L.)	1B-DH	100	376	56	94	14	0	27	72	.250	29	127	0	766	54	6	.993
1997—	Detroit (A.L.)	1B-DH	159	580	105	160	28	3	32	117	.276	93	144	1	*1422	100	10	.993
Major league totals (3 years)			286	1057	171	278	47	4	62	200	.263	130	301	1	2441	172	20	.992

CLARK, WILL — 1B — RANGERS

PERSONAL: Born March 13, 1964, in New Orleans. ... 6-1/200. ... Bats left, throws left. ... Full name: William Nuschler Clark Jr.
HIGH SCHOOL: Jesuit (New Orleans).
COLLEGE: Mississippi State.
TRANSACTIONS/CAREER NOTES: Selected by Kansas City Royals organization in fourth round of free-agent draft (June 7, 1982); did not sign. ... Selected by San Francisco Giants organization in first round (second pick overall) of free-agent draft (June 3, 1985). ... On San Francisco disabled list (June 4-July 24, 1986); included rehabilitation assignment to Phoenix (July 7-24). ... On disabled list (August 26-September 10, 1993). ... Granted free agency (October 25, 1993). ... Signed by Texas Rangers (November 22, 1993). ... On Texas disabled list (June 8-23, June 30-July 15 and July 17-August 4, 1996); included rehabilitation assignment to Tulsa (August 1-4). ... On disabled list (March 28-April 18 and August 25, 1997-remainder of season).
HONORS: Named designated hitter on THE SPORTING NEWS college All-America team (1984). ... Named Golden Spikes Award winner by USA Baseball (1985). ... Named first baseman on THE SPORTING NEWS college All-America team (1985). ... Named first baseman on THE SPORTING NEWS N.L. All-Star team (1988-89 and 1991). ... Named first baseman on THE SPORTING NEWS N.L. Silver Slugger team (1989 and 1991). ... Won N.L. Gold Glove at first base (1991).
STATISTICAL NOTES: Led N.L. first basemen with 130 double plays in 1987, 126 in 1988, 118 in 1990, 115 in 1991 and 130 in 1992. ... Led N.L. with 27 intentional bases on balls received in 1988. ... Led N.L. first basemen with 1,608 total chances in 1988, 1,566 in 1989 and 1,587 in 1990. ... Led N.L. with .536 slugging percentage and tied for lead with 303 total bases in 1991. ... Led A.L. first basemen with 1,051 total chances in 1994. ... Career major league grand slams: 3.
MISCELLANEOUS: Member of 1984 U.S. Olympic baseball team. ... Hit home run in first minor league at-bat (June 21, 1985) and first major league at-bat (April 8, 1986); both were on the first swing.

							BATTING								FIELDING		
Year	Team (League)	Pos.	G	AB	R	H	2B	3B	HR	RBI	Avg.	BB	SO	SB	PO	A	E	Avg.
1985—	Fresno (California)	1B-OF	65	217	41	67	14	0	10	48	.309	62	46	11	523	51	6	.990
1986—	San Francisco (N.L.)	1B	111	408	66	117	27	2	11	41	.287	34	76	4	942	72	11	.989
	Phoenix (PCL)	DH	6	20	3	5	0	0	0	1	.250	4	2	1	...	...	...	...

Year Team (League)	Pos.	G	AB	R	H	2B	3B	HR	RBI	Avg.	BB	SO	SB	PO	A	E	Avg.
1987— San Francisco (N.L.) ..	1B	150	529	89	163	29	5	35	91	.308	49	98	5	1253	103	13	.991
1988— San Francisco (N.L.) ..	1B	*162	575	102	162	31	6	29	*109	.282	*100	129	9	*1492	104	12	.993
1989— San Francisco (N.L.) ..	1B	159	588	•104	196	38	9	23	111	.333	74	103	8	*1445	111	10	.994
1990— San Francisco (N.L.) ..	1B	154	600	91	177	25	5	19	95	.295	62	97	8	*1456	119	12	.992
1991— San Francisco (N.L.) ..	1B	148	565	84	170	32	7	29	116	.301	51	91	4	1273	110	4	*.997
1992— San Francisco (N.L.) ..	1B	144	513	69	154	40	1	16	73	.300	73	82	12	1275	105	10	.993
1993— San Francisco (N.L.) ..	1B	132	491	82	139	27	2	14	73	.283	63	68	2	1078	88	14	.988
1994— Texas (A.L.)■	1B-DH	110	389	73	128	24	2	13	80	.329	71	59	5	*968	73	•10	.990
1995— Texas (A.L.)	1B-DH	123	454	85	137	27	3	16	92	.302	68	50	0	1076	88	7	.994
1996— Texas (A.L.)	1B	117	436	69	124	25	1	13	72	.284	64	67	2	956	73	4	.996
—Tulsa (Texas)	1B	3	9	3	2	0	0	0	0	.222	2	0	0	21	3	0	1.000
1997— Texas (A.L.)	1B-DH	110	393	56	128	29	1	12	51	.326	49	62	0	880	62	4	.996
American League totals (4 years)		460	1672	283	517	105	7	54	295	.309	252	238	7	3880	296	25	.994
National League totals (8 years)		1160	4269	687	1278	249	37	176	709	.299	506	744	52	10214	812	86	.992
Major league totals (12 years)		1620	5941	970	1795	354	44	230	1004	.302	758	982	59	14094	1108	111	.993

DIVISION SERIES RECORD

Year Team (League)	Pos.	G	AB	R	H	2B	3B	HR	RBI	Avg.	BB	SO	SB	PO	A	E	Avg.
1996— Texas (A.L.)	1B	4	16	1	2	0	0	0	0	.125	4	2	0	35	4	0	1.000

CHAMPIONSHIP SERIES RECORD

RECORDS: Holds single-series record for most hits—13. ... Shares single-series record for most total bases—24 (1989). ... Holds single-game record for most runs batted in—6 (October 4, 1989). ... Shares single-game record for most runs—8 (1989). ... Shares single-game records for most runs—4; and most grand slams—1 (October 4, 1989). ... Shares record for most runs batted in in one inning—4 (October 4, 1989, fourth inning). ... Shares N.L. single-series record for most consecutive hits—5 (1989). ... Shares N.L. single-game record for most hits—4 (October 4, 1989).

NOTES: Named N.L. Championship Series Most Valuable Player (1989).

Year Team (League)	Pos.	G	AB	R	H	2B	3B	HR	RBI	Avg.	BB	SO	SB	PO	A	E	Avg.
1987— San Francisco (N.L.) ..	1B	7	25	3	9	2	0	1	3	.360	3	6	1	63	7	1	.986
1989— San Francisco (N.L.) ..	1B	5	20	8	13	3	1	2	8	.650	2	2	0	43	6	0	1.000
Championship series totals (2 years)		12	45	11	22	5	1	3	11	.489	5	8	1	106	13	1	.992

WORLD SERIES RECORD

Year Team (League)	Pos.	G	AB	R	H	2B	3B	HR	RBI	Avg.	BB	SO	SB	PO	A	E	Avg.
1989— San Francisco (N.L.) ..	1B	4	16	2	4	1	0	0	0	.250	1	3	0	40	2	0	1.000

ALL-STAR GAME RECORD

Year League	Pos.	AB	R	H	2B	3B	HR	RBI	Avg.	BB	SO	SB	PO	A	E	Avg.
1988— National	1B	2	0	0	0	0	0	0	.000	0	0	0	4	1	0	1.000
1989— National	1B	2	0	0	0	0	0	0	.000	0	1	0	5	0	0	1.000
1990— National	1B	3	0	1	0	0	0	0	.333	0	0	0	6	0	0	1.000
1991— National	1B	2	0	1	0	0	0	0	.500	1	0	0	2	0	0	1.000
1992— National	PH-1B	2	1	1	0	0	1	3	.500	0	1	0	1	0	0	1.000
1994— American	1B	2	0	2	0	0	0	0	1.000	0	0	1	7	0	0	1.000
All-Star Game totals (6 years)		13	1	5	0	0	1	3	.385	1	2	1	25	1	0	1.000

CLAYTON, ROYCE   SS   CARDINALS

PERSONAL: Born January 2, 1970, in Burbank, Calif. ... 6-0/183. ... Bats right, throws right. ... Full name: Royce Spencer Clayton.
HIGH SCHOOL: St. Bernard (Inglewood, Calif.).
TRANSACTIONS/CAREER NOTES: Selected by San Francisco Giants organization in first round (15th pick overall) of free-agent draft (June 1, 1988); pick received as compensation for Cincinnati Reds signing Type B free-agent OF Eddie Milner. ... Traded by Giants with a player to be named later to St. Louis Cardinals for P Allen Watson, P Rich DeLucia and P Doug Creek (December 14, 1995); Cardinals acquired 2B Chris Wimmer to complete deal (January 16, 1996).
STATISTICAL NOTES: Led Texas League shortstops with 80 double plays in 1991. ... Led N.L. shortstops with 103 double plays in 1993. ... Led N.L. shortstops with 654 total chances in 1995.

Year Team (League)	Pos.	G	AB	R	H	2B	3B	HR	RBI	Avg.	BB	SO	SB	PO	A	E	Avg.
1988— Everett (N'west)	SS	60	212	35	55	4	0	3	29	.259	27	54	10	75	166	35	.873
1989— Clinton (Midwest)	SS	104	385	39	91	13	3	0	24	.236	39	101	28	182	332	31	.943
—San Jose (Calif.)	SS	28	92	5	11	2	0	0	4	.120	13	27	10	53	71	8	.939
1990— San Jose (Calif.)	SS	123	460	80	123	15	10	4	71	.267	68	98	32	*202	358	37	.938
1991— Shreveport (Texas)	SS	126	485	84	136	22	8	•5	68	.280	61	104	36	174	379	29	.950
—San Francisco (N.L.) ..	SS	9	26	0	3	1	0	0	2	.115	1	6	0	16	6	3	.880
1992— San Francisco (N.L.) ..	SS-3B	98	321	31	72	7	4	4	24	.224	26	63	8	142	257	11	.973
—Phoenix (PCL)	SS	48	192	30	46	6	2	3	18	.240	17	25	15	81	150	7	.971
1993— San Francisco (N.L.) ..	SS	153	549	54	155	21	5	6	70	.282	38	91	11	251	449	27	.963
1994— San Francisco (N.L.) ..	SS	108	385	38	91	14	6	3	30	.236	30	74	23	177	330	14	.973
1995— San Francisco (N.L.) ..	SS	138	509	56	124	29	3	5	58	.244	38	109	24	*223	•411	20	.969
1996— St. Louis (N.L.)■	SS	129	491	64	136	20	4	6	35	.277	33	89	33	171	347	15	.972
1997— St. Louis (N.L.)	SS	154	576	75	153	39	5	9	61	.266	33	109	30	228	*452	19	.973
Major league totals (7 years)		789	2857	318	734	131	27	33	280	.257	199	541	129	1208	2252	109	.969

DIVISION SERIES RECORD

Year Team (League)	Pos.	G	AB	R	H	2B	3B	HR	RBI	Avg.	BB	SO	SB	PO	A	E	Avg.
1996— St. Louis (N.L.)	SS	2	6	1	2	0	0	0	0	.333	3	1	0	4	5	0	1.000

Year	Team (League)	Pos.	G	AB	R	H	2B	3B	HR	RBI	Avg.	BB	SO	SB	PO	A	E	Avg.
							BATTING									FIELDING		
1996—	St. Louis (N.L.)...........	SS	5	20	4	7	0	0	0	1	.350	1	4	1	5	16	2	.913

ALL-STAR GAME RECORD

Year	League	Pos.	AB	R	H	2B	3B	HR	RBI	Avg.	BB	SO	SB	PO	A	E	Avg.
						BATTING									FIELDING		
1997—	National......................	SS	1	0	0	0	0	0	0	.000	0	1	0	0	1	0	1.000

CLEMENS, ROGER   P   BLUE JAYS

C

PERSONAL: Born August 4, 1962, in Dayton, Ohio. ... 6-4/230. ... Throws right, bats right. ... Full name: William Roger Clemens.

HIGH SCHOOL: Spring Woods (Houston).

JUNIOR COLLEGE: San Jacinto (North) College (Texas).

COLLEGE: Texas.

TRANSACTIONS/CAREER NOTES: Selected by New York Mets organization in 12th round of free-agent draft (June 8, 1981); did not sign. ... Selected by Boston Red Sox organization in first round (19th pick overall) of free-agent draft (June 6, 1983). ... On disabled list (July 8-August 3 and August 21, 1985-remainder of season). ... On suspended list (April 26-May 3, 1991). ... On Boston disabled list (June 19-July 16, 1993); included rehabilitation assignment to Pawtucket (July 11-16). ... On Boston disabled list (April 16-June 2, 1995); included rehabilitation assignments to Sarasota (May 25-28) and Pawtucket (May 28-June 2). ... Granted free agency (November 5, 1996). ... Signed by Toronto Blue Jays (December 13, 1996).

RECORDS: Holds major league single-game record for most strikeouts (nine-inning game)—20 (April 29, 1986 and September 18, 1996). ... Shares major league record for most putouts by pitcher in one inning—3 (June 27, 1992, sixth inning). ... Shares A.L. record for most consecutive seasons with 200 or more strikeouts—7 (1986-92). ... Shares A.L. single-game record for most consecutive strikeouts—8 (April 29, 1986).

HONORS: Named Major League Player of the Year by THE SPORTING NEWS (1986). ... Named A.L. Pitcher of the Year by THE SPORTING NEWS (1986, 1991 and 1997). ... Named righthanded pitcher on THE SPORTING NEWS A.L. All-Star team (1986-87, 1991 and 1997). ... Named A.L. Most Valuable Player by Baseball Writers' Association of America (1986). ... Named A.L. Cy Young Award winner by Baseball Writers' Association of America (1986-87, 1991 and 1997).

STATISTICAL NOTES: Struck out 15 batters in one game (August 21, 1984 and July 9, 1988). ... Struck out 20 batters in one game (April 29, 1986 and September 18, 1996). ... Struck out 16 batters in one game (May 9 and July 15, 1988 and July 12, 1997). ... Pitched 6-0 one-hit, complete-game victory against Cleveland (September 10, 1988). ... Led A.L. with 14 hit batsmen in 1995.

MISCELLANEOUS: Singled in only appearance as pinch-hitter (1996).

Year	Team (League)	W	L	Pct.	ERA	G	GS	CG	ShO	Sv.	IP	H	R	ER	BB	SO
1983—	Winter Haven (FSL)............	3	1	.750	1.24	4	4	3	1	0	29	22	4	4	0	36
—	New Britain (East.)	4	1	.800	1.38	7	7	1	1	0	52	31	8	8	12	59
1984—	Pawtucket (Int'l)	2	3	.400	1.93	7	6	3	1	0	46²/₃	39	12	10	14	50
—	Boston (A.L.)	9	4	.692	4.32	21	20	5	1	0	133¹/₃	146	67	64	29	126
1985—	Boston (A.L.)	7	5	.583	3.29	15	15	3	1	0	98¹/₃	83	38	36	37	74
1986—	Boston (A.L.)	*24	4	*.857	2.48	33	33	10	1	0	254	179	77	70	67	238
1987—	Boston (A.L.)	•20	9	.690	2.97	36	36	*18	*7	0	281²/₃	248	100	93	83	256
1988—	Boston (A.L.)	18	12	.600	2.93	35	35	*14	*8	0	264	217	93	86	62	*291
1989—	Boston (A.L.)	17	11	.607	3.13	35	35	8	3	0	253¹/₃	215	101	88	93	230
1990—	Boston (A.L.)	21	6	.778	*1.93	31	31	7	*4	0	228¹/₃	193	59	49	54	209
1991—	Boston (A.L.)	18	10	.643	*2.62	35	•35	13	*4	0	*271¹/₃	219	93	79	65	*241
1992—	Boston (A.L.)	18	11	.621	*2.41	32	32	11	*5	0	246²/₃	203	80	66	62	208
1993—	Boston (A.L.)	11	14	.440	4.46	29	29	6	1	0	191²/₃	175	99	95	67	160
—	Pawtucket (Int'l)	0	0	...	0.00	1	1	0	0	0	3²/₃	1	0	0	4	8
1994—	Boston (A.L.)	9	7	.563	2.85	24	24	3	1	0	170²/₃	124	62	54	71	168
1995—	Sarasota (Florida State)......	0	0	...	0.00	1	1	0	0	0	4	0	0	0	2	7
—	Pawtucket (Int'l)	0	0	...	0.00	1	1	0	0	0	5	1	0	0	3	5
—	Boston (A.L.)	10	5	.667	4.18	23	23	0	0	0	140	141	70	65	60	132
1996—	Boston (A.L.)	10	13	.435	3.63	34	34	6	2	0	242²/₃	216	106	98	106	*257
1997—	Toronto (A.L.)	*21	7	.750	*2.05	34	34	•9	•3	0	•264	204	65	60	68	*292
	Major league totals (14 years)....	213	118	.644	2.97	417	416	109	41	0	3040	2563	1110	1003	924	2882

DIVISION SERIES RECORD

Year	Team (League)	W	L	Pct.	ERA	G	GS	CG	ShO	Sv.	IP	H	R	ER	BB	SO
1995—	Boston (A.L.)......................	0	0	...	3.86	1	1	0	0	0	7	5	3	3	1	5

CHAMPIONSHIP SERIES RECORD

RECORDS: Holds single-series record for most hits allowed—22 (1986). ... Shares single-series record for most earned runs allowed—11 (1986). ... Shares single-game records for most earned runs allowed—7 (October 7, 1986); and most consecutive strikeouts—4 (October 6, 1988). ... Holds A.L. single-series record for most innings pitched—22 ²/₃ (1986). ... Shares A.L. single-game record for most runs allowed—8 (October 7, 1986).

Year	Team (League)	W	L	Pct.	ERA	G	GS	CG	ShO	Sv.	IP	H	R	ER	BB	SO
1986—	Boston (A.L.)......................	1	1	.500	4.37	3	3	0	0	0	22²/₃	22	12	11	7	17
1988—	Boston (A.L.)......................	0	0	...	3.86	1	1	0	0	0	7	6	3	3	0	8
1990—	Boston (A.L.)......................	0	1	.000	3.52	2	2	0	0	0	7²/₃	7	3	3	5	4
	Champ. series totals (3 years)	1	2	.333	4.10	6	6	0	0	0	37¹/₃	35	18	17	12	29

WORLD SERIES RECORD

Year	Team (League)	W	L	Pct.	ERA	G	GS	CG	ShO	Sv.	IP	H	R	ER	BB	SO
1986—	Boston (A.L.)......................	0	0	...	3.18	2	2	0	0	0	11¹/₃	9	5	4	6	11

ALL-STAR GAME RECORD

NOTES: Named Most Valuable Player (1986).

Year	League	W	L	Pct.	ERA	GS	CG	ShO	Sv.	IP	H	R	ER	BB	SO
1986—	American	1	0	1.000	0.00	1	0	0	0	3	0	0	0	0	2
1988—	American	0	0	...	0.00	0	0	0	0	1	0	0	0	0	1

Year League	W	L	Pct.	ERA	GS	CG	ShO	Sv.	IP	H	R	ER	BB	SO
1990— American							Did not play.							
1991— American	0	0	...	9.00	0	0	0	0	1	1	1	1	0	0
1992— American	0	0	...	0.00	0	0	0	0	1	2	0	0	0	0
1997— American	0	0	...	0.00	0	0	0	1	1	0	0	0	0	0
All-Star totals (5 years)	1	0	1.000	1.29	1	0	0	0	7	4	1	1	0	3

CLEMENT, MATT — P — PADRES

PERSONAL: Born August 12, 1974, in McCandless Township, Pa. ... 6-3/180. ... Throws right, bats right. ... Full name: Matthew Paul Clement.
HIGH SCHOOL: Butler (Pa.).
TRANSACTIONS/CAREER NOTES: Selected by San Diego Padres organization in third round of free-agent draft (June 3, 1993).

Year Team (League)	W	L	Pct.	ERA	G	GS	CG	ShO	Sv.	IP	H	R	ER	BB	SO
1993—								Did not play.							
1994— Peoria (Arizona)	•8	5	.615	4.43	13	13	0	0	0	67	65	38	33	17	76
— Spokane (N'west)	1	1	.500	6.14	2	2	0	0	0	7 1/3	8	7	5	11	4
1995— Rancho Cuca. (Calif.)	3	4	.429	4.24	12	12	0	0	0	57 1/3	61	37	27	49	33
1996— Clinton (Midwest)	8	3	.727	2.80	16	16	1	•1	0	96 1/3	66	31	30	52	109
— Rancho Cucamonga (Cal.) .	4	5	.444	5.59	11	11	0	0	0	56 1/3	61	40	35	26	75
1997— Rancho Cucamonga (Cal.) .	6	3	.667	1.60	14	14	2	1	0	101	74	30	18	31	109
— Mobile (Southern)	6	5	.545	2.56	13	13	1	1	0	88	83	37	25	32	92

CLEMONS, CHRIS — P — DIAMONDBACKS

PERSONAL: Born October 31, 1972, in Baytown, Texas. ... 6-4/215. ... Throws right, bats right.
HIGH SCHOOL: McGregor (Texas).
COLLEGE: Texas A&M.
TRANSACTIONS/CAREER NOTES: Selected by Chicago White Sox organization in 21st round of free-agent draft (June 3, 1991); did not sign. ... Selected by Chicago White Sox organization in supplemental round ("sandwich pick" between first and second round, 33rd pick overall) of free-agent draft (June 2, 1994); pick recieved as compensation for Colorado Rockies signing Type A free-agent OF Ellis Burks. ... Selected by Arizona Diamondbacks in second round (43rd pick overall) of expansion draft (November 18, 1997).

Year Team (League)	W	L	Pct.	ERA	G	GS	CG	ShO	Sv.	IP	H	R	ER	BB	SO
1994— GC White Sox (GCL)	0	1	.000	3.86	2	2	0	0	0	7	5	3	3	1	5
— Hickory (S. Atl.)	4	2	.667	4.41	12	12	0	0	0	69 1/3	74	37	34	18	42
1995— Prince William (Caro.)	7	12	.368	4.73	27	27	1	0	0	137	136	78	72	64	92
1996— Prince William (Caro.)	1	4	.200	2.25	6	6	0	0	0	36	36	16	9	8	26
— Birmingham (Southern)	5	2	.714	3.15	19	16	1	0	0	94 1/3	91	39	33	40	69
1997— Nashville (A.A.)	5	5	.500	4.55	22	21	1	1	0	124 2/3	115	73	63	65	70
— Chicago (A.L.)	0	2	.000	8.53	5	2	0	0	0	12 2/3	19	13	12	11	8
Major league totals (1 year)	0	2	.000	8.53	5	2	0	0	0	12 2/3	19	13	12	11	8

CLINE, PAT — C — CUBS

PERSONAL: Born October 9, 1974, in Bradenton, Fla. ... 6-3/225. ... Throws right, bats right. ... Full name: James Patrick Cline.
HIGH SCHOOL: Manatee (Bradenton, Fla.).
TRANSACTIONS/CAREER NOTES: Selected by Chicago Cubs organization in sixth round of free-agent draft (June 3, 1993). ... On Gulf Coast Cubs disabled list (June 20-27, 1994). ... On Huntington disabled list (July 20-September 8, 1994).
STATISTICAL NOTES: Led Appalachian League with 17 passed balls in 1993. ... Tied for Midwest League lead with 18 passed balls in 1995. ... Led Florida State League catchers with 783 total chances in 1996.

Year Team (League)	Pos.	G	AB	R	H	2B	3B	HR	RBI	Avg.	BB	SO	SB	PO	A	E	Avg.
														BATTING			FIELDING
1993— Huntington (Appal.)	C	33	96	17	18	6	0	2	13	.188	17	28	0	174	10	5	.974
1994— GC Cubs (GCL)	C	3	3	0	0	0	0	0	0	.000	0	0	0	2	0	0	1.000
1995— Rockford (Midwest)	C	112	390	65	106	17	0	13	77	.272	58	93	6	549	64	17	.973
1996— Daytona (Fla. St.)	C	124	434	75	121	30	2	17	76	.279	54	79	10	*697	70	16	.980
1997— Orlando (South.)	C	78	271	39	69	19	0	7	37	.255	27	78	2	416	35	5	.989
— Iowa (Am. Assoc.)	C	27	95	6	21	2	0	3	10	.221	10	24	0	188	11	2	.990

CLONTZ, BRAD — P — BRAVES

PERSONAL: Born April 25, 1971, in Stuart, Va. ... 6-1/180. ... Throws right, bats right. ... Full name: John Bradley Clontz.
HIGH SCHOOL: Patrick County (Stuart, Va.).
COLLEGE: Virginia Tech.
TRANSACTIONS/CAREER NOTES: Selected by Atlanta Braves organization in 10th round of free-agent draft (June 1, 1992).
HONORS: Named Southern League Outstanding Pitcher (1994).

Year Team (League)	W	L	Pct.	ERA	G	GS	CG	ShO	Sv.	IP	H	R	ER	BB	SO
1992— Pulaski (Appalachian)	0	0	...	1.59	4	0	0	0	1	5 2/3	3	1	1	2	7
— Macon (S. Atl.)	2	1	.667	3.91	17	0	0	0	2	23	19	14	10	10	18
1993— Durham (Carolina)	1	7	.125	2.75	51	0	0	0	10	75 1/3	69	32	23	26	79
1994— Greenville (Southern)	1	2	.333	1.20	39	0	0	0	*27	45	32	13	6	10	49
— Richmond (Int'l)	0	0	...	2.10	24	0	0	0	11	25 2/3	19	6	6	9	21
1995— Atlanta (N.L.)	8	1	.889	3.65	59	0	0	0	4	69	71	29	28	22	55
1996— Atlanta (N.L.)	6	3	.667	5.69	*81	0	0	0	1	80 2/3	78	53	51	33	49
1997— Atlanta (N.L.)	5	1	.833	3.75	51	0	0	0	1	48	52	24	20	18	42
— Richmond (Int'l)	0	0	...	0.00	16	0	0	0	6	22	10	1	0	2	24
Major league totals (3 years)	19	5	.792	4.51	191	0	0	0	6	197 2/3	201	106	99	73	146

DIVISION SERIES RECORD

Year — Team (League)	W	L	Pct.	ERA	G	GS	CG	ShO	Sv.	IP	H	R	ER	BB	SO
1995— Atlanta (N.L.)	0	0	...	0.00	1	0	0	0	0	1 1/3	0	0	0	0	2
1996— Atlanta (N.L.)								Did not play.							
Div. series totals (1 years)	0	0	...	0.00	1	0	0	0	0	1 1/3	0	0	0	0	2

CHAMPIONSHIP SERIES RECORD

Year — Team (League)	W	L	Pct.	ERA	G	GS	CG	ShO	Sv.	IP	H	R	ER	BB	SO
1995— Atlanta (N.L.)	0	0	...	0.00	1	0	0	0	0	1/3	1	0	0	0	0
1996— Atlanta (N.L.)	0	0	...	0.00	1	0	0	0	0	2/3	0	0	0	0	0
Champ. series totals (2 years)	0	0	...	0.00	2	0	0	0	0	1	1	0	0	0	0

WORLD SERIES RECORD

NOTES: Member of World Series championship team (1995).

Year — Team (League)	W	L	Pct.	ERA	G	GS	CG	ShO	Sv.	IP	H	R	ER	BB	SO
1995— Atlanta (N.L.)	0	0	...	2.70	2	0	0	0	0	3 1/3	2	1	1	0	2
1996— Atlanta (N.L.)	0	0	...	0.00	3	0	0	0	0	1 2/3	1	0	0	2	2
World Series totals (2 years)	0	0	...	1.80	5	0	0	0	0	5	3	1	1	2	4

CLOUDE, KEN   P   MARINERS

PERSONAL: Born January 9, 1975, in Baltimore. ... 6-1/180. ... Throws right, bats right. ... Full name: Kenneth Brian Cloude.
HIGH SCHOOL: McDonogh (Owings Mills, Md.).
TRANSACTIONS/CAREER NOTES: Selected by Seattle Mariners organization in sixth round of free-agent draft (June 3, 1993).

Year — Team (League)	W	L	Pct.	ERA	G	GS	CG	ShO	Sv.	IP	H	R	ER	BB	SO
1994— Ariz. Mariners (Ariz.)	3	4	.429	2.06	12	7	0	0	0	52 1/3	36	22	12	19	61
1995— Wis. Rap. (Midw.)	9	8	.529	3.24	25	25	4	0	0	161	137	64	58	63	140
1996— Lancaster (Calif.)	15	4	.789	4.22	28	28	1	0	0	168 1/3	167	94	79	60	161
1997— Memphis (Southern)	11	7	.611	3.87	22	22	3	•2	0	132 2/3	131	62	57	48	124
— Seattle (A.L.)	4	2	.667	5.12	10	9	0	0	0	51	41	32	29	26	46
Major league totals (1 year)	4	2	.667	5.12	10	9	0	0	0	51	41	32	29	26	46

CLYBURN, DANNY   OF   ORIOLES

PERSONAL: Born April 6, 1974, in Lancaster, S.C. ... 6-3/220. ... Bats right, throws right.
HIGH SCHOOL: Lancaster (S.C.).
TRANSACTIONS/CAREER NOTES: Selected by Pittsburgh Pirates organization in second round of free-agent draft (June 1, 1992). ... On disabled list (April 7-17, 1994). ... Traded by Pirates organization to Cincinnati Reds organization for OF Jacob Brumfield (October 11, 1994). ... Traded by Reds organization with P Tony Nieto to Baltimore Orioles organization for P Brad Pennington (June 16, 1995). ... On Bowie disabled list (July 17-24, 1996).

Year — Team (League)	Pos.	G	AB	R	H	2B	3B	HR	RBI	Avg.	BB	SO	SB	PO	A	E	Avg.
1992— GC Pirates (GCL)	OF	39	149	26	51	9	0	4	25	.342	5	20	7	41	0	3	.932
1993— Augusta (S. Atl.)	OF	127	457	55	121	21	4	9	66	.265	37	97	5	156	9	7	.959
1994— Salem (Carolina)	OF	118	461	57	126	19	0	22	90	.273	20	96	4	135	6	12	.922
1995— Win.-Salem (Car.)■	OF	59	227	27	59	10	2	11	41	.260	13	59	2	66	6	4	.947
— Frederick (Carolina)■	OF	15	45	4	9	4	0	0	4	.200	4	18	1	13	0	1	.929
— High Desert (Calif.)	OF	45	160	20	45	3	1	12	37	.281	17	41	2	63	6	5	.932
1996— Bowie (Eastern)	OF	95	365	51	92	14	5	18	55	.252	17	88	4	103	4	12	.899
1997— Rochester (Int'l)	OF	•137	520	91	156	33	5	20	76	.300	53	107	14	241	5	*10	.961
— Baltimore (A.L.)	OF	2	3	0	0	0	0	0	0	.000	0	2	0	0	0	0	...
Major league totals (1 year)		2	3	0	0	0	0	0	0	.000	0	2	0	0	0	0	...

COGGIN, DAVE   P   PHILLIES

PERSONAL: Born October 30, 1976, in Covina, Calif. ... 6-4/195. ... Throws right, bats right. ... Full name: David Raymond Coggin.
HIGH SCHOOL: Upland (Calif.).
TRANSACTIONS/CAREER NOTES: Selected by Philadelphia Phillies organization in supplemental round ("sandwich pick" between first and second round, 30th pick overall) of free-agent draft (June 1, 1995).
STATISTICAL NOTES: Led Florida State League with 24 wild pitches in 1997.

Year — Team (League)	W	L	Pct.	ERA	G	GS	CG	ShO	Sv.	IP	H	R	ER	BB	SO
1995— Martinsville (App.)	5	3	.625	3.00	11	11	0	0	0	48	45	25	16	31	37
1996— Piedmont (South Atlantic)	9	12	.429	4.31	28	•28	3	3	0	169 1/3	156	87	*81	46	129
1997— Clearwater (Fla. St.)	11	8	.579	4.70	27	27	3	2	0	155	160	96	81	86	110

COLBERT, CRAIG   C   PADRES

PERSONAL: Born February 13, 1965, in Iowa City, Ia. ... 6-0/214. ... Bats right, throws right. ... Full name: Craig Charles Colbert.
HIGH SCHOOL: Manhattan (Kan.).
COLLEGE: Oral Roberts.
TRANSACTIONS/CAREER NOTES: Selected by San Francisco Giants organization in 20th round of free-agent draft (June 2, 1986). ... On disabled list (May 3-June 5 and June 22-August 11, 1991). ... On San Francisco disabled list (August 6-21, 1992). ... On San Francisco disabled list (June 4-August 22, 1993); included rehabilitation assignment to Phoenix (July 23-30, August 9-11 and August 16-22). ... Released by Giants (November 18, 1993). ... Signed by Cleveland Indians organization (December 14, 1993). ... On disabled list (July 31-August 10, 1994). ... Granted free agency (October 15, 1994). ... Signed by Oklahoma City, Texas Rangers organization (January 21, 1995). ... Released by Rangers organization (March 6, 1995). ... Signed by San Diego Padres organization (March 23, 1995). ... Granted free agency (October 16, 1995). ... Re-signed by Padres organization (February 26, 1996). ... Granted free agency (October 15, 1996). ... Re-signed by Padres organization prior to 1997 season. ... On disabled list (April 3-15, April 21-July 12 and July 18, 1997-remainder of season). ... Granted free agency (October 15, 1997). ... Re-signed by Padres organization (October 27, 1997).
STATISTICAL NOTES: Tied for California League lead in double plays by third baseman with 22 in 1987.

Year Team (League)	Pos.	G	AB	R	H	2B	3B	HR	RBI	Avg.	BB	SO	SB	PO	A	E	Avg.
1986—Clinton (Midwest)......	3B	72	263	26	60	12	0	1	17	.228	23	53	4	49	153	15	.931
1987—Fresno (California)......	3B	115	388	41	95	12	4	6	51	.245	22	89	5	86	225	34	.901
1988—Clinton (Midwest)........	3B-1B-OF	124	455	56	106	19	2	11	64	.233	41	100	8	541	158	25	.965
1989—Shreveport (Texas)......	S-3-O-1	106	363	47	94	19	3	7	34	.259	23	67	3	122	203	23	.934
1990—Phoenix (PCL)........	3-C-S-1	111	400	41	112	22	2	8	47	.280	31	80	4	281	166	18	.961
1991—Phoenix (PCL)........	C-3-O-1-S	42	142	9	35	6	2	2	13	.246	11	38	0	130	127	6	.977
1992—San Francisco (N.L.)..	C-3B-2B	49	126	10	29	5	2	1	16	.230	9	22	1	147	24	1	.994
—Phoenix (PCL)........	3-C-S-O	36	140	16	45	8	1	1	12	.321	3	16	0	61	50	5	.957
1993—San Francisco (N.L.)..	C-2B-3B	23	37	2	6	2	0	1	5	.162	3	13	0	52	5	1	.983
—Phoenix (PCL)........	C-3B-1B	13	45	5	10	2	1	1	7	.222	0	11	0	73	9	2	.976
1994—Charlotte (Int'l)■........	O-3-C-1-2	69	182	19	47	7	1	4	25	.258	19	40	1	91	43	6	.957
1995—Las Vegas (PCL)■........	C-1-O-P-3	74	241	30	60	8	1	1	24	.249	21	44	1	352	43	7	.983
1996—Las Vegas (PCL)	C-3B-OF	65	200	18	50	8	0	5	19	.250	8	48	3	308	33	5	.986
1997—Las Vegas (PCL)	PH	2	2	0	2	1	0	0	0	1.000	0	0	0				...
Major league totals (2 years)		72	163	12	35	7	2	2	21	.215	12	35	1	199	29	2	.991

RECORD AS PITCHER

Year Team (League)	W	L	Pct.	ERA	G	GS	CG	ShO	Sv.	IP	H	R	ER	BB	SO
1995—Las Vegas (PCL)■	0	0	...	0.00	1	0	0	0	0	1	1	0	0	1	1

COLBRUNN, GREG   1B   ROCKIES

PERSONAL: Born July 26, 1969, in Fontana, Calif. ... 6-0/200. ... Bats right, throws right. ... Full name: Gregory Joseph Colbrunn.
HIGH SCHOOL: Fontana (Calif.).
TRANSACTIONS/CAREER NOTES: Selected by Montreal Expos organization in sixth round of free-agent draft (June 2, 1987). ... On disabled list (April 10, 1991-entire season). ... On Indianapolis disabled list (April 9-May 5, 1992). ... On Montreal disabled list (August 2-18, 1992); included rehabilitation assignment to Indianapolis (August 13-18). ... On Montreal disabled list (April 5-21, 1993); included rehabilitation assignment to West Palm Beach (April 9-20). ... On Montreal disabled list (July 12, 1993-remainder of season); included rehabilitation assignment to Ottawa (July 27-August 2). ... Claimed on waivers by Florida Marlins (October 7, 1993). ... On Florida disabled list (April 9-May 27, and July 15-30, 1994); included rehabilitation assignments to Brevard County (May 12-18 and July 28-30) and Edmonton (May 18-27). ... On disabled list (July 24-August 8, 1996). ... Granted free agency (December 20, 1996). ... Signed by Minnesota Twins organization (January 24, 1997). ... Traded by Twins to Atlanta Braves for a player to be named later (August 14, 1997); Twins acquired OF Marc Lewis to complete deal (October 1, 1997). ... Granted free agency (October 23, 1997). ... Signed by Colorado Rockies organization (December 23, 1997).
STATISTICAL NOTES: Had 21-game hitting streak (May 31-June 23, 1996). ... Career major league grand slams: 2.

Year Team (League)	Pos.	G	AB	R	H	2B	3B	HR	RBI	Avg.	BB	SO	SB	PO	A	E	Avg.
1988—Rockford (Midwest) ...	C	115	417	55	111	18	2	7	46	.266	22	60	5	595	81	15	.978
1989—W.P. Beach (FSL)........	C	59	228	20	54	8	0	0	25	.237	6	29	3	376	49	5	.988
—Jacksonville (South.)..	C	55	178	21	49	11	1	3	18	.275	13	33	0	304	34	4	.988
1990—Jacksonville (South.)..	C	125	458	57	138	29	1	13	76	.301	38	78	1	698	58	15	.981
1991—							Did not play.										
1992—Indianapolis (A.A.)......	1B	57	216	32	66	19	1	11	48	.306	7	41	1	441	27	4	.992
—Montreal (N.L.)........	1B	52	168	12	45	8	0	2	18	.268	6	34	3	363	29	3	.992
1993—W.P. Beach (FSL)........	1B	8	31	6	12	2	1	1	5	.387	4	1	0	74	5	1	.988
—Montreal (N.L.)..........	1B	70	153	15	39	9	0	4	23	.255	6	33	4	372	27	2	.995
—Ottawa (Int'l)........	1B	6	22	4	6	1	0	0	4	.273	1	2	1	50	1	0	1.000
1994—Florida (N.L.)..........	1B	47	155	17	47	10	0	6	31	.303	9	21	1	304	26	4	.988
—Brevard County (FSL).	1B	7	11	3	6	2	0	1	2	.545	1	0	0	16	1	1	.944
—Edmonton (PCL)	1B	7	17	2	4	0	0	1	2	.235	0	1	0	28	1	1	.967
1995—Florida (N.L.)..........	1B	138	528	70	146	22	1	23	89	.277	22	69	11	1066	90	5	.996
1996—Florida (N.L.)..........	1B	141	511	60	146	26	2	16	69	.286	25	76	4	1169	101	6	.995
1997—Minnesota (A.L.)■......	1B-DH	70	217	24	61	14	0	5	26	.281	8	38	1	475	35	6	.988
—Atlanta (N.L.)■..........	1B-DH	28	54	3	15	3	0	2	9	.278	2	11	0	54	6	1	.984
American League totals (1 year)		70	217	24	61	14	0	5	26	.281	8	38	1	475	35	6	.988
National League totals (6 years)		476	1569	177	438	78	3	53	239	.279	70	250	23	3328	279	21	.994
Major league totals (6 years)		546	1786	201	499	92	3	58	265	.279	78	288	24	3803	314	27	.993

DIVISION SERIES RECORD

Year Team (League)	Pos.	G	AB	R	H	2B	3B	HR	RBI	Avg.	BB	SO	SB	PO	A	E	Avg.
1997—Atlanta (N.L.)..............	PH	1	1	0	1	0	0	0	2	1.000	0	0	0	0	0	0	...

CHAMPIONSHIP SERIES RECORD

Year Team (League)	Pos.	G	AB	R	H	2B	3B	HR	RBI	Avg.	BB	SO	SB	PO	A	E	Avg.
1997—Atlanta (N.L.)..............	PH	3	3	0	2	0	0	0	0	.667	0	0	0	0	0	0	...

COLEMAN, MICHAEL   OF   RED SOX

PERSONAL: Born August 16, 1975, in Nashville, Tenn. ... 5-11/180. ... Bats right, throws right. ... Full name: Michael D. Coleman.
HIGH SCHOOL: Stratford (Nashville, Tenn.).
TRANSACTIONS/CAREER NOTES: Selected by Boston Red Sox organization in 18th round of free-agent draft (June 2, 1994).

Year Team (League)	Pos.	G	AB	R	H	2B	3B	HR	RBI	Avg.	BB	SO	SB	PO	A	E	Avg.
1994—Fort Myers (GCL)	OF	25	95	15	26	6	1	3	15	.274	10	20	5	32	0	0	1.000
—Utica (N.Y.-Penn)........	OF	23	65	16	11	2	0	1	3	.169	14	21	11	35	2	2	.949
1995—Michigan (Midwest) ...	OF	112	422	70	113	16	2	11	61	.268	40	93	29	251	5	5	.981
1996—Sarasota (Fla. St.)	OF	110	407	54	100	20	5	1	36	.246	38	86	24	261	9	2	*.993
1997—Trenton (Eastern)	OF	102	385	56	116	17	8	14	58	.301	41	89	20	259	6	5	.981
—Pawtucket (Int'l)........	OF	28	113	27	36	9	2	7	19	.319	12	27	4	53	2	4	.932
—Boston (A.L.)..........	OF	8	24	2	4	1	0	0	2	.167	0	11	1	16	0	1	.941
Major league totals (1 year)		8	24	2	4	1	0	0	2	.167	0	11	1	16	0	1	.941

PERSONAL: Born September 22, 1961, in Jacksonville. ... 6-1/185. ... Bats both, throws right. ... Full name: Vincent Maurice Coleman. ... Cousin of Greg Coleman, punter, Cleveland Browns and Minnesota Vikings (1977-88).

HIGH SCHOOL: Raines (Jacksonville).

COLLEGE: Florida A&M (degree in physical education).

TRANSACTIONS/CAREER NOTES: Selected by Philadelphia Phillies organization in 20th round of free-agent draft (June 8, 1981); did not sign. ... Selected by St. Louis Cardinals organization in 10th round of free-agent draft (June 7, 1982). ... Granted free agency (November 5, 1990). ... Signed by New York Mets (December 5, 1990). ... On disabled list (June 15-July 25 and August 14-September 27, 1991). ... On New York disabled list (April 10-May 1, 1992). ... On New York disabled list (May 2-28, 1992); included rehabilitation assignment to St. Lucie (May 23-28). ... On New York disabled list (June 27-July 27, 1992). ... Traded by Mets with cash to Kansas City Royals for OF Kevin McReynolds (January 5, 1994). ... Granted free agency (October 20, 1994). ... Re-signed by Omaha, Royals organization (April 26, 1995). ... Traded by Royals to Seattle Mariners for a player to be named later (August 15, 1995); Royals acquired P Jim Converse to complete deal (August 18, 1995). ... Granted free agency (October 31, 1995). ... Signed by Indianapolis, Cincinnati Reds organization (January 20, 1996). ... Released by Reds (June 18, 1996). ... Signed by Vancouver, California Angels organization (June 30, 1996). ... Granted free agency (October 15, 1996). ... Signed by Detroit Tigers organization (January 9, 1997). ... Released by Tigers (April 16, 1997).

RECORDS: Holds major league rookie-season records for most stolen bases—110; and most times caught stealing—25 (1985). ... Holds major league career record for most consecutive stolen bases without being caught stealing—50 (September 18, 1988 through July 26, 1989). ... Shares major league single-game record for most sacrifice flies—3 (May 1, 1986). ... Shares N.L. record for most consecutive seasons leading league in stolen bases—6 (1985-90). ... Shares A.L. single-season record for fewest times caught stealing (50 or more stolen bases)—8 (1994).

HONORS: Named South Atlantic League Most Valuable Player (1983). ... Named N.L. Rookie Player of the Year by THE SPORTING NEWS (1985). ... Named N.L. Rookie of the Year by Baseball Writers' Association of America (1985).

STATISTICAL NOTES: Led South Atlantic League in caught stealing with 31 in 1983. ... Led American Association in caught stealing with 36 in 1984. ... Led American Association outfielders with 381 total chances in 1984. ... Led N.L. in caught stealing with 25 in 1985, 22 in 1987 and tied for lead with 27 in 1988. ... Career major league grand slams: 1.

							BATTING							FIELDING		
Year Team (League)	Pos.	G	AB	R	H	2B	3B	HR	RBI	Avg.	BB	SO	SB	PO	A	E	Avg.
1982— Johnson City (App.) ...	OF	58	212	40	53	2	1	0	16	.250	29	49	•43	123	7	8	.942
1983— Macon (S. Atl.)	OF	113	446	99	156	8	7	0	53	*.350	56	85	*145	225	18	8	.968
1984— Louisville (A.A.)	OF	152	*608	*97	156	21	7	4	48	.257	55	112	*101	357	14	•10	.974
1985— Louisville (A.A.)	OF	5	21	1	3	0	0	0	0	.143	0	2	0	8	0	0	1.000
— St. Louis (N.L.)	OF	151	636	107	170	20	10	1	40	.267	50	115	*110	305	16	7	.979
1986— St. Louis (N.L.)	OF	154	600	94	139	13	8	0	29	.232	60	98	*107	300	12	•9	.972
1987— St. Louis (N.L.)	OF	151	623	121	180	14	10	3	43	.289	70	126	*109	274	16	9	.970
1988— St. Louis (N.L.)	OF	153	616	77	160	20	10	3	38	.260	49	111	*81	290	14	9	.971
1989— St. Louis (N.L.)	OF	145	563	94	143	21	9	2	28	.254	50	90	*65	247	5	•10	.962
1990— St. Louis (N.L.)	OF	124	497	73	145	18	9	6	39	.292	35	88	*77	244	12	5	.981
1991— New York (N.L.)■	OF	72	278	45	71	7	5	1	17	.255	39	47	37	132	5	3	.979
1992— New York (N.L.)	OF	71	229	37	63	11	1	2	21	.275	27	41	24	112	2	1	.991
— St. Lucie (Fla. St.)	OF	6	22	4	8	0	0	0	2	.364	2	6	3	9	0	0	1.000
1993— New York (N.L.)	OF	92	373	64	104	14	8	2	25	.279	21	58	38	162	5	3	.982
1994— Kansas City (A.L.)■ ...	OF-DH	104	438	61	105	14	12	2	33	.240	29	72	50	164	11	7	.962
1995— Omaha (A.A.)	OF	9	38	7	15	2	0	1	5	.395	2	6	3	19	0	1	.950
— Kansas City (A.L.)	OF-DH	75	293	39	84	13	4	4	20	.287	27	48	26	107	7	3	.974
— Seattle (A.L.)■	OF	40	162	27	47	10	2	1	9	.290	10	32	16	83	2	1	.988
1996— Cincinnati (N.L.)■	OF	33	84	10	13	1	1	1	4	.155	9	31	12	28	2	1	.968
— Indianapolis (A.A.)	OF	7	26	2	2	0	0	0	1	.077	1	5	0	6	0	0	1.000
— Vancouver (PCL)■	OF	21	87	9	18	2	1	0	5	.207	9	15	4	24	0	1	.960
1997— Detroit (A.L.)■	OF-DH	6	14	0	1	0	0	0	0	.071	1	3	0	3	0	0	1.000
American League totals (3 years)		225	907	127	237	37	18	7	62	.261	67	155	92	357	20	11	.972
National League totals (10 years)		1146	4499	722	1188	139	71	21	284	.264	410	805	660	2094	89	57	.975
Major league totals (13 years)		1371	5406	849	1425	176	89	28	346	.264	477	960	752	2451	109	68	.974

DIVISION SERIES RECORD

							BATTING							FIELDING		
Year Team (League)	Pos.	G	AB	R	H	2B	3B	HR	RBI	Avg.	BB	SO	SB	PO	A	E	Avg.
1995— Seattle (A.L.)	OF	5	23	6	5	0	1	1	1	.217	2	4	1	14	0	0	1.000

CHAMPIONSHIP SERIES RECORD

RECORDS: Shares N.L. career record for most times caught stealing—4.

							BATTING							FIELDING		
Year Team (League)	Pos.	G	AB	R	H	2B	3B	HR	RBI	Avg.	BB	SO	SB	PO	A	E	Avg.
1985— St. Louis (N.L.)	OF	3	14	2	4	0	0	0	1	.286	0	2	1	8	0	0	1.000
1987— St. Louis (N.L.)	OF	7	26	3	7	1	0	0	4	.269	4	6	1	9	1	0	1.000
1995— Seattle (A.L.)	OF-PH	6	20	0	2	0	0	0	0	.100	2	6	4	12	0	0	1.000
Championship series totals (3 years)		16	60	5	13	1	0	0	5	.217	6	14	6	29	1	0	1.000

WORLD SERIES RECORD

							BATTING							FIELDING		
Year Team (League)	Pos.	G	AB	R	H	2B	3B	HR	RBI	Avg.	BB	SO	SB	PO	A	E	Avg.
1985— St. Louis (N.L.)								Did not play.									
1987— St. Louis (N.L.)	OF	7	28	5	4	2	0	0	2	.143	2	10	6	10	2	0	1.000
World Series total (1 year)...		7	28	5	4	2	0	0	2	.143	2	10	6	10	2	0	1.000

ALL-STAR GAME RECORD

						BATTING							FIELDING		
Year League	Pos.	AB	R	H	2B	3B	HR	RBI	Avg.	BB	SO	SB	PO	A	E	Avg.
1988— National	OF	2	1	1	0	0	0	0	.500	0	0	1	3	0	0	1.000
1989— National	PR-OF	0	0	0	0	0	0	0	...	0	0	0	0	0	0	...
All-Star Game totals (2 years)		2	1	1	0	0	0	0	.500	0	0	1	3	0	0	1.000

COLES, DARNELL   OF/3B   ROCKIES

PERSONAL: Born June 2, 1962, in San Bernardino, Calif. ... 6-1/185. ... Bats right, throws right.
HIGH SCHOOL: Eisenhower (Rialto, Calif.).
COLLEGE: Orange Coast College (Calif.).
TRANSACTIONS/CAREER NOTES: Selected by Seattle Mariners organization in first round (sixth pick overall) of free-agent draft (June 3, 1980). ... On Seattle disabled list (March 29-April 24, 1984); included rehabilitation assignment to Salt Lake (April 12-24). ... On Calgary disabled list (August 8-September 9, 1985). ... Traded by Mariners to Detroit Tigers for P Rich Monteleone (December 12, 1985). ... On disabled list (June 16-July 1, 1986). ... On Detroit disabled list (May 25-June 27, 1987); included rehabilitation assignment to Toledo (June 16-27). ... Traded by Tigers organization with a player to be named later to Pittsburgh Pirates for 3B Jim Morrison (August 7, 1987); Pirates organization acquired P Morris Madden to complete deal (August 12, 1987). ... Traded by Pirates to Mariners for OF Glenn Wilson (July 22, 1988). ... Traded by Mariners to Tigers for OF Tracy Jones (June 18, 1990). ... Granted free agency (November 5, 1990). ... Signed by Phoenix, San Francisco Giants organization (March 30, 1991). ... Granted free agency (October 16, 1991). ... Signed by Cincinnati Reds organization (November 12, 1991). ... On Cincinnati disabled list (August 26, 1992-remainder of season). ... Granted free agency (October 28, 1992). ... Signed by Toronto Blue Jays (November 27, 1992). ... Granted free agency (October 14, 1994). ... Signed by Louisville, St. Louis Cardinals organization (March 9, 1995). ... Released by Cardinals (August 25, 1995). ... Signed by Chunichi Dragons of Japan Central League (February 12, 1996). ... Signed by Colorado Rockies organization (January 24, 1997). ... Contract sold by Rockies to Hanshin Tigers of the Japan Central League (May 23, 1997).
STATISTICAL NOTES: Led Midwest League shortstops with 66 double plays in 1981. ... Hit three home runs in one game (September 30, 1987, second game; and July 5, 1994). ... Career major league grand slams: 3.

Year Team (League)	Pos.	G	AB	R	H	2B	3B	HR	RBI	Avg.	BB	SO	SB	PO	A	E	Avg.
										BATTING					FIELDING		
1980— Bellingham (N'west)...	SS	35	117	23	25	3	1	2	12	.214	22	24	1	37	80	*28	.807
1981— Wausau (Midwest)	SS	111	354	53	97	20	3	9	48	.274	42	67	9	154	335	52	.904
1982— Bakersfield (Calif.)	SS	136	482	91	146	24	4	11	55	.303	68	61	27	200	419	*73	.895
1983— Chattanooga (Sou.)	SS	72	261	49	75	10	4	5	24	.287	41	39	12	131	232	30	.924
—Salt Lake (PCL)	SS	61	234	43	74	12	5	10	41	.316	20	19	11	100	178	25	.917
—Seattle (A.L.)	3B	27	92	9	26	7	0	1	6	.283	7	12	0	17	47	4	.941
1984— Salt Lake (PCL)	3B	69	242	57	77	22	3	14	68	.318	48	41	7	45	164	16	.929
—Seattle (A.L.)	3B-OF-DH	48	143	15	23	3	1	0	6	.161	17	26	2	31	63	8	.922
1985— Calgary (PCL)	3B-SS-OF	31	97	16	31	8	0	4	24	.320	17	15	2	16	49	5	.929
—Seattle (A.L.)	S-3-O-DH	27	59	8	14	4	0	1	5	.237	9	17	0	25	44	6	.920
1986— Detroit (A.L.)■......	3-DH-O-S	142	521	67	142	30	2	20	86	.273	45	84	6	111	242	23	.939
1987— Detroit (A.L.) 3-1-O-DH-S		53	149	14	27	5	1	4	15	.181	15	23	0	84	67	17	.899
—Toledo (Int'l)	3B-OF-SS	10	37	7	12	5	0	1	8	.324	4	2	0	7	8	1	.938
—Pittsburgh (N.L.)■......	OF-3B-1B	40	119	20	27	8	0	6	24	.227	19	20	1	39	20	3	.952
1988— Pittsburgh (N.L.)	OF-1B-3B	68	211	20	49	13	1	5	36	.232	20	41	1	100	0	2	.980
—Seattle (A.L.)■..........	OF-DH-1B	55	195	32	57	10	1	10	34	.292	17	26	3	66	3	1	.986
1989— Seattle (A.L.)	O-3-1-DH	146	535	54	135	21	3	10	59	.252	27	61	5	317	76	12	.970
1990— Seattle (A.L.)	3B-OF-DH	37	107	9	23	5	1	2	16	.215	4	17	0	34	0	6	.850
—Detroit (A.L.)■..........	DH-O-3-1	52	108	13	22	2	0	1	4	.204	12	21	0	35	22	3	.950
1991— Phoenix (PCL)■.......	3B-OF-1B	83	328	43	95	23	2	6	65	.290	27	43	0	102	118	17	.928
—San Francisco (N.L.) ..	OF-1B	11	14	1	3	0	0	0	0	.214	0	2	0	4	0	0	1.000
1992— Nashville (A.A.)■.......	3B-1B	22	81	19	24	5	0	6	16	.296	8	13	1	69	35	5	.954
—Cincinnati (N.L.)	3B-1B-OF	55	141	16	44	11	2	3	18	.312	3	15	1	161	42	0	1.000
1993— Toronto (A.L.)■.........	O-3-DH-1	64	194	26	49	9	1	4	26	.253	16	29	1	77	20	7	.933
1994— Toronto (A.L.)	O-1-3-DH	48	143	15	30	6	1	4	15	.210	10	25	0	103	9	4	.966
1995— St. Louis (N.L.)■......	3B-1B-OF	63	138	13	31	7	0	3	16	.225	16	20	0	136	33	3	.983
1996— Chunichi (Jp. Cn.)■....	...	130	513	...	155	15	1	29	79	.302	54	79	0	...	...	...	...
1997— Colorado (N.L.)■......	3B-OF	21	22	1	7	1	0	1	2	.318	0	6	0	0	3	0	1.000
American League totals (10 years)		699	2246	262	548	102	11	57	272	.244	179	341	17	900	593	91	.943
National League totals (6 years)		258	645	71	161	40	3	18	96	.250	58	104	3	440	98	8	.985
Major league totals (14 years)		957	2891	333	709	142	14	75	368	.245	237	445	20	1340	691	99	.954

CHAMPIONSHIP SERIES RECORD

Year Team (League)	Pos.	G	AB	R	H	2B	3B	HR	RBI	Avg.	BB	SO	SB	PO	A	E	Avg.
										BATTING					FIELDING		
1993— Toronto (A.L.)								Did not play.									

WORLD SERIES RECORD

NOTES: Member of World Series championship team (1993).

Year Team (League)	Pos.	G	AB	R	H	2B	3B	HR	RBI	Avg.	BB	SO	SB	PO	A	E	Avg.
										BATTING					FIELDING		
1993— Toronto (A.L.)								Did not play.									

COLLIER, LOU   SS   PIRATES

PERSONAL: Born August 21, 1973, in Chicago. ... 5-10/180. ... Bats right, throws right. ... Full name: Louis Keith Collier.
HIGH SCHOOL: Vocational (Chicago).
JUNIOR COLLEGE: Triton Community College (River Grove, Ill.).
TRANSACTIONS/CAREER NOTES: Selected by Pittsburgh Pirates organization in 31st round of free-agent draft (June 1, 1992).

Year Team (League)	Pos.	G	AB	R	H	2B	3B	HR	RBI	Avg.	BB	SO	SB	PO	A	E	Avg.
										BATTING					FIELDING		
1993— Welland (NYP)...........	SS	50	201	35	61	6	2	1	19	.303	12	31	8	74	138	27	.887
1994— Augusta (S. Atl.)........	SS	85	318	48	89	17	4	7	40	.280	25	53	32	106	262	34	.915
—Salem (Carolina)........	SS	43	158	25	42	4	1	6	16	.266	15	29	5	65	129	11	.946
1995— Lynchburg (Caro.).......	SS	114	399	68	110	19	3	4	38	.276	51	60	31	156	361	35	.937
1996— Carolina (Southern)....	SS	119	443	76	124	20	3	3	49	.280	48	73	29	189	310	30	.943
1997— Calgary (PCL)............	SS-2B	112	397	65	131	31	5	1	48	.330	37	47	12	187	315	34	.937
—Pittsburgh (N.L.)..........	SS	18	37	3	5	0	0	0	3	.135	1	11	1	9	36	0	1.000
Major league totals (1 year)		18	37	3	5	0	0	0	3	.135	1	11	1	9	36	0	1.000

COLON, BARTOLO   P   INDIANS

PERSONAL: Born May 24, 1975, in Altamira, Dominican Republic. ... 6-0/185. ... Throws right, bats right.
TRANSACTIONS/CAREER NOTES: Signed as non-drafted free agent by Cleveland Indians organization (June 26, 1993). ... On Canton/Akron disabled list (May 30-July 24, 1996).
HONORS: Named Carolina League Pitcher of the Year (1995).
STATISTICAL NOTES: Pitched 4-0 no-hit victory against New Orleans (June 20, 1997).

Year Team (League)	W	L	Pct.	ERA	G	GS	CG	ShO	Sv.	IP	H	R	ER	BB	SO
1993— Santiago (DSL)	6	1	.857	2.59	11	10	2	1	1	66	44	24	19	33	48
1994— Burlington (Appalachian)	7	4	.636	3.14	12	12	0	0	0	66	46	32	23	44	84
1995— Kinston (Carolina)	13	3	*.813	1.96	21	21	0	0	0	128 2/3	91	31	28	39	*152
1996— Cant./Akr. (Eastern)	2	2	.500	1.74	13	12	0	0	0	62	44	17	12	25	56
— Buffalo (A.A.)	0	0	...	6.00	8	0	0	0	0	15	16	10	10	8	19
1997— Cleveland (A.L.)	4	7	.364	5.65	19	17	1	0	0	94	107	66	59	45	66
— Buffalo (A.A.)	7	1	.875	2.22	10	10	1	1	0	56 2/3	45	15	14	23	54
Major league totals (1 year)	4	7	.364	5.65	19	17	1	0	0	94	107	66	59	45	66

CONE, DAVID   P   YANKEES

C

PERSONAL: Born January 2, 1963, in Kansas City, Mo. ... 6-1/190. ... Throws right, bats left. ... Full name: David Brian Cone.
HIGH SCHOOL: Rockhurst (Kansas City, Mo.).
TRANSACTIONS/CAREER NOTES: Selected by Kansas City Royals organization in third round of free-agent draft (June 8, 1981). ... On disabled list (April 8, 1983-entire season). ... Traded by Royals with C Chris Jelic to New York Mets for C Ed Hearn, P Rick Anderson and P Mauro Gozzo (March 27, 1987). ... On New York disabled list (May 28-August 14, 1987); included rehabilitation assignment to Tidewater (July 30-August 14). ... Traded by Mets to Toronto Blue Jays for IF Jeff Kent and a player to be named later (August 27, 1992); Mets acquired OF Ryan Thompson to complete deal (September 1, 1992). ... Granted free agency (October 30, 1992). ... Signed by Royals (December 8, 1992). ... Traded by Royals to Blue Jays for P David Sinnes, IF Chris Stynes and IF Tony Medrano (April 6, 1995). ... Traded by Blue Jays to New York Yankees for P Marty Janzen, P Jason Jarvis and P Mike Gordon (July 28, 1995). ... Granted free agency (November 3, 1995). ... Re-signed by Yankees (December 21, 1995). ... On New York disabled list (May 3-September 2, 1996); included rehabilitation assignment to Norwich (August 21-September 1). ... On disabled list (August 18-September 20, 1997).
RECORDS: Shares major league record for striking out side on nine pitches (August 30, 1991, seventh inning). ... Shares N.L. single-game record for most strikeouts—19 (October 6, 1991).
HONORS: Named righthanded pitcher on THE SPORTING NEWS A.L. All-Star team (1994). ... Named A.L. Cy Young Award winner by Baseball Writers' Association of America (1994).
STATISTICAL NOTES: Led Southern League with 27 wild pitches in 1984. ... Pitched 6-0 one-hit, complete-game victory against San Diego (August 29, 1988). ... Tied for N.L. lead with 10 balks in 1988. ... Pitched 1-0 one-hit, complete-game victory against St. Louis (September 20, 1991). ... Struck out 19 batters in one game (October 6, 1991). ... Pitched 4-0 one-hit, complete-game victory against California (May 22, 1994). ... Led A.L. with 229.1 innings pitched in 1995. ... Struck out 16 batters in one game (June 23, 1997). ... Tied for A.L. lead with 14 wild pitches in 1997.
MISCELLANEOUS: Singled in only appearance as pinch-hitter (1990).

Year Team (League)	W	L	Pct.	ERA	G	GS	CG	ShO	Sv.	IP	H	R	ER	BB	SO
1981— GC Royals-Bl. (GCL)	6	4	.600	2.55	14	12	0	0	0	67	52	24	19	33	45
1982— Charleston, S.C. (S. Atl.)	9	2	.818	2.06	16	16	1	1	0	104 2/3	84	38	24	47	87
— Fort Myers (Fla. St.)	7	1	.875	2.12	10	9	6	1	0	72 1/3	56	21	17	25	57
1983—								Did not play.							
1984— Memphis (Southern)	8	12	.400	4.28	29	29	9	1	0	178 2/3	162	103	85	114	110
1985— Omaha (Am. Assoc.)	9	15	.375	4.65	28	27	5	1	0	158 2/3	157	90	82	*93	115
1986— Omaha (Am. Assoc.)	8	4	.667	2.79	39	2	2	0	14	71	60	23	22	25	63
— Kansas City (A.L.)	0	0	...	5.56	11	0	0	0	0	22 2/3	29	14	14	13	21
1987— New York (N.L.)■	5	6	.455	3.71	21	13	1	0	1	99 1/3	87	46	41	44	68
— Tidewater (Int'l)	0	1	.000	5.73	3	3	0	0	0	11	10	8	7	6	7
1988— New York (N.L.)	20	3	*.870	2.22	35	28	8	4	0	231 1/3	178	67	57	80	213
1989— New York (N.L.)	14	8	.636	3.52	34	33	7	2	0	219 2/3	183	92	86	74	190
1990— New York (N.L.)	14	10	.583	3.23	31	30	6	2	0	211 2/3	177	84	76	65	*233
1991— New York (N.L.)	14	14	.500	3.29	34	34	5	2	0	232 2/3	204	95	85	73	*241
1992— New York (N.L.)	13	7	.650	2.88	27	27	7	•5	0	196 2/3	162	75	63	*82	214
— Toronto (A.L.)■	4	3	.571	2.55	8	7	0	0	0	53	39	16	15	29	47
1993— Kansas City (A.L.)■	11	14	.440	3.33	34	34	6	1	0	254	205	102	94	114	191
1994— Kansas City (A.L.)■	16	5	.762	2.94	23	23	4	3	0	171 2/3	130	60	56	54	132
1995— Toronto (A.L.)■	9	6	.600	3.38	17	17	5	2	0	130 1/3	113	53	49	41	102
— New York (A.L.)	9	2	.818	3.82	13	13	1	0	0	§99	82	42	42	47	89
1996— New York (A.L.)	7	2	.778	2.88	11	11	1	0	0	72	50	25	23	34	71
— Norwich (Eastern)	0	0	...	0.90	2	2	0	0	0	10	9	3	1	1	13
1997— New York (A.L.)	12	6	.667	2.82	29	29	1	0	0	195	155	67	61	86	222
A.L. totals (7 years)	68	38	.642	3.19	146	134	18	6	0	997 2/3	803	379	354	418	875
N.L. totals (6 years)	80	48	.625	3.08	182	165	34	15	1	1191 1/3	991	459	408	418	1159
Major league totals (12 years)	148	86	.632	3.13	328	299	52	21	1	2189	1794	838	762	836	2034

DIVISION SERIES RECORD

RECORDS: Holds career records for most runs allowed—20; most earned runs allowed—20; hits allowed—30; and bases on balls allowed—10. ... Holds A.L. career record for most innings pitched—25.

Year Team (League)	W	L	Pct.	ERA	G	GS	CG	ShO	Sv.	IP	H	R	ER	BB	SO
1995— New York (A.L.)	1	0	1.000	4.60	2	2	0	0	0	15 2/3	15	8	8	9	14
1996— New York (A.L.)	0	1	.000	9.00	2	1	0	0	0	6	8	6	6	2	8
1997— New York (A.L.)	0	0	...	16.20	1	1	0	0	0	3 1/3	7	6	6	2	2
Div. series totals (3 years)	1	1	.500	7.20	5	4	0	0	0	25	30	20	20	13	24

CHAMPIONSHIP SERIES RECORD

Year Team (League)	W	L	Pct.	ERA	G	GS	CG	ShO	Sv.	IP	H	R	ER	BB	SO
1988— New York (N.L.)	1	1	.500	4.50	3	2	1	0	0	12	10	6	6	5	9
1992— Toronto (A.L.)	1	1	.500	3.00	2	2	0	0	0	12	11	7	4	5	9
1996— New York (A.L.)	0	0	...	3.00	1	1	0	0	0	6	5	2	2	5	5
Champ. series totals (3 years)	2	2	.500	3.60	6	5	1	0	0	30	26	15	12	15	23

WORLD SERIES RECORD

NOTES: Member of World Series championship team (1992 and 1996).

Year— Team (League)	W	L	Pct.	ERA	G	GS	CG	ShO	Sv.	IP	H	R	ER	BB	SO
1992— Toronto (A.L.)	0	0	...	3.48	2	2	0	0	0	10 1/3	9	5	4	8	8
1996— New York (A.L.)	1	0	1.000	1.50	1	1	0	0	0	6	4	1	1	4	3
World Series totals (2 years)	1	0	1.000	2.76	3	3	0	0	0	16 1/3	13	6	5	12	11

ALL-STAR GAME RECORD

Year— League	W	L	Pct.	ERA	GS	CG	ShO	Sv.	IP	H	R	ER	BB	SO
1988— National	0	0	...	0.00	0	0	0	0	1	0	0	0	0	1
1992— National	0	0	...	0.00	0	0	0	0	1	0	0	0	0	1
1994— American	0	0	...	13.50	0	0	0	0	2	4	3	3	0	3
1997— American	0	0	...	0.00	0	0	0	0	1	0	0	0	2	0
All-Star totals (4 years)	0	0	...	5.40	0	0	0	0	5	4	3	3	2	5

C

CONINE, JEFF — OF — ROYALS

PERSONAL: Born June 27, 1966, in Tacoma, Wash. ... 6-1/220. ... Bats right, throws right. ... Full name: Jeffrey Guy Conine.

HIGH SCHOOL: Eisenhower (Rialto, Calif.).

COLLEGE: UCLA.

TRANSACTIONS/CAREER NOTES: Selected by Kansas City Royals organization in 58th round of free-agent draft (June 2, 1987). ... On disabled list (June 28, 1991-remainder of season). ... Selected by Florida Marlins in first round (22nd pick overall) of expansion draft (November 17, 1992). ... Traded by Marlins to Royals for P Blaine Mull (November 20, 1997).

RECORDS: Shares major league rookie-season record for most games—162 (1993).

HONORS: Named Southern League Most Valuable Player (1990).

STATISTICAL NOTES: Led Southern League first basemen with 1,164 putouts, 95 assists, 22 errors, 1,281 total chances and 108 double plays in 1990. ... Led N.L. with 12 sacrifice flies in 1995. ... Career major league grand slams: 3.

MISCELLANEOUS: Holds Florida Marlins all-time records for most hits (737), most runs (337), highest career batting average (.291), most runs batted in (422) and most doubles (122).

Year Team (League)	Pos.	G	AB	R	H	2B	3B	HR	RBI	Avg.	BB	SO	SB	PO	A	E	Avg.
1988— Baseball City (FSL)	1B-3B	118	415	63	113	23	9	10	59	.272	46	77	26	661	51	22	.970
1989— Baseball City (FSL)	1B	113	425	68	116	12	7	14	60	.273	40	91	32	830	65	18	.980
1990— Memphis (Southern)	1B-3B	137	487	89	156	37	8	15	95	.320	94	88	21	†1164	†95	†22	.983
— Kansas City (A.L.)	1B	9	20	3	5	2	0	0	2	.250	2	5	0	39	4	1	.977
1991— Omaha (A.A.)	1B-OF	51	171	23	44	9	1	3	15	.257	26	39	0	392	41	7	.984
1992— Omaha (A.A.)	1B-OF	110	397	69	120	24	5	20	72	.302	54	67	4	845	60	6	.993
— Kansas City (A.L.)	OF-1B	28	91	10	23	5	2	0	9	.253	8	23	0	75	3	0	1.000
1993— Florida (N.L.)■	OF-1B	*162	595	75	174	24	3	12	79	.292	52	135	2	403	25	2	.995
1994— Florida (N.L.)	OF-1B	115	451	60	144	27	6	18	82	.319	40	92	1	408	24	6	.986
1995— Florida (N.L.)	OF-1B	133	483	72	146	26	2	25	105	.302	66	94	2	292	18	6	.981
1996— Florida (N.L.)	OF-1B	157	597	84	175	32	2	26	95	.293	62	121	1	478	48	8	.985
1997— Florida (N.L.)	1B-OF	151	405	46	98	13	1	17	61	.242	57	89	2	897	104	8	.992
American League totals (2 years)		37	111	13	28	7	2	0	11	.252	10	28	0	114	7	1	.992
National League totals (5 years)		718	2531	337	737	122	14	98	422	.291	277	531	8	2478	219	30	.989
Major league totals (7 years)		755	2642	350	765	129	16	98	433	.290	287	559	8	2592	226	31	.989

DIVISION SERIES RECORD

Year Team (League)	Pos.	G	AB	R	H	2B	3B	HR	RBI	Avg.	BB	SO	SB	PO	A	E	Avg.
1997— Florida (N.L.)	1B	3	11	3	4	1	0	0	0	.364	1	0	0	24	3	1	.964

CHAMPIONSHIP SERIES RECORD

Year Team (League)	Pos.	G	AB	R	H	2B	3B	HR	RBI	Avg.	BB	SO	SB	PO	A	E	Avg.
1997— Florida (N.L.)	1B	6	18	1	2	0	0	0	1	.111	1	4	0	34	5	0	1.000

WORLD SERIES RECORD

NOTES: Member of World Series championship team (1997).

Year Team (League)	Pos.	G	AB	R	H	2B	3B	HR	RBI	Avg.	BB	SO	SB	PO	A	E	Avg.
1997— Florida (N.L.)	1B-PH	6	13	1	3	0	0	0	2	.231	0	0	0	30	2	0	1.000

ALL-STAR GAME RECORD

NOTES: Hit home run in first at-bat (July 11, 1995). ... Named Most Valuable Player (1995).

Year League	Pos.	AB	R	H	2B	3B	HR	RBI	Avg.	BB	SO	SB	PO	A	E	Avg.
1994— National								Did not play.								
1995— National	PH	1	1	1	0	0	1	1	1.000	0	0	0	...	...	...	...
All-Star Game totals (1 year)		1	1	1	0	0	1	1	1.000	0	0	0	...	...	...	...

CONNER, DECOMBA — OF — MARINERS

PERSONAL: Born July 17, 1973, in Mooresville, N.C. ... 5-10/185. ... Bats right, throws right. ... Full name: Decomba Kawasaki Conner.

HIGH SCHOOL: Mooresville (N.C.).

JUNIOR COLLEGE: North Greenville (S.C.) College.

TRANSACTIONS/CAREER NOTES: Selected by Cincinnati Reds organization in seventh round of free-agent draft (June 2, 1994). ... Traded by Reds with P Ben Bailey to Detroit Tigers for OF Ruben Sierra (October 28, 1996). ... On Jacksonville disabled list (April 13-30, 1997). ... Claimed on waivers by Seattle Mariners (October 17, 1997).

STATISTICAL NOTES: Tied for Appalachian League lead in double plays by outfielder with three in 1994. ... Led Carolina League outfielders with 321 total chances in 1996.

Year Team (League)	Pos.	G	AB	R	H	2B	3B	HR	RBI	Avg.	BB	SO	SB	PO	A	E	Avg.
1994— Princeton (Appal.)	OF	46	158	45	53	7	5	7	19	.335	24	39	30	85	5	8	.918
1995— Char., W.Va. (SAL)	OF	91	308	55	81	10	7	5	5	.263	39	77	22	184	3	2	.989
— Princeton (Appal.)	OF	6	16	2	2	2	0	0	5	.125	3	3	2	18	2	0	1.000
1996— Win.-Salem (Car.)■	OF	129	512	77	144	18	5	20	63	.281	43	117	33	*308	6	7	.978
1997— Jacksonv. (South.)■ ..	OF	47	154	22	32	6	3	4	17	.208	30	45	5	96	1	4	.960
— Lakeland (Fla. St.)	OF	56	201	35	64	7	4	7	29	.318	21	47	9	133	1	0	1.000

CONVERSE, JIM   P

PERSONAL: Born August 17, 1971, in San Francisco. ... 5-9/185. ... Throws right, bats right. ... Full name: James Daniel Converse.
HIGH SCHOOL: Orangevale (Calif.)-Casa Roble.
TRANSACTIONS/CAREER NOTES: Selected by Seattle Mariners organization in 16th round of free-agent draft (June 4, 1990). ... Traded by Mariners to Kansas City Royals (August 18, 1995); completing deal in which Mariners acquired OF Vince Coleman for a player to be named later (August 15, 1995). ... On disabled list (March 22, 1996-entire season). ... Granted free agency (October 15, 1996). ... Signed by Omaha, Royals organization (December 27, 1996). ... Released by Royals (June 2, 1997) ... Signed by Oneonta, Yankees organization (June 9, 1997). ... On Columbus disabled list (June 15-July 11, 1997) ... Granted free agency (October 15, 1997).
HONORS: Named Southern League co-Pitcher of the Year (1992).
STATISTICAL NOTES: Led Northwest League with 10 balks in 1990. ... Tied for Pacific Coast League lead in balks with four in 1995.

Year Team (League)	W	L	Pct.	ERA	G	GS	CG	ShO	Sv.	IP	H	R	ER	BB	SO
1990— Bellingham (N'west)	2	4	.333	3.92	12	12	0	0	0	66²/₃	50	31	29	32	75
1991— Peninsula (Caro.)	6	15	.286	4.97	26	26	1	0	0	137²/₃	143	90	76	97	137
1992— Jacksonville (Southern)	12	7	.632	2.66	27	26	2	0	0	159	134	61	47	*82	*157
1993— Calgary (PCL)	7	8	.467	5.40	23	22	•4	0	0	121²/₃	144	86	73	64	78
— Seattle (A.L.)	1	3	.250	5.31	4	4	0	0	0	20¹/₃	23	12	12	14	10
1994— Calgary (PCL)	5	3	.625	5.11	14	14	0	0	0	74	105	48	42	21	53
— Seattle (A.L.)	0	5	.000	8.69	13	8	0	0	0	48²/₃	73	49	47	40	39
1995— Seattle (A.L.)	0	3	.000	7.36	6	1	0	0	1	11	16	9	9	8	9
— Tacoma (PCL)	4	7	.364	5.99	17	12	0	0	0	73²/₃	96	57	49	36	43
— Omaha (Am. Assoc.)■	1	0	1.000	0.00	4	0	0	0	0	5	1	0	0	1	9
— Kansas City (A.L.)	1	0	1.000	5.84	9	0	0	0	0	12¹/₃	12	8	8	8	5
1996—							Did not play.								
1997— Omaha (Am. Assoc.)■	2	1	.667	6.75	6	3	0	0	0	17¹/₃	18	13	13	9	13
— Kansas City (A.L.)	0	0	...	3.60	3	0	0	0	0	5	4	2	2	5	3
— GC Yankees (GCL)■	0	0	...	1.93	3	3	0	0	0	4²/₃	5	1	1	1	8
— Columbus (Int'l)	0	2	.000	3.32	10	1	0	0	1	19	22	8	7	11	13
Major league totals (4 years)	2	11	.154	7.21	35	13	0	0	1	97¹/₃	128	80	78	75	66

COOK, DENNIS   P   METS

PERSONAL: Born October 4, 1962, in Lamarque, Texas. ... 6-3/190. ... Throws left, bats left. ... Full name: Dennis Bryan Cook.
HIGH SCHOOL: Dickinson (Texas).
JUNIOR COLLEGE: Angelina College (Texas).
COLLEGE: Texas.
TRANSACTIONS/CAREER NOTES: Selected by San Diego Padres organization in sixth round of free-agent draft (January 11, 1983); did not sign. ... Selected by San Francisco Giants organization in 18th round of free-agent draft (June 3, 1985). ... Traded by Giants with P Terry Mulholland and 3B Charlie Hayes to Philadelphia Phillies for P Steve Bedrosian and a player to be named later (June, 18, 1989); Giants organization acquired IF Rick Parker to complete deal (August 7, 1989). ... Traded by Phillies to Los Angeles Dodgers for C Darrin Fletcher (September 13, 1990). ... Traded by Dodgers with P Mike Christopher to Cleveland Indians for P Rudy Seanez (December 10, 1991). ... Granted free agency (October 15, 1993). ... Signed by Chicago White Sox organization (January 5, 1994). ... Claimed on waivers by Indians (October 17, 1994). ... Traded by Indians to Texas Rangers for SS Guillermo Mercedes (June 22, 1995). ... Granted free agency (October 29, 1996). ... Signed by Florida Marlins (December 10, 1996). ... On suspended list (July 4-5, 1997). ... Traded by Marlins to New York Mets for OF Fletcher Bates and P Scott Comer (December 18, 1997).
HONORS: Named Texas League Pitcher of the Year (1987).
STATISTICAL NOTES: Led A.L. with five balks in 1992.
MISCELLANEOUS: Appeared in one game as pinch-runner with Philadelphia (1989). ... Singled once and scored once in five games as pinch-hitter and appeared in one game as pinch-runner with Philadelphia (1990). ... Appeared in one game as pinch-runner (1997). ... Singled twice, scored once and had an RBI in two games as pinch-hitter (1997).

Year Team (League)	W	L	Pct.	ERA	G	GS	CG	ShO	Sv.	IP	H	R	ER	BB	SO
1985— Clinton (Midwest)	5	4	.556	3.36	13	13	1	0	0	83	73	35	31	27	40
1986— Fresno (California)	12	7	.632	3.97	27	25	2	1	1	170	141	92	75	100	*173
1987— Shreveport (Texas)	9	2	.818	2.13	16	16	1	0	0	105²/₃	94	32	25	20	98
— Phoenix (PCL)	2	5	.286	5.23	12	11	1	0	0	62	72	45	36	26	24
1988— Phoenix (PCL)	11	9	.550	3.88	26	25	5	1	0	141¹/₃	138	73	61	51	110
— San Francisco (N.L.)	2	1	.667	2.86	4	4	1	1	0	22	9	8	7	11	13
1989— Phoenix (PCL)	7	4	.636	3.12	12	12	3	1	0	78	73	29	27	19	85
— San Francisco (N.L.)	1	0	1.000	1.80	2	2	1	0	0	15	13	3	3	5	9
— Philadelphia (N.L.)■	6	8	.429	3.99	21	16	1	1	0	106	97	56	47	33	58
1990— Philadelphia (N.L.)■	8	3	.727	3.56	42	13	2	1	1	141²/₃	132	61	56	54	58
— Los Angeles (N.L.)■	1	1	.500	7.53	5	3	0	0	0	14¹/₃	23	13	12	2	6
1991— Albuquerque (PCL)	7	3	.700	3.63	14	14	1	0	0	91²/₃	73	46	37	32	84
— Los Angeles (N.L.)	1	0	1.000	0.51	20	1	0	0	0	17²/₃	12	3	1	7	8
— San Antonio (Tex.)	1	3	.250	2.49	7	7	1	0	0	50²/₃	43	20	14	10	45
1992— Cleveland (A.L.)■	5	7	.417	3.82	32	25	0	0	0	158	156	79	67	50	96
1993— Cleveland (A.L.)	5	5	.500	5.67	25	6	0	0	0	54	62	36	34	16	34
— Charlotte (Int'l)	3	2	.600	5.06	12	6	0	0	0	42²/₃	46	26	24	6	40

Year Team (League)	W	L	Pct.	ERA	G	GS	CG	ShO	Sv.	IP	H	R	ER	BB	SO
1994— Chicago (A.L.)■	3	1	.750	3.55	38	0	0	0	0	33	29	17	13	14	26
1995— Cleveland (A.L.)■	0	0	...	6.39	11	0	0	0	0	12 2/3	16	9	9	10	13
— Texas (A.L.)■	0	2	.000	4.00	35	1	0	0	2	45	47	23	20	16	40
1996— Texas (A.L.)	5	2	.714	4.09	60	0	0	0	0	70 1/3	53	34	32	35	64
1997— Florida (N.L.)■	1	2	.333	3.90	59	0	0	0	0	62 1/3	64	28	27	28	63
A.L. totals (5 years)	18	17	.514	4.22	201	32	1	0	2	373	363	198	175	141	273
N.L. totals (5 years)	20	15	.571	3.63	153	39	5	3	1	379	350	172	153	140	215
Major league totals (10 years)	38	32	.543	3.93	354	71	6	3	3	752	713	370	328	281	488

DIVISION SERIES RECORD

Year Team (League)	W	L	Pct.	ERA	G	GS	CG	ShO	Sv.	IP	H	R	ER	BB	SO
1996— Texas (A.L.)	0	0	...	0.00	2	0	0	0	0	1 1/3	0	0	0	1	0
1997— Florida (N.L.)	1	0	1.000	0.00	2	0	0	0	0	3	0	0	0	1	3
Div. series totals (2 years)	1	0	1.000	0.00	4	0	0	0	0	4 1/3	0	0	0	2	3

CHAMPIONSHIP SERIES RECORD

Year Team (League)	W	L	Pct.	ERA	G	GS	CG	ShO	Sv.	IP	H	R	ER	BB	SO
1997— Florida (N.L.)	0	0	...	0.00	2	0	0	0	0	2 1/3	0	0	0	0	2

WORLD SERIES RECORD

NOTES: Member of World Series championship team (1997).

Year Team (League)	W	L	Pct.	ERA	G	GS	CG	ShO	Sv.	IP	H	R	ER	BB	SO
1997— Florida (N.L.)	1	0	1.000	0.00	3	0	0	0	0	3 2/3	1	0	0	1	5

C

COOKE, STEVE   P   REDS

PERSONAL: Born January 14, 1970, in Kauai, Hawaii. ... 6-6/230. ... Throws left, bats right. ... Full name: Stephen Montague Cooke.
HIGH SCHOOL: Tigard (Ore.).
COLLEGE: Southern Idaho.
TRANSACTIONS/CAREER NOTES: Selected by Philadelphia Phillies organization in 53rd round of free-agent draft (June 1, 1988); did not sign. ... Selected by Pittsburgh Pirates organization in 35th round of free-agent draft (June 5, 1989). ... On Buffalo disabled list (May 18-28, 1992). ... On Pittsburgh disabled list (April 16, 1995-entire season); included rehabilitation assignments to Augusta (July 18) and Carolina (July 24-26). ... On Pittsburgh disabled list (March 30-June 19, 1996); included rehabilitation assignment to Carolina (May 27-June 19). ... On Carolina disabled list (August 23-September 2, 1996). ... Granted free agency (October 29, 1996). ... Re-signed by Pirates (November 20, 1996). ... Released by Pirates (December 15, 1997). ... Signed by Cincinnati Reds (December 22, 1997).

Year Team (League)	W	L	Pct.	ERA	G	GS	CG	ShO	Sv.	IP	H	R	ER	BB	SO
1990— Welland (N.Y.-Penn)	2	3	.400	2.35	11	11	0	0	0	46	36	21	12	17	43
1991— Augusta (S. Atl.)	5	4	.556	2.82	11	11	1	0	0	60 2/3	50	28	19	35	52
— Salem (Carolina)	1	0	1.000	4.85	2	2	0	0	0	13	14	8	7	2	5
— Carolina (Southern)	0	0	...	2.84	3	9	1	1	0	12 2/3	9	4	4	7	18
1992— Carolina (Southern)	2	2	.500	3.00	6	6	0	0	0	36	31	13	12	12	38
— Buffalo (A.A.)	6	3	.667	3.75	13	13	0	0	0	74 1/3	71	35	31	36	52
— Pittsburgh (N.L.)	2	0	1.000	3.52	11	0	0	0	1	23	22	9	9	4	10
1993— Pittsburgh (N.L.)	10	10	.500	3.89	32	32	3	1	0	210 2/3	207	101	91	59	132
1994— Pittsburgh (N.L.)	4	11	.267	5.02	25	23	2	0	0	134 1/3	157	79	75	46	74
1995— Augusta (S. Atl.)	1	0	1.000	0.00	1	1	0	0	0	5	2	0	0	1	6
— Carolina (Southern)	0	0	...	7.20	1	1	0	0	0	5	5	4	4	5	4
1996— Carolina (Southern)	1	5	.167	4.36	12	12	0	0	0	53 2/3	56	34	26	26	45
— Pittsburgh (N.L.)	0	0	...	7.56	3	0	0	0	0	8 1/3	11	7	7	5	7
1997— Pittsburgh (N.L.)	9	15	.375	4.30	32	32	0	0	0	167 1/3	184	95	80	77	109
Major league totals (5 years)	25	36	.410	4.34	103	87	5	1	1	543 2/3	581	291	262	191	332

COOLBAUGH, MIKE   3B   ROCKIES

PERSONAL: Born June 5, 1972, in Binghamton, N.Y. ... 6-1/185. ... Bats right, throws right. ... Full name: Michael Robert Coolbaugh.
HIGH SCHOOL: Theodore Roosevelt (San Antonio).
TRANSACTIONS/CAREER NOTES: Selected by Toronto Blue Jays organization in 16th round of free-agent draft (June 4, 1990). ... On disabled list (June 23-August 21, 1993). ... Selected by Texas Rangers organization in Rule 5 minor league draft (December 4, 1996). ... Granted free agency (October 15, 1996). ... Signed by Oakland Athletics organization (November 4, 1996). ... Granted free agency (October 15, 1997). ... Signed by Colorado Rockies organization prior to 1998 season.
STATISTICAL NOTES: Led Southern League with 303 total bases in 1997. ... Led Southern League third basemen with .943 fielding percentage, 94 putouts, 302 assists, 420 total chances and 35 double plays in 1997.

Year Team (League)	Pos.	G	AB	R	H	2B	3B	HR	RBI	Avg.	BB	SO	SB	PO	A	E	Avg.
														FIELDING			
1990— Medicine Hat (Pio.)	SS-2B-3B	58	211	21	40	9	0	2	16	.190	13	47	3	77	136	33	.866
1991— St. Catharines (NYP)	1-2-3-O	71	256	28	59	13	2	3	25	.230	17	40	4	461	75	12	.978
1992— St. Catharines (NYP)	3B-OF	15	49	3	14	1	0	2	2	.286	3	12	0	16	16	4	.889
1993— Hagerstown (SAL)	2-3-1-O	112	389	58	95	23	1	16	62	.244	32	94	4	213	173	17	.958
1994— Dunedin (Fla. St.)	3-S-O-1-2	122	456	53	120	33	3	16	66	.263	28	94	3	85	293	22	.945
1995— Knoxville (Southern)	3-1-2-O	•142	500	71	120	32	2	9	56	.240	37	110	7	159	296	25	.948
1996— Charlotte (Fla. St.)	S-1-3-O-P	124	449	76	129	33	4	15	75	.287	42	80	8	366	180	22	.961
— Tulsa (Texas)	2B-1B	7	23	6	8	3	0	2	9	.348	2	3	1	31	23	0	1.000
1997— Huntsville (Sou.)■	3B-SS-2B	*139	*559	100	172	37	2	•30	*132	.308	52	105	8	†106	†330	26	†.944

RECORD AS PITCHER

Year Team (League)	W	L	Pct.	ERA	G	GS	CG	ShO	Sv.	IP	H	R	ER	BB	SO
1996— Charlotte (Fla. St.)■	0	0	...	36.00	124	0	0	0	0	1	5	4	4	0	2

COOMER, RON   3B   TWINS

PERSONAL: Born November 18, 1966, in Crest Hill, Ill. ... 5-11/225. ... Bats right, throws right. ... Full name: Ronald Bryan Coomer.
HIGH SCHOOL: Lockport (Ill.) Township.
COLLEGE: Taft (Calif.) College.
TRANSACTIONS/CAREER NOTES: Selected by Oakland Athletics organization in 14th round of free-agent draft (June 2, 1987). ... Released by A's organization (August 1, 1990). ... Signed by Chicago White Sox organization (March 18, 1991). ... On disabled list (June 5-19, 1992). ... On Birmingham disabled list (June 12-21, 1993). ... Traded by White Sox organization to Los Angeles Dodgers organization for P Isidro Martinez (December 27, 1993). ... Traded by Dodgers with P Greg Hansell, P Jose Parra and a player to be named later to Minnesota Twins for P Kevin Tapani and P Mark Guthrie (July 31, 1995); Twins acquired OF Chris Latham to complete deal (October 30, 1995).
STATISTICAL NOTES: Led Southern League with eight sacrifice flies and tied for lead in grounding into double plays with 21 in 1991. ... Led Southern League third basemen with 94 putouts, 396 total chances, 24 double plays and tied for lead with 26 errors in 1991. ... Led Pacific Coast League with 293 total bases in 1994. ... Led Pacific Coast League third basemen with .952 fielding percentage, 399 total chances and 299 assists in 1994.

						BATTING								FIELDING		
Year Team (League)	Pos.	G	AB	R	H	2B	3B	HR	RBI	Avg.	BB	SO	SB	PO	A	E	Avg.
1987—Medford (N'west)	3B-1B	45	168	23	58	10	2	1	26	.345	19	22	1	54	78	11	.923
1988—Modesto (California) ..	3B-1B	131	495	67	138	23	2	17	85	.279	60	88	2	78	105	16	.920
1989—Madison (Midwest) ...	3B-1B	61	216	28	69	15	0	4	28	.319	30	34	0	67	64	6	.956
1990—Huntsville (Southern) .	2B-1B-3B	66	194	22	43	7	0	3	27	.222	21	40	3	200	100	11	.965
1991—Birmingham (Sou.)■ .	3B-1B	137	505	*81	129	27	5	13	76	.255	59	78	0	†113	278	‡26	.938
1992—Vancouver (PCL)	3B	86	262	29	62	10	0	9	40	.237	16	36	3	49	115	13	.927
1993—Birmingham (Sou.)	3B-1B	69	262	44	85	18	0	13	50	.324	15	43	1	43	106	11	.931
—Nashville (A.A.)	3B	59	211	34	66	19	0	13	51	.313	10	29	1	30	107	16	.895
1994—Albuquerque (PCL)■..	3B-2B	127	535	89	181	34	6	22	*123	.338	26	62	4	81	†299	19	†.952
1995—Albuquerque (PCL)	3B-1B	85	323	54	104	23	2	16	76	.322	18	28	5	335	93	9	.979
—Minnesota (A.L.)■	1-3-DH-O	37	101	15	26	3	1	5	19	.257	9	11	0	138	32	2	.988
1996—Minnesota (A.L.)	1-O-3-DH	95	233	34	69	12	1	12	41	.296	17	24	3	275	42	4	.988
1997—Minnesota (A.L.)	3-1-DH-O	140	523	63	156	30	2	13	85	.298	22	91	4	123	223	11	.969
Major league totals (3 years)		272	857	112	251	45	4	30	145	.293	48	126	7	536	297	17	.980

COOPER, BRIAN   P   ANGELS

PERSONAL: Born August 19, 1974, in North Hollywood, Calif. ... 6-1/175. ... Throws right, bats right.
HIGH SCHOOL: Glendora (Calif.).
COLLEGE: Southern California.
TRANSACTIONS/CAREER NOTES: Selected by California Angels organization in fourth round of free-agent draft (June 1, 1995). ... Angels franchise renamed Anaheim Angels for 1997 season.

Year Team (League)	W	L	Pct.	ERA	G	GS	CG	ShO	Sv.	IP	H	R	ER	BB	SO
1995—Boise (Northwest)	3	2	.600	3.92	13	11	0	0	1	62	60	31	27	22	66
1996—Lake Elsinore (Calif.)	7	9	.438	4.21	26	23	1	1	0	162⅓	177	100	76	39	155
1997—Lake Elsinore (Calif.)	7	3	.700	3.54	17	17	1	0	0	117	111	56	46	27	104

COOPER, SCOTT   3B   RANGERS

PERSONAL: Born October 13, 1967, in St. Louis. ... 6-3/205. ... Bats left, throws right. ... Full name: Scott Kendrick Cooper.
HIGH SCHOOL: Pattonville (Maryland Heights, Mo.).
TRANSACTIONS/CAREER NOTES: Selected by Boston Red Sox organization in third round of free-agent draft (June 2, 1986). ... On disabled list (August 4, 1994-remainder of season). ... Traded by Red Sox with P Cory Bailey and a player to be named later to St. Louis Cardinals for P Rheal Cormier and OF Mark Whiten (April 8, 1995). ... Granted free agency (December 21, 1995). ... Signed by Seibu Lions of Japan Pacific League (January 26, 1996). ... Released by Lions after 1996 season. ... Signed by Kansas City Royals organization (December 16, 1996). ... On disabled list (July 23-September 1, 1997). ... Granted free agency (October 3, 1997). ... Signed by Texas Rangers organization (December 23, 1997).
STATISTICAL NOTES: Led Carolina League with 234 total bases in 1988. ... Led International League third basemen with 94 putouts and tied for lead with 240 assists in 1990. ... Led International League with 11 intentional bases on balls received in 1991. ... Led International League third basemen with 106 putouts, 232 assists, 26 errors and 364 total chances in 1991. ... Hit for the cycle (April 12, 1994). ... Career major league grand slams: 1.

						BATTING								FIELDING		
Year Team (League)	Pos.	G	AB	R	H	2B	3B	HR	RBI	Avg.	BB	SO	SB	PO	A	E	Avg.
1986—Elmira (N.Y.-Penn)......	3B	51	191	23	55	9	0	4	43	.288	19	32	1	22	62	9	.903
1987—Greensboro (S. Atl.) ...	3B-1B-P	119	370	52	93	21	2	15	63	.251	58	69	1	150	153	21	.935
1988—Lynchburg (Caro.)	3B-1B-OF	130	497	90	*148	*45	7	9	73	.298	58	74	0	116	198	27	.921
1989—New Britain (Eastern) .	3B	124	421	50	104	24	2	7	39	.247	55	84	1	91	212	22	.932
1990—Pawtucket (Int'l)	3B-SS	124	433	56	115	17	1	12	44	.266	39	75	2	†96	‡244	22	.939
—Boston (A.L.)	PH-PR	2	1	0	0	0	0	0	0	.000	0	1	0	...	...	...	...
1991—Pawtucket (Int'l)	3B-SS	137	483	55	134	21	2	15	72	.277	50	58	3	†115	†241	†26	.932
—Boston (A.L.)	3B	14	35	6	16	4	2	0	7	.457	2	2	0	6	22	2	.933
1992—Boston (A.L.) 1-3-DH-S-2		123	337	34	93	21	0	5	33	.276	37	33	1	472	136	9	.985
1993—Boston (A.L.)	3B-1B-SS	156	526	67	147	29	3	9	63	.279	58	81	5	112	244	24	.937
1994—Boston (A.L.)	3B	104	369	49	104	16	4	13	53	.282	30	65	0	51	219	16	.944
1995—St. Louis (N.L.)■	3B	118	374	29	86	18	2	3	40	.230	49	85	0	65	243	18	.945
1996—Seibu (Jp. Pac.)■		81	276	27	67	13	0	7	27	.243	37	51	1	...	...	...	...
1997—Kansas City (A.L.)■ ...	3B-1B-DH	75	159	12	32	6	1	3	15	.201	17	32	1	48	55	0	1.000
American League totals (6 years)		474	1427	168	392	76	10	30	171	.275	144	214	7	689	676	51	.964
National League totals (1 year)		118	374	29	86	18	2	3	40	.230	49	85	0	65	243	18	.945
Major league totals (7 years)		592	1801	197	478	94	12	33	211	.265	193	299	7	754	919	69	.960

C

Year	League	Pos.	AB	R	H	2B	3B	HR	RBI	Avg.	BB	SO	SB	PO	A	E	Avg.
1993—	American	3B	2	0	0	0	0	0	0	.000	0	1	0	1	0	0	1.000
1994—	American	3B	2	1	1	1	0	0	1	.500	0	0	0	0	2	0	1.000
All-Star Game totals (2 years)			4	1	1	1	0	0	1	.250	0	1	0	1	2	0	1.000

RECORD AS PITCHER

Year	Team (League)	W	L	Pct.	ERA	G	GS	CG	ShO	Sv.	IP	H	R	ER	BB	SO
1987—	Greensboro (S. Atl.)	0	0	...	0.00	2	0	0	0	0	2	2	1	0	2	3

COPPINGER, ROCKY   P   ORIOLES

PERSONAL: Born March 19, 1974, in El Paso, Texas. ... 6-5/225. ... Throws right, bats right. ... Full name: John Thomas Coppinger. ... Name pronounced COP-in-jer.
HIGH SCHOOL: Coronado (El Paso, Texas).
JUNIOR COLLEGE: Hillsboro (Texas).
TRANSACTIONS/CAREER NOTES: Selected by Baltimore Orioles in 17th round of free-agent draft (June 3, 1993). ... On Baltimore disabled list (March 31-April 15, 1997); included rehabilitation assignments to Rochester (May 14-22), Gulf Coast Orioles (July 1-12) and Bowie (July 17-27). ... On Baltimore disabled list (May 10, 1997-remainder of season).

Year	Team (League)	W	L	Pct.	ERA	G	GS	CG	ShO	Sv.	IP	H	R	ER	BB	SO
1994—	Bluefield (Appalachian)	4	3	.571	2.45	14	13	0	0	0	73 1/3	51	24	20	40	88
1995—	Frederick (Carolina)	7	1	.875	1.57	11	11	2	1	0	68 2/3	46	16	12	24	91
—	Bowie (Eastern)	6	2	.750	2.69	13	13	2	2	0	83 2/3	58	33	25	43	62
—	Rochester (Int'l)	3	0	1.000	1.04	5	5	0	0	0	34 2/3	23	5	4	17	19
1996—	Rochester (Int'l)	6	4	.600	4.19	12	12	0	0	0	73	65	36	34	39	81
—	Baltimore (A.L.)	10	6	.625	5.18	23	22	0	0	0	125	126	76	72	60	104
1997—	Baltimore (A.L.)	1	1	.500	6.30	5	4	0	0	0	20	21	14	14	16	22
—	Rochester (Int'l)	1	2	.333	5.52	3	3	0	0	0	14 2/3	16	10	9	11	9
—	GC Orioles (GCL)	0	0	...	1.80	3	3	0	0	0	10	7	3	2	0	13
—	Bowie (Eastern)	1	1	.500	4.80	3	3	0	0	0	15	15	9	8	3	15
Major league totals (2 years)		11	7	.611	5.34	28	26	0	0	0	145	147	90	86	76	126

CHAMPIONSHIP SERIES RECORD

Year	Team (League)	W	L	Pct.	ERA	G	GS	CG	ShO	Sv.	IP	H	R	ER	BB	SO
1996—	Baltimore (A.L.)	0	1	.000	8.44	1	1	0	0	0	5 1/3	6	5	5	1	3

COQUILLETTE, TRACE   2B   EXPOS

PERSONAL: Born June 4, 1974, in Orangevale, Calif. ... 5-11/175. ... Bats right, throws right. ... Full name: Trace Robert Coquillette. ... Name pronounced COE-kill-ette.
HIGH SCHOOL: Casa Roble (Orangevale, Calif.).
JUNIOR COLLEGE: Sacramento City College.
TRANSACTIONS/CAREER NOTES: Selected by Montreal Expos organization in 10th round of free-agent draft (June 3, 1993). ... On West Palm Beach disabled list (June 2-August 1, 1996).
STATISTICAL NOTES: Led New York-Pennsylvania League second basemen with 366 total chances in 1994.

							BATTING								FIELDING		
Year	Team (League)	Pos.	G	AB	R	H	2B	3B	HR	RBI	Avg.	BB	SO	SB	PO	A	E	Avg.
1993—	G.C. Expos (GCL)	2B	44	159	27	40	4	3	2	11	.252	37	28	16	80	123	•12	.944
—	W.P. Beach (FSL)	2B	6	18	2	5	3	0	0	3	.278	2	5	0	8	16	1	.960
1994—	Burl. (Midw.)	2B	5	17	2	3	1	0	0	0	.176	1	4	1	6	14	1	.952
—	Vermont (NYP)	2B	70	252	54	77	11	5	9	52	.306	23	40	7	125	216	*25	.932
1995—	Albany (S. Atl.)	2B	128	458	67	123	27	4	3	57	.269	64	91	17	252	292	14	.975
1996—	G.C. Expos (GCL)	2B-3B	7	25	4	4	1	0	0	0	.160	4	6	1	16	16	1	.970
—	W.P. Beach (FSL)	2B-3B	72	266	39	67	17	4	1	27	.252	27	72	9	100	142	22	.917
1997—	Harrisburg (Eastern) ..	2B-3B	81	293	46	76	17	3	10	51	.259	25	40	9	116	169	16	.947
—	W.P. Beach (FSL)	2B-3B-OF	53	188	34	60	18	2	8	33	.319	27	27	8	90	111	7	.966

CORA, JOEY   2B   MARINERS

PERSONAL: Born May 14, 1965, in Caguas, Puerto Rico. ... 5-8/155. ... Bats both, throws right. ... Full name: Jose Manuel Cora. ... Brother of Alex Cora, shortstop, Los Angeles Dodgers organization.
COLLEGE: Vanderbilt.
TRANSACTIONS/CAREER NOTES: Selected by San Diego Padres organization in first round (23rd pick overall) of free-agent draft (June 3, 1985); pick received as compensation for New York Yankees signing free-agent P Ed Whitson. ... On disabled list (June 22-August 15, 1986). ... Traded by Padres with IF Kevin Garner and OF Warren Newson to Chicago White Sox for P Adam Peterson and P Steve Rosenberg (March 31, 1991). ... On Chicago disabled list (June 22-July 11, 1991); included rehabilitation assignment to South Bend (July 9-11). ... On Chicago disabled list (June 30-July 15, 1994); included rehabilitation assignment to South Bend (July 11-15). ... Granted free agency (December 23, 1994). ... Signed by Seattle Mariners (April 6, 1995). ... Granted free agency (November 6, 1997). ... Re-signed by Mariners (November 18, 1997).
RECORDS: Holds A.L. single-season record for most consecutive games batted safely by switch-hitter—24 (1997).
STATISTICAL NOTES: Led Pacific Coast League second basemen with 24 errors in 1988 and 1989. ... Led A.L. with 19 sacrifice hits in 1993. ... Led A.L. second basemen with 19 errors in 1993 and 22 in 1995. ... Had 24-game hitting streak (May 2-29, 1997).

							BATTING								FIELDING		
Year	Team (League)	Pos.	G	AB	R	H	2B	3B	HR	RBI	Avg.	BB	SO	SB	PO	A	E	Avg.
1985—	Spokane (N'west)	2B	43	170	48	55	11	2	3	26	.324	27	24	13	92	123	9	.960
1986—	Beaumont (Texas)	2B-SS	81	315	54	96	5	5	3	41	.305	47	29	24	217	267	19	.962

Year	Team (League)	Pos.	G	AB	R	H	2B	3B	HR	RBI	Avg.	BB	SO	SB	PO	A	E	Avg.
1987—	San Diego (N.L.)	2B-SS	77	241	23	57	7	2	0	13	.237	28	26	15	123	200	10	.970
—	Las Vegas (PCL)	2B-SS	81	293	50	81	9	1	1	24	.276	62	39	12	186	249	9	.980
1988—	Las Vegas (PCL)	2B-3B-OF	127	460	73	136	15	3	3	55	.296	44	19	31	285	346	†26	.960
1989—	Las Vegas (PCL)	2B-SS	119	507	79	157	25	4	0	37	.310	42	31	*40	245	349	†27	.957
—	San Diego (N.L.)	SS-3B-2B	12	19	5	6	1	0	0	1	.316	1	0	1	11	15	2	.929
1990—	San Diego (N.L.)	SS-2B-C	51	100	12	27	3	0	0	2	.270	6	9	8	59	49	11	.908
—	Las Vegas (PCL)	SS-2B	51	211	41	74	13	9	0	24	.351	29	16	15	125	148	14	.951
1991—	Chicago (A.L.)■	2B-SS-DH	100	228	37	55	2	3	0	18	.241	20	21	11	107	192	10	.968
—	South Bend (Mid.)......	2B	1	5	1	1	0	0	0	0	.200	0	1	1	2	4	0	1.000
1992—	Chicago (A.L.)	2-DH-S-3	68	122	27	30	7	1	0	9	.246	22	13	10	60	84	3	.980
1993—	Chicago (A.L.)	2B-3B	153	579	95	155	15	13	2	51	.268	67	63	20	296	413	†19	.974
1994—	Chicago (A.L.)	2B-DH	90	312	55	86	13	4	2	30	.276	38	32	8	162	195	8	.978
—	South Bend (Mid.)......	2B	3	11	3	5	1	0	0	1	.455	2	1	1	4	8	1	.923
1995—	Seattle (A.L.)■	2B-SS	120	427	64	127	19	2	3	39	.297	37	31	18	205	262	†23	.953
1996—	Seattle (A.L.)	2B-3B	144	530	90	154	37	6	6	45	.291	35	32	5	296	314	13	.979
1997—	Seattle (A.L.)	2B	149	574	105	172	40	4	11	54	.300	53	49	6	*307	310	17	.973
	American League totals (7 years)		824	2772	473	779	133	33	24	246	.281	272	241	78	1433	1770	93	.972
	National League totals (3 years)		140	360	40	90	11	2	0	16	.250	35	35	24	193	264	23	.952
	Major league totals (10 years)		964	3132	513	869	144	35	24	262	.277	307	276	102	1626	2034	116	.969

DIVISION SERIES RECORD

Year	Team (League)	Pos.	G	AB	R	H	2B	3B	HR	RBI	Avg.	BB	SO	SB	PO	A	E	Avg.
1995—	Seattle (A.L.)	2B	5	19	7	6	1	0	1	1	.316	3	0	1	10	12	1	.957
1997—	Seattle (A.L.)	2B	4	17	1	3	0	0	0	0	.176	0	4	0	7	11	0	1.000
	Division series totals (2 years)		9	36	8	9	1	0	1	1	.250	3	4	1	17	23	1	.976

CHAMPIONSHIP SERIES RECORD

Year	Team (League)	Pos.	G	AB	R	H	2B	3B	HR	RBI	Avg.	BB	SO	SB	PO	A	E	Avg.
1993—	Chicago (A.L.)	2B	6	22	1	3	0	0	0	1	.136	3	6	0	18	20	3	.927
1995—	Seattle (A.L.)	2B	6	23	3	4	1	0	0	0	.174	1	0	2	15	12	1	.964
	Championship series totals (2 years)		12	45	4	7	1	0	0	1	.156	4	6	2	33	32	4	.942

ALL-STAR GAME RECORD

Year	League	Pos.	AB	R	H	2B	3B	HR	RBI	Avg.	BB	SO	SB	PO	A	E	Avg.
1997—	American	PR-2B	1	0	0	0	0	0	0	.000	0	0	0	0	1	0	1.000

CORBIN, ARCHIE   P   PADRES

PERSONAL: Born December 30, 1967, in Beaumont, Texas. ... 6-4/187. ... Throws right, bats right. ... Full name: Archie Ray Corbin.

HIGH SCHOOL: Pellard (Beaumont, Texas).

TRANSACTIONS/CAREER NOTES: Selected by New York Mets organization in 16th round of free-agent draft (June 2, 1986). ... On disabled list (April 6-May 4, 1990). ... Traded by Mets organization to Kansas City Royals organization for 1B/OF Pat Tabler (August 31, 1990). ... On Memphis disabled list (April 13-21, 1992). ... Traded by Royals with 3B Sean Berry to Montreal Expos for P Bill Sampen and P Chris Haney (August 29, 1992). ... Traded by Expos to Milwaukee Brewers for a player to be named later (November 20, 1992). ... Contract sold to Brewers to Expos (February 5, 1993). ... On temporarily inactive list (July 13-August 2, 1993). ... Granted free agency (October 15, 1993). ... Signed by Buffalo, Pittsburgh Pirates organization (November 22, 1993). ... On disabled list (July 18-August 4, 1995). ... Granted free agency (October 16, 1995). ... Signed by Oakland A's organization (November 29, 1995). ... Released by Edmonton, A's organization (March 31, 1996). ... Signed by Rochester, Baltimore Orioles organization (May 7, 1996). ... On disabled list (April 17-May 3, 1997). ... Released by Orioles following 1997 season. ... Signed by San Diego Padres (November 7, 1997).

Year	Team (League)	W	L	Pct.	ERA	G	GS	CG	ShO	Sv.	IP	H	R	ER	BB	SO
1986—	Kingsport (Appalachian).....	1	1	.500	4.75	18	1	0	0	0	30 1/3	31	23	16	28	30
1987—	Kingsport (Appalachian).....	2	3	.400	6.31	6	6	0	0	0	25 2/3	24	21	18	26	17
1988—	Kingsport (Appalachian).....	7	2	.778	1.56	11	10	4	1	0	69 1/3	47	23	12	17	47
1989—	Columbia (S. Atl.)............	9	9	.500	4.51	27	23	4	2	1	153 2/3	149	86	77	72	130
1990—	St. Lucie (Fla. St.)	7	8	.467	2.97	20	18	3	0	0	118	97	47	39	59	105
1991—	Memphis (Southern)■	8	8	.500	4.66	28	25	1	0	0	156 1/3	139	90	*81	90	166
—	Kansas City (A.L.)	0	0	. . .	3.86	2	0	0	0	0	2 1/3	3	1	1	2	1
1992—	Memphis (Southern)	7	8	.467	4.73	27	20	2	0	0	112 1/3	115	64	59	73	100
—	Harrisburg (Eastern)■	0	0	. . .	0.00	1	1	0	0	0	3	2	0	0	1	3
1993—	Harrisburg (Eastern)	5	3	.625	3.68	42	2	0	0	4	73 1/3	43	31	30	59	91
1994—	Buffalo (A.A.)■	0	0	. . .	4.76	14	1	0	0	0	22 2/3	14	13	12	18	23
1995—	Calgary (PCL)..................	1	5	.167	8.56	47	1	0	0	1	61	76	63	58	55	54
1996—	Reynoso (Mexican)■	0	0	. . .	9.31	9	0	0	0	0	9 2/3	10	10	10	7	13
—	Rochester (Int'l)■.............	0	2	.000	4.74	20	5	0	0	1	43 2/3	44	25	23	25	47
—	Baltimore (A.L.)................	2	0	1.000	2.30	18	0	0	0	0	27 1/3	22	7	7	22	20
1997—	Rochester (Int'l)	4	3	.571	4.00	43	1	0	0	5	69 2/3	47	32	31	62	66
	Major league totals (2 years)......	2	0	1.000	2.43	20	0	0	0	0	29 2/3	25	8	8	24	21

CORDERO, FRANCISCO   P   TIGERS

PERSONAL: Born August 11, 1977, in Santo Domingo, Dominican Republic. ... 6-2/160. ... Throws right, bats right. ... Full name: Francisco Javier Cordero.

HIGH SCHOOL: Colegio Luz de Arroyo Hondo (Dominican Republic)..

TRANSACTIONS/CAREER NOTES: Signed as non-drafted free agent by Detroit Tigers organization (June 18, 1994). ... On Jamestown disabled list (June 28, 1996-remainder of season).

Year— Team (League)	W	L	Pct.	ERA	G	GS	CG	ShO	Sv.	IP	H	R	ER	BB	SO
1994— Dom. Tigers (DSL)	4	3	.571	3.90	12	12	0	0	0	60	65	47	26	27	36
1995— Fayetteville (S. Atl.)	0	3	.000	6.30	4	4	0	0	0	20	26	16	14	12	19
—Jamestown (NYP)	4	7	.364	5.22	15	14	0	0	0	88	96	62	51	37	54
1996— Fayetteville (S. Atl.)	0	0	...	2.57	2	1	0	0	0	7	2	2	2	6	7
—Jamestown (NYP)	0	0	...	0.82	2	2	0	0	0	11	5	1	1	2	10
1997— West. Mich. (Mid.)	6	1	.857	0.99	50	0	0	0	*35	54 1/3	36	13	6	15	67

CORDERO, WIL   SS

PERSONAL: Born October 3, 1971, in Mayaguez, Puerto Rico. ... 6-2/195. ... Bats right, throws right. ... Full name: Wilfredo Nieva Cordero. ... Name pronounced cor-DARE-oh.
HIGH SCHOOL: Centro de Servicios Education de Mayaguez (Puerto Rico).
TRANSACTIONS/CAREER NOTES: Signed as non-drafted free agent by Montreal Expos organization (May 24, 1988). ... On Indianapolis disabled list (August 1, 1991-remainder of season; and May 12-June 11 and July 7-20, 1992). ... Traded by Expos with P Bryan Eversgerd to Boston Red Sox for P Rheal Cormier, 1B Ryan McGuire and P Shayne Bennett (January 10, 1996). ... On Boston disabled list (May 21-August 12, 1996); included rehabilitation assignments to Gulf Coast Red Sox (July 23-27) and Pawtucket (July 27-August 6). ... Released by Red Sox (September 28, 1997).
HONORS: Named shortstop on THE SPORTING NEWS N.L. Silver Slugger team (1994).
STATISTICAL NOTES: Career major league grand slams: 1.

Year— Team (League)	Pos.	G	AB	R	H	2B	3B	HR	RBI	Avg.	BB	SO	SB	PO	A	E	Avg.
1988— Jamestown (NYP)	SS	52	190	18	49	3	0	2	22	.258	15	44	3	82	159	31	.886
1989— W.P. Beach (FSL)	SS	78	289	37	80	12	2	6	29	.277	33	58	2	121	224	29	.922
—Jacksonville (South.)	SS	39	121	9	26	6	1	3	17	.215	12	33	1	62	93	7	.957
1990— Jacksonville (South.)	SS	131	444	63	104	18	4	7	40	.234	56	122	9	179	349	41	.928
1991— Indianapolis (A.A.)	SS	98	360	48	94	16	4	11	52	.261	26	89	9	157	287	27	.943
1992— Indianapolis (A.A.)	SS	52	204	32	64	11	1	6	27	.314	24	54	6	75	146	12	.948
—Montreal (N.L.)	SS-2B	45	126	17	38	4	1	2	8	.302	9	31	0	51	92	8	.947
1993— Montreal (N.L.)	SS-3B	138	475	56	118	32	2	10	58	.248	34	60	12	163	373	36	.937
1994— Montreal (N.L.)	SS	110	415	65	122	30	3	15	63	.294	41	62	16	124	316	22	.952
1995— Montreal (N.L.)	SS-OF	131	514	64	147	35	2	10	49	.286	36	88	9	168	281	22	.953
1996— Boston (A.L.)■	2B-DH-1B	59	198	29	57	14	0	3	37	.288	11	31	2	82	110	10	.950
—GC Red Sox (GCL)	2B	3	10	1	3	0	0	1	3	.300	0	2	1	1	1	0	1.000
—Pawtucket (Int'l)	2B	4	10	2	3	1	0	1	2	.300	2	3	0	2	6	0	1.000
1997— Boston (A.L.)	OF-DH-2B	140	570	82	160	26	3	18	72	.281	31	122	1	248	11	2	.992
American League totals (2 years)		199	768	111	217	40	3	21	109	.283	42	153	3	330	121	12	.974
National League totals (4 years)		424	1530	202	425	101	8	37	178	.278	120	241	37	506	1062	88	.947
Major league totals (6 years)		623	2298	313	642	141	11	58	287	.279	162	394	40	836	1183	100	.953

ALL-STAR GAME RECORD

Year— League	Pos.	AB	R	H	2B	3B	HR	RBI	Avg.	BB	SO	SB	PO	A	E	Avg.
1994— National	SS	2	0	0	0	0	0	0	.000	0	0	0	1	1	0	1.000

CORDOVA, FRANCISCO   P   PIRATES

PERSONAL: Born April 26, 1972, in Veracruz, Mexico. ... 6-1/171. ... Throws right, bats right.
TRANSACTIONS/CAREER NOTES: Signed as non-drafted free agent by Pittsburgh Pirates organization (January 18, 1996).
STATISTICAL NOTES: Pitched nine innings, combining with Ricardo Rincon (one inning) in 3-0 no-hit victory against Houston (July 12, 1997).

Year— Team (League)	W	L	Pct.	ERA	G	GS	CG	ShO	Sv.	IP	H	R	ER	BB	SO
1992— M.C. Red Devils (Mex.)	3	0	1.000	5.79	16	1	0	0	0	28	28	19	18	14	15
1993— M.C. Red Devils (Mex.)	9	2	.818	3.23	43	4	1	0	4	89	66	44	38	47	71
1994— M.C. Red Devils (Mex.)	15	4	.789	2.33	41	15	6	3	8	150 1/3	122	43	39	43	104
1995— M.C. Red Devils (Mex.)	13	0	*1.000	3.10	27	20	1	0	4	125	131	52	43	42	88
1996— Pittsburgh (N.L.)■	4	7	.364	4.09	59	6	0	0	12	99	103	49	45	20	95
1997— Pittsburgh (N.L.)	11	8	.579	3.63	29	29	2	2	0	178 2/3	175	80	72	49	121
Major league totals (2 years)	15	15	.500	3.79	88	35	2	2	12	277 2/3	278	129	117	69	216

CORDOVA, MARTY   OF   TWINS

PERSONAL: Born July 10, 1969, in Las Vegas. ... 6-0/201. ... Bats right, throws right. ... Full name: Martin Keevin Cordova.
HIGH SCHOOL: Bishop Gorman (Las Vegas).
JUNIOR COLLEGE: Orange Coast College (Calif.).
COLLEGE: UNLV.
TRANSACTIONS/CAREER NOTES: Selected by San Diego Padres organization in eighth round of free-agent draft (June 2, 1987); did not sign. ... Selected by Minnesota Twins organization in 10th round of free-agent draft (June 5, 1989). ... On disabled list (April 12-May 20, 1991 and April 7-May 11, 1994). ... On Minnesota disabled list (April 11-May 26, 1997); included rehabilitation assignment to Salt Lake (May 20-26).
HONORS: Named California League Most Valuable Player (1992). ... Named A.L. Rookie of the Year by Baseball Writers' Association of America (1995).
STATISTICAL NOTES: Led California League with 302 total bases and .589 slugging percentage and tied for lead in grounding into double plays with 20 in 1992. ... Had 23-game hitting streak (June 5-29, 1996).

Year— Team (League)	Pos.	G	AB	R	H	2B	3B	HR	RBI	Avg.	BB	SO	SB	PO	A	E	Avg.
1989— Elizabethton (App.)	OF-3B	38	148	32	42	2	3	8	29	.284	14	29	2	6	9	4	.789
1990— Kenosha (Midwest)	OF	81	269	35	58	7	5	7	25	.216	28	73	6	87	5	5	.948

Year Team (League)	Pos.	G	AB	R	H	2B	3B	HR	RBI	Avg.	BB	SO	SB	PO	A	E	Avg.
1991— Visalia (California)......	OF	71	189	31	40	6	1	7	19	.212	17	46	2	58	2	5	.923
1992— Visalia (California)......	OF	134	513	103	175	31	6	*28	*131	.341	76	99	13	173	10	3	.984
1993— Nashville (Southern) ..	OF	138	508	83	127	30	5	19	77	.250	64	*153	10	209	7	2	*.991
1994— Salt Lake (PCL)	OF	103	385	69	138	25	4	19	66	.358	39	63	17	187	13	8	.962
1995— Minnesota (A.L.)	OF	137	512	81	142	27	4	24	84	.277	52	111	20	345	12	5	.986
1996— Minnesota (A.L.)	OF	145	569	97	176	46	1	16	111	.309	53	96	11	328	9	3	.991
1997— Minnesota (A.L.)	OF-DH	103	378	44	93	18	4	15	51	.246	30	92	5	217	12	2	.991
— Salt Lake (PCL)	OF	6	24	5	9	4	0	1	4	.375	2	3	1	3	0	1	.750
Major league totals (3 years)		385	1459	222	411	91	9	55	246	.282	135	299	36	890	33	10	.989

COREY, BRYAN — P — DIAMONDBACKS

PERSONAL: Born October 21, 1973, in Thousand Oaks, Calif. ... 6-0/160. ... Throws right, bats right. ... Full name: Bryan Scott Corey.
HIGH SCHOOL: Thousand Oaks (Calif.).
JUNIOR COLLEGE: Los Angeles Pierce Junior College.
TRANSACTIONS/CAREER NOTES: Selected by Detroit Tigers organization in 12th round of free-agent draft (June 3, 1993). ... Selected by Arizona Diamondbacks in third round (63rd pick overall) of expansion draft (November 18, 1997).

Year Team (League)	W	L	Pct.	ERA	G	GS	CG	ShO	Sv.	IP	H	R	ER	BB	SO
1995— Jamestown (NYP)	2	2	.500	3.86	29	0	0	0	10	28	21	14	12	12	41
1996— Fayetteville (S. Atl.)	6	4	.600	1.21	60	0	0	0	34	82	50	19	11	17	101
1997— Jacksonville (Southern)......	3	8	.273	4.76	52	0	0	0	9	68	74	42	36	21	37

RECORD AS POSITION PLAYER

Year Team (League)	Pos.	G	AB	R	H	2B	3B	HR	RBI	Avg.	BB	SO	SB	PO	A	E	Avg.
1993— Bristol (Appal.)..........	SS-2B	39	95	14	10	3	0	0	3	.105	26	35	2	53	80	10	.930
1994— Jamestown (NYP)	2B-SS-3B	41	85	14	13	1	1	0	3	.153	13	27	1	38	64	10	.911

CORMIER, RHEAL — P — INDIANS

PERSONAL: Born April 23, 1967, in Moncton, New Brunswick, Canada. ... 5-10/187. ... Throws left, bats left. ... Full name: Rheal Paul Cormier. ... Name pronounced ree-AL COR-mee-AY.
HIGH SCHOOL: Polyvalente Louis J. Robichaud.
JUNIOR COLLEGE: Community College of Rhode Island.
TRANSACTIONS/CAREER NOTES: Selected by St. Louis Cardinals organization in sixth round of free-agent draft (June 6, 1988). ... On Louisville disabled list (April 10-29, 1991). ... On disabled list (August 12-September 7, 1993). ... On St. Louis disabled list (April 28-May 13 and May 21-August 3, 1994); included rehabilitation assignments to Arkansas (July 7-18) and Louisville (July 18-30). ... Traded by Cardinals with OF Mark Whiten to Boston Red Sox for 3B Scott Cooper, P Cory Bailey and a player to be named later (April 8, 1995). ... Traded by Red Sox with 1B Ryan McGuire and P Shayne Bennett to Montreal Expos for SS Wil Cordero and P Bryan Eversgerd (Jauary 10, 1996). ... On disabled list (August 26-September 10, 1996). ... Granted free agency (October 30, 1997). ... Signed by Cleveland Indians organization (December 18, 1997).
MISCELLANEOUS: Member of 1988 Canadian Olympic baseball team.

Year Team (League)	W	L	Pct.	ERA	G	GS	CG	ShO	Sv.	IP	H	R	ER	BB	SO
1989— St. Petersburg (FSL)	12	7	.632	2.23	26	26	4	1	0	169 2/3	141	63	42	33	122
1990— Arkansas (Texas)................	5	•12	.294	5.04	22	21	3	1	0	121 1/3	133	81	68	30	102
— Louisville (A.A.)..................	1	1	.500	2.25	4	4	0	0	0	24	18	8	6	3	9
1991— Louisville (A.A.)	7	9	.438	4.23	21	21	3	*3	0	127 2/3	140	64	60	31	74
— St. Louis (N.L.)...................	4	5	.444	4.12	11	10	2	0	0	67 2/3	74	35	31	8	38
1992— Louisville (A.A.)	0	1	.000	6.75	1	1	0	0	0	4	8	4	3	0	1
— St. Louis (N.L.)...................	10	10	.500	3.68	31	30	3	0	0	186	194	83	76	33	117
1993— St. Louis (N.L.)...................	7	6	.538	4.33	38	21	1	0	0	145 1/3	163	80	70	27	75
1994— St. Louis (N.L.)...................	3	2	.600	5.45	7	7	0	0	0	39 2/3	40	24	24	7	26
— Arkansas (Texas)................	1	0	1.000	1.93	2	2	0	0	0	9 1/3	9	2	2	0	11
— Louisville (A.A.).................	1	2	.333	4.50	3	3	1	0	0	22	21	11	11	8	13
1995— Boston (A.L.)■...................	7	5	.583	4.07	48	12	0	0	0	115	131	60	52	31	69
1996— Montreal (N.L.)■..............	7	10	.412	4.17	33	27	1	1	0	159 2/3	165	80	74	41	100
1997— Montreal (N.L.).................	0	1	.000	33.75	1	1	0	0	0	1 1/3	4	5	5	1	0
A.L. totals (1 year)	7	5	.583	4.07	48	12	0	0	0	115	131	60	52	31	69
N.L. totals (6 years)	31	34	.477	4.20	121	96	7	1	0	599 2/3	640	307	280	117	356
Major league totals (7 years)	38	39	.494	4.18	169	108	7	1	0	714 2/3	771	367	332	148	425

DIVISION SERIES RECORD

Year Team (League)	W	L	Pct.	ERA	G	GS	CG	ShO	Sv.	IP	H	R	ER	BB	SO
1995— Boston (A.L.).......................	0	0	...	13.50	2	0	0	0	0	2/3	2	1	1	1	2

CORSI, JIM — P — RED SOX

PERSONAL: Born September 9, 1961, in Newton, Mass. ... 6-1/220. ... Throws right, bats right. ... Full name: James Bernard Corsi.
HIGH SCHOOL: Newton (Mass.) North.
COLLEGE: St. Leo (Fla.) College (bachelor of arts degree in management).
TRANSACTIONS/CAREER NOTES: Selected by New York Yankees organization in 25th round of free-agent draft (June 7, 1982). ... On Fort Lauderdale disabled list (April 8-May 11, 1983). ... Released by Yankees organization (April 3, 1984). ... Signed by Greensboro, Boston Red Sox organization (April 1, 1985). ... Released by Red Sox organization (January 31, 1986). ... Re-signed by Red Sox organization (April 5, 1986). ... Released by Red Sox organization (April 2, 1987). ... Signed by Modesto, Oakland Athletics organization (April 12, 1987). ... On Oakland disabled list (March 29, 1990-entire season); included rehabilitation assignment to Tacoma (June 29-July 25). ... Granted free agency (December 20, 1990). ... Signed by Tucson, Houston Astros organization (March 19, 1991). ... Released by Astros (November 18, 1991). ... Signed by Tacoma, A's organization (March 16, 1992). ... Selected by Florida Marlins in second round (49th pick overall) of expansion draft (November 17, 1992). ... On Florida disabled list (March 27-April 30, 1993); included rehabilitation assignment to High Desert (April 20-30).

C

... On Florida disabled list (July 6, 1993-remainder of season). ... Granted free agency (October 15, 1993). ... Re-signed by Marlins organization (January 24, 1994). ... On Brevard County disabled list (April 11-July 5, 1994). ... Granted free agency (October 15, 1994). ... Signed by Edmonton, A's organization (January 20, 1995). ... On Oakland disabled list (June 22-August 8, 1995). ... On Oakland disabled list (April 28-May 18, 1996); included rehabilitation assignment to Modesto (May 17-18). ... Granted free agency (November 4, 1996). ... Signed by Red Sox organization (February 3, 1997). ... On Boston disabled list (June 2-July 1, 1997); included rehabilitation assignment to Gulf Coast Red Sox (June 23-30). ... Granted free agency (October 28, 1997). ... Re-signed by Red Sox (December 3, 1997).

Year Team (League)	W	L	Pct.	ERA	G	GS	CG	ShO	Sv.	IP	H	R	ER	BB	SO
1982— Oneonta (N.Y.-Penn)	0	0	...	10.80	1	0	0	0	0	3 1/3	5	4	4	2	6
—Paintsville (Appal.)	0	2	.000	2.90	8	4	0	0	0	31	32	11	10	13	20
1983— Greensboro (S. Atl.)	2	2	.500	4.09	12	7	1	0	1	50 2/3	59	37	23	33	37
—Oneonta (N.Y.-Penn)	3	6	.333	4.25	11	10	2	0	0	59 1/3	76	38	28	21	47
1984—						Out of organized baseball.									
1985— Greensboro (S. Atl.)■	5	8	.385	4.23	41	2	1	0	9	78 2/3	94	49	37	23	84
1986— New Britain (East.)	2	3	.400	2.28	29	0	0	0	3	51 1/3	52	13	13	20	38
1987— Modesto (California)■	3	1	.750	3.60	19	0	0	0	6	30	23	16	12	10	45
—Huntsville (Southern)	8	1	.889	2.81	28	0	0	0	4	48	30	17	15	15	33
1988— Tacoma (PCL)	2	5	.286	2.75	50	0	0	0	16	59	60	25	18	23	48
—Oakland (A.L.)	0	1	.000	3.80	11	1	0	0	0	21 1/3	20	10	9	6	10
1989— Tacoma (PCL)	2	3	.400	4.13	23	0	0	0	8	28 1/3	40	17	13	9	23
—Oakland (A.L.)	1	2	.333	1.88	22	0	0	0	0	38 1/3	26	8	8	10	21
1990— Tacoma (PCL)	0	0	...	1.50	5	0	0	0	0	6	9	2	1	1	3
1991— Tucson (PCL)■	0	0	...	0.00	2	0	0	0	0	3	2	0	0	0	4
—Houston (N.L.)	0	5	.000	3.71	47	0	0	0	0	77 2/3	76	37	32	23	53
1992— Tacoma (PCL)■	0	0	...	1.23	26	0	0	0	12	29 1/3	22	8	4	10	21
—Oakland (A.L.)	4	2	.667	1.43	32	0	0	0	0	44	44	12	7	18	19
1993— High Desert (Calif.)■	0	1	.000	3.00	3	3	0	0	0	9	11	3	3	2	6
—Florida (N.L.)	0	2	.000	6.64	15	0	0	0	0	20 1/3	28	15	15	10	7
1994— Brevard County (FSL)	0	1	.000	1.64	6	0	0	0	0	11	8	3	2	0	11
—Edmonton (PCL)	0	1	.000	4.50	15	0	0	0	0	22	29	15	11	10	15
1995— Edmonton (PCL)■	0	0	...	0.00	3	0	0	0	3	3	0	0	0	1	3
—Oakland (A.L.)	2	4	.333	2.20	38	0	0	0	2	45	31	14	11	26	26
1996— Oakland (A.L.)	6	0	1.000	4.03	56	0	0	0	3	73 2/3	71	33	33	34	43
—Modesto (California)	0	0	...	0.00	1	1	0	0	0	1	0	0	0	0	2
1997— Pawtucket (Int'l)■	0	0	...	0.00	2	0	0	0	1	2 1/3	2	0	0	1	3
—Boston (A.L.)	5	3	.625	3.43	52	0	0	0	2	57 2/3	56	26	22	21	40
—GC Red Sox (GCL)	1	0	1.000	0.00	3	2	0	0	0	4	2	1	0	0	6
A.L. totals (6 years)	18	12	.600	2.89	211	1	0	0	7	280	248	103	90	115	159
N.L. totals (2 years)	0	7	.000	4.32	62	0	0	0	0	98	104	52	47	33	60
Major league totals (8 years)	18	19	.486	3.26	273	1	0	0	7	378	352	155	137	148	219

CHAMPIONSHIP SERIES RECORD

Year Team (League)	W	L	Pct.	ERA	G	GS	CG	ShO	Sv.	IP	H	R	ER	BB	SO
1992— Oakland (A.L.)	0	0	...	0.00	3	0	0	0	0	2	2	0	0	3	0

COUNSELL, CRAIG   2B   MARLINS

PERSONAL: Born August 21, 1970, in South Bend, Ind. ... 6-0/170. ... Bats left, throws right. ... Full name: Craig John Counsell. ... Son of John Counsell, outfielder, Minnesota Twins organization (1964-68).

HIGH SCHOOL: Whitefish Bay (Milwaukee).

COLLEGE: Notre Dame.

TRANSACTIONS/CAREER NOTES: Selected by Colorado Rockies organization in 11th round of free-agent draft (June 1, 1992). ... On disabled list (April 7-May 13, July 30-August 6 and August 7-27, 1994). ... On disabled list (May 1-July 15 and July 18-September 3, 1996). ... Traded by Rockies to Florida Marlins for P Mark Hutton (July 27, 1997).

STATISTICAL NOTES: Led California League shortstops with 621 total chances in 1993. ... Led Pacific Coast League shortstops with 598 total chances and 86 double plays in 1995. ... Career major league grand slams: 1.

Year Team (League)	Pos.	G	AB	R	H	2B	3B	HR	RBI	Avg.	BB	SO	SB	PO	A	E	Avg.
1992— Bend (Northwest)	2B-SS	18	61	11	15	6	1	0	8	.246	9	10	1	23	36	2	.967
1993— Central Valley (Cal.)	SS	131	471	79	132	26	3	5	59	.280	95	68	14	*233	353	35	.944
1994— New Haven (Eastern)	SS-2B	83	300	47	84	20	1	5	37	.280	37	32	4	122	242	27	.931
1995— Colo. Springs (PCL)	SS	118	399	60	112	22	6	5	53	.281	34	47	10	182	386	30	.950
—Colorado (N.L.)	SS	3	1	0	0	0	0	0	0	.000	1	0	0	1	1	0	1.000
1996— Colo. Springs (PCL)	2B-3B-SS	25	75	17	18	3	0	2	10	.240	24	7	4	35	64	4	.961
1997— Colo. Springs (PCL)	2B-SS	96	376	77	126	31	6	5	63	.335	45	38	12	213	260	9	.981
—Colorado (N.L.)	PR	1	0	0	0	0	0	0	0	...	0	0	0	0	0	0	...
—Florida (N.L.)■	2B	51	164	20	49	9	2	1	16	.299	18	17	1	124	149	3	.989
Major league totals (2 years)		55	165	20	49	9	2	1	16	.297	19	17	1	125	150	3	.989

DIVISION SERIES RECORD

Year Team (League)	Pos.	G	AB	R	H	2B	3B	HR	RBI	Avg.	BB	SO	SB	PO	A	E	Avg.
1997— Florida (N.L.)	2B	3	5	0	2	1	0	0	1	.400	1	0	0	5	2	1	.875

CHAMPIONSHIP SERIES RECORD

Year Team (League)	Pos.	G	AB	R	H	2B	3B	HR	RBI	Avg.	BB	SO	SB	PO	A	E	Avg.
1997— Florida (N.L.)	2B-PH	5	14	0	6	0	0	0	2	.429	3	3	0	7	9	1	.941

WORLD SERIES RECORD

NOTES: Member of World Series championship team (1997).

Year Team (League)	Pos.	G	AB	R	H	2B	3B	HR	RBI	Avg.	BB	SO	SB	PO	A	E	Avg.
1997— Florida (N.L.)	2B	7	22	4	4	1	0	0	2	.182	6	5	1	18	15	1	.971

COX, STEVE   1B   DEVIL RAYS

PERSONAL: Born October 31, 1974, in Delano, Calif. ... 6-4/223. ... Bats left, throws left. ... Full name: Charles Steven Cox.
HIGH SCHOOL: Monache (Porterville, Calif.).
TRANSACTIONS/CAREER NOTES: Selected by Oakland Athletics organization in fifth round of free-agent draft (June 1, 1992). ... On disabled list (July 23, 1993-remainder of season). ... Selected by Tampa Bay Devil Rays in second round (46th pick overall) of expansion draft (November 18, 1997).
STATISTICAL NOTES: Led California League with 10 sacrifice flies in 1995. ... Tied for Pacific Coast League lead with nine sacrifice flies in 1997.

							BATTING						FIELDING		
Year Team (League)	Pos.	G	AB	R	H	2B	3B	HR	RBI	Avg.	BB	SO	SB	PO	A	E	Avg.
1992— Scottsdale (Ariz.)........	1B	52	184	30	43	4	1	1	35	.234	27	51	2	407	28	11	.975
1993— S. Oregon (N'west).....	1B	15	57	10	18	4	1	2	16	.316	5	15	0	104	11	2	.983
1994— W. Mich. (Mid.)	1B-OF	99	311	37	75	19	2	6	32	.241	41	95	2	727	49	10	.987
1995— Modesto (California) ..	1B	132	483	95	144	29	3	*30	*110	.298	84	88	5	991	77	17	.984
1996— Huntsville (Southern) .	1B	104	381	59	107	21	1	12	61	.281	51	65	2	909	72	15	.985
1997— Edmonton (PCL)	1B	131	467	84	128	34	1	15	93	.274	*88	90	1	1043	70	*10	.991

CRABTREE, TIM   P   BLUE JAYS

PERSONAL: Born October 13, 1969, in Jackson, Mich. ... 6-4/200. ... Throws right, bats right. ... Full name: Timothy Lyle Crabtree.
HIGH SCHOOL: Grass Lake (Mich.).
COLLEGE: Michigan State.
TRANSACTIONS/CAREER NOTES: Selected by Toronto Blue Jays organization in second round of free-agent draft (June 1, 1992). ... On disabled list (August 16-September 6, 1996). ... On Toronto disabled list (June 4-August 3, 1997); included rehabilitation assignments to St. Catherines (July 22-July 24) and Syracuse (July 27-August 4).

Year Team (League)	W	L	Pct.	ERA	G	GS	CG	ShO	Sv.	IP	H	R	ER	BB	SO
1992— St. Catharines (NYP)	6	3	.667	1.57	12	12	2	0	0	69	45	19	12	22	47
— Knoxville (Southern)	0	2	.000	0.95	3	3	1	0	0	19	14	8	2	4	13
1993— Knoxville (Southern)	9	14	.391	4.08	27	27	2	2	0	158 2/3	178	93	72	59	67
1994— Syracuse (Int'l).................	2	6	.250	4.17	51	9	0	0	2	108	125	58	50	49	58
1995— Syracuse (Int'l).................	0	2	.000	5.40	26	0	0	0	5	31 2/3	38	25	19	12	22
— Toronto (A.L.)....................	0	2	.000	3.09	31	0	0	0	0	32	30	16	11	13	21
1996— Toronto (A.L.)....................	5	3	.625	2.54	53	0	0	0	1	67 1/3	59	26	19	22	57
1997— Toronto (A.L.)....................	3	3	.500	7.08	37	0	0	0	2	40 2/3	65	32	32	17	26
— St. Catharines (NYP)	0	0	...	3.00	2	1	0	0	0	3	3	2	1	0	3
— Syracuse (Int'l).................	0	0	...	9.82	3	0	0	0	1	3 2/3	7	4	4	1	3
Major league totals (3 years)......	8	8	.500	3.99	121	0	0	0	3	140	154	74	62	52	104

CRAWFORD, JOE   P

PERSONAL: Born May 2, 1970, in Gainesville, Fla. ... 6-3/225. ... Throws left, bats left. ... Full name: Joseph Randal Crawford.
HIGH SCHOOL: Hillsboro (Ohio).
COLLEGE: Kent.
TRANSACTIONS/CAREER NOTES: Selected by New York Mets organization in 17th round of free-agent draft (June 3, 1991). ... On disabled list (April 28-May 30, 1992). ... Selected by Boston Red Sox from Mets organization in Rule 5 major league draft (December 4, 1995). ... Traded by Red Sox to New York Mets for cash (March 26, 1996). ... Released by Mets (January 8, 1998).
STATISTICAL NOTES: Pitched 1-0 no-hit victory against Trenton (May 5, 1996, second game).
MISCELLANEOUS: Struck out in only appearance as pinch-hitter (1997).

Year Team (League)	W	L	Pct.	ERA	G	GS	CG	ShO	Sv.	IP	H	R	ER	BB	SO
1991— Kingsport (Appalachian).....	0	0	...	1.11	19	0	0	0	11	32 1/3	16	5	4	8	43
— Columbia (S. Atl.)...............	0	0	...	0.00	3	0	0	0	0	3	0	0	0	0	6
1992— St. Lucie (Fla. St.)	3	3	.500	2.06	25	1	0	0	3	43 2/3	29	18	10	15	32
1993— St. Lucie (Fla. St.)	3	3	.500	3.65	34	0	0	0	5	37	38	15	15	14	24
1994— St. Lucie (Fla. St.)	1	1	.500	1.48	33	0	0	0	5	42 2/3	22	8	7	9	31
— Binghamton (Eastern)	1	0	1.000	5.52	13	0	0	0	0	14 2/3	20	10	9	8	9
1995— Binghamton (Eastern)	7	2	.778	2.23	42	1	0	0	0	60 2/3	48	17	15	17	43
— Norfolk (Int'l)	1	1	.500	1.93	8	0	0	0	1	18 2/3	9	5	4	4	13
1996— Norfolk (Int'l)	6	5	.545	3.44	20	16	2	1	0	96 2/3	98	45	37	20	68
— Binghamton (Eastern)	5	1	.833	1.45	7	7	1	1	0	49 2/3	34	10	8	9	34
1997— Norfolk (Int'l)	8	2	.800	3.52	16	16	0	0	0	99 2/3	109	45	39	31	72
— New York (N.L.).................	4	3	.571	3.30	19	2	0	0	0	46 1/3	36	18	17	13	25
Major league totals (1 year)......	4	3	.571	3.30	19	2	0	0	0	46 1/3	36	18	17	13	25

CREEK, DOUG   P

PERSONAL: Born March 1, 1969, in Winchester, Va. ... 6-0/210. ... Throws left, bats left. ... Full name: Paul Douglas Creek.
HIGH SCHOOL: Martinsburg (W.Va.).
COLLEGE: Georgia Tech.
TRANSACTIONS/CAREER NOTES: Selected by California Angels organization in fifth round of free-agent draft (June 4, 1990); did not sign. ... Selected by St. Louis Cardinals organization in seventh round of free-agent draft (June 3, 1991). ... On Arkansas disabled list (April 10-May 21, 1992; July 25-August 1, 1993; and June 25-July 10, 1994). ... Traded by Cardinals with P Allen Watson and P Rich DeLucia to San Francisco Giants for SS Royce Clayton and a player to be named later (December 14, 1995); Cardinals acquired 2B Chris Wimmer to complete deal (January 16, 1996). ... Contract purchased by Chicago White Sox (November 7, 1997). ... Contract sold by White Sox to Hanshin Tigers of Japanese Pacific League (December 4, 1997).

Year Team (League)	W	L	Pct.	ERA	G	GS	CG	ShO	Sv.	IP	H	R	ER	BB	SO
1991—Hamilton (NYP)	3	2	.600	5.12	9	5	0	0	1	38 2/3	39	22	22	18	45
—Savannah (S. Atl.)	2	1	.667	4.45	5	5	0	0	0	28 1/3	24	14	14	17	32
1992—Springfield (Mid.)	4	1	.800	2.58	6	6	0	0	0	38 1/3	32	11	11	13	43
—St. Petersburg (FSL)	5	4	.556	2.82	13	13	0	0	0	73 1/3	57	31	23	37	63
1993—Louisville (A.A.)	0	0	...	3.21	2	2	0	0	0	14	10	5	5	9	9
—Arkansas (Texas)	11	10	.524	4.02	25	25	1	1	0	147 2/3	142	75	66	48	128
1994—Louisville (A.A.)	1	4	.200	8.54	7	7	0	0	0	26 1/3	37	26	25	23	16
—Arkansas (Texas)	3	10	.231	4.40	17	17	1	0	0	92	96	54	45	36	65
1995—Louisville (A.A.)	3	2	.600	3.23	26	0	0	0	0	30 2/3	20	12	11	21	29
—Arkansas (Texas)	4	2	.667	2.88	26	0	0	0	1	34 1/3	24	12	11	16	50
—St. Louis (N.L.)	0	0	...	0.00	6	0	0	0	0	6 2/3	2	0	0	3	10
1996—San Francisco (N.L.)■	0	2	.000	6.52	63	0	0	0	0	48 1/3	45	41	35	32	38
1997—Phoenix (PCL)	8	6	.571	4.93	25	23	2	1	0	129 2/3	140	76	71	66	*137
—San Francisco (N.L.)	1	2	.333	6.75	3	3	0	0	0	13 1/3	12	12	10	14	14
Major league totals (3 years)	1	4	.200	5.93	72	3	0	0	0	68 1/3	59	53	45	49	62

CREEK, RYAN — P — ASTROS

PERSONAL: Born September 24, 1972, in Winchester, Va. ... 6-1/180. ... Throws right, bats right. ... Full name: Ryan Matthew Creek.

JUNIOR COLLEGE: Louisburg (N.C.) College.

TRANSACTIONS/CAREER NOTES: Selected by Houston Astros organization in 34th round of free-agent draft (June 1, 1992). ... On disabled list (July 17-September 2, 1997).

Year Team (League)	W	L	Pct.	ERA	G	GS	CG	ShO	Sv.	IP	H	R	ER	BB	SO
1993—GC Astros (GCL)	•7	3	.700	2.34	12	11	2	1	1	69 1/3	53	22	18	30	62
1994—Quad City (Midwest)	3	5	.375	4.99	21	15	0	0	0	74	86	62	41	41	66
1995—Jackson (Texas)	9	7	.563	3.63	26	24	1	1	0	143 2/3	137	74	58	64	120
1996—Jackson (Texas)	7	15	.318	5.26	27	26	1	0	0	142	139	95	83	*121	119
1997—Jackson (Texas)	10	5	.667	4.11	19	19	0	0	0	105	95	57	48	74	88

CRESPO, FELIPE — IF — BLUE JAYS

PERSONAL: Born March 5, 1973, in Rio Piedras, Puerto Rico. ... 5-11/200. ... Bats both, throws right. ... Full name: Felipe Javier Clauso Crespo.

HIGH SCHOOL: Notre Dame (Caguas, Puerto Rico).

TRANSACTIONS/CAREER NOTES: Selected by Toronto Blue Jays organization in third round of free-agent draft (June 4, 1990). ... On disabled list (May 26-July 2, 1995). ... On Toronto disabled list (April 1-24, 1996); included rehabilitation assignment to Dunedin (April 12-24).

STATISTICAL NOTES: Led Southern League third basemen with 127 putouts and 42 errors in 1994.

Year Team (League)	Pos.	G	AB	R	H	2B	3B	HR	RBI	Avg.	BB	SO	SB	PO	A	E	Avg.
1991—Medicine Hat (Pio.)	2B	49	184	40	57	11	4	4	31	.310	25	31	6	*97	133	*23	.909
1992—Myrtle Beach (SAL)	2B-3B	81	263	43	74	14	3	1	29	.281	58	38	7	161	149	22	.934
1993—Dunedin (Fla. St.)	2B	96	345	51	103	16	8	6	39	.299	47	40	18	198	269	25	.949
1994—Knoxville (Southern)	3B-2B	129	502	74	135	30	4	8	49	.269	57	95	20	†127	270	†42	.904
1995—Syracuse (Int'l)	2B	88	347	56	102	20	5	13	41	.294	41	56	12	160	220	*25	.938
1996—Dunedin (Fla. St.)	2B	9	34	3	11	1	0	2	6	.324	2	3	1	18	18	2	.947
—Toronto (A.L.)	2B-3B-1B	22	49	6	9	4	0	0	4	.184	12	13	1	34	38	1	.986
—Syracuse (Int'l)	2-0-3-1	98	355	53	100	25	0	8	58	.282	56	39	10	220	143	19	.950
1997—Toronto (A.L.)	3B-DH-2B	12	28	3	8	0	1	1	5	.286	2	4	0	9	9	1	.947
—Syracuse (Int'l)	0-2-1-3	80	290	53	75	12	0	12	26	.259	46	38	7	247	103	2	.967
Major league totals (2 years)		34	77	9	17	4	1	1	9	.221	14	17	1	43	47	2	.978

CROMER, BRANDON — SS — MARLINS

PERSONAL: Born January 25, 1974, in Lake City, S.C. ... 6-2/175. ... Bats left, throws right. ... Full name: Brandon Eugene Cromer. ... Son of Roy Cromer former scout with St. Louis Cardinals and minor league pitcher/second baseman (1960-63); brother of Tripp Cromer, infielder, Los Angeles Dodgers; brother of D.T. Cromer, first baseman/outfielder, Oakland Athletics organization; and brother of Burke Cromer, pitcher, Atlanta Braves organization (1992-93).

HIGH SCHOOL: Lexington (S.C.).

TRANSACTIONS/CAREER NOTES: Selected by Toronto Blue Jays organization in supplemental round ("sandwich pick" between first and second round, 34th pick overall) of free-agent draft (June 1, 1992); pick received as part of compensation for Los Angeles Dodgers signing Type A free agent P Tom Candiotti. ... Traded by Blue Jays with P Jose Silva and P Jose Pett and three players to be named later to Pittsburgh Pirates organization for OF Orlando Merced, IF Carlos Garcia and P Don Plesac (November 14, 1996); Pirates acquired P Mike Halperin, IF Abraham Nunez and C/OF Craig Wilson to complete deal (December 11, 1996). ... Claimed on waivers by Florida Marlins (December 5, 1997).

Year Team (League)	Pos.	G	AB	R	H	2B	3B	HR	RBI	Avg.	BB	SO	SB	PO	A	E	Avg.
1992—GC Jays (GCL)	SS	49	180	26	51	12	3	1	21	.283	14	26	7	65	127	14	.932
1993—St. Catharines (NYP)	SS	75	278	29	64	9	2	5	21	.230	21	64	2	82	204	24	.923
1994—Hagerstown (SAL)	SS	80	259	25	35	8	5	6	26	.135	25	98	0	102	220	17	.950
1995—Dunedin (Fla. St.)	SS	106	329	40	78	11	3	6	43	.237	43	84	0	146	259	15	.964
1996—Knoxville (Southern)	SS-3B-2B	98	318	56	88	15	8	7	32	.277	60	84	3	94	239	16	.954
1997—Calgary (PCL)■	SS-2B-3B	68	228	30	53	15	2	8	36	.232	19	46	3	95	196	11	.964
—Carolina (Southern)	SS-2B	55	193	23	44	12	4	4	14	.228	29	50	1	94	165	12	.956

CROMER, D.T.   1B/OF   ATHLETICS

PERSONAL: Born March 19, 1971, in Lake City, S.C. ... 6-2/190. ... Bats left, throws left. ... Full name: David Thomas Cromer. ... Son of Roy Cromer, former scout with St. Louis Cardinals and minor league pitcher/second baseman (1960-63); brother of Brandon Cromer, shortstop, Florida Marlins organization; brother of Tripp Cromer, Los Angeles Dodgers; and brother of Burke Cromer, pitcher, Atlanta Braves organization (1992-93).
HIGH SCHOOL: Lexington (S.C.).
COLLEGE: South Carolina.
TRANSACTIONS/CAREER NOTES: Selected by Oakland Athletics organization in 11th round of free-agent draft (June 1, 1992).
HONORS: Named California League Most Valuable Player (1996).
STATISTICAL NOTES: Led California League with 316 total bases and .626 slugging percentage in 1996. ... Led Southern League first basemen with 1,167 putouts, 18 errors, 1,285 total chances and 129 double plays in 1997.

Year Team (League)	Pos.	G	AB	R	H	2B	3B	HR	RBI	Avg.	BB	SO	SB	PO	A	E	Avg.
1992—S. Oregon (N'west).....	OF	50	168	17	35	7	0	4	26	.208	13	34	4	61	6	5	.931
1993—Madison (Midwest)....	OF-1B	98	321	37	84	20	4	4	41	.262	22	72	8	233	8	7	.972
1994—W. Mich. (Mid.).........	OF-1B	102	349	50	89	20	5	10	58	.255	33	76	11	328	28	10	.973
1995—Modesto (California)..	OF-1B	108	378	59	98	18	5	14	52	.259	36	66	5	160	16	8	.957
1996—Modesto (California)..	1B-OF	124	505	100	166	40	10	30	130	.329	32	67	20	549	67	14	.978
1997—Huntsville (Southern).	1B-OF	134	545	100	*176	*40	6	15	121	.323	60	102	12	†1169	101	†18	.986

CROMER, TRIPP   SS   DODGERS   C

PERSONAL: Born November 21, 1967, in Lake City, S.C. ... 6-2/165. ... Bats right, throws right. ... Full name: Roy Bunyan Cromer III. ... Son of Roy Cromer, former scout with St. Louis Cardinals and minor league pitcher/second baseman (1960-63); brother of Brandon Cromer, shortstop, Florida Marlins organization; brother of D.T. Cromer, first baseman/outfielder, Oakland Athletics organization; and brother of Burke Cromer, pitcher, Atlanta Braves organization (1992-93).
HIGH SCHOOL: Lake City (S.C.).
COLLEGE: South Carolina.
TRANSACTIONS/CAREER NOTES: Selected by St. Louis Cardinals organization in third round of free-agent draft (June 5, 1989). ... On Arkansas disabled list (May 14-26, 1992). ... On Louisville disabled list (April 30-May 28 and July 5-August 3, 1993). ... On disabled list (May 20-27, 1996). ... Claimed on waivers by Los Angeles Dodgers (October 10, 1996). ... On disabled list (July 31, 1997-remainder of season).

Year Team (League)	Pos.	G	AB	R	H	2B	3B	HR	RBI	Avg.	BB	SO	SB	PO	A	E	Avg.
1989—Hamilton (NYP)..........	SS	35	137	18	36	6	3	0	6	.263	17	30	4	66	85	11	.932
1990—St. Petersburg (FSL)..	SS	121	408	53	88	12	5	5	38	.216	46	78	7	202	334	32	.944
1991—St. Petersburg (FSL)..	SS	43	137	11	28	3	1	0	10	.204	9	17	0	79	134	3	.986
—Arkansas (Texas)........	SS	73	227	28	52	12	1	1	18	.229	15	37	0	117	198	10	.969
1992—Arkansas (Texas)........	SS	110	339	30	81	16	6	7	29	.239	22	82	4	135	315	18	*.962
—Louisville (A.A.).........	SS	6	25	5	5	1	1	1	7	.200	1	6	0	13	20	0	1.000
1993—Louisville (A.A.)........	SS	85	309	39	85	8	4	11	33	.275	15	60	1	123	253	12	.969
—St. Louis (N.L.).........	SS	10	23	1	2	0	0	0	0	.087	1	6	0	13	18	3	.912
1994—Louisville (A.A.)........	SS	124	419	53	115	23	9	9	50	.274	33	85	5	165	370	12	*.978
—St. Louis (N.L.).........	SS	2	0	1	0	0	0	0	0	....	0	0	0	0	0	1	.000
1995—St. Louis (N.L.)..........	SS-2B	105	345	36	78	19	0	5	18	.226	14	66	0	126	292	17	.961
1996—Louisville (A.A.)........	SS-2B	80	244	28	55	4	4	4	25	.225	22	47	3	124	238	5	.986
1997—Albuquerque (PCL)■..	SS	43	140	25	45	8	6	5	24	.321	14	34	6	65	106	6	.966
—Los Angeles (N.L.).....	2B-SS-3B	28	86	8	25	3	0	4	20	.291	6	16	0	47	61	3	.973
Major league totals (4 years)		145	454	46	105	22	0	9	38	.231	21	88	0	186	371	24	.959

CROUSHORE, RICH   P   CARDINALS

PERSONAL: Born August 7, 1970, in Lakehurst, N.J. ... 6-4/210. ... Throws right, bats right. ... Full name: Richard S. Croushore.
HIGH SCHOOL: Mount Vernon (Texas).
JUNIOR COLLEGE: Hutchinson (Kan.) Community College.
TRANSACTIONS/CAREER NOTES: Signed as non-drafted free agent by St. Louis Cardinals organization (June 12, 1993). ... On disabled list (April 6-June 19, 1995).

Year Team (League)	W	L	Pct.	ERA	G	GS	CG	ShO	Sv.	IP	H	R	ER	BB	SO
1993—Glens Falls (NYP)..............	4	1	.800	3.05	31	0	0	0	1	41 1/3	38	16	14	22	36
1994—Madison (Midwest)...........	6	6	.500	4.10	•62	0	0	0	0	94 1/3	90	49	43	46	103
1995—St. Petersburg (FSL)...........	6	4	.600	3.51	12	11	0	0	0	59	44	25	23	32	57
1996—Arkansas (Texas)...............	5	10	.333	4.92	34	17	2	0	3	108	113	75	59	51	85
1997—Arkansas (Texas)...............	7	5	.583	4.18	17	16	1	0	0	92 2/3	111	52	43	37	67
—Louisville (A.A.).............	1	2	.333	2.47	14	6	0	0	1	43 2/3	37	14	12	13	41

CROW, DEAN   P   TIGERS

PERSONAL: Born August 21, 1972, in Garland, Texas. ... 6-4/215. ... Throws right, bats left. ... Full name: Paul Dean Crow Jr.
HIGH SCHOOL: Stratford (Texas).
JUNIOR COLLEGE: San Jacinto College (Texas).
COLLEGE: Miami of Ohio, then Baylor.
TRANSACTIONS/CAREER NOTES: Selected by Seattle Mariners organization in 10th round of free-agent draft (June 3, 1993). ... On disabled list (June 15-26 and July 18, 1994-remainder of season). ... Traded by Mariners with P Scott Sanders and 3B Carlos Villalobos to Detroit Tigers for P Omar Olivares and P Felipe Lira (July 18, 1997).

Year	Team (League)	W	L	Pct.	ERA	G	GS	CG	ShO	Sv.	IP	H	R	ER	BB	SO
1993—	Bellingham (N'west)	5	3	.625	1.89	25	0	0	0	4	47²/₃	31	14	10	21	38
1994—	Appleton (Midwest)	2	4	.333	7.04	16	0	0	0	2	15¹/₃	25	15	12	7	11
1995—	Riverside (California)	3	4	.429	2.63	51	0	0	0	22	61²/₃	54	21	18	13	46
1996—	Port City (Southern)	2	3	.400	3.04	60	0	0	0	26	68	64	35	23	20	43
1997—	Tacoma (PCL)	4	2	.667	4.78	33	0	0	0	7	43¹/₃	56	25	23	19	36
—	Toledo (Int'l)■	3	0	1.000	7.85	18	0	0	0	2	18¹/₃	26	16	16	10	10

CROWELL, JIM — P — REDS

PERSONAL: Born May 14, 1974, in Minneapolis. ... 6-4/225. ... Throws left, bats left. ... Full name: James E. Crowell.
HIGH SCHOOL: Valparaiso (Ind.).
COLLEGE: Indianapolis.
TRANSACTIONS/CAREER NOTES: Signed as non-drafted free agent by Cleveland Indians organization (June 17, 1995). ... Traded by Indians with P Danny Graves, P Scott Winchester and IF Damian Jackson to Cincinnati Reds for P John Smiley and IF Jeff Branson (July 31, 1997).

Year	Team (League)	W	L	Pct.	ERA	G	GS	CG	ShO	Sv.	IP	H	R	ER	BB	SO
1995—	Watertown (NYP)	5	2	.714	2.86	12	9	0	0	0	56²/₃	50	22	18	27	48
1996—	Columbus (S. Atl.)	7	10	.412	4.14	28	•28	3	0	0	165¹/₃	163	89	76	69	104
1997—	Kinston (Carolina)	9	4	.692	2.37	17	17	0	0	0	114	96	41	30	26	94
—	Akron (Eastern)	1	0	1.000	4.50	3	3	0	0	0	18	13	12	9	11	7
—	Chattanooga (Southern)■	2	1	.667	2.84	3	3	0	0	0	19	19	6	6	5	14
—	Indianapolis (A.A.)	1	1	.500	2.75	3	3	1	1	0	19²/₃	19	7	6	8	6
—	Cincinnati (N.L.)	0	1	.000	9.95	2	1	0	0	0	6¹/₃	12	7	7	5	3
Major league totals (1 year)		0	1	.000	9.95	2	1	0	0	0	6¹/₃	12	7	7	5	3

CRUZ, DEIVI — SS — TIGERS

PERSONAL: Born June 11, 1975, in Bani, Dominican Republic. ... 5-11/160. ... Bats right, throws right. ... Full name: Deivi Garcia Cruz.
TRANSACTIONS/CAREER NOTES: Signed as non-drafted free agent by San Francisco Giants (April 23, 1993). ... Selected by Los Angeles Dodgers organization from Giants organization in Rule 5 major league draft (December 9, 1996). ... Traded by Dodgers with OF Juan Hernaiz to Detroit Tigers for 2B Jeff Berblinger (December 9, 1996).
STATISTICAL NOTES: Led Northwest League third basemen with 47 putouts and .941 fielding percentage in 1995. ... Led Midwest League shortstops with 427 assists and .980 fielding percentage in 1996.

Year	Team (League)	Pos.	G	AB	R	H	2B	3B	HR	RBI	Avg.	BB	SO	SB	PO	A	E	Avg.
										BATTING					FIELDING			
1993—	Ariz. Giants (Ariz.)	3B-SS-1B	28	82	8	28	3	0	0	15	.341	4	5	3	17	52	2	.972
1994—	Ariz. Giants (Ariz.)	SS-3B	18	53	10	16	8	0	0	5	.302	5	3	0	11	37	1	.980
1995—	Burl. (Midw.)	2B-3B-SS	16	58	2	8	1	0	1	9	.138	4	7	1	20	42	2	.969
—	Bellingham (N'west)	3B-2B	62	223	32	66	17	0	3	28	.296	19	21	6	†55	124	10	†.947
1996—	Burlington (Midw.)	SS-3B	127	517	72	152	27	2	9	64	.294	35	49	12	159	†444	13	†.979
1997—	Detroit (A.L.)■	SS	147	436	35	105	26	0	2	40	.241	14	55	3	192	420	13	.979
Major league totals (1 year)			147	436	35	105	26	0	2	40	.241	14	55	3	192	420	13	.979

CRUZ, IVAN — 1B — YANKEES

PERSONAL: Born May 3, 1968, in Fajardo, Puerto Rico. ... 6-3/210. ... Bats left, throws left. ... Full name: Luis Ivan Cruz.
HIGH SCHOOL: Colegio Santiago (Fajardo, Puerto Rico).
COLLEGE: Jacksonville.
TRANSACTIONS/CAREER NOTES: Selected by Detroit Tigers organization in 28th round of free-agent draft (June 5, 1989). ... Granted free agency (October 16, 1995). ... Signed by New York Yankees organization (November 27, 1996).
STATISTICAL NOTES: Tied for Florida State League lead in double plays by first baseman with 75 in 1990. ... Led Southern League with .564 slugging percentage in 1995. ... Tied for Southern League lead in intentional bases on balls received with 15 in 1995. ... Led International League second basemen with 1,028 total chances and 88 double plays in 1996.

Year	Team (League)	Pos.	G	AB	R	H	2B	3B	HR	RBI	Avg.	BB	SO	SB	PO	A	E	Avg.
										BATTING					FIELDING			
1989—	Niag. Falls (NYP)	1B	64	226	43	62	11	2	7	40	.274	27	29	2	439	30	5	.989
1990—	Lakeland (Fla. St.)	1B	118	414	61	118	23	2	11	73	.285	49	71	8	938	44	11	.989
1991—	London (Eastern)	1B	121	443	46	110	21	0	9	47	.248	36	73	3	845	49	12	.987
—	Toledo (Int'l)	1B	8	29	2	4	0	0	1	4	.138	2	12	0	70	7	0	1.000
1992—	London (Eastern)	1B	134	*524	71	143	25	1	14	*104	.273	37	102	1	549	35	8	.986
1993—	Toledo (Int'l)	1B	115	402	44	91	18	4	13	50	.226	30	85	1	268	27	2	.993
1994—	Toledo (Int'l)	1B	97	303	36	75	11	2	15	43	.248	28	83	1	411	37	6	.987
1995—	Toledo (Int'l)	1B	11	36	5	7	2	0	0	3	.194	6	9	0	89	6	3	.969
—	Jacksonville (South.)	1B	108	397	65	112	17	1	*31	93	.282	60	94	0	795	60	7	.992
1996—	Columbus (Int'l)	1B	130	446	84	115	26	0	28	96	.258	48	99	2	*1028	*94	5	*.996
1997—	Columbus (Int'l)	1B	116	417	69	125	35	1	24	95	.300	65	78	4	974	83	8	.992
—	New York (A.L.)	DH-1B-OF	11	20	0	5	1	0	0	3	.250	2	4	0	8	0	0	1.000
Major league totals (1 year)			11	20	0	5	1	0	0	3	.250	2	4	0	8	0	0	1.000

CRUZ, JACOB — OF — GIANTS

PERSONAL: Born January 28, 1973, in Oxnard, Calif. ... 6-0/179. ... Bats left, throws left.
HIGH SCHOOL: Channel Islands (Oxnard, Calif.).
COLLEGE: Arizona State.

C

TRANSACTIONS/CAREER NOTES: Selected by California Angels organization in 45th round of free-agent draft (June 3, 1991); did not sign. ... Selected by San Francisco Giants organization in supplemental round ("sandwich pick" between first and second round; 32nd pick overall) of free-agent draft (June 2, 1994); pick received as part of compensation for Texas Rangers signing Type A free agent 1B Will Clark.

STATISTICAL NOTES: Led Pacific Coast League with 11 sacrifice flies in 1996. ... Led Pacific Coast League with .434 on-base percentage and tied for league lead with nine intentional bases on balls in 1997.

Year	Team (League)	Pos.	G	AB	R	H	2B	3B	HR	RBI	Avg.	BB	SO	SB	PO	A	E	Avg.
1994—	San Jose (Calif.).........	OF	31	118	14	29	7	0	0	12	.246	9	22	0	42	2	2	.957
1995—	Shreveport (Texas).....	OF	127	458	88	136	33	1	13	77	.297	57	72	9	235	16	1	*.996
1996—	Phoenix (PCL)............	OF	121	435	60	124	26	4	7	75	.285	62	77	5	249	11	3	.989
	— San Francisco (N.L.) ..	OF	33	77	10	18	3	0	3	10	.234	12	24	0	41	1	1	.977
1997—	Phoenix (PCL)............	OF	127	493	97	178	*45	3	12	95	*.361	64	64	18	239	*16	8	.970
	— San Francisco (N.L.) ..	OF	16	25	3	4	1	0	0	3	.160	3	4	0	12	2	1	.933
Major league totals (2 years)			49	102	13	22	4	0	3	13	.216	15	28	0	53	3	2	.966

CRUZ, JOSE — OF — BLUE JAYS

PERSONAL: Born April 19, 1974, in Arroyo, Puerto Rico. ... 6-0/190. ... Bats both, throws right. ... Full name: Jose Cruz Jr. ... Son of Jose Cruz Sr., outfielder, St. Louis Cardinals, Houston Astros and New York Yankees (1970-88); nephew of Hector Cruz, major league outfielder/third baseman with four teams (1973, 1975-82); and nephew of Tommy Cruz, coach, Peoria Mariners, and outfielder, St. Louis Cardinals and Chicago White Sox (1973 and 1977) and Nippon Ham Fighters of Japan League (1980-85).

HIGH SCHOOL: Bellaire (Houston).

COLLEGE: Rice.

TRANSACTIONS/CAREER NOTES: Selected by Atlanta Braves organization in 15th round of free-agent draft (June 1, 1992); did not sign. ... Selected by Seattle Mariners organization in first round (third pick overall) of free-agent draft (June 1, 1995). ... Traded by Mariners to Toronto Blue Jays for P Mike Timlin and P Paul Spoljaric (July 31, 1997).

STATISTICAL NOTES: Switch-hit home runs in one game (August 24, 1997).

Year	Team (League)	Pos.	G	AB	R	H	2B	3B	HR	RBI	Avg.	BB	SO	SB	PO	A	E	Avg.
1995—	Everett (N'west).........	OF	3	11	6	5	0	0	0	2	.455	3	3	1	7	0	0	1.000
	— Riverside (Calif.).........	OF	35	144	34	37	7	1	7	29	.257	24	50	3	70	4	3	.961
1996—	Lancaster (Calif.).........	OF	53	203	38	66	17	1	6	43	.325	39	33	7	62	7	1	.986
	— Port City (Southern)...	OF	47	181	39	51	10	2	3	31	.282	27	38	5	90	6	1	.990
	— Tacoma (PCL)	OF	22	76	15	18	1	2	6	15	.237	18	12	1	36	4	0	1.000
1997—	Tacoma (PCL)	OF	50	190	33	51	16	2	6	30	.268	34	44	3	70	3	0	1.000
	— Seattle (A.L.)	OF	49	183	28	49	12	1	12	34	.268	13	45	1	83	1	3	.966
	— Toronto (A.L.)■.........	OF	55	212	31	49	7	0	14	34	.231	28	72	6	98	3	2	.981
Major league totals (1 year)			104	395	59	98	19	1	26	68	.248	41	117	7	181	4	5	.974

CRUZ, NELSON — P — WHITE SOX

PERSONAL: Born September 13, 1972, in Puerta Plata, Dominican Republic. ... 6-1/175. ... Throws right, bats right.

HIGH SCHOOL: Liceo Jose Castellanos (Puerto Plaza, Dominican Republic).

TRANSACTIONS/CAREER NOTES: Signed as non-drafted free agent by Montreal Expos organization (July 5, 1989). ... Released by Expos organization (March 27, 1992). ... Signed by Chicago White Sox organization (December 10, 1994).

Year	Team (League)	W	L	Pct.	ERA	G	GS	CG	ShO	Sv.	IP	H	R	ER	BB	SO
1990—	DSL Expos (DSL)	9	2	.818	2.62	16	16	0	0	0	103	105	49	30	42	83
1991—	GC Expos (GCL)	2	4	.333	2.40	12	8	1	•1	0	48²/₃	40	18	13	19	34
1992—	....							Out of organized baseball.								
1993—	....							Out of organized baseball.								
1994—	....							Out of organized baseball.								
1995—	Bristol (Appalachian)■.......	0	0	....	9.00	1	0	0	0	0	1	2	1	1	0	0
	— Hickory (S. Atl.)	2	7	.222	2.70	44	0	0	0	9	66²/₃	65	31	20	15	68
	— Prince William (Caro.)	2	1	.667	0.47	9	0	0	0	1	19¹/₃	12	1	1	6	15
1996—	Birmingham (Southern)	6	6	.500	3.20	37	18	2	1	1	149	150	65	53	41	142
1997—	Nashville (A.A.)	11	7	.611	5.11	21	20	1	0	0	123¹/₃	139	75	70	31	93
	— Chicago (A.L.)	0	2	.000	6.49	19	0	0	0	0	26¹/₃	29	19	19	9	23
Major league totals (1 year)........		0	2	.000	6.49	19	0	0	0	0	26¹/₃	29	19	19	9	23

CUMBERLAND, CHRIS — P — TWINS

PERSONAL: Born January 15, 1973, in Clearwater, Fla. ... 6-1/190. ... Throws left, bats right. ... Full name: Christopher Mark Cumberland.

JUNIOR COLLEGE: Pasco-Hernando (Fla.).

TRANSACTIONS/CAREER NOTES: Selected by New York Yankees organization in 48th round of free-agent draft (June 1, 1992). ... On Greensboro disabled list (April 6-August 12, 1995). ... Signed by Minnesota Twins organization (August 30, 1997).

STATISTICAL NOTES: Teid for Eastern League lead with four balks in 1997.

Year	Team (League)	W	L	Pct.	ERA	G	GS	CG	ShO	Sv.	IP	H	R	ER	BB	SO
1993—	Oneonta (N.Y.-Penn)	4	4	.500	3.34	15	15	0	0	0	89	*109	43	33	28	62
1994—	Greensboro (S. Atl.)	14	5	.737	2.94	22	22	1	1	0	137²/₃	123	55	45	41	95
1995—	GC Yankees (GCL).............	0	1	.000	1.29	4	4	0	0	0	7	3	1	1	1	7
	— Tampa (Florida State)	1	2	.333	1.82	5	5	0	0	0	24²/₃	28	10	5	5	10
1996—	Columbus (Int'l)	2	7	.222	6.52	12	12	1	0	0	58	86	45	42	23	35
	— Norwich (Eastern)	5	7	.417	5.27	16	16	2	1	0	95²/₃	112	73	56	37	44
1997—	Norwich (Eastern)	11	10	.524	4.02	25	25	3	1	0	154²/₃	188	100	69	59	81
	— New Britain (East.)■	1	0	1.000	3.18	1	1	0	0	0	5²/₃	5	2	2	2	2

CUMMINGS, JOHN   P   INDIANS

PERSONAL: Born May 10, 1969, in Torrance, Calif. ... 6-3/200. ... Throws left, bats left. ... Full name: John Russell Cummings.
HIGH SCHOOL: Canyon (Anaheim, Calif.).
COLLEGE: Southern California.
TRANSACTIONS/CAREER NOTES: Selected by New York Yankees organization in 32nd round of free-agent draft (June 1, 1988); did not sign. ... Selected by Seattle Mariners organization in eighth round of free-agent draft (June 4, 1990). ... On Calgary disabled list (August 1-8, 1993). ... On Seattle disabled list (May 11-28, 1994); included rehabilitation assignment to Appleton (May 23-26). ... Claimed on waivers by Los Angeles Dodgers (May 25, 1995). ... Traded by Dodgers with P Joey Eischen to Detroit Tigers for OF Chad Curtis (July 31, 1996). ... Granted free agency (October 15, 1997). ... Signed by Cleveland Indians organization (January 8, 1998).
HONORS: Named Carolina League Pitcher of the Year (1992).

Year	Team (League)	W	L	Pct.	ERA	G	GS	CG	ShO	Sv.	IP	H	R	ER	BB	SO
1990—	Bellingham (N'west)	1	1	.500	2.12	6	6	0	0	0	34	25	11	8	9	39
	—San Bernardino (Calif.)	2	4	.333	4.20	7	7	1	0	0	40 2/3	47	27	19	20	30
1991—	San Bernardino (Calif.)	4	10	.286	4.06	29	20	0	0	1	124	129	79	56	61	120
1992—	Peninsula (Caro.)	*16	6	.727	2.57	27	27	4	1	0	168 1/3	149	71	48	63	*144
1993—	Seattle (A.L.)	0	6	.000	6.02	10	8	1	0	0	46 1/3	59	34	31	16	19
	—Jacksonville (Southern)	2	2	.500	3.15	7	7	0	0	0	45 2/3	50	24	16	9	35
	—Calgary (PCL)	3	4	.429	4.13	11	10	0	0	0	65 1/3	69	40	30	21	42
1994—	Seattle (A.L.)	2	4	.333	5.63	17	8	0	0	0	64	66	43	40	37	33
	—Appleton (Midwest)	0	0	...	3.00	1	1	0	0	0	3	2	1	1	0	6
	—Calgary (PCL)	1	0	1.000	1.50	1	1	0	0	0	6	3	1	1	2	4
	—Riverside (California)	0	1	.000	6.75	1	1	0	0	0	2 2/3	5	2	2	1	2
1995—	Seattle (A.L.)	0	0	...	11.81	4	0	0	0	0	5 1/3	8	8	7	7	4
	—Tacoma (PCL)	0	1	.000	7.71	1	1	0	0	0	2 1/3	6	4	2	3	3
	—San Antonio (Tex.)■	0	2	.000	3.95	6	5	0	0	0	27 1/3	28	13	12	7	13
	—Los Angeles (N.L.)	3	1	.750	3.00	35	0	0	0	0	39	38	16	13	10	21
1996—	Los Angeles (N.L.)	0	1	.000	6.75	4	0	0	0	0	5 1/3	12	7	4	2	5
	—Albuquerque (PCL)	2	6	.250	4.14	27	9	0	0	2	78 1/3	91	47	36	28	49
	—Detroit (A.L.)■	3	3	.500	5.12	21	0	0	0	0	31 2/3	36	20	18	20	24
1997—	Detroit (A.L.)	2	0	1.000	5.47	19	0	0	0	0	24 2/3	32	22	15	14	8
	—Toledo (Int'l)	2	1	.667	2.76	19	0	0	0	0	16 1/3	13	6	5	6	7
A.L. totals (5 years)		7	13	.350	5.81	71	16	1	0	0	172	201	127	111	94	88
N.L. totals (2 years)		3	2	.600	3.45	39	0	0	0	0	44 1/3	50	23	17	12	26
Major league totals (5 years)		10	15	.400	5.33	110	16	1	0	0	216 1/3	251	150	128	106	114

DIVISION SERIES RECORD

Year	Team (League)	W	L	Pct.	ERA	G	GS	CG	ShO	Sv.	IP	H	R	ER	BB	SO
1995—	Los Angeles (N.L.)	0	0	...	20.25	2	0	0	0	0	1 1/3	3	3	3	2	3

CUMMINGS, MIDRE   OF   PHILLIES

PERSONAL: Born October 14, 1971, in St. Croix, Virgin Islands. ... 6-0/195. ... Bats left, throws right. ... Full name: Midre Almeric Cummings.
HIGH SCHOOL: Miami Edison Senior.
TRANSACTIONS/CAREER NOTES: Selected by Minnesota Twins organization in supplemental round ("sandwich pick" between first and second round, 29th pick overall) of free-agent draft (June 4, 1990); pick received as part of compensation for Boston Red Sox signing Type A free-agent P Jeff Reardon. ... Traded by Twins organization with P Denny Neagle to Pittsburgh Pirates organization for P John Smiley (March 17, 1992). ... On Buffalo disabled list (April 21-June 6, 1994). ... On Calgary disabled list (June 17-July 1, 1995). ... Claimed on waivers by Philadelphia Phillies (July 8, 1997).
MISCELLANEOUS: Batted as switch-hitter (1990-92).

Year	Team (League)	Pos.	G	AB	R	H	2B	3B	HR	RBI	Avg.	BB	SO	SB	PO	A	E	Avg.
1990—	GC Twins (GCL)	OF	47	177	28	56	3	4	5	28	.316	13	32	14	73	2	6	.926
1991—	Kenosha (Midwest)	OF	106	382	59	123	20	4	4	54	*.322	22	66	28	166	6	•13	.930
1992—	Salem (Carolina)■	OF	113	420	55	128	20	5	14	75	.305	35	67	23	151	10	6	.964
1993—	Carolina (Southern)	OF	63	237	33	70	17	2	6	26	.295	14	23	5	99	7	4	.964
	—Buffalo (A.A.)	OF	60	232	36	64	12	1	9	21	.276	22	45	5	90	1	2	.978
	—Pittsburgh (N.L.)	OF	13	36	5	4	1	0	0	3	.111	4	9	0	21	0	0	1.000
1994—	Buffalo (A.A.)	OF	49	183	23	57	12	4	2	22	.311	13	26	5	117	2	0	1.000
	—Pittsburgh (N.L.)	OF	24	86	11	21	4	0	1	12	.244	4	18	0	49	1	2	.962
1995—	Pittsburgh (N.L.)	OF	59	152	13	37	7	1	2	15	.243	13	30	1	79	2	1	.988
	—Calgary (PCL)	OF	45	159	19	44	9	1	1	16	.277	6	27	1	96	4	6	.943
1996—	Calgary (PCL)	OF	97	368	60	112	24	3	8	55	.304	21	60	6	176	9	5	.974
	—Pittsburgh (N.L.)	OF	24	85	11	19	3	1	3	7	.224	0	16	0	49	0	1	.980
1997—	Pittsburgh (N.L.)	OF	52	106	11	20	6	2	3	8	.189	8	26	0	37	1	0	1.000
	—Philadelphia (N.L.)■	OF	63	208	24	63	16	4	1	23	.303	23	30	2	113	1	1	.991
Major league totals (5 years)			235	673	75	164	37	8	10	68	.244	52	129	3	348	5	5	.986

CUNNANE, WILL   P   PADRES

PERSONAL: Born April 24, 1974, in Suffern, N.Y. ... 6-2/175. ... Throws right, bats right. ... Full name: William Cunnane.
HIGH SCHOOL: Clarkstown North (New City, N.Y.).
TRANSACTIONS/CAREER NOTES: Signed as non-drafted free agent by Florida Marlins organization (August 18, 1992). ... On Portland disabled list (August 7-23, 1996). ... Selected by San Diego Padres organization from Marlins organization in Rule 5 major league draft (December 9, 1996).
MISCELLANEOUS: Appeared in one game as pinch-runner (1997).

Year Team (League)	W	L	Pct.	ERA	G	GS	CG	ShO	Sv.	IP	H	R	ER	BB	SO
1993— GC Marlins (GCL)	3	3	.500	2.70	16	9	0	0	2	66²/₃	75	32	20	8	64
1994— Kane County (Midwest)	11	3	.786	*1.43	32	16	5	*4	1	138²/₃	110	27	22	23	106
1995— Portland (Eastern)	9	2	*.818	3.67	21	21	1	1	0	117²/₃	120	48	48	34	83
1996— Portland (Eastern)	10	12	.455	3.74	25	25	4	0	0	151²/₃	156	73	63	30	101
1997— San Diego (N.L.)■	6	3	.667	5.81	54	8	0	0	0	91¹/₃	114	69	59	49	79
Major league totals (1 year)........	6	3	.667	5.81	54	8	0	0	0	91¹/₃	114	69	59	49	79

CURTIS, CHAD   OF   YANKEES

PERSONAL: Born November 6, 1968, in Marion, Ind. ... 5-10/185. ... Bats right, throws right. ... Full name: Chad David Curtis.
HIGH SCHOOL: Benson (Ariz.) Union.
JUNIOR COLLEGE: Yavapai College (Ariz.), then Cochise County Community College (Ariz.).
COLLEGE: Grand Canyon (Ariz.).
TRANSACTIONS/CAREER NOTES: Selected by California Angels organization in 45th round of free-agent draft (June 5, 1989). ... On disabled list (June 5-20, 1991). ... On suspended list (June 8-12, 1993). ... Traded by Angels to Detroit Tigers for OF/3B Tony Phillips (April 12, 1995). ... Traded by Tigers to Los Angeles Dodgers for P Joey Eischen and P John Cummings (July 31, 1996). ... Granted free agency (October 15, 1996). ... Signed by Cleveland Indians (December 18, 1996). ... On Cleveland disabled list (May 14-June 9, 1997). ... Traded by Indians to New York Yankees for P David Weathers (June 9, 1997); on disabled list when acquired by Yankees and activated on June 11.
RECORDS: Shares A.L. single-season record for fewest errors by outfielder who led league in errors—9 (1993).
STATISTICAL NOTES: Led Midwest League with 223 total bases in 1990. ... Tied for A.L. lead in caught stealing with 24 in 1993. ... Led A.L. outfielders with 448 total chances and tied for lead with nine errors in 1993. ... Led A.L. outfielders with 345 total chances in 1994. ... Career major league grand slams: 1.

Year Team (League)	Pos.	G	AB	R	H	2B	3B	HR	RBI	Avg.	BB	SO	SB	PO	A	E	Avg.
1989— Ariz. Angels (Ariz.)	2B-OF	32	122	30	37	4	4	3	20	.303	14	20	17	62	58	6	.952
— Quad City (Midwest) ..	OF	23	78	7	19	3	0	2	11	.244	6	17	7	34	1	1	.972
1990— Quad City (Midwest) ..	2B-OF	135	*492	87	*151	28	1	14	65	.307	57	76	64	216	221	26	.944
1991— Edmonton (PCL)	3B-OF	115	431	81	136	28	7	9	61	.316	51	56	46	124	220	25	.932
1992— California (A.L.)	OF-DH	139	441	59	114	16	2	10	46	.259	51	71	43	250	*16	6	.978
1993— California (A.L.)	OF-2B	152	583	94	166	25	3	6	59	.285	70	89	48	426	13	‡9	.980
1994— California (A.L.)	OF	114	453	67	116	23	4	11	50	.256	37	69	25	*332	9	4	.988
1995— Detroit (A.L.)■	OF	144	586	96	157	29	3	21	67	.268	70	93	27	362	5	3	.992
1996— Detroit (A.L.)	OF	104	400	65	105	20	1	10	37	.263	53	73	16	243	6	9	.965
— Los Angeles (N.L.)■ ..	OF	43	104	20	22	5	0	2	9	.212	17	15	2	62	2	1	.985
1997— Cleveland (A.L.)■	OF	22	29	8	6	1	0	3	5	.207	7	10	0	20	0	0	1.000
— Akron (Eastern)	OF	4	18	5	7	1	0	3	6	.389	0	3	0	5	2	0	1.000
— New York (A.L.)■.......	OF	93	320	51	93	21	1	12	50	.291	36	49	12	168	6	4	.978
American League totals (6 years)		768	2812	440	757	135	14	73	314	.269	324	454	171	1801	55	35	.981
National League totals (1 year)		43	104	20	22	5	0	2	9	.212	17	15	2	62	2	1	.985
Major league totals (6 years)		811	2916	460	779	140	14	75	323	.267	341	469	173	1863	57	36	.982

DIVISION SERIES RECORD

Year Team (League)	Pos.	G	AB	R	H	2B	3B	HR	RBI	Avg.	BB	SO	SB	PO	A	E	Avg.
1996— Los Angeles (N.L.)	OF	1	2	0	0	0	0	0	0	.000	1	1	0	2	0	0	1.000
1997— New York (A.L.)	OF-PR	4	6	0	1	0	0	0	0	.167	3	1	0	4	0	0	1.000
Division series totals (2 years)		5	8	0	1	0	0	0	0	.125	4	2	0	6	0	0	1.000

D'AMICO, JEFF   P   BREWERS

PERSONAL: Born December 27, 1975, in St. Petersburg, Fla. ... 6-7/245. ... Throws right, bats right. ... Full name: Jeffrey Charles D'Amico.
HIGH SCHOOL: Northeast (St. Petersburg, Fla.).
TRANSACTIONS/CAREER NOTES: Selected by Milwaukee Brewers organization in first round (23rd pick overall) of free-agent draft (June 3, 1993). ... On disabled list (June 24-September 1, 1994). ... On Milwaukee disabled list (July 28-September 2, 1997).

Year Team (League)	W	L	Pct.	ERA	G	GS	CG	ShO	Sv.	IP	H	R	ER	BB	SO
1994—					Did not play.										
1995— Beloit (Midwest)	13	3	*.813	2.39	21	20	3	1	0	132	102	40	35	31	119
1996— El Paso (Texas)	5	4	.556	3.19	13	13	3	0	0	96	89	42	34	13	76
— Milwaukee (A.L.)	6	6	.500	5.44	17	17	0	0	0	86	88	53	52	31	53
1997— Milwaukee (A.L.)	9	7	.563	4.71	23	23	1	1	0	135²/₃	139	81	71	43	94
— Beloit (Midwest)	0	0	...	0.00	1	1	0	0	0	3	0	0	0	1	7
Major league totals (2 years)......	15	13	.536	4.99	40	40	1	1	0	221²/₃	227	134	123	74	147

D'AMICO, JEFF   P   ATHLETICS

PERSONAL: Born November 9, 1974, in Inglewood, Calif. ... 6-3/195. ... Throws right, bats right. ... Full name: Jeffrey Michael D'Amico.
HIGH SCHOOL: Redmond (Wash.).
TRANSACTIONS/CAREER NOTES: Selected by Oakland Athletics organization in second round of free-agent draft (June 3, 1993). ... On West Michigan disabled list (April 22-September 19, 1994).

Year Team (League)	W	L	Pct.	ERA	G	GS	CG	ShO	Sv.	IP	H	R	ER	BB	SO
1996— Modesto (California)	0	0	...	18.00	1	0	0	0	0	1	3	3	2	1	0
— Arizona A's (Arizona)	3	0	1.000	1.42	8	0	0	0	0	19	14	3	3	2	15
1997— Modesto (California)	7	3	.700	3.80	20	13	0	0	1	97	115	57	41	34	89
— Edmonton (PCL)	1	2	.333	8.22	10	7	0	0	1	30²/₃	42	29	28	6	19

C
D

RECORD AS POSITION PLAYER

Year Team (League)	Pos.	G	AB	R	H	2B	3B	HR	RBI	Avg.	BB	SO	SB	PO	A	E	Avg.
1993— S. Oregon (N'west).....	SS-3B	33	114	12	30	9	0	3	15	.263	9	25	2	43	67	14	.887
1994— W. Mich. (Mid.).........	SS	9	36	5	10	3	0	0	3	.278	4	7	2	14	25	1	.975
1995— W. Mich. (Mid.)	SS-3B	125	434	56	98	24	1	7	55	.226	56	94	8	120	304	37	.920
1996— Modesto (California) ..	3-2-S-P	47	172	28	46	7	1	4	21	.267	19	31	3	36	101	19	.878

DAAL, OMAR　　　　　　　　P　　　　　　　　DIAMONDBACKS

PERSONAL: Born March 1, 1972, in Maracaibo, Venezuela. ... 6-3/185. ... Throws left, bats left. ... Full name: Omar Jose Cordaro Daal.
HIGH SCHOOL: Valencia (Venezuela) Superior.
TRANSACTIONS/CAREER NOTES: Signed as non-drafted free agent by Los Angeles Dodgers organization (August 24, 1990). ... Traded by Dodgers to Montreal Expos for P Rick Clelland (December 14, 1995). ... Claimed on waivers by Toronto Blue Jays (July 25, 1997). ... Selected by Arizona Diamondbacks in second round (31st pick overall) of expansion draft (November 18, 1997).

Year Team (League)	W	L	Pct.	ERA	G	GS	CG	ShO	Sv.	IP	H	R	ER	BB	SO
1990— Dom. Dodgers (DSL)	3	6	.333	1.18	17	13	6	0	2	91 2/3	61	29	12	29	91
1991— Dom. Dodgers (DSL)	7	2	.778	1.16	13	13	0	0	0	93	30	17	12	32	81
1992— Albuquerque (PCL)............	0	2	.000	7.84	12	0	0	0	0	10 1/3	14	9	9	11	9
— San Antonio (Tex.)	2	6	.250	5.02	35	5	0	0	5	57 1/3	60	39	32	33	52
1993— Albuquerque (PCL)............	1	1	.500	3.38	6	0	0	0	2	5 1/3	5	2	2	3	2
— Los Angeles (N.L.)	2	3	.400	5.09	47	0	0	0	0	35 1/3	36	20	20	21	19
1994— Albuquerque (PCL)............	4	2	.667	5.19	11	5	0	0	1	34 2/3	38	20	20	16	28
— Los Angeles (N.L.)	0	0	...	3.29	24	0	0	0	0	13 2/3	12	5	5	5	9
1995— Albuquerque (PCL)............	2	3	.400	4.05	17	9	0	0	1	53 1/3	56	28	24	26	46
— Los Angeles (N.L.)	4	0	1.000	7.20	28	0	0	0	0	20	29	16	16	15	11
1996— Montreal (N.L.)■..............	4	5	.444	4.02	64	6	0	0	0	87 1/3	74	40	39	37	82
1997— Montreal (N.L.)	1	2	.333	9.79	33	0	0	0	1	30 1/3	48	35	33	15	16
— Ottawa (Int'l)	0	1	.000	5.63	2	2	0	0	0	8	10	6	5	1	9
— Toronto (A.L.)■..............	1	1	.500	4.00	9	3	0	0	0	27	34	13	12	6	28
— Syracuse (Int'l)	3	0	1.000	0.53	5	5	1	1	0	33 2/3	18	2	2	10	29
A.L. totals (1 year)	1	1	.500	4.00	9	3	0	0	0	27	34	13	12	6	28
N.L. totals (5 years)	11	10	.524	5.45	196	6	0	0	1	186 2/3	199	116	113	93	137
Major league totals (5 years)......	12	11	.522	5.27	205	9	0	0	1	213 2/3	233	129	125	99	165

DALE, CARL　　　　　　　　P　　　　　　　　ATHLETICS

PERSONAL: Born December 7, 1972, in Indianapolis. ... 6-2/215. ... Throws right, bats right. ... Full name: James Carl Dale.
HIGH SCHOOL: Cookeville (Tenn.).
COLLEGE: Winthrop (S.C.).
TRANSACTIONS/CAREER NOTES: Selected by St. Louis Cardinals organization in second round of free-agent draft (June 2, 1994). ... Traded by Cardinals with OF Allen Battle, P Bret Wagner and P Jay Witasick to Oakland Athletics for P Todd Stottlemyre (January 6, 1996). ... On temporarily inactive list (June 12-19, 1996).

Year Team (League)	W	L	Pct.	ERA	G	GS	CG	ShO	Sv.	IP	H	R	ER	BB	SO
1994— New Jersey (NYP)	2	7	.222	4.56	15	•15	0	0	0	73	79	44	37	38	75
1995— Peoria (Midwest)	9	9	.500	2.94	24	24	2	1	0	143 2/3	124	66	47	62	104
1996— Modesto (California)■..........	8	2	.800	4.28	26	24	0	0	0	128 1/3	124	79	61	72	102
1997— Huntsville (Southern)	6	4	.600	5.38	20	16	0	0	0	85 1/3	95	61	51	43	57

DAMON, JOHNNY　　　　　　　　OF　　　　　　　　ROYALS

PERSONAL: Born November 5, 1973, in Fort Riley, Kan. ... 6-2/190. ... Bats left, throws left. ... Full name: Johnny David Damon.
HIGH SCHOOL: Dr. Phillips (Orlando).
TRANSACTIONS/CAREER NOTES: Selected by Kansas City Royals organization in supplemental round ("sandwich pick" between first and second round, 35th pick overall) of free-agent draft (June 1, 1992); pick received as part of compensation for San Diego Padres signing Type A free-agent IF Kurt Stillwell. ... On suspended list (September 5-7, 1997).
HONORS: Named Texas League Player of the Year (1995).
STATISTICAL NOTES: Led Gulf Coast League with 109 total bases in 1992. ... Led Midwest League outfielders with five double plays in 1993. ... Led Texas League with .434 on-base percentage in 1995. ... Led Texas League with .534 slugging percentage in 1995. ... Led Texas League with 13 intentional bases on balls received in 1995. ... Career major league grand slams: 1.

Year Team (League)	Pos.	G	AB	R	H	2B	3B	HR	RBI	Avg.	BB	SO	SB	PO	A	E	Avg.
1992— GC Royals (GCL)	OF	50	192	*58	67	12	*9	4	24	*.349	31	21	33	77	7	1	.988
— Baseball City (FSL)........	OF	1	1	0	0	0	0	0	0	.000	0	0	0	0	0	0	...
1993— Rockford (Midwest) ...	OF	127	511	82	148	25	*13	5	50	.290	52	83	59	240	14	6	.977
1994— Wilmington (Caro.).....	OF	119	472	96	149	25	13	6	75	.316	62	55	44	273	9	3	.989
1995— Wichita (Texas)	OF	111	423	83	145	15	9	16	54	.343	67	35	26	296	11	5	.984
— Kansas City (A.L.)	OF	47	188	32	53	11	5	3	23	.282	12	22	7	110	0	1	.991
1996— Kansas City (A.L.)	OF-DH	145	517	61	140	22	5	6	50	.271	31	64	25	350	5	6	.983
1997— Kansas City (A.L.)	OF-DH	146	472	70	130	12	8	8	48	.275	42	70	16	322	5	4	.988
Major league totals (3 years)		338	1177	163	323	45	18	17	121	.274	85	156	48	782	10	11	.986

DARENSBOURG, VIC　　　　　　　　P　　　　　　　　MARLINS

PERSONAL: Born November 13, 1970, in Los Angeles. ... 5-10/165. ... Throws left, bats left. ... Full name: Victor Anthony Darensbourg.
HIGH SCHOOL: Westchester (Los Angeles).

COLLEGE: Lewis & Clark (Ore.).
TRANSACTIONS/CAREER NOTES: Signed as non-drafted free agent by Florida Marlins organization (June 11, 1992). ... On Florida disabled list (September 15, 1995-remainder of season). ... On Portland disabled list (April 4-15, 1996).

Year Team (League)	W	L	Pct.	ERA	G	GS	CG	ShO	Sv.	IP	H	R	ER	BB	SO
1992—GC Marlins (GCL)	2	1	.667	0.64	8	4	0	0	2	42	28	5	3	11	37
1993—Kane County (Midwest)	9	1	.900	2.14	46	0	0	0	16	71 1/3	58	17	17	28	89
—High Desert (Calif.)	0	0	...	0.00	1	0	0	0	0	1	0	0	0	0	1
1994—Portland (Eastern)	10	7	.588	3.81	35	21	1	1	4	149	146	76	63	60	103
1995—							Did not play.								
1996—Brevard County (FSL)	0	0	...	0.00	2	0	0	0	0	3	1	0	0	1	5
—Charlotte (Int'l)	1	5	.167	3.69	47	0	0	0	7	63 1/3	61	30	26	32	66
1997—Charlotte (Int'l)	4	2	.667	4.38	27	0	0	0	2	24 2/3	22	12	12	15	21

DARR, MIKE — OF — PADRES

PERSONAL: Born March 21, 1976, in Corona, Calif. ... 6-3/205. ... Bats left, throws right. ... Full name: Michael C. Darr Jr.
HIGH SCHOOL: Corona (Calif.).
TRANSACTIONS/CAREER NOTES: Selected by Detroit Tigers organization in second round of free-agent draft (June 2, 1994). ... Traded by Tigers with P Mike Skrmetta to San Diego Padres for 2B Jody Reed (March 22, 1997). ... On disabled list (April 4-May 28, 1996).

Year Team (League)	Pos.	G	AB	R	H	2B	3B	HR	RBI	Avg.	BB	SO	SB	PO	A	E	Avg.
1994—Bristol (Appal.)	OF	44	149	23	41	6	0	1	18	.275	23	22	4	59	4	4	.940
1995—Fayetteville (SAL)	OF	112	395	58	114	21	2	5	66	.289	58	88	5	123	15	9	.939
1996—Lakeland (Fla. St.)	OF	85	311	26	77	14	7	0	38	.248	28	64	7	128	8	3	.978
1997—Rancho Cuca. (Cal.)■	OF	134	521	104	179	32	11	15	94	.344	57	90	23	176	12	8	.959

DARWIN, DANNY — P — GIANTS

PERSONAL: Born October 25, 1955, in Bonham, Texas. ... 6-3/200. ... Throws right, bats right. ... Full name: Daniel Wayne Darwin. ... Brother of Jeff Darwin, pitcher with Seattle Mariners (1994) and Chicago White Sox (1996-97).
HIGH SCHOOL: Bonham (Texas).
COLLEGE: Grayson County (Texas) College.
TRANSACTIONS/CAREER NOTES: Signed as non-drafted free agent by Texas Rangers organization (May 10, 1976). ... On disabled list (April 25-May 4 and May 22-June 11, 1977; June 5-26, 1980; March 25-April 10 and August 9-September 1, 1983). ... Traded by Rangers with a player to be named later to Milwaukee Brewers as part of a six-player, four-team deal in which Kansas City Royals acquired C Jim Sundberg from Brewers, Rangers acquired C Don Slaught from Royals, New York Mets organization acquired P Frank Wills from Royals and Brewers organization acquired P Tim Leary from Mets (January 18, 1985); Brewers organization acquired C Bill Hance from Rangers to complete deal (January 30, 1985). ... Granted free agency (November 12, 1985). ... Re-signed by Brewers (December 22, 1985). ... Traded by Brewers organization to Houston Astros for P Don August and a player to be named later (August 15, 1986); Brewers organization acquired P Mark Knudson to complete deal (August 21, 1986). ... Granted free agency (November 9, 1987). ... Re-signed by Astros (January 8, 1988). ... Granted free agency (December 7, 1990). ... Signed by Boston Red Sox (December 19, 1990). ... On disabled list (April 23-May 22 and July 5, 1991-remainder of season; and June 16, 1994-remainder of season). ... Granted free agency (October 21, 1994). ... Signed by Toronto Blue Jays (April 10, 1995). ... Released by Blue Jays (July 18, 1995). ... Signed by Oklahoma City, Rangers organization (July 31, 1995). ... Granted free agency (November 11, 1995). ... Signed by Carolina, Pittsburgh Pirates organization (February 4, 1996). ... Traded by Pirates to Astros for P Rich Loiselle (July 23, 1996). ... On Houston suspended list (August 16-21, 1996). ... Granted free agency (November 6, 1996). ... Signed by Chicago White Sox organization (February 7, 1997). ... Traded by White Sox with P Wilson Alvarez and P Roberto Hernandez to San Francisco Giants for SS Michael Caruso, OF Brian Manning, P Lorenzo Barcelo, P Keith Foulke, P Bobby Howry and P Ken Vining (July 31, 1997). ... Granted free agency (October 30, 1997). ... Re-signed by Giants (December 6, 1997).
STATISTICAL NOTES: Tied for Western Carolinas League lead with five balks in 1976. ... Tied for Texas League lead with eight hit batsmen in 1977. ... Pitched 5-0 one-hit, complete-game victory against Boston (April 29, 1981). ... Pitched 4-1 one-hit, complete-game victory against Minnesota (August 19, 1985). ... Tied for A.L. lead with 34 home runs allowed in 1985. ... Pitched 5-0 one-hit, complete-game victory against Chicago (August 18, 1993).
MISCELLANEOUS: Appeared in four games as pinch-runner (1990).

Year Team (League)	W	L	Pct.	ERA	G	GS	CG	ShO	Sv.	IP	H	R	ER	BB	SO
1976—Asheville (W. Caro.)	6	3	.667	3.62	16	16	6	1	0	102	96	54	41	48	76
1977—Tulsa (Texas)	13	4	.765	2.51	23	23	6	•4	0	154	130	53	43	72	129
1978—Tucson (PCL)	8	9	.471	6.26	23	23	4	0	0	125	147	100	87	83	126
—Texas (A.L.)	1	0	1.000	4.00	3	1	0	0	0	9	11	4	4	1	8
1979—Tucson (PCL)	6	6	.500	3.60	13	13	4	1	0	95	89	43	38	42	65
—Texas (A.L.)	4	4	.500	4.04	20	6	1	0	0	78	50	36	35	30	58
1980—Texas (A.L.)	13	4	.765	2.62	53	2	0	0	8	110	98	37	32	50	104
1981—Texas (A.L.)	9	9	.500	3.64	22	22	6	2	0	146	115	67	59	57	98
1982—Texas (A.L.)	10	8	.556	3.44	56	1	0	0	7	89	95	38	34	37	61
1983—Texas (A.L.)	8	13	.381	3.49	28	26	9	2	0	183	175	86	71	62	92
1984—Texas (A.L.)	8	12	.400	3.94	35	32	5	2	0	223 2/3	249	110	98	54	123
1985—Milwaukee (A.L.)■	8	18	.308	3.80	39	29	11	1	2	217 2/3	212	112	92	65	125
1986—Milwaukee (A.L.)	6	8	.429	3.52	27	14	5	1	0	130 1/3	120	62	51	35	80
—Houston (N.L.)■	5	2	.714	2.32	12	8	1	0	0	54 1/3	50	19	14	9	40
1987—Houston (N.L.)	9	10	.474	3.59	33	30	3	1	0	195 2/3	184	87	78	69	134
1988—Houston (N.L.)	8	13	.381	3.84	44	20	3	0	3	192	189	86	82	48	129
1989—Houston (N.L.)	11	4	.733	2.36	68	0	0	0	7	122	92	34	32	33	104
1990—Houston (N.L.)	11	4	.733	*2.21	48	17	3	0	2	162 2/3	136	42	40	31	109
1991—Boston (A.L.)■	3	6	.333	5.16	12	12	0	0	0	68	71	39	39	15	42
1992—Boston (A.L.)	9	9	.500	3.96	51	15	2	0	3	161 1/3	159	76	71	53	124
1993—Boston (A.L.)	15	11	.577	3.26	34	34	2	1	0	229 1/3	196	93	83	49	130
1994—Boston (A.L.)	7	5	.583	6.30	13	13	0	0	0	75 2/3	101	54	53	24	54
1995—Toronto (A.L.)■	1	8	.111	7.62	13	11	1	0	0	65	91	60	55	24	36
—Oklahoma City (A.A.)■	0	0	...	0.00	1	1	0	0	0	3	1	0	0	0	4
—Texas (A.L.)	2	2	.500	7.15	7	4	0	0	0	34	40	27	27	7	22

D

Year Team (League)	W	L	Pct.	ERA	G	GS	CG	ShO	Sv.	IP	H	R	ER	BB	SO
1996— Pittsburgh (N.L.)■............	7	9	.438	3.02	19	19	0	0	0	122 1/3	117	48	41	16	69
—Houston (N.L.)■...............	3	2	.600	5.95	15	6	0	0	0	42 1/3	43	31	28	11	27
1997—Chicago (A.L.)■.............	4	8	.333	4.13	21	17	1	0	0	113 1/3	130	60	52	31	62
—San Francisco (N.L.)■	1	3	.250	4.91	10	7	0	0	0	44	51	26	24	14	30
A.L. totals (15 years)	108	125	.464	3.98	434	239	43	9	20	1933 1/3	1913	961	856	594	1219
N.L. totals (7 years)	55	47	.539	3.26	249	107	10	1	12	935 1/3	862	373	339	231	642
Major league totals (20 years)....	163	172	.487	3.75	683	346	53	10	32	2868 2/3	2775	1334	1195	825	1861

DARWIN, JEFF   P   GIANTS

PERSONAL: Born July 6, 1969, in Sherman, Texas. ... 6-3/180. ... Throws right, bats right. ... Full name: Jeffrey Scott Darwin. ... Brother of Danny Darwin, pitcher, San Francisco Giants.
HIGH SCHOOL: Bonham (Texas).
JUNIOR COLLEGE: Alvin (Texas) Community College.
TRANSACTIONS/CAREER NOTES: Selected by Seattle Mariners organization in 46th round of free-agent draft (June 2, 1987); did not sign. ... Selected by Mariners organization in 13th round of free-agent draft (June 1, 1988). ... On disabled list (June 3-August 2, 1991). ... Traded by Mariners with OF Henry Cotto to Florida Marlins for 3B Dave Magadan (June 27, 1993). ... Traded by Marlins with cash to Mariners for 3B Dave Magadan (November 9, 1993). ... Traded by Mariners organization to Chicago White Sox organization (October 9, 1995), completing deal in which Mariners acquired OF Warren Newson from White Sox for a player to be named later (July 18, 1995). ... Released by White Sox (November 26, 1997). ... Signed by San Francisco Giants organization (January 12, 1998).
STATISTICAL NOTES: Led Carolina League with nine balks in 1990.

Year Team (League)	W	L	Pct.	ERA	G	GS	CG	ShO	Sv.	IP	H	R	ER	BB	SO
1989—Bellingham (N'west)	1	7	.125	4.92	12	12	0	0	0	64	73	42	35	24	47
1990—Peninsula (Caro.)	8	•14	.364	4.01	25	25	1	0	0	150 1/3	153	86	67	57	89
1991—San Bernardino (Calif.)	3	9	.250	6.20	16	14	0	0	0	74	80	53	51	31	58
1992—Peninsula (Caro.)	5	11	.313	3.35	32	20	4	•2	3	139 2/3	132	58	52	40	122
1993—Jacksonville (Southern)......	3	5	.375	2.97	27	0	0	0	7	36 1/3	29	17	12	17	39
—Edmonton (PCL)■.............	2	2	.500	8.51	25	0	0	0	2	30 2/3	50	34	29	10	22
1994—Calgary (PCL)...............	1	2	.333	3.44	42	0	0	0	11	70 2/3	60	32	27	28	54
—Seattle (A.L.)	0	0	...	13.50	2	0	0	0	0	4	7	6	6	3	1
1995—Tacoma (PCL)	7	2	.778	2.70	46	0	0	0	12	63 1/3	51	21	19	21	51
1996—Nashville (A.A.)■............	5	2	.714	3.55	25	6	0	0	3	63 1/3	52	31	25	17	33
—Chicago (A.L.)...............	0	1	.000	2.93	22	0	0	0	0	30 2/3	26	10	10	9	15
1997—Nashville (A.A.)	4	3	.571	4.53	47	0	0	0	22	53 2/3	60	32	27	24	44
—Chicago (A.L.)...............	0	1	.000	5.27	14	0	0	0	0	13 2/3	17	8	8	7	9
Major league totals (3 years)......	0	2	.000	4.47	38	0	0	0	0	48 1/3	50	24	24	19	25

DAULTON, DARREN   C

PERSONAL: Born January 3, 1962, in Arkansas City, Kan. ... 6-2/207. ... Bats left, throws right. ... Full name: Darren Arthur Daulton.
HIGH SCHOOL: Arkansas City (Kan.).
JUNIOR COLLEGE: Cowley County (Kan.) Community College.
TRANSACTIONS/CAREER NOTES: Selected by Philadelphia Phillies organization in 25th round of free-agent draft (June 3, 1980). ... On disabled list (July 20-August 28, 1984). ... On Philadelphia disabled list (May 17-August 9, 1985); included rehabilitation assignment to Portland (July 20-August 7). ... On Philadelphia disabled list (June 22, 1986-remainder of season; April 1-16, 1987; August 28, 1988-remainder of season; and May 6-21, 1991). ... On Philadelphia disabled list (May 28-June 18 and September 7, 1991-remainder of season); included rehabilitation assignments to Scranton/Wilkes-Barre (June 15-17) and Reading (June 17-18). ... On disabled list (June 29, 1994-remainder of season and August 26, 1995-remainder of season). ... On Philadelphia disabled list (April 7, 1996-remainder of season); included rehabilitation assignment to Clearwater (June 24-25). ... Traded by Phillies to Florida Marlins for OF Billy McMillon (July 21, 1997). ... Granted free agency (October 31, 1997).
HONORS: Named catcher on The Sporting News N.L. All-Star team (1992). ... Named catcher on The Sporting News N.L. Silver Slugger team (1992). ... Named N.L. Comeback Player of the Year by The Sporting News (1997).
STATISTICAL NOTES: Tied for Eastern League lead with 10 sacrifice flies in 1983. ... Tied for N.L. lead in double plays by catcher with 10 in 1990. ... Led N.L. catchers with 1,057 total chances and 19 double plays in 1993. ... Career major league grand slams: 5.

Year Team (League)	Pos.	G	AB	R	H	2B	3B	HR	RBI	Avg.	BB	SO	SB	PO	A	E	Avg.
1980—Helena (Pioneer)	C	37	100	13	20	2	1	1	10	.200	23	29	5	224	17	4	.984
1981—Spartanburg (SAL)	C-OF-3B	98	270	44	62	11	1	3	29	.230	56	35	14	378	34	4	.990
1982—Peninsula (Caro.)	C-1B	110	324	65	78	21	2	11	44	.241	89	51	17	654	63	9	.988
1983—Reading (Eastern)	C-1B-OF	113	362	77	95	16	4	19	83	.262	106	87	28	557	57	14	.978
—Philadelphia (N.L.)......	C	2	3	1	1	0	0	0	0	.333	1	1	0	8	0	0	1.000
1984—Portland (PCL)	C	80	252	45	75	19	4	7	38	.298	57	49	3	322	26	6	.983
1985—Portland (PCL)	C	23	64	13	19	5	3	2	10	.297	16	13	6	110	9	0	1.000
—Philadelphia (N.L.)......	C	36	103	14	21	3	1	4	11	.204	16	37	3	160	15	1	.994
1986—Philadelphia (N.L.)......	C	49	138	18	31	4	0	8	21	.225	38	41	2	244	21	4	.985
1987—Clearwater (FSL)	C-1B	9	22	1	5	3	0	1	5	.227	4	3	0	27	5	5	.914
—Maine (Int'l)...............	C-1B	20	70	9	15	1	1	3	10	.214	16	15	5	138	12	0	1.000
—Philadelphia (N.L.)......	C-1B	53	129	10	25	6	0	3	13	.194	16	37	0	210	13	2	.991
1988—Philadelphia (N.L.)......	C-1B	58	144	13	30	6	0	1	12	.208	17	26	2	205	15	6	.973
1989—Philadelphia (N.L.)......	C	131	368	29	74	12	2	8	44	.201	52	58	2	627	56	11	.984
1990—Philadelphia (N.L.)......	C	143	459	62	123	30	1	12	57	.268	72	72	7	683	•70	8	.989
1991—Philadelphia (N.L.)......	C	89	285	36	56	12	0	12	42	.196	41	66	5	493	33	8	.985
—Scran./W.B. (Int'l)......	C	2	9	1	2	0	0	1	1	.222	0	0	0	14	1	0	1.000
—Reading (Eastern)	C	1	4	0	1	0	0	0	0	.250	1	0	0	6	2	0	1.000
1992—Philadelphia (N.L.)......	C	145	485	80	131	32	5	27	*109	.270	88	103	11	760	69	11	.987
1993—Philadelphia (N.L.)......	C	147	510	90	131	35	4	24	105	.257	117	111	5	*981	67	9	.991
1994—Philadelphia (N.L.)......	C	69	257	43	77	17	1	15	56	.300	33	43	4	435	42	3	.994
1995—Philadelphia (N.L.)......	C	98	342	44	85	19	3	9	55	.249	55	52	3	631	45	4	.994

Year Team (League)	Pos.	G	AB	R	H	2B	3B	HR	RBI	Avg.	BB	SO	SB	PO	A	E	Avg.
1996— Philadelphia (N.L.)......	OF	5	12	3	2	0	0	0	0	.167	7	5	0	6	0	0	1.000
— Clearwater (FSL)	1B	1	1	1	0	0	0	0	0	.000	0	0	0	5	1	0	1.000
1997— Philadelphia (N.L.)......	OF-DH-1B	84	269	46	71	13	6	11	42	.264	54	57	4	162	6	3	.982
— Florida (N.L.)■..........	1B-OF-DH	52	126	22	33	8	2	3	21	.262	22	17	2	229	17	4	.984
Major league totals (14 years)		1161	3630	511	891	197	25	137	588	.245	629	726	50	5834	469	74	.988

CHAMPIONSHIP SERIES RECORD

RECORDS: Shares single-game record for most bases on balls received—4 (October 10, 1993).

Year Team (League)	Pos.	G	AB	R	H	2B	3B	HR	RBI	Avg.	BB	SO	SB	PO	A	E	Avg.
1993— Philadelphia (N.L.)......	C	6	19	2	5	1	0	1	3	.263	6	3	0	54	3	0	1.000
1997— Florida (N.L.)	PH-1B	3	4	1	1	1	0	0	1	.250	1	2	0	8	1	0	1.000
Championship series totals (2 years)		9	23	3	6	2	0	1	4	.261	7	5	0	62	4	0	1.000

WORLD SERIES RECORD

NOTES: Member of World Series championship team (1997).

Year Team (League)	Pos.	G	AB	R	H	2B	3B	HR	RBI	Avg.	BB	SO	SB	PO	A	E	Avg.
1993— Philadelphia (N.L.)......	C	6	23	4	5	2	0	1	4	.217	4	5	0	31	4	0	1.000
1997— Florida (N.L.)	1B-PH-DH	7	18	7	7	2	0	1	2	.389	3	0	1	28	4	0	1.000
World Series totals (2 years)		13	41	11	12	4	0	2	6	.293	7	5	1	59	8	0	1.000

ALL-STAR GAME RECORD

Year League	Pos.	AB	R	H	2B	3B	HR	RBI	Avg.	BB	SO	SB	PO	A	E	Avg.
1992— National	C	3	1	0	0	0	0	0	.000	0	0	0	5	0	0	1.000
1993— National	C	3	0	0	0	0	0	0	.000	0	1	0	4	0	0	1.000
1995— National	C	0	0	0	0	0	0	0	...	0	0	0	3	0	0	1.000
All-Star Game totals (3 years)		6	1	0	0	0	0	0	.000	0	1	0	12	0	0	1.000

DAVEY, TOM — P — BLUE JAYS

PERSONAL: Born September 11, 1973, in Garden City, Mich. ... 6-7/215. ... Throws right, bats right. ... Full name: Thomas Joseph Davey.
HIGH SCHOOL: Plymouth-Salem (Canton, Mich.).
JUNIOR COLLEGE: Henry Ford Community College (Mich.).
TRANSACTIONS/CAREER NOTES: Selected by Toronto Blue Jays organization in fifth round of free-agent draft (June 2, 1994). ... Selected by Baltimore Orioles organization from Blue Jays organization in Rule 5 major league draft (December 9, 1996). ... Returned to Blue Jays (March 20, 1997).

Year Team (League)	W	L	Pct.	ERA	G	GS	CG	ShO	Sv.	IP	H	R	ER	BB	SO
1994— Medicine Hat (Pio.)	2	•8	.200	5.12	14	14	0	0	0	65	76	59	37	*59	35
1995— St. Catharines (NYP)	4	3	.571	3.32	7	7	0	0	0	38	27	19	14	21	29
— Hagerstown (S. Atl.)	4	1	.800	3.38	8	8	0	0	0	37 1/3	29	23	14	31	25
1996— Hagerstown (S. Atl.)	10	9	.526	3.87	26	26	2	1	0	155 2/3	132	76	67	91	98
1997— Dunedin (Fla. St.)	1	3	.250	4.31	7	6	0	0	0	39 2/3	44	21	19	15	36
— Knoxville (Southern)	6	7	.462	5.83	20	16	0	0	0	92 2/3	108	65	60	50	72

DAVIDSON, CLEATUS — 2B — TWINS

PERSONAL: Born November 1, 1976, in Bartow, Fla. ... 5-10/160. ... Bats both, throws right. ... Full name: Cleatus Lavon Davidson.
HIGH SCHOOL: Lake Wales (Fla.).
TRANSACTIONS/CAREER NOTES: Selected by Minnesota Twins organization in second round of free-agent draft (June 2, 1994).
STATISTICAL NOTES: Led Appalachian League shortstops with 33 double plays and 335 total chances in 1996. ... Led Midwest League second basemen with 271 putouts, 405 assists, 696 total chances and 98 double plays in 1997.

Year Team (League)	Pos.	G	AB	R	H	2B	3B	HR	RBI	Avg.	BB	SO	SB	PO	A	E	Avg.
1994— GC Twins (GCL).........	SS-OF	24	85	8	15	1	0	0	5	.176	9	19	3	15	65	11	.879
1995— GC Twins (GCL).........	SS-2B	21	75	11	15	2	1	0	5	.200	10	17	8	38	74	7	.941
— Elizabethton (App.).....	SS	39	152	27	45	6	2	3	27	.296	11	31	10	54	113	22	.884
1996— Fort Wayne (Midw.).....	SS	59	203	20	36	8	3	0	30	.177	23	45	2	86	185	24	.919
— Elizabethton (App.).....	SS	95	248	•53	71	10	6	6	31	.286	39	45	17	*100	*200	*35	.896
1997— Fort Wayne (Midw.).....	2B-OF	124	478	80	122	16	8	6	52	.255	52	100	39	†272	†405	20	.971

DAVIS, BEN — C — PADRES

PERSONAL: Born March 10, 1977, in San Diego. ... 6-4/195. ... Bats both, throws right. ... Full name: Benjamin Matthew Davis.
HIGH SCHOOL: Malvern Prep (Pa.).
TRANSACTIONS/CAREER NOTES: Selected by San Diego Padres organization in first round (second pick overall) of free-agent draft (June 3, 1995).

Year Team (League)	Pos.	G	AB	R	H	2B	3B	HR	RBI	Avg.	BB	SO	SB	PO	A	E	Avg.
1995— Idaho Falls (Pio.)........	C	52	197	36	55	8	3	5	46	.279	17	36	0	*362	44	6	.985
1996— Rancho Cuca. (Cal.) ...	C	98	353	35	71	10	1	6	41	.201	31	89	1	642	51	9	.987
1997— Rancho Cuca. (Cal.) ...	C-1B	122	474	67	132	30	1	17	76	.278	28	107	3	993	103	14	.987

PERSONAL: Born January 17, 1960, in Kingston, Jamaica. ... 6-3/217. ... Bats both, throws right. ... Full name: Charles Theodore Davis.
HIGH SCHOOL: Dorsey (Los Angeles).
TRANSACTIONS/CAREER NOTES: Selected by San Francisco Giants organization in 11th round of free-agent draft (June 7, 1977). ... On Phoenix disabled list (August 19-28, 1981). ... Granted free agency (November 9, 1987). ... Signed by California Angels (December 1, 1987). ... On disabled list (July 17-August 9, 1990). ... Granted free agency (December 7, 1990). ... Signed by Minnesota Twins (January 29, 1991). ... Granted free agency (November 3, 1992). ... Signed by Angels (December 11, 1992). ... On disabled list (June 20-July 18, 1995). ... Traded by Angels to Kansas City Royals for P Mark Gubicza and P Mike Bovee (October 28, 1996). ... On disabled list (March 23-April 14, 1997). ... Granted free agency (October 29, 1997). ... Signed by New York Yankees (December 10, 1997).
RECORDS: Shares A.L. single-season record for most games with switch-hit home runs—2 (1994).
STATISTICAL NOTES: Switch-hit home runs in one game 10 times (June 5, 1983; June 27 and September 15, 1987; July 30, 1988; July 1, 1989; October 2, 1992; May 11 and July 30, 1994; August 21, 1996 and June 7, 1997). ... Tied for A.L. lead with 10 sacrifice flies in 1988. ... Career major league grand slams: 7.
MISCELLANEOUS: Original nickname was Chili Bowl, which was prompted by a friend who saw Davis after he received a haircut in the sixth grade. The nickname was later shortened to Chili.

Year Team (League)	Pos.	G	AB	R	H	2B	3B	HR	RBI	Avg.	BB	SO	SB	PO	A	E	Avg.
1978—Cedar Rap. (Midw.)....	C-OF	124	424	63	119	18	5	16	73	.281	36	103	15	365	45	25	.943
1979—Fresno (California)....	OF-C	134	490	91	132	24	5	21	95	.269	80	91	30	339	43	20	.950
1980—Shreveport (Texas)....	OF-C	129	442	50	130	30	4	12	67	.294	52	94	19	184	20	12	.944
1981—San Francisco (N.L.) ..	OF	8	15	1	2	0	0	0	0	.133	1	2	2	7	0	0	1.000
—Phoenix (PCL)...........	OF	88	334	76	117	16	6	19	75	.350	46	54	40	175	7	6	.968
1982—San Francisco (N.L.) ..	OF	154	641	86	167	27	6	19	76	.261	45	115	24	404	•16	12	.972
1983—San Francisco (N.L.) ..	OF	137	486	54	113	21	2	11	59	.233	55	108	10	357	7	9	.976
—Phoenix (PCL)...........	OF	10	44	12	13	2	0	2	9	.295	4	6	5	15	0	2	.882
1984—San Francisco (N.L.) ..	OF	137	499	87	157	21	6	21	81	.315	42	74	12	292	9	9	.971
1985—San Francisco (N.L.) ..	OF	136	481	53	130	25	2	13	56	.270	62	74	15	279	10	6	.980
1986—San Francisco (N.L.) ..	OF	153	526	71	146	28	3	13	70	.278	84	96	16	303	9	•9	.972
1987—San Francisco (N.L.) ..	OF	149	500	80	125	22	1	24	76	.250	72	109	16	265	6	7	.975
1988—California (A.L.)■.....	OF-DH	158	600	81	161	29	3	21	93	.268	56	118	9	299	10	*19	.942
1989—California (A.L.).........	OF-DH	154	560	81	152	24	1	22	90	.271	61	109	3	270	5	6	.979
1990—California (A.L.).........	DH-OF	113	412	58	109	17	1	12	58	.265	61	89	1	77	5	3	.965
1991—Minnesota (A.L.)■	DH-OF	153	534	84	148	34	1	29	93	.277	95	117	5	2	0	0	1.000
1992—Minnesota (A.L.)	DH-OF-1B	138	444	63	128	27	2	12	66	.288	73	76	4	6	0	0	1.000
1993—California (A.L.).........	DH-P	153	573	74	139	32	0	27	112	.243	71	135	4	0	0	0	....
1994—California (A.L.).........	DH-OF	108	392	72	122	18	1	26	84	.311	69	84	3	5	0	0	1.000
1995—California (A.L.).........	DH	119	424	81	135	23	0	20	86	.318	89	79	3	...	...	...	...
1996—California (A.L.).........	DH	145	530	73	155	24	0	28	95	.292	86	99	5	...	...	...	...
1997—Kansas City (A.L.)■ ...	DH	140	477	71	133	20	0	30	90	.279	85	96	6	...	...	...	...
American League totals (10 years)		1381	4946	738	1382	248	9	227	867	.279	746	1002	43	659	20	28	.960
National League totals (7 years)		874	3148	432	840	144	20	101	418	.267	361	578	95	1907	57	52	.974
Major league totals (17 years)		2255	8094	1170	2222	392	29	328	1285	.275	1107	1580	138	2566	77	80	.971

CHAMPIONSHIP SERIES RECORD

Year Team (League)	Pos.	G	AB	R	H	2B	3B	HR	RBI	Avg.	BB	SO	SB	PO	A	E	Avg.
1987—San Francisco (N.L.) ..	OF	6	20	2	3	1	0	0	0	.150	1	4	0	11	1	1	.923
1991—Minnesota (A.L.)	DH	5	17	3	5	2	0	0	2	.294	5	8	1	...	...	...	...
Championship series totals (2 years)		11	37	5	8	3	0	0	2	.216	6	12	1	11	1	1	.923

WORLD SERIES RECORD

NOTES: Member of World Series championship team (1991).

Year Team (League)	Pos.	G	AB	R	H	2B	3B	HR	RBI	Avg.	BB	SO	SB	PO	A	E	Avg.
1991—Minnesota (A.L.)	DH-PH-OF	6	18	4	4	0	0	2	4	.222	2	3	0	1	0	0	1.000

ALL-STAR GAME RECORD

Year League	Pos.	AB	R	H	2B	3B	HR	RBI	Avg.	BB	SO	SB	PO	A	E	Avg.
1984—National	PH	1	0	0	0	0	0	0	.000	0	0	0	...	...	...	...
1986—National	OF	1	0	0	0	0	0	0	.000	0	1	0	0	0	0	...
1994—American	PH	1	0	0	0	0	0	0	.000	0	0	0	...	...	...	...
All-Star Game totals (3 years)		3	0	0	0	0	0	0	.000	0	1	0	0	0	0	...

RECORD AS PITCHER

Year Team (League)	W	L	Pct.	ERA	G	GS	CG	ShO	Sv.	IP	H	R	ER	BB	SO
1993—California (A.L.)■..............	0	0	...	0.00	1	0	0	0	0	2	0	0	0	0	0

PERSONAL: Born May 29, 1962, in Los Angeles. ... 6-3/185. ... Bats right, throws right. ... Full name: Eric Keith Davis.
HIGH SCHOOL: Fremont (Los Angeles).
TRANSACTIONS/CAREER NOTES: Selected by Cincinnati Reds organization in eighth round of free-agent draft (June 3, 1980). ... On Cincinnati disabled list (August 16-September 1, 1984; May 3-18, 1989; April 25-May 19, 1990; June 12-27 and July 31, 1991). ... Traded by Reds with P Kip Gross to Los Angeles Dodgers for P Tim Belcher and P John Wetteland (November 27, 1991). ... On disabled list (May 23-June 19 and August 2-25, 1992). ... Granted free agency (November 3, 1992). ... Re-signed by Dodgers (December 1, 1992). ... Traded by Dodgers to Detroit Tigers for a player to be named later (August 31, 1993); Dodgers acquired P John DeSilva to complete deal (September 7, 1993). ... Granted free agency (October 28, 1993). ... Re-signed by Tigers (November 1, 1993). ... On disabled list (May 23-July 19 and July 27, 1994-remainder of season). ... Granted free agency (October 20, 1994). ... On retired list (October 20, 1994-January 2,

1996). ... Signed by Reds organization (January 2, 1996). ... On disabled list (May 26-June 10, 1996). ... Granted free agency (October 28, 1996). ... Signed by Baltimore Orioles (December 19, 1996). ... On disabled list (May 26-September 15, 1997).

RECORDS: Holds major league career record for highest stolen-base percentage (300 or more attempts)—.861. ... Shares major league record for most grand slams in two consecutive games—2 (May 4 and 5, 1996); and most strikeouts in two consecutive games—9 (April 24 [4] and 25 [5], 1987, 21 innings). ... Shares major league single-month record for most grand slams—3 (May 1987). ... Holds N.L. career record for highest stolen-base percentage (300 or more attempts)—.861. ... Shares major league record for most grand slams in two consecutive games—2 (August 13 and 14, 1991).

HONORS: Named outfielder on THE SPORTING NEWS N.L. All-Star team (1987 and 1989). ... Named outfielder on THE SPORTING NEWS N.L. Silver Slugger team (1987 and 1989). ... Won N.L. Gold Glove as outfielder (1987-89). ... Named N.L. Comeback Player of the Year by THE SPORTING NEWS (1996).

STATISTICAL NOTES: Hit three home runs in one game (September 10, 1986 and May 3, 1987). ... Led N.L. outfielders with 394 total chances in 1987. ... Led N.L. with 21 game-winning RBIs in 1988. ... Hit for the cycle (June 2, 1989). ... Career major league grand slams: 9.

							BATTING							FIELDING			
Year Team (League)	Pos.	G	AB	R	H	2B	3B	HR	RBI	Avg.	BB	SO	SB	PO	A	E	Avg.
1980— Eugene (Northwest) ...	SS-2B-OF	33	73	12	16	1	0	1	11	.219	14	26	10	29	36	11	.855
1981— Eugene (Northwest) ...	OF	62	214	*67	69	10	4	11	39	.322	57	59	*40	94	11	4	.963
1982— Cedar Rap. (Midw.)	OF	111	434	80	120	20	5	15	56	.276	51	103	53	239	9	9	.965
1983— Waterbury (Eastern)...	OF	89	293	56	85	13	1	15	43	.290	65	75	39	214	8	2	.991
— Indianapolis (A.A.).....	OF	19	77	18	23	4	0	7	19	.299	8	22	9	61	1	1	.984
1984— Wichita (A.A.)............	OF	52	194	42	61	9	5	14	34	.314	25	55	27	110	5	5	.958
— Cincinnati (N.L.)..........	OF	57	174	33	39	10	1	10	30	.224	24	48	10	125	4	1	.992
1985— Cincinnati (N.L.)...........	OF	56	122	26	30	3	3	8	18	.246	7	39	16	75	3	1	.987
— Denver (A.A.).............	OF	64	206	48	57	10	2	15	38	.277	29	67	35	94	5	3	.971
1986— Cincinnati (N.L.)........	OF	132	415	97	115	15	3	27	71	.277	68	100	80	274	2	7	.975
1987— Cincinnati (N.L.)........	OF	129	474	120	139	23	4	37	100	.293	84	134	50	*380	10	4	.990
1988— Cincinnati (N.L.)........	OF	135	472	81	129	18	3	26	93	.273	65	124	35	300	2	6	.981
1989— Cincinnati (N.L.)........	OF	131	462	74	130	14	2	34	101	.281	68	116	21	298	2	5	.984
1990— Cincinnati (N.L.)........	OF	127	453	84	118	26	2	24	86	.260	60	100	21	257	11	2	.993
1991— Cincinnati (N.L.)........	OF	89	285	39	67	10	0	11	33	.235	48	92	14	190	5	3	.985
1992— Los Angeles (N.L.)■..	OF	76	267	21	61	8	1	5	32	.228	36	71	19	123	0	5	.961
1993— Los Angeles (N.L.)	OF	108	376	57	88	17	0	14	53	.234	41	88	33	221	7	2	.991
— Detroit (A.L.)■..........	OF-DH	23	75	14	19	1	1	6	15	.253	14	18	2	52	0	1	.981
1994— Detroit (A.L.)	OF	37	120	19	22	4	0	3	13	.183	18	45	5	85	1	1	.989
1995—								Did not play.									
1996— Cincinnati (N.L.)■......	OF-1B	129	415	81	119	20	0	26	83	.287	70	121	23	279	3	3	.989
1997— Baltimore (A.L.)■......	OF-DH	42	158	29	48	11	0	8	25	.304	14	47	6	39	0	1	.975
American League totals (3 years)		102	353	62	89	16	1	17	53	.252	46	110	13	176	1	3	.983
National League totals (11 years)		1169	3915	713	1035	164	19	222	700	.264	571	1033	322	2522	49	39	.985
Major league totals (13 years)		1271	4268	775	1124	180	20	239	753	.263	617	1143	335	2698	50	42	.985

DIVISION SERIES RECORD

							BATTING							FIELDING			
Year Team (League)	Pos.	G	AB	R	H	2B	3B	HR	RBI	Avg.	BB	SO	SB	PO	A	E	Avg.
1997— Baltimore (A.L.).........	OF	3	9	0	2	0	0	0	2	.222	0	5	0	1	0	0	1.000

CHAMPIONSHIP SERIES RECORD

							BATTING							FIELDING			
Year Team (League)	Pos.	G	AB	R	H	2B	3B	HR	RBI	Avg.	BB	SO	SB	PO	A	E	Avg.
1990— Cincinnati (N.L.)	OF	6	23	2	4	1	0	0	2	.174	1	9	0	12	1	0	1.000
1997— Baltimore (A.L.)	OF-DH	6	13	1	2	0	0	1	1	.154	1	3	0	3	0	0	1.000
Championship series totals (2 years)		12	36	3	6	1	0	1	3	.167	2	12	0	15	1	0	1.000

WORLD SERIES RECORD

NOTES: Hit home run in first at-bat (October 16, 1990). ... Member of World Series championship team (1990).

							BATTING							FIELDING			
Year Team (League)	Pos.	G	AB	R	H	2B	3B	HR	RBI	Avg.	BB	SO	SB	PO	A	E	Avg.
1990— Cincinnati (N.L.)	OF	4	14	3	4	0	0	1	5	.286	0	0	0	4	0	0	1.000

ALL-STAR GAME RECORD

						BATTING							FIELDING			
Year League	Pos.	AB	R	H	2B	3B	HR	RBI	Avg.	BB	SO	SB	PO	A	E	Avg.
1987— National	OF	3	0	0	0	0	0	0	.000	0	1	0	1	0	0	1.000
1989— National	OF	2	0	0	0	0	0	0	.000	1	0	1	1	0	0	1.000
All-Star Game totals (2 years)		5	0	0	0	0	0	0	.000	1	1	1	2	0	0	1.000

DAVIS, JEFF — P — RANGERS

PERSONAL: Born August 20, 1972, in Fall River, Mass. ... 6-0/170. ... Throws right, bats right. ... Full name: Jeff Marc Davis.
HIGH SCHOOL: Durfee (Fall River, Mass.).
JUNIOR COLLEGE: Massasoit Community College (Mass.).
TRANSACTIONS/CAREER NOTES: Selected by Texas Rangers organization in 28th round of free-agent draft (June 3, 1993). ... On disabled list (June 25-September 17, 1996). ... On Tulsa disabled list (June 4-12 and June 16, 1997-remainder of season).

Year Team (League)	W	L	Pct.	ERA	G	GS	CG	ShO	Sv.	IP	H	R	ER	BB	SO
1993— Erie (N.Y.-Penn)................	0	5	.000	3.65	27	0	0	0	13	37	32	18	15	10	41
1994— Charleston, S.C. (S. Atl.)	2	3	.400	3.99	45	0	0	0	19	49²/₃	53	25	22	11	72
1995— Charlotte (Fla. St.).............	12	7	.632	2.89	26	.26	0	0	0	165¹/₃	159	74	53	37	105
— Tulsa (Texas)...................	1	0	1.000	0.00	1	1	0	0	0	7	2	0	0	1	4
1996— Tulsa (Texas)...................	7	2	.778	4.59	16	15	3	0	0	98	110	57	50	20	51
1997— Tulsa (Texas)...................	4	6	.400	3.65	11	11	2	•1	0	69	76	41	28	17	25

D

DAVIS, KANE — P — PIRATES

PERSONAL: Born June 25, 1975, in Ripley, W.Va. ... 6-3/190. ... Throws right, bats right. ... Full name: Kane Thomas Davis.
HIGH SCHOOL: Spencer (W.Va.).
TRANSACTIONS/CAREER NOTES: Selected by Pittsburgh Pirates organization in 13th round of free-agent draft (June 3, 1993).

Year Team (League)	W	L	Pct.	ERA	G	GS	CG	ShO	Sv.	IP	H	R	ER	BB	SO
1993— GC Pirates (GCL)	0	4	.000	7.07	11	4	0	0	0	28	34	30	22	19	24
1994— Welland (N.Y.-Penn)	5	5	.500	2.65	15	•15	0	0	0	98 1/3	90	36	29	32	74
1995— Augusta (S. Atl.)	12	6	.667	3.75	26	25	1	0	0	139 1/3	136	73	58	43	78
1996— Lynchburg (Carolina)	11	9	.550	4.29	26	26	3	1	0	157 1/3	160	84	75	56	116
1997— Carolina (Southern)	0	3	.000	3.77	6	6	0	0	0	28 2/3	22	17	12	16	23

DAVIS, MARK — P — DIAMONDBACKS

PERSONAL: Born October 19, 1960, in Livermore, Calif. ... 6-4/215. ... Throws left, bats left. ... Full name: Mark William Davis.
HIGH SCHOOL: Granada (Livermore, Calif.).
COLLEGE: Chabot College (Calif.).
TRANSACTIONS/CAREER NOTES: Selected by New York Mets organization in 21st round of free-agent draft (June 6, 1978); did not sign. ... Selected by Philadelphia Phillies organization in secondary phase of free-agent draft (January 9, 1979). ... On Oklahoma City disabled list (April 14-June 11, 1981 and August 3-30, 1982). ... Traded by Phillies organization with P Mike Krukow and OF Charles Penigar to San Francisco Giants for 2B Joe Morgan and P Al Holland (December 14, 1982). ... Traded by Giants with 3B Chris Brown, P Keith Comstock and P Mark Grant to San Diego Padres for P Dave Dravecky, P Craig Lefferts and IF Kevin Mitchell (July 4, 1987). ... Granted free agency (November 13, 1989). ... Signed by Kansas City Royals (December 11, 1989). ... On disabled list (August 10-September 5, 1990). ... On Kansas City disabled list (April 20-May 5 and June 18-August 5, 1991); included rehabilitation assignment to Omaha (July 6-August 4). ... Traded by Royals to Atlanta Braves for P Juan Berenguer (July 21, 1992). ... Traded by Braves to Philadelphia Phillies for P Brad Hassinger (April 13, 1993). ... Released by Phillies (July 2, 1993). ... Signed by Padres (July 10, 1993). ... Released by Padres (May 24, 1994). ... Signed by Brevard County, Florida Marlins organization (July 30, 1995). ... Granted free agency (October 16, 1995). ... Re-signed by Marlins organization (December 13, 1995). ... Released by Charlotte, Marlins organization (March 23, 1996). ... Signed by Arizona Diamondbacks organization (February 7, 1997). ... Loaned by Diamondbacks to Tucson, Milwaukee Brewers organization (July 1-August 14, 1997). ... Traded by Diamondbacks organization to Brewers for a player to be named later (August 14, 1997). ... Granted free agency (October 30, 1997). ... Signed by Diamondbacks organization (January 11, 1998).
HONORS: Named Eastern League Most Valuable Player (1980). ... Named N.L. Pitcher of the Year by The Sporting News (1989). ... Named N.L. Fireman of the Year by The Sporting News (1989). ... Named lefthanded pitcher on The Sporting News N.L. All-Star team (1989). ... Named N.L. Cy Young Award winner by Baseball Writers' Association of America (1989).
STATISTICAL NOTES: Led Western Carolinas League with 18 home runs allowed and tied for lead with five balks in 1979.

Year Team (League)	W	L	Pct.	ERA	G	GS	CG	ShO	Sv.	IP	H	R	ER	BB	SO
1979— Spartan. (W. Car.)	11	9	.550	3.20	26	26	9	•5	0	166	147	76	59	49	135
1980— Reading (Eastern)	*19	6	.760	*2.47	28	•28	8	•4	0	*193	140	63	53	75	*185
— Philadelphia (N.L.)	0	0	. . .	2.57	2	1	0	0	0	7	4	2	2	5	5
1981— Oklahoma City (A.A.)	5	2	.714	3.88	13	13	1	0	0	65	66	34	28	47	56
— Philadelphia (N.L.)	1	4	.200	7.74	9	9	0	0	0	43	49	37	37	24	29
1982— Oklahoma City (A.A.)	5	12	.294	6.24	21	19	3	1	0	96 2/3	111	75	67	50	95
1983— Phoenix (PCL)■	6	3	.667	6.32	13	13	1	1	0	72 2/3	89	57	51	33	64
— San Francisco (N.L.)	6	4	.600	3.49	20	20	2	2	0	111	93	51	43	50	83
1984— San Francisco (N.L.)	5	17	.227	5.36	46	27	1	0	0	174 2/3	201	113	*104	54	124
1985— San Francisco (N.L.)	5	12	.294	3.54	77	1	0	0	7	114 1/3	89	49	45	41	131
1986— San Francisco (N.L.)	5	7	.417	2.99	67	2	0	0	4	84 1/3	63	33	28	34	90
1987— San Francisco (N.L.)■	4	5	.444	4.71	20	11	1	0	0	70 2/3	72	38	37	28	51
— San Diego (N.L.)	5	3	.625	3.18	43	0	0	0	2	62 1/3	51	26	22	31	47
1988— San Diego (N.L.)	5	10	.333	2.01	62	0	0	0	28	98 1/3	70	24	22	42	102
1989— San Diego (N.L.)	4	3	.571	1.85	70	0	0	0	*44	92 2/3	66	21	19	31	92
1990— Kansas City (A.L.)■	2	7	.222	5.11	53	3	0	0	6	68 2/3	71	43	39	52	73
1991— Kansas City (A.L.)	6	3	.667	4.45	29	5	0	0	1	62 2/3	55	36	31	39	47
— Omaha (Am. Assoc.)	4	1	.800	2.02	6	6	0	0	0	35 2/3	27	11	8	9	36
1992— Kansas City (A.L.)	1	3	.250	7.18	13	6	0	0	0	36 1/3	42	31	29	28	19
— Atlanta (N.L.)■	1	0	1.000	7.02	14	0	0	0	0	16 2/3	22	13	13	13	15
1993— Philadelphia (N.L.)■	1	2	.333	5.17	25	0	0	0	0	31 1/3	35	22	18	24	28
— San Diego (N.L.)■	0	3	.000	3.52	35	0	0	0	4	38 1/3	44	15	15	20	42
1994— San Diego (N.L.)	0	1	.000	8.82	20	0	0	0	0	16 1/3	20	18	16	13	15
1995— Brevard County (FSL)■	0	0	. . .	0.00	3	0	0	0	0	5	2	0	0	0	4
— Charlotte (Int'l)	0	0	. . .	5.00	9	0	0	0	0	9	13	8	5	1	5
1996—							Did not play.								
1997— High Desert (Calif.)■	3	1	.750	2.66	16	0	0	0	0	20 1/3	17	6	6	4	28
— Tucson (PCL)■	0	2	.000	3.57	17	0	0	0	2	22 2/3	19	9	9	12	19
— Milwaukee (A.L.)	0	0	. . .	5.51	19	0	0	0	0	16 1/3	21	10	10	5	14
A.L. totals (4 years)	9	13	.409	5.33	114	14	0	0	7	184	189	120	109	124	153
N.L. totals (12 years)	42	71	.372	3.94	510	71	4	2	89	961	879	462	421	410	854
Major league totals (15 years)	51	84	.378	4.17	624	85	4	2	96	1145	1068	582	530	534	1007

ALL-STAR GAME RECORD

Year League	W	L	Pct.	ERA	GS	CG	ShO	Sv.	IP	H	R	ER	BB	SO
1988— National	0	0	. . .	0.00	0	0	0	0	2/3	1	0	0	0	0
1989— National	0	0	. . .	0.00	0	0	0	0	1	0	0	0	0	2
All-Star totals (2 years)	0	0	. . .	0.00	0	0	0	0	1 2/3	1	0	0	0	2

DAVIS, RUSS — 3B — MARINERS

PERSONAL: Born September 13, 1969, in Birmingham, Ala. ... 6-0/195. ... Bats right, throws right. ... Full name: Russell Stuart Davis.
HIGH SCHOOL: Hueytown (Ala.).
JUNIOR COLLEGE: Shelton State Junior College (Ala.).

TRANSACTIONS/CAREER NOTES: Selected by New York Yankees organization in 29th round of free-agent draft (June 1, 1988). ... On disabled list (July 13-August 1, 1993). ... On Columbus disabled list (April 7-15 and August 26, 1994-remainder of season). ... Traded by Yankees with P Sterling Hitchcock to Seattle Mariners for 1B Tino Martinez, P Jeff Nelson and P Jim Mecir (December 7, 1995). ... On disabled list (June 8, 1996-remainder of season and August 25-September 26, 1997).
HONORS: Named Eastern League Most Valuable Player (1992).
STATISTICAL NOTES: Tied for New York-Pennsylvania League lead with 11 double plays by third baseman in 1989. ... Led Carolina League third basemen with 336 total chances and 18 double plays in 1990. ... Tied for Eastern League lead with .917 fielding percentage, 83 putouts, 205 assists, 26 errors and 314 total chances by third basemen in 1991. ... Led Eastern League with 237 total bases and .483 slugging percentage in 1992. ... Led International League third basemen with 25 errors in 1993.

							BATTING								FIELDING		
Year	Team (League)	Pos.	G	AB	R	H	2B	3B	HR	RBI	Avg.	BB	SO	SB	PO	A	E	Avg.
1988— GC Yankees (GCL)......		2B-3B	58	213	33	49	11	3	2	30	.230	16	39	6	64	105	15	.918
1989— Fort Lauderdale (FSL)		3B-2B	48	147	8	27	5	1	2	22	.184	11	38	3	32	72	17	.860
— Oneonta (NYP)...........		3B	65	236	33	68	7	5	7	42	.288	19	44	3	27	87	17	.870
1990— Prince William (Car.) ..		3B	137	510	55	127	*37	3	16	71	.249	37	136	3	*68	*244	24	.929
1991— Alb./Colon. (Eastern)..		3B-2B	135	473	57	103	23	3	8	58	.218	50	102	3	‡83	‡206	‡26	‡.917
1992— Alb./Colon. (Eastern)..		3B	132	491	77	140	23	4	22	71	.285	49	93	3	78	185	23	.920
1993— Columbus (Int'l)		3B-SS	113	424	63	108	24	1	26	83	.255	40	118	1	85	245	†26	.927
1994— Columbus (Int'l)		3B-1B	117	416	76	115	30	2	25	69	.276	62	93	3	86	250	23	.936
— New York (A.L.).........		3B	4	14	0	2	0	0	0	1	.143	0	4	0	2	6	0	1.000
1995— Columbus (Int'l)		3B-1B	20	76	12	19	4	1	2	15	.250	17	23	0	17	31	7	.873
— New York (A.L.)		3B-DH-1B	40	98	14	27	5	2	2	12	.276	10	26	0	16	45	2	.968
1996— Seattle (A.L.)■......		3B	51	167	24	39	9	0	5	18	.234	17	50	2	31	67	7	.933
1997— Seattle (A.L.)		3B-DH	119	420	57	114	29	1	20	63	.271	27	100	6	56	219	18	.939
Major league totals (4 years)			214	699	95	182	43	3	27	94	.260	54	180	8	105	337	27	.942

DIVISION SERIES RECORD

							BATTING								FIELDING		
Year	Team (League)	Pos.	G	AB	R	H	2B	3B	HR	RBI	Avg.	BB	SO	SB	PO	A	E	Avg.
1995— New York (A.L.)..........		3B	2	5	0	1	0	0	0	0	.200	0	2	0	0	1	0	1.000

DAVIS, TIM   P   MARINERS

PERSONAL: Born July 14, 1970, in Marianna, Fla. ... 5-11/165. ... Throws left, bats left. ... Full name: Timothy Howard Davis.
HIGH SCHOOL: Liberty County (Bristol, Fla.).
JUNIOR COLLEGE: Gulf Coast Community College (Fla.).
COLLEGE: Florida State.
TRANSACTIONS/CAREER NOTES: Selected by Minnesota Twins organization in 34th round of free-agent draft (June 3, 1991); did not sign. ... Selected by Seattle Mariners organization in sixth round of free-agent draft (June 1, 1992). ... On Tacoma disabled list (June 7-September 8, 1995). ... On Seattle disabled list (September 8, 1995-remainder of season). ... On Seattle disabled list (May 27-July 11, 1996); included rehabilitation assignment to Everett (July 8-11). ... On Seattle disabled list (April 24, 1997-remainder of season).

Year	Team (League)	W	L	Pct.	ERA	G	GS	CG	ShO	Sv.	IP	H	R	ER	BB	SO
1993— Appleton (Midwest)............		10	2	.833	1.85	16	10	3	2	2	77 2/3	54	20	16	33	89
— Riverside (California)..........		3	0	1.000	1.76	18	0	0	0	7	30 2/3	14	6	6	9	56
1994— Seattle (A.L.)		2	2	.500	4.01	42	1	0	0	2	49 1/3	57	25	22	25	28
— Calgary (PCL).......................		3	1	.750	1.82	6	6	1	0	0	39 2/3	35	13	8	8	43
1995— Seattle (A.L.)		2	1	.667	6.38	5	5	0	0	0	24	30	21	17	18	19
— Tacoma (PCL)		0	1	.000	5.40	2	2	0	0	0	13 1/3	15	8	8	4	13
1996— Tacoma (PCL)		0	1	.000	5.29	8	1	0	0	0	17	19	12	10	10	19
— Seattle (A.L.)		2	2	.500	4.01	40	0	0	0	0	42 2/3	43	21	19	17	34
— Everett (Northwest)............		0	0	. . .	0.00	1	1	0	0	0	2	0	0	0	1	5
1997— Tacoma (PCL)		1	0	1.000	3.60	1	1	0	0	0	5	4	2	2	3	5
— Seattle (A.L.)		0	0	. . .	6.75	2	0	0	0	0	6 2/3	6	5	5	4	10
Major league totals (4 years)......		6	5	.545	4.62	89	6	0	0	2	122 2/3	136	72	63	64	91

DECKER, STEVE   C   PIRATES

PERSONAL: Born October 25, 1965, in Rock Island, Ill. ... 6-3/220. ... Bats right, throws right. ... Full name: Steven Michael Decker.
HIGH SCHOOL: Rock Island (Ill.).
COLLEGE: Lewis-Clark State College (Idaho).
TRANSACTIONS/CAREER NOTES: Selected by San Francisco Giants organization in 21st round of free-agent draft (June 1, 1988). ... Selected by Florida Marlins in second round (35th pick overall) of expansion draft (November 17, 1992). ... On disabled list (May 18, 1993-remainder of season). ... On disabled list (April 8-May 14, 1994). ... Granted free agency (October 16, 1995). ... Signed by San Francisco Giants (April 5, 1996). ... Contract sold to Colorado Rockies (August 21, 1996). ... Released by Rockies (March 26, 1997). ... Signed by Tacoma, Seattle Mariners organization (April 4, 1997). ... Released by Mariners (September 3, 1997). ... Signed by Pittsburgh Pirates (November 24, 1997).
STATISTICAL NOTES: Led Pacific Coast League catchers with 626 putouts and 694 total chances in 1992.

							BATTING								FIELDING		
Year	Team (League)	Pos.	G	AB	R	H	2B	3B	HR	RBI	Avg.	BB	SO	SB	PO	A	E	Avg.
1988— Everett (N'west).........		C	13	42	11	22	2	0	2	13	.524	7	5	0	37	3	2	.952
— San Jose (Calif.)........		C	47	175	31	56	9	0	4	34	.320	21	21	0	199	26	5	.978
1989— San Jose (Calif.).........		C-1B	64	225	27	65	12	0	3	46	.289	44	36	8	417	51	7	.985
— Shreveport (Texas).....		C	44	142	19	46	8	0	1	18	.324	11	24	0	229	22	5	.980
1990— Shreveport (Texas).....		C	116	403	52	118	22	1	15	80	.293	40	64	3	650	71	10	.986
— San Francisco (N.L.) ..		C	15	54	5	16	2	0	3	8	.296	1	10	0	75	11	1	.989
1991— San Francisco (N.L.) ..		C	79	233	11	48	7	1	5	24	.206	16	44	0	385	41	7	.984
— Phoenix (PCL)...........		C	31	111	20	28	5	1	6	14	.252	13	29	0	156	16	1	.994
1992— Phoenix (PCL)...........		C-1B	125	450	50	127	22	2	8	74	.282	47	64	2	†650	65	5	.993
— San Francisco (N.L.) ..		C	15	43	3	7	1	0	0	1	.163	6	7	0	94	4	0	1.000

Year Team (League)	Pos.	G	AB	R	H	2B	3B	HR	RBI	Avg.	BB	SO	SB	PO	A	E	Avg.
1993—Florida (N.L.)■..........	C	8	15	0	0	0	0	0	1	.000	3	3	0	28	2	1	.968
1994—Edmonton (PCL)	C-1B	73	259	38	101	23	0	11	48	.390	27	24	0	295	34	8	.976
1995—Florida (N.L.)............	C-1B	51	133	12	30	2	1	3	13	.226	19	22	1	299	24	5	.985
1996—San Fran. (N.L.)■.......	C-1B-3B	57	122	16	28	1	0	1	12	.230	15	26	0	203	17	0	1.000
—Colo. Springs (PCL)■	C	7	25	4	10	1	0	0	3	.400	4	3	0	56	4	1	.984
—Colorado (N.L.)	C	10	25	8	8	2	0	1	8	.320	3	3	1	51	6	0	1.000
1997—Tacoma (PCL)■........	C-3B-1B	99	350	44	104	25	1	10	52	.297	22	37	0	400	68	6	.987
Major league totals (6 years)		235	625	55	137	15	2	13	67	.219	63	115	2	1135	105	14	.989

DeHART, RICK — P — EXPOS

PERSONAL: Born March 21, 1970, in Topeka, Kan. ... 6-1/180. ... Throws left, bats left. ... Full name: Richard Allen DeHart.
HIGH SCHOOL: Seaman (Topeka, Kan.).
COLLEGE: Washburn.
TRANSACTIONS/CAREER NOTES: Signed as non-drafted free agent by Montreal Expos organization (March 24, 1992).

Year Team (League)	W	L	Pct.	ERA	G	GS	CG	ShO	Sv.	IP	H	R	ER	BB	SO
1992—Albany (S. Atl.)................	9	6	.600	2.46	38	10	1	1	3	117	91	42	32	40	133
1993—San Bernardino (Calif.).......	4	3	.571	3.04	9	9	0	0	0	53 1/3	56	26	18	25	44
—Harrisburg (Eastern)	2	4	.333	7.68	12	7	0	0	0	34	45	31	29	19	18
—W.P. Beach (FSL)...............	1	3	.250	3.00	7	7	1	1	0	42	42	14	14	17	33
1994—W.P. Beach (FSL).............	9	7	.563	3.37	30	20	3	2	0	136 1/3	132	61	51	34	68
1995—Harrisburg (Eastern)	6	7	.462	4.84	35	12	0	0	0	93	94	62	50	39	64
1996—Harrisburg (Eastern)	1	2	.333	2.68	30	2	0	0	1	43 2/3	46	19	13	19	30
1997—Ottawa (Int'l)...................	0	4	.000	4.00	43	0	0	0	2	63	60	33	28	22	57
—Montreal (N.L.).................	2	1	.667	5.52	23	0	0	0	0	29 1/3	33	21	18	14	29
Major league totals (1 year)........	2	1	.667	5.52	23	0	0	0	0	29 1/3	33	21	18	14	29

DeJEAN, MIKE — P — ROCKIES

PERSONAL: Born September 28, 1970, in Baton Rouge, La. ... 6-2/205. ... Throws right, bats right. ... Full name: Michel DeJean.
HIGH SCHOOL: Walker (La.).
COLLEGE: Livingston (La.).
TRANSACTIONS/CAREER NOTES: Selected by New York Yankees organization in 24th round of free-agent draft (June 1, 1992). ... On disabled list (June 4-July 21 and July 26, 1993-remainder of season). ... Traded by Yankees with a player to be named later to Colorado Rockies for C Joe Girardi (November 20, 1995); Rockies acquired P Steve Shoemaker to complete deal (December 6, 1995). ... On disabled list (July 18-August 8, 1997); included rehabilitation assignment to New Haven (July 30-August 8).

Year Team (League)	W	L	Pct.	ERA	G	GS	CG	ShO	Sv.	IP	H	R	ER	BB	SO
1992—Oneonta (N.Y.-Penn)	0	0	...	0.44	20	0	0	0	16	20 2/3	12	3	1	3	20
1993—Greensboro (S. Atl.)	2	3	.400	5.00	20	0	0	0	9	18	22	12	10	8	16
1994—Tampa (Florida State)........	0	2	.000	2.38	34	0	0	0	16	34	39	15	9	13	22
—Albany (Eastern)................	0	2	.000	4.38	16	0	0	0	4	24 2/3	22	14	12	15	13
1995—Norwich (Eastern)	5	5	.500	2.99	59	0	0	0	20	78 1/3	58	29	26	34	57
1996—Colo. Springs (PCL)■.......	0	2	.000	5.13	30	0	0	0	1	40 1/3	52	24	23	21	31
—New Haven (Eastern).........	0	0	...	3.22	16	0	0	0	11	22 1/3	20	9	8	8	12
1997—Colo. Springs (PCL)	0	1	.000	5.40	10	0	0	0	4	10	17	6	6	7	9
—Colorado (N.L.)	5	0	1.000	3.99	55	0	0	0	2	67 2/3	74	34	30	24	38
—New Haven (Eastern).........	0	1	.000	6.00	2	0	0	0	0	3	3	2	2	2	2
Major league totals (1 year)........	5	0	1.000	3.99	55	0	0	0	2	67 2/3	74	34	30	24	38

DE LA CRUZ, YNOCENCIO — P — DIAMONDBACKS

PERSONAL: Born February 28, 1977, in Puerta Plata, Dominican Republic. ... 6-2/160. ... Throws right, bats right.
TRANSACTIONS/CAREER NOTES: Signed as non-drafted free agent by New York Mets organization (October 14, 1993). ... Selected by Arizona Diamondbacks from Mets organization in Rule 5 major league draft (December 15, 1997).

Year Team (League)	W	L	Pct.	ERA	G	GS	CG	ShO	Sv.	IP	H	R	ER	BB	SO
1994—Dom. Mets (DSL)..............	4	1	.800	4.55	14	10	1	0	1	57 1/3	68	42	29	23	32
1995—Dom. Mets (DSL)..............	5	1	.833	3.38	14	13	3	0	0	69 1/3	69	36	26	24	60
1996—Dom. Mets (DSL)..............	2	0	1.000	2.38	7	5	1	0	0	34	30	19	9	6	33
1997—Gulf Coast Mets (GCL)........	3	3	.500	1.55	6	5	0	0	0	39	31	12	5	3	42
—Kingsport (Appal.).............	2	3	.400	6.61	6	6	0	0	0	31 1/3	46	30	23	8	31

DE LA MAZA, ROLAND — P — ROYALS

PERSONAL: Born November 11, 1971, in Granada Hills, Calif. ... 6-2/195. ... Throws right, bats right. ... Full name: Roland Robert De La Maza.
COLLEGE: Cal State Sacramento.
TRANSACTIONS/CAREER NOTES: Selected by Cleveland Indians in 15th round of free-agent draft (June 3, 1993). ... Traded by Indians to Kansas City Royals for IF/OF Bip Roberts (August 31, 1997).

Year Team (League)	W	L	Pct.	ERA	G	GS	CG	ShO	Sv.	IP	H	R	ER	BB	SO
1993—Watertown (NYP)..............	10	3	.769	2.52	15	15	1	0	0	100	90	39	28	14	81
1994—Columbus (S. Atl.)............	13	2	.867	2.96	21	21	1	0	0	112 2/3	102	59	37	25	97
1995—Kinston (Carolina)	6	0	1.000	2.37	26	12	0	0	1	110 1/3	99	31	29	28	100
—Cant./Akr. (Eastern)...........	2	1	.667	4.10	7	7	0	0	0	37 1/3	35	19	17	18	27
1996—Cant./Akr. (Eastern)	9	7	.563	4.38	40	14	0	0	1	139 2/3	122	75	68	49	132

Year	Team (League)	W	L	Pct.	ERA	G	GS	CG	ShO	Sv.	IP	H	R	ER	BB	SO
1997— Buffalo (A.A.)		9	4	.692	2.90	34	14	2	0	2	115	104	42	37	43	73
— Kansas City (A.L.)■		0	0	...	4.50	1	0	0	0	0	2	1	1	1	1	1
Major league totals (1 year)		0	0	...	4.50	1	0	0	0	0	2	1	1	1	1	1

DE LA ROSA, MAXIMO   P   INDIANS

PERSONAL: Born July 12, 1971, in Villa Mella, Dominican Republic. ... 5-11/170. ... Throws right, bats right.
HIGH SCHOOL: Ramon Mella (Villa Mella, Dominican Republic).
TRANSACTIONS/CAREER NOTES: Signed as non-drafted free agent by Cleveland Indians organization (February 24, 1990).

Year	Team (League)	W	L	Pct.	ERA	G	GS	CG	ShO	Sv.	IP	H	R	ER	BB	SO
1993— Burlington (Appalachian)		7	2	.778	3.77	14	•14	2	1	0	76 1/3	53	38	32	37	69
1994— Kinston (Carolina)		0	11	.000	5.04	13	13	0	0	0	69 2/3	82	56	39	38	53
— Columbus (S. Atl.)		4	2	.667	3.35	14	14	0	0	0	75 1/3	49	33	28	38	71
1995— Kinston (Carolina)		5	2	.714	2.19	43	0	0	0	8	61 2/3	46	23	15	37	61
— Cant./Akr. (Eastern)		0	0	...	54.00	1	0	0	0	0	1/3	1	2	2	1	0
1996— Cant./Akr. (Eastern)		11	5	.688	3.91	40	15	0	0	3	119 2/3	104	60	52	81	109
1997— Buffalo (A.A.)		2	2	.500	6.49	15	4	0	0	0	43	43	34	31	33	31
— Akron (Eastern)		4	9	.308	4.44	17	13	5	0	0	97 1/3	112	63	48	32	70

RECORD AS POSITION PLAYER

						BATTING								FIELDING		
Year	Team (League)	Pos.	G	AB	R	H	2B	3B	HR	RBI	Avg.	BB	SO	SB	PO	A	E	Avg.
---	---	---	---	---	---	---	---	---	---	---	---	---	---	---	---	---	---	---
1990— Dom. Inds. (DSL)		OF	61	225	51	63	14	1	1	31	.280	36	24	15	...	...	...	...
1991— Dom. Inds. (DSL)		OF	60	219	43	67	8	2	4	36	.306	28	23	15	...	...	...	...
1992— Burlington (Appal.)		OF	62	222	27	54	5	1	1	30	.243	24	52	4	100	3	4	.963
1996— Cant./Akr. (Eastern)		P	40	0	0	0	0	0	0	0	...	0	0	0	7	15	2	.917

DELGADO, CARLOS   1B/OF   BLUE JAYS

D

PERSONAL: Born June 25, 1972, in Aguadilla, Puerto Rico. ... 6-3/225. ... Bats left, throws right. ... Full name: Carlos Juan Delgado.
HIGH SCHOOL: Jose de Diego (Aguadilla, Puerto Rico).
TRANSACTIONS/CAREER NOTES: Signed as non-drafted free agent by Toronto Blue Jays organization (October 9, 1988).
HONORS: Named Florida State League Most Valuable Player (1992). ... Named Southern League Most Valuable Player (1993).
STATISTICAL NOTES: Led New York-Pennsylvania League catchers with 540 total chances and six double plays in 1990. ... Led South Atlantic League with 29 passed balls in 1991. ... Led Florida State League with 281 total bases, .579 slugging percentage, .402 on-base percentage and 11 intentional bases on balls received in 1992. ... Led Florida State League catchers with 784 total chances in 1992. ... Led Southern League with .524 slugging percentage, .430 on-base percentage and 18 intentional bases on balls received in 1993. ... Led Southern League catchers with 800 total chances in 1993. ... Led International League with .610 slugging percentage in 1995. ... Led International League with seven intentional bases on balls received in 1995. ... Career major league grand slams: 3.

						BATTING								FIELDING		
Year	Team (League)	Pos.	G	AB	R	H	2B	3B	HR	RBI	Avg.	BB	SO	SB	PO	A	E	Avg.
---	---	---	---	---	---	---	---	---	---	---	---	---	---	---	---	---	---	---
1989— St. Catharines (NYP)		C	31	89	9	16	5	0	0	11	.180	23	39	0	63	13	2	.974
1990— St. Catharines (NYP)		C	67	228	30	64	13	0	6	39	.281	35	65	2	*471	*62	7	.987
1991— Myrtle Beach (SAL)		C	132	441	72	126	18	2	18	70	.286	75	97	9	679	*100	19	.976
— Syracuse (Int'l)		C	1	3	0	0	0	0	0	0	.000	0	2	0	5	0	0	1.000
1992— Dunedin (Fla. St.)		C	133	485	83	*157	•30	2	*30	*100	.324	59	91	2	*684	89	11	.986
1993— Knoxville (Southern)		C	140	468	91	142	28	0	*25	*102	.303	*102	98	10	*683	*103	*14	.983
— Toronto (A.L.)		DH-C	2	1	0	0	0	0	0	0	.000	1	0	0	2	0	0	1.000
1994— Toronto (A.L.)		OF-C	43	130	17	28	2	0	9	24	.215	25	46	1	56	2	2	.967
— Syracuse (Int'l)		C-1B	85	307	52	98	11	0	19	58	.319	42	58	1	235	25	7	.974
1995— Toronto (A.L.)		OF-DH-1B	37	91	7	15	3	0	3	11	.165	6	26	0	54	2	0	1.000
— Syracuse (Int'l)		1B-OF	91	333	59	106	23	4	22	74	.318	45	78	0	724	49	4	.995
1996— Toronto (A.L.)		DH-1B	138	488	68	132	28	2	25	92	.270	58	139	0	221	13	4	.983
1997— Toronto (A.L.)		1B-DH	153	519	79	136	42	3	30	91	.262	64	133	0	962	67	12	.988
Major league totals (5 years)			373	1229	171	311	75	5	67	218	.253	154	344	1	1295	84	18	.987

DELGADO, WILSON   SS   GIANTS

PERSONAL: Born July 15, 1975, in San Cristobal, Dominican Republic. ... 5-11/155. ... Bats both, throws right. ... Full name: Wilson Duran Delgado.
TRANSACTIONS/CAREER NOTES: Signed as non-drafted free agent by Seattle Mariners organization (October 29, 1992). ... Traded by Mariners with P Shawn Estes to San Francisco Giants for P Salomon Torres (May 21, 1995).
STATISTICAL NOTES: Led Pacific Coast League shortstops with 197 putouts, 547 total chances and 86 double plays in 1997.

						BATTING								FIELDING		
Year	Team (League)	Pos.	G	AB	R	H	2B	3B	HR	RBI	Avg.	BB	SO	SB	PO	A	E	Avg.
---	---	---	---	---	---	---	---	---	---	---	---	---	---	---	---	---	---	---
1993— Dom. Mariners (DSL)		IF	60	171	19	50	8	0	0	26	.292	34	25	5	96	148	16	.938
1994— Ariz. Mariners (Ariz.)		SS-2B	39	149	30	56	5	4	0	10	*.376	15	24	13	58	114	10	.945
1995— Wis. Rap. (Mid.)		SS	19	70	13	17	3	0	0	7	.243	3	15	3	29	65	6	.940
— Burlington (Mid.)■		SS	93	365	52	113	20	3	5	37	.310	32	57	9	127	285	19	.956
1996— San Jose (Calif.)		SS	121	462	59	124	19	6	2	54	.268	48	89	8	192	343	24	.957
— Phoenix (PCL)		SS	12	43	1	6	0	1	0	1	.140	3	7	0	30	47	2	.975
— San Francisco (N.L.)		SS	6	22	3	8	0	0	0	2	.364	1	5	1	12	12	1	.960
1997— San Francisco (N.L.)		2B-SS	8	7	1	1	1	0	0	0	.143	0	2	0	2	3	0	1.000
— Phoenix (PCL)		SS-2B	119	416	47	120	22	4	9	59	.288	24	70	9	208	347	18	.969
Major league totals (2 years)			14	29	4	9	1	0	0	2	.310	1	7	1	14	15	1	.967

DELLUCCI, DAVID — OF — DIAMONDBACKS

PERSONAL: Born October 31, 1973, in Baton Rouge, La. ... 5-10/180. ... Bats left, throws left. ... Full name: David Michael Dellucci.
HIGH SCHOOL: Catholic (Baton Rouge, La.).
COLLEGE: Mississippi.
TRANSACTIONS/CAREER NOTES: Selected by Baltimore Orioles organization in 10th round of free agent draft (June 1, 1995). ... Selected by Arizona Diamondbacks in second round (45th pick overall) of expansion draft (November 18, 1997).

							BATTING								FIELDING			
Year Team (League)	Pos.	G	AB	R	H	2B	3B	HR	RBI	Avg.	BB	SO	SB	PO	A	E	Avg.
1995—Frederick (Carolina)....	OF	28	96	16	27	3	0	1	10	.281	12	10	1	26	2	1	.966
— Bluefield (Appal.)........	OF	20	69	11	23	5	1	2	12	.333	6	7	3	11	0	2	.846
1996—Frederick (Carolina)....	OF	59	185	33	60	11	1	4	28	.324	38	34	5	100	4	3	.972
— Bowie (Eastern).........	OF	66	251	27	73	14	1	2	33	.291	28	56	2	134	5	3	.979
1997—Bowie (Eastern).........	OF	107	385	71	126	29	3	20	55	.327	58	69	11	162	2	1	.994
— Baltimore (A.L.)..........	OF-DH	17	27	3	6	1	0	1	3	.222	4	7	0	20	1	0	1.000
Major league totals (1 year)		17	27	3	6	1	0	1	3	.222	4	7	0	20	1	0	1.000

DE LOS SANTOS, LUIS — P — YANKEES

PERSONAL: Born November 1, 1977, in Santo Domingo, Dominican Republic. ... 6-2/187. ... Throws right, bats right.
TRANSACTIONS/CAREER NOTES: Signed as non-drafted free agent by New York Yankees organization (February 11, 1995).
STATISTICAL NOTES: Pitched 4-0 no-hit victory against Batavia (July 28, 1996).

Year Team (League)	W	L	Pct.	ERA	G	GS	CG	ShO	Sv.	IP	H	R	ER	BB	SO
1995—Tampa (Florida State).........	0	0	...	0.00	2	0	0	0	0	5	5	2	0	2	6
1996—Oneonta (NYP)................	4	4	.500	3.72	10	10	3	2	0	58	44	28	24	21	62
— Greensboro (S. Atl.)..........	4	1	.800	4.83	7	6	0	0	0	31 2/3	39	17	17	11	21
1997—Greensboro (S. Atl.).........	5	6	.455	3.05	14	14	1	0	0	88 2/3	91	45	30	13	62
— Tampa (Florida State).........	5	0	1.000	2.34	10	10	0	0	0	61 2/3	49	19	16	8	39
— Norwich (Eastern)............	1	1	.500	2.52	4	4	0	0	0	25	23	9	7	7	15

DE LOS SANTOS, VALERIO — P — BREWERS

PERSONAL: Born September 6, 1975, in Las Matas, Dominican Republic. ... 6-2/180. ... Throws left, bats left. ... Full name: Valerio Lorenzo De Los Santos.
TRANSACTIONS/CAREER NOTES: Signed as non-drafted free agent by Milwaukee Brewers organization (January 26, 1993).

Year Team (League)	W	L	Pct.	ERA	G	GS	CG	ShO	Sv.	IP	H	R	ER	BB	SO
1993—Dom. Dodgers (DSL)	1	7	.125	6.50	19	6	1	0	0	63 2/3	91	57	46	37	39
1994—Dom. Dodgers (DSL)	7	6	.538	3.69	17	•16	1	1	0	90 1/3	90	52	37	35	50
1995—Ariz. Brewers (Ariz.)	4	6	.400	2.20	14	12	0	0	0	82	81	34	20	12	57
1996—Beloit (Midwest)................	10	8	.556	3.55	33	23	5	1	4	164 2/3	164	83	65	59	137
1997—El Paso (Texas).................	6	10	.375	5.75	26	16	1	0	2	114 1/3	146	83	73	38	61

DeLUCIA, RICH — P — ANGELS

PERSONAL: Born October 7, 1964, in Reading, Pa. ... 6-0/190. ... Throws right, bats right. ... Full name: Richard Anthony DeLucia. ... Name pronounced duh-LOO-sha.
HIGH SCHOOL: Wyomissing (Pa.) Area.
COLLEGE: Tennessee.
TRANSACTIONS/CAREER NOTES: Selected by Toronto Blue Jays organization in 15th round of free-agent draft (June 3, 1985); did not sign. ... Selected by Seattle Mariners organization in sixth round of free-agent draft (June 2, 1986). ... On disabled list (April 10, 1987-remainder of season). ... On disabled list (May 31-July 2 and July 7, 1989-remainder of season). ... On Seattle disabled list (August 5-September 1, 1992); included rehabilitation assignment to Calgary (August 26-31). ... On Seattle disabled list (June 28-July 22, 1993); included rehabilitation assignment to Calgary (July 16-22). ... Released by Mariners (March 29, 1994). ... Signed by Cincinnati Reds organization (April 2, 1994). ... Granted free agency (October 15, 1994). ... Signed by Rochester, Baltimore Orioles organization (November 17, 1994). ... Selected by St. Louis Cardinals from Orioles organization in Rule 5 major league draft (December 5, 1994). ... Traded by Cardinals with P Allen Watson and P Doug Creek to San Francisco Giants for SS Royce Clayton and a player to be named later (December 14, 1995); Cardinals acquired 2B Chris Wimmer to complete deal (January 16, 1996). ... On San Francisco disabled list (March 25-May 2 and July 27-August 23, 1996); included rehabilitation assignments to San Jose (April 25-May 2 and August 18-23). ... Traded by Giants to Anaheim Angels for a player to be named later (April 14, 1997); Giants acquired P Travis Thurmond to complete deal (May 22, 1997). ... On Anaheim disabled list (July 15-September 2, 1997). ... Granted free agency (October 31, 1997). ... Re-signed by Angels (December 6, 1997).
STATISTICAL NOTES: Pitched seven-inning, 1-0 no-hit victory against Everett (July 17, 1986). ... Led A.L. with 31 home runs allowed in 1991.

Year Team (League)	W	L	Pct.	ERA	G	GS	CG	ShO	Sv.	IP	H	R	ER	BB	SO
1986—Bellingham (N'west)	8	2	.800	*1.70	13	11	1	•1	0	74	44	20	14	24	69
1987—Salinas (Calif.)	0	0	...	9.00	1	1	0	0	0	1	2	1	1	0	1
1988—San Bernardino (Calif.)	7	8	.467	3.10	22	22	0	0	0	127 2/3	110	57	44	59	118
1989—Williamsport (Eastern)	3	4	.429	3.79	10	10	0	0	0	54 2/3	59	28	23	13	41
1990—San Bernardino (Calif.)	4	1	.800	2.05	5	5	1	0	0	30 2/3	19	9	7	3	35
—Williamsport (Eastern)	6	6	.500	2.11	18	18	2	1	0	115	92	30	27	30	76
—Calgary (PCL)	2	2	.500	3.62	5	5	1	0	0	32 1/3	30	17	13	12	23
—Seattle (A.L.)	1	2	.333	2.00	5	5	1	0	0	36	30	9	8	9	20
1991—Seattle (A.L.)	12	13	.480	5.09	32	31	0	0	0	182	176	107	103	78	98
1992—Seattle (A.L.)	3	6	.333	5.49	30	11	0	0	1	83 2/3	100	55	51	35	66
—Calgary (PCL)	4	2	.667	2.45	8	5	2	1	1	40 1/3	32	11	11	14	38
1993—Seattle (A.L.)	3	6	.333	4.64	30	1	0	0	0	42 2/3	46	24	22	23	48
—Calgary (PCL)	1	5	.167	5.73	8	7	0	0	1	44	45	30	28	20	38
1994—Indianapolis (A.A.)■	5	1	.833	2.30	36	0	0	0	19	43	22	12	11	24	52
—Cincinnati (N.L.)	0	0	...	4.22	8	0	0	0	0	10 2/3	9	6	5	5	15

Year—Team (League)	W	L	Pct.	ERA	G	GS	CG	ShO	Sv.	IP	H	R	ER	BB	SO
1995— St. Louis (N.L.)■	8	7	.533	3.39	56	1	0	0	0	82 1/3	63	38	31	36	76
1996— San Jose (California)■	0	0	...	2.45	5	4	0	0	0	7 1/3	5	2	2	3	11
— San Francisco (N.L.)	3	6	.333	5.84	56	0	0	0	0	61 2/3	62	44	40	31	55
1997— San Francisco (N.L.)	0	0	...	10.80	3	0	0	0	0	1 2/3	6	3	2	0	2
— Anaheim (A.L.)■	6	4	.600	3.61	33	0	0	0	3	42 1/3	29	18	17	27	42
A.L. totals (5 years)	25	31	.446	4.68	130	48	1	0	4	386 2/3	381	213	201	172	274
N.L. totals (4 years)	11	13	.458	4.49	123	1	0	0	0	156 1/3	140	91	78	72	148
Major league totals (8 years)	36	44	.450	4.62	253	49	1	0	4	543	521	304	279	244	422

DESCHENES, MARC   P   DODGERS

PERSONAL: Born January 6, 1973, in Lowell, Mass. ... 6-0/175. ... Throws right, bats right. ... Full name: Marc A. Deschenes.
HIGH SCHOOL: Dracut (Mass.).
COLLEGE: Massachusetts-Lowell.
TRANSACTIONS/CAREER NOTES: Selected by Cleveland Indians organization in 20th round of free-agent draft (June 1, 1995). ... Selected by Los Angeles Dodgers from Indians organization in Rule 5 major league draft (December 15, 1997).

Year—Team (League)	W	L	Pct.	ERA	G	GS	CG	ShO	Sv.	IP	H	R	ER	BB	SO
1996— Columbus (S. Atl.)	5	2	.714	3.40	16	16	0	00	0	76 2/3	70	38	29	44	67
1997— Columbus (S. Atl.)	2	2	.500	1.90	40	0	0	0	19	42 2/3	31	11	9	21	69
— Kinston (Carolina)	2	0	1.000	0.81	20	0	0	0	10	22 1/3	9	2	2	4	39

RECORD AS POSITION PLAYER

Year—Team (League)	Pos.	G	AB	R	H	2B	3B	HR	RBI	Avg.	BB	SO	SB	PO	A	E	Avg.
1995— Watertown (NYP)	2B-SS	42	144	18	30	4	1	1	14	.208	18	45	6	69	125	9	.956

DeSHIELDS, DELINO   2B   CARDINALS

PERSONAL: Born January 15, 1969, in Seaford, Del. ... 6-1/175. ... Bats left, throws right. ... Full name: Delino Lamont DeShields. ... Name pronounced duh-LINE-oh.
HIGH SCHOOL: Seaford (Del.).
COLLEGE: Villanova.
TRANSACTIONS/CAREER NOTES: Selected by Montreal Expos organization in first round (12th pick overall) of free-agent draft (June 2, 1987). ... On disabled list (June 16-July 12, 1990 and August 12-September 11, 1993). ... Traded by Expos to Los Angeles Dodgers for P Pedro J. Martinez (November 19, 1993). ... On disabled list (May 26-June 20, 1994). ... Granted free agency (October 29, 1996). ... Signed by St. Louis Cardinals (November 20, 1996).
RECORDS: Shares modern N.L. record for most hits in first major league game—4 (April 9, 1990). ... Shares major league single-game record (nine innings) for most strikeouts—5 (September 17, 1991, second game).
STATISTICAL NOTES: Led Gulf Coast League shortstops with 22 errors in 1987. ... Had 21-game hitting streak (June 28-July 21, 1993). ... Career major league grand slams: 1.

Year—Team (League)	Pos.	G	AB	R	H	2B	3B	HR	RBI	Avg.	BB	SO	SB	PO	A	E	Avg.
1987— GC Expos (GCL)	SS-3B	31	111	17	24	5	2	1	4	.216	21	30	16	47	90	†22	.862
— Jamestown (NYP)	SS	34	96	16	21	1	2	1	5	.219	24	28	14	25	57	21	.796
1988— Rockford (Midwest)	SS	129	460	97	116	26	6	12	46	.252	95	110	59	173	344	42	.925
1989— Jacksonville (South.)	SS	93	307	55	83	10	6	3	35	.270	76	80	37	127	218	34	.910
— Indianapolis (A.A.)	SS	47	181	29	47	8	4	2	14	.260	16	53	16	73	101	13	.930
1990— Montreal (N.L.)	2B	129	499	69	144	28	6	4	45	.289	66	96	42	236	371	12	.981
1991— Montreal (N.L.)	2B	151	563	83	134	15	4	10	51	.238	95	*151	56	285	405	*27	.962
1992— Montreal (N.L.)	2B	135	530	82	155	19	8	7	56	.292	54	108	46	251	360	15	.976
1993— Montreal (N.L.)	2B	123	481	75	142	17	7	2	29	.295	72	64	43	243	381	11	.983
1994— Los Angeles (N.L.)■	2B-SS	89	320	51	80	11	3	2	33	.250	54	53	27	156	282	7	.984
1995— Los Angeles (N.L.)	2B	127	425	66	109	18	3	8	37	.256	63	83	39	204	330	•11	.980
1996— Los Angeles (N.L.)	2B	154	581	75	130	12	8	5	41	.224	53	124	48	274	400	17	.975
1997— St. Louis (N.L.)■	2B	150	572	92	169	26	*14	11	58	.295	55	72	55	272	398	19	.972
Major league totals (8 years)		1058	3971	593	1063	146	53	49	350	.268	512	751	356	1921	2927	119	.976

DIVISION SERIES RECORD

Year—Team (League)	Pos.	G	AB	R	H	2B	3B	HR	RBI	Avg.	BB	SO	SB	PO	A	E	Avg.
1995— Los Angeles (N.L.)	2B	3	12	1	3	0	0	0	0	.250	1	3	0	8	7	0	1.000
1996— Los Angeles (N.L.)	2B	2	4	0	0	0	0	0	0	.000	0	1	0	3	2	0	1.000
Division series totals (2 years)		5	16	1	3	0	0	0	0	.188	1	4	0	11	9	0	1.000

DESSENS, ELMER   P   PIRATES

PERSONAL: Born January 13, 1972, in Hermosillo, Mexico ... 6-0/185. ... Throws right, bats right. ... Name pronounced DAH-cenz.
TRANSACTIONS/CAREER NOTES: Signed as non-drafted free agent by Pittsburgh Pirates organization (January 27, 1993). ... Loaned by Pirates organization to Mexico City Red Devils of Mexican League for 1993 and 1994 seasons; returned to Pirates organization for 1995 season. ... Loaned by Pirates organization to Red Devils (May 7, 1996). ... Returned to Pirates organization (June 21, 1996). ... On Pittsburgh disabled list (July 31-September 10, 1996); included rehabilitation assignment to Carolina (August 16-September 10). ... Loaned to Red Devils of Mexican League (March 24, 1997). ... Returned to Pirates (September 5, 1997).

Year—Team (League)	W	L	Pct.	ERA	G	GS	CG	ShO	Sv.	IP	H	R	ER	BB	SO
1993— M.C. Red Devils (Mex.)	3	1	.750	2.35	14	0	0	0	2	30 2/3	31	8	8	5	16
1994— M.C. Red Devils (Mex.)	11	4	.733	2.04	37	15	4	1	3	127 2/3	121	37	29	32	51
1995— Carolina (Southern)	*15	8	.652	*2.49	27	27	1	0	0	152	170	62	42	21	68

Year Team (League)	W	L	Pct.	ERA	G	GS	CG	ShO	Sv.	IP	H	R	ER	BB	SO
1996—Calgary (PCL)	2	2	.500	3.15	6	6	0	0	0	34 1/3	40	14	12	15	15
—M.C. Red Devils (Mex.)■	7	0	1.000	1.26	7	7	1	0	0	50	44	12	7	10	17
—Pittsburgh (N.L.)■	0	2	.000	8.28	15	3	0	0	0	25	40	23	23	4	13
—Carolina (Southern)	0	1	.000	5.40	5	1	0	0	0	11 2/3	15	8	7	4	7
1997—Pittsburgh (N.L.)■	0	0	...	0.00	3	0	0	0	0	3 1/3	2	0	0	0	2
—M.C. Red Devils (Mex.)■	16	5	.762	3.56	26	25	3	1	0	159 1/3	156	73	63	51	61
Major league totals (2 years)	0	2	.000	7.31	18	3	0	0	0	28 1/3	42	23	23	4	15

DEVEREAUX, MIKE — OF — DODGERS

PERSONAL: Born April 10, 1963, in Casper, Wyo. ... 6-0/195. ... Bats right, throws right. ... Full name: Michael Devereaux. ... Name pronounced DEH-ver-oh.

HIGH SCHOOL: Kelly Walsh (Casper, Wyo.).

JUNIOR COLLEGE: Mesa (Ariz.) Community College.

COLLEGE: Arizona State (bachelor of arts degree in finance).

TRANSACTIONS/CAREER NOTES: Selected by Cleveland Indians organization in 26th round of free-agent draft (June 4, 1984); did not sign. ... Selected by Los Angeles Dodgers organization in fifth round of free-agent draft (June 3, 1985). ... Traded by Dodgers to Baltimore Orioles for P Mike Morgan (March 12, 1989). ... On Baltimore disabled list (May 17-June 15, 1990); included rehabilitation assignments to Frederick (June 9-10) and Hagerstown (June 11-15). ... On Baltimore disabled list (May 3-27, 1993); included rehabilitation assignment to Bowie (May 25-27). ... On disabled list (June 16-July 1, 1994). ... Signed by Chicago White Sox (April 8, 1995). ... Traded by White Sox to Atlanta Braves for OF Andre King (August 25, 1995). ... Granted free agency (November 3, 1995). ... Signed by Orioles (January 11, 1996). ... Granted free agency (October 29, 1996). ... Signed by Texas Rangers (January 6, 1997). ... Released by Rangers (June 12, 1997). ... Signed by Dodgers organization (January 16, 1998).

HONORS: Named outfielder on THE SPORTING NEWS A.L. All-Star team (1992).

STATISTICAL NOTES: Led Pioneer League with 152 total bases in 1985. ... Led Texas League with 11 sacrifice flies in 1987. ... Led Texas League outfielders with 349 total chances in 1987. ... Career major league grand slams: 3.

Year Team (League)	Pos.	G	AB	R	H	2B	3B	HR	RBI	Avg.	BB	SO	SB	PO	A	E	Avg.
1985—Great Falls (Pio.)	OF	•70	*289	*73	*103	17	10	4	*67	.356	32	29	*40	100	4	5	.954
1986—San Antonio (Tex.)	OF	115	431	69	130	22	2	10	53	.302	58	47	31	292	13	4	.987
1987—San Antonio (Tex.)	OF	*135	*562	90	169	28	9	26	91	.301	48	65	33	*339	7	3	*.991
—Albuquerque (PCL)	OF	3	11	2	3	1	0	1	1	.273	0	2	1	4	1	0	1.000
—Los Angeles (N.L.)	OF	19	54	7	12	3	0	0	4	.222	3	10	3	21	1	0	1.000
1988—Albuquerque (PCL)	OF	109	423	88	144	26	4	13	76	.340	44	46	33	211	5	7	.969
—Los Angeles (N.L.)	OF	30	43	4	5	1	0	0	2	.116	2	10	0	29	0	0	1.000
1989—Baltimore (A.L.)■	OF-DH	122	391	55	104	14	3	8	46	.266	36	60	22	288	1	5	.983
1990—Baltimore (A.L.)	OF-DH	108	367	48	88	18	1	12	49	.240	28	48	13	281	4	5	.983
—Frederick (Carolina)	OF	2	8	3	4	0	0	1	3	.500	1	2	0	4	2	0	1.000
—Hagerstown (Eastern)	OF	4	20	4	5	3	0	0	3	.250	0	1	0	13	0	1	.929
1991—Baltimore (A.L.)	OF	149	608	82	158	27	10	19	59	.260	47	115	16	399	10	3	.993
1992—Baltimore (A.L.)	OF	156	653	76	180	29	11	24	107	.276	44	94	10	431	5	5	.989
1993—Baltimore (A.L.)	OF	131	527	72	132	31	3	14	75	.250	43	99	3	311	8	4	.988
—Bowie (Eastern)	OF	2	7	1	2	1	0	0	2	.286	0	2	0	5	0	0	1.000
1994—Baltimore (A.L.)	OF-DH	85	301	35	61	8	2	9	33	.203	22	72	1	203	3	1	.995
1995—Chicago (A.L.)■	OF	92	333	48	102	21	1	10	55	.306	25	51	6	187	4	3	.985
—Atlanta (N.L.)■	OF	29	55	7	14	3	0	1	8	.255	2	11	2	41	0	0	1.000
1996—Baltimore (A.L.)	OF-DH	127	323	49	74	11	2	8	34	.229	34	53	8	170	7	3	.983
1997—Texas (A.L.)■	OF	29	72	8	15	3	0	0	7	.208	7	10	1	40	0	0	1.000
American League totals (9 years)		999	3575	473	914	162	33	104	465	.256	286	602	80	2310	42	29	.988
National League totals (3 years)		78	152	18	31	7	0	1	14	.204	7	31	5	91	1	0	1.000
Major league totals (11 years)		1077	3727	491	945	169	33	105	479	.254	293	633	85	2401	43	29	.988

DIVISION SERIES RECORD

Year Team (League)	Pos.	G	AB	R	H	2B	3B	HR	RBI	Avg.	BB	SO	SB	PO	A	E	Avg.
1995—Atlanta (N.L.)	OF-PH	4	5	1	1	0	0	0	0	.200	0	0	0	2	0	0	1.000
1996—Baltimore (A.L.)	OF-PR	4	1	0	0	0	0	0	0	.000	0	0	0	2	0	0	1.000
Division series totals (2 years)		8	6	1	1	0	0	0	0	.167	0	0	0	4	0	0	1.000

CHAMPIONSHIP SERIES RECORD

NOTES: Named N.L. Championship Series Most Valuable Player (1995).

Year Team (League)	Pos.	G	AB	R	H	2B	3B	HR	RBI	Avg.	BB	SO	SB	PO	A	E	Avg.
1995—Atlanta (N.L.)	OF	4	13	2	4	1	0	1	5	.308	1	2	0	2	0	0	1.000
1996—Baltimore (A.L.)	OF	3	2	0	0	0	0	0	0	.000	0	1	0	1	0	0	1.000
Championship series totals (2 years)		7	15	2	4	1	0	1	5	.267	1	3	0	3	0	0	1.000

WORLD SERIES RECORD

NOTES: Member of World Series championship team (1995).

Year Team (League)	Pos.	G	AB	R	H	2B	3B	HR	RBI	Avg.	BB	SO	SB	PO	A	E	Avg.
1995—Atlanta (N.L.)	OF-PH-DH	5	4	0	1	0	0	0	1	.250	2	1	0	0	0	1	.000

DIAZ, ALEX — OF

PERSONAL: Born October 5, 1968, in Brooklyn, N.Y. ... 5-11/180. ... Bats both, throws right. ... Full name: Alexis Diaz. ... Son of Mario Caballero Diaz, minor league infielder (1959-64).

HIGH SCHOOL: Manuel Mendez Licihea (Puerto Rico).

TRANSACTIONS/CAREER NOTES: Signed as non-drafted free agent by New York Mets organization (August 24, 1986). ... Traded by Mets with OF Darren Reed to Montreal Expos for OF Terrel Hansen and P David Sommer (April 2, 1991). ... On suspended list (August 30, 1991; remainder of season). ... Traded by Expos organization to Milwaukee Brewers organization for IF George Canale (October 15, 1991). ... On

Milwaukee disabled list (May 3-August 30, 1993); included rehabilitation assignment to New Orleans (August 13-30). ... Granted free agency (December 20, 1993). ... Re-signed by Brewers (December 21, 1993). ... On disabled list (July 31, 1994-remainder of season). ... Claimed on waivers by Seattle Mariners (October 14, 1994). ... On Seattle disabled list (June 5-August 4 and August 12-September 2, 1996); included rehabilitation assignments to Tacoma (July 15-August 4 and August 31-September 2). ... Granted free agency (October 8, 1996). ... Signed by Mets organization (November 19, 1996). ... Released by Norfolk, Mets organization (April 13, 1997). ... Signed by Oklahoma City, Texas Rangers organization (April 16, 1997). ... Granted free agency (October 15, 1997).

Year Team (League)	Pos.	G	AB	R	H	2B	3B	HR	RBI	Avg.	BB	SO	SB	PO	A	E	Avg.
1987—Kingsport (Appal.)	SS	54	212	29	56	9	1	0	13	.264	16	31	*34	67	126	18	.915
—Little Falls (NYP)	SS	12	47	7	16	4	1	0	8	.340	2	3	2	13	22	4	.897
1988—Columbia (S. Atl.)	SS	123	481	82	126	14	*11	0	37	.262	21	49	28	175	299	*72	.868
—St. Lucie (Fla. St.)	SS	3	6	2	0	0	0	0	1	.000	0	4	0	3	3	3	.667
1989—St. Lucie (Fla. St.)	SS-OF	102	416	54	106	11	10	1	33	.255	20	38	43	151	244	28	.934
—Jackson (Texas)	SS	23	95	11	26	5	1	2	9	.274	3	11	3	25	65	3	.968
1990—Tidewater (Int'l)	OF-2B-SS	124	437	55	112	15	2	1	36	.256	30	39	23	196	101	11	.964
1991—Indianapolis (A.A.)■	O-S-3-2	108	370	48	90	14	4	1	21	.243	27	46	17	207	45	8	.969
1992—Denver (A.A.)■	OF-2B-SS	106	455	67	122	17	4	1	41	.268	24	36	42	240	43	7	.976
—Milwaukee (A.L.)	OF-DH	22	9	5	1	0	0	0	1	.111	0	0	3	10	0	0	1.000
1993—Milwaukee (A.L.)	OF-DH	32	69	9	22	2	0	0	1	.319	0	12	5	46	1	1	.979
—New Orleans (A.A.)	OF	16	55	8	16	2	0	0	5	.291	3	6	7	38	1	0	1.000
1994—Milwaukee (A.L.)	OF-2B-DH	79	187	17	47	5	7	1	17	.251	10	19	5	138	11	2	.987
1995—Seattle (A.L.)■	OF	103	270	44	67	14	0	3	27	.248	13	27	18	145	4	2	.987
—Tacoma (PCL)	OF	10	40	3	10	1	0	0	4	.250	2	5	1	15	1	0	1.000
1996—Seattle (A.L.)	OF-DH	38	79	11	19	2	0	1	5	.241	2	8	6	55	1	1	.982
—Tacoma (PCL)	OF-3B	44	176	19	43	5	0	0	7	.244	7	20	5	76	5	2	.976
1997—Norfolk (Int'l)■	OF	7	26	0	2	1	0	0	1	.077	2	3	0	10	2	1	.923
—Okla. City (A.A.)■	O-2-P-S	1	426	65	122	25	2	12	49	.286	33	53	26	180	52	10	.959
—Texas (A.L.)	OF-1B-2B	28	90	8	20	4	0	2	12	.222	5	13	1	54	3	1	.983
Major league totals (6 years)		302	704	94	176	27	7	7	63	.250	30	79	38	448	20	7	.985

DIVISION SERIES RECORD

Year Team (League)	Pos.	G	AB	R	H	2B	3B	HR	RBI	Avg.	BB	SO	SB	PO	A	E	Avg.
1995—Seattle (A.L.)	OF-PH	2	3	0	1	0	0	0	0	.333	1	1	0	1	1	0	1.000

CHAMPIONSHIP SERIES RECORD

Year Team (League)	Pos.	G	AB	R	H	2B	3B	HR	RBI	Avg.	BB	SO	SB	PO	A	E	Avg.
1995—Seattle (A.L.)	PH-OF	4	7	0	3	1	0	0	0	.429	1	1	0	1	0	0	1.000

RECORD AS PITCHER

Year Team (League)	W	L	Pct.	ERA	G	GS	CG	ShO	Sv.	IP	H	R	ER	BB	SO
1997—Oklahoma City (A.A.)■	0	0	...	0.00	1	0	0	0	0	1	0	1	0	3	1

DIAZ, EDDY   IF   BREWERS

PERSONAL: Born September 29, 1971, in Barquisimeto, Venezuela. ... 5-10/160. ... Bats right, throws right. ... Full name: Eddy Javier Diaz.
TRANSACTIONS/CAREER NOTES: Signed as non-drafted free agent by Seattle Mariners organization (February 15, 1990). ... Granted free agency (October 15, 1996). ... Signed by Milwaukee Brewers organization (November 26, 1996).
STATISTICAL NOTES: Led Northwest League second basemen with .973 fielding percentage in 1991.

Year Team (League)	Pos.	G	AB	R	H	2B	3B	HR	RBI	Avg.	BB	SO	SB	PO	A	E	Avg.
1991—Bellingham (N'west)	2B-SS	61	246	48	68	14	1	3	23	.276	24	33	9	104	160	9	†.967
1992—San Bern. (Calif.)	2B-SS	114	436	80	119	15	2	9	39	.273	38	46	33	214	373	24	.961
1993—Jacksonville (South.)	0-2-3-1	77	259	36	65	16	0	6	26	.251	17	31	6	96	56	5	.968
—Appleton (Midwest)	2-S-0-3	46	189	28	63	14	2	3	33	.333	15	13	13	84	112	6	.970
1994—Jacksonville (South.)	0-3-2-S-P	104	340	43	84	20	0	8	42	.247	21	23	13	106	118	20	.918
1995—Tacoma (PCL)	2B-3B	11	36	5	12	2	0	0	5	.333	4	2	0	12	23	1	.972
—Port City (Southern)	SS-2B-3B	110	421	66	110	22	0	16	47	.261	40	39	9	165	285	22	.953
1996—Tacoma (PCL)	S-2-3-0-1	107	422	63	118	28	4	13	58	.280	15	38	3	143	277	14	.968
1997—Tucson (PCL)■	3-S-2-0	94	356	65	117	24	3	9	70	.329	26	25	0	58	199	16	.941
—Milwaukee (A.L.)	2B-3B-SS	16	50	4	11	2	1	0	7	.220	1	5	0	27	35	0	1.000
Major league totals (1 year)		16	50	4	11	2	1	0	7	.220	1	5	0	27	35	0	1.000

RECORD AS PITCHER

Year Team (League)	W	L	Pct.	ERA	G	GS	CG	ShO	Sv.	IP	H	R	ER	BB	SO
1994—Jacksonville (Southern)	0	0	...	0.00	1	0	0	0	0	2/3	1	0	0	0	0

DIAZ, EDWIN   2B   DIAMONDBACKS

PERSONAL: Born January 15, 1975, in Bayamon, Puerto Rico. ... 5-11/172. ... Bats right, throws right.
TRANSACTIONS/CAREER NOTES: Selected by Texas Rangers organization in second round of free-agent draft (June 3, 1993); pick received as compensation for Chicago Cubs signing Type A free agent Jose Guzman. ... Selected by Arizona Diamondbacks in first round (11th pick overall) of expansion draft (November 18, 1997).

Year Team (League)	Pos.	G	AB	R	H	2B	3B	HR	RBI	Avg.	BB	SO	SB	PO	A	E	Avg.
1993—GC Rangers (GCL)	2B	43	154	27	47	10	5	1	23	.305	19	21	12	78	100	6	.967
1994—Char., S.C. (S. Atl.)	2B-SS	122	443	52	109	22	7	11	60	.246	22	107	11	204	303	31	.942
1995—Charlotte (Fla. St.)	2B-SS	115	450	48	128	26	5	8	56	.284	33	94	8	213	277	16	.968
1996—Tulsa (Texas)	2B	121	500	70	132	33	6	16	65	.264	25	122	8	238	322	19	.967
1997—Oklahoma City (A.A.)	2B	20	73	6	8	3	1	1	4	.110	2	27	1	37	48	6	.934
—Tulsa (Texas)	2B	105	440	65	121	31	1	15	46	.275	33	102	6	170	312	*19	.962

DIAZ, EINAR   C   INDIANS

PERSONAL: Born December 28, 1972, in Chiniqui, Panama. ... 5-10/165. ... Bats right, throws right. ... Full name: Einar Antonio Diaz.
TRANSACTIONS/CAREER NOTES: Signed as non-drafted free agent by Cleveland Indians organization (October 5, 1990).
STATISTICAL NOTES: Led Appalachian League third basemen with 125 assists and .959 fielding percentage in 1992. ... Led Appalachian League catchers with 54 assists and nine errors in 1993. ... Led South Atlantic League in grounding into double plays with 18 in 1994. ... Led South Atlantic League catchers with 966 total chances, 845 putouts, 112 assists and tied for lead with eight double plays in 1994. ... Led Carolina League catchers with 107 assists and .992 fielding percentage in 1995. ... Led Eastern League catchers with 15 errors in 1996. ... Led American Association catchers with 18 errors in 1997.

Year Team (League)	Pos.	G	AB	R	H	2B	3B	HR	RBI	Avg.	BB	SO	SB	PO	A	E	Avg.
1991—Dom. Inds. (DSL)......	...	62	239	35	67	6	3	1	29	.280	14	5	10	...	...	...	...
1992—Burlington (Appal.).....	3B-SS	52	178	19	37	3	0	1	14	.208	20	9	2	27	†137	7	†.959
1993—Burlington (Appal.)......	C-3B	60	231	40	69	15	3	5	33	.299	8	7	7	315	†55	†10	.974
—Columbus (S. Atl.)......	C	1	5	0	0	0	0	0	0	.000	0	1	0	3	1	0	1.000
1994—Columbus (S. Atl.)......	C-3B	120	491	67	137	23	2	16	71	.279	17	34	4	†848	†134	9	.991
1995—Kinston (Carolina)......	C-3B	104	373	46	98	21	0	6	43	.263	12	29	3	676	†111	7	†.991
1996—Cant./Akr. (Eastern)......	C-3B	104	395	47	111	26	2	3	35	.281	12	22	3	765	88	†15	.983
—Cleveland (A.L.)..........	C	4	1	0	0	0	0	0	0	.000	0	0	0	4	0	0	1.000
1997—Buffalo (A.A.)......	C-3B	109	336	40	86	18	2	3	31	.256	18	34	2	653	67	†19	.974
—Cleveland (A.L.)..........	C	5	7	1	1	1	0	0	1	.143	0	2	0	18	3	1	.955
Major league totals (2 years)		9	8	1	1	1	0	0	1	.125	0	2	0	22	3	1	.962

DICKSON, JASON   P   ANGELS

PERSONAL: Born March 30, 1973, in London, Ont. ... 6-0/190. ... Throws right, bats left. ... Full name: Jason Royce Dickson.
HIGH SCHOOL: James M. Hill (Chatham, N.B.).
JUNIOR COLLEGE: Northeastern Oklahoma A&M.
TRANSACTIONS/CAREER NOTES: Selected by California Angels organization in sixth round of free-agent draft (June 2, 1994). ... Angels franchise renamed Anaheim Angels for 1997 season.
HONORS: Named A.L. Rookie Pitcher of the Year by THE SPORTING NEWS (1997).

Year Team (League)	W	L	Pct.	ERA	G	GS	CG	ShO	Sv.	IP	H	R	ER	BB	SO
1994—Boise (Northwest)	3	1	.750	3.86	9	7	0	0	1	44 1/3	40	22	19	18	37
1995—Cedar Rapids (Midw.)	14	6	.700	2.86	25	25	*9	1	0	173	151	71	55	45	134
1996—Midland (Texas)	5	2	.714	3.58	8	8	3	1	0	55 1/3	55	27	22	10	40
—Vancouver (PCL)	7	11	.389	3.80	18	18	*7	0	0	130 1/3	134	73	55	40	70
—California (A.L.)	1	4	.200	4.57	7	7	0	0	0	43 1/3	52	22	22	18	20
1997—Anaheim (A.L.)	13	9	.591	4.29	33	32	2	1	0	203 2/3	236	111	97	56	115
Major league totals (2 years)	14	13	.519	4.34	40	39	2	1	0	247	288	133	119	74	135

ALL-STAR GAME RECORD

Year League	W	L	Pct.	ERA	GS	CG	ShO	Sv.	IP	H	R	ER	BB	SO
1997—American				Did not play.										

DIFELICE, MIKE   C   DEVIL RAYS

PERSONAL: Born May 28, 1969, in Philadelphia. ... 6-2/205. ... Bats right, throws right. ... Full name: Michael William Difelice.
HIGH SCHOOL: Bearden (Knoxville, Tenn.).
COLLEGE: Tennessee.
TRANSACTIONS/CAREER NOTES: Selected by St. Louis Cardinals organization in 11th round of free-agent draft (June 3, 1991). ... Selected by Tampa Bay Devil Rays in first round (20th pick overall) of expansion draft (November 18, 1997).
STATISTICAL NOTES: Tied for N.L. lead in passed balls with 12 in 1997.

Year Team (League)	Pos.	G	AB	R	H	2B	3B	HR	RBI	Avg.	BB	SO	SB	PO	A	E	Avg.
1991—Hamilton (NYP).........	C	43	157	10	33	5	0	4	15	.210	9	40	1	297	40	9	.974
1992—Hamilton (NYP).........	C-1B	18	58	11	20	3	0	2	9	.345	4	7	2	135	19	5	.969
—St. Petersburg (FSL) ..	C	17	53	0	12	3	0	0	4	.226	3	11	0	73	11	2	.977
1993—Springfield (Midw.)	C	8	20	5	7	1	0	0	3	.350	2	3	0	52	9	0	1.000
—St. Petersburg (FSL) ..	C	30	97	5	22	2	0	0	8	.227	11	13	1	165	23	7	.964
1994—Arkansas (Texas).......	C	71	200	19	50	11	2	2	15	.250	12	48	0	419	40	6	.987
1995—Arkansas (Texas).......	C	62	176	14	47	10	1	1	24	.267	23	29	0	327	48	6	.984
—Louisville (A.A.).........	C	21	63	8	17	4	0	0	3	.270	5	11	1	111	10	2	.984
1996—Louisville (A.A.).........	C	79	246	25	70	13	0	9	33	.285	20	43	0	455	48	8	.984
—St. Louis (N.L.)..........	C	4	7	0	2	1	0	0	2	.286	0	1	0	15	1	0	1.000
1997—Arkansas (Texas).......	C	1	3	0	1	0	0	0	0	.333	1	0	0	6	2	0	1.000
—St. Louis (N.L.)..........	C-1B	93	260	16	62	10	1	4	30	.238	19	61	1	587	64	6	.991
—Louisville (A.A.).........	C	1	4	1	1	0	0	1	1	.250	0	1	0	3	1	0	1.000
Major league totals (2 years)		97	267	16	64	11	1	4	32	.240	19	62	1	602	65	6	.991

DiPOTO, JERRY   P   ROCKIES

PERSONAL: Born May 24, 1968, in Jersey City, N.J. ... 6-2/200. ... Throws right, bats right. ... Full name: Gerard Peter DiPoto III.
HIGH SCHOOL: Toms River (N.J.).
COLLEGE: Virginia Commonwealth.
TRANSACTIONS/CAREER NOTES: Selected by Cleveland Indians organization in third round of free-agent draft (June 5, 1989). ... On Cleveland disabled list (March 25-June 12, 1994); included rehabilitation assignment to Charlotte (May 10-June 8). ... Traded by Indians with

P Paul Byrd, P Dave Mlicki and a player to be named later to New York Mets for OF Jeromy Burnitz and P Joe Roa (November 18, 1994); Mets acquired 2B Jesus Azuaje to complete deal (December 6, 1994). ... Traded by Mets to Colorado Rockies for P Armando Reynoso (November 27, 1996).

STATISTICAL NOTES: Led Eastern League with 15 wild pitches and tied for lead with three balks in 1991.

Year Team (League)	W	L	Pct.	ERA	G	GS	CG	ShO	Sv.	IP	H	R	ER	BB	SO
1989— Watertown (NYP)	6	5	.545	3.61	14	14	1	0	0	87 1/3	75	42	35	39	98
1990— Kinston (Carolina)	11	4	.733	3.78	24	24	1	0	0	145 1/3	129	75	61	77	143
—Cant./Akr. (Eastern)	1	0	1.000	2.57	3	2	0	0	0	14	11	5	4	4	12
1991— Cant./Akr. (Eastern)	6	11	.353	3.81	28	26	2	0	0	156	143	83	66	74	97
1992— Colo. Springs (PCL)	9	9	.500	4.94	50	9	0	0	2	122	148	78	67	66	62
1993— Charlotte (Int'l)	6	3	.667	1.93	34	0	0	0	12	46 2/3	34	10	10	13	44
—Cleveland (A.L.)	4	4	.500	2.40	46	0	0	0	11	56 1/3	57	21	15	30	41
1994— Charlotte (Int'l)	3	2	.600	3.15	25	2	0	0	9	34 1/3	37	13	12	12	26
—Cleveland (A.L.)	0	0	. . .	8.04	7	0	0	0	0	15 2/3	26	14	14	10	9
1995— New York (N.L.)■	4	6	.400	3.78	58	0	0	0	2	78 2/3	77	41	33	29	49
1996— New York (N.L.)	7	2	.778	4.19	57	0	0	0	0	77 1/3	91	44	36	45	52
1997— Colorado (N.L.)■	5	3	.625	4.70	74	0	0	0	16	95 2/3	108	56	50	33	74
A.L. totals (2 years)	4	4	.500	3.63	53	0	0	0	11	72	83	35	29	40	50
N.L. totals (3 years)	16	11	.593	4.26	189	0	0	0	18	251 2/3	276	141	119	107	175
Major league totals (5 years)	20	15	.571	4.12	242	0	0	0	29	323 2/3	359	176	148	147	225

DiSARCINA, GARY   SS   ANGELS

PERSONAL: Born November 19, 1967, in Malden, Mass. ... 6-1/178. ... Bats right, throws right. ... Full name: Gary Thomas DiSarcina. ... Brother of Glenn DiSarcina, shortstop, Chicago White Sox organization (1991-96). ... Name pronounced DEE-sar-SEE-na.

HIGH SCHOOL: Billerica (Mass.) Memorial.

COLLEGE: Massachusetts.

TRANSACTIONS/CAREER NOTES: Selected by California Angels organization in sixth round of free-agent draft (June 1, 1988). ... On disabled list (August 27, 1993-remainder of season and August 4-September 17, 1995). ... Angels franchise renamed Anaheim Angels for 1997 season.

RECORDS: Holds A.L. single-season record for fewest putouts by shortstop (150 or more games)—212 (1996).

STATISTICAL NOTES: Led Pacific Coast League shortstops with .968 fielding percentage and 419 assists in 1991. ... Led A.L. shortstops with 761 total chances in 1992.

						BATTING								FIELDING		
Year Team (League)	Pos.	G	AB	R	H	2B	3B	HR	RBI	Avg.	BB	SO	SB	PO	A	E	Avg.
1988— Bend (Northwest)	SS	71	295	40	90	11	•5	2	39	.305	27	34	7	104	*237	27	.927
1989— Midland (Texas)	SS	126	441	65	126	18	7	4	54	.286	24	54	11	206	*411	30	*.954
—California (A.L.)	SS	2	0	0	0	0	0	0	0	. . .	0	0	0	0	0	0	. . .
1990— Edmonton (PCL)	SS	97	330	46	70	12	2	4	37	.212	25	46	5	165	289	24	.950
—California (A.L.)	SS-2B	18	57	8	8	1	1	0	0	.140	3	10	1	17	57	4	.949
1991— Edmonton (PCL)	SS-2B	119	390	61	121	21	4	4	58	.310	29	32	16	191	†425	20	†.969
—California (A.L.)	SS-2B-3B	18	57	5	12	2	0	0	3	.211	3	4	0	29	45	4	.949
1992— California (A.L.)	SS	157	518	48	128	19	0	3	42	.247	20	50	9	250	*486	•25	.967
1993— California (A.L.)	SS	126	416	44	99	20	1	3	45	.238	15	38	5	193	362	14	.975
1994— California (A.L.)	SS	112	389	53	101	14	2	3	33	.260	18	28	3	159	*358	9	.983
1995— California (A.L.)	SS	99	362	61	111	28	6	5	41	.307	20	25	7	146	275	6	.986
1996— California (A.L.)	SS	150	536	62	137	26	4	5	48	.256	21	36	2	212	460	20	.971
1997— Anaheim (A.L.)	SS	154	549	52	135	28	2	4	47	.246	17	29	7	227	421	15	.977
Major league totals (9 years)		836	2884	333	731	138	16	23	259	.253	117	220	34	1233	2464	97	.974

ALL-STAR GAME RECORD

					BATTING							FIELDING		
Year League	Pos.	AB	R	H	2B	3B	HR	RBI	Avg.	BB	SO	SB	PO	A	E	Avg.
1995— American	PR-SS	1	0	0	0	0	0	0	.000	0	0	0	0	0	0	. . .

DISHMAN, GLENN   P   TIGERS

PERSONAL: Born November 5, 1970, in Baltimore. ... 6-1/195. ... Throws left, bats right. ... Full name: Glenelg Edward Dishman.

HIGH SCHOOL: Moreau (Hayward, Calif.).

COLLEGE: Texas Christian.

TRANSACTIONS/CAREER NOTES: Signed as non-drafted free agent by San Diego Padres organization (June 10, 1993). ... Claimed on waivers by Philadelphia Phillies (September 12, 1996). ... Claimed on waivers by Detroit Tigers (October 3, 1996).

STATISTICAL NOTES: Pitched 1-0 no-hit victory for Spokane against Yakima (July 17, 1993).

Year Team (League)	W	L	Pct.	ERA	G	GS	CG	ShO	Sv.	IP	H	R	ER	BB	SO
1993— Spokane (N'west)	6	3	.667	2.20	12	12	2	•2	0	77 2/3	59	25	19	13	79
—Rancho Cucamonga (Cal.)	0	1	.000	7.15	2	2	0	0	0	11 1/3	14	9	9	5	6
1994— Wichita (Texas)	11	8	.579	2.82	27	•27	1	0	0	169 1/3	156	73	53	42	*165
—Las Vegas (PCL)	1	1	.500	3.46	2	2	0	0	0	13	15	7	5	1	12
1995— Las Vegas (PCL)	6	3	.667	2.55	14	14	3	1	0	106	91	37	30	20	64
—San Diego (N.L.)	4	8	.333	5.01	19	16	0	0	0	97	104	60	54	34	43
1996— Las Vegas (PCL)	6	8	.429	5.57	26	26	3	1	0	155	177	103	96	43	115
—San Diego (N.L.)	0	0	. . .	7.71	2 1/3	3	2	2	1	0
—Philadelphia (N.L.)■	0	0	. . .	7.71	4	1	0	0	0	7	9	6	6	2	3
1997— Toledo (Int'l)■	7	6	.538	3.87	21	18	1	0	1	114	112	53	49	32	77
—Detroit (A.L.)	1	2	.333	5.28	7	4	0	0	0	29	30	18	17	8	20
A.L. totals (1 year)	1	2	.333	5.28	7	4	0	0	0	29	30	18	17	8	20
N.L. totals (2 years)	4	8	.333	5.25	26	17	0	0	0	106 1/3	116	68	62	37	46
Major league totals (3 years)	5	10	.333	5.25	33	21	0	0	0	135 1/3	146	86	79	45	66

DOSTER, DAVE   2B   PHILLIES

PERSONAL: Born October 8, 1970, in Fort Wayne, Ind. ... 5-10/185. ... Bats right, throws right. ... Full name: David Eric Doster.
HIGH SCHOOL: New Haven (Ind.).
COLLEGE: Indiana State.
TRANSACTIONS/CAREER NOTES: Selected by Philadelphia Phillies organization in 27th round of free-agent draft (June 3, 1993).
STATISTICAL NOTES: Led Florida State League second basemen with 743 total chances and 115 double plays in 1994. ... Led Eastern League with 254 total bases in 1995. ... Led Eastern League second basemen with 420 assists, 693 total chances and 91 double plays in 1995.

Year	Team (League)	Pos.	G	AB	R	H	2B	3B	HR	RBI	Avg.	BB	SO	SB	PO	A	E	Avg.
															BATTING			**FIELDING**
1993—	Spartanburg (SAL)	2B	60	223	34	61	15	0	3	20	.274	25	36	1	111	205	13	.960
	—Clearwater (FSL)	2B-3B	9	28	4	10	3	1	0	2	.357	2	2	2	16	29	5	.900
1994—	Clearwater (FSL)	2B	131	480	76	135	*42	4	13	74	.281	54	71	12	*278	*445	20	.973
1995—	Reading (Eastern)	2B-OF	139	*551	84	146	39	3	21	79	.265	51	61	11	261	†420	12	.983
1996—	Scran./W.B. (Int'l)......	2B	88	322	37	83	20	0	7	48	.258	26	54	7	197	203	6	.985
	—Philadelphia (N.L.).....	2B-3B	39	105	14	28	8	0	1	8	.267	7	21	0	52	57	3	.973
1997—	Scran./W.B. (Int'l)......	2B-3B	108	410	70	129	32	2	16	79	.315	30	60	5	152	248	14	.966
Major league totals (1 year)			39	105	14	28	8	0	1	8	.267	7	21	0	52	57	3	.973

DOTEL, OCTAVIO   P   METS

PERSONAL: Born November 25, 1975, in Santo Domingo, Dominican Republic. ... 6-0/175. ... Throws right, bats right.
TRANSACTIONS/CAREER NOTES: Signed as non-drafted free agent by New York Mets organization (March 20, 1993). ... On disabled list (July 18-August 16, 1996).

Year	Team (League)	W	L	Pct.	ERA	G	GS	CG	ShO	Sv.	IP	H	R	ER	BB	SO
1993—	Dominican Mets (DSL)......	6	2	.750	4.10		11	0	0	0	59 1/3	46	30	27	38	48
1994—	Dominican Mets (DSL)......	5	0	1.000	4.32	15	14	1	0	0	81 1/3	84	53	39	31	95
1995—	GC Mets (GCL)	•7	4	.636	2.18	13	12	2	0	0	*74 1/3	48	23	18	17	*86
	—St. Lucie (Fla. St.)	1	0	1.000	5.63	3	0	0	0	0	8	10	5	5	4	9
1996—	Columbia (South Atlantic)..	11	3	.786	3.59	22	19	0	0	0	115 1/3	89	49	46	49	142
1997—	St. Lucie (Fla. St.)	5	2	.714	2.52	9	8	1	1	0	50	44	18	14	23	39
	—Binghamton (Eastern)	3	4	.429	5.98	12	12	0	0	0	55 2/3	66	50	37	38	40
	—GC Mets (GCL)	0	0	...	0.96	3	2	0	0	1	9 1/3	9	1	1	2	7

DRABEK, DOUG   P   ORIOLES

PERSONAL: Born July 25, 1962, in Victoria, Texas. ... 6-1/185. ... Throws right, bats right. ... Full name: Douglas Dean Drabek. ... Name pronounced DRAY-bek.
HIGH SCHOOL: St. Joseph (Victoria, Texas).
COLLEGE: Houston.
TRANSACTIONS/CAREER NOTES: Selected by Cleveland Indians organization in fourth round of free-agent draft (June 3, 1980); did not sign. ... Selected by Chicago White Sox organization in 11th round of free-agent draft (June 6, 1983). ... Traded by White Sox with P Kevin Hickey to New York Yankees organization (August 13, 1984), completing deal in which Yankees traded IF Roy Smalley to White Sox for two players to be named later (July 18, 1984). ... Traded by Yankees with P Brian Fisher and P Logan Easley to Pittsburgh Pirates for P Rick Rhoden, P Cecilio Guante and P Pat Clements (November 26, 1986). ... On disabled list (April 26-May 18, 1987). ... Granted free agency (October 26, 1992). ... Signed by Houston Astros (December 1, 1992). ... On suspended list (September 12-17, 1995). ... On disabled list (August 23-September 8, 1996). ... Granted free agency (November 18, 1996). ... Signed by White Sox (January 14, 1997). ... Granted free agency (October 30, 1997). ... Signed by Baltimore Orioles (December 11, 1997).
RECORDS: Shares major league single-season record for fewest double plays by pitcher who led league in double plays—4 (1992).
HONORS: Named N.L. Pitcher of the Year by THE SPORTING NEWS (1990). ... Named righthanded pitcher on THE SPORTING NEWS N.L. All-Star team (1990). ... Named N.L. Cy Young Award winner by Baseball Writers' Association of America (1990).
STATISTICAL NOTES: Pitched 11-0 one-hit, complete-game victory against Philadelphia (August 3, 1990). ... Pitched 8-0 one-hit, complete-game victory against St. Louis (May 27, 1991).
MISCELLANEOUS: Appeared in five games as pinch-runner (1989). ... Appeared in one game as pinch-runner (1991). ... Made an out in only appearance as pinch-hitter (1992). ... Appeared in one game as pinch-runner (1994). ... Appeared in two games as pinch-runner (1995). ... Appeared in two games as pinch-runner (1996). ... Appeared in one game as pinch-runner (1997).

Year	Team (League)	W	L	Pct.	ERA	G	GS	CG	ShO	Sv.	IP	H	R	ER	BB	SO
1983—	Niagara Falls (NYP)	6	7	.462	3.65	16	13	3	0	0	103 2/3	99	52	42	48	103
1984—	Appleton (Midwest)...........	1	0	1.000	1.80	1	1	0	0	0	5	3	1	1	3	6
	—Glens Falls (Eastern)	12	5	.706	2.24	19	17	7	3	0	124 2/3	90	34	31	44	75
	—Nashville (Southern)■	1	2	.333	2.32	4	4	2	0	0	31	30	11	8	10	22
1985—	Alb./Colon. (Eastern)	13	7	.650	2.99	26	26	9	2	0	*192 2/3	153	71	64	55	*153
1986—	Columbus (Int'l)	1	4	.200	7.29	8	8	0	0	0	42	50	36	34	25	23
	—New York (A.L.)...............	7	8	.467	4.10	27	21	0	0	0	131 2/3	126	64	60	50	76
1987—	Pittsburgh (N.L.)■	11	12	.478	3.88	29	28	1	1	0	176 1/3	165	86	76	46	120
1988—	Pittsburgh (N.L.)	15	7	.682	3.08	33	32	3	1	0	219 1/3	194	83	75	50	127
1989—	Pittsburgh (N.L.)	14	12	.538	2.80	35	34	8	5	0	244 1/3	215	83	76	69	123
1990—	Pittsburgh (N.L.)	*22	6	.786	2.76	33	33	9	3	0	231 1/3	190	78	71	56	131
1991—	Pittsburgh (N.L.)	15	14	.517	3.07	35	35	5	2	0	234 2/3	245	92	80	62	142
1992—	Pittsburgh (N.L.)	15	11	.577	2.77	34	34	10	4	0	256 2/3	218	84	79	54	177
1993—	Houston (N.L.)■	9	*18	.333	3.79	34	34	7	2	0	237 2/3	242	108	100	60	157
1994—	Houston (N.L.)	12	6	.667	2.84	23	23	6	2	0	164 2/3	132	58	52	45	121
1995—	Houston (N.L.)	10	9	.526	4.77	31	•31	2	1	0	185	205	104	98	54	143
1996—	Houston (N.L.)	7	9	.438	4.57	30	30	1	0	0	175 1/3	208	102	89	60	137
1997—	Chicago (A.L.)■	12	11	.522	5.74	31	31	0	0	0	169 1/3	170	109	108	69	85
A.L. totals (2 years)		19	19	.500	5.02	58	52	0	0	0	301	296	173	168	119	161
N.L. totals (10 years)		130	104	.556	3.37	317	314	52	21	0	2125 1/3	2014	878	796	556	1378
Major league totals (12 years)		149	123	.548	3.58	375	366	52	21	0	2426 1/3	2310	1051	964	675	1539

RECORDS: Holds single-series record for most games lost—3 (1992). ... Shares N.L. career record for most complete games pitched—2.

Year	Team (League)	W	L	Pct.	ERA	G	GS	CG	ShO	Sv.	IP	H	R	ER	BB	SO
1990—Pittsburgh (N.L.)		1	1	.500	1.65	2	2	1	0	0	16 1/3	12	4	3	3	13
1991—Pittsburgh (N.L.)		1	1	.500	0.60	2	2	1	0	0	15	10	1	1	5	10
1992—Pittsburgh (N.L.)		0	3	.000	3.71	3	3	0	0	0	17	18	11	7	6	10
Champ. series totals (3 years)	....	2	5	.286	2.05	7	7	2	0	0	48 1/3	40	16	11	14	33

ALL-STAR GAME RECORD

Year	League	W	L	Pct.	ERA	GS	CG	ShO	Sv.	IP	H	R	ER	BB	SO
1994—National		0	0	...	13.50	0	0	0	0	2/3	4	3	1	0	1

DREIFORT, DARREN — P — DODGERS

PERSONAL: Born May 3, 1972, in Wichita, Kan. ... 6-2/205. ... Throws right, bats right. ... Full name: Darren John Dreifort. ... Name pronounced DRY-fert.

HIGH SCHOOL: Wichita (Kan.) Heights.

COLLEGE: Wichita State.

TRANSACTIONS/CAREER NOTES: Selected by New York Mets organization in 11th round of free-agent draft (June 4, 1990); did not sign. ... Selected by Los Angeles Dodgers organization in first round (second pick overall) of free-agent draft (June 3, 1993). ... On San Antonio disabled list (July 7-28, 1994). ... On Albuquerque disabled list (August 27, 1994-remainder of season). ... On disabled list (April 23, 1995-entire season). ... On Los Angeles disabled list (March 25-May 16, 1996); included rehabilitation assignment to Albuquerque (April 18-May 15). ... On disabled list (May 12-June 17, 1997).

HONORS: Named righthanded pitcher on THE SPORTING NEWS college All-America team (1992-93). ... Named Golden Spikes Award winner by USA Baseball (1993).

MISCELLANEOUS: Member of 1992 U.S. Olympic baseball team. ... Singled with an RBI in one game as pinch-hitter with Los Angeles (1994). ... Made an out in only appearance as pinch-hitter (1996).

Year	Team (League)	W	L	Pct.	ERA	G	GS	CG	ShO	Sv.	IP	H	R	ER	BB	SO
1993—								Did not play.								
1994—Los Angeles (N.L.)		0	5	.000	6.21	27	0	0	0	6	29	45	21	20	15	22
—San Antonio (Tex.)		3	1	.750	2.80	8	8	0	0	0	35 1/3	36	14	11	13	32
—Albuquerque (PCL)		1	0	1.000	5.68	1	1	0	0	0	6 1/3	8	4	4	3	3
1995—								Did not play.								
1996—Albuquerque (PCL)		5	6	.455	4.17	18	18	0	0	0	86 1/3	88	49	40	52	75
—Los Angeles (N.L.)		1	4	.200	4.94	19	0	0	0	0	23 2/3	23	13	13	12	24
1997—Los Angeles (N.L.)		5	2	.714	2.86	48	0	0	0	4	63	45	21	20	34	63
—Albuquerque (PCL)		0	0	...	1.59	2	2	0	0	0	5 2/3	2	1	1	1	3
Major league totals (3 years)	......	6	11	.353	4.12	94	0	0	0	10	115 2/3	113	55	53	61	109

DIVISION SERIES RECORD

Year	Team (League)	W	L	Pct.	ERA	G	GS	CG	ShO	Sv.	IP	H	R	ER	BB	SO
1996—Los Angeles (N.L.)		0	0	...	0.00	1	0	0	0	0	2/3	0	0	0	0	0

DREWS, MATT — P — TIGERS

PERSONAL: Born August 29, 1974, in Sarasota, Fla. ... 6-8/230. ... Throws right, bats right. ... Full name: Matthew Ross Drews. ... Grandson of Karl Drews, pitcher with four major league baseball teams (1946-49 and 1951-54).

HIGH SCHOOL: Sarasota (Fla.).

TRANSACTIONS/CAREER NOTES: Selected by New York Yankees organization in first round (13th pick overall) of free-agent draft (June 3, 1993). ... Traded by Yankees with OF Ruben Sierra to Detroit Tigers for 1B/DH Cecil Fielder (July 31, 1996). ... Selected by Arizona Diamondbacks in second round (39th pick overall) of expansion draft (November 18, 1997). ... Traded by Diamondbacks with IF Joe Randa and IF Gabe Alvarez to Tigers for IF Travis Fryman (November 18, 1997).

STATISTICAL NOTES: Led Southern League with 16 hit batsmen in 1997.

Year	Team (League)	W	L	Pct.	ERA	G	GS	CG	ShO	Sv.	IP	H	R	ER	BB	SO
1994—Oneonta (N.Y.-Penn)		7	6	.538	2.10	14	14	1	0	0	90	76	31	21	19	69
1995—Tampa (Florida State)		*15	7	.682	2.27	28	*28	3	0	0	182	142	73	46	58	140
1996—Columbus (Int'l)		0	4	.000	8.41	7	7	0	0	0	20 1/3	18	27	19	27	7
—Tampa (Florida State)		0	3	.000	7.13	4	4	0	0	0	17 2/3	26	20	14	12	12
—Norwich (Eastern)		1	3	.250	4.50	9	9	0	0	0	46	40	26	23	33	37
—Jacksonville (Southern)■	..	0	4	.000	4.35	6	6	1	0	0	31	26	18	15	19	40
1997—Jacksonville (Southern)	......	8	11	.421	5.49	24	24	4	1	0	144 1/3	160	109	88	50	85
—Toledo (Int'l)		0	2	.000	6.60	3	3	0	0	0	15	14	11	11	14	7

DRISKILL, TRAVIS — P

PERSONAL: Born August 1, 1971, in Omaha, Neb. ... 6-0/185. ... Throws right, bats right. ... Full name: Travis Corey Driskill.

HIGH SCHOOL: L.C. Anderson (Austin, Texas).

COLLEGE: Texas Tech.

TRANSACTIONS/CAREER NOTES: Selected by Houston Astros organization in 76th round of free-agent draft (June 4, 1990); did not sign. ... Selected by Cleveland Indians organization in fourth round of free-agent draft (June 3, 1993). ... Contract sold by Indians to Yakult Swallows of Japanese Central League (January 6, 1998).

Year	Team (League)	W	L	Pct.	ERA	G	GS	CG	ShO	Sv.	IP	H	R	ER	BB	SO
1993—Watertown (NYP)		5	4	.556	4.14	21	8	0	0	3	63	62	38	29	21	53
1994—Columbus (S. Atl.)		5	5	.500	2.52	•62	0	0	0	35	64 1/3	51	25	18	30	88
1995—Kinston (Carolina)		2	2	.000	2.74	15	0	0	0	0	23	17	7	7	5	24
—Cant./Akr. (Eastern)		3	4	.429	4.66	33	0	0	0	4	46 1/3	46	24	24	19	39
1996—Cant./Akr. (Eastern)		13	7	.650	3.61	29	24	4	2	0	172	169	89	69	63	148
1997—Buffalo (A.A.)		8	7	.533	4.65	29	24	1	0	0	147	159	86	76	60	102

DRUMRIGHT, MIKE P TIGERS

PERSONAL: Born April 19, 1974, in Salina, Kan. ... 6-4/210. ... Throws right, bats left. ... Full name: Michael R. Drumright.
HIGH SCHOOL: Valley Center (Kan.).
COLLEGE: Wichita State.
TRANSACTIONS/CAREER NOTES: Selected by Baltimore Orioles organization in 45th round of free-agent draft (June 1, 1992); did not sign. ... Selected by Detroit Tigers organization in first round (11th pick overall) of free-agent draft (June 1, 1995).
STATISTICAL NOTES: Led Southern League with six balks in 1996. ... Tied for International League lead with four balks in 1997.

Year Team (League)	W	L	Pct.	ERA	G	GS	CG	ShO	Sv.	IP	H	R	ER	BB	SO
1995— Lakeland (Fla. St.)	1	1	.500	4.29	5	5	0	0	0	21	19	11	10	9	19
— Jacksonville (Southern)	0	1	.000	3.69	5	5	0	0	0	31 2/3	30	13	13	15	34
1996— Jacksonville (Southern)	6	4	.600	3.97	18	18	1	1	0	99 2/3	80	51	44	48	109
1997— Jacksonville (Southern)	1	1	.500	1.57	5	5	0	0	0	28 2/3	16	7	5	13	24
— Toledo (Int'l)	5	10	.333	5.06	23	23	0	0	0	133 1/3	134	78	75	•91	115

DUCEY, ROB OF MARINERS

PERSONAL: Born May 24, 1965, in Toronto. ... 6-2/180. ... Bats left, throws right. ... Full name: Robert Thomas Ducey.
HIGH SCHOOL: Glenview Park (Toronto).
JUNIOR COLLEGE: Seminole Community College (Fla.).
TRANSACTIONS/CAREER NOTES: Signed as non-drafted free agent by Toronto Blue Jays organization (May 16, 1984). ... On Toronto disabled list (June 9-September 2, 1989); included rehabilitation assignments to Syracuse (July 5-14 and August 24-September 2). ... Traded by Blue Jays with C Greg Myers to California Angels for P Mark Eichhorn (July 30, 1992). ... Released by Angels (November 19, 1992). ... Signed by Texas Rangers organization (December 18, 1992). ... On Oklahoma City disabled list (April 21-May 16, 1993). ... Released by Rangers (October 14, 1994). ... Signed by Nippon Ham Fighters of Japan Pacific League prior to 1995 season. ... Signed by Seattle Mariners organization (January 22, 1997). ... On Seattle disabled list (August 3-21, 1997).
STATISTICAL NOTES: Tied for Southern League lead in double plays by outfielder with six in 1986. ... Tied for International League lead in double plays by outfielder with four in 1990.

Year Team (League)	Pos.	G	AB	R	H	2B	3B	HR	RBI	Avg.	BB	SO	SB	PO	A	E	Avg.
1984— Medicine Hat (Pio.)	OF-1B	63	235	49	71	10	3	12	49	.302	41	61	13	185	11	6	.970
1985— Florence (S. Atl.)	OF-1B	134	529	78	133	22	2	13	86	.251	49	103	12	228	8	9	.963
1986— Ventura (Calif.)	OF-1B	47	178	36	60	11	3	12	38	.337	21	24	17	97	3	2	.980
— Knoxville (Southern)	OF	88	344	49	106	22	3	11	58	.308	29	59	7	186	10	6	.970
1987— Syracuse (Int'l)	OF	100	359	62	102	14	•10	10	60	.284	61	89	8	171	13	6	.968
— Toronto (A.L.)	OF-DH	34	48	12	9	1	0	1	6	.188	8	10	2	31	0	0	1.000
1988— Syracuse (Int'l)	OF	90	317	40	81	14	4	7	42	.256	43	81	7	233	6	4	.984
— Toronto (A.L.)	OF-DH	27	54	15	17	4	1	0	6	.315	5	7	1	35	1	0	1.000
1989— Toronto (A.L.)	OF-DH	41	76	5	16	4	0	0	7	.211	9	25	2	56	3	0	1.000
— Syracuse (Int'l)	OF	10	29	0	3	0	1	0	3	.103	10	13	0	14	0	1	.933
1990— Syracuse (Int'l)	OF	127	438	53	117	32	7	7	47	.267	60	87	13	262	13	13	.955
— Toronto (A.L.)	OF	19	53	7	16	5	0	0	7	.302	7	15	1	37	0	0	1.000
1991— Syracuse (Int'l)	OF	72	266	53	78	10	3	8	40	.293	51	58	5	120	1	0	1.000
— Toronto (A.L.)	OF-DH	39	68	8	16	2	2	1	4	.235	6	26	2	32	1	4	.892
1992— Toronto (A.L.)	OF-DH	23	21	3	1	1	0	0	2	.048	0	10	0	11	0	0	1.000
— California (A.L.)■	OF-DH	31	59	4	14	3	0	0	2	.237	5	12	2	32	2	2	.944
1993— Okla. City (A.A.)■	OF	105	389	68	118	17	•10	17	56	.303	46	97	17	244	8	7	.973
— Texas (A.L.)	OF	27	85	15	24	6	3	2	9	.282	10	17	2	51	1	0	1.000
1994— Oklahoma City (A.A.)	OF	115	403	69	108	27	9	17	65	.268	75	91	9	221	9	4	.983
— Texas (A.L.)	OF	11	29	1	5	1	0	0	1	.172	2	1	0	15	0	2	.882
1995— Nippon (Japan)■	...	117	425	61	106	19	4	25	61	.249	54	103	7	...	...	...	...
1996— Nippon (Japan)	...	120	427	68	105	17	5	26	59	.246	86	90	3	...	...	...	...
1997— Tacoma (PCL)■	OF	23	74	8	24	8	0	0	11	.324	8	15	0	44	3	3	.940
— Seattle (A.L.)	OF	76	143	25	41	15	2	5	10	.287	° 6	31	3	66	3	1	.986
Major league totals (9 years)		328	636	95	159	42	8	9	52	.250	58	154	15	366	11	9	.977

DIVISION SERIES RECORD

Year Team (League)	Pos.	G	AB	R	H	2B	3B	HR	RBI	Avg.	BB	SO	SB	PO	A	E	Avg.
1997— Seattle (A.L.)	PH-OF	2	4	0	2	0	0	0	1	.500	0	0	0	0	0	0	...

CHAMPIONSHIP SERIES RECORD

Year Team (League)	Pos.	G	AB	R	H	2B	3B	HR	RBI	Avg.	BB	SO	SB	PO	A	E	Avg.
1989— Toronto (A.L.)								Did not play.									
1991— Toronto (A.L.)	PR-OF	1	1	0	0	0	0	0	0	.000	0	0	0	0	0	0	...
Championship series totals (1 year)		1	1	0	0	0	0	0	0	.000	0	0	0	0	0	0	...

DUNCAN, COURTNEY P CUBS

PERSONAL: Born October 9, 1974, in Mobile, Ala. ... 6-0/180. ... Throws right, bats left. ... Full name: Courtney Demond Duncan.
HIGH SCHOOL: Daphne (Ala.).
COLLEGE: Grambling State.
TRANSACTIONS/CAREER NOTES: Selected by Chicago Cubs organization in 20th round of free-agent draft (June 2, 1996).

Year Team (League)	W	L	Pct.	ERA	G	GS	CG	ShO	Sv.	IP	H	R	ER	BB	SO
1996— Williamsport (NYP)	*11	1	*.917	2.19	15	•15	1	0	0	90 1/3	58	28	22	34	91
1997— Daytona (Fla. St.)	8	4	.667	*1.63	19	19	1	0	0	121 2/3	90	35	26	35	120
— Orlando (South.)	2	2	.500	3.40	8	8	0	0	0	45	37	28	17	29	45

D

PERSONAL: Born March 13, 1963, in San Pedro de Macoris, Dominican Republic. ... 6-0/185. ... Bats right, throws right.
TRANSACTIONS/CAREER NOTES: Signed as non-drafted free agent by Los Angeles Dodgers organization (January 17, 1982). ... On Los Angeles disabled list (August 19-September 17, 1986; June 19-July 4 and August 16, 1987-remainder of season; May 28-June 12 and July 1-16, 1989). ... Traded by Dodgers with P Tim Leary to Cincinnati Reds for OF Kal Daniels and IF Lenny Harris (July 18, 1989). ... On disabled list (May 14-30, 1990 and August 8-23, 1991). ... Granted free agency (October 30, 1991). ... Signed by Philadelphia Phillies (December 10, 1991). ... On disabled list (July 3-18, 1993 and July 24-August 8, 1994). ... On suspended list (September 20-24, 1993). ... Granted free agency (October 18, 1994). ... Re-signed by Phillies organization (April 14, 1995). ... Claimed on waivers by Reds (August 8, 1995). ... Granted free agency (October 31, 1995). ... Signed by New York Yankees (December 11, 1995). ... On New York disabled list (May 5-23, 1996); included rehabilitation assignment to Columbus (May 17-19). ... Traded with P Kenny Rogers and P Kevin Henthorne to San Diego Padres for OF Greg Vaughn, P Kerry Taylor and P Chris Clark (July 4, 1997); trade later voided because Vaughn failed physical (July 6). ... Traded by Yankees with cash to Toronto Blue Jays for OF Angel Ramirez (July 29, 1997). ... On Toronto disabled list (September 18-28, 1997). ... Granted free agency (October 28, 1997). ... Signed by Yomiuri Giants of Japan Central League (January 15, 1998).
STATISTICAL NOTES: Led Texas League second basemen with 84 double plays in 1984. ... Led N.L. shortstops with 21 errors in 1987. ... Career major league grand slams: 3.
MISCELLANEOUS: Batted as switch-hitter (1982-88).

							BATTING								FIELDING		
Year Team (League)	Pos.	G	AB	R	H	2B	3B	HR	RBI	Avg.	BB	SO	SB	PO	A	E	Avg.
1982—Lethbridge (Pioneer) ..	SS-2B	30	55	9	13	3	1	1	8	.236	8	21	1	23	35	15	.795
1983—Vero Beach (FSL)	OF-SS-2B	109	384	73	102	10	*15	0	42	.266	44	87	*56	169	157	37	.898
1984—San Antonio (Tex.)	2B-OF-SS	125	502	80	127	14	•11	2	44	.253	41	110	41	283	335	22	.966
1985—Los Angeles (N.L.)	SS-2B	142	562	74	137	24	6	6	39	.244	38	113	38	224	430	30	.956
1986—Los Angeles (N.L.)	SS	109	407	47	93	7	0	8	30	.229	30	78	48	172	317	25	.951
1987—Los Angeles (N.L.)	SS-2B-OF	76	261	31	56	8	1	6	18	.215	17	62	11	101	213	†21	.937
—Albuquerque (PCL).....	SS	6	22	6	6	0	0	0	0	.273	2	5	3	8	15	2	.920
1988—Albuquerque (PCL)	SS-2B	56	227	48	65	4	8	0	25	.286	10	40	33	104	153	18	.935
1989—Los Angeles (N.L.)	SS-2B	49	84	9	21	5	1	0	8	.250	1	15	3	28	44	5	.935
—Cincinnati (N.L.)■.....	SS-OF-2B	45	174	23	43	10	1	3	13	.247	8	36	6	73	111	9	.953
1990—Cincinnati (N.L.)	2B-SS-OF	125	435	67	133	22	*11	10	55	.306	24	67	13	265	303	18	.969
1991—Cincinnati (N.L.)	2B-SS-OF	100	333	46	86	7	4	12	40	.258	12	57	5	169	212	9	.977
1992—Philadelphia (N.L.)■..	O-2-S-3	142	574	71	153	40	3	8	50	.267	17	108	23	256	210	16	.967
1993—Philadelphia (N.L.)	2B-SS	124	496	68	140	26	4	11	73	.282	12	88	6	180	304	21	.958
1994—Philadelphia (N.L.)	2-3-S-1	88	347	49	93	22	1	8	48	.268	17	72	10	147	188	12	.965
1995—Philadelphia (N.L.)	2-S-1-3	52	196	20	56	12	1	3	23	.286	0	43	1	156	119	10	.965
—Cincinnati (N.L.)■	2-1-S-O	29	69	16	20	2	1	3	13	.290	5	19	0	59	26	1	.988
1996—New York (A.L.)■......	2-3-0-DH	109	400	62	136	34	3	8	56	.340	9	77	4	187	239	12	.973
—Columbus (Int'l)	2B	2	5	0	1	0	0	0	2	.200	0	2	0	1	5	0	1.000
1997—New York (A.L.)	2B-OF-DH	50	172	16	42	8	0	1	13	.244	6	39	2	72	100	5	.972
—Toronto (A.L.)■..........	2B	39	167	20	38	6	0	0	12	.228	6	39	4	74	111	3	.984
American League totals (2 years)		198	739	98	216	48	3	9	81	.292	21	155	10	333	450	20	.975
National League totals (10 years)		1081	3938	521	1031	185	34	78	410	.262	180	758	164	1830	2477	177	.961
Major league totals (12 years)		1279	4677	619	1247	233	37	87	491	.267	201	913	174	2163	2927	197	.963

DIVISION SERIES RECORD

							BATTING								FIELDING		
Year Team (League)	Pos.	G	AB	R	H	2B	3B	HR	RBI	Avg.	BB	SO	SB	PO	A	E	Avg.
1995—Cincinnati (N.L.)	PH-2B	2	3	1	2	0	0	0	1	.667	0	0	1	0	1	0	1.000
1996—New York (A.L.)	2B	4	16	0	5	0	0	0	3	.313	0	4	0	9	13	0	1.000
Division series totals (2 years)		6	19	1	7	0	0	0	4	.368	0	4	1	9	14	0	1.000

CHAMPIONSHIP SERIES RECORD

RECORDS: Holds single-game record for most triples—2 (October 9, 1993). ... Shares single-series record for most triples—2 (1993). ... Shares N.L. career record for most triples—3.

							BATTING								FIELDING		
Year Team (League)	Pos.	G	AB	R	H	2B	3B	HR	RBI	Avg.	BB	SO	SB	PO	A	E	Avg.
1985—Los Angeles (N.L.)	SS	5	18	2	4	2	1	0	1	.222	1	3	1	7	16	1	.958
1990—Cincinnati (N.L.)	2B	6	20	1	6	0	0	1	4	.300	0	8	0	6	11	1	.944
1993—Philadelphia (N.L.)......	2B	3	15	3	4	0	2	0	0	.267	0	5	0	5	6	1	.917
1995—Cincinnati (N.L.)	PH-1B	3	3	0	0	0	0	0	0	.000	1	1	0	9	0	0	1.000
1996—New York (A.L.)	2B	4	15	0	3	2	0	0	0	.200	0	3	0	5	7	1	.923
Championship series totals (5 years)		21	71	6	17	4	3	1	5	.239	2	20	1	32	40	4	.947

WORLD SERIES RECORD

NOTES: Member of World Series championship team (1990 and 1996).

							BATTING								FIELDING		
Year Team (League)	Pos.	G	AB	R	H	2B	3B	HR	RBI	Avg.	BB	SO	SB	PO	A	E	Avg.
1990—Cincinnati (N.L.)	2B	4	14	1	2	0	0	0	1	.143	2	2	1	9	9	0	1.000
1993—Philadelphia (N.L.)......	2B-DH	6	29	5	10	0	1	0	2	.345	1	7	3	11	17	1	.966
1996—New York (A.L.)	2B	6	19	1	1	0	0	0	0	.053	0	4	0	9	14	2	.920
World Series totals (3 years)		16	62	7	13	0	1	0	3	.210	3	13	4	29	40	3	.958

ALL-STAR GAME RECORD

					BATTING								FIELDING		
Year League	Pos.	AB	R	H	2B	3B	HR	RBI	Avg.	BB	SO	SB	PO	A	E	Avg.
1994—National	2B	1	0	0	0	0	0	0	.000	0	0	0	0	2	0	1.000

PERSONAL: Born July 29, 1970, in Tulsa, Okla. ... 6-5/220. ... Bats right, throws right. ... Full name: Todd Kent Dunn.
HIGH SCHOOL: Bishop Kenny (Jacksonville).

COLLEGE: Georgia Tech (did not play baseball), then North Florida.
TRANSACTIONS/CAREER NOTES: Selected by Milwaukee Brewers organization in supplemental round ("sandwich pick" between first and second round, 35th pick overall) of free-agent draft (June 3, 1993); pick received as compensation for Toronto Blue Jays signing Type A free-agent DH Paul Molitor. ... On disabled list (July 9-September 1, 1995). ... On El Paso disabled list (April 16-May 11, 1996).
STATISTICAL NOTES: Led Texas League with .593 slugging percentage in 1996.

											BATTING					FIELDING		
Year	Team (League)	Pos.	G	AB	R	H	2B	3B	HR	RBI	Avg.	BB	SO	SB	PO	A	E	Avg.
1993—	Helena (Pioneer)	OF-1B	43	150	33	46	11	2	10	42	.307	22	52	5	91	1	4	.958
1994—	Beloit (Midwest)	OF	129	429	72	94	13	2	23	63	.219	50	131	18	236	14	9	.965
1995—	Stockton (California)	OF	67	249	44	73	20	2	7	40	.293	19	67	14	116	6	4	.968
1996—	El Paso (Texas)	OF	98	359	72	122	24	5	19	78	*.340	45	84	13	108	2	7	.940
	—Milwaukee (A.L.)	OF	6	10	2	3	1	0	0	1	.300	0	3	0	6	0	0	1.000
1997—	Tucson (PCL)	OF	93	332	66	101	31	4	18	66	.304	39	83	5	143	6	4	.961
	—Milwaukee (A.L.)	OF-DH	44	118	17	27	5	0	3	9	.229	2	39	3	39	1	4	.909
Major league totals (2 years)			50	128	19	30	6	0	3	10	.234	2	42	3	45	1	4	.920

DUNSTON, SHAWON   SS

PERSONAL: Born March 21, 1963, in Brooklyn, N.Y. ... 6-1/180. ... Bats right, throws right. ... Full name: Shawon Donnell Dunston.
HIGH SCHOOL: Thomas Jefferson (Brooklyn, N.Y.).
TRANSACTIONS/CAREER NOTES: Selected by Chicago Cubs organization in first round (first pick overall) of free-agent draft (June 7, 1982). ... On disabled list (May 31-June 10, 1983). ... On Chicago disabled list (June 16-August 21, 1987); included rehabilitation assignment to Iowa (August 14-21). ... On disabled list (May 5, 1992-remainder of season and March 27-September 1, 1993). ... On suspended list (September 8-12, 1995). ... Granted free agency (October 31, 1995). ... Signed by San Francisco Giants (January 9, 1996). ... On disabled list (April 24-May 13 and August 5-October 1, 1996). ... Granted free agency (November 18, 1996). ... Signed by Cubs (December 7, 1996). ... On Chicago disabled list (June 9-24, 1997). ... Traded by Cubs to Pittsburgh Pirates for a player to be named later (August 31, 1997). ... Granted free agency (October 28, 1997).
RECORDS: Shares modern major league single-game record for most triples—3 (July 28, 1990).
HONORS: Named shortstop on The Sporting News N.L. All-Star team (1989).
STATISTICAL NOTES: Led N.L. shortstops with 817 total chances and tied for lead in double plays with 96 in 1986. ... Career major league grand slams: 2.

											BATTING					FIELDING		
Year	Team (League)	Pos.	G	AB	R	H	2B	3B	HR	RBI	Avg.	BB	SO	SB	PO	A	E	Avg.
1982—	GC Cubs (GCL)	SS-3B	53	190	27	61	11	0	2	28	.321	11	22	32	61	129	24	.888
1983—	Quad Cities (Mid.)	SS	117	455	65	141	17	8	4	62	.310	7	51	58	172	326	47	.914
1984—	Midland (Texas)	SS	73	298	44	98	13	3	3	34	.329	11	38	11	164	203	32	.920
	—Iowa (Am. Assoc.)	SS	61	210	25	49	11	1	7	27	.233	4	40	9	90	165	26	.907
1985—	Chicago (N.L.)	SS	74	250	40	65	12	4	4	18	.260	19	42	11	144	248	17	.958
	—Iowa (Am. Assoc.)	SS	73	272	24	73	9	6	2	28	.268	5	48	17	138	176	12	.963
1986—	Chicago (N.L.)	SS	150	581	66	145	36	3	17	68	.250	21	114	13	*320	*465	*32	.961
1987—	Chicago (N.L.)	SS	95	346	40	85	18	3	5	22	.246	10	68	12	160	271	14	.969
	—Iowa (Am. Assoc.)	SS	5	19	1	8	1	0	0	2	.421	0	3	1	6	12	1	.947
1988—	Chicago (N.L.)	SS	155	575	69	143	23	6	9	56	.249	16	108	30	*257	455	20	.973
1989—	Chicago (N.L.)	SS	138	471	52	131	20	6	9	60	.278	30	86	19	213	379	17	.972
1990—	Chicago (N.L.)	SS	146	545	73	143	22	8	17	66	.262	15	87	25	255	392	20	.970
1991—	Chicago (N.L.)	SS	142	492	59	128	22	7	12	50	.260	23	64	21	*261	383	21	.968
1992—	Chicago (N.L.)	SS	18	73	8	23	3	1	0	2	.315	3	13	2	28	42	1	.986
1993—	Chicago (N.L.)	SS	7	10	3	4	2	0	0	2	.400	0	1	0	5	0	0	1.000
1994—	Chicago (N.L.)	SS	88	331	38	92	19	0	11	35	.278	16	48	3	121	218	12	.966
1995—	Chicago (N.L.)	SS	127	477	58	141	30	6	14	69	.296	10	75	10	187	336	17	.969
1996—	San Fran. (N.L.)■	SS	82	287	27	86	12	2	5	25	.300	13	40	8	116	217	15	.957
1997—	Chicago (N.L.)■	SS-OF	114	419	57	119	18	4	9	41	.284	8	64	29	179	227	12	.971
	—Pittsburgh (N.L.)■	SS	18	71	14	28	4	1	5	16	.394	0	11	3	28	55	3	.965
Major league totals (13 years)			1354	4928	604	1333	241	51	117	530	.270	184	821	186	2274	3688	201	.967

CHAMPIONSHIP SERIES RECORD

											BATTING					FIELDING		
Year	Team (League)	Pos.	G	AB	R	H	2B	3B	HR	RBI	Avg.	BB	SO	SB	PO	A	E	Avg.
1989—	Chicago (N.L.)	SS	5	19	2	6	0	0	0	0	.316	1	1	1	10	14	1	.960

ALL-STAR GAME RECORD

							BATTING							FIELDING		
Year	League	Pos.	AB	R	H	2B	3B	HR	RBI	Avg.	BB	SO	SB	PO	A	E	Avg.
1988—	National							Did not play.									
1990—	National	SS	2	0	0	0	0	0	0	.000	0	0	0	0	0	0	...
All-Star Game totals (1 year)			2	0	0	0	0	0	0	.000	0	0	0	0	0	0	...

DUNWOODY, TODD   OF   MARLINS

PERSONAL: Born April 11, 1975, in Lafayette, Ind. ... 6-1/195. ... Bats left, throws left.
HIGH SCHOOL: West Lafayette (Ind.) Harrison.
TRANSACTIONS/CAREER NOTES: Selected by Florida Marlins organization in seventh round of free-agent draft (June 3, 1993).
STATISTICAL NOTES: Led Eastern League with 267 total bases in 1996.

											BATTING					FIELDING		
Year	Team (League)	Pos.	G	AB	R	H	2B	3B	HR	RBI	Avg.	BB	SO	SB	PO	A	E	Avg.
1993—	GC Marlins (GCL)	OF	31	109	13	21	2	2	0	7	.193	7	28	5	45	1	1	.979
1994—	GC Marlins (GCL)	OF	46	169	32	44	6	6	1	25	.260	21	28	11	91	1	1	.989
	—Kane County (Midw.)	OF	15	45	7	5	0	0	1	1	.111	5	17	1	21	2	0	1.000
1995—	Kane County (Midw.)	OF	132	494	89	140	20	8	14	89	.283	52	105	39	284	6	5	.983
1996—	Portland (Eastern)	OF	138	*552	88	153	30	6	24	93	.277	45	*149	24	254	2	1	*.996

Year	Team (League)	Pos.	G	AB	R	H	2B	3B	HR	RBI	Avg.	BB	SO	SB	PO	A	E	Avg.
1997—Charlotte (Int'l)..........		OF	107	401	74	105	16	7	23	62	.262	39	129	25	231	5	2	.992
—Florida (N.L.)...............		OF	19	50	7	13	2	2	2	7	.260	7	21	2	26	0	2	.929
Major league totals (1 year)			19	50	7	13	2	2	2	7	.260	7	21	2	26	0	2	.929

DURAN, ROBERTO   P   TIGERS

PERSONAL: Born March 6, 1973, in Moca, Dominican Republic. ... 6-0/167. ... Throws left, bats left.
HIGH SCHOOL: Liceo Domingo Fantino (Moca, Dominican Republic).
TRANSACTIONS/CAREER NOTES: Signed as non-drafted free agent by Los Angeles Dodgers organization (February 10, 1990). ... On disabled list (May 8, 1991-remainder of season). ... Claimed on waivers by Toronto Blue Jays (March 14, 1996). ... Traded by Blue Jays to Detroit Tigers for OF Anton French (December 11, 1996).

Year	Team (League)	W	L	Pct.	ERA	G	GS	CG	ShO	Sv.	IP	H	R	ER	BB	SO
1990—Dom. Dodgers (DSL)		0	2	.000	13.27	9	8	0	0	0	19 2/3	18	31	29	36	23
1991—Dom. Dodgers (DSL)		1	1	.500	3.18	3	3	0	0	0	11 1/3	8	8	4	8	22
1992—Vero Beach (FSL)		0	0	. . .	9.00	2	1	0	0	0	5	6	5	5	4	5
—GC Dodgers (GCL)		4	3	.571	2.79	9	8	0	0	0	38 2/3	22	17	12	31	57
1993—Vero Beach (FSL)		1	1	.500	3.72	8	0	0	0	0	9 2/3	10	4	4	8	9
—Yakima (N'west)		2	2	.500	6.98	20	3	0	0	0	40	37	34	31	42	50
1994—Bakersfield (California).......		6	5	.545	4.82	42	4	0	0	10	65 1/3	61	43	35	48	86
1995—Vero Beach (FSL)		7	4	.636	3.38	23	22	0	0	0	101 1/3	82	42	38	70	114
1996—Knoxville (Southern)■		4	6	.400	5.13	19	16	0	0	0	80 2/3	72	52	46	61	74
—Dunedin (Fla. St.)..............		3	1	.750	1.12	8	8	1	1	0	48 1/3	31	9	6	19	54
1997—Jacksonville (Sou.)■		4	2	.667	2.37	50	0	0	0	16	60 2/3	41	19	16	39	95
—Detroit (A.L.)		0	0	. . .	7.59	13	0	0	0	0	10 2/3	7	9	9	15	11
Major league totals (1 year)........		0	0	. . .	7.59	13	0	0	0	0	10 2/3	7	9	9	15	11

DURANT, MIKE   C   TWINS

PERSONAL: Born September 14, 1969, in Columbus, Ohio. ... 6-2/202. ... Bats right, throws right. ... Full name: Michael Joseph Durant.
HIGH SCHOOL: Watterson (Columbus, Ohio).
COLLEGE: Ohio State.
TRANSACTIONS/CAREER NOTES: Selected by Houston Astros organization in 19th round of free-agent draft (June 1, 1988); did not sign. ... Selected by Minnesota Twins organization in second round of free-agent draft (June 3, 1991).
STATISTICAL NOTES: Led Southern League catchers with .992 fielding percentage in 1993.

Year	Team (League)	Pos.	G	AB	R	H	2B	3B	HR	RBI	Avg.	BB	SO	SB	PO	A	E	Avg.
1991—Kenosha (Midwest)		C-3B-OF	66	217	27	44	10	0	2	20	.203	25	35	20	335	50	12	.970
1992—Visalia (California)		C	119	418	61	119	18	2	6	57	.285	55	35	19	672	79	14	.982
1993—Nashville (Southern) ..		C-OF	123	437	58	106	23	1	8	57	.243	44	68	17	591	61	5	†.992
1994—Salt Lake (PCL)		C	103	343	67	102	24	4	4	51	.297	35	47	9	569	44	*11	.982
1995—Salt Lake (PCL)		C-OF-1B	85	295	40	74	15	3	2	51	.251	20	31	11	370	30	5	.988
1996—Salt Lake (PCL)		C-1B	31	101	21	29	7	0	1	12	.287	11	21	7	101	12	2	.983
—Minnesota (A.L.)		C	40	81	15	17	3	0	0	5	.210	10	15	3	183	13	5	.975
1997—Salt Lake (PCL)		C	66	223	33	46	13	1	8	36	.206	21	42	4	326	23	0	1.000
Major league totals (1 year)			40	81	15	17	3	0	0	5	.210	10	15	3	183	13	5	.975

DURHAM, RAY   2B   WHITE SOX

PERSONAL: Born November 30, 1971, in Charlotte. ... 5-8/170. ... Bats both, throws right.
HIGH SCHOOL: Harding (Charlotte).
TRANSACTIONS/CAREER NOTES: Selected by Chicago White Sox organization in fifth round of free-agent draft (June 4, 1990). ... On Utica suspended list (April 1-May 22, 1992). ... On Sarasota disabled list (June 16-July 9, 1992).
RECORDS: Holds major league single-season record for fewest putouts by second baseman (150 or more games)—236 (1996); and fewest chances accepted by second baseman (150 or more games)—659 (1996).
STATISTICAL NOTES: Led Southern League in caught stealing with 25 in 1993. ... Led Southern League second basemen with 541 total chances in 1993. ... Led American Association with 261 total bases in 1994. ... Led American Association second basemen with 701 total chances and 92 double plays in 1994. ... Career major league grand slams: 2.

Year	Team (League)	Pos.	G	AB	R	H	2B	3B	HR	RBI	Avg.	BB	SO	SB	PO	A	E	Avg.
1990—GC Whi. Sox (GCL)		2B-SS	35	116	18	32	3	3	0	13	.276	15	36	23	61	85	15	.907
1991—Utica (N.Y.-Penn)........		2B	39	142	29	36	2	7	0	17	.254	25	44	12	54	101	12	.928
—GC Whi. Sox (GCL)		2B	6	23	3	7	1	0	0	4	.304	3	5	5	18	15	0	1.000
1992—Sarasota (Fla. St.)		2B	57	202	37	55	6	3	0	7	.272	32	36	28	66	107	10	.945
—GC Whi. Sox (GCL)		2B	5	13	3	7	2	0	0	2	.538	3	1	1	4	3	0	1.000
1993—Birmingham (Sou.)......		2B	137	528	83	143	22	*10	3	37	.271	42	100	39	227	284	*30	.945
1994—Nashville (A.A.)...........		2B	133	527	89	156	33	*12	16	66	.296	46	91	34	*254	*429	*19	.973
1995—Chicago (A.L.)		2B-DH	125	471	68	121	27	6	7	51	.257	31	83	18	245	298	15	.973
1996—Chicago (A.L.)		2B-DH	156	557	79	153	33	5	10	65	.275	58	95	30	236	423	11	.984
1997—Chicago (A.L.)		2B-DH	155	634	106	172	27	5	11	53	.271	61	96	33	270	395	*18	.974
Major league totals (3 years)			436	1662	253	446	87	16	28	169	.268	150	274	81	751	1116	44	.977

DUROCHER, JAYSON   P   EXPOS

PERSONAL: Born August 18, 1974, in Hartford. ... 6-2/185. ... Throws right, bats right. ... Full name: Jayson Paul Durocher.
HIGH SCHOOL: Horizon (Scottsdale, Ariz.).

D

TRANSACTIONS/CAREER NOTES: Selected by Montreal Expos organization in ninth round of free-agent draft (June 3, 1993). ... Selected by Chicago White Sox from Expos organization in Rule 5 major league draft (December 9, 1996). ... Returned by White Sox organization to Expos organization (March 31, 1997). ... On disabled list (April 3-20, 1997).

Year	Team (League)	W	L	Pct.	ERA	G	GS	CG	ShO	Sv.	IP	H	R	ER	BB	SO
1993—	GC Expos (GCL)	2	3	.400	3.46	7	7	*3	*2	0	39	32	23	15	13	21
1994—	Vermont (NYP)	•9	2	.818	3.09	15	•15	•3	1	0	•99	92	40	34	44	74
1995—	Albany (S. Atl.)	3	7	.300	3.91	24	22	1	0	0	122	105	67	53	56	88
1996—	W.P. Beach (FSL)	7	6	.538	3.34	23	23	1	1	0	129 1/3	118	65	48	44	101
1997—	W.P. Beach (FSL)	6	4	.600	3.83	25	17	0	0	0	87	84	58	37	39	71

DUVALL, MIKE — P — DEVIL RAYS

PERSONAL: Born October 11, 1974, in Warrenton, Va. ... 6-1/185. ... Throws left, bats left. ... Full name: Michael Duvall.
JUNIOR COLLEGE: Potomac State College (W.Va.).
TRANSACTIONS/CAREER NOTES: Selected by Florida Marlins organization in 19th round of free-agent draft (June 1, 1995). ... Selected by Tampa Bay Devil Rays in second round (32nd pick overall) of expansion draft (November 18, 1997).

Year	Team (League)	W	L	Pct.	ERA	G	GS	CG	ShO	Sv.	IP	H	R	ER	BB	SO
1995—	GC Marlins (GCL)	5	0	1.000	2.22	16	1	0	0	1	28 1/3	15	8	7	12	34
1996—	Kane County (Midwest)	4	1	.800	2.06	41	0	0	0	8	48	43	20	11	21	46
1997—	Brevard County (FSL)	1	0	1.000	0.73	11	0	0	0	6	12 1/3	7	1	1	3	9
—	Portland (Eastern)	4	6	.400	1.84	45	0	0	0	18	68 1/3	63	20	14	20	49

DYE, JERMAINE — OF — ROYALS

PERSONAL: Born January 28, 1974, in Oakland. ... 6-4/210. ... Bats right, throws right. ... Full name: Jermaine Terrell Dye.
JUNIOR COLLEGE: Cosumnes River (Calif.) College.
TRANSACTIONS/CAREER NOTES: Selected by Atlanta Braves organization in 17th round of free-agent draft (June 3, 1993). ... On disabled list (July 13-August 9, 1995). ... Traded by Braves with P Jamie Walker to Kansas City Royals for OF Michael Tucker and IF Keith Lockhart (March 27, 1997). ... On Kansas City disabled list (April 17-May 3, 1997); included rehabilitation assignment to Omaha (May 1-3, 1997). ... On Kansas City disabled list (July 10-August 13, 1997); included rehabilitation assignment to Omaha (July 27-August 13).
STATISTICAL NOTES: Led South Atlantic League outfielders with six double plays in 1994. ... Career major league grand slams: 1.
MISCELLANEOUS: Hit home run in first major league at-bat (May 17, 1996).

Year	Team (League)	Pos.	G	AB	R	H	2B	3B	HR	RBI	Avg.	BB	SO	SB	PO	A	E	Avg.
1993—	GC Braves (GCL)	OF-3B	31	124	17	43	14	0	0	27	.347	5	13	5	46	9	3	.948
—	Danville (Appal.)	OF	25	94	6	26	6	1	2	12	.277	8	10	19	51	1	2	.963
1994—	Macon (S. Atl.)	OF	135	506	73	151	*41	4	15	98	.298	33	82	19	263	*22	9	.969
1995—	Greenville (Southern)	OF	104	403	50	115	26	4	15	71	.285	27	74	4	234	*22	5	.981
1996—	Richmond (Int'l)	OF	36	142	25	33	7	1	6	19	.232	5	25	3	83	2	4	.955
—	Atlanta (N.L.)	OF	98	292	32	82	16	0	12	37	.281	8	67	1	150	2	8	.950
1997—	Kansas City (A.L.)■	OF	75	263	26	62	14	0	7	22	.236	17	51	2	164	7	6	.966
—	Omaha (A.A.)	OF	39	144	21	44	6	0	10	25	.306	9	25	0	41	2	0	1.000
American League totals (1 year)			75	263	26	62	14	0	7	22	.236	17	51	2	164	7	6	.966
National League totals (1 year)			98	292	32	82	16	0	12	37	.281	8	67	1	150	2	8	.950
Major league totals (2 years)			173	555	58	144	30	0	19	59	.259	25	118	3	314	9	14	.958

DIVISION SERIES RECORD

Year	Team (League)	Pos.	G	AB	R	H	2B	3B	HR	RBI	Avg.	BB	SO	SB	PO	A	E	Avg.
1996—	Atlanta (N.L.)	OF	3	11	1	2	0	0	1	1	.182	0	6	1	11	1	0	1.000

CHAMPIONSHIP SERIES RECORD

RECORDS: Shares N.L. single-game record for most at-bats—6 (October 14, 1996).

Year	Team (League)	Pos.	G	AB	R	H	2B	3B	HR	RBI	Avg.	BB	SO	SB	PO	A	E	Avg.
1996—	Atlanta (N.L.)	OF	7	28	2	6	1	0	0	4	.214	1	7	0	14	0	0	1.000

WORLD SERIES RECORD

Year	Team (League)	Pos.	G	AB	R	H	2B	3B	HR	RBI	Avg.	BB	SO	SB	PO	A	E	Avg.
1996—	Atlanta (N.L.)	OF	5	17	0	2	0	0	0	1	.118	1	1	0	15	0	1	.938

DYKSTRA, LENNY — OF — PHILLIES

PERSONAL: Born February 10, 1963, in Santa Ana, Calif. ... 5-10/188. ... Bats left, throws left. ... Full name: Leonard Kyle Dykstra. ... Grandson of Pete Leswick, National Hockey League player (1936-37 and 1944-45); and nephew of Tony Leswick, NHL player (1945-46 through 1955-56 and 1957-58). ... Name pronounced DIKE-struh.
HIGH SCHOOL: Garden Grove (Calif.).
TRANSACTIONS/CAREER NOTES: Selected by New York Mets organization in 12th round of free-agent draft (June 8, 1981). ... Traded by Mets with P Roger McDowell and a player to be named later to Philadelphia Phillies for OF Juan Samuel (June 18, 1989); Phillies organization acquired P Tom Edens to complete deal (July 27, 1989). ... On disabled list (May 6-July 15 and August 27, 1991-remainder of season; April 8-24, June 29-July 16 and August 16, 1992-remainder of season). ... On Philadelphia disabled list (June 18-July 23, 1994); included rehabilitation assignment to Scranton/Wilkes-Barre (July 19-23). ... On disabled list (June 4-June 24 and July 28, 1995-remainder of season). ... On disabled list (May 19, 1996-remainder of season). ... On disabled list (March 29, 1997-entire season).
RECORDS: Shares N.L. single-season record for fewest assists by outfielder (150 or more games)—2 (1993).
HONORS: Named Carolina League Player of the Year (1983). ... Named outfielder on THE SPORTING NEWS N.L. All-Star team (1993). ... Named outfielder on THE SPORTING NEWS N.L. Silver Slugger team (1993).

STATISTICAL NOTES: Led Carolina League in caught stealing with 23 in 1983. ... Had 23-game hitting streak (May 15-June 10, 1990). ... Led N.L. outfielders with 452 total chances in 1990 and 481 in 1993. ... Led N.L. with .418 on-base percentage in 1990. ... Career major league grand slams: 1.

						BATTING								FIELDING		
Year Team (League)	Pos.	G	AB	R	H	2B	3B	HR	RBI	Avg.	BB	SO	SB	PO	A	E	Avg.
1981— Shelby (S. Atl.)...........	OF-SS	48	157	34	41	7	2	0	18	.261	37	31	15	86	3	4	.957
1982— Shelby (S. Atl.)...........	OF	120	413	95	120	13	7	3	38	.291	95	40	77	239	11	14	.947
1983— Lynchburg (Caro.).....	OF	•136	*525	*132	*188	24	*14	8	81	.358	*107	35	*105	268	9	7	.975
1984— Jackson (Texas)........	OF	131	501	*100	138	25	7	6	52	.275	73	45	53	256	5	2	*.992
1985— Tidewater (Int'l).........	OF	58	229	44	71	8	6	1	25	.310	31	20	26	184	4	5	.974
— New York (N.L.).........	OF	83	236	40	60	9	3	1	19	.254	30	24	15	165	6	1	.994
1986— New York (N.L.).........	OF	147	431	77	127	27	7	8	45	.295	58	55	31	283	8	3	.990
1987— New York (N.L.).........	OF	132	431	86	123	37	3	10	43	.285	40	67	27	239	4	3	.988
1988— New York (N.L.).........	OF	126	429	57	116	19	3	8	33	.270	30	43	30	270	3	1	.996
1989— New York (N.L.).........	OF	56	159	27	43	12	1	3	13	.270	23	15	13	124	1	2	.984
— Philadelphia (N.L.)■ ..	OF	90	352	39	78	20	3	4	19	.222	37	38	17	208	9	2	.991
1990— Philadelphia (N.L.)......	OF	149	590	106	•192	35	3	9	60	.325	89	48	33	*439	7	6	.987
1991— Philadelphia (N.L.)......	OF	63	246	48	73	13	5	3	12	.297	37	20	24	167	3	4	.977
1992— Philadelphia (N.L.)......	OF	85	345	53	104	18	0	6	39	.301	40	32	30	253	6	3	.989
1993— Philadelphia (N.L.)......	OF	161	*637	*143	*194	44	6	19	66	.305	*129	64	37	*469	2	10	.979
1994— Philadelphia (N.L.)......	OF	84	315	68	86	26	5	5	24	.273	68	44	15	235	4	4	.984
— Scran./W.B. (Int'l)......	OF	3	7	1	2	1	1	0	1	.286	1	1	0	2	0	0	1.000
1995— Philadelphia (N.L.)......	OF	62	254	37	67	15	1	2	18	.264	33	28	10	153	2	2	.987
1996— Philadelphia (N.L.)......	OF	40	134	21	35	6	3	3	13	.261	26	25	3	103	3	0	1.000
1997—							Did not play.										
Major league totals (12 years)		1278	4559	802	1298	281	43	81	404	.285	640	503	285	3108	58	41	.987

CHAMPIONSHIP SERIES RECORD

RECORDS: Shares single-series record for most times hit by pitch—2 (1988).

						BATTING								FIELDING		
Year Team (League)	Pos.	G	AB	R	H	2B	3B	HR	RBI	Avg.	BB	SO	SB	PO	A	E	Avg.
1986— New York (N.L.).........	OF-PH	6	23	3	7	1	1	1	3	.304	2	4	1	10	0	0	1.000
1988— New York (N.L.).........	OF-PH	7	14	6	6	3	0	1	3	.429	4	0	0	9	0	0	1.000
1993— Philadelphia (N.L.)......	OF	6	25	5	7	1	0	2	2	.280	5	8	0	13	0	0	1.000
Championship series totals (3 years)		19	62	14	20	5	1	4	8	.323	11	12	1	32	0	0	1.000

WORLD SERIES RECORD

NOTES: Member of World Series championship team (1986).

						BATTING								FIELDING		
Year Team (League)	Pos.	G	AB	R	H	2B	3B	HR	RBI	Avg.	BB	SO	SB	PO	A	E	Avg.
1986— New York (N.L.).........	OF-PH	7	27	4	8	0	0	2	3	.296	2	7	0	14	0	0	1.000
1993— Philadelphia (N.L.)......	OF	6	23	9	8	1	0	4	8	.348	7	4	4	18	1	0	1.000
World Series totals (2 years)		13	50	13	16	1	0	6	11	.320	9	11	4	32	1	0	1.000

ALL-STAR GAME RECORD

				BATTING								FIELDING		
Year League	Pos.	AB	R	H	2B	3B	HR	RBI	Avg.	BB	SO	SB	PO	A	E	Avg.
1990— National......................	OF	4	0	1	0	0	0	0	.250	0	0	0	3	0	0	1.000
1994— National......................						Selected, did not play—injured.										
1995— National......................	OF	2	0	0	0	0	0	0	.000	1	0	0	1	0	0	1.000
All-Star Game totals (2 years)		6	0	1	0	0	0	0	.167	1	0	0	4	0	0	1.000

EASLEY, DAMION   2B   TIGERS

PERSONAL: Born November 11, 1969, in New York. ... 5-11/185. ... Bats right, throws right. ... Full name: Jacinto Damion Easley.
HIGH SCHOOL: Lakewood (Calif.).
JUNIOR COLLEGE: Long Beach (Calif.) City College.
TRANSACTIONS/CAREER NOTES: Selected by California Angels organization in 30th round of free-agent draft (June 1, 1988). ... On disabled list (June 19-July 4 and July 28, 1993-remainder of season; and May 30-June 17, 1994). ... On California disabled list (April 1-May 10, 1996); included rehabilitation assignment to Vancouver (April 30-May 10). ... Traded by Angels to Detroit Tigers for P Greg Gohr (July 31, 1996).

						BATTING								FIELDING		
Year Team (League)	Pos.	G	AB	R	H	2B	3B	HR	RBI	Avg.	BB	SO	SB	PO	A	E	Avg.
1989— Bend (Northwest).......	2B	36	131	34	39	5	1	4	21	.298	25	21	9	49	89	22	.863
1990— Quad City (Midwest) ..	SS	103	365	59	100	19	3	10	56	.274	41	60	25	136	206	41	.893
1991— Midland (Texas).........	SS	127	452	73	115	24	5	6	57	.254	58	67	23	186	388	*47	.924
1992— Edmonton (PCL).........	SS-3B	108	429	61	124	18	3	3	44	.289	31	44	26	152	342	30	.943
— California (A.L.)..........	3B-SS	47	151	14	39	5	0	1	12	.258	8	26	9	30	102	5	.964
1993— California (A.L.).........	2B-3B-DH	73	230	33	72	13	2	2	22	.313	28	35	6	111	157	6	.978
1994— California (A.L.).........	3B-2B	88	316	41	68	16	1	6	30	.215	29	48	4	122	179	7	.977
1995— California (A.L.).........	2B-SS	114	357	35	77	14	2	4	35	.216	32	47	5	186	276	10	.979
1996— Vancouver (PCL).........	SS-2B-3B	12	48	13	15	2	1	2	8	.313	9	6	4	20	26	2	.958
— Midland (Texas).........	3B-SS	4	14	1	6	2	0	0	2	.429	0	0	1	5	12	1	.944
— California (A.L.).........S-2-3-DH-O		28	45	4	7	1	0	2	7	.156	6	12	0	23	39	3	.954
— Detroit (A.L.)■.............	2-S-3-DH	21	67	10	23	1	0	2	10	.343	4	13	3	22	47	3	.958
1997— Detroit (A.L.).............	2B-SS-DH	151	527	97	139	37	3	22	72	.264	68	102	28	244	405	12	.982
Major league totals (6 years)		522	1693	234	425	87	8	39	188	.251	175	283	55	738	1205	46	.977

D
E

EBERT, DERRIN   P   BRAVES

PERSONAL: Born August 21, 1976, in Anaheim, Calif. ... 6-3/175. ... Throws left, bats right. ... Full name: Derrin Lee Ebert.
HIGH SCHOOL: Hesperia (Calif.).
TRANSACTIONS/CAREER NOTES: Selected by Atlanta Braves organization in 18th round of free-agent draft (June 2, 1994).
STATISTICAL NOTES: Pitched 6-0 seven-inning no-hit victory against Gulf Coast Marlins (August 12, 1994).

Year Team (League)	W	L	Pct.	ERA	G	GS	CG	ShO	Sv.	IP	H	R	ER	BB	SO
1994— GC Braves (GCL)	1	3	.250	2.93	10	7	1	1	0	43	40	18	14	8	25
1995— Macon (S. Atl.)	*14	5	.737	3.31	28	28	0	0	0	*182	*184	87	67	46	124
1996— Durham (Carolina)	12	9	.571	4.00	27	27	2	0	0	166 1/3	189	102	74	37	99
1997— Greenville (Southern)	11	8	.579	4.10	27	25	0	0	0	175 2/3	191	95	80	48	101

ECHEVARRIA, ANGEL   OF   ROCKIES

PERSONAL: Born May 25, 1971, in Bridgeport, Conn. ... 6-3/219. ... Bats right, throws right.
HIGH SCHOOL: Bassick (Bridgeport, Conn.).
COLLEGE: Rutgers.
TRANSACTIONS/CAREER NOTES: Selected by Colorado Rockies organization in 17th round of free-agent draft (June 1, 1992). ... On Colorado disabled list (July 29-August 16, 1997).

Year Team (League)	Pos.	G	AB	R	H	2B	3B	HR	RBI	Avg.	BB	SO	SB	PO	A	E	Avg.
1992— Bend (Northwest)	OF	57	205	24	46	4	1	5	30	.224	19	54	8	65	7	0	1.000
1993— Central Valley (Cal.)	OF	104	358	45	97	16	2	6	52	.271	44	74	6	141	8	6	.961
1994— Central Valley (Cal.)	OF	50	192	25	58	8	1	6	35	.302	9	25	2	52	3	1	.982
—New Haven (Eastern)	OF	58	205	25	52	6	0	6	32	.254	15	46	2	91	5	2	.980
1995— New Haven (Eastern)	OF	124	453	78	136	30	1	21	*100	.300	56	93	8	202	*20	5	.978
1996— Colo. Springs (PCL)	OF	110	415	67	140	19	2	16	74	.337	38	81	4	168	8	4	.978
—Colorado (N.L.)	OF	26	21	2	6	0	0	0	6	.286	2	5	0	1	0	0	1.000
1997— Colo. Springs (PCL)	OF-1B	77	295	59	95	24	0	13	80	.322	28	47	6	135	9	1	.993
—Colorado (N.L.)	OF	15	20	4	5	2	0	0	0	.250	2	5	0	4	1	0	1.000
Major league totals (2 years)		41	41	6	11	2	0	0	6	.268	4	10	0	5	1	0	1.000

ECKERSLEY, DENNIS   P   RED SOX

PERSONAL: Born October 3, 1954, in Oakland. ... 6-2/195. ... Throws right, bats right. ... Full name: Dennis Lee Eckersley.
HIGH SCHOOL: Washington (Fremont, Calif.).
TRANSACTIONS/CAREER NOTES: Selected by Cleveland Indians organization in third round of free-agent draft (June 6, 1972). ... Traded by Indians with C Fred Kendall to Boston Red Sox for P Rick Wise, P Mike Paxton, 3B Ted Cox and C Bo Diaz (March 30, 1978). ... Traded by Red Sox with OF Mike Brumley to Chicago Cubs for 1B/OF Bill Buckner (May 25, 1984). ... Granted free agency (November 8, 1984). ... Re-signed by Cubs (November 28, 1984). ... On disabled list (August 11-September 7, 1985). ... Traded by Cubs with IF Dan Rohn to Oakland Athletics for OF Dave Wilder, IF Brian Guinn and P Mark Leonette (April 3, 1987). ... On disabled list (May 29-July 13, 1989). ... Granted free agency (October 25, 1994). ... Re-signed by A's (April 3, 1995). ... Traded by A's to St. Louis Cardinals for P Steve Montgomery (February 13, 1996). ... On disabled list (May 19-June 13, 1996). ... Granted free agency (October 29, 1997). ... Signed by Red Sox (December 9, 1997).
RECORDS: Holds A.L. career records for most saves—323; and most consecutive errorless games by pitcher—470 (May 1, 1987 through May 4, 1995).
HONORS: Named A.L. Rookie Pitcher of the Year by THE SPORTING NEWS (1975). ... Named A.L. Fireman of the Year by THE SPORTING NEWS (1988 and 1992). ... Named A.L. co-Fireman of the Year by THE SPORTING NEWS (1991). ... Named A.L. Most Valuable Player by Baseball Writers' Association of America (1992). ... Named A.L. Cy Young Award winner by Baseball Writers' Association of America (1992).
STATISTICAL NOTES: Led Texas League with 10 hit batsmen in 1974. ... Pitched 1-0 no-hit victory against California (May 30, 1977). ... Pitched 2-0 one-hit, complete-game victory against Milwaukee (August 12, 1977, first game). ... Led A.L. with 30 home runs allowed in 1978. ... Pitched 3-1 one-hit, complete-game victory against Toronto (September 26, 1980).
MISCELLANEOUS: Holds Oakland Athletics all-time records for lowest earned run average (2.74), most games pitched (525) and most saves (320).

Year Team (League)	W	L	Pct.	ERA	G	GS	CG	ShO	Sv.	IP	H	R	ER	BB	SO
1972— Reno (California)	5	5	.500	4.80	12	12	3	1	0	75	87	46	40	33	56
1973— Reno (California)	12	8	.600	3.65	31	*31	11	•5	0	202	182	97	82	91	218
1974— San Antonio (Tex.)	•14	3	*.824	3.40	23	23	10	2	0	167	141	66	63	60	*163
1975— Cleveland (A.L.)	13	7	.650	2.60	34	24	6	2	2	187	147	61	54	90	152
1976— Cleveland (A.L.)	13	12	.520	3.44	36	30	9	3	1	199	155	82	76	78	200
1977— Cleveland (A.L.)	14	13	.519	3.53	33	33	12	3	0	247	214	100	97	54	191
1978— Boston (A.L.)■	20	8	.714	2.99	35	35	16	3	0	268	258	99	89	71	162
1979— Boston (A.L.)	17	10	.630	2.99	33	33	17	2	0	247	234	89	82	59	150
1980— Boston (A.L.)	12	14	.462	4.27	30	30	8	0	0	198	188	101	94	44	121
1981— Boston (A.L.)	9	8	.529	4.27	23	23	8	2	0	154	160	82	73	35	79
1982— Boston (A.L.)	13	13	.500	3.73	33	33	11	3	0	224 1/3	228	101	93	43	127
1983— Boston (A.L.)	9	13	.409	5.61	28	28	2	0	0	176 1/3	223	119	110	39	77
1984— Boston (A.L.)	4	4	.500	5.01	9	9	2	0	0	64 2/3	71	38	36	13	33
—Chicago (N.L.)■	10	8	.556	3.03	24	24	2	0	0	160 1/3	152	59	54	36	81
1985— Chicago (N.L.)	11	7	.611	3.08	25	25	6	2	0	169 1/3	145	61	58	19	117
1986— Chicago (N.L.)	6	11	.353	4.57	33	32	1	0	0	201	226	109	102	43	137
1987— Oakland (A.L.)■	6	8	.429	3.03	54	2	0	0	16	115 2/3	99	41	39	17	113
1988— Oakland (A.L.)	4	2	.667	2.35	60	0	0	0	45	72 2/3	52	20	19	11	70
1989— Oakland (A.L.)	4	0	1.000	1.56	51	0	0	0	33	57 2/3	32	10	10	3	55
1990— Oakland (A.L.)	4	2	.667	0.61	63	0	0	0	48	73 1/3	41	9	5	4	73
1991— Oakland (A.L.)	5	4	.556	2.96	67	0	0	0	43	76	60	26	25	9	87
1992— Oakland (A.L.)	7	1	.875	1.91	69	0	0	0	*51	80	62	17	17	11	93

E

Year Team (League)	W	L	Pct.	ERA	G	GS	CG	ShO	Sv.	IP	H	R	ER	BB	SO
1993—Oakland (A.L.)	2	4	.333	4.16	64	0	0	0	36	67	67	32	31	13	80
1994—Oakland (A.L.)	5	4	.556	4.26	45	0	0	0	19	44 1/3	49	26	21	13	47
1995—Oakland (A.L.)	4	6	.400	4.83	52	0	0	0	29	50 1/3	53	29	27	11	40
1996—St. Louis (N.L.)■	0	6	.000	3.30	63	0	0	0	30	60	65	26	22	6	49
1997—St. Louis (N.L.)	1	5	.167	3.91	57	0	0	0	36	53	49	24	23	8	45
A.L. totals (19 years)	165	133	.554	3.45	819	280	91	18	323	2602 1/3	2393	1082	998	618	1950
N.L. totals (5 years)	28	37	.431	3.62	202	81	9	2	66	643 2/3	637	279	259	112	429
Major league totals (23 years)	193	170	.532	3.49	1021	361	100	20	389	3246	3030	1361	1257	730	2379

DIVISION SERIES RECORD

Year Team (League)	W	L	Pct.	ERA	G	GS	CG	ShO	Sv.	IP	H	R	ER	BB	SO
1996—St. Louis (N.L.)	0	0	...	0.00	3	0	0	0	3	3 2/3	3	0	0	0	2

CHAMPIONSHIP SERIES RECORD

RECORDS: Holds career record for most saves—11. ... Holds single-series record for most saves—4 (1988). ... Holds A.L. career record for most saves—10. ... Shares A.L. career records for most games pitched—14; and most games as relief pitcher—14.

NOTES: Named A.L. Championship Series Most Valuable Player (1988).

Year Team (League)	W	L	Pct.	ERA	G	GS	CG	ShO	Sv.	IP	H	R	ER	BB	SO
1984—Chicago (N.L.)	0	1	.000	8.44	1	1	0	0	0	5 1/3	9	5	5	0	0
1988—Oakland (A.L.)	0	0	...	0.00	4	0	0	0	4	6	1	0	0	2	5
1989—Oakland (A.L.)	0	0	...	1.59	4	0	0	0	3	5 2/3	4	1	1	0	2
1990—Oakland (A.L.)	0	0	...	0.00	3	0	0	0	2	3 1/3	2	0	0	0	3
1992—Oakland (A.L.)	0	0	...	6.00	3	0	0	0	1	3	8	2	2	0	2
1996—St. Louis (N.L.)	1	0	1.000	0.00	3	0	0	0	1	3 1/3	2	0	0	0	4
Champ. series totals (6 years)	1	1	.500	2.70	18	1	0	0	11	26 2/3	26	8	8	2	16

WORLD SERIES RECORD

NOTES: Member of World Series championship team (1989).

Year Team (League)	W	L	Pct.	ERA	G	GS	CG	ShO	Sv.	IP	H	R	ER	BB	SO
1988—Oakland (A.L.)	0	1	.000	10.80	2	0	0	0	0	1 2/3	2	2	2	1	2
1989—Oakland (A.L.)	0	0	...	0.00	2	0	0	0	1	1 2/3	0	0	0	0	0
1990—Oakland (A.L.)	0	1	.000	6.75	2	0	0	0	0	1 1/3	3	1	1	0	1
World Series totals (3 years)	0	2	.000	5.79	6	0	0	0	1	4 2/3	5	3	3	1	3

ALL-STAR GAME RECORD

Year League	W	L	Pct.	ERA	GS	CG	ShO	Sv.	IP	H	R	ER	BB	SO
1977—American	0	0	...	0.00	0	0	0	0	2	0	0	0	0	1
1982—American	0	1	.000	9.00	1	0	0	0	3	2	3	3	2	1
1988—American	0	0	...	0.00	0	0	0	1	1	0	0	0	0	1
1990—American	0	0	...	0.00	0	0	0	1	1	1	0	0	0	1
1991—American	0	0	...	0.00	0	0	0	1	1	1	0	0	0	1
1992—American	0	0	...	0.00	0	0	0	0	2/3	3	2	0	0	2
All-Star totals (6 years)	0	1	.000	3.12	1	0	0	3	8 2/3	6	5	3	2	7

EDMONDS, JIM — OF — ANGELS

E

PERSONAL: Born June 27, 1970, in Fullerton, Calif. ... 6-1/190. ... Bats left, throws left. ... Full name: James Patrick Edmonds. ... Name pronounced ED-muns.

HIGH SCHOOL: Diamond Bar (Calif.).

TRANSACTIONS/CAREER NOTES: Selected by California Angels organization in seventh round of free-agent draft (June 1, 1988). ... On disabled list (June 19-September 2, 1989; April 10-May 7 and May 23, 1991-remainder of season). ... On Vancouver disabled list (June 29-July 19, 1993). ... On California disabled list (May 26-June 10 and June 12-July 18, 1996); included rehabilitation assignment to Lake Elsinore (July 13-18). ... Angels franchise renamed Anaheim Angels for 1997 season. ... On disabled list (August 1-16, 1997).

HONORS: Named outfielder on The Sporting News A.L. All-Star team (1995). ... Won A.L. Gold Glove as outfielder (1997).

STATISTICAL NOTES: Had 23-game hitting streak (June 4-29, 1995). ... Career major league grand slams: 1.

Year Team (League)	Pos.	G	AB	R	H	2B	3B	HR	RBI	Avg.	BB	SO	SB	PO	A	E	Avg.
1988—Bend (Northwest)	OF	35	122	23	27	4	0	0	13	.221	20	44	4	59	1	1	.984
1989—Quad City (Midwest)	OF	31	92	11	24	4	0	1	4	.261	7	34	1	47	2	3	.942
1990—Palm Springs (Cal.)	OF	91	314	36	92	18	6	3	56	.293	27	75	5	199	9	10	.954
1991—Palm Springs (Cal.)	OF-1B-P	60	187	28	55	15	1	2	27	.294	40	57	2	97	6	0	1.000
1992—Midland (Texas)	OF	70	246	42	77	15	2	8	32	.313	41	83	3	139	6	5	.967
—Edmonton (PCL)	OF	50	194	37	58	15	2	6	36	.299	14	55	3	79	5	1	.988
1993—Vancouver (PCL)	OF	95	356	59	112	28	4	9	74	.315	41	81	6	167	4	3	.983
—California (A.L.)	OF	18	61	5	15	4	1	0	4	.246	2	16	0	47	4	1	.981
1994—California (A.L.)	OF-1B	94	289	35	79	13	1	5	37	.273	30	72	8	301	20	3	.991
1995—California (A.L.)	OF	141	558	120	162	30	4	33	107	.290	51	130	1	401	8	1	.998
1996—California (A.L.)	OF-DH	114	431	73	131	28	3	27	66	.304	46	101	4	280	6	1	.997
—Lake Elsinore (Calif.)	OF	5	15	4	6	2	0	1	4	.400	1	1	0	5	0	0	1.000
1997—Anaheim (A.L.)	OF-1B-DH	133	502	82	146	27	0	26	80	.291	60	80	5	395	16	5	.988
Major league totals (5 years)		500	1841	315	533	102	9	91	294	.290	189	399	14	1424	54	11	.993

ALL-STAR GAME RECORD

Year League	Pos.	AB	R	H	2B	3B	HR	RBI	Avg.	BB	SO	SB	PO	A	E	Avg.
1995—American	PH-OF	1	0	0	0	0	0	0	.000	0	1	0	0	0	0	...

RECORD AS PITCHER

Year Team (League)	W	L	Pct.	ERA	G	GS	CG	ShO	Sv.	IP	H	R	ER	BB	SO
1991—Palm Springs (California)	0	0	...	0.00	1	0	0	0	0	2	1	0	0	3	2

EDSELL, GEOFF   P   ANGELS

PERSONAL: Born December 12, 1971, in Butler, Pa. ... 6-2/190. ... Throws right, bats right. ... Full name: Geoffrey Scott Edsell.
HIGH SCHOOL: Montoursville (Pa.).
COLLEGE: Old Dominion.
TRANSACTIONS/CAREER NOTES: Selected by Minnesota Twins organization in 33rd round of free-agent draft (June 4, 1990); did not sign. ... Selected by California Angels organization in sixth round of free-agent draft (June 3, 1993). ... On Midland suspended list (June 5-7, 1996). ... Angels franchise renamed Anaheim Angels for 1997 season.
STATISTICAL NOTES: Tied for Pacific Coast League lead with 12 hit batsmen in 1997.

Year	Team (League)	W	L	Pct.	ERA	G	GS	CG	ShO	Sv.	IP	H	R	ER	BB	SO
1993—	Boise (Northwest)	4	3	.571	6.89	13	13	1	0	0	64	64	52	49	40	63
1994—	Cedar Rapids (Midw.)	11	5	.688	3.02	17	17	4	1	0	125 1/3	109	54	42	65	84
	—Lake Elsinore (Calif.)	2	2	.500	4.05	9	7	0	0	0	40	38	21	18	24	26
1995—	Lake Elsinore (Calif.)	8	12	.400	3.67	23	22	1	1	0	139 2/3	127	81	57	67	134
	—Midland (Texas)	2	3	.400	5.91	5	5	1	0	0	32	39	26	21	16	19
1996—	Midland (Texas)	5	5	.500	4.70	14	14	0	0	0	88	84	53	46	47	60
	—Vancouver (PCL)	4	6	.400	3.43	15	15	3	•2	0	105	93	45	40	45	48
1997—	Vancouver (PCL)	14	11	.560	5.15	30	*29	*6	1	0	*183 1/3	196	121	105	*96	95

EENHOORN, ROBERT   SS   ANGELS

PERSONAL: Born February 9, 1968, in Rotterdam, The Netherlands. ... 6-3/185. ... Bats right, throws right. ... Full name: Robert F. Eenhoorn.
COLLEGE: Davidson (N.C.).
TRANSACTIONS/CAREER NOTES: Selected by New York Yankees organization in second round of free-agent draft (June 4, 1990); pick received as compensation for Pittsburgh Pirates signing Type B free-agent P Walt Terrell. ... On Prince William disabled list (May 30-June 28 and July 1-September 2, 1991). ... On disabled list (July 28, 1993-remainder of season). ... Claimed on waivers by California Angels (September 6, 1996). ... Angels franchise renamed Anaheim Angels for 1997 season.
STATISTICAL NOTES: Tied for Pacific Coast League lead with 12 sacrifice hits in 1997.
MISCELLANEOUS: Member of The Netherlands' 1988 Olympic baseball team.

Year	Team (League)	Pos.	G	AB	R	H	2B	3B	HR	RBI	Avg.	BB	SO	SB	PO	A	E	Avg.
1990—	Oneonta (NYP)	SS	57	220	30	59	9	3	2	18	.268	18	29	11	83	135	9	*.960
1991—	GC Yankees (GCL)	SS	13	40	6	14	4	1	1	7	.350	3	8	1	12	29	4	.911
	—Prince William (Car.)	SS	29	108	15	26	6	1	1	12	.241	13	21	0	45	69	6	.950
1992—	Fort Lauderdale (FSL)	SS	57	203	23	62	5	2	4	33	.305	19	25	6	60	138	16	.925
	—Alb./Colon. (Eastern)	SS	60	196	24	46	11	2	1	23	.235	10	17	2	88	153	13	.949
1993—	Alb./Colon. (Eastern)	SS	82	314	48	88	24	3	6	46	.280	21	39	3	143	221	31	.922
1994—	Columbus (Int'l)	SS-2B	99	343	38	82	10	2	5	39	.239	14	43	2	135	325	17	.964
	—New York (A.L.)	SS	3	4	1	2	1	0	0	0	.500	0	0	0	0	1	0	1.000
1995—	Columbus (Int'l)	2B-3B-SS	92	318	36	80	11	3	5	32	.252	20	54	2	168	231	8	.980
	—New York (A.L.)	2B-SS	5	14	1	2	1	0	0	2	.143	1	3	0	11	8	1	.950
1996—	New York (A.L.)	2B-3B	12	14	2	1	0	0	0	2	.071	2	3	0	17	12	0	1.000
	—Columbus (Int'l)	SS-2B	55	172	28	58	14	1	1	16	.337	21	18	7	76	160	13	.948
	—California (A.L.)■	SS-2B	6	15	1	4	0	0	0	0	.267	0	2	0	5	10	2	.882
1997—	Vancouver (PCL)	SS-2B	120	455	77	140	29	5	12	58	.308	25	59	1	157	302	21	.956
	—Anaheim (A.L.)	3B-2B-SS	11	20	2	7	1	0	1	6	.350	0	2	0	8	8	3	.842
Major league totals (4 years)			37	67	7	16	3	0	1	10	.239	3	10	0	41	39	6	.930

EILAND, DAVE   P   DEVIL RAYS

PERSONAL: Born July 5, 1966, in Dade City, Fla. ... 6-3/212. ... Throws right, bats right. ... Full name: David William Eiland. ... Name pronounced EYE-land.
HIGH SCHOOL: Zephyrhills (Fla.).
COLLEGE: South Florida, then Florida.
TRANSACTIONS/CAREER NOTES: Selected by New York Yankees organization in seventh round of free-agent draft (June 2, 1987). ... On New York disabled list (May 28-July 12, 1991); included rehabilitation assignment to Columbus (June 16-July 12). ... Released by Yankees (January 19, 1992). ... Signed by San Diego Padres organization (January 27, 1992). ... On San Diego disabled list (May 4-June 26, 1992); included rehabilitation assignment to Las Vegas (May 27-June 25). ... On San Diego disabled list (July 5-August 26, 1992); included rehabilitation assignment to Las Vegas (July 28-August 26). ... Granted free agency (December 7, 1992). ... Signed by Wichita, Padres organization (February 28, 1993). ... Granted free agency (May 27, 1993). ... Signed by Charlotte, Cleveland Indians organization (May 29, 1993). ... Traded by Indians organization to Texas Rangers organization for P Gerald Alexander and P Allan Anderson (August 4, 1993). ... Granted free agency (October 15, 1993). ... Signed by Columbus, Yankees organization (March 12, 1994). ... Granted free agency (October 3, 1995). ... Signed by St. Louis Cardinals organization (December 6, 1995). ... On Louisville temporarily inactive list (April 10-18, 1996). ... On Louisville disabled list (May 14-22 and June 3-15, 1996). ... Released by Cardinals (June 15, 1996). ... Signed by Yankees organization (June 18, 1996). ... Granted free agency (October 15, 1996). ... Re-signed by Yankees organization (December 23, 1996). ... On Columbus disabled list (May 14-25, 1997). ... Granted free agency (October 15, 1997). ... Signed by Tampa Bay Devil Rays (December 19, 1997).
HONORS: Named International League Most Valuable Pitcher (1990).
STATISTICAL NOTES: Hit home run in first major league at-bat (April 10, 1992).

Year	Team (League)	W	L	Pct.	ERA	G	GS	CG	ShO	Sv.	IP	H	R	ER	BB	SO
1987—	Oneonta (N.Y.-Penn)	4	0	1.000	1.84	5	5	0	0	0	29 1/3	20	6	6	3	16
	—Fort Lauderdale (FSL)	5	3	.625	1.88	8	8	4	1	0	62 1/3	57	17	13	8	28
1988—	Alb./Colon. (Eastern)	9	5	.643	2.56	18	18	•7	2	0	119 1/3	95	39	34	22	66
	—Columbus (Int'l)	1	1	.500	2.59	4	4	0	0	0	24 1/3	25	8	7	6	13
	—New York (A.L.)	0	0	...	6.39	3	3	0	0	0	12 2/3	15	9	9	4	7
1989—	Columbus (Int'l)	9	4	.692	3.76	18	18	2	0	0	103	107	47	43	21	46
	—New York (A.L.)	1	3	.250	5.77	6	6	0	0	0	34 1/3	44	25	22	13	11
1990—	Columbus (Int'l)	*16	5	.762	2.87	27	26	*11	•3	0	175 1/3	155	63	56	32	96
	—New York (A.L.)	2	1	.667	3.56	5	5	0	0	0	30 1/3	31	14	12	5	16

Year	Team (League)	W	L	Pct.	ERA	G	GS	CG	ShO	Sv.	IP	H	R	ER	BB	SO
1991—	New York (A.L.)................	2	5	.286	5.33	18	13	0	0	0	72²/₃	87	51	43	23	18
	— Columbus (Int'l)	6	1	.857	2.40	9	9	2	0	0	60	54	22	16	7	18
1992—	San Diego (N.L.)■.............	0	2	.000	5.67	7	7	0	0	0	27	33	21	17	5	10
	— Las Vegas (PCL)	4	5	.444	5.23	14	14	0	0	0	63²/₃	78	43	37	11	31
1993—	San Diego (N.L.)	0	3	.000	5.21	10	9	0	0	0	48¹/₃	58	33	28	17	14
	— Charlotte (Int'l)	1	3	.250	5.30	8	8	0	0	0	35²/₃	42	22	21	12	13
	— Oklahoma City (A.A.)■.......	3	1	.750	4.29	7	7	1	0	0	35²/₃	39	18	17	9	15
1994—	Columbus (Int'l).................	9	6	.600	3.58	26	26	0	0	0	140²/₃	141	72	56	33	84
1995—	Columbus (Int'l)	8	7	.533	3.14	19	18	1	1	0	109	109	44	38	22	62
	— New York (A.L.)	1	1	.500	6.30	4	1	0	0	0	10	16	10	7	3	6
1996—	Louisville (A.A.)■.............	0	1	.000	5.55	8	6	0	0	0	24¹/₃	27	17	15	8	17
	— Columbus (Int'l)■.............	8	4	.667	2.92	15	15	3	0	0	92¹/₃	77	37	30	13	76
1997—	Columbus (Int'l)	4	2	.667	6.64	13	11	0	0	0	62¹/₃	80	47	46	14	43
	— GC Yankees (GCL)	0	1	.000	9.00	2	1	0	0	0	7	12	8	7	0	5
	— Tampa (Florida State)	1	0	1.000	3.75	3	3	0	0	0	12	11	5	5	0	11
A.L. totals (5 years)		6	10	.375	5.23	36	28	0	0	0	160	193	109	93	48	58
N.L. totals (2 years)		0	5	.000	5.38	17	16	0	0	0	75¹/₃	91	54	45	22	24
Major league totals (7 years)		6	15	.286	5.28	53	44	0	0	0	235¹/₃	284	163	138	70	82

EINERTSON, DARRELL   P   YANKEES

PERSONAL: Born September 4, 1972, in Rhinelander, Wis. ... 6-2/190. ... Throws right, bats right. ... Full name: Darrell Lee Einertson.
HIGH SCHOOL: Urbandale (Iowa).
JUNIOR COLLEGE: Indian Hills Community College (Iowa).
COLLEGE: Cameron, then Iowa Wesleyan.
TRANSACTIONS/CAREER NOTES: Selected by New York Yankees organization in 11th round of free-agent draft (June 1, 1995).

Year	Team (League)	W	L	Pct.	ERA	G	GS	CG	ShO	Sv.	IP	H	R	ER	BB	SO
1995—	Oneonta (N.Y.-Penn)	0	4	.000	1.88	25	0	0	0	0	38¹/₃	32	20	8	15	35
1996—	Greensboro (S. Atl.)	3	9	.250	2.70	48	0	0	0	0	70	69	29	21	19	48
1997—	Tampa (Florida State)	5	4	.556	2.15	45	0	0	0	6	71	63	24	17	19	55

EISCHEN, JOEY   P

PERSONAL: Born May 25, 1970, in West Covina, Calif. ... 6-1/200. ... Throws left, bats left. ... Full name: Joseph Raymond Eischen. ... Name pronounced EYE-shen.
HIGH SCHOOL: West Covina (Calif.).
JUNIOR COLLEGE: Pasadena (Calif.) City College.
TRANSACTIONS/CAREER NOTES: Selected by Chicago White Sox organization in fifth round of free-agent draft (June 1, 1988); did not sign. ... Selected by Texas Rangers organization in fourth round of free-agent draft (June 5, 1989). ... Traded by Rangers organization with P Jonathan Hurst and a player to be named later to Montreal Expos organization for P Oil Can Boyd (July 21, 1991); Expos organization acquired P Travis Buckley to complete deal (September 1, 1991). ... Traded by Expos with OF Roberto Kelly to Los Angeles Dodgers for OF Henry Rodriguez and IF Jeff Treadway (May 23, 1995). ... Traded by Dodgers with P John Cummings to Detroit Tigers for OF Chad Curtis (July 31, 1996). ... Traded by Tigers with P Cam Smith to San Diego Padres for C Brian Johnson and P Willie Blair (December 17, 1996). ... Traded by Padres to Cincinnati Reds for a player to be named later (March 16, 1997); Padres acquired IF Ray Brown to complete deal (March 19, 1997). ... On disabled list (March 25-April 26 and April 29-July 18, 1997); included rehabilitation assignment to Indianapolis (April 13-26). ... Granted free agency (December 21, 1997).
HONORS: Named Eastern League Pitcher of the Year (1993).
STATISTICAL NOTES: Led Pioneer League with 11 balks in 1989. ... Led Florida State League with 86 runs allowed in 1991. ... Pitched 5-0 no-hit victory against Vero Beach (June 16, 1992, first game).

Year	Team (League)	W	L	Pct.	ERA	G	GS	CG	ShO	Sv.	IP	H	R	ER	BB	SO
1989—	Butte (Pioneer)..................	3	7	.300	5.30	12	12	0	0	0	52²/₃	50	45	31	38	57
1990—	Gastonia (S. Atl.)...............	3	7	.300	2.70	17	14	0	0	0	73¹/₃	51	36	22	40	69
1991—	Charlotte (Fla. St.).............	4	10	.286	3.41	18	18	1	0	0	108¹/₃	99	59	41	55	80
	— W.P. Beach (FSL)■.............	4	2	.667	5.17	8	8	1	0	0	38¹/₃	35	§27	22	24	26
1992—	W.P. Beach (FSL)	9	8	.529	3.08	27	26	3	2	0	169²/₃	128	68	58	*83	167
1993—	Harrisburg (Eastern)	*14	4	*.778	3.62	20	20	0	0	0	119¹/₃	122	62	48	60	110
	— Ottawa (Int'l)	2	2	.500	3.54	6	6	0	0	0	40²/₃	34	18	16	15	29
1994—	Ottawa (Int'l)	2	6	.250	4.94	48	2	0	0	2	62	54	38	34	40	57
	— Montreal (N.L.)..................	0	0	...	54.00	1	0	0	0	0	²/₃	4	4	4	0	1
1995—	Ottawa (Int'l)	2	1	.667	1.72	11	0	0	0	0	15²/₃	9	4	3	8	13
	— Los Angeles (N.L.)■............	0	0	...	3.10	17	0	0	0	0	20¹/₃	19	9	7	11	15
	— Albuquerque (PCL).............	3	0	1.000	0.00	13	0	0	0	2	16¹/₃	8	0	0	3	14
1996—	Los Angeles (N.L.)	0	1	.000	4.78	28	0	0	0	0	43¹/₃	48	25	23	20	36
	— Detroit (A.L.)■..................	1	1	.500	3.24	24	0	0	0	0	25	27	11	9	14	15
1997—	Cincinnati (N.L.)■..............	0	0	...	6.75	1	0	0	0	0	1¹/₃	2	2	1	1	2
	— Indianapolis (A.A.).............	1	0	1.000	1.27	26	5	0	0	2	42²/₃	41	7	6	13	26
A.L. totals (1 year)		1	1	.500	3.24	24	0	0	0	0	25	27	11	9	14	15
N.L. totals (4 years)		0	1	.000	4.80	47	0	0	0	0	65²/₃	73	40	35	32	54
Major league totals (4 years)		1	2	.333	4.37	71	0	0	0	0	90²/₃	100	51	44	46	69

EISENREICH, JIM   OF   MARLINS

PERSONAL: Born April 18, 1959, in St. Cloud, Minn. ... 5-11/195. ... Bats left, throws left. ... Full name: James Michael Eisenreich. ... Name pronounced EYES-en-rike.
HIGH SCHOOL: Technical (St. Cloud, Minn.).
COLLEGE: St. Cloud (Minn.) State.

TRANSACTIONS/CAREER NOTES: Selected by Minnesota Twins organization in 16th round of free-agent draft (June 3, 1980). ... On disabled list (May 6-28 and June 18-September 1, 1982). ... On disabled list (April 7, 1983); then transferred to voluntarily retired list (May 27, 1983-remainder of season). ... On disabled list (April 26-May 18, 1984). ... On voluntarily retired list (June 4, 1984-September 29, 1986). ... Claimed on waivers by Kansas City Royals (October 2, 1986). ... On Kansas City disabled list (August 25-September 9, 1987 and July 22-August 6, 1989). ... Granted free agency (October 30, 1991). ... Re-signed by Royals (January 31, 1992). ... On disabled list (August 12-September 7, 1992). ... Granted free agency (October 30, 1992). ... Signed by Philadelphia Phillies (January 20, 1993). ... Granted free agency (October 29, 1993). ... Re-signed by Phillies (November 24, 1993). ... Granted free agency (November 1, 1995). ... Re-signed by Phillies (December 7, 1995). ... Granted free agency (November 18, 1996). ... Signed by Florida Marlins (December 3, 1996).
HONORS: Named Appalachian League co-Player of the Year (1980).
STATISTICAL NOTES: Career major league grand slams: 3.

Year Team (League)	Pos.	G	AB	R	H	2B	3B	HR	RBI	Avg.	BB	SO	SB	PO	A	E	Avg.
1980— Elizabethton (App.).....	OF	67	258	47	77	12	•4	3	41	.298	35	32	12	151	7	3	.981
—Wis. Rap. (Mid.).........	DH	5	16	4	7	0	0	0	5	.438	1	0	1	...	...	...	...
1981— Wis. Rap. (Mid.).........	OF	*134	489	101	•152	*27	6	23	99	.311	84	70	9	*295	17	9	.972
1982— Minnesota (A.L.)........	OF	34	99	10	30	6	0	2	9	.303	11	13	0	72	0	2	.973
1983— Minnesota (A.L.)........	OF	2	7	1	2	1	0	0	0	.286	1	1	0	6	1	0	1.000
1984— Minnesota (A.L.)........	OF-DH	12	32	1	7	1	0	0	3	.219	2	4	2	5	0	0	1.000
1985—						Out of organized baseball.											
1986—						Out of organized baseball.											
1987— Memphis (Sou.)■......	DH	70	275	60	105	36	•10	11	57	.382	47	44	13	...	...	...	...
—Kansas City (A.L.)........	DH	44	105	10	25	8	2	4	21	.238	7	13	1	...	...	...	...
1988— Kansas City (A.L.)......	OF-DH	82	202	26	44	8	1	1	19	.218	6	31	9	109	0	4	.965
—Omaha (A.A.)..............	OF	36	142	28	41	8	3	4	14	.289	9	20	9	73	1	1	.987
1989— Kansas City (A.L.)......	OF-DH	134	475	64	139	33	7	9	59	.293	37	44	27	273	4	3	.989
1990— Kansas City (A.L.)......	OF-DH	142	496	61	139	29	7	5	51	.280	42	51	12	261	6	1	*.996
1991— Kansas City (A.L.).....	OF-1B-DH	135	375	47	113	22	3	2	47	.301	20	35	5	243	12	5	.981
1992— Kansas City (A.L.)......	OF-DH	113	353	31	95	13	3	2	28	.269	24	36	11	180	1	1	.995
1993— Philadelphia (N.L.)■..	OF-1B	153	362	51	115	17	4	7	54	.318	26	36	5	223	6	1	.996
1994— Philadelphia (N.L.)......	OF	104	290	42	87	15	4	4	43	.300	33	31	6	179	4	2	.989
1995— Philadelphia (N.L.)......	OF	129	377	46	119	22	2	10	55	.316	38	44	10	205	2	0	*1.000
1996— Philadelphia (N.L.)......	OF	113	338	45	122	24	3	3	41	.361	31	32	11	167	3	4	.977
1997— Florida (N.L.)■........	OF-1B-DH	120	293	36	82	19	1	2	34	.280	30	28	0	211	13	2	.991
American League totals (9 years)		698	2144	251	594	121	23	25	237	.277	150	228	67	1149	24	16	.987
National League totals (5 years)		619	1660	220	525	97	14	26	227	.316	158	171	32	985	28	9	.991
Major league totals (14 years)		1317	3804	471	1119	218	37	51	464	.294	308	399	99	2134	52	25	.989

DIVISION SERIES RECORD

Year Team (League)	Pos.	G	AB	R	H	2B	3B	HR	RBI	Avg.	BB	SO	SB	PO	A	E	Avg.
1997— Florida (N.L.).............	PH	2	0	0	0	0	0	0	0	...	2	0	0	0	0	0	...

CHAMPIONSHIP SERIES RECORD

Year Team (League)	Pos.	G	AB	R	H	2B	3B	HR	RBI	Avg.	BB	SO	SB	PO	A	E	Avg.
1993— Philadelphia (N.L.)......	OF-PH	6	15	0	2	1	0	0	1	.133	0	2	0	6	0	0	1.000
1997— Florida (N.L.).............	OF	1	3	0	0	0	0	0	0	.000	0	0	0	2	0	0	1.000
Championship series totals (2 years)		7	18	0	2	1	0	0	1	.111	0	2	0	8	0	0	1.000

WORLD SERIES RECORD

NOTES: Member of World Series championship team (1997).

Year Team (League)	Pos.	G	AB	R	H	2B	3B	HR	RBI	Avg.	BB	SO	SB	PO	A	E	Avg.
1993— Philadelphia (N.L.)......	OF	6	26	3	6	0	0	1	7	.231	2	4	0	18	0	0	1.000
1997— Florida (N.L.).............	PH-DH-1B	5	8	1	4	0	0	1	3	.500	3	1	0	3	1	0	1.000
World Series totals (2 years)		11	34	4	10	0	0	2	10	.294	5	5	0	21	1	0	1.000

ELARTON, SCOTT — P — ASTROS

PERSONAL: Born February 23, 1976, in Lamar, Colo. ... 6-7/240. ... Throws right, bats right. ... Full name: Vincent Scott Elarton.
HIGH SCHOOL: Lamar (Colo.).
TRANSACTIONS/CAREER NOTES: Selected by Houston Astros organization in first round (25th pick overall) of free-agent draft (June 2, 1994).

Year Team (League)	W	L	Pct.	ERA	G	GS	CG	ShO	Sv.	IP	H	R	ER	BB	SO
1994— GC Astros (GCL)	4	0	1.000	0.00	5	5	0	0	0	28	9	0	0	5	28
—Quad City (Midwest)	4	1	.800	3.29	9	9	0	0	0	54²/₃	42	23	20	18	42
1995— Quad City (Midwest)	13	7	.650	4.45	26	26	0	0	0	149²/₃	149	86	74	71	112
1996— Kissimmee (Florida State)..	12	7	.632	2.92	27	27	3	1	0	172¹/₃	154	67	56	54	130
1997— Jackson (Texas)	7	4	.636	3.24	20	20	2	0	0	133¹/₃	103	57	48	47	141
—New Orleans (A.A.)............	4	4	.500	5.33	9	9	0	0	0	54	51	36	32	17	50

ELDRED, CAL — P — BREWERS

PERSONAL: Born November 24, 1967, in Cedar Rapids, Iowa. ... 6-4/235. ... Throws right, bats right. ... Full name: Calvin John Eldred.
HIGH SCHOOL: Urbana (Iowa) Community.
COLLEGE: Iowa.
TRANSACTIONS/CAREER NOTES: Selected by Milwaukee Brewers organization in first round (17th pick overall) of free-agent draft (June 5, 1989). ... On disabled list (May 15, 1995-remainder of season). ... On Milwaukee disabled list (March 29-July 14, 1996); included rehabilitation assignment to New Orleans (June 10-July 9).

STATISTICAL NOTES: Led American Association with 12 hit batsmen in 1991.

Year Team (League)	W	L	Pct.	ERA	G	GS	CG	ShO	Sv.	IP	H	R	ER	BB	SO
1989— Beloit (Midwest)	2	1	.667	2.30	5	5	0	0	0	31 1/3	23	10	8	11	32
1990— Stockton (California)	4	2	.667	1.62	7	7	3	1	0	50	31	12	9	19	75
— El Paso (Texas)	5	4	.556	4.49	19	19	0	0	0	110 1/3	126	61	55	47	93
1991— Denver (Am. Assoc.)	13	9	.591	3.75	29	*29	3	1	0	*185	161	82	77	84	*168
— Milwaukee (A.L.)	2	0	1.000	4.50	3	3	0	0	0	16	20	9	8	6	10
1992— Denver (Am. Assoc.)	10	6	.625	3.00	19	19	4	1	0	141	122	49	47	42	99
— Milwaukee (A.L.)	11	2	.846	1.79	14	14	2	1	0	100 1/3	76	21	20	23	62
1993— Milwaukee (A.L.)	16	16	.500	4.01	36	•36	8	1	0	*258	232	120	115	91	180
1994— Milwaukee (A.L.)	11	11	.500	4.68	25	•25	6	0	0	179	158	96	93	84	98
1995— Milwaukee (A.L.)	1	1	.500	3.42	4	4	0	0	0	23 2/3	24	10	9	10	18
1996— New Orleans (A.A.)	2	2	.500	3.34	6	6	0	0	0	32 1/3	24	12	12	17	30
— Milwaukee (A.L.)	4	4	.500	4.46	15	15	0	0	0	84 2/3	82	43	42	38	50
1997— Milwaukee (A.L.)	13	•15	.464	4.99	34	34	1	1	0	202	207	118	112	89	122
Major league totals (7 years)	**58**	**49**	**.542**	**4.16**	**131**	**131**	**17**	**3**	**0**	**863 2/3**	**799**	**417**	**399**	**341**	**540**

ELSTER, KEVIN   SS   RANGERS

PERSONAL: Born August 3, 1964, in San Pedro, Calif. ... 6-2/200. ... Bats right, throws right. ... Full name: Kevin Daniel Elster.

HIGH SCHOOL: Marina (Huntington Beach, Calif.).

JUNIOR COLLEGE: Golden West College (Calif.).

TRANSACTIONS/CAREER NOTES: Selected by New York Mets organization in second round of free-agent draft (January 17, 1984). ... On Jackson disabled list (August 11, 1985-remainder of season). ... On disabled list (August 4, 1990-remainder of season; May 6-21, 1991; and April 13, 1992-remainder of season). ... Granted free agency (December 19, 1992). ... Signed by Los Angeles Dodgers organization (January 12, 1993). ... On Albuquerque disabled list (April 8-May 2, 1993). ... Released by Dodgers (May 17, 1993). ... Signed by Florida Marlins organization (May 22, 1993). ... Released by Edmonton, Marlins organization (June 4, 1993). ... Signed by San Diego Padres organization (December 17, 1993). ... Released by Las Vegas, Padres organization (March 21, 1994). ... Signed by Columbus, New York Yankees organization (May 1, 1994). ... On Columbus temporarily inactive list (May 1-June 1, 1994). ... On New York disabled list (July 7, 1994-remainder of season; included rehabilitation assignment to Albany (August 1-20). ... Released by Yankees (June 8, 1995). ... Signed by Omaha, Kansas City Royals organization (June 29, 1995). ... Released by Omaha, Royals organization (July 3, 1995). ... Signed by Scranton/Wilkes-Barre, Philadelphia Phillies organization (July 7, 1995). ... Granted free agency (October 5, 1995). ... Signed by Texas Rangers organization (January 16, 1996). ... Granted free agency (October 31, 1996). ... Signed by Pittsburgh Pirates (December 20, 1996). ... On disabled list (May 17, 1997-remainder of season). ... Granted free agency (October 28, 1997). ... Signed by Rangers (December 8, 1997).

RECORDS: Holds major league single-season record for fewest putouts by shortstop who led league in putouts—235 (1989). ... Holds N.L. career record for most consecutive errorless games by shortstop—88 (July 20, 1988 through May 8, 1989).

HONORS: Named A.L. Comeback Player of the Year by THE SPORTING NEWS (1996).

STATISTICAL NOTES: Led New York-Pennsylvania League shortstops with 358 total chances and 45 double plays in 1984. ... Led Texas League shortstops with 589 total chances and 83 double plays in 1986. ... Career major league grand slams: 2.

						BATTING									FIELDING		
Year Team (League)	Pos.	G	AB	R	H	2B	3B	HR	RBI	Avg.	BB	SO	SB	PO	A	E	Avg.
1984— Little Falls (NYP)	SS	71	257	35	66	7	3	3	35	.257	35	41	13	*128	214	16	*.955
1985— Lynchburg (Caro.)	SS	59	224	41	66	9	0	7	26	.295	33	21	8	82	195	16	.945
— Jackson (Texas)	SS	59	214	30	55	13	0	2	22	.257	19	29	2	107	220	10	.970
1986— Jackson (Texas)	SS	127	435	69	117	19	3	2	52	.269	61	46	6	*196	*365	28	*.952
— New York (N.L.)	SS	19	30	3	5	1	0	0	0	.167	3	8	0	16	35	2	.962
1987— Tidewater (Int'l)	SS	134	*549	83	*170	33	7	8	74	.310	35	62	7	219	419	21	.968
— New York (N.L.)	SS	5	10	1	4	2	0	0	1	.400	0	1	0	4	6	1	.909
1988— New York (N.L.)	SS	149	406	41	87	11	1	9	37	.214	35	47	2	196	345	13	.977
1989— New York (N.L.)	SS	151	458	52	106	25	2	10	55	.231	34	77	4	*235	374	15	.976
1990— New York (N.L.)	SS	92	314	36	65	20	1	9	45	.207	30	54	2	159	251	17	.960
1991— New York (N.L.)	SS	115	348	33	84	16	2	6	36	.241	40	53	2	149	299	14	.970
1992— New York (N.L.)	SS	6	18	0	4	0	0	0	0	.222	0	2	0	8	10	0	1.000
1993— San Antonio (Tex.)■..	SS	10	39	5	11	2	1	0	7	.282	4	4	0	14	31	4	.918
1994— Tampa (Fla. St.)■	2B-3B	3	11	2	2	1	0	0	2	.182	2	2	0	4	7	1	.917
— Alb./Colon. (Eastern)..	SS-3B-2B	41	135	19	33	7	0	2	21	.244	21	16	2	64	112	7	.962
— New York (A.L.)	SS	7	20	0	0	0	0	0	0	.000	1	6	0	5	27	0	1.000
1995— New York (A.L.)	SS-2B	10	17	1	2	1	0	0	0	.118	1	5	0	10	14	0	1.000
— Omaha (A.A.)■	SS	11	42	5	10	4	0	0	6	.238	5	8	0	22	30	0	1.000
— Scran./W.B. (Int'l)■..	SS	5	17	2	5	3	0	0	2	.294	2	3	0	6	12	1	.947
— Philadelphia (N.L.)	SS-1B-3B	26	53	10	11	4	1	1	9	.208	7	14	0	37	38	1	.987
1996— Texas (A.L.)■	SS	157	515	79	130	32	2	24	99	.252	52	138	4	*285	441	14	.981
1997— Pittsburgh (N.L.)■....	SS	39	138	14	31	6	2	7	25	.225	21	39	0	54	123	1	.994
American League totals (3 years)		174	552	80	132	33	2	24	99	.239	54	149	4	300	482	14	.982
National League totals (9 years)		602	1775	190	397	85	9	42	208	.224	170	295	10	858	1481	64	.973
Major league totals (11 years)		776	2327	270	529	118	11	66	307	.227	224	444	14	1158	1963	78	.976

DIVISION SERIES RECORD

						BATTING									FIELDING		
Year Team (League)	Pos.	G	AB	R	H	2B	3B	HR	RBI	Avg.	BB	SO	SB	PO	A	E	Avg.
1996— Texas (A.L.)	SS	4	12	2	4	2	0	0	0	.333	3	2	1	6	7	1	.929

CHAMPIONSHIP SERIES RECORD

						BATTING									FIELDING		
Year Team (League)	Pos.	G	AB	R	H	2B	3B	HR	RBI	Avg.	BB	SO	SB	PO	A	E	Avg.
1986— New York (N.L.)	SS-PR	4	3	0	0	0	0	0	0	.000	0	1	0	2	3	0	1.000
1988— New York (N.L.)	SS-PR	5	8	1	2	1	0	0	1	.250	3	0	0	7	7	2	.875
Championship series totals (2 years)		9	11	1	2	1	0	0	1	.182	3	1	0	9	10	2	.905

E

WORLD SERIES RECORD

NOTES: Member of World Series championship team (1986).

			BATTING											FIELDING		
Year Team (League)	**Pos.**	**G**	**AB**	**R**	**H**	**2B**	**3B**	**HR**	**RBI**	**Avg.**	**BB**	**SO**	**SB**	**PO**	**A**	**E**	**Avg.**
1986— New York (N.L.)..........	SS	1	1	0	0	0	0	0	0	.000	0	0	0	3	3	1	.857

EMBREE, ALAN — P — BRAVES

PERSONAL: Born January 23, 1970, in Vancouver, Wash. ... 6-2/190. ... Throws left, bats left. ... Full name: Alan Duane Embree.
HIGH SCHOOL: Prairie (Vancouver, Wash.).
TRANSACTIONS/CAREER NOTES: Selected by Cleveland Indians organization in fifth round of free-agent draft (June 5, 1989). ... On Cleveland disabled list (April 1-June 2 and June 2, 1993-remainder of season); included rehabilitation assignment to Canton/Akron (June 2-15). ... On Cleveland disabled list (August 1-September 7, 1996); included rehabilitation assignment to Buffalo (August 6-September 4). ... Traded by Indians with OF Kenny Lofton to Atlanta Braves for OF Marquis Grissom and OF Dave Justice (March 25, 1997).

Year Team (League)	W	L	Pct.	ERA	G	GS	CG	ShO	Sv.	IP	H	R	ER	BB	SO
1990— Burlington (Appalachian)....	4	4	.500	2.64	15	•15	0	0	0	81 2/3	87	36	24	30	58
1991— Columbus (S. Atl.)............	10	8	.556	3.59	27	26	3	1	0	155 1/3	126	80	62	77	137
1992— Kinston (Carolina)............	10	5	.667	3.30	15	15	1	0	0	101	89	48	37	32	115
— Cant./Akr. (Eastern)...........	7	2	.778	2.28	12	12	0	0	0	79	61	24	20	28	56
— Cleveland (A.L.)..................	0	2	.000	7.00	4	4	0	0	0	18	19	14	14	8	12
1993— Cant./Akr. (Eastern)...........	0	0	...	3.38	1	1	0	0	0	5 1/3	3	2	2	3	4
1994— Cant./Akr. (Eastern)...........	9	•16	.360	5.50	30	27	2	1	0	157	183	106	96	64	81
1995— Buffalo (A.A.).....................	3	4	.429	0.89	30	0	0	0	5	40 2/3	31	10	4	19	56
— Cleveland (A.L.)..................	3	2	.600	5.11	23	0	0	0	1	24 2/3	23	16	14	16	23
1996— Cleveland (A.L.).................	1	1	.500	6.39	24	0	0	0	0	31	30	26	22	21	33
— Buffalo (A.A.)......................	4	1	.800	3.93	20	0	0	0	5	34 1/3	26	16	15	14	46
1997— Atlanta (N.L.)■.................	3	1	.750	2.54	66	0	0	0	0	46	36	13	13	20	45
A.L. totals (3 years)....................	4	5	.444	6.11	51	4	0	0	1	73 2/3	72	56	50	45	68
N.L. totals (1 year)......................	3	1	.750	2.54	66	0	0	0	0	46	36	13	13	20	45
Major league totals (4 years)......	7	6	.538	4.74	117	4	0	0	1	119 2/3	108	69	63	65	113

DIVISION SERIES RECORD

Year Team (League)	W	L	Pct.	ERA	G	GS	CG	ShO	Sv.	IP	H	R	ER	BB	SO
1996— Cleveland (A.L.).................	0	0	...	9.00	3	0	0	0	0	1	0	1	1	0	1

CHAMPIONSHIP SERIES RECORD

Year Team (League)	W	L	Pct.	ERA	G	GS	CG	ShO	Sv.	IP	H	R	ER	BB	SO
1995— Cleveland (A.L.).................	0	0	...	0.00	1	0	0	0	0	1/3	0	0	0	0	1
1997— Atlanta (N.L.).....................	0	0	...	0.00	1	0	0	0	0	1	0	0	0	1	1
Champ. series totals (2 years)....	0	0	...	0.00	2	0	0	0	0	1 1/3	0	0	0	1	2

WORLD SERIES RECORD

Year Team (League)	W	L	Pct.	ERA	G	GS	CG	ShO	Sv.	IP	H	R	ER	BB	SO
1995— Cleveland (A.L.).................	0	0	...	2.70	4	0	0	0	0	3 1/3	2	1	1	2	2

ENCARNACION, ANGELO — C — ANGELS

PERSONAL: Born April 18, 1973, in Santo Domingo, Dominican Republic. ... 5-8/180. ... Bats right, throws right. ... Full name: Angelo Benjamin Encarnacion.
HIGH SCHOOL: Francisco Espaillat College (Dominican Republic).
TRANSACTIONS/CAREER NOTES: Signed as non-drafted free agent by Pittsburgh Pirates organization (June 1, 1990). ... On Salem disabled list (June 28-July 16, 1993). ... On disabled list (July 27, 1994-remainder of season). ... On Calgary disabled list (June 16-July 1, 1996). ... Traded by Pirates with OF Trey Beamon to San Diego Padres for OF Mark Smith and P Hal Garrett (March 29, 1997). ... Traded by Padres to Anaheim Angels for IF/OF Aaron Guiel (August 23, 1997).
STATISTICAL NOTES: Led South Atlantic League catchers with 15 double plays in 1992.

			BATTING											FIELDING			
Year Team (League)	**Pos.**	**G**	**AB**	**R**	**H**	**2B**	**3B**	**HR**	**RBI**	**Avg.**	**BB**	**SO**	**SB**	**PO**	**A**	**E**	**Avg.**
1990— Dom. Pirates (DSL)....	...	30	96	18	32	2	0	0	19	.333	6	5	8	...	...	...	...
1991— Welland (NYP)............	C	50	181	21	46	3	2	0	15	.254	5	27	4	366	74	*18	.961
1992— Augusta (S. Atl.).........	C	94	314	39	80	14	3	1	29	.255	25	37	2	676	*121	*22	.973
1993— Salem (Carolina).........	C	70	238	20	61	12	1	3	24	.256	13	27	1	450	82	*21	.962
— Buffalo (A.A.)...............	C-OF	3	9	1	3	0	0	0	2	.333	0	0	0	14	1	0	1.000
1994— Carolina (Southern)....	C	67	227	26	66	17	0	3	32	.291	11	28	2	400	71	*15	.969
1995— Calgary (PCL)............	C	21	80	8	20	3	0	1	6	.250	1	12	1	113	14	2	.984
— Pittsburgh (N.L.)........	C	58	159	18	36	7	2	2	10	.226	13	28	1	278	43	7	.979
1996— Calgary (PCL)............	C	75	263	38	84	18	0	4	31	.319	10	19	6	314	63	4	.990
— Pittsburgh (N.L.)........	C	7	22	3	7	2	0	0	1	.318	0	5	0	35	4	2	.951
1997— Las Vegas (PCL)■.....	C-OF	79	253	27	62	12	1	3	23	.245	15	32	1	455	61	10	.981
— Anaheim (A.L.)■........	C	11	17	2	7	1	0	1	4	.412	0	1	2	43	4	3	.940
American League totals (1 year)		11	17	2	7	1	0	1	4	.412	0	1	2	43	4	3	.940
National League totals (2 years)		65	181	21	43	9	2	2	11	.238	13	33	1	313	47	9	.976
Major league totals (3 years)		76	198	23	50	10	2	3	15	.253	13	34	3	356	51	12	.971

ENCARNACION, JUAN — OF — TIGERS

PERSONAL: Born March 22, 1976, in Las Matas de Faran, Dominican Republic. ... 6-2/160. ... Bats right, throws right. ... Full name: Juan DeDios Encarnacion.
HIGH SCHOOL: Liceo Mercedes Maria Mateo (Las Matas de Faran, Dominican Republic).

TRANSACTIONS/CAREER NOTES: Signed as non-drafted free agent by Detroit Tigers organization (December 27, 1992).
STATISTICAL NOTES: Led Southern League in being hit by pitch with 12 in 1997.

Year — Team (League)	Pos.	G	AB	R	H	2B	3B	HR	RBI	Avg.	BB	SO	SB	PO	A	E	Avg.
1993— Dom. Tigers (DSL)	OF	72	251	36	63	13	4	13	49	.251	15	65	6	110	13	17	.879
1994— Bristol (Appal.)	OF	54	197	16	49	7	1	4	31	.249	13	54	9	83	*9	3	.968
— Fayetteville (SAL)	OF	24	83	6	16	1	1	1	4	.193	8	36	1	22	1	2	.920
— Lakeland (Fla. St.)	OF	3	6	1	2	0	0	0	0	.333	0	3	0	0	0	0	...
1995— Fayetteville (SAL)	OF	124	457	62	129	31	7	16	72	.282	30	113	30	143	10	7	.956
1996— Lakeland (Fla. St.)	OF	131	499	54	120	31	2	15	58	.240	24	104	11	233	12	6	.976
1997— Jacksonville (South.)..	OF	131	493	91	159	31	4	26	90	.323	43	86	17	208	12	3	.987
— Detroit (A.L.)	OF	11	33	3	7	1	1	1	5	.212	3	12	3	22	0	0	1.000
Major league totals (1 year)		11	33	3	7	1	1	1	5	.212	3	12	3	22	0	0	1.000

ERDOS, TODD — P — DIAMONDBACKS

PERSONAL: Born November 21, 1973, in Washington, Pa. ... 6-1/190. ... Throws right, bats right. ... Full name: Todd Michael Erdos.
HIGH SCHOOL: Meadville (Pa.).
TRANSACTIONS/CAREER NOTES: Selected by San Diego Padres organization in ninth round of free-agent draft (June 1, 1992). ... On disabled list (June 4-September 16, 1994). ... Selected by Arizona Diamondbacks in second round (41st pick overall) of expansion draft (November 18, 1997).
STATISTICAL NOTES: Led Northwest League with 13 home runs allowed in 1993.

Year — Team (League)	W	L	Pct.	ERA	G	GS	CG	ShO	Sv.	IP	H	R	ER	BB	SO
1992— Ariz. Padres (Ariz.)	3	4	.429	2.65	12	9	1	0	0	57²/₃	36	28	17	18	61
— Spokane (N'west)	1	0	1.000	0.69	2	2	0	0	0	13	9	2	1	5	11
1993— Spokane (N'west)	5	6	.455	3.19	16	15	0	0	0	90¹/₃	73	39	32	•53	64
— Waterloo (Midw.)	1	9	.100	8.31	11	11	0	0	0	47²/₃	64	51	44	31	27
1994— Ariz. Padres (Ariz.)							Did not play.								
1995— Idaho Falls (Pioneer)	5	3	.625	3.48	32	0	0	0	0	41¹/₃	34	19	16	30	48
1996— Rancho Cucamonga (Cal.) .	3	3	.500	3.74	55	0	0	0	17	67¹/₃	63	33	28	37	82
1997— Mobile (Southern)	1	4	.200	3.36	55	0	0	0	27	59	45	22	22	22	49
— San Diego (N.L.)	2	0	1.000	5.27	11	0	0	0	0	13²/₃	17	9	8	4	13
Major league totals (1 year)	2	0	1.000	5.27	11	0	0	0	0	13²/₃	17	9	8	4	13

ERICKS, JOHN — P — INDIANS

PERSONAL: Born September 16, 1967, in Oak Lawn, Ill. ... 6-7/250. ... Throws right, bats right. ... Full name: John Edward Ericks III.
HIGH SCHOOL: Chicago Christian (Palos Heights, Ill.).
COLLEGE: Illinois.
TRANSACTIONS/CAREER NOTES: Selected by St. Louis Cardinals organization in first round (22nd pick overall) of free-agent draft (June 1, 1988); pick received as part of compensation for New York Yankees signing Type A free-agent 1B Jack Clark. ... On Arkansas disabled list (May 19, 1990-remainder of season). ... On disabled list (May 11-23 and July 7-September 8, 1992). ... Released by Cardinals (September 8, 1992). ... Signed by Carolina, Pittsburgh Pirates organization (February 12, 1993). ... On disabled list (April 8, 1993-entire season). ... On Carolina disabled list (August 8-19, 1994). ... On Calgary disabled list (May 22-June 7, 1996). ... On disabled list (April 29, 1997-remainder of season); included rehabilitation assignments to Gulf Coast Pirates (September 17-August 10) and Calgary (August 12-27). ... Granted free agency (October 15, 1997). ... Signed by Cleveland Indians organization (January 8, 1998).

Year — Team (League)	W	L	Pct.	ERA	G	GS	CG	ShO	Sv.	IP	H	R	ER	BB	SO
1988— Johnson City (App.)	3	2	.600	3.73	9	9	1	0	0	41	27	20	17	27	41
1989— Savannah (S. Atl.)	11	10	.524	2.04	28	28	1	0	0	167¹/₃	90	59	38	101	*211
1990— St. Petersburg (FSL)	2	1	.667	1.57	4	4	0	0	0	23	16	5	4	6	25
— Arkansas (Texas)	1	2	.333	9.39	4	4	1	0	0	15¹/₃	17	19	16	19	19
1991— Arkansas (Texas)	5	14	.263	4.77	25	25	1	0	0	139²/₃	138	94	74	84	103
1992— Arkansas (Texas)	2	6	.250	4.08	13	13	1	0	0	75	69	36	34	29	71
1993—							Did not play.								
1994— Salem (Carolina)■	4	2	.667	3.10	17	5	0	0	1	52¹/₃	42	22	18	20	71
— Carolina (Southern)	2	4	.333	2.68	11	11	0	0	0	57	42	22	17	19	64
1995— Calgary (PCL)	2	1	.667	2.48	5	5	0	0	0	29	20	8	8	13	25
— Pittsburgh (N.L.)	3	9	.250	4.58	19	18	1	0	0	106	108	59	54	50	80
1996— Pittsburgh (N.L.)	4	5	.444	5.79	28	4	0	0	8	46²/₃	56	35	30	19	46
— Calgary (PCL)	1	2	.333	4.20	14	4	0	0	1	30	31	15	14	15	40
1997— Pittsburgh (N.L.)	1	0	1.000	1.93	10	0	0	0	6	9¹/₃	7	3	2	4	6
— GC Pirates (GCL)	0	0	...	3.46	9	8	0	0	0	13	5	5	5	5	18
— Calgary (PCL)	0	0	...	12.86	6	0	0	0	0	7	14	11	10	1	10
Major league totals (3 years)	8	14	.364	4.78	57	22	1	0	14	162	171	97	86	73	132

ERICKSON, SCOTT — P — ORIOLES

PERSONAL: Born February 2, 1968, in Long Beach, Calif. ... 6-4/230. ... Throws right, bats right. ... Full name: Scott Gavin Erickson.
HIGH SCHOOL: Homestead (Cupertino, Calif.).
JUNIOR COLLEGE: San Jose City College.
COLLEGE: Arizona.
TRANSACTIONS/CAREER NOTES: Selected by New York Mets organization in 36th round of free-agent draft (June 2, 1986); did not sign. ... Selected by Houston Astros organization in 34th round of free-agent draft (June 2, 1987); did not sign. ... Selected by Toronto Blue Jays organization in 44th round of free-agent draft (June 1, 1988); did not sign. ... Selected by Minnesota Twins organization in fourth round of free-agent draft (June 5, 1989). ... On disabled list (June 30-July 15, 1991; April 3-18, 1993 and May 15-31, 1994). ... Traded by Twins to Baltimore Orioles for P Scott Klingenbeck and a player to be named later (July 7, 1995); Twins acquired OF Kim Bartee to complete deal (September 18, 1995).
STATISTICAL NOTES: Pitched 5-0 one-hit, complete-game victory against Boston (July 24, 1992, first game). ... Pitched 6-0 no-hit victory against Milwaukee (April 27, 1994). ... Tied for A.L. lead with nine hit batsmen in 1994.

Year Team (League)	W	L	Pct.	ERA	G	GS	CG	ShO	Sv.	IP	H	R	ER	BB	SO
1989— Visalia (California)	3	4	.429	2.97	12	12	2	0	0	78²/₃	79	29	26	22	59
1990— Orlando (South.)	8	3	.727	3.03	15	15	3	1	0	101	75	38	34	24	69
— Minnesota (A.L.)	8	4	.667	2.87	19	17	1	0	0	113	108	49	36	51	53
1991— Minnesota (A.L.)	•20	8	.714	3.18	32	32	5	3	0	204	189	80	72	71	108
1992— Minnesota (A.L.)	13	12	.520	3.40	32	32	5	3	0	212	197	86	80	83	101
1993— Minnesota (A.L.)	8	*19	.296	5.19	34	34	1	0	0	218²/₃	*266	*138	126	71	116
1994— Minnesota (A.L.)	8	11	.421	5.44	23	23	2	1	0	144	173	95	87	59	104
1995— Minnesota (A.L.)	4	6	.400	5.95	15	15	0	0	0	87²/₃	102	61	58	32	45
— Baltimore (A.L.)■	9	4	.692	3.89	17	16	7	2	0	108²/₃	111	47	47	35	61
1996— Baltimore (A.L.)	13	12	.520	5.02	34	34	6	0	0	222¹/₃	262	137	124	66	100
1997— Baltimore (A.L.)	16	7	.696	3.69	34	33	3	2	0	221²/₃	218	100	91	61	131
Major league totals (8 years)	99	83	.544	4.24	240	236	30	11	0	1532	1626	793	721	529	819

DIVISION SERIES RECORD

Year Team (League)	W	L	Pct.	ERA	G	GS	CG	ShO	Sv.	IP	H	R	ER	BB	SO
1996— Baltimore (A.L.)	0	0	...	4.05	1	1	0	0	0	6²/₃	6	3	3	2	6
1997— Baltimore (A.L.)	1	0	1.000	4.05	1	1	0	0	0	6²/₃	7	3	3	2	6
Div. series totals (2 years)	1	0	1.000	4.05	2	2	0	0	0	13¹/₃	13	6	6	4	12

CHAMPIONSHIP SERIES RECORD

RECORDS: Shares A.L. record for most runs allowed in one inning—6 (October 13, 1996, third inning). ... Holds record for most home runs allowed in one inning—3 (October 13, 1996, third inning).

Year Team (League)	W	L	Pct.	ERA	G	GS	CG	ShO	Sv.	IP	H	R	ER	BB	SO
1991— Minnesota (A.L.)	0	0	...	4.50	1	1	0	0	0	4	3	2	2	5	2
1996— Baltimore (A.L.)	0	1	.000	2.38	2	2	0	0	0	11¹/₃	14	9	3	4	8
1997— Baltimore (A.L.)	1	0	1.000	4.26	2	2	0	0	0	12²/₃	15	7	6	1	6
Champ. series totals (3 years)	1	1	.500	3.54	5	5	0	0	0	28	32	18	11	10	16

WORLD SERIES RECORD

NOTES: Member of World Series championship team (1991).

Year Team (League)	W	L	Pct.	ERA	G	GS	CG	ShO	Sv.	IP	H	R	ER	BB	SO
1991— Minnesota (A.L.)	0	0	...	5.06	2	2	0	0	0	10²/₃	10	7	6	4	5

ERSTAD, DARIN — OF — ANGELS

PERSONAL: Born June 4, 1974, in Jamestown, N.D. ... 6-2/210. ... Bats left, throws left. ... Full name: Darin Charles Erstad.
HIGH SCHOOL: Jamestown (N.D.).
COLLEGE: Nebraska.
TRANSACTIONS/CAREER NOTES: Selected by New York Mets organization in 13th round of free-agent draft (June 1, 1992); did not sign. ... Selected by California Angels organization in first round (first pick overall) of free-agent draft (June 1, 1995). ... Angels franchise renamed Anaheim Angels for 1997 season.

Year Team (League)	Pos.	G	AB	R	H	2B	3B	HR	RBI	Avg.	BB	SO	SB	PO	A	E	Avg.
1995— Ariz. Angels (Ariz.)	OF	4	18	2	10	1	0	0	1	.556	1	1	1	3	0	0	1.000
— Lake Elsinore (Calif.)	OF	25	113	24	41	7	2	5	24	.363	6	22	3	65	2	1	.985
1996— Vancouver (PCL)	OF-1B	85	351	63	107	22	5	6	41	.305	44	53	11	184	10	1	.995
— California (A.L.)	OF	57	208	34	59	5	1	4	20	.284	17	29	3	121	2	3	.976
1997— Anaheim (A.L.)	1B-DH-OF	139	539	99	161	34	4	16	77	.299	51	86	23	1003	64	11	.990
Major league totals (2 years)		196	747	133	220	39	5	20	97	.295	68	115	26	1124	66	14	.988

ESCOBAR, KELVIM — P — BLUE JAYS

PERSONAL: Born April 11, 1976, in La Guaira, Venezuela. ... 6-1/205. ... Throws right, bats right. ... Full name: Kelvim Jose Bolivar Escobar.
TRANSACTIONS/CAREER NOTES: Signed as non-drafted free agent by Toronto Blue Jays organization (July 9, 1992).

Year Team (League)	W	L	Pct.	ERA	G	GS	CG	ShO	Sv.	IP	H	R	ER	BB	SO
1993— Dom. B. Jays (DSL)	2	1	.667	4.13	8	7	0	0	0	32²/₃	34	17	15	25	31
1994— GC Blue Jays (GCL)	4	4	.500	2.35	11	10	1	0	1	65	56	23	17	18	64
1995— Dom. B. Jays (DSL)	0	1	.000	1.72	3	2	0	0	0	15²/₃	14	3	3	5	20
— Medicine Hat (Pio.)	3	3	.500	5.71	14	14	1	•1	0	69¹/₃	66	47	44	33	75
1996— Dunedin (Fla. St.)	9	5	.643	2.69	18	18	1	0	0	110¹/₃	101	44	33	33	113
— Knoxville (Southern)	3	4	.429	5.33	10	10	0	0	0	54	61	36	32	24	44
1997— Knoxville (Southern)	2	1	.667	3.70	5	5	1	0	0	24¹/₃	20	13	10	16	31
— Dunedin (Fla. St.)	0	1	.000	3.75	3	2	0	0	0	12	16	9	5	3	16
— Toronto (A.L.)	3	2	.600	2.90	27	0	0	0	14	31	28	12	10	19	36
Major league totals (1 year)	3	2	.600	2.90	27	0	0	0	14	31	28	12	10	19	36

ESHELMAN, VAUGHN — P — DEVIL RAYS

PERSONAL: Born May 22, 1969, in Philadelphia. ... 6-3/215. ... Throws left, bats left. ... Full name: Vaughn Michael Eshelman.
HIGH SCHOOL: Westfield (Houston).
JUNIOR COLLEGE: Blinn College (Texas).
COLLEGE: Houston.
TRANSACTIONS/CAREER NOTES: Selected by Baltimore Orioles organization in fourth round of free-agent draft (June 3, 1991). ... On disabled list (April 9, 1992-entire season). ... Selected by Boston Red Sox from Orioles organization in Rule 5 major league draft (December 5, 1994). ... On Boston disabled list (May 25-June 13, July 6-24 and August 25-September 9, 1995); included rehabilitation assignment to Trenton (July 14-24). ... On Boston disabled list (March 29-April 27, 1996); included rehabilitation assignment to Pawtucket (April 15-27). ... Claimed on waivers by Oakland Athletics (October 15, 1997). ... Selected by Tampa Bay Devil Rays in third round (70th pick overall) of expansion draft (November 18, 1997).

Year	Team (League)	W	L	Pct.	ERA	G	GS	CG	ShO	Sv.	IP	H	R	ER	BB	SO
1991—	Bluefield (Appalachian)	1	0	1.000	0.64	3	3	0	0	0	14	10	1	1	9	15
—	Kane County (Midwest)......	5	3	.625	2.32	11	11	2	1	0	77²/₃	57	23	20	35	90
1992—	....							Did not play.								
1993—	Frederick (Carolina).............	7	10	.412	3.89	24	24	2	1	0	143¹/₃	128	70	62	59	122
1994—	Bowie (Eastern)................	11	9	.550	4.00	27	25	2	2	0	166¹/₃	175	81	74	60	133
1995—	Boston (A.L.)■..................	6	3	.667	4.85	23	14	0	0	0	81²/₃	86	47	44	36	41
—	Trenton (Eastern)	0	1	.000	0.00	2	2	0	0	0	7	3	1	0	0	7
1996—	Pawtucket (Int'l)................	1	2	.333	4.33	7	7	1	0	0	43²/₃	40	21	21	19	28
—	Boston (A.L.)..................	6	3	.667	7.08	39	10	0	0	0	87¹/₃	112	79	69	58	59
1997—	Pawtucket (Int'l)................	3	4	.429	4.86	14	13	0	0	1	66²/₃	63	38	36	22	57
—	Boston (A.L.)..................	3	3	.500	6.33	21	6	0	0	0	42²/₃	58	32	30	17	18
Major league totals (3 years)......		**15**	**9**	**.625**	**6.07**	**83**	**30**	**0**	**0**	**0**	**212**	**256**	**158**	**143**	**111**	**118**

ESPINAL, JOSE   P   CUBS

PERSONAL: Born August 31, 1976, in Santo Domingo, Dominican Republic. ... 6-1/165. ... Throws right, bats right. ... Full name: Jose Ramon Espinal (Feliz).

HIGH SCHOOL: Pedro Hernandez (Santo Domingo, Dominican Republic).

TRANSACTIONS/CAREER NOTES: Signed as non-drafted free agent by Chicago Cubs organization (March 31, 1994).

Year	Team (League)	W	L	Pct.	ERA	G	GS	CG	ShO	Sv.	IP	H	R	ER	BB	SO
1994—	Dom. Cubs (DSL)...............	1	4	.200	4.63	6	6	0	0	0	23¹/₃	23	19	12	13	25
1995—	GC Cubs (GCL).................	3	2	.600	1.75	13	5	0	0	1	36	29	20	7	10	27
1996—	GC Cubs (GCL).................	4	1	.800	2.21	11	7	0	0	0	61	46	20	15	18	57
1997—	Rockford (Midwest)	10	10	.500	4.92	24	24	1	0	0	120²/₃	147	83	66	41	107

ESPINOZA, ALVARO   SS/2B

PERSONAL: Born February 19, 1962, in Valencia, Carabobo, Venezuela. ... 6-0/190. ... Bats right, throws right. ... Full name: Alvaro Alberto Ramirez Espinoza. ... Name pronounced ESS-pin-OH-zuh.

HIGH SCHOOL: Valencia (Carabobo, Venezuela).

TRANSACTIONS/CAREER NOTES: Signed as non-drafted free agent by Houston Astros organization (October 30, 1978). ... Released by Astros organization (September 30, 1980). ... Signed by Wisconsin Rapids, Minnesota Twins organization (March 18, 1982). ... On Toledo disabled list (June 7-25, 1984 and June 6-July 2, 1985). ... Granted free agency (October 15, 1987). ... Signed by Columbus, New York Yankees organization (November 17, 1987). ... Released by Yankees (March 17, 1992). ... Signed by Colorado Springs, Cleveland Indians organization (April 3, 1992). ... Granted free agency (November 2, 1995). ... Re-signed by Indians organization (December 7, 1995). ... Traded by Indians with 2B Carlos Baerga to New York Mets for IF Jose Vizcaino and IF Jeff Kent (July 29, 1996). ... Released by Mets (March 26, 1997). ... Signed by Seattle Mariners (April 2, 1997). ... On disabled list (May 29-June 13, 1997); included rehabilitation assignment to Tacoma (June 6-13). ... Released by Mariners (July 14, 1997).

RECORDS: Shares major league single-season record for fewest runs batted in (150 or more games)—20 (1990).

STATISTICAL NOTES: Led Gulf Coast League shortstops with 114 putouts, 217 assists, 25 errors, 356 total chances and 33 double plays in 1980. ... Led California League shortstops with 660 total chances in 1983. ... Tied for International League lead with 16 sacrifice hits in 1984. ... Led International League shortstops with 159 putouts in 1986. ... Led Pacific Coast League shortstops with 631 total chances and 112 double plays in 1992.

Year	Team (League)	Pos.	G	AB	R	H	2B	3B	HR	RBI	Avg.	BB	SO	SB	PO	A	E	Avg.
1979—	GC Astros (GCL)	SS-2B-3B	11	32	3	7	0	0	0	5	.219	4	6	0	18	27	1	.978
1980—	GC Ast.-Or. (GCL)	SS-3B	59	200	24	43	5	0	0	14	.215	15	18	6	†114	†219	‡25	.930
1981—	....						Out of organized baseball.											
1982—	Wis. Rap. (Mid.)■....	SS-3B-1B	112	379	41	101	9	0	5	29	.266	16	66	9	237	241	33	.935
1983—	Visalia (California)	SS	130	486	57	155	20	1	4	57	.319	14	50	6	*256	364	40	.939
1984—	Toledo (Int'l)	SS	104	344	22	80	12	5	0	30	.233	3	49	3	157	293	19	.959
—	Minnesota (A.L.)	SS	1	0	0	0	0	0	0	0	...	0	0	0	0	0	0	...
1985—	Toledo (Int'l)	SS	82	266	24	61	11	0	1	33	.229	14	30	1	132	245	16	.959
—	Minnesota (A.L.)	SS	32	57	5	15	2	0	0	9	.263	1	9	0	25	69	5	.949
1986—	Toledo (Int'l)	SS-2B	73	253	18	71	8	1	2	27	.281	6	30	1	†170	205	12	.969
—	Minnesota (A.L.)	2B-SS	37	42	4	9	1	0	0	1	.214	1	10	0	23	52	4	.949
1987—	Portland (PCL)	SS-3B-1B	91	291	28	80	3	2	4	28	.275	12	37	2	158	236	20	.952
1988—	Columbus (Int'l)■	SS-2B-3B	119	435	42	107	10	5	2	30	.246	7	53	4	221	404	19	.970
—	New York (A.L.)	2B-SS	3	3	0	0	0	0	0	0	.000	0	0	0	5	2	0	1.000
1989—	New York (A.L.)	SS	146	503	51	142	23	1	0	41	.282	14	60	3	237	471	22	.970
1990—	New York (A.L.)	SS	150	438	31	98	12	2	2	20	.224	16	54	1	268	447	17	.977
1991—	New York (A.L.)	SS-3B-P	148	480	51	123	23	2	5	33	.256	16	57	4	225	*414	21	.969
1992—	Colo. Springs (PCL)■	SS	122	483	64	145	36	6	9	36	.300	21	55	2	191	*414	26	.959
1993—	Cleveland (A.L.)	3B-SS-2B	129	263	34	73	15	0	4	27	.278	8	36	2	66	157	12	.949
1994—	Cleveland (A.L.)	3-S-2-1	90	231	27	55	13	0	1	19	.238	6	33	1	93	210	10	.968
1995—	Cleveland (A.L.)	2-3-S-1-DH	66	143	15	36	4	0	2	17	.252	2	16	0	50	101	5	.968
1996—	Cleveland (A.L.)	3-1-S-2-DH	59	112	12	25	4	2	4	11	.223	6	18	1	125	59	3	.984
—	New York (N.L.)■	3-S-2-1	48	134	19	41	7	2	4	16	.306	4	19	0	24	66	8	.918
1997—	Seattle (A.L.)■	SS-2B-3B	33	72	3	13	1	0	0	7	.181	2	12	1	42	57	3	.971
—	Tacoma (PCL)	2B-3B-SS	4	12	1	4	0	0	0	1	.333	2	1	0	5	4	2	.818
American League totals (12 years)			**894**	**2344**	**233**	**589**	**98**	**7**	**18**	**185**	**.251**	**72**	**305**	**13**	**1159**	**2066**	**102**	**.969**
National League totals (1 year)			**48**	**134**	**19**	**41**	**7**	**2**	**4**	**16**	**.306**	**4**	**19**	**0**	**24**	**66**	**8**	**.918**
Major league totals (12 years)			**942**	**2478**	**252**	**630**	**105**	**9**	**22**	**201**	**.254**	**76**	**324**	**13**	**1183**	**2132**	**110**	**.968**

DIVISION SERIES RECORD

					BATTING										FIELDING			
Year	Team (League)	Pos.	G	AB	R	H	2B	3B	HR	RBI	Avg.	BB	SO	SB	PO	A	E	Avg.
1995—	Cleveland (A.L.)..........	3B	1	1	0	0	0	0	0	0	.000	0	0	0	0	0	0	...

E

CHAMPIONSHIP SERIES RECORD

							BATTING									FIELDING		
Year Team (League)	Pos.	G	AB	R	H	2B	3B	HR	RBI	Avg.	BB	SO	SB		PO	A	E	Avg.
1995—Cleveland (A.L.)..........	3B	4	8	1	1	0	0	0	0	.125	0	3	0		3	3	1	.750

WORLD SERIES RECORD

							BATTING									FIELDING		
Year Team (League)	Pos.	G	AB	R	H	2B	3B	HR	RBI	Avg.	BB	SO	SB		PO	A	E	Avg.
1995—Cleveland (A.L.)..........	PR-3B	2	2	1	1	0	0	0	0	.500	0	0	0		1	1	0	1.000

RECORD AS PITCHER

Year Team (League)	W	L	Pct.	ERA	G	GS	CG	ShO	Sv.	IP	H	R	ER	BB	SO
1991—New York (A.L.)................	0	0	...	0.00	1	0	0	0	0	2/3	0	0	0	0	0
Major league totals (1 year)........	0	0	...	0.00	1	0	0	0	0	2/3	0	0	0	0	0

ESTALELLA, BOBBY   C   PHILLIES

PERSONAL: Born August 23, 1974, in Hialeah, Fla. ... 6-1/195. ... Bats right, throws right. ... Full name: Robert M. Estalella. ... Grandson of Bobby Estalella, outfielder with Washington Senators (1935-36, 1939 and 1942), St. Louis Browns (1941), and Philadelphia Athletics (1943-45 and 1949).
HIGH SCHOOL: Cooper City (Fla.).
JUNIOR COLLEGE: Miami-Dade (South) Community College.
TRANSACTIONS/CAREER NOTES: Selected by Philadelphia Phillies organization in 23rd round of free-agent draft (June 1, 1992).
STATISTICAL NOTES: Tied for South Atlantic League lead in double plays by catcher with eight in 1994. ... Led Florida State League catchers with 864 total chances in 1995. ... Led International League with 928 total chances and tied for league lead in double plays by catcher with nine in 1997. ... Hit three home runs in one game (September 4, 1997).

							BATTING									FIELDING		
Year Team (League)	Pos.	G	AB	R	H	2B	3B	HR	RBI	Avg.	BB	SO	SB		PO	A	E	Avg.
1993—Martinsville (App.)......	C	35	122	14	36	11	0	3	19	.295	14	24	0		210	25	6	.975
—Clearwater (FSL)	C	11	35	4	8	0	0	0	4	.229	2	3	0		47	8	0	1.000
1994—Spartanburg (SAL).....	C	86	299	34	65	19	1	9	41	.217	31	85	0		592	87	10	.985
—Clearwater (FSL)	C	13	46	3	12	1	0	2	9	.261	3	17	0		92	5	1	.990
1995—Clearwater (FSL)	C	117	404	61	105	24	1	15	58	.260	56	76	0		*771	82	11	.987
—Reading (Eastern)	C	10	34	5	8	1	0	2	9	.235	4	7	0		60	9	1	.986
1996—Reading (Eastern)	C	111	365	48	89	14	2	23	72	.244	67	104	2		775	84	14	.984
—Scran./W.B. (Int'l)......	C	11	36	7	9	3	0	3	8	.250	5	10	0		55	6	2	.968
—Philadelphia (N.L.)......	C	7	17	5	6	0	0	2	4	.353	1	6	1		24	1	0	1.000
1997—Scran./W.B. (Int'l)......	C	123	433	63	101	32	0	16	65	.233	56	109	3		*844	71	13	.986
—Philadelphia (N.L.)......	C	13	29	9	10	1	0	4	9	.345	7	7	0		49	3	0	1.000
Major league totals (2 years)		20	46	14	16	1	0	6	13	.348	8	13	1		73	4	0	1.000

ESTES, SHAWN   P   GIANTS

PERSONAL: Born February 18, 1973, in San Bernardino, Calif. ... 6-2/195. ... Throws left, bats left. ... Full name: Aaron Shawn Estes.
HIGH SCHOOL: Douglas (Minden, Nev.).
TRANSACTIONS/CAREER NOTES: Selected by Seattle Mariners organization in first round (11th pick overall) of free-agent draft (June 3, 1991). ... On disabled list (August 19, 1993-remainder of season). ... On Appleton disabled list (April 8-July 19 and July 25-August 15, 1994). ... Traded by Mariners with IF Wilson Delgado to San Francisco Giants for P Salomon Torres (May 21, 1995). ... On disabled list (March 23-April 6, 1997).
MISCELLANEOUS: Appeared in four games as pinch-runner with San Francisco (1996). ... Appeared in four games as pinch-runner (1997).

Year Team (League)	W	L	Pct.	ERA	G	GS	CG	ShO	Sv.	IP	H	R	ER	BB	SO
1991—Bellingham (N'west)...........	1	3	.250	6.88	9	9	0	0	0	34	27	33	26	55	35
1992—Bellingham (N'west)...........	3	3	.500	4.32	15	15	0	0	0	77	84	55	37	45	77
1993—Appleton (Midwest)..........	5	9	.357	7.24	19	18	0	0	0	83 1/3	108	85	67	52	65
1994—Appleton (Midwest)..........	0	2	.000	4.58	5	4	0	0	0	19 2/3	19	13	10	17	28
—Ariz. Mariners (Ariz.).........	0	3	.000	3.15	5	5	0	0	0	20	16	9	7	6	31
1995—Wis. Rap. (Midw.)..........	0	0	...	0.90	2	2	0	0	0	10	5	1	1	5	11
—Burlington (Midw.)■..........	0	0	...	4.11	4	4	0	0	0	15 1/3	13	8	7	12	22
—San Jose (California).........	5	2	.714	2.17	9	8	0	0	0	49 2/3	32	13	12	17	61
—Shreveport (Texas).........	2	0	1.000	2.01	4	4	0	0	0	22 1/3	14	5	5	10	18
—San Francisco (N.L.)	0	3	.000	6.75	3	3	0	0	0	17 1/3	16	14	13	5	14
1996—Phoenix (PCL).............	9	3	.750	3.43	18	18	0	0	0	110 1/3	92	43	42	38	95
—San Francisco (N.L.)	3	5	.375	3.60	11	11	0	0	0	70	63	30	28	39	60
1997—San Francisco (N.L.)	19	5	.792	3.18	32	32	3	2	0	201	162	80	71	*100	181
Major league totals (3 years)......	22	13	.629	3.50	46	46	3	2	0	288 1/3	241	124	112	144	255

DIVISION SERIES RECORD

Year Team (League)	W	L	Pct.	ERA	G	GS	CG	ShO	Sv.	IP	H	R	ER	BB	SO
1997—San Francisco (N.L.)	0	0	...	15.00	1	1	0	0	0	3	5	5	5	4	3

ALL-STAR GAME RECORD

Year League	W	L	Pct.	ERA	GS	CG	ShO	Sv.	IP	H	R	ER	BB	SO
1997—National.............	0	1	.000	18.00	0	0	0	0	1	1	2	2	1	1

ESTRADA, HORACIO   P   BREWERS

PERSONAL: Born October 19, 1975, in San Joaquin, Venezuela. ... 6-0/160. ... Throws left, bats left. ... Full name: Horacio J. Estrada.
TRANSACTIONS/CAREER NOTES: Signed as non-drafted free agent by Milwaukee Brewers organization (July 3, 1992).

E

Year—Team (League)	W	L	Pct.	ERA	G	GS	CG	ShO	Sv.	IP	H	R	ER	BB	SO
1993—Dom. Brewers (DSL)..........	1	2	.333	4.41	22	3	0	0	0	51	39	33	25	37	60
1994—Dom. Brewers (DSL)..........	3	4	.429	2.67	26	2	0	0	7	60²/₃	41	27	18	46	52
1995—Ariz. Brewers (Ariz.)...........	0	1	.000	3.71	8	1	0	0	2	17	13	9	7	8	21
—Helena (Pioneer).................	1	2	.333	5.40	13	0	0	0	0	30	27	21	18	24	30
1996—Beloit (Midwest).................	2	1	.667	1.23	17	0	0	0	1	29¹/₃	21	8	4	11	34
—Stockton (California)..........	1	3	.250	4.59	29	0	0	0	3	51	43	29	26	21	62
1997—El Paso (Texas)...................	8	10	.444	4.74	29	23	1	0	1	153²/₃	174	93	81	70	127

EUSEBIO, TONY   C   ASTROS

PERSONAL: Born April 27, 1967, in San Jose de Los Llames, Dominican Republic. ... 6-2/210. ... Bats right, throws right. ... Full name: Raul Antonio Eusebio. ... Name pronounced you-SAY-bee-o.

HIGH SCHOOL: San Rafael (Dominican Republic).

TRANSACTIONS/CAREER NOTES: Signed as non-drafted free agent by Houston Astros organization (May 30, 1985). ... On disabled list (August 5, 1990-remainder of season); April 16-23, 1992 and August 24, 1993-remainder of season). ... On Houston disabled list (May 8-June 17 and June 22-August 7, 1996); included rehabilitation assignments to Tucson (June 10-17 and July 29-August 7).

STATISTICAL NOTES: Tied for Southern League lead in double plays by catcher with eight in 1989. ... Led Texas League catchers with .9963 fielding percentage and 12 double plays in 1992. ... Career major league grand slams: 2.

							BATTING								FIELDING		
Year—Team (League)	Pos.	G	AB	R	H	2B	3B	HR	RBI	Avg.	BB	SO	SB	PO	A	E	Avg.
1985—GC Astros (GCL)	C	1	1	0	0	0	0	0	0	.000	0	0	0	4	0	0	1.000
1985—					Dominican Summer League statistics unavailable.												
1986—					Dominican Summer League statistics unavailable.												
1987—GC Astros (GCL)	C-1B	42	125	26	26	1	2	1	15	.208	18	19	8	204	24	4	.983
1988—Osceola (Fla. St.)........	C-OF	118	392	45	96	6	3	0	40	.245	40	69	19	611	66	8	.988
1989—Columbus (Southern).	C	65	203	20	38	6	1	0	18	.187	38	47	7	355	46	7	.983
—Osceola (Fla. St.)........	C	52	175	22	50	6	3	0	30	.286	19	27	5	290	40	5	.985
1990—Columbus (Southern).	C	92	318	36	90	18	0	4	37	.283	21	80	6	558	69	4	*.994
1991—Jackson (Texas)	C	66	222	27	58	8	3	2	31	.261	25	54	3	424	48	7	.985
—Tucson (PCL)	C	5	20	5	8	1	0	0	2	.400	3	3	1	40	1	0	1.000
—Houston (N.L.)	C	10	19	4	2	1	0	0	0	.105	6	8	0	49	4	1	.981
1992—Jackson (Texas)	C	94	339	33	104	9	3	5	44	.307	25	58	1	493	51	2	*.996
1993—Tucson (PCL)	C	78	281	39	91	20	1	1	43	.324	22	40	1	450	46	3	.994
1994—Houston (N.L.)	C	55	159	18	47	9	1	5	30	.296	8	33	0	263	24	2	.993
1995—Houston (N.L.)	C	113	368	46	110	21	1	6	58	.299	31	59	0	645	49	5	.993
1996—Houston (N.L.)	C	58	152	15	41	7	2	1	19	.270	18	20	0	255	24	1	.996
—Tucson (PCL)	C	15	53	8	22	4	0	0	14	.415	2	7	0	45	1	0	1.000
1997—Houston (N.L.)	C	60	164	12	45	2	0	1	18	.274	19	27	0	297	16	4	.987
Major league totals (5 years)		296	862	95	245	40	4	13	125	.284	82	147	0	1509	117	13	.992

DIVISION SERIES RECORD

							BATTING								FIELDING		
Year—Team (League)	Pos.	G	AB	R	H	2B	3B	HR	RBI	Avg.	BB	SO	SB	PO	A	E	Avg.
1997—Houston (N.L.)	C	1	3	1	2	0	0	0	0	.667	0	1	1	6	1	0	1.000

EVANS, BART   P   ROYALS

PERSONAL: Born December 30, 1970, in Springfield, Mo. ... 6-1/190. ... Throws right, bats right. ... Full name: Bart Steven Evans.

HIGH SCHOOL: Mansfield (Mo.).

COLLEGE: Southwest Missouri State.

TRANSACTIONS/CAREER NOTES: Selected by Kansas City Royals organization in ninth round of free-agent draft (June 1, 1992). ... On disabled list (June 17, 1993-remainder of season). ... On Wichita temporarily inactive list (April 24-May 10, 1995). ... On disabled list (June 14-September 19, 1996).

HONORS: Named Southern League Pitcher of the Year (1994).

Year—Team (League)	W	L	Pct.	ERA	G	GS	CG	ShO	Sv.	IP	H	R	ER	BB	SO
1992—Eugene (Northwest)	1	1	.500	6.23	13	1	0	0	0	26	17	20	18	31	39
1993—Rockford (Midwest)	10	4	.714	4.36	27	16	0	0	0	99	95	52	48	60	120
1994—Wilmington (Caro.).............	10	3	.769	2.98	26	26	0	0	0	145	107	53	48	61	145
1995—Wichita (Texas)	0	4	.000	10.48	7	7	0	0	0	22¹/₃	22	28	26	45	13
—Wilmington (Caro.)	4	1	.800	2.89	16	6	0	0	2	46²/₃	30	21	15	44	47
1996—Wichita (Texas)	1	2	.333	11.84	9	7	0	0	0	24¹/₃	31	38	32	36	16
1997—Wilmington (Caro.).............	0	1	.000	6.53	16	2	0	0	0	20²/₃	22	18	15	15	22
—Wichita (Texas)	1	2	.333	4.59	32	0	0	0	6	33¹/₃	45	20	17	8	28

EVANS, TOM   3B   BLUE JAYS

PERSONAL: Born July 9, 1974, in Kirkland, Wash. ... 6-1/208. ... Bats right, throws right. ... Full name: Thomas John Evans.

HIGH SCHOOL: Juanita (Kirkland, Wash.).

TRANSACTIONS/CAREER NOTES: Selected by Toronto Blue Jays organization in fourth round of free-agent draft (June 1, 1992). ... On disabled list (April 7-May 17, 1994). ... On Toronto disabled list (September 14-28, 1997).

STATISTICAL NOTES: Led Florida State League third basemen with 435 total chances in 1995. ... Led Southern League with .453 on-base percentage in 1996. ... Led International league third basemen with 337 total chances and 27 double plays in 1997.

							BATTING								FIELDING		
Year—Team (League)	Pos.	G	AB	R	H	2B	3B	HR	RBI	Avg.	BB	SO	SB	PO	A	E	Avg.
1992—Medicine Hat (Pio.)	3B	52	166	17	36	3	0	1	21	.217	33	29	4	53	115	20	.894
1993—Hagerstown (SAL)......	3B-1B-SS	119	389	47	100	25	1	7	54	.257	53	92	9	92	181	27	.910

Year	Team (League)	Pos.	G	AB	R	H	2B	3B	HR	RBI	Avg.	BB	SO	SB	PO	A	E	Avg.
1994— Hagerstown (SAL)......		3B	95	322	52	88	16	2	13	48	.273	51	80	2	60	196	36	.877
1995— Dunedin (Fla. St.)......		3B	130	444	63	124	29	3	9	66	.279	51	80	7	*92	*309	34	.922
1996— Knoxville (Southern) ..		3B-1B	120	394	87	111	27	1	17	65	.282	*115	113	4	52	146	12	.943
1997— Dunedin (Fla. St.).......		3B	15	42	8	11	2	0	2	4	.262	11	10	0	6	12	2	.900
— Syracuse (Int'l)............		3B	107	376	60	99	17	1	15	65	.263	53	104	1	*83	*242	12	*.964
— Toronto (A.L.).............		3B	12	38	7	11	2	0	1	2	.289	2	10	0	9	24	3	.917
Major league totals (1 year)			12	38	7	11	2	0	1	2	.289	2	10	0	9	24	3	.917

EVERETT, CARL   OF   ASTROS

PERSONAL: Born June 3, 1971, in Tampa. ... 6-0/190. ... Bats both, throws right. ... Full name: Carl Edward Everett.
HIGH SCHOOL: Hillsborough (Tampa).
TRANSACTIONS/CAREER NOTES: Selected by New York Yankees organization in first round (10th pick overall) of free-agent draft (June 4, 1990). ... On Fort Lauderdale disabled list (July 7-August 15, 1992). ... Selected by Florida Marlins in second round (27th pick overall) of expansion draft (November 17, 1992). ... On High Desert disabled list (April 8-13, 1993). ... On Florida disabled list (July 23-August 10, 1994). ... On Edmonton suspended list (August 29, 1994-remainder of season). ... Traded by Marlins to New York Mets for 2B Quilvio Veras (November 29, 1994). ... On disabled list (April 12-27, 1996). ... Traded by Mets to Houston Astros for P John Hudek (December 22, 1997).
STATISTICAL NOTES: Led South Atlantic League in being hit by pitch with 23 in 1991. ... Switch-hit home runs in one game three times (June 6, 1994; September 12, 1996 and April 20, 1997, first game). ... Career major league grand slams: 3.

Year	Team (League)	Pos.	G	AB	R	H	2B	3B	HR	RBI	Avg.	BB	SO	SB	PO	A	E	Avg.
1990— GC Yankees (GCL)......		OF	48	185	28	48	8	5	1	14	.259	15	38	15	64	5	5	.932
1991— Greensboro (S. Atl.) ...		OF	123	468	96	127	18	0	4	40	.271	57	122	28	250	14	7	.974
1992— Fort Lauderdale (FSL)		OF	46	183	30	42	8	2	2	9	.230	12	40	11	111	5	3	.975
— Prince William (Car.) ..		OF	6	22	7	7	0	0	4	9	.318	5	7	1	12	1	0	1.000
1993— High Desert (Calif.)■ .		OF	59	253	48	73	12	6	10	52	.289	22	73	24	124	6	2	.985
— Florida (N.L.)...........		OF	11	19	0	2	0	0	0	0	.105	1	9	1	6	0	1	.857
— Edmonton (PCL)		OF	35	136	28	42	13	4	6	16	.309	19	45	12	69	12	2	.976
1994— Edmonton (PCL)		OF	78	321	63	108	17	2	11	47	.336	19	65	16	167	11	2	.989
— Florida (N.L.)..........		OF	16	51	7	11	1	0	2	6	.216	3	15	4	28	2	0	1.000
1995— New York (N.L.)■......		OF	79	289	48	75	13	1	12	54	.260	39	67	2	148	9	3	.981
— Norfolk (Int'l)		OF-SS	67	260	52	78	16	4	6	35	.300	20	47	12	133	7	0	1.000
1996— New York (N.L.).........		OF	101	192	29	46	8	1	1	16	.240	21	53	6	96	4	7	.935
1997— New York (N.L.).........		OF	142	443	58	110	28	3	14	57	.248	32	102	17	226	8	7	.971
Major league totals (5 years)			349	994	142	244	50	5	29	133	.245	96	246	30	504	23	18	.967

EVERSGERD, BRYAN   P

PERSONAL: Born February 11, 1969, in Centralia, Ill. ... 6-1/190. ... Throws left, bats right. ... Full name: Bryan David Eversgerd.
HIGH SCHOOL: Carlyle (Ill.).
JUNIOR COLLEGE: Kaskaskia Community College (Ill.).
TRANSACTIONS/CAREER NOTES: Signed as non-drafted free agent by St. Louis Cardinals organization (June 14, 1989). ... Traded by Cardinals with P Kirk Bullinger and OF Darond Stovall to Montreal Expos for P Ken Hill (April 5, 1995). ... Traded by Expos with SS Wil Cordero to Boston Red Sox for P Rheal Cormier, 1B Ryan McGuire and P Shayne Bennett (January 10, 1996). ... Traded by Red Sox organization to Texas Rangers organization for a player to be named later (April 18, 1996); Red Sox acquired OF Rudy Pemberton to complete deal (April 24, 1996). ... Granted free agency (October 15, 1996). ... Signed by San Diego Padres organization (December 2, 1996). ... Released by Padres (March 22, 1997). ... Signed by Texas Rangers organization (May 1, 1997). ... Granted free agency (October 27, 1997).

Year	Team (League)	W	L	Pct.	ERA	G	GS	CG	ShO	Sv.	IP	H	R	ER	BB	SO
1989— Johnson City (App.)		2	3	.400	3.64	16	1	0	0	0	29²/₃	30	16	12	12	19
1990— Springfield (Mid.)		6	8	.429	4.14	20	15	2	0	0	104¹/₃	123	60	48	26	55
1991— Savannah (S. Atl.)		1	5	.167	3.47	72	0	0	0	1	93¹/₃	71	43	36	34	97
1992— St. Petersburg (FSL)		3	2	.600	2.68	57	1	0	0	0	74	65	25	22	25	57
— Arkansas (Texas)		0	1	.000	6.75	6	0	0	0	0	5¹/₃	7	4	4	2	4
1993— Arkansas (Texas)		4	4	.500	2.18	*62	0	0	0	0	66	60	24	16	19	68
1994— Louisville (A.A.)		1	1	.500	4.50	9	0	0	0	0	12	11	7	6	8	8
— St. Louis (N.L.)..................		2	3	.400	4.52	40	1	0	0	0	67²/₃	75	36	34	20	47
1995— Montreal (N.L.)■..............		0	0	. . .	5.14	25	0	0	0	0	21	22	13	12	9	8
— Ottawa (Int'l)		6	2	.750	2.38	38	0	0	0	2	53	49	21	14	26	45
1996— Trenton (Eastern)■		1	0	1.000	2.57	4	0	0	0	0	7	6	2	2	4	2
— Oklahoma City (A.A.)■......		3	3	.500	2.74	38	5	0	0	4	65²/₃	57	21	20	14	60
1997— Oklahoma City (A.A.)		1	3	.250	4.24	26	7	0	0	0	76¹/₃	91	48	36	24	43
— Texas (A.L.)		0	2	.000	20.25	3	0	0	0	0	1¹/₃	5	3	3	3	2
A.L. totals (1 year)		0	2	.000	20.25	3	0	0	0	0	1¹/₃	5	3	3	3	2
N.L. totals (2 years)		2	3	.400	4.67	65	1	0	0	0	88²/₃	97	49	46	29	55
Major league totals (3 years)		2	5	.286	4.90	68	1	0	0	0	90	102	52	49	32	57

EYRE, SCOTT   P   WHITE SOX

PERSONAL: Born May 30, 1972, in Inglewood, Calif. ... 6-1/160. ... Throws left, bats left. ... Full name: Scott Alan Eyre.
HIGH SCHOOL: Cyprus (Magna, Utah).
JUNIOR COLLEGE: College of Southern Idaho.
TRANSACTIONS/CAREER NOTES: Selected by Texas Rangers organization in ninth round of free-agent draft (June 3, 1991). ... Traded by Rangers organization to Chicago White Sox organization for SS Esteban Beltre (March 28, 1994). ... On disabled list (April 8-27, 1994). ... On Prince William disabled list (April 6-September 7, 1995).
HONORS: Named Southern League Most Outstanding Pitcher (1997).

E

Year— Team (League)	W	L	Pct.	ERA	G	GS	CG	ShO	Sv.	IP	H	R	ER	BB	SO
1992— Butte (Pioneer)	7	3	.700	2.90	15	14	2	1	0	80 2/3	71	30	26	39	94
1993— Charleston, S.C. (S. Atl.)	11	7	.611	3.45	26	26	0	0	0	143 2/3	115	74	55	59	154
1994— South Bend (Mid.)■	8	4	.667	3.47	19	18	2	0	0	111 2/3	108	56	43	37	111
1995— GC White Sox (GCL)	0	2	.000	2.30	9	9	0	0	0	27 1/3	16	7	7	12	40
1996— Birmingham (Southern)	12	7	.632	4.38	27	27	0	0	0	158 1/3	170	90	77	79	137
1997— Birmingham (Southern)	•13	5	.722	3.84	22	22	0	0	0	126 2/3	110	61	54	55	127
— Chicago (A.L.)	4	4	.500	5.04	11	11	0	0	0	60 2/3	62	36	34	31	36
Major league totals (1 year)	4	4	.500	5.04	11	11	0	0	0	60 2/3	62	36	34	31	36

FABREGAS, JORGE   C   DIAMONDBACKS

PERSONAL: Born March 13, 1970, in Miami. ... 6-3/205. ... Bats left, throws right.
HIGH SCHOOL: Christopher Columbus (Miami).
COLLEGE: Miami (Fla.).
TRANSACTIONS/CAREER NOTES: Selected by Cleveland Indians organization in 11th round of free-agent draft (June 1, 1988); did not sign. ... Selected by California Angels organization in supplemental round ("sandwich pick" between first and second round, 34th pick overall) of free-agent draft (June 3, 1991); pick received as part of compensation for Minnesota Twins signing Type A free-agent OF/DH Chili Davis. ... On disabled list (April 12-May 4 and July 28-September 5, 1992). ... Angels franchise renamed Anaheim Angels for 1997 season. ... Traded by Angels with P Chuck McElroy to Chicago White Sox for OF Tony Phillips and C Chad Kreuter (May 18, 1997). ... Selected by Arizona Diamondbacks in first round (seventh pick overall) of expansion draft (November 18, 1997).
STATISTICAL NOTES: Led Texas League with 17 passed balls in 1993.

Year— Team (League)	Pos.	G	AB	R	H	2B	3B	HR	RBI	Avg.	BB	SO	SB	PO	A	E	Avg.
1992— Palm Springs (Calif.)	C	70	258	35	73	13	0	0	40	.283	30	27	0	436	63	*17	.967
1993— Midland (Texas)	C	113	409	63	118	26	3	6	56	.289	31	60	1	620	99	•11	.985
— Vancouver (PCL)	C	4	13	1	3	1	0	0	1	.231	1	3	0	30	3	0	1.000
1994— Vancouver (PCL)	C	66	211	17	47	6	1	1	24	.223	12	25	1	365	41	4	.990
— California (A.L.)	C	43	127	12	36	3	0	0	16	.283	7	18	2	217	16	3	.987
1995— California (A.L.)	C	73	227	24	56	10	0	1	22	.247	17	28	0	391	36	6	.986
— Vancouver (PCL)	C	21	73	9	18	3	0	4	10	.247	9	12	0	112	12	4	.969
1996— California (A.L.)	C-DH	90	254	18	73	6	0	2	26	.287	17	27	0	502	46	6	.989
— Vancouver (PCL)	C-1B	10	37	4	11	3	0	0	5	.297	4	4	0	27	2	0	1.000
1997— Anaheim (A.L.)	C	21	38	2	3	1	0	0	3	.079	3	3	0	81	5	1	.989
— Chicago (A.L.)■	C-1B	100	322	31	90	10	1	7	48	.280	11	43	1	520	46	7	.988
Major league totals (4 years)		327	968	87	258	30	1	10	115	.267	55	119	3	1711	149	23	.988

FALTEISEK, STEVE   P   EXPOS

PERSONAL: Born January 28, 1972, in Mineola, N.Y. ... 6-2/200. ... Throws right, bats right. ... Full name: Steven James Falteisek.
HIGH SCHOOL: Memorial (Floral Park, N.Y.).
COLLEGE: South Alabama.
TRANSACTIONS/CAREER NOTES: Selected by Montreal Expos organization in 10th round of free-agent draft (June 1, 1992).

Year— Team (League)	W	L	Pct.	ERA	G	GS	CG	ShO	Sv.	IP	H	R	ER	BB	SO
1992— Jamestown (NYP)	3	*8	.273	3.56	15	•15	2	0	0	*96	84	47	38	31	82
1993— Burlington (Midw.)	3	5	.375	5.90	14	14	0	0	0	76 1/3	86	59	50	35	63
1994— W.P. Beach (FSL)	9	4	.692	2.54	27	24	0	0	0	159 2/3	144	72	45	49	91
1995— Harrisburg (Eastern)	9	6	.600	2.95	25	25	•5	0	0	168	152	74	55	64	112
— Ottawa (Int'l)	2	0	1.000	1.17	3	3	1	1	0	23	17	4	3	5	18
1996— Ottawa (Int'l)	2	5	.286	6.36	12	12	0	0	0	58	75	45	41	25	26
— Harrisburg (Eastern)	6	5	.545	3.81	17	17	1	0	0	115 2/3	111	60	49	48	62
1997— Ottawa (Int'l)	6	9	.400	3.96	22	22	1	0	0	125	135	67	55	54	56
— Montreal (N.L.)	0	0	. . .	3.38	5	0	0	0	0	8	8	4	3	3	2
Major league totals (1 year)	0	0	. . .	3.38	5	0	0	0	0	8	8	4	3	3	2

FASANO, SAL   C   ROYALS

PERSONAL: Born August 10, 1971, in Chicago. ... 6-2/220. ... Bats right, throws right. ... Full name: Salvatore Frank Fasano.
HIGH SCHOOL: Hoffman Estates (Ill.).
COLLEGE: Evansville.
TRANSACTIONS/CAREER NOTES: Selected by Kansas City Royals organization in 37th round of free-agent draft (June 3, 1993).
STATISTICAL NOTES: Led Northwest League catchers with seven double plays in 1993.

Year— Team (League)	Pos.	G	AB	R	H	2B	3B	HR	RBI	Avg.	BB	SO	SB	PO	A	E	Avg.
1993— Eugene (Northwest)	C	49	176	25	47	11	1	10	36	.267	19	49	4	276	38	1	.997
1994— Rockford (Midwest)	C-1B	97	345	61	97	16	1	25	81	.281	33	66	8	527	86	12	.981
— Wilmington (Caro.)	C-1B	23	90	15	29	7	0	7	32	.322	13	24	0	80	9	4	.957
1995— Wilmington (Caro.)	C-1B	23	88	12	20	2	1	2	7	.227	5	16	0	132	12	0	1.000
— Wichita (Texas)	C-1B	87	317	60	92	19	2	20	66	.290	27	61	3	589	64	14	.979
1996— Kansas City (A.L.)	C	51	143	20	29	2	0	6	19	.203	14	25	1	291	14	5	.984
— Omaha (A.A.)	C-1B-3B	29	104	12	24	4	0	4	15	.231	6	21	0	198	21	4	.982
1997— Omaha (A.A.)	C	49	152	17	25	7	0	4	14	.164	12	53	0	296	34	4	.988
— Kansas City (A.L.)	C-DH	13	38	4	8	2	0	1	1	.211	1	12	0	53	3	1	.982
— Wichita (Texas)	C-1B	40	131	27	31	5	0	13	27	.237	20	35	0	232	21	4	.984
Major league totals (2 years)		64	181	24	37	4	0	7	20	.204	15	37	1	344	17	6	.984

E
F

FASSERO, JEFF   P   MARINERS

PERSONAL: Born January 5, 1963, in Springfield, Ill. ... 6-1/195. ... Throws left, bats left. ... Full name: Jeffrey Joseph Fassero. ... Name pronounced fuh-SAIR-oh.

HIGH SCHOOL: Griffin (Springfield, Ill.).

JUNIOR COLLEGE: Lincoln Land Community College (Ill.).

COLLEGE: Mississippi.

TRANSACTIONS/CAREER NOTES: Selected by St. Louis Cardinals organization in 22nd round of free-agent draft (June 4, 1984). ... Selected by Chicago White Sox organization from Cardinals organization in Rule 5 minor league draft (December 5, 1989). ... Released by White Sox organization (April 3, 1990). ... Signed by Cleveland Indians organization (April 9, 1990). ... Granted free agency (October 15, 1990). ... Signed by Indianapolis, Montreal Expos organization (January 3, 1991). ... On disabled list (July 24-August 11, 1994). ... Traded by Expos with P Alex Pacheco to Seattle Mariners for C Chris Widger, P Trey Moore and P Matt Wagner (October 29, 1996).

STATISTICAL NOTES: Pitched 5-0 no-hit victory for Arkansas against Jackson (June 12, 1989).

Year — Team (League)	W	L	Pct.	ERA	G	GS	CG	ShO	Sv.	IP	H	R	ER	BB	SO
1984— Johnson City (App.)	4	7	.364	4.59	13	11	2	0	1	66²/₃	65	42	34	39	59
1985— Springfield (Mid.)	4	8	.333	4.01	29	15	1	0	1	119	125	78	53	45	65
1986— St. Petersburg (FSL)	13	7	.650	2.45	26	•26	6	1	0	*176	156	63	48	56	112
1987— Arkansas (Texas)	10	7	.588	4.10	28	27	2	1	0	151¹/₃	168	90	69	67	118
1988— Arkansas (Texas)	5	5	.500	3.58	70	1	0	0	17	78	97	48	31	41	72
1989— Louisville (A.A.)	3	10	.231	5.22	22	19	0	0	1	112	136	79	65	47	73
— Arkansas (Texas)	4	1	.800	1.64	6	6	2	1	0	44	32	11	8	12	38
1990— Cant./Akr. (Eastern)■	5	4	.556	2.80	*61	0	0	0	6	64¹/₃	66	24	20	24	61
1991— Indianapolis (A.A.)■	3	0	1.000	1.47	18	0	0	0	4	18¹/₃	11	3	3	7	12
— Montreal (N.L.)	2	5	.286	2.44	51	0	0	0	8	55¹/₃	39	17	15	17	42
1992— Montreal (N.L.)	8	7	.533	2.84	70	0	0	0	1	85²/₃	81	35	27	34	63
1993— Montreal (N.L.)	12	5	.706	2.29	56	15	1	0	1	149²/₃	119	50	38	54	140
1994— Montreal (N.L.)	8	6	.571	2.99	21	21	1	0	0	138²/₃	119	54	46	40	119
1995— Montreal (N.L.)	13	14	.481	4.33	30	30	1	0	0	189	207	102	91	74	164
1996— Montreal (N.L.)	15	11	.577	3.30	34	34	5	1	0	231²/₃	217	95	85	55	222
1997— Seattle (A.L.)■	16	9	.640	3.61	35	•35	2	1	0	234¹/₃	226	108	94	84	189
A.L. totals (1 year)	16	9	.640	3.61	35	35	2	1	0	234¹/₃	226	108	94	84	189
N.L. totals (6 years)	58	48	.547	3.20	262	100	8	1	10	850	782	353	302	274	750
Major league totals (7 years)	74	57	.565	3.29	297	135	10	2	10	1084¹/₃	1008	461	396	358	939

DIVISION SERIES RECORD

Year — Team (League)	W	L	Pct.	ERA	G	GS	CG	ShO	Sv.	IP	H	R	ER	BB	SO
1997— Seattle (A.L.)	1	0	1.000	1.13	1	1	0	0	0	8	3	1	1	4	3

FEBLES, CARLOS   2B   ROYALS

PERSONAL: Born May 24, 1976, in El Seybo, Dominican Republic. ... 5-11/170. ... Bats right, throws right. ... Full name: Carlos Manuel Febles.

HIGH SCHOOL: Sagrado Corazon de Jesus (Dominican Republic).

TRANSACTIONS/CAREER NOTES: Signed as non-drafted free-agent by Kansas City Royals (November 2, 1993).

STATISTICAL NOTES: Led Gulf Coast League second basemen with 230 total chances and 39 double plays in 1995. ... Led Carolina League with 590 total chances and 85 double plays in 1997.

Year — Team (League)	Pos.	G	AB	R	H	2B	3B	HR	RBI	Avg.	BB	SO	SB	PO	A	E	Avg.
1994— Dom. Royals (DSL)	2B	56	184	38	61	9	3	2	37	.332	38	27	12	113	113	16	.934
1995— GC Royals (GCL)	2B	54	188	40	53	13	5	3	20	.282	26	30	16	*117	101	12	.948
1996— Lansing (Midwest)	2B-SS	102	363	84	107	23	5	5	43	.295	66	64	30	206	292	19	.963
1997— Wilmington (Caro.)	2B	122	438	78	104	27	6	3	29	.237	51	95	49	212	*355	*23	.961

FELIX, PEDRO   3B   GIANTS

PERSONAL: Born April 27, 1977, in Azua, Dominican Republic. ... 6-1/180. ... Bats right, throws right.

TRANSACTIONS/CAREER NOTES: Signed as non-drafted free agent by San Francisco Giants organization (February 7, 1994).

STATISTICAL NOTES: Led California League third basemen with 457 total chances and 39 double plays in 1997.

Year — Team (League)	Pos.	G	AB	R	H	2B	3B	HR	RBI	Avg.	BB	SO	SB	PO	A	E	Avg.
1994— Ariz. Giants (Ariz.)	3B	38	119	7	23	0	0	3	.193	2	20	2	19	82	5	.953	
1995— Bellingham (N'west)	3B-1B	43	113	14	31	2	1	0	16	.274	7	33	1	30	37	2	.971
1996— Bellingham (N'west)	3B-1B	93	321	36	85	12	2	5	36	.265	18	65	5	66	186	17	.937
1997— Bakersfield (Calif.)	3B	135	515	59	140	25	4	14	56	.272	23	90	5	*112	*322	23	*.950

FERMIN, RAMON   P   REDS

PERSONAL: Born November 25, 1972, in San Francisco de Macoris, Dominican Republic. ... 6-3/180. ... Throws right, bats right. ... Full name: Ramon Antonio Ventura Fermin. ... Name pronounced fair-MEEN.

TRANSACTIONS/CAREER NOTES: Signed as non-drafted free agent by Oakland Athletics organization (December 1, 1989). ... Traded by Athletics with IF Fausto Cruz to Detroit Tigers for OF Phil Plantier (March 22, 1996). ... Granted free agency (October 15, 1997). ... Signed by Cincinnati Reds organization (November 27, 1997).

Year — Team (League)	W	L	Pct.	ERA	G	GS	CG	ShO	Sv.	IP	H	R	ER	BB	SO
1991— Arizona A's (Arizona)	3	0	1.000	2.13	7	3	1	0	0	25¹/₃	20	6	6	4	11
— Modesto (California)	1	0	1.000	4.38	3	2	0	0	0	12¹/₃	16	7	6	3	5
1992— Madison (Midwest)	5	5	.500	2.43	14	14	1	0	0	77²/₃	66	33	21	35	37
— Modesto (California)	2	3	.400	5.70	14	5	0	0	1	42²/₃	50	31	27	19	18

Year— Team (League)	W	L	Pct.	ERA	G	GS	CG	ShO	Sv.	IP	H	R	ER	BB	SO
1993— Modesto (California)	4	6	.400	6.15	31	5	0	0	1	67 1/3	78	56	46	37	47
1994— Modesto (California)	9	6	.600	3.59	29	18	0	0	5	133	129	71	53	42	120
1995— Huntsville (Southern)	6	7	.462	3.86	32	13	0	0	7	100 1/3	105	53	43	45	58
—Oakland (A.L.)	0	0	...	13.50	1	0	0	0	0	1 1/3	4	2	2	1	0
1996— Jacksonville (Southern)■ ..	6	6	.500	4.50	46	6	0	0	3	84	82	56	42	46	48
1997— Toledo (Int'l)	4	2	.667	4.93	41	8	0	0	0	80 1/3	103	53	44	33	46
Major league totals (1 year)........	0	0	...	13.50	1	0	0	0	0	1 1/3	4	2	2	1	0

FERNANDEZ, ALEX — P — MARLINS

PERSONAL: Born August 13, 1969, in Miami Beach, Fla. ... 6-1/215. ... Throws right, bats right. ... Full name: Alexander Fernandez.
HIGH SCHOOL: Pace (Miami).
JUNIOR COLLEGE: Miami-Dade (South) Community College.
COLLEGE: Miami (Fla.).
TRANSACTIONS/CAREER NOTES: Selected by Milwaukee Brewers organization in first round (24th pick overall) of free-agent draft (June 1, 1988); did not sign. ... Selected by Chicago White Sox organization in first round (fourth pick overall) of free-agent draft (June 4, 1990). ... Granted free agency (December 7, 1996). ... Signed by Florida Marlins (December 9, 1996).
HONORS: Named Golden Spikes Award winner by USA Baseball (1990).
STATISTICAL NOTES: Pitched 7-0 one-hit, complete-game victory for Chicago against Milwaukee (May 4, 1992). ... Pitched 1-0 one-hit, complete-game victory against Chicago (April 10, 1997).
MISCELLANEOUS: Had a sacrifice hit in only appearance as pinch-hitter (1997).

Year— Team (League)	W	L	Pct.	ERA	G	GS	CG	ShO	Sv.	IP	H	R	ER	BB	SO
1990— GC White Sox (GCL)	1	0	1.000	3.60	2	2	0	0	0	10	11	4	4	1	16
—Sarasota (Florida State)......	1	1	.500	1.84	2	2	0	0	0	14 2/3	8	4	3	3	23
—Birmingham (Southern)	3	0	1.000	1.08	4	4	0	0	0	25	20	7	3	6	27
—Chicago (A.L.)	5	5	.500	3.80	13	13	3	0	0	87 2/3	89	40	37	34	61
1991— Chicago (A.L.)	9	13	.409	4.51	34	32	2	0	0	191 2/3	186	100	96	88	145
1992— Chicago (A.L.)	8	11	.421	4.27	29	29	4	2	0	187 2/3	199	100	89	50	95
—Vancouver (PCL)	2	1	.667	0.94	4	3	2	1	0	28 2/3	15	8	3	6	27
1993— Chicago (A.L.)	18	9	.667	3.13	34	34	3	1	0	247 1/3	221	95	86	67	169
1994— Chicago (A.L.)	11	7	.611	3.86	24	24	4	3	0	170 1/3	163	83	73	50	122
1995— Chicago (A.L.)	12	8	.600	3.80	30	30	5	2	0	203 2/3	200	98	86	65	159
1996— Chicago (A.L.)	16	10	.615	3.45	35	35	6	1	0	258	248	110	99	72	200
1997— Florida (N.L.)■	17	12	.586	3.59	32	32	5	1	0	220 2/3	193	93	88	69	183
A.L. totals (7 years)	79	63	.556	3.78	199	197	27	9	0	1346 1/3	1306	626	566	449	951
N.L. totals (1 year)	17	12	.586	3.59	32	32	5	1	0	220 2/3	193	93	88	69	183
Major league totals (8 years).....	96	75	.561	3.76	231	229	32	10	0	1567	1499	719	654	495	1134

DIVISION SERIES RECORD

Year— Team (League)	W	L	Pct.	ERA	G	GS	CG	ShO	Sv.	IP	H	R	ER	BB	SO
1997— Florida (N.L.)	1	0	1.000	2.57	1	1	0	0	0	7	7	2	2	0	5

CHAMPIONSHIP SERIES RECORD

Year— Team (League)	W	L	Pct.	ERA	G	GS	CG	ShO	Sv.	IP	H	R	ER	BB	SO
1993— Chicago (A.L.)	0	2	.000	1.80	2	2	0	0	0	15	15	6	3	6	10
1997— Florida (N.L.)	0	1	.000	16.88	1	1	0	0	0	2 2/3	6	5	5	1	3
Champ. series totals (2 years)	0	3	.000	4.08	3	3	0	0	0	17 2/3	21	11	8	7	13

WORLD SERIES RECORD

NOTES: Member of World Series championship team (1997); inactive due to injury.

Year— Team (League)	W	L	Pct.	ERA	G	GS	CG	ShO	Sv.	IP	H	R	ER	BB	SO
1997— Florida (N.L.)						Did not play.									

FERNANDEZ, JOSE — 3B — EXPOS

PERSONAL: Born November 2, 1974, in La Vega, Dominican Republic. ... 6-2/190. ... Bats right, throws right. ... Full name: Jose Mayobanex Fernandez.
HIGH SCHOOL: Instituto Evangelico (Santo Domingo, Dominican Republic).
COLLEGE: Universidad Madre y Maestra (Santiago, Dominican Republic).
TRANSACTIONS/CAREER NOTES: Signed as non-drafted free agent by Montreal Expos organization (March 2, 1993).

						BATTING								FIELDING			
Year— Team (League)	Pos.	G	AB	R	H	2B	3B	HR	RBI	Avg.	BB	SO	SB	PO	A	E	Avg.
1993— Dom. Expos (DSL)	IF	65	251	40	80	8	1	10	49	.319	32	23	2	103	223	25	.929
1994— G.C. Expos (GCL)	3B-1B	45	172	27	40	8	0	5	23	.233	14	35	11	87	77	9	.948
1995— Vermont (NYP).........	3B	66	270	38	74	6	7	4	41	.274	13	51	29	48	157	21	.907
1996— Delmarva (S. Atl.).......	3B	126	421	72	115	23	6	12	70	.273	50	76	23	*102	239	35	.907
1997— Harrisburg (Eastern) ..	3B-1B	29	96	10	22	3	1	4	11	.229	11	28	2	41	31	6	.923
—W.P. Beach (FSL)........	3B-1B	97	350	49	108	21	3	9	58	.309	37	76	22	89	193	15	.949

FERNANDEZ, OSVALDO — P — GIANTS

PERSONAL: Born November 4, 1968, in Holguin, Cuba. ... 6-2/193. ... Throws right, bats right.
HIGH SCHOOL: Universidad de Holguin (Holguin, Cuba).
TRANSACTIONS/CAREER NOTES: Signed as non-drafted free agent by San Francisco Giants organization (January 16, 1996). ... On disabled list (May 20-June 19 and June 26-September 28, 1997); included rehabilitation assignmet to Phoenix (June 11-20).
MISCELLANEOUS: Appeared in three games as pinch-runner (1996). ... Appeared in one game as pinch-runner with San Francisco (1997).

F

Year	Team (League)	W	L	Pct.	ERA	G	GS	CG	ShO	Sv.	IP	H	R	ER	BB	SO
1996—San Francisco (N.L.)		7	13	.350	4.61	30	28	2	0	0	171 2/3	193	95	88	57	106
1997—San Francisco (N.L.)		3	4	.429	4.95	11	11	0	0	0	56 1/3	74	39	31	15	31
—Phoenix (PCL)		0	0	...	3.00	2	2	0	0	0	12	10	5	4	3	4
Major league totals (2 years)......		**10**	**17**	**.370**	**4.70**	**41**	**39**	**2**	**0**	**0**	**228**	**267**	**134**	**119**	**72**	**137**

FERNANDEZ, SID   P

PERSONAL: Born October 12, 1962, in Honolulu. ... 6-1/230. ... Throws left, bats left. ... Full name: Charles Sidney Fernandez.

HIGH SCHOOL: Kaiser (Honolulu).

TRANSACTIONS/CAREER NOTES: Selected by Los Angeles Dodgers organization in third round of free-agent draft (June 8, 1981). ... Traded by Dodgers with IF Ross Jones to New York Mets for P Carlos Diaz and a player to be named later (December 8, 1983); Dodgers acquired IF Bob Bailor to complete deal (December 12, 1983). ... On disabled list (August 4-22, 1987). ... On New York disabled list (March 12-July 18, 1991); included rehabilitation assignment to St. Lucie (June 22-27), Tidewater (June 27-July 7 and July 14-16) and Williamsport (July 7-14). ... On New York disabled list (May 1-July 29, 1993); included rehabilitation assignment to St. Lucie (July 11-17) and Binghamton (July 17-29). ... Granted free agency (October 25, 1993). ... Signed by Baltimore Orioles (November 22, 1993). ... On Baltimore disabled list (March 25-April 17 and June 19-July 4, 1994); included rehabilitation assignments to Albany (April 7-12) and Rochester (April 12-17). ... On Baltimore disabled list (June 5-28, 1995); included rehabilitation assignment to Bowie (June 14-28). ... Released by Orioles (July 10, 1995). ... Signed by Philadelphia Phillies (July 13, 1995). ... Granted free agency (November 3, 1995). ... Re-signed by Phillies (November 20, 1995). ... On Philadelphia disabled list (May 19-June 12 and June 24-September 3, 1996); included rehabilitation assignment to Clearwater (August 21-September 3). ... Granted free agency (October 28, 1996). ... Signed by Houston Astros (December 2, 1996). ... On disabled list (April 23-August 1, 1997); included rehabilitation assignment to New Orleans (May 10-21). ... Announced retirement (August 1, 1997).

HONORS: Named Texas League Pitcher of the Year (1983).

STATISTICAL NOTES: Pitched 5-0 no-hit victory for Vero Beach against Winter Haven (April 24, 1982). ... Pitched 1-0 no-hit victory for Vero Beach against Fort Lauderdale (June 8, 1982). ... Struck out 16 batters in one game (July 14, 1989).

Year	Team (League)	W	L	Pct.	ERA	G	GS	CG	ShO	Sv.	IP	H	R	ER	BB	SO
1981—Lethbridge (Pioneer)		5	1	.833	*1.54	11	11	2	1	0	76	43	21	13	31	*128
1982—Vero Beach (FSL)		8	1	.889	1.91	12	12	5	4	0	84 2/3	38	19	18	38	*137
—Albuquerque (PCL)		6	5	.545	5.42	13	13	5	0	0	88	76	54	53	52	86
1983—San Antonio (Tex.)		•13	4	.765	*2.82	24	24	4	1	0	153	111	61	48	96	*209
—Los Angeles (N.L.)		0	1	.000	6.00	2	1	0	0	0	6	7	4	4	7	9
1984—Tidewater (Int'l)■		6	5	.545	2.56	17	17	3	0	0	105 2/3	69	39	30	63	123
—New York (N.L.)		6	6	.500	3.50	15	15	0	0	0	90	74	40	35	34	62
1985—Tidewater (Int'l)		4	1	.800	2.04	5	5	1	0	0	35 1/3	17	8	8	21	42
—New York (N.L.)		9	9	.500	2.80	26	26	3	0	0	170 1/3	108	56	53	80	180
1986—New York (N.L.)		16	6	.727	3.52	32	31	2	1	0	204 1/3	161	82	80	91	200
1987—New York (N.L.)		12	8	.600	3.81	28	27	3	1	0	156	130	75	66	67	134
1988—New York (N.L.)		12	10	.545	3.03	31	31	1	1	0	187	127	69	63	70	189
1989—New York (N.L.)		14	5	.737	2.83	35	32	6	2	0	219 1/3	157	73	69	75	198
1990—New York (N.L.)		9	14	.391	3.46	30	30	2	1	0	179 1/3	130	79	69	67	181
1991—St. Lucie (Fla. St.)		0	0	...	0.00	1	1	0	0	0	3	1	0	0	1	4
—Tidewater (Int'l)		1	0	1.000	1.15	3	3	0	0	0	15 2/3	9	2	2	6	22
—Williamsport (Eastern)		0	0	...	0.00	1	1	0	0	0	6	3	0	0	1	5
—New York (N.L.)		1	3	.250	2.86	8	8	0	0	0	44	36	18	14	9	31
1992—New York (N.L.)		14	11	.560	2.73	32	32	5	2	0	214 2/3	162	67	65	67	193
1993—New York (N.L.)		5	6	.455	2.93	18	18	1	1	0	119 2/3	82	42	39	36	81
—St. Lucie (Fla. St.)		0	0	...	4.50	1	1	0	0	0	4	3	2	2	1	7
—Binghamton (Eastern)		0	1	.000	1.80	2	2	0	0	0	10	6	2	2	3	11
1994—Albany (S. Atl.)■		0	0	...	0.00	1	1	0	0	0	3	0	0	0	2	4
—Rochester (Int'l)		0	0	...	4.50	1	1	0	0	0	4	3	2	2	1	4
—Baltimore (A.L.)		6	6	.500	5.15	19	19	2	0	0	115 1/3	109	66	66	46	95
1995—Baltimore (A.L.)		0	4	.000	7.39	8	7	0	0	0	28	36	26	23	17	31
—Bowie (Eastern)		1	0	1.000	0.75	2	2	1	1	0	12	4	2	1	3	10
—Philadelphia (N.L.)■		6	1	.857	3.34	11	11	0	0	0	64 2/3	48	25	24	21	79
1996—Philadelphia (N.L.)		3	6	.333	3.43	11	11	0	0	0	63	50	25	24	26	77
—Clearwater (Fla. St.)		0	0	...	0.00	1	1	0	0	0	3	0	0	0	0	5
1997—Houston (N.L.)■		1	0	1.000	3.60	1	1	0	0	0	5	4	2	2	2	5
—New Orleans (A.A.)		0	1	.000	4.32	2	2	0	0	0	8 1/3	7	4	4	3	7
A.L. totals (2 years)		**6**	**10**	**.375**	**5.59**	**27**	**26**	**2**	**0**	**0**	**143 1/3**	**145**	**92**	**89**	**63**	**126**
N.L. totals (14 years)		**108**	**86**	**.557**	**3.17**	**280**	**274**	**23**	**9**	**1**	**1723 1/3**	**1276**	**657**	**607**	**652**	**1617**
Major league totals (15 years)....		**114**	**96**	**.543**	**3.36**	**307**	**300**	**25**	**9**	**1**	**1866 2/3**	**1421**	**749**	**696**	**715**	**1743**

CHAMPIONSHIP SERIES RECORD

Year	Team (League)	W	L	Pct.	ERA	G	GS	CG	ShO	Sv.	IP	H	R	ER	BB	SO
1986—New York (N.L.)		0	1	.000	4.50	1	1	0	0	0	6	3	3	3	1	5
1988—New York (N.L.)		0	1	.000	13.50	1	1	0	0	0	4	7	6	6	1	5
Champ. series totals (2 years)		**0**	**2**	**.000**	**8.10**	**2**	**2**	**0**	**0**	**0**	**10**	**10**	**9**	**9**	**2**	**10**

WORLD SERIES RECORD

NOTES: Member of World Series championship team (1986).

Year	Team (League)	W	L	Pct.	ERA	G	GS	CG	ShO	Sv.	IP	H	R	ER	BB	SO
1986—New York (N.L.)		0	0	...	1.35	3	0	0	0	0	6 2/3	6	1	1	1	10

ALL-STAR GAME RECORD

Year	League	W	L	Pct.	ERA	GS	CG	ShO	Sv.	IP	H	R	ER	BB	SO
1986—National		0	0	...	0.00	0	0	0	0	1	0	0	0	2	3
1987—National		0	0	...	0.00	0	0	0	1	1	0	0	0	1	1
All-Star totals (2 years)		**0**	**0**	**...**	**0.00**	**0**	**0**	**0**	**1**	**2**	**0**	**0**	**0**	**3**	**4**

F

PERSONAL: Born June 30, 1962, in San Pedro de Macoris, Dominican Republic. ... 6-2/175. ... Bats both, throws right. ... Full name: Octavio Antonio Castro Fernandez.

HIGH SCHOOL: Gasto Fernando (San Pedro de Macoris, Dominican Republic).

TRANSACTIONS/CAREER NOTES: Signed as non-drafted free agent by Toronto Blue Jays organization (April 24, 1979). ... On Syracuse disabled list (August 10-27, 1981). ... On disabled list (April 8-May 2, 1989). ... Traded by Blue Jays with 1B Fred McGriff to San Diego Padres for OF Joe Carter and 2B Roberto Alomar (December 5, 1990). ... Traded by Padres to New York Mets for P Wally Whitehurst, OF D.J. Dozier and a player to be named later (October 26, 1992); Padres acquired C Raul Casanova from Mets to complete deal (December 7, 1992). ... Traded by Mets to Blue Jays for OF Darrin Jackson (June 11, 1993). ... Granted free agency (November 3, 1993). ... Signed by Cincinnati Reds organization (March 8, 1994). ... Granted free agency (October 13, 1994). ... Signed by New York Yankees (December 15, 1994). ... On disabled list (May 21-June 8, 1995). ... On disabled list (March 24, 1996-remainder of season). ... Granted free agency (November 18, 1996). ... Signed by Cleveland Indians (December 28, 1996). ... Granted free agency (October 30, 1997). ... Signed by Blue Jays (December 8, 1997).

RECORDS: Shares major league career record for highest fielding percentage by shortstop (1,000 or more games)—.980. ... Shares major league record for most times caught stealing in one inning—2 (June 26, 1992, fifth inning). ... Holds A.L. career record for highest fielding percentage by shortstop (1,000 or more games)—.982. ... Holds A.L. single-season record for most games by shortstop—163 (1986). ... Shares A.L. single-season record for most games by switch-hitter—163 (1986).

HONORS: Named shortstop on THE SPORTING NEWS A.L. All-Star team (1986). ... Won A.L. Gold Glove at shortstop (1986-89).

STATISTICAL NOTES: Led International League shortstops with 87 double plays in 1983. ... Led A.L. shortstops with 791 total chances in 1985 and 786 in 1990. ... Led N.L. third basemen with .991 fielding percentage in 1994. ... Hit for the cycle (September 3, 1995, 10 innings). ... Career major league grand slams: 2.

MISCELLANEOUS: Holds Toronto Blue Jays all-time record for most triples (70).

Year Team (League)	Pos.	G	AB	R	H	2B	3B	HR	RBI	Avg.	BB	SO	SB	PO	A	E	Avg.
1980—Kinston (Carolina)	SS	62	187	28	52	6	2	0	12	.278	28	17	7	93	205	28	.914
1981—Kinston (Carolina)	SS	75	280	57	89	10	6	1	13	.318	49	20	15	121	227	19	.948
—Syracuse (Int'l)	SS	31	115	13	32	6	2	1	9	.278	7	15	9	69	80	3	.980
1982—Syracuse (Int'l)	SS	134	523	78	158	21	6	4	56	.302	42	31	22	*246	364	23	*.964
1983—Syracuse (Int'l)	SS	117	437	65	131	18	6	5	38	.300	57	27	35	*211	361	26	.957
—Toronto (A.L.)	SS-DH	15	34	5	9	1	1	0	2	.265	2	2	0	16	17	0	1.000
1984—Syracuse (Int'l)	SS	26	94	12	24	1	0	0	6	.255	13	9	1	46	72	5	.959
—Toronto (A.L.)	SS-3B-DH	88	233	29	63	5	3	3	19	.270	17	15	5	119	195	9	.972
1985—Toronto (A.L.)	SS	161	564	71	163	31	10	2	51	.289	43	41	13	283	*478	30	.962
1986—Toronto (A.L.)	SS	*163	*687	91	213	33	9	10	65	.310	27	52	25	*294	445	13	*.983
1987—Toronto (A.L.)	SS	146	578	90	186	29	8	5	67	.322	51	48	32	*270	396	14	.979
1988—Toronto (A.L.)	SS	154	648	76	186	41	4	5	70	.287	45	65	15	247	470	14	.981
1989—Toronto (A.L.)	SS	140	573	64	147	25	9	11	64	.257	29	51	22	260	475	6	*.992
1990—Toronto (A.L.)	SS	161	635	84	175	27	*17	4	66	.276	71	70	26	*297	*480	9	.989
1991—San Diego (N.L.)■......	SS	145	558	81	152	27	5	4	38	.272	55	74	23	247	440	20	.972
1992—San Diego (N.L.)	SS	155	622	84	171	32	4	4	37	.275	56	62	20	240	405	11	.983
1993—New York (N.L.)■......	SS	48	173	20	39	5	2	1	14	.225	25	19	6	83	150	6	.975
—Toronto (A.L.)■......	SS	94	353	45	108	18	9	4	50	.306	31	26	15	196	260	7	.985
1994—Cincinnati (N.L.)	3B-SS-2B	104	366	50	102	18	6	8	50	.279	44	40	12	67	195	4	†.985
1995—New York (A.L.)■.......	SS-2B	108	384	57	94	20	2	5	45	.245	42	40	6	148	283	10	.977
1996—									Did not play.								
1997—Cleveland (A.L.)■.......	2B-SS-DH	120	409	55	117	21	1	11	44	.286	22	47	6	219	322	11	.980
American League totals (11 years)		1350	5098	667	1461	251	73	60	543	.287	380	457	165	2349	3821	123	.980
National League totals (4 years)		452	1719	235	464	82	17	17	139	.270	180	195	61	637	1190	41	.978
Major league totals (14 years)		1802	6817	902	1925	333	90	77	682	.282	560	652	226	2986	5011	164	.980

DIVISION SERIES RECORD

Year Team (League)	Pos.	G	AB	R	H	2B	3B	HR	RBI	Avg.	BB	SO	SB	PO	A	E	Avg.
1995—New York (A.L.)	SS	5	21	0	5	2	0	0	0	.238	2	2	0	9	15	0	1.000
1997—Cleveland (A.L.)	2B-PH	4	11	0	2	1	0	0	4	.182	0	0	0	8	9	0	1.000
Division series totals (2 years)		9	32	0	7	3	0	0	4	.219	2	2	0	17	24	0	1.000

CHAMPIONSHIP SERIES RECORD

Year Team (League)	Pos.	G	AB	R	H	2B	3B	HR	RBI	Avg.	BB	SO	SB	PO	A	E	Avg.
1985—Toronto (A.L.)	SS	7	24	2	8	2	0	0	2	.333	1	2	0	11	15	2	.929
1989—Toronto (A.L.)	SS	5	20	6	7	3	0	0	1	.350	1	2	5	9	15	0	1.000
1993—Toronto (A.L.)	SS	6	22	1	7	0	0	0	1	.318	2	4	0	12	8	0	1.000
1997—Cleveland (A.L.)	2B-PH	5	14	1	5	1	0	1	2	.357	1	2	0	9	10	1	.950
Championship series totals (4 years)		23	80	10	27	6	0	1	6	.338	5	10	5	41	48	3	.967

WORLD SERIES RECORD

NOTES: Member of World Series championship team (1993).

Year Team (League)	Pos.	G	AB	R	H	2B	3B	HR	RBI	Avg.	BB	SO	SB	PO	A	E	Avg.
1993—Toronto (A.L.)	SS	6	21	2	7	1	0	0	9	.333	3	3	0	11	8	0	1.000
1997—Cleveland (A.L.)	2B-PH	5	17	1	8	1	0	0	4	.471	0	1	0	9	14	2	.920
World Series totals (2 years)		11	38	3	15	2	0	0	13	.395	3	4	0	20	22	2	.955

ALL-STAR GAME RECORD

Year League	Pos.	AB	R	H	2B	3B	HR	RBI	Avg.	BB	SO	SB	PO	A	E	Avg.
1986—American	SS	0	0	0	0	0	0	0	...	0	0	0	0	0	0	...
1987—American	SS	2	0	0	0	0	0	0	.000	0	0	0	1	3	0	1.000
1989—American	PR-SS	1	0	0	0	0	0	0	.000	0	0	0	2	2	0	1.000
1992—National	SS	2	1	1	0	0	0	0	.500	0	0	0	3	0	0	1.000
All-Star Game totals (4 years)		5	1	1	0	0	0	0	.200	0	0	0	6	5	0	1.000

F

FETTERS, MIKE — P — ATHLETICS

PERSONAL: Born December 19, 1964, in Van Nuys, Calif. ... 6-4/224. ... Throws right, bats right. ... Full name: Michael Lee Fetters.
HIGH SCHOOL: Iolani (Honolulu, Hawaii).
COLLEGE: Pepperdine.
TRANSACTIONS/CAREER NOTES: Selected by Los Angeles Dodgers organization in 22nd round of free-agent draft (June 6, 1983); did not sign. ... Selected by California Angels organization in supplemental round ("sandwich pick" between first and second round, 27th pick overall) of free-agent draft (June 2, 1986); pick received as compensation for Baltimore Orioles signing Type A free-agent OF/IF Juan Beniquez. ... Traded by Angels with P Glenn Carter to Milwaukee Brewers for P Chuck Crim (December 10, 1991). ... On disabled list (May 3-19, 1992 and May 25-June 9, 1995). ... On disabled list (April 4-May 5, 1997); including rehabilitation assignment to Tucson (April 30-May 5). ... Traded by Brewers with P Ben McDonald and P Ron Villone to Cleveland Indians for OF Marquis Grissom and P Jeff Juden (December 8, 1997). ... Traded by Indians to Oakland Athletics for P Steve Karsay (December 8, 1997).

Year	Team (League)	W	L	Pct.	ERA	G	GS	CG	ShO	Sv.	IP	H	R	ER	BB	SO
1986—	Salem (Northwest)	4	2	.667	3.38	12	12	1	0	0	72	60	39	27	51	72
1987—	Palm Springs (California)	9	7	.563	3.57	19	19	2	0	0	116	106	62	46	73	105
1988—	Midland (Texas)	8	8	.500	5.92	20	20	2	0	0	114	116	78	75	67	101
	—Edmonton (PCL)	2	0	1.000	1.93	2	2	1	0	0	14	8	3	3	10	11
1989—	Edmonton (PCL)	12	8	.600	3.80	26	26	•6	2	0	168	160	80	71	72	*144
	—California (A.L.)	0	0	...	8.10	1	0	0	0	0	3 1/3	5	4	3	1	4
1990—	Edmonton (PCL)	1	1	.500	0.99	5	5	1	1	0	27 1/3	22	9	3	13	26
	—California (A.L.)	1	1	.500	4.12	26	2	0	0	1	67 2/3	77	33	31	20	35
1991—	Edmonton (PCL)	2	7	.222	4.87	11	11	1	0	0	61	65	39	33	26	43
	—California (A.L.)	2	5	.286	4.84	19	4	0	0	0	44 2/3	53	29	24	28	24
1992—	Milwaukee (A.L.)■	5	1	.833	1.87	50	0	0	0	2	62 2/3	38	15	13	24	43
1993—	Milwaukee (A.L.)	3	3	.500	3.34	45	0	0	0	0	59 1/3	59	29	22	22	23
1994—	Milwaukee (A.L.)	1	4	.200	2.54	42	0	0	0	17	46	41	16	13	27	31
1995—	Milwaukee (A.L.)	0	0	.000	3.38	40	0	0	0	22	34 2/3	40	16	13	20	33
1996—	Milwaukee (A.L.)	3	3	.500	3.38	61	0	0	0	32	61 1/3	65	28	23	26	53
1997—	Milwaukee (A.L.)	1	5	.167	3.45	51	0	0	0	6	70 1/3	62	30	27	33	62
	—Tucson (PCL)	0	0	...	10.80	2	0	0	0	0	1 2/3	1	2	2	1	0
Major league totals (9 years)		16	25	.390	3.38	335	6	0	0	80	450	440	200	169	201	308

FIELDER, CECIL — DH/1B — ANGELS

PERSONAL: Born September 21, 1963, in Los Angeles. ... 6-3/250. ... Bats right, throws right. ... Full name: Cecil Grant Fielder.
HIGH SCHOOL: Nogales (La Puente, Calif.).
COLLEGE: UNLV.
TRANSACTIONS/CAREER NOTES: Selected by Baltimore Orioles organization in 31st round of free-agent draft (June 8, 1981); did not sign. ... Selected by Kansas City Royals organization in secondary phase of free-agent draft (June 7, 1982). ... Traded by Royals organization to Toronto Blue Jays organization for OF Leon Roberts (February 4, 1983). ... Contract sold by Blue Jays to Hanshin Tigers of Japan Central League (December 22, 1988). ... Signed as free agent by Detroit Tigers (January 15, 1990). ... Traded by Tigers to New York Yankees for OF Ruben Sierra and P Matt Drews (July 31, 1996). ... On disabled list (July 16-September 16). ... Granted free agency (October 27, 1997). ... Signed by Anaheim Angels (December 19, 1997).
RECORDS: Shares major league career record for most times hitting three or more consecutive home runs in a game—3. ... Shares major league records for most consecutive years leading league in runs batted in—3 (1990-92); and most years without a stolen base (150 games or more per year)—4. ... Shares major league single-season record for most games with three home runs—2 (1990).
HONORS: Named A.L. Player of the Year by THE SPORTING NEWS (1990). ... Named first baseman on THE SPORTING NEWS A.L. All-Star team (1990-91). ... Named first baseman on THE SPORTING NEWS A.L. Silver Slugger team (1990-91).
STATISTICAL NOTES: Led Pioneer League with 176 total bases and in being hit by pitch with eight in 1982. ... Led A.L. with 339 total bases and .592 slugging percentage in 1990. ... Led A.L. first basemen with 137 double plays in 1990. ... Hit three home runs in one game (May 6, 1990; and April 16, 1996). ... Career major league grand slams: 10.

Year	Team (League)	Pos.	G	AB	R	H	2B	3B	HR	RBI	Avg.	BB	SO	SB	PO	A	E	Avg.
1982—	Butte (Pioneer)	1B	69	273	73	88	*28	0	*20	68	.322	37	62	3	247	18	4	.985
1983—	Florence (S. Atl.)■	1B	140	500	81	156	28	2	16	94	.312	58	90	2	957	64	16	.985
1984—	Kinston (Carolina)	1B	61	222	42	63	12	1	19	49	.284	28	44	2	533	24	9	.984
	—Knoxville (Southern)	1B	64	236	33	60	12	2	9	44	.254	22	48	0	173	10	4	.979
1985—	Knoxville (Southern)	1B	96	361	52	106	26	2	18	81	.294	45	83	0	444	26	6	.987
	—Toronto (A.L.)	1B	30	74	6	23	4	0	4	16	.311	6	16	0	171	17	4	.979
1986—	Toronto (A.L.)	DH-1-3-O	34	83	7	13	2	0	4	13	.157	6	27	0	37	4	1	.976
	—Syracuse (Int'l)	OF-1B	88	325	47	91	13	3	18	68	.280	32	91	0	117	5	1	.992
1987—	Toronto (A.L.)	DH-1B-3B	82	175	30	47	7	1	14	32	.269	20	48	0	98	6	0	1.000
1988—	Toronto (A.L.)	DH-1-3-2	74	174	24	40	6	1	9	23	.230	14	53	0	101	12	1	.991
1989—	Hanshin (Jp. Cn.)■	...	106	384	60	116	11	0	38	81	.302	67	107	0	...	...	...	...
1990—	Detroit (A.L.)■	1B-DH	159	573	104	159	25	1	*51	*132	.277	90	*182	0	1190	111	14	.989
1991—	Detroit (A.L.)	1B-DH	•162	624	102	163	25	0	•44	*133	.261	78	151	0	1055	83	8	.993
1992—	Detroit (A.L.)	1B-DH	155	594	80	145	22	0	35	*124	.244	73	151	0	957	92	10	.991
1993—	Detroit (A.L.)	1B-DH	154	573	80	153	23	0	30	117	.267	90	125	0	971	78	10	.991
1994—	Detroit (A.L.)	1B-DH	109	425	67	110	16	2	28	90	.259	50	110	0	887	*108	7	.993
1995—	Detroit (A.L.)	1B-DH	136	494	70	120	18	1	31	82	.243	75	116	0	631	73	5	.993
1996—	Detroit (A.L.)	1B-DH	107	391	55	97	12	0	26	80	.248	63	91	0	589	59	7	.989
	—New York (A.L.)■	DH-1B	53	200	30	52	8	0	13	37	.260	24	48	2	74	4	0	1.000
1997—	New York (A.L.)	DH-1B	98	361	40	94	15	0	13	61	.260	51	87	0	59	6	0	1.000
Major league totals (12 years)			1353	4741	695	1216	183	6	302	940	.256	640	1205	2	6820	653	67	.991

DIVISION SERIES RECORD

Year	Team (League)	Pos.	G	AB	R	H	2B	3B	HR	RBI	Avg.	BB	SO	SB	PO	A	E	Avg.
1996—	New York (A.L.)	DH	3	11	2	4	0	0	1	4	.364	1	2	0	0	0	0	...
1997—	New York (A.L.)	DH	2	8	0	1	0	0	0	1	.125	0	3	0	0	0	0	...
Division series totals (2 years)			5	19	2	5	0	0	1	5	.263	1	5	0	0	0	0	...

CHAMPIONSHIP SERIES RECORD

							BATTING								FIELDING		
Year	Team (League)	Pos.	G	AB	R	H	2B	3B	HR	RBI	Avg.	BB	SO	SB	PO	A	E	Avg.
1985— Toronto (A.L.).............		PH	3	3	0	1	1	0	0	0	.333	0	0	0	...	...	...	...
1996— New York (A.L.)..........		DH	5	18	3	3	0	0	2	8	.167	5	5	0	0	0	0	...
Championship series totals (2 years)			8	21	3	4	1	0	2	8	.190	5	5	0	0	0	0	...

WORLD SERIES RECORD

NOTES: Member of World Series championship team (1996).

							BATTING								FIELDING		
Year	Team (League)	Pos.	G	AB	R	H	2B	3B	HR	RBI	Avg.	BB	SO	SB	PO	A	E	Avg.
1996— New York (A.L.)..........		DH-1B	6	23	1	9	2	0	0	2	.391	2	2	0	21	5	0	1.000

ALL-STAR GAME RECORD

					BATTING								FIELDING		
Year	League	Pos.	AB	R	H	2B	3B	HR	RBI	Avg.	BB	SO	SB	PO	A	E	Avg.
1990— American....................		PH-1B	1	0	0	0	0	0	0	.000	0	0	0	3	1	0	1.000
1991— American....................		1B	3	0	0	0	0	0	0	.000	0	1	0	6	2	0	1.000
1993— American....................		1B	1	0	0	0	0	0	0	.000	0	0	0	4	0	0	1.000
All-Star Game totals (3 years)			5	0	0	0	0	0	0	.000	0	1	0	13	3	0	1.000

FIGGA, MIKE — C — YANKEES

PERSONAL: Born July 31, 1970, in Tampa. ... 6-0/200. ... Bats right, throws right. ... Full name: Michael Anthony Figga.
JUNIOR COLLEGE: Central Florida Community College.
TRANSACTIONS/CAREER NOTES: Selected by New York Yankees organization in 44th round of free-agent draft (June 5, 1989). ... On disabled list (August 31, 1996-remainder of season).
STATISTICAL NOTES: Led Gulf Coast League catchers with 296 total chances in 1990.

						BATTING								FIELDING		
Year	Team (League)	Pos.	G	AB	R	H	2B	3B	HR	RBI	Avg.	BB	SO	SB	PO	A	E	Avg.
1990— GC Yankees (GCL)......	C	40	123	19	35	1	1	2	18	.285	17	33	4	*270	19	7	.976
1991— Prince William (Car.) ..	C	55	174	15	34	6	0	3	17	.195	19	51	2	278	33	5	.984
1992— Fort Lauderdale (FSL) .	C	80	249	12	44	13	0	1	15	.177	13	78	3	568	71	12	.982
— Prince William (Car.) ..	C	3	10	0	2	1	0	0	0	.200	2	3	1	27	1	0	1.000
1993— San Bern. (Calif.)........	C	83	308	48	82	17	1	25	71	.266	17	84	2	491	70	12	.979
— Alb./Colon. (Eastern)..	C	6	22	3	5	0	0	2	2	.227	2	9	1	31	2	1	.971
1994— Tampa (Florida State) .	C	111	420	48	116	17	5	15	75	.276	22	94	3	703	79	10	.987
— Alb./Colon. (Eastern)..	C	1	2	1	1	1	0	0	0	.500	0	1	0	5	0	0	1.000
1995— Norwich (Eastern)......	C	109	399	59	108	22	4	13	61	.271	43	90	1	640	92	11	.985
— Columbus (Int'l)........	C	8	25	2	7	1	0	1	3	.280	3	5	0	29	4	0	1.000
1996— Columbus (Int'l)........	C	4	11	3	3	1	0	0	0	.273	1	3	0	17	2	0	1.000
1997— Columbus (Int'l)........	C	110	390	48	95	14	4	12	54	.244	18	104	3	706	62	11	.986
— New York (A.L.)..........	DH-C	2	4	0	0	0	0	0	0	.000	0	3	0	6	0	0	1.000
Major league totals (1 year)		2	4	0	0	0	0	0	0	.000	0	3	0	6	0	0	1.000

FINLEY, CHUCK — P — ANGELS

PERSONAL: Born November 26, 1962, in Monroe, La. ... 6-6/214. ... Throws left, bats left. ... Full name: Charles Edward Finley.
HIGH SCHOOL: West Monroe (La.).
COLLEGE: Northeast Louisiana.
TRANSACTIONS/CAREER NOTES: Selected by California Angels organization in 15th round of free-agent draft (June 4, 1984); did not sign. ... Selected by Angels organization in secondary phase of free-agent draft (January 9, 1985). ... On disabled list (August 22-September 15, 1989 and April 6-22, 1992). ... Granted free agency (November 7, 1995). ... Re-signed by Angels (January 4, 1996). ... Angels franchise renamed Anaheim Angels for 1997 season. ... On disabled list (March 23-April 15, 1997 and August 20, 1997-remainder of season); included rehabilitation assignment to Lake Elsinore (April 5-10).
HONORS: Named lefthanded pitcher on THE SPORTING NEWS A.L. All-Star team (1989-90).
STATISTICAL NOTES: Pitched 5-0 one-hit, complete-game victory against Boston (May 26, 1989). ... Struck out 15 batters in one game (June 24, 1989 and May 23, 1995). ... Led A.L. with 17 wild pitches in 1996.
MISCELLANEOUS: Holds Anaheim Angels franchise all-time records for most wins (142), most innings pitched (2238 1/3) and games pitched (369).

Year	Team (League)	W	L	Pct.	ERA	G	GS	CG	ShO	Sv.	IP	H	R	ER	BB	SO
1985— Salem (Northwest)	3	1	.750	4.66	18	0	0	0	5	29	34	21	15	10	32
1986— Quad Cities (Midw.)............	1	0	1.000	0.00	10	0	0	0	6	12	4	0	0	3	16
— California (A.L.)..................	3	1	.750	3.30	25	0	0	0	0	46 1/3	40	17	17	23	37
1987— California (A.L.)..................	2	7	.222	4.67	35	3	0	0	0	90 2/3	102	54	47	43	63
1988— California (A.L.)..................	9	15	.375	4.17	31	31	2	0	0	194 1/3	191	95	90	82	111
1989— California (A.L.)..................	16	9	.640	2.57	29	29	9	1	0	199 2/3	171	64	57	82	156
1990— California (A.L.)..................	18	9	.667	2.40	32	32	7	2	0	236	210	77	63	81	177
1991— California (A.L.)..................	18	9	.667	3.80	34	34	4	2	0	227 1/3	205	102	96	101	171
1992— California (A.L.)..................	7	12	.368	3.96	31	31	4	1	0	204 1/3	212	99	90	98	124
1993— California (A.L.)..................	16	14	.533	3.15	35	35	*13	2	0	251 1/3	243	108	88	82	187
1994— California (A.L.)..................	10	10	.500	4.32	25	*25	7	2	0	*183 1/3	178	95	88	71	148
1995— California (A.L.)..................	15	12	.556	4.21	32	32	2	1	0	203	192	106	95	93	195
1996— California (A.L.)..................	15	16	.484	4.16	35	35	4	1	0	238	241	124	110	94	215
1997— Anaheim (A.L.)..................	13	6	.684	4.23	25	25	3	1	0	164	152	79	77	65	155
— Lake Elsinore (Calif.)	0	0	...	2.00	2	2	0	0	0	9	5	3	2	4	12
Major league totals (12 years)....	142	120	.542	3.69	369	312	55	13	0	2238 1/3	2137	1020	918	915	1739

F

CHAMPIONSHIP SERIES RECORD

Year Team (League)	W	L	Pct.	ERA	G	GS	CG	ShO	Sv.	IP	H	R	ER	BB	SO
1986— California (A.L.).................	0	0	...	0.00	3	0	0	0	0	2	1	0	0	0	1

ALL-STAR GAME RECORD

Year League	W	L	Pct.	ERA	GS	CG	ShO	Sv.	IP	H	R	ER	BB	SO
1989— American..........................						Did not play.								
1990— American..........................	0	0	...	0.00	0	0	0	0	1	0	0	0	1	1
1995— American..........................						Did not play.								
1996— American..........................	0	0	...	4.50	0	0	0	0	2	3	1	1	0	4
All-Star totals (2 years)	0	0	...	3.00	0	0	0	0	3	3	1	1	1	5

FINLEY, STEVE — OF — PADRES

PERSONAL: Born March 12, 1965, in Union City, Tenn. ... 6-2/180. ... Bats left, throws left. ... Full name: Steven Allen Finley.
HIGH SCHOOL: Paducah (Ky.) Tilghman.
COLLEGE: Southern Illinois (degree in physiology).
TRANSACTIONS/CAREER NOTES: Selected by Atlanta Braves organization in 11th round of free-agent draft (June 2, 1986); did not sign. ... Selected by Baltimore Orioles organization in 13th round of free-agent draft (June 2, 1987). ... On Baltimore disabled list (April 4-22, 1989). ... On Baltimore disabled list (July 29-September 1, 1989); included rehabilitation assignment to Hagerstown (August 21-23). ... Traded by Orioles with P Pete Harnisch and P Curt Schilling to Houston Astros for 1B Glenn Davis (January 10, 1991). ... On disabled list (April 25-May 14, 1993). ... On Houston disabled list (June 13-July 3, 1994); included rehabilitation assignment to Jackson (June 28-July 3). ... Traded by Astros with 3B Ken Caminiti, SS Andujar Cedeno, 1B Roberto Petagine, P Brian Williams and a player to be named later to San Diego Padres for OF Phil Plantier, OF Derek Bell, P Pedro Martinez, P Doug Brocail, IF Craig Shipley and SS Ricky Gutierrez (December 28, 1994); Padres acquired P Sean Fesh to complete deal (May 1, 1995). ... On San Diego disabled list (April 20-May 6, 1997); included rehabilitation assignment to Rancho Cucamonga (April 25-May 6).
HONORS: Won N.L. Gold Glove as outfielder (1995-96).
STATISTICAL NOTES: Led International League outfielders with 315 total chances in 1988. ... Had 21-game hitting streak (June 20-July 14, 1996). ... Hit three home runs in one game (May 19 and June 23, 1997). ... Career major league grand slams: 5.

Year Team (League)	Pos.	G	AB	R	H	2B	3B	HR	RBI	Avg.	BB	SO	SB	PO	A	E	Avg.
1987— Newark (NY-Penn)......	OF	54	222	40	65	13	2	3	33	.293	22	24	26	122	7	4	.970
— Hagerstown (Car.)	OF	15	65	9	22	3	2	1	5	.338	1	6	7	32	3	0	1.000
1988— Hagerstown (Car.)	OF	8	28	2	6	2	0	0	3	.214	4	3	4	17	0	0	1.000
— Charlotte (Southern) ..	OF	10	40	7	12	4	2	1	6	.300	4	3	2	14	0	0	1.000
— Rochester (Int'l)	OF	120	456	61	*143	19	7	5	54	*.314	28	55	20	*289	14	*12	.962
1989— Baltimore (A.L.)........	OF-DH	81	217	35	54	5	2	2	25	.249	15	30	17	144	1	2	.986
— Rochester (Int'l)	OF	7	25	2	4	0	0	2	2	.160	1	3	5	17	2	0	1.000
— Hagerstown (Eastern)	OF	11	48	11	20	3	1	0	7	.417	4	3	4	35	2	3	.925
1990— Baltimore (A.L.)........	OF-DH	142	464	46	119	16	4	3	37	.256	32	53	22	298	4	7	.977
1991— Houston (N.L.)■........	OF	159	596	84	170	28	10	8	54	.285	42	65	34	323	13	5	.985
1992— Houston (N.L.)........	OF	•162	607	84	177	29	13	5	55	.292	58	63	44	417	8	3	.993
1993— Houston (N.L.)........	OF	142	545	69	145	15	*13	8	44	.266	28	65	19	329	12	4	.988
1994— Houston (N.L.)........	OF	94	373	64	103	16	5	11	33	.276	28	52	13	214	9	4	.982
— Jackson (Texas)........	OF	5	13	3	4	0	0	0	0	.308	4	0	1	6	0	0	1.000
1995— San Diego (N.L.)■	OF	139	562	104	167	23	8	10	44	.297	59	62	36	291	8	7	.977
1996— San Diego (N.L.)........	OF	161	655	126	195	45	9	30	95	.298	56	87	22	385	7	7	.982
1997— San Diego (N.L.)........	OF	143	560	101	146	26	5	28	92	.261	43	92	15	338	10	4	.989
— Rancho Cuca. (Cal.) ...	OF	4	14	3	4	0	0	2	3	.286	3	2	1	0	0	0	...
— Mobile (Southern)......	DH	1	4	1	2	0	0	1	2	.500	1	2	0	0	0	0	...
American League totals (2 years)		223	681	81	173	21	6	5	62	.254	47	83	39	442	5	9	.980
National League totals (7 years)		1000	3898	632	1103	182	63	100	417	.283	314	486	183	2297	67	34	.986
Major league totals (9 years)		1223	4579	713	1276	203	69	105	479	.279	361	569	222	2739	72	43	.985

DIVISION SERIES RECORD

Year Team (League)	Pos.	G	AB	R	H	2B	3B	HR	RBI	Avg.	BB	SO	SB	PO	A	E	Avg.
1996— San Diego (N.L.)	OF	3	12	0	1	0	0	0	1	.083	0	4	1	10	0	0	1.000

ALL-STAR GAME RECORD

Year League	Pos.	AB	R	H	2B	3B	HR	RBI	Avg.	BB	SO	SB	PO	A	E	Avg.
1997— National....................	OF	1	0	0	0	0	0	0	.000	0	1	0	1	0	0	1.000

FIORE, TONY — P — PHILLIES

PERSONAL: Born October 12, 1971, in Oak Park, Ill. ... 6-4/210. ... Throws right, bats right. ... Full name: Anthony James Fiore.
HIGH SCHOOL: Holy Cross (River Grove, Ill.).
JUNIOR COLLEGE: Triton College (Ill.).
TRANSACTIONS/CAREER NOTES: Selected by Philadelphia Phillies organization in 28th round of free-agent draft (June 1, 1992). ... On disabled list (April 2-20, 1995).

Year Team (League)	W	L	Pct.	ERA	G	GS	CG	ShO	Sv.	IP	H	R	ER	BB	SO
1992— Martinsville (App.)...............	2	3	.400	4.18	17	2	0	0	0	32 1/3	32	20	15	31	30
1993— Batavia (N.Y.-Penn)	2	•8	.200	3.05	16	•16	1	0	0	97 1/3	82	51	33	40	55
1994— Spartanburg (SAL)	12	13	.480	4.10	28	•28	*9	1	0	166 2/3	162	94	76	77	113
1995— Clearwater (Fla. St.)	6	2	.750	3.71	24	10	0	0	0	70 1/3	70	41	29	44	45
1996— Clearwater (Fla. St.)	8	4	.667	3.16	22	22	3	1	0	128	102	61	45	56	80
— Reading (Eastern)	1	2	.333	4.35	5	5	0	0	0	31	32	21	15	18	19
1997— Reading (Eastern)	8	3	.727	3.01	9	16	0	0	0	104 2/3	89	47	35	40	64
— Scran./W.B. (Int'l)...............	3	5	.375	3.86	9	9	1	0	0	60 2/3	60	34	26	26	56

FLAHERTY, JOHN   C   DEVIL RAYS

PERSONAL: Born October 21, 1967, in New York. ... 6-1/205. ... Bats right, throws right. ... Full name: John Timothy Flaherty.
HIGH SCHOOL: St. Joseph's Regional (Montvale, N.J.).
COLLEGE: George Washington.
TRANSACTIONS/CAREER NOTES: Selected by Boston Red Sox organization in 25th round of free-agent draft (June 1, 1988). ... Traded by Red Sox to Detroit Tigers for C Rich Rowland (April 1, 1994). ... Traded by Tigers with SS Chris Gomez to San Diego Padres for C Brad Ausmus, SS Andujar Cedeno and P Russ Spear (June 18, 1996). ... Traded by Padres to Tampa Bay Devil Rays for P Brian Boehringer and IF Andy Sheets (November 18, 1997).
STATISTICAL NOTES: Tied for Florida State League lead with 19 passed balls in 1989. ... Had 27-game hitting streak (June 21-July 27, 1996). ... Career major league grand slams: 1.

Year	Team (League)	Pos.	G	AB	R	H	2B	3B	HR	RBI	Avg.	BB	SO	SB	PO	A	E	Avg.
																BATTING		FIELDING
1988—Elmira (N.Y.-Penn).....		C	46	162	17	38	3	0	3	16	.235	12	23	2	235	39	7	.975
1989—Winter Haven (FSL)....		C-1B	95	334	31	87	14	2	4	28	.260	20	44	1	369	60	9	.979
1990—Pawtucket (Int'l)........		C-3B	99	317	35	72	18	0	4	32	.227	24	43	1	509	59	10	.983
—Lynchburg (Caro.).......		C	1	4	0	0	0	0	0	1	.000	0	1	0	3	2	0	1.000
1991—New Britain (Eastern).		C	67	225	27	65	9	0	3	18	.289	31	22	0	337	46	9	.977
—Pawtucket (Int'l)........		C	45	156	18	29	7	0	3	13	.186	15	14	0	270	18	•9	.970
1992—Boston (A.L.).............		C	35	66	3	13	2	0	0	2	.197	3	7	0	102	7	2	.982
—Pawtucket (Int'l)........		C	31	104	11	26	3	0	0	7	.250	5	8	0	158	17	4	.978
1993—Pawtucket (Int'l)........		C	105	365	29	99	22	0	6	35	.271	26	41	0	626	78	10	.986
—Boston (A.L.).............		C	13	25	3	3	2	0	0	2	.120	2	6	0	35	9	0	1.000
1994—Toledo (Int'l)■..........		C	44	151	20	39	10	2	7	17	.258	6	21	3	286	24	2	.994
—Detroit (A.L.).............		C-DH	34	40	2	6	1	0	0	4	.150	1	11	0	78	9	0	1.000
1995—Detroit (A.L.)..........		C	112	354	39	86	22	1	11	40	.243	18	47	0	569	33	*11	.982
1996—Detroit (A.L.).........		C	47	152	18	38	12	0	4	23	.250	8	25	1	243	13	5	.981
—San Diego (N.L.)■		C	72	264	22	80	12	0	9	41	.303	9	36	2	471	29	5	.990
1997—San Diego (N.L.).......		C	129	439	38	120	21	1	9	46	.273	33	62	4	753	65	11	.987
American League totals (5 years)			241	637	65	146	39	1	15	71	.229	32	96	1	1027	71	18	.984
National League totals (2 years)			201	703	60	200	33	1	18	87	.284	42	98	6	1224	94	16	.988
Major league totals (6 years)			442	1340	125	346	72	2	33	158	.258	74	194	7	2251	165	34	.986

DIVISION SERIES RECORD

Year	Team (League)	Pos.	G	AB	R	H	2B	3B	HR	RBI	Avg.	BB	SO	SB	PO	A	E	Avg.
								BATTING									FIELDING	
1996—San Diego (N.L.)		C	2	4	0	0	0	0	0	0	.000	0	1	0	9	0	0	1.000

FLENER, HUCK   P

PERSONAL: Born February 25, 1969, in Austin, Texas. ... 5-11/190. ... Throws left, bats both. ... Full name: Gregory Alan Flener. ... Name pronounced FLENN-er.
HIGH SCHOOL: Armijo (Fairfield, Calif.).
COLLEGE: Cal State Fullerton.
TRANSACTIONS/CAREER NOTES: Selected by Toronto Blue Jays organization in 10th round of free-agent draft (June 4, 1990). ... On Syracuse disabled list (June 7-27, 1996). ... Granted free agency (October 15, 1997).
STATISTICAL NOTES: Led Southern League with eight balks in 1993.

Year	Team (League)	W	L	Pct.	ERA	G	GS	CG	ShO	Sv.	IP	H	R	ER	BB	SO
1990—St. Catharines (NYP)		4	3	.571	3.36	14	7	0	0	1	61 2/3	45	29	23	33	46
1991—Myrtle Beach (SAL)...........		6	4	.600	1.82	55	0	0	0	13	79	58	28	16	41	107
1992—Dunedin (Fla. St.)..............		7	3	.700	2.24	41	8	0	0	8	112 1/3	70	35	28	50	93
1993—Knoxville (Southern)		•13	6	.684	3.30	38	16	2	2	4	136 1/3	130	56	50	39	114
—Toronto (A.L.).................		0	0	...	4.05	6	0	0	0	0	6 2/3	7	3	3	4	2
1994—Syracuse (Int'l).................		0	3	.000	4.62	6	6	0	0	0	37	38	22	19	8	20
1995—Syracuse (Int'l).................		6	11	.353	3.94	30	23	1	0	0	134 2/3	131	70	59	41	83
1996—Syracuse (Int'l).................		7	3	.700	2.28	14	14	0	0	0	86 2/3	73	27	22	23	62
—Toronto (A.L.).................		3	2	.600	4.58	15	11	0	0	0	70 2/3	68	40	36	33	44
1997—Syracuse (Int'l).................		6	6	.500	4.14	20	20	1	1	0	124	126	71	57	43	58
—Toronto (A.L.).................		0	1	.000	9.87	8	1	0	0	0	17 1/3	40	19	19	6	9
Major league totals (3 years)......		3	3	.500	5.51	29	12	0	0	0	94 2/3	115	62	58	43	55

FLETCHER, DARRIN   C   BLUE JAYS

PERSONAL: Born October 3, 1966, in Elmhurst, Ill. ... 6-1/200. ... Bats left, throws right. ... Full name: Darrin Glen Fletcher. ... Son of Tom Fletcher, pitcher, Detroit Tigers (1962).
HIGH SCHOOL: Oakwood (Ill.).
COLLEGE: Illinois.
TRANSACTIONS/CAREER NOTES: Selected by Los Angeles Dodgers organization in sixth round of free-agent draft (June 2, 1987). ... Traded by Dodgers to Philadelphia Phillies for P Dennis Cook (September 13, 1990). ... Traded by Phillies with cash to Montreal Expos for P Barry Jones (December 9, 1991). ... On Montreal disabled list (May 12-June 15, 1992); included rehabilitation assignment to Indianapolis (May 31-June 14). ... On disabled list (June 18-July 3, 1997). ... Granted free agency (October 27, 1997). ... Signed by Toronto Blue Jays (November 26, 1997).
STATISTICAL NOTES: Tied for Texas League lead in double plays by catcher with nine in 1988. ... Led Pacific Coast League catchers with 787 total chances in 1990. ... Led N.L. with 12 sacrifice flies in 1994. ... Career major league grand slams: 2.

Year	Team (League)	Pos.	G	AB	R	H	2B	3B	HR	RBI	Avg.	BB	SO	SB	PO	A	E	Avg.
								BATTING									FIELDING	
1987—Vero Beach (FSL)		C	43	124	13	33	7	0	0	15	.266	22	12	0	212	35	3	.988
1988—San Antonio (Tex.)		C	89	279	19	58	8	0	1	20	.208	17	42	2	529	64	5	*.992

F

Year Team (League)	Pos.	G	AB	R	H	2B	3B	HR	RBI	Avg.	BB	SO	SB	PO	A	E	Avg.
1989—Albuquerque (PCL).....	C	100	315	34	86	16	1	5	44	.273	30	38	1	632	63	9	.987
—Los Angeles (N.L.).....	C	5	8	1	4	0	0	1	2	.500	1	0	0	16	1	0	1.000
1990—Albuquerque (PCL).....	C	105	350	58	102	23	1	13	65	.291	40	37	1	*715	64	8	.990
—Los Angeles (N.L.).....	C	2	1	0	0	0	0	0	0	.000	0	1	0	0	0	0	...
—Philadelphia (N.L.)■..	C	9	22	3	3	1	0	0	1	.136	1	5	0	30	3	0	1.000
1991—Scran./W.B. (Int'l)......	C-1B	90	306	39	87	13	1	8	50	.284	23	29	1	491	44	5	.991
—Philadelphia (N.L.).....	C	46	136	5	31	8	0	1	12	.228	5	15	0	242	22	2	.992
1992—Montreal (N.L.)■........	C	83	222	13	54	10	2	2	26	.243	14	28	0	360	33	2	.995
—Indianapolis (A.A.)......	C	13	51	2	13	2	0	1	9	.255	2	10	0	65	7	1	.986
1993—Montreal (N.L.)..........	C	133	396	33	101	20	1	9	60	.255	34	40	0	620	41	8	.988
1994—Montreal (N.L.)..........	C	94	285	28	74	18	1	10	57	.260	25	23	0	479	20	2	.996
1995—Montreal (N.L.)..........	C	110	350	42	100	21	1	11	45	.286	32	23	0	613	44	4	.994
1996—Montreal (N.L.)..........	C	127	394	41	105	22	0	12	57	.266	27	42	0	721	30	6	.992
1997—Montreal (N.L.)..........	C	96	310	39	86	20	1	17	55	.277	17	35	1	606	26	4	.994
Major league totals (9 years)		705	2124	205	558	120	6	63	315	.263	156	212	1	3687	220	28	.993

ALL-STAR GAME RECORD

Year League	Pos.	AB	R	H	2B	3B	HR	RBI	Avg.	BB	SO	SB	PO	A	E	Avg.
1994—National....................	C	0	0	0	0	0	0	0	...	0	0	0	3	0	0	1.000

FLORES, IGNACIO   P   DODGERS

PERSONAL: Born May 8, 1975, in Baja California Sur, Mexico. ... 6-2/180. ... Throws right, bats right. ... Full name: Jose Ignacio Flores.
HIGH SCHOOL: Conalep Colegio Nacional (Baja California Sur, Mexico).
TRANSACTIONS/CAREER NOTES: Signed as non-drafted free agent by Los Angeles Dodgers organization (April 6, 1995).

Year Team (League)	W	L	Pct.	ERA	G	GS	CG	ShO	Sv.	IP	H	R	ER	BB	SO
1995—Great Falls (Pio.).............	6	4	.600	4.72	16	12	0	0	0	68 2/3	66	42	36	38	76
1996—Saltillo (Mexican).............	5	10	.333	5.09	26	25	3	1	0	141 1/3	144	92	80	108	82
—Torreon (Mexican).............	1	1	.500	5.83	18	2	0	0	0	29 1/3	24	22	19	27	21
1997—San Antonio (Tex.)...........	10	7	.588	3.25	27	18	0	0	1	133	125	59	48	39	102

FLORIE, BRYCE   P   TIGERS

PERSONAL: Born May 21, 1970, in Charleston, S.C. ... 5-11/190. ... Throws right, bats right. ... Full name: Bryce Bettencourt Florie.
HIGH SCHOOL: Hanahan (Charleston, S.C.).
COLLEGE: Trident Technical College (S.C.).
TRANSACTIONS/CAREER NOTES: Selected by San Diego Padres organization in fifth round of free-agent draft (June 1, 1988). ... Traded by Padres with P Ron Villone and OF Marc Newfield to Milwaukee Brewers for OF Greg Vaughn and a player to be named later (July 31, 1996); Padres acquired OF Gerald Parent to complete deal (September 16, 1996). ... Traded by Brewers with a player to be named later to Detroit Tigers for P Mike Myers, P Rick Greene and SS Santiago Perez (November 20, 1997). ... On disabled list (August 31-September 8, 1997).
STATISTICAL NOTES: Led Texas League with 25 wild pitches in 1993.

Year Team (League)	W	L	Pct.	ERA	G	GS	CG	ShO	Sv.	IP	H	R	ER	BB	SO
1988—Ariz. Padres (Ariz.).....	4	5	.444	7.98	11	6	0	0	0	38 1/3	52	44	34	22	29
1989—Spokane (N'west).............	4	5	.444	7.08	14	14	0	0	0	61	79	•66	48	40	50
—Charleston, S.C. (S. Atl.).....	1	7	.125	6.95	12	12	0	0	0	44	54	47	34	42	22
1990—Waterloo (Midw.).............	4	5	.444	4.39	14	14	0	0	0	65 2/3	60	37	32	37	38
1991—Waterloo (Midw.).............	7	6	.538	3.92	23	23	2	0	0	133	119	66	58	79	90
1992—High Desert (Calif.).....	9	7	.563	4.12	26	24	0	0	0	137 2/3	99	79	63	*114	106
—Charleston, S.C. (S. Atl.).....	0	1	.000	1.80	1	1	0	0	0	5	3	1	0	5	5
1993—Wichita (Texas)............	11	8	.579	3.96	27	•27	0	0	0	154 2/3	128	80	68	*100	133
1994—Las Vegas (PCL)............	2	5	.286	5.15	50	0	0	0	1	71 2/3	76	47	41	47	67
—San Diego (N.L.)............	0	0	...	0.96	9	0	0	0	0	9 1/3	8	1	1	3	8
1995—San Diego (N.L.)............	2	2	.500	3.01	47	0	0	0	0	68 2/3	49	30	23	38	68
1996—San Diego (N.L.)............	2	2	.500	4.01	39	0	0	0	0	49 1/3	45	24	22	27	51
—Milwaukee (A.L.)■............	0	1	.000	6.63	15	0	0	0	0	19	20	16	14	13	12
1997—Milwaukee (A.L.).............	4	4	.500	4.32	32	8	0	0	0	75	74	43	36	42	53
A.L. totals (2 years)..................	4	5	.444	4.79	47	8	0	0	0	94	94	59	50	55	65
N.L. totals (3 years)..................	4	4	.500	3.25	95	0	0	0	1	127 1/3	102	55	46	68	127
Major league totals (4 years)......	8	9	.471	3.90	142	8	0	0	1	221 1/3	196	114	96	123	192

FLOYD, CLIFF   OF   MARLINS

PERSONAL: Born December 5, 1972, in Chicago. ... 6-4/235. ... Bats left, throws right. ... Full name: Cornelius Clifford Floyd.
HIGH SCHOOL: Thornwood (South Holland, Ill.).
TRANSACTIONS/CAREER NOTES: Selected by Montreal Expos organization in first round (14th pick overall) of free-agent draft (June 3, 1991). ... On disabled list (May 16-September 11, 1995). ... Traded by Expos to Florida Marlins for OF Joe Orsulak and P Dustin Hermanson (March 26, 1997). ... On disabled list (May 9-24, 1997). ... On disabled list (June 21-September 1, 1997); included rehabilitation assignment to Charlotte (July 20-September 1, 1997).
HONORS: Named Minor League Player of the Year by THE SPORTING NEWS (1993). ... Named Eastern League Most Valuable Player (1993).
STATISTICAL NOTES: Led South Atlantic League with 261 total bases and nine intentional bases on balls received in 1992. ... Led Eastern League with .600 slugging percentage and 12 intentional bases on balls received in 1993.

Year Team (League)	Pos.	G	AB	R	H	2B	3B	HR	RBI	Avg.	BB	SO	SB	PO	A	E	Avg.
1991—GC Expos (GCL).........	1B	56	214	35	56	9	3	6	30	.262	19	37	13	451	27	*15	.970
1992—Albany (S. Atl.)...........	OF-1B	134	516	83	157	24	*16	16	*97	.304	45	75	32	423	29	17	.964
—W.P. Beach (FSL)........	OF	1	4	0	0	0	0	0	1	.000	0	1	0	2	0	0	1.000

Year Team (League)	Pos.	G	AB	R	H	2B	3B	HR	RBI	Avg.	BB	SO	SB	PO	A	E	Avg.
1993—Harrisburg (Eastern)..	1B-OF	101	380	82	125	17	4	•26	*101	.329	54	71	31	564	27	19	.969
—Ottawa (Int'l)	1B	32	125	12	30	2	2	2	18	.240	16	34	2	272	23	5	.983
—Montreal (N.L.)	1B	10	31	3	7	0	0	1	2	.226	0	9	0	79	4	0	1.000
1994—Montreal (N.L.)	1B-OF	100	334	43	94	19	4	4	41	.281	24	63	10	565	42	6	.990
1995—Montreal (N.L.)	1B-OF	29	69	6	9	1	0	1	8	.130	7	22	3	146	12	3	.981
1996—Ottawa (Int'l)	OF-3B	20	76	7	23	3	1	1	8	.303	7	20	2	38	1	2	.951
—Montreal (N.L.)	OF-1B	117	227	29	55	15	4	6	26	.242	30	52	7	109	2	5	.957
1997—Florida (N.L.)■	OF-1B	61	137	23	32	9	1	1	6	.234	24	33	6	96	5	3	.971
—Charlotte (Int'l)	OF-1B	39	131	27	48	10	0	9	33	.366	10	29	7	79	5	1	.988
Major league totals (5 years)		317	798	104	197	44	9	18	96	.247	85	179	26	995	65	17	.984

WORLD SERIES RECORD

NOTES: Member of World Series championship team (1997).

Year Team (League)	Pos.	G	AB	R	H	2B	3B	HR	RBI	Avg.	BB	SO	SB	PO	A	E	Avg.
1997—Florida (N.L.)	PH-DH	4	2	1	0	0	0	0	0	.000	1	1	0	0	0	0	...

FLURY, PATRICK   P   ROYALS

PERSONAL: Born March 14, 1973, in Reno, Nev. ... 6-1/220. ... Throws right, bats right. ... Full name: Patrick Shannon Flury.
HIGH SCHOOL: Edward C. Reed (Sparks, Nev.).
JUNIOR COLLEGE: College of Southern Idaho.
COLLEGE: UNLV.
TRANSACTIONS/CAREER NOTES: Selected by Kansas City Royals organization in seventh round of free-agent draft (June 3, 1993).

Year Team (League)	W	L	Pct.	ERA	G	GS	CG	ShO	Sv.	IP	H	R	ER	BB	SO
1993—Eugene (Northwest)	2	2	.500	3.27	27	0	0	0	7	33	25	15	12	22	34
1994—Rockford (Midwest)	1	3	.250	3.93	34	0	0	0	2	55	61	27	24	33	41
1995—Springfield (Mid.)	2	6	.250	4.31	34	0	0	0	1	54 1/3	65	32	26	24	35
—Wilmington (Caro.)	1	0	1.000	2.45	15	0	0	0	1	22	18	6	6	9	14
1996—Wilmington (Caro.)	7	2	.778	1.92	45	0	0	0	5	84 1/3	66	22	18	29	67
1997—Wichita (Texas)	8	3	.727	3.56	42	0	0	0	5	48	47	26	19	18	47
—Omaha (Am. Assoc.)	1	0	1.000	6.08	18	0	0	0	0	26 2/3	29	18	18	16	24

FONTENOT, JOE   P   MARLINS

PERSONAL: Born March 20, 1977, in Lafeyette, La. ... 6-2/185. ... Throws right, bats right. ... Full name: Joseph Fontenot.
HIGH SCHOOL: Acadiana (Lafeytte, La.).
TRANSACTIONS/CAREER NOTES: Selected by San Francisco Giants organization in first round (16th pick overall) of free-agent draft (June 1, 1995). ... Traded by Giants with P Mike Villano and P Mick Pageler to Florida Marlins for P Robb Nen (November 18, 1997).
STATISTICAL NOTES: Led Texas League in hit batsmen with 12 in 1997.

Year Team (League)	W	L	Pct.	ERA	G	GS	CG	ShO	Sv.	IP	H	R	ER	BB	SO
1995—Bellingham (N'west)	0	3	.000	1.93	6	6	0	0	0	18 2/3	14	5	4	10	14
1996—San Jose (California)	9	4	.692	4.44	26	23	0	0	0	144	137	87	71	74	124
1997—Shreveport (Texas)	10	11	.476	5.53	26	26	1	0	0	151 1/3	171	105	93	65	103

FONVILLE, CHAD   SS/2B   INDIANS

PERSONAL: Born March 5, 1971, in Jacksonville, N.C. ... 5-6/155. ... Bats both, throws right. ... Full name: Chad Everette Fonville.
HIGH SCHOOL: White Oak (Jacksonville, N.C.).
JUNIOR COLLEGE: Louisburg (N.C.).
TRANSACTIONS/CAREER NOTES: Selected by San Francisco Giants organization in 11th round of free-agent draft (June 1, 1992). ... On disabled list (April 8-June 10, 1994). ... Selected by Montreal Expos from Giants organization in Rule 5 major league draft (December 5, 1994). ... Claimed on waivers by Los Angeles Dodgers (May 31, 1995). ... Traded by Dodgers to Chicago White Sox (September 2, 1997), completing trade in which White Sox traded OF Darren Lewis to Dodgers for a player to be named later (August 27, 1997). ... Claimed on waivers by Cleveland Indians (November 25, 1997).
STATISTICAL NOTES: Led Northwest League second basemen with 131 putouts and tied for lead with 17 errors in 1992.

Year Team (League)	Pos.	G	AB	R	H	2B	3B	HR	RBI	Avg.	BB	SO	SB	PO	A	E	Avg.
1992—Everett (N'west)	2B-SS	63	260	56	71	9	1	1	33	.273	31	39	36	†134	141	‡18	.939
1993—Clinton (Midwest)	SS-3B-2B	120	447	80	137	16	10	1	44	.306	40	48	52	167	319	36	.931
1994—San Jose (Calif.)	SS-2B-OF	68	283	58	87	9	6	0	26	.307	34	34	22	119	203	22	.936
1995—Montreal (N.L.)■	2B	14	12	2	4	0	0	0	0	.333	0	3	0	0	0	0	...
—Los Angeles (N.L.)■	SS-2B-OF	88	308	41	85	6	1	0	16	.276	23	39	20	125	195	11	.967
1996—Los Angeles (N.L.)	O-2-S-3	103	201	34	41	4	1	0	13	.204	17	31	7	84	71	6	.963
—Albuquerque (PCL)	SS-2B-OF	25	96	17	23	1	0	0	5	.240	8	13	7	42	70	6	.949
1997—Los Angeles (N.L.)	2B	9	14	1	2	0	0	0	1	.143	2	3	0	0	5	1	.833
—Albuquerque (PCL)	OF-2B-SS	102	371	49	81	5	2	0	22	.218	30	39	23	173	149	15	.955
—Chicago (A.L.)■	O-2-S-DH	9	9	1	1	0	0	0	1	.111	1	1	2	9	3	1	.923
American League totals (1 year)		9	9	1	1	0	0	0	1	.111	1	1	2	9	3	1	.923
National League totals (3 years)		214	535	78	132	10	2	0	30	.247	42	76	27	209	271	18	.964
Major league totals (3 years)		223	544	79	133	10	2	0	31	.244	43	77	29	218	274	19	.963

DIVISION SERIES RECORD

Year Team (League)	Pos.	G	AB	R	H	2B	3B	HR	RBI	Avg.	BB	SO	SB	PO	A	E	Avg.
1995—Los Angeles (N.L.)	SS	3	12	1	6	0	0	0	0	.500	0	1	0	1	7	1	.889

F

FORD, BEN — P — DIAMONDBACKS

PERSONAL: Born August 15, 1975, in Cedar Rapids, Iowa. ... 6-7/200. ... Throws right, bats right. ... Full name: Benjamin Ford.
HIGH SCHOOL: George Washington (Cedar Rapids, Iowa).
JUNIOR COLLEGE: Indian Hills Community College (Iowa).
TRANSACTIONS/CAREER NOTES: Selected by New York Yankees organization in 20th round of free-agent draft (June 2, 1994). ... Selected by Arizona Diamondbacks in first round (17th pick overall) of expansion draft (November 18, 1997).

Year Team (League)	W	L	Pct.	ERA	G	GS	CG	ShO	Sv.	IP	H	R	ER	BB	SO
1994—GC Yankees (GCL)	2	2	.500	2.38	18	0	0	0	3	34	27	13	9	8	31
1995—Oneonta (N.Y.-Penn)	5	0	1.000	0.87	29	0	0	0	0	52	39	23	5	16	50
—Greensboro (S. Atl.)	0	0	...	5.14	7	0	0	0	0	7	4	4	4	5	8
1996—Greensboro (S. Atl.)	2	6	.250	4.26	43	0	0	0	2	82 1/3	75	48	39	33	84
1997—Tampa (Florida State)	4	0	1.000	1.93	32	0	0	0	18	37 1/3	27	8	8	14	37
—Norwich (Eastern)	4	3	.571	4.22	28	0	0	0	1	42 2/3	35	28	20	19	38

FORDHAM, TOM — P — WHITE SOX

PERSONAL: Born February 20, 1974, in San Diego. ... 6-2/210. ... Throws left, bats left.
HIGH SCHOOL: Granite Hills (El Cajon, Calif.).
JUNIOR COLLEGE: Grossmont College (Calif.).
TRANSACTIONS/CAREER NOTES: Selected by Chicago White Sox organization in 11th round of free-agent draft (June 3, 1993).

Year Team (League)	W	L	Pct.	ERA	G	GS	CG	ShO	Sv.	IP	H	R	ER	BB	SO
1993—Sara. W. Sox (GCL)	1	1	.500	1.80	3	0	0	0	0	10	9	2	2	3	12
—Sarasota (Florida State)	0	0	...	0.00	2	0	0	0	0	5	3	1	0	3	5
—Hickory (S. Atl.)	4	3	.571	3.88	8	8	1	0	0	48 2/3	36	21	21	21	27
1994—Hickory (S. Atl.)	10	5	.667	3.14	17	17	1	1	0	109	101	47	38	30	121
—South Bend (Mid.)	4	4	.500	4.34	11	11	1	1	0	74 2/3	82	46	36	14	48
1995—Prince William (Caro.)	9	0	1.000	2.04	13	13	1	1	0	84	66	20	19	35	78
—Birmingham (Southern)	6	3	.667	3.38	14	14	2	1	0	82 2/3	79	35	31	28	61
1996—Birmingham (Southern)	2	1	.667	2.65	6	6	0	0	0	37 1/3	26	13	11	14	37
—Nashville (A.A.)	10	8	.556	3.45	22	22	3	0	0	140 2/3	117	60	54	69	118
1997—Nashville (A.A.)	6	7	.462	4.74	21	20	2	0	0	114	113	64	60	53	90
—Chicago (A.L.)	0	1	.000	6.23	7	1	0	0	0	17 1/3	17	13	12	10	10
Major league totals (1 year)	0	1	.000	6.23	7	1	0	0	0	17 1/3	17	13	12	10	10

FORDYCE, BROOK — C — REDS

PERSONAL: Born May 7, 1970, in New London, Conn. ... 6-1/185. ... Bats right, throws right. ... Full name: Brook Alexander Fordyce. ... Name pronounced FOR-dice.
HIGH SCHOOL: St. Bernard's (Uncasville, Conn.).
TRANSACTIONS/CAREER NOTES: Selected by New York Mets organization in third round of free-agent draft (June 5, 1989). ... On disabled list (June 19-July 2 and July 18-August 30, 1994).... On suspended list (August 30-September 1, 1994). ... Claimed on waivers by Cleveland Indians (May 15, 1995). ... Granted free agency (October 16, 1995). ... Signed by Cincinnati Reds organization (December 7, 1995). ... On disabled list (July 16-August 5, 1997); included rehabilitation assignment to Indianapolis (July 21-August 5).
STATISTICAL NOTES: Led Appalachian League catchers with .991 fielding percentage in 1989. ... Led South Atlantic League in slugging percentage with .478 and tied for lead in grounding into double plays with 18 in 1990. ... Led South Atlantic League with 30 passed balls in 1990. ... Led Eastern League catchers with 795 total chances in 1992. ... Led International League catchers with 810 total chances and tied for lead in double plays by catcher with 11 in 1993.

Year Team (League)	Pos.	G	AB	R	H	2B	3B	HR	RBI	Avg.	BB	SO	SB	PO	A	E	Avg.
1989—Kingsport (Appal.)	C-OF-3B	69	226	45	74	15	0	9	38	.327	30	26	10	311	28	4	†.988
1990—Columbia (S. Atl.)	C	104	372	45	117	29	1	10	54	.315	39	42	4	574	63	15	.977
1991—St. Lucie (Fla. St.)	C	115	406	42	97	19	3	7	55	.239	37	50	4	630	87	13	.982
1992—Binghamton (East.)	C	118	425	59	118	30	0	11	61	.278	37	78	1	*713	*79	3	*.996
1993—Norfolk (Int'l)	C	116	409	33	106	21	2	2	41	.259	26	62	2	*735	67	8	.990
1994—Norfolk (Int'l)	C	66	229	26	60	13	3	3	32	.262	19	26	1	330	33	7	.981
1995—New York (N.L.)	...	4	2	1	1	1	0	0	0	.500	1	0	0	0	0	0	...
—Buffalo (A.A.)■	C-OF	58	176	18	44	13	0	0	9	.250	14	20	1	306	18	3	.991
1996—Indianapolis (A.A.)■ ..	C-1B	107	374	48	103	20	3	16	64	.275	25	56	2	620	49	4	*.994
—Cincinnati (N.L.)	C	4	7	0	2	1	0	0	1	.286	3	1	0	18	0	0	1.000
1997—Cincinnati (N.L.)	C-DH	47	96	7	20	5	0	1	8	.208	8	15	2	162	12	3	.983
—Indianapolis (A.A.)	C	12	47	7	11	2	0	2	6	.234	5	6	1	73	8	0	1.000
Major league totals (3 years)		55	105	8	23	7	0	1	9	.219	12	16	2	180	12	3	.985

FOSSAS, TONY — P — MARINERS

PERSONAL: Born September 23, 1957, in Havana, Cuba. ... 6-0/198. ... Throws left, bats left. ... Full name: Emilio Anthony Fossas.
HIGH SCHOOL: St. Mary's (Brookline, Mass.).
COLLEGE: South Florida.
TRANSACTIONS/CAREER NOTES: Selected by Minnesota Twins organization in ninth round of free-agent draft (June 6, 1978); did not sign. ... Selected by Texas Rangers organization in 12th round of free-agent draft (June 5, 1979). ... Released by Rangers organization (February 18, 1982). ... Signed by Midland, Chicago Cubs organization (March 11, 1982). ... Loaned by Cubs organization to Tabasco of Mexican League (March 15-April 7, 1982). ... Released by Cubs organization (April 7, 1982). ... Signed by Burlington, Rangers organization (May 3, 1982). ... Granted free agency (October 15, 1985). ... Signed by Edmonton, California Angels organization (December 13, 1985). ... On disabled list (June 2, 1986-remainder of season). ... Granted free agency (October 15, 1987). ... Signed by Oklahoma City, Rangers organization (December 1, 1987). ... Granted free agency (October 15, 1988). ... Signed by Denver, Milwaukee Brewers organization (January 21, 1989).

... Released by Brewers organization (December 6, 1990). ... Signed by Boston Red Sox organization (January 23, 1991). ... Released by Red Sox (December 11, 1992). ... Re-signed by Red Sox organization (January 18, 1993). ... Granted free agency (December 20, 1993). ... Re-signed by Red Sox organization (January 20, 1994). ... Granted free agency (December 23, 1994). ... Signed by New Jersey, St. Louis Cardinals organization (April 11, 1995). ... Granted free agency (October 27, 1997). ... Signed by Seattle Mariners (December 16, 1997).

Year	Team (League)	W	L	Pct.	ERA	G	GS	CG	ShO	Sv.	IP	H	R	ER	BB	SO
1979—	GC Rangers (GCL)	6	3	.667	3.00	10	9	1	0	0	60	54	28	20	26	49
—	Tulsa (Texas)	1	1	.500	6.55	2	2	0	0	0	11	14	10	8	4	3
1980—	Asheville (S. Atl.)	8	2	.800	3.15	30	•27	8	2	2	*197	*187	84	69	69	140
1981—	Tulsa (Texas)	5	6	.455	4.16	38	12	1	1	2	106	113	65	49	44	57
1982—	Tabasco (Mexican)■	0	3	.000	5.56	3	3	0	0	0	11 1/3	15	14	7	10	6
—	Burlington (Midw.)■	8	9	.471	3.08	25	18	10	1	0	146 1/3	121	63	50	33	115
1983—	Tulsa (Texas)	8	7	.533	4.20	24	16	6	1	0	133	123	77	62	46	103
—	Oklahoma City (A.A.)	1	2	.333	7.90	10	5	0	0	0	35 1/3	55	33	31	12	23
1984—	Tulsa (Texas)	0	1	.000	4.50	4	0	0	0	2	10	12	5	5	3	7
—	Oklahoma City (A.A.)	5	9	.357	4.31	29	15	3	0	0	121	143	65	58	34	74
1985—	Oklahoma City (A.A.)	7	6	.538	4.75	30	13	2	0	2	110	121	65	58	36	49
1986—	Edmonton (PCL)■	3	3	.500	4.57	7	7	2	1	0	43 1/3	53	23	22	12	15
1987—	Edmonton (PCL)■	6	8	.429	4.99	40	15	1	0	0	117 1/3	152	76	65	29	54
1988—	Oklahoma City (A.A.)■	3	0	1.000	2.84	52	0	0	0	4	66 2/3	64	21	21	16	42
—	Texas (A.L.)	0	0	. . .	4.76	5	0	0	0	0	5 2/3	11	3	3	2	0
1989—	Denver (Am. Assoc.)■	5	1	.833	2.04	24	1	0	0	0	35 1/3	27	9	8	11	35
—	Milwaukee (A.L.)	2	2	.500	3.54	51	0	0	0	1	61	57	27	24	22	42
1990—	Milwaukee (A.L.)	2	3	.400	6.44	32	0	0	0	0	29 1/3	44	23	21	10	24
—	Denver (Am. Assoc.)	5	2	.714	1.51	25	0	0	0	4	35 2/3	29	8	6	10	45
1991—	Boston (A.L.)■	3	2	.600	3.47	64	0	0	0	0	57	49	27	22	28	29
1992—	Boston (A.L.)	1	2	.333	2.43	60	0	0	0	2	29 2/3	31	9	8	14	19
1993—	Boston (A.L.)	1	1	.500	5.18	71	0	0	0	0	40	38	28	23	15	39
1994—	Boston (A.L.)	2	0	1.000	4.76	44	0	0	0	1	34	35	18	18	15	31
—	Pawtucket (Int'l)	2	0	1.000	0.00	11	0	0	0	0	9 2/3	4	1	0	3	8
1995—	St. Louis (N.L.)■	3	0	1.000	1.47	58	0	0	0	0	36 2/3	28	6	6	10	40
1996—	St. Louis (N.L.)	0	4	.000	2.68	65	0	0	0	2	47	43	19	14	21	36
1997—	St. Louis (N.L.)	2	7	.222	3.83	71	0	0	0	0	51 2/3	62	32	22	26	41
A.L. totals (7 years)		11	10	.524	4.17	327	0	0	0	5	256 2/3	265	135	119	106	184
N.L. totals (3 years)		5	11	.313	2.79	194	0	0	0	2	135 1/3	133	57	42	57	117
Major league totals (10 years)		16	21	.432	3.70	521	0	0	0	7	392	398	192	161	163	301

DIVISION SERIES RECORD

Year	Team (League)	W	L	Pct.	ERA	G	GS	CG	ShO	Sv.	IP	H	R	ER	BB	SO
1996—	St. Louis (N.L.)							Did not play.								

CHAMPIONSHIP SERIES RECORD

Year	Team (League)	W	L	Pct.	ERA	G	GS	CG	ShO	Sv.	IP	H	R	ER	BB	SO
1996—	St. Louis (N.L.)	0	0	. . .	2.08	5	0	0	0	0	4 1/3	1	1	1	4	1

FOSTER, KEVIN   P   CUBS

PERSONAL: Born January 13, 1969, in Evanston, Ill. ... 6-1/165. ... Throws right, bats right. ... Full name: Kevin Christopher Foster.
HIGH SCHOOL: Evanston (Ill.) Township.
COLLEGE: Kishwaukee College (Ill.).
TRANSACTIONS/CAREER NOTES: Selected by Montreal Expos organization in 29th round of free-agent draft (June 2, 1987). ... On Albany (Ga.) suspended list (April 9-May 6, 1992). ... Traded by Expos organization to Seattle Mariners for IF Frank Bolick and a player to be named later (November 20, 1992); Expos organization acquired C Miah Bradbury to complete deal (December 8, 1992). ... Traded by Mariners to Philadelphia Phillies for P Bob Ayrault (June 12, 1993). ... Traded by Phillies to Chicago Cubs for P Shawn Boskie (April 12, 1994). ... On disabled list (August 17-September 1, 1997).
STATISTICAL NOTES: Led N.L. with 32 home runs allowed in 1995.
MISCELLANEOUS: Appeared in three games as pinch-runner (1995). ... Appeared in two games as pinch-runner for Chicago (1996). ... Struck out three times and had a sacrifice hit in four games as pinch-hitter (1997).

Year	Team (League)	W	L	Pct.	ERA	G	GS	CG	ShO	Sv.	IP	H	R	ER	BB	SO
1990—	GC Expos (GCL)	2	0	1.000	5.06	4	0	0	0	0	10 2/3	9	6	6	6	11
—	Gate City (Pioneer)	1	7	.125	4.58	10	10	0	0	0	55	43	42	28	34	52
1991—	Sumter (S. Atl.)	10	4	.714	2.74	34	11	1	1	1	102	62	36	31	68	111
1992—	W.P. Beach (FSL)	7	2	.778	1.95	16	11	0	0	0	69 1/3	45	19	15	31	66
1993—	Jacksonville (Southern)■	4	4	.500	3.97	12	12	1	1	0	65 2/3	53	32	29	29	72
—	Scran./W.B. (Int'l)■	1	1	.500	3.93	17	9	1	0	0	71	63	32	31	29	59
—	Philadelphia (N.L.)	0	1	.000	14.85	2	1	0	0	0	6 2/3	13	11	11	7	6
1994—	Reading (Eastern)	0	1	.000	6.00	1	1	0	0	0	6	7	4	4	1	3
—	Orlando (South.)■	1	0	1.000	0.95	3	3	1	1	0	19	8	2	2	2	21
—	Iowa (Am. Assoc.)	3	1	.750	4.28	6	6	1	0	0	33 2/3	28	17	16	14	35
—	Chicago (N.L.)	3	4	.429	2.89	13	13	0	0	0	81	70	31	26	35	75
1995—	Chicago (N.L.)	12	11	.522	4.51	30	28	0	0	0	167 2/3	149	90	84	65	146
1996—	Chicago (N.L.)	7	6	.538	6.21	17	16	1	0	0	87	98	63	60	35	53
—	Iowa (Am. Assoc.)	7	6	.538	4.30	18	18	3	1	0	115	106	56	55	46	87
1997—	Chicago (N.L.)	10	7	.588	4.61	26	25	1	0	0	146 1/3	141	79	75	66	118
Major league totals (5 years)		32	29	.525	4.71	88	83	2	0	0	488 2/3	471	274	256	208	398

RECORD AS POSITION PLAYER

Year	Team (League)	Pos.	G	AB	R	H	2B	3B	HR	RBI	Avg.	BB	SO	SB	PO	A	E	Avg.
1988—	GC Expos (GCL)	3B-2B-SS	49	164	21	42	10	1	2	21	.256	21	33	16	38	92	18	.878
1989—	Rockford (Midwest)	3B-2B	44	117	9	19	3	2	1	15	.162	18	44	1	29	70	12	.892
1990—	W.P. Beach (FSL)	3B	3	6	0	1	0	1	0	2	.167	1	1	0	2	1	0	1.000

F

FOULKE, KEITH — P — WHITE SOX

PERSONAL: Born October 19, 1972, in San Diego. ... 6-0/195. ... Throws right, bats right. ... Full name: Keith Charles Foulke.
HIGH SCHOOL: Hargrave (Huffman, Texas).
JUNIOR COLLEGE: Lewis & Clark State (Idaho).
COLLEGE: Galveston (Texas) College.
TRANSACTIONS/CAREER NOTES: Selected by San Francisco Giants organization in ninth round of free-agent draft (June 2, 1994). ... Traded by Giants with SS Michael Caruso, OF Brian Manning, P Lorenzo Barcelo, P Bobby Howry and P Ken Vining to Chicago White Sox for P Wilson Alvarez, P Danny Darwin and P Roberto Hernandez (July 31, 1997).

Year — Team (League)	W	L	Pct.	ERA	G	GS	CG	ShO	Sv.	IP	H	R	ER	BB	SO
1994— Everett (Northwest)	2	0	1.000	0.93	4	4	0	0	0	19 1/3	17	4	2	3	22
1995— San Jose (California)	13	6	.684	3.50	28	26	2	1	0	177 1/3	166	85	69	32	168
1996— Shreveport (Texas)	12	7	.632	*2.76	27	27	4	2	0	*182 2/3	149	61	56	35	129
1997— Phoenix (PCL)	5	4	.556	4.50	12	12	0	0	0	76	79	38	38	15	54
— San Francisco (N.L.)	1	5	.167	8.26	11	8	0	0	0	44 2/3	60	41	41	18	33
— Nashville (A.A.)■	0	0	...	5.79	1	1	0	0	0	4 2/3	8	3	3	0	4
— Chicago (A.L.)	3	0	1.000	3.45	16	0	0	0	3	28 2/3	28	11	11	5	21
A.L. totals (1 year)	3	0	1.000	3.45	16	0	0	0	3	28 2/3	28	11	11	5	21
N.L. totals (1 year)	1	5	.167	8.26	11	8	0	0	0	44 2/3	60	41	41	18	33
Major league totals (1 year)	4	5	.444	6.38	27	8	0	0	3	73 1/3	88	52	52	23	54

FOX, ANDY — 3B — YANKEES

PERSONAL: Born January 12, 1971, in Sacramento. ... 6-4/205. ... Bats left, throws right. ... Full name: Andrew Junipero Fox.
HIGH SCHOOL: Christian Brothers (Sacramento).
TRANSACTIONS/CAREER NOTES: Selected by New York Yankees organization in second round of free-agent draft (June 5, 1989). ... On disabled list (June 11-21, 1991; April 9-22, 1992 and June 10-August 1, 1993).
STATISTICAL NOTES: Led Carolina League third basemen with 96 putouts in 1992. ... Led Eastern League third basemen with 30 errors in 1994. ... Led International League third basemen with 22 double plays in 1995.

Year — Team (League)	Pos.	G	AB	R	H	2B	3B	HR	RBI	Avg.	BB	SO	SB	PO	A	E	Avg.
1989— GC Yankees (GCL)	3B	40	141	26	35	9	2	3	25	.248	31	29	6	37	78	10	.920
1990— Greensboro (S. Atl.)	3B	134	455	68	99	19	4	9	55	.218	92	132	26	93	238	*45	.880
1991— Prince William (Car.)	3B	126	417	60	96	22	2	10	46	.230	81	104	15	85	247	*29	.920
1992— Prince William (Car.)	3B-SS	125	473	75	113	18	3	7	42	.239	54	81	28	†97	304	27	.937
1993— Alb./Colon. (Eastern)	3B	65	236	44	65	16	1	3	24	.275	32	54	12	59	150	19	.917
1994— Alb./Colon. (Eastern)	3B-SS-2B	121	472	75	105	20	3	11	43	.222	62	102	22	110	261	†34	.916
1995— Norwich (Eastern)	SS	44	175	23	36	3	5	5	17	.206	19	36	8	77	127	9	.958
— Columbus (Int'l)	3-S-O-2	82	302	61	105	16	6	9	37	.348	43	41	22	84	211	9	.970
1996— New York (A.L.)	2-3-S-DH-O	113	189	26	37	4	0	3	13	.196	20	28	11	96	158	12	.955
1997— Columbus (Int'l)	3-2-S-O	95	318	66	87	11	4	6	33	.274	54	64	28	111	218	14	.959
— New York (A.L.)	3-2-DH-S-O	22	31	13	7	1	0	0	1	.226	7	9	2	19	30	1	.980
Major league totals (2 years)		135	220	39	44	5	0	3	14	.200	27	37	13	115	188	13	.959

DIVISION SERIES RECORD

Year — Team (League)	Pos.	G	AB	R	H	2B	3B	HR	RBI	Avg.	BB	SO	SB	PO	A	E	Avg.
1996— New York (A.L.)	DH-PR	2	0	0	0	0	0	0	0	...	0	0	0	...	...	...	...
1997— New York (A.L.)	2B-PR	2	0	0	0	0	0	0	0	...	0	0	0	0	0	0	...
Division series totals (2 years)		4	0	0	0	0	0	0	0	...	0	0	0	0	0	0	...

CHAMPIONSHIP SERIES RECORD

Year — Team (League)	Pos.	G	AB	R	H	2B	3B	HR	RBI	Avg.	BB	SO	SB	PO	A	E	Avg.
1996— New York (A.L.)	DH-PR	2	0	0	0	0	0	0	0	...	0	0	0	...	...	...	...

WORLD SERIES RECORD

NOTES: Member of World Series championship team (1996).

Year — Team (League)	Pos.	G	AB	R	H	2B	3B	HR	RBI	Avg.	BB	SO	SB	PO	A	E	Avg.
1996— New York (A.L.)	2B-PR-3B	4	0	1	0	0	0	0	0	...	0	0	0	1	0	0	1.000

FOX, CHAD — P — BREWERS

PERSONAL: Born September 3, 1970, in Conroe, Texas. ... 6-3/183. ... Throws right, bats right. ... Full name: Chad Douglas Fox.
HIGH SCHOOL: Westfield (Houston).
COLLEGE: Tarleton State (Texas).
TRANSACTIONS/CAREER NOTES: Selected by Cincinnati Reds organization in 23rd round of free-agent draft (June 1, 1992). ... Traded by Reds organization with a player to be named later to Atlanta Braves for OF Mike Kelly (January 9, 1996); Braves acquired P Ray King to complete deal (June 11, 1996). ... On disabled list (July 16-September 3, 1996). ... Traded by Braves to Milwaukee Brewers for OF Gerald Williams (December 11, 1997).
STATISTICAL NOTES: Led Carolina League with 20 wild pitches in 1994.

Year — Team (League)	W	L	Pct.	ERA	G	GS	CG	ShO	Sv.	IP	H	R	ER	BB	SO
1992— Princeton (Appalachian)	4	2	.667	4.74	15	8	0	0	0	49 1/3	55	43	26	34	37
1993— Char., W.Va. (S. Atl.)	9	12	.429	5.37	27	26	0	0	0	135 2/3	138	100	81	97	81
1994— Win.-Salem (Car.)	12	5	.706	3.86	25	25	1	0	0	156 1/3	121	77	67	*94	137
1995— Chattanooga (Southern)	4	5	.444	5.06	20	17	0	0	0	80	76	49	45	52	56
1996— Richmond (Int'l)■	3	10	.231	4.73	18	18	1	0	0	93 1/3	91	57	49	49	87

Year Team (League)	W	L	Pct.	ERA	G	GS	CG	ShO	Sv.	IP	H	R	ER	BB	SO
1997— Richmond (Int'l)	1	0	1.000	3.70	13	0	0	0	0	24 1/3	24	10	10	14	25
— Atlanta (N.L.)	0	1	.000	3.29	30	0	0	0	0	27 1/3	24	12	10	16	28
Major league totals (1 year)	0	1	.000	3.29	30	0	0	0	0	27 1/3	24	12	10	16	28

FRANCO, JOHN P METS

PERSONAL: Born September 17, 1960, in Brooklyn, N.Y. ... 5-10/185. ... Throws left, bats left. ... Full name: John Anthony Franco.
HIGH SCHOOL: Lafayette (Brooklyn, N.Y.).
COLLEGE: St. John's.
TRANSACTIONS/CAREER NOTES: Selected by Los Angeles Dodgers organization in fifth round of free-agent draft (June 8, 1981). ... Traded by Dodgers organization with P Brett Wise to Cincinnati Reds organization for IF Rafael Landestoy (May 9, 1983). ... Traded by Reds with OF Don Brown to New York Mets for P Randy Myers and P Kip Gross (December 6, 1989). ... On disabled list (June 30-August 1 and August 26, 1992-remainder of season; April 17-May 7 and August 3-26, 1993). ... Granted free agency (October 18, 1994). ... Re-signed by Mets (April 5, 1995).
HONORS: Named N.L. Fireman of the Year by THE SPORTING NEWS (1988, 1990 and 1994).
MISCELLANEOUS: Holds Cincinnati Reds all-time record for most saves (148). ... Holds New York Mets all-time record for most saves (211).

Year Team (League)	W	L	Pct.	ERA	G	GS	CG	ShO	Sv.	IP	H	R	ER	BB	SO
1981— Vero Beach (FSL)	7	4	.636	3.53	13	11	3	0	0	79	78	41	31	41	60
1982— Albuquerque (PCL)	1	2	.333	7.24	5	5	0	0	0	27 1/3	41	22	22	15	24
— San Antonio (Tex.)	10	5	.667	4.96	17	17	3	0	0	105 1/3	137	70	58	46	76
1983— Albuquerque (PCL)	0	0	. . .	5.40	11	0	0	0	0	15	10	11	9	11	8
— Indianapolis (A.A.)■	6	10	.375	4.85	23	18	2	0	2	115	148	69	62	42	54
1984— Wichita (Am. Assoc.)	1	0	1.000	5.79	6	0	0	0	0	9 1/3	8	6	6	4	11
— Cincinnati (N.L.)	6	2	.750	2.61	54	0	0	0	4	79 1/3	74	28	23	36	55
1985— Cincinnati (N.L.)	12	3	.800	2.18	67	0	0	0	12	99	83	27	24	40	61
1986— Cincinnati (N.L.)	6	6	.500	2.94	74	0	0	0	29	101	90	40	33	44	84
1987— Cincinnati (N.L.)	8	5	.615	2.52	68	0	0	0	32	82	76	26	23	27	61
1988— Cincinnati (N.L.)	6	6	.500	1.57	70	0	0	0	*39	86	60	18	15	27	46
1989— Cincinnati (N.L.)	4	8	.333	3.12	60	0	0	0	32	80 2/3	77	35	28	36	60
1990— New York (N.L.)■	5	3	.625	2.53	55	0	0	0	*33	67 2/3	66	22	19	21	56
1991— New York (N.L.)	5	9	.357	2.93	52	0	0	0	30	55 1/3	61	27	18	18	45
1992— New York (N.L.)	6	2	.750	1.64	31	0	0	0	15	33	24	6	6	11	20
1993— New York (N.L.)	4	3	.571	5.20	35	0	0	0	10	36 1/3	46	24	21	19	29
1994— New York (N.L.)	1	4	.200	2.70	47	0	0	0	*30	50	47	20	15	19	42
1995— New York (N.L.)	5	3	.625	2.44	48	0	0	0	29	51 2/3	48	17	14	17	41
1996— New York (N.L.)	4	3	.571	1.83	51	0	0	0	28	54	54	15	11	21	48
1997— New York (N.L.)	5	3	.625	2.55	59	0	0	0	36	60	60	49	18	17	20	53
Major league totals (14 years)	77	60	.562	2.57	771	0	0	0	359	936	855	323	267	356	701

ALL-STAR GAME RECORD

Year League	W	L	Pct.	ERA	GS	CG	ShO	Sv.	IP	H	R	ER	BB	SO
1986— National						Did not play.								
1987— National	0	0	. . .	0.00	0	0	0	0	2/3	0	0	0	0	0
1989— National						Did not play.								
1990— National	0	0	. . .	0.00	0	0	0	0	1	0	0	0	0	0
1991— National						Did not play.								
All-Star totals (2 years)	0	0	. . .	0.00	0	0	0	0	1 2/3	0	0	0	0	0

FRANCO, JULIO DH/1B/2B

F

PERSONAL: Born August 23, 1961, in San Pedro de Macoris, Dominican Republic. ... 6-1/200. ... Bats right, throws right. ... Full name: Julio Cesar Franco.
HIGH SCHOOL: Divine Providence (San Pedro de Macoris, Dominican Republic).
TRANSACTIONS/CAREER NOTES: Signed as non-drafted free agent by Philadelphia Phillies organization (June 23, 1978). ... Traded by Phillies with 2B Manny Trillo, OF George Vukovich, P Jay Baller and C Jerry Willard to Cleveland Indians for OF Von Hayes (December 9, 1982). ... On disabled list (July 13-August 8, 1987). ... Traded by Indians to Texas Rangers for 1B Pete O'Brien, OF Oddibe McDowell and 2B Jerry Browne (December 6, 1988). ... On disabled list (March 28-April 19, May 4-June 1 and July 9, 1992-remainder of season). ... Granted free agency (October 27, 1993). ... Signed by Chicago White Sox (December 15, 1993). ... Granted free agency (October 21, 1994). ... Signed by Chiba Lotte Marines of Japan Pacific League (December 28, 1994). ... Signed as free agent by Indians (December 7, 1995). ... On disabled list (July 7-25 and August 4-30, 1996). ... Released by Indians (August 13, 1997). ... Signed by Milwaukee Brewers (August 13, 1997). ... Granted free agency (October 28, 1997).
HONORS: Named Carolina League Most Valuable Player (1980). ... Named second baseman on THE SPORTING NEWS A.L. Silver Slugger team (1988-1991). ... Named second baseman on THE SPORTING NEWS A.L. All-Star team (1989-1991). ... Named designated hitter on THE SPORTING NEWS A.L. Silver Slugger team (1994).
STATISTICAL NOTES: Led Northwest League with 153 total bases in 1979. ... Led Northwest League shortstops with 45 double plays in 1979. ... Led Carolina League shortstops with 73 double plays in 1980. ... Led American Association shortstops with 42 errors in 1982. ... Led A.L. shortstops with 35 errors in 1985. ... Led A.L. in grounding into double plays with 28 in 1986 and 27 in 1989. ... Had 21-game hitting streak (May 11-June 3, 1988). ... Had 22-game hitting streak (July 3-27, 1988). ... Career major league grand slams: 6.

Year Team (League)	Pos.	G	AB	R	H	2B	3B	HR	RBI	Avg.	BB	SO	SB	PO	A	E	Avg.
1978— Butte (Pioneer)	SS	47	141	34	43	5	2	3	28	.305	17	30	4	37	52	25	.781
1979— Cen. Oregon (NWL)....	SS	•71	299	57	*98	15	5	•10	45	.328	24	59	22	103	*256	31	.921
1980— Peninsula (Caro.)	SS	•140	*555	105	178	25	6	11	*99	.321	33	66	44	179	*412	42	.934
1981— Reading (Eastern)	SS	*139	*532	70	160	17	3	8	74	.301	52	60	27	246	437	30	.958
1982— Oklahoma City (A.A.)..	SS-3B	120	463	80	139	19	5	21	66	.300	39	56	33	211	350	†42	.930
— Philadelphia (N.L.)......	SS-3B	16	29	3	8	1	0	0	3	.276	2	4	0	8	25	0	1.000
1983— Cleveland (A.L.)■.......	SS	149	560	68	153	24	8	8	80	.273	27	50	32	247	438	28	.961
1984— Cleveland (A.L.)..........	SS-DH	160	*658	82	188	22	5	3	79	.286	43	68	19	280	481	*36	.955

Year	Team (League)	Pos.	G	AB	R	H	2B	3B	HR	RBI	Avg.	BB	SO	SB	PO	A	E	Avg.
1985—Cleveland (A.L.)	SS-2B-DH	160	636	97	183	33	4	6	90	.288	54	74	13	252	437	†36	.950
1986—Cleveland (A.L.)	SS-2B-DH	149	599	80	183	30	5	10	74	.306	32	66	10	248	413	19	.972
1987—Cleveland (A.L.)	SS-2B-DH	128	495	86	158	24	3	8	52	.319	57	56	32	175	313	18	.964
1988—Cleveland (A.L.)	2B-DH	152	613	88	186	23	6	10	54	.303	56	72	25	310	434	14	.982
1989—Texas (A.L.)■	2B-DH	150	548	80	173	31	5	13	92	.316	66	69	21	256	386	13	.980
1990—Texas (A.L.)	2B-DH	157	582	96	172	27	1	11	69	.296	82	83	31	310	444	•19	.975
1991—Texas (A.L.)	2B	146	589	108	201	27	3	15	78	*.341	65	78	36	294	372	14	.979
1992—Texas (A.L.)	DH-2B-OF	35	107	19	25	7	0	2	8	.234	15	17	1	21	17	3	.927
1993—Texas (A.L.)	DH	144	532	85	154	31	3	14	84	.289	62	95	9	...	...	...	...
1994—Chicago (A.L.)■	DH-1B	112	433	72	138	19	2	20	98	.319	62	75	8	88	7	3	.969
1995—Chiba Lot. (J.P.)■	1B	127	474	60	145	25	3	10	58	.306	...	...	11	...	...	...	...
1996—Cleveland (A.L.)■	1B-DH	112	432	72	139	20	1	14	76	.322	61	82	8	852	77	9	.990
1997—Cleveland (A.L.)	DH-2B-1B	78	289	46	82	13	1	3	25	.284	38	75	8	70	107	3	.983
—Milwaukee (A.L.)■	DH-1B	42	141	22	34	3	0	4	19	.241	31	41	7	108	11	1	.992
American League totals (14 years)		1874	7214	1101	2169	334	45	141	978	.301	751	1001	260	3511	3937	216	.972
National League totals (1 year)		16	29	3	8	1	0	0	3	.276	2	4	0	8	25	0	1.000
Major league totals (15 years)		1890	7243	1104	2177	335	47	141	981	.301	753	1005	260	3519	3962	216	.972

DIVISION SERIES RECORD

Year	Team (League)	Pos.	G	AB	R	H	2B	3B	HR	RBI	Avg.	BB	SO	SB	PO	A	E	Avg.
1996—Cleveland (A.L.)	1B-DH	4	15	1	2	0	0	0	1	.133	1	6	0	18	1	0	1.000

ALL-STAR GAME RECORD

NOTES: Named Most Valuable Player (1990).

Year	League	Pos.	AB	R	H	2B	3B	HR	RBI	Avg.	BB	SO	SB	PO	A	E	Avg.
1989—American	2B	3	0	1	0	0	0	0	.333	0	0	0	1	1	0	1.000
1990—American	PH-2B	3	0	1	1	0	0	2	.333	0	0	0	1	0	0	1.000
1991—American								Did not play.									
All-Star Game totals (2 years)		6	0	2	1	0	0	2	.333	0	0	0	2	1	0	1.000

FRANCO, MATT — 3B — METS

PERSONAL: Born August 19, 1969, in Santa Monica, Calif. ... 6-2/210. ... Bats left, throws right. ... Full name: Matthew Neil Franco.
HIGH SCHOOL: Westlake (Calif.) Village.
TRANSACTIONS/CAREER NOTES: Selected by Chicago Cubs organization in seventh round of free-agent draft (June 2, 1987). ... On disabled list (May 6-13, 1994). ... Traded by Cubs to New York Mets organization for a player to be named later (April 8, 1996); Cubs acquired P Chris DeWitt to complete deal (June 11, 1996). ... On Norfolk disabled list (April 8-11, 1996). ... Granted free agency (October 15, 1996). ... Re-signed by Mets organization (November 21, 1997).
STATISTICAL NOTES: Led Midwest League in grounding into double plays with 19 in 1990.

Year	Team (League)	Pos.	G	AB	R	H	2B	3B	HR	RBI	Avg.	BB	SO	SB	PO	A	E	Avg.
1987—Wytheville (App.)	3B-1B-2B	62	202	25	50	10	1	1	21	.248	26	41	4	95	88	23	.888
1988—Wytheville (App.)	3B-1B	20	79	14	31	9	1	0	16	.392	7	5	0	31	24	6	.902
—Geneva (NY-Penn)	3B-1B	44	164	19	42	2	0	3	21	.256	19	13	2	190	43	14	.943
1989—Char., W.Va. (SAL)	3-1-O-S	109	377	42	102	16	1	5	48	.271	57	40	2	113	189	22	.932
—Peoria (Midwest)	3B	16	58	4	13	4	0	0	9	.224	5	5	0	11	32	6	.878
1990—Peoria (Midwest)	1B-3B	123	443	52	125	*33	2	6	65	.282	43	39	4	810	75	18	.980
1991—Win.-Salem (Car.)	1B-3B-SS	104	307	47	66	12	1	4	41	.215	46	42	4	711	53	11	.986
1992—Charlotte (Southern)	3B-1B-OF	108	343	35	97	18	3	2	31	.283	26	46	3	248	69	13	.961
1993—Orlando (South.)	1B-3B	68	237	31	75	20	1	7	37	.316	29	30	3	444	40	4	.992
—Iowa (Am. Assoc.)	1-0-2-P	62	199	24	58	17	4	5	29	.291	16	30	4	450	39	2	.996
1994—Iowa (Am. Assoc.)	1B-3B-OF	128	437	63	121	32	4	11	71	.277	52	66	3	976	81	7	.993
1995—Iowa (Am. Assoc.)	3-1-P-C	121	455	51	128	28	5	6	58	.281	37	44	1	283	179	19	.960
—Chicago (N.L.)	2B-1B-3B	16	17	3	5	1	0	0	1	.294	0	4	0	2	2	0	1.000
1996—Norfolk (Int'l)■	3B-1B	133	508	74	*164	*40	2	7	81	.323	36	55	5	383	167	22	.962
—New York (N.L.)	3B-1B	14	31	3	6	1	0	1	2	.194	1	5	0	15	12	3	.900
1997—Norfolk (Int'l)	OF-1B-3B	7	26	5	7	2	0	0	0	.269	2	2	0	13	4	0	1.000
—New York (N.L.)	3-1-DH-O	112	163	21	45	5	0	5	24	.276	13	23	1	61	52	4	.954
Major league totals (3 years)		142	211	27	56	7	0	6	24	.265	14	32	1	78	66	7	.954

RECORD AS PITCHER

Year	Team (League)	W	L	Pct.	ERA	G	GS	CG	ShO	Sv.	IP	H	R	ER	BB	SO
1993—Iowa (Am. Assoc.)	0	0	...	36.00	1	0	0	0	0	1	5	4	4	1	1
1995—Iowa (Am. Assoc.)	0	0	...	0.00	1	0	0	0	0	1	1	0	0	1	1

FRANKLIN, MICAH — OF

PERSONAL: Born April 25, 1972, in San Francisco. ... 6-0/200. ... Bats both, throws right. ... Full name: Micah Ishanti Franklin.
HIGH SCHOOL: Lincoln (San Francisco).
TRANSACTIONS/CAREER NOTES: Selected by New York Mets organization in third round of free-agent draft (June 4, 1990). ... On Pittsfield suspended list (July 20-24, 1991). ... Released by Pittsfield, Mets organization (March 11, 1992). ... Signed by Cincinnati Reds organization (March 27, 1992). ... Traded by Reds organization to Pittsburgh Pirates organization (October 13, 1994), completing deal in which Pirates traded 1B Brian R. Hunter to Reds for a player to be named later (July 27, 1994). ... Claimed on waivers by Detroit Tigers (November 20, 1995). ... Traded by Tigers with P Brian Maxcy to St. Louis Cardinals for P Tom Urbani and IF Miguel Inzunza (June 7, 1996). ... Granted free agency (October 15, 1997).
STATISTICAL NOTES: Led Pioneer League with 17 caught stealing and tied for lead with three intentional bases on balls received in 1992.

Year Team (League)	Pos.	G	AB	R	H	2B	3B	HR	RBI	Avg.	BB	SO	SB	PO	A	E	Avg.
1990— Kingsport (Appal.)......	2B	39	158	29	41	10	3	7	25	.259	8	44	5	72	98	13	.929
1991— Pittsfield (NYP)	2B	26	94	17	27	4	2	0	14	.287	21	20	12	48	81	14	.902
— Erie (N.Y.-Penn)..........	OF-2B	39	153	28	37	4	0	2	8	.242	25	35	4	45	9	6	.900
1992— Billings (Pioneer)■	OF	*75	251	58	84	13	2	11	60	.335	53	65	18	42	3	2	.957
1993— Char., W.Va. (SAL)......	OF	102	343	56	90	14	4	17	68	.262	47	109	6	134	5	7	.952
— Win.-Salem (Car.)......	OF	20	69	10	16	1	1	3	6	.232	10	19	0	36	1	1	.974
1994— Chattanooga (Sou.)	OF	79	279	46	77	17	0	10	40	.276	33	79	2	112	3	6	.950
— Win.-Salem (Car.)■...	OF	42	150	44	45	7	0	21	44	.300	27	48	7	65	3	4	.944
1995— Calgary (PCL)■..........	OF	110	358	64	105	28	0	21	71	.293	47	95	3	162	3	6	.965
1996— Toledo (Int'l)...........	OF	53	179	32	44	10	1	7	21	.246	27	60	3	93	2	0	1.000
— Louisville (A.A.)■......	OF	86	289	43	67	18	3	15	53	.232	40	71	2	159	11	4	.977
1997— Louisville (A.A.).........	OF	99	326	49	72	14	1	12	48	.221	51	74	2	128	7	3	.978
— St. Louis (N.L.)...........	OF	17	34	6	11	0	0	2	2	.324	3	10	0	13	0	0	1.000
Major league totals (1 year)		17	34	6	11	0	0	2	2	.324	3	10	0	13	0	0	1.000

FRASCATORE, JOHN   P   CARDINALS

PERSONAL: Born February 4, 1970, in Queens, N.Y. ... 6-1/210. ... Throws right, bats right. ... Full name: John Vincent Frascatore. ... Name pronounced FRASS-kuh-TOR-ee.

HIGH SCHOOL: Oceanside (N.Y.).

COLLEGE: C.W. Post (N.Y.).

TRANSACTIONS/CAREER NOTES: Selected by St. Louis Cardinals organization in 24th round of free-agent draft (June 3, 1991).

Year Team (League)	W	L	Pct.	ERA	G	GS	CG	ShO	Sv.	IP	H	R	ER	BB	SO
1991— Hamilton (NYP)	2	7	.222	9.20	30	1	0	0	1	30 1/3	44	38	31	22	18
1992— Savannah (S. Atl.)	5	7	.417	3.84	50	0	0	0	23	58 2/3	49	32	25	29	56
1993— Springfield (Mid.)	7	12	.368	3.78	27	26	2	1	0	157 1/3	157	84	66	33	126
1994— Arkansas (Texas)	7	3	.700	3.10	12	12	4	1	0	78 1/3	76	37	27	15	63
— Louisville (A.A.)	8	3	.727	3.39	13	12	2	1	0	85	82	34	32	33	58
— St. Louis (N.L.)....................	0	1	.000	16.20	1	1	0	0	0	3 1/3	7	6	6	2	2
1995— Louisville (A.A.).................	2	8	.200	3.95	28	10	1	0	5	82	89	54	36	34	55
— St. Louis (N.L.)....................	1	1	.500	4.41	14	4	0	0	0	32 2/3	39	19	16	16	21
1996— Louisville (A.A.).................	6	13	.316	5.18	36	21	3	0	0	156 1/3	180	106	90	42	95
1997— St. Louis (N.L.).................	5	2	.714	2.48	59	0	0	0	0	80	74	25	22	33	58
Major league totals (3 years)......	6	4	.600	3.41	74	5	0	0	0	116	120	50	44	51	81

FREEHILL, MIKE   P   ANGELS

PERSONAL: Born June 1, 1971, in Phoenix. ... 6-3/185. ... Throws right, bats right. ... Full name: Michael Thomas Freehill.

HIGH SCHOOL: Cortez (Phoenix).

JUNIOR COLLEGE: Phoenix Community College.

COLLEGE: San Diego.

TRANSACTIONS/CAREER NOTES: Selected by California Angels organization in 15th round of free-agent draft (June 2, 1994). ... Angels franchise renamed Anaheim Angels for 1997 season.

Year Team (League)	W	L	Pct.	ERA	G	GS	CG	ShO	Sv.	IP	H	R	ER	BB	SO
1994— Boise (Northwest)	3	6	.333	3.20	28	0	0	0	8	45	37	20	16	10	38
1995— Cedar Rapids (Midw.)	4	5	.444	2.62	54	0	0	0	28	55	54	25	16	12	47
1996— Midland (Texas)................	7	6	.538	3.42	47	0	0	0	17	50	49	25	19	21	48
— Vancouver (PCL)................	1	1	.500	9.90	7	0	0	0	0	10	16	11	11	8	5
1997— Midland (Texas)................	0	7	.000	7.05	35	0	0	0	10	37	46	33	29	20	32
— Lake Elsinore (Calif.)	0	1	.000	1.99	21	0	0	0	8	22 2/3	18	7	5	8	20

FREEL, RYAN   SS   BLUE JAYS

PERSONAL: Born March 8, 1976, in Jacksonville. ... 5-10/175. ... Bats right, throws right. ... Full name: Ryan Paul Freel.

HIGH SCHOOL: Englewood (Fla.).

JUNIOR COLLEGE: Tallahassee (Fla.) Community College.

TRANSACTIONS/CAREER NOTES: Selected by Toronto Blue Jays organization in 10th round of free-agent draft (June 1, 1995). ... On Dunedin disabled list (July 2-18 and July 23-30, 1997).

Year Team (League)	Pos.	G	AB	R	H	2B	3B	HR	RBI	Avg.	BB	SO	SB	PO	A	E	Avg.
1995— St. Catharines (NYP) ..	2B	65	243	30	68	10	5	3	29	.280	22	49	12	118	181	*19	.940
1996— Dunedin (Fla. St.)	2B-3B	104	381	64	97	23	3	4	41	.255	33	76	19	193	276	20	.959
1997— Knoxville (Southern) ..	SS	33	94	18	19	1	1	0	4	.202	19	13	5	44	92	13	.913
— Dunedin (Fla. St.)	S-O-2-3	61	181	42	51	8	2	3	17	.282	46	28	24	88	93	18	.910

FRIAS, HANLEY   SS   DIAMONDBACKS

PERSONAL: Born December 5, 1973, in Villa Atiagracia, Dominican Republic. ... 6-0/160. ... Bats both, throws right. ... Full name: Hanley Acevedo Frias.

TRANSACTIONS/CAREER NOTES: Signed as non-drafted free agent by Texas Rangers organization (July 3, 1990). ... Selected by Arizona Diamondbacks in second round (51st pick overall) of expansion draft (November 18, 1997).

STATISTICAL NOTES: Tied for American Association lead in caught stealing with 15 in 1997. ... Led Americam Association shortstops with 623 total chances in 1997.

F

Year Team (League)	Pos.	G	AB	R	H	2B	3B	HR	RBI	Avg.	BB	SO	SB	PO	A	E	Avg.
1991—					Dominican Summer League statistics unavailable.												
1992—GC Rangers (GCL).....	2B-SS	58	205	37	50	9	2	0	28	.244	27	30	28	90	143	11	.955
1993—Char., S.C. (S. Atl.).....	2-O-S-3	132	473	61	109	20	4	4	37	.230	40	108	27	211	249	25	.948
1994—High Desert (Calif.).....	SS	124	452	70	115	17	6	3	59	.254	41	74	37	169	*404	37	.939
1995—Charlotte (Fla. St.)......	SS	33	120	23	40	6	3	0	14	.333	15	11	8	45	106	11	.932
—Tulsa (Texas).............	SS	93	360	44	101	18	4	0	27	.281	45	53	14	137	301	24	.948
1996—Tulsa (Texas).............	SS	134	505	73	145	24	12	2	41	.287	30	73	9	197	*417	23	.964
1997—Oklahoma City (A.A.)..	SS	132	484	64	128	17	4	5	46	.264	56	72	35	*176	*414	33	.947
—Texas (A.L.)................	SS-2B	14	26	4	5	1	0	0	1	.192	1	4	0	12	13	0	1.000
Major league totals (1 year)		14	26	4	5	1	0	0	1	.192	1	4	0	12	13	0	1.000

FRYE, JEFF   2B   RED SOX

PERSONAL: Born August 31, 1966, in Oakland. ... 5-9/165. ... Bats right, throws right. ... Full name: Jeffrey Dustin Frye.
HIGH SCHOOL: Panama (Okla.).
COLLEGE: Southeastern Oklahoma State.
TRANSACTIONS/CAREER NOTES: Selected by Texas Rangers organization in 30th round of free-agent draft (June 1, 1988). ... On Texas disabled list (March 27, 1993-entire season; June 9-24, 1994; and June 3-18 and June 21-July 6, 1995). ... Granted free agency (December 21, 1995). ... Re-signed by Rangers organization (March 25, 1996). ... Released by Rangers organization (June 5, 1996). ... Signed by Boston Red Sox (June 5, 1996).
STATISTICAL NOTES: Led Pioneer League second basemen with 44 double plays in 1988. ... Tied for American Association lead in being hit by pitch with 11 in 1992.

Year Team (League)	Pos.	G	AB	R	H	2B	3B	HR	RBI	Avg.	BB	SO	SB	PO	A	E	Avg.
1988—Butte (Pioneer)..........	2B	54	185	47	53	7	1	0	14	.286	35	25	16	96	149	7	.972
1989—Gastonia (S. Atl.)......	2B	464	85	145	26	3	1	40	*.313	72	53	33	242	340	14	*.977	
1990—Charlotte (Fla. St.)......	2B	131	503	77	137	16	7	0	50	.272	80	66	29	252	350	13	*.979
1991—Tulsa (Texas).............	2B	131	503	92	152	32	11	4	41	.302	71	60	15	262	322	*26	.957
1992—Oklahoma City (A.A.)..	2B	87	337	64	101	26	2	2	28	.300	51	39	11	212	248	7	.985
—Texas (A.L.)................	2B	67	199	24	51	9	1	1	12	.256	16	27	1	120	196	7	.978
1993—						Did not play.											
1994—Oklahoma City (A.A.)..	2B	17	68	7	19	3	0	1	5	.279	6	7	2	28	44	1	.986
—Texas (A.L.)................	2B-DH-3B	57	205	37	67	20	3	0	18	.327	29	23	6	90	136	4	.983
1995—Texas (A.L.)................	2B	90	313	38	87	15	2	4	29	.278	24	45	3	173	248	11	.975
1996—Oklahoma City (A.A.)..	2-O-S-3	49	181	25	43	10	0	1	18	.238	24	21	10	94	148	8	.968
—Boston (A.L.)■..........	2-O-S-DH	105	419	74	120	27	2	4	41	.286	54	57	18	211	317	9	.983
1997—Boston (A.L.).............2-3-O-DH-S-1		127	404	56	126	36	2	3	51	.312	27	44	19	227	264	12	.976
Major league totals (5 years)		446	1540	229	451	107	10	12	151	.293	150	196	47	821	1161	43	.979

FRYMAN, TRAVIS   3B   INDIANS

PERSONAL: Born March 25, 1969, in Lexington, Ky. ... 6-1/194. ... Bats right, throws right. ... Full name: David Travis Fryman.
HIGH SCHOOL: Tate (Gonzalez, Fla.).
TRANSACTIONS/CAREER NOTES: Selected by Detroit Tigers organization in supplemental round ("sandwich pick" between first and second round, 30th pick overall) of free-agent draft (June 2, 1987); pick received as compensation for Philadelphia Phillies signing Type A free-agent C Lance Parrish. ... Traded by Tigers to Arizona Diamondbacks for 3B Joe Randa, P Matt Drews and 3B Gabe Alvarez (November 18, 1997). ... Traded by Diamondbacks with P Tom Martin and cash to Cleveland Indians for 3B Matt Williams (December 1, 1997).
HONORS: Named shortstop on THE SPORTING NEWS A.L. All-Star team (1992). ... Named shortstop on THE SPORTING NEWS A.L. Silver Slugger team (1992). ... Named third baseman on THE SPORTING NEWS A.L. All-Star team (1993).
STATISTICAL NOTES: Led Appalachian League shortstops with 313 total chances in 1987. ... Hit for the cycle (July 28, 1993). ... Tied for A.L. lead with 13 sacrifice flies in 1994. ... Led A.L. third basemen with 313 total chances in 1994 and 337 in 1995. ... Led A.L. third basemen with 38 double plays in 1995. ... Led A.L. third basemen with 133 putouts and .979 fielding percentage in 1996. ... Career major league grand slams: 4.

Year Team (League)	Pos.	G	AB	R	H	2B	3B	HR	RBI	Avg.	BB	SO	SB	PO	A	E	Avg.
1987—Bristol (Appal.)...........	SS	67	248	25	58	9	0	2	20	.234	22	39	6	*103	187	•23	.927
1988—Fayetteville (SAL)	SS-2B	123	411	44	96	17	4	0	47	.234	24	83	16	174	390	32	.946
1989—London (Eastern)	SS	118	426	52	113	*30	1	9	56	.265	19	78	5	192	346	*27	.952
1990—Toledo (Int'l)..............	SS	87	327	38	84	22	2	10	53	.257	17	59	4	128	277	26	.940
—Detroit (A.L.)............	3B-SS-DH	66	232	32	69	11	1	9	27	.297	17	51	3	47	145	14	.932
1991—Detroit (A.L.)............	3B-SS-DH	149	557	65	144	36	3	21	91	.259	40	149	12	153	354	23	.957
1992—Detroit (A.L.)............	SS-3B	161	*659	87	175	31	4	20	96	.266	45	144	8	220	489	22	.970
1993—Detroit (A.L.)............	SS-3B-DH	151	607	98	182	37	5	22	97	.300	77	128	9	169	382	23	.960
1994—Detroit (A.L.)............	3B	114	*464	66	122	34	5	18	85	.263	45	*128	2	78	*221	14	.955
1995—Detroit (A.L.)............	3B	144	567	79	156	21	5	15	81	.275	63	100	4	107	*337	14	.969
1996—Detroit (A.L.)............	3B-SS	157	616	90	165	32	3	22	100	.268	57	118	4	149	†354	10	†.981
1997—Detroit (A.L.)............	3B	154	595	90	163	27	3	22	102	.274	46	113	16	•126	312	10	*.978
Major league totals (8 years)		1096	4297	607	1176	229	29	149	679	.274	390	931	58	1049	2594	130	.966

ALL-STAR GAME RECORD

Year League	Pos.	AB	R	H	2B	3B	HR	RBI	Avg.	BB	SO	SB	PO	A	E	Avg.
1992—American	SS	1	1	1	0	0	0	1	1.000	1	0	0	1	3	0	1.000
1993—American	SS	1	0	0	0	0	0	0	.000	0	0	0	1	1	0	1.000
1994—American	PH	1	0	0	0	0	0	0	.000	0	1	0	...	...	...	...
1996—American	PH-3B	1	0	0	0	0	0	0	.000	0	1	0	0	1	0	1.000
All-Star Game totals (4 years)		4	1	1	0	0	0	1	.250	1	2	0	1	5	0	1.000

F

FULLMER, BRAD   1B   EXPOS

PERSONAL: Born January 17, 1975, in Chatsworth, Calif. ... 6-1/190. ... Bats left, throws right. ... Full name: Bradley Ryan Fullmer.
HIGH SCHOOL: Montclair Prep (Van Nuys, Calif.).
TRANSACTIONS/CAREER NOTES: Selected by Montreal Expos organization in second round of free-agent draft (June 3, 1993). ... On disabled list (June 20-September 26, 1994).
STATISTICAL NOTES: Hit home run in first major league at-bat (September 2, 1997).

| | | | | | | | BATTING | | | | | | | FIELDING | | |
Year Team (League)	Pos.	G	AB	R	H	2B	3B	HR	RBI	Avg.	BB	SO	SB	PO	A	E	Avg.
1994—							Did not play.										
1995— Albany (S. Atl.).........	3B-1B	123	468	69	•151	38	4	8	67	.323	36	33	10	269	66	30	.918
1996— W.P. Beach (FSL)........	OF-1B	102	380	52	115	29	1	5	63	.303	32	43	4	197	10	7	.967
— Harrisburg (Eastern) ..	OF-1B	24	98	11	27	4	1	4	14	.276	3	8	0	43	1	2	.957
1997— Harrisburg (Eastern) ...	1B-OF	94	357	60	111	24	2	19	62	.311	30	25	6	538	41	6	.990
— Ottawa (Int'l)............	1B-OF	24	91	13	27	7	0	3	17	.297	3	10	1	173	12	1	.995
— Montreal (N.L.)...........	1B-OF	19	40	4	12	2	0	3	8	.300	2	7	0	50	7	2	.966
Major league totals (1 year)		19	40	4	12	2	0	3	8	.300	2	7	0	50	7	2	.966

FUSSELL, CHRIS   P   ORIOLES

PERSONAL: Born May 19, 1976, in Oregon, Ohio. ... 6-2/185. ... Throws right, bats right. ... Full name: Christopher Wren Fussell.
HIGH SCHOOL: Clay (Ohio).
TRANSACTIONS/CAREER NOTES: Selected by Baltimore Orioles organization in ninth round of free-agent draft (June 2, 1994). ... On disabled list (July 13, 1996-remainder of season).

Year Team (League)	W	L	Pct.	ERA	G	GS	CG	ShO	Sv.	IP	H	R	ER	BB	SO
1994— GC Orioles (GCL)...............	2	3	.400	4.15	14	8	0	0	0	56 1/3	53	30	26	24	65
1995— Bluefield (Appalachian)	9	1	.900	2.19	12	12	1	1	0	65 2/3	37	18	16	32	98
1996— Frederick (Carolina)..........	5	2	.714	2.81	15	14	1	1	0	86 1/3	71	36	27	44	94
1997— Bowie (Eastern)................	1	8	.111	7.11	19	18	0	0	0	82 1/3	102	71	65	58	71
— Frederick (Carolina)..........	3	3	.500	3.96	9	9	1	1	0	50	42	23	22	31	54

GAETTI, GARY   3B   CARDINALS

PERSONAL: Born August 19, 1958, in Centralia, Ill. ... 6-0/205. ... Bats right, throws right. ... Full name: Gary Joseph Gaetti. ... Name pronounced guy-ETT-ee.
HIGH SCHOOL: Centralia (Ill.).
JUNIOR COLLEGE: Lake Land College (Ill.).
COLLEGE: Northwest Missouri State.
TRANSACTIONS/CAREER NOTES: Selected by St. Louis Cardinals organization in fourth round of free-agent draft (January 10, 1978); did not sign. ... Selected by Chicago White Sox organization in secondary phase of free-agent draft (June 6, 1978); did not sign. ... Selected by Minnesota Twins organization in secondary phase of free-agent draft (June 5, 1979). ... Granted free agency (November 9, 1987). ... Re-signed by Twins (January 7, 1988). ... On disabled list (August 21-September 5, 1988 and August 26-September 13, 1989). ... Granted free agency (December 7, 1990). ... Signed by California Angels (January 23, 1991). ... Released by Angels (June 3, 1993). ... Signed by Kansas City Royals (June 19, 1993). ... Granted free agency (October 25, 1993). ... Re-signed by Royals organization (December 16, 1993). ... On disabled list (May 5-20, 1994). ... Granted free agency (October 28, 1994). ... Re-signed by Omaha, Royals organization (December 20, 1994). ... Granted free agency (November 3, 1995). ... Signed by Cardinals (December 18, 1995). ... On disabled list (April 28-May 14, 1996). ... Granted free agency (October 27, 1997). ... Re-signed by Cardinals (December 6, 1997).
RECORDS: Shares major league rookie-season record for most sacrifice flies—13 (1982).
HONORS: Won A.L. Gold Glove at third base (1986-89). ... Named third baseman on THE SPORTING NEWS A.L. Silver Slugger team (1995).
STATISTICAL NOTES: Tied for Appalachian League lead in errors by third baseman with 18 in 1979. ... Led Midwest League third basemen with 492 total chances and 35 double plays in 1980. ... Led Southern League third basemen with 122 putouts, 281 assists, 32 errors and 435 total chances in 1981. ... Hit home run in first major-league at-bat (September 20, 1981). ... Led A.L. with 13 sacrifice flies in 1982. ... Led A.L. third basemen with 131 putouts in 1983, 142 in 1984 and 146 in 1985. ... Led A.L. third basemen with 46 double plays in 1983, 36 in 1986 and 1990 and 39 in 1991. ... Led A.L. third basemen with 496 total chances in 1984, 473 in 1986, 438 in 1990 and 481 in 1991. ... Led A.L. third basemen with 334 assists in both 1984 and 1986 and 318 in 1990. ... Tied for A.L. lead in errors by third basemen with 20 in 1984. ... Led A.L. in grounding into double plays with 25 in 1987. ... Led A.L. third basemen with .982 fielding percentage in 1994. ... Led N.L. third basemen with .978 fielding percentage in 1997. ... Career major league grand slams: 9.

| | | | | | | | BATTING | | | | | | | FIELDING | | |
Year Team (League)	Pos.	G	AB	R	H	2B	3B	HR	RBI	Avg.	BB	SO	SB	PO	A	E	Avg.
1979— Elizabethton (App.).....	3B-SS	66	230	50	59	15	2	14	42	.257	43	40	6	70	134	‡21	.907
1980— Wis. Rap. (Mid.).........	3B	138	503	77	134	27	3	*22	82	.266	67	120	24	*94	*363	•35	.929
1981— Orlando (South.).........	3B-1B	137	495	92	137	19	2	30	93	.277	58	105	15	†143	†283	†32	.930
— Minnesota (A.L.).........	3B-DH	9	26	4	5	0	0	2	3	.192	0	6	0	5	17	0	1.000
1982— Minnesota (A.L.).........	3B-SS-DH	145	508	59	117	25	4	25	84	.230	37	107	0	106	291	17	.959
1983— Minnesota (A.L.).........	3B-SS-DH	157	584	81	143	30	3	21	78	.245	54	121	7	†131	361	17	.967
1984— Minnesota (A.L.).........	3B-OF-SS	•162	588	55	154	29	4	5	65	.262	44	81	11	†163	†335	‡21	.960
1985— Minnesota (A.L.).........	3-0-1-DH	160	560	71	138	31	0	20	63	.246	37	89	13	†162	316	18	.964
1986— Minnesota (A.L.).........	3-S-O-2	157	596	91	171	34	1	34	108	.287	52	108	14	120	†335	21	.956
1987— Minnesota (A.L.).........	3B-DH	154	584	95	150	36	2	31	109	.257	37	92	10	•134	261	11	.973
1988— Minnesota (A.L.).........	3B-DH-SS	133	468	66	141	29	2	28	88	.301	36	85	7	105	191	7	.977
1989— Minnesota (A.L.).........	3B-DH-1B	130	498	63	125	11	4	19	75	.251	25	87	6	115	253	10	.974
1990— Minnesota (A.L.).........	3B-SS	154	577	61	132	27	5	16	85	.229	36	101	6	125	†319	18	.961
1991— California (A.L.)■......	3B	152	586	58	144	22	1	18	66	.246	33	104	5	111	*353	17	.965
1992— California (A.L.)........	3B-1B-DH	130	456	41	103	13	2	12	48	.226	21	79	3	423	196	22	.966
1993— California (A.L.)........	3B-1B-DH	20	50	3	9	2	0	0	4	.180	5	12	1	38	7	1	.978
— Kansas City (A.L.)■■...	3B-1B-DH	82	281	37	72	18	1	14	46	.256	16	75	0	147	146	6	.980
1994— Kansas City (A.L.)	3B-1B	90	327	53	94	15	3	12	57	.287	19	63	0	99	166	4	†.985

F
G

Year	Team (League)	Pos.	G	AB	R	H	2B	3B	HR	RBI	Avg.	BB	SO	SB	PO	A	E	Avg.
						BATTING									**FIELDING**			
1995—Kansas City (A.L.)	3B-1B-DH	137	514	76	134	27	0	35	96	.261	47	91	3	182	228	16	.962
1996—St. Louis (N.L.)■	3B-1B	141	522	71	143	27	4	23	80	.274	35	97	2	148	231	10	.974
1997—St. Louis (N.L.)	3B-1B-P	148	502	63	126	24	1	17	69	.251	36	88	7	133	250	7	†.982
American League totals (15 years)		1972	7203	914	1832	349	32	292	1075	.254	499	1301	86	2166	3775	206	.966
National League totals (2 years)		289	1024	134	269	51	5	40	149	.263	71	185	9	281	481	17	.978
Major league totals (17 years)		2261	8227	1048	2101	400	37	332	1224	.255	570	1486	95	2447	4256	223	.968

DIVISION SERIES RECORD

Year	Team (League)	Pos.	G	AB	R	H	2B	3B	HR	RBI	Avg.	BB	SO	SB	PO	A	E	Avg.
						BATTING									**FIELDING**			
1996—St. Louis (N.L.)	3B	3	11	1	1	0	0	1	3	.091	0	3	0	1	3	0	1.000

CHAMPIONSHIP SERIES RECORD

NOTES: Hit home run in first at-bat (October 7, 1987). ... Named A.L. Championship Series Most Valuable Player (1987).

Year	Team (League)	Pos.	G	AB	R	H	2B	3B	HR	RBI	Avg.	BB	SO	SB	PO	A	E	Avg.
						BATTING									**FIELDING**			
1987—Minnesota (A.L.)	3B	5	20	5	6	1	0	2	5	.300	1	3	0	8	7	0	1.000
1996—St. Louis (N.L.)	3B	7	24	1	7	0	0	1	4	.292	1	5	0	4	12	0	1.000
Championship series totals (2 years)		12	44	6	13	1	0	3	9	.295	2	8	0	12	19	0	1.000

WORLD SERIES RECORD

NOTES: Member of World Series championship team (1987).

Year	Team (League)	Pos.	G	AB	R	H	2B	3B	HR	RBI	Avg.	BB	SO	SB	PO	A	E	Avg.
						BATTING									**FIELDING**			
1987—Minnesota (A.L.)	3B	7	27	4	7	2	1	1	4	.259	2	5	2	6	15	0	1.000

ALL-STAR GAME RECORD

Year	League	Pos.	AB	R	H	2B	3B	HR	RBI	Avg.	BB	SO	SB	PO	A	E	Avg.
						BATTING								**FIELDING**			
1988—American	PH	1	0	0	0	0	0	0	.000	0	0	0	...	...	...	...
1989—American	3B	1	0	0	0	0	0	0	.000	0	1	0	1	0	0	1.000
All-Star Game totals (2 years)		2	0	0	0	0	0	0	.000	0	1	0	1	0	0	1.000

RECORD AS PITCHER

Year	Team (League)	W	L	Pct.	ERA	G	GS	CG	ShO	Sv.	IP	H	R	ER	BB	SO
1997—St. Louis (N.L.)	0	0	...	0.00	1	0	0	0	0	1/3	1	0	0	0	0

GAGNE, GREG — SS

PERSONAL: Born November 12, 1961, in Fall River, Mass. ... 5-11/180. ... Bats right, throws right. ... Full name: Gregory Carpenter Gagne. ... Name pronounced GAG-nee.

HIGH SCHOOL: Somerset (Mass.).

TRANSACTIONS/CAREER NOTES: On disabled list (September 4-22, 1980). ... Traded by Yankees organization with P Ron Davis, P Paul Boris and cash to Minnesota Twins for SS Roy Smalley (April 10, 1982). ... On Toledo disabled list (June 13-July 18, 1984). ... On disabled list (August 10-September 1, 1985). ... Granted free agency (October 27, 1992). ... Signed by Kansas City Royals (December 8, 1992). ... On disabled list (June 22-July 13, 1995). ... Granted free agency (November 7, 1995). ... Signed by Los Angeles Dodgers (November 30, 1995). ... On Los Angeles disabled list (May 18-June 20, 1996); included rehabilitation assignment to Albuquerque (June 16-20). ... Granted free agency (October 9, 1997).

RECORDS: Shares major league single-game record for most inside-the-park home runs—2 (October 4, 1986).

STATISTICAL NOTES: Led International League shortstops with 599 total chances in 1983. ... Led A.L. shortstops with 26 errors in 1986. ... Led A.L. in caught stealing with 17 in 1994. ... Career major league grand slams: 2.

Year	Team (League)	Pos.	G	AB	R	H	2B	3B	HR	RBI	Avg.	BB	SO	SB	PO	A	E	Avg.
							BATTING									**FIELDING**			
1979—Paintsville (Appal.)	SS	41	106	10	19	2	3	0	7	.179	13	25	2	28	62	14	.865
1980—Greensboro (S. Atl.)	SS-3B-2B	98	337	39	91	20	5	3	32	.270	22	46	8	133	233	35	.913
1981—Greensboro (S. Atl.)	2B-SS-3B	104	364	71	108	21	3	9	48	.297	49	72	14	172	280	25	.948
1982—Fort Lauder. (FSL)	SS	1	3	0	1	0	0	0	0	.333	1	1	0	3	5	0	1.000
—Orlando (South.)■	SS-2B	136	504	73	117	23	5	11	57	.232	57	100	8	185	403	39	.938
1983—Toledo (Int'l)	SS	119	392	61	100	22	4	17	66	.255	36	70	6	201	*364	*34	.943
—Minnesota (A.L.)	SS	10	27	2	3	1	0	0	3	.111	0	6	0	10	14	2	.923
1984—Toledo (Int'l)	3B-SS-2B	70	236	31	66	7	2	9	27	.280	34	52	2	58	168	20	.919
—Minnesota (A.L.)	PR-PH	2	1	0	0	0	0	0	0	.000	0	0	0	...	...	...	...
1985—Minnesota (A.L.)	SS-DH	114	293	37	66	15	3	2	23	.225	20	57	10	149	269	14	.968
1986—Minnesota (A.L.)	SS-2B	156	472	63	118	22	6	12	54	.250	30	108	12	228	381	†26	.959
1987—Minnesota (A.L.)	S-O-2-DH	137	437	68	116	28	7	10	40	.265	25	84	6	196	391	18	.970
1988—Minnesota (A.L.)	S-O-2-3	149	461	70	109	20	6	14	48	.236	27	110	15	202	373	18	.970
1989—Minnesota (A.L.)	SS-OF	149	460	69	125	29	7	9	48	.272	17	80	11	218	389	18	.971
1990—Minnesota (A.L.)	SS-OF	138	388	38	91	22	3	7	38	.235	24	76	8	184	377	14	.976
1991—Minnesota (A.L.)	SS-3B-DH	139	408	52	108	23	3	8	42	.265	26	72	11	181	377	9	.984
1992—Minnesota (A.L.)	SS	146	439	53	108	23	0	7	39	.246	19	83	6	208	438	18	.973
1993—Kansas City (A.L.)■	SS	159	540	66	151	32	3	10	57	.280	33	93	10	266	451	10	*.986
1994—Kansas City (A.L.)	SS	107	375	39	97	23	3	7	51	.259	27	79	10	*189	323	12	.977
1995—Kansas City (A.L.)	SS-DH	120	430	58	110	25	4	6	49	.256	38	60	3	174	389	•18	.969
1996—Los Angeles (N.L.)■	SS	128	428	48	109	13	2	10	55	.255	50	93	4	184	404	21	.966
—Albuquerque (PCL)	SS	4	11	1	3	1	0	0	1	.273	1	1	0	7	9	0	1.000
1997—Los Angeles (N.L.)	SS	144	514	49	129	20	3	9	57	.251	31	120	2	175	357	16	.971
American League totals (13 years)		1526	4731	615	1202	263	45	92	492	.254	286	908	102	2205	4172	177	.973
National League totals (2 years)		272	942	97	238	33	5	19	112	.253	81	213	6	359	761	37	.968
Major league totals (15 years)		1798	5673	712	1440	296	50	111	604	.254	367	1121	108	2564	4933	214	.972

G

DIVISION SERIES RECORD

					BATTING										FIELDING			
Year	Team (League)	Pos.	G	AB	R	H	2B	3B	HR	RBI	Avg.	BB	SO	SB	PO	A	E	Avg.
1996— Los Angeles (N.L.)		SS	3	11	2	3	1	0	0	0	.273	0	5	0	3	9	0	1.000

CHAMPIONSHIP SERIES RECORD

					BATTING										FIELDING			
Year	Team (League)	Pos.	G	AB	R	H	2B	3B	HR	RBI	Avg.	BB	SO	SB	PO	A	E	Avg.
1987— Minnesota (A.L.)		SS	5	18	5	5	3	0	2	3	.278	3	4	0	9	13	2	.917
1991— Minnesota (A.L.)		SS	5	17	1	4	0	0	0	1	.235	1	5	0	9	9	2	.900
Championship series totals (2 years)			10	35	6	9	3	0	2	4	.257	4	9	0	18	22	4	.909

RECORDS: Shares record for most at-bats in one inning—2 (October 18, 1987, fourth inning).
NOTES: Member of World Series championship teams (1987 and 1991).

WORLD SERIES RECORD

					BATTING										FIELDING			
Year	Team (League)	Pos.	G	AB	R	H	2B	3B	HR	RBI	Avg.	BB	SO	SB	PO	A	E	Avg.
1987— Minnesota (A.L.)		SS	7	30	5	6	1	0	1	3	.200	1	6	0	6	20	2	.929
1991— Minnesota (A.L.)		SS	7	24	1	4	1	0	1	3	.167	0	7	0	13	24	0	1.000
World Series totals (2 years)			14	54	6	10	2	0	2	6	.185	1	13	0	19	44	2	.969

GAILLARD, EDDIE P TIGERS

PERSONAL: Born August 13, 1970, in Camden, N.J. ... 6-1/180. ... Throws right, bats right. ... Full name: Julian Edward Gaillard III. ... Name pronounced GAY-lard.
HIGH SCHOOL: Forest Hill (West Palm Beach, Fla.).
JUNIOR COLLEGE: Palm Beach Community College (Fla.).
COLLEGE: Florida Southern.
TRANSACTIONS/CAREER NOTES: Selected by Detroit Tigers organization in 13th round of free-agent draft (June 3, 1993).

Year	Team (League)	W	L	Pct.	ERA	G	GS	CG	ShO	Sv.	IP	H	R	ER	BB	SO
1993— Niagara Falls (NYP)		1	2	.333	3.68	3	3	0	0	0	14 2/3	15	6	6	4	12
— Fayetteville (S. Atl.)		5	2	.714	4.09	11	11	0	0	0	61 2/3	64	30	28	20	41
1994— Lakeland (Fla. St.)		6	1	.857	2.84	30	9	0	0	2	92	82	37	29	29	51
1995— Jacksonville (Southern)......		0	1	.000	5.63	8	0	0	0	0	8	11	5	5	5	4
— Lakeland (Fla. St.)		2	4	.333	1.31	43	0	0	0	25	55	48	13	8	18	51
1996— Jacksonville (Southern)......		9	6	.600	3.38	56	0	0	0	1	88	82	40	33	50	76
1997— Toledo (Int'l)		1	4	.200	4.25	55	0	0	0	*28	53	52	27	25	24	54
— Detroit (A.L.)		1	0	1.000	5.31	16	0	0	0	1	20 1/3	16	12	12	10	12
Major league totals (1 year)........		1	0	1.000	5.31	16	0	0	0	1	20 1/3	16	12	12	10	12

GALARRAGA, ANDRES 1B BRAVES

PERSONAL: Born June 18, 1961, in Caracas, Venezuela. ... 6-3/235. ... Bats right, throws right. ... Full name: Andres Jose Galarraga. ... Name pronounced GAHL-ah-RAH-guh.
HIGH SCHOOL: Enrique Felmi (Caracas, Venezuela).
TRANSACTIONS/CAREER NOTES: Signed as non-drafted free agent by Montreal Expos organization (January 19, 1979). ... On disabled list (July 10-August 19 and August 20-September 4, 1986; and May 26-July 4, 1991). ... Traded by Expos to St. Louis Cardinals for P Ken Hill (November 25, 1991). ... On St. Louis disabled list (April 8-May 22, 1992); included rehabilitation assignment to Louisville (May 13-22). ... Granted free agency (October 27, 1992). ... Signed by Colorado Rockies (November 16, 1992). ... On disabled list (May 10-27 and July 25-August 21, 1993). ... Granted free agency (October 25, 1993). ... Re-signed by Rockies (December 6, 1993). ... On disabled list (July 29, 1994-remainder of season). ... On suspended list (August 3-5, 1997). ... Granted free agency (October 27, 1997). ... Signed by Atlanta Braves (November 20, 1997).
HONORS: Named Southern League Most Valuable Player (1984). ... Named first baseman on THE SPORTING NEWS N.L. Silver Slugger team (1988 and 1996). ... Won N.L. Gold Glove at first base (1989-90). ... Named N.L. Comeback Player of the Year by THE SPORTING NEWS (1993).
STATISTICAL NOTES: Led Southern League with 271 total bases, .508 slugging percentage and 10 intentional bases on balls received and tied for lead in being hit by pitch with nine in 1984. ... Led Southern League first basemen with 1,428 total chances and 130 double plays in 1984. ... Led N.L. in being hit by pitch with 10 in 1987 and tied for lead with 13 in 1989. ... Led N.L. with 329 total bases in 1988. ... Hit three home runs in one game (June 25, 1995). ... Collected six hits in one game (July 3, 1995). ... Led N.L. first basemen with 1,432 total chances and 129 double plays in 1995. ... Led N.L. first basemen with 1,528 putouts, 1,658 total chances and 154 double plays in 1996. ... Led N.L. first basemen with 1,590 total chances and 176 double plays in 1997. ... Career major league grand slams: 9.
MISCELLANEOUS: Holds Colorado Rockies all-time records for most home runs (172), most runs batted in (575), highest career batting average (.316) and most runs (476).

G

					BATTING										FIELDING			
Year	Team (League)	Pos.	G	AB	R	H	2B	3B	HR	RBI	Avg.	BB	SO	SB	PO	A	E	Avg.
1979— W.P. Beach (FSL)........		1B	7	23	3	3	0	0	0	1	.130	2	11	0	2	1	0	1.000
— Calgary (Pioneer)		1B-3B-C	42	112	14	24	3	1	4	16	.214	9	42	1	187	21	5	.977
1980— Calgary (Pioneer)		1-3-C-O	59	190	27	50	11	4	4	22	.263	7	55	3	287	52	21	.942
1981— Jamestown (NYP)		C-1-O-3	47	154	24	40	5	4	6	26	.260	15	44	0	154	15	0	1.000
1982— W.P. Beach (FSL)........		1B-OF	105	338	39	95	20	2	14	51	.281	34	77	2	462	36	9	.982
1983— W.P. Beach (FSL)........		1B-OF-3B	104	401	55	116	18	3	10	66	.289	33	68	7	861	77	13	.986
1984— Jacksonville (South.)..		1B	143	533	81	154	28	4	27	87	.289	59	122	2	*1302	*110	16	.989
1985— Indianapolis (A.A.)......		1B-OF	121	439	*75	118	15	8	25	87	.269	45	103	9	930	63	14	.986
— Montreal (N.L.)............		1B	24	75	9	14	1	0	2	4	.187	3	18	1	173	22	1	.995
1986— Montreal (N.L.)............		1B	105	321	39	87	13	0	10	42	.271	30	79	6	805	40	4	.995
1987— Montreal (N.L.)............		1B	147	551	72	168	40	3	13	90	.305	41	127	7	*1300	103	10	.993
1988— Montreal (N.L.)............		1B	157	609	99	*184	*42	8	29	92	.302	39	*153	13	1464	103	15	.991
1989— Montreal (N.L.)............		1B	152	572	76	147	30	1	23	85	.257	48	*158	12	1335	91	11	.992
1990— Montreal (N.L.)............		1B	155	579	65	148	29	0	20	87	.256	40	*169	10	1300	94	10	.993

Year— Team (League)	Pos.	G	AB	R	H	2B	3B	HR	RBI	Avg.	BB	SO	SB	PO	A	E	Avg.
1991— Montreal (N.L.)...........	1B	107	375	34	82	13	2	9	33	.219	23	86	5	887	80	9	.991
1992— St. Louis (N.L.)■	1B	95	325	38	79	14	2	10	39	.243	11	69	5	777	62	8	.991
— Louisville (A.A.)	1B	11	34	3	6	0	1	2	3	.176	0	8	1	61	7	2	.971
1993— Colorado (N.L.)■	1B	120	470	71	174	35	4	22	98	*.370	24	73	2	1018	103	11	.990
1994— Colorado (N.L.)	1B	103	417	77	133	21	0	31	85	.319	19	93	8	953	65	8	.992
1995— Colorado (N.L.)	1B	143	554	89	155	29	3	31	106	.280	32	*146	12	*1299	120	*13	.991
1996— Colorado (N.L.)	1B-3B	159	626	119	190	39	3	*47	*150	.304	40	157	18	*1528	116	14	.992
1997— Colorado (N.L.)	1B	154	600	120	191	31	3	41	*140	.318	54	141	15	*1458	117	*15	.991
Major league totals (13 years)		1621	6074	908	1752	337	29	268	1051	.288	404	1469	114	14297	1116	129	.992

DIVISION SERIES RECORD

Year— Team (League)	Pos.	G	AB	R	H	2B	3B	HR	RBI	Avg.	BB	SO	SB	PO	A	E	Avg.
1995— Colorado (N.L.)	1B	4	18	1	5	1	0	0	2	.278	0	6	0	41	2	0	1.000

ALL-STAR GAME RECORD

Year— League	Pos.	AB	R	H	2B	3B	HR	RBI	Avg.	BB	SO	SB	PO	A	E	Avg.
1988— National	1B	2	0	0	0	0	0	0	.000	0	1	0	6	0	0	1.000
1993— National	1B	1	0	0	0	0	0	0	.000	0	0	0	0	0	0	...
1997— National	PH-DH	1	0	0	0	0	0	0	.000	0	1	0	0	0	0	...
All-Star Game totals (3 years)		4	0	0	0	0	0	0	.000	0	2	0	6	0	0	1.000

GALLEGO, MIKE   IF

PERSONAL: Born October 31, 1960, in Whittier, Calif. ... 5-8/175. ... Bats right, throws right. ... Full name: Michael Anthony Gallego. ... Name pronounced guy-YAY-go.

HIGH SCHOOL: St. Paul (Sante Fe Springs, Calif.).

COLLEGE: UCLA.

TRANSACTIONS/CAREER NOTES: Selected by Oakland Athletics organization in second round of free-agent draft (June 8, 1981); pick received as compensation for Chicago White Sox signing free-agent C/1B Jim Essian. ... On Tacoma temporarily inactive list (April 10-May 20, 1983). ... On Oakland disabled list (June 13-July 29, 1987). ... Granted free agency (October 28, 1991). ... Signed by New York Yankees (January 9, 1992). ... On New York disabled list (March 28-May 17, 1992); included rehabilitation assignment to Fort Lauderdale (May 14-17). ... On New York disabled list (July 8-September 18, 1992; June 11-26, 1993 and June 29-July 19, 1994). ... Granted free agency (October 24, 1994). ... Signed by A's (April 12, 1995). ... On Oakland disabled list (May 18-August 10, 1995); included rehabilitation assignment to Edmonton (August 3-10). ... Granted free agency (November 1, 1995). ... Signed by St. Louis Cardinals (January 11, 1996). ... On St. Louis disabled list (March 22-April 12, 1996); included rehabilitation assignment to St. Petersburg (June 24-July 11). ... Released by Cardinals (July 29, 1997).

STATISTICAL NOTES: Led Pacific Coast League in being hit by pitch with eight in 1986. ... Tied for A.L. lead with 17 sacrifice hits in 1990. ... Career major league grand slams: 1.

Year— Team (League)	Pos.	G	AB	R	H	2B	3B	HR	RBI	Avg.	BB	SO	SB	PO	A	E	Avg.
1981— Modesto (California) ..	2B	60	202	38	55	9	3	0	23	.272	31	31	9	127	161	13	.957
1982— West Haven (East.).......	2B-SS	54	139	17	25	1	0	0	5	.180	13	25	3	85	111	4	.980
— Tacoma (PCL)	2B-3B-SS	44	136	12	30	3	1	0	11	.221	7	12	4	73	111	8	.958
1983— Tacoma (PCL)	2B	2	2	0	0	0	0	0	0	.000	0	1	0	0	1	0	1.000
— Alb./Colon. (Eastern) ..	2B-SS-3B	90	274	31	61	6	0	0	18	.223	43	25	3	184	260	4	.991
1984— Tacoma (PCL)	2B-SS-3B	101	288	29	70	8	1	0	18	.243	27	39	7	167	231	13	.968
1985— Oakland (A.L.)	2B-SS-3B	76	77	13	16	5	1	1	9	.208	12	14	1	57	94	1	.993
— Modesto (California) ..	2B-SS-3B	6	25	1	5	1	0	0	2	.200	2	8	1	12	11	1	.958
1986— Tacoma (PCL)	SS-3B-2B	132	443	58	122	16	5	4	46	.275	39	58	3	197	417	23	.964
— Oakland (A.L.)	2B-3B-SS	20	37	2	10	2	0	0	4	.270	1	6	0	24	51	1	.987
1987— Tacoma (PCL)	2B	10	41	6	11	0	2	0	6	.268	10	7	1	15	25	1	.976
— Oakland (A.L.)	2B-3B-SS	72	124	18	31	6	0	2	14	.250	12	21	0	75	122	8	.961
1988— Oakland (A.L.)	2B-SS-3B	129	277	38	58	8	0	2	20	.209	34	53	2	155	254	8	.981
1989— Oakland (A.L.)	S-2-3-DH	133	357	45	90	14	2	3	30	.252	35	43	7	211	363	19	.968
1990— Oakland (A.L.) 2-S-3-O-DH		140	389	36	80	13	2	3	34	.206	35	50	5	207	379	13	.978
1991— Oakland (A.L.)	2B-SS	159	482	67	119	15	4	12	49	.247	67	84	6	283	446	12	.984
1992— Fort Lauderdale (FSL)■	SS	3	10	0	2	1	0	0	2	.200	1	4	1	3	5	0	1.000
— New York (A.L.)..........	2B-SS	53	173	24	44	7	1	3	14	.254	20	22	0	112	153	6	.978
1993— New York (A.L.)	S-2-3-DH	119	403	63	114	20	1	10	54	.283	50	65	3	169	368	13	.976
1994— New York (A.L.)	SS-2B	89	306	39	73	17	1	6	41	.239	38	46	0	143	311	11	.976
1995— Oakland (A.L.)■	2B-SS-3B	43	120	11	28	0	0	6	8	.233	9	24	0	46	90	5	.965
— Edmonton (PCL)	SS	6	18	1	5	1	0	0	1	.278	0	3	0	8	8	0	1.000
1996— St. Petersburg (FSL)■	2B-3B-SS	14	51	7	15	0	0	0	5	.294	7	4	0	19	44	2	.969
— St. Louis (N.L.)...........	2B-3B-SS	51	143	12	30	2	0	4	5	.210	12	31	0	90	126	3	.986
1997— Louisville (PCL)..........	SS	6	18	0	5	1	0	0	1	.278	3	5	1	8	13	1	.955
— St. Louis (N.L.)...........	2B-3B-SS	27	43	6	7	2	0	0	1	.163	1	6	0	15	41	1	.982
American League totals (11 years)		1033	2745	356	663	107	12	42	277	.242	313	428	24	1482	2631	97	.977
National League totals (2 years)		78	186	18	37	4	0	4	5	.199	13	37	0	105	167	4	.986
Major league totals (13 years)		1111	2931	374	700	111	12	42	282	.239	326	465	24	1587	2798	101	.977

DIVISION SERIES RECORD

Year— Team (League)	Pos.	G	AB	R	H	2B	3B	HR	RBI	Avg.	BB	SO	SB	PO	A	E	Avg.
1996— St. Louis (N.L.)...........	2B-3B	2	1	0	0	0	0	0	0	.000	0	1	0	0	0	0	...

CHAMPIONSHIP SERIES RECORD

RECORDS: Shares A.L. single-series record for most sacrifice hits—2 (1989).

G

Year Team (League)	Pos.	G	AB	R	H	2B	3B	HR	RBI	Avg.	BB	SO	SB	PO	A	E	Avg.
1988—Oakland (A.L.)............	2B	4	12	1	1	0	0	0	0	.083	0	3	0	7	6	0	1.000
1989—Oakland (A.L.)............	SS-2B	4	11	3	3	1	0	0	1	.273	0	2	0	6	14	0	1.000
1990—Oakland (A.L.)............	SS-2B	4	10	1	4	1	0	0	2	.400	1	1	0	8	9	0	1.000
1996—St. Louis (N.L.)...........	3B-2B	7	14	1	2	0	0	0	0	.143	1	3	0	8	12	1	.952
Championship series totals (4 years)		19	47	6	10	2	0	0	3	.213	2	9	0	29	41	1	.986

WORLD SERIES RECORD

NOTES: Member of World Series championship team (1989).

Year Team (League)	Pos.	G	AB	R	H	2B	3B	HR	RBI	Avg.	BB	SO	SB	PO	A	E	Avg.
1988—Oakland (A.L.)............	PR-2B	1	0	0	0	0	0	0	0	...	0	0	0	0	0	0	...
1989—Oakland (A.L.)............	2B-PH-3B	2	1	0	0	0	0	0	0	.000	0	0	0	0	0	0	...
1990—Oakland (A.L.)............	SS	4	11	0	1	0	0	0	1	.091	1	3	1	7	10	1	.944
World Series totals (3 years)		7	12	0	1	0	0	0	1	.083	1	3	1	7	10	1	.944

GANDARILLAS, GUS   P   TWINS

PERSONAL: Born July 19, 1971, in Coral Gables, Fla. ... 6-0/183. ... Throws right, bats right. ... Full name: Gustavo Gandarillas. ... Name pronounced gan-dar-REE-yas..
HIGH SCHOOL: Hialeah (Fla.)-Miami Lakes.
JUNIOR COLLEGE: Miami-Dade (South) Community College.
COLLEGE: Miami (Fla.).
TRANSACTIONS/CAREER NOTES: Selected by Minnesota Twins organization in third round of free-agent draft (June 1, 1992). ... On Salt Lake disabled list (April 4-August 10, 1996).

Year Team (League)	W	L	Pct.	ERA	G	GS	CG	ShO	Sv.	IP	H	R	ER	BB	SO
1992—Elizabethton (Appal.)..........	1	2	.333	3.00	*29	0	0	0	•13	36	24	14	12	10	34
1993—Fort Wayne (Midw.).............	5	5	.500	3.26	52	0	0	0	25	66 1/3	66	37	24	22	59
1994—Fort Myers (Fla. St.)..........	4	1	.800	0.77	37	0	0	0	20	46 2/3	37	7	4	13	39
—Nashville (Southern)	2	2	.500	3.16	28	0	0	0	8	37	34	13	13	10	29
1995—Salt Lake (PCL).................	2	3	.400	6.44	22	0	0	0	2	29 1/3	34	23	21	19	17
—New Britain (East.).............	2	4	.333	6.12	25	0	0	0	7	32 1/3	38	26	22	16	25
1996—GC Twins (GCL).................	0	0	...	1.00	3	1	0	0	2	9	10	3	1	3	14
—Fort Myers (Fla. St.)	0	0	...	9.00	4	0	0	0	1	6	9	7	6	8	3
1997—New Britain (East.).............	2	4	.333	4.70	17	7	1	0	0	61 1/3	67	34	32	15	29
—Salt Lake (PCL)	1	0	1.000	3.18	11	2	0	0	2	22 2/3	22	8	8	6	13

GANT, RON   OF   CARDINALS

PERSONAL: Born March 2, 1965, in Victoria, Texas. ... 6-0/200. ... Bats right, throws right. ... Full name: Ronald Edwin Gant.
HIGH SCHOOL: Victoria (Texas).
TRANSACTIONS/CAREER NOTES: Selected by Atlanta Braves organization in fourth round of free-agent draft (June 6, 1983). ... On suspended list (July 31, 1991). ... Released by Braves (March 15, 1994). ... Signed by Cincinnati Reds (June 21, 1994). ... On Cincinnati disabled list (June 21, 1994-remainder of season). ... On suspended list (September 11-15, 1995). ... Granted free agency (October 30, 1995). ... Signed by St. Louis Cardinals (December 23, 1995). ... On disabled list (May 11-June 14, 1996).
HONORS: Named outfielder on THE SPORTING NEWS N.L. All-Star team (1991). ... Named outfielder on THE SPORTING NEWS N.L. Silver Slugger team (1991). ... Named N.L. Comeback Player of the Year by THE SPORTING NEWS (1995).
STATISTICAL NOTES: Led South Atlantic League second basemen with 75 double plays in 1984. ... Led Carolina League with 271 total bases in 1986. ... Led Southern League second basemen with 783 total chances and 108 double plays in 1987. ... Led N.L. second basemen with 26 errors in 1988. ... Career major league grand slams: 4.

Year Team (League)	Pos.	G	AB	R	H	2B	3B	HR	RBI	Avg.	BB	SO	SB	PO	A	E	Avg.
1983—GC Braves (GCL).......	SS	56	193	32	45	2	2	1	14	.233	41	34	4	68	134	22	.902
1984—Anderson (S. Atl.)	2B	105	359	44	85	14	6	3	38	.237	29	65	13	248	263	31	.943
1985—Sumter (S. Atl.)..........	2B-SS-OF	102	305	46	78	14	4	7	37	.256	33	59	19	160	200	10	.973
1986—Durham (Carolina).......	2B	137	512	108	142	31	10	*26	102	.277	78	85	35	240	384	26	.960
1987—Greenville (Southern) .	2B	140	527	78	130	27	3	14	82	.247	59	91	24	*328	*434	21	*.973
—Atlanta (N.L.)........	2B	21	83	9	22	4	0	2	9	.265	1	11	4	45	59	3	.972
1988—Richmond (Int'l)	2B	12	45	3	14	2	2	0	4	.311	2	10	1	22	23	5	.900
—Atlanta (N.L.)	2B-3B	146	563	85	146	28	8	19	60	.259	46	118	19	316	417	†31	.959
1989—Atlanta (N.L.)	3B-OF	75	260	26	46	8	3	9	25	.177	20	63	9	70	103	17	.911
—Sumter (S. Atl.)	OF	12	39	13	15	4	1	1	5	.385	11	3	4	19	1	2	.909
—Richmond (Int'l)	OF-3B	63	225	42	59	13	2	11	27	.262	29	42	6	111	14	5	.962
1990—Atlanta (N.L.).............	OF	152	575	107	174	34	3	32	84	.303	50	86	33	357	7	8	.978
1991—Atlanta (N.L.).............	OF	154	561	101	141	35	4	32	105	.251	71	104	34	338	7	6	.983
1992—Atlanta (N.L.).............	OF	153	544	74	141	22	6	17	80	.259	45	101	32	277	5	4	.986
1993—Atlanta (N.L.).............	OF	157	606	113	166	27	4	36	117	.274	67	117	26	271	5	*11	.962
1994—								Did not play.									
1995—Cincinnati (N.L.)■......	OF	119	410	79	113	19	4	29	88	.276	74	108	23	191	7	3	.985
1996—St. Louis (N.L.)■........	OF	122	419	74	103	14	2	30	82	.246	73	98	13	216	4	5	.978
1997—St. Louis (N.L.)...........	OF-DH	139	502	68	115	21	4	17	62	.229	58	162	14	247	4	6	.977
Major league totals (10 years)		1238	4523	736	1167	212	37	223	712	.258	505	968	207	2328	618	94	.969

DIVISION SERIES RECORD

Year Team (League)	Pos.	G	AB	R	H	2B	3B	HR	RBI	Avg.	BB	SO	SB	PO	A	E	Avg.
1995—Cincinnati (N.L.).........	OF	3	13	3	3	0	0	1	2	.231	0	3	0	8	1	0	1.000
1996—St. Louis (N.L.)...........	OF	3	10	3	4	1	0	1	4	.400	2	0	2	5	0	0	1.000
Division series totals (2 years)		6	23	6	7	1	0	2	6	.304	2	3	2	13	1	0	1.000

G

RECORDS: Shares single-game record for most grand slams—1 (October 7, 1992). ... Shares records for most runs batted in in one inning—4 (October 7, 1992, fifth inning); and most stolen bases in one inning—2 (October 10, 1991, third inning). ... Holds N.L. career record for most strikeouts—26. ... Holds N.L. single-series record for most stolen bases—7 (1991). ... Shares N.L. single-game record for most stolen bases—3 (October 10, 1991).

									BATTING							FIELDING		
Year	Team (League)	Pos.	G	AB	R	H	2B	3B	HR	RBI	Avg.	BB	SO	SB	PO	A	E	Avg.
1991— Atlanta (N.L.).............		OF	7	27	4	7	1	0	1	3	.259	2	4	7	15	2	0	1.000
1992— Atlanta (N.L.).............		OF	7	22	5	4	0	0	2	6	.182	4	4	1	16	0	0	1.000
1993— Atlanta (N.L.).............		OF	6	27	4	5	3	0	0	3	.185	2	9	0	10	1	1	.917
1995— Cincinnati (N.L.)........		OF	4	16	1	3	0	0	0	1	.188	0	3	0	9	0	0	1.000
1996— St. Louis (N.L.)..........		OF	7	25	3	6	1	0	2	4	.240	2	6	0	12	0	0	1.000
Championship series totals (5 years)			31	117	17	25	5	0	5	17	.214	10	26	8	62	3	1	.985

WORLD SERIES RECORD

							BATTING							FIELDING		
Year	Team (League)	Pos.	G	AB	R	H	2B	3B	HR	RBI	Avg.	BB	SO	SB	PO	A	E	Avg.
1991— Atlanta (N.L.).............		OF	7	30	3	8	0	1	0	4	.267	2	3	1	19	0	0	1.000
1992— Atlanta (N.L.).............		OF-PR-PH	4	8	2	1	1	0	0	0	.125	1	2	2	3	1	0	1.000
World Series totals (2 years)			11	38	5	9	1	1	0	4	.237	3	5	3	22	1	0	1.000

ALL-STAR GAME RECORD

						BATTING						FIELDING		
Year	League	Pos.	AB	R	H	2B	3B	HR	RBI	Avg.	BB	SO	SB	PO	A	E	Avg.
1992— National		PH-OF	2	0	0	0	0	0	0	.000	0	0	0	1	0	0	1.000
1995— National		DH	2	0	0	0	0	0	0	.000	0	1	0	...	...	...	...
All-Star Game totals (2 years)			4	0	0	0	0	0	0	.000	0	1	0	1	0	0	1.000

GARCES, RICHARD   P   RED SOX

PERSONAL: Born May 18, 1971, in Maracay, Venezuela. ... 6-0/215. ... Throws right, bats right. ... Full name: Richard Aron Garces Jr. ... Name pronounced gar-SESS.

HIGH SCHOOL: Jose Felix Rivas (Maracay, Venezuela).

COLLEGE: Venezuela Universidad.

TRANSACTIONS/CAREER NOTES: Signed as non-drafted free agent by Minnesota Twins organization (December 29, 1987). ... On Portland suspended list (May 17-September 16, 1991). ... On Portland disabled list (July 28, 1991-remainder of season). ... Granted free agency (October 15, 1994). ... Signed by Iowa, Chicago Cubs organization (January 30, 1995). ... Claimed on waivers by Florida Marlins (August 9, 1995). ... Granted free agency (October 16, 1995). ... Signed by Boston Red Sox (April 25, 1996). ... On Boston disabled list (July 25-August 20 and August 24, 1996-remainder of season); included rehabilitation assignment to Pawtucket (August 9-20). ... On disabled list (March 27-April 27, 1997); included rehabilitation assignment to Pawtucket (April 18-21 and April 25-27). ... On disabled list (June 2-23, 1997); included rehabilitation assignment to Pawtucket (June 12-23).

Year	Team (League)	W	L	Pct.	ERA	G	GS	CG	ShO	Sv.	IP	H	R	ER	BB	SO
1988— Elizabethton (Appal.)		5	4	.556	2.29	17	3	1	0	5	59	51	22	15	27	69
1989— Kenosha (Midwest)		9	10	.474	3.41	24	24	4	1	0	142 2/3	117	70	54	62	84
1990— Visalia (California)		2	2	.500	1.81	47	0	0	0	*28	54 2/3	33	14	11	16	75
—Orlando (South.)		2	1	.667	2.08	15	0	0	0	8	17 1/3	17	4	4	14	22
—Minnesota (A.L.)		0	0	...	1.59	5	0	0	0	2	5 2/3	4	2	1	4	1
1991— Portland (PCL)		0	1	.000	4.85	10	0	0	0	3	13	10	7	7	8	13
—Orlando (South.)		2	1	.667	3.31	10	0	0	0	0	16 1/3	12	6	6	14	17
1992— Orlando (South.)		3	3	.500	4.54	58	0	0	0	13	73 1/3	76	46	37	39	72
1993— Portland (PCL)		1	3	.250	8.33	35	7	0	0	0	54	70	55	50	64	48
—Minnesota (A.L.)		0	0	...	0.00	3	0	0	0	0	4	4	2	0	2	3
1994— Nashville (Southern)		4	5	.444	3.72	40	1	0	0	3	77 1/3	70	40	32	31	76
1995— Iowa (Am. Assoc.)■		0	2	.000	2.86	23	0	0	0	7	28 1/3	25	10	9	8	36
—Chicago (N.L.)		0	0	...	3.27	7	0	0	0	0	11	11	6	4	3	6
—Florida (N.L.)■		0	2	.000	5.40	11	0	0	0	0	13 1/3	14	9	8	8	16
1996— Pawtucket (Int'l)■		4	0	1.000	2.30	10	0	0	0	0	15 2/3	10	4	4	5	13
—Boston (A.L.)		3	2	.600	4.91	37	0	0	0	0	44	42	26	24	33	55
1997— Boston (A.L.)		0	1	.000	4.61	12	0	0	0	0	13 2/3	14	9	7	9	12
—Pawtucket (Int'l)		2	1	.667	1.45	26	0	0	0	5	31	24	5	5	13	42
A.L. totals (4 years)		3	3	.500	4.28	57	0	0	0	2	67 1/3	64	39	32	48	71
N.L. totals (1 year)		0	2	.000	4.44	18	0	0	0	0	24 1/3	25	15	12	11	22
Major league totals (5 years)		3	5	.375	4.32	75	0	0	0	2	91 2/3	89	54	44	59	93

G

GARCIA, AMAURY   2B   MARLINS

PERSONAL: Born May 20, 1975, in Santo Domingo, Dominican Republic. ... 5-10/160. ... Bats right, throws right.

HIGH SCHOOL: Colegio Discipulos de Jesus (Santo Domingo, Dominican Republic).

TRANSACTIONS/CAREER NOTES: Signed as non-drafted free agent by Florida Marlins organization (December 4, 1992).

							BATTING							FIELDING		
Year	Team (League)	Pos.	G	AB	R	H	2B	3B	HR	RBI	Avg.	BB	SO	SB	PO	A	E	Avg.
1993— Dom. Marlins (DSL) ...		IF	64	237	35	67	5	3	4	29	.283	31	41	9	129	112	19	.927
1994— GC Marlins (GCL).......		3B-2B-OF	58	208	46	65	9	3	0	25	.313	33	49	10	44	113	17	.902
1995— Kane County (Midw.)..		3B-2B	26	58	19	14	4	1	1	5	.241	18	12	5	11	31	13	.764
—Elmira (N.Y.-Penn)......		2B	62	231	40	63	7	3	0	17	.273	34	50	*41	128	178	18	.944
1996— Kane County (Midw.)..		2B	106	395	65	104	19	7	6	36	.263	62	84	37	219	286	19	.964
1997— Brevard Co. (Fla. St.)..		2B	124	479	77	138	30	2	7	44	.288	49	97	45	246	329	16	.973

GARCIA, APOSTOL   P   TIGERS

PERSONAL: Born August 3, 1976, in Las Matas de Faran, Dominican Republic. ... 6-0/155. ... Throws right, bats right.
HIGH SCHOOL: Liceo Mercedes Maria Mateo (Las Matas de Faran, Dominican Republic).
TRANSACTIONS/CAREER NOTES: Signed as non-drafted free agent by Detroit Tigers organization (December 6, 1992).

Year Team (League)	W	L	Pct.	ERA	G	GS	CG	ShO	Sv.	IP	H	R	ER	BB	SO
1997— West. Mich. (Mid.)	7	2	.778	3.02	33	5	0	0	1	65 2/3	48	26	22	31	52

RECORD AS POSITION PLAYER

Year Team (League)	Pos.	G	AB	R	H	2B	3B	HR	RBI	Avg.	BB	SO	SB	PO	A	E	Avg.
1993— Dom. Tigers (DSL)	OF-IF	65	150	24	29	2	0	0	6	.193	15	32	14	107	26	13	.911
1994— Bristol (Appal.)	SS-2B	47	130	20	20	3	0	0	8	.154	18	35	18	68	107	9	.951
— Lakeland (Fla. St.)	SS	6	15	0	4	0	0	0	0	.267	0	3	1	3	10	2	.867
1995— Jamestown (NYP)	SS-2B	60	200	25	47	8	3	0	21	.235	10	36	10	66	189	28	.901
1996— Fayetteville (SAL)	SS-2B	74	242	33	47	7	1	2	17	.194	21	77	12	105	181	30	.905

GARCIA, CARLOS   2B   INDIANS

PERSONAL: Born October 15, 1967, in Tachira, Venezuela. ... 6-1/197. ... Bats right, throws right. ... Full name: Carlos Jesus Garcia.
HIGH SCHOOL: Bolivar (Venezuela).
TRANSACTIONS/CAREER NOTES: Signed as non-drafted free agent by Pittsburgh Pirates organization (January 9, 1987). ... On disabled list (July 28-August 14, 1995). ... On Pittsburgh disabled list (May 2-17 and July 22-August 27, 1996); included rehabilitation assignment to Calgary (August 23-25). ... Traded by Pirates with OF Orlando Merced and P Dan Plesac to Toronto Blue Jays for P Jose Silva, P Jose Pett, IF Brandon Cromer and three players to be named later (November 14, 1996); Pirates acquired P Mike Halperin, IF Abraham Nunez and C/OF Craig Wilson to complete deal (December 11, 1996). ... Granted free agency (December 21, 1997). ... Signed by Cleveland Indians (January 6, 1998).
STATISTICAL NOTES: Led N.L. second basemen with 80 double plays in 1994. ... Had 21-game hitting streak (June 5-27, 1995).

Year Team (League)	Pos.	G	AB	R	H	2B	3B	HR	RBI	Avg.	BB	SO	SB	PO	A	E	Avg.
1987— Macon (S. Atl.)	SS	110	373	44	95	14	3	3	38	.255	23	80	20	161	262	42	.910
1988— Augusta (S. Atl.)	SS	73	269	32	78	13	2	1	45	.290	22	46	11	138	207	29	.922
— Salem (Carolina)	SS	62	236	21	65	9	3	1	28	.275	10	32	8	131	151	24	.922
1989— Salem (Carolina)	SS	81	304	45	86	12	4	7	49	.283	18	51	19	137	262	32	.926
— Harrisburg (Eastern) ..	SS	54	188	28	53	5	5	3	25	.282	8	36	6	84	131	7	.968
1990— Harrisburg (Eastern) ..	SS	65	242	36	67	11	2	5	25	.277	16	36	12	101	209	14	.957
— Buffalo (A.A.)	SS	63	197	23	52	10	0	5	18	.264	16	41	7	106	170	19	.936
— Pittsburgh (N.L.)	SS	4	4	1	2	0	0	0	0	.500	0	2	0	4	0	0	1.000
1991— Buffalo (A.A.)	SS	127	463	62	123	21	6	7	60	.266	33	78	30	*212	332	*31	.946
— Pittsburgh (N.L.)	SS-3B-2B	12	24	2	6	0	2	0	1	.250	1	8	0	11	18	1	.967
1992— Buffalo (A.A.)	SS-2B	113	426	73	129	28	9	13	70	.303	24	64	21	192	314	28	.948
— Pittsburgh (N.L.)	2B-SS	22	39	4	8	1	0	0	4	.205	0	9	0	25	35	2	.968
1993— Pittsburgh (N.L.)	2B-SS	141	546	77	147	25	5	12	47	.269	31	67	18	299	347	11	.983
1994— Pittsburgh (N.L.)	2B	98	412	49	114	15	2	6	28	.277	16	67	18	•225	315	12	.978
1995— Pittsburgh (N.L.)	2B-SS	104	367	41	108	24	2	6	50	.294	25	55	8	234	298	15	.973
1996— Pittsburgh (N.L.)	2B-SS-3B	101	390	66	111	18	4	6	44	.285	23	58	16	160	284	11	.976
— Calgary (PCL)	2B-SS	2	6	0	2	0	1	0	0	.333	0	0	0	3	5	0	1.000
1997— Toronto (A.L.)■	2B-SS-3B	103	350	29	77	18	2	3	23	.220	15	60	11	171	256	10	.977
American League totals (1 year)		103	350	29	77	18	2	3	23	.220	15	60	11	171	256	10	.977
National League totals (7 years)		482	1782	240	496	83	15	30	174	.278	96	266	60	954	1301	52	.977
Major league totals (8 years)		585	2132	269	573	101	17	33	197	.269	111	326	71	1125	1557	62	.977

CHAMPIONSHIP SERIES RECORD

Year Team (League)	Pos.	G	AB	R	H	2B	3B	HR	RBI	Avg.	BB	SO	SB	PO	A	E	Avg.
1992— Pittsburgh (N.L.)	2B	1	1	0	0	0	0	0	0	.000	0	0	0	0	0	0	...

ALL-STAR GAME RECORD

Year League	Pos.	AB	R	H	2B	3B	HR	RBI	Avg.	BB	SO	SB	PO	A	E	Avg.
1994— National	2B	2	0	1	0	0	0	0	.500	0	0	0	0	1	0	1.000

GARCIA, FREDDY   P   ASTROS

PERSONAL: Born October 6, 1976, in Caracas, Venezuela. ... 6-4/235. ... Throws right, bats right.
TRANSACTIONS/CAREER NOTES: Signed as non-drafted free agent by Houston Astros organization (October 21, 1993).

Year Team (League)	W	L	Pct.	ERA	G	GS	CG	ShO	Sv.	IP	H	R	ER	BB	SO
1994— Dom. Astros (DSL)............	4	6	.400	5.29	16	15	0	0	0	85	80	61	50	38	68
1995— GC Astros (GCL)	6	3	.667	4.47	11	11	0	0	0	58 1/3	60	32	29	14	58
1996— Quad City (Midwest)	5	4	.556	3.12	13	13	0	0	0	60 2/3	57	27	21	27	50
1997— Kissimmee (Florida State) ..	10	8	.556	2.56	27	27	5	2	0	179	165	63	51	49	131

GARCIA, FREDDY   3B   PIRATES

PERSONAL: Born August 1, 1972, in La Romana, Dominican Republic. ... 6-2/205. ... Bats right, throws right. ... Full name: Freddy Adrian Garcia.
TRANSACTIONS/CAREER NOTES: Signed as non-drafted free agent by Toronto Blue Jays organization (May 16, 1991). ... Selected by Pittsburgh Pirates from Blue Jays organization in Rule 5 major league draft (December 5, 1994).

G

STATISTICAL NOTES: Led Pioneer League third basemen with 267 total chances and tied for lead in double plays with 18 in 1993. ... Led New York-Pennsylvania League third basemen with 257 total chances and 18 double plays in 1994. ... Tied for Carolina League lead with 12 sacrifice flies in 1996. ... Led Carolina League third basemen with 29 double plays in 1996.

Year Team (League)	Pos.	G	AB	R	H	2B	3B	HR	RBI	Avg.	BB	SO	SB	PO	A	E	Avg.
1991— Villa Mella (DSL)	IF	53	154	28	39	4	1	1	19	.253	39	36	8	...	—	—	...
1992— Blue Jays East (DSL)..	IF	70	249	56	73	13	2	12	62	.293	61	52	5	146	32	5	.973
1993— Medicine Hat (Pio.) ...	3B	72	264	47	63	8	2	11	42	.239	31	71	4	*63	*175	•29	.891
1994— St. Catharines (NYP) ..	3B	73	260	46	74	10	2	*13	40	.285	33	57	1	63	*169	25	.903
1995— Pittsburgh (N.L.)■	OF-3B	42	57	5	8	1	1	0	1	.140	8	17	0	19	15	1	.971
1996— Lynchburg (Caro.)	3B	129	474	79	145	*39	3	•21	86	.306	44	86	4	96	285	*35	.916
1997— Calgary (PCL)	3B	35	121	21	29	6	0	5	17	.240	9	20	0	18	53	12	.855
— Pittsburgh (N.L.)	3B-1B	20	40	4	6	1	0	3	5	.150	2	17	0	21	9	3	.909
— Carolina (Southern)....	3B-1B	73	282	47	82	17	4	19	57	.291	18	56	0	93	155	22	.919
Major league totals (2 years)		62	97	9	14	2	1	3	6	.144	10	34	0	40	24	4	.941

GARCIA, KARIM — OF — DIAMONDBACKS

PERSONAL: Born October 29, 1975, in Ciudad Obregon, Mexico. ... 6-0/172. ... Bats left, throws left. ... Full name: Gustavo Garcia.
HIGH SCHOOL: Preparatoria Abierta (Ciudad Obregon, Mexico).
TRANSACTIONS/CAREER NOTES: Signed as non-drafted free agent by Los Angeles Dodgers organization (July 16, 1992). ... On Los Angeles disabled list (September 19, 1997-remainder of season). ... Selected by Arizona Diamondbacks in first round (ninth pick overall) of expansion draft (November 18, 1997).
HONORS: Named Minor League Player of the Year by THE SPORTING NEWS (1995).

Year Team (League)	Pos.	G	AB	R	H	2B	3B	HR	RBI	Avg.	BB	SO	SB	PO	A	E	Avg.
1993— Bakersfield (California)	OF	123	460	61	111	20	9	19	54	.241	37	109	5	193	12	*13	.940
1994— Vero Beach (FSL)	OF	121	452	72	120	28	10	*21	84	.265	37	112	8	229	12	5	.980
1995— Albuquerque (PCL).....	OF	124	474	88	151	26	10	20	•91	.319	38	102	12	185	7	*14	.932
— Los Angeles (N.L.)	OF	13	20	1	4	0	0	0	0	.200	0	4	0	5	2	0	1.000
1996— Albuquerque (PCL).....	OF	84	327	54	97	17	0	13	58	.297	29	67	6	148	4	13	.921
— San Antonio (Tex.)	OF	35	129	21	32	6	1	5	22	.248	9	38	1	60	6	2	.971
— Los Angeles (N.L.)	OF	1	1	0	0	0	0	0	0	.000	0	1	0	0	0	0	...
1997— Albuquerque (PCL).....	OF	71	262	53	80	17	6	20	66	.305	23	70	11	97	3	5	.952
— Los Angeles (N.L.)	OF	15	39	5	5	0	0	1	8	.128	6	14	0	13	0	0	1.000
Major league totals (3 years)		29	60	6	9	0	0	1	8	.150	6	19	0	18	2	0	1.000

GARCIA, LUIS — IF — TIGERS

PERSONAL: Born May 20, 1975, in San Francisco De Macoris, Dominican Republic. ... 6-0/175. ... Bats right, throws right. ... Full name: Luis Rafael Garcia.
TRANSACTIONS/CAREER NOTES: Signed as non-drafted free agent Detroit Tigers organization (February 3, 1993).
STATISTICAL NOTES: Led Southern League shortstops with 676 total chances in 1996.

Year Team (League)	Pos.	G	AB	R	H	2B	3B	HR	RBI	Avg.	BB	SO	SB	PO	A	E	Avg.
1993— Bristol (Appal.)	2B-SS-3B	24	57	7	12	1	0	1	7	.211	3	11	3	33	15	3	.946
1994— Jamestown (NYP)	SS	67	239	21	47	8	2	1	19	.197	8	48	6	115	205	*27	.922
1995— Lakeland (Fla. St.)	SS-2B	102	361	39	101	10	4	2	35	.280	8	42	9	167	302	34	.932
— Jacksonville (South.)..	SS-3B	17	47	6	13	0	0	0	5	.277	1	8	2	19	46	5	.929
1996— Jacksonville (South.)..	SS	131	522	68	128	22	4	9	46	.245	12	90	15	*205	*435	*36	*.947
1997— Jacksonville (South.)..	SS	126	456	55	122	19	1	5	48	.268	10	59	3	176	370	30	.948

GARCIA, RAMON — P — ASTROS

PERSONAL: Born December 9, 1969, in Guanare, Venezuela. ... 6-2/200. ... Throws right, bats right. ... Full name: Ramon Antonio Garcia.
HIGH SCHOOL: Cesar Lizardo (Guanare, Venezuela).
TRANSACTIONS/CAREER NOTES: Signed as free agent by Chicago White Sox organization (June 30, 1987). ... On disabled list (May 28, 1993-remainder of season). ... Released by White Sox (September 15, 1993). ... Signed by Ottawa, Montreal Expos organization (February 11, 1995). ... Released by Ottawa (April 3, 1995). ... Signed by Milwaukee Brewers (April 3, 1996). ... Granted free agency (October 15, 1996). ... Re-signed by New Orleans, Brewers organization (November 4, 1996). ... Selected by Houston Astros organization from Brewers organization in Rule 5 major league draft (December 9, 1996).
STATISTICAL NOTES: Pitched 2-0 no-hit victory against Sarasota (August 3, 1989). ... Led Florida State League with 10 home runs allowed in 1990.

Year Team (League)	W	L	Pct.	ERA	G	GS	CG	ShO	Sv.	IP	H	R	ER	BB	SO
1987— GC White Sox (GCL)	1	0	1.000	1.50	6	0	0	0	0	12	8	3	2	5	6
1988— GC White Sox (GCL)	2	1	.667	2.45	13	0	0	0	0	22	15	9	6	4	17
1989— GC White Sox (GCL)	6	4	.600	3.06	14	7	2	•1	0	53	34	21	18	17	52
1990— Sarasota (Florida State)......	9	*14	.391	3.95	26	26	1	0	0	157 1/3	155	84	69	45	130
— Vancouver (PCL)	0	0	...	0.00	1	0	0	0	0	1	2	0	0	0	1
1991— Birmingham (Southern)	4	0	1.000	0.93	6	6	2	1	0	38 2/3	27	5	4	11	38
— Vancouver (PCL)	2	2	.500	4.05	4	4	0	0	0	26 2/3	24	13	12	7	17
— Chicago (A.L.)	4	4	.500	5.40	16	15	0	0	0	78 1/3	79	50	47	31	40
1992— Vancouver (PCL)	9	11	.450	3.71	28	•28	2	1	0	170	165	83	70	56	79
1993— Nashville (A.A.)	4	1	.800	4.01	7	7	1	1	0	42 2/3	45	22	19	11	23
1994—						Out of organized baseball.									
1995—						Out of organized baseball.									
1996— New Orleans (A.A.)■.........	2	1	.667	1.88	11	5	0	0	0	38 1/3	31	10	8	12	32
— Milwaukee (A.L.)	4	4	.500	6.66	37	2	0	0	4	75 2/3	84	58	56	21	40

G

Year Team (League)	W	L	Pct.	ERA	G	GS	CG	ShO	Sv.	IP	H	R	ER	BB	SO
1997—Houston (N.L.)■	9	8	.529	3.69	42	20	1	1	1	158²/₃	155	71	65	52	120
A.L. totals (2 years)	8	8	.500	6.02	53	17	0	0	4	154	163	108	103	52	80
N.L. totals (1 year)	9	8	.529	3.69	42	20	1	1	1	158²/₃	155	71	65	52	120
Major league totals (3 years)......	17	16	.515	4.84	95	37	1	1	5	312²/₃	318	179	168	104	200

DIVISION SERIES RECORD

Year Team (League)	W	L	Pct.	ERA	G	GS	CG	ShO	Sv.	IP	H	R	ER	BB	SO
1997—Houston (N.L.)	0	0	...	0.00	2	0	0	0	0	1	1	2	0	1	1

GARCIAPARRA, NOMAR   SS   RED SOX

PERSONAL: Born July 23, 1973, in Whittier, Calif. ... 6-0/167. ... Bats right, throws right. ... Full name: Anthony Nomar Garciaparra.
HIGH SCHOOL: St. John Bosco (Bellflower, Calif.).
COLLEGE: Georgia Tech.
TRANSACTIONS/CAREER NOTES: Selected by Milwaukee Brewers organization in fifth round of free-agent draft (June 3, 1991); did not sign. ... Selected by Boston Red Sox organization in first round (12th pick overall) of free-agent draft (June 2, 1994). ... On Pawtucket disabled list (April 4-15 and April 19-July 11, 1996).
RECORDS: Holds A.L. rookie-season record for most consecutive games batted safely—30 (1997). ... Holds major league rookie-season record for most consecutive games batted safely—34 (August 25-October 2, 1987).
HONORS: Named A.L. Rookie Player of the Year by THE SPORTING NEWS (1997). ... Named shortstop on THE SPORTING NEWS A.L. All-Star team (1997). ... Named shortstop on THE SPORTING NEWS A.L. Silver Slugger team (1997). ... Named A.L. Rookie of the Year by Baseball Writers' Association of America (1997).
STATISTICAL NOTES: Led Eastern League shortstops with 624 total chances in 1994. ... Had 30-game hitting streak (July 26-August 29, 1997). ... Led A.L. shortstops in total chances with 720 and double plays with 113 in 1997.
MISCELLANEOUS: Member of 1992 U.S. Olympic baseball team.

						BATTING								FIELDING			
Year Team (League)	Pos.	G	AB	R	H	2B	3B	HR	RBI	Avg.	BB	SO	SB	PO	A	E	Avg.
1994—Sarasota (Fla. St.)	SS	28	105	20	31	8	1	1	16	.295	10	6	5	42	72	3	.974
1995—Trenton (Eastern)	SS	125	513	77	137	20	8	8	47	.267	50	42	35	205	*396	23	.963
1996—Pawtucket (Int'l)	SS	43	172	40	59	15	2	16	46	.343	14	21	3	63	120	5	.973
— GC Red Sox (GCL)	SS	5	14	4	4	2	1	0	5	.286	1	0	0	7	12	1	.950
— Boston (A.L.)	SS-DH-2B	24	87	11	21	2	3	4	16	.241	4	14	5	37	51	1	.989
1997—Boston (A.L.)	SS	153	*684	122	*209	44	*11	30	98	.306	35	92	22	*249	450	21	.971
Major league totals (2 years)		177	771	133	230	46	14	34	114	.298	39	106	27	286	501	22	.973

ALL-STAR GAME RECORD

				BATTING								FIELDING			
Year League	Pos.	AB	R	H	2B	3B	HR	RBI	Avg.	BB	SO	SB	PO	A	E	Avg.
1997—American	SS	1	0	0	0	0	0	0	.000	0	0	0	1	0	0	1.000

GARDNER, MARK   P   GIANTS

PERSONAL: Born March 1, 1962, in Los Angeles. ... 6-1/215. ... Throws right, bats right. ... Full name: Mark Allan Gardner.
HIGH SCHOOL: Clovis (Calif.).
JUNIOR COLLEGE: Fresno (Calif.) City College.
COLLEGE: Fresno State.
TRANSACTIONS/CAREER NOTES: Selected by California Angels organization in sixth round of free-agent draft (January 11, 1983); did not sign. ... Selected by Cleveland Indians organization in 17th round of free-agent draft (June 4, 1984); did not sign. ... Selected by Montreal Expos organization in eighth round of free-agent draft (June 3, 1985). ... On disabled list (September 20, 1990-remainder of season). ... On Montreal disabled list (April 2-May 14, 1991); included rehabilitation assignment to Indianapolis (April 11-May 8). ... Traded by Expos with P Doug Piatt to Kansas City Royals for C Tim Spehr and P Jeff Shaw (December 9, 1992). ... On Kansas City disabled list (July 7-August 27, 1993); included rehabilitation assignment to Omaha (July 28-August 26). ... Released by Royals (December 8, 1993). ... Signed by Edmonton, Florida Marlins organization (January 6, 1994). ... On Florida disabled list (June 8-26, 1994); included rehabilitation assignment to Brevard County (June 18-22). ... Granted free agency (February 17, 1995). ... Re-signed by Marlins (April 7, 1995). ... Granted free agency (October 16, 1995). ... Re-signed by Marlins organization (December 8, 1995) ... Granted free agency (March 28, 1996). ... Signed by San Francisco Giants (March 29, 1996). ... On San Francisco disabled list (July 3-21, 1996); included rehabilitation assignment to San Jose (July 17-21).
RECORDS: Shares major league record for most hit batsmen in one inning—3 (August 15, 1992, first inning).
HONORS: Named American Association Pitcher of the Year (1989).
STATISTICAL NOTES: Led N.L. with nine hit batsmen in 1990. ... Pitched nine hitless innings against Los Angeles Dodgers, but gave up two hits in 10th inning and lost, 1-0, when reliever Jeff Fassero gave up game-winning hit in 10th (July 26, 1991).
MISCELLANEOUS: Struck out once in two games as pinch-hitter for Montreal (1991). ... Had two sacrifice hits in three games as pinch-hitter for San Francisco (1996).

Year Team (League)	W	L	Pct.	ERA	G	GS	CG	ShO	Sv.	IP	H	R	ER	BB	SO
1985—Jamestown (NYP)	0	0	...	2.77	3	3	0	0	0	13	9	4	4	4	16
— W.P. Beach (FSL)................	5	4	.556	2.37	10	9	4	0	0	60²/₃	54	24	16	18	44
1986—Jacksonville (Southern)...	10	11	.476	3.84	29	28	3	1	0	168²/₃	144	88	72	90	140
1987—Indianapolis (A.A.)...........	3	3	.500	5.67	9	9	0	0	0	46	48	32	29	28	41
— Jacksonville (Southern)...	4	6	.400	4.19	17	17	1	0	0	101	101	50	47	42	78
1988—Jacksonville (Southern)...	6	3	.667	1.60	15	15	4	2	0	112¹/₃	72	24	20	36	130
— Indianapolis (A.A.)...........	4	2	.667	2.77	13	13	3	1	0	84¹/₃	65	30	26	32	71
1989—Indianapolis (A.A.)...........	12	4	*.750	2.37	24	23	4	2	0	163¹/₃	122	51	43	59	*175
— Montreal (N.L.)................	0	3	.000	5.13	7	4	0	0	0	26¹/₃	26	16	15	11	21
1990—Montreal (N.L.)................	7	9	.438	3.42	27	26	3	3	0	152²/₃	129	62	58	61	135
1991—Indianapolis (A.A.)...........	2	0	1.000	3.48	6	6	0	0	0	31	26	13	12	16	38
— Montreal (N.L.)................	9	11	.450	3.85	27	27	0	0	0	168¹/₃	139	78	72	75	107
1992—Montreal (N.L.)................	12	10	.545	4.36	33	30	0	0	0	179²/₃	179	91	87	60	132
1993—Kansas City (A.L.)■..........	4	6	.400	6.19	17	16	0	0	0	91²/₃	92	65	63	36	54
— Omaha (Am. Assoc.)..........	4	2	.667	2.79	8	8	1	0	0	48¹/₃	34	17	15	19	41

G

Year Team (League)	W	L	Pct.	ERA	G	GS	CG	ShO	Sv.	IP	H	R	ER	BB	SO
1994—Florida (N.L.)■	4	4	.500	4.87	20	14	0	0	0	92⅓	97	53	50	30	57
—Edmonton (PCL)	1	0	1.000	0.00	1	1	0	0	0	6	4	0	0	1	11
—Brevard County (FSL)	1	0	1.000	0.00	1	1	0	0	0	5	1	0	0	1	3
1995—Florida (N.L.)	5	5	.500	4.49	39	11	1	1	1	102⅓	109	60	51	43	87
1996—San Francisco (N.L.)■	12	7	.632	4.42	30	28	4	1	0	179⅓	200	105	88	57	145
—San Jose (California)	0	0	...	3.18	1	1	0	0	0	5⅔	4	2	2	0	7
1997—San Francisco (N.L.)	12	9	.571	4.29	30	30	2	1	0	180⅓	188	92	86	57	136
A.L. totals (1 year)	4	6	.400	6.19	17	16	0	0	0	91⅔	92	65	63	36	54
N.L. totals (8 years)	61	58	.513	4.22	213	170	10	6	1	1081⅓	1067	557	507	394	820
Major league totals (9 years)	65	64	.504	4.37	230	186	10	6	1	1173	1159	622	570	430	874

GATES, BRENT　　　2B　　　TWINS

PERSONAL: Born March 14, 1970, in Grand Rapids, Mich. ... 6-1/191. ... Bats both, throws right. ... Full name: Brent Robert Gates.
HIGH SCHOOL: Grandville (Mich.).
COLLEGE: Minnesota.
TRANSACTIONS/CAREER NOTES: Selected by Oakland Athletics organization in first round (26th pick overall) of free-agent draft (June 3, 1991). ... On disabled list (April 10-May 5 and July 17, 1994-remainder of season). ... On disabled list (June 16, 1996-remainder of season). ... Released by A's (March 11, 1997). ... Signed by Seattle Mariners (March 16, 1997). ... Released by Mariners (December 15, 1997). ... Signed by Minnesota Twins organization (December 23, 1997).
STATISTICAL NOTES: Led California League second basemen with 735 total chances and 105 double plays in 1992.

| | | | | | | | | BATTING | | | | | | | FIELDING | | |
Year Team (League)	Pos.	G	AB	R	H	2B	3B	HR	RBI	Avg.	BB	SO	SB	PO	A	E	Avg.
1991—S. Oregon (N'west)	SS-2B-3B	58	219	41	63	11	0	3	26	.288	30	33	8	77	177	15	.944
—Madison (Midwest)	SS-3B	4	12	4	4	2	0	0	1	.333	3	2	1	6	10	0	1.000
1992—Modesto (California)	2B	133	505	94	162	39	2	10	88	.321	85	60	9	*293	*420	*22	.970
1993—Huntsville (Southern)	2B	12	45	7	15	4	0	1	11	.333	7	9	0	32	28	0	1.000
—Tacoma (PCL)	2B	12	44	7	15	7	0	1	4	.341	4	6	2	27	36	1	.984
—Oakland (A.L.)	2B	139	535	64	155	29	2	7	69	.290	56	75	7	281	431	14	.981
1994—Oakland (A.L.)	2B-1B	64	233	29	66	11	1	2	24	.283	21	32	3	113	159	8	.971
1995—Oakland (A.L.)	2B-DH-1B	136	524	60	133	24	4	5	56	.254	46	84	3	241	428	12	.982
1996—Oakland (A.L.)	2B	64	247	26	65	19	2	2	30	.263	18	35	1	140	183	9	.973
1997—Seattle (A.L.)■	3-2-S-DH-1-O	65	151	18	36	8	0	3	20	.238	14	21	0	26	82	5	.956
—Tacoma (PCL)	2B-SS	7	33	7	15	3	0	0	6	.455	4	2	0	10	12	4	.846
Major league totals (5 years)		468	1690	197	455	91	9	19	199	.269	155	247	14	801	1283	48	.977

DIVISION SERIES RECORD

| | | | | | | | | BATTING | | | | | | | FIELDING | | |
Year Team (League)	Pos.	G	AB	R	H	2B	3B	HR	RBI	Avg.	BB	SO	SB	PO	A	E	Avg.
1997—Seattle (A.L.)	3B-PH	2	4	0	0	0	0	0	0	.000	0	0	0	1	2	0	1.000

GIAMBI, JASON　　　1B　　　ATHLETICS

PERSONAL: Born January 8, 1971, in West Covina, Calif. ... 6-2/218. ... Bats left, throws right. ... Full name: Jason Gilbert Giambi. ... Name pronounced GEE-om-bee..
HIGH SCHOOL: South Hills (Covina, Calif.).
COLLEGE: Long Beach State.
TRANSACTIONS/CAREER NOTES: Selected by Milwaukee Brewers organization in 43rd round of free-agent draft (June 5, 1989); did not sign. ... Selected by Oakland Athletics organization in second round of free-agent draft (June 1, 1992). ... On disabled list (July 27-August 28, 1993). ... On Huntsville disabled list (April 7-14, 1994).
STATISTICAL NOTES: Had 25-game hitting streak (May 12-June 23, 1997). ... Career major league grand slams: 1.
MISCELLANEOUS: Member of 1992 U.S. Olympic baseball team.

| | | | | | | | | BATTING | | | | | | | FIELDING | | |
Year Team (League)	Pos.	G	AB	R	H	2B	3B	HR	RBI	Avg.	BB	SO	SB	PO	A	E	Avg.
1992—S. Oregon (N'west)	3B	13	41	9	13	3	0	3	13	.317	9	6	1	5	20	1	.962
1993—Modesto (California)	3B	89	313	72	91	16	2	12	60	.291	73	47	2	49	145	19	.911
1994—Huntsville (Southern)	3B-1B	56	193	31	43	9	0	6	30	.223	27	31	0	111	77	11	.945
—Tacoma (PCL)	3B-SS	52	176	28	56	20	0	4	38	.318	25	32	1	39	110	8	.949
1995—Edmonton (PCL)	3B-1B	55	190	34	65	26	1	3	41	.342	34	26	0	38	98	9	.938
—Oakland (A.L.)	3B-1B-DH	54	176	27	45	7	0	6	25	.256	28	31	2	194	55	4	.984
1996—Oakland (A.L.)	1-O-3-DH	140	536	84	156	40	1	20	79	.291	51	95	0	478	117	11	.984
1997—Oakland (A.L.)	OF-1B-DH	142	519	66	152	41	2	20	81	.293	55	89	0	501	44	7	.987
Major league totals (3 years)		336	1231	177	353	88	3	46	185	.287	134	215	2	1173	216	22	.984

GIBBS, KEVIN　　　OF　　　DODGERS

PERSONAL: Born April 3, 1974, in Washington D.C. ... 6-2/185. ... Bats both, throws right. ... Full name: Kevin Casey Gibbs.
HIGH SCHOOL: St. John's College.
COLLEGE: Old Dominion.
TRANSACTIONS/CAREER NOTES: Selected by Los Angeles Dodgers in sixth round of free-agent draft (June 1, 1995). ... On disabled list (April 20-May 1 and July 19-26, 1997).
STATISTICAL NOTES: Tied for Florida State League lead in caught stealing with 19 in 1996. ... Tied for Florida State League lead in double plays by outfielder with four in 1996.

| | | | | | | | | BATTING | | | | | | | FIELDING | | |
Year Team (League)	Pos.	G	AB	R	H	2B	3B	HR	RBI	Avg.	BB	SO	SB	PO	A	E	Avg.
1995—Vero Beach (FSL)	OF	7	20	1	5	1	0	0	2	.250	0	0	1	12	0	0	1.000
—San Bern. (Calif.)	OF	5	13	1	3	1	0	0	0	.231	0	2	1	5	0	0	1.000
—Yakima (N'west)	OF	52	182	36	57	6	*4	1	18	.313	36	46	*38	71	1	2	.973
1996—Vero Beach (FSL)	OF	118	423	69	114	9	*11	0	33	.270	65	80	*60	252	11	4	.985
1997—San Antonio (Tex.)	OF	101	358	89	120	21	6	2	34	.335	72	48	49	215	2	4	.982

GIBRALTER, STEVE   OF   REDS

PERSONAL: Born October 9, 1972, in Dallas. ... 6-0/190. ... Bats right, throws right. ... Full name: Stephan Benson Gibralter. ... Brother of David Gibralter, third baseman, Boston Red Sox organization.
HIGH SCHOOL: Duncanville (Texas).
TRANSACTIONS/CAREER NOTES: Selected by Cincinnati Reds organization in sixth round of free-agent draft (June 4, 1990). ... On Indianapolis disabled list (July 16, 1995-remainder of season). ... On Cincinnati disabled list (February 27, 1997-remainder of season); including rehabilitation assignment to Chattanooga (April 25-May 25 and May 29-June 5). ... Granted free agency (December 21, 1997). ... Re-signed by Reds organization (January 14, 1998).
HONORS: Named Midwest League Most Valuable Player (1992).
STATISTICAL NOTES: Led Gulf Coast League outfielders with 115 total chances in 1990. ... Tied for South Atlantic League lead in double plays by outfielder with three in 1991. ... Led Midwest League with 257 total bases in 1992. ... Led Southern League outfielders with 334 total chances in 1993.

						BATTING							FIELDING			
Year Team (League)	Pos.	G	AB	R	H	2B	3B	HR	RBI	Avg.	BB	SO	SB	PO	A	E	Avg.
1990— GC Reds (GCL)..........	OF	52	174	26	45	11	3	4	27	.259	23	30	9	100	•9	6	.948
1991— Char., W.Va. (SAL)......	OF	*140	*544	72	145	*36	7	6	71	.267	31	117	11	234	15	10	.961
1992— Cedar Rap. (Midw.)	OF	•137	529	*92	*162	32	3	*19	*99	.306	51	99	12	*311	7	7	.978
1993— Chattanooga (Sou.).....	OF	132	477	65	113	25	3	11	47	.237	20	108	7	*319	7	8	.976
1994— Chattanooga (Sou.)....	OF	133	460	71	124	28	3	14	63	.270	47	114	10	304	7	5	.984
1995— Indianapolis (A.A.)......	OF	79	263	49	83	19	3	18	63	.316	25	70	0	207	2	5	.977
— Cincinnati (N.L.)....	OF	4	3	0	1	0	0	0	0	.333	0	0	0	1	0	0	1.000
1996— Indianapolis (A.A.)......	OF	126	447	58	114	29	2	11	54	.255	26	114	2	262	10	7	.975
— Cincinnati (N.L.)....	OF	2	2	0	0	0	0	0	0	.000	0	2	0	0	0	1	.000
1997— Chattanooga (Sou.)....	OF	30	97	20	25	9	0	2	12	.258	13	22	0	35	0	1	.972
Major league totals (2 years)		6	5	0	1	0	0	0	0	.200	0	2	0	1	0	1	.500

GIBSON, DERRICK   OF   ROCKIES

PERSONAL: Born February 5, 1975, in Winter Haven, Fla. ... 6-2/230. ... Bats right, throws right. ... Full name: Derrick Lamont Gibson.
HIGH SCHOOL: Haines City (Fla.).
TRANSACTIONS/CAREER NOTES: Selected by Colorado Rockies organization in 13th round of free-agent draft (June 3, 1993).

						BATTING							FIELDING			
Year Team (League)	Pos.	G	AB	R	H	2B	3B	HR	RBI	Avg.	BB	SO	SB	PO	A	E	Avg.
1993— Ariz. Rockies (Ariz.)....	OF	34	119	13	18	2	2	0	10	.151	5	55	3	22	1	5	.821
1994— Bend (Northwest)....	OF	73	284	47	75	19	5	•12	57	.264	29	*102	14	82	*10	9	.911
1995— Asheville (S. Atl.)........	OF	135	506	91	148	16	10	•32	*115	.292	29	136	31	190	11	9	.957
1996— New Haven (Eastern)..	OF	122	449	58	115	21	4	15	62	.256	31	125	3	168	10	*13	.932
1997— New Haven (Eastern)..	OF	119	461	91	146	24	2	23	75	.317	36	100	20	188	8	*11	.947
— Colo. Springs (PCL) ...	OF	21	78	14	33	7	0	3	12	.423	5	9	0	30	0	1	.968

GIL, BENJI   SS   WHITE SOX

PERSONAL: Born October 6, 1972, in Tijuana, Mexico. ... 6-2/182. ... Bats right, throws right. ... Full name: Romar Benjamin Gil.
HIGH SCHOOL: Castle Park (Chula Vista, Calif.).
TRANSACTIONS/CAREER NOTES: Selected by Texas Rangers organization in first round (19th pick overall) of free-agent draft (June 3, 1991). ... On Texas disabled list (March 22-May 22, 1996); included rehabilitation assigments to Charlotte (May 2-17) and Oklahoma City (May 17-21). ... Traded by Rangers to Chicago White Sox for P Al Levine and P Larry Thomas (December 19, 1997).
STATISTICAL NOTES: Led American Association shortstops with 660 total chances and 85 double plays in 1994. ... Career major league grand slams: 1.

						BATTING							FIELDING			
Year Team (League)	Pos.	G	AB	R	H	2B	3B	HR	RBI	Avg.	BB	SO	SB	PO	A	E	Avg.
1991— Butte (Pioneer)..........	SS	32	129	25	37	4	3	2	15	.287	14	36	9	61	88	14	.914
1992— Gastonia (S. Atl.)........	SS	132	482	75	132	21	1	9	55	.274	50	106	26	226	384	45	.931
1993— Texas (A.L.)	SS	22	57	3	7	0	0	0	2	.123	5	22	1	27	76	5	.954
— Tulsa (Texas)	SS	101	342	45	94	9	1	17	59	.275	35	89	20	159	285	19	.959
1994— Oklahoma City (A.A.)..	SS	*139	487	62	121	20	6	10	55	.248	33	120	14	*222	*401	*37	.944
1995— Texas (A.L.)	SS	130	415	36	91	20	3	9	46	.219	26	147	2	226	409	17	.974
1996— Charlotte (Fla. St.)......	SS	11	31	2	8	6	0	1	7	.258	3	7	0	6	21	2	.931
— Oklahoma City (A.A.)..	SS	84	292	32	65	15	1	6	28	.223	21	90	4	121	267	21	.949
— Texas (A.L.)..............	SS	5	5	0	2	0	0	0	1	.400	1	1	0	5	7	1	.923
1997— Texas (A.L.)	SS-DH	110	317	35	71	13	2	5	31	.224	17	96	1	163	328	19	.963
Major league totals (4 years)		267	794	74	171	33	5	14	80	.215	49	266	4	421	820	42	.967

GILBERT, SHAWN   IF   METS

PERSONAL: Born March 12, 1965, in Camden, N.J. ... 5-9/170. ... Bats right, throws right. ... Full name: Albert Shawn Gilbert Jr.
HIGH SCHOOL: Agua Fria Union (Avondale, Ariz.).
JUNIOR COLLEGE: Golden West College (Calif.).
COLLEGE: Fresno State.
TRANSACTIONS/CAREER NOTES: Selected by Los Angeles Dodgers organization in 21st round of free-agent draft (June 6, 1983). ... Selected by Cincinnati Reds organization in secondary phase of free-agent draft (January 9, 1985). ... Selected by Minnesota Twins organization in secondary phase of free-agent draft (June 5, 1985). ... Selected by Twins organization in 12th round of free-agent draft (June 2, 1987). ... Claimed on waivers by Chicago White Sox (November 12, 1992). ... Granted free agency (October 15, 1993). ... Signed by Scranton/Wilkes-Barre, Philadelphia Phillies organization (January 5, 1994). ... Granted free agency (October 16, 1995). ... Signed by New York Mets organization (January 30, 1996). ... On New York disabled list (June 16-30, 1997). ... Granted free agency (October 15, 1997). ... Re-signed by Mets organization (December 19, 1997).
STATISTICAL NOTES: Led Midwest League shortstops with 80 double plays in 1988. ... Led Southern League in caught stealing with 19 in 1991.

G

Year Team (League)	Pos.	G	AB	R	H	2B	3B	HR	RBI	Avg.	BB	SO	SB	PO	A	E	Avg.
1987—Visalia (California)	SS	82	272	39	61	5	0	5	27	.224	34	59	6	122	214	30	.918
1988—Visalia (California)	SS-2B	14	43	10	16	3	2	0	8	.372	10	7	1	18	34	10	.839
—Kenosha (Midwest)	SS	108	402	80	112	21	2	3	44	.279	63	61	49	151	325	41	.921
1989—Visalia (California)	SS	125	453	52	113	17	1	2	43	.249	54	70	42	204	382	39	.938
1990—Orlando (South.)	SS	123	433	68	110	18	2	4	44	.254	61	69	31	157	*361	41	.927
1991—Orlando (South.)	O-S-2-3	138	529	69	136	12	5	3	38	.257	53	71	*43	247	250	20	.961
1992—Portland (PCL)	S-O-2-3	138	444	60	109	17	2	3	52	.245	36	55	31	214	303	25	.954
1993—Nashville (A.A.)■	3-O-S-2	104	278	28	63	17	2	0	17	.227	12	41	6	81	123	17	.923
1994—Scran./W.B. (Int'l)■....	SS-OF-2B	*141	*547	81	139	33	4	7	52	.254	66	86	20	215	275	27	.948
1995—Scran./W.B. (Int'l)	SS-OF-3B	136	536	84	141	26	2	2	42	.263	64	102	16	213	361	28	.953
1996—Norfolk (Int'l)■	3-2-S-O	131	493	76	126	28	1	9	50	.256	46	97	17	174	312	25	.951
1997—Norfolk (Int'l)	S-O-2-3	78	288	53	76	13	1	8	33	.264	43	64	16	124	134	16	.942
—New York (N.L.)..........	2-S-3-O	29	22	3	3	0	0	1	1	.136	1	8	1	11	8	1	.950
Major league totals (1 year)		**29**	**22**	**3**	**3**	**0**	**0**	**1**	**1**	**.136**	**1**	**8**	**1**	**11**	**8**	**1**	**.950**

GILES, BRIAN — OF — INDIANS

PERSONAL: Born January 21, 1971, in El Cajon, Calif. ... 5-11/200. ... Bats left, throws left. ... Full name: Brian S. Giles.
HIGH SCHOOL: Granite Hills (El Cajon, Calif.).
TRANSACTIONS/CAREER NOTES: Selected by Cleveland Indians organization in 17th round of free-agent draft (June 5, 1989). ... On Canton/Akron disabled list (May 15-July 7, 1992).
STATISTICAL NOTES: Led International League with 10 intentional bases on balls received in 1994. ... Led International League outfielders with five double plays in 1994.

Year Team (League)	Pos.	G	AB	R	H	2B	3B	HR	RBI	Avg.	BB	SO	SB	PO	A	E	Avg.
1989—Burlington (Appal.).....	OF	36	129	18	40	7	0	0	20	.310	11	19	6	52	3	1	.982
1990—Watertown (NYP)	OF	70	246	44	71	15	2	1	23	.289	48	23	11	108	8	1	.991
1991—Kinston (Carolina)	OF	125	394	71	122	14	0	4	47	.310	68	70	19	187	10	5	.975
1992—Cant./Akr. (Eastern)	OF	23	74	6	16	4	0	0	3	.216	10	10	3	45	0	0	1.000
—Kinston (Carolina)	OF	42	140	28	37	5	1	3	18	.264	30	21	3	74	3	1	.987
1993—Cant./Akr. (Eastern)	OF	123	425	64	139	17	6	6	64	.327	57	43	18	186	3	5	.974
1994—Charlotte (Int'l)	OF	128	434	74	136	18	3	16	58	.313	55	61	8	242	12	4	.984
1995—Buffalo (A.A.)	OF	123	413	67	128	18	•8	15	67	.310	54	40	7	248	4	5	.981
—Cleveland (A.L.)..........	OF-DH	6	9	6	5	0	0	1	3	.556	0	1	0	2	1	0	1.000
1996—Buffalo (A.A.)	OF	83	318	65	100	17	6	20	64	.314	42	29	1	132	5	2	.986
—Cleveland (A.L.)..........	DH-OF	51	121	26	43	14	1	5	27	.355	19	13	3	26	0	0	1.000
1997—Cleveland (A.L.)..........	OF-DH	130	377	62	101	15	3	17	61	.268	63	50	13	201	7	6	.972
Major league totals (3 years)		**187**	**507**	**94**	**149**	**29**	**4**	**23**	**91**	**.294**	**82**	**64**	**16**	**229**	**8**	**6**	**.975**

DIVISION SERIES RECORD

Year Team (League)	Pos.	G	AB	R	H	2B	3B	HR	RBI	Avg.	BB	SO	SB	PO	A	E	Avg.
1996—Cleveland (A.L.)..........	PH	1	1	0	0	0	0	0	0	.000	0	1	0	0	0	0	...
1997—Cleveland (A.L.)..........	OF	3	7	0	1	0	0	0	0	.143	0	1	0	4	1	0	1.000
Division series totals (2 years)		**4**	**8**	**0**	**1**	**0**	**0**	**0**	**0**	**.125**	**0**	**2**	**0**	**4**	**1**	**0**	**1.000**

CHAMPIONSHIP SERIES RECORD

Year Team (League)	Pos.	G	AB	R	H	2B	3B	HR	RBI	Avg.	BB	SO	SB	PO	A	E	Avg.
1997—Cleveland (A.L.)..........	OF	6	16	1	3	0	0	0	0	.188	2	6	0	9	0	0	1.000

WORLD SERIES RECORD

Year Team (League)	Pos.	G	AB	R	H	2B	3B	HR	RBI	Avg.	BB	SO	SB	PO	A	E	Avg.
1997—Cleveland (A.L.)..........	PH-OF	5	4	1	2	1	0	0	2	.500	4	1	0	2	0	0	1.000

GILKEY, BERNARD — OF — METS

PERSONAL: Born September 24, 1966, in St. Louis. ... 6-0/200. ... Bats right, throws right. ... Full name: Otis Bernard Gilkey.
HIGH SCHOOL: University City (Mo.).
TRANSACTIONS/CAREER NOTES: Signed as non-drafted free agent by St. Louis Cardinals organization (August 22, 1984). ... On disabled list (April 10-25, 1986 and May 29, 1987-remainder of season). ... On St. Louis disabled list (June 14-July 11, 1991 and April 29-May 14, 1993). ... On suspended list (July 8-9, 1994). ... Granted free agency (April 7, 1995). ... Re-signed by Cardinals (April 8, 1995). ... On St. Louis disabled list (June 28-July 17, 1995); included rehabilitation assignment to Louisville (July 15-17). ... Traded by Cardinals to New York Mets for P Eric Ludwick, P Erik Hiljus and OF Yudith Ozorio (January 22, 1996).
STATISTICAL NOTES: Led New York-Pennsylvania League outfielders with 185 total chances in 1985. ... Led Texas League in caught stealing with 22 in 1989. ... Led American Association in caught stealing with 33 in 1990. ... Led N.L. outfielders with 19 assists in 1993. ... Tied for N.L. lead in double plays by outfielder with four in 1995. ... Tied for N.L. lead with 12 sacrifice flies in 1997.

Year Team (League)	Pos.	G	AB	R	H	2B	3B	HR	RBI	Avg.	BB	SO	SB	PO	A	E	Avg.
1985—Erie (N.Y.-Penn)..........	OF	•77	*294	57	60	9	1	7	27	.204	55	57	34	*164	*13	*8	.957
1986—Savannah (S. Atl.)	OF	105	374	64	88	15	4	6	36	.235	84	57	32	220	7	5	.978
1987—Springfield (Midw.)	OF	46	162	30	37	5	0	0	9	.228	39	28	18	79	5	4	.955
1988—Springfield (Midw.)	OF	125	491	84	120	18	7	6	36	.244	65	54	54	165	10	6	.967
1989—Arkansas (Texas)........	OF	131	500	*104	139	25	3	6	57	.278	70	54	*53	236	*22	9	.966
1990—Louisville (A.A.)..........	OF	132	499	83	147	26	8	3	46	.295	*75	49	45	236	18	•11	.958
—St. Louis (N.L.)..........	OF	18	64	11	19	5	2	1	3	.297	8	5	6	47	2	2	.961
1991—St. Louis (N.L.)..........	OF	81	268	28	58	7	2	5	20	.216	39	33	14	164	6	1	.994
—Louisville (A.A.)..........	OF	11	41	5	6	2	0	0	2	.146	6	10	1	33	1	0	1.000

G

Year Team (League)	Pos.	G	AB	R	H	2B	3B	HR	RBI	Avg.	BB	SO	SB	PO	A	E	Avg.
1992—St. Louis (N.L.)	OF	131	384	56	116	19	4	7	43	.302	39	52	18	217	9	5	.978
1993—St. Louis (N.L.)	OF-1B	137	557	99	170	40	5	16	70	.305	56	66	15	251	†20	8	.971
1994—St. Louis (N.L.)	OF	105	380	52	96	22	1	6	45	.253	39	65	15	168	9	3	.983
1995—St. Louis (N.L.)	OF	121	480	73	143	33	4	17	69	.298	42	70	12	206	10	3	.986
—Louisville (A.A.)	OF	2	6	3	2	1	0	1	1	.333	1	0	0	2	0	0	1.000
1996—New York (N.L.)■	OF	153	571	108	181	44	3	30	117	.317	73	125	17	309	*18	6	.982
1997—New York (N.L.)	OF-DH	145	518	85	129	31	1	18	78	.249	70	111	7	251	*17	3	.989
Major league totals (8 years)		891	3222	512	912	201	22	100	445	.283	366	527	104	1613	91	31	.982

GIOVANOLA, ED   IF   PADRES

PERSONAL: Born March 4, 1969, in Los Gatos, Calif. ... 5-10/170. ... Bats left, throws right. ... Full name: Edward Thomas Giovanola.
HIGH SCHOOL: Bellarmine College Prepatory (San Jose, Calif.).
COLLEGE: Santa Clara.
TRANSACTIONS/CAREER NOTES: Selected by Atlanta Braves organization in seventh round of free-agent draft (June 4, 1990). ... On disabled list (May 29-June 5 and June 23-July 23, 1992). ... On Richmond disabled list (June 28-July 21, 1995). ... Claimed on waivers by San Diego Padres (October 13, 1997).
STATISTICAL NOTES: Led International League with .417 on-base percentage in 1995.

Year Team (League)	Pos.	G	AB	R	H	2B	3B	HR	RBI	Avg.	BB	SO	SB	PO	A	E	Avg.
1990—Idaho Falls (Pio.)	2B	25	98	25	38	6	0	0	13	.388	17	9	6	32	72	2	.981
—Sumter (S. Atl.)	2B	35	119	20	29	4	0	0	8	.244	34	17	8	61	125	3	.984
1991—Durham (Carolina)	3-S-2-O	101	299	50	76	9	0	6	27	.254	57	39	18	112	182	15	.951
1992—Greenville (Southern)	3B	75	270	39	72	5	0	5	30	.267	29	40	4	35	168	18	.919
1993—Greenville (Southern)	3B-2B	120	384	70	108	21	5	5	43	.281	84	49	6	94	281	14	.964
1994—Greenville (Southern)	3B	25	84	13	20	6	1	4	16	.238	10	12	2	20	41	2	.968
—Richmond (Int'l)	3-S-2-O	98	344	48	97	16	2	6	30	.282	31	49	7	94	211	16	.950
1995—Richmond (Int'l)	SS-3B	99	321	45	103	18	2	4	36	.321	55	37	8	125	286	15	.965
—Atlanta (N.L.)	2B-3B-SS	13	14	2	1	0	0	0	0	.071	3	5	0	9	7	0	1.000
1996—Richmond (Int'l)	S-2-3-O	62	210	29	62	15	1	3	16	.295	37	34	2	77	155	11	.955
—Atlanta (N.L.)	SS-3B-2B	43	82	10	19	2	0	0	7	.232	8	13	1	24	56	1	.988
1997—Richmond (Int'l)	3B-SS-OF	116	395	65	115	23	5	2	46	.291	64	56	2	87	227	16	.952
—Atlanta (N.L.)	3B-2B-SS	14	8	0	2	0	0	0	0	.250	2	1	0	0	6	0	1.000
Major league totals (3 years)		70	104	12	22	2	0	0	7	.212	13	19	1	33	69	1	.990

GIPSON, CHARLES   IF/OF   MARINERS

PERSONAL: Born December 16, 1972, in Orange, Calif. ... 6-2/180. ... Bats right, throws right. ... Full name: Charles Wells Gipson Jr.
HIGH SCHOOL: Loara (Anaheim, Calif.).
JUNIOR COLLEGE: Cypress (Calif.) College.
TRANSACTIONS/CAREER NOTES: Selected by Seattle Mariners organization in 63rd round of free-agent draft (June 3, 1991). ... On disabled list (May 4-19, 1993).
STATISTICAL NOTES: Led Midwest League in being hit by pitch with 27 in 1993. ... Tied for Southern League lead in double plays by outfielder with four in 1995. ... Tied for Southern League lead in caught stealing with 15 in 1996.

Year Team (League)	Pos.	G	AB	R	H	2B	3B	HR	RBI	Avg.	BB	SO	SB	PO	A	E	Avg.
1992—Ariz. Mariners (Ariz.)	SS	39	124	30	29	2	0	0	14	.234	13	19	11	49	114	•23	.876
1993—Appleton (Midwest)	2B-OF-SS	109	348	53	89	13	1	0	20	.256	61	76	21	192	201	28	.933
1994—Riverside (Calif.)	OF	128	481	*102	141	12	3	1	41	.293	76	67	34	293	14	9	.972
1995—Port City (Southern)	OF-2B	112	391	36	87	11	2	0	29	.223	30	66	10	235	19	6	.977
1996—Port City (Southern)	OF-SS	119	407	54	109	12	3	1	30	.268	41	62	15	210	162	15	.961
1997—Memphis (Southern)	S-3-2-O	88	320	56	79	9	4	1	28	.247	34	71	31	143	211	23	.939
—Tacoma (PCL)	3-0-2-S	11	35	5	11	2	0	0	5	.314	4	3	0	15	16	3	.912

GIRARDI, JOE   C   YANKEES

PERSONAL: Born October 14, 1964, in Peoria, Ill. ... 5-11/195. ... Bats right, throws right. ... Full name: Joseph Elliott Girardi. ... Name pronounced jeh-RAR-dee.
HIGH SCHOOL: Spalding Institute (Peoria, Ill.).
COLLEGE: Northwestern (degree in industrial engineering, 1986).
TRANSACTIONS/CAREER NOTES: Selected by Chicago Cubs organization in fifth round of free-agent draft (June 2, 1986). ... On disabled list (August 27, 1986-remainder of season and August 7, 1988-remainder of season). ... On Chicago disabled list (April 17-August 6, 1991); included rehabilitation assignment to Iowa (July 23-August 6). ... Selected by Colorado Rockies in first round (19th pick overall) of expansion draft (November 17, 1992). ... On Colorado disabled list (June 5-August 11, 1993); included rehabilitation assignment to Colorado Springs (August 1-11). ... On disabled list (July 11-26, 1994). ... Traded by Rockies to New York Yankees for P Mike DeJean and a player to be named later (November 20, 1995). ... Rockies acquired P Steve Shoemaker to complete deal (December 6, 1995). ... Granted free agency (November 5, 1996). ... Re-signed by Yankees (December 3, 1996).
STATISTICAL NOTES: Led Carolina League catchers with 661 total chances and tied for lead with 17 passed balls in 1987. ... Led Eastern League catchers with .992 fielding percentage, 448 putouts, 76 assists and 528 total chances and tied for lead with five double plays in 1988. ... Tied for N.L. lead with 16 passed balls in 1990.

Year Team (League)	Pos.	G	AB	R	H	2B	3B	HR	RBI	Avg.	BB	SO	SB	PO	A	E	Avg.
1986—Peoria (Midwest)	C	68	230	36	71	13	1	3	28	.309	17	36	6	405	34	5	.989
1987—Win.-Salem (Car.)	C	99	364	51	102	9	8	8	46	.280	33	64	9	*569	*74	18	.973
1988—Pittsfield (Eastern)	C-OF	104	357	44	97	14	1	7	41	.272	29	51	7	†460	†76	6	†.989

Year Team (League)	Pos.	G	AB	R	H	2B	3B	HR	RBI	Avg.	BB	SO	SB	PO	A	E	Avg.
								BATTING							FIELDING		
1989— Chicago (N.L.)	C	59	157	15	39	10	0	1	14	.248	11	26	2	332	28	7	.981
— Iowa (Am. Assoc.)......	C	32	110	12	27	4	2	2	11	.245	5	19	3	172	21	1	.995
1990— Chicago (N.L.)	C	133	419	36	113	24	2	1	38	.270	17	50	8	653	61	11	.985
1991— Chicago (N.L.)	C	21	47	3	9	2	0	0	6	.191	6	6	0	95	11	3	.972
— Iowa (Am. Assoc.)......	C	12	36	3	8	1	0	0	4	.222	4	8	2	62	5	3	.957
1992— Chicago (N.L.)	C	91	270	19	73	3	1	1	12	.270	19	38	0	369	51	4	.991
1993— Colorado (N.L.)■	C	86	310	35	90	14	5	3	31	.290	24	41	6	478	46	6	.989
— Colo. Springs (PCL) ...	C	8	31	6	15	1	1	1	6	.484	0	3	1	40	3	1	.977
1994— Colorado (N.L.)	C	93	330	47	91	9	4	4	34	.276	21	48	3	549	56	5	.992
1995— Colorado (N.L.)	C	125	462	63	121	17	2	8	55	.262	29	76	3	730	60	10	.988
1996— New York (A.L.)■	C-DH	124	422	55	124	22	3	2	45	.294	30	55	13	803	46	3	.996
1997— New York (A.L.).........	C	112	398	38	105	23	1	1	50	.264	26	53	2	829	55	5	.994
American League totals (2 years)		236	820	93	229	45	4	3	95	.279	56	108	15	1632	101	8	.995
National League totals (7 years)		608	1995	218	536	79	14	18	190	.269	127	285	22	3206	313	46	.987
Major league totals (9 years)		844	2815	311	765	124	18	21	285	.272	183	393	37	4838	414	54	.990

DIVISION SERIES RECORD

Year Team (League)	Pos.	G	AB	R	H	2B	3B	HR	RBI	Avg.	BB	SO	SB	PO	A	E	Avg.
								BATTING							FIELDING		
1995— Colorado (N.L.)	C	4	16	0	2	0	0	0	0	.125	0	2	0	25	3	1	.966
1996— New York (A.L.).........	C-PR	4	9	1	2	0	0	0	0	.222	4	1	0	28	1		1.000
1997— New York (A.L.).........	C	5	15	2	2	0	0	0	0	.133	1	3	0	21	2	0	1.000
Division series totals (3 years)		13	40	3	6	0	0	0	0	.150	5	6	0	74	6	1	.988

CHAMPIONSHIP SERIES RECORD

Year Team (League)	Pos.	G	AB	R	H	2B	3B	HR	RBI	Avg.	BB	SO	SB	PO	A	E	Avg.
								BATTING							FIELDING		
1989— Chicago (N.L.)	C	4	10	1	1	0	0	0	0	.100	1	2	0	20	0	0	1.000
1996— New York (A.L.)	C-PH	4	12	1	3	0	1	0	0	.250	1	3	0	22	0	0	1.000
Championship series totals (2 years)		8	22	2	4	0	1	0	0	.182	2	5	0	42	0	0	1.000

WORLD SERIES RECORD

NOTES: Member of World Series championship team (1996).

Year Team (League)	Pos.	G	AB	R	H	2B	3B	HR	RBI	Avg.	BB	SO	SB	PO	A	E	Avg.
								BATTING							FIELDING		
1996— New York (A.L.).........	C	4	10	1	2	0	1	0	1	.200	1	2	0	23	4	0	1.000

GLANVILLE, DOUG   OF   PHILLIES

PERSONAL: Born August 25, 1970, in Hackensack, N.J. ... 6-2/175. ... Bats right, throws right. ... Full name: Douglas Metunwa Glanville.
HIGH SCHOOL: Teaneck (N.J.).
COLLEGE: Pennsylvania.
TRANSACTIONS/CAREER NOTES: Selected by Chicago Cubs organization in first round (12th pick overall) of free-agent draft (June 3, 1991). ... Traded by Cubs to Philadelphia Phillies for 2B Mickey Morandini (December 23, 1997).
STATISTICAL NOTES: Led Carolina League outfielders with 312 total chances in 1992. ... Led Southern League in caught stealing with 20 in 1994. ... Led Southern League outfielders with 339 total chances in 1994.

Year Team (League)	Pos.	G	AB	R	H	2B	3B	HR	RBI	Avg.	BB	SO	SB	PO	A	E	Avg.
								BATTING							FIELDING		
1991— Geneva (NY-Penn)......	OF	36	152	29	46	8	0	2	12	.303	11	25	17	77	4	0	1.000
1992— Win.-Salem (Car.).......	OF	120	485	72	125	18	4	4	36	.258	40	78	32	*293	12	7	.978
1993— Daytona (Fla. St.)	OF	61	239	47	70	10	1	2	21	.293	28	24	18	123	11	7	.950
— Orlando (South.)	OF	73	296	42	78	14	4	9	40	.264	12	41	15	168	8	5	.972
1994— Orlando (South.)	OF	130	483	53	127	22	2	5	52	.263	24	49	26	*322	14	3	.991
1995— Iowa (Am. Assoc.)......	OF	112	419	48	113	16	2	4	37	.270	16	64	13	209	9	4	.982
1996— Iowa (Am. Assoc.)......	OF	90	373	53	115	23	3	3	34	.308	12	35	15	217	6	3	.987
— Chicago (N.L.)	OF	49	83	10	20	5	1	1	10	.241	3	11	2	35	1	1	.973
1997— Chicago (N.L.)	OF	146	474	79	142	22	5	4	35	.300	24	46	19	247	12	3	.989
Major league totals (2 years)		195	557	89	162	27	6	5	45	.291	27	57	21	282	13	4	.987

GLAUBER, KEITH   P   REDS

PERSONAL: Born January 8, 1972, in Brooklyn, N.Y. ... 6-2/190. ... Throws right, bats right. ... Full name: Keith H. Glauber.
HIGH SCHOOL: Marlboro (N.J.)
COLLEGE: Montclair (N.J.) State.
TRANSACTIONS/CAREER NOTES: Selected by St. Louis Cardinals organization in 42nd round of free-agent draft (June 2, 1994). ... Selected by Cincinnati Reds from Cardinals organization in Rule 5 major league draft (December 15, 1997).

Year Team (League)	W	L	Pct.	ERA	G	GS	CG	ShO	Sv.	IP	H	R	ER	BB	SO
1994— New Jersey (NYP).............	4	6	.400	4.19	17	10	0	0	0	68²/₃	67	36	32	26	51
1995— Savannah (S. Atl.)	2	1	.667	3.73	40	0	0	0	0	62²/₃	50	29	26	36	62
1996— Peoria (Midwest)...............	3	3	.500	3.09	54	0	0	0	0	64	54	31	22	26	80
1997— Arkansas (Texas)...............	5	7	.417	2.75	50	0	0	0	3	59	48	22	18	25	53
— Louisville (A.A.)...............	1	3	.250	5.17	15	0	0	0	5	15²/₃	18	14	9	4	14

GLAVINE, TOM   ,   P   BRAVES

PERSONAL: Born March 25, 1966, in Concord, Mass. ... 6-1/185. ... Throws left, bats left. ... Full name: Thomas Michael Glavine. ... Brother of Michael Glavine, first baseman, Cleveland Indians organization. ... Name pronounced GLAV-in.

HIGH SCHOOL: Billerica (Mass.).
TRANSACTIONS/CAREER NOTES: Selected by Atlanta Braves organization in second round of free-agent draft (June 4, 1984).
HONORS: Named N.L. Pitcher of the Year by THE SPORTING NEWS (1991). ... Named lefthanded pitcher on THE SPORTING NEWS N.L. All-Star team (1991-92). ... Named pitcher on THE SPORTING NEWS N.L. Silver Slugger team (1991, 1995 and 1996). ... Named N.L. Cy Young Award winner by Baseball Writers' Association of America (1991).
STATISTICAL NOTES: Led Gulf Coast League with 12 wild pitches in 1984.
MISCELLANEOUS: Selected by Los Angeles Kings in fourth round (69th pick overall) of NHL entry draft (June 9, 1984). ... Appeared in eight games as pinch-runner (1988). ... Appeared in one game as pinch-runner (1989). ... Appeared in one game as pinch-runner (1990). ... Received a base on balls and scored once in one game as pinch-hitter and appeared in one game as pinch-runner (1991). ... Singled and struck out in two games as pinch-hitter (1992). ... Struck out in only appearance as pinch-hitter (1994). ... Singled and struck out in three games as pinch-hitter (1996).

Year Team (League)	W	L	Pct.	ERA	G	GS	CG	ShO	Sv.	IP	H	R	ER	BB	SO
1984— GC Braves (GCL)	2	3	.400	3.34	8	7	0	0	0	32 1/3	29	17	12	13	34
1985— Sumter (S. Atl.)	9	6	.600	*2.35	26	26	2	1	0	168 2/3	114	58	44	73	174
1986— Greenville (Southern)	11	6	.647	3.41	22	22	2	1	0	145 1/3	129	62	55	70	114
— Richmond (Int'l)	1	5	.167	5.63	7	7	1	1	0	40	40	29	25	27	12
1987— Richmond (Int'l)	6	12	.333	3.35	22	22	4	1	0	150 1/3	142	70	56	56	91
— Atlanta (N.L.)	2	4	.333	5.54	9	9	0	0	0	50 1/3	55	34	31	33	20
1988— Atlanta (N.L.)	7	*17	.292	4.56	34	34	1	0	0	195 1/3	201	111	99	63	84
1989— Atlanta (N.L.)	14	8	.636	3.68	29	29	6	4	0	186	172	88	76	40	90
1990— Atlanta (N.L.)	10	12	.455	4.28	33	33	1	0	0	214 1/3	232	111	102	78	129
1991— Atlanta (N.L.)	•20	11	.645	2.55	34	34	•9	1	0	246 2/3	201	83	70	69	192
1992— Atlanta (N.L.)	•20	8	.714	2.76	33	33	7	•5	0	225	197	81	69	70	129
1993— Atlanta (N.L.)	•22	6	.786	3.20	36	•36	4	2	0	239 1/3	236	91	85	90	120
1994— Atlanta (N.L.)	13	9	.591	3.97	25	25	2	0	0	165 1/3	173	76	73	70	140
1995— Atlanta (N.L.)	16	7	.696	3.08	29	29	3	1	0	198 2/3	182	76	68	66	127
1996— Atlanta (N.L.)	15	10	.600	2.98	36	*36	1	0	0	235 1/3	222	91	78	85	181
1997— Atlanta (N.L.)	14	7	.667	2.96	33	33	5	2	0	240	197	86	79	79	152
Major league totals (11 years)	153	99	.607	3.40	331	331	39	15	0	2196 1/3	2068	928	830	743	1364

DIVISION SERIES RECORD

RECORDS: Holds N.L. career record for most bases on balls allowed—9.

Year Team (League)	W	L	Pct.	ERA	G	GS	CG	ShO	Sv.	IP	H	R	ER	BB	SO
1995— Atlanta (N.L.)	0	0	...	2.57	1	1	0	0	0	7	5	3	2	1	3
1996— Atlanta (N.L.)	1	0	1.000	1.35	1	1	0	0	0	6 2/3	5	1	1	3	7
1997— Atlanta (N.L.)	1	0	1.000	4.50	1	1	0	0	0	6	5	3	3	5	4
Div. series totals (3 years)	2	0	1.000	2.75	3	3	0	0	0	19 2/3	15	7	6	9	14

CHAMPIONSHIP SERIES RECORD

RECORDS: Holds records for most runs allowed in one inning—8 (October 13, 1992, second inning); and most earned runs allowed in one inning—7 (October 13, 1992, second inning). ... Shares single-game record for most earned runs allowed—7 (October 13, 1992 and October 14, 1997). ... Holds career record for most earned runs allowed—29; and most hits allowed—61. ... Shares record for most hits allowed in one inning—6 (October 13, 1992, second inning). ... Shares career N.L. record for most batsmen—4. ... Shares career record for most series with one team—6 (Atlanta, 1991-93 and 1995-97). ... Shares N.L. single-series record for most hit batsmen—2 (1992).

Year Team (League)	W	L	Pct.	ERA	G	GS	CG	ShO	Sv.	IP	H	R	ER	BB	SO
1991— Atlanta (N.L.)	0	2	.000	3.21	2	2	0	0	0	14	12	5	5	6	11
1992— Atlanta (N.L.)	0	2	.000	12.27	2	2	0	0	0	7 1/3	13	11	10	3	2
1993— Atlanta (N.L.)	1	0	1.000	2.57	1	1	0	0	0	7	6	2	2	0	5
1995— Atlanta (N.L.)	0	0	...	1.29	1	1	0	0	0	7	7	1	1	2	5
1996— Atlanta (N.L.)	1	1	.500	2.08	2	2	0	0	0	13	10	3	3	0	9
1997— Atlanta (N.L.)	1	1	.500	5.40	2	2	0	0	0	13 1/3	13	8	8	11	9
Champ. series totals (6 years)	3	6	.333	4.23	10	10	0	0	0	61 2/3	61	30	29	22	41

WORLD SERIES RECORD

RECORDS: Shares records for most bases on balls allowed in one inning—4 (October 24, 1991, sixth inning); and most consecutive bases on balls allowed in one inning—3 (October 24, 1991, sixth inning).
NOTES: Named Most Valuable Player (1995). ... Member of World Series championship team (1995).

Year Team (League)	W	L	Pct.	ERA	G	GS	CG	ShO	Sv.	IP	H	R	ER	BB	SO
1991— Atlanta (N.L.)	1	1	.500	2.70	2	2	1	0	0	13 1/3	8	6	4	7	8
1992— Atlanta (N.L.)	1	1	.500	1.59	2	2	2	0	0	17	10	3	3	4	8
1995— Atlanta (N.L.)	2	0	1.000	1.29	2	2	0	0	0	14	4	2	2	6	11
1996— Atlanta (N.L.)	0	1	.000	1.29	1	1	0	0	0	7	4	2	1	3	8
World Series totals (4 years)	4	3	.571	1.75	7	7	3	0	0	51 1/3	26	13	10	20	35

ALL-STAR GAME RECORD

RECORDS: Holds single-game record for most hits allowed—9 (July 14, 1992). ... Holds record for most hits allowed in one inning—7 (July 14, 1992, first inning).

Year League	W	L	Pct.	ERA	GS	CG	ShO	Sv.	IP	H	R	ER	BB	SO
1991— National	0	0	...	0.00	1	0	0	0	2	1	0	0	1	3
1992— National	0	1	.000	27.00	1	0	0	0	1 2/3	9	5	5	0	2
1993— National						Did not play.								
1996— National	0	0	...	0.00	0	0	0	0	1	0	0	0	0	1
1997— National						Did not play.								
All-Star totals (3 years)	0	1	.000	9.64	2	0	0	0	4 2/3	10	5	5	1	6

GLOVER, GARY   P   BLUE JAYS

G

PERSONAL: Born December 3, 1976, in Cleveland. ... 6-5/180. ... Throws right, bats right. ... Full name: John Gary Glover.
HIGH SCHOOL: DeLand (Fla.).
TRANSACTIONS/CAREER NOTES: Selected by Toronto Blue Jays organization in 15th round of free-agent draft (June 2, 1994). ... On disabled list (August 10-September 8, 1994).

Year Team (League)	W	L	Pct.	ERA	G	GS	CG	ShO	Sv.	IP	H	R	ER	BB	SO
1994— GC Blue Jays (GCL)............	0	0	...	47.25	2	0	0	0	0	1 1/3	4	8	7	4	2
1995— GC Blue Jays (GCL)............	3	7	.300	4.91	12	10	2	0	0	62 1/3	62	48	34	26	46
1996— Medicine Hat (Pio.)	3	*12	.200	7.75	15	•15	*2	0	0	83 2/3	*119	*94	72	29	54
1997— Hagerstown (S. Atl.)..........	6	*17	.261	3.73	28	28	3	0	0	173 2/3	165	94	72	58	155

GLYNN, RYAN   P   RANGERS

PERSONAL: Born November 1, 1974, in Portsmouth, Va. ... 6-3/200. ... Throws right, bats right. ... Full name: Ryan David Glynn.
HIGH SCHOOL: Churchland (Portsmouth, Va.).
COLLEGE: VMI.
TRANSACTIONS/CAREER NOTES: Selected by Texas Rangers organization in fourth round of free-agent draft (June 1, 1995).

Year Team (League)	W	L	Pct.	ERA	G	GS	CG	ShO	Sv.	IP	H	R	ER	BB	SO
1995— Hudson Valley (NYP).........	3	3	.500	4.70	9	8	0	0	0	44	56	27	23	16	21
1996— Charleston, S.C. (S. Atl.)....	8	7	.533	4.54	19	19	2	1	0	121	118	70	61	59	72
1997— Charlotte (Fla. St.).............	8	7	.533	4.97	23	22	5	1	1	134	148	81	74	44	96
— Tulsa (Texas)	1	1	.500	3.38	3	3	0	0	0	21 1/3	21	9	8	10	18

GOMES, WAYNE   P   PHILLIES

PERSONAL: Born January 15, 1973, in Hampton, Va. ... 6-2/205. ... Throws right, bats right. ... Full name: Wayne M. Gomes.
HIGH SCHOOL: Phoebus (Hampton, Va.).
COLLEGE: Old Dominion.
TRANSACTIONS/CAREER NOTES: Selected by Philadelphia Phillies organization in first round (fourth pick overall) of free-agent draft (June 3, 1993). ... On disabled list (May 12-June 23, 1995).
STATISTICAL NOTES: Led Florida State League with 27 wild pitches in 1994. ... Tied for Eastern League lead with six balks in 1995.

Year Team (League)	W	L	Pct.	ERA	G	GS	CG	ShO	Sv.	IP	H	R	ER	BB	SO
1993— Batavia (N.Y.-Penn)	1	0	1.000	1.23	5	0	0	0	0	7 1/3	1	1	1	8	11
— Clearwater (Fla. St.)	0	0	...	1.17	9	0	0	0	4	7 2/3	4	1	1	9	13
1994— Clearwater (Fla. St.)	6	8	.429	4.74	23	21	1	1	0	104 1/3	85	63	55	82	102
1995— Reading (Eastern)	7	4	.636	3.96	22	22	1	1	0	104 2/3	89	54	46	70	102
1996— Reading (Eastern)	0	4	.000	4.48	*67	0	0	0	24	64 1/3	53	35	32	48	79
1997— Scran./W.B. (Int'l)..............	3	1	.750	2.37	26	0	0	0	7	38	31	11	10	24	36
— Philadelphia (N.L.).............	5	1	.833	5.27	37	0	0	0	0	42 2/3	45	26	25	24	24
Major league totals (1 year)........	5	1	.833	5.27	37	0	0	0	0	42 2/3	45	26	25	24	24

GOMEZ, CHRIS   SS   PADRES

PERSONAL: Born June 16, 1971, in Los Angeles. ... 6-1/195. ... Bats right, throws right. ... Full name: Christopher Cory Gomez.
HIGH SCHOOL: Lakewood (Calif.).
COLLEGE: Long Beach State.
TRANSACTIONS/CAREER NOTES: Selected by California Angels organization in 37th round of free-agent draft (June 5, 1989); did not sign. ... Selected by Detroit Tigers organization in third round of free-agent draft (June 1, 1992). ... Traded by Tigers with C John Flaherty to San Diego Padres for C Brad Ausmus, SS Andujar Cedeno and P Russ Spear (June 18, 1996).

Year Team (League)	Pos.	G	AB	R	H	2B	3B	HR	RBI	Avg.	BB	SO	SB	PO	A	E	Avg.
1992— London (Eastern)	SS	64	220	20	59	13	2	1	19	.268	20	34	1	100	174	14	.951
1993— Toledo (Int'l)..............	SS	87	277	29	68	12	2	0	20	.245	23	37	6	133	261	16	.961
— Detroit (A.L.)..............	SS-2B-DH	46	128	11	32	7	1	0	11	.250	9	17	2	69	118	5	.974
1994— Detroit (A.L.)	SS-2B	84	296	32	76	19	0	8	53	.257	33	64	5	140	210	8	.978
1995— Detroit (A.L.)	SS-2B-DH	123	431	49	96	20	2	11	50	.223	41	96	4	210	361	15	.974
1996— Detroit (A.L.)	SS	48	128	21	31	5	0	1	16	.242	18	20	1	77	114	6	.970
— San Diego (N.L.)■......	SS	89	328	32	86	16	1	3	29	.262	39	64	2	124	261	13	.967
1997— San Diego (N.L.)	SS	150	522	62	132	19	2	5	54	.253	53	114	5	226	433	15	.978
American League totals (4 years)		301	983	113	235	51	3	20	130	.239	101	197	12	496	803	34	.974
National League totals (2 years)		239	850	94	218	35	3	8	83	.256	92	178	7	350	694	28	.974
Major league totals (5 years)		540	1833	207	453	86	6	28	213	.247	193	375	19	846	1497	62	.974

DIVISION SERIES RECORD

Year Team (League)	Pos.	G	AB	R	H	2B	3B	HR	RBI	Avg.	BB	SO	SB	PO	A	E	Avg.
1996— San Diego (N.L.)	SS	3	12	0	2	0	0	0	1	.167	0	4	0	8	5	0	1.000

GONZALES, RENE   IF   ROCKIES

PERSONAL: Born September 3, 1961, in Austin, Texas. ... 6-3/220. ... Bats right, throws right. ... Full name: Rene Adrian Gonzales.
HIGH SCHOOL: Rosemead (Calif.).
JUNIOR COLLEGE: Glendale (Calif.) College.
COLLEGE: Cal State Los Angeles.
TRANSACTIONS/CAREER NOTES: Selected by Montreal Expos organization in fifth round of free-agent draft (June 7, 1982). ... Traded by Expos to Baltimore Orioles (December 16, 1986), completing deals in which Orioles traded P Dennis Martinez (June 16, 1986) and C John Stefero (December 8, 1986) to Expos for a player to be named later. ... Traded by Orioles to Toronto Blue Jays for P Rob Blumberg (January 15, 1991). ... Granted free agency (November 18, 1991). ... Signed by California Angels organization (January 10, 1992). ... On disabled list (August 12, 1992-remainder of season). ... Granted free agency (October 26, 1992). ... Re-signed by Angels (December 18, 1992). ... Granted free agency (October 29, 1993). ... Signed by Orioles organization (February 3, 1994). ... Released by Rochester, Orioles organization (April 6, 1994). ... Signed by Charlotte, Cleveland Indians organization (April 6, 1994). ... Granted free agency (October 25, 1994). ... Signed by

G

Midland, Angels organization (April 16, 1995). ... On Vancouver disabled list (April 25-May 2, 1995). ... Granted free agency (October 30, 1995). ... Signed by Texas Rangers organization (January 9, 1996). ... Granted free agency (October 29, 1996). ... Signed by San Diego Padres organization (December 2, 1996). ... Released by Las Vegas, Padres organization (April 22, 1997). ... Signed by Colorado Springs, Colorado Rockies organization (May 3, 1997).

STATISTICAL NOTES: Led Southern League shortstops with 102 double plays in 1983. ... Led American Association shortstops with 79 double plays in 1985.

Year Team (League)	Pos.	G	AB	R	H	2B	3B	HR	RBI	Avg.	BB	SO	SB	PO	A	E	Avg.
1982— Memphis (Southern)..	SS	56	183	10	39	3	1	1	11	.213	9	44	2	77	183	14	.949
1983— Memphis (Southern)..	SS	144	476	67	128	12	2	2	44	.269	40	53	5	*258	449	20	*.972
1984— Indianapolis (A.A.)......	SS-3B-2B	114	359	41	84	12	2	2	32	.234	20	33	10	161	349	13	.975
— Montreal (N.L.)..........	SS	29	30	5	7	1	0	0	2	.233	2	5	0	17	28	2	.957
1985— Indianapolis (A.A.)......	SS	130	340	21	77	11	1	0	25	.226	22	49	3	203	*345	23	.960
1986— Indianapolis (A.A.)......	3B-SS-2B	116	395	57	108	14	2	3	43	.273	41	47	8	208	297	23	.956
— Montreal (N.L.)..........	SS-3B	11	26	1	3	0	0	0	0	.115	2	7	0	7	19	0	1.000
1987— Baltimore (A.L.)■......	3B-2B-SS	37	60	14	16	2	1	1	7	.267	3	11	1	22	43	2	.970
— Rochester (Int'l)	3-S-2-1-O	42	170	20	51	9	3	0	24	.300	13	17	4	72	108	3	.984
1988— Baltimore (A.L.)..........	3-2-S-1-O	92	237	13	51	6	0	2	15	.215	13	32	2	66	185	8	.969
1989— Baltimore (A.L.)..........	2B-3B-SS	71	166	16	36	4	0	1	11	.217	12	30	5	103	146	7	.973
1990— Baltimore (A.L.)..........	2-3-S-O	67	103	13	22	3	1	1	12	.214	12	14	1	68	114	2	.989
1991— Toronto (A.L.)■..........	S-3-2-1	71	118	16	23	3	0	1	6	.195	12	22	0	61	118	7	.962
1992— California (A.L.)..........	3-2-1-S	104	329	47	91	17	1	7	38	.277	41	46	7	191	229	9	.979
1993— California (A.L.)..........	3-1-S-2-P	118	335	34	84	17	0	2	31	.251	49	45	5	234	170	12	.971
1994— Charlotte (Int'l)■........	S-3-1-O	42	133	26	30	4	0	2	17	.226	38	21	1	79	106	3	.984
— Cleveland (A.L.)........	3-1-S-2	22	23	6	8	1	1	1	5	.348	5	3	2	17	21	1	.974
1995— Midland (Texas)■........	2B	5	17	1	3	0	0	0	2	.176	4	1	0	11	16	1	.964
— Vancouver (PCL)........	S-3-2-1	50	165	27	45	12	0	4	18	.273	24	25	0	53	120	10	.945
— California (A.L.)........	3B-2B-SS	30	18	1	6	1	0	1	3	.333	0	4	0	6	12	0	1.000
1996— Okla. City (A.A.)■........	SS-3B-1B	42	154	21	40	8	2	3	13	.260	26	23	1	55	142	10	.952
— Texas (A.L.)	1-3-S-2-O	51	92	19	20	4	0	2	5	.217	10	11	0	109	61	2	.988
1997— Las Vegas (PCL)■........	3B	13	43	2	8	1	0	0	3	.186	6	6	0	4	25	2	.935
— Colo. Springs (PCL)■	2-1-S-3	85	296	48	88	20	1	3	39	.297	37	43	2	240	156	17	.959
— Colorado (N.L.)	3B	2	2	0	1	0	0	0	1	.500	0	0	0	0	0	0	...
American League totals (10 years)		663	1481	179	357	58	4	19	133	.241	157	218	23	877	1099	50	.975
National League totals (3 years)		42	58	6	11	1	0	0	3	.190	4	12	0	24	47	2	.973
Major league totals (13 years)		705	1539	185	368	59	4	19	136	.239	161	230	23	901	1146	52	.975

DIVISION SERIES RECORD

Year Team (League)	Pos.	G	AB	R	H	2B	3B	HR	RBI	Avg.	BB	SO	SB	PO	A	E	Avg.
1996— Texas (A.L.)	PR	1	0	0	0	0	0	0	0	...	0	0	0	...	...	...	...

CHAMPIONSHIP SERIES RECORD

Year Team (League)	Pos.	G	AB	R	H	2B	3B	HR	RBI	Avg.	BB	SO	SB	PO	A	E	Avg.
1991— Toronto (A.L.).............	PR-1B-SS	2	0	0	0	0	0	0	0	...	0	0	0	2	0	0	1.000

RECORD AS PITCHER

Year Team (League)	W	L	Pct.	ERA	G	GS	CG	ShO	Sv.	IP	H	R	ER	BB	SO
1993— California (A.L.)	0	0	...	0.00	1	0	0	0	0	1	0	0	0	0	0

GONZALEZ, ALEX   IF   MARLINS

PERSONAL: Born February 15, 1977, in Cagua, Venezuela. ... 6-0/170. ... Bats right, throws right.
HIGH SCHOOL: Liceo Ramon Bastidas.
TRANSACTIONS/CAREER NOTES: Signed as non-drafted free agent by Florida Marlins organization (April 18, 1994). ... On Kane County disabled list (April 5-August 17, 1996). ... On Portland disabled list (September 7, 1996-remainder of season).

Year Team (League)	Pos.	G	AB	R	H	2B	3B	HR	RBI	Avg.	BB	SO	SB	PO	A	E	Avg.
1994— Dom. Marlins (DSL) ...	SS	54	239	30	54	7	3	3	31	.226	15	36	4	140	222	34	.914
1995— GC Marlins (GCL).......	SS	53	187	30	55	7	4	2	30	.294	19	27	11	65	168	17	.932
— Brevard Co. (Fla. St.)..	SS	17	59	6	12	2	1	0	8	.203	1	14	1	26	51	8	.906
1996— Portland (Eastern)	SS	11	34	4	8	0	1	0	1	.235	2	10	0	17	38	7	.887
— Kane County (Midw.)..	SS	4	10	2	2	0	0	0	0	.200	2	4	0	2	10	0	1.000
— GC Marlins (GCL).......	SS	10	41	6	16	3	0	0	6	.390	2	4	1	14	30	5	.898
1997— Portland (Eastern)	SS	133	449	69	114	16	4	19	65	.254	27	83	4	192	423	*37	.943

GONZALEZ, ALEX   SS   BLUE JAYS

PERSONAL: Born April 8, 1973, in Miami. ... 6-0/190. ... Bats right, throws right. ... Full name: Alexander Scott Gonzalez.
HIGH SCHOOL: Miami Killian.
TRANSACTIONS/CAREER NOTES: Selected by Toronto Blue Jays organization in 14th round of free-agent draft (June 3, 1991). ... On Toronto disabled list (April 29-May 27, 1994); included rehabilitation assignment to Syracuse (May 14-27). ... On disabled list (August 13-September 14, 1997).
RECORDS: Shares A.L. record for most assists by shortstop in nine-inning game—13 (1996).
STATISTICAL NOTES: Led Gulf Coast League shortstops with 247 total chances in 1991. ... Led Southern League with 253 total bases in 1993. ... Led Southern League shortstops with 682 total chances and 92 double plays in 1993. ... Led International League shortstops with 542 total chances in 1994. ... Led A.L. shortstops with 765 total chances and 122 double plays in 1996.

G

Year Team (League)	Pos.	G	AB	R	H	2B	3B	HR	RBI	Avg.	BB	SO	SB	PO	A	E	Avg.
1991— GC Jays (GCL)	SS	53	191	29	40	5	4	0	10	.209	12	41	7	66	*160	21	.915
1992— Myrtle Beach (SAL)	SS	134	535	83	145	22	9	10	62	.271	38	119	26	*248	*406	48	.932
1993—Knoxville (S. Atl.)	SS	*142	561	*93	162	29	7	16	69	.289	39	110	38	*224	*428	30	*.956
1994—Toronto (A.L.)	SS	15	53	7	8	3	1	0	1	.151	4	17	3	18	49	6	.918
—Syracuse (Int'l)	SS	110	437	69	124	22	4	12	57	.284	53	92	23	*163	*348	*31	.943
1995—Toronto (A.L.)	SS-3B-DH	111	367	51	89	19	4	10	42	.243	44	114	4	164	227	19	.954
1996—Toronto (A.L.)	SS	147	527	64	124	30	5	14	64	.235	45	127	16	279	465	21	.973
1997—Toronto (A.L.)	SS	126	426	46	102	23	2	12	35	.239	34	94	15	209	341	8	*.986
Major league totals (4 years)		399	1373	168	323	75	12	36	142	.235	127	352	38	670	1082	54	.970

GONZALEZ, JEREMI — P — CUBS

PERSONAL: Born January 8, 1975, in Maracaibo, Venezuela. ... 6-1/180. ... Throws right, bats right. ... Full name: Geremis Segundo Acosta Gonzalez.

HIGH SCHOOL: Colegro La Chinita (Maracaibo, Venezuela).

TRANSACTIONS/CAREER NOTES: Signed as non-drafted free agent by Chicago Cubs organization (October 21, 1991). ... On disabled list (July 6-August 10, 1996).

STATISTICAL NOTES: Led Arizona League with 10 hit batsmen in 1992.

Year Team (League)	W	L	Pct.	ERA	G	GS	CG	ShO	Sv.	IP	H	R	ER	BB	SO
1992—Arizona Cubs (Arizona)	0	5	.000	7.80	14	7	0	0	0	45	65	59	39	22	39
1993—Huntington (Appal.)	3	9	.250	6.25	12	12	1	0	0	67 2/3	82	59	47	38	42
1994—Peoria (Midwest)	1	7	.125	5.55	13	13	1	0	0	71 1/3	86	53	44	32	39
—Williamsport (NYP)	4	6	.400	4.24	16	12	1	1	1	80 2/3	83	46	38	29	64
1995—Rockford (Midwest)	4	4	.500	5.10	12	12	1	0	0	65 1/3	63	43	37	28	36
—Daytona (Fla. St.)	5	1	.833	1.22	19	2	0	0	4	44 1/3	34	15	6	13	30
1996—Orlando (South.)	6	3	.667	3.34	17	14	0	0	0	97	95	39	36	28	85
1997—Iowa (Am. Assoc.)	2	2	.500	3.48	10	10	1	1	0	62	47	27	24	21	58
—Chicago (N.L.)	11	9	.550	4.25	23	23	1	1	0	144	126	73	68	69	93
Major league totals (1 year)	11	9	.550	4.25	23	23	1	1	0	144	126	73	68	69	93

GONZALEZ, JUAN — OF — RANGERS

PERSONAL: Born October 16, 1969, in Vega Baja, Puerto Rico. ... 6-3/220. ... Bats right, throws right. ... Full name: Juan Alberto Vazquez Gonzalez.

HIGH SCHOOL: Vega Baja (Puerto Rico).

TRANSACTIONS/CAREER NOTES: Signed as non-drafted free agent by Texas Rangers organization (May 30, 1986). ... On disabled list (April 27-June 17, 1988; March 30-April 26, 1991; April 16-June 1 and July 27-August 16, 1995; May 8-June 1, 1996; and March 24-May 2, 1997).

HONORS: Named American Association Most Valuable Player (1990). ... Named outfielder on THE SPORTING NEWS A.L. Silver Slugger team (1992-93, 1996 and 1997). ... Named outfielder on THE SPORTING NEWS A.L. All-Star team (1993 and 1996). ... Named A.L. Most Valuable Player by Baseball Writers' Association of America (1996).

STATISTICAL NOTES: Led Texas League with 254 total bases in 1989. ... Led American Association with 252 total bases in 1990. ... Hit three home runs in one game (June 7, 1992 and August 28, 1993). ... Led A.L. with .632 slugging percentage in 1993. ... Had 21-game hitting streaks (June 25-July 19 and August 8-31, 1996). ... Career major league grand slams: 5.

MISCELLANEOUS: Holds Texas Rangers all-time records for most home runs (256) and most runs batted in (790).

Year Team (League)	Pos.	G	AB	R	H	2B	3B	HR	RBI	Avg.	BB	SO	SB	PO	A	E	Avg.
1986—GC Rangers (GCL)	OF	60	*233	24	56	4	1	0	36	.240	21	54	7	89	6	•6	.941
1987—Gastonia (S. Atl.)	OF	127	509	69	135	21	2	14	74	.265	30	92	9	234	10	12	.953
1988—Charlotte (Fla. St.)	OF	77	277	25	71	14	3	8	43	.256	25	64	5	139	5	4	.973
1989—Tulsa (Texas)	OF	133	502	73	147	30	7	21	85	.293	31	98	1	292	15	9	.972
—Texas (A.L.)	OF	24	60	6	9	3	0	1	7	.150	6	17	0	53	0	2	.964
1990—Oklahoma City (A.A.)	OF	128	496	78	128	29	4	*29	*101	.258	32	109	2	220	7	8	.966
—Texas (A.L.)	OF-DH	25	90	11	26	7	1	4	12	.289	2	18	0	33	0	0	1.000
1991—Texas (A.L.)	OF-DH	142	545	78	144	34	1	27	102	.264	42	118	4	310	6	6	.981
1992—Texas (A.L.)	OF-DH	155	584	77	152	24	2	*43	109	.260	35	143	0	379	9	10	.975
1993—Texas (A.L.)	OF-DH	140	536	105	166	33	1	*46	118	.310	37	99	4	265	5	4	.985
1994—Texas (A.L.)	OF	107	422	57	116	18	4	19	85	.275	30	66	6	223	9	2	.991
1995—Texas (A.L.)	DH-OF	90	352	57	104	20	2	27	82	.295	17	66	0	6	1	0	1.000
1996—Texas (A.L.)	OF-DH	134	541	89	170	33	2	47	144	.314	45	82	2	163	6	2	.988
1997—Texas (A.L.)	DH-OF	133	533	87	158	24	3	42	131	.296	33	107	0	128	6	4	.971
Major league totals (9 years)		950	3663	567	1045	196	16	256	790	.285	247	716	16	1560	42	30	.982

DIVISION SERIES RECORD

RECORDS: Shares single-game record for most home runs—2 (October 2, 1996). ... Shares career record for most home runs—5.

NOTES: Shares postseason single-series record for most home runs—5 (1996).

Year Team (League)	Pos.	G	AB	R	H	2B	3B	HR	RBI	Avg.	BB	SO	SB	PO	A	E	Avg.
1996—Texas (A.L.)	OF	4	16	5	7	0	0	5	9	.438	4	2	0	8	0	0	1.000

ALL-STAR GAME RECORD

Year League	Pos.	AB	R	H	2B	3B	HR	RBI	Avg.	BB	SO	SB	PO	A	E	Avg.
1993—American	OF	1	0	0	0	0	0	0	.000	1	1	0	1	0	0	1.000

GONZALEZ, LARIEL — P — ROCKIES

PERSONAL: Born May 25, 1976, in San Cristobal, Dominican Republic. ... 6-1/180. ... Throws right, bats right. ... Full name: Lariel Alfonso Gonzalez.

G

TRANSACTIONS/CAREER NOTES: Signed as non-drafted free agent by Colorado Rockies (May 19, 1993).
STATISTICAL NOTES: Tied for Northwest League lead with five balks in 1995.

Year	Team (League)	W	L	Pct.	ERA	G	GS	CG	ShO	Sv.	IP	H	R	ER	BB	SO
1993—DSL Rockies......................		0	4	.000	9.38	14	7	0	0	1	24	32	34	25	46	17
1994—Ariz. Rockies (Ariz.)...........		3	2	.600	4.71	16	1	0	0	0	28 2/3	28	24	15	21	23
1995—Portland (Northwest)........		3	4	.429	4.06	15	11	0	0	2	57 2/3	44	31	26	43	48
1996—Asheville (S. Atl.)...............		1	1	.500	3.60	35	0	0	0	4	45	37	21	18	37	53
1997—Salem (Carolina)		5	0	1.000	2.53	44	0	0	0	8	57	42	19	16	23	79

GONZALEZ, LUIS — OF — TIGERS

PERSONAL: Born September 3, 1967, in Tampa. ... 6-2/185. ... Bats left, throws right. ... Full name: Luis Emilio Gonzalez.
HIGH SCHOOL: Jefferson (Tampa).
COLLEGE: South Alabama.
TRANSACTIONS/CAREER NOTES: Selected by Houston Astros organization in fourth round of free-agent draft (June 1, 1988). ... On disabled list (May 26-July 5, 1989 and August 29-September 13, 1991). ... On Houston disabled list (July 21-August 5, 1992). ... Traded by Astros with C Scott Servais to Chicago Cubs for C Rick Wilkins (June 28, 1995). ... Granted free agency (December 7, 1996). ... Signed by Astros (December 19, 1996). ... Granted free agency (October 28, 1997). ... Signed by Detroit Tigers (December 9, 1997).
STATISTICAL NOTES: Tied for Southern League lead with 12 sacrifice flies and nine intentional bases on balls received in 1990. ... Led N.L. with 10 sacrifice flies in 1993. ... Had 23-game hitting streak (May 26-June 20, 1997). ... Career major league grand slams: 1.

Year	Team (League)	Pos.	G	AB	R	H	2B	3B	HR	RBI	Avg.	BB	SO	SB	PO	A	E	Avg.
1988—Asheville (S. Atl.)........		3B	31	115	13	29	7	1	2	14	.252	12	17	2	19	62	6	.931
—Auburn (NY-Penn)..		3B-SS-1B	39	157	32	49	10	3	5	27	.312	12	19	2	37	83	13	.902
1989—Osceola (Fla. St.).........		DH	86	287	46	82	16	7	6	38	.286	37	49	2	...	...	...	...
1990—Columbus (Southern).		1B-3B	138	495	86	131	30	6	•24	89	.265	54	100	27	1039	88	23	.980
—Houston (N.L.)		3B-1B	12	21	1	4	2	0	0	0	.190	2	5	0	22	10	0	1.000
1991—Houston (N.L.)............		OF	137	473	51	120	28	9	13	69	.254	40	101	10	294	6	5	.984
1992—Houston (N.L.)............		OF	122	387	40	94	19	3	10	55	.243	24	52	7	261	5	2	.993
—Tucson (PCL)		OF	13	44	11	19	4	2	1	9	.432	5	7	4	26	0	1	.963
1993—Houston (N.L.)		OF	154	540	82	162	34	3	15	72	.300	47	83	20	347	10	8	.978
1994—Houston (N.L.)		OF	112	392	57	107	29	4	8	67	.273	49	57	15	228	5	2	.991
1995—Houston (N.L.)		OF	56	209	35	54	10	4	6	35	.258	18	30	1	94	2	2	.980
—Chicago (N.L.)■........		OF	77	262	34	76	19	4	7	34	.290	39	33	5	172	5	4	.978
1996—Chicago (N.L.)............		OF-1B	146	483	70	131	30	4	15	79	.271	61	49	9	244	7	3	.988
1997—Houston (N.L.)■........		OF-1B	152	550	78	142	31	2	10	68	.258	71	67	10	266	10	5	.982
Major league totals (8 years)			968	3317	448	890	202	33	84	479	.268	351	477	77	1928	60	31	.985

DIVISION SERIES RECORD

Year	Team (League)	Pos.	G	AB	R	H	2B	3B	HR	RBI	Avg.	BB	SO	SB	PO	A	E	Avg.
1997—Houston (N.L.)		OF	3	12	0	4	0	0	0	0	.333	0	1	0	13	1	1	.933

GOOCH, ARNOLD — P — METS

PERSONAL: Born November 11, 1976, in Levittown, Pa. ... 6-2/195. ... Throws right, bats right. ... Full name: Arnold Walter Gooch.
HIGH SCHOOL: Neshaminy (Langhorne, Pa.).
TRANSACTIONS/CAREER NOTES: Selected by Colorado Rockies organization in ninth round of free-agent draft (June 3, 1994). ... Traded by Rockies to New York Mets for P Bret Saberhagen and a player to be named later (July 31, 1995); Rockies acquired P David Swanson to complete deal (August 4, 1995).

Year	Team (League)	W	L	Pct.	ERA	G	GS	CG	ShO	Sv.	IP	H	R	ER	BB	SO
1994—Ariz. Rockies (Ariz.)...........		2	4	.333	2.64	15	9	0	0	0	58	45	28	17	16	66
1995—Asheville (S. Atl.)..............		5	8	.385	2.94	21	21	1	1	0	128 2/3	111	51	42	57	117
—Columbia (S. Atl.)■..........		2	3	.400	4.46	6	6	0	0	0	38 1/3	39	25	19	15	34
1996—St. Lucie (Fla. St.)		12	12	.500	2.58	26	26	2	0	0	167 2/3	131	74	48	51	141
1997—Binghamton (Eastern)		10	•12	.455	5.09	27	27	4	1	0	161	179	106	91	76	98

GOODEN, DWIGHT — P — INDIANS

PERSONAL: Born November 16, 1964, in Tampa. ... 6-3/210. ... Throws right, bats right. ... Full name: Dwight Eugene Gooden. ... Uncle of Gary Sheffield, outfielder, Florida Marlins.
HIGH SCHOOL: Hillsborough (Tampa).
TRANSACTIONS/CAREER NOTES: Selected by New York Mets organization in first round (fifth pick overall) of free-agent draft (June 7, 1982). ... On New York disabled list (April 1-June 5, 1987); included rehabilitation assignment to Tidewater (May 12-17 and May 21-June 1). ... On disabled list (July 2-September 2, 1989; August 24, 1991-remainder of season and July 18-August 8, 1992). ... On suspended list (September 2-7, 1993). ... On New York disabled list (April 22-June 9, 1994); included rehabilitation assignments to Norfolk (May 30-June 4) and Binghamton (June 4-9). ... On suspended list (June 28, 1994-remainder of season). ... Granted free agency (October 24, 1994). ... On suspended list (November 4, 1994-entire 1995 season). ... Signed by New York Yankees (February 20, 1996). ... On New York disabled list (April 11-June 15, 1997); included rehabilitation assignment to Norwich (May 18-June 2). ... Granted free agency (November 1, 1997). ... Signed by Cleveland Indians (December 8, 1997).
RECORDS: Holds major league rookie-season record for most strikeouts—276 (1984). ... Shares modern major league record for most strikeouts in two consecutive games—32 (September 12 [16] and 17 [16], 1984). ... Holds N.L. record for most strikeouts in three consecutive games—43 (September 7 [11], 12 [16] and 17 [16], 1984).
HONORS: Named Carolina League Pitcher of the Year (1983). ... Named N.L. Rookie Pitcher of the Year by THE SPORTING NEWS (1984). ... Named N.L. Rookie of the Year by Baseball Writers' Association of America (1984). ... Named N.L. Pitcher of the Year by THE SPORTING NEWS (1985). ... Named righthanded pitcher on THE SPORTING NEWS N.L. All-Star team (1985). ... Named N.L. Cy Young Award winner by Baseball Writers' Association of America (1985). ... Named pitcher on THE SPORTING NEWS N.L. Silver Slugger team (1992).

G

STATISTICAL NOTES: Pitched 10-0 one-hit, complete-game victory against Chicago (September 7, 1984). ... Struck out 16 batters in one game (September 12 and September 17, 1984; August 20, 1985). ... Tied for N.L. lead with seven balks in 1984. ... Struck out 15 batters in one game (May 11, 1990). ... Pitched 2-0 no-hit victory against Seattle (May 14, 1996).
MISCELLANEOUS: Appeared in one game as pinch-runner (1990). ... Singled and made an out in two games as pinch-hitter (1992). ... Tripled with an RBI in one game as pinch-hitter (1993).

Year Team (League)	W	L	Pct.	ERA	G	GS	CG	ShO	Sv.	IP	H	R	ER	BB	SO
1982— Kingsport (Appalachian).....	5	4	.556	2.47	9	9	4	2	0	65 2/3	53	34	18	25	66
— Little Falls (NYP)	0	1	.000	4.15	2	2	0	0	0	13	11	6	6	3	18
1983— Lynchburg (Carolina)	*19	4	.826	*2.50	27	27	10	*6	0	191	121	58	53	*112	*300
1984— New York (N.L.)................	17	9	.654	2.60	31	31	7	3	0	218	161	72	63	73	*276
1985— New York (N.L.)................	*24	4	.857	*1.53	35	35	*16	8	0	*276 2/3	198	51	47	69	*268
1986— New York (N.L.)................	17	6	.739	2.84	33	33	12	2	0	250	197	92	79	80	200
1987— Tidewater (Int'l)	3	0	1.000	2.05	4	4	1	0	0	22	20	7	5	9	24
— Lynchburg (Carolina)	0	0	. . .	0.00	1	1	0	0	0	4	2	0	0	2	3
— New York (N.L.)................	15	7	.682	3.21	25	25	7	3	0	179 2/3	162	68	64	53	148
1988— New York (N.L.)................	18	9	.667	3.19	34	34	10	3	0	248 1/3	242	98	88	57	175
1989— New York (N.L.)................	9	4	.692	2.89	19	17	0	0	1	118 1/3	93	42	38	47	101
1990— New York (N.L.)................	19	7	.731	3.83	34	34	2	1	0	232 2/3	229	106	99	70	223
1991— New York (N.L.)................	13	7	.650	3.60	27	27	3	1	0	190	185	80	76	56	150
1992— New York (N.L.)................	10	13	.435	3.67	31	31	3	0	0	206	197	93	84	70	145
1993— New York (N.L.)................	12	15	.444	3.45	29	29	7	2	0	208 2/3	188	89	80	61	149
1994— New York (N.L.)................	3	4	.429	6.31	7	7	0	0	0	41 1/3	46	32	29	15	40
— Norfolk (Int'l)	0	0	. . .	0.00	1	1	0	0	0	3	0	0	0	1	4
— Binghamton (Eastern)	1	0	1.000	0.00	1	1	0	0	0	5	2	0	0	1	4
1995—				Out of organized baseball.											
1996— New York (A.L.)■.............	11	7	.611	5.01	29	29	1	1	0	170 2/3	169	101	95	88	126
1997— New York (A.L.)................	9	5	.643	4.91	20	19	0	0	0	106 1/3	116	61	58	53	66
— Norwich (Eastern)	3	0	1.000	3.00	3	3	0	0	0	18	13	6	6	5	14
— Columbus (Int'l)	1	1	.500	3.75	2	2	0	0	0	12	7	5	5	4	10
A.L. totals (2 years)	20	12	.625	4.97	49	48	1	1	0	277	285	162	153	141	192
N.L. totals (11 years)	157	85	.649	3.10	305	303	67	23	1	2169 2/3	1898	823	747	651	1875
Major league totals (13 years)....	177	97	.646	3.31	354	351	68	24	1	2446 2/3	2183	985	900	792	2067

DIVISION SERIES RECORD

Year Team (League)	W	L	Pct.	ERA	G	GS	CG	ShO	Sv.	IP	H	R	ER	BB	SO
1997— New York (A.L.)................	0	0	. . .	1.59	1	1	0	0	0	5 2/3	5	1	1	3	5

CHAMPIONSHIP SERIES RECORD

RECORDS: Holds single-series record for most strikeouts—20 (1988). ... Shares N.L. single-game record for most innings pitched—10 (October 14, 1986).

Year Team (League)	W	L	Pct.	ERA	G	GS	CG	ShO	Sv.	IP	H	R	ER	BB	SO
1986— New York (N.L.)................	0	1	.000	1.06	2	2	0	0	0	17	16	2	2	5	9
1988— New York (N.L.)................	0	0	. . .	2.95	3	2	0	0	0	18 1/3	10	6	6	8	20
Champ. series totals (2 years)	0	1	.000	2.04	5	4	0	0	0	35 1/3	26	8	8	13	29

WORLD SERIES RECORD

NOTES: Member of World Series championship team (1986). ... Member of World Series championship team (1996); inactive.

Year Team (League)	W	L	Pct.	ERA	G	GS	CG	ShO	Sv.	IP	H	R	ER	BB	SO
1986— New York (N.L.)................	0	2	.000	8.00	2	2	0	0	0	9	17	10	8	4	9

ALL-STAR GAME RECORD

RECORDS: Holds career record for most balks—2. ... Shares career record for most games lost—2.

Year League	W	L	Pct.	ERA	GS	CG	ShO	Sv.	IP	H	R	ER	BB	SO
1984— National	0	0	. . .	0.00	0	0	0	0	2	1	0	0	0	3
1985— National				Did not play.										
1986— National	0	1	.000	6.00	1	0	0	0	3	3	2	2	0	2
1988— National	0	1	.000	3.00	1	0	0	0	3	3	1	1	1	1
All-Star totals (3 years)	0	2	.000	3.38	2	0	0	0	8	7	3	3	1	6

GOODWIN, CURTIS · OF · ROCKIES

PERSONAL: Born September 30, 1972, in Oakland. ... 5-11/180. ... Bats left, throws left. ... Full name: Curtis LaMar Goodwin.
HIGH SCHOOL: San Leandro (Calif.).
TRANSACTIONS/CAREER NOTES: Selected by Baltimore Orioles organization in 12th round of free-agent draft (June 3, 1991). ... On Baltimore disabled list (August 20-September 4, 1995). ... Traded by Orioles with OF Trovin Valdez to Cincinnati Reds for P David Wells (December 26, 1995). ... Traded by Reds to Colorado Rockies for P Mark Hutton (December 10, 1997).
STATISTICAL NOTES: Led Midwest League outfielders with 327 total chances and seven double plays in 1992. ... Led Eastern League with 13 sacrifice hits in 1994. ... Led Eastern League outfielders with 323 total chances in 1994.

Year Team (League)	Pos.	G	AB	R	H	2B	3B	HR	RBI	Avg.	BB	SO	SB	PO	A	E	Avg.
1991— GC Orioles (GCL)........	OF	48	151	32	39	5	0	0	9	.258	38	25	26	77	5	1	.988
1992— Kane County (Midw.)..	OF	134	*542	85	153	7	5	0	42	.282	38	106	52	301	15	11	.966
1993— Frederick (Carolina)....	OF	•138	*555	*98	•156	15	*10	2	42	.281	52	90	*61	271	9	7	.976
1994— Bowie (Eastern)........	OF	*142	*597	*105	*171	18	8	2	37	.286	40	78	*59	*301	12	10	.969
1995— Rochester (Int'l)	OF	36	140	24	37	3	3	0	7	.264	12	15	17	81	1	3	.965
— Baltimore (A.L.)	OF-DH	87	289	40	76	11	3	1	24	.263	15	53	22	202	1	2	.990
1996— Indianapolis (A.A.)■ ..	OF	91	337	57	88	19	4	2	30	.261	54	67	*40	172	4	4	.978
— Cincinnati (N.L.).........	OF	49	136	20	31	3	0	0	5	.228	19	34	15	64	0	2	.970
1997— Indianapolis (A.A.)......	OF	30	116	14	32	4	1	0	7	.276	15	20	11	57	2	0	1.000
— Cincinnati (N.L.).........	OF	85	265	27	67	11	0	1	12	.253	24	53	22	159	3	0	1.000
American League totals (1 year)		87	289	40	76	11	3	1	24	.263	15	53	22	202	1	2	.990
National League totals (2 years)		134	401	47	98	14	0	1	17	.244	43	87	37	223	3	2	.991
Major league totals (3 years)		221	690	87	174	25	3	2	41	.252	58	140	59	425	4	4	.991

G

PERSONAL: Born July 27, 1968, in Fresno, Calif. ... 6-1/175. ... Bats left, throws right. ... Full name: Thomas Jones Goodwin.

HIGH SCHOOL: Central (Fresno, Calif.).

COLLEGE: Fresno State.

TRANSACTIONS/CAREER NOTES: Selected by Pittsburgh Pirates organization in sixth round of free-agent draft (June 2, 1986); did not sign. ... Selected by Los Angeles Dodgers organization in first round (22nd pick overall) of free-agent draft (June 5, 1989). ... Claimed on waivers by Kansas City Royals (January 6, 1994). ... Traded by Royals to Texas Rangers for 3B Dean Palmer (July 25, 1997).

HONORS: Named outfielder on THE SPORTING NEWS college All-America team (1989).

STATISTICAL NOTES: Tied for Pacific Coast League lead in caught stealing with 23 in 1991. ... Led American Association in caught stealing with 20 in 1994. ... Led A.L. in sacrifice hits with 14 in 1995 and 21 in 1996. ... Led A.L. in caught stealing with 22 in 1996.

MISCELLANEOUS: Member of 1988 U.S. Olympic baseball team.

							BATTING								FIELDING		
Year Team (League)	Pos.	G	AB	R	H	2B	3B	HR	RBI	Avg.	BB	SO	SB	PO	A	E	Avg.
1989—Great Falls (Pio.)	OF	63	240	*55	74	12	3	2	33	.308	28	30	*60	67	3	1	.986
1990—San Antonio (Tex.)	OF	102	428	76	119	15	4	0	28	.278	38	72	*60	264	7	3	*.989
—Bakersfield (Calif.)	OF	32	134	24	39	6	2	0	13	.291	11	22	22	55	2	0	1.000
1991—Albuquerque (PCL)	OF	132	509	84	139	19	4	1	45	.273	59	83	48	284	6	3	.990
—Los Angeles (N.L.)	OF	16	7	3	1	0	0	0	0	.143	0	0	1	8	0	0	1.000
1992—Albuquerque (PCL)	OF	82	319	48	96	10	4	2	28	.301	37	47	27	184	5	1	.995
—Los Angeles (N.L.)	OF	57	73	15	17	1	1	0	3	.233	6	10	7	43	0	0	1.000
1993—Los Angeles (N.L.)	OF	30	17	6	5	1	0	0	1	.294	1	4	1	8	0	0	1.000
—Albuquerque (PCL)	OF	85	289	48	75	5	5	1	28	.260	30	51	21	145	1	2	.986
1994—Kansas City (A.L.)■	DH-OF	2	2	0	0	0	0	0	0	.000	0	1	0	1	0	0	1.000
—Omaha (A.A.)	OF	113	429	67	132	17	7	2	34	.308	23	60	*50	276	3	2	.993
1995—Kansas City (A.L.)	OF-DH	133	480	72	138	16	3	4	28	.288	38	72	50	292	6	3	.990
1996—Kansas City (A.L.)	OF-DH	143	524	80	148	14	4	1	35	.282	39	79	66	303	7	5	.984
1997—Kansas City (A.L.)	OF	97	367	51	100	13	4	2	22	.272	19	51	34	232	3	1	.996
—Texas (A.L.)■	OF	53	207	39	49	13	2	0	17	.237	25	37	16	138	3	2	.986
American League totals (4 years)		428	1580	242	435	56	13	7	102	.275	121	240	166	966	19	11	.989
National League totals (3 years)		103	97	24	23	2	1	0	4	.237	7	14	9	59	0	0	1.000
Major league totals (7 years)		531	1677	266	458	58	14	7	106	.273	128	254	175	1025	19	11	.990

PERSONAL: Born November 18, 1967, in Sebring, Fla. ... 5-9/180. ... Throws right, bats right. ... Full name: Thomas Gordon. ... Brother of Tony Gordon, minor league pitcher (1988-94).

HIGH SCHOOL: Avon Park (Fla.).

TRANSACTIONS/CAREER NOTES: Selected by Kansas City Royals organization in sixth round of free-agent draft (June 2, 1986). ... On disabled list (August 12-September 1, 1992 and May 8-24, 1995). ... Granted free agency (October 30, 1995). ... Signed by Boston Red Sox (December 21, 1995).

HONORS: Named A.L. Rookie Pitcher of the Year by THE SPORTING NEWS (1989).

STATISTICAL NOTES: Tied for Northwest League lead with four balks in 1987.

MISCELLANEOUS: Appeared in one game as pinch-runner (1991). ... Appeared in one game as pinch-runner (1995).

Year Team (League)	W	L	Pct.	ERA	G	GS	CG	ShO	Sv.	IP	H	R	ER	BB	SO
1986—GC Royals (GCL)	3	1	.750	1.02	9	7	2	1	0	44	31	12	5	23	47
—Omaha (Am. Assoc.)	0	0	...	47.25	1	0	0	0	0	$1\frac{1}{3}$	6	7	7	2	3
1987—Eugene (Northwest)	•9	0	•1.000	2.86	15	13	0	0	1	$72\frac{1}{3}$	48	33	23	47	91
—Fort Myers (Fla. St.)	1	0	1.000	2.63	3	3	0	0	0	$13\frac{2}{3}$	5	4	4	17	11
1988—Appleton (Midwest)	7	5	.583	2.06	17	17	5	1	0	118	69	30	27	43	*172
—Memphis (Southern)	6	0	1.000	0.38	6	6	2	2	0	$47\frac{1}{3}$	16	3	2	17	62
—Omaha (Am. Assoc.)	3	0	1.000	1.33	3	3	0	0	0	$20\frac{1}{3}$	11	3	3	15	29
—Kansas City (A.L.)	0	2	.000	5.17	5	2	0	0	0	$15\frac{2}{3}$	16	9	9	7	18
1989—Kansas City (A.L.)	17	9	.654	3.64	49	16	1	1	1	163	122	67	66	86	153
1990—Kansas City (A.L.)	12	11	.522	3.73	32	32	6	1	0	$195\frac{1}{3}$	192	99	81	99	175
1991—Kansas City (A.L.)	9	14	.391	3.87	45	14	1	0	1	158	129	76	68	87	167
1992—Kansas City (A.L.)	6	10	.375	4.59	40	11	0	0	0	$117\frac{2}{3}$	116	67	60	55	98
1993—Kansas City (A.L.)	12	6	.667	3.58	48	14	2	0	1	$155\frac{1}{3}$	125	65	62	77	143
1994—Kansas City (A.L.)	11	7	.611	4.35	24	24	0	0	0	$155\frac{1}{3}$	136	79	75	87	126
1995—Kansas City (A.L.)	12	12	.500	4.43	31	31	2	0	0	189	204	110	93	89	119
1996—Boston (A.L.)■	12	9	.571	5.59	34	34	4	1	0	$215\frac{2}{3}$	249	143	*134	105	171
1997—Boston (A.L.)	6	10	.375	3.74	42	25	2	1	11	$182\frac{2}{3}$	155	85	76	78	159
Major league totals (10 years)	97	90	.519	4.21	350	203	18	4	14	1548	1444	800	724	770	1329

G

PERSONAL: Born August 27, 1973, in Evergreen Park, Ill. ... 6-3/167. ... Throws right, bats right. ... Full name: Richard Gorecki.

HIGH SCHOOL: Oak Forest (Ill.).

TRANSACTIONS/CAREER NOTES: Selected by Los Angeles Dodgers organization in 10th round of free-agent draft (June 3, 1991). ... On disabled list (May 27-June 3 and June 20-July 17, 1994). ... On Los Angeles disabled list (April 23, 1995-entire season); included rehabilitation assignments to Vero Beach (June 26-29 and July 9-August 3). ... On disabled list (March 25, 1996-entire season). ... Selected by Tampa Bay Devil Rays in second round (40th pick overall) of expansion draft (November 18, 1997).

Year— Team (League)	W	L	Pct.	ERA	G	GS	CG	ShO	Sv.	IP	H	R	ER	BB	SO
1991— Great Falls (Pio.)	0	3	.000	4.41	13	10	0	0	0	51	44	34	25	27	56
1992— Bakersfield (California)	11	7	.611	4.05	25	24	0	0	0	129	122	68	58	90	115
1993— San Antonio (Tex.)	6	9	.400	3.35	26	26	0	0	0	156	136	76	58	62	118
1994— Albuquerque (PCL)	8	6	.571	5.07	22	21	0	0	0	103	119	65	58	60	73
1995— Vero Beach (FSL)	1	2	.333	0.67	6	5	0	0	0	27	19	6	2	9	24
1996—								Did not play.							
1997— San Bernardino (Calif.)	2	3	.400	3.88	14	14	0	0	0	51	38	22	22	32	58
— San Antonio (Tex.)	4	2	.667	1.39	7	7	0	0	0	45 1/3	26	8	7	15	33
— Los Angeles (N.L.)	1	0	1.000	15.00	4	1	0	0	0	6	9	10	10	6	6
Major league totals (1 year)	1	0	1.000	15.00	4	1	0	0	0	6	9	10	10	6	6

GRACE, MARK — 1B — CUBS

PERSONAL: Born June 28, 1964, in Winston-Salem, N.C. ... 6-2/195. ... Bats left, throws left. ... Full name: Mark Eugene Grace.
HIGH SCHOOL: Tustin (Calif.).
JUNIOR COLLEGE: Saddleback Community College (Calif.).
COLLEGE: San Diego State.
TRANSACTIONS/CAREER NOTES: Selected by Minnesota Twins organization in 15th round of free-agent draft (January 17, 1984); did not sign. ... Selected by Chicago Cubs organization in 24th round of free-agent draft (June 3, 1985). ... On disabled list (June 5-23, 1989). ... Granted free agency (October 15, 1994). ... Re-signed by Cubs (April 7, 1995). ... Granted free agency (November 3, 1995). ... Re-signed by Cubs (December 19, 1995). ... On disabled list (June 11-28, 1996 and April 4-19, 1997).
RECORDS: Shares major league record for most assists by first baseman in one inning—3 (May 23, 1990, fourth inning). ... Holds N.L. single-season record for most assists by first baseman—180 (1990).
HONORS: Named Eastern League Most Valuable Player (1987). ... Named N.L. Rookie Player of the Year by THE SPORTING NEWS (1988). ... Won N.L. Gold Glove at first base (1992-93 and 1995-96).
STATISTICAL NOTES: Led Midwest League first basemen with 103 double plays in 1986. ... Led Eastern League with .545 slugging percentage in 1987. ... Led N.L. first basemen with 1,695 total chances in 1991, 1,725 in 1992 and 1,573 in 1993. ... Tied for N.L. lead in grounding into double plays with 25 in 1993. ... Led N.L. first basemen with 134 double plays in 1993. ... Hit for the cycle (May 9, 1993).

Year— Team (League)	Pos.	G	AB	R	H	2B	3B	HR	RBI	Avg.	BB	SO	SB	PO	A	E	Avg.
1986— Peoria (Midwest)	1B-OF	126	465	81	159	30	4	15	95	*.342	60	28	6	1050	69	13	.989
1987— Pittsfield (Eastern)	1B	123	453	81	151	29	8	17	*101	.333	48	24	5	1054	*96	6	*.995
1988— Iowa (Am. Assoc.)	1B	21	67	11	17	4	0	0	14	.254	13	4	1	189	20	1	.995
— Chicago (N.L.)	1B	134	486	65	144	23	4	7	57	.296	60	43	3	1182	87	•17	.987
1989— Chicago (N.L.)	1B	142	510	74	160	28	3	13	79	.314	80	42	14	1230	126	6	.996
1990— Chicago (N.L.)	1B	157	589	72	182	32	1	9	82	.309	59	54	15	1324	*180	12	.992
1991— Chicago (N.L.)	1B	160	*619	87	169	28	5	8	58	.273	70	53	3	*1520	*167	8	.995
1992— Chicago (N.L.)	1B	158	603	72	185	37	5	9	79	.307	72	36	6	*1580	*141	4	.998
1993— Chicago (N.L.)	1B	155	594	86	193	39	4	14	98	.325	71	32	8	*1456	112	5	.997
1994— Chicago (N.L.)	1B	106	403	55	120	23	3	6	44	.298	48	41	0	925	78	7	.993
1995— Chicago (N.L.)	1B	143	552	97	180	*51	3	16	92	.326	65	46	6	1211	114	7	.995
1996— Chicago (N.L.)	1B	142	547	88	181	39	1	9	75	.331	62	41	2	1259	107	4	.997
1997— Chicago (N.L.)	1B	151	555	87	177	32	5	13	78	.319	88	45	2	1202	120	6	.995
Major league totals (10 years)		1448	5458	783	1691	332	34	104	742	.310	675	433	59	12889	1232	76	.995

CHAMPIONSHIP SERIES RECORD

NOTES: Hit home run in first at-bat (October 4, 1989).

Year— Team (League)	Pos.	G	AB	R	H	2B	3B	HR	RBI	Avg.	BB	SO	SB	PO	A	E	Avg.
1989— Chicago (N.L.)	1B	5	17	3	11	3	1	1	8	.647	4	1	1	44	3	0	1.000

ALL-STAR GAME RECORD

Year— League	Pos.	AB	R	H	2B	3B	HR	RBI	Avg.	BB	SO	SB	PO	A	E	Avg.
1993— National	DH	3	0	0	0	0	0	0	.000	0	0	0	...	...	...	...
1995— National	1B	0	0	0	0	0	0	0	...	0	0	0	1	0	0	1.000
1997— National	1B	1	0	0	0	0	0	0	.000	0	0	0	1	0	0	1.000
All-Star Game totals (3 years)		4	0	0	0	0	0	0	.000	0	0	0	2	0	0	1.000

G

GRACE, MIKE — P — PHILLIES

PERSONAL: Born June 20, 1970, in Joliet, Ill. ... 6-4/220. ... Throws right, bats right. ... Full name: Michael James Grace.
HIGH SCHOOL: Joliet (Ill.) Catholic.
COLLEGE: Bradley.
TRANSACTIONS/CAREER NOTES: Selected by Philadelphia Phillies organization in 10th round of free-agent draft (June 3, 1991). ... On disabled list (April 9-June 8, July 8-20 and July 27, 1992-remainder of season; April 8, 1993-entire season; April 7-June 14, 1994; and June 3, 1996-remainder of season). ... On Philadelphia disabled list (March 27-June 25, 1997); included rehabilitation assignments to Reading (May 28-June 14) and Scranton/Wilkes-Barre (June 14-25).

Year— Team (League)	W	L	Pct.	ERA	G	GS	CG	ShO	Sv.	IP	H	R	ER	BB	SO
1991— Batavia (N.Y.-Penn)	1	2	.333	1.39	6	6	0	0	0	32 1/3	20	9	5	14	36
— Spartanburg (SAL)	3	1	.750	1.89	6	6	0	0	0	33 1/3	24	7	7	9	23
1992— Spartanburg (SAL)	0	1	.000	4.94	6	6	0	0	0	27 1/3	25	16	15	8	21
1993—								Did not play.							
1994— Spartanburg (SAL)	5	5	.500	4.82	15	15	0	0	0	80 1/3	84	50	43	20	45
1995— Reading (Eastern)	13	6	.684	3.54	24	24	2	0	0	147 1/3	137	65	58	35	118

Year	Team (League)	W	L	Pct.	ERA	G	GS	CG	ShO	Sv.	IP	H	R	ER	BB	SO
— Scran./W.B. (Int'l)		2	0	1.000	1.59	2	2	1	0	0	17	17	3	3	2	13
— Philadelphia (N.L.)		1	1	.500	3.18	2	2	0	0	0	11 1/3	10	4	4	4	7
1996— Philadelphia (N.L.)		7	2	.778	3.49	12	12	1	1	0	80	72	33	31	16	49
1997— Reading (Eastern)		1	3	.250	5.75	4	4	0	0	0	20 1/3	28	17	13	6	10
— Scran./W.B. (Int'l)		5	6	.455	4.56	12	12	4	0	0	75	84	43	38	27	55
— Philadelphia (N.L.)		3	2	.600	3.46	6	6	1	1	0	39	32	16	15	10	26
Major league totals (3 years)		11	5	.688	3.45	20	20	2	2	0	130 1/3	114	53	50	30	82

GRAFFANINO, TONY — 2B — BRAVES

PERSONAL: Born June 6, 1972, in Amityville, N.Y. ... 6-1/175. ... Bats right, throws right. ... Full name: Anthony Joseph Graffanino. ... Name pronounced GRAF-uh-NEE-noh..
HIGH SCHOOL: East Islip (Islip Terrace, N.Y.).
TRANSACTIONS/CAREER NOTES: Selected by Atlanta Braves organization in 10th round of free-agent draft (June 4, 1990). ... On disabled list (July 3, 1995-remainder of season).
STATISTICAL NOTES: Led Pioneer League shortstops with 41 double plays in 1991. ... Led Carolina League second basemen with .968 fielding percentage in 1993. ... Led International League second basemen with 441 total chances in 1996.

							BATTING								FIELDING		
Year	Team (League)	Pos.	G	AB	R	H	2B	3B	HR	RBI	Avg.	BB	SO	SB	PO	A	E	Avg.
1990— Pulaski (Appalachian).	SS	42	131	23	27	5	1	0	11	.206	26	17	6	60	105	24	.873
1991— Idaho Falls (Pio.)	SS	66	274	53	95	16	4	4	56	.347	27	37	19	112	187	*29	.912
1992— Macon (S. Atl.)	2B	112	400	50	96	15	5	10	31	.240	50	84	9	178	239	17	.961
1993— Durham (Carolina)	2B-SS	123	459	78	126	30	5	15	69	.275	45	78	24	186	263	15	†.968
1994— Greenville (Southern).	2B	124	440	66	132	28	3	7	52	.300	50	53	29	254	326	14	.976
1995— Richmond (Int'l)	2B	50	179	20	34	6	0	4	17	.190	15	49	2	102	127	4	.983
1996— Richmond (Int'l)	2B	96	353	57	100	29	2	7	33	.283	34	72	11	*215	216	10	.977
— Atlanta (N.L.)	2B	22	46	7	8	1	1	0	2	.174	4	13	0	24	39	2	.969
1997— Atlanta (N.L.)	2-3-S-1	104	186	33	48	9	1	8	20	.258	26	46	6	90	180	5	.982
Major league totals (2 years)		126	232	40	56	10	2	8	22	.241	30	59	6	114	219	7	.979

DIVISION SERIES RECORD

							BATTING								FIELDING		
Year	Team (League)	Pos.	G	AB	R	H	2B	3B	HR	RBI	Avg.	BB	SO	SB	PO	A	E	Avg.
1997— Atlanta (N.L.)	2B	3	3	0	0	0	0	0	0	.000	2	1	0	1	6	0	1.000

CHAMPIONSHIP SERIES RECORD

							BATTING								FIELDING		
Year	Team (League)	Pos.	G	AB	R	H	2B	3B	HR	RBI	Avg.	BB	SO	SB	PO	A	E	Avg.
1997— Atlanta (N.L.)	2B	3	8	1	2	1	0	0	0	.250	0	3	0	4	2	0	1.000

GRANGER, JEFF — P — PIRATES

PERSONAL: Born December 16, 1971, in San Pedro, Calif. ... 6-4/200. ... Throws left, bats right. ... Full name: Jeffrey Adam Granger.
HIGH SCHOOL: Orangefield (Texas).
COLLEGE: Texas A&M.
TRANSACTIONS/CAREER NOTES: Selected by Minnesota Twins organization in 14th round of free-agent draft (June 4, 1990); did not sign. ... Selected by Kansas City Royals organization in first round (fifth pick overall) of free-agent draft (June 3, 1993). ... On disabled list (June 20-July 3, 1995). ... Traded by Royals with 3B Joe Randa, P Jeff Martin and P Jeff Wallace to Pittsburgh Pirates for SS Jay Bell and 1B Jeff King (December 13, 1996).
HONORS: Named lefthanded pitcher on THE SPORTING NEWS college All-America team (1993).
STATISTICAL NOTES: Tied for Southern League lead with 14 wild pitches in 1994.

Year	Team (League)	W	L	Pct.	ERA	G	GS	CG	ShO	Sv.	IP	H	R	ER	BB	SO
1993— Eugene (Northwest)	3	3	.500	3.00	8	7	0	0	0	36	28	17	12	10	56
— Kansas City (A.L.)	0	0	...	27.00	1	0	0	0	0	1	3	3	3	2	1
1994— Memphis (Southern)	7	7	.500	3.87	25	25	0	0	0	139 2/3	155	72	60	61	112
— Kansas City (A.L.)	0	1	.000	6.75	2	2	0	0	0	9 1/3	13	8	7	6	3
1995— Wichita (Texas)	4	7	.364	5.93	18	18	0	0	0	95 2/3	122	76	63	40	81
1996— Omaha (Am. Assoc.)	5	3	.625	2.34	45	0	0	0	4	77	65	24	20	29	68
— Kansas City (A.L.)	0	0	...	6.61	15	0	0	0	0	16 1/3	21	13	12	10	11
1997— Pittsburgh (N.L.)■	0	0	...	18.00	9	0	0	0	0	5	10	10	10	8	4
— Calgary (PCL)	1	7	.125	5.55	30	12	0	0	1	82 2/3	111	63	51	33	68
A.L. totals (3 years)	0	1	.000	7.43	18	2	0	0	0	26 2/3	37	24	22	18	15
N.L. totals (1 year)	0	0	...	18.00	9	0	0	0	0	5	10	10	10	8	4
Major league totals (4 years)	0	1	.000	9.09	27	2	0	0	0	31 2/3	47	34	32	26	19

GRAVES, DANNY — P — REDS

PERSONAL: Born August 7, 1973, in Saigon, Vietnam. ... 5-11/200. ... Throws right, bats right.
HIGH SCHOOL: Brandon (Fla.).
COLLEGE: Miami (Fla.).
TRANSACTIONS/CAREER NOTES: Selected by Cleveland Indians organization in fourth round of free-agent draft (June 2, 1994). ... Traded by Indians with P Jim Crowell, P Scott Winchester and IF Damian Jackson to Cincinnati Reds for P John Smiley and IF Jeff Branson (July 31, 1997).
MISCELLANEOUS: Injured knee during 1994 College World Series and did not play professional baseball during 1994 season.

Year	Team (League)	W	L	Pct.	ERA	G	GS	CG	ShO	Sv.	IP	H	R	ER	BB	SO
1994—					Did not play.											
1995— Kinston (Carolina)	3	1	.750	0.82	38	0	0	0	21	44	30	11	4	12	46
— Cant./Akr. (Eastern)	1	0	1.000	0.00	17	0	0	0	10	23 1/3	10	1	0	2	11
— Buffalo (A.A.)	0	0	...	3.00	3	0	0	0	0	3	5	4	1	1	2

G

Year Team (League)	W	L	Pct.	ERA	G	GS	CG	ShO	Sv.	IP	H	R	ER	BB	SO
1996— Buffalo (A.A.)	4	3	.571	1.48	43	0	0	0	19	79	57	14	13	24	46
—Cleveland (A.L.)	2	0	1.000	4.55	15	0	0	0	0	29 2/3	29	18	15	10	22
1997— Buffalo (A.A.)	2	3	.400	4.19	19	3	0	0	2	43	45	21	20	11	21
—Cleveland (A.L.)	0	0	...	4.76	5	0	0	0	0	11 1/3	15	8	6	9	4
—Indianapolis (A.A.)■	1	0	1.000	3.09	11	0	0	0	5	11 2/3	7	4	4	5	5
—Cincinnati (N.L.)	0	0	...	6.14	10	0	0	0	0	14 2/3	26	14	10	11	7
A.L. totals (2 years)	2	0	1.000	4.61	20	0	0	0	0	41	44	26	21	19	26
N.L. totals (1 year)	0	0	...	6.14	10	0	0	0	0	14 2/3	26	14	10	11	7
Major league totals (2 years)	2	0	1.000	5.01	30	0	0	0	0	55 2/3	70	40	31	30	33

GREBECK, CRAIG — IF — BLUE JAYS

PERSONAL: Born December 29, 1964, in Johnstown, Pa. ... 5-7/148. ... Bats right, throws right. ... Full name: Craig Allen Grebeck. ... Name pronounced GRAY-bek.
HIGH SCHOOL: Lakewood (Calif.).
COLLEGE: Cal State Dominguez Hills.
TRANSACTIONS/CAREER NOTES: Signed as non-drafted free agent by Chicago White Sox organization (August 13, 1986). ... On disabled list (August 9, 1992-remainder of season). ... On Chicago disabled list (May 21-June 30, 1994); included rehabilitation assignment at Nashville (June 23-30). ... Granted free agency (December 21, 1995). ... Signed by Florida Marlins organization (December 22, 1995). ... On disabled list (July 4-August 13, 1996). ... Granted free agency (October 31, 1996). ... Signed by Anaheim Angels (December 6, 1996). ... Granted free agency (October 9, 1997). ... Signed by Toronto Blue Jays organization (November 27, 1997).
STATISTICAL NOTES: Led Southern League in grounding into double plays with 15 in 1989. ... Career major league grand slams: 1.

Year Team (League)	Pos.	G	AB	R	H	2B	3B	HR	RBI	Avg.	BB	SO	SB	PO	A	E	Avg.
1987—Peninsula (Caro.)	SS-3B	104	378	63	106	22	3	15	67	.280	37	62	3	137	278	16	.963
1988—Birmingham (Sou.)	2B	133	450	57	126	21	1	9	53	.280	65	72	5	238	368	19	.970
1989—Birmingham (Sou.)	SS-3B-2B	•143	•533	85	*153	25	4	5	80	.287	63	77	14	234	364	28	.955
1990—Chicago (A.L.)	3B-SS-2B	59	119	7	20	3	1	1	9	.168	8	24	0	36	98	3	.978
—Vancouver (PCL)	SS-3B-2B	12	41	8	8	0	0	1	3	.195	6	7	1	28	26	1	.982
1991—Chicago (A.L.)	3B-2B-SS	107	224	37	63	16	3	6	31	.281	38	40	1	104	183	10	.966
1992—Chicago (A.L.)	SS-3B-OF	88	287	24	77	21	2	3	35	.268	30	34	0	112	283	8	.980
1993—Chicago (A.L.)	SS-2B-3B	72	190	25	43	5	0	1	12	.226	26	26	1	91	185	5	.982
1994—Chicago (A.L.)	2B-SS-3B	35	97	17	30	5	0	0	4	.309	12	5	0	44	65	2	.982
—Nashville (A.A.)	SS	5	15	3	6	2	0	0	4	.400	1	2	0	5	12	1	.944
1995—Chicago (A.L.)	SS-3B-2B	53	154	19	40	12	0	1	18	.260	21	23	0	76	127	7	.967
1996—Florida (N.L.)■	2B-SS-3B	50	95	8	20	1	0	1	9	.211	4	14	0	67	66	2	.985
1997—Anaheim (A.L.)■	2-S-3-O-DH	63	126	12	34	9	0	1	6	.270	18	11	0	68	88	2	.987
American League totals (7 years)		477	1197	141	307	71	6	13	116	.256	153	163	2	531	1029	37	.977
National League totals (1 year)		50	95	8	20	1	0	1	9	.211	4	14	0	67	66	2	.985
Major league totals (8 years)		527	1292	149	327	72	6	14	125	.253	157	177	2	598	1095	39	.977

CHAMPIONSHIP SERIES RECORD

Year Team (League)	Pos.	G	AB	R	H	2B	3B	HR	RBI	Avg.	BB	SO	SB	PO	A	E	Avg.
1993—Chicago (A.L.)	PH-3B	1	1	0	1	0	0	0	0	1.000	0	0	0	0	0	0	...

GREEN, SCARBOROUGH — OF — CARDINALS

PERSONAL: Born June 9, 1974, in Creve Coeur, Mo. ... 5-10/170. ... Bats right, throws right. ... Full name: Bertrum Scarborough Green.
HIGH SCHOOL: Lafayette (Ballwin, Mo.).
JUNIOR COLLEGE: St. Louis Community College at Meramec.
TRANSACTIONS/CAREER NOTES: Selected by St. Louis Cardinals organization in 10th round of free-agent draft (June 1, 1992).
STATISTICAL NOTES: Tied for Texas League lead with four intentional bases on balls in 1997.

Year Team (League)	Pos.	G	AB	R	H	2B	3B	HR	RBI	Avg.	BB	SO	SB	PO	A	E	Avg.
1993— Ariz. Cardinals (Ariz.)	SS	33	95	16	21	3	1	0	11	.221	7	17	3	35	87	14	.897
1994— Johnson City (App.)	SS-OF	54	199	32	48	5	0	0	11	.241	25	61	22	58	140	22	.900
1995— Savannah (S. Atl.)	SS	132	429	48	98	7	6	1	25	.228	55	101	26	*205	358	51	.917
1996— St. Petersburg (FSL)	OF	36	140	26	41	4	1	1	11	.293	21	22	13	90	4	2	.979
—Arkansas (Texas)	OF	92	300	45	60	6	3	3	24	.200	38	58	21	194	7	2	.990
1997— Arkansas (Texas)	OF	76	251	45	77	14	4	2	29	.307	36	48	11	170	8	1	.994
—Louisville (A.A.)	OF	52	209	26	53	11	2	3	13	.254	22	55	10	138	7	1	.993
—St. Louis (N.L.)	OF	20	31	5	3	0	0	0	1	.097	2	5	0	19	1	1	.952
Major league totals (1 year)		20	31	5	3	0	0	0	1	.097	2	5	0	19	1	1	.952

GREEN, SHAWN — OF — BLUE JAYS

PERSONAL: Born November 10, 1972, in Des Plaines, Ill. ... 6-4/195. ... Bats left, throws left. ... Full name: Shawn David Green.
HIGH SCHOOL: Tustin (Calif.).
TRANSACTIONS/CAREER NOTES: Selected by Toronto Blue Jays organization in first round (16th pick overall) of free-agent draft (June 3, 1991); pick received as compensation for San Francisco Giants signing Type A free-agent P Bud Black. ... On disabled list (June 30-July 23, 1992). ... On Knoxville disabled list (June 11-July 24, 1993).
STATISTICAL NOTES: Tied for Florida State League lead with eight sacrifice flies in 1992.

G

Year Team (League)	Pos.	G	AB	R	H	2B	3B	HR	RBI	Avg.	BB	SO	SB	PO	A	E	Avg.
1992—Dunedin (Fla. St.)	OF	114	417	44	114	21	3	1	49	.273	28	66	22	182	3	5	.974
1993—Knoxville (Southern) ..	OF	99	360	40	102	14	2	4	34	.283	26	72	4	172	3	8	.956
—Toronto (A.L.)	OF-DH	3	6	0	0	0	0	0	0	.000	0	1	0	1	0	0	1.000
1994—Syracuse (Int'l)..........	OF	109	433	82	149	27	3	13	61	*.344	40	54	19	220	5	1	*.996
—Toronto (A.L.)	OF	14	33	1	3	1	0	0	1	.091	1	8	1	12	2	0	1.000
1995—Toronto (A.L.).............	OF	121	379	52	109	31	4	15	54	.288	20	68	1	207	9	6	.973
1996—Toronto (A.L.).............	OF-DH	132	422	52	118	32	3	11	45	.280	33	75	5	254	10	2	.992
1997—Toronto (A.L.)..............	OF-DH	135	429	57	123	22	4	16	53	.287	36	99	14	173	6	3	.984
Major league totals (5 years)		405	1269	162	353	86	11	42	153	.278	90	251	21	647	27	11	.984

GREEN, TYLER — P — PHILLIES

PERSONAL: Born February 18, 1970, in Springfield, Ohio. ... 6-5/211. ... Throws right, bats right. ... Full name: Tyler Scott Green.
HIGH SCHOOL: Thomas Jefferson (Denver).
COLLEGE: Wichita State.
TRANSACTIONS/CAREER NOTES: Selected by Cincinnati Reds organization in third round of free-agent draft (June 1, 1988); did not sign. ... Selected by Philadelphia Phillies organization in first round (10th pick overall) of free-agent draft (June 3, 1991). ... On Clearwater disabled list (August 7, 1991-remainder of season). ... On Scranton/Wilkes-Barre disabled list (July 10, 1992-remainder of season and May 3-22, 1993). ... On disabled list (March 23, 1996-entire season). ... On Philadelphia disabled list (March 27-June 1, 1997); included rehabilitation assignment to Scranton/Wilkes-Barre (April 29-May 25).
STATISTICAL NOTES: Pitched 3-1 no-hit victory for Scranton/Wilkes-Barre against Ottawa (July 4, 1993, first game). ... Led International League with 12 hit batsmen in 1994.
MISCELLANEOUS: Appeared in one game as pinch-runner (1995).

Year—Team (League)	W	L	Pct.	ERA	G	GS	CG	ShO	Sv.	IP	H	R	ER	BB	SO
1991—Batavia (N.Y.-Penn)	1	0	1.000	1.20	3	3	0	0	0	15	7	2	2	6	19
—Clearwater (Fla. St.)	2	0	1.000	1.38	2	2	0	0	0	13	3	2	2	8	20
1992—Reading (Eastern)	6	3	.667	1.88	12	12	0	0	0	62 1/3	46	16	13	20	67
—Scran./W.B. (Int'l)	0	1	.000	6.10	2	2	0	0	0	10 1/3	7	7	7	12	15
1993—Philadelphia (N.L.)..............	0	0	...	7.36	3	2	0	0	0	7 1/3	16	9	6	5	7
—Scran./W.B. (Int'l)	6	10	.375	3.95	28	14	4	0	0	118 1/3	102	62	52	43	87
1994—Scran./W.B. (Int'l)	7	*16	.304	5.56	27	26	4	0	0	162	179	*110	*100	*77	95
1995—Philadelphia (N.L.)..............	8	9	.471	5.31	26	25	4	2	0	140 2/3	157	86	83	66	85
1996—							Did not play.								
1997—Scran./W.B. (Int'l)	4	8	.333	6.10	12	12	3	0	0	72 1/3	80	54	49	29	40
—Philadelphia (N.L.)..............	4	4	.500	4.93	14	14	0	0	0	76 2/3	72	50	42	45	58
Major league totals (3 years)	12	13	.480	5.25	43	41	4	2	0	224 2/3	245	145	131	116	150

ALL-STAR GAME RECORD

Year League	W	L	Pct.	ERA	GS	CG	ShO	Sv.	IP	H	R	ER	BB	SO
1995—National	0	0	...	0.00	0	0	0	0	1	2	0	0	0	1

GREENE, CHARLIE — C — ORIOLES

PERSONAL: Born January 23, 1971, in Miami. ... 6-2/190. ... Bats right, throws right. ... Full name: Charles P. Greene.
HIGH SCHOOL: Miami Killian.
JUNIOR COLLEGE: Miami-Dade (South) Community College.
TRANSACTIONS/CAREER NOTES: Selected by San Diego Padres organization in 19th round of free-agent draft (June 3, 1991). ... Selected by Norfolk, New York Mets organization, from Padres organization in Rule 5 minor league draft (December 13, 1993). ... Claimed on waivers by Baltimore Orioles (September 11, 1997).
STATISTICAL NOTES: Tied for Midwest League lead in double plays by catcher with 11 in 1993.

Year Team (League)	Pos.	G	AB	R	H	2B	3B	HR	RBI	Avg.	BB	SO	SB	PO	A	E	Avg.
1991—Ariz. Padres (Ariz.)	C-1B-3B	49	183	27	52	15	1	5	38	.284	16	26	6	334	30	3	.992
1992—Char., S.C. (S. Atl.)	C-3B	98	298	22	55	9	1	1	24	.185	11	60	1	561	119	14	.980
1993—Waterloo (Midw.)	C-1-3-S	84	213	19	38	8	0	2	20	.178	13	33	0	460	96	16	.972
1994—St. Lucie (Fla. St.)■...	C	69	224	23	57	4	0	0	21	.254	9	31	0	380	65	13	.972
—Binghamton (East.)	C	30	106	13	18	4	0	0	2	.170	6	18	0	190	30	3	.987
1995—Binghamton (East.)	C	100	346	26	82	13	0	2	34	.237	15	47	2	670	54	4	*.995
—Norfolk (Int'l)	C	27	88	6	17	3	0	0	4	.193	3	28	0	157	25	0	1.000
1996—Binghamton (East.)	C	100	336	35	82	17	0	2	27	.244	17	52	2	550	75	3	.995
—New York (N.L.)..........	C	2	1	0	0	0	0	0	0	.000	0	0	0	1	0	0	1.000
1997—Norfolk (Int'l)	C	76	238	27	49	7	0	8	28	.206	9	54	1	475	49	8	.985
—Baltimore (A.L.)■.......	C	5	2	0	0	0	0	0	1	.000	0	1	0	4	0	0	1.000
American League totals (1 year)		5	2	0	0	0	0	0	1	.000	0	1	0	4	0	0	1.000
National League totals (1 year)		2	1	0	0	0	0	0	0	.000	0	0	0	1	0	0	1.000
Major league totals (2 years)		7	3	0	0	0	0	0	1	.000	0	1	0	5	0	0	1.000

GREENE, RICK — P — BREWERS

PERSONAL: Born January 2, 1971, in Fort Knox, Ky. ... 6-5/200. ... Throws right, bats right. ... Full name: Richard Douglas Greene Jr.
HIGH SCHOOL: Coral Gables (Fla.).
COLLEGE: Louisiana State.
TRANSACTIONS/CAREER NOTES: Selected by Detroit Tigers organization in first round (16th pick overall) of free-agent draft (June 1, 1992). ... Missed entire 1992 season due to injury. ... On disabled list (May 23-July 17, 1995). ... Traded by Tigers with P Mike Myers and SS Santiago Perez to Milwaukee Brewers for P Bryce Florie (November 20, 1997).
MISCELLANEOUS: Member of 1992 U.S. Olympic baseball team.

G

Year	Team (League)	W	L	Pct.	ERA	G	GS	CG	ShO	Sv.	IP	H	R	ER	BB	SO
1992—	....							Did not play.								
1993—	Lakeland (Fla. St.)............	2	3	.400	6.20	26	0	0	0	2	40 2/3	57	28	28	16	32
	— London (Eastern)............	2	2	.500	6.52	23	0	0	0	0	29	31	22	21	20	19
1994—	Trenton (Eastern)..............	1	1	.500	7.91	20	0	0	0	3	19 1/3	17	17	17	21	5
	— Lakeland (Fla. St.)...........	0	4	.000	4.32	19	2	0	0	4	33 1/3	50	23	16	10	28
1995—	Jacksonville (Southern)......	6	2	.750	3.49	32	0	0	0	0	38 2/3	45	19	15	15	29
1996—	Jacksonville (Southern)......	2	7	.222	4.98	57	0	0	0	30	56	67	44	31	39	42
1997—	Toledo (International).........	6	8	.429	2.83	57	0	0	0	1	70	49	29	22	32	51

GREENE, TODD   C   ANGELS

PERSONAL: Born May 8, 1971, in Augusta, Ga. ... 5-9/195. ... Bats right, throws right. ... Full name: Todd Anthony Greene.
HIGH SCHOOL: Evans (Ga.).
COLLEGE: Georgia Southern.
TRANSACTIONS/CAREER NOTES: Selected by Atlanta Braves organization in 27th round of free-agent draft (June 5, 1989); did not sign. ... Selected by California Angels organization in 12th round of free-agent draft (June 3, 1993). ... On Vancouver disabled list (April 11-May 25, 1996). ... Angels franchise renamed Anaheim Angels for 1997 season. ... On Anaheim disabled list (August 20, 1997-remainder of season).
HONORS: Named California League Most Valuable Player (1994). ... Named California League Rookie of the Year (1994).
STATISTICAL NOTES: Led California League with 306 total bases, 12 intentional bases on balls received and .584 slugging percentage in 1994. ... Led California League catchers with 15 errors, 13 double plays and 44 passed balls in 1994.

Year	Team (League)	Pos.	G	AB	R	H	2B	3B	HR	RBI	Avg.	BB	SO	SB	PO	A	E	Avg.
								BATTING							FIELDING			
1993—	Boise (Northwest)	OF	•76	*305	55	82	15	3	*15	*71	.269	34	44	4	136	4	3	.979
1994—	Lake Elsinore (Calif.) ..	C-OF-1B	133	524	98	158	*39	2	*35	*124	.302	64	96	10	624	90	†15	.979
1995—	Midland (Texas)........	C-1B	82	318	59	104	19	1	26	57	.327	17	55	3	314	44	3	.992
	— Vancouver (PCL)	C	43	168	28	42	3	1	14	35	.250	11	36	1	175	17	1	.995
1996—	Vancouver (PCL)	C	60	223	27	68	18	0	5	33	.305	16	36	0	219	37	3	.988
	— California (A.L.).........	C-DH	29	79	9	15	1	0	2	9	.190	4	11	2	119	19	0	1.000
1997—	Anaheim (A.L.)	C-DH	34	124	24	36	6	0	9	24	.290	7	25	2	153	7	0	1.000
	— Vancouver (PCL)	C-1B-OF	64	260	51	92	22	0	25	75	.354	20	31	5	331	43	3	.992
Major league totals (2 years)			63	203	33	51	7	0	11	33	.251	11	36	4	272	26	0	1.000

GREENE, TOMMY   P   BRAVES

PERSONAL: Born April 6, 1967, in Lumberton, N.C. ... 6-5/225. ... Throws right, bats right. ... Full name: Ira Thomas Greene.
HIGH SCHOOL: Whiteville (N.C.).
TRANSACTIONS/CAREER NOTES: Selected by Atlanta Braves organization in first round (14th pick overall) of free-agent draft (June 3, 1985). ... Traded by Braves to Scranton/Wilkes-Barre, Philadelphia Phillies organization (August 9, 1990), as partial completion of deal in which Braves traded OF Dale Murphy and a player to be named later to Phillies for P Jeff Parrett and two players to be named later (August 3, 1990); Braves acquired OF Jim Vatcher (August 9, 1990) and SS Victor Rosario (September 4, 1990) to complete deal. ... On Philadelphia disabled list (May 13-September 1, 1992); included rehabilitation assignments to Scranton/Wilkes-Barre (May 29-June 4, August 12-20 and August 21-September 1) and Reading (August 20-21). ... On disabled list (July 28-August 12, 1993). ... On Philadelphia disabled list (April 8-26, 1994); included rehabilitation assignment to Clearwater (April 21-26). ... On Philadelphia disabled list (May 23, 1994-remainder of season); included rehabilitation assignments to Scranton/Wilkes-Barre (July 27) and Reading (July 28-August 11). ... On Philadelphia disabled list (April 19-June 29, July 4-August 5 and August 28-September 12, 1995); included rehabilitation assignments to Clearwater (June 13-28) and Scranton/Wilkes-Barre (July 14-August 3 and September 1-11). ... On Scranton/Wilkes-Barre disabled list (April 4-June 3, 1996). ... Granted free agency (October 15, 1996). ... Signed by Houston Astros organization (February 4, 1997). ... On Houston disabled list (July 10, 1997-remainder of season). ... Released by Astros following 1997 season. ... Signed by Braves organization (January 23, 1998).
STATISTICAL NOTES: Pitched 2-0 no-hit victory against Montreal (May 23, 1991). ... Led N.L. with 15 wild pitches in 1993.
MISCELLANEOUS: Made two outs in two games as pinch-hitter (1991). ... Appeared in one game as pinch-runner (1993).

Year	Team (League)	W	L	Pct.	ERA	G	GS	CG	ShO	Sv.	IP	H	R	ER	BB	SO
1985—	Pulaski (Appalachian).........	2	5	.286	7.64	12	12	1	1	0	50 2/3	49	45	43	27	32
1986—	Sumter (S. Atl.).................	11	7	.611	4.69	28	*28	5	•3	0	174 2/3	162	95	91	82	169
1987—	Greenville (Southern)	11	8	.579	3.29	23	23	4	2	0	142 1/3	103	60	52	66	101
1988—	Richmond (Int'l)	7	17	.292	4.77	29	29	4	•3	0	177 1/3	169	98	94	70	130
1989—	Richmond (Int'l)................	9	12	.429	3.61	26	26	2	1	0	152	136	74	61	50	125
	— Atlanta (N.L.).................	1	2	.333	4.10	4	4	1	1	0	26 1/3	22	12	12	6	17
1990—	Atlanta (N.L.)...................	1	0	1.000	8.03	5	2	0	0	0	12 1/3	14	11	11	9	4
	— Richmond (Int'l).............	5	8	.385	3.72	19	18	2	0	0	109	88	49	45	65	65
	— Philadelphia (N.L.)..........	2	3	.400	4.15	10	7	0	0	0	39	36	20	18	17	17
1991—	Philadelphia (N.L.)............	13	7	.650	3.38	36	27	3	2	0	207 2/3	177	85	78	66	154
1992—	Philadelphia (N.L.)............	3	3	.500	5.32	13	12	0	0	0	64 1/3	75	39	38	34	39
	— Reading (Eastern)	0	0	. . .	9.00	1	1	0	0	0	2	3	2	2	2	2
	— Scran./W.B. (Int'l)..........	2	1	.667	2.49	5	5	1	1	0	21 2/3	15	7	6	4	21
1993—	Philadelphia (N.L.)............	16	4	.800	3.42	31	30	7	2	0	200	175	84	76	62	167
1994—	Philadelphia (N.L.)............	2	0	1.000	4.54	7	7	0	0	0	35 2/3	37	20	18	22	28
	— Clearwater (Fla. St.)	0	0	. . .	0.00	1	1	0	0	0	5	2	0	0	1	4
	— Scran./W.B. (Int'l)..........	0	0	. . .	0.00	1	1	0	0	0	4	3	1	0	1	6
	— Reading (Eastern)	1	0	1.000	4.35	2	2	0	0	0	10 1/3	12	5	5	3	12
1995—	Clearwater (Fla. St.)	0	3	.000	3.15	3	3	0	0	0	20	12	7	7	7	20
	— Philadelphia (N.L.)..........	0	5	.000	8.29	11	6	0	0	0	33 2/3	45	32	31	20	24
	— Scran./W.B. (Int'l)...........	3	0	1.000	2.22	4	4	0	0	0	28 1/3	18	8	7	6	19
1996—	New Orleans (A.A.)■..........	2	0	1.000	3.77	5	5	0	0	0	31	31	13	13	7	26
	— Clearwater (Fla. St.)	1	1	.500	2.00	7	4	0	0	0	27	25	8	6	4	23
1997—	New Orleans (A.A.)■..........	5	3	.625	3.38	13	13	0	0	0	74 2/3	59	30	28	25	75
	— Houston (N.L.)	0	1	.000	7.00	2	2	0	0	0	9	10	7	7	5	11
Major league totals (8 years)		38	25	.603	4.14	119	97	11	5	0	628	591	310	289	241	461

G

CHAMPIONSHIP SERIES RECORD

RECORDS: Shares single-game record for most earned runs allowed—7 (October 7, 1993).

Year Team (League)	W	L	Pct.	ERA	G	GS	CG	ShO	Sv.	IP	H	R	ER	BB	SO
1993— Philadelphia (N.L.)...............	1	1	.500	9.64	2	2	0	0	0	9 1/3	12	10	10	7	7

WORLD SERIES RECORD

Year Team (League)	W	L	Pct.	ERA	G	GS	CG	ShO	Sv.	IP	H	R	ER	BB	SO
1993— Philadelphia (N.L.)...............	0	0	...	27.00	1	1	0	0	0	2 1/3	7	7	7	4	1

GREENE, WILLIE   3B   REDS

PERSONAL: Born September 23, 1971, in Milledgeville, Ga. ... 5-11/185. ... Bats left, throws right. ... Full name: Willie Louis Greene.
HIGH SCHOOL: Jones County (Gray, Ga.).
TRANSACTIONS/CAREER NOTES: Selected by Pittsburgh Pirates organization in first round (18th pick overall) of free-agent draft (June 5, 1989). ... Traded by Pirates organization with P Scott Ruskin and a player to be named later to Montreal Expos organization for P Zane Smith (August 8, 1990). ... Expos acquired OF Moises Alou to complete deal (August 16, 1990). ... Traded by Expos organization with OF Dave Martinez and P Scott Ruskin to Cincinnati Reds organization for P John Wetteland and P Bill Risley (December 11, 1991). ... On Cincinnati disabled list (August 21, 1993-remainder of season). ... On Indianapolis disabled list (June 7-19, 1995). ... On disabled list (June 27-July 12, 1996).
STATISTICAL NOTES: Led Florida State League third basemen with 31 errors in 1991. ... Led Southern League third basemen with 24 double plays in 1992. ... Led American Association third basemen with 23 errors in 1993. ... Hit three home runs in one game (September 24, 1996). ... Career major league grand slams: 3.

Year Team (League)	Pos.	G	AB	R	H	2B	3B	HR	RBI	Avg.	BB	SO	SB	PO	A	E	Avg.
1989— Princeton (Appal.)	SS	39	136	22	44	6	4	2	24	.324	9	29	4	33	69	19	.843
— GC Pirates (GCL)........	SS	23	86	17	24	3	3	5	11	.279	9	6	4	25	49	3	.961
1990— Augusta (S. Atl.).........	SS-2B	86	291	59	75	12	4	11	47	.258	61	58	7	117	209	34	.906
— Salem (Carolina)	SS	17	60	9	11	1	1	3	9	.183	7	18	0	22	43	2	.970
— Rockford (Midwest)■	SS	11	35	4	14	3	0	0	2	.400	6	7	2	14	37	4	.927
1991— W.P. Beach (FSL).......	3B-SS	99	322	46	70	9	3	12	43	.217	50	93	10	72	184	†32	.889
1992— Cedar Rap. (Midw.)■.	3B	34	120	26	34	8	2	12	40	.283	18	27	3	13	60	8	.901
— Chattanooga (Sou.) ...	3B	96	349	47	97	19	2	15	66	.278	46	90	9	*77	174	14	*.947
— Cincinnati (N.L.)	3B	29	93	10	25	5	2	2	13	.269	10	23	0	15	40	3	.948
1993— Indianapolis (A.A.)	3B-SS	98	341	62	91	19	0	22	58	.267	51	83	2	77	171	†23	.915
— Cincinnati (N.L.)	SS-3B	15	50	7	8	1	1	2	5	.160	2	19	0	19	37	1	.982
1994— Cincinnati (N.L.)	3B-OF	16	37	5	8	2	0	0	3	.216	6	14	0	2	21	1	.958
— Indianapolis (A.A.)......	3B-SS	114	435	77	124	24	1	23	80	.285	56	88	8	93	249	17	.953
1995— Cincinnati (N.L.)	3B	8	19	1	2	0	0	0	0	.105	3	7	1	1	13	0	1.000
— Indianapolis (A.A.)......	3B-SS-OF	91	325	57	79	12	2	19	45	.243	38	67	3	60	160	12	.948
1996— Cincinnati (N.L.)	3-0-1-S-2	115	287	48	70	5	5	19	63	.244	36	88	0	57	149	16	.928
1997— Cincinnati (N.L.)	3-0-1-S	151	495	62	125	22	1	26	91	.253	78	111	6	176	175	17	.954
Major league totals (6 years)		334	981	133	238	35	9	49	175	.243	135	262	6	270	435	38	.949

GREER, RUSTY   OF   RANGERS

PERSONAL: Born January 21, 1969, in Fort Rucker, Ala. ... 6-0/190. ... Bats left, throws left. ... Full name: Thurman Clyde Greer III.
HIGH SCHOOL: Albertville (Ala.).
COLLEGE: Montevallo (Ala.).
TRANSACTIONS/CAREER NOTES: Selected by Texas Rangers organization in 10th round of free-agent draft (June 4, 1990). ... On disabled list (July 31-August 22, 1992).
RECORDS: Shares major league record for fewest double plays by outfielder (150 or more games)—0 (1997).
STATISTICAL NOTES: Led Florida State League with .395 on-base percentage in 1991. ... Career major league grand slams: 4.

Year Team (League)	Pos.	G	AB	R	H	2B	3B	HR	RBI	Avg.	BB	SO	SB	PO	A	E	Avg.
1990— Butte (Pioneer)	OF	62	226	48	78	12	6	10	50	.345	41	23	9	84	5	*8	.918
1991— Charlotte (Fla. St.)......	OF-1B	111	388	52	114	25	1	5	48	.294	66	48	12	213	15	7	.970
— Tulsa (Texas)	OF	20	64	12	19	3	2	3	12	.297	17	6	2	34	0	0	1.000
1992— Tulsa (Texas)	1B-OF	106	359	47	96	22	4	5	37	.267	60	63	2	814	50	11	.987
1993— Tulsa (Texas)	1B	129	474	76	138	25	6	15	59	.291	53	79	10	1055	93	8	.993
— Oklahoma City (A.A.)..	OF	8	27	6	6	2	0	1	4	.222	6	7	0	16	0	0	1.000
1994— Oklahoma City (A.A.)..	OF-1B	31	111	18	35	12	1	3	13	.315	18	24	1	52	3	3	.948
— Texas (A.L.)	OF-1B	80	277	36	87	16	1	10	46	.314	46	46	0	216	4	6	.973
1995— Texas (A.L.)	OF-1B	131	417	58	113	21	2	13	61	.271	55	66	3	240	9	6	.976
1996— Texas (A.L.)	OF-DH-1B	139	542	96	180	41	6	18	100	.332	62	86	9	304	6	5	.984
1997— Texas (A.L.)	OF-DH	157	601	112	193	42	3	26	87	.321	83	87	9	318	9	*12	.965
Major league totals (4 years)		507	1837	302	573	120	12	67	294	.312	246	285	21	1078	28	29	.974

DIVISION SERIES RECORD

Year Team (League)	Pos.	G	AB	R	H	2B	3B	HR	RBI	Avg.	BB	SO	SB	PO	A	E	Avg.
1996— Texas (A.L.)	OF	4	16	2	2	0	0	0	0	.125	3	3	0	12	0	0	1.000

GREGG, TOMMY   OF/1B   BRAVES

PERSONAL: Born July 29, 1963, in Boone, N.C. ... 6-1/190. ... Bats left, throws left. ... Full name: William Thomas Gregg Jr.
HIGH SCHOOL: R.J. Reynolds (Winston-Salem, N.C.).
COLLEGE: Wake Forest.

G

TRANSACTIONS/CAREER NOTES: Selected by Cleveland Indians organization in ninth round of free-agent draft (June 8, 1981); did not sign. ... Selected by Indians organization in 32nd round of free-agent draft (June 4, 1984); did not sign. ... Selected by Pittsburgh Pirates organization in seventh round of free-agent draft (June 3, 1985). ... Traded by Pirates to Atlanta Braves (September 1, 1988), completing deal in which Braves traded IF Ken Oberkfell and cash to Pirates for a player to be named later (August 28, 1988). ... On disabled list (April 20-June 2, 1989). ... On Atlanta disabled list (April 28-June 9, 1991); included rehabilitation assignment to Richmond (June 5-9). ... On Atlanta disabled list (March 24-July 21, 1992); included rehabilitation assignments to Richmond (May 30-June 7, July 8-13 and July 16-20). ... Claimed on waivers by Cincinnati Reds (December 1, 1992). ... Released by Indianapolis, Reds organization (March 26, 1993). ... Re-signed by Indianapolis (March 27, 1993). ... On Indianapolis disabled list (May 15-22 and June 7-17, 1993). ... Granted free agency (August 30, 1993). ... Signed by Buffalo, Pittsburgh Pirates organization (April 30, 1995). ... Loaned by Buffalo to Mexico City Red Devils of Mexican League (April 30, 1995). ... Granted free agency (October 15, 1994). ... Signed by Charlotte, Florida Marlins organization (January 11, 1995). ... On Florida disabled list (August 11-September 1, 1995); included rehabilitation assignment to Charlotte (August 26-September 1). ... Granted free agency (October 16, 1995). ... Re-signed by Marlins organization (November 2, 1995). ... Granted free agency (October 15, 1996). ... Signed by Houston Astros organization (February 5, 1997). ... Released by Astros (March 20, 1997). ... Signed by Braves organization (March 22, 1997).

STATISTICAL NOTES: Led Eastern League with 14 intentional bases on balls received in 1987. ... Career major league grand slams: 1.

Year Team (League)	Pos.	G	AB	R	H	2B	3B	HR	RBI	Avg.	BB	SO	SB	PO	A	E	Avg.
1985— Macon (S. Atl.)..........	OF	72	259	43	81	14	2	1	18	.313	49	38	16	117	4	1	.992
1986— Nashua (Eastern).......	OF-1B	126	421	55	113	13	4	1	29	.268	66	48	11	216	7	4	.982
1987— Harrisburg (Eastern) ..	OF	133	461	99	171	22	9	10	82	*.371	84	47	35	242	12	7	.973
— Pittsburgh (N.L.).........	OF	10	8	3	2	1	0	0	0	.250	0	2	0	1	0	0	1.000
1988— Buffalo (A.A.)............	OF	72	252	34	74	12	0	6	27	.294	25	26	7	134	3	2	.986
— Pittsburgh (N.L.)	OF	14	15	4	3	1	0	1	3	.200	1	4	0	4	0	0	1.000
— Atlanta (N.L.)■..........	OF	11	29	1	10	3	0	0	4	.345	2	2	0	22	1	0	1.000
1989— Atlanta (N.L.)...........	OF-1B	102	276	24	67	8	0	6	23	.243	18	45	3	321	17	2	.994
1990— Atlanta (N.L.)...........	1B-OF	124	239	18	63	13	1	5	32	.264	24	39	4	356	34	6	.985
1991— Atlanta (N.L.)...........	OF-1B	72	107	13	20	8	1	1	4	.187	12	24	2	121	9	0	1.000
— Richmond (Int'l).........	OF	3	13	3	6	0	0	1	4	.462	1	2	1	5	0	0	1.000
1992— Richmond (Int'l)........	OF	39	125	17	36	9	2	0	12	.288	19	27	3	53	0	2	.964
— Atlanta (N.L.)...........	OF	18	19	1	5	0	0	1	1	.263	1	7	1	15	0	0	1.000
1993— Indianapolis (A.A.)■ ..	1B-OF	71	198	34	63	12	5	7	30	.318	26	28	3	330	29	7	.981
— Cincinnati (N.L.).........	OF	10	12	1	2	0	0	0	1	.167	0	0	0	2	0	0	1.000
1994— M.C. R. Dev. (Mex.)■.	1B	85	287	69	101	19	3	7	64	.352	56	28	12	703	46	8	.989
1995— Charlotte (Int'l)■........	1B-OF	34	124	30	48	10	1	9	32	.387	21	13	7	140	13	1	.994
— Florida (N.L.)...........	OF-1B	72	156	20	37	5	0	6	20	.237	16	33	3	80	1	1	.988
1996— Charlotte (Int'l)..........	1B-OF	119	405	69	116	24	0	22	80	.286	49	62	10	569	46	3	.995
1997— Richmond (Int'l)■.......	OF-1B	115	385	52	128	36	1	9	54	*.332	46	64	3	230	12	2	.992
— Atlanta (N.L.)...........	OF-1B	13	19	1	5	2	0	0	0	.263	1	2	1	5	0	0	1.000
Major league totals (9 years)		446	880	86	214	41	2	20	88	.243	75	158	14	927	62	9	.991

CHAMPIONSHIP SERIES RECORD

Year Team (League)	Pos.	G	AB	R	H	2B	3B	HR	RBI	Avg.	BB	SO	SB	PO	A	E	Avg.
1991— Atlanta (N.L.).............	PH	4	4	0	1	0	0	0	0	.250	0	2	0	...	...	...	...
1997— Atlanta (N.L.).............	PH	4	4	0	0	0	0	0	0	.000	0	1	0	0	0	0	...
Championship series totals (2 years)		8	8	0	1	0	0	0	0	.125	0	3	0	0	0	0	...

WORLD SERIES RECORD

Year Team (League)	Pos.	G	AB	R	H	2B	3B	HR	RBI	Avg.	BB	SO	SB	PO	A	E	Avg.
1991— Atlanta (N.L.)..............	PH	4	3	0	0	0	0	0	0	.000	0	2	0	...	...	...	...

GRIEVE, BEN   OF   ATHLETICS

PERSONAL: Born May 4, 1976, in Arlington, Texas. ... 6-4/200. ... Bats left, throws right. ... Full name: Benjamin Grieve. ... Son of Tom Grieve, outfielder with four major league teams (1970-79).

HIGH SCHOOL: James W. Martin (Arlington, Texas).

TRANSACTIONS/CAREER NOTES: Selected by Oakland Athletics organization in first round (second overall pick) of free-agent draft (June 2, 1994).

HONORS: Named Minor League Player of the Year by THE SPORTING NEWS (1997). ... Named Southern League Most Valuable Player (1997).

STATISTICAL NOTES: Tied for Northwest League lead with seven intentional bases on balls received in 1994. ... Led Southern League with .455 on-base percentage in 1997.

Year Team (League)	Pos.	G	AB	R	H	2B	3B	HR	RBI	Avg.	BB	SO	SB	PO	A	E	Avg.
1994— S. Oregon (N'west).....	OF	72	252	44	83	13	0	7	50	.329	51	48	2	133	8	6	.959
1995— W. Mich. (Mid.)...........	OF	102	371	53	97	16	1	4	62	.261	60	75	11	125	6	8	.942
— Modesto (California) ..	OF	28	107	17	28	5	0	2	14	.262	14	15	2	37	2	2	.951
1996— Modesto (California) ..	OF	72	281	61	100	20	1	11	51	.356	38	52	8	104	5	5	.956
— Huntsville (Southern).	OF	63	232	34	55	8	1	8	32	.237	35	53	0	79	2	4	.953
1997— Huntsville (Southern).	OF	100	372	100	122	29	2	24	108	.328	81	75	5	193	6	•8	.961
— Edmonton (PCL)	OF	27	108	27	46	11	1	7	28	.426	12	16	0	51	2	2	.964
— Oakland (A.L.)	OF	24	93	12	29	6	0	3	24	.312	13	25	0	39	1	0	1.000
Major league totals (1 year)		24	93	12	29	6	0	3	24	.312	13	25	0	39	1	0	1.000

GRIFFEY JR., KEN   OF   MARINERS

PERSONAL: Born November 21, 1969, in Donora, Pa. ... 6-3/205. ... Bats left, throws left. ... Full name: George Kenneth Griffey Jr. ... Son of Ken Griffey Sr., hitting coach, Cincinnati Reds, and major league outfielder with four teams (1973-91); and brother of Craig Griffey, outfielder, Seattle Mariners organization.

HIGH SCHOOL: Moeller (Cincinnati).

G

TRANSACTIONS/CAREER NOTES: Selected by Seattle Mariners organization in first round (first pick overall) of free-agent draft (June 2, 1987). ... On San Bernardino disabled list (June 9-August 15, 1988). ... On disabled list (July 24-August 20, 1989; June 9-25, 1992; and June 20-July 13, 1996). ... On Seattle disabled list (May 27-August 15, 1995); included rehabilitation assignment to Tacoma (August 13-15).

RECORDS: Shares major league record for most consecutive games with one or more home runs—8 (July 20 through July 28, 1993).

HONORS: Won A.L. Gold Glove as outfielder (1990-97). ... Named outfielder on THE SPORTING NEWS A.L. All-Star team (1991, 1993-94 and 1996-97). ... Named outfielder on THE SPORTING NEWS A.L. Silver Slugger team (1991, 1993-94, 1996 and 1997). ... Named Major League Player of the Year by THE SPORTING NEWS (1997). ... Named A.L. Most Valuable Player by Baseball Writers' Association of America (1997).

STATISTICAL NOTES: Led A.L. outfielders with six double plays in 1989. ... Led A.L. with 359 total bases in 1993 and 393 in 1997. ... Hit three home runs in one game (May 24, 1996 and April 25, 1997). ... Led A.L. with 23 intentional bases on balls received in 1997. ... Led A.L. in slugging percentage with .646 in 1997. ... Career major league grand slams: 9.

MISCELLANEOUS: Holds Seattle Mariners franchise all-time record for most runs (820), most hits (1,389), most home runs (294) and most runs batted in (872).

							BATTING								FIELDING		
Year Team (League)	Pos.	G	AB	R	H	2B	3B	HR	RBI	Avg.	BB	SO	SB	PO	A	E	Avg.
1987—Bellingham (N'west)...	OF	54	182	43	57	9	1	14	40	.313	44	42	13	117	4	1	*.992
1988—San Bern. (Calif.)........	OF	58	219	50	74	13	3	11	42	.338	34	39	32	145	3	2	.987
—Vermont (Eastern)......	OF	17	61	10	17	5	1	2	10	.279	5	12	4	40	2	1	.977
1989—Seattle (A.L.)	OF-DH	127	455	61	120	23	0	16	61	.264	44	83	16	302	12	•10	.969
1990—Seattle (A.L.)	OF	155	597	91	179	28	7	22	80	.300	63	81	16	330	8	7	.980
1991—Seattle (A.L.)	OF-DH	154	548	76	179	42	1	22	100	.327	71	82	18	360	15	4	.989
1992—Seattle (A.L.)	OF-DH	142	565	83	174	39	4	27	103	.308	44	67	10	359	8	1	.997
1993—Seattle (A.L.)	OF-DH-1B	156	582	113	180	38	3	45	109	.309	96	91	17	317	8	3	.991
1994—Seattle (A.L.)	OF-DH	111	433	94	140	24	4	*40	90	.323	56	73	11	225	12	4	.983
1995—Seattle (A.L.)	OF-DH	72	260	52	67	7	0	17	42	.258	52	53	4	190	5	2	.990
—Tacoma (PCL)	DH	1	3	0	0	0	0	0	0	.000	0	1	0	...	...	...	...
1996—Seattle (A.L.)	OF-DH	140	545	125	165	26	2	49	140	.303	78	104	16	375	10	4	.990
1997—Seattle (A.L.)	OF-DH	157	608	*125	185	34	3	*56	*147	.304	76	121	15	388	9	6	.985
Major league totals (9 years)		1214	4593	820	1389	261	24	294	872	.302	580	755	123	2846	87	41	.986

DIVISION SERIES RECORD

RECORDS: Shares single-game record for most home runs—2 (October 3, 1995). ... Shares career record for most home runs—5.

NOTES: Shares postseason single-series record for most home runs—5 (1995).

							BATTING								FIELDING		
Year Team (League)	Pos.	G	AB	R	H	2B	3B	HR	RBI	Avg.	BB	SO	SB	PO	A	E	Avg.
1995—Seattle (A.L.)	OF	5	23	9	9	0	0	5	7	.391	2	4	1	15	1	0	1.000
1997—Seattle (A.L.)	OF	4	15	0	2	0	0	0	2	.133	1	3	2	12	1	0	1.000
Division series totals (2 years)		9	38	9	11	0	0	5	9	.289	3	7	3	27	2	0	1.000

CHAMPIONSHIP SERIES RECORD

							BATTING								FIELDING		
Year Team (League)	Pos.	G	AB	R	H	2B	3B	HR	RBI	Avg.	BB	SO	SB	PO	A	E	Avg.
1995—Seattle (A.L.)	OF	6	21	2	7	2	0	1	2	.333	4	4	2	13	0	1	.929

ALL-STAR GAME RECORD

NOTES: Named Most Valuable Player (1992).

						BATTING								FIELDING		
Year League	Pos.	AB	R	H	2B	3B	HR	RBI	Avg.	BB	SO	SB	PO	A	E	Avg.
1990—American..................	OF	2	0	0	0	0	0	0	.000	1	0	0	2	0	0	1.000
1991—American..................	OF	3	0	2	0	0	0	0	.667	0	0	0	2	0	0	1.000
1992—American..................	OF	3	2	3	1	0	1	2	1.000	0	0	0	1	0	0	1.000
1993—American..................	OF	3	1	1	0	0	0	1	.333	0	1	0	2	0	0	1.000
1994—American..................	OF	3	0	2	1	0	0	1	.667	0	0	0	2	0	0	1.000
1995—American..................					Selected, did not play—injured.											
1996—American..................					Selected, did not play—injured.											
1997—American..................	OF	4	0	0	0	0	0	0	.000	0	2	0	0	0	0	...
All-Star Game totals (6 years)		18	3	8	2	0	1	4	.444	1	3	0	9	0	0	1.000

GRISSOM, MARQUIS   OF   BREWERS

PERSONAL: Born April 17, 1967, in Atlanta. ... 5-11/190. ... Bats right, throws right. ... Full name: Marquis Dean Grissom. ... Name pronounced mar-KEESE.

HIGH SCHOOL: Lakeshore (College Park, Ga.).

COLLEGE: Florida A&M.

TRANSACTIONS/CAREER NOTES: Selected by Montreal Expos organization in third round of free-agent draft (June 1, 1988). ... On Montreal disabled list (May 29-June 30, 1990); included rehabilitation assignment to Indianapolis (June 25-30). ... Traded by Expos to Atlanta Braves for OF Roberto Kelly, OF Tony Tarasco and P Esteban Yan (April 6, 1995). ... Traded by Braves with OF Dave Justice to Cleveland Indians for OF Kenny Lofton and P Alan Embree (March 25, 1997). ... On disabled list (April 22-May 5, 1997). ... Traded by Indians with P Jeff Juden to Milwaukee Brewers for P Ben McDonald, P Mike Fetters and P Ron Villone (December 8, 1997).

HONORS: Won N.L. Gold Glove as outfielder (1993-96).

STATISTICAL NOTES: Led New York-Pennsylvania League with 146 total bases in 1988. ... Led N.L. outfielders with 333 total chances in 1994. ... Had 28-game hitting streak (July 25-August 24, 1996). ... Career major league grand slams: 3.

							BATTING								FIELDING		
Year Team (League)	Pos.	G	AB	R	H	2B	3B	HR	RBI	Avg.	BB	SO	SB	PO	A	E	Avg.
1988—Jamestown (NYP)	OF	74	*291	*69	94	14	7	8	39	.323	35	39	23	123	•11	3	.978
1989—Jacksonville (South.)..	OF	78	278	43	83	15	4	3	31	.299	24	31	24	141	7	3	.980
—Indianapolis (A.A.)......	OF	49	187	28	52	10	4	2	21	.278	14	23	16	106	5	0	1.000
—Montreal (N.L.)...........	OF	26	74	16	19	2	0	1	2	.257	12	21	1	32	1	2	.943
1990—Montreal (N.L.)...........	OF	98	288	42	74	14	2	3	29	.257	27	40	22	165	5	2	.988
—Indianapolis (A.A.)......	OF	5	22	3	4	0	0	2	3	.182	0	5	1	16	0	0	1.000

G

Year Team (League)	Pos.	G	AB	R	H	2B	3B	HR	RBI	Avg.	BB	SO	SB	PO	A	E	Avg.
1991— Montreal (N.L.)	OF	148	558	73	149	23	9	6	39	.267	34	89	*76	350	•15	6	.984
1992— Montreal (N.L.)	OF	159	*653	99	180	39	6	14	66	.276	42	81	*78	401	7	7	.983
1993— Montreal (N.L.)	OF	157	630	104	188	27	2	19	95	.298	52	76	53	416	8	7	.984
1994— Montreal (N.L.)	OF	110	475	96	137	25	4	11	45	.288	41	66	36	*321	7	5	.985
1995— Atlanta (N.L.)■	OF	139	551	80	142	23	3	12	42	.258	47	61	29	309	9	2	.994
1996— Atlanta (N.L.)	OF	158	671	106	207	32	10	23	74	.308	41	73	28	338	10	1	.997
1997— Cleveland (A.L.)■	OF	144	558	74	146	27	6	12	66	.262	43	89	22	356	7	3	.992
American League totals (1 year)		144	558	74	146	27	6	12	66	.262	43	89	22	356	7	3	.992
National League totals (8 years)		995	3900	616	1096	185	36	89	392	.281	296	507	323	2332	62	32	.987
Major league totals (9 years)		1139	4458	690	1242	212	42	101	458	.279	339	596	345	2688	69	35	.987

DIVISION SERIES RECORD

RECORDS: Holds single-game record for most hits—5 (October 7, 1995). ... Shares single-game record for most home runs—2 (October 4, 1995). ... Shares career record for most triples—1.

Year Team (League)	Pos.	G	AB	R	H	2B	3B	HR	RBI	Avg.	BB	SO	SB	PO	A	E	Avg.
1995— Atlanta (N.L.)	OF	4	21	5	11	2	0	3	4	.524	0	3	2	9	0	0	1.000
1996— Atlanta (N.L.)	OF	3	12	2	1	0	0	0	0	.083	1	2	1	4	0	1	.800
1997— Cleveland (A.L.)	OF	5	17	3	4	0	1	0	0	.235	1	2	0	14	0	0	1.000
Division series totals (3 years)		12	50	10	16	2	1	3	4	.320	2	7	3	27	0	1	.964

CHAMPIONSHIP SERIES RECORD

RECORDS: Holds single-series record for most at-bats—35 (1996). ... Shares N.L. single-game record for most at-bats—6 (October 14 and 17, 1996).

NOTES: Named A.L. Championship Series Most Valuable Player (1997).

Year Team (League)	Pos.	G	AB	R	H	2B	3B	HR	RBI	Avg.	BB	SO	SB	PO	A	E	Avg.
1995— Atlanta (N.L.)	OF	4	19	2	5	0	1	0	0	.263	1	4	0	8	0	1	.889
1996— Atlanta (N.L.)	OF	7	35	7	10	1	0	1	3	.286	0	8	2	17	0	1	.944
1997— Cleveland (A.L.)	OF	6	23	2	6	0	0	1	4	.261	1	9	3	13	1	0	1.000
Championship series totals (3 years)		17	77	11	21	1	1	2	7	.273	2	21	5	38	1	2	.951

WORLD SERIES RECORD

NOTES: Member of World Series championship team (1995).

Year Team (League)	Pos.	G	AB	R	H	2B	3B	HR	RBI	Avg.	BB	SO	SB	PO	A	E	Avg.
1995— Atlanta (N.L.)	OF	6	25	3	9	1	0	0	1	.360	1	3	3	13	0	0	1.000
1996— Atlanta (N.L.)	OF	6	27	4	12	2	1	0	5	.444	1	2	1	7	0	1	.875
1997— Cleveland (A.L.)	OF	7	25	5	9	1	0	0	2	.360	4	4	0	19	0	1	.950
World Series totals (3 years)		19	77	12	30	4	1	0	8	.390	6	9	4	39	0	2	.951

ALL-STAR GAME RECORD

Year League	Pos.	AB	R	H	2B	3B	HR	RBI	Avg.	BB	SO	SB	PO	A	E	Avg.
1993— National	OF	3	0	0	0	0	0	0	.000	0	1	0	1	0	0	1.000
1994— National	OF	1	1	1	0	0	1	1	1.000	1	0	0	2	1	0	1.000
All-Star Game totals (2 years)		4	1	1	0	0	1	1	.250	1	1	0	3	1	0	1.000

GROOM, BUDDY   P   ATHLETICS

PERSONAL: Born July 10, 1965, in Dallas. ... 6-2/205. ... Throws left, bats left. ... Full name: Wedsel Gary Groom Jr.
HIGH SCHOOL: Red Oak (Texas).
COLLEGE: Mary Hardin-Baylor (Texas).
TRANSACTIONS/CAREER NOTES: Selected by Chicago White Sox organization in 12th round of free-agent draft (June 2, 1987). ... Selected by Detroit Tigers organization from White Sox organization in Rule 5 minor league draft (December 3, 1990). ... Traded by Tigers to Florida Marlins for a player to be named later (August 7, 1995); Tigers acquired P Mike Myers to complete deal (August 9, 1995). ... Granted free agency (October 16, 1995). ... Signed by Oakland Athletics organization (November 27, 1995).

Year Team (League)	W	L	Pct.	ERA	G	GS	CG	ShO	Sv.	IP	H	R	ER	BB	SO
1987— GC White Sox (GCL)	1	0	1.000	0.75	4	1	0	0	1	12	12	1	1	2	8
— Daytona Beach (FSL)	7	2	.778	3.59	11	10	2	0	0	67 2/3	60	30	27	33	29
1988— Tampa (Florida State)	13	10	.565	2.54	27	27	8	0	0	*195	181	69	55	51	118
1989— Birmingham (Southern)	13	8	.619	4.52	26	26	3	1	0	167 1/3	172	101	84	78	94
1990— Birmingham (Southern)	6	8	.429	5.07	20	20	0	0	0	115 1/3	135	81	65	48	66
1991— Toledo (Int'l)■	2	5	.286	4.32	24	6	0	0	1	75	75	39	36	25	49
— London (Eastern)	7	1	.875	3.48	11	7	0	0	0	51 2/3	51	20	20	12	39
1992— Toledo (Int'l)	7	7	.500	2.80	16	16	1	0	0	109 1/3	102	41	34	23	71
— Detroit (A.L.)	0	5	.000	5.82	12	7	0	0	1	38 2/3	48	28	25	22	15
1993— Toledo (Int'l)	9	3	.750	2.74	16	15	0	0	0	102	98	34	31	30	78
— Detroit (A.L.)	0	2	.000	6.14	19	3	0	0	0	36 2/3	48	25	25	13	15
1994— Toledo (Int'l)	0	0	...	2.25	5	0	0	0	0	4	2	1	1	0	6
— Detroit (A.L.)	0	1	.000	3.94	40	0	0	0	1	32	31	14	14	13	27
1995— Detroit (A.L.)	1	3	.250	7.52	23	4	0	0	1	40 2/3	55	35	34	26	23
— Toledo (Int'l)	2	3	.400	1.91	6	5	1	0	0	33	31	14	7	4	24
— Florida (N.L.)■	1	2	.333	7.20	14	0	0	0	0	15	26	12	12	6	12
1996— Oakland (A.L.)■	5	0	1.000	3.84	72	1	0	0	2	77 1/3	85	37	33	34	57
1997— Oakland (A.L.)	2	2	.500	5.15	78	0	0	0	3	64 2/3	75	38	37	24	45
A.L. totals (6 years)	8	13	.381	5.21	244	15	0	0	8	290	342	177	168	132	182
N.L. totals (1 year)	1	2	.333	7.20	14	0	0	0	0	15	26	12	12	6	12
Major league totals (6 years)	9	15	.375	5.31	258	15	0	0	8	305	368	189	180	138	194

G

GROSS, KEVIN — P

PERSONAL: Born June 8, 1961, in Downey, Calif. ... 6-5/227. ... Throws right, bats right. ... Full name: Kevin Frank Gross.
HIGH SCHOOL: Fillmore (Calif.).
JUNIOR COLLEGE: Oxnard (Calif.) College.
COLLEGE: California Lutheran College.
TRANSACTIONS/CAREER NOTES: Selected by Baltimore Orioles organization in 32nd round of free-agent draft (June 5, 1979); did not sign. ... Selected by Philadelphia Phillies organization in secondary phase of free-agent draft (January 13, 1981). ... Traded by Phillies to Montreal Expos for P Floyd Youmans and P Jeff Parrett (December 6, 1988). ... On disabled list (June 28-July 20, 1990). ... Granted free agency (November 5, 1990). ... Signed by Los Angeles Dodgers (December 3, 1990). ... Granted free agency (October 20, 1994). ... Signed by Texas Rangers (December 13, 1994). ... On Texas disabled list (May 18-June 4 and July 15-August 3, 1996); included rehabilitation assignment to Oklahoma City (July 28-August 3). ... Granted free agency (October 31, 1996). ... Re-signed by Rangers (March 17, 1997). ... Released by Rangers (April 30, 1997). ... Signed by Anaheim Angels organization (June 5, 1997). ... Released by Angels (July 28, 1997).
STATISTICAL NOTES: Led N.L. with 28 home runs allowed in 1986. ... Led N.L. with 11 hit batsmen in 1988 and tied for lead with eight in 1986 and 10 in 1987. ... Pitched 2-0 no-hit victory against San Francisco (August 17, 1992).
MISCELLANEOUS: Made an out in only appearance as pinch-hitter (1990). ... Singled, scored and struck out in two games as pinch-hitter (1991).

Year	Team (League)	W	L	Pct.	ERA	G	GS	CG	ShO	Sv.	IP	H	R	ER	BB	SO
1981—	Spartanburg (SAL)	13	12	.520	3.56	28	•28	8	2	0	192	173	94	76	62	123
1982—	Reading (Eastern)	10	15	.400	4.23	26	24	8	2	0	151	138	81	71	89	136
1983—	Portland (PCL)	3	5	.375	6.75	15	15	0	0	0	80	82	60	60	45	61
	—Philadelphia (N.L.)	4	6	.400	3.56	17	17	1	1	0	96	100	46	38	35	66
1984—	Philadelphia (N.L.)	8	5	.615	4.12	44	14	1	0	1	129	140	66	59	44	84
1985—	Philadelphia (N.L.)	15	13	.536	3.41	38	31	6	2	0	205 2/3	194	86	78	81	151
1986—	Philadelphia (N.L.)	12	12	.500	4.02	37	36	7	2	0	241 2/3	240	115	108	94	154
1987—	Philadelphia (N.L.)	9	16	.360	4.35	34	33	3	1	0	200 2/3	205	107	97	87	110
1988—	Philadelphia (N.L.)	12	14	.462	3.69	33	33	5	1	0	231 2/3	209	101	95	*89	162
1989—	Montreal (N.L.)■	11	12	.478	4.38	31	31	4	3	0	201 1/3	188	105	*98	88	158
1990—	Montreal (N.L.)	9	12	.429	4.57	31	26	2	1	0	163 1/3	171	86	83	65	111
1991—	Los Angeles (N.L.)■	10	11	.476	3.58	46	10	0	0	3	115 2/3	123	55	46	50	95
1992—	Los Angeles (N.L.)	8	13	.381	3.17	34	30	4	3	0	204 2/3	182	82	72	77	158
1993—	Los Angeles (N.L.)	13	13	.500	4.14	33	32	3	0	0	202 1/3	224	110	93	74	150
1994—	Los Angeles (N.L.)	9	7	.563	3.60	25	23	1	0	1	157 1/3	162	64	63	43	124
1995—	Texas (A.L.)■	9	•15	.375	5.54	31	30	4	0	0	183 2/3	200	124	113	89	106
1996—	Texas (A.L.)	11	8	.579	5.22	28	19	1	0	0	129 1/3	151	78	75	50	78
	—Oklahoma City (A.A.)	0	0	. . .	6.75	1	1	0	0	0	4	6	4	3	2	3
1997—	Oklahoma City (A.A.)	2	3	.400	4.83	6	6	0	0	0	31 2/3	35	18	17	6	26
	—Vancouver (PCL)■	1	0	1.000	1.64	2	2	0	0	0	11	7	2	2	0	5
	—Anaheim (A.L.)	2	1	.667	6.75	12	3	0	0	0	25 1/3	30	20	19	20	20
A.L. totals (3 years)		22	24	.478	5.51	71	52	5	0	0	338 1/3	381	222	207	159	204
N.L. totals (12 years)		120	134	.472	3.89	403	316	37	14	5	2149 1/3	2138	1023	930	827	1523
Major league totals (15 years)		142	158	.473	4.11	474	368	42	14	5	2487 2/3	2519	1245	1137	986	1727

WORLD SERIES RECORD

Year	Team (League)	W	L	Pct.	ERA	G	GS	CG	ShO	Sv.	IP	H	R	ER	BB	SO
1983—	Philadelphia (N.L.)							Did not play.								

ALL-STAR GAME RECORD

Year	League	W	L	Pct.	ERA	GS	CG	ShO	Sv.	IP	H	R	ER	BB	SO
1988—	National	0	0	. . .	0.00	0	0	0	0	1	0	0	0	0	1

GRUDZIELANEK, MARK — SS — EXPOS

PERSONAL: Born June 30, 1970, in Milwaukee. ... 6-1/185. ... Bats right, throws right. ... Full name: Mark James Grudzielanek. ... Name pronounced gruzz-ELL-uh-neck..
HIGH SCHOOL: J.M. Hanks (El Paso, Texas).
JUNIOR COLLEGE: Trinidad (Colo.) State Junior College.
TRANSACTIONS/CAREER NOTES: Selected by New York Mets organization in 17th round of free-agent draft (June 5, 1989); did not sign. ... Selected by Montreal Expos organization in 11th round of free-agent draft (June 3, 1991). ... On disabled list (July 13-August 9, 1993 and May 12-19, 1994).
RECORDS: Holds major league single-season record for fewest chances accepted by shortstop who led league in chances accepted—683 (1997). ... Shares major league single-season record for fewest putouts by shortstop (150 or more games)—180 (1996).
HONORS: Named Eastern League Most Valuable Player (1994).
STATISTICAL NOTES: Led Eastern League shortstops with .959 fielding percentage in 1994. ... Led N.L. shortstops with 715 total chances and 99 double plays in 1997.

							BATTING								FIELDING		
Year	Team (League)	Pos.	G	AB	R	H	2B	3B	HR	RBI	Avg.	BB	SO	SB	PO	A	E	Avg.
1991—	Jamestown (NYP)	SS	72	275	44	72	9	3	2	32	.262	18	43	14	112	206	23	.933
1992—	Rockford (Midwest)	SS	128	496	64	122	12	5	5	54	.246	22	59	25	173	290	41	.919
1993—	W.P. Beach (FSL)	2-S-O-3	86	300	41	80	11	6	1	34	.267	14	42	17	105	135	13	.949
1994—	Harrisburg (Eastern)	SS-3B	122	488	92	157	•37	3	11	66	.322	43	66	32	178	344	23	†.958
1995—	Montreal (N.L.)	SS-3B-2B	78	269	27	66	12	2	1	20	.245	14	47	8	94	198	10	.967
	—Ottawa (Int'l)	SS	49	181	26	54	9	1	1	22	.298	10	17	12	58	156	14	.939
1996—	Montreal (N.L.)	SS	153	657	99	201	34	4	6	49	.306	26	83	33	180	453	27	.959
1997—	Montreal (N.L.)	SS	156	*649	76	177	*54	3	4	51	.273	23	76	25	237	446	*32	.955
Major league totals (3 years)			387	1575	202	444	100	9	11	120	.282	63	206	66	511	1097	69	.959

ALL-STAR GAME RECORD

					BATTING								FIELDING		
Year	League	Pos.	AB	R	H	2B	3B	HR	RBI	Avg.	BB	SO	SB	PO	A	E	Avg.
1996—	National	3B	1	0	0	0	0	0	0	.000	0	0	0	0	0	0	. . .

G

GRUNDT, KENNETH — P

PERSONAL: Born August 26, 1969, in Melrose Park, Ill. ... 6-3/195. ... Throws left, bats left. ... Full name: Kenneth Allan Grundt.
HIGH SCHOOL: Luther North (Chicago).
COLLEGE: Missouri Southern.
TRANSACTIONS/CAREER NOTES: Selected by San Francisco Giants organization in 53rd round of free-agent draft (June 3, 1991). ... On San Jose disabled list (April 8-September 7, 1993). ... Released by Giants organization (September 14, 1993). ... Signed by Sioux Falls of Northern League (1993). ... Sold by Sioux Falls to Colorado Rockies organization (June 25, 1995). ... Granted free agency (October 15, 1995). ... Signed by Boston Red Sox organization (November 9, 1995). ... Granted free agency (October 15, 1996). ... Re-signed by Red Sox (January 23, 1997). ... Granted free agency (October 15, 1997).

Year Team (League)	W	L	Pct.	ERA	G	GS	CG	ShO	Sv.	IP	H	R	ER	BB	SO
1991— Everett (Northwest)	4	5	.444	2.33	*29	0	0	0	4	54	55	27	14	16	58
1992— Clinton (Midwest)	5	3	.625	0.62	40	0	0	0	16	57 2/3	39	11	4	11	59
— San Jose (California)	1	0	1.000	1.02	11	0	0	0	3	17 2/3	9	3	2	7	17
1993— Arizona Giants (Ariz.)	0	0	...	2.25	4	0	0	0	0	4	5	1	1	0	2
1994— Sioux Falls (Nor.)■	3	3	.500	1.64	26	0	0	0	2	44	44	15	8	21	35
1995— Asheville (S. Atl.)■	0	0	...	0.30	20	0	0	0	1	30 1/3	18	1	1	7	38
— New Haven (Eastern)	2	2	.500	2.13	28	0	0	0	3	38	26	14	9	10	27
— Colo. Springs (PCL)	0	0	...	4.76	9	0	0	0	0	5 2/3	9	5	3	4	5
1996— Trenton (Eastern)■	1	0	1.000	0.00	12	0	0	0	0	12 2/3	6	0	0	6	13
— Pawtucket (Int'l)	9	4	.692	4.20	44	0	0	0	2	64 1/3	72	32	30	16	46
— Boston (A.L.)	0	0	...	27.00	1	0	0	0	0	1/3	1	1	1	0	0
1997— Pawtucket (Int'l)	4	2	.667	5.32	49	1	0	0	3	47 1/3	59	30	28	22	28
— Boston (A.L.)	0	0	...	9.00	2	0	0	0	0	3	5	3	3	0	0
Major league totals (2 years)	0	0	...	10.80	3	0	0	0	0	3 1/3	6	4	4	0	0

GRZANICH, MIKE — P — ASTROS

PERSONAL: Born August 24, 1972, in Canton, Ill. ... 6-1/180. ... Throws right, bats right. ... Full name: Michael Edward Grzanich.
JUNIOR COLLEGE: Parkland College (Ill.).
TRANSACTIONS/CAREER NOTES: Selected by Houston Astros organization in 19th round of free-agent draft (June 1, 1992).
STATISTICAL NOTES: Led New York-Pennsylvania League with 11 home runs allowed in 1993.

Year Team (League)	W	L	Pct.	ERA	G	GS	CG	ShO	Sv.	IP	H	R	ER	BB	SO
1992— GC Astros (GCL)	2	5	.286	4.54	17	17	0	0	3	33 2/3	38	21	17	14	29
1993— Auburn (N.Y.-Penn)	5	•8	.385	4.82	16	14	•4	•1	0	93 1/3	106	*63	50	27	71
1994— Quad City (Midwest)	11	7	.611	3.09	23	22	3	0	0	142 2/3	145	55	49	43	101
1995— Jackson (Texas)	5	3	.625	2.74	50	0	0	0	8	65 2/3	55	22	20	38	44
1996— Jackson (Texas)	5	4	.556	3.98	57	0	0	0	6	72 1/3	60	47	32	43	80
1997— Jackson (Texas)	7	6	.538	4.96	38	13	0	0	12	101 2/3	114	68	56	46	73

GUARDADO, EDDIE — P — TWINS

PERSONAL: Born October 2, 1970, in Stockton, Calif. ... 6-0/195. ... Throws left, bats right. ... Full name: Edward Adrian Guardado. ... Name pronounced gwar-DAH-doh.
HIGH SCHOOL: Franklin (Stockton, Calif.).
COLLEGE: San Joaquin Delta College (Calif.).
TRANSACTIONS/CAREER NOTES: Selected by Minnesota Twins organization in 21st round of free-agent draft (June 4, 1990).
STATISTICAL NOTES: Pitched 5-0 no-hit victory against Pulaski (August 26, 1991).

Year Team (League)	W	L	Pct.	ERA	G	GS	CG	ShO	Sv.	IP	H	R	ER	BB	SO
1991— Elizabethton (Appal.)	8	4	.667	1.86	14	13	3	•1	0	92	67	30	19	31	*106
1992— Kenosha (Midwest)	5	10	.333	4.37	18	18	2	1	0	101	106	57	49	30	103
— Visalia (California)	7	0	1.000	1.64	7	7	1	1	0	49 1/3	47	13	9	10	39
1993— Nashville (Southern)	4	0	1.000	1.24	10	10	2	2	0	65 1/3	53	10	9	10	57
— Minnesota (A.L.)	3	8	.273	6.18	19	16	0	0	0	94 2/3	123	68	65	36	46
1994— Salt Lake (PCL)	12	7	.632	4.83	24	24	2	0	0	151	171	90	81	51	87
— Minnesota (A.L.)	0	2	.000	8.47	4	4	0	0	0	17	26	16	16	4	8
1995— Minnesota (A.L.)	4	9	.308	5.12	51	5	0	0	2	91 1/3	99	54	52	45	71
1996— Minnesota (A.L.)	6	5	.545	5.25	•83	0	0	0	4	73 2/3	61	45	43	33	74
1997— Minnesota (A.L.)	0	4	.000	3.91	69	0	0	0	1	46	45	23	20	17	54
Major league totals (5 years)	13	28	.317	5.47	226	25	0	0	7	322 2/3	354	206	196	135	253

G

GUBICZA, MARK — P — DODGERS

PERSONAL: Born August 14, 1962, in Philadelphia. ... 6-5/230. ... Throws right, bats right. ... Full name: Mark Steven Gubicza. ... Son of Anthony Gubicza, minor league pitcher (1950-51). ... Name pronounced GOO-ba-zah.
HIGH SCHOOL: William Penn Charter (Philadelphia).
TRANSACTIONS/CAREER NOTES: Selected by Kansas City Royals organization in second round of free-agent draft (June 8, 1981); pick received as compensation for St. Louis Cardinals signing free-agent C Darrell Porter. ... On disabled list (June 29, 1982-remainder of season; June 6-21, 1986; and July 1, 1990-remainder of season). ... On Kansas City disabled list (March 30-May 14, 1991); included rehabilitation assignment to Omaha (April 20-May 13). ... On Kansas City disabled list (July 11, 1992-remainder of season). ... Granted free agency (October 30, 1992). ... Re-signed by Royals (November 25, 1992). ... Granted free agency (November 3, 1993). ... Re-signed by Royals (December 7, 1993). ... Granted free agency (October 18, 1994). ... Re-signed by Royals (December 12, 1994). ... Granted free agency (October 31, 1995). ... Re-signed by Royals (December 7, 1995). ... On disabled list (July 6, 1996-remainder of season). ... Traded by Royals with P Mike Bovee to California Angels for DH Chili Davis (October 28, 1996). ... Angels franchise renamed Anaheim Angels for 1997 season. ... On disabled list (April 12, 1997-remainder of season). ... Granted free agency (October 30, 1997). ... Re-signed by Angels (December 6, 1997); contract voided under terms mutually agreed upon by Angels and Gubicza. ... Signed by Los Angeles Dodgers (January 12, 1998).

STATISTICAL NOTES: Pitched 7-0 one-hit, complete-game victory against Oakland (June 15, 1995).
MISCELLANEOUS: Holds Kansas City Royals all-time record for most strikeouts (1,366).

Year	Team (League)	W	L	Pct.	ERA	G	GS	CG	ShO	Sv.	IP	H	R	ER	BB	SO
1981—	GC Royals-Gd. (GCL)	•8	1	.889	2.25	11	11	0	0	0	56	39	18	14	23	40
1982—	Fort Myers (Fla. St.)	2	5	.286	4.13	11	11	0	0	0	48	49	33	22	25	36
1983—	Jacksonville (Southern)......	14	12	.538	3.08	28	28	5	0	0	196	146	81	67	93	*146
1984—	Kansas City (A.L.)	10	14	.417	4.05	29	29	4	2	0	189	172	90	85	75	111
1985—	Kansas City (A.L.)	14	10	.583	4.06	29	28	0	0	0	177 1/3	160	88	80	77	99
1986—	Kansas City (A.L.)	12	6	.667	3.64	35	24	3	2	0	180 2/3	155	77	73	84	118
1987—	Kansas City (A.L.)	13	18	.419	3.98	35	35	10	2	0	241 2/3	231	114	107	120	166
1988—	Kansas City (A.L.)	20	8	.714	2.70	35	35	8	4	0	269 2/3	237	94	81	83	183
1989—	Kansas City (A.L.)	15	11	.577	3.04	36	•36	8	2	0	255	252	100	86	63	173
1990—	Kansas City (A.L.)	4	7	.364	4.50	16	16	2	0	0	94	101	48	47	38	71
1991—	Omaha (Am. Assoc.)	2	1	.667	3.31	3	3	0	0	0	16 1/3	20	7	6	4	12
—	Kansas City (A.L.)	9	12	.429	5.68	26	26	0	0	0	133	168	90	84	42	89
1992—	Kansas City (A.L.)	7	6	.538	3.72	18	18	2	1	0	111 1/3	110	47	46	36	81
1993—	Kansas City (A.L.)	5	8	.385	4.66	49	6	0	0	2	104 1/3	128	61	54	43	80
1994—	Kansas City (A.L.)	7	9	.438	4.50	22	22	0	0	0	130	158	74	65	26	59
1995—	Kansas City (A.L.)	12	14	.462	3.75	33	*33	3	2	0	213 1/3	222	97	89	62	81
1996—	Kansas City (A.L.)	4	12	.250	5.13	19	19	2	1	0	119 1/3	132	70	68	34	55
1997—	Anaheim (A.L.)■	0	1	.000	25.07	2	2	0	0	0	4 2/3	13	13	13	3	5
—	Lake Elsinore (Calif.)	0	1	.000	15.75	2	2	0	0	0	4	12	7	7	1	1
Major league totals (14 years)....		132	136	.493	3.96	384	329	42	16	2	2223 1/3	2239	1063	978	786	1371

CHAMPIONSHIP SERIES RECORD

Year	Team (League)	W	L	Pct.	ERA	G	GS	CG	ShO	Sv.	IP	H	R	ER	BB	SO
1985—	Kansas City (A.L.)	1	0	1.000	3.24	2	1	0	0	0	8 1/3	4	3	3	4	4

WORLD SERIES RECORD

NOTES: Member of World Series championship team (1985).

Year	Team (League)	W	L	Pct.	ERA	G	GS	CG	ShO	Sv.	IP	H	R	ER	BB	SO
1985—	Kansas City (A.L.)							Did not play.								

ALL-STAR GAME RECORD

Year	League	W	L	Pct.	ERA	GS	CG	ShO	Sv.	IP	H	R	ER	BB	SO
1988—	American	0	0	. . .	4.50	0	0	0	0	2	3	1	1	0	2
1989—	American	0	0	. . .	0.00	0	0	0	0	1	0	0	0	0	1
All-Star totals (2 years)		0	0	. . .	3.00	0	0	0	0	3	3	1	1	0	3

GUERRERO, VLADIMIR OF EXPOS

PERSONAL: Born February 9, 1976, in Nizao Bani, Dominican Republican ... 6-2/195. ... Bats right, throws right. ... Brother of Wilton Guerrero, infielder, Los Angeles Dodgers.
TRANSACTIONS/CAREER NOTES: Signed as non-drafted free agent by Montreal Expos organization (March 1, 1993). ... On disabled list (March 30-May 2, 1997); included rehabilitation assignment to West Palm Beach (April 29-May 2). ... On Montreal disabled list (June 5-21 and July 12-27, 1997); included rehabilitation assignment to West Palm Beach (April 29-May 2).
HONORS: Named Eastern League Most Valuable Player (1996). ... Named Minor League Player of the Year by THE SPORTING NEWS (1996).
STATISTICAL NOTES: Tied for South Atlantic League lead in double plays by outfielder with four in 1995. ... Led Eastern League with .438 on-base percentage and 13 intentional bases on balls received in 1996.

							BATTING								FIELDING		
Year	Team (League)	Pos.	G	AB	R	H	2B	3B	HR	RBI	Avg.	BB	SO	SB	PO	A	E	Avg.
1993—	Dom. Expos (DSL)	OF-IF-P	34	105	19	35	4	0	1	14	.333	8	13	4	75	7	5	.943
1994—	Dom. Expos (DSL)	OF	25	92	34	39	11	0	12	35	.424	21	6	5	38	6	2	.957
—	GC Expos (GCL)	OF	37	137	24	43	13	3	5	25	.314	11	18	0	64	9	1	.986
1995—	Albany (S. Atl.)	OF	110	421	77	140	21	10	16	63	*.333	30	45	12	207	15	11	.953
1996—	W.P. Beach (FSL)........	OF	20	80	16	29	8	0	5	18	.363	3	10	2	28	5	3	.917
—	Harrisburg (Eastern) ..	OF	118	417	84	150	32	8	19	78	*.360	51	42	17	184	13	8	.961
—	Montreal (N.L.)	OF	9	27	2	5	0	0	1	1	.185	0	3	0	11	0	0	1.000
1997—	W.P. Beach (FSL)........	OF	3	10	0	4	2	0	0	2	.400	1	0	1	4	1	0	1.000
—	Montreal (N.L.)	OF	90	325	44	98	22	2	11	40	.302	19	39	3	148	10	*12	.929
Major league totals (2 years)			99	352	46	103	22	2	12	41	.293	19	42	3	159	10	12	.934

RECORD AS PITCHER

Year	Team (League)	W	L	Pct.	ERA	G	GS	CG	ShO	Sv.	IP	H	R	ER	BB	SO
1993—	DSL Expos (DSL)	0	0	. . .	2.25	3	0	0	0	0	8	10	3	2	4	6

GUERRERO, WILTON 2B DODGERS

G

PERSONAL: Born October 24, 1974, in Don Gregorio, Dominican Republic. ... 5-11/145. ... Bats right, throws right. ... Brother of Vladimir Guerrero, outfielder, Montreal Expos.
HIGH SCHOOL: Escuela Primaria (Don Gregorio, Dominican Republic).
TRANSACTIONS/CAREER NOTES: Signed as non-drafted free agent by Los Angeles Dodgers organization (October 8, 1991). ... On Albuquerque disabled list (June 26-July 5 and July 26-August 23, 1996). ... On suspended list (June 2-9, 1997).
STATISTICAL NOTES: Led Florida State League in caught stealing with 20 in 1994. ... Led Texas League in caught stealing with 22 in 1995.

							BATTING								FIELDING		
Year	Team (League)	Pos.	G	AB	R	H	2B	3B	HR	RBI	Avg.	BB	SO	SB	PO	A	E	Avg.
1992—	Dom. Dodgers (DSL) .	SS	61	225	52	87	7	4	0	38	.387	34	21	15	104	215	21	.938
1993—	Great Falls (Pio.)	SS	66	256	44	76	5	1	0	21	.297	24	33	20	76	184	21	.925
—	Dom. Dodgers (DSL) .	SS	8	31	6	11	0	1	0	4	.355	4	3	2	15	18	1	.971
1994—	Vero Beach (FSL)	SS	110	402	55	118	11	4	1	32	.294	29	71	23	111	292	17	.960

Year Team (League)	Pos.	G	AB	R	H	2B	3B	HR	RBI	Avg.	BB	SO	SB	PO	A	E	Avg.
1995—San Antonio (Tex.)	SS	95	382	53	133	13	6	0	26	*.348	26	63	21	121	263	19	.953
—Albuquerque (PCL).....	SS-OF	14	49	10	16	1	1	0	2	.327	1	7	2	13	39	9	.852
1996—Albuquerque (PCL).....	2B-SS	98	425	79	146	17	12	2	38	.344	26	48	26	183	306	19	.963
—Los Angeles (N.L.).....	OF	5	2	1	0	0	0	0	0	.000	0	2	0	0	0	0	...
1997—Los Angeles (N.L.).....	2B-SS	111	357	39	104	10	9	4	32	.291	8	52	6	148	231	4	.990
—Albuquerque (PCL).....	SS-2B	10	45	9	18	0	1	0	5	.400	2	3	3	16	38	5	.915
Major league totals (2 years)		116	359	40	104	10	9	4	32	.290	8	54	6	148	231	4	.990

GUEVARA, GIOMAR 2B/SS MARINERS

PERSONAL: Born October 23, 1972, in Miranda, Venezuela. ... 5-8/150. ... Bats both, throws right. ... Full name: Giomar Antonio Guevara.
TRANSACTIONS/CAREER NOTES: Signed as non-drafted free agent by Seattle Mariners organization (November 13, 1990). ... On disabled list (June 14-July 21, 1995).

Year Team (League)	Pos.	G	AB	R	H	2B	3B	HR	RBI	Avg.	BB	SO	SB	PO	A	E	Avg.
1991—						Dominican Summer League statistics unavailable.											
1992—Dom. Dodgers (DSL) .	IF	45	163	30	51	13	4	1	24	.313	19	30	14	37	103	10	.933
1993—Bellingham (N'west)...	SS	62	211	31	48	8	3	1	23	.227	34	46	4	83	172	16	.941
1994—Appleton (Midwest)....	SS-2B	110	385	57	116	23	3	8	46	.301	42	77	9	171	270	23	.950
—Jacksonville (Sou.).....	SS	7	20	2	4	2	0	1	3	.200	2	9	0	12	25	3	.925
1995—Riverside (Calif.).....	SS	83	292	53	71	12	3	2	34	.243	30	71	7	123	231	27	.929
1996—Port City (Southern)...	SS-2B	119	414	60	110	18	2	2	41	.266	54	102	21	187	350	35	.939
1997—Tacoma (PCL)	2B-SS	54	176	29	43	5	1	2	13	.244	5	39	3	102	129	11	.955
—Memphis (Southern)..	SS	65	228	30	60	10	4	4	28	.263	20	42	5	80	217	13	.958
—Seattle (A.L.).............	DH-2B-SS	5	4	0	0	0	0	0	0	.000	0	2	1	2	6	1	.889
Major league totals (1 year)		5	4	0	0	0	0	0	0	.000	0	2	1	2	6	1	.889

GUILLEN, CARLOS SS ASTROS

PERSONAL: Born September 30, 1975, in Maracay, Venezuela. ... 6-1/180. ... Bats right, throws right.
TRANSACTIONS/CAREER NOTES: Signed as non-drafted free agent by Houston Astros organization (September 19, 1992). ... On disabled list (June 1-September 12, 1994). ... On disabled list (May 21-September 11, 1996).

Year Team (League)	Pos.	G	AB	R	H	2B	3B	HR	RBI	Avg.	BB	SO	SB	PO	A	E	Avg.
1993—Dom. Astros (DSL).....	IF	18	56	12	14	4	2	0	8	.250	8	12	0	37	6	2	.956
1994—						Did not play.											
1995—Dom. Astros (DSL).....	DH	30	105	17	31	4	2	2	15	.295	9	17	17	...	...	...	...
1996—Quad City (Midwest)..	SS	29	112	23	37	7	1	3	17	.330	16	25	13	47	71	9	.929
1997—Jackson (Texas)	SS	115	390	47	99	16	1	10	39	.254	38	78	6	169	313	35	.932
—New Orleans (A.A.).....	SS	3	13	3	4	1	0	0	0	.308	0	4	0	5	6	0	1.000

GUILLEN, JOSE OF PIRATES

PERSONAL: Born May 17, 1976, in San Cristobal, Dominican Republic. ... 5-11/185. ... Bats right, throws right. ... Full name: Jose Manuel Guillen.
TRANSACTIONS/CAREER NOTES: Signed as non-drafted free agent by Pittsburgh Pirates organization (August 19, 1992).
HONORS: Named Carolina League Most Valuable Player (1996).
STATISTICAL NOTES: Led Carolina League with 263 total bases and grounding into double plays with 16 in 1996. ... Led Carolina League outfielders with 6 double plays in 1996.

Year Team (League)	Pos.	G	AB	R	H	2B	3B	HR	RBI	Avg.	BB	SO	SB	PO	A	E	Avg.
1993—Dom. Pirates (DSL)....	OF	63	234	39	53	3	4	11	41	.226	21	55	10	112	12	7	.947
1994—Bra. Pirates (GCL)......	OF	30	110	17	29	4	1	4	11	.264	7	15	2	59	5	2	.970
1995—Erie (N.Y.-Penn)..........	OF	66	258	41	81	17	1	*12	46	.314	10	44	1	107	10	13	.900
—Augusta (S. Atl.).........	OF	10	34	6	8	1	1	2	6	.235	2	9	0	5	0	0	1.000
1996—Lynchburg (Caro.)......	OF	136	*528	78	*170	30	0	•21	94	.322	20	73	24	224	16	*13	.949
1997—Pittsburgh (N.L.).......	OF	143	498	58	133	20	5	14	70	.267	17	88	1	226	9	9	.963
Major league totals (1 year)		143	498	58	133	20	5	14	70	.267	17	88	1	226	9	9	.963

G

GUILLEN, OZZIE SS

PERSONAL: Born January 20, 1964, in Ocular del Tuy, Miranda, Venezuela. ... 5-11/164. ... Bats left, throws right. ... Full name: Oswaldo Jose Barrios Guillen. ... Name pronounced GHEE-un.
TRANSACTIONS/CAREER NOTES: Signed as non-drafted free agent by San Diego Padres organization (December 17, 1980). ... Traded by Padres organization with P Tim Lollar, P Bill Long and 3B Luis Salazar to Chicago White Sox for P LaMarr Hoyt, P Kevin Kristan and P Todd Simmons (December 6, 1984). ... On disabled list (April 22, 1992-remainder of season). ... Granted free agency (October 31, 1997).
RECORDS: Holds major league single-season record for fewest bases on balls received (150 or more games)—10 (1996). ... Holds A.L. single-season record for fewest putouts by shortstop (150 or more games)—220 (1985).
HONORS: Named A.L. Rookie Player of the Year by THE SPORTING NEWS (1985). ... Named A.L. Rookie of the Year by Baseball Writers' Association of America (1985). ... Won A.L. Gold Glove at shortstop (1990).
STATISTICAL NOTES: Tied for California League lead with 14 sacrifice hits in 1982. ... Led Pacific Coast League shortstops with 362 assists and 549 total chances in 1984. ... Led A.L. shortstops with 760 total chances in 1987 and 863 in 1988. ... Led A.L. shortstops with 105 double plays in 1987. ... Career major league grand slams: 1.
MISCELLANEOUS: Batted as switch-hitter (1981-84).

Year — Team (League)	Pos.	G	AB	R	H	2B	3B	HR	RBI	Avg.	BB	SO	SB	PO	A	E	Avg.
						BATTING									FIELDING		
1981— GC Padres (GCL).......	SS-2B	55	189	26	49	4	1	0	16	.259	13	24	8	105	135	15	.941
1982— Reno (California)	SS	130	528	*103	*183	33	1	2	54	.347	16	53	25	*240	399	41	.940
1983— Beaumont (Texas)	SS	114	427	62	126	20	4	2	48	.295	15	29	7	185	327	*38	.931
1984— Las Vegas (PCL)	SS-2B	122	463	81	137	26	6	5	53	.296	13	40	9	172	†364	17	.969
1985— Chicago (A.L.)■........	SS	150	491	71	134	21	9	1	33	.273	12	36	7	220	382	12	*.980
1986— Chicago (A.L.)	SS-DH	159	547	58	137	19	4	2	47	.250	12	52	8	261	459	22	.970
1987— Chicago (A.L.)	SS	149	560	64	156	22	7	2	51	.279	22	52	25	266	475	19	.975
1988— Chicago (A.L.)	SS	156	566	58	148	16	7	0	39	.261	25	40	25	273	*570	20	.977
1989— Chicago (A.L.)	SS	155	597	63	151	20	8	1	54	.253	15	48	36	272	512	22	.973
1990— Chicago (A.L.)	SS	160	516	61	144	21	4	1	58	.279	26	37	13	252	474	17	.977
1991— Chicago (A.L.)	SS	154	524	52	143	20	3	3	49	.273	11	38	21	249	439	21	.970
1992— Chicago (A.L.)	SS	12	40	5	8	4	0	0	7	.200	1	5	1	20	39	0	1.000
1993— Chicago (A.L.)	SS	134	457	44	128	23	4	4	50	.280	10	41	5	189	361	16	.972
1994— Chicago (A.L.)	SS	100	365	46	105	9	5	1	39	.288	14	35	5	139	237	16	.959
1995— Chicago (A.L.)	SS-DH	122	415	50	103	20	3	1	41	.248	13	25	6	167	319	12	.976
1996— Chicago (A.L.)	SS-OF	150	499	62	131	24	8	4	45	.263	10	27	6	222	348	11	.981
1997— Chicago (A.L.)	SS	142	490	59	120	21	6	4	52	.245	22	24	5	207	348	15	.974
Major league totals (13 years)		1743	6067	693	1608	240	68	24	565	.265	193	460	163	2737	4963	203	.974

CHAMPIONSHIP SERIES RECORD

Year — Team (League)	Pos.	G	AB	R	H	2B	3B	HR	RBI	Avg.	BB	SO	SB	PO	A	E	Avg.
						BATTING									FIELDING		
1993— Chicago (A.L.)	SS	6	22	4	6	1	0	0	2	.273	0	2	1	12	14	0	1.000

ALL-STAR GAME RECORD

NOTES: Named to A.L. All-Star team; replaced by Kurt Stillwell due to injury (1988).

Year — League	Pos.	AB	R	H	2B	3B	HR	RBI	Avg.	BB	SO	SB	PO	A	E	Avg.
						BATTING								FIELDING		
1988— American...................					Selected, did not play—injured.											
1990— American...................	SS	2	0	0	0	0	0	0	.000	0	0	0	0	2	0	1.000
1991— American...................	SS	0	0	0	0	0	0	0	...	0	0	0	1	0	0	1.000
All-Star Game totals (2 years)		2	0	0	0	0	0	0	.000	0	0	0	1	2	0	1.000

GULAN, MIKE   3B   CARDINALS

PERSONAL: Born December 18, 1970, in Steubenville, Ohio. ... 6-1/192. ... Bats right, throws right. ... Full name: Michael W. Gulan. ... Name pronounced GOO-len..
HIGH SCHOOL: Catholic Central (Steubenville, Ohio).
COLLEGE: Kent.
TRANSACTIONS/CAREER NOTES: Selected by St. Louis Cardinals organization in second round of free-agent draft (June 1, 1992). ... On disabled list (April 27-May 12, 1994). ... On disabled list (April 4-8, 1996).
STATISTICAL NOTES: Led American Association third basemen with 24 errors in 1996. ... Led American Association third basemen with .948 fielding percentage in 1997.

Year — Team (League)	Pos.	G	AB	R	H	2B	3B	HR	RBI	Avg.	BB	SO	SB	PO	A	E	Avg.
						BATTING									FIELDING		
1992— Hamilton (NYP).........	3B-1B	62	242	33	66	8	4	7	36	.273	23	53	12	51	113	11	.937
1993— Springfield (Midw.).....	3B	132	455	81	118	28	4	23	76	.259	34	135	8	78	*255	28	.922
1994— St. Petersburg (FSL) ..	3B	120	466	39	113	30	2	8	56	.242	26	108	2	86	218	26	.921
1995— Arkansas (Texas).......	3B	64	242	47	76	16	3	12	48	.314	11	52	4	33	150	14	.929
— Louisville (A.A.).........	3B	58	195	21	46	10	4	5	27	.236	10	53	2	38	90	7	.948
1996— Louisville (A.A.).........	3B-1B	123	419	47	107	27	4	17	55	.255	26	119	7	67	240	†24	.927
1997— Louisville (A.A.).........	3B-1B-OF	116	412	50	110	20	6	14	61	.267	28	121	5	78	221	16	*.949
— St. Louis (N.L.)...........	3B	5	9	2	0	0	0	0	1	.000	1	5	0	1	1	0	1.000
Major league totals (1 year)		5	9	2	0	0	0	0	1	.000	1	5	0	1	1	0	1.000

GUNDERSON, ERIC   P   RANGERS

PERSONAL: Born March 29, 1966, in Portland, Ore. ... 6-0/190. ... Throws left, bats right. ... Full name: Eric Andrew Gunderson.
HIGH SCHOOL: Aloha (Portland, Ore.).
COLLEGE: Portland (Ore.) State.
TRANSACTIONS/CAREER NOTES: Selected by San Francisco Giants organization in second round of free-agent draft (June 2, 1987). ... Released by Giants (March 31, 1992). ... Signed by Jacksonville, Seattle Mariners organization (April 10, 1992). ... On Jacksonville disabled list (April 10-17, 1992). ... On Seattle suspended list (September 30-October 4, 1992). ... Released by Mariners (April 29, 1993). ... Signed by Binghamton, New York Mets organization (June 10, 1993). ... Granted free agency (October 15, 1993). ... Signed by San Diego Padres organization (December 24, 1993). ... Released by Las Vegas (April 2, 1994). ... Signed by St. Lucie, Mets organization (May 5, 1994). ... Claimed on waivers by Mariners (August 4, 1995). ... Claimed on waivers by Boston Red Sox (August 10, 1995). ... Granted free agency (October 7, 1996). ... Signed by Texas Rangers organization (January 24, 1997). ... On disabled list (August 26-September 7, 1997).
STATISTICAL NOTES: Led California League with 17 hit batsmen in 1988.

Year — Team (League)	W	L	Pct.	ERA	G	GS	CG	ShO	Sv.	IP	H	R	ER	BB	SO
1987— Everett (Northwest)...........	8	4	.667	2.46	15	•15	*5	•3	0	98 2/3	80	34	27	34	*99
1988— San Jose (California).........	12	5	.706	2.65	20	20	5	•4	0	149 1/3	131	56	44	52	151
— Shreveport (Texas).............	1	2	.333	5.15	7	6	0	0	0	36 2/3	45	25	21	13	28
1989— Shreveport (Texas)............	8	2	*.800	2.72	11	11	2	1	0	72 2/3	68	24	22	23	61
— Phoenix (PCL)	2	4	.333	5.04	14	14	2	1	0	85 2/3	93	51	48	36	56
1990— San Francisco (N.L.)	1	2	.333	5.49	7	4	0	0	0	19 2/3	24	14	12	11	14
— Phoenix (PCL)	5	7	.417	8.23	16	16	0	0	0	82	137	87	75	46	41
— Shreveport (Texas).............	2	2	.500	3.25	8	8	1	1	0	52 2/3	51	24	19	17	44

G

Year — Team (League)	W	L	Pct.	ERA	G	GS	CG	ShO	Sv.	IP	H	R	ER	BB	SO
1991— San Francisco (N.L.)	0	0	...	5.40	2	0	0	0	1	3 1/3	6	4	2	1	2
— Phoenix (PCL)	7	6	.538	6.14	40	14	0	0	3	107	153	85	73	44	53
1992— Jacksonville (Southern)■ ..	2	0	1.000	2.31	15	0	0	0	2	23 1/3	18	10	6	7	23
— Calgary (PCL).....................	0	2	.000	6.02	27	1	0	0	5	52 1/3	57	37	35	31	50
— Seattle (A.L.)	2	1	.667	8.68	9	0	0	0	0	9 1/3	12	12	9	5	2
1993— Calgary (PCL).................	0	1	.000	18.90	5	0	0	0	0	6 2/3	14	15	14	8	3
— Binghamton (Eastern)■	2	1	.667	5.24	20	1	0	0	1	22 1/3	20	14	13	14	26
— Norfolk (Int'l)	3	2	.600	3.71	6	5	1	0	0	34	41	16	14	9	26
1994— St. Lucie (Fla. St.)	1	0	1.000	0.00	3	0	0	0	1	4 2/3	4	0	0	0	6
— Norfolk (Int'l)	3	1	.750	3.68	19	2	1	1	1	36 2/3	25	16	15	17	31
— New York (N.L.)...............	0	0	...	0.00	14	0	0	0	0	9	5	0	0	4	4
1995— New York (N.L.)	1	1	.500	3.70	30	0	0	0	0	24 1/3	25	10	10	8	19
— Boston (A.L.)■................	2	1	.667	5.11	19	0	0	0	0	12 1/3	13	7	7	9	9
1996— Pawtucket (Int'l)	2	1	.667	3.48	26	1	0	0	2	33 2/3	38	15	13	9	34
— Boston (A.L.).................	0	1	.000	8.31	28	0	0	0	0	17 1/3	21	17	16	8	7
1997— Texas (A.L.)■.................	2	1	.667	3.26	60	0	0	0	1	49 2/3	45	19	18	15	31
A.L. totals (4 years)	6	4	.600	5.08	116	0	0	0	1	88 2/3	91	55	50	37	49
N.L. totals (4 years)	2	3	.400	3.83	53	4	0	0	1	56 1/3	60	28	24	24	39
Major league totals (7 years)......	8	7	.533	4.59	169	4	0	0	2	145	151	83	74	61	88

GUTHRIE, MARK — P — DODGERS

PERSONAL: Born September 22, 1965, in Buffalo. ... 6-4/207. ... Throws left, bats right. ... Full name: Mark Andrew Guthrie.
HIGH SCHOOL: Venice (Fla.).
COLLEGE: Louisiana State.
TRANSACTIONS/CAREER NOTES: Selected by St. Louis Cardinals organization in fourth round of free-agent draft (June 2, 1986); did not sign. ... Selected by Minnesota Twins organization in seventh round of free-agent draft (June 2, 1987). ... On disabled list (May 29, 1993-remainder of season). ... Traded by Twins with P Kevin Tapani to Los Angeles Dodgers for 1B/3B Ron Coomer, P Greg Hansell, P Jose Parra and a player to be named later (July 31, 1995); Twins acquired OF Chris Latham to complete deal (October 30, 1995). ... Granted free agency (October 29, 1996). ... Re-signed by Dodgers (November 6, 1996).
MISCELLANEOUS: Appeared in one game as pinch-runner (1991).

Year — Team (League)	W	L	Pct.	ERA	G	GS	CG	ShO	Sv.	IP	H	R	ER	BB	SO
1987— Visalia (California)	2	1	.667	4.50	4	1	0	0	0	12	10	7	6	5	9
1988— Visalia (California)	12	9	.571	3.31	25	25	4	1	0	171 1/3	169	81	63	86	182
1989— Orlando (South.)	8	3	.727	1.97	14	14	0	0	0	96	75	32	21	38	103
— Portland (PCL)	3	4	.429	3.65	7	7	1	0	0	44 1/3	45	21	18	16	35
— Minnesota (A.L.)	2	4	.333	4.55	13	8	0	0	0	57 1/3	66	32	29	21	38
1990— Minnesota (A.L.)	7	9	.438	3.79	24	21	3	1	0	144 2/3	154	65	61	39	101
— Portland (PCL)	1	3	.250	2.98	9	8	1	0	0	42 1/3	47	19	14	12	39
1991— Minnesota (A.L.)	7	5	.583	4.32	41	12	0	0	2	98	116	52	47	41	72
1992— Minnesota (A.L.)	2	3	.400	2.88	54	0	0	0	5	75	59	27	24	23	76
1993— Minnesota (A.L.)	2	1	.667	4.71	22	0	0	0	0	21	20	11	11	16	15
1994— Minnesota (A.L.)	4	2	.667	6.14	50	2	0	0	1	51 1/3	65	43	35	18	38
1995— Minnesota (A.L.)	5	3	.625	4.46	36	0	0	0	0	42 1/3	47	22	21	16	48
— Los Angeles (N.L.)■........	0	2	.000	3.66	24	0	0	0	0	19 2/3	19	11	8	9	19
1996— Los Angeles (N.L.)	2	3	.400	2.22	66	0	0	0	0	73	65	21	18	22	56
1997— Los Angeles (N.L.)	1	4	.200	5.32	62	0	0	0	1	69 1/3	71	44	41	30	42
A.L. totals (7 years)	29	27	.518	4.19	240	43	3	1	8	489 2/3	527	252	228	174	388
N.L. totals (3 years)	3	9	.250	3.72	152	0	0	0	2	162	155	76	67	61	117
Major league totals (9 years)......	32	36	.471	4.07	392	43	3	1	10	651 2/3	682	328	295	235	505

DIVISION SERIES RECORD

Year — Team (League)	W	L	Pct.	ERA	G	GS	CG	ShO	Sv.	IP	H	R	ER	BB	SO
1995— Los Angeles (N.L.)	0	0	...	6.75	3	0	0	0	0	1 1/3	2	1	1	1	1
1996— Los Angeles (N.L.)	0	0	...	0.00	1	0	0	0	0	1/3	0	0	0	1	1
Div. series totals (2 years)	0	0	...	5.40	4	0	0	0	0	1 2/3	2	1	1	2	2

CHAMPIONSHIP SERIES RECORD

Year — Team (League)	W	L	Pct.	ERA	G	GS	CG	ShO	Sv.	IP	H	R	ER	BB	SO
1991— Minnesota (A.L.)	1	0	1.000	0.00	2	0	0	0	0	2 2/3	0	0	0	0	0

WORLD SERIES RECORD

NOTES: Member of World Series championship team (1991).

Year — Team (League)	W	L	Pct.	ERA	G	GS	CG	ShO	Sv.	IP	H	R	ER	BB	SO
1991— Minnesota (A.L.)	0	1	.000	2.25	4	0	0	0	0	4	3	1	1	4	3

G

GUTIERREZ, RICKY — SS — ASTROS

PERSONAL: Born May 23, 1970, in Miami. ... 6-1/175. ... Bats right, throws right. ... Full name: Ricardo Gutierrez.
HIGH SCHOOL: American (Hialeah, Fla.).
TRANSACTIONS/CAREER NOTES: Selected by Baltimore Orioles organization in supplemental round ("sandwich pick" between first and second round, 28th pick overall) of free-agent draft (June 1, 1988); pick received as compensation for Orioles failing to sign 1987 No. 1 pick P Brad DuVall. ... Traded by Orioles to San Diego Padres (September 4, 1992), completing deal in which Padres traded P Craig Lefferts to Orioles for P Erik Schullstrom and a player to be named later (August 31, 1992). ... Traded by Padres with OF Phil Plantier, OF Derek Bell, P Pedro Martinez, P Doug Brocail and IF Craig Shipley to Houston Astros for 3B Ken Caminiti, OF Steve Finley, SS Andujar Cedeno, 1B Robert Petagine, P Brian Williams and a player to be named later (December 28, 1994); Padres acquired P Sean Fesh to complete deal (May 1, 1995). ... On disabled list (March 31-May 6, 1997); included rehabilitation assignment to New Orleans (April 29-May 6).
STATISTICAL NOTES: Led Appalachian League shortstops with 309 total chances in 1988.

Year	Team (League)	Pos.	G	AB	R	H	2B	3B	HR	RBI	Avg.	BB	SO	SB	PO	A	E	Avg.
1988—	Bluefield (Appal.)........	SS	62	208	35	51	8	2	2	19	.245	44	40	5	*100	175	34	.890
1989—	Frederick (Carolina)....	SS	127	456	48	106	16	2	3	41	.232	39	89	15	190	372	34	*.943
1990—	Frederick (Carolina)....	SS	112	425	54	117	16	4	1	46	.275	38	59	12	192	286	26	.948
	—Hagerstown (Eastern)	SS	20	64	4	15	0	1	0	6	.234	3	8	2	31	36	4	.944
1991—	Hagerstown (Eastern)	SS	84	292	47	69	6	4	0	30	.236	57	52	11	158	196	22	.941
	—Rochester (Int'l)	SS-3B	49	157	23	48	5	3	0	15	.306	24	27	4	61	129	8	.960
1992—	Rochester (Int'l)	2B-SS	125	431	54	109	9	3	0	41	.253	53	77	14	251	283	15	.973
	—Las Vegas (PCL)■	SS	3	6	0	1	0	0	0	1	.167	1	3	0	1	8	0	1.000
1993—	Las Vegas (PCL)	2B-SS	5	24	4	10	4	0	0	4	.417	0	4	4	11	14	2	.926
	—San Diego (N.L.)	S-2-O-3	133	438	76	110	10	5	5	26	.251	50	97	4	194	305	14	.973
1994—	San Diego (N.L.)	SS-2B	90	275	27	66	11	2	1	28	.240	32	54	2	93	202	22	.931
1995—	Houston (N.L.)■	SS-3B	52	156	22	43	6	0	0	12	.276	10	33	5	64	108	8	.956
	—Tucson (PCL)	SS	64	236	46	71	12	4	1	26	.301	28	28	9	91	167	6	.977
1996—	Houston (N.L.)	SS-3B-2B	89	218	28	62	8	1	1	15	.284	23	42	6	86	149	12	.951
1997—	New Orleans (A.A.)......	SS	7	27	2	5	1	0	0	4	.185	2	4	0	12	21	1	.971
	—Houston (N.L.)	SS-3B-2B	102	303	33	79	14	4	3	34	.261	21	50	5	104	191	8	.974
Major league totals (5 years)			466	1390	186	360	49	12	10	115	.259	136	276	22	541	955	64	.959

DIVISION SERIES RECORD

Year	Team (League)	Pos.	G	AB	R	H	2B	3B	HR	RBI	Avg.	BB	SO	SB	PO	A	E	Avg.
1997—	Houston (N.L.)	SS	3	8	0	1	0	0	0	0	.125	2	1	0	5	5	0	1.000

GUZMAN, DOMINGO   P   PADRES

PERSONAL: Born April 5, 1975, in San Cristobal, Dominican Republic. ... 6-0/180. ... Throws right, bats right. ... Full name: Domingo Serrano Guzman.

TRANSACTIONS/CAREER NOTES: Signed as non-drafted free agent by San Diego Padres organization (June 15, 1993). ... On Clinton suspended list (May 15-18, 1997).

STATISTICAL NOTES: Pitched 6-0 no-hit victory vs. Butte (August 15, 1996).

Year	Team (League)	W	L	Pct.	ERA	G	GS	CG	ShO	Sv.	IP	H	R	ER	BB	SO
1994—	Ariz. Padres (Ariz.)	•8	4	.667	4.11	13	13	0	0	0	70	65	39	32	25	55
1995—	Idaho Falls (Pioneer)	2	1	.667	6.66	27	0	0	0	•11	25 2/3	25	22	19	25	33
1996—	Idaho Falls (Pioneer)	4	2	.667	4.13	15	10	1	•1	0	65 1/3	52	41	30	29	75
	—Clinton (Midwest)..............	0	5	.000	12.63	6	5	0	0	0	20 2/3	32	33	29	19	18
1997—	Clinton (Midwest)..............	4	5	.444	3.19	12	12	5	0	0	79	66	36	28	25	91
	—Rancho Cucamonga (Cal.) .	3	2	.600	5.45	6	6	0	0	0	38	42	23	23	16	39

GUZMAN, JUAN   P   BLUE JAYS

PERSONAL: Born October 28, 1966, in Santo Domingo, Dominican Republic. ... 5-11/195. ... Throws right, bats right. ... Full name: Juan Andres Correa Guzman.

HIGH SCHOOL: Liceo Las Americas (Dominican Republic).

TRANSACTIONS/CAREER NOTES: Signed as non-drafted free agent by Los Angeles Dodgers organization (March 16, 1985). ... Traded by Dodgers to Toronto Blue Jays organization for IF Mike Sharperson (September 22, 1987). ... On Toronto disabled list (August 4-29, 1992); included rehabilitation assignment to Syracuse (August 24-25). ... On Toronto disabled list (May 16-June 5 and August 10-29, 1995); included rehabilitation assignment to Syracuse (August 25-26). ... On Toronto disabled list (May 23-June 7, 1996). ... On Toronto disabled list (May 29-June 26 and July 16-September 28, 1997).

RECORDS: Holds A.L. single-season record for most wild pitches—26 (1993).

HONORS: Named A.L. Rookie Pitcher of the Year by THE SPORTING NEWS (1991).

STATISTICAL NOTES: Led Gulf Coast League with 15 wild pitches in 1985. ... Led Florida State League with 16 wild pitches in 1986. ... Led Southern League with 21 wild pitches in 1990. ... Led A.L. with 26 wild pitches in 1993 and tied for lead with 13 in 1994.

Year	Team (League)	W	L	Pct.	ERA	G	GS	CG	ShO	Sv.	IP	H	R	ER	BB	SO
1985—	GC Dodgers (GCL)	5	1	.833	3.86	21	3	0	0	4	42	39	26	18	25	43
1986—	Vero Beach (FSL)	10	9	.526	3.49	20	24	3	0	0	131 1/3	114	69	51	90	96
1987—	Bakersfield (California)	5	6	.455	4.75	22	21	0	0	0	110	106	71	58	84	113
1988—	Knoxville (Southern)■	4	5	.444	2.36	46	2	0	0	6	84	52	29	22	61	90
1989—	Syracuse (Int'l)	1	1	.500	3.98	14	0	0	0	0	20 1/3	13	9	9	30	28
	—Knoxville (Southern)	1	4	.200	6.23	22	8	0	0	0	47 2/3	34	36	33	60	50
1990—	Knoxville (Southern)	11	9	.550	4.24	37	21	2	0	1	157	145	84	74	80	138
1991—	Syracuse (Int'l)	4	5	.444	4.03	12	11	0	0	0	67	46	39	30	42	67
	—Toronto (A.L.)..................	10	3	.769	2.99	23	23	1	0	0	138 2/3	98	53	46	66	123
1992—	Toronto (A.L.)..................	16	5	.762	2.64	28	28	1	0	0	180 2/3	135	56	53	72	165
	—Syracuse (Int'l)................	0	0	. . .	6.00	1	1	0	0	0	3	6	2	2	1	3
1993—	Toronto (A.L.)..................	14	3	*.824	3.99	33	33	2	1	0	221	211	107	98	110	194
1994—	Toronto (A.L.)..................	12	11	.522	5.68	25	•25	2	0	0	147 1/3	165	102	93	76	124
1995—	Toronto (A.L.)..................	4	14	.222	6.32	24	24	3	0	0	135 1/3	151	101	95	73	94
	—Syracuse (Int'l)	0	0	. . .	0.00	1	1	0	0	0	5	1	0	0	3	5
1996—	Toronto (A.L.)..................	11	8	.579	*2.93	27	27	4	1	0	187 2/3	158	68	61	53	165
1997—	Toronto (A.L.)..................	3	6	.333	4.95	13	13	0	0	0	60	48	42	33	31	52
	—Dunedin (Fla. St.)	0	0	. . .	0.00	2	2	0	0	0	4	3	0	0	1	3
Major league totals (7 years)		70	50	.583	4.03	173	173	13	2	0	1070 2/3	966	529	479	481	917

CHAMPIONSHIP SERIES RECORD

Year	Team (League)	W	L	Pct.	ERA	G	GS	CG	ShO	Sv.	IP	H	R	ER	BB	SO
1991—	Toronto (A.L.)..................	1	0	1.000	3.18	1	1	0	0	0	5 2/3	4	2	2	4	2
1992—	Toronto (A.L.)..................	2	0	1.000	2.08	2	2	0	0	0	13	12	3	3	5	11
1993—	Toronto (A.L.)..................	2	0	1.000	2.08	2	2	0	0	0	13	8	4	3	9	9
Champ. series totals (3 years)	....	5	0	1.000	2.27	5	5	0	0	0	31 2/3	24	9	8	18	22

G

WORLD SERIES RECORD

NOTES: Member of World Series championship teams (1992 and 1993).

Year	Team (League)	W	L	Pct.	ERA	G	GS	CG	ShO	Sv.	IP	H	R	ER	BB	SO
1992— Toronto (A.L.)		0	0	...	1.13	1	1	0	0	0	8	8	2	1	1	7
1993— Toronto (A.L.)		0	1	.000	3.75	2	2	0	0	0	12	10	6	5	8	12
World Series totals (2 years)		0	1	.000	2.70	3	3	0	0	0	20	18	8	6	9	19

ALL-STAR GAME RECORD

Year	League	W	L	Pct.	ERA	GS	CG	ShO	Sv.	IP	H	R	ER	BB	SO
1992— American		0	0	...	0.00	0	0	0	0	1	2	0	0	1	2

GWYNN, TONY   OF   PADRES

PERSONAL: Born May 9, 1960, in Los Angeles. ... 5-11/220. ... Bats left, throws left. ... Full name: Anthony Keith Gwynn. ... Brother of Chris Gwynn, outfielder with Los Angeles Dodgers (1987-1991 and 1994-95), Kansas City Royals (1992-93) and San Diego Padres (1996).
HIGH SCHOOL: Long Beach (Calif.) Polytechnic.
COLLEGE: San Diego State.
TRANSACTIONS/CAREER NOTES: Selected by San Diego Padres organization in third round of free-agent draft (June 8, 1981). ... On San Diego disabled list (August 26-September 10, 1982). ... On San Diego disabled list (March 26-June 21, 1983); included rehabilitation to Las Vegas (May 31-June 20). ... On disabled list (May 8-29, 1988 and July 2-August 6, 1996).
RECORDS: Holds N.L. career record for most years leading league in singles—7 (1984, 1986-87, 1989, 1994, 1995 and 1997). ... Holds N.L. single-season record for lowest batting average by leader—.313 (1988). ... Shares N.L. single-season record for most times collecting five or more hits in one game—4 (1993). ... Shares N.L. career record for most years leading league in batting average—8.
HONORS: Named Northwest League Most Valuable Player (1981). ... Named outfielder on THE SPORTING NEWS N.L. All-Star team (1984, 1986-87, 1989, 1994 and 1997). ... Named outfielder on THE SPORTING NEWS N.L. Silver Slugger team (1984, 1986-87, 1989, 1994-95 and 1997). ... Won N.L. Gold Glove as outfielder (1986-87 and 1989-91).
STATISTICAL NOTES: Had 25-game hitting streak (August 21-September 18, 1983). ... Led N.L. with .410 on-base percentage in 1984. ... Led N.L. outfielders with 360 total chances in 1986. ... Collected six hits in one game (August 4, 1993, 12 innings). ... Led N.L. in grounding into double plays with 20 in 1994. ... Had 20-game hitting streak (May 20-June 10, 1997). ... Tied for N.L. lead with 12 sacrifice flies in 1997. ... Career major league grand slams: 2.
MISCELLANEOUS: Holds San Diego Padres all-time records for most runs (1,237), most hits (2,780), most doubles (460), most triples (84), highest career batting average (.340), most runs batted in (973) and most stolen bases (308). ... Selected by San Diego Clippers in 10th round (210th pick overall) of 1981 NBA draft (June 9, 1981).

Year Team (League)	Pos.	G	AB	R	H	2B	3B	HR	RBI	Avg.	BB	SO	SB	PO	A	E	Avg.
1981— Walla Walla (NWL)	OF	42	178	46	59	12	1	12	37	*.331	23	21	17	76	2	3	.963
—Amarillo (Texas)	OF	23	91	22	42	8	2	4	19	.462	5	7	5	41	1	0	1.000
1982— Hawaii (PCL)	OF	93	366	65	120	23	2	5	46	.328	18	18	14	208	11	4	.982
—San Diego (N.L.)	OF	54	190	33	55	12	2	1	17	.289	14	16	8	110	1	1	.991
1983— Las Vegas (PCL)	OF	17	73	15	25	6	0	0	7	.342	6	5	3	23	2	3	.893
—San Diego (N.L.)	OF	86	304	34	94	12	2	1	37	.309	23	21	7	163	9	1	.994
1984— San Diego (N.L.)	OF	158	606	88	*213	21	10	5	71	*.351	59	23	33	345	11	4	.989
1985— San Diego (N.L.)	OF	154	622	90	197	29	5	6	46	.317	45	33	14	337	14	4	.989
1986— San Diego (N.L.)	OF	160	*642	•107	*211	33	7	14	59	.329	52	35	37	*337	19	4	.989
1987— San Diego (N.L.)	OF	157	589	119	*218	36	13	7	54	*.370	82	35	56	298	13	6	.981
1988— San Diego (N.L.)	OF	133	521	64	163	22	5	7	70	*.313	51	40	26	264	8	5	.982
1989— San Diego (N.L.)	OF	158	604	82	*203	27	7	4	62	*.336	56	30	40	353	13	6	.984
1990— San Diego (N.L.)	OF	141	573	79	177	29	10	4	72	.309	44	23	17	327	11	5	.985
1991— San Diego (N.L.)	OF	134	530	69	168	27	11	4	62	.317	34	19	8	291	8	3	.990
1992— San Diego (N.L.)	OF	128	520	77	165	27	3	6	41	.317	46	16	3	270	9	5	.982
1993— San Diego (N.L.)	OF	122	489	70	175	41	3	7	59	.358	36	19	14	244	8	5	.981
1994— San Diego (N.L.)	OF	110	419	79	*165	35	1	12	64	*.394	48	19	5	191	6	3	.985
1995— San Diego (N.L.)	OF	135	535	82	•197	33	1	9	90	*.368	35	15	17	245	8	2	.992
1996— San Diego (N.L.)	OF	116	451	67	159	27	2	3	50	*.353	39	17	11	182	2	2	.989
1997— San Diego (N.L.)	OF-DH	149	592	97	*220	49	2	17	119	*.372	43	28	12	218	8	4	.983
Major league totals (16 years)		2095	8187	1237	2780	460	84	107	973	.340	707	389	308	4175	148	60	.986

DIVISION SERIES RECORD

Year Team (League)	Pos.	G	AB	R	H	2B	3B	HR	RBI	Avg.	BB	SO	SB	PO	A	E	Avg.
1996— San Diego (N.L.)	OF	3	13	0	4	1	0	0	1	.308	0	2	1	2	0	0	1.000

CHAMPIONSHIP SERIES RECORD

Year Team (League)	Pos.	G	AB	R	H	2B	3B	HR	RBI	Avg.	BB	SO	SB	PO	A	E	Avg.
1984— San Diego (N.L.)	OF	5	19	6	7	3	0	0	3	.368	1	2	0	9	0	0	1.000

WORLD SERIES RECORD

Year Team (League)	Pos.	G	AB	R	H	2B	3B	HR	RBI	Avg.	BB	SO	SB	PO	A	E	Avg.
1984— San Diego (N.L.)	OF	5	19	1	5	0	0	0	0	.263	3	2	1	12	1	1	.929

ALL-STAR GAME RECORD

RECORDS: Shares single-game record for most at-bats in nine-inning game—5 (July 12, 1994). ... Named to All-Star team for 1996 game; replaced by Henry Rodriguez due to injury.

Year League	Pos.	AB	R	H	2B	3B	HR	RBI	Avg.	BB	SO	SB	PO	A	E	Avg.
1984— National	OF	3	0	1	0	0	0	0	.333	0	0	0	0	0	0	...
1985— National	OF	1	0	0	0	0	0	0	.000	0	0	0	1	0	0	1.000
1986— National	OF	3	0	0	0	0	0	0	.000	0	0	0	1	0	0	1.000
1987— National	PH	1	0	0	0	0	0	0	.000	0	0	0	...	...	...	...

G

Year League	Pos.	AB	R	H	2B	3B	HR	RBI	Avg.	BB	SO	SB	PO	A	E	Avg.
						BATTING								FIELDING		
1989— National	OF	2	1	1	0	0	0	0	.500	1	1	1	2	0	0	1.000
1990— National	PH	0	0	0	0	0	0	0	...	1	0	0	...	...	...	...
1991— National	OF	4	1	2	0	0	0	0	.500	0	0	0	6	0	0	1.000
1992— National	OF	2	0	0	0	0	0	0	.000	1	0	0	0	2	0	1.000
1993— National	OF	1	0	0	0	0	0	0	.000	0	0	0	0	0	0	...
1994— National	OF	5	2	2	1	0	0	2	.400	0	0	0	2	0	0	1.000
1995— National	OF	2	0	0	0	0	0	0	.000	0	0	0	1	0	0	1.000
1996— National						Selected, did not play—injured.										
1997— National	DH	3	0	0	0	0	0	0	.000	0	0	0	0	0	0	...
All-Star Game totals (12 years)		27	4	6	1	0	0	2	.222	3	1	1	13	2	0	1.000

HACKMAN, LUTHER — P — ROCKIES

PERSONAL: Born October 6, 1974, in Lawndale, Miss. ... 6-4/195. ... Throws right, bats right. ... Full name: Luther G. Hackman.
HIGH SCHOOL: Columbus (Miss.).
TRANSACTIONS/CAREER NOTES: Selected by Colorado Rockies organization in sixth round of free-agent draft (June 2, 1994). ... On disabled list (June 1-July 10, 1996).

Year Team (League)	W	L	Pct.	ERA	G	GS	CG	ShO	Sv.	IP	H	R	ER	BB	SO
1994— Ariz. Rockies (Ariz.)	1	3	.250	2.10	12	12	0	0	0	55 2/3	50	21	13	16	63
1995— Asheville (S. Atl.)	11	11	.500	4.64	28	28	2	0	0	165	162	*95	*85	65	108
1996— Carolina (Southern)	5	7	.417	4.24	21	21	1	0	0	110 1/3	93	60	52	69	83
1997— New Haven (Eastern)■	0	6	.000	7.82	10	10	0	0	0	50 2/3	58	49	44	34	34
— Salem (Carolina)	1	4	.200	5.80	15	15	2	0	0	80 2/3	99	60	52	37	59

HALAMA, JOHN — P — ASTROS

PERSONAL: Born February 22, 1972, in Brooklyn, N.Y. ... 6-5/195. ... Throws left, bats left. ... Full name: John Thadeuz Halama. ... Name pronounced ha-LA-ma.
HIGH SCHOOL: Bishop Ford (Brooklyn, N.Y.).
COLLEGE: St. Francis (N.Y.).
TRANSACTIONS/CAREER NOTES: Selected by Houston Astros organization in 23rd round of free-agent draft (June 3, 1994).

Year Team (League)	W	L	Pct.	ERA	G	GS	CG	ShO	Sv.	IP	H	R	ER	BB	SO
1994— Auburn (N.Y.-Penn)	4	1	.800	1.29	6	3	0	0	1	28	18	5	4	5	27
— Quad City (Midwest)	3	4	.429	4.56	9	9	1	1	0	51 1/3	63	31	26	18	37
1995— Quad City (Midwest)	1	2	.333	2.02	55	0	0	0	2	62 1/3	48	16	14	22	56
1996— Jackson (Texas)	9	10	.474	3.21	27	27	0	0	0	162 2/3	151	77	58	59	110
1997— New Orleans (A.A.)	13	3	*.813	2.58	26	24	1	0	0	171	150	57	49	32	126

HALE, CHIP — IF — ANGELS

PERSONAL: Born December 2, 1964, in Santa Clara, Calif. ... 5-11/186. ... Bats left, throws right. ... Full name: Walter William Hale III.
HIGH SCHOOL: Campolindo (Moraga, Calif.).
COLLEGE: Arizona (received degree).
TRANSACTIONS/CAREER NOTES: Selected by Minnesota Twins organization in 17th round of free-agent draft (June 2, 1987). ... Granted free agency (October 4, 1996). ... Signed by Los Angeles Dodgers (October 30, 1996). ... Released by Dodgers (September 3, 1997). ... Signed by Anaheim Angels organization (December 22, 1997).
STATISTICAL NOTES: Led Pacific Coast League second basemen with 332 assists in 1989. ... Led Pacific Coast League second basemen with .982 fielding percentage, 311 putouts, 679 total chances and 101 double plays in 1990. ... Led Pacific Coast League second basemen with 552 total chances and 85 double plays in 1991. ... Led Pacific Coast League second basemen with .986 fielding percentage and 273 putouts in 1992.

Year Team (League)	Pos.	G	AB	R	H	2B	3B	HR	RBI	Avg.	BB	SO	SB	PO	A	E	Avg.
							BATTING							FIELDING			
1987— Kenosha (Midwest)	2B	87	339	65	117	12	7	7	65	*.345	33	26	3	164	233	10	.975
1988— Orlando (South.)	2B	133	482	62	126	20	1	11	65	.261	64	31	6	254	322	*23	.962
1989— Portland (PCL)	2B-3B	108	411	49	112	16	9	2	34	.273	35	55	3	217	†333	10	.982
— Minnesota (A.L.)	2B	28	67	6	14	3	0	0	4	.209	1	6	0	15	40	1	.982
1990— Portland (PCL)	2B-SS-3B	130	479	71	134	24	2	3	40	.280	68	57	6	†312	362	13	†.981
— Minnesota (A.L.)	2B	1	2	0	0	0	0	0	2	.000	0	1	0	2	6	0	1.000
1991— Portland (PCL)	2B	110	352	45	85	16	3	1	37	.241	47	22	3	*236	306	10	*.982
1992— Portland (PCL)	2B-OF-P	132	474	77	135	25	8	1	53	.285	73	45	3	†278	361	9	†.986
1993— Portland (PCL)	2B-3B-SS	55	211	37	59	15	3	1	24	.280	21	13	2	79	134	11	.951
— Minnesota (A.L.)	2-DH-3-S-1	69	186	25	62	6	1	3	27	.333	18	17	2	39	63	4	.962
1994— Minnesota (A.L.)	3-DH-1-2-O	67	118	13	31	9	0	1	11	.263	16	14	0	45	51	3	.970
1995— Minnesota (A.L.)	DH-2-3-1	69	103	10	27	4	0	2	18	.262	11	20	0	16	6	0	1.000
— Salt Lake (PCL)	3B-2B-1B	16	49	5	14	4	0	0	2	.286	7	5	0	33	26	0	1.000
1996— Minnesota (A.L.)	2-DH-1-3-O	85	87	8	24	5	0	1	16	.276	10	6	0	17	16	0	1.000
1997— Los Angeles (N.L.)■	3B	14	12	0	1	0	0	0	0	.083	2	4	0	1	0	0	1.000
— Albuquerque (PCL)	1-2-3-O	88	247	43	66	16	0	2	30	.267	58	26	3	427	99	3	.994
American League totals (6 years)		319	563	62	158	27	1	7	78	.281	56	64	2	134	182	8	.975
National League totals (1 year)		14	12	0	1	0	0	0	0	.083	2	4	0	1	0	0	1.000
Major league totals (7 years)		333	575	62	159	27	1	7	78	.277	58	68	2	135	182	8	.975

RECORD AS PITCHER

Year Team (League)	W	L	Pct.	ERA	G	GS	CG	ShO	Sv.	IP	H	R	ER	BB	SO
1992— Portland (PCL)	0	0	...	18.00	1	0	0	0	0	1	5	4	2	0	0

G
H

PERSONAL: Born July 14, 1964, in Marysville, Ohio. ... 6-3/205. ... Throws right, bats right. ... Full name: Michael Darren Hall.
HIGH SCHOOL: Nimitz (Irving, Texas).
COLLEGE: Dallas Baptist.
TRANSACTIONS/CAREER NOTES: Selected by Toronto Blue Jays organization in 28th round of free-agent draft (June 2, 1986). ... On disabled list (June 26, 1990-remainder of season; June 19-July 4 and July 24, 1995-remainder of season). ... Granted free agency (October 16, 1995). ... Signed by Los Angeles Dodgers (November 1, 1995). ... On Los Angeles disabled list (April 25-September 9, 1996); included rehabilitation assignment to Yakima (September 3-9).
STATISTICAL NOTES: Tied for Pioneer League lead with 12 wild pitches in 1986.

Year Team (League)	W	L	Pct.	ERA	G	GS	CG	ShO	Sv.	IP	H	R	ER	BB	SO
1986— Medicine Hat (Pio.)	5	7	.417	3.83	17	•16	1	1	0	89⅓	91	64	38	47	60
1987— Myrtle Beach (SAL)	5	5	.500	3.51	41	0	0	0	6	66⅔	57	31	26	28	68
1988— Dunedin (Fla. St.)	1	1	.500	1.93	4	0	0	0	1	9⅓	6	2	2	5	15
— Knoxville (Southern)	3	2	.600	2.23	37	0	0	0	17	40⅓	28	11	10	17	33
1989— Dunedin (Fla. St.)	1	4	.200	3.53	16	14	0	0	0	51	46	25	20	21	42
— Knoxville (Southern)	0	2	.000	3.66	13	0	0	0	1	19⅔	21	12	8	10	10
1990— Knoxville (Southern)	3	5	.375	4.86	28	0	0	0	1	33⅓	29	23	18	33	28
1991— Knoxville (Southern)	5	3	.625	2.60	42	0	0	0	1	69⅓	56	23	20	27	78
1992— Syracuse (Int'l)	4	6	.400	4.30	55	0	0	0	5	69	62	36	33	35	49
1993— Syracuse (Int'l)	6	7	.462	5.33	60	0	0	0	13	79⅓	75	51	47	31	68
1994— Syracuse (Int'l)	1	0	1.000	1.59	6	0	0	0	3	5⅔	5	2	1	2	7
— Toronto (A.L.)	2	3	.400	3.41	30	0	0	0	17	31⅔	26	12	12	14	28
1995— Toronto (A.L.)	0	2	.000	4.41	17	0	0	0	3	16⅓	21	9	8	9	11
1996— Los Angeles (N.L.)■	0	2	.000	6.00	9	0	0	0	0	12	13	9	8	5	12
— Yakima (N'west)	0	1	.000	3.00	2	2	0	0	0	3	5	2	1	0	4
1997— Los Angeles (N.L.)	3	2	.600	2.30	63	0	0	0	2	54⅔	58	15	14	26	39
A.L. totals (2 years)	2	5	.286	3.75	47	0	0	0	20	48	47	21	20	23	39
N.L. totals (2 years)	3	4	.429	2.97	72	0	0	0	2	66⅔	71	24	22	31	51
Major league totals (4 years)	5	9	.357	3.30	119	0	0	0	22	114⅔	118	45	42	54	90

PERSONAL: Born March 6, 1966, in Paducah, Ky. ... 6-0/180. ... Bats right, throws right. ... Full name: Joseph Geroy Hall.
HIGH SCHOOL: Saint Mary (Paducah, Ky.).
COLLEGE: Southern Illinois.
TRANSACTIONS/CAREER NOTES: Selected by St. Louis Cardinals organization in 10th round of free-agent draft (June 1, 1988). ... Traded by Cardinals organization to Chicago White Sox organization for OF Willie Magallanes (April 3, 1991). ... On disabled list (July 30-August 15, 1992 and July 30-August 12, 1993). ... On Chicago disabled list (May 14-July 21, 1994); included rehabilitation assignments to South Bend (June 9-19 and June 22-29). ... Released by White Sox (April 22, 1995). ... Signed by Toledo, Detroit Tigers organization (May 8, 1995). ... Granted free agency (October 16, 1995). ... Signed by Rochester, Baltimore Orioles organizaiton (November 13, 1995). ... Granted free agency (October 15, 1996). ... Granted free agency (October 15, 1997). ... Signed by Texas Rangers organization (December 22, 1997).
STATISTICAL NOTES: Led Florida State League in caught stealing with 28 in 1989. ... Led Pacific Coast League third basemen with .938 fielding percentage in 1991.

Year Team (League)	Pos.	G	AB	R	H	2B	3B	HR	RBI	Avg.	BB	SO	SB	PO	A	E	Avg.
1988— Hamilton (NYP)	0-1-C-3	70	274	46	78	9	1	2	37	.285	30	37	30	291	21	4	.987
— Springfield (Midw.)	3B-OF	1	1	0	0	0	0	0	0	.000	0	1	0	0	0	0	...
1989— St. Petersburg (FSL)	3B-OF-2B	134	504	72	147	9	3	0	54	.292	60	57	45	190	147	25	.931
1990— Arkansas (Texas)	0-3-1-C	115	399	44	108	13	4	4	44	.271	35	41	21	179	40	15	.936
1991— Vancouver (PCL)■	3-0-1-C	118	427	41	106	16	1	4	39	.248	23	45	11	114	205	19	‡.944
1992— Vancouver (PCL)	3-0-C-1	112	367	46	104	19	7	6	56	.283	60	44	11	160	101	16	.942
1993— Nashville (A.A.)	0-3-C-P	116	424	66	123	33	5	10	58	.290	52	56	10	189	66	7	.973
1994— Chicago (A.L.)	OF-DH	17	28	6	11	3	0	1	5	.393	2	4	0	11	0	1	.917
— Birmingham (Sou.)	OF-C-3B	19	67	9	14	6	0	0	6	.209	5	11	0	31	7	0	1.000
— Nashville (A.A.)	0-C-1-3	22	72	14	21	7	0	4	21	.292	16	10	0	57	8	0	1.000
1995— Toledo (Int'l)■	OF-3B-2B	91	319	52	102	19	2	11	47	.320	36	50	4	148	26	4	.978
— Detroit (A.L.)	OF-DH	7	15	2	2	0	0	0	0	.133	2	3	0	11	1	0	1.000
1996— Rochester (Int'l)■	OF	131	479	96	138	26	•10	19	95	.288	67	69	15	203	*15	5	.978
1997— Toledo (Int'l)■	OF-1B	75	271	35	68	18	2	6	30	.251	22	48	2	135	15	1	.993
— Detroit (A.L.)	OF	2	4	1	2	1	0	0	3	.500	0	0	0	1	0	0	1.000
Major league totals (3 years)		26	47	9	15	4	0	1	8	.319	4	7	0	23	1	1	.960

RECORD AS PITCHER

Year Team (League)	W	L	Pct.	ERA	G	GS	CG	ShO	Sv.	IP	H	R	ER	BB	SO
1993— Nashville (A.A.)	0	0	...	0.00	1	0	0	0	0	1	1	0	0	0	1

PERSONAL: Born May 14, 1977, in Denver. ... 6-6/200. ... Throws right, bats right. ... Full name: Harry Leroy Halladay.
HIGH SCHOOL: Arvada West (Arvada, Colo.).
TRANSACTIONS/CAREER NOTES: Selected by Toronto Blue Jays organization in first round (17th pick overall) of free-agent draft (June 1, 1995).

Year Team (League)	W	L	Pct.	ERA	G	GS	CG	ShO	Sv.	IP	H	R	ER	BB	SO
1995— GC Blue Jays (GCL)	3	5	.375	3.40	10	8	0	0	0	50⅓	35	25	19	16	48
1996— Dunedin (Fla. St.)	15	7	.682	2.73	27	27	2	•2	0	164⅔	158	75	50	46	109
1997— Knoxville (Southern)	2	3	.400	5.40	7	7	0	0	0	36⅔	46	26	22	11	30
— Syracuse (Int'l)	7	10	.412	4.58	22	22	2	2	0	125⅔	132	74	64	53	64

H

HALTER, SHANE · SS · ROYALS

PERSONAL: Born November 8, 1969, in La Plata, Md. ... 5-10/160. ... Bats right, throws right. ... Full name: Shane David Halter.
HIGH SCHOOL: Hooks (Texas).
JUNIOR COLLEGE: Seminole (Okla.) Junior College.
COLLEGE: Texas.
TRANSACTIONS/CAREER NOTES: Selected by Cincinnati Reds organization in 16th round of free-agent draft (June 4, 1990); did not sign. ... Selected by Kansas City Royals organization in fifth round of free-agent draft (June 3, 1991).
STATISTICAL NOTES: Led Midwest League shortstops with 64 double plays in 1992. ... Led American Association with 19 sacrifice hits in 1995.

							BATTING								FIELDING		
Year Team (League)	Pos.	G	AB	R	H	2B	3B	HR	RBI	Avg.	BB	SO	SB	PO	A	E	Avg.
1991—Eugene (Northwest) ...	SS	64	236	41	55	9	1	1	18	.233	49	60	12	*118	154	21	.928
1992—Appleton (Midwest)....	SS	80	313	50	83	22	3	3	33	.265	41	54	21	150	227	16	.959
—Baseball City (FSL).....	SS	44	117	11	28	1	0	1	14	.239	24	31	5	70	115	6	.969
1993—Wilmington (Caro.).....	SS	54	211	44	63	8	5	5	32	.299	27	55	5	84	146	15	.939
—Memphis (Southern)..	SS	81	306	50	79	7	0	4	20	.258	30	74	4	142	229	16	.959
1994—Memphis (Southern)...	SS	129	494	61	111	23	1	6	35	.225	39	102	10	177	369	29	.950
1995—Omaha (A.A.)..............	SS-2B	124	392	42	90	19	3	8	39	.230	40	97	2	225	355	19	.968
1996—Omaha (A.A.)..............	O-3-S-2-P	93	299	43	77	24	0	3	33	.258	31	49	7	130	75	13	.940
—Charlotte (Int'l)..........	0-2-3-1	16	41	3	12	1	0	0	4	.293	2	8	0	15	10	1	.962
1997—Omaha (A.A.)..............	3-0-2-S	14	49	10	13	1	1	2	9	.265	6	10	0	22	14	2	.947
—Kansas City (A.L.) O-2-3-S-DH		74	123	16	34	5	1	2	10	.276	10	28	4	63	40	1	.990
Major league totals (1 year)		74	123	16	34	5	1	2	10	.276	10	28	4	63	40	1	.990

RECORD AS PITCHER

Year Team (League)	W	L	Pct.	ERA	G	GS	CG	ShO	Sv.	IP	H	R	ER	BB	SO
1996—Omaha (Am. Assoc.)..........	0	0	...	9.00	93	0	0	0	0	1	2	1	1	1	0

HAMELIN, BOB · DH/1B · BREWERS

PERSONAL: Born November 29, 1967, in Elizabeth, N.J. ... 6-0/235. ... Bats left, throws left. ... Full name: Robert James Hamelin III.
HIGH SCHOOL: Irvine (Calif.).
JUNIOR COLLEGE: Rancho Santiago College (Calif.).
COLLEGE: UCLA.
TRANSACTIONS/CAREER NOTES: Selected by Kansas City Royals organization in second round of free-agent draft (June 1, 1988). ... On disabled list (June 25-July 2 and August 3, 1989-remainder of season; August 8, 1990-remainder of season; and May 27, 1991-remainder of season). ... On Omaha disabled list (April 9-June 10, 1992). ... On Kansas City disabled list (June 17-July 15, 1996); included rehabilitation assignment to Omaha (July 11-15). ... Released by Royals (March 26, 1997). ... Signed by Detroit Tigers organization (April 8, 1997). ... Granted free agency (December 21, 1997). ... Signed by Milwaukee Brewers organization (January 14, 1998).
RECORDS: Shares major league single-game record (nine innings) for most strikeouts—5 (May 24, 1995).
HONORS: Named A.L. Rookie Player of the Year by THE SPORTING NEWS (1994). ... Named A.L. Rookie of the Year by Baseball Writers' Association of America (1994).
STATISTICAL NOTES: Led Northwest League first basemen with 682 total chances in 1988. ... Led American Association first basemen with 1,205 total chances and 116 double plays in 1993.

							BATTING								FIELDING		
Year Team (League)	Pos.	G	AB	R	H	2B	3B	HR	RBI	Avg.	BB	SO	SB	PO	A	E	Avg.
1988—Eugene (Northwest) ...	1B	70	235	42	70	19	1	*17	61	.298	56	67	9	*642	25	*15	.978
1989—Memphis (Southern)..	1B	68	211	45	62	12	5	16	47	.294	52	52	3	487	27	8	.985
1990—Omaha (A.A.)...............	1B	90	271	31	63	11	2	8	30	.232	62	78	2	396	32	4	.991
1991—Omaha (A.A.)...............	1B	37	127	13	24	3	1	4	19	.189	16	32	0	55	4	0	1.000
1992—Baseball City (FSL)......	1B	11	44	7	12	0	1	1	6	.273	2	11	0	18	1	3	.864
—Memphis (Southern)..	1B	35	120	23	40	8	0	6	22	.333	26	17	0	173	9	2	.989
—Omaha (A.A.)...............	1B	27	95	9	19	3	1	5	15	.200	14	15	0	230	13	3	.988
1993—Omaha (A.A.)..............	1B	•137	479	77	124	19	3	29	84	.259	*82	94	8	*1104	*90	•11	.991
—Kansas City (A.L.)	1B	16	49	2	11	3	0	2	5	.224	6	15	0	129	9	2	.986
1994—Kansas City (A.L.)	DH-1B	101	312	64	88	25	1	24	65	.282	56	62	4	234	18	2	.992
1995—Kansas City (A.L.)	DH-1B	72	208	20	35	7	1	7	25	.168	26	56	0	66	9	0	1.000
—Omaha (A.A.)...............	1B	36	119	25	35	12	0	10	32	.294	31	34	2	157	19	6	.967
1996—Kansas City (A.L.)	DH-1B	89	239	31	61	14	1	9	40	.255	54	58	5	232	20	4	.984
—Omaha (A.A.)...............	1B	4	16	4	5	1	1	0	0	.313	1	4	1	37	1	0	1.000
1997—Toledo (Int'l)■..........	1B	27	91	14	22	7	0	6	24	.242	27	24	0	121	5	2	.984
—Detroit (A.L.)............	DH-1B	110	318	47	86	15	0	18	52	.270	48	72	2	29	1	0	1.000
Major league totals (5 years)		388	1126	164	281	64	3	60	187	.250	190	263	11	690	57	8	.989

HAMILTON, DARRYL · OF · GIANTS

PERSONAL: Born December 3, 1964, in Baton Rouge, La. ... 6-1/185. ... Bats left, throws right. ... Full name: Darryl Quinn Hamilton.
HIGH SCHOOL: University (Baton Rouge, La.).
COLLEGE: Nicholls State (La.).
TRANSACTIONS/CAREER NOTES: Selected by Milwaukee Brewers organization in 11th round of free-agent draft (June 2, 1986). ... On disabled list (May 22-June 15, 1991; May 6-24, 1992; May 2-17, 1993; May 11-26 and June 10, 1994-remainder of season). ... Granted free agency (November 1, 1995). ... Signed by Texas Rangers (December 14, 1995). ... Granted free agency (November 18, 1996). ... Signed by San Francisco Giants (January 10, 1997). ... On San Francisco disabled list (April 18-May 8, 1997); included rehabilitation assignment to Phoenix (May 5-8, 1997).
STATISTICAL NOTES: Led California League with nine intentional bases on balls received in 1987. ... Career major league grand slams: 2.

H

Year Team (League)	Pos.	G	AB	R	H	2B	3B	HR	RBI	Avg.	BB	SO	SB	PO	A	E	Avg.
1986— Helena (Pioneer)	OF	65	248	*72	•97	12	•6	0	35	*.391	51	18	34	132	9	0	*1.000
1987— Stockton (California) ..	OF	125	494	102	162	17	6	8	61	.328	74	59	42	221	8	1	*.996
1988— Denver (A.A.).............	OF	72	277	55	90	11	4	0	32	.325	39	28	28	160	2	2	.988
—Milwaukee (A.L.)	OF-DH	44	103	14	19	4	0	1	11	.184	12	9	7	75	1	0	1.000
1989— Denver (A.A.).............	OF	129	497	72	142	24	4	2	40	.286	42	58	20	263	11	0	*1.000
1990— Milwaukee (A.L.)	OF-DH	89	156	27	46	5	0	1	18	.295	9	12	10	120	1	1	.992
1991— Milwaukee (A.L.)	OF	122	405	64	126	15	6	1	57	.311	33	38	16	234	3	1	.996
1992— Milwaukee (A.L.)	OF	128	470	67	140	19	7	5	62	.298	45	42	41	279	10	0	*1.000
1993— Milwaukee (A.L.)	OF-DH	135	520	74	161	21	1	9	48	.310	45	62	21	340	10	3	.992
1994— Milwaukee (A.L.)	OF-DH	36	141	23	37	10	1	1	13	.262	15	17	3	60	2	0	1.000
1995— Milwaukee (A.L.)	OF-DH	112	398	54	108	20	6	5	44	.271	47	35	11	262	4	3	.989
1996— Texas (A.L.)■............	OF	148	627	94	184	29	4	6	51	.293	54	66	15	387	2	0	•1.000
1997— San Fran. (N.L.)■......	OF	125	460	78	124	23	3	5	43	.270	61	61	15	243	1	5	.980
—Phoenix (PCL)	OF	3	14	1	4	1	0	1	2	.286	0	2	0	6	0	0	1.000
American League totals (8 years)		814	2820	417	821	123	25	29	304	.291	260	281	124	1757	33	8	.996
National League totals (1 year)		125	460	78	124	23	3	5	43	.270	61	61	15	243	1	5	.980
Major league totals (9 years)		939	3280	495	945	146	28	34	347	.288	321	342	139	2000	34	13	.994

DIVISION SERIES RECORD

Year Team (League)	Pos.	G	AB	R	H	2B	3B	HR	RBI	Avg.	BB	SO	SB	PO	A	E	Avg.
1996— Texas (A.L.)	OF	4	19	0	3	0	0	0	0	.158	0	2	0	16	1	0	1.000
1997— San Francisco (N.L.) ..	OF	2	5	1	0	0	0	0	0	.000	0	1	0	3	0	0	1.000
Division series totals (2 years)		6	24	1	3	0	0	0	0	.125	0	3	0	19	1	0	1.000

HAMILTON, JOEY   P   PADRES

PERSONAL: Born September 9, 1970, in Statesboro, Ga. ... 6-4/230. ... Throws right, bats right. ... Full name: Johns Joseph Hamilton.
HIGH SCHOOL: Statesboro (Ga.).
COLLEGE: Georgia Southern.
TRANSACTIONS/CAREER NOTES: Selected by Baltimore Orioles organization in 28th round of free-agent draft (June 1, 1988); did not sign. ... Selected by San Diego Padres organization in first round (eighth pick overall) of free-agent draft (June 3, 1991). ... On Rancho Cucamonga disabled list (April 5-20, 1993). ... On disabled list (April 24-May 17, 1997).
HONORS: Named righthanded pitcher on The Sporting News college All-America second team (1990).

Year Team (League)	W	L	Pct.	ERA	G	GS	CG	ShO	Sv.	IP	H	R	ER	BB	SO
1992— Charleston, S.C. (S. Atl.)	2	2	.500	3.38	7	7	0	0	0	34 2/3	37	24	13	4	35
—High Desert (Calif.)............	4	3	.571	2.74	9	8	0	0	0	49 1/3	46	20	15	18	43
—Wichita (Texas)...............	3	0	1.000	2.86	6	6	0	0	0	34 2/3	33	12	11	11	26
1993— Rancho Cuca. (Calif.)	1	0	1.000	4.09	2	2	0	0	0	11	11	5	5	2	6
—Wichita (Texas)...............	4	9	.308	3.97	15	15	0	0	0	90 2/3	101	55	40	36	20
—Las Vegas (PCL)..............	3	2	.600	4.40	8	8	0	0	0	47	49	25	23	22	33
1994— Las Vegas (PCL)	3	5	.375	2.73	9	9	1	1	0	59 1/3	69	25	18	22	32
—San Diego (N.L.)	9	6	.600	2.98	16	16	1	1	0	108 2/3	98	40	36	29	61
1995— San Diego (N.L.)	6	9	.400	3.08	31	30	2	2	0	204 1/3	189	89	70	56	123
1996— San Diego (N.L.)	15	9	.625	4.17	34	33	3	1	0	211 2/3	206	100	98	83	184
1997— San Diego (N.L.)	12	7	.632	4.25	31	29	1	0	0	192 2/3	199	100	91	69	124
Major league totals (4 years)......	42	31	.575	3.70	112	108	7	4	0	717 1/3	692	329	295	237	492

DIVISION SERIES RECORD

Year Team (League)	W	L	Pct.	ERA	G	GS	CG	ShO	Sv.	IP	H	R	ER	BB	SO
1996— San Diego (N.L.)	0	1	.000	4.50	1	1	0	0	0	6	5	3	3	0	6

HAMMOND, CHRIS   P   ROYALS

PERSONAL: Born January 21, 1966, in Atlanta. ... 6-1/195. ... Throws left, bats left. ... Full name: Christopher Andrew Hammond. ... Brother of Steve Hammond, outfielder, Kansas City Royals (1982).
HIGH SCHOOL: Vestavia Hills (Birmingham, Ala.).
JUNIOR COLLEGE: Gulf Coast Community College (Fla.).
COLLEGE: Alabama-Birmingham.
TRANSACTIONS/CAREER NOTES: Selected by Cincinnati Reds organization in sixth round of free-agent draft (January 14, 1986). ... On disabled list (July 27-September 1, 1991). ... Traded by Reds to Florida Marlins for 3B Gary Scott and a player to be named later (March 27, 1993); Reds acquired P Hector Carrasco to complete deal (September 10, 1993). ... On Florida disabled list (June 11-August 3, 1994); included rehabilitation assignments to Portland (June 24-25) and Brevard County (July 25-30). ... On Florida disabled list (April 16-May 13 and August 3-19, 1995); included rehabilitation assignments to Brevard County (May 4-9) and Charlotte (May 9-13). ... On Florida disabled list (June 9-July 14, 1996); included rehabilitation assignments to Brevard County (July 1-5) and Charlotte (July 5-14). ... Granted free agency (October 4, 1996). ... Signed by Boston Red Sox (December 17, 1996). ... On disabled list (June 30-remainder of 1997 season). ... Granted free agency (October 30, 1997). ... Signed by Kansas City Royals organization (January 12, 1998).
HONORS: Named American Association Pitcher of the Year (1990).
STATISTICAL NOTES: Career major league grand slams: 1.
MISCELLANEOUS: Appeared in two games as pinch-runner (1992). ... Struck out in one game as pinch-hitter (1993).

Year Team (League)	W	L	Pct.	ERA	G	GS	CG	ShO	Sv.	IP	H	R	ER	BB	SO
1986— GC Reds (GCL).................	3	2	.600	2.81	7	7	1	0	0	41 2/3	27	21	13	17	53
—Tampa (Florida State).........	0	2	.000	3.32	5	5	0	0	0	21 2/3	25	8	8	13	5
1987— Tampa (Florida State).........	11	11	.500	3.55	25	24	6	0	0	170	174	81	67	60	126
1988— Chattanooga (Southern)	*16	5	.762	*1.72	26	26	4	2	0	182 2/3	127	48	35	77	127
1989— Nashville (A.A.)	11	7	.611	3.38	24	24	3	1	0	157 1/3	144	69	59	96	142
1990— Nashville (A.A.)	*15	1	*.938	*2.17	24	24	5	*3	0	149	118	43	36	63	*149
—Cincinnati (N.L.)	0	2	.000	6.35	3	3	0	0	0	11 1/3	13	9	8	12	4
1991— Cincinnati (N.L.)	7	7	.500	4.06	20	18	0	0	0	99 2/3	92	51	45	48	50

H

Year Team (League)	W	L	Pct.	ERA	G	GS	CG	ShO	Sv.	IP	H	R	ER	BB	SO
1992—Cincinnati (N.L.)	7	10	.412	4.21	28	26	0	0	0	147 1/3	149	75	69	55	79
1993—Florida (N.L.)■	11	12	.478	4.66	32	32	1	0	0	191	207	106	99	66	108
1994—Florida (N.L.)	4	4	.500	3.07	13	13	1	1	0	73 1/3	79	30	25	23	40
—Portland (Eastern)	0	0	...	0.00	1	1	0	0	0	2	0	0	0	0	2
—Brevard County (FSL)	0	0	...	1.23	2	2	0	0	0	7 1/3	4	3	1	3	5
1995—Brevard County (FSL)	0	0	...	0.00	1	1	0	0	0	4	3	1	0	0	4
—Charlotte (Int'l)	0	0	...	0.00	1	1	0	0	0	4	3	1	0	2	3
—Florida (N.L.)	9	6	.600	3.80	25	24	3	2	0	161	157	73	68	47	126
1996—Florida (N.L.)	5	8	.385	6.56	38	9	0	0	0	81	104	65	59	27	50
—Brevard County (FSL)	0	0	...	0.00	1	1	0	0	0	4	3	0	0	0	8
—Charlotte (Int'l)	1	0	1.000	7.20	1	1	0	0	0	5	5	4	4	0	3
1997—Boston (A.L.)■	3	4	.429	5.92	29	8	0	0	1	65 1/3	81	45	43	27	48
A.L. totals (1 year)	3	4	.429	5.92	29	8	0	0	1	65 1/3	81	45	43	27	48
N.L. totals (7 years)	43	49	.467	4.39	159	125	5	3	0	764 2/3	801	409	373	278	457
Major league totals (8 years)	46	53	.465	4.51	188	133	5	3	1	830	882	454	416	305	505

HAMMONDS, JEFFREY   OF   ORIOLES

PERSONAL: Born March 5, 1971, in Plainfield, N.J. ... 6-0/195. ... Bats right, throws right. ... Full name: Jeffrey Bryan Hammonds. ... Brother of Reggie Hammonds, outfielder, Pittsburgh Pirates organization (1984-86).

HIGH SCHOOL: Scotch Plains (N.J.)-Fanwood.

COLLEGE: Stanford.

TRANSACTIONS/CAREER NOTES: Selected by Toronto Blue Jays organization in ninth round of free-agent draft (June 5, 1989); did not sign. ... Selected by Baltimore Orioles organization in first round (fourth pick overall) of free-agent draft (June 1, 1992). ... On Hagerstown temporarily inactive list (August 6-September 14, 1992). ... On Rochester disabled list (May 17-28, 1993). ... On Baltimore disabled list (August 8-September 1, 1993); included rehabilitation assignment to Bowie (August 28-September 1). ... On Baltimore disabled list (September 28, 1993-remainder of season; May 4-June 16, 1994; July 18-September 3, 1995; and August 17-September 22, 1996).

HONORS: Named outfielder on THE SPORTING NEWS college All-America team (1990 and 1992).

MISCELLANEOUS: Member of 1992 U.S. Olympic baseball team.

Year Team (League)	Pos.	G	AB	R	H	2B	3B	HR	RBI	Avg.	BB	SO	SB	PO	A	E	Avg.
1992—								Did not play.									
1993—Bowie (Eastern)	OF	24	92	13	26	3	0	3	10	.283	9	18	4	48	2	0	1.000
—Rochester (Int'l)	OF	36	151	25	47	9	1	5	23	.311	5	27	6	72	1	0	1.000
—Baltimore (A.L.)	OF-DH	33	105	10	32	8	0	3	19	.305	2	16	4	47	2	2	.961
1994—Baltimore (A.L.)	OF	68	250	45	74	18	2	8	31	.296	17	39	5	147	5	6	.962
1995—Baltimore (A.L.)	OF-DH	57	178	18	43	9	1	4	23	.242	9	30	4	88	1	1	.989
—Bowie (Eastern)	OF	9	31	7	12	3	1	1	11	.387	10	7	3	12	0	1	.923
1996—Baltimore (A.L.)	OF-DH	71	248	38	56	10	1	9	27	.226	23	53	3	145	3	3	.980
—Rochester (Int'l)	OF	34	125	24	34	4	2	3	19	.272	19	19	3	75	1	1	.987
1997—Baltimore (A.L.)	OF-DH	118	397	71	105	19	3	21	55	.264	32	73	15	240	4	5	.980
Major league totals (5 years)		347	1178	182	310	64	7	45	155	.263	83	211	31	667	15	17	.976

DIVISION SERIES RECORD

Year Team (League)	Pos.	G	AB	R	H	2B	3B	HR	RBI	Avg.	BB	SO	SB	PO	A	E	Avg.
1997—Baltimore (A.L.)	OF-PR	4	10	3	1	1	0	0	2	.100	2	2	1	8	1	0	1.000

CHAMPIONSHIP SERIES RECORD

Year Team (League)	Pos.	G	AB	R	H	2B	3B	HR	RBI	Avg.	BB	SO	SB	PO	A	E	Avg.
1997—Baltimore (A.L.)	PH-OF-PR	5	3	0	0	0	0	0	0	.000	1	2	1	2	0	0	1.000

HAMPTON, MIKE   P   ASTROS

PERSONAL: Born September 9, 1972, in Brooksville, Fla. ... 5-10/180. ... Throws left, bats right. ... Full name: Michael William Hampton.

HIGH SCHOOL: Crystal River (Fla.).

TRANSACTIONS/CAREER NOTES: Selected by Seattle Mariners organization in sixth round of free-agent draft (June 4, 1990). ... Traded by Mariners with OF Mike Felder to Houston Astros for OF Eric Anthony (December 10, 1993). ... On disabled list (May 15-June 13, 1995).

STATISTICAL NOTES: Led Arizona League with 10 wild pitches in 1990. ... Pitched 6-0 no-hit victory for San Bernardino against Visalia (May 31, 1991).

MISCELLANEOUS: Appeared in two games as pinch-runner (1996).

Year Team (League)	W	L	Pct.	ERA	G	GS	CG	ShO	Sv.	IP	H	R	ER	BB	SO
1990—Ariz. Mariners (Ariz.)	•7	2	.778	2.66	14	•13	0	0	0	64 1/3	52	32	19	40	59
1991—San Bernardino (Calif.)	1	7	.125	5.25	18	15	1	1	0	73 2/3	71	58	43	47	57
—Bellingham (N'west)	5	2	.714	1.58	9	9	0	0	0	57	32	15	10	26	65
1992—San Bernardino (Calif.)	13	8	.619	3.12	25	25	6	•2	0	170	163	75	59	66	132
—Jacksonville (Southern)	0	1	.000	4.35	2	2	1	0	0	10 1/3	13	5	5	1	6
1993—Seattle (A.L.)	1	3	.250	9.53	13	3	0	0	1	17	28	20	18	17	8
—Jacksonville (Southern)	6	4	.600	3.71	15	14	1	0	0	87 1/3	71	43	36	33	84
1994—Houston (N.L.)■	2	1	.667	3.70	44	0	0	0	0	41 1/3	46	19	17	16	24
1995—Houston (N.L.)	9	8	.529	3.35	24	24	0	0	0	150 2/3	141	73	56	49	115
1996—Houston (N.L.)	10	10	.500	3.59	27	27	2	1	0	160 1/3	175	79	64	49	101
1997—Houston (N.L.)	15	10	.600	3.83	34	34	7	2	0	223	217	105	95	77	139
A.L. totals (1 year)	1	3	.250	9.53	13	3	0	0	1	17	28	20	18	17	8
N.L. totals (4 years)	36	29	.554	3.63	129	85	9	3	0	575 1/3	579	276	232	191	379
Major league totals (5 years)	37	32	.536	3.80	142	88	9	3	1	592 1/3	607	296	250	208	387

DIVISION SERIES RECORD

Year Team (League)	W	L	Pct.	ERA	G	GS	CG	ShO	Sv.	IP	H	R	ER	BB	SO
1997—Houston (N.L.)	0	1	.000	11.57	1	1	0	0	0	4 2/3	2	6	6	8	2

H

HANCOCK, RYAN — P — PADRES

PERSONAL: Born November 11, 1971, in Santa Clara, Calif. ... 6-2/215. ... Throws right, bats right. ... Full name: Ryan Lee Hancock.
HIGH SCHOOL: Monta Vista (Cupertino, Calif.).
COLLEGE: Brigham Young.
TRANSACTIONS/CAREER NOTES: Selected by California Angels organization in second round of free-agent draft (June 3, 1993). ... Angels franchise renamed Anaheim Angels for 1997 season. ... Traded by Angels with P Stevenson Agosto and a player to be named later to San Diego Padres for OF Rickey Henderson (August 13, 1997); Padres acquired 3B George Arias to complete deal (August 19, 1997).
MISCELLANEOUS: Singled and scored a run in only appearance as pinch-hitter with California (1996).

Year Team (League)	W	L	Pct.	ERA	G	GS	CG	ShO	Sv.	IP	H	R	ER	BB	SO
1993— Boise (Northwest)	1	0	1.000	3.31	3	3	0	0	0	16 1/3	14	9	6	8	18
1994— Lake Elsinore (Calif.)	9	6	.600	3.79	18	18	3	1	0	116 1/3	113	62	49	36	95
— Midland (Texas)	3	4	.429	5.81	8	8	0	0	0	48	63	34	31	11	35
1995— Midland (Texas)	12	9	.571	4.56	28	*28	*5	1	0	*175 2/3	*222	*107	*89	45	79
1996— Vancouver (PCL)	4	6	.400	3.70	19	11	1	0	0	80 1/3	69	38	33	38	65
— California (A.L.)	4	1	.800	7.48	11	4	0	0	0	27 2/3	34	23	23	17	19
1997— Vancouver (PCL)	3	3	.500	3.63	39	2	0	0	2	74 1/3	72	37	30	36	60
— Las Vegas (PCL)■	0	0	...	12.60	4	0	0	0	0	5	9	7	7	4	3
Major league totals (1 year)	4	1	.800	7.48	11	4	0	0	0	27 2/3	34	23	23	17	19

HANEY, CHRIS — P — ROYALS

PERSONAL: Born November 16, 1968, in Baltimore. ... 6-3/205. ... Throws left, bats left. ... Full name: Christopher Deane Haney. ... Son of Larry Haney, major league catcher with five teams (1966-70 and 1972-78) and coach, Milwaukee Brewers (1978-91).
HIGH SCHOOL: Orange County (Va.).
COLLEGE: UNC Charlotte.
TRANSACTIONS/CAREER NOTES: Selected by Milwaukee Brewers organization in 25th round of free-agent draft (June 2, 1987); did not sign. ... Selected by Montreal Expos organization in second round of free-agent draft (June 4, 1990). ... On Indianapolis disabled list (June 17-25, 1992). ... Traded by Expos with P Bill Sampen to Kansas City Royals for 3B Sean Berry and P Archie Corbin (August 29, 1992). ... On disabled list (July 13, 1995-remainder of season). ... On Kansas City disabled list (April 15-June 17 and June 27-September 3, 1997); included rehabilitation assignments to Omaha (May 31-June 13) and Wichita (August 25-29).
MISCELLANEOUS: Appeared in one game as pinch-runner with Montreal (1992).

Year Team (League)	W	L	Pct.	ERA	G	GS	CG	ShO	Sv.	IP	H	R	ER	BB	SO
1990— Jamestown (NYP)	3	0	1.000	0.96	6	5	0	0	1	28	17	3	3	10	26
— Rockford (Midwest)	2	4	.333	2.21	8	8	3	0	0	53	40	15	13	6	45
— Jacksonville (Southern)	1	0	1.000	0.00	1	1	0	0	0	6	6	0	0	3	6
1991— Harrisburg (Eastern)	5	3	.625	2.16	12	12	3	0	0	83 1/3	65	21	20	31	68
— Montreal (N.L.)	3	7	.300	4.04	16	16	0	0	0	84 2/3	94	49	38	43	51
— Indianapolis (A.A.)	1	1	.500	4.35	2	2	0	0	0	10 1/3	14	10	5	6	8
1992— Montreal (N.L.)	2	3	.400	5.45	9	6	1	1	0	38	40	25	23	10	27
— Indianapolis (A.A.)	5	2	.714	5.14	15	15	0	0	0	84	88	50	48	42	61
— Kansas City (A.L.)■	2	3	.400	3.86	7	7	1	1	0	42	35	18	18	16	27
1993— Omaha (Am. Assoc.)	6	1	.857	2.27	8	7	2	0	0	47 2/3	43	13	12	14	32
— Kansas City (A.L.)	9	9	.500	6.02	23	23	1	0	0	124	141	87	83	53	65
1994— Kansas City (A.L.)	2	2	.500	7.31	6	6	0	0	0	28 1/3	36	25	23	11	18
— Omaha (Am. Assoc.)	8	7	.533	5.25	18	18	1	0	0	104 2/3	125	77	61	37	78
1995— Kansas City (A.L.)	3	4	.429	3.65	16	13	1	0	0	81 1/3	78	35	33	33	31
1996— Kansas City (A.L.)	10	14	.417	4.70	35	35	4	1	0	228	*267	136	119	51	115
1997— Kansas City (A.L.)	1	2	.333	4.38	8	3	0	0	0	24 2/3	29	16	12	5	16
— Omaha (Am. Assoc.)	1	0	1.000	3.79	4	3	0	0	0	19	16	12	8	6	7
— Wichita (Texas)	0	1	.000	2.70	2	2	0	0	0	6 2/3	5	3	2	0	2
A.L. totals (6 years)	27	34	.443	4.91	95	87	7	3	0	528 1/3	586	317	288	169	272
N.L. totals (2 years)	5	10	.333	4.48	25	22	1	1	0	122 2/3	134	74	61	53	78
Major league totals (7 years)	32	44	.421	4.82	120	109	8	4	0	651	720	391	349	222	350

HANEY, TODD — 2B — METS

PERSONAL: Born July 30, 1965, in Galveston, Texas. ... 5-9/165. ... Bats right, throws right. ... Full name: Todd Michael Haney.
HIGH SCHOOL: Richfield (Waco, Texas).
JUNIOR COLLEGE: Panola Junior College (Texas).
COLLEGE: Texas.
TRANSACTIONS/CAREER NOTES: Selected by Seattle Mariners organization in 38th round of free-agent draft (June 2, 1987). ... Traded by Mariners organization to Detroit Tigers organization for P Dave Richards (January 21, 1991). ... Released by Tigers organization (April 4, 1991). ... Signed by Montreal Expos organization (April 7, 1991). ... On Indianapolis disabled list (April 12-July 16, 1992). ... Granted free agency (October 15, 1993). ... Signed by Chicago Cubs organization (December 14, 1993). ... Granted free agency (October 15, 1994). ... Re-signed by Cubs organization (January 9, 1995). ... Granted free agency (October 15, 1996). ... Signed by Mariners organization (December 12, 1996). ... On Tacoma disabled list (April 11-24, 1997). ... Traded by Marlins to Houston Astros organization for a player to be named later (April 24, 1997). ... Granted free agency (October 15, 1997). ... Signed by New York Mets (December 6, 1997).
STATISTICAL NOTES: Led Midwest League second basemen with 29 double plays in 1988. ... Led American Association second basemen with .974 fielding percentage, 381 assists and 74 double plays in 1991.

Year Team (League)	Pos.	G	AB	R	H	2B	3B	HR	RBI	Avg.	BB	SO	SB	PO	A	E	Avg.
1987— Bellingham (N'west)	2B	66	252	57	64	11	2	5	27	.254	44	33	18	148	170	16	.952
1988— Wausau (Midwest)	2B-SS	132	452	66	127	23	2	7	52	.281	56	54	35	282	318	30	.952
1989— San Bern. (Calif.)	2B	25	107	10	27	5	0	0	7	.252	7	14	2	47	14	3	.953
— Williamsport (East.)	2B	115	401	59	108	20	4	2	31	.269	49	43	13	213	313	*18	.967
1990— Williamsport (East.)	2B	1	2	0	1	1	0	0	0	.500	1	0	0	1	1	0	1.000
— Calgary (PCL)	2B	108	419	81	142	15	6	1	36	.339	37	38	16	206	292	15	.971

H

Year Team (League)	Pos.	G	AB	R	H	2B	3B	HR	RBI	Avg.	BB	SO	SB	PO	A	E	Avg.
							BATTING								FIELDING		
1991—Indianapolis (A.A.)■ ..	2B-SS	132	510	68	159	32	3	2	39	.312	47	49	12	232	†385	16	†.975
1992—Indianapolis (A.A.)......	2B	57	200	30	53	14	0	6	33	.265	37	34	1	113	161	7	.975
—Montreal (N.L.)..........	2B	7	10	0	3	1	0	0	1	.300	0	0	0	2	6	0	1.000
1993—Ottawa (Int'l)............	2B-SS	136	506	69	147	30	4	3	46	.291	36	56	11	245	401	15	.977
1994—Iowa (Am. Assoc.)■ ..	2B-OF	83	305	48	89	22	1	3	35	.292	28	29	9	159	199	8	.978
—Chicago (N.L.)	2B-3B	17	37	6	6	0	0	1	2	.162	3	3	2	20	28	1	.980
1995—Iowa (Am. Assoc.)......	2-S-3-O	90	326	38	102	20	2	4	30	.313	28	21	2	123	182	10	.968
—Chicago (N.L.)	2B-3B	25	73	11	30	8	0	2	6	.411	7	11	0	34	61	2	.979
1996—Chicago (N.L.)	2B-3B-SS	49	82	11	11	1	0	0	3	.134	7	15	1	32	65	3	.970
—Iowa (Am. Assoc.)......	2-3-S-P-O	66	240	20	59	13	0	2	19	.246	19	24	3	108	158	11	.960
1997—Tacoma (PCL)■	3B-SS-OF	4	17	3	6	4	0	2	2	.353	2	2	0	5	9	0	1.000
—New Orleans (A.A.)■..	2B-3B	115	454	63	128	25	0	2	63	.282	43	50	5	213	260	5	*.990
Major league totals (4 years)		98	202	28	50	10	0	3	12	.248	17	29	3	88	160	6	.976

RECORD AS PITCHER

Year Team (League)	W	L	Pct.	ERA	G	GS	CG	ShO	Sv.	IP	H	R	ER	BB	SO
1996—Iowa (Am. Assoc.).............	0	0	...	0.00	1	0	0	0	0	1	2	0	0	0	0

HANSELL, GREG P DIAMONDBACKS

PERSONAL: Born March 12, 1971, in Bellflower, Calif. ... 6-5/224. ... Throws right, bats right. ... Full name: Gregory Michael Hansell.

HIGH SCHOOL: John F. Kennedy (La Palma, Calif.).

TRANSACTIONS/CAREER NOTES: Selected by Boston Red Sox organization in 10th round of free-agent draft (June 5, 1989). ... Traded by Red Sox organization with OF Ed Perozo and a player to be named later to New York Mets organization for 1B Mike Marshall (July 27, 1990); Mets acquired C Paul Williams to complete deal (November 19, 1990). ... Traded by Mets organization with P Bob Ojeda to Los Angeles Dodgers organization for OF Hubie Brooks (December 15, 1990). ... On disabled list (June 19-July 8, 1993). ... Traded by Dodgers with 3B/1B Ron Coomer, P Jose Parra and a player to be named later to Minnesota Twins for P Kevin Tapani and P Mark Guthrie (July 31, 1995); Twins acquired OF Chris Latham to complete deal (October 30, 1995). ... Claimed on waivers by Boston Red Sox (October 11, 1996). ... Signed by Milwaukee Brewers organization (March 31, 1997). ... Released by Brewers (August 2, 1997). ... Granted free agency (October 15, 1997). ... Signed by Arizona Diamondbacks organization (December 18, 1997).

STATISTICAL NOTES: Tied for Florida State League lead with 14 losses in 1990. ... Tied for Florida State League lead with 27 games started in 1990.

Year Team (League)	W	L	Pct.	ERA	G	GS	CG	ShO	Sv.	IP	H	R	ER	BB	SO
1989—GC Red Sox (GCL)	3	2	.600	2.53	10	8	0	0	2	57	51	23	16	23	44
1990—Winter Haven (FSL)........	7	10	.412	3.59	21	21	2	1	0	115 1/3	95	63	46	64	79
—St. Lucie (Fla. St.)■	2	§4	.333	2.84	6	‡6	0	0	0	38	34	22	12	15	16
1991—Bakersfield (California)■....	14	5	.737	2.87	25	25	0	0	0	150 2/3	142	56	48	42	132
1992—San Antonio (Tex.)	6	4	.600	2.83	14	14	0	0	0	92 1/3	80	40	29	33	64
—Albuquerque (PCL).............	1	5	.167	5.24	13	13	0	0	0	68 2/3	84	46	40	35	38
1993—Albuquerque (PCL).............	5	10	.333	6.93	26	20	0	0	0	101 1/3	131	86	78	60	60
1994—Albuquerque (PCL).............	10	2	*.833	2.99	47	6	0	0	8	123 1/3	109	44	41	31	101
1995—Los Angeles (N.L.)	0	1	.000	7.45	20	0	0	0	0	19 1/3	29	17	16	6	13
—Albuquerque (PCL).............	1	1	.500	8.44	8	1	0	0	1	16	25	15	15	6	15
—Salt Lake (PCL)■	3	1	.750	5.01	7	5	0	0	0	32 1/3	39	20	18	4	17
1996—Minnesota (A.L.)	3	0	1.000	5.69	50	0	0	0	3	74 1/3	83	48	47	31	46
1997—Tucson (PCL)■	2	3	.400	4.64	40	9	0	0	2	87 1/3	99	52	45	27	76
—Milwaukee (A.L.)	0	0	...	9.64	3	0	0	0	0	4 2/3	5	5	5	1	5
A.L. totals (2 years)	3	0	1.000	5.92	53	0	0	0	3	79	88	53	52	32	51
N.L. totals (1 year)	0	1	.000	7.45	20	0	0	0	0	19 1/3	29	17	16	6	13
Major league totals (3 years)	3	1	.750	6.22	73	0	0	0	3	98 1/3	117	70	68	38	64

HANSEN, DAVE 3B

PERSONAL: Born November 24, 1968, in Long Beach, Calif. ... 6-0/195. ... Bats left, throws right. ... Full name: David Andrew Hansen.

HIGH SCHOOL: Rowland (Long Beach, Calif.).

TRANSACTIONS/CAREER NOTES: Selected by Los Angeles Dodgers organization in second round of free-agent draft (June 2, 1986). ... On disabled list (May 9-28, 1994). ... Granted free agency (November 27, 1996). ... Signed by Chicago Cubs organization (January 22, 1997). ... Granted free agency (October 27, 1997).

STATISTICAL NOTES: Led California League third basemen with 45 errors in 1987. ... Led Florida State League with 210 total bases and tied for lead with nine sacrifice flies in 1988. ... Led Florida State League third basemen with 383 total chances and 24 double plays in 1988. ... Led Pacific Coast League third basemen with .926 fielding percentage, 254 assists, 349 total chances and 25 double plays in 1990. ... Career major league grand slams: 1.

Year Team (League)	Pos.	G	AB	R	H	2B	3B	HR	RBI	Avg.	BB	SO	SB	PO	A	E	Avg.
							BATTING								FIELDING		
1986—Great Falls (Pio.)	0-3-C-2	61	204	39	61	7	3	1	36	.299	27	28	9	54	10	7	.901
1987—Bakersfield (Calif.)	3B-OF	132	432	68	113	22	1	3	38	.262	65	61	4	79	198	†45	.860
1988—Vero Beach (FSL)	3B	135	512	68	*149	•28	6	7	*81	.291	56	46	2	*102	*263	18	*.953
1989—San Antonio (Tex.)	3B	121	464	72	138	21	4	6	52	.297	50	44	3	*92	208	16	*.949
—Albuquerque (PCL)	3B	6	30	6	8	1	0	2	10	.267	2	3	0	3	8	3	.786
1990—Albuquerque (PCL)	3B-OF-SS	135	487	90	154	20	3	11	92	.316	*90	54	9	71	†255	26	†.926
—Los Angeles (N.L.)	3B	5	7	0	1	0	0	0	1	.143	0	0	0	0	1	1	.500
1991—Albuquerque (PCL)	3B-SS	68	254	42	77	11	1	5	40	.303	49	33	4	43	125	6	.966
—Los Angeles (N.L.)	3B-SS	53	56	3	15	4	0	1	5	.268	2	12	1	5	19	0	1.000
1992—Los Angeles (N.L.)	3B	132	341	30	73	11	0	6	22	.214	34	49	0	61	183	8	*.968
1993—Los Angeles (N.L.)	3B	84	105	13	38	3	0	4	30	.362	21	13	0	11	27	3	.927
1994—Los Angeles (N.L.)	3B	40	44	3	15	3	0	0	5	.341	5	5	0	6	1	1	.857
1995—Los Angeles (N.L.)	3B	100	181	19	52	10	0	1	14	.287	28	28	0	27	70	7	.933
1996—Los Angeles (N.L.)	3B-1B	80	104	7	23	1	0	0	6	.221	11	22	0	60	23	1	.988
1997—Chicago (N.L.)■	3B-1B-2B	90	151	19	47	8	2	3	21	.311	31	32	1	45	47	7	.929
Major league totals (8 years)		584	989	94	264	40	2	15	104	.267	132	161	2	209	376	28	.954

H

Year Team (League)	Pos.	G	AB	R	H	2B	3B	HR	RBI	Avg.	BB	SO	SB	PO	A	E	Avg.
1995— Los Angeles (N.L.)	PH	3	3	0	2	0	0	0	0	.667	0	0	0	...	...	...	...
1996— Los Angeles (N.L.)	PH-3B	2	2	0	0	0	0	0	0	.000	0	0	0	1	0	0	1.000
Division series totals (2 years)		5	5	0	2	0	0	0	0	.400	0	0	0	1	0	0	1.000

HANSEN, JED — 2B — ROYALS

PERSONAL: Born August 19, 1972, in Tacoma, Wash. ... 6-1/180. ... Bats right, throws right. ... Full name: Jed Ramon Hansen.
HIGH SCHOOL: Capital (Olympia, Wash.).
COLLEGE: Stanford.
TRANSACTIONS/CAREER NOTES: Selected by Cleveland Indians organization in 21st round of free-agent draft (June 3, 1991); did not sign. ... Selected by Kansas City Royals organization in second round of free-agent draft (June 2, 1994).
STATISTICAL NOTES: Led Northwest League second basemen with 337 total chances in 1994. ... Tied for American Association lead in errors by second baseman with 17 in 1997.

Year Team (League)	Pos.	G	AB	R	H	2B	3B	HR	RBI	Avg.	BB	SO	SB	PO	A	E	Avg.
1994— Eugene (Northwest) ...	2B	66	235	26	57	8	2	3	17	.243	24	56	6	*141	*189	7	*.979
1995— Springfield (Midw.) ...	2B	122	414	86	107	27	7	9	50	.258	78	73	44	220	*345	22	.963
1996— Wichita (Texas)	2B-OF	99	405	60	116	27	4	12	50	.286	29	72	14	196	276	10	.979
— Omaha (A.A.)	2B	29	99	14	23	4	0	3	9	.232	12	22	2	66	75	7	.953
1997— Omaha (A.A.)..............	2B-SS-3B	114	380	43	102	20	2	11	44	.268	32	78	8	205	323	‡23	.958
— Kansas City (A.L.)	2B	34	94	11	29	6	1	1	14	.309	13	29	3	56	77	1	.993
Major league totals (1 year)		34	94	11	29	6	1	1	14	.309	13	29	3	56	77	1	.993

HANSON, ERIK — P — BLUE JAYS

PERSONAL: Born May 18, 1965, in Kinnelon, N.J. ... 6-6/215. ... Throws right, bats right. ... Full name: Erik Brian Hanson.
HIGH SCHOOL: Peddie Prep (Highstown, N.J.).
COLLEGE: Wake Forest.
TRANSACTIONS/CAREER NOTES: Selected by Montreal Expos organization in seventh round of free-agent draft (June 6, 1983); did not sign. ... Selected by Seattle Mariners organization in second round of free-agent draft (June 2, 1986). ... On inactive list (June 12-August 18, 1986). ... On Seattle disabled list (May 25-August 4, 1989); included rehabilitation assignments to Calgary (June 14-22 and July 24-August 4). ... On Seattle disabled list (May 12-28 and May 29-June 22, 1991); included rehabilitation assignment to Calgary (June 16-20). ... On disabled list (August 23-September 12, 1992). ... Traded by Mariners with 2B Bret Boone to Cincinnati Reds for P Bobby Ayala and C Dan Wilson (November 2, 1993). ... On disabled list (August 9, 1994-remainder of season). ... Granted free agency (October 31, 1994). ... Signed by Boston Red Sox (April 11, 1995). ... Granted free agency (November 1, 1995). ... Signed by Toronto Blue Jays (December 22, 1995). ... On disabled list (March 24-April 17, 1997); included rehabilitation assignment to Dunedin (April 5-12). ... On disabled list (April 24-September 14, 1997).
STATISTICAL NOTES: Pitched 5-0 no-hit victory for Calgary against Las Vegas (August 21, 1988, second game).
MISCELLANEOUS: Scored once in two games as pinch-runner; after pinch-running in one game, became designated hitter but made no plate appearance (1993).

Year Team (League)	W	L	Pct.	ERA	G	GS	CG	ShO	Sv.	IP	H	R	ER	BB	SO
1986— Chattanooga (Southern).....	0	0	...	3.86	3	2	0	0	0	9 1/3	10	4	4	4	11
1987— Chattanooga (Southern).....	8	10	.444	2.60	21	21	1	0	0	131 1/3	102	56	38	43	131
— Calgary (PCL)......................	1	3	.250	3.61	8	7	0	0	0	47 1/3	38	23	19	21	43
1988— Calgary (PCL)......................	12	7	.632	4.23	27	26	2	1	0	161 2/3	167	92	76	57	*154
— Seattle (A.L.)......................	2	3	.400	3.24	6	6	0	0	0	41 2/3	35	17	15	12	36
1989— Seattle (A.L.)......................	9	5	.643	3.18	17	17	1	0	0	113 1/3	103	44	40	32	75
— Calgary (PCL)......................	4	2	.667	6.87	8	8	1	0	0	38	51	30	29	11	37
1990— Seattle (A.L.)......................	18	9	.667	3.24	33	33	5	1	0	236	205	88	85	68	211
1991— Seattle (A.L.)......................	8	8	.500	3.81	27	27	2	1	0	174 2/3	182	82	74	56	143
— Calgary (PCL)......................	0	0	...	1.50	1	1	0	0	0	6	1	1	1	2	5
1992— Seattle (A.L.)......................	8	*17	.320	4.82	31	30	6	1	0	186 2/3	209	110	100	57	112
1993— Seattle (A.L.)......................	11	12	.478	3.47	31	30	7	0	0	215	215	91	83	60	163
1994— Cincinnati (N.L.)■.............	5	5	.500	4.11	22	21	0	0	0	122 2/3	137	60	56	23	101
1995— Boston (A.L.)■.................	15	5	.750	4.24	29	29	1	1	0	186 2/3	187	94	88	59	139
1996— Toronto (A.L.)■.................	13	17	.433	5.41	35	35	4	1	0	214 2/3	243	143	129	102	156
1997— Dunedin (Fla. St.).............	0	0	...	1.29	2	2	0	0	0	7	7	5	1	1	5
— Toronto (A.L.)...................	0	0	...	7.80	3	2	0	0	0	15	15	13	13	6	18
A.L. totals (9 years)	84	76	.525	4.08	212	209	26	5	0	1383 2/3	1394	682	627	452	1053
N.L. totals (1 year)	5	5	.500	4.11	22	21	0	0	0	122 2/3	137	60	56	23	101
Major league totals (10 years)....	89	81	.524	4.08	234	230	26	5	0	1506 1/3	1531	742	683	475	1154

DIVISION SERIES RECORD

Year Team (League)	W	L	Pct.	ERA	G	GS	CG	ShO	Sv.	IP	H	R	ER	BB	SO
1995— Boston (A.L.)......................	0	1	.000	4.50	1	1	1	0	0	8	4	4	4	4	5

ALL-STAR GAME RECORD

Year League	W	L	Pct.	ERA	GS	CG	ShO	Sv.	IP	H	R	ER	BB	SO
1995— American...........................						Did not play.								

HARDTKE, JASON — 2B — CUBS

PERSONAL: Born September 15, 1971, in Milwaukee. ... 5-10/175. ... Bats both, throws right. ... Full name: Jason Robert Hardtke.
HIGH SCHOOL: Leland (San Jose, Calif.).

TRANSACTIONS/CAREER NOTES: Selected by Cleveland Indians organization in third round of free-agent draft (June 4, 1990). ... Traded by Indians organization with a player to be named later to San Diego Padres organization for OF Thomas Howard (April 14, 1992); Padres acquired C Christopher Maffett to complete deal (July 10, 1992). ... Selected by New York Mets organization from Padres organization in Rule 5 minor league draft (December 5, 1994). ... On Norfolk disabled list (July 1-30, 1996). ... Granted free agency (October 15, 1996). ... Re-signed by Mets organization (November 21, 1996). ... Claimed on waivers by Chicago Cubs (October 15, 1997).
STATISTICAL NOTES: Tied for Eastern League lead with nine sacrifice flies in 1995. ... Led International League with 516 total chances in 1997.

Year Team (League)	Pos.	G	AB	R	H	2B	3B	HR	RBI	Avg.	BB	SO	SB	PO	A	E	Avg.
1990— Burlington (Appal.).....	SS-2B	39	142	18	38	7	0	4	16	.268	23	19	11	36	118	9	.945
1991— Columbus (S. Atl.).....	SS-2B	139	534	•104	*155	26	8	12	81	.290	75	48	23	194	345	41	.929
1992— Waterloo (Midw.)■	2B	110	411	75	125	27	4	8	47	.304	38	33	9	225	256	15	*.970
— High Desert (Calif.)....	DH	10	41	9	11	1	0	2	8	.268	4	4	1	...	...	...	...
1993— Rancho Cuca. (Cal.)	2B-3B-1B	130	*523	96	167	38	7	11	85	.319	61	54	7	248	337	23	.962
1994— Wichita (Texas)	3B-2B	75	255	26	60	15	1	5	29	.235	21	44	1	57	102	11	.935
— Rancho Cuca. (Cal.)	2B-3B	4	13	2	4	0	0	0	0	.308	3	2	0	9	7	0	1.000
1995— Norfolk (Int'l)■	2B	4	7	1	2	1	0	0	0	.286	2	0	1	5	2	0	1.000
— Binghamton (East.)	2B-3B	121	455	65	130	*42	4	4	52	.286	66	58	6	201	356	19	.967
1996— Binghamton (East.)	2B	35	137	23	36	11	0	3	16	.263	16	16	0	61	100	6	.964
— Norfolk (Int'l)	2B	71	257	49	77	17	2	9	35	.300	29	29	4	149	175	5	.985
— New York (N.L.).........	2B	19	57	3	11	5	0	0	6	.193	2	12	0	26	34	0	1.000
1997— Norfolk (Int'l)	2B	97	388	46	107	23	3	11	45	.276	40	54	3	187	*319	10	.981
— New York (N.L.).........	2B-3B	30	56	9	15	2	0	2	8	.268	4	6	1	25	26	1	.981
— Binghamton (East.)	2B	6	26	3	10	2	0	1	4	.385	2	2	0	13	20	0	1.000
Major league totals (2 years)		49	113	12	26	7	0	2	14	.230	6	18	1	51	60	1	.991

HARKEY, MIKE   P

PERSONAL: Born October 25, 1966, in San Diego. ... 6-5/235. ... Throws right, bats right. ... Full name: Michael Anthony Harkey.
HIGH SCHOOL: Ganesha (Pomona, Calif.).
COLLEGE: Cal State Fullerton.
TRANSACTIONS/CAREER NOTES: Selected by San Diego Padres organization in 18th round of free-agent draft (June 4, 1984); did not sign. ... Selected by Chicago Cubs organization in first round (fourth pick overall) of free-agent draft (June 2, 1987). ... On disabled list (April 5-28 and July 4, 1989-remainder of season; May 29-June 13, 1990; and April 27, 1991-remainder of season). ... On Chicago disabled list (March 28-July 20, 1992); included rehabilitation assignments to Peoria (June 9-13 and June 19-20), Iowa (June 20-July 9) and Charlotte (July 15-16). ... On Chicago disabled list (March 27-April 14, 1993); included rehabilitation assignment to Orlando (April 9-10). ... On Chicago disabled list (June 13-July 5, 1993). ... Granted free agency (December 20, 1993). ... Signed by Colorado Rockies (January 4, 1994). ... Granted free agency (October 18, 1994). ... Signed by Edmonton, Oakland Athletics organization (March 8, 1995). ... Claimed on waivers by California Angels (July 19, 1995). ... Granted free agency (December 21, 1995). ... Signed by Albuquerque, Los Angeles Dodgers organization (February 16, 1996). ... Granted free agency (October 15, 1996). ... Re-signed by Dodgers organization (February 18, 1997). ... Granted free agency (October 6, 1997).
RECORDS: Shares major league record for most putouts by pitcher in one inning—3 (May 23, 1990, fourth inning).
HONORS: Named N.L. Rookie Pitcher of the Year by THE SPORTING NEWS (1990).

Year Team (League)	W	L	Pct.	ERA	G	GS	CG	ShO	Sv.	IP	H	R	ER	BB	SO
1987— Peoria (Midwest)................	2	3	.400	3.55	12	12	3	0	0	76	81	45	30	28	48
— Pittsfield (Eastern)..............	0	0	...	0.00	1	0	0	0	0	2	1	0	0	0	2
1988— Pittsfield (Eastern).............	9	2	*.818	1.37	13	13	3	1	0	85²/₃	66	29	13	35	73
— Iowa (Am. Assoc.).............	7	2	.778	3.55	12	12	3	1	0	78²/₃	55	36	31	33	62
— Chicago (N.L.).................	0	3	.000	2.60	5	5	0	0	0	34²/₃	33	14	10	15	18
1989— Iowa (Am. Assoc.).............	2	7	.222	4.43	12	12	0	0	0	63	67	37	31	35	37
1990— Chicago (N.L.)..............	12	6	.667	3.26	27	27	2	1	0	173²/₃	153	71	63	59	94
1991— Chicago (N.L.)..............	0	2	.000	5.30	4	4	0	0	0	18²/₃	21	11	11	6	15
1992— Peoria (Midwest)..............	1	0	1.000	3.00	2	2	0	0	0	12	15	6	4	3	17
— Iowa (Am. Assoc.).............	0	1	.000	5.56	4	4	0	0	0	22²/₃	21	15	14	13	16
— Charlotte (Southern)..........	0	1	.000	5.63	1	1	0	0	0	8	9	5	5	0	5
— Chicago (N.L.).................	4	0	1.000	1.89	7	7	0	0	0	38	34	13	8	15	21
1993— Orlando (South.)	0	0	...	1.69	1	1	0	0	0	5¹/₃	4	1	1	2	5
— Chicago (N.L.).................	10	10	.500	5.26	28	28	1	0	0	157¹/₃	187	100	92	43	67
1994— Colorado (N.L.)■.............	1	6	.143	5.79	24	13	0	0	0	91²/₃	125	61	59	35	39
— Colo. Springs (PCL)..........	1	1	.500	12.60	2	2	0	0	0	10	19	14	14	3	4
1995— Oakland (A.L.)■.............	4	6	.400	6.27	14	12	0	0	0	66	75	46	46	31	28
— California (A.L.)■.............	4	3	.571	4.55	12	8	1	0	0	61¹/₃	80	32	31	16	28
1996— Albuquerque (PCL)■..........	7	11	.389	5.38	49	13	0	0	13	118²/₃	146	79	71	39	90
1997— Albuquerque (PCL)...........	2	2	.500	2.10	47	0	0	0	15	55²/₃	50	14	13	11	57
— Los Angeles (N.L.)	1	0	1.000	4.30	10	0	0	0	0	14²/₃	12	8	7	5	6
A.L. totals (1 year)	8	9	.471	5.44	26	20	1	0	0	127¹/₃	155	78	77	47	56
N.L. totals (7 years)	28	27	.509	4.26	105	84	3	1	0	528²/₃	565	278	250	178	260
Major league totals (8 years)	36	36	.500	4.49	131	104	4	1	0	656	720	356	327	225	316

HARNISCH, PETE   P   REDS

PERSONAL: Born September 23, 1966, in Commack, N.Y. ... 6-0/207. ... Throws right, bats right. ... Full name: Peter Thomas Harnisch.
HIGH SCHOOL: Commack (N.Y.).
COLLEGE: Fordham.
TRANSACTIONS/CAREER NOTES: Selected by Baltimore Orioles organization in supplemental round ("sandwich pick" between first and second round, 27th pick overall) of free-agent draft (June 2, 1987); pick received as compensation for Cleveland Indians signing Type A free-agent C Rick Dempsey. ... Traded by Orioles with P Curt Schilling and OF Steve Finley to Houston Astros for 1B Glenn Davis (January 10, 1991). ... On suspended list (July 7-9, 1992). ... On Houston disabled list (May 23-June 30, 1994); included rehabilitation assignment to Tucson (June 25-26). ... Traded by Astros to New York Mets for two players to be named later (November 28, 1994); Astros acquired P Andy Beckerman (December 6, 1994) and P Juan Castillo (April 12, 1995) to complete deal. ... Granted free agency (December 23, 1994). ... Re-signed by Mets (April 7, 1995). ... On disabled list (August 2, 1995-remainder of season). ... On New York disabled list (March 26-April 14,

H

1996); included rehabilitation assignment to St. Lucie (March 30-April 14). ... On New York suspended list (May 22-31, 1996). ... On New York disabled list (April 2-August 5, 1997). ... Traded by Mets to Milwaukee Brewers for OF Donny Moore (August 31, 1997). ... Granted free agency (October 27, 1997). ... Signed by Cincinnati Reds (January 22, 1998).

RECORDS: Shares major league record for striking out side on nine pitches (September 6, 1991, seventh inning). ... Shares N.L. record for most consecutive home runs allowed in one inning—4 (July 23, 1996, first inning).

STATISTICAL NOTES: Pitched 4-0 one-hit, complete-game victory against Chicago (July 10, 1993). ... Pitched 3-0 one-hit, complete-game victory against San Diego (September 17, 1993).

MISCELLANEOUS: Appeared in one game as pinch-runner with Houston (1994). ... Appeared in one game as pinch-runner with New York (1996).

Year	Team (League)	W	L	Pct.	ERA	G	GS	CG	ShO	Sv.	IP	H	R	ER	BB	SO
1987—	Bluefield (Appalachian)	3	1	.750	2.56	9	9	0	0	0	52 2/3	38	19	15	26	64
	—Hagerstown (Caro.)	1	2	.333	2.25	4	4	0	0	0	20	17	7	5	14	18
1988—	Charlotte (Southern)	7	6	.538	2.58	20	20	4	2	0	132 1/3	113	55	38	52	141
	—Rochester (Int'l)	4	1	.800	2.16	7	7	3	2	0	58 1/3	44	16	14	14	43
	—Baltimore (A.L.)■	0	2	.000	5.54	2	2	0	0	0	13	13	8	8	9	10
1989—	Baltimore (A.L.)	5	9	.357	4.62	18	17	2	0	0	103 1/3	97	55	53	64	70
	—Rochester (Int'l)	5	5	.500	2.58	12	12	3	1	0	87 1/3	60	27	25	35	59
1990—	Baltimore (A.L.)	11	11	.500	4.34	31	31	3	0	0	188 2/3	189	96	91	86	122
1991—	Houston (N.L.)■■	12	9	.571	2.70	33	33	4	2	0	216 2/3	169	71	65	83	172
1992—	Houston (N.L.)	9	10	.474	3.70	34	34	0	0	0	206 2/3	182	92	85	64	164
1993—	Houston (N.L.)	16	9	.640	2.98	33	33	5	*4	0	217 2/3	171	84	72	79	185
1994—	Houston (N.L.)	8	5	.615	5.40	17	17	1	0	0	95	100	59	57	39	62
	—Tucson (PCL)	0	0	. . .	0.00	1	1	0	0	0	5	2	0	0	1	1
1995—	New York (N.L.)■	2	8	.200	3.68	18	18	0	0	0	110	111	55	45	24	82
1996—	St. Lucie (Fla. St.)	1	0	1.000	2.77	2	2	0	0	0	13	11	4	4	0	12
	—New York (N.L.)	8	12	.400	4.21	31	31	2	1	0	194 2/3	195	103	91	61	114
1997—	GC Mets (GCL)	0	0	. . .	12.00	1	1	0	0	0	3	7	4	4	0	5
	—St. Lucie (Fla. St.)	1	0	1.000	3.00	2	2	0	0	0	12	5	5	4	4	7
	—Norfolk (Int'l)	1	1	.500	5.40	3	3	0	0	0	16 2/3	16	12	10	10	16
	—New York (N.L.)	0	1	.000	8.06	6	5	0	0	0	25 2/3	35	24	23	11	12
	—Milwaukee (A.L.)■	1	1	.500	5.14	4	3	0	0	0	14	13	9	8	12	10
A.L. totals (4 years)		17	23	.425	4.51	55	53	5	0	0	319	312	168	160	171	212
N.L. totals (7 years)		55	54	.505	3.70	172	171	12	7	0	1066 1/3	963	488	438	361	791
Major league totals (10 years)....		72	77	.483	3.88	227	224	17	7	0	1385 1/3	1275	656	598	532	1003

ALL-STAR GAME RECORD

Year	League	W	L	Pct.	ERA	GS	CG	ShO	Sv.	IP	H	R	ER	BB	SO
1991—	National	0	0	. . .	0.00	0	0	0	0	1	2	0	0	0	1

HARRIS, JEFF   P   TWINS

PERSONAL: Born July 4, 1974, in Alameda, Calif. ... 6-0/180. ... Throws right, bats right. ... Full name: Jeffrey Austin Harris.
HIGH SCHOOL: Pinole Valley (Pinole, Calif.).
JUNIOR COLLEGE: Contra Costa College (Calif.).
COLLEGE: San Francisco.
TRANSACTIONS/CAREER NOTES: Selected by Minnesota Twins organization in 28th round of free-agent draft (June 1, 1995).

Year	Team (League)	W	L	Pct.	ERA	G	GS	CG	ShO	Sv.	IP	H	R	ER	BB	SO
1995—	Elizabethton (Appal.)	1	3	.250	3.82	21	0	0	0	10	33	42	15	14	13	27
1996—	Fort Wayne (Midw.)	8	3	.727	3.11	42	0	0	0	3	89 2/3	90	35	31	33	85
1997—	Fort Myers (Fla. St.)	2	4	.333	2.14	24	0	0	0	1	42	30	11	10	15	32
	—New Britain (East.)	2	1	.667	2.34	28	0	0	0	3	42 1/3	30	15	11	16	44

HARRIS, LENNY   OF/IF   REDS

PERSONAL: Born October 28, 1964, in Miami. ... 5-10/210. ... Bats left, throws right. ... Full name: Leonard Anthony Harris.
HIGH SCHOOL: Jackson (Miami).
JUNIOR COLLEGE: Miami-Dade (North) Community College.
TRANSACTIONS/CAREER NOTES: Selected by Cincinnati Reds organization in fifth round of free-agent draft (June 6, 1983). ... Loaned by Reds organization to Glens Falls, Detroit Tigers organization (May 6-28, 1988). ... Traded by Reds with OF Kal Daniels to Los Angeles Dodgers for P Tim Leary and SS Mariano Duncan (July 18, 1989). ... Granted free agency (October 8, 1993). ... Signed by Reds (December 1, 1993). ... Granted free agency (October 31, 1996). ... Re-signed by Reds (November 13, 1996).
STATISTICAL NOTES: Led Florida State League third basemen with 34 double plays in 1985. ... Led Eastern League third basemen with 116 putouts, 28 errors and 360 total chances in 1986. ... Led American Association in caught stealing with 22 in 1988. ... Led American Association second basemen with 23 errors in 1988. ... Career major league grand slams: 2.

							BATTING							FIELDING		
Year	Team (League)	Pos.	G	AB	R	H	2B	3B	HR	RBI	Avg.	BB	SO	SB	PO	A	E	Avg.
1983—	Billings (Pioneer)........	3B	56	224	37	63	8	1	1	26	.281	13	35	7	34	95	22	.854
1984—	Cedar Rap. (Midw.)	3B	132	468	52	115	15	3	6	53	.246	42	59	31	111	204	*34	.903
1985—	Tampa (Florida State).	3B	132	499	66	129	11	8	3	51	.259	37	57	15	89	*277	*35	.913
1986—	Vermont (Eastern)......	3B-SS	119	450	68	114	17	2	10	52	.253	29	38	36	†119	220	†28	.924
1987—	Nashville (A.A.)	SS-3B	120	403	45	100	12	3	2	31	.248	27	43	30	124	210	34	.908
1988—	Nashville (A.A.)	2B-SS-3B	107	422	46	117	20	2	0	35	.277	22	36	*45	203	247	†25	.947
	—Glens Falls (East.)■...	2B	17	65	9	22	5	1	1	7	.338	9	6	4	40	49	5	.947
	—Cincinnati (N.L.)■....	3B-2B	16	43	7	16	1	0	0	8	.372	5	4	4	14	33	1	.979
1989—	Cincinnati (N.L.)	2B-SS-3B	61	188	17	42	4	0	2	11	.223	9	20	10	92	134	13	.946
	—Nashville (A.A.)	2B	8	34	6	9	2	0	3	6	.265	0	5	0	23	20	0	1.000
	—Los Angeles (N.L.)■..	O-2-3-S	54	147	19	37	6	1	1	15	.252	11	13	4	55	34	2	.978
1990—	Los Angeles (N.L.)	3-2-O-S	137	431	61	131	16	4	2	29	.304	29	31	15	140	205	11	.969
1991—	Los Angeles (N.L.)	3-2-S-O	145	429	59	123	16	1	3	38	.287	37	32	12	125	250	20	.949
1992—	Los Angeles (N.L.)	2-3-O-S	135	347	28	94	11	0	0	30	.271	24	24	19	199	248	27	.943

Year Team (League)	Pos.	G	AB	R	H	2B	3B	HR	RBI	Avg.	BB	SO	SB	PO	A	E	Avg.
1993—Los Angeles (N.L.)	2-3-S-O	107	160	20	38	6	1	2	11	.238	15	15	3	61	99	3	.982
1994—Cincinnati (N.L.)■	3-1-0-2	66	100	13	31	3	1	0	14	.310	5	13	7	27	29	6	.903
1995—Cincinnati (N.L.)	3-1-0-2	101	197	32	41	8	3	2	16	.208	14	20	10	147	68	4	.982
1996—Cincinnati (N.L.)	O-3-1-2	125	302	33	86	17	2	5	32	.285	21	31	14	199	66	6	.978
1997—Cincinnati (N.L.)	O-2-3-1	120	238	32	65	13	1	3	28	.273	18	18	4	120	57	3	.983
Major league totals (10 years)		1067	2582	321	704	101	14	20	232	.273	188	221	102	1179	1223	96	.962

CHAMPIONSHIP SERIES RECORD

Year Team (League)	Pos.	G	AB	R	H	2B	3B	HR	RBI	Avg.	BB	SO	SB	PO	A	E	Avg.
1995—Cincinnati (N.L.)	PH	3	2	0	2	0	0	0	1	1.000	0	0	1	0	0	0	...

HARRIS, PEP — P — ANGELS

PERSONAL: Born September 23, 1972, in Lancaster, S.C. ... 6-2/185. ... Throws right, bats right. ... Full name: Hernando Petrocelli Harris.
HIGH SCHOOL: Lancaster (S.C.).
TRANSACTIONS/CAREER NOTES: Selected by Cleveland Indians organization in seventh round of free-agent draft (June 3, 1991). ... On disabled list (June 4-15, 1992 and April 9-May 1, 1993). ... Traded by Indians with P Jason Grimsley to California Angels for P Brian Anderson (February 15, 1996). ... Angels franchise renamed Anaheim Angels for 1997 season.

Year Team (League)	W	L	Pct.	ERA	G	GS	CG	ShO	Sv.	IP	H	R	ER	BB	SO
1991—Burlington (Appalachian)	4	3	.571	3.29	13	13	0	0	0	65⅔	67	30	24	31	47
1992—Columbus (S. Atl.)	7	4	.636	3.67	18	17	0	0	0	90⅔	88	51	37	51	57
1993—Columbus (S. Atl.)	7	8	.467	4.24	26	17	0	0	0	119	113	67	56	44	82
1994—Cant./Akr. (Eastern)	2	0	1.000	2.21	24	0	0	0	12	20⅓	9	5	5	13	15
—Kinston (Carolina)	4	1	.800	1.93	27	0	0	0	8	32⅔	21	14	7	16	37
1995—Cant./Akr. (Eastern)	6	3	.667	2.39	32	7	0	0	10	83	78	34	22	23	40
—Buffalo (A.A.)	2	1	.667	2.48	14	0	0	0	0	32⅔	32	11	9	15	18
1996—Midland (Texas)■	2	2	.500	5.31	6	6	1	0	0	39	47	27	23	9	28
—Vancouver (PCL)	9	3	.750	4.56	18	18	1	0	0	118⅓	135	67	60	46	61
—California (A.L.)	2	0	1.000	3.90	11	3	0	0	0	32⅓	31	16	14	17	20
1997—Anaheim (A.L.)	5	4	.556	3.62	61	0	0	0	0	79⅔	82	33	32	38	56
Major league totals (2 years)	7	4	.636	3.70	72	3	0	0	0	112	113	49	46	55	76

HARRIS, REGGIE — P — ASTROS

PERSONAL: Born August 12, 1968, in Waynesboro, Va. ... 6-2/212. ... Throws right, bats right. ... Full name: Reginald Allen Harris. ... Cousin of Dell Curry, guard with Charlotte Hornets.
HIGH SCHOOL: Waynesboro (Va.).
TRANSACTIONS/CAREER NOTES: Selected by Boston Red Sox organization in first round (26th pick overall) of free-agent draft (June 2, 1987). ... Selected by Oakland Athletics from Red Sox organization in Rule 5 major league draft (December 4, 1989). ... On Oakland disabled list (March 29-July 3, 1990); included rehabilitation assignment to Huntsville (May 26-June 24). ... On Tacoma disabled list (June 17-August 4, 1991). ... Selected by Seattle Mariners from A's organization in Rule 5 major league draft (December 7, 1992). ... On Jacksonville disabled list (May 19-28, 1993). ... On Calgary temporarily inactive list (July 21-August 1, 1993). ... Granted free agency (October 15, 1993). ... Re-signed by Mariners (November 11, 1993). ... Granted free agency (October 3, 1994). ... Signed by Omaha, Kansas City Royals organization (February 4, 1995). ... On disabled list (April 6-18, 1995). ... Released by Royals organization (April 25, 1995). ... Signed by Colorado Rockies organization (February 14, 1996). ... Released by Rockies (March 26, 1996). ... Signed by Boston Red Sox organization (May 7, 1996). ... On Trenton disabled list (June 12-24, 1996). ... Released by Red Sox (December 5, 1996). ... Signed by Philadelphia Phillies organization (December 23, 1996). ... On suspended list (August 29-September 1, 1997). ... Released by Phillies following 1997 season. ... Signed by Houston Astros organization (January 9, 1998).
STATISTICAL NOTES: Led Pacific Coast League with 20 wild pitches in 1992.

Year Team (League)	W	L	Pct.	ERA	G	GS	CG	ShO	Sv.	IP	H	R	ER	BB	SO
1987—Elmira (N.Y.-Penn)	2	3	.400	5.01	9	8	1	1	0	46⅔	50	29	26	22	25
1988—Lynchburg (Caroline)	1	8	.111	7.45	17	11	0	0	0	64	86	60	53	34	48
—Elmira (N.Y.-Penn)	3	6	.333	5.30	10	10	0	0	0	54⅓	56	37	32	28	46
1989—Winter Haven (FSL)	10	13	.435	3.99	29	26	1	0	0	153⅓	144	81	68	77	85
1990—Huntsville (Southern)■	0	2	.000	3.03	5	5	0	0	0	29⅔	26	12	10	16	34
—Oakland (A.L.)	1	0	1.000	3.48	16	1	0	0	0	41⅓	25	16	16	21	31
1991—Tacoma (PCL)	5	4	.556	4.99	16	15	0	0	0	83	83	55	46	58	72
—Oakland (A.L.)	0	0	...	12.00	2	0	0	0	0	3	5	4	4	3	2
1992—Tacoma (PCL)	6	*16	.273	5.71	29	•28	1	0	0	149⅔	141	*108	*95	*117	111
1993—Jacksonville (Southern)■	1	4	.200	4.78	9	8	0	0	0	37⅔	33	24	20	22	30
—Calgary (PCL)	8	6	.571	5.20	17	15	1	0	0	88⅓	74	55	51	61	75
1994—Calgary (PCL)	6	9	.400	8.12	20	18	0	0	0	98⅔	137	99	89	51	73
1995—Omaha (Am. Assoc.)■	0	1	.000	18.00	2	0	0	0	0	2	5	4	4	1	2
1996—Trenton (Eastern)■	2	1	.667	1.46	33	0	0	0	17	37	17	6	6	19	43
—Boston (A.L.)	0	0	...	12.46	4	0	0	0	0	4⅓	7	6	6	5	4
1997—Philadelphia (N.L.)■	1	3	.250	5.30	50	0	0	0	0	54⅓	55	33	32	43	45
A.L. totals (3 years)	1	0	1.000	4.81	22	1	0	0	0	48⅔	37	26	26	29	37
N.L. totals (1 year)	1	3	.250	5.30	50	0	0	0	0	54⅓	55	33	32	43	45
Major league totals (4 years)	2	3	.400	5.07	72	1	0	0	0	103	92	59	58	72	82

HARVEY, BRYAN — P — ASTROS

PERSONAL: Born June 2, 1963, in Chattanooga, Tenn. ... 6-2/212. ... Throws right, bats right. ... Full name: Bryan Stanley Harvey.
HIGH SCHOOL: Bandys (Catawba, N.C.).
COLLEGE: UNC Charlotte.

H

TRANSACTIONS/CAREER NOTES: Signed as non-drafted free agent by California Angels organization (August 20, 1984). ... On disabled list (April 12-22, 1985; June 7-22 and July 1, 1992-remainder of season). ... Selected by Florida Marlins in first round (20th pick overall) of expansion draft (November 17, 1992). ... On Florida disabled list (April 26-May 25, May 26-June 22 and June 30, 1994-remainder of season); included rehabilitation assignments to Brevard County (May 9-10, May 25 and June 9-22). ... On disabled list (April 29, 1995-remainder of season). ... Granted free agency (October 30, 1995). ... Signed by Angels (December 20, 1995). ... On disabled list (March 24, 1996-entire season). ... Granted free agency (October 10, 1996). ... Signed by Atlanta Braves (December 6, 1996). ... On disabled list (March 24-July 6, 1997); included rehabilitation assignments to Greenville (April 12-May 4, May 18-28, June 5-17 and June 24-29). ... Signed by Marlins organization (July 19, 1997). ... Granted free agency (October 15, 1997). ... Signed by Houston Astros organization (December 30, 1997).
HONORS: Named A.L. Rookie Pitcher of the Year by THE SPORTING NEWS (1988). ... Named A.L. co-Fireman of the Year by THE SPORTING NEWS (1991).
MISCELLANEOUS: Holds Anaheim Angels franchise all-time record for most saves (126).

Year Team (League)	W	L	Pct.	ERA	G	GS	CG	ShO	Sv.	IP	H	R	ER	BB	SO
1985— Quad City (Midwest)	5	6	.455	3.53	30	7	0	0	4	81 2/3	66	37	32	37	111
1986— Palm Springs (California)...	3	4	.429	2.68	43	0	0	0	15	57	38	24	17	38	68
1987— Midland (Texas).................	2	2	.500	2.04	43	0	0	0	20	53	40	14	12	28	78
— California (A.L.)	0	0	...	0.00	3	0	0	0	0	5	6	0	0	2	3
1988— Edmonton (PCL)	0	0	...	3.18	5	0	0	0	2	5 2/3	7	2	2	4	10
— California (A.L.)	7	5	.583	2.13	50	0	0	0	17	76	59	22	18	20	67
1989— California (A.L.)	3	3	.500	3.44	51	0	0	0	25	55	36	21	21	41	78
1990— California (A.L.)	4	4	.500	3.22	54	0	0	0	25	64 1/3	45	24	23	35	82
1991— California (A.L.)	2	4	.333	1.60	67	0	0	0	*46	78 2/3	51	20	14	17	101
1992— California (A.L.)	0	4	.000	2.83	25	0	0	0	13	28 2/3	22	12	9	11	34
1993— Florida (N.L.)■...................	1	5	.167	1.70	59	0	0	0	45	69	45	14	13	13	73
1994— Florida (N.L.)	0	0	...	5.23	12	0	0	0	6	10 1/3	12	6	6	4	10
— Brevard County (FSL)........	0	0	...	1.50	7	1	0	0	0	6	2	1	1	2	6
1995— Florida (N.L.)	0	0	...	...	1	0	0	0	0	0	2	3	3	1	0
1996—								Did not play.							
1997— Greenville (Southern)■.......	1	1	.500	5.18	22	8	0	0	0	24 1/3	23	15	14	16	18
— Brevard County (FSL)■.......	0	1	.000	4.91	4	4	0	0	0	11	11	9	6	1	11
— Charlotte (Int'l)	0	0	...	0.00	2	0	0	0	0	1 1/3	0	0	0	0	0
A.L. totals (6 years)	16	20	.444	2.49	250	0	0	0	126	307 2/3	219	99	85	126	365
N.L. totals (3 years)	1	5	.167	2.50	72	0	0	0	51	79 1/3	59	23	22	18	83
Major league totals (9 years)......	17	25	.405	2.49	322	0	0	0	177	387	278	122	107	144	448

ALL-STAR GAME RECORD

Year League	W	L	Pct.	ERA	GS	CG	ShO	Sv.	IP	H	R	ER	BB	SO
1991— American.............................							Did not play.							
1993— National.............................	0	0	...	0.00	0	0	0	0	1	1	0	0	0	2
All-Star totals (1 years)	0	0	...	0.00	0	0	0	0	1	1	0	0	0	2

HASEGAWA, SHIGETOSHI — P — ANGELS

PERSONAL: Born August 1, 1968, in Kobe, Japan ... 5-11/160. ... Throws right, bats right. ... Name pronounced SHE-geh-TOE-she HAH-seh-GAH-wah.
COLLEGE: Ritsumeikan University (Kyoto, Japan).
TRANSACTIONS/CAREER NOTES: ... Played for Orix Blue Wave of Japan Pacific League (1991-96). ... Signed by Anaheim Angels (January 9, 1997).

Year Team (League)	W	L	Pct.	ERA	G	GS	CG	ShO	Sv.	IP	H	R	ER	BB	SO
1991— Orix (Jap. Pacific)..............	12	9	.571	3.55	28	25	11	3	1	185	184	76	73	50	111
1992— Orix (Jap. Pacific)..............	6	8	.429	3.27	24	19	4	0	1	143 1/3	138	60	52	51	86
1993— Orix (Jap. Pacific)..............	12	6	.667	2.71	23	22	9	3	0	159 2/3	146	61	48	48	86
1994— Orix (Jap. Pacific)..............	11	9	.550	3.11	25	22	8	3	1	156 1/3	169	61	54	46	86
1995— Orix (Jap. Pacific)..............	12	7	.632	2.89	24	23	9	4	0	171	167	62	55	51	91
1996— Orix (Jap. Pacific)..............	4	6	.400	5.34	18	16	2	0	1	87 2/3	109	60	52	40	55
1997— Anaheim (A.L.)■................	3	7	.300	3.93	50	7	0	0	0	116 2/3	118	60	51	46	83
Major league totals (1 year)........	3	7	.300	3.93	50	7	0	0	0	116 2/3	118	60	51	46	83

HASELMAN, BILL — C — RANGERS

PERSONAL: Born May 25, 1966, in Long Branch, N.J. ... 6-3/223. ... Bats right, throws right. ... Full name: William Joseph Haselman.
HIGH SCHOOL: Saratoga (Calif.).
COLLEGE: UCLA.
TRANSACTIONS/CAREER NOTES: Selected by Texas Rangers organization in first round (23rd pick overall) of free-agent draft (June 2, 1987); pick received as compensation for New York Yankees signing Type A free-agent OF Gary Ward. ... On disabled list (March 28-May 4, 1992). ... Claimed on waivers by Seattle Mariners (May 29, 1992). ... On suspended list (July 22-25, 1993). ... Granted free agency (October 15, 1994). ... Signed by Boston Red Sox (November 7, 1994). ... On disabled list (June 30-August 8, 1997); included rehabilitation assignment to Gulf Coast Red Sox (July 29-August 1) and Trenton (August 1-8). ... Traded by Red Sox with P Aaron Sele and C Bill Haselman to Rangers for C Jim Leyritz and OF Damon Buford (November 6, 1997).
RECORDS: Shares A.L. single-game record for most chances accepted by catcher (nine-inning game)—20 (September 18, 1996).
STATISTICAL NOTES: Led Texas League with 12 passed balls in 1989. ... Led Texas League catchers with 676 putouts, 90 assists, 20 errors, 786 total chances and 20 passed balls in 1990. ... Led American Association catchers with 673 putouts and 751 total chances in 1991. ... Tied for A.L. lead in passed balls with 17 in 1997. ... Career major league grand slams: 1.

Year Team (League)	Pos.	G	AB	R	H	2B	3B	HR	RBI	Avg.	BB	SO	SB	PO	A	E	Avg.
1987— Gastonia (S. Atl.)........	C	61	235	35	72	13	1	8	33	.306	19	46	1	26	2	2	.933
1988— Charlotte (Fla. St.)......	C	122	453	56	111	17	2	10	54	.245	45	99	8	249	30	6	.979
1989— Tulsa (Texas)	C	107	352	38	95	17	2	7	36	.270	40	88	5	508	63	9	.984
1990— Tulsa (Texas)	C-1-O-3	120	430	68	137	39	2	18	80	.319	43	96	3	†722	†93	†20	.976
— Texas (A.L.)	DH-C	7	13	0	2	0	0	0	3	.154	1	5	0	8	0	0	1.000

H

Year	Team (League)	Pos.	G	AB	R	H	2B	3B	HR	RBI	Avg.	BB	SO	SB	PO	A	E	Avg.
1991—	Oklahoma City (A.A.)..	C-O-1-3	126	442	57	113	22	2	9	60	.256	61	89	10	†706	71	11	.986
1992—	Oklahoma City (A.A.)..	OF-C	17	58	8	14	5	0	1	9	.241	13	12	1	45	7	3	.945
—	Calgary (PCL)■........	C-OF	88	302	49	77	14	2	19	53	.255	41	89	3	227	23	6	.977
—	Seattle (A.L.)............	C-OF	8	19	1	5	0	0	0	0	.263	0	7	0	19	2	0	1.000
1993—	Seattle (A.L.)	C-DH-OF	58	137	21	35	8	0	5	16	.255	12	19	2	236	17	2	.992
1994—	Seattle (A.L.)	C-DH-OF	38	83	11	16	7	1	1	8	.193	3	11	1	157	6	3	.982
—	Calgary (PCL)	C-1B	44	163	44	54	10	0	15	46	.331	30	33	1	219	16	5	.979
1995—	Boston (A.L.)■............	C-DH-1-3	64	152	22	37	6	1	5	23	.243	17	30	0	259	16	3	.989
1996—	Boston (A.L.).............	C-DH-1B	77	237	33	65	13	1	8	34	.274	19	52	4	507	33	3	.994
1997—	Boston (A.L.)	C	67	212	22	50	15	0	6	26	.236	15	44	0	373	40	7	.983
—	GC Red Sox (GCL)	DH	4	16	2	2	0	0	0	1	.125	0	1	1	0	0	0	...
—	Trenton (Eastern)	C	7	26	3	6	1	0	2	3	.231	2	2	0	30	2	0	1.000
Major league totals (7 years)			319	853	110	210	49	3	25	110	.246	67	168	7	1559	114	18	.989

DIVISION SERIES RECORD

Year	Team (League)	Pos.	G	AB	R	H	2B	3B	HR	RBI	Avg.	BB	SO	SB	PO	A	E	Avg.
1995—	Boston (A.L.)..............	C	1	2	0	0	0	0	0	0	.000	0	0	0	6	0	0	1.000

HASSELHOFF, DEREK   P   WHITE SOX

PERSONAL: Born October 10, 1973, in Baltimore. ... 6-2/185. ... Throws right, bats right. ... Full name: Derek Carl Hasselhoff.
HIGH SCHOOL: Chesapeake (Pasadena, Md.).
COLLEGE: Towson State.
TRANSACTIONS/CAREER NOTES: Selected by Chicago White Sox organization in 17th round of free-agent draft (June 1, 1995). ... On Winston-Salem suspended list (April 22-25, 1997).

Year	Team (League)	W	L	Pct.	ERA	G	GS	CG	ShO	Sv.	IP	H	R	ER	BB	SO
1995—	Bristol (Appalachian)..........	7	3	.700	3.66	12	11	0	0	0	66 1/3	66	32	27	14	46
1996—	South Bend (Mid.)...............	6	3	.667	3.02	5	0	0	0	10	47 2/3	46	18	16	17	39
—	Prince William (Caro.)	0	1	.000	5.23	5	0	0	0	1	10 1/3	14	7	6	6	9
1997—	Win.-Salem (Car.)	3	2	.600	1.56	20	0	0	0	3	34 2/3	22	10	6	15	41
—	Birmingham (Southern)	5	2	.714	2.41	18	0	0	0	3	33 2/3	35	10	9	11	22
—	Nashville (A.A.)	1	1	.500	9.82	6	0	0	0	0	7 1/3	9	8	8	7	2

HATTEBERG, SCOTT   C   RED SOX

PERSONAL: Born December 14, 1969, in Salem, Ore. ... 6-1/195. ... Bats left, throws right. ... Full name: Scott Allen Hatteberg. ... Name pronounced HAT-ee-berg.
HIGH SCHOOL: Eisenhower (Yakima, Wash.).
COLLEGE: Washington State.
TRANSACTIONS/CAREER NOTES: Selected by Philadelphia Phillies organization in 12th round of free-agent draft (June 1, 1988); did not sign. ... Selected by Boston Red Sox organization in supplemental round ("sandwich pick" between first and second round, 43rd pick overall) of free-agent draft (June 3, 1991); pick received as part of compensation for Kansas City signing Type A free-agent P Mike Boddicker. ... On disabled list (July 27-August 3, 1992).
STATISTICAL NOTES: Tied for A.L. lead in double plays by catcher with 13 and in passed balls with 17 in 1997.

Year	Team (League)	Pos.	G	AB	R	H	2B	3B	HR	RBI	Avg.	BB	SO	SB	PO	A	E	Avg.
1991—	Winter Haven (FSL)....	C	56	191	21	53	7	3	1	25	.277	22	22	1	261	35	5	.983
—	Lynchburg (Caro.)	C	8	25	4	5	1	0	0	2	.200	7	6	0	35	2	0	1.000
1992—	New Britain (Eastern) .	C	103	297	28	69	13	2	1	30	.232	41	49	1	473	44	11	.979
1993—	New Britain (Eastern) .	C	68	227	35	63	10	2	1	28	.278	42	38	1	410	45	10	.978
—	Pawtucket (Int'l)	C	18	53	6	10	0	0	1	2	.189	6	12	0	131	4	5	.964
1994—	New Britain (Eastern) .	C	20	68	6	18	4	1	1	9	.265	7	9	0	125	14	1	.993
—	Pawtucket (Int'l)	C	78	238	26	56	14	0	7	19	.235	32	49	2	467	36	7	.986
1995—	Pawtucket (Int'l)	C	85	251	36	68	15	1	7	27	.271	40	39	2	446	45	•8	.984
—	Boston (A.L.)..............	C	2	2	1	1	0	0	0	0	.500	0	0	0	4	0	0	1.000
1996—	Pawtucket (Int'l)	C	90	287	52	77	16	0	12	49	.268	58	66	1	566	42	6	.990
—	Boston (A.L.)..............	C	10	11	3	2	1	0	0	0	.182	3	2	0	32	2	0	1.000
1997—	Boston (A.L.)..............	C-DH	114	350	46	97	23	1	10	44	.277	40	70	0	574	46	11	.983
Major league totals (3 years)			126	363	50	100	24	1	10	44	.275	43	72	0	610	48	11	.984

HAUGHT, GARY   P   ATHLETICS

PERSONAL: Born September 29, 1970, in Choctaw, Okla. ... 6-1/180. ... Throws right, bats both. ... Full name: Gary Allen Haught.
HIGH SCHOOL: Choctaw (Okla.).
COLLEGE: Southwestern Louisiana.
TRANSACTIONS/CAREER NOTES: Selected by Oakland Athletics organization in 22nd round of free-agent draft (June 1, 1992).

Year	Team (League)	W	L	Pct.	ERA	G	GS	CG	ShO	Sv.	IP	H	R	ER	BB	SO
1992—	S. Oregon (N'west)..........	8	2	.800	1.98	19	4	0	0	2	68 1/3	58	18	15	14	69
1993—	Madison (Midwest)	7	1	.875	2.58	17	12	2	0	0	83 2/3	62	27	24	29	75
—	Modesto (California)	0	1	.000	5.09	12	0	0	0	0	23	25	14	13	17	15
1994—	Modesto (California)	4	3	.571	4.33	39	1	0	0	2	70 2/3	66	35	34	26	52
1995—	Modesto (California)	9	5	.643	2.60	34	4	0	0	4	86 2/3	76	29	25	24	81
—	Huntsville (Southern)	1	1	.500	4.30	9	3	0	0	0	23	23	14	11	8	20
1996—	Huntsville (Southern)	3	1	.600	3.90	45	0	0	0	4	67	67	33	29	24	52
1997—	Huntsville (Southern)	0	1	.000	5.59	6	0	0	0	0	9 2/3	15	6	6	2	6
—	Edmonton (PCL)	1	1	.500	3.59	30	2	0	0	11	42 2/3	37	20	17	13	35
—	Oakland (A.L.)	0	0	...	7.15	6	0	0	0	0	11 1/3	12	9	9	6	11
Major league totals (1 year)........		0	0	...	7.15	6	0	0	0	0	11 1/3	12	9	9	6	11

H

PERSONAL: Born December 21, 1972, in Gary, Ind. ... 6-5/201. ... Throws right, bats right.
HIGH SCHOOL: West Side (Gary, Ind.).
TRANSACTIONS/CAREER NOTES: Selected by Minnesota Twins organization in seventh round of free-agent draft (June 3, 1991).
STATISTICAL NOTES: Tied for A.L. lead with three balks in 1997.

Year	Team (League)	W	L	Pct.	ERA	G	GS	CG	ShO	Sv.	IP	H	R	ER	BB	SO
1991—	GC Twins (GCL)	4	3	.571	4.75	11	11	0	0	0	55	62	34	29	26	47
1992—	GC Twins (GCL)	3	2	.600	3.22	6	6	1	0	0	36⅓	36	19	13	10	35
	—Elizabethton (Appal.)	0	1	.000	3.38	5	5	1	0	0	26⅔	21	12	10	11	36
1993—	Fort Wayne (Midw.)	•15	5	.750	*2.06	26	23	4	•3	0	157⅓	110	53	36	41	*179
1994—	Fort Myers (Fla. St.)	4	0	1.000	2.33	6	6	1	1	0	38⅔	32	10	10	6	36
	—Nashville (Southern)	9	2	*.818	2.33	11	11	1	0	0	73⅓	50	23	19	28	53
	—Salt Lake (PCL)	5	4	.556	4.08	12	12	1	0	0	81⅔	92	42	37	33	37
1995—	Minnesota (A.L.)	2	3	.400	8.67	6	6	1	0	0	27	39	29	26	12	9
	—Salt Lake (PCL)	9	7	.563	3.55	22	22	4	1	0	144⅓	150	63	57	40	74
1996—	Minnesota (A.L.)	1	1	.500	8.20	7	6	0	0	0	26⅓	42	24	24	9	24
	—Salt Lake (PCL)	9	8	.529	3.92	20	20	4	1	0	137⅔	138	66	60	31	99
1997—	Salt Lake (PCL)	9	4	.692	5.45	14	13	2	1	0	76	100	53	46	16	53
	—Minnesota (A.L.)	6	12	.333	5.84	20	20	0	0	0	103⅓	134	71	67	47	58
Major league totals (3 years)		9	16	.360	6.72	33	32	1	0	0	156⅔	215	124	117	68	91

PERSONAL: Born May 29, 1965, in Hattiesburg, Miss. ... 6-0/215. ... Bats right, throws right. ... Full name: Charles Dewayne Hayes.
HIGH SCHOOL: Forrest County Agricultural (Brooklyn, Miss.).
TRANSACTIONS/CAREER NOTES: Selected by San Francisco Giants organization in fourth round of free-agent draft (June 6, 1983). ... On disabled list (July 20, 1983-remainder of season). ... Traded by Giants with P Dennis Cook and P Terry Mulholland to Philadelphia Phillies for P Steve Bedrosian and a player to be named later (June 18, 1989); Giants organization acquired IF Rick Parker to complete deal (August 7, 1989). ... Traded by Phillies to New York Yankees (February 19, 1992), completing deal in which Yankees traded P Darrin Chapin to Phillies for a player to be named later (January 8, 1992). ... Selected by Colorado Rockies in first round (third pick overall) of expansion draft (November 17, 1992). ... On suspended list (August 10-13, 1993). ... Granted free agency (December 23, 1994). ... Signed by Phillies (April 6, 1995). ... Granted free agency (November 2, 1995). ... Signed by Pittsburgh Pirates (December 28, 1995). ... Traded by Pirates to Yankees for a player to be named later (August 30, 1996); Pirates acquired P Chris Corn to complete deal (August 31, 1996). ... Traded by Yankees with cash to Giants for OF Chris Singleton and P Alberto Castillo (November 11, 1997).
STATISTICAL NOTES: Led Texas League third basemen with 27 double plays in 1986. ... Led Texas League third basemen with 334 total chances in 1987. ... Led Pacific Coast League in grounding into double plays with 19 in 1988. ... Led N.L. third basemen with 324 assists and tied for lead with 465 total chances in 1990. ... Tied for A.L. lead in double plays by third baseman with 29 in 1992. ... Tied for N.L. lead in grounding into double plays with 25 in 1993. ... Led N.L. in grounding into double plays with 23 in 1995. ... Career major league grand slams: 3.

							BATTING								FIELDING		
Year	Team (League)	Pos.	G	AB	R	H	2B	3B	HR	RBI	Avg.	BB	SO	SB	PO	A	E	Avg.
1983—	Great Falls (Pio.)	3B-OF	34	111	9	29	4	2	0	9	.261	7	26	1	13	32	9	.833
1984—	Clinton (Midwest)	3B	116	392	41	96	17	2	2	51	.245	34	110	4	68	216	28	.910
1985—	Fresno (California)	3B	131	467	73	132	17	2	4	68	.283	56	95	7	*100	233	18	*.949
1986—	Shreveport (Texas)	3B	121	434	52	107	23	2	5	45	.247	28	83	1	89	*259	25	.933
1987—	Shreveport (Texas)	3B	128	487	66	148	33	3	14	75	.304	26	76	5	*100	*212	22	*.934
1988—	Phoenix (PCL)	OF-3B	131	492	71	151	26	4	7	71	.307	34	91	4	206	100	23	.930
	—San Francisco (N.L.)	OF-3B	7	11	0	1	0	0	0	0	.091	0	3	0	5	0	0	1.000
1989—	Phoenix (PCL)	3-O-1-S-2	61	229	25	65	15	1	7	27	.284	15	48	5	76	76	8	.950
	—San Francisco (N.L.)	3B	3	5	0	1	0	0	0	0	.200	0	1	0	2	1	0	1.000
	—Scran./W.B. (Int'l)■	3B	7	27	4	11	3	1	1	3	.407	0	3	0	8	8	0	1.000
	—Philadelphia (N.L.)	3B	84	299	26	77	15	1	8	43	.258	11	49	3	49	173	22	.910
1990—	Philadelphia (N.L.)	3B-1B-2B	152	561	56	145	20	0	10	57	.258	28	91	4	151	†329	20	.960
1991—	Philadelphia (N.L.)	3B-SS	142	460	34	106	23	1	12	53	.230	16	75	3	88	240	15	.956
1992—	New York (A.L.)■	3B-1B	142	509	52	131	19	2	18	66	.257	28	100	3	125	249	13	.966
1993—	Colorado (N.L.)■	3B-SS	157	573	89	175	*45	2	25	98	.305	43	82	11	123	292	20	.954
1994—	Colorado (N.L.)	3B	113	423	46	122	23	4	10	50	.288	36	71	3	72	216	17	.944
1995—	Philadelphia (N.L.)■	3B	141	529	58	146	30	3	11	85	.276	50	88	5	•104	264	14	.963
1996—	Pittsburgh (N.L.)■	3B	128	459	51	114	21	2	10	62	.248	36	78	6	66	275	18	.950
	—New York (A.L.)■	3B	20	67	7	19	3	0	2	13	.284	1	12	0	14	30	0	1.000
1997—	New York (A.L.)	3B-2B	100	353	39	91	16	0	11	53	.258	40	66	3	67	169	13	.948
American League totals (3 years)			262	929	98	241	38	2	31	132	.259	69	178	6	206	448	26	.962
National League totals (8 years)			927	3320	360	887	177	13	86	448	.267	220	538	35	660	1790	126	.951
Major league totals (10 years)			1189	4249	458	1128	215	15	117	580	.265	289	716	41	866	2238	152	.953

DIVISION SERIES RECORD

							BATTING								FIELDING		
Year	Team (League)	Pos.	G	AB	R	H	2B	3B	HR	RBI	Avg.	BB	SO	SB	PO	A	E	Avg.
1996—	New York (A.L.)	3B-DH	3	5	0	1	0	0	0	1	.200	0	0	0	1	3	0	1.000
1997—	New York (A.L.)	3B-2B	5	15	0	5	0	0	0	1	.333	0	2	0	3	9	3	.800
Division series totals (2 years)			8	20	0	6	0	0	0	2	.300	0	2	0	4	12	3	.842

CHAMPIONSHIP SERIES RECORD

							BATTING								FIELDING		
Year	Team (League)	Pos.	G	AB	R	H	2B	3B	HR	RBI	Avg.	BB	SO	SB	PO	A	E	Avg.
1996—	New York (A.L.)	PH-3B-DH	4	7	0	1	0	0	0	0	.143	2	2	0	0	3	0	1.000

WORLD SERIES RECORD

NOTES: Member of World Series championship team (1996).

Year Team (League)	Pos.	G	AB	R	H	2B	3B	HR	RBI	Avg.	BB	SO	SB	PO	A	E	Avg.
1996— New York (A.L.).........3B-PH-DH-1B		5	16	2	3	0	0	0	1	.188	1	5	0	3	6	0	1.000

HAYNES, JIMMY — P — ATHLETICS

PERSONAL: Born September 5, 1972, in La Grange, Ga. ... 6-4/185. ... Throws right, bats right. ... Full name: Jimmy Wayne Haynes.
HIGH SCHOOL: Troup (La Grange, Ga.).
TRANSACTIONS/CAREER NOTES: Selected by Baltimore Orioles organization in seventh round of free-agent draft (June 3, 1991). ... Traded by Orioles with a player to be named later to Oakland Athletics for OF Geronimo Berroa (June 27, 1997); A's acquired P Mark Seaver to complete deal (September 2, 1997).

Year Team (League)	W	L	Pct.	ERA	G	GS	CG	ShO	Sv.	IP	H	R	ER	BB	SO
1991— GC Orioles (GCL)	3	2	.600	1.60	14	8	1	0	2	62	44	27	11	21	67
1992— Kane County (Midwest)	7	11	.389	2.56	24	24	4	0	0	144	131	66	41	45	141
1993— Frederick (Carolina)	12	8	.600	3.03	27	27	2	1	0	172 1/3	139	73	58	61	174
1994— Bowie (Eastern)	13	8	.619	2.90	25	25	5	1	0	173 2/3	154	67	56	46	*177
— Rochester (Int'l)	1	0	1.000	6.75	3	3	0	0	0	13 1/3	20	12	10	6	14
1995— Rochester (Int'l)	•12	8	.600	3.29	26	25	3	1	0	167	162	77	61	49	*140
— Baltimore (A.L.)	2	1	.667	2.25	4	3	0	0	0	24	11	6	6	12	22
1996— Baltimore (A.L.)	3	6	.333	8.29	26	11	0	0	1	89	122	84	82	58	65
— Rochester (Int'l)	1	1	.500	5.65	5	5	0	0	0	28 2/3	31	19	18	18	24
1997— Rochester (Int'l)	5	4	.556	3.44	16	16	2	1	0	102	89	49	39	55	113
— Edmonton (PCL)■	0	2	.000	4.85	5	5	0	0	0	29 2/3	36	22	16	11	24
— Oakland (A.L.)	3	6	.333	4.42	13	13	0	0	0	73 1/3	74	38	36	40	65
Major league totals (3 years)	8	13	.381	5.99	43	27	0	0	1	186 1/3	207	128	124	110	152

HEFLIN, BRONSON — P — PHILLIES

PERSONAL: Born August 29, 1971, in Clarksville, Tenn. ... 6-3/200. ... Throws right, bats right. ... Full name: Bronson Wayne Heflin.
HIGH SCHOOL: Donnelson Christian Academy (Nashville).
JUNIOR COLLEGE: Central Florida Community College.
COLLEGE: Tennessee.
TRANSACTIONS/CAREER NOTES: Selected by New York Yankees organization in 45th round of free-agent (June 3, 1991); did not sign. ... Selected by Philadelphia Phillies organization in 37th round of free-agent draft (June 2, 1994). ... On disabled list (April 21-June 13, 1997).

Year Team (League)	W	L	Pct.	ERA	G	GS	CG	ShO	Sv.	IP	H	R	ER	BB	SO
1994— Batavia (N.Y.-Penn)	6	5	.545	3.58	14	13	1	0	0	83	85	38	33	20	71
1995— Clearwater (Fla. St.)	2	3	.400	2.95	57	0	0	0	0	61	52	25	20	21	84
— Reading (Eastern)	0	0	...	0.00	1	0	0	0	0	1	0	0	0	1	2
1996— Reading (Eastern)	2	2	.500	5.22	25	0	0	0	1	29 1/3	37	20	17	15	27
— Scran./W.B. (Int'l)	4	0	1.000	2.61	30	0	0	0	12	38	25	11	11	3	23
— Philadelphia (N.L.)	0	0	...	6.75	3	0	0	0	0	6 2/3	11	7	5	3	4
1997— Scran./W.B. (Int'l)	1	1	.500	2.28	35	0	0	0	13	43 1/3	29	17	11	25	36
Major league totals (1 year)	0	0	...	6.75	3	0	0	0	0	6 2/3	11	7	5	3	4

HEISERMAN, RICK — P — CARDINALS

PERSONAL: Born February 22, 1973, in Atlantic, Iowa. ... 6-7/225. ... Throws right, bats right. ... Full name: Richard M. Heiserman.
HIGH SCHOOL: Millard South (Omaha, Neb.).
COLLEGE: Creighton.
TRANSACTIONS/CAREER NOTES: Selected by Cleveland Indians organization in third round of free-agent draft (June 2, 1994). ... Traded by Indians with C Pepe McNeal and IF David Bell to St. Louis Cardinals for P Ken Hill (July 27, 1995).

Year Team (League)	W	L	Pct.	ERA	G	GS	CG	ShO	Sv.	IP	H	R	ER	BB	SO
1994— Watertown (NYP)	1	0	1.000	2.31	7	0	0	0	0	11 2/3	6	3	3	5	6
1995— Kinston (Carolina)	9	3	.750	3.74	19	19	1	0	0	113	97	55	47	42	86
— St. Petersburg (FSL)■	2	3	.400	5.46	6	5	0	0	0	28	28	18	17	11	18
1996— St. Petersburg (FSL)	10	8	.556	3.24	26	26	1	1	0	155 1/3	168	68	56	41	104
1997— Arkansas (Texas)	5	8	.385	4.17	34	20	1	•1	4	131 2/3	151	73	61	36	90
— Louisville (A.A.)	0	0	...	4.50	1	0	0	0	0	2	2	1	1	1	0

HELD, DAN — 1B — PHILLIES

PERSONAL: Born August 29, 1971, in Hartford, Wis. ... 6-1/200. ... Bats right, throws right. ... Full name: Daniel Richard Held.
HIGH SCHOOL: Hartford (Wis.).
JUNIOR COLLEGE: Waukesha County Technical (Wis.).
TRANSACTIONS/CAREER NOTES: Selected by Philadelphia Phillies organization in 42nd round of free-agent draft (June 3, 1993).
STATISTICAL NOTES: Led Eastern League in being hit by pitch with 22 in 1996. ... Led Eastern League first basemen with 111 double plays in 1996. ... Led Eastern League in being hit by pitch with 18 in 1997.

Year Team (League)	Pos.	G	AB	R	H	2B	3B	HR	RBI	Avg.	BB	SO	SB	PO	A	E	Avg.
1993— Batavia (NY-Penn)	1B	45	151	18	31	8	1	3	16	.205	16	40	2	356	22	5	.987
1994— Spartanburg (SAL)	1B	130	484	69	123	32	1	18	69	.254	52	119	2	681	37	8	.989
1995— Clearwater (FSL)	1B	•134	489	82	133	*35	1	*21	82	.272	56	127	2	1115	72	12	.990
— Reading (Eastern)	1B-OF	2	4	2	2	1	0	1	3	.500	2	1	1	8	0	0	1.000
1996— Reading (Eastern)	1B	136	497	77	121	17	5	26	92	.243	60	141	3	1115	81	*12	.990
1997— Reading (Eastern)	1B-3B	138	525	80	143	31	4	26	86	.272	42	116	1	1127	86	8	.993

HELLING, RICK — P — RANGERS

PERSONAL: Born December 15, 1970, in Devils Lake, N.D. ... 6-3/220. ... Throws right, bats right. ... Full name: Ricky Allen Helling.
HIGH SCHOOL: Shanley (Fargo, N.D.), then Lakota (N.D.).
JUNIOR COLLEGE: Kishwaukee College (Ill.).
COLLEGE: North Dakota, then Stanford.
TRANSACTIONS/CAREER NOTES: Selected by New York Mets organization in 50th round of free-agent draft (June 4, 1990); did not sign. ... Selected by Texas Rangers organization in first round (22nd pick overall) of free-agent draft (June 1, 1992). ... Traded by Rangers to Florida Marlins (September 3, 1996); completing deal in which Marlins traded P John Burkett to Rangers for P Ryan Dempster and a player to be named later (August 8, 1996). ... Traded by Marlins to Rangers for P Ed Vosberg (August 12, 1997).
STATISTICAL NOTES: Pitched 4-0 no-hit victory against Nashville (August 13, 1996).
MISCELLANEOUS: Member of 1992 U.S. Olympic baseball team.

Year Team (League)	W	L	Pct.	ERA	G	GS	CG	ShO	Sv.	IP	H	R	ER	BB	SO
1992— Charlotte (Fla. St.)	1	1	.500	2.29	3	3	0	0	0	19²/₃	13	5	5	4	20
1993— Tulsa (Texas)	12	8	.600	3.60	26	26	2	•2	0	177¹/₃	150	76	71	46	*188
— Oklahoma City (A.A.)	1	1	.500	1.64	2	2	1	0	0	11	5	3	2	3	17
1994— Texas (A.L.)	3	2	.600	5.88	9	9	1	1	0	52	62	34	34	18	25
— Oklahoma City (A.A.)	4	12	.250	5.78	20	20	2	0	0	132¹/₃	153	93	85	43	85
1995— Texas (A.L.)	0	2	.000	6.57	3	3	0	0	0	12¹/₃	17	11	9	8	5
— Oklahoma City (A.A.)	4	8	.333	5.33	20	20	3	0	0	109²/₃	132	73	65	41	80
1996— Oklahoma City (A.A.)	12	4	.750	2.96	23	22	2	1	0	140	124	54	46	38	157
— Florida (N.L.)■	1	2	.333	7.52	6	2	0	0	0	20¹/₃	23	17	17	9	16
1997— Florida (N.L.)	2	1	.667	1.95	5	4	0	0	0	27²/₃	14	6	6	7	26
— Texas (A.L.)■	2	6	.250	4.38	31	8	0	0	0	76	61	38	37	48	53
	3	3	.500	4.58	10	8	0	0	0	55	47	29	28	21	46
A.L. totals (4 years)	7	9	.438	5.67	28	22	1	1	0	139²/₃	149	91	88	56	92
N.L. totals (2 years)	4	7	.364	3.73	36	12	0	0	0	103²/₃	75	44	43	55	79
Major league totals (4 years)	11	16	.407	4.85	64	34	1	1	0	243¹/₃	224	135	131	111	171

HELMS, WES — 3B — BRAVES

PERSONAL: Born May 12, 1976, in Gastonia, N.C. ... 6-4/210. ... Bats right, throws right. ... Full name: Wesley Ray Helms.
HIGH SCHOOL: Ashbrook (Gastonia, N.C.).
TRANSACTIONS/CAREER NOTES: Selected by Atlanta Braves organization in 10th round of free-agent draft (June 2, 1994).
STATISTICAL NOTES: Led South Atlantic League third basemen with 25 double plays in 1995.

Year Team (League)	Pos.	G	AB	R	H	2B	3B	HR	RBI	Avg.	BB	SO	SB	PO	A	E	Avg.
1994— GC Braves (GCL)	3B	56	184	22	49	15	1	4	29	.266	22	36	6	•47	93	20	.875
1995— Macon (S. Atl.)	3B	136	*539	89	149	32	1	11	85	.276	50	107	2	91	*269	40	.900
1996— Durham (Carolina)	3B	67	258	40	83	19	2	13	54	.322	12	51	1	40	133	15	.920
— Greenville (Southern)	3B	64	231	24	59	13	2	4	22	.255	13	48	2	50	96	12	.924
1997— Richmond (Int'l)	3B	32	110	11	21	4	0	3	15	.191	10	34	1	18	65	9	.902
— Greenville (Southern)	3B	86	314	50	93	14	1	11	44	.296	33	50	3	60	147	11	.950

HELTON, TODD — 1B — ROCKIES

PERSONAL: Born August 20, 1973, in Knoxville, Tenn. ... 6-2/190. ... Bats left, throws left. ... Full name: Todd Lynn Helton.
HIGH SCHOOL: Knoxville Central (Tenn.).
COLLEGE: Tennessee.
TRANSACTIONS/CAREER NOTES: Selected by San Diego Padres organization in second round of free-agent draft (June 1, 1992); did not sign. ... Selected by Colorado Rockies organization in first round (eighth pick overall) of free-agent draft (June 3, 1995). ... On New Haven disabled list (June 15-24, 1996).

Year Team (League)	Pos.	G	AB	R	H	2B	3B	HR	RBI	Avg.	BB	SO	SB	PO	A	E	Avg.
1995— Asheville (S. Atl.)	1B	54	201	24	51	11	1	1	15	.254	25	32	1	388	21	4	.990
1996— New Haven (Eastern)	1B	93	319	46	106	24	2	7	51	.332	51	37	2	788	61	5	.994
— Colo. Springs (PCL)	1B-OF	21	71	13	25	4	1	2	13	.352	11	12	0	144	17	2	.988
1997— Colo. Springs (PCL)	1B-OF	99	392	87	138	31	2	16	88	.352	61	68	3	622	64	9	.987
— Colorado (N.L.)	OF-1B	35	93	13	26	2	1	5	11	.280	8	11	0	84	12	0	1.000
Major league totals (1 year)		35	93	13	26	2	1	5	11	.280	8	11	0	84	12	0	1.000

HEMPHILL, BRET — C — ANGELS

PERSONAL: Born December 17, 1971, in Santa Clara, Calif. ... 6-3/200. ... Bats both, throws right.
HIGH SCHOOL: Cupertino (Calif.).
COLLEGE: Cal State Fullerton.
TRANSACTIONS/CAREER NOTES: Selected by Houston Astros organization in 29th round of free-agent draft (June 4, 1990); did not sign. ... Selected by California Angels in 14th round of free-agent draft (June 2, 1994). ... Angels franchise renamed Anaheim Angels for 1997 season. ... On disabled list (June 12-29 and August 8, 1997-remainder of season).
STATISTICAL NOTES: Led Northwest League catchers with 534 putouts, 68 assists and 613 total chances and tied for lead in double plays with four in 1994. ... Led California League catchers with 989 total chances in 1996.

Year Team (League)	Pos.	G	AB	R	H	2B	3B	HR	RBI	Avg.	BB	SO	SB	PO	A	E	Avg.
1994— Boise (Northwest)	C-1B	71	252	44	74	16	1	3	36	.294	40	53	1	†548	†69	11	.982
1995— Cedar Rap. (Midw.)	C	72	234	36	59	11	1	8	28	.252	21	54	0	429	69	4	.992
— Lake Elsinore (Calif.)	C	45	146	12	29	7	0	1	17	.199	18	36	2	354	47	10	.976
1996— Lake Elsinore (Calif.)	C	108	399	64	105	21	3	17	64	.263	52	93	4	*879	*92	18	.982
1997— Midland (Texas)	C	78	266	46	82	15	2	10	63	.308	47	56	0	425	48	7	.985

H

PERSONAL: Born December 25, 1958, in Chicago. ... 5-10/190. ... Bats right, throws left. ... Full name: Rickey Henley Henderson.

HIGH SCHOOL: Technical (Oakland).

TRANSACTIONS/CAREER NOTES: Selected by Oakland Athletics organization in fourth round of free-agent draft (June 8, 1976). ... Traded by A's with P Bert Bradley and cash to New York Yankees for OF Stan Javier, P Jay Howell, P Jose Rijo, P Eric Plunk and P Tim Birtsas (December 5, 1984). ... On New York disabled list (March 30-April 22, 1985); included rehabilitation assignment to Fort Lauderdale (April 19-22). ... On disabled list (June 5-29 and July 26-September 1, 1987). ... Traded by Yankees to A's for P Greg Cadaret, P Eric Plunk and OF Luis Polonia (June 21, 1989). ... Granted free agency (November 13, 1989). ... Re-signed by A's (November 28, 1989). ... On disabled list (April 12-27, 1991; May 28-June 17 and June 30-July 16, 1992). ... Traded by A's to Toronto Blue Jays for P Steve Karsay and a player to be named later (July 31, 1993); A's acquired OF Jose Herrera to complete deal (August 6, 1993). ... Granted free agency (October 29, 1993). ... Signed by A's (December 17, 1993). ... On disabled list (May 11-27, 1994). ... Granted free agency (October 30, 1995). ... Signed by San Diego Padres (December 29, 1995). ... On San Diego disabled list (May 9-24, 1997). ... Traded by Padres to Anaheim Angels for P Ryan Hancock, P Stevenson Agosto and a player to be named later (August 13, 1997); Padres acquired 3B George Arias to complete deal (August 19, 1997). ... Granted free agency (October 27, 1997). ... Signed by A's (January 22, 1998).

RECORDS: Holds major league career records for most stolen bases—1,231; and most home runs as leadoff batter—72. ... Holds major league single-season records for most stolen bases—130 (1982); and most times caught stealing—42 (1982). ... Holds major league record for most years leading league in stolen bases—11. ... Holds A.L. career records for most stolen bases—1,165; most home runs as leadoff batter—68; and most times caught stealing—269. ... Holds A.L. records for most years with 50 or more stolen bases—11; and most consecutive years with 50 or more stolen bases—7 (1980-86). ... Shares A.L. single-season record for fewest times caught stealing (50 or more stolen bases)—8 (1993). ... Shares A.L. record for most stolen bases in two consecutive games—7 (July 3 [4], 15 innings, and 4 [3], 1983).

HONORS: Named outfielder on THE SPORTING NEWS A.L. All-Star team (1981, 1985 and 1990). ... Named outfielder on THE SPORTING NEWS A.L. Silver Slugger team (1981, 1985 and 1990). ... Won A.L. Gold Glove as outfielder (1981). ... Won THE SPORTING NEWS Silver Shoe Award (1982). ... Won THE SPORTING NEWS Golden Shoe Award (1983). ... Named A.L. Most Valuable Player by Baseball Writers' Association of America (1990).

STATISTICAL NOTES: Led California League in caught stealing with 22 in 1977. ... Led Eastern League in caught stealing with 28 in 1978. ... Led Eastern League outfielders with four double plays in 1978. ... Led A.L. in caught stealing with 26 in 1980, 22 in 1981, 42 in 1982, 19 in 1983 and tied for lead with 18 in 1986. ... Led A.L. outfielders with 341 total chances in 1981. ... Tied for A.L. lead in double plays by outfielder with five in 1988. ... Led A.L. with 77 stolen bases and 126 bases on balls in 1989. ... Tied for A.L. lead with 113 runs scored in 1989. ... Led A.L. with .439 on-base percentage in 1990. ... Career major league grand slams: 1.

MISCELLANEOUS: Holds Oakland Athletics all-time records for most runs (1,169), most hits (1,640), most doubles (273), most stolen bases (801) and highest batting average (.293). ... Holds New York Yankees all-time record for most stolen bases (326).

					BATTING									FIELDING			
Year Team (League)	Pos.	G	AB	R	H	2B	3B	HR	RBI	Avg.	BB	SO	SB	PO	A	E	Avg.
1976— Boise (Northwest)	OF	46	140	34	47	13	2	3	23	.336	33	32	29	99	3	*12	.895
1977— Modesto (California)	OF	134	481	120	166	18	4	11	69	.345	104	67	*95	278	15	*20	.936
1978— Jersey City (East.)	OF	133	455	81	141	14	4	0	34	.310	83	67	*81	305	•15	7	.979
1979— Ogden (PCL)	OF	71	259	66	80	11	8	3	26	.309	53	41	44	149	6	6	.963
— Oakland (A.L.)	OF	89	351	49	96	13	3	1	26	.274	34	39	33	215	5	6	.973
1980— Oakland (A.L.)	OF-DH	158	591	111	179	22	4	9	53	.303	117	54	*100	407	15	7	.984
1981— Oakland (A.L.)	OF	108	423	*89	*135	18	7	6	35	.319	64	68	*56	*327	7	7	.979
1982— Oakland (A.L.)	OF-DH	149	536	119	143	24	4	10	51	.267	*116	94	*130	379	2	9	.977
1983— Oakland (A.L.)	OF-DH	145	513	105	150	25	7	9	48	.292	*103	80	*108	349	9	3	.992
1984— Oakland (A.L.)	OF	142	502	113	147	27	4	16	58	.293	86	81	*66	341	7	11	.969
1985— Fort Laud. (FSL)■	OF	3	6	5	1	0	1	0	3	.167	5	2	1	6	0	0	1.000
— New York (A.L.)	OF-DH	143	547	*146	172	28	5	24	72	.314	99	65	*80	439	7	9	.980
1986— New York (A.L.)	OF-DH	153	608	*130	160	31	5	28	74	.263	89	81	*87	426	4	6	.986
1987— New York (A.L.)	OF-DH	95	358	78	104	17	3	17	37	.291	80	52	41	189	3	4	.980
1988— New York (A.L.)	OF	140	554	118	169	30	2	6	50	.305	82	54	*93	320	7	12	.965
1989— New York (A.L.)	OF	65	235	41	58	13	1	3	22	.247	56	29	25	144	3	1	.993
— Oakland (A.L.)■	OF-DH	85	306	§72	90	13	2	9	35	.294	§70	39	§52	191	3	3	.985
1990— Oakland (A.L.)	OF-DH	136	489	*119	159	33	3	28	61	.325	97	60	*65	289	5	5	.983
1991— Oakland (A.L.)	OF-DH	134	470	105	126	17	1	18	57	.268	98	73	*58	249	10	8	.970
1992— Oakland (A.L.)	OF-DH	117	396	77	112	18	3	15	46	.283	95	56	48	231	9	4	.984
1993— Oakland (A.L.)	OF-DH	90	318	77	104	19	1	17	47	.327	85	46	31	182	5	5	.974
— Toronto (A.L.)■	OF	44	163	37	35	3	1	4	12	.215	35	19	22	76	1	2	.975
1994— Oakland (A.L.)■	OF-DH	87	296	66	77	13	0	6	20	.260	72	45	22	166	4	4	.977
1995— Oakland (A.L.)	OF-DH	112	407	67	122	31	1	9	54	.300	72	66	32	162	5	2	.988
1996— San Diego (N.L.)■	OF	148	465	110	112	17	2	9	29	.241	125	90	37	228	3	6	.975
1997— San Diego (N.L.)	OF	88	288	63	79	11	0	6	27	.274	71	62	29	160	4	7	.959
— Anaheim (A.L.)■	DH-OF	32	115	21	21	3	0	2	7	.183	26	23	16	26	0	0	1.000
American League totals (18 years)		2224	8178	1740	2359	398	57	237	865	.288	1576	1124	1165	5108	111	108	.980
National League totals (2 years)		236	753	173	191	28	2	15	56	.254	196	152	66	388	7	13	.968
Major league totals (19 years)		2460	8931	1913	2550	426	59	252	921	.286	1772	1276	1231	5496	118	121	.979

DIVISION SERIES RECORD

					BATTING									FIELDING			
Year Team (League)	Pos.	G	AB	R	H	2B	3B	HR	RBI	Avg.	BB	SO	SB	PO	A	E	Avg.
1981— Oakland (A.L.)	OF	3	11	3	2	0	0	0	0	.182	2	0	2	8	0	0	1.000
1996— San Diego (N.L.)	OF	3	12	2	4	0	0	1	1	.333	2	3	0	4	0	0	1.000
Division series totals (2 years)		6	23	5	6	0	0	1	1	.261	4	3	2	12	0	0	1.000

CHAMPIONSHIP SERIES RECORD

RECORDS: Holds career record for most stolen bases—16. ... Holds single-series record for most stolen bases—8 (1989). ... Holds single-game record for most stolen bases—4 (October 4, 1989). ... Shares records for most at-bats in one inning—2; most hits in one inning—2; most singles in one inning—2 (October 6, 1990, ninth inning); and most stolen bases in one inning—2 (October 4, 1989, fourth and seventh innings). ... Shares single-series record for most runs—8 (1989). ... Shares A.L. career record for most bases on balls received—17. ... Shares A.L. single-game record for most at-bats—6 (October 5, 1993).

NOTES: Named A.L. Championship Series Most Valuable Player (1989).

H

Year Team (League)	Pos.	G	AB	R	H	2B	3B	HR	RBI	Avg.	BB	SO	SB	PO	A	E	Avg.
						BATTING								FIELDING			
1981—Oakland (A.L.)	OF	3	11	0	4	2	1	0	1	.364	1	2	2	6	0	1	.857
1989—Oakland (A.L.)	OF	5	15	8	6	1	1	2	5	.400	7	0	8	13	0	1	.929
1990—Oakland (A.L.)	OF	4	17	1	5	0	0	0	3	.294	1	2	2	10	0	1	1.000
1992—Oakland (A.L.)	OF	6	23	5	6	0	0	0	1	.261	4	4	2	15	0	3	.833
1993—Toronto (A.L.)	OF	6	25	4	3	2	0	0	0	.120	4	5	2	9	0	1	.900
Championship series totals (5 years)		24	91	18	24	5	2	2	10	.264	17	13	16	53	0	6	.898

WORLD SERIES RECORD

RECORDS: Shares single-game record for most at-bats—6 (October 28, 1989).
NOTES: Member of World Series championship teams (1989 and 1993).

Year Team (League)	Pos.	G	AB	R	H	2B	3B	HR	RBI	Avg.	BB	SO	SB	PO	A	E	Avg.
						BATTING								FIELDING			
1989—Oakland (A.L.)	OF	4	19	4	9	1	2	1	3	.474	2	2	3	9	0	0	1.000
1990—Oakland (A.L.)	OF	4	15	2	5	2	0	1	3	.333	3	4	3	12	1	0	1.000
1993—Toronto (A.L.)	OF	6	22	6	5	2	0	0	2	.227	5	2	1	8	0	0	1.000
World Series totals (3 years)		14	56	12	19	5	2	2	6	.339	10	8	7	29	1	0	1.000

ALL-STAR GAME RECORD

RECORDS: Shares single-game record for most singles—3 (July 13, 1982).

Year League	Pos.	AB	R	H	2B	3B	HR	RBI	Avg.	BB	SO	SB	PO	A	E	Avg.
					BATTING								FIELDING			
1980—American	OF	1	0	0	0	0	0	0	.000	0	1	0	0	0	0	...
1982—American	OF	4	1	3	0	0	0	0	.750	0	0	1	3	0	1	.750
1983—American	OF	1	0	0	0	0	0	1	.000	0	0	0	0	0	0	...
1984—American	OF	2	0	0	0	0	0	0	.000	0	0	0	0	0	0	...
1985—American	OF	3	1	1	0	0	0	0	.333	0	1	1	1	0	0	1.000
1986—American	OF	3	0	0	0	0	0	0	.000	0	1	0	2	0	0	1.000
1987—American	OF	3	0	1	0	0	0	0	.333	0	0	0	0	0	0	...
1988—American	OF	2	0	1	0	0	0	0	.500	1	0	0	1	0	0	1.000
1990—American	OF	3	0	0	0	0	0	0	.000	0	1	0	1	0	0	1.000
1991—American	OF	2	1	1	0	0	0	0	.500	0	0	0	2	0	0	...
All-Star Game totals (10 years)		24	3	7	0	0	0	1	.292	1	4	2	9	0	1	.900

HENLEY, BOB   C   EXPOS

PERSONAL: Born January 30, 1973, in Mobile, Ala. ... 6-2/190. ... Throws right, bats right. ... Full name: Robert Clifton Henley.
HIGH SCHOOL: Mobile County (Grand Bay, Ala.).
JUNIOR COLLEGE: Okaloosa-Walton Community College (Fla.).
TRANSACTIONS/CAREER NOTES: Selected by Montreal Expos organization in 26th round of free-agent draft (June 13, 1991). ... On Gulf Coast Expos disabled list (June 18-August 31, 1992). ... On disabled list (July 20-30 and July 31, 1997-remainder of season).
STATISTICAL NOTES: Led South Atlantic League catchers with nine double plays in 1995. ... Tied for Eastern League lead with 11 double plays by catcher in 1996.

Year Team (League)	Pos.	G	AB	R	H	2B	3B	HR	RBI	Avg.	BB	SO	SB	PO	A	E	Avg.
						BATTING								FIELDING			
1992—							Did not play.										
1993—Jamestown (NYP)	C	60	206	25	53	10	4	7	29	.257	20	60	0	143	36	4	.978
1994—Burl. (Midw.)	C-1B	98	346	72	104	20	1	20	67	.301	49	91	1	322	64	11	.972
1995—Albany (S. Atl.)	C	102	335	45	94	20	1	3	46	.281	83	57	1	684	*111	•14	.983
1996—Harrisburg (Eastern)	C	103	289	33	66	12	1	3	27	.228	70	78	1	565	*92	9	.986
1997—Harrisburg (Eastern)	C	79	280	41	85	19	0	12	49	.304	32	40	5	574	77	3	*.995

HENRIQUEZ, OSCAR   P   MARLINS

PERSONAL: Born January 28, 1974, in LaGuaria, Venezuela. ... 6-6/220. ... Throws right, bats right. ... Full name: Oscar Eduardo Henriquez.
TRANSACTIONS/CAREER NOTES: Signed as non-drafted free agent by Houston Astros organization (May 28, 1991). ... On disabled list (June 15, 1994-remainder of season). ... Traded by Astros with P Manuel Barrios and a player to be named later to Florida Marlins for OF Moises Alou (November 11, 1997).

Year Team (League)	W	L	Pct.	ERA	G	GS	CG	ShO	Sv.	IP	H	R	ER	BB	SO
1992—				Dominican League statistics unavailable.											
1993—Asheville (S. Atl.)	9	10	.474	4.44	27	26	2	1	0	150	154	95	74	70	117
1994—				Did not play.											
1995—Kissimmee (Florida State)	3	4	.429	5.04	20	0	0	0	1	44 2/3	40	29	25	30	36
1996—Kissimmee (Florida State)	0	4	.000	3.97	37	0	0	0	15	34	28	18	15	29	40
1997—New Orleans (A.A.)	4	5	.444	2.80	*60	0	0	0	12	74	65	28	23	27	80
—Houston (N.L.)	0	1	.000	4.50	4	0	0	0	0	4	2	2	2	3	3
Major league totals (1 year)	0	1	.000	4.50	4	0	0	0	0	4	2	2	2	3	3

HENRY, BUTCH   P   RED SOX

PERSONAL: Born October 7, 1968, in El Paso, Texas. ... 6-1/205. ... Throws left, bats left. ... Full name: Floyd Bluford Henry III.
HIGH SCHOOL: Eastwood (El Paso, Texas).
TRANSACTIONS/CAREER NOTES: Selected by Cincinnati Reds organization in 15th round of free-agent draft (June 2, 1987). ... On disabled list (April 28, 1989-remainder of season). ... Traded by Reds with C Terry McGriff and P Keith Kaiser to Houston Astros, completing deal in which Astros traded 2B Bill Doran to Reds for three players to be named later (August 30, 1990). ... Selected by Colorado Rockies in second round (36th pick overall) of expansion draft (November 17, 1992). ... Traded by Rockies to Montreal Expos for P Kent Bottenfield (July 16, 1993). ... On disabled list (August 16, 1995-remainder of season). ... Claimed on waivers by Boston Red Sox (October 13, 1995). ... On disabled list (March 22, 1996-entire season). ... On disabled list (May 5-June 23, 1997); included rehabilitation assignment to Sarasota (June 14-23).

Year Team (League)	W	L	Pct.	ERA	G	GS	CG	ShO	Sv.	IP	H	R	ER	BB	SO
1987—Billings (Pioneer)	4	0	1.000	4.63	9	5	0	0	1	35	37	21	18	12	38
1988—Cedar Rapids (Midw.)	16	2	*.889	2.26	27	27	1	1	0	187	144	59	47	56	163
1989—Chattanooga (Southern)	1	3	.250	3.42	7	7	0	0	0	26 1/3	22	12	10	12	19
1990—Chattanooga (Southern)	8	8	.500	4.21	24	22	2	0	0	143 1/3	151	74	67	58	95
1991—Tucson (PCL)■	10	11	.476	4.80	27	27	2	0	0	153 2/3	192	92	82	42	97
1992—Houston (N.L.)	6	9	.400	4.02	28	28	2	1	0	165 2/3	185	81	74	41	96
1993—Colorado (N.L.)■	2	8	.200	6.59	20	15	1	0	0	84 2/3	117	66	62	24	39
—Montreal (N.L.)■	1	1	.500	3.93	10	1	0	0	0	18 1/3	18	10	8	4	8
—Ottawa (Int'l)	3	1	.750	3.73	5	5	1	0	0	31 1/3	34	15	13	1	25
1994—Ottawa (Int'l)	2	0	1.000	0.00	2	2	1	1	0	14	11	0	0	2	11
—Montreal (N.L.)	8	3	.727	2.43	24	15	0	0	1	107 1/3	97	30	29	20	70
1995—Montreal (N.L.)	7	9	.438	2.84	21	21	1	1	0	126 2/3	133	47	40	28	60
1996—							Did not play.								
1997—Boston (A.L.)■	7	3	.700	3.52	36	5	0	0	6	84 1/3	89	36	33	19	51
—Sarasota (Florida State)	0	1	.000	5.40	2	2	0	0	0	8 1/3	8	5	5	0	7
A.L. totals (1 year)	7	3	.700	3.52	36	5	0	0	6	84 1/3	89	36	33	19	51
N.L. totals (4 years)	24	30	.444	3.81	103	80	4	2	1	502 2/3	550	234	213	117	273
Major league totals (5 years)	31	33	.484	3.77	139	85	4	2	7	587	639	270	246	136	324

HENRY, DOUG P ASTROS

PERSONAL: Born December 10, 1963, in Sacramento. ... 6-4/205. ... Throws right, bats right. ... Full name: Richard Douglas Henry.
HIGH SCHOOL: Tennyson (Hayward, Calif.).
COLLEGE: Arizona State.
TRANSACTIONS/CAREER NOTES: Selected by New York Mets organization in 16th round of free-agent draft (June 7, 1982); did not sign. ... Selected by Milwaukee Brewers organization in eighth round of free-agent draft (June 3, 1985). ... On El Paso disabled list (April 5-June 5 and June 18-August 9, 1989). ... On Milwaukee disabled list (March 25-April 26, 1994); included rehabilitation assignments to El Paso (April 8-22) and New Orleans (April 22-26). ... Traded by Brewers to New York Mets for two players to be named later (November 30, 1994); Brewers acquired C Javier Gonzales (December 6, 1994) and IF Fernando Vina (December 22, 1994) to complete deal. ... Released by Mets (November 25, 1996). ... Signed by San Francisco Giants (January 8, 1997). Granted free agency (October 27, 1997). ... Signed by Houston Astros (November 26, 1997).
STATISTICAL NOTES: Combined with Michael Ignasiak in 6-3 no-hit victory for Stockton against San Jose (April 15, 1990, first game).

Year Team (League)	W	L	Pct.	ERA	G	GS	CG	ShO	Sv.	IP	H	R	ER	BB	SO
1986— Beloit (Midwest)	7	8	.467	4.65	27	24	4	1	1	143 1/3	153	95	74	56	115
1987— Beloit (Midwest)	8	9	.471	4.88	31	15	1	0	2	132 2/3	145	83	72	51	106
1988— Stockton (California)	7	1	.875	1.78	23	1	1	0	7	70 2/3	46	19	14	31	71
— El Paso (Texas)	4	0	1.000	3.15	14	3	3	1	0	45 2/3	33	16	16	19	50
1989— Stockton (California)	0	1	.000	0.00	4	3	0	0	1	11	9	4	0	3	9
— El Paso (Texas)	0	0	...	13.50	1	1	0	0	0	2	3	3	3	3	2
1990— Stockton (California)	1	0	1.000	1.13	4	0	0	0	1	8	4	1	1	3	13
— El Paso (Texas)	1	0	1.000	2.93	15	0	0	0	9	30 2/3	31	13	10	11	25
— Denver (Am. Assoc.)	2	3	.400	4.44	27	0	0	0	8	50 2/3	46	26	25	27	54
1991— Denver (Am. Assoc.)	3	2	.600	2.18	32	0	0	0	14	57 2/3	47	16	14	20	47
— Milwaukee (A.L.)	2	1	.667	1.00	32	0	0	0	15	36	16	4	4	14	28
1992— Milwaukee (A.L.)	1	4	.200	4.02	68	0	0	0	29	65	64	34	29	24	52
1993— Milwaukee (A.L.)	4	4	.500	5.56	54	0	0	0	17	55	67	37	34	25	38
1994— El Paso (Texas)	1	0	1.000	5.40	6	0	0	0	3	8 1/3	7	5	5	2	10
— New Orleans (A.A.)	1	0	1.000	1.84	10	0	0	0	3	14 2/3	5	3	3	10	10
— Milwaukee (A.L.)	2	3	.400	4.60	25	0	0	0	0	31 1/3	32	17	16	23	20
1995— New York (N.L.)■	3	6	.333	2.96	51	0	0	0	4	67	48	23	22	25	62
1996— New York (N.L.)	2	8	.200	4.68	58	0	0	0	9	75	82	48	39	36	58
1997— San Francisco (N.L.)■	4	5	.444	4.71	75	0	0	0	3	70 2/3	70	45	37	41	69
A.L. totals (4 years)	9	12	.429	3.99	179	0	0	0	61	187 1/3	179	92	83	86	138
N.L. totals (3 years)	9	19	.321	4.15	184	0	0	0	16	212 2/3	200	116	98	102	189
Major league totals (7 years)	18	31	.367	4.07	363	0	0	0	77	400	379	208	181	188	327

DIVISION SERIES RECORD

Year Team (League)	W	L	Pct.	ERA	G	GS	CG	ShO	Sv.	IP	H	R	ER	BB	SO
1997— San Francisco (N.L.)	0	0	...	0.00	1	0	0	0	0	2	1	0	0	3	2

HENTGEN, PAT P BLUE JAYS

PERSONAL: Born November 13, 1968, in Detroit. ... 6-2/200. ... Throws right, bats right. ... Full name: Patrick George Hentgen. ... Name pronounced HENT-ghen.
HIGH SCHOOL: Fraser (Mich.).
TRANSACTIONS/CAREER NOTES: Selected by Toronto Blue Jays organization in fifth round of free-agent draft (June 2, 1986). ... On Toronto disabled list (August 13-September 29, 1992); included rehabilitation assignment to Syracuse (September 1-8).
HONORS: Named A.L. Pitcher of the Year by THE SPORTING NEWS (1996). ... Named righthanded pitcher on THE SPORTING NEWS A.L. All-Star team (1996). ... Named A.L. Cy Young Award winner by Baseball Writers' Association of America (1996).
STATISTICAL NOTES: Combined with relievers Willie Blair and Enrique Burgos in 2-1 no-hit victory against Osceola (May 10, 1988).

Year Team (League)	W	L	Pct.	ERA	G	GS	CG	ShO	Sv.	IP	H	R	ER	BB	SO
1986— St. Catharines (NYP)	0	4	.000	4.50	13	11	0	0	1	40	38	27	20	30	30
1987— Myrtle Beach (SAL)	11	5	.688	2.35	32	*31	2	2	0	*188	145	62	49	60	131
1988— Dunedin (Fla. St.)	3	12	.200	3.45	31	*30	0	0	0	151 1/3	139	80	58	65	125
1989— Dunedin (Fla. St.)	9	8	.529	2.68	29	28	0	0	0	151 1/3	123	53	45	71	148
1990— Knoxville (Southern)	9	5	.643	3.05	28	26	0	0	0	153 1/3	121	57	52	68	142
1991— Syracuse (Int'l)	8	9	.471	4.47	31	•28	1	0	0	171	146	91	85	*90	*155
— Toronto (A.L.)	0	0	...	2.45	3	1	0	0	0	7 1/3	5	2	2	3	3

H

Year Team (League)	W	L	Pct.	ERA	G	GS	CG	ShO	Sv.	IP	H	R	ER	BB	SO
1992— Toronto (A.L.)	5	2	.714	5.36	28	2	0	0	0	50 1/3	49	30	30	32	39
—Syracuse (Int'l)	1	2	.333	2.66	4	4	0	0	0	20 1/3	15	6	6	8	17
1993— Toronto (A.L.)	19	9	.679	3.87	34	32	3	0	0	216 1/3	215	103	93	74	122
1994— Toronto (A.L.)	13	8	.619	3.40	24	24	6	3	0	174 2/3	158	74	66	59	147
1995— Toronto (A.L.)	10	14	.417	5.11	30	30	2	0	0	200 2/3	*236	*129	*114	90	135
1996— Toronto (A.L.)	20	10	.667	3.22	35	35	*10	•3	0	*265 2/3	238	105	95	94	177
1997— Toronto (A.L.)■	15	10	.600	3.68	35	•35	•9	•3	0	•264	253	116	108	71	160
Major league totals (7 years)	82	53	.607	3.88	189	159	30	9	0	1179	1154	559	508	423	783

CHAMPIONSHIP SERIES RECORD

Year Team (League)	W	L	Pct.	ERA	G	GS	CG	ShO	Sv.	IP	H	R	ER	BB	SO
1993— Toronto (A.L.)	0	1	.000	18.00	1	1	0	0	0	3	9	6	6	2	3

WORLD SERIES RECORD

NOTES: Member of World Series championship team (1993).

Year Team (League)	W	L	Pct.	ERA	G	GS	CG	ShO	Sv.	IP	H	R	ER	BB	SO
1993— Toronto (A.L.)	1	0	1.000	1.50	1	1	0	0	0	6	5	1	1	3	6

ALL-STAR GAME RECORD

Year League	W	L	Pct.	ERA	GS	CG	ShO	Sv.	IP	H	R	ER	BB	SO
1993— American			...				Did not play.							
1994— American	0	0	...	0.00	0	0	0	0	1	1	0	0	0	0
1997— American	0	0	...	0.00	0	0	0	0	1	0	0	0	0	0
All-Star totals (2 years)	0	0	...	0.00	0	0	0	0	2	1	0	0	0	0

HEREDIA, FELIX — P — MARLINS

PERSONAL: Born June 18, 1976, in Barahona, Dominican Republic. ... 6-0/175. ... Throws left, bats left.
HIGH SCHOOL: Escuela Dominical (Barahona, Dominican Republic).
TRANSACTIONS/CAREER NOTES: Signed as non-drafted free agent by Florida Marlins organization (November 22, 1992).

Year Team (League)	W	L	Pct.	ERA	G	GS	CG	ShO	Sv.	IP	H	R	ER	BB	SO
1993— GC Marlins (GCL)	5	1	.833	2.47	12	•12	0	0	0	62	50	18	17	11	53
1994— Kane County (Midwest)	4	5	.444	5.69	24	8	1	0	3	68	86	55	43	14	65
1995— Brevard County (FSL)	6	4	.600	3.57	34	8	0	0	1	95 2/3	101	52	38	36	76
1996— Portland (Eastern)	8	1	.889	1.50	55	0	0	0	5	60	48	11	10	15	42
—Florida (N.L.)	1	1	.500	4.32	21	0	0	0	0	16 2/3	21	8	8	10	10
1997— Florida (N.L.)	5	3	.625	4.29	56	0	0	0	0	56 2/3	53	30	27	30	54
Major league totals (2 years)	6	4	.600	4.30	77	0	0	0	0	73 1/3	74	38	35	40	64

CHAMPIONSHIP SERIES RECORD

Year Team (League)	W	L	Pct.	ERA	G	GS	CG	ShO	Sv.	IP	H	R	ER	BB	SO
1997— Florida (N.L.)	0	0	...	5.40	2	0	0	0	0	3 1/3	3	2	2	2	4

WORLD SERIES RECORD

NOTES: Member of World Series championship team (1997).

Year Team (League)	W	L	Pct.	ERA	G	GS	CG	ShO	Sv.	IP	H	R	ER	BB	SO
1997— Florida (N.L.)	0	0	...	0.00	4	0	0	0	0	5 1/3	2	0	0	1	5

HEREDIA, WILSON — P

PERSONAL: Born March 30, 1972, in La Romana, Dominican Republic. ... 6-0/175. ... Throws right, bats right.
TRANSACTIONS/CAREER NOTES: Signed as non-drafted free agent by Texas Rangers organization (February 28, 1990). ... On disabled list (June 3-August 17, 1994). ... Traded by Rangers to Florida Marlins (August 11, 1995), completing deal in which Rangers acquired P Bobby Witt for two players to be named later (August 8, 1995); Marlins acquired OF Scott Podsednik to complete deal (October 2, 1995). ... On disabled list (March 29-September 30, 1996). ... Claimed on waivers by Rangers (October 3, 1996). ... Granted free agency (December 21, 1997).

Year Team (League)	W	L	Pct.	ERA	G	GS	CG	ShO	Sv.	IP	H	R	ER	BB	SO
1990— San Pedro (DSL)	5	7	.417	4.86	15	15	8	1	0	111	119	69	60	48	58
1991— GC Rangers (GCL)	2	4	.333	2.14	17	0	0	0	4	25 2/3	25	18	8	20	22
1992— Gastonia (S. Atl.)	1	2	.333	5.12	39	1	0	0	5	63 1/3	71	45	36	30	64
1993— Charlotte (Fla. St.)	1	5	.167	3.76	34	0	0	0	15	38 1/3	30	17	16	20	26
1994— Tulsa (Texas)	3	2	.600	3.77	18	1	0	0	0	43	35	23	18	8	53
1995— Texas (A.L.)	0	1	.000	3.75	6	0	0	0	0	12	9	5	5	15	14
—Oklahoma City (A.A.)	1	4	.200	6.82	8	7	0	0	0	31 2/3	40	26	24	25	21
—Tulsa (Texas)	4	2	.667	3.18	8	7	1	1	1	45 1/3	42	19	16	21	34
—Portland (Eastern)■	4	0	1.000	2.00	4	4	0	0	0	27	22	7	6	14	19
1996—							Did not play.								
1997—Oklahoma City (A.A.)■	7	12	.368	4.97	27	26	2	0	0	168 1/3	167	106	93	70	113
—Texas (A.L.)	1	0	1.000	3.20	10	0	0	0	0	19 2/3	14	9	7	16	8
Major league totals (2 years)	1	1	.500	3.41	16	0	0	0	0	31 2/3	23	14	12	31	14

HERMANSEN, CHAD — OF/2B — PIRATES

PERSONAL: Born September 10, 1977, in Salt Lake City. ... 6-2/185. ... Bats right, throws right. ... Full name: Chad B. Hermansen.
HIGH SCHOOL: Green Valley (Henderson, Nev.).
TRANSACTIONS/CAREER NOTES: Selected by Pittsburgh Pirates organization in first round (10th pick overall) of free-agent draft (June 1, 1995).
STATISTICAL NOTES: Tied for Southern League lead in errors by outfielder with eight in 1997.

H

Year Team (League)	Pos.	G	AB	R	H	2B	3B	HR	RBI	Avg.	BB	SO	SB	PO	A	E	Avg.
1995—Bra. Pirates (GCL)	SS	24	92	14	28	10	1	3	17	.304	9	19	0	20	56	10	.884
—Erie (N.Y.-Penn).........	SS	44	165	30	45	8	3	6	25	.273	18	39	4	52	104	30	.839
1996—Augusta (S. Atl.).........	SS	62	226	41	57	11	3	14	41	.252	38	65	11	71	135	25	.892
—Lynchburg (Caro.)......	SS	66	251	40	69	11	3	10	46	.275	29	56	5	75	168	28	.897
1997—Carolina (Southern)....	OF-SS-2B	129	487	87	134	31	4	20	70	.275	69	*136	18	194	125	‡39	.891

HERMANSON, DUSTIN   P   EXPOS

PERSONAL: Born December 21, 1972, in Springfield, Ohio. ... 6-2/195. ... Throws right, bats right. ... Full name: Dustin Michael Hermanson.
HIGH SCHOOL: Kenton Ridge (Springfield, Ohio).
COLLEGE: Kent.
TRANSACTIONS/CAREER NOTES: Selected by Pittsburgh Pirates organization in 39th round of free-agent draft (June 3, 1991); did not sign. ... Selected by San Diego Padres organization in first round (third pick overall) of free-agent draft (June 2, 1994). ... Traded by Padres to Florida Marlins for 2B Quilvio Veras (November 21, 1996). ... Traded by Marlins with OF Joe Orsulak to Montreal Expos for OF/1B Cliff Floyd (March 26, 1997).
STATISTICAL NOTES: Hit home run in first major league at-bat (April 16, 1997).

Year Team (League)	W	L	Pct.	ERA	G	GS	CG	ShO	Sv.	IP	H	R	ER	BB	SO
1994—Wichita (Texas)	1	0	1.000	0.43	16	0	0	0	8	21	13	1	1	6	30
—Las Vegas (PCL)	0	0	...	6.14	7	0	0	0	3	7 1/3	6	5	5	5	6
1995—Las Vegas (PCL)	0	1	.000	3.50	31	0	0	0	11	36	35	23	14	29	42
—San Diego (N.L.)..............	3	1	.750	6.82	26	0	0	0	0	31 2/3	35	26	24	22	19
1996—Las Vegas (PCL)	1	4	.200	3.13	42	0	0	0	21	46	41	20	16	27	54
—San Diego (N.L.)..............	1	0	1.000	8.56	8	0	0	0	0	13 2/3	18	15	13	4	11
1997—Montreal (N.L.)■..............	8	8	.500	3.69	32	28	1	1	0	158 1/3	134	68	65	66	136
Major league totals (3 years)......	**12**	**9**	**.571**	**4.51**	**66**	**28**	**1**	**1**	**0**	**203 2/3**	**187**	**109**	**102**	**92**	**166**

HERNANDEZ, CARLOS   2B   ASTROS

PERSONAL: Born December 12, 1975, in Caracas, Venezuela. ... 5-9/175. ... Bats right, throws right.
TRANSACTIONS/CAREER NOTES: Signed as non-drafted free agent by Houston Astros organization (July 2, 1992). ... On disabled list (August 1, 1997-remainder of season).
STATISTICAL NOTES: Tied for Midwest League lead in double plays by second baseman with 79 in 1996.

Year Team (League)	Pos.	G	AB	R	H	2B	3B	HR	RBI	Avg.	BB	SO	SB	PO	A	E	Avg.
1993—Dom. Astros (DSL).....	IF	67	245	52	75	13	4	1	36	.306	27	29	36	181	134	21	.938
1994—GC Astros (GCL)	2B-SS	51	192	45	62	10	1	0	23	.323	19	22	25	89	149	8	.967
1995—Quad City (Midwest) ..	2B-SS	126	470	74	122	19	6	4	40	.260	39	68	*58	188	349	21	.962
1996—Quad City (Midwest) ..	2B-SS	112	456	67	123	15	7	5	49	.270	27	71	41	238	336	19	.968
1997—Jackson (Texas)	2B	91	363	62	106	12	1	4	33	.292	33	59	17	187	269	8	.983

HERNANDEZ, CARLOS   C   PADRES

PERSONAL: Born May 24, 1967, in San Felix, Bolivar, Venezuela. ... 5-11/215. ... Bats right, throws right. ... Full name: Carlos Alberto Hernandez.
HIGH SCHOOL: Escuela Tecnica Industrial (San Felix, Bolivar, Venezuela).
TRANSACTIONS/CAREER NOTES: Signed as non-drafted free agent by Los Angeles Dodgers organization (October 10, 1984). ... On Albuquerque disabled list (May 27-June 20, 1990). ... On disabled list (April 4-22, 1994). ... On Los Angeles disabled list (May 17-June 14, 1996); included rehabilitation assignment to Albuquerque (June 5-14). ... Granted free agency (October 15, 1996). ... Signed by San Diego Padres organization (December 2, 1996). ... On San Diego disabled list (July 13-August 15, 1997). ... Granted free agency (October 31, 1997). ... Re-signed by Padres (November 12, 1997).
STATISTICAL NOTES: Tied for Gulf Coast League lead in double plays by catcher with three in 1986. ... Led Texas League catchers with 737 total chances in 1989. ... Led Pacific Coast League catchers with 684 total chances in 1991.

Year Team (League)	Pos.	G	AB	R	H	2B	3B	HR	RBI	Avg.	BB	SO	SB	PO	A	E	Avg.
1985—GC Dodgers (GCL)	3B-1B	22	49	3	12	1	0	0	0	.245	3	8	0	48	16	2	.970
1986—GC Dodgers (GCL)	C-3B	57	205	19	64	7	0	1	31	.312	5	18	1	217	36	10	.962
1987—Bakersfield (Calif.)......	C	48	162	22	37	6	1	3	22	.228	14	23	8	181	26	8	.963
1988—Bakersfield (Calif.)......	C	92	333	37	103	15	2	5	52	.309	16	39	3	480	88	14	.976
—Albuquerque (PCL).....	C	3	8	0	1	0	0	0	1	.125	0	0	0	11	0	1	.917
1989—San Antonio (Tex.)	C	99	370	37	111	16	3	8	41	.300	12	46	2	*629	*90	*18	.976
—Albuquerque (PCL).....	C	4	14	1	3	0	0	0	1	.214	2	1	0	23	3	3	.897
1990—Albuquerque (PCL).....	C	52	143	11	45	8	1	0	16	.315	8	25	2	207	31	8	.967
—Los Angeles (N.L.).....	C	10	20	2	4	1	0	0	1	.200	0	2	0	37	2	0	1.000
1991—Albuquerque (PCL).....	C	95	345	60	119	24	2	8	44	.345	24	36	5	*592	*77	*15	.978
—Los Angeles (N.L.).....	C-3B	15	14	1	3	1	0	0	1	.214	0	5	1	24	4	1	.966
1992—Los Angeles (N.L.).....	C	69	173	11	45	4	0	3	17	.260	11	21	0	295	37	7	.979
1993—Los Angeles (N.L.).....	C	50	99	6	25	5	0	2	7	.253	2	11	0	181	15	7	.966
1994—Los Angeles (N.L.).....	C	32	64	6	14	2	0	2	6	.219	1	14	0	104	13	0	1.000
1995—Los Angeles (N.L.).....	C	45	94	3	14	1	0	0	8	.149	7	25	0	210	25	4	.983
1996—Los Angeles (N.L.).....	C	13	14	1	4	0	0	0	0	.286	2	2	0	31	1	0	1.000
—Albuquerque (PCL).....	C-1B-3B	66	233	19	56	11	0	5	30	.240	11	49	5	331	38	9	.976
1997—San Diego (N.L.)■.....	C-1B	50	134	15	42	7	1	3	14	.313	3	27	0	239	29	3	.989
—Las Vegas (PCL)	C	3	10	1	4	0	0	1	5	.400	1	3	0	15	2	0	1.000
—Rancho Cuca. (Cal.) ...	C	1	4	0	1	0	0	0	0	.250	0	1	0	11	1	0	1.000
Major league totals (8 years)		**284**	**612**	**45**	**151**	**21**	**1**	**12**	**54**	**.247**	**26**	**107**	**1**	**1121**	**126**	**22**	**.983**

H

HERNANDEZ, ELVIN — P — PIRATES

PERSONAL: Born August 20, 1977, in Ranchete, Dominican Republic. ... 6-1/165. ... Throws right, bats right. ... Full name: Elvin Radhames Hernandez.

TRANSACTIONS/CAREER NOTES: Signed as non-drafted free agent by Pittsburgh Pirates organization (June 29, 1993). ... On Carolina disabled list (July 18-August 10, 1997).

Year Team (League)	W	L	Pct.	ERA	G	GS	CG	ShO	Sv.	IP	H	R	ER	BB	SO
1994— DSL Pirates (DSL)	4	5	.444	2.70	11	10	2	0	0	70	62	28	21	13	68
1995— Erie (N.Y.-Penn)	6	1	.857	2.89	14	14	2	0	0	90 1/3	82	40	29	22	54
1996— Augusta (S. Atl.)	*17	5	.773	3.14	27	27	2	1	0	157 2/3	140	60	55	16	171
1997— Carolina (Southern)	2	7	.222	5.73	17	17	0	0	0	92 2/3	104	67	59	26	66
— Lynchburg (Caroline)	0	0	...	1.80	3	0	0	0	1	5	4	1	1	1	5

HERNANDEZ, FERNANDO — P

PERSONAL: Born June 16, 1971, in Santiago, Dominican Republic. ... 6-2/185. ... Throws right, bats right.

TRANSACTIONS/CAREER NOTES: Signed as non-drafted free agent by Cleveland Indians organization (January 5, 1990). ... Traded by Indians with OF Tracy Sanders to San Diego Padres organization for P Jeremy Hernandez (June 1, 1993). ... Claimed on waivers by Detroit Tigers (September 18, 1996). ... Granted free agency (December 21, 1997).

Year Team (League)	W	L	Pct.	ERA	G	GS	CG	ShO	Sv.	IP	H	R	ER	BB	SO
1990— GC Indians (GCL)	4	4	.500	4.00	11	11	2	0	0	69 2/3	61	36	31	30	43
1991— Burlington (Appalachian)	4	4	.500	2.92	14	13	0	0	0	77	74	33	25	19	86
1992— Kinston (Carolina)	1	3	.250	4.54	8	8	1	0	0	41 2/3	36	23	21	22	32
— Columbus (S. Atl.)	4	5	.444	1.57	11	11	1	1	0	68 2/3	42	16	12	33	70
1993— Kinston (Carolina)	2	3	.400	1.76	8	8	0	0	0	51	34	15	10	18	53
— Cant./Akr. (Eastern)	0	1	.000	11.74	2	2	0	0	0	7 2/3	14	11	10	5	8
— Rancho Cuca. (Calif.)■	7	5	.583	4.15	17	17	1	0	0	99 2/3	90	54	46	67	121
1994— Wichita (Texas)	7	9	.438	4.80	23	23	1	1	0	131 1/3	124	82	70	77	95
1995— Memphis (Southern)	4	6	.400	5.16	12	12	0	0	0	66 1/3	72	46	38	42	74
— Las Vegas (PCL)	1	6	.143	7.65	8	8	0	0	0	37 2/3	43	32	32	31	40
1996— Memphis (Southern)	11	10	.524	4.64	27	27	0	0	0	147 1/3	128	83	76	85	161
1997— Detroit (A.L.)■	0	0	...	40.50	2	0	0	0	0	1 1/3	5	6	6	3	2
— Toledo (Int'l)	6	5	.545	4.11	55	1	0	0	0	4	76 2/3	71	44	35	51	98
Major league totals (1 year)	0	0	...	40.50	2	0	0	0	0	1 1/3	5	6	6	3	2

HERNANDEZ, JOSE — IF — CUBS

PERSONAL: Born July 14, 1969, in Vega Alta, Puerto Rico. ... 6-1/180. ... Bats right, throws right. ... Full name: Jose Antonio Hernandez.
HIGH SCHOOL: Maestro Ladi (Vega Alta, Puerto Rico).
COLLEGE: American University (Puerto Rico).
TRANSACTIONS/CAREER NOTES: Signed as non-drafted free agent by Texas Rangers organization (January 13, 1987). ... Claimed on waivers by Cleveland Indians (April 3, 1992). ... Traded by Indians to Chicago Cubs for P Heathcliff Slocumb (June 1, 1993).
STATISTICAL NOTES: Led Gulf Coast League third basemen with .950 fielding percentage, 47 putouts and 11 double plays in 1988. ... Led Florida State League shortstops with .959 fielding percentage in 1990. ... Career major league grand slams: 1.

Year Team (League)	Pos.	G	AB	R	H	2B	3B	HR	RBI	Avg.	BB	SO	SB	PO	A	E	Avg.
1987— GC Rangers (GCL)	SS	24	52	5	9	1	1	0	2	.173	9	25	2	30	38	5	.932
1988— GC Rangers (GCL)	3-2-S-1-O	55	162	19	26	7	1	1	13	.160	12	36	4	†68	115	8	†.958
1989— Gastonia (S. Atl.)	3-S-2-O	91	215	35	47	7	6	1	16	.219	33	67	9	101	169	17	.941
1990— Charlotte (Fla. St.)	SS-OF	121	388	43	99	14	7	1	44	.255	50	122	11	192	372	25	†.958
1991— Tulsa (Texas)	SS	91	301	36	72	17	4	1	20	.239	26	75	4	151	300	15	*.968
— Oklahoma City (A.A.)	SS	14	46	6	14	1	1	1	3	.304	4	10	0	32	43	3	.962
— Texas (A.L.)	SS-3B	45	98	8	18	2	1	0	4	.184	3	31	0	49	111	4	.976
1992— Cant./Akr. (Eastern)■	SS	130	404	56	103	16	4	3	46	.255	37	108	7	*226	320	*40	.932
— Cleveland (A.L.)	SS	3	4	0	0	0	0	0	0	.000	0	2	0	3	3	1	.857
1993— Cant./Akr. (Eastern)	SS-3B	45	150	19	30	6	0	2	17	.200	10	39	0	75	135	7	.968
— Orlando (South.)■	SS	71	263	42	80	8	3	8	33	.304	20	60	8	136	205	14	.961
— Iowa (Am. Assoc.)	SS	6	24	3	6	1	0		3	.250	0	2	0	14	26	1	.976
1994— Chicago (N.L.)	3-S-2-O	56	132	18	32	2	3	1	9	.242	8	29	2	46	86	4	.971
1995— Chicago (N.L.)	SS-2B-3B	93	245	37	60	11	4	13	40	.245	13	69	1	113	189	9	.971
1996— Chicago (N.L.)	S-3-2-O	131	331	52	80	14	1	10	41	.242	24	97	4	148	248	20	.952
1997— Chicago (N.L.)	3-S-2-O-DH-1	121	183	33	50	8	5	7	26	.273	14	42	2	79	91	8	.955
American League totals (2 years)		48	102	8	18	2	1	0	4	.176	3	33	0	52	114	5	.971
National League totals (4 years)		401	891	140	222	35	13	31	116	.249	59	237	9	386	614	41	.961
Major league totals (6 years)		449	993	148	240	37	14	31	120	.242	62	270	9	438	728	46	.962

HERNANDEZ, LIVAN — P — MARLINS

PERSONAL: Born February 20, 1975, in Villa Clara, Cuba. ... 6-2/220. ... Throws right, bats right. ... Full name: Eisler Hernandez.
TRANSACTIONS/CAREER NOTES: Signed as non-drafted free agent by Florida Marlins orgaization (January 13, 1996).
MISCELLANEOUS: Member of Cuban national team (1994-95).
STATISTICAL NOTES: Led International League with four balks in 1996.

Year Team (League)	W	L	Pct.	ERA	G	GS	CG	ShO	Sv.	IP	H	R	ER	BB	SO
1996— Charlotte (Int'l)	2	4	.333	5.14	10	10	0	0	0	49	61	32	28	34	45
— Florida (N.L.)	0	0	...	0.00	1	0	0	0	0	3	3	0	0	2	2
1997— Portland (Eastern)	0	0	...	2.25	1	1	0	0	0	4	2	1	1	7	2
— Charlotte (Int'l)	5	3	.625	3.98	14	14	0	0	0	81 1/3	76	39	36	38	58
— Florida (N.L.)	9	3	.750	3.18	17	17	0	0	0	96 1/3	81	39	34	38	72
Major league totals (2 years)	9	3	.750	3.08	18	17	0	0	0	99 1/3	84	39	34	40	74

H

DIVISION SERIES RECORD

Year Team (League)	W	L	Pct.	ERA	G	GS	CG	ShO	Sv.	IP	H	R	ER	BB	SO
1997—Florida (N.L.)	0	0	...	2.25	1	0	0	0	0	4	3	1	1	0	3

CHAMPIONSHIP SERIES RECORD

NOTES: Named N.L. Championship Series Most Valuable Player (1997).

Year Team (League)	W	L	Pct.	ERA	G	GS	CG	ShO	Sv.	IP	H	R	ER	BB	SO
1997—Florida (N.L.)	2	0	1.000	0.84	2	1	1	0	0	10²/₃	5	1	1	2	16

WORLD SERIES RECORD

NOTES: Named Most Valuable Player (1997). ... Member of World Series championship team (1997).

Year Team (League)	W	L	Pct.	ERA	G	GS	CG	ShO	Sv.	IP	H	R	ER	BB	SO
1997—Florida (N.L.)	2	0	1.000	5.27	2	2	0	0	0	13²/₃	15	9	8	10	7

HERNANDEZ, RAMON   C   ATHLETICS

PERSONAL: Born May 20, 1976, in Caracas, Venezuela. ... 6-0/170. ... Throws right, bats right. ... Full name: Ramon Jose Marin Hernandez.
TRANSACTIONS/CAREER NOTES: Signed as non-drafted free agent by Oakland Athletics organization (February 18, 1994).
HONORS: Named Arizona League Most Valuable Player (1995).
STATISTICAL NOTES: Led Arizona League catchers with a .982 fielding percentage in 1995. ... Led Midwest League catchers with 877 putouts and 981 totals chances and tied for lead with 20 errors in 1996. ... Led California League with .427 on-base percentage in 1997. ... Led California League catchers with 16 errors in 1997.

							BATTING								FIELDING		
Year Team (League)	Pos.	G	AB	R	H	2B	3B	HR	RBI	Avg.	BB	SO	SB	PO	A	E	Avg.
1994—Dom. Athletics (DSL) .	C	42	134	24	33	2	0	2	18	.246	18	10	1	182	28	2	.991
1995—Arizona A's (Ariz.)	C-1B-3B	48	143	37	52	9	6	4	37	.364	39	16	6	358	61	12	†.972
1996—W. Mich. (Mid.)	C-1B	123	447	62	114	26	2	12	68	.255	69	62	2	†917	85	‡20	.980
1997—Visalia (California)	C-1B	86	332	57	120	21	2	15	85	*.361	35	47	2	577	80	†16	.976
—Huntsville (Southern) .	C-1B-3B	44	161	27	31	3	0	4	24	.193	18	23	0	274	27	1	.997

HERNANDEZ, ROBERTO   P   DEVIL RAYS

PERSONAL: Born November 11, 1964, in Santurce, Puerto Rico. ... 6-4/235. ... Throws right, bats right. ... Full name: Roberto Manuel Hernandez.
HIGH SCHOOL: New Hampton (N.H.) Prep.
COLLEGE: South Carolina-Aiken.
TRANSACTIONS/CAREER NOTES: Selected by California Angels organization in first round (16th pick overall) of free-agent draft (June 2, 1986); pick received as compensation for Baltimore Orioles signing Type A free-agent OF/IF Juan Beniquez. ... On disabled list (May 6-21 and June 4-August 14, 1987). ... Traded by Angels with OF Mark Doran to Chicago White Sox organization for OF Mark Davis (August 2, 1989). ... On Vancouver disabled list (May 17-August 10, 1991). ... Traded by White Sox with P Wilson Alvarez and P Danny Darwin to San Francisco Giants for SS Michael Caruso, OF Brian Manning, P Lorenzo Barcelo, P Keith Foulke, P Bobby Howry and P Ken Vining (July 31, 1997). ... Granted free agency (October 30, 1997). ... Signed by Tampa Bay Devil Rays (November 18, 1997).

Year Team (League)	W	L	Pct.	ERA	G	GS	CG	ShO	Sv.	IP	H	R	ER	BB	SO
1986—Salem (Northwest)	2	2	.500	4.58	10	10	0	0	0	55	57	37	28	42	38
1987—Quad City (Midwest)	2	3	.400	6.86	7	6	0	0	1	21	24	21	16	12	21
1988—Quad City (Midwest)	9	10	.474	3.17	24	24	6	1	0	164²/₃	157	70	58	48	114
—Midland (Texas)	0	2	.000	6.57	3	3	0	0	0	12¹/₃	16	13	9	8	7
1989—Midland (Texas)	2	7	.222	6.89	12	12	0	0	0	64	94	57	49	30	42
—Palm Springs (California)	1	4	.200	4.64	7	7	0	0	0	42²/₃	49	27	22	16	33
—South Bend (Mid.)■	1	1	.500	3.33	4	4	0	0	0	24¹/₃	19	9	9	7	17
1990—Birmingham (Southern)	8	5	.615	3.67	17	17	1	0	0	108	103	57	44	43	62
—Vancouver (PCL)	3	5	.375	2.84	11	11	3	1	0	79¹/₃	73	33	25	26	49
1991—Birmingham (Southern)	2	1	.667	1.99	4	4	0	0	0	22²/₃	11	5	5	6	25
—Vancouver (PCL)	4	1	.800	3.22	7	7	0	0	0	44²/₃	41	17	16	23	40
—GC White Sox (GCL)	0	0	...	0.00	1	1	0	0	0	6	2	0	0	0	7
—Chicago (A.L.)	1	0	1.000	7.80	9	3	0	0	0	15	18	15	13	7	6
1992—Chicago (A.L.)	7	3	.700	1.65	43	0	0	0	12	71	45	15	13	20	68
—Vancouver (PCL)	3	3	.500	2.61	9	0	0	0	2	20²/₃	13	9	6	11	23
1993—Chicago (A.L.)	3	4	.429	2.29	70	0	0	0	38	78²/₃	66	21	20	20	71
1994—Chicago (A.L.)	4	4	.500	4.91	45	0	0	0	14	47²/₃	44	29	26	19	50
1995—Chicago (A.L.)	3	7	.300	3.92	60	0	0	0	32	59²/₃	63	30	26	28	84
1996—Chicago (A.L.)	6	5	.545	1.91	72	0	0	0	38	84²/₃	65	21	18	38	85
1997—Chicago (A.L.)	5	1	.833	2.44	46	0	0	0	27	48	38	15	13	24	47
—San Francisco (N.L.)■	5	2	.714	2.48	28	0	0	0	4	32²/₃	29	9	9	14	35
A.L. totals (7 years)	29	24	.547	2.87	345	3	0	0	161	404²/₃	339	146	129	156	411
N.L. totals (1 year)	5	2	.714	2.48	28	0	0	0	4	32²/₃	29	9	9	14	35
Major league totals (7 years)	34	26	.567	2.84	373	3	0	0	165	437¹/₃	368	155	138	170	446

DIVISION SERIES RECORD

Year Team (League)	W	L	Pct.	ERA	G	GS	CG	ShO	Sv.	IP	H	R	ER	BB	SO
1997—San Francisco (N.L.)	0	1	.000	20.25	3	0	0	0	0	1¹/₃	5	3	3	3	1

CHAMPIONSHIP SERIES RECORD

Year Team (League)	W	L	Pct.	ERA	G	GS	CG	ShO	Sv.	IP	H	R	ER	BB	SO
1993—Chicago (A.L.)	0	0	...	0.00	4	0	0	0	1	4	4	0	0	0	1

ALL-STAR GAME RECORD

Year League	W	L	Pct.	ERA	GS	CG	ShO	Sv.	IP	H	R	ER	BB	SO
1996—American	0	0	...	0.00	0	0	0	0	1	1	0	0	0	0

H

HERNANDEZ, SANTOS   P   DEVIL RAYS

PERSONAL: Born November 3, 1972, in Chirqui, Panama. ... 6-2/180. ... Throws right, bats right. ... Full name: Santos Secundino Hernandez.
TRANSACTIONS/CAREER NOTES: Signed as non-drafted free agent by San Francisco Giants organization (September 7, 1994). ... Selected by Tampa Bay Devil Rays in second round (56th pick overall) of expansion draft (November 18, 1997).

Year Team (League)	W	L	Pct.	ERA	G	GS	CG	ShO	Sv.	IP	H	R	ER	BB	SO
1994— Clinton (Midwest)	5	7	.417	3.75	32	0	0	0	4	48	47	23	20	10	48
1995— Burlington (Midw.)	5	8	.385	2.66	44	0	0	0	9	64 1/3	54	27	19	20	85
1996— Burlington (Midw.)	3	3	.500	1.89	*61	0	0	0	*35	66 2/3	39	15	14	13	79
1997— San Jose (California)	2	6	.250	3.47	47	0	0	0	15	57	51	26	22	14	87
— Shreveport (Texas)	1	1	.500	2.30	11	0	0	0	6	15 2/3	13	4	4	3	14

HERNANDEZ, XAVIER   P   RANGERS

PERSONAL: Born August 16, 1965, in Port Arthur, Texas. ... 6-2/195. ... Throws right, bats left. ... Full name: Francis Xavier Hernandez.
HIGH SCHOOL: Thomas Jefferson (Port Arthur, Texas).
COLLEGE: Southwestern Louisiana.
TRANSACTIONS/CAREER NOTES: Selected by Toronto Blue Jays organization in fourth round of free-agent draft (June 2, 1986). ... On disabled list (June 7-27, 1987). ... Selected by Houston Astros from Blue Jays organization in Rule 5 major league draft (December 4, 1989). ... On Houston disabled list (June 3-26, 1991); included rehabilitation assignment to Tucson (June 14-26). ... Traded by Astros to New York Yankees for P Domingo Jean and IF Andy Stankiewicz (November 27, 1993). ... On disabled list (July 27-August 11, 1994). ... Granted free agency (November 28, 1994). ... Signed by Cincinnati Reds (December 1, 1994). ... Released by Reds (April 17, 1996). ... Signed by Astros (April 24, 1996). ... Granted free agency (October 31, 1996). ... Signed by Texas Rangers (December 17, 1996). ... On disabled list (August 2-remainder of 1997 season).
MISCELLANEOUS: Appeared in two games as pinch-runner (1990).

Year Team (League)	W	L	Pct.	ERA	G	GS	CG	ShO	Sv.	IP	H	R	ER	BB	SO
1986— St. Catharines (NYP)	5	5	.500	2.67	13	10	1	1	0	70 2/3	55	27	21	16	69
1987— St. Catharines (NYP)	3	3	.500	5.07	13	11	0	0	0	55	57	39	31	16	49
1988— Myrtle Beach (SAL)	13	6	.684	2.55	23	22	2	2	0	148	116	52	42	28	111
— Knoxville (Southern)	2	4	.333	2.90	11	11	2	0	0	68 1/3	73	32	22	15	33
1989— Knoxville (Southern)	1	1	.500	4.13	4	4	1	0	0	24	25	11	11	11	17
— Syracuse (Int'l)	5	6	.455	3.53	15	15	2	1	0	99 1/3	95	42	39	22	47
— Toronto (A.L.)	1	0	1.000	4.76	7	0	0	0	0	22 2/3	25	15	12	8	7
1990— Houston (N.L.)■	2	1	.667	4.62	34	1	0	0	0	62 1/3	60	34	32	24	24
1991— Houston (N.L.)	2	7	.222	4.71	32	6	0	0	3	63	66	34	33	32	55
— Tucson (PCL)	2	1	.667	2.75	16	3	0	0	4	36	35	16	11	9	34
1992— Houston (N.L.)	9	1	.900	2.11	77	0	0	0	7	111	81	31	26	42	96
1993— Houston (N.L.)	4	5	.444	2.61	72	0	0	0	9	96 2/3	75	37	28	28	101
1994— New York (A.L.)■	4	4	.500	5.85	31	0	0	0	6	40	48	27	26	21	27
1995— Cincinnati (N.L.)■	7	2	.778	4.60	59	0	0	0	3	90	95	47	46	31	84
1996— Cincinnati (N.L.)	0	0	...	13.50	3	0	0	0	0	3 1/3	8	6	5	2	3
— Houston (N.L.)■	5	5	.500	4.22	58	0	0	0	6	74 2/3	69	39	35	26	78
1997— Texas (A.L.)■	0	4	.000	4.56	44	0	0	0	0	49 1/3	51	27	25	22	36
A.L. totals (3 years)	5	8	.385	5.06	82	0	0	0	6	112	124	69	63	51	80
N.L. totals (6 years)	29	21	.580	3.68	335	7	0	0	28	501	454	228	205	185	441
Major league totals (9 years)	34	29	.540	3.93	417	7	0	0	34	613	578	297	268	236	521

CHAMPIONSHIP SERIES RECORD

Year Team (League)	W	L	Pct.	ERA	G	GS	CG	ShO	Sv.	IP	H	R	ER	BB	SO
1995— Cincinnati (N.L.)	0	0	...	27.00	1	0	0	0	0	2/3	3	2	2	0	0

HERSHISER, OREL   P   GIANTS

PERSONAL: Born September 16, 1958, in Buffalo. ... 6-3/195. ... Throws right, bats right. ... Full name: Orel Leonard Hershiser IV. ... Brother of Gordie Hershiser, minor league pitcher (1987-88). ... Name pronounced her-SHY-zer.
HIGH SCHOOL: Cherry Hill (N.J.) East.
COLLEGE: Bowling Green State.
TRANSACTIONS/CAREER NOTES: Selected by Los Angeles Dodgers organization in 17th round of free-agent draft (June 5, 1979). ... On disabled list (April 27, 1990-remainder of season). ... On Los Angeles disabled list (March 31-May 29, 1991); included rehabilitation assignments to Bakersfield (May 8-13 and May 18-24), Albuquerque (May 13-18) and San Antonio (May 24-29). ... Granted free agency (November 1, 1991). ... Re-signed by Dodgers (December 3, 1991). ... Granted free agency (October 17, 1994). ... Signed by Cleveland Indians (April 8, 1995). ... On disabled list (June 22-July 7, 1995). ... On disabled list (July 29-August 13, 1997). ... Granted free agency (October 29, 1997). ... Signed by San Francisco Giants (December 9, 1997).
RECORDS: Holds major league single-season record for most consecutive scoreless innings—59 (August 30, sixth inning through September 28, 10th inning, 1988). ... Shares N.L. single-season record for fewest games lost by pitcher who led league in games lost—15 (1989 and 1992). ... Shares N.L. record for most shutouts in one month—5 (September 1988).
HONORS: Named Major League Player of the Year by THE SPORTING NEWS (1988). ... Named N.L. Pitcher of the Year by THE SPORTING NEWS (1988). ... Named righthanded pitcher on THE SPORTING NEWS N.L. All-Star team (1988). ... Won N.L. Gold Glove at pitcher (1988). ... Named N.L. Cy Young Award winner by Baseball Writers' Association of America (1988). ... Named pitcher on THE SPORTING NEWS N.L. Silver Slugger team (1993).
STATISTICAL NOTES: Pitched 2-0 one-hit, complete-game victory against San Diego (April 26, 1985). ... Pitched 6-0 one-hit, complete-game victory against Pittsburgh (July 23, 1985). ... Tied for N.L. lead with 19 sacrifice hits in 1988.
MISCELLANEOUS: Had sacrifice hit in only appearance as pinch-hitter (1988). ... Singled once in two games as pinch-hitter (1992). ... Started one game at third base but was replaced before first plate appearance and never played in field (1993).

Year Team (League)	W	L	Pct.	ERA	G	GS	CG	ShO	Sv.	IP	H	R	ER	BB	SO
1979— Clinton (Midwest)	4	0	1.000	2.09	15	4	1	0	2	43	33	15	10	17	33
1980— San Antonio (Tex.)	5	9	.357	3.55	49	3	1	0	14	109	120	59	43	59	75
1981— San Antonio (Tex.)	7	6	.538	4.68	42	4	3	0	*15	102	94	54	53	50	95

H

Year Team (League)	W	L	Pct.	ERA	G	GS	CG	ShO	Sv.	IP	H	R	ER	BB	SO
1982— Albuquerque (PCL)............	9	6	.600	3.71	47	7	2	0	4	123²/₃	121	73	51	63	93
1983— Albuquerque (PCL)............	10	8	.556	4.09	49	10	6	0	16	134¹/₃	132	73	61	57	95
— Los Angeles (N.L.)...........	0	0	...	3.38	8	0	0	0	1	8	7	6	3	6	5
1984— Los Angeles (N.L.)...........	11	8	.579	2.66	45	20	8	•4	2	189²/₃	160	65	56	50	150
1985— Los Angeles (N.L.)...........	19	3	*.864	2.03	36	34	9	5	0	239²/₃	179	72	54	68	157
1986— Los Angeles (N.L.)...........	14	14	.500	3.85	35	35	8	1	0	231¹/₃	213	112	99	86	153
1987— Los Angeles (N.L.)...........	16	16	.500	3.06	37	35	10	1	1	*264²/₃	247	105	90	74	190
1988— Los Angeles (N.L.)...........	•23	8	.742	2.26	35	34	•15	*8	1	*267	208	73	67	73	178
1989— Los Angeles (N.L.)...........	15	•15	.500	2.31	35	33	8	4	0	*256²/₃	226	75	66	77	178
1990— Los Angeles (N.L.)...........	1	1	.500	4.26	4	4	0	0	0	25¹/₃	26	12	12	4	16
1991— Bakersfield (California).......	2	0	1.000	0.82	2	2	0	0	0	11	5	2	1	1	6
— Albuquerque (PCL)...........	0	0	...	0.00	1	1	0	0	0	5	5	0	0	0	5
— San Antonio (Tex.)	0	1	.000	2.57	1	1	0	0	0	7	11	3	2	1	5
— Los Angeles (N.L.)...........	7	2	.778	3.46	21	21	0	0	0	112	112	43	43	32	73
1992— Los Angeles (N.L.)...........	10	•15	.400	3.67	33	33	1	0	0	210²/₃	209	101	86	69	130
1993— Los Angeles (N.L.)...........	12	14	.462	3.59	33	33	5	1	0	215²/₃	201	106	86	72	141
1994— Los Angeles (N.L.)...........	6	6	.500	3.79	21	21	1	0	0	135¹/₃	146	67	57	42	72
1995— Cleveland (A.L.)■....	16	6	.727	3.87	26	26	1	1	0	167¹/₃	151	76	72	51	111
1996— Cleveland (A.L.)...............	15	9	.625	4.24	33	33	1	0	0	206	238	115	97	58	125
1997— Cleveland (A.L.)...............	14	6	.700	4.47	32	32	1	0	0	195¹/₃	199	105	97	69	107
A.L. totals (3 years)	45	21	.682	4.21	91	91	3	1	0	568²/₃	588	296	266	178	343
N.L. totals (12 years)	134	102	.568	3.00	343	303	65	24	5	2156	1934	837	719	653	1443
Major league totals (15 years)....	179	123	.593	3.25	434	394	68	25	5	2724²/₃	2522	1133	985	831	1786

DIVISION SERIES RECORD

Year Team (League)	W	L	Pct.	ERA	G	GS	CG	ShO	Sv.	IP	H	R	ER	BB	SO
1995— Cleveland (A.L.)...............	1	0	1.000	0.00	1	1	0	0	0	7¹/₃	3	0	0	2	7
1996— Cleveland (A.L.)...............	0	0	...	5.40	1	1	0	0	0	5	7	4	3	3	3
1997— Cleveland (A.L.)...............	0	0	...	3.97	2	2	0	0	0	11¹/₃	14	5	5	2	4
Div. series totals (3 years)	1	0	1.000	3.04	4	4	0	0	0	23²/₃	24	9	8	7	14

CHAMPIONSHIP SERIES RECORD

RECORDS: Holds single-series record for most innings pitched—24²/₃ (1988). ... Holds N.L. single-game record for most hit batsmen—2 (October 12, 1988). ... Shares N.L. career record for most complete games—2. ... Shares N.L. single-series record for most hit batsmen—2 (1988).

NOTES: Named N.L. Championship Series Most Valuable Player (1988). ... Named A.L. Championship Series Most Valuable Player (1995).

Year Team (League)	W	L	Pct.	ERA	G	GS	CG	ShO	Sv.	IP	H	R	ER	BB	SO
1983— Los Angeles (N.L.)							Did not play.								
1985— Los Angeles (N.L.)	1	0	1.000	3.52	2	2	1	0	0	15¹/₃	17	6	6	6	5
1988— Los Angeles (N.L.)	1	0	1.000	1.09	4	3	1	1	1	24²/₃	18	5	3	7	15
1995— Cleveland (A.L.)................	2	0	1.000	1.29	2	2	0	0	0	14	9	3	2	3	15
1997— Cleveland (A.L.)................	0	0	...	0.00	1	1	0	0	0	7	4	0	0	1	7
Champ. series totals (4 years)	4	0	1.000	1.62	9	8	2	1	1	61	48	14	11	17	42

WORLD SERIES RECORD

RECORDS: Shares single-game record for most earned runs allowed—7 (October 18, 1997).

NOTES: Named Most Valuable Player (1988). ... Member of World Series championship team (1988).

Year Team (League)	W	L	Pct.	ERA	G	GS	CG	ShO	Sv.	IP	H	R	ER	BB	SO
1988— Los Angeles (N.L.)	2	0	1.000	1.00	2	2	2	1	0	18	7	2	2	6	17
1995— Cleveland (A.L.)................	1	1	.500	2.57	2	2	0	0	0	14	8	5	4	4	13
1997— Cleveland (A.L.)................	0	2	.000	11.70	2	2	0	0	0	10	15	13	13	6	5
World Series totals (3 years)	3	3	.500	4.07	6	6	2	1	0	42	30	20	19	16	35

ALL-STAR GAME RECORD

Year League	W	L	Pct.	ERA	GS	CG	ShO	Sv.	IP	H	R	ER	BB	SO
1987— National..............................	0	0	...	0.00	0	0	0	0	2	1	0	0	1	0
1988— National..............................	0	0	...	0.00	0	0	0	0	1	0	0	0	0	0
1989— National..............................						Did not play.								
All-Star totals (2 years)	0	0	...	0.00	0	0	0	0	3	1	0	0	1	0

HIDALGO, RICHARD   OF   ASTROS

PERSONAL: Born July 2, 1975, in Caracas, Venezuela. ... 6-3/190. ... Bats right, throws right. ... Full name: Richard Jose Hidalgo.
TRANSACTIONS/CAREER NOTES: Signed as non-drafted free agent by Houston Astros organization (July 2, 1991).
STATISTICAL NOTES: Led Texas League in grounding into double plays with 24 in 1996.

					BATTING								FIELDING		
Year Team (League)	Pos.	G	AB	R	H	2B	3B	HR	RBI	Avg.	BB	SO	SB	PO	A	E	Avg.
1992— GC Astros (GCL)	OF	51	184	20	57	7	3	1	27	.310	13	27	14	67	6	0	1.000
1993— Asheville (S. Atl.)........	OF	111	403	49	109	23	3	10	55	.270	30	76	21	197	*30	6	.974
1994— Quad City (Midwest) ..	OF	124	476	68	139	*47	6	12	76	.292	23	80	12	202	*23	11	.953
1995— Jackson (Texas)	OF	133	489	59	130	28	6	14	59	.266	32	76	8	238	14	5	.981
1996— Jackson (Texas)	OF	130	513	66	151	34	2	14	78	.294	29	55	11	302	14	6	.981
1997— New Orleans (A.A.).....	OF	134	526	74	147	*37	5	11	78	.279	35	57	6	261	*15	9	.968
— Houston (N.L.).............	OF	19	62	8	19	5	0	2	6	.306	4	18	1	28	0	0	1.000
Major league totals (1 year)		19	62	8	19	5	0	2	6	.306	4	18	1	28	0	0	1.000

DIVISION SERIES RECORD

					BATTING								FIELDING		
Year Team (League)	Pos.	G	AB	R	H	2B	3B	HR	RBI	Avg.	BB	SO	SB	PO	A	E	Avg.
1997— Houston (N.L.)	OF	2	5	1	0	0	0	0	0	.000	1	2	0	5	0	0	1.000

H

HIGGINSON, BOBBY   OF   TIGERS

PERSONAL: Born August 18, 1970, in Philadelphia. ... 5-11/180. ... Bats left, throws right. ... Full name: Robert Leigh Higginson.
COLLEGE: Temple.
TRANSACTIONS/CAREER NOTES: Selected by Detroit Tigers organization in 12th round of free-agent draft (June 1, 1992). ... On Detroit disabled list (May 11-June 7, 1996); included rehabilitation assignment to Toledo (June 4-7). ... On disabled list (June 15-26, 1997). ... On suspended list for one game (September 26, 1997).
RECORDS: Shares major league record for most consecutive home runs—4 (June 30 [3], July 1 [1], 1997).
STATISTICAL NOTES: Hit three home runs in one game (June 30, 1997). ... Tied for A.L. lead in double plays by outfielder with five in 1997. ... Career major league grand slams: 3.

							BATTING								FIELDING		
Year Team (League)	Pos.	G	AB	R	H	2B	3B	HR	RBI	Avg.	BB	SO	SB	PO	A	E	Avg.
1992— Niag. Falls (NYP)	OF	70	232	35	68	17	4	2	37	.293	33	47	12	109	5	2	.983
1993— Lakeland (Fla. St.)	OF	61	223	42	67	11	7	3	25	.300	40	31	8	88	7	2	.979
— London (Eastern)	OF	63	224	25	69	15	4	4	35	.308	19	37	3	100	11	2	.982
1994— Toledo (Int'l)	OF	137	476	81	131	28	3	23	67	.275	46	99	16	282	10	8	.973
1995— Detroit (A.L.)	OF-DH	131	410	61	92	17	5	14	43	.224	62	107	6	247	*13	4	.985
1996— Detroit (A.L.)	OF-DH	130	440	75	141	35	0	26	81	.320	65	66	6	227	9	9	.963
— Toledo (Int'l)	OF	3	13	4	4	0	1	0	1	.308	3	0	0	3	0	0	1.000
1997— Detroit (A.L.)	OF-DH	146	546	94	163	30	5	27	101	.299	70	85	12	287	*20	9	.972
Major league totals (3 years)		407	1396	230	396	82	10	67	225	.284	197	258	24	761	42	22	.973

HILL, GLENALLEN   OF   MARINERS

PERSONAL: Born March 22, 1965, in Santa Cruz, Calif. ... 6-2/225. ... Bats right, throws right.
HIGH SCHOOL: Santa Cruz (Calif.).
TRANSACTIONS/CAREER NOTES: Selected by Toronto Blue Jays organization in ninth round of free-agent draft (June 6, 1983). ... On disabled list (July 6-21, 1990). ... Traded by Blue Jays with P Denis Boucher, OF Mark Whiten and a player to be named later to Cleveland Indians for P Tom Candiotti and OF Turner Ward (June 27, 1991); Indians acquired cash instead of player to complete deal (October 15, 1991). ... On Cleveland disabled list (September 8, 1991-remainder of season). ... On Cleveland disabled list (April 23-May 22, 1992); included rehabilitation assignment to Canton/Akron (May 18-22). ... Traded by Indians to Chicago Cubs for OF Candy Maldonado (August 19, 1993). ... Granted free agency (October 27, 1993). ... Re-signed by Cubs (November 24, 1993). ... Granted free agency (April 7, 1995). ... Signed by San Francisco Giants (April 9, 1995). ... On San Francisco disabled list (May 27-August 5, 1996); included rehabilitation assignment to Phoenix (July 29-August 5). ... Granted free agency (October 29, 1997). ... Signed by Seattle Mariners organization (January 7, 1998).
STATISTICAL NOTES: Led Southern League with 287 total bases and tied for lead with 13 sacrifice flies in 1986. ... Led International League with 279 total bases and .578 slugging percentage in 1989. ... Career major league grand slams: 3.

							BATTING								FIELDING		
Year Team (League)	Pos.	G	AB	R	H	2B	3B	HR	RBI	Avg.	BB	SO	SB	PO	A	E	Avg.
1983— Medicine Hat (Pio.)	OF	46	133	34	63	3	4	6	27	.474	17	49	4	63	3	6	.917
1984— Florence (S. Atl.)	OF	129	440	75	105	19	5	16	64	.239	63	*150	30	281	9	16	.948
1985— Kinston (Carolina)	OF	131	466	57	98	13	0	20	56	.210	57	*211	42	234	12	13	.950
1986— Knoxville (Southern)	OF	141	*570	87	159	23	6	*31	96	.279	39	*153	18	230	9	*21	.919
1987— Syracuse (Int'l)	OF	*137	536	65	126	25	6	16	77	.235	25	*152	22	176	10	10	.949
— Knoxville (Southern)	OF	79	269	37	71	13	2	12	38	.264	28	75	10	130	6	5	.965
1988— Syracuse (Int'l)	OF	51	172	21	40	7	0	4	19	.233	15	59	7	101	2	1	.990
1989— Syracuse (Int'l)	OF	125	483	*86	*155	31	*15	*21	72	.321	34	107	21	242	3	*7	.972
— Toronto (A.L.)	OF-DH	19	52	4	15	0	0	1	7	.288	3	12	2	27	0	1	.964
1990— Toronto (A.L.)	OF-DH	84	260	47	60	11	3	12	32	.231	18	62	8	115	4	2	.983
1991— Toronto (A.L.)	DH-OF	35	99	14	25	5	2	3	11	.253	7	24	2	29	0	1	.967
— Cleveland (A.L.)■	OF-DH	37	122	15	32	3	0	5	14	.262	16	30	4	89	0	2	.978
1992— Cleveland (A.L.)	OF-DH	102	369	38	89	16	1	18	49	.241	20	73	9	126	5	6	.956
— Cant./Akr. (Eastern)	OF	3	9	1	1	1	0	0	1	.111	2	4	0	4	0	1	.800
1993— Cleveland (A.L.)	OF-DH	66	174	19	39	7	2	5	25	.224	11	50	7	62	1	4	.940
— Chicago (N.L.)■	OF	31	87	14	30	7	0	10	22	.345	6	21	1	42	2	2	.957
1994— Chicago (N.L.)	OF	89	269	48	80	12	1	10	38	.297	29	57	19	149	0	2	.987
1995— San Fran. (N.L.)■	OF	132	497	71	131	29	4	24	86	.264	39	98	25	226	10	10	.959
1996— San Francisco (N.L.)	OF	98	379	56	106	26	0	19	67	.280	33	95	6	160	6	7	.960
— Phoenix (PCL)	OF	5	17	4	6	1	0	2	2	.353	0	3	1	8	0	0	1.000
1997— San Francisco (N.L.)	OF-DH	128	398	47	104	28	4	11	64	.261	19	87	7	158	2	9	.947
American League totals (5 years)		343	1076	137	260	42	8	44	138	.242	75	251	32	448	10	16	.966
National League totals (5 years)		478	1630	236	451	102	9	74	277	.277	126	358	58	735	20	30	.962
Major league totals (9 years)		821	2706	373	711	144	17	118	415	.263	201	609	90	1183	30	46	.963

DIVISION SERIES RECORD

							BATTING								FIELDING		
Year Team (League)	Pos.	G	AB	R	H	2B	3B	HR	RBI	Avg.	BB	SO	SB	PO	A	E	Avg.
1997— San Francisco (N.L.)	OF-PH	3	7	0	0	0	0	0	0	.000	2	2	0	2	0	0	1.000

HILL, KEN   P   ANGELS

PERSONAL: Born December 14, 1965, in Lynn, Mass. ... 6-2/205. ... Throws right, bats right. ... Full name: Kenneth Wade Hill.
HIGH SCHOOL: Classical (Lynn, Mass.).
COLLEGE: North Adams (Mass.) State.
TRANSACTIONS/CAREER NOTES: Signed as non-drafted free agent by Detroit Tigers organization (February 14, 1985). ... Traded by Tigers with a player to be named later to St. Louis Cardinals for C Mike Heath (August 10, 1986); Cardinals acquired 1B Mike Laga to complete deal (September 2, 1986). ... On St. Louis disabled list (March 26-May 9, 1988). ... On St. Louis disabled list (August 11-September 1, 1991); included rehabilitation assignment to Louisville (August 29-30). ... Traded by Cardinals to Montreal Expos for 1B Andres Galarraga (November

H

25, 1991). ... On Montreal disabled list (June 26-July 17, 1993); included rehabilitation assignment to Ottawa (July 12-15). ... Traded by Expos to Cardinals for P Brian Eversgerd, P Kirk Bullinger and OF Darond Stovall (April 5, 1995). ... Traded by Cardinals to Cleveland Indians for 3B/2B David Bell, P Rick Heiserman and C Pepe McNeal (July 27, 1995). ... Granted free agency (November 1, 1995). ... Signed by Texas Rangers (December 22, 1995). ... Traded by Rangers to Anaheim Angels for C Jim Leyritz and a player to be named later (July 29, 1997); Rangers acquired IF Rob Sasser to complete deal (October 31, 1997). ... On disabled list (May 1-24, 1997); included rehabilitation assignment to Tulsa (May 20-24). ... Granted free agency (November 7, 1997). ... Re-signed by Angels (November 15, 1997).

RECORDS: Shares N.L. single-season record for fewest games lost by pitcher who led league in games lost—15 (1989).

STATISTICAL NOTES: Pitched 6-0 one-hit, complete-game victory against New York (June 8, 1992). ... Led N.L. with 16 sacrifice hits in 1994. ... Pitched 11-0 one-hit, complete-game victory against Detroit (May 3, 1996). ... Led A.L. with four balks in 1996. ... Led A.L. with 95 bases on balls in 1997.

MISCELLANEOUS: Made an out in one game as pinch-hitter with Montreal (1993). ... Had sacrifice hit in one game as pinch-hitter (1994).

Year Team (League)	W	L	Pct.	ERA	G	GS	CG	ShO	Sv.	IP	H	R	ER	BB	SO
1985—Gastonia (S. Atl.)	3	6	.333	4.96	15	12	0	0	0	69	60	51	38	57	48
1986—Gastonia (S. Atl.)	9	5	.643	2.79	22	16	1	0	0	122^2/$_3$	95	51	38	80	86
—Glens Falls (Eastern)	0	1	.000	5.14	1	1	0	0	0	7	4	4	4	6	4
—Arkansas (Texas)■	1	2	.333	4.50	3	3	1	0	0	18	18	10	9	7	9
1987—Arkansas (Texas)	3	5	.375	5.20	18	8	0	0	2	53^2/$_3$	60	33	31	30	48
—St. Petersburg (FSL)	1	3	.250	4.17	18	4	0	0	2	41	38	19	19	17	32
1988—St. Louis (N.L.)	0	1	.000	5.14	4	1	0	0	0	14	16	9	8	6	6
—Arkansas (Texas)	9	9	.500	4.92	22	22	3	1	0	115^1/$_3$	129	76	63	50	107
1989—Louisville (A.A.)	0	2	.000	3.50	3	3	0	0	0	18	13	8	7	10	18
—St. Louis (N.L.)	7	•15	.318	3.80	33	33	2	1	0	196^2/$_3$	186	92	83	*99	112
1990—St. Louis (N.L.)	5	6	.455	5.49	17	14	1	0	0	78^2/$_3$	79	49	48	33	58
—Louisville (A.A.)	6	1	.857	1.79	12	12	2	1	0	85^1/$_3$	47	20	17	27	104
1991—St. Louis (N.L.)	11	10	.524	3.57	30	30	0	0	0	181^1/$_3$	147	76	72	67	121
—Louisville (A.A.)	0	0	. . .	0.00	1	1	0	0	0	1	0	0	0	0	2
1992—Montreal (N.L.)■	16	9	.640	2.68	33	33	3	3	0	218	187	76	65	75	150
1993—Montreal (N.L.)	9	7	.563	3.23	28	28	2	0	0	183^2/$_3$	163	84	66	74	90
—Ottawa (Int'l)	0	0	. . .	0.00	1	1	0	0	0	4	1	0	0	1	0
1994—Montreal (N.L.)	•16	5	.762	3.32	23	23	2	1	0	154^2/$_3$	145	61	57	44	85
1995—St. Louis (N.L.)■	6	7	.462	5.06	18	18	0	0	0	110^1/$_3$	125	71	62	45	50
—Cleveland (A.L.)■	4	1	.800	3.98	12	11	1	0	0	74^2/$_3$	77	36	33	32	48
1996—Texas (A.L.)■	16	10	.615	3.63	35	35	7	•3	0	250^2/$_3$	250	110	101	95	170
1997—Texas (A.L.)	5	8	.385	5.19	19	19	0	0	0	111	129	69	64	56	68
—Tulsa (Texas)	0	0	. . .	0.00	1	1	0	0	0	5	2	0	0	1	3
—Anaheim (A.L.)■	4	4	.500	3.65	12	12	1	0	0	79	65	34	32	§39	38
A.L. totals (3 years)	29	23	.558	4.02	78	77	9	3	0	515^1/$_3$	521	249	230	222	324
N.L. totals (8 years)	70	60	.538	3.65	186	180	10	5	0	1137^1/$_3$	1048	518	461	443	672
Major league totals (10 years)	99	83	.544	3.76	264	257	19	8	0	1652^2/$_3$	1569	767	691	665	996

DIVISION SERIES RECORD

Year Team (League)	W	L	Pct.	ERA	G	GS	CG	ShO	Sv.	IP	H	R	ER	BB	SO
1995—Cleveland (A.L.)	1	0	1.000	0.00	1	0	0	0	0	1^1/$_3$	1	0	0	0	2
1996—Texas (A.L.)	0	0	. . .	4.50	1	1	0	0	0	6	5	3	3	3	1
Div. series totals (2 years)	1	0	1.000	3.68	2	1	0	0	0	7^1/$_3$	6	3	3	3	3

CHAMPIONSHIP SERIES RECORD

Year Team (League)	W	L	Pct.	ERA	G	GS	CG	ShO	Sv.	IP	H	R	ER	BB	SO
1995—Cleveland (A.L.)	1	0	1.000	0.00	1	1	0	0	0	7	5	0	0	3	6

WORLD SERIES RECORD

Year Team (League)	W	L	Pct.	ERA	G	GS	CG	ShO	Sv.	IP	H	R	ER	BB	SO
1995—Cleveland (A.L.)	0	1	.000	4.26	2	1	0	0	0	6^1/$_3$	7	3	3	4	1

ALL-STAR GAME RECORD

Year League	W	L	Pct.	ERA	GS	CG	ShO	Sv.	IP	H	R	ER	BB	SO
1994—National	0	0	. . .	0.00	0	0	0	0	2	0	0	0	1	0

HINCH, A.J.   C   ATHLETICS

PERSONAL: Born May 15, 1974, in Waverly, Iowa. ... 6-1/195. ... Bats right, throws right. ... Full name: Andrew Jay Hinch.
HIGH SCHOOL: Midwest City (Okla.).
COLLEGE: Stanford.
TRANSACTIONS/CAREER NOTES: Selected by Chicago White Sox organization in second round of free-agent draft (June 2, 1992); did not sign. ... Selected by Minnesota Twins organization in third round of free-agent draft (June 1, 1995); did not sign. ... Selected by Oakland Athletics organization in third round of free-agent draft (June 4, 1996). ... On Modesto suspended list (June 7-9, 1997).
STATISTICAL NOTES: Led California League catchers with .996 fielding percentage in 1997.
MISCELLANEOUS: Member of 1996 U.S. Olympic baseball team.

Year Team (League)	Pos.	G	AB	R	H	2B	3B	HR	RBI	Avg.	BB	SO	SB	PO	A	E	Avg.
1996—							Did not play.										
1997—Modesto (California)	C-1B	95	333	70	103	25	3	20	73	.309	42	68	8	622	66	3	†.996
—Edmonton (PCL)	C-OF	39	125	23	47	7	0	4	24	.376	20	13	2	201	7	3	.986

HINCHLIFFE, BRETT   P   MARINERS

PERSONAL: Born July 21, 1974, in Detroit. ... 6-5/190. ... Throws right, bats right.
HIGH SCHOOL: Bishop Gallagher (Harper Woods, Mich.).
TRANSACTIONS/CAREER NOTES: Selected by Seattle Mariners organization in 16th round of free-agent draft (June 1, 1992).
STATISTICAL NOTES: Pitched 12-0 no-hit victory against Cedar Rapids (June 28, 1994).

H

Year	Team (League)	W	L	Pct.	ERA	G	GS	CG	ShO	Sv.	IP	H	R	ER	BB	SO
1992—	Ariz. Mariners (Ariz.)	5	4	.556	2.31	*24	0	0	0	3	35	42	17	9	9	26
1993—	Ariz. Mariners (Ariz.)	0	4	.000	5.08	10	9	0	0	0	44 1/3	55	32	25	5	29
1994—	Appleton (Midwest)	11	7	.611	3.21	27	27	3	1	0	173 2/3	140	79	62	50	160
1995—	Riverside (California)	3	8	.273	6.61	15	15	0	0	0	77 2/3	110	69	57	35	68
1996—	Lancaster (Calif.)	11	10	.524	4.24	27	26	0	0	0	163 1/3	179	105	77	64	146
1997—	Memphis (Southern)	10	10	.500	4.45	24	24	*5	1	0	145 2/3	159	81	72	45	107

HITCHCOCK, STERLING　　　　　P　　　　　PADRES

PERSONAL: Born April 29, 1971, in Fayetteville, N.C. ... 6-1/192. ... Throws left, bats left. ... Full name: Sterling Alex Hitchcock.
HIGH SCHOOL: Armwood (Seffner, Fla.).
TRANSACTIONS/CAREER NOTES: Selected by New York Yankees organization in ninth round of free-agent draft (June 5, 1989). ... On disabled list (June 26-August 14, 1991). ... On Columbus disabled list (May 23-July 21, 1993). ... Traded by Yankees with 3B Russ Davis to Seattle Mariners for 1B Tino Martinez, P Jeff Nelson and P Jim Mecir (December 7, 1995). ... Traded by Mariners to San Diego Padres for P Scott Sanders (December 6, 1996). ... On disabled list (June 6-July 3, 1997).
STATISTICAL NOTES: Pitched 1-0 no-hit victory against Sumter (July 16, 1990).

Year	Team (League)	W	L	Pct.	ERA	G	GS	CG	ShO	Sv.	IP	H	R	ER	BB	SO
1989—	GC Yankees (GCL)	*9	1	.900	1.64	13	•13	0	0	0	76 2/3	48	16	14	27	*98
1990—	Greensboro (S. Atl.)	12	12	.500	2.91	27	27	6	*5	0	173 1/3	122	68	56	60	*171
1991—	Prince William (Caro.)	7	7	.500	2.64	19	19	2	0	0	119 1/3	111	49	35	26	101
1992—	Alb./Colon. (Eastern)	6	9	.400	2.58	24	24	2	0	0	146 2/3	116	51	42	42	*155
—New York (A.L.)		0	2	.000	8.31	3	3	0	0	0	13	23	12	12	6	6
1993—	Columbus (Int'l)	3	5	.375	4.81	16	16	0	0	0	76 2/3	80	43	41	28	85
—New York (A.L.)		1	2	.333	4.65	6	6	0	0	0	31	32	18	16	14	26
1994—	New York (A.L.)	4	1	.800	4.20	23	5	1	0	2	49 1/3	48	24	23	29	37
—Columbus (Int'l)		3	4	.429	4.32	10	9	1	0	0	50	53	30	24	18	47
—Alb./Colon. (Eastern)		1	0	1.000	1.80	1	1	0	0	0	5	4	1	1	0	7
1995—	New York (A.L.)	11	10	.524	4.70	27	27	4	1	0	168 1/3	155	91	88	68	121
1996—	Seattle (A.L.)■	13	9	.591	5.35	35	35	0	0	0	196 2/3	245	131	117	73	132
1997—	San Diego (N.L.)■	10	11	.476	5.20	32	28	1	0	0	161	172	102	93	55	106
A.L. totals (5 years)		29	24	.547	5.03	94	76	5	1	2	458 1/3	503	276	256	190	322
N.L. totals (1 year)		10	11	.476	5.20	32	28	1	0	0	161	172	102	93	55	106
Major league totals (6 years)		39	35	.527	5.07	126	104	6	1	2	619 1/3	675	378	349	245	428

					DIVISION SERIES RECORD											
Year	Team (League)	W	L	Pct.	ERA	G	GS	CG	ShO	Sv.	IP	H	R	ER	BB	SO
1995—	New York (A.L.)	0	0	...	5.40	2	0	0	0	0	1 2/3	2	2	1	2	1

HOCKING, DENNY　　　　　SS　　　　　TWINS

PERSONAL: Born April 2, 1970, in Torrance, Calif. ... 5-10/180. ... Bats both, throws right. ... Full name: Dennis Lee Hocking.
HIGH SCHOOL: West Torrance (Calif.).
COLLEGE: El Camino College (Calif.).
TRANSACTIONS/CAREER NOTES: Selected by Minnesota Twins organization in 52nd round of free-agent draft (June 5, 1989). ... On Nashville disabled list (April 8-29, 1993). ... On Minnesota disabled list (March 22-April 30, May 30-June 29 and July 31-September 8, 1996); included rehabilitation assignments to Salt Lake (April 4-30, June 21-29 and August 24-September 8).
STATISTICAL NOTES: Led California League shortstops with 721 total chances in 1992. ... Led Pacific Coast League shortstops with .966 fielding percentage and 390 assists in 1995.

Year	Team (League)	Pos.	G	AB	R	H	2B	3B	HR	RBI	Avg.	BB	SO	SB	PO	A	E	Avg.
1990—	Elizabethton (App.)	SS-2B-3B	54	201	45	59	6	2	6	30	.294	40	26	14	77	179	20	.928
1991—	Kenosha (Midwest)	SS	125	432	72	110	17	8	2	36	.255	77	69	22	193	308	42	.923
1992—	Visalia (California)	SS	135	*550	117	*182	34	9	7	81	.331	72	77	38	214	*469	38	.947
1993—	Nashville (Southern)	SS-2B	107	409	54	109	9	4	8	50	.267	34	66	15	144	300	30	.937
—Minnesota (A.L.)		SS-2B	15	36	7	5	1	0	0	0	.139	6	8	1	19	23	1	.977
1994—	Salt Lake (PCL)	SS	112	394	61	110	14	6	5	57	.279	28	57	13	143	342	26	.949
—Minnesota (A.L.)		SS	11	31	3	10	3	0	0	2	.323	0	4	2	11	27	0	1.000
1995—	Salt Lake (PCL)	SS-2B	117	397	51	112	24	2	8	75	.282	25	41	12	173	†393	20	†.966
—Minnesota (A.L.)		SS	9	25	4	5	0	2	0	3	.200	2	2	1	13	20	1	.971
1996—	Minnesota (A.L.)	O-S-2-DH-1	49	127	16	25	6	0	1	10	.197	8	24	3	67	9	1	.987
—Salt Lake (PCL)		S-0-1-2-3	37	130	18	36	6	2	3	22	.277	10	17	2	51	69	3	.976
1997—	Minnesota (A.L.)	S-3-0-2-DH-1	115	253	28	65	12	4	2	25	.257	18	51	3	124	146	4	.985
Major league totals (5 years)			199	472	58	110	22	6	3	40	.233	34	89	10	234	225	7	.985

HOFFMAN, TREVOR　　　　　P　　　　　PADRES

PERSONAL: Born October 13, 1967, in Bellflower, Calif. ... 6-0/205. ... Throws right, bats right. ... Full name: Trevor William Hoffman. ... Brother of Glenn Hoffman, minor league field coordinator, Los Angeles Dodgers, and major league infielder with Boston Red Sox, Dodgers and California Angels (1980-89).
HIGH SCHOOL: Savanna (Anaheim, Calif.).
JUNIOR COLLEGE: Cypress (Calif.) College.
COLLEGE: Arizona.
TRANSACTIONS/CAREER NOTES: Selected by Cincinnati Reds organization in 11th round of free-agent draft (June 5, 1989). ... Selected by Florida Marlins in first round (eighth pick overall) of expansion draft (November 17, 1992). ... Traded by Marlins with P Jose Martinez and P Andres Berumen to San Diego Padres for 3B Gary Sheffield and P Rich Rodriguez (June 24, 1993).
HONORS: Named N.L. Fireman of the Year by THE SPORTING NEWS (1996).
MISCELLANEOUS: Holds San Diego Padres all-time record for most saves (133).

H

Year Team (League)	W	L	Pct.	ERA	G	GS	CG	ShO	Sv.	IP	H	R	ER	BB	SO
1991—Cedar Rapids (Midw.)	1	1	.500	1.87	27	0	0	0	12	33²/₃	22	8	7	13	52
—Chattanooga (Southern).....	1	0	1.000	1.93	14	0	0	0	8	14	10	4	3	7	23
1992—Chattanooga (Southern).....	3	0	1.000	1.52	6	6	0	0	0	29²/₃	22	6	5	11	31
—Nashville (A.A.)	4	6	.400	4.27	42	5	0	0	6	65¹/₃	57	32	31	32	63
1993—Florida (N.L.)■...............	2	2	.500	3.28	28	0	0	0	2	35²/₃	24	13	13	19	26
—San Diego (N.L.)■.............	2	4	.333	4.31	39	0	0	0	3	54¹/₃	56	30	26	20	53
1994—San Diego (N.L.)	4	4	.500	2.57	47	0	0	0	20	56	39	16	16	20	68
1995—San Diego (N.L.)	7	4	.636	3.88	55	0	0	0	31	53¹/₃	48	25	23	14	52
1996—San Diego (N.L.)	9	5	.643	2.25	70	0	0	0	42	88	50	23	22	31	111
1997—San Diego (N.L.)	6	4	.600	2.66	70	0	0	0	37	81¹/₃	59	25	24	24	111
Major league totals (5 years)	30	23	.566	3.03	309	0	0	0	135	368²/₃	276	132	124	128	421

DIVISION SERIES RECORD

Year Team (League)	W	L	Pct.	ERA	G	GS	CG	ShO	Sv.	IP	H	R	ER	BB	SO
1996—San Diego (N.L.)	0	1	.000	10.80	2	0	0	0	0	1²/₃	3	2	2	1	2

RECORD AS POSITION PLAYER

						BATTING								FIELDING		
Year Team (League)	Pos.	G	AB	R	H	2B	3B	HR	RBI	Avg.	BB	SO	SB	PO	A	E	Avg.
1989—Billings (Pioneer)........	SS	61	201	22	50	5	0	1	20	.249	19	40	1	*116	140	•25	.911
1990—Char., W.Va. (SAL)......	SS-3B	103	278	41	59	10	1	2	23	.212	38	53	3	114	209	30	.915

HOILES, CHRIS   C   ORIOLES

PERSONAL: Born March 20, 1965, in Bowling Green, Ohio. ... 6-0/215. ... Bats right, throws right. ... Full name: Christopher Allen Hoiles.
HIGH SCHOOL: Elmwood (Wayne, Ohio).
COLLEGE: Eastern Michigan.
TRANSACTIONS/CAREER NOTES: Selected by Detroit Tigers organization in 19th round of free-agent draft (June 2, 1986). ... Traded by Tigers organization with P Cesar Mejia and P Robinson Garces to Baltimore Orioles (September 9, 1988), completing deal in which Orioles traded OF Fred Lynn to Tigers for three players to be named later (August 31, 1988). ... On Rochester disabled list (June 18-July 7, 1989). ... On Baltimore disabled list (June 22-August 18, 1992); included rehabilitation assignment to Hagerstown (August 11-18). ... On disabled list (August 3-24, 1993 and July 16-31, 1995). ... On Baltimore disabled list (June 17-July 18, 1997); included rehabilitation assignment to Bowie (July 15-18).
STATISTICAL NOTES: Led Appalachian League first basemen with .996 fielding percentage, 515 putouts and 551 total chances in 1986. ... Led Appalachian League with 143 total bases in 1986. ... Led Eastern League with .500 slugging percentage in 1988. ... Tied for Eastern League lead in double plays by catcher with five in 1988. ... Led A.L. catchers with .998 fielding percentage in 1991 and 1.000 in 1997. ... Led A.L. catchers with 658 total chances in 1994. ... Career major league grand slams: 5.

						BATTING								FIELDING		
Year Team (League)	Pos.	G	AB	R	H	2B	3B	HR	RBI	Avg.	BB	SO	SB	PO	A	E	Avg.
1986—Bristol (Appal.)...........	1B-C	•68	253	42	81	*19	2	13	*57	.320	30	20	10	†563	38	4	†.993
1987—Glens Falls (Eastern) ..	C-1B-3B	108	380	47	105	12	0	13	53	.276	35	37	1	406	88	11	.978
1988—Glens Falls (Eastern) ..	C-1B	103	360	67	102	21	3	•17	73	.283	50	56	4	438	57	7	.986
—Toledo (Int'l)............	C	22	69	4	11	1	0	2	6	.159	2	12	1	71	2	1	.986
1989—Rochester (Int'l)■	C-1B	96	322	41	79	19	1	10	51	.245	31	58	1	431	33	7	.985
—Baltimore (A.L.).........	C-DH	6	9	0	1	1	0	0	1	.111	1	3	0	11	0	0	1.000
1990—Rochester (Int'l)	C-1B	74	247	52	86	20	1	18	56	.348	44	48	4	268	13	5	.983
—Baltimore (A.L.).........	C-DH-1B	23	63	7	12	3	0	1	6	.190	5	12	0	62	6	0	1.000
1991—Baltimore (A.L.).........	C-1B	107	341	36	83	15	0	11	31	.243	29	61	0	443	44	1	†.998
1992—Baltimore (A.L.).........	C-DH	96	310	49	85	10	1	20	40	.274	55	60	0	500	31	3	.994
—Hagerstown (East.).....	C	7	24	7	11	1	0	1	5	.458	2	5	0	16	5	0	1.000
1993—Baltimore (A.L.).........	C-DH	126	419	80	130	28	0	29	82	.310	69	94	1	696	64	5	.993
1994—Baltimore (A.L.).........	C	99	332	45	82	10	0	19	53	.247	63	73	2	*615	36	7	.989
1995—Baltimore (A.L.).........	C-DH	114	352	53	88	15	1	19	58	.250	67	80	1	659	33	3	*.996
1996—Baltimore (A.L.).........	C-1B	127	407	64	105	13	0	25	73	.258	57	97	0	777	42	7	.992
1997—Baltimore (A.L.).........	C-DH-1-3	99	320	45	83	15	0	12	49	.259	51	86	1	622	31	0	†1.000
—Bowie (Eastern).........	C	3	7	1	1	1	0	0	2	.143	3	2	0	12	0	0	1.000
Major league totals (9 years)		797	2553	379	669	110	2	136	393	.262	397	566	5	4385	287	26	.994

DIVISION SERIES RECORD

						BATTING								FIELDING		
Year Team (League)	Pos.	G	AB	R	H	2B	3B	HR	RBI	Avg.	BB	SO	SB	PO	A	E	Avg.
1996—Baltimore (A.L.)..........	C-PH	4	7	1	1	0	0	0	0	.143	4	3	0	14	3	0	1.000
1997—Baltimore (A.L.)..........	C	3	7	1	1	0	0	1	1	.143	2	1	0	23	0	0	1.000
Division series totals (2 years)		7	14	2	2	0	0	1	1	.143	6	4	0	37	3	0	1.000

CHAMPIONSHIP SERIES RECORD

						BATTING								FIELDING		
Year Team (League)	Pos.	G	AB	R	H	2B	3B	HR	RBI	Avg.	BB	SO	SB	PO	A	E	Avg.
1996—Baltimore (A.L.)..........	C-PH	4	12	1	2	0	0	1	2	.167	1	3	0	23	2	0	1.000
1997—Baltimore (A.L.)..........	C	4	14	1	2	0	0	0	0	.143	2	5	0	47	2	0	1.000
Championship series totals (2 years)		8	26	2	4	0	0	1	2	.154	3	8	0	70	4	0	1.000

HOLBERT, AARON   SS/2B   MARINERS

PERSONAL: Born January 9, 1973, in Torrance, Calif. ... 6-0/160. ... Bats right, throws right. ... Full name: Aaron Keith Holbert. ... Brother of Ray Holbert, shortstop, Detroit Tigers organization.
HIGH SCHOOL: David Starr Jordan (Long Beach, Calif.).
TRANSACTIONS/CAREER NOTES: Selected by St. Louis Cardinals organization in first round (18th pick overall) of free-agent draft (June 4, 1990); pick received as part of compensation for Boston Red Sox signing Type A free-agent C Tony Pena. ... On disabled list (June 5-July 17,

H

1991). ... On Arkansas disabled list (May 10-July 30, 1994). ... On disabled list (May 15-22 and July 28-August 4, 1995). ... On suspended list (May 23-25, 1995). ... Granted free agency (October 15, 1997). ... Signed by Seattle Mariners organization (December 2, 1997).

STATISTICAL NOTES: Led Florida State League in caught stealing with 22 in 1993. ... Led American Association in caught stealing with 14 in 1996. ... Led American Association second basemen with 18 errors in 1996.

Year Team (League)	Pos.	G	AB	R	H	2B	3B	HR	RBI	Avg.	BB	SO	SB	PO	A	E	Avg.
1990— Johnson City (App.) ...	SS	54	174	27	30	4	1	1	18	.172	24	31	4	87	136	*30	.881
1991— Springfield (Midw.)	SS	59	215	22	48	5	1	1	24	.223	15	28	5	112	181	15	.951
1992— Savannah (S. Atl.)	SS	119	438	53	117	17	4	1	34	.267	40	57	62	190	314	47	.915
1993— St. Petersburg (FSL) ..	SS-2B	121	457	60	121	18	3	2	31	.265	28	61	45	220	351	32	.947
1994— Arkansas (Texas)........	SS	59	233	41	69	10	6	2	19	.296	14	25	9	94	192	17	.944
— Ariz. Cardinals (Ariz.) .	SS	5	12	3	2	0	0	0	0	.167	2	2	2	2	17	1	.950
1995— Louisville (A.A.)..........	SS	112	401	57	103	16	4	9	40	.257	20	60	14	153	302	*31	.936
1996— Louisville (A.A.)..........	2B-SS	112	436	54	115	16	6	4	32	.264	21	61	20	185	340	30	.946
— St. Louis (N.L.)............	2B	1	3	0	0	0	0	0	0	.000	0	0	0	1	0	0	1.000
1997— Louisville (A.A.)..........	SS-2B	93	314	32	80	14	3	4	32	.255	15	56	9	129	261	27	.935
Major league totals (1 year)		1	3	0	0	0	0	0	0	.000	0	0	0	1	0	0	1.000

HOLDRIDGE, DAVID   P   MARINERS

PERSONAL: Born February 5, 1969, in Wayne, Mich. ... 6-3/185. ... Throws right, bats right. ... Full name: David Allen Holdridge.

HIGH SCHOOL: Ocean View (Huntington Beach, Calif.).

TRANSACTIONS/CAREER NOTES: Selected by California Angels organization in supplemental round ("sandwich pick" between first and second round, 31st pick overall) of free-agent draft (June 2, 1987); pick received as compensation for Oakland Athletics signing Type A free-agent DH/OF Reggie Jackson. ... Traded by Angels organization to Philadelphia Phillies organization (October 3, 1988). ... On Reading disabled list (May 27-June 25, 1991). ... Selected by Angels from Phillies organization in Rule 5 major league draft (December 9, 1991). ... Granted free agency (October 3, 1996). ... Signed by Seattle Mariners organization (December 13, 1996).

STATISTICAL NOTES: Tied for Florida State League lead with 11 home runs allowed in 1989. ... Tied for Eastern League lead with 13 home runs allowed in 1990. ... Led California League with 21 wild pitches in 1992.

Year Team (League)	W	L	Pct.	ERA	G	GS	CG	ShO	Sv.	IP	H	R	ER	BB	SO
1988— Quad City (Midwest)	6	12	.333	3.87	28	28	0	0	0	153²/₃	151	92	66	66	110
1989— Clearwater (Fla. St.)■	7	10	.412	5.71	24	24	3	0	0	132¹/₃	147	*100	*84	77	77
1990— Reading (Eastern)	8	12	.400	4.58	24	24	1	0	0	127²/₃	114	74	65	*79	78
1991— Reading (Eastern)	0	2	.000	5.47	7	7	0	0	0	26¹/₃	26	24	16	34	19
— Clearwater (Fla. St.)	0	0	...	7.56	15	0	0	0	1	25	34	23	21	21	23
1992— Palm Springs (Calif.)■......	12	12	.500	4.25	28	27	3	•2	0	159	169	99	75	87	135
1993— Midland (Texas)...............	8	10	.444	6.08	27	•27	1	1	0	151	*202	*117	*102	55	123
1994— Midland (Texas)...............	7	4	.636	3.93	38	2	0	0	2	66¹/₃	66	33	29	23	59
— Vancouver (PCL)	0	0	...	5.14	4	0	0	0	0	7	12	7	4	4	4
1995— Vancouver (PCL)	0	2	.000	4.61	11	0	0	0	1	13²/₃	18	10	7	7	13
— Lake Elsinore (Calif.)	3	0	1.000	0.98	12	0	0	0	0	18¹/₃	13	3	2	5	24
— Midland (Texas)	1	0	1.000	1.78	14	0	0	0	1	25¹/₃	20	8	5	8	23
1996— Vancouver (PCL)	2	1	.667	4.63	29	0	0	0	1	35	39	19	18	23	26
— Lake Elsinore (Calif.)	0	0	...	2.08	12	0	0	0	6	13	11	3	3	2	21
1997— Memphis (Southern)■	0	3	.000	3.34	30	0	0	0	17	35	31	14	13	17	37
— Tacoma (PCL)	1	1	.500	2.96	15	0	0	0	1	24¹/₃	21	9	8	13	24

HOLLANDSWORTH, TODD   OF   DODGERS

PERSONAL: Born April 20, 1973, in Dayton, Ohio. ... 6-2/193. ... Bats left, throws left. ... Full name: Todd Mathew Hollandsworth.

HIGH SCHOOL: Newport (Bellevue, Wash.).

TRANSACTIONS/CAREER NOTES: Selected by Los Angeles Dodgers organization in third round of free-agent draft (June 3, 1991); pick received as part of compensation for Kansas City Royals signing Type B free-agent OF/DH Kirk Gibson. ... On Los Angeles disabled list (May 3-July 7 and August 9-September 12, 1995); included rehabilitation assignments to San Bernardino (June 6-7) and Albuquerque (June 27-July 7). ... On Los Angeles disabled list (August 2-16 and August 17-September 6, 1997).

HONORS: Named N.L. Rookie of the Year by Baseball Writers' Association of America (1996).

Year Team (League)	Pos.	G	AB	R	H	2B	3B	HR	RBI	Avg.	BB	SO	SB	PO	A	E	Avg.
1991— Yakima (N'west)	OF	56	203	34	48	5	1	8	33	.236	27	57	11	106	1	7	.939
1992— Bakersfield (Calif.)	OF	119	430	70	111	23	5	13	58	.258	50	113	27	230	8	6	.975
1993— San Antonio (Tex.)	OF	126	474	57	119	24	9	17	63	.251	29	101	24	246	13	12	.956
1994— Albuquerque (PCL).....	OF	132	505	80	144	31	5	19	91	.285	46	96	15	237	5	13	.949
1995— Los Angeles (N.L.)	OF	41	103	16	24	2	0	5	13	.233	10	29	2	60	1	4	.938
— San Bern. (Calif.)........	OF	1	2	0	1	0	0	0	0	.500	0	1	0	0	0	0	...
— Albuquerque (PCL)......	OF	10	38	9	9	2	0	2	4	.237	6	8	1	19	3	0	1.000
1996— Los Angeles (N.L.)	OF	149	478	64	139	26	4	12	59	.291	41	93	21	217	7	5	.978
1997— Los Angeles (N.L.)	OF	106	296	39	73	20	2	4	31	.247	17	60	5	185	2	3	.984
— Albuquerque (PCL)......	OF	13	56	13	24	4	3	1	14	.429	4	4	2	32	1	0	1.000
— San Bern. (Calif.)........	OF	2	8	1	2	0	1	0	2	.250	1	2	0	2	1	0	1.000
Major league totals (3 years)		296	877	119	236	48	6	21	103	.269	68	182	28	462	10	12	.975

DIVISION SERIES RECORD

RECORDS: Shares N.L. career record for most doubles—3.

Year Team (League)	Pos.	G	AB	R	H	2B	3B	HR	RBI	Avg.	BB	SO	SB	PO	A	E	Avg.
1995— Los Angeles (N.L.)	OF-PH	2	2	0	0	0	0	0	0	.000	0	0	0	0	0	0	...
1996— Los Angeles (N.L.)	OF	3	12	1	4	3	0	0	1	.333	0	3	0	4	0	0	1.000
Division series totals (2 years)		5	14	1	4	3	0	0	1	.286	0	3	0	4	0	0	1.000

H

HOLLINS, DAMON — OF — BRAVES

PERSONAL: Born June 12, 1974, in Fairfield, Calif. ... 5-11/180. ... Bats right, throws left. ... Full name: Damon Jamall Hollins.
HIGH SCHOOL: Vallejo (Calif.).
TRANSACTIONS/CAREER NOTES: Selected by Atlanta Braves organization in fourth round of free-agent draft (June 1, 1992). ... On disabled list (May 28-September 3, 1996).
STATISTICAL NOTES: Led Southern League outfielders with 356 total chances in 1995.

										BATTING					FIELDING		
Year — Team (League)	Pos.	G	AB	R	H	2B	3B	HR	RBI	Avg.	BB	SO	SB	PO	A	E	Avg.
1992— GC Braves (GCL)	OF	49	179	35	41	12	1	1	15	.229	30	22	15	83	6	1	.989
1993— Danville (Appal.)	OF	62	240	37	77	15	2	7	51	.321	19	30	10	95	*11	6	.946
1994— Durham (Carolina)	OF	131	485	76	131	28	0	23	88	.270	45	115	12	279	11	*13	.957
1995— Greenville (Southern) .	OF	129	466	64	115	26	2	18	77	.247	44	120	6	*330	18	8	.978
1996— Richmond (Int'l)	OF	42	146	16	29	9	0	0	8	.199	16	37	2	116	6	3	.976
1997— Richmond (Int'l)	OF	134	498	73	132	31	3	20	63	.265	45	84	7	319	14	8	.977

HOLLINS, DAVE — 3B — ANGELS

PERSONAL: Born May 25, 1966, in Buffalo. ... 6-1/210. ... Bats both, throws right. ... Full name: David Michael Hollins.
HIGH SCHOOL: Orchard Park (N.Y.).
COLLEGE: South Carolina.
TRANSACTIONS/CAREER NOTES: Selected by San Diego Padres organization in sixth round of free-agent draft (June 2, 1987). ... Selected by Philadelphia Phillies from Padres organization in Rule 5 major league draft (December 4, 1989). ... On Philadelphia disabled list (August 16-September 6, 1991); included rehabilitation assignment to Scranton/Wilkes-Barre (September 2-5). ... On suspended list (September 29-October 3, 1992). ... On disabled list (June 11-28, 1993). ... On Philadelphia disabled list (May 23-July 23 and July 25, 1994-remainder of season); included rehabilitation assignment to Scranton/Wilkes-Barre (July 16-23). ... On Philadelphia disabled list (June 12-27, 1995). ... Traded by Phillies to Boston Red Sox for OF Mark Whiten (July 24, 1995). ... On Boston disabled list (August 9, 1995-remainder of season). ... Granted free agency (December 21, 1995). ... Signed by Minnesota Twins (December 23, 1995). ... Traded by Twins to Seattle Mariners for a player to be named later (August 29, 1996); Twins acquired 1B David Arias to complete deal (September 13, 1996). ... Granted free agency (October 31, 1996). ... Signed by Anaheim Angels (November 20, 1996).
STATISTICAL NOTES: Led Northwest League with seven intentional bases on balls received in 1987. ... Led Northwest League third basemen with 241 total chances in 1987. ... Led Texas League with 10 sacrifice flies in 1989. ... Led N.L. in being hit by pitch with 19 in 1992. ... Led A.L. third basemen with 29 errors in 1997. ... Career major league grand slams: 3.

										BATTING					FIELDING		
Year — Team (League)	Pos.	G	AB	R	H	2B	3B	HR	RBI	Avg.	BB	SO	SB	PO	A	E	Avg.
1987— Spokane (N'west)	3B	75	278	52	86	14	4	2	44	.309	53	36	20	*59	*167	11	*.938
1988— Riverside (Calif.)	3B-1B-SS	139	516	90	157	32	1	9	92	.304	82	67	13	102	248	29	.923
1989— Wichita (Texas)	3B	131	459	69	126	29	4	9	79	.275	63	88	8	77	209	25	.920
1990— Philadelphia (N.L.)■ ..	3B-1B	72	114	14	21	0	0	5	15	.184	10	28	0	27	37	4	.941
1991— Philadelphia (N.L.)	3B-1B	56	151	18	45	10	2	6	21	.298	17	26	1	67	62	8	.942
— Scran./W.B. (Int'l)	3B-1B	72	229	37	61	11	6	8	35	.266	43	43	4	67	105	10	.945
1992— Philadelphia (N.L.)	3B-1B	156	586	104	158	28	4	27	93	.270	76	110	9	120	253	18	.954
1993— Philadelphia (N.L.)	3B	143	543	104	148	30	4	18	93	.273	85	109	2	73	215	27	.914
1994— Philadelphia (N.L.)	3B-OF	44	162	28	36	7	1	4	26	.222	23	32	1	39	48	11	.888
— Scran./W.B. (Int'l)	OF	6	19	6	4	0	0	1	3	.211	5	4	0	12	1	2	.867
1995— Philadelphia (N.L.)	1B	65	205	46	47	12	2	7	25	.229	53	38	1	532	30	7	.988
— Boston (A.L.)■	DH-OF	5	13	2	2	0	0	0	1	.154	4	7	0	3	0	0	1.000
1996— Minnesota (A.L.)■	3B-DH-SS	121	422	71	102	26	0	13	53	.242	71	102	6	81	206	15	.950
— Seattle (A.L.)■	3B-1B	28	94	17	33	3	0	3	25	.351	13	15	0	21	53	3	.961
1997— Anaheim (A.L.)■	3B-1B	149	572	101	165	29	2	16	85	.288	62	124	16	208	249	†29	.940
American League totals (3 years)		303	1101	191	302	58	2	32	164	.274	150	248	22	313	508	47	.946
National League totals (6 years)		536	1761	314	455	87	13	67	273	.258	264	343	14	858	645	75	.952
Major league totals (8 years)		839	2862	505	757	145	15	99	437	.265	414	591	36	1171	1153	122	.950

CHAMPIONSHIP SERIES RECORD

										BATTING					FIELDING		
Year — Team (League)	Pos.	G	AB	R	H	2B	3B	HR	RBI	Avg.	BB	SO	SB	PO	A	E	Avg.
1993— Philadelphia (N.L.)	3B	6	20	2	4	1	0	2	4	.200	5	4	1	5	4	0	1.000

WORLD SERIES RECORD

										BATTING					FIELDING		
Year — Team (League)	Pos.	G	AB	R	H	2B	3B	HR	RBI	Avg.	BB	SO	SB	PO	A	E	Avg.
1993— Philadelphia (N.L.)	3B	6	23	5	6	1	0	0	2	.261	6	5	0	9	9	0	1.000

ALL-STAR GAME RECORD

								BATTING					FIELDING		
Year — League	Pos.	AB	R	H	2B	3B	HR	RBI	Avg.	BB	SO	SB	PO	A	E	Avg.
1993— National	3B	1	0	1	1	0	0	0	1.000	0	0	0	1	0	0	1.000

HOLLINS, STACY — P — ATHLETICS

PERSONAL: Born July 31, 1972, in Conroe, Texas. ... 6-3/180. ... Throws right, bats right. ... Full name: Stacy Evan Hollins.
HIGH SCHOOL: Willis (Texas).
JUNIOR COLLEGE: San Jacinto College (Texas).
TRANSACTIONS/CAREER NOTES: Selected by Oakland Athletics organization in 43rd round of free-agent draft (June 1, 1992). ... On Huntsville temporarily inactive list (April 18-May 6, 1995).
STATISTICAL NOTES: Led Midwest League with 12 home runs allowed in 1993. ... Pitched 3-0 no-hit victory against Springfield (July 7, 1993).

H

Year Team (League)	W	L	Pct.	ERA	G	GS	CG	ShO	Sv.	IP	H	R	ER	BB	SO
1992— Arizona A's (Arizona)	6	3	.667	3.39	15	14	3	2	0	*93	*89	47	35	19	*93
1993— Madison (Midwest)	10	11	.476	5.14	26	26	2	1	0	150 2/3	145	100	*86	52	105
1994— Modesto (California)	13	6	.684	3.39	29	22	0	0	0	143 1/3	133	57	54	55	131
1995— Huntsville (Southern)	3	8	.273	5.33	15	15	0	0	0	82 2/3	80	52	49	42	62
—Edmonton (PCL)	0	7	.000	10.31	7	7	0	0	0	29 2/3	47	43	34	21	25
1996— Huntsville (Southern)	9	9	.500	5.11	28	26	3	•2	0	141	149	100	80	56	102
1997— Huntsville (Southern)	5	4	.556	5.37	32	17	0	0	2	114	110	77	68	72	68
—Edmonton (PCL)	0	0	...	10.13	1	1	0	0	0	2 2/3	5	4	3	3	2

HOLMES, DARREN   P   YANKEES

PERSONAL: Born April 25, 1966, in Asheville, N.C. ... 6-0/202. ... Throws right, bats right. ... Full name: Darren Lee Holmes.
HIGH SCHOOL: T.C. Roberson (Asheville, N.C.).
TRANSACTIONS/CAREER NOTES: Selected by Los Angeles Dodgers organization in 16th round of free-agent draft (June 4, 1984). ... On disabled list (June 5, 1986-remainder of season). ... Loaned by Dodgers organization to San Luis Potosi (1988). ... Traded by Dodgers to Milwaukee Brewers for C Bert Heffernan (December 20, 1990). ... On Milwaukee disabled list (July 3-18, 1991); included rehabilitation assignment to Beloit (July 13-18). ... Selected by Colorado Rockies in first round (fifth pick overall) of expansion draft (November 17, 1992). ... On Colorado disabled list (May 30-June 24 and July 21-August 11, 1994); included rehabilitation assignments to Asheville (June 14-19) and Colorado Springs (June 20). ... On disabled list (April 30-May 15, 1997). ... Granted free agency (October 27, 1997). ... Signed by New York Yankees (December 22, 1997).

Year Team (League)	W	L	Pct.	ERA	G	GS	CG	ShO	Sv.	IP	H	R	ER	BB	SO
1984— Great Falls (Pio.)	2	5	.286	6.65	18	6	1	0	0	44 2/3	53	41	33	30	29
1985— Vero Beach (FSL)	4	3	.571	3.11	33	0	0	0	2	63 2/3	57	31	22	35	46
1986— Vero Beach (FSL)	3	6	.333	2.92	11	10	0	0	0	64 2/3	55	30	21	39	59
1987— Vero Beach (FSL)	6	4	.600	4.52	19	19	1	0	0	99 2/3	111	60	50	53	46
1988— San Luis Potosi (Mex.)■	9	9	.500	4.64	23	23	7	1	0	139 2/3	151	88	72	92	110
—Albuquerque (PCL)■	0	1	.000	5.06	2	1	0	0	0	5 1/3	6	3	3	1	1
1989— San Antonio (Tex.)	5	8	.385	3.83	17	16	3	2	1	110 1/3	102	59	47	44	81
—Albuquerque (PCL)	1	4	.200	7.45	9	8	0	0	0	38 2/3	50	32	32	18	31
1990— Albuquerque (PCL)	12	2	*.857	3.11	56	0	0	0	13	92 2/3	78	34	32	39	99
—Los Angeles (N.L.)	0	1	.000	5.19	14	0	0	0	0	17 1/3	15	10	10	11	19
1991— Denver (Am. Assoc.)■	0	0	...	9.00	1	0	0	0	0	1	1	1	1	2	2
—Milwaukee (A.L.)	1	4	.200	4.72	40	0	0	0	3	76 1/3	90	43	40	27	59
—Beloit (Midwest)	0	0	...	0.00	2	0	0	0	2	2	0	0	0	0	3
1992— Denver (Am. Assoc.)	0	0	...	1.38	12	0	0	0	7	13	7	2	2	1	12
—Milwaukee (A.L.)	4	4	.500	2.55	41	0	0	0	6	42 1/3	35	12	12	11	31
1993— Colorado (N.L.)■	3	3	.500	4.05	62	0	0	0	25	66 2/3	56	31	30	20	60
—Colo. Springs (PCL)	1	0	1.000	0.00	3	2	0	0	0	8 2/3	1	1	0	1	9
1994— Colorado (N.L.)	0	3	.000	6.35	29	0	0	0	3	28 1/3	35	25	20	24	33
—Colo. Springs (PCL)	0	1	.000	8.22	4	2	0	0	0	7 2/3	11	7	7	3	12
—Asheville (S. Atl.)	0	0	...	0.00	2	1	0	0	0	3	1	0	0	0	7
1995— Colorado (N.L.)	6	1	.857	3.24	68	0	0	0	14	66 2/3	59	26	24	28	61
1996— Colorado (N.L.)	5	4	.556	3.97	62	0	0	0	1	77	78	41	34	28	73
1997— Colorado (N.L.)	9	2	.818	5.34	42	6	0	0	3	89 1/3	113	58	53	36	70
A.L. totals (2 years)	5	8	.385	3.94	81	0	0	0	9	118 2/3	125	55	52	38	90
N.L. totals (6 years)	23	14	.622	4.46	277	6	0	0	46	345 1/3	356	191	171	147	316
Major league totals (8 years)	28	22	.560	4.33	358	6	0	0	55	464	481	246	223	185	406

DIVISION SERIES RECORD

Year Team (League)	W	L	Pct.	ERA	G	GS	CG	ShO	Sv.	IP	H	R	ER	BB	SO
1995— Colorado (N.L.)	1	0	1.000	0.00	3	0	0	0	0	1 2/3	6	2	0	9	2

HOLT, CHRIS   P   ASTROS

PERSONAL: Born September 18, 1971, in Dallas. ... 6-4/205. ... Throws right, bats right. ... Full name: Christopher Michael Holt.
COLLEGE: Navarro College (Texas).
TRANSACTIONS/CAREER NOTES: Selected by Houston Astros organization in third round of free-agent draft (June 1, 1992).

Year Team (League)	W	L	Pct.	ERA	G	GS	CG	ShO	Sv.	IP	H	R	ER	BB	SO
1992— Auburn (N.Y.-Penn)	2	5	.286	4.45	14	14	0	0	0	83	75	48	41	24	81
1993— Quad City (Midwest)	11	10	.524	2.27	26	26	*10	•3	0	*186 1/3	162	70	47	54	176
1994— Jackson (Texas)	10	9	.526	3.45	26	25	5	•2	0	167	169	78	64	22	111
1995— Jackson (Texas)	2	2	.500	1.67	5	5	1	1	0	32 1/3	27	8	6	5	24
—Tucson (PCL)	5	8	.385	4.10	20	19	0	0	0	118 2/3	155	65	54	32	69
1996— Tucson (PCL)	9	6	.600	3.62	28	27	4	1	0	*186 1/3	208	87	75	38	137
—Houston (N.L.)	0	1	.000	5.79	4	0	0	0	0	4 2/3	5	3	3	3	0
1997— Houston (N.L.)	8	12	.400	3.52	33	32	0	0	0	209 2/3	211	98	82	61	95
Major league totals (2 years)	8	13	.381	3.57	37	32	0	0	0	214 1/3	216	101	85	64	95

HOLTZ, MIKE   P   ANGELS

PERSONAL: Born October 10, 1972, in Arlington, Va. ... 5-9/175. ... Throws left, bats left. ... Full name: Michael James Holtz.
HIGH SCHOOL: Central Cambria (Ebensburg, Pa.).
COLLEGE: Clemson.
TRANSACTIONS/CAREER NOTES: Selected by California Angels organization in 17th round of free-agent draft (June 2, 1994). ... Angels franchise renamed Anaheim Angels for 1997 season.

Year Team (League)	W	L	Pct.	ERA	G	GS	CG	ShO	Sv.	IP	H	R	ER	BB	SO
1994— Boise (Northwest)	0	0	...	0.51	22	0	0	0	11	35	22	4	2	11	59
1995— Lake Elsinore (Calif.)	4	4	.500	2.29	*56	0	0	0	3	82 2/3	70	26	21	23	101

H

Year Team (League)	W	L	Pct.	ERA	G	GS	CG	ShO	Sv.	IP	H	R	ER	BB	SO
1996— Midland (Texas).................	1	2	.333	4.17	33	0	0	0	2	41	52	34	19	9	41
— California (A.L.).................	3	3	.500	2.45	30	0	0	0	0	29 1/3	21	11	8	19	31
1997— Anaheim (A.L.).................	3	4	.429	3.32	66	0	0	0	0	43 1/3	38	21	16	15	40
Major league totals (2 years)......	6	7	.462	2.97	96	0	0	0	2	72 2/3	59	32	24	34	71

HOLZEMER, MARK   P   MARINERS

PERSONAL: Born August 20, 1969, in Littleton, Colo. ... 6-0/165. ... Throws left, bats left. ... Full name: Mark Harold Holzemer. ... Name pronounced HOLE-zeh-mer.
HIGH SCHOOL: J.K. Mullen (Denver).
JUNIOR COLLEGE: Seminole (Okla.) Junior College.
TRANSACTIONS/CAREER NOTES: Selected by California Angels organization in fourth round of free-agent draft (June 2, 1987). ... On Midland disabled list (July 2-September 18, 1990; April 12-May 25 and June 7-26, 1991). ... On California disabled list (June 10-September 1, 1996); included rehabilitation assignment to Lake Elsinore (August 16-September 1). ... Granted free agency (October 15, 1996). ... Signed by Seattle Mariners organization (December 11, 1996).
STATISTICAL NOTES: Led Pacific Coast League with 15 wild pitches in 1994.

Year Team (League)	W	L	Pct.	ERA	G	GS	CG	ShO	Sv.	IP	H	R	ER	BB	SO
1988— Bend (Northwest).................	4	6	.400	5.24	13	13	1	1	0	68 2/3	59	51	40	47	72
1989— Quad City (Midwest)	12	7	.632	3.36	25	25	3	1	0	139 1/3	122	68	52	64	131
1990— Midland (Texas).................	1	7	.125	5.26	15	15	1	0	0	77	92	55	45	41	54
1991— Midland (Texas).................	0	0	...	1.42	2	2	0	0	0	6 1/3	3	2	1	5	7
— Palm Springs (California)...	0	4	.000	2.86	6	6	0	0	0	22	15	14	7	16	19
1992— Palm Springs (California)...	3	2	.600	3.00	5	5	2	0	0	30	23	10	10	13	32
— Midland (Texas).................	2	5	.286	3.83	7	7	2	0	0	44 2/3	45	22	19	13	36
— Edmonton (PCL)	5	7	.417	6.67	17	16	4	0	0	89	114	69	66	55	49
1993— Vancouver (PCL)	9	6	.600	4.82	24	23	2	0	0	145 2/3	158	94	78	70	80
— California (A.L.)..............	0	3	.000	8.87	5	4	0	0	0	23 1/3	34	24	23	13	10
1994— Vancouver (PCL)	5	10	.333	6.60	29	17	0	0	0	117 1/3	144	93	86	58	77
1995— Vancouver (PCL)	3	2	.600	2.47	28	4	0	0	2	54 2/3	45	18	15	24	35
— California (A.L.)..............	0	1	.000	5.40	12	0	0	0	0	8 1/3	11	6	5	7	5
1996— California (A.L.)..............	1	0	1.000	8.76	25	0	0	0	0	24 2/3	35	28	24	8	20
— Lake Elsinore (Calif.)	0	1	.000	2.38	9	3	0	0	0	11 1/3	10	3	3	4	10
1997— Tacoma (PCL)■	1	0	1.000	2.20	37	0	0	0	13	41	32	10	10	10	38
— Seattle (A.L.)	0	0	...	6.00	14	0	0	0	1	9	9	6	6	8	7
Major league totals (4 years)......	1	4	.200	7.99	56	4	0	0	1	65 1/3	89	64	58	36	42

HONEYCUTT, RICK   P

PERSONAL: Born June 29, 1954, in Chattanooga, Tenn. ... 6-1/191. ... Throws left, bats left. ... Full name: Frederick Wayne Honeycutt.
HIGH SCHOOL: Lakeview (Fort Oglethorpe, Ga.).
COLLEGE: Tennessee (degree in health education).
TRANSACTIONS/CAREER NOTES: Selected by Baltimore Orioles organization in 14th round of free-agent draft (June 6, 1972); did not sign. ... Selected by Pittsburgh Pirates organization in 17th round of free-agent draft (June 8, 1976). ... Traded by Pirates organization to Seattle Mariners (August 22, 1977), completing deal in which Mariners traded P Dave Pagan to Pirates for a player to be named later (July 27, 1977). ... On disabled list (May 20-June 26, 1978). ... Traded by Mariners with C Larry Cox, OF Willie Horton, OF Leon Roberts and SS Mario Mendoza to Texas Rangers for P Brian Allard, P Ken Clay, P Steve Finch, P Jerry Don Gleaton, SS Rick Auerbach and OF Richie Zisk (December 12, 1980). ... Traded by Rangers to Los Angeles Dodgers for P Dave Stewart and a player to be named later (August 19, 1983); Rangers acquired P Ricky Wright to complete deal (September 16, 1983). ... Traded by Dodgers to Oakland Athletics for a player to be named later (August 29, 1987); Dodgers acquired P Tim Belcher to complete deal (September 3, 1987). ... Granted free agency (November 4, 1988). ... Re-signed by A's (December 21, 1988). ... On Oakland disabled list (April 1-June 16, 1991); included rehabilitation assignments to Modesto (June 6-14) and Madison (June 14-16). ... Granted free agency (October 30, 1992). ... Re-signed by A's (December 7, 1992). ... On disabled list (June 15-July 24, 1993). ... Granted free agency (November 1, 1993). ... Signed by Rangers (November 24, 1993). ... On disabled list (June 22-July 15, 1994). ... Granted free agency (October 25, 1994). ... Signed by Edmonton, A's organization (April 8-9, 1995). ... Contract sold by A's to New York Yankees (September 25, 1995). ... Contract sold by Yankees to St. Louis Cardinals (December 21, 1995). ... On disabled list (March 29-April 25 and May 3-remainder of 1997 season). ... Announced retirement (September 26, 1997).
STATISTICAL NOTES: Pitched 1-0 one-hit, complete-game victory against San Diego (April 27, 1984).
MISCELLANEOUS: Played two games as first baseman and one game as shortstop (1976). ... Appeared as shortstop with no chances with Shreveport (1977). ... Made an out in both appearances as pinch-hitter and appeared in one game as pinch-runner (1990).

Year Team (League)	W	L	Pct.	ERA	G	GS	CG	ShO	Sv.	IP	H	R	ER	BB	SO
1976— Niagara Falls (NYP)..........	5	3	.625	2.60	13	12	•7	0	0	*97	91	36	28	20	*98
1977— Shreveport (Texas).............	10	6	.625	*2.47	21	21	6	0	0	135	144	53	37	42	82
— Seattle (A.L.)■	0	1	.000	4.34	10	3	0	0	0	29	26	16	14	11	17
1978— Seattle (A.L.).................	5	11	.313	4.90	26	24	4	1	0	134	150	81	73	49	50
1979— Seattle (A.L.).................	11	12	.478	4.04	33	28	8	0	0	194	201	103	87	67	83
1980— Seattle (A.L.).................	10	17	.370	3.95	30	30	9	2	0	203	221	99	89	60	79
1981— Texas (A.L.)■.................	11	6	.647	3.30	20	20	8	2	0	128	120	49	47	17	40
1982— Texas (A.L.).................	5	17	.227	5.27	30	26	4	1	0	164	201	103	96	54	64
1983— Texas (A.L.).................	14	8	.636	*2.42	25	25	5	2	0	174 2/3	168	59	47	37	56
— Los Angeles (N.L.)■.........	2	3	.400	5.77	9	7	1	0	0	39	46	26	25	13	18
1984— Los Angeles (N.L.).........	10	9	.526	2.84	29	28	6	2	0	183 2/3	180	72	58	51	75
1985— Los Angeles (N.L.).........	8	12	.400	3.42	31	25	1	0	1	142	141	71	54	49	67
1986— Los Angeles (N.L.).........	11	9	.550	3.32	32	28	0	0	0	171	164	71	63	45	100
1987— Los Angeles (N.L.).........	2	12	.143	4.59	27	20	1	1	0	115 2/3	133	74	59	45	92
— Oakland (A.L.)■.............	1	4	.200	5.32	7	4	0	0	0	23 2/3	25	17	14	9	10
1988— Oakland (A.L.).............	3	2	.600	3.50	55	0	0	0	7	79 2/3	74	36	31	25	47
1989— Oakland (A.L.).............	2	2	.500	2.35	64	0	0	0	12	76 2/3	56	26	20	26	52
1990— Oakland (A.L.).............	2	2	.500	2.70	63	0	0	0	7	63 1/3	46	23	19	22	38
1991— Oakland (A.L.).............	2	4	.333	3.58	43	0	0	0	0	37 2/3	37	16	15	20	26
— Modesto (California)	0	0	...	0.00	3	3	0	0	0	5	4	1	0	1	5
— Madison (Midwest)	0	1	.000	18.00	1	1	0	0	0	1	4	2	2	0	2

H

Year Team (League)	W	L	Pct.	ERA	G	GS	CG	ShO	Sv.	IP	H	R	ER	BB	SO
1992— Oakland (A.L.)	1	4	.200	3.69	54	0	0	0	3	39	41	19	16	10	32
1993— Oakland (A.L.)	1	4	.200	2.81	52	0	0	0	1	41²/₃	30	18	13	20	21
1994— Texas (A.L.)■	1	2	.333	7.20	42	0	0	0	1	25	37	21	20	9	18
1995— Oakland (A.L.)■	5	1	.833	2.42	49	0	0	0	2	44²/₃	37	13	12	9	21
— New York (A.L.)■	0	0	. . .	27.00	3	0	0	0	0	1	2	3	3	1	0
1996— St. Louis (N.L.)■	2	1	.667	2.85	61	0	0	0	4	47¹/₃	42	15	15	7	30
1997— St. Louis (N.L.)	0	0	. . .	13.50	2	0	0	0	0	2	5	3	3	1	2
A.L. totals (16 years)	74	97	.433	3.80	606	160	38	8	33	1459	1472	702	616	446	654
N.L. totals (7 years)	35	46	.432	3.56	191	108	9	3	5	700²/₃	711	332	277	211	384
Major league totals (21 years)....	109	143	.433	3.72	797	268	47	11	38	2159²/₃	2183	1034	893	657	1038

DIVISION SERIES RECORD

Year Team (League)	W	L	Pct.	ERA	G	GS	CG	ShO	Sv.	IP	H	R	ER	BB	SO
1996— St. Louis (N.L.)	1	0	1.000	3.38	3	0	0	0	0	2²/₃	3	1	1	2	2

CHAMPIONSHIP SERIES RECORD

RECORDS: Holds career records for most games pitched—20; and most games as relief pitcher—20.

Year Team (League)	W	L	Pct.	ERA	G	GS	CG	ShO	Sv.	IP	H	R	ER	BB	SO
1983— Los Angeles (N.L.)	0	0	. . .	21.60	2	0	0	0	0	1²/₃	4	4	4	0	2
1985— Los Angeles (N.L.)	0	0	. . .	13.50	2	0	0	0	0	1¹/₃	4	2	2	2	1
1988— Oakland (A.L.)	1	0	1.000	0.00	3	0	0	0	0	2	0	0	0	2	0
1989— Oakland (A.L.)	0	0	. . .	32.40	3	0	0	0	0	1²/₃	6	6	6	5	1
1990— Oakland (A.L.)	0	0	. . .	0.00	3	0	0	0	1	1²/₃	0	0	0	0	0
1992— Oakland (A.L.)	0	0	. . .	0.00	2	0	0	0	0	2	0	0	0	0	1
1996— St. Louis (N.L.)	0	0	. . .	9.00	5	0	0	0	0	4	5	4	4	3	3
Champ. series totals (7 years) ...	1	0	1.000	10.05	20	0	0	0	1	14¹/₃	19	16	16	12	8

WORLD SERIES RECORD

NOTES: Member of World Series championship team (1989).

Year Team (League)	W	L	Pct.	ERA	G	GS	CG	ShO	Sv.	IP	H	R	ER	BB	SO
1988— Oakland (A.L.)	1	0	1.000	0.00	3	0	0	0	0	3¹/₃	0	0	0	0	5
1989— Oakland (A.L.)	0	0	. . .	6.75	3	0	0	0	0	2²/₃	4	2	2	0	2
1990— Oakland (A.L.)	0	0	. . .	0.00	1	0	0	0	0	1²/₃	2	0	0	1	0
World Series totals (3 years)	1	0	1.000	2.35	7	0	0	0	0	7²/₃	6	2	2	1	7

ALL-STAR GAME RECORD

Year League	W	L	Pct.	ERA	GS	CG	ShO	Sv.	IP	H	R	ER	BB	SO
1980— American...................							Did not play.							
1983— American...................	0	0	. . .	9.00	0	0	0	0	2	5	2	2	0	0
All-Star totals (1 years)	0	0	. . .	9.00	0	0	0	0	2	5	2	2	0	0

HOUSTON, TYLER   C   CUBS

PERSONAL: Born January 17, 1971, in Las Vegas. ... 6-1/205. ... Bats left, throws right. ... Full name: Tyler Sam Houston.
HIGH SCHOOL: Valley (Las Vegas).
TRANSACTIONS/CAREER NOTES: Selected by Atlanta Braves organization in first round (second pick overall) of free-agent draft (June 5, 1989). ... On Greenville disabled list (June 25-July 5, 1993). ... Traded by Braves to Chicago Cubs for P Ismael Villegas (June 27, 1996). ... On disabled list (May 3-19, 1997); included rehabilitation assignment to Iowa (May 14-19, 1997). ... On Chicago disabled list (June 11-July 11, 1997); included rehabilitation assignment to Rockford (July 9-11). ... On suspended list for one game (September 16, 1997).
STATISTICAL NOTES: Led Pioneer League with 14 passed balls in 1989.

Year Team (League)	Pos.	G	AB	R	H	2B	3B	HR	RBI	Avg.	BB	SO	SB	PO	A	E	Avg.
1989— Idaho Falls (Pio.)........	C	50	176	30	43	11	0	4	24	.244	25	41	4	148	15	5	.970
1990— Sumter (S. Atl.)	C	117	442	58	93	14	3	13	56	.210	49	101	6	498	55	*18	.968
1991— Macon (S. Atl.)	C	107	351	41	81	16	3	8	47	.231	39	70	10	591	75	10	.985
1992— Durham (Carolina)......	C-3B-1B	117	402	39	91	17	1	7	38	.226	20	89	5	493	65	15	.974
1993— Greenville (Southern) .	C-OF	84	262	27	73	14	1	5	33	.279	13	50	5	410	34	9	.980
— Richmond (Int'l)	C	13	36	4	5	1	1	1	3	.139	1	8	0	69	2	3	.959
1994— Richmond (Int'l)	1B-C-OF	97	312	33	76	15	2	4	33	.244	16	44	3	619	54	7	.990
1995— Richmond (Int'l)	1-C-O-3	103	349	41	89	10	3	12	42	.255	18	62	3	579	69	11	.983
1996— Atlanta (N.L.)	1B-OF-3B	33	27	3	6	2	1	1	8	.222	1	9	0	16	1	0	1.000
— Chicago (N.L.)■	C-3-2-1	46	115	18	39	7	0	2	19	.339	8	18	3	139	25	3	.982
1997— Chicago (N.L.)	C-3-1-2-S	72	196	15	51	10	0	2	28	.260	9	35	1	280	37	5	.984
— Iowa (Am. Assoc.)......	3B-C	6	23	0	5	2	0	0	4	.217	0	2	0	6	9	2	.882
— Rockford (Midwest) ...	C-3B	2	6	1	3	1	0	0	1	.500	0	0	0	5	0	0	1.000
Major league totals (2 years)		151	338	36	96	19	1	5	55	.284	18	62	4	435	63	8	.984

HOWARD, DAVID   IF/OF   CARDINALS

PERSONAL: Born February 26, 1967, in Sarasota, Fla. ... 6-0/175. ... Bats both, throws right. ... Full name: David Wayne Howard. ... Son of Bruce Howard, pitcher, Chicago White Sox, Baltimore Orioles and Washington Senators (1963-68).
HIGH SCHOOL: Riverview (Sarasota, Fla.).
JUNIOR COLLEGE: Manatee Junior College (Fla.).
TRANSACTIONS/CAREER NOTES: Selected by Kansas City Royals organization in 32nd round of free-agent draft (June 2, 1986). ... On disabled list (May 12-31 and July 23-August 9, 1989). ... On Kansas City disabled list (April 22-July 6, 1992); included rehabilitation assignments to Baseball City (June 16-20) and Omaha (June 20-July 5). ... On Kansas City disabled list (April 19-May 17, 1993); included rehabilitation assignment to Omaha (May 10-17). ... On Kansas City disabled list (June 7-August 10, 1993); included rehabilitation assignments to Omaha (July 15-23 and July 31-August 10). ... On disabled list (May 27-June 17, 1995). ... On disabled list (August 14-September 1, 1997). ... Granted free agency (October 28, 1997). ... Signed by St. Louis Cardinals (December 4, 1997).
STATISTICAL NOTES: Led A.L. shortstops with .982 fielding percentage in 1996.

H

Year Team (League)	Pos.	G	AB	R	H	2B	3B	HR	RBI	Avg.	BB	SO	SB	PO	A	E	Avg.
1987—Fort Myers (FSL)	SS	89	289	26	56	9	4	1	19	.194	30	68	11	123	273	28	.934
1988—Appleton (Midwest)....	SS	110	368	48	82	9	4	1	22	.223	25	80	10	151	275	43	.908
1989—Baseball City (FSL)	S-O-3-2	83	267	36	63	7	3	3	30	.236	23	44	12	141	225	18	.953
1990—Memphis (Southern)..	SS-2B	116	384	41	96	10	4	5	44	.250	39	73	15	194	321	32	.941
1991—Omaha (A.A.).............	SS-2B	14	41	2	5	0	0	0	2	.122	7	11	1	30	43	3	.961
— Kansas City (A.L.) S-2-3-0-DH		94	236	20	51	7	0	1	17	.216	16	45	3	129	248	12	.969
1992—Kansas City (A.L.)	SS-OF	74	219	19	49	6	2	1	18	.224	15	43	3	124	204	8	.976
— Baseball City (FSL).....	SS	3	9	3	4	1	0	0	0	.444	2	0	0	3	7	1	.909
— Omaha (A.A.).............	SS	19	68	5	8	1	0	0	5	.118	3	8	1	25	52	8	.906
1993—Kansas City (A.L.)	2-S-3-0	15	24	5	8	0	1	0	2	.333	2	5	1	17	28	3	.938
— Omaha (A.A.).............	SS	47	157	15	40	8	2	0	18	.255	7	20	3	76	137	8	.964
1994—Kansas City (A.L.) 3-S-2-DH-P-O		46	83	9	19	4	0	1	13	.229	11	23	3	27	79	1	.991
1995—Kansas City (A.L.) 2-S-O-DH-1		95	255	23	62	13	4	0	19	.243	24	41	6	167	195	29	.926
1996—Kansas City (A.L.) S-2-1-DH-O		143	420	51	92	14	5	4	48	.219	40	74	5	210	411	11	†.983
1997—Kansas City (A.L.) 2-O-S-3-DH		80	162	24	39	8	1	1	13	.241	10	31	2	96	109	7	.967
Major league totals (7 years)		547	1399	151	320	52	13	8	130	.229	118	262	23	770	1274	71	.966

HOWARD, THOMAS — OF — DODGERS

PERSONAL: Born December 11, 1964, in Middletown, Ohio. ... 6-2/205. ... Bats both, throws right. ... Full name: Thomas Sylvester Howard.
HIGH SCHOOL: Valley View (Germantown, Ohio).
COLLEGE: Ball State.
TRANSACTIONS/CAREER NOTES: Selected by San Diego Padres organization in first round (11th pick overall) of free-agent draft (June 2, 1986). ... On disabled list (June 5-July 17, 1989). ... Traded by Padres to Cleveland Indians for SS Jason Hardtke and a player to be named later (April 14, 1992); Padres acquired C Christopher Maffett to complete deal (July 10, 1992). ... Traded by Indians to Cincinnati Reds (August 20, 1993), completing deal in which Reds traded 1B Randy Milligan to Indians for a player to be named later (August 17, 1993). ... On Cincinnati disabled list (March 23-April 20, 1996); included rehabilitation assignments to Chattanooga (April 11-19) and Indianapolis (April 19-20). ... Released by Reds (November 18, 1996). ... Signed by Houston Astros (December 4, 1996). ... Granted free agency (October 28, 1997). ... Signed by Los Angeles Dodgers organization (January 8, 1998).
HONORS: Named outfielder on THE SPORTING NEWS college All-America team (1986).

Year Team (League)	Pos.	G	AB	R	H	2B	3B	HR	RBI	Avg.	BB	SO	SB	PO	A	E	Avg.
1986—Spokane (N'west).......	OF	13	55	16	23	3	3	2	17	.418	3	9	2	24	3	0	1.000
— Reno (California)	OF	61	223	35	57	7	3	10	39	.256	34	49	10	104	5	6	.948
1987—Wichita (Texas)	OF	113	401	72	133	27	4	14	60	.332	36	72	26	226	6	6	.975
1988—Wichita (Texas)	OF	29	103	15	31	9	2	0	16	.301	13	14	6	51	2	2	.964
— Las Vegas (PCL)	OF	44	167	29	42	9	1	0	15	.251	12	31	3	74	3	2	.975
1989—Las Vegas (PCL)	OF	80	303	45	91	18	3	3	31	.300	30	56	22	178	7	2	.989
1990—Las Vegas (PCL)	OF	89	341	58	112	26	8	5	51	.328	44	63	27	159	6	2	.988
— San Diego (N.L.)	OF	20	44	4	12	2	0	0	0	.273	0	11	0	19	0	1	.950
1991—San Diego (N.L.)	OF	106	281	30	70	12	3	4	22	.249	24	57	10	182	4	1	.995
— Las Vegas (PCL)	OF	25	94	22	29	3	1	2	16	.309	10	16	11	54	2	2	.966
1992—San Diego (N.L.)	PH	5	3	1	1	0	0	0	0	.333	0	0	0	...	...	...	...
— Cleveland (A.L.)■.......	OF-DH	117	358	36	99	15	2	2	32	.277	17	60	15	185	5	2	.990
1993—Cleveland (A.L.)	OF-DH	74	178	26	42	7	0	3	23	.236	12	42	5	81	3	2	.977
— Cincinnati (N.L.)■.......	OF	38	141	22	39	8	3	4	13	.277	12	21	5	73	4	1	.987
1994—Cincinnati (N.L.)	OF	83	178	24	47	11	0	5	24	.264	10	30	4	80	2	3	.965
1995—Cincinnati (N.L.)	OF	113	281	42	85	15	2	3	26	.302	20	37	17	127	2	2	.985
1996—Cincinnati (N.L.)	OF	121	360	50	88	19	10	6	42	.244	17	51	6	160	7	3	.982
— Chattanooga (Sou.)....	OF	8	30	4	10	1	0	1	2	.333	2	7	1	8	0	0	1.000
— Indianapolis (A.A.)	OF	1	6	2	2	0	0	1	2	.333	0	0	0	3	0	0	1.000
1997—Houston (N.L.)■.......	OF	107	255	24	63	16	1	3	22	.247	26	48	1	107	5	0	1.000
American League totals (2 years)		191	536	62	141	22	2	5	55	.263	29	102	20	266	8	4	.986
National League totals (8 years)		593	1543	197	405	83	19	25	149	.262	109	255	43	748	24	11	.986
Major league totals (8 years)		784	2079	259	546	105	21	30	204	.263	138	357	63	1014	32	15	.986

DIVISION SERIES RECORD

Year Team (League)	Pos.	G	AB	R	H	2B	3B	HR	RBI	Avg.	BB	SO	SB	PO	A	E	Avg.
1995—Cincinnati (N.L.)	OF	3	10	0	1	1	0	0	0	.100	0	2	0	5	0	0	1.000
1997—Houston (N.L.)	PH	2	1	0	0	0	0	0	0	.000	1	1	0	0	0	0	...
Division series totals (2 years)		5	11	0	1	1	0	0	0	.091	1	3	0	5	0	0	1.000

CHAMPIONSHIP SERIES RECORD

Year Team (League)	Pos.	G	AB	R	H	2B	3B	HR	RBI	Avg.	BB	SO	SB	PO	A	E	Avg.
1995—Cincinnati (N.L.)	PH-OF	4	8	0	2	1	0	0	1	.250	2	0	0	2	0	0	1.000

HOWELL, JACK — 3B — ASTROS

PERSONAL: Born August 18, 1961, in Tucson, Ariz. ... 6-0/190. ... Bats left, throws right. ... Full name: Jack Robert Howell.
HIGH SCHOOL: Palo Verde (Tucson, Ariz.).
JUNIOR COLLEGE: Pima Community College (Ariz.).
COLLEGE: Arizona.
TRANSACTIONS/CAREER NOTES: Signed as free agent by California Angels organization (August 6, 1983). ... On Edmonton disabled list (June 21-July 7, 1985). ... On California disabled list (May 23-June 9, 1990 and May 5-28, 1991). ... Traded by Angels to San Diego Padres for OF Shawn Abner (July 30, 1991). ... Granted free agency (October 28, 1991). ... Signed by Yakult Swallows of Japan Central League (December 8, 1991). ... Signed by Yomiuri Giants of Japan Central League (December 7, 1994). ... Signed by Angels organization (December

H

5, 1995). ... On California disabled list (June 16-July 19, 1996); included rehabilitation assignment to Lake Elsinore (July 13-19). ... Granted free agency (November 18, 1996). ... Re-signed by Angels organization (December 20, 1996). ... Angels franchise renamed Anaheim Angels for 1997 season. ... Granted free agency (October 30, 1997). ... Signed by Houston Astros (December 9, 1997).
STATISTICAL NOTES: Led California League third basemen with .943 fielding percentage, 259 assists, 368 total chances and 23 double plays in 1984. ... Led A.L. third basemen with .974 fielding percentage, 322 assists and 428 total chances in 1989. ... Career major league grand slams: 1.

Year Team (League)	Pos.	G	AB	R	H	2B	3B	HR	RBI	Avg.	BB	SO	SB	PO	A	E	Avg.
1983— Salem (Northwest).....	3B-2B	21	76	23	30	2	5	3	12	.395	17	11	26	19	32	11	.823
1984— Redwood (Calif.)........	3B-1B	135	451	62	111	21	5	5	64	.246	44	95	12	96	†260	21	†.944
1985— Edmonton (PCL)........	3B-SS	79	284	55	106	22	3	13	48	.373	52	57	3	67	130	12	.943
— California (A.L.).........	3B	43	137	19	27	4	0	5	18	.197	16	33	1	33	75	8	.931
1986— Edmonton (PCL)........	3B	44	156	39	56	17	3	3	28	.359	38	29	1	28	84	8	.933
— California (A.L.).........	3B-DH-OF	63	151	26	41	14	2	4	21	.272	19	28	2	38	57	2	.979
1987— California (A.L.).........	OF-3B-2B	138	449	64	110	18	5	23	64	.245	57	118	4	185	95	7	.976
1988— California (A.L.).........	3B-OF	154	500	59	127	32	2	16	63	.254	46	130	2	97	249	17	.953
1989— California (A.L.).........	3B-OF	144	474	56	108	19	4	20	52	.228	52	125	0	97	†322	11	†.974
1990— California (A.L.).........	3B-SS-1B	105	316	35	72	19	1	8	33	.228	46	61	3	76	196	18	.938
— Edmonton (PCL).........	3B	20	75	14	25	7	1	2	15	.333	7	13	3	22	33	1	.982
1991— California (A.L.).........2-0-1-3-DH		32	81	11	17	2	0	2	7	.210	11	11	1	53	55	2	.982
— San Diego (N.L.)■.....	3B	58	160	24	33	3	1	6	16	.206	18	33	0	33	98	2	.985
1992— Yakult (Jp. Cen.)■......	3B	113	387	67	128	...	...	*38	87	*.331	41	86	3	...			
1993— Yakult (Jp. Cen.)........	...	121	396	72	117	15	1	28	88	.295	86	83	3	...			
1994— Yakult (Jp. Cen.)........	IF	105	363	54	91	14	0	20	56	.251	62	74	4	...			
1995— Yomiuri (Jp. Cen.)■.....	IF	66	219	35	61	10	0	14	41	.279	37	66	1	...			
1996— California (A.L.)■........	3-DH-1-2	66	126	20	34	4	1	8	21	.270	10	30	0	28	44	9	.889
— Lake Elsinore (Calif.)..	3B	4	12	2	2	1	0	1	3	.167	3	4	0	3	8	1	.917
1997— Anaheim (A.L.)..........	3B-DH-1B	77	174	25	45	7	0	14	34	.259	13	36	1	58	33	3	.968
American League totals (9 years)		822	2408	315	581	119	15	100	313	.241	270	572	14	665	1126	77	.959
National League totals (1 year)		58	160	24	33	3	1	6	16	.206	18	33	0	33	98	2	.985
Major league totals (9 years)		880	2568	339	614	122	16	106	329	.239	288	605	14	698	1224	79	.961

CHAMPIONSHIP SERIES RECORD

Year Team (League)	Pos.	G	AB	R	H	2B	3B	HR	RBI	Avg.	BB	SO	SB	PO	A	E	Avg.
1986— California (A.L.).........	PH	2	1	0	0	0	0	0	0	.000	1	1	0	...	...	...	...

HOWRY, BOBBY P WHITE SOX

PERSONAL: Born August 4, 1973, in Phoenix. ... 6-5/210. ... Throws right, bats left. ... Full name: Bobby Dean Howry.
HIGH SCHOOL: Deer Valley (Phoenix).
JUNIOR COLLEGE: Yavapai College (Ariz.).
COLLEGE: McNeese State.
TRANSACTIONS/CAREER NOTES: Selected by San Francisco Giants organization in fifth round of free-agent draft (June 2, 1994). ... Traded with SS Mike Caruso, OF Brian Manning, P Keith Foulke, P Lorenzo Barcelo and P Ken Vining by Giants to Chicago White Sox for P Wilson Alvarez, P Danny Darwin and P Roberto Hernandez (July 31, 1997).

Year Team (League)	W	L	Pct.	ERA	G	GS	CG	ShO	Sv.	IP	H	R	ER	BB	SO
1994— Everett (Northwest)...........	0	4	.000	4.74	5	5	0	0	0	19	29	15	10	10	16
— Clinton (Midwest)..............	1	8	.250	4.20	9	8	0	0	0	49 1/3	61	29	23	16	22
1995— San Jose (California).......	12	10	.545	3.54	27	25	1	0	0	165 1/3	171	79	65	54	107
1996— Shreveport (Texas)............	12	10	.545	4.65	27	27	0	0	0	156 2/3	163	90	81	56	57
1997— Shreveport (Texas)............	6	3	.667	4.91	48	0	0	0	*22	55	58	35	30	21	43
— Birmingham (Southern)■..	0	0	...	2.84	12	0	0	0	0	12 2/3	16	4	4	3	3

HUBBARD, MIKE C CUBS

PERSONAL: Born February 16, 1971, in Lynchburg, Va. ... 6-1/200. ... Bats right, throws right. ... Full name: Michael Wayne Hubbard.
HIGH SCHOOL: Amherst (Va.) County.
COLLEGE: James Madison.
TRANSACTIONS/CAREER NOTES: Selected by Chicago Cubs organization in eighth round of free-agent draft (June 1, 1992).

Year Team (League)	Pos.	G	AB	R	H	2B	3B	HR	RBI	Avg.	BB	SO	SB	PO	A	E	Avg.
1992— Geneva (NY-Penn)......	C	50	183	25	44	4	4	3	25	.240	7	29	6	325	27	5	.986
1993— Daytona (Fla. St.)........	C-2B	68	245	25	72	10	3	1	20	.294	18	41	10	354	66	9	.979
1994— Orlando (South.)........	C-3B-1B	104	357	52	102	13	3	11	39	.286	29	58	7	498	78	12	.980
1995— Iowa (Am. Assoc.).......	C-3B	75	254	28	66	6	3	5	23	.260	26	60	6	447	34	9	.982
— Chicago (N.L.).............	C	15	23	2	4	0	0	0	1	.174	2	2	0	33	0	1	.971
1996— Iowa (Am. Assoc.).......	C-3B-OF	67	232	38	68	12	0	7	33	.293	10	56	2	372	27	5	.988
— Chicago (N.L.).............	C	21	38	1	4	0	0	1	4	.105	0	15	0	53	3	0	1.000
1997— Iowa (Am. Assoc.).......	C-OF	50	186	24	52	15	1	6	26	.280	11	23	2	310	22	2	.994
— Chicago (N.L.).........	C-3B	29	64	4	13	0	0	1	2	.203	2	21	0	120	8	1	.992
Major league totals (3 years)		65	125	7	21	0	0	2	7	.168	4	38	0	206	11	2	.991

HUBBARD, TRENIDAD OF DODGERS

PERSONAL: Born May 11, 1966, in Chicago. ... 5-8/183. ... Bats right, throws right. ... Full name: Trenidad Aviel Hubbard. ... Cousin of Joe Cribbs, running back, Buffalo Bills (1980-83 and 1985).
HIGH SCHOOL: South Shore (Chicago).
COLLEGE: Southern (La.).

H

TRANSACTIONS/CAREER NOTES: Selected by Houston Astros organization in 12th round of free-agent draft (June 2, 1986). ... Granted free agency (October 15, 1992). ... Signed by Colorado Rockies organization (October 30, 1992). ... On disabled list (June 15-24, 1993). ... Granted free agency (October 15, 1993). ... Re-signed by Rockies organization (December 3, 1993). ... Granted free agency (October 15, 1994). ... Re-signed by Colorado Springs, Rockies organization (November 14, 1994). ... Claimed on waivers by San Francisco Giants (August 21, 1996). ... On San Francisco disabled list (September 13, 1996-remainder of season). ... Traded by Giants to Cleveland Indians for P Joe Roa (December 16, 1996), completing deal in which Indians traded IF Jeff Kent, IF Jose Vizcaino, P Julian Tavarez and a player to be named later to Giants for 3B Matt Williams and a player to be named later (November 13, 1996). ... Signed by Los Angeles Dodgers (December 3, 1997).

STATISTICAL NOTES: Led Texas League second basemen with 296 putouts, 653 total chances and 81 double plays in 1991. ... Tied for Pacific Coast League lead in caught stealing with 18 in 1993. ... Led Pacific Coast League with .416 on-base percentage in 1995.

MISCELLANEOUS: Batted lefthanded on occasion though not a switch-hitter (1986-91).

Year	Team (League)	Pos.	G	AB	R	H	2B	3B	HR	RBI	Avg.	BB	SO	SB	PO	A	E	Avg.
1986—Auburn (NY-Penn)	2B-OF	70	242	42	75	12	1	1	32	.310	28	42	35	131	110	18	.931
1987—Asheville (S. Atl.)	2-O-C-3-P	101	284	39	67	8	1	1	35	.236	28	42	28	124	108	14	.943
1988—Osceola (Fla. St.)	2-C-O-3-1	130	446	68	116	15	11	3	65	.260	61	72	44	261	150	12	.972
1989—Columbus (Sou.)	2-C-O-3	104	348	55	92	7	8	3	37	.264	43	53	28	321	122	15	.967
—Tucson (PCL)	OF-3B-C	21	50	3	11	2	0	0	2	.220	1	10	3	20	9	1	.967
1990—Columbus (Sou.)	2-O-C-3	95	335	39	84	14	4	4	35	.251	32	51	17	216	116	11	.968
—Tucson (PCL)	2B-3B-C	12	27	5	6	2	2	0	2	.222	3	6	1	20	22	3	.933
1991—Jackson (Texas)	2-0-1-P	126	455	78	135	21	3	2	41	.297	65	81	39	†299	338	21	.968
—Tucson (PCL)	2B	2	4	0	0	0	0	0	0	.000	0	0	0	1	2	0	1.000
1992—Tucson (PCL)	2B-3B	115	420	69	130	16	4	2	33	.310	45	68	34	238	353	18	.970
1993—Colo. Springs (PCL)■	0-2-3-S	117	439	83	138	24	8	7	56	.314	47	57	33	208	29	6	.975
1994—Colo. Springs (PCL)	OF	79	278	78	116	22	5	8	38	.363	44	40	28	183	5	7	.964
—Colorado (N.L.)	OF	18	25	3	7	1	1	1	3	.280	3	4	0	4	0	0	1.000
1995—Colo. Springs (PCL)	OF	123	480	*102	163	29	7	12	66	.340	61	59	*37	285	11	6	.980
—Colorado (N.L.)	OF	24	58	13	18	4	0	3	9	.310	8	6	2	16	1	0	1.000
1996—Colorado (N.L.)	OF	45	60	12	13	5	1	1	12	.217	9	22	2	32	0	0	1.000
—Colo. Springs (PCL)	0-2-3-C	50	188	41	59	15	5	6	16	.314	28	14	6	89	55	4	.973
—San Fran. (N.L.)■	OF	10	29	3	6	0	1	1	2	.207	2	5	0	19	1	0	1.000
1997—Buffalo (A.A.)■	OF-3B	103	375	71	117	22	1	16	60	.312	57	52	26	236	26	2	.992
—Cleveland (A.L.)	OF	7	12	3	3	1	0	0	0	.250	1	3	2	3	0	0	1.000
American League totals (1 year)		7	12	3	3	1	0	0	0	.250	1	3	2	3	0	0	1.000
National League totals (3 years)		97	172	31	44	10	3	6	26	.256	22	37	4	71	2	0	1.000
Major league totals (4 years)		104	184	34	47	11	3	6	26	.255	23	40	6	74	2	0	1.000

DIVISION SERIES RECORD

Year	Team (League)	Pos.	G	AB	R	H	2B	3B	HR	RBI	Avg.	BB	SO	SB	PO	A	E	Avg.
1995—Colorado (N.L.)	PH	3	2	0	0	0	0	0	0	.000	0	0	0	...	...	...	...

RECORD AS PITCHER

Year	Team (League)	W	L	Pct.	ERA	G	GS	CG	ShO	Sv.	IP	H	R	ER	BB	SO
1987—Asheville (S. Atl.)		0	0	...	0.00	1	0	0	0	0	1	1	0	0	1	0
1991—Jackson (Texas)		0	0	...	0.00	1	0	0	0	0	1	0	0	0	2	0

HUDEK, JOHN — P — METS

PERSONAL: Born August 8, 1966, in Tampa. ... 6-1/200. ... Throws right, bats both. ... Full name: John Raymond Hudek. ... Name pronounced HOO-dek.

HIGH SCHOOL: H.B. Plant (Tampa).

COLLEGE: Florida Southern.

TRANSACTIONS/CAREER NOTES: Selected by Texas Rangers organization in 30th round of free-agent draft (June 3, 1985); did not sign. ... Selected by Chicago White Sox organization in 10th round of free-agent draft (June 1, 1988). ... Selected by Detroit Tigers from White Sox organization in Rule 5 major league draft (December 7, 1992). ... Claimed on waivers by Houston Astros (July 29, 1993). ... On disabled list (June 26, 1995-remainder of season). ... On Houston disabled list (March 22-July 15, 1996); included rehabilitation assignments to Kissimmee (June 21-30) and Tucson (June 30-July 15). ... Traded by Astros to New York Mets for OF Carl Everett (December 22, 1997).

STATISTICAL NOTES: Combined with starter Jose Ventura and Chris Howard in 4-1 no-hit victory against Charlotte (April 18, 1991).

Year	Team (League)	W	L	Pct.	ERA	G	GS	CG	ShO	Sv.	IP	H	R	ER	BB	SO
1988—South Bend (Mid.)	7	2	.778	1.98	26	0	0	0	8	54 2/3	45	19	12	21	35
1989—Sarasota (Florida State)	1	3	.250	1.67	27	0	0	0	15	43	22	10	8	13	39
—Birmingham (Southern)	1	1	.500	4.24	18	0	0	0	11	17	14	8	8	9	10
1990—Birmingham (Southern)	6	6	.500	4.58	42	10	0	0	4	92 1/3	84	59	47	52	67
1991—Birmingham (Southern)	5	10	.333	3.84	51	0	0	0	13	65 2/3	58	39	28	28	49
1992—Birmingham (Southern)	0	1	.000	2.31	5	0	0	0	1	11 2/3	9	4	3	11	9
—Vancouver (PCL)	8	1	.889	3.16	39	3	1	1	2	85 1/3	69	36	30	45	61
1993—Toledo (Int'l)■	1	3	.250	5.82	16	5	0	0	0	38 2/3	44	26	25	22	32
—Tucson (PCL)■	3	1	.750	3.79	13	1	0	0	0	19	17	11	8	11	18
1994—Tucson (PCL)	0	0	...	4.91	6	0	0	0	2	7 1/3	3	4	4	3	14
—Houston (N.L.)	0	2	.000	2.97	42	0	0	0	16	39 1/3	24	14	13	18	39
1995—Houston (N.L.)	2	2	.500	5.40	19	0	0	0	7	20	19	12	12	5	29
1996—Kissimmee (Florida State)	0	0	...	0.00	2	1	0	0	0	3	2	0	0	2	3
—Tucson (PCL)	1	0	1.000	3.10	17	2	0	0	4	20 1/3	17	8	7	8	26
—Houston (N.L.)	2	0	1.000	2.81	15	0	0	0	2	16	12	5	5	5	14
1997—Houston (N.L.)	1	3	.250	5.98	40	0	0	0	4	40 2/3	38	27	27	33	36
—New Orleans (A.A.)	0	0	...	0.44	19	0	0	0	7	20 2/3	3	1	1	3	26
Major league totals (4 years)	5	7	.417	4.42	116	0	0	0	29	116	93	58	57	61	118

ALL-STAR GAME RECORD

Year	League	W	L	Pct.	ERA	GS	CG	ShO	Sv.	IP	H	R	ER	BB	SO
1994—National	0	0	...	27.00	0	0	0	0	2/3	1	2	2	1	1

H

PERSONAL: Born September 2, 1960, in Tempe, Ariz. ... 6-0/195. ... Bats right, throws right. ... Full name: Rex Allen Hudler.
HIGH SCHOOL: Bullard (Fresno, Calif.).
TRANSACTIONS/CAREER NOTES: Selected by New York Yankees organization in first round (18th pick overall) of free-agent draft (June 6, 1978); pick received as compensation for Chicago White Sox signing free-agent DH/OF Ron Blomberg. ... On Fort Lauderdale disabled list (May 18-31, 1979; May 10-June 15, 1980; and May 11-June 11, 1981). ... Traded by Yankees with P Rich Bordi to Baltimore Orioles for OF Gary Roenicke and a player to be named later (December 12, 1985); Yankees acquired OF Leo Hernandez to complete deal (December 16, 1985). ... On Baltimore disabled list (March 23-June 16, 1987; included rehabilitation assignment to Rochester (May 28-June 16). ... Granted free agency (October 15, 1987). ... Signed by Indianapolis, Montreal Expos organization (December 18, 1987). ... Traded by Expos to St. Louis Cardinals for P John Costello (April 23, 1990). ... On disabled list (May 7-June 29, 1992). ... Released by Cardinals (December 7, 1992). ... Signed by Yakult Swallows of Japan Central League (1993). ... Signed as free agent by San Francisco Giants organization (December 20, 1993). ... Released by Phoenix, Giants organization (March 22, 1994). ... Signed by California Angels (March 28, 1994). ... On disabled list (May 28-June 14, 1994). ... Granted free agency (October 18, 1994). ... Re-signed by Angels (December 6, 1994). ... Granted free agency (October 28, 1996). ... Signed by Philadelphia Phillies (November 21, 1996). ... On disabled list (April 12-May 6 and June 9-August 6, 1997); included rehabilitation assignments to Reading (April 25-28 and May 3-7), Clearwater (July 23-August 2) and Scranton/Wilkes-Barre (August 5-6).
STATISTICAL NOTES: Led International League second basemen with 95 double plays in 1984.

							BATTING							FIELDING		
Year Team (League)	Pos.	G	AB	R	H	2B	3B	HR	RBI	Avg.	BB	SO	SB	PO	A	E	Avg.
1978—Oneonta (NYP)	SS	58	221	33	62	5	5	0	24	.281	21	29	16	123	21	22	.867
1979—Fort Lauderdale (FSL)	S-3-2-O	116	414	37	104	14	1	1	25	.251	15	73	23	164	314	45	.914
1980—Fort Lauderdale (FSL)	3-2-O-1	37	125	14	26	4	0	0	6	.208	2	25	2	55	71	5	.962
—Greensboro (S. Atl.) ...	2B	20	75	7	17	3	1	2	9	.227	4	14	1	51	52	5	.954
1981—Fort Lauderdale (FSL)	2-S-3-O	79	259	35	77	11	1	2	26	.297	13	31	6	104	238	19	.947
1982—Nashville (Southern) ..	2B-SS-OF	89	299	27	71	14	1	0	24	.237	9	51	9	136	219	20	.947
—Fort Lauderdale (FSL)	2B	9	32	2	8	1	0	1	6	.250	4	5	0	23	25	2	.960
1983—Fort Lauderdale (FSL)	2B-SS	91	345	55	93	15	2	2	50	.270	26	44	30	195	245	15	.967
—Columbus (Int'l)	2B-3B-SS	40	118	17	36	5	0	1	11	.305	6	25	1	55	95	4	.974
1984—Columbus (Int'l)	2B	114	394	49	115	26	1	1	35	.292	16	61	11	266	348	16	.975
—New York (A.L.)............	2B	9	7	2	1	1	0	0	0	.143	1	5	0	4	7	0	1.000
1985—Columbus (Int'l)	2-S-O-3-1	106	380	62	95	13	4	3	18	.250	17	51	29	192	234	17	.962
—New York (A.L.)........	2B-1B-SS	20	51	4	8	0	1	0	1	.157	1	9	0	42	51	2	.979
1986—Rochester (Int'l)■....	2-3-O-S	77	219	29	57	12	3	2	13	.260	16	32	12	135	191	15	.956
—Baltimore (A.L.)........	2B-3B	14	1	1	0	0	0	0	0	.000	0	0	1	2	3	1	.833
1987—Rochester (Int'l)	OF-2B-SS	31	106	22	27	5	1	5	10	.255	2	15	9	51	15	2	.971
1988—Indianapolis (A.A.)■..	O-2-S-3	67	234	36	71	11	3	7	25	.303	10	35	14	102	96	4	.980
—Montreal (N.L.)........	2B-SS-OF	77	216	38	59	14	2	4	14	.273	10	34	29	116	168	10	.966
1989—Montreal (N.L.)..........	2B-OF-SS	92	155	21	38	7	0	6	13	.245	6	23	15	59	59	7	.944
1990—Montreal (N.L.)..........	PH	4	3	1	1	0	0	0	0	.333	0	1	0	0	0	0	...
—St. Louis (N.L.)■....	O-2-1-3-S	89	217	30	61	11	2	7	22	.281	12	31	18	158	42	5	.976
1991—St. Louis (N.L.)..........	OF-1B-2B	101	207	21	47	10	2	1	15	.227	10	29	12	130	6	2	.986
1992—St. Louis (N.L.)..........	2B-OF-1B	61	98	17	24	4	0	3	5	.245	2	23	2	44	39	3	.965
1993—Yakult (Jp. Cen.)■......	...	120	410	48	123	26	3	14	64	.300	32	77	1	...	...	...	...
1994—California (A.L.)■.......2-O-DH-1		56	124	17	37	8	0	8	20	.298	6	28	2	71	61	5	.964
1995—California (A.L.)	2-O-DH-1	84	223	30	59	16	0	6	27	.265	10	48	13	122	115	4	.983
1996—California (A.L.)	2-O-DH-1	92	302	60	94	20	3	16	40	.311	9	54	14	173	117	6	.980
1997—Reading (Eastern)■....	OF-2B	6	23	5	8	2	0	1	5	.348	1	2	0	4	1	0	1.000
—Philadelphia (N.L.)......	OF-2B	50	122	17	27	4	0	5	10	.221	6	28	1	61	10	3	.959
—Clearwater (FSL)	OF-2B	9	34	8	11	2	1	3	6	.324	0	8	1	10	2	0	1.000
—Scran./W.B. (Int'l).......	2B	3	9	0	3	0	0	0	0	.333	0	0	0	1	5	0	1.000
American League totals (6 years)		275	708	114	199	45	4	30	88	.281	27	144	30	414	354	18	.977
National League totals (6 years)		474	1018	145	257	50	6	26	79	.252	46	169	77	568	324	30	.967
Major league totals (12 years)		749	1726	259	456	95	10	56	167	.264	73	313	107	982	678	48	.972

PERSONAL: Born September 29, 1970, in Philadelphia. ... 6-1/180. ... Throws right, bats right. ... Full name: Joseph Paul Hudson.
HIGH SCHOOL: Holy Cross (Delran, N.J.).
COLLEGE: West Virginia.
TRANSACTIONS/CAREER NOTES: Selected by Boston Red Sox organization in 27th round of free-agent draft (June 1, 1992).

Year Team (League)	W	L	Pct.	ERA	G	GS	CG	ShO	Sv.	IP	H	R	ER	BB	SO
1992—Elmira (N.Y.-Penn).......	3	3	.500	4.38	19	7	0	0	0	72	76	46	35	33	38
1993—Lynchburg (Caroline)	8	6	.571	4.06	49	1	0	0	0	84 1/3	97	49	38	38	62
1994—Sarasota (Florida State)......	3	1	.750	2.23	30	0	0	0	7	48 1/3	42	20	12	27	33
—New Britain (East.)	5	3	.625	3.92	23	0	0	0	0	39	49	18	17	18	24
1995—Trenton (Eastern)	0	1	.000	1.71	22	0	0	0	8	31 2/3	20	8	6	17	24
—Boston (A.L.)................	0	1	.000	4.11	39	0	0	0	1	46	53	21	21	23	29
1996—Pawtucket (Int'l)..............	1	1	.500	3.51	25	0	0	0	5	33 1/3	29	19	13	21	18
—Boston (A.L.)................	3	5	.375	5.40	36	0	0	0	1	45	57	35	27	32	19
1997—Pawtucket (Int'l)................	2	1	.667	2.25	29	0	0	0	7	32	25	22	8	23	14
—Boston (A.L.)................	3	1	.750	3.53	26	0	0	0	0	35 2/3	39	16	14	14	14
Major league totals (3 years)......	6	7	.462	4.41	101	0	0	0	2	126 2/3	149	72	62	69	62

DIVISION SERIES RECORD

Year Team (League)	W	L	Pct.	ERA	G	GS	CG	ShO	Sv.	IP	H	R	ER	BB	SO
1995—Boston (A.L.)................	0	0	...	0.00	1	0	0	0	0	1	2	0	0	1	0

H

HUGHES, BOBBY   C   BREWERS

PERSONAL: Born March 10, 1971, in Burbank, Calif. ... 6-4/237. ... Bats right, throws right. ... Full name: Robert E. Hughes.
HIGH SCHOOL: Notre Dame (Sherman Oaks, Calif.).
JUNIOR COLLEGE: College of the Canyons (Calif.).
COLLEGE: Loyola Marymount, then Southern California.
TRANSACTIONS/CAREER NOTES: Selected by Detroit Tigers organization in 47th round of free-agent draft (June 3, 1991); did not sign. ... Selected by Milwaukee Brewers organization in second round of free-agent draft (June 1, 1992). ... On disabled list (April 3-11 and May 4-20, 1997).
STATISTICAL NOTES: Led Midwest League catchers with 17 errors in 1993. ... Led Pacific Coast League catchers with 12 errors in 1997.

									BATTING					FIELDING		
Year Team (League)	Pos.	G	AB	R	H	2B	3B	HR	RBI	Avg.	BB	SO	SB	PO	A	E	Avg.
1992—Helena (Pioneer)	OF-C	11	40	5	7	1	1	0	6	.175	4	14	0	64	9	1	.986
1993—Beloit (Midwest)	C-1B	98	321	42	89	11	3	17	56	.277	23	76	1	573	67	†18	.973
1994—Stockton (California) ..	C-1B-3B	95	322	54	81	24	3	11	53	.252	33	83	2	517	63	8	.986
—El Paso (Texas)..........	C	12	36	3	10	4	1	0	12	.278	5	7	0	52	8	1	.984
1995—Stockton (California) ..	C-1B	52	179	22	42	9	2	8	31	.235	17	41	2	252	50	4	.987
—El Paso (Texas)..........	C	51	173	11	46	12	0	7	27	.266	12	30	0	299	29	8	.976
1996—New Orleans (A.A.)	C-1B-3B	37	125	11	25	5	0	4	15	.200	4	31	1	176	27	5	.976
—El Paso (Texas)..........	C	67	237	43	72	18	1	15	39	.304	30	40	3	250	32	6	.979
1997—Tucson (PCL)	C-3B	89	290	43	90	29	2	7	51	.310	24	46	0	455	48	†12	.977

HUISMAN, RICK   P   GIANTS

PERSONAL: Born May 17, 1969, in Oak Park, Ill. ... 6-3/210. ... Throws right, bats right. ... Full name: Richard Allen Huisman. ... Name pronounced HIGHS-man..
HIGH SCHOOL: Timothy Christian (Elmhurst, Ill.).
COLLEGE: Lewis (Ill.).
TRANSACTIONS/CAREER NOTES: Selected by San Francisco Giants organization in third round of free-agent draft (June 4, 1990). ... On Phoenix disabled list (April 8-May 18, 1993). ... Claimed on waivers by Houston Astros (August 27, 1993). ... Traded by Astros to Kansas City Royals (August 17, 1995), completing deal in which Astros acquired C Pat Borders for a player to be named later (August 12, 1995). ... On disabled list (March 23-June 6, 1997); included rehabilitation assignment to Omaha (May 19-June 6). ... Released by Royals following 1997 season. ... Signed by Giants organization (January 12, 1998).
HONORS: Named California League Pitcher of the Year (1991).

Year Team (League)	W	L	Pct.	ERA	G	GS	CG	ShO	Sv.	IP	H	R	ER	BB	SO
1990—Everett (Northwest)	0	0	...	4.50	1	0	0	0	0	2	3	1	1	2	2
—Clinton (Midwest)	6	5	.545	2.05	14	13	0	0	0	79	56	19	18	33	103
1991—San Jose (California).........	*16	4	.800	*1.83	26	26	7	*4	0	*182 1/3	126	45	37	73	*216
1992—Shreveport (Texas)	7	4	.636	2.35	17	16	1	1	0	103 1/3	79	33	27	31	100
—Phoenix (PCL)	3	2	.600	2.41	9	8	0	0	0	56	45	16	15	24	44
1993—San Jose (California)	2	1	.667	2.31	4	4	1	0	0	23 1/3	19	6	6	12	15
—Phoenix (PCL)	3	4	.429	5.97	14	14	0	0	0	72 1/3	78	54	48	45	59
—Tucson (PCL)■	1	0	1.000	7.36	2	0	0	0	0	3 2/3	6	5	3	1	4
1994—Jackson (Texas)	3	0	1.000	1.61	49	0	0	0	31	50 1/3	32	10	9	24	63
1995—Tucson (PCL)	6	1	.857	4.45	42	0	0	0	6	54 2/3	58	33	27	28	47
—Omaha (Am. Assoc.)■......	0	0	...	1.80	5	0	0	0	1	5	3	1	1	1	13
—Kansas City (A.L.)	0	0	...	7.45	7	0	0	0	0	9 2/3	14	8	8	1	12
1996—Omaha (Am. Assoc.)	2	4	.333	4.87	27	4	0	0	6	57 1/3	54	32	31	24	50
—Kansas City (A.L.)	2	1	.667	4.60	22	0	0	0	1	29 1/3	25	15	15	18	23
1997—Omaha (Am. Assoc.)	1	5	.167	3.62	37	1	0	0	2	59 2/3	59	29	24	35	57
Major league totals (2 years)......	2	1	.667	5.31	29	0	0	0	1	39	39	23	23	19	35

HUNDLEY, TODD   C   METS

PERSONAL: Born May 27, 1969, in Martinsville, Va. ... 5-11/185. ... Bats both, throws right. ... Full name: Todd Randolph Hundley. ... Son of Randy Hundley, major league catcher with four teams (1964-77).
HIGH SCHOOL: William Fremd (Palatine, Ill.).
COLLEGE: William Rainey Harper College (Ill.).
TRANSACTIONS/CAREER NOTES: Selected by New York Mets organization in second round of free-agent draft (June 2, 1987); pick received as compensation for Baltimore Orioles signing Type B free-agent 3B/1B Ray Knight. ... On Tidewater disabled list (June 29-July 6, 1991). ... On disabled list (July 23, 1995-remainder of season).
RECORDS: Holds major league single-season record for most home runs by catcher—41 (1996). ... Holds N.L. record for most home runs by switchhitter in two consecutive seasons—71. ... Holds N.L. single-season record for most home runs by switch-hitter—41 (1996); and most strikeouts by switch hitter—146 (1996).
STATISTICAL NOTES: Led South Atlantic League in intentional bases on balls received with 10 and in grounding into double plays with 20 in 1989. ... Led South Atlantic League catchers with 826 putouts and 930 total chances in 1989. ... Tied for International League lead in errors by catcher with nine and double plays with 12 in 1991. ... Switch-hit home runs in one game five times (June 18, 1994; May 18; June 10, 1996; May 5 and July 20, 1997). ... Career major league grand slams: 4.

									BATTING					FIELDING		
Year Team (League)	Pos.	G	AB	R	H	2B	3B	HR	RBI	Avg.	BB	SO	SB	PO	A	E	Avg.
1987—Little Falls (NYP)	C	34	103	12	15	4	0	1	10	.146	12	27	0	181	25	7	.967
1988—Little Falls (NYP)	C	52	176	23	33	8	0	2	18	.188	16	31	1	345	54	8	.980
—St. Lucie (Fla. St.)	C	1	1	0	0	0	0	0	0	.000	2	1	0	4	0	1	.800
1989—Columbia (S. Atl.).......	C-OF	125	439	67	118	23	4	11	66	.269	54	67	6	†829	91	13	.986
1990—Jackson (Texas)	C-3B	81	279	27	74	12	2	1	35	.265	34	44	5	474	63	9	.984
—New York (N.L.)...........	C	36	67	8	14	6	0	0	2	.209	6	18	0	162	8	2	.988
1991—Tidewater (Int'l)..........	C-1B	125	454	62	124	24	4	14	66	.273	51	95	1	585	63	‡9	.986
—New York (N.L.)..........	C	21	60	5	8	0	1	1	7	.133	6	14	0	85	11	0	1.000

– 265 –

H

Year Team (League)	Pos.	G	AB	R	H	2B	3B	HR	RBI	Avg.	BB	SO	SB	PO	A	E	Avg.
1992— New York (N.L.).........	C	123	358	32	75	17	0	7	32	.209	19	76	3	700	48	3	.996
1993— New York (N.L.).........	C	130	417	40	95	17	2	11	53	.228	23	62	1	592	63	8	.988
1994— New York (N.L.).........	C	91	291	45	69	10	1	16	42	.237	25	73	2	448	28	5	.990
1995— New York (N.L.).........	C	90	275	39	77	11	0	15	51	.280	42	64	1	488	29	7	.987
1996— New York (N.L.).........	C	153	540	85	140	32	1	41	112	.259	79	146	1	911	72	8	.992
1997— New York (N.L.).........	C-DH	132	417	78	114	21	2	30	86	.273	83	116	2	678	54	10	.987
Major league totals (8 years)		776	2425	332	592	114	7	121	385	.244	283	569	10	4064	313	43	.990

ALL-STAR GAME RECORD

Year League	Pos.	AB	R	H	2B	3B	HR	RBI	Avg.	BB	SO	SB	PO	A	E	Avg.
1997— National....................							Selected, did not play—injured.									

HUNTER, BRIAN OF TIGERS

PERSONAL: Born March 5, 1971, in Portland, Ore. ... 6-4/180. ... Bats right, throws right. ... Full name: Brian Lee Hunter.
HIGH SCHOOL: Fort Vancouver (Vancouver, Wash.).
TRANSACTIONS/CAREER NOTES: Selected by Houston Astros organization in second round of free-agent draft (June 5, 1989); pick received as part of compensation for Texas Rangers signing Type A free-agent P Nolan Ryan. ... On Houston disabled list (July 5-23, 1995); included rehabilitation assignment to Jackson (July 21-23). ... On Houston disabled list (June 29-July 27, 1996); included rehabilitation assignment to Tucson (July 23-27). ... Traded by Astros with IF Orlando Miller, P Doug Brocail, P Todd Jones and a player to be named later to Detroit Tigers for C Brad Ausmus, P Jose Lima, P C.J. Nitkowski, P Trever Miller and IF Daryle Ward (December 10, 1996).
RECORDS: Shares major league record for fewest double plays by outfielder (150 or more games)—0 (1997).
STATISTICAL NOTES: Tied for American Association lead with 249 total bases in 1997. ... Led A.L. in caught stealing with 18 in 1997. ... Led A.L. outfielders in total chances with 402 in 1997. ... Career major league grand slams: 1.

Year Team (League)	Pos.	G	AB	R	H	2B	3B	HR	RBI	Avg.	BB	SO	SB	PO	A	E	Avg.
1989— GC Astros (GCL)	OF	51	206	15	35	2	0	0	13	.170	7	42	12	95	4	2	.980
1990— Asheville (S. Atl.)........	OF	127	444	84	111	14	6	0	16	.250	60	72	45	219	13	11	.955
1991— Osceola (Fla. St.)........	OF	118	392	51	94	15	3	1	30	.240	45	75	32	250	7	9	.966
1992— Osceola (Fla. St.)........	OF	131	489	62	146	18	9	1	62	.299	31	76	39	295	10	9	.971
1993— Jackson (Texas)	OF	133	523	84	154	22	5	10	52	.294	34	85	*35	276	9	*14	.953
1994— Tucson (PCL)	OF	128	513	*113	*191	28	9	10	51	*.372	52	52	*49	244	14	5	.981
— Houston (N.L.)	OF	6	24	2	6	1	0	0	0	.250	1	6	2	14	1	1	.938
1995— Tucson (PCL)	OF	38	155	28	51	5	1	1	16	.329	17	13	11	91	1	0	1.000
— Houston (N.L.)	OF	78	321	52	97	14	5	2	28	.302	21	52	24	182	8	9	.955
— Jackson (Texas)	OF	2	6	1	3	0	0	0	0	.500	1	0	0	5	0	0	1.000
1996— Houston (N.L.)	OF	132	526	74	145	27	2	5	35	.276	17	92	35	279	11	•12	.960
— Tucson (PCL)	OF	3	14	3	5	0	1	0	1	.357	0	2	3	8	0	0	1.000
1997— Detroit (A.L.)■..........	OF	•162	658	112	177	29	7	4	45	.269	66	121	*74	*408	8	4	.990
American League totals (1 year)		162	658	112	177	29	7	4	45	.269	66	121	74	408	8	4	.990
National League totals (3 years)		216	871	128	248	42	7	7	63	.285	39	150	61	475	20	22	.957
Major league totals (4 years)		378	1529	240	425	71	14	11	108	.278	105	271	135	883	28	26	.972

HUNTER, RICH P PHILLIES

PERSONAL: Born September 25, 1974, in Pasadena, Calif. ... 6-1/185. ... Throws right, bats right. ... Full name: Richard Thomas Hunter.
HIGH SCHOOL: The Linfield School (Temecula, Calif.).
TRANSACTIONS/CAREER NOTES: Selected by Philadelphia Phillies organization in 14th round of free-agent draft (June 3, 1993).
MISCELLANEOUS: Appeared in one game as pinch-runner with Philadelphia (1996).

Year Team (League)	W	L	Pct.	ERA	G	GS	CG	ShO	Sv.	IP	H	R	ER	BB	SO
1993— Martinsville (App.).........	0	6	.000	9.55	13	9	0	0	0	49	82	61	*52	27	36
1994— Martinsville (App.).........	3	2	.600	4.50	18	0	0	0	5	38	31	19	19	9	39
1995— Piedmont (S. Atl.)	10	2	.833	2.77	15	15	3	2	0	104	79	37	32	19	80
— Clearwater (Fla. St.)	6	0	1.000	2.93	9	9	0	0	0	58 1/3	62	23	19	7	46
— Reading (Eastern)	3	0	1.000	2.05	3	3	0	0	0	22	14	6	5	6	17
1996— Philadelphia (N.L.)..........	3	7	.300	6.49	14	14	0	0	0	69 1/3	84	54	50	33	32
— Scran./W.B. (Int'l)	2	4	.333	6.69	8	7	1	0	0	40 1/3	39	31	30	22	22
— Reading (Eastern)	4	3	.571	3.17	10	10	2	0	0	71	69	26	25	12	40
1997— Reading (Eastern)	6	11	.353	4.69	29	28	1	1	0	163	191	100	85	60	104
Major league totals (1 year)........	3	7	.300	6.49	14	14	0	0	0	69 1/3	84	54	50	33	32

HUNTER, SCOTT OF METS

PERSONAL: Born December 17, 1975, in Philadelphia. ... 6-2/195. ... Full name: Scott William Hunter.
HIGH SCHOOL: Northeast (Philadelphia).
TRANSACTIONS/CAREER NOTES: Selected by Los Angeles Dodgers organization in fifth round of free-agent draft (June 3, 1993). ... Traded with OF Dwight Maness by Dodgers to New York Mets organization for OF Brett Butler (August 18, 1995). ... On disabled list (June 29-remainder of 1997 season).
STATISTICAL NOTES: Led Pioneer League third basemen with 33 errors in 1994.

Year Team (League)	Pos.	G	AB	R	H	2B	3B	HR	RBI	Avg.	BB	SO	SB	PO	A	E	Avg.
1994— Great Falls (Pio.)	3B-OF-SS	64	237	45	75	12	4	2	28	.316	25	40	17	38	113	†33	.821
1995— San Bern. (Calif.)	OF	113	379	68	108	19	3	11	59	.285	36	83	27	177	7	9	.953
— Columbia (S. Atl.)■.......	OF	12	40	2	10	0	0	0	1	.250	2	11	3	21	1	1	.957
1996— St. Lucie (Fla. St.)	OF	127	475	71	122	19	1	2	38	.257	38	68	12	167	13	9	.952
1997— Binghamton (East.)	OF	80	289	45	74	12	2	10	31	.256	25	52	24	109	7	1	.991

H

HUNTER, TORII   OF   TWINS

PERSONAL: Born July 18, 1975, in Pine Bluff, Ark. ... 6-2/205. ... Bats right, throws right. ... Full name: Torii Kedar Hunter. ... Name pronounced TORE-ee.
HIGH SCHOOL: Pine Bluff (Ark.).
TRANSACTIONS/CAREER NOTES: Selected by Minnesota Twins organization in first round (20th pick overall) of free-agent draft (June 3, 1993); pick recieved as part of compensation for Cincinnati Reds signing Type A free-agent P John Smiley. ... On New Britain disabled list (April 4-May 10, 1996).
STATISTICAL NOTES: Led Florida State League outfielders with seven double plays in 1995. ... Tied for Eastern League lead for double plays by an outfielder with four in 1997.

Year Team (League)	Pos.	G	AB	R	H	2B	3B	HR	RBI	Avg.	BB	SO	SB	PO	A	E	Avg.
1993— GC Twins (GCL).........	OF	28	100	6	19	3	0	0	8	.190	4	23	4	50	1	•6	.895
1994— Fort Wayne (Midw.)....	OF	91	335	57	98	17	1	10	50	.293	25	80	8	224	12	7	.971
1995— Fort Myers (FSL).......	OF	113	391	64	96	15	2	7	36	.246	38	77	7	242	15	7	.973
1996— New Britain (Eastern).	OF	99	342	49	90	20	3	7	33	.263	28	60	7	207	11	4	.982
—Fort Myers (FSL)........	OF	4	16	1	3	0	0	0	1	.188	2	5	1	9	0	0	1.000
1997— New Britain (Eastern).	OF	127	471	57	109	22	2	8	56	.231	47	94	8	252	7	7	.974
—Minnesota (A.L.)	PR	1	0	0	0	0	0	0	0	...	0	0	0	...	...	...	...
Major league totals (1 year)		1	0	0	0	0	0	0	0	...	0	0	0	...	...	...	...

HURST, BILL   P   TIGERS

PERSONAL: Born April 28, 1970, in Miami Beach, Fla. ... 6-7/220. ... Throws right, bats right. ... Full name: William H. Hurst.
HIGH SCHOOL: Miami Palmetto.
JUNIOR COLLEGE: Central Florida Community College.
TRANSACTIONS/CAREER NOTES: Selected by St. Louis Cardinals organization in 20th round of free-agent draft (June 5, 1989). ... On Savannah disabled list (August 10, 1990-remainder of season). ... On disabled list (April 29, 1991-remainder of season and April 10, 1992-entire season). ... Released by Cardinals organization (December 10, 1992). ... Signed by Florida Marlins organization (March 12, 1995). ... On Portland disabled list (August 1-9, 1996). ... On disabled list (August 30, 1997-remainder of season). ... Claimed on waivers by Detroit Tigers (October 14, 1997).

Year Team (League)	W	L	Pct.	ERA	G	GS	CG	ShO	Sv.	IP	H	R	ER	BB	SO
1990— Johnson City (App.)	0	0	...	1.64	2	2	0	0	0	11	5	2	2	6	12
—Savannah (S. Atl.)	2	1	.667	3.38	7	7	0	0	0	32	??	17	12	27	14
1991— Johnson City (App.)	0	0	...	10.80	2	0	0	0	0	1 2/3	0	2	2	2	2
1992—							Did not play.								
1993—							Did not play.								
1994—							Did not play.								
1995— Brevard County (FSL)■.....	1	4	.200	3.02	39	4	0	0	12	50 2/3	33	20	17	41	35
1996— Portland (Eastern)...............	2	3	.400	2.20	45	0	0	0	*30	49	45	22	12	31	46
—Florida (N.L.)......................	0	0	...	0.00	2	0	0	0	0	2	3	0	0*	1	1
1997— Charlotte (Int'l)...................	1	2	.333	7.76	27	0	0	0	3	29	39	27	25	22	15
—Portland (Eastern).............	0	0	...	0.00	2	0	0	0	0	2	1	0	0	0	2
Major league totals (1 year)........	0	0	...	0.00	2	0	0	0	0	2	3	0	0	1	1

HURST, JIMMY   OF   RED SOX

PERSONAL: Born March 1, 1972, in Druid City, Ala. ... 6-6/225. ... Bats right, throws right.
HIGH SCHOOL: Central High of Tuscaloosa (Ala.).
JUNIOR COLLEGE: Three Rivers Community College (Mo.).
TRANSACTIONS/CAREER NOTES: Selected by Chicago White Sox organization in 12th round of free-agent draft (June 4, 1990). ... Claimed on waivers by Detroit Tigers (March 26, 1997). ... Contract sold by Tigers to Boston Red Sox (November 24, 1997).
STATISTICAL NOTES: Tied for Midwest League lead in errors by outfielder with 12 in 1993.

Year Team (League)	Pos.	G	AB	R	H	2B	3B	HR	RBI	Avg.	BB	SO	SB	PO	A	E	Avg.
1991— GC Whi. Sox (GCL)	OF	36	121	14	31	4	0	0	12	.256	13	32	6	37	4	1	.976
1992— Utica (N.Y.-Penn)....	OF	68	220	31	50	8	5	6	35	.227	27	78	11	81	6	6	.935
1993— South Bend (Mid.)......	OF-1B	123	464	79	113	26	0	20	79	.244	37	141	15	98	8	‡12	.898
1994— Prince William (Car.) ..	OF	127	455	90	126	31	6	25	91	.277	72	128	15	145	6	5	.968
1995— Birmingham (Sou.).....	OF	91	301	47	57	11	0	12	34	.189	33	95	12	131	3	10	.931
1996— Birmingham (Sou.).....	OF	126	472	62	125	23	1	18	88	.265	53	128	19	234	11	7	.972
—Nashville (A.A.)	OF	3	6	2	2	1	0	1	2	.333	1	3	0	2	0	0	1.000
1997— Jacksonv. (Sou.)■.....	OF	5	17	5	8	2	0	2	6	.471	3	6	0	3	0	0	1.000
—Toledo (Int'l).............	OF	110	377	51	102	11	3	18	58	.271	47	115	14	210	*18	9	.962
—Detroit (A.L.)	OF-DH	13	17	1	3	1	0	1	1	.176	2	6	0	12	0	0	1.000
Major league totals (1 year)		13	17	1	3	1	0	1	1	.176	2	6	0	12	0	0	1.000

HURTADO, EDWIN   P   MARINERS

PERSONAL: Born February 1, 1970, in Barquisimeto, Venezuela. ... 6-3/215. ... Throws right, bats right. ... Full name: Edwin Amilgar Hurtado.
TRANSACTIONS/CAREER NOTES: Signed as non-drafted free agent by Toronto Blue Jays organization (December 10, 1990). ... Traded by Blue Jays with P Paul Menhart to Seattle Mariners for P Bill Risley and 2B Miguel Cairo (December 18, 1995). ... On Tacoma disabled list (July 11-September 1, 1996). ... On Seattle disabled list (September 1, 1996-remainder of season).

Year Team (League)	W	L	Pct.	ERA	G	GS	CG	ShO	Sv.	IP	H	R	ER	BB	SO
1991— Dom. Dodgers (DSL)	7	1	.875	1.61	13	13	2	1	0	84	59	21	15	48	92
1992— Dom. Dodgers (DSL)	11	0	*1.000	1.36	16	15	2	1	0	92 1/3	65	17	14	37	110

H

Year Team (League)	W	L	Pct.	ERA	G	GS	CG	ShO	Sv.	IP	H	R	ER	BB	SO
1993— St. Catharines (NYP)	10	2	.833	2.50	15	15	3	•1	0	101	69	34	28	34	87
1994— Hagerstown (S. Atl.)	11	2	.846	2.95	33	16	1	0	2	134⅓	118	53	44	46	121
1995— Knoxville (Southern)	2	4	.333	4.45	11	11	0	0	0	54⅔	54	34	27	25	38
— Toronto (A.L.)	5	2	.714	5.45	14	10	1	0	0	77⅔	81	50	47	40	33
1996— Seattle (A.L.)■	2	5	.286	7.74	16	4	0	0	2	47⅔	61	42	41	30	36
— Tacoma (PCL)	1	2	.333	3.73	5	4	0	0	0	31⅓	23	13	13	12	26
1997— Seattle (A.L.)	1	2	.333	9.00	13	1	0	0	0	19	25	19	19	15	10
— Tacoma (PCL)	10	6	.625	*3.88	20	20	5	*3	0	132⅓	139	60	57	37	100
Major league totals (3 years)	8	9	.471	6.67	43	15	1	0	2	144⅓	167	111	107	85	79

HUSKEY, BUTCH — OF/1B — METS

PERSONAL: Born November 10, 1971, in Anadarko, Okla. ... 6-3/244. ... Bats right, throws right. ... Full name: Robert Leon Huskey.
HIGH SCHOOL: Eisenhower (Lawton, Okla.).
TRANSACTIONS/CAREER NOTES: Selected by New York Mets in seventh round of free-agent draft (June 5, 1989). ... On disabled list (August 6-September 1, 1996).
HONORS: Named International League Most Valuable Player (1995).
STATISTICAL NOTES: Led Gulf Coast League third basemen with 50 putouts and 23 errors in 1989. ... Led Appalachian League third basemen with 217 total chances and tied for lead with 11 double plays in 1990. ... Led South Atlantic League with 256 total bases in 1991. ... Led South Atlantic League third basemen with 21 double plays in 1991. ... Led Florida State League third basemen with 456 total chances and 28 double plays in 1992. ... Led Eastern League third basemen with 101 putouts, 297 assists, 34 errors and 432 total chances in 1993. ... Led International League third basemen with 31 double plays in 1994. ... Had 20-game hitting streak (August 22-September 13, 1997).

Year Team (League)	Pos.	G	AB	R	H	2B	3B	HR	RBI	Avg.	BB	SO	SB	PO	A	E	Avg.
1989— GC Mets (GCL)	3B-1B	54	190	27	50	14	2	6	34	.263	14	36	4	†73	106	‡23	.886
1990— Kingsport (Appal.)	3B	*72	*279	39	75	13	0	14	53	.269	24	74	7	45	*150	•22	.899
1991— Columbia (S. Atl.)	3B	134	492	88	141	27	5	*26	*99	.287	54	89	22	*102	218	31	.912
1992— St. Lucie (Fla. St.)	3B	134	493	65	125	17	1	18	75	.254	33	74	7	*108	*310	*38	.917
1993— Binghamton (East.)	3B-SS	*139	*526	72	132	23	1	25	98	.251	48	102	11	†101	†297	†34	.921
— New York (N.L.)	3B	13	41	2	6	1	0	0	3	.146	1	13	0	9	27	3	.923
1994— Norfolk (Int'l)	3B	127	474	59	108	23	3	10	57	.228	37	88	16	*95	297	25	.940
1995— Norfolk (Int'l)	3B-OF-1B	109	394	66	112	18	1	*28	87	.284	39	88	8	248	132	13	.967
— New York (N.L.)	3B-OF	28	90	8	17	1	0	3	11	.189	10	16	1	16	60	6	.927
1996— New York (N.L.)	1B-OF-3B	118	414	43	115	16	2	15	60	.278	27	77	1	638	54	15	.979
1997— New York (N.L.)	O-1-3-DH	142	471	61	135	26	2	24	81	.287	25	84	8	377	38	15	.965
Major league totals (4 years)		301	1016	114	273	44	4	42	155	.269	63	190	10	1040	179	39	.969

HUSON, JEFF — IF — MARINERS

PERSONAL: Born August 15, 1964, in Scottsdale, Ariz. ... 6-3/180. ... Bats left, throws right. ... Full name: Jeffrey Kent Huson. ... Name pronounced HYOO-son.
HIGH SCHOOL: Mingus Union (Cottonwood, Ariz.).
JUNIOR COLLEGE: Glendale (Ariz.) Community College.
COLLEGE: Wyoming.
TRANSACTIONS/CAREER NOTES: Signed as non-drafted free agent by Montreal Expos organization (August 18, 1985). ... Traded by Expos to Oklahoma City, Texas Rangers organization, for P Drew Hall (April 2, 1990). ... On Texas disabled list (August 8-31, 1991); included rehabilitation assignment to Oklahoma City (August 29-31). ... On Texas disabled list (March 27-May 27, 1993); included rehabilitation assignment to Oklahoma City (May 24-27). ... On Texas disabled list (June 5-July 15, 1993); included rehabilitation assignment to Oklahoma City (July 10-15). ... On Texas disabled list (July 24-August 23, 1993); included rehabilitation assignment to Oklahoma City (July 31-August 19). ... On Texas disabled list (March 25-June 6, 1994); included rehabilitation assignment to Oklahoma City (May 17-June 5). ... Released by Rangers (November 30, 1994). ... Signed by Rochester, Baltimore Orioles organization (December 31, 1994). ... On Baltimore disabled list (May 18-July 15, 1996); included rehabilitation assignment to Frederick (June 27-July 15). ... Released by Orioles (August 13, 1996). ... Signed by Colorado Springs, Colorado Rockies organization (August 19, 1996). ... Traded by Rockies to Milwaukee Brewers for a player to be named later (April 23, 1997). ... Granted free agency (October 28, 1997). ... Signed by Rockies organization (November 18, 1997). ... Selected by Seattle Mariners from Rockies organization in Rule 5 major league draft (December 15, 1997).

Year Team (League)	Pos.	G	AB	R	H	2B	3B	HR	RBI	Avg.	BB	SO	SB	PO	A	E	Avg.
1986— Burl. (Midw.)	SS-3B-2B	133	457	85	132	19	1	16	72	.289	76	68	32	183	324	37	.932
— Jacksonville (South.)..	3B	1	4	0	0	0	0	0	0	.000	0	0	0	0	1	0	1.000
1987— W.P. Beach (FSL)	SS-OF-2B	131	455	54	130	15	4	1	53	.286	50	30	33	234	347	34	.945
1988— Jacksonville (South.)..	S-2-O-3	128	471	72	117	18	1	0	34	.248	59	45	*56	217	285	26	.951
— Montreal (N.L.)	S-2-3-O	20	42	7	13	2	0	0	3	.310	4	3	2	18	41	4	.937
1989— Indianapolis (A.A.)	SS-OF-2B	102	378	70	115	17	4	3	35	.304	50	26	30	172	214	17	.958
— Montreal (N.L.)	SS-2B-3B	32	74	1	12	5	0	0	2	.162	6	6	3	40	65	8	.929
1990— Texas (A.L.)■	SS-3B-2B	145	396	57	95	12	2	0	28	.240	46	54	12	183	304	19	.962
1991— Texas (A.L.)	SS-2B-3B	119	268	36	57	8	3	2	26	.213	39	32	8	143	269	15	.965
— Oklahoma City (A.A.)..	SS	2	6	0	3	1	0	0	2	.500	0	1	0	5	3	0	1.000
1992— Texas (A.L.)	S-2-O-DH	123	318	49	83	14	3	4	24	.261	41	43	18	178	250	9	.979
1993— Oklahoma City (A.A.)..	S-3-S-2-O	24	76	11	22	5	0	1	10	.289	13	10	1	39	52	3	.968
— Texas (A.L.)	S-2-DH-3	23	45	3	6	1	1	0	2	.133	0	10	0	25	42	6	.918
1994— Oklahoma City (A.A.)..	2-3-O-S	83	302	47	91	20	2	1	27	.301	30	32	18	140	165	7	.978
1995— Rochester (Int'l)■......	SS-2B	60	223	28	56	9	0	3	21	.251	26	29	16	110	203	7	.978
— Baltimore (A.L.)	3-2-DH-S	66	161	24	40	4	2	1	19	.248	15	20	5	59	89	1	.993
1996— Baltimore (A.L.)..........	2B-3B-OF	17	28	5	9	1	0	0	2	.321	1	3	0	20	17	1	.974
— Rochester (Int'l)	OF	2	8	0	2	0	0	0	1	.250	0	2	0	4	0	0	1.000
— Frederick (Carolina)....	OF	4	16	4	7	2	0	1	1	.438	2	0	0	6	0	0	1.000
— Bowie (Eastern)..........	OF-3B	3	13	3	5	2	0	0	0	.385	1	0	0	4	4	0	1.000
— Colo. Springs (PCL)■	2B-SS	14	61	10	18	4	0	0	8	.295	3	1	6	36	42	1	.987

H

Year	Team (League)	Pos.	G	AB	R	H	2B	3B	HR	RBI	Avg.	BB	SO	SB	PO	A	E	Avg.
1997—Colo. Springs (PCL) ...		3B-2B	9	20	3	7	3	0	1	5	.350	2	2	0	5	8	0	1.000
—Milwaukee (A.L.)■		..2-1-0-DH-3	84	143	12	29	3	0	0	11	.203	5	15	3	109	52	1	.994
American League totals (7 years)			577	1359	186	319	43	11	7	112	.235	147	177	46	717	1023	52	.971
National League totals (2 years)			52	116	8	25	7	0	0	5	.216	10	9	5	58	106	12	.932
Major league totals (9 years)			629	1475	194	344	50	11	7	117	.233	157	186	51	775	1129	64	.967

HUTCHINS, NORM OF ANGELS

PERSONAL: Born November 20, 1975, in White Plains, N.Y. ... 6-1/185. ... Bats right, throws left. ... Full name: Norman Hutchins.
HIGH SCHOOL: Lincoln (N.Y.).
TRANSACTIONS/CAREER NOTES: Selected by California Angels organization in second round of free-agent draft (June 2, 1994). ... Angels franchise renamed Anaheim Angels for 1997 season.

Year	Team (League)	Pos.	G	AB	R	H	2B	3B	HR	RBI	Avg.	BB	SO	SB	PO	A	E	Avg.
1994—Mes. Roc./Cubs (Ar.)..		OF	43	136	8	26	4	1	0	7	.191	3	44	5	70	0	6	.921
1995—Mes. Roc./Cubs (Ar.)..		OF	14	59	9	16	1	1	0	7	.271	4	10	8	17	0	2	.895
—Boise (Northwest)		OF	45	176	34	44	6	2	2	11	.250	15	44	10	92	3	2	.979
1996—Cedar Rapids (Mid.) ...		OF	126	466	59	105	13	*16	2	52	.225	28	110	22	*303	2	14	.956
1997—Lake Elsinore (Calif.)..		OF	132	564	82	163	31	12	15	69	.289	23	147	39	266	9	•13	.955

HUTTON, MARK P REDS

PERSONAL: Born February 6, 1970, in South Adelaide, Australia. ... 6-6/240. ... Throws right, bats right. ... Full name: Mark Steven Hutton.
HIGH SCHOOL: Scotch College Private School (Adelaide, Australia).
TRANSACTIONS/CAREER NOTES: Signed as non-drafted free agent by New York Yankees organization (December 15, 1988). ... On Columbus disabled list (April 23-May 15, 1993). ... On Columbus temporarily inactive list (April 11-16, 1994). ... On Columbus disabled list (June 2-11, July 5-August 12, August 18-27 and August 28-September 4, 1994) ... On disabled list (June 8-26 and July 11, 1995-remainder of season). ... On New York disabled list (April 15-May 29, 1996); included rehabilitation assignments to Tampa (May 16-23) and Columbus (May 23-29). ... Traded by Yankees to Florida Marlins for P David Weathers (July 31, 1996). ... Traded by Marlins to Colorado Rockies for IF Craig Counsell (July 27, 1997). ... Traded by Rockies to Cincinnati Reds for OF Curtis Goodwin (December 10, 1997).

Year	Team (League)	W	L	Pct.	ERA	G	GS	CG	ShO	Sv.	IP	H	R	ER	BB	SO
1989—Oneonta (N.Y.-Penn)	6	2	.750	4.07	12	12	0	0	0	66 1/3	70	39	30	24	62
1990—Greensboro (S. Atl.)	1	10	.091	6.31	21	19	0	0	0	81 1/3	77	78	57	62	72
1991—Fort Lauderdale (FSL)	5	8	.385	2.45	24	24	3	0	0	147	98	54	40	65	117
—Columbus (Int'l)	1	0	1.000	1.50	1	1	0	0	0	6	3	2	1	5	5
1992—Alb./Colon. (Eastern)	13	7	.650	3.59	26	25	1	0	0	165 1/3	146	75	66	66	128
—Columbus (Int'l)	0	1	.000	5.40	1	0	0	0	0	5	7	4	3	2	4
1993—Columbus (Int'l)	10	4	.714	3.18	21	21	0	0	0	133	98	52	47	53	112
—New York (A.L.)	1	1	.500	5.73	7	4	0	0	0	22	24	17	14	17	12
1994—Columbus (Int'l)	2	5	.286	3.63	22	5	0	0	3	34 2/3	31	16	14	12	27
—New York (A.L.)	0	0	...	4.91	2	0	0	0	0	3 2/3	4	3	2	0	1
1995—Columbus (Int'l)	2	6	.250	8.43	11	11	0	0	0	52 1/3	64	51	49	24	23
1996—New York (A.L.)	0	2	.000	5.04	12	2	0	0	0	30 1/3	32	19	17	18	25
—Tampa (Florida State)	0	0	...	1.80	3	2	0	0	0	5	2	1	1	1	6
—Columbus (Int'l)	0	0	...	0.00	2	0	0	0	0	2	0	0	0	2	3
—Florida (N.L.)■	5	1	.833	3.67	13	9	0	0	0	56 1/3	47	23	23	18	31
1997—Florida (N.L.)	3	1	.750	3.78	32	0	0	0	0	47 2/3	50	24	20	19	29
—Colorado (N.L.)■	0	1	.000	7.11	8	1	0	0	0	12 2/3	22	10	10	7	10
A.L. totals (3 years)	1	3	.250	5.30	21	6	0	0	0	56	60	39	33	35	38
N.L. totals (2 years)	8	3	.727	4.09	53	10	0	0	0	116 2/3	119	57	53	44	70
Major league totals (4 years)	9	6	.600	4.48	74	16	0	0	0	172 2/3	179	96	86	79	108

HYZDU, ADAM OF RED SOX

PERSONAL: Born December 6, 1971, in San Jose, Calif. ... 6-2/210. ... Bats right, throws right. ... Full name: Adam Davis Hyzdu. ... Name pronounced HIZE-doo.
HIGH SCHOOL: Moeller (Cincinnati).
TRANSACTIONS/CAREER NOTES: Selected by San Francisco Giants organization in first round (15th pick overall) of free-agent draft (June 4, 1990); pick received as compensation for Houston Astros signing Type B free-agent IF Ken Oberkfell. ... Selected by Cincinnati Reds from Giants organization in Rule 5 major league draft (December 13, 1993). ... Released by Reds (March 23, 1996). ... Signed by Boston Red Sox organization (April 26, 1996).
STATISTICAL NOTES: Led Eastern League with .618 slugging percentage in 1996.

Year	Team (League)	Pos.	G	AB	R	H	2B	3B	HR	RBI	Avg.	BB	SO	SB	PO	A	E	Avg.
1990—Everett (N'west)..........		OF	69	253	31	62	16	1	6	34	.245	28	78	2	128	2	5	.963
1991—Clinton (Midwest).......		OF	124	410	47	96	13	5	5	50	.234	64	131	4	185	8	9	.955
1992—San Jose (Calif.).......		OF	128	457	60	127	25	5	9	60	.278	55	134	10	193	8	5	.976
1993—San Jose (Calif.)........		OF	44	165	35	48	11	3	13	38	.291	29	53	1	72	5	3	.963
—Shreveport (Texas)......		OF	86	302	30	61	17	0	6	25	.202	20	82	0	136	8	4	.973
1994—Chattanooga (Sou.)■..		OF-1B	38	133	17	35	10	0	3	9	.263	8	21	0	70	4	4	.949
—Indianapolis (A.A.).....		OF	12	25	3	3	2	0	0	3	.120	1	5	0	10	1	1	.917
—Win.-Salem (Car.).....		OF	55	210	30	58	11	1	15	39	.276	18	33	1	67	2	4	.945
1995—Chattanooga (Sou.)...		OF	102	312	55	82	14	1	13	48	.263	45	56	3	182	4	1	*.995
1996—Trenton (Eastern)■...		OF-C	109	374	71	126	24	3	25	80	.337	56	75	1	135	9	3	.980
1997—Pawtucket (Int'l)........		OF	119	413	77	114	21	1	23	84	.276	72	113	10	170	10	4	.978

H

IBANEZ, RAUL   OF   MARINERS

PERSONAL: Born June 2, 1972, in New York. ... 6-2/200. ... Bats left, throws right. ... Full name: Raul Javier Ibanez.
HIGH SCHOOL: Sunset (Miami).
JUNIOR COLLEGE: Miami-Dade (South) Community College.
TRANSACTIONS/CAREER NOTES: Selected by Seattle Mariners organization in 36th round of free-agent draft (June 1, 1992). ... On disabled list (June 4-July 16, 1994).
STATISTICAL NOTES: Led California League with .612 slugging percentage in 1995. ... Led California League with 25 passed balls in 1995.

Year Team (League)	Pos.	G	AB	R	H	2B	3B	HR	RBI	Avg.	BB	SO	SB	PO	A	E	Avg.
1992—Ariz. Mariners (Ariz.)..	1B-C-OF	33	120	25	37	8	2	1	16	.308	9	18	1	51	3	4	.931
1993—Appleton (Midwest)....	1B-C-OF	52	157	26	43	9	0	5	21	.274	24	31	0	98	2	2	.980
—Bellingham (N'west)...	C	43	134	16	38	5	2	0	15	.284	21	23	0	137	15	1	.993
1994—Appleton (Midwest)....	C-1B-OF	91	327	55	102	30	3	7	59	.312	32	37	10	304	28	10	.971
1995—Riverside (Calif.)........	C-1B	95	361	59	120	23	9	20	108	.332	41	49	4	465	54	12	.977
1996—Tacoma (PCL)	OF-1B	111	405	59	115	20	3	11	47	.284	44	56	7	201	12	11	.951
—Port City (Southern)...	OF-C-1B	19	76	12	28	8	1	1	13	.368	8	7	3	36	2	4	.905
—Seattle (A.L.)........	DH	4	5	0	0	0	0	0	0	.000	0	1	0	0	0	0	...
1997—Tacoma (PCL)	OF	111	438	84	133	30	5	15	84	.304	32	75	7	192	12	5	.976
—Seattle (A.L.)..........	OF-DH	11	26	3	4	0	1	1	4	.154	0	6	0	9	0	0	1.000
Major league totals (2 years)		15	31	3	4	0	1	1	4	.129	0	7	0	9	0	0	1.000

INCAVIGLIA, PETE   OF

PERSONAL: Born April 2, 1964, in Pebble Beach, Calif. ... 6-1/230. ... Bats right, throws right. ... Full name: Peter Joseph Incaviglia. ... Son of Tom Incaviglia, minor league infielder (1948-55); and brother of Tony Incaviglia, minor league third baseman (1979-83).
HIGH SCHOOL: Monterey (Pebble Beach, Calif.).
COLLEGE: Oklahoma State.
TRANSACTIONS/CAREER NOTES: Selected by San Francisco Giants organization in 10th round of free-agent draft (June 7, 1982); did not sign. ... Selected by Montreal Expos organization in first round (eighth pick overall) of free-agent draft (June 3, 1985). ... Traded by Expos to Texas Rangers organization for P Bob Sebra and IF Jim Anderson (November 2, 1985). ... On disabled list (June 15-30, 1989). ... Released by Rangers (March 29, 1991). ... Signed by Detroit Tigers (April 7, 1991). ... On disabled list (June 13-July 5 and July 25-August 11, 1991). ... Granted free agency (October 31, 1991). ... Signed by Tucson, Houston Astros organization (January 27, 1992). ... Granted free agency (November 3, 1992). ... Signed by Philadelphia Phillies (December 8, 1992). ... Granted free agency (October 18, 1994). ... Signed by Chiba Lotte Marines of Japan Pacific League (December 28, 1994). ... Signed by Phillies organization (December 13, 1995). ... Traded by Phillies with 3B Todd Zeile to Baltimore Orioles for two players to be named later (August 29, 1996); Phillies acquired P Calvin Maduro and P Garrett Stephenson to complete deal (September 4, 1996). ... Granted free agency (October 31, 1996). ... Re-signed by Orioles (December 19, 1996). ... On Baltimore disabled list (March 31-April 7, 1997). ... Released by Orioles (July 14, 1997). ... Signed by New York Yankees organization (July 25, 1997). ... Released by Yankees (August 15, 1997).
RECORDS: Shares major league record for most doubles in one inning—2 (May 11, 1986, second game, fourth inning).
HONORS: Named designated hitter on THE SPORTING NEWS college All-America team (1985).
STATISTICAL NOTES: Career major league grand slams: 7.

Year Team (League)	Pos.	G	AB	R	H	2B	3B	HR	RBI	Avg.	BB	SO	SB	PO	A	E	Avg.
1986—Texas (A.L.)	OF-DH	153	540	82	135	21	2	30	88	.250	55	*185	3	157	6	•14	.921
1987—Texas (A.L.)	OF-DH	139	509	85	138	26	4	27	80	.271	48	168	9	216	8	•13	.945
1988—Texas (A.L.)	OF-DH	116	418	59	104	19	3	22	54	.249	39	•153	6	172	12	2	.989
1989—Texas (A.L.)	OF-DH	133	453	48	107	27	4	21	81	.236	32	136	5	213	7	6	.973
1990—Texas (A.L.)	OF-DH	153	529	59	123	27	0	24	85	.233	45	146	3	290	12	8	.974
1991—Detroit (A.L.)■	OF-DH	97	337	38	72	12	1	11	38	.214	36	92	1	106	4	3	.973
1992—Houston (N.L.)■	OF	113	349	31	93	22	1	11	44	.266	25	99	2	188	8	6	.970
1993—Philadelphia (N.L.)■..	OF	116	368	60	101	16	3	24	89	.274	21	82	1	164	4	5	.971
1994—Philadelphia (N.L.).....	OF	80	244	28	56	10	1	13	32	.230	16	71	1	90	2	2	.979
1995—Chiba Lot. (Jp. Pac.)■	OF	...	243	25	44	...	...	10	31	.181	...	...	...	...	...	...	...
1996—Philadelphia (N.L.)■..	OF	99	269	33	63	7	2	16	42	.234	30	82	2	91	4	3	.969
—Baltimore (A.L.)■.......	OF-DH	12	33	4	10	2	0	2	8	.303	0	7	0	9	1	0	1.000
1997—Baltimore (A.L.)..........	DH-OF	48	138	18	34	4	0	5	12	.246	11	43	0	20	0	1	.952
—Columbus (Int'l)■......	OF	3	13	1	4	1	0	0	2	.308	0	4	0	7	1	0	1.000
—New York (A.L.).........	DH	5	16	1	4	0	0	0	0	.250	0	3	0	0	0	0	...
American League totals (8 years)		856	2973	394	727	138	14	142	446	.245	266	933	27	1183	50	47	.963
National League totals (4 years)		408	1230	152	313	55	7	64	207	.254	92	334	6	533	18	16	.972
Major league totals (11 years)		1264	4203	546	1040	193	21	206	653	.247	358	1267	33	1716	68	63	.966

DIVISION SERIES RECORD

Year Team (League)	Pos.	G	AB	R	H	2B	3B	HR	RBI	Avg.	BB	SO	SB	PO	A	E	Avg.
1996—Baltimore (A.L.)..........	OF-PR	2	5	1	1	0	0	0	0	.200	0	4	0	0	0	0	...

CHAMPIONSHIP SERIES RECORD

Year Team (League)	Pos.	G	AB	R	H	2B	3B	HR	RBI	Avg.	BB	SO	SB	PO	A	E	Avg.
1993—Philadelphia (N.L.)......	OF	3	12	2	2	0	0	1	1	.167	0	3	0	8	0	0	1.000
1996—Baltimore (A.L.)..........	DH	1	2	1	1	0	0	0	0	.500	0	0	0	00	0		...
Championship series totals (2 years)		4	14	3	3	0	0	1	1	.214	0	3	0	8	0	0	1.000

WORLD SERIES RECORD

Year Team (League)	Pos.	G	AB	R	H	2B	3B	HR	RBI	Avg.	BB	SO	SB	PO	A	E	Avg.
1993—Philadelphia (N.L.)......	OF-PH	4	8	0	1	0	0	0	1	.125	0	4	0	7	0	0	1.000

INGRAM, DARRON — OF/1B — REDS

PERSONAL: Born June 7, 1976, in Lexington, Ky. ... 6-3/210. ... Bats right, throws right. ... Full name: Darron Scott Ingram.
HIGH SCHOOL: Bryan Station (Lexington, Ky.).
TRANSACTIONS/CAREER NOTES: Selected by Cincinnati Reds organization in 12th round of free-agent draft (June 2, 1994).

							BATTING								FIELDING		
Year Team (League)	Pos.	G	AB	R	H	2B	3B	HR	RBI	Avg.	BB	SO	SB	PO	A	E	Avg.
1994— Princeton (Appal.)	OF-2B	46	131	13	26	5	1	2	11	.198	19	50	1	38	1	3	.929
1995— Princeton (Appal.)	OF	60	233	37	64	6	3	14	53	.275	11	78	3	98	2	5	.952
1996— Char., W.Va. (SAL)	OF	15	48	5	9	3	0	1	6	.188	8	19	0	4	0	0	1.000
— Billings (Pioneer)	OF	65	251	49	74	13	0	•17	56	.295	34	988	7	4	0	0	1.000

INGRAM, GAREY — 2B — DODGERS

PERSONAL: Born July 25, 1970, in Columbus, Ga. ... 5-11/185. ... Bats right, throws right. ... Full name: Garey Lamar Ingram.
HIGH SCHOOL: Columbus (Ga.).
JUNIOR COLLEGE: Middle Georgia College.
TRANSACTIONS/CAREER NOTES: Selected by Los Angeles Dodgers organization in 43rd round of free-agent draft (June 1, 1988); did not sign. ... Selected by Dodgers organization in 44th round of free-agent draft (June 5, 1989). ... On Bakersfield disabled list (June 28-July 6, 1991). ... On San Antonio disabled list (April 14-June 16, 1992; April 26-May 3, May 14-June 10 and July 29-August 8, 1993). ... On Albuquerque disabled list (April 14-September 17, 1996). ... On Los Angeles disabled list (September 29, 1996-remainder of season).
STATISTICAL NOTES: Tied for California League lead in being hit by pitch with 14 in 1991. ... Led Texas League in being hit by pitch with 12 in 1992. ... Tied for Texas League lead in errors by second baseman with 27 in 1993.
MISCELLANEOUS: Hit home run in first major league at-bat (May 19, 1994).

							BATTING								FIELDING		
Year Team (League)	Pos.	G	AB	R	H	2B	3B	HR	RBI	Avg.	BB	SO	SB	PO	A	E	Avg.
1990— Great Falls (Pio.)	DH	56	198	43	68	12	*8	2	21	.343	22	37	10				
1991— Bakersfield (Calif.)	OF	118	445	75	132	16	4	9	61	.297	52	70	30	174	5	9	.952
— San Antonio (Tex.)	OF	1	1	0	0	0	0	0	1	1.000	0	1	0	2	0	0	1.000
1992— San Antonio (Tex.)	OF	65	198	34	57	9	5	2	17	.288	28	43	11	112	4	4	.967
1993— San Antonio (Tex.)	2B-OF	84	305	43	82	14	5	6	33	.269	31	50	19	101	184	‡27	.913
1994— San Antonio (Tex.)	2B-OF-SS	99	345	68	89	24	3	8	28	.258	43	61	19	152	205	8	.978
— Los Angeles (N.L.)	2B	26	78	10	22	1	0	3	8	.282	7	22	0	44	68	2	.982
— Albuquerque (PCL)	OF	2	8	2	2	0	0	0	0	.250	0	1	1	0	0	0	...
1995— Los Angeles (N.L.)	3B-2B-OF	44	55	5	11	2	0	0	3	.200	9	8	3	17	26	8	.843
— Albuquerque (PCL)	2B-OF	63	232	28	57	11	4	1	30	.246	21	40	10	115	144	6	.977
1996— Albuquerque (PCL)	2B	6	10	1	1	0	0	0	0	.100	1	2	0	3	1	1	.800
1997— San Antonio (Tex.)	2B-OF-3B	92	348	68	104	28	7	12	52	.299	37	50	16	154	192	13	.964
— Los Angeles (N.L.)	OF	12	9	2	4	0	0	1	1	.444	1	3	1	4	0	0	1.000
Major league totals (3 years)		82	142	17	37	3	0	3	12	.261	17	33	4	65	94	10	.941

IRABU, HIDEKI — P — YANKEES

PERSONAL: Born May 5, 1969, in Hyogo, Japan. ... 6-4/240. ... Throws right, bats right.
TRANSACTIONS/CAREER NOTES: Rights acquired by San Diego Padres from Chiba Lotte Marines of Japan Pacific League (January 16, 1997) . ... Traded by Padres with 2B Homer Bush, OF Gordon Amerson and a player to be named later to New York Yankees for OF Ruben Rivera, P Rafael Medina and cash (April 22, 1997); Padres traded OF Vernon Maxwell to Yankees to complete deal (June 9). ... Signed by Yankees (May 29, 1997).
STATISTICAL NOTES: Tied for A.L. lead with three balks in 1997.

Year Team (League)	W	L	Pct.	ERA	G	GS	CG	ShO	Sv.	IP	H	R	ER	BB	SO
1988— Lotte (Jap. Pac.)	2	5	.286	3.89	14	...	...	...	1	39 1/3	...	...	17	...	21
1989— Lotte (Jap. Pac.)	0	2	.000	3.53	33	...	...	...	9	51	...	...	20	...	50
1990— Lotte (Jap. Pac.)	8	5	.615	3.78	34	...	...	...	0	123 2/3	...	...	52	...	102
1991— Lotte (Jap. Pac.)	3	8	.273	6.88	24	...	...	...	0	100 2/3	...	...	77	...	78
1992— Chiba Lotte (Jp. Pac.)■	0	5	.000	3.86	28	...	...	...	0	77	...	...	33	...	55
1993— Chiba Lotte (Jp. Pac.)	8	7	.533	3.10	32	...	...	...	1	142 1/3	...	...	49	...	160
1994— Chiba Lotte (Jp. Pac.)	*15	10	.600	3.04	27	...	...	...	0	207 1/3	...	...	70	...	239
1995— Chiba Lotte (Jp. Pac.)	11	11	.500	*2.53	28	...	...	...	0	203	...	...	57	...	239
1996— Chiba Lotte (Jp. Pac.)	12	6	.667	*2.40	23	...	3	...	0	157 1/3	...	...	42	...	167
1997— Tampa (Florida State)■	1	0	1.000	0.00	2	2	0	0	0	9	4	0	0	0	12
— Norwich (Eastern)	1	1	.500	4.50	2	2	0	0	0	10	13	5	5	0	9
— Columbus (Int'l)	2	0	1.000	1.67	4	4	1	1	0	27	19	7	5	5	28
— New York (A.L.)	5	4	.556	7.09	13	9	0	0	0	53 1/3	69	47	42	20	56
Major league totals (1 year)	5	4	.556	7.09	13	9	0	0	0	53 1/3	69	47	42	20	56

ISRINGHAUSEN, JASON — P — METS

PERSONAL: Born September 7, 1972, in Brighton, Ill. ... 6-3/196. ... Throws right, bats right. ... Full name: Jason Derek Isringhausen.
HIGH SCHOOL: Piasa (Ill.) Southwestern.
JUNIOR COLLEGE: Lewis & Clark (Ill.).
TRANSACTIONS/CAREER NOTES: Selected by New York Mets organization in 44th round of free-agent draft (June 3, 1991). ... On disabled list (August 13-September 1, 1996). ... On disabled list (March 24-August 27, 1997); included rehabilitation assignment to Norfolk (April 6-11).
HONORS: Named International League Most Valuable Pitcher (1995).

Year Team (League)	W	L	Pct.	ERA	G	GS	CG	ShO	Sv.	IP	H	R	ER	BB	SO
1992— GC Mets (GCL)	2	4	.333	4.34	6	6	0	0	0	29	26	19	14	17	25
— Kingsport (Appalachian)	4	1	.800	3.25	7	6	1	1	0	36	32	22	13	12	24

Year Team (League)	W	L	Pct.	ERA	G	GS	CG	ShO	Sv.	IP	H	R	ER	BB	SO
1993— Pittsfield (NYP)	7	4	.636	3.29	15	15	2	0	0	90 1/3	68	45	33	28	*104
1994— St. Lucie (Fla. St.)	6	4	.600	2.23	14	14	•6	•3	0	101	76	31	25	27	59
— Binghamton (Eastern)	5	4	.556	3.02	14	14	2	0	0	92 1/3	78	35	31	23	69
1995— Binghamton (Eastern)	2	1	.667	2.85	6	6	1	0	0	41	26	15	13	12	59
— Norfolk (Int'l)	9	1	*.900	1.55	12	12	3	*3	0	87	64	17	15	24	75
— New York (N.L.)	9	2	.818	2.81	14	14	1	0	0	93	88	29	29	31	55
1996— New York (N.L.)	6	14	.300	4.77	27	27	2	1	0	171 2/3	190	103	91	73	114
1997— Norfolk (Int'l)	0	2	.000	4.05	3	3	0	0	0	20	20	10	9	8	17
— St. Lucie (Fla. St.)	1	0	1.000	0.00	2	2	0	0	0	12	8	1	0	5	15
— GC Mets (GCL)	1	0	1.000	1.93	1	0	0	0	0	4 2/3	2	1	1	1	7
— New York (N.L.)	2	2	.500	7.58	6	6	0	0	0	29 2/3	40	27	25	22	25
Major league totals (3 years)	17	18	.486	4.43	47	47	3	1	0	294 1/3	318	159	145	126	194

JACKSON, DAMIAN · SS · REDS

PERSONAL: Born August 16, 1973, in Los Angeles. ... 5-10/160. ... Bats right, throws right. ... Full name: Damian Jacques Jackson.
HIGH SCHOOL: Ygnacio (Concord, Calif.).
JUNIOR COLLEGE: Laney (Calif.).
TRANSACTIONS/CAREER NOTES: Selected by Cleveland Indians organization in 44th round of free-agent draft (June 3, 1991). ... Traded by Indians with P Danny Graves, P Jim Crowell and P Scott Winchester to Cincinnati Reds for P John Smiley and IF Jeff Branson (July 31, 1997).
STATISTICAL NOTES: Led Appalachian League shortstops with 342 total chances and 45 double plays in 1992. ... Led Eastern League shortstops with 241 putouts, 446 assists, 54 errors, 741 total chances and 85 double plays in 1994. ... Led Eastern League in caught stealing with 22 in 1995. ... Tied for Eastern League lead in double plays by shortstop with 80 in 1995. ... Led American Association shortstops with 635 total chances and 84 double plays in 1996.

Year Team (League)							BATTING								FIELDING		
Year Team (League)	Pos.	G	AB	R	H	2B	3B	HR	RBI	Avg.	BB	SO	SB	PO	A	E	Avg.
1992— Burlington (Appal.)	SS	62	226	32	56	12	1	0	23	.248	32	31	29	*102	*217	23	.933
1993— Columbus (S. Atl.)	SS	108	350	70	94	19	3	6	45	.269	41	61	26	191	324	52	.908
1994— Cant./Akr. (Eastern)	SS-OF	138	531	85	143	29	5	5	60	.269	60	121	37	†241	†446	†54	.927
1995— Cant./Akr. (Eastern)	SS	131	484	67	120	20	2	3	34	.248	65	103	40	*220	337	*36	.939
1996— Buffalo (A.A.)	SS	133	452	77	116	15	1	12	49	.257	48	78	24	*203	*403	29	.954
— Cleveland (A.L.)	SS	5	10	2	3	2	0	0	1	.300	1	4	0	3	13	0	1.000
1997— Buffalo (A.A.)	SS-2B-OF	73	266	51	78	10	0	4	13	.293	37	45	20	128	246	23	.942
— Cleveland (A.L.)	SS-2B	8	9	2	1	0	0	0	0	.111	0	1	1	7	7	0	1.000
— Indianapolis (A.A.)■	2B-SS	19	71	12	19	6	1	0	7	.268	10	17	4	36	55	5	.948
— Cincinnati (N.L.)	SS-2B	12	27	6	6	2	1	1	2	.222	4	7	1	12	21	1	.971
American League totals (2 years)		13	19	4	4	2	0	0	1	.211	1	5	1	10	20	0	1.000
National League totals (1 year)		12	27	6	6	2	1	1	2	.222	4	7	1	12	21	1	.971
Major league totals (2 years)		25	46	10	10	4	1	1	3	.217	5	12	2	22	41	1	.984

JACKSON, DANNY · P

PERSONAL: Born January 5, 1962, in San Antonio. ... 6-0/220. ... Throws left, bats right. ... Full name: Danny Lynn Jackson.
HIGH SCHOOL: Central (Aurora, Colo.).
JUNIOR COLLEGE: Trinidad State Junior College (Colo.).
COLLEGE: Oklahoma.
TRANSACTIONS/CAREER NOTES: Selected by Oakland Athletics organization in 24th round of free-agent draft (June 3, 1980); did not sign. ... Selected by Kansas City Royals organization in secondary phase of free-agent draft (January 17, 1982). ... On Jacksonville disabled list (September 8, 1982-remainder of season). ... On disabled list (April 4-21, 1986). ... Traded by Royals with SS Angel Salazar to Cincinnati Reds for P Ted Power and SS Kurt Stillwell (November 6, 1987). ... On disabled list (June 18-July 6 and July 25-September 1, 1989). ... On Cincinnati disabled list (April 30-May 17, 1990); included rehabilitation assignment to Nashville (May 13-17). ... On Cincinnati disabled list (July 18-August 8, 1990); included rehabilitation assignment to Charleston, W.Va. (August 5-8). ... On Cincinnati disabled list (August 14-30, 1990); included rehabilitation assignment to Nashville (August 30). ... Granted free agency (November 5, 1990). ... Signed by Chicago Cubs (November 21, 1990). ... On Chicago disabled list (April 20-June 9, 1991). ... On Chicago disabled list (June 20-August 3, 1991); included rehabilitation assignment to Iowa (July 29-30). ... Traded by Cubs to Pittsburgh Pirates for 3B Steve Buechele (July 11, 1992). ... Selected by Florida Marlins in third round (53rd pick overall) of expansion draft (November 17, 1992). ... Traded by Marlins to Philadelphia Phillies for P Joel Adamson and P Matt Whisenant (November 17, 1992). ... Granted free agency (October 17, 1994). ... Signed by St. Louis Cardinals (December 12, 1994). ... On St. Louis disabled list (June 8-26 and August 12, 1995-remainder of season); included rehabilitation assignment to Louisville (June 20-26). ... On St. Louis disabled list (March 19-August 3, 1996); included rehabilitation assignments to St. Petersburg (July 15-19) and Louisville (July 19-August 3). ... On St. Louis disabled list (March 23-May 20, 1997); included rehabilitation assignment to Louisville (April 28-May 16). ... Traded by Cardinals with P Rich Batchelor and OF Mark Sweeney to San Diego Padres for P Fernando Valenzuela, 3B Scott Livingstone and OF Phil Plantier (June 13, 1997). ... Announced retirement (August 10, 1997).
HONORS: Named lefthanded pitcher on THE SPORTING NEWS N.L. All-Star team (1988 and 1994).
MISCELLANEOUS: Appeared in one game as pinch-runner (1989). ... Appeared in one game as pinch-runner (1994).

Year Team (League)	W	L	Pct.	ERA	G	GS	CG	ShO	Sv.	IP	H	R	ER	BB	SO
1982— Charleston, S.C. (S. Atl.)	10	1	.909	2.62	13	13	3	0	0	96 1/3	80	37	28	39	62
— Jacksonville (Southern)	7	2	.778	2.39	14	14	3	1	0	98	78	30	26	42	74
1983— Omaha (Am. Assoc.)	7	8	.467	3.97	23	22	5	•2	0	136	126	74	60	73	93
— Kansas City (A.L.)	1	1	.500	5.21	4	3	0	0	0	19	26	12	11	6	9
1984— Kansas City (A.L.)	2	6	.250	4.26	15	11	1	0	0	76	84	41	36	35	40
— Omaha (Am. Assoc.)	5	8	.385	3.67	16	16	•10	•3	0	110 1/3	91	50	45	45	82
1985— Kansas City (A.L.)	14	12	.538	3.42	32	32	4	3	0	208	209	94	79	76	114
1986— Kansas City (A.L.)	11	12	.478	3.20	32	27	4	1	1	185 2/3	177	83	66	79	115
1987— Kansas City (A.L.)	9	18	.333	4.02	36	34	11	2	0	224	219	115	100	109	152
1988— Cincinnati (N.L.)■	•23	8	.742	2.73	35	35	•15	6	0	260 2/3	206	86	79	71	161
1989— Cincinnati (N.L.)	6	11	.353	5.60	20	20	1	0	0	115 2/3	122	78	72	57	70
1990— Cincinnati (N.L.)	6	6	.500	3.61	22	21	0	0	0	117 1/3	119	54	47	40	76
— Nashville (A.A.)	1	0	1.000	0.00	2	2	0	0	0	11	9	0	0	4	3
— Char., W.Va. (S. Atl.)	0	0	. . .	6.00	1	1	0	0	0	3	2	2	2	1	2

Year Team (League)	W	L	Pct.	ERA	G	GS	CG	ShO	Sv.	IP	H	R	ER	BB	SO
1991—Chicago (N.L.)■	1	5	.167	6.75	17	14	0	0	0	70 2/3	89	59	53	48	31
—Iowa (Am. Assoc.)	0	0	...	1.80	1	1	0	0	0	5	2	1	1	2	4
1992—Chicago (N.L.)	4	9	.308	4.22	19	19	0	0	0	113	117	59	53	48	51
—Pittsburgh (N.L.)■	4	4	.500	3.36	15	15	0	0	0	88 1/3	94	40	33	29	46
1993—Philadelphia (N.L.)■	12	11	.522	3.77	32	32	2	1	0	210 1/3	214	105	88	80	120
1994—Philadelphia (N.L.)	14	6	.700	3.26	25	25	4	1	0	179 1/3	183	71	65	46	129
1995—St. Louis (N.L.)■	2	12	.143	5.90	19	19	2	1	0	100 2/3	120	82	66	48	52
—Louisville (A.A.)■	1	0	1.000	1.29	1	1	1	0	0	7	8	1	1	2	2
1996—St. Petersburg (FSL)	0	0	...	0.00	1	1	0	0	0	4	2	0	0	0	3
—Louisville (A.A.)	0	0	...	3.46	8	1	0	0	0	13	14	6	5	5	10
—St. Louis (N.L.)	1	1	.500	4.46	13	4	0	0	0	36 1/3	33	18	18	16	27
1997—Louisville (A.A.)	1	0	1.000	1.80	4	4	0	0	0	25	20	6	5	8	14
—St. Louis (N.L.)	1	2	.333	7.71	4	4	0	0	0	18 2/3	26	17	16	8	13
—San Diego (N.L.)■	1	7	.125	7.53	13	9	0	0	0	49	72	47	41	20	19
A.L. totals (5 years)	37	49	.430	3.69	119	107	20	6	1	712 2/3	715	345	292	305	430
N.L. totals (10 years)	75	82	.478	4.18	234	217	24	9	0	1360	1395	716	631	511	795
Major league totals (15 years)	112	131	.461	4.01	353	324	44	15	1	2072 2/3	2110	1061	923	816	1225

DIVISION SERIES RECORD

Year Team (League)	W	L	Pct.	ERA	G	GS	CG	ShO	Sv.	IP	H	R	ER	BB	SO
1996— St. Louis (N.L.)						Did not play.									

CHAMPIONSHIP SERIES RECORD

Year Team (League)	W	L	Pct.	ERA	G	GS	CG	ShO	Sv.	IP	H	R	ER	BB	SO
1985— Kansas City (A.L.)	1	0	1.000	0.00	2	1	1	1	0	10	10	0	0	1	7
1990— Cincinnati (N.L.)	1	0	1.000	2.38	2	2	0	0	0	11 1/3	8	3	3	7	8
1992— Pittsburgh (N.L.)	0	1	.000	21.60	1	1	0	0	0	1 2/3	4	4	4	2	0
1993— Philadelphia (N.L.)	1	0	1.000	1.17	1	1	0	0	0	7 2/3	9	1	1	2	6
1996— St. Louis (N.L.)	0	0	...	9.00	1	0	0	0	0	3	7	3	3	3	3
Champ. series totals (5 years)	3	1	.750	2.94	7	5	1	1	0	33 2/3	38	11	11	15	24

WORLD SERIES RECORD

RECORDS: Shares record for most consecutive strikeouts (by batter) in one series—5 (October 19 [2] and 24 [3], 1985).

NOTES: Member of World Series championship teams (1985 and 1990).

Year Team (League)	W	L	Pct.	ERA	G	GS	CG	ShO	Sv.	IP	H	R	ER	BB	SO
1985— Kansas City (A.L.)	1	1	.500	1.69	2	2	1	0	0	16	9	3	3	5	12
1990— Cincinnati (N.L.)	0	0	...	10.13	1	1	0	0	0	2 2/3	6	4	3	2	0
1993— Philadelphia (N.L.)	0	1	.000	7.20	1	1	0	0	0	5	6	4	4	1	1
World Series totals (3 years)	1	2	.333	3.80	4	4	1	0	0	23 2/3	21	11	10	8	13

ALL-STAR GAME RECORD

Year League	W	L	Pct.	ERA	GS	CG	ShO	Sv.	IP	H	R	ER	BB	SO
1988— National						Did not play.								
1994— National	0	0	...	...	0	0	0	0	3	1	1	0	0	0
All-Star totals (1 years)	0	0	...	...	0	0	0	0	3	1	1	0	0	0

J

JACKSON, DARRIN   OF   BREWERS

PERSONAL: Born August 22, 1963, in Los Angeles. ... 6-0/185. ... Bats right, throws right. ... Full name: Darrin Jay Jackson.

HIGH SCHOOL: Culver City (Calif.).

TRANSACTIONS/CAREER NOTES: Selected by Chicago Cubs organization in second round of free-agent draft (June 8, 1981). ... Traded by Cubs with P Calvin Schiraldi and a player to be named later to San Diego Padres for OF Marvell Wynne and IF Luis Salazar (August 30, 1989); Padres acquired 1B Phil Stephenson to complete deal (September 5, 1989). ... Traded by Padres to Toronto Blue Jays for OF Derek Bell and OF Stoney Briggs (March 30, 1993). ... Traded by Blue Jays to New York Mets for SS Tony Fernandez (June 11, 1993). ... On New York disabled list (July 19-September 1, 1993). ... Granted free agency (December 20, 1993). ... Signed by Chicago White Sox organization (December 28, 1993). ... Granted free agency (October 15, 1994). ... Played with Seibu of Japan Pacific League (1995 and 1996). ... Signed by San Francisco Giants organization (December 20, 1996). ... Released by Giants (March 31, 1997). ... Signed by Minnesota Twins organization (April 24, 1997). ... Traded by Twins to Milwaukee Brewers for a player to be named later (August 30, 1997); Twins acquired P Mick Fieldbinder to complete deal (September 4, 1997). ... Granted free agency (October 27, 1997). ... Re-signed by Brewers (December 6, 1997).

STATISTICAL NOTES: Led Gulf Coast League outfielders with 127 total chances in 1981. ... Tied for Texas League lead in double plays by outfielder with six in 1984. ... Tied for American Association lead in double plays by outfielder with six in 1987. ... Led N.L. in grounding into double plays with 21 in 1992. ... Led N.L. outfielders with 455 total chances and nine double plays in 1992. ... Career major league grand slams: 3.

Year Team (League)	Pos.	G	AB	R	H	2B	3B	HR	RBI	Avg.	BB	SO	SB	PO	A	E	Avg.
1981—GC Cubs (GCL)	OF	62	210	29	39	5	0	4	15	.186	28	53	18	*121	5	1	.992
1982—Quad Cities (Mid.)	OF	132	529	86	146	23	5	5	48	.276	47	106	58	266	9	8	.972
1983—Salinas (Calif.)	OF	129	509	70	126	18	5	6	54	.248	38	111	36	237	15	13	.951
1984—Midland (Texas)	OF	132	496	63	134	18	2	15	54	.270	49	102	13	286	*19	8	.974
1985—Iowa (Am. Assoc.)	OF	10	40	0	7	2	1	0	1	.175	3	10	1	19	0	0	1.000
—Pittsfield (Eastern)	OF	91	325	38	82	10	1	3	30	.252	34	64	8	221	5	0	1.000
—Chicago (N.L.)	OF	5	11	0	1	0	0	0	0	.091	0	3	0	7	0	0	1.000
1986—Pittsfield (Eastern)	OF	137	•520	82	139	28	2	15	64	.267	43	110	42	320	*16	7	.980
1987—Iowa (Am. Assoc.)	OF	132	474	81	130	32	5	23	81	.274	26	110	13	290	15	6	.981
—Chicago (N.L.)	OF	7	5	2	4	1	0	0	0	.800	0	0	0	1	0	0	1.000
1988—Chicago (N.L.)	OF	100	188	29	50	11	3	6	20	.266	5	28	4	116	1	2	.983
1989—Chicago (N.L.)	OF	45	83	7	19	4	0	1	8	.229	6	17	1	61	3	2	.970
—Iowa (Am. Assoc.)	OF	30	120	18	31	4	1	7	17	.258	7	22	4	66	12	0	1.000
—San Diego (N.L.)■	OF	25	87	10	18	3	0	3	12	.207	7	17	0	60	2	3	.954
1990—San Diego (N.L.)	OF	58	113	10	29	3	0	3	9	.257	5	24	3	63	1	1	.985
—Las Vegas (PCL)	OF	29	98	14	27	4	0	5	15	.276	9	21	3	61	4	0	1.000
1991—San Diego (N.L.)	OF-P	122	359	51	94	12	1	21	49	.262	27	66	5	243	2	2	.992

Year Team (League)	Pos.	G	AB	R	H	2B	3B	HR	RBI	Avg.	BB	SO	SB	PO	A	E	Avg.
1992—San Diego (N.L.)	OF	155	587	72	146	23	5	17	70	.249	26	106	14	436	*18	2	.996
1993—Toronto (A.L.)■	OF	46	176	15	38	8	0	5	19	.216	8	53	0	86	2	1	.989
—New York (N.L.)■	OF	31	87	4	17	1	0	1	7	.195	2	22	0	51	4	0	1.000
1994—Chicago (A.L.)■	OF	104	369	43	115	17	3	10	51	.312	27	56	7	223	2	1	.996
1995—Seibu (Jp. Pac.)■	...	128	506	66	146	28		20	68	.289	34	104	9				...
1996—Seibu (Jp. Pac.)..........	...	126	489	42	130	21	3	19	64	.266	30	70	10				...
1997—Salt Lake (PCL)■	OF	19	80	14	24	3	3	1	12	.300	5	17	3	26	2	0	1.000
—Minnesota (A.L.)■	OF	49	130	19	33	2	1	3	21	.254	4	21	2	93	4	1	.990
—Milwaukee (A.L.)■	OF	26	81	7	22	7	0	2	15	.272	2	10	2	55	2	0	1.000
American League totals (3 years)		225	756	84	208	34	4	20	106	.275	41	140	11	457	10	3	.994
National League totals (8 years)		548	1520	185	378	58	9	52	175	.249	78	283	27	1038	31	12	.989
Major league totals (10 years)		773	2276	269	586	92	13	72	281	.257	119	423	38	1495	41	15	.990

RECORD AS PITCHER

Year Team (League)	W	L	Pct.	ERA	G	GS	CG	ShO	Sv.	IP	H	R	ER	BB	SO
1991—San Diego (N.L.)	0	0	...	9.00	1	0	0	0	0	2	3	2	2	2	0

JACKSON, MIKE — P — INDIANS

PERSONAL: Born December 22, 1964, in Houston. ... 6-2/225. ... Throws right, bats right. ... Full name: Michael Ray Jackson.
HIGH SCHOOL: Forest Brook (Houston).
JUNIOR COLLEGE: Hill Junior College (Texas).
TRANSACTIONS/CAREER NOTES: Selected by Philadelphia Phillies organization in 29th round of free-agent draft (June 6, 1983); did not sign. ... Selected by Phillies organization in secondary phase of free-agent draft (January 17, 1984). ... On Philadelphia disabled list (August 6-21, 1987). ... Traded by Phillies organization with OF Glenn Wilson and OF Dave Brundage to Seattle Mariners for OF Phil Bradley and P Tim Fortugno (December 9, 1987). ... Traded by Mariners with P Bill Swift and P Dave Burba to San Francisco Giants for OF Kevin Mitchell and P Mike Remlinger (December 11, 1991). ... On disabled list (July 24-August 9, 1993; June 17-July 2 and July 7, 1994-remainder of season). ... Granted free agency (October 17, 1994). ... Signed by Cincinnati Reds (April 8, 1995). ... On Cincinnati disabled list (April 20-June 5, 1995); included rehabilitation assignments to Chattanooga (May 21-30) and Indianapolis (May 30-June 5). ... Granted free agency (November 3, 1995). ... Signed by Mariners (February 2, 1996). ... Granted free agency (October 30, 1996). ... Signed by Cleveland Indians (December 12, 1996).
STATISTICAL NOTES: Led Carolina League with seven balks in 1985. ... Tied for N.L. lead with eight balks in 1987.

Year Team (League)	W	L	Pct.	ERA	G	GS	CG	ShO	Sv.	IP	H	R	ER	BB	SO
1984—Spartanburg (SAL)	7	2	.778	2.68	14	0	0	0	0	80 2/3	53	35	24	50	77
1985—Peninsula (Caro.)	7	9	.438	4.60	31	18	0	0	1	125 1/3	127	71	64	53	96
1986—Reading (Eastern)	2	3	.400	1.66	30	0	0	0	6	43 1/3	25	9	8	22	42
—Portland (PCL)	3	1	.750	3.18	17	0	0	0	3	22 2/3	18	8	8	13	23
—Philadelphia (N.L.)	0	0	...	3.38	9	0	0	0	0	13 1/3	12	5	5	4	3
1987—Philadelphia (N.L.)	3	10	.231	4.20	55	7	0	0	1	109 1/3	88	55	51	56	93
—Maine (International)	1	0	1.000	0.82	2	2	0	0	0	11	9	2	1	5	13
1988—Seattle (A.L.)■	6	5	.545	2.63	62	0	0	0	4	99 1/3	74	37	29	43	76
1989—Seattle (A.L.)	4	6	.400	3.17	65	0	0	0	7	99 1/3	81	43	35	54	94
1990—Seattle (A.L.)	5	7	.417	4.54	63	0	0	0	3	77 1/3	64	42	39	44	69
1991—Seattle (A.L.)	7	7	.500	3.25	72	0	0	0	14	88 2/3	64	35	32	34	74
1992—San Francisco (N.L.)■	6	6	.500	3.73	67	0	0	0	2	82	76	35	34	33	80
1993—San Francisco (N.L.)	6	6	.500	3.03	*81	0	0	0	1	77 1/3	58	28	26	24	70
1994—San Francisco (N.L.)	3	2	.600	1.49	36	0	0	0	4	42 1/3	23	8	7	11	51
1995—Chattanooga (Southern)■..	0	0	...	0.00	3	2	0	0	0	3	2	0	0	0	2
—Indianapolis (A.A.)	0	0	...	0.00	2	1	0	0	0	2	0	0	0	0	1
—Cincinnati (N.L.)	6	1	.857	2.39	40	0	0	0	2	49	38	13	13	19	41
1996—Seattle (A.L.)■	1	1	.500	3.63	73	0	0	0	6	72	61	32	29	24	70
1997—Cleveland (A.L.)■	2	5	.286	3.24	71	0	0	0	15	75	59	33	27	29	74
A.L. totals (6 years)	25	31	.446	3.36	406	0	0	0	49	511 2/3	403	222	191	228	457
N.L. totals (6 years)	24	25	.490	3.28	288	7	0	0	10	373 1/3	295	144	136	147	338
Major league totals (12 years)....	49	56	.467	3.33	694	7	0	0	59	885	698	366	327	375	795

DIVISION SERIES RECORD

Year Team (League)	W	L	Pct.	ERA	G	GS	CG	ShO	Sv.	IP	H	R	ER	BB	SO
1995—Cincinnati (N.L.)	0	0	...	0.00	3	0	0	0	0	3 2/3	4	0	0	0	1
1997—Cleveland (A.L.)	1	0	1.000	0.00	4	0	0	0	0	4 1/3	3	0	0	1	5
Div. series totals (2 years)	1	0	1.000	0.00	7	0	0	0	0	8	7	0	0	1	6

CHAMPIONSHIP SERIES RECORD

Year Team (League)	W	L	Pct.	ERA	G	GS	CG	ShO	Sv.	IP	H	R	ER	BB	SO
1995—Cincinnati (N.L.)	0	1	.000	23.14	3	0	0	0	0	2 1/3	5	6	6	4	1
1997—Cleveland (A.L.)	0	0	...	0.00	5	0	0	0	0	4 1/3	1	0	0	1	7
Champ. series totals (2 years)	0	1	.000	8.10	8	0	0	0	0	6 2/3	6	6	6	5	8

WORLD SERIES RECORD

Year Team (League)	W	L	Pct.	ERA	G	GS	CG	ShO	Sv.	IP	H	R	ER	BB	SO
1997—Cleveland (A.L.)	0	0	...	1.93	4	0	0	0	0	4 2/3	5	1	1	3	4

JACKSON, RYAN — OF — MARLINS

PERSONAL: Born November 11, 1971, in Sarasota, Fla. ... 6-3/185. ... Bats left, throws left.
COLLEGE: Duke.
TRANSACTIONS/CAREER NOTES: Selected by Florida Marlins organization in seventh round of free-agent draft (June 2, 1994). ... On Kane County disabled list (April 5-August 1, 1996). ... On Portland disabled list (August 1-26, 1996).

Year Team (League)	Pos.	G	AB	R	H	2B	3B	HR	RBI	Avg.	BB	SO	SB	PO	A	E	Avg.
						BATTING									FIELDING		
1994— Elmira (N.Y.-Penn)......	OF-1B	72	276	46	80	18	1	6	41	.290	22	40	4	176	15	7	.965
1995— Kane County (Midw.)..	OF-1B	132	471	78	138	*39	6	10	82	.293	67	74	13	571	32	7	.989
1996— Brevard Co. (Fla. St.)..	1B	6	26	4	8	2	0	1	4	.308	1	7	1	28	2	2	.938
— GC Marlins (GCL).......	1B-OF	8	26	5	9	0	0	0	7	.346	1	3	2	35	3	0	1.000
1997— Portland (Eastern)......	OF-1B	134	491	87	153	28	4	26	98	.312	51	85	2	227	9	5	.979

JACOBS, DWAYNE — P — BRAVES

PERSONAL: Born July 17, 1976, in Jacksonville. ... 6-6/185. ... Throws right, bats right. ... Full name: Dwayne Allen Jacobs.
HIGH SCHOOL: First Coast (Jacksonville).
TRANSACTIONS/CAREER NOTES: Selected by Atlanta Braves organization in 24th round of free-agent draft (June 2, 1994). ... On restricted list (June 12, 1995-remainder of season). ... On disabled list (April 22-May 11, 1996).

Year Team (League)	W	L	Pct.	ERA	G	GS	CG	ShO	Sv.	IP	H	R	ER	BB	SO
1994— GC Braves (GCL)................	1	2	.333	8.16	12	1	0	0	0	28²/₃	35	29	26	19	14
1995—								Did not play.							
1996— Macon (S. Atl.)..............	2	7	.222	6.80	26	15	0	0	0	82	85	82	62	76	76
1997— Durham (Carolina).............	4	8	.333	5.01	25	24	1	1	0	116²/₃	112	78	65	85	115

JACOBS, RUSSELL — P — DIAMONDBACKS

PERSONAL: Born January 2, 1975, in Winter Haven, Fla. ... 6-6/205. ... Throws right, bats right.
HIGH SCHOOL: Winter Haven (Fla.).
TRANSACTIONS/CAREER NOTES: Selected by Seattle Mariners organization in 23rd round of free-agent draft (June 3, 1993). ... On disabled list (May 30-July 6, 1996). ... Selected by Arizona Diamondbacks from Mariners organization in Rule 5 major league draft (December 15, 1997).

Year Team (League)	W	L	Pct.	ERA	G	GS	CG	ShO	Sv.	IP	H	R	ER	BB	SO
1994— Ariz. Mariners (Ariz.).........	0	0	...	2.70	8	2	0	0	0	13⅓	9	4	4	5	12
1995— Ariz. Mariners (Ariz.).........	6	2	.750	2.88	12	11	0	0	0	56⅓	47	29	18	31	54
1996— Wisconsin (Midwest).........	4	4	.500	5.27	24	10	0	0	2	68⅓	67	48	40	53	63
1997— Wisconsin (Midwest).........	4	2	.667	4.44	21	9	0	0	1	77	62	41	38	58	76

JACOME, JASON — P — INDIANS

PERSONAL: Born November 24, 1970, in Tulsa, Okla. ... 6-1/185. ... Throws left, bats left. ... Full name: Jason James Jacome.
HIGH SCHOOL: Rincon (Tucson, Ariz.).
JUNIOR COLLEGE: Pima Community College (Ariz.).
TRANSACTIONS/CAREER NOTES: Selected by New York Mets organization in 12th round of free-agent draft (June 3, 1991). ... On Norfolk disabled list (June 5-16 and June 17-July 21, 1995). ... Traded by Mets with P Allen McDill to Kansas City Royals for P Derek Wallace and a player to be named later (July 21, 1995); Mets acquired P John Carter to complete deal (November 16, 1995). ... Claimed on waivers by Cleveland Indians (May 8, 1997).

Year Team (League)	W	L	Pct.	ERA	G	GS	CG	ShO	Sv.	IP	H	R	ER	BB	SO
1991— Kingsport (Appalachian).....	5	4	.556	1.63	12	7	3	•1	2	55¹/₃	35	18	10	13	48
1992— Columbia (S. Atl.).............	4	1	.800	1.03	8	8	1	0	0	52²/₃	40	7	6	15	49
— St. Lucie (Fla. St.)	6	7	.462	2.83	17	17	5	1	0	114¹/₃	98	45	36	30	66
1993— St. Lucie (Fla. St.)	6	3	.667	3.08	14	14	2	2	0	99¹/₃	106	37	34	23	66
— Binghamton (Eastern)	8	4	.667	3.21	14	14	0	0	0	87	85	36	31	38	56
1994— Norfolk (Int'l)	8	6	.571	2.84	19	19	4	1	0	126²/₃	138	57	40	42	80
— New York (N.L.)..................	4	3	.571	2.67	8	8	1	1	0	54	54	17	16	17	30
1995— New York (N.L.).................	0	4	.000	10.29	5	5	0	0	0	21	33	24	24	15	11
— Norfolk (Int'l)	2	4	.333	3.92	8	8	0	0	0	43²/₃	40	21	19	13	31
— Kansas City (A.L.)■.........	4	6	.400	5.36	15	14	1	0	0	84	101	52	50	21	39
1996— Kansas City (A.L.).............	0	4	.000	4.72	49	2	0	0	0	47²/₃	67	27	25	22	32
1997— Kansas City (A.L.).............	0	0	...	9.45	7	0	0	0	0	6²/₃	13	7	7	5	3
— Cleveland (A.L.)■..............	2	0	1.000	5.27	21	4	0	0	0	42²/₃	45	26	25	15	24
— Buffalo (A.A.).....................	3	1	.750	3.16	7	7	1	0	0	37	41	14	13	10	23
A.L. totals (3 years)	6	10	.375	5.32	92	20	1	0	1	181	226	112	107	63	98
N.L. totals (2 years)	4	7	.364	4.80	13	13	1	1	0	75	87	41	40	32	41
Major league totals (4 years)......	10	17	.370	5.17	105	33	2	1	1	256	313	153	147	95	139

JAHA, JOHN — 1B — BREWERS

PERSONAL: Born May 27, 1966, in Portland, Ore. ... 6-1/222. ... Bats right, throws right. ... Full name: John Emile Jaha. ... Name pronounced JAH-ha.
HIGH SCHOOL: David Douglas (Portland, Ore.).
TRANSACTIONS/CAREER NOTES: Selected by Milwaukee Brewers organization in 14th round of free-agent draft (June 4, 1984). ... On disabled list (April 6-August 1, 1990 and May 21-June 6, 1995). ... On Milwaukee disabled list (June 24-July 27, 1995); included rehabilitation assignments to Beloit (July 16-20) and New Orleans (July 20-27). ... On disabled list (June 3, 1997-remainder of season).
HONORS: Named Texas League Most Valuable Player (1991).
STATISTICAL NOTES: Led Northwest League with 144 total bases and tied for lead with four intentional bases on balls received in 1986. ... Led Texas League with 301 total bases, .619 slugging percentage and .438 on-base percentage in 1991. ... Led Texas League first basemen with 87 assists in 1991. ... Career major league grand slams: 4.

Year Team (League)	Pos.	G	AB	R	H	2B	3B	HR	RBI	Avg.	BB	SO	SB	PO	A	E	Avg.
						BATTING									FIELDING		
1985— Helena (Pioneer)	3B	24	68	13	18	3	0	2	14	.265	14	23	4	9	32	1	.976
1986— Tri-Cities (NWL)	1B-3B	•73	258	65	82	13	2	*15	67	.318	*70	75	9	352	101	18	.962

J

Year Team (League)	Pos.	G	AB	R	H	2B	3B	HR	RBI	Avg.	BB	SO	SB	PO	A	E	Avg.
														BATTING			FIELDING
1987— Beloit (Midwest)	3B-1B-SS	122	376	68	101	22	0	7	47	.269	102	86	10	493	113	18	.971
1988— Stockton (California)	1B	99	302	58	77	14	6	8	54	.255	69	85	10	793	60	5	*.994
1989— Stockton (California)	1B-3B	140	479	83	140	26	5	25	91	.292	*112	115	8	1081	62	8	.993
1990— Stockton (California)	DH	26	84	12	22	5	0	4	19	.262	18	25	0	...	...	...	...
1991— El Paso (Texas)	1B-3B	130	486	*121	167	38	3	*30	*134	.344	78	101	12	883	†87	10	.990
1992— Denver (A.A.)	1B	79	274	61	88	18	2	18	69	.321	50	60	6	654	50	7	.990
— Milwaukee (A.L.)	1B-DH-OF	47	133	17	30	3	1	2	10	.226	12	30	10	286	22	0	1.000
1993— Milwaukee (A.L.)	1B-3B-2B	153	515	78	136	21	0	19	70	.264	51	109	13	1187	128	10	.992
1994— Milwaukee (A.L.)	1B-DH	84	291	45	70	14	0	12	39	.241	32	75	3	660	47	8	.989
— New Orleans (A.A.)	1B	18	62	8	25	7	1	2	16	.403	12	8	2	122	14	1	.993
1995— Milwaukee (A.L.)	1B-DH	88	316	59	99	20	2	20	65	.313	36	66	2	649	60	2	.997
— Beloit (Midwest)	DH	1	4	1	0	0	0	0	0	.000	0	1	0	0	0	0	...
— New Orleans (A.A.)	1B	3	10	2	4	1	0	1	3	.400	2	1	0	9	2	0	1.000
1996— Milwaukee (A.L.)	1B-DH	148	543	108	163	28	1	34	118	.300	85	118	3	676	58	6	.992
1997— Milwaukee (A.L.)	1B-DH	46	162	25	40	7	0	11	26	.247	25	40	1	220	14	2	.992
Major league totals (6 years)		566	1960	332	538	93	4	98	328	.274	241	438	32	3678	329	28	.993

JAMES, MIKE — P — ANGELS

PERSONAL: Born August 15, 1967, in Fort Walton Beach, Fla. ... 6-4/216. ... Throws right, bats right. ... Full name: Michael Elmo James.
HIGH SCHOOL: Fort Walton Beach (Fla.).
JUNIOR COLLEGE: Lurleen B. Wallace State Junior College (Ala.).
TRANSACTIONS/CAREER NOTES: Selected by Los Angeles Dodgers organization in 43rd round of free-agent draft (June 2, 1987). ... On Albuquerque disabled list (July 12-August 26, 1992). ... On Vero Beach disabled list (July 2-9, 1993). ... Traded by Dodgers to California Angels for OF Reggie Williams (October 26, 1993). ... On California disabled list (May 11-June 1, 1995); included rehabilitation assignment to Lake Elsinore (May 25-June 1). ... Angels franchise renamed Anaheim Angels for 1997 season. ... On disabled list (July 3-27, 1997).

Year Team (League)	W	L	Pct.	ERA	G	GS	CG	ShO	Sv.	IP	H	R	ER	BB	SO
1988— Great Falls (Pio.)	7	1	*.875	3.76	14	12	0	0	0	67	61	36	28	41	59
1989— Bakersfield (California)	11	8	.579	3.78	27	27	1	1	0	159 2/3	144	82	67	78	127
1990— San Antonio (Tex.)	11	4	.733	3.32	26	26	3	0	0	157	144	73	58	78	97
1991— Albuquerque (PCL)	1	3	.250	6.60	13	8	0	0	0	45	51	36	33	30	39
— San Antonio (Tex.)	9	5	.643	4.53	15	15	2	1	0	89 1/3	88	54	45	51	74
1992— Albuquerque (PCL)	2	1	.667	5.59	18	6	0	0	1	46 2/3	55	35	29	22	33
— San Antonio (Tex.)	2	1	.667	2.67	8	8	0	0	0	54	39	16	16	20	52
1993— Albuquerque (PCL)	1	0	1.000	7.47	16	0	0	0	2	31 1/3	38	28	26	19	32
— Vero Beach (FSL)	2	3	.400	4.92	30	1	0	0	5	60 1/3	54	37	33	33	60
1994— Vancouver (PCL)■	5	3	.625	5.22	37	10	0	0	8	91 1/3	101	56	53	34	66
1995— California (A.L.)	3	0	1.000	3.88	46	0	0	0	1	55 2/3	49	27	24	26	36
— Lake Elsinore (Calif.)	0	0	...	9.53	5	1	0	0	0	5 2/3	9	6	6	3	8
1996— California (A.L.)	5	5	.500	2.67	69	0	0	0	1	81	62	27	24	42	65
1997— Anaheim (A.L.)	5	5	.500	4.31	58	0	0	0	7	62 2/3	69	32	30	28	57
Major league totals (3 years)	13	10	.565	3.52	173	0	0	0	9	199 1/3	180	86	78	96	158

JANZEN, MARTY — P — DIAMONDBACKS

PERSONAL: Born May 31, 1973, in Homestead, Fla. ... 6-3/200. ... Throws right, bats right. ... Full name: Martin Thomas Janzen.
HIGH SCHOOL: Gainesville (Fla.).
TRANSACTIONS/CAREER NOTES: Signed as non-drafted free agent by New York Yankees organization (August 8, 1991). ... On disabled list (June 17, 1993-remainder of season). ... Traded by Yankees organization with P Jason Jarvis and P Mike Gordon to Toronto Blue Jays organization for P David Cone (July 28, 1995). ... Selected by Arizona Diamondbacks in third round (69th pick overall) of expansion draft (November 18, 1997).

Year Team (League)	W	L	Pct.	ERA	G	GS	CG	ShO	Sv.	IP	H	R	ER	BB	SO
1992— GC Yankees (GCL)	7	2	.778	2.36	12	•11	0	0	0	68 2/3	55	21	18	15	73
— Greensboro (S. Atl.)	0	0	...	3.60	2	0	0	0	1	5	5	2	2	1	5
1993— GC Yankees (GCL)	0	1	.000	1.21	5	5	0	0	0	22 1/3	20	5	3	3	19
1994— Greensboro (S. Atl.)	3	7	.300	3.89	17	17	0	0	0	104	98	57	45	25	92
1995— Tampa (Florida State)	10	3	.769	2.61	18	18	1	0	0	113 2/3	102	38	33	30	104
— Norwich (Eastern)	1	2	.333	4.95	3	3	0	0	0	20	17	11	11	7	16
— Knoxville (Southern)■	5	1	.833	2.63	7	7	2	1	0	48	35	14	14	14	44
1996— Syracuse (Int'l)	3	4	.429	7.76	10	10	0	0	0	55 2/3	74	54	48	24	34
— Toronto (A.L.)	4	6	.400	7.33	15	11	0	0	0	73 2/3	95	65	60	38	29
1997— Syracuse (Int'l)	0	5	.000	7.20	22	9	0	0	1	65	76	58	52	36	56
— Toronto (A.L.)	2	1	.667	3.60	12	0	0	0	0	25	23	11	10	13	17
Major league totals (2 years)	6	7	.462	6.39	27	11	0	0	0	98 2/3	118	76	70	51	64

JARVIS, KEVIN — P

PERSONAL: Born August 1, 1969, in Lexington, Ky. ... 6-2/200. ... Throws right, bats left. ... Full name: Kevin Thomas Jarvis.
HIGH SCHOOL: Tates Creek (Lexington, Ky.).
COLLEGE: Wake Forest.
TRANSACTIONS/CAREER NOTES: Selected by Cincinnati Reds organization in 21st round of free-agent draft (June 3, 1991). ... Claimed on waivers by Detroit Tigers (May 2, 1997). ... Claimed on waivers by Minnesota Twins (May 9, 1997). ... Claimed on waivers by Tigers (June 17, 1997). ... On Detroit disabled list (June 25-July 14, 1997); included rehabilitation assignment to Toledo (July 4-14). ... Released by Tigers (December 12, 1997). ... Signed to play for Chunichi Dragons of Japan Central League for 1998 season (January 23, 1998).

Year Team (League)	W	L	Pct.	ERA	G	GS	CG	ShO	Sv.	IP	H	R	ER	BB	SO
1991— Princeton (Appalachian)	5	6	.455	2.42	13	13	4	•1	0	85 2/3	73	34	23	29	79
1992— Cedar Rapids (Midw.)	0	0	...	0.00	1	1	0	0	0	1	1	0	0	0	0
— Char., W.Va. (S. Atl.)	6	8	.429	3.11	28	18	2	1	0	133	123	59	46	37	131
1993— Win.-Salem (Car.)	8	7	.533	3.41	21	20	2	1	0	145	133	68	55	48	101

Year	Team (League)	W	L	Pct.	ERA	G	GS	CG	ShO	Sv.	IP	H	R	ER	BB	SO
	—Chattanooga (Southern)....	3	1	.750	1.69	7	3	2	0	0	37 1/3	26	7	7	11	18
1994—	Cincinnati (N.L.)................	1	1	.500	7.13	6	3	0	0	0	17 2/3	22	14	14	5	10
	—Indianapolis (A.A.).............	10	2	•.833	3.54	21	20	2	0	0	132 1/3	136	55	52	34	90
1995—	Indianapolis (A.A.).............	4	2	.667	4.45	10	10	2	1	0	60 2/3	62	33	30	18	37
	—Cincinnati (N.L.)................	3	4	.429	5.70	19	11	1	1	0	79	91	56	50	32	33
1996—	Indianapolis (A.A.).............	4	3	.571	5.06	8	8	0	0	0	42 2/3	45	27	24	12	32
	—Cincinnati (N.L.)................	8	9	.471	5.98	24	20	2	1	0	120 1/3	152	93	80	43	63
1997—	Cincinnati (N.L.)................	0	1	.000	10.13	9	0	0	0	1	13 1/3	21	16	15	7	12
	—Toledo (Int'l)■................	0	1	.000	6.75	2	2	0	0	0	8	7	6	6	4	5
	—Minnesota (A.L.)■.............	0	0	. . .	12.46	6	2	0	0	0	13	23	18	18	8	9
	—Detroit (A.L.)■................	0	3	.000	5.40	17	3	0	0	0	41 2/3	55	28	25	14	27
A.L. totals (1 year)		0	3	.000	7.08	23	5	0	0	0	54 2/3	78	46	43	22	36
N.L. totals (4 years)		12	15	.444	6.21	58	34	3	2	1	230 1/3	286	179	159	87	118
Major league totals (4 years)......		12	18	.400	6.38	81	39	3	2	1	285	364	225	202	109	154

JAVIER, STAN   OF   GIANTS

J

PERSONAL: Born January 9, 1964, in San Francisco de Macoris, Dominican Republic. ... 6-0/195. ... Bats both, throws right. ... Full name: Stanley Julian Javier. ... Son of Julian Javier, infielder, St. Louis Cardinals and Cincinnati Reds (1960-72). ... Name pronounced HA-vee-AIR.

HIGH SCHOOL: La Altagracia (San Francisco de Macoris, Dominican Republic).

TRANSACTIONS/CAREER NOTES: Signed as non-drafted free agent by St. Louis Cardinals organization (March 26, 1981). ... Traded by Cardinals organization with SS Bobby Meacham to New York Yankees organization for OF Bob Helsom, P Marty Mason and P Steve Fincher (December 14, 1982). ... Traded by Yankees organization with P Jay Howell, P Jose Rijo, P Eric Plunk and P Tim Birtsas to Oakland A's for OF Rickey Henderson, P Bert Bradley and cash (December 5, 1984). ... On Oakland disabled list (August 3-September 1, 1987); included rehabilitation assignment to Tacoma (August 20-September 1). ... On disabled list (August 18-September 2, 1988 and July 7-24, 1989). ... Traded by A's to Los Angeles Dodgers for 2B Willie Randolph (May 13, 1990). ... Traded by Dodgers to Philadelphia Phillies for P Steve Searcy and a player to be named later (July 2, 1992); Dodgers acquired IF Julio Peguero to complete deal (July 28, 1992). ... Granted free agency (October 27, 1992). ... Signed by California Angels organization (January 15, 1993). ... Granted free agency (October 29, 1993). ... Signed by A's (December 7, 1993). ... Granted free agency (November 2, 1995). ... Signed by San Francisco Giants (December 8, 1995). ... On San Francisco disabled list (April 13-29 and July 17, 1996-remainder of season); included rehabilitation assignment to San Jose (April 26-29). ... Granted free agency (October 28, 1997). ... Re-signed by Giants (November 26, 1997).

STATISTICAL NOTES: Led A.L. outfielders with 1.000 fielding percentage in 1995.

								BATTING						FIELDING			
Year	Team (League)	Pos.	G	AB	R	H	2B	3B	HR	RBI	Avg.	BB	SO	SB	PO	A	E	Avg.
1981—	Johnson City (App.) ...	OF	53	144	30	36	5	4	3	19	.250	40	33	2	53	2	3	.948
1982—	Johnson City (App.) ...	OF	57	185	45	51	3	•4	8	36	.276	42	55	11	94	8	4	.962
1983—	Greensboro (S. Atl.)■	OF	129	489	109	152	*34	6	12	77	.311	75	95	33	250	10	15	.945
1984—	New York (A.L.)..........	OF	7	7	1	1	0	0	0	0	.143	0	1	0	3	0	0	1.000
	—Nashville (Southern) ..	OF	76	262	40	76	17	4	7	38	.290	39	57	17	202	4	7	.967
	—Columbus (Int'l)	OF	32	99	12	22	3	1	0	7	.222	12	26	1	77	4	2	.976
1985—	Huntsville (Sou.)■	OF	140	486	105	138	22	8	9	64	.284	*112	92	61	363	8	7	.981
1986—	Tacoma (PCL)	OF-1B	69	248	50	81	16	2	4	51	.327	47	46	18	172	9	6	.968
	—Oakland (A.L.)	OF-DH	59	114	13	23	8	0	0	8	.202	16	27	8	118	1	0	1.000
1987—	Oakland (A.L.)	OF-1B-DH	81	151	22	28	3	1	2	9	.185	19	33	3	149	5	3	.981
	—Tacoma (PCL)	OF-1B	15	51	6	11	2	0	0	2	.216	4	12	3	26	0	2	.929
1988—	Oakland (A.L.)	OF-1B-DH	125	397	49	102	13	3	2	35	.257	32	63	20	274	7	5	.983
1989—	Oakland (A.L.)	OF-2B-1B	112	310	42	77	12	3	1	28	.248	31	45	12	221	8	2	.991
1990—	Oakland (A.L.)	OF-DH	19	33	4	8	0	2	0	3	.242	3	6	0	19	0	0	1.000
	—Los Angeles (N.L.)■	OF	104	276	56	84	9	4	3	24	.304	37	44	15	204	2	0	1.000
1991—	Los Angeles (N.L.)	OF-1B	121	176	21	36	5	3	1	11	.205	16	36	7	90	4	3	.969
1992—	Los Angeles (N.L.)	OF	56	58	6	11	3	0	1	5	.190	6	11	1	17	0	0	1.000
	—Philadelphia (N.L.)■ ...	OF	74	276	36	72	14	1	0	24	.261	31	43	17	212	7	3	.986
1993—	California (A.L.)■........	O-1-2-DH	92	237	33	69	10	4	3	28	.291	27	33	12	167	4	4	.977
1994—	Oakland (A.L.)■........	OF-1B-3B	109	419	75	114	23	0	10	44	.272	49	76	24	274	4	4	.986
1995—	Oakland (A.L.)	OF-3B	130	442	81	123	20	2	8	56	.278	49	63	36	332	3	0	†1.000
1996—	San Fran. (N.L.)■........	OF	71	274	44	74	25	0	2	22	.270	25	51	14	180	2	3	.984
	—San Jose (Calif.)	OF	3	5	1	2	0	0	0	1	.400	1	1	0	1	0	0	1.000
1997—	San Fran. (N.L.)	OF-1B	142	440	69	126	16	4	8	50	.286	56	70	25	279	2	7	.976
American League totals (9 years)			734	2110	320	545	89	15	26	211	.258	226	347	115	1557	32	18	.989
National League totals (5 years)			568	1500	232	403	72	12	15	136	.269	171	255	79	982	17	16	.984
Major league totals (13 years)			1302	3610	552	948	161	27	41	347	.263	397	602	194	2539	49	34	.987

DIVISION SERIES RECORD

								BATTING						FIELDING			
Year	Team (League)	Pos.	G	AB	R	H	2B	3B	HR	RBI	Avg.	BB	SO	SB	PO	A	E	Avg.
1997—	San Francisco (N.L.) ..	OF	3	12	2	5	1	0	0	1	.417	0	2	1	11	0	0	1.000

CHAMPIONSHIP SERIES RECORD

								BATTING						FIELDING			
Year	Team (League)	Pos.	G	AB	R	H	2B	3B	HR	RBI	Avg.	BB	SO	SB	PO	A	E	Avg.
1988—	Oakland (A.L.)	OF-PR	2	4	0	2	0	0	0	1	.500	1	0	0	5	0	0	1.000
1989—	Oakland (A.L.)	OF	1	2	0	0	0	0	0	0	.000	0	1	0	1	0	0	1.000
Championship series totals (2 years)			3	6	0	2	0	0	0	1	.333	1	1	0	6	0	0	1.000

WORLD SERIES RECORD

NOTES: Member of World Series championship team (1989).

								BATTING						FIELDING			
Year	Team (League)	Pos.	G	AB	R	H	2B	3B	HR	RBI	Avg.	BB	SO	SB	PO	A	E	Avg.
1988—	Oakland (A.L.)	PR-OF	3	4	0	2	0	0	0	2	.500	0	1	0	1	0	0	1.000
1989—	Oakland (A.L.)	OF	1	0	0	0	0	0	0	0	. . .	0	0	0	0	0	0	. . .
World Series totals (2 years)			4	4	0	2	0	0	0	2	.500	0	1	0	1	0	0	1.000

JEFFERIES, GREGG   OF   PHILLIES

PERSONAL: Born August 1, 1967, in Burlingame, Calif. ... 5-10/184. ... Bats both, throws right. ... Full name: Gregory Scott Jefferies.
HIGH SCHOOL: Serra (San Mateo, Calif.).
TRANSACTIONS/CAREER NOTES: Selected by New York Mets organization in first round (20th pick overall) of free-agent draft (June 3, 1985). ... On disabled list (April 27-May 13, 1991). ... Traded by Mets with OF Kevin McReynolds and 2B Keith Miller to Kansas City Royals for P Bret Saberhagen and IF Bill Pecota (December 11, 1991). ... Traded by Royals with OF Ed Gerald to St. Louis Cardinals for OF Felix Jose and IF/OF Craig Wilson (February 12, 1993). ... Granted free agency (October 18, 1994). ... Signed by Philadelphia Phillies (December 14, 1994). ... On disabled list (June 17-July 2, 1995). ... On Philadelphia disabled list (April 5-June 4, 1996); included rehabilitation assignment to Scranton/Wilkes-Barre (May 30-June 4). ... On disabled list (August 18-September 2, 1997).
HONORS: Named Appalachian League Player of the Year (1985). ... Named Carolina League Most Valuable Player (1986). ... Named Texas League Most Valuable Player (1987).
STATISTICAL NOTES: Led Carolina League with .549 slugging percentage in 1986. ... Led Texas League with 18 intentional bases on balls received in 1987. ... Tied for International League lead with 10 intentional bases on balls received in 1988. ... Led International League third basemen with 240 assists in 1988. ... Led A.L. third basemen with 26 errors in 1992. ... Tied for N.L. lead with 94 double plays by first basemen in 1994 ... Hit for the cycle (August 25, 1995). ... Career major league grand slams: 2.

Year	Team (League)	Pos.	G	AB	R	H	2B	3B	HR	RBI	Avg.	BB	SO	SB	PO	A	E	Avg.
1985—Kingsport (Appal.)......		SS-2B	47	166	27	57	18	2	3	29	.343	14	16	21	78	130	21	.908
—Columbia (S. Atl.)......		2B-SS	20	64	7	18	2	2	1	12	.281	4	4	7	28	26	2	.964
1986—Columbia (S. Atl.).......		SS	25	112	29	38	6	1	5	24	.339	9	10	13	36	83	7	.944
—Lynchburg (Caro.)......		SS	95	390	66	138	25	9	11	80	*.354	33	29	43	138	273	20	.954
—Jackson (Texas).........		SS-3B	5	19	1	8	1	1	0	7	.421	2	2	1	7	9	1	.941
1987—Jackson (Texas).........		SS-3B	134	510	81	187	*48	5	20	101	.367	49	43	26	167	388	35	.941
—New York (N.L.).........		PH	6	6	0	3	1	0	0	2	.500	0	0	0	...	...	...	...
1988—Tidewater (Int'l).........		3-S-2-O	132	504	62	142	28	4	7	61	.282	32	35	32	110	†330	27	.942
—New York (N.L.).........		3B-2B	29	109	19	35	8	2	6	17	.321	8	10	5	33	46	2	.975
1989—New York (N.L.).........		2B-3B	141	508	72	131	28	2	12	56	.258	39	46	21	242	280	14	.974
1990—New York (N.L.).........		2B-3B	153	604	96	171	*40	3	15	68	.283	46	40	11	242	341	16	.973
1991—New York (N.L.).........		2B-3B	136	486	59	132	19	2	9	62	.272	47	38	26	170	271	17	.963
1992—Kansas City (A.L.)■		3B-DH-2B	152	604	66	172	36	3	10	75	.285	43	29	19	96	304	†26	.939
1993—St. Louis (N.L.)■......		1B-2B	142	544	89	186	24	3	16	83	.342	62	32	46	1281	77	9	.993
1994—St. Louis (N.L.) ..		1B	103	397	52	129	27	1	12	55	.325	45	26	12	889	53	7	.993
1995—Philadelphia (N.L.)■		1B-OF	114	480	69	147	31	2	11	56	.306	35	26	9	579	36	3	.995
1996—Philadelphia (N.L.)......		1B-OF	104	404	55	118	17	3	7	51	.292	36	21	20	522	39	1	.998
—Scran./W.B. (Int'l)......		1B	4	17	1	2	0	1	0	0	.118	1	3	0	22	4	1	.962
1997—Philadelphia (N.L.)......		OF	130	476	68	122	25	3	11	48	.256	53	27	12	211	5	3	.986
American League totals (1 year)			152	604	66	172	36	3	10	75	.285	43	29	19	96	304	26	.939
National League totals (10 years)			1058	4014	583	1174	220	21	99	498	.292	371	266	162	4169	1148	72	.987
Major league totals (11 years)			1210	4618	649	1346	256	24	109	573	.291	414	295	181	4265	1452	98	.983

CHAMPIONSHIP SERIES RECORD

Year	Team (League)	Pos.	G	AB	R	H	2B	3B	HR	RBI	Avg.	BB	SO	SB	PO	A	E	Avg.
1988—New York (N.L.)..........		3B	7	27	2	9	2	0	0	1	.333	4	0	0	5	8	1	.929

ALL-STAR GAME RECORD

Year	League	Pos.	AB	R	H	2B	3B	HR	RBI	Avg.	BB	SO	SB	PO	A	E	Avg.
1993—National		PH-DH	1	0	0	0	0	0	0	.000	0	1	0	...	...	...	...
1994—National		1B	1	2	1	1	0	0	0	1.000	0	0	0	6	0	0	1.000
All-Star Game totals (2 years)			2	2	1	1	0	0	0	.500	0	1	0	6	0	0	1.000

JEFFERSON, REGGIE   DH/1B   RED SOX

PERSONAL: Born September 25, 1968, in Tallahassee, Fla. ... 6-4/215. ... Bats left, throws left. ... Full name: Reginald Jirod Jefferson.
HIGH SCHOOL: Lincoln (Tallahassee, Fla.).
TRANSACTIONS/CAREER NOTES: Selected by Cincinnati Reds organization in third round of free-agent draft (June 2, 1986). ... On disabled list (May 25, 1990-remainder of season). ... Traded by Reds to Cleveland Indians for 1B Tim Costo (June 14, 1991). ... On Cleveland disabled list (June 24-July 1, 1991); included rehabilitation assignment to Canton/Akron (June 25-July 1). ... On Cleveland disabled list (March 28-July 4, 1992); included rehabilitation assignment to Colorado Springs (June 15-July 4). ... On Colorado Springs suspended list (September 6-9, 1992). ... Traded by Indians with SS Felix Fermin and cash to Seattle Mariners for SS Omar Vizquel (December 20, 1993). ... On disabled list (May 21-June 10, 1994). ... Granted free agency (March 11, 1995). ... Signed by Boston Red Sox (April 9, 1995). ... On disabled list (July 10-September 19, 1995).
STATISTICAL NOTES: Led Gulf Coast League first basemen with 624 total chances in 1986. ... Had 22-game hitting streak (July 13-August 8, 1997). ... Career major league grand slams: 2.
MISCELLANEOUS: Batted as switch-hitter (1986 and 1989-May 1994).

Year	Team (League)	Pos.	G	AB	R	H	2B	3B	HR	RBI	Avg.	BB	SO	SB	PO	A	E	Avg.
1986—GC Reds (GCL)..........		1B	59	208	28	54	4	*5	3	33	.260	24	40	10	*581	*36	4	.989
1987—Billings (Pioneer)........		1B	8	22	10	8	1	0	1	9	.364	4	2	1	21	1	0	1.000
—Cedar Rap. (Midw.)....		1B	15	54	9	12	5	0	3	11	.222	1	12	1	120	11	1	.992
1988—Cedar Rap. (Midw.)....		1B	135	517	76	149	26	2	18	*90	.288	40	89	1	1084	91	13	.989
1989—Chattanooga (Sou.).....		1B	135	487	66	140	19	3	17	80	.287	43	73	2	1004	79	16	.985
1990—Nashville (A.A.).........		1B	37	126	24	34	11	2	5	23	.270	14	30	1	314	20	4	.988
1991—Nashville (A.A.)		1B	28	103	15	33	3	1	3	20	.320	10	22	3	196	13	2	.991
—Cincinnati (N.L.)......		1B	5	7	1	1	0	0	1	1	.143	1	2	0	14	1	0	1.000
—Cleveland (A.L.)■......		1B	26	101	10	20	3	0	2	12	.198	2	22	0	252	24	2	.993
—Cant./Akr. (Eastern) ...		1B	6	25	2	7	1	0	0	4	.280	1	5	0	46	3	0	1.000
—Colo. Springs (PCL) ...		1B	39	136	29	42	11	0	3	21	.309	16	28	0	289	25	3	.991
1992—Colo. Springs (PCL) ...		1B	57	218	49	68	11	4	11	44	.312	29	50	1	363	34	5	.988
—Cleveland (A.L.)..........		1B-DH	24	89	8	30	6	2	1	6	.337	1	17	0	129	12	1	.993

Year	Team (League)	Pos.	G	AB	R	H	2B	3B	HR	RBI	Avg.	BB	SO	SB	PO	A	E	Avg.
1993—	Cleveland (A.L.)..........	DH-1B	113	366	35	91	11	2	10	34	.249	28	78	1	112	10	3	.976
1994—	Seattle (A.L.)■...........	DH-1B-OF	63	162	24	53	11	0	8	32	.327	17	32	0	95	10	2	.981
1995—	Boston (A.L.)■...........	DH-1B-OF	46	121	21	35	8	0	5	26	.289	9	24	0	28	4	0	1.000
1996—	Boston (A.L.).............	DH-OF-1B	122	386	67	134	30	4	19	74	.347	25	89	0	178	17	3	.985
1997—	Boston (A.L.).............	DH-1B	136	489	74	156	33	1	13	67	.319	24	93	1	74	5	2	.975
American League totals (7 years)			530	1714	239	519	102	9	58	251	.303	107	355	2	868	82	13	.987
National League totals (1 year)			5	7	1	1	0	0	1	1	.143	1	2	0	14	1	0	1.000
Major league totals (7 years)			535	1721	240	520	102	9	59	252	.302	108	357	2	882	83	13	.987

DIVISION SERIES RECORD

Year	Team (League)	Pos.	G	AB	R	H	2B	3B	HR	RBI	Avg.	BB	SO	SB	PO	A	E	Avg.
1995—	Boston (A.L.).............	DH	1	4	1	1	0	0	0	0	.250	0	1	0	...	...	...	...

JENKINS, GEOFF — OF — BREWERS

PERSONAL: Born July 21, 1974, in Olympia, Wash. ... 6-1/200. ... Bats left, throws right. ... Full name: Geoff Scott Jenkins.
HIGH SCHOOL: Rancho Cordova (Calif.).
COLLEGE: Southern California.
TRANSACTIONS/CAREER NOTES: Selected by Milwaukee Brewers organization in first round (ninth pick overall) of free-agent draft (June 1, 1995). ... On El Paso disabled list (May 8-July 23, 1996). ... On disabled list (July 4-August 11, 1997).

Year	Team (League)	Pos.	G	AB	R	H	2B	3B	HR	RBI	Avg.	BB	SO	SB	PO	A	E	Avg.
1995—	Helena (Pioneer)	OF	7	26	2	9	0	1	0	9	.346	3	11	0	15	1	0	1.000
	—Stockton (California) ..	OF	13	47	13	12	2	0	3	12	.255	10	12	2	14	3	2	.895
	—El Paso (Texas)..........	OF	22	79	12	22	4	2	1	13	.278	8	23	3	41	1	7	.857
1996—	El Paso (Texas)...........	DH	22	77	17	22	5	4	1	11	.286	12	21	1	...	...	...	...
	—Stockton (California) ..	OF	37	138	27	48	8	4	3	25	.348	20	32	3	2	0	0	1.000
1997—	Tucson (PCL)	OF-SS	93	347	44	82	24	3	10	56	.236	33	87	0	115	7	5	.961

JENNINGS, ROBIN — OF — CUBS

PERSONAL: Born April 11, 1972, in Singapore. ... 6-2/210. ... Bats left, throws left. ... Full name: Robin Christopher Jennings.
HIGH SCHOOL: Annandale (Va.).
JUNIOR COLLEGE: Manatee (Fla.).
TRANSACTIONS/CAREER NOTES: Selected by Baltimore Orioles organization in 30th round of free-agent draft (June 4, 1990); did not sign. ... Selected by Chicago Cubs organization in 33rd round of free-agent draft (June 3, 1991). ... On Iowa disabled list (May 31-June 11 and August 10-20, 1996).
STATISTICAL NOTES: Tied for New York-Pennsylvania League lead in double plays by outfielder with two in 1992. ... Led Midwest League outfielders with 20 assists in 1993.

Year	Team (League)	Pos.	G	AB	R	H	2B	3B	HR	RBI	Avg.	BB	SO	SB	PO	A	E	Avg.
1992—	Geneva (NY-Penn)......	OF	72	275	39	82	12	2	7	47	.298	20	43	10	96	*9	4	.963
1993—	Peoria (Midwest)........	OF-1B	132	474	64	146	29	5	3	65	.308	46	73	11	219	†31	7	.973
1994—	Daytona (Fla. St.)	OF	128	476	54	133	24	5	8	60	.279	45	54	2	165	8	8	.956
1995—	Orlando (South.)	OF	132	490	71	145	27	7	17	79	.296	44	61	7	242	15	10	.963
1996—	Iowa (Am. Assoc.)......	OF	86	331	53	94	15	6	18	56	.284	32	53	2	156	5	3	.982
	—Chicago (N.L.)...........	OF	31	58	7	13	5	0	0	4	.224	3	9	1	19	2	0	1.000
1997—	Iowa (Am. Assoc.)......	OF	126	464	67	128	25	5	20	71	.276	56	73	5	197	10	3	.986
	—Chicago (N.L.)...........	OF	9	18	1	3	1	0	0	2	.167	0	2	0	5	0	0	1.000
Major league totals (2 years)			40	76	8	16	6	0	0	6	.211	3	11	1	24	2	0	1.000

JENSEN, MARCUS — C — TIGERS

PERSONAL: Born December 14, 1972, in Oakland. ... 6-4/204. ... Bats both, throws right. ... Full name: Marcus C. Jensen.
HIGH SCHOOL: Skyline (Oakland).
TRANSACTIONS/CAREER NOTES: Selected by San Francisco Giants organization in supplemental round ("sandwich pick" between first and second round, 33rd pick overall) of free-agent draft (June 4, 1990); pick received as part of compensation for San Diego Padres signing Type A free-agent P Craig Lefferts. ... On disabled list (June 1-14, 1993). ... Traded by Giants to Detroit Tigers for C Brian Johnson (July 16, 1997). ... Granted free agency (July 22, 1997). ... Re-signed by Tigers (July 26, 1997).
STATISTICAL NOTES: Tied for Arizona League lead with three intentional bases on balls received in 1991. ... Led California League catchers with 722 total chances in 1994. ... Led Texas League catchers with 546 total chances in 1995.

Year	Team (League)	Pos.	G	AB	R	H	2B	3B	HR	RBI	Avg.	BB	SO	SB	PO	A	E	Avg.
1990—	Everett (N'west).........	C	51	171	21	29	3	0	2	12	.170	24	60	0	191	27	3	.986
1991—	Ariz. Giants (Ariz.)	C-1B	48	155	28	44	8	3	2	30	.284	34	22	4	226	29	7	.973
1992—	Clinton (Midwest).......	C-1B	86	264	35	62	14	0	4	33	.235	54	87	4	493	68	10	.982
1993—	Clinton (Midwest).......	C	104	324	53	85	24	2	11	56	.262	66	98	1	641	73	7	.990
1994—	San Jose (Calif.).........	C	118	418	56	101	18	0	7	47	.242	61	100	1	*627	86	9	.988
1995—	Shreveport (Texas)	C	95	321	55	91	22	8	4	45	.283	41	68	0	*471	70	5	.991
1996—	Phoenix (PCL)	C	120	405	41	107	22	4	5	53	.264	44	95	1	568	65	8	.988
	—San Francisco (N.L.) ..	C	9	19	4	4	1	0	0	4	.211	8	7	0	37	5	2	.955
1997—	San Francisco (N.L.) ..	C	30	74	5	11	2	0	1	3	.149	7	23	0	106	10	2	.983
	—Toledo (Int'l)■............	C	24	80	5	14	5	0	0	9	.175	9	25	0	149	6	1	.994
	—Detroit (A.L.).............	C	8	11	1	2	0	0	0	1	.182	1	5	0	26	1	1	.964
American League totals (1 year)			8	11	1	2	0	0	0	1	.182	1	5	0	26	1	1	.964
National League totals (2 years)			39	93	9	15	3	0	1	7	.161	15	30	0	143	15	4	.975
Major league totals (2 years)			47	104	10	17	3	0	1	8	.163	16	35	0	169	16	5	.974

JERZEMBECK, MIKE   P   YANKEES

PERSONAL: Born May 18, 1972, in Queens, N.Y. ... 6-1/185. ... Throws right, bats right. ... Full name: Michael Joseph Jerzembeck.
HIGH SCHOOL: Archbishop Molloy (Jamaica, N.Y.).
COLLEGE: North Carolina.
TRANSACTIONS/CAREER NOTES: Selected by New York Yankees organization in fifth round of free-agent draft (June 3, 1993). ... On disabled list (May 8-29 and June 13-July 16, 1994). ... On disabled list (April 18-September 8, 1995).

Year Team (League)	W	L	Pct.	ERA	G	GS	CG	ShO	Sv.	IP	H	R	ER	BB	SO
1993— Oneonta (N.Y.-Penn)	8	4	.667	2.68	14	14	0	0	0	77 1/3	70	25	23	26	76
1994— Tampa (Florida State)	4	3	.571	3.15	16	16	0	0	0	68 2/3	59	27	24	22	45
1995— Tampa (Florida State)	0	1	.000	9.00	2	0	0	0	0	3	5	4	3	2	1
1996— Columbus (Int'l)	0	0	...	5.40	1	0	0	0	0	1 2/3	1	1	1	1	0
— Norwich (Eastern)	3	6	.333	4.52	14	13	1	1	0	69 2/3	74	38	35	26	65
— Tampa (Florida State)	4	2	.667	2.95	12	12	0	0	0	73 1/3	67	26	24	13	60
1997— Norwich (Eastern)	2	1	.667	1.71	8	8	0	0	0	42	21	10	8	16	42
— Columbus (Int'l)	7	5	.583	3.59	20	20	2	0	0	130 1/3	125	55	52	37	118

JETER, DEREK   SS   YANKEES

PERSONAL: Born June 26, 1974, in Pequannock, N.J. ... 6-3/185. ... Bats right, throws right.
HIGH SCHOOL: Central (Kalamazoo, Mich.).
COLLEGE: Michigan.
TRANSACTIONS/CAREER NOTES: Selected by New York Yankees organization in first round (sixth pick overall) of free-agent draft (June 1, 1992).
HONORS: Named Minor League Player of the Year by THE SPORTING NEWS (1994). ... Named A.L. Rookie Player of the Year by THE SPORTING NEWS (1996). ... Named A.L. Rookie of the Year by Baseball Writers' Association of America (1996).

Year Team (League)	Pos.	G	AB	R	H	2B	3B	HR	RBI	Avg.	BB	SO	SB	PO	A	E	Avg.
1992— GC Yankees (GCL)	SS	47	173	19	35	10	0	3	25	.202	19	36	2	67	132	12	.943
— Greensboro (S. Atl.)	SS	11	37	4	9	0	0	1	4	.243	7	16	0	14	25	9	.813
1993— Greensboro (S. Atl.)	SS	128	515	85	152	14	11	5	71	.295	56	95	18	158	292	56	.889
1994— Tampa (Florida State)	SS	69	292	61	96	13	8	0	39	.329	23	30	28	93	204	12	.961
— Alb./Colon. (Eastern)	SS	34	122	17	46	7	2	2	13	.377	15	16	12	42	105	6	.961
— Columbus (Int'l)	SS	35	126	25	44	7	1	3	16	.349	20	15	10	54	93	7	.955
1995— Columbus (Int'l)	SS	123	486	*96	154	27	9	2	45	.317	61	56	20	189	394	*29	.953
— New York (A.L.)	SS	15	48	5	12	4	1	0	7	.250	3	11	0	17	34	2	.962
1996— New York (A.L.)	SS	157	582	104	183	25	6	10	78	.314	48	102	14	244	444	22	.969
1997— New York (A.L.)	SS	159	654	116	190	31	7	10	70	.291	74	125	23	243	*457	18	.975
Major league totals (3 years)		331	1284	225	385	60	14	20	155	.300	125	238	37	504	935	42	.972

DIVISION SERIES RECORD

Year Team (League)	Pos.	G	AB	R	H	2B	3B	HR	RBI	Avg.	BB	SO	SB	PO	A	E	Avg.
1996— New York (A.L.)	SS	4	17	2	7	1	0	0	1	.412	0	2	0	8	10	2	.900
1997— New York (A.L.)	SS	5	21	6	7	1	0	2	2	.333	3	5	1	12	15	0	1.000
Division series totals (2 years)		9	38	8	14	2	0	2	3	.368	3	7	1	20	25	2	.957

CHAMPIONSHIP SERIES RECORD

Year Team (League)	Pos.	G	AB	R	H	2B	3B	HR	RBI	Avg.	BB	SO	SB	PO	A	E	Avg.
1996— New York (A.L.)	SS	5	24	5	10	2	0	1	1	.417	0	5	2	6	13	0	1.000

WORLD SERIES RECORD

NOTES: Member of World Series championship team (1996).

Year Team (League)	Pos.	G	AB	R	H	2B	3B	HR	RBI	Avg.	BB	SO	SB	PO	A	E	Avg.
1996— New York (A.L.)	SS	6	20	5	5	0	0	0	1	.250	4	6	1	15	22	2	.949

JOHNSON, BRIAN   C   GIANTS

PERSONAL: Born January 8, 1968, in Oakland. ... 6-2/210. ... Bats right, throws right. ... Full name: Brian David Johnson.
HIGH SCHOOL: Skyline (Oakland).
COLLEGE: Stanford.
TRANSACTIONS/CAREER NOTES: Selected by Montreal Expos organization in 36th round of free-agent draft (June 2, 1986); did not sign. ... Selected by New York Yankees organization in 16th round of free-agent draft (June 5, 1989). ... Selected by Las Vegas, San Diego Padres organization from Albany/Colonie, Yankees organization, in Rule 5 minor league draft (December 9, 1991). ... On disabled list (April 22-May 16, 1992). ... Traded by Padres with P Willie Blair to Detroit Tigers for P Joey Eischen and P Cam Smith (December 17, 1996). ... Traded by Tigers to San Francisco Giants for C Marcus Jensen (July 16, 1997).
STATISTICAL NOTES: Led South Atlantic League catchers with 752 putouts and 844 total chances in 1990. ... Led Florida State League catchers with 654 putouts in 1991. ... Career major league grand slams: 3.

Year Team (League)	Pos.	G	AB	R	H	2B	3B	HR	RBI	Avg.	BB	SO	SB	PO	A	E	Avg.
1989— GC Yankees (GCL)	C	17	61	7	22	1	1	0	8	.361	4	5	0	84	14	1	.990
1990— Greensboro (S. Atl.)	C-3B-1B	137	496	58	118	15	0	7	51	.238	57	65	4	†773	91	13	.985
1991— Alb./Colon. (Eastern)	C-1B	2	8	0	0	0	0	0	0	.000	0	2	0	10	2	0	1.000
— Fort Lauderdale (FSL)	C-1B-3B	113	394	35	94	19	0	1	44	.239	34	67	4	†738	65	13	.984
1992— Wichita (Texas)■	C-3B	75	245	30	71	20	0	3	26	.290	22	32	3	472	40	3	.994
1993— Las Vegas (PCL)	C-3B-OF	115	416	58	141	35	6	10	71	.339	41	53	0	513	67	9	.985
1994— San Diego (N.L.)	C-1B	36	93	7	23	4	1	3	16	.247	5	21	0	185	15	0	1.000
— Las Vegas (PCL)	C	15	51	6	11	1	0	2	9	.216	8	6	0	61	5	0	1.000

Year—Team (League)	Pos.	G	AB	R	H	2B	3B	HR	RBI	Avg.	BB	SO	SB	PO	A	E	Avg.
1995—San Diego (N.L.)	C-1B	68	207	20	52	9	0	3	29	.251	11	39	0	403	32	4	.991
1996—San Diego (N.L.)	C-1B-3B	82	243	18	66	13	1	8	35	.272	4	36	0	456	21	5	.990
1997—Detroit (A.L.)■	C-DH	45	139	13	33	6	1	2	18	.237	5	19	1	217	9	3	.987
—Toledo (Int'l)	C	7	21	0	3	2	0	0	1	.143	0	2	0	38	4	0	1.000
—San Fran. (N.L.)■......	C-1B	56	179	19	50	7	2	11	27	.279	14	26	0	352	24	2	.995
American League totals (1 year)		45	139	13	33	6	1	2	18	.237	5	19	1	217	9	3	.987
National League totals (4 years)		242	722	64	191	33	4	25	107	.265	34	122	0	1396	92	11	.993
Major league totals (4 years)		287	861	77	224	39	5	27	125	.260	39	141	1	1613	101	14	.992

DIVISION SERIES RECORD

Year—Team (League)	Pos.	G	AB	R	H	2B	3B	HR	RBI	Avg.	BB	SO	SB	PO	A	E	Avg.
1996—San Diego (N.L.)	C	2	8	2	3	1	0	0	0	.375	0	1	0	15	3	0	1.000
1997—San Francisco (N.L.) ..	C	3	10	2	1	0	0	1	1	.100	1	4	0	18	0	0	1.000
Division series totals (2 years)		5	18	4	4	1	0	1	1	.222	1	5	0	33	3	0	1.000

J

JOHNSON, CHARLES — C — MARLINS

PERSONAL: Born July 20, 1971, in Fort Pierce, Fla. ... 6-2/220. ... Bats right, throws right. ... Full name: Charles Edward Johnson Jr.
HIGH SCHOOL: Westwood (Fort Pierce, Fla.).
COLLEGE: Miami (Fla.).
TRANSACTIONS/CAREER NOTES: Selected by Montreal Expos organization in first round (10th pick overall) of free-agent draft (June 5, 1989); did not sign. ... Selected by Florida Marlins organization in first round (28th pick overall) of free-agent draft (June 1, 1992). ... On Florida disabled list (August 9-September 1, 1995); included rehabilitation assignment to Portland (August 30-September 1). ... On disabled list (July 28-September 1, 1996).
RECORDS: Holds major league career records for most consecutive errorless games by catcher—159 (June 24, 1996 through September 28, 1997); and most consecutive chances accepted by catcher without an error—1,294 (June 23, 1996 through September 28, 1997). ... Holds major league single-season records for most consecutive errorless games by catcher—123 (April 1 through September 28, 1997); and most chances accepted without an error by catcher—973 (April 1 through September 28, 1997). ... Shares major league single-season record for highest fielding average by catcher (100 or more games)—1.000 (1997); and fewest errors (100 or more games)—0 (1997).
HONORS: Named catcher on THE SPORTING NEWS college All-America team (1992). ... Won N.L. Gold Glove at catcher (1995-97).
STATISTICAL NOTES: Led Midwest League with 230 total bases in 1993. ... Led Midwest League catchers with 1,004 total chances in 1993. ... Led N.L. catchers with 12 double plays in 1996.
MISCELLANEOUS: Member of 1992 U.S. Olympic baseball team.

Year—Team (League)	Pos.	G	AB	R	H	2B	3B	HR	RBI	Avg.	BB	SO	SB	PO	A	E	Avg.
1993—Kane County (Midw.)..	C	135	488	74	134	29	5	19	*94	.275	62	111	9	*852	*140	12	.988
1994—Portland (Eastern)	C	132	443	64	117	29	1	*28	80	.264	*74	97	4	713	*84	7	.991
—Florida (N.L.)	C	4	11	5	5	1	0	1	4	.455	1	4	0	18	2	0	1.000
1995—Florida (N.L.)	C	97	315	40	79	15	1	11	39	.251	46	71	0	641	•63	6	.992
—Portland (Eastern)	C	2	7	0	0	0	0	0	0	.000	1	3	0	21	2	1	.958
1996—Florida (N.L.)	C	120	386	34	84	13	1	13	37	.218	40	91	1	751	70	4	*.995
1997—Florida (N.L.)	C	124	416	43	104	26	1	19	63	.250	60	109	0	901	73	0	*1.000
Major league totals (4 years)		345	1128	122	272	55	3	44	143	.241	147	275	1	2311	208	10	.996

DIVISION SERIES RECORD

Year—Team (League)	Pos.	G	AB	R	H	2B	3B	HR	RBI	Avg.	BB	SO	SB	PO	A	E	Avg.
1997—Florida (N.L.)	C	3	8	5	2	1	0	1	2	.250	3	2	0	21	3	0	1.000

CHAMPIONSHIP SERIES RECORD

Year—Team (League)	Pos.	G	AB	R	H	2B	3B	HR	RBI	Avg.	BB	SO	SB	PO	A	E	Avg.
1997—Florida (N.L.)	C	6	17	1	2	2	0	0	5	.118	3	8	0	52	3	2	.965

WORLD SERIES RECORD

NOTES: Member of World Series championship team (1997).

Year—Team (League)	Pos.	G	AB	R	H	2B	3B	HR	RBI	Avg.	BB	SO	SB	PO	A	E	Avg.
1997—Florida (N.L.)	C	7	28	4	10	0	0	1	3	.357	1	6	0	49	2	0	1.000

ALL-STAR GAME RECORD

Year—League	Pos.	AB	R	H	2B	3B	HR	RBI	Avg.	BB	SO	SB	PO	A	E	Avg.
1997—National	C	1	0	0	0	0	0	0	.000	0	1	0	2	0	0	1.000

JOHNSON, DANE — P — BLUE JAYS

PERSONAL: Born February 10, 1963, in Coral Gables, Fla. ... 6-5/205. ... Throws right, bats right. ... Full name: Dane Edward Johnson.
HIGH SCHOOL: Southwest Miami (Miami).
COLLEGE: St. Thomas (Fla.).
TRANSACTIONS/CAREER NOTES: Selected by Toronto Blue Jays organization in second round of free-agent draft (June 4, 1984). ... On disabled list (July 1, 1985-remainder of season). ... Released by Blue Jays (June 12, 1989). ... Played in Taiwan (1990-92). ... Signed by El Paso, Milwaukee Brewers organization (June 5, 1993). ... Granted free agency (October 15, 1993). ... Signed by Chicago White Sox organization (January 26, 1994). ... Granted free agency (October 16, 1995). ... Signed by Syracuse, Blue Jays organization (February 10, 1996). ... On Syracuse disabled list (May 27-June 11, 1996). ... Claimed on waivers by Oakland Athletics (October 2, 1996). ... Claimed on waivers by Blue Jays (October 29, 1997).

Year	Team (League)	W	L	Pct.	ERA	G	GS	CG	ShO	Sv.	IP	H	R	ER	BB	SO
1984— Medicine Hat (Pio.)	1	5	.167	8.42	10	10	0	0	0	41 2/3	43	48	39	59	15
1985— Florence (S. Atl.)	0	4	.000	6.29	10	7	0	0	1	34 1/3	27	31	24	37	25
1986— Florence (S. Atl.)	8	12	.400	6.99	31	24	0	0	0	123 2/3	136	*116	*96	•114	68
1987— Dunedin (Fla. St.)	2	5	.286	5.80	18	13	0	0	0	59	68	44	38	49	25
1988— Dunedin (Fla. St.)	11	6	.647	4.73	32	19	0	0	0	104 2/3	91	73	55	89	73
1989— Myrtle Beach (SAL)	0	0	. . .	1.59						5 2/3	5	1	1	4	5
1990—					Taiwan League statistics unavailable.										
1991—					Taiwan League statistics unavailable.										
1992—					Taiwan League statistics unavailable.										
1993— El Paso (Texas)■	2	2	.500	3.91	15	1	0	0	1	25 1/3	23	12	11	10	26
— New Orleans (A.A.)	0	0	. . .	2.40	13	0	0	0	6	15	11	4	4	4	10
1994— Nashville (A.A.)■	1	5	.167	2.25	39	0	0	0	24	44	40	13	11	18	40
— Chicago (A.L.)	2	1	.667	6.57	15	0	0	0	0	12 1/3	16	9	9	11	7
1995— Nashville (A.A.)	4	4	.500	2.41	46	0	0	0	15	56	48	24	15	28	51
1996— Syracuse (Int'l)■	3	2	.600	2.45	43	0	0	0	22	51 1/3	37	14	14	17	51
— Toronto (A.L.)	0	0	. . .	3.00	10	0	0	0	0	9	5	3	3	5	7
1997— Edmonton (PCL)■	1	1	.500	5.63	14	0	0	0	6	16	17	11	10	8	13
— Oakland (A.L.)	4	1	.800	4.53	38	0	0	0	2	45 2/3	49	28	23	31	43
Major league totals (3 years)......	**6**	**2**	**.750**	**4.70**	**63**	**0**	**0**	**0**	**2**	**67**	**70**	**40**	**35**	**47**	**57**

JOHNSON, EARL   OF   TIGERS

PERSONAL: Born October 3, 1971, in Detroit. ... 5-10/165. ... Bats both, throws right. ... Full name: Earl R. Johnson.
HIGH SCHOOL: Osborn (Detroit).
JUNIOR COLLEGE: Henry Ford Community College (Mich.).
TRANSACTIONS/CAREER NOTES: Signed as non-drafted free agent by San Diego Padres organization (August 24, 1991). ... On Rancho Cucamonga disabled list (July 20-August 2, 1995). ... On disabled list (July 20-August 21, 1996). ... Traded by Padres to Detroit Tigers for IF Dave Hajek (July 16, 1997).
STATISTICAL NOTES: Tied for Midwest League lead in double plays by outfielder with four in 1994.

							BATTING						FIELDING			
Year	Team (League)	Pos.	G	AB	R	H	2B	3B	HR	RBI	Avg.	BB	SO	SB	PO	A	E	Avg.
1992— Ariz. Padres (Ariz.)	OF	35	101	20	17	1	0	0	1	.168	10	28	19	60	5	0	1.000
1993— Spokane (N'west)	OF	63	199	33	49	3	1	0	14	.246	16	49	19	139	8	5	.967
1994— Springfield (Midw.)	OF	136	533	80	149	11	3	1	43	.280	37	94	*80	277	15	10	.967
1995— Rancho Cuca. (Cal.) ...	OF	81	341	51	100	11	3	0	25	.293	25	51	34	225	16	7	.972
— Memphis (Southern)..	OF	2	10	0	2	0	0	0	0	.200	1	0	0	4	0	1	.800
1996— Memphis (Southern) ...	OF	82	337	50	85	10	6	2	33	.252	18	59	15	204	9	3	.986
1997— Jacksonville (Sou.)	OF	36	146	24	33	3	1	2	13	.226	9	19	7	69	4	1	.986
— Mobile (Southern)	OF	78	307	52	78	11	3	1	22	.254	21	56	35	189	8	3	.985

JOHNSON, J.J.   OF   TWINS

PERSONAL: Born August 31, 1973, in Sharon, Conn. ... 6-0/213. ... Bats right, throws right. ... Full name: Jermaine Jay Johnson.
HIGH SCHOOL: Stissing Mount (Pine Plains, N.Y.).
TRANSACTIONS/CAREER NOTES: Selected by Boston Red Sox organization in supplemental round ("sandwich pick" between first and second round, 37th pick overall) of free-agent draft (June 3, 1991); pick received as part of compensation for San Diego Padres signing Type A free-agent P Larry Andersen. ... Traded by Red Sox organization to Minnesota Twins organization (October 11, 1995), completing deal in which Twins traded P Rick Aguilera to Red Sox for P Frank Rodriguez and a player to be named later (July 6, 1995).

							BATTING						FIELDING			
Year	Team (League)	Pos.	G	AB	R	H	2B	3B	HR	RBI	Avg.	BB	SO	SB	PO	A	E	Avg.
1991— GC Red Sox (GCL)	OF	31	110	14	19	1	0	0	9	.173	10	16	3	40	3	2	.956
1992— Elmira (N.Y.-Penn)	OF	30	114	8	26	3	1	1	12	.228	4	32	8	44	1	3	.938
1993— Utica (N.Y.-Penn)	OF	43	170	33	49	17	4	2	27	.288	9	34	5	87	3	4	.957
— Lynchburg (Caro.)	OF	25	94	10	24	3	0	4	17	.255	7	20	1	38	2	2	.952
1994— Lynchburg (Caro.)	OF	131	515	66	120	28	4	14	51	.233	36	132	4	209	9	7	.969
1995— Sarasota (Fla. St.)	OF	107	391	49	108	162	16	4	43	.276	26	74	7	159	8	8	.954
— Trenton (Eastern)	OF	2	6	1	3	0	0	0	1	.500	0	0	0	1	0	0	1.000
1996— New Britain (East.)■ ..	OF	119	440	62	120	23	3	16	59	.273	40	90	10	201	9	9	.959
— Salt Lake (PCL)	OF	13	56	8	19	3	1	1	13	.339	1	11	0	20	0	1	.952
1997— Salt Lake (PCL)	OF	26	82	6	12	1	1	0	5	.146	4	24	2	22	1	1	.958
— New Britain (Eastern) .	OF	103	356	60	84	11	3	3	42	.236	38	94	13	168	5	4	.977

JOHNSON, JASON   P   DEVIL RAYS

PERSONAL: Born October 27, 1973, in Santa Barbara, Calif. ... 6-6/215. ... Throws right, bats right. ... Full name: Jason Michael Johnson.
HIGH SCHOOL: Conner (Hebron, Ky.).
TRANSACTIONS/CAREER NOTES: Signed as non-drafted free agent by Pittsburgh Pirates organization (July 21, 1992). ... Selected by Tampa Bay Devil Rays in first round (14th pick overall) of expansion draft (November 18, 1997).

Year	Team (League)	W	L	Pct.	ERA	G	GS	CG	ShO	Sv.	IP	H	R	ER	BB	SO
1992— GC Pirates (GCL)	2	0	1.000	3.68	5	0	0	0	0	7 1/3	6	3	3	6	3
1993— GC Pirates (GCL)	1	4	.200	2.33	9	9	0	0	0	54	48	22	14	14	39
— Welland (N.Y.-Penn)	1	5	.167	4.63	6	6	1	0	0	35	33	24	18	9	19
1994— Augusta (S. Atl.)	2	12	.143	4.03	20	19	1	0	0	102 2/3	119	67	46	32	69
1995— Augusta (S. Atl.)	3	5	.375	4.36	11	11	1	0	0	53 2/3	57	32	26	17	42
— Lynchburg (Carolina)	1	2	.333	2.05	5	4	0	0	0	22	23	6	5	5	9

Year — Team (League)	W	L	Pct.	ERA	G	GS	CG	ShO	Sv.	IP	H	R	ER	BB	SO
1996— Lynchburg (Carolina)	1	4	.200	6.50	15	5	0	0	0	44 1/3	56	37	32	12	27
— Augusta (S. Atl.).................	4	4	.500	3.11	14	14	1	1	0	84	82	40	29	25	83
1997— Lynchburg (Carolina)	8	4	.667	3.71	17	17	0	0	0	99 1/3	98	43	41	30	92
— Carolina (Southern)	3	3	.500	4.08	9	9	1	0	0	57 1/3	56	31	26	16	63
— Pittsburgh (N.L.)	0	0	. . .	6.00	3	0	0	0	0	6	10	4	4	1	3
Major league totals (1 year)........	0	0	. . .	6.00	3	0	0	0	0	6	10	4	4	1	3

JOHNSON, JONATHON   P   RANGERS

PERSONAL: Born July 16, 1974, in LaGrange, Ga. ... 6-0/180. ... Throws right, bats right. ... Full name: Jonathon Kent Johnson.
HIGH SCHOOL: Forest (Ocala, Fla.).
COLLEGE: Florida State.
TRANSACTIONS/CAREER NOTES: Selected by Texas Rangers organization in first round (seventh pick overall) of free-agent draft (June 1, 1995).

Year — Team (League)	W	L	Pct.	ERA	G	GS	CG	ShO	Sv.	IP	H	R	ER	BB	SO
1995— Charlotte (Fla. St.)	1	5	.167	2.70	8	7	1	0	0	43	34	14	13	16	25
1996— Tulsa (Texas)	*13	10	.565	3.56	26	25	*6	0	0	174 1/3	176	86	69	41	97
— Oklahoma City (A.A.)..........	1	0	1.000	0.00	1	1	1	1	0	9	2	0	0	1	6
1997— Oklahoma City (A.A.)..........	1	8	.111	7.29	13	12	1	0	1	58	83	54	47	29	33
— Tulsa (Texas)	5	4	.556	3.52	10	10	4	0	0	71 2/3	70	35	28	15	47

JOHNSON, LANCE   OF   CUBS

PERSONAL: Born July 6, 1963, in Lincoln Heights, Ohio. ... 5-11/160. ... Bats left, throws left. ... Full name: Kenneth Lance Johnson.
HIGH SCHOOL: Princeton (Cincinnati).
JUNIOR COLLEGE: Triton College (Ill.).
COLLEGE: South Alabama.
TRANSACTIONS/CAREER NOTES: Selected by Pittsburgh Pirates organization in 30th round of free-agent draft (June 8, 1981); did not sign. ... Selected by Seattle Mariners organization in 31st round of free-agent draft (June 7, 1982); did not sign. ... Selected by St. Louis Cardinals organization in sixth round of free-agent draft (June 4, 1984). ... Traded by Cardinals with P Rick Horton and cash to Chicago White Sox for P Jose DeLeon (February 9, 1988). ... Granted free agency (November 8, 1995). ... Signed by New York Mets (December 14, 1995). ... On New York disabled list (May 2-June 16, 1997). ... Traded by Mets with two players to be named later to Chicago Cubs for OF Brian McRae, P Mel Rojas and P Turk Wendell (August 8, 1997); Mets traded P Mark Clark (August 11) and IF Manny Alexander (August 14) to Cubs to complete deal.
RECORDS: Holds major league record for most consecutive years leading league in triples—4 (1991-94). ... Shares A.L. single-season record for fewest errors by outfielder who led league in errors—9 (1993). ... Shares A.L. single-game record for most triples—3 (September 23, 1995).
HONORS: Named American Association Most Valuable Player (1987).
STATISTICAL NOTES: Led New York-Pennsylvania League outfielders with 201 total chances in 1984. ... Led Texas League in caught stealing with 15 in 1986. ... Led American Association outfielders with 333 total chances in 1987. ... Led Pacific Coast League outfielders with five double plays in 1988. ... Led Pacific Coast League outfielders with 273 total chances in 1989. ... Led Pacific Coast League in caught stealing with 18 in 1989. ... Led A.L. in caught stealing with 22 in 1990. ... Led N.L. outfielders with 412 total chances in 1996. ... Had 25-game hitting streak (July 16-August 11, 1992). ... Collected six hits in one game (September 23, 1995). ... Career major league grand slams: 1.

						BATTING								FIELDING		
Year — Team (League)	Pos.	G	AB	R	H	2B	3B	HR	RBI	Avg.	BB	SO	SB	PO	A	E	Avg.
1984— Erie (N.Y.-Penn).........	OF	71	283	*63	*96	7	5	1	28	.339	45	20	29	*188	5	8	.960
1985— St. Petersburg (FSL) ..	OF	129	497	68	134	17	10	2	55	.270	58	39	33	338	16	5	.986
1986— Arkansas (Texas).......	OF	127	445	82	128	24	6	2	33	.288	59	57	*49	262	11	7	.975
1987— Louisville (A.A.).........	OF	116	477	89	159	21	11	5	50	.333	49	45	42	*319	6	*8	.976
— St. Louis (N.L.).........	OF	33	59	4	13	2	1	0	7	.220	4	6	6	27	0	2	.931
1988— Chicago (A.L.)■......	OF-DH	33	124	11	23	4	1	0	6	.185	6	11	6	63	1	2	.970
— Vancouver (PCL)........	OF	100	411	71	126	12	6	2	36	.307	42	52	49	262	9	5	.982
1989— Vancouver (PCL)........	OF	106	408	69	124	11	7	0	28	.304	46	36	33	*261	7	5	.982
— Chicago (A.L.)..........	OF-DH	50	180	28	54	8	2	0	16	.300	17	24	16	113	0	2	.983
1990— Chicago (A.L.)..........	OF-DH	151	541	76	154	18	9	1	51	.285	33	45	36	353	5	10	.973
1991— Chicago (A.L.)..........	OF	159	588	72	161	14	•13	0	49	.274	26	58	26	425	11	2	.995
1992— Chicago (A.L.)..........	OF	157	567	67	158	15	*12	3	47	.279	34	33	41	433	11	6	.987
1993— Chicago (A.L.)..........	OF	147	540	75	168	18	*14	0	47	.311	36	33	35	*427	7	•9	.980
1994— Chicago (A.L.)..........	OF-DH	106	412	56	114	11	*14	3	54	.277	26	23	26	317	1	0	*1.000
1995— Chicago (A.L.)..........	OF-DH	142	*607	98	*186	18	12	10	57	.306	32	31	40	338	8	3	.991
1996— New York (N.L.)■	OF	160	*682	117	*227	31	*21	9	69	.333	33	40	50	*391	9	•12	.971
1997— New York (N.L.)........	OF	72	265	43	82	10	6	1	24	.309	33	21	15	152	4	4	.975
— Chicago (N.L.)■........	OF-DH	39	145	17	44	6	2	4	15	.303	9	10	5	79	0	3	.963
American League totals (8 years)		945	3559	483	1018	106	77	17	327	.286	210	258	226	2469	44	34	.987
National League totals (3 years)		304	1151	181	366	49	30	14	115	.318	79	77	76	649	13	21	.969
Major league totals (11 years)		1249	4710	664	1384	155	107	31	442	.294	289	335	302	3118	57	55	.983

CHAMPIONSHIP SERIES RECORD

						BATTING								FIELDING		
Year — Team (League)	Pos.	G	AB	R	H	2B	3B	HR	RBI	Avg.	BB	SO	SB	PO	A	E	Avg.
1987— St. Louis (N.L.)..........	PR	1	0	1	0	0	0	0	0	. . .	0	0	1	. . .	. . .	. . .	. . .
1993— Chicago (A.L.)	OF	6	23	2	5	1	1	1	6	.217	2	1	1	15	0	0	1.000
Championship series totals (2 years)		7	23	3	5	1	1	1	6	.217	2	1	2	15	0	0	1.000

WORLD SERIES RECORD

						BATTING								FIELDING		
Year — Team (League)	Pos.	G	AB	R	H	2B	3B	HR	RBI	Avg.	BB	SO	SB	PO	A	E	Avg.
1987— St. Louis (N.L.)...........	PR	1	0	0	0	0	0	0	0	. . .	0	0	1	. . .	. . .	. . .	. . .

– 283 –

JOHNSON, MARK — C — WHITE SOX

PERSONAL: Born September 12, 1975, in Wheat Ridge, Colo. ... 6-0/185. ... Bats left, throws right. ... Full name: Mark Landon Johnson.
HIGH SCHOOL: Warner Robins (Ga.).
TRANSACTIONS/CAREER NOTES: Selected by Chicago White Sox organization in first round (26th pick overall) of free-agent draft (June 2, 1994).
STATISTICAL NOTES: Led Carolina League with .420 on-base percentage in 1997. ... Led Carolina League catchers with 1000 total chances and tied for league lead with eight double plays in 1997.

							BATTING							FIELDING		
Year Team (League)	Pos.	G	AB	R	H	2B	3B	HR	RBI	Avg.	BB	SO	SB	PO	A	E	Avg.
1994— GC Whi. Sox (GCL)	C	32	87	10	21	5	0	0	14	.241	14	15	1	182	22	3	.986
1995— Hickory (S. Atl.)	C	107	319	31	58	9	0	2	17	.182	59	52	3	*681	67	11	.986
1996— South Bend (Mid.)	C	67	214	29	55	14	3	2	27	.257	39	25	3	408	37	9	.980
— Prince William (Car.) ..	C	18	58	9	14	3	0	0	3	.241	13	6	0	112	8	1	.992
1997— Win.-Salem (Car.).......	C	120	375	59	95	27	4	4	46	.253	*106	85	4	*899	90	11	*.989

JOHNSON, MARK — 1B — REDS

PERSONAL: Born October 17, 1967, in Worcester, Mass. ... 6-4/230. ... Bats left, throws left. ... Full name: Mark Patrick Johnson.
HIGH SCHOOL: Holy Name (Worcester, Mass.).
COLLEGE: Dartmouth.
TRANSACTIONS/CAREER NOTES: Selected by Pittsburgh Pirates organization in 42nd round of free-agent draft (June 5, 1989); did not sign. ... Selected by Pirates organization in 20th round of free-agent draft (June 4, 1990). ... On Calgary disabled list (August 26-September 8, 1995). ... Calimed on waivers by Cincinnati Reds (August 29, 1997).
HONORS: Named Southern League Most Valuable Player (1994).
STATISTICAL NOTES: Led Southern League with 11 intentional bases on balls received in 1994. ... Career major league grand slams: 1.

							BATTING							FIELDING		
Year Team (League)	Pos.	G	AB	R	H	2B	3B	HR	RBI	Avg.	BB	SO	SB	PO	A	E	Avg.
1990— Welland (NYP)...........	1B	5	8	2	4	1	0	0	2	.500	2	0	0	2	1	0	1.000
— Augusta (S. Atl.)..........	1B	43	144	12	36	7	0	0	19	.250	24	18	4	240	18	5	.981
1991— Augusta (S. Atl.).........	1B	49	139	23	36	7	4	2	25	.259	29	1	15	319	33	9	.975
— Salem (Carolina) ..	1B-OF-3B	37	103	12	26	2	0	2	13	.252	18	25	0	32	28	3	.952
1992— Carolina (Southern)....	1B	122	383	40	89	16	1	7	45	.232	55	94	16	610	41	8	.988
1993— Carolina (Southern)....	1B-OF	125	399	48	93	18	4	14	52	.233	66	93	6	500	40	4	.993
1994— Carolina (Southern)....	1B-OF	111	388	69	107	20	2	*23	85	.276	67	89	6	570	52	6	.990
1995— Pittsburgh (N.L.)	1B	79	221	32	46	6	1	13	28	.208	37	66	5	527	36	8	.986
— Calgary (PCL)	1B	9	23	7	7	4	0	2	8	.304	6	4	1	65	5	2	.972
1996— Pittsburgh (N.L.)	1B-OF	127	343	55	94	24	0	13	47	.274	44	64	6	778	73	6	.993
1997— Pittsburgh (N.L.)	1B-DH	78	219	30	47	10	0	4	29	.215	43	78	1	542	44	5	.992
— Calgary (PCL)	1B-OF	34	115	28	39	11	1	6	16	.339	22	28	4	183	25	0	1.000
— Indianapolis (A.A.)■ ..	1B	3	4	0	0	0	0	0	0	.000	2	2	0	17	2	0	1.000
Major league totals (3 years)		284	783	117	187	40	1	30	104	.239	124	208	12	1847	153	19	.991

JOHNSON, MIKE — P — EXPOS

PERSONAL: Born October 3, 1975, in Edmonton. ... 6-2/175. ... Throws right, bats left. ... Full name: Michael Keith Johnson.
HIGH SCHOOL: Salisbury Composite (Edmonton).
TRANSACTIONS/CAREER NOTES: Selected by Toronto Blue Jays organization in 17th round of free-agent draft (June 3, 1993). ... Selected by San Francisco Giants organization from Toronto Blue Jays organization in Rule 5 major league draft (December 9, 1996). ... Traded by Giants to Baltimore Orioles for cash considerations (December 9, 1996). ... Traded by Orioles to Montreal Expos for a player to be named later (July 31, 1997); Orioles acquired P Everett Stull to complete deal (October 31, 1997).

Year Team (League)	W	L	Pct.	ERA	G	GS	CG	ShO	Sv.	IP	H	R	ER	BB	SO
1993— GC Blue Jays (GCL)...........	0	2	.000	4.87	16	1	0	0	1	44 1/3	51	40	24	22	31
1994— Medicine Hat (Pio.)	1	3	.250	4.46	9	9	0	0	0	36 1/3	48	31	18	22	8
1995— GC Blue Jays (GCL)...........	0	2	.000	7.20	3	3	0	0	0	15	20	15	12	8	13
— Medicine Hat (Pio.)	4	1	.800	3.86	19	0	0	0	3	49	46	26	21	25	32
1996— Hagerstown (S. Atl.)............	11	8	.579	3.15	29	23	5	3	0	162 2/3	157	74	57	39	155
1997— Baltimore (A.L.)■■............	0	1	.000	7.94	14	5	0	0	2	39 2/3	52	36	35	16	29
— Montreal (N.L.)■■...............	2	5	.286	5.94	11	11	0	0	0	50	54	34	33	21	28
A.L. totals (1 year)	0	1	.000	7.94	14	5	0	0	2	39 2/3	52	36	35	16	29
N.L. totals (1 year)	2	5	.286	5.94	11	11	0	0	0	50	54	34	33	21	28
Major league totals (1 year)........	2	6	.250	6.83	25	16	0	0	2	89 2/3	106	70	68	37	57

JOHNSON, RANDY — P — MARINERS

PERSONAL: Born September 10, 1963, in Walnut Creek, Calif. ... 6-10/225. ... Throws left, bats right. ... Full name: Randall David Johnson.
HIGH SCHOOL: Livermore (Calif.).
COLLEGE: Southern California.
TRANSACTIONS/CAREER NOTES: Selected by Atlanta Braves organization in third round of free-agent draft (June 7, 1982); did not sign. ... Selected by Montreal Expos organization in second round of free-agent draft (June 3, 1985). ... Traded by Expos organization with P Brian Holman and P Gene Harris to Seattle Mariners for P Mark Langston and a player to be named later (May 25, 1989); Indianapolis, Expos organization, acquired P Mike Campbell to complete deal (July 31, 1989). ... On disabled list (June 11-27, 1992). ... On Seattle disabled list (May 15-August 6 and August 27, 1996-remainder of season); included rehabilitation assignment to Everett (August 3-6).
RECORDS: Shares major league single-game record for most strikeouts by lefthander—19 (June 24 and August 8, 1997). ... Shares A.L. record for most strikeouts in two consecutive games—32 (August 8 [19] and 15 [13], 1997, 17 innings).

HONORS: Named A.L. Pitcher of the Year by THE SPORTING NEWS (1995). ... Named lefthanded pitcher on THE SPORTING NEWS A.L. All-Star team (1995 and 1997). ... Named A.L. Cy Young Award winner by Baseball Writers' Association of America (1995).

STATISTICAL NOTES: Led American Association with 20 balks in 1988. ... Pitched 2-0 no-hit victory against Detroit (June 2, 1990). ... Pitched 4-0 one-hit, complete-game victory against Oakland (August 14, 1991). ... Struck out 15 batters in one game (September 16, 1992; June 14 and September 16, 1993; June 4 and August 11, 1994; June 24 and September 23, 1995; May 28 and June 8, 1997). ... Struck out 18 batters in one game (September 27, 1992). ... Led A.L. with 18 hit batsmen in 1992 and 16 in 1993. ... Pitched 7-0 one-hit, complete-game victory against Oakland (May 16, 1993). ... Struck out 16 batters in one game (July 15, 1995 and July 18, 1997). ... Struck out 19 batters in one game (June 24 and August 8, 1997).

MISCELLANEOUS: Holds Seattle Mariners franchise all-time records for lowest earned-run average (3.37), most innings pitched (1,678 $^1/_3$), most strikeouts (1,949), most shutouts (17) and highest winning percentage (.654). ... Appeared in one game as outfielder with no chances (1993).

Year Team (League)	W	L	Pct.	ERA	G	GS	CG	ShO	Sv.	IP	H	R	ER	BB	SO
1985—Jamestown (NYP)	0	3	.000	5.93	8	8	0	0	0	27 $^1/_3$	29	22	18	24	21
1986—W.P. Beach (FSL)	8	7	.533	3.16	26	•26	2	1	0	119 $^2/_3$	89	49	42	*94	133
1987—Jacksonville (Southern)	11	8	.579	3.73	25	24	0	0	0	140	100	63	58	128	*163
1988—Indianapolis (A.A.)	8	7	.533	3.26	20	19	0	0	0	113 $^1/_3$	85	52	41	72	111
—Montreal (N.L.)	3	0	1.000	2.42	4	4	1	0	0	26	23	8	7	7	25
1989—Montreal (N.L.)	0	4	.000	6.67	7	6	0	0	0	29 $^2/_3$	29	25	22	26	26
—Indianapolis (A.A.)	1	1	.500	2.00	3	3	0	0	0	18	13	5	4	9	17
—Seattle (A.L.)■	7	9	.438	4.40	22	22	2	0	0	131	118	75	64	70	104
1990—Seattle (A.L.)	14	11	.560	3.65	33	33	5	2	0	219 $^2/_3$	174	103	89	*120	194
1991—Seattle (A.L.)	13	10	.565	3.98	33	33	2	1	0	201 $^1/_3$	151	96	89	*152	228
1992—Seattle (A.L.)	12	14	.462	3.77	31	31	6	2	0	210 $^1/_3$	154	104	88	*144	*241
1993—Seattle (A.L.)	19	8	.704	3.24	35	34	10	3	1	255 $^1/_3$	185	97	92	99	*308
1994—Seattle (A.L.)	13	6	.684	3.19	23	23	*9	*4	0	172	132	65	61	72	*204
1995—Seattle (A.L.)	18	2	*.900	*2.48	30	30	6	3	0	214 $^1/_3$	159	65	59	65	*294
1996—Seattle (A.L.)	5	0	1.000	3.67	14	8	0	0	1	61 $^1/_3$	48	27	25	25	85
—Everett (Northwest)	0	0	...	0.00	1	1	0	0	0	2	0	0	0	0	5
1997—Seattle (A.L.)	20	4	*.833	2.28	30	29	5	2	0	213	147	60	54	77	291
A.L. totals (9 years)	121	64	.654	3.33	251	243	45	17	2	1678 $^1/_3$	1268	692	621	824	1949
N.L. totals (2 years)	3	4	.429	4.69	11	10	1	0	0	55 $^2/_3$	52	33	29	33	51
Major league totals (10 years)	124	68	.646	3.37	262	253	46	17	2	1734	1320	725	650	857	2000

DIVISION SERIES RECORD

RECORDS: Holds single-game record for most strikeouts—13 (October 5, 1997). ... Holds career record for most strikeouts—32.

Year Team (League)	W	L	Pct.	ERA	G	GS	CG	ShO	Sv.	IP	H	R	ER	BB	SO
1995—Seattle (A.L.)	2	0	1.000	2.70	2	1	0	0	0	10	5	3	3	6	16
1997—Seattle (A.L.)	0	2	.000	5.54	2	2	1	0	0	13	14	8	8	6	16
Div. series totals (2 years)	2	2	.500	4.30	4	3	1	0	0	23	19	11	11	12	32

CHAMPIONSHIP SERIES RECORD

Year Team (League)	W	L	Pct.	ERA	G	GS	CG	ShO	Sv.	IP	H	R	ER	BB	SO
1995—Seattle (A.L.)	0	1	.000	2.35	2	2	0	0	0	15 $^1/_3$	12	6	4	2	13

ALL-STAR GAME RECORD

Year League	W	L	Pct.	ERA	GS	CG	ShO	Sv.	IP	H	R	ER	BB	SO
1990— American				Did not play.										
1993— American	0	0	...	0.00	0	0	0	0	2	0	0	0	0	1
1994— American	0	0	...	9.00	0	0	0	0	1	2	1	1	0	0
1995— American	0	0	...	0.00	1	0	0	0	2	0	0	0	1	3
1997— American	0	0	...	0.00	1	0	0	0	2	0	0	0	1	2
All-Star totals (4 years)	0	0	...	1.29	2	0	0	0	7	2	1	1	2	6

JOHNSON, RUSS   3B   ASTROS

PERSONAL: Born February 22, 1973, in Baton Rouge, La. ... 5-10/180. ... Bats right, throws right.
HIGH SCHOOL: Denham Springs (La.)
COLLEGE: Louisiana State.
TRANSACTIONS/CAREER NOTES: Selected by Houston Astros organization in supplemental round ("sandwich pick" between first and second round, 30th pick overall) of free-agent draft (June 2, 1994); pick received as part of compensation for San Francisco Giants signing Type A free-agent P Mark Portugal.
STATISTICAL NOTES: Led Texas League shortstops with 664 total chances and 87 double plays in 1995.

Year Team (League)	Pos.	G	AB	R	H	2B	3B	HR	RBI	Avg.	BB	SO	SB	PO	A	E	Avg.
1995—Jackson (Texas)	SS	132	475	65	118	16	2	9	53	.248	50	60	10	182	383	13	.978
1996—Jackson (Texas)	SS	132	496	86	154	24	5	15	74	.310	56	50	5	219	411	34	.949
1997—New Orleans (A.A.)	3B-SS	122	445	72	123	16	6	4	49	.276	66	78	7	86	269	21	.944
—Houston (N.L.)	3B-2B	21	60	7	18	1	0	2	9	.300	6	14	1	13	24	1	.974
Major league totals (1 year)		21	60	7	18	1	0	2	9	.300	6	14	1	13	24	1	.974

DIVISION SERIES RECORD

Year Team (League)	Pos.	G	AB	R	H	2B	3B	HR	RBI	Avg.	BB	SO	SB	PO	A	E	Avg.
1997—Houston (N.L.)	PH	1	1	0	0	0	0	0	0	.000	0	1	0	0	0	0	...

JOHNSTONE, JOHN   P   GIANTS

PERSONAL: Born November 25, 1968, in Liverpool, N.Y. ... 6-3/195. ... Throws right, bats right. ... Full name: John William Johnstone.
HIGH SCHOOL: Bishop Ludden (Syracuse, N.Y.).
JUNIOR COLLEGE: Onondaga Community College (N.Y.).

TRANSACTIONS/CAREER NOTES: Selected by New York Mets organization in 20th round of free-agent draft (June 2, 1987). ... On disabled list (June 24-July 7, 1992). ... Selected by Florida Marlins in second round (31st pick overall) of expansion draft (November 17, 1992). ... On disabled list (May 8, 1995-remainder of season). ... Granted free agency (December 21, 1995). ... Signed by Houston Astros organization (December 28, 1995). ... Granted free agency (September 30, 1996). ... Signed by San Francisco Giants organization (December 17, 1996). ... Claimed on waivers by Oakland Athletics (August 7, 1997). ... Granted free agency (August 31, 1997). ... Signed by Giants organization (September 1, 1997).

Year Team (League)	W	L	Pct.	ERA	G	GS	CG	ShO	Sv.	IP	H	R	ER	BB	SO
1987— Kingsport (Appalachian)	1	1	.500	7.45	17	1	0	0	0	29	42	28	24	20	21
1988— GC Mets (GCL)	3	4	.429	2.68	12	12	3	0	0	74	65	29	22	25	57
1989— Pittsfield (NYP)	*11	2	.846	2.77	15	15	2	1	0	104	101	47	32	28	60
1990— St. Lucie (Fla. St.)	*15	6	.714	2.24	25	25	*9	3	0	172 2/3	145	53	43	60	120
1991— Williamsport (Eastern)	7	9	.438	3.97	27	•27	2	0	0	165 1/3	159	94	73	79	100
1992— Binghamton (Eastern)	7	7	.500	3.74	24	24	2	0	0	149 1/3	132	66	62	36	121
1993— Edmonton (PCL)■	4	*15	.211	5.18	30	21	1	0	4	144 1/3	167	95	83	59	126
— Florida (N.L.)	0	2	.000	5.91	7	0	0	0	0	10 2/3	16	8	7	7	5
1994— Edmonton (PCL)	5	3	.625	4.46	29	0	0	0	4	42 1/3	46	23	21	9	43
— Florida (N.L.)	1	2	.333	5.91	17	0	0	0	0	21 1/3	23	20	14	16	23
1995— Florida (N.L.)	0	0	...	3.86	4	0	0	0	0	4 2/3	7	2	2	2	3
1996— Tucson (PCL)■	3	3	.500	3.42	45	1	0	0	5	55 1/3	59	27	21	22	70
— Houston (N.L.)	1	0	1.000	5.54	9	0	0	0	0	13	17	8	8	5	5
1997— Phoenix (PCL)■	0	3	.000	4.03	38	0	0	0	*24	38	34	17	17	15	30
— San Francisco (N.L.)	0	0	...	3.38	13	0	0	0	0	18 2/3	15	7	7	7	15
— Oakland (A.L.)■	0	0	...	2.84	5	0	0	0	0	6 1/3	7	2	2	7	4
A.L. totals (1 year)	0	0	...	2.84	5	0	0	0	0	6 1/3	7	2	2	7	4
N.L. totals (5 years)	2	4	.333	5.00	50	0	0	0	0	68 1/3	78	45	38	37	51
Major league totals (5 years)	2	4	.333	4.82	55	0	0	0	0	74 2/3	85	47	40	44	55

JONES, ANDRUW — OF — BRAVES

PERSONAL: Born April 23, 1977, in Wellemstad, Curacao. ... 6-1/185. ... Bats right, throws right. ... Full name: Andruw Rudolf Jones.
HIGH SCHOOL: St. Paulus (Willemstad, Curacao).
TRANSACTIONS/CAREER NOTES: Signed as non-drafted free agent by Atlanta Braves organization (July 1, 1993).
HONORS: Named South Atlantic League Most Valuable Player (1995).
STATISTICAL NOTES: Led South Atlantic League with nine sacrifice flies in 1995. ... Led South Atlantic League outfielders with 246 total chances and tied for lead with four double plays in 1995. ... Career major league grand slams: 1.

Year Team (League)	Pos.	G	AB	R	H	2B	3B	HR	RBI	Avg.	BB	SO	SB	PO	A	E	Avg.
1994— GC Braves (GCL)	OF	27	95	22	21	5	1	2	10	.221	16	19	5	90	0	3	.968
— Danville (Appal.)	OF	36	143	20	48	9	2	1	16	.336	9	25	16	81	3	2	.977
1995— Macon (S. Atl.)	OF	•139	537	*104	149	41	5	25	100	.277	70	122	*56	*332	10	4	.988
1996— Durham (Carolina)	OF	66	243	65	76	14	3	17	43	.313	42	54	16	174	9	7	.963
— Greenville (Southern)	OF	38	157	39	58	10	1	12	37	.369	17	34	12	129	7	1	.993
— Richmond (Int'l)	OF	12	45	11	17	3	1	5	12	.378	1	9	2	34	1	1	.972
— Atlanta (N.L.)	OF	31	106	11	23	7	1	5	13	.217	7	29	3	73	4	2	.975
1997— Atlanta (N.L.)	OF	153	399	60	92	18	1	18	70	.231	56	107	20	287	14	7	.977
Major league totals (2 years)		184	505	71	115	25	2	23	83	.228	63	136	23	360	18	9	.977

DIVISION SERIES RECORD

Year Team (League)	Pos.	G	AB	R	H	2B	3B	HR	RBI	Avg.	BB	SO	SB	PO	A	E	Avg.
1996— Atlanta (N.L.)	OF-PR	3	0	0	0	0	0	0	0	...	1	0	0	2	0	0	1.000
1997— Atlanta (N.L.)	OF	3	5	1	0	0	0	0	1	.000	1	1	0	10	0	0	1.000
Division series totals (2 years)		6	5	1	0	0	0	0	1	.000	2	1	0	12	0	0	1.000

CHAMPIONSHIP SERIES RECORD

Year Team (League)	Pos.	G	AB	R	H	2B	3B	HR	RBI	Avg.	BB	SO	SB	PO	A	E	Avg.
1996— Atlanta (N.L.)	OF-PR-PH	5	9	3	2	0	0	1	3	.222	3	2	0	5	0	0	1.000
1997— Atlanta (N.L.)	OF-PH	5	9	0	4	0	0	0	1	.444	1	1	0	12	1	0	1.000
Championship series totals (2 years)		10	18	3	6	0	0	1	4	.333	4	3	0	17	1	0	1.000

WORLD SERIES RECORD

RECORDS: Shares record for most home runs in two consecutive innings—2 (October 20, 1996, second and third innings).
NOTES: Hit home runs in first two at-bats (October 20, 1996, second and third innings).

Year Team (League)	Pos.	G	AB	R	H	2B	3B	HR	RBI	Avg.	BB	SO	SB	PO	A	E	Avg.
1996— Atlanta (N.L.)	OF	6	20	4	8	1	0	2	6	.400	3	6	1	7	1	0	1.000

JONES, BOBBY — P — METS

PERSONAL: Born February 10, 1970, in Fresno, Calif. ... 6-4/225. ... Throws right, bats right. ... Full name: Robert Joseph Jones.
HIGH SCHOOL: Fresno (Calif.).
COLLEGE: Fresno State.
TRANSACTIONS/CAREER NOTES: Selected by New York Mets organization in supplemental round ("sandwich pick" between first and second round, 36th pick overall) of free-agent draft (June 3, 1991); pick received as part of compensation for Los Angeles Dodgers signing Type A free-agent OF Darryl Strawberry.
HONORS: Named Eastern League Pitcher of the Year (1992).
STATISTICAL NOTES: Led International League with 11 hit batsmen in 1993. ... Led N.L. with 18 sacrifice hits in 1995.

Year Team (League)	W	L	Pct.	ERA	G	GS	CG	ShO	Sv.	IP	H	R	ER	BB	SO
1991— Columbia (S. Atl.)	3	1	.750	1.85	5	5	5	0	0	24 1/3	20	5	5	3	35
1992— Binghamton (Eastern)	12	4	.750	*1.88	24	24	4	*4	0	158	118	40	33	43	143
1993— Norfolk (Int'l)	12	10	.545	3.63	24	24	6	*3	0	166	149	72	67	32	126
— New York (N.L.)	2	4	.333	3.65	9	9	0	0	0	61 2/3	61	35	25	22	35
1994— New York (N.L.)	12	7	.632	3.15	24	24	1	1	0	160	157	75	56	56	80
1995— New York (N.L.)	10	10	.500	4.19	30	30	3	1	0	195 2/3	209	107	91	53	127
1996— New York (N.L.)	12	8	.600	4.42	31	31	3	1	0	195 2/3	219	102	96	46	116
1997— New York (N.L.)	15	9	.625	3.63	30	30	2	1	0	193 1/3	177	88	78	63	125
Major league totals (5 years)	51	38	.573	3.86	124	124	9	4	0	806 1/3	823	407	346	240	483

ALL-STAR GAME RECORD

Year League	W	L	Pct.	ERA	GS	CG	ShO	Sv.	IP	H	R	ER	BB	SO
1997— National	0	0	...	0.00	0	0	0	0	1	1	0	0	0	2

JONES, BOBBY   P   ROCKIES

PERSONAL: Born April 11, 1972, in Orange, N.J. ... 6-0/175. ... Throws left, bats right. ... Full name: Robert M. Jones.
HIGH SCHOOL: Rutherford (N.J.).
JUNIOR COLLEGE: Chipola Junior College (Fla.).
TRANSACTIONS/CAREER NOTES: Selected by Milwaukee Brewers organization in 44th round of free-agent draft (June 3, 1991). ... Selected by Colorado Rockies organization from Brewers organization in Rule 5 minor league draft (December 5, 1994).
STATISTICAL NOTES: Tied for Pacific Coast League lead with 12 hit batsmen in 1997.

Year Team (League)	W	L	Pct.	ERA	G	GS	CG	ShO	Sv.	IP	H	R	ER	BB	SO
1992— Helena (Pioneer)	5	4	.556	4.36	14	13	1	0	0	76 1/3	93	51	37	23	53
1993— Beloit (Midwest)	10	10	.500	4.11	25	25	4	0	0	144 2/3	159	82	66	65	115
1994— Stockton (California)	6	12	.333	4.21	26	26	2	0	0	147 2/3	131	90	69	64	147
1995— New Haven (Eastern)■	5	2	.714	2.58	27	8	0	0	3	73 1/3	61	27	21	36	70
— Colo. Springs (PCL)	1	2	.333	7.30	11	8	0	0	0	40 2/3	50	38	33	33	48
1996— Colo. Springs (PCL)	2	8	.200	4.97	57	0	0	0	3	88 2/3	88	54	49	63	78
1997— Colo. Springs (PCL)	7	11	.389	5.14	25	21	0	0	0	133	135	89	76	71	104
— Colorado (N.L.)	1	1	.500	8.38	4	4	0	0	0	19 1/3	30	18	18	12	5
Major league totals (1 year)	1	1	.500	8.38	4	4	0	0	0	19 1/3	30	18	18	12	5

JONES, CHIPPER   3B   BRAVES

PERSONAL: Born April 24, 1972, in De Land, Fla. ... 6-3/195. ... Bats both, throws right. ... Full name: Larry Wayne Jones.
HIGH SCHOOL: The Bolles School (Jacksonville).
TRANSACTIONS/CAREER NOTES: Selected by Atlanta Braves organization in first round (first pick overall) of free-agent draft (June 4, 1990). ... On Atlanta disabled list (March 20, 1994-entire season). ... On disabled list (March 22-April 6, 1996).
HONORS: Named N.L. Rookie Player of the Year by THE SPORTING NEWS (1995).
STATISTICAL NOTES: Led South Atlantic League with 10 sacrifice flies in 1991. ... Led South Atlantic League shortstops with 692 total chances and 71 double plays in 1991. ... Led International League with 268 total bases in 1993. ... Led International League shortstops with 619 total chances in 1993. ... Career major league grand slams: 3.

Year Team (League)	Pos.	G	AB	R	H	2B	3B	HR	RBI	Avg.	BB	SO	SB	PO	A	E	Avg.
1990— GC Braves (GCL)	SS	44	140	20	32	1	1	1	18	.229	14	25	5	64	140	18	.919
1991— Macon (S. Atl.)	SS	136	473	*104	154	24	11	15	98	.326	69	70	40	*217	*419	56	.919
1992— Durham (Carolina)	SS	70	264	43	73	22	1	4	31	.277	31	34	10	106	200	14	.956
— Greenville (Southern)	SS	67	266	43	92	17	11	9	42	.346	11	32	14	92	218	18	.945
1993— Richmond (Int'l)	SS	139	536	*97	*174	31	*12	13	89	.325	57	70	23	195	381	*43	.931
— Atlanta (N.L.)	SS	8	3	2	2	1	0	0	0	.667	1	1	0	1	1	0	1.000
1994—								Did not play.									
1995— Atlanta (N.L.)	3B-OF	140	524	87	139	22	3	23	86	.265	73	99	8	103	255	25	.935
1996— Atlanta (N.L.)	3B-SS-OF	157	598	114	185	32	5	30	110	.309	87	88	14	103	288	17	.958
1997— Atlanta (N.L.)	3B-OF	157	597	100	176	41	3	21	111	.295	76	88	20	83	241	15	.956
Major league totals (4 years)		462	1722	303	502	96	11	74	307	.292	237	276	42	290	785	57	.950

DIVISION SERIES RECORD

RECORDS: Shares single-game record for most home runs—2 (October 3, 1995). ... Holds N.L. career records for highest slugging percentage (20 or more at-bats)—.771; most hits—13; most home runs—4; and most bases on balls—8. ... Shares N.L. career records for most games—10; and most runs 9.

Year Team (League)	Pos.	G	AB	R	H	2B	3B	HR	RBI	Avg.	BB	SO	SB	PO	A	E	Avg.
1995— Atlanta (N.L.)	3B	4	18	4	7	2	0	2	4	.389	2	2	0	3	4	0	1.000
1996— Atlanta (N.L.)	3B	3	9	2	2	0	0	1	2	.222	3	4	1	1	3	0	1.000
1997— Atlanta (N.L.)	3B	3	8	3	4	0	0	1	2	.500	3	2	1	2	3	1	.833
Division series totals (3 years)		10	35	9	13	2	0	4	8	.371	8	8	2	6	10	1	.941

CHAMPIONSHIP SERIES RECORD

RECORDS: Shares single-series record for most singles—9 (1996). ... Shares single-game record for most singles—4 (October 9, 1996). ... Holds N.L. career record for highest batting average—.385.

Year Team (League)	Pos.	G	AB	R	H	2B	3B	HR	RBI	Avg.	BB	SO	SB	PO	A	E	Avg.
1995— Atlanta (N.L.)	3B	4	16	3	7	0	0	1	3	.438	3	1	1	4	13	0	1.000
1996— Atlanta (N.L.)	3B	7	25	6	11	2	0	0	4	.440	2	1	1	5	7	1	.923
1997— Atlanta (N.L.)	3B	6	24	5	7	1	0	2	4	.292	2	3	0	1	8	0	1.000
Championship series totals (3 years)		17	65	14	25	3	0	3	11	.385	8	5	2	10	28	1	.974

WORLD SERIES RECORD

NOTES: Member of World Series championship team (1995).

Year Team (League)	Pos.	G	AB	R	H	2B	3B	HR	RBI	Avg.	BB	SO	SB	PO	A	E	Avg.
1995—Atlanta (N.L.)	3B	6	21	3	6	3	0	0	1	.286	4	3	0	6	12	1	.947
1996—Atlanta (N.L.)	3B-SS	6	21	3	6	3	0	0	3	.286	4	2	0	4	7	0	1.000
World Series totals (2 years)		12	42	6	12	6	0	0	4	.286	8	5	0	10	19	1	.967

ALL-STAR GAME RECORD

Year League	Pos.	AB	R	H	2B	3B	HR	RBI	Avg.	BB	SO	SB	PO	A	E	Avg.
1997—National	3B	1	0	0	0	0	0	0	.000	0	0	0	0	1	0	1.000

J

JONES, CHRIS OF DIAMONDBACKS

PERSONAL: Born December 16, 1965, in Utica, N.Y. ... 6-2/205. ... Bats right, throws right. ... Full name: Christopher Carlos Jones.
HIGH SCHOOL: Liverpool (N.Y.).
TRANSACTIONS/CAREER NOTES: Selected by Cincinnati Reds organization in third round of free-agent draft (June 4, 1984). ... Released by Reds (December 13, 1991). ... Signed by Houston Astros organization (December 19, 1991). ... Granted free agency (October 16, 1992). ... Signed by Colorado Rockies (October 26, 1992). ... Granted free agency (December 20, 1993). ... Re-signed by Rockies organization (December 22, 1993). ... Granted free agency (October 15, 1994). ... Signed by New York Mets (December 7, 1994). ... Granted free agency (October 15, 1996). ... Signed by San Diego Padres (November 4, 1996). ... On disabled list (May 22-June 10, 1997). ... Granted free agency (October 6, 1997). ... Signed by Arizona Diamondbacks (November 19, 1997).

Year Team (League)	Pos.	G	AB	R	H	2B	3B	HR	RBI	Avg.	BB	SO	SB	PO	A	E	Avg.
1984—Billings (Pioneer)	3B	21	73	8	11	2	0	2	13	.151	2	24	4	6	27	5	.868
1985—Billings (Pioneer)	OF	63	240	43	62	12	5	4	33	.258	19	72	13	112	4	*13	.899
1986—Cedar Rap. (Midw.)	OF	128	473	65	117	13	9	20	78	.247	20	126	23	218	15	11	.955
1987—Vermont (Eastern)	OF	113	383	50	88	11	4	10	39	.230	23	99	13	207	12	8	.965
1988—Chattanooga (Sou.)	OF	116	410	50	111	20	7	4	61	.271	29	102	11	185	15	8	.962
1989—Chattanooga (Sou.)	OF	103	378	47	95	18	2	10	54	.251	23	68	10	197	8	7	.967
—Nashville (A.A.)	OF	21	49	8	8	1	0	2	5	.163	0	16	2	25	0	1	.962
1990—Nashville (A.A.)	OF	134	436	53	114	23	3	10	52	.261	23	86	12	209	17	8	.966
1991—Nashville (A.A.)	OF	73	267	29	65	5	4	9	33	.243	19	65	10	110	5	6	.950
—Cincinnati (N.L.)	OF	52	89	14	26	1	2	2	6	.292	2	31	2	27	1	0	1.000
1992—Houston (N.L.)■	OF	54	63	7	12	2	1	1	4	.190	7	21	3	27	0	2	.931
—Tucson (PCL)	OF	45	170	25	55	9	8	3	28	.324	18	34	7	86	7	2	.979
1993—Colo. Springs (PCL)■	OF	46	168	41	47	5	5	12	40	.280	19	47	8	107	5	3	.974
—Colorado (N.L.)	OF	86	209	29	57	11	4	6	31	.273	10	48	9	114	2	2	.983
1994—Colo. Springs (PCL)	OF	98	386	77	124	22	4	20	75	.321	35	72	12	191	11	*15	.931
—Colorado (N.L.)	OF	21	40	6	12	2	1	0	2	.300	2	14	0	16	0	1	.941
1995—Norfolk (Int'l)■	OF	33	114	20	38	12	1	3	19	.333	11	20	5	62	4	1	.985
—New York (N.L.)	OF-1B	79	182	33	51	6	2	8	31	.280	13	45	2	122	6	2	.985
1996—New York (N.L.)	OF-1B	89	149	22	36	7	0	4	18	.242	12	42	1	83	1	3	.966
1997—San Diego (N.L.)■	OF	92	152	24	37	9	0	7	25	.243	16	45	7	73	4	4	.951
Major league totals (7 years)		473	884	135	231	38	10	28	117	.261	62	246	24	462	14	14	.971

JONES, DAX OF ASTROS

PERSONAL: Born August 4, 1970, in Pittsburgh. ... 6-0/180. ... Bats right, throws right. ... Full name: Dax Xenos Jones.
HIGH SCHOOL: Waukegan (Ill.) West.
COLLEGE: Creighton.
TRANSACTIONS/CAREER NOTES: Selected by Toronto Blue Jays organization in 49th round of free-agent draft (June 1, 1988); did not sign. ... Selected by San Francisco Giants organization in eighth round of free-agent draft (June 3, 1991). ... On Clinton disabled list (May 22-June 13, 1992). ... On disabled list (July 7-28, 1994). ... Granted free agency (October 15, 1997). ... Signed by Houston Astros organization (December 22, 1997).
STATISTICAL NOTES: Tied for Northwest League lead in double plays by outfielder with two in 1991.

Year Team (League)	Pos.	G	AB	R	H	2B	3B	HR	RBI	Avg.	BB	SO	SB	PO	A	E	Avg.
1991—Everett (N'west)	OF	53	180	42	55	5	•6	5	29	.306	27	26	15	77	•10	6	.935
1992—Clinton (Midwest)	OF	79	295	45	88	12	4	1	42	.298	21	32	18	159	13	8	.956
—Shreveport (Texas)	OF	19	66	10	20	0	2	1	7	.303	4	6	2	24	3	3	.900
1993—Shreveport (Texas)	OF	118	436	59	124	19	5	4	36	.284	26	53	13	236	13	7	.973
1994—Phoenix (PCL)	OF	111	399	55	111	25	5	4	52	.278	21	42	16	283	*21	7	.977
1995—Phoenix (PCL)	OF	112	404	47	108	21	3	2	45	.267	31	52	11	284	9	6	.980
1996—Phoenix (PCL)	OF	74	298	52	92	20	6	6	41	.309	19	21	13	178	9	0	1.000
—San Francisco (N.L.)	OF	34	58	7	10	0	2	1	7	.172	8	12	2	46	1	0	1.000
1997—Phoenix (PCL)	OF	93	271	48	69	7	5	3	28	.255	39	39	9	146	6	5	.968
Major league totals (1 year)		34	58	7	10	0	2	1	7	.172	8	12	2	46	1	0	1.000

JONES, DOUG P BREWERS

PERSONAL: Born June 24, 1957, in Covina, Calif. ... 6-2/225. ... Throws right, bats right. ... Full name: Douglas Reid Jones.
HIGH SCHOOL: Lebanon (Ind.).
JUNIOR COLLEGE: Central Arizona College.
COLLEGE: Butler.

TRANSACTIONS/CAREER NOTES: Selected by Milwaukee Brewers organization in third round of free-agent draft (January 10, 1978). ... On disabled list (June 20-July 12, 1978). ... On Vancouver disabled list (April 11-September 1, 1983 and April 25-May 30, 1984). ... Granted free agency (October 15, 1984). ... Signed by Waterbury, Cleveland Indians organization (April 3, 1985). ... Granted free agency (December 20, 1991). ... Signed by Houston Astros organization (January 24, 1992). ... Traded by Astros with P Jeff Juden to Philadelphia Phillies for P Mitch Williams (December 2, 1993). ... Granted free agency (October 15, 1994). ... Signed by Baltimore Orioles (April 8, 1995). ... Granted free agency (November 3, 1995). ... Signed by Chicago Cubs (December 28, 1995). ... Released by Cubs (June 15, 1996). ... Signed by New Orleans, Brewers organization (June 28, 1996). ... Granted free agency (November 6, 1996). ... Re-signed by Brewers (December 7, 1996). ... On disabled list (July 16-August 3, 1997). ... Granted free agency (October 27, 1997). ... Re-signed by Brewers (November 18, 1997).

HONORS: Named N.L. co-Fireman of the Year by THE SPORTING NEWS (1992).

MISCELLANEOUS: Holds Cleveland Indians all-time record for most saves (128).

Year Team (League)	W	L	Pct.	ERA	G	GS	CG	ShO	Sv.	IP	H	R	ER	BB	SO
1978— Newark (N.Y.-Penn)	2	4	.333	5.21	15	3	1	0	2	38	49	30	22	15	27
1979— Burlington (Midw.)	10	10	.500	*1.75	28	20	*16	•3	0	*190	144	63	37	73	115
1980— Stockton (California)	6	2	.750	2.84	11	11	5	1	0	76	63	32	24	31	54
— Vancouver (PCL)	3	2	.600	3.23	8	8	1	1	0	53	52	19	19	15	28
— Holyoke (Eastern)	5	3	.625	2.90	8	8	4	2	0	62	57	23	20	26	39
1981— El Paso (Texas)	5	7	.417	5.80	15	15	3	1	0	90	121	67	58	28	62
— Vancouver (PCL)	5	3	.625	3.04	11	10	2	0	0	80	79	29	27	22	38
1982— Milwaukee (A.L.)	0	0	. . .	10.13	4	0	0	0	0	2 2/3	5	3	3	1	1
— Vancouver (PCL)	5	8	.385	2.97	23	9	4	0	2	106	109	48	35	31	60
1983— Vancouver (PCL)	0	1	.000	10.29	3	1	0	0	0	7	10	8	8	5	4
1984— Vancouver (PCL)	1	0	1.000	10.13	3	0	0	0	0	8	9	9	9	3	2
— El Paso (Texas)	6	8	.429	4.28	16	16	7	0	0	109 1/3	120	61	52	35	62
1985— Waterbury (Eastern)■	9	4	.692	3.65	39	1	0	0	7	116	123	59	47	36	113
1986— Maine (International)	5	6	.455	*2.09	43	3	0	0	9	116 1/3	105	35	27	27	98
— Cleveland (A.L.)	1	0	1.000	2.50	11	0	0	0	1	18	18	5	5	6	12
1987— Cleveland (A.L.)	6	5	.545	3.15	49	0	0	0	8	91 1/3	101	45	32	24	87
— Buffalo (A.A.)	5	2	.714	2.04	23	0	0	0	7	61 2/3	49	18	14	12	61
1988— Cleveland (A.L.)	3	4	.429	2.27	51	0	0	0	37	83 1/3	69	26	21	16	72
1989— Cleveland (A.L.)	7	10	.412	2.34	59	0	0	0	32	80 2/3	76	25	21	13	65
1990— Cleveland (A.L.)	5	5	.500	2.56	66	0	0	0	43	84 1/3	66	26	24	22	55
1991— Cleveland (A.L.)	4	8	.333	5.54	36	4	0	0	7	63 1/3	87	42	39	17	48
— Colo. Springs (PCL)	2	2	.500	3.28	17	2	1	1	7	35 2/3	30	14	13	5	29
1992— Houston (N.L.)■	11	8	.579	1.85	80	0	0	0	36	111 2/3	96	29	23	17	93
1993— Houston (N.L.)	4	10	.286	4.54	71	0	0	0	26	85 1/3	102	46	43	21	66
1994— Philadelphia (N.L.)■	2	4	.333	2.17	47	0	0	0	27	54	55	14	13	6	38
1995— Baltimore (A.L.)■	0	4	.000	5.01	52	0	0	0	22	46 2/3	55	30	26	16	42
1996— Chicago (N.L.)■	2	2	.500	5.01	28	0	0	0	2	32 1/3	41	20	18	7	26
— New Orleans (A.A.)■	0	3	.000	3.75	13	0	0	0	6	24	28	10	10	6	17
— Milwaukee (A.L.)	5	0	1.000	3.41	24	0	0	0	1	31 2/3	31	13	12	13	34
1997— Milwaukee (A.L.)	6	6	.500	2.02	75	0	0	0	36	80 1/3	62	20	18	9	82
A.L. totals (10 years)	37	42	.468	3.11	427	4	0	0	187	582 1/3	570	235	201	137	498
N.L. totals (4 years)	19	24	.442	3.08	226	0	0	0	91	283 1/3	294	109	97	51	223
Major league totals (13 years)	56	66	.459	3.10	653	4	0	0	278	865 2/3	864	344	298	188	721

ALL-STAR GAME RECORD

Year League	W	L	Pct.	ERA	GS	CG	ShO	Sv.	IP	H	R	ER	BB	SO
1988— American	0	0	. . .	0.00	0	0	0	0	2/3	0	0	0	0	1
1989— American	0	0	. . .	0.00	0	0	0	1	1 1/3	1	0	0	0	0
1990— American							Did not play.							
1992— National	0	0	. . .	27.00	0	0	0	0	1	4	3	3	0	2
1994— National	1	0	1.000	0.00	0	0	0	0	1	2	0	0	0	2
All-Star totals (4 years)	1	0	1.000	6.75	0	0	0	1	4	7	3	3	0	5

JONES, JACQUE   OF   TWINS

PERSONAL: Born April 25, 1975, in San Diego. ... 5-10/175. ... Bats left, throws left. ... Full name: Jacque Dewayne Jones.
HIGH SCHOOL: San Diego.
COLLEGE: Southern California.
TRANSACTIONS/CAREER NOTES: Selected by Minnesota Twins organization in second round of free-agent draft (June 2, 1996).

Year Team (League)	Pos.	G	AB	R	H	2B	3B	HR	RBI	Avg.	BB	SO	SB	PO	A	E	Avg.
1996— Fort Myers (FSL)	OF	1	3	0	2	1	0	0	1	.667	0	0	0	. . .	. . .	. . .	. . .
1997— Fort Myers (FSL)	OF	131	539	84	*160	33	6	15	82	.297	33	110	24	313	8	7	.979

JONES, RYAN   1B   BLUE JAYS

PERSONAL: Born November 5, 1974, in Torrance, Calif. ... 6-3/225. ... Bats right, throws right. ... Full name: Ryan Matthew Jones.
HIGH SCHOOL: Irvine (Calif.).
TRANSACTIONS/CAREER NOTES: Selected by Toronto Blue Jays organization in second round of free-agent draft (June 3, 1993); pick received as part of compensation for Texas Rangers signing Type B free agent IF Manny Lee.
STATISTICAL NOTES: Led South Atlantic League first basemen with 90 double plays in 1994. ... Tied for Southern League lead with 116 double plays in 1996.

Year Team (League)	Pos.	G	AB	R	H	2B	3B	HR	RBI	Avg.	BB	SO	SB	PO	A	E	Avg.
1993— Medicine Hat (Pio.)	1B	47	171	20	42	5	0	3	27	.246	12	46	1	385	17	7	.983
1994— Hagerstown (SAL)	1B	115	402	60	96	29	0	18	72	.239	45	124	1	937	57	13	.987
1995— Knoxville (Southern)	1B	134	506	70	137	26	3	20	97	.271	60	88	2	1054	76	9	.992
1996— Knoxville (Southern)	1B	134	506	70	137	26	3	20	97	.271	60	88	2	1054	76	9	.992
1997— Syracuse (Int'l)	1B	41	123	8	17	5	1	3	16	.138	15	28	0	333	16	3	.991
— Knoxville (Southern)	1B	86	328	41	84	19	3	12	51	.256	27	63	0	546	26	9	.985

JONES, TERRY — OF — EXPOS

PERSONAL: Born February 15, 1971, in Birmingham, Ala. ... 5-10/165. ... Bats both, throws right. ... Full name; Terry Lee Jones
HIGH SCHOOL: Pinson Valley (Pinson, Ala.).
JUNIOR COLLEGE: Wallace State Community College (Ala.).
COLLEGE: North Alabama.
TRANSACTIONS/CAREER NOTES: Selected by Colorado Rockies organization in 40th round of free-agent draft (June 3, 1993). ... Traded by Rockies with a player to be named later to Montreal Expos for P Dave Veres and a player to be named later (December 10, 1997).
STATISTICAL NOTES: Led California League outfielders with 342 total chances and tied for lead with four double plays in 1994. ... Led Pacific Coast League outfielders with 311 total chances in 1996.

| | | | | | | | BATTING | | | | | | | | FIELDING | | |
Year Team (League)	Pos.	G	AB	R	H	2B	3B	HR	RBI	Avg.	BB	SO	SB	PO	A	E	Avg.
1993— Bend (Northwest).......	OF	33	138	21	40	5	4	0	18	.290	12	19	16	57	7	1	.985
—Central Valley (Cal.)....	OF	21	73	16	21	1	0	0	7	.288	10	15	5	36	2	1	.974
1994— Central Valley (Cal.)....	OF	129	*536	94	157	20	1	2	34	.293	42	85	44	*312	*16	14	.959
1995— New Haven (Eastern)..	OF	124	472	78	127	12	1	1	26	.269	39	104	*51	264	18	*10	.966
1996— Colo. Springs (PCL) ...	OF	128	497	75	143	7	4	0	33	.288	37	80	26	281	14	*16	.949
—Colorado (N.L.)........	OF	12	10	6	3	0	0	0	1	.300	0	3	0	5	0	0	1.000
1997— Colo. Springs (PCL) ...	OF	92	363	70	98	14	4	1	25	.270	25	49	*36	139	11	1	.993
Major league totals (1 year)		12	10	6	3	0	0	0	1	.300	0	3	0	5	0	0	1.000

JONES, TODD — P — TIGERS

PERSONAL: Born April 24, 1968, in Marietta, Ga. ... 6-3/200. ... Throws right, bats left. ... Full name: Todd Barton Jones.
HIGH SCHOOL: Osborne (Ga.).
COLLEGE: Jacksonville (Ala.) State.
TRANSACTIONS/CAREER NOTES: Selected by New York Mets organization in 41st round of free-agent draft (June 2, 1986); did not sign. ... Selected by Houston Astros organization in supplemental round ("sandwich pick" between first and second round, 27th pick overall) of free-agent draft (June 5, 1989); pick received as part of compensation for Texas Rangers signing Type A free-agent P Nolan Ryan. ... On suspended list (September 14-16, 1993). ... On Houston disabled list (July 19-August 12 and August 18-September 12, 1996); included rehabilitation assignment to Tucson (August 9-12). ... Traded by Astros with OF Brian Hunter, IF Orlando Miller, P Doug Brocail and a player to be named later to Detroit Tigers for C Brad Ausmus, P Jose Lima, P C.J. Nitkowski, P Trever Miller and IF Daryle Ward (December 10, 1996).

Year Team (League)	W	L	Pct.	ERA	G	GS	CG	ShO	Sv.	IP	H	R	ER	BB	SO
1989— Auburn (N.Y.-Penn)...........	2	3	.400	5.44	11	9	1	0	0	49 2/3	47	39	30	42	71
1990— Osceola (Florida St.)..........	12	10	.545	3.51	27	•27	1	0	0	151 1/3	124	81	59	*109	106
1991— Osceola (Florida St.)..........	4	4	.500	4.35	14	14	0	0	0	72 1/3	69	38	35	35	51
—Jackson (Texas)	4	3	.571	4.88	10	10	0	0	0	55 1/3	51	37	30	39	37
1992— Jackson (Texas)	3	7	.300	3.14	*61	0	0	0	25	66	52	28	23	44	60
—Tucson (PCL)	0	1	.000	4.50	3	0	0	0	0	4	1	2	2	10	4
1993— Tucson (PCL)	4	2	.667	4.44	41	0	0	0	12	48 2/3	49	26	24	31	45
—Houston (N.L.)	1	2	.333	3.13	27	0	0	0	2	37 1/3	28	14	13	15	25
1994— Houston (N.L.)	5	2	.714	2.72	48	0	0	0	5	72 2/3	52	23	22	26	63
1995— Houston (N.L.)	6	5	.545	3.07	68	0	0	0	15	99 2/3	89	38	34	52	96
1996— Houston (N.L.)	6	3	.667	4.40	51	0	0	0	17	57 1/3	61	30	28	32	44
—Tucson (PCL)	0	0	. . .	0.00	1	0	0	0	0	2	1	1	0	2	0
1997— Detroit (A.L.)■	5	4	.556	3.09	68	0	0	0	31	70	60	29	24	35	70
A.L. totals (1 year)	5	4	.556	3.09	68	0	0	0	31	70	60	29	24	35	70
N.L. totals (4 years)	18	12	.600	3.27	194	0	0	0	39	267	230	105	97	125	228
Major league totals (5 years)	23	16	.590	3.23	262	0	0	0	70	337	290	134	121	160	298

JORDAN, BRIAN — OF — CARDINALS

PERSONAL: Born March 29, 1967, in Baltimore. ... 6-1/205. ... Bats right, throws right. ... Full name: Brian O'Neal Jordan.
HIGH SCHOOL: Milford (Baltimore).
COLLEGE: Richmond.
TRANSACTIONS/CAREER NOTES: Selected by Cleveland Indians organization in 20th round of free-agent draft (June 3, 1985); did not sign. ... Selected by St. Louis Cardinals organization in supplemental round ("sandwich pick" between first and second round, 30th pick overall) of free-agent draft (June 1, 1988). ... On disabled list (May 1-8 and June 3-10, 1991). ... On temporarily inactive list (July 3, 1991-remainder of season). ... On St. Louis disabled list (May 23-June 22, 1992); included rehabilitation assignment to Louisville (June 10-22). ... On Louisville disabled list (June 7-14, 1993). ... On disabled list (July 10, 1994-remainder of season). ... On disabled list (March 31-April 15, 1996). ... On St.Louis disabled list (May 6-June 13, June 26-August 10 and August 25-remainder of 1997 season); included rehabilitation assignment to Louisville (June 5-13).
STATISTICAL NOTES: Career major league grand slams: 2.

| | | | | | | | BATTING | | | | | | | | FIELDING | | |
Year Team (League)	Pos.	G	AB	R	H	2B	3B	HR	RBI	Avg.	BB	SO	SB	PO	A	E	Avg.
1988— Hamilton (NYP)..........	OF	19	71	12	22	3	1	4	12	.310	6	15	3	32	1	1	.971
1989— St. Petersburg (FSL) ..	OF	11	43	7	15	4	1	2	11	.349	0	8	0	22	2	0	1.000
1990— Arkansas (Texas)........	OF	16	50	4	8	1	0	0	0	.160	0	11	0	28	0	2	.933
—St. Petersburg (FSL) ..	OF	9	30	3	5	0	1	0	1	.167	2	11	0	23	0	0	1.000
1991— Louisville (A.A.).........	OF	61	212	35	56	11	4	4	24	.264	17	41	10	144	3	3	.987
1992— Louisville (A.A.).........	OF	43	155	23	45	3	1	4	16	.290	8	21	13	89	3	1	.989
—St. Louis (N.L.)..........	OF	55	193	17	40	9	4	5	22	.207	10	48	7	101	4	1	.991
1993— St. Louis (N.L.)..........	OF	67	223	33	69	10	6	10	44	.309	12	35	6	140	4	4	.973
—Louisville (A.A.).........	OF	38	144	24	54	13	2	5	35	.375	16	17	9	75	2	0	1.000
1994— St. Louis (N.L.)..........	OF-1B	53	178	14	46	8	2	5	15	.258	16	40	4	105	6	1	.991
1995— St. Louis (N.L.)..........	OF	131	490	83	145	20	4	22	81	.296	22	79	24	267	4	1	.996
1996— St. Louis (N.L.)..........	OF-1B	140	513	82	159	36	1	17	104	.310	29	84	22	310	9	2	.994

J

Year	Team (League)	Pos.	G	AB	R	H	2B	3B	HR	RBI	Avg.	BB	SO	SB	PO	A	E	Avg.
								BATTING								FIELDING		
1997— St. Louis (N.L.)...........		OF	47	145	17	34	5	0	0	10	.234	10	21	6	82	2	0	1.000
— Louisville (A.A.).........		OF	6	20	1	3	0	0	0	2	.150	1	2	0	6	0	0	1.000
Major league totals (6 years)			493	1742	246	493	88	17	59	276	.283	99	307	69	1005	29	9	.991

DIVISION SERIES RECORD

Year	Team (League)	Pos.	G	AB	R	H	2B	3B	HR	RBI	Avg.	BB	SO	SB	PO	A	E	Avg.
								BATTING								FIELDING		
1996— St. Louis (N.L.)..........		OF	3	12	4	4	0	0	1	3	.333	1	3	1	5	0	0	1.000

CHAMPIONSHIP SERIES RECORD

Year	Team (League)	Pos.	G	AB	R	H	2B	3B	HR	RBI	Avg.	BB	SO	SB	PO	A	E	Avg.
								BATTING								FIELDING		
1996— St. Louis (N.L.)..........		OF	7	25	3	6	1	1	1	2	.240	2	3	0	13	0	0	1.000

JORDAN, KEVIN   IF   PHILLIES

PERSONAL: Born October 9, 1969, in San Francisco. ... 6-1/193. ... Bats right, throws right. ... Full name: Kevin Wayne Jordan.
HIGH SCHOOL: Lowell (San Francisco).
JUNIOR COLLEGE: Canada College (Calif.).
COLLEGE: Nebraska.
TRANSACTIONS/CAREER NOTES: Selected by Los Angeles Dodgers organization in 10th round of free-agent draft (June 5, 1989); did not sign. ... Selected by New York Yankees organization in 20th round of free-agent draft (June 4, 1990). ... Traded by Yankees with P Bobby Munoz and P Ryan Karp to Philadelphia Phillies for P Terry Mulholland and a player to be named later (February 9, 1994). ... On disabled list (May 1-June 20, 1994 and June 17, 1996-remainder of season).
STATISTICAL NOTES: Led Eastern League with 234 total bases in 1993. ... Led Eastern League second basemen with 93 double plays in 1993.

Year	Team (League)	Pos.	G	AB	R	H	2B	3B	HR	RBI	Avg.	BB	SO	SB	PO	A	E	Avg.
								BATTING								FIELDING		
1990— Oneonta (NYP)..........		2B	73	276	47	92	13	•7	4	54	.333	23	31	19	131	158	8	.973
1991— Fort Lauderdale (FSL)		2B-1B	121	448	61	122	25	5	4	53	.272	37	66	14	182	306	16	.968
1992— Prince William (Car.) ..		2B-3B	112	438	67	136	29	8	8	63	.311	27	54	6	192	288	20	.960
1993— Alb./Colon. (Eastern)..		2B	135	513	87	145	*33	4	16	87	.283	41	53	8	261	359	21	.967
1994— Scran./W.B. (Int'l)■..		2B-3B	81	314	44	91	22	1	12	57	.290	29	28	0	160	237	16	.961
1995— Scran./W.B. (Int'l).......		2B	106	410	61	127	29	4	5	60	.310	28	36	3	217	279	12	.976
— Philadelphia (N.L.)......		2B-3B	24	54	6	10	1	0	2	6	.185	2	9	0	29	35	1	.985
1996— Philadelphia (N.L.)......		1B-2B-3B	43	131	15	37	10	0	3	12	.282	5	20	2	243	27	0	1.000
1997— Scran./W.B. (Int'l).......		3B-2B-1B	7	30	5	9	2	2	0	2	.300	2	6	2	23	18	1	.976
— Philadelphia (N.L.)......		1-3-2-DH	84	177	19	47	8	0	6	30	.266	3	26	0	157	31	6	.969
Major league totals (3 years)			151	362	40	94	19	0	11	48	.260	10	55	2	429	93	7	.987

JORDAN, RICARDO   P   REDS

PERSONAL: Born June 27, 1970, in Boynton Beach, Fla. ... 6-0/180. ... Throws left, bats left.
HIGH SCHOOL: Atlantic (Delray Beach, Fla.).
JUNIOR COLLEGE: Miami-Dade (South) Community College.
TRANSACTIONS/CAREER NOTES: Selected by Toronto Blue Jays organization in 37th round of free-agent draft (June 4, 1990). ... Traded by Blue Jays with 3B Howard Battle to Philadelphia Phillies for P Paul Quantrill (December 6, 1995). ... Traded by Phillies with P Toby Borland to New York Mets for 1B Rico Brogna (November 27, 1996). ... Granted free agency (October 15, 1997). ... Signed by Cincinnati Reds organization (November 27, 1997).

Year	Team (League)	W	L	Pct.	ERA	G	GS	CG	ShO	Sv.	IP	H	R	ER	BB	SO
1990— Dunedin (Fla. St.)...............	0	2	.000	2.38	13	2	0	0	0	22 2/3	15	9	6	19	16
1991— Myrtle Beach (SAL).............	9	8	.529	2.74	29	23	3	1	1	144 2/3	101	58	44	79	152
1992— Dunedin (Fla. St.)...............	0	5	.000	3.83	45	0	0	0	15	47	44	26	20	28	49
1993— Knoxville (Southern)	1	4	.200	2.45	25	0	0	0	2	36 2/3	33	17	10	18	35
— Dunedin (Fla. St.)..............	2	0	1.000	4.38	15	0	0	0	1	24 2/3	20	13	12	15	24
1994— Knoxville (Southern)	4	3	.571	2.66	53	0	0	0	17	64 1/3	54	25	19	23	70
1995— Syracuse (Int'l)...................	0	0	....	6.57	13	0	0	0	1	12 1/3	15	9	9	7	17
— Toronto (A.L.).....................	1	0	1.000	6.60	15	0	0	0	1	15	18	11	11	13	10
1996— Scran./W.B. (Int'l)■..........	3	3	.500	5.26	32	0	0	0	1	39 1/3	40	30	23	22	40
— Philadelphia (N.L.).............	2	2	.500	1.80	26	0	0	0	0	25	18	6	5	12	17
1997— New York (N.L.)■	1	2	.333	5.33	22	0	0	0	0	27	31	17	16	15	19
— Norfolk (Int'l).....................	0	1	.000	2.79	34	0	0	0	1	29	20	11	9	24	34
A.L. totals (1 year)	1	0	1.000	6.60	15	0	0	0	1	15	18	11	11	13	10
N.L. totals (2 years)	3	4	.429	3.63	48	0	0	0	0	52	49	23	21	27	36
Major league totals (3 years)......	4	4	.500	4.30	63	0	0	0	1	67	67	34	32	40	46

JOYNER, WALLY   1B   PADRES

PERSONAL: Born June 16, 1962, in Atlanta. ... 6-2/200. ... Bats left, throws left. ... Full name: Wallace Keith Joyner.
HIGH SCHOOL: Redan (Stone Mountain, Ga.).
COLLEGE: Brigham Young.
TRANSACTIONS/CAREER NOTES: Selected by California Angels organization in third round of free-agent draft (June 6, 1983); pick received as compensation for New York Yankees signing free-agent DH Don Baylor. ... On disabled list (July 12, 1990-remainder of season). ... Granted free agency (October 28, 1991). ... Signed by Kansas City Royals (December 9, 1991). ... On disabled list (June 26-July 14, 1994). ... Traded by Royals with P Aaron Dorlarque to San Diego Padres for 2B/OF Bip Roberts and P Bryan Wolff (December 21, 1995). ... On San Diego disabled list (June 3-July 11, 1996); included rehabilitation assignment to Rancho Cucamonga (July 7-11). ... On disabled list (April 28-May 13, 1997); included rehabilitation assignment to Las Vegas (May 8-12).
RECORDS: Shares major league record for most home runs in month of October—4 (1987).

STATISTICAL NOTES: Tied for Eastern League lead with eight intentional bases on balls received in 1984. ... Led Pacific Coast League first basemen with 1,229 total chances and 121 double plays in 1985. ... Led A.L. with 12 sacrifice flies in 1986. ... Hit three home runs in one game (October 3, 1987). ... Led A.L. first basemen with 1,520 total chances in 1988 and 1,441 in 1991. ... Led A.L. first basemen with 148 double plays in 1988 and 138 in 1992. ... Career major league grand slams: 5.

Year Team (League)	Pos.	G	AB	R	H	2B	3B	HR	RBI	Avg.	BB	SO	SB	PO	A	E	Avg.
1983— Peoria (Midwest)	1B	54	192	25	63	16	2	3	33	.328	19	25	1	480	45	6	.989
1984— Waterbury (Eastern)	1B-OF	134	467	81	148	24	7	12	72	.317	67	60	0	906	86	9	.991
1985— Edmonton (PCL)	1B	126	477	68	135	29	5	12	73	.283	60	64	2	*1107	*107	•15	.988
1986— California (A.L.)	1B	154	593	82	172	27	3	22	100	.290	57	58	5	1222	139	15	.989
1987— California (A.L.)	1B	149	564	100	161	33	1	34	117	.285	72	64	8	1276	92	10	.993
1988— California (A.L.)	1B	158	597	81	176	31	2	13	85	.295	55	51	8	*1369	*143	8	.995
1989— California (A.L.)	1B	159	593	78	167	30	2	16	79	.282	46	58	3	*1487	99	4	*.997
1990— California (A.L.)	1B	83	310	35	83	15	0	8	41	.268	41	34	2	727	62	4	.995
1991— California (A.L.)	1B	143	551	79	166	34	3	21	96	.301	52	66	2	*1335	98	8	.994
1992— Kansas City (A.L.)■	1B-DH	149	572	66	154	36	2	9	66	.269	55	50	11	1236	137	10	.993
1993— Kansas City (A.L.)	1B	141	497	83	145	36	3	15	65	.292	66	67	5	1116	145	7	.994
1994— Kansas City (A.L.)	1B-DH	97	363	52	113	20	3	8	57	.311	47	43	3	777	64	8	.991
1995— Kansas City (A.L.)	1B-DH	131	465	69	144	28	0	12	83	.310	69	65	3	1111	118	3	*.998
1996— San Diego (N.L.)■	1B	121	433	59	120	29	1	8	65	.277	69	71	5	1059	89	3	*.997
— Rancho Cuca. (Cal.)	1B	3	10	1	3	1	0	0	2	.300	1	1	0	14	2	0	1.000
1997— San Diego (N.L.)	1B	135	455	59	149	29	2	13	83	.327	51	51	3	1027	89	4	*.996
— Las Vegas (PCL)	1B	3	8	1	2	0	0	0	1	.250	1	1	0	16	1	0	1.000
American League totals (10 years)		1364	5105	725	1481	290	19	158	789	.290	560	556	50	11656	1097	77	.994
National League totals (2 years)		256	888	118	269	58	3	21	148	.303	120	122	8	2086	178	7	.997
Major league totals (12 years)		1620	5993	843	1750	348	22	179	937	.292	680	678	58	13742	1275	84	.994

DIVISION SERIES RECORD

Year Team (League)	Pos.	G	AB	R	H	2B	3B	HR	RBI	Avg.	BB	SO	SB	PO	A	E	Avg.
1996— San Diego (N.L.)	1B	3	9	0	1	0	0	0	0	.111	0	2	0	12	2	0	1.000

CHAMPIONSHIP SERIES RECORD

Year Team (League)	Pos.	G	AB	R	H	2B	3B	HR	RBI	Avg.	BB	SO	SB	PO	A	E	Avg.
1986— California (A.L.)	1B	3	11	3	5	2	0	1	2	.455	2	0	0	24	1	0	1.000

ALL-STAR GAME RECORD

Year League	Pos.	AB	R	H	2B	3B	HR	RBI	Avg.	BB	SO	SB	PO	A	E	Avg.
1986— American	1B	1	0	0	0	0	0	0	.000	0	0	0	3	1	0	1.000

JUDD, MIKE — P — DODGERS

PERSONAL: Born June 30, 1975, in San Diego. ... 6-1/200. ... Throws right, bats right. ... Full name: Michael Galen Judd.
HIGH SCHOOL: Helix (La Mesa, Calif.).
JUNIOR COLLEGE: Grossmont.
TRANSACTIONS/CAREER NOTES: Selected by New York Yankees organization in ninth round of free-agent draft (June 1, 1995). ... Traded by Yankees to Los Angeles Dodgers for P Billy Brewer (June 22, 1996).

Year Team (League)	W	L	Pct.	ERA	G	GS	CG	ShO	Sv.	IP	H	R	ER	BB	SO
1995— GC Yankees (GCL)	1	1	.500	1.11	21	0	0	0	8	32 1/3	18	5	4	6	30
— Greensboro (S. Atl.)	0	0	...	0.00	1	0	0	0	0	2 2/3	2	0	0	0	1
1996— Greensboro (S. Atl.)	2	2	.500	3.81	29	0	0	0	10	28 1/3	22	14	12	8	36
— Savannah (S. Atl.)■	4	2	.667	2.44	15	8	1	0	3	55 1/3	40	21	15	15	62
1997— Vero Beach (FSL)	6	5	.545	3.53	14	14	1	0	0	86 2/3	67	37	34	39	104
— San Antonio (Tex.)	4	2	.667	2.73	12	12	0	0	0	79	69	27	24	33	65
— Los Angeles (N.L.)	0	0	...	0.00	1	0	0	0	0	2 2/3	4	0	0	0	4
Major league totals (1 year)	0	0	...	0.00	1	0	0	0	0	2 2/3	4	0	0	0	4

JUDEN, JEFF — P — BREWERS

PERSONAL: Born January 19, 1971, in Salem, Mass. ... 6-8/265. ... Throws right, bats right. ... Full name: Jeffrey Daniel Juden. ... Cousin of Daniel Juden, right winger, Tampa Bay Lightning organization. ... Name pronounced JOO-den.
HIGH SCHOOL: Salem (Mass.).
TRANSACTIONS/CAREER NOTES: Selected by Houston Astros organization in first round (12th pick overall) of free-agent draft (June 5, 1989). ... On disabled list (June 14-21, 1992). ... Traded by Astros with P Doug Jones to Philadelphia Phillies for P Mitch Williams (December 2, 1993). ... On Scranton/Wilkes-Barre disabled list (June 22-July 24 and July 25, 1994-remainder of season). ... Traded by Phillies with OF/1B Tommy Eason to San Francisco Giants for IF Mike Benjamin (October 6, 1995). ... Claimed on waivers by Montreal Expos (July 11, 1996). ... On Montreal suspended list (September 4-7, 1996). ... Traded by Expos to Cleveland Indians for P Steve Kline and a player to be named later (July 31, 1997). ... Traded by Indians with OF Marquis Grissom to Milwaukee Brewers for P Ben McDonald, P Mike Fetters and P Ron Villone (December 8, 1997).
STATISTICAL NOTES: Led Pacific Coast League with seven balks in 1992. ... Career major league grand slams: 1.

Year Team (League)	W	L	Pct.	ERA	G	GS	CG	ShO	Sv.	IP	H	R	ER	BB	SO
1989— Sarasota (Florida State)	1	4	.200	3.40	9	8	0	0	0	39 2/3	33	21	15	17	49
1990— Osceola (Florida St.)	10	1	*.909	2.27	15	15	2	1	0	91	72	37	23	42	85
— Columbus (Southern)	1	3	.250	5.37	11	11	0	0	0	52	55	36	31	42	40
1991— Jackson (Texas)	6	3	.667	3.10	16	16	0	0	0	95 2/3	84	43	33	44	75
— Tucson (PCL)	3	2	.600	3.18	10	10	0	0	0	56 2/3	56	28	20	25	51
— Houston (N.L.)	0	2	.000	6.00	4	3	0	0	0	18	19	14	12	7	11

Year Team (League)	W	L	Pct.	ERA	G	GS	CG	ShO	Sv.	IP	H	R	ER	BB	SO
1992— Tucson (PCL)	9	10	.474	4.04	26	26	0	0	0	147	149	84	66	71	120
1993— Tucson (PCL)	11	6	.647	4.63	27	27	0	0	0	169	174	102	87	*76	156
— Houston (N.L.)	0	1	.000	5.40	2	0	0	0	0	5	4	3	3	4	7
1994— Philadelphia (N.L.)■	1	4	.200	6.18	6	5	0	0	0	27²/₃	29	25	19	12	22
— Scran./W.B. (Int'l)	2	2	.500	8.53	6	6	0	0	0	25¹/₃	30	28	24	19	28
1995— Scran./W.B. (Int'l)	6	4	.600	4.10	14	13	0	0	0	83¹/₃	73	43	38	33	65
— Philadelphia (N.L.)	2	4	.333	4.02	13	10	1	0	0	62²/₃	53	31	28	31	47
1996— San Francisco (N.L.)■	4	0	1.000	4.10	36	0	0	0	0	41²/₃	39	23	19	20	35
— Montreal (N.L.)■	1	0	1.000	2.20	22	0	0	0	0	32²/₃	22	12	8	14	26
1997— Montreal (N.L.)	11	5	.688	4.22	22	22	3	0	0	130	125	64	61	57	107
— Cleveland (A.L.)■	0	1	.000	5.46	8	5	0	0	0	31¹/₃	32	21	19	15	29
A.L. totals (1 year)	0	1	.000	5.46	8	5	0	0	0	31¹/₃	32	21	19	15	29
N.L. totals (6 years)	19	16	.543	4.25	105	40	4	0	0	317²/₃	291	172	150	145	255
Major league totals (6 years)	19	17	.528	4.36	113	45	4	0	0	349	323	193	169	160	284

CHAMPIONSHIP SERIES RECORD

Year Team (League)	W	L	Pct.	ERA	G	GS	CG	ShO	Sv.	IP	H	R	ER	BB	SO
1997— Cleveland (A.L.)	0	0	...	0.00	3	0	0	0	0	1	2	0	0	2	2

WORLD SERIES RECORD

Year Team (League)	W	L	Pct.	ERA	G	GS	CG	ShO	Sv.	IP	H	R	ER	BB	SO
1997— Cleveland (A.L.)	0	0	...	4.50	2	0	0	0	0	2	2	1	1	2	0

JUSTICE, DAVID — OF — INDIANS

PERSONAL: Born April 14, 1966, in Cincinnati. ... 6-3/200. ... Bats left, throws left. ... Full name: David Christopher Justice.

HIGH SCHOOL: Covington (Ky.) Latin.

COLLEGE: Thomas More College (Ky.).

TRANSACTIONS/CAREER NOTES: Selected by Atlanta Braves organization in fourth round of free-agent draft (June 3, 1985). ... On Atlanta disabled list (June 27-August 20, 1991); included rehabilitation assignment to Macon (August 16-20). ... On disabled list (April 12-27, 1992; June 2-17, 1995 and May 16, 1996-remainder of season). ... Traded by Braves with OF Marquis Grissom to Cleveland Indians for OF Kenny Lofton and P Alan Embree (March 25, 1997). ... On disabled list (June 24-July 10, 1997).

RECORDS: Holds major league single-season record for fewest errors by outfielder who led league in errors—8 (1992).

HONORS: Named N.L. Rookie Player of the Year by THE SPORTING NEWS (1990). ... Named N.L. Rookie of the Year by Baseball Writers' Association of America (1990). ... Named outfielder on THE SPORTING NEWS N.L. All-Star team (1993). ... Named outfielder on THE SPORTING NEWS N.L. Silver Slugger team (1993). ... Named outfielder on THE SPORTING NEWS A.L. Silver Slugger team (1997). ... Named A.L. Comeback Player of the Year by THE SPORTING NEWS (1997). ... Named outfielder on THE SPORTING NEWS A.L. All-Star team (1997).

STATISTICAL NOTES: Tied for Appalachian League lead with five sacrifice flies in 1985. ... Career major league grand slams: 2.

						BATTING								FIELDING		
Year Team (League)	Pos.	G	AB	R	H	2B	3B	HR	RBI	Avg.	BB	SO	SB	PO	A	E	Avg.
1985— Pulaski (Appalachian)	OF	66	204	39	50	8	0	•10	46	.245	40	30	0	86	2	4	.957
1986— Sumter (S. Atl.)	OF	61	220	48	66	16	0	10	61	.300	48	28	10	124	7	4	.970
— Durham (Carolina)	OF-1B	67	229	47	64	9	1	12	44	.279	46	24	2	163	5	1	.994
1987— Greenville (Southern)	OF	93	348	38	79	12	4	6	40	.227	53	48	3	199	4	8	.962
1988— Richmond (Int'l)	OF	70	227	27	46	9	1	8	28	.203	39	55	4	136	5	4	.972
— Greenville (Southern)	OF	58	198	34	55	13	1	9	37	.278	37	41	6	100	3	5	.954
1989— Richmond (Int'l)	OF-1B	115	391	47	102	24	3	12	58	.261	59	66	12	220	15	6	.975
— Atlanta (N.L.)	OF	16	51	7	12	3	0	1	3	.235	3	9	2	24	0	0	1.000
1990— Richmond (Int'l)	OF-1B	12	45	7	16	5	1	2	7	.356	7	6	0	23	4	2	.931
— Atlanta (N.L.)	1B-OF	127	439	76	124	23	2	28	78	.282	64	92	11	604	42	14	.979
1991— Atlanta (N.L.)	OF	109	396	67	109	25	1	21	87	.275	65	81	8	204	9	7	.968
— Macon (S. Atl.)	OF	3	10	2	2	0	0	2	5	.200	2	1	0	1	0	0	1.000
1992— Atlanta (N.L.)	OF	144	484	78	124	19	5	21	72	.256	79	85	2	313	8	*8	.976
1993— Atlanta (N.L.)	OF	157	585	90	158	15	4	40	120	.270	78	90	3	323	9	5	.985
1994— Atlanta (N.L.)	OF	104	352	61	110	16	2	19	59	.313	69	45	2	192	6	*11	.947
1995— Atlanta (N.L.)	OF	120	411	73	104	17	2	24	78	.253	73	68	4	233	8	4	.984
1996— Atlanta (N.L.)	OF	40	140	23	45	9	0	6	25	.321	21	22	1	88	3	0	1.000
1997— Cleveland (A.L.)■	OF-DH	139	495	84	163	31	1	33	101	.329	80	79	3	120	3	2	.984
American League totals (1 year)		139	495	84	163	31	1	33	101	.329	80	79	3	120	3	2	.984
National League totals (8 years)		817	2858	475	786	127	16	160	522	.275	452	492	33	1981	85	49	.977
Major league totals (9 years)		956	3353	559	949	158	17	193	623	.283	532	571	36	2101	88	51	.977

DIVISION SERIES RECORD

						BATTING								FIELDING		
Year Team (League)	Pos.	G	AB	R	H	2B	3B	HR	RBI	Avg.	BB	SO	SB	PO	A	E	Avg.
1995— Atlanta (N.L.)	OF	4	13	2	3	0	0	0	0	.231	5	2	0	6	0	1	.857
1997— Cleveland (A.L.)	DH	5	19	3	5	2	0	1	2	.263	2	3	0	0	0	0	...
Division series totals (2 years)		9	32	5	8	2	0	1	2	.250	7	5	0	6	0	1	.857

CHAMPIONSHIP SERIES RECORD

						BATTING								FIELDING		
Year Team (League)	Pos.	G	AB	R	H	2B	3B	HR	RBI	Avg.	BB	SO	SB	PO	A	E	Avg.
1991— Atlanta (N.L.)	OF	7	25	4	5	1	0	1	2	.200	3	7	0	17	0	1	.944
1992— Atlanta (N.L.)	OF	7	25	5	7	1	0	2	6	.280	6	2	0	19	3	0	1.000
1993— Atlanta (N.L.)	OF	6	21	2	3	1	0	0	4	.143	3	3	0	14	0	1	.933
1995— Atlanta (N.L.)	OF	3	11	1	3	0	0	0	1	.273	2	1	0	0	0	0	...
1997— Cleveland (A.L.)	DH	6	21	3	7	1	0	0	0	.333	2	4	0	...	...	...	...
Championship series totals (5 years)		29	103	15	25	4	0	3	13	.243	16	17	0	50	3	2	.964

WORLD SERIES RECORD

NOTES: Member of World Series championship team (1995).

Year Team (League)	Pos.	G	AB	R	H	2B	3B	HR	RBI	Avg.	BB	SO	SB	PO	A	E	Avg.
1991—Atlanta (N.L.).............	OF	7	27	5	7	0	0	2	6	.259	5	5	2	21	1	1	.957
1992—Atlanta (N.L.).............	OF	6	19	4	3	0	0	1	3	.158	6	5	1	15	0	1	.938
1995—Atlanta (N.L.).............	OF	6	20	3	5	1	0	1	5	.250	5	1	0	16	0	0	1.000
1997—Cleveland (A.L.).........	OF-DH	7	27	4	5	0	0	0	4	.185	6	8	0	9	0	0	1.000
World Series totals (4 years)		26	93	16	20	1	0	4	18	.215	22	19	3	61	1	2	.969

ALL-STAR GAME RECORD

Year League	Pos.	AB	R	H	2B	3B	HR	RBI	Avg.	BB	SO	SB	PO	A	E	Avg.
1993— National	OF	3	0	1	0	0	0	0	.333	0	0	0	1	0	1	.500
1994— National	OF	2	0	0	0	0	0	0	.000	0	0	0	1	0	0	1.000
1997— American...................							Selected, did not play—injured.									
All-Star Game totals (2 years)		5	0	1	0	0	0	0	.200	0	0	0	2	0	1	.667

KAMIENIECKI, SCOTT   P   ORIOLES

PERSONAL: Born April 19, 1964, in Mt. Clemens, Mich. ... 6-0/195. ... Throws right, bats right. ... Full name: Scott Andrew Kamieniecki. ... Name pronounced KAM-ah-NIK-ee.
HIGH SCHOOL: Redford St. Mary's (Detroit).
COLLEGE: Michigan (degree in physical education).
TRANSACTIONS/CAREER NOTES: Selected by Detroit Tigers organization in second round of free-agent draft (June 7, 1982); did not sign. ... Selected by Milwaukee Brewers organization in 23rd round of free-agent draft (June 3, 1985); did not sign. ... Selected by New York Yankees organization in 14th round of free-agent draft (June 2, 1986). ... On New York disabled list (August 3, 1991-remainder of season). ... On New York disabled list (April 2-29, 1992); included rehabilitation assignments to Fort Lauderdale (April 9-17) and Columbus (April 17-29). ... On New York disabled list (May 6-July 15, 1995); included rehabilitation assignments to Tampa (July 5-10) and Columbus (July 10-12). ... On New York disabled list (March 27-April 24 and July 31, 1996-remainder of season); included rehabilitation assignment to Tampa (April 6-24). ... On Columbus disabled list (June 20-July 31, 1996). ... Granted free agency (December 20, 1996). ... Signed by Baltimore Orioles organization (January 22, 1997). ... Granted free agency (October 30, 1997). ... Re-signed by Orioles (December 5, 1997).

Year Team (League)	W	L	Pct.	ERA	G	GS	CG	ShO	Sv.	IP	H	R	ER	BB	SO
1987—Alb./Colon. (Eastern).........	1	3	.250	5.35	10	7	0	0	0	37	41	25	22	33	19
—Prince William (Caro.).......	9	5	.643	4.17	19	19	1	0	0	112 1/3	91	61	52	78	84
1988—Prince William (Caro.).......	6	7	.462	4.40	15	15	•7	2	0	100 1/3	115	62	49	50	72
—Fort Lauderdale (FSL)........	3	6	.333	3.62	12	11	1	1	0	77	71	36	31	40	51
1989—Alb./Colon. (Eastern).........	10	9	.526	3.70	24	23	6	3	1	151	142	67	62	57	*140
1990—Alb./Colon. (Eastern).........	10	9	.526	3.20	22	21	3	1	0	132	113	55	47	61	99
1991—Columbus (Int'l).............	6	3	.667	2.36	11	11	3	1	0	76 1/3	61	25	20	20	58
—New York (A.L.).............	4	4	.500	3.90	9	9	0	0	0	55 1/3	54	24	24	22	34
1992—Fort Lauderdale (FSL).......	1	0	1.000	1.29	1	1	1	0	0	7	8	1	1	0	3
—Columbus (Int'l).............	1	0	1.000	0.69	2	2	0	0	0	13	6	1	1	4	12
—New York (A.L.).............	6	14	.300	4.36	28	28	4	0	0	188	193	100	91	74	88
1993—New York (A.L.).............	10	7	.588	4.08	30	20	2	0	1	154 1/3	163	73	70	59	72
—Columbus (Int'l).............	1	0	1.000	1.50	1	1	0	0	0	6	5	1	1	0	4
1994—New York (A.L.).............	8	6	.571	3.76	22	16	1	0	0	117 1/3	115	53	49	59	71
1995—New York (A.L.).............	7	6	.538	4.01	17	16	1	0	0	89 2/3	83	43	40	49	43
—Tampa (Florida State)........	1	0	1.000	1.80	1	1	0	0	0	5	6	2	1	1	2
—Columbus (Int'l).............	1	0	1.000	0.00	1	1	0	0	0	6 2/3	2	0	0	1	10
1996—Tampa (Florida State)........	2	1	.667	1.17	3	3	1	0	0	23	20	6	3	4	17
—New York (A.L.).............	1	2	.333	11.12	7	5	0	0	0	22 2/3	36	30	28	19	15
—Columbus (Int'l).............	2	1	.667	5.64	5	5	2	0	0	30 1/3	33	21	19	8	27
1997—Baltimore (A.L.)■..............	10	6	.625	4.01	30	30	0	0	0	179 1/3	179	83	80	67	109
Major league totals (7 years)......	46	45	.505	4.26	143	124	8	0	1	806 2/3	823	406	382	349	432

DIVISION SERIES RECORD

Year Team (League)	W	L	Pct.	ERA	G	GS	CG	ShO	Sv.	IP	H	R	ER	BB	SO
1995— New York (A.L.).................	0	0	...	7.20	1	1	0	0	0	5	9	5	4	4	4

CHAMPIONSHIP SERIES RECORD

Year Team (League)	W	L	Pct.	ERA	G	GS	CG	ShO	Sv.	IP	H	R	ER	BB	SO
1997— Baltimore (A.L.).................	1	0	1.000	0.00	2	1	0	0	0	8	4	0	0	2	5

KAPLER, GABRIEL   OF   TIGERS

PERSONAL: Born August 31, 1975, in Hollywood, Calif. ... 6-2/190. ... Bats right, throws right. ... Full name: Gabriel Stefan Kapler. ... Name pronounced CAP-ler.
HIGH SCHOOL: Taft (Calif.) Union.
JUNIOR COLLEGE: Moorpark (Calif.) College.
TRANSACTIONS/CAREER NOTES: Selected by Detroit Tigers organization in 57th round of free-agent draft (June 1, 1995).
STATISTICAL NOTES: Led South Atlantic League with 280 total bases in 1996. ... Led Florida State League with 262 total bases in 1997.

Year Team (League)	Pos.	G	AB	R	H	2B	3B	HR	RBI	Avg.	BB	SO	SB	PO	A	E	Avg.
1995—Jamestown (NYP)	OF	63	236	38	68	19	4	4	34	.288	23	37	1	103	9	9	.926
1996—Fayetteville (SAL)	OF-3B	138	524	81	*157	*45	0	26	99	.300	62	73	14	195	14	7	.968
1997—Lakeland (Fla. St.)	OF	137	519	87	153	*40	6	19	87	.295	54	68	8	232	14	6	.978

KARCHNER, MATT   P   WHITE SOX

PERSONAL: Born June 28, 1967, in Berwick, Pa. ... 6-4/210. ... Throws right, bats right. ... Full name: Matthew Dean Karchner.
HIGH SCHOOL: Berwick (Pa.).
COLLEGE: Bloomsburg (Pa.).

TRANSACTIONS/CAREER NOTES: Selected by Kansas City Royals organization in eighth round of free-agent draft (June 5, 1989). ... On disabled list (August 1-8, 1991). ... Selected by Montreal Expos from Royals organization in Rule 5 major league draft (December 9, 1991). ... Returned to Royals (April 4, 1992). ... On disabled list (September 2-18, 1992 and May 10, 1993-remainder of season). ... Selected by Nashville, Chicago White Sox organization, from Memphis, Royals organization, in Rule 5 minor league draft (December 13, 1993). ... On Chicago disabled list (August 11-September 1, 1996); included rehabilitation assignment to Nashville (August 30-September 1).

Year Team (League)	W	L	Pct.	ERA	G	GS	CG	ShO	Sv.	IP	H	R	ER	BB	SO
1989— Eugene (Northwest)	1	1	.500	3.90	8	5	0	0	0	30	30	19	13	8	25
1990— Appleton (Midwest)	2	7	.222	4.82	27	11	1	0	0	71	70	42	38	31	58
1991— Baseball City (FSL)	6	3	.667	1.97	38	0	0	0	5	73	49	28	16	25	65
1992— Memphis (Southern)	8	8	.500	4.47	33	18	2	0	1	141	161	83	70	35	88
1993— Memphis (Southern)	3	2	.600	4.20	6	5	0	0	0	30	34	16	14	4	14
1994— Birmingham (Southern)■..	5	2	.714	1.26	39	0	0	0	6	43	36	10	6	14	29
—Nashville (A.A.)	4	2	.667	1.37	17	0	0	0	2	26 1/3	18	5	4	7	19
1995— Nashville (A.A.)	3	3	.500	1.45	28	0	0	0	9	37 1/3	39	7	6	10	29
—Chicago (A.L.)	4	2	.667	1.69	31	0	0	0	0	32	33	8	6	12	24
1996— Chicago (A.L.)	7	4	.636	5.76	50	0	0	0	1	59 1/3	61	42	38	41	46
—Nashville (A.A.)	0	0	. . .	0.00	1	0	0	0	0	2/3	0	0	0	0	0
1997— Nashville (A.A.)	2	1	.667	1.93	13	0	0	0	3	18 2/3	12	5	4	6	11
—Chicago (A.L.)	3	1	.750	2.91	52	0	0	0	15	52 2/3	50	18	17	26	30
Major league totals (3 years)......	**14**	**7**	**.667**	**3.81**	**133**	**0**	**0**	**0**	**16**	**144**	**144**	**68**	**61**	**79**	**100**

KARKOVICE, RON　　　　C　　　　INDIANS

PERSONAL: Born August 8, 1963, in Union, N.J. ... 6-1/219. ... Bats right, throws right. ... Full name: Ronald Joseph Karkovice. ... Name pronounced CAR-ko-VICE.
HIGH SCHOOL: Boone (Orlando).
TRANSACTIONS/CAREER NOTES: Selected by Chicago White Sox organization in first round (14th pick overall) of free-agent draft (June 7, 1982). ... On disabled list (May 20-July 3, 1991; June 20-July 6, 1993 and July 18, 1994-remainder of season). ... Granted free agency (October 31, 1997). ... Signed by Cleveland Indians organization (January 13, 1998).
STATISTICAL NOTES: Led Gulf Coast League catchers with 394 total chances and tied for lead with five double plays in 1982. ... Led Midwest League catchers with .996 fielding percentage in 1983. ... Led Eastern League catchers with 13 double plays in 1985. ... Career major league grand slams: 5.

Year Team (League)	Pos.	G	AB	R	H	2B	3B	HR	RBI	Avg.	BB	SO	SB	PO	A	E	Avg.
1982— GC Whi. Sox (GCL)	C	60	214	34	56	6	0	7	32	.262	29	*73	5	*331	*51	12	.970
1983— Appleton (Midwest)....	C-OF	97	326	54	78	17	3	13	48	.239	31	90	10	682	91	4	†.995
1984— Glens Falls (Eastern) ..	C	88	260	37	56	9	1	13	39	.215	25	102	3	442	*68	11	.979
—Denver (A.A.)	C	31	86	7	19	1	0	2	10	.221	8	25	1	149	28	3	.983
1985— Glens Falls (Eastern) ..	C	99	324	37	70	9	3	11	37	.216	49	104	6	573	*103	*14	.980
1986— Birmingham (Sou.).....	C	97	319	63	90	13	1	20	53	.282	61	109	2	463	72	10	.982
—Chicago (A.L.)	C	37	97	13	24	7	0	4	13	.247	9	37	1	227	19	1	.996
1987— Chicago (A.L.)	C-DH	39	85	7	6	0	0	2	7	.071	7	40	3	147	20	3	.982
—Hawaii (PCL)	C-OF	34	104	15	19	3	0	4	11	.183	8	37	3	108	13	3	.976
1988— Vancouver (PCL)	C	39	116	12	29	10	0	2	13	.250	8	26	2	202	16	3	.986
—Chicago (A.L.)	C	46	115	10	20	4	0	3	9	.174	7	30	4	190	24	1	.995
1989— Chicago (A.L.)	C-DH	71	182	21	48	9	2	3	24	.264	10	56	0	299	47	5	.986
1990— Chicago (A.L.)	C-DH	68	183	30	45	10	0	6	20	.246	16	52	2	296	31	2	.994
1991— Chicago (A.L.)	C-OF	75	167	25	41	13	0	5	22	.246	15	42	0	309	28	4	.988
1992— Chicago (A.L.)	C-OF	123	342	39	81	12	1	13	50	.237	30	89	10	536	53	6	.990
1993— Chicago (A.L.)	C	128	403	60	92	17	1	20	54	.228	29	126	2	769	63	5	.994
1994— Chicago (A.L.)	C	77	207	33	44	9	1	11	29	.213	36	68	0	417	19	3	.993
1995— Chicago (A.L.)	C	113	323	44	70	14	1	13	51	.217	39	84	2	629	42	6	.991
1996— Chicago (A.L.)	C	111	355	44	78	22	0	10	38	.220	24	93	0	680	45	5	.993
1997— Chicago (A.L.)	C	51	138	10	25	3	0	6	18	.181	11	32	0	261	13	1	.996
Major league totals (12 years)		**939**	**2597**	**336**	**574**	**120**	**6**	**96**	**335**	**.221**	**233**	**749**	**24**	**4760**	**404**	**42**	**.992**

CHAMPIONSHIP SERIES RECORD

Year Team (League)	Pos.	G	AB	R	H	2B	3B	HR	RBI	Avg.	BB	SO	SB	PO	A	E	Avg.
1993— Chicago (A.L.)	C-PR	6	15	0	0	0	0	0	0	.000	1	7	0	30	2	0	1.000

KARL, SCOTT　　　　P　　　　BREWERS

PERSONAL: Born August 9, 1971, in Riverside, Calif. ... 6-2/195. ... Throws left, bats left. ... Full name: Randall Scott Karl.
HIGH SCHOOL: Carlsbad (Calif.).
COLLEGE: Hawaii.
TRANSACTIONS/CAREER NOTES: Selected by Milwaukee Brewers organization in sixth round of free-agent draft (June 1, 1992). ... On New Orleans disabled list (April 27-May 31, 1994).
STATISTICAL NOTES: Tied for Texas League lead with seven balks in 1993.

Year Team (League)	W	L	Pct.	ERA	G	GS	CG	ShO	Sv.	IP	H	R	ER	BB	SO
1992— Helena (Pioneer)	7	0	•1.000	*1.46	9	9	1	1	0	61 2/3	54	13	10	16	57
1993— El Paso (Texas)..................	13	8	.619	2.45	27	•27	•4	•2	0	*180	172	67	49	35	95
1994— New Orleans (A.A.).............	5	5	.500	3.84	15	13	2	0	0	89	92	38	38	33	54
—El Paso (Texas)..............	5	1	.833	2.96	8	8	3	0	0	54 2/3	44	21	18	15	51
1995— New Orleans (A.A.).............	3	4	.429	3.30	8	6	1	1	0	46 1/3	47	18	17	12	29
—Milwaukee (A.L.)	6	7	.462	4.14	25	18	1	0	0	124	141	65	57	50	59
1996— Milwaukee (A.L.)	13	9	.591	4.86	32	32	3	1	0	207 1/3	220	124	112	72	121
1997— Milwaukee (A.L.)	10	13	.435	4.47	32	32	1	0	0	193 1/3	212	103	96	67	119
Major league totals (3 years)......	**29**	**29**	**.500**	**4.55**	**89**	**82**	**5**	**1**	**0**	**524 2/3**	**573**	**292**	**265**	**189**	**299**

K

KARP, RYAN
P

PERSONAL: Born April 5, 1970, in Los Angeles. ... 6-4/214. ... Throws left, bats left. ... Full name: Ryan Jason Karp.
HIGH SCHOOL: Beverly Hills (Calif.).
JUNIOR COLLEGE: Los Angeles Harbor.
COLLEGE: Miami (Fla.), then Florida International.
TRANSACTIONS/CAREER NOTES: Selected by Houston Astros organization in 73rd round of free-agent draft (June 5, 1989); did not sign. ... Selected by New York Yankees organization in ninth round of free-agent draft (June 1, 1992). ... Traded by Yankees organization with P Bobby Munoz and 2B Kevin Jordan to Philadelphia Phillies organization for P Terry Mulholland and a player to be named later (February 9, 1994); Yankees acquired P Jeff Patterson to complete deal (November 8, 1994). ... On disabled list (May 13-June 25, 1994). ... On Scranton/Wilkes-Barre disabled list (April 17-May 12, 1995 and May 10-September 6, 1996). ... Selected by Tampa Bay Devil Rays in second round (54th pick overall) of expansion draft (November 18, 1997). ... Granted free agency (December 21, 1997).
HONORS: Named South Atlantic League Most Outstanding Pitcher (1993).

Year Team (League)	W	L	Pct.	ERA	G	GS	CG	ShO	Sv.	IP	H	R	ER	BB	SO
1992— Oneonta (N.Y.-Penn)	6	4	.600	4.09	14	13	1	1	0	70 1/3	66	38	32	30	58
1993— Greensboro (S. Atl.)	13	1	*.929	1.81	17	17	0	0	0	109 1/3	73	26	22	40	132
— Prince William (Caro.)	3	2	.600	2.20	8	8	1	1	0	49	35	17	12	12	34
— Albany (Eastern)................	0	0	...	4.15	3	3	0	0	0	13	13	7	6	9	10
1994— Reading (Eastern)■	4	11	.267	4.45	21	21	0	0	0	121 1/3	123	67	60	54	96
1995— Reading (Eastern)............	1	2	.333	3.06	7	7	0	0	0	47	44	18	16	15	37
— Philadelphia (N.L.).............	0	0	...	4.50	1	0	0	0	0	2	1	1	1	3	2
— Scran./W.B. (Int'l).............	7	1	.875	4.20	13	13	0	0	0	81 1/3	81	43	38	31	73
1996— Scran./W.B. (Int'l).............	1	1	.500	3.07	7	7	0	0	0	41	35	14	14	14	30
1997— Scran./W.B. (Int'l).............	4	3	.571	4.19	32	5	0	0	1	73	72	35	34	42	55
— Philadelphia (N.L.).............	1	1	.500	5.40	15	1	0	0	0	15	12	12	9	9	18
Major league totals (2 years)......	1	1	.500	5.29	16	1	0	0	0	17	13	13	10	12	20

KARROS, ERIC
1B   **DODGERS**

PERSONAL: Born November 4, 1967, in Hackensack, N.J. ... 6-4/222. ... Bats right, throws right. ... Full name: Eric Peter Karros. ... Name pronounced CARE-ose.
HIGH SCHOOL: Patrick Henry (San Diego).
COLLEGE: UCLA.
TRANSACTIONS/CAREER NOTES: Selected by Los Angeles Dodgers organization in sixth round of free-agent draft (June 1, 1988).
HONORS: Named N.L. Rookie Player of the Year by THE SPORTING NEWS (1992). ... Named N.L. Rookie of the Year by Baseball Writers' Association of America (1992). ... Named first baseman on THE SPORTING NEWS N.L. All-Star team (1995). ... Named first baseman on THE SPORTING NEWS N.L. Silver Slugger team (1995).
STATISTICAL NOTES: Tied for Pioneer League lead in errors by first baseman with 14 in 1988. ... Led California League first basemen with 1,232 putouts, 110 assists and 1,358 total chances in 1989. ... Led Texas League with 282 total bases in 1990. ... Led Texas League first basemen with 1,337 total chances and 129 double plays in 1990. ... Led Pacific Coast League with 269 total bases in 1991. ... Tied for Pacific Coast League lead with eight intentional bases on balls received in 1991. ... Led Pacific Coast League first basemen with 1,095 putouts, 109 assists and 1,215 total chances in 1991. ... Led N.L. in grounding into double plays with 27 in 1996.

Year Team (League)	Pos.	G	AB	R	H	2B	3B	HR	RBI	Avg.	BB	SO	SB	PO	A	E	Avg.
1988— Great Falls (Pio.)	1B-3B	66	268	68	98	12	1	12	55	.366	32	35	8	516	31	‡19	.966
1989— Bakersfield (Calif.)......	1B-3B	*142	545	86	*165	*40	1	15	86	.303	63	99	18	†1238	†113	19	.986
1990— San Antonio (Tex.).....	1B	•131	509	91	*179	*45	2	18	78	*.352	57	79	8	*1223	†106	8	.994
1991— Albuquerque (PCL).....	1B-3B	132	488	88	154	33	8	22	101	.316	58	80	3	†1095	†109	11	.991
— Los Angeles (N.L.)....	1B	14	14	0	1	1	0	0	1	.071	1	6	0	33	2	0	1.000
1992— Los Angeles (N.L.)....	1B	149	545	63	140	30	1	20	88	.257	37	103	2	1211	126	9	.993
1993— Los Angeles (N.L.)....	1B	158	619	74	153	27	2	23	80	.247	34	82	0	1335	*147	12	.992
1994— Los Angeles (N.L.)....	1B	111	406	51	108	21	1	14	46	.266	29	53	2	896	118	•9	.991
1995— Los Angeles (N.L.)....	1B	143	551	83	164	29	3	32	105	.298	61	115	4	1234	109	7	.995
1996— Los Angeles (N.L.)....	1B	154	608	84	158	29	1	34	111	.260	53	121	8	1314	121	15	.990
1997— Los Angeles (N.L.)....	1B	•162	628	86	167	28	0	31	104	.266	61	116	15	1317	121	11	.992
Major league totals (7 years)		891	3371	441	891	165	8	154	535	.264	276	596	31	7340	744	63	.992

DIVISION SERIES RECORD

RECORDS: Shares single-game record for most home runs—2 (October 4, 1995).

Year Team (League)	Pos.	G	AB	R	H	2B	3B	HR	RBI	Avg.	BB	SO	SB	PO	A	E	Avg.
1995— Los Angeles (N.L.)	1B	3	12	3	6	1	0	2	4	.500	1	0	0	14	0	0	1.000
1996— Los Angeles (N.L.)	1B	3	9	0	0	0	0	0	0	.000	2	3	0	28	2	0	1.000
Division series totals (2 years)		6	21	3	6	1	0	2	4	.286	3	3	0	42	2	0	1.000

KARSAY, STEVE
P   **INDIANS**

PERSONAL: Born March 24, 1972, in College Point, N.Y. ... 6-3/205. ... Throws right, bats right. ... Full name: Stefan Andrew Karsay. ... Name pronounced CAR-say..
HIGH SCHOOL: Christ the King (Queens, N.Y.).
TRANSACTIONS/CAREER NOTES: Selected by Toronto Blue Jays organization in first round (22nd pick overall) of free-agent draft (June 4, 1990). ... On Knoxville disabled list (July 3-16, 1993). ... Traded by Blue Jays with a player to be named later to Oakland Athletics for OF Rickey Henderson (July 31, 1993); A's acquired OF Jose Herrera to complete deal (August 6, 1993). ... On disabled list (April 26, 1994-remainder of season and April 24, 1995-entire season). ... On disabled list (August 6-October 7, 1997). ... Traded by A's to Cleveland Indians for P Mike Fetters (December 8, 1997).
MISCELLANEOUS: Appeared in one game as pinch-runner (1997).

Year Team (League)	W	L	Pct.	ERA	G	GS	CG	ShO	Sv.	IP	H	R	ER	BB	SO
1990— St. Catharines (NYP).........	1	1	.500	0.79	5	5	0	0	0	22 2/3	11	4	2	12	25
1991— Myrtle Beach (SAL)...........	4	9	.308	3.58	20	20	1	0	0	110 2/3	96	58	44	48	100
1992— Dunedin (Fla. St.).............	6	3	.667	2.73	16	16	3	2	0	85 2/3	56	32	26	29	87
1993— Knoxville (Southern).........	8	4	.667	3.38	19	18	1	0	0	104	98	42	39	32	100
— Huntsville (Southern)■......	0	0	...	5.14	2	2	0	0	0	14	13	8	8	3	22
— Oakland (A.L.)..............	3	3	.500	4.04	8	8	0	0	0	49	49	23	22	16	33
1994— Oakland (A.L.).................	1	1	.500	2.57	4	4	1	0	0	28	26	8	8	8	15
1995—							Did not play.								
1996— Modesto (California)..........	0	1	.000	2.65	14	14	0	0	0	34	35	16	10	1	31
1997— Oakland (A.L.).................	3	12	.200	5.77	24	24	0	0	0	132 2/3	166	92	85	47	92
Major league totals (3 years)......	7	16	.304	4.94	36	36	1	0	0	209 2/3	241	123	115	71	140

KASHIWADA, TAKASHI — P

PERSONAL: Born May 14, 1971, in Yatsushiro, Japan. ... 5-11/165. ... Throws left, bats left.
HIGH SCHOOL: Yatsushiro (Japan) Industrial High School
TRANSACTIONS/CAREER NOTES: Played for Yomiuri Giants of Japan Central League (1994-96). ... Sold by Giants to New York Mets organization (April 3, 1997). ... Released by Mets (October 10, 1997).

Year Team (League)	W	L	Pct.	ERA	G	GS	CG	ShO	Sv.	IP	H	R	ER	BB	SO
1994— Yomiuri (Jp. Cn.).................	1	0	1.000	3.50	16	...	...	...	...	18	...	...	7	...	10
1995— Yomiuri (Jp. Cn.).................	0	0	...	6.75	2	...	...	...	...	4	...	...	3	...	4
1996— Yomiuri (Jp. Cn.).................	0	1	.000	3.27	8	...	0	0	0	11	...	...	4	...	1
1997— Norfolk (Int'l)■.................	0	1	.000	4.73	14	0	0	0	0	13 1/3	11	9	7	5	12
— New York (N.L.)...................	3	1	.750	4.31	35	0	0	0	0	31 1/3	35	15	15	18	19
Major league totals (1 year)........	3	1	.750	4.31	35	0	0	0	0	31 1/3	35	15	15	18	19

KEAGLE, GREG — P — TIGERS

PERSONAL: Born June 20, 1971, in Corning, N.Y. ... 6-1/185. ... Throws right, bats right. ... Full name: Gregory Charles Keagle.
HIGH SCHOOL: Horseheads (N.Y.) Central.
TRANSACTIONS/CAREER NOTES: Selected by San Diego Padres organization in sixth round of free-agent draft (June 3, 1993). ... Traded by Padres organization to Seattle Mariners organization (September 16, 1995), completing deal in which Padres traded P Andy Benes and a player to be named later to Mariners for P Ron Villone and OF Marc Newfield (July 31, 1995). ... Selected by Detroit Tigers from Mariners organization in Rule 5 major league draft (December 4, 1995). ... On Detroit disabled list (July 7-August 21, 1996); included rehabilitation assignment to Toledo (July 22-August 20).

Year Team (League)	W	L	Pct.	ERA	G	GS	CG	ShO	Sv.	IP	H	R	ER	BB	SO
1993— Spokane (N'west).............	3	3	.500	3.25	15	15	1	0	0	83	80	37	30	40	77
1994— Rancho Cucamonga (Cal.) .	11	1	.917	2.05	14	14	1	1	0	92	62	23	21	41	91
— Wichita (Texas)	3	9	.250	6.27	13	13	0	0	0	70 1/3	84	53	49	32	57
1995— Memphis (Southern).........	4	9	.308	5.11	15	15	1	0	0	81	82	52	46	41	82
— Rancho Cucamonga (Cal.) .	0	0	...	4.50	2	2	0	0	0	14	14	9	7	2	11
— Las Vegas (PCL)................	7	6	.538	4.28	14	13	0	0	0	75 2/3	76	47	36	42	49
1996— Detroit (A.L.)■...............	3	6	.333	7.39	26	6	0	0	0	87 2/3	104	76	72	68	70
— Toledo (Int'l)......................	2	3	.400	10.00	6	6	0	0	0	27	42	32	30	11	24
1997— Toledo (Int'l).................	11	7	.611	3.81	23	23	3	1	0	151 1/3	136	68	64	61	140
— Detroit (A.L.).....................	3	5	.375	6.55	11	10	0	0	0	45 1/3	58	33	33	18	33
Major league totals (2 years)......	6	11	.353	7.11	37	16	0	0	0	133	162	109	105	86	103

KELLY, JEFF — P — PIRATES

PERSONAL: Born January 11, 1975, in Staten Island, N.Y. ... 6-6/240. ... Throws left, bats left. ... Full name: Jeffrey Michael Kelly.
HIGH SCHOOL: McKee Tech (Staten Island, N.Y.).
TRANSACTIONS/CAREER NOTES: Selected by Pittsburgh Pirates organization in 15th round of free-agent draft (June 2, 1994). ... On Lynchburg suspended list (August 21-25, 1996).

Year Team (League)	W	L	Pct.	ERA	G	GS	CG	ShO	Sv.	IP	H	R	ER	BB	SO
1994— GC Pirates (GCL)...............	0	5	.000	4.08	11	7	0	0	0	46 1/3	54	26	21	12	24
1995— Augusta (S. Atl.)................	6	11	.353	3.47	26	26	0	0	0	142 2/3	134	68	55	51	114
1996— Augusta (S. Atl.)................	6	3	.667	3.32	14	14	0	0	0	84	76	39	31	27	68
— Lynchburg (Carolina)	4	5	.444	3.60	13	13	0	0	0	75	77	45	30	24	57
1997— Carolina (Southern)...........	6	11	.353	4.65	31	19	0	0	0	127 2/3	134	79	66	*85	83

KELLY, MIKE — OF — DEVIL RAYS

PERSONAL: Born June 2, 1970, in Los Angeles. ... 6-4/195. ... Bats right, throws right. ... Full name: Michael Raymond Kelly.
HIGH SCHOOL: Los Alamitos (Calif.).
COLLEGE: Arizona State.
TRANSACTIONS/CAREER NOTES: Selected by New York Mets organization in 24th round of free-agent draft (June 1, 1988); did not sign. ... Selected by Atlanta Braves organization in first round (second pick overall) of free-agent draft (June 3, 1991). ... Traded by Braves to Cincinnati Reds organization for P Chad Fox and a player to be named later (January 9, 1996); Braves acquired P Ray King to complete deal (June 11, 1996). ... Traded by Reds to Tampa Bay Devil Rays for a player to be named later (November 11, 1997); Reds acquired 1B Dmitri Young to complete deal (November 18).

HONORS: Named College Player of the Year by THE SPORTING NEWS (1990). ... Named outfielder on THE SPORTING NEWS college All-America team (1990). ... Named Golden Spikes Award winner by USA Baseball (1991).

Year Team (League)	Pos.	G	AB	R	H	2B	3B	HR	RBI	Avg.	BB	SO	SB	PO	A	E	Avg.
1991— Durham (Carolina)......	OF	35	124	29	31	6	1	6	17	.250	19	47	6	4	0	0	1.000
1992— Greenville (Southern).	OF	133	471	83	108	18	4	25	71	.229	65	*162	22	244	7	3	.988
1993— Richmond (Int'l)........	OF	123	424	63	103	13	1	19	58	.243	36	109	11	270	6	2	*.993
1994— Atlanta (N.L.).............	OF	30	77	14	21	10	1	2	9	.273	2	17	0	25	0	1	.962
— Richmond (Int'l)......	OF	81	313	46	82	14	4	15	45	.262	32	96	9	181	5	1	.995
1995— Richmond (Int'l)........	OF	15	45	5	13	1	0	2	8	.289	5	17	0	24	0	1	1.000
— Atlanta (N.L.)..........	OF	97	137	26	26	6	1	3	17	.190	11	49	7	63	0	4	.940
1996— Cincinnati (N.L.)■......	OF	19	49	5	9	4	0	1	7	.184	9	11	4	34	1	1	.972
— Indianapolis (A.A.)......	OF	88	292	43	61	10	1	8	30	.209	30	80	13	132	2	4	.971
1997— Chattanooga (Sou.)....	OF	15	60	14	21	7	0	3	12	.350	3	16	3	32	2	0	1.000
— Indianapolis (A.A.)......	OF	27	92	28	32	8	0	7	18	.348	23	23	7	51	1	2	.963
— Cincinnati (N.L.)........	OF-DH	73	140	27	41	13	2	6	19	.293	10	30	6	88	2	2	.978
Major league totals (4 years)		219	403	72	97	33	4	12	52	.241	32	107	17	210	3	8	.964

KELLY, PAT — 2B — BLUE JAYS

PERSONAL: Born October 14, 1967, in Philadelphia. ... 6-0/182. ... Bats right, throws right. ... Full name: Patrick Franklin Kelly.
HIGH SCHOOL: Catashuqua (Pa.).
COLLEGE: West Chester (Pa.).
TRANSACTIONS/CAREER NOTES: Selected by New York Yankees organization in ninth round of free-agent draft (June 1, 1988). ... On New York disabled list (April 21-May 7, 1992); included rehabilitation assignment to Albany/Colonie (May 5-7). ... On New York disabled list (June 22-July 7, 1994); included rehabilitation assignment to Albany/Colonie (July 6-7). ... On New York disabled list (May 27-July 7, 1995); included rehabilitation assignments to Gulf Coast Yankees (July 3-4) and Tampa (July 4-7). ... On New York disabled list (March 27-July 26; July 27-August 7, 1996 and August 23-September 7, 1996); included rehabilitation assignments to Gulf Coast Yankees (July 1-5), Tampa (July 5-8 and July 11-16), Columbus (July 16-26) and Norwich (August 8-12). ... On New York disabled list (May 10-June 3 and August 17-September 1, 1997); included rehabilitation assignment to Columbus (May 21-June 2). ... Granted free agency (November 7, 1997). ... Signed by Toronto Blue Jays organization (November 27, 1997).
STATISTICAL NOTES: Led Carolina League second basemen with 76 double plays and tied for lead with 641 total chances in 1989. ... Led Eastern League second basemen with 667 total chances and 97 double plays in 1990. ... Led A.L. with 14 sacrifice hits in 1994.

Year Team (League)	Pos.	G	AB	R	H	2B	3B	HR	RBI	Avg.	BB	SO	SB	PO	A	E	Avg.
1988— Oneonta (NYP)..........	2B-SS	71	280	49	92	11	6	2	34	.329	15	45	25	124	207	16	.954
1989— Prince William (Car.)..	2B	124	436	61	116	21	*7	3	45	.266	32	79	31	244	*372	25	.961
1990— Alb./Colon. (Eastern)..	2B	126	418	67	113	19	6	8	44	.270	37	79	31	*266	*381	*20	.970
1991— Columbus (Int'l)........	2B	31	116	27	39	9	2	3	19	.336	9	16	8	53	97	4	.974
— New York (A.L.).........	3B-2B	96	298	35	72	12	4	3	23	.242	15	52	12	78	204	18	.940
1992— New York (A.L.).........	2B-DH	106	318	38	72	22	2	7	27	.226	25	72	8	203	296	11	.978
— Alb./Colon. (Eastern)..	2B	2	6	1	0	0	0	0	0	.000	2	4	0	4	8	0	1.000
1993— New York (A.L.).........	2B	127	406	49	111	24	1	7	51	.273	24	68	14	245	369	14	.978
1994— New York (A.L.).........	2B	93	286	35	80	21	2	3	41	.280	19	51	6	180	258	10	.978
— Alb./Colon. (Eastern)..	2B	1	4	1	1	0	0	0	0	.250	0	1	1	2	2	0	1.000
1995— New York (A.L.).........	2B-DH	89	270	32	64	12	1	4	29	.237	23	65	8	161	255	7	.983
— GC Yankees (GCL)......	2B	1	2	2	0	0	0	0	0	1.000	1	0	0	3	3	0	1.000
— Tampa (Florida State).	2B	3	17	0	4	1	0	0	2	.235	0	1	0	8	14	0	1.000
1996— GC Yankees (GCL)......	2B	5	17	7	6	2	0	1	1	.353	3	2	3	5	5	0	1.000
— Tampa (Florida State).	2B	6	22	6	6	0	0	1	2	.273	1	7	0	15	9	2	.923
— Columbus (Int'l).........	2B	8	37	6	14	1	1	2	7	.378	2	11	3	19	19	0	1.000
— New York (A.L.).........	2B-DH	13	21	4	3	0	0	0	2	.143	2	9	0	8	24	1	.970
— Norwich (Eastern)......	2B	4	17	3	5	2	1	0	0	.294	0	2	1	7	13	1	.952
1997— New York (A.L.).........	2B-DH	67	120	25	29	6	1	2	10	.242	14	37	8	63	92	3	.981
— Columbus (Int'l).........	2B	11	44	8	15	4	0	2	6	.341	4	6	1	15	39	0	1.000
Major league totals (7 years)		591	1719	218	431	97	11	26	183	.251	122	354	56	938	1498	64	.974

DIVISION SERIES RECORD

Year Team (League)	Pos.	G	AB	R	H	2B	3B	HR	RBI	Avg.	BB	SO	SB	PO	A	E	Avg.
1995— New York (A.L.)..........	2B-PR	5	3	3	0	0	0	0	1	.000	1	3	0	2	4	0	1.000

KELLY, ROBERTO — OF — RANGERS

PERSONAL: Born October 1, 1964, in Panama City, Panama. ... 6-2/198. ... Bats right, throws right. ... Full name: Roberto Conrado Kelly.
HIGH SCHOOL: Panama City (Panama).
COLLEGE: Jose Dolores Moscote College (Panama).
TRANSACTIONS/CAREER NOTES: Signed as non-drafted free agent by New York Yankees organization (February 21, 1982). ... On disabled list (July 10-August 23, 1986). ... On New York disabled list (June 29-September 1, 1988; May 26-June 12, 1989; and July 6-August 13, 1991). ... Traded by Yankees to Cincinnati Reds for OF Paul O'Neill and 1B Joe DeBerry (November 3, 1992). ... On disabled list (July 14, 1993-remainder of season). ... Traded by Reds with P Roger Etheridge to Atlanta Braves for OF Deion Sanders (May 29, 1994). ... Traded by Braves with OF Tony Tarasco and P Esteban Yan to Montreal Expos for OF Marquis Grissom (April 6, 1995). ... Traded by Expos with P Joey Eischen to Los Angeles Dodgers for OF Henry Rodriguez and IF Jeff Treadway (May 23, 1995). ... Granted free agency (November 6, 1995). ... Signed by Minnesota Twins (January 29, 1996). ... On disabled list (June 27-July 12, 1996). ... On disabled list (March 24-April 16, 1997); included rehabilitation assignment to Fort Myers (April 11-16). ... Traded by Twins to Seattle Mariners for two players to be named later (August 20, 1997); Twins acquired P Joe Mays and P Jeromy Palki to complete deal (October 9, 1997). ... Granted free agency (October 31, 1997). ... Signed by Texas Rangers (December 9, 1997).
RECORDS: Holds major league single-season record for most times reaching base on catcher's interference—8 (1992). ... Shares major league single-season record for fewest double plays by outfielder (150 or more games)—0 (1990).
STATISTICAL NOTES: Led International League outfielders with 345 total chances in 1987. ... Led A.L. outfielders with 430 total chances in 1990. ... Career major league grand slams: 1.
MISCELLANEOUS: Batted as switch-hitter (1985).

Year Team (League)	Pos.	G	AB	R	H	2B	3B	HR	RBI	Avg.	BB	SO	SB	PO	A	E	Avg.
1982— GC Yankees (GCL)......	SS-OF	31	86	13	17	1	1	1	18	.198	10	18	3	47	79	19	.869
1983— Oneonta (NYP)..........	OF-3B	48	167	17	36	1	2	2	17	.216	12	20	12	70	3	5	.936
— Greensboro (S. Atl.) ...	OF-SS	20	49	6	13	0	0	0	3	.265	3	5	3	30	2	0	1.000
1984— Greensboro (S. Atl.) ...	OF-1B	111	361	68	86	13	2	1	26	.238	57	49	42	228	5	4	.983
1985— Fort Lauderdale (FSL)	OF	114	417	86	103	4	*13	3	38	.247	58	70	49	187	1	1	.995
1986— Alb./Colon. (Eastern)..	OF	86	299	42	87	11	4	2	43	.291	29	63	10	206	8	7	.968
1987— Columbus (Int'l)........	OF	118	471	77	131	19	8	13	62	.278	33	116	*51	*331	4	10	.971
— New York (A.L.).......	OF-DH	23	52	12	14	3	0	1	7	.269	5	15	9	42	0	2	.955
1988— New York (A.L.).......	OF-DH	38	77	9	19	4	1	1	7	.247	3	15	5	70	1	1	.986
— Columbus (Int'l)........	OF	30	120	25	40	8	1	3	16	.333	6	29	11	51	1	0	1.000
1989— New York (A.L.).......	OF	137	441	65	133	18	3	9	48	.302	41	89	35	353	9	6	.984
1990— New York (A.L.).........	OF	*162	641	85	183	32	4	15	61	.285	33	148	42	420	5	5	.988
1991— New York (A.L.).......	OF	126	486	68	130	22	2	20	69	.267	45	77	32	268	8	4	.986
1992— New York (A.L.).......	OF	152	580	81	158	31	2	10	66	.272	41	96	28	389	8	1	.995
1993— Cincinnati (N.L.)■.....	OF	78	320	44	102	17	3	9	35	.319	17	43	21	198	3	1	.995
1994— Cincinnati (N.L.)■.....	OF	47	179	29	54	8	0	3	21	.302	11	35	9	118	2	1	.992
— Atlanta (N.L.)■........	OF	63	255	44	73	15	3	6	24	.286	24	36	10	128	3	2	.985
1995— Montreal (N.L.)■ ...	OF	24	95	11	26	4	0	1	9	.274	7	14	4	42	1	0	1.000
— Los Angeles (N.L.)■ ..	OF	112	409	47	114	19	2	6	48	.279	15	65	15	183	2	6	.969
1996— Minnesota (A.L.)■	OF-DH	98	322	41	104	17	4	6	47	.323	23	53	10	203	4	2	.990
1997— Fort Myers (FSL)	OF	4	11	2	4	0	0	1	3	.364	4	1	0	6	0	0	1.000
— Minnesota (A.L.)........	OF-DH	75	247	39	71	19	2	5	37	.287	17	50	7	101	1	0	1.000
— Seattle (A.L.)■	OF-DH	30	121	19	36	7	0	7	22	.298	5	17	2	53	1	0	1.000
American League totals (8 years)		841	2967	419	848	153	18	74	364	.286	213	560	170	1899	37	27	.986
National League totals (3 years)		324	1258	175	369	63	8	25	137	.293	74	193	59	669	11	10	.986
Major league totals (11 years)		1165	4225	594	1217	216	26	99	501	.288	287	753	229	2568	48	37	.986

DIVISION SERIES RECORD

Year Team (League)	Pos.	G	AB	R	H	2B	3B	HR	RBI	Avg.	BB	SO	SB	PO	A	E	Avg.
1995— Los Angeles (N.L.)	OF	3	11	0	4	0	0	0	0	.364	1	0	0	8	0	1	.889
1997— Seattle (A.L.)	OF-PH	4	13	1	4	3	0	0	1	.308	0	3	0	4	0	0	1.000
Division series totals (2 years)		7	24	1	8	3	0	0	1	.333	1	3	0	12	0	1	.923

ALL-STAR GAME RECORD

Year League	Pos.	AB	R	H	2B	3B	HR	RBI	Avg.	BB	SO	SB	PO	A	E	Avg.
1992— American	OF	2	0	1	1	0	0	2	.500	0	1	0	1	0	0	1.000
1993— National	OF	1	0	0	0	0	0	0	.000	0	1	0	0	1	0	1.000
All-Star Game totals (2 years)		3	0	1	1	0	0	2	.333	0	2	0	1	1	0	1.000

KENDALL, JASON   C   PIRATES

PERSONAL: Born June 26, 1974, in San Diego. ... 6-0/190. ... Bats right, throws right. ... Full name: Jason Daniel Kendall. ... Son of Fred Kendall, catcher/first baseman with San Diego Padres, Cleveland Indians and Boston Red Sox (1969-80).

HIGH SCHOOL: Torrance (Calif.).

TRANSACTIONS/CAREER NOTES: Selected by Pittsburgh Pirates organization in first round (23rd pick overall) of free-agent draft (June 1, 1992).

HONORS: Named Southern League Most Valuable Player (1995). ... Named N.L. Rookie Player of the Year by THE SPORTING NEWS (1996).

STATISTICAL NOTES: Led Gulf Coast League with 13 passed balls in 1992. ... Led Southern League with .414 on-base percentage in 1995. ... Led Southern League catchers with 754 total chances in 1995. ... Led N.L. catchers in double plays with 20 in 1997.

Year Team (League)	Pos.	G	AB	R	H	2B	3B	HR	RBI	Avg.	BB	SO	SB	PO	A	E	Avg.
1992— GC Pirates (GCL)........	C	33	111	7	29	2	0	0	10	.261	8	9	2	182	36	5	.978
1993— Augusta (S. Atl.)........	C	102	366	43	101	17	4	1	40	.276	22	30	8	472	65	20	.964
1994— Salem (Carolina)	C	101	371	68	118	19	2	7	66	.318	47	21	14	409	33	9	.980
— Carolina (Southern)....	C	13	47	6	11	2	0	0	6	.234	2	3	0	54	9	2	.969
1995— Carolina (Southern)....	C	117	429	87	140	26	1	8	71	.326	56	22	10	*692	54	8	.989
1996— Pittsburgh (N.L.)	C	130	414	54	124	23	5	3	42	.300	35	30	5	797	71	*18	.980
1997— Pittsburgh (N.L.)	C	144	486	71	143	36	4	8	49	.294	49	53	18	952	*103	11	.990
Major league totals (2 years)		274	900	125	267	59	9	11	91	.297	84	83	23	1749	174	29	.985

ALL-STAR GAME RECORD

Year League	Pos.	AB	R	H	2B	3B	HR	RBI	Avg.	BB	SO	SB	PO	A	E	Avg.
1996— National	C	0	0	0	0	0	0	0	...	0	0	0	0	0	0	...

KENT, JEFF   2B   GIANTS

PERSONAL: Born March 7, 1968, in Bellflower, Calif. ... 6-1/190. ... Bats right, throws right. ... Full name: Jeffrey Franklin Kent.

HIGH SCHOOL: Edison (Huntington Beach, Calif.).

COLLEGE: California.

TRANSACTIONS/CAREER NOTES: Selected by Toronto Blue Jays organization in 20th round of free-agent draft (June 5, 1989). ... Traded by Blue Jays with a player to be named later to New York Mets for P David Cone (August 27, 1992); Mets acquired OF Ryan Thompson to complete deal (September 1, 1992). ... On disabled list (July 6-21, 1995). ... Traded by New York Mets with IF Jose Vizcaino to Cleveland Indians for 2B Carlos Baerga and IF Alvaro Espinoza (July 29, 1996). ... Traded by Indians with IF Jose Vizcaino, P Julian Tavarez and a player to be named later to San Francisco Giants for 3B Matt Williams and a player to be named later (November 13, 1996); Indians traded P Joe Roa to Giants for OF Trenidad Hubbard to complete deal (December 16, 1996). ...On suspended list (August 22-25, 1997)

– 299 –

STATISTICAL NOTES: Led Florida State League second basemen with 680 total chances and 83 double plays in 1990. ... Led Southern League second basemen with 673 total chances and 96 double plays in 1991. ... Led N.L. second basemen with 18 errors in 1993. ... Career major league grand slams: 5.

Year Team (League)	Pos.	G	AB	R	H	2B	3B	HR	RBI	Avg.	BB	SO	SB	PO	A	E	Avg.
1989— St. Catharines (NYP) ..	SS-3B	73	268	34	60	14	1	*13	37	.224	33	81	5	103	178	29	.906
1990— Dunedin (Fla. St.)	2B	132	447	72	124	32	2	16	60	.277	53	98	17	*261	*404	15	.978
1991— Knoxville (Southern) ..	2B	•139	445	68	114	*34	1	2	61	.256	80	104	25	249	*395	*29	.957
1992— Toronto (A.L.)	3B-2B-1B	65	192	36	46	13	1	8	35	.240	20	47	2	62	112	11	.941
—New York (N.L.)■ ..	2B-SS-3B	37	113	16	27	8	1	3	15	.239	7	29	0	62	93	3	.981
1993— New York (N.L.)	2B-3B-SS	140	496	65	134	24	0	21	80	.270	30	88	4	261	341	†22	.965
1994— New York (N.L.)	2B	107	415	53	121	24	5	14	68	.292	23	84	1	222	337	•14	.976
1995— New York (N.L.)	2B	125	472	65	131	22	3	20	65	.278	29	89	3	245	354	10	.984
1996— New York (N.L.)	3B	89	335	45	97	20	1	9	39	.290	21	56	4	75	184	21	.925
—Cleveland (A.L.)■	1-2-3-DH	39	102	16	27	7	0	3	16	.265	10	22	2	125	46	1	.994
1997— San Fran. (N.L.)■	2B-1B	155	580	90	145	38	2	29	121	.250	48	133	11	405	429	16	.981
American League totals (2 years)		104	294	52	73	20	1	11	51	.248	30	69	4	187	158	12	.966
National League totals (6 years)		653	2411	334	655	136	12	96	388	.272	158	479	23	1270	1738	86	.972
Major league totals (6 years)		757	2705	386	728	156	13	107	439	.269	188	548	27	1457	1896	98	.972

DIVISION SERIES RECORD

RECORDS: Shares single-game record for most home runs—2 (October 3, 1997).

Year Team (League)	Pos.	G	AB	R	H	2B	3B	HR	RBI	Avg.	BB	SO	SB	PO	A	E	Avg.
1996— Cleveland (A.L.)	2-1-PR-3	4	8	2	1	1	0	0	0	.125	0	0	0	3	3	0	1.000
1997— San Francisco (N.L.) ..	2B-1B	3	10	2	3	0	0	2	2	.300	2	1	0	19	7	0	1.000
Division series totals (2 years)		7	18	4	4	1	0	2	2	.222	2	1	0	22	10	0	1.000

KEY, JIMMY — P — ORIOLES

PERSONAL: Born April 22, 1961, in Huntsville, Ala. ... 6-1/185. ... Throws left, bats right. ... Full name: James Edward Key.
HIGH SCHOOL: Butler (Huntsville, Ala.).
COLLEGE: Clemson.
TRANSACTIONS/CAREER NOTES: Selected by Chicago White Sox organization in 10th round of free-agent draft (June 5, 1979); did not sign. ... Selected by Toronto Blue Jays organization in third round of free-agent draft (June 7, 1982). ... On Toronto disabled list (April 15-June 29, 1988); included rehabilitation assignment to Dunedin (June 10-27). ... On disabled list (August 4-19, 1989). ... On Toronto disabled list (May 23-June 22, 1990); included rehabilitation assignment to Dunedin (June 7-18). ... Granted free agency (October 27, 1992). ... Signed by New York Yankees (December 10, 1992). ... On disabled list (May 17, 1995-remainder of season). ... On New York disabled list (May 16-31 and June 11-26, 1996); included rehabilitation assignment to Tampa (May 21-31) and Gulf Coast Yankees (June 22-23). ... Granted free agency (December 7, 1996). ... Signed by Baltimore Orioles (December 10, 1996).
HONORS: Named A.L. Pitcher of the Year by THE SPORTING NEWS (1987 and 1994). ... Named lefthanded pitcher on THE SPORTING NEWS A.L. All-Star team (1987 and 1993-94).
STATISTICAL NOTES: Pitched 5-0 one-hit, complete-game victory against Chicago (May 22, 1986). ... Pitched 5-0 one-hit, complete-game victory against California (April 27, 1993).
MISCELLANEOUS: Appeared in one game as pinch-runner (1985).

Year Team (League)	W	L	Pct.	ERA	G	GS	CG	ShO	Sv.	IP	H	R	ER	BB	SO
1982— Medicine Hat (Pio.)	2	1	.667	2.30	5	5	1	0	0	31 1/3	27	12	8	10	25
—Florence (S. Atl.)	5	2	.714	3.72	9	9	0	0	0	58	59	33	24	18	49
1983— Knoxville (Southern)	6	5	.545	2.85	14	14	2	0	0	101	86	35	32	40	57
—Syracuse (Int'l)	4	8	.333	4.13	16	15	2	0	0	89 1/3	87	58	41	33	71
1984— Toronto (A.L.)	4	5	.444	4.65	63	0	0	0	10	62	70	37	32	32	44
1985— Toronto (A.L.)	14	6	.700	3.00	35	32	3	0	0	212 2/3	188	77	71	50	85
1986— Toronto (A.L.)	14	11	.560	3.57	36	35	4	2	0	232	222	98	92	74	141
1987— Toronto (A.L.)	17	8	.680	*2.76	36	36	8	1	0	261	210	93	80	66	161
1988— Toronto (A.L.)	12	5	.706	3.29	21	21	2	2	0	131 1/3	127	55	48	30	65
—Dunedin (Fla. St.)	2	0	1.000	0.00	4	4	0	0	0	21 1/3	15	2	0	1	11
1989— Toronto (A.L.)	13	14	.481	3.88	33	33	5	1	0	216	226	99	93	27	118
1990— Toronto (A.L.)	13	7	.650	4.25	27	27	0	0	0	154 2/3	169	79	73	22	88
—Dunedin (Fla. St.)	2	0	1.000	2.50	3	3	0	0	0	18	21	7	5	3	14
1991— Toronto (A.L.)	16	12	.571	3.05	33	33	2	2	0	209 1/3	207	84	71	44	125
1992— Toronto (A.L.)	13	13	.500	3.53	33	33	2	0	0	216 2/3	205	88	85	59	117
1993— New York (A.L.)■	18	6	.750	3.00	34	34	4	2	0	236 2/3	219	84	79	43	173
1994— New York (A.L.)	*17	4	.810	3.27	25	•25	1	0	0	168	177	68	61	52	97
1995— New York (A.L.)	1	2	.333	5.64	5	5	0	0	0	30 1/3	40	20	19	6	14
1996— New York (A.L.)	12	11	.522	4.68	30	30	0	0	0	169 1/3	171	93	88	58	116
—Tampa (Florida State)	0	0	...	2.77	2	2	0	0	0	13	10	4	4	1	11
—GC Yankees (GCL)	1	0	1.000	0.00	1	1	0	0	0	5	3	2	0	0	10
1997— Baltimore (A.L.)■	16	10	.615	3.43	34	34	1	1	0	212 1/3	210	90	81	82	141
Major league totals (14 years)	180	114	.612	3.49	445	378	34	13	10	2512 1/3	2441	1065	973	645	1485

DIVISION SERIES RECORD

Year Team (League)	W	L	Pct.	ERA	G	GS	CG	ShO	Sv.	IP	H	R	ER	BB	SO
1996— New York (A.L.)	0	0	...	3.60	1	1	0	0	0	5	5	2	2	1	3
1997— Baltimore (A.L.)	0	1	.000	3.86	1	1	0	0	0	4 2/3	8	2	2	0	4
Div. series totals (2 years)	0	1	.000	3.72	2	2	0	0	0	9 2/3	13	4	4	1	7

CHAMPIONSHIP SERIES RECORD

RECORDS: Shares single-series record for most hit batsmen—3 (1997).

Year Team (League)	W	L	Pct.	ERA	G	GS	CG	ShO	Sv.	IP	H	R	ER	BB	SO
1985— Toronto (A.L.)	0	1	.000	5.19	2	2	0	0	0	8 2/3	15	5	5	2	5
1989— Toronto (A.L.)	1	0	1.000	4.50	1	1	0	0	0	6	7	3	3	2	2

Year Team (League)	W	L	Pct.	ERA	G	GS	CG	ShO	Sv.	IP	H	R	ER	BB	SO
1991— Toronto (A.L.)	0	0	...	3.00	1	1	0	0	0	6	5	2	2	1	1
1992— Toronto (A.L.)	0	0	...	0.00	1	0	0	0	0	3	2	0	0	2	1
1996— New York (A.L.)	1	0	1.000	2.25	1	1	0	0	0	8	3	2	2	1	5
1997— Baltimore (A.L.)	0	0	...	2.57	2	1	0	0	0	7	5	2	2	3	7
Champ. series totals (6 years)	2	1	.667	3.26	8	6	0	0	0	38 2/3	37	14	14	11	21

WORLD SERIES RECORD

NOTES: Member of World Series championship team (1992 and 1996).

Year Team (League)	W	L	Pct.	ERA	G	GS	CG	ShO	Sv.	IP	H	R	ER	BB	SO
1992— Toronto (A.L.)	2	0	1.000	1.00	2	1	0	0	0	9	6	2	1	0	6
1996— New York (A.L.)	1	1	.500	3.97	2	2	0	0	0	11 1/3	15	5	5	5	1
World Series totals (2 years)	3	1	.750	2.66	4	3	0	0	0	20 1/3	21	7	6	5	7

ALL-STAR GAME RECORD

Year League	W	L	Pct.	ERA	GS	CG	ShO	Sv.	IP	H	R	ER	BB	SO
1985— American	0	0	...	0.00	0	0	0	0	1/3	0	0	0	0	0
1991— American	1	0	1.000	0.00	0	0	0	0	1	1	0	0	0	1
1993— American	0	0	...	9.00	0	0	0	0	1	2	1	1	0	1
1994— American	0	0	...	4.50	1	0	0	0	2	1	1	1	0	1
All-Star totals (4 years)	1	0	1.000	4.15	1	0	0	0	4 1/3	4	2	2	0	3

KIESCHNICK, BROOKS   OF   DEVIL RAYS

K

PERSONAL: Born June 6, 1972, in Robstown, Texas. ... 6-4/230. ... Bats left, throws right. ... Full name: Michael Brooks Kieschnick. ... Name pronounced KEY-shnik..
HIGH SCHOOL: Carroll (Corpus Christi, Texas).
COLLEGE: Texas.
TRANSACTIONS/CAREER NOTES: Selected by Chicago Cubs organization in first round (10th pick overall) of free-agent draft (June 3, 1993). ... Selected by Tampa Bay Devil Rays in third round (64th pick overall) of expansion draft (November 18, 1997).
STATISTICAL NOTES: Led American Association with 250 total bases in 1995.

Year Team (League)	Pos.	G	AB	R	H	2B	3B	HR	RBI	Avg.	BB	SO	SB	PO	A	E	Avg.
1993— GC Cubs (GCL)	OF	3	9	0	2	1	0	0	0	.222	0	1	0	3	1	0	1.000
— Daytona (Fla. St.)	OF	6	22	1	4	2	0	0	2	.182	1	4	0	9	1	0	1.000
— Orlando (South.)	OF	25	91	12	31	8	0	2	10	.341	7	19	1	22	1	3	.885
1994— Orlando (South.)	OF-1B-3B	126	468	57	132	25	3	14	55	.282	33	78	3	259	14	6	.978
1995— Iowa (Am. Assoc.)	OF-1B	138	505	61	*149	30	1	*23	73	.295	58	91	2	179	15	2	.990
1996— Chicago (N.L.)	OF	25	29	6	10	2	0	1	6	.345	3	8	0	5	0	1	.833
— Iowa (Am. Assoc.)	1B-OF	117	441	47	114	20	1	18	64	.259	37	108	0	498	28	8	.985
1997— Iowa (Am. Assoc.)	1B-OF-3B	97	360	57	93	21	0	21	66	.258	36	89	0	562	54	8	.987
— Chicago (N.L.)	OF	39	90	9	18	2	0	4	12	.200	12	21	1	39	1	2	.952
Major league totals (2 years)		64	119	15	28	4	0	5	18	.235	15	29	1	44	1	3	.938

KILE, DARRYL   P   ROCKIES

PERSONAL: Born December 2, 1968, in Garden Grove, Calif. ... 6-5/185. ... Throws right, bats right. ... Full name: Darryl Andrew Kile.
JUNIOR COLLEGE: Chaffey College (Calif.).
TRANSACTIONS/CAREER NOTES: Selected by Houston Astros organization in 30th round of free-agent draft (June 2, 1987). ... On Tucson disabled list (June 25-July 5, 1992). ... Granted free agency (October 28, 1997). ... Signed by Colorado Rockies (December 4, 1997).
RECORDS: Shares modern N.L. record for most hit batsmen in nine-inning game—4 (June 2, 1996).
STATISTICAL NOTES: Led N.L. with 15 hit batsmen in 1993. ... Pitched 7-1 no-hit victory against New York (September 8, 1993). ... Tied for N.L. lead with 10 wild pitches in 1994. ... Tied for N.L. lead with 16 hit batsmen in 1996.
MISCELLANEOUS: Appeared in two games as pinch-runner (1996).

Year Team (League)	W	L	Pct.	ERA	G	GS	CG	ShO	Sv.	IP	H	R	ER	BB	SO
1988— GC Astros (GCL)	5	3	.625	3.17	12	12	0	0	0	59 2/3	48	34	21	33	54
1989— Columbus (Southern)	11	6	.647	2.58	20	20	6	•2	0	125 2/3	74	47	36	68	108
— Tucson (PCL)	2	1	.667	5.96	6	6	1	1	0	25 2/3	33	20	17	13	18
1990— Tucson (PCL)	5	10	.333	6.64	26	23	1	0	0	123 1/3	147	97	91	68	77
1991— Houston (N.L.)	7	11	.389	3.69	37	22	0	0	0	153 2/3	144	81	63	84	100
1992— Houston (N.L.)	5	10	.333	3.95	22	22	2	0	0	125 1/3	124	61	55	63	90
— Tucson (PCL)	4	1	.800	3.99	9	9	0	0	0	56 1/3	50	31	25	32	43
1993— Houston (N.L.)	15	8	.652	3.51	32	26	4	2	0	171 2/3	152	73	67	69	141
1994— Houston (N.L.)	9	6	.600	4.57	24	24	0	0	0	147 2/3	153	84	75	*82	105
1995— Houston (N.L.)	4	12	.250	4.96	25	21	0	0	0	127	114	81	70	73	113
— Tucson (PCL)	2	1	.667	8.51	4	4	0	0	0	24 1/3	29	23	23	12	15
1996— Houston (N.L.)	12	11	.522	4.19	35	33	4	0	0	219	233	113	102	97	219
1997— Houston (N.L.)	19	7	.731	2.57	34	34	6	4	0	255 2/3	208	87	73	94	205
Major league totals (7 years)	71	65	.522	3.79	209	182	16	6	0	1200	1128	580	505	562	973

DIVISION SERIES RECORD

Year Team (League)	W	L	Pct.	ERA	G	GS	CG	ShO	Sv.	IP	H	R	ER	BB	SO
1997— Houston (N.L.)	0	1	.000	2.57	1	1	0	0	0	7	2	2	2	2	4

ALL-STAR GAME RECORD

Year League	W	L	Pct.	ERA	GS	CG	ShO	Sv.	IP	H	R	ER	BB	SO
1993— National						Did not play.								
1997— National						Did not play.								

KING, BILL   P   ATHLETICS

PERSONAL: Born February 18, 1973, in Tallahassee, Fla. ... 6-5/215. ... Throws right, bats right. ... Full name: William Byron King.
HIGH SCHOOL: Carroll (Ozark, Ala.).
COLLEGE: Birmingham-Southern.
TRANSACTIONS/CAREER NOTES: Selected by Oakland Athletics organization in third round of free-agent draft (June 2, 1994).

Year Team (League)	W	L	Pct.	ERA	G	GS	CG	ShO	Sv.	IP	H	R	ER	BB	SO
1994— S. Oregon (N'west)	0	0	...	0.00	1	1	0	0	0	3	1	0	0	1	2
— West. Mich. (Mid.)	2	1	.667	1.81	17	1	0	0	4	44²/₃	35	11	9	19	25
1995— West. Mich. (Mid.)	9	7	.563	3.34	30	18	0	0	2	148¹/₃	152	75	55	41	95
1996— Modesto (California)	16	4	.800	4.75	29	27	0	0	1	163	193	102	86	40	100
1997— Huntsville (Southern)	9	7	.563	4.19	28	27	1	0	0	•176	*216	99	82	28	103

KING, CESAR   C   RANGERS

PERSONAL: Born February 28, 1978, in LaRomana, Dominican Republic. ... 6-0/175. ... Bats right, throws right.
TRANSACTIONS/CAREER NOTES: Signed as non-drafted free agent by Texas Rangers organization (September 4, 1994).
STATISTICAL NOTES: Led Florida State League catchers with 10 double plays in 1997.

Year Team (League)	Pos.	G	AB	R	H	2B	3B	HR	RBI	Avg.	BB	SO	SB	PO	A	E	Avg.
1995— Dom. Rangers (DSL)	C	54	182	33	55	9	0	3	22	.302	22	34	3	277	43	11	.967
1996— Char., S.C. (S. Atl.)	C	84	276	35	69	10	1	7	28	.250	21	58	8	399	71	14	.971
1997— Charlotte (Fla. St.)	C-3B	91	307	51	91	14	4	6	37	.296	35	58	8	553	84	10	.985
— Tulsa (Texas)	C	14	45	6	16	1	0	1	8	.356	5	3	0	85	8	3	.969

KING, CURTIS   P   CARDINALS

PERSONAL: Born October 25, 1970, in Norristown, Pa. ... 6-5/200. ... Throws right, bats right. ... Full name: Curtis Albert King.
HIGH SCHOOL: Plymouth-Whitemarsh (Plymouth Meeting, Pa.).
COLLEGE: Philadelphia Textile.
TRANSACTIONS/CAREER NOTES: Selected by St. Louis Cardinals organization in fifth round of free-agent draft (June 2, 1994).

Year Team (League)	W	L	Pct.	ERA	G	GS	CG	ShO	Sv.	IP	H	R	ER	BB	SO
1994— New Jersey (NYP)	1	0	1.000	2.61	5	4	0	0	0	20²/₃	19	7	6	11	14
— Savannah (S. Atl.)	4	1	.800	1.87	8	8	2	2	0	53	37	14	11	9	40
1995— St. Petersburg (FSL)	7	8	.467	2.58	28	21	3	0	0	136	117	49	39	49	65
1996— Arkansas (Texas)	0	1	.000	19.80	5	0	0	0	0	5	15	12	11	6	5
— St. Petersburg (FSL)	3	3	.500	2.75	48	0	0	0	1	55²/₃	41	20	17	24	27
1997— Arkansas (Texas)	2	3	.400	4.46	32	0	0	0	30	36¹/₃	38	19	18	10	29
— Louisville (A.A.)	2	1	.667	2.05	16	0	0	0	16	22	19	5	5	6	9
— St. Louis (N.L.)	4	2	.667	2.76	30	0	0	0	3	29¹/₃	38	14	9	11	13
Major league totals (1 year)	4	2	.667	2.76	30	0	0	0	3	29¹/₃	38	14	9	11	13

KING, JEFF   1B   ROYALS

PERSONAL: Born December 26, 1964, in Marion, Ind. ... 6-1/188. ... Bats right, throws right. ... Full name: Jeffrey Wayne King. ... Son of Jack King, minor league catcher (1954-55).
HIGH SCHOOL: Rampart (Colorado Springs, Colo.).
COLLEGE: Arkansas.
TRANSACTIONS/CAREER NOTES: Selected by Chicago Cubs organization in 23rd round of free-agent draft (June 6, 1983); did not sign. ... Selected by Pittsburgh Pirates organization in first round (first pick overall) of free-agent draft (June 2, 1986). ... On Pittsburgh disabled list (May 5-31, 1991); included rehabilitation assignment to Buffalo (May 25-31). ... On Pittsburgh disabled list (June 13-October 7, 1991); included rehabilitation assignment to Buffalo (August 28-September 6). ... On disabled list (May 25-June 9, 1994 and June 16-July 1, 1995). ... Traded by Pirates with SS Jay Bell to Kansas City Royals for 3B Joe Randa, P Jeff Granger, P Jeff Martin and P Jeff Wallace (December 13, 1996).
RECORDS: Shares major league single-inning record for most home runs—2 (August 8, 1995, second inning and April 30, 1996, fourth inning).
HONORS: Named College Player of the Year by The Sporting News (1986). ... Named third baseman on The Sporting News college All-America team (1986).
STATISTICAL NOTES: Led Carolina League with .565 slugging percentage in 1987. ... Led N.L. third basemen with 27 double plays in 1994. ... Led A.L. first basemen in double plays with 135 in 1997. ... Career major league grand slams: 8.

Year Team (League)	Pos.	G	AB	R	H	2B	3B	HR	RBI	Avg.	BB	SO	SB	PO	A	E	Avg.
1986— Prince William (Car.)	3B	37	132	18	31	4	1	6	20	.235	19	34	1	25	50	8	.904
1987— Salem (Carolina)	1B-3B	90	310	68	86	9	1	26	71	.277	61	88	6	572	106	13	.981
— Harrisburg (Eastern)	1B	26	100	12	24	7	0	2	25	.240	4	27	0	107	10	1	.992
1988— Harrisburg (Eastern)	3B	117	411	49	105	21	1	14	66	.255	46	87	5	97	208	24	.927
1989— Buffalo (A.A.)	1B-3B	51	169	26	43	5	2	6	29	.254	57	60	11	213	61	8	.972
— Pittsburgh (N.L.)	1-3-2-S	75	215	31	42	13	3	5	19	.195	20	34	4	403	59	4	.991
1990— Pittsburgh (N.L.)	3B-1B	127	371	46	91	17	1	14	53	.245	21	50	3	61	215	18	.939
1991— Pittsburgh (N.L.)	3B	33	109	16	26	1	1	4	18	.239	14	15	3	15	62	2	.975
— Buffalo (A.A.)	3B	9	18	3	4	1	1	0	2	.222	6	3	1	2	8	1	.909
1992— Pittsburgh (N.L.)	3-2-1-S-O	130	480	56	111	21	2	14	65	.231	27	56	4	368	234	12	.980
— Buffalo (A.A.)	3B-1B-2B	7	29	6	10	2	0	2	5	.345	2	2	1	21	12	0	1.000
1993— Pittsburgh (N.L.)	3B-SS-2B	158	611	82	180	35	3	9	98	.295	59	54	8	108	†362	18	.963
1994— Pittsburgh (N.L.)	3B-2B	94	339	36	89	23	0	5	42	.263	30	38	3	61	198	13	.952
1995— Pittsburgh (N.L.)	3-1-2-S	122	445	61	118	27	2	18	87	.265	55	63	7	352	206	17	.970

Year Team (League)	Pos.	G	AB	R	H	2B	3B	HR	RBI	Avg.	BB	SO	SB	PO	A	E	Avg.
						BATTING								FIELDING			
1996— Pittsburgh (N.L.)	1B-2B-3B	155	591	91	160	36	4	30	111	.271	70	95	15	896	252	11	.991
1997— Kansas City (A.L.)■ ...	1B-DH	155	543	84	129	30	1	28	112	.238	89	96	16	1217	*147	5	*.996
American League totals (1 year)		155	543	84	129	30	1	28	112	.238	89	96	16	1217	147	5	.996
National League totals (8 years)		894	3161	419	817	173	16	99	493	.258	296	405	47	2264	1588	95	.976
Major league totals (9 years)		1049	3704	503	946	203	17	127	605	.255	385	501	63	3481	1735	100	.981

CHAMPIONSHIP SERIES RECORD

Year Team (League)	Pos.	G	AB	R	H	2B	3B	HR	RBI	Avg.	BB	SO	SB	PO	A	E	Avg.
						BATTING								FIELDING			
1990— Pittsburgh (N.L.)	3B-PH	5	10	0	1	0	0	0	0	.100	1	5	0	1	4	0	1.000
1992— Pittsburgh (N.L.)	3B	7	29	4	7	4	0	0	2	.241	0	1	0	11	19	1	.968
Championship series totals (2 years)		12	39	4	8	4	0	0	2	.205	1	6	0	12	23	1	.972

KINGSALE, GENE   OF   ORIOLES

PERSONAL: Born August 20, 1976, in Aruba. ... 6-3/170. ... Bats both, throws right. ... Full name: Eugene Humphrey Kingsale.
HIGH SCHOOL: John F. Kennedy Technical School (Dranjestad, Aruba).
TRANSACTIONS/CAREER NOTES: Signed as non-drafted free agent by Baltimore Orioles organization (June 19, 1993). ... On Frederick disabled list (May 29-August 31, 1996). ... On Bowie disabled list (April 8-August 8, 1997).
STATISTICAL NOTES: Tied for Gulf Coast League lead in double plays by outfielder with two in 1994.

Year Team (League)	Pos.	G	AB	R	H	2B	3B	HR	RBI	Avg.	BB	SO	SB	PO	A	E	Avg.
						BATTING								FIELDING			
1994— GC Orioles (GCL)	OF-2B	50	168	26	52	2	3	0	9	.310	18	24	15	100	2	3	.971
1995— Bluefield (Appal.)	OF	47	171	45	54	11	4	0	16	.316	27	31	20	95	3	*11	.899
1996— Frederick (Carolina)	OF	49	166	26	45	6	4	0	9	.271	19	32	23	100	1	4	.962
—Baltimore (A.L.)	OF	3	0	0	0	0	0	0	0	...	0	0	0	2	0	0	1.000
1997— Bowie (Eastern)	OF	13	46	8	19	6	0	0	4	.413	5	4	5	23	0	1	.958
—GC Orioles (GCL)	OF	6	17	2	5	0	0	0	0	.294	2	2	1	16	0	1	.941
Major league totals (1 year)		3	0	0	0	0	0	0	0	...	0	0	0	2	0	0	1.000

KINKADE, MIKE   3B   BREWERS

PERSONAL: Born May 6, 1973, in Livonia, Mich. ... 6-1/210. ... Bats right, throws right. ... Full name: Michael A. Kinkade.
COLLEGE: Washington State.
TRANSACTIONS/CAREER NOTES: Selected by Milwaukee Brewers organization in ninth round of free-agent draft (June 1, 1995).
HONORS: Named Texas League Player of the Year (1997).
STATISTICAL NOTES: Led Texas League with .455 on-base percentage and tied for league lead with 275 total bases in 1997.

Year Team (League)	Pos.	G	AB	R	H	2B	3B	HR	RBI	Avg.	BB	SO	SB	PO	A	E	Avg.
						BATTING								FIELDING			
1995— Helena (Pioneer)	3B-1B-C	69	266	76	94	19	1	4	39	.353	43	38	26	291	79	10	.974
1996— Beloit (Midwest)	3B-C-1B	135	499	105	151	33	4	15	100	.303	47	69	23	148	310	39	.922
1997— El Paso (Texas)	3B	125	468	•112	*180	35	12	12	*109	*.385	52	66	17	*79	249	*60	.845

KIRBY, WAYNE   OF

PERSONAL: Born January 22, 1964, in Williamsburg, Va. ... 5-10/190. ... Bats left, throws right. ... Full name: Wayne Edward Kirby. ... Brother of Terry Kirby, running back, San Francisco 49ers; and cousin of Chris Slade, linebacker, New England Patriots.
HIGH SCHOOL: Tabb (Va.).
COLLEGE: Newport News (Va.) Apprentice School.
TRANSACTIONS/CAREER NOTES: Selected by Los Angeles Dodgers organization in 13th round of free-agent draft (January 11, 1983). ... Granted free agency (October 15, 1990). ... Signed by Cleveland Indians organization (December 3, 1990). ... Granted free agency (October 15, 1991). ... Re-signed by Colorado Springs, Indians organization (December 12, 1991). ... Released by Indians (June 19, 1996). ... Claimed on waivers by Dodgers (June 24, 1996). ... Granted free agency (October 3, 1997).
STATISTICAL NOTES: Led Pacific Coast League in caught stealing with 20 in 1992.

Year Team (League)	Pos.	G	AB	R	H	2B	3B	HR	RBI	Avg.	BB	SO	SB	PO	A	E	Avg.
						BATTING								FIELDING			
1983— GC Dodgers (GCL)	OF	60	216	43	63	7	1	0	13	.292	34	19	23	89	9	1	.990
1984— Vero Beach (FSL)	OF	76	224	39	61	6	3	0	21	.272	21	30	11	101	3	5	.954
—Great Falls (Pio.)	OF	20	84	19	26	2	2	1	11	.310	12	9	19	35	3	2	.950
—Bakersfield (Calif.)	OF	23	84	14	23	3	0	0	10	.274	4	5	8	10	1	3	.786
1985— Vero Beach (FSL)	OF	122	437	70	123	9	3	0	28	.281	41	41	31	231	10	4	.984
1986— Vero Beach (FSL)	OF-2B	114	387	60	101	9	4	2	31	.261	37	30	28	264	18	4	.986
1987— Bakersfield (Calif.)	OF	105	416	77	112	14	3	0	34	.269	49	42	56	213	13	12	.950
—San Antonio (Tex.)	OF	24	80	7	19	1	2	1	9	.238	4	7	6	47	1	3	.941
1988— Bakersfield (Calif.)	OF	12	47	12	13	0	1	0	4	.277	11	4	9	20	2	2	.917
—San Antonio (Tex.)	OF	100	334	50	80	9	2	0	21	.240	21	43	26	181	4	2	.989
1989— San Antonio (Tex.)	OF	44	140	14	30	3	1	0	7	.214	18	17	11	77	3	4	.952
—Albuquerque (PCL)	OF	78	310	62	106	18	8	0	30	.342	26	27	29	149	8	2	.987
1990— Albuquerque (PCL)	OF	119	342	56	95	14	5	0	30	.278	28	36	29	185	11	9	.956
1991— Colo. Springs (PCL)■	OF-2B	118	385	66	113	14	4	1	39	.294	34	36	29	227	14	6	.976
—Cleveland (A.L.)	OF	21	43	4	9	2	0	0	5	.209	2	6	1	40	1	0	1.000
1992— Colo. Springs (PCL)	OF	123	470	•101	*162	18	*16	11	74	.345	36	28	51	274	14	7	.976
—Cleveland (A.L.)	DH-OF	21	18	9	3	1	0	1	1	.167	3	2	0	3	0	0	1.000

Year Team (League)	Pos.	G	AB	R	H	2B	3B	HR	RBI	Avg.	BB	SO	SB	PO	A	E	Avg.
1993— Charlotte (Int'l)	OF	17	76	10	22	6	2	3	7	.289	3	10	4	38	1	0	1.000
— Cleveland (A.L.)	OF-DH	131	458	71	123	19	5	6	60	.269	37	58	17	273	*19	5	.983
1994— Cleveland (A.L.)	OF-DH	78	191	33	56	6	0	5	23	.293	13	30	11	92	2	4	.959
1995— Cleveland (A.L.)	OF-DH	101	188	29	39	10	2	1	14	.207	13	32	10	94	2	1	.990
1996— Cleveland (A.L.)	OF-DH	27	16	3	4	1	0	0	1	.250	2	2	0	8	0	0	1.000
— Los Angeles (N.L.)■	OF	65	188	23	51	10	1	1	11	.271	17	17	4	93	2	3	.969
1997— Los Angeles (N.L.)	OF	46	65	6	11	2	0	0	4	.169	10	12	0	36	1	0	1.000
— Albuquerque (PCL)	OF	68	269	57	90	16	5	10	43	.335	26	33	18	138	9	5	.967
American League totals (6 years)		379	914	149	234	39	7	13	104	.256	70	130	39	510	24	10	.982
National League totals (2 years)		111	253	29	62	12	1	1	15	.245	27	29	4	129	3	3	.978
Major league totals (7 years)		490	1167	178	296	51	8	14	119	.254	97	159	43	639	27	13	.981

DIVISION SERIES RECORD

Year Team (League)	Pos.	G	AB	R	H	2B	3B	HR	RBI	Avg.	BB	SO	SB	PO	A	E	Avg.
							BATTING									FIELDING	
1995— Cleveland (A.L.)	PR-OF	3	1	0	1	0	0	0	0	1.000	0	0	0	0	0	0	
1996— Los Angeles (N.L.)	OF-PH	3	8	1	1	0	0	0	0	.125	2	1	0	4	0	0	1.000
Division series totals (2 years)		6	9	1	2	0	0	0	0	.222	2	1	0	4	0	0	1.000

CHAMPIONSHIP SERIES RECORD

Year Team (League)	Pos.	G	AB	R	H	2B	3B	HR	RBI	Avg.	BB	SO	SB	PO	A	E	Avg.
							BATTING									FIELDING	
1995— Cleveland (A.L.)	OF-PR	5	5	2	1	0	0	0	0	.200	0	0	1	3	0	0	1.000

WORLD SERIES RECORD

K

Year Team (League)	Pos.	G	AB	R	H	2B	3B	HR	RBI	Avg.	BB	SO	SB	PO	A	E	Avg.
							BATTING									FIELDING	
1995— Cleveland (A.L.)	PH-PR-OF	3	1	0	0	0	0	0	0	.000	0	1	0	1	0	0	1.000

KIRKREIT, DARON — P — REDS

PERSONAL: Born August 7, 1972, in Anaheim, Calif. ... 6-6/225. ... Throws right, bats right. ... Full name: Daron Jon Kirkreit.
COLLEGE: California-Riverside.
TRANSACTIONS/CAREER NOTES: Selected by Cleveland Indians organization in first round (11th pick overall) of free-agent draft (June 3, 1993). ... On Kinston disabled list (July 10, 1995-remainder of season). ... On Cleveland disabled list (March 31-September 12, 1996). ... Granted free agency (October 15, 1997). ... Signed by Cincinnati Reds organization (November 27, 1997).
MISCELLANEOUS: Member of 1992 U.S. Olympic baseball team.

Year Team (League)	W	L	Pct.	ERA	G	GS	CG	ShO	Sv.	IP	H	R	ER	BB	SO
1993— Watertown (NYP)	4	1	.800	2.23	7	7	1	0	0	36 1/3	33	14	9	11	44
1994— Kinston (Carolina)	8	7	.533	2.68	20	19	4	0	0	127 2/3	92	48	38	40	116
— Cant./Akr. (Eastern)	3	5	.375	6.22	9	9	0	0	0	46 1/3	53	35	32	25	54
1995— Kinston (Carolina)	0	1	.000	5.93	3	3	0	0	0	13 2/3	14	9	9	6	14
— Cant./Akr. (Eastern)	2	9	.182	5.69	14	14	1	0	0	80 2/3	74	54	51	46	67
1996— Kinston (Carolina)	2	0	1.000	1.93	6	6	0	0	0	32 2/3	23	7	7	10	19
1997— Akron (Eastern)	8	9	.471	5.20	26	20	1	0	0	117 2/3	131	96	68	69	83
— Buffalo (A.A.)	1	0	1.000	0.00	1	1	1	1	0	7	3	0	0	1	2

KLASSEN, DANNY — SS — DIAMONDBACKS

PERSONAL: Born September 22, 1975, in Learington, Ont. ... 6-0/175. ... Bats right, throws right. ... Full name: Daniel V. Klassen.
HIGH SCHOOL: John Carroll (Fort Pierce, Fla.).
TRANSACTIONS/CAREER NOTES: Selected by Milwaukee Brewers organization in second round of free-agent draft (June 3, 1993). ... On disabled list (April 7-June 23, 1995 and April 11-22, 1996). ... Selected by Arizona Diamondbacks in second round (37th pick overall) of expansion draft (November 18, 1997).
STATISTICAL NOTES: Tied for Arizona League lead in intentional bases on balls received with three in 1994.

Year Team (League)	Pos.	G	AB	R	H	2B	3B	HR	RBI	Avg.	BB	SO	SB	PO	A	E	Avg.
								BATTING									FIELDING	
1993— Ariz. Brewers (Ariz.)	SS	38	117	26	26	5	0	2	20	.222	24	28	14	45	97	12	.922
— Helena (Pioneer)	SS	18	45	8	9	1	0	0	3	.200	7	11	2	25	42	7	.905
1994— Beloit (Midwest)	SS	133	458	61	119	20	3	6	54	.260	58	123	28	177	328	40	.927
1995— Beloit (Midwest)	SS-3B	59	218	27	60	15	2	2	25	.275	16	43	12	73	133	18	.920
1996— Stockton (California)	SS	118	432	58	116	22	4	2	46	.269	34	77	14	186	373	*33	.944
1997— El Paso (Texas)	SS	135	519	112	172	30	6	14	81	.331	48	104	16	177	399	*50	.920

KLESKO, RYAN — OF — BRAVES

PERSONAL: Born June 12, 1971, in Westminster, Calif. ... 6-3/220. ... Bats left, throws left. ... Full name: Ryan Anthony Klesko.
HIGH SCHOOL: Westminster (Calif.).
TRANSACTIONS/CAREER NOTES: Selected by Atlanta Braves organization in fifth round of free-agent draft (June 5, 1989). ... On Atlanta disabled list (May 3-18, 1995); included rehabilitation assignment to Greenville (May 13-17).
HONORS: Named Southern League Most Valuable Player (1991).
STATISTICAL NOTES: Career major league grand slams: 5.

Year Team (League)	Pos.	G	AB	R	H	2B	3B	HR	RBI	Avg.	BB	SO	SB	PO	A	E	Avg.
								BATTING									FIELDING	
1989— GC Braves (GCL)	DH	17	57	14	23	5	4	1	16	.404	6	6	4	...	...	...	...
— Sumter (S. Atl.)	1B	25	90	17	26	6	0	1	12	.289	11	14	1	173	11	4	.979
1990— Sumter (S. Atl.)	1B	63	231	41	85	15	1	10	38	.368	31	30	13	575	43	14	.978
— Durham (Carolina)	1B	77	292	40	80	16	1	7	47	.274	32	53	10	490	34	13	.976
								BATTING									FIELDING	

Year Team (League)	Pos.	G	AB	R	H	2B	3B	HR	RBI	Avg.	BB	SO	SB	PO	A	E	Avg.
1991—Greenville (Southern).	1B	126	419	64	122	22	3	14	67	.291	75	60	14	1043	57	*17	.985
1992—Richmond (Int'l)........	1B	123	418	63	105	22	2	17	59	.251	41	72	3	947	51	*11	.989
—Atlanta (N.L.)............	1B	13	14	0	0	0	0	0	1	.000	0	5	0	25	0	0	1.000
1993—Richmond (Int'l).......	1B-OF	98	343	59	94	14	2	22	74	.274	47	69	4	587	45	12	.981
—Atlanta (N.L.)............	1B-OF	22	17	3	6	1	0	2	5	.353	3	4	0	8	0	0	1.000
1994—Atlanta (N.L.)...........	OF-1B	92	245	42	68	13	3	17	47	.278	26	48	1	89	3	7	.929
1995—Atlanta (N.L.)...........	OF-1B	107	329	48	102	25	2	23	70	.310	47	72	5	131	4	8	.944
—Greenville (Southern).	OF	4	13	1	3	0	0	1	4	.231	2	1	0	2	0	0	1.000
1996—Atlanta (N.L.)...........	OF-1B	153	528	90	149	21	4	34	93	.282	68	129	6	204	8	5	.977
1997—Atlanta (N.L.)...........	OF-1B	143	467	67	122	23	6	24	84	.261	48	130	4	245	6	6	.977
Major league totals (6 years)		530	1600	250	447	83	15	100	300	.279	192	388	16	702	21	26	.965

DIVISION SERIES RECORD

RECORDS: Shares N.L. career record for most games—10; and most strikeouts—9.

| | | | | | BATTING | | | | | | | | FIELDING | | | |
Year Team (League)	Pos.	G	AB	R	H	2B	3B	HR	RBI	Avg.	BB	SO	SB	PO	A	E	Avg.
1995—Atlanta (N.L.).............	OF	4	15	5	7	1	0	1	1	.467	0	3	0	3	0	0	1.000
1996—Atlanta (N.L.).............	OF	3	8	1	1	0	0	1	1	.125	3	4	1	2	1	0	.667
1997—Atlanta (N.L.).............	OF	3	8	2	2	1	0	1	1	.250	0	2	0	3	0	1	.750
Division series totals (3 years)		10	31	8	10	2	0	2	3	.323	3	9	1	8	0	2	.800

CHAMPIONSHIP SERIES RECORD

| | | | | | BATTING | | | | | | | | FIELDING | | | |
Year Team (League)	Pos.	G	AB	R	H	2B	3B	HR	RBI	Avg.	BB	SO	SB	PO	A	E	Avg.
1995—Atlanta (N.L.).............	OF-PH	4	7	0	0	0	0	0	0	.000	3	4	0	1	0	0	1.000
1996—Atlanta (N.L.).............	OF	6	16	1	4	0	0	1	3	.250	2	6	0	13	0	0	1.000
1997—Atlanta (N.L.).............	OF	5	17	2	4	0	0	2	4	.235	2	3	0	5	0	0	1.000
Championship series totals (3 years)		15	40	3	8	0	0	3	7	.200	7	13	0	19	0	0	1.000

WORLD SERIES RECORD

NOTES: Member of World Series championship team (1995).

| | | | | | BATTING | | | | | | | | FIELDING | | | |
Year Team (League)	Pos.	G	AB	R	H	2B	3B	HR	RBI	Avg.	BB	SO	SB	PO	A	E	Avg.
1995—Atlanta (N.L.).............	OF-DH	6	16	4	5	0	0	3	4	.313	3	4	0	1	0	0	1.000
1996—Atlanta (N.L.)............DH-O-1-PH	5	10	2	1	0	0	0	1	.100	3	4	0	1	0	1	.500
World Series totals (2 years)		11	26	6	6	0	0	3	5	.231	6	8	0	2	0	1	.667

KLINE, STEVE   P   EXPOS

PERSONAL: Born August 22, 1972, in Sunbury, Pa. ... 6-2/200. ... Throws left, bats both. ... Full name: Steven James Kline.
COLLEGE: West Virginia.
TRANSACTIONS/CAREER NOTES: Selected by Cleveland Indians organization in eighth round of free-agent draft (June 3, 1993). ... On disabled list (May 23-August 5, 1995). ... On temporarily inactive list (April 5-20, 1996). ... Traded by Indians with a player to be named later to Montreal Expos for P Jeff Juden (July 31, 1997).

Year Team (League)	W	L	Pct.	ERA	G	GS	CG	ShO	Sv.	IP	H	R	ER	BB	SO
1993—Burlington (Appalachian)....	1	1	.500	4.91	2	1	0	0	0	7 1/3	11	4	4	2	4
—Watertown (NYP)	5	4	.556	3.19	13	13	2	1	0	79	77	36	28	12	45
1994—Columbus (S. Atl.)...............	*18	5	.783	3.01	28	•28	2	1	0	*185 2/3	175	67	62	36	*174
1995—Cant./Akr. (Eastern)............	2	3	.400	2.42	14	14	0	0	0	89 1/3	86	34	24	30	45
1996—Cant./Akr. (Eastern)	8	12	.400	5.46	25	24	0	0	0	146 2/3	168	98	89	55	107
1997—Cleveland (A.L.)...............	3	1	.750	5.81	20	1	0	0	0	26 1/3	42	19	17	13	17
—Buffalo (A.A.).................	3	3	.500	4.03	20	4	0	0	1	51 1/3	53	26	23	13	41
—Montreal (N.L.)■..............	1	3	.250	6.15	26	0	0	0	0	26 1/3	31	18	18	10	20
A.L. totals (1 year)	3	1	.750	5.81	20	1	0	0	0	26 1/3	42	19	17	13	17
N.L. totals (1 year)	1	3	.250	6.15	26	0	0	0	0	26 1/3	31	18	18	10	20
Major league totals (1 year)........	4	4	.500	5.98	46	1	0	0	0	52 2/3	73	37	35	23	37

KLINGENBECK, SCOTT   P   REDS

PERSONAL: Born February 3, 1971, in Cincinnati. ... 6-2/205. ... Throws right, bats right. ... Full name: Scott Edward Klingenbeck.
HIGH SCHOOL: Oak Hills (Cincinnati).
COLLEGE: Ohio State.
TRANSACTIONS/CAREER NOTES: Selected by Detroit Tigers organization in 57th round of free-agent draft (June 5, 1989); did not sign. ... Selected by Baltimore Orioles organization in fifth round of free-agent draft (June 1, 1992). ... On Bowie disabled list (July 11-30, 1994). ... Traded by Orioles with a player to be named later to Minnesota Twins for P Scott Erickson (July 7, 1995); Twins acquired OF Kimera Bartee to complete deal (September 18, 1995). ... Traded by Twins to Cincinnati Reds organization for future considerations (April 8, 1997).
STATISTICAL NOTES: Led American Association with 23 home runs allowed in 1997.

Year Team (League)	W	L	Pct.	ERA	G	GS	CG	ShO	Sv.	IP	H	R	ER	BB	SO
1992—Kane County (Midwest)......	3	4	.429	2.63	11	11	0	0	0	68 1/3	50	31	20	28	64
1993—Frederick (Carolina)...........	13	4	*.765	2.98	23	23	0	0	0	139	151	62	46	35	146
1994—Bowie (Eastern).................	7	5	.583	3.63	25	25	3	0	0	143 2/3	151	76	58	37	120
—Baltimore (Eastern)...........	1	0	1.000	3.86	1	1	0	0	0	7	6	4	3	4	5
1995—Rochester (Int'l)...............	3	1	.750	2.72	8	7	0	0	0	43	46	14	13	10	29
—Baltimore (A.L.).................	2	2	.500	4.88	6	5	0	0	0	31 1/3	32	17	17	18	15
—Minnesota (A.L.)■	0	2	.000	8.57	18	4	0	0	0	48 1/3	69	48	46	24	27
1996—Salt Lake (PCL)..............	9	3	.750	3.11	22	22	5	•2	0	150 2/3	159	64	52	41	100
—Minnesota (A.L.)	1	1	.500	7.85	10	3	0	0	0	28 2/3	42	28	25	10	15
1997—Salt Lake (PCL)	0	0	. . .	1.29	1	1	0	0	0	7	6	1	1	0	6
—Indianapolis (A.A.)■	12	8	.600	3.96	27	27	2	0	0	170 2/3	180	85	75	41	119
Major league totals (3 years)......	4	5	.444	7.10	35	13	0	0	0	115 1/3	149	97	91	56	62

KNIGHT, BRANDON — P — RANGERS

PERSONAL: Born October 1, 1975, in Oxnard, Calif. ... 6-0/170. ... Throws left, bats left. ... Full name: Brandon M. Knight.
HIGH SCHOOL: Buena (Ventura, Calif.).
JUNIOR COLLEGE: Ventura.
TRANSACTIONS/CAREER NOTES: Selected by Texas Rangers organization in 14th round of free-agent draft (June 1, 1995).

Year Team (League)	W	L	Pct.	ERA	G	GS	CG	ShO	Sv.	IP	H	R	ER	BB	SO
1995— GC Rangers (GCL)	2	1	.667	5.25	3	2	0	0	0	12	12	7	7	6	11
—Charleston, S.C. (SAL)	4	2	.667	3.13	9	9	0	0	0	54²/₃	37	22	19	21	52
1996— Charlotte (Fla. St.)	4	10	.286	5.12	19	17	2	0	0	102	118	65	58	45	74
—Hudson Valley (NYP)	2	2	.500	4.42	9	9	0	0	0	53	59	26	26	21	52
1997— Charlotte (Fla. St.)	7	4	.636	2.23	14	12	3	1	0	92²/₃	82	33	23	22	91
—Tulsa (Texas)	6	4	.600	4.50	14	14	2	•1	0	90	83	52	45	35	84

KNOBLAUCH, CHUCK — 2B — TWINS

PERSONAL: Born July 7, 1968, in Houston. ... 5-9/169. ... Bats right, throws right. ... Full name: Edward Charles Knoblauch. ... Son of Ray Knoblauch, minor league pitcher (1947-56); and nephew of Ed Knoblauch, minor league outfielder (1938-42 and 1947-55). ... Name pronounced NOB-lock.
HIGH SCHOOL: Bellaire (Houston).
COLLEGE: Texas A&M.
TRANSACTIONS/CAREER NOTES: Selected by Philadelphia Phillies organization in 18th round of free-agent draft (June 2, 1986); did not sign. ... Selected by Minnesota Twins organization in first round (25th pick overall) of free-agent draft (June 5, 1989).
HONORS: Named A.L. Rookie Player of the Year by THE SPORTING NEWS (1991). ... Named A.L. Rookie of the Year by Baseball Writers' Association of America (1991). ... Named second baseman on THE SPORTING NEWS A.L. All-Star team (1994 and 1997). ... Named second baseman on THE SPORTING NEWS A.L. Silver Slugger team (1995 and 1997). ... Won A.L. Gold Glove at second base (1997).
STATISTICAL NOTES: Had 20-game hitting streak (September 2-25, 1991). ... Led A.L. second basemen with 424 assists, 101 double plays and 718 total chances in 1997. ... Career major league grand slams: 1.
MISCELLANEOUS: Holds Minnesota Twins all-time record for most stolen bases (276).

Year Team (League)	Pos.	G	AB	R	H	2B	3B	HR	RBI	Avg.	BB	SO	SB	PO	A	E	Avg.
1989— Kenosha (Midwest)	SS	51	196	29	56	13	1	2	19	.286	32	23	9	60	124	21	.898
—Visalia (California)	SS	18	77	20	28	10	0	0	21	.364	6	11	4	23	52	10	.882
1990— Orlando (South.)	2B	118	432	74	125	23	6	2	53	.289	63	31	23	275	300	20	.966
1991— Minnesota (A.L.)	2B	151	565	78	159	24	6	1	50	.281	59	40	25	249	460	18	.975
1992— Minnesota (A.L.)	2B-DH-SS	155	600	104	178	19	6	2	56	.297	88	60	34	306	415	6	.992
1993— Minnesota (A.L.)	2B-SS-OF	153	602	82	167	27	4	2	41	.277	65	44	29	302	431	9	.988
1994— Minnesota (A.L.)	2B-SS	109	445	85	139	*45	3	5	51	.312	41	56	35	191	285	3	.994
1995— Minnesota (A.L.)	2B-SS	136	538	107	179	34	8	11	63	.333	78	95	46	254	400	10	.985
1996— Minnesota (A.L.)	2B-DH	153	578	140	197	35	*14	13	72	.341	98	74	45	271	390	8	*.988
1997— Minnesota (A.L.)	2B-DH-SS	156	611	117	178	26	10	9	58	.291	84	84	62	285	†428	12	.983
Major league totals (7 years)		1013	3939	713	1197	210	51	43	391	.304	513	453	276	1858	2809	66	.986

CHAMPIONSHIP SERIES RECORD

Year Team (League)	Pos.	G	AB	R	H	2B	3B	HR	RBI	Avg.	BB	SO	SB	PO	A	E	Avg.
1991— Minnesota (A.L.)	2B	5	20	5	7	2	0	0	3	.350	3	3	2	8	14	0	1.000

WORLD SERIES RECORD

NOTES: Member of World Series championship team (1991).

Year Team (League)	Pos.	G	AB	R	H	2B	3B	HR	RBI	Avg.	BB	SO	SB	PO	A	E	Avg.
1991— Minnesota (A.L.)	2B	7	26	3	8	1	0	0	2	.308	4	2	4	15	14	1	.967

ALL-STAR GAME RECORD

Year League	Pos.	AB	R	H	2B	3B	HR	RBI	Avg.	BB	SO	SB	PO	A	E	Avg.
1992— American	PH-2B	1	0	0	0	0	0	0	.000	1	0	0	0	0	0	
1994— American	2B	3	1	0	0	0	0	0	.000	0	2	0	1	2	0	1.000
1996— American	2B	1	0	1	0	0	0	0	1.000	0	0	0	3	1	0	1.000
1997— American	2B	0	0	0	0	0	0	0	. . .	0	0	0	1	1	0	1.000
All-Star Game totals (4 years)		5	1	1	0	0	0	0	.200	1	2	0	5	4	0	1.000

KNORR, RANDY — C — ASTROS

PERSONAL: Born November 12, 1968, in San Gabriel, Calif. ... 6-2/215. ... Bats right, throws right. ... Full name: Randy Duane Knorr. ... Name pronounced NOR.
HIGH SCHOOL: Baldwin Park (Calif.).
TRANSACTIONS/CAREER NOTES: Selected by Toronto Blue Jays organization in 10th round of free-agent draft (June 2, 1986). ... On disabled list (June 24-July 4, 1986 and May 10, 1989-remainder of season). ... On Syracuse disabled list (May 11-23, 1992). ... On Toronto disabled list (August 20-September 30, 1992). ... On Toronto disabled list (July 1-August 11, 1995); included rehabilitation assignment to Syracuse (July 21-August 9). ... Traded by Blue Jays to Houston Astros for cash (May 17, 1996). ... Granted free agency (December 20, 1996). ... Re-signed by Astros organization (December 23, 1996). ... On Houston disabled list (August 29-September 6, 1997); included rehabilitation assignment to New Orleans (August 29-September 6).
STATISTICAL NOTES: Led South Atlantic League catchers with 960 total chances and 25 passed balls in 1988.

Year	Team (League)	Pos.	G	AB	R	H	2B	3B	HR	RBI	Avg.	BB	SO	SB	PO	A	E	Avg.
1986— Medicine Hat (Pio.)		1B	55	215	21	58	13	0	4	52	.270	17	53	0	451	29	10	.980
1987— Myrtle Beach (SAL)....		C-1B-2B	46	129	17	34	4	0	6	21	.264	6	46	0	95	7	1	.990
— Medicine Hat (Pio.)		C	26	106	21	31	7	0	10	24	.292	5	26	0	70	5	4	.949
1988— Myrtle Beach (SAL)		C	117	364	43	85	13	0	9	42	.234	41	91	0	*870	75	15	.984
1989— Dunedin (Fla. St.)		C	33	122	13	32	6	0	6	23	.262	6	21	0	186	20	2	.990
1990— Knoxville (Southern) ..		C	116	392	51	108	12	1	13	64	.276	31	83	0	599	72	15	.978
1991— Knoxville (Southern) ..		C-1B	24	74	7	13	4	0	0	4	.176	10	18	2	136	16	2	.987
— Syracuse (Int'l)		C	91	342	29	89	20	0	5	44	.260	23	58	1	477	49	7	.987
— Toronto (A.L.)		C	3	1	0	0	0	0	0	0	.000	1	1	0	6	1	0	1.000
1992— Syracuse (Int'l)		C	61	228	27	62	13	1	11	27	.272	17	38	1	220	22	3	.988
— Toronto (A.L.)		C	8	19	1	5	0	0	1	2	.263	1	5	0	33	3	0	1.000
1993— Toronto (A.L.)		C	39	101	11	25	3	2	4	20	.248	9	29	0	168	20	0	1.000
1994— Toronto (A.L.)		C	40	124	20	30	2	0	7	19	.242	10	35	0	247	21	2	.993
1995— Toronto (A.L.)		C	45	132	18	28	8	0	3	16	.212	11	28	0	243	22	8	.971
— Syracuse (Int'l)		C	18	67	6	18	5	1	1	6	.269	5	14	0	129	14	3	.979
1996— Syracuse (Int'l)		C	12	36	1	10	5	0	0	5	.278	5	8	0	53	2	0	1.000
— Houston (N.L.)■		C	37	87	7	17	5	0	1	7	.195	5	18	0	204	14	0	1.000
1997— New Orleans (A.A.).....		C	72	244	22	58	10	0	5	27	.238	22	38	0	502	54	9	.984
— Houston (N.L.)		C-1B	4	8	1	3	0	0	1	1	.375	0	2	0	19	3	0	1.000
American League totals (5 years)			135	377	50	88	13	2	15	57	.233	32	98	0	697	67	10	.987
National League totals (2 years)			41	95	8	20	5	0	2	8	.211	5	20	0	223	17	0	1.000
Major league totals (7 years)			176	472	58	108	18	2	17	65	.229	37	118	0	920	84	10	.990

CHAMPIONSHIP SERIES RECORD

Year	Team (League)	Pos.	G	AB	R	H	2B	3B	HR	RBI	Avg.	BB	SO	SB	PO	A	E	Avg.
1992— Toronto (A.L.)									Did not play.									
1993— Toronto (A.L.)									Did not play.									
Championship series totals (year)			0	0	0	0	0	0	0	0	...	0	0	0	0	0	0	...

WORLD SERIES RECORD

NOTES: Member of World Series championship teams (1992 and 1993).

Year	Team (League)	Pos.	G	AB	R	H	2B	3B	HR	RBI	Avg.	BB	SO	SB	PO	A	E	Avg.
1992— Toronto (A.L.)									Did not play.									
1993— Toronto (A.L.).............		C	1	0	0	0	0	0	0	0	...	0	0	0	3	0	0	1.000
World Series totals (1 year).			1	0	0	0	0	0	0	0	...	0	0	0	3	0	0	1.000

KOLB, DAN   P   RANGERS

PERSONAL: Born March 29, 1975, in Sterling, Ill. ... 6-4/185. ... Throws right, bats right. ... Full name: Daniel L. Kolb.
HIGH SCHOOL: Walnut (Ill.).
JUNIOR COLLEGE: Sauk Valley Community College (Ill.).
TRANSACTIONS/CAREER NOTES: Selected by Minnesota Twins organization in 17th round of free-agent draft (June 3, 1993); did not sign. ... Selected by Texas Rangers organization in sixth round of free-agent draft (June 3, 1995).
STATISTICAL NOTES: Pitched six-inning, 3-0 no-hit victory against Columbus (June 12, 1996). ... Tied for Appalachian League lead with 22 hit batsmen in 1996.

Year	Team (League)	W	L	Pct.	ERA	G	GS	CG	ShO	Sv.	IP	H	R	ER	BB	SO
1995— GC Twins (GCL).................		1	7	.125	2.21	12	11	0	0	0	53	38	22	13	28	46
1996— Charleston, S.C. (S. Atl.)		8	6	.571	2.57	20	20	4	2	0	126	80	50	36	60	127
— Charlotte (Fla. St.)		2	2	.500	4.26	6	6	0	0	0	38	38	18	18	14	28
— Tulsa (Texas)		1	0	1.000	0.77	2	2	0	0	0	11 2/3	5	1	1	8	7
1997— Charlotte (Fla. St.)		4	10	.286	4.87	24	23	3	0	0	133	146	91	72	62	83
— Tulsa (Texas)		0	2	.000	4.76	2	2	0	0	0	11 1/3	7	7	6	11	6

KONERKO, PAUL   3B/1B   DODGERS

PERSONAL: Born March 5, 1976, in Providence, R.I. ... 6-3/205. ... Throws right, bats right. ... Full name: Paul Henry Konerko.
HIGH SCHOOL: Chaparral (Scottsdale, Ariz.).
TRANSACTIONS/CAREER NOTES: Selected by Los Angeles Dodgers organization in first round (13th pick overall) of free-agent draft (June 2, 1994).
HONORS: Named Pacific Coast League Most Valuable Player in 1997.
STATISTICAL NOTES: Led Northwest League with seven sacrifice flies in 1994. ... Led Pacific Coast League with 300 total bases and .621 slugging percentage in 1997.

Year	Team (League)	Pos.	G	AB	R	H	2B	3B	HR	RBI	Avg.	BB	SO	SB	PO	A	E	Avg.
1994— Yakima (N'west)		C	67	257	25	74	15	2	6	*58	.288	36	52	1	271	33	5	.984
1995— San Bern. (Calif.)........		C	118	448	7	124	21	1	19	77	.277	59	88	3	676	68	11	.985
1996— San Antonio (Tex.)		1B	133	470	78	141	23	2	29	86	.300	72	85	1	1114	92	14	.989
— Albuquerque (PCL).........		1B	4	14	2	6	0	0	1	2	.429	1	2	0	30	0	0	1.000
1997— Albuquerque (PCL).....		3B-1B-2B	130	483	97	156	31	1	*37	*127	.323	64	61	2	257	216	24	.952
— Los Angeles (N.L.)		1B-3B	6	7	0	1	0	0	0	0	.143	1	2	0	3	0	0	1.000
Major league totals (1 year)			6	7	0	1	0	0	0	0	.143	1	2	0	3	0	0	1.000

K

KOSKIE, COREY — 3B — TWINS

PERSONAL: Born June 28, 1973, in Winnipeg, Man. ... 6-3/215. ... Throws right, bats left. ... Full name: Cordel Leonard Koskie.
HIGH SCHOOL: Springfield Collegiate (Oakbank, Man.).
JUNIOR COLLEGE: Des Moines Area Community College (Iowa).
COLLEGE: Kwantlen (B.C.).
TRANSACTIONS/CAREER NOTES: Selected by Minnesota Twins organization in 26th round of free-agent draft (June 2, 1994). ... On Fort Myers disabled list (May 10-28 and June 25-July 4, 1996).
STATISTICAL NOTES: Tied for Eastern League lead with 10 intentional bases on balls in 1997.

Year Team (League)	Pos.	G	AB	R	H	2B	3B	HR	RBI	Avg.	BB	SO	SB	PO	A	E	Avg.
1994—Elizabethton (App.).....	3B	34	107	13	25	2	1	3	10	.234	18	27	0	23	84	8	.930
1995—Fort Wayne (Midw.)....	3B	123	462	64	143	37	5	16	78	.310	38	79	2	80	244	36	.900
1996—Fort Myers (FSL)........	3B	95	338	43	88	19	4	9	55	.260	40	76	1	62	176	19	.926
1997—New Britain (Eastern) .	3B	131	437	88	125	26	6	23	79	.286	90	106	9	72	234	22	.933

KOTSAY, MARK — OF — MARLINS

PERSONAL: Born December 2, 1975, in Woodier, Calif. ... 6-0/180. ... Bats left, throws left. ... Full name: Mark Steven Kotsay.
HIGH SCHOOL: Santa Fe Springs (Calif.).
COLLEGE: Cal State Fullerton.
TRANSACTIONS/CAREER NOTES: Selected by Florida Marlins organization in first round (ninth pick overall) of free-agent draft (June 4, 1996).
HONORS: Named Golden Spikes Award winner by USA Baseball (1995). ... Named Most Outstanding Player of College World Series (1995).
STATISTICAL NOTES: Tied for Eastern League lead for double plays by outfielder with four in 1997.
MISCELLANEOUS: Member of 1996 U.S. Olympic baseball team.

Year Team (League)	Pos.	G	AB	R	H	2B	3B	HR	RBI	Avg.	BB	SO	SB	PO	A	E	Avg.
1996—Kane County (Midw.)..	OF	17	60	16	17	5	0	2	8	.283	16	8	3	37	2	0	1.000
1997—Portland (Eastern)......	OF	114	438	*103	134	27	2	20	77	.306	75	65	17	230	12	2	*.992
—Florida (N.L.)..............	OF	14	52	5	10	1	1	0	4	.192	4	7	3	31	2	0	1.000
Major league totals (1 year)		14	52	5	10	1	1	0	4	.192	4	7	3	31	2	0	1.000

KRAUSE, SCOTT — OF — BREWERS

PERSONAL: Born August 16, 1973, in Willowick, Ohio. ... 6-1/180. ... Bats right, throws right.
COLLEGE: New Orleans.
TRANSACTIONS/CAREER NOTES: Selected by Milwaukee Brewers organization in 10th round of free-agent draft (June 2, 1994).
STATISTICAL NOTES: Led Midwest League outfielders with .985 fielding percentage and tied for for lead in double plays with three in 1995.

Year Team (League)	Pos.	G	AB	R	H	2B	3B	HR	RBI	Avg.	BB	SO	SB	PO	A	E	Avg.
1994—Helena (Pioneer)	OF	63	252	51	90	18	3	4	52	.357	18	49	13	77	6	4	.954
1995—Beloit (Midwest).........	OF-2B-1B	134	481	83	119	30	4	13	76	.247	50	126	24	179	14	3	†.985
1996—Stockton (California) ..	OF-1B	108	427	82	128	22	4	19	83	.300	32	101	25	209	12	5	.978
—El Paso (Texas)..........	OF	24	85	16	27	5	2	3	11	.318	2	19	2	36	4	0	1.000
1997—El Paso (Texas)..........	OF-1B	125	474	97	171	33	11	16	88	.361	20	108	13	196	13	7	.968

KREUTER, CHAD — C — WHITE SOX

PERSONAL: Born August 26, 1964, in Greenbrae, Calif. ... 6-2/200. ... Bats both, throws right. ... Full name: Chad Michael Kreuter. ... Name pronounced CREW-ter.
HIGH SCHOOL: Redwood (Calif.).
COLLEGE: Pepperdine.
TRANSACTIONS/CAREER NOTES: Selected by Texas Rangers organization in fifth round of free-agent draft (June 3, 1985). ... Granted free agency (October 15, 1991). ... Signed by Toledo, Detroit Tigers organization (January 2, 1992). ... Granted free agency (December 23, 1994). ... Signed by Seattle Mariners (April 8, 1995). ... On Seattle disabled list (June 19-July 6, 1995). ... On Tacoma disabled list (August 4-25, 1995). ... Granted free agency (October 16, 1995). ... Signed by Chicago White Sox organization (December 11, 1995). ... On disabled list (July 20, 1996-remainder of season). ... Granted free agency (October 14, 1996). ... Re-signed by White Sox organization (January 29, 1997). ... Traded by White Sox with OF Tony Phillips to Anaheim Angels for P Chuck McElroy and C Jorge Fabregas (May 18, 1997). ... Granted free agency (November 1, 1997). ... Signed by White Sox (December 10, 1997).
RECORDS: Shares major league single-game record for most sacrifice flies—3 (July 30, 1994). ... Shares major league record for most hits in one inning in first major league game—2 (September 14, 1988, fifth inning).
STATISTICAL NOTES: Led Carolina League catchers with 21 errors and 17 double plays and tied for lead with 113 assists in 1986. ... Tied for Texas League lead in double plays by catcher with nine in 1988. ... Led A.L. with 21 passed balls in 1989. ... Switch-hit home runs in one game (September 7, 1993). ... Career major league grand slams: 1.
MISCELLANEOUS: Batted righthanded only (1985 and 1990).

Year Team (League)	Pos.	G	AB	R	H	2B	3B	HR	RBI	Avg.	BB	SO	SB	PO	A	E	Avg.
1985—Burl. (Midw.)	C	69	199	25	53	9	0	4	26	.266	38	48	3	349	34	8	.980
1986—Salem (Carolina)	C-OF-3B	125	387	55	85	21	2	6	49	.220	67	82	5	613	†115	†21	.972
1987—Charlotte (Fla. St.)......	C-OF-3B	85	281	36	61	18	1	9	40	.217	31	32	1	380	54	8	.982
1988—Tulsa (Texas).............	C	108	358	46	95	24	6	3	51	.265	55	66	2	603	71	•13	.981
—Texas (A.L.)	C	16	51	3	14	2	1	1	5	.275	7	13	0	93	8	1	.990
1989—Texas (A.L.)	C	87	158	16	24	3	0	5	9	.152	27	40	0	453	26	4	.992
—Oklahoma City (A.A.)..	C	26	87	10	22	3	0	0	6	.253	13	11	1	146	14	2	.988

Year	Team (League)	Pos.	G	AB	R	H	2B	3B	HR	RBI	Avg.	BB	SO	SB	PO	A	E	Avg.
1990—	Texas (A.L.)	C	22	22	2	1	1	0	0	2	.045	8	9	0	39	4	1	.977
	—Oklahoma City (A.A.)..	C	92	291	41	65	17	1	7	35	.223	52	80	0	559	64	10	.984
1991—	Texas (A.L.)	C	3	4	0	0	0	0	0	0	.000	0	1	0	5	0	0	1.000
	—Oklahoma City (A.A.)..	C	24	70	14	19	6	0	1	12	.271	18	16	2	146	23	7	.960
	—Tulsa (Texas)	C	42	128	23	30	5	1	2	10	.234	29	23	1	269	27	4	.987
1992—	Detroit (A.L.)■	C-DH	67	190	22	48	9	0	2	16	.253	20	38	0	271	22	5	.983
1993—	Detroit (A.L.)	C-DH-1B	119	374	59	107	23	3	15	51	.286	49	92	2	522	70	7	.988
1994—	Detroit (A.L.)	C-1B-OF	65	170	17	38	8	0	1	19	.224	28	36	0	280	22	4	.987
1995—	Seattle (A.L.)■	C	26	75	12	17	5	0	1	8	.227	5	22	0	151	12	4	.976
	—Tacoma (PCL)	C	15	48	6	14	5	0	1	11	.292	8	11	0	70	10	1	.988
1996—	Chicago (A.L.)■	C-1B-DH	46	114	14	25	8	0	3	18	.219	13	29	0	182	12	2	.990
1997—	Chicago (A.L.)■	C-1B	19	37	6	8	2	1	1	3	.216	8	9	0	59	4	2	.969
	—Anaheim (A.L.)■	C-DH	70	218	19	51	7	1	4	18	.234	21	57	0	431	29	3	.994
Major league totals (10 years)			540	1413	170	333	68	6	33	149	.236	186	346	2	2486	209	33	.988

KRIVDA, RICK   P   ORIOLES

K

PERSONAL: Born January 19, 1970, in McKeesport, Pa. ... 6-1/180. ... Throws left, bats right. ... Full name: Rick Michael Krivda.
HIGH SCHOOL: McKeesport (Pa.) Area.
COLLEGE: California (Pa.).
TRANSACTIONS/CAREER NOTES: Selected by Baltimore Orioles organization in 23rd round of free-agent draft (June 3, 1991).

Year	Team (League)	W	L	Pct.	ERA	G	GS	CG	ShO	Sv.	IP	H	R	ER	BB	SO
1991—	Bluefield (Appalachian)	7	1	.875	1.88	15	8	0	0	1	67	48	20	14	24	79
1992—	Kane County (Midwest)	12	5	.706	3.03	18	18	2	0	0	121 2/3	108	53	41	41	124
	—Frederick (Carolina)	5	1	.833	2.98	9	9	1	1	0	57 1/3	51	23	19	15	64
1993—	Bowie (Eastern)	7	5	.583	3.08	22	22	0	0	0	125 2/3	114	46	43	50	108
	—Rochester (Int'l)	3	0	1.000	1.89	5	5	0	0	0	33 1/3	20	7	7	16	23
1994—	Rochester (Int'l)	9	10	.474	3.53	28	26	3	2	0	163	149	75	64	73	122
1995—	Rochester (Int'l)	6	5	.545	3.19	16	16	1	0	0	101 2/3	96	44	36	32	74
	—Baltimore (A.L.)	2	7	.222	4.54	13	13	1	0	0	75 1/3	76	40	38	25	53
1996—	Rochester (Int'l)	3	1	.750	4.30	8	8	0	0	0	44	51	24	21	15	34
	—Baltimore (A.L.)	3	5	.375	4.96	22	11	0	0	0	81 2/3	89	48	45	39	54
1997—	Rochester (Int'l)	14	2	.875	3.39	22	21	*6	*3	0	146	122	61	55	34	128
	—Baltimore (A.L.)	4	2	.667	6.30	10	10	0	0	0	50	67	36	35	18	29
Major league totals (3 years)		9	14	.391	5.13	45	34	1	0	0	207	232	124	118	82	136

KROON, MARC   P   PADRES

PERSONAL: Born April 2, 1973, in Bronx, N.Y. ... 6-2/195. ... Throws right, bats right. ... Full name: Marc Jason Kroon.
HIGH SCHOOL: South Mountain (Phoenix).
TRANSACTIONS/CAREER NOTES: Selected by New York Mets organization in supplemental round ("sandwich pick" between second and third round) of free-agent draft (June 3, 1991); pick received as part of compensation for Toronto Blue Jays signing Type C free-agent 1B/DH Pat Tabler. ... Traded by Mets organization to San Diego Padres organization (December 13, 1993), completing deal in which Mets traded OF Randy Curtis and a player to named later to Padres for P Frank Seminara, OF Tracy Jones and SS Pablo Martinez (December 10, 1993).

Year	Team (League)	W	L	Pct.	ERA	G	GS	CG	ShO	Sv.	IP	H	R	ER	BB	SO
1991—	GC Mets (GCL)	2	3	.400	4.53	12	10	1	0	0	47 2/3	39	33	24	22	39
1992—	Kingsport (Appalachian)	3	5	.375	4.10	12	12	0	0	0	68	52	41	31	57	60
1993—	Capital City (S. Atl.)	2	11	.154	3.47	29	19	0	0	2	124 1/3	123	65	48	70	122
1994—	Rancho Cuca. (Cal.)■	11	6	.647	4.83	26	26	0	0	0	143 1/3	143	86	77	81	153
1995—	Memphis (Southern)	7	5	.583	3.51	22	19	0	0	2	115 1/3	90	49	45	61	123
	—San Diego (N.L.)	0	1	.000	10.80	2	0	0	0	0	1 2/3	1	2	2	2	2
1996—	Memphis (Southern)	2	4	.333	2.89	44	0	0	0	22	46 2/3	33	19	15	28	56
1997—	Las Vegas (PCL)■	1	3	.250	4.54	46	0	0	0	15	41 2/3	34	22	21	22	53
	—San Diego (N.L.)	0	1	.000	7.15	12	0	0	0	0	11 1/3	14	9	9	5	12
Major league totals (2 years)		0	2	.000	7.62	14	0	0	0	0	13	15	11	11	7	14

KUBINSKI, TIM   P   ATHLETICS

PERSONAL: Born January 20, 1972, in Pullman, Wash. ... 6-4/205. ... Throws left, bats left. ... Full name: Timothy Mark Kubinski.
HIGH SCHOOL: San Luis Obispo (Calif.).
COLLEGE: UCLA.
TRANSACTIONS/CAREER NOTES: Selected by Oakland Athletics organization in seventh round of free-agent draft (June 3, 1993).
STATISTICAL NOTES: Led Midwest League with 10 balks in 1994.

Year	Team (League)	W	L	Pct.	ERA	G	GS	CG	ShO	Sv.	IP	H	R	ER	BB	SO
1993—	Arizona A's (Arizona)	0	1	.000	6.00	1	1	0	0	0	3	5	2	2	0	3
	—S. Oregon (N'west)	5	5	.500	2.83	12	12	1	0	0	70	67	36	22	18	51
1994—	West. Mich. (Mid.)	14	6	.700	3.63	30	23	1	0	0	158 2/3	168	82	64	36	126
1995—	Modesto (California)	6	10	.375	4.95	25	17	0	0	2	109	126	73	60	24	83
	—Edmonton (PCL)	1	2	.333	4.78	6	5	0	0	0	32	34	18	17	10	12
1996—	Huntsville (Southern)	8	7	.533	2.38	43	3	0	0	3	102	84	41	27	36	78
	—Edmonton (PCL)	0	0	...	0.00	1	0	0	0	0	1	1	0	0	1	0
1997—	Edmonton (PCL)	4	4	.500	4.50	47	0	0	0	7	76	64	39	38	34	53
	—Oakland (A.L.)	0	0	...	5.68	11	0	0	0	0	12 2/3	12	9	8	6	10
Major league totals (1 year)		0	0	...	5.68	11	0	0	0	0	12 2/3	12	9	8	6	10

LACY, KERRY   P   RED SOX

PERSONAL: Born August 7, 1972, in Chattanooga, Tenn. ... 6-2/215. ... Throws right, bats right. ... Full name: Kerry Ardeen Lacy.
HIGH SCHOOL: North Sand Mountain (Higdon, Ala.).
COLLEGE: Chattanooga (Tenn.) State.
TRANSACTIONS/CAREER NOTES: Selected by Texas Rangers organization in 15th round of free-agent draft (June 3, 1991). ... Traded by Rangers with P Mark Brandenburg to Boston Red Sox for P Mike Stanton and a player to be named later (July 31, 1996); Rangers received OF Dwayne Hosey to complete deal (July 31, 1996).

Year Team (League)	W	L	Pct.	ERA	G	GS	CG	ShO	Sv.	IP	H	R	ER	BB	SO
1991—Butte (Pioneer)	2	1	.667	5.59	24	2	0	0	1	48⅓	47	34	30	36	45
1992—Gastonia (S. Atl.)	3	7	.300	3.88	49	1	0	0	17	55⅔	55	35	24	42	57
1993—Charleston, S.C. (S. Atl.)	0	6	.000	3.15	58	0	0	0	36	60	49	25	21	32	54
—Charlotte (Fla. St.)	0	0	...	1.93	4	0	0	0	2	4⅔	2	2	1	3	3
1994—Tulsa (Texas)	2	6	.250	3.68	41	0	0	0	12	63⅔	49	30	26	37	46
1995—Tulsa (Texas)	2	7	.222	4.28	28	7	0	0	9	82	94	47	39	39	49
—Oklahoma City (A.A.)	0	0	...	0.00	1	0	0	0	1	2⅓	0	0	0	0	1
1996—Tulsa (Texas)	0	0	...	0.00	2	0	0	0	2	4	3	0	0	0	1
—Oklahoma City (A.A.)	3	3	.500	2.89	37	0	0	0	6	56	48	21	18	15	31
—Pawtucket (Int'l)■	0	0	...	0.00	7	0	0	0	4	8	1	0	0	2	8
—Boston (A.L.)	2	0	1.000	3.38	11	0	0	0	0	10⅔	15	5	4	8	9
1997—Pawtucket (Int'l)■	5	3	.625	4.73	23	0	0	0	8	32⅓	36	18	17	11	21
—Boston (A.L.)	1	1	.500	6.11	33	0	0	0	3	45⅔	60	34	31	22	18
Major league totals (2 years)	3	1	.750	5.59	44	0	0	0	3	56⅓	75	39	35	30	27

LAKER, TIM   C   DEVIL RAYS

PERSONAL: Born November 27, 1969, in Encino, Calif. ... 6-3/200. ... Bats right, throws right. ... Full name: Timothy John Laker.
HIGH SCHOOL: Simi Valley (Calif.).
COLLEGE: Oxnard (Calif.) College.
TRANSACTIONS/CAREER NOTES: Selected by Kansas City Royals organization in 49th round of free-agent draft (June 2, 1987); did not sign. ... Selected by Montreal Expos organization in sixth round of free-agent draft (June 1, 1988). ... On Ottawa disabled list (April 30-May 14, 1993). ... On disabled list (March 29, 1996-entire season). ... Claimed on waivers by Baltimore Orioles (March 25, 1997). ... On Rochester disabled list (June 5-16, 1997). ... Granted free agency (October 15, 1997). ... Signed by Tampa Bay Devil Rays (December 19, 1997).
STATISTICAL NOTES: Led New York-Pennsylvania League with 16 passed balls in 1989. ... Led Midwest League catchers with 125 assists, 18 errors and 944 total chances in 1990. ... Tied for International League lead in errors by catcher with 11 in 1993. ... Led International League with 20 passed balls in 1994.

Year Team (League)	Pos.	G	AB	R	H	2B	3B	HR	RBI	Avg.	BB	SO	SB	PO	A	E	Avg.
1988—Jamestown (NYP)	C-OF	47	152	14	34	9	0	0	17	.224	8	30	2	236	22	2	.992
1989—Rockford (Midwest)	C	14	48	4	11	1	1	0	4	.229	3	6	1	91	6	4	.960
—Jamestown (NYP)	C	58	216	25	48	9	1	2	24	.222	16	40	8	437	61	8	.984
1990—Rockford (Midwest)	C-OF	120	425	46	94	18	3	7	57	.221	32	83	7	802	†125	†18	.981
—W.P. Beach (FSL)	C	2	3	0	0	0	0	0	0	.000	0	1	0	0	0	0	1.000
1991—Harrisburg (Eastern)	C	11	35	4	10	1	0	1	5	.286	2	5	0	67	4	3	.959
—W.P. Beach (FSL)	C	100	333	35	77	15	2	5	33	.231	22	51	10	560	87	*14	.979
1992—Harrisburg (Eastern)	C	117	409	55	99	19	3	15	68	.242	39	89	3	630	62	*14	.980
—Montreal (N.L.)	C	28	46	8	10	3	0	0	4	.217	2	14	1	102	8	1	.991
1993—Montreal (N.L.)	C	43	86	3	17	2	1	0	7	.198	2	16	2	186	18	2	.987
—Ottawa (Int'l)	C-1B	56	204	26	47	10	0	4	23	.230	21	41	3	341	37	‡11	.972
1994—Ottawa (Int'l)	C	118	424	68	131	32	2	12	71	.309	47	96	11	643	*89	•11	.985
1995—Montreal (N.L.)	C	64	141	17	33	8	1	3	20	.234	14	38	0	265	27	7	.977
1996—							Did not play.										
1997—Rochester (Int'l)■	C	79	290	45	75	11	1	11	37	.259	34	49	1	283	17	6	.980
—Baltimore (A.L.)	C	7	14	0	0	0	0	0	1	.000	2	9	0	28	0	1	.966
American League totals (1 year)		7	14	0	0	0	0	0	1	.000	2	9	0	28	0	1	.966
National League totals (3 years)		135	273	28	60	13	2	3	31	.220	18	68	3	503	53	10	.982
Major league totals (4 years)		142	287	28	60	13	2	3	32	.209	20	77	3	531	53	11	.982

LAMPKIN, TOM   C   CARDINALS

PERSONAL: Born March 4, 1964, in Cincinnati. ... 5-11/185. ... Bats left, throws right. ... Full name: Thomas Michael Lampkin.
HIGH SCHOOL: Blanchet (Seattle).
COLLEGE: Portland.
TRANSACTIONS/CAREER NOTES: Selected by Cleveland Indians organization in 11th round of free-agent draft (June 2, 1986). ... On disabled list (July 6, 1989-remainder of season). ... Traded by Indians organization to San Diego Padres for OF Alex Cole (July 11, 1990). ... Traded by Padres to Milwaukee Brewers for cash (March 25, 1993). ... Granted free agency (December 20, 1993). ... Signed by San Francisco Giants organization (January 5, 1994). ... On San Francisco disabled list (March 31-April 24 and August 26, 1996-remainder of season); included rehabilitation assignment to San Jose (April 22-24). ... Traded by Giants to St. Louis Cardinals for a player to be named later or cash (December 19, 1996); Giants acquired P Rene Arocha to complete deal (February 12, 1997).
STATISTICAL NOTES: Led Pacific Coast League catchers with 11 double plays in 1992. ... Led Pacific Coast League catchers with 595 putouts in 1994.

Year Team (League)	Pos.	G	AB	R	H	2B	3B	HR	RBI	Avg.	BB	SO	SB	PO	A	E	Avg.
1986—Batavia (NY-Penn)	C	63	190	24	49	5	1	1	20	.258	31	14	4	323	36	8	.978
1987—Waterloo (Midw.)	C	118	398	49	106	19	2	7	55	.266	34	41	5	689	*100	15	.981
1988—Williamsport (East.)	C	80	263	38	71	10	0	3	23	.270	25	20	1	431	60	9	.982
—Colo. Springs (PCL)	C	34	107	14	30	5	0	0	7	.280	9	2	0	171	28	5	.975
—Cleveland (A.L.)	C	4	4	0	0	0	0	0	0	.000	1	0	0	3	0	0	1.000

Year Team (League)	Pos.	G	AB	R	H	2B	3B	HR	RBI	Avg.	BB	SO	SB	PO	A	E	Avg.
1989—Colo. Springs (PCL)...	C	63	209	26	67	10	3	4	32	.321	10	18	4	305	21	8	.976
1990—Colo. Springs (PCL)...	C-2B	69	199	32	44	7	5	1	18	.221	19	19	7	312	36	12	.967
—San Diego (N.L.)■.....	C	26	63	4	14	0	1	1	4	.222	4	9	0	91	10	3	.971
—Las Vegas (PCL)........	C	1	2	0	1	0	0	0	0	.500	0	1	0	3	0	0	1.000
1991—San Diego (N.L.).......	C	38	58	4	11	3	1	0	3	.190	3	9	0	49	5	0	1.000
—Las Vegas (PCL)........	C-1B-OF	45	164	25	52	11	1	2	29	.317	10	19	2	211	26	6	.975
1992—Las Vegas (PCL).......	C	108	340	45	104	17	4	3	48	.306	53	27	15	506	*64	12	.979
—San Diego (N.L.).......	C-OF	9	17	3	4	0	0	0	0	.235	6	1	2	30	3	0	1.000
1993—New Orleans (A.A.)■..	C-OF	25	80	18	26	5	0	2	10	.325	18	4	5	152	12	3	.982
—Milwaukee (A.L.).......	C-OF-DH	73	162	22	32	8	0	4	25	.198	20	26	7	242	24	6	.978
1994—Phoenix (PCL)■........	C-OF	118	453	76	136	32	8	8	70	.300	42	49	8	†595	59	10	.985
1995—San Francisco (N.L.) ..	C-OF	65	76	8	21	2	0	1	9	.276	9	8	2	62	5	0	1.000
1996—San Jose (Calif.)........	C	2	7	2	2	0	1	0	2	.286	1	2	0	10	1	0	1.000
—San Francisco (N.L.) ..	C	66	177	26	41	8	0	6	29	.232	20	22	1	342	27	3	.992
1997—St. Louis (N.L.)■	C	108	229	28	56	8	1	7	22	.245	28	30	2	413	37	5	.989
American League totals (2 years)		77	166	22	32	8	0	4	25	.193	21	26	7	245	24	6	.978
National League totals (6 years)		312	620	73	147	21	3	15	67	.237	70	79	7	987	87	11	.990
Major league totals (8 years)		389	786	95	179	29	3	19	92	.228	91	105	14	1232	111	17	.988

LANDRY, TODD   1B   BREWERS

PERSONAL: Born September 21, 1972, in Baton Rouge, La. ... 6-4/215. ... Throws left, bats right.
HIGH SCHOOL: Ascension Catholic (Donaldsville, La.).
JUNIOR COLLEGE: Lassen College (Calif.).
COLLEGE: Arizona.
TRANSACTIONS/CAREER NOTES: Selected by Milwaukee Brewers organization in 31st round of free-agent draft (June 3, 1993).
STATISTICAL NOTES: Led Texas League in grounding into double plays with 20 in 1995. ... Led Texas League first basemen with 123 assists in 1995. ... Led American Association first basemen with 86 assists in 1996.

Year Team (League)	Pos.	G	AB	R	H	2B	3B	HR	RBI	Avg.	BB	SO	SB	PO	A	E	Avg.
1993—Helena (Pioneer)	1B-OF	29	124	27	39	10	1	5	24	.315	8	20	5	174	24	6	.971
—Beloit (Midwest).........	1B-OF	38	149	26	45	6	0	4	24	.302	4	36	4	277	30	3	.990
1994—Stockton (California) ..	1B	105	356	55	95	12	6	8	49	.267	28	53	4	781	*83	4	.995
1995—El Paso (Texas)...........	1B-OF	132	511	76	149	33	4	16	79	.292	33	100	9	1027	†124	15	.987
1996—New Orleans (A.A.).....	1B-OF	113	391	41	94	19	2	5	44	.240	32	61	14	783	88	9	.990
1997—El Paso (Texas)...........	1B-OF	106	346	43	109	24	3	7	69	.315	15	52	5	530	46	2	.997

LANE, RYAN   SS/2B   TWINS

PERSONAL: Born July 6, 1974, in Bellefontaine, Ohio. ... 6-1/185. ... Throws right, bats right. ... Full name: Ryan Jeffrey Lane.
HIGH SCHOOL: Bellefontaine (Ohio).
TRANSACTIONS/CAREER NOTES: Selected by Minnesota Twins organization in eighth round of free-agent draft (June 3, 1993).
STATISTICAL NOTES: Led Appalachian League shortstops with .926 fielding percentage and 34 double plays in 1994. ... Tied for Eastern League lead with seven sacrifice flies in 1997. ... Led Eastern League second basemen with 94 double plays in 1997.

Year Team (League)	Pos.	G	AB	R	H	2B	3B	HR	RBI	Avg.	BB	SO	SB	PO	A	E	Avg.
1993—GC Twins (GCL).........	SS	43	138	15	20	3	2	0	5	.145	15	38	3	50	94	11	.929
1994—Elizabethton (App.)......	SS-2B	59	202	32	48	13	0	3	18	.238	26	47	5	78	170	19	†.929
1995—Fort Wayne (Midw.)....	SS-2B	115	432	69	115	37	1	6	56	.266	65	92	17	176	314	25	.951
1996—Fort Myers (FSL)........	2B-SS	106	404	74	110	20	7	9	62	.272	60	96	21	233	300	19	.966
—New Britain (Eastern).	SS-2B	33	117	13	26	5	1	2	12	.222	8	29	3	55	77	11	.923
1997—New Britain (Eastern).	2B-SS	128	444	63	115	26	2	5	56	.259	43	79	18	246	374	16	.975

LANGSTON, MARK   P   PADRES

PERSONAL: Born August 20, 1960, in San Diego. ... 6-2/184. ... Throws left, bats right. ... Full name: Mark Edward Langston.
HIGH SCHOOL: Buchser (Santa Clara, Calif.).
COLLEGE: San Jose State.
TRANSACTIONS/CAREER NOTES: Selected by Chicago Cubs organization in 15th round of free-agent draft (June 6, 1978); did not sign. ... Selected by Seattle Mariners organization in third round of free-agent draft (June 8, 1981); pick received as compensation for Texas Rangers signing free-agent IF Bill Stein. ... On disabled list (June 7-July 22, 1985). ... Traded by Mariners with a player to be named later to Montreal Expos for P Randy Johnson, P Brian Holman and P Gene Harris (May 25, 1989); Indianapolis, Expos organization, acquired P Mike Campbell to complete deal (July 31, 1989). ... Granted free agency (November 13, 1989). ... Signed by California Angels (December 1, 1989). ... On disabled list (April 10-May 11, 1994). ... On California disabled list (May 6-31, July 12-28 and August 11, 1996-remainder of season); included rehabilitation assignment to Lake Elsinore (May 26-31). ... Angels franchise renamed Anaheim Angels for 1997 season. ... On disabled list (May 20-August 20 and August 21, 1997-remainder of season). ... Granted free agency (October 28, 1997). ... Signed by San Diego Padres organization (January 7, 1998).
RECORDS: Holds major league single-season record for fewest assists by pitcher who led league in assists—42 (1990).
HONORS: Named A.L. Rookie Pitcher of the Year by THE SPORTING NEWS (1984). ... Won A.L. Gold Glove at pitcher (1987-88 and 1991-95).
STATISTICAL NOTES: Pitched seven innings, combining with Mike Witt (two innings) in 1-0 no-hit victory against Seattle (April 11, 1990). ... Struck out 15 batters in one game (June 25, 1986). ... Struck out 16 batters in one game (May 10, 1988). ... Pitched 3-0 one-hit, complete-game victory against Texas (September 24, 1988).
MISCELLANEOUS: Scored in only appearance as pinch-runner and struck out twice in two appearances as designated hitter (1992).

Year Team (League)	W	L	Pct.	ERA	G	GS	CG	ShO	Sv.	IP	H	R	ER	BB	SO
1981— Bellingham (N'west)	7	3	.700	3.39	13	13	5	1	0	85	81	37	32	46	97
1982— Bakersfield (California)	12	7	.632	2.54	26	26	7	3	0	177⅓	143	71	50	102	161
1983— Chattanooga (Southern)	14	9	.609	3.59	28	28	10	0	0	198	187	104	79	102	142
1984— Seattle (A.L.)	17	10	.630	3.40	35	33	5	2	0	225	188	99	85	*118	*204
1985— Seattle (A.L.)	7	14	.333	5.47	24	24	2	0	0	126⅔	122	85	77	91	72
1986— Seattle (A.L.)	12	14	.462	4.85	37	36	9	0	0	239⅓	234	*142	*129	123	*245
1987— Seattle (A.L.)	19	13	.594	3.84	35	35	14	3	0	272	242	132	116	114	*262
1988— Seattle (A.L.)	15	11	.577	3.34	35	35	9	3	0	261⅓	222	108	97	110	235
1989— Seattle (A.L.)	4	5	.444	3.56	10	10	2	1	0	73⅓	60	30	29	19	60
—Montreal (N.L.)■	12	9	.571	2.39	24	24	6	4	0	176⅔	138	57	47	93	175
1990— California (A.L.)■	10	17	.370	4.40	33	33	5	1	0	223	215	120	109	104	195
1991— California (A.L.)	19	8	.704	3.03	34	34	7	0	0	246⅓	190	89	82	96	183
1992— California (A.L.)	13	14	.481	3.66	32	32	9	2	0	229	206	103	93	74	174
1993— California (A.L.)	16	11	.593	3.20	35	35	7	0	0	256⅓	220	100	91	85	196
1994— California (A.L.)	7	8	.467	4.68	18	18	2	1	0	119⅓	121	67	62	54	109
1995— California (A.L.)	15	7	.682	4.63	31	31	2	1	0	200⅓	212	109	103	64	142
1996— California (A.L.)	6	5	.545	4.82	18	18	2	0	0	123⅓	116	68	66	45	83
—Lake Elsinore (Calif.)	0	0	. . .	0.00	1	1	0	0	0	4	3	0	0	0	5
1997— Anaheim (A.L.)	2	4	.333	5.85	9	9	0	0	0	47⅔	61	34	31	29	30
—Lake Elsinore (Calif.)	0	2	.000	3.21	3	3	0	0	0	14	11	7	5	2	10
A.L. totals (14 years)	162	141	.535	3.98	386	383	75	14	0	2643	2409	1286	1170	1126	2190
N.L. totals (1 year)	12	9	.571	2.39	24	24	6	4	0	176⅔	138	57	47	93	175
Major league totals (14 years)	174	150	.537	3.88	410	407	81	18	0	2819⅔	2547	1343	1217	1219	2365

ALL-STAR GAME RECORD

Year League	W	L	Pct.	ERA	GS	CG	ShO	Sv.	IP	H	R	ER	BB	SO
1987— American	0	0	. . .	0.00	0	0	0	0	2	0	0	0	0	3
1991— American						Did not play.								
1992— American	0	0	. . .	9.00	0	0	0	0	1	2	1	1	0	1
1993— American	0	0	. . .	9.00	1	0	0	0	2	3	2	2	1	2
All-Star totals (3 years)	0	0	. . .	5.40	1	0	0	0	5	5	3	3	1	6

LANKFORD, FRANK   P   DODGERS*

PERSONAL: Born March 26, 1971, in Atlanta. ... 6-2/190. ... Throws right, bats right.
HIGH SCHOOL: Westminster (Atlanta).
COLLEGE: Virginia.
TRANSACTIONS/CAREER NOTES: Selected by New York Yankees organization in 17th round of free-agent draft (June 3, 1993). ... Selected by Los Angeles Dodgers from Yankees organization in Rule 5 major league draft (December 15, 1997).

Year Team (League)	W	L	Pct.	ERA	G	GS	CG	ShO	Sv.	IP	H	R	ER	BB	SO
1993— Oneonta (New York-Penn.)	4	5	.444	3.34	16	7	0	0	0	64⅔	60	41	24	22	61
1994— Greensboro (S. Atl.)	7	6	.538	2.95	54	0	0	0	7	82⅓	79	37	27	18	74
1995— Tampa (Florida State)	4	6	.400	2.59	55	0	0	0	15	73	64	29	21	22	58
1996— Norwich (Eastern)	7	8	.467	2.66	61	0	0	0	4	88	82	42	26	40	61
1997— Norwich (Eastern)	4	2	.667	2.90	11	11	2	0	0	68⅓	58	28	22	15	39
—Columbus (International)	7	4	.636	2.69	15	13	1	1	0	93⅔	84	33	28	22	40

LANKFORD, RAY   OF   CARDINALS

PERSONAL: Born June 5, 1967, in Modesto, Calif. ... 5-11/198. ... Bats left, throws left. ... Full name: Raymond Lewis Lankford.
HIGH SCHOOL: Grace Davis (Modesto, Calif.).
JUNIOR COLLEGE: Modesto (Calif.) Junior College.
TRANSACTIONS/CAREER NOTES: Selected by Chicago Cubs organization in third round of free-agent draft (January 14, 1986); did not sign. ... Selected by St. Louis Cardinals organization in third round of free-agent draft (June 2, 1987). ... On disabled list (June 24-July 9, 1993). ... On St. Louis disabled list (March 27-April 22, 1997); included rehabilitation assignment to Prince William (April 14-22).
RECORDS: Shares major league single-season record for fewest double plays by outfielder (150 or more games)—0 (1992).
HONORS: Named Texas League Most Valuable Player (1989).
STATISTICAL NOTES: Led Appalachian League outfielders with 155 total chances in 1987. ... Led Appalachian League in caught stealing with 11 in 1987. ... Led Midwest League with 242 total bases in 1988. ... Led Texas League outfielders with 387 total chances in 1989. ... Led American Association outfielders with 352 total chances in 1990. ... Tied for American Association lead with nine intentional bases on balls received in 1990. ... Hit for the cycle (September 15, 1991). ... Led N.L. in caught stealing with 24 in 1992. ... Career major league grand slams: 3.

Year Team (League)	Pos.	G	AB	R	H	2B	3B	HR	RBI	Avg.	BB	SO	SB	PO	A	E	Avg.
1987— Johnson City (App.)	OF	66	253	45	78	17	4	3	32	.308	19	43	14	*143	7	5	.968
1988— Springfield (Midw.)	OF	135	532	90	151	26	*16	11	66	.284	60	92	33	284	5	7	.976
1989— Arkansas (Texas)	OF	*134	498	98	*158	28	*12	11	98	.317	65	57	38	*367	9	11	.972
1990— Louisville (A.A.)	OF	132	473	61	123	25	8	10	72	.260	72	81	30	*333	8	•11	.969
—St. Louis (N.L.)	OF	39	126	12	36	10	1	3	12	.286	13	27	8	92	1	1	.989
1991— St. Louis (N.L.)	OF	151	566	83	142	23	*15	9	69	.251	41	114	44	367	7	6	.984
1992— St. Louis (N.L.)	OF	153	598	87	175	40	6	20	86	.293	72	*147	42	*438	5	2	.996
1993— St. Louis (N.L.)	OF	127	407	64	97	17	3	7	45	.238	81	111	14	312	6	7	.978
1994— St. Louis (N.L.)	OF	109	416	89	111	25	5	19	57	.267	58	113	11	260	5	5	.978
1995— St. Louis (N.L.)	OF	132	483	81	134	35	2	25	82	.277	63	110	24	300	7	3	.990
1996— St. Louis (N.L.)	OF	149	545	100	150	36	8	21	86	.275	79	133	35	356	9	1	*.997
1997— Prince William (Car.)	OF	4	13	3	4	1	0	0	4	.308	4	5	1	6	0	0	1.000
—St. Louis (N.L.)	OF	133	465	94	137	36	3	31	98	.295	95	125	21	293	4	9	.971
Major league totals (8 years)		993	3606	610	982	222	43	135	535	.272	502	880	199	2418	44	35	.986

Year	Team (League)	Pos.	G	AB	R	H	2B	3B	HR	RBI	Avg.	BB	SO	SB	PO	A	E	Avg.
							BATTING									FIELDING		
1996— St. Louis (N.L.)...........		OF-PH	1	2	1	1	0	0	0	0	.500	1	0	0	4	0	0	1.000

CHAMPIONSHIP SERIES RECORD

RECORDS: Holds N.L. career record for most at-bats without a hit—13 (1996).

Year	Team (League)	Pos.	G	AB	R	H	2B	3B	HR	RBI	Avg.	BB	SO	SB	PO	A	E	Avg.
							BATTING									FIELDING		
1996— St. Louis (N.L.)...........		OF-PH	5	13	1	0	0	0	0	1	.000	1	4	0	7	0	0	1.000

ALL-STAR GAME RECORD

Year	League	Pos.	AB	R	H	2B	3B	HR	RBI	Avg.	BB	SO	SB	PO	A	E	Avg.
						BATTING									FIELDING		
1997— National....................		OF	2	0	0	0	0	0	0	.000	1	1	0	0	0	0	...

LANSING, MIKE   2B   ROCKIES

PERSONAL: Born April 3, 1968, in Rawlins, Wyo. ... 6-0/185. ... Bats right, throws right. ... Full name: Michael Thomas Lansing.
HIGH SCHOOL: Natrona County (Casper, Wyo.).
COLLEGE: Wichita State.
TRANSACTIONS/CAREER NOTES: Selected by Baltimore Orioles organization in ninth round of free-agent draft (June 5, 1989); did not sign. ... Selected by Miami, independent, in sixth round of free-agent draft (June 4, 1990). ... On disabled list (April 29-May 9, 1991). ... Contract sold by Miami to Montreal Expos organization (September 18, 1991). ... On disabled list (May 31-June 15, 1995). ... Traded by Expos to Colorado Rockies for P Jake Westbrook, P John Nicholson and OF Mark Hamlin (November 18, 1997).
STATISTICAL NOTES: Led Eastern League shortstops with 76 double plays in 1992. ... Career major league grand slams: 2.

Year	Team (League)	Pos.	G	AB	R	H	2B	3B	HR	RBI	Avg.	BB	SO	SB	PO	A	E	Avg.
							BATTING									FIELDING		
1990— Miami (Fla. St.)		SS	61	207	20	50	5	2	2	11	.242	29	35	15	104	166	10	.964
1991— Miami (Fla. St.)		SS-2B	104	384	54	110	20	7	6	55	.286	40	75	29	148	273	27	.940
1992— Harrisburg (East.)■..		SS	128	483	66	135	20	6	6	54	.280	52	64	46	189	*373	20	*.966
1993— Montreal (N.L.)..........		3B-SS-2B	141	491	64	141	29	1	3	45	.287	46	56	23	136	336	24	.952
1994— Montreal (N.L.)..........		2B-3B-SS	106	394	44	105	21	2	5	35	.266	30	37	12	164	283	10	.978
1995— Montreal (N.L.)..........		2B-SS	127	467	47	119	30	2	10	62	.255	28	65	27	306	373	6	.991
1996— Montreal (N.L.)..........		2B-SS	159	641	99	183	40	2	11	53	.285	44	85	23	349	395	11	.985
1997— Montreal (N.L.)..........		2B	144	572	86	161	45	2	20	70	.281	45	92	11	279	395	9	.987
Major league totals (5 years)			677	2565	340	709	165	9	49	265	.276	193	335	96	1234	1782	60	.980

LARKIN, ANDY   P   MARLINS

PERSONAL: Born June 27, 1974, in Chelan, Wash. ... 6-4/190. ... Throws right, bats right.
HIGH SCHOOL: South Medford (Medford, Ore.).
TRANSACTIONS/CAREER NOTES: Selected by Florida Marlins organization in 25th round of free-agent draft (June 1, 1992). ... On disabled list (June 14-August 23, 1995). ... On Portland disabled list (April 4-May 11, 1996). ... On Florida disabled list (May 11-July 17, 1996); included rehabilitation assignment to Brevard County (June 18-July 17).
STATISTICAL NOTES: Pitched 6-0 no-hit victory against Welland (July 25, 1993). ... Led New York-Pennsylvania League with 12 hit batsmen in 1993. ... Led Midwest League with 19 hit batsmen in 1994. ... Led International League with 15 hit batsmen in 1997.

Year	Team (League)	W	L	Pct.	ERA	G	GS	CG	ShO	Sv.	IP	H	R	ER	BB	SO
1992— GC Marlins (GCL)...............	1	2	.333	5.23	14	4	0	0	2	41 1/3	41	26	24	19	20
1993— Elmira (N.Y.-Penn).............	5	7	.417	2.97	14	14	•4	•1	0	88	74	43	29	23	89
1994— Kane County (Midwest)......	9	7	.563	2.83	21	21	3	1	0	140	125	53	44	27	125
1995— Portland (Eastern)..............	1	2	.333	3.38	9	9	0	0	0	40	29	16	15	11	23
1996— Brevard County (FSL)........	0	4	.000	4.23	6	6	0	0	0	27 2/3	34	20	13	7	18
— Portland (Eastern).............	4	1	.800	3.10	8	8	0	0	0	49 1/3	45	18	17	10	40
— Florida (N.L.)..................	0	0	...	1.80	1	1	0	0	0	5	3	1	1	4	2
1997— Charlotte (Int'l)..................	6	11	.353	6.05	28	27	3	0	0	144 1/3	166	109	97	76	103
Major league totals (1 year)........	0	0	...	1.80	1	1	0	0	0	5	3	1	1	4	2

LARKIN, BARRY   SS   REDS

PERSONAL: Born April 28, 1964, in Cincinnati. ... 6-0/195. ... Bats right, throws right. ... Full name: Barry Louis Larkin. ... Cousin of Nathan Davis, defensive tackle, Atlanta Falcons.
HIGH SCHOOL: Moeller (Cincinnati).
COLLEGE: Michigan.
TRANSACTIONS/CAREER NOTES: Selected by Cincinnati Reds organization in second round of free-agent draft (June 7, 1982); did not sign. ... Selected by Reds organization in first round (fourth pick overall) of free-agent draft (June 3, 1985). ... On disabled list (April 13-May 2, 1987). ... On Cincinnati disabled list (July 11-September 1, 1989); included rehabilitation assignment to Nashville (August 27-September 1). ... On disabled list (May 18-June 4, 1991; April 19-May 8, 1992; and August 5, 1993-remainder of season). ... On disabled list (June 17-August 2 and September 1, 1997-remainder of season).
RECORDS: Holds major league single-season record for fewest putouts by shortstop for leader—230 (1996). ... Shares major league record for most home runs in two consecutive games—5 (June 27 [2] and 28 [3], 1991).
HONORS: Named shortstop on THE SPORTING NEWS college All-America team (1985). ... Named American Association Most Valuable Player (1986). ... Named shortstop on THE SPORTING NEWS N.L. All-Star team (1988-92 and 1994-96). ... Named shortstop on THE SPORTING NEWS N.L. Silver Slugger team (1988-92 and 1995-96). ... Won N.L. Gold Glove at shortstop (1994-96). ... Named N.L. Most Valuable Player by Baseball Writers' Association of America (1995).
STATISTICAL NOTES: Led American Association with .525 slugging percentage in 1986. ... Had 21-game hitting streak (September 10-October 2, 1988). ... Tied for N.L. lead in double plays by shortstop with 86 in 1990. ... Hit three home runs in one game (June 28, 1991).
MISCELLANEOUS: Member of 1984 U.S. Olympic baseball team.

Year Team (League)	Pos.	G	AB	R	H	2B	3B	HR	RBI	Avg.	BB	SO	SB	PO	A	E	Avg.
1985—Vermont (Eastern)......	SS	72	255	42	68	13	2	1	31	.267	23	21	12	110	166	17	.942
1986—Denver (A.A.)............	SS-2B	103	413	67	136	31	10	10	51	.329	31	43	19	172	287	18	.962
—Cincinnati (N.L.).........	SS-2B	41	159	27	45	4	3	3	19	.283	9	21	8	51	125	4	.978
1987—Cincinnati (N.L.)........	SS	125	439	64	107	16	2	12	43	.244	36	52	21	168	358	19	.965
1988—Cincinnati (N.L.)........	SS	151	588	91	174	32	5	12	56	.296	41	24	40	231	470	•29	.960
1989—Cincinnati (N.L.)........	SS	97	325	47	111	14	4	4	36	.342	20	23	10	142	267	10	.976
—Nashville (A.A.).........	SS	2	5	2	5	1	0	0	0	1.000	0	0	0	1	3	0	1.000
1990—Cincinnati (N.L.)........	SS	158	614	85	185	25	6	7	67	.301	49	49	30	254	*469	17	.977
1991—Cincinnati (N.L.)........	SS	123	464	88	140	27	4	20	69	.302	55	64	24	226	372	15	.976
1992—Cincinnati (N.L.)........	SS	140	533	76	162	32	6	12	78	.304	63	58	15	233	408	11	.983
1993—Cincinnati (N.L.)........	SS	100	384	57	121	20	3	8	51	.315	51	33	14	159	281	16	.965
1994—Cincinnati (N.L.)........	SS	110	427	78	119	23	5	9	52	.279	64	58	26	*178	312	10	.980
1995—Cincinnati (N.L.)........	SS	131	496	98	158	29	6	15	66	.319	61	49	51	192	341	11	.980
1996—Cincinnati (N.L.)........	SS	152	517	117	154	32	4	33	89	.298	96	52	36	*230	426	17	.975
1997—Cincinnati (N.L.)........	SS-DH	73	224	34	71	17	3	4	20	.317	47	24	14	77	171	5	.980
Major league totals (12 years)		1401	5170	862	1547	271	51	139	646	.299	592	507	289	2141	4000	164	.974

DIVISION SERIES RECORD

Year Team (League)	Pos.	G	AB	R	H	2B	3B	HR	RBI	Avg.	BB	SO	SB	PO	A	E	Avg.
1995—Cincinnati (N.L.)	SS	3	13	2	5	0	0	1	1	.385	1	2	4	3	8	0	1.000

CHAMPIONSHIP SERIES RECORD

Year Team (League)	Pos.	G	AB	R	H	2B	3B	HR	RBI	Avg.	BB	SO	SB	PO	A	E	Avg.
1990—Cincinnati (N.L.)	SS	6	23	5	6	2	0	0	1	.261	3	1	3	21	15	1	.973
1995—Cincinnati (N.L.)	SS	4	18	1	7	2	1	0	0	.389	1	1	1	10	15	1	.962
Championship series totals (2 years)		10	41	6	13	4	1	0	1	.317	4	2	4	31	30	2	.968

WORLD SERIES RECORD

RECORDS: Shares record for most at-bats in one inning—2 (October 19, 1990, third inning).
NOTES: Member of World Series championship team (1990).

Year Team (League)	Pos.	G	AB	R	H	2B	3B	HR	RBI	Avg.	BB	SO	SB	PO	A	E	Avg.
1990—Cincinnati (N.L.)	SS	4	17	3	6	1	1	0	1	.353	2	0	0	1	14	0	1.000

ALL-STAR GAME RECORD

Year League	Pos.	AB	R	H	2B	3B	HR	RBI	Avg.	BB	SO	SB	PO	A	E	Avg.
1988—National....................	SS	2	0	0	0	0	0	0	.000	0	1	0	0	1	0	1.000
1989—National....................							Did not play.									
1990—National....................	PR-SS	0	0	0	0	0	0	0	...	0	0	1	1	2	0	1.000
1991—National....................	SS	1	0	0	0	0	0	0	.000	0	0	0	0	2	0	1.000
1993—National....................	SS	2	0	0	0	0	0	1	.000	0	1	0	2	1	0	1.000
1994—National....................							Selected, did not play—injured.									
1995—National....................	SS	3	0	0	0	0	0	0	.000	0	0	0	2	3	0	1.000
1996—National....................	SS	3	1	1	0	0	0	0	.333	0	0	0	0	2	0	1.000
1997—National....................							Selected, did not play—injured.									
All-Star Game totals (6 years)		11	1	1	0	0	0	1	.091	0	2	1	5	11	0	1.000

LaRUE, JASON   C   REDS

PERSONAL: Born March 19, 1974, in Houston. ... 5-11/190. ... Bats right, throws right. ... Full name: Michael Jason LaRue.
HIGH SCHOOL: Smithson Valley (Spring Branch, Texas)
COLLEGE: Dallas Baptist.
TRANSACTIONS/CAREER NOTES: Selected by Cincinnati Reds organization in fifth round of free-agent draft (June 1, 1995). ... On disabled list (June 30-September 13, 1996).
STATISTICAL NOTES: Tied for Pioneer League lead in being hit by pitch with 12 in 1995. ... Led Pioneer League catchers with seven double plays in 1995.

Year Team (League)	Pos.	G	AB	R	H	2B	3B	HR	RBI	Avg.	BB	SO	SB	PO	A	E	Avg.
1995—Billings (Pioneer)........	C	58	183	35	50	8	1	5	31	.273	16	28	3	346	46	8	.980
1996—Char., W.Va. (SAL)......	C-1B	37	123	17	26	8	0	2	14	.211	11	28	3	234	48	6	.979
1997—Char., W.Va. (SAL).....C-1B-3B-OF	132	473	78	149	*50	3	8	81	.315	47	90	14	711	84	19	.977

LATHAM, CHRIS   OF   TWINS

PERSONAL: Born May 26, 1973, in Coeur d'Alene, Idaho. ... 6-0/185. ... Bats both, throws right. ... Full name: Christopher Joseph Latham.
HIGH SCHOOL: Basic Technical (Las Vegas).
TRANSACTIONS/CAREER NOTES: Selected by Los Angeles Dodgers organization in 11th round of free-agent draft (June 3, 1991). ... Traded by Dodgers organization to Minnesota Twins (October 30, 1995), completing deal in which Twins traded P Mark Guthrie and P Kevin Tapani to Dodgers for 1B/3B Ron Coomer, P Greg Hansell, P Jose Parra and a player to be named later (July 31, 1995). ... On disabled list (August 30-September 9, 1996).
STATISTICAL NOTES: Led Northwest League with 148 total bases and 20 caught stealing in 1994. ... Tied for Northwest League lead with seven intentional bases on balls received in 1994. ... Led Northwest League outfielders with 154 total chances in 1994. ... Led Pacific Coast League lead in caught stealing with 19 in 1997.

Year — Team (League)	Pos.	G	AB	R	H	2B	3B	HR	RBI	Avg.	BB	SO	SB	PO	A	E	Avg.
1991— GC Dodgers (GCL)	2B	43	109	17	26	2	1	0	11	.239	16	45	14	47	63	10	.917
1992— Great Falls (Pio.)	2B	17	37	8	12	2	0	0	3	.324	8	8	1	17	24	6	.872
— GC Dodgers (GCL)	2B-SS-3B	14	48	4	11	2	0	0	2	.229	4	5	17	2	26	14	1	.976
1993— Yakima (N'west)	OF	54	192	46	50	2	*6	4	17	.260	39	53	25	83	5	6	.936
— Bakersfield (Calif.)	OF	6	27	1	5	1	0	0	3	.185	4	5	2	12	0	1	.923
1994— Bakersfield (Calif.)	OF	52	191	29	41	5	2	2	15	.215	28	49	28	88	4	7	.929
— Yakima (N'west)	OF	71	288	*69	*98	19	*8	5	32	*.340	55	66	33	*144	6	4	.974
1995— Vero Beach (FSL)	OF	71	259	53	74	13	4	6	39	.286	56	54	42	125	5	7	.949
— San Antonio (Tex.)	OF	58	214	38	64	14	5	9	37	.299	33	59	11	135	2	4	.972
— Albuquerque (PCL).....	OF	5	18	2	3	0	1	0	3	.167	1	4	1	7	0	0	1.000
1996— Salt Lake (PCL)■......	OF	115	376	59	103	16	6	9	50	.274	36	91	26	235	9	9	.964
1997— Salt Lake (PCL)	OF	118	492	78	152	22	5	8	58	.309	58	110	21	262	6	11	.961
— Minnesota (A.L.)	OF	15	22	4	4	1	0	0	1	.182	0	8	0	11	0	1	.917
Major league totals (1 year)		15	22	4	4	1	0	0	1	.182	0	8	0	11	0	1	.917

LAWRENCE, SEAN — P — PIRATES

PERSONAL: Born September 2, 1970, in Oak Park, Ill. ... 6-4/200. ... Throws left, bats left. ... Full name: Sean Christopher Lawrence.
COLLEGE: St. Francis (Ill.).
TRANSACTIONS/CAREER NOTES: Selected by Pittsburgh Pirates organization in sixth round of free-agent draft (June 1, 1992). ... On disabled list (June 14-September 8, 1994).

Year — Team (League)	W	L	Pct.	ERA	G	GS	CG	ShO	Sv.	IP	H	R	ER	BB	SO
1992— Welland (N.Y.-Penn)	3	6	.333	5.23	15	•15	0	0	0	74	75	55	43	34	71
1993— Salem (Northwest)	1	3	.250	10.20	4	4	0	0	0	15	25	19	17	9	14
— Augusta (S. Atl.)...............	6	8	.429	3.12	22	22	0	0	0	121	108	59	42	50	96
1994— Salem (Carolina)	4	2	.667	2.63	12	12	0	0	0	72	76	38	21	18	66
1995— Carolina (Southern)............	0	2	.000	5.48	12	3	0	0	0	21 1/3	27	13	13	8	19
— Lynchburg (Carolina)	5	8	.385	4.22	20	19	0	00	0	111	115	56	52	25	82
1996— Carolina (Southern)............	3	5	.375	3.95	37	9	0	0	2	82	80	40	36	36	81
1997— Calgary (PCL).....................	8	9	.471	4.21	26	26	2	0	0	143 1/3	154	83	67	57	116

LAWTON, MATT — OF — TWINS

L

PERSONAL: Born November 3, 1971, in Gulfport, Miss. ... 5-10/200. ... Bats left, throws right. ... Full name: Matthew Lawton III.
HIGH SCHOOL: Harrison Central (Gulfport, Miss.).
JUNIOR COLLEGE: Gulf Coast Community College (Fla.).
TRANSACTIONS/CAREER NOTES: Selected by Minnesota Twins organization in 12th round of free-agent draft (June 3, 1991).
STATISTICAL NOTES: Led Florida State League with .407 on-base percentage in 1994. ... Career major league grand slams: 1.

Year — Team (League)	Pos.	G	AB	R	H	2B	3B	HR	RBI	Avg.	BB	SO	SB	PO	A	E	Avg.
1992— GC Twins (GCL)..........	2B	53	173	39	45	8	3	2	26	.260	27	27	20	129	142	12	.958
1993— Fort Wayne (Midw.).....	OF	111	340	50	97	21	3	9	38	.285	65	42	23	65	6	3	.959
1994— Fort Myers (FSL)	OF	122	446	79	134	30	1	7	51	.300	80	64	42	188	13	6	.971
1995— New Britain (Eastern)..	OF	114	412	75	111	19	5	13	54	.269	56	70	26	221	12	2	*.991
— Minnesota (A.L.)	OF-DH	21	60	11	19	4	1	1	12	.317	7	11	1	34	1	1	.972
1996— Minnesota (A.L.)	OF-DH	79	252	34	65	7	1	6	42	.258	28	28	4	196	4	3	.985
— Salt Lake (PCL)	OF	53	212	40	63	16	1	7	33	.297	26	34	2	88	0	6	.936
1997— Minnesota (A.L.)	OF	142	460	74	114	29	3	14	60	.248	76	81	7	278	9	7	.976
Major league totals (3 years)		242	772	119	198	40	5	21	114	.256	111	120	12	508	14	11	.979

LEDEE, RICKY — OF — YANKEES

PERSONAL: Born November 22, 1973, in Ponce, Puerto Rico. ... 6-1/160. ... Bats left, throws left. ... Full name: Ricardo Alberto Ledee.
HIGH SCHOOL: Colonel Nuestra Sonora de Valvanera (Coano, Puerto Rico).
TRANSACTIONS/CAREER NOTES: Selected by New York Yankees organization in 16th round of free-agent draft (June 3, 1990). ... On Tampa disabled list (April 6-May 27, 1996). ... On Columbus disabled list (May 5-16 and May 22-August 4, 1997).

Year — Team (League)	Pos.	G	AB	R	H	2B	3B	HR	RBI	Avg.	BB	SO	SB	PO	A	E	Avg.
1990— GC Yankees (GCL)......	OF	19	37	5	4	2	0	0	1	.108	6	18	2	18	1	0	1.000
1991— GC Yankees (GCL)......	OF	47	165	22	44	6	2	0	18	.267	22	40	3	79	6	6	.934
1992— GC Yankees (GCL)......	OF	52	179	25	41	9	2	2	23	.229	24	47	1	62	4	2	.971
1993— Oneonta (NYP)	OF	52	192	32	49	7	6	8	20	.255	25	46	7	91	6	3	.970
1994— Greensboro (S. Atl.) ...	OF	134	484	87	121	23	9	22	71	.250	91	126	10	170	10	5	.973
1995— Greensboro (S. Atl.) ...	OF	89	335	65	90	16	6	14	49	.269	51	66	10	160	7	3	.982
1996— Norwich (Eastern)	OF	39	137	27	50	11	1	8	37	.365	16	25	2	48	2	1	.980
— Columbus (Int'l)	OF	96	358	79	101	22	6	21	64	.282	44	95	6	97	3	5	.952
1997— Columbus (Int'l)	OF	43	170	38	52	12	1	10	39	.306	21	49	4	56	0	2	.966
— GC Yankees (GCL)......	OF	7	21	3	7	1	0	0	2	.333	2	4	0	1	0	0	1.000

LEDESMA, AARON — IF — DEVIL RAYS

PERSONAL: Born June 3, 1971, in Union City, Calif. ... 6-2/200. ... Bats right, throws right. ... Full name: Aaron David Ledesma.
HIGH SCHOOL: James Logan (Union City, Calif.).
COLLEGE: Chabot College (Calif.).

TRANSACTIONS/CAREER NOTES: Selected by New York Mets organization in second round of free-agent draft (June 4, 1990). ... On disabled list (April 13-May 24, 1991 and July 19, 1993-remainder of season). ... On suspended list (July 29-31, 1994). ... Traded by Mets to California Angels for OF Kevin Flora (January 18, 1996). ... Granted free agency (October 15, 1996). ... Signed by Rochester, Baltimore Orioles organization (January 17, 1997). ... Selected by Tampa Bay Devil Rays in third round (62nd pick overall) of expansion draft (November 18, 1997).
STATISTICAL NOTES: Led Florida State League shortstops with 641 total chances and 79 double plays in 1992. ... Led International League shortstops with 68 double plays in 1994. ... Led Pacific Coast League in grounding into double plays with 18 in 1996.

Year — Team (League)	Pos.	G	AB	R	H	2B	3B	HR	RBI	Avg.	BB	SO	SB	PO	A	E	Avg.
1990— Kingsport (Appal.)......	SS	66	243	50	81	11	1	5	38	.333	30	28	27	78	*170	24	.912
1991— Columbia (S. Atl.)......	SS	33	115	19	39	8	0	1	14	.339	8	16	3	44	64	10	.915
1992— St. Lucie (Fla. St.)	SS	134	456	51	120	17	2	2	50	.263	46	66	20	185	*411	45	.930
1993— Binghamton (East.)	SS	66	206	23	55	12	0	5	22	.267	14	43	2	36	65	10	.910
1994— Norfolk (Int'l)	SS	119	431	49	118	20	1	3	57	.274	28	41	18	157	347	26	*.951
1995— Norfolk (Int'l)	3B-1B-SS	56	201	26	60	12	1	0	28	.299	10	22	6	73	94	10	.944
— New York (N.L.)........	3B-1B-SS	21	33	4	8	0	0	0	3	.242	6	7	0	5	12	2	.895
1996— Vancouver (PCL)■......	SS-3B	109	440	60	134	27	4	1	51	.305	32	59	2	150	261	20	.954
1997— Rochester (Int'l)■......	SS-1B	85	326	40	106	26	1	3	43	.325	35	48	12	121	185	13	.959
— Baltimore (A.L.)........	2-3-1-S	43	88	24	31	5	1	2	11	.352	13	9	1	68	52	3	.976
American League totals (1 year)		43	88	24	31	5	1	2	11	.352	13	9	1	68	52	3	.976
National League totals (1 year)		21	33	4	8	0	0	0	3	.242	6	7	0	5	12	2	.895
Major league totals (2 years)		64	121	28	39	5	1	2	14	.322	19	16	1	73	64	5	.965

LEE, COREY — P — RANGERS

PERSONAL: Born December 26, 1974, in Raleigh, N.C. ... 6-2/180. ... Throws left, bats both. ... Full name: Corey W. Lee.
HIGH SCHOOL: Clayton (N.C.).
COLLEGE: North Carolina State.
TRANSACTIONS/CAREER NOTES: Selected by Texas Rangers organization in supplemental round ("sandwich pick" between first and second round, 32nd pick overall) of free-agent draft (June 2, 1996); pick received as compensation for New York Yankees signing Type A free-agent P Kenny Rogers.

Year — Team (League)	W	L	Pct.	ERA	G	GS	CG	ShO	Sv.	IP	H	R	ER	BB	SO
1996— Hudson Valley (NYP)..........	1	4	.200	3.29	9	9	0	0	0	54 2/3	42	24	20	21	59
1997— Charlotte (Fla. St.)	*15	5	.750	3.47	23	23	6	2	0	160 2/3	132	66	62	60	147

LEE, DERREK — 1B — MARLINS

PERSONAL: Born September 6, 1975, in Sacramento. ... 6-5/205. ... Throws right, bats right. ... Full name: Derrek Leon Lee. ... Son of Leon Lee, infielder, St. Louis Cardinals organization (1969-71) and Lotte Orions (1978-82), Taiyo Whales (1983-85) and Yakult Swallows (1986-87) of Japanese League and nephew of Leron Lee, outfielder, four major league teams (1969-1976) and Lotte Orions (1977-87) of Japanese league.
HIGH SCHOOL: El Camino (Sacramento).
TRANSACTIONS/CAREER NOTES: Selected by San Diego Padres in first round (14th pick overall) of free-agent draft (June 2, 1994). ... Traded by Padres with P Rafael Medina and P Steve Hoff to Florida Marlins for P Kevin Brown (December 15, 1997).
HONORS: Named Southern League Most Valuable Player (1996).
STATISTICAL NOTES: Led Southern League with 285 total bases in 1996. ... Led Southern League first basemen with 1,121 putouts in 1996. ... Led Pacific Coast League first basemen with 1,189 total chances and 108 double plays in 1997.

Year — Team (League)	Pos.	G	AB	R	H	2B	3B	HR	RBI	Avg.	BB	SO	SB	PO	A	E	Avg.
1993— Ariz. Padres (Ariz.)	1B	15	52	11	17	1	1	2	5	.327	6	7	4	115	14	2	.985
— Rancho Cuca. (Cal.) ...	1B	20	73	13	20	5	1	1	10	.274	10	20	0	115	6	5	.960
1994— Rancho Cuca. (Cal.) ...	1B	126	442	66	118	19	2	8	53	.267	42	95	18	289	27	4	.988
1995— Rancho Cuca. (Cal.) ...	1B	128	502	82	151	25	2	23	95	.301	49	130	14	970	86	*18	.983
— Memphis (Southern)..	1B	2	9	0	1	0	0	0	1	.111	0	2	0	16	3	0	1.000
1996— Memphis (Southern)..	1B-3B	134	500	98	140	39	2	34	*104	.280	65	*170	13	†1121	77	11	.991
1997— Las Vegas (PCL)	1B	125	472	86	153	29	2	13	64	.324	60	116	17	*1069	*111	9	*.992
— San Diego (N.L.)	1B	22	54	9	14	3	0	1	4	.259	9	24	0	131	13	0	1.000
Major league totals (1 year)		22	54	9	14	3	0	1	4	.259	9	24	0	131	13	0	1.000

LEITER, AL — P — MARLINS

PERSONAL: Born October 23, 1965, in Toms River, N.J. ... 6-3/220. ... Throws left, bats left. ... Full name: Alois Terry Leiter. ... Brother of Mark Leiter, pitcher, Philadelphia Phillies; and brother of Kurt Leiter, minor league pitcher (1982-84 and 1986). ... Name pronounced LIE-ter.
HIGH SCHOOL: Central Regional (Bayville, N.J.).
TRANSACTIONS/CAREER NOTES: Selected by New York Yankees organization in second round of free-agent draft (June 4, 1984). ... On New York disabled list (June 22-July 26, 1988); included rehabilitation assignment to Columbus (July 17-25). ... Traded by Yankees to Toronto Blue Jays for OF Jesse Barfield (April 30, 1989). ... On Toronto disabled list (May 11, 1989-remainder of season); included rehabilitation assignment to Dunedin (August 12-29). ... On Syracuse disabled list (May 20-June 13, 1990). ... On Toronto disabled list (April 27, 1991-remainder of season); included rehabilitation assignments to Dunedin (May 20-28 and July 19-August 7). ... On disabled list (April 24-May 9, 1993 and June 9-24, 1994). ... Granted free agency (November 6, 1995). ... Signed by Florida Marlins (December 14, 1995). ... On disabled list (May 1-20 and August 13-29, 1997).
HONORS: Named lefthanded pitcher on THE SPORTING NEWS N.L. All-Star team (1996).
STATISTICAL NOTES: Tied for A.L. lead with five balks in 1994. ... Led A.L. with 14 wild pitches in 1995. ... Pitched 11-0 no-hit victory against Colorado (May 11, 1996).

Year — Team (League)	W	L	Pct.	ERA	G	GS	CG	ShO	Sv.	IP	H	R	ER	BB	SO
1984— Oneonta (N.Y.-Penn)	3	2	.600	3.63	10	10	0	0	0	57	52	32	23	26	48
1985— Oneonta (N.Y.-Penn)	3	2	.600	2.37	6	6	2	0	0	38	27	14	10	25	34
— Fort Lauderdale (FSL)	1	6	.143	6.48	17	17	1	0	0	82	87	70	59	57	44

Year Team (League)	W	L	Pct.	ERA	G	GS	CG	ShO	Sv.	IP	H	R	ER	BB	SO
1986— Fort Lauderdale (FSL)	4	8	.333	4.05	22	21	1	1	0	117 2/3	96	64	53	90	101
1987— Columbus (Int'l)	1	4	.200	6.17	5	5	0	0	0	23 1/3	21	18	16	15	23
—Alb./Colon. (Eastern)	3	3	.500	3.35	15	14	2	0	0	78	64	34	29	37	71
—New York (A.L.)	2	2	.500	6.35	4	4	0	0	0	22 2/3	24	16	16	15	28
1988— New York (A.L.)	4	4	.500	3.92	14	14	0	0	0	57 1/3	49	27	25	33	60
—Columbus (Int'l)	0	2	.000	3.46	4	4	0	0	0	13	5	7	5	14	12
1989— New York (A.L.)	1	2	.333	6.08	4	4	0	0	0	26 2/3	23	20	18	21	22
—Toronto (A.L.)■................	0	0	...	4.05	1	1	0	0	0	6 2/3	9	3	3	2	4
—Dunedin (Fla. St.)	0	2	.000	5.63	3	3	0	0	0	8	11	5	5	5	4
1990— Dunedin (Fla. St.)	0	0	...	2.63	6	6	0	0	0	24	18	8	7	12	14
—Syracuse (Int'l)	3	8	.273	4.62	15	14	1	1	0	78	59	43	40	68	69
—Toronto (A.L.)	0	0	...	0.00	4	0	0	0	0	6 1/3	1	0	0	2	5
1991— Toronto (A.L.)	0	0	...	27.00	3	0	0	0	0	1 2/3	3	5	5	5	1
—Dunedin (Fla. St.)	0	0	...	1.86	4	3	0	0	0	9 2/3	5	2	2	7	5
1992— Syracuse (Int'l)	8	9	.471	3.86	27	27	2	0	0	163 1/3	159	82	70	64	108
—Toronto (A.L.)	0	0	...	9.00	1	0	0	0	0	1	1	1	1	2	0
1993— Toronto (A.L.)	9	6	.600	4.11	34	12	1	1	2	105	93	52	48	56	66
1994— Toronto (A.L.)	6	7	.462	5.08	20	20	1	0	0	111 2/3	125	68	63	65	100
1995— Toronto (A.L.)	11	11	.500	3.64	28	28	2	1	0	183	162	80	74	*108	153
1996— Florida (N.L.)■................	16	12	.571	2.93	33	33	2	1	0	215 1/3	153	74	70	*119	200
1997— Florida (N.L.)	11	9	.550	4.34	27	27	0	0	0	151 1/3	133	78	73	91	132
A.L. totals (9 years)	33	32	.508	4.36	113	83	4	2	2	522	490	272	253	309	439
N.L. totals (2 years)	27	21	.563	3.51	60	60	2	1	0	366 2/3	286	152	143	210	332
Major league totals (11 years)....	60	53	.531	4.01	173	143	6	3	2	888 2/3	776	424	396	519	771

DIVISION SERIES RECORD

Year Team (League)	W	L	Pct.	ERA	G	GS	CG	ShO	Sv.	IP	H	R	ER	BB	SO
1997— Florida (N.L.)	0	0	...	9.00	1	1	0	0	0	4	7	4	4	3	3

CHAMPIONSHIP SERIES RECORD

Year Team (League)	W	L	Pct.	ERA	G	GS	CG	ShO	Sv.	IP	H	R	ER	BB	SO
1993— Toronto (A.L.)......................	0	0	...	3.38	2	0	0	0	0	2 2/3	4	1	1	2	2
1997— Florida (N.L.)	0	1	.000	4.32	2	1	0	0	0	8 1/3	13	4	4	2	6
Champ. series totals (2 years)	0	1	.000	4.09	4	1	0	0	0	11	17	5	5	4	8

WORLD SERIES RECORD

RECORDS: Shares record for most bases on balls allowed in one inning—4 (October 21, 1997, fourth inning).

NOTES: Member of World Series championship team (1993 and 1997).

Year Team (League)	W	L	Pct.	ERA	G	GS	CG	ShO	Sv.	IP	H	R	ER	BB	SO
1993— Toronto (A.L.)	1	0	1.000	7.71	3	0	0	0	0	7	12	6	6	2	5
1997— Florida (N.L.)	0	0	...	5.06	2	2	0	0	0	10 2/3	10	9	6	10	10
World Series totals (2 years)	1	0	1.000	6.11	5	2	0	0	0	17 2/3	22	15	12	12	15

ALL-STAR GAME RECORD

Year League	W	L	Pct.	ERA	GS	CG	ShO	Sv.	IP	H	R	ER	BB	SO
1996— National	0	0	...	0.00	0	0	0	0	1/3	0	0	0	0	0

LEITER, MARK   P   PHILLIES

PERSONAL: Born April 13, 1963, in Joliet, Ill. ... 6-3/210. ... Throws right, bats right. ... Full name: Mark Edward Leiter. ... Brother of Al Leiter, pitcher, Florida Marlins; and brother of Kurt Leiter, minor league pitcher (1982-84 and 1986). ... Name pronounced LIE-ter.

HIGH SCHOOL: Central Regional (Bayville, N.J.).

JUNIOR COLLEGE: Connors State College (Okla.).

COLLEGE: Ramapo College of New Jersey.

TRANSACTIONS/CAREER NOTES: Selected by Baltimore Orioles organization in fourth round of free-agent draft (January 11, 1983). ... On disabled list (April 10, 1986-entire season; April 10, 1987-entire season; and April 10-June 13, 1988). ... Released by Orioles organization (June 13, 1988). ... Signed by Fort Lauderdale, New York Yankees organization (September 29, 1988). ... Traded by Yankees to Detroit Tigers for IF Torey Lovullo (March 19, 1991). ... On Detroit disabled list (June 6-23, 1991; July 24-August 24, 1992; and August 4-September 1, 1993). ... Released by Tigers (March 15, 1994). ... Signed by California Angels (March 21, 1994). ... Granted free agency (December 23, 1994). ... Signed by Phoenix, San Francisco Giants organization (April 10, 1995). ... Traded by Giants to Montreal Expos for P Tim Scott and P Kirk Rueter (July 30, 1996). ... Granted free agency (November 5, 1996). ... Signed by Philadelphia Phillies (December 12, 1996). ... On disabled list (June 21-July 5, 1997).

STATISTICAL NOTES: Tied for A.L. lead with nine hit batsmen in 1994. ... Led N.L. with 17 hit batsmen in 1995 and tied for lead with 16 in 1996. ... Led N.L. with 37 home runs allowed in 1996.

Year Team (League)	W	L	Pct.	ERA	G	GS	CG	ShO	Sv.	IP	H	R	ER	BB	SO
1983— Bluefield (Appalachian)	2	1	.667	2.70	6	6	2	0	0	36 2/3	33	17	11	13	35
—Hagerstown (Caro.)	1	5	.167	7.25	8	8	0	0	0	36	42	31	29	28	18
1984— Hagerstown (Caro.)	8	•13	.381	5.62	27	24	5	1	0	139 1/3	132	96	87	*108	105
1985— Hagerstown (Caro.)	2	8	.200	3.46	34	6	1	0	8	83 1/3	77	44	32	29	82
—Charlotte (Southern)	0	1	.000	1.42	5	0	0	0	1	6 1/3	3	1	1	2	8
1986—					Did not play.										
1987—					Did not play.										
1988—					Did not play.										
1989— Fort Lauderdale (FSL)■	2	2	.500	1.53	6	4	1	0	1	35 1/3	27	9	6	5	22
—Columbus (Int'l)	9	6	.600	5.00	22	12	0	0	0	90	102	50	50	34	70
1990— Columbus (Int'l)	9	4	.692	3.60	30	14	2	1	1	122 2/3	114	56	49	27	115
—New York (A.L.)	1	1	.500	6.84	8	3	0	0	0	26 1/3	33	20	20	9	21
1991— Toledo (Int'l)■...................	1	0	1.000	0.00	5	0	0	0	1	6 2/3	6	0	0	3	7
—Detroit (A.L.)	9	7	.563	4.21	38	15	1	0	1	134 2/3	125	66	63	50	103
1992— Detroit (A.L.)	8	5	.615	4.18	35	14	1	0	0	112	116	57	52	43	75
1993— Detroit (A.L.)	6	6	.500	4.73	27	13	1	0	0	106 2/3	111	61	56	44	70
1994— California (A.L.)■...............	4	7	.364	4.72	40	7	0	0	2	95 1/3	99	56	50	35	71

– 317 –

Year Team (League)	W	L	Pct.	ERA	G	GS	CG	ShO	Sv.	IP	H	R	ER	BB	SO
1995— San Francisco (N.L.)■	10	12	.455	3.82	30	29	7	1	0	195 2/3	185	91	83	55	129
1996— San Francisco (N.L.)	4	10	.286	5.19	23	22	1	0	0	135 1/3	151	93	78	50	118
— Montreal (N.L.)■	4	2	.667	4.39	12	12	1	0	0	69 2/3	68	35	34	19	46
1997— Philadelphia (N.L.)■	10	*17	.370	5.67	31	31	3	0	0	182 2/3	216	*132	*115	64	148
A.L. totals (5 years)	28	26	.519	4.57	148	52	3	0	3	475	484	260	241	181	340
N.L. totals (3 years)	28	41	.406	4.78	96	94	12	1	0	583 1/3	620	351	310	188	441
Major league totals (8 years)	56	67	.455	4.69	244	146	15	1	3	1058 1/3	1104	611	551	369	781

LEMKE, MARK — 2B

PERSONAL: Born August 13, 1965, in Utica, N.Y. ... 5-9/167. ... Bats both, throws right. ... Full name: Mark Alan Lemke. ... Name pronounced LEM-kee.

HIGH SCHOOL: Notre Dame (Utica, N.Y.).

TRANSACTIONS/CAREER NOTES: Selected by Atlanta Braves organization in 27th round of free-agent draft (June 6, 1983). ... On Atlanta disabled list (May 29-July 17, 1990); included rehabilitation assignment to Gulf Coast Braves (July 9-17). ... On disabled list (June 25-July 18, 1995 and May 27-June 13, 1996). ... Granted free agency (October 30, 1996). ... Re-signed by Braves (December 18, 1996). ... On disabled list (August 22, 1997-remainder of season). ... Granted free agency (November 5, 1997).

STATISTICAL NOTES: Led Gulf Coast League second basemen with .977 fielding percentage, 175 putouts, 207 assists, 391 total chances and 39 double plays in 1984. ... Led Carolina League second basemen with .982 fielding percentage, 355 assists and 83 double plays in 1987. ... Led Southern League with 239 total bases in 1988. ... Led Southern League second basemen with 739 total chances and 105 double plays in 1988. ... Led International League second basemen with 731 total chances and 105 double plays in 1989. ... Led N.L. second basemen with 785 total chances and 100 double plays in 1993.

Year Team (League)	Pos.	G	AB	R	H	2B	3B	HR	RBI	Avg.	BB	SO	SB	PO	A	E	Avg.
1983— GC Braves (GCL)	2B	53	209	37	55	6	0	0	19	.263	30	19	10	81	101	11	.943
1984— Anderson (S. Atl.)	2B-3B	42	121	18	18	2	0	0	5	.149	14	14	3	67	83	4	.974
— GC Braves (GCL)	2B-SS	•63	*243	41	67	11	0	3	32	.276	29	14	2	†175	†209	9	†.977
1985— Sumter (S. Atl.)	2B	90	231	25	50	6	0	0	20	.216	34	22	2	119	174	11	.964
1986— Sumter (S. Atl.)	3B-2B	126	448	99	122	24	2	18	66	.272	87	31	11	134	274	16	.962
1987— Durham (Carolina)	2B-3B	127	489	75	143	28	3	20	68	.292	54	45	10	248	†355	11	†.982
— Greenville (Southern)	3B	6	26	0	6	0	0	0	4	.231	0	4	0	4	12	1	.941
1988— Greenville (Southern)	2B	•143	*567	81	*153	30	4	16	80	.270	52	92	18	*281	*440	18	.976
— Atlanta (N.L.)	2B	16	58	8	13	4	0	0	2	.224	4	5	0	47	51	3	.970
1989— Richmond (Int'l)	2B	*146	*518	69	143	22	7	5	61	.276	66	45	4	*299	*417	*15	.979
— Atlanta (N.L.)	2B	14	55	4	10	2	1	2	10	.182	5	7	0	25	40	0	1.000
1990— Atlanta (N.L.)	3B-2B-SS	102	239	22	54	13	0	0	21	.226	21	22	0	90	193	4	.986
— GC Braves (GCL)	2B-3B	4	11	2	4	0	0	1	5	.364	1	3	0	5	11	1	.941
1991— Atlanta (N.L.)	2B-3B	136	269	36	63	11	2	2	23	.234	29	27	1	162	215	10	.974
1992— Atlanta (N.L.)	2B-3B	155	427	38	97	7	4	6	26	.227	50	39	0	236	335	9	.984
1993— Atlanta (N.L.)	2B	151	493	52	124	19	2	7	49	.252	65	50	1	*329	442	14	.982
1994— Atlanta (N.L.)	2B	104	350	40	103	15	0	3	31	.294	38	37	0	209	300	3	*.994
1995— Atlanta (N.L.)	2B	116	399	42	101	16	5	5	38	.253	44	40	2	205	305	5	.990
1996— Atlanta (N.L.)■	2B	135	498	64	127	17	0	5	37	.255	53	48	5	228	410	15	.977
1997— Atlanta (N.L.)	2B	109	351	33	86	17	1	2	26	.245	33	51	2	191	309	10	.980
Major league totals (10 years)		1038	3139	339	778	121	15	32	263	.248	342	326	11	1722	2600	73	.983

DIVISION SERIES RECORD

Year Team (League)	Pos.	G	AB	R	H	2B	3B	HR	RBI	Avg.	BB	SO	SB	PO	A	E	Avg.
1995— Atlanta (N.L.)	2B	4	19	3	4	1	0	0	1	.211	1	3	0	8	16	0	1.000
1996— Atlanta (N.L.)	2B	3	12	1	2	1	0	0	2	.167	0	1	0	4	8	0	1.000
Division series totals (2 years)		7	31	4	6	2	0	0	3	.194	1	4	0	12	24	0	1.000

CHAMPIONSHIP SERIES RECORD

RECORDS: Holds N.L. career record for most games with one club—31. ... Shares single-series record for most singles—9 (1996).

Year Team (League)	Pos.	G	AB	R	H	2B	3B	HR	RBI	Avg.	BB	SO	SB	PO	A	E	Avg.
1991— Atlanta (N.L.)	2B	7	20	1	4	1	0	0	1	.200	4	0	0	12	10	1	.957
1992— Atlanta (N.L.)	2B-3B	7	21	2	7	1	0	0	2	.333	5	3	0	11	17	0	1.000
1993— Atlanta (N.L.)	2B	6	24	2	5	2	0	0	4	.208	1	6	0	6	19	2	.926
1995— Atlanta (N.L.)	2B	4	18	2	3	0	0	0	1	.167	1	0	0	13	16	0	1.000
1996— Atlanta (N.L.)■	2B	7	27	4	12	2	0	1	5	.444	4	2	0	9	18	0	1.000
Championship series totals (5 years)		31	110	11	31	6	0	1	13	.282	15	11	0	51	80	3	.978

WORLD SERIES RECORD

RECORDS: Shares single-game record for most triples—2 (October 24, 1991).

NOTES: Member of World Series championship team (1995).

Year Team (League)	Pos.	G	AB	R	H	2B	3B	HR	RBI	Avg.	BB	SO	SB	PO	A	E	Avg.
1991— Atlanta (N.L.)	2B	6	24	4	10	1	3	0	4	.417	2	4	0	14	19	1	.971
1992— Atlanta (N.L.)	2B	6	19	0	4	0	0	0	2	.211	1	3	0	18	12	0	1.000
1995— Atlanta (N.L.)	2B	6	22	1	6	0	0	0	0	.273	3	2	0	10	24	1	.971
1996— Atlanta (N.L.)	2B	6	26	2	6	1	0	0	2	.231	0	3	0	11	24	00	1.000
World Series totals (4 years)		24	91	7	26	2	3	0	8	.286	6	12	0	53	79	2	.985

LENNON, PATRICK — OF

PERSONAL: Born April 27, 1968, in Whiteville, N.C. ... 6-2/220. ... Bats right, throws right. ... Full name: Patrick Orlando Lennon.

HIGH SCHOOL: Whiteville (N.C.).

TRANSACTIONS/CAREER NOTES: Selected by Seattle Mariners organization in first round (eighth pick overall) of free-agent draft (June 2, 1986). ... On Calgary disabled list (May 18, 1992-remainder of season). ... Granted free agency (October 15, 1992). ... Signed by Colorado Rockies (October 29, 1992). ... Released by Colorado Springs, Rockies organization (April 2, 1993). ... Signed by Torreon of Mexican League (1993). ... Signed by Canton/Akron, Cleveland Indians organization (July 19, 1993). ... Granted free agency (October 15, 1993). ... Signed by New Britain, Boston Red Sox organization (March 7, 1994). ... On disabled list (August 4-12, 1994). ... Released by Red Sox organization (July 20, 1995). ... Signed by Salt Lake, Minnesota Twins organization (July 22, 1995). ... Granted free agency (October 16, 1995). ... Signed by Kansas City Royals (March 31, 1996). ... Released by Royals (April 29, 1996). ... Signed by Edmonton, Oakland Athletics organization (June 1, 1996). ... On Edmonton disabled list (September 10-18, 1996). ... On Oakland disabled list (August 20-September 12, 1997); included rehabilitation assignments to Modesto (August 28-September 3) and Edmonton (Septmeber 3-12). ... Released by A's (December 15, 1997).

STATISTICAL NOTES: Led Midwest League third basemen with 39 errors in 1987.

Year Team (League)	Pos.	G	AB	R	H	2B	3B	HR	RBI	Avg.	BB	SO	SB	PO	A	E	Avg.
1986— Bellingham (N'west)...	SS-3B	51	169	35	41	5	2	3	27	.243	36	50	8	57	90	27	.845
1987— Wausau (Midwest)	3B-SS	98	319	54	80	21	3	7	34	.251	45	82	25	73	190	†40	.868
1988— Vermont (Eastern)......	3B	95	321	44	83	9	3	9	40	.259	21	87	15	81	143	*28	.889
1989— Williamsport (East.) ...	OF-3B	66	248	32	65	14	2	3	31	.262	23	53	7	67	20	14	.861
1990— San Bern. (Calif.)........	3B-OF	44	163	29	47	6	2	8	30	.288	15	51	6	29	40	7	.908
— Williamsport (East.) ...	OF-3B	49	167	24	49	6	4	5	22	.293	10	37	10	62	40	10	.911
1991— Calgary (PCL).............	OF-3B	112	416	75	137	29	5	15	74	.329	46	68	12	114	3	6	.951
— Seattle (A.L.).............	DH-OF	9	8	2	1	1	0	0	1	.125	3	1	0	2	0	0	1.000
1992— Seattle (A.L.).............	1B	1	2	0	0	0	0	0	0	.000	0	0	0	5	0	0	1.000
— Calgary (PCL).............	OF-3B	13	48	8	17	3	0	1	9	.354	6	10	4	12	0	1	.923
1993— Torreon (Mexican)■...	OF	27	97	18	34	5	0	5	15	.351	11	31	0	27	1	0	1.000
— Cant./Akr. (Eastern)■.	OF-1B	45	152	24	39	7	1	4	23	.257	30	45	4	45	3	4	.923
1994— New Britain (East.)■ ..	OF-1B	114	429	80	140	30	5	17	67	.326	48	96	13	189	12	3	.985
1995— Pawtucket (Int'l).........	OF	40	128	20	35	6	2	3	20	.273	16	42	6	54	4	3	.951
— Trenton (Eastern)	OF	27	98	19	39	7	0	1	8	.398	14	22	7	32	2	3	.919
— Salt Lake (PCL)■	OF	34	115	26	46	15	0	6	29	.400	12	29	2	10	0	0	1.000
1996— Kansas City (A.L.)■ ...	OF-DH	14	30	5	7	3	0	0	1	.233	7	10	0	18	0	1	.947
— Edmonton (PCL)■	OF	68	251	37	82	16	2	12	42	.327	28	82	3	57	5	4	.939
1997— Edmonton (PCL)	OF	39	134	28	46	7	0	9	35	.343	22	34	0	13	1	0	1.000
— Oakland (A.L.)	OF-DH	56	116	14	34	6	1	1	14	.293	15	35	0	55	0	3	.948
— Modesto (California) ..	OF	5	16	3	3	1	0	1	4	.188	3	5	0	2	0	0	1.000
Major league totals (4 years)		80	156	21	42	10	1	1	16	.269	25	46	0	80	0	4	.952

LeROY, JOHN — P — DEVIL RAYS

PERSONAL: Born April 19, 1975, in Bellevue, Wash. ... 6-3/175. ... Throws right, bats right. ... Full name: John Michael LeRoy.
HIGH SCHOOL: Sammanish (Bellevue, Wash.).
TRANSACTIONS/CAREER NOTES: Selected by Atlanta Braves organization in 15th round of free-agent draft (June 3, 1993). ... Selected by Tampa Bay Devil Rays in second round (34th pick overall) of expansion draft (November 18, 1997).

Year Team (League)	W	L	Pct.	ERA	G	GS	CG	ShO	Sv.	IP	H	R	ER	BB	SO
1993— GC Braves (GCL)...............	2	2	.500	2.05	10	2	0	0	1	26 1/3	21	9	6	8	32
1994— Macon (S. Atl.)..................	3	3	.500	4.46	10	9	0	0	0	40 1/3	36	21	20	20	44
1995— Durham (Carolina)..............	6	9	.400	5.44	24	22	1	0	0	125 2/3	128	82	76	57	77
1996— Durham (Carolina)..............	7	4	.636	3.50	19	19	0	0	0	110 2/3	91	47	43	52	94
— Greenville (Southern)	1	1	.500	2.98	8	8	0	0	0	45 1/3	43	18	15	18	38
1997— Greenville (Southern)	5	5	.500	5.03	29	14	0	0	1	98 1/3	105	59	55	43	84
— Atlanta (N.L.).....................	1	0	1.000	0.00	1	0	0	0	0	2	1	0	0	3	3
Major league totals (1 year)........	1	0	1.000	0.00	1	0	0	0	0	2	1	0	0	3	3

LESHER, BRIAN — OF — ATHLETICS

PERSONAL: Born March 5, 1971, in Antwerp, Belgium. ... 6-5/205. ... Bats right, throws left. ... Full name: Brian Herbert Lesher.
COLLEGE: Delaware.
TRANSACTIONS/CAREER NOTES: Selected by Oakland Athletics organization in 25th round of free-agent draft (June 1, 1992).

Year Team (League)	Pos.	G	AB	R	H	2B	3B	HR	RBI	Avg.	BB	SO	SB	PO	A	E	Avg.
1992— S. Oregon (N'west).....	OF-1B	46	136	21	26	7	1	3	18	.191	12	35	3	63	3	4	.943
1993— Madison (Midwest)	OF	119	394	63	108	13	5	5	47	.274	46	102	20	193	9	5	.976
1994— Modesto (California) ..	OF-1B	117	393	76	114	21	0	14	68	.290	81	84	11	332	20	11	.970
1995— Huntsville (Southern).	OF-1B	127	471	78	123	23	2	19	71	.261	64	110	7	198	7	6	.972
1996— Edmonton (PCL)	1B-OF	109	414	57	119	29	2	18	75	.287	36	108	6	699	44	9	.988
— Oakland (A.L.)	OF-1B	26	82	11	19	3	0	5	16	.232	5	17	0	46	2	1	.980
1997— Edmonton (PCL)	OF-1B	110	415	85	134	27	5	21	78	.323	64	86	14	220	6	6	.974
— Oakland (A.L.)	OF-DH-1B	46	131	17	30	4	1	4	16	.229	9	30	4	87	5	3	.968
Major league totals (2 years)		72	213	28	49	7	1	9	32	.230	14	47	4	133	7	4	.972

LESKANIC, CURTIS — P — ROCKIES

PERSONAL: Born April 2, 1968, in Homestead, Pa. ... 6-0/180. ... Throws right, bats right. ... Full name: Curtis John Leskanic.
HIGH SCHOOL: Steel Valley (Munhall, Pa.).
COLLEGE: Louisiana State.
TRANSACTIONS/CAREER NOTES: Selected by Cleveland Indians organization in eighth round of free-agent draft (June 5, 1989). ... On disabled list (April 23-June 25, 1990). ... Traded by Indians organization with P Oscar Munoz to Minnesota Twins organization for 1B Paul Sorrento (March 28, 1992). ... Selected by Colorado Rockies in third round (66th pick overall) of expansion draft (November 17, 1992). ... Loaned by Rockies organization to Wichita, Padres organization (April 7-May 20, 1993). ... On Colorado disabled list (May 30-June 28, 1996); included rehabilitation assignment to Colorado Springs (June 22-27). ... On Colorado disabled list (March 23-April 12, 1997); included rehabilitation assignment to Salem (April 6-8).

Year Team (League)	W	L	Pct.	ERA	G	GS	CG	ShO	Sv.	IP	H	R	ER	BB	SO
1990— Kinston (Carolina)	6	5	.545	3.68	14	14	2	0	0	73 1/3	61	34	30	30	71
1991— Kinston (Carolina)	•15	8	.652	2.79	28	28	0	0	0	174 1/3	143	63	54	91	*163
1992— Orlando (South.)■	9	11	.450	4.30	26	23	3	0	0	152 2/3	158	84	73	64	126
— Portland (PCL)	1	2	.333	9.98	5	3	0	0	0	15 1/3	16	17	17	8	14
1993— Wichita (Texas)■	3	2	.600	3.45	7	7	0	0	0	44 1/3	37	20	17	17	42
— Colo. Springs (PCL)■	4	3	.571	4.47	9	7	1	1	0	44 1/3	39	24	22	26	38
— Colorado (N.L.)	1	5	.167	5.37	18	8	0	0	0	57	59	40	34	27	30
1994— Colo. Springs (PCL)	5	7	.417	3.31	21	21	2	0	0	130 1/3	129	60	48	54	98
— Colorado (N.L.)■	1	1	.500	5.64	8	3	0	0	0	22 1/3	27	14	14	10	17
1995— Colorado (N.L.)	6	3	.667	3.40	*76	0	0	0	10	98	83	38	37	33	107
1996— Colorado (N.L.)	7	5	.583	6.23	70	0	0	0	6	73 2/3	82	51	51	38	76
— Colo. Springs (PCL)	0	0	...	3.00	3	0	0	0	0	3	5	1	1	1	2
1997— Salem (Carolina)	0	0	...	3.86	2	1	0	0	0	2 1/3	5	2	1	1	3
— Colorado (N.L.)	4	0	1.000	5.55	55	0	0	0	2	58 1/3	59	36	36	24	53
— Colo. Springs (PCL)	0	0	...	3.79	10	3	0	0	2	19	11	9	8	18	20
Major league totals (5 years)	19	14	.576	5.00	227	11	0	0	18	309 1/3	310	179	172	132	283

DIVISION SERIES RECORD

Year Team (League)	W	L	Pct.	ERA	G	GS	CG	ShO	Sv.	IP	H	R	ER	BB	SO
1995— Colorado (N.L.)	0	1	.000	6.00	3	0	0	0	0	3	3	2	2	0	4

LEVINE, ALAN   P   RANGERS

PERSONAL: Born May 22, 1968, in Park Ridge, Ill. ... 6-3/180. ... Throws right, bats left. ... Full name: Alan Brian Levine.
COLLEGE: Southern Illinois-Carbondale.
TRANSACTIONS/CAREER NOTES: Selected by Chicago White Sox in 11th round of free-agent draft (June 3, 1991). ... Traded by White Sox with P Larry Thomas to Texas Rangers for SS Benji Gil (December 19, 1997).

Year Team (League)	W	L	Pct.	ERA	G	GS	CG	ShO	Sv.	IP	H	R	ER	BB	SO
1991— Utica (N.Y.-Penn)	6	4	.600	3.18	16	12	2	1	1	85	75	45	30	26	83
1992— South Bend (Mid.)	9	5	.643	2.81	23	23	2	0	0	156 2/3	151	67	49	36	131
— Sarasota (Florida State)	0	2	.000	4.02	3	2	0	0	0	15 2/3	17	11	7	5	11
1993— Sarasota (Florida State)	11	8	.579	3.68	27	26	5	1	0	161 1/3	169	87	66	50	*129
1994— Birmingham (Southern)	5	9	.357	3.31	18	18	1	0	0	114 1/3	117	50	42	44	94
— Nashville (A.A.)	0	2	.000	7.88	8	4	0	0	0	24	34	23	21	11	24
1995— Nashville (A.A.)	0	2	.000	5.14	3	3	0	0	0	14	20	10	8	7	14
— Birmingham (Southern)	4	3	.571	2.34	43	1	0	0	7	73	61	22	19	25	68
1996— Nashville (A.A.)	4	5	.444	3.65	43	0	0	0	12	61 2/3	58	27	25	24	45
— Chicago (A.L.)	0	1	.000	5.40	16	0	0	0	0	18 1/3	22	14	11	7	12
1997— Chicago (A.L.)	2	2	.500	6.91	25	0	0	0	0	27 1/3	35	22	21	16	22
— Nashville (A.A.)	1	1	.500	7.13	26	0	0	0	2	35 1/3	58	32	28	11	29
Major league totals (2 years)	2	3	.400	6.31	41	0	0	0	0	45 2/3	57	36	32	23	34

LEVIS, JESSE   C   BREWERS

PERSONAL: Born April 14, 1968, in Philadelphia. ... 5-9/180. ... Bats left, throws right.
HIGH SCHOOL: Northeast (Philadelphia).
COLLEGE: North Carolina.
TRANSACTIONS/CAREER NOTES: Selected by Philadelphia Phillies organization in 36th round of free-agent draft (June 2, 1986); did not sign. ... Selected by Cleveland Indians organization in fourth round of free-agent draft (June 5, 1989). ... Traded by Indians to Milwaukee Brewers for P Scott Nate and a player to be named later (April 4, 1996); Indians acquired P Jared Camp to complete deal (June 9, 1996).
STATISTICAL NOTES: Led Eastern League catchers with 733 total chances in 1991.

Year Team (League)	Pos.	G	AB	R	H	2B	3B	HR	RBI	Avg.	BB	SO	SB	PO	A	E	Avg.
1989— Burlington (Appal.)	C	27	93	11	32	4	0	4	16	.344	10	7	1	189	27	2	.991
— Kinston (Carolina)	C	27	87	11	26	6	0	2	11	.299	12	15	1	95	17	2	.982
— Colo. Springs (PCL)	PH	1	1	0	0	0	0	0	0	.000	0	0	0	...	...	...	...
1990— Kinston (Carolina)	C	107	382	63	113	18	3	7	64	.296	64	42	4	517	63	5	.991
1991— Cant./Akr. (Eastern)	C	115	382	31	101	17	3	6	45	.264	40	36	2	*644	*77	12	.984
1992— Colo. Springs (PCL)	C	87	253	39	92	20	1	6	44	.364	37	25	1	375	47	4	.991
— Cleveland (A.L.)	C-DH	28	43	2	12	4	0	1	3	.279	0	5	0	59	5	1	.985
1993— Charlotte (Int'l)	C	47	129	10	32	6	1	2	20	.248	15	12	0	266	22	4	.986
— Cleveland (A.L.)	C	31	63	7	11	2	0	0	4	.175	2	10	0	109	7	1	.991
1994— Charlotte (Int'l)	C	111	375	55	107	20	0	10	59	.285	55	39	2	452	34	4	.992
— Cleveland (A.L.)	PH	1	1	0	1	0	0	0	0	1.000	0	0	0	...	...	...	...
1995— Buffalo (A.A.)	C	66	196	26	61	16	0	4	20	.311	32	11	0	338	20	2	.994
— Cleveland (A.L.)	C	12	18	1	6	2	0	0	3	.333	1	0	0	33	5	0	1.000
1996— Milwaukee (A.L.)■	C-DH	104	233	27	55	6	1	1	21	.236	38	15	0	373	26	1	*.998
1997— Milwaukee (A.L.)	C-DH	99	200	19	57	7	0	1	19	.285	24	17	1	296	19	2	.994
Major league totals (6 years)		275	558	56	142	21	1	3	50	.254	65	47	1	870	62	5	.995

LEWIS, DARREN   OF   RED SOX

PERSONAL: Born August 28, 1967, in Berkeley, Calif. ... 6-0/189. ... Bats right, throws right. ... Full name: Darren Joel Lewis.
HIGH SCHOOL: Moreau (Hayward, Calif.).
JUNIOR COLLEGE: Chabot College (Calif.).
COLLEGE: California.
TRANSACTIONS/CAREER NOTES: Selected by Los Angeles Dodgers organization in sixth round of free-agent draft (January 14, 1986); did not sign. ... Selected by Toronto Blue Jays organization in 45th round of free-agent draft (June 2, 1987); did not sign. ... Selected by Oakland

Athletics organization in 18th round of free-agent draft (June 1, 1988). ... Traded by A's with a player to be named later to San Francisco Giants for IF Ernest Riles (December 4, 1990); Giants acquired P Pedro Pena to complete deal (December 17, 1990). ... On disabled list (August 20-September 4, 1993). ... Traded by Giants with P Mark Portugal and P Dave Burba to Cincinnati Reds for OF Deion Sanders, P John Roper, P Ricky Pickett, P Scott Service and IF Dave McCarty (July 21, 1995). ... Released by Reds (December 1, 1995). ... Signed by Chicago White Sox (December 14, 1995). ... Traded by White Sox to Los Angeles Dodgers for a player to be named later (August 27, 1997); White Sox acquired IF Chad Fonville to complete deal (September 2, 1997). ... Granted free agency (October 27, 1997). ... Signed by Boston Red Sox (December 23, 1997).

RECORDS: Holds major league records for most consecutive errorless games by outfielder—392 (August 21, 1990 through June 29, 1994); and most consecutive chances accepted without an error by outfielder—938 (August 21, 1990 through June 29, 1994). ... Holds N.L. records for most consecutive errorless games by outfielder—369 (July 13, 1991 through June 29, 1994); and most consecutive chances accepted without an error by outfielder—905 (July 13, 1991 through June 29, 1994).

HONORS: Won N.L. Gold Glove as outfielder (1994).

STATISTICAL NOTES: Led California League outfielders with 324 total chances in 1989. ... Career major league grand slams: 1.

Year Team (League)	Pos.	G	AB	R	H	2B	3B	HR	RBI	Avg.	BB	SO	SB	PO	A	E	Avg.
1988—Arizona A's (Ariz.)	OF	5	15	8	5	3	0	0	4	.333	6	5	4	15	1	0	1.000
—Madison (Midwest)	OF-2B	60	199	38	49	4	1	0	11	.246	46	37	31	195	3	4	.980
1989—Modesto (California)	OF	129	503	74	150	23	5	4	39	.298	59	84	27	*311	8	5	.985
—Huntsville (Southern)	OF	9	31	7	10	1	1	1	7	.323	2	6	0	16	0	0	1.000
1990—Huntsville (Southern)	OF	71	284	52	84	11	3	3	23	.296	36	28	21	186	6	0	1.000
—Tacoma (PCL)	OF	60	247	32	72	5	2	2	26	.291	16	35	16	132	9	2	.986
—Oakland (A.L.)	OF-DH	25	35	4	8	0	0	0	1	.229	7	4	2	33	0	0	1.000
1991—Phoenix (PCL)■	OF	81	315	63	107	12	10	2	52	.340	41	36	32	243	5	2	.992
—San Francisco (N.L.)	OF	72	222	41	55	5	3	1	15	.248	36	30	13	159	2	0	1.000
1992- -San Francisco (N.L.)	OF	100	320	38	74	8	1	1	18	.231	29	46	28	225	3	0	1.000
—Phoenix (PCL)	OF	42	158	22	36	5	2	0	6	.228	11	15	9	93	2	0	1.000
1993—San Francisco (N.L.)	OF	136	522	84	132	17	7	2	48	.253	30	40	46	344	4	0	•1.000
1994—San Francisco (N.L.)	OF	114	451	70	116	15	•9	4	29	.257	53	50	30	279	5	2	.993
1995—San Francisco (N.L.)	OF	74	309	47	78	10	3	1	16	.252	17	37	21	200	2	1	.995
—Cincinnati (N.L.)■	OF	58	163	19	40	3	0	0	8	.245	17	20	11	121	3	1	.992
1996—Chicago (A.L.)■	OF	141	337	55	77	12	2	4	53	.228	45	40	21	287	0	3	.990
1997—Chicago (A.L.)	OF-DH	81	77	15	18	1	0	0	5	.234	11	14	11	90	1	0	1.000
—Los Angeles (N.L.)■	OF	26	77	7	23	3	1	1	10	.299	6	17	3	49	1	1	.980
American League totals (3 years)		247	449	74	103	13	2	4	59	.229	63	58	34	410	1	3	.993
National League totals (6 years)		580	2064	306	518	61	24	10	144	.251	188	240	152	1377	20	5	.996
Major league totals (8 years)		827	2513	380	621	74	26	14	203	.247	251	298	186	1787	21	8	.996

DIVISION SERIES RECORD

Year Team (League)	Pos.	G	AB	R	H	2B	3B	HR	RBI	Avg.	BB	SO	SB	PO	A	E	Avg.
1995—Cincinnati (N.L.)	OF-PH	3	3	0	0	0	0	0	0	.000	0	1	0	3	0	0	1.000

CHAMPIONSHIP SERIES RECORD

Year Team (League)	Pos.	G	AB	R	H	2B	3B	HR	RBI	Avg.	BB	SO	SB	PO	A	E	Avg.
1995—Cincinnati (N.L.)	OF-PR	2	1	0	0	0	0	0	0	.000	0	0	0	2	0	0	1.000

LEWIS, MARC   OF   TWINS

PERSONAL: Born May 20, 1975, in Decatur, Ala. ... 6-2/175. ... Bats right, throws right. ... Full name: Marc Devarey Lewis.
HIGH SCHOOL: Decatur (Ala.).
JUNIOR COLLEGE: John C. Calhoun Community College (Ala.).
TRANSACTIONS/CAREER NOTES: Selected by Boston Red Sox organization in 25th round of free-agent draft (June 2, 1994). ... Traded by Red Sox with P Mike Jacobs to Braves (August 31, 1995); completing deal in which Red Sox traded two players to be named later to Braves for P Mike Stanton and player to be named later (July 31, 1995); Red Sox acquired P Matt Murray to complete deal (August 31, 1995). ... Traded by Braves to Minnesota Twins (October 1, 1997), completing deal in which Twins traded 1B Greg Colbrunn to Braves for a player to be named later (August 14, 1997).

Year Team (League)	Pos.	G	AB	R	H	2B	3B	HR	RBI	Avg.	BB	SO	SB	PO	A	E	Avg.
1994—GC Red Sox (GCL)	OF	50	197	32	64	13	2	3	32	.325	10	19	16	87	4	3	.968
—Lynchburg (Caro.)	OF	8	32	3	6	1	0	1	5	.188	3	4	0	17	1	1	.947
1995—Michigan (Midwest)	OF	36	92	14	14	2	1	1	5	.152	9	16	10	48	3	1	.981
—Utica (N.Y.-Penn)	OF	69	272	47	82	15	5	5	39	.301	17	32	24	135	11	4	.973
1996—Macon (S. Atl.)■	OF	66	241	36	76	14	3	5	28	.315	21	31	25	102	7	4	.965
—Durham (Carolina)	OF	68	262	43	78	12	2	6	26	.298	24	37	25	122	7	2	.985
1997—Greenville (Southern)	OF	135	512	64	140	17	3	17	67	.273	25	84	21	275	4	5	.982

LEWIS, MARK   3B/2B   PHILLIES

PERSONAL: Born November 30, 1969, in Hamilton, Ohio. ... 6-1/185. ... Bats right, throws right. ... Full name: Mark David Lewis.
HIGH SCHOOL: Hamilton (Ohio).
TRANSACTIONS/CAREER NOTES: Selected by Cleveland Indians organization in first round (second pick overall) of free-agent draft (June 1, 1988). ... On Kinston disabled list (May 29-June 20, 1989). ... Traded by Indians to Cincinnati Reds for IF Tim Costo (December 14, 1994). ... Traded by Reds to Detroit Tigers (November 16, 1995), completing deal in which Reds acquired P David Wells for P C.J. Nitkowski, P David Tuttle and a player to be named later (July 31, 1995). ... Traded by Tigers to San Francisco Giants for 1B Jesus Ibarra (December 16, 1996). ... On disabled list (March 31-April 12, 1997). ... Granted free agency (December 21, 1997). ... Signed by Philadelphia Phillies (December 23, 1997).

STATISTICAL NOTES: Tied for A.L. lead in errors by shortstop with 25 in 1992. ... Tied for International League lead in grounding into double plays with 19 in 1993. ... Led International League shortstops with 81 double plays in 1993. ... Career major league grand slams: 1.

Year Team (League)	Pos.	G	AB	R	H	2B	3B	HR	RBI	Avg.	BB	SO	SB	PO	A	E	Avg.
1988—Burlington (Appal.)	SS	61	227	39	60	13	1	7	43	.264	25	44	14	70	*177	23	.915
1989—Kinston (Carolina)	SS	93	349	50	94	16	3	1	32	.269	34	50	17	130	244	32	.921
—Cant./Akr. (Eastern)	SS	7	25	4	5	1	0	0	1	.200	1	3	0	15	28	2	.956
1990—Cant./Akr. (Eastern)	SS	102	390	55	106	19	3	10	60	.272	23	49	8	152	286	31	.934
—Colo. Springs (PCL)	SS	34	124	16	38	8	1	1	21	.306	9	13	2	52	84	11	.925
1991—Colo. Springs (PCL)	SS-2B-3B	46	179	29	50	10	3	2	31	.279	18	23	3	65	135	10	.952
—Cleveland (A.L.)	2B-SS	84	314	29	83	15	1	0	30	.264	15	45	2	129	231	9	.976
1992—Cleveland (A.L.)	SS-3B	122	413	44	109	21	0	5	30	.264	25	69	4	184	336	‡26	.952
1993—Charlotte (Int'l)	SS	126	507	93	144	30	4	17	67	.284	34	76	9	168	*403	23	.961
—Cleveland (A.L.)	SS	14	52	6	13	2	0	1	5	.250	0	7	3	22	31	2	.964
1994—Cleveland (A.L.)	SS-3B-2B	20	73	6	15	5	0	1	8	.205	2	13	1	17	40	6	.905
—Charlotte (Int'l)	SS-2B-3B	86	328	56	85	16	1	8	34	.259	35	48	2	117	199	12	.963
1995—Cincinnati (N.L.)■	3B-2B-SS	81	171	25	58	13	1	3	30	.339	21	33	0	19	107	4	.969
1996—Detroit (A.L.)■	2B-DH	145	545	69	147	30	3	11	55	.270	42	109	6	264	413	9	.987
1997—San Fran. (N.L.)■	3B-2B-DH	118	341	50	91	14	6	10	42	.267	23	62	3	74	157	14	.943
American League totals (5 years)		385	1397	154	367	73	4	18	128	.263	84	243	16	616	1051	52	.970
National League totals (2 years)		199	512	75	149	27	7	13	72	.291	44	95	3	93	264	18	.952
Major league totals (7 years)		584	1909	229	516	100	11	31	200	.270	128	338	19	709	1315	70	.967

DIVISION SERIES RECORD

Year Team (League)	Pos.	G	AB	R	H	2B	3B	HR	RBI	Avg.	BB	SO	SB	PO	A	E	Avg.
1995—Cincinnati (N.L.)	3B-PH	2	2	2	1	0	0	1	5	.500	1	0	0	0	0	1	.000
1997—San Francisco (N.L.)	2B	1	5	0	3	0	0	0	1	.600	0	0	0	1	3	0	1.000
Division series totals (2 years)		3	7	2	4	0	0	1	6	.571	1	0	0	1	3	1	.800

CHAMPIONSHIP SERIES RECORD

Year Team (League)	Pos.	G	AB	R	H	2B	3B	HR	RBI	Avg.	BB	SO	SB	PO	A	E	Avg.
1995—Cincinnati (N.L.)	3B	2	4	0	1	0	0	0	0	.250	1	1	0	2	3	0	1.000

LEWIS, RICHIE   P

PERSONAL: Born January 25, 1966, in Muncie, Ind. ... 5-10/175. ... Throws right, bats right. ... Full name: Richie Todd Lewis.

HIGH SCHOOL: South Side (Muncie, Ind.).

COLLEGE: Florida State (received degree, 1987).

TRANSACTIONS/CAREER NOTES: Selected by Montreal Expos organization in second round of free-agent draft (June 2, 1987). ... On disabled list (June 2-August 12 and August 22, 1988-remainder of season; and July 28, 1989-remainder of season). ... On Jacksonville disabled list (June 1-8 and June 11, 1990-remainder of season). ... Traded by Expos to Baltimore Orioles for P Chris Myers (August 24, 1991). ... Selected by Florida Marlins in second round (51st pick overall) of expansion draft (November 17, 1992). ... On Jacksonville disabled list (April 6-25, 1995). ... Granted free agency (October 16, 1995). ... Signed by Las Vegas, San Diego Padres organization (January 18, 1996). ... Traded by Padres with OF Melvin Nieves and C Raul Casanova to Detroit Tigers for P Sean Bergman, P Cade Gaspar and OF Todd Steverson (March 22, 1996). ... On Detroit disabled list (June 21-July 11, 1996); included rehabilitation assignment to Toledo (July 6-11). ... Released by Tigers (November 20, 1996). ... Signed by Oakland Athletics organization (January 6, 1997). ... Released by A's (June 19, 1997). ... Signed by Indianapolis, Reds organization (June 20, 1997); released following 1997 season. ... Signed by Philadelphia Phillies organization (January 14, 1998).

HONORS: Named righthanded pitcher on The Sporting News college All-America team (1987).

STATISTICAL NOTES: Tied for N.L. lead with 10 wild pitches in 1994.

MISCELLANEOUS: Made an out in only appearance as pinch-hitter with Detroit (1996).

Year Team (League)	W	L	Pct.	ERA	G	GS	CG	ShO	Sv.	IP	H	R	ER	BB	SO
1987—Indianapolis (A.A.)	0	0	...	9.82	2	0	0	0	0	3²/₃	6	4	4	2	3
1988—Jacksonville (Southern)	5	3	.625	3.38	12	12	1	0	0	61¹/₃	37	32	23	56	60
1989—Jacksonville (Southern)	5	4	.556	2.58	17	17	0	0	0	94¹/₃	80	37	27	55	105
1990—W.P. Beach (FSL)	0	1	.000	4.80	10	0	0	0	2	15	12	12	8	11	14
—Jacksonville (Southern)	0	0	...	1.26	11	0	0	0	5	14¹/₃	7	2	2	5	14
1991—Harrisburg (Eastern)	6	5	.545	3.74	34	6	0	0	5	74²/₃	67	33	31	40	82
—Indianapolis (A.A.)	1	0	1.000	3.58	5	4	0	0	0	27²/₃	35	12	11	20	22
—Rochester (Int'l)■	1	0	1.000	2.81	2	2	0	0	0	16	13	5	5	7	18
1992—Rochester (Int'l)	10	9	.526	3.28	24	23	6	1	0	159¹/₃	136	63	58	61	154
—Baltimore (A.L.)	1	1	.500	10.80	2	2	0	0	0	6²/₃	13	8	8	7	4
1993—Florida (N.L.)■	6	3	.667	3.26	57	0	0	0	0	77¹/₃	68	37	28	43	65
1994—Florida (N.L.)	1	4	.200	5.67	45	0	0	0	0	54	62	44	38	45	45
1995—Charlotte (Int'l)	5	2	.714	3.20	17	8	1	0	0	59	50	22	21	20	45
—Florida (N.L.)	0	1	.000	3.75	21	1	0	0	0	36	30	15	15	15	32
1996—Detroit (A.L.)■	4	6	.400	4.18	72	0	0	0	2	90¹/₃	78	45	42	65	78
—Toledo (Int'l)	0	0	...	2.25	2	0	0	0	0	4	1	1	1	1	4
1997—Oakland (A.L.)■	2	0	1.000	9.64	14	0	0	0	0	18²/₃	24	21	20	15	12
—Edmonton (PCL)	1	1	.500	5.85	11	1	0	0	0	20	24	13	13	14	25
—Indianapolis (A.A.)■	0	1	.000	1.52	27	0	0	0	9	29²/₃	22	7	5	7	33
—Cincinnati (N.L.)	0	0	...	6.35	4	0	0	0	0	5²/₃	4	5	4	3	4
A.L. totals (3 years)	7	7	.500	5.45	88	2	0	0	2	115²/₃	115	74	70	87	94
N.L. totals (4 years)	7	8	.467	4.21	127	1	0	0	0	173	164	101	81	99	146
Major league totals (6 years)	14	15	.483	4.71	215	3	0	0	2	288²/₃	279	175	151	186	240

LEYRITZ, JIM   C/DH   RED SOX

PERSONAL: Born December 27, 1963, in Lakewood, Ohio. ... 6-0/195. ... Bats right, throws right. ... Full name: James Joseph Leyritz. ... Name pronounced LAY-rits.

JUNIOR COLLEGE: Middle Georgia College.

COLLEGE: Kentucky.

TRANSACTIONS/CAREER NOTES: Signed as non-drafted free agent by New York Yankees organization (August 24, 1985). ... Traded by Yankees to Anaheim Angels for two players to be named later (December 5, 1996); Yankees acquired 3B Ryan Kane and P Jeremy Blevins to complete deal (December 9, 1996). ... Traded by Angels with a player to be named later to Texas Rangers for P Ken Hill (July 29, 1997); Rangers acquired IF Rob Sasser to complete deal (October 31, 1997). ... Traded by Rangers with OF Damon Buford to Boston Red Sox for P Aaron Sele, P Mark Brandenburg and C Bill Haselman (November 6, 1997).

STATISTICAL NOTES: Led Florida State League with 25 passed balls in 1987. ... Tied for Eastern League lead in being hit by pitch with nine in 1989. ... Career major league grand slams: 2.

Year Team (League)	Pos.	G	AB	R	H	2B	3B	HR	RBI	Avg.	BB	SO	SB	PO	A	E	Avg.
1986— Oneonta (NYP)	C	23	91	12	33	3	1	4	15	.363	5	10	1	170	21	2	.990
— Fort Lauderdale (FSL)	C	12	34	3	10	1	1	0	1	.294	4	5	0	32	8	1	.976
1987— Fort Lauderdale (FSL)	C	102	374	48	115	22	0	6	51	.307	38	54	2	458	*76	13	.976
1988— Alb./Colon. (Eastern)..	C-3B-1B	112	382	40	92	18	3	5	50	.241	43	62	3	418	73	6	.988
1989— Alb./Colon. (Eastern)..	C-OF-3B	114	375	53	118	18	2	10	66	*.315	65	51	2	421	41	3	.994
1990— Columbus (Int'l)	3-2-1-0-C	59	204	36	59	11	1	8	32	.289	37	33	4	75	96	13	.929
— New York (A.L.)	3B-OF-C	92	303	28	78	13	1	5	25	.257	27	51	2	117	107	13	.945
1991— New York (A.L.)	3-C-1-DH	32	77	8	14	3	0	0	4	.182	13	15	0	38	21	3	.952
— Columbus (Int'l)	C-3-S-2	79	270	50	72	24	1	11	48	.267	38	50	1	209	48	5	.981
1992— New York (A.L.)	DH-C-O-3-1-2	63	144	17	37	6	0	7	26	.257	14	22	0	96	15	1	.991
1993— New York (A.L.)	1-O-DH-C	95	259	43	80	14	0	14	53	.309	37	59	0	333	15	2	.994
1994— New York (A.L.)	C-DH-1B	75	249	47	66	12	0	17	58	.265	35	61	0	282	15	0	1.000
1995— New York (A.L.)	C-1B-DH	77	264	37	71	12	0	7	37	.269	37	73	1	417	24	3	.993
1996— New York (A.L.)	C-DH-3-1-O-2	88	265	23	70	10	0	7	40	.264	30	68	2	387	31	6	.986
1997— Anaheim (A.L.) ■	C-1B-DH	84	294	47	81	7	0	11	50	.276	37	56	1	440	45	2	.996
— Texas (A.L.) ■	C-DH-1B	37	85	11	24	4	0	0	14	.282	23	22	1	116	7	1	.992
Major league totals (8 years)		643	1940	261	521	81	1	68	307	.269	253	427	7	2226	280	31	.988

DIVISION SERIES RECORD

Year Team (League)	Pos.	G	AB	R	H	2B	3B	HR	RBI	Avg.	BB	SO	SB	PO	A	E	Avg.
1995— New York (A.L.)	C-PH	2	7	1	1	0	0	1	2	.143	0	1	0	13	0	0	1.000
1996— New York (A.L.)	C-DH	2	3	0	0	0	0	0	1	.000	0	1	0	4	0	0	1.000
Division series totals (2 years)		4	10	1	1	0	0	1	3	.100	0	2	0	17	0	0	1.000

CHAMPIONSHIP SERIES RECORD

Year Team (League)	Pos.	G	AB	R	H	2B	3B	HR	RBI	Avg.	BB	SO	SB	PO	A	E	Avg.
1996— New York (A.L.)	C-OF-PH	3	8	1	2	0	0	1	2	.250	1	4	0	11	2	0	1.000

WORLD SERIES RECORD

NOTES: Member of World Series championship team (1996).

Year Team (League)	Pos.	G	AB	R	H	2B	3B	HR	RBI	Avg.	BB	SO	SB	PO	A	E	Avg.
1996— New York (A.L.)	C-PH	4	8	1	3	0	0	1	3	.375	4	2	1	15	0	0	1.000

LIDLE, CORY — P — DIAMONDBACKS

PERSONAL: Born March 22, 1972, in Hollywood, Calif. ... 5-11/180. ... Throws right, bats right. ... Full name: Cory Fulton Lidle. ... Twin brother of Kevin Lidle, catcher, Detroit Tigers organization.

HIGH SCHOOL: South Hills (Covina, Calif.).

TRANSACTIONS/CAREER NOTES: Signed as non-drafted free agent by Minnesota Twins organization (August 25, 1990). ... Released by Elizabethton, Twins organization (April 1, 1993). ... Signed by Pocatello, independent (May 28, 1993). ... Purchased by Milwaukee Brewers organization from Pocatello (September 17, 1993). ... Traded by Brewers to New York Mets organization for C Kelly Stinnett (January 17, 1996). ... Selected by Arizona Diamondbacks in first round (13th pick overall) of expansion draft (November 18, 1997).

Year Team (League)	W	L	Pct.	ERA	G	GS	CG	ShO	Sv.	IP	H	R	ER	BB	SO
1991— GC Twins (GCL)	1	1	.500	5.79	4	0	0	0	0	4 2/3	5	3	3	0	5
1992— Elizabethton (Appal.)	2	1	.667	3.71	19	2	0	0	6	43 2/3	40	29	18	21	32
1993— Pocatello (Pioneer) ■	•8	4	.667	4.13	17	16	3	0	1	106 2/3	104	59	49	54	91
1994— Stockton (California) ■	1	2	.333	4.43	25	1	0	0	4	42 2/3	60	32	21	13	38
— Beloit (Midwest)	3	4	.429	2.61	13	9	1	1	0	69	65	24	20	11	62
1995— El Paso (Texas)	5	4	.556	3.36	45	9	0	0	2	109 2/3	126	52	41	36	78
1996— Binghamton (Eastern) ■	14	10	.583	3.31	27	27	•6	1	0	*190 1/3	186	78	70	49	141
1997— Norfolk (Int'l)	4	2	.667	3.64	7	7	1	0	0	42	46	20	17	10	34
— New York (N.L.)	7	2	.778	3.53	54	2	0	0	2	81 2/3	86	38	32	20	54
Major league totals (1 year)	7	2	.778	3.53	54	2	0	0	2	81 2/3	86	38	32	20	54

LIEBER, JON — P — PIRATES

PERSONAL: Born April 2, 1970, in Council Bluffs, Iowa. ... 6-2/220. ... Throws right, bats left. ... Full name: Jonathan Ray Lieber. ... Name pronounced LEE-ber..

HIGH SCHOOL: Abraham Lincoln (Council Bluffs, Iowa.).

JUNIOR COLLEGE: Iowa Western Community College-Council Bluffs.

COLLEGE: South Alabama.

TRANSACTIONS/CAREER NOTES: Selected by Chicago Cubs organization in ninth round of free-agent draft (June 3, 1991); did not sign. ... Selected by Kansas City Royals organization in second round of free-agent draft (June 1, 1992); pick received as part of compensation for New York Yankees signing Type A free-agent OF Danny Tartabull. ... Traded by Royals organization with P Dan Miceli to Pittsburgh Pirates organization for P Stan Belinda (July 31, 1993).

Year	Team (League)	W	L	Pct.	ERA	G	GS	CG	ShO	Sv.	IP	H	R	ER	BB	SO
1992—	Eugene (Northwest)	3	0	1.000	1.16	5	5	0	0	0	31	26	6	4	2	23
——	Baseball City (FSL)............	3	3	.500	4.65	7	6	0	0	0	31	45	20	16	8	19
1993—	Wilmington (Caro.)............	9	3	.750	2.67	17	16	2	0	0	114²/₃	125	47	34	9	89
——	Memphis (Southern).........	2	1	.667	6.86	4	4	0	0	0	21	32	16	16	6	17
——	Carolina (Southern)■......	4	2	.667	3.97	6	6	0	0	0	34	39	15	15	10	28
1994—	Carolina (Southern)...........	2	0	1.000	1.29	3	3	1	1	0	21	13	4	3	2	21
——	Buffalo (A.A.)....................	1	1	.500	1.69	3	3	0	0	0	21¹/₃	16	4	4	1	21
——	Pittsburgh (N.L.)...............	6	7	.462	3.73	17	17	1	0	0	108²/₃	116	62	45	25	71
1995—	Pittsburgh (N.L.)...............	4	7	.364	6.32	21	12	0	0	0	72²/₃	103	56	51	14	45
——	Calgary (PCL)...................	1	5	.167	7.01	14	14	0	0	0	77	122	69	60	19	34
1996—	Pittsburgh (N.L.)...............	9	5	.643	3.99	51	15	0	0	1	142	156	70	63	28	94
1997—	Pittsburgh (N.L.)...............	11	14	.440	4.49	33	32	1	0	0	188¹/₃	193	102	94	51	160
Major league totals (4 years)......		**30**	**33**	**.476**	**4.45**	**122**	**76**	**2**	**0**	**1**	**511²/₃**	**568**	**290**	**253**	**118**	**370**

LIEBERTHAL, MIKE   C   PHILLIES

PERSONAL: Born January 18, 1972, in Glendale, Calif. ... 6-0/178. ... Bats right, throws right. ... Full name: Michael Scott Lieberthal. ... Name pronounced LEE-ber-thal..

HIGH SCHOOL: Westlake (Westlake Village, Calif.).

TRANSACTIONS/CAREER NOTES: Selected by Philadelphia Phillies organization in first round (third pick overall) of free-agent draft (June 4, 1990). ... On Scranton/Wilkes-Barre disabled list (August 31, 1992-remainder of season). ... On disabled list (August 22, 1996-remainder of season).

STATISTICAL NOTES: Tied for N.L. lead in passed balls with 12 in 1997. ... Career major league grand slams: 1.

Year	Team (League)	Pos.	G	AB	R	H	2B	3B	HR	RBI	Avg.	BB	SO	SB	PO	A	E	Avg.
1990—	Martinsville (App.)......	C	49	184	26	42	9	0	4	22	.228	11	40	2	421	*52	5	*.990
1991—	Spartanburg (SAL)	C	72	243	34	74	17	0	0	31	.305	23	25	1	565	68	10	.984
——	Clearwater (FSL)	C	16	52	7	15	2	0	0	7	.288	3	12	0	128	9	1	.993
1992—	Reading (Eastern)	C	86	309	30	88	16	1	2	37	.285	19	26	4	524	48	7	.988
——	Scran./W.B. (Int'l)......	C	16	45	4	9	1	0	0	4	.200	2	5	0	86	6	1	.989
1993—	Scran./W.B. (Int'l)......	C	112	382	35	100	17	0	7	40	.262	24	32	2	659	75	•11	.985
1994—	Scran./W.B. (Int'l)......	C	84	296	23	69	16	0	1	32	.233	21	29	1	472	50	9	.983
——	Philadelphia (N.L.)......	C	24	79	6	21	3	1	1	5	.266	3	5	0	122	4	4	.969
1995—	Philadelphia (N.L.)......	C	16	47	1	12	2	0	0	4	.255	5	5	0	95	10	1	.991
——	Scran./W.B. (Int'l)......	C-3B	85	278	44	78	20	2	6	42	.281	44	26	1	503	46	5	.991
1996—	Philadelphia (N.L.)......	C	50	166	21	42	8	0	7	23	.253	10	30	0	284	20	3	.990
1997—	Philadelphia (N.L.)......	C-DH	134	455	59	112	27	1	20	77	.246	44	76	3	934	73	12	.988
Major league totals (4 years)			**224**	**747**	**87**	**187**	**40**	**2**	**28**	**109**	**.250**	**62**	**116**	**3**	**1435**	**107**	**20**	**.987**

LIEFER, JEFF   3B/OF   WHITE SOX

PERSONAL: Born August 17, 1974, in Upland, Calif. ... 6-3/195. ... Bats left, throws right.

HIGH SCHOOL: Upland (Calif.).

COLLEGE: Long Beach State.

TRANSACTIONS/CAREER NOTES: Selected by Cleveland Indians organization in sixth round of free-agent draft (June 1, 1992); did not sign. ... Selected by Chicago White Sox organization in first round (25th pick overall) of free-agent draft (June 1, 1995).

Year	Team (League)	Pos.	G	AB	R	H	2B	3B	HR	RBI	Avg.	BB	SO	SB	PO	A	E	Avg.
1996—	South Bend (Mid.)......	3B	74	277	60	90	14	0	15	58	.325	30	62	6	31	62	23	.802
——	Prince William (Car.)..	DH	37	147	17	33	6	0	1	13	.224	11	27	0	0	0	0	...
1997—	Birmingham (Sou.).....	OF	119	474	67	113	24	9	15	71	.238	38	115	2	166	2	•8	.955

LIGTENBERG, KERRY   P   BRAVES

PERSONAL: Born May 11, 1971, in Rapid City, S.D. ... 6-2/205. ... Throws right, bats right. ... Full name: Kerry Dale Ligtenberg.

HIGH SCHOOL: Park (Cottage Grove, Minn.).

COLLEGE: Minnesota-Morris, then Minnesota.

TRANSACTIONS/CAREER NOTES: Contract purchased by Atlanta Braves organization from Minneapolis of the Prairie League (March 28, 1995). ... Signed by Minneapolis of Prairie League prior to 1994 season.

Year	Team (League)	W	L	Pct.	ERA	G	GS	CG	ShO	Sv.	IP	H	R	ER	BB	SO
1994—	Minneapolis (Prairie)..........	5	5	.500	3.31	19	19	2	...	0	114¹/₃	103	47	42	44	94
1995—	Minneapolis (Prairie)..........	11	2	.846	2.73	17	15	4	...	0	108²/₃	101	41	33	26	100
1996—	Durham (Carolina)■	7	4	.636	2.41	49	0	0	0	20	59²/₃	58	20	16	16	76
1997—	Greenville (Southern)	3	1	.750	2.04	31	0	0	0	16	35¹/₃	20	8	8	14	43
——	Richmond (Int'l)	0	3	.000	4.32	14	0	0	0	1	25	21	13	12	2	35
——	Atlanta (N.L.)....................	1	0	1.000	3.00	15	0	0	0	1	15	12	5	5	4	19
Major league totals (1 year)........		**1**	**0**	**1.000**	**3.00**	**15**	**0**	**0**	**0**	**1**	**15**	**12**	**5**	**5**	**4**	**19**

	CHAMPIONSHIP SERIES RECORD															
Year	Team (League)	W	L	Pct.	ERA	G	GS	CG	ShO	Sv.	IP	H	R	ER	BB	SO
1997—	Atlanta (N.L.).....................	0	0	...	0.00	2	0	0	0	0	3	1	0	0	0	4

LIMA, JOSE   P   ASTROS

PERSONAL: Born September 30, 1972, in Santiago, Dominican Republic. ... 6-2/170. ... Throws right, bats right. ... Full name: Jose D. Lima.

TRANSACTIONS/CAREER NOTES: Signed as non-drafted free agent by Detroit Tigers organization (July 5, 1989). ... Traded by Tigers with C Brad Ausmus, P C.J. Nitkowski, P Trever Miller and IF Daryle Ward to Houston Astros for OF Brian Hunter, IF Orlando Miller, P Doug Brocail, P Todd Jones and a player to be named later (December 10, 1996).

STATISTICAL NOTES: Led Florida State League with 14 home runs allowed in 1992. ... Led Eastern League with 13 balks in 1993. ... Pitched 3-0 no-hit victory for Toledo against Pawtucket (August 17, 1994).

Year Team (League)	W	L	Pct.	ERA	G	GS	CG	ShO	Sv.	IP	H	R	ER	BB	SO
1990— Bristol (Appalachian)..........	3	8	.273	5.02	14	12	1	0	1	75 1/3	89	49	42	22	64
1991— Lakeland (Fla. St.).............	0	1	.000	10.38	4	1	0	0	0	8 2/3	16	10	10	2	5
— Fayetteville (S. Atl.)............	1	3	.250	4.97	18	7	0	0	0	58	53	38	32	25	60
1992— Lakeland (Fla. St.).............	5	11	.313	3.16	25	25	5	2	0	151	132	57	53	21	137
1993— London (Eastern)	8	•13	.381	4.07	27	27	2	0	0	177	160	96	80	59	138
1994— Toledo (Int'l)...................	7	9	.438	3.60	23	22	3	2	0	142 1/3	124	70	57	48	117
— Detroit (A.L.).......................	0	1	.000	13.50	3	1	0	0	0	6 2/3	11	10	10	3	7
1995— Lakeland (Fla. St.)	3	1	.750	2.57	4	4	0	0	0	21	23	11	6	0	20
— Toledo (Int'l).......................	5	3	.625	3.01	11	11	1	0	0	74 2/3	69	26	25	14	40
— Detroit (A.L.).......................	3	9	.250	6.11	15	15	0	0	0	73 2/3	85	52	50	18	37
1996— Toledo (Int'l)...................	5	4	.556	6.78	12	12	0	0	0	69	93	53	52	12	57
— Detroit (A.L.).......................	5	6	.455	5.70	39	4	0	0	3	72 2/3	87	48	46	22	59
1997— Houston (N.L.)■................	1	6	.143	5.28	52	1	0	0	2	75	79	45	44	16	63
A.L. totals (3 years)....................	8	16	.333	6.24	57	20	0	0	3	153	183	110	106	43	103
N.L. totals (1 year).....................	1	6	.143	5.28	52	1	0	0	2	75	79	45	44	16	63
Major league totals (4 years)......	9	22	.290	5.92	109	21	0	0	5	228	262	155	150	59	166

DIVISION SERIES RECORD

Year Team (League)	W	L	Pct.	ERA	G	GS	CG	ShO	Sv.	IP	H	R	ER	BB	SO
1997— Houston (N.L.)	0	0	...	0.00	1	0	0	0	0	1	0	0	0	1	1

LIRA, FELIPE   P   MARINERS

PERSONAL: Born April 26, 1972, in Miranda, Venezuela. ... 6-0/170. ... Throws right, bats right. ... Full name: Antonio Felipe Lira.

TRANSACTIONS/CAREER NOTES: Signed as non-drafted free agent by Detroit Tigers organization (February 20, 1990). ... On Lakeland disabled list (April 10-June 10, 1991). ... Traded by Tigers with P Omar Olivares to Seattle Mariners for P Scott Sanders, P Dean Crow and 3B Carlos Villalobos (July 18, 1997).

STATISTICAL NOTES: Pitched seven-inning, 4-0 no-hit victory against Columbus (May 4, 1994). ... Led International League with 16 wild pitches in 1994.

Year Team (League)	W	L	Pct.	ERA	G	GS	CG	ShO	Sv.	IP	H	R	ER	BB	SO
1990— Bristol (Appalachian)..........	5	5	.500	2.41	13	10	2	1	1	78 1/3	70	26	21	16	71
— Lakeland (Fla. St.)	0	0	...	5.40	1	0	0	0	0	1 2/3	3	1	1	3	4
1991— Fayetteville (S. Atl.)..........	5	5	.500	4.66	15	13	0	0	1	73 1/3	79	43	38	19	56
1992— Lakeland (Fla. St.)	11	5	.688	2.39	32	8	2	1	1	109	95	36	29	16	84
1993— London (Eastern)	10	4	.714	3.38	22	22	2	0	0	152	157	63	57	39	122
— Toledo (Int'l)......................	1	2	.333	4.60	5	5	0	0	0	31 1/3	32	18	16	11	23
1994— Toledo (Int'l)...................	7	12	.368	4.70	26	26	1	1	0	151 1/3	171	91	79	45	110
1995— Detroit (A.L.)....................	9	13	.409	4.31	37	22	0	0	1	146 1/3	151	74	70	56	89
1996— Detroit (A.L.)....................	6	14	.300	5.22	32	32	3	2	0	194 2/3	204	123	113	66	113
1997— Detroit (A.L.)....................	5	7	.417	5.77	20	15	1	1	0	92	101	61	59	45	64
— Seattle (A.L.)■....................	0	4	.000	9.16	8	3	0	0	0	18 2/3	31	21	19	10	9
— Everett (Northwest).............	1	0	1.000	3.60	1	1	0	0	0	5	6	3	2	2	9
— Tacoma (PCL).....................	2	0	1.000	3.43	3	3	0	0	0	21	21	8	8	5	17
Major league totals (3 years)......	20	38	.345	5.20	97	72	4	3	1	451 2/3	487	279	261	177	275

LIRIANO, NELSON   2B   ROCKIES

PERSONAL: Born June 3, 1964, in Puerto Plata, Dominican Republic. ... 5-10/185. ... Bats both, throws right. ... Full name: Nelson Arturo Liriano. ... Name pronounced LEER-ee-ON-oh.

HIGH SCHOOL: Jose Debeaw (Puerto Plata, Dominican Republic).

TRANSACTIONS/CAREER NOTES: Signed as non-drafted free agent by Toronto Blue Jays organization (November 1, 1982). ... Traded by Blue Jays with OF Pedro Munoz to Minnesota Twins for P John Candelaria (July 27, 1990). ... Released by Twins (April 2, 1991). ... Signed by Omaha, Kansas City Royals organization (May 1, 1991). ... Granted free agency (October 15, 1991). ... Signed by Colorado Springs, Cleveland Indians organization (January 31, 1992). ... Granted free agency (October 15, 1992). ... Re-signed by Rockies organization (October 26, 1992). ... On Colorado Springs disabled list (April 7-30, 1993). ... Claimed on waivers by Pittsburgh Pirates (October 14, 1994). ... Claimed on waivers by Los Angeles Dodgers (November 20, 1996). ... On disabled list (March 24-April 13, 1997). ... Granted free agency (October 3, 1997). ... Signed by Rockies organization (December 19, 1997).

STATISTICAL NOTES: Led Carolina League second basemen with 79 double plays in 1985. ... Led International League second basemen with 611 total chances and 96 double plays in 1987. ... Career major league grand slams: 1.

Year Team (League)	Pos.	G	AB	R	H	2B	3B	HR	RBI	Avg.	BB	SO	SB	PO	A	E	Avg.
1983— Florence (S. Atl.)	2B	129	478	87	124	24	5	6	57	.259	70	81	27	214	323	34	.940
1984— Kinston (Carolina)	2B	132	*512	68	126	22	4	5	50	.246	46	86	10	260	*357	*21	.967
1985— Kinston (Carolina)	2B	134	451	68	130	23	1	6	36	.288	39	55	25	*261	328	25	.959
1986— Knoxville (Southern) ..	2B-3B-SS	135	557	88	159	25	*15	7	59	.285	48	63	35	239	324	22	.962
1987— Syracuse (Int'l)	2B	130	531	72	133	19	•10	10	55	.250	44	76	36	*246	*346	*19	.969
— Toronto (A.L.)............	2B	37	158	29	38	6	2	2	10	.241	16	22	13	83	107	1	.995
1988— Toronto (A.L.)............	2B-DH-3B	99	276	36	73	6	2	3	23	.264	11	40	12	121	177	12	.961
— Syracuse (Int'l).........	2B	8	31	2	6	1	1	0	1	.194	2	4	2	14	23	0	1.000
1989— Toronto (A.L.)............	2B-DH	132	418	51	110	26	3	5	53	.263	43	51	16	267	330	12	.980
1990— Toronto (A.L.)............	2B	50	170	16	36	7	2	1	15	.212	16	20	3	93	132	4	.983
— Minnesota (A.L.)■...	2B-DH-SS	53	185	30	47	5	7	0	13	.254	22	24	5	83	128	7	.968
1991— Omaha (A.A.)...........	2B-SS	86	292	50	80	16	9	2	36	.274	31	39	6	149	218	9	.976
— Kansas City (A.L.)	2B	10	22	5	9	0	0	0	1	.409	0	2	0	11	23	0	1.000
1992— Colo. Springs (PCL)■	2B-3B-SS	106	361	73	110	19	9	5	52	.305	48	50	20	144	230	9	.977
1993— Central Valley (Cal.)...	3B-SS-2B	6	22	3	8	0	2	0	4	.364	6	0	0	4	10	0	1.000
— Colo. Springs (PCL)...	2B-SS-3B	79	293	48	105	23	6	6	46	.358	32	34	9	143	232	15	.962
— Colorado (N.L.)	SS-2B-3B	48	151	28	46	6	3	2	15	.305	18	22	6	65	103	6	.96

Year Team (League)	Pos.	G	AB	R	H	2B	3B	HR	RBI	Avg.	BB	SO	SB	PO	A	E	Avg.
									BATTING						FIELDING		
1994— Colorado (N.L.)	2B-SS-3B	87	255	39	65	17	5	3	31	.255	42	44	0	145	225	10	.974
1995— Pittsburgh (N.L.)■	2B-3B-SS	107	259	29	74	12	1	5	38	.286	24	34	2	130	137	5	.982
1996— Pittsburgh (N.L.)	2B-3B-SS	112	217	23	58	14	2	3	30	.267	14	22	2	58	98	3	.981
1997— Los Angeles (N.L.)■ ..	2-1-3-S	76	88	10	20	6	0	1	11	.227	6	12	0	19	24	2	.956
American League totals (5 years)		381	1229	167	313	50	16	11	115	.255	108	159	49	658	897	36	.977
National League totals (5 years)		430	970	129	263	55	11	14	125	.271	104	134	10	417	587	26	.975
Major league totals (10 years)		811	2199	296	576	105	27	25	240	.262	212	293	59	1075	1484	62	.976

CHAMPIONSHIP SERIES RECORD

Year Team (League)	Pos.	G	AB	R	H	2B	3B	HR	RBI	Avg.	BB	SO	SB	PO	A	E	Avg.
									BATTING						FIELDING		
1989— Toronto (A.L.)............	2B	3	7	1	3	0	0	0	1	.429	2	0	3	4	3	1	.875

LISTACH, PAT — SS — MARINERS

PERSONAL: Born September 12, 1967, in Natchitoches, La. ... 5-9/180. ... Bats both, throws right. ... Full name: Patrick Alan Listach. ... Name pronounced LISS-tatch.
HIGH SCHOOL: Natchitoches (La.) Central.
JUNIOR COLLEGE: McLennan Community College (Texas).
COLLEGE: Arizona State.
TRANSACTIONS/CAREER NOTES: Selected by Seattle Mariners organization in 23rd round of free-agent draft (June 2, 1987); did not sign. ... Selected by Milwaukee Brewers organization in fifth round of free-agent draft (June 1, 1988). ... On Milwaukee disabled list (June 2-July 18, 1993); included rehabilitation assignment to Beloit (July 14-18, 1993). ... On Milwaukee disabled list (April 24, 1994-remainder of season); included rehabilitation assignment to New Orleans (August 5-7). ... On Milwaukee disabled list (June 26-July 11, 1996); included rehabilitation assignment to Beloit (July 8-9). ... Traded by Brewers with P Graeme Lloyd to New York Yankees for OF Gerald Williams and P Bob Wickman (August 23, 1996). ... On New York disabled list (August 23, 1996-remainder of season). ... Returned by Yankees to Brewers as part of a compensation agreement (October 2, 1996). ... Granted free agency (October 2, 1996). ... Signed by Houston Astros (December 2, 1996). ... Released by Astros (July 1, 1997). ... Signed by Cleveland Indians organization (July 25, 1997). ... Granted free agency (October 15, 1997). ... Signed by Mariners (December 16, 1997).
HONORS: Named A.L. Rookie Player of the Year by THE SPORTING NEWS (1992). ... Named A.L. Rookie of the Year by Baseball Writers' Association of America (1992).
STATISTICAL NOTES: Led California League second basemen with 276 putouts in 1990.
MISCELLANEOUS: Batted righthanded only (1988-89 and 1991).

Year Team (League)	Pos.	G	AB	R	H	2B	3B	HR	RBI	Avg.	BB	SO	SB	PO	A	E	Avg.
									BATTING						FIELDING		
1988— Beloit (Midwest).........	SS	53	200	40	48	5	1	1	18	.240	18	20	20	66	117	24	.884
1989— Stockton (California) ..	2B-SS	132	480	73	110	11	4	2	34	.229	58	106	37	250	351	29	.954
1990— Stockton (California) ..	2B-SS-OF	•139	503	*116	137	21	6	2	39	.272	*105	122	78	†319	356	25	.964
1991— El Paso (Texas).........	SS-2B	49	186	40	47	5	2	0	13	.253	25	56	14	86	131	22	.908
— Denver (A.A.)............	2B-SS-OF	89	286	51	72	10	4	1	31	.252	45	66	23	182	237	9	.979
1992— Milwaukee (A.L.).......	SS-OF-2B	149	579	93	168	19	6	1	47	.290	55	124	54	238	449	24	.966
1993— Milwaukee (A.L.).......	SS-OF	98	356	50	87	15	1	3	30	.244	37	70	18	135	267	10	.976
— Beloit (Midwest).........	SS	4	12	2	3	0	0	0	1	.250	1	2	2	3	7	0	1.000
1994— Milwaukee (A.L.).......	SS	16	54	8	16	3	0	0	2	.296	3	8	2	18	51	3	.958
— New Orleans (A.A.)......	OF	2	5	1	2	0	0	0	0	.400	0	0	0	0	0	0	...
1995— Milwaukee (A.L.).......	2-S-O-3	101	334	35	73	8	2	0	25	.219	25	61	13	169	273	6	.987
1996— Milwaukee (A.L.).......	O-2-S-DH	87	317	51	76	16	2	1	33	.240	36	51	25	192	42	5	.979
— Beloit (Midwest).........	SS	1	5	2	2	0	0	0	0	.400	0	1	0	2	3	1	.833
1997— Houston (N.L.)■.......	SS-OF	52	132	13	24	2	2	0	6	.182	11	24	4	35	71	6	.946
— Buffalo (A.A.)■.........	S-O-3-2	25	73	3	19	1	1	0	2	.260	12	10	6	34	42	4	.950
American League totals (5 years)		451	1640	237	420	61	11	5	137	.256	156	314	112	752	1082	48	.974
National League totals (1 year)		52	132	13	24	2	2	0	6	.182	11	24	4	35	71	6	.946
Major league totals (6 years)		503	1772	250	444	63	13	5	143	.251	167	338	116	787	1153	54	.973

LITTLE, MARK — OF — RANGERS

PERSONAL: Born July 11, 1972, in Edwardsville, Ill. ... 6-0/195. ... Throws right, bats right. ... Full name: Mark Travis Little.
HIGH SCHOOL: Edwardsville (Ill.).
COLLEGE: Memphis.
TRANSACTIONS/CAREER NOTES: Selected by Texas Rangers organization in eighth round of free-agent draft (June 2, 1994). ... On disabled list (August 5-September 5, 1996).
STATISTICAL NOTES: Led American Association outfielders with 280 putouts and 297 total chances in 1997.

Year Team (League)	Pos.	G	AB	R	H	2B	3B	HR	RBI	Avg.	BB	SO	SB	PO	A	E	Avg.
									BATTING						FIELDING		
1994— Hudson Valley (NYP)..	OF	54	208	33	61	15	5	3	27	.293	22	38	14	136	3	6	.959
1995— Charlotte (Fla. St.)	OF	115	438	75	112	31	8	9	50	.256	51	108	20	274	8	10	.966
1996— Tulsa (Texas)	OF	101	409	69	119	24	2	13	50	.291	48	88	22	263	9	9	.968
1997— Oklahoma City (A.A.)..	OF-1B	121	415	72	109	23	4	15	45	.263	39	100	21	†282	9	8	.973

LIVINGSTONE, SCOTT — 3B — EXPOS

PERSONAL: Born July 15, 1965, in Dallas. ... 6-0/190. ... Bats left, throws right. ... Full name: Scott Louis Livingstone.
HIGH SCHOOL: Lake Highlands (Dallas).
COLLEGE: Texas A&M.

TRANSACTIONS/CAREER NOTES: Selected by Toronto Blue Jays organization in sixth round of free-agent draft (June 4, 1984); did not sign. ... Selected by New York Yankees organization in 26th round of free-agent draft (June 2, 1986); did not sign. ... Selected by Oakland Athletics organization in third round of free-agent draft (June 2, 1987); did not sign. ... Selected by Detroit Tigers organization in second round of free-agent draft (June 1, 1988). ... On disabled list (July 14-23 and July 28-August 7, 1990). ... Traded by Tigers with SS Jorge Velandia to San Diego Padres for P Gene Harris (May 11, 1994). ... On disabled list (June 3-23, 1996). ... On San Diego disabled list (April 29-May 26, 1997); included rehabilitation assignment to Rancho Cucamonga (May 10-12). ... Traded by Padres with P Fernando Valenzuela and OF Phil Plantier to St. Louis Cardinals for P Danny Jackson, P Rich Batchelor and OF Mark Sweeney (June 13, 1997). ... Granted free agency (November 7, 1997). ... Signed by Montreal Expos organization (January 16, 1998).

HONORS: Named designated hitter on THE SPORTING NEWS college All-America team (1987-88).

STATISTICAL NOTES: Tied for Eastern League lead in total chances by third baseman with 360 in 1989.

						BATTING								FIELDING			
Year Team (League)	Pos.	G	AB	R	H	2B	3B	HR	RBI	Avg.	BB	SO	SB	PO	A	E	Avg.
1988— Lakeland (Fla. St.)	3B	53	180	28	51	8	1	2	25	.283	11	25	1	30	115	8	.948
1989— London (Eastern)	3B-SS	124	452	46	98	18	1	14	71	.217	52	67	1	100	265	25	.936
1990— Toledo (Int'l)	3B	103	345	44	94	19	0	6	36	.272	21	40	1	66	181	13	.950
1991— Toledo (Int'l)	3B-1B	92	331	48	100	13	3	3	62	.302	40	52	2	65	137	16	.927
— Detroit (A.L.)	3B	44	127	19	37	5	0	2	11	.291	10	25	2	32	67	2	.980
1992— Detroit (A.L.)	3B	117	354	43	100	21	0	4	46	.282	21	36	1	67	189	10	.962
1993— Detroit (A.L.)	3B-DH	98	304	39	89	10	2	2	39	.293	19	32	1	33	94	6	.955
1994— Detroit (A.L.)	DH-1B-3B	15	23	0	5	1	0	0	1	.217	1	4	0	6	3	0	1.000
— San Diego (N.L.)■	3B	57	180	11	49	12	1	2	10	.272	6	22	2	20	78	6	.942
1995— San Diego (N.L.)	1B-3B-2B	99	196	26	66	15	0	5	32	.337	15	22	2	300	33	3	.991
1996— San Diego (N.L.)	1B-3B	102	172	20	51	4	1	2	20	.297	9	22	0	143	34	2	.989
1997— San Diego (N.L.)	3B-1B-2B	23	26	1	4	1	0	0	3	.154	2	1	0	17	9	2	.929
— Rancho Cuca. (Cal.)	DH	3	8	2	2	0	0	0	0	.250	3	0	0	0	0	0	...
— St. Louis (N.L.)■	3B-DH-OF	42	41	3	7	1	0	0	3	.171	1	10	1	0	1	0	1.000
— Louisville (A.A.)	1B	9	25	4	9	1	0	0	2	.360	2	3	0	31	3	1	.971
American League totals (4 years)		274	808	101	231	37	2	8	97	.286	51	97	4	138	353	18	.965
National League totals (4 years)		323	615	61	177	33	2	9	68	.288	33	77	5	480	155	13	.980
Major league totals (7 years)		597	1423	162	408	70	4	17	165	.287	84	174	9	618	508	31	.973

DIVISION SERIES RECORD

						BATTING								FIELDING			
Year Team (League)	Pos.	G	AB	R	H	2B	3B	HR	RBI	Avg.	BB	SO	SB	PO	A	E	Avg.
1996— San Diego (N.L.)	PH	2	2	1	1	0	0	0	0	.500	0	0	0	0	0	0	...

LLOYD, GRAEME — P — YANKEES

PERSONAL: Born April 9, 1967, in Victoria, Australia. ... 6-7/234. ... Throws left, bats left. ... Full name: Graeme John Lloyd. ... Name pronounced GRAM.

HIGH SCHOOL: Geelong Technical School (Victoria, Australia).

TRANSACTIONS/CAREER NOTES: Signed as non-drafted free agent by Toronto Blue Jays organization (January 26, 1988). ... On Myrtle Beach disabled list (June 29-September 1, 1989). ... Selected by Philadelphia Phillies from Blue Jays organization in Rule 5 major league draft (December 7, 1992). ... Traded by Phillies to Milwaukee Brewers for P John Trisler (December 8, 1992). ... On disabled list (August 20-September 4, 1993 and July 25-September 10, 1995). ... On suspended list (September 5-9, 1993). ... Traded by Brewers with OF Pat Listach to New York Yankees for OF Gerald Williams and P Bob Wickman (August 23, 1996).

Year Team (League)	W	L	Pct.	ERA	G	GS	CG	ShO	Sv.	IP	H	R	ER	BB	SO
1988— Myrtle Beach (SAL)	3	2	.600	3.62	41	0	0	0	2	59 2/3	71	33	24	30	43
1989— Dunedin (Fla. St.)	0	0	...	10.13	2	0	0	0	0	2 2/3	6	3	3	1	0
— Myrtle Beach (SAL)	0	0	...	5.40	1	1	0	0	0	5	5	4	3	0	3
1990— Myrtle Beach (SAL)	5	2	.714	2.72	19	6	0	0	6	49 2/3	51	20	15	16	42
1991— Dunedin (Fla. St.)	2	5	.286	2.24	50	0	0	0	24	60 1/3	54	17	15	25	39
— Knoxville (Southern)	0	0	...	0.00	2	0	0	0	0	1 2/3	1	0	0	1	2
1992— Knoxville (Southern)	4	8	.333	1.96	49	7	1	0	14	92	79	30	20	25	65
1993— Milwaukee (A.L.)■	3	4	.429	2.83	55	0	0	0	0	63 2/3	64	24	20	13	31
1994— Milwaukee (A.L.)	2	3	.400	5.17	43	0	0	3	0	47	49	28	27	15	31
1995— Milwaukee (A.L.)	0	5	.000	4.50	33	0	0	0	4	32	28	16	16	8	13
1996— Milwaukee (A.L.)	2	4	.333	2.82	52	0	0	0	0	51	49	19	16	17	24
— New York (A.L.)■	0	2	.000	17.47	13	0	0	0	0	5 2/3	12	11	11	5	6
1997— New York (A.L.)	1	1	.500	3.31	46	0	0	0	1	49	55	24	18	20	26
Major league totals (5 years)	8	19	.296	3.91	242	0	0	0	8	248 1/3	257	122	108	78	131

DIVISION SERIES RECORD

Year Team (League)	W	L	Pct.	ERA	G	GS	CG	ShO	Sv.	IP	H	R	ER	BB	SO
1996— New York (A.L.)	0	0	...	0.00	2	0	0	0	0	1	1	0	0	0	0
1997— New York (A.L.)	0	0	...	0.00	2	0	0	0	0	1 1/3	0	0	0	0	1
Div. series totals (2 years)	0	0	...	0.00	4	0	0	0	0	2 1/3	1	0	0	0	1

CHAMPIONSHIP SERIES RECORD

Year Team (League)	W	L	Pct.	ERA	G	GS	CG	ShO	Sv.	IP	H	R	ER	BB	SO
1996— New York (A.L.)	0	0	...	0.00	2	0	0	0	0	1 2/3	0	0	0	0	1

WORLD SERIES RECORD

NOTES: Member of World Series championship team (1996).

Year Team (League)	W	L	Pct.	ERA	G	GS	CG	ShO	Sv.	IP	H	R	ER	BB	S
1996— New York (A.L.)	1	0	1.000	0.00	4	0	0	0	0	2 2/3	0	0	0	0	0

LOAIZA, ESTEBAN — P — PIRAT[...]

PERSONAL: Born December 31, 1971, in Tijuana, Mexico. ... 6-2/195. ... Throws right, bats right. ... Full name: Esteban Antonio Lo[...] Name pronounced low-WAY-zah..

HIGH SCHOOL: Mar Vista (Imperial Beach, Calif.).
TRANSACTIONS/CAREER NOTES: Signed as non-drafted free agent by Pittsburgh Pirates organization (March 21, 1991). ... Loaned by Pirates organization to Mexico City Red Devils of the Mexican League (May 7, 1993). ... Returned to Pirates organization (May 28, 1993). ... On disabled list (April 7-28 and July 7-14, 1994). ... Loaned to Red Devils of the Mexican League (June 19, 1996). ... Returned to Pirates organization (August 14, 1996).
MISCELLANEOUS: Made an out in only appearance as pinch-hitter (1995). ... Had sacrifice hit in only appearance as pinch-hitter (1996).

Year Team (League)	W	L	Pct.	ERA	G	GS	CG	ShO	Sv.	IP	H	R	ER	BB	SO
1991— GC Pirates (GCL)	5	1	.833	2.26	11	11	1	•1	0	51 2/3	48	17	13	14	41
1992— Augusta (S. Atl.)	10	8	.556	3.89	26	25	3	0	0	143 1/3	134	72	62	60	123
1993— Salem (Carolina)	6	7	.462	3.39	17	17	3	0	0	109	113	53	41	30	61
— Carolina (Southern)	2	1	.667	3.77	7	7	1	0	0	43	39	18	18	12	40
— M.C. Red Devils (Mex.)■	1	1	.500	5.18	4	3	0	0	0	24 1/3	32	18	14	4	15
1994— Carolina (Southern)■	10	5	.667	3.79	24	24	3	0	0	154 1/3	169	69	65	30	115
1995— Pittsburgh (N.L.)	8	9	.471	5.16	32	•31	1	0	0	172 2/3	205	*115	*99	55	85
1996— Calgary (PCL)	3	4	.429	4.02	12	11	1	1	0	69 1/3	61	34	31	25	38
— M.C. Red Devils (Mex.)■	2	0	1.000	2.43	5	5	0	0	0	33 1/3	28	12	9	14	16
— Pittsburgh (N.L.)■	2	3	.400	4.96	10	10	1	1	0	52 2/3	65	32	29	19	32
1997— Pittsburgh (N.L.)	11	11	.500	4.13	33	32	1	0	0	196 1/3	214	99	90	56	122
Major league totals (3 years)	21	23	.477	4.65	75	73	3	1	0	421 2/3	484	246	218	130	239

LOCKHART, KEITH — 2B — BRAVES

PERSONAL: Born November 10, 1964, in Whittier, Calif. ... 5-10/170. ... Bats left, throws right. ... Full name: Keith Virgil Lockhart.
HIGH SCHOOL: Northview (Covina, Calif.).
JUNIOR COLLEGE: Mount San Antonio.
COLLEGE: Oral Roberts.
TRANSACTIONS/CAREER NOTES: Selected by Cincinnati Reds organization in 11th round of free-agent draft (June 2, 1986). ... Contract sold by Reds organization to Tacoma, Oakland Athletics organization (February 4, 1992). ... Granted free agency (October 15, 1992). ... Signed by St. Louis Cardinals organization (December 12, 1992). ... Granted free agency (October 15, 1993). ... Signed by San Diego Padres organization (January 7, 1994). ... Granted free agency (October 15, 1994). ... Signed by Omaha, Kansas City Royals organization (November 14, 1994). ... Traded by Royals with OF Michael Tucker to Atlanta Braves for OF Jermaine Dye and P Jamie Walker (March 27, 1997). ... On disabled list (August 6-22, 1997).
STATISTICAL NOTES: Led Midwest League third basemen with 33 double plays in 1987. ... Led Southern League with 11 sacrifice flies in 1988. ... Led American Association second basemen with 631 total chances in 1989. ... Order of frequency of positions played in 1994 for Las Vegas: OF-SS-2B-3B-P-C. ... Career major league grand slams: 1.

Year Team (League)	Pos.	G	AB	R	H	2B	3B	HR	RBI	Avg.	BB	SO	SB	PO	A	E	Avg.
1986— Billings (Pioneer)	2B-3B	53	202	51	70	11	3	7	31	.347	35	22	4	81	150	17	.931
— Cedar Rap. (Midw.)	2B-3B	13	42	4	8	2	0	0	1	.190	6	6	1	17	15	0	1.000
1987— Cedar Rap. (Midw.)	3B-2B	*140	511	101	160	37	5	23	84	.313	86	70	20	85	292	28	.931
1988— Chattanooga (Sou.)	3B-2B	139	515	74	137	27	3	12	67	.266	61	59	7	102	323	36	.922
1989— Nashville (A.A.)	2B	131	479	77	128	21	6	14	58	.267	61	41	4	*279	*335	17	.973
1990— Nashville (A.A.)	2B-3B-OF	126	431	48	112	25	4	9	63	.260	51	74	8	173	248	9	.979
1991— Nashville (A.A.)	3B-2B-OF	116	411	53	107	25	3	8	36	.260	24	64	3	153	241	13	.968
1992— Tacoma (PCL)■	2B-3B-SS	107	363	44	101	25	3	5	37	.278	29	21	5	199	239	11	.976
1993— Louisville (A.A.)■	3-2-0-1	132	467	66	140	24	3	13	68	.300	60	43	3	157	239	12	.971
1994— San Diego (N.L.)■	3-2-S-0	27	43	4	9	0	0	2	6	.209	4	10	1	10	21	1	.969
— Las Vegas (PCL)	O-I-P-C	89	331	61	106	15	5	7	43	.320	26	37	3	143	113	10	.962
1995— Omaha (A.A.)■	3B	44	148	24	56	7	1	5	19	.378	16	10	1	31	72	8	.928
— Kansas City (A.L.)	2B-3B-DH	94	274	41	88	19	3	6	33	.321	14	21	8	111	178	8	.973
1996— Kansas City (A.L.)	2B-3B-DH	138	433	49	118	33	3	7	55	.273	30	40	11	137	281	13	.970
1997— Atlanta (N.L.)	2B-3B-DH	96	147	25	41	5	3	6	32	.279	14	17	0	24	48	3	.960
American League totals (2 years)		232	707	90	206	52	6	13	88	.291	44	61	19	248	459	21	.971
National League totals (2 years)		123	190	29	50	5	3	8	38	.263	18	27	1	34	69	4	.963
Major league totals (4 years)		355	897	119	256	57	9	21	126	.285	62	88	20	282	528	25	.970

DIVISION SERIES RECORD

Year Team (League)	Pos.	G	AB	R	H	2B	3B	HR	RBI	Avg.	BB	SO	SB	PO	A	E	Avg.
1997— Atlanta (N.L.)	2B	2	6	0	0	0	0	0	0	.000	0	1	0	1	8	1	.900

CHAMPIONSHIP SERIES RECORD

Year Team (League)	Pos.	G	AB	R	H	2B	3B	HR	RBI	Avg.	BB	SO	SB	PO	A	E	Avg.
1997— Atlanta (N.L.)	2B-PH	5	16	4	8	1	1	0	3	.500	1	1	0	14	5	0	1.000

RECORD AS PITCHER

Year Team (League)	W	L	Pct.	ERA	G	GS	CG	ShO	Sv.	IP	H	R	ER	BB	SO
1994— Las Vegas (PCL)	0	0	...	0.00	1	1	0	0	0	1	0	0	0	0	0

LoDUCA, PAUL — C — DODGERS

PERSONAL: Born April 12, 1972, in Brooklyn, N.Y. ... 5-10/185. ... Bats right, throws right. ... Full name: Paul Anthony LoDuca.
HIGH SCHOOL: Apollo (Glendale, Ariz.).
JUNIOR COLLEGE: Glendale (Ariz.) Community College.
COLLEGE: Arizona State.
TRANSACTIONS/CAREER NOTES: Selected by Los Angeles Dodgers organization in 25th round of free-agent draft (June 3, 1993).
STATISTICAL NOTES: Led Florida State League with .400 on-base percentage in 1996. ... Led Florida State League catchers with 17 errors in Led Texas League catchers with .990 fielding percentage, 84 assists and 667 total chances in 1997.

Year Team (League)	Pos.	G	AB	R	H	2B	3B	HR	RBI	Avg.	BB	SO	SB	PO	A	E	Avg.
1993— Vero Beach (FSL)	C	39	134	17	42	6	0	0	13	.313	13	22	0	209	26	2	.992
1994— Bakersfield (Calif.)	1B-C	123	455	65	144	32	1	6	68	.316	52	49	16	657	59	5	.993
1995— San Antonio (Tex.)	C-1B-3B	61	199	27	49	8	0	1	8	.246	26	25	5	353	43	11	.973
1996— Vero Beach (FSL)	C-1B-3B	124	439	54	134	22	0	3	66	.305	70	38	8	747	116	†18	.980
1997— San Antonio (Tex.)	C-1B	105	385	63	126	28	2	7	69	.327	46	27	16	636	†91	7	†.990

LOEWER, CARLTON P PHILLIES

PERSONAL: Born September 24, 1973, in Lafayette, La. ... 6-6/220. ... Throws right, ... Full name: Carlton Edward Loewer.
HIGH SCHOOL: St. Edmund (Eunice, La.).
COLLEGE: Mississippi State.
TRANSACTIONS/CAREER NOTES: Selected by Toronto Blue Jays organization in seventh round of free-agent draft (June 3, 1991); did not sign. ... Selected by Philadelphia Phillies organization in first round (23rd pick overall) of free-agent draft (June 2, 1994).
STATISTICAL NOTES: Led Eastern League with 24 home runs allowed in 1996.

Year Team (League)	W	L	Pct.	ERA	G	GS	CG	ShO	Sv.	IP	H	R	ER	BB	SO
1995— Clearwater (Fla. St.)	7	5	.583	3.30	20	20	1	0	0	114²/₃	124	59	42	36	83
— Reading (Eastern)	4	1	.800	2.16	8	8	0	0	0	50	42	17	12	31	35
1996— Reading (Eastern)	7	10	.412	5.26	27	27	3	1	0	171	*191	115	100	57	119
1997— Scran./W.B. (Int'l)...............	5	13	.278	4.60	29	*29	4	0	0	184	*198	*120	94	50	152

LOFTON, KENNY OF INDIANS

PERSONAL: Born May 31, 1967, in East Chicago, Ind. ... 6-0/190. ... Bats left, throws left. ... Full name: Kenneth Lofton.
HIGH SCHOOL: Washington (East Chicago, Ind.).
COLLEGE: Arizona.
TRANSACTIONS/CAREER NOTES: Selected by Houston Astros organization in 17th round of free-agent draft (June 1, 1988). ... Traded by Astros with IF Dave Rohde to Cleveland Indians for P Willie Blair and C Eddie Taubensee (December 10, 1991). ... On disabled list (July 17-August 1, 1995). ... Traded by Indians with P Alan Embree to Atlanta Braves for OF Marquis Grissom and OF Dave Justice (March 25, 1997). ... On disabled list (June 18-July 5 and July 6-28, 1997). ... Granted free agency (October 28, 1997). ... Signed by Indians (December 8, 1997).
RECORDS: Holds A.L. rookie-season record for most stolen bases—66 (1992). ... Shares A.L. single-season record for fewest errors by outfielder who led league in errors—9 (1993).
HONORS: Won A.L. Gold Glove as outfielder (1993-96).
STATISTICAL NOTES: Tied for Pacific Coast League lead in caught stealing with 23 in 1991. ... Led Pacific Coast League outfielders with 344 total chances in 1991. ... Led N.L. in caught stealing with 20 in 1997. ... Career major league grand slams: 1.

Year Team (League)	Pos.	G	AB	R	H	2B	3B	HR	RBI	Avg.	BB	SO	SB	PO	A	E	Avg.
1988— Auburn (NY-Penn)......	OF	48	187	23	40	6	1	1	14	.214	19	51	26	94	5	4	.961
1989— Auburn (NY-Penn)......	OF	34	110	21	29	3	1	0	8	.264	14	30	26	37	4	8	.837
— Asheville (S. Atl.)........	OF	22	82	14	27	2	0	1	9	.329	12	10	14	38	1	2	.951
1990— Osceola (Fla. St.)........	OF	124	481	98	*159	15	5	2	35	.331	61	77	62	246	13	7	.974
1991— Tucson (PCL)	OF	130	*545	93	*168	19	*17	2	50	.308	52	95	40	*308	*27	9	.974
— Houston (N.L.)........	OF	20	74	9	15	1	0	0	0	.203	5	19	2	41	1	1	.977
1992— Cleveland (A.L.)■.......	OF	148	576	96	164	15	8	5	42	.285	68	54	*66	420	14	8	.982
1993— Cleveland (A.L.).........	OF	148	569	116	185	28	8	1	42	.325	81	83	*70	402	11	•9	.979
1994— Cleveland (A.L.).........	OF	112	459	105	*160	32	9	12	57	.349	52	56	*60	276	•13	2	.993
1995— Cleveland (A.L.).........	OF-DH	118	481	93	149	22	*13	7	53	.310	40	49	*54	248	•11	8	.970
1996— Cleveland (A.L.).........	OF	154	*662	132	210	35	4	14	67	.317	61	82	*75	376	13	10	.975
1997— Atlanta (N.L.)■.........	OF	122	493	90	164	20	6	5	48	.333	64	83	27	290	5	5	.983
American League totals (5 years)		680	2747	542	868	132	42	39	261	.316	302	324	325	1722	62	37	.980
National League totals (2 years)		142	567	99	179	21	6	5	48	.316	69	102	29	331	6	6	.983
Major league totals (7 years)		822	3314	641	1047	153	48	44	309	.316	371	426	354	2053	68	43	.980

DIVISION SERIES RECORD

Year Team (League)	Pos.	G	AB	R	H	2B	3B	HR	RBI	Avg.	BB	SO	SB	PO	A	E	Avg.
1995— Cleveland (A.L.)..........	OF	3	13	1	2	0	0	0	0	.154	1	3	0	9	0	2	.818
1996— Cleveland (A.L.)..........	OF	4	18	3	3	0	0	1	1	.167	2	3	5	10	0	0	1.000
1997— Atlanta (N.L.).............	OF	3	13	2	2	1	0	0	0	.154	1	2	0	6	1	0	1.000
Division series totals (3 years)		10	44	6	7	1	0	1	1	.159	4	8	5	25	1	2	.929

CHAMPIONSHIP SERIES RECORD

Year Team (League)	Pos.	G	AB	R	H	2B	3B	HR	RBI	Avg.	BB	SO	SB	PO	A	E	Avg.
1995— Cleveland (A.L.)..........	OF	6	24	4	11	0	2	0	3	.458	4	6	5	15	0	0	1.000
1997— Atlanta (N.L.).............	OF	6	27	3	5	0	1	0	1	.185	1	7	1	9	1	2	.833
Championship series totals (2 years)		12	51	7	16	0	3	0	4	.314	5	13	6	24	1	2	.926

WORLD SERIES RECORD

RECORDS: Shares record for most stolen bases in one inning—2 (October 21, 1995).

Year Team (League)	Pos.	G	AB	R	H	2B	3B	HR	RBI	Avg.	BB	SO	SB	PO	A	E
1995— Cleveland (A.L.)..........	OF	6	25	6	5	1	0	0	0	.200	3	1	6	12	0	0

ALL-STAR GAME RECORD

RECORDS: Shares single-game record for most stolen bases—2 (July 9, 1996).

Year	League	Pos.	AB	R	H	2B	3B	HR	RBI	Avg.	BB	SO	SB	PO	A	E	Avg.
								BATTING							FIELDING		
1994— American		OF	2	0	1	0	0	0	2	.500	0	1	1	1	0	0	1.000
1995— American		OF	3	0	0	0	0	0	0	.000	0	1	0	0	0	0	...
1996— American		OF	3	0	2	0	0	0	0	.667	0	0	2	0	0	0	...
1997— National								Selected, did not play—injured.									
All-Star Game totals (3 years)			8	0	3	0	0	0	2	.375	0	2	3	1	0	0	1.000

LOISELLE, RICH   P   PIRATES

PERSONAL: Born January 12, 1972, in Neenah, Wis. ... 6-5/240. ... Throws right, bats right. ... Full name: Richard Frank Loiselle.
HIGH SCHOOL: Lawton (Okla.).
JUNIOR COLLEGE: Odessa (Texas) College.
TRANSACTIONS/CAREER NOTES: Selected by San Diego Padres organization in 38th round of free-agent draft (June 3, 1991). ... Traded by Padres organization with P Jeff Tabaka to Houston Astros organization for OF Phil Plantier (July 19, 1995). ... On Tucson disabled list (August 2, 1995-remainder of season). ... Traded by Astros to Pittsburgh Pirates for P Danny Darwin (July 23, 1996).

Year	Team (League)	W	L	Pct.	ERA	G	GS	CG	ShO	Sv.	IP	H	R	ER	BB	SO
1991— Ariz. Padres (Ariz.)		2	3	.400	3.52	12	12	0	0	0	61 1/3	72	40	24	26	47
1992— Charleston (A.A.)		4	8	.333	3.71	19	19	2	2	0	97	93	51	40	42	64
1993— Waterloo (Midw.)		1	5	.167	3.94	14	10	1	1	0	59 1/3	55	28	26	29	47
— Rancho Cucamonga (Cal.)		5	8	.385	5.77	14	14	1	0	0	82 2/3	109	64	53	34	53
1994— Rancho Cucamonga (Cal.)		9	10	.474	3.96	27	27	0	0	0	156 2/3	160	83	69	76	120
1995— Memphis (Southern)		6	3	.667	3.55	13	13	1	0	0	78 2/3	82	46	31	33	48
— Las Vegas (PCL)		2	2	.500	7.24	8	7	1	1	0	27 1/3	36	27	22	9	16
— Tucson (PCL)■		0	0	...	2.61	2	1	0	0	0	10 1/3	8	4	3	4	4
1996— Jackson (Texas)		7	4	.636	3.47	16	16	2	0	0	98 2/3	107	46	38	27	65
— Tucson (PCL)		2	2	.500	2.43	5	5	1	1	0	33 1/3	28	20	9	11	31
— Calgary (PCL)■		2	2	.500	4.09	8	8	0	0	0	50 2/3	64	28	23	16	41
— Pittsburgh (N.L.)		1	0	1.000	3.05	5	3	0	0	0	20 2/3	22	8	7	8	9
1997— Pittsburgh (N.L.)		1	5	.167	3.10	72	0	0	0	29	72 2/3	76	29	25	24	66
Major league totals (2 years)		2	5	.286	3.09	77	3	0	0	29	93 1/3	98	37	32	32	75

LOMBARD, GEORGE   OF   BRAVES

PERSONAL: Born September 14, 1975, in Atlanta. ... 6-0/210. ... Throws right, bats left. ... Full name: George Paul Lombard.
HIGH SCHOOL: Lovett (Atlanta).
TRANSACTIONS/CAREER NOTES: Selected by Atlanta Braves organization in second round of free-agent draft (June 2, 1994). ... On disabled list (August 16-September 25, 1996).
STATISTICAL NOTES: Tied for South Atlantic League lead in caught stealing with 13 in 1995. ... Led Carolina League outfielders with 284 total chances in 1997.

Year	Team (League)	Pos.	G	AB	R	H	2B	3B	HR	RBI	Avg.	BB	SO	SB	PO	A	E	Avg.
								BATTING								FIELDING		
1994— GC Braves (GCL)		OF	40	129	10	18	2	0	0	5	.140	18	47	10	33	1	2	.944
1995— Eugene (Northwest)		OF	68	262	38	66	5	3	5	19	.252	23	91	35	71	5	3	.962
— Macon (S. Atl.)		OF	49	180	32	37	6	1	3	16	.206	27	44	16	44	2	2	.958
1996— Macon (S. Atl.)		OF	116	444	76	109	16	8	15	51	.245	36	122	24	229	2	7	.971
1997— Durham (Carolina)		OF	131	462	65	122	25	7	14	72	.264	66	145	35	*270	5	9	.968

LONG, JOEY   P

PERSONAL: Born July 15, 1970, in Sidney, Ohio. ... 6-2/220. ... Throws left, bats right.
HIGH SCHOOL: Graham (St. Paris, Ohio).
COLLEGE: Kent.
TRANSACTIONS/CAREER NOTES: Selected by San Diego Padres organization in fifth round of free-agent draft (June 3, 1991). ... On Chandler disabled list (June 24, 1992-remainder of season). ... On Las Vegas disabled list (June 29-September 1, 1996). ... Granted free agency (October 15, 1997).

Year	Team (League)	W	L	Pct.	ERA	G	GS	CG	ShO	Sv.	IP	H	R	ER	BB	SO
1991— Spokane (N'west)		1	*9	.100	6.99	13	11	0	0	0	56 2/3	78	57	44	39	40
1992—								Did not play.								
1993— Waterloo (Midw.)		4	3	.571	4.86	33	7	0	0	0	96 1/3	96	56	52	36	90
1994— Rancho Cucamonga (Cal.)		2	4	.333	4.67	46	0	0	0	3	52	69	36	27	22	52
1995— Las Vegas (PCL)		1	3	.250	4.60	25	0	0	0	0	31 1/3	38	22	16	16	13
— Memphis (Southern)		0	2	.000	3.32	25	0	0	0	0	21 2/3	28	15	8	10	18
1996— Memphis (Southern)		2	0	1.000	2.00	10	0	0	0	0	18	16	4	4	11	14
— Las Vegas (PCL)		3	3	.500	4.24	32	0	0	0	1	34	39	21	16	23	23
1997— Las Vegas (PCL)		0	0	...	4.82	16	0	0	0	0	18 2/3	17	10	10	12	13
— San Diego (N.L.)		0	0	...	8.18	10	0	0	0	0	11	17	11	10	8	8
Major league totals (1 year)		0	0	...	8.18	10	0	0	0	0	11	17	11	10	8	8

LONG, RYAN   OF   ROYALS

ʀSONAL: Born February 3, 1973, in Houston. ... 6-2/215. ... Bats right, throws right. ... Full name: Ryan Marcus Long.
ʜ SCHOOL: Dobie (Houston).
ᴺSACTIONS/CAREER NOTES: Selected by Kansas City Royals organization in second round of free-agent draft (June 3, 1991); pick ʳᵈ as part of compensation for New York Yankees signing Type A free agent P Steve Farr.
ᴛICAL NOTES: Led Northwest League third basemen with 24 errors in 1992.

Year Team (League)	Pos.	G	AB	R	H	2B	3B	HR	RBI	Avg.	BB	SO	SB	PO	A	E	Avg.
1991— GC Royals (GCL)	3B	48	177	17	55	2	2	0	20	.311	10	20	6	32	71	19	.844
1992— Eugene (Northwest) ...	3-S-O-1	54	183	19	42	5	2	0	18	.230	3	33	7	32	77	†25	.813
1993— Rockford (Midwest) ...	3B-SS-2B	107	396	46	115	27	6	8	68	.290	16	76	16	64	192	34	.883
1994— Wilmington (Caro.)......	3B	123	494	69	130	25	5	11	68	.263	16	72	7	75	212	33	.897
1995— Wichita (Texas)	3B-OF	102	342	36	79	26	4	5	34	.231	10	48	4	83	135	17	.928
1996— Wichita (Texas)	OF	122	442	64	125	29	1	20	78	.283	17	71	6	150	6	5	.969
1997— Omaha (A.A.).............	OF	113	411	48	109	26	0	19	56	.265	18	98	2	186	9	9	.956
— Kansas City (A.L.)	OF	6	9	2	2	0	0	0	2	.222	0	3	0	6	0	0	1.000
Major league totals (1 year)		6	9	2	2	0	0	0	2	.222	0	3	0	6	0	0	1.000

LONG, TERRENCE — OF — METS

PERSONAL: Born February 29, 1976, in Montgomery, Ala. ... 6-1/180. ... Bats left, throws left. ... Full name: Terrence Dean Long.
HIGH SCHOOL: Stanhope Elmore (Millbrook, Ala.).
TRANSACTIONS/CAREER NOTES: Selected by New York Mets organization in first round (20th pick overall) of free-agent draft (June 2, 1994); pick received as compensation for Baltimore Orioles signing Type A free-agent P Sid Fernandez. ... On disabled list (May 15-27, 1996).

Year Team (League)	Pos.	G	AB	R	H	2B	3B	HR	RBI	Avg.	BB	SO	SB	PO	A	E	Avg.
1994— Kingsport (Appal.)......	OF-1B	60	215	39	50	9	2	12	39	.233	32	52	9	237	5	5	.980
1995— Capital City (SAL).......	OF	55	178	27	35	1	2	2	13	.197	28	43	8	69	5	5	.937
— Pittsfield (NYP)	OF	51	187	24	48	9	4	4	31	.257	18	36	11	111	3	1	*.991
1996— Columbia (S. Atl.)......	OF	123	473	66	136	26	9	12	78	.288	36	120	32	246	8	5	.981
1997— St. Lucie (Fla. St.)	OF	126	470	52	118	29	7	8	61	.251	40	102	24	235	7	7	.972

LOOPER, BRADEN — P — CARDINALS

PERSONAL: Born October 28, 1974, in Weatherford, Okla. ... 6-4/220. ... Throws right, bats right. ... Full name: Braden LaVern Looper. ... Name pronounced BRAY-dun.
HIGH SCHOOL: Mangum (Okla.).
COLLEGE: Wichita State.
TRANSACTIONS/CAREER NOTES: Selected by St. Louis Cardinals organization in first round (third pick overall) of free-agent draft (June 2, 1996).

Year Team (League)	W	L	Pct.	ERA	G	GS	CG	ShO	Sv.	IP	H	R	ER	BB	SO
1996—							Did not play.								
1997— Prince William (Caro.)........	3	6	.333	4.48	12	12	0	0	0	64 1/3	71	38	32	25	58
— Arkansas (Texas)................	1	4	.200	5.91	19	0	0	0	5	21 1/3	24	14	14	7	20

LOPEZ, ALBIE — P — DEVIL RAYS

PERSONAL: Born August 18, 1971, in Mesa, Ariz. ... 6-2/235. ... Throws right, bats right. ... Full name: Albert Anthony Lopez.
HIGH SCHOOL: Westwood (Mesa, Ariz.).
JUNIOR COLLEGE: Mesa (Ariz.) Community College.
TRANSACTIONS/CAREER NOTES: Selected by San Francisco Giants organization in 46th round of free-agent draft (June 5, 1989); did not sign. ... Selected by Seattle Mariners organization in 19th round of free-agent draft (June 4, 1990); did not sign. ... Selected by Cleveland Indians organization in 20th round of free-agent draft (June 3, 1991). ... On Cleveland disabled list (July 2-28 and August 13-September 1, 1997). ... Selected by Tampa Bay Devil Rays in second round (48th pick overall) of expansion draft (November 18, 1997).
STATISTICAL NOTES: Led American Association with 10 hit batsmen and tied for lead with three balks in 1996.

Year Team (League)	W	L	Pct.	ERA	G	GS	CG	ShO	Sv.	IP	H	R	ER	BB	SO
1991— Burlington (Appalachian)....	4	5	.444	3.44	13	13	0	0	0	73 1/3	61	33	28	23	81
1992— Columbus (S. Atl.)............	7	2	.778	2.88	16	16	1	0	0	97	80	41	31	33	117
— Kinston (Carolina)	5	2	.714	3.52	10	10	1	1	0	64	56	28	25	26	44
1993— Cant./Akr. (Eastern)	9	4	.692	3.11	16	16	2	0	0	110	79	44	38	47	80
— Cleveland (A.L.)	3	1	.750	5.98	9	9	0	0	0	49 2/3	49	34	33	32	25
— Charlotte (Int'l)	1	0	1.000	2.25	3	2	0	0	0	12	8	3	3	2	7
1994— Charlotte (Int'l)	13	3	.813	3.94	22	22	3	0	0	144	136	68	63	42	105
— Cleveland (A.L.)	1	2	.333	4.24	4	4	1	0	0	17	20	11	8	6	18
1995— Buffalo (A.A.)...................	5	10	.333	4.44	18	18	1	1	0	101 1/3	101	57	50	51	82
— Cleveland (A.L.)	0	0	. . .	3.13	6	2	0	0	0	23	17	8	8	7	22
1996— Buffalo (A.A.)...................	10	2	.833	3.87	17	17	2	0	0	104 2/3	90	54	45	40	89
— Cleveland (A.L.)	5	4	.556	6.39	13	10	0	0	0	62	80	47	44	22	45
1997— Cleveland (A.L.)	3	7	.300	6.93	37	6	0	0	0	76 2/3	101	61	59	40	63
— Buffalo (A.A.)...................	1	0	1.000	0.00	7	0	0	0	1	11 1/3	6	0	0	2	13
— Akron (Eastern)................	0	0	. . .	0.00	1	0	0	0	0	1	2	0	0	0	2
Major league totals (5 years)......	12	14	.462	5.99	69	31	1	1	0	228 1/3	267	161	152	107	173

LOPEZ, JAVY — C — BRAVES

PERSONAL: Born November 5, 1970, in Ponce, Puerto Rico. ... 6-3/200. ... Bats right, throws right. ... Full name: Javier Torres Lopez.
HIGH SCHOOL: Academia Cristo Rey (Urb la Ramble Ponce, Puerto Rico).
TRANSACTIONS/CAREER NOTES: Signed as non-drafted free agent by Atlanta Braves organization (November 6, 1987). ... On Greenville disabled list (July 18-August 2, 1992). ... On disabled list (July 6-22, 1997).
HONORS: Named Southern League Most Valuable Player (1992).
STATISTICAL NOTES: Led Midwest League catchers with 11 double plays and 31 passed balls in 1990. ... Led Carolina League catchers with 701 total chances and 14 double plays in 1991. ... Led Southern League catchers with 763 total chances and 19 passed balls in 1992. ... International League catchers with 15 passed balls in 1993. ... Tied for N.L. lead with 10 passed balls in 1994. ... Career major league grand slams: 1.

Year Team (League)	Pos.	G	AB	R	H	2B	3B	HR	RBI	Avg.	BB	SO	SB	PO	A	E	Avg.
									BATTING						FIELDING		
1988—GC Braves (GCL)	C	31	94	8	18	4	0	1	9	.191	3	19	1	131	30	7	.958
1989—Pulaski (Appalachian)	C	51	153	27	40	8	1	3	27	.261	5	35	3	264	26	5	.983
1990—Burlington (Midw.)	C	116	422	48	112	17	3	11	55	.265	14	84	0	724	79	11	.986
1991—Durham (Carolina)	C	113	384	43	94	14	2	11	51	.245	25	88	10	*610	85	6	.991
1992—Greenville (Southern)	C	115	442	63	142	28	3	16	60	.321	24	47	7	*680	75	8	.990
—Atlanta (N.L.)	C	9	16	3	6	2	0	0	2	.375	0	1	0	28	2	0	1.000
1993—Richmond (Int'l)	C	100	380	56	116	23	2	17	74	.305	12	53	1	718	70	10	.987
—Atlanta (N.L.)	C	8	16	1	6	1	1	1	2	.375	0	2	0	37	2	1	.975
1994—Atlanta (N.L.)	C	80	277	27	68	9	0	13	35	.245	17	61	0	559	35	3	.995
1995—Atlanta (N.L.)	C	100	333	37	105	11	4	14	51	.315	14	57	0	625	50	8	.988
1996—Atlanta (N.L.)	C	138	489	56	138	19	1	23	69	.282	28	84	1	993	*81	6	.994
1997—Atlanta (N.L.)	C	123	414	52	122	28	1	23	68	.295	40	82	1	792	56	6	.993
Major league totals (6 years)		458	1545	176	445	70	7	74	227	.288	99	287	2	3034	226	24	.993

DIVISION SERIES RECORD

Year Team (League)	Pos.	G	AB	R	H	2B	3B	HR	RBI	Avg.	BB	SO	SB	PO	A	E	Avg.
1995—Atlanta (N.L.)	C	3	9	0	4	0	0	0	3	.444	0	3	0	22	3	0	1.000
1996—Atlanta (N.L.)	C	2	7	1	2	0	0	1	1	.286	1		1	21	1	1	.957
1997—Atlanta (N.L.)	C	2	7	3	2	2	0	0	1	.286	2	1	0	18	0	0	1.000
Division series totals (3 years)		7	23	4	8	2	0	1	5	.348	3	4	1	61	4	1	.985

CHAMPIONSHIP SERIES RECORD

RECORDS: Shares N.L. single-game record for most runs—4 (October 14, 1996). ... Holds N.L. single-series record for most runs—8 (1996). ... Shares N.L. single-series record for most consecutive hits—5 (1996). ... Holds single-series record for most doubles—5 (1996). ... Shares single-series record for most total bases—24 (1996). ... Holds single-series record for most long hits—7 (1996).

NOTES: Named N.L. Championship Series Most Valuable Player (1996).

Year Team (League)	Pos.	G	AB	R	H	2B	3B	HR	RBI	Avg.	BB	SO	SB	PO	A	E	Avg.
1992—Atlanta (N.L.)	C	1	1	0	0	0	0	0	0	.000	0	0	0	2	0	0	1.000
1995—Atlanta (N.L.)	C	3	14	2	5	1	0	1	3	.357	0	1	0	28	2	0	1.000
1996—Atlanta (N.L.)	C	7	24	8	13	5	0	2	6	.542	4	1	1	48	3	0	1.000
1997—Atlanta (N.L.)	C-PH	5	17	0	1	1	0	0	2	.059	1	7	0	40	3	0	1.000
Championship series totals (4 years)		16	56	10	19	7	0	3	11	.339	5	9	1	118	8	0	1.000

WORLD SERIES RECORD

NOTES: Member of World Series championship team (1995).

Year Team (League)	Pos.	G	AB	R	H	2B	3B	HR	RBI	Avg.	BB	SO	SB	PO	A	E	Avg.
1992—Atlanta (N.L.)								Did not play.									
1995—Atlanta (N.L.)	C-PH	6	17	1	3	2	0	1	3	.176	1	1	0	32	4	0	1.000
1996—Atlanta (N.L.)	C	6	21	3	4	0	0	0	1	.190	3	4	0	41	4	0	1.000
World Series totals (2 years)		12	38	4	7	2	0	1	4	.184	4	5	0	73	8	0	1.000

ALL-STAR GAME RECORD

RECORDS: Hit home run in first at-bat (July 8, 1997).

Year League	Pos.	AB	R	H	2B	3B	HR	RBI	Avg.	BB	SO	SB	PO	A	E	Avg.
1997—National	C	1	1	1	0	0	1	1	1.000	0	0	0	4	1	0	1.000

LOPEZ, LUIS   SS   METS

PERSONAL: Born September 4, 1970, in Cidra, Puerto Rico. ... 5-11/175. ... Bats both, throws right. ... Full name: Luis Santos Lopez.

HIGH SCHOOL: San Jose (Caguas, Puerto Rico).

TRANSACTIONS/CAREER NOTES: Signed as non-drafted free agent by San Diego Padres organization (September 9, 1987). ... On Las Vegas disabled list (July 3-14, 1994). ... Granted free agency (October 15, 1994). ... Re-signed by Padres (April 20, 1995). ... On disabled list (April 24, 1995-entire season). ... On San Diego disabled list (March 29-April 18 and July 31-September 1, 1996); included rehabilitation assignments to Las Vegas (March 30-April 18 and August 17-September 1). ... Traded by Padres to Houston Astros for P Sean Runyan (March 15, 1997). ... Traded by Astros to New York Mets for IF Tim Bogar (March 31, 1997).

STATISTICAL NOTES: Led South Atlantic League shortstops with 703 total chances and 78 double plays in 1989. ... Led Pacific Coast League shortstops with 30 errors in 1992. ... Tied for Pacific Coast League lead with 13 sacrifice hits in 1993. ... Career major league grand slams: 1.

Year Team (League)	Pos.	G	AB	R	H	2B	3B	HR	RBI	Avg.	BB	SO	SB	PO	A	E	Avg.
1988—Spokane (N'west)	SS	70	312	50	95	13	1	0	35	.304	18	59	14	*118	217	*47	.877
1989—Char., S.C. (S. Atl.)	SS	127	460	50	102	15	1	1	29	.222	17	85	12	*256	*373	*74	.895
1990—Riverside (Calif.)	SS	14	46	5	17	3	1	1	4	.370	3	3	4	18	38	6	.903
1991—Wichita (Texas)	2B-SS	125	452	43	121	17	1	1	41	.268	18	70	6	274	339	26	.959
1992—Las Vegas (PCL)	SS-OF	120	395	44	92	8	1	3	31	.233	19	65	6	200	358	†30	.949
1993—Las Vegas (PCL)	SS-2B	131	491	52	150	36	6	6	58	.305	27	62	8	230	380	29	.955
—San Diego (N.L.)	2B	17	43	1	5	1	0	0	1	.116	0	8	0	23	34	1	.983
1994—Las Vegas (PCL)	2B	12	49	2	10	2	2	0	6	.204	1	5	0	28	43	2	.973
—San Diego (N.L.)	SS-2B-3B	77	235	29	65	16	1	2	20	.277	15	39	3	101	174	14	.952
1995—								Did not play.									
1996—Las Vegas (PCL)	2B-SS	18	68	4	14	3	0	1	12	.206	2	15	0	39	43	2	.976
—San Diego (N.L.)	SS-2B-3B	63	139	10	25	3	0	2	11	.180	9	35	0	57	100	4	.975
1997—Norfolk (Int'l)■	SS-2B	48	203	32	67	12	1	4	19	.330	9	29	2	79	123	14	.935
—New York (N.L.)	SS-2B-3B	78	178	19	48	12	1	1	19	.270	12	42	2	79	156	9	.963
Major league totals (4 years)		235	595	59	143	32	2	5	51	.240	36	124	5	260	464	28	.963

DIVISION SERIES RECORD

				BATTING												FIELDING		
Year	Team (League)	Pos.	G	AB	R	H	2B	3B	HR	RBI	Avg.	BB	SO	SB	PO	A	E	Avg.
1996— San Diego (N.L.)		PR	1	0	0	0	0	0	0	0	...	0	0	0	0	0	0	...

LOPEZ, MENDY — SS — ROYALS

PERSONAL: Born October 15, 1974, in Santo Domingo, Dominican Republic. ... 6-2/165. ... Bats right, throws right.
HIGH SCHOOL: Liceo Los Trinitanos (Santo Domingo, Dominican Republic).
TRANSACTIONS/CAREER NOTES: Signed as non-drafted free agent by Kansas City Royals organization (February 26, 1992).
STATISTICAL NOTES: Led Gulf Coast League shortstops with .971 fielding percentage, 80 putouts, 154 assists, 241 total chances and 39 double plays in 1994. ... Tied for Texas League lead with 28 double plays by third baseman in 1996.

				BATTING												FIELDING		
Year	Team (League)	Pos.	G	AB	R	H	2B	3B	HR	RBI	Avg.	BB	SO	SB	PO	A	E	Avg.
1992— Dom. Royals (DSL)		SS	49	145	22	40	1	0	1	23	.276	22	15	7	81	155	26	.901
1993— Dom. Royals (DSL)		IF	28	98	15	27	5	2	0	20	.276	11	5	2	52	75	15	.894
1994— GC Royals (GCL)		SS-3B-2B	59	*235	56	85	*19	3	5	*50	.362	22	27	10	†84	†195	12	†.959
1995— Wilmington (Caro.)....		3B-SS	130	428	42	116	29	3	2	36	.271	28	73	18	84	335	25	.944
1996— Wichita (Texas)		3B-SS	93	327	47	92	20	5	6	32	.281	26	67	14	80	265	24	.935
1997— Omaha (A.A.)..............		3B	17	52	6	12	2	0	1	6	.231	8	21	0	15	38	6	.898
— Wichita (Texas)		SS	101	357	56	83	16	3	5	42	.232	36	70	7	193	296	26	.961

LORETTA, MARK — IF — BREWERS

PERSONAL: Born August 14, 1971, in Santa Monica, Calif. ... 6-0/175. ... Bats right, throws right. ... Full name: Mark David Loretta.
HIGH SCHOOL: St. Francis (La Canada, Calif.).
COLLEGE: Northwestern.
TRANSACTIONS/CAREER NOTES: Selected by Milwaukee Brewers organization in seventh round of free-agent draft (June 3, 1993). ... On New Orleans suspended list (May 17-20, 1996).
STATISTICAL NOTES: Led American Association shortstops with 200 putouts and 591 total chances in 1995.

				BATTING												FIELDING		
Year	Team (League)	Pos.	G	AB	R	H	2B	3B	HR	RBI	Avg.	BB	SO	SB	PO	A	E	Avg.
1993— Helena (Pioneer)		SS	6	28	5	9	1	0	1	8	.321	1	4	0	11	18	0	1.000
— Stockton (California) ..		SS-3B	53	201	36	73	4	1	4	31	.363	22	17	8	75	173	15	.943
1994— El Paso (Texas)...........		SS-P	77	302	50	95	13	6	0	38	.315	27	33	8	125	271	11	.973
— New Orleans (A.A.)....		SS-2B	43	138	16	29	7	0	1	14	.210	12	13	2	68	121	11	.945
1995— New Orleans (A.A.)....		SS-3B-2B	127	479	48	137	22	5	7	79	.286	34	47	8	†204	376	25	.959
— Milwaukee (A.L.)		SS-2B-DH	19	50	13	13	3	0	1	3	.260	4	7	1	18	42	1	.984
1996— New Orleans (A.A.)....		SS	19	71	10	18	5	1	0	11	.254	9	8	1	31	60	5	.948
— Milwaukee (A.L.)		2B-3B-SS	73	154	20	43	3	0	1	13	.279	14	15	2	63	116	2	.989
1997— Milwaukee (A.L.)		2-S-1-3-DH	132	418	56	120	17	5	5	47	.287	47	60	5	334	277	15	.976
Major league totals (3 years)			224	622	89	176	23	5	7	63	.283	65	82	8	415	435	18	.979

RECORD AS PITCHER

Year	Team (League)	W	L	Pct.	ERA	G	GS	CG	ShO	Sv.	IP	H	R	ER	BB	SO
1994— El Paso (Texas).................		0	0	...	...	1	0	0	0	0	0	0	1	1	1	0

LORRAINE, ANDREW — P — ATHLETICS

PERSONAL: Born August 11, 1972, in Los Angeles. ... 6-3/195. ... Throws left, bats left. ... Full name: Andrew Jason Lorraine.
HIGH SCHOOL: William S. Hart (Newhall, Calif.).
COLLEGE: Stanford.
TRANSACTIONS/CAREER NOTES: Selected by New York Mets organization in 38th round of free-agent draft (June 4, 1990); did not sign. ... Selected by California Angels organization in fourth round of free-agent draft (June 3, 1993). ... Traded by Angels with OF McKay Christensen, P Bill Simas and P John Snyder to Chicago White Sox for P Jim Abbott and P Tim Fortugno (July 27, 1995). ... Traded by White Sox with OF Charles Poe to Oakland Athletics for OF/DH Danny Tartabull (January 22, 1996).

Year	Team (League)	W	L	Pct.	ERA	G	GS	CG	ShO	Sv.	IP	H	R	ER	BB	SO
1993— Boise (Northwest)		4	1	.800	1.29	6	6	3	1	0	42	33	6	6	6	39
1994— Vancouver (PCL)		12	4	.750	3.42	22	22	•4	•2	0	142	156	63	54	34	90
— California (A.L.)		0	2	.000	10.61	4	3	0	0	0	18 2/3	30	23	22	11	10
1995— Vancouver (PCL)		6	6	.500	3.96	18	18	4	1	0	97 2/3	105	49	43	30	51
— Nashville (A.A.)■		4	1	.800	6.00	7	7	0	0	0	39	51	29	26	12	26
— Chicago (A.L.)		0	0	...	3.38	5	0	0	0	0	8	3	3	3	2	5
1996— Edmonton (PCL)■		8	10	.444	5.68	30	25	0	0	0	141	181	95	89	46	73
1997— Edmonton (PCL)		8	6	.571	4.74	23	20	2	2	0	117 2/3	143	72	62	34	75
— Oakland (A.L.)		3	1	.750	6.37	12	6	0	0	0	29 2/3	45	22	21	15	18
Major league totals (3 years)......		3	3	.500	7.35	21	9	0	0	0	56 1/3	78	48	46	28	33

LOVULLO, TOREY — IF — INDIANS

PERSONAL: Born July 25, 1965, in Santa Monica, Calif. ... 6-0/185. ... Bats both, throws right. ... Full name: Salvatore Anthony Lovullo Name pronounced leh-VOO-lo.
HIGH SCHOOL: Montclair Prep (Van Nuys, Calif.).
COLLEGE: UCLA (degree in psychology).
TRANSACTIONS/CAREER NOTES: Selected by Kansas City Royals organization in 27th round of free-agent draft (June 2, 1986); did n[e]... ... Selected by Detroit Tigers organization in fifth round of free-agent draft (June 2, 1987). ... Traded by Tigers to New York Yanke[e] Mark Leiter (March 19, 1991). ... Granted free agency (October 16, 1992). ... Signed by California Angels (November 19, 1992). ... on waivers by Seattle Mariners (April 1, 1994). ... Granted free agency (October 15, 1994). ... Signed by Cleveland Indians (Nove[...]

L

1994). ... Granted free agency (October 16, 1995). ... Signed by Oakland Athletics organization (December 5, 1995). ... Granted free agency (October 15, 1996). ... Signed by Ottawa, Expos organization (December 17, 1996). ... Released by Expos (May 20, 1997). ... Signed by Buffalo, Indians organization (May 20, 1997). ... Granted free agency (October 15, 1997). ... Re-signed by Indians organization (December 19, 1997).

HONORS: Named second baseman on THE SPORTING NEWS college All-America team (1987).
STATISTICAL NOTES: Tied for International League lead with 10 intentional bases on balls received in 1989. ... Led International League with .509 slugging percentage in 1992.

Year Team (League)	Pos.	G	AB	R	H	2B	3B	HR	RBI	Avg.	BB	SO	SB	PO	A	E	Avg.
1987—Fayetteville (SAL)	3B-2B	55	191	34	49	13	0	8	32	.257	37	30	6	41	133	22	.888
—Lakeland (Fla. St.)	3B	18	60	11	16	3	0	1	16	.267	10	8	0	11	30	2	.953
1988—Glens Falls (Eastern)	3B-2B	78	270	37	74	17	1	9	50	.274	36	44	2	63	173	21	.918
—Toledo (Int'l)	2B-3B-SS	57	177	18	41	8	1	5	20	.232	9	24	2	120	149	5	.982
—Detroit (A.L.)	2B-3B	12	21	2	8	1	1	1	2	.381	1	2	0	12	19	0	1.000
1989—Toledo (Int'l)	1-3-2-S	112	409	48	94	23	2	10	52	.230	44	57	2	217	257	20	.960
—Detroit (A.L.)	1B-2B	29	87	8	10	2	0	1	4	.115	14	20	1	134	24	1	.994
1990—Toledo (Int'l)	2B-3B-1B	141	486	71	131	*38	1	14	58	.270	61	74	4	280	352	18	.972
1991—New York (A.L.)■	3B	22	51	0	9	2	0	0	2	.176	5	7	0	14	33	3	.940
—Columbus (Int'l)	3-1-2-O	106	395	74	107	24	5	10	75	.271	59	54	4	277	164	16	.965
1992—Columbus (Int'l)	2-3-1-O	131	468	69	138	*33	5	19	89	.295	64	65	9	187	206	8	.980
1993—California (A.L.)■	2-3-S-O-DH-1	116	367	42	92	20	0	6	30	.251	36	49	7	208	249	11	.976
1994—Seattle (A.L.)■	2B-3B-DH	36	72	9	16	5	0	2	7	.222	9	13	1	19	49	1	.986
—Calgary (PCL)	SS-2B-3B	54	211	43	62	18	1	11	47	.294	34	28	2	85	165	9	.965
1995—Buffalo (A.A.)■	2-3-1-S	132	474	84	121	20	5	16	61	.255	70	62	3	235	303	18	.968
1996—Oakland (A.L.)■	1-3-DH-2-S-O	65	82	15	18	4	0	3	9	.220	11	17	1	134	21	1	.994
—Edmonton (PCL)	1-2-3-P-O-S	26	93	18	26	4	0	4	19	.280	18	12	0	112	39	3	.981
1997—Ottawa (Int'l)■	2B-3B	28	64	6	9	3	0	0	6	.141	6	13	0	31	42	0	1.000
—Buffalo (A.A.)■	3-2-1-S	97	321	40	73	18	0	12	40	.227	51	64	0	115	203	12	.964
Major league totals (6 years)		280	680	76	153	34	1	13	54	.225	76	108	10	521	395	17	.982

RECORD AS PITCHER

Year Team (League)	W	L	Pct.	ERA	G	GS	CG	ShO	Sv.	IP	H	R	ER	BB	SO
1996—Edmonton (PCL)	0	0	...	4.50	26	0	0	0	0	4	3	2	2	3	0

L

LOWE, DEREK   P   RED SOX

PERSONAL: Born June 1, 1973, in Dearborn, Mich. ... 6-6/170. ... Throws right, bats right. ... Full name: Derek Christopher Lowe.
HIGH SCHOOL: Edsel Ford (Dearborn, Mich.).
TRANSACTIONS/CAREER NOTES: Selected by Seattle Mariners organization in eighth round of free-agent draft (June 3, 1991). ... Traded by Mariners with C Jason Varitek to Boston Red Sox for P Heathcliff Slocumb (July 31, 1997).
STATISTICAL NOTES: Led Southern League with seven balks in 1994.

Year Team (League)	W	L	Pct.	ERA	G	GS	CG	ShO	Sv.	IP	H	R	ER	BB	SO
1991—Ariz. Mariners (Ariz.)	5	3	.625	2.41	12	12	0	0	0	71	58	26	19	21	60
1992—Bellingham (N'west)	7	3	.700	2.42	14	13	2	•1	0	85 2/3	69	34	23	22	66
1993—Riverside (California)	12	9	.571	5.26	27	26	3	2	0	154	189	104	90	60	80
1994—Jacksonville (Southern)	7	10	.412	4.94	26	26	2	0	0	151 1/3	177	92	83	50	75
1995—Port City (Southern)	1	6	.143	6.08	10	10	1	0	0	53 1/3	70	41	36	22	30
—Ariz. Mariners (Ariz.)	1	0	1.000	0.93	2	2	0	0	0	9 2/3	5	1	1	2	11
1996—Port City (Southern)	5	3	.625	3.05	10	10	0	0	0	65	56	27	22	17	33
—Tacoma (PCL)	6	9	.400	4.54	17	16	1	1	0	105	118	64	53	37	54
1997—Tacoma (PCL)	3	4	.429	3.45	10	9	1	0	0	57 1/3	53	26	22	20	49
—Seattle (A.L.)	2	4	.333	6.96	12	9	0	0	0	53	59	43	41	20	39
—Pawtucket (Int'l)■	4	0	1.000	2.37	6	5	0	0	0	30 1/3	23	8	8	11	21
—Boston (A.L.)	0	2	.000	3.38	8	0	0	0	0	16	15	6	6	3	13
Major league totals (1 year)	2	6	.250	6.13	20	9	0	0	0	69	74	49	47	23	52

LOWE, SEAN   P   CARDINALS

PERSONAL: Born March 29, 1971, in Dallas. ... 6-2/205. ... Throws right, bats right. ... Full name: Jonathon Sean Lowe.
HIGH SCHOOL: Mesquite (Texas).
JUNIOR COLLEGE: McLennan Community College (Texas).
COLLEGE: Arizona State.
TRANSACTIONS/CAREER NOTES: Selected by Cincinnati Reds organization in 43rd round of free-agent draft (June 5, 1989); did not sign. ... Selected by Oakland Athletics organization in 43rd round of free-agent draft (June 4, 1990); did not sign. ... Selected by St. Louis Cardinals organization in first round (15th pick overall) of free-agent draft (June 1, 1992). ... On St. Petersburg disabled list (July 19-August 8, 1994). ... On Arkansas disabled list (May 28-June 4, 1996). ... On Louisville disabled list (April 9-18, 1997).
STATISTICAL NOTES: Tied for American Association lead with 10 hit batsmen in 1997.

Year Team (League)	W	L	Pct.	ERA	G	GS	CG	ShO	Sv.	IP	H	R	ER	BB	SO
1992—Hamilton (NYP)	2	0	1.000	1.61	5	5	0	0	0	28	14	8	5	14	22
1993—St. Petersburg (FSL)	6	11	.353	4.27	25	25	0	0	0	132 2/3	152	80	63	62	87
1994—St. Petersburg (FSL)	5	6	.455	3.47	21	21	0	0	0	114	119	51	44	37	92
—Arkansas (Texas)	2	1	.667	1.40	3	3	0	0	0	19 1/3	13	3	3	8	11
1995—Arkansas (Texas)	9	8	.529	4.88	24	24	0	0	0	129	143	84	70	64	77
—Louisville (A.A.)	8	9	.471	4.70	25	18	0	0	0	115	127	72	60	51	76
1996—Arkansas (Texas)	2	3	.400	6.00	6	6	0	0	0	33	32	24	22	15	25
—Louisville (A.A.)	6	10	.375	4.37	26	23	1	0	1	131 2/3	142	74	64	53	117
1997—St. Louis (N.L.)	0	2	.000	9.35	6	4	0	0	0	17 1/3	27	21	18	10	8
Major league totals (1 year)	0	2	.000	9.35	6	4	0	0	0	17 1/3	27	21	18	10	8

LOWELL, MIKE　　　3B　　　YANKEES

PERSONAL: Born February 24, 1974, in San Juan, Puerto Rico. ... 6-4/195. ... Bats right, throws right. ... Full name: Michael A. Lowell.
HIGH SCHOOL: Coral Gables (Fla.).
COLLEGE: Florida International.
TRANSACTIONS/CAREER NOTES: Selected by New York Yankees organization in 20th round of free-agent draft (June 1, 1995).
STATISTICAL NOTES: Led New York-Pennsylvania League third basemen with 271 total chances in 1995. ... Led South Atlantic League third basemen with .926 fielding percentage, 301 putouts and 421 total chances in 1996.

Year Team (League)	Pos.	G	AB	R	H	2B	3B	HR	RBI	Avg.	BB	SO	SB	PO	A	E	Avg.
1995—Oneonta (NYP)	3B	72	281	36	73	18	0	1	27	.260	23	34	3	59	188	24	.911
1996—Greensboro (S. Atl.)	3B-SS	113	433	58	122	33	0	8	64	.282	46	43	10	91	†302	32	.925
—Tampa (Florida State)	3B	24	78	8	22	5	0	0	11	.282	3	13	1	22	40	3	.954
1997—Norwich (Eastern)	3B-SS	78	285	60	98	17	0	15	47	.344	48	30	2	57	133	15	.927
—Columbus (Int'l)	3B-SS	57	210	36	58	13	1	15	45	.276	23	34	2	31	73	5	.954

LOWERY, TERRELL　　　OF　　　CUBS

PERSONAL: Born October 25, 1970, in Oakland. ... 6-3/180. ... Bats right, throws right. ... Full name: Quenton Terrell Lowery. ... Brother of Josh Lowery, minor league shortstop (1989-90).
HIGH SCHOOL: Oakland Technical.
COLLEGE: Loyola Marymount.
TRANSACTIONS/CAREER NOTES: Selected by Texas Rangers organization in second round of free-agent draft (June 3, 1991). ... On Butte disabled list (June 17-27, 1992). ... On restricted list (June 27, 1992-February 5, 1993). ... On Oklahoma City disabled list (April 6-August 24, 1995). ... Traded by Rangers to New York Mets for OF Damon Buford (January 25, 1996). ... Selected by Chicago Cubs organization from Mets organization in Rule 5 major league draft (December 9, 1996).
STATISTICAL NOTES: Led Texas League outfielders with 303 total chances in 1994. ... Led American Association with .401 on-base percentage in 1997.

Year Team (League)	Pos.	G	AB	R	H	2B	3B	HR	RBI	Avg.	BB	SO	SB	PO	A	E	Avg.
1991—Butte (Pioneer)	OF	54	214	38	64	10	7	3	33	.299	29	44	23	92	7	6	.943
1992—								Did not play.									
1993—Charlotte (Fla. St.)	OF	65	257	46	77	7	9	3	36	.300	46	47	14	156	5	4	.976
—Tulsa (Texas)	OF	66	258	29	62	5	1	3	14	.240	28	50	10	152	6	2	.988
1994—Tulsa (Texas)	OF	129	496	89	142	34	8	8	54	.286	59	113	33	*280	16	7	.977
1995—GC Rangers (GCL)	OF	10	34	10	9	3	1	3	7	.265	6	7	1	7	0	0	1.000
—Charlotte (Fla. St.)	OF	11	35	4	9	2	2	0	4	.257	6	6	1	18	0	1	1.000
1996—Norfolk (Int'l)■	OF	62	193	25	45	7	2	4	21	.233	22	44	6	106	4	1	.991
—Binghamton (East.)	OF	62	211	34	58	13	4	7	32	.275	44	44	5	97	3	3	.971
1997—Iowa (Am. Assoc.)■	OF	110	386	69	116	28	3	17	71	.301	65	97	9	244	8	3	.988
—Chicago (N.L.)	OF	9	14	2	4	0	0	0	0	.286	3	3	1	7	2	0	1.000
Major league totals (1 year)		9	14	2	4	0	0	0	0	.286	3	3	1	7	2	0	1.000

LUDWICK, ERIC　　　P　　　MARLINS

PERSONAL: Born December 14, 1971, in Whiteman AFB, Mo. ... 6-5/220. ... Throws right, bats right. ... Full name: Eric D. Ludwick.
HIGH SCHOOL: El Dorado (Las Vegas).
COLLEGE: California, then UNLV.
TRANSACTIONS/CAREER NOTES: Selected by New York Mets organization in second round of free-agent draft (June 3, 1993). ... Traded by Mets with P Erik Hiljus and OF Yudith Ozorio to St. Louis Cardinals for OF Bernard Gilkey (January 22, 1996). ... Traded by Cardinals with P T.J. Mathews and P Blake Stein to Oakland Athletics for 1B Mark McGwire (July 31, 1997). ... Traded by A's to Florida Marlins for IF Kurt Abbott (December 19, 1997).

Year Team (League)	W	L	Pct.	ERA	G	GS	CG	ShO	Sv.	IP	H	R	ER	BB	SO
1993—Pittsfield (NYP)	4	4	.500	3.18	10	10	1	0	0	51	51	27	18	18	40
1994—St. Lucie (Fla. St.)	7	13	.350	4.55	27	27	3	0	0	150 1/3	162	*102	76	77	77
1995—Binghamton (Eastern)	12	5	.706	2.95	23	22	3	2	0	143 1/3	108	52	47	68	131
—Norfolk (Int'l)	1	1	.500	5.85	4	3	0	0	0	20	22	15	13	7	9
1996—Louisville (A.A.)■	3	4	.429	2.83	11	11	0	0	0	60 1/3	55	24	19	24	73
—St. Louis (N.L.)	0	1	.000	9.00	6	1	0	0	0	10	11	11	10	3	12
1997—St. Louis (N.L.)	0	1	.000	9.45	5	0	0	0	0	6 2/3	12	7	7	6	7
—Louisville (A.A.)	6	8	.429	2.93	24	11	1	0	4	80	67	31	26	26	85
—Edmonton (PCL)■	1	1	.500	3.32	6	3	0	0	0	19	22	7	7	4	20
—Oakland (A.L.)	1	4	.200	8.25	6	5	0	0	0	24	32	24	22	16	14
A.L. totals (1 year)	1	4	.200	8.25	6	5	0	0	0	24	32	24	22	16	14
N.L. totals (2 years)	0	2	.000	9.18	11	1	0	0	0	16 2/3	23	18	17	9	19
Major league totals (2 years)	1	6	.143	8.63	17	6	0	0	0	40 2/3	55	42	39	25	?

LUKE, MATT　　　OF　　　DODGERS

PERSONAL: Born February 26, 1971, in Long Beach, Calif. ... 6-5/220. ... Bats left, throws left. ... Full name: Matthew Clifford Luke.
HIGH SCHOOL: El Dorado (Calif.).
COLLEGE: California.
TRANSACTIONS/CAREER NOTES: Selected by New York Yankees organization in eighth round of free-agent draft (June 1, 1992). .. disabled list (April 22-May 9, 1994). .. On Columbus disabled list (April 5-May 1 and May 12-June 2, 1996). ... On temporarily (April 3-May 13, 1997) ... Claimed on waivers by Los Angeles Dodgers (September 25, 1997).
STATISTICAL NOTES: Led South Atlantic League with 267 total bases in 1993.

Year Team (League)	Pos.	G	AB	R	H	2B	3B	HR	RBI	Avg.	BB	SO	SB	PO	A	E	Avg.
1992—Oneonta (NYP)	OF-1B	69	271	30	67	11	*7	2	34	.247	19	32	4	230	16	7	.972
1993—Greensboro (S. Atl.) ..	OF	135	*549	83	•157	37	5	21	91	.286	47	79	11	218	11	3	*.987
1994—Tampa (Florida State) .	OF	57	222	52	68	11	2	16	42	.306	28	27	4	100	12	5	.957
—Alb./Colon. (Eastern) ..	OF-1B	63	236	34	67	11	2	8	40	.284	28	50	6	158	8	3	.982
1995—Norwich (Eastern)	OF	93	365	48	95	17	5	8	53	.260	20	68	5	178	12	4	.979
—Columbus (Int'l)	OF	23	77	11	23	4	1	3	12	.299	2	12	1	36	1	2	.949
1996—New York (A.L.)..........	PR	1	0	1	0	0	0	0	0	...	0	0	0	...	...	...	...
—Columbus (Int'l)	OF-1B	74	264	46	74	14	2	19	70	.280	17	52	1	159	8	2	.988
—Tampa (Florida State) .	OF	2	7	1	2	0	0	0	1	.286	1	1	0	3	0	0	1.000
1997—Columbus (Int'l)	OF-1B	87	337	42	77	19	3	8	45	.228	29	64	0	263	23	4	.986
Major league totals (1 year)		1	0	1	0	0	0	0	0	...	0	0	0	...	...	...	...

LUNAR, FERNANDO   C   BRAVES

PERSONAL: Born May 25, 1977, in Cantanura, Venezuela. ... 6-1/190. ... Bats right, throws right. ... Full name: Fernando Jose Lunar.
TRANSACTIONS/CAREER NOTES: Signed as non-drafted free agent by Atlanta Braves organization (March 15, 1994). ... On disabled list (April 16-24, 1995).
STATISTICAL NOTES: Tied for Gulf Coast League lead in double plays by catcher with three in 1994. ... Led South Atlantic League catchers with 11 double plays in 1996. ... Led South Atlantic League with 1,026 total chances in 1997.

Year Team (League)	Pos.	G	AB	R	H	2B	3B	HR	RBI	Avg.	BB	SO	SB	PO	A	E	Avg.
1994—GC Braves (GCL)	C	33	100	9	24	5	0	2	12	.240	1	13	0	203	32	7	.971
1995—Macon (S. Atl.)	C	39	134	13	24	2	0	0	9	.179	10	38	1	261	35	10	.967
1996—Macon (S. Atl.)	C	104	343	33	63	9	0	7	33	.184	20	65	3	648	112	12	.984
1997—Macon (S. Atl.)	C	105	380	41	99	26	2	7	37	.261	18	42	0	*888	*135	13	.987

LYONS, CURT   P   REDS

PERSONAL: Born October 17, 1974, in Greencastle, Ind. ... 6-5/240. ... Throws right, bats right. ... Full name: Curt Russell Lyons.
HIGH SCHOOL: Madison Central (Richmond, Ky.).
TRANSACTIONS/CAREER NOTES: Selected by Cincinnati Reds organization in sixth round of free-agent draft (June 1, 1992). ... Traded by Reds to Chicago Cubs for OF Ozzie Timmons and P Jayson Peterson (March 31, 1997). ... On Iowa disabled list (June 10-September 11, 1997). ... Claimed on waivers by Reds (October 3, 1997).
HONORS: Named Southern League Most Outstanding Pitcher (1996).
STATISTICAL NOTES: Tied for South Atlantic League lead with 15 hit batsmen in 1995.

Year Team (League)	W	L	Pct.	ERA	G	GS	CG	ShO	Sv.	IP	H	R	ER	BB	SO
1992—Princeton (Appalachian).....	5	3	.625	2.77	11	11	0	0	0	55 1/3	61	36	17	17	33
1993—Billings (Pioneer).............	7	3	.700	3.00	15	12	2	0	0	84	89	35	28	20	64
1994—Princeton (Appalachian).....	1	1	.500	1.98	4	4	0	0	0	27 1/3	16	9	6	2	28
—Char., W.Va. (S. Atl.)	3	6	.333	3.86	12	11	0	0	0	65 1/3	64	30	28	22	55
1995—Win.-Salem (Car.)	9	9	.500	2.98	26	26	0	0	0	160 1/3	139	66	53	67	122
1996—Chattanooga (Southern)	13	4	.765	2.41	24	24	1	0	0	141 2/3	113	48	38	52	*176
—Cincinnati (N.L.)	2	0	1.000	4.50	3	3	0	0	0	16	17	8	8	7	14
1997—Iowa (Am. Assoc.) ■	0	2	.000	6.37	8	8	0	0	0	29 2/3	35	23	21	21	26
—Orlando (South.)	0	0	...	7.50	2	2	0	0	0	6	6	5	5	2	8
Major league totals (1 year).......	2	0	1.000	4.50	3	3	0	0	0	16	17	8	8	7	14

MABRY, JOHN   OF/1B   CARDINALS

PERSONAL: Born October 17, 1970, in Wilmington, Del. ... 6-4/195. ... Bats left, throws right. ... Full name: John Steven Mabry. ... Name pronounced MAY-bree.
HIGH SCHOOL: Bohemia Manor (Chesapeake City, Md.).
COLLEGE: West Chester (Pa.).
TRANSACTIONS/CAREER NOTES: Selected by St. Louis Cardinals organization in sixth round of free-agent draft (June 3, 1991). ... On disabled list (April 22-30 and May 6-18, 1992). ... On disabled list (August 20-September 24, 1997).
STATISTICAL NOTES: Led Texas League in grounding into double plays with 17 in 1993. ... Led Texas League outfielders with six double plays in 1993. ... Hit for the cycle (May 18, 1996). ... Had 20-game hitting streak (May 19-June 9, 1997).

Year Team (League)	Pos.	G	AB	R	H	2B	3B	HR	RBI	Avg.	BB	SO	SB	PO	A	E	Avg.
1991—Hamilton (NYP)	OF	49	187	25	58	11	0	1	31	.310	17	18	9	73	*10	5	.943
—Savannah (S. Atl.)	OF	22	86	10	20	6	1	0	8	.233	7	12	1	36	1	1	.974
1992—Springfield (Midw.)	OF	115	438	63	115	13	6	11	57	.263	24	39	2	171	14	6	.969
1993—Arkansas (Texas)........	OF	*136	528	68	153	32	2	16	72	.290	27	68	7	262	15	3	*.989
—Louisville (A.A.)...........	OF	4	7	0	1	0	0	0	1	.143	0	1	0	3	0	0	1.000
1994—Louisville (A.A.)...........	OF	122	477	76	125	30	1	15	68	.262	32	67	2	237	4	2	.992
—St. Louis (N.L.)..........	OF	6	23	2	7	3	0	0	3	.304	2	4	0	16	0	0	1.000
1995—St. Louis (N.L.)..........	1B-OF	129	388	35	119	21	1	5	41	.307	24	45	0	652	58	4	.994
—Louisville (A.A.)...........	OF	4	12	0	1	0	0	0	0	.083	0	0	0	8	0	1	.889
1996—St. Louis (N.L.)..........	1B-OF	151	543	63	161	30	4	13	74	.297	37	84	3	1182	76	8	.994
1997—St. Louis (N.L.)..........	OF-1B-3B	116	388	40	110	19	0	5	36	.284	39	77	0	455	30	1	.998
League totals (4 years)		402	1342	140	397	73	3	23	154	.296	102	210	3	2305	164	13	.995

DIVISION SERIES RECORD

RECORDS: Shares career record for most triples—1.

(League)	Pos.	G	AB	R	H	2B	3B	HR	RBI	Avg.	BB	SO	SB	PO	A	E	Avg.
—St. Louis (N.L.)..........	1B	3	10	1	3	0	1	0	1	.300	2	1	0	20	1	0	1.000

L
M

CHAMPIONSHIP SERIES RECORD

Year	Team (League)	Pos.	G	AB	R	H	2B	3B	HR	RBI	Avg.	BB	SO	SB	PO	A	E	Avg.
				BATTING											FIELDING			
1996—	St. Louis (N.L.)..........	1B-OF	7	23	1	6	0	0	0	0	.261	0	6	0	45	1	0	1.000

MACFARLANE, MIKE C ROYALS

PERSONAL: Born April 12, 1964, in Stockton, Calif. ... 6-1/210. ... Bats right, throws right. ... Full name: Michael Andrew Macfarlane.

HIGH SCHOOL: Lincoln (Stockton, Calif.).

COLLEGE: Santa Clara.

TRANSACTIONS/CAREER NOTES: Selected by Kansas City Royals organization in fourth round of free-agent draft (June 3, 1985). ... On disabled list (April 9-July 9, 1986 and July 16-September 14, 1991). ... Granted free agency (October 17, 1994). ... Signed by Boston Red Sox (April 8, 1995). ... Granted free agency (November 6, 1995). ... Signed by Royals (December 16, 1995). ... On disabled list (March 29-April 13 and May 3-23, 1997). ... Granted free agency (October 28, 1997). ... Re-signed by Royals (November 25, 1997).

STATISTICAL NOTES: Tied for A.L. lead in being hit by pitch with 15 in 1992. ... Led A.L. in being hit by pitch with 18 in 1994. ... Led A.L. catchers with nine double plays in 1994. ... Led A.L. with 26 passed balls in 1995. ... Career major league grand slams: 4.

Year	Team (League)	Pos.	G	AB	R	H	2B	3B	HR	RBI	Avg.	BB	SO	SB	PO	A	E	Avg.
				BATTING											FIELDING			
1985—	Memphis (Southern)..	C	65	223	29	60	15	4	8	39	.269	11	30	0	295	24	9	.973
1986—	Memphis (Southern)..	OF	40	141	26	34	7	2	12	29	.241	10	26	0	0	0	0	...
1987—	Omaha (A.A.).............	C	87	302	53	79	25	1	13	50	.262	22	50	0	408	37	6	.987
	— Kansas City (A.L.)	C	8	19	0	4	1	0	0	3	.211	2	2	0	29	2	0	1.000
1988—	Kansas City (A.L.)	C	70	211	25	56	15	0	4	26	.265	21	37	0	309	18	2	.994
	— Omaha (A.A.).............	C	21	76	8	18	7	2	2	8	.237	4	15	0	85	5	1	.989
1989—	Kansas City (A.L.)	C-DH	69	157	13	35	6	0	2	19	.223	7	27	0	249	17	1	.996
1990—	Kansas City (A.L.)	C-DH	124	400	37	102	24	4	6	58	.255	25	69	1	660	23	6	.991
1991—	Kansas City (A.L.)	C-DH	84	267	34	74	18	2	13	41	.277	17	52	1	391	28	3	.993
1992—	Kansas City (A.L.)	C-DH	129	402	51	94	28	3	17	48	.234	30	89	1	527	43	4	.993
1993—	Kansas City (A.L.)	C	117	388	55	106	27	0	20	67	.273	40	83	2	647	68	11	.985
1994—	Kansas City (A.L.)	C-DH	92	314	53	80	17	3	14	47	.255	35	71	1	498	39	4	.993
1995—	Boston (A.L.)■..........	C-DH	115	364	45	82	18	1	15	51	.225	38	78	2	618	49	5	.993
1996—	Kansas City (A.L.)■ ...	C-DH	112	379	58	104	24	2	19	54	.274	31	57	3	511	35	4	.993
1997—	Kansas City (A.L.)	C	82	257	34	61	14	2	8	35	.237	24	47	0	439	20	4	.991
Major league totals (11 years)			1002	3158	405	798	192	17	118	449	.253	270	612	11	4878	342	44	.992

DIVISION SERIES RECORD

Year	Team (League)	Pos.	G	AB	R	H	2B	3B	HR	RBI	Avg.	BB	SO	SB	PO	A	E	Avg.
				BATTING											FIELDING			
1995—	Boston (A.L.)............	C	3	9	0	3	0	0	0	1	.333	0	3	0	18	0	2	.900

MACHADO, ROBERT C WHITE SOX

PERSONAL: Born June 3, 1973, in Caracas, Venezuela. ... 6-1/205. ... Throws right, bats right. ... Full name: Robert Alexis Machado.

TRANSACTIONS/CAREER NOTES: Signed as non-drafted free agent by Chicago White Sox organization (August 10, 1989).

STATISTICAL NOTES: Led Gulf Coast League catchers with 349 total chances in 1991. ... Tied for Southern League lead in double plays by catcher with 10 in 1996. ... Tied for American Association lead in passed balls with nine in 1997.

Year	Team (League)	Pos.	G	AB	R	H	2B	3B	HR	RBI	Avg.	BB	SO	SB	PO	A	E	Avg.
				BATTING											FIELDING			
1991—	GC Whi. Sox (GCL)	C	38	126	11	31	4	1	0	15	.246	6	21	2	*287	*54	8	.977
1992—	Utica (N.Y.-Penn)........	C	45	161	16	44	13	1	2	20	.273	5	26	1	279	30	12	.963
1993—	South Bend (Mid.)......	C	75	281	34	86	14	3	2	33	.306	19	59	1	490	66	12	.979
1994—	Prince William (Car.) ..	C	93	312	45	81	17	1	11	47	.260	27	68	0	562	66	*16	.975
1995—	Nashville (A.A.)	C	16	49	7	7	3	0	1	5	.143	7	12	0	87	17	3	.972
	— Prince William (Car.) ..	C	83	272	37	69	14	0	6	31	.254	40	47	0	548	78	5	.992
1996—	Birmingham (Sou.).....	C	87	309	35	74	16	0	6	28	.239	20	56	1	502	67	5	.991
	— Chicago (A.L.)	C	4	6	1	4	1	0	0	2	.667	0	0	0	6	0	0	1.000
1997—	Nashville (A.A.)	C	84	308	43	83	18	0	8	30	.269	12	61	5	461	49	6	.988
	— Chicago (A.L.)	C	10	15	1	3	0	1	0	2	.200	1	6	0	34	3	0	1.000
Major league totals (2 years)			14	21	2	7	1	1	0	4	.333	1	6	0	40	3	0	1.000

MACK, SHANE OF ATHLETICS

PERSONAL: Born December 7, 1963, in Los Angeles. ... 6-0/190. ... Bats right, throws right. ... Full name: Shane Lee Mack. ... Brother of Quinn Mack, outfielder, Seattle Mariners (1994).

HIGH SCHOOL: Gahr (Cerritos, Calif.).

COLLEGE: UCLA.

TRANSACTIONS/CAREER NOTES: Selected by Kansas City Royals organization in fourth round of free-agent draft (June 8, 1981); did not sign. ... Selected by San Diego Padres organization in first round (11th pick overall) of free-agent draft (June 4, 1984). ... On San Diego disabled list (March 25-May 4, 1989). ... Selected by Minnesota Twins from Padres organization in Rule 5 major league draft (December 4, 1989). ... On disabled list (May 15-30, 1993 and March 29-May 3, 1994). ... Granted free agency (October 19, 1994). ... Signed by Yomiuri Giants of Japan Central League (January 4, 1995). ... Signed by Boston Red Sox (December 14, 1996). ... On disabled list (August 7-September 1, 1997). ... Granted free agency (October 28, 1997). ... Signed by Oakland Athletics (December 22, 1997).

HONORS: Named outfielder on The Sporting News college All-America team (1984).

STATISTICAL NOTES: Tied for Texas League lead in being hit by pitch with seven in 1986. ... Led Texas League outfielders with four doubl plays in 1986. ... Had 22-game hitting streak (July 26-August 18, 1992). ... Tied for A.L. lead in being hit by pitch with 15 in 1992. ... Care major league grand slams: 4.

MISCELLANEOUS: Member of 1984 U.S. Olympic baseball team.

Year Team (League)	Pos.	G	AB	R	H	2B	3B	HR	RBI	Avg.	BB	SO	SB	PO	A	E	Avg.
1985—Beaumont (Texas)	OF-3B	125	430	59	112	23	3	6	55	.260	38	89	12	252	12	7	.974
1986—Beaumont (Texas)	OF	115	452	61	127	26	3	15	68	.281	21	79	14	255	•14	8	.971
— Las Vegas (PCL)	OF	19	69	13	25	1	6	0	6	.362	2	13	3	43	0	2	.956
1987— Las Vegas (PCL)	OF	39	152	38	51	11	1	5	26	.336	19	32	13	97	3	1	.990
— San Diego (N.L.)	OF	105	238	28	57	11	3	4	25	.239	18	47	4	159	1	3	.982
1988— Las Vegas (PCL)	OF	55	196	43	68	7	1	10	40	.347	29	44	7	116	7	3	.976
— San Diego (N.L.)	OF	56	119	13	29	3	0	0	12	.244	14	21	5	110	4	2	.983
1989— Las Vegas (PCL)	OF	24	80	10	18	3	1	1	8	.225	14	19	4	59	3	1	.984
1990— Minnesota (A.L.)■	OF-DH	125	313	50	102	10	4	8	44	.326	29	69	13	230	8	3	.988
1991— Minnesota (A.L.)	OF-DH	143	442	79	137	27	8	18	74	.310	34	79	13	290	6	7	.977
1992— Minnesota (A.L.)	OF	156	600	101	189	31	6	16	75	.315	64	106	26	322	9	4	.988
1993— Minnesota (A.L.)	OF	128	503	66	139	30	4	10	61	.276	41	76	15	347	8	5	.986
1994— Minnesota (A.L.)	OF-DH	81	303	55	101	21	2	15	61	.333	32	51	4	201	2	2	.990
1995— Yomiuri (Jp. Cen.)■	...	120	477	...	131	...	...	20	52	.275	...	...	...	...	...	...	...
1996— Yomiuri (Jp. Cen.)	...	127	484	71	142	28	0	22	75	.293	...	...	12	...	...	...	...
1997— Boston (A.L.)■...........	OF-DH	60	130	13	41	7	0	3	17	.315	9	24	2	75	0	0	1.000
American League totals (6 years)		693	2291	364	709	126	24	70	332	.309	209	405	73	1465	33	21	.986
National League totals (2 years)		161	357	41	86	14	3	4	37	.241	32	68	9	269	5	5	.982
Major league totals (8 years)		854	2648	405	795	140	27	74	369	.300	241	473	82	1734	38	26	.986

CHAMPIONSHIP SERIES RECORD

Year Team (League)	Pos.	G	AB	R	H	2B	3B	HR	RBI	Avg.	BB	SO	SB	PO	A	E	Avg.
1991— Minnesota (A.L.)	OF	5	18	4	6	1	0	0	3	.333	2	4	2	3	0	1	.750

WORLD SERIES RECORD

NOTES: Member of World Series championship team (1991).

Year Team (League)	Pos.	G	AB	R	H	2B	3B	HR	RBI	Avg.	BB	SO	SB	PO	A	E	Avg.
1991— Minnesota (A.L.)	OF	6	23	0	3	1	0	0	1	.130	0	7	0	11	0	0	1.000

MADDUX, GREG   P   BRAVES

PERSONAL: Born April 14, 1966, in San Angelo, Texas. ... 6-0/175. ... Throws right, bats right. ... Full name: Gregory Alan Maddux. ... Brother of Mike Maddux, major league pitcher with seven teams (1986-97).

HIGH SCHOOL: Valley (Las Vegas).

TRANSACTIONS/CAREER NOTES: Selected by Chicago Cubs organization in second round of free-agent draft (June 4, 1984). ... Granted free agency (October 26, 1992). ... Signed by Atlanta Braves (December 9, 1992).

RECORDS: Holds major league single-season record for fewest complete games by pitcher who led league in complete games—8 (1993). ... Shares major league career record for most years leading league in putouts by pitcher—5; most years leading league in double plays by pitcher—5; and most years leading league in total chances by pitcher—8. ... Shares major league single-game record for most putouts by pitcher—7 (April 29, 1990). ... Shares N.L. career record for most years leading league in assists by pitcher—5. ... Shares modern N.L. single-season record for most putouts by pitcher—39 (each in 1990-91 and 1993).

HONORS: Won N.L. Gold Glove at pitcher (1990-97). ... Named righthanded pitcher on The Sporting News N.L. All-Star team (1992-95). ... Named N.L. Cy Young Award winner by Baseball Writers' Association of America (1992-95). ... Named N.L. Pitcher of the Year by The Sporting News (1993-95).

STATISTICAL NOTES: Led Appalachian League with eight hit batsmen in 1984. ... Led American Association with 12 hit batsmen in 1986. ... Led N.L. with 14 hit batsmen in 1992. ... Pitched 3-1 one-hit, complete-game victory against Houston (May 28, 1995). ... Pitched 2-0 one-hit, complete-game victory against San Diego (April 27, 1997).

MISCELLANEOUS: Appeared in three games as pinch-runner (1988). ... Singled and scored and struck out in two appearances as pinch-hitter (1991).

Year Team (League)	W	L	Pct.	ERA	G	GS	CG	ShO	Sv.	IP	H	R	ER	BB	SO
1984—Pikeville (Appal.)	6	2	.750	2.63	14	12	2	•2	0	85 2/3	63	35	25	41	62
1985—Peoria (Midwest)	13	9	.591	3.19	27	27	6	0	0	186	176	86	66	52	125
1986—Pittsfield (Eastern)	4	3	.571	2.73	8	8	4	2	0	62 2/3	49	22	19	15	35
— Iowa (Am. Assoc.)............	10	1	*.909	3.02	18	18	5	•2	0	128 1/3	127	49	43	30	65
— Chicago (N.L.)............	2	4	.333	5.52	6	5	1	0	0	31	44	20	19	11	20
1987— Chicago (N.L.)	6	14	.300	5.61	30	27	1	1	0	155 2/3	181	111	97	74	101
— Iowa (Am. Assoc.)............	3	0	1.000	0.98	4	4	2	•2	0	27 2/3	17	3	3	12	22
1988— Chicago (N.L.)	18	8	.692	3.18	34	34	9	3	0	249	230	97	88	81	140
1989— Chicago (N.L.)	19	12	.613	2.95	35	35	7	1	0	238 1/3	222	90	78	82	135
1990— Chicago (N.L.)	15	15	.500	3.46	35	•35	8	2	0	237	*242	*116	91	71	144
1991— Chicago (N.L.)	15	11	.577	3.35	37	*37	7	2	0	*263	232	113	98	66	198
1992— Chicago (N.L.)	•20	11	.645	2.18	35	•35	9	4	0	*268	201	68	65	70	199
1993—Atlanta (N.L.)■............	20	10	.667	*2.36	36	•36	*8	1	0	*267	228	85	70	52	197
1994—Atlanta (N.L.)............	•16	6	.727	*1.56	25	25	*10	•3	0	*202	150	44	35	31	156
1995—Atlanta (N.L.)............	*19	2	*.905	*1.63	28	28	*10	•3	0	•209 2/3	147	39	38	23	181
1996—Atlanta (N.L.)............	15	11	.577	2.72	35	35	5	1	0	245	225	85	74	28	172
1997—Atlanta (N.L.)............	19	4	*.826	2.20	33	33	5	2	0	232 2/3	200	58	57	20	177
Major league totals (12 years)	184	108	.630	2.81	369	365	80	23	0	2598 1/3	2302	926	810	609	1820

DIVISION SERIES RECORD

RECORDS: Holds career records for most innings pitched—30; and hits allowed—30. ... Shares career record for most wins—3.

Year Team (League)	W	L	Pct.	ERA	G	GS	CG	ShO	Sv.	IP	H	R	ER	BB	SO
1995—Atlanta (N.L.)............	1	0	1.000	4.50	2	2	0	0	0	14	19	7	7	2	7
996—Atlanta (N.L.)............	1	0	1.000	0.00	1	1	0	0	0	7	3	2	0	0	7
997—Atlanta (N.L.)............	1	0	1.000	1.00	1	1	1	0	0	9	7	1	1	1	6
iv. series totals (3 years)	3	0	1.000	2.40	4	4	1	0	0	30	29	10	8	3	20

M

CHAMPIONSHIP SERIES RECORD

RECORDS: Shares single-series record for most earned runs allowed—11 (1989). ... Holds N.L. single-series record for most runs allowed—12 (1989). ... Holds career record for most runs allowed—37.

NOTES: Scored once in one game as pinch-runner (1989).

Year Team (League)	W	L	Pct.	ERA	G	GS	CG	ShO	Sv.	IP	H	R	ER	BB	SO
1989—Chicago (N.L.)	0	1	.000	13.50	2	2	0	0	0	7 1/3	13	12	11	4	5
1993—Atlanta (N.L.)	1	1	.500	4.97	2	2	0	0	0	12 2/3	11	8	7	7	11
1995—Atlanta (N.L.)	1	0	1.000	1.13	1	1	0	0	0	8	7	1	1	2	4
1996—Atlanta (N.L.)	1	1	.500	2.51	2	2	0	0	0	14 1/3	15	9	4	3	10
1997—Atlanta (N.L.)	0	2	.000	1.38	2	2	0	0	0	13	9	7	2	4	16
Champ. series totals (5 years)	3	5	.375	4.07	9	9	0	0	0	55 1/3	55	37	25	20	46

WORLD SERIES RECORD

NOTES: Member of World Series championship team (1995).

Year Team (League)	W	L	Pct.	ERA	G	GS	CG	ShO	Sv.	IP	H	R	ER	BB	SO
1995—Atlanta (N.L.)	1	1	.500	2.25	2	2	1	0	0	16	9	6	4	3	8
1996—Atlanta (N.L.)	1	1	.500	1.72	2	2	0	0	0	15 2/3	14	3	3	1	5
World Series totals (2 years)	2	2	.500	1.99	4	4	1	0	0	31 2/3	23	9	7	4	13

ALL-STAR GAME RECORD

Year League	W	L	Pct.	ERA	GS	CG	ShO	Sv.	IP	H	R	ER	BB	SO
1988— National					Did not play.									
1992— National	0	0	...	6.75	0	0	0	0	1 1/3	1	1	1	0	0
1994— National	0	0	...	3.00	1	0	0	0	3	3	1	1	0	2
1995— National					Selected, did not play—injured.									
1996— National					Did not play.									
1997— National	0	0	...	4.50	1	0	0	0	2	2	1	1	0	0
All-Star totals (3 years)	0	0	...	4.26	2	0	0	0	6 1/3	6	3	3	0	2

MADDUX, MIKE   P

PERSONAL: Born August 27, 1961, in Dayton, Ohio. ... 6-2/185. ... Throws right, bats left. ... Full name: Michael Ausley Maddux. ... Brother of Greg Maddux, pitcher, Atlanta Braves.

HIGH SCHOOL: Rancho (Las Vegas).

COLLEGE: Texas-El Paso.

TRANSACTIONS/CAREER NOTES: Selected by Cincinnati Reds organization in 36th round of free-agent draft (June 5, 1979); did not sign. ... Selected by Philadelphia Phillies organization in fifth round of free-agent draft (June 7, 1982). ... On Philadelphia disabled list (April 21-June 1, 1988); included rehabilitation assignment to Maine (May 13-22). ... Released by Phillies organization (November 20, 1989). ... Signed by Los Angeles Dodgers (December 21, 1989). ... Granted free agency (October 15, 1990). ... Signed by San Diego Padres (March 30, 1991). ... On disabled list (April 5-26, 1992). ... Traded by Padres to New York Mets for P Roger Mason and P Mike Freitas (December 17, 1992). ... On disabled list (April 27-May 13, 1994). ... Granted free agency (October 18, 1994). ... Signed by Calgary, Pittsburgh Pirates organization (April 10, 1995). ... Released by Pirates (May 16, 1995). ... Signed by Boston Red Sox (May 30, 1995). ... Granted free agency (November 6, 1995). ... Re-signed by Red Sox (December 15, 1995). ... On Boston disabled list (May 6-August 2, 1996); included rehabilitation assignments to Pawtucket (May 24-25, July 12-16 and July 25-31). ... Granted free agency (November 1, 1996). ... Re-signed by Red Sox (December 7, 1996). ... Released by Red Sox (March 26, 1997). ... Signed by Everett, Seattle Mariners organization (April 11, 1997). ... On Seattle disabled list (June 22-July 13, 1997). ... Released by Mariners (July 23, 1997). ... Signed by Las Vegas, Padres organization (August 19, 1997). ... Granted free agency (October 15, 1997).

MISCELLANEOUS: Appeared in one game as pinch-runner with Philadelphia (1988).

Year Team (League)	W	L	Pct.	ERA	G	GS	CG	ShO	Sv.	IP	H	R	ER	BB	SO
1982—Bend (Northwest)	3	6	.333	3.99	11	10	3	0	0	65 1/3	68	35	29	26	59
1983—Spartanburg (SAL)	4	6	.400	5.44	13	13	3	0	0	84 1/3	98	62	51	47	85
—Peninsula (Caro.)	8	4	.667	3.62	14	14	6	0	0	99 1/3	92	46	40	35	78
—Reading (Eastern)	0	0	...	6.00	1	1	0	0	0	3	4	2	2	1	2
1984—Reading (Eastern)	3	•12	.200	5.04	20	19	4	0	0	116	143	82	65	49	77
—Portland (PCL)	2	4	.333	5.84	8	8	1	0	0	44 2/3	58	32	29	17	22
1985—Portland (PCL)	9	12	.429	5.31	27	26	6	1	0	166	195	106	98	51	96
1986—Portland (PCL)	5	2	.714	2.36	12	12	3	0	0	84	70	26	22	22	65
—Philadelphia (N.L.)	3	7	.300	5.42	16	16	0	0	0	78	88	56	47	34	44
1987—Maine (International)	6	6	.500	4.35	18	16	3	1	0	103 1/3	116	58	50	26	71
—Philadelphia (N.L.)	2	0	1.000	2.65	7	2	0	0	0	17	17	5	5	5	15
1988—Philadelphia (N.L.)	4	3	.571	3.76	25	11	0	0	0	88 2/3	91	41	37	34	59
—Maine (International)	0	2	.000	4.18	5	3	1	0	0	23 2/3	25	18	11	10	18
1989—Philadelphia (N.L.)	1	3	.250	5.15	16	4	2	1	1	43 2/3	52	29	25	14	26
—Scran./W.B. (Int'l)	7	7	.500	3.66	19	17	3	1	0	123	119	55	50	26	100
1990—Albuquerque (PCL)■	8	5	.615	4.25	20	19	2	0	0	108	122	59	51	32	85
—Los Angeles (N.L.)	0	1	.000	6.53	11	2	0	0	0	20 2/3	24	15	15	4	11
1991—San Diego (N.L.)■	7	2	.778	2.46	64	1	0	0	5	98 2/3	78	30	27	27	57
1992—San Diego (N.L.)	2	2	.500	2.37	50	1	0	0	5	79 2/3	71	25	21	24	60
1993—New York (N.L.)■	3	8	.273	3.60	58	0	0	0	5	75	67	34	30	27	57
1994—New York (N.L.)■	2	1	.667	5.11	27	0	0	0	2	44	45	25	25	13	32
1995—Pittsburgh (N.L.)■	1	0	1.000	9.00	8	0	0	0	0	9	14	9	9	3	4
—Boston (A.L.)■	4	1	.800	3.61	36	4	0	0	1	89 2/3	86	40	36	15	65
1996—Boston (A.L.)	3	2	.600	4.48	23	7	0	0	0	64 1/3	76	37	32	27	32
—Pawtucket (Int'l)	2	0	1.000	3.21	3	3	0	0	0	14	13	5	5	2	9
1997—Tacoma (PCL)■	0	0	...	0.00	1	1	0	0	0	5	1	0	0	2	5
—Seattle (A.L.)	1	0	1.000	10.13	6	0	0	0	0	10 2/3	20	12	12	8	
—Las Vegas (PCL)■	0	2	.000	5.63	3	3	0	0	0	16	23	11	10	9	
A.L. totals (3 years)	8	3	.727	4.37	65	11	0	0	1	164 2/3	182	89	80	50	
N.L. totals (10 years)	25	27	.481	3.91	282	37	2	1	18	554 1/3	547	269	241	185	
Major league totals (12 years)	33	30	.524	4.02	347	48	2	1	19	719	729	358	321	235	

DIVISION SERIES RECORD

Year Team (League)	W	L	Pct.	ERA	G	GS	CG	ShO	Sv.	IP	H	R	ER	BB
1995—Boston (A.L.)	0	0	...	0.00	2	0	0	0	0	3	2	0	0	

MADURO, CALVIN   P   PHILLIES

PERSONAL: Born September 5, 1974, in Santa Cruz, Aruba. ... 6-0/175. ... Throws right, bats right. ... Full name: Calvin Gregory Maduro.
HIGH SCHOOL: Tourist Economy School (Santa Cruz, Aruba).
TRANSACTIONS/CAREER NOTES: Signed as non-drafted free agent by Baltimore Orioles organization (September 9, 1991). ... Traded by Orioles with P Garrett Stephenson to Philadelphia Phillies (September 4, 1996), completing deal in which Phillies traded 3B Todd Zeile and OF Pete Incaviglia to Orioles for two players to be named later (August 29, 1996).
STATISTICAL NOTES: Pitched 5-0 no-hit victory for Bowie against Portland (May 28, 1996, first game).
MISCELLANEOUS: Appeared in one game as pinch-runner with Philadelphia (1997).

Year Team (League)	W	L	Pct.	ERA	G	GS	CG	ShO	Sv.	IP	H	R	ER	BB	SO
1992—GC Orioles (GCL)	1	4	.200	2.27	13	•12	1	1	0	71 1/3	56	29	18	26	66
1993—Bluefield (Appalachian)	•9	4	.692	3.96	14	•14	*3	1	0	*91	90	46	40	17	*83
1994—Frederick (Carolina)	9	8	.529	4.25	27	26	0	0	0	152 1/3	132	86	72	59	137
1995—Frederick (Carolina)	8	5	.615	2.94	20	20	2	2	0	122 1/3	109	43	40	34	120
—Bowie (Eastern)	0	6	.000	5.09	7	7	0	0	0	35 1/3	39	28	20	27	26
1996—Bowie (Eastern)	9	7	.563	3.26	19	19	4	*3	0	124 1/3	116	50	45	36	87
—Rochester (Int'l)	3	5	.375	4.74	8	8	0	0	0	43 2/3	49	25	23	18	40
—Philadelphia (N.L.)■	0	1	.000	3.52	4	2	0	0	0	15 1/3	13	6	6	3	11
1997—Philadelphia (N.L.)	3	7	.300	7.23	15	13	0	0	0	71	83	59	57	41	31
—Scran./W.B. (Int'l)	6	4	.600	4.99	13	13	2	0	0	79 1/3	71	48	44	57	53
Major league totals (2 years)	3	8	.273	6.57	19	15	0	0	0	86 1/3	96	65	63	44	42

MAGADAN, DAVE   3B/1B   ATHLETICS

PERSONAL: Born September 30, 1962, in Tampa. ... 6-4/210. ... Bats left, throws right. ... Full name: David Joseph Magadan. ... Cousin of Lou Piniella, manager, Seattle Mariners, and major league outfielder/designated hitter with four teams (1964 and 1968-84). ... Name pronounced MAG-uh-dun.
HIGH SCHOOL: Jesuit (Tampa).
COLLEGE: Alabama.
TRANSACTIONS/CAREER NOTES: Selected by Boston Red Sox organization in 12th round of free-agent draft (June 3, 1980); did not sign. ... Selected by New York Mets organization in second round of free-agent draft (June 6, 1983). ... On disabled list (August 7-September 10, 1984; March 29-April 17, 1987; May 5-20, 1988; and August 9, 1992-remainder of season). ... Granted free agency (October 27, 1992). ... Signed by Florida Marlins organization (December 8, 1992). ... Traded by Marlins to Seattle Mariners for OF Henry Cotto and P Jeff Darwin (June 27, 1993). ... Traded by Mariners to Marlins for P Jeff Darwin and cash (November 9, 1993). ... On disabled list (March 29-April 13 and July 21, 1994-remainder of season). ... Granted free agency (October 19, 1994). ... Signed by Houston Astros (April 15, 1995). ... Granted free agency (October 30, 1995). ... Signed by Chicago Cubs (December 26, 1995). ... On Chicago disabled list (March 22-April 16 and April 17-May 31, 1996); included rehabilitation assignment to Daytona (May 17-29). ... Granted free agency (November 18, 1996). ... Signed by Oakland Athletics organization (January 23, 1997). ... Granted free agency (October 27, 1997). ... Re-signed by A's (November 12, 1997).
HONORS: Named Golden Spikes Award winner by USA Baseball (1983). ... Named designated hitter on THE SPORTING NEWS college All-America team (1983).
STATISTICAL NOTES: Led Carolina League with 10 intentional bases on balls received in 1984. ... Led Texas League third basemen with 87 putouts, 275 assists, 393 total chances and 31 errors in 1985. ... Led International League third basemen with .934 fielding percentage, 283 assists and 31 double plays in 1986. ... Led N.L. first basemen with .998 fielding percentage in 1990.

Year Team (League)	Pos.	G	AB	R	H	2B	3B	HR	RBI	Avg.	BB	SO	SB	PO	A	E	Avg.
1983—Columbia (S. Atl.)	1B	64	220	41	74	13	1	3	32	.336	51	29	2	520	37	7	.988
1984—Lynchburg (Caro.)	1B	112	371	78	130	22	4	0	62	*.350	104	43	2	896	64	16	.984
1985—Jackson (Texas)	3B-1B	134	466	84	144	22	0	0	76	.309	*106	57	0	†106	†276	†31	.925
1986—Tidewater (Int'l)	3B-1B	133	473	68	147	33	6	1	64	.311	84	45	2	†284	25		†.935
—New York (N.L.)	1B	10	18	3	8	0	0	0	3	.444	3	1	0	48	5	0	1.000
1987—New York (N.L.)	3B-1B	85	192	21	61	13	1	3	24	.318	22	22	0	88	92	4	.978
1988—New York (N.L.)	1B-3B	112	314	39	87	15	0	1	35	.277	60	39	0	459	99	10	.982
1989—New York (N.L.)	1B-3B	127	374	47	107	22	3	4	41	.286	49	37	0	587	89	7	.990
1990—New York (N.L.)	1B-3B	144	451	74	148	28	6	6	72	.328	74	55	2	837	99	3	†.997
1991—New York (N.L.)	1B	124	418	58	108	23	0	4	51	.258	83	50	1	1035	90	5	.996
1992—New York (N.L.)	3B-1B	99	321	33	91	9	1	3	28	.283	56	44	1	54	136	11	.945
1993—Florida (N.L.)■	3B-1B	66	227	22	65	12	0	4	29	.286	44	30	0	55	122	7	.962
—Seattle (A.L.)■	1B-3B-DH	71	228	27	59	11	0	1	21	.259	36	33	2	325	72	5	.988
1994—Florida (N.L.)■	3B-1B	74	211	30	58	7	0	1	17	.275	39	25	0	127	78	4	.981
1995—Houston (N.L.)■	3B-1B	127	348	44	109	24	0	2	51	.313	71	56	2	121	163	18	.940
1996—Daytona (Fla. St.)■	3B	7	20	5	6	1	0	0	3	.300	7	2	0	6	1		.857
—Iowa (Am. Assoc.)	3B	3	9	0	2	1	0	0	1	.222	1	2	0	3	3	0	1.000
—Chicago (N.L.)	3B-1B	78	169	23	43	10	0	3	17	.254	29	23	0	75	67	3	.979
1997—Oakland (A.L.)■	3B-1B-DH	128	271	38	82	10	1	4	30	.303	50	40	1	148	65	5	.977
American League totals (2 years)		199	499	65	141	21	1	5	50	.283	86	73	3	473	137	10	.984
National League totals (11 years)		1046	3043	394	885	163	11	31	368	.291	530	382	7	3486	1040	72	.984
Major league totals (12 years)		1245	3542	459	1026	184	12	36	419	.290	616	455	10	3959	1177	82	.984

CHAMPIONSHIP SERIES RECORD

Year Team (League)	Pos.	G	AB	R	H	2B	3B	HR	RBI	Avg.	BB	SO	SB	PO	A	E	Avg.
1988—New York (N.L.)	PH	3	3	0	0	0	0	0	0	.000	0	2	0	...	...	...	...

MAGEE, WENDELL   OF   PHILLIES

[PER]SONAL: Born August 3, 1972, in Hattiesburg, Miss. ... 6-0/220. ... Bats right, throws right. ... Full name: Wendell Errol Magee.
[HIGH] SCHOOL: Hattiesburg (Miss.).
[COLLE]GE: Samford.
[TRANS]ACTIONS/CAREER NOTES: Selected by Philadelphia Phillies organization in 12th round of free-agent draft (June 2, 1994).

Year	Team (League)	Pos.	BATTING												FIELDING		
			G	AB	R	H	2B	3B	HR	RBI	Avg.	BB	SO	SB	PO	A	E	Avg.
1994— Batavia (NY-Penn)		OF	63	229	42	64	12	4	2	35	.279	16	24	10	115	7	6	.953
1995— Clearwater (FSL)		OF	96	388	67	137	24	5	6	46	*.353	33	40	7	166	12	5	.973
— Reading (Eastern)		OF	39	136	17	40	9	1	3	21	.294	21	17	3	65	4	5	.932
1996— Reading (Eastern)		OF	71	270	38	79	15	5	6	30	.293	24	40	10	101	8	3	.973
— Scran./W.B. (Int'l)......		OF	44	155	31	44	9	2	10	32	.284	21	31	3	92	2	4	.959
— Philadelphia (N.L.)......		OF	38	142	9	29	7	0	2	14	.204	9	33	0	88	2	2	.978
1997— Philadelphia (N.L.)......		OF	38	115	7	23	4	0	1	9	.200	9	20	1	95	2	4	.960
— Scran./W.B. (Int'l)......		OF	83	294	39	72	20	1	10	39	.245	30	56	4	167	3	3	.983
Major league totals (2 years)			76	257	16	52	11	0	3	23	.202	18	53	1	183	4	6	.969

MAGNANTE, MIKE — P — ASTROS

PERSONAL: Born June 17, 1965, in Glendale, Calif. ... 6-1/195. ... Throws left, bats left. ... Full name: Michael Anthony Magnante. ... Name pronounced mag-NAN-tee.
HIGH SCHOOL: John Burroughs (Burbank, Calif.).
COLLEGE: UCLA (bachelor of science in applied mathematics).
TRANSACTIONS/CAREER NOTES: Selected by Kansas City Royals organization in 11th round of free-agent draft (June 1, 1988). ... On disabled list (June 17, 1990-remainder of season; July 2-20, 1992; and July 16-31, 1994). ... On Kansas City disabled list (May 19-June 13, 1996); included rehabilitation assignment to Omaha (June 8-13). ... Released by Royals (October 2, 1996). ... Signed by Houston Astros organization (December 19, 1996).
RECORDS: Shares major league record for striking out side on nine pitches (August 22, 1997, ninth inning).

Year	Team (League)	W	L	Pct.	ERA	G	GS	CG	ShO	Sv.	IP	H	R	ER	BB	SO
1988— Eugene (Northwest)	1	1	.500	0.56	3	3	0	0	0	16	10	6	1	2	26
— Appleton (Midwest)............	3	2	.600	3.21	9	8	0	0	0	47 2/3	48	20	17	15	40
— Baseball City (FSL).............	1	1	.500	4.13	4	4	1	0	0	24	19	12	11	8	19
1989— Memphis (Southern)	8	9	.471	3.66	26	26	4	1	0	157 1/3	137	70	64	53	118
— Omaha (Am. Assoc.)	2	5	.286	4.11	13	13	2	0	0	76 2/3	72	39	35	25	56
1990— Omaha (Am. Assoc.)	6	1	.857	3.02	10	10	2	0	0	65 2/3	53	23	22	23	50
— Kansas City (A.L.)	0	1	.000	2.45	38	0	0	0	0	55	55	19	15	23	42
1992— Kansas City (A.L.)	4	9	.308	4.94	44	12	0	0	0	89 1/3	115	53	49	35	31
1993— Omaha (Am. Assoc.)	2	6	.250	3.67	33	13	0	0	2	105 1/3	97	46	43	29	74
— Kansas City (A.L.)	1	2	.333	4.08	7	6	0	0	0	35 1/3	37	16	16	11	16
1994— Kansas City (A.L.)	2	3	.400	4.60	36	1	0	0	0	47	55	27	24	16	21
1995— Omaha (Am. Assoc.)	5	1	.833	2.84	15	8	0	0	0	57	55	23	18	13	38
— Kansas City (A.L.)	1	1	.500	4.23	28	0	0	0	0	44 2/3	45	23	21	16	28
1996— Kansas City (A.L.)	2	2	.500	5.67	38	0	0	0	0	54	58	38	34	24	32
— Omaha (Am. Assoc.)	1	0	1.000	0.00	1	0	0	0	0	3	3	1	0	0	6
1997— New Orleans (A.A.)■.........	2	3	.400	4.50	17	0	0	0	1	24	31	14	12	5	23
— Houston (N.L.)	3	1	.750	2.27	40	0	0	0	1	47 2/3	39	16	12	11	43
A.L. totals (6 years)	10	18	.357	4.40	191	19	0	0	0	325 1/3	365	176	159	125	170
N.L. totals (1 year).....................	3	1	.750	2.27	40	0	0	0	1	47 2/3	39	16	12	11	43
Major league totals (7 years)	13	19	.406	4.13	231	19	0	0	1	373	404	192	171	136	213

DIVISION SERIES RECORD

Year	Team (League)	W	L	Pct.	ERA	G	GS	CG	ShO	Sv.	IP	H	R	ER	BB	SO
1997— Houston (N.L.)	0	0	...	4.50	2	0	0	0	0	2	4	3	1	0	2

MAHAFFEY, ALAN — P — CUBS

PERSONAL: Born February 2, 1974, in Altus, Okla. ... 6-1/200. ... Throws left, bats left. ... Full name: Alan Lee Mahaffey.
HIGH SCHOOL: Kickapoo (Springfield, Mo.).
TRANSACTIONS/CAREER NOTES: Selected by Minnesota Twins organization in 16th round of free-agent draft (June 1, 1995). ... Selected by Chicago Cubs from Twins organization in Rule 5 major league draft (December 15, 1997).

Year	Team (League)	W	L	Pct.	ERA	G	GS	CG	ShO	Sv.	IP	H	R	ER	BB	SO
1995— Elizabethton (Appal.)	5	6	.455	3.47	13	12	1	0	0	70	66	42	27	21	73
1996— Fort Wayne (Midw.)...........	7	10	.412	4.84	30	19	2	0	0	126 1/3	139	84	68	35	75
1997— Fort Myers (Fla. St.)	1	2	.333	4.10	38	0	0	0	1	48 1/3	46	27	22	8	55
— New Britain (East.)	1	2	.333	3.57	13	1	0	0	1	22 2/3	19	11	9	10	29

MAHAY, RON — P — RED SOX

PERSONAL: Born June 28, 1971, in Crestwood, Ill. ... 6-2/190. ... Throws left, bats left. ... Full name: Ronald Matthew Mahay.
HIGH SCHOOL: Alan B. Shepard (Palos Heights, Ill.).
JUNIOR COLLEGE: South Suburban (Ill.).
TRANSACTIONS/CAREER NOTES: Selected by Boston Red Sox organization in 18th round of free-agent draft (June 3, 1991). ... On disabled list (May 5-September 28, 1992). ... On Lynchburg disabled list (August 6-September 9, 1993). ... On disabled list (August 23-September 1, 1994). ... On Pawtucket temporarily inactive list (April 19-25, 1995). ... On Sarasota disabled list (April 4-25, 1996).

Year	Team (League)	W	L	Pct.	ERA	G	GS	CG	ShO	Sv.	IP	H	R	ER	BB	SO
1996— Sarasota (Florida State)......	2	2	.500	3.82	31	4	0	0	2	70 2/3	61	33	30	35	68
— Trenton (Eastern)	0	1	.000	29.45	1	1	0	0	0	3 2/3	12	13	12	6	4
1997— Trenton (Eastern)	3	3	.500	3.10	17	4	0	0	5	40 2/3	29	16	14	13	4
— Pawtucket (Int'l)................	1	0	1.000	0.00	2	0	0	0	0	4 2/3	3	0	0	1	
— Boston (A.L.)...................	3	0	1.000	2.52	28	0	0	0	0	25	19	7	7	11	
Major league totals (1 year)........	3	0	1.000	2.52	28	0	0	0	0	25	19	7	7	11	

M

Year Team (League)	Pos.	G	AB	R	H	2B	3B	HR	RBI	Avg.	BB	SO	SB	PO	A	E	Avg.
1991—GC Red Sox (GCL)	OF	54	187	30	51	6	5	1	29	.273	33	40	2	97	2	3	.971
1992—Winter Haven (FSL)....	OF	19	63	6	16	2	1	0	4	.254	2	19	0	33	2	1	.972
1993—Lynchburg (Caro.)......	OF-C	73	254	28	54	8	1	5	23	.213	11	63	1	174	7	5	.973
—New Britain (Eastern) .	OF	8	25	2	3	0	0	1	2	.120	1	6	1	15	1	2	.889
1994—Sarasota (Fla. St.)	OF	105	367	43	102	18	0	4	46	.278	39	67	3	189	16	4	.981
1995—Pawtucket (Int'l)........	OF	11	44	5	14	4	0	0	3	.318	4	9	1	30	2	1	1.000
—Trenton (Eastern)	OF	93	310	37	73	12	3	5	28	.235	44	90	5	187	9	6	.970
—Boston (A.L.)..........	OF	5	20	3	4	2	0	1	3	.200	1	6	0	9	0	0	1.000
1996—Sarasota (Fla. St.).........	P	31	0	0	0	0	0	0	0	...	0	0	0	6	9	2	.882
Major league totals (1 year)		5	20	3	4	2	0	1	3	.200	1	6	0	9	0	0	1.000

MAHOMES, PAT — P — RED SOX

PERSONAL: Born August 9, 1970, in Bryan, Texas. ... 6-4/212. ... Throws right, bats right. ... Full name: Patrick Lavon Mahomes. ... Name pronounced muh-HOMES.

HIGH SCHOOL: Lindale (Texas).

TRANSACTIONS/CAREER NOTES: Selected by Minnesota Twins organization in sixth round of free-agent draft (June 1, 1988). ... On disabled list (July 6-23, 1994). ... Traded by Twins to Boston Red Sox for a player to be named later (August 26, 1996); Twins acquired P Brian Looney to complete deal (December 17, 1996).

MISCELLANEOUS: Appeared in one game as pinch-runner (1994).

Year Team (League)	W	L	Pct.	ERA	G	GS	CG	ShO	Sv.	IP	H	R	ER	BB	SO
1988—Elizabethton (Appal.)	6	3	.667	3.69	13	13	3	0	0	78	66	45	32	51	93
1989—Kenosha (Midwest)	13	7	.650	3.28	25	25	3	1	0	156 1/3	120	66	57	•100	167
1990—Visalia (California)	11	11	.500	3.30	28	*28	5	1	0	•185 1/3	136	77	68	*118	178
1991—Orlando (South.)	8	5	.615	*1.78	18	17	2	0	0	116	77	30	23	57	136
—Portland (PCL)	3	5	.375	3.44	9	9	2	0	0	55	50	26	21	36	41
1992—Minnesota (A.L.)	3	4	.429	5.04	14	13	0	0	0	69 2/3	73	41	39	37	44
—Portland (PCL)	9	5	.643	3.41	17	16	3	*3	1	111	97	43	42	43	87
1993—Minnesota (A.L.)	1	5	.167	7.71	12	5	0	0	0	37 1/3	47	34	32	16	23
—Portland (PCL)	11	4	•.733	*3.03	17	16	3	1	0	115 2/3	89	47	39	54	94
1994—Minnesota (A.L.)	9	5	.643	4.73	21	21	0	0	0	120	121	68	63	62	53
1995—Minnesota (A.L.)	4	10	.286	6.37	47	7	0	0	3	94 2/3	100	74	67	47	67
1996—Minnesota (A.L.)	1	4	.200	7.20	20	5	0	0	0	45	63	38	36	27	30
—Salt Lake (PCL)	3	1	.750	3.74	22	2	0	0	7	33 2/3	32	14	14	12	41
—Boston (A.L.)■..................	2	0	1.000	5.84	11	0	0	0	2	12 1/3	9	8	8	6	6
1997—Boston (A.L.)	1	0	1.000	8.10	10	0	0	0	0	10	15	10	9	10	5
—Pawtucket (Int'l)	5	1	.833	2.84	18	1	0	0	7	31 2/3	22	11	10	17	40
Major league totals (6 years)......	21	28	.429	5.88	135	51	0	0	5	389	428	273	254	205	228

MALAVE, JOSE — OF — RED SOX

PERSONAL: Born May 31, 1971, in Cumana, Venezuela. ... 6-2/212. ... Bats right, throws right. ... Full name: Jose Francisco Malave. ... Brother of Omar Malave, manager, Knoxville, Toronto Blue Jays organization, and minor league infielder (1981-89). ... Name pronounced muh-LAH-vee.

HIGH SCHOOL: Modesto Silva (Cumana, Venezuela).

TRANSACTIONS/CAREER NOTES: Signed as non-drafted free agent by Boston Red Sox organization (August 15, 1989). ... On disabled list (May 29-June 26 and August 3, 1993-remainder of season; and April 25-May 16, 1995). ... On Boston disabled list (July 19-August 7, 1996); included rehabilitation assignment to Pawtucket (August 3-7).

STATISTICAL NOTES: Led Eastern League with .563 slugging percentage and 262 total bases in 1994.

Year Team (League)	Pos.	G	AB	R	H	2B	3B	HR	RBI	Avg.	BB	SO	SB	PO	A	E	Avg.
1990—Elmira (N.Y.-Penn)......	OF	13	29	4	4	1	0	0	3	.138	2	12	1	4	0	1	.800
1991—GC Red Sox (GCL)	1B-OF	37	146	24	47	4	2	2	28	.322	10	23	6	277	8	7	.976
1992—Winter Haven (FSL)....	OF	8	25	1	4	0	0	0	0	.160	0	11	0	8	0	1	.889
—Elmira (N.Y.-Penn)......	OF-1B	65	268	44	87	9	1	12	46	.325	14	48	8	306	22	5	.985
1993—Lynchburg (Caro.)......	OF	82	312	42	94	27	1	8	54	.301	36	54	2	129	10	10	.933
1994—New Britain (Eastern) .	OF	122	465	87	139	•37	7	24	*92	.299	52	81	4	166	5	*11	.940
1995—Pawtucket (Int'l)........	OF	91	318	55	86	12	1	23	57	.270	30	67	0	113	2	4	.966
1996—Pawtucket (Int'l)	OF	41	155	30	42	6	0	8	29	.271	12	37	2	68	0	1	.986
—Boston (A.L.)............	OF	41	102	12	24	3	0	4	17	.235	2	25	0	43	1	1	.978
1997—Pawtucket (Int'l)	OF-1B	115	427	87	127	24	2	17	70	.297	55	78	12	259	12	6	.978
—Boston (A.L.)............	OF	4	4	0	0	0	0	0	0	.000	0	2	0	3	0	0	1.000
Major league totals (2 years)		45	106	12	24	3	0	4	17	.226	2	27	0	46	1	1	.979

MALLOY, MARTY — 2B — BRAVES

PERSONAL: Born April 6, 1972, in Gainesville, Fla. ... 5-10/160. ... Throws right, bats left. ... Full name: Marty Thomas Malloy.

HIGH SCHOOL: Trenton (Fla.).

JUNIOR COLLEGE: Santa Fe Community College (Fla.).

TRANSACTIONS/CAREER NOTES: Signed as non-drafted free agent by Atlanta Braves organization (June 25, 1992).

Team (League)	Pos.	G	AB	R	H	2B	3B	HR	RBI	Avg.	BB	SO	SB	PO	A	E	Avg.
—Idaho Falls (Pio.)........	2B-SS	62	251	45	79	18	1	2	28	.315	11	43	8	127	143	17	.941
—Macon (S. Atl.)..........	2B-SS-OF	109	376	55	110	19	3	2	36	.293	39	70	24	187	264	19	.960

Year	Team (League)	Pos.	G	AB	R	H	2B	3B	HR	RBI	Avg.	BB	SO	SB	PO	A	E	Avg.
1994—Durham (Carolina)......		2B-SS	118	428	53	113	22	1	6	35	.264	52	69	18	193	317	19	.964
1995—Greenville (Southern).		2B	124	461	73	128	20	3	10	59	.278	39	58	11	246	321	16	.973
1996—Greenville (Southern).		2B	111	429	82	134	27	2	4	36	.312	54	50	11	209	278	14	.972
—Richmond (Int'l)........		2B-SS	18	64	7	13	2	1	0	8	.203	5	7	3	34	40	2	.974
1997—Richmond (Int'l)........		2B	108	414	66	118	19	5	2	25	.285	41	61	17	*195	278	•12	.975

MALONEY, SEAN   P   BREWERS

PERSONAL: Born May 25, 1971, in South Kingstown, R.I. ... 6-7/210. ... Throws right, bats right.
HIGH SCHOOL: South Kingstown, (R.I.).
COLLEGE: Georgetown (D.C.); bachelor's degree in business administration.
TRANSACTIONS/CAREER NOTES: Selected by Milwaukee Brewers organization in 19th round of free-agent draft (June 3, 1993). ... On Tucson disabled list (May 8-24 and June 12-September 2, 1997).

Year	Team (League)	W	L	Pct.	ERA	G	GS	CG	ShO	Sv.	IP	H	R	ER	BB	SO
1993—Helena (Pioneer)		2	2	.500	4.34	17	3	1	0	0	47 2/3	55	31	23	11	35
1994—Beloit (Midwest).................		2	6	.250	5.49	51	0	0	0	22	59	73	42	36	10	53
1995—El Paso (Texas).................		7	5	.583	4.18	43	0	0	0	15	64 2/3	69	41	30	28	54
1996—El Paso (Texas).................		3	2	.600	1.43	51	0	0	0	*38	56 2/3	49	11	9	12	57
1997—Tucson (PCL).................		0	2	.000	4.82	15	0	0	0	5	18 2/3	24	10	10	3	21
—Milwaukee (A.L.).................		0	0	. . .	5.14	3	0	0	0	0	7	7	4	4	2	5
Major league totals (1 year).......		0	0	. . .	5.14	3	0	0	0	0	7	7	4	4	2	5

MANTEI, MATT   P   MARLINS

PERSONAL: Born July 7, 1973, in Tampa. ... 6-1/190. ... Throws right, bats right. ... Full name: Matthew Bruce Mantei. ... Name pronounced MAN-tay..
HIGH SCHOOL: River Valley (Three Oaks, Mich.).
TRANSACTIONS/CAREER NOTES: Selected by Seattle Mariners organization in 25th round of free-agent draft (June 3, 1991). ... Selected by Florida Marlins from Mariners organization in Rule 5 major league draft (December 5, 1994). ... On Florida disabled list (April 20-June 18 and July 29-September 1, 1995); included rehabilitation assignments to Portland and Charlotte (May 13-June 18). ... On Florida disabled list (June 19, 1996-remainder of season). ... On disabled list (March 31, 1997-entire season). ... Granted free agency (December 21, 1997). ... Re-signed by Marlins organization (December 21, 1997).

Year	Team (League)	W	L	Pct.	ERA	G	GS	CG	ShO	Sv.	IP	H	R	ER	BB	SO
1991—Ariz. Mariners (Ariz.)..........		1	4	.200	6.69	17	5	0	0	0	40 1/3	54	40	30	28	29
1992—Ariz. Mariners (Ariz.)..........		1	1	.500	5.63	3	3	0	0	0	16	18	10	10	5	19
1993—Bellingham (N'west)...........		1	1	.500	5.96	26	0	0	0	*12	25 2/3	26	19	17	15	34
1994—Appleton (Midwest)...........		5	1	.833	2.06	48	0	0	0	26	48	42	14	11	21	70
1995—Portland (Eastern)■...........		1	0	1.000	2.38	8	0	0	0	1	11 1/3	10	3	3	5	15
—Charlotte (Int'l)...........		0	1	.000	2.57	6	0	0	0	0	7	1	3	2	5	10
—Florida (N.L.)...........		0	1	.000	4.73	12	0	0	0	0	13 1/3	12	8	7	13	15
1996—Florida (N.L.)...........		1	0	1.000	6.38	14	0	0	0	0	18 1/3	13	13	13	21	25
—Charlotte (Int'l)...........		0	2	.000	4.70	7	0	0	0	2	7 2/3	6	4	4	7	8
1997—Brevard County (FSL)........		0	0	. . .	6.00	4	0	0	0	0	6	4	4	4	6	11
—Portland (Eastern)...........		1	0	1.000	6.75	5	0	0	0	0	4	1	3	3	8	7
Major league totals (2 years)......		1	1	.500	5.68	26	0	0	0	0	31 2/3	25	21	20	34	40

MANTO, JEFF   3B   INDIANS

PERSONAL: Born August 23, 1964, in Bristol, Pa. ... 6-3/210. ... Bats right, throws right. ... Full name: Jeffrey Paul Manto.
HIGH SCHOOL: Bristol (Pa.).
COLLEGE: Temple.
TRANSACTIONS/CAREER NOTES: Selected by New York Yankees organization in 35th round of free-agent draft (June 7, 1982); did not sign. ... Selected by California Angels organization in 14th round of free-agent draft (June 3, 1985). ... On disabled list (July 16, 1986-remainder of season). ... Traded by Angels organization with P Colin Charland to Cleveland Indians for P Scott Bailes (January 9, 1990). ... Released by Indians (November 27, 1991). ... Signed by Richmond, Atlanta Braves organization (January 23, 1992). ... On disabled list (May 4-14, 1992). ... Granted free agency (October 15, 1992). ... Signed by Philadelphia Phillies organization (December 16, 1992). ... Granted free agency (October 15, 1993). ... Signed by New York Mets organization (December 16, 1993). ... Traded by Mets organization to Baltimore Orioles organization for future considerations (May 19, 1994). ... On Baltimore disabled list (June 26-July 13, 1995); included rehabilitation assignments to Bowie (July 9-10) and Frederick (July 10-13). ... Signed by Yomiuri Giants of Japan Central League (January 25, 1996). ... Released by Giants (April 23, 1996). ... Signed by Boston Red Sox organization (May 7, 1996). ... On Boston disabled list (May 26-June 27, 1996); included rehabilitation assignment to Trenton (June 21-27). ... Claimed on waivers by Red Sox (August 29, 1996). ... Granted free agency (October 4, 1996). ... Signed by Red Sox to Seattle Mariners for IF Arquimedez Pozo (July 23, 1996). ... Released by Mariners (August 29, 1996). ... . Signed by Syracuse, Blue Jays organization (February 17, 1997). ... On Syracuse disabled list (May 26-June 2, 1997). ... Traded by Blue Jays organization to Cleveland Indians organization for OF Ryan Thompson (June 6, 1997).
RECORDS: Shares major league record for most consecutive home runs in three games—4 (June 8 [1], 9 [2] and 10 [1], 1995).
HONORS: Named Texas League Most Valuable Player (1988). ... Named International League Most Valuable Player (1994).
STATISTICAL NOTES: Led California League third basemen with 245 assists and 365 total chances in 1987. ... Tied for Texas League lead in errors by third baseman with 32 in 1988. ... Led Texas League in grounding into double plays with 17 in 1988. ... Led Pacific Coast League with .446 on-base percentage in 1990. ... Led Pacific Coast League third basemen with .943 fielding percentage, 265 assists and 22 double plays in 1989. ... Led International League with 12 sacrifice flies in 1992. ... Led International League with .404 on-base percentage, 260 total bases, 31 home runs, 100 RBIs and tied for lead in being hit by pitch with 11 in 1994.

Year	Team (League)	Pos.	G	AB	R	H	2B	3B	HR	RBI	Avg.	BB	SO	SB	PO	A	E
1985—Quad Cities (Mid.)		OF-3B	74	233	34	46	5	2	11	34	.197	40	74	3	87	8	3
1986—Quad Cities (Mid.)		3B	73	239	31	59	13	0	8	49	.247	37	70	2	48	114	28

M

Year — Team (League)	Pos.	G	AB	R	H	2B	3B	HR	RBI	Avg.	BB	SO	SB	PO	A	E	Avg.
1987— Palm Springs (Cal.)....	3B-1B	112	375	61	96	21	4	7	63	.256	102	85	8	93	†246	37	·902
1988— Midland (Texas)........	3B-2B-1B	120	408	88	123	23	3	24	101	.301	62	76	7	82	208	‡32	.901
1989— Edmonton (PCL)........	3B-1B	127	408	89	113	25	3	23	67	.277	91	81	4	140	†266	21	†.951
1990— Colo. Springs (PCL)■	3B-1B	96	316	73	94	27	4	18	82	.297	78	65	10	340	131	10	.979
— Cleveland (A.L.)........	1B-3B	30	76	12	17	5	1	2	14	.224	21	18	0	185	24	2	.991
1991— Cleveland (A.L.)........	3-1-C-O	47	128	15	27	7	0	2	13	.211	14	22	2	109	63	8	.956
— Colo. Springs (PCL) ...	3-1-C-S-O	43	153	36	49	16	0	6	36	.320	33	24	1	169	53	11	.953
1992— Richmond (Int'l)........	3B-2B-1B	127	450	65	131	24	1	13	68	.291	57	63	1	89	245	23	.936
1993— Scran./W.B. (Int'l)■....	3B-1B-C	106	388	62	112	30	1	17	88	.289	55	58	4	401	134	8	.985
— Philadelphia (N.L.).....	3B-SS	8	18	0	1	0	0	0	0	.056	0	3	0	2	8	0	1.000
1994— Norfolk (Int'l)■........	3B-1B-2B	37	115	20	30	6	0	4	17	.261	27	28	1	73	46	4	.967
— Rochester (Int'l)■......	3B-1B	94	329	61	102	25	2	§27	§83	.310	43	47	2	277	102	15	.962
1995— Baltimore (A.L.).........	3B-DH-1B	89	254	31	65	9	0	17	38	.256	24	69	0	68	103	6	.966
— Bowie (Eastern)......	DH	1	4	1	1	0	0	0	0	.250	0	2	0	0	0	0	...
— Frederick (Carolina)	3B	2	8	1	3	0	0	1	3	.375	0	1	0	0	2	0	1.000
1996— Yomiuri (Jp. Cen.)■ ...	...	...	27	1	3	...	...	0	1	.111	...	...	...	...	...	...	...
— Pawtucket (Int'l)■......	3B-2B	12	45	6	11	5	0	2	6	.244	5	8	1	13	29	2	.955
— Boston (A.L.).........	3-2-S-1	22	48	8	10	3	1	2	6	.208	8	12	0	25	47	4	.947
— Trenton (Eastern)	3B-2B-SS	6	21	3	6	0	0	0	5	.286	1	5	0	5	5	3	.769
— Seattle (A.L.)■........	3B-DH-OF	21	54	7	10	3	0	1	4	.185	9	12	0	8	26	1	.971
1997— Syracuse (Int'l)■........	3B-OF-1B	40	132	18	27	5	1	3	11	.205	22	30	1	23	19	1	.977
— Buffalo (A.A.)■	3B-1B-OF	54	187	37	60	11	0	20	54	.321	31	43	0	59	54	6	.950
— Cleveland (A.L.)■......	3B-1B-OF	16	30	3	8	3	0	2	7	.267	1	10	0	35	5	0	1.000
American League totals (5 years)		225	590	76	137	30	2	26	82	.232	77	143	2	430	268	21	.971
National League totals (1 year)		8	18	0	1	0	0	0	0	.056	0	3	0	2	8	0	1.000
Major league totals (6 years)		233	608	76	138	30	2	26	82	.227	77	146	2	432	276	21	.971

MANUEL, BARRY   P   DIAMONDBACKS

PERSONAL: Born August 12, 1965, in Mamou, La. ... 5-11/185. ... Throws right, bats right. ... Full name: Barry Paul Manuel. ... Brother of Ferral Manuel, minor league catcher (1989).

HIGH SCHOOL: Mamou (La.).

COLLEGE: Louisiana State.

TRANSACTIONS/CAREER NOTES: Selected by Texas Rangers organization in second round of free-agent draft (June 2, 1987). ... On Texas disabled list (March 27-June 20, 1993); included rehabilitation assignment to Charlotte (June 11-20). ... Claimed on waivers by Baltimore Orioles (August 9, 1993). ... Granted free agency (October 15, 1994). ... Signed by Ottawa, Montreal Expos organization (February 19, 1995). ... Granted free agency (October 16, 1995). ... Re-signed by Expos (March 31, 1996). ... Traded by Expos to New York Mets for cash (March 28, 1997). ... Granted free agency (October 15, 1997). ... Signed by Arizona Diamondbacks organization (December 18, 1997).

STATISTICAL NOTES: Pitched one inning, combining with Cedric Shaw (seven innings) and Everett Cunningham (one inning) in 2-0 no-hit victory for Tulsa against Arkansas (April 18, 1991).

Year — Team (League)	W	L	Pct.	ERA	G	GS	CG	ShO	Sv.	IP	H	R	ER	BB	SO
1987— GC Rangers (GCL)........	0	0	...	18.00	1	0	0	0	0	1	3	2	2	1	1
— Charlotte (Fla. St.).............	1	2	.333	6.60	13	5	0	0	0	30	33	24	22	18	19
1988— Charlotte (Fla. St.).............	4	3	.571	2.54	37	0	0	0	4	60 1/3	47	24	17	32	55
1989— Tulsa (Texas)	3	4	.429	7.48	11	11	0	0	0	49 1/3	49	44	41	39	40
— Charlotte (Fla. St.).............	4	7	.364	4.72	15	14	0	0	0	76 1/3	77	43	40	30	51
1990— Charlotte (Fla. St.).............	1	5	.167	2.88	57	0	0	0	*36	56 1/3	39	23	18	30	60
1991— Tulsa (Texas)	2	7	.222	3.29	56	0	0	0	*25	68 1/3	63	29	25	34	45
— Texas (A.L.)	1	0	1.000	1.13	8	0	0	0	0	16	7	2	2	6	5
1992— Oklahoma City (A.A.).........	1	8	.111	5.27	27	0	0	0	5	27 1/3	32	24	16	26	11
— Texas (A.L.)	1	0	1.000	4.76	3	0	0	0	0	5 2/3	6	3	3	1	9
— Tulsa (Texas)	2	0	1.000	4.00	16	1	0	0	2	27	28	12	12	16	28
1993— Charlotte (Fla. St.).............	0	0	...	0.00	3	0	0	0	0	4 2/3	6	0	0	2	4
— Oklahoma City (A.A.).........	2	2	.500	7.99	21	0	0	0	0	23 2/3	29	21	21	16	19
— Rochester (Int'l)	1	1	.500	3.66	9	0	0	0	0	19 2/3	14	8	8	7	11
1994— Rochester (Int'l)	11	8	.579	5.48	35	20	1	0	4	139 2/3	161	87	85	58	107
1995— Ottawa (Int'l)■	5	12	.294	4.59	35	22	1	0	1	127 1/3	125	71	65	50	85
1996— Montreal (N.L.)■	4	1	.800	3.24	53	0	0	0	0	86	70	34	31	26	62
1997— New York (N.L.)■	0	1	.000	5.26	19	0	0	0	0	25 2/3	35	18	15	13	21
— Norfolk (Int'l)	2	5	.286	4.87	19	8	0	0	0	61	60	36	33	21	52
A.L. totals (2 years)	2	0	1.000	2.08	11	0	0	0	0	21 2/3	13	5	5	7	14
N.L. totals (2 years)	4	2	.667	3.71	72	0	0	0	0	111 2/3	105	52	46	39	83
Major league totals (4 years)	6	2	.750	3.44	83	0	0	0	0	133 1/3	118	57	51	46	97

MANWARING, KIRT   C   ROCKIES

PERSONAL: Born July 15, 1965, in Elmira, N.Y. ... 5-11/203. ... Bats right, throws right. ... Full name: Kirt Dean Manwaring.

HIGH SCHOOL: Horseheads (N.Y.).

COLLEGE: Coastal Carolina (S.C.).

TRANSACTIONS/CAREER NOTES: Selected by Boston Red Sox organization in 12th round of free-agent draft (June 6, 1983); did not sign. ... Selected by San Francisco Giants organization in second round of free-agent draft (June 2, 1986). ... On disabled list (August 31-September 15, 1989 and June 24-July 18, 1990). ... On San Francisco disabled list (May 30-July 11, 1991); included rehabilitation assignments to Phoenix (July 1-8) and San Jose (July 8-11). ... On San Francisco disabled list (July 22-August 6, 1992). ... On San Francisco disabled list (April 10-May 23, 1996); included rehabilitation assignment to Phoenix (May 18-23). ... Traded by Giants to Houston Astros for C Rick Wilkins and cash (July 27, 1996). ... Granted free agency (October 28, 1996). ... Signed by Colorado Rockies (December 9, 1996).

HONORS: Won N.L. Gold Glove at catcher (1993).

STATISTICAL NOTES: Led Texas League catchers with 688 total chances and eight double plays in 1987. ... Led N.L. catchers with 12 double [plays] in 1992 and 10 in 1994.

Year Team (League)	Pos.	G	AB	R	H	2B	3B	HR	RBI	Avg.	BB	SO	SB	PO	A	E	Avg.
1986—Clinton (Midwest).......	C	49	147	18	36	7	1	2	16	.245	14	26	1	243	31	5	.982
1987—Shreveport (Texas).....	C	98	307	27	82	13	2	2	22	.267	19	33	1	603	*81	4	.994
—San Francisco (N.L.) ..	C	6	7	0	1	0	0	0	0	.143	0	1	0	9	1	1	.909
1988—Phoenix (PCL)	C	81	273	29	77	12	2	2	35	.282	14	32	3	411	51	6	.987
—San Francisco (N.L.) ..	C	40	116	12	29	7	0	1	15	.250	2	21	0	162	24	4	.979
1989—San Francisco (N.L.) ..	C	85	200	14	42	4	2	0	18	.210	11	28	2	289	32	6	.982
1990—Phoenix (PCL)	C	74	247	20	58	10	2	3	14	.235	24	34	0	352	45	4	*.990
—San Francisco (N.L.) ..	C	8	13	0	2	0	1	0	1	.154	0	3	0	22	3	0	1.000
1991—San Francisco (N.L.) ..	C	67	178	16	40	9	0	0	19	.225	9	22	1	315	28	4	.988
—Phoenix (PCL)	C	24	81	8	18	0	0	4	14	.222	8	15	0	100	15	3	.975
—San Jose (Calif.)	C	1	3	1	0	0	0	0	0	.000	1	1	0	16	0	0	1.000
1992—San Francisco (N.L.) ..	C	109	349	24	85	10	5	4	26	.244	29	42	2	564	68	4	.994
1993—San Francisco (N.L.) ..	C	130	432	48	119	15	1	5	49	.275	41	76	1	739	70	2	*.998
1994—San Francisco (N.L.) ..	C	97	316	30	79	17	1	1	29	.250	25	50	1	541	52	4	.993
1995—San Francisco (N.L.) ..	C	118	379	21	95	15	2	4	36	.251	27	72	1	607	55	7	.990
1996—San Francisco (N.L.) ..	C	49	145	9	34	6	0	1	14	.234	16	24	0	268	26	2	.993
--Phoenix (PCL)	C	4	11	1	2	0	0	0	1	.182	2	0	0	15	3	0	1.000
—Houston (N.L.)■	C	37	82	5	18	3	0	0	4	.220	3	16	0	171	21	1	.995
1997—Colorado (N.L.)■	C	104	337	22	76	6	4	1	27	.226	30	78	1	488	40	3	.994
Major league totals (11 years)		850	2554	201	620	92	16	17	238	.243	193	433	9	4175	420	38	.992

CHAMPIONSHIP SERIES RECORD

Year Team (League)	Pos.	G	AB	R	H	2B	3B	HR	RBI	Avg.	BB	SO	SB	PO	A	E	Avg.
1989—San Francisco (N.L.) ..	C-PH	3	2	0	0	0	0	0	0	.000	0	0	0	5	0	0	1.000

WORLD SERIES RECORD

Year Team (League)	Pos.	G	AB	R	H	2B	3B	HR	RBI	Avg.	BB	SO	SB	PO	A	E	Avg.
1989—San Francisco (N.L.) ..	C	1	1	1	1	1	0	0	0	1.000	0	0	0	0	0	0	...

MANZANILLO, JOSIAS   P

PERSONAL: Born October 16, 1967, in San Pedro de Macoris, Dominican Republic. ... 6-0/190. ... Throws right, bats right. ... Brother of Ravelo Manzanillo, pitcher, Seattle Mariners organization. ... Name pronounced hose-EYE-ess MAN-zan-EE-oh..

TRANSACTIONS/CAREER NOTES: Signed as non-drafted free agent by Boston Red Sox organization (January 10, 1983). ... On disabled list (June 8, 1987-remainder of season and April 8, 1988-entire season). ... Granted free agency (March 24, 1992). ... Signed by Omaha, Kansas City Royals organization (April 3, 1992). ... Granted free agency (October 15, 1992). ... Signed by Milwaukee Brewers (November 20, 1992). ... Traded by Brewers to New York Mets for OF Wayne Housie (June 12, 1993). ... On New York disabled list (July 27, 1994-remainder of season). ... Claimed on waivers by New York Yankees (June 5, 1995). ... On New York Yankees disabled list (July 6, 1995-remainder of season). ... Granted free agency (October 16, 1995). ... Missed entire 1996 season due to injury. ... Signed by Seattle Mariners organization (December 21, 1996). ... On Seattle disabled list (April 9-May 6 and May 25-July 1, 1997); included rehabilitation assignments to Memphis (May 1-6) and Tacoma (May 25-July 1). ... Released by Mariners organization (July 17, 1997). ... Signed by New Orleans, Houston Astros organization (July 27, 1997). ... Granted free agency (October 15, 1997).

Year Team (League)	W	L	Pct.	ERA	G	GS	CG	ShO	Sv.	IP	H	R	ER	BB	SO
1983—Elmira (N.Y.-Penn).............	1	5	.167	7.98	12	4	0	0	0	38 1/3	52	44	34	20	19
1984—Elmira (N.Y.-Penn).............	2	3	.400	5.26	14	0	0	0	1	25 2/3	27	24	15	26	15
1985—Greensboro (S. Atl.)	1	1	.500	9.75	7	0	0	0	0	12	12	13	13	18	10
—Elmira (N.Y.-Penn)............	2	4	.333	3.86	19	4	0	0	1	39 2/3	36	19	17	36	43
1986—Winter Haven (FSL)...........	13	5	.722	2.27	23	21	3	2	0	142 2/3	110	51	36	81	102
1987—New Britain (East.)	2	0	1.000	4.50	2	2	0	0	0	10	8	5	5	8	12
1988—								Did not play.							
1989—New Britain (East.)	9	10	.474	3.66	26	•26	3	1	0	147 2/3	129	78	60	85	93
1990—New Britain (East.)	4	4	.500	3.41	12	12	2	1	0	74	66	34	28	37	51
—Pawtucket (Int'l)	4	7	.364	5.55	15	15	5	0	0	82 2/3	75	57	51	45	77
1991—Pawtucket (Int'l)	5	5	.500	5.61	20	16	0	0	0	102 2/3	109	69	64	53	65
—New Britain (East.)	2	2	.500	2.90	7	7	0	0	0	49 2/3	37	25	16	28	35
—Boston (A.L.)	0	0	...	18.00	1	0	0	0	0	1	2	2	2	3	1
1992—Omaha (Am. Assoc.)■.........	7	10	.412	4.36	26	21	0	0	0	136 1/3	138	76	66	71	114
—Memphis (Southern)	0	2	.000	7.36	2	0	0	0	0	7 1/3	6	6	6	6	8
1993—Milwaukee (A.L.)■	1	1	.500	9.53	10	1	0	0	1	17	22	20	18	10	10
—New Orleans (A.A.)	0	1	.000	9.00	1	0	0	0	0	1	1	1	1	0	3
—Norfolk (Int'l)■	1	5	.167	3.11	14	12	2	1	0	84	82	40	29	25	79
—New York (N.L.).................	0	0	...	3.00	6	0	0	0	0	6	8	7	4	9	11
1994—Norfolk (Int'l)	0	1	.000	4.38	8	0	0	0	3	12 1/3	12	6	6	6	10
—New York (N.L.).................	3	2	.600	2.66	37	0	0	0	2	47 1/3	34	15	14	13	48
1995—New York (N.L.)	1	2	.333	7.88	12	0	0	0	0	16	18	15	14	6	14
—New York (A.L.)■	0	0	...	2.08	11	0	0	0	0	17 1/3	19	4	4	9	14
1996—								Did not play.							
1997—Seattle (A.L.)■	0	1	.000	5.40	16	0	0	0	0	18 1/3	19	13	11	11	17
—Memphis (Southern)	0	0	...	3.00	2	0	0	0	0	3	1	1	1	0	
—Tacoma (PCL)	0	0	...	6.43	11	0	0	0	1	14	16	10	10	8	
—New Orleans (A.A.)■	0	0	...	4.40	11	0	0	0	0	14 1/3	17	7	7	6	
A.L. totals (4 years)	1	2	.333	5.87	38	1	0	0	1	53 2/3	62	39	35	33	
N.L. totals (3 years)	4	4	.500	3.82	55	0	0	0	2	75 1/3	60	37	32		
Major league totals (5 years)......	5	6	.455	4.67	93	1	0	0	3	129	122	76	67		

MARRERO, ELI — C — CARDINALS

PERSONAL: Born November 17, 1973, in Havana, Cuba. ... 6-1/180. ... Bats right, throws right. ... Full name: Elieser Marrero.
HIGH SCHOOL: Coral Gables (Fla.).
TRANSACTIONS/CAREER NOTES: Selected by St. Louis Cardinals organization in third round of free-agent draft (June 3, 1993).
STATISTICAL NOTES: Led Texas League catchers with 746 total chances in 1996. ... Led American Association catchers with 750 total chances in 1997.

Year Team (League)	Pos.	G	AB	R	H	2B	3B	HR	RBI	Avg.	BB	SO	SB	PO	A	E	Avg.
1993—Johnson City (App.) ...	C	18	61	10	22	8	0	2	14	.361	12	9	2	154	18	1	.994
1994—Savannah (S. Atl.)	C	116	421	71	110	16	3	21	79	.261	39	92	5	821	92	•15	.984
1995—St. Petersburg (FSL) ..	C	107	383	43	81	16	1	10	55	.211	23	55	9	574	52	10	.984
1996—Arkansas (Texas)........	C	116	374	65	101	17	3	19	65	.270	32	55	9	*676	67	3	*.996
1997—Louisville (A.A.).........	C	112	395	60	108	21	7	20	68	.273	25	53	4	*675	*68	7	.991
— St. Louis (N.L.)...........	C	17	45	4	11	2	0	2	7	.244	2	13	4	82	12	3	.969
Major league totals (1 year)		17	45	4	11	2	0	2	7	.244	2	13	4	82	12	3	.969

MARTE, DAMASO — P — MARINERS

PERSONAL: Born February 14, 1975, in Santo Domingo, Dominican Republic. ... 6-0/170. ... Throws left, bats left.
TRANSACTIONS/CAREER NOTES: Signed as non-drafted free agent by Seattle Mariners organization (October 28, 1992). ... On disabled list (April 3-17, 1997).

Year Team (League)	W	L	Pct.	ERA	G	GS	CG	ShO	Sv.	IP	H	R	ER	BB	SO
1993—Dom. Mariners (DSL)........	2	5	.286	6.55	17	15	2	0	0	56 1/3	62	48	41	50	29
1994—Dom. Mariners (DSL)........	7	0	1.000	3.86	17	13	0	0	0	65 1/3	53	41	28	48	80
1995—Everett (Northwest)	2	2	.500	2.21	11	11	5	0	0	36 2/3	25	11	9	10	39
1996—Wis. Rap. (Midw.)	8	6	.571	4.49	26	26	2	1	0	142 1/3	134	82	71	75	115
1997—Lancaster (Calif.).............	8	8	.500	4.13	25	25	2	1	0	139 1/3	144	75	64	62	127

MARTIN, AL — OF — PIRATES

PERSONAL: Born November 24, 1967, in West Covina, Calif. ... 6-2/210. ... Bats left, throws left. ... Full name: Albert Lee Martin. ... Formerly known as Albert Scales-Martin.
HIGH SCHOOL: Rowland Heights (Calif.).
COLLEGE: Southern California.
TRANSACTIONS/CAREER NOTES: Selected by Atlanta Braves organization in eighth round of free-agent draft (June 3, 1985). ... Granted free agency (October 15, 1991). ... Signed by Pittsburgh Pirates organization (November 11, 1991). ... On suspended list (September 17-20, 1993). ... On disabled list (July 11, 1994-remainder of season). ... On Pittsburgh disabled list (May 22-June 24, 1997); included rehabilitaion assignment to Carolina (June 21-23).
RECORDS: Shares major league record for fewest double plays by outfielder (150 or more games)—0 (1996). ... Holds modern N.L. single-season record for fewest putouts by outfielder (150 or more games)—217 (1996). ... Holds N.L. single-season record for fewest chances accepted by outfielder (150 or more games)—222 (1997).
STATISTICAL NOTES: Led Gulf Coast League first basemen with 15 errors in 1985. ... Led American Association with .557 slugging percentage in 1992. ... Led American Association outfielders with six double plays in 1992. ... Career major league grand slams: 1.

Year Team (League)	Pos.	G	AB	R	H	2B	3B	HR	RBI	Avg.	BB	SO	SB	PO	A	E	Avg.
1985—GC Braves (GCL)	1B-OF	40	138	16	32	3	0	0	9	.232	19	36	1	246	13	†15	.945
1986—Sumter (S. Atl.)	1B	44	156	23	38	5	0	1	24	.244	23	36	6	299	12	8	.975
— Idaho Falls (Pio.)........	OF-1B	63	242	39	80	17	•6	4	44	.331	20	53	11	272	15	8	.973
1987—Sumter (S. Atl.)	OF-1B	117	375	59	95	18	5	12	64	.253	44	69	27	137	7	9	.941
1988—Burl. (Midw.)..........	OF	123	480	69	134	21	3	7	42	.279	30	88	40	224	4	8	.966
1989—Durham (Carolina)......	OF	128	457	*84	124	26	3	9	48	.271	34	107	27	169	7	7	.962
1990—Greenville (Southern) .	OF	133	455	64	110	17	4	11	50	.242	43	102	20	200	8	7	.967
1991—Greenville (Southern) .	OF-1B	86	301	38	73	13	3	7	38	.243	32	84	19	134	7	6	.959
— Richmond (Int'l)........	OF	44	151	20	42	11	1	5	18	.278	7	33	11	73	4	2	.975
1992—Buffalo (A.A.)■	OF	125	420	85	128	16	*15	20	59	.305	35	93	20	222	10	8	.967
— Pittsburgh (N.L.)	OF	12	12	1	2	0	1	0	2	.167	0	5	0	6	0	0	1.000
1993—Pittsburgh (N.L.)	OF	143	480	85	135	26	8	18	64	.281	42	122	16	268	6	7	.975
1994—Pittsburgh (N.L.)	OF	82	276	48	79	12	4	9	33	.286	34	56	15	129	8	3	.979
1995—Pittsburgh (N.L.)	OF	124	439	70	124	25	3	13	41	.282	44	92	20	206	8	5	.977
1996—Pittsburgh (N.L.)	OF	155	630	101	189	40	1	18	72	.300	54	116	38	217	5	8	.965
1997—Pittsburgh (N.L.)	OF	113	423	64	123	24	7	13	59	.291	45	83	23	125	8	6	.957
— Carolina (Southern)....	OF	3	9	0	1	0	0	0	0	.111	0	0	0	2	0	0	1.000
Major league totals (6 years)		629	2260	369	652	127	24	71	271	.288	219	474	112	951	35	29	.971

MARTIN, NORBERTO — IF — ANGELS

PERSONAL: Born December 10, 1966, in Santo Domingo, Dominican Republic. ... 5-10/164. ... Bats right, throws right. ... Full name: Norberto ...onal Martin. ... Name pronounced mar-TEEN.
...NSACTIONS/CAREER NOTES: Signed as non-drafted free agent by Chicago White Sox organization (March 27, 1984). ... On Peninsula ...led list (April 10-May 5, 1986). ... On Appleton disabled list (May 14, 1986-remainder of season). ... On disabled list (April 7, 1989-entire ... and May 5-June 9, 1991). ... On Chicago disabled list (April 6-June 5, 1996); included rehabilitation assignment to Nashville (May ... 1). ... On disabled list (June 20-July 3 and July 21-August 8, 1997). ... Granted free agency (December 21, 1997). ... Signed by ... Angels (January 10, 1998).
...CAL NOTES: Led Gulf Coast League shortstops with 37 errors in 1984. ... Led Pacific Coast League second basemen with 681 total ... 1992. ... Led American Association second basemen with 291 putouts, 438 assists, 18 errors and 747 total chances in 1993. ... ... r league grand slams: 1.

M

Year Team (League)	Pos.	G	AB	R	H	2B	3B	HR	RBI	Avg.	BB	SO	SB	PO	A	E	Avg.
1984— GC Whi. Sox (GCL)	SS-OF	56	205	36	56	8	2	1	30	.273	21	31	18	66	149	†37	.853
1985— Appleton (Midwest)....	SS	30	196	15	19	2	0	0	5	.097	9	23	2	39	86	12	.912
— Niag. Falls (NYP)........	SS	60	217	22	55	9	0	1	13	.253	7	41	6	85	173	35	.881
1986— Appleton (Midwest)....	SS	9	33	4	10	2	0	0	2	.303	2	5	1	13	16	6	.829
— GC Whi. Sox (GCL)	PR	1	0	0	0	0	0	0	0	...	0	0	0	...	...	...	...
1987— Char., W.Va. (SAL).....	SS-OF-2B	68	250	44	78	14	1	5	35	.312	17	40	14	84	152	25	.904
— Peninsula (Caro.)	2B	41	162	21	42	6	1	1	18	.259	18	19	11	94	108	15	.931
1988— Tampa (Florida State).	2B	101	360	44	93	10	4	2	33	.258	17	49	24	196	268	20	.959
1989—							Did not play.										
1990— Vancouver (PCL)........	2B	130	508	77	135	20	4	3	45	.266	27	63	10	283	324	17	.973
1991— Vancouver (PCL)........	2B-SS	93	338	39	94	9	0	0	20	.278	21	38	11	196	265	16	.966
1992— Vancouver (PCL)........	2B	135	497	72	143	12	7	0	29	.288	29	44	29	266	*395	•20	.971
1993— Nashville (A.A.).........	2B-SS	•137	*580	87	*179	21	6	9	74	.309	26	59	31	†292	†442	†18	.976
— Chicago (A.L.)	2B-DH	8	14	3	5	0	0	0	2	.357	1	1	0	13	9	1	.957
1994— Nashville (A.A.).........	S-3-2-O	43	172	26	44	8	0	2	12	.256	10	14	4	47	72	10	.922
— Chicago (A.L.) 2-S-3-0-DH		45	131	19	36	7	1	1	16	.275	9	16	4	58	77	2	.985
1995— Chicago (A.L.) 2-0-DH-3-S		72	160	17	43	7	4	2	17	.269	3	25	5	52	67	7	.944
1996— Chicago (A.L.)	S-DH-2-3	70	140	30	49	7	0	1	14	.350	6	17	10	61	79	6	.959
— Nashville (A.A.)	2B-SS-3B	17	68	9	14	3	0	2	8	.206	4	10	1	27	43	2	.972
1997— Chicago (A.L.)	S-3-2-DH	71	213	24	64	7	1	2	27	.300	6	31	1	50	97	5	.967
Major league totals (5 years)		266	658	93	197	28	6	6	76	.299	25	90	20	234	329	21	.964

MARTIN, TOM — P — INDIANS

PERSONAL: Born May 21, 1970, in Charleston, S.C. ... 6-1/185. ... Throws left, bats left. ... Full name: Thomas Edgar Martin.

HIGH SCHOOL: Bay (Panama City, Fla.).

TRANSACTIONS/CAREER NOTES: Selected by Baltimore Orioles organization in sixth round of free-agent draft (June 1, 1988). ... Traded by Orioles with 3B Craig Worthington to San Diego Padres organization for P Jim Lewis and OF Steve Martin (February 17, 1992). ... Selected by Richmond, Atlanta Braves organization, from Wichita, Padres organization, in Rule 5 minor league draft (December 13, 1993). ... Signed by Jackson, Houston Astros organization (February 21, 1996). ... On disabled list (May 30-June 15, 1997). ... Selected by Arizona Diamondbacks in second round (29th pick overall) of expansion draft (November 18, 1997). ... Traded by Diamondbacks with 3B Travis Fryman and cash to Cleveland Indians for 3B Matt Williams (December 1, 1997).

Year Team (League)	W	L	Pct.	ERA	G	GS	CG	ShO	Sv.	IP	H	R	ER	BB	SO
1989— Bluefield (Appalachian)	3	3	.500	4.62	8	8	0	0	0	39	36	28	20	25	31
— Erie (N.Y.-Penn).................	0	5	.000	6.64	7	7	0	0	0	40 2/3	42	39	30	25	44
1990— Wausau (Midwest)...........	2	3	.400	2.48	9	9	0	0	0	40	31	25	11	27	45
1991— Kane County (Midwest).....	4	10	.286	3.64	38	10	0	0	6	99	92	50	40	56	106
1992— High Desert (Calif.)■	0	2	.000	9.37	11	0	0	0	0	16 1/3	23	19	17	16	10
— Waterloo (Midw.).............	2	6	.250	4.25	39	2	0	0	3	55	62	38	26	22	57
1993— Rancho Cucamonga (Cal.) .	1	4	.200	5.61	47	1	0	0	0	59 1/3	72	41	37	39	53
1994— Greenville (Southern)■......	5	6	.455	4.62	36	6	0	0	0	74	82	40	38	27	51
1995— Richmond (Int'l)................	0	0	...	9.00	7	0	0	0	0	9	10	9	9	10	3
1996— Tucson (PCL)■.................	0	0	...	0.00	5	0	0	0	0	6	6	0	0	2	1
— Jackson (Texas)	6	2	.750	3.24	57	0	0	0	3	75	71	35	27	42	58
1997— Houston (N.L.)	5	3	.625	2.09	55	0	0	0	2	56	52	13	13	23	36
Major league totals (1 year)........	5	3	.625	2.09	55	0	0	0	2	56	52	13	13	23	36

DIVISION SERIES RECORD

Year Team (League)	W	L	Pct.	ERA	G	GS	CG	ShO	Sv.	IP	H	R	ER	BB	SO
1997— Houston (N.L.)	0	0	...	0.00	2	0	0	0	0	2/3	1	1	0	1	0

MARTINEZ, DAVE — OF — DEVIL RAYS

PERSONAL: Born September 26, 1964, in New York. ... 5-10/175. ... Bats left, throws left. ... Full name: David Martinez.

HIGH SCHOOL: Lake Howell (Casselberry, Fla.).

JUNIOR COLLEGE: Valencia Community College (Fla.).

TRANSACTIONS/CAREER NOTES: Selected by Texas Rangers organization in 40th round of free-agent draft (June 7, 1982); did not sign. ... Selected by Chicago Cubs organization in secondary phase of free-agent draft (January 11, 1983). ... On disabled list (April 27, 1984-remainder of season). ... Traded by Cubs to Montreal Expos for OF Mitch Webster (July 14, 1988). ... On disqualified list (October 4-5, 1991). ... Traded by Expos with P Scott Ruskin and SS Willie Greene to Cincinnati Reds for P John Wetteland and P Bill Risley (December 11, 1991). ... Granted free agency (October 27, 1992). ... Signed by San Francisco Giants (December 9, 1992). ... On San Francisco disabled list (April 30-June 4, 1993); included rehabilitation assignment to Phoenix (June 1-4). ... Granted free agency (October 14, 1994). ... Signed by Chicago White Sox (April 5, 1995). ... Granted free agency (November 3, 1995). ... Re-signed by White Sox (November 14, 1995). ... Granted free agency (October 27, 1997). ... Signed by Tampa Bay Devil Rays (December 4, 1997).

RECORDS: Shares single-game major league record for most unassisted double plays by first baseman—2 (June 21, 1997).

STATISTICAL NOTES: Career major league grand slams: 2.

Year Team (League)	Pos.	G	AB	R	H	2B	3B	HR	RBI	Avg.	BB	SO	SB	PO	A	E	Avg.
1983— Quad Cities (Mid.)	OF	44	119	17	29	6	2	0	10	.244	26	30	10	47	8	1	.982
— Geneva (NY-Penn)......	OF	64	241	35	63	15	2	5	33	.261	40	52	16	132	6	8	.945
1984— Quad Cities (Mid.)	OF	12	41	6	9	2	2	0	5	.220	9	13	3	13	2	1	.938
1985— Win.-Salem (Car.).......	OF	115	386	52	132	14	4	5	54	*.342	62	35	38	206	11	7	.96
1986— Iowa (Am. Assoc.).......	OF	83	318	52	92	11	5	5	32	.289	36	34	42	214	7	2	.9?
— Chicago (N.L.)...........	OF	53	108	13	15	1	1	1	7	.139	6	22	4	77	2	1	.9?
1987— Chicago (N.L.)...........	OF	142	459	70	134	18	8	8	36	.292	57	96	16	283	10	6	
1988— Chicago (N.L.)...........	OF	75	256	27	65	10	1	4	34	.254	21	46	7	162	2	5	
— Montreal (N.L.)■.......	OF	63	191	24	49	3	5	2	12	.257	17	48	16	119	2	1	
1989— Montreal (N.L.)..........	OF	126	361	41	99	16	7	3	27	.274	27	57	23	199	7	7	

M

Year Team (League)	Pos.	G	AB	R	H	2B	3B	HR	RBI	Avg.	BB	SO	SB	PO	A	E	Avg.
1990— Montreal (N.L.)..........	OF-P	118	391	60	109	13	5	11	39	.279	24	48	13	257	6	3	.989
1991— Montreal (N.L.)..........	OF	124	396	47	117	18	5	7	42	.295	20	54	16	213	10	4	.982
1992— Cincinnati (N.L.).■...	OF-1B	135	393	47	100	20	5	3	31	.254	42	54	12	382	18	6	.985
1993— San Fran. (N.L.).■......	OF	91	241	28	58	12	1	5	27	.241	27	39	6	131	6	1	.993
— Phoenix (PCL).............	OF	3	15	4	7	0	0	0	2	.467	1	1	1	5	1	0	1.000
1994— San Francisco (N.L.) ..	OF-1B	97	235	23	58	9	3	4	27	.247	21	22	3	256	18	3	.989
1995— Chicago (A.L.).■........	O-1-DH-P	119	303	49	93	16	4	5	37	.307	32	41	8	392	25	3	.993
1996— Chicago (A.L.)............	OF-1B	146	440	85	140	20	8	10	53	.318	52	52	15	368	16	6	.985
1997— Chicago (A.L.)	OF-1B-DH	145	504	78	144	16	6	12	55	.286	55	69	12	485	30	7	.987
American League totals (3 years)		410	1247	212	377	52	18	27	145	.302	139	162	35	1245	71	16	.988
National League totals (9 years)		1024	3031	380	804	120	41	48	282	.265	262	486	116	2079	81	37	.983
Major league totals (12 years)		1434	4278	592	1181	172	59	75	427	.276	401	648	151	3324	152	53	.985

RECORD AS PITCHER

Year Team (League)	W	L	Pct.	ERA	G	GS	CG	ShO	Sv.	IP	H	R	ER	BB	SO
1990— Montreal (N.L.).................	0	0	...	54.00	1	0	0	0	0	1/3	2	2	2	2	0
1995— Chicago (A.L.).■................	0	0	...	0.00	1	0	0	0	0	1	0	0	0	2	0
A.L. totals (1 year)......................	0	0	...	0.00	1	0	0	0	0	1	0	0	0	2	0
N.L. totals (1 year)......................	0	0	...	54.00	1	0	0	0	0	1/3	2	2	2	2	0
Major league totals (2 years)......	0	0	...	13.50	2	0	0	0	0	1 1/3	2	2	2	4	0

MARTINEZ, DENNIS   P

PERSONAL: Born May 14, 1955, in Granada, Nicaragua. ... 6-1/185. ... Throws right, bats right. ... Full name: Jose Dennis Martinez.

TRANSACTIONS/CAREER NOTES: Signed as non-drafted free agent by Baltimore Orioles organization (December 10, 1973). ... On Baltimore disabled list (March 28-April 20, 1980). ... On Baltimore disabled list (June 3-July 10, 1980); included rehabilitation assignment to Miami (July 1-10). ... On Baltimore disabled list (April 28-June 16, 1986); included rehabilitation assignment to Rochester (May 21-June 10). ... Traded by Orioles to Montreal Expos for a player to be named later (June 16, 1986); Orioles acquired IF Rene Gonzales to complete deal (December 16, 1986). ... Granted free agency (November 12, 1986). ... Signed by Miami, independent (April 14, 1987). ... Released by Miami (May 6, 1987). ... Signed by Expos organization (May 6, 1987). ... Granted free agency (November 9, 1987). ... Re-signed by Expos (December 18, 1987). ... Granted free agency (October 25, 1993). ... Signed by Cleveland Indians (December 2, 1993). ... On disabled list (June 29-July 24, July 31-August 27 and August 30, 1996-remainder of season). ... Granted free agency (November 18, 1996). ... Signed by Seattle Mariners organization (February 20, 1997). ... Released by Mariners (May 24, 1997).

RECORDS: Shares major league single-season record for fewest complete games by pitcher who led league in complete games—9 (1991).

HONORS: Named International League Pitcher of the Year (1976).

STATISTICAL NOTES: Pitched 4-0 one-hit, complete-game victory against California (June 5, 1985). ... Tied for N.L. lead with 10 balks in 1988. ... Pitched 2-0 perfect game against Los Angeles (July 28, 1991).

MISCELLANEOUS: Had sacrifice hit in one game as pinch-hitter (1991). ... Had sacrifice fly in one game as pinch-hitter (1993).

Year Team (League)	W	L	Pct.	ERA	G	GS	CG	ShO	Sv.	IP	H	R	ER	BB	SO
1974— Miami (Florida St.)	15	6	.714	2.06	25	25	10	4	0	179	124	48	41	53	162
1975— Miami (Florida St.)	12	4	.750	2.61	20	20	9	3	0	145	125	54	42	35	114
— Asheville (South.)	4	1	.800	2.60	6	6	4	1	0	45	45	16	13	12	18
— Rochester (Int'l)	0	0	...	5.40	2	0	0	0	0	5	7	4	3	2	4
1976— Rochester (Int'l)	*14	8	.636	*2.50	25	23	*16	1	0	180	148	64	50	50	*140
— Baltimore (A.L.)	1	2	.333	2.57	4	2	1	0	0	28	23	8	8	8	18
1977— Baltimore (A.L.)	14	7	.667	4.10	42	13	5	0	4	167	157	86	76	64	107
1978— Baltimore (A.L.)	16	11	.593	3.52	40	38	15	2	0	276	257	121	108	93	142
1979— Baltimore (A.L.)	15	16	.484	3.67	40	*39	*18	3	0	*292	279	129	119	78	132
1980— Baltimore (A.L.)	6	4	.600	3.96	25	12	2	0	1	100	103	44	44	44	42
— Miami (Florida St.)	0	0	...	0.00	2	2	0	0	0	12	3	1	0	5	7
1981— Baltimore (A.L.)	*14	5	.737	3.32	25	24	9	2	0	179	173	84	66	62	88
1982— Baltimore (A.L.)	16	12	.571	4.21	40	39	10	2	0	252	262	123	118	87	111
1983— Baltimore (A.L.)	7	16	.304	5.53	32	25	4	0	0	153	209	108	94	45	71
1984— Baltimore (A.L.)	6	9	.400	5.02	34	20	2	0	0	141 2/3	145	81	79	37	77
1985— Baltimore (A.L.)	13	11	.542	5.15	33	31	3	1	0	180	203	110	103	63	68
1986— Baltimore (A.L.)	0	0	...	6.75	4	0	0	0	0	6 2/3	11	5	5	2	2
— Rochester (Int'l)	2	1	.667	6.05	4	4	0	0	0	19 1/3	18	14	13	9	14
— Montreal (N.L.)■.............	3	6	.333	4.59	19	15	1	1	0	98	103	52	50	28	63
1987— Miami (Florida St.)■.........	1	1	.500	6.16	3	3	0	0	0	19	21	14	13	3	11
— Indianapolis (A.A.)■........	3	2	.600	4.46	7	7	1	1	0	38 1/3	32	20	19	13	30
— Montreal (N.L.)■.............	11	4	*.733	3.30	22	22	2	1	0	144 2/3	133	59	53	40	84
1988— Montreal (N.L.).................	15	13	.536	2.72	34	34	9	2	0	235 1/3	215	94	71	55	120
1989— Montreal (N.L.).................	16	7	.696	3.18	34	33	5	2	0	232	227	88	82	49	142
1990— Montreal (N.L.).................	10	11	.476	2.95	32	32	7	2	0	226	191	80	74	49	156
1991— Montreal (N.L.).................	14	11	.560	*2.39	31	31	•9	*5	0	222	187	70	59	62	123
1992— Montreal (N.L.).................	16	11	.593	2.47	32	32	6	0	0	226 1/3	172	75	62	60	147
1993— Montreal (N.L.).................	15	9	.625	3.85	35	34	2	0	1	224 2/3	211	110	96	64	138
1994— Cleveland (A.L.)■.............	11	6	.647	3.52	24	24	7	3	0	176 2/3	166	75	69	44	92
1995— Cleveland (A.L.)...............	12	5	.706	3.08	28	28	3	2	0	187	174	71	64	46	99
1996— Cleveland (A.L.)...............	9	6	.600	4.50	20	20	1	1	0	112	122	63	56	37	48
1997— Seattle (A.L.)■.................	1	5	.167	7.71	9	9	0	0	0	49	65	46	42	29	17
A.L. totals (15 years)	141	115	.551	4.11	400	324	80	16	5	2300	2349	1154	1051	739	1114
N.L. totals (8 years)	100	72	.581	3.06	239	233	41	13	1	1609	1439	628	547	407	973
Major league totals (22 years)....	241	187	.563	3.68	639	557	121	29	6	3909	3788	1782	1598	1146	2087

DIVISION SERIES RECORD

Team (League)	W	L	Pct.	ERA	G	GS	CG	ShO	Sv.	IP	H	R	ER	BB	SO
— Cleveland (A.L.)	0	0	...	3.00	1	1	0	0	0	6	5	2	2	0	2

M

CHAMPIONSHIP SERIES RECORD

Year Team (League)	W	L	Pct.	ERA	G	GS	CG	ShO	Sv.	IP	H	R	ER	BB	SO
1979— Baltimore (A.L.)................	0	0	...	3.24	1	1	0	0	0	8 1/3	8	3	3	0	4
1983— Baltimore (A.L.)						Did not play.									
1995— Cleveland (A.L.)...............	1	1	.500	2.03	2	2	0	0	0	13 1/3	10	3	3	3	7
Champ. series totals (2 years)	1	1	.500	2.49	3	3	0	0	0	21 2/3	18	6	6	3	11

WORLD SERIES RECORD

NOTES: Member of World Series championship team (1983).

Year Team (League)	W	L	Pct.	ERA	G	GS	CG	ShO	Sv.	IP	H	R	ER	BB	SO
1979— Baltimore (A.L.)................	0	0	...	18.00	2	1	0	0	0	2	6	4	4	0	0
1983— Baltimore (A.L.)						Did not play.									
1995— Cleveland (A.L.)...............	0	1	.000	3.48	2	2	0	0	0	10 1/3	12	4	4	8	5
World Series totals (2 years)	0	1	.000	5.84	4	3	0	0	0	12 1/3	18	8	8	8	5

ALL-STAR GAME RECORD

Year League	W	L	Pct.	ERA	GS	CG	ShO	Sv.	IP	H	R	ER	BB	SO
1990— National	0	0	...	0.00	0	0	0	0	1	0	0	0	0	1
1991— National	0	1	.000	13.50	0	0	0	0	2	4	3	3	0	0
1992— National	0	0	...	0.00	0	0	0	0	1	0	0	0	1	1
1995-- American	0	0	...	4.50	0	0	0	0	2	1	1	1	0	0
All-Star totals (4 years) ...	0	1	.000	6.00	0	0	0	0	6	5	4	4	1	2

MARTINEZ, EDGAR   DH   MARINERS

PERSONAL: Born January 2, 1963, in New York. ... 5-11/190. ... Bats right, throws right. ... Cousin of Carmelo Martinez, major league first baseman/outfielder with six teams (1983-91).

HIGH SCHOOL: Dorado (Puerto Rico).

COLLEGE: American College (Puerto Rico).

TRANSACTIONS/CAREER NOTES: Signed as non-drafted free agent by Seattle Mariners organization (December 19, 1982). ... On Seattle disabled list (April 4-May 17, 1993). ... On Seattle disabled list (June 15-July 21, 1993); included rehabilitation assignment to Jacksonville (July 17-21). ... On Seattle disabled list (August 17, 1993-remainder of season). ... On disabled list (April 16-May 6, 1994 and July 21-August 12, 1996).

RECORDS: Shares A.L. single-game record for most errors by third baseman—4 (May 6, 1990).

HONORS: Named third baseman on The Sporting News A.L. All-Star team (1992). ... Named third baseman on The Sporting News A.L. Silver Slugger team (1992). ... Named designated hitter on The Sporting News A.L. All-Star team (1995 and 1997). ... Named designated hitter on The Sporting News A.L. Silver Slugger team (1995 and 1997).

STATISTICAL NOTES: Led Southern League third basemen with 360 total chances and 34 double plays in 1985. ... Led Southern League with 12 sacrifice flies in 1985. ... Led Southern League third basemen with .960 fielding percentage in 1986. ... Led Pacific Coast League third basemen with 389 total chances and 31 double plays in 1987. ... Led A.L. with .479 on-base percentage in 1995. ... Hit three home runs in one game (July 6, 1996). ... Career major league grand slams: 2.

MISCELLANEOUS: Holds Seattle Mariners franchise all-time records for most doubles (291) and highest batting average (.317).

Year Team (League)	Pos.	G	AB	R	H	2B	3B	HR	RBI	Avg.	BB	SO	SB	PO	A	E	Avg.
1983— Bellingham (N'west)...	3B	32	104	14	18	1	1	0	5	.173	18	24	1	22	58	6	.930
1984— Wausau (Midwest)	3B	126	433	72	131	32	2	15	66	.303	84	57	11	85	246	25	.930
1985— Chattanooga (Sou.)....	3B	111	357	43	92	15	5	3	47	.258	71	30	1	*94	*247	19	*.947
— Calgary (PCL)............	3B-2B	20	68	8	24	7	1	0	14	.353	12	7	1	15	44	4	.937
1986— Chattanooga (Sou.)....	3B-2B	132	451	71	119	29	5	6	74	.264	89	35	2	94	263	15	†.960
1987— Calgary (PCL)............	3B	129	438	75	144	31	1	10	66	.329	82	47	3	*91	*278	20	.949
— Seattle (A.L.)	3B-DH	13	43	6	16	5	2	0	5	.372	2	5	0	13	19	0	1.000
1988— Calgary (PCL)............	3B-2B	95	331	63	120	19	4	8	64	*.363	66	40	9	48	185	20	.921
— Seattle (A.L.)	3B	14	32	0	9	4	0	0	5	.281	4	7	0	5	8	1	.929
1989— Seattle (A.L.)	3B	65	171	20	41	5	0	2	20	.240	17	26	2	40	72	6	.949
— Calgary (PCL)............	3B-2B	32	113	30	39	11	4	3	23	.345	22	13	2	22	56	12	.867
1990— Seattle (A.L.)	3B-DH	144	487	71	147	27	2	11	49	.302	74	62	1	89	259	*27	.928
1991— Seattle (A.L.)	3B	150	544	98	167	35	1	14	52	.307	84	72	0	84	299	15	.962
1992— Seattle (A.L.)	3B-DH-1B	135	528	100	181	•46	3	18	73	*.343	54	61	14	88	211	17	.946
1993— Seattle (A.L.)	DH-3B	42	135	20	32	7	0	4	13	.237	28	19	0	5	11	2	.889
— Jacksonville (South.)..	3B	4	14	2	5	0	0	1	3	.357	2	0	0	...	...	...	...
1994— Seattle (A.L.)	3B-DH	89	326	47	93	23	1	13	51	.285	53	42	6	44	128	9	.950
1995— Seattle (A.L.)	DH-3B-1B	•145	511	•121	182	•52	0	29	113	*.356	116	87	4	30	4	2	.944
1996— Seattle (A.L.)	DH-1-3-0	139	499	121	163	52	2	26	103	.327	123	84	3	29	1	1	.968
1997— Seattle (A.L.)	DH-1B-3B	155	542	104	179	35	1	28	108	.330	119	86	2	68	4	1	.986
Major league totals (11 years)		1091	3818	708	1210	291	12	145	592	.317	674	551	32	495	1016	81	.949

DIVISION SERIES RECORD

RECORDS: Holds single-game record for most runs batted in—7 (October 7, 1995). ... Shares single-game record for most home runs—2 (October 7, 1995). ... Holds career record for highest slugging percentage (20 or more at-bats)—.811. ... Shares career record for most runs batted in—13.

NOTES: Holds postseason single-game record for most RBIs—7 (October 7, 1995).

Year Team (League)	Pos.	G	AB	R	H	2B	3B	HR	RBI	Avg.	BB	SO	SB	PO	A	E	Avg.
1995— Seattle (A.L.)	DH	5	21	6	12	3	0	2	10	.571	6	2	0	...	...	...	...
1997— Seattle (A.L.)	DH	4	16	2	3	0	0	2	3	.188	0	3	0	...	...	...	...
Division series totals (2 years)		9	37	8	15	3	0	4	13	.405	6	5	0	...	...	...	...

CHAMPIONSHIP SERIES RECORD

Year Team (League)	Pos.	G	AB	R	H	2B	3B	HR	RBI	Avg.	BB	SO	SB	PO	A	E	A
1995— Seattle (A.L.)	DH	6	23	0	2	0	0	0	0	.087	2	5	1	...	...	...	

M

Year League	Pos.	AB	R	H	2B	3B	HR	RBI	Avg.	BB	SO	SB	PO	A	E	Avg.
1992— American	PH	1	0	0	0	0	0	0	.000	0	0	0	...	...	...	...
1995— American	DH	3	0	0	0	0	0	0	.000	0	1	0	...	...	...	...
1996— American	PH	1	0	0	0	0	0	0	.000	0	0	0	...	...	...	...
1997— American	DH	2	1	2	0	0	1	1	1.000	0	0	0	...	...	...	...
All-Star Game totals (4 years)		7	1	2	0	0	1	1	.286	0	1	0				

MARTINEZ, FELIX   SS   ROYALS

PERSONAL: Born May 18, 1974, in Nagua, Dominican Republic. ... 6-0/170. ... Throws right, bats both.
HIGH SCHOOL: Solome Urena (Nagua, Dominican Republic).
TRANSACTIONS/CAREER NOTES: Purchased by Kansas City Royals organization from Hiroshima Toyo Carp of Japan (March 5, 1993).
STATISTICAL NOTES: Led Texas League shortstops with 643 total chances in 1993.

Year Team (League)	Pos.	G	AB	R	H	2B	3B	HR	RBI	Avg.	BB	SO	SB	PO	A	E	Avg.
1993—GC Royals (GCL)	SS-2B-3B	57	165	23	42	5	1	0	12	.255	17	26	22	79	136	30	.878
1994—Wilmington (Caro.).....	SS	117	400	65	107	16	4	2	43	.268	30	91	19	177	329	30	.944
1995—Wichita (Texas)	SS	127	426	53	112	15	3	3	30	.263	31	71	*44	*222	371	*50	.922
1996—Omaha (A.A.).............	SS	118	395	54	93	13	3	5	35	.235	44	79	18	177	374	*42	.929
1997—Omaha (A.A.).............	SS	112	410	55	104	19	4	2	36	.254	29	86	21	175	312	*36	.931
—Kansas City (A.L.)	SS-DH	16	31	3	7	1	1	0	3	.226	6	8	0	17	22	1	.975
Major league totals (1 year)		16	31	3	7	1	1	0	3	.226	6	8	0	17	22	1	.975

MARTINEZ, GABBY   SS   YANKEES

PERSONAL: Born January 7, 1974, in San Juan, Puerto Rico. ... 6-2/170. ... Bats both, throws right. ... Full name: Gabriel Martinez.
HIGH SCHOOL: Luchetti (Santurce, Puerto Rico).
TRANSACTIONS/CAREER NOTES: Selected by Milwaukee Brewers organization in supplemental round ("sandwich pick" between first and second round, 38th pick overall) of free-agent draft (June 1, 1992). ... Traded by Brewers to New York Yankees (November 5, 1996), completing deal in which Brewers traded P Ricky Bones and a player to be named later to Yankees (August 29, 1996) for compensation of injury status of OF Pat Listach who was traded by Brewers to Yankees with P Graeme Lloyd for OF Gerald Williams and P Bob Wickman (August 23, 1996). ... On Norwich disabled list (June 22-July 11, 1997) ... On New York disabled list (September 9, 1997-remainder of season).

Year Team (League)	Pos.	G	AB	R	H	2B	3B	HR	RBI	Avg.	BB	SO	SB	PO	A	E	Avg.
1992—Ariz. Brewers (Ariz.) ...	SS	48	165	29	43	7	2	0	24	.261	12	19	7	58	129	21	.899
1993—Beloit (Midwest)........	SS	94	285	40	69	14	5	0	24	.242	14	52	22	109	242	23	.939
1994—Stockton (California) ..	SS-OF	112	364	37	90	18	3	0	32	.247	17	66	19	151	236	32	.924
1995—Stockton (California) ..	SS	64	213	25	55	13	3	1	20	.258	10	25	13	96	158	21	.924
—El Paso (Texas)...........	SS	44	133	13	37	3	2	0	11	.278	2	22	5	65	103	9	.949
1996—El Paso (Texas)..........	SS	91	338	44	85	11	8	0	37	.251	18	57	8	102	239	32	.914
1997—Norwich (Eastern)	SS-2B	77	312	49	100	12	5	6	54	.321	11	44	21	99	209	17	.948
—GC Yankees (GCL)......	2B	2	5	3	2	0	0	1	2	.400	1	0	2	3	5	0	1.000

MARTINEZ, JAVIER   P   PIRATES

PERSONAL: Born February 5, 1977, in Bayamon, Puerto Rico. ... 6-2/210. ... Throws right, bats right. ... Full name: Javier Antonio Martinez.
HIGH SCHOOL: Liceo (Bayamon, Puerto Rico).
TRANSACTIONS/CAREER NOTES: Selected by Chicago Cubs organization in third round of free-agent draft (June 2, 1994). ... On Rockford disabled list (April 5-July 10, 1996). ... Selected by Oakland Athletics from Cubs organization in Rule 5 major league draft (December 15, 1997). ... Traded by A's to Pittsburgh Pirates for cash (December 15, 1997).

Year Team (League)	W	L	Pct.	ERA	G	GS	CG	ShO	Sv.	IP	H	R	ER	BB	SO
1994—Huntington (Appal.)...........	2	1	.667	3.55	8	8	0	0	0	33	21	18	13	19	28
1995—Rockford (Midwest)	6	6	.500	3.97	18	18	1	0	0	104 1/3	100	56	46	39	53
1996—GC Cubs (GCL).................	2	1	.667	0.60	3	3	0	0	0	15	11	4	1	6	15
—Rockford (Midwest)	4	3	.571	3.36	10	10	3	0	0	59	49	26	22	30	53
1997—Daytona (Fla. St.)	2	6	.250	5.79	9	9	2	0	0	51 1/3	65	40	33	26	34
—Rockford (Midwest)	1	7	.125	5.70	17	17	1	0	0	79	85	61	50	50	70

MARTINEZ, JESUS   P   MARLINS

PERSONAL: Born March 13, 1974, in Santo Domingo, Dominican Republic. ... 6-2/145. ... Throws left, bats left. ... Brother of Ramon J. Martinez, pitcher, Los Angeles Dodgers; and brother of Pedro J. Martinez, pitcher, Boston Red Sox.
HIGH SCHOOL: Liceo Las Americas (Santo Domingo, Dominican Republic).
TRANSACTIONS/CAREER NOTES: Signed as non-drafted free agent by Los Angeles Dodgers organization (August 22, 1990). ... Selected by Arizona Diamondbacks in third round (59th pick overall) of expansion draft (November 18, 1997). ... Traded by Diamondbacks to Florida Marlins for OF Devon White (November 18, 1997).
STATISTICAL NOTES: Tied for Texas League lead with four balks in 1995. ... Led Texas League with 20 wild pitches in 1996.

Year Team (League)	W	L	Pct.	ERA	G	GS	CG	ShO	Sv.	IP	H	R	ER	BB	SO
1991—Dom. Dodgers (DSL)	3	2	.600	3.57	14	14	0	0	0	70 2/3	58	34	28	45	83
1992—GC Dodgers (GCL)	1	4	.200	3.29	7	7	1	0	0	41	38	19	15	11	39
—Great Falls (Pio.)	0	3	.000	13.25	6	6	0	0	0	18 1/3	36	30	27	21	23
1993—Bakersfield (California)	4	*13	.235	4.14	30	21	0	0	0	145 2/3	144	95	67	75	108
1994—Vero Beach (FSL)	7	9	.438	6.26	18	18	1	1	0	87 2/3	91	65	61	43	69
—San Antonio (Tex.)	0	1	.000	4.50	1	1	0	0	0	4	3	2	2	2	3

M

Year	Team (League)	W	L	Pct.	ERA	G	GS	CG	ShO	Sv.	IP	H	R	ER	BB	SO
1995—	San Antonio (Tex.)	6	9	.400	3.54	24	24	1	0	0	139 2/3	129	64	55	71	83
—	Albuquerque (PCL)	1	1	.500	4.50	2	0	0	0	0	4	4	2	2	4	5
1996—	San Antonio (Tex.)	10	13	.435	4.40	27	27	0	0	0	161 2/3	157	90	79	92	124
1997—	Albuquerque (PCL)	7	1	.875	6.21	26	12	0	0	0	84	112	64	58	52	80

MARTINEZ, MANNY — OF — PIRATES

PERSONAL: Born October 3, 1970, in San Pedro de Macoris, Dominican Republic. ... 6-2/170. ... Throws right, bats right. ... Full name: Manuel DeJesus Martinez.

TRANSACTIONS/CAREER NOTES: Signed as non-drafted free agent by Oakland Athletics organization (March 9, 1988). ... Played in Dominican Summer League (1988-89). ... Granted free agency (October 15, 1994). ... Signed by Chicago Cubs organization (February 13, 1995). ... Granted free agency (October 15, 1995). ... Signed by Seattle Mariners organization (January 29, 1996). ... Claimed on waivers by Philadelphia Phillies organization (July 11, 1996). ... Granted free agency (October 15, 1996). ... Signed by Pittsburgh Pirates organization (December 19, 1996) ... On Calgary disabled list (April 30-May 8 and June 20-27, 1997).

STATISTICAL NOTES: Tied for Northwest League lead in double plays by outfielder with three in 1990. ... Led American Association outfielders with 302 total chances in 1995.

							BATTING								FIELDING			
Year	Team (League)	Pos.	G	AB	R	H	2B	3B	HR	RBI	Avg.	BB	SO	SB	PO	A	E	Avg.
1990—	S. Oregon (N'west)	OF-P	66	244	36	60	5	0	2	17	.246	16	59	6	124	9	6	.957
1991—	Modesto (California)	OF	125	502	73	136	32	3	3	55	.271	34	80	26	267	13	8	.972
1992—	Modesto (California)	OF	121	495	70	125	23	1	9	45	.253	39	75	17	232	12	10	.961
1993—	San Bern. (Calif.)	OF	109	459	88	148	26	3	11	52	.322	41	60	28	222	15	4	.983
—	Tacoma (PCL)	OF	20	59	9	18	2	0	1	6	.305	4	12	2	33	6	0	1.000
1994—	Tacoma (PCL)	OF	*137	*536	76	137	25	5	9	60	.256	28	72	18	*322	11	9	.974
1995—	Iowa (Am. Assoc.)■	OF	122	397	63	115	17	•8	8	49	.290	20	64	11	*281	16	5	.983
1996—	Tacoma (PCL)■	OF	66	277	54	87	15	1	4	24	.314	23	41	14	181	11	5	.975
—	Seattle (A.L.)	OF	9	17	3	4	2	1	0	3	.235	3	5	2	12	2	0	1.000
—	Scran./W.B. (Int'l)■	OF	17	67	8	14	1	1	0	5	.209	4	17	3	40	0	1	.976
—	Philadelphia (N.L.)	OF	13	36	2	8	0	2	0	0	.222	1	11	2	20	1	1	.955
1997—	Calgary (PCL)■	OF	109	420	78	139	34	1	16	66	.331	33	80	17	196	7	5	.976
American League totals (1 year)			9	17	3	4	2	1	0	3	.235	3	5	2	12	2	0	1.000
National League totals (1 year)			13	36	2	8	0	2	0	0	.222	1	11	2	20	1	1	.955
Major league totals (1 year)			22	53	5	12	2	3	0	3	.226	4	16	4	32	3	1	.972

RECORD AS PITCHER

Year	Team (League)	W	L	Pct.	ERA	G	GS	CG	ShO	Sv.	IP	H	R	ER	BB	SO
1990—	S. Oregon (N'west)	0	0	...	45.00	66	0	0	0	0	1	5	5	5	2	0

MARTINEZ, PEDRO A. — P

PERSONAL: Born November 29, 1968, in Santo Domingo, Dominican Republic. ... 6-2/185. ... Throws left, bats right. ... Full name: Pedro Aquino Martinez. ... Formerly known as Pedro Aquino.

HIGH SCHOOL: Ramon Matia Melle (Santo Domingo, Dominican Republic).

TRANSACTIONS/CAREER NOTES: Signed as non-drafted free agent by San Diego Padres organization (September 30, 1986). ... Traded by Padres with OF Phil Plantier, OF Derek Bell, P Doug Brocail, IF Craig Shipley and SS Ricky Gutierrez to Houston Astros for 3B Ken Caminiti, OF Steve Finley, SS Andujar Cedeno, 1B Robert Petagine, P Brian Williams and a player to be named later (December 28, 1994); Padres acquired P Sean Fesh to complete deal (May 1, 1995). ... Traded by Astros to Padres for SS Ray Holbert (October 10, 1995). ... Traded by Padres to New York Mets for OF Jeff Barry (December 15, 1995). ... Claimed on waivers by Cincinnati Reds (September 13, 1996). ... Granted free agency (October 7, 1997).

Year	Team (League)	W	L	Pct.	ERA	G	GS	CG	ShO	Sv.	IP	H	R	ER	BB	SO
1987—	Spokane (N'west)	4	1	.800	3.83	18	5	1	0	0	51 2/3	57	31	22	36	42
1988—	Spokane (N'west)	8	3	.727	4.24	15	15	1	0	0	99 2/3	108	55	47	32	89
1989—	Charleston, S.C. (S. Atl.)	•14	8	.636	*1.97	27	27	5	2	0	*187	147	53	41	64	158
1990—	Wichita (Texas)	6	10	.375	4.80	24	23	2	0	0	129 1/3	139	83	69	70	88
1991—	Wichita (Texas)	11	10	.524	5.23	26	26	3	2	0	156 2/3	169	99	*91	57	95
1992—	Wichita (Texas)	7	11	.611	2.99	26	26	1	0	0	168 1/3	153	66	56	52	142
1993—	Las Vegas (PCL)	3	5	.375	4.72	15	14	1	0	0	87 2/3	94	49	46	40	65
—	San Diego (N.L.)	3	1	.750	2.43	32	0	0	0	0	37	23	11	10	13	32
1994—	San Diego (N.L.)	3	2	.600	2.90	48	1	0	0	3	68 1/3	52	31	22	49	52
1995—	Houston (N.L.)■	0	0	...	7.40	25	0	0	0	0	20 2/3	29	18	17	16	17
—	Tucson (PCL)	1	1	.500	6.62	20	3	0	0	2	34	44	28	25	13	21
1996—	Norfolk (Int'l)■	4	4	.500	3.02	34	5	0	0	0	56 2/3	45	29	19	20	37
—	New York (N.L.)	0	0	...	6.43	9	0	0	0	0	7	8	7	5	7	6
—	Cincinnati (N.L.)■	0	0	...	6.00	4	0	0	0	0	3	5	2	2	1	3
1997—	Indianapolis (A.A.)	4	3	.571	3.47	28	11	1	1	0	80 1/3	70	37	31	35	36
—	Cincinnati (N.L.)	1	1	.500	9.45	8	0	0	0	0	6 2/3	8	9	7	7	4
Major league totals (5 years)		7	4	.636	3.97	122	1	0	0	3	142 2/3	125	78	63	93	114

MARTINEZ, PEDRO J. — P — RED SOX

PERSONAL: Born July 25, 1971, in Manoguayabo, Dominican Republic. ... 5-11/175. ... Throws right, bats right. ... Full name: Pedro Jaime Martinez. ... Brother of Ramon J. Martinez, pitcher, Los Angeles Dodgers; and brother of Jesus Martinez, pitcher, Florida Marlins.

COLLEGE: Ohio Dominican College (Dominican Republic).

TRANSACTIONS/CAREER NOTES: Signed as non-drafted free agent by Los Angeles Dodgers organization (June 18, 1988). ... On Albuquerque disabled list (June 20-July 2 and July 13-August 25, 1992). ... Traded by Dodgers to Montreal Expos for 2B Delino DeShields (November 19, 1993). ... On suspended list (April 1-9, 1997). ... Traded by Expos to Boston Red Sox for P Carl Pavano and a player to be named later (November 18, 1997); Expos acquired P Tony Armas Jr. to complete deal (December 18, 1997).

M

HONORS: Named Minor League Player of the Year by THE SPORTING NEWS (1991). ... Named N.L. Pitcher of the Year by THE SPORTING NEWS (1997). ... Named righthanded pitcher on THE SPORTING NEWS N.L. All-Star team (1997). ... Named N.L. Cy Young Award winner by Baseball Writers' Association of America (1997).

STATISTICAL NOTES: Led N.L. with 11 hit batsmen in 1994. ... Pitched nine perfect innings against San Diego, before being relieved after yielding leadoff double in 10th inning (June 3, 1995). ... Tied for N.L. lead with 16 sacrifice hits in 1996. ... Pitched 2-0 one-hit, complete-game victory against Cincinnati (July 13, 1997).

MISCELLANEOUS: Started one game at third base for Los Angeles, but replaced before first plate appearance and never played in field (1993).

Year	Team (League)	W	L	Pct.	ERA	G	GS	CG	ShO	Sv.	IP	H	R	ER	BB	SO
1988—	Dom. Dodgers (DSL)	5	1	.833	3.10	8	7	1	0	0	49 1/3	45	25	17	16	28
1989—	Dom. Dodgers (DSL)	7	2	.778	2.73	13	7	2	3	1	85 2/3	59	30	26	25	63
1990—	Great Falls (Pio.)	8	3	.727	3.62	14	•14	0	0	0	77	74	39	31	40	82
1991—	Bakersfield (California)	8	0	1.000	2.05	10	10	0	0	0	61 1/3	41	17	14	19	83
	— San Antonio (Tex.)	7	5	.583	1.76	12	12	4	•3	0	76 2/3	57	21	15	31	74
	— Albuquerque (PCL)	3	3	.500	3.66	6	6	0	0	0	39 1/3	28	17	16	16	35
1992—	Albuquerque (PCL)	7	6	.538	3.81	20	20	3	1	0	125 1/3	104	57	53	57	124
	— Los Angeles (N.L.)	0	1	.000	2.25	2	1	0	0	0	8	6	2	2	1	8
1993—	Albuquerque (PCL)	0	0	. . .	3.00	1	1	0	0	0	3	1	1	1	1	4
	— Los Angeles (N.L.)	10	5	.667	2.61	65	2	0	0	2	107	76	34	31	57	119
1994—	Montreal (N.L.)■	11	5	.688	3.42	24	23	1	1	1	144 2/3	115	58	55	45	142
1995—	Montreal (N.L.)	14	10	.583	3.51	30	30	2	2	0	194 2/3	158	79	76	66	174
1996—	Montreal (N.L.)	13	10	.565	3.70	33	33	4	1	0	216 2/3	189	100	89	70	222
1997—	Montreal (N.L.)	17	8	.680	*1.90	31	31	*13	4	0	241 1/3	158	65	51	67	305
Major league totals (6 years)		65	39	.625	3.00	185	120	20	8	3	912 1/3	702	338	304	306	970

ALL-STAR GAME RECORD

Year	League	W	L	Pct.	ERA	GS	CG	ShO	Sv.	IP	H	R	ER	BB	SO
1996—	National	0	0	. . .	0.00	0	0	0	0	1	2	0	0	0	1
1997—	National	0	0	. . .	0.00	0	0	0	0	1	0	0	0	0	2
All-Star totals (2 years)		0	0	. . .	0.00	0	0	0	0	2	2	0	0	0	3

MARTINEZ, RAMON E.   2B   GIANTS

PERSONAL: Born October 10, 1972, in Philadelphia. ... 6-1/170. ... Bats right, throws right. ... Full name: Ramon E. Martinez.

HIGH SCHOOL: Escuela Superior Catholica (Bayamon, Puerto Rico).

JUNIOR COLLEGE: Vernon (Texas) Regional Junior College.

TRANSACTIONS/CAREER NOTES: Signed as non-drafted free agent by Kansas City Royals organization (January 15, 1994). ... Traded by Royals to San Francisco Giants (December 9, 1996); completing deal in which Giants traded P Jamie Brewington to Royals for a player to be named later (November 26, 1996).

STATISTICAL NOTES: Led Texas League with 18 sacrifice hits and nine sacrifice flies in 1995. ... Led Texas League second basemen with .984 fielding percentage in 1995. ... Led American Association with 13 sacrifice hits in 1996.

									BATTING						FIELDING		
Year	Team (League)	Pos.	G	AB	R	H	2B	3B	HR	RBI	Avg.	BB	SO	SB	PO	A	E	Avg.
1993—	GC Royals (GCL)	2B-OF	57	165	23	42	5	1	0	12	.255	17	26	22	72	108	6	.968
	— Wilmington (Caro.)	2B-SS	24	75	8	19	4	0	0	6	.253	11	9	1	52	72	6	.954
1994—	Wilmington (Caro.)	2B	90	325	40	87	13	2	2	35	.268	35	25	6	176	249	16	.964
	— Rockford (Midwest)	2B	6	18	3	5	0	0	0	3	.278	4	2	1	9	12	1	.955
1995—	Wichita (Texas)	2B-SS	103	393	58	108	20	2	3	51	.275	42	50	11	186	311	9	†.982
1996—	Omaha (A.A.)	2B	85	320	35	81	12	3	6	41	.253	21	34	3	163	207	12	.969
	— Wichita (Texas)	2B	26	93	16	32	4	1	1	8	.344	7	8	4	47	84	6	.956
1997—	Shreveport (Texas)■	SS	105	404	72	129	32	4	5	54	.319	40	48	4	167	370	18	.968
	— Phoenix (PCL)	2B-SS	18	57	6	16	2	0	1	7	.281	5	9	1	26	44	3	.959

MARTINEZ, RAMON J.   P   DODGERS

PERSONAL: Born March 22, 1968, in Santo Domingo, Dominican Republic. ... 6-4/186. ... Throws right, bats both. ... Full name: Ramon Jaime Martinez. ... Brother of Pedro J. Martinez, pitcher, Boston Red Sox; and brother of Jesus Martinez, pitcher, Florida Marlins.

HIGH SCHOOL: Liceo Secunderia Las Americas (Dominican Republic).

TRANSACTIONS/CAREER NOTES: Signed as non-drafted free agent by Los Angeles Dodgers organization (September 1, 1984). ... On suspended list (July 8-12, 1993). ... Granted free agency (November 1, 1995). ... Re-signed by Dodgers (November 16, 1995). ... On Los Angeles disabled list (April 7-May 14, 1996); included rehabilitation assignments to San Antonio (May 4-9) and Vero Beach (May 9-14). ... On disabled list (June 15-August 20, 1997); included rehabilitation assignment to San Bernardino (July 26-August 20, 1997).

STATISTICAL NOTES: Struck out 18 batters in one game (June 4, 1990). ... Pitched 7-0 no-hit victory against Florida (July 14, 1995).

MISCELLANEOUS: Member of 1984 Dominican Republic Olympic baseball team. ... Appeared in one game as pinch-runner (1989). ... Appeared in one game as pinch-runner (1992). ... Appeared in one game as pinch-hitter and appeared in one game as pinch-runner with Los Angeles (1996).

Year	Team (League)	W	L	Pct.	ERA	G	GS	CG	ShO	Sv.	IP	H	R	ER	BB	SO
1985—	GC Dodgers (GCL)	4	1	.800	2.59	23	6	0	0	1	59	57	30	17	23	42
1986—	Bakersfield (California)	4	8	.333	4.75	20	20	2	1	0	106	119	73	56	63	78
1987—	Vero Beach (FSL)	16	5	.762	2.17	25	25	6	1	0	170 1/3	128	45	41	78	148
1988—	San Antonio (Tex.)	8	4	.667	2.46	14	14	2	1	0	95	79	29	26	34	89
	— Albuquerque (PCL)	5	2	.714	2.76	10	10	1	1	0	58 2/3	43	24	18	32	49
	— Los Angeles (N.L.)	1	3	.250	3.79	9	6	0	0	0	35 2/3	27	17	15	22	23
1989—	Albuquerque (PCL)	10	2	.833	2.79	18	18	2	1	0	113	92	40	35	50	127
	— Los Angeles (N.L.)	6	4	.600	3.19	15	15	2	2	0	98 2/3	79	39	35	41	89
1990—	Los Angeles (N.L.)	20	6	.769	2.92	33	33	*12	3	0	234 1/3	191	89	76	67	223
1991—	Los Angeles (N.L.)	17	13	.567	3.27	33	33	6	4	0	220 1/3	190	89	80	69	150
1992—	Los Angeles (N.L.)	8	11	.421	4.00	25	25	1	1	0	150 2/3	141	82	67	69	101
1993—	Los Angeles (N.L.)	10	12	.455	3.44	32	32	4	3	0	211 2/3	202	88	81	*104	127
1994—	Los Angeles (N.L.)	12	7	.632	3.97	24	24	4	•3	0	170	160	83	75	56	119
1995—	Los Angeles (N.L.)	17	7	.708	3.66	30	30	4	2	0	206 1/3	176	95	84	*81	138

M

Royce Clayton of the Cardinals goes high to turn two.
(Photo by THE SPORTING NEWS)

Mark Grace of the Cubs.
(Photo by Albert Dickson/THE SPORTING NEWS)

Kenny Lofton digs down the line.
(Photo by Robert Seale/THE SPORTING NEWS)

Bernie Williams of the Yankees closes in for a catch.
(Photo by Ezra O. Shaw for THE SPORTING NEWS)

Tony Womack puts on the brakes.
(Photo by Ed Nessen/THE SPORTING NEWS)

Dean Palmer's caught in a rundown.
(Photo by Ed Nessen/THE SPORTING NEWS)

Terry Tata tosses the Pirates' Mark Smith.
(Photo by Ed Nessen/THE SPORTING NEWS)

Tim Bogar keeps his eye on the runner, his foot on the bag and gets the force. (Photo by Ed Nessen/ THE SPORTING NEWS)

Year Team (League)	W	L	Pct.	ERA	G	GS	CG	ShO	Sv.	IP	H	R	ER	BB	SO
1996—San Antonio (Tex.)	0	0	...	0.00	1	1	0	0	0	2²/₃	0	0	0	3	1
—Vero Beach (FSL)	1	0	1.000	0.00	1	1	0	0	0	7	5	1	0	0	10
—Los Angeles (N.L.)	15	6	.714	3.42	29	27	2	2	0	168²/₃	153	76	64	86	133
1997—Los Angeles (N.L.)	10	5	.667	3.64	22	22	1	0	0	133²/₃	123	64	54	68	120
—San Bernardino	0	1	.000	1.15	4	4	0	0	0	15²/₃	10	2	2	4	16
Major league totals (10 years)....	**116**	**74**	**.611**	**3.48**	**252**	**247**	**36**	**20**	**0**	**1630**	**1442**	**722**	**631**	**663**	**1223**

DIVISION SERIES RECORD

Year Team (League)	W	L	Pct.	ERA	G	GS	CG	ShO	Sv.	IP	H	R	ER	BB	SO
1995—Los Angeles (N.L.)	0	1	.000	14.54	1	1	0	0	0	4¹/₃	10	7	7	2	3
1996—Los Angeles (N.L.)	0	0	...	1.13	1	1	0	0	0	8	3	1	1	3	6
Div. series totals (2 years)	**0**	**1**	**.000**	**5.84**	**2**	**2**	**0**	**0**	**0**	**12¹/₃**	**13**	**8**	**8**	**5**	**9**

MARTINEZ, SANDY · C · CUBS

PERSONAL: Born October 3, 1972, in Villa Mella, Dominican Republic. ... 6-2/205. ... Bats left, throws right. ... Full name: Angel Sandy Martinez.

TRANSACTIONS/CAREER NOTES: Signed as non-drafted free agent by Toronto Blue Jays organization (January 10, 1990). ... On disabled list (May 15-June 8, 1993). ... On Toronto disabled list (August 17-September 1, 1996); included rehabilitation assignment to Knoxville (August 26-September 1). ... On Syracuse disabled list (June 14-24, 1997). ... Traded by Blue Jays to Chicago Cubs for a player to be named later (December 11, 1997).

STATISTICAL NOTES: Led Pioneer League with 24 passed balls in 1992. ... Led Florida State League catchers with 14 errors in 1994.

							BATTING								FIELDING		
Year Team (League)	Pos.	G	AB	R	H	2B	3B	HR	RBI	Avg.	BB	SO	SB	PO	A	E	Avg.
1990—Dom. Dodgers (DSL) .	C	44	145	21	35	2	0	0	10	.241	18	15	1	...	...	...	...
1991—Dunedin (Fla. St.)	C	12	38	3	7	1	0	0	3	.184	7	7	0	82	9	2	.978
—Medicine Hat (Pio.)	C	34	98	8	17	1	0	2	16	.173	12	29	0	141	19	3	.982
1992—Dunedin (Fla. St.)	C	4	15	4	3	1	0	2	4	.200	0	3	0	11	2	1	.929
—Medicine Hat (Pio.)	C-1B-SS	57	206	27	52	15	0	4	39	.252	14	62	0	275	58	5	.985
1993—Hagerstown (SAL)	C	94	338	41	89	16	1	9	46	.263	19	71	1	493	68	14	.976
1994—Dunedin (Fla. St.)	C-1B	122	450	50	117	14	6	7	52	.260	22	79	1	615	79	†14	.980
1995—Knoxville (Southern) ..	C	41	144	14	33	8	1	2	22	.229	6	34	0	219	30	5	.980
—Toronto (A.L.)	C	62	191	12	46	12	0	2	25	.241	7	45	0	329	28	5	.986
1996—Toronto (A.L.).............	C	76	229	17	52	9	3	3	18	.227	16	58	0	413	33	3	.993
—Knoxville (Southern) ..	C	4	16	2	3	0	0	0	0	.188	0	5	0	17	2	1	.950
1997—Syracuse (Int'l)...........	C	96	322	28	72	12	1	4	29	.224	27	76	7	588	50	9	.986
—Toronto (A.L.).............	C	3	2	1	0	0	0	0	0	.000	1	1	0	12	2	1	.933
Major league totals (3 years)		**141**	**422**	**30**	**98**	**21**	**3**	**5**	**43**	**.232**	**24**	**104**	**0**	**754**	**63**	**9**	**.989**

MARTINEZ, TINO · 1B · YANKEES

PERSONAL: Born December 7, 1967, in Tampa. ... 6-2/210. ... Bats left, throws right. ... Full name: Constantino Martinez.

HIGH SCHOOL: Jefferson (Tampa).

COLLEGE: Tampa (Fla.).

TRANSACTIONS/CAREER NOTES: Selected by Boston Red Sox organization in third round of free-agent draft (June 3, 1985); did not sign. ... Selected by Seattle Mariners organization in first round (14th pick overall) of free-agent draft (June 1, 1988). ... On disabled list (August 10, 1993-remainder of season). ... Traded by Mariners with P Jeff Nelson and P Jim Mecir to New York Yankees for P Sterling Hitchcock and 3B Russ Davis (December 7, 1995).

HONORS: Named first baseman on The Sporting News college All-America team (1988). ... Named Pacific Coast League Most Valuable Player (1991). ... Named first baseman on The Sporting News A.L. All-Star team (1997). ... Named first baseman on The Sporting News A.L. Silver Slugger team (1997).

STATISTICAL NOTES: Led Eastern League with 13 intentional bases on balls received in 1989. ... Led Eastern League first basemen with 1,348 total chances and 106 double plays in 1989. ... Tied for Pacific Coast League lead with 11 intentional bases on balls received in 1990. ... Led Pacific Coast League first basemen with .991 fielding percentage, 1,051 putouts, 98 assists, 1,159 total chances and 117 double plays in 1990. ... Led Pacific Coast League first basemen with .992 fielding percentage and 122 double plays in 1991. ... Hit three home runs in one game (April 2, 1997). ... Led A.L. with 13 sacrifice flies in 1997. ... Career major league grand slams: 5.

MISCELLANEOUS: Member of 1988 U.S. Olympic baseball team.

							BATTING								FIELDING		
Year Team (League)	Pos.	G	AB	R	H	2B	3B	HR	RBI	Avg.	BB	SO	SB	PO	A	E	Avg.
1989—Williamsport (East.) ...	1B	*137	*509	51	131	29	2	13	64	.257	59	54	7	*1260	*81	7	*.995
1990—Calgary (PCL).............	1B-3B	128	453	83	145	28	1	17	93	.320	74	37	8	†1051	†98	10	†.991
—Seattle (A.L.)	1B	24	68	4	15	4	0	0	5	.221	9	9	0	155	12	0	1.000
1991—Calgary (PCL).............	1B-3B	122	442	94	144	34	5	18	86	.326	82	44	3	1078	106	9	†.992
—Seattle (A.L.)	1B-DH	36	112	11	23	2	0	4	9	.205	11	24	0	249	22	2	.993
1992—Seattle (A.L.)	1B-DH	136	460	53	118	19	2	16	66	.257	42	77	2	678	58	4	.995
1993—Seattle (A.L.)	1B-DH	109	408	48	108	25	1	17	60	.265	45	56	0	932	60	3	.997
1994—Seattle (A.L.)	1B-DH	97	329	42	86	21	0	20	61	.261	29	52	1	705	45	2	.997
1995—Seattle (A.L.)	1B-DH	141	519	92	152	35	3	31	111	.293	62	91	0	1048	101	8	.993
1996—New York (A.L.)■......	1B-DH	155	595	82	174	28	0	25	117	.292	68	85	2	1238	83	5	*.996
1997—New York (A.L.)..........	1B-DH	158	594	96	176	31	2	44	141	.296	75	75	3	1302	105	8	.994
Major league totals (8 years)		**856**	**3085**	**428**	**852**	**165**	**8**	**157**	**570**	**.276**	**341**	**469**	**8**	**6307**	**486**	**32**	**.995**

DIVISION SERIES RECORD

RECORDS: Holds career records for most games—14; and most at-bats—55.

							BATTING								FIELDING		
Year Team (League)	Pos.	G	AB	R	H	2B	3B	HR	RBI	Avg.	BB	SO	SB	PO	A	E	Avg.
1995—Seattle (A.L.)	1B	5	22	4	9	1	0	1	5	.409	3	4	0	39	5	0	1.000
1996—New York (A.L.)..........	1B	4	15	3	4	2	0	0	0	.267	4	1	0	33	3	0	1.000
1997—New York (A.L.)..........	1B	5	18	1	4	1	0	1	4	.222	2	4	0	48	6	0	1.000
Division series totals (3 years)		**14**	**55**	**8**	**17**	**4**	**0**	**2**	**9**	**.309**	**9**	**9**	**0**	**120**	**14**	**0**	**1.000**

M

CHAMPIONSHIP SERIES RECORD

Year	Team (League)	Pos.	G	AB	R	H	2B	3B	HR	RBI	Avg.	BB	SO	SB	PO	A	E	Avg.
1995—	Seattle (A.L.)	1B	6	22	1	3	0	0	0	0	.136	3	7	0	45	5	1	.980
1996—	New York (A.L.)	1B	5	22	3	4	1	0	0	0	.182	0	2	0	49	2	0	1.000
	Championship series totals (2 years)		11	44	4	7	1	0	0	0	.159	3	9	0	94	7	1	.990

WORLD SERIES RECORD

NOTES: Member of World Series championship team (1996).

Year	Team (League)	Pos.	G	AB	R	H	2B	3B	HR	RBI	Avg.	BB	SO	SB	PO	A	E	Avg.
1996—	New York (A.L.)	1B-PH	6	11	0	1	0	0	0	0	.091	2	5	0	27	0	0	1.000

ALL-STAR GAME RECORD

Year	League	Pos.	AB	R	H	2B	3B	HR	RBI	Avg.	BB	SO	SB	PO	A	E	Avg.
1995—	American	PH	1	0	1	0	0	0	0	1.000	0	0	0	...	...	...	...
1997—	American	1B	2	0	0	0	0	0	0	.000	0	0	0	10	0	0	1.000
	All-Star Game totals (2 years)		3	0	1	0	0	0	0	.333	0	0	0	10	0	0	1.000

MARTINEZ, WILLY — P — INDIANS

PERSONAL: Born January 4, 1978, in Barquisimeto, Venezuela. ... 6-2/165. ... Throws right, bats right. ... Full name: William Martinez.
TRANSACTIONS/CAREER NOTES: Signed as non-drafted free agent by Cleveland Indians organization (January 16, 1995).

Year	Team (League)	W	L	Pct.	ERA	G	GS	CG	ShO	Sv.	IP	H	R	ER	BB	SO
1995—	Burlington (Appalachian)....	0	7	.000	9.45	11	11	0	0	0	40	64	50	42	25	36
1996—	Watertown (NYP)	6	5	.545	2.40	14	14	1	1	0	90	79	25	24	21	92
1997—	Kinston (Carolina)	8	2	.800	3.09	23	23	1	0	0	137	125	61	47	42	120

MARZANO, JOHN — C — MARINERS

PERSONAL: Born February 14, 1963, in Philadelphia. ... 5-11/195. ... Bats right, throws right. ... Full name: John Robert Marzano.
HIGH SCHOOL: Central (Philadelphia).
COLLEGE: Temple.
TRANSACTIONS/CAREER NOTES: Selected by Minnesota Twins organization in third round of free-agent draft (June 8, 1981, did not sign); pick received as compensation for California Angels signing free-agent P Geoff Zahn. ... Selected by Boston Red Sox organization in first round (14th pick overall) of free-agent draft (June 4, 1984). ... On disabled list (June 13-28, 1986). ... On Boston disabled list (April 6-July 26, 1992); included rehabilitation assignment to Pawtucket (July 7-26). ... Released by Red Sox (March 24, 1993). ... Signed by Charlotte, Cleveland Indians organization (May 5, 1993). ... On disabled list (May 12-23, 1993). ... Released by Charlotte (May 23, 1993). ... Signed by Philadelphia Phillies organization (December 14, 1993). ... Granted free agency (October 15, 1994). ... Signed by Oklahoma City, Texas Rangers organization (April 2, 1995). ... On Oklahoma City suspended list (June 8-10, 1995). ... Granted free agency (October 16, 1995). ... Signed by Seattle Mariners organization (December 14, 1995). ... On suspended list (September 3-5, 1996). ... Granted free agency (October 29, 1997). ... Re-signed by Mariners organization (December 8, 1997).
HONORS: Named catcher on THE SPORTING NEWS college All-America team (1984).
STATISTICAL NOTES: Led Eastern League in being hit by pitch with 12 in 1986. ... Led American Association catchers with 620 total chances and 12 double plays in 1995.
MISCELLANEOUS: Member of 1984 U.S. Olympic baseball team.

Year	Team (League)	Pos.	G	AB	R	H	2B	3B	HR	RBI	Avg.	BB	SO	SB	PO	A	E	Avg.
1985—	New Britain (Eastern) .	C	103	350	36	86	14	6	4	51	.246	19	43	4	530	70	12	.980
1986—	New Britain (Eastern) .	C-3B	118	445	55	126	28	2	10	62	.283	24	66	2	509	76	14	.977
1987—	Pawtucket (Int'l)	C	70	255	46	72	22	0	10	35	.282	21	50	2	326	36	8	.978
	—Boston (A.L.)	C	52	168	20	41	11	0	5	24	.244	7	41	0	337	24	5	.986
1988—	Boston (A.L.)	C	10	29	3	4	1	0	0	1	.138	1	3	0	77	4	0	1.000
	—Pawtucket (Int'l)	C	33	111	7	22	2	1	0	5	.198	8	17	1	151	24	8	.956
	—New Britain (Eastern) .	C	35	112	11	23	6	1	0	5	.205	10	13	1	117	11	3	.977
1989—	Pawtucket (Int'l)	C	106	322	27	68	11	0	8	36	.211	15	53	1	574	62	10	.985
	—Boston (A.L.)	C	7	18	5	8	3	0	1	3	.444	0	2	0	29	4	0	1.000
1990—	Boston (A.L.)	C	32	83	8	20	4	0	0	6	.241	5	10	0	153	14	0	1.000
	—Pawtucket (Int'l)	C-3B	26	75	16	24	4	1	2	8	.320	11	9	6	100	12	0	1.000
1991—	Boston (A.L.)	C	49	114	10	30	8	0	0	9	.263	1	16	0	174	20	3	.985
1992—	Pawtucket (Int'l)	C	35	62	5	18	1	0	2	12	.290	3	11	0	53	4	2	.966
	—Boston (A.L.)	C-DH	19	50	4	4	2	1	0	1	.080	2	12	0	81	9	3	.968
1993—	Charlotte (Int'l)■......	C	3	9	0	1	0	0	0	0	.111	1	1	0	12	1	1	.929
1994—	Scran./W.B. (Int'l)■...	C-OF	88	280	25	59	19	2	1	19	.211	24	32	2	311	31	7	.980
1995—	Okla. City (A.A.)■......	C	120	427	55	132	*41	3	9	56	.309	33	54	3	*551	*64	5	.992
	—Texas (A.L.)	C	2	6	1	2	0	0	0	0	.333	0	0	0	7	1	0	1.000
1996—	Seattle (A.L.)■............	C	41	106	8	26	6	0	0	6	.245	7	15	0	194	10	3	.986
1997—	Seattle (A.L.)	C-DH	39	87	7	25	3	0	1	10	.287	7	15	0	191	13	5	.976
	Major league totals (9 years)		251	661	66	160	38	1	7	60	.242	30	114	0	1243	99	19	.986

MASHORE, DAMON — OF

PERSONAL: Born October 31, 1969, in Ponce, Puerto Rico. ... 5-11/195. ... Throws right, bats right. ... Full name: Damon Wayne Mashore. ... Son of Clyde Mashore, major league outfielder with Cincinnati Reds (1969) and Montreal Expos (1970-73). ... Name pronounced MAY-shore.
HIGH SCHOOL: Clayton Valley (Concord, Calif.).
COLLEGE: Arizona.

TRANSACTIONS/CAREER NOTES: Selected by Oakland Athletics organization in ninth round of free-agent draft (June 3, 1991). ... On disabled list (July 13-September 8, 1993). ... On Huntsville disabled list (May 23-August 2, 1994). ... On Oakland disabled list (August 13, 1996-remainder of season). ... On disabled list (July 27, 1997-remainder of season). ... Granted free agency (October 15, 1997).
STATISTICAL NOTES: Tied for Northwest League lead in double plays by outfielder with two in 1991.

						BATTING								FIELDING			
Year Team (League)	Pos.	G	AB	R	H	2B	3B	HR	RBI	Avg.	BB	SO	SB	PO	A	E	Avg.
1991— S. Oregon (N'west).....	OF	73	264	48	72	17	6	6	31	.273	34	94	15	93	6	3	.971
1992— Modesto (California) ..	OF	124	471	91	133	22	3	18	64	.282	73	*136	29	212	12	8	.966
1993— Huntsville (Southern) .	OF	70	253	35	59	7	2	3	20	.233	25	64	18	167	9	3	.983
1994— Scottsdale (Ariz.)........	OF	11	34	6	14	2	00	0	6	.412	4	3	1	15	0	0	1.000
—Huntsville (Southern) .	OF	59	21	24	47	11	2	3	21	2.238	13	53	6	97	2	5	.952
1995— Edmonton (PCL)	OF	117	337	50	101	19	5	1	37	.300	42	77	17	197	12	4	.981
1996— Edmonton (PCL)	OF	50	183	32	49	9	1	8	29	.268	19	48	6	74	7	1	.988
—Oakland (A.L.)	OF	50	105	20	28	7	1	3	12	.267	16	31	4	65	1	1	.985
1997— Oakland (A.L.)	OF	92	279	55	69	10	2	3	18	.247	50	82	5	203	10	2	.991
Major league totals (2 years)		142	384	75	97	17	3	6	30	.253	66	113	9	268	11	3	.989

MATEO, RUBEN   OF   RANGERS

PERSONAL: Born February 10, 1978, in San Cristobal, Dominican Republic. ... 6-0/170. ... Throws right, bats right. ... Full name: Ruben Amaurys Mateo.
TRANSACTIONS/CAREER NOTES: Signed as non-drafted free agent by Texas Rangers organization (October 24, 1994).

						BATTING								FIELDING			
Year Team (League)	Pos.	G	AB	R	H	2B	3B	HR	RBI	Avg.	BB	SO	SB	PO	A	E	Avg.
1995— Dom. Rangers (DSL)..	OF	48	176	30	53	9	3	4	42	.301	20	23	1	55	1	1	.982
1996— Char., S.C. (S. Atl.)	OF	134	496	65	129	30	8	8	58	.260	26	78	30	215	15	7	.970
1997— Charlotte (Fla. St.)	OF	99	385	63	121	23	8	12	67	.314	22	55	20	174	10	8	.958

MATHENY, MIKE   C   BREWERS

PERSONAL: Born September 22, 1970, in Columbus, Ohio. ... 6-3/205. ... Bats right, throws right. ... Full name: Michael Scott Matheny.
HIGH SCHOOL: Reynoldsburg (Ohio).
COLLEGE: Michigan.
TRANSACTIONS/CAREER NOTES: Selected by Toronto Blue Jays organization in 31st round of free-agent draft (June 1, 1988); did not sign. ... Selected by Milwaukee Brewers organization in eighth round of free-agent draft (June 3, 1991). ... On Milwaukee suspended list (June 20-23, 1996).
STATISTICAL NOTES: Led California League catchers with 20 double plays in 1992. ... Led Texas League catchers with 18 double plays in 1993. ... Career major league grand slams: 2.

						BATTING								FIELDING			
Year Team (League)	Pos.	G	AB	R	H	2B	3B	HR	RBI	Avg.	BB	SO	SB	PO	A	E	Avg.
1991— Helena (Pioneer)	C	64	253	35	72	14	0	2	34	.285	19	52	2	456	68	5	*.991
1992— Stockton (California) ..	C	106	333	42	73	13	2	6	46	.219	35	81	2	582	114	8	*.989
1993— El Paso (Texas)..........	C	107	339	39	86	21	2	2	28	.254	17	73	1	524	*100	9	.986
1994— Milwaukee (A.L.)	C	28	53	3	12	3	0	1	2	.226	3	13	0	81	8	1	.989
—New Orleans (A.A.).....	C-1B	57	177	20	39	10	1	4	21	.220	16	39	1	345	43	5	.987
1995— New Orleans (A.A.)	C	6	17	3	6	2	0	3	4	.353	0	5	0	30	4	0	1.000
—Milwaukee (A.L.)	C	80	166	13	41	9	1	0	21	.247	12	28	2	261	18	4	.986
1996— Milwaukee (A.L.)	C-DH	106	313	31	64	15	2	8	46	.204	14	80	3	475	40	8	.985
—New Orleans (A.A.)	C	20	66	3	15	4	0	1	6	.227	2	17	1	87	6	0	1.000
1997— Milwaukee (A.L.)	C-1B	123	320	29	78	16	1	4	32	.244	17	68	0	697	58	5	.993
Major league totals (4 years)		337	852	76	195	43	4	13	101	.229	46	189	5	1514	124	18	.989

MATHEWS, T.J.   P   ATHLETICS

PERSONAL: Born January 19, 1970, in Belleville, Ill. ... 6-2/200. ... Throws right, bats right. ... Full name: Timothy Jay Mathews. ... Son of Nelson Mathews, outfielder, Chicago Cubs and Kansas City Athletics (1960-65).
HIGH SCHOOL: Columbia (Ill.).
COLLEGE: UNLV.
TRANSACTIONS/CAREER NOTES: Selected by St. Louis Cardinals organization in 36th round of free-agent draft (June 1, 1992). ... On Louisville disabled list (May 30-June 6, 1995). ... On suspended list (April 1-7, 1997). ... Traded by Cardinals with P Eric Ludwick and P Blake Stein to Oakland Athletics for 1B Mark McGwire (July 31, 1997).
STATISTICAL NOTES: Pitched 4-0 no-hit victory against Burlington (August 13, 1993).

Year Team (League)	W	L	Pct.	ERA	G	GS	CG	ShO	Sv.	IP	H	R	ER	BB	SO
1992— Hamilton (NYP).................	10	1	*.909	2.18	14	14	1	0	0	86 2/3	70	25	21	30	89
1993— Springfield (Mid.).............	12	9	.571	2.71	25	25	5	2	0	159 1/3	121	59	48	29	144
1994— St. Petersburg (FSL)	5	5	.500	2.44	11	11	1	0	0	66 1/3	52	22	18	23	62
—Arkansas (Texas)................	5	5	.500	3.15	16	16	1	0	0	97	83	37	34	24	93
1995— Louisville (A.A.)................	9	4	.692	2.70	32	7	0	0	1	66 2/3	60	35	20	27	50
—St. Louis (N.L.)................	1	1	.500	1.52	23	0	0	0	2	29 2/3	21	7	5	11	28
1996— St. Louis (N.L.)................	2	6	.250	3.01	67	0	0	0	6	83 2/3	62	32	28	32	80
1997— St. Louis (N.L.)................	4	4	.500	2.15	40	0	0	0	0	46	41	14	11	18	46
—Oakland (A.L.)■................	6	2	.750	4.40	24	0	0	0	3	28 2/3	34	18	14	12	24
A.L. totals (1 year)	6	2	.750	4.40	24	0	0	0	3	28 2/3	34	18	14	12	24
N.L. totals (3 years)	7	11	.389	2.49	130	0	0	0	8	159 1/3	124	53	44	61	154
Major league totals (3 years)	13	13	.500	2.78	154	0	0	0	11	188	158	71	58	73	178

M

DIVISION SERIES RECORD

Year	Team (League)	W	L	Pct.	ERA	G	GS	CG	ShO	Sv.	IP	H	R	ER	BB	SO
1996— St. Louis (N.L.)		1	0	1.000	0.00	1	0	0	0	0	1	1	0	0	0	2

CHAMPIONSHIP SERIES RECORD

Year	Team (League)	W	L	Pct.	ERA	G	GS	CG	ShO	Sv.	IP	H	R	ER	BB	SO
1996— St. Louis (N.L.)		0	0	...	0.00	2	0	0	0	0	$2/3$	2	0	0	2	2

MATHEWS, TERRY   P   ORIOLES

PERSONAL: Born October 5, 1964, in Alexandria, La. ... 6-2/225. ... Throws right, bats left. ... Full name: Terry Alan Mathews.
HIGH SCHOOL: Menard (Alexandria, La.).
COLLEGE: Northeast Louisiana.
TRANSACTIONS/CAREER NOTES: Selected by Texas Rangers organization in fifth round of free-agent draft (June 2, 1987). ... On Texas disabled list (July 29-September 12, 1992). ... Released by Rangers organization (April 4, 1993). ... Signed by Houston Astros organization (April 4, 1993). ... Granted free agency (October 15, 1993). ... Signed by Edmonton, Florida Marlins organization (November 9, 1993). ... On Florida disabled list (August 19-September 3, 1995); included rehabilitation assignment to Charlotte (August 29-September 1). ... On Florida disabled list (April 2-17, 1996). ... Traded by Marlins to Baltimore Orioles for a player to be named later (August 21, 1996); Marlins acquired C Greg Zaun to complete deal (August 23, 1996).
MISCELLANEOUS: Grounded into double play in only appearance as pinch-hitter with Florida (1995).

Year	Team (League)	W	L	Pct.	ERA	G	GS	CG	ShO	Sv.	IP	H	R	ER	BB	SO
1987— Gastonia (S. Atl.)		3	3	.500	5.59	34	1	0	0	0	$48 1/3$	53	35	30	32	46
1988— Charlotte (Fla. St.)		13	6	.684	2.80	27	26	2	1	0	$163 2/3$	141	68	51	49	94
1989— Tulsa (Texas)		2	5	.286	6.15	10	10	1	0	0	$45 1/3$	53	40	31	24	32
— Charlotte (Fla. St.)		4	2	.667	3.64	10	10	0	0	0	$59 1/3$	55	28	24	17	30
1990— Tulsa (Texas)		5	7	.417	4.27	14	14	4	2	0	$86 1/3$	88	50	41	36	48
— Oklahoma City (A.A.)		2	7	.222	3.69	12	11	1	1	0	$70 2/3$	81	39	29	15	36
1991— Oklahoma City (A.A.)		5	6	.455	3.49	18	13	1	0	1	$95 1/3$	98	39	37	34	63
— Texas (A.L.)		4	0	1.000	3.61	34	2	0	0	1	$57 1/3$	54	24	23	18	51
1992— Texas (A.L.)		2	4	.333	5.95	40	0	0	0	0	$42 1/3$	48	29	28	31	26
— Oklahoma City (A.A.)		1	1	.500	4.32	9	2	0	0	1	$16 2/3$	17	8	8	7	13
1993— Jackson (Texas)■		6	5	.545	3.67	17	17	0	0	0	103	116	55	42	29	74
— Tucson (PCL)		5	0	1.000	3.55	16	4	0	0	2	33	40	14	13	11	34
1994— Edmonton (PCL)■		4	4	.500	4.29	13	12	3	0	0	84	88	43	40	22	46
— Florida (N.L.)		2	1	.667	3.35	24	2	0	0	0	43	45	16	16	9	21
1995— Florida (N.L.)		4	4	.500	3.38	57	0	0	0	3	$82 2/3$	70	32	31	27	72
— Charlotte (Int'l)		0	0	...	4.91	2	0	0	0	0	$3 2/3$	5	2	2	0	5
1996— Florida (N.L.)		2	4	.333	4.91	57	0	0	0	4	55	59	33	30	27	49
— Baltimore (A.L.)■		2	2	.500	3.38	14	0	0	0	0	$18 2/3$	20	7	7	7	13
1997— Baltimore (A.L.)		4	4	.500	4.41	57	0	0	0	1	$63 1/3$	63	35	31	36	39
A.L. totals (4 years)		12	10	.545	4.41	145	2	0	0	2	$181 2/3$	185	95	89	92	129
N.L. totals (3 years)		8	9	.471	3.84	138	2	0	0	7	$180 2/3$	174	81	77	63	142
Major league totals (6 years)		20	19	.513	4.12	283	4	0	0	9	$362 1/3$	359	176	166	155	271

DIVISION SERIES RECORD

Year	Team (League)	W	L	Pct.	ERA	G	GS	CG	ShO	Sv.	IP	H	R	ER	BB	SO
1996— Baltimore (A.L.)		0	0	...	0.00	3	0	0	0	0	$2 2/3$	3	0	0	1	2
1997— Baltimore (A.L.)		0	0	...	18.00	1	0	0	0	0	1	2	2	2	0	1
Div. series totals (2 years)		0	0	...	4.91	4	0	0	0	0	$3 2/3$	5	2	2	1	3

CHAMPIONSHIP SERIES RECORD

Year	Team (League)	W	L	Pct.	ERA	G	GS	CG	ShO	Sv.	IP	H	R	ER	BB	SO
1996— Baltimore (A.L.)		0	0	...	0.00	3	0	0	0	0	$2 1/3$	0	0	0	2	3

MATOS, PASCUAL   C   BRAVES

PERSONAL: Born December 23, 1973, in Barahona, Dominican Republic. ... 6-2/160. ... Bats right, throws right. ... Full name: Pascual Cuevas Matos.
HIGH SCHOOL: Colegio Divino Tesoro (Barahona, Dominican Republic).
TRANSACTIONS/CAREER NOTES: Signed as non-drafted free agent by Atlanta Braves organization (March 5, 1992).
STATISTICAL NOTES: Led Pioneer League catchers with three double plays in 1994. ... Led Carolina League catchers with 26 passed balls and tied for league lead with eight double plays in 1997.

										BATTING					FIELDING			
Year	Team (League)	Pos.	G	AB	R	H	2B	3B	HR	RBI	Avg.	BB	SO	SB	PO	A	E	Avg.
1992— Dom. Braves (DSL)		C	19	58	6	19	4	1	1	14	.328	6	12	0	105	15	3	.976
— GC Braves (GCL)		C	13	33	3	5	1	0	0	0	.152	10	12	0	97	11	0	1.000
1993— GC Braves (GCL)		C	36	119	12	27	5	1	0	15	.227	3	32	3	259	39	10	.968
1994— Idaho Falls (Pio.)		C	43	157	22	40	7	1	7	29	.255	2	39	7	226	48	13	.955
— Macon (S. Atl.)		C	11	29	1	5	2	0	0	2	.172	0	10	1	48	5	6	.898
1995— Macon (S. Atl.)		C	72	238	23	44	11	1	5	26	.185	11	86	2	498	76	9	.985
1996— Durham (Carolina)		C	67	219	24	49	9	3	6	28	.224	7	70	6	394	54	8	.982
1997— Durham (Carolina)		C	117	430	51	104	18	3	18	50	.242	14	122	4	783	*109	*13	.986

MATTHEWS, GARY   OF   PADRES

PERSONAL: Born August 25, 1974, in Canoga Park, Calif. ... 6-2/185. ... Bats both, throws right. ... Full name: Gary Nathaniel Matthews Jr. ... Son of Gary Matthews, outfielder with five major league teams (1972-87).
HIGH SCHOOL: Granada Hills (Calif.).
JUNIOR COLLEGE: Los Angeles Mission.
TRANSACTIONS/CAREER NOTES: Selected by San Diego Padres organization in 13th round of free-agent draft (June 3, 1993).

Year Team (League)	Pos.	G	AB	R	H	2B	3B	HR	RBI	Avg.	BB	SO	SB	PO	A	E	Avg.
1994— Spokane (N'west)	OF-2B	52	191	23	40	6	1	0	18	.209	19	58	3	96	2	4	.961
1995— Clinton (Midwest)	OF	128	421	57	100	18	4	2	40	.238	68	109	28	245	9	9	.966
1996— Rancho Cuca. (Cal.)	OF	123	435	65	118	21	11	7	54	.271	60	102	7	218	7	16	.934
1997— Rancho Cuca. (Cal.)	OF	69	268	66	81	15	4	8	40	.302	49	57	10	110	6	5	.959
— Mobile (Southern)	OF	28	90	14	22	4	1	2	12	.244	15	29	3	45	3	2	.960

MATTHEWS, MIKE — P — INDIANS

PERSONAL: Born October 24, 1973, in Fredericksburg, Va. ... 6-2/175. ... Throws left, bats left. ... Full name: Michael Scott Matthews.
HIGH SCHOOL: Woodbridge Senior (Va.).
JUNIOR COLLEGE: Montgomery-Rockville (Md.).
TRANSACTIONS/CAREER NOTES: Selected by Cleveland Indians organization in second round of free-agent draft (June 1, 1992). ... On Watertown disabled list (June 17-September 12, 1993). ... On disabled list (June 7-28, 1995).
STATISTICAL NOTES: Tied for Eastern League lead with four balks in 1997.

Year Team (League)	W	L	Pct.	ERA	G	GS	CG	ShO	Sv.	IP	H	R	ER	BB	SO
1992— Burlington (Appalachian)	7	0	•1.000	*1.01	10	10	0	0	0	62 1/3	33	13	7	27	55
— Watertown (NYP)	1	0	1.000	3.27	2	2	2	0	0	11	10	4	4	8	5
1993—							Did not play.								
1994— Columbus (S. Atl.)	6	8	.429	3.08	23	23	0	0	0	119 2/3	120	53	41	44	99
1995— Cant./Akr. (Eastern)	5	8	.385	5.93	15	15	1	0	0	74 1/3	82	62	49	43	37
1996— Cant./Akr. (Eastern)	9	11	.450	4.66	27	27	3	0	0	162 1/3	178	96	84	74	112
1997— Buffalo (A.A.)	0	2	.000	7.71	5	5	0	0	0	21	32	19	18	10	17
— Akron (Eastern)	6	8	.429	3.82	19	19	3	1	0	113	116	62	48	57	69

MAXWELL, JASON — SS — CUBS

PERSONAL: Born March 21, 1972, in Lewisburg, Tenn. ... 6-1/175. ... Bats right, throws right. ... Full name: Jason Ramond Maxwell.
HIGH SCHOOL: Marshall County (Lewisburg, Tenn.).
COLLEGE: Middle Tennessee.
TRANSACTIONS/CAREER NOTES: Selected by Chicago Cubs organization in 74th round of free-agent draft (June 3, 1993).
STATISTICAL NOTES: Led Southern League with nine sacrifice flies in 1997.

Year Team (League)	Pos.	G	AB	R	H	2B	3B	HR	RBI	Avg.	BB	SO	SB	PO	A	E	Avg.
1993— Hunting. (Appal.)	SS	61	179	50	52	7	2	7	38	.291	35	39	6	60	140	9	.957
1994— Daytona (Fla. St.)	SS	116	368	71	85	18	2	10	31	.231	55	96	7	167	333	*38	.929
1995— Daytona (Fla. St.)	SS	117	388	66	102	13	3	10	58	.263	63	68	12	181	325	16	*.969
1996— Orlando (South.)	SS-2B-3B	126	433	64	115	20	1	9	45	.266	56	77	19	188	336	29	.948
1997— Orlando (South.)	SS-2B	122	409	87	114	22	6	14	58	.279	82	72	12	176	376	28	.952

MAY, DARRELL — P — ANGELS

PERSONAL: Born June 13, 1972, in San Bernardino, Calif. ... 6-2/170. ... Throws left, bats left. ... Full name: Darrell Kevin May.
HIGH SCHOOL: Rogue River (Ore.).
COLLEGE: Sacramento City College.
TRANSACTIONS/CAREER NOTES: Selected by Atlanta Braves organization in 46th round of free-agent draft (June 1, 1992). ... Claimed on waivers by Pittsburgh Pirates (April 4, 1996). ... Claimed on waivers by California Angels (September 6, 1996). ... Angels franchise renamed Anaheim Angels for 1997 season.
STATISTICAL NOTES: Pitched 4-0 no-hit victory against Colorado Springs (April 30, 1997, second game).

Year Team (League)	W	L	Pct.	ERA	G	GS	CG	ShO	Sv.	IP	H	R	ER	BB	SO
1992— GC Braves (GCL)	4	3	.571	1.36	12	7	0	0	1	53	34	13	8	13	61
1993— Macon (S. Atl.)	10	4	.714	2.24	17	17	0	0	0	104 1/3	81	29	26	22	111
— Durham (Carolina)	5	2	.714	2.09	9	9	0	0	0	51 2/3	44	18	12	16	47
1994— Greenville (Southern)	5	3	.625	3.11	11	11	1	0	0	63 2/3	61	25	22	17	42
— Durham (Carolina)	8	2	*.800	3.01	12	12	1	0	0	74 2/3	74	29	25	17	73
1995— Greenville (Southern)	2	8	.200	3.55	15	15	0	0	0	91 1/3	81	44	36	20	79
— Richmond (Int'l)	4	2	.667	3.71	9	9	0	0	0	51	53	21	21	16	42
— Atlanta (N.L.)	0	0	...	11.25	2	0	0	0	0	4	10	5	5	0	1
1996— Calgary (PCL)■	7	6	.538	4.10	23	22	1	1	0	131 2/3	146	64	60	36	75
— Pittsburgh (N.L.)	0	1	.000	9.35	5	2	0	0	0	8 2/3	15	10	9	4	5
— California (A.L.)■	0	0	...	10.13	5	0	0	0	0	2 2/3	3	3	3	2	1
1997— Vancouver (PCL)	7	5	.583	3.26	13	12	2	2	0	80	65	31	29	31	62
— Anaheim (A.L.)	2	1	.667	5.23	29	2	0	0	0	51 2/3	56	31	30	25	42
A.L. totals (2 years)	2	1	.667	5.47	34	2	0	0	0	54 1/3	59	34	33	27	43
N.L. totals (2 years)	0	1	.000	9.95	7	2	0	0	0	12 2/3	25	15	14	4	6
Major league totals (3 years)	2	2	.500	6.31	41	4	0	0	0	67	84	49	47	31	49

M

MAY, DERRICK — OF — EXPOS

PERSONAL: Born July 14, 1968, in Rochester, N.Y. ... 6-4/225. ... Bats left, throws right. ... Full name: Derrick Brant May. ... Son of Dave May, major league outfielder with five teams (1967-78).
HIGH SCHOOL: Newark (Del.).
TRANSACTIONS/CAREER NOTES: Selected by Chicago Cubs organization in first round (ninth pick overall) of free-agent draft (June 2, 1986). ... On Iowa disabled list (April 14-May 27 and June 6-24, 1991). ... Granted free agency (April 7, 1995). ... Signed by New Orleans, Milwaukee Brewers organization (April 12, 1995). ... Traded by Brewers to Houston Astros for a player to be named later (June 21, 1995); Brewers acquired IF Tommy Nevers to complete deal (July 21, 1996). ... On disabled list (June 20-July 5, 1996). ... Granted free agency (December 20, 1996). ... Signed by Philadelphia Phillies organization (January 29, 1997). ... Released by Phillies (August 6, 1997) ... Signed by Montreal Expos organization (January 6, 1998).
STATISTICAL NOTES: Tied for Carolina League lead in double plays by outfielder with four in 1988. ... Career major league grand slams: 2.

Year Team (League)	Pos.	G	AB	R	H	2B	3B	HR	RBI	Avg.	BB	SO	SB	PO	A	E	Avg.
1986— Wytheville (App.)........	OF	54	178	25	57	6	1	0	23	.320	16	15	17	47	3	5	.909
1987— Peoria (Midwest)........	OF	128	439	60	131	19	8	9	52	.298	42	106	5	181	13	8	.960
1988— Win.-Salem (Car.)......	OF	130	485	76	•148	29	*9	8	65	.305	37	82	13	209	13	10	.957
1989— Charlotte (Southern) ..	OF	136	491	72	145	26	5	9	70	.295	34	77	19	239	8	•13	.950
1990— Iowa (Am. Assoc.)......	OF-1B	119	459	55	136	27	1	8	69	.296	23	50	5	159	10	8	.955
—Chicago (N.L.)......	OF	17	61	8	15	3	0	1	11	.246	2	7	1	34	1	1	.972
1991— Iowa (Am. Assoc.)......	OF	82	310	47	92	18	4	3	49	.297	19	38	7	130	2	5	.964
—Chicago (N.L.)...........	OF	15	22	4	5	2	0	1	3	.227	2	1	0	11	1	0	1.000
1992— Iowa (Am. Assoc.)......	OF	8	30	6	11	4	1	2	8	.367	3	3	0	11	1	0	1.000
—Chicago (N.L.)...........	OF	124	351	33	96	11	0	8	45	.274	14	40	5	153	3	5	.969
1993— Chicago (N.L.)...........	OF	128	465	62	137	25	2	10	77	.295	31	41	10	220	8	7	.970
1994— Chicago (N.L.)...........	OF	100	345	43	98	19	2	8	51	.284	30	34	3	155	4	1	.994
1995— Milwaukee (A.L.)■.....	OF	32	113	15	28	3	1	1	9	.248	5	18	0	65	1	2	.971
—Houston (N.L.)■......	OF-1B	78	206	29	62	15	1	8	41	.301	19	24	5	74	0	2	.974
1996— Houston (N.L.)...........	OF	109	259	24	65	12	3	5	33	.251	30	33	2	125	5	4	.970
1997— Philadelphia (N.L.)■ ..	OF	83	149	8	34	5	1	1	13	.228	8	26	4	69	4	3	.961
American League totals (1 year)		32	113	15	28	3	1	1	9	.248	5	18	0	65	1	2	.971
National League totals (8 years)		654	1858	211	512	92	9	42	274	.276	136	206	30	841	26	23	.974
Major league totals (8 years)		686	1971	226	540	95	10	43	283	.274	141	224	30	906	27	25	.974

MAYNE, BRENT   C   GIANTS

PERSONAL: Born April 19, 1968, in Loma Linda, Calif. ... 6-1/190. ... Bats left, throws right. ... Full name: Brent Danem Mayne.
HIGH SCHOOL: Costa Mesa (Calif.).
JUNIOR COLLEGE: Orange Coast College (Calif.).
COLLEGE: Cal State Fullerton.
TRANSACTIONS/CAREER NOTES: Selected by Kansas City Royals organization in first round (13th pick overall) of free-agent draft (June 5, 1989). ... On disabled list (July 24, 1989-remainder of season). ... Traded by Royals to New York Mets for OF Al Shirley (December 19, 1995). ... Granted free agency (December 7, 1996). ... Signed by Seattle Mariners organization (January 10, 1997). ... Released by Mariners (March 28, 1997). ... Signed by Edmonton, A's organization (April 8, 1997). ... Granted free agency (October 30, 1997). ... Signed by San Francisco Giants (November 21, 1997).
STATISTICAL NOTES: Led A.L. catchers with 11 double plays in 1995. ... Career major league grand slams: 1.

Year Team (League)	Pos.	G	AB	R	H	2B	3B	HR	RBI	Avg.	BB	SO	SB	PO	A	E	Avg.
1989— Baseball City (FSL).....	C	7	24	5	13	3	1	0	8	.542	0	3	0	31	2	0	1.000
1990— Memphis (Southern)..	C	115	412	48	110	16	3	2	61	.267	52	51	5	591	61	11	.983
—Kansas City (A.L.)	C	5	13	2	3	0	0	0	1	.231	3	3	0	29	3	1	.970
1991— Kansas City (A.L.)	C-DH	85	231	22	58	8	0	3	31	.251	23	42	2	425	38	6	.987
1992— Kansas City (A.L.)	C-3B-DH	82	213	16	48	10	0	0	18	.225	11	26	0	281	33	3	.991
1993— Kansas City (A.L.)	C-DH	71	205	22	52	9	1	2	22	.254	18	31	3	356	27	2	.995
1994— Kansas City (A.L.)	C-DH	46	144	19	37	5	1	2	20	.257	14	27	1	246	14	1	.996
1995— Kansas City (A.L.)	C	110	307	23	77	18	1	1	27	.251	25	41	0	540	40	3	.995
1996— New York (N.L.)■......	C	70	99	9	26	6	0	1	6	.263	12	22	0	85	3	0	1.000
1997— Edmonton (PCL)■	C	2	3	0	0	0	0	0	0	.000	0	1	0	5	0	0	1.000
—Oakland (A.L.)	C	85	256	29	74	12	0	6	22	.289	18	33	1	419	36	2	.996
American League totals (7 years)		484	1369	133	349	62	3	14	141	.255	112	203	7	2296	191	18	.993
National League totals (1 year)		70	99	9	26	6	0	1	6	.263	12	22	0	85	3	0	1.000
Major league totals (8 years)		554	1468	142	375	68	3	15	147	.255	124	225	7	2381	194	18	.993

McANDREW, JAMIE   P   INDIANS

PERSONAL: Born September 2, 1967, in Williamsport, Pa. ... 6-2/190. ... Throws right, bats right. ... Full name: James Brian McAndrew. ... Son of Jim McAndrew, pitcher with New York Mets and San Diego Padres (1968-74).
HIGH SCHOOL: Ponderosa (Fla.).
COLLEGE: Florida.
TRANSACTIONS/CAREER NOTES: Selected by Seattle Mariners organization in 23rd round of free-agent draft (June 2, 1986); did not sign. ... Selected by Los Angeles Dodgers organization in supplemental round ("sandwich pick" between first and second round, 28th pick overall) of free-agent draft (June 5, 1989); pick received as part of compensation for New York Yankees signing Type A free-agent 2B Steve Sax. ... On San Antonio disabled list (May 2-July 6, 1992). ... Selected by Florida Marlins in third round (57th pick overall) of expansion draft (November 17, 1992). ... Traded by Marlins to Milwaukee Brewers for P Tom McGraw (April 2, 1993). ... On New Orleans disabled list (April 7, 1994-entire season). ... On Milwaukee disabled list (August 29-September 28, 1995 and March 29, 1996-entire season). ... Granted free agency (October 15, 1997). ... Signed by Cleveland Indians organization (January 8, 1998).
STATISTICAL NOTES: Led Pacific Coast League with four balks in 1997.

Year Team (League)	W	L	Pct.	ERA	G	GS	CG	ShO	Sv.	IP	H	R	ER	BB	SO
1989— Great Falls (Pio.)	*11	0	*1.000	1.65	13	13	1	0	0	76 1/3	49	16	14	27	72
1990— San Antonio (Tex.)	7	3	.700	1.93	12	12	0	0	0	79 1/3	68	28	17	32	50
—Bakersfield (California).......	10	3	.769	2.27	14	14	1	1	0	95	88	31	24	29	82
1991— Albuquerque (PCL).............	12	10	.545	5.04	28	26	0	0	1	155 1/3	167	105	87	76	91
1992— Albuquerque (PCL).............	1	3	.250	5.83	5	5	0	0	0	29 1/3	41	20	19	14	22
—San Antonio (Tex.)	3	4	.429	3.58	11	8	0	0	0	50 1/3	50	26	20	19	35
1993— New Orleans (A.A.)■........	11	6	.647	3.94	27	25	5	1	0	166 2/3	172	78	73	45	97
1994—							Did not play.								
1995— New Orleans (A.A.)............	7	5	.583	3.97	17	17	3	1	0	104 1/3	102	48	46	44	62
—Milwaukee (A.L.)	2	3	.400	4.71	10	4	0	0	0	36 1/3	37	21	19	12	19
1996—							Did not play.								
1997— Milwaukee (A.L.)	1	1	.500	8.38	5	4	0	0	0	19 1/3	24	19	18	23	13
—Tucson (PCL)	7	8	.467	6.79	22	21	0	0	0	108 2/3	132	87	82	65	63
Major league totals (2 years)......	3	4	.429	5.98	15	8	0	0	0	55 2/3	61	40	37	35	27

M

McCALL, ROD   1B   CUBS

PERSONAL: Born November 4, 1971, in Anaheim, Calif. ... 6-7/235. ... Bats left, throws right.
HIGH SCHOOL: Rancho Alamitos (Garden Grove, Calif.).
JUNIOR COLLEGE: Orange Coast (Costa Mesa, Calif.).
TRANSACTIONS/CAREER NOTES: Selected by Cleveland Indians organization in ninth round of free-agent draft (June 4, 1990). ... On disabled list (August 23-September 12, 1993). ... Traded by Indians organization to Chicago Cubs organization for IF Bobby Morris (June 2, 1997).

Year Team (League)	Pos.	G	AB	R	H	2B	3B	HR	RBI	Avg.	BB	SO	SB	PO	A	E	Avg.
1990— Burlington (Appal.).....	1B	31	92	8	15	5	0	1	11	.163	10	43	0	286	12	15	.952
— GC Indians (GCL)	1B	10	36	5	10	2	0	0	6	.278	5	10	0	85	6	1	.989
1991— Columbus (S. Atl.)......	1B	103	323	34	70	14	1	5	35	.217	61	128	2	767	56	*19	.977
1992— Columbus (S. Atl.)......	OF	116	404	55	97	15	0	20	80	.240	68	121	1	912	62	14	.986
1993— Kinston (Carolina)	1B	71	245	32	51	13	0	9	33	.208	32	85	3	396	30	5	.988
1994— Cant./Akr. (Eastern)	1B	20	66	8	13	4	0	3	9	.197	2	27	0	175	12	3	.984
— High Desert (Calif.)	1B	48	183	40	51	14	0	17	43	.279	20	63	2	414	14	11	.975
— Kinston (Carolina)	1B	58	205	32	44	14	0	11	27	.215	26	75	1	266	35	9	.971
1995— Bakersfield (Calif.)......	1B	96	345	61	114	19	1	20	70	.330	40	90	2	490	26	11	.979
— Cant./Akr. (Eastern)	1B	26	95	16	26	5	0	9	18	.274	12	21	1	111	17	1	.992
1996— Cant./Akr. (Eastern)	1B	120	440	80	132	29	2	27	85	.300	52	118	2	250	19	2	.993
1997— Buffalo (A.A.).............	1B	36	107	12	25	5	0	6	20	.234	9	37	0	74	3	0	1.000
— Orlando (South.)■.....	1B	19	70	11	21	2	0	6	20	.300	10	24	0	125	7	3	.978
— Iowa (Am. Assoc.)......	1B	49	148	26	42	5	0	14	35	.284	22	53	1	176	8	1	.995

McCARTHY, GREG   P   MARINERS

PERSONAL: Born October 30, 1968, in Norwalk, Conn. ... 6-2/215. ... Throws left, bats left. ... Full name: Gregory O'Neil McCarthy.
HIGH SCHOOL: Bridgeport (Conn.) Central.
TRANSACTIONS/CAREER NOTES: Selected by Philadelphia Phillies organization in 36th round of free-agent draft (June 2, 1987). ... Selected by Montreal Expos from Phillies organization in Rule 5 major league draft (December 3, 1990). ... On disabled list (March 29, 1991-entire season). ... Selected by Colorado Springs, Cleveland Indians organization, from Harrisburg, Expos organization, in Rule 5 minor league draft (December 9, 1991). ... On disabled list (July 5-September 9, 1992). ... Granted free agency (December 20, 1993). ... Signed by Charlotte, Cleveland Indians organization (January 6, 1994). ... Granted free agency (October 15, 1994). ... Signed by Nashville, Chicago White Sox organization (November 24, 1994). ... On Birmingham disabled list (May 16-23 and May 28-July 4, 1995). ... Granted free agency (October 16, 1995). ... Signed by Seattle Mariners organization (November 3, 1995).

Year Team (League)	W	L	Pct.	ERA	G	GS	CG	ShO	Sv.	IP	H	R	ER	BB	SO
1987— Utica (N.Y.-Penn)................	4	1	.800	0.91	20	0	0	0	3	29 2/3	14	9	3	23	40
1988— Spartanburg (SAL)	4	2	.667	4.04	34	1	0	0	2	64 2/3	52	36	29	52	65
1989— Spartanburg (SAL)	5	8	.385	4.18	24	15	2	1	0	112	90	58	52	80	115
1990— Clearwater (Fla. St.)	1	3	.250	3.47	42	1	0	0	5	59 2/3	47	33	23	38	67
1991—						Did not play.									
1992— Kinston (Carolina)■..........	3	0	1.000	0.00	23	0	0	0	12	27 1/3	14	0	0	9	37
1993— Kinston (Carolina)	0	0	...	1.69	9	0	0	0	2	10 2/3	8	4	2	13	14
— Cant./Akr. (Eastern)	2	3	.400	4.72	33	0	0	0	6	34 1/3	28	18	18	37	39
1994— Cant./Akr. (Eastern)	2	3	.400	2.25	22	0	0	0	9	32	19	12	8	23	39
— Charlotte (Int'l)...................	1	0	1.000	6.94	18	0	0	0	0	23 1/3	17	22	18	28	21
1995— Birmingham (Southern)■..	3	3	.500	5.04	38	0	0	0	3	44 2/3	37	28	25	29	48
1996— Tacoma (PCL)■..................	4	2	.667	3.29	39	0	0	0	4	68 1/3	58	31	25	53	90
— Seattle (A.L.)	0	0	...	1.86	10	0	0	0	0	9 2/3	8	2	2	4	7
1997— Tacoma (PCL)	2	1	.667	3.27	22	0	0	0	3	22	21	8	8	16	34
— Seattle (A.L.)	1	1	.500	5.46	37	0	0	0	0	29 2/3	26	21	18	16	34
Major league totals (2 years)......	1	1	.500	4.58	47	0	0	0	0	39 1/3	34	23	20	20	41

McCRACKEN, QUINTON   OF   DEVIL RAYS

PERSONAL: Born March 16, 1970, in Wilmington, N.C. ... 5-7/173. ... Bats both, throws right. ... Full name: Quinton Antoine McCracken.
HIGH SCHOOL: South Brunswick (Southport, N.C.).
COLLEGE: Duke.
TRANSACTIONS/CAREER NOTES: Selected by Colorado Rockies organization in 25th round of free-agent draft (June 1, 1992). ... Selected by Tampa Bay Devil Rays in first round (fourth pick overall) of expansion draft (November 18, 1997).
STATISTICAL NOTES: Led California League with 12 sacrifice hits in 1993. ... Led Eastern League in caught stealing with 19 in 1994.

Year Team (League)	Pos.	G	AB	R	H	2B	3B	HR	RBI	Avg.	BB	SO	SB	PO	A	E	Avg.
1992— Bend (Northwest)	2B-OF	67	232	37	65	13	2	0	27	.280	25	39	18	98	129	17	.930
1993— Central Valley (Cal.).....	OF-2B	127	483	94	141	17	7	2	58	.292	78	90	60	153	75	13	.946
1994— New Haven (Eastern)..	OF	136	544	94	151	27	4	5	39	.278	48	72	36	273	6	8	.972
1995— New Haven (Eastern)..	OF	55	221	33	79	11	4	1	26	.357	21	32	26	92	10	3	.971
— Colo. Springs (PCL) ...	OF	61	244	55	88	14	6	3	28	.361	23	30	17	104	5	1	.991
— Colorado (N.L.)	OF	3	1	0	0	0	0	0	0	.000	0	1	0	0	0	0	...
1996— Colorado (N.L.)	OF	124	283	50	82	13	6	3	40	.290	32	62	17	131	3	6	.957
1997— Colorado (N.L.)	OF	147	325	69	95	11	1	3	36	.292	42	62	28	195	5	4	.980
Major league totals (3 years)		274	609	119	177	24	7	6	76	.291	74	125	45	326	8	10	.971

M

McCURRY, JEFF   P   PIRATES

PERSONAL: Born January 21, 1970, in Tokyo, Japan. ... 6-7/210. ... Throws right, bats right. ... Full name: Jeffrey Dee McCurry.
HIGH SCHOOL: St. Thomas (Houston).
COLLEGE: San Jacinto (North) College (Texas).
TRANSACTIONS/CAREER NOTES: Selected by Pittsburgh Pirates organization in 20th round of free-agent draft (June 5, 1989); did not sign. ... Selected by Pirates organization in 14th round of free-agent draft (June 4, 1990). ... On Welland disabled list (June 19-July 12, 1991). ... Claimed on waivers by Detroit Tigers (November 20, 1995). ... Selected by Colorado Rockies from Tigers organization in Rule 5 minor league draft (December 9, 1996). ... Released by Rockies following 1997 season. ... Signed by Pirates organization (December 18, 1997).

Year Team (League)	W	L	Pct.	ERA	G	GS	CG	ShO	Sv.	IP	H	R	ER	BB	SO
1991—GC Pirates (GCL)	1	0	1.000	2.57	6	1	0	0	0	14	19	10	4	4	8
—Welland (N.Y.-Penn)	2	1	.667	0.57	9	0	0	0	0	15 2/3	11	4	1	10	18
1992—Augusta (S. Atl.)	2	1	.667	3.30	19	0	0	0	7	30	36	14	11	15	34
—Salem (Carolina)	6	2	.750	2.87	30	0	0	0	3	62 2/3	49	22	20	24	52
1993—Salem (Carolina)	1	4	.200	3.89	41	0	0	0	22	44	41	21	19	15	32
—Carolina (Southern)	2	1	.667	2.79	23	0	0	0	0	29	24	11	9	14	14
1994—Carolina (Southern)	6	5	.545	3.21	48	2	0	0	11	81 1/3	74	35	29	30	60
1995—Calgary (PCL)	0	0	...	1.80	3	0	0	0	0	5	3	1	1	2	2
—Pittsburgh (N.L.)	1	4	.200	5.02	55	0	0	0	1	61	82	38	34	30	27
1996—Toledo (Int'l)■	1	4	.200	4.76	39	0	0	0	2	58 2/3	66	37	31	26	56
—Detroit (A.L.)	0	0	...	24.30	2	0	0	0	0	3 1/3	9	9	9	2	0
1997—Colorado (N.L.)	1	4	.200	4.43	33	0	0	0	0	40 2/3	43	22	20	20	19
—Colo. Springs (PCL)	1	1	.500	5.09	16	0	0	0	3	17 2/3	17	12	10	6	13
A.L. totals (1 year)	0	0	...	24.30	2	0	0	0	0	3 1/3	9	9	9	2	0
N.L. totals (2 years)	2	8	.200	4.78	88	0	0	0	1	101 2/3	125	60	54	50	46
Major league totals (3 years)	2	8	.200	5.40	90	0	0	0	1	105	134	69	63	52	46

McDILL, ALLEN   P   ROYALS

PERSONAL: Born August 23, 1971, in Greenvill, Miss. ... 6-0/155. ... Throws left, bats left. ... Full name: Allen Gabriel McDill.
HIGH SCHOOL: Lake Hamilton (Ark.).
TRANSACTIONS/CAREER NOTES: Selected by New York Mets organization in 20th round of free-agent draft (June 1, 1992). ... Traded by Mets organization with P Jason Jacome to Kansas City Royals organization for P Derek Wallace and a player to be named later (July 21, 1995); Mets acquired P John Carter to complete deal (November 16, 1995).

Year Team (League)	W	L	Pct.	ERA	G	GS	CG	ShO	Sv.	IP	H	R	ER	BB	SO
1992—GC Mets (GCL)	3	4	.429	2.70	10	9	0	0	0	53 1/3	36	23	16	15	60
—Kingsport (Appalachian)	0	0	...	0.00	1	0	0	0	0	1/3	0	0	0	2	0
1993—Kingsport (Appalachian)	5	2	.714	2.19	9	9	0	0	0	53 1/3	52	19	13	14	42
—Pittsfield (NYP)	2	3	.400	5.40	5	5	0	0	0	28 1/3	31	22	17	15	24
1994—Columbia (S. Atl.)	9	6	.600	3.55	19	19	1	0	0	111 2/3	101	52	44	38	102
1995—Binghamton (Eastern)	3	5	.375	4.56	12	12	1	0	0	73	69	42	37	38	44
—St. Lucie (Fla. St.)	4	2	.667	1.64	7	7	1	1	0	49 1/3	36	11	9	13	28
—Wichita (Texas)■	1	0	1.000	2.11	12	1	0	0	1	21 1/3	16	7	5	5	20
1996—Wichita (Texas)	1	5	.167	5.54	54	0	0	0	11	65	79	43	40	21	62
—Omaha (Am. Assoc.)	0	1	.000	54.00	2	0	0	0	0	1/3	3	2	2	1	1
1997—Omaha (Am. Assoc.)	5	2	.714	5.88	23	6	0	0	2	64 1/3	80	42	42	26	51
—Kansas City (A.L.)	0	0	...	13.50	3	0	0	0	0	4	3	6	6	8	2
—Wichita (Texas)	0	1	.000	3.12	16	0	0	0	3	17 1/3	18	7	6	7	14
Major league totals (1 year)	0	0	...	13.50	3	0	0	0	0	4	3	6	6	8	2

McDONALD, BEN   P   INDIANS

PERSONAL: Born November 24, 1967, in Baton Rouge, La. ... 6-7/214. ... Throws right, bats right. ... Full name: Larry Benard McDonald.
HIGH SCHOOL: Denham Springs (La.).
COLLEGE: Louisiana State.
TRANSACTIONS/CAREER NOTES: Selected by Atlanta Braves organization in 27th round of free-agent draft (June 2, 1986); did not sign. ... Selected by Baltimore Orioles organization in first round (first pick overall) of free-agent draft (June 5, 1989). ... On Baltimore disabled list (April 6-May 22, 1990); included rehabilitation assignments to Hagerstown (April 24-29 and May 14) and Rochester (April 30-May 13 and May 15-21). ... On Baltimore disabled list (March 29-April 19, 1991). ... On Baltimore disabled list (May 23-July 1, 1991); included rehabilitation assignment to Rochester (June 19-July 1). ... On Baltimore disabled list (June 17-July 14 and July 20-September 11, 1995); included rehabilitation assignment to Rochester (August 31-September 11). ... Granted free agency (December 21, 1995). ... Signed by Milwaukee Brewers (January 23, 1996). ... On disabled list (July 20, 1997-remainder of season). ... Traded by Brewers with P Mike Fetters and P Ron Villone to Cleveland Indians for OF Marquis Grissom and P Jeff Juden (December 8, 1997).
HONORS: Named Golden Spikes Award winner by USA Baseball (1989). ... Named College Player of the Year by THE SPORTING NEWS (1989). ... Named righthanded pitcher on THE SPORTING NEWS college All-America team (1989).
STATISTICAL NOTES: Pitched 7-0 one-hit, complete-game victory against Kansas City (July 20, 1993). ... Pitched 4-0 one-hit, complete-game victory against Milwaukee (August 5, 1994).
MISCELLANEOUS: Member of 1988 U.S. Olympic baseball team.

Year Team (League)	W	L	Pct.	ERA	G	GS	CG	ShO	Sv.	IP	H	R	ER	BB	SO
1989—Frederick (Carolina)	0	0	...	2.00	2	2	0	0	0	9	10	2	2	0	9
—Baltimore (A.L.)	1	0	1.000	8.59	6	0	0	0	0	7 1/3	8	7	7	4	3
1990—Hagerstown (Eastern)	0	1	.000	6.55	3	3	0	0	0	11	11	8	8	3	15
—Rochester (Int'l)	3	3	.500	2.86	7	7	0	0	0	44	33	18	14	21	37
—Baltimore (A.L.)	8	5	.615	2.43	21	15	3	2	0	118 2/3	88	36	32	35	65
1991—Baltimore (A.L.)	6	8	.429	4.84	21	21	1	0	0	126 1/3	126	71	68	43	85
—Rochester (Int'l)	0	1	.000	7.71	2	2	0	0	0	7	10	7	6	5	7
1992—Baltimore (A.L.)	13	13	.500	4.24	35	35	4	2	0	227	213	113	107	74	158
1993—Baltimore (A.L.)	13	14	.481	3.39	34	34	7	1	0	220 1/3	185	92	83	86	171

Year	Team (League)	W	L	Pct.	ERA	G	GS	CG	ShO	Sv.	IP	H	R	ER	BB	SO
1994—	Baltimore (A.L.)	14	7	.667	4.06	24	24	5	1	0	157 1/3	151	75	71	54	94
1995—	Baltimore (A.L.)	3	6	.333	4.16	14	13	1	0	0	80	67	40	37	38	62
—	Rochester (Int'l)	0	0	...	2.45	1	1	0	0	0	3 2/3	1	2	1	4	1
1996—	Milwaukee (A.L.)■	12	10	.545	3.90	35	35	2	0	0	221 1/3	228	104	96	67	146
1997—	Milwaukee (A.L.)	8	7	.533	4.06	21	21	1	0	0	133	120	68	60	36	110
Major league totals (9 years)		78	70	.527	3.91	211	198	24	6	0	1291 1/3	1186	606	561	437	894

McDONALD, DONZELL — OF — YANKEES

PERSONAL: Born February 20, 1975, in Long Beach, Calif. ... 5-11/185. ... Bats both, throws right.
HIGH SCHOOL: Cherry Creek (Colo.).
JUNIOR COLLEGE: Yavapai College (Ariz.).
TRANSACTIONS/CAREER NOTES: Selected by New York Yankees organization in 22nd round of free-agent draft (June 1, 1995). ... On disabled list (July 3-August 6, 1997).
STATISTICAL NOTES: Led New York-Pennsylvania League outfielders with 179 total chances in 1996.

						BATTING								FIELDING		
Year	Team (League)	Pos.	G	AB	R	H	2B	3B	HR	RBI	Avg.	BB	SO	SB	PO	A	E	Avg.
1995—	GC Yankees (GCL)	OF	28	110	23	26	5	1	0	9	.236	16	24	11	44	0	3	.936
1996—	Oneonta (NYP)	OF	74	282	57	78	8	*10	2	30	.277	43	62	*54	*169	4	6	.966
1997—	Tampa (Florida State)	OF	77	297	69	88	23	8	3	23	.296	48	75	39	173	3	4	.978

McDONALD, JASON — SS/OF — ATHLETICS

PERSONAL: Born March 20, 1972, in Modesto, Calif. ... 5-8/185. ... Bats both, throws right. ... Full name: Jason Adam McDonald.
HIGH SCHOOL: Elk Grove (Calif.) Unified School.
COLLEGE: Houston.
TRANSACTIONS/CAREER NOTES: Selected by Oakland Athletics organization in fourth round of free-agent draft (June 3, 1993).
STATISTICAL NOTES: Led California League shortstops with 43 errors in 1995. ... Tied for Pacific Coast League lead in being hit by pitch with 15 in 1996. ... Led Pacific Coast League second basemen with 254 putouts, 352 assists, 24 errors, 630 total chances and 75 double plays in 1996.

						BATTING								FIELDING		
Year	Team (League)	Pos.	G	AB	R	H	2B	3B	HR	RBI	Avg.	BB	SO	SB	PO	A	E	Avg.
1993—	S. Oregon (N'west)	2B	35	112	26	33	5	2	0	8	.295	31	17	22	70	77	7	.955
1994—	W. Mich. (Mid.)	2B-OF-SS	116	404	67	96	11	*9	2	31	.238	81	87	52	253	167	21	.952
1995—	Modesto (California)	SS-OF-2B	133	493	109	129	25	7	6	50	.262	*110	84	*70	247	246	†50	.908
1996—	Edmonton (PCL)	2B-OF	137	479	71	114	7	5	8	46	.238	63	82	33	†302	†352	†25	.963
1997—	Edmonton (PCL)	OF	79	276	74	73	14	6	4	30	.264	74	58	31	187	10	5	.975
—	Oakland (A.L.)	OF	78	236	47	62	11	4	4	14	.263	36	49	13	151	3	5	.969
Major league totals (1 year)			78	236	47	62	11	4	4	14	.263	36	49	13	151	3	5	.969

McDOWELL, JACK — P

PERSONAL: Born January 16, 1966, in Van Nuys, Calif. ... 6-5/190. ... Throws right, bats right. ... Full name: Jack Burns McDowell.
HIGH SCHOOL: Notre Dame (Van Nuys, Calif.).
COLLEGE: Stanford.
TRANSACTIONS/CAREER NOTES: Selected by Boston Red Sox organization in 20th round of free-agent draft (June 4, 1984); did not sign. ... Selected by Chicago White Sox organization in first round (fifth pick overall) of free-agent draft (June 2, 1987). ... On suspended list (August 20-24, 1991). ... Traded by White Sox to New York Yankees for P Keith Heberling and a player to be named later (December 14, 1994); White Sox acquired OF Lyle Mouton to complete deal (April 22, 1995). ... Granted free agency (October 31, 1995). ... Signed by Cleveland Indians (December 14, 1995). ... On disabled list (July 22-August 9, 1996). ... On disabled list (May 13, 1997-remainder of season). ... Granted free agency (November 5, 1997).
HONORS: Named righthanded pitcher on THE SPORTING NEWS A.L. All-Star team (1992-93). ... Named A.L. Pitcher of the Year by THE SPORTING NEWS (1993). ... Named A.L. Cy Young Award winner by Baseball Writers' Association of America (1993).
STATISTICAL NOTES: Pitched 15-1 one-hit, complete-game victory against Milwaukee (July 14, 1991).

Year	Team (League)	W	L	Pct.	ERA	G	GS	CG	ShO	Sv.	IP	H	R	ER	BB	SO
1987—	GC White Sox (GCL)	0	1	.000	2.57	2	1	0	0	0	7	4	3	2	1	12
—	Birmingham (Southern)	1	2	.333	7.84	4	4	1	1	0	20 2/3	19	20	18	8	17
—	Chicago (A.L.)	3	0	1.000	1.93	4	4	0	0	0	28	16	6	6	6	15
1988—	Chicago (A.L.)	5	10	.333	3.97	26	26	1	0	0	158 2/3	147	85	70	68	84
1989—	Vancouver (PCL)	5	6	.455	6.13	16	16	1	0	0	86 2/3	97	60	59	50	65
—	GC White Sox (GCL)	2	0	1.000	0.75	4	4	0	0	0	24	19	2	2	4	25
1990—	Chicago (A.L.)	14	9	.609	3.82	33	33	4	0	0	205	189	93	87	77	165
1991—	Chicago (A.L.)	17	10	.630	3.41	35	•35	*15	3	0	253 2/3	212	97	96	82	191
1992—	Chicago (A.L.)	20	10	.667	3.18	34	34	*13	1	0	260 2/3	247	95	92	75	178
1993—	Chicago (A.L.)	*22	10	.688	3.37	34	34	10	*4	0	256 2/3	261	104	96	69	158
1994—	Chicago (A.L.)	10	9	.526	3.73	25	•25	6	2	0	181	186	82	75	42	127
1995—	New York (A.L.)■	15	10	.600	3.93	30	30	*8	2	0	217 2/3	211	106	95	78	157
1996—	Cleveland (A.L.)■	13	9	.591	5.11	30	30	5	1	0	192	214	119	109	67	141
1997—	Cleveland (A.L.)	3	3	.500	5.09	8	6	0	0	0	40 2/3	44	25	23	18	38
Major league totals (10 years)		122	80	.604	3.76	259	257	62	13	0	1794	1727	812	749	582	1254

DIVISION SERIES RECORD

Year	Team (League)	W	L	Pct.	ERA	G	GS	CG	ShO	Sv.	IP	H	R	ER	BB	SO
1995—	New York (A.L.)	0	2	.000	9.00	2	1	0	0	0	7	8	7	7	4	6
1996—	Cleveland (A.L.)	0	0	...	6.35	1	1	0	0	0	5 2/3	6	4	4	1	5
Div. series totals (2 years)		0	2	.000	7.82	3	2	0	0	0	12 2/3	14	11	11	5	11

RECORDS: Holds single-game record for most hits allowed—13 (October 5, 1993). ... Shares single-game record for most earned runs allowed—7 (October 5, 1993).

Year	Team (League)	W	L	Pct.	ERA	G	GS	CG	ShO	Sv.	IP	H	R	ER	BB	SO
1993—	Chicago (A.L.)	0	2	.000	10.00	2	2	0	0	0	9	18	10	10	5	5

ALL-STAR GAME RECORD

Year	League	W	L	Pct.	ERA	GS	CG	ShO	Sv.	IP	H	R	ER	BB	SO
1991—	American	0	0	...	0.00	0	0	0	0	2	1	0	0	2	0
1992—	American	0	0	...	0.00	0	0	0	0	1	0	0	0	0	0
1993—	American	1	0	1.000	0.00	0	0	0	0	1	0	0	0	0	0
All-Star totals (3 years)		1	0	1.000	0.00	0	0	0	0	4	1	0	0	2	0

McELROY, CHUCK — P — ROCKIES

PERSONAL: Born October 1, 1967, in Port Arthur, Texas. ... 6-0/195. ... Throws left, bats left. ... Full name: Charles Dwayne McElroy. ... Name pronounced MACK-il-roy.

HIGH SCHOOL: Lincoln (Port Arthur, Texas).

TRANSACTIONS/CAREER NOTES: Selected by Philadelphia Phillies organization in eighth round of free-agent draft (June 2, 1986). ... Traded by Phillies with P Bob Scanlan to Chicago Cubs for P Mitch Williams (April 7, 1991). ... Traded by Cubs to Cincinnati Reds for P Larry Luebbers, P Mike Anderson and C Darron Cox (December 10, 1993). ... On disabled list (June 7-23, 1995). ... On Cincinnati disabled list (March 28-April 28, 1996); included rehabilitation assignment to Indianapolis (April 12-28). ... Traded by Reds to California Angels for P Lee Smith (May 27, 1996). ... On California disabled list (August 11-28, 1996). ... Angels franchise renamed Anaheim Angels for 1997 season. ... Traded by Angels with C Jorge Fabregas to Chicago White Sox for OF Tony Phillips and C Chad Kreuter (May 18, 1997). ... Selected by Arizona Diamondbacks in third round (67th pick overall) of expansion draft (November 18, 1997). ... Traded by Diamondbacks to Colorado Rockies for OF Harvey Pulliam (November 18, 1997).

MISCELLANEOUS: Appeared in one game as pinch-runner with Chicago (1997).

Year	Team (League)	W	L	Pct.	ERA	G	GS	CG	ShO	Sv.	IP	H	R	ER	BB	SO
1986—	Utica (N.Y.-Penn)	4	6	.400	2.95	14	14	5	1	0	94 2/3	85	40	31	28	91
1987—	Spartanburg (SAL)	14	4	.778	3.11	24	21	5	2	0	130 1/3	117	51	45	48	115
—	Clearwater (Fla. St.)	1	0	1.000	0.00	2	2	0	0	0	7 1/3	1	1	0	4	7
1988—	Reading (Eastern)	9	12	.429	4.50	28	26	4	2	0	160	•173	89	*80	70	92
1989—	Reading (Eastern)	3	1	.750	2.68	32	0	0	0	12	47	39	14	14	14	39
—	Scran./W.B. (Int'l)	1	2	.333	2.93	14	0	0	0	3	15 1/3	13	6	5	11	12
—	Philadelphia (N.L.)	0	0	...	1.74	11	0	0	0	0	10 1/3	12	2	2	4	8
1990—	Scran./W.B. (Int'l)	6	8	.429	2.72	57	1	0	0	7	76	62	24	23	34	78
—	Philadelphia (N.L.)	0	1	.000	7.71	16	0	0	0	0	14	24	13	12	10	16
1991—	Chicago (N.L.)■	6	2	.750	1.95	71	0	0	0	3	101 1/3	73	33	22	57	92
1992—	Chicago (N.L.)	4	7	.364	3.55	72	0	0	0	6	83 2/3	73	40	33	51	83
1993—	Chicago (N.L.)	2	2	.500	4.56	49	0	0	0	0	47 1/3	51	30	24	25	31
—	Iowa (Am. Assoc.)	0	1	.000	4.60	9	0	0	0	2	15 2/3	19	10	8	9	13
1994—	Cincinnati (N.L.)■	1	2	.333	2.34	52	0	0	0	5	57 2/3	52	15	15	15	38
1995—	Cincinnati (N.L.)	3	4	.429	6.02	44	0	0	0	0	40 1/3	46	29	27	15	27
1996—	Indianapolis (A.A.)	1	1	.500	2.70	5	3	0	0	0	13 1/3	11	4	4	4	10
—	Cincinnati (N.L.)	2	0	1.000	6.57	12	0	0	0	0	12 1/3	13	10	9	10	13
—	California (N.L.)■	5	1	.833	2.95	40	0	0	0	0	36 2/3	32	12	12	13	32
1997—	Anaheim (A.L.)	0	0	...	3.45	13	0	0	0	0	15 2/3	17	7	6	3	10
—	Chicago (A.L.)■	1	3	.250	3.94	48	0	0	0	1	59 1/3	56	29	26	19	44
A.L. totals (2 years)		6	4	.600	3.55	101	0	0	0	1	111 2/3	105	48	44	35	94
N.L. totals (8 years)		18	18	.500	3.53	327	0	0	0	14	367	344	172	144	187	308
Major league totals (9 years)		24	22	.522	3.53	428	0	0	0	15	478 2/3	449	220	188	222	402

McGEE, WILLIE — OF — CARDINALS

PERSONAL: Born November 2, 1958, in San Francisco. ... 6-1/185. ... Bats both, throws right. ... Full name: Willie Dean McGee.

HIGH SCHOOL: Ellis (Richmond, Calif.).

COLLEGE: Diablo Valley College (Calif.).

TRANSACTIONS/CAREER NOTES: Selected by Chicago White Sox organization in seventh round of free-agent draft (June 8, 1976); did not sign. ... Selected by New York Yankees organization in secondary phase of free-agent draft (January 11, 1977). ... On disabled list (May 22-June 7 and July 14-August 7, 1980; and April 24-June 4, 1981). ... Traded by Yankees organization to St. Louis Cardinals organization for P Bob Sykes (October 21, 1981). ... On Louisville disabled list (April 13-23, 1982). ... On St. Louis disabled list (March 30-April 29, 1983); included rehabilitation assignment to Arkansas (April 18-29). ... On disabled list (July 12-27, 1984 and August 3-27, 1986). ... On disabled list (June 7-July 18, 1989); included rehabilitation assignment to Louisville (July 8-18). ... On St. Louis disabled list (July 26-August 14, 1989). ... Traded by Cardinals to Oakland Athletics for OF Felix Jose, 3B Stan Royer and P Daryl Green (August 29, 1990). ... Granted free agency (November 5, 1990). ... Signed by San Francisco Giants (December 3, 1990). ... On San Francisco disabled list (July 12-August 1, 1991); included rehabilitation assignment to Phoenix (July 28-August 1). ... On disabled list (July 10-30, 1993 and June 8, 1994-remainder of season). ... Granted free agency (October 14, 1994). ... Signed by Pawtucket, Boston Red Sox organization (June 6, 1995). ... Granted free agency (November 3, 1995). ... Signed by Cardinals (December 15, 1995). ... Granted free agency (November 13, 1996). ... Re-signed by Cardinals (December 4, 1996). ... On disabled list (July 12-29, 1997). ... Granted free agency (October 29, 1997). ... Re-signed by Cardinals (December 5, 1997).

RECORDS: Holds modern N.L. single-season record for highest batting average by switch-hitter (100 or more games)—.353 (1985). ... Shares major league single-season record for fewest double plays by outfielder who led league in double plays—3 (1991).

HONORS: Won N.L. Gold Glove as outfielder (1983, 1985-86). ... Named N.L. Player of the Year by THE SPORTING NEWS (1985). ... Named outfielder on THE SPORTING NEWS N.L. All-Star team (1985). ... Named outfielder on THE SPORTING NEWS N.L. Silver Slugger team (1985). ... Named N.L. Most Valuable Player by Baseball Writers' Association of America (1985).

STATISTICAL NOTES: Hit for the cycle (June 23, 1984). ... Led N.L. in grounding into double plays with 24 in 1987. ... Had 22-game hitting streak (July 5-August 1, 1990). ... Tied for N.L. lead in double plays by outfielder with three in 1991. ... Career major league grand slams: 2.

Year Team (League)	Pos.	G	AB	R	H	2B	3B	HR	RBI	Avg.	BB	SO	SB	PO	A	E	Avg.
1977— Oneonta (NYP)	OF	65	225	31	53	4	3	2	22	.236	13	65	13	103	5	10	.915
1978— Fort Lauderdale (FSL)	OF	124	423	62	106	6	6	0	37	.251	50	78	25	243	12	9	.966
1979— West Haven (East.).....	OF	49	115	21	28	3	1	1	8	.243	13	17	7	88	3	3	.968
— Fort Lauderdale (FSL)	OF	46	176	25	56	8	3	1	18	.318	17	34	16	103	3	2	.981
1980— Nashville (Southern) ..	OF	78	223	35	63	4	5	1	22	.283	19	39	7	127	6	6	.957
1981— Nashville (Southern) ..	OF	100	388	77	125	20	5	7	63	.322	24	46	24	203	10	6	.973
1982— Louisville (A.A.)■..	OF	13	55	11	16	2	2	1	3	.291	2	7	5	40	0	1	.976
— St. Louis (N.L.)..........	OF	123	422	43	125	12	8	4	56	.296	12	58	24	245	3	11	.958
1983— St. Louis (N.L.)..........	OF	147	601	75	172	22	8	5	75	.286	26	98	39	385	7	5	.987
— Arkansas (Texas)........	OF	7	29	5	8	1	1	0	2	.276	4	6	1	7	0	0	1.000
1984— St. Louis (N.L.)..........	OF	145	571	82	166	19	11	6	50	.291	29	80	43	374	10	6	.985
1985— St. Louis (N.L.)..........	OF	152	612	114	*216	26	*18	10	82	*.353	34	86	56	382	11	9	.978
1986— St. Louis (N.L.)..........	OF	124	497	65	127	22	7	7	48	.256	37	82	19	325	9	3	*.991
1987— St. Louis (N.L.)..........	OF-SS	153	620	76	177	37	11	11	105	.285	24	90	16	354	10	7	.981
1988— St. Louis (N.L.)..........	OF	137	562	73	164	24	6	3	50	.292	32	84	41	348	9	9	.975
1989— St. Louis (N.L.)..........	OF	58	199	23	47	10	2	3	17	.236	10	34	8	118	2	3	.976
— Louisville (A.A.)..........	OF	8	27	5	11	4	0	0	4	.407	3	4	3	20	1	1	.955
1990— St. Louis (N.L.)..........	OF	125	501	76	168	32	5	3	62	*.335	38	86	28	341	13	*16	.957
— Oakland (A.L.)■..........	OF-DH	29	113	23	31	3	2	0	15	.274	10	18	3	72	1	1	.986
1991— San Fran. (N.L.)■......	OF	131	497	67	155	30	3	4	43	.312	34	74	17	259	6	6	.978
— Phoenix (PCL)	OF	4	10	4	5	1	0	0	1	.500	3	1	2	10	0	1	.909
1992— San Francisco (N.L.) ..	OF	138	474	56	141	20	2	1	36	.297	29	88	13	231	11	6	.976
1993— San Francisco (N.L.) ..	OF	130	475	53	143	28	1	4	46	.301	38	67	10	224	9	5	.979
1994— San Francisco (N.L.) ..	OF	45	156	19	44	3	0	5	23	.282	15	24	3	80	2	1	.988
1995— Pawtucket (Int'l)■.....	OF	5	21	9	10	0	0	0	2	.476	0	4	2	7	0	1	.875
— Boston (A.L.)..............	OF	67	200	32	57	11	3	2	15	.285	9	41	5	101	7	3	.973
1996— St. Louis (N.L.)■	OF-1B	123	309	52	95	15	2	5	41	.307	18	60	5	142	10	5	.968
1997— St. Louis (N.L.)..........	OF-DH	122	300	29	90	19	4	3	38	.300	22	59	8	99	6	2	.981
American League totals (2 years)		96	313	55	88	14	5	2	30	.281	19	59	8	173	8	4	.978
National League totals (15 years)		1853	6796	903	2030	319	88	74	772	.299	398	1070	330	3907	118	94	.977
Major league totals (16 years)		1949	7109	958	2118	333	93	76	802	.298	417	1129	338	4080	126	98	.977

DIVISION SERIES RECORD

Year Team (League)	Pos.	G	AB	R	H	2B	3B	HR	RBI	Avg.	BB	SO	SB	PO	A	E	Avg.
1995— Boston (A.L.)............	OF-PH	2	4	0	1	0	0	0	1	.250	0	2	0	0	0	0	...
1996— St. Louis (N.L.)..........	OF	3	10	1	1	0	0	0	1	.100	1	3	0	9	0	1	.900
Division series totals (2 years)		5	14	1	2	0	0	0	2	.143	1	5	0	9	0	1	.900

CHAMPIONSHIP SERIES RECORD

RECORDS: Shares single-series record for most triples—2 (1982). ... Shares N.L. career records for most triples—3; and most times caught stealing—4. ... Shares N.L. single-series record for most times caught stealing—3 (1985).

Year Team (League)	Pos.	G	AB	R	H	2B	3B	HR	RBI	Avg.	BB	SO	SB	PO	A	E	Avg.
1982— St. Louis (N.L.)..........	OF	3	13	4	4	0	2	1	5	.308	0	5	0	12	0	1	.923
1985— St. Louis (N.L.)..........	OF	6	26	6	7	1	0	0	3	.269	3	6	2	18	0	0	1.000
1987— St. Louis (N.L.)..........	OF	7	26	2	8	1	1	0	2	.308	0	5	0	16	0	0	1.000
1990— Oakland (A.L.)	OF-PR-DH	3	9	3	2	1	0	0	0	.222	1	2	2	2	0	0	1.000
1996— St. Louis (N.L.)..........	OF-PH	6	15	0	5	0	0	0	0	.333	0	3	0	5	0	1	.833
Championship series totals (5 years)		25	89	15	26	3	3	1	10	.292	4	21	4	53	0	2	.964

WORLD SERIES RECORD

NOTES: Member of World Series championship team (1982).

Year Team (League)	Pos.	G	AB	R	H	2B	3B	HR	RBI	Avg.	BB	SO	SB	PO	A	E	Avg.
1982— St. Louis (N.L.)..........	OF	6	25	6	6	0	0	2	5	.240	1	3	2	24	0	0	1.000
1985— St. Louis (N.L.)..........	OF	7	27	2	7	2	0	1	2	.259	1	3	1	15	0	0	1.000
1987— St. Louis (N.L.)..........	OF	7	27	2	10	2	0	0	4	.370	0	9	0	21	1	1	.957
1990— Oakland (A.L.)	OF-PH	4	10	1	2	1	0	0	0	.200	0	2	1	5	0	0	1.000
World Series totals (4 years)		24	89	11	25	5	0	3	11	.281	2	17	4	65	1	1	.985

ALL-STAR GAME RECORD

Year League	Pos.	AB	R	H	2B	3B	HR	RBI	Avg.	BB	SO	SB	PO	A	E	Avg.
1983— National	OF	2	0	1	0	0	0	0	.500	0	0	0	2	0	0	1.000
1985— National	OF	2	0	1	1	0	0	2	.500	0	1	0	1	0	0	1.000
1987— National	OF	4	0	0	0	0	0	0	.000	0	0	0	2	0	0	1.000
1988— National	PR-OF	2	0	0	0	0	0	0	.000	0	1	0	1	0	0	1.000
All-Star Game totals (4 years)		10	0	2	1	0	0	2	.200	0	0	0	6	0	0	1.000

M

McGRAW, TOM   P

PERSONAL: Born December 8, 1967, in Portland, Ore. ... 6-2/195. ... Throws left, bats left. ... Full name: Thomas Virgil McGraw.
HIGH SCHOOL: Battleground (Wash.)
COLLEGE: Washington State.
TRANSACTIONS/CAREER NOTES: Selected by Milwaukee Brewers organization in sixth round of free-agent draft (June 4, 1990). ... Traded to Florida Marlins organization for P Jamie McAndrew (April 2, 1993). ... Signed by Boston Red Sox organization (June 10, 1996). ... Granted free agency (October 15, 1996). ... Signed by St. Louis Cardinals organization (December 10, 1996). ... Granted free agency (October 15, 1997).

Year Team (League)	W	L	Pct.	ERA	G	GS	CG	ShO	Sv.	IP	H	R	ER	BB	SO
1990— Beloit (Midwest)	7	3	.700	1.93	12	12	1	1	0	70	49	33	15	34	61
1991— El Paso (Texas)	1	1	.500	5.80	9	7	0	0	1	35 2/3	43	28	23	21	28
— Stockton (California)	3	0	1.000	2.30	11	7	0	0	0	47	35	15	12	13	39
1992— Stockton (California)	6	4	.600	2.68	15	15	1	0	0	97 1/3	97	44	29	31	70
— El Paso (Texas)	6	0	1.000	2.73	11	10	1	0	0	69 1/3	75	24	21	26	53
1993— High Desert (Calif.)■	2	3	.400	3.55	6	6	1	0	0	38	38	17	15	7	31
— Edmonton (PCL)	2	0	1.000	5.59	5	2	0	0	0	9 2/3	12	7	6	4	8
1994— Portland (Eastern)	3	5	.375	4.62	37	7	0	0	2	74	91	44	38	35	56
1995— Portland (Eastern)	5	0	1.000	1.81	51	0	0	0	2	74 2/3	69	21	15	31	60
1996— Trenton (Eastern)■	3	4	.429	3.18	30	0	0	0	2	34	34	15	12	19	32
1997— Louisville (A.A.)■	1	4	.200	5.33	45	0	0	0	0	49	55	34	29	26	39
— St. Louis (N.L.)	0	0	. . .	0.00	2	0	0	0	0	1 2/3	2	0	0	1	0
Major league totals (1 year)	0	0	. . .	0.00	2	0	0	0	0	1 2/3	2	0	0	1	0

McGRIFF, FRED — 1B — DEVIL RAYS

PERSONAL: Born October 31, 1963, in Tampa. ... 6-3/215. ... Bats left, throws left. ... Full name: Frederick Stanley McGriff. ... Cousin of Terry McGriff, catcher with four major league teams (1987-90, 1993 and 1994); and uncle of Charles Johnson, catcher, Florida Marlins.
HIGH SCHOOL: Jefferson (Tampa).
TRANSACTIONS/CAREER NOTES: Selected by New York Yankees organization in ninth round of free-agent draft (June 8, 1981). ... Traded by Yankees organization with OF Dave Collins, P Mike Morgan and cash to Toronto Blue Jays for OF/C Tom Dodd and P Dale Murray (December 9, 1982). ... On disabled list (June 5-August 14, 1985). ... Traded by Blue Jays with SS Tony Fernandez to San Diego Padres for OF Joe Carter and 2B Roberto Alomar (December 5, 1990). ... On suspended list (June 23-26, 1992). ... Traded by Padres to Atlanta Braves for OF Melvin Nieves, P Donnie Elliott and OF Vince Moore (July 18, 1993). ... Granted free agency (November 6, 1995). ... Re-signed by Braves (December 2, 1995). ... Traded by Braves to Tampa Bay Devil Rays for a player to be named later (November 18, 1997).
RECORDS: Shares major league record for most grand slams in two consecutive games—2 (August 13 and 14, 1991). ... Shares N.L. single-season record for fewest errors by first baseman who led league in errors—12 (1992).
HONORS: Named first baseman on THE SPORTING NEWS A.L. All-Star team (1989). ... Named first baseman on THE SPORTING NEWS A.L. Silver Slugger team (1989). ... Named first baseman on THE SPORTING NEWS N.L. All-Star team (1992-93). ... Named first baseman on THE SPORTING NEWS N.L. Silver Slugger team (1992-93).
STATISTICAL NOTES: Led International League first basemen with .992 fielding percentage, 1,219 putouts, 85 assists, 1,314 total chances and 108 double plays in 1986. ... Tied for International League lead in intentional bases on balls received with eight and in grounding into double plays with 16 in 1986. ... Led A.L. first basemen with 1,592 total chances and 148 double plays in 1989. ... Led N.L. with 26 intentional base on balls received in 1991. ... Led N.L. first basemen with 1,077 total chances in 1994. ... Led N.L. in grounding into double plays with 22 in 1997. ... Career major league grand slams: 5.

Year Team (League)	Pos.	G	AB	R	H	2B	3B	HR	RBI	Avg.	BB	SO	SB	PO	A	E	Avg.
1981— GC Yankees (GCL)	1B	29	81	6	12	2	0	0	9	.148	11	20	0	176	8	7	.963
1982— GC Yankees (GCL)	1B	62	217	38	59	11	1	*9	•41	.272	*48	63	6	514	*56	8	.986
1983— Florence (S. Atl.)■	1B	33	119	26	37	3	1	7	26	.311	20	35	3	250	14	8	.978
— Kinston (Carolina)	1B	94	350	53	85	14	1	21	57	.243	55	112	3	784	57	10	.988
1984— Knoxville (Southern)	1B	56	189	29	47	13	2	9	25	.249	29	55	0	481	45	10	.981
— Syracuse (Int'l)	1B	70	238	28	56	10	1	13	28	.235	26	89	4	644	45	3	.996
1985— Syracuse (Int'l)	1B	51	176	19	40	8	2	5	20	.227	23	53	0	433	37	5	.989
1986— Syracuse (Int'l)	1B-OF	133	468	69	121	23	4	19	74	.259	83	119	0	†1219	†85	10	†.992
— Toronto (A.L.)	DH-1B	3	5	1	1	0	0	0	0	.200	0	2	0	3	0	0	1.000
1987— Toronto (A.L.)	DH-1B	107	295	58	73	16	0	20	43	.247	60	104	3	108	7	2	.983
1988— Toronto (A.L.)	1B	154	536	100	151	35	4	34	82	.282	79	149	6	1344	93	5	*.997
1989— Toronto (A.L.)	1B-DH	161	551	98	148	27	3	*36	92	.269	119	131	7	1460	115	*17	.989
1990— Toronto (A.L.)	1B-DH	153	557	91	167	21	1	35	88	.300	94	108	5	1246	126	6	.996
1991— San Diego (N.L.)■	1B	153	528	84	147	19	1	31	106	.278	105	135	4	1370	87	14	.990
1992— San Diego (N.L.)	1B	152	531	79	152	30	4	*35	104	.286	96	108	8	1219	108	•12	.991
1993— San Diego (N.L.)	1B	83	302	52	83	11	1	18	46	.275	42	55	4	640	47	12	.983
— Atlanta (N.L.)■	1B	68	255	59	79	18	1	19	55	.310	34	51	1	563	45	5	.992
1994— Atlanta (N.L.)	1B	113	424	81	135	25	1	34	94	.318	50	76	7	*1004	66	7	.994
1995— Atlanta (N.L.)	1B	•144	528	85	148	27	1	27	93	.280	65	99	3	1285	96	5	.996
1996— Atlanta (N.L.)	1B	159	617	81	182	37	1	28	107	.295	68	116	7	1416	124	12	.992
1997— Atlanta (N.L.)	1B	152	564	77	156	25	1	22	97	.277	68	112	5	1191	96	13	.990
American League totals (5 years)		578	1944	348	540	99	8	125	305	.278	352	494	21	4161	341	30	.993
National League totals (7 years)		1024	3749	598	1082	192	11	214	702	.289	528	752	39	8688	669	80	.992
Major league totals (12 years)		1602	5693	946	1622	291	19	339	1007	.285	880	1246	60	12849	1010	110	.992

DIVISION SERIES RECORD

RECORDS: Holds N.L. single-game record for most runs batted in—5 (October 7, 1995). ... Holds N.L. career record for most at-bats—36. ... Shares N.L. career records for most games—10; most runs—9; and most runs batted in—10.

Year Team (League)	Pos.	G	AB	R	H	2B	3B	HR	RBI	Avg.	BB	SO	SB	PO	A	E	Avg.
1995— Atlanta (N.L.)	1B	4	18	4	6	0	0	2	6	.333	2	3	0	39	2	0	1.000
1996— Atlanta (N.L.)	1B	3	9	1	3	1	0	1	3	.333	2	1	0	25	3	0	1.000
1997— Atlanta (N.L.)	1B	3	9	4	2	0	0	0	1	.222	3	2	0	27	3	0	1.000
Division series totals (3 years)		10	36	9	11	1	0	3	10	.306	7	6	0	91	8	0	1.000

CHAMPIONSHIP SERIES RECORD

RECORDS: Shares N.L. single-game record for most at-bats—6 (October 14, 1996). ... Shares N.L. single-game record for most runs—4 (October 17, 1996). ... Shares career record for most doubles—7.

Year Team (League)	Pos.	G	AB	R	H	2B	3B	HR	RBI	Avg.	BB	SO	SB	PO	A	E	Avg.
1989— Toronto (A.L.)	1B	5	21	1	3	0	0	0	3	.143	0	4	0	35	2	1	.974
1993— Atlanta (N.L.)	1B	6	23	6	10	2	0	1	4	.435	4	7	0	49	4	0	1.000

M

Year Team (League)	Pos.	G	AB	R	H	2B	3B	HR	RBI	Avg.	BB	SO	SB	PO	A	E	Avg.
1995—Atlanta (N.L.)	1B	4	16	5	7	4	0	0	0	.438	3	0	0	42	4	0	1.000
1996—Atlanta (N.L.)	1B	7	28	6	7	0	1	2	7	.250	3	5	0	55	2	1	.983
1997—Atlanta (N.L.)	1B	6	21	0	7	1	0	0	4	.333	2	7	0	41	2	1	.977
Championship series totals (5 years)		28	109	18	34	7	1	3	18	.312	12	23	0	222	14	3	.987

WORLD SERIES RECORD

NOTES: Hit home run in first at-bat (October 21, 1995). ... Member of World Series championship team (1995).

Year Team (League)	Pos.	G	AB	R	H	2B	3B	HR	RBI	Avg.	BB	SO	SB	PO	A	E	Avg.
1995—Atlanta (N.L.)	1B	6	23	5	6	2	0	2	3	.261	3	7	1	68	2	1	.986
1996—Atlanta (N.L.)	1B	6	20	4	6	0	0	2	6	.300	6	4	0	62	5	0	1.000
World Series totals (2 years)		12	43	9	12	2	0	4	9	.279	9	11	1	130	7	1	.993

ALL-STAR GAME RECORD

NOTES: Named Most Valuable Player (1994).

Year League	Pos.	AB	R	H	2B	3B	HR	RBI	Avg.	BB	SO	SB	PO	A	E	Avg.
1992—National	1B	3	0	2	0	0	0	1	.667	0	0	0	7	1	0	1.000
1994—National	PH-1B	1	1	1	0	0	1	2	1.000	0	0	0	0	0	0	...
1995—National	1B	3	0	0	0	0	0	0	.000	0	2	0	5	0	0	1.000
1996—National	1B	2	0	0	0	0	0	0	.000	0	2	0	2	1	0	1.000
All-Star Game totals (4 years)		9	1	3	0	0	1	3	.333	0	4	0	14	2	0	1.000

McGUIRE, RYAN   1B   EXPOS

PERSONAL: Born November 23, 1971, in Wilson, N.C. ... 6-2/210. ... Bats left, throws left. ... Full name: Ryan B. McGuire.

HIGH SCHOOL: El Camino Real (Woodland Hills, Calif.).

COLLEGE: UCLA.

TRANSACTIONS/CAREER NOTES: Selected by Boston Red Sox organization in third round of free-agent draft (June 3, 1993). ... Traded by Red Sox with P Rheal Cormier and P Shayne Bennett to Montreal Expos for SS Wil Cordero and P Bryan Eversgerd (January 10, 1996).

STATISTICAL NOTES: Led Carolina League first basemen with 1,312 total chances in 1994.

Year Team (League)	Pos.	G	AB	R	H	2B	3B	HR	RBI	Avg.	BB	SO	SB	PO	A	E	Avg.
1993—Fort Lauderdale (FSL)	1B	56	213	23	69	12	2	4	38	.324	27	34	2	513	61	5	.991
1994—Lynchburg (Caro.)	1B	*137	489	70	133	29	0	10	73	.272	79	77	10	*1165	*129	18	.986
1995—Trenton (Eastern)	1B	109	414	59	138	29	1	7	59	.333	58	51	11	708	55	10	.987
1996—Ottawa (Int'l)■	1B-OF	134	451	62	116	21	2	12	60	.257	59	80	11	987	73	8	.993
1997—Ottawa (Int'l)	1B	50	184	37	55	11	1	3	15	.299	36	29	5	421	52	2	.996
—Montreal (N.L.)	OF-1B-DH	84	199	22	51	15	2	3	17	.256	19	34	1	226	19	3	.988
Major league totals (1 year)		84	199	22	51	15	2	3	17	.256	19	34	1	226	19	3	.988

McGWIRE, MARK   1B   CARDINALS

M

PERSONAL: Born October 1, 1963, in Pomona, Calif. ... 6-5/250. ... Bats right, throws right. ... Full name: Mark David McGwire. ... Brother of Dan McGwire, quarterback with Seattle Seahawks (1991-94) and Miami Dolphins (1995).

HIGH SCHOOL: Damien (Claremont, Calif.).

COLLEGE: Southern California.

TRANSACTIONS/CAREER NOTES: Selected by Montreal Expos organization in eighth round of free-agent draft (June 8, 1981); did not sign. ... Selected by Oakland Athletics organization in first round (10th pick overall) of free-agent draft (June 4, 1984). ... On disabled list (April 11-26, 1989 and August 22-September 11, 1992). ... Granted free agency (October 26, 1992). ... Re-signed by A's (December 24, 1992). ... On disabled list (May 14-September 3, 1993; April 30-June 18 and July 27, 1994-remainder of season). ... On suspended list (September 4-8, 1993). ... On disabled list (July 18-August 2 and August 5-26, 1995). ... On disabled list (March 22-April 23, 1996). ... Traded by A's to St. Louis Cardinals for P T.J. Mathews, P Eric Ludwick and P Blake Stein (July 31, 1997).

RECORDS: Holds major league rookie-season records for most home runs—49; and extra bases on long hits—183 (1987). ... Holds major league record for most home runs by righthander in consecutive years—110 (1996-1997). ... Shares major league single-season records for most home runs by righthander—58 (1997). ... Shares major league records for most home runs by first baseman—58 (1997).. ... Shares major league records for most consecutive years with 50 or more home runs—2; most home runs in two consecutive games—5 (June 27 [3] and 28 [2], 1987 and June 10 [2] and 11 [3], 1995); and most home runs in one inning—2 (September 22, 1996, fifth inning). ... Shares modern major league record for most runs in two consecutive games—9 (June 27 and 28, 1987). ... Holds A.L. rookie-season record for highest slugging percentage—.618 (1987).

HONORS: Named College Player of the Year by THE SPORTING NEWS (1984). ... Named first baseman on THE SPORTING NEWS college All-America team (1984). ... Named A.L. Rookie Player of the Year by THE SPORTING NEWS (1987). ... Named A.L. Rookie of the Year by Baseball Writers' Association of America (1987). ... Won A.L. Gold Glove at first base (1990). ... Named first baseman on THE SPORTING NEWS A.L. All-Star team (1992 and 1996). ... Named first baseman on THE SPORTING NEWS A.L. Silver Slugger team (1992 and 1996). ... Named Sportsman of the Year by THE SPORTING NEWS (1997).

STATISTICAL NOTES: Led California League third basemen with 239 assists and 354 total chances in 1985. ... Hit three home runs in one game (June 27, 1987 and June 11, 1995). ... Led A.L. in slugging percentage with .618 in 1987, .585 in 1992 and .730 in 1996. ... Led A.L. first basemen with 1,429 total chances in 1990. ... Led A.L. with .467 on-base percentage in 1996. ... Led major leagues with 58 home runs in 1997. ... Career major league grand slams: 9.

MISCELLANEOUS: Holds Oakland Athletics all-time records for most home runs (363) and most runs batted in (941). ... Member of 1984 U.S. Olympic baseball team.

Year Team (League)	Pos.	G	AB	R	H	2B	3B	HR	RBI	Avg.	BB	SO	SB	PO	A	E	Avg.
1984—Modesto (California)	1B	16	55	7	11	3	0	1	1	.200	8	21	0	107	6	1	.991
1985—Modesto (California)	3B-1B	138	489	95	134	23	3	•24	•106	.274	96	108	1	105	†240	33	.913

Year Team (League)	Pos.	G	AB	R	H	2B	3B	HR	RBI	Avg.	BB	SO	SB	PO	A	E	Avg.
1986—Huntsville (Southern) .	3B	55	195	40	59	15	0	10	53	.303	46	45	3	34	124	16	.908
—Tacoma (PCL)	3B	78	280	42	89	21	5	13	59	.318	42	67	1	53	126	25	.877
—Oakland (A.L.)	3B	18	53	10	10	1	0	3	9	.189	4	18	0	10	20	6	.833
1987—Oakland (A.L.)	1B-3B-OF	151	557	97	161	28	4	*49	118	.289	71	131	1	1176	101	13	.990
1988—Oakland (A.L.)	1B-OF	155	550	87	143	22	1	32	99	.260	76	117	0	1228	88	9	.993
1989—Oakland (A.L.)	1B-DH	143	490	74	113	17	0	33	95	.231	83	94	1	1170	114	6	.995
1990—Oakland (A.L.)	1B-DH	156	523	87	123	16	0	39	108	.235	*110	116	2	*1329	95	5	.997
1991—Oakland (A.L.)	1B	154	483	62	97	22	0	22	75	.201	93	116	2	1191	•101	4	.997
1992—Oakland (A.L.)	1B	139	467	87	125	22	0	42	104	.268	90	105	0	1118	71	6	.995
1993—Oakland (A.L.)	1B	27	84	16	28	6	0	9	24	.333	21	19	0	197	14	0	1.000
1994—Oakland (A.L.)	1B-DH	47	135	26	34	3	0	9	25	.252	37	40	0	307	18	4	.988
1995—Oakland (A.L.)	1B-DH	104	317	75	87	13	0	39	90	.274	88	77	1	775	64	*12	.986
1996—Oakland (A.L.)	1B-DH	130	423	104	132	21	0	*52	113	.312	116	112	0	913	60	10	.990
1997—Oakland (A.L.)	1B	105	366	48	104	24	0	34	81	.284	58	98	1	884	60	6	.994
—St. Louis (N.L.) ■	1B	51	174	38	44	3	0	§24	42	.253	43	61	2	438	34	1	.998
American League totals (12 years)		1329	4448	773	1157	195	5	363	941	.260	847	1043	8	10298	806	81	.993
National League totals (1 year)		51	174	38	44	3	0	24	42	.253	43	61	2	438	34	1	.998
Major league totals (12 years)		1380	4622	811	1201	198	5	387	983	.260	890	1104	10	10736	840	82	.993

CHAMPIONSHIP SERIES RECORD

Year Team (League)	Pos.	G	AB	R	H	2B	3B	HR	RBI	Avg.	BB	SO	SB	PO	A	E	Avg.
1988—Oakland (A.L.)	1B	4	15	4	5	0	0	1	3	.333	1	5	0	24	2	0	1.000
1989—Oakland (A.L.)	1B	5	18	3	7	1	0	1	3	.389	1	4	0	46	1	1	.979
1990—Oakland (A.L.)	1B	4	13	2	2	0	0	0	2	.154	3	3	0	40	0	0	1.000
1992—Oakland (A.L.)	1B	6	20	1	3	0	0	1	3	.150	5	4	0	46	2	1	.980
Championship series totals (4 years)		19	66	10	17	1	0	3	11	.258	10	16	0	156	5	2	.988

NOTES: Member of World Series championship team (1989).

WORLD SERIES RECORD

Year Team (League)	Pos.	G	AB	R	H	2B	3B	HR	RBI	Avg.	BB	SO	SB	PO	A	E	Avg.
1988—Oakland (A.L.)	1B	5	17	1	1	0	0	1	1	.059	3	4	0	40	3	0	1.000
1989—Oakland (A.L.)	1B	4	17	0	5	1	0	0	1	.294	1	3	0	28	2	0	1.000
1990—Oakland (A.L.)	1B	4	14	1	3	0	0	0	0	.214	2	4	0	42	1	2	.956
World Series totals (3 years)		13	48	2	9	1	0	1	2	.188	6	11	0	110	6	2	.983

ALL-STAR GAME RECORD

NOTES: Named to A.L. All-Star team for 1991 game; replaced by Rafael Palmeiro due to injury.

Year League	Pos.	AB	R	H	2B	3B	HR	RBI	Avg.	BB	SO	SB	PO	A	E	Avg.
1987—American	1B	3	0	0	0	0	0	0	.000	0	0	0	7	0	1	.875
1988—American	1B	2	0	1	0	0	0	0	.500	0	1	0	8	0	0	1.000
1989—American	1B	3	0	1	0	0	0	0	.333	0	0	0	5	0	0	1.000
1990—American	1B	2	0	0	0	0	0	0	.000	0	2	0	7	0	0	1.000
1991—American					Selected, did not play—injured.											
1992—American	1B	3	1	1	0	0	0	2	.333	0	0	0	4	0	0	1.000
1995—American					Selected, did not play—injured.											
1996—American	1B	1	0	1	0	0	0	0	1.000	0	0	0	2	1	0	1.000
1997—American	1B	2	0	0	0	0	0	0	.000	0	2	0	4	0	0	1.000
All-Star Game totals (7 years)		16	1	4	0	0	0	2	.250	0	5	0	37	1	1	.974

McKEEL, WALT   C   RED SOX

PERSONAL: Born January 17, 1972, in Wilson, N.C. ... 6-0/200. ... Bats right, throws right. ... Full name: Walt Thomas McKeel.
HIGH SCHOOL: Greene Central (Snow Hill, N.C.).
TRANSACTIONS/CAREER NOTES: Selected by Boston Red Sox organization in third round of free-agent draft (June 4, 1990).
STATISTICAL NOTES: Led Carolina League with 22 passed balls in 1992. ... Led Eastern League with 17 passed balls and tied for lead with 11 double plays in 1996. ... Led International League with 10 passed balls in 1997.

Year Team (League)	Pos.	G	AB	R	H	2B	3B	HR	RBI	Avg.	BB	SO	SB	PO	A	E	Avg.
1990—GC Red Sox (GCL)	C	13	44	2	11	3	0	0	6	.250	3	8	0	42	5	2	.959
1991—GC Red Sox (GCL)	C-1B	35	113	10	15	0	1	2	12	.133	17	20	0	150	52	4	.981
1992—Lynchburg (Caro.)	C	96	288	33	64	11	0	12	33	.222	22	77	2	525	90	17	.973
1993—Lynchburg (Caro.)	C	80	247	28	59	17	2	5	32	.239	26	40	0	390	59	8	.982
1994—Sarasota (Fla. St.)	C	37	137	15	38	8	1	2	15	.277	8	19	1	220	44	8	.971
—New Britain (Eastern) .	C	50	164	10	30	6	1	1	17	.183	7	35	0	281	46	12	.965
1995—Trenton (Eastern)	C-1B	29	84	11	20	3	1	2	11	.238	8	15	2	88	11	2	.980
—Sarasota (Fla. St.)	C	62	198	26	66	14	0	8	35	.333	25	28	6	326	51	9	.977
1996—Trenton (Eastern)	C-1B-3B	128	464	86	140	19	1	16	78	.302	60	52	2	835	100	10	.989
—Boston (A.L.)	C	1	0	0	0	0	0	0	0	...	0	0	0	0	0	0	...
1997—Pawtucket (Int'l)	C-1B	66	237	34	60	15	0	6	30	.253	34	39	0	447	39	6	.988
—Boston (A.L.)	C-1B	5	3	0	0	0	0	0	0	.000	0	1	0	6	0	1	1.000
—Trenton (Eastern)	C-1B	7	25	0	4	2	0	0	4	.160	1	2	0	17	1	0	1.000
Major league totals (2 years)		6	3	0	0	0	0	0	0	.000	0	1	0	6	0	1	1.000

PERSONAL: Born October 4, 1964, in San Diego. ... 5-11/207. ... Bats both, throws right. ... Full name: Mark Tremell McLemore.
HIGH SCHOOL: Morse (San Diego).
TRANSACTIONS/CAREER NOTES: Selected by California Angels organization in ninth round of free-agent draft (June 7, 1982). ... On disabled list (May 15-27, 1985). ... On California disabled list (May 24-August 2, 1988); included rehabilitation assignments to Palm Springs (July 7-21) and Edmonton (July 22-27). ... On California disabled list (May 17-August 17, 1990); included rehabilitation assignments to Edmonton (May 24-June 6) and Palm Springs (August 9-13). ... Traded by Angels to Colorado Springs, Cleveland Indians organization (August 17, 1990), completing deal in which Indians traded C Ron Tingley to Angels for a player to be named later (September 6, 1989). ... Released by Indians organization (December 13, 1990). ... Signed by Tucson, Houston Astros organization (March 6, 1991). ... On Houston disabled list (May 9-June 25, 1991); included rehabilitation assignments to Tucson (May 24-29) and Jackson (June 14-22). ... Released by Astros (June 25, 1991). ... Signed by Baltimore Orioles organization (July 5, 1991). ... Granted free agency (October 15, 1991). ... Re-signed by Orioles organization (February 5, 1992). ... Granted free agency (December 19, 1992). ... Re-signed by Rochester, Orioles organization (January 6, 1993). ... Granted free agency (October 18, 1994). ... Signed by Texas Rangers (December 13, 1994). ... Granted free agency (December 7, 1996). ... Re-signed by Rangers (December 13, 1996). ... On Texas disabled list (May 15-June 12 and August 19-September 28, 1997); included rehabilitation assignments to Charlotte (June 7-8) and Oklahoma City (June 9-12).
STATISTICAL NOTES: Led California League second basemen with 400 assists and 84 double plays in 1984. ... Led Pacific Coast League second basemen with 597 total chances and 95 double plays in 1989. ... Led A.L. second basemen with 473 assists and 798 total chances in 1996.

								BATTING						FIELDING		
Year	Team (League)	Pos.	G	AB	R	H	2B	3B	HR	RBI	Avg.	BB	SO	SB	PO	A	E	Avg.
1982—	Salem (Northwest)	2B-SS	55	165	42	49	6	2	0	25	.297	39	38	14	81	125	11	.949
1983—	Peoria (Midwest)	2B-SS	95	329	42	79	7	3	0	18	.240	53	64	15	170	250	24	.946
1984—	Redwood (Calif.)	2B-SS	134	482	102	142	8	3	0	45	.295	106	75	59	274	†429	25	.966
1985—	Midland (Texas)	2B-SS	117	458	80	124	17	6	2	46	.271	66	59	31	301	339	19	.971
1986—	Midland (Texas)	2B	63	237	54	75	9	1	1	29	.316	48	18	38	155	194	13	.964
—	Edmonton (PCL)	2B	73	286	41	79	13	1	0	23	.276	39	30	29	173	215	7	.982
—	California (A.L.)	2B	5	4	0	0	0	0	0	0	.000	1	2	0	3	10	0	1.000
1987—	California (A.L.)	2B-SS-DH	138	433	61	102	13	3	3	41	.236	48	72	25	293	363	17	.975
1988—	California (A.L.)	2B-3B-DH	77	233	38	56	11	2	2	16	.240	25	25	13	108	178	6	.979
—	Palm Springs (Cal.)	2B	11	44	9	15	3	1	0	6	.341	11	7	7	18	24	1	.977
—	Edmonton (PCL)	2B	12	45	7	12	3	0	0	6	.267	4	4	7	35	33	1	.986
1989—	Edmonton (PCL)	2B	114	430	60	105	13	2	2	34	.244	49	67	26	*264	323	10	*.983
—	California (A.L.)	2B-DH	32	103	12	25	3	1	0	14	.243	7	19	6	55	88	5	.966
1990—	California (A.L.)	2B	20	48	4	7	2	0	0	2	.146	4	9	1	14	15	0	1.000
—	Edmonton (PCL)	2B-SS	9	39	4	10	2	0	0	3	.256	6	10	0	24	32	4	.933
—	Palm Springs (Cal.)	2B	6	22	3	6	0	0	0	2	.273	3	7	0	20	22	0	1.000
—	Colo. Springs (PCL)■	2B-3B-SS	14	54	11	15	2	0	1	7	.278	11	8	5	23	40	2	.969
—	Cleveland (A.L.)	SS-3B-2B	8	12	2	2	0	0	0	1	.167	0	6	0	23	24	4	.922
1991	Houston (N.L.)■	2B	21	61	6	9	1	0	0	2	.148	6	13	0	25	54	2	.975
—	Tucson (PCL)	2B	4	14	2	5	1	0	0	0	.357	2	1	0	8	6	0	1.000
—	Jackson (Texas)	2B	7	22	6	5	3	0	1	4	.227	6	3	1	27	24	0	1.000
—	Rochester (Int'l)■	2B	57	228	32	64	11	4	1	28	.281	27	29	12	134	166	5	.984
1992—	Baltimore (A.L.)	2B-DH	101	228	40	56	7	2	0	27	.246	21	26	11	126	186	7	.978
1993—	Baltimore (A.L.)	O-2-3-DH	148	581	81	165	27	5	4	72	.284	64	92	21	335	80	6	.986
1994—	Baltimore (A.L.)	2B-OF-DH	104	343	44	88	11	1	3	29	.257	51	50	20	219	269	9	.982
1995—	Texas (A.L.)■	OF-2B-DH	129	467	73	122	20	5	5	41	.261	59	71	21	248	184	4	.991
1996—	Texas (A.L.)	2B-OF	147	517	84	150	23	4	5	46	.290	87	69	27	313	†473	12	.985
1997—	Texas (A.L.)	2B-OF	89	349	47	91	17	2	1	25	.261	40	54	7	148	254	8	.980
—	Charlotte (Fla. St.)	2B	2	7	1	4	1	0	0	3	.571	2	1	1	3	3	0	1.000
—	Oklahoma City (A.A.)	2B	3	10	0	1	0	0	0	1	.100	1	1	1	2	3	0	1.000
American League totals (11 years)			998	3318	486	864	134	25	23	313	.260	407	495	152	1885	2124	78	.981
National League totals (1 year)			21	61	6	9	1	0	0	2	.148	6	13	0	25	54	2	.975
Major league totals (12 years)			1019	3379	492	873	135	25	23	315	.258	413	508	152	1910	2178	80	.981

DIVISION SERIES RECORD

								BATTING						FIELDING		
Year	Team (League)	Pos.	G	AB	R	H	2B	3B	HR	RBI	Avg.	BB	SO	SB	PO	A	E	Avg.
1996—	Texas (A.L.)	2B	4	15	1	2	0	0	0	2	.133	0	4	0	10	16	0	1.000

McMICHAEL, GREG   P   METS

PERSONAL: Born December 1, 1966, in Knoxville, Tenn. ... 6-3/215. ... Throws right, bats right. ... Full name: Gregory Winston McMichael.
HIGH SCHOOL: Webb School of Knoxville (Knoxville, Tenn.).
COLLEGE: Tennessee.
TRANSACTIONS/CAREER NOTES: Selected by Cleveland Indians organization in seventh round of free-agent draft (June 1, 1988). ... Released by Colorado Springs, Indians organization (April 4, 1991). ... Signed by Durham, Atlanta Braves organization (April 16, 1991). ... Traded by Braves to New York Mets for P Paul Byrd and a player to be named later (November 25, 1996); Braves acquired P Andy Zwirchitz to complete deal (May 25, 1997).

Year	Team (League)	W	L	Pct.	ERA	G	GS	CG	ShO	Sv.	IP	H	R	ER	BB	SO
1988—	Burlington (Appalachian)	2	0	1.000	2.57	3	3	1	1	0	21	17	9	6	4	20
—	Kinston (Carolina)	4	2	.667	2.68	11	11	2	0	0	77 1/3	57	31	23	18	35
1989—	Cant./Akr. (Eastern)	11	11	.500	3.49	26	•26	8	•5	0	170	164	81	66	64	101
1990—	Cant./Akr. (Eastern)	2	3	.400	3.35	13	4	0	0	0	40 1/3	39	17	15	17	19
—	Colo. Springs (PCL)	2	3	.400	5.80	12	12	1	1	0	59	72	45	38	30	34
1991—	Durham (Carolina)■	5	6	.455	3.62	36	6	0	0	2	79 2/3	83	34	32	29	82
1992—	Greenville (Southern)	4	2	.667	1.36	15	4	0	0	1	46 1/3	37	14	7	13	53
—	Richmond (Int'l)	6	5	.545	4.38	19	13	0	0	0	90 1/3	89	52	44	34	86
1993—	Atlanta (N.L.)	2	3	.400	2.06	74	0	0	0	19	91 2/3	68	22	21	29	89
1994—	Atlanta (N.L.)	4	6	.400	3.84	51	0	0	0	21	58 2/3	66	29	25	19	47

Year — Team (League)	W	L	Pct.	ERA	G	GS	CG	ShO	Sv.	IP	H	R	ER	BB	SO
1995— Atlanta (N.L.)	7	2	.778	2.79	67	0	0	0	2	80⅔	64	27	25	32	74
1996— Atlanta (N.L.)	5	3	.625	3.22	73	0	0	0	2	86⅔	84	37	31	27	78
1997— New York (N.L.)■	7	10	.412	2.98	73	0	0	0	7	87⅔	73	34	29	27	81
Major league totals (5 years)	25	24	.510	2.91	338	0	0	0	51	405⅓	355	149	131	134	369

DIVISION SERIES RECORD

Year — Team (League)	W	L	Pct.	ERA	G	GS	CG	ShO	Sv.	IP	H	R	ER	BB	SO
1995— Atlanta (N.L.)	0	0	...	6.75	2	0	0	0	0	1⅓	1	1	1	2	1
1996— Atlanta (N.L.)	0	0	...	6.75	2	0	0	0	0	1⅓	1	1	1	1	3
Div. series totals (2 years)	0	0	...	6.75	4	0	0	0	0	2⅔	2	2	2	3	4

CHAMPIONSHIP SERIES RECORD

Year — Team (League)	W	L	Pct.	ERA	G	GS	CG	ShO	Sv.	IP	H	R	ER	BB	SO
1993— Atlanta (N.L.)	0	1	.000	6.75	4	0	0	0	0	4	7	3	3	2	1
1995— Atlanta (N.L.)	1	0	1.000	0.00	3	0	0	0	1	2⅔	0	0	0	1	2
1996— Atlanta (N.L.)	0	1	.000	9.00	3	0	0	0	0	2	4	2	2	1	3
Champ. series totals (3 years)	1	2	.333	5.19	10	0	0	0	1	8⅔	11	5	5	4	6

WORLD SERIES RECORD

NOTES: Member of World Series championship team (1995).

Year — Team (League)	W	L	Pct.	ERA	G	GS	CG	ShO	Sv.	IP	H	R	ER	BB	SO
1995— Atlanta (N.L.)	0	0	...	2.70	3	0	0	0	0	3⅓	3	2	1	2	2
1996— Atlanta (N.L.)	0	0	...	27.00	2	0	0	0	0	1	5	3	3	0	1
World Series totals (2 years)	0	0	...	8.31	5	0	0	0	0	4⅓	8	5	4	2	3

McMILLON, BILLY — OF — PHILLIES

PERSONAL: Born November 17, 1971, in Otero, N.M. ... 5-11/180. ... Bats left, throws left. ... Full name: William E. McMillon.
HIGH SCHOOL: Bishopville (S.C.).
COLLEGE: Clemson.
TRANSACTIONS/CAREER NOTES: Selected by Florida Marlins organization in eighth round of free-agent draft (June 3, 1993). ... On Charlotte disabled list (April 20-29, 1997). ... Traded by Marlins to Philadelphia Phillies for OF/1B Darren Daulton (July 21, 1997).
STATISTICAL NOTES: Tied for New York-Pennsylvania League lead with four intentional bases on balls received in 1993. ... Tied for Midwest League lead with nine sacrifice flies in 1994. ... Led Eastern League with .423 on-base percentage in 1995. ... Led International League with .418 on-base percentage in 1996. ... Career major league grand slams: 1.

Year — Team (League)	Pos.	G	AB	R	H	2B	3B	HR	RBI	Avg.	BB	SO	SB	PO	A	E	Avg.
1993— Elmira (N.Y.-Penn)	OF	57	226	38	69	14	2	6	35	.305	31	43	5	66	1	5	.931
1994— Kane County (Midw.)	OF	•137	496	88	125	25	3	17	*101	.252	*84	99	7	187	9	7	.966
1995— Portland (Eastern)	OF	*141	518	92	*162	29	3	14	93	.313	*96	90	15	207	14	4	.982
1996— Charlotte (Int'l)	OF	97	347	72	122	32	2	17	70	*.352	36	76	5	135	10	4	.973
— Florida (N.L.)	OF	28	51	4	11	0	0	4	4	.216	5	14	0	17	0	0	1.000
1997— Charlotte (Int'l)	OF	57	204	34	57	18	0	8	26	.279	32	51	8	84	5	2	.978
— Florida (N.L.)	OF	13	18	0	2	1	0	0	1	.111	0	7	0	4	0	0	1.000
— Scran./W.B. (Int'l)■	OF	26	92	18	27	8	1	4	21	.293	12	24	2	49	3	0	1.000
— Philadelphia (N.L.)	OF	24	72	10	21	4	1	2	13	.292	6	17	2	42	2	2	.957
Major league totals (2 years)		65	141	14	34	5	1	2	18	.241	11	38	2	63	2	2	.970

McRAE, BRIAN — OF — METS

PERSONAL: Born August 27, 1967, in Bradenton, Fla. ... 6-0/195. ... Bats both, throws right. ... Full name: Brian Wesley McRae. ... Son of Hal McRae, hitting coach, Philadelphia Phillies; outfielder/designated hitter, Reds and Kansas City Royals (1968 and 1970-87); coach, Royals (1987) and Montreal Expos (1990-91); and manager, Royals (1991-94).
HIGH SCHOOL: Blue Springs (Mo.).
TRANSACTIONS/CAREER NOTES: Selected by Kansas City Royals organization in first round (17th pick overall) of free-agent draft (June 3, 1985). ... Traded by Royals to Chicago Cubs for P Derek Wallace and P Geno Morones (April 5, 1995). ... Traded by Cubs with P Mel Rojas and P Turk Wendell to New York Mets for OF Lance Johnson and two players to be named later (August 8, 1997); Mets traded P Mark Clark (August 11) and IF Manny Alexander (August 14) to Cubs to complete deal.
RECORDS: Shares major league single-season record for fewest double plays by outfielder (150 or more games)—0 (1991). ... Shares major league single-game record for most unassisted double plays by outfielder—1 (August 23, 1992). ... Shares N.L. single-season record for fewest assists by outfielder (150 or more games)—2 (1996).
STATISTICAL NOTES: Led Northwest League second basemen with 373 total chances in 1986. ... Tied for Southern League lead in double plays by outfielder with five in 1989. ... Had 22-game hitting streak (July 20-August 13, 1991). ... Led N.L. outfielders with 352 total chances in 1995. ... Career major league grand slams: 4.

Year — Team (League)	Pos.	G	AB	R	H	2B	3B	HR	RBI	Avg.	BB	SO	SB	PO	A	E	Avg.
1985— GC Royals (GCL)	2B-SS	60	217	40	58	6	5	0	23	.267	28	34	27	116	142	18	.935
1986— Eugene (Northwest)	2B	72	306	*66	82	10	3	1	29	.268	41	49	28	146	*214	13	*.965
1987— Fort Myers (FSL)	2B	131	481	62	121	14	1	1	31	.252	22	70	33	*284	346	18	.972
1988— Baseball City (FSL)	2B	30	107	18	33	2	0	1	11	.308	9	11	8	70	103	4	.977
— Memphis (Southern)	2B	91	288	33	58	13	1	4	15	.201	16	60	13	147	231	18	.955
1989— Memphis (Southern)	OF	138	*533	72	121	18	8	5	42	.227	43	65	23	249	11	5	.981
1990— Memphis (Southern)	OF	116	470	78	126	24	6	10	64	.268	44	66	21	265	8	7	.975
— Kansas City (A.L.)	OF	46	168	21	48	8	3	2	23	.286	9	29	4	120	1	0	1.000
1991— Kansas City (A.L.)	OF	152	629	86	164	28	9	8	64	.261	24	99	20	405	2	3	.993
1992— Kansas City (A.L.)	OF	149	533	63	119	23	5	4	52	.223	42	88	18	419	8	3	.993
1993— Kansas City (A.L.)	OF	153	627	78	177	28	9	12	69	.282	37	105	23	394	4	7	.983
1994— Kansas City (A.L.)	OF-DH	114	436	71	119	22	6	4	40	.273	54	67	28	252	2	3	.988

Year Team (League)	Pos.	G	AB	R	H	2B	3B	HR	RBI	Avg.	BB	SO	SB	PO	A	E	Avg.
1995—Chicago (N.L.)■	OF	137	*580	92	167	38	7	12	48	.288	47	92	27	*345	4	3	.991
1996—Chicago (N.L.)	OF	157	624	111	172	32	5	17	66	.276	73	84	37	345	2	5	.986
1997—Chicago (N.L.)	OF	108	417	63	100	27	5	6	28	.240	52	62	14	242	3	1	.996
—New York (N.L.)■	OF	45	145	23	36	5	2	5	15	.248	13	22	3	65	1	3	.957
American League totals (5 years)		614	2393	319	627	109	32	30	248	.262	166	388	93	1590	17	16	.990
National League totals (3 years)		447	1766	289	475	102	19	40	157	.269	185	260	81	997	10	12	.988
Major league totals (8 years)		1061	4159	608	1102	211	51	70	405	.265	351	648	174	2587	27	28	.989

MEADOWS, BRIAN   P   MARLINS

PERSONAL: Born November 21, 1975, in Montgomery, Ala. ... 6-4/200. ... Throws right, bats right.
HIGH SCHOOL: Charles Henderson (Troy, Ala.).
TRANSACTIONS/CAREER NOTES: Selected by Florida Marlins organization in third round of free-agent draft (June 2, 1994); choice received as compensation for Colorado Rockies signing Type-B free agent SS Walt Weiss.

Year Team (League)	W	L	Pct.	ERA	G	GS	CG	ShO	Sv.	IP	H	R	ER	BB	SO
1994—GC Marlins (GCL)	3	0	1.000	1.95	8	7	0	0	0	37	34	9	8	6	33
1995—Kane County (Midwest)	9	9	.500	4.22	26	26	1	1	0	147	163	90	69	41	103
1996—Portland (Eastern)	0	1	.000	4.33	4	4	1	0	0	27	26	15	13	4	13
—Brevard County (FSL)	8	7	.533	3.58	24	23	3	1	0	146	129	73	58	25	69
1997—Portland (Eastern)	9	7	.563	4.61	29	*29	4	0	0	175²/₃	204	99	90	48	115

MEARES, PAT   SS   TWINS

PERSONAL: Born September 6, 1968, in Salina, Kan. ... 6-0/187. ... Bats right, throws right. ... Full name: Patrick James Meares.
HIGH SCHOOL: Sacred Heart (Salina, Kan.).
COLLEGE: Wichita State.
TRANSACTIONS/CAREER NOTES: Selected by Minnesota Twins organization in 15th round of free-agent draft (June 4, 1990). ... On disabled list (June 22-July 7, 1994). ... On disabled list (August 11-26, 1997).
RECORDS: Holds major league single-season record for fewest assists by shortstop (150 or more games)—344 (1996).

Year Team (League)	Pos.	G	AB	R	H	2B	3B	HR	RBI	Avg.	BB	SO	SB	PO	A	E	Avg.
1990—Kenosha (Midwest)	3B-2B	52	197	26	47	10	2	4	22	.239	25	45	2	35	94	16	.890
1991—Visalia (California)	2B-3B-OF	89	360	53	109	21	4	6	44	.303	24	63	15	155	224	26	.936
1992—Orlando (South.)	SS	81	300	42	76	19	0	3	23	.253	11	57	5	91	190	35	.889
1993—Portland (PCL)	SS	18	54	6	16	5	0	0	3	.296	3	11	0	28	48	5	.938
—Minnesota (A.L.)	SS	111	346	33	87	14	3	0	33	.251	7	52	4	165	304	19	.961
1994—Minnesota (A.L.)	SS	80	229	29	61	12	1	2	24	.266	14	50	5	133	209	13	.963
1995—Minnesota (A.L.)	SS-OF	116	390	57	105	19	4	12	49	.269	15	68	10	187	317	•18	.966
1996—Minnesota (A.L.)	SS-OF	152	517	66	138	26	7	8	67	.267	17	90	9	257	344	22	.965
1997—Minnesota (A.L.)	SS	134	439	63	121	23	3	10	60	.276	18	86	7	211	415	20	.969
Major league totals (5 years)		593	1921	248	512	94	18	32	233	.267	71	346	35	953	1589	92	.965

MECIR, JIM   P   DEVIL RAYS

PERSONAL: Born May 16, 1970, in Queens, N.Y. ... 6-1/195. ... Throws right, bats both. ... Full name: James Jason Mecir.
HIGH SCHOOL: Smithtown East (St. James, N.Y.).
COLLEGE: Eckerd (Fla.).
TRANSACTIONS/CAREER NOTES: Selected by Seattle Mariners organization in third round of free-agent draft (June 3, 1991). ... On disabled list (June 25-August 25, 1992). ... Traded by Mariners with 1B Tino Martinez and P Jeff Nelson to New York Yankees for P Sterling Hitchcock and 3B Russ Davis (December 7, 1995). ... Traded by Yankees to Boston Red Sox (September 29, 1997), completing deal in which Yankees traded P Tony Armas and a player to be named later to Red Sox for C Mike Stanley and IF Randy Brown (August 13, 1997). ... Selected by Tampa Bay Devil Rays in second round (36th pick overall) of expansion draft (November 18, 1997).
STATISTICAL NOTES: Led California League with 15 hit batsmen in 1993.

Year Team (League)	W	L	Pct.	ERA	G	GS	CG	ShO	Sv.	IP	H	R	ER	BB	SO
1991—San Bernardino (Calif.)	3	5	.375	4.22	14	12	0	0	1	70¹/₃	72	40	33	37	48
1992—San Bernardino (Calif.)	4	5	.444	4.67	14	11	0	0	0	61²/₃	72	40	32	26	53
1993—Riverside (California)	9	11	.450	4.33	26	26	1	0	0	145¹/₃	160	89	70	58	85
1994—Jacksonville (Southern)	6	5	.545	2.69	46	0	0	0	13	80¹/₃	73	28	24	35	53
1995—Tacoma (PCL)	1	4	.200	3.10	40	0	0	0	8	69²/₃	63	29	24	28	46
—Seattle (A.L.)	0	0	. . .	0.00	2	0	0	0	0	4²/₃	5	1	0	2	3
1996—Columbus (Int'l)■	3	3	.500	2.27	33	0	0	0	7	47²/₃	37	14	12	15	52
—New York (A.L.)	1	1	.500	5.13	26	0	0	0	0	40¹/₃	42	24	23	23	38
1997—Columbus (Int'l)	1	1	.500	1.00	24	0	0	0	11	27	14	4	3	6	34
—New York (A.L.)	0	4	.000	5.88	25	0	0	0	0	33²/₃	36	23	22	10	25
Major league totals (3 years)	1	5	.167	5.15	53	0	0	0	0	78²/₃	83	48	45	35	66

MEDINA, RAFAEL   P   MARLINS

PERSONAL: Born February 15, 1975, in Panama City, Panama. ... 6-3/195. ... Throws right, bats right. ... Brother of Ricardo Medina, third baseman with Chicago Cubs organization (1989-94).
TRANSACTIONS/CAREER NOTES: Signed as non-drafted free agent by New York Yankees organization (September 6, 1992). ... On disabled list (July 11-22 and August 5-September 30, 1996). ... Traded by Yankees with OF Ruben Rivera and $3 million to San Diego Padres for rights to P Hideki Irabu, 2B Homer Bush, OF Gordon Amerson and a player to be named later (April 22, 1997); Padres traded OF Vernon Maxwell to Yankees to complete deal (June 9). ... Traded by Padres with P Steve Hoff and 1B Derrek Lee to Florida Marlins for P Kevin Brown (December 15, 1997).

Year	Team (League)	W	L	Pct.	ERA	G	GS	CG	ShO	Sv.	IP	H	R	ER	BB	SO
1993—	GC Yankees (GCL)	2	0	1.000	0.66	5	5	0	0	0	27 1/3	16	6	2	12	21
1994—	Oneonta (N.Y.-Penn)	3	7	.300	4.66	14	14	1	0	0	73 1/3	67	54	38	35	59
1995—	Greensboro (S. Atl.)	4	4	.500	4.01	19	19	1	0	0	98 2/3	86	48	44	38	108
—	Tampa (Florida State)	2	2	.500	2.37	6	6	0	0	0	30 1/3	29	12	8	12	25
1996—	Norwich (Eastern)	5	8	.385	3.06	19	19	1	0	0	103	78	48	35	55	112
1997—	Rancho Cuca. (Cal.)■	2	0	1.000	2.00	3	3	0	0	0	18	13	4	4	5	14
—	Las Vegas (PCL)	4	5	.444	7.56	13	13	0	0	0	66 2/3	90	60	56	39	50

MEJIA, MIGUEL — OF

PERSONAL: Born March 25, 1975, in San Pedro de Macoris, Dominican Republic. ... 6-1/155. ... Bats right, throws right.
TRANSACTIONS/CAREER NOTES: Signed as non-drafted free agent by Baltimore Orioles organization (January 22, 1992). ... Selected by Kansas City Royals from Orioles organization in Rule 5 major league draft (December 4, 1995). ... Traded by Royals to St. Louis Cardinals as part of a three-team deal in which Cardinals sent OF Andre King to Cincinnati Reds for SS Luis Ordaz. Reds then sent P Mike Remlinger to Royals to complete deal (December 4, 1995). ... On St. Louis disabled list (August 2-September 1, 1996); included rehabilitation assignment to St. Petersburg (August 19-31). ... On Prince William disabled list (April 9-23 and April 25-May 13, 1997). ... Granted free agency (December 21, 1997).

Year	Team (League)	Pos.	G	AB	R	H	2B	3B	HR	RBI	Avg.	BB	SO	SB	PO	A	E	Avg.
1992—	Dom. Orioles (DSL)	OF	51	187	42	63	11	0	1	31	.337	30	19	30	93	12	14	.882
1993—	Albany (S. Atl.)	OF	23	79	11	13	0	0	2	.165	4	22	7	37	1	3	.927
—	GC Orioles (GCL)	OF	35	130	21	32	3	3	0	12	.246	13	23	18	80	3	2	.976
1994—	Albany (S. Atl.)	OF	22	58	6	10	1	1	0	3	.172	5	20	5	41	4	3	.938
—	Bluefield (Appal.)	OF	50	191	34	51	5	5	2	24	.267	17	39	33	86	6	6	.940
1995—	Bluefield (Appal.)	OF	51	181	50	54	6	3	3	30	.298	18	30	36	74	5	5	.940
—	High Desert (Calif.)	OF	37	119	14	32	6	1	0	12	.269	14	17	16	58	2	3	.952
1996—	St. Louis (N.L.)■	OF	45	23	10	2	0	0	0	0	.087	0	10	6	14	0	1	.933
—	St. Petersburg (FSL)	OF	8	26	2	3	0	0	0	0	.115	1	12	2	14	0	0	1.000
1997—	Prince William (Car.)	OF	39	136	17	29	2	0	0	9	.213	10	25	7	70	7	2	.975
—	New Jersey (NYP)	OF	30	124	22	41	8	1	0	14	.331	6	27	11	55	3	4	.935
Major league totals (1 year)			45	23	10	2	0	0	0	0	.087	0	10	6	14	0	1	.933

DIVISION SERIES RECORD

Year	Team (League)	Pos.	G	AB	R	H	2B	3B	HR	RBI	Avg.	BB	SO	SB	PO	A	E	Avg.
1996—	St. Louis (N.L.)	PR	1	0	0	0	0	0	0	0	...	0	0	0	...	...	...	...

CHAMPIONSHIP SERIES RECORD

Year	Team (League)	Pos.	G	AB	R	H	2B	3B	HR	RBI	Avg.	BB	SO	SB	PO	A	E	Avg.
1996—	St. Louis (N.L.)	PR-OF	3	1	1	0	0	0	0	0	.000	0	1	0	2	0	0	1.000

MEJIA, ROBERTO — 2B — CARDINALS

M

PERSONAL: Born April 14, 1972, in Hato Mayor, Dominican Republic. ... 5-11/165. ... Bats right, throws right. ... Full name: Roberto Antonio Diaz Mejia.
HIGH SCHOOL: Colegio Adventista (Dominican Republic).
TRANSACTIONS/CAREER NOTES: Signed as non-drafted free agent by Los Angeles Dodgers organization (November 21, 1988). ... On disabled list (April 29-May 19 and August 18, 1992-remainder of season). ... Selected by Colorado Rockies in second round (30th pick overall) of expansion draft (November 17, 1992). ... On Colorado Springs suspended list (June 26-28, 1995). ... Granted free agency (December 21, 1995). ... Signed by Cincinnati Reds organization (January 2, 1996). ... Traded by Reds with P Brad Tweedlie to Boston Red Sox for OF Kevin Mitchell (July 30, 1996). ... Released by Red Sox (February 3, 1997). ... Signed by St. Louis Cardinals organization (February 14, 1997). ... On St. Louis disabled list (April 12, 1997-remainder of season); included rehabilitation assignment to Louisville (April 24-May 1). ... Released by Cardinals (December 16, 1997). ... Re-signed by Cardinals organization (January 12, 1998).

Year	Team (League)	Pos.	G	AB	R	H	2B	3B	HR	RBI	Avg.	BB	SO	SB	PO	A	E	Avg.
1989—	Dom. Dodgers (DSL)	...	43	136	18	30	5	3	0	20	.221	24	22	7	...	...	...	...
1990—	Dom. Dodgers (DSL)	...	67	246	61	74	19	1	8	74	.301	48	30	9	...	...	...	...
1991—	Great Falls (Pio.)	2B	23	84	17	22	6	2	2	14	.262	7	22	3	33	54	3	.967
1992—	Vero Beach (FSL)	2B	96	330	42	82	17	1	12	40	.248	37	60	14	148	212	15	.960
1993—	Colo. Springs (PCL)■	2B	77	291	51	87	15	2	14	48	.299	18	56	12	166	204	8	.979
—	Colorado (N.L.)	2B	65	229	31	53	14	5	5	20	.231	13	63	4	126	184	12	.963
1994—	Colorado (N.L.)	2B	38	116	11	28	8	1	4	14	.241	15	33	3	69	94	7	.959
—	Colo. Springs (PCL)	2B	73	283	54	80	24	2	6	37	.283	21	49	7	172	213	12	.970
1995—	Colo. Springs (PCL)	2B	38	143	18	42	10	2	2	14	.294	7	29	0	80	97	5	.973
—	Colorado (N.L.)	2B	23	52	5	8	1	0	1	4	.154	0	17	0	35	30	2	.970
1996—	Indianapolis (A.A.)■	2B-3B	101	374	55	109	24	*9	13	58	.291	29	79	13	208	261	12	.975
—	Pawtucket (Int'l)■	2B-OF	21	74	9	19	4	0	0	4	.257	5	18	4	27	52	3	.963
1997—	St. Louis (N.L.)	2B-OF	7	14	0	1	1	0	0	2	.071	0	5	0	3	6	1	.900
—	Louisville (A.A.)	2B-3B	6	21	3	7	1	0	1	2	.333	0	4	0	9	8	1	.944
Major league totals (4 years)			133	411	47	90	24	6	10	40	.219	28	118	7	233	314	22	.961

MELO, JUAN — SS — PADRES

PERSONAL: Born May 11, 1976, in Bani, Dominican Republic. ... 6-1/160. ... Throws right, bats both.
HIGH SCHOOL: Colegio Redentol (Bani, Dominican Republic).
TRANSACTIONS/CAREER NOTES: Signed as non-drafted free agent San Diego Padres organization (June 15, 1993). ... On suspended list (July 9-13, 1996).
STATISTICAL NOTES: Tied for Midwest League lead in double plays by shortstop with 70 in 1995. ... Led California League shortstops with 613 total chances and 92 double plays in 1996.

Year Team (League)	Pos.	G	AB	R	H	2B	3B	HR	RBI	Avg.	BB	SO	SB	PO	A	E	Avg.
1994— Ariz. Padres (Ariz.)	SS	37	145	20	41	3	3	0	15	.283	10	36	3	46	117	13	.926
— Spokane (N'west)	SS	3	11	4	4	1	0	1	2	.364	1	3	0	2	11	2	.867
1995— Clinton (Midwest)	SS	134	479	65	135	32	1	5	46	.282	33	88	12	183	372	47	.922
1996— Rancho Cuca. (Cal.) ...	SS	128	503	75	153	27	6	8	75	.304	22	102	6	*209	*378	26	.958
1997— Mobile (Southern)	SS	113	456	52	131	22	2	7	67	.287	29	90	7	182	307	28	.946
— Las Vegas (PCL)	SS	12	48	6	13	4	0	1	6	.271	1	10	0	11	33	3	.936

MELUSKEY, MITCH   C   ASTROS

PERSONAL: Born September 18, 1973, in Yakima, Wash. ... 6-0/185. ... Bats both, throws right. ... Full name: Mitchell Wade Meluskey.
HIGH SCHOOL: Eisenhower (Yakima, Wash.).
TRANSACTIONS/CAREER NOTES: Selected by Cleveland Indians organization in 12th round of free-agent draft (June 1, 1992). ... Traded by Indians to Houston Astros organization for OF Buck McNabb (April 27, 1995).
STATISTICAL NOTES: Led South Atlantic catchers with nine double plays in 1993. ... Tied for Texas League lead with four intentional bases on balls in 1997.

Year Team (League)	Pos.	G	AB	R	H	2B	3B	HR	RBI	Avg.	BB	SO	SB	PO	A	E	Avg.
1992— Burlington (Appal.).....	C	43	126	23	29	7	0	3	16	.230	29	36	3	227	29	4	.985
1993— Columbus (S. Atl.)......	C	101	342	36	84	18	3	3	47	.246	35	69	1	639	87	7	.990
1994— Kinston (Carolina)	C	100	319	36	77	16	1	3	41	.241	49	62	3	458	40	6	.988
1995— Kinston (Carolina)	C	8	29	5	7	5	0	0	2	.241	2	9	0	58	6	1	.985
— Kissimmee (Fla. St.)■	C	78	261	23	56	18	1	3	31	.215	27	33	3	443	40	10	.980
1996— Kissimmee (Fla. St.) ...	C	74	231	29	77	19	0	1	31	.333	29	26	1	315	27	9	.974
— Jackson (Texas)	C	38	134	18	42	11	0	0	21	.313	18	24	0	207	18	5	.978
1997— Jackson (Texas)	C	73	241	49	82	18	0	14	46	.340	31	39	1	356	43	6	.985
— New Orleans (A.A.).....	C	51	172	22	43	7	0	3	21	.250	25	38	0	323	26	4	.989

MENDOZA, CARLOS   OF   DEVIL RAYS

PERSONAL: Born November 4, 1974, in Ciudad Bolivar, Venezuela ... 5-11/160. ... Bats left, throws left.
TRANSACTIONS/CAREER NOTES: Signed as non-drafted free agent by New York Mets organization (November 10, 1992). ... On disabled list (May 27-June 9, 1996). ... On Binghamton disabled list (April 17-June 22, 1997). ... Selected by Tampa Bay Devil Rays in second round (52nd pick overall) of expansion draft (November 18, 1997).

Year Team (League)	Pos.	G	AB	R	H	2B	3B	HR	RBI	Avg.	BB	SO	SB	PO	A	E	Avg.
1993— Dominican Mets (DSL)	OF	36	96	25	23	1	0	1	14	.240	23	10	7	17	3	1	.952
1994— Dominican Mets (DSL)	OF	67	197	66	69	11	1	1	25	.350	68	13	15	74	6	3	.964
1995— Kingsport (Appal.)......	OF	51	179	*56	63	9	0	1	24	.328	27	24	28	54	4	3	.951
1996— Columbia (South Atlantic)	OF	85	304	61	102	10	2	0	37	*.336	57	47	31	54	6	2	.968
1997— Binghamton (East.)	OF	59	228	36	87	12	2	1	13	.382	14	25	14	79	5	1	.988
— Norfolk (Int'l)	OF	10	35	3	5	0	1	0	0	.143	3	4	1	17	0	0	1.000
— New York (N.L.)..........	OF	15	12	6	3	0	0	0	1	.250	4	2	0	5	0	0	1.000
Major league totals (1 year)		15	12	6	3	0	0	0	1	.250	4	2	0	5	0	0	1.000

MENDOZA, RAMIRO   P   YANKEES

PERSONAL: Born June 15, 1972, in Los Santos, Panama. ... 6-2/154. ... Throws right, bats right.
TRANSACTIONS/CAREER NOTES: Signed as non-drafted free agent by New York Yankees organization (November 13, 1991).

Year Team (League)	W	L	Pct.	ERA	G	GS	CG	ShO	Sv.	IP	H	R	ER	BB	SO
1992— Dominican Yankees (DSL)..	10	2	.833	2.13	15	15	5	0	0	109²/₃	93	37	26	28	79
1993— GC Yankees (GCL)..............	4	5	.444	2.79	15	9	0	0	1	67²/₃	59	26	21	7	61
— Greensboro (S. Atl.)	0	1	.000	2.45	2	0	0	0	0	3²/₃	3	1	1	5	3
1994— Tampa (Florida State)	12	6	.667	3.01	22	21	1	0	0	134¹/₃	133	54	45	35	110
1995— Norwich (Eastern)	5	6	.455	3.21	19	19	2	1	0	89²/₃	87	39	32	33	68
— Columbus (Int'l)	1	0	1.000	2.57	2	2	0	0	0	14	10	4	4	2	13
1996— Columbus (Int'l)	6	2	.750	2.51	15	15	0	0	0	97	96	30	27	19	61
— New York (A.L.).■	4	5	.444	6.79	12	11	0	0	0	53	80	43	40	10	34
1997— Columbus (Int'l)	0	0	. . .	5.68	1	1	0	0	0	6¹/₃	7	6	4	1	4
— New York (A.L.)................	8	6	.571	4.24	39	15	0	0	2	133²/₃	157	67	63	28	82
Major league totals (2 years)......	12	11	.522	4.97	51	26	0	0	2	186²/₃	237	110	103	38	116

DIVISION SERIES RECORD

Year Team (League)	W	L	Pct.	ERA	G	GS	CG	ShO	Sv.	IP	H	R	ER	BB	SO
1997— New York (A.L.).................	1	1	.500	2.45	2	0	0	0	0	3²/₃	3	1	1	0	2

MENHART, PAUL   P   PADRES

PERSONAL: Born March 25, 1969, in St. Louis. ... 6-2/190. ... Throws right, bats right. ... Full name: Paul Gerard Menhart.
HIGH SCHOOL: Robert E. Fitch Senior (Groton, Conn.).
COLLEGE: Western Carolina.
TRANSACTIONS/CAREER NOTES: Selected by Toronto Blue Jays organization in ninth round of free-agent draft (June 4, 1990). ... On disabled list (August 12-27, 1993 and March 26, 1994-entire season). ... Traded by Blue Jays with P Edwin Hurtado to Seattle Mariners for P Bill Risley and 2B Miguel Cairo (December 18, 1995). ... On Seattle disabled list (August 14, 1996-remainder of season). ... Traded by Mariners to San Diego Padres for P Andres Berumen (June 10, 1997).
STATISTICAL NOTES: Pitched 1-0 one-hit, complete-game loss for Toronto against Baltimore (August 2, 1995).

M

Year Team (League)	W	L	Pct.	ERA	G	GS	CG	ShO	Sv.	IP	H	R	ER	BB	SO
1990— St. Catharines (NYP)	0	5	.000	4.05	8	8	0	0	0	40	34	27	18	19	38
— Myrtle Beach (SAL)	3	0	1.000	0.59	5	4	1	0	0	30 2/3	18	5	2	5	18
1991— Dunedin (Fla. St.)	10	6	.625	2.66	20	20	3	0	0	128 1/3	114	42	38	34	114
1992— Knoxville (Southern)	10	11	.476	3.85	28	28	2	1	0	177 2/3	181	85	76	38	104
1993— Syracuse (Int'l)	9	10	.474	3.64	25	25	4	0	0	151	143	74	61	67	108
1994—								Did not play.							
1995— Toronto (A.L.)	1	4	.200	4.92	21	9	1	0	0	78 2/3	72	49	43	47	50
— Syracuse (Int'l)	2	4	.333	6.31	10	10	0	0	0	51 1/3	62	42	36	25	30
1996— Seattle (A.L.)■	2	2	.500	7.29	11	6	0	0	0	42	55	36	34	25	18
— Tacoma (PCL)	0	3	.000	11.08	6	6	0	0	0	26	53	33	32	16	12
1997— Tacoma (PCL)	4	7	.364	6.16	15	10	0	0	1	61 1/3	76	46	42	34	51
— Las Vegas (PCL)■	0	7	.000	5.97	11	11	1	0	0	66 1/3	78	46	44	21	44
— San Diego (N.L.)	2	3	.400	4.70	9	8	0	0	0	44	42	23	23	13	22
A.L. totals (2 years)	3	6	.333	5.74	32	15	1	0	0	120 2/3	127	85	77	72	68
N.L. totals (1 year)	2	3	.400	4.70	9	8	0	0	0	44	42	23	23	13	22
Major league totals (3 years)	5	9	.357	5.47	41	23	1	0	0	164 2/3	169	108	100	85	90

MERCADO, HECTOR — P — METS

PERSONAL: Born April 29, 1974, in Catano, Puerto Rico. ... 6-3/205. ... Throws left, bats left.
HIGH SCHOOL: Jose S. Alegria (Dorado, Puerto Rico).
TRANSACTIONS/CAREER NOTES: Selected by Houston Astros organization in 13th round of free-agent draft (June 1, 1992). ... Selected by Florida Marlins organization in Rule 5 minor league draft (December 9, 1996). ... Selected by Philadelphia Phillies from Marlins organization in Rule 5 major league draft (December 15, 1997). ... Traded by Phillies to New York Mets for P Mike Welch (December 15, 1997).

Year Team (League)	W	L	Pct.	ERA	G	GS	CG	ShO	Sv.	IP	H	R	ER	BB	SO
1992— GC Astros (GCL)	1	2	.333	4.20	13	3	0	0	0	30	22	17	14	36	
1993— GC Astros (GCL)	5	4	.556	2.42	11	11	1	1	0	67	49	26	18	29	59
— Osceola (Florida St.)	1	1	.500	5.19	2	2	0	0	0	8 2/3	9	7	5	6	5
1994— Osceola (Florida St.)	6	•13	.316	3.95	25	25	1	1	0	136 2/3	123	75	60	79	88
1995— Kissimmee (Florida State)..	6	8	.429	3.46	19	17	2	0	0	104	96	50	40	37	75
— Jackson (Texas)	1	4	.200	7.80	8	7	0	0	0	30	36	33	26	32	20
1996— Kissimmee (Florida State)..	3	5	.375	4.16	56	0	0	0	3	80	78	43	37	48	68
1997— Portland (Eastern)■	11	3	.786	3.96	31	17	1	1	0	129 2/3	129	66	57	54	125
— Charlotte (Int'l)	0	1	.000	9.00	1	1	0	0	0	5	5	5	5	5	1

MERCED, ORLANDO — OF/1B — TWINS

PERSONAL: Born November 2, 1966, in San Juan, Puerto Rico. ... 5-11/190. ... Bats left, throws right. ... Full name: Orlando Luis Merced. ... Name pronounced mer-SED.
HIGH SCHOOL: University Garden (San Juan, Puerto Rico).
TRANSACTIONS/CAREER NOTES: Signed as non-drafted free agent by Pittsburgh Pirates organization (February 22, 1985). ... On Macon disabled list (April 18-28, 1987). ... On Watertown disabled list (June 23, 1987-remainder of season). ... On disabled list (May 1-18, August 1-16 and August 22-September 6, 1996). ... Traded by Pirates with IF Carlos Garcia and P Dan Plesac to Toronto Blue Jays for P Jose Silva, P Jose Pett, IF Brandon Cromer and three players to be named later (November 14, 1996); Pirates acquired P Mike Halperin, IF Abraham Nunez and C/OF Craig Wilson to complete deal (December 11, 1996). ... On disabled list (July 29-September 28, 1997). ... Granted free agency (October 27, 1997). ... Signed by Minnesota Twins organization (January 12, 1998).
STATISTICAL NOTES: Led N.L. outfielders in double plays with five in 1993 and five in 1996. ... Career major league grand slams: 2.
MISCELLANEOUS: Batted as switch-hitter (1985-92).

Year Team (League)	Pos.	G	AB	R	H	2B	3B	HR	RBI	Avg.	BB	SO	SB	PO	A	E	Avg.
1985— GC Pirates (GCL)	SS-3B-1B	40	136	16	31	6	0	1	13	.228	9	9	3	46	78	28	.816
1986— Macon (S. Atl.)	OF-3B	65	173	20	34	4	1	2	24	.197	12	38	5	53	15	13	.840
— Watertown (NYP)	3B-1B-OF	27	89	12	16	0	1	3	9	.180	14	21	6	49	28	10	.885
1987— Macon (S. Atl.)	OF	4	4	1	0	0	0	0	0	.000	1	3	0	1	1	0	1.000
— Watertown (NYP)	2B	4	12	4	5	0	1	0	3	.417	1	1	1	11	7	2	.900
1988— Augusta (S. Atl.)	2B-3B-SS	37	136	19	36	6	3	1	17	.265	7	20	2	35	39	7	.914
— Salem (Carolina)	3-2-O-S	80	298	47	87	12	7	7	42	.292	27	64	13	77	183	31	.893
1989— Harrisburg (Eastern) ..	1B-OF-3B	95	341	43	82	16	4	6	48	.240	32	66	13	435	32	10	.979
— Buffalo (A.A.)	1B-OF-3B	35	129	18	44	5	3	1	16	.341	7	26	0	173	15	3	.984
1990— Buffalo (A.A.)	1B-3B-OF	101	378	52	99	12	6	9	55	.262	46	63	14	689	83	20	.975
— Pittsburgh (N.L.)	OF-C	25	24	3	5	1	0	0	0	.208	1	9	0	4	1	0	1.000
1991— Buffalo (A.A.)	1B	3	12	1	2	0	0	0	0	.167	1	4	1	29	2	0	1.000
— Pittsburgh (N.L.)	1B-OF	120	411	83	113	17	2	10	50	.275	64	81	8	916	60	12	.988
1992— Pittsburgh (N.L.)	1B-OF	134	405	50	100	28	5	6	60	.247	52	63	5	906	75	5	.995
1993— Pittsburgh (N.L.)	OF-1B	137	447	68	140	26	4	8	70	.313	77	64	3	485	31	10	.981
1994— Pittsburgh (N.L.)	OF-1B	108	386	48	105	21	3	9	51	.272	42	58	4	508	29	5	.991
1995— Pittsburgh (N.L.)	OF-1B	132	487	75	146	29	4	15	83	.300	52	74	7	374	23	6	.985
1996— Pittsburgh (N.L.)	OF-1B	120	453	69	130	24	1	17	80	.287	51	74	8	242	15	3	.988
1997— Toronto (A.L.)■	OF-DH-1B	98	368	45	98	23	2	9	40	.266	47	62	7	193	10	3	.985
American League totals (1 year)		98	368	45	98	23	2	9	40	.266	47	62	7	193	10	3	.985
National League totals (7 years)		776	2613	396	739	146	19	65	394	.283	339	423	35	3431	233	41	.989
Major league totals (8 years)		874	2981	441	837	169	21	74	434	.281	386	485	42	3624	243	44	.989

CHAMPIONSHIP SERIES RECORD

NOTES: Hit home run in first at-bat (October 12, 1991).

Year Team (League)	Pos.	G	AB	R	H	2B	3B	HR	RBI	Avg.	BB	SO	SB	PO	A	E	Avg.
1991— Pittsburgh (N.L.)	1B-PH	3	9	1	2	0	0	1	1	.222	0	1	0	13	0	1	.929
1992— Pittsburgh (N.L.)	1B-PH	4	10	0	1	1	0	0	2	.100	2	4	0	27	2	1	.967
Championship series totals (2 years)		7	19	1	3	1	0	1	3	.158	2	5	0	40	2	2	.955

M

MERCEDES, HENRY   C   GIANTS

PERSONAL: Born July 23, 1969, in Santo Domingo, Dominican Republic. ... 6-1/210. ... Bats right, throws right. ... Full name: Henry Felipe Perez Mercedes.

TRANSACTIONS/CAREER NOTES: Signed as non-drafted free agent by Oakland Athletics organization (June 22, 1987). ... Granted free agency (October 15, 1994). ... Signed by Omaha, Kansas City Royals organization (November 11, 1994). ... Granted free agency (October 12, 1996). ... Signed by Texas Rangers (November 18, 1996). ... Granted free agency (October 27, 1997). ... Signed by San Francisco Giants organization (January 12, 1998).

STATISTICAL NOTES: Led California League catchers with 21 errors in 1991. ... Led Pacific Coast League catchers with 12 errors and 10 double plays in 1993.

Year Team (League)	Pos.	G	AB	R	H	2B	3B	HR	RBI	Avg.	BB	SO	SB	PO	A	E	Avg.
1987—																	
1988—Arizona A's (Ariz.).......	C	2	5	1	2	0	0	0	0	.400	0	0	0	13	2	0	1.000
1989—S. Oregon (N'west).......	C-3B	22	61	6	10	0	1	0	1	.164	10	24	0	129	15	3	.980
—Modesto (California) ..	C	16	37	6	3	0	0	1	3	.081	7	22	0	81	9	4	.957
—Madison (Midwest)	C	51	152	11	32	3	0	2	13	.211	22	46	0	304	40	5	.986
1990—Madison (Midwest) ..	C-3-2-O	90	282	29	64	13	2	3	37	.227	30	100	6	555	110	9	.987
—Tacoma (PCL)	C	12	31	3	6	1	0	0	2	.194	3	7	0	46	4	0	1.000
1991—Modesto (California)..	C-3B-P	116	388	55	100	17	3	4	61	.258	68	110	5	551	86	†24	.964
1992—Tacoma (PCL)	C	85	246	36	57	9	2	0	20	.232	26	60	1	476	62	9	.984
—Oakland (A.L.)	C	9	5	1	4	0	1	0	1	.800	0	1	0	7	0	1	.875
1993—Tacoma (PCL)	C-3B-OF	85	256	37	61	13	1	4	32	.238	31	53	1	332	74	†18	.958
—Oakland (A.L.)	C-DH	20	47	5	10	2	0	0	3	.213	2	15	1	66	10	1	.987
1994—Tacoma (PCL)	C-3-1-O	66	205	16	39	5	1	1	17	.190	13	60	1	216	33	8	.969
1995—Omaha (A.A.)■	C-3B	86	275	37	59	12	0	11	37	.215	22	90	2	419	71	8	.984
—Kansas City (A.L.)	C	23	43	7	11	2	0	0	9	.256	8	13	0	62	8	1	.986
1996—Omaha (A.A.).........	C-P	72	223	28	48	9	1	8	35	.215	28	60	0	401	49	3	.993
—Kansas City (A.L.)	C	4	4	1	1	0	0	0	0	.250	0	1	0	2	0	0	1.000
1997—Texas (A.L.)■.........	C	23	47	4	10	4	0	0	4	.213	6	25	0	78	4	1	.988
—Oklahoma City (A.A.)..	C	16	57	6	14	3	0	1	4	.246	9	12	0	78	13	1	.989
Major league totals (5 years)		**79**	**146**	**18**	**36**	**8**	**1**	**0**	**17**	**.247**	**16**	**55**	**1**	**215**	**22**	**4**	**.983**

RECORD AS PITCHER

Year Team (League)	W	L	Pct.	ERA	G	GS	CG	ShO	Sv.	IP	H	R	ER	BB	SO
1991—Modesto (California)	0	1	.000	81.00	1	0	0	0	0	1	4	9	9	6	2
1996—Omaha (Am. Assoc.)..........	0	0	...	0.00	72	0	0	0	0	1 1/3	0	0	0	0	0

MERCEDES, JOSE   P   BREWERS

PERSONAL: Born March 5, 1971, in El Seibo, Dominican Republic. ... 6-1/199. ... Throws right, bats right. ... Full name: Jose Miguel Mercedes.

TRANSACTIONS/CAREER NOTES: Signed as non-drafted free agent by Baltimore Orioles organization (August 10, 1989). ... Selected by Milwaukee Brewers from Orioles organization in Rule 5 major league draft (December 13, 1993). ... On Milwaukee disabled list (April 2-May 30, 1994); included rehabilitation assignments to El Paso (April 30-May 14) and New Orleans (May 14-28). ... On disabled list (May 14, 1995-remainder of season).

Year Team (League)	W	L	Pct.	ERA	G	GS	CG	ShO	Sv.	IP	H	R	ER	BB	SO
1990—															
1991—															
1992—GC Orioles (GCL)........	2	3	.400	1.78	8	5	2	0	0	35 1/3	31	12	7	13	21
—Kane County (Midwest)......	3	2	.600	2.66	8	8	2	•2	0	47 1/3	40	26	14	15	45
1993—Bowie (Eastern).................	6	8	.429	4.78	26	23	3	0	0	147	170	86	78	65	75
1994—El Paso (Texas)■.............	2	0	1.000	4.66	3	0	0	0	0	9 2/3	13	6	5	4	8
—New Orleans (A.A.).............	0	0	...	4.91	3	3	0	0	0	18 1/3	19	10	10	8	7
—Milwaukee (A.L.).................	2	0	1.000	2.32	19	0	0	0	0	31	22	9	8	16	11
1995—Milwaukee (A.L.).................	0	1	.000	9.82	5	0	0	0	0	7 1/3	12	9	8	8	6
1996—New Orleans (A.A.).............	3	7	.300	3.56	25	15	0	0	1	101	109	58	40	28	47
—Milwaukee (A.L.).................	0	2	.000	9.18	11	0	0	0	0	16 2/3	20	18	17	5	6
1997—Milwaukee (A.L.).................	7	10	.412	3.79	29	23	2	1	0	159	146	76	67	53	80
Major league totals (4 years)......	**9**	**13**	**.409**	**4.21**	**64**	**23**	**2**	**1**	**0**	**214**	**200**	**112**	**100**	**82**	**103**

MERCKER, KENT   P   CARDINALS

PERSONAL: Born February 1, 1968, in Dublin, Ohio. ... 6-2/195. ... Throws left, bats left. ... Full name: Kent Franklin Mercker.

HIGH SCHOOL: Dublin (Ohio).

TRANSACTIONS/CAREER NOTES: Selected by Atlanta Braves organization in first round (fifth pick overall) of free-agent draft (June 2, 1986). ... On Richmond disabled list (March 30-May 6, 1990). ... On disabled list (August 9-24, 1991). ... Traded by Braves to Baltimore Orioles for P Joe Borowski and P Rachaad Stewart (December 17, 1995). ... Traded by Orioles to Cleveland Indians for 1B Eddie Murray (July 21, 1996). ... Granted free agency (November 4, 1996). ... Signed by Cincinnati Reds (December 10, 1996). ... On disabled list (August 17-September 2, 1997). ... Granted free agency (October 27, 1997). ... Signed by St. Louis Cardinals (December 16, 1997).

HONORS: Named Carolina League co-Pitcher of the Year (1988).

STATISTICAL NOTES: Pitched six innings, combining with Mark Wohlers (two innings) and Alejandro Pena (one inning) in 1-0 no-hit victory against San Diego (September 11, 1991). ... Pitched 6-0 no-hit victory against Los Angeles (April 8, 1994).

MISCELLANEOUS: Had a sacrifice hit and received a base on balls in two games as pinch-hitter (1991). ... Appeared in one game as pinch-runner (1997).

Year Team (League)	W	L	Pct.	ERA	G	GS	CG	ShO	Sv.	IP	H	R	ER	BB	SO
1986—GC Braves (GCL)...............	4	3	.571	2.47	9	8	0	0	0	47 1/3	37	21	13	16	42
1987—Durham (Carolina).............	0	1	.000	5.40	3	3	0	0	0	11 2/3	11	8	7	6	14

M

Year Team (League)	W	L	Pct.	ERA	G	GS	CG	ShO	Sv.	IP	H	R	ER	BB	SO
1988—Durham (Carolina)...........	11	4	.733	*2.75	19	19	5	0	0	127²/₃	102	44	39	47	159
— Greenville (Southern)........	3	1	.750	3.35	9	9	0	0	0	48¹/₃	36	20	18	26	60
1989—Richmond (Int'l)..........	9	12	.429	3.20	27	•27	4	0	0	168²/₃	107	66	60	*95	*144
—Atlanta (N.L.)................	0	0	...	12.46	2	1	0	0	0	4¹/₃	8	6	6	6	4
1990—Richmond (Int'l)..........	5	4	.556	3.55	12	10	0	0	1	58¹/₃	60	30	23	27	69
—Atlanta (N.L.)................	4	7	.364	3.17	36	0	0	0	7	48¹/₃	43	22	17	24	39
1991—Atlanta (N.L.)............	5	3	.625	2.58	50	4	0	0	6	73¹/₃	56	23	21	35	62
1992—Atlanta (N.L.)............	3	2	.600	3.42	53	0	0	0	6	68¹/₃	51	27	26	35	49
1993—Atlanta (N.L.)............	3	1	.750	2.86	43	6	0	0	0	66	52	24	21	36	59
1994—Atlanta (N.L.)............	9	4	.692	3.45	20	17	2	1	0	112¹/₃	90	46	43	45	111
1995—Atlanta (N.L.)............	7	8	.467	4.15	29	26	0	0	0	143	140	73	66	61	102
1996—Baltimore (A.L.)■....	3	6	.333	7.76	14	12	0	0	0	58	73	56	50	35	22
—Buffalo (A.A.)■....	0	2	.000	3.94	3	3	0	0	0	16	11	7	7	9	11
—Cleveland (A.L.)....	1	0	1.000	3.09	10	0	0	0	0	11²/₃	10	7	7	9	11
1997—Cincinnati (N.L.)■....	8	11	.421	3.92	28	25	0	0	0	144²/₃	135	65	63	62	75
A.L. totals (1 year)...........	4	6	.400	6.98	24	12	0	0	0	69²/₃	83	60	54	38	29
N.L. totals (8 years).........	39	36	.520	3.58	261	79	2	1	19	660¹/₃	575	286	263	304	501
Major league totals (9 years).....	43	42	.506	3.91	285	91	2	1	19	730	658	346	317	342	530

DIVISION SERIES RECORD

Year Team (League)	W	L	Pct.	ERA	G	GS	CG	ShO	Sv.	IP	H	R	ER	BB	SO
1995—Atlanta (N.L.).....................	0	0	...	0.00	1	0	0	0	0	¹/₃	0	0	0	0	0

CHAMPIONSHIP SERIES RECORD

Year Team (League)	W	L	Pct.	ERA	G	GS	CG	ShO	Sv.	IP	H	R	ER	BB	SO
1991—Atlanta (N.L.).....................	0	1	.000	13.50	1	0	0	0	0	²/₃	0	1	1	2	0
1992—Atlanta (N.L.).....................	0	0	...	0.00	2	0	0	0	0	3	1	0	1	1	1
1993—Atlanta (N.L.).....................	0	0	...	1.80	5	0	0	0	0	5	3	1	1	2	4
Champ. series totals (3 years)....	0	1	.000	2.08	8	0	0	0	0	8²/₃	4	2	2	5	5

WORLD SERIES RECORD

NOTES: Member of World Series championship team (1995).

Year Team (League)	W	L	Pct.	ERA	G	GS	CG	ShO	Sv.	IP	H	R	ER	BB	SO
1991—Atlanta (N.L.).....................	0	0	...	0.00	2	0	0	0	0	1	0	0	0	0	1
1995—Atlanta (N.L.).....................	0	0	...	4.50	1	0	0	0	0	2	1	1	1	1	2
World Series totals (2 years)......	0	0	...	3.00	3	0	0	0	0	3	1	1	1	2	3

MESA, JOSE P INDIANS

PERSONAL: Born May 22, 1966, in Azua, Dominican Republic. ... 6-3/230. ... Throws right, bats right. ... Full name: Jose Ramon Mesa.
HIGH SCHOOL: Santa School (Azua, Dominican Republic).
TRANSACTIONS/CAREER NOTES: Signed as non-drafted free agent by Toronto Blue Jays organization (October 31, 1981). ... On Kinston disabled list (August 27, 1984-remainder of season). ... Traded by Blue Jays organization to Baltimore Orioles (September 4, 1987), completing deal in which Orioles traded P Mike Flanagan to Blue Jays for P Oswald Peraza and a player to be named later (August 31, 1987). ... On Rochester disabled list (April 18-May 16 and June 30, 1988-remainder of season; May 27, 1989-remainder of season; and August 21-September 5, 1991). ... Traded by Orioles to Cleveland Indians for OF Kyle Washington (July 14, 1992). ... On suspended list (April 5-8, 1993).
HONORS: Named A.L. Fireman of the Year by THE SPORTING NEWS (1995).
STATISTICAL NOTES: Tied for Carolina League lead with nine hit batsmen in 1985.
MISCELLANEOUS: Appeared in one game as pinch-runner for Baltimore (1991).

Year Team (League)	W	L	Pct.	ERA	G	GS	CG	ShO	Sv.	IP	H	R	ER	BB	SO
1982—GC Blue Jays (GCL)........	6	4	.600	2.70	13	12	6	*3	1	83¹/₃	58	34	25	20	40
1983—Florence (S. Atl.)	6	12	.333	5.48	28	27	1	0	0	141¹/₃	153	*116	86	93	91
1984—Florence (S. Atl.)	4	3	.571	3.76	7	7	0	0	0	38¹/₃	38	24	16	25	35
— Kinston (Carolina)	5	2	.714	3.91	10	9	0	0	0	50²/₃	51	23	22	28	24
1985—Kinston (Carolina)	5	10	.333	6.16	30	20	0	0	1	106²/₃	110	89	73	79	71
1986—Vent. County (Cal.)...........	10	6	.625	3.86	24	24	2	1	0	142¹/₃	141	71	61	58	113
—Knoxville (Southern)	2	2	.500	4.35	9	8	2	1	0	41¹/₃	40	32	20	23	30
1987—Knoxville (Southern)	10	•13	.435	5.21	35	*35	4	2	0	*193¹/₃	*206	*131	*112	104	115
—Baltimore (A.L.)■............	1	3	.250	6.03	6	5	0	0	0	31¹/₃	38	23	21	15	17
1988—Rochester (Int'l)...........	0	3	.000	8.62	11	2	0	0	0	15²/₃	21	20	15	14	15
1989—Rochester (Int'l)...........	0	2	.000	5.40	7	1	0	0	0	10	10	6	6	6	3
—Hagerstown (Eastern)	0	0	...	1.38	3	3	0	0	0	13	9	2	2	4	12
1990—Hagerstown (Eastern)	5	5	.500	3.42	15	15	3	1	0	79	77	35	30	30	72
—Rochester (Int'l)...........	1	2	.333	2.42	4	4	0	0	0	26	21	11	7	12	23
—Baltimore (A.L.)....	3	2	.600	3.86	7	7	0	0	0	46²/₃	37	20	20	27	24
1991—Baltimore (A.L.)....	6	11	.353	5.97	23	23	2	1	0	123²/₃	151	86	82	62	64
—Rochester (Int'l)...........	3	3	.500	3.86	8	8	1	1	0	51¹/₃	37	25	22	30	48
1992—Baltimore (A.L.)....	3	8	.273	5.19	13	12	0	0	0	67²/₃	77	41	39	27	22
—Cleveland (A.L.)■....	4	4	.500	4.16	15	15	1	1	0	93	92	45	43	43	40
1993—Cleveland (A.L.)....	10	12	.455	4.92	34	33	3	0	0	208²/₃	232	122	114	62	118
1994—Cleveland (A.L.)....	7	5	.583	3.82	51	0	0	0	0	73	71	33	31	26	63
1995—Cleveland (A.L.)....	3	0	1.000	1.13	62	0	0	0	*46	64	49	9	8	17	58
1996—Cleveland (A.L.)....	2	7	.222	3.73	69	0	0	0	39	72¹/₃	69	32	30	28	64
1997—Cleveland (A.L.)....	4	4	.500	2.40	66	0	0	0	16	82¹/₃	83	28	22	28	69
Major league totals (9 years)......	43	56	.434	4.28	346	95	6	2	103	862²/₃	899	439	410	335	539

DIVISION SERIES RECORD

Year Team (League)	W	L	Pct.	ERA	G	GS	CG	ShO	Sv.	IP	H	R	ER	BB	SO
1995—Cleveland (A.L.)........	0	0	...	0.00	2	0	0	0	0	2	0	0	0	2	0
1996—Cleveland (A.L.)........	0	1	.000	3.86	2	0	0	0	0	4²/₃	8	2	2	0	7
1997—Cleveland (A.L.)........	0	0	...	2.70	2	0	0	0	1	3¹/₃	5	1	1	1	2
Div. series totals (3 years)	0	1	.000	2.70	6	0	0	0	1	10	13	3	3	3	9

CHAMPIONSHIP SERIES RECORD

Year Team (League)	W	L	Pct.	ERA	G	GS	CG	ShO	Sv.	IP	H	R	ER	BB	SO
1995— Cleveland (A.L.)	0	0	...	2.25	4	0	0	0	1	4	3	1	1	1	1
1997— Cleveland (A.L.)	1	0	1.000	3.38	4	0	0	0	2	5 1/3	5	2	2	3	5
Champ. series totals (2 years)	1	0	1.000	2.89	8	0	0	0	3	9 1/3	8	3	3	4	6

WORLD SERIES RECORD

Year Team (League)	W	L	Pct.	ERA	G	GS	CG	ShO	Sv.	IP	H	R	ER	BB	SO
1995— Cleveland (A.L.)	1	0	1.000	4.50	2	0	0	0	1	4	5	2	2	1	4
1997— Cleveland (A.L.)	0	0	...	5.40	5	0	0	0	1	5	10	3	3	1	5
World Series totals (2 years)	1	0	1.000	5.00	7	0	0	0	2	9	15	5	5	2	9

ALL-STAR GAME RECORD

Year League	W	L	Pct.	ERA	GS	CG	ShO	Sv.	IP	H	R	ER	BB	SO
1995— American	0	0	...	0.00	0	0	0	0	1	0	0	0	0	1
1996— American							Did not play.							
All-Star totals (1 year)	0	0	...	0.00	0	0	0	0	1	0	0	0	0	1

METCALFE, MIKE   2B   DODGERS

PERSONAL: Born January 2, 1973, in Qunatico, Va. ... 5-10/175. ... Bats right, throws right. ... Full name: Michael Henry Metcalfe Jr.
HIGH SCHOOL: Colonial (Orlando).
COLLEGE: Miami (Fla.).
TRANSACTIONS/CAREER NOTES: Selected by Los Angeles Dodgers organization in third round of free-agent draft (June 2, 1994). ... On disabled list (June 17-August 23 and August 27, 1996-remainder of season).
STATISTICAL NOTES: Led Florida State League in caught stealing with 27 in 1995. ... Led California League in caught stealing with 32 in 1997.

										BATTING					FIELDING		
Year Team (League)	Pos.	G	AB	R	H	2B	3B	HR	RBI	Avg.	BB	SO	SB	PO	A	E	Avg.
1994— Bakersfield (Calif.)	SS	69	275	44	78	10	0	0	18	.284	28	34	41	98	208	17	.947
1995— San Antonio (Tex.)	SS	10	41	10	10	1	0	0	2	.244	7	2	1	14	31	2	.957
— Vero Beach (FSL)	SS	120	435	86	131	13	3	3	35	.301	60	37	*60	153	301	*40	.919
1996— Vero Beach (FSL)	DH	2	5	0	0	0	0	0	0	.000	0	0	0	...	...	...	...
1997— San Bern. (Calif.)	2B	132	519	83	147	28	7	3	47	.283	55	79	67	*228	324	12	*.979

MEULENS, HENSLEY   OF

PERSONAL: Born June 23, 1967, in Curacao, Netherlands Antilles. ... 6-3/210. ... Bats right, throws right. ... Full name: Hensley Filemon Meulens.
TRANSACTIONS/CAREER NOTES: Signed as non-drafted free agent by New York Yankees organization (October 31, 1985). ... Released by Yankees (November 26, 1993). ... Signed by Chiba Lotte Marines of Japan Pacific League (November 26, 1993). ... Signed by Yakult Swallows of Japan Central League for 1995 and 1996 seasons. ... Signed by Atlanta Braves organization (December 20, 1996). ... Released by Braves (March 20, 1997). ... Signed by Montreal Expos organization (April 17, 1997). ... Granted free agency (October 6, 1997).
HONORS: Named International League Most Valuable Player (1990).
STATISTICAL NOTES: Led Gulf Coast League third basemen with 178 total chances in 1986. ... Tied for Eastern League lead in double plays by third baseman with 18 in 1988. ... Tied for Eastern League lead in being hit by pitch with nine in 1989. ... Led International League with 245 total bases in 1990 and 257 in 1992. ... Led International League third basemen with 88 putouts, 30 errors and 373 total chances in 1992.

										BATTING					FIELDING		
Year Team (League)	Pos.	G	AB	R	H	2B	3B	HR	RBI	Avg.	BB	SO	SB	PO	A	E	Avg.
1986— GC Yankees (GCL)	3B	59	219	36	51	10	4	4	31	.233	28	*66	4	*40	*118	20	.888
1987— Prince William (Car.)	3B-OF	116	430	76	129	23	2	28	103	.300	53	124	14	96	224	*37	.896
— Fort Lauderdale (FSL)	3B	17	58	2	10	3	0	0	2	.172	7	25	0	18	37	7	.887
1988— Alb./Colon. (Eastern)	3B	79	278	50	68	9	1	13	40	.245	37	96	3	57	162	23	.905
— Columbus (Int'l)	3B	55	209	27	48	9	1	6	22	.230	14	61	0	39	114	11	.915
1989— Alb./Colon. (Eastern)	3B	104	335	55	86	8	2	11	45	.257	61	108	3	67	172	*29	.892
— Columbus (Int'l)	3B	14	45	8	13	4	0	1	3	.289	8	13	0	11	27	3	.927
— New York (A.L.)	3B	8	28	2	5	0	0	0	1	.179	2	8	0	5	23	4	.875
1990— Columbus (Int'l)	OF-1B-3B	136	480	81	137	20	5	26	96	.285	66	132	6	359	51	13	.969
— New York (A.L.)	OF	23	83	12	20	7	0	3	10	.241	9	25	1	49	3	2	.963
1991— New York (A.L.)	OF-DH-1B	96	288	37	64	8	1	6	29	.222	18	97	3	179	5	6	.968
1992— Columbus (Int'l)	3B-2B	141	534	*96	147	28	2	*26	*100	.275	60	*168	15	†88	255	†30	.920
— New York (A.L.)	3B	2	5	1	3	0	0	1	1	.600	1	0	0	0	3	0	1.000
1993— Columbus (Int'l)	OF-1B-3B	75	279	39	57	14	0	14	45	.204	32	92	6	264	20	19	.937
— New York (A.L.)	OF-1B-3B	30	53	8	9	1	1	2	5	.170	8	19	0	32	0	0	1.000
1994— Chiba Lotte (Jp.Pc.)■	...	122	431	...	107	...	...	...	23	69	.248	...	...	8	...	...	...	...
1995— Yakult (Jp. Cent.)■	...	130	438	...	107	...	...	...	29	80	.244	...	...	6	...	...	...	...
1996— Yakult (Jp. Cent.)	...	128	439	...	108	...	...	...	25	67	.246	...	...	1	...	...	...	...
1997— W.P. Beach (FSL)■	3B	1	4	0	1	1	0	0	0	.250	0	2	0	0	2	0	1.000
— Ottawa (Int'l)	3B-1B-OF	121	423	81	116	20	2	24	75	.274	62	119	19	384	114	20	.961
— Montreal (N.L.)	OF-1B	16	24	6	7	1	0	2	6	.292	4	10	0	15	0	0	1.000
American League totals (5 years)		159	457	60	101	16	2	12	46	.221	38	149	4	265	34	12	.961
National League totals (1 year)		16	24	6	7	1	0	2	6	.292	4	10	0	15	0	0	1.000
Major league totals (6 years)		175	481	66	108	17	2	14	52	.225	42	159	4	280	34	12	.963

MICELI, DAN   P   PADRES

PERSONAL: Born September 9, 1970, in Newark, N.J. ... 6-0/216. ... Throws right, bats right. ... Full name: Daniel Miceli.
HIGH SCHOOL: Dr. Phillips (Orlando).

TRANSACTIONS/CAREER NOTES: Signed as non-drafted free agent by Kansas City Royals organization (March 7, 1990). ... Traded by Royals with P Jon Lieber to Pittsburgh Pirates for P Stan Belinda (July 31, 1993). ... Traded by Pirates to Detroit Tigers for P Clint Sodowsky (November 1, 1996). ... Traded by Tigers with P Donne Wall and 3B Ryan Balfe to San Diego Padres for P Tim Worrell and OF Trey Beamon (November 19, 1997).

Year Team (League)	W	L	Pct.	ERA	G	GS	CG	ShO	Sv.	IP	H	R	ER	BB	SO
1990— GC Royals (GCL)	3	4	.429	3.91	*27	0	0	0	4	53	45	27	23	29	48
1991— Eugene (Northwest)	0	1	.000	2.14	25	0	0	0	10	33²/₃	18	8	8	18	43
1992— Appleton (Midwest)	1	1	.500	1.93	23	0	0	0	9	23¹/₃	12	6	5	4	44
— Memphis (Southern)	3	0	1.000	1.91	32	0	0	0	4	37²/₃	20	10	8	13	46
1993— Memphis (Southern)	6	4	.600	4.60	40	0	0	0	7	58²/₃	54	30	30	39	68
— Carolina (Southern)■	0	2	.000	5.11	13	0	0	0	10	12¹/₃	11	8	7	4	19
— Pittsburgh (N.L.)	0	0	...	5.06	9	0	0	0	0	5¹/₃	6	3	3	3	4
1994— Buffalo (A.A.)	1	1	.500	1.88	19	0	0	0	2	24	15	5	5	6	31
— Pittsburgh (N.L.)	2	1	.667	5.93	28	0	0	0	2	27¹/₃	28	19	18	11	27
1995— Pittsburgh (N.L.)	4	4	.500	4.66	58	0	0	0	21	58	61	30	30	28	56
1996— Pittsburgh (N.L.)	2	10	.167	5.78	44	9	0	0	1	85²/₃	99	65	55	45	66
— Carolina (Southern)	1	0	1.000	1.00	3	0	0	0	1	9	4	1	1	1	17
1997— Detroit (A.L.)■	3	2	.600	5.01	71	0	0	0	3	82²/₃	77	49	46	38	79
A.L. totals (1 year)	3	2	.600	5.01	71	0	0	0	3	82²/₃	77	49	46	38	79
N.L. totals (4 years)	8	15	.348	5.41	139	9	0	0	24	176¹/₃	194	117	106	87	153
Major league totals (5 years)	11	17	.393	5.28	210	9	0	0	27	259	271	166	152	125	232

MIENTKIEWICZ, DOUG — 1B — TWINS

PERSONAL: Born June 19, 1974, in Toledo, Ohio. ... 6-2/195. ... Bats left, throws right. ... Full name: Douglas Andrew Mientkiewicz.
HIGH SCHOOL: Westminster Christian (Miami).
COLLEGE: Florida State.
TRANSACTIONS/CAREER NOTES: Selected by Minnesota Twins organization in fifth round of free-agent draft (June 1, 1995).
STATISTICAL NOTES: Led Florida State League first basemen with 1,271 total chances and 113 double plays in 1996. ... Led Eastern League first basemen with .995 fielding percentage in 1997.

Year Team (League)	Pos.	G	AB	R	H	2B	3B	HR	RBI	Avg.	BB	SO	SB	PO	A	E	Avg.
1995— Fort Myers (FSL)	1B	38	110	9	27	6	1	1	15	.245	18	19	2	160	12	1	.994
1996— Fort Myers (FSL)	1B	133	492	69	143	•36	4	5	79	.291	66	47	12	*1183	85	3	*.998
1997— New Britain (Eastern)	1B-OF	132	467	87	119	28	2	15	61	.255	*98	67	21	989	63	5	†.995

MIESKE, MATT — OF — CUBS

PERSONAL: Born February 13, 1968, in Midland, Mich. ... 6-0/192. ... Bats right, throws right. ... Full name: Matthew Todd Mieske. ... Name pronounced MEE-skee.
HIGH SCHOOL: Bay City Western (Auburn, Mich.).
COLLEGE: Western Michigan.
TRANSACTIONS/CAREER NOTES: Selected by Oakland Athletics organization in 20th round of free-agent draft (June 5, 1989); did not sign. ... Selected by San Diego Padres organization in 17th round of free-agent draft (June 4, 1990). ... Traded by Padres organization with P Ricky Bones and SS Jose Valentin to Milwaukee Brewers organization for 3B Gary Sheffield and P Geoff Kellogg (March 27, 1992). ... On New Orleans disabled list (May 25-June 10 and June 13-July 29, 1993). ... On disabled list (August 9-September 2, 1997). ... Granted free agency (December 21, 1997). ... Signed by Chicago Cubs (December 29, 1997).
HONORS: Named Northwest League Most Valuable Player (1990). ... Named California League Most Valuable Player (1991).
STATISTICAL NOTES: Led Northwest League with 155 total bases in 1990. ... Led Northwest League outfielders with 148 total chances in 1990. ... Led California League with 261 total bases and .456 on-base percentage in 1991. ... Career major league grand slams: 2.

Year Team (League)	Pos.	G	AB	R	H	2B	3B	HR	RBI	Avg.	BB	SO	SB	PO	A	E	Avg.
1990— Spokane (N'west)	OF	*76	*291	*59	99	20	0	*12	*63	.340	45	43	26	*134	7	7	.953
1991— High Desert (Calif.)	OF	•133	492	108	*168	*36	6	15	119	*.341	*94	82	39	258	14	*15	.948
1992— Denver (A.A.)	OF	134	*524	80	140	29	11	19	77	.267	39	90	13	252	*23	*13	.955
1993— New Orleans (A.A.)	OF	60	219	36	57	14	2	8	22	.260	27	46	6	114	4	2	.983
— Milwaukee (A.L.)	OF	23	58	9	14	0	0	3	7	.241	4	14	0	43	1	3	.936
1994— Milwaukee (A.L.)	OF-DH	84	259	39	67	13	1	10	38	.259	21	62	3	154	7	4	.976
— New Orleans (A.A.)	OF	2	8	2	2	0	0	1	3	.250	1	1	1	2	0	0	1.000
1995— Milwaukee (A.L.)	OF-DH	117	267	42	67	13	1	12	48	.251	27	45	2	177	7	4	.979
1996— Milwaukee (A.L.)	OF	127	374	46	104	24	3	14	64	.278	26	76	1	250	7	1	.996
1997— Milwaukee (A.L.)	OF-DH	84	253	39	63	15	3	5	21	.249	19	50	1	121	6	5	.962
Major league totals (5 years)		435	1211	175	315	65	8	44	178	.260	97	247	7	745	28	17	.978

MILLAR, KEVIN — 1B/3B — MARLINS

PERSONAL: Born September 24, 1971, in Los Angeles. ... 6-0/185. ... Bats right, throws right.
JUNIOR COLLEGE: Los Angeles Community College.
TRANSACTIONS/CAREER NOTES: Purchased by Florida Marlins organization from St. Paul of Northern League (September 20, 1993). ... Granted free agency (December 21, 1997). ... Re-signed by Marlins (December 21, 1997).
HONORS: Named Eastern League Player of the Year (1997).
STATISTICAL NOTES: Led Midwest League with 240 total bases in 1994. ... Led Florida State League with 10 sacrifice flies in 1995. ... Led Florida State League first basemen with 1,320 total chances in 1995. ... Led Eastern League with 309 total bases and .423 on-base percentage and tied for league lead with seven sacrifice flies in 1997. ... Led Eastern League first basemen with 93 assists and 116 double plays in 1997.

Year Team (League)	Pos.	G	AB	R	H	2B	3B	HR	RBI	Avg.	BB	SO	SB	PO	A	E	Avg.
1993—St. Paul (Northern).....	3B-2B	63	227	33	59	11	1	5	30	.260	24	27	2	51	133	18	.911
1994—Kane County (Midw.)■	1B	135	477	75	144	35	2	19	93	.302	74	88	3	1010	64	11	.990
1995—Brevard Co. (Fla. St.)..	1B	129	459	53	132	32	2	13	68	.288	70	66	4	*1213	95	12	.991
1996—Portland (Eastern).....	1B-3B	130	472	69	150	32	0	18	86	.318	37	53	6	753	134	15	.983
1997—Portland (Eastern).....	1B-3B	135	511	94	*175	•34	2	32	*131	*.342	66	53	2	1146	†121	17	.987

MILLER, DAMIAN — C — DIAMONDBACKS

PERSONAL: Born October 13, 1969, in LaCrosse, Wis. ... 6-3/202. ... Throws right, bats right. ... Full name: Damian Donald Miller.
HIGH SCHOOL: West Salem (Wis.).
COLLEGE: Viterbo (Wis.).
TRANSACTIONS/CAREER NOTES: Selected by Minnesota Twins organization in 20th round of free-agent draft (June 4, 1990). ... Selected by Arizona Diamondbacks in second round (47th pick overall) of expansion draft (November 18, 1997).
STATISTICAL NOTES: Led Pacific Coast League catchers with .998 fielding percentage in 1995. ... Led Pacific Coast League catchers with 70 assists and 695 total chances in 1996. ... Career major league grand slams: 1.

Year Team (League)	Pos.	G	AB	R	H	2B	3B	HR	RBI	Avg.	BB	SO	SB	PO	A	E	Avg.
1990—Elizabethton (App.).....	C	14	45	7	10	1	0	1	6	.222	9	3	1	102	6	2	.982
1991—Kenosha (Midwest)	C-1B-OF	80	267	28	62	11	1	3	34	.232	24	53	3	357	52	4	.990
1992—Kenosha (Midwest)	C	115	377	53	110	27	2	5	56	.292	53	66	6	696	89	9	.989
1993—Fort Myers (FSL)........	C	87	325	31	69	12	1	1	26	.212	31	44	6	465	62	8	.985
—Nashville (Southern) ..	C	4	13	0	3	0	0	0	0	.231	2	4	0	...	...	...	...
1994—Nashville (Southern) ..	C	103	328	36	88	10	0	8	35	.268	35	51	4	628	81	8	.989
1995—Salt Lake (PCL)	C-OF	83	295	39	84	23	1	3	41	.285	15	39	2	395	52	1	†.998
1996—Salt Lake (PCL)	C	104	385	54	110	27	1	7	55	.286	25	58	1	619	†70	6	.991
1997—Salt Lake (PCL)	C	85	314	48	106	19	3	11	82	.338	29	62	6	445	35	6	.988
—Minnesota (A.L.)	C-DH	25	66	5	18	1	0	2	13	.273	2	12	0	85	3	0	1.000
Major league totals (1 year)		25	66	5	18	1	0	2	13	.273	2	12	0	85	3	0	1.000

MILLER, KURT — P — CUBS

PERSONAL: Born August 24, 1972, in Tucson, Ariz. ... 6-5/220. ... Throws right, bats right. ... Full name: Kurt Everett Miller.
HIGH SCHOOL: Bowie (Texas), then Tulsa (Okla.) Union, and then West (Bakersfield, Calif.).
TRANSACTIONS/CAREER NOTES: Selected by Pittsburgh Pirates organization in first round (fifth pick overall) of free-agent draft (June 4, 1990). ... On Augusta disabled list (July 10-August 3, 1991). ... Traded by Pirates with a player to be named later to Texas Rangers for 3B Steve Buechele (August 30, 1991); Rangers acquired P Hector Fajardo to complete deal (September 6, 1991). ... Traded by Rangers with P Robb Nen to Florida Marlins for P Cris Carpenter (July 17, 1993). ... On disabled list (March 31-September 1, 1997); included rehabilitation assignments to Brevard County (April 13-18) and Charlotte (May 27-September 1, 1997). ... Traded by Marlins to Chicago Cubs for a player to be named later (November 18, 1997).
STATISTICAL NOTES: Tied for Texas League lead with four balks in 1992.

Year Team (League)	W	L	Pct.	ERA	G	GS	CG	ShO	Sv.	IP	H	R	ER	BB	SO
1990—Welland (N.Y.-Penn)..........	3	2	.600	3.29	14	12	0	0	0	65 2/3	59	39	24	37	62
1991—Augusta (S. Atl.)..............	6	7	.462	2.50	21	21	2	2	0	115 1/3	89	49	32	57	103
1992—Charlotte (Fla. St.)..........	5	4	.556	2.39	12	12	0	0	0	75 1/3	51	23	20	29	58
—Tulsa (Texas)	7	5	.583	3.68	16	15	0	0	0	88	82	42	36	35	73
1993—Tulsa (Texas)	6	8	.429	5.06	18	18	0	0	0	96	102	69	54	45	68
—Edmonton (PCL)■	3	3	.500	4.50	9	9	0	0	0	48	42	24	24	34	19
1994—Edmonton (PCL)............	7	*13	.350	6.88	23	23	0	0	0	125 2/3	164	105	96	64	58
—Florida (N.L.)................	1	3	.250	8.10	4	4	0	0	0	20	26	18	18	7	11
1995—Charlotte (Int'l)............	8	11	.421	4.62	22	22	0	0	0	126 2/3	143	76	65	55	83
1996—Charlotte (Int'l)............	3	5	.375	4.66	12	12	2	0	0	65 2/3	77	39	34	26	38
—Florida (N.L.)................	1	3	.250	6.80	26	5	0	0	0	46 1/3	57	41	35	33	30
1997—Brevard County (FSL)........	0	0	. . .	1.80	2	2	0	0	0	5	6	1	1	2	7
—Charlotte (Int'l)............	2	1	.667	3.58	21	0	0	0	0	27 2/3	25	12	11	22	31
—Florida (N.L.)................	0	1	.000	9.82	7	0	0	0	0	7 1/3	12	8	8	7	7
Major league totals (3 years)......	2	7	.222	7.45	37	9	0	0	0	73 2/3	95	67	61	47	48

MILLER, ORLANDO — SS

PERSONAL: Born January 13, 1969, in Changuinola, Panama. ... 6-1/180. ... Bats right, throws right. ... Full name: Orlando Salmon Miller.
TRANSACTIONS/CAREER NOTES: Signed as non-drafted free agent by New York Yankees organization (September 17, 1987). ... Traded by Yankees organization to Houston Astros organization for IF Dave Silvestri and a player to be named later (March 13, 1990); Yankees acquired P Daven Bond to complete deal (June 11, 1990). ... On Jackson disabled list (May 10-June 8, 1991). ... On disabled list (April 8-24, 1993 and August 26-September 10, 1995). ... Traded by Astros with OF Brian Hunter, P Doug Brocail, P Todd Jones and a player to be named later to Detroit Tigers for C Brad Ausmus, P Jose Lima, P C.J. Nitkowski, P Trever Miller and IF Daryle Ward (December 10, 1996). ... On Detroit disabled list (March 25-June 10, 1997); included rehabilitation assignment to Lakeland (May 18-June 10). ... Claimed on waivers by Kansas City Royals (December 1, 1997). ... Granted free agency (December 21, 1997).
STATISTICAL NOTES: Led South Atlantic League shortstops with 93 double plays in 1990.

Year Team (League)	Pos.	G	AB	R	H	2B	3B	HR	RBI	Avg.	BB	SO	SB	PO	A	E	Avg.
1988—Fort Lauderdale (FSL)	SS	3	11	0	3	0	0	0	1	.273	0	1	0	4	4	0	1.000
—GC Yankees (GCL)......	2B-SS	14	44	5	8	1	0	0	5	.182	3	10	1	19	30	5	.907
1989—Oneonta (NYP)	2-S-3-0	58	213	29	62	5	2	1	25	.291	6	37	8	96	124	9	.961
1990—Asheville (S. Atl.)■	SS	121	438	60	137	29	6	4	62	.313	25	52	12	208	348	*47	.922
1991—Jackson (Texas)	SS	23	70	5	13	6	0	1	5	.186	5	13	0	31	66	12	.890
—Osceola (Fla. St.)........	SS	74	272	27	81	11	2	0	36	.298	13	30	1	106	205	24	.928

M

Year Team (League)	Pos.	G	AB	R	H	2B	3B	HR	RBI	Avg.	BB	SO	SB	PO	A	E	Avg.
						BATTING								FIELDING			
1992—Jackson (Texas)	SS	115	379	51	100	26	5	5	53	.264	16	75	7	132	254	22	.946
—Tucson (PCL)	SS	10	37	4	9	0	0	2	8	.243	1	2	0	10	26	1	.973
1993—Tucson (PCL)	SS	122	471	86	143	29	16	16	89	.304	20	95	2	180	389	*33	.945
1994—Tucson (PCL)	SS-2B	93	338	54	87	16	6	10	55	.257	16	77	3	154	296	29	.939
—Houston (N.L.)	SS-2B	16	40	3	13	0	1	2	9	.325	2	12	1	12	30	0	1.000
1995—Houston (N.L.)	SS	92	324	36	85	20	1	5	36	.262	22	71	3	131	270	15	.964
1996—Houston (N.L.)	SS-3B	139	468	43	120	26	2	15	58	.256	14	116	3	147	320	21	.957
1997—Lakeland (Fla. St.)■	SS	5	21	1	4	1	1	0	0	.190	1	4	0	3	11	1	.933
—Jacksonville (South.)	SS	3	11	2	4	1	0	1	3	.364	1	1	0	3	8	2	.846
—Toledo (Int'l)	SS	8	30	3	8	1	0	1	5	.267	2	5	2	10	12	1	.957
—Detroit (A.L.)	S-DH-3-1	50	111	13	26	7	1	2	10	.234	5	24	1	37	71	3	.973
American League totals (1 year)		50	111	13	26	7	1	2	10	.234	5	24	1	37	71	3	.973
National League totals (3 years)		247	832	82	218	46	4	22	103	.262	38	199	7	290	620	36	.962
Major league totals (4 years)		297	943	95	244	53	5	24	113	.259	43	223	8	327	691	39	.963

MILLER, TRAVIS　　　P　　　TWINS

PERSONAL: Born November 2, 1972, in Dayton, Ohio. ... 6-3/207. ... Throws left, bats right. ... Full name: Travis Eugene Miller.
HIGH SCHOOL: National Trail (New Paris, Ohio).
COLLEGE: Kent.
TRANSACTIONS/CAREER NOTES: Selected by Minnesota Twins organization in supplemental round ("sandwich pick" between first and second round, 34th pick overall) of free-agent draft (June 2, 1994); pick received as compensation for Twins failing to sign 1993 first-round pick C Jason Varitek.

Year Team (League)	W	L	Pct.	ERA	G	GS	CG	ShO	Sv.	IP	H	R	ER	BB	SO
1994—Fort Wayne (Midw.)	4	1	.800	2.60	11	9	1	0	0	55 1/3	52	17	16	12	50
—Nashville (Southern)	0	0	...	2.84	1	1	0	0	0	6 1/3	3	3	2	2	4
1995—New Britain (East.)	7	9	.438	4.37	28	27	1	1	0	162 2/3	*172	93	79	65	151
1996—Minnesota (A.L.)	1	2	.333	9.23	7	7	0	0	0	26 1/3	45	29	27	9	15
—Salt Lake (PCL)	8	10	.444	4.83	27	27	1	0	0	160 1/3	187	97	86	57	*143
1997—Salt Lake (PCL)	10	6	.625	4.73	21	21	0	0	0	125 2/3	140	73	66	57	86
—Minnesota (A.L.)	1	5	.167	7.63	13	7	0	0	0	48 1/3	64	49	41	23	26
Major league totals (2 years)	2	7	.222	8.20	20	14	0	0	0	74 2/3	109	78	68	32	41

MILLER, TREVER　　　P　　　ASTROS

PERSONAL: Born May 29, 1973, in Louisville, Ky. ... 6-3/175. ... Throws left, bats right. ... Full name: Trever Douglas Miller.
HIGH SCHOOL: Trinity (Louisville, Ky.).
TRANSACTIONS/CAREER NOTES: Selected by Detroit Tigers organization in supplemental round ("sandwich pick" between first and second round, 41st pick overall) of free-agent draft (June 3, 1991); pick received as part of compensation for Atlanta Braves signing Type A free-agent C Mike Heath. ... Traded by Tigers with C Brad Ausmus, P Jose Lima, P C.J. Nitkowski and IF Daryle Ward to Houston Astros for OF Brian Hunter, IF Orlando Miller, P Doug Brocail, P Todd Jones and a player to be named later (December 10, 1996).
STATISTICAL NOTES: Tied for Appalachian League lead with seven home runs allowed in 1991.

Year Team (League)	W	L	Pct.	ERA	G	GS	CG	ShO	Sv.	IP	H	R	ER	BB	SO
1991—Bristol (Appalachian)	2	7	.222	5.67	13	13	0	0	0	54	60	44	34	29	46
1992—Bristol (Appalachian)	3	•8	.273	4.93	12	12	1	0	0	69 1/3	75	45	38	27	64
1993—Fayetteville (S. Atl.)	8	13	.381	4.19	28	28	2	0	0	161	151	99	75	67	116
1994—Trenton (Eastern)	7	•16	.304	4.39	26	26	*6	0	0	174 1/3	*198	95	85	51	73
1995—Jacksonville (Southern)	8	2	.800	2.72	31	16	3	2	0	122 1/3	122	46	37	34	77
1996—Toledo (Int'l)	13	6	.684	4.90	27	27	0	0	0	165 1/3	167	98	90	65	115
—Detroit (A.L.)	0	4	.000	9.18	5	4	0	0	0	16 2/3	28	17	17	9	8
1997—New Orleans (A.A.)■	6	7	.462	3.30	29	27	2	0	0	163 2/3	177	71	60	54	99
Major league totals (1 year)	0	4	.000	9.18	5	4	0	0	0	16 2/3	28	17	17	9	8

MILLIARD, RALPH　　　2B　　　MARLINS

PERSONAL: Born December 30, 1973, in Willemstad, Curacao. ... 5-11/170. ... Throws right, bats right. ... Full name: Ralph Gregory Milliard.
HIGH SCHOOL: Aamsvdorda Technical School (Soest, The Netherlands).
TRANSACTIONS/CAREER NOTES: Signed as non-drafted free agent by Florida Marlins organization (July 26, 1992). ... On Charlotte disabled list (April 22-May 7, 1997).
STATISTICAL NOTES: Led Gulf Coast League second basemen with 111 putouts, 142 assists, 257 total chances and .984 fielding percentage in 1993. ... Led Midwest League second basemen with 659 total chances and 72 double plays in 1994.

Year Team (League)	Pos.	G	AB	R	H	2B	3B	HR	RBI	Avg.	BB	SO	SB	PO	A	E	Avg.
						BATTING								FIELDING			
1993—GC Marlins (GCL)	2B-3B	53	192	35	45	15	0	0	25	.234	30	17	11	†114	†145	5	.981
1994—Kane County (Midw.)	2B	133	515	*97	153	34	2	8	67	.297	68	63	10	*248	*390	21	.968
1995—Portland (Eastern)	2B	128	464	*104	124	22	3	11	40	.267	85	83	22	*299	357	17	.975
1996—Portland (Eastern)	2B	6	20	2	4	0	1	0	2	.200	1	5	1	12	18	0	1.000
—Charlotte (Int'l)	2B	69	250	47	69	15	2	6	26	.276	38	43	8	154	188	5	.986
—Florida (N.L.)	2B	24	62	7	10	2	0	0	1	.161	14	16	2	42	65	5	.955
1997—Charlotte (Int'l)	2B	33	132	19	35	5	1	4	18	.265	9	21	5	71	91	1	.994
—Florida (N.L.)	2B	8	30	2	6	0	0	0	2	.200	3	3	1	14	32	0	1.000
—Portland (Eastern)	2B	19	69	13	19	1	2	0	5	.275	7	8	3	37	53	1	.968
Major league totals (2 years)		32	92	9	16	2	0	0	3	.174	17	19	3	56	97	5	.968

M

MILLS, ALAN   P   ORIOLES

PERSONAL: Born October 18, 1966, in Lakeland, Fla. ... 6-1/195. ... Throws right, bats both. ... Full name: Alan Bernard Mills.
HIGH SCHOOL: Kathleen (Fla.).
JUNIOR COLLEGE: Polk Community College (Fla.).
TRANSACTIONS/CAREER NOTES: Selected by Boston Red Sox organization in first round (13th pick overall) of free-agent draft (January 14, 1986); did not sign. ... Selected by California Angels organization in secondary phase of free-agent draft (June 2, 1986). ... Traded by Angels organization to New York Yankees organization (June 22, 1987), completing deal in which Angels traded P Ron Romanick and a player to be named later to Yankees for C Butch Wynegar (December 19, 1986). ... Traded by Yankees to Baltimore Orioles for two players to be named later (February 29, 1992); Yankees acquired P Francisco de la Rosa (February 29, 1992) and P Mark Carper (June 8, 1992) to complete deal. ... On suspended list (June 26-30, 1993). ... On Rochester disabled list (July 4-September 16, 1995). ... On disabled list (March 22-May 12, 1996). ... On disabled list (April 10-June 15, 1997).

Year	Team (League)	W	L	Pct.	ERA	G	GS	CG	ShO	Sv.	IP	H	R	ER	BB	SO
1986—	Salem (Northwest)	6	6	.500	4.63	14	14	1	0	0	83 2/3	77	58	43	60	50
1987—	Prince William (Caro.)■	2	11	.154	6.09	35	8	0	0	1	85 2/3	102	75	58	64	53
1988—	Prince William (Caro.)	3	8	.273	4.13	42	5	0	0	4	93 2/3	93	56	43	43	59
1989—	Prince William (Caro.)	6	1	.857	0.91	26	0	0	0	7	39 2/3	22	5	4	13	44
	Fort Lauderdale (FSL)	1	4	.200	3.77	22	0	0	0	6	31	40	15	13	9	25
1990—	New York (A.L.)	1	5	.167	4.10	36	0	0	0	0	41 2/3	48	21	19	33	24
	Columbus (Int'l)	3	3	.500	3.38	17	0	0	0	6	29 1/3	22	11	11	14	30
1991—	Columbus (Int'l)	7	5	.583	4.43	38	15	0	0	8	113 2/3	109	65	56	75	77
	New York (A.L.)	1	1	.500	4.41	6	2	0	0	0	16 1/3	16	9	8	8	11
1992—	Rochester (Int'l)■	0	1	.000	5.40	3	0	0	0	1	5	6	3	3	2	8
	Baltimore (A.L.)	10	4	.714	2.61	35	3	0	0	2	103 1/3	78	33	30	54	60
1993—	Baltimore (A.L.)	5	4	.556	3.23	45	0	0	0	4	100 1/3	80	39	36	51	68
1994—	Baltimore (A.L.)	3	3	.500	5.16	47	0	0	0	2	45 1/3	43	26	26	24	44
1995—	Baltimore (A.L.)	3	0	1.000	7.43	21	0	0	0	0	23	30	20	19	18	16
	Rochester (Int'l)	0	1	.000	0.00	1	1	0	0	0	2 2/3	2	6	0	5	2
	GC Orioles (GCL)	0	0	. . .	0.00	1	1	0	0	0	2	3	0	0	2	1
1996—	Baltimore (A.L.)	3	2	.600	4.28	49	0	0	0	3	54 2/3	40	26	26	35	50
1997—	Baltimore (A.L.)	2	3	.400	4.89	39	0	0	0	0	38 2/3	41	23	21	33	32
Major league totals (8 years)		**28**	**22**	**.560**	**3.93**	**278**	**8**	**0**	**0**	**11**	**423 1/3**	**376**	**197**	**185**	**256**	**305**

DIVISION SERIES RECORD

Year	Team (League)	W	L	Pct.	ERA	G	GS	CG	ShO	Sv.	IP	H	R	ER	BB	SO
1997—	Baltimore (A.L.)	0	0	. . .	0.00	1	0	0	0	0	1	1	0	0	0	1

CHAMPIONSHIP SERIES RECORD

Year	Team (League)	W	L	Pct.	ERA	G	GS	CG	ShO	Sv.	IP	H	R	ER	BB	SO
1996—	Baltimore (A.L.)	0	0	. . .	3.86	3	0	0	0	0	2 1/3	3	1	1	1	3
1997—	Baltimore (A.L.)	0	1	.000	2.70	3	0	0	0	0	3 1/3	1	1	1	2	3
Champ. series totals (2 years)		**0**	**1**	**.000**	**3.18**	**6**	**0**	**0**	**0**	**0**	**5 2/3**	**4**	**2**	**2**	**3**	**6**

MILLWOOD, KEVIN   P   BRAVES

PERSONAL: Born December 24, 1974, in Gastonia, N.C. ... 6-4/205. ... Throws right, bats right. ... Full name: Kevin Austin Millwood.
HIGH SCHOOL: Bessemer City (N.C.).
TRANSACTIONS/CAREER NOTES: Selected by Atlanta Braves organization in 11th round of free-agent draft (June 3, 1993).

Year	Team (League)	W	L	Pct.	ERA	G	GS	CG	ShO	Sv.	IP	H	R	ER	BB	SO
1993—	GC Braves (GCL)	3	3	.500	3.06	12	9	0	0	0	50	36	27	17	28	49
1994—	Danville (Appalachian)	3	3	.500	3.72	13	5	0	0	1	46	42	25	19	34	56
	Macon (S. Atl.)	0	5	.000	5.79	12	4	0	0	1	32 2/3	31	31	21	32	24
1995—	Macon (S. Atl.)	5	6	.455	4.63	29	12	0	0	0	103	86	65	53	57	89
1996—	Durham (Carolina)	6	9	.400	4.28	33	20	1	0	1	149 1/3	138	77	71	58	139
1997—	Greenville (Southern)	3	5	.375	4.11	11	11	0	0	0	61 1/3	59	37	28	24	61
	Richmond (Int'l)	7	0	1.000	1.93	9	9	1	0	0	60 2/3	38	13	13	16	46
	Atlanta (N.L.)	5	3	.625	4.03	12	8	0	0	0	51 1/3	55	26	23	21	42
Major league totals (1 year)		**5**	**3**	**.625**	**4.03**	**12**	**8**	**0**	**0**	**0**	**51 1/3**	**55**	**26**	**23**	**21**	**42**

MILTON, ERIC   P   YANKEES

PERSONAL: Born August 4, 1975, in State College, Pa. ... 6-3/200. ... Throws left, bats left.
COLLEGE: Maryland.
TRANSACTIONS/CAREER NOTES: Selected by New York Yankees organization in first round (20th pick overall) of free-agent draft (June 2, 1996).
STATISTICAL NOTES: Tied for Eastern League lead with four balks in 1997.

Year	Team (League)	W	L	Pct.	ERA	G	GS	CG	ShO	Sv.	IP	H	R	ER	BB	SO
1997—	Tampa (Florida State)	8	3	.727	3.09	14	14	1	0	0	93 1/3	78	35	32	14	95
	Norwich (Eastern)	6	3	.667	3.13	14	14	1	0	0	77 2/3	59	29	27	36	67

MIMBS, MARK   P   METS

PERSONAL: Born February 13, 1969, in Macon, Ga. ... 6-2/180. ... Throws left, bats left. ... Full name: Mark Ivey Mimbs. ... Twin brother of Mike Mimbs, pitcher, Philadelphia Phillies.
HIGH SCHOOL: Windsor Academy (Macon, Ga.).
COLLEGE: Mercer (Ga.).

TRANSACTIONS/CAREER NOTES: Selected by Los Angeles Dodgers organization in 25th round of free-agent draft (June 4, 1990). ... On Albuquerque disabled list (April 7-May 5 and May 20, 1994-remainder of season). ... On disabled list (July 16-August 26, 1995). ... Selected by Texas Rangers from Dodgers organization in Rule 5 major league draft (December 4, 1995). ... Returned by Rangers to Dodgers for cash (March 21, 1996). ... Granted free agency (October 15, 1996). ... Signed by Boston Red Sox organization (November 25, 1996). ... Traded by Pawtucket, Red Sox organization to New Orleans, Houston Astros organization (June 23, 1997). ... Granted free agency (October 15, 1997). ... Signed by New York Mets (December 6, 1997).

Year Team (League)	W	L	Pct.	ERA	G	GS	CG	ShO	Sv.	IP	H	R	ER	BB	SO
1990— Great Falls (Pio.)	7	4	.636	3.23	14	•14	0	0	0	78	69	32	28	29	*94
1991— Bakersfield (California)	12	6	.667	2.22	27	25	0	0	0	170	134	49	42	59	164
1992— Albuquerque (PCL)	0	4	.000	6.10	12	7	0	0	0	48 2/3	58	34	33	19	32
— San Antonio (Tex.)	1	5	.167	3.61	13	13	0	0	0	82 1/3	78	43	33	22	55
1993— Albuquerque (PCL)	0	1	.000	10.13	19	1	0	0	1	18 2/3	20	21	21	16	12
— San Antonio (Tex.)	3	3	.500	1.60	49	0	0	0	10	67 2/3	49	21	12	18	77
1994— Albuquerque (PCL)	1	0	1.000	4.05	6	0	0	0	0	6 2/3	8	3	3	0	9
— Bakersfield (California)	0	0	...	0.00	1	0	0	0	0	1 2/3	3	0	0	0	0
1995— Albuquerque (PCL)	6	5	.545	2.97	23	16	1	0	0	106	105	40	35	22	96
1996— Albuquerque (PCL)	8	8	.500	4.59	34	23	1	1	0	151	165	93	77	43	136
1997— Pawtucket (Int'l)■	3	8	.273	5.06	15	14	0	0	0	83 2/3	97	58	47	35	81
— New Orleans (A.A.)■	1	2	.333	4.36	22	3	0	0	1	33	36	19	16	9	26

MIMBS, MIKE — P — PHILLIES

PERSONAL: Born February 13, 1969, in Macon, Ga. ... 6-2/190. ... Throws left, bats left. ... Full name: Michael Randall Mimbs. ... Twin brother of Mark Mimbs, pitcher, New York Mets.
HIGH SCHOOL: Windsor Academy (Macon, Ga.).
COLLEGE: Mercer (Ga.).
TRANSACTIONS/CAREER NOTES: Selected by Los Angeles Dodgers organization in 24th round of free-agent draft (June 4, 1990). ... Released by Albuquerque, Dodgers organization (March 31, 1993). ... Signed by St. Paul, independent (May 1993). ... Signed by Harrisburg, Montreal Expos organization (January 24, 1994). ... Selected by Philadelphia Phillies from Expos organization in Rule 5 major league draft (December 5, 1994). ... On Philadelphia disabled list (August 7-September 2, 1996); included rehabilitation assignment to Scranton/Wilkes-Barre (August 26-September 2).

Year Team (League)	W	L	Pct.	ERA	G	GS	CG	ShO	Sv.	IP	H	R	ER	BB	SO
1990— Great Falls (Pio.)	0	0	...	4.05	3	0	0	0	0	6 2/3	4	5	3	5	7
— Yakima (N'west)	4	3	.571	3.88	12	12	0	0	0	67 1/3	58	36	29	39	72
1991— Vero Beach (FSL)	•12	4	.750	2.67	24	22	1	1	0	141 2/3	124	52	42	70	132
1992— San Antonio (Tex.)	10	8	.556	4.23	24	22	0	0	1	129 2/3	132	65	61	73	87
1993— St. Paul (Northern)■	8	2	.800	3.20	20	16	1	0	0	98 1/3	94	48	35	45	97
1994— Harrisburg (Eastern)■	11	4	.733	3.46	32	21	2	1	0	153 2/3	130	69	59	61	145
1995— Philadelphia (N.L.)	9	7	.563	4.15	35	19	2	1	1	136 2/3	127	70	63	75	93
1996— Philadelphia (N.L.)	3	9	.250	5.53	21	17	0	0	0	99 1/3	116	66	61	41	56
— Scran./W.B. (Int'l)	2	1	.667	2.48	7	3	0	0	0	29	27	8	8	5	20
1997— Philadelphia (N.L.)	0	3	.000	7.53	17	1	0	0	0	28 2/3	31	27	24	27	29
— Scran./W.B. (Int'l)	4	2	.667	5.98	11	8	1	0	0	43 2/3	52	33	29	20	41
Major league totals (3 years)	12	19	.387	5.03	73	37	2	1	1	264 2/3	274	163	148	143	178

MINCHEY, NATE — P

PERSONAL: Born August 31, 1969, in Austin, Texas. ... 6-7/225. ... Throws right, bats right. ... Full name: Nathan Derek Minchey.
HIGH SCHOOL: Pflugerville (Texas).
TRANSACTIONS/CAREER NOTES: Selected by Montreal Expos organization in second round of free-agent draft (June 2, 1987); pick received as compensation for Chicago Cubs signing Type A free-agent OF Andre Dawson. ... Traded by Expos with P Sergio Valdez and OF Kevin Dean to Atlanta Braves organization for P Zane Smith (July 2, 1989). ... Loaned by Braves organization to Miami, independent (April 10-June 19, 1991). ... Traded by Braves with OF Sean Ross to Boston Red Sox for P Jeff Reardon (August 30, 1992). ... Traded by Red Sox with OF Jeff McNeely to St. Louis Cardinals for 2B Luis Alicea (December 7, 1994). ... On suspended list (May 15-17, 1995). ... Granted free agency (October 16, 1995). ... Signed by Pawtucket, Red Sox organization (December 17, 1995). ... On Boston disabled list (June 28, 1996-remainder of season). ... Granted free agency (October 11, 1996).
STATISTICAL NOTES: Led Midwest League with 81 earned runs allowed and 22 wild pitches in 1989.

Year Team (League)	W	L	Pct.	ERA	G	GS	CG	ShO	Sv.	IP	H	R	ER	BB	SO
1987— GC Expos (GCL)	3	4	.429	4.94	12	11	2	0	0	54 2/3	62	45	30	28	61
1988— Rockford (Midwest)	11	12	.478	4.79	28	27	0	0	0	150 1/3	148	93	80	87	63
1989— Rockford (Midwest)	3	6	.333	4.76	15	15	0	0	0	87	85	51	*46	54	53
— Burlington (Midw.)■	2	6	.250	4.57	11	11	1	0	0	69	69	37	*35	28	34
1990— Durham (Carolina)	4	11	.267	3.79	25	24	2	2	0	133	143	75	56	46	100
1991— Durham (Carolina)	6	6	.500	2.84	15	12	3	0	0	88 2/3	72	31	28	29	77
— Miami (Florida St.)■	5	3	.625	1.89	13	13	4	1	0	95 1/3	81	31	20	31	61
1992— Greenville (Southern)■	•13	8	.684	2.30	28	25	5	•4	0	172	137	51	44	40	115
— Pawtucket (Int'l)■	2	0	1.000	0.00	2	0	0	0	0	7	3	0	0	4	4
1993— Pawtucket (Int'l)	7	*14	.333	4.02	•29	29	*7	2	0	*194 2/3	182	*103	87	50	113
— Boston (A.L.)	1	2	.333	3.55	5	5	1	0	0	33	35	16	13	8	18
1994— Pawtucket (Int'l)	11	5	.688	3.03	23	22	6	2	0	151 1/3	128	65	51	51	93
— Boston (A.L.)	2	3	.400	8.61	6	5	0	0	0	23	44	26	22	14	15
1995— Louisville (A.A.)■	8	7	.533	3.73	26	24	1	0	0	147 1/3	153	77	61	42	67
1996— Pawtucket (Int'l)■	7	4	.636	2.96	14	13	6	1	0	97 1/3	89	32	32	21	61
— Boston (A.L.)	0	2	.000	15.00	2	2	0	0	0	6	16	11	10	5	4
1997— Colo. Springs (PCL)■	*15	6	.714	4.51	27	21	3	0	0	157 2/3	172	87	79	53	107
— Colorado (N.L.)	0	0	...	13.50	2	0	0	0	0	2	5	3	3	1	1
A.L. totals (3 years)	3	7	.300	6.53	13	12	1	0	0	62	95	53	45	27	37
N.L. totals (1 year)	0	0	...	13.50	2	0	0	0	0	2	5	3	3	1	1
Major league totals (4 years)	3	7	.300	6.75	15	12	1	0	0	64	100	56	48	28	38

M

MINOR, BLAS   P

PERSONAL: Born March 20, 1966, in Merced, Calif. ... 6-3/203. ... Throws right, bats right. ... Name pronounced BLOSS.
HIGH SCHOOL: Atwater (Calif.).
JUNIOR COLLEGE: Merced (Calif.) College.
COLLEGE: Arizona State.
TRANSACTIONS/CAREER NOTES: Selected by Kansas City Royals organization in 11th round of free-agent draft (January 9, 1985); did not sign. ... Selected by Philadelphia Phillies organization in secondary phase of free-agent draft (June 3, 1985); did not sign. ... Selected by Phillies organization in secondary phase of free-agent draft (January 14, 1986); did not sign. ... Selected by Pittsburgh Pirates organization in sixth round of free-agent draft (June 1, 1988). ... On Buffalo disabled list (June 8-24 and June 28-August 12, 1991). ... On suspended list (September 3-8, 1993). ... Claimed on waivers by New York Mets (November 4, 1994). ... On disabled list (July 24-August 24, 1995). ... Traded by Mets to Seattle Mariners for IF Randy Vickers (June 9, 1996). ... Granted free agency (October 15, 1996). ... Signed by Houston Astros organization (November 22, 1996). ... Granted free agency (July 17, 1997). ... Signed by Tucson, Milwaukee Brewers organization (July 24, 1997). ... Granted free agency (October 15, 1997).

Year	Team (League)	W	L	Pct.	ERA	G	GS	CG	ShO	Sv.	IP	H	R	ER	BB	SO
1988—	Princeton (Appalachian).....	0	1	.000	4.41	15	0	0	0	7	16 1/3	18	10	8	5	23
1989—	Salem (Carolina)	3	5	.375	3.63	39	4	0	0	0	86 2/3	91	43	35	31	62
1990—	Harrisburg (Eastern)	6	4	.600	3.06	38	6	0	0	5	94	81	41	32	29	98
	—Buffalo (A.A.)....................	0	1	.000	3.38	1	0	0	0	0	2 2/3	2	1	1	2	2
1991—	Buffalo (A.A.)....................	2	2	.500	5.75	17	3	0	0	0	36	46	27	23	15	25
	—Carolina (Southern)	0	0	...	2.84	3	2	0	0	0	12 2/3	9	4	4	7	18
1992—	Buffalo (A.A.)....................	5	4	.556	2.43	45	7	0	0	18	96 1/3	72	30	26	26	60
	—Pittsburgh (N.L.)	0	0	...	4.50	1	0	0	0	0	2	3	2	1	0	0
1993—	Pittsburgh (N.L.)	8	6	.571	4.10	65	0	0	0	2	94 1/3	94	43	43	26	84
1994—	Pittsburgh (N.L.)	0	1	.000	8.05	17	0	0	0	1	19	27	17	17	9	17
	—Buffalo (A.A.)....................	1	2	.333	2.98	33	3	0	0	11	51 1/3	47	17	17	12	61
1995—	New York (N.L.)■	4	2	.667	3.66	35	0	0	0	1	46 2/3	44	21	19	13	43
1996—	New York (N.L.)	0	0	...	3.51	17	0	0	0	0	25 2/3	23	11	10	6	20
	—Seattle (A.L.)■	0	1	.000	4.97	11	0	0	0	0	25 1/3	27	14	14	11	14
	—Tacoma (PCL)	1	2	.333	8.38	7	0	0	0	1	9 2/3	15	11	9	3	8
1997—	New Orleans (A.A.)■...........	3	3	.500	2.27	23	0	0	0	6	31 2/3	20	8	8	9	27
	—Houston (N.L.)	1	0	1.000	4.50	11	0	0	0	1	12	13	7	6	5	6
	—Tucson (PCL)■	2	2	.500	4.03	12	3	0	0	1	29	36	21	13	15	21
	A.L. totals (1 year)	0	1	.000	4.97	11	0	0	0	0	25 1/3	27	14	14	11	14
	N.L. totals (6 years)	13	9	.591	4.33	146	0	0	0	5	199 2/3	204	101	96	59	170
	Major league totals (6 years)......	13	10	.565	4.40	157	0	0	0	5	225	231	115	110	70	184

MINOR, RYAN   3B   ORIOLES

PERSONAL: Born January 5, 1974, in Canton, Ohio. ... 6-7/225. ... Bats right, throws right. ... Full name: Ryan Dale Minor. ... Brother of Damon Minor, infielder, San Francisco Giants organization.
HIGH SCHOOL: Hammon (Okla.).
COLLEGE: Oklahoma.
TRANSACTIONS/CAREER NOTES: Selected by Baltimore Orioles organization in 15th round of free-agent draft (June 1, 1992); did not sign. ... Selected by Orioles organization in 33rd round of free-agent draft (June 4, 1996).
MISCELLANEOUS: Selected by Philadelphia 76ers in second round (32nd pick overall) of 1996 NBA draft. ... Played in Continental Basketball Association with Oklahoma City Calvary (1996-97 season).

							BATTING							FIELDING		
Year	Team (League)	Pos.	G	AB	R	H	2B	3B	HR	RBI	Avg.	BB	SO	SB	PO	A	E	Avg.
1996—	Bluefield (Appal.)........	3B-SS	25	87	14	22	6	0	4	9	.253	7	32	1	13	45	5	.921
1997—	Delmarva (S. Atl.).......	3B-1B	134	488	83	150	42	1	24	97	.307	51	102	7	193	209	34	.922

MIRABELLI, DOUG   C   GIANTS

PERSONAL: Born October 18, 1970, in Kingman, Ariz. ... 6-0/215. ... Bats right, throws right. ... Full name: Douglas Anthony Mirabelli.
HIGH SCHOOL: Valley (Las Vegas).
COLLEGE: Wichita State.
TRANSACTIONS/CAREER NOTES: Selected by Detroit Tigers organization in sixth round of free-agent draft (June 5, 1989); did not sign. ... Selected by San Francisco Giants organization in fifth round of free-agent draft (June 1, 1992). ... On Phoenix disabled list (May 16-23, 1995).
STATISTICAL NOTES: Led Texas League with .419 on-base percentage in 1996. ... Led Pacific Coast League catchers with 680 total chances in 1997.

							BATTING							FIELDING		
Year	Team (League)	Pos.	G	AB	R	H	2B	3B	HR	RBI	Avg.	BB	SO	SB	PO	A	E	Avg.
1992—	San Jose (Calif.)........	C	53	177	30	41	11	1	0	21	.232	24	18	1	321	38	10	.973
1993—	San Jose (Calif.)........	C	113	371	58	100	19	2	1	48	.270	72	55	0	737	99	9	.989
1994—	Shreveport (Texas).....	C-1B	85	255	23	56	8	0	4	24	.220	36	48	3	391	51	3	.993
1995—	Shreveport (Texas).....	C-1B	40	126	14	38	13	0	0	16	.302	20	14	1	193	21	3	.986
	—Phoenix (PCL)	C	23	66	3	11	0	1	0	7	.167	12	10	1	115	17	2	.985
1996—	Shreveport (Texas).....	C-1B	115	380	60	112	23	0	21	70	.295	76	49	0	548	56	7	.989
	—Phoenix (PCL)	C	14	47	10	14	7	0	0	7	.298	4	7	0	97	10	2	.982
	—San Francisco (N.L.) ..	C	9	18	2	4	1	0	0	1	.222	3	4	0	29	2	0	1.000
1997—	Phoenix (PCL)	C	100	332	49	88	23	2	8	48	.265	58	69	1	*629	47	4	.994
	—San Francisco (N.L.) ..	C	6	7	0	1	0	0	0	0	.143	1	3	0	16	0	0	1.000
	Major league totals (2 years)		15	25	2	5	1	0	0	1	.200	4	7	0	45	2	0	1.000

MIRANDA, ANGEL　　　　P

PERSONAL: Born November 9, 1969, in Arecibo, Puerto Rico. ... 6-1/195. ... Throws left, bats left. ... Full name: Angel Luis Miranda.
HIGH SCHOOL: Maria Cadillo (Arecibo, Puerto Rico).
TRANSACTIONS/CAREER NOTES: Signed as non-drafted free agent by Milwaukee Brewers organization (March 4, 1987). ... Loaned by Brewers organization to Butte, independent (March 4, 1987). ... On Milwaukee disabled list (March 27-June 1, 1993); included rehabilitation assignment to New Orleans (May 4-June 1). ... On Milwaukee disabled list (March 21-June 28, 1994); included rehabilitation assignments to Beloit (June 4-11) and New Orleans (June 11-25). ... On disabled list (June 27-July 29, 1995). ... On Milwaukee disabled list (April 29-May 18, 1997); included rehabilitation assignment to Stockton (May 16-18). ... Released by Brewers (June 17, 1997). ... Signed by Cleveland Indians organization (July 3, 1997). ... Released by Indians organization (August 14, 1997). ... Signed by Texas Rangers organization (August 25, 1997). ... Granted free agency (October 15, 1997).
STATISTICAL NOTES: Led American Association with six balks in 1992.

Year　Team (League)	W	L	Pct.	ERA	G	GS	CG	ShO	Sv.	IP	H	R	ER	BB	SO
1987— Butte (Pioneer)	1	1	.500	3.74	12	0	0	0	0	21 2/3	15	13	9	10	28
— Helena (Pioneer)■	0	1	.000	2.49	13	0	0	0	3	21 2/3	12	9	6	16	32
1988— Stockton (California)	0	1	.000	7.18	16	0	0	0	2	26 1/3	20	30	21	37	36
— Helena (Pioneer)	5	2	.714	3.86	14	11	0	0	0	60 2/3	54	32	26	58	75
1989— Beloit (Midwest)	6	5	.545	0.86	43	0	0	0	16	63	39	13	6	32	88
1990— Stockton (California)	9	4	.692	2.66	52	9	2	1	24	108 1/3	75	37	32	49	138
1991— El Paso (Texas)	4	2	.667	2.54	38	0	0	0	11	74 1/3	55	27	21	41	86
— Denver (Am. Assoc.)	0	1	.000	6.17	11	0	0	0	2	11 2/3	10	9	8	17	14
1992— Denver (Am. Assoc.)	6	12	.333	4.77	28	27	1	1	0	160 1/3	183	100	85	*77	122
1993— New Orleans (A.A.)	0	1	.000	3.44	9	2	0	0	0	18 1/3	11	8	7	10	24
— Milwaukee (A.L.)	4	5	.444	3.30	22	17	2	0	0	120	100	53	44	52	88
1994— Beloit (Midwest)	0	0	...	2.70	2	2	0	0	0	10	11	3	3	1	14
— New Orleans (A.A.)	0	1	.000	3.46	3	3	0	0	0	13	11	5	5	7	9
— Milwaukee (A.L.)	2	5	.286	5.28	8	8	1	0	0	46	39	28	27	27	24
1995— Milwaukee (A.L.)	4	5	.444	5.23	30	10	0	0	1	74	83	47	43	49	45
1996— Milwaukee (A.L.)	7	6	.538	4.94	46	12	0	0	1	109 1/3	116	68	60	69	78
1997— Milwaukee (A.L.)	0	0	...	3.86	10	0	0	0	0	14	17	6	6	9	8
— Stockton (California)	0	0	...	0.00	1	1	0	0	0	2	0	0	0	2	2
— Buffalo (A.A.)■	0	2	.000	10.03	9	0	0	0	0	11 2/3	20	14	13	5	9
— Oklahoma City (A.A.)■	0	1	.000	16.88	2	0	0	0	0	2 2/3	4	5	5	1	2
Major league totals (5 years)	**17**	**21**	**.447**	**4.46**	**116**	**47**	**3**	**0**	**2**	**363 1/3**	**355**	**202**	**180**	**206**	**243**

MISURACA, MIKE　　　　P

PERSONAL: Born August 21, 1968, in Long Beach, Calif. ... 6-0/188. ... Throws right, bats right. ... Full name: Michael William Misuraca.
HIGH SCHOOL: Glendora (Calif.).
TRANSACTIONS/CAREER NOTES: Signed as non-drafted free agent by Minnesota Twins organization (July 20, 1988). ... On temporarily inactive list (May 1-June 1, 1991). ... Granted free agency (December 21, 1995). ... Re-signed by Twins organization (January 12, 1996). ... Traded by Twins organization to Milwaukee Brewers organization (June 1, 1996). ... Granted free agency (October 14, 1996). ... Re-signed by Brewers organization (January 26, 1997). ... Granted free agency (October 15, 1997).
STATISTICAL NOTES: Led Pacific Coast League with eight hit batsmen in 1995.

Year　Team (League)	W	L	Pct.	ERA	G	GS	CG	ShO	Sv.	IP	H	R	ER	BB	SO
1989— Kenosha (Midwest)	1	5	.167	5.28	9	9	0	0	0	46	47	32	27	15	30
— Elizabethton (Appal.)	•10	3	.769	2.53	13	13	9	*2	0	*103	92	34	29	33	89
1990— Kenosha (Midwest)	9	9	.500	3.33	26	26	1	0	0	167 1/3	164	81	62	57	116
1991— Visalia (California)	7	9	.438	4.27	21	19	2	1	0	116	131	65	55	39	82
1992— Miracle (Florida State)	7	14	.333	3.61	28	*28	3	1	0	157	163	84	63	63	107
1993— Nashville (Southern)	6	6	.500	3.82	25	17	2	1	0	113	103	57	48	40	80
1994— Nashville (Southern)	8	4	.667	3.63	17	17	0	0	0	106 2/3	115	56	43	22	80
— Salt Lake (PCL)	3	5	.375	5.21	10	10	1	0	0	65 2/3	88	43	38	13	51
1995— Salt Lake (PCL)	9	6	.600	5.34	31	19	1	0	0	143 1/3	174	93	85	36	67
1996— Salt Lake (PCL)	1	2	.333	6.27	18	2	0	0	1	37 1/3	50	33	26	16	25
— New Orleans (A.A.)■	2	7	.222	4.13	23	12	0	0	2	80 2/3	93	42	37	31	57
1997— Tucson (PCL)	8	7	.533	4.98	33	10	0	0	1	108 1/3	119	68	60	39	62
— Milwaukee (A.L.)	0	0	...	11.32	5	0	0	0	0	10 1/3	15	13	13	7	10
Major league totals (1 year)	**0**	**0**	**...**	**11.32**	**5**	**0**	**0**	**0**	**0**	**10 1/3**	**15**	**13**	**13**	**7**	**10**

MITCHELL, KEVIN　　　　OF

PERSONAL: Born January 13, 1962, in San Diego. ... 5-11/244. ... Bats right, throws right. ... Full name: Kevin Darrell Mitchell. ... Cousin of Keith Mitchell, outfielder, Cincinnati Reds organization.
HIGH SCHOOL: Clairmont (San Diego).
TRANSACTIONS/CAREER NOTES: Signed as non-drafted free agent by New York Mets organization (November 16, 1980). ... On disabled list (July 21, 1982-remainder of season and July 12-30, 1985). ... Traded by Mets with OF Shawn Abner, OF Stanley Jefferson, P Kevin Armstrong and P Kevin Brown to San Diego Padres for OF Kevin McReynolds, P Gene Walter and IF Adam Ging (December 11, 1986). ... Traded by Padres with P Dave Dravecky and P Craig Lefferts to San Francisco Giants for 3B Chris Brown, P Keith Comstock, P Mark Davis and P Mark Grant (July 4, 1987). ... On suspended list for one game (May 3, 1991). ... On disabled list (June 3-25, 1991). ... Traded by Giants with P Mike Remlinger to Seattle Mariners for P Bill Swift, P Mike Jackson and P Dave Burba (December 11, 1991). ... On disabled list (August 8-23 and September 2, 1992-remainder of season). ... Traded by Mariners to Cincinnati Reds for P Norm Charlton (November 17, 1992). ... On disabled list (July 9-24, 1993). ... Suspended by Reds for two games (July 24-25, 1993). ... On disabled list (September 10, 1993-remainder of season). ... Granted free agency (October 25, 1994). ... Played in Japan (1995). ... Signed by Boston Red Sox (March 8, 1996). ... On Boston disabled list (April 23-May 9 and May 30-July 16, 1996); included rehabilitation assignments to Pawtucket (May 7-9 and June 14-17). ... Traded by Red Sox to Reds for IF Robert Mejia and P Brad Tweedlie (July 30, 1996). ... Granted free agency (November 18, 1996). ... Signed by Cleveland Indians organization (December 13, 1996). ... Released by Indians (June 3, 1997).
RECORDS: Holds major league single-season record for most intentional bases on balls received by righthanded batter—32 (1989).

HONORS: Named Major League Player of the Year by THE SPORTING NEWS (1989). ... Named N.L. Player of the Year by THE SPORTING NEWS (1989). ... Named outfielder on THE SPORTING NEWS N.L. All-Star team (1989). ... Named outfielder on THE SPORTING NEWS N.L. Silver Slugger team (1989). ... Named N.L. Most Valuable Player by Baseball Writers' Association of America (1989).

STATISTICAL NOTES: Led Texas League third basemen with 224 assists in 1983. ... Led International League third basemen with 215 assists in 1984. ... Led International League third basemen with 22 errors in 1985. ... Led N.L. with 345 total bases, 32 intentional bases on balls received and .635 slugging percentage in 1989. ... Hit three home runs in one game (May 25, 1990). ... Had 20-game hitting streak (June 1-30, 1993). ... Career major league grand slams: 1.

Year — Team (League)	Pos.	G	AB	R	H	2B	3B	HR	RBI	Avg.	BB	SO	SB	PO	A	E	Avg.
1981— Kingsport (Appal.)	3B-OF	62	221	39	74	9	2	7	45	.335	22	31	5	44	102	18	.890
1982— Lynchburg (Caro.)	3B	29	85	19	27	5	1	1	16	.318	13	25	0	11	33	10	.815
1983— Jackson (Texas)	3B-OF	120	441	75	132	25	2	15	85	.299	48	84	11	81	†224	21	.936
1984— Tidewater (Int'l)	3B-1B-OF	120	432	51	105	21	3	10	54	.243	25	89	1	114	†220	22	.938
— New York (N.L.)	3B	7	14	0	3	0	0	0	1	.214	0	3	0	1	4	1	.833
1985— Tidewater (Int'l)	3B-1B	95	348	44	101	24	2	9	43	.290	32	60	3	56	209	†22	.923
1986— New York (N.L.)	O-S-3-1	108	328	51	91	22	2	12	43	.277	33	61	3	158	69	10	.958
1987— San Diego (N.L.)■	3B-OF	62	196	19	48	7	1	7	26	.245	20	38	0	32	108	8	.946
— San Fran. (N.L.)■	3B-SS-OF	69	268	49	82	13	1	15	44	.306	28	50	9	44	132	7	.962
1988— San Francisco (N.L.)	3B-OF	148	505	60	127	25	7	19	80	.251	48	85	5	118	205	22	.936
1989— San Francisco (N.L.)	OF-3B	154	543	100	158	34	6	*47	*125	.291	87	115	3	305	10	7	.978
1990— San Francisco (N.L.)	OF	140	524	90	152	24	2	35	93	.290	58	87	4	295	9	9	.971
1991— San Francisco (N.L.)	OF-1B	113	371	52	95	13	1	27	69	.256	43	57	2	188	6	6	.970
1992— Seattle (A.L.)■	OF-DH	99	360	48	103	24	0	9	67	.286	35	46	0	130	4	0	1.000
1993— Cincinnati (N.L.)■	OF	93	323	56	110	21	3	19	64	.341	25	48	1	149	7	7	.957
1994— Cincinnati (N.L.)	OF-1B	95	310	57	101	18	1	30	77	.326	59	62	2	139	10	4	.974
1995— Fukuoka (Jp. Pac.)■	OF	37	130	...	39	...	...	8	28	.300	...	...	...	...	...	...	...
1996— Boston (A.L.)■	OF-DH	27	92	9	28	4	0	2	13	.304	11	14	0	29	0	2	.935
— Pawtucket (Int'l)	OF	5	16	1	2	0	0	0	0	.125	1	5	0	2	0	1	.667
— Cincinnati (N.L.)■	OF-1B	37	114	18	37	11	0	6	26	.325	26	16	0	73	2	2	.974
1997— Cleveland (A.L.)	DH-OF	20	59	7	9	1	0	4	11	.153	9	11	1	0	0	1	1.000
American League totals (3 years)		146	511	64	140	29	0	15	91	.274	55	71	1	159	4	3	.982
National League totals (10 years)		1026	3496	552	1004	188	24	217	648	.287	427	622	29	1502	562	83	.961
Major league totals (12 years)		1172	4007	616	1144	217	24	232	739	.286	482	693	30	1661	566	86	.963

CHAMPIONSHIP SERIES RECORD

Year — Team (League)	Pos.	G	AB	R	H	2B	3B	HR	RBI	Avg.	BB	SO	SB	PO	A	E	Avg.
1986— New York (N.L.)	OF	2	8	1	2	0	0	0	0	.250	0	1	0	3	0	0	1.000
1987— San Francisco (N.L.)	3B	7	30	2	8	1	0	1	2	.267	0	3	1	4	11	1	.938
1989— San Francisco (N.L.)	OF	5	17	5	6	0	0	2	7	.353	3	0	0	15	1	1	.941
Championship series totals (3 years)		14	55	8	16	1	0	3	9	.291	3	4	1	22	12	2	.944

WORLD SERIES RECORD

NOTES: Member of World Series championship team (1986).

Year — Team (League)	Pos.	G	AB	R	H	2B	3B	HR	RBI	Avg.	BB	SO	SB	PO	A	E	Avg.
1986— New York (N.L.)	PH-OF-DH	5	8	1	2	0	0	0	0	.250	0	3	0	2	0	0	1.000
1989— San Francisco (N.L.)	OF	4	17	2	5	0	0	1	2	.294	0	3	0	10	0	1	.909
World Series totals (2 years)		9	25	3	7	0	0	1	2	.280	0	6	0	10	2	1	.923

ALL-STAR GAME RECORD

Year League	Pos.	AB	R	H	2B	3B	HR	RBI	Avg.	BB	SO	SB	PO	A	E	Avg.
1989— National	OF	4	1	2	0	0	0	1	.500	0	2	0	0	0	0	...
1990— National	OF	2	0	0	0	0	0	0	.000	0	1	0	1	0	1	1.000
All-Star Game totals (2 years)		6	1	2	0	0	0	1	.333	0	3	0	1	0	0	1.000

MITCHELL, LARRY   P   YANKEES

PERSONAL: Born October 16, 1971, in Flint, Mich. ... 6-1/219. ... Throws right, bats right. ... Full name: Larry Paul Mitchell II.

HIGH SCHOOL: Charlottesville (Va.).

COLLEGE: James Madison.

TRANSACTIONS/CAREER NOTES: Selected by Philadelphia Phillies organization in fifth round of free-agent draft (June 1, 1992). ... Claimed on waivers by New York Yankees (March 27, 1997).

STATISTICAL NOTES: Led Eastern League with 15 wild pitches in 1994.

Year — Team (League)	W	L	Pct.	ERA	G	GS	CG	ShO	Sv.	IP	H	R	ER	BB	SO
1992— Martinsville (App.)	1	0	1.000	1.42	3	3	0	0	0	19	17	8	3	6	18
— Batavia (N.Y.-Penn)	7	2	.778	2.63	10	10	3	1	0	65	63	25	19	11	58
1993— Spartanburg (SAL)	6	6	.500	4.10	19	19	4	*2	0	116 1/3	113	55	53	54	114
— Clearwater (Fla. St.)	4	4	.500	3.00	9	9	1	0	0	57	50	23	19	21	45
1994— Reading (Eastern)	10	13	.435	3.97	30	*30	2	0	0	165 1/3	143	91	73	*103	128
1995— Reading (Eastern)	6	11	.353	5.54	25	24	1	1	0	128 1/3	136	85	79	72	107
1996— Reading (Eastern)	3	6	.333	5.21	34	2	0	0	0	57	55	39	33	44	71
— Scran./W.B. (Int'l)	1	1	.500	2.55	11	0	0	0	1	24 2/3	19	8	7	10	24
— Philadelphia (N.L.)	0	0	...	4.50	7	0	0	0	0	12	14	6	6	5	7
1997— Norwich (Eastern)■	9	9	.500	3.49	57	0	0	0	0	95 1/3	98	45	37	37	99
Major league totals (1 year)	0	0	...	4.50	7	0	0	0	0	12	14	6	6	5	7

M

MLICKI, DAVE   P   METS

PERSONAL: Born June 8, 1968, in Cleveland. ... 6-4/205. ... Throws right, bats right. ... Full name: David John Mlicki. ... Brother of Doug Mlicki, pitcher, Houston Astros organization. ... Name pronounced muh-LICK-ee.
HIGH SCHOOL: Cheyenne Mountain (Colorado Springs, Colo.).
COLLEGE: Oklahoma State.
TRANSACTIONS/CAREER NOTES: Selected by Seattle Mariners organization in 23rd round of free-agent draft (June 5, 1989); did not sign. ... Selected by Cleveland Indians organization in 17th round of free-agent draft (June 4, 1990). ... On Cleveland disabled list (April 4-August 4, 1993); included rehabilitation assignment to Canton/Akron (July 19-August 4). ... Traded by Indians organization with P Jerry DiPoto, P Paul Byrd and a player to be named later to New York Mets organization for OF Jeromy Burnitz and P Joe Roa (November 18, 1994); Mets acquired 2B Jesus Azuaje to complete deal (December 6, 1994).
STATISTICAL NOTES: Led International League with 26 home runs allowed in 1994.
MISCELLANEOUS: Struck out in only appearance as pinch-hitter (1996). ... Appeared in one game as pinch-runner (1997).

Year Team (League)	W	L	Pct.	ERA	G	GS	CG	ShO	Sv.	IP	H	R	ER	BB	SO
1990— Burlington (Appalachian)....	3	1	.750	3.50	8	1	0	0	0	18	16	11	7	6	17
— Watertown (NYP)	3	0	1.000	3.38	7	4	0	0	0	32	33	15	12	11	28
1991— Columbus (S. Atl.)............	8	6	.571	4.20	22	19	2	0	0	115²/₃	101	70	54	70	136
1992— Cant./Akr. (Eastern)	11	9	.550	3.60	27	*27	2	0	0	172²/₃	143	77	69	•80	146
— Cleveland (A.L.)..................	0	2	.000	4.98	4	4	0	0	0	21²/₃	23	14	12	16	16
1993— Cant./Akr. (Eastern)	2	1	.667	0.39	6	6	0	0	0	23	15	2	1	8	21
— Cleveland (A.L.).................	0	0	...	3.38	3	3	0	0	0	13¹/₃	11	6	5	6	7
1994— Charlotte (Int'l)...............	6	10	.375	4.25	28	28	0	0	0	165¹/₃	179	85	78	64	152
1995— New York (N.L.)■..........	9	7	.563	4.26	29	25	0	0	0	160²/₃	160	82	76	54	123
1996— New York (N.L.)...........	6	7	.462	3.30	51	2	0	0	1	90	95	46	33	33	83
1997— New York (N.L.)...........	8	12	.400	4.00	32	32	1	1	0	193²/₃	194	89	86	76	157
A.L. totals (2 years)	0	2	.000	4.37	7	7	0	0	0	35	34	20	17	22	23
N.L. totals (3 years)	23	26	.469	3.95	112	59	1	1	1	444¹/₃	449	217	195	163	363
Major league totals (5 years)	23	28	.451	3.98	119	66	1	1	1	479¹/₃	483	237	212	185	386

MLICKI, DOUG   P   ASTROS

PERSONAL: Born April 12, 1971, in Cleveland. ... 6-3/175. ... Throws right, bats right. ... Full name: Douglas James Mlicki. ... Brother of Dave Mlicki, pitcher, New York Mets. ... Name pronounced muh-LICK-ee.
COLLEGE: Ohio University.
TRANSACTIONS/CAREER NOTES: Selected by Houston Astros organization in 12th round of free-agent draft (June 1, 1992).
STATISTICAL NOTES: Led Florida State League with 16 home runs allowed in 1993.

Year Team (League)	W	L	Pct.	ERA	G	GS	CG	ShO	Sv.	IP	H	R	ER	BB	SO
1992— Auburn (N.Y.-Penn)	1	6	.143	2.99	14	13	0	0	0	81¹/₃	50	35	27	30	83
1993— Osceola (Florida St.)..........	11	10	.524	3.91	26	23	0	0	0	158²/₃	158	81	69	65	111
1994— Jackson (Texas)	13	7	.650	3.38	23	23	1	0	0	138²/₃	107	62	52	54	130
1995— Jackson (Texas)	8	3	.727	2.79	16	16	2	0	0	96²/₃	73	41	30	33	72
— Tucson (PCL)	1	2	.333	5.56	6	6	0	0	0	34	44	27	21	6	22
1996— Tucson (PCL)	5	11	.313	4.72	26	26	0	0	0	137¹/₃	171	89	72	41	98
1997— New Orleans (A.A.)..........	4	3	.571	3.60	14	3	0	0	0	30	27	12	12	10	18
— Kissimmee (Florida State)..	0	0	...	0.00	1	1	0	0	0	4	4	0	0	0	2
— Jackson (Texas)	4	4	.500	5.36	9	9	0	0	0	48²/₃	69	36	29	20	35

MOEHLER, BRIAN   P   TIGERS

PERSONAL: Born December 31, 1971, in Rockingham, N.C. ... 6-3/195. ... Throws right, bats right. ... Full name: Brian Merritt Moehler.
HIGH SCHOOL: Richmond (N.C.) South
COLLEGE: North Carolina-Greensboro.
TRANSACTIONS/CAREER NOTES: Selected by Detroit Tigers organization in sixth round of free-agent draft (June 3, 1993). ... On disabled list (August 9-22, 1997).

Year Team (League)	W	L	Pct.	ERA	G	GS	CG	ShO	Sv.	IP	H	R	ER	BB	SO
1993— Niagara Falls (NYP)	6	5	.545	3.22	12	11	0	0	0	58²/₃	51	33	21	27	38
1994— Lakeland (Fla. St.)	12	12	.500	3.01	26	25	5	2	0	164²/₃	153	66	55	65	92
1995— Jacksonville (Southern)......	8	10	.444	4.82	28	27	0	0	0	162¹/₃	176	94	87	52	89
1996— Detroit (A.L.)	0	1	.000	4.35	2	2	0	0	0	10¹/₃	11	10	5	8	7
— Jacksonville (Southern)......	15	6	.714	3.48	28	28	1	0	0	173¹/₃	186	80	67	50	120
1997— Detroit (A.L.)	11	12	.478	4.67	31	31	2	1	0	175¹/₃	198	97	91	61	97
Major league totals (2 years)	11	13	.458	4.65	33	33	2	1	0	185²/₃	209	107	96	69	99

MOHLER, MIKE   P   ATHLETICS

PERSONAL: Born July 26, 1968, in Dayton, Ohio. ... 6-2/209. ... Throws left, bats right. ... Full name: Michael Ross Mohler.
HIGH SCHOOL: East Ascension (Gonzales, La.).
COLLEGE: Nicholls State (La.).
TRANSACTIONS/CAREER NOTES: Selected by Oakland Athletics organization in 42nd round of free-agent draft (June 5, 1989). ... On Tacoma disabled list (April 7-May 24, 1994).
MISCELLANEOUS: Appeared in two games as pinch-runner (1997).

Year Team (League)	W	L	Pct.	ERA	G	GS	CG	ShO	Sv.	IP	H	R	ER	BB	SO
1990— Madison (Midwest)	1	1	.500	3.41	42	2	0	0	1	63¹/₃	56	34	24	32	72
1991— Modesto (California)	9	4	.692	2.86	21	20	1	0	0	122²/₃	106	48	39	45	98
— Huntsville (Southern)	4	2	.667	3.57	8	8	0	0	0	53	55	22	21	20	27
1992— Huntsville (Southern)	3	8	.273	3.59	44	6	0	0	3	80¹/₃	72	41	32	39	56

M

Year— Team (League)	W	L	Pct.	ERA	G	GS	CG	ShO	Sv.	IP	H	R	ER	BB	SO
1993— Oakland (A.L.)	1	6	.143	5.60	42	9	0	0	0	64 1/3	57	45	40	44	42
1994— Modesto (California)	1	1	.500	2.76	7	5	0	0	1	29 1/3	21	9	9	6	29
— Tacoma (PCL)	1	3	.250	3.53	17	11	0	0	0	63 2/3	66	31	25	21	50
— Oakland (A.L.)	0	1	.000	7.71	1	1	0	0	0	2 1/3	2	3	2	2	4
1995— Edmonton (PCL)	2	1	.667	2.60	29	0	0	0	5	45	40	16	13	20	28
— Oakland (A.L.)	1	1	.500	3.04	28	0	0	0	1	23 2/3	16	8	8	18	15
1996— Oakland (A.L.)	6	3	.667	3.67	72	0	0	0	7	81	79	36	33	41	64
1997— Oakland (A.L.)	1	10	.091	5.13	62	10	0	0	1	101 2/3	116	65	58	54	66
Major league totals (5 years)......	**9**	**21**	**.300**	**4.65**	**205**	**20**	**0**	**0**	**9**	**273**	**270**	**157**	**141**	**159**	**191**

MOLINA, IZZY — C

PERSONAL: Born June 3, 1971, in New York. ... 6-1/214. ... Bats right, throws right. ... Full name: Islay Molina.
HIGH SCHOOL: Christopher Columbus (Miami).
TRANSACTIONS/CAREER NOTES: Selected by Oakland Athletics organization in 22nd round of free-agent draft (June 4, 1990). ... Granted free agency (December 21, 1997).
STATISTICAL NOTES: Tied for Arizona League lead in errors by catcher with six in 1990. ... Tied for Midwest League lead in double plays by catcher with eight in 1991. ... Tied for California League lead in grounding into double plays with 20 in 1992. ... Led California League catchers with 871 total chances and 28 passed balls in 1992. ... Led California League catchers with 740 putouts, 119 assists, 15 errors, 874 total chances, 11 double plays and 20 passed balls in 1993. ... Led Southern League catchers with 831 total chances and 14 passed balls in 1994. ... Led Southern League catchers with 74 assists and 11 double plays in 1995.

Year— Team (League)	Pos.	G	AB	R	H	2B	3B	HR	RBI	Avg.	BB	SO	SB	PO	A	E	Avg.
1990— Arizona A's (Ariz.)	C-1B	39	127	20	43	12	2	0	18	.339	9	22	5	261	17	‡6	.979
1991— Madison (Midwest)	C	95	316	35	89	16	1	3	45	.282	15	38	6	560	63	8	.987
1992— Reno (California)	C	116	436	71	113	17	2	10	75	.259	39	57	8	*716	*139	16	.982
— Tacoma (PCL)	C	10	36	3	7	0	1	0	5	.194	2	6	1	52	4	0	1.000
1993— Modesto (California) .	C-OF	125	444	61	116	26	5	6	69	.261	44	85	2	†740	†119	†15	.983
1994— Huntsville (Southern) .	C	116	388	31	84	17	2	8	50	.216	16	47	5	*703	*116	12	.986
1995— Edmonton (PCL)	C	2	6	0	1	0	0	0	0	.167	0	2	0	9	1	0	1.000
— Huntsville (Southern) .	C-1B	83	301	38	78	16	1	8	26	.259	26	62	3	462	†75	12	.978
1996— Edmonton (PCL)	C-1B	98	342	45	90	12	3	12	56	.263	25	55	2	582	65	7	.989
— Oakland (A.L.)	C-DH	14	25	0	5	2	0	0	1	.200	1	3	0	31	1	0	1.000
1997— Oakland (A.L.)	C	48	111	6	22	3	1	3	7	.198	3	17	0	218	17	2	.992
— Edmonton (PCL)	C-P	1	218	33	57	11	3	6	34	.261	12	27	2	330	32	2	.995
Major league totals (2 years)		**62**	**136**	**6**	**27**	**5**	**1**	**3**	**8**	**.199**	**4**	**20**	**0**	**249**	**18**	**2**	**.993**

RECORD AS PITCHER

Year— Team (League)	W	L	Pct.	ERA	G	GS	CG	ShO	Sv.	IP	H	R	ER	BB	SO
1997— Edmonton (PCL)	0	0	. . .	0.00	1	0	0	0	0	1/3	0	0	0	0	0

MOLITOR, PAUL — DH/1B — TWINS

M

PERSONAL: Born August 22, 1956, in St. Paul, Minn. ... 6-0/193. ... Bats right, throws right. ... Full name: Paul Leo Molitor.
HIGH SCHOOL: Cretin (St. Paul).
COLLEGE: Minnesota.
TRANSACTIONS/CAREER NOTES: Selected by St. Louis Cardinals organization in 28th round of free-agent draft (June 5, 1974); did not sign. ... Selected by Milwaukee Brewers organization in first round (third pick overall) of free-agent draft (June 7, 1977). ... On disabled list (June 24-July 18, 1980; May 3-August 12, 1981; May 2, 1984-remainder of season; August 13-28, 1985; May 10-30, June 2-17 and June 19-July 8, 1986; and April 30-May 26 and June 27-July 16, 1987). ... Granted free agency (November 9, 1987). ... Re-signed by Brewers (January 5, 1988). ... On disabled list (March 30-April 14, 1989). ... On Milwaukee disabled list (April 2-27, 1990). ... On Milwaukee disabled list (June 17-July 30, 1990); included rehabilitation assignment to Beloit (July 28). ... Granted free agency (October 30, 1992). ... Signed by Toronto Blue Jays (December 7, 1992). ... Granted free agency (November 3, 1995). ... Signed by Minnesota Twins (December 5, 1995). ... On disabled list (April 17-May 2, 1997). ... Granted free agency (October 28, 1997). ... Re-signed by Twins (December 6, 1997).
RECORDS: Shares major league record for most stolen bases in one inning—3 (July 26, 1987, first inning). ... Holds A.L. single-season record for most stolen bases without being caught stealing—20 (1994).
HONORS: Named shortstop on The Sporting News college All-America team (1977). ... Named Midwest League Most Valuable Player (1977). ... Named A.L. Rookie Player of the Year by The Sporting News (1978). ... Named designated hitter on The Sporting News A.L. All-Star team (1987 and 1993-96). ... Named designated hitter on The Sporting News A.L. Silver Slugger team (1987-88, 1993 and 1996).
STATISTICAL NOTES: Hit three home runs in one game (May 12, 1982). ... Led A.L. third basemen with 29 errors and 48 double plays in 1982. ... Had 39-game hitting streak (July 16-August 25, 1987). ... Hit for the cycle (May 15, 1991). ... Career major league grand slams: 3.
MISCELLANEOUS: Holds Milwaukee Brewers all-time record for highest batting average (.303) and most stolen bases (412). ... Holds Toronto Blue Jays all-time record for highest batting average (.315).

Year— Team (League)	Pos.	G	AB	R	H	2B	3B	HR	RBI	Avg.	BB	SO	SB	PO	A	E	Avg.
1977— Burl. (Midw.)	SS	64	228	52	79	12	0	8	50	.346	47	25	14	83	207	28	.912
1978— Milwaukee (A.L.)	2B-S-DH-3	125	521	73	142	26	4	6	45	.273	19	54	30	253	401	22	.967
1979— Milwaukee (A.L.)	2B-SS-DH	140	584	88	188	27	16	9	62	.322	48	48	33	309	440	16	.979
1980— Milwaukee (A.L.)	2-S-DH-3	111	450	81	137	29	2	9	37	.304	48	48	34	260	336	20	.968
1981— Milwaukee (A.L.)	OF-DH	64	251	45	67	11	0	2	19	.267	25	29	10	119	4	3	.976
1982— Milwaukee (A.L.)	3B-DH-SS	160	*666	*136	201	26	8	19	71	.302	69	93	41	134	350	†32	.938
1983— Milwaukee (A.L.)	3B-DH	152	608	95	164	28	6	15	47	.270	59	74	41	105	343	16	.966
1984— Milwaukee (A.L.)	3B-DH	13	46	3	10	1	0	0	6	.217	2	8	1	7	21	2	.933
1985— Milwaukee (A.L.)	3B-DH	140	576	93	171	28	3	10	48	.297	54	80	21	126	263	19	.953
1986— Milwaukee (A.L.)	3B-DH-OF	105	437	62	123	24	6	9	55	.281	40	81	20	86	171	15	.945
1987— Milwaukee (A.L.)	DH-3B-2B	118	465	*114	164	*41	5	16	75	.353	69	67	45	60	113	5	.972
1988— Milwaukee (A.L.)	3B-DH-2B	154	609	115	190	34	6	13	60	.312	71	54	41	87	188	17	.942
1989— Milwaukee (A.L.)	3B-DH-2B	155	615	84	194	35	4	11	56	.315	64	67	27	106	287	18	.956

Year Team (League)	Pos.	G	AB	R	H	2B	3B	HR	RBI	Avg.	BB	SO	SB	PO	A	E	Avg.
1990— Milwaukee (A.L.)	2-1-DH-3	103	418	64	119	27	6	12	45	.285	37	51	18	463	222	10	.986
— Beloit (Midwest)	DH	1	4	1	2	0	0	1	1	.500	0	0	0	...	...	...	...
1991— Milwaukee (A.L.)	DH-1B	158	*665	*133	*216	32	•13	17	75	.325	77	62	19	389	32	6	.986
1992— Milwaukee (A.L.)	DH-1B	158	609	89	195	36	7	12	89	.320	73	66	31	461	26	2	.996
1993— Toronto (A.L.)■	DH-1B	160	636	121	*211	37	5	22	111	.332	77	71	22	178	14	3	.985
1994— Toronto (A.L.)	DH-1B	*115	454	86	155	30	4	14	75	.341	55	48	20	47	3	0	1.000
1995— Toronto (A.L.)	DH	130	525	63	142	31	2	15	60	.270	61	57	12	...	...	...	...
1996— Minnesota (A.L.)■	DH-1B	161	660	99	*225	41	8	9	113	.341	56	72	18	138	13	1	.993
1997— Minnesota (A.L.)	DH-1B	135	538	63	164	32	4	10	89	.305	45	73	11	99	7	1	.991
Major league totals (20 years)		2557	10333	1707	3178	576	109	230	1238	.308	1049	1203	495	3427	3234	208	.970

DIVISION SERIES RECORD

Year Team (League)	Pos.	G	AB	R	H	2B	3B	HR	RBI	Avg.	BB	SO	SB	PO	A	E	Avg.
1981— Milwaukee (A.L.)	OF	5	20	2	5	0	0	1	1	.250	2	5	0	12	0	0	1.000

CHAMPIONSHIP SERIES RECORD

RECORDS: Holds single-series record for most consecutive hits—6 (1993). ... Shares career record for most consecutive hits—6 (1993).

Year Team (League)	Pos.	G	AB	R	H	2B	3B	HR	RBI	Avg.	BB	SO	SB	PO	A	E	Avg.
1982— Milwaukee (A.L.)	3B	5	19	4	6	1	0	2	5	.316	2	3	1	4	11	2	.882
1993— Toronto (A.L.)	DH	6	23	7	9	2	1	1	5	.391	3	3	0	...	...	...	...
Championship series totals (2 years)		11	42	11	15	3	1	3	10	.357	5	6	1	4	11	2	.882

WORLD SERIES RECORD

RECORDS: Holds single-game records for most hits—5; and most singles—5 (October 12, 1982). ... Shares single-series record for most runs—10 (1993). ... Shares single-game record (nine innings) for most at-bats—6 (October 12, 1982).

NOTES: Named Most Valuable Player (1993). ... Member of World Series championship team (1993).

Year Team (League)	Pos.	G	AB	R	H	2B	3B	HR	RBI	Avg.	BB	SO	SB	PO	A	E	Avg.
1982— Milwaukee (A.L.)	3B	7	31	5	11	0	0	0	3	.355	2	4	1	4	9	0	1.000
1993— Toronto (A.L.)	DH-3B-1B	6	24	10	12	2	2	2	8	.500	3	0	1	7	3	0	1.000
World Series totals (2 years)		13	55	15	23	2	2	2	11	.418	5	4	2	11	12	0	1.000

ALL-STAR GAME RECORD

Year League	Pos.	AB	R	H	2B	3B	HR	RBI	Avg.	BB	SO	SB	PO	A	E	Avg.
1980— American					Selected, did not play—injured.											
1985— American	3B-OF	1	0	0	0	0	0	0	.000	0	0	0	0	0	0	...
1988— American	2B	3	0	0	0	0	0	0	.000	0	1	0	1	2	0	1.000
1991— American	3B	0	0	0	0	0	0	0	...	0	0	0	0	0	0	...
1992— American	PH-1B	2	0	1	0	0	0	0	.500	0	1	0	5	0	1	.833
1993— American	DH	1	0	0	0	0	0	0	.000	1	0	0	...	...	...	...
1994— American	PH	1	0	0	0	0	0	0	.000	0	0	0	...	...	...	...
All-Star Game totals (6 years)		8	0	1	0	0	0	0	.125	1	2	0	6	2	1	.889

M

MONAHAN, SHANE OF MARINERS

PERSONAL: Born August 12, 1974, in Syosset, N.Y. ... 6-0/195. ... Bats left, throws right. ... Full name: Shane Hartland Monahan. ... Son of Hartland Monahan, right winger with six NHL teams (1973-74 through 1980-81); great-grandson Howie Morenz, Hockey Hall of Fame center with three NHL teams (1923-24 through 1936-37); grandson of Bernie "Boom Boom" Geoffrion, Hockey Hall of Fame right winger with Montreal Canadiens and New York Rangers (1950-51 through 1967-68).

HIGH SCHOOL: Wheeler (Marietta, Ga.).

COLLEGE: Clemson.

TRANSACTIONS/CAREER NOTES: Selected by Seattle Mariners organization in second round of free-agent draft (June 1, 1995).

STATISTICAL NOTES: Led California League outfielders with 265 total chances in 1996.

Year Team (League)	Pos.	G	AB	R	H	2B	3B	HR	RBI	Avg.	BB	SO	SB	PO	A	E	Avg.
1995— Wisconsin (Midwest)	OF	59	233	34	66	9	6	1	32	.283	11	40	9	100	0	3	.971
1996— Lancaster (Calif.)	OF	132	*584	107	164	31	*12	14	97	.281	30	124	19	*248	10	7	.974
1997— Tacoma (PCL)	OF	21	85	15	25	4	0	2	12	.294	5	21	5	46	3	2	.961
— Memphis (Southern)	OF	107	401	52	121	24	6	12	76	.302	30	100	14	139	10	3	.980

MONDESI, RAUL OF DODGERS

PERSONAL: Born March 12, 1971, in San Cristobal, Dominican Republic. ... 5-11/212. ... Bats right, throws right. ... Name pronounced MON-de-see.

HIGH SCHOOL: Liceo Manuel Maria Valencia (Dominican Republic).

TRANSACTIONS/CAREER NOTES: Signed as non-drafted free agent by Los Angeles Dodgers organization (June 6, 1988). ... On Bakersfield disabled list (May 8-July 5, 1991). ... On Albuquerque disabled list (May 8-16, 1992). ... On San Antonio disabled list (June 2-16, June 24-August 10 and August 24, 1992-remainder of season).

HONORS: Named N.L. Rookie Player of the Year by THE SPORTING NEWS (1994). ... Named N.L. Rookie of the Year by Baseball Writers' Association of America (1994). ... Won N.L. Gold Glove as outfielder (1995 and 1997).

STATISTICAL NOTES: Career major league grand slams: 1.

Year Team (League)	Pos.	G	AB	R	H	2B	3B	HR	RBI	Avg.	BB	SO	SB	PO	A	E	Avg.
1990— Great Falls (Pio.)	OF	44	175	35	53	10	4	8	31	.303	11	30	30	65	4	1	.986
1991— Bakersfield (Calif.)	OF	28	106	23	30	7	2	3	13	.283	5	21	9	42	5	3	.940

Year Team (League)	Pos.	G	AB	R	H	2B	3B	HR	RBI	Avg.	BB	SO	SB	PO	A	E	Avg.
—San Antonio (Tex.)	OF	53	213	32	58	11	5	5	26	.272	8	47	8	101	6	4	.964
—Albuquerque (PCL).....	OF	2	9	3	3	0	1	0	0	.333	0	1	1	0	0	1	.000
1992—Albuquerque (PCL).....	OF	35	138	23	43	4	7	4	15	.312	9	35	2	89	8	7	.933
—San Antonio (Tex.)	OF	18	68	8	18	2	2	2	14	.265	1	24	3	31	6	1	.974
1993—Albuquerque (PCL).....	OF	110	425	65	119	22	7	12	65	.280	18	85	13	211	10	10	.957
—Los Angeles (N.L.)	OF	42	86	13	25	3	1	4	10	.291	4	16	4	55	3	3	.951
1994—Los Angeles (N.L.)	OF	112	434	63	133	27	8	16	56	.306	16	78	11	206	*16	8	.965
1995—Los Angeles (N.L.)	OF	139	536	91	153	23	6	26	88	.285	33	96	27	282	*16	6	.980
1996—Los Angeles (N.L.)	OF	157	634	98	188	40	7	24	88	.297	32	122	14	337	11	•12	.967
1997—Los Angeles (N.L.)	OF	159	616	95	191	42	5	30	87	.310	44	105	32	338	10	4	.989
Major league totals (5 years)		609	2306	360	690	135	27	100	329	.299	129	417	88	1218	56	33	.975

DIVISION SERIES RECORD

Year Team (League)	Pos.	G	AB	R	H	2B	3B	HR	RBI	Avg.	BB	SO	SB	PO	A	E	Avg.
1995—Los Angeles (N.L.)	OF	3	9	0	2	0	0	0	1	.222	0	2	0	8	0	0	1.000
1996—Los Angeles (N.L.)	OF	3	11	0	2	2	0	0	1	.182	0	4	0	2	0	0	1.000
Division series totals (2 years)		6	20	0	4	2	0	0	2	.200	0	6	0	10	0	0	1.000

ALL-STAR GAME RECORD

Year League	Pos.	AB	R	H	2B	3B	HR	RBI	Avg.	BB	SO	SB	PO	A	E	Avg.
1995—National	OF	1	0	0	0	0	0	0	.000	0	0	0	2	0	0	1.000

MONDS, WONDERFUL   OF   ROCKIES

PERSONAL: Born January 11, 1973, in Fort Pierce, Fla. ... 6-3/190. ... Bats right, throws right. ... Full name: Wonderful Terrific Monds.
HIGH SCHOOL: Westwood (Fort Pierce, Fla.).
COLLEGE: Tennessee State.
TRANSACTIONS/CAREER NOTES: Selected by Atlanta Braves organization in 50th round of free-agent draft (June 3, 1993). ... On Durham disabled list (May 19-July 3, 1995). ... On Greenville disabled list (April 21-August 6, 1996 and May 5-July 20, 1997). ... Released by Braves (September 2, 1997). ... Signed by Colorado Rockies organization (November 14, 1997).

Year Team (League)	Pos.	G	AB	R	H	2B	3B	HR	RBI	Avg.	BB	SO	SB	PO	A	E	Avg.
1993—Idaho Falls (Pio.)........	OF	60	214	47	64	13	8	4	35	.299	25	43	16	73	8	7	.920
1994—Macon (S. Atl.)...........	OF	104	365	70	106	23	12	10	41	.290	22	82	41	180	17	5	.975
—Durham (Carolina)......	OF	18	53	7	11	2	0	2	10	.208	2	11	5	21	1	0	1.000
1995—GC Braves (GCL)........	OF	4	15	1	2	0	0	0	1	.133	1	8	2	8	0	0	1.000
—Durham (Carolina)......	OF	81	297	44	83	17	0	6	33	.279	17	63	28	112	9	2	.984
1996—Greenville (Southern).	OF	32	110	17	33	9	1	2	14	.300	9	17	7	62	2	2	.970
—GC Braves (GCL)........	OF	3	5	3	2	0	0	2	3	.400	2	1	0	7	0	0	1.000
1997—Greenville (Southern).	OF	27	89	21	28	5	0	8	15	.315	20	23	6	61	3	4	.941
—GC Braves (GCL)........	OF	2	4	2	1	0	0	1	1	.250	1	1	0	0	0	0	...

MONTANE, IVAN   P   MARINERS

PERSONAL: Born June 3, 1973, in Santurce, Puerto Rico. ... 6-2/195. ... Throws right, bats right. ... Full name: Ivan Carlos Montane.
HIGH SCHOOL: Kilian (Miami).
JUNIOR COLLEGE: Miami-Dade (South) Community College.
TRANSACTIONS/CAREER NOTES: Selected by Seattle Mariners organization in ninth round of free-agent draft (June 1, 1992).
STATISTICAL NOTES: Led Arizona League with 18 wild pitches in 1992.

Year Team (League)	W	L	Pct.	ERA	G	GS	CG	ShO	Sv.	IP	H	R	ER	BB	SO
1992—Ariz. Mariners (Ariz.).........	1	3	.250	5.67	13	11	0	0	0	46	44	39	29	*44	48
1993—Bellingham (N'west).........	5	4	.556	3.93	15	15	1	0	0	73 1/3	55	36	32	37	53
1994—Appleton (Midwest)...........	8	9	.471	3.85	29	26	1	1	0	159	132	79	68	82	155
1995—Riverside (California).........	5	5	.500	5.63	24	16	0	0	0	92 2/3	101	67	58	71	79
1996—Lancaster (Calif.)...........	2	2	.500	3.64	11	0	0	0	0	59 1/3	57	37	24	43	54
—Port City (Southern).........	3	8	.273	5.20	18	18	0	0	0	100 1/3	96	67	58	75	81
1997—Memphis (Southern).........	0	8	.000	7.53	22	12	0	0	0	71 2/3	83	70	60	51	63
—Lancaster (Calif.)...............	1	2	.333	5.29	6	6	0	0	0	32 1/3	40	25	19	13	34

MONTGOMERY, JEFF   P   ROYALS

PERSONAL: Born January 7, 1962, in Wellston, Ohio. ... 5-11/180. ... Throws right, bats right. ... Full name: Jeffrey Thomas Montgomery.
HIGH SCHOOL: Wellston (Ohio).
COLLEGE: Marshall (bachelor of science degree in computer science, 1984).
TRANSACTIONS/CAREER NOTES: Selected by Cincinnati Reds organization in ninth round of free-agent draft (June 6, 1983). ... Traded by Reds to Kansas City Royals for OF Van Snider (February 15, 1988). ... Granted free agency (November 8, 1995). ... Re-signed by Royals (December 15, 1995). ... On Kansas City disabled list (April 18-May 3, 1997); included rehabilitation assignment to Omaha (April 29-May 3).
RECORDS: Shares major league record for striking out side on nine pitches (April 29, 1990, eighth inning).
HONORS: Named A.L. Fireman of the Year by THE SPORTING NEWS (1993).
MISCELLANEOUS: Holds Kansas City Royals all-time record for most saves (256).

Year Team (League)	W	L	Pct.	ERA	G	GS	CG	ShO	Sv.	IP	H	R	ER	BB	SO
1983—Billings (Pioneer)...............	6	2	.750	2.42	20	0	0	0	5	44 2/3	31	13	12	13	90
1984—Tampa (Florida State)........	5	3	.625	2.44	31	0	0	0	•14	44 1/3	29	15	12	30	56
—Vermont (Eastern).............	2	0	1.000	2.13	22	0	0	0	4	25 1/3	14	7	6	24	20
1985—Vermont (Eastern).............	5	3	.625	2.05	*53	1	0	0	9	101	63	25	23	48	89

M

Year	Team (League)	W	L	Pct.	ERA	G	GS	CG	ShO	Sv.	IP	H	R	ER	BB	SO
1986—	Denver (Am. Assoc.)	11	7	.611	4.39	30	22	2	2	1	151 2/3	162	88	74	57	78
1987—	Nashville (A.A.)	8	5	.615	4.14	24	21	1	0	0	139	132	76	64	51	121
—	Cincinnati (N.L.)■	2	2	.500	6.52	14	1	0	0	0	19 1/3	25	15	14	9	13
1988—	Omaha (Am. Assoc.)■	1	2	.333	1.91	20	0	0	0	13	28 1/3	15	6	6	11	36
—	Kansas City (A.L.)	7	2	.778	3.45	45	0	0	0	1	62 2/3	54	25	24	30	47
1989—	Kansas City (A.L.)	7	3	.700	1.37	63	0	0	0	18	92	66	16	14	25	94
1990—	Kansas City (A.L.)	6	5	.545	2.39	73	0	0	0	24	94 1/3	81	36	25	34	94
1991—	Kansas City (A.L.)	4	4	.500	2.90	67	0	0	0	33	90	83	32	29	28	77
1992—	Kansas City (A.L.)	1	6	.143	2.18	65	0	0	0	39	82 2/3	61	23	20	27	69
1993—	Kansas City (A.L.)	7	5	.583	2.27	69	0	0	0	•45	87 1/3	65	22	22	23	66
1994—	Kansas City (A.L.)	2	3	.400	4.03	42	0	0	0	27	44 2/3	48	21	20	15	50
1995—	Kansas City (A.L.)	2	3	.400	3.43	54	0	0	0	31	65 2/3	60	27	25	25	49
1996—	Kansas City (A.L.)	4	6	.400	4.26	48	0	0	0	24	63 1/3	59	31	30	19	45
1997—	Kansas City (A.L.)	1	4	.200	3.49	55	0	0	0	14	59 1/3	53	24	23	18	48
—	Omaha (Am. Assoc.)	0	0	...	0.00	2	0	0	0	0	2	1	0	0	1	2
A.L. totals (10 years)		41	41	.500	2.81	581	0	0	0	256	742	630	257	232	244	639
N.L. totals (1 year)		2	2	.500	6.52	14	1	0	0	0	19 1/3	25	15	14	9	13
Major league totals (11 years)		43	43	.500	2.91	595	1	0	0	256	761 1/3	655	272	246	253	652

ALL-STAR GAME RECORD

Year	League	W	L	Pct.	ERA	GS	CG	ShO	Sv.	IP	H	R	ER	BB	SO
1992—	American	0	0	...	27.00	0	0	0	0	2/3	2	2	2	0	0
1993—	American	0	0	...	0.00	0	0	0	0	1	0	0	0	0	1
1996—	American							Did not play.							
All-Star totals (2 years)		0	0	...	10.80	0	0	0	0	1 2/3	2	2	2	0	1

MONTGOMERY, RAY — OF — ASTROS

PERSONAL: Born August 8, 1969, in Bronxville, N.Y. ... 6-3/195. ... Bats right, throws right. ... Full name: Raymond James Montgomery.
COLLEGE: Fordham.
TRANSACTIONS/CAREER NOTES: Selected by Houston Astros organization in 13th round of free-agent draft (June 4, 1990). ... On disabled list (April 10-17 and June 3-July 24, 1992). ... On Houston disabled list (June 18, 1997-remainder of season).

Year	Team (League)	Pos.	G	AB	R	H	2B	3B	HR	RBI	Avg.	BB	SO	SB	PO	A	E	Avg.
1990—	Auburn (NY-Penn)	OF-1B	61	193	19	45	8	1	0	13	.233	23	32	12	245	14	8	.970
1991—	Burlington (Midw.)	OF	120	433	60	109	24	3	3	57	.252	37	65	16	249	12	4	.985
1992—	Jackson (Texas)	OF	51	148	13	31	4	1	1	10	.209	7	27	4	76	3	2	.975
1993—	Jackson (Texas)	OF	100	338	50	95	16	3	10	59	.281	36	54	12	151	9	6	.964
—	Tucson (PCL)	OF	15	50	9	17	3	1	2	6	.340	5	7	1	33	1	0	1.000
1994—	Tucson (PCL)	OF	103	332	51	85	19	6	7	51	.256	35	54	5	179	11	8	.960
1995—	Jackson (Texas)	OF-1B	35	127	24	38	8	1	10	24	.299	13	13	6	102	10	1	.991
—	Tucson (PCL)	OF	88	291	48	88	19	0	11	68	.302	24	58	5	182	10	7	.965
1996—	Tucson (PCL)	OF-1B	100	360	70	110	20	0	22	75	.306	59	54	7	182	8	4	.979
—	Houston (N.L.)	OF	12	14	4	3	1	0	1	4	.214	1	5	0	6	0	0	1.000
1997—	Houston (N.L.)	OF	29	68	8	16	4	1	0	4	.235	5	18	0	25	2	0	1.000
—	New Orleans (A.A.)	OF	20	73	17	21	5	0	6	13	.288	11	15	1	33	0	1	.971
Major league totals (2 years)			41	82	12	19	5	1	1	8	.232	6	23	0	31	2	0	1.000

MONTGOMERY, STEVE — P — INDIANS

PERSONAL: Born December 25, 1970, in Westminster, Calif. ... 6-4/212. ... Throws right, bats right. ... Full name: Steven L. Montgomery.
HIGH SCHOOL: Fountain Valley (Calif.).
COLLEGE: Pepperdine.
TRANSACTIONS/CAREER NOTES: Selected by St. Louis Cardinals organization in third round of free-agent draft (June 1, 1992). ... Traded by Cardinals to Oakland Athletics for P Dennis Eckersley (February 13, 1996). ... Released by A's (September 18, 1996). ... Claimed on waivers by Cleveland Indians organization (August 7, 1997).

Year	Team (League)	W	L	Pct.	ERA	G	GS	CG	ShO	Sv.	IP	H	R	ER	BB	SO
1993—	St. Petersburg (FSL)	2	1	.667	2.66	14	5	0	0	3	40 1/3	33	14	12	9	34
—	Arkansas (Texas)	3	3	.500	3.94	6	6	0	0	0	32	34	17	14	12	19
1994—	Arkansas (Texas)	4	5	.444	3.28	50	9	0	0	2	107	97	43	39	33	73
1995—	Arkansas (Texas)	5	2	.714	3.25	*55	0	0	0	*36	61	52	22	22	22	56
1996—	Oakland (A.L.)■	1	0	1.000	9.22	8	0	0	0	0	13 2/3	18	14	14	13	8
—	Edmonton (PCL)	2	0	1.000	2.89	37	0	0	0	1	56	51	19	18	12	40
1997—	Edmonton (PCL)	2	1	.667	5.79	30	0	0	0	3	46 2/3	61	30	30	17	38
—	Oakland (A.L.)	0	1	.000	9.95	4	0	0	0	0	6 1/3	10	7	7	8	1
—	Buffalo (A.A.)■	1	2	.333	5.63	7	0	0	0	1	8	12	6	5	3	5
Major league totals (2 years)		1	1	.500	9.45	12	0	0	0	0	20	28	21	21	21	9

MOODY, ERIC — P — RANGERS

PERSONAL: Born January 6, 1971, in Greenville, S.C. ... 6-6/185. ... Throws right, bats right. ... Full name: Eric Lane Moody.
HIGH SCHOOL: Palmetto (Williamston, S.C.).
COLLEGE: Erskine, S.C. (degree in physical education).
TRANSACTIONS/CAREER NOTES: Selected by Texas Rangers organization in 24th round of free-agent draft (June 3, 1993).

Year	Team (League)	W	L	Pct.	ERA	G	GS	CG	ShO	Sv.	IP	H	R	ER	BB	SO
1993—	Erie (N.Y.-Penn)	3	3	.500	3.83	17	7	0	0	0	54	54	30	23	13	33
1994—	Hudson Valley (NYP)	7	3	.700	2.83	15	12	1	0	0	89	82	32	28	18	68
1995—	Charlotte (Fla. St.)	5	5	.500	2.75	13	13	2	2	0	88 1/3	84	30	27	13	72
1996—	Tulsa (Texas)	8	4	.667	3.57	44	5	0	0	16	95 2/3	92	40	38	23	80
1997—	Oklahoma City (A.A.)	5	6	.455	3.46	35	10	1	1	1	112	114	49	43	21	72
—	Texas (A.L.)	0	1	.000	4.26	10	1	0	0	0	19	26	10	9	2	12
Major league totals (1 year)		0	1	.000	4.26	10	1	0	0	0	19	26	10	9	2	12

M

MOORE, MARCUS — P — INDIANS

PERSONAL: Born November 2, 1970, in Oakland. ... 6-5/195. ... Throws right, bats both. ... Full name: Marcus Braymont Moore.
HIGH SCHOOL: John F. Kennedy (Richmond, Calif.).
TRANSACTIONS/CAREER NOTES: Selected by California Angels organization in 17th round of free-agent draft (June 1, 1988). ... Traded by Angels organization to Toronto Blue Jays organization for C Ken Rivers (December 4, 1990); completing deal in which Angels traded OF Devon White, P Willie Fraser and a player to be named later to Blue Jays for OF Junior Felix, IF Luis Sojo and a player to be named later (December 2, 1990). ... Selected by Colorado Rockies in third round (56th pick overall) of expansion draft (November 17, 1992). ... Traded by Rockies to Cincinnati Reds for IF Chris Sexton (April 10, 1995). ... Released by Reds organization (October 4, 1996). ... Signed by Akron, Cleveland Indians organization (April 18, 1997). ... On Akron disabled list (April 18-May 1, 1997).

Year — Team (League)	W	L	Pct.	ERA	G	GS	CG	ShO	Sv.	IP	H	R	ER	BB	SO
1989— Bend (Northwest)	2	5	.286	4.52	14	14	1	0	0	81²/₃	84	55	41	51	74
1990— Quad City (Midwest)	*16	5	.762	3.31	27	27	2	1	0	160¹/₃	150	83	59	106	160
1991— Dunedin (Fla. St.)■	6	13	.316	3.70	27	25	2	0	0	160²/₃	139	78	66	*99	115
1992— Knoxville (Southern)	5	10	.333	5.59	36	14	1	0	0	106¹/₃	110	82	66	79	85
1993— Central Valley (Cal.)■	1	0	1.000	0.75	8	0	0	0	2	12	7	3	1	9	15
— Colo. Springs (PCL)	1	5	.167	4.47	30	0	0	0	4	44¹/₃	54	26	22	29	38
— Colorado (N.L.)	3	1	.750	6.84	27	0	0	0	0	26¹/₃	30	25	20	20	13
1994— Colorado (N.L.)	1	1	.500	6.15	29	0	0	0	0	33²/₃	33	26	23	21	33
— Colo. Springs (PCL)	3	4	.429	8.00	19	8	0	0	0	54	67	59	48	61	54
1995— Indianapolis (A.A.)■	1	0	1.000	4.97	7	1	0	0	1	12²/₃	13	8	7	14	6
— Chattanooga (Southern)	6	1	.857	4.98	36	0	0	0	2	43¹/₃	31	24	24	34	57
1996— Indianapolis (A.A.)	4	7	.364	3.45	15	15	0	0	0	88²/₃	72	41	34	38	70
— Cincinnati (N.L.)	3	3	.500	5.81	23	0	0	0	2	26¹/₃	26	21	17	22	27
1997— Akron (Eastern)■	3	5	.375	4.94	13	10	1	0	0	71	84	50	39	32	63
— Buffalo (A.A.)	5	3	.625	2.54	10	10	3	1	0	71	54	26	20	31	72
Major league totals (3 years)	7	5	.583	6.25	79	0	0	0	2	86¹/₃	89	72	60	63	73

MOORE, TREY — P — EXPOS

PERSONAL: Born October 2, 1972, in Houston. ... 6-1/200. ... Throws left, bats left. ... Full name: Warren Neal Moore III.
HIGH SCHOOL: Keller (Texas).
COLLEGE: Texas A&M.
TRANSACTIONS/CAREER NOTES: Selected by Seattle Mariners organization in second round of free-agent draft (June 2, 1994). ... Traded by Mariners with C Chris Widger and P Matt Wagner to Montreal Expos for P Alex Pacheco and P Jeff Fassero (October 29, 1996).

Year — Team (League)	W	L	Pct.	ERA	G	GS	CG	ShO	Sv.	IP	H	R	ER	BB	SO
1994— Bellingham (N'west)	5	2	.714	2.63	11	10	1	0	0	61²/₃	48	18	18	24	73
1995— Riverside (California)	14	6	.700	3.09	24	24	0	0	0	148¹/₃	122	65	51	58	134
1996— Port City (Southern)	1	6	.143	7.71	11	11	0	0	0	53²/₃	73	54	46	33	42
— Lancaster (Calif.)	7	5	.583	4.10	15	15	2	0	0	94¹/₃	106	57	43	31	77
1997— Harrisburg (Eastern)■	11	6	.647	4.15	27	27	2	•2	0	162²/₃	152	91	75	66	137

MORANDINI, MICKEY — 2B — CUBS

PERSONAL: Born April 22, 1966, in Leechburg, Pa. ... 5-11/176. ... Bats left, throws right. ... Full name: Michael Robert Morandini. ... Name pronounced MOR-an-DEEN-ee.
HIGH SCHOOL: Leechburg (Pa.) Area.
COLLEGE: Indiana.
TRANSACTIONS/CAREER NOTES: Selected by Pittsburgh Pirates organization in seventh round of free-agent draft (June 2, 1987); did not sign. ... Selected by Philadelphia Phillies organization in fifth round of free-agent draft (June 1, 1988). ... On disabled list (June 15-30, 1996). ... Traded by Phillies to Chicago Cubs for OF Doug Glanville (December 23, 1997).
STATISTICAL NOTES: Led International League second basemen with 271 putouts, 419 assists and 701 total chances in 1990.
MISCELLANEOUS: Member of 1988 U.S. Olympic baseball team. ... Turned unassisted triple play while playing second base (September 20, 1992, sixth inning); ninth player ever to accomplish feat and first ever by second baseman during regular season.

						BATTING								FIELDING		
Year — Team (League)	Pos.	G	AB	R	H	2B	3B	HR	RBI	Avg.	BB	SO	SB	PO	A	E	Avg.
1989— Spartanburg (SAL)	SS	63	231	43	78	19	1	1	30	.338	35	45	18	87	198	10	.966
— Clearwater (FSL)	SS	17	63	14	19	4	1	0	4	.302	7	8	3	20	59	2	.975
— Reading (Eastern)	SS	48	188	39	66	12	1	5	29	.351	23	32	5	73	137	10	.955
1990— Scran./W.B. (Int'l)	2B-SS	139	503	76	131	24	*10	1	31	.260	60	90	16	†271	†419	11	.984
— Philadelphia (N.L.)	2B	25	79	9	19	4	0	1	3	.241	6	19	3	37	61	1	.990
1991— Scran./W.B. (Int'l)	2B	12	46	7	12	4	0	1	6	.261	5	6	2	19	38	1	.983
— Philadelphia (N.L.)	2B	98	325	38	81	11	4	1	20	.249	29	45	13	183	254	6	.986
1992— Philadelphia (N.L.)	2B-SS	127	422	47	112	8	8	3	30	.265	25	64	8	239	336	6	.990
1993— Philadelphia (N.L.)	2B	120	425	57	105	19	9	3	33	.247	34	73	13	208	288	5	.990
1994— Philadelphia (N.L.)	2B	87	274	40	80	16	5	2	26	.292	34	33	10	167	216	6	.985
1995— Philadelphia (N.L.)	2B	127	494	65	140	34	7	6	49	.283	42	80	9	269	336	7	.989
1996— Philadelphia (N.L.)	2B	140	539	64	135	24	6	3	32	.250	49	87	26	286	352	12	.982
1997— Philadelphia (N.L.)	2B-SS	150	553	83	163	40	2	1	39	.295	62	91	16	254	350	6	.990
Major league totals (8 years)		874	3111	403	835	156	41	20	232	.268	281	492	98	1643	2193	49	.987

CHAMPIONSHIP SERIES RECORD

						BATTING								FIELDING		
Year — Team (League)	Pos.	G	AB	R	H	2B	3B	HR	RBI	Avg.	BB	SO	SB	PO	A	E	Avg.
1993— Philadelphia (N.L.)	2B-PH	4	16	1	4	0	1	0	2	.250	0	3	1	8	9	1	.944

M

WORLD SERIES RECORD

Year	Team (League)	Pos.	G	AB	R	H	2B	3B	HR	RBI	Avg.	BB	SO	SB	PO	A	E	Avg.
1993—	Philadelphia (N.L.)......	PH-2B	3	5	1	1	0	0	0	0	.200	1	2	0	2	0	0	1.000

ALL-STAR GAME RECORD

Year	League	Pos.	AB	R	H	2B	3B	HR	RBI	Avg.	BB	SO	SB	PO	A	E	Avg.
1995—	National.....................	2B	1	0	0	0	0	0	0	.000	0	1	0	0	1	0	1.000

MORDECAI, MIKE　　　3B　　　EXPOS

PERSONAL: Born December 13, 1967, in Birmingham, Ala. ... 5-11/175. ... Bats right, throws right. ... Full name: Michael Howard Mordecai.
HIGH SCHOOL: Hewitt-Trussville (Ala.).
COLLEGE: South Alabama.
TRANSACTIONS/CAREER NOTES: Selected by Pittsburgh Pirates organization in 33rd round of free-agent draft (June 2, 1986); did not sign. ... Selected by Atlanta Braves organization in sixth round of free-agent draft (June 5, 1989). ... On disabled list (April 8-29, 1993). ... On Atlanta disabled list (April 19-May 11, 1996); included rehabilitation assignment to Richmond (May 8-11). ... Granted free agency (December 21, 1997). ... Signed by Montreal Expos organization (January 16, 1998).

Year	Team (League)	Pos.	G	AB	R	H	2B	3B	HR	RBI	Avg.	BB	SO	SB	PO	A	E	Avg.
1989—	Burlington (Midw.)	SS-3B	65	241	39	61	11	1	1	22	.253	33	43	12	80	163	21	.920
—Greenville (Southern) .	3B-2B	4	8	0	3	0	0	0	1	.375	1	1	0	4	6	0	1.000
1990—	Durham (Carolina)......	SS	72	271	42	76	11	7	3	36	.280	42	45	10	111	221	29	.920
1991—	Durham (Carolina)......	SS	109	397	52	104	15	2	4	42	.262	40	58	30	164	302	27	.945
1992—	Greenville (Southern) .	SS	65	222	31	58	13	1	4	31	.261	29	31	9	93	204	11	.964
—Richmond (Int'l)........	SS-2B-3B	36	118	12	29	3	0	1	6	.246	5	19	0	48	101	10	.937
1993—	Richmond (Int'l).......	2-S-3-O-C-1	72	205	29	55	8	1	2	14	.268	14	33	10	98	145	9	.964
1994—	Richmond (Int'l).......	SS-1B-3B	99	382	67	107	25	1	14	57	.280	35	50	14	117	279	22	.947
—Atlanta (N.L.)............	SS	4	4	1	1	0	0	1	3	.250	1	0	0	1	4	0	1.000
1995—	Atlanta (N.L.)............	2-1-3-S-O	69	75	10	21	6	0	3	11	.280	9	16	0	39	31	0	1.000
1996—	Atlanta (N.L.)............	2-3-S-1	66	108	12	26	5	0	2	8	.241	9	24	1	33	52	2	.977
—Richmond (Int'l)........	SS	3	11	2	2	0	0	1	2	.182	0	3	0	3	13	0	1.000
1997—	Atlanta (N.L.)............	3-2-S-1-DH-O	61	81	8	14	2	1	0	3	.173	6	16	0	26	17	0	1.000
—Richmond (Int'l)........	2B-3B-SS	31	122	23	38	10	0	3	15	.311	9	17	0	29	61	1	.989
Major league totals (4 years)		200	268	31	62	13	1	6	25	.231	25	56	1	99	104	2	.990

DIVISION SERIES RECORD

Year	Team (League)	Pos.	G	AB	R	H	2B	3B	HR	RBI	Avg.	BB	SO	SB	PO	A	E	Avg.
1995—	Atlanta (N.L.).............	PH-SS	2	3	1	2	1	0	0	2	.667	0	0	0	1	0	0	1.000
1996—	Atlanta (N.L.)									Did not play.								
Division series totals (1 year)		2	3	1	2	1	0	0	2	.667	0	0	0	1	0	0	1.000

CHAMPIONSHIP SERIES RECORD

Year	Team (League)	Pos.	G	AB	R	H	2B	3B	HR	RBI	Avg.	BB	SO	SB	PO	A	E	Avg.
1995—	Atlanta (N.L.).............	PH-SS	2	2	0	0	0	0	0	0	.000	0	1	0	0	0	0	...
1996—	Atlanta (N.L.).............	3B-PH-2B	4	4	1	1	0	0	0	0	.250	0	1	0	1	1	0	1.000
Championship series totals (2 years)		6	6	1	1	0	0	0	0	.167	0	2	0	1	1	0	1.000

WORLD SERIES RECORD

NOTES: Member of World Series championship team (1995).

Year	Team (League)	Pos.	G	AB	R	H	2B	3B	HR	RBI	Avg.	BB	SO	SB	PO	A	E	Avg.
1995—	Atlanta (N.L.).............	SS-DH	3	3	0	1	0	0	0	0	.333	0	1	0	0	6	0	1.000
1996—	Atlanta (N.L.).............	PH	1	1	0	0	0	0	0	0	.000	0	0	0	...	...	...	...
World Series totals (2 years)		4	4	0	1	0	0	0	0	.250	0	1	0	0	6	0	1.000

MOREL, RAMON　　　P　　　CUBS

PERSONAL: Born August 15, 1974, in Villa Gonzalez, Dominican Republic. ... 6-2/200. ... Throws right, bats right. ... Full name: Ramon Rafael Morel.
HIGH SCHOOL: Milagro Hernandez (Dominican Republic).
TRANSACTIONS/CAREER NOTES: Signed as non-drafted free agent by Pittsburgh Pirates organization (May 29, 1991). ... On Calgary disabled list (July 23-31, 1997). ... Claimed on waivers by Chicago Cubs (September 10, 1997).

Year	Team (League)	W	L	Pct.	ERA	G	GS	CG	ShO	Sv.	IP	H	R	ER	BB	SO
1991—	DSL Pirates (DSL).............	3	3	.500	3.60	16	1	0	0	0	25	25	20	10	16	14
1992—	DSL Pirates (DSL).............	2	0	1.000	1.06	3	3	0	0	0	17	12	2	2	7	9
—GC Pirates (GCL)..............	2	2	.500	4.34	14	2	1	1	0	45 2/3	49	26	22	11	29
1993—	Welland (N.Y.-Penn)..........	7	8	.467	4.21	16	16	0	0	0	77	90	45	36	21	51
1994—	Augusta (S. Atl.)................	10	7	.588	2.83	28	27	2	1	0	168 2/3	157	69	53	24	152
1995—	Lynchburg (Carolina)	3	7	.300	3.47	12	12	1	1	0	72 2/3	80	35	28	13	44
—Carolina (Southern)..........	3	3	.500	3.52	10	10	0	0	0	69	71	31	27	10	34
—Pittsburgh (N.L.)..............	0	1	.000	2.84	5	0	0	0	0	6 1/3	6	2	2	2	3
1996—	Carolina (Southern)..........	2	5	.286	5.09	11	11	0	0	0	63 2/3	75	42	36	16	44
—Pittsburgh (N.L.)..............	2	1	.667	5.36	29	0	0	0	0	42	57	27	25	19	22
1997—	Calgary (PCL)...................	6	7	.462	5.75	27	18	0	0	0	101 2/3	131	71	65	42	72
—Pittsburgh (N.L.)..............	0	0	...	4.70	5	0	0	0	0	7 2/3	11	4	4	4	4
—Chicago (N.L.)■...............	0	0	...	4.91	3	0	0	0	0	3 2/3	3	2	2	3	3
Major league totals (3 years)......	2	2	.500	4.98	42	0	0	0	0	59 2/3	77	35	33	28	32

M

MORENO, JULIO   P   ORIOLES

PERSONAL: Born October 23, 1975, in San Pedro de Macoris, Dominican Republic. ... 6-1/145. ... Throws right, bats right. ... Full name: Julio Cesar Moreno.
TRANSACTIONS/CAREER NOTES: Signed as non-drafted free agent by Baltimore Orioles organization (January 15, 1993). ... On disabled list (April 24-May 4, 1997).

Year Team (League)	W	L	Pct.	ERA	G	GS	CG	ShO	Sv.	IP	H	R	ER	BB	SO
1993— Dom. Orioles (DSL)	1	2	.333	12.54	16	2	0	0	0	28	45	42	39	28	11
1994— Dom. Orioles (DSL)	2	1	.667	3.61	8	8	2	1	0	47⅓	35	31	19	33	25
— GC Orioles (GCL)	0	22	.000	11.88	4	2	0	0	0	8⅓	14	14	11	1	6
1995— GC Orioles (GCL)	3	2	.600	1.59	5	5	1	1	0	34	17	9	6	7	29
— Bluefield (Appalachian)	4	3	.571	4.20	9	8	0	0	0	49⅓	61	31	23	12	36
1996— Frederick (Carolina)	9	10	.474	3.50	28	26	0	0	0	162	167	80	63	38	147
1997— Bowie (Eastern)	9	6	.600	3.83	27	25	1	0	0	138⅔	141	76	59	64	106

MORGAN, KEVIN   IF   METS

PERSONAL: Born December 3, 1969, in Lafayette, La. ... 6-1/170. ... Bats right, throws right. ... Full name: Kevin Lee Morgan.
HIGH SCHOOL: Acadiana (Lafayette, La.).
TRANSACTIONS/CAREER NOTES: Selected by Detroit Tigers organization in 30th round of free-agent draft (June 3, 1991). ... Traded to New York Mets organization for IF Joe Dellicarri (February 18, 1994).

							BATTING								FIELDING		
Year Team (League)	Pos.	G	AB	R	H	2B	3B	HR	RBI	Avg.	BB	SO	SB	PO	A	E	Avg.
1991— Niag. Falls (NYP)	SS-2B-3B	70	252	23	60	13	0	0	26	.238	22	49	8	116	206	20	.942
1992— Fayetteville (SAL)	SS	123	466	55	106	19	2	0	37	.227	49	61	15	158	294	48	.904
1993— Lakeland (Fla. St.)	SS	112	417	45	99	12	2	2	34	.237	32	84	9	184	365	29	.950
1994— St. Lucie (Fla. St.)■	2B-SS	132	448	63	122	8	3	1	47	.272	37	62	7	286	434	22	.970
1995— Binghamton (East.)	SS	114	430	63	119	21	1	4	51	.277	44	52	9	192	340	21	.962
— Norfolk (Int'l)	2B-SS	19	62	10	20	1	00	0	8	.323	4	8	1	37	55	1	.989
1996— Norfolk (Int'l)	2B	29	82	7	11	3	0	0	3	.134	9	14	3	49	73	3	.976
— Binghamton (East.)	SS	107	409	61	103	11	2	6	35	.252	53	59	13	170	330	23	.956
1997— Binghamton (East.)	SS-2B	51	191	16	37	7	0	1	10	.194	19	25	11	112	174	14	.953
— Norfolk (Int'l)	SS-2B	71	256	34	70	11	1	2	20	.273	27	26	6	100	213	16	.951
— New York (N.L.)	3B	1	1	0	0	0	0	0	0	.000	0	0	0	0	1	0	1.000
Major league totals (1 year)		1	1	0	0	0	0	0	0	.000	0	0	0	0	1	0	1.000

MORGAN, MIKE   P   TWINS

PERSONAL: Born October 8, 1959, in Tulare, Calif. ... 6-2/220. ... Throws right, bats right. ... Full name: Michael Thomas Morgan.
HIGH SCHOOL: Valley (Las Vegas).
TRANSACTIONS/CAREER NOTES: Selected by Oakland Athletics organization in first round (fourth pick overall) of free-agent draft (June 6, 1978). ... On disabled list (May 14-June 27, 1980). ... Traded by A's organization to New York Yankees for SS Fred Stanley and a player to be named later (November 3, 1980); A's acquired 2B Brian Doyle to complete deal (November 17, 1980). ... On disabled list (April 9-22, 1981). ... Traded by Yankees with OF/1B Dave Collins, 1B Fred McGriff and cash to Toronto Blue Jays for P Dale Murray and OF/C Tom Dodd (December 9, 1982). ... On Toronto disabled list (July 2-August 23, 1983); included rehabilitation assignment to Syracuse (August 1-18). ... Selected by Seattle Mariners from Blue Jays organization in Rule 5 major league draft (December 3, 1984). ... On Seattle disabled list (April 17, 1985-remainder of season); included rehabilitation assignment to Calgary (July 19-22). ... Traded by Mariners to Baltimore Orioles for P Ken Dixon (December 9, 1987). ... On Baltimore disabled list (June 9-July 19, 1988); included rehabilitation assignment to Rochester (June 30-July 17). ... On Baltimore disabled list (August 12, 1988-remainder of season). ... Traded by Orioles to Los Angeles Dodgers for OF Mike Devereaux (March 12, 1989). ... Granted free agency (October 28, 1991). ... Signed by Chicago Cubs (December 3, 1991). ... On disabled list (June 14-29, 1993; May 9-27, June 2-22 and July 28, 1994-remainder of season). ... On Chicago disabled list (April 24-May 25, 1995); included rehabilitation assignment to Orlando (May 15-25). ... Traded by Cubs with 3B/OF Paul Torres and C Francisco Morales to St. Louis Cardinals for 3B Todd Zeile and cash (June 16, 1995). ... On St. Louis disabled list (July 4-24, 1995). ... Granted free agency (November 6, 1995). ... Re-signed by Cardinals (December 7, 1995). ... On St. Louis disabled list (March 22-May 18, 1996); included rehabilitation assignment to St. Petersburg (April 20-May 15). ... Released by Cardinals (August 28, 1996). ... Signed by Cincinnati Reds (September 4, 1996). ... On disabled list (June 8-24, 1997). ... Granted free agency (October 28, 1997). ... Signed by Minnesota Twins (December 16, 1997).

Year Team (League)	W	L	Pct.	ERA	G	GS	CG	ShO	Sv.	IP	H	R	ER	BB	SO
1978— Oakland (A.L.)	0	3	.000	7.50	3	3	1	0	0	12	19	12	10	8	0
— Vancouver (PCL)	5	6	.455	5.58	14	14	5	1	0	92	109	67	57	54	31
1979— Ogden (Pac. Coast)	5	5	.500	3.48	13	13	6	0	0	101	93	48	39	49	42
— Oakland (A.L.)	2	10	.167	5.96	13	13	2	0	0	77	102	57	51	50	17
1980— Ogden (Pac. Coast)	6	9	.400	5.40	20	20	3	0	0	115	135	79	69	77	46
1981— Nashville (Southern)■	8	7	.533	4.42	26	26	7	0	0	169	164	97	83	83	100
1982— New York (A.L.)	7	11	.389	4.37	30	23	2	0	0	150⅓	167	77	73	67	71
1983— Toronto (A.L.)	0	3	.000	5.16	16	4	0	0	0	45⅓	48	26	26	21	22
— Syracuse (Int'l)	0	3	.000	5.59	5	4	0	0	1	19⅓	20	12	12	13	17
1984— Syracuse (Int'l)	13	11	.542	4.07	34	28	10	•4	1	*185⅔	167	•101	84	•100	105
1985— Seattle (A.L.)■	1	1	.500	12.00	2	2	0	0	0	6	11	8	8	5	2
— Calgary (PCL)	0	0	...	4.50	1	1	0	0	0	2	3	1	1	0	0
1986— Seattle (A.L.)	11	•17	.393	4.53	37	33	9	1	1	216⅓	243	122	109	86	116
1987— Seattle (A.L.)	12	17	.414	4.65	34	31	8	2	0	207	245	117	107	53	85
1988— Baltimore (A.L.)■	1	6	.143	5.43	22	10	2	0	1	71⅓	70	45	43	23	29
— Rochester (Int'l)	0	2	.000	4.76	3	3	0	0	0	17	19	10	9	6	7
1989— Los Angeles (N.L.)■	8	11	.421	2.53	40	19	0	0	0	152⅔	130	51	43	33	72
1990— Los Angeles (N.L.)	11	15	.423	3.75	33	33	6	•4	0	211	216	100	88	60	106
1991— Los Angeles (N.L.)	14	10	.583	2.78	34	33	5	1	1	236⅓	197	85	73	61	140
1992— Chicago (N.L.)■	16	8	.667	2.55	34	34	6	1	0	240	203	80	68	79	123
1993— Chicago (N.L.)	10	15	.400	4.03	32	32	1	1	0	207⅔	206	100	93	74	111

M

Year Team (League)	W	L	Pct.	ERA	G	GS	CG	ShO	Sv.	IP	H	R	ER	BB	SO
1994— Chicago (N.L.)	2	10	.167	6.69	15	15	1	0	0	80 2/3	111	65	60	35	57
1995— Orlando (South.)	0	2	.000	7.59	2	2	0	0	0	10 2/3	13	9	9	7	5
— Chicago (N.L.)	2	1	.667	2.19	4	4	0	0	0	24 2/3	19	8	6	9	15
— St. Louis (N.L.)■	5	6	.455	3.88	17	17	1	0	0	106 2/3	114	48	46	25	46
1996— St. Petersburg (FSL)	1	0	1.000	0.00	1	1	0	0	0	5 2/3	4	0	0	1	4
— Louisville (A.A.)	1	3	.250	7.04	4	4	1	0	0	23	29	18	18	11	10
— St. Louis (N.L.)	4	8	.333	5.24	18	18	0	0	0	103	118	63	60	40	55
— Cincinnati (N.L.)■	2	3	.400	2.30	5	5	0	0	0	27 1/3	28	9	7	7	19
1997— Cincinnati (N.L.)	9	12	.429	4.78	31	30	1	0	0	162	165	91	86	49	103
A.L. totals (8 years)	34	68	.333	4.89	157	119	24	3	2	785 1/3	905	464	427	313	342
N.L. totals (9 years)	83	99	.456	3.65	263	240	21	7	1	1552	1507	700	630	472	847
Major league totals (17 years)	117	167	.412	4.07	420	359	45	10	3	2337 1/3	2412	1164	1057	785	1189

ALL-STAR GAME RECORD

Year League	W	L	Pct.	ERA	GS	CG	ShO	Sv.	IP	H	R	ER	BB	SO
1991— National	0	0	...	0.00	0	0	0	0	1	0	0	0	0	1

MORGAN, SCOTT · OF · INDIANS

PERSONAL: Born July 19, 1973, in Westlake, Calif. ... 6-7/230. ... Bats right, throws right.
HIGH SCHOOL: Lompoc (Calif.).
JUNIOR COLLEGE: Allan Hancock College (Calif.).
COLLEGE: Gonzaga.
TRANSACTIONS/CAREER NOTES: Selected by Milwaukee Brewers organization in 45th round of free-agent draft (June 1, 1992); did not sign. ... Selected by Cleveland Indians organization in seventh round of free-agent draft (June 1, 1995). ... On disabled list (July 11, 1996-remainder of season).
STATISTICAL NOTES: Led Carolina League with .606 slugging percentage in 1997.

Year Team (League)	Pos.	G	AB	R	H	2B	3B	HR	RBI	Avg.	BB	SO	SB	PO	A	E	Avg.
1995— Watertown (NYP)	OF	66	244	42	64	18	0	2	33	.262	26	63	6	50	3	3	.946
1996— Columbus (S. Atl.)	OF	87	305	62	95	25	1	22	80	.311	46	70	9	106	6	4	.966
1997— Kinston (Carolina)	OF	95	368	*86	116	32	3	23	67	.315	47	87	4	143	7	2	.987
— Akron (Eastern)	OF	21	69	11	12	3	0	2	6	.174	8	20	1	37	4	1	.976

MORMAN, ALVIN · P · INDIANS

PERSONAL: Born January 6, 1969, in Rockingham, N.C. ... 6-3/210. ... Throws left, bats left.
HIGH SCHOOL: Richmond Senior (Rockingham, N.C.).
COLLEGE: Wingate (N.C.).
TRANSACTIONS/CAREER NOTES: Selected by Houston Astros organization in 39th round of free-agent draft (June 3, 1991). ... On disabled list (August 26, 1993-remainder of season and May 23-June 14, 1995). ... On temporarily inactive list (July 25-August 2, 1994). ... Traded by Astros to Cleveland Indians for P Jose Cabrera (May 9, 1997). ... On Cleveland disabled list (July 28-September 1, 1997).

Year Team (League)	W	L	Pct.	ERA	G	GS	CG	ShO	Sv.	IP	H	R	ER	BB	SO
1991— GC Astros (GCL)	1	0	1.000	2.16	11	0	0	0	1	16 2/3	15	7	4	5	24
— Osceola (Florida St.)	0	0	...	1.50	3	0	0	0	0	6	5	3	1	2	3
1992— Asheville (S. Atl.)	8	0	1.000	1.55	57	0	0	0	15	75 1/3	60	17	13	26	70
1993— Jackson (Texas)	8	2	*.800	2.96	19	19	0	0	0	97 1/3	77	35	32	28	101
1994— Tucson (PCL)	3	7	.300	5.11	58	0	0	0	5	74	84	51	42	26	49
1995— Tucson (PCL)	5	1	.833	3.91	45	0	0	0	3	48 1/3	50	26	21	20	36
1996— Houston (N.L.)	4	1	.800	4.93	53	0	0	0	0	42	43	24	23	24	31
1997— New Orleans (A.A.)	0	1	.000	4.50	8	0	0	0	0	10	11	5	5	2	14
— Cleveland (A.L.)■	0	0	...	5.89	34	0	0	0	2	18 1/3	19	13	12	14	13
— Buffalo (A.A.)	0	0	...	0.00	3	0	0	0	0	3 1/3	2	0	0	0	3
A.L. totals (1 year)	0	0	...	5.89	34	0	0	0	2	18 1/3	19	13	12	14	13
N.L. totals (1 year)	4	1	.800	4.93	53	0	0	0	0	42	43	24	23	24	31
Major league totals (2 years)	4	1	.800	5.22	87	0	0	0	2	60 1/3	62	37	35	38	44

DIVISION SERIES RECORD

Year Team (League)	W	L	Pct.	ERA	G	GS	CG	ShO	Sv.	IP	H	R	ER	BB	SO
1997— Cleveland (A.L.)	0	0	...	...	1	0	0	0	0	0	0	0	0	1	0

CHAMPIONSHIP SERIES RECORD

Year Team (League)	W	L	Pct.	ERA	G	GS	CG	ShO	Sv.	IP	H	R	ER	BB	SO
1997— Cleveland (A.L.)	0	0	...	0.00	2	0	0	0	0	1 1/3	0	0	0	0	1

WORLD SERIES RECORD

Year Team (League)	W	L	Pct.	ERA	G	GS	CG	ShO	Sv.	IP	H	R	ER	BB	SO
1997— Cleveland (A.L.)	0	0	...	0.00	2	0	0	0	0	1/3	0	2	0	2	1

MORMAN, RUSS · 1B/OF

PERSONAL: Born April 28, 1962, in Independence, Mo. ... 6-4/215. ... Bats right, throws right. ... Full name: Russell Lee Morman.
HIGH SCHOOL: William Chrisman (Independence, Mo.).
JUNIOR COLLEGE: Iowa Western Community College.
COLLEGE: Wichita State.
TRANSACTIONS/CAREER NOTES: Selected by Kansas City Royals organization in seventh round of free-agent draft (January 13, 1981); did not sign. ... Selected by Chicago White Sox organization in first round (28th pick overall) of free-agent draft (June 6, 1983); pick received as compensation for Oakland Athletics signing Type B free-agent SS Bill Almon. ... Released by White Sox (November 20, 1989). ... Signed by

Omaha, Kansas City Royals organization (December 21, 1989). ... Granted free agency (October 16, 1991). ... Signed by Cincinnati Reds organization (November 12, 1991). ... Released by Nashville, Reds organization (March 26, 1992). ... Re-signed by Nashville (May 22, 1992). ... Released by Nashville (September 25, 1992). ... Signed by Pittsburgh Pirates organization (January 12, 1993). ... On disabled list (June 23-30, 1993). ... Granted free agency (October 15, 1993). ... Signed by Edmonton, Florida Marlins organization (February 4, 1994). ... On Florida disabled list (July 29-August 19, 1995); included rehabilitation assignment to Charlotte (August 14-18). ... Granted free agency (October 16, 1995). ... Re-signed by Marlins organization (November 7, 1995). ... Granted free agency (October 15, 1996). ... Re-signed by Marlins organization (January 16, 1997). ... on Charlotte disabled list (May 10-17, 1997). ... Granted free agency (October 15, 1997).

RECORDS: Shares major league record for most hits in one inning in first major league game—2 (August 3, 1986, fourth inning).

HONORS: Named first baseman on THE SPORTING NEWS college All-America team (1983).

STATISTICAL NOTES: Led Eastern League with .512 slugging percentage in 1985. ... Led Eastern League first basemen with .988 fielding percentage and 79 assists in 1985. ... Led American Association third basemen with 23 double plays in 1986. ... Led International League with .623 slugging percentage in 1997.

								BATTING						FIELDING		
Year Team (League)	Pos.	G	AB	R	H	2B	3B	HR	RBI	Avg.	BB	SO	SB	PO	A	E	Avg.
1983— Glens Falls (Eastern) ..	1B	71	233	29	57	9	1	3	32	.245	40	65	8	591	43	7	.989
1984— Appleton (Midwest)....	1B-OF	122	424	68	111	17	7	7	80	.262	80	93	29	823	43	10	.989
1985— Glens Falls (Eastern) ..	1B-3B-OF	119	422	64	131	24	5	17	81	.310	65	51	11	905	†81	12	†.988
— Buffalo (A.A.)..........	1B	21	64	16	19	3	1	7	14	.297	10	16	2	144	7	2	.987
1986— Buffalo (A.A.)..........	3B-OF	106	365	52	97	17	2	13	57	.266	54	58	3	87	201	24	.923
— Chicago (A.L.)...........	1B	49	159	18	40	5	0	4	17	.252	16	36	1	342	26	4	.989
1987— Hawaii (PCL)...........	1B-OF	89	294	52	79	19	2	9	53	.269	60	56	5	410	28	3	.993
1988— Vancouver (PCL)	1B-OF	69	257	40	77	8	1	5	45	.300	32	48	4	370	21	3	.992
— Chicago (A.L.)	1B-OF-DH	40	75	8	18	2	0	0	3	.240	3	17	0	114	5	2	.983
1989— Vancouver (PCL)	1B-OF	61	216	18	60	14	1	1	23	.278	18	41	1	163	12	3	.983
— Chicago (A.L.)	1B	37	58	5	13	2	0	0	8	.224	6	16	1	157	13	2	.988
1990— Omaha (A.A.)■	1-0-3-2	121	436	67	130	14	9	13	81	.298	51	78	21	665	59	5	.993
— Kansas City (A.L.)	OF-1B-DH	12	37	5	10	4	2	1	3	.270	3	3	0	27	4	0	1.000
1991— Kansas City (A.L.)	1B-OF-DH	12	23	1	6	0	0	0	1	.261	1	5	0	47	3	0	1.000
— Omaha (A.A.)■	1B-OF-P	88	316	46	83	15	3	7	50	.263	43	53	10	564	41	7	.989
1992— Nashville (A.A.)■	1B	101	384	53	119	31	2	14	63	.310	36	60	5	773	59	8	.990
1993— Buffalo (A.A.)■	1B	119	409	79	131	34	2	22	77	.320	48	59	0	814	60	8	.991
1994— Edmonton (PCL)■	1B-3B-P	114	406	69	142	30	2	19	82	.350	36	62	9	818	80	6	.993
— Florida (N.L.)...........	1B	13	33	2	7	0	1	1	2	.212	2	9	0	66	9	1	.987
1995— Charlotte (Int'l)...........	1B-OF	44	169	28	53	7	1	6	36	.314	14	22	2	416	23	2	.995
— Florida (N.L.)...........	OF-1B	34	72	9	20	2	1	3	7	.278	3	12	0	31	2	1	.971
1996— Charlotte (Int'l)...........	1B	80	289	59	96	18	1	18	77	.332	29	51	2	533	25	4	.993
— Florida (N.L.)...........	1B	6	6	0	1	1	0	0	0	.167	1	2	0	2	0	0	1.000
1997— Charlotte (Int'l)...........	1B-OF	117	395	82	126	17	2	*33	99	.319	58	89	3	398	29	5	.988
— Florida (N.L.)...........	OF-1B	4	7	3	2	1	0	1	2	.286	0	2	1	3	1	0	1.000
American League totals (5 years)		150	352	37	87	13	2	5	32	.247	29	77	2	687	51	8	.989
National League totals (4 years)		57	118	14	30	4	2	5	11	.254	6	25	1	102	12	2	.983
Major league totals (9 years)		207	470	51	117	17	4	10	43	.249	35	102	3	789	63	10	.988

RECORD AS PITCHER

Year Team (League)	W	L	Pct.	ERA	G	GS	CG	ShO	Sv.	IP	H	R	ER	BB	SO
1991— Omaha (Am. Assoc.)..........	0	0	...	0.00	1	0	0	0	0	1	0	0	0	0	0
1994— Edmonton (PCL)■	0	0	...	54.00	1	0	0	0	0	1/3	0	2	2	3	0

M

MORRIS, HAL   1B   ROYALS

PERSONAL: Born April 9, 1965, in Fort Rucker, Ala. ... 6-4/210. ... Bats left, throws left. ... Full name: William Harold Morris. ... Brother of Bobby Morris, second baseman, Cleveland Indians organization.

HIGH SCHOOL: Munster (Ind.).

COLLEGE: Michigan.

TRANSACTIONS/CAREER NOTES: Selected by New York Yankees organization in eighth round of free-agent draft (June 2, 1986). ... On Albany/Colonie disabled list (August 14, 1986-remainder of season). ... Traded by Yankees with P Rodney Imes to Cincinnati Reds for P Tim Leary and OF Van Snider (December 12, 1989). ... On Cincinnati disabled list (April 16-May 17, 1992); included rehabilitation assignment to Nashville (May 14-17). ... On Cincinnati disabled list (August 5-21, 1992). ... On Cincinnati disabled list (March 27-June 7, 1993); included rehabilitation assignment to Indianapolis (June 4-7). ... On suspended list (August 10, 1993). ... On Cincinnati disabled list (June 18-July 13, 1995); included rehabilitation assignment to Indianapolis (July 7-10). ... Granted free agency (November 2, 1995). ... Re-signed by Reds (December 6, 1995). ... On Cincinnati disabled list (July 2-17, 1996); included rehabilitation assignment to Indianapolis (July 16-17). ... On Cincinnati disabled list (July 31-September 10, 1997). ... Granted free agency (October 29, 1997). ... Signed by Kansas City Royals (December 22, 1997).

RECORDS: Shares major league single-inning record for most doubles—2 (August 17, 1996, eighth inning).

STATISTICAL NOTES: Had 29-game hitting streak (August 27-September 29, 1996). ... Career major league grand slams: 1.

								BATTING						FIELDING		
Year Team (League)	Pos.	G	AB	R	H	2B	3B	HR	RBI	Avg.	BB	SO	SB	PO	A	E	Avg.
1986— Oneonta (NYP)	1B	36	127	26	48	9	2	3	30	.378	18	15	1	317	26	3	.991
— Alb./Colon. (Eastern) ..	1B	25	79	7	17	5	0	0	4	.215	4	10	0	203	19	2	.991
1987— Alb./Colon. (Eastern) ..	1B-OF	135	*530	65	*173	31	4	5	73	.326	36	43	7	1086	79	17	.986
1988— Columbus (Int'l).........	OF-1B	121	452	41	134	19	4	3	38	.296	36	62	8	543	26	8	.986
— New York (A.L.).........	OF-DH	15	20	1	2	0	0	0	0	.100	0	9	0	7	0	0	1.000
1989— Columbus (Int'l).........	1B-OF	111	417	70	136	24	1	17	66	*.326	28	47	5	636	67	9	.987
— New York (A.L.).........	OF-1B-DH	15	18	2	5	0	0	0	4	.278	1	4	0	12	0	0	1.000
1990— Cincinnati (N.L.)■.....	1B-OF	107	309	50	105	22	3	7	36	.340	21	32	9	595	53	4	.994
— Nashville (A.A.)	OF	16	64	8	22	5	0	1	10	.344	5	10	4	23	1	1	.960
1991— Cincinnati (N.L.).........	1B-OF	136	478	72	152	33	1	14	59	.318	46	61	10	979	100	9	.992
1992— Cincinnati (N.L.).........	1B	115	395	41	107	21	3	6	53	.271	45	53	6	841	86	1	*.999
— Nashville (A.A.)	1B	2	6	1	1	1	0	0	0	.167	2	1	0	13	3	0	1.000
1993— Indianapolis (A.A.)......	1B	3	13	4	6	0	1	1	5	.462	1	2	0	26	3	0	1.000
— Cincinnati (N.L.)	1B	101	379	48	120	18	0	7	49	.317	34	51	2	746	75	5	.994

Year Team (League)	Pos.	G	AB	R	H	2B	3B	HR	RBI	Avg.	BB	SO	SB	PO	A	E	Avg.
1994— Cincinnati (N.L.)	1B	112	436	60	146	30	4	10	78	.335	34	62	6	901	80	6	.994
1995— Cincinnati (N.L.)	1B	101	359	53	100	25	2	11	51	.279	29	58	1	757	72	5	.994
— Indianapolis (A.A.)......	1B	2	5	2	2	0	0	0	1	.400	1	0	0	13	2	0	1.000
1996— Cincinnati (N.L.)	1B	142	528	82	165	32	4	16	80	.313	50	76	7	1129	91	8	.993
— Indianapolis (A.A.)......	1B	1	4	1	2	1	0	1	1	.500	0	1	0	2	0	0	1.000
1997— Cincinnati (N.L.)	1B	96	333	42	92	20	1	1	33	.276	23	43	3	672	52	7	.990
American League totals (2 years)		30	38	3	7	0	0	0	4	.184	1	13	0	19	0	0	1.000
National League totals (8 years)		910	3217	448	987	201	18	72	439	.307	282	436	44	6620	609	45	.994
Major league totals (10 years)		940	3255	451	994	201	18	72	443	.305	283	449	44	6639	609	45	.994

DIVISION SERIES RECORD

Year Team (League)	Pos.	G	AB	R	H	2B	3B	HR	RBI	Avg.	BB	SO	SB	PO	A	E	Avg.
1995— Cincinnati (N.L.)	1B	3	10	5	5	1	0	0	2	.500	3	1	1	22	2	0	1.000

CHAMPIONSHIP SERIES RECORD

Year Team (League)	Pos.	G	AB	R	H	2B	3B	HR	RBI	Avg.	BB	SO	SB	PO	A	E	Avg.
1990— Cincinnati (N.L.)	1B-PH	5	12	3	5	1	0	0	1	.417	1	0	0	20	2	0	1.000
1995— Cincinnati (N.L.)	1B-PH	4	12	0	2	1	0	0	1	.167	1	1	1	27	3	0	1.000
Championship series totals (2 years)		9	24	3	7	2	0	0	2	.292	2	1	1	47	5	0	1.000

WORLD SERIES RECORD

NOTES: Member of World Series championship team (1990).

Year Team (League)	Pos.	G	AB	R	H	2B	3B	HR	RBI	Avg.	BB	SO	SB	PO	A	E	Avg.
1990— Cincinnati (N.L.)	1B-DH	4	14	0	1	0	0	0	2	.071	1	1	0	18	1	0	1.000

MORRIS, MATT — P — CARDINALS

PERSONAL: Born August 9, 1974, in Middletown, N.Y. ... 6-5/210. ... Throws right, bats right. ... Full name: Matthew Christian Morris.
HIGH SCHOOL: Valley Central (Montgomery, N.Y.).
COLLEGE: Seton Hall.
TRANSACTIONS/CAREER NOTES: Selected by Milwaukee Brewers organization in 25th round of free-agent draft (June 1, 1992); did not sign. ... Selected by St. Louis Cardinals organization in first round (12th pick overall) of free-agent draft (June 1, 1995).
HONORS: Named N.L. Rookie Pitcher of the Year by THE SPORTING NEWS (1997).
MISCELLANEOUS: Struck out in only appearance as pinch-hitter (1997).

Year Team (League)	W	L	Pct.	ERA	G	GS	CG	ShO	Sv.	IP	H	R	ER	BB	SO
1995— New Jersey (NYP)	2	0	1.000	1.64	2	2	0	0	0	11	12	3	2	3	13
— St. Petersburg (FSL)	3	2	.600	2.38	6	6	1	1	0	34	22	16	9	11	31
1996— Arkansas (Texas)	12	12	.500	3.88	27	27	4	*4	0	167	178	79	72	48	120
— Louisville (A.A.)	0	1	.000	3.38	1	1	0	0	0	8	8	3	3	1	9
1997— St. Louis (N.L.)	12	9	.571	3.19	33	33	3	0	0	217	208	88	77	69	149
Major league totals (1 year)	12	9	.571	3.19	33	33	3	0	0	217	208	88	77	69	149

MOSQUERA, JULIO — C — BLUE JAYS

PERSONAL: Born January 29, 1972, in Panama City, Panama. ... 6-0/190. ... Bats right, throws right. ... Full name: Julio Alberto Mosquera.
TRANSACTIONS/CAREER NOTES: Signed as non-drafted free agent by Toronto Blue Jays organization (May 16, 1991).
STATISTICAL NOTES: Led Pioneer League with 13 passed balls in 1994. ... Led South Atlantic League catchers with .991 fielding percentage in 1995. ... Led Southern League with 19 passed balls in 1996.

Year Team (League)	Pos.	G	AB	R	H	2B	3B	HR	RBI	Avg.	BB	SO	SB	PO	A	E	Avg.
1991— Dom. B. Jays (DSL) ...	C	42	136	20	29	3	0	0	10	.213	8	12	3	...	...	...	...
1992— Dom. B. Jays (DSL)	C	67	235	47	85	12	1	3	39	.362	17	20	17	207	94	14	.956
1993— GC Jays (GCL)	C-SS	35	108	9	28	3	2	0	15	.259	8	16	3	180	39	8	.965
1994— Medicine Hat (Pio.)	C	59	229	33	78	17	1	2	34	.341	18	35	3	299	*70	11	.971
1995— Hagerstown (SAL)......	C-1B	108	406	64	118	22	5	3	46	.291	29	53	5	641	103	7	†.991
1996— Knoxville (Southern) ..	C	92	318	36	73	17	0	2	31	.230	29	55	6	679	63	7	.991
— Syracuse (Int'l)...........	C	23	72	6	18	1	0	0	5	.250	6	14	0	164	9	3	.983
— Toronto (A.L.)...........	C	8	22	2	5	2	0	0	2	.227	0	4	0	48	1	0	1.000
1997— Knoxville (Southern) ..	C	87	309	47	90	23	1	5	50	.291	22	56	3	587	56	7	.989
— Syracuse (Int'l)..........	C	10	35	5	8	1	0	0	1	.229	2	5	0	55	5	1	.984
— Toronto (A.L.)...........	C	3	8	0	2	1	0	0	0	.250	0	2	0	11	1	0	1.000
Major league totals (2 years)		11	30	2	7	3	0	0	2	.233	0	5	0	59	2	0	1.000

MOSS, DAMIAN — P — BRAVES

PERSONAL: Born November 24, 1976, in Darlinghurst, Australia. ... 6-0/187. ... Throws right, bats left. ... Full name: Damian Joseph Moss.
TRANSACTIONS/CAREER NOTES: Signed as non-drafted free agent by Atlanta Braves organization (July 1, 1993).
STATISTICAL NOTES: Led Appalachian League with 14 hit batsmen in 1994.

Year Team (League)	W	L	Pct.	ERA	G	GS	CG	ShO	Sv.	IP	H	R	ER	BB	SO
1994— Danville (Appalachian)........	2	5	.286	3.58	12	12	1	1	0	60⅓	30	28	24	55	77
1995— Macon (S. Atl.)	9	10	.474	3.56	27	27	0	0	0	149⅓	134	73	59	70	•177
1996— Durham (Carolina)..............	9	1	*.900	2.25	14	14	0	0	0	84	52	25	21	40	89
— Greenville (Southern)	2	5	.286	4.97	11	10	0	0	0	58	57	41	32	35	48
1997— Greenville (Southern)	6	8	.429	5.35	21	19	1	0	0	112⅔	111	73	67	58	116

PERSONAL: Born December 29, 1968, in Denver. ... 5-9/175. ... Bats right, throws right. ... Full name: James Raleigh Mouton. ... Name pronounced MOO-tawn.

HIGH SCHOOL: Luther Burbank Senior (Sacramento).

COLLEGE: St. Mary's (Calif.).

TRANSACTIONS/CAREER NOTES: Selected by New York Yankees organization in 42nd round of free-agent draft (June 2, 1987); did not sign. ... Selected by Minnesota Twins organization in eighth round of free-agent draft (June 4, 1990); did not sign. ... Selected by Houston Astros organization in seventh round of free-agent draft (June 3, 1991). ... On Houston disabled list (June 12-30, 1995); included rehabilitation assignment to Tucson (June 27-30). ... Traded by Astros to San Diego Padres for P Sean Bergman (January 15, 1998).

HONORS: Named Pacific Coast League Most Valuable Player (1993).

STATISTICAL NOTES: Led New York-Pennsylvania League in caught stealing with 18 in 1991. ... Led New York-Pennsylvania League second basemen with 382 total chances in 1991. ... Led Florida State League second basemen with 623 total chances in 1992. ... Led Pacific Coast League with 286 total bases and tied for lead in caught stealing with 18 in 1993. ... Led Pacific Coast League second basemen with 674 total chances and 75 double plays in 1993. ... Career major league grand slams: 1.

Year Team (League)	Pos.	G	AB	R	H	2B	3B	HR	RBI	Avg.	BB	SO	SB	PO	A	E	Avg.
1991— Auburn (NY-Penn)......	2B	76	288	71	76	15	*10	2	40	.264	55	32	*60	*170	184	*28	.927
1992— Osceola (Fla. St.)........	2B	133	507	*110	143	•30	6	11	62	.282	71	78	*51	*288	294	*41	.934
1993— Tucson (PCL)	2B	134	*546	*126	*172	*42	12	16	92	.315	72	82	40	*277	*354	*43	.936
1994— Houston (N.L.)	OF	99	310	43	76	11	0	2	16	.245	27	69	24	163	5	3	.982
— Tucson (PCL)	OF	4	17	2	7	1	0	1	1	.412	2	3	1	7	1	0	1.000
1995— Tucson (PCL)	OF	3	11	1	5	0	0	1	1	.455	0	2	0	1	0	1	.500
— Houston (N.L.)	OF	104	298	42	78	18	2	4	27	.262	25	59	25	136	4	0	1.000
1996— Houston (N.L.)	OF	122	300	40	79	15	1	3	34	.263	38	55	21	158	7	5	.971
— Tucson (PCL)	OF	1	4	1	1	0	0	0	0	.250	1	0	0	2	0	0	1.000
1997— Houston (N.L.)	OF	86	180	24	38	9	1	3	23	.211	18	30	9	86	1	0	1.000
Major league totals (4 years)		411	1088	149	271	53	4	12	100	.249	108	213	79	543	17	8	.986

MOUTON, LYLE   OF

PERSONAL: Born May 13, 1969, in Lafayette, La. ... 6-4/240. ... Bats right, throws right. ... Full name: Lyle Joseph Mouton. ... Name pronounced MOO-tawn.

HIGH SCHOOL: St. Thomas More (Lafayette, La.).

COLLEGE: Louisiana State.

TRANSACTIONS/CAREER NOTES: Selected by New York Yankees organization in fifth round of free-agent draft (June 3, 1991). ... Traded by Yankees to Chicago White Sox (April 22, 1995), completing deal in which White Sox traded P Jack McDowell to Yankees for P Keith Heberling and a player to be named later (December 14, 1994). ... On Chicago disabled list (May 11-27, 1997); included rehabilitation assignment to Birmingham (May 25-27). ... Contract sold to Yakult Swallows of the Japan Central League (November 21, 1997).

Year Team (League)	Pos.	G	AB	R	H	2B	3B	HR	RBI	Avg.	BB	SO	SB	PO	A	E	Avg.
1991— Oneonta (NYP)	OF	70	272	53	84	11	2	7	41	.309	31	38	15	106	5	5	.957
1992— Prince William (Car.) ..	OF	50	189	28	50	14	1	6	34	.265	17	42	4	49	5	4	.931
— Albany (Eastern)........	OF	64	214	25	46	12	2	2	27	.215	24	55	1	102	1	0	1.000
1993— Albany (Eastern)........	OF	135	491	74	125	22	3	16	76	.255	50	125	18	189	9	5	.975
1994— Alb./Colon. (Eastern)..	OF-3B	74	274	42	84	23	1	12	42	.307	27	62	7	118	4	2	.984
— Columbus (Int'l)........	OF	59	204	26	64	14	5	4	32	.314	14	45	5	99	5	1	.990
1995— Nashville (A.A.)■	OF	71	267	40	79	17	0	8	41	.296	23	58	10	123	8	3	.978
— Chicago (A.L.)	OF-DH	58	179	23	54	16	0	5	27	.302	19	46	1	93	5	1	.990
1996— Chicago (A.L.)	OF-DH	87	214	25	63	8	1	7	39	.294	22	50	3	64	1	2	.970
1997— Chicago (A.L.)	OF-DH	88	242	26	65	9	0	5	23	.269	14	66	4	126	1	4	.969
— Birmingham (Sou.).....	OF	3	11	1	2	0	0	1	1	.182	1	4	0	5	0	0	1.000
		233	635	74	182	33	1	17	89	.287	55	162	8	283	7	7	.976

Major league totals (3 years)

MOYER, JAMIE   P   MARINERS

PERSONAL: Born November 18, 1962, in Sellersville, Pa. ... 6-0/170. ... Throws left, bats left. ... Son-in-law of Digger Phelps, ESPN college basketball analyst, and Notre Dame basketball coach (1971-72 through 1990-91).

HIGH SCHOOL: Souderton (Pa.) Area.

COLLEGE: St. Joseph's (Pa.).

TRANSACTIONS/CAREER NOTES: Selected by Chicago Cubs organization in sixth round of free-agent draft (June 4, 1984). ... Traded by Cubs with OF Rafael Palmeiro and P Drew Hall to Texas Rangers for P Mitch Williams, P Paul Kilgus, P Steve Wilson, IF Curtis Wilkerson, IF Luis Benitez and OF Pablo Delgado (December 5, 1988). ... On Texas disabled list (May 31-September 1, 1989); included rehabilitation assignments to Gulf Coast Rangers (August 5-14) and Tulsa (August 15-24). ... Released by Rangers (November 13, 1990). ... Signed by Louisville, St. Louis Cardinals organization (January 9, 1991). ... Released by Cardinals (October 14, 1991). ... Signed by Cubs organization (January 8, 1992). ... Released by Iowa, Cubs organization (March 30, 1992). ... Signed by Toledo, Detroit Tigers organization (May 24, 1992). ... Granted free agency (December 8, 1992). ... Signed by Baltimore Orioles organization (December 14, 1992). ... Granted free agency (November 1, 1995). ... Signed by Boston Red Sox (January 2, 1996). ... Traded by Red Sox to Seattle Mariners for OF Darren Bragg (July 30, 1996). ... Granted free agency (October 29, 1996). ... Re-signed by Mariners (November 20, 1996). ... On Seattle disabled list (March 23-April 29, 1997); included rehabilitation assignment to Tacoma (April 24-29).

STATISTICAL NOTES: Led American Association with 16 home runs allowed in 1991. ... Led A.L. with .813 winning percentage in 1996.

Year Team (League)	W	L	Pct.	ERA	G	GS	CG	ShO	Sv.	IP	H	R	ER	BB	SO
1984— Geneva (N.Y.-Penn)	•9	3	.750	1.89	14	14	5	2	0	*104 2/3	59	27	22	31	*120
1985— Win.-Salem (Car.).......	8	2	.800	2.30	12	12	6	2	0	94	82	36	24	22	94
— Pittsfield (Eastern)........	7	6	.538	3.72	15	15	3	0	0	96 2/3	99	49	40	32	51
1986— Pittsfield (Eastern).......	3	1	.750	0.88	6	6	0	0	0	41	27	10	4	16	42
— Iowa (Am. Assoc.)........	3	2	.600	2.55	6	6	2	0	0	42 1/3	25	14	12	11	25
— Chicago (N.L.)	7	4	.636	5.05	16	16	1	1	0	87 1/3	107	52	49	42	45

Year— Team (League)	W	L	Pct.	ERA	G	GS	CG	ShO	Sv.	IP	H	R	ER	BB	SO
1987— Chicago (N.L.)	12	15	.444	5.10	35	33	1	0	0	201	210	127	*114	97	147
1988— Chicago (N.L.)	9	15	.375	3.48	34	30	3	1	0	202	212	84	78	55	121
1989— Texas (A.L.)■	4	9	.308	4.86	15	15	1	0	0	76	84	51	41	33	44
— GC Rangers (GCL)	1	0	1.000	1.64	3	3	0	0	0	11	8	4	2	1	18
— Tulsa (Texas)	1	1	.500	5.11	2	2	1	1	0	12 1/3	16	8	7	3	9
1990— Texas (A.L.)	2	6	.250	4.66	33	10	1	0	0	102 1/3	115	59	53	39	58
1991— St. Louis (N.L.)■	0	5	.000	5.74	8	7	0	0	0	31 1/3	38	21	20	16	20
— Louisville (A.A.)	5	10	.333	3.80	20	20	1	0	0	125 2/3	125	64	53	43	69
1992— Toledo (Int'l)■	10	8	.556	2.86	21	20	5	0	0	138 2/3	128	48	44	37	80
1993— Rochester (Int'l)■	6	0	1.000	1.67	8	8	1	1	0	54	42	13	10	13	41
— Baltimore (A.L.)	12	9	.571	3.43	25	25	3	1	0	152	154	63	58	38	90
1994— Baltimore (A.L.)	5	7	.417	4.77	23	23	0	0	0	149	158	81	79	38	87
1995— Baltimore (A.L.)	8	6	.571	5.21	27	18	0	0	0	115 2/3	117	70	67	30	65
1996— Boston (A.L.)	7	1	.875	4.50	23	10	0	0	0	90	111	50	45	27	50
— Seattle (A.L.)■	6	2	§.750	3.31	11	11	0	0	0	70 2/3	66	36	26	19	29
1997— Tacoma (PCL)	1	0	1.000	0.00	1	1	0	0	0	5	1	0	0	0	6
— Seattle (A.L.)	17	5	.773	3.86	30	30	2	0	0	188 2/3	187	82	81	43	113
A.L. totals (7 years)	61	45	.575	4.29	187	142	7	1	0	944 1/3	992	491	450	267	536
N.L. totals (4 years)	28	39	.418	4.50	93	86	5	2	0	521 2/3	567	284	261	210	333
Major league totals (11 years)	89	84	.514	4.36	280	228	12	3	0	1466	1559	776	711	477	869

DIVISION SERIES RECORD

Year— Team (League)	W	L	Pct.	ERA	G	GS	CG	ShO	Sv.	IP	H	R	ER	BB	SO
1997— Seattle (A.L.)	0	1	.000	5.79	1	1	0	0	0	4 2/3	5	3	3	1	2

MUELLER, BILL　　　　　　3B　　　　　　GIANTS

PERSONAL: Born March 17, 1971, in Maryland Heights, Mo. ... 5-10/170. ... Bats both, throws right. ... Full name: William Mueller. ... Name pronounced MILLER.

HIGH SCHOOL: DeSmet (Creve Coeur, Mo.).

COLLEGE: Southwest Missouri State.

TRANSACTIONS/CAREER NOTES: Selected by San Francisco Giants organization in 15th round of free-agent draft (June 3, 1993). ... On disabled list (July 1-16, 1997).

STATISTICAL NOTES: Led California League with .435 on-base percentage in 1994. ... Led Pacific Coast League third basemen with 25 double plays in 1996.

							BATTING							FIELDING		
Year— Team (League)	Pos.	G	AB	R	H	2B	3B	HR	RBI	Avg.	BB	SO	SB	PO	A	E	Avg.
1993— Everett (N'west)	2B	58	200	31	60	8	2	1	24	.300	42	17	13	86	143	8	.966
1994— San Jose (Calif.)	3B-2B-SS	120	431	79	130	20	•9	5	72	.302	*103	47	4	83	276	29	.925
1995— Shreveport (Texas)	3B-2B	88	330	56	102	16	2	1	39	.309	53	36	6	52	169	5	.978
— Phoenix (PCL)	3B-2B	41	172	23	51	13	6	2	19	.297	19	31	0	26	85	7	.941
1996— Phoenix (PCL)	3B-SS-2B	106	440	73	133	14	6	4	36	.302	44	40	2	92	250	11	.969
— San Francisco (N.L.)	3B-2B	55	200	31	66	15	1	0	19	.330	24	26	0	51	99	6	.962
1997— San Francisco (N.L.)	3B	128	390	51	114	26	3	7	44	.292	48	71	4	85	218	14	.956
Major league totals (2 years)		183	590	82	180	41	4	7	63	.305	72	97	4	136	317	20	.958

DIVISION SERIES RECORD

							BATTING							FIELDING		
Year— Team (League)	Pos.	G	AB	R	H	2B	3B	HR	RBI	Avg.	BB	SO	SB	PO	A	E	Avg.
1997— San Francisco (N.L.)	3B	3	12	1	3	0	1	1	1	.250	0	0	0	2	9	0	1.000

MULHOLLAND, TERRY　　　　　　P

PERSONAL: Born March 9, 1963, in Uniontown, Pa. ... 6-3/212. ... Throws left, bats right. ... Full name: Terence John Mulholland.

HIGH SCHOOL: Laurel Highlands (Uniontown, Pa.).

COLLEGE: Marietta College (Ohio).

TRANSACTIONS/CAREER NOTES: Selected by San Francisco Giants organization in first round (24th pick overall) of free-agent draft (June 4, 1984); pick received as compensation for Detroit Tigers signing free-agent IF Darrell Evans. ... On San Francisco disabled list (August 1, 1988-remainder of season). ... Traded by Giants with P Dennis Cook and 3B Charlie Hayes to Philadelphia Phillies for P Steve Bedrosian and a player to be named later (June 18, 1989); Giants organization acquired IF Rick Parker to complete deal (August 7, 1989). ... On Philadelphia disabled list (June 12-28, 1990); included rehabilitation assignment to Scranton/Wilkes-Barre (June 23-24). ... Traded by Phillies with a player to be named later to New York Yankees for P Bobby Munoz, 2B Kevin Jordan and P Ryan Karp (February 9, 1994); Yankees acquired P Jeff Patterson to complete deal (November 8, 1994). ... Granted free agency (October 17, 1994). ... Signed by Giants (April 8, 1995). ... On San Francisco disabled list (June 4-July 4, 1995); included rehabilitation assignment to Phoenix (June 23-July 4). ... Granted free agency (November 3, 1995). ... Signed by Reading, Phillies organization (February 17, 1996). ... Traded by Phillies to Seattle Mariners for IF Desi Relaford (July 31, 1996). ... Granted free agency (October 28, 1996). ... Signed by Chicago Cubs (December 10, 1996). ... Claimed on waivers by Giants (August 8, 1997). ... Granted free agency (October 27, 1997).

STATISTICAL NOTES: Pitched 6-0 no-hit victory for Philadelphia against San Francisco (August 15, 1990).

MISCELLANEOUS: Appeared in one game as pinch-runner (1991). ... Appeared in one game as pinch-runner with San Francisco (1995).

Year— Team (League)	W	L	Pct.	ERA	G	GS	CG	ShO	Sv.	IP	H	R	ER	BB	SO
1984— Everett (Northwest)	1	0	1.000	0.00	3	3	0	0	0	19	10	2	0	4	15
— Fresno (California)	5	2	.714	2.95	9	9	0	0	0	42 2/3	32	17	14	36	39
1985— Shreveport (Texas)	9	8	.529	2.90	26	26	8	*3	0	176 2/3	166	79	57	87	122
1986— Phoenix (PCL)	8	5	.615	4.46	17	17	3	0	0	111	112	60	55	56	77
— San Francisco (N.L.)	1	7	.125	4.94	15	10	0	0	0	54 2/3	51	33	30	35	27
1987— Phoenix (PCL)	7	12	.368	5.07	37	*29	3	1	0	172 1/3	200	*124	•97	90	94
1988— Phoenix (PCL)	7	3	.700	3.58	19	14	3	2	0	100 2/3	116	45	40	44	57
— San Francisco (N.L.)	2	1	.667	3.72	9	6	2	1	0	46	50	20	19	7	18
1989— San Francisco (N.L.)	0	0	...	4.09	5	1	0	0	0	11	15	5	5	4	6
— Phoenix (PCL)	4	5	.444	2.99	13	10	0	0	0	78 1/3	67	30	26	26	61

Year Team (League)	W	L	Pct.	ERA	G	GS	CG	ShO	Sv.	IP	H	R	ER	BB	SO
— Philadelphia (N.L.)■	4	7	.364	5.00	20	17	2	1	0	104 1/3	122	61	58	32	60
1990— Philadelphia (N.L.).............	9	10	.474	3.34	33	26	6	1	0	180 2/3	172	78	67	42	75
— Scran./W.B. (Int'l).............	0	1	.000	3.00	1	1	0	0	0	6	9	4	2	2	2
1991— Philadelphia (N.L.).............	16	13	.552	3.61	34	34	8	3	0	232	231	100	93	49	142
1992— Philadelphia (N.L.).............	13	11	.542	3.81	32	32	*12	2	0	229	227	101	97	46	125
1993— Philadelphia (N.L.).............	12	9	.571	3.25	29	28	7	2	0	191	177	80	69	40	116
1994— New York (A.L.)■.............	6	7	.462	6.49	24	19	2	0	0	120 2/3	150	94	87	37	72
1995— San Francisco (N.L.)■	5	13	.278	5.80	29	24	2	0	0	149	190	112	96	38	65
— Phoenix (PCL).................	0	0	...	2.25	1	1	0	0	0	4	4	3	1	1	4
1996— Philadelphia (N.L.)■..........	8	7	.533	4.66	21	21	3	0	0	133 1/3	157	74	69	21	52
— Seattle (A.L.)■.................	5	4	.556	4.67	12	12	0	0	0	69 1/3	75	38	36	28	34
1997— Chicago (N.L.)■..........	6	12	.333	4.07	25	25	1	0	0	157	162	79	71	45	74
— San Francisco (N.L.)■...	0	1	.000	5.16	15	2	0	0	0	29 2/3	28	21	17	6	25
A.L. totals (2 years)	11	11	.500	5.83	36	31	2	0	0	190	225	132	123	65	106
N.L. totals (10 years)..................	76	91	.455	4.10	267	226	43	10	0	1517 2/3	1582	764	691	365	785
Major league totals (11 years).......	87	102	.460	4.29	303	257	45	10	0	1707 2/3	1807	896	814	430	891

CHAMPIONSHIP SERIES RECORD

Year Team (League)	W	L	Pct.	ERA	G	GS	CG	ShO	Sv.	IP	H	R	ER	BB	SO
1993— Philadelphia (N.L.).............	0	1	.000	7.20	1	1	0	0	0	5	9	5	4	1	2

WORLD SERIES RECORD

Year Team (League)	W	L	Pct.	ERA	G	GS	CG	ShO	Sv.	IP	H	R	ER	BB	SO
1993— Philadelphia (N.L.).............	1	0	1.000	6.75	2	2	0	0	0	10 2/3	14	8	8	3	5

ALL-STAR GAME RECORD

Year League	W	L	Pct.	ERA	GS	CG	ShO	Sv.	IP	H	R	ER	BB	SO
1993— National	0	0	...	4.50	1	0	0	0	2	1	1	1	2	0

MULL, BLAINE   P   MARLINS

PERSONAL: Born August 14, 1976, in Morganton, N.C. ... 6-4/210. ... Throws right, bats right. ... Full name: Blaine Edward Mull.
HIGH SCHOOL: Freedom (Morganton, N.C.).
TRANSACTIONS/CAREER NOTES: Selected by Kansas City Royals organization in sixth round of free-agent draft (June 2, 1994). ... Traded by Royals to Florida Marlins for 1B Jeff Conine (November 21, 1997).

Year Team (League)	W	L	Pct.	ERA	G	GS	CG	ShO	Sv.	IP	H	R	ER	BB	SO
1994— GC Royals (GCL)................	2	0	1.000	0.00	3	3	0	0	0	15	8	1	0	2	9
1995— Springfield (Mid.).............	4	10	.286	4.88	25	25	0	0	0	125 1/3	142	79	68	50	71
1996— Lansing (Midwest)	15	8	.652	3.25	28	28	1	0	0	174 2/3	186	91	63	40	114
1997— Wichita (Texas)	1	2	.333	6.65	8	8	0	0	0	44 2/3	66	41	33	23	16
— Wilmington (Caro.).............	8	6	.571	3.56	19	19	0	0	0	111 1/3	126	55	44	33	64

MUNOZ, BOBBY   P

M

PERSONAL: Born March 3, 1968, in Rio Piedras, Puerto Rico. ... 6-8/259. ... Throws right, bats right. ... Full name: Roberto Munoz.
HIGH SCHOOL: Hialeah (Fla.) Miami Lakes.
JUNIOR COLLEGE: Palm Beach Junior College (Fla.) and Polk Community College (Fla.).
TRANSACTIONS/CAREER NOTES: Selected by New York Yankees organization in 15th round of free-agent draft (June 1, 1988). ... Traded by Yankees with 2B Kevin Jordan and P Ryan Karp to Philadelphia Phillies for P Terry Mulholland and a player to be named later (February 9, 1994). ... Yankees acquired P Jeff Patterson to complete deal (November 8, 1994). ... On Philadelphia disabled list (April 18-July 22 and August 3, 1995-remainder of season); included rehabilitation assignments to Reading (June 19-July 10) and Scranton/Wilkes-Barre (July 10-17). ... On Philadelphia disabled list (March 23-June 11, June 17-July 22 and August 8, 1996-remainder of season); included rehabilitation assignments to Clearwater (May 21-June 11), Scranton/Wilkes-Barre (June 22-July 19) and Reading (August 13-September 2). ... Granted free agency (May 19, 1997). ... Signed by San Diego Padres organization (May 29, 1997). ... Released by Padres organization (July 15, 1997) ... Signed by Albuquerque, Los Angeles Dodgers organization (July 21, 1997). ... Granted free agency (October 15, 1997).

Year Team (League)	W	L	Pct.	ERA	G	GS	CG	ShO	Sv.	IP	H	R	ER	BB	SO
1989— GC Yankees (GCL).............	1	1	.500	3.48	2	2	0	0	0	10 1/3	5	4	4	4	13
— Fort Lauderdale (FSL)	1	2	.333	4.73	3	3	0	0	0	13 1/3	16	8	7	7	2
1990— Greensboro (S. Atl.)........	5	12	.294	3.73	25	24	0	0	0	132 2/3	133	70	55	58	100
1991— Fort Lauderdale (FSL).......	5	8	.385	2.33	19	19	4	2	0	108	91	45	28	40	53
— Columbus (Int'l).................	0	1	.000	24.00	1	1	0	0	0	3	8	8	8	3	2
1992— Alb./Colon. (Eastern)	7	5	.583	3.28	22	22	0	0	0	112 1/3	96	55	41	70	66
1993— Columbus (Int'l)...............	3	1	.750	1.44	22	1	0	0	10	31 1/3	24	6	5	8	16
— New York (A.L.).................	3	3	.500	5.32	38	0	0	0	0	45 2/3	48	27	27	26	33
1994— Philadelphia (N.L.)■........	7	5	.583	2.67	21	14	1	0	1	104 1/3	101	40	31	35	59
— Scran./W.B. (Int'l).............	2	3	.400	2.12	6	5	0	0	0	34	27	9	8	14	24
1995— Reading (Eastern)	0	4	.000	10.80	4	4	0	0	0	15	28	19	18	3	8
— Scran./W.B. (Int'l).............	1	0	1.000	0.56	2	2	1	1	0	16	8	2	1	3	10
— Philadelphia (N.L.).............	0	2	.000	5.74	3	3	0	0	0	15 2/3	15	13	10	9	6
1996— Clearwater (Fla. St.)	1	1	.500	1.93	2	2	0	0	0	14	15	4	3	2	7
— Scran./W.B. (Int'l).............	4	2	.667	3.91	8	8	0	0	0	50 2/3	50	24	22	7	34
— Philadelphia (N.L.).............	0	3	.000	7.82	6	6	0	0	0	25 1/3	42	28	22	7	8
— Reading (Eastern)	0	1	.000	2.93	4	4	0	0	0	27 2/3	24	13	9	8	29
1997— Philadelphia (N.L.).............	1	5	.167	8.91	8	7	0	0	0	33 1/3	47	35	33	15	20
— Las Vegas (PCL)■.........	0	2	.000	9.93	17	1	0	0	0	22 2/3	30	26	25	11	13
— Albuquerque (PCL)■.........	0	3	.000	4.35	18	0	0	0	0	31	43	17	15	15	20
A.L. totals (1 year)	3	3	.500	5.32	38	0	0	0	0	45 2/3	48	27	27	26	33
N.L. totals (4 years)	8	15	.348	4.84	38	30	1	0	1	178 2/3	205	116	96	66	93
Major league totals (5 years)......	11	18	.379	4.93	76	30	1	0	1	224 1/3	253	143	123	92	126

MUNOZ, JUAN — OF — CARDINALS

PERSONAL: Born March 27, 1974, in Diriamba, Nicaragua. ... 5-10/170. ... Bats left, throws left. ... Full name: Juan A. Munoz.
HIGH SCHOOL: Miami (Fla.) Senior.
COLLEGE: Florida International.
TRANSACTIONS/CAREER NOTES: Selected by St. Louis Cardinals organization in 33rd round of free-agent draft (June 1, 1995).

							BATTING							FIELDING		
Year Team (League)	Pos.	G	AB	R	H	2B	3B	HR	RBI	Avg.	BB	SO	SB	PO	A	E	Avg.
1995— Johnson City (App.) ...	OF	57	190	43	66	12	1	7	31	.347	27	17	13	101	*14	2	.983
1996— Peoria (Midwest)........	OF	30	107	19	38	9	0	0	18	.355	14	13	4	45	3	0	1.000
— St. Petersburg (FSL) ..	OF	90	330	41	80	12	3	1	46	.242	38	35	6	132	10	2	.986
1997— Prince William (Car.) ..	OF	66	256	41	80	16	7	4	48	.313	19	25	3	115	7	3	.976
— Arkansas (Texas)........	OF	58	215	28	60	9	2	6	31	.279	16	26	6	107	11	0	1.000

MUNOZ, MIKE — P — ROCKIES

PERSONAL: Born July 12, 1965, in Baldwin Park, Calif. ... 6-2/192. ... Throws left, bats left. ... Full name: Michael Anthony Munoz.
HIGH SCHOOL: Bishop Amat (La Puente, Calif.).
COLLEGE: Cal Poly Pomona.
TRANSACTIONS/CAREER NOTES: Selected by Los Angeles Dodgers organization in third round of free-agent draft (June 2, 1986). ... Traded by Dodgers organization to Detroit Tigers for P Mike Wilkins (September 30, 1990). ... Granted free agency (May 12, 1993). ... Signed by Colorado Springs, Colorado Rockies organization (May 14, 1993). ... On Colorado disabled list (July 27-August 15, 1996); included rehabilitation assignment to Colorado Springs (August 10-15). ... Granted free agency (October 27, 1997).

Year Team (League)	W	L	Pct.	ERA	G	GS	CG	ShO	Sv.	IP	H	R	ER	BB	SO
1986— Great Falls (Pio.)	4	4	.500	3.21	14	14	2	2	0	81 1/3	85	44	29	38	49
1987— Bakersfield (California).......	8	7	.533	3.74	52	12	2	0	9	118	125	68	49	43	80
1988— San Antonio (Tex.)	7	2	.778	1.00	56	0	0	0	14	71 2/3	63	18	8	24	71
1989— Albuquerque (PCL)	6	4	.600	3.08	60	0	0	0	6	79	72	32	27	40	81
— Los Angeles (N.L.)	0	0	. . .	16.88	3	0	0	0	0	2 2/3	5	5	5	2	3
1990— Los Angeles (N.L.)	0	1	.000	3.18	8	0	0	0	0	5 2/3	6	2	2	3	2
— Albuquerque (PCL)	4	1	.800	4.25	49	0	0	0	6	59 1/3	65	33	28	19	40
1991— Toledo (Int'l)■.....................	2	3	.400	3.83	38	1	0	0	8	54	44	30	23	35	38
— Detroit (A.L.)	0	0	. . .	9.64	6	0	0	0	0	9 1/3	14	10	10	5	3
1992— Detroit (A.L.)	1	2	.333	3.00	65	0	0	0	2	48	44	16	16	25	23
1993— Detroit (A.L.)	0	1	.000	6.00	8	0	0	0	0	3	4	2	2	6	1
— Colo. Springs (PCL)■	1	2	.333	1.67	40	0	0	0	3	37 2/3	46	10	7	9	30
— Colorado (N.L.)	2	1	.667	4.50	21	0	0	0	0	18	21	12	9	9	16
1994— Colorado (N.L.)	4	2	.667	3.74	57	0	0	0	1	45 2/3	37	22	19	31	32
1995— Colorado (N.L.)	2	4	.333	7.42	64	0	0	0	2	43 2/3	54	38	36	27	37
1996— Colorado (N.L.)	2	2	.500	6.65	54	0	0	0	0	44 2/3	55	33	33	16	45
— Colo. Springs (PCL)	1	1	.500	2.03	10	0	0	0	3	13 1/3	8	3	3	6	13
1997— Colorado (N.L.)	3	3	.500	4.53	64	0	0	0	2	45 2/3	52	25	23	13	26
A.L. totals (3 years)	1	3	.250	4.18	79	0	0	0	2	60 1/3	62	28	28	36	27
N.L. totals (7 years)	13	13	.500	5.55	271	0	0	0	5	206	230	137	127	101	161
Major league totals (9 years)......	14	16	.467	5.24	350	0	0	0	7	266 1/3	292	165	155	137	188

DIVISION SERIES RECORD

Year Team (League)	W	L	Pct.	ERA	G	GS	CG	ShO	Sv.	IP	H	R	ER	BB	SO
1995— Colorado (N.L.)	0	1	.000	13.50	4	0	0	0	0	1 1/3	4	2	2	1	1

MUNRO, PETER — P — RED SOX

PERSONAL: Born June 14, 1975, in Flushing, N.Y. ... 6-2/195. ... Throws right, bats right. ... Full name: Peter Daniel Munro.
HIGH SCHOOL: Benjamin Cardozo (Bayside, N.Y.).
JUNIOR COLLEGE: Okaloosa-Walton Community College (Fla.).
TRANSACTIONS/CAREER NOTES: Signed as non-drafted free agent by Boston Red Sox organization (May 25, 1994).

Year Team (League)	W	L	Pct.	ERA	G	GS	CG	ShO	Sv.	IP	H	R	ER	BB	SO
1995— Utica (N.Y.-Penn)................	5	4	.556	2.60	14	14	0	0	0	90	79	38	26	33	74
1996— Sarasota (Florida State).......	11	6	.647	3.60	27	25	2	•2	1	155	153	76	62	62	115
1997— Trenton (Eastern)	7	10	.412	4.95	22	22	1	0	0	116 1/3	113	76	64	47	109

MURRAY, CALVIN — OF — GIANTS

PERSONAL: Born July 30, 1971, in Dallas. ... 5-11/175. ... Bats right, throws right. ... Full name: Calvin Duane Murray.
HIGH SCHOOL: Warren Travis White (Dallas).
COLLEGE: Texas.
TRANSACTIONS/CAREER NOTES: Selected by San Francisco Giants organization in first round (seventh pick overall) of free-agent draft (June 1, 1992).
STATISTICAL NOTES: Tied for Texas League lead in double plays by outfielder with four in 1997.
MISCELLANEOUS: Member of 1992 U.S. Olympic Baseball team.

							BATTING							FIELDING		
Year Team (League)	Pos.	G	AB	R	H	2B	3B	HR	RBI	Avg.	BB	SO	SB	PO	A	E	Avg.
1993— San Jose (Calif.).........	OF	85	345	61	97	24	1	9	42	.281	40	63	42	203	9	2	.991
— Shreveport (Texas)	OF	37	138	15	26	6	0	0	6	.188	14	29	12	79	2	2	.976
— Phoenix (PCL)	OF	5	19	4	6	1	1	0	0	.316	2	5	1	13	0	2	.867
1994— Shreveport (Texas)	OF	480	480	67	111	19	5	2	35	.231	47	81	33	268	5	3	.989

M

Year	Team (League)	Pos.	G	AB	R	H	2B	3B	HR	RBI	Avg.	BB	SO	SB	PO	A	E	Avg.
1995— Phoenix (PCL)	OF	13	50	8	9	1	0	4	10	.180	4	6	2	19	2	0	1.000
— Shreveport (Texas)	OF	110	441	77	104	17	3	2	29	.236	59	70	26	286	9	2	.993
1996— Shreveport (Texas)	OF	50	169	32	44	7	0	7	24	.260	25	33	6	89	4	3	.969
— Phoenix (PCL)	OF	83	311	50	76	16	6	3	28	.244	43	60	12	207	3	2	.991
1997— Shreveport (Texas)	OF	122	419	83	114	25	3	10	56	.272	66	73	*52	214	9	5	.978

MURRAY, EDDIE — DH/1B

PERSONAL: Born February 24, 1956, in Los Angeles. ... 6-2/220. ... Bats both, throws right. ... Full name: Eddie Clarence Murray. ... Brother of Rich Murray, first baseman, San Francisco Giants (1980 and 1983); brother of Leon Murray, minor league first baseman (1970); brother of Charles Murray, minor league outfielder (1962-66 and 1969); and brother of Venice Murray, minor league first baseman (1978).

HIGH SCHOOL: Locke (Los Angeles).

COLLEGE: Cal State Los Angeles.

TRANSACTIONS/CAREER NOTES: Selected by Baltimore Orioles organization in third round of free-agent draft (June 5, 1973). ... On disabled list (July 10-August 7, 1986). ... Traded by Orioles to Los Angeles Dodgers for P Brian Holton, P Ken Howell and SS Juan Bell (December 4, 1988). ... Granted free agency (October 29, 1991). ... Signed by New York Mets (November 27, 1991). ... Granted free agency (November 1, 1993). ... Signed by Cleveland Indians (December 2, 1993). ... On disabled list (July 3-August 1, 1995). ... Granted free agency (November 6, 1995). ... Re-signed by Indians (December 7, 1995). ... Traded by Indians to Orioles for P Kent Mercker (July 21, 1996). ... Granted free agency (November 18, 1996). ... Signed by Anaheim Angels (December 18, 1996). ... On Anaheim disabled list (June 12-August 3, 1997); included rehabilitation assignment to Lake Elsinore (July 16-17, 1997). ... Released by Angels (August 14, 1997). ... Signed by Dodgers organization (August 20, 1997). ... Granted free agency (October 30, 1997).

RECORDS: Holds major league career records for most games with switch-hit home runs—11; most sacrifice flies—128; most games by first baseman—2,413; and most assists by first baseman—1,865. ... Holds major league record for most consecutive games with switch-hit home runs—2 (May 8-9, 1987). ... Holds A.L. career record for most game-winning RBIs—117. ... Holds A.L. single-season record for most intentional bases on balls by switch-hitter—25 (1984). ... Shares A.L. single-season record for most games with switch-hit home runs—2 (1982, 1987). ... Holds N.L. single-season record for fewest double plays by first baseman (150 or more games)—88 (1990). ... Shares N.L. single-season record for fewest errors by first baseman who led league in errors—12 (1992).

HONORS: Named Appalachian League Player of the Year (1973). ... Named A.L. Rookie of the Year by Baseball Writers' Association of America (1977). ... Won A.L. Gold Glove at first base (1982-84). ... Named first baseman on THE SPORTING NEWS A.L. All-Star team (1983). ... Named first baseman on THE SPORTING NEWS A.L. Silver Slugger team (1983-84). ... Named first baseman on THE SPORTING NEWS N.L. All-Star team (1990). ... Named first baseman on THE SPORTING NEWS N.L. Silver Slugger team (1990).

STATISTICAL NOTES: Led Florida State League with 212 total bases in 1974. ... Led Florida State League first basemen with 113 double plays in 1974. ... Switch-hit home runs in one game 11 times (August 3, 1977; August 29, 1979, second game, two righthanded and one lefthanded; August 16, 1981; April 24 and August 26, 1982; August 26, 1985, two lefthanded and one righthanded; May 8 and May 9, 1987; April 18 and June 9, 1990; and April 21, 1994). ... Led A.L. first basemen with 1,615 total chances in 1978, 1,694 in 1984 and 1,526 in 1987. ... Led A.L. first basemen with 1,504 putouts in 1978. ... Hit three home runs in one game (August 29, 1979, second game; September 14, 1980, 13 innings; and August 26, 1985). ... Tied for A.L. lead with 18 intentional bases on balls received in 1984. ... Had 22-game hitting streak (August 17-September 10, 1984). ... Led A.L. with .410 on-base percentage and 19 game-winning RBIs in 1984. ... Led A.L. with 25 intentional bases on balls received in 1984. ... Led A.L. first basemen with 152 double plays in 1984, 146 in 1987 and tied for lead with 154 in 1985. ... Led N.L. first basemen with .996 fielding percentage, 137 assists and 122 double plays in 1989. ... Tied for N.L. lead with 21 intentional bases on balls received in 1990. ... Career major league grand slams: 19.

Year	Team (League)	Pos.	G	AB	R	H	2B	3B	HR	RBI	Avg.	BB	SO	SB	PO	A	E	Avg.
1973— Bluefield (Appal.)	1B	50	188	34	54	6	0	11	32	.287	19	46	6	421	14	13	.971
1974— Miami (Fla. St.)	1B	131	460	64	133	*29	7	12	63	.289	58	85	4	*1114	*51	*25	.979
— Asheville (South.)	1B	2	7	1	2	2	0	0	2	.286	1	1	0	17	0	0	1.000
1975— Asheville (South.)	1B-3B	124	436	66	115	13	5	17	46	.264	53	79	7	637	58	15	.979
1976— Charlotte (Southern)	1B	88	299	46	89	15	2	12	46	.298	43	41	11	746	45	9	.989
— Rochester (Int'l)	1B-OF-3B	54	168	35	46	6	2	11	40	.274	34	27	3	291	13	5	.984
1977— Baltimore (A.L.)	DH-1B	160	611	81	173	29	2	27	88	.283	48	104	0	482	20	4	.992
1978— Baltimore (A.L.)	1B-3B-DH	161	610	85	174	32	3	27	95	.285	70	97	6	†1507	112	6	.996
1979— Baltimore (A.L.)	1B-DH	159	606	90	179	30	2	25	99	.295	72	78	10	*1456	107	10	.994
1980— Baltimore (A.L.)	1B-DH	158	621	100	186	36	2	32	116	.300	54	71	7	1369	77	9	.994
1981— Baltimore (A.L.)	1B	99	378	57	111	21	2	*22	*78	.294	40	43	2	899	*91	1	*.999
1982— Baltimore (A.L.)	1B-DH	151	550	87	174	30	1	32	110	.316	70	82	5	1269	97	4	*.997
1983— Baltimore (A.L.)	1B-DH	156	582	115	178	30	3	33	111	.306	86	90	5	1393	114	10	.993
1984— Baltimore (A.L.)	1B-DH	*162	588	97	180	26	3	29	110	.306	*107	87	10	*1538	*143	13	.992
1985— Baltimore (A.L.)	1B-DH	156	583	111	173	37	1	31	124	.297	84	68	5	1338	152	*19	.987
1986— Baltimore (A.L.)	1B-DH	137	495	61	151	25	1	17	84	.305	78	49	3	1045	88	13	.989
1987— Baltimore (A.L.)	1B-DH	160	618	89	171	28	3	30	91	.277	73	80	1	1371	145	10	.993
1988— Baltimore (A.L.)	1B-DH	161	603	75	171	27	2	28	84	.284	75	78	5	867	106	11	.989
1989— Los Angeles (N.L.)■	1B-3B	160	594	66	147	29	1	20	88	.247	87	85	7	1316	†137	6	†.996
1990— Los Angeles (N.L.)	1B	155	558	96	184	22	3	26	95	.330	82	64	8	1180	113	10	.992
1991— Los Angeles (N.L.)	1B-3B	153	576	69	150	23	1	19	96	.260	55	74	10	1327	128	7	.995
1992— New York (N.L.)■	1B	156	551	64	144	37	2	16	93	.261	66	74	4	1283	96	*12	.991
1993— New York (N.L.)	1B	154	610	77	174	28	1	27	100	.285	40	61	2	1319	111	18	.988
1994— Cleveland (A.L.)■	DH-1B	108	433	57	110	21	1	17	76	.254	31	53	8	243	14	3	.988
1995— Cleveland (A.L.)	DH-1B	113	436	68	141	21	0	21	82	.323	39	65	5	160	22	3	.984
1996— Cleveland (A.L.)	DH-1B	88	336	33	88	9	1	12	45	.262	34	45	3	10	1	0	1.000
— Baltimore (A.L.)	DH	64	230	36	59	12	0	10	34	.257	27	42	1	...	...	...	...
1997— Anaheim (A.L.)■	DH	46	160	13	35	7	0	3	15	.219	13	24	1	...	...	...	...
— Lake Elsinore (Calif.)	DH	2	8	1	4	0	0	1	2	.500	0	0	0	...	...	...	...
— Albuquerque (PCL)■	1B	9	26	4	8	1	0	2	9	.308	3	3	0	56	1	2	.966
— Los Angeles (N.L.)■	PH	9	7	0	2	0	0	0	3	.286	2	2	0	...	...	...	...
American League totals (16 years)		2239	8440	1255	2454	421	27	396	1442	.291	1001	1156	79	14947	1289	116	.992
National League totals (6 years)		787	2896	372	801	139	8	108	475	.277	332	360	31	6425	585	53	.992
Major league totals (21 years)		3026	11336	1627	3255	560	35	504	1917	.287	1333	1516	110	21372	1874	169	.993

M

RECORDS: Shares career record for most triples—1.

Year Team (League)	Pos.	G	AB	R	H	2B	3B	HR	RBI	Avg.	BB	SO	SB	PO	A	E	Avg.
1995— Cleveland (A.L.)..........	DH	3	13	3	5	0	1	1	3	.385	2	1	0	...	...	...	...
1996— Baltimore (A.L.)..........	DH	4	15	1	6	1	0	0	1	.400	5	4	1	...	...	...	...
Division series totals (2 years)		7	28	4	11	1	1	1	4	.393	7	5	1	...	...	...	...

CHAMPIONSHIP SERIES RECORD

RECORDS: Shares single-game record for most runs—4 (October 7, 1983).

Year Team (League)	Pos.	G	AB	R	H	2B	3B	HR	RBI	Avg.	BB	SO	SB	PO	A	E	Avg.
1979— Baltimore (A.L.)..........	1B	4	12	3	5	0	0	1	5	.417	5	2	0	44	3	2	.959
1983— Baltimore (A.L.)..........	1B	4	15	5	4	0	0	1	3	.267	3	3	1	34	3	1	.974
1995— Cleveland (A.L.)..........	DH	6	24	2	6	1	0	1	3	.250	2	3	0	...	...	...	...
1996— Baltimore (A.L.)..........	DH	5	15	1	4	0	0	1	2	.267	2	2	0	0	...	...	...
Championship series totals (4 years)		19	66	11	19	1	0	4	13	.288	12	10	1	78	6	3	.966

WORLD SERIES RECORD

NOTES: Member of World Series championship team (1983).

Year Team (League)	Pos.	G	AB	R	H	2B	3B	HR	RBI	Avg.	BB	SO	SB	PO	A	E	Avg.
1979— Baltimore (A.L.)..........	1B	7	26	3	4	1	0	1	2	.154	4	4	1	60	7	0	1.000
1983— Baltimore (A.L.)..........	1B	5	20	2	5	0	0	2	3	.250	1	4	0	46	1	1	.979
1995— Cleveland (A.L.)..........	1B-DH	6	19	1	2	0	0	1	3	.105	5	4	0	27	0	0	1.000
World Series totals (3 years)		18	65	6	11	1	0	4	8	.169	10	12	1	133	8	1	.993

ALL-STAR GAME RECORD

Year League	Pos.	AB	R	H	2B	3B	HR	RBI	Avg.	BB	SO	SB	PO	A	E	Avg.
1978— American....................							Did not play.									
1981— American....................	PH-1B	2	0	0	0	0	0	0	.000	0	0	0	2	1	0	1.000
1982— American....................	PH-1B	1	0	0	0	0	0	0	.000	1	0	0	4	0	0	1.000
1983— American....................	1B	2	0	0	0	0	0	0	.000	0	0	0	4	0	0	1.000
1984— American....................	1B	2	0	1	1	0	0	0	.500	0	1	0	3	0	0	1.000
1985— American....................	1B	3	0	0	0	0	0	0	.000	0	0	0	5	2	0	1.000
1986— American....................							Did not play.									
1991— National....................	1B	1	0	0	0	0	0	0	.000	0	1	0	3	0	0	1.000
All-Star Game totals (6 years)		11	0	1	1	0	0	0	.091	1	2	0	21	3	0	1.000

MURRAY, HEATH — P — PADRES

PERSONAL: Born April 19, 1973, in Troy, Ohio. ... 6-4/205. ... Throws left, bats left. ... Full name: Heath Robertson Murray.
HIGH SCHOOL: Troy (Ohio).
COLLEGE: Michigan.
TRANSACTIONS/CAREER NOTES: Selected by San Diego Padres organization in third round of free-agent draft (June 2, 1994). ... On San Diego disabled list (June 23-July 10, 1997).

Year Team (League)	W	L	Pct.	ERA	G	GS	CG	ShO	Sv.	IP	H	R	ER	BB	SO
1994— Spokane (N'west)..............	5	6	.455	2.90	15	15	•2	•1	0	*99 1/3	101	46	32	18	78
1995— Rancho Cucamonga (Cal.) .	9	4	.692	3.12	14	14	4	•2	0	92 1/3	80	37	32	38	81
— Memphis (Southern)	5	4	.556	3.38	14	14	0	0	0	77 1/3	83	36	29	42	71
1996— Memphis (Southern)	13	9	.591	3.21	27	27	1	1	0	174	154	83	62	60	156
1997— Las Vegas (PCL)	6	8	.429	5.45	19	19	2	1	0	109	142	72	66	41	99
— San Diego (N.L.)	1	2	.333	6.75	17	3	0	0	0	33 1/3	50	25	25	21	16
Major league totals (1 year)........	1	2	.333	6.75	17	3	0	0	0	33 1/3	50	25	25	21	16

MUSSINA, MIKE — P — ORIOLES

PERSONAL: Born December 8, 1968, in Williamsport, Pa. ... 6-1/180. ... Throws right, bats right. ... Full name: Michael Cole Mussina. ... Name pronounced myoo-SEEN-uh.
HIGH SCHOOL: Montoursville (Pa.).
COLLEGE: Stanford (degree in economics, 1990).
TRANSACTIONS/CAREER NOTES: Selected by Baltimore Orioles organization in 11th round of free-agent draft (June 2, 1987); did not sign. ... Selected by Orioles organization in first round (20th pick overall) of free-agent draft (June 4, 1990). ... On Rochester disabled list (May 5-12, 1991). ... On Baltimore disabled list (July 22-August 20, 1993); included rehabilitation assignment to Bowie (August 9-20).
HONORS: Named International League Most Valuable Pitcher (1991). ... Named righthanded pitcher on The Sporting News A.L. All-Star team (1995). ... Won A.L. Gold Glove at pitcher (1996-97).
STATISTICAL NOTES: Pitched 8-0 one-hit, complete-game victory against Texas (July 17, 1992). ... Pitched 3-0 one-hit, complete-game victory against Cleveland (May 30, 1997).
MISCELLANEOUS: Holds Baltimore Orioles all-time record for highest winning percentage (.682).

Year Team (League)	W	L	Pct.	ERA	G	GS	CG	ShO	Sv.	IP	H	R	ER	BB	SO
1990— Hagerstown (Eastern)	3	0	1.000	1.49	7	7	2	1	0	42 1/3	34	10	7	7	40
— Rochester (Int'l)	0	0	...	1.35	2	2	0	0	0	13 1/3	8	2	2	4	15
1991— Rochester (Int'l)	10	4	.714	2.87	19	19	3	1	0	122 1/3	108	42	39	31	107
— Baltimore (A.L.)...............	4	5	.444	2.87	12	12	2	0	0	87 2/3	77	31	28	21	52
1992— Baltimore (A.L.)...............	18	5	*.783	2.54	32	32	8	4	0	241	212	70	68	48	130
1993— Baltimore (A.L.)...............	14	6	.700	4.46	25	25	3	2	0	167 2/3	163	84	83	44	117
— Bowie (Eastern)................	1	0	1.000	2.25	2	2	0	0	0	8	5	2	2	1	10

Year Team (League)	W	L	Pct.	ERA	G	GS	CG	ShO	Sv.	IP	H	R	ER	BB	SO
1994— Baltimore (A.L.)	16	5	.762	3.06	24	24	3	0	0	176 1/3	163	63	60	42	99
1995— Baltimore (A.L.)	*19	9	.679	3.29	32	32	7	*4	0	221 2/3	187	86	81	50	158
1996— Baltimore (A.L.)	19	11	.633	4.81	36	*36	4	1	0	243 1/3	264	137	130	69	204
1997— Baltimore (A.L.)	15	8	.652	3.20	33	33	4	1	0	224 2/3	197	87	80	54	218
Major league totals (7 years)	105	49	.682	3.50	194	194	31	12	0	1362 1/3	1263	558	530	328	978

DIVISION SERIES RECORD

Year Team (League)	W	L	Pct.	ERA	G	GS	CG	ShO	Sv.	IP	H	R	ER	BB	SO
1996— Baltimore (A.L.)	0	0	...	4.50	1	1	0	0	0	6	7	4	3	2	6
1997— Baltimore (A.L.)	2	0	1.000	1.93	2	2	0	0	0	14	7	3	3	3	16
Div. series totals (2 years)	2	0	1.000	2.70	3	3	0	0	0	20	14	7	6	5	22

CHAMPIONSHIP SERIES RECORD

Year Team (League)	W	L	Pct.	ERA	G	GS	CG	ShO	Sv.	IP	H	R	ER	BB	SO
1996— Baltimore (A.L.)	0	1	.000	5.87	1	1	0	0	0	7 2/3	8	5	5	2	6
1997— Baltimore (A.L.)	0	0	...	0.60	2	2	0	0	0	15	4	1	1	4	25
Champ. series totals (2 years)	0	1	.000	2.38	3	3	0	0	0	22 2/3	12	6	6	6	31

ALL-STAR GAME RECORD

Year League	W	L	Pct.	ERA	GS	CG	ShO	Sv.	IP	H	R	ER	BB	SO
1992— American	0	0	...	0.00	0	0	0	0	1	0	0	0	0	0
1993— American							Did not play.							
1994— American	0	0	...	0.00	0	0	0	0	1	1	0	0	0	1
1997— National							Did not play.							
All-Star totals (2 years)	0	0	...	0.00	0	0	0	0	2	1	0	0	0	1

MYERS, GREG   C   PADRES

PERSONAL: Born April 14, 1966, in Riverside, Calif. ... 6-2/208. ... Bats left, throws right. ... Full name: Gregory Richard Myers.
HIGH SCHOOL: Riverside (Calif.) Polytechnical.
TRANSACTIONS/CAREER NOTES: Selected by Toronto Blue Jays organization in third round of free-agent draft (June 4, 1984). ... On disabled list (June 17, 1988-remainder of season). ... On Toronto disabled list (March 26-June 5, 1989); included rehabilitation assignment to Knoxville (May 17-June 5). ... On Toronto disabled list (May 5-25, 1990); included rehabilitation assignment to Syracuse (May 21-24). ... Traded by Blue Jays with OF Rob Ducey to California Angels for P Mark Eichhorn (July 30, 1992). ... On California disabled list (August 27, 1992-remainder of season). ... On California disabled list (April 24-June 21, 1994); included rehabilitation assignments to Lake Elsinore (May 20-June 6 and June 13-21). ... On disabled list (April 21-May 6, June 1-21 and September 30, 1995-remainder of season). ... Granted free agency (November 3, 1995). ... Signed by Minnesota Twins (December 8, 1995). ... On disabled list (July 14-August 2, 1996). ... On Minnesota disabled list (August 9-24, 1997). ... Traded by Twins to Atlanta Braves for a player to be named later (September 5, 1997); Twins acquired 1B Steve Hacker to complete deal (December 18, 1997). ... Granted free agency (October 28, 1997). ... Signed by San Diego Padres (November 25, 1997).
STATISTICAL NOTES: Led California League catchers with 967 total chances in 1986. ... Led International League catchers with 698 total chances in 1987.

							BATTING								FIELDING		
Year Team (League)	Pos.	G	AB	R	H	2B	3B	HR	RBI	Avg.	BB	SO	SB	PO	A	E	Avg.
1984— Medicine Hat (Pio.)	C	38	133	20	42	9	0	2	20	.316	16	6	0	216	24	4	.984
1985— Florence (S. Atl.)	C	134	489	52	109	19	2	5	62	.223	39	54	0	551	61	7	*.989
1986— Ventura (Calif.)	C	124	451	65	133	23	4	20	79	.295	43	46	9	*849	99	19	.980
1987— Syracuse (Int'l)	C	107	342	35	84	19	1	10	47	.246	22	46	3	*637	50	11	.984
— Toronto (A.L.)	C	7	9	1	1	0	0	0	0	.111	0	3	0	24	1	0	1.000
1988— Syracuse (Int'l)	C	34	120	18	34	7	1	7	21	.283	8	24	1	63	9	1	.986
1989— Knoxville (Southern)	C	29	90	11	30	10	0	5	19	.333	3	16	1	130	12	1	.993
— Toronto (A.L.)	C-DH	17	44	0	5	2	0	0	1	.114	2	9	0	46	6	0	1.000
— Syracuse (Int'l)	C	24	89	8	24	6	0	1	11	.270	4	9	1	60	7	1	.985
1990— Toronto (A.L.)	C	87	250	33	59	7	1	5	22	.236	22	33	0	411	30	3	.993
— Syracuse (Int'l)	C	3	11	0	2	1	0	0	2	.182	1	1	0	14	0	0	1.000
1991— Toronto (A.L.)	C	107	309	25	81	22	0	8	36	.262	21	45	0	484	37	11	.979
1992— Toronto (A.L.)	C	22	61	4	14	6	0	1	13	.230	5	5	0	92	13	1	.991
— California (A.L.)■	C-DH	8	17	0	4	1	0	0	0	.235	0	6	0	33	3	0	1.000
1993— California (A.L.)	C-DH	108	290	27	74	10	0	7	40	.255	17	47	3	369	44	6	.986
1994— California (A.L.)	C-DH	45	126	10	31	6	0	2	8	.246	10	27	0	194	28	2	.991
— Lake Elsinore (Calif.)	C	10	32	4	8	2	0	0	5	.250	2	6	0	31	3	0	1.000
1995— California (A.L.)	C-DH	85	273	35	71	12	2	9	38	.260	17	49	0	341	21	4	.989
1996— Minnesota (A.L.)■	C	97	329	37	94	22	3	6	28	.286	19	52	0	488	27	8	.985
1997— Minnesota (A.L.)	C-DH	62	165	24	44	11	1	5	28	.267	16	29	0	196	11	3	.986
— Atlanta (N.L.)■	C	9	9	0	1	0	0	0	1	.111	1	3	0	11	2	0	1.000
American League totals (10 years)		645	1873	196	478	99	7	43	233	.255	129	305	3	2678	221	38	.987
National League totals (1 year)		9	9	0	1	0	0	0	1	.111	1	3	0	11	2	0	1.000
Major league totals (10 years)		654	1882	196	479	99	7	43	234	.255	130	308	3	2689	223	38	.987

CHAMPIONSHIP SERIES RECORD

							BATTING								FIELDING		
Year Team (League)	Pos.	G	AB	R	H	2B	3B	HR	RBI	Avg.	BB	SO	SB	PO	A	E	Avg.
1991— Toronto (A.L.)								Did not play.									

MYERS, MIKE   P   BREWERS

PERSONAL: Born June 26, 1969, in Arlington Heights, Ill. ... 6-3/197. ... Throws left, bats left. ... Full name: Michael Stanley Myers.
HIGH SCHOOL: Crystal Lake (Ill.) Central.
COLLEGE: Iowa State.

TRANSACTIONS/CAREER NOTES: Selected by San Francisco Giants organization in fourth round of free-agent draft (June 4, 1990). ... On Clinton disabled list (June 3-September 16, 1991; April 9-June 2 and June 21-July 6, 1992). ... Selected by Florida Marlins from Giants organization in Rule 5 major league draft (December 7, 1992). ... On Edmonton disabled list (April 13-June 7, 1994). ... On Florida disabled list (June 7-August 5, 1994); included rehabilitation assignment to Brevard County (June 23-July 11). ... Traded by Marlins to Detroit Tigers (August 9, 1995), completing deal in which Marlins acquired P Buddy Groom for a player to be named later (August 7, 1995). ... Traded by Tigers with P Rick Greene and SS Santiago Perez to Milwaukee Brewers for P Bryce Florie and a player to be named later (November 20, 1997).

STATISTICAL NOTES: Led Pacific Coast League with 10 hit batsmen in 1993.

Year Team (League)	W	L	Pct.	ERA	G	GS	CG	ShO	Sv.	IP	H	R	ER	BB	SO
1990— Everett (Northwest)	4	5	.444	3.90	15	14	1	0	0	85 1/3	91	43	37	30	73
1991— Clinton (Midwest)	5	3	.625	2.62	11	11	1	0	0	65 1/3	61	23	19	18	59
1992— San Jose (California)	5	1	.833	2.30	8	8	0	0	0	54 2/3	43	20	14	17	40
— Clinton (Midwest)	1	2	.333	1.19	7	7	0	0	0	37 2/3	28	11	5	8	32
1993— Edmonton (PCL)■	7	14	.333	5.18	27	27	3	0	0	161 2/3	195	109	93	52	112
1994— Edmonton (PCL)	1	5	.167	5.55	12	11	0	0	0	60	78	42	37	21	55
— Brevard County (FSL)	0	0	...	0.79	3	2	0	0	0	11 1/3	7	1	1	4	15
1995— Charlotte (Int'l)	0	5	.000	5.65	37	0	0	0	0	36 2/3	41	25	23	15	24
— Florida (N.L.)	0	0	...	0.00	2	0	0	0	0	2	1	0	0	3	0
— Toledo (Int'l)■	0	0	...	4.32	6	0	0	0	0	8 1/3	6	4	4	3	8
— Detroit (A.L.)	1	0	1.000	9.95	11	0	0	0	0	6 1/3	10	7	7	4	4
1996— Detroit (A.L.)	1	5	.167	5.01	•83	0	0	0	6	64 2/3	70	41	36	34	69
1997— Detroit (A.L.)	0	4	.000	5.70	•88	0	0	0	2	53 2/3	58	36	34	25	50
A.L. totals (3 years)	2	9	.182	5.56	182	0	0	0	8	124 2/3	138	84	77	63	123
N.L. totals (1 year)	0	0	...	0.00	2	0	0	0	0	2	1	0	0	3	0
Major league totals (3 years)	2	9	.182	5.47	184	0	0	0	8	126 2/3	139	84	77	66	123

MYERS, RANDY   P   BLUE JAYS

PERSONAL: Born September 19, 1962, in Vancouver, Wash. ... 6-1/225. ... Throws left, bats left. ... Full name: Randall Kirk Myers.

HIGH SCHOOL: Evergreen (Vancouver, Wash.).

JUNIOR COLLEGE: Clark Community College (Wash.).

TRANSACTIONS/CAREER NOTES: Selected by Cincinnati Reds organization in third round of free-agent draft (January 12, 1982); did not sign. ... Selected by New York Mets organization in secondary phase of free-agent draft (June 7, 1982). ... Traded by Mets with P Kip Gross to Cincinnati Reds for P John Franco and OF Don Brown (December 6, 1989). ... Traded by Reds to San Diego Padres for OF/2B Bip Roberts and a player to be named later (December 8, 1991); Reds acquired OF Craig Pueschner to complete deal (December 9, 1991). ... Granted free agency (October 26, 1992). ... Signed by Chicago Cubs (December 9, 1992). ... Granted free agency (November 3, 1995). ... Signed by Baltimore Orioles (December 14, 1995). ... Granted free agency (October 27, 1997). ... Signed by Toronto Blue Jays (November 26, 1997).

RECORDS: Shares N.L. single-game record for most consecutive strikeouts by relief pitcher—6 (September 8, 1990). ... Holds N.L. single-season record for most saves—53 (1993).

HONORS: Named Carolina League Pitcher of the Year (1984). ... Named N.L. Fireman of the Year by The Sporting News (1993 and 1995).

STATISTICAL NOTES: Tied for Appalachian League lead with three balks in 1982.

MISCELLANEOUS: Had sacrifice hit in one game as pinch-hitter (1992). ... Grounded into a double play in one game as pinch-hitter (1993).

Year Team (League)	W	L	Pct.	ERA	G	GS	CG	ShO	Sv.	IP	H	R	ER	BB	SO
1982— Kingsport (Appalachian)	6	3	.667	4.12	13	•13	1	0	0	74 1/3	68	49	34	69	•86
1983— Columbia (S. Atl.)	14	10	.583	3.63	28	•28	3	0	0	173 1/3	146	94	70	108	164
1984— Lynchburg (Carolina)	13	5	.722	*2.06	23	22	•7	1	0	157	123	46	36	61	171
— Jackson (Texas)	2	1	.667	2.06	5	5	1	0	0	35	29	14	8	16	35
1985— Jackson (Texas)	4	8	.333	3.96	19	19	2	1	0	120 1/3	99	61	53	69	116
— Tidewater (Int'l)	1	1	.500	1.84	8	7	0	0	0	44	40	13	9	20	25
— New York (N.L.)	0	0	...	0.00	1	0	0	0	0	2	0	0	0	1	2
1986— Tidewater (Int'l)	6	7	.462	2.35	45	0	0	0	12	65	44	19	17	44	79
— New York (N.L.)	0	0	...	4.22	10	0	0	0	0	10 2/3	11	5	5	9	13
1987— New York (N.L.)	3	6	.333	3.96	54	0	0	0	6	75	61	36	33	30	92
— Tidewater (Int'l)	0	0	...	4.91	5	0	0	0	3	7 1/3	6	4	4	4	13
1988— New York (N.L.)	7	3	.700	1.72	55	0	0	0	26	68	45	15	13	17	69
1989— New York (N.L.)	7	4	.636	2.35	65	0	0	0	24	84 1/3	62	23	22	40	88
1990— Cincinnati (N.L.)■	4	6	.400	2.08	66	0	0	0	31	86 2/3	59	24	20	38	98
1991— Cincinnati (N.L.)	6	13	.316	3.55	58	12	1	0	6	132	116	61	52	80	108
1992— San Diego (N.L.)■	3	6	.333	4.29	66	0	0	0	38	79 2/3	84	38	38	34	66
1993— Chicago (N.L.)■	2	4	.333	3.11	73	0	0	0	*53	75 1/3	65	26	26	26	86
1994— Chicago (N.L.)	1	5	.167	3.79	38	0	0	0	21	40 1/3	40	18	17	16	32
1995— Chicago (N.L.)	1	2	.333	3.88	57	0	0	0	*38	55 2/3	49	25	24	28	59
1996— Baltimore (A.L.)■	4	4	.500	3.53	62	0	0	0	31	58 2/3	60	24	23	29	74
1997— Baltimore (A.L.)	2	3	.400	1.51	61	0	0	0	*45	59 2/3	47	12	10	22	56
A.L. totals (2 years)	6	7	.462	2.51	123	0	0	0	76	118 1/3	107	36	33	51	130
N.L. totals (11 years)	34	49	.410	3.17	543	12	1	0	243	709 2/3	592	271	250	319	713
Major league totals (13 years)	40	56	.417	3.08	666	12	1	0	319	828	699	307	283	370	843

DIVISION SERIES RECORD

RECORDS: Shares A.L. career record for most saves—3.

Year Team (League)	W	L	Pct.	ERA	G	GS	CG	ShO	Sv.	IP	H	R	ER	BB	SO
1996— Baltimore (A.L.)	0	0	...	0.00	3	0	0	0	2	3	0	0	0	0	3
1997— Baltimore (A.L.)	0	0	...	0.00	2	0	0	0	1	2	0	0	0	0	5
Div. series totals (2 years)	0	0	...	0.00	5	0	0	0	3	5	0	0	0	0	8

CHAMPIONSHIP SERIES RECORD

RECORDS: Shares N.L. single-series record for most saves—3 (1990).

NOTES: Named N.L. Championship Series co-Most Valuable Player (1990).

Year Team (League)	W	L	Pct.	ERA	G	GS	CG	ShO	Sv.	IP	H	R	ER	BB	SO
1988— New York (N.L.)	2	0	1.000	0.00	3	0	0	0	0	4 2/3	1	0	0	2	0
1990— Cincinnati (N.L.)	0	0	...	0.00	4	0	0	0	3	5 2/3	2	0	0	3	7

M

Year	Team (League)	W	L	Pct.	ERA	G	GS	CG	ShO	Sv.	IP	H	R	ER	BB	SO
1996— Baltimore (A.L.)		0	1	.000	2.25	3	0	0	0	0	4	4	1	1	3	2
1997— Baltimore (A.L.)		0	1	.000	5.06	4	0	0	0	1	5 1/3	6	3	3	3	7
Champ. series totals (4 years)		2	2	.500	1.83	14	0	0	0	4	19 2/3	13	4	4	11	16

WORLD SERIES RECORD

NOTES: Member of World Series championship team (1990).

Year	Team (League)	W	L	Pct.	ERA	G	GS	CG	ShO	Sv.	IP	H	R	ER	BB	SO
1990— Cincinnati (N.L.)		0	0	. . .	0.00	3	0	0	0	1	3	2	0	0	0	3

ALL-STAR GAME RECORD

Year	League	W	L	Pct.	ERA	GS	CG	ShO	Sv.	IP	H	R	ER	BB	SO
1990— National		0	0	. . .	0.00	0	0	0	0	1	1	0	0	2	0
1994— National		0	0	. . .	0.00	0	0	0	0	1	1	0	0	0	1
1995— National		0	0	. . .	0.00	0	0	0	1	1	1	0	0	1	0
1997— National		0	0	. . .	0.00	0	0	0	0	1	1	0	0	0	2
All-Star totals (4 years)		0	0	. . .	0.00	0	0	0	1	4	4	2	0	3	3

MYERS, ROD   OF   ROYALS

PERSONAL: Born January 14, 1973, in Conroe, Texas. ... 6-1/190. ... Bats left, throws left. ... Full name: Roderick Demond Myers.

HIGH SCHOOL: Conroe (Texas).

TRANSACTIONS/CAREER NOTES: Selected by Kansas City Royals organization in 13th round of free-agent draft (June 3, 1991). ... On disabled list (March 23-July 10, 1997); included rehabilitation assignment to Wichita (July 3-10).

							BATTING								FIELDING		
Year	Team (League)	Pos.	G	AB	R	H	2B	3B	HR	RBI	Avg.	BB	SO	SB	PO	A	E	Avg.
1991— GC Royals (GCL)		OF	44	133	14	37	2	3	1	18	.278	6	27	12	45	2	1	.979
— Baseball City (FSL)		OF	4	11	1	2	0	0	0	0	.182	0	5	1	4	0	0	1.000
1992— Appleton (Midwest)		OF	71	218	31	48	10	2	4	30	.220	39	67	25	132	5	10	.932
1993— Rockford (Midwest)		OF	129	474	69	123	24	5	9	68	.259	58	117	49	208	10	7	.969
1994— Wilmington (Caro.)		OF	126	457	76	120	20	4	12	65	.263	67	93	31	168	5	7	.961
1995— Wichita (Texas)		OF-1B	131	499	71	*153	22	6	7	62	.307	34	77	29	262	8	10	.964
1996— Omaha (A.A.)		OF	112	411	68	120	27	1	16	54	.292	49	106	37	263	5	2	*.993
— Kansas City (A.L.)		OF	22	63	9	18	7	0	1	11	.286	7	16	3	33	0	0	1.000
1997— Wichita (Texas)		OF	4	16	3	5	2	0	0	3	.313	3	3	0	8	0	0	1.000
— Kansas City (A.L.)		OF	31	101	14	26	7	0	2	9	.257	17	22	4	55	1	1	.982
— Omaha (A.A.)		OF	38	142	21	36	10	0	2	10	.254	15	37	6	89	3	1	.989
Major league totals (2 years)			53	164	23	44	14	0	3	20	.268	24	38	7	88	1	1	.989

MYERS, ROD   P   CUBS

PERSONAL: Born June 26, 1969, in Rockford, Ill. ... 6-1/210. ... Throws right, bats right. ... Full name: Rodney Luther Myers.

HIGH SCHOOL: Rockford (Ill.) East.

COLLEGE: Wisconsin.

TRANSACTIONS/CAREER NOTES: Selected by Kansas City Royals organization in 12th round of free-agent draft (June 4, 1990). ... On disabled list (May 17-June 3 and June 21-September 15, 1994; and June 30-July 21, 1995). ... Selected by Chicago Cubs from Royals organization in Rule 5 major league draft (December 4, 1995).

Year	Team (League)	W	L	Pct.	ERA	G	GS	CG	ShO	Sv.	IP	H	R	ER	BB	SO
1990— Eugene (Northwest)		0	2	.000	1.19	6	4	0	0	0	22 2/3	19	9	3	13	17
1991— Appleton (Midwest)		1	1	.500	2.60	9	4	0	0	0	27 2/3	22	9	8	26	29
1992— Lethbridge (Pioneer)		5	•8	.385	4.01	15	15	*5	0	0	*103 1/3	93	57	46	61	76
1993— Rockford (Midwest)		7	3	.700	1.79	12	12	5	2	0	85 1/3	65	22	17	18	65
— Memphis (Southern)		3	6	.333	5.62	12	12	1	1	0	65 2/3	73	46	41	32	42
1994— Wilmington (Caro.)		1	1	.500	4.82	4	0	0	0	1	9 1/3	9	6	5	1	9
— Memphis (Southern)		5	1	.833	1.03	42	0	0	0	9	69 2/3	45	20	8	29	53
1995— Omaha (Am. Assoc.)		4	5	.444	4.10	38	0	0	0	2	48 1/3	52	26	22	19	38
1996— Chicago (N.L.)■		2	1	.667	4.68	45	0	0	0	0	67 1/3	61	38	35	38	50
1997— Iowa (Am. Assoc.)		7	8	.467	4.09	24	23	1	0	0	140 2/3	140	76	64	38	79
— Chicago (N.L.)		0	0	. . .	6.00	5	1	0	0	0	9	12	6	6	7	6
Major league totals (2 years)		2	1	.667	4.83	50	1	0	0	0	76 1/3	73	44	41	45	56

NAEHRING, TIM   3B   RED SOX

PERSONAL: Born February 1, 1967, in Cincinnati. ... 6-2/203. ... Bats right, throws right. ... Full name: Timothy James Naehring. ... Name pronounced NAIR-ring.

HIGH SCHOOL: LaSalle (Cincinnati).

COLLEGE: Miami of Ohio.

TRANSACTIONS/CAREER NOTES: Selected by Boston Red Sox organization in eighth round of free-agent draft (June 1, 1988). ... On Boston disabled list (August 16, 1990-remainder of season and May 18, 1991-remainder of season). ... On Boston disabled list (July 25-September 3, 1992); included rehabilitation assignment to Pawtucket (August 22-September 3). ... On Boston disabled list (April 1-July 2, 1993); included rehabilitation assignment to Pawtucket (June 13-July 2). ... On Boston disabled list (June 7-July 6, 1994); included rehabilitation assignment to Pawtucket (July 2-6). ... On Boston disabled list (April 15-May 3, 1996); included rehabilitation assignment to Trenton (April 29-May 3). ... Granted free agency (December 7, 1996). ... Re-signed by Red Sox (December 13, 1996). ... On disabled list (June 30, 1997-remainder of season).

STATISTICAL NOTES: Career major league grand slams: 2.

Year Team (League)	Pos.	G	AB	R	H	2B	3B	HR	RBI	Avg.	BB	SO	SB	PO	A	E	Avg.
1988— Elmira (N.Y.-Penn)......	SS	19	59	6	18	3	0	1	13	.305	8	11	0	25	51	6	.927
—Winter Haven (FSL)....	SS	42	141	17	32	7	0	0	10	.227	19	24	1	77	136	20	.914
1989—Lynchburg (Caro.)......	SS	56	209	24	63	7	1	4	37	.301	23	30	2	72	131	12	.944
—Pawtucket (Int'l)........	SS-3B	79	273	32	75	16	1	3	31	.275	27	41	2	118	192	21	.937
1990—Pawtucket (Int'l)......	SS-3B-2B	82	290	45	78	16	1	15	47	.269	37	56	0	126	240	16	.958
—Boston (A.L.)..........	SS-3B-2B	24	85	10	23	6	0	2	12	.271	8	15	0	36	66	9	.919
1991—Boston (A.L.)..........	SS-3B-2B	20	55	1	6	1	0	0	3	.109	6	15	1	17	53	3	.959
1992—Boston (A.L.)...........S-2-3-DH-O		72	186	12	43	8	0	3	14	.231	18	31	0	95	170	3	.989
—Pawtucket (Int'l)......	2B	11	34	7	10	0	0	2	5	.294	8	6	1	22	39	3	.953
1993—Pawtucket (Int'l)......	3B-SS-2B	55	202	38	62	9	1	7	36	.307	35	27	0	79	133	4	.981
—Boston (A.L.)..........	2-DH-3-S	39	127	14	42	10	0	1	17	.331	10	26	1	45	44	2	.978
1994—Boston (A.L.)...........2-3-1-S-DH		80	297	41	82	18	1	7	42	.276	30	56	1	190	183	6	.984
—Pawtucket (Int'l)......	2B-3B	4	15	2	2	2	0	0	3	.133	1	2	0	2	5	1	.875
1995—Boston (A.L.)..........	3B-DH	126	433	61	133	27	2	10	57	.307	77	66	0	85	244	16	.954
1996—Boston (A.L.)..........	3B-2B	116	430	77	124	16	0	17	65	.288	49	63	2	82	206	11	.963
—Trenton (Eastern)	3B	3	9	2	2	1	0	1	2	.222	1	3	0	1	2	1	.750
1997—Boston (A.L.)..........	3B-DH	70	259	38	74	18	1	9	40	.286	38	40	1	40	111	3	.981
Major league totals (8 years)		547	1872	254	527	104	4	49	250	.282	236	312	5	590	1077	53	.969

DIVISION SERIES RECORD

Year Team (League)	Pos.	G	AB	R	H	2B	3B	HR	RBI	Avg.	BB	SO	SB	PO	A	E	Avg.
1995—Boston (A.L.).............	3B	3	13	2	4	0	0	1	1	.308	0	1	0	5	5	0	1.000

NAGY, CHARLES   P   INDIANS

PERSONAL: Born May 5, 1967, in Fairfield, Conn. ... 6-3/200. ... Throws right, bats left. ... Full name: Charles Harrison Nagy. ... Name pronounced NAG-ee.

HIGH SCHOOL: Roger Ludlowe (Fairfield, Conn.).

COLLEGE: Connecticut.

TRANSACTIONS/CAREER NOTES: Selected by Cleveland Indians organization in first round (17th pick overall) of free-agent draft (June 1, 1988); pick received as part of compensation for San Francisco Giants signing Type A free-agent OF Brett Butler. ... On Cleveland disabled list (May 16-October 1, 1993); included rehabilitation assignment to Canton/Akron (June 10-24).

HONORS: Named Carolina League Pitcher of the Year (1989).

STATISTICAL NOTES: Pitched 6-0 one-hit, complete-game victory against Baltimore (August 8, 1992).

MISCELLANEOUS: Member of 1988 U.S. Olympic baseball team.

Year Team (League)	W	L	Pct.	ERA	G	GS	CG	ShO	Sv.	IP	H	R	ER	BB	SO
1989—Kinston (Carolina)	8	4	.667	1.51	13	13	6	*4	0	95 1/3	69	22	16	24	99
—Cant./Akr. (Eastern)	4	5	.444	3.35	15	14	2	0	0	94	102	44	35	32	65
1990—Cant./Akr. (Eastern)	13	8	.619	2.52	23	23	•9	0	0	175	132	62	49	39	99
—Cleveland (A.L.)..................	2	4	.333	5.91	9	8	0	0	0	45 2/3	58	31	30	21	26
1991—Cleveland (A.L.)..................	10	15	.400	4.13	33	33	6	1	0	211 1/3	228	103	97	66	109
1992—Cleveland (A.L.)..................	17	10	.630	2.96	33	33	10	3	0	252	245	91	83	57	169
1993—Cleveland (A.L.)..................	2	6	.250	6.29	9	9	1	0	0	48 2/3	66	38	34	13	30
—Cant./Akr. (Eastern)	0	0	...	1.13	2	2	0	0	0	8	8	1	1	2	4
1994—Cleveland (A.L.)..................	10	8	.556	3.45	23	23	3	0	0	169 1/3	175	76	65	48	108
1995—Cleveland (A.L.)..................	16	6	.727	4.55	29	29	2	1	0	178	194	95	90	61	139
1996—Cleveland (A.L.)..................	17	5	.773	3.41	32	32	5	0	0	222	217	89	84	61	167
1997—Cleveland (A.L.)..................	15	11	.577	4.28	34	34	1	1	0	227	253	115	108	77	149
Major league totals (8 years)......	89	65	.578	3.93	202	201	28	6	0	1354	1436	638	591	404	897

DIVISION SERIES RECORD

Year Team (League)	W	L	Pct.	ERA	G	GS	CG	ShO	Sv.	IP	H	R	ER	BB	SO
1995—Cleveland (A.L.).................	1	0	1.000	1.29	1	1	0	0	0	7	4	1	1	5	6
1996—Cleveland (A.L.).................	0	1	.000	7.15	2	2	0	0	0	11 1/3	15	9	9	5	13
1997—Cleveland (A.L.).................	0	1	.000	9.82	1	1	0	0	0	3 2/3	2	5	4	6	1
Div. series totals (3 years)	1	2	.333	5.73	4	4	0	0	0	22	21	15	14	16	20

CHAMPIONSHIP SERIES RECORD

RECORDS: Shares A.L. single-game record for most consecutive strikeouts—4 (October 13, 1995).

Year Team (League)	W	L	Pct.	ERA	G	GS	CG	ShO	Sv.	IP	H	R	ER	BB	SO
1995—Cleveland (A.L.).................	0	0	...	1.13	1	1	0	0	0	8	5	2	1	0	6
1997—Cleveland (A.L.).................	0	0	...	2.77	2	2	0	0	0	13	17	4	4	5	5
Champ. series totals (2 years)	0	0	...	2.14	3	3	0	0	0	21	22	6	5	5	11

WORLD SERIES RECORD

RECORDS: Shares record for most consecutive bases on balls allowed in one inning—3 (October 21, 1997, third inning).

Year Team (League)	W	L	Pct.	ERA	G	GS	CG	ShO	Sv.	IP	H	R	ER	BB	SO
1995—Cleveland (A.L.).................	0	0	...	6.43	1	1	0	0	0	7	8	5	5	1	4
1997—Cleveland (A.L.).................	0	1	.000	6.43	2	1	0	0	0	7	8	6	5	5	5
World Series totals (2 years)	0	1	.000	6.43	3	2	0	0	0	14	16	11	10	6	9

ALL-STAR GAME RECORD

Year League	W	L	Pct.	ERA	GS	CG	ShO	Sv.	IP	H	R	ER	BB	SO
1992—American	0	0	...	0.00	0	0	0	0	1	0	0	0	0	1
1996—American	0	1	.000	13.50	1	0	0	0	2	4	3	3	0	1
All-Star totals (2 years)	0	1	.000	9.00	1	0	0	0	3	4	3	3	0	2

N

NATAL, BOB   C

PERSONAL: Born November 13, 1965, in Long Beach, Calif. ... 5-11/190. ... Bats right, throws right. ... Full name: Robert Marcel Natal.
HIGH SCHOOL: Hilltop (Chula Vista, Calif.).
COLLEGE: UC San Diego.
TRANSACTIONS/CAREER NOTES: Selected by Montreal Expos organization in 13th round of free-agent draft (June 2, 1987). ... Selected by Florida Marlins in third round (55th pick overall) of expansion draft (November 17, 1992). ... On Florida disabled list (June 2-23, 1993); included rehabilitation assignment to Edmonton (June 14-23). ... Granted free agency (October 15, 1996). ... Re-signed by Marlins organization (January 16, 1997). ... Released by Marlins (November 20, 1997).
STATISTICAL NOTES: Led Florida State League catchers with 765 total chances in 1988.

Year Team (League)	Pos.	G	AB	R	H	2B	3B	HR	RBI	Avg.	BB	SO	SB	PO	A	E	Avg.
1987—Jamestown (NYP)	C	57	180	26	58	8	4	7	32	.322	12	25	6	321	52	6	.984
1988—W.P. Beach (FSL)	C	113	387	47	93	17	0	6	51	.240	29	50	3	*671	77	17	.978
1989—Jacksonville (South.)	C	46	141	12	29	8	1	0	11	.206	9	24	2	324	37	7	.981
—W.P. Beach (FSL)	C	15	48	5	6	0	0	1	2	.125	9	9	1	68	24	3	.968
1990—Jacksonville (South.)	C	62	171	23	42	7	1	7	25	.246	14	42	0	344	46	10	.975
1991—Indianapolis (A.A.)	C	16	41	2	13	4	0	0	9	.317	6	9	1	62	5	2	.971
—Harrisburg (Eastern)	C	100	336	47	86	16	3	13	53	.256	49	90	1	453	45	4	.992
1992—Indianapolis (A.A.)	C-OF	96	344	50	104	19	3	12	50	.302	28	42	3	468	54	5	.991
—Montreal (N.L.)	C	5	6	0	0	0	0	0	0	.000	1	1	0	10	0	1	.909
1993—Edmonton (PCL)■	C	17	66	16	21	6	1	3	16	.318	8	10	0	119	19	2	.986
—Florida (N.L.)	C	41	117	3	25	4	1	1	6	.214	6	22	1	196	18	0	1.000
1994—Edmonton (PCL)	C	37	115	12	32	5	2	3	19	.278	9	18	1	184	31	1	.995
—Florida (N.L.)	C	10	29	2	8	2	0	0	2	.276	5	5	1	50	9	1	.983
1995—Florida (N.L.)	C	16	43	2	10	2	1	2	6	.233	1	9	0	80	3	1	.988
—Charlotte (Int'l)	C-3B-1B	53	191	23	60	14	0	3	24	.314	11	23	0	271	49	2	.994
1996—Florida (N.L.)	C	44	90	4	12	1	1	0	2	.133	15	31	0	187	14	5	.976
1997—Charlotte (Int'l)	C-OF	78	251	34	67	17	2	11	49	.267	19	37	2	401	34	4	.991
—Florida (N.L.)	C	4	4	2	2	1	0	1	3	.500	2	0	0	16	0	0	1.000
Major league totals (6 years)		120	289	13	57	10	3	4	19	.197	30	68	2	539	44	8	.986

NATHAN, JOE   P   GIANTS

PERSONAL: Born November 22, 1974, in Houston. ... 6-4/195. ... Throws right, bats right. ... Full name: Joseph M. Nathan.
HIGH SCHOOL: Pine Bush (N.Y.).
COLLEGE: New York State-Stony Brook.
TRANSACTIONS/CAREER NOTES: Selected by San Francisco Giants organization in sixth round of free-agent draft (June 1, 1995).

Year Team (League)	W	L	Pct.	ERA	G	GS	CG	ShO	Sv.	IP	H	R	ER	BB	SO
1996—							Did not play.								
1997—Salem-Kaizer (Northwest)	2	1	.667	2.47	18	5	0	0	2	62	53	22	17	26	44

RECORD AS POSITION PLAYER

Year Team (League)	Pos.	G	AB	R	H	2B	3B	HR	RBI	Avg.	BB	SO	SB	PO	A	E	Avg.
1995—Bellingham (N'west)	SS	56	177	23	41	7	2	3	20	.232	22	48	3	76	150	26	.897

NAULTY, DAN   P   TWINS

PERSONAL: Born January 6, 1970, in Los Angeles. ... 6-6/223. ... Throws right, bats right. ... Full name: Daniel Naulty.
HIGH SCHOOL: Ocean View (Huntington Beach, Calif.).
COLLEGE: Cal State-Fullerton.
TRANSACTIONS/CAREER NOTES: Selected by Minnesota Twins organization in 14th round of free-agent draft (June 1, 1992). ... On disabled list (August 5-September 30, 1996). ... On Minnesota disabled list (May 26-September 1, 1997); included rehabilitation assignments to Gulf Coast Twins (July 24-26) and Salt Lake (July 28-August 31).

Year Team (League)	W	L	Pct.	ERA	G	GS	CG	ShO	Sv.	IP	H	R	ER	BB	SO
1992—Kenosha (Midwest)	0	1	.000	5.50	6	2	0	0	0	18	22	12	11	7	14
1993—Fort Myers (Fla. St.)	0	3	.000	5.70	7	6	0	0	0	30	41	22	19	14	20
—Fort Wayne (Midw.)	6	8	.429	3.26	18	18	3	2	0	116	101	45	42	48	96
1994—Fort Myers (Fla. St.)	8	4	.667	2.95	16	15	1	0	0	88 1/3	78	35	29	32	83
—Nashville (Southern)	0	7	.000	5.89	9	9	0	0	0	47 1/3	48	32	31	22	29
1995—Salt Lake (PCL)	2	6	.250	5.18	42	8	0	0	4	90 1/3	92	55	52	2	76
1996—Minnesota (A.L.)	3	2	.600	3.79	49	0	0	0	4	57	43	26	24	35	56
1997—Minnesota (A.L.)	1	1	.500	5.87	29	0	0	0	1	30 2/3	29	20	20	10	23
—GC Twins (GCL)	0	0	. . .	2.25	2	2	0	0	0	4	2	1	1	3	3
—Salt Lake (PCL)	0	1	.000	11.37	6	0	0	0	0	6 1/3	11	10	8	2	5
Major league totals (2 years)	4	3	.571	4.52	78	0	0	0	5	87 2/3	72	46	44	45	79

N

NAVARRO, JAIME   P   WHITE SOX

PERSONAL: Born March 27, 1968, in Bayamon, Puerto Rico. ... 6-5/235. ... Throws right, bats right. ... Son of Julio Navarro, pitcher, Los Angeles Angels, Detroit Tigers and Atlanta Braves (1962-66 and 1970).
HIGH SCHOOL: Luis Pales Matos (Bayamon, Puerto Rico).
JUNIOR COLLEGE: Miami-Dade Community College-New World Center.
TRANSACTIONS/CAREER NOTES: Selected by Baltimore Orioles organization in second round of free-agent draft (January 14, 1986); did not sign. ... Selected by Orioles organization in secondary phase of free-agent draft (June 2, 1986); did not sign. ... Selected by Milwaukee

Brewers organization in third round of free-agent draft (June 2, 1987). ... Granted free agency (April 7, 1995). ... Signed by Chicago Cubs (April 9, 1995). ... Granted free agency (November 1, 1995). ... Re-signed by Cubs (December 8, 1995). ... Granted free agency (November 1, 1996). ... Signed by Chicago White Sox (December 11, 1996).

RECORDS: Shares major league record for most errors by pitcher in one inning—3 (August 18, 1996, third inning). ... Shares A.L. single-season record for most sacrifice flies allowed—17 (1993).

STATISTICAL NOTES: Led A.L. with five balks in 1990. ... Tied for A.L. lead with 14 wild pitches in 1997.

Year Team (League)	W	L	Pct.	ERA	G	GS	CG	ShO	Sv.	IP	H	R	ER	BB	SO
1987—Helena (Pioneer)	4	3	.571	3.57	13	13	3	0	0	85 2/3	87	37	34	18	95
1988—Stockton (California)	15	5	.750	3.09	26	23	8	2	0	174 2/3	148	70	60	74	151
1989—El Paso (Texas)	5	2	.714	2.47	11	11	1	0	0	76 2/3	61	29	21	35	78
—Denver (Am. Assoc.)	1	1	.500	3.60	3	3	1	0	0	20	24	8	8	7	17
—Milwaukee (A.L.)	7	8	.467	3.12	19	17	1	0	0	109 2/3	119	47	38	32	56
1990—Milwaukee (A.L.)	8	7	.533	4.46	32	22	3	0	1	149 1/3	176	83	74	41	75
—Denver (Am. Assoc.)	2	3	.400	4.20	6	6	1	0	0	40 2/3	41	27	19	14	28
1991—Milwaukee (A.L.)	15	12	.556	3.92	34	34	10	2	0	234	237	117	102	73	114
1992—Milwaukee (A.L.)	17	11	.607	3.33	34	34	5	3	0	246	224	98	91	64	100
1993—Milwaukee (A.L.)	11	12	.478	5.33	35	34	5	1	0	214 1/3	254	135	*127	73	114
1994—Milwaukee (A.L.)	4	9	.308	6.62	29	10	0	0	0	89 2/3	115	71	66	35	65
1995—Chicago (N.L.)■	14	6	.700	3.28	29	29	1	1	0	200 1/3	194	79	73	56	128
1996—Chicago (N.L.)	15	12	.556	3.92	35	35	4	1	0	*236 2/3	244	116	103	72	158
1997—Chicago (A.L.)■	9	14	.391	5.79	33	33	2	0	0	209 2/3	*267	*155	*135	73	142
A.L. totals (7 years)	71	73	.493	4.55	216	184	26	6	1	1252 2/3	1392	706	633	391	666
N.L. totals (2 years)	29	18	.617	3.62	64	64	5	2	0	437	438	195	176	128	286
Major league totals (9 years)	100	91	.524	4.31	280	248	31	8	1	1689 2/3	1830	901	809	519	952

NEAGLE, DENNY　　　　　P　　　　　BRAVES

PERSONAL: Born September 13, 1968, in Gambrills, Md. ... 6-2/225. ... Throws left, bats left. ... Full name: Dennis Edward Neagle Jr. ... Name pronounced NAY-ghul.

HIGH SCHOOL: Arundel (Gambrills, Md.).

COLLEGE: Minnesota.

TRANSACTIONS/CAREER NOTES: Selected by Minnesota Twins organization in third round of free-agent draft (June 5, 1989). ... On Portland disabled list (April 5-23, 1991). ... On Minnesota disabled list (July 28-August 12, 1991). ... Traded by Twins with OF Midre Cummings to Pittsburgh Pirates for P John Smiley (March 17, 1992). ... Traded by Pirates to Atlanta Braves for 1B Ron Wright and a player to be named later (August 28, 1996); Pirates acquired P Jason Schmidt to complete deal (August 30, 1996).

HONORS: Named lefthanded pitcher on THE SPORTING NEWS N.L. All-Star team (1997).

STATISTICAL NOTES: Tied for N.L. lead with 16 sacrifice hits in 1996. ... Career major league grand slams: 1.

MISCELLANEOUS: Appeared in one game as pinch-runner (1992). ... Appeared in one game as pinch-runner (1995). ... Doubled and had a sacrifice hit in three games as pinch-hitter with Pittsburgh (1996).

Year Team (League)	W	L	Pct.	ERA	G	GS	CG	ShO	Sv.	IP	H	R	ER	BB	SO
1989—Elizabethton (Appal.)	1	2	.333	4.50	6	3	0	0	1	22	20	11	11	8	32
—Kenosha (Midwest)	2	1	.667	1.65	6	6	1	1	0	43 2/3	25	9	8	16	40
1990—Visalia (California)	8	0	1.000	1.43	10	10	0	0	0	63	39	13	10	16	92
—Orlando (South.)	12	3	.800	2.45	17	17	4	1	0	121 1/3	94	40	33	31	94
1991—Portland (PCL)	9	4	.692	3.27	19	17	1	1	0	104 2/3	101	41	38	32	94
—Minnesota (A.L.)	0	1	.000	4.05	7	3	0	0	0	20	28	9	9	7	14
1992—Pittsburgh (N.L.)■	4	6	.400	4.48	55	6	0	0	2	86 1/3	81	46	43	43	77
1993—Pittsburgh (N.L.)	3	5	.375	5.31	50	7	0	0	1	81 1/3	82	49	48	37	73
—Buffalo (A.A.)	0	0	...	0.00	3	0	0	0	0	3 1/3	3	0	0	2	6
1994—Pittsburgh (N.L.)	9	10	.474	5.12	24	24	2	0	0	137	135	80	78	49	122
1995—Pittsburgh (N.L.)	13	8	.619	3.43	31	•31	5	1	0	•209 2/3	*221	91	80	45	150
1996—Pittsburgh (N.L.)	14	6	.700	3.05	27	27	1	0	0	182 2/3	186	67	62	34	131
—Atlanta (N.L.)■	2	3	.400	5.59	6	6	1	0	0	38 2/3	40	26	24	14	18
1997—Atlanta (N.L.)	*20	5	.800	2.97	34	34	4	4	0	233 1/3	204	87	77	49	172
A.L. totals (1 year)	0	1	.000	4.05	7	3	0	0	0	20	28	9	9	7	14
N.L. totals (6 years)	65	43	.602	3.83	227	135	13	5	3	969	949	446	412	271	743
Major league totals (7 years)	65	44	.596	3.83	234	138	13	5	3	989	977	455	421	278	757

CHAMPIONSHIP SERIES RECORD

Year Team (League)	W	L	Pct.	ERA	G	GS	CG	ShO	Sv.	IP	H	R	ER	BB	SO
1992—Pittsburgh (N.L.)	0	0	...	27.00	2	0	0	0	0	1 2/3	4	5	5	3	0
1996—Atlanta (N.L.)	0	0	...	2.35	2	1	0	0	0	7 2/3	2	2	2	3	8
1997—Atlanta (N.L.)	1	0	1.000	0.00	2	1	1	1	0	12	5	0	0	1	9
Champ. series totals (3 years)	1	0	1.000	2.95	6	2	1	1	0	21 1/3	11	7	7	7	17

WORLD SERIES RECORD

Year Team (League)	W	L	Pct.	ERA	G	GS	CG	ShO	Sv.	IP	H	R	ER	BB	SO
1996—Atlanta (N.L.)	0	0	...	3.00	2	1	0	0	0	6	5	3	2	4	3

ALL-STAR GAME RECORD

Year League	W	L	Pct.	ERA	GS	CG	ShO	Sv.	IP	H	R	ER	BB	SO
1995—National	0	0	...	0.00	0	0	0	0	1	1	0	0	0	1
1997—National						Did not play.								
All-Star totals (1 year)	0	0	...	0.00	0	0	0	0	1	1	0	0	0	1

NELSON, JEFF　　　　　P　　　　　YANKEES

PERSONAL: Born November 17, 1966, in Baltimore. ... 6-8/235. ... Throws right, bats right. ... Full name: Jeffrey Allen Nelson.

HIGH SCHOOL: Catonsville (Md.).

JUNIOR COLLEGE: Catonsville (Md.) Community College.

TRANSACTIONS/CAREER NOTES: Selected by Los Angeles Dodgers organization in 22nd round of free-agent draft (June 4, 1984). ... On disabled list (April 10-June 4, 1986). ... Selected by Calgary, Seattle Mariners organization from Dodgers organization in Rule 5 minor league draft (December 9, 1986). ... On disabled list (July 16, 1989-remainder of season). ... Traded by Mariners with 1B Tino Martinez and P Jim Mecir to New York Yankees for P Sterling Hitchcock and 3B Russ Davis (December 7, 1995). ... On suspended list (September 3-5, 1996).

MISCELLANEOUS: Appeared in one game as outfielder with no chances with Seattle (1993).

Year Team (League)	W	L	Pct.	ERA	G	GS	CG	ShO	Sv.	IP	H	R	ER	BB	SO
1984— Great Falls (Pio.)	0	0	...	54.00	1	0	0	0	0	$2/3$	3	4	4	3	1
— GC Dodgers (GCL)	0	0	...	1.35	9	0	0	0	0	$13 1/3$	6	3	2	6	7
1985— GC Dodgers (GCL)	0	5	.000	5.51	14	7	0	0	0	$47 1/3$	72	50	29	32	31
1986— Great Falls (Pio.)	0	0	...	13.50	3	0	0	0	0	2	5	3	3	3	1
— Bakersfield (California)	0	7	.000	6.69	24	11	0	0	0	$71 1/3$	79	83	53	84	37
1987— Salinas (Calif.)■	3	7	.300	5.74	17	16	1	0	0	80	80	61	51	71	43
1988— San Bernardino (Calif.)	8	9	.471	5.54	27	27	1	1	0	$149 1/3$	163	115	92	91	94
1989— Williamsport (Eastern)	7	5	.583	3.31	15	15	2	0	0	$92 1/3$	72	41	34	53	61
1990— Williamsport (Eastern)	1	4	.200	6.44	10	10	0	0	0	$43 1/3$	65	35	31	18	14
— Peninsula (Caro.)	2	2	.500	3.15	18	7	1	1	6	60	47	21	21	25	49
1991— Jacksonville (Southern)	4	0	1.000	1.27	21	0	0	0	12	$28 1/3$	23	5	4	9	34
— Calgary (PCL)	3	4	.429	3.90	28	0	0	0	21	$32 1/3$	39	19	14	15	26
1992— Calgary (PCL)	1	0	1.000	0.00	2	0	0	0	0	$3 2/3$	0	0	0	1	0
— Seattle (A.L.)	1	7	.125	3.44	66	0	0	0	6	81	71	34	31	44	46
1993— Calgary (PCL)	1	0	1.000	1.17	5	0	0	0	1	$7 2/3$	6	1	1	2	6
— Seattle (A.L.)	5	3	.625	4.35	71	0	0	0	1	60	57	30	29	34	61
1994— Seattle (A.L.)	0	0	...	2.76	28	0	0	0	0	$42 1/3$	35	18	13	20	44
— Calgary (PCL)	1	4	.200	2.84	18	0	0	0	8	$25 1/3$	21	9	8	7	30
1995— Seattle (A.L.)	7	3	.700	2.17	62	0	0	0	2	$78 2/3$	58	21	19	27	96
1996— New York (A.L.)■	4	4	.500	4.36	73	0	0	0	2	$74 1/3$	75	38	36	36	91
1997— New York (A.L.)	3	7	.300	2.86	77	0	0	0	2	$78 2/3$	53	32	25	37	81
Major league totals (6 years)	20	24	.455	3.32	377	0	0	0	13	415	349	173	153	198	419

DIVISION SERIES RECORD

Year Team (League)	W	L	Pct.	ERA	G	GS	CG	ShO	Sv.	IP	H	R	ER	BB	SO
1995— Seattle (A.L.)	0	1	.000	3.18	3	0	0	0	0	$5 2/3$	7	2	2	3	7
1996— New York (A.L.)	1	0	1.000	0.00	2	0	0	0	0	$3 2/3$	2	0	0	3	5
1997— New York (A.L.)	0	0	...	0.00	4	0	0	0	0	4	4	0	0	2	0
Div. series totals (3 years)	1	1	.500	1.35	9	0	0	0	0	$13 1/3$	13	2	2	8	12

CHAMPIONSHIP SERIES RECORD

Year Team (League)	W	L	Pct.	ERA	G	GS	CG	ShO	Sv.	IP	H	R	ER	BB	SO
1995— Seattle (A.L.)	0	0	...	0.00	3	0	0	0	0	3	3	0	0	5	3
1996— New York (A.L.)	0	1	.000	11.57	2	0	0	0	0	$2 1/3$	5	3	3	0	2
Champ. series totals (2 years)	0	1	.000	5.06	5	0	0	0	0	$5 1/3$	8	3	3	5	5

WORLD SERIES RECORD

NOTES: Member of World Series championship team (1996).

Year Team (League)	W	L	Pct.	ERA	G	GS	CG	ShO	Sv.	IP	H	R	ER	BB	SO
1996— New York (A.L.)	0	0	...	0.00	3	0	0	0	0	$4 1/3$	1	0	0	1	5

NEN, ROBB   P   GIANTS

PERSONAL: Born November 28, 1969, in San Pedro, Calif. ... 6-5/210. ... Throws right, bats right. ... Full name: Robert Allen Nen. ... Son of Dick Nen, first baseman, Los Angeles Dodgers, Washington Senators and Chicago Cubs (1963, 1965-68 and 1970).

HIGH SCHOOL: Los Alamitos (Calif.).

TRANSACTIONS/CAREER NOTES: Selected by Texas Rangers organization in 32nd round of free-agent draft (June 2, 1987). ... On Charlotte disabled list (beginning of season-April 26 and May 6-May 24, 1990). ... On disabled list (April 23-June 10, June 28-July 8 and July 11-September 3, 1991; and May 7-September 9, 1992). ... On Texas disabled list (June 12-July 17, 1993); included rehabilitation assignment to Oklahoma City (June 21-July 17). ... Traded by Rangers with P Kurt Miller to Florida Marlins for P Cris Carpenter (July 17, 1993). ... Traded by Marlins to San Francisco Giants for P Mike Villano, P Joe Fontenot and P Mick Pageler (November 18, 1997).

MISCELLANEOUS: Holds Florida Marlins all-time records for most games pitched (269) and most saves (108).

Year Team (League)	W	L	Pct.	ERA	G	GS	CG	ShO	Sv.	IP	H	R	ER	BB	SO
1987— GC Rangers (GCL)	0	0	...	7.71	2	0	0	0	0	$2 1/3$	4	2	2	3	4
1988— Gastonia (S. Atl.)	0	5	.000	7.45	14	10	0	0	0	$48 1/3$	69	57	40	45	36
— Butte (Pioneer)	4	5	.444	8.75	14	13	0	0	0	$48 1/3$	65	55	47	45	30
1989— Gastonia (S. Atl.)	7	4	.636	2.41	24	24	1	1	0	$138 1/3$	96	47	37	76	146
1990— Charlotte (Fla. St.)	1	4	.200	3.69	11	11	1	0	0	$53 2/3$	44	28	22	36	38
— Tulsa (Texas)	0	5	.000	5.06	7	7	0	0	0	$26 2/3$	23	20	15	21	21
1991— Tulsa (Texas)	0	2	.000	5.79	6	6	0	0	0	28	24	21	18	20	23
1992— Tulsa (Texas)	1	1	.500	2.16	4	4	1	0	0	25	21	7	6	2	20
1993— Texas (A.L.)	1	1	.500	6.35	9	3	0	0	0	$22 2/3$	28	17	16	26	12
— Oklahoma City (A.A.)	0	2	.000	6.67	6	5	0	0	0	$28 1/3$	45	22	21	18	12
— Florida (N.L.)■	1	0	1.000	7.02	15	1	0	0	0	$33 1/3$	35	28	26	20	27
1994— Florida (N.L.)	5	5	.500	2.95	44	0	0	0	15	58	46	20	19	17	60
1995— Florida (N.L.)	0	7	.000	3.29	62	0	0	0	23	$65 2/3$	62	26	24	23	68
1996— Florida (N.L.)	5	1	.833	1.95	75	0	0	0	35	83	67	21	18	21	92
1997— Florida (N.L.)	9	3	.750	3.89	73	0	0	0	35	74	72	35	32	40	81
A.L. totals (1 year)	1	1	.500	6.35	9	3	0	0	0	$22 2/3$	28	17	16	26	12
N.L. totals (5 years)	20	16	.556	3.41	269	1	0	0	108	314	282	130	119	121	328
Major league totals (5 years)	21	17	.553	3.61	278	4	0	0	108	$336 2/3$	310	147	135	147	340

DIVISION SERIES RECORD

Year Team (League)	W	L	Pct.	ERA	G	GS	CG	ShO	Sv.	IP	H	R	ER	BB	SO
1997— Florida (N.L.)	1	0	1.000	0.00	2	0	0	0	0	2	1	1	0	2	2

Year Team (League)	W	L	Pct.	ERA	G	GS	CG	ShO	Sv.	IP	H	R	ER	BB	SO
CHAMPIONSHIP SERIES RECORD															
1997— Florida (N.L.)	0	0	...	0.00	2	0	0	0	2	2	0	0	0	0	0

WORLD SERIES RECORD

NOTES: Member of World Series championship team (1997).

Year Team (League)	W	L	Pct.	ERA	G	GS	CG	ShO	Sv.	IP	H	R	ER	BB	SO
1997— Florida (N.L.)	0	0	...	7.71	4	0	0	0	2	4 2/3	8	5	4	2	7

NEVIN, PHIL — OF/3B/1B — ANGELS

PERSONAL: Born January 19, 1971, in Fullerton, Calif. ... 6-2/180. ... Bats right, throws right. ... Full name: Phillip Joseph Nevin.
HIGH SCHOOL: El Dorado (Placentia, Calif.).
COLLEGE: Cal State Fullerton.
TRANSACTIONS/CAREER NOTES: Selected by Los Angeles Dodgers organization in third round of free-agent draft (June 5, 1989); did not sign. ... Selected by Houston Astros organization in first round (first pick overall) of free-agent draft (June 1, 1992). ... On Tucson disabled list (July 12-30, 1995). ... Traded by Astros to Detroit Tigers (August 15, 1995), completing deal in which Astros acquired P Mike Henneman for a player to be named later (August 10, 1995). ... On Detroit disabled list (March 21-April 16, 1997); included rehabilitation assignment to Lakeland (April 8-16). ... Traded by Tigers with C Matt Walbeck to Anaheim Angels for P Nick Skuse (November 20, 1997).
HONORS: Named Golden Spikes Award winner by USA Baseball (1992). ... Named third baseman on THE SPORTING NEWS college All-America team (1992). ... Named Most Outstanding Player of College World Series (1992).
STATISTICAL NOTES: Led Pacific Coast League third basemen with .891 fielding percentage in 1993. ... Led Pacific Coast League in grounding into double plays with 21 in 1994. ... Led Pacific Coast League third basemen with 31 errors and 32 double plays in 1994.
MISCELLANEOUS: Member of 1992 U.S. Olympic baseball team.

Year Team (League)	Pos.	G	AB	R	H	2B	3B	HR	RBI	Avg.	BB	SO	SB	PO	A	E	Avg.
							BATTING								**FIELDING**		
1993— Tucson (PCL)	3B-OF	123	448	67	128	21	3	10	93	.286	52	99	8	68	187	29	†.898
1994— Tucson (PCL)	3B-OF	118	445	67	117	20	1	12	79	.263	55	101	3	73	240	†32	.907
1995— Tucson (PCL)	3B	62	223	31	65	16	0	7	41	.291	27	39	2	39	128	14	.923
— Houston (N.L.)	3B	18	60	4	7	1	0	0	1	.117	7	13	1	10	32	3	.933
— Toledo (Int'l)■	OF	7	23	3	7	2	0	1	3	.304	1	5	0	2	0	0	1.000
— Detroit (A.L.)	OF-DH	29	96	9	21	3	1	2	12	.219	11	27	0	50	2	2	.963
1996— Jacksonville (South.)	C-3-O-1	98	344	77	101	18	1	24	69	.294	60	83	6	384	76	11	.977
— Detroit (A.L.)	3-O-C-DH	38	120	15	35	5	0	8	19	.292	8	39	1	45	51	5	.950
1997— Lakeland (Fla. St.)	1B-3B	3	9	3	5	1	0	1	4	.556	3	2	0	9	4	1	.929
— Toledo (Int'l)	3B	6	19	1	3	0	0	1	3	.158	2	9	0	19	4	0	1.000
— Detroit (A.L.)	O-DH-3-1-C	93	251	32	59	16	1	9	35	.235	25	68	0	94	18	2	.982
American League totals (3 years)		160	467	56	115	24	2	19	66	.246	44	134	1	189	71	9	.967
National League totals (1 year)		18	60	4	7	1	0	0	1	.117	7	13	1	10	32	3	.933
Major league totals (3 years)		178	527	60	122	25	2	19	67	.231	51	147	2	199	103	12	.962

NEWFIELD, MARC — OF — BREWERS

PERSONAL: Born October 19, 1972, in Sacramento. ... 6-4/205. ... Bats right, throws right. ... Full name: Marc Alexander Newfield.
HIGH SCHOOL: Marina (Huntington Beach, Calif.).
TRANSACTIONS/CAREER NOTES: Selected by Seattle Mariners organization in first round (sixth pick overall) of free-agent draft (June 4, 1990). ... On disabled list (June 3, 1992-remainder of season). ... Traded by Mariners with P Ron Villone to San Diego Padres for P Andy Benes and a player to be named later (July 31, 1995); Mariners acquired P Greg Keagle to complete deal (September 16, 1995). ... Traded by Padres with P Bryce Florie and P Ron Villone to Milwaukee Brewers for OF Greg Vaughn and a player to be named later (July 31, 1996); Padres acquired OF Gerald Parent to complete deal (September 16, 1996). ... On Milwaukee disabled list (May 29-July 5 and July 23, 1997-remainder of season); included rehabilitation assignment to Tucson (June 25-July 3).
HONORS: Named Arizona League Most Valuable Player (1990).

Year Team (League)	Pos.	G	AB	R	H	2B	3B	HR	RBI	Avg.	BB	SO	SB	PO	A	E	Avg.
							BATTING								**FIELDING**		
1990— Ariz. Mariners (Ariz.)	1B-OF	51	192	34	60	•13	2	6	38	.313	25	20	4	358	13	5	.987
1991— San Bern. (Calif.)	OF-1B	125	440	64	132	22	3	11	68	.300	59	90	12	245	10	8	.970
— Jacksonville (South.)	OF-1B	6	26	4	6	3	0	0	2	.231	0	8	0	16	0	1	.941
1992— Jacksonville (South.)	OF	45	162	15	40	12	0	4	19	.247	12	34	1	17	1	0	1.000
1993— Jacksonville (South.)	1B-OF	91	336	48	103	18	0	19	51	.307	33	35	1	435	21	3	.993
— Seattle (A.L.)	DH-OF	22	66	5	15	3	0	1	7	.227	2	8	0	0	0	0	...
1994— Calgary (PCL)	OF	107	430	89	150	*44	2	19	83	.349	42	58	0	136	1	9	.938
— Seattle (A.L.)	DH-OF	12	38	3	7	1	0	1	4	.184	2	4	0	2	0	0	1.000
1995— Tacoma (PCL)	OF	53	198	30	55	11	0	5	30	.278	19	30	1	55	1	2	.966
— Seattle (A.L.)	OF	24	85	7	16	3	0	3	14	.188	3	16	0	44	0	0	1.000
— Las Vegas (PCL)■	OF-1B	20	70	10	24	5	1	3	12	.343	3	11	2	54	2	1	.982
— San Diego (N.L.)	OF	21	55	6	17	5	1	1	7	.309	2	8	0	24	1	0	1.000
1996— San Diego (N.L.)	1B-OF	84	191	27	48	11	0	5	26	.251	16	44	1	73	1	3	.961
— Milwaukee (A.L.)■	OF	49	179	21	55	15	0	7	31	.307	11	26	0	96	3	1	.990
1997— Milwaukee (A.L.)	OF-DH	50	157	14	36	8	0	1	18	.229	14	27	0	43	0	1	.977
— Tucson (PCL)	DH	8	31	4	10	1	0	1	3	.323	4	6	0	...	...	...	...
American League totals (5 years)		157	525	50	129	30	0	13	74	.246	32	81	0	185	3	2	.989
National League totals (2 years)		105	246	33	65	16	1	6	33	.264	18	52	1	97	2	3	.971
Major league totals (5 years)		262	771	83	194	46	1	19	107	.252	50	133	1	282	5	5	.983

NEWSON, WARREN — OF

PERSONAL: Born July 3, 1964, in Newnan, Ga. ... 5-7/202. ... Bats left, throws left. ... Full name: Warren Dale Newson.
HIGH SCHOOL: Newnan (Ga.).
COLLEGE: Middle Georgia College.

TRANSACTIONS/CAREER NOTES: Selected by San Diego Padres organization in fourth round of free-agent draft (January 14, 1986). ... Traded by Padres with IF Joey Cora and IF Kevin Garner to Chicago White Sox organization for P Adam Peterson and P Steve Rosenberg (March 31, 1991). ... On Nashville disabled list (April 29-May 22, 1993). ... Traded by White Sox to Seattle Mariners for a player to be named later (July 18, 1995); White Sox acquired P Jeff Darwin to complete deal (October 9, 1995). ... Released by Mariners (November 16, 1995). ... Signed by Texas Rangers (December 6, 1995). ... On Texas disabled list (April 2-20 and August 25, 1997-remainder of season); included rehabilitation assignment to Tulsa (April 17-20). ... Granted free agency (October 2, 1997).
STATISTICAL NOTES: Led Texas League with 10 intentional bases on balls received in 1989.

							BATTING								FIELDING		
Year Team (League)	Pos.	G	AB	R	H	2B	3B	HR	RBI	Avg.	BB	SO	SB	PO	A	E	Avg.
1986— Spokane (N'west)	OF	54	159	29	37	8	1	2	31	.233	47	37	3	54	3	3	.950
1987— Char., S.C. (S. Atl.)	OF	58	191	50	66	12	2	7	32	.346	52	35	13	81	4	2	.977
— Reno (California)	OF	51	165	44	51	7	2	6	28	.309	39	34	2	60	5	8	.890
1988— Riverside (Calif.)	OF	130	438	99	130	23	•7	*22	91	.297	107	102	36	182	7	11	.945
1989— Wichita (Texas)	OF	128	427	94	130	20	6	18	70	.304	*103	99	20	191	15	5	.976
1990— Las Vegas (PCL)	OF	123	404	80	123	20	3	13	58	.304	83	110	13	146	4	10	.938
1991— Vancouver (PCL)■	OF	33	111	19	41	12	1	2	19	.369	30	26	5	53	1	0	1.000
— Chicago (A.L.)	OF-DH	71	132	20	39	5	0	4	25	.295	28	34	2	48	3	2	.962
1992— Chicago (A.L.)	OF-DH	63	136	19	30	3	0	1	11	.221	37	38	3	67	5	0	1.000
— Vancouver (PCL)	OF	19	59	7	15	0	0	0	9	.254	16	21	3	42	1	1	.977
1993— Nashville (A.A.)	OF	61	176	40	60	8	2	4	21	.341	38	38	5	74	7	1	.988
— Chicago (A.L.)	DH-OF	26	40	9	12	0	0	2	6	.300	9	12	0	5	0	0	1.000
1994— Chicago (A.L.)	OF-DH	63	102	16	26	5	0	2	7	.255	14	23	1	46	1	1	.979
1995— Chicago (A.L.)	OF-DH	51	85	19	20	0	2	3	9	.235	23	27	1	44	1	1	.978
— Seattle (A.L.)■	OF	33	72	15	21	2	0	2	6	.292	16	18	1	33	1	1	.971
1996— Texas (A.L.)■	OF-DH	91	235	34	60	14	1	10	31	.255	37	82	3	122	5	1	.992
1997— Chicago (A.L.)	OF-DH	81	169	23	36	10	1	10	23	.213	31	53	3	93	1	5	.949
— Tulsa (Texas)	DH	2	7	1	1	0	0	1	2	.143	2	1	0	...	...	...	...
Major league totals (7 years)		479	971	155	244	39	4	34	118	.251	195	287	14	458	17	11	.977

DIVISION SERIES RECORD

							BATTING								FIELDING		
Year Team (League)	Pos.	G	AB	R	H	2B	3B	HR	RBI	Avg.	BB	SO	SB	PO	A	E	Avg.
1995— Seattle (A.L.)	PH	1	1	0	0	0	0	0	0	.000	0	1	0	...	...	...	...
1996— Texas (A.L.)	PH	2	1	0	0	0	0	0	0	.000	1	0	0	...	...	...	...
Division series totals (2 years)		3	2	0	0	0	0	0	0	.000	1	1	0	...	...	...	...

CHAMPIONSHIP SERIES RECORD

							BATTING								FIELDING		
Year Team (League)	Pos.	G	AB	R	H	2B	3B	HR	RBI	Avg.	BB	SO	SB	PO	A	E	Avg.
1993— Chicago (A.L.)	DH-PH	2	5	1	1	0	0	1	1	.200	0	1	0	...	...	...	...

NIEVES, JOSE   SS/2B   CUBS

PERSONAL: Born June 16, 1975, in Guacara, Venezuela. ... 6-1/170. ... Bats right, throws right. ... Full name: Jose Miguel Nieves (Pinto).
HIGH SCHOOL: Enrique Delgado Palacios (Carabobo, Venezuela).
TRANSACTIONS/CAREER NOTES: Signed as non-drafted free agent by Milwaukee Brewers organization (June 10, 1992). ... Released by Brewers organization (October 19, 1993). ... Signed by Chicago Cubs organization (June 30, 1994). ... On disabled list (May 29-June 12, 1997).

							BATTING								FIELDING		
Year Team (League)	Pos.	G	AB	R	H	2B	3B	HR	RBI	Avg.	BB	SO	SB	PO	A	E	Avg.
1992— Dom. Brewers (DSL)	IF	8	15	2	5	0	0	1	3	.333	4	4	0	9	13	5	.815
1993— Dom. Brewers (DSL)	IF	54	144	21	29	4	3	2	14	.201	22	25	6	43	78	19	.864
1994— Dom. Cubs (DSL)■	2B	37	137	21	39	6	1	4	24	.285	13	23	5	50	76	9	.933
1995— Will. (NYP)	SS-2B	69	276	46	59	13	1	4	44	.214	21	39	11	85	193	33	.894
1996— Rockford (Midwest)	SS-2B-3B	113	396	55	96	20	4	5	57	.242	33	59	17	156	318	37	.928
1997— Daytona (Fla. St.)	SS-2B	85	331	51	91	20	1	4	42	.275	17	55	16	151	218	27	.932

NIEVES, MELVIN   OF   REDS

N

PERSONAL: Born December 28, 1971, in San Juan, Puerto Rico. ... 6-2/210. ... Bats both, throws right. ... Full name: Melvin Ramos Nieves. ... Name pronounced nee-EV-es.
HIGH SCHOOL: Ivis Pales Matos (Santa Rosa, Puerto Rico).
TRANSACTIONS/CAREER NOTES: Signed as non-drafted free agent by Atlanta Braves organization (May 20, 1988). ... On disabled list (April 11-June 13, 1991). ... On Richmond disabled list (May 18-26, 1993). ... Traded by Braves with P Donnie Elliott and OF Vince Moore to San Diego Padres for 1B Fred McGriff (July 18, 1993). ... Traded by Padres with P Richie Lewis and C Raul Casanova to Detroit Tigers for P Sean Bergman, P Cade Gaspar and OF Todd Steverson (March 22, 1996). ... On disabled list (June 5-20 and August 2-19, 1996). ... On disabled list (August 4-19, 1997). ... Traded by Tigers to Cincinnati Reds for C Paul Bako and P Donne Wall (November 11, 1997).
RECORDS: Holds A.L. single-season record for most games with switch-hit home runs—2 (1996).
STATISTICAL NOTES: Switch-hit home runs in one game two times (July 15 and August 20, 1996). ... Career major league grand slams: 2.

							BATTING								FIELDING		
Year Team (League)	Pos.	G	AB	R	H	2B	3B	HR	RBI	Avg.	BB	SO	SB	PO	A	E	Avg.
1988— GC Braves (GCL)	OF	56	170	16	30	6	0	1	12	.176	20	53	5	100	1	2	.981
1989— Pulaski (Appalachian)	OF	64	231	43	64	16	3	9	46	.277	30	59	6	45	1	6	.885
1990— Sumter (S. Atl.)	OF	126	459	60	130	24	7	9	59	.283	53	125	10	227	7	11	.955
1991— Durham (Carolina)	OF	64	201	31	53	11	0	9	25	.264	40	53	3	75	8	5	.943
1992— Durham (Carolina)	OF	31	106	18	32	9	1	8	32	.302	17	33	4	61	4	2	.970
— Greenville (Southern)	OF	100	350	61	99	23	5	18	76	.283	52	98	6	127	9	5	.965
— Atlanta (N.L.)	OF	12	19	0	4	1	0	0	1	.211	2	7	0	8	0	3	.727
1993— Richmond (Int'l)	OF	78	273	38	76	10	3	10	36	.278	25	84	4	124	5	7	.949
— Las Vegas (PCL)■	OF	43	159	31	49	10	1	7	24	.308	18	42	2	79	4	1	.988
— San Diego (N.L.)	OF	19	47	4	9	0	0	2	3	.191	3	21	0	27	0	2	.931

Year Team (League)	Pos.	G	AB	R	H	2B	3B	HR	RBI	Avg.	BB	SO	SB	PO	A	E	Avg.
1994—Las Vegas (PCL)	OF-1B	111	406	81	125	17	6	25	92	.308	58	*138	1	170	4	10	.946
— San Diego (N.L.)	OF	10	19	2	5	1	0	1	4	.263	3	10	0	11	1	0	1.000
1995—San Diego (N.L.)	OF-1B	98	234	32	48	6	1	14	38	.205	19	88	2	106	5	2	.982
1996—Detroit (A.L.)■	OF-DH	120	431	71	106	23	4	24	60	.246	44	158	1	207	9	*13	.943
1997—Detroit (A.L.)	OF-DH	116	359	46	82	18	1	20	64	.228	39	157	1	187	4	4	.979
American League totals (2 years)		236	790	117	188	41	5	44	124	.238	83	315	2	394	13	17	.960
National League totals (4 years)		139	319	38	66	8	1	17	46	.207	27	126	2	152	6	7	.958
Major league totals (6 years)		375	1109	155	254	49	6	61	170	.229	110	441	4	546	19	24	.959

NILSSON, DAVE   1B   BREWERS

PERSONAL: Born December 14, 1969, in Brisbane, Queensland, Australia. ... 6-3/231. ... Bats left, throws right. ... Full name: David Wayne Nilsson.

HIGH SCHOOL: Kedron (Brisbane, Australia).

TRANSACTIONS/CAREER NOTES: Signed as non-drafted free agent by Milwaukee Brewers organization (February 9, 1987). ... On disabled list (April 30-May 26, 1990). ... On Denver disabled list (August 13, 1991-remainder of season). ... On Milwaukee disabled list (July 6-24, 1992); included rehabilitation assignment to Denver (July 16-24). ... On Milwaukee disabled list (March 27-April 14, 1993); included rehabilitation assignment to El Paso (April 5-14). ... On Milwaukee disabled list (May 18-June 22, 1993); included rehabilitation assignment to New Orleans (May 26-June 13). ... On Milwaukee disabled list (April 16, 1995); included rehabilitation assignments to Beloit (June 10-14), El Paso (June 14-21) and New Orleans (June 21-24). ... On Milwaukee disabled list (April 4-May 8, 1996); included rehabilitation assignment to New Orleans (May 2-8).

RECORDS: Shares major league record for most home runs in one inning—2 (May 17, 1996, sixth inning).

STATISTICAL NOTES: Career major league grand slams: 2.

Year Team (League)	Pos.	G	AB	R	H	2B	3B	HR	RBI	Avg.	BB	SO	SB	PO	A	E	Avg.
1987—Helena (Pioneer)	C	55	188	36	74	13	0	1	21	.394	5	7	0	329	28	7	.981
1988—Beloit (Midwest).........	C-1B	95	332	28	74	15	2	4	41	.223	25	49	2	526	64	6	.990
1989—Stockton (California) ..	C-2B	125	472	59	115	16	6	5	56	.244	50	76	2	703	66	13	.983
1990—Stockton (California) ..	C-1B-3B	107	359	70	104	22	3	7	47	.290	43	36	6	600	86	12	.983
1991—El Paso (Texas)..........	C-3B	65	249	52	104	24	3	5	57	.418	27	14	4	348	46	8	.980
— Denver (A.A.).............	C-1B-3B	28	95	10	22	8	0	1	14	.232	17	16	1	146	16	2	.988
1992—Denver (A.A.).............	C-1B-3B	66	240	38	76	16	7	3	39	.317	23	19	10	350	51	6	.985
— Milwaukee (A.L.)........	C-1B-DH	51	164	15	38	8	0	4	25	.232	17	18	2	231	16	2	.992
1993—El Paso (Texas).........	C	5	17	5	8	1	0	1	7	.471	2	4	1	31	9	0	1.000
— Milwaukee (A.L.)........	C-DH-1B	100	296	35	76	10	2	7	40	.257	37	36	3	457	33	9	.982
— New Orleans (A.A.)......	C	17	61	9	21	6	0	1	9	.344	5	6	0	55	7	1	.984
1994—Milwaukee (A.L.)........	C-DH-1B	109	397	51	109	28	3	12	69	.275	34	61	1	315	15	2	.994
1995—Beloit (Midwest)........	DH	3	11	2	6	3	0	1	7	.545	2	0	1	...	...	...	...
— El Paso (Texas).........	OF	5	15	1	7	1	0	1	4	.467	0	1	1	4	0	0	1.000
— New Orleans (A.A.)......	OF	3	9	1	4	0	0	1	4	.444	2	0	0	2	0	0	1.000
— Milwaukee (A.L.)........	O-DH-1-C	81	263	41	73	12	1	12	53	.278	24	41	2	117	7	2	.984
1996—New Orleans (A.A.)......	1B	7	26	3	7	1	0	1	2	.269	4	3	0	25	3	0	1.000
— Milwaukee (A.L.)........	O-DH-1-C	123	453	81	150	33	2	17	84	.331	57	68	2	252	19	7	.975
1997—Milwaukee (A.L.)........	1B-DH-OF	156	554	71	154	33	0	20	81	.278	65	88	2	641	39	6	.991
Major league totals (6 years)		620	2127	294	600	124	8	72	352	.282	234	312	12	2013	129	28	.987

NITKOWSKI, C.J.   P   ASTROS

PERSONAL: Born March 3, 1973, in Suffren, N.Y. ... 6-3/190. ... Throws left, bats left. ... Full name: Christopher J. Nitkowski.

HIGH SCHOOL: Don Bosco (N.J.).

COLLEGE: St. John's.

TRANSACTIONS/CAREER NOTES: Selected by Cincinnati Reds organization in first round (ninth pick overall) of free-agent draft (June 2, 1994). ... Traded by Reds with P David Tuttle and a player to be named later to Detroit Tigers for P David Wells (July 31, 1995); Tigers acquired IF Mark Lewis to complete deal (November 16, 1995). ... On Detroit disabled list (August 11-29, 1996). ... Traded by Tigers with C Brad Ausmus, P Jose Lima, P Trever Miller and IF Daryle Ward to Houston Astros for OF Brian Hunter, IF Orlando Miller, P Doug Brocail, P Todd Jones and a player to be named later (December 10, 1996).

Year Team (League)	W	L	Pct.	ERA	G	GS	CG	ShO	Sv.	IP	H	R	ER	BB	SO
1994—Chattanooga (Southern).....	6	3	.667	3.50	14	14	0	0	0	74 2/3	61	30	29	40	60
1995—Chattanooga (Southern).....	4	2	.667	2.50	8	8	0	0	0	50 1/3	39	20	14	20	52
— Indianapolis (A.A.)............	0	2	.000	5.20	6	6	0	0	0	27 2/3	28	16	16	10	21
— Cincinnati (N.L.).............	1	3	.250	6.12	9	7	0	0	0	32 1/3	41	25	22	15	18
— Detroit (A.L.)■	1	4	.200	7.09	11	11	0	0	0	39 1/3	53	32	31	20	13
1996—Toledo (Int'l).............	4	6	.400	4.46	19	19	1	0	0	111	104	60	55	53	103
— Detroit (A.L.)...............	2	3	.400	8.08	11	8	0	0	0	45 2/3	62	44	41	38	36
1997—New Orleans (A.A.)■........	8	10	.444	3.98	28	28	1	0	0	174 1/3	183	82	77	56	*141
A.L. totals (2 years)	3	7	.300	7.62	22	19	0	0	0	85	115	76	72	58	49
N.L. totals (1 year)	1	3	.250	6.12	9	7	0	0	0	32 1/3	41	25	22	15	18
Major league totals (2 years)	4	10	.286	7.21	31	26	0	0	0	117 1/3	156	101	94	73	67

NIXON, OTIS   OF   TWINS

PERSONAL: Born January 9, 1959, in Evergreen, N.C. ... 6-2/180. ... Bats both, throws right. ... Full name: Otis Junior Nixon. ... Brother of Donell Nixon, outfielder with Seattle Mariners, San Francisco Giants and Baltimore Orioles (1985, 1987-89 and 1990).

HIGH SCHOOL: Columbus (N.C.).

COLLEGE: Louisburg (N.C.) College.

TRANSACTIONS/CAREER NOTES: Selected by Cincinnati Reds organization in 21st round of free-agent draft (June 6, 1978); did not sign. ... Selected by California Angels organization in secondary phase of free-agent draft (January 9, 1979); did not sign. ... Selected by New York Yankees organization in secondary phase of free-agent draft (June 5, 1979). ... Traded by Yankees with P George Frazier and a player to be named later to Cleveland Indians for 3B Toby Harrah and a player to be named later (February 5, 1984); Yankees organization acquired P Rick Browne and Indians organization acquired P Guy Elston to complete deal (February 8, 1984). ... Granted free agency (October 15, 1987). ... Signed by Indianapolis, Montreal Expos organization (March 5, 1988). ... Traded by Expos with 3B Boi Rodriguez to Atlanta Braves for C Jimmy Kremers and a player to be named later (April 1, 1991); Sumter, Expos organization, acquired P Keith Morrison to complete deal (June 3, 1991). ... On suspended list (August 13-16, 1991). ... On disqualified list (September 16, 1991-April 24, 1992). ... Granted free agency (November 11, 1991). ... Re-signed by Braves (December 12, 1991). ... Granted free agency (October 25, 1993). ... Signed by Boston Red Sox (December 7, 1993). ... Traded by Red Sox with 3B Luis Ortiz to Texas Rangers for DH/OF Jose Canseco (December 9, 1994). ... Granted free agency (November 3, 1995). ... Signed by Toronto Blue Jays (December 7, 1995). ... On disabled list (June 11-26, 1996). ... Traded by Blue Jays to Los Angeles Dodgers for C Bobby Cripps (August 12, 1997). ... Granted free agency (October 27, 1997). ... Signed by Minnesota Twins (December 11, 1997).

RECORDS: Shares modern major league single-game record for most stolen bases—6 (June 16, 1991).

STATISTICAL NOTES: Led Appalachian League third basemen with .945 fielding percentage, 52 putouts, 120 assists, 182 total chances and 12 double plays in 1979. ... Led International League in caught stealing with 29 in 1983. ... Led International League outfielders with .992 fielding percentage, 363 putouts and 371 total chances in 1983. ... Had 20-game hitting streak (July 11-31, 1991). ... Led A.L. in caught stealing with 21 in 1995.

							BATTING								FIELDING		
Year Team (League)	Pos.	G	AB	R	H	2B	3B	HR	RBI	Avg.	BB	SO	SB	PO	A	E	Avg.
1979— Paintsville (Appal.)	3B-SS	63	203	58	58	10	3	1	25	.286	*57	40	5	†54	†122	11	†.941
1980— Greensboro (S. Atl.) ..	3B-SS	136	493	*124	137	12	5	3	48	.278	*113	88	*67	164	308	36	.929
1981— Nashville (Southern) ..	SS	127	407	89	102	9	2	0	20	.251	*110	101	71	198	348	*56	.907
1982— Nashville (Southern) ..	SS-2B	72	283	47	80	3	2	0	20	.283	59	56	61	126	211	23	.936
— Columbus (Int'l)	2B-SS	59	207	43	58	4	0	0	14	.280	49	41	46	104	169	14	.951
1983— Columbus (Int'l)	OF-2B	138	*557	*129	*162	11	6	0	41	.291	96	83	*94	†385	24	4	†.990
— New York (A.L.)	OF	13	14	2	2	0	0	0	0	.143	1	5	2	14	1	1	.938
1984— Cleveland (A.L.)■	OF	49	91	16	14	0	0	0	1	.154	8	11	12	81	3	0	1.000
— Maine (Int'l)	OF	72	253	42	70	5	1	0	22	.277	44	45	39	206	7	1	.995
1985— Cleveland (A.L.)	OF-DH	104	162	34	38	4	0	3	9	.235	8	27	20	129	5	4	.971
1986— Cleveland (A.L.)	OF-DH	105	95	33	25	4	1	0	8	.263	13	12	23	90	3	3	.969
1987— Cleveland (A.L.)	OF-DH	19	17	2	1	0	0	0	1	.059	3	4	2	21	0	0	1.000
— Buffalo (A.A.)	OF	59	249	51	71	13	4	2	23	.285	34	30	36	170	3	3	.983
1988— Indianapolis (A.A.)■ ..	OF	67	235	52	67	6	3	0	19	.285	43	28	40	130	1	1	.992
— Montreal (N.L.)	OF	90	271	47	66	8	2	0	15	.244	28	42	46	176	2	1	.994
1989— Montreal (N.L.)	OF	126	258	41	56	7	2	0	21	.217	33	36	37	160	2	2	.988
1990— Montreal (N.L.)	OF-SS	119	231	46	58	6	2	1	20	.251	28	33	50	149	6	1	.994
1991— Atlanta (N.L.)■	OF	124	401	81	119	10	1	0	26	.297	47	40	72	218	6	3	.987
1992— Atlanta (N.L.)	OF	120	456	79	134	14	2	2	22	.294	39	54	41	333	6	3	.991
1993— Atlanta (N.L.)	OF	134	461	77	124	12	3	1	24	.269	61	63	47	308	4	3	.990
1994— Boston (A.L.)	OF	103	398	60	109	15	1	0	25	.274	55	65	42	254	4	3	.989
1995— Texas (A.L.)■	OF	139	589	87	174	21	2	0	45	.295	58	85	50	357	4	4	.989
1996— Toronto (A.L.)■	OF	125	496	87	142	15	1	1	29	.286	71	68	54	342	5	2	.994
1997— Toronto (A.L.)■	OF-DH	103	401	54	105	12	1	1	26	.262	52	54	47	254	1	1	.996
— Los Angeles (N.L.)■ ..	OF	42	175	30	48	6	2	1	18	.274	13	24	12	97	1	1	.990
American League totals (9 years)		760	2263	375	610	71	6	5	144	.270	269	331	252	1542	26	18	.989
National League totals (7 years)		755	2253	401	605	63	14	5	146	.269	249	292	305	1441	27	14	.991
Major league totals (15 years)		1515	4516	776	1215	134	20	10	290	.269	518	623	557	2983	53	32	.990

CHAMPIONSHIP SERIES RECORD

RECORDS: Shares N.L. single-game record for most hits—4 (October 10, 1992).

							BATTING								FIELDING		
Year Team (League)	Pos.	G	AB	R	H	2B	3B	HR	RBI	Avg.	BB	SO	SB	PO	A	E	Avg.
1992— Atlanta (N.L.)	OF	7	28	5	8	2	0	0	2	.286	4	4	3	16	0	0	1.000
1993— Atlanta (N.L.)	OF	6	23	3	8	2	0	0	4	.348	5	6	0	13	0	0	1.000
Championship series totals (2 years)		13	51	8	16	4	0	0	6	.314	9	10	3	29	0	0	1.000

WORLD SERIES RECORD

							BATTING								FIELDING		
Year Team (League)	Pos.	G	AB	R	H	2B	3B	HR	RBI	Avg.	BB	SO	SB	PO	A	E	Avg.
1992— Atlanta (N.L.)	OF	6	27	3	8	1	0	0	1	.296	1	3	5	18	0	0	1.000

NIXON, TROT   OF   RED SOX

PERSONAL: Born April 11, 1974, in Durham, N.C. ... 6-2/196. ... Bats left, throws left. ... Full name: Christopher Trotman Nixon.

HIGH SCHOOL: New Hanover (Wilmington, N.C.).

TRANSACTIONS/CAREER NOTES: Selected by Boston Red Sox organization in first round (seventh pick overall) of free-agent draft (June 3, 1993). ... On disabled list (July 12, 1994-remainder of season).

STATISTICAL NOTES: Tied for Eastern League lead with four double plays by outfielders in 1996.

							BATTING								FIELDING		
Year Team (League)	Pos.	G	AB	R	H	2B	3B	HR	RBI	Avg.	BB	SO	SB	PO	A	E	Avg.
1994— Lynchburg (Caro.)	OF	71	264	33	65	12	0	12	43	.246	44	53	10	143	8	4	.974
1995— Sarasota (Fla. St.)	OF	73	264	43	80	11	4	5	39	.303	45	46	7	140	4	2	.986
— Trenton (Eastern)	OF	25	94	9	15	3	1	2	8	.160	7	20	2	66	2	0	1.000
1996— Trenton (Eastern)	OF	123	438	55	110	11	4	11	63	.251	50	65	7	224	*14	5	.979
— Boston (A.L.)	OF	2	4	2	2	1	0	0	0	.500	0	1	1	3	0	0	1.000
1997— Pawtucket (Int'l)	OF	130	475	80	116	18	3	20	61	.244	63	86	11	268	10	4	.986
Major league totals (1 year)		2	4	2	2	1	0	0	0	.500	0	1	1	3	0	0	1.000

PERSONAL: Born August 31, 1968, in Osaka, Japan. ... 6-2/210. ... Throws right, bats right.
TRANSACTIONS/CAREER NOTES: Selected by Kintetsu Buffaloes in first round of 1989 Japanese free-agent draft. ... Signed as free agent by Los Angeles Dodgers organization (February 8, 1995). ... On Albuquerque temporarily inactive list (April 3-27, 1995).
HONORS: Named N.L. Rookie Pitcher of the Year by THE SPORTING NEWS (1995). ... Named N.L. Rookie of the Year by Baseball Writers' Association of America (1995).
STATISTICAL NOTES: Struck out 16 batters in one game (June 14, 1995). ... Pitched 3-0 one-hit, complete-game victory against San Francisco (August 5, 1995). ... Led N.L. with 19 wild pitches and five balks in 1995. ... Led N.L. with five balks in 1995 and four in 1997. ... Struck out 17 batters in one game (April 13, 1996). ... Pitched 9-0 no-hit victory against Colorado (September 17, 1996).
MISCELLANEOUS: Member of 1988 Japanese Olympic baseball team.

Year Team (League)	W	L	Pct.	ERA	G	GS	CG	ShO	Sv.	IP	H	R	ER	BB	SO
1990—Kintetsu (Jap. Pac.)	*18	8	.692	*2.91	29	27	21	2	0	235	167	...	76	*109	*287
1991—Kintetsu (Jap. Pac.)	*17	11	.607	3.05	31	29	22	*4	1	242⅓	183	...	82	*128	*287
1992—Kintetsu (Jap. Pac.)	*18	8	.692	2.66	30	29	17	*5	0	216⅔	150	...	64	*117	*228
1993—Kintetsu (Jap. Pac.)	*17	12	.586	3.70	32	32	14	2	0	243⅓	*201	...	100	*148	*276
1994—Kintetsu (Jap. Pac.)	8	7	.533	3.63	17	17	6	0	0	114	...	...	46	86	126
1995—Bakersfield (California)■	0	1	.000	3.38	1	1	0	0	0	5⅓	6	2	2	1	6
—Los Angeles (N.L.)	13	6	.684	2.54	28	28	4	*3	0	191⅓	124	63	54	78	*236
1996—Los Angeles (N.L.)	16	11	.593	3.19	33	33	3	2	0	228⅓	180	93	81	85	234
1997—Los Angeles (N.L.)	14	12	.538	4.25	33	33	1	0	0	207⅓	193	104	98	92	233
Major league totals (3 years)	43	29	.597	3.34	94	94	8	5	0	627	497	260	233	255	703

DIVISION SERIES RECORD

RECORDS: Holds N.L. career records for most runs allowed—10; and most earned runs allowed—10.

Year Team (League)	W	L	Pct.	ERA	G	GS	CG	ShO	Sv.	IP	H	R	ER	BB	SO
1995—Los Angeles (N.L.)	0	1	.000	9.00	1	1	0	0	0	5	7	5	5	2	6
1996—Los Angeles (N.L.)	0	1	.000	12.27	1	1	0	0	0	3⅔	5	5	5	3	3
Div. series totals (2 years)	0	2	.000	10.38	2	2	0	0	0	8⅔	12	10	10	7	9

ALL-STAR GAME RECORD

Year League	W	L	Pct.	ERA	GS	CG	ShO	Sv.	IP	H	R	ER	BB	SO
1995—National	0	0	...	0.00	1	0	0	0	2	1	0	0	0	3

NORMAN, LES   OF   RANGERS

PERSONAL: Born February 25, 1969, in Warren, Mich. ... 6-1/185. ... Bats right, throws right. ... Full name: Leslie Eugene Norman.
HIGH SCHOOL: Reed-Custer (Braidwood, Ill.).
COLLEGE: College of St. Francis (Ill.).
TRANSACTIONS/CAREER NOTES: Selected by Boston Red Sox organization in 26th round of free-agent draft (June 4, 1990); did not sign. ... Selected by Kansas City Royals organization in 25th round of free-agent draft (June 3, 1991). ... On Kansas City disabled list (June 6-August 2, 1996); included rehabilitation assignment to Omaha (July 13-August 1). ... Granted free agency (November 20, 1996). ... Signed by Cleveland Indians organization (December 19, 1996). ... Granted free agency (October 15, 1997). ... Signed by Texas Rangers organization (December 16, 1997).
STATISTICAL NOTES: Led Southern League outfielders with 17 assists in 1993. ... Led Southern League outfielders with .996 fielding percentage in 1994.

Year Team (League)	Pos.	G	AB	R	H	2B	3B	HR	RBI	Avg.	BB	SO	SB	PO	A	E	Avg.
1991—Eugene (Northwest)	OF	30	102	14	25	4	1	2	18	.245	9	18	2	65	5	3	.959
1992—Appleton (Midwest)	OF-1B-3B	59	218	38	82	17	1	4	47	.376	22	18	8	119	20	3	.979
—Memphis (Southern)	OF	72	271	32	74	14	5	3	20	.273	22	37	4	124	9	4	.971
1993—Memphis (Southern)	OF-1B	133	484	78	141	32	5	17	81	.291	50	88	11	273	†17	10	.967
1994—Memphis (Southern)	OF-1B	106	383	53	101	19	4	13	55	.264	36	44	7	242	14	2	†.992
1995—Omaha (A.A.)	OF-1B	83	313	46	89	19	3	9	33	.284	18	48	5	180	9	4	.979
—Kansas City (A.L.)	OF-DH	24	40	6	9	0	1	0	4	.225	6	6	0	22	1	1	.958
1996—Kansas City (A.L.)	OF-DH	54	49	9	6	0	0	0	0	.122	6	14	1	44	1	0	1.000
—Omaha (A.A.)	OF-1B	24	77	8	20	6	0	1	13	.260	6	8	0	56	1	4	.934
1997—Buffalo (A.A.)■	OF-1B	118	428	71	111	20	1	17	56	.259	43	80	7	223	7	1	.996
Major league totals (2 years)		78	89	15	15	0	1	0	4	.169	12	20	1	66	2	1	.986

N

NORTON, GREG   3B   WHITE SOX

PERSONAL: Born July 6, 1972, in San Leandro, Calif. ... 6-1/190. ... Bats both, throws right. ... Full name: Gregory Norton.
HIGH SCHOOL: Bishop O'dowd (Oakland).
COLLEGE: Oklahoma.
TRANSACTIONS/CAREER NOTES: Selected by San Francisco Giants organization in seventh round of free-agent draft (June 4, 1990); did not sign. ... Selected by Chicago White Sox organization in second round of free-agent draft (June 3, 1993).
STATISTICAL NOTES: Led Midwest League third basemen with 387 total chances in 1994. ... Led American Association with .534 slugging percentage in 1997. ... Led American Association third basemen with 29 errors in 1997.

Year Team (League)	Pos.	G	AB	R	H	2B	3B	HR	RBI	Avg.	BB	SO	SB	PO	A	E	Avg.
1993—GC Whi. Sox (GCL)	3B	3	9	1	2	0	0	0	2	.222	1	1	0	1	7	0	1.000
—Hickory (S. Atl.)	3B-SS	71	254	36	62	12	2	4	36	.244	41	44	0	57	161	17	.928
1994—South Bend (Mid.)	3B	127	477	73	137	22	2	6	64	.287	62	71	5	92	*265	30	.922
1995—Birmingham (Sou.)	3B	133	469	65	162	23	2	6	60	.345	64	90	19	102	277	25	*.938
1996—Birmingham (Sou.)	SS	76	287	40	81	14	3	8	44	.282	33	55	5	104	214	17	.949
—Nashville (A.A.)	SS-3B	43	164	28	47	14	2	7	26	.287	17	42	2	43	95	13	.914
—Chicago (A.L.)	SS-3B-DH	11	23	4	5	0	0	2	3	.217	4	6	0	8	5	2	.867
1997—Nashville (A.A.)	3B-SS-2B	114	414	82	114	27	1	26	76	.275	57	101	3	83	247	†38	.897
—Chicago (A.L.)	3B-DH	18	34	5	9	2	2	0	1	.265	2	8	0	4	15	3	.864
Major league totals (2 years)		29	57	9	14	2	2	2	4	.246	6	14	0	12	20	5	.865

NUNEZ, ABRAHAM — SS — PIRATES

PERSONAL: Born March 16, 1976, in Santo Domingo, Dominican Republic. ... 5-11/170. ... Bats both, throws right. ... Full name: Abraham Orlando Nunez.

TRANSACTIONS/CAREER NOTES: Signed as non-drafted free agent by Toronto Blue Jays organization (May 5, 1994). ... Traded Blue Jays with P Mike Halperin and C/OF Craig Wilson to Pittsburgh Pirates (December 11, 1996), completing deal in which Blue Jays traded P Jose Silva, P Jose Pett, IF Brandon Cromer and three players to be named later to Pirates for OF/1B Orlando Merced, IF Carlos Garcia, and P Dan Plesac (November 14, 1996).

STATISTICAL NOTES: Tied for New York-Pennsylvania League lead in caught stealing with 14 in 1996. ... Led New York-Pennsylvania League shortstops in fielding with .953 in 1996.

Year Team (League)	Pos.	G	AB	R	H	2B	3B	HR	RBI	Avg.	BB	SO	SB	PO	A	E	Avg.
1994—Dom. B. Jays (DSL) ...	2B	59	188	31	47	5	0	0	15	.250	42	37	22	155	27	12	.938
1995—Dom. B. Jays (DSL) ...	2B	54	186	49	56	10	3	4	25	.301	30	27	24	80	97	7	.962
1996—St. Catharines (NYP)..	SS-2B	75	*297	43	83	6	4	3	26	.279	31	43	37	136	239	15	•.962
1997—Lynchburg (Caro.)■...	SS	78	304	45	79	9	4	3	32	.260	23	47	29	100	219	15	.955
—Carolina (Southern)....	SS	47	198	31	65	6	1	1	14	.328	20	28	10	76	129	11	.949
—Pittsburgh (N.L.).......	SS-2B	19	40	3	9	2	2	0	6	.225	3	10	1	14	37	0	1.000
Major league totals (1 year)		19	40	3	9	2	2	0	6	.225	3	10	1	14	37	0	1.000

NUNEZ, SERGIO — 2B — WHITE SOX

PERSONAL: Born January 3, 1975, in Santo Domingo, Dominican Republic. ... 5-11/155. ... Bats right, throws right. ... Full name: Sergio Augusto Nunez.

HIGH SCHOOL: Lico Secuonderio Las Americas (Santo Domingo, Dominican Republic).

TRANSACTIONS/CAREER NOTES: Signed as non-drafted free agent by Kansas City Royals organization (November 15, 1991). ... On Wichita disabled list (April 20-July 17, 1997). ... Claimed on waivers by Chicago White Sox (December 8, 1997).

STATISTICAL NOTES: Tied for Dominican Summer League lead with seven intentional bases on balls received in 1993. ... Led Gulf Coast League with 130 total bases, .560 slugging percentage and .474 on-base percentage in 1994. ... Tied for Gulf Coast League lead in caught stealing with 12 in 1994.

Year Team (League)	Pos.	G	AB	R	H	2B	3B	HR	RBI	Avg.	BB	SO	SB	PO	A	E	Avg.
1992—Dom. Royals (DSL)	2B-SS	62	202	49	61	4	5	0	30	.302	31	21	29	123	169	24	.924
1993—Dom. Royals (DSL)	IF	70	249	63	85	18	2	2	35	.341	50	17	32	171	214	16	.960
1994—GC Royals (GCL)	2B	59	232	*64	*92	9	7	5	24	*.397	32	17	*37	123	176	10	.968
1995—Wilmington (Caro.).....	2B	124	460	63	109	10	2	4	25	.237	51	66	33	231	313	26	.954
1996—Wilmington (Caro.).....	2B	105	402	60	109	23	6	3	40	.271	38	54	*44	228	254	14	.972
1997—Wichita (Texas)	2B	34	137	18	38	1	1	1	11	.277	6	17	12	56	93	9	.943
—GC Royals (GCL)	2B-1B	5	14	3	4	1	1	0	0	.286	0	4	2	12	2	0	1.000

NUNEZ, VLADIMIR — P — DIAMONDBACKS

PERSONAL: Born March 15, 1975, in Havana, Cuba. ... 6-4/235. ... Throws right, bats right.

TRANSACTIONS/CAREER NOTES: Signed as non-drafted free agent by Arizona Diamondbacks organization (February 1, 1996).

STATISTICAL NOTES: Led California League with 36 home runs allowed in 1997.

Year Team (League)	W	L	Pct.	ERA	G	GS	CG	ShO	Sv.	IP	H	R	ER	BB	SO
1996—Visalia (California).............	1	6	.143	5.43	12	10	0	0	0	53	64	45	32	17	37
—Lethbridge (Pioneer)	*10	0	*1.000	*2.22	14	13	0	0	0	85	78	25	21	10	*93
1997—High Desert (Calif.).............	8	5	.615	5.17	28	28	1	1	0	158 1/3	169	102	91	40	142

NUNNALLY, JON — OF — REDS

PERSONAL: Born November 9, 1971, in Pelham, N.C. ... 5-10/190. ... Bats left, throws right. ... Full name: Jonathan Keith Nunnally.

HIGH SCHOOL: Hargrave Military Institute (Chatham, Va.).

JUNIOR COLLEGE: Miami-Dade (South) Community College.

TRANSACTIONS/CAREER NOTES: Selected by Baltimore Orioles organization in 39th round of free-agent draft (June 4, 1990); did not sign. ... Selected by Cleveland Indians organization in third round of free-agent draft (June 1, 1992). ... Selected by Kansas City Royals from Indians organization in Rule 5 major league draft (December 5, 1994). ... Traded by Royals with IF/OF Chris Stynes to Cincinnati Reds for P Hector Carrasco and P Scott Service (July 15, 1997).

STATISTICAL NOTES: Tied for American Association lead with eight bases on balls received in 1996. ... Tied for American Association lead with five double plays by outfielder in 1996. ... Career major league grand slams: 1.

MISCELLANEOUS: Hit home run in first major league at-bat (April 29, 1995).

Year Team (League)	Pos.	G	AB	R	H	2B	3B	HR	RBI	Avg.	BB	SO	SB	PO	A	E	Avg.
1992—Watertown (NYP)	OF	69	246	39	59	10	4	5	43	.240	32	55	12	146	2	8	.949
1993—Columbus (S. Atl.)......	2B-OF	125	438	81	110	15	2	15	56	.251	63	108	17	226	202	25	.945
1994—Kinston (Carolina)	OF	132	483	70	129	29	2	22	74	.267	64	125	23	263	*14	9	.969
1995—Kansas City (A.L.)■...	OF-DH	119	303	51	74	15	6	14	42	.244	51	86	6	197	5	6	.971
1996—Kansas City (A.L.)......	OF-DH	35	90	16	19	5	1	5	17	.211	13	25	0	61	0	2	.968
—Omaha (A.A.)..............	OF	103	345	76	97	21	4	25	77	.281	47	100	10	182	12	4	.980
1997—Omaha (A.A.)..............	OF	68	230	35	64	11	1	15	33	.278	39	67	8	173	8	7	.963
—Kansas City (A.L.)	OF	13	29	8	7	0	1	1	4	.241	5	7	0	12	0	0	1.000
—Cincinnati (N.L.)■......	OF	65	201	38	64	12	3	13	35	.318	26	51	7	120	3	2	.984
American League totals (3 years)		167	422	75	100	20	8	20	63	.237	69	118	6	270	5	8	.972
National League totals (1 year)		65	201	38	64	12	3	13	35	.318	26	51	7	120	3	2	.984
Major league totals (3 years)		232	623	113	164	32	11	33	98	.263	95	169	13	390	8	10	.975

NYE, RYAN   P   PHILLIES

PERSONAL: Born June 24, 1973, in Biloxi, Miss. ... 6-2/195. ... Throws right, bats right. ... Full name: Ryan Craig Nye.
HIGH SCHOOL: Cameron (Okla.).
JUNIOR COLLEGE: Westark Community College (Ark.).
COLLEGE: Texas Tech.
TRANSACTIONS/CAREER NOTES: Selected by Seattle Mariners organization in 43rd round of free-agent draft (June 3, 1991); did not sign. ... Selected by Seattle Mariners organization in 22nd round of free-agent draft (June 1, 1992); did not sign. ... Selected by Philadelphia Phillies organization in second round of free-agent draft (June 2, 1994). ... On Philadelphia disabled list (June 23-July 18, 1997).

Year—Team (League)	W	L	Pct.	ERA	G	GS	CG	ShO	Sv.	IP	H	R	ER	BB	SO
1994—Batavia (N.Y.-Penn)	7	2	.778	2.64	13	12	1	0	0	71 2/3	64	27	21	15	71
1995—Clearwater (Fla. St.)	12	7	.632	3.40	27	27	5	1	0	167	164	71	63	33	116
1996—Reading (Eastern)	8	2	.800	3.84	14	14	0	0	0	86 2/3	76	41	37	30	90
—Scran./W.B. (Int'l)	5	2	.714	5.02	14	14	0	0	0	80 2/3	97	52	45	30	51
1997—Scran./W.B. (Int'l)	4	10	.286	5.52	17	17	0	0	0	109 1/3	117	70	67	32	85
—Philadelphia (N.L.)	0	2	.000	8.25	4	2	0	0	0	12	20	11	11	9	7
Major league totals (1 year)	0	2	.000	8.25	4	2	0	0	0	12	20	11	11	9	7

OBANDO, SHERMAN   OF   ROCKIES

PERSONAL: Born January 23, 1970, in Bocas del Toro, Panama. ... 6-4/220. ... Bats right, throws right. ... Full name: Sherman Omar Obando.
TRANSACTIONS/CAREER NOTES: Signed as non-drafted free agent by New York Yankees organization (September 17, 1987). ... On Prince William disabled list (May 3-July 25, 1991). ... On disabled list (April 9-May 11, 1992). ... Selected by Baltimore Orioles from Yankees organization in Rule 5 major league draft (December 7, 1992). ... On Baltimore disabled list (May 25-June 24, 1993); included rehabilitation assignment to Bowie (June 4-23). ... On Baltimore disabled list (June 26-July 11, 1993). ... Traded by Orioles to Montreal Expos for OF Tony Tarasco (March 13, 1996). ... On disabled list (July 21-August 9, 1996). ... On Montreal disabled list (July 27, 1997-remainder of season). ... Granted free agency (October 8, 1997). ... Signed by Colorado Rockies organization (December 19, 1997).
STATISTICAL NOTES: Led International League with .603 slugging percentage in 1994.

Year—Team (League)	Pos.	G	AB	R	H	2B	3B	HR	RBI	Avg.	BB	SO	SB	PO	A	E	Avg.
1988—GC Yankees (GCL)	OF	49	172	26	44	10	2	4	27	.256	16	32	8	55	3	3	.951
1989—Oneonta (NYP)	OF	70	276	50	86	*23	3	6	45	.312	16	45	8	50	0	6	.893
1990—Prince William (Car.)	OF	121	439	67	117	24	6	10	67	.267	42	85	5	156	4	7	.958
1991—GC Yankees (GCL)	DH	4	17	3	5	2	0	0	1	.294	1	2	0	...	...	...	...
—Prince William (Car.)	OF	42	140	25	37	11	1	7	31	.264	19	28	0	19	1	0	1.000
1992—Alb./Colon. (Eastern)	1B	109	381	71	107	19	3	17	56	.281	32	67	3	430	32	11	.977
1993—Baltimore (A.L.)■	DH-OF	31	92	8	25	2	0	3	15	.272	4	26	0	13	0	1	.929
—Bowie (Eastern)	OF-1B	19	58	8	14	2	0	3	12	.241	9	11	1	32	0	1	.970
1994—Rochester (Int'l)	OF	109	403	67	133	*36	7	20	69	.330	30	53	1	97	5	3	.971
1995—Baltimore (A.L.)	DH-OF	16	38	0	10	1	0	0	3	.263	2	12	1	12	0	1	.923
—Rochester (Int'l)	OF-1B	85	324	42	96	26	6	9	53	.296	29	57	1	184	15	8	.961
1996—Montreal (N.L.)■	OF	89	178	30	44	9	0	8	22	.247	22	48	2	74	2	3	.962
1997—Montreal (N.L.)	OF-DH	41	47	3	6	1	0	2	9	.128	6	14	0	11	0	0	1.000
—Ottawa (Int'l)	OF	7	21	5	5	0	0	3	8	.238	5	7	0	3	0	0	1.000
American League totals (2 years)		47	130	8	35	3	0	3	18	.269	6	38	1	25	0	2	.926
National League totals (2 years)		130	225	33	50	10	0	10	31	.222	28	62	2	85	2	3	.967
Major league totals (4 years)		177	355	41	85	13	0	13	49	.239	34	100	3	110	2	5	.957

O'BRIEN, CHARLIE   C   WHITE SOX

PERSONAL: Born May 1, 1961, in Tulsa, Okla. ... 6-2/205. ... Bats right, throws right. ... Full name: Charles Hugh O'Brien. ... Brother of John O'Brien, minor league first baseman, St. Louis Cardinals organization (1991-93).
HIGH SCHOOL: Bishop Kelley (Tulsa, Okla.).
JUNIOR COLLEGE: McLennan Community College (Texas).
COLLEGE: Wichita State.
TRANSACTIONS/CAREER NOTES: Selected by Texas Rangers organization in 14th round of free-agent draft (June 6, 1978); did not sign. ... Selected by Seattle Mariners organization in 21st round of free-agent draft (June 8, 1981); did not sign. ... Selected by Oakland Athletics organization in fifth round of free-agent draft (June 7, 1982). ... On disabled list (July 31, 1983-remainder of season). ... On Albany/Colonie disabled list (April 13-May 15, 1984). ... Traded by A's organization with IF Steve Kiefer, P Mike Fulmer and P Pete Kendrick to Milwaukee Brewers for P Moose Haas (March 30, 1986). ... Traded by Brewers with a player to be named later to New York Mets for two players to be named later (August 30, 1990); Brewers acquired P Julio Machado and P Kevin Brown (September 7, 1990) and Mets acquired P Kevin Carmody (September 11, 1990) to complete deal. ... Granted free agency (October 29, 1993). ... Signed by Atlanta Braves (November 26, 1993). ... Granted free agency (October 30, 1995). ... Signed by Toronto Blue Jays (December 14, 1995). ... Granted free agency (October 27, 1997). ... Signed by Chicago White Sox (December 10, 1997).
STATISTICAL NOTES: Career major league grand slams: 1.

Year—Team (League)	Pos.	G	AB	R	H	2B	3B	HR	RBI	Avg.	BB	SO	SB	PO	A	E	Avg.
1982—Medford (N'west)	C	17	60	11	17	3	0	3	14	.283	10	10	0	116	18	4	.971
—Modesto (California)	C	41	140	23	42	6	0	3	32	.300	20	19	7	239	44	5	.983
1983—Alb./Colon. (Eastern)	C-1B	92	285	50	83	12	1	14	56	.291	52	39	3	478	82	11	.981
1984—Modesto (California)	C	9	32	8	9	2	0	1	5	.281	2	4	1	41	8	0	1.000
—Tacoma (PCL)	C-OF	69	195	33	44	11	0	9	22	.226	28	31	0	260	39	0	1.000
1985—Huntsville (Southern)	C	33	115	20	24	5	0	7	16	.209	16	20	0	182	29	5	.977
—Oakland (A.L.)	C	16	11	3	3	1	0	0	1	.273	3	3	0	23	0	1	.958
—Modesto (California)	C	9	27	5	8	4	1	1	2	.296	2	5	0	33	8	1	.976
—Tacoma (PCL)	C	18	57	5	9	4	0	1	7	.158	6	17	0	110	9	3	.975
1986—Vancouver (PCL)■■	C	6	17	1	2	0	0	0	1	.118	4	4	0	22	3	2	.926
—El Paso (Texas)	C-OF-1B	92	336	72	109	20	3	15	75	.324	50	30	0	437	43	4	.992

N
O

Year — Team (League)	Pos.	G	AB	R	H	2B	3B	HR	RBI	Avg.	BB	SO	SB	PO	A	E	Avg.
1987—Denver (A.A.)	C	80	266	37	75	12	1	8	35	.282	41	33	5	415	53	6	.987
—Milwaukee (A.L.)	C	10	35	2	7	3	1	0	0	.200	4	4	0	78	11	0	1.000
1988—Denver (A.A.)	C	48	153	16	43	5	0	4	25	.281	19	19	1	243	44	3	.990
—Milwaukee (A.L.)	C	40	118	12	26	6	0	2	9	.220	5	16	0	210	20	2	.991
1989—Milwaukee (A.L.)	C	62	188	22	44	10	0	6	35	.234	21	11	0	314	36	5	.986
1990—Milwaukee (A.L.)	C	46	145	11	27	7	2	0	11	.186	11	26	0	217	24	2	.992
—New York (N.L.)■	C	28	68	6	11	3	0	0	9	.162	10	8	0	191	21	3	.986
1991—New York (N.L.)	C	69	168	16	31	6	0	2	14	.185	17	25	0	396	37	4	.991
1992—New York (N.L.)	C	68	156	15	33	12	0	2	13	.212	16	18	0	287	44	7	.979
1993—New York (N.L.)	C	67	188	15	48	11	0	4	23	.255	14	14	1	325	39	5	.986
1994—Atlanta (N.L.)■	C	51	152	24	37	11	0	8	28	.243	15	24	0	308	26	3	.991
1995—Atlanta (N.L.)	C	67	198	18	45	7	0	9	23	.227	29	40	0	446	23	4	.992
1996—Toronto (A.L.)■	C	109	324	33	77	17	0	13	44	.238	29	68	0	613	37	3	.995
1997—Toronto (A.L.)	C	69	225	22	49	15	1	4	27	.218	22	45	0	543	41	3	.995
American League totals (7 years)		352	1046	105	233	59	4	25	127	.223	95	173	0	1998	169	16	.993
National League totals (6 years)		350	930	94	205	50	0	25	110	.220	101	129	1	1953	190	26	.988
Major league totals (12 years)		702	1976	199	438	109	4	50	237	.222	196	302	1	3951	359	42	.990

DIVISION SERIES RECORD

Year — Team (League)	Pos.	G	AB	R	H	2B	3B	HR	RBI	Avg.	BB	SO	SB	PO	A	E	Avg.
1995—Atlanta (N.L.)	C	2	5	0	1	0	0	0	0	.200	1	1	0	8	1	0	1.000

CHAMPIONSHIP SERIES RECORD

Year — Team (League)	Pos.	G	AB	R	H	2B	3B	HR	RBI	Avg.	BB	SO	SB	PO	A	E	Avg.
1995—Atlanta (N.L.)	C-PH	2	5	1	2	0	0	1	3	.400	0	1	0	3	1	0	1.000

WORLD SERIES RECORD

NOTES: Member of World Series championship team (1995).

Year — Team (League)	Pos.	G	AB	R	H	2B	3B	HR	RBI	Avg.	BB	SO	SB	PO	A	E	Avg.
1995—Atlanta (N.L.)	C	2	3	0	0	0	0	0	0	.000	0	0	0	7	2	0	1.000

OCHOA, ALEX — OF — TWINS

PERSONAL: Born March 29, 1972, in Miami Lakes, Fla. ... 6-0/185. ... Bats right, throws right.

HIGH SCHOOL: Hialeah (Fla.) Miami Lakes.

TRANSACTIONS/CAREER NOTES: Selected by Baltimore Orioles organization in third round of free-agent draft (June 3, 1991). ... Traded by Orioles with OF Damon Buford to New York Mets for 3B/OF Bobby Bonilla and a player to be named later (July 28, 1995); Orioles acquired P Jimmy Williams to complete deal (August 17, 1995). ... Traded by Mets to Minnesota Twins for OF Rich Becker (December 17, 1997).

STATISTICAL NOTES: Led Carolina League in grounding into double plays with 15 in 1993. ... Led Eastern League with 12 sacrifice flies in 1994. ... Tied for Eastern League lead in double plays by outfielder with five in 1994. ... Led International League outfielders with 249 putouts and 266 total chances in 1995. ... Hit for the cycle (July 3, 1996). ... Tied for International League lead in double plays by outfielder with three in 1996.

Year — Team (League)	Pos.	G	AB	R	H	2B	3B	HR	RBI	Avg.	BB	SO	SB	PO	A	E	Avg.
1991—GC Orioles (GCL)	OF	53	179	26	55	8	3	1	30	.307	16	14	11	45	3	2	.960
1992—Kane County (Midw.)	OF	133	499	65	147	22	7	1	59	.295	58	55	31	225	•17	•12	.953
1993—Frederick (Carolina)	OF	137	532	84	147	29	5	13	90	.276	46	67	34	169	13	11	.943
1994—Bowie (Eastern)	OF	134	519	77	156	25	2	14	82	.301	49	67	28	237	*22	6	.977
1995—Rochester (Int'l)	OF	91	336	41	92	18	2	8	46	.274	26	50	17	183	9	5	.975
—Norfolk (Int'l)■	OF	34	123	17	38	6	2	2	15	.309	14	12	7	‡66	1	2	.971
—New York (N.L.)	OF	11	37	7	11	1	0	0	0	.297	2	10	1	20	1	0	1.000
1996—Norfolk (Int'l)	OF	67	233	45	79	12	4	8	39	.339	32	22	5	110	9	5	.960
—New York (N.L.)	OF	82	282	37	83	19	3	4	33	.294	17	30	4	135	8	5	.966
1997—New York (N.L.)	OF-DH	113	238	31	58	14	1	3	22	.244	18	32	3	104	7	3	.982
Major league totals (3 years)		206	557	75	152	34	4	7	55	.273	37	72	8	259	16	7	.975

OFFERMAN, JOSE — 2B — ROYALS

PERSONAL: Born November 8, 1968, in San Pedro de Macoris, Dominican Republic. ... 6-0/190. ... Bats both, throws right. ... Full name: Jose Antonio Dono Offerman.

HIGH SCHOOL: Colegio Biblico Cristiano (Dominican Republic).

TRANSACTIONS/CAREER NOTES: Signed as non-drafted free agent by Los Angeles Dodgers organization (July 24, 1986). ... Traded by Dodgers to Kansas City Royals for P Billy Brewer (December 17, 1995). ... On Kansas City disabled list (April 6-29, July 10-22 and August 14-September 6, 1997).

HONORS: Named Minor League Player of the Year by The Sporting News (1990). ... Named Pacific Coast League Player of the Year (1990).

STATISTICAL NOTES: Tied for Pioneer League lead in caught stealing with 10 in 1988. ... Tied for Pacific Coast League lead in caught stealing with 18 in 1990. ... Led Pacific Coast League shortstops with 36 errors in 1990. ... Hit home run in first major league at-bat (August 19, 1990). ... Led N.L. with 25 sacrifice hits in 1993.

Year — Team (League)	Pos.	G	AB	R	H	2B	3B	HR	RBI	Avg.	BB	SO	SB	PO	A	E	Avg.
1987—							Dominican Summer League statistics unavailable.										
1988—Great Falls (Pio.)	SS	60	251	75	83	11	5	2	28	.331	38	42	*57	82	143	18	*.926
1989—Bakersfield (Calif.)	SS	62	245	53	75	9	4	2	22	.306	35	48	37	94	179	30	.901
—San Antonio (Tex.)	SS	78	278	47	80	6	3	2	22	.288	40	39	32	106	168	20	.932
1990—Albuquerque (PCL)	SS-2B	117	454	104	148	16	11	0	56	.326	71	81	*60	174	361	†36	.937
—Los Angeles (N.L.)	SS	29	58	7	9	0	0	1	7	.155	4	14	1	30	40	4	.946
1991—Albuquerque (PCL)	SS	79	289	58	86	8	4	0	29	.298	47	58	32	126	241	17	.956
—Los Angeles (N.L.)	SS	52	113	10	22	2	0	0	3	.195	25	32	3	50	121	10	.945
1992—Los Angeles (N.L.)	SS	149	534	67	139	20	8	1	30	.260	57	98	23	208	398	*42	.935
1993—Los Angeles (N.L.)	SS	158	590	77	159	21	6	1	62	.269	71	75	30	250	454	*37	.950

Year Team (League)	Pos.	G	AB	R	H	2B	3B	HR	RBI	Avg.	BB	SO	SB	PO	A	E	Avg.
1994— Los Angeles (N.L.)	SS	72	243	27	51	8	4	1	25	.210	38	38	2	123	195	11	.967
—Albuquerque (PCL).....	SS	56	224	43	74	7	5	1	31	.330	37	48	9	91	196	13	.957
1995— Los Angeles (N.L.)	SS	119	429	69	123	14	6	4	33	.287	69	67	2	165	312	*35	.932
1996— Kansas City (A.L.)■	1-2-S-O	151	561	85	170	33	8	5	47	.303	74	98	24	920	234	16	.986
1997— Kansas City (A.L.)	2B-DH	106	424	59	126	23	6	2	39	.297	41	64	9	201	254	9	.981
American League totals (2 years)		257	985	144	296	56	14	7	86	.301	115	162	33	1121	488	25	.985
National League totals (6 years)		579	1967	257	503	65	24	8	160	.256	264	324	61	826	1520	139	.944
Major league totals (8 years)		836	2952	401	799	121	38	15	246	.271	379	486	94	1947	2008	164	.960

DIVISION SERIES RECORD

Year Team (League)	Pos.	G	AB	R	H	2B	3B	HR	RBI	Avg.	BB	SO	SB	PO	A	E	Avg.
1995— Los Angeles (N.L.)	PR	1	0	0	0	0	0	0	0	...	0	0	0	...	...	...	...

ALL-STAR GAME RECORD

Year League	Pos.	AB	R	H	2B	3B	HR	RBI	Avg.	BB	SO	SB	PO	A	E	Avg.
1995— National	SS	0	0	0	0	0	0	0	...	0	0	0	0	0	0	...

OGDEN, JAMIE   1B/OF   TWINS

PERSONAL: Born January 19, 1972, in South St. Paul, Minn. ... 6-5/233. ... Bats left, throws left. ... Full name: Jamie Jason Ogden.
HIGH SCHOOL: White Bear Lake (Minn.).
TRANSACTIONS/CAREER NOTES: Selected by Minnesota Twins organization in third round of free-agent draft (June 4, 1990); pick recieved as part of compensation for Pittsburgh Pirates signing Type C free-agent 2B Wally Backman.

Year Team (League)	Pos.	G	AB	R	H	2B	3B	HR	RBI	Avg.	BB	SO	SB	PO	A	E	Avg.
1990— GC Twins (GCL).........	1B	28	101	11	20	1	2	0	5	.198	7	41	2	199	19	5	.978
1991— GC Twins (GCL).........	1B-OF	37	122	22	39	9	•7	2	25	.320	11	30	8	257	12	6	.978
1992— Kenosha (Midwest)	OF	108	372	36	91	14	3	3	51	.245	52	108	9	126	7	6	.957
1993— Fort Myers (FSL).......	OF	118	396	37	96	22	4	8	46	.242	34	89	7	217	16	7	.971
1994— Fort Myers (FSL).......	OF	69	251	32	66	12	0	7	22	.263	16	52	12	74	4	2	.975
1995— New Britain (Eastern) .	OF	117	384	54	109	22	1	13	61	.284	48	90	6	660	44	9	.987
1996— Salt Lake (PCL)	1B-OF	123	448	80	118	22	2	18	74	.263	45	105	17	840	47	10	.989
1997— Salt Lake (PCL)	OF-1B	97	367	67	105	18	5	14	53	.286	35	99	14	324	19	1	.997

OGEA, CHAD   P   INDIANS

PERSONAL: Born November 9, 1970, in Lake Charles, La. ... 6-2/220. ... Throws right, bats left. ... Full name: Chad Wayne Ogea. ... Name pronounced OH-jay.
HIGH SCHOOL: St. Louis (Lake Charles, La.).
COLLEGE: Louisiana State.
TRANSACTIONS/CAREER NOTES: Selected by Cleveland Indians organization in third round of free-agent draft (June 3, 1991). ... On Cleveland disabled list (April 28-May 28, 1996); included rehabilitation assignment to Buffalo (May 15-June 8). ... On Cleveland disabled list (June 24-September 1, 1997).
STATISTICAL NOTES: Led International League with 26 home runs allowed in 1993.

Year Team (League)	W	L	Pct.	ERA	G	GS	CG	ShO	Sv.	IP	H	R	ER	BB	SO
1992— Kinston (Carolina)	13	3	.813	3.49	21	21	•5	•2	0	139 1/3	135	61	54	29	123
—Cant./Akr. (Eastern)	6	1	.857	2.20	7	7	1	1	0	49	38	12	12	12	40
1993— Charlotte (Int'l)...................	•13	8	.619	3.82	29	•29	0	0	0	181 1/3	169	91	77	54	135
1994— Charlotte (Int'l)...................	9	10	.474	3.85	24	23	6	0	1	163 2/3	146	80	70	34	113
—Cleveland (A.L.)..................	0	1	.000	6.06	4	1	0	0	0	16 1/3	21	11	11	10	11
1995— Buffalo (A.A.)...................	0	1	.000	4.58	4	4	0	0	0	17 2/3	16	12	9	8	11
—Cleveland (A.L.)..................	8	3	.727	3.05	20	14	1	0	0	106 1/3	95	38	36	29	57
1996— Cleveland (A.L.)..................	10	6	.625	4.79	29	21	1	1	0	146 2/3	151	82	78	42	101
—Buffalo (A.A.)...................	0	1	.000	5.26	5	5	0	0	0	25 2/3	27	15	15	6	20
1997— Cleveland (A.L.)..................	8	9	.471	4.99	21	21	0	0	0	126 1/3	139	79	70	47	65
—Buffalo (A.A.)...................	1	1	.500	4.29	4	4	0	0	0	21	24	10	10	6	11
Major league totals (4 years)......	26	19	.578	4.44	74	57	3	1	0	395 2/3	406	210	195	128	249

DIVISION SERIES RECORD

Year Team (League)	W	L	Pct.	ERA	G	GS	CG	ShO	Sv.	IP	H	R	ER	BB	SO
1996— Cleveland (A.L.).................	0	0	...	0.00	1	0	0	0	0	1/3	0	0	0	2	0
1997— Cleveland (A.L.).................	0	0	...	1.69	1	0	0	0	0	5 1/3	2	1	1	0	1
Div. series totals (2 years)	0	0	...	1.59	2	0	0	0	0	5 2/3	2	1	1	2	1

CHAMPIONSHIP SERIES RECORD

Year Team (League)	W	L	Pct.	ERA	G	GS	CG	ShO	Sv.	IP	H	R	ER	BB	SO
1995— Cleveland (A.L.).................	0	0	...	0.00	1	0	0	0	0	2/3	1	0	0	0	2
1997— Cleveland (A.L.).................	0	2	.000	3.21	2	2	0	0	0	14	12	5	5	5	7
Champ. series totals (2 years)	0	2	.000	3.07	3	2	0	0	0	14 2/3	13	5	5	5	9

WORLD SERIES RECORD

Year Team (League)	W	L	Pct.	ERA	G	GS	CG	ShO	Sv.	IP	H	R	ER	BB	SO
1997— Cleveland (A.L.)..................	2	0	1.000	1.54	2	2	0	0	0	11 2/3	11	2	2	3	5

0

PERSONAL: Born December 24, 1968, in Kalamazoo, Mich. ... 6-2/210. ... Throws left, bats left. ... Full name: Kirt Stanley Ojala. ... Name pronounced oh-JAH-la.
HIGH SCHOOL: Portage (Mich.) Central.
COLLEGE: Michigan.
TRANSACTIONS/CAREER NOTES: Selected by New York Yankees organization in fourth round of free-agent draft (June 4, 1990). ... On disabled list (April 9-23, 1992). ... Selected by Oakland Athletics from Yankees organization in Rule 5 major league draft (December 7, 1992). ... Returned to Yankees organization (March 27, 1993). ... Granted free agency (April 5, 1996). ... Signed by Indianapolis, Cincinnati Reds organization (April 11, 1996). ... Claimed on waivers by Florida Marlins organization (March 27, 1997). ... Granted free agency (October 15, 1997). ... Signed by Arizona Diamondbacks (November 26, 1997).

Year Team (League)	W	L	Pct.	ERA	G	GS	CG	ShO	Sv.	IP	H	R	ER	BB	SO
1990— Oneonta (N.Y.-Penn)	7	2	.778	2.16	14	14	1	0	0	79	75	28	19	43	87
1991— Prince William (Caro.)	8	7	.533	2.53	25	23	1	0	0	156²/₃	120	52	44	61	112
1992— Alb./Colon. (Eastern)	12	8	.600	3.62	24	23	2	1	0	151¹/₃	130	71	61	•80	116
1993— Columbus (Int'l)	8	9	.471	5.50	31	20	0	0	0	126	145	85	77	71	83
— Alb./Colon. (Eastern)	1	0	1.000	0.00	1	1	0	0	0	6¹/₃	5	0	0	2	6
1994— Columbus (Int'l)	11	7	.611	3.83	25	23	1	1	0	148	157	78	63	46	81
1995— Columbus (Int'l)	8	7	.533	3.95	32	20	0	0	1	145²/₃	138	74	64	54	107
1996— Indianapolis (A.A.)■	7	7	.500	3.77	22	21	3	0	0	133²/₃	143	67	56	31	92
1997— Charlotte (Int'l)■	8	7	.533	3.50	25	24	0	0	0	149	148	74	58	55	119
— Florida (N.L.)	1	2	.333	3.14	7	5	0	0	0	28²/₃	28	10	10	18	19
Major league totals (1 year)	1	2	.333	3.14	7	5	0	0	0	28²/₃	28	10	10	18	19

PERSONAL: Born August 4, 1969, in Compton, Calif. ... 6-0/198. ... Bats left, throws left. ... Full name: Troy Franklin O'Leary.
HIGH SCHOOL: Cypress (Calif.).
TRANSACTIONS/CAREER NOTES: Selected by Milwaukee Brewers organization in 13th round of free-agent draft (June 2, 1987). ... Claimed on waivers by Boston Red Sox (April 14, 1995).
HONORS: Named Texas League Most Valuable Player (1992).
STATISTICAL NOTES: Led Pioneer League with 144 total bases in 1989. ... Led Texas League with 227 total bases and .399 on-base percentage in 1992. ... Led Texas League outfielders with 242 total chances in 1992. ... Career major league grand slams: 3.

Year Team (League)	Pos.	G	AB	R	H	2B	3B	HR	RBI	Avg.	BB	SO	SB	PO	A	E	Avg.
1987— Helena (Pioneer)	OF	3	5	0	2	0	0	0	1	.400	0	0	0	0	0	0	...
1988— Helena (Pioneer)	OF	67	203	40	70	11	1	0	27	.345	30	32	10	64	4	3	.958
1989— Beloit (Midwest)	OF	42	115	7	21	4	0	0	8	.183	15	20	1	55	1	1	.982
— Helena (Pioneer)	OF	•68	263	54	•89	16	3	11	•56	.338	28	43	9	92	6	3	.970
1990— Beloit (Midwest)	OF	118	436	73	130	29	1	6	62	.298	41	90	12	184	14	8	.961
— Stockton (California) ..	OF	2	6	1	3	1	0	0	0	.500	2	1	0	3	0	1	.750
1991— Stockton (California) ..	OF	126	418	63	110	20	4	5	46	.263	73	96	4	163	4	3	.982
1992— El Paso (Texas)	OF	*135	*506	*92	*169	27	8	5	79	*.334	59	87	28	*220	11	*11	.955
1993— New Orleans (A.A.)	OF-1B	111	388	65	106	32	1	7	59	.273	43	61	6	189	8	6	.970
— Milwaukee (A.L.)	OF	19	41	3	12	3	0	0	3	.293	5	9	0	32	1	0	1.000
1994— New Orleans (A.A.)	OF-1B	63	225	44	74	18	5	8	43	.329	32	37	10	99	10	2	.982
— Milwaukee (A.L.)	OF-DH	27	66	9	18	1	1	2	7	.273	5	12	1	37	2	0	1.000
1995— Boston (A.L.)■	OF-DH	112	399	60	123	31	6	10	49	.308	29	64	5	196	6	5	.976
1996— Boston (A.L.)	OF	149	497	68	129	28	5	15	81	.260	47	80	3	227	8	7	.971
1997— Boston (A.L.)	OF-DH	146	499	65	154	32	4	15	80	.309	39	70	0	267	8	6	.979
Major league totals (5 years)		453	1502	205	436	95	16	42	220	.290	125	235	9	759	25	18	.978

PERSONAL: Born August 5, 1968, in Seattle. ... 6-5/220. ... Bats left, throws left. ... Full name: John Garrett Olerud. ... Son of John E. Olerud, minor league catcher (1965-70). ... Name pronounced OH-luh-rude.
HIGH SCHOOL: Interlake (Bellevue, Wash.).
COLLEGE: Washington State.
TRANSACTIONS/CAREER NOTES: Selected by New York Mets organization in 27th round of free-agent draft (June 2, 1986); did not sign. ... Selected by Toronto Blue Jays organization in third round of free-agent draft (June 5, 1989). ... Traded by Blue Jays with cash to Mets for P Robert Person (December 20, 1996). ... Granted free agency (October 27, 1997). ... Re-signed by Mets (November 24, 1997).
RECORDS: Shares A.L. single-season records for most intentional bases on balls received—33 (1993); and most intentional bases on balls received by lefthanded hitter—33 (1993).
STATISTICAL NOTES: Tied for A.L. lead with 10 sacrifice flies in 1991. ... Had 26-game hitting streak (May 26-June 22, 1993). ... Led A.L. with 33 intentional bases on balls received and .473 on-base percentage in 1993. ... Hit for the cycle (September 11, 1997). ... Career major league grand slams: 3.

Year Team (League)	Pos.	G	AB	R	H	2B	3B	HR	RBI	Avg.	BB	SO	SB	PO	A	E	Avg.
1989— Toronto (A.L.)	1B-DH	6	8	2	3	0	0	0	0	.375	0	1	0	19	2	0	1.000
1990— Toronto (A.L.)	DH-1B	111	358	43	95	15	1	14	48	.265	57	75	0	133	10	2	.986
1991— Toronto (A.L.)	1B-DH	139	454	64	116	30	1	17	68	.256	68	84	0	1120	78	5	.996
1992— Toronto (A.L.)	1B-DH	138	458	68	130	28	0	16	66	.284	70	61	1	1057	81	7	.994
1993— Toronto (A.L.)	1B-DH	158	551	109	200	*54	2	24	107	*.363	114	65	0	1160	97	10	.992
1994— Toronto (A.L.)	1B-DH	108	384	47	114	29	2	12	67	.297	61	53	1	824	68	6	.993
1995— Toronto (A.L.)	1B	135	492	72	143	32	0	8	54	.291	84	54	0	1099	89	4	.997
1996— Toronto (A.L.)	1B-DH	125	398	59	109	25	0	18	61	.274	60	37	1	781	56	2	.998
1997— New York (N.L.)■	1B	154	524	90	154	34	1	22	102	.294	85	67	0	1292	120	7	.995
American League totals (8 years)		920	3103	464	910	213	6	109	471	.293	514	430	3	6193	481	36	.995
National League totals (1 year)		154	524	90	154	34	1	22	102	.294	85	67	0	1292	120	7	.995
Major league totals (9 years)		1074	3627	554	1064	247	7	131	573	.293	599	497	3	7485	601	43	.995

O

CHAMPIONSHIP SERIES RECORD

Year Team (League)	Pos.	G	AB	R	H	2B	3B	HR	RBI	Avg.	BB	SO	SB	PO	A	E	Avg.
1991— Toronto (A.L.).............	1B	5	19	1	3	0	0	0	3	.158	3	1	0	40	3	0	1.000
1992— Toronto (A.L.).............	1B	6	23	4	8	2	0	1	4	.348	2	5	0	51	1	0	1.000
1993— Toronto (A.L.).............	1B	6	23	5	8	1	0	0	3	.348	4	1	0	48	9	1	.983
Championship series totals (3 years)		17	65	10	19	3	0	1	10	.292	9	7	0	139	13	1	.993

WORLD SERIES RECORD

NOTES: Member of World Series championship teams (1992 and 1993).

Year Team (League)	Pos.	G	AB	R	H	2B	3B	HR	RBI	Avg.	BB	SO	SB	PO	A	E	Avg.
1992— Toronto (A.L.).............	1B	4	13	2	4	0	0	0	0	.308	0	4	0	25	3	0	1.000
1993— Toronto (A.L.).............	1B	5	17	5	4	1	0	1	2	.235	4	1	0	36	0	0	1.000
World Series totals (2 years)		9	30	7	8	1	0	1	2	.267	4	5	0	61	3	0	1.000

ALL-STAR GAME RECORD

Year League	Pos.	AB	R	H	2B	3B	HR	RBI	Avg.	BB	SO	SB	PO	A	E	Avg.
1993— American	1B	2	0	0	0	0	0	0	.000	0	0	0	4	0	0	1.000

OLIVARES, OMAR   P   ANGELS

PERSONAL: Born July 6, 1967, in Mayaguez, Puerto Rico. ... 6-1/193. ... Throws right, bats right. ... Full name: Omar Palqu Olivares. ... Son of Ed Olivares, outfielder, St. Louis Cardinals (1960-61).

HIGH SCHOOL: Hostos (Mayaguez, Puerto Rico).

TRANSACTIONS/CAREER NOTES: Signed as non-drafted free agent by San Diego Padres organization (September 15, 1986). ... Traded by Padres organization to St. Louis Cardinals for OF Alex Cole and P Steve Peters (February 27, 1990). ... On St. Louis disabled list (May 27-June 13, 1992 and June 4-20, 1993). ... Granted free agency (April 7, 1995). ... Signed by Colorado Rockies (April 9, 1995). ... Claimed on waivers by Philadelphia Phillies (July 11, 1995). ... Granted free agency (October 16, 1995). ... Signed by Detroit Tigers (December 20, 1995). ... On Detroit disabled list (April 16-May 30, 1996); included rehabilitation assignment to Toledo (May 24-30). ... Traded by Tigers with P Felipe Lira to Seattle Mariners for P Scott Sanders, P Dean Crow and 3B Carlos Villalobos (July 18, 1997). ... Granted free agency (October 30, 1997). ... Signed by Anaheim Angels (December 11, 1997).

RECORDS: Shares major league single-season record for fewest double plays by pitcher who led league in double plays—4 (1992).

STATISTICAL NOTES: Tied for Texas League lead with 10 hit batsmen in 1989.

MISCELLANEOUS: Appeared in one game as pinch-runner and singled and scored in three games as pinch-hitter (1992). ... Appeared in one game as pinch-runner and made an out in one game as pinch-hitter (1993). ... Made an out in one game as pinch-hitter with St. Louis (1994). ... Appeared in one game as pinch-runner with Colorado (1995). ... Hit two-run home run in only game as pinch-hitter with Philadelphia (1995). ... Appeared in three games as pinch-runner with Detroit (1997).

Year Team (League)	W	L	Pct.	ERA	G	GS	CG	ShO	Sv.	IP	H	R	ER	BB	SO
1987— Charleston, S.C. (S. Atl.)....	4	14	.222	4.60	31	24	5	0	0	170 1/3	182	107	87	57	86
1988— Charleston, S.C. (S. Atl.)....	13	6	.684	2.23	24	24	*10	3	0	185 1/3	166	63	46	43	94
— Riverside (California).........	3	0	1.000	1.16	4	3	1	0	0	23 1/3	18	9	3	9	16
1989— Wichita (Texas)...............	12	11	.522	3.39	26	26	6	1	0	*185 2/3	175	87	70	61	79
1990— Louisville (A.A.)■.............	10	11	.476	2.82	23	23	5	2	0	159 1/3	127	58	50	59	88
— St. Louis (N.L.)................	1	1	.500	2.92	9	6	0	0	0	49 1/3	45	17	16	17	20
1991— St. Louis (N.L.)................	11	7	.611	3.71	28	24	0	0	1	167 1/3	148	72	69	61	91
— Louisville (A.A.)...............	1	2	.333	3.47	6	6	0	0	0	36 1/3	39	15	14	16	27
1992— St. Louis (N.L.)................	9	9	.500	3.84	32	30	1	0	0	197	189	84	84	63	124
1993— St. Louis (N.L.)................	5	3	.625	4.17	58	9	0	0	1	118 2/3	134	60	55	54	63
1994— Louisville (A.A.)...............	2	1	.667	4.37	9	9	0	0	0	47 1/3	47	24	23	16	38
— St. Louis (N.L.)................	3	4	.429	5.74	14	12	1	0	1	73 2/3	84	53	47	37	26
1995— Colo. Springs (PCL)■.......	0	1	.000	5.40	3	2	0	0	0	11 2/3	14	7	7	2	6
— Colorado (N.L.)..............	1	3	.250	7.39	11	6	0	0	0	31 2/3	44	28	26	21	15
— Philadelphia (N.L.)■........	0	1	.000	5.40	5	0	0	0	0	10	11	6	6	2	7
— Scran./W.B. (Int'l)............	0	3	.000	4.87	7	7	0	0	0	44 1/3	49	25	24	20	28
1996— Detroit (A.L.)■...............	7	11	.389	4.89	25	25	4	0	0	160	169	90	87	75	81
— Toledo (Int'l).................	1	0	1.000	8.44	1	1	0	0	0	5 1/3	4	5	5	3	5
1997— Detroit (A.L.).................	5	6	.455	4.70	19	19	3	2	0	115	110	68	60	53	74
— Seattle (A.L.)■...............	1	4	.200	5.49	13	12	0	0	0	62 1/3	81	41	38	28	29
A.L. totals (2 years)	13	21	.382	4.94	57	56	7	2	0	337 1/3	360	199	185	156	184
N.L. totals (6 years)	30	28	.517	4.21	157	87	2	0	3	647 2/3	655	320	303	255	346
Major league totals (8 years)	43	49	.467	4.46	214	143	9	2	3	985	1015	519	488	411	530

OLIVER, DARREN   P   RANGERS

PERSONAL: Born October 6, 1970, in Kansas City, Mo. ... 6-2/200. ... Throws left, bats right. ... Full name: Darren Christopher Oliver. ... Son of Bob Oliver, major league first baseman/outfielder with five teams (1965 and 1969-75).

HIGH SCHOOL: Rio Linda (Calif.) Senior.

TRANSACTIONS/CAREER NOTES: Selected by Texas Rangers organization in third round of free-agent draft (June 1, 1988). ... On Gulf Coast Rangers disabled list (April 6-August 9, 1990). ... On disabled list (May 1, 1991-remainder of season). ... On Tulsa disabled list (July 1, 1992-remainder of season). ... On disabled list (June 27, 1995-remainder of season).

Year Team (League)	W	L	Pct.	ERA	G	GS	CG	ShO	Sv.	IP	H	R	ER	BB	SO
1988— GC Rangers (GCL).............	5	1	.833	2.15	12	9	0	0	0	54 1/3	39	16	13	18	59
1989— Gastonia (S. Atl.)...............	8	7	.533	3.16	24	23	2	1	0	122 1/3	86	54	43	82	108
1990— GC Rangers (GCL).............	0	0	...	0.00	3	3	0	0	0	6	1	1	0	1	7
— Gastonia (S. Atl.).............	0	0	...	13.50	1	1	0	0	0	2	1	3	3	4	2

Year Team (League)	W	L	Pct.	ERA	G	GS	CG	ShO	Sv.	IP	H	R	ER	BB	SO
1991— Charlotte (Fla. St.).............	0	1	.000	4.50	2	2	0	0	0	8	6	4	4	3	12
1992— Charlotte (Fla. St.).............	1	0	1.000	0.72	8	2	1	1	2	25	11	2	2	10	33
— Tulsa (Texas)	0	1	.000	3.14	3	3	0	0	0	14 1/3	15	9	5	4	14
1993— Tulsa (Texas)	7	5	.583	1.96	46	0	0	0	6	73 1/3	51	18	16	41	77
— Texas (A.L.)	0	0	...	2.70	2	0	0	0	0	3 1/3	2	1	1	1	4
1994— Texas (A.L.)	4	0	1.000	3.42	43	0	0	0	2	50	40	24	19	35	50
— Oklahoma City (A.A.).........	0	0	...	0.00	6	0	0	0	1	7 1/3	1	0	0	3	6
1995— Texas (A.L.)	4	2	.667	4.22	17	7	0	0	0	49	47	25	23	32	39
1996— Charlotte (Fla. St.).............	0	1	.000	3.00	2	1	0	0	0	12	8	4	4	3	9
— Texas (A.L.)	14	6	.700	4.66	30	30	1	1	0	173 2/3	190	97	90	76	112
1997— Texas (A.L.)	13	12	.520	4.20	32	32	3	1	0	201 1/3	213	111	94	82	104
Major league totals (5 years)......	35	20	.636	4.28	124	69	4	2	2	477 1/3	492	258	227	226	309

DIVISION SERIES RECORD

Year Team (League)	W	L	Pct.	ERA	G	GS	CG	ShO	Sv.	IP	H	R	ER	BB	SO
1996— Texas (A.L.)	0	1	.000	3.38	1	1	0	0	0	8	6	3	3	2	3

OLIVER, JOE — C — TIGERS

PERSONAL: Born July 24, 1965, in Memphis. ... 6-3/220. ... Bats right, throws right. ... Full name: Joseph Melton Oliver.
HIGH SCHOOL: Boone (Orlando).
TRANSACTIONS/CAREER NOTES: Selected by Cincinnati Reds organization in second round of free-agent draft (June 6, 1983); pick received as compensation for New York Yankees signing Type A free-agent P Bob Shirley. ... On disabled list (April 23-May 6, 1986 and April 12, 1994-remainder of season). ... Released by Reds (November 3, 1994). ... Signed by New Orleans, Milwaukee Brewers organization (March 24, 1995). ... On Milwaukee disabled list (July 14-August 15, 1995); included rehabilitation assignment to New Orleans (August 10-15). ... Granted free agency (October 31, 1995). ... Signed by Reds (February 26, 1996). ... Granted free agency (November 18, 1996). ... Re-signed by Reds organization (February 8, 1997). ... Granted free agency (October 30, 1997). ... Signed by Detroit Tigers organization (December 22, 1997).
STATISTICAL NOTES: Led Pioneer League catchers with .989 fielding percentage, 425 putouts, 38 assists and 468 total chances in 1983. ... Led Midwest League catchers with 855 total chances and 30 passed balls in 1984. ... Led Florida State League catchers with 84 assists and 33 passed balls in 1985. ... Led American Association catchers with 13 errors in 1989. ... Tied for N.L. lead with 16 passed balls in 1990. ... Led N.L. catchers with 925 putouts and 997 total chances in 1992. ... Career major league grand slams: 4.

Year Team (League)	Pos.	G	AB	R	H	2B	3B	HR	RBI	Avg.	BB	SO	SB	PO	A	E	Avg.
1983— Billings (Pioneer)........	C-1B	56	186	21	40	4	0	4	28	.215	15	47	1	†426	†39	5	†.989
1984— Cedar Rap. (Midw.)	C	102	335	34	73	11	0	3	29	.218	17	83	2	*757	85	13	.985
1985— Tampa (Florida State).	C-1B	112	386	38	104	23	2	7	62	.269	32	75	1	615	†94	16	.978
1986— Vermont (Eastern)......	C	84	282	32	78	18	1	6	41	.277	21	47	2	383	62	14	.969
1987— Vermont (Eastern)......	C-1B	66	236	31	72	13	2	10	60	.305	17	30	0	247	35	10	.966
1988— Nashville (A.A.)	C	73	220	19	45	7	2	4	24	.205	18	39	0	413	37	7	.985
— Chattanooga (Sou.)	C	28	105	9	26	6	0	3	12	.248	5	19	0	176	15	0	1.000
1989— Nashville (A.A.)	C-1B	71	233	22	68	13	0	6	31	.292	13	35	0	388	37	†13	.970
— Cincinnati (N.L.)........	C	49	151	13	41	8	0	3	23	.272	6	28	0	260	21	4	.986
1990— Cincinnati (N.L.)........	C	121	364	34	84	23	0	8	52	.231	37	75	1	686	59	6	*.992
1991— Cincinnati (N.L.)........	C	94	269	21	58	11	0	11	41	.216	18	53	0	496	40	11	.980
1992— Cincinnati (N.L.)........	C-1B	143	485	42	131	25	1	10	57	.270	35	75	2	†926	64	8	.992
1993— Cincinnati (N.L.)........	C-1B-OF	139	482	40	115	28	0	14	75	.239	27	91	0	825	70	7	.992
1994— Cincinnati (N.L.)........	C	6	19	1	4	0	0	1	5	.211	2	3	0	48	2	1	.980
1995— Milwaukee (A.L.)■......	C-DH-1B	97	337	43	92	20	0	12	51	.273	27	66	2	414	40	8	.983
— New Orleans (A.A.).......	C	4	13	0	1	1	0	0	0	.077	0	3	0	14	7	0	1.000
1996— Cincinnati (N.L.)■......	C-1B-OF	106	289	31	70	12	1	11	46	.242	28	54	2	583	45	5	.992
1997— Indianapolis (A.A.)......	C	2	9	1	3	0	0	1	1	.333	0	1	0	21	4	0	1.000
— Cincinnati (N.L.)........	C-1B	111	349	28	90	13	0	14	43	.258	25	58	1	681	55	7	.991
American League totals (1 year)		97	337	43	92	20	0	12	51	.273	27	66	2	414	40	8	.983
National League totals (8 years)		769	2408	210	593	120	2	72	342	.246	178	437	6	4505	356	49	.990
Major league totals (9 years)		866	2745	253	685	140	2	84	393	.250	205	503	8	4919	396	57	.989

CHAMPIONSHIP SERIES RECORD

Year Team (League)	Pos.	G	AB	R	H	2B	3B	HR	RBI	Avg.	BB	SO	SB	PO	A	E	Avg.
1990— Cincinnati (N.L.).........	C	5	14	1	2	0	0	0	0	.143	0	2	0	27	1	0	1.000

WORLD SERIES RECORD

NOTES: Member of World Series championship team (1990).

Year Team (League)	Pos.	G	AB	R	H	2B	3B	HR	RBI	Avg.	BB	SO	SB	PO	A	E	Avg.
1990— Cincinnati (N.L.).........	C	4	18	2	6	3	0	0	2	.333	0	1	0	27	1	3	.903

OLSEN, JASON — P — WHITE SOX

PERSONAL: Born March 16, 1975, in Fairfield, Calif. ... 6-4/210. ... Throws right, bats right.
JUNIOR COLLEGE: Napa (Calif.) Valley College.
TRANSACTIONS/CAREER NOTES: Selected by Chicago White Sox organization in 44th round of free-agent draft (June 2, 1994).

Year Team (League)	W	L	Pct.	ERA	G	GS	CG	ShO	Sv.	IP	H	R	ER	BB	SO
1996— Hickory (S. Atl.)	2	1	.667	1.37	4	4	1	0	0	26 1/3	19	5	4	6	32
— South Bend (Mid.).............	4	1	.800	1.75	9	9	0	0	0	56 2/3	39	16	11	13	55
— Prince William (Caro.)........	6	4	.600	3.87	12	12	0	0	0	79	74	39	34	31	55
1997— Birmingham (Southern)	9	14	.391	4.88	28	27	1	1	0	160 1/3	183	101	87	58	121

O

OLSON, GREGG   P

PERSONAL: Born October 11, 1966, in Omaha, Neb. ... 6-4/212. ... Throws right, bats right. ... Full name: Gregg William Olson.
HIGH SCHOOL: Northwest (Omaha, Neb.).
COLLEGE: Auburn.
TRANSACTIONS/CAREER NOTES: Selected by Baltimore Orioles organization in first round (fourth pick overall) of free-agent draft (June 1, 1988). ... On disabled list (August 9-September 20, 1993). ... Granted free agency (December 20, 1993). ... Signed by Atlanta Braves (February 8, 1994). ... On Atlanta disabled list (March 26-May 30, 1994); included rehabilitation assignment to Richmond (May 14-30). ... Granted free agency (December 23, 1994). ... Signed by Cleveland Indians organization (March 24, 1995). ... On Buffalo disabled list (April 6-14, 1995). ... Contract sold by Buffalo to Kansas City Royals (July 24, 1995). ... Granted free agency (November 1, 1995). ... Signed by St. Louis Cardinals organization (January 23, 1996). ... Released by Louisville, Cardinals organization (March 26, 1996). ... Signed by Indianapolis, Cincinnati Reds organization (March 26, 1996). ... Traded by Reds to Detroit Tigers for IF Yuri Sanchez (April 26, 1996). ... Traded by Tigers to Houston Astros for two players to be named later (August 26, 1996); Tigers acquired P Kevin Gallaher and IF Pedro Santana to complete deal (August 27, 1996). ... Granted free agency (October 28, 1996). ... Signed by Minnesota Twins organization (December 20, 1996). ... Released by Twins (May 16, 1997). ... Signed by Royals organization (May 25, 1997). ... Granted free agency (October 28, 1997).
RECORDS: Holds A.L. rookie-season record for most saves—27 (1989).
HONORS: Named righthanded pitcher on THE SPORTING NEWS college All-America team (1988). ... Named A.L. Rookie of the Year by Baseball Writers' Association of America (1989).
STATISTICAL NOTES: Pitched one inning, combining with starter Bob Milacki (six innings), Mike Flanagan (one inning) and Mark Williamson (one inning) in 2-0 no-hit victory against Oakland (July 13, 1991).
MISCELLANEOUS: Holds Baltimore Orioles all-time record for most saves (160). ... Struck out in only plate appearance (1993).

Year Team (League)	W	L	Pct.	ERA	G	GS	CG	ShO	Sv.	IP	H	R	ER	BB	SO
1988—Hagerstown (Caro.)	1	0	1.000	2.00	8	0	0	0	4	9	5	2	2	2	9
—Charlotte (Southern)	0	1	.000	5.87	8	0	0	0	1	15 1/3	24	13	10	6	22
—Baltimore (A.L.)	1	1	.500	3.27	10	0	0	0	0	11	10	4	4	10	9
1989—Baltimore (A.L.)	5	2	.714	1.69	64	0	0	0	27	85	57	17	16	46	90
1990—Baltimore (A.L.)	6	5	.545	2.42	64	0	0	0	37	74 1/3	57	20	20	31	74
1991—Baltimore (A.L.)	4	6	.400	3.18	72	0	0	0	31	73 2/3	74	28	26	29	72
1992—Baltimore (A.L.)	1	5	.167	2.05	60	0	0	0	36	61 1/3	46	14	14	24	58
1993—Baltimore (A.L.)	0	2	.000	1.60	50	0	0	0	29	45	37	9	8	18	44
1994—Richmond (Int'l)■	0	0	...	1.59	8	2	0	0	2	11 1/3	8	3	2	8	13
—Atlanta (N.L.)	0	2	.000	9.20	16	0	0	0	0	14 2/3	19	15	15	13	10
1995—Buffalo (A.A.)■	1	0	1.000	2.49	18	0	0	0	13	21 2/3	16	6	6	9	25
—Cleveland (A.L.)	0	0	...	13.50	3	0	0	0	0	2 2/3	5	4	4	2	0
—Omaha (Am. Assoc.)■	0	0	...	0.00	1	0	0	0	0	1	0	0	0	1	1
—Kansas City (A.L.)	3	3	.500	3.26	20	0	0	0	3	30 1/3	23	11	11	17	21
1996—Indianapolis (A.A.)■	0	0	...	4.26	7	0	0	0	4	6 1/3	6	4	3	6	4
—Detroit (A.L.)■	3	0	1.000	5.02	43	0	0	0	8	43	43	25	24	28	29
—Houston (N.L.)■	1	0	1.000	4.82	9	0	0	0	0	9 1/3	12	5	5	7	8
1997—Minnesota (A.L.)■	0	0	...	18.36	11	0	0	0	0	8 1/3	19	17	17	11	6
—Omaha (Am. Assoc.)■	3	1	.750	3.31	9	5	0	0	0	35 1/3	30	13	13	10	20
—Kansas City (A.L.)	4	3	.571	3.02	34	0	0	0	1	41 2/3	39	18	14	17	28
A.L. totals (9 years)	27	27	.500	2.99	431	0	0	0	172	476 1/3	410	167	158	233	431
N.L. totals (2 years)	1	2	.333	7.50	25	0	0	0	1	24	31	20	20	20	18
Major league totals (10 years)	28	29	.491	3.20	456	0	0	0	173	500 1/3	441	187	178	253	449

ALL-STAR GAME RECORD

Year League	W	L	Pct.	ERA	GS	CG	ShO	Sv.	IP	H	R	ER	BB	SO
1990—American							Did not play.							

O'NEILL, PAUL   OF   YANKEES

PERSONAL: Born February 25, 1963, in Columbus, Ohio. ... 6-4/215. ... Bats left, throws left. ... Full name: Paul Andrew O'Neill. ... Son of Charles O'Neill, minor league pitcher (1945-48).
HIGH SCHOOL: Brookhaven (Columbus, Ohio).
COLLEGE: Otterbein College (Ohio).
TRANSACTIONS/CAREER NOTES: Selected by Cincinnati Reds organization in fourth round of free-agent draft (June 8, 1981). ... On Denver disabled list (May 10-July 16, 1986). ... On Cincinnati disabled list (July 21-September 1, 1989); included rehabilitation assignment to Nashville (August 27-September 1). ... Traded by Reds with 1B Joe DeBerry to New York Yankees for OF Roberto Kelly (November 3, 1992). ... On disabled list (May 7-23, 1995). ... On suspended list (September 6-8, 1996).
STATISTICAL NOTES: Led American Association outfielders with 20 assists and eight double plays in 1985. ... Hit three home runs in one game (August 31, 1995). ... Career major league grand slams: 3.

Year Team (League)	Pos.	G	AB	R	H	2B	3B	HR	RBI	Avg.	BB	SO	SB	PO	A	E	Avg.
1981—Billings (Pioneer)	OF	66	241	37	76	7	2	3	29	.315	21	35	6	87	4	5	.948
1982—Cedar Rap. (Midw.)	OF	116	386	50	105	19	2	8	71	.272	21	79	12	137	7	8	.947
1983—Tampa (Florida State)	OF-1B	121	413	62	115	23	7	8	51	.278	56	70	20	218	14	10	.959
—Waterbury (Eastern)	OF	14	43	6	12	0	0	0	6	.279	6	8	2	26	0	0	1.000
1984—Vermont (Eastern)	OF	134	475	70	126	31	5	16	76	.265	52	72	29	246	5	7	.973
1985—Denver (A.A.)	OF-1B	*137	*509	63	*155	*32	3	7	74	.305	28	73	5	248	†20	7	.975
—Cincinnati (N.L.)	OF	5	12	1	4	1	0	0	1	.333	0	2	0	3	1	0	1.000
1986—Cincinnati (N.L.)	PH	3	2	0	0	0	0	0	0	.000	1	1	0	...	...	...	
—Denver (A.A.)	OF	55	193	20	49	9	2	5	27	.254	9	28	1	98	7	4	.963
1987—Cincinnati (N.L.)	OF-1B-P	84	160	24	41	14	1	7	28	.256	18	29	2	90	2	4	.958
—Nashville (A.A.)	OF	11	37	12	11	0	0	3	6	.297	5	5	1	19	1	0	1.000
1988—Cincinnati (N.L.)	OF-1B	145	485	58	122	25	3	16	73	.252	38	65	8	410	13	6	.986
1989—Cincinnati (N.L.)	OF	117	428	49	118	24	2	15	74	.276	46	64	20	223	7	4	.983
—Nashville (A.A.)	OF	4	11	4	0	0	0	0		.333	3	1	1	7	1	0	1.000
1990—Cincinnati (N.L.)	OF	145	503	59	136	28	0	16	78	.270	53	103	13	271	12	2	.993
1991—Cincinnati (N.L.)	OF	152	532	71	136	36	0	28	91	.256	73	107	12	301	13	2	.994

O

Year Team (League)	Pos.	G	AB	R	H	2B	3B	HR	RBI	Avg.	BB	SO	SB	PO	A	E	Avg.
								BATTING							FIELDING		
1992—Cincinnati (N.L.).........	OF	148	496	59	122	19	1	14	66	.246	77	85	6	291	12	1	*.997
1993—New York (A.L.)■...	OF-DH	141	498	71	155	34	1	20	75	.311	44	69	2	230	7	2	.992
1994—New York (A.L.).........	OF-DH	103	368	68	132	25	1	21	83	*.359	72	56	5	203	7	1	.995
1995—New York (A.L.).........	OF-DH	127	460	82	138	30	4	22	96	.300	71	76	1	220	3	3	.987
1996—New York (A.L.).........	OF-DH-1B	150	546	89	165	35	1	19	91	.302	102	76	0	293	7	0	•1.000
1997—New York (A.L.).........	OF-DH-1B	149	553	89	179	42	0	21	117	.324	75	92	10	293	7	5	.984
American League totals (5 years)		670	2425	399	769	166	7	103	462	.317	364	369	18	1239	31	11	.991
National League totals (8 years)		799	2618	321	679	147	7	96	411	.259	306	456	61	1589	60	19	.989
Major league totals (13 years)		1469	5043	720	1448	313	14	199	873	.287	670	825	79	2828	91	30	.990

DIVISION SERIES RECORD

Year Team (League)	Pos.	G	AB	R	H	2B	3B	HR	RBI	Avg.	BB	SO	SB	PO	A	E	Avg.
								BATTING							FIELDING		
1995—New York (A.L.).........	OF-PH	5	18	5	6	0	0	3	6	.333	5	5	0	13	0	0	1.000
1996—New York (A.L.).........	OF	4	15	0	2	0	0	0	0	.133	0	2	0	13	0	0	1.000
1997—New York (A.L.).........	OF	5	19	5	8	2	0	2	7	.421	3	0	0	9	0	0	1.000
Division series totals (3 years)		14	52	10	16	2	0	5	13	.308	8	7	0	35	0	0	1.000

CHAMPIONSHIP SERIES RECORD

Year Team (League)	Pos.	G	AB	R	H	2B	3B	HR	RBI	Avg.	BB	SO	SB	PO	A	E	Avg.
								BATTING							FIELDING		
1990—Cincinnati (N.L.).........	OF	5	17	1	8	3	0	1	4	.471	1	1	1	9	2	0	1.000
1996—New York (A.L.).........	OF	4	11	1	3	0	0	1	2	.273	3	2	0	9	1	0	1.000
Championship series totals (2 years)		9	28	2	11	3	0	2	6	.393	4	3	1	18	3	0	1.000

WORLD SERIES RECORD

NOTES: Member of World Series championship teams (1990 and 1996).

Year Team (League)	Pos.	G	AB	R	H	2B	3B	HR	RBI	Avg.	BB	SO	SB	PO	A	E	Avg.
								BATTING							FIELDING		
1990—Cincinnati (N.L.).........	OF	4	12	2	1	0	0	0	1	.083	5	2	1	11	0	0	1.000
1996—New York (A.L.).........	OF-PH	5	12	1	2	2	0	0	0	.167	3	2	0	12	0	0	1.000
World Series totals (2 years)		9	24	3	3	2	0	0	1	.125	8	4	1	23	0	0	1.000

ALL-STAR GAME RECORD

Year League	Pos.	AB	R	H	2B	3B	HR	RBI	Avg.	BB	SO	SB	PO	A	E	Avg.
						BATTING								FIELDING		
1991—National.....................	OF	2	0	0	0	0	0	0	.000	0	1	0	0	0	0	...
1994—American..................	PH	1	0	0	0	0	0	0	.000	0	0	0	...	...	...	...
1995—American..................	OF	1	0	0	0	0	0	0	.000	0	0	0	0	0	0	...
1997—American..................	OF	2	0	0	0	0	0	0	.000	0	1	0	1	0	0	1.000
All-Star Game totals (4 years)		6	0	0	0	0	0	0	.000	0	2	0	1	0	0	1.000

RECORD AS PITCHER

Year Team (League)	W	L	Pct.	ERA	G	GS	CG	ShO	Sv.	IP	H	R	ER	BB	SO
1987—Cincinnati (N.L.)	0	0	...	13.50	1	0	0	0	0	2	2	3	3	4	2

OQUIST, MIKE   P   ATHLETICS

PERSONAL: Born May 30, 1968, in La Junta, Colo. ... 6-2/170. ... Throws right, bats right. ... Full name: Michael Lee Oquist. ... Name pronounced OH-kwist.

HIGH SCHOOL: La Junta (Colo.).

COLLEGE: Arkansas.

TRANSACTIONS/CAREER NOTES: Selected by Baltimore Orioles organization in 13th round of free-agent draft (June 5, 1989). ... Granted free agency (October 16, 1995). ... Signed by Las Vegas, San Diego Padres organization (December 21, 1995). ... On Las Vegas disabled list (April 4-11, 1996). ... Granted free agency (October 15, 1996). ... Signed by Oakland Athletics organization (November 19, 1996). ... On Oakland disabled list (July 14-August 20, 1997); included rehabilitation assignment to Modesto (August 12-20).

MISCELLANEOUS: Appeared in two games as pinch-runner with Oakland (1997).

Year Team (League)	W	L	Pct.	ERA	G	GS	CG	ShO	Sv.	IP	H	R	ER	BB	SO
1989—Erie (N.Y.-Penn)...................	7	4	.636	3.59	15	15	1	1	0	97²/₃	86	43	39	25	109
1990—Frederick (Carolina)............	9	8	.529	2.81	25	25	3	1	0	166¹/₃	134	64	52	48	*170
1991—Hagerstown (Eastern)	10	9	.526	4.06	27	26	1	0	0	166¹/₃	168	82	75	62	136
1992—Rochester (Int'l)	10	12	.455	4.11	26	24	5	0	0	153¹/₃	164	80	70	45	111
1993—Rochester (Int'l)	9	8	.529	3.50	28	21	2	1	0	149¹/₃	144	62	58	41	128
—Baltimore (A.L.)................	0	0	...	3.86	5	0	0	0	0	11²/₃	12	5	5	4	8
1994—Rochester (Int'l)	3	2	.600	3.73	13	8	0	0	3	50²/₃	54	23	21	15	36
—Baltimore (A.L.)................	3	3	.500	6.17	15	9	0	0	0	58¹/₃	75	41	40	30	39
1995—Baltimore (A.L.).................	2	1	.667	4.17	27	0	0	0	0	54	51	27	25	41	27
—Rochester (Int'l)	0	0	...	5.25	7	0	0	0	2	12	17	8	7	5	11
1996—Las Vegas (PCL)■............	9	4	.692	2.89	27	20	2	0	1	140¹/₃	136	55	45	44	110
—San Diego (N.L.)	0	0	...	2.35	8	0	0	0	0	7²/₃	6	2	2	4	4
1997—Edmonton (PCL)■............	6	1	.857	3.25	9	9	1	0	0	52²/₃	57	23	19	16	37
—Oakland (A.L.)	4	6	.400	5.02	19	17	0	0	0	107²/₃	111	62	60	43	72
—Modesto (California)	0	0	...	4.91	2	2	0	0	0	3²/₃	5	2	2	1	5
A.L. totals (4 years)	9	10	.474	5.05	66	26	1	0	0	231²/₃	249	135	130	118	146
N.L. totals (1 year)	0	0	...	2.35	8	0	0	0	0	7²/₃	6	2	2	4	4
Major league totals (5 years)......	9	10	.474	4.96	74	26	1	0	0	239¹/₃	255	137	132	122	150

ORDAZ, LUIS — SS — CARDINALS

PERSONAL: Born August 12, 1975, in Maracaibo, Venezuela. ... 5-11/170. ... Bats right, throws right. ... Full name: Luis Javier Ordaz.
HIGH SCHOOL: Santa Maria Gorette (Maracaibo, Venezuela).
TRANSACTIONS/CAREER NOTES: Signed as non-drafted free agent by Cincinnati Reds organization (January 27, 1993). ... Traded by Reds to St. Louis Cardinals as part of three-team deal in which Reds sent P Mike Remlinger to Kansas City Royals, Cardinals sent OF Andre King to Reds and Royals sent OF Miguel Mejia to Cardinals (December 4, 1995).
STATISTICAL NOTES: Led Appalachian League shortstops with 277 total chances and 24 errors and tied for lead with 173 assists in 1994. ... Led Texas League in grounding into double plays with 19 in 1997.

Year Team (League)	Pos.	G	AB	R	H	2B	3B	HR	RBI	Avg.	BB	SO	SB	PO	A	E	Avg.
1993—Princeton (Appal.)	3B-SS-2B	57	217	28	65	9	7	2	39	.300	7	32	3	58	117	13	.931
1994—Char., W.Va. (SAL)	SS	9	31	3	7	0	0	0	0	.226	1	4	1	16	18	7	.829
—Princeton (Appal.)	SS-2B	60	211	33	52	12	3	0	12	.246	10	27	7	81	‡173	†24	.914
1995—Char., W.Va. (SAL)	SS	112	359	43	83	14	7	2	42	.231	13	47	12	164	290	22	.954
1996—St. Peters. (FSL)■	SS	126	423	46	115	13	3	3	49	.272	30	53	10	228	317	21	.963
1997—Arkansas (Texas)	SS	115	390	44	112	20	6	4	58	.287	22	39	11	149	327	33	.935
—St. Louis (N.L.)	SS	12	22	3	6	1	0	0	1	.273	1	2	3	9	17	1	.963
Major league totals (1 year)		12	22	3	6	1	0	0	1	.273	1	2	3	9	17	1	.963

ORDONEZ, MAGGLIO — OF — WHITE SOX

PERSONAL: Born January 28, 1974, in Caracas, Venezuela. ... 5-11/170. ... Bats right, throws right.
TRANSACTIONS/CAREER NOTES: Signed as non-drafted free agent by Chicago White Sox organization (May 18, 1991).
HONORS: Named American Association Most Valuable Player (1997).
STATISTICAL NOTES: Led American Association with nine sacrifice flies and tied for league lead with 249 total bases in 1997.

Year Team (League)	Pos.	G	AB	R	H	2B	3B	HR	RBI	Avg.	BB	SO	SB	PO	A	E	Avg.
1992—GC Whi. Sox (GCL)	OF	38	111	17	20	10	2	1	14	.180	13	26	6	26	2	0	1.000
1993—Hickory (S. Atl.)	OF	84	273	32	59	14	4	3	20	.216	26	66	5	131	10	6	.959
1994—Hickory (S. Atl.)	OF	132	490	86	144	24	5	11	69	.294	45	57	16	275	16	6	.980
1995—Prince William (Car.)	OF	131	487	61	116	24	2	12	65	.238	41	71	11	256	5	6	.978
1996—Birmingham (Sou.)	OF	130	479	66	126	41	0	18	67	.263	39	74	9	231	12	6	.976
1997—Nashville (A.A.)	OF	135	523	65	*172	29	3	14	90	*.329	32	61	14	278	8	5	.983
—Chicago (A.L.)	OF	21	69	12	22	6	0	4	11	.319	2	8	1	43	1	0	1.000
Major league totals (1 year)		21	69	12	22	6	0	4	11	.319	2	8	1	43	1	0	1.000

ORDONEZ, REY — SS — METS

PERSONAL: Born November 11, 1972, in Havana, Cuba. ... 5-9/159. ... Bats right, throws right. ... Full name: Reynaldo Ordonez.
HIGH SCHOOL: Espa (Cuba).
COLLEGE: Fajardo College (Havana, Cuba).
TRANSACTIONS/CAREER NOTES: Played with St. Paul Saints of Northern League (1993). ... Acquired by New York Mets organization in lottery of Cuban defectors (October 29, 1993). ... Signed by Mets organization (February 8, 1994). ... On disabled list (June 2-July 11, 1997).
HONORS: Won N.L. Gold Glove at shortstop (1997).
STATISTICAL NOTES: Led International League shortstops in total chances with 645 in 1995. ... Led N.L. shortstops with 705 total chances and 102 double plays in 1996.

Year Team (League)	Pos.	G	AB	R	H	2B	3B	HR	RBI	Avg.	BB	SO	SB	PO	A	E	Avg.
1994—St. Lucie (Fla. St.)	SS	79	314	47	97	21	2	2	40	.309	14	28	11	141	291	15	.966
—Binghamton (East.)	SS	48	191	22	50	10	2	1	20	.262	4	18	4	57	139	8	.961
1995—Norfolk (Int'l)	SS	125	439	49	94	21	4	2	50	.214	27	50	11	188	*436	21	.967
1996—New York (N.L.)	SS	151	502	51	129	12	4	1	30	.257	22	53	1	228	450	27	.962
1997—New York (N.L.)	SS	120	356	35	77	5	3	1	33	.216	18	36	11	171	355	9	*.983
Major league totals (2 years)		271	858	86	206	17	7	2	63	.240	40	89	12	399	805	36	.971

ORIE, KEVIN — 3B — CUBS

PERSONAL: Born September 1, 1972, in West Chester, Pa. ... 6-4/210. ... Bats right, throws right. ... Full name: Kevin Leonard Orie.
HIGH SCHOOL: Upper St. Clair (Pa.).
COLLEGE: Indiana.
TRANSACTIONS/CAREER NOTES: Selected by Chicago Cubs organization in supplemental round ("sandwich pick" between first and second round, 29th pick overall) of free-agent draft (June 3, 1993); pick received as part of compensation for Atlanta Braves signing Type A free-agent P Greg Maddux. ... On disabled list (May 3, 1994-remainder of season). ... On Iowa disabled list (July 27-August 19, 1996). ... On Chicago disabled list (April 30-May 30, 1997); included rehabilitation assignment to Orlando (May 16-20) and Iowa (May 20-30).

Year Team (League)	Pos.	G	AB	R	H	2B	3B	HR	RBI	Avg.	BB	SO	SB	PO	A	E	Avg.
1993—Peoria (Midwest)	SS-OF	65	238	28	64	17	1	7	45	.269	21	51	3	77	149	12	.950
1994—Daytona (Fla. St.)	DH	6	17	4	7	3	1	1	5	.412	8	4	0	...	...	...	...
1995—Daytona (Fla. St.)	3B	119	409	54	100	17	4	9	51	.244	42	71	5	80	204	26	.916
1996—Orlando (South.)	3B	82	296	42	93	25	0	8	58	.314	48	52	2	60	144	14	.936
—Iowa (Am. Assoc.)	3B	14	48	5	10	1	0	2	6	.208	6	10	0	11	26	1	.974
1997—Chicago (N.L.)	3B-SS	114	364	40	100	23	5	8	44	.275	39	57	2	91	213	9	.971
—Orlando (South.)	DH	3	13	3	5	2	0	2	6	.385	2	1	0	...	...	...	...
—Iowa (Am. Assoc.)	3B	9	32	7	12	4	0	1	8	.375	5	5	0	2	13	1	.938
Major league totals (1 year)		114	364	40	100	23	5	8	44	.275	39	57	2	91	213	9	.971

PERSONAL: Born April 21, 1957, in Santa Barbara, Calif. ... 6-2/205. ... Throws left, bats right. ... Name pronounced oh-ROSS-koh.
HIGH SCHOOL: Santa Barbara (Calif.).
COLLEGE: Santa Barbara (Calif.) City College.
TRANSACTIONS/CAREER NOTES: Selected by St. Louis Cardinals organization in seventh round of free-agent draft (January 11, 1977); did not sign. ... Selected by Minnesota Twins organization in second round of free-agent draft (January 10, 1978). ... Traded by Twins organization to New York Mets (February 7, 1979), completing deal in which Twins traded P Greg Field and a player to be named later to Mets for P Jerry Koosman (December 8, 1978). ... Traded by Mets as part of an eight-player, three-team deal in which Mets sent Orosco to Oakland Athletics (December 11, 1987); A's then traded Orosco, SS Alfredo Griffin and P Jay Howell to Los Angeles Dodgers for P Bob Welch, P Matt Young and P Jack Savage; A's then traded Savage, P Wally Whitehurst and P Kevin Tapani to Mets. ... Granted free agency (November 4, 1988). ... Signed by Cleveland Indians (December 3, 1988). ... Traded by Indians to Milwaukee Brewers for a player to be named later (December 6, 1991); deal settled in cash. ... Granted free agency (November 5, 1992). ... Re-signed by Brewers (December 4, 1992). ... Granted free agency (October 15, 1994). ... Signed by Baltimore Orioles (April 9, 1995). ... Granted free agency (October 27, 1996). ... Re-signed by Orioles (November 15, 1996).
MISCELLANEOUS: Appeared in one game as outfielder with one putout (1986). ... Struck out in only plate appearance (1993).

Year Team (League)	W	L	Pct.	ERA	G	GS	CG	ShO	Sv.	IP	H	R	ER	BB	SO
1978— Elizabethton (Appal.)	4	4	.500	1.13	20	0	0	0	6	40	29	7	5	20	48
1979— Tidewater (Int'l)■	4	4	.500	3.89	16	15	1	0	0	81	82	45	35	43	55
— New York (N.L.)	1	2	.333	4.89	18	2	0	0	0	35	33	20	19	22	22
1980— Jackson (Texas)	4	4	.500	3.68	37	1	0	0	3	71	52	36	29	62	85
1981— Tidewater (Int'l)	9	5	.643	3.31	46	10	0	0	8	87	80	39	32	32	81
— New York (N.L.)	0	1	.000	1.59	8	0	0	0	1	17	13	4	3	6	18
1982— New York (N.L.)	4	10	.286	2.72	54	2	0	0	4	109 1/3	92	37	33	40	89
1983— New York (N.L.)	13	7	.650	1.47	62	0	0	0	17	110	76	27	18	38	84
1984— New York (N.L.)	10	6	.625	2.59	60	0	0	0	31	87	58	29	25	34	85
1985— New York (N.L.)	8	6	.571	2.73	54	0	0	0	17	79	66	26	24	34	68
1986— New York (N.L.)	8	6	.571	2.33	58	0	0	0	21	81	64	23	21	35	62
1987— New York (N.L.)	3	9	.250	4.44	58	0	0	0	16	77	78	41	38	31	78
1988— Los Angeles (N.L.)■	3	2	.600	2.72	55	0	0	0	9	53	41	18	16	30	43
1989— Cleveland (A.L.)■	3	4	.429	2.08	69	0	0	0	3	78	54	20	18	26	79
1990— Cleveland (A.L.)	5	4	.556	3.90	55	0	0	0	2	64 2/3	58	35	28	38	55
1991— Cleveland (A.L.)	2	0	1.000	3.74	47	0	0	0	0	45 2/3	52	20	19	15	36
1992— Milwaukee (A.L.)■	3	1	.750	3.23	59	0	0	0	1	39	33	15	14	13	40
1993— Milwaukee (A.L.)	3	5	.375	3.18	57	0	0	0	8	56 2/3	47	25	20	17	67
1994— Milwaukee (A.L.)	3	1	.750	5.08	40	0	0	0	0	39	32	26	22	26	36
1995— Baltimore (A.L.)■	2	4	.333	3.26	*65	0	0	0	3	49 2/3	28	19	18	27	58
1996— Baltimore (A.L.)	3	1	.750	3.40	66	0	0	0	0	55 2/3	42	22	21	28	52
1997— Baltimore (A.L.)	6	3	.667	2.32	71	0	0	0	0	50 1/3	29	13	13	30	46
A.L. totals (9 years)	30	23	.566	3.25	529	0	0	0	17	478 2/3	375	195	173	220	469
N.L. totals (9 years)	50	49	.505	2.73	427	4	0	0	116	648 1/3	521	225	197	270	549
Major league totals (18 years)	80	72	.526	2.95	956	4	0	0	133	1127	896	420	370	490	1018

DIVISION SERIES RECORD

Year Team (League)	W	L	Pct.	ERA	G	GS	CG	ShO	Sv.	IP	H	R	ER	BB	SO
1996— Baltimore (A.L.)	0	1	.000	36.00	4	0	0	0	0	1	2	4	4	3	2
1997— Baltimore (A.L.)	0	0	...	0.00	2	0	0	0	0	1 1/3	1	0	0	0	1
Div. series totals (2 years)	0	1	.000	15.43	6	0	0	0	0	2 1/3	3	4	4	3	3

CHAMPIONSHIP SERIES RECORD

RECORDS: Holds single-series record for most games won—3 (1986).

Year Team (League)	W	L	Pct.	ERA	G	GS	CG	ShO	Sv.	IP	H	R	ER	BB	SO
1986— New York (N.L.)	3	0	1.000	3.38	4	0	0	0	0	8	5	3	3	2	10
1988— Los Angeles (N.L.)	0	0	...	7.71	4	0	0	0	0	2 1/3	4	2	2	3	0
1996— Baltimore (A.L.)	0	0	...	4.50	4	0	0	0	0	2	2	1	1	2	2
1997— Baltimore (A.L.)	0	0	...	0.00	2	0	0	0	0	1 1/3	0	0	0	1	1
Champ. series totals (4 years)	3	0	1.000	3.95	14	0	0	0	0	13 2/3	11	6	6	8	13

WORLD SERIES RECORD

NOTES: Member of World Series championship teams (1986 and 1988).

Year Team (League)	W	L	Pct.	ERA	G	GS	CG	ShO	Sv.	IP	H	R	ER	BB	SO
1986— New York (N.L.)	0	0	...	0.00	4	0	0	0	2	5 2/3	2	0	0	0	6
1988— Los Angeles (N.L.)							Did not play.								
World Series totals (1 year)	0	0	...	0.00	4	0	0	0	2	5 2/3	2	0	0	0	6

ALL-STAR GAME RECORD

Year League	W	L	Pct.	ERA	GS	CG	ShO	Sv.	IP	H	R	ER	BB	SO
1983— National	0	0	...	0.00	0	0	0	0	1/3	0	0	0	0	1
1984— National							Did not play.							
All-Star totals (1 year)	0	0	...	0.00	0	0	0	0	1/3	0	0	0	0	1

ORSULAK, JOE   OF

PERSONAL: Born May 31, 1962, in Glen Ridge, N.J. ... 6-1/210. ... Bats left, throws left. ... Full name: Joseph Michael Orsulak. ... Name pronounced OR-suh-lack.
HIGH SCHOOL: Parsippany (N.J.).
TRANSACTIONS/CAREER NOTES: Selected by Pittsburgh Pirates organization in sixth round of free-agent draft (June 3, 1980). ... On temporarily inactive list (July 10-27, 1981). ... On disabled list (May 25-June 9, 1985). ... On Pittsburgh disabled list (March 31-May 22, 1987); included rehabilitation assignment to Vancouver (May 4-22). ... Traded by Pirates to Baltimore Orioles for SS Terry Crowley Jr. and 3B Rico

Rossy (November 6, 1987). ... On disabled list (August 16-September 1, 1992). ... Granted free agency (October 28, 1992). ... Signed by New York Mets (December 18, 1992). ... Granted free agency (November 11, 1995). ... Signed by Florida Marlins (December 5, 1995). ... Traded by Marlins with P Dustin Hermanson to Montreal Expos for OF/1B Cliff Floyd (March 26, 1997). ... Granted free agency (October 6, 1997).
STATISTICAL NOTES: Tied for South Atlantic League lead in double plays by outfielder with four in 1981. ... Led Pacific Coast League outfielders with 367 total chances and eight double plays in 1983. ... Had 21-game hitting streak (August 2-25, 1991). ... Career major league grand slams: 2.

							BATTING							FIELDING		
Year Team (League)	Pos.	G	AB	R	H	2B	3B	HR	RBI	Avg.	BB	SO	SB	PO	A	E	Avg.
1981— Greenwood (SAL)......	OF	118	460	80	145	18	8	6	70	.315	29	32	18	249	16	4	*.985
1982— Alexandria (Caro.)	OF-1B	129	463	92	134	18	4	14	65	.289	47	46	28	286	7	10	.967
1983— Hawaii (PCL)	OF	139	538	87	154	12	•13	10	58	.286	48	41	38	*341	•18	8	.978
— Pittsburgh (N.L.)	OF	7	11	0	2	0	0	0	1	.182	0	2	0	2	2	0	1.000
1984— Hawaii (PCL)	OF	98	388	51	110	19	12	3	53	.284	29	38	14	258	6	2	.992
— Pittsburgh (N.L.)	OF	32	67	12	17	1	2	0	3	.254	1	7	3	41	1	0	1.000
1985— Pittsburgh (N.L.)	OF	121	397	54	119	14	6	0	21	.300	26	27	24	229	10	6	.976
1986— Pittsburgh (N.L.)	OF	138	401	60	100	19	6	2	19	.249	28	38	24	193	11	4	.981
1987— Vancouver (PCL)	OF	39	143	20	33	6	1	1	12	.231	17	21	2	58	2	2	.968
1988— Baltimore (A.L.)■........	OF	125	379	48	109	21	3	8	27	.288	23	30	9	228	6	5	.979
1989— Baltimore (A.L.)........	OF-DH	123	390	59	111	22	5	7	55	.285	41	35	5	250	10	4	.985
1990— Baltimore (A.L.)........	OF-DH	124	413	49	111	14	3	11	57	.269	46	48	6	267	5	3	.989
1991— Baltimore (A.L.)........	OF-DH	143	486	57	135	22	1	5	43	.278	28	45	6	273	*22	1	.997
1992— Baltimore (A.L.)........	OF-DH	117	391	45	113	18	3	4	39	.289	28	34	5	228	9	4	.983
1993— New York (N.L.)■.......	OF-1B	134	409	59	116	15	4	8	35	.284	28	25	5	231	10	5	.980
1994— New York (N.L.)........	OF-1B	96	292	39	76	3	0	8	42	.260	16	21	4	148	8	3	.981
1995— New York (N.L.)........	OF-1B	108	290	41	82	19	2	1	37	.283	19	35	1	111	4	4	.966
1996— Florida (N.L.)■.........	OF-1B	120	217	23	48	6	1	2	19	.221	16	38	1	84	7	4	.958
1997— Montreal (N.L.)■.......	OF-1B-DH	106	150	13	34	12	1	1	7	.227	18	17	0	153	13	1	.994
American League totals (5 years)		632	2059	258	579	97	15	35	221	.281	166	192	31	1246	52	17	.987
National League totals (9 years)		862	2234	301	594	89	22	22	184	.266	152	210	62	1192	66	27	.979
Major league totals (14 years)		1494	4293	559	1173	186	37	57	405	.273	318	402	93	2438	118	44	.983

ORTIZ, DAVID   1B   TWINS

PERSONAL: Born November 18, 1975, in Santo Domingo, Dominican Republic. ... 6-4/230. ... Bats left, throws left. ... Full name: David Americo Ortiz.
HIGH SCHOOL: Estudia Espallat (Dominican Republic).
TRANSACTIONS/CAREER NOTES: Signed as non-drafted free agent by Seattle Mariners organization (November 28, 1992). ... Traded by Mariners to Minnesota Twins (September 13, 1996); completing deal in which Twins traded 3B Dave Hollins to Mariners for a player to be named later (August 29, 1996).
STATISTICAL NOTES: Led Arizona League first basemen with 393 total chances in 1994.

							BATTING							FIELDING		
Year Team (League)	Pos.	G	AB	R	H	2B	3B	HR	RBI	Avg.	BB	SO	SB	PO	A	E	Avg.
1994— Ariz. Mariners (Ariz.)..	1B	53	167	14	41	10	1	2	20	.246	14	46	1	*372	15	6	.985
1995— Ariz. Mariners (Ariz.)..	1B	48	184	30	61	18	4	4	37	.332	23	52	2	436	*27	5	*.989
1996— Wis. Rap. (Mid.).........	1B-3B	129	485	89	156	34	2	18	93	.322	52	108	3	1126	80	13	.989
1997— Fort Myers (FSL).........	1B	61	239	45	79	15	0	13	58	.331	22	53	2	524	44	9	.984
— New Britain (Eastern).	1B	69	258	40	83	22	2	14	56	.322	21	78	2	268	16	3	.990
— Salt Lake (PCL)	1B	10	42	5	9	1	0	4	10	.214	2	11	0	71	2	0	1.000
— Minnesota (A.L.)	1B-DH	15	49	10	16	3	0	1	6	.327	2	19	0	84	10	1	.989
Major league totals (1 year)		15	49	10	16	3	0	1	6	.327	2	19	0	84	10	1	.989

ORTIZ, RAMON   P   ANGELS

PERSONAL: Born May 23, 1976, in Cotui, Dominican Republic. ... 6-0/165. ... Throws left, bats left. ... Full name: Ramon Diogenes Ortiz.
HIGH SCHOOL: 8th Intermedian (Dominican Republic).
TRANSACTIONS/CAREER NOTES: Signed as non-drafted free agent by California Angels organization (June 20, 1995). ... Angels franchise renamed Anaheim Angels for 1997 season.
STATISTICAL NOTES: Pitched 12-0 no-hit victory against Quad City (August 7, 1997).

Year Team (League)	W	L	Pct.	ERA	G	GS	CG	ShO	Sv.	IP	H	R	ER	BB	SO
1996— Arizona Angels(Arizona).....	5	4	.556	2.12	16	8	2	2	1	68	55	28	16	27	78
— Boise (Northwest)	1	1	.500	3.66	3	3	0	0	0	19²/₃	21	10	8	6	18
1997— Cedar Rapids (Midw.)	11	10	.524	3.58	27	•27	*8	*4	0	181	156	78	72	53	*225

ORTIZ, RUSS   P   GIANTS

PERSONAL: Born June 5, 1974, in Encino, Calif. ... 6-1/190. ... Throws right, bats right. ... Full name: Russell R. Ortiz.
HIGH SCHOOL: Montclair Prep (Van Nuys, Calif.).
COLLEGE: Oklahoma.
TRANSACTIONS/CAREER NOTES: Selected by San Francisco Giants organization in fourth round of free-agent draft (June 1, 1995).

Year Team (League)	W	L	Pct.	ERA	G	GS	CG	ShO	Sv.	IP	H	R	ER	BB	SO
1995— Bellingham (N'west)..........	2	0	1.000	0.52	25	0	0	0	11	34¹/₃	19	4	2	13	55
— San Jose (California)..........	0	1	.000	1.50	5	0	0	0	0	6	4	1	1	2	7
1996— San Jose (California)..........	0	0	. . .	0.25	34	0	0	0	23	36²/₃	16	2	1	20	63
— Shreveport (Texas).............	1	2	.333	4.05	26	0	0	0	13	26²/₃	22	14	12	21	29
1997— Shreveport (Texas).............	2	3	.400	4.13	12	12	0	0	0	56²/₃	52	28	26	37	50
— Phoenix (PCL)	4	3	.571	5.51	14	14	0	0	0	85	96	57	52	34	70

O

OSBORNE, DONOVAN   P   CARDINALS

PERSONAL: Born June 21, 1969, in Roseville, Calif. ... 6-2/195. ... Throws left, bats left. ... Full name: Donovan Alan Osborne.
HIGH SCHOOL: Carson (Carson City, Nev.).
COLLEGE: UNLV.
TRANSACTIONS/CAREER NOTES: Selected by Montreal Expos organization in ninth round of free-agent draft (June 2, 1987); did not sign. ... Selected by St. Louis Cardinals organization in first round (13th pick overall) of free-agent draft (June 4, 1990). ... On St. Louis disabled list (April 2, 1994-entire season). ... On St. Louis disabled list (May 15-July 14, 1995); included rehabilitation assignments to Arkansas and Louisville (June 28-July 14). ... On St. Louis disabled list (March 25-April 17, 1996); included rehabilitation assignments to St. Petersburg (April 7-12) and Louisville (April 12-17). ... On St. Louis disabled list (May 3-July 29, 1997).
HONORS: Named lefthanded pitcher on THE SPORTING NEWS college All-America team (1989).
STATISTICAL NOTES: Career major league grand slams: 1.
MISCELLANEOUS: Appeared in three games as pinch-runner (1993).

Year — Team (League)	W	L	Pct.	ERA	G	GS	CG	ShO	Sv.	IP	H	R	ER	BB	SO
1990— Hamilton (NYP)	0	2	.000	3.60	4	4	0	0	0	20	21	8	8	5	14
— Savannah (S. Atl.)	2	2	.500	2.61	6	6	1	0	0	41 1/3	40	20	12	7	28
1991— Arkansas (Texas)	8	12	.400	3.63	26	26	3	0	0	166	178	82	67	43	130
1992— St. Louis (N.L.)	11	9	.550	3.77	34	29	0	0	0	179	193	91	75	38	104
1993— St. Louis (N.L.)	10	7	.588	3.76	26	26	1	0	0	155 2/3	153	73	65	47	83
1994— St. Louis (N.L.)							Did not play.								
1995— St. Louis (N.L.)	4	6	.400	3.81	19	19	0	0	0	113 1/3	112	58	48	34	82
— Arkansas (Texas)	0	1	.000	2.45	2	2	0	0	0	11	12	4	3	2	6
— Louisville (A.A.)	0	1	.000	3.86	1	1	0	0	0	7	8	3	3	0	3
1996— St. Petersburg (FSL)	1	0	1.000	0.00	1	1	0	0	0	6	2	0	0	0	2
— Louisville (A.A.)	1	0	1.000	2.57	1	1	0	0	0	7	6	2	2	2	3
— St. Louis (N.L.)	13	9	.591	3.53	30	30	2	1	0	198 2/3	191	87	78	57	134
1997— St. Louis (N.L.)	3	7	.300	4.93	14	14	0	0	0	80 1/3	84	46	44	23	51
— Louisville (A.A.)	0	1	.000	4.73	3	3	0	0	0	13 1/3	13	7	7	5	13
Major league totals (5 years)	**41**	**38**	**.519**	**3.84**	**123**	**118**	**3**	**1**	**0**	**727**	**733**	**355**	**310**	**199**	**454**

DIVISION SERIES RECORD

Year — Team (League)	W	L	Pct.	ERA	G	GS	CG	ShO	Sv.	IP	H	R	ER	BB	SO
1996— St. Louis (N.L.)	0	0	...	9.00	1	1	0	0	0	4	7	4	4	0	5

CHAMPIONSHIP SERIES RECORD

Year — Team (League)	W	L	Pct.	ERA	G	GS	CG	ShO	Sv.	IP	H	R	ER	BB	SO
1996— St. Louis (N.L.)	1	1	.500	9.39	2	2	0	0	0	7 2/3	12	8	8	4	6

OSIK, KEITH   C   PIRATES

PERSONAL: Born October 22, 1968, in Port Jefferson, N.Y. ... 6-0/190. ... Bats right, throws right. ... Full name: Keith Richard Osik. ... Name pronounced OH-sik.
HIGH SCHOOL: Shoreham (N.Y.) Wading River.
COLLEGE: Louisiana State.
TRANSACTIONS/CAREER NOTES: Selected by Texas Rangers organization in 47th round of free-agent draft (June 2, 1987); did not sign. ... Selected by Pittsburgh Pirates organization in 24th round of free-agent draft (June 4, 1990). ... On Pittsburgh disabled list (July 16-August 13, 1996); included rehabilitation assignment to Erie (August 10-13).

						BATTING									FIELDING		
Year — Team (League)	Pos.	G	AB	R	H	2B	3B	HR	RBI	Avg.	BB	SO	SB	PO	A	E	Avg.
1990— Welland (NYP)	3-C-1-2-S	29	97	13	27	4	0	1	20	.278	11	12	2	59	29	2	.978
1991— Salem (Carolina)	C-3B-2B	87	300	31	81	12	1	6	35	.270	38	48	2	307	85	12	.970
— Carolina (Southern)	C-3B	17	43	9	13	3	1	0	5	.302	5	5	0	84	13	2	.980
1992— Carolina (Southern)	3-C-2-P	129	425	41	110	17	1	5	45	.259	52	69	2	222	195	19	.956
1993— Carolina (Southern)	C-3B	103	371	47	104	21	2	10	47	.280	30	46	0	662	69	6	.992
1994— Buffalo (A.A.)	C-0-1-P-2	83	260	27	55	16	0	5	33	.212	28	41	0	403	50	8	.983
1995— Calgary (PCL)	C-1-O-P-3	90	301	40	101	25	1	10	59	.336	21	42	2	458	35	4	.992
1996— Pittsburgh (N.L.)	C-3B-OF	48	140	18	41	14	1	1	14	.293	14	22	1	237	25	6	.978
— Erie (N.Y.-Penn)	C	3	10	1	3	1	0	0	2	.300	1	2	0	19	2	0	1.000
1997— Pittsburgh (N.L.)	C-2-1-3	49	105	10	27	9	1	0	7	.257	9	21	0	163	14	2	.989
Major league totals (2 years)		**97**	**245**	**28**	**68**	**23**	**2**	**1**	**21**	**.278**	**23**	**43**	**1**	**400**	**39**	**8**	**.982**

RECORD AS PITCHER

Year — Team (League)	W	L	Pct.	ERA	G	GS	CG	ShO	Sv.	IP	H	R	ER	BB	SO
1992— Carolina (Southern)	0	0	...	0.00	2	0	0	0	0	2 2/3	2	0	0	0	3
1994— Buffalo (A.A.)	0	1	.000	13.50	1	0	0	0	0	2/3	2	1	1	0	1
1995— Calgary (PCL)	0	0	...	4.50	2	0	0	0	0	2	1	1	1	1	3

OSUNA, ANTONIO   P   DODGERS

PERSONAL: Born April 12, 1973, in Sinaloa, Mexico. ... 5-11/160. ... Throws right, bats right. ... Full name: Antonio Pedro Osuna.
HIGH SCHOOL: Secondaria Federal (Mexico).
TRANSACTIONS/CAREER NOTES: Signed as non-drafted free agent by Los Angeles Dodgers organization (June 12, 1991). ... On suspended list (April 8-July 17, 1993). ... On San Antonio disabled list (April 8-June 6, 1994). ... On Los Angeles disabled list (May 19-June 16, 1995); included rehabilitation assignment to San Bernardino (June 6-16).

Year — Team (League)	W	L	Pct.	ERA	G	GS	CG	ShO	Sv.	IP	H	R	ER	BB	SO
1991— GC Dodgers (GCL)	0	0	...	0.82	8	0	0	0	4	11	8	5	1	0	13
— Yakima (N'west)	0	0	...	3.20	13	0	0	0	5	25 1/3	18	10	9	8	39
1992— M.C. Tigers (Mex.)	13	7	.650	4.05	28	26	3	1	0	166 2/3	181	80	75	74	129
1993— Bakersfield (California)	0	2	.000	4.91	14	2	0	0	2	18 1/3	19	10	10	5	20

O

Year Team (League)	W	L	Pct.	ERA	G	GS	CG	ShO	Sv.	IP	H	R	ER	BB	SO
1994—San Antonio (Tex.)	1	2	.333	0.98	35	0	0	0	19	46	19	6	5	18	53
—Albuquerque (PCL)	0	0	...	0.00	6	0	0	0	4	6	5	1	0	1	8
1995—Los Angeles (N.L.)	2	4	.333	4.43	39	0	0	0	0	44 2/3	39	22	22	20	46
—San Bernardino (Calif.)	0	0	...	1.29	5	0	0	0	0	7	3	1	1	5	11
—Albuquerque (PCL)	0	1	.000	4.42	19	0	0	0	11	18 1/3	15	9	9	9	19
1996—Albuquerque (PCL)	0	0	...	0.00	1	0	0	0	0	1	2	0	0	0	1
—Los Angeles (N.L.)	9	6	.600	3.00	73	0	0	0	4	84	65	33	28	32	85
1997—Albuquerque (PCL)	1	1	.500	1.93	13	0	0	0	6	14	9	3	3	4	26
—Los Angeles (N.L.)	3	4	.429	2.19	48	0	0	0	0	61 2/3	46	15	15	19	68
Major league totals (3 years)	14	14	.500	3.07	160	0	0	0	4	190 1/3	150	70	65	71	199

DIVISION SERIES RECORD

Year Team (League)	W	L	Pct.	ERA	G	GS	CG	ShO	Sv.	IP	H	R	ER	BB	SO
1995—Los Angeles (N.L.)	0	1	.000	2.70	3	0	0	0	0	3 1/3	3	1	1	1	3
1996—Los Angeles (N.L.)	0	1	.000	4.50	2	0	0	0	0	2	3	1	1	1	4
Div. series totals (2 years)	0	2	.000	3.38	5	0	0	0	0	5 1/3	6	2	2	2	7

OTANEZ, WILLIS — 3B

PERSONAL: Born April 19, 1973, in Cotui, Dominican Republic. ... 5-11/150. ... Bats right, throws right. ... Full name: Willis A. Otanez.
HIGH SCHOOL: Liceo Miguel Angel Garcia (Cotui, Dominican Republic).
TRANSACTIONS/CAREER NOTES: Signed as non-drafted free agent by Los Angeles Dodgers organization (February 10, 1990). ... On disabled list (August 3-September 10, 1993). ... Traded by Dodgers with 2B Miguel Cairo to Seattle Mariners for 3B Mike Blowers (November 29, 1995). ... Claimed on waivers by Baltimore Orioles (February 12, 1996). ... On Rochester disabled list (May 15-July 24, 1997). ... Granted free agency (December 21, 1997).
STATISTICAL NOTES: Led Eastern League second basemen with 106 putouts in 1996.

Year Team (League)	Pos.	G	AB	R	H	2B	3B	HR	RBI	Avg.	BB	SO	SB	PO	A	E	Avg.
1990—Dom. Dodgers (DSL)	...	70	267	44	84	18	0	1	46	.315	51	24	4	...	...	...	...
1991—Great Falls (Pio.)	SS-3B	58	222	38	64	9	2	6	39	.288	19	34	3	...	...	...	...
1992—Vero Beach (FSL)	SS-3B	117	390	27	86	18	0	3	27	.221	24	60	2	64	124	22	.895
1993—Bakersfield (Calif.)	3B-SS-2B	95	325	34	85	11	2	10	39	.262	29	63	1	76	211	25	.920
1994—Vero Beach (FSL)	3B	131	476	77	132	27	1	19	72	.277	53	98	4	*109	302	23	.947
1995—Vero Beach (FSL)	3B	92	354	39	92	24	0	10	53	.260	28	59	1	59	186	20	.925
—San Antonio (Tex.)	3B	27	100	8	24	4	1	1	7	.240	6	25	0	18	48	3	.957
1996—Bowie (Eastern)■	3B-SS	138	506	60	134	27	2	24	75	.265	45	97	3	†106	279	24	.941
1997—Rochester (Int'l)	3B-1B	49	168	20	35	9	0	5	25	.208	15	35	0	67	68	12	.918
—Bowie (Eastern)	3B	19	78	13	26	9	0	3	13	.333	9	19	0	1	20	1	.955
—GC Orioles (GCL)	DH	8	25	5	8	2	0	2	3	.320	2	4	0	...	...	...	...

OTERO, RICKY — OF — PHILLIES

PERSONAL: Born April 15, 1972, in Vega Baja, Puerto Rico. ... 5-5/150. ... Bats both, throws right. ... Full name: Ricardo Otero.
HIGH SCHOOL: Lino Padron Rivera (Vega Baja, Puerto Rico).
TRANSACTIONS/CAREER NOTES: Selected by Toronto Blue Jays organization in 65th round of free-agent draft (June 5, 1989); did not sign. ... Selected by New York Mets organization in 45th round of free-agent draft (June 4, 1990). ... On suspended list (April 17-29 and August 27-29, 1994). ... Traded by Mets to Philadelphia Phillies for OF Phil Geisler (December 14, 1995). ... On Scranton/Wilkes-Barre disabled list (April 6-25, 1997).
STATISTICAL NOTES: Led Appalachian League with six sacrifice flies and tied for league lead with five intentional bases on balls received and two double plays by outfielder in 1991. ... Tied for International League lead in caught stealing with 13 in 1995. ... Led International League outfielders with five double plays in 1995.

Year Team (League)	Pos.	G	AB	R	H	2B	3B	HR	RBI	Avg.	BB	SO	SB	PO	A	E	Avg.
1991—Kingsport (Appal.)	OF	66	236	47	*81	16	3	7	52	*.343	35	32	12	122	7	2	.985
—Pittsfield (NYP)	OF	6	24	4	7	0	0	0	2	.292	2	1	4	11	1	1	.923
1992—Columbia (S. Atl.)	OF	90	353	57	106	24	4	8	60	.300	38	53	39	203	15	10	.956
—St. Lucie (Fla. St.)	OF	40	151	20	48	8	4	0	19	.318	9	11	10	94	6	1	.990
1993—Binghamton (East.)	OF	124	503	63	133	21	10	2	54	.264	38	57	29	238	9	6	.976
1994—Binghamton (East.)	OF	128	531	96	156	31	*9	7	57	.294	50	49	33	264	6	4	.985
1995—New York (N.L.)	OF	35	51	5	7	2	0	0	1	.137	3	10	2	31	1	0	1.000
—Norfolk (Int'l)	OF	72	295	37	79	8	6	1	23	.268	27	33	16	147	12	5	.970
1996—Scran./W.B. (Int'l)■	OF	46	177	38	53	9	8	1	9	.299	28	13	15	121	4	3	.977
—Philadelphia (N.L.)	OF	104	411	54	112	11	7	2	32	.273	34	30	16	247	8	4	.985
1997—Scran./W.B. (Int'l)	OF	38	160	24	53	10	5	1	15	.331	13	13	5	90	5	2	.979
—Philadelphia (N.L.)	OF	50	151	20	38	6	2	0	3	.252	19	15	0	95	4	0	1.000
Major league totals (3 years)		189	613	79	157	19	9	2	36	.256	56	55	18	373	13	4	.990

OWENS, ERIC — IF/OF — REDS

PERSONAL: Born February 3, 1971, in Danville, Va. ... 6-1/185. ... Bats right, throws right. ... Full name: Eric Blake Owens.
HIGH SCHOOL: Tunstall (Dry Fork, Va.).
COLLEGE: Ferrum (Va.).
TRANSACTIONS/CAREER NOTES: Selected by Cincinnati Reds organization in fourth round of free-agent draft (June 1, 1992). ... On Indianapolis disabled list (August 20-September 11, 1995).
HONORS: Named American Association Most Valuable Player (1995).
STATISTICAL NOTES: Led Pioneer League shortstops with 29 errors in 1992. ... Tied for American Association lead in errors by second baseman with 17 in 1997.

O

Year Team (League)	Pos.	G	AB	R	H	2B	3B	HR	RBI	Avg.	BB	SO	SB	PO	A	E	Avg.
1992—Billings (Pioneer)........	SS-3B	67	239	41	72	10	3	3	26	.301	23	22	15	82	164	†29	.895
1993—Win.-Salem (Car.).......	SS	122	487	74	132	25	4	10	63	.271	53	69	21	*215	347	34	.943
1994—Chattanooga (Sou.).....	3B-2B	134	523	73	133	17	3	3	36	.254	54	86	38	151	266	40	.912
1995—Indianapolis (A.A.).....	2B	108	427	*86	134	24	•8	12	63	.314	52	61	*33	219	274	*17	.967
—Cincinnati (N.L.)........	3B	2	2	0	2	0	0	0	1	1.000	0	0	0	0	0	0	...
1996—Indianapolis (A.A.).....	S-3-2-0	33	128	24	41	8	2	4	14	.320	11	16	6	44	64	6	.947
—Cincinnati (N.L.)........	OF-2B-3B	88	205	26	41	6	0	0	9	.200	23	38	16	76	14	2	.978
1997—Cincinnati (N.L.)........	OF-2B	27	57	8	15	0	0	0	3	.263	4	11	3	15	0	1	.938
—Indianapolis (A.A.).....	2-S-O-3	104	391	56	112	15	4	11	44	.286	42	55	23	184	241	‡27	.940
Major league totals (3 years)		117	264	34	58	6	0	0	13	.220	27	49	19	91	14	3	.972

PADILLA, ROY   OF   RED SOX

PERSONAL: Born August 4, 1975, in Panama City, Panama. ... 6-5/225. ... Bats left, throws left. ... Full name: Roy R. Padilla.
TRANSACTIONS/CAREER NOTES: Signed as non-drafted free agent by Boston Red Sox organization (September 30, 1992).
STATISTICAL NOTES: Led Florida State League outfielders with 347 total chances in 1997.

Year Team (League)	Pos.	G	AB	R	H	2B	3B	HR	RBI	Avg.	BB	SO	SB	PO	A	E	Avg.
1996—Sarasota (Fla. St.)	OF	8	27	2	8	2	0	0	2	.296	2	3	4	17	0	1	.944
—Michigan (Midwest) ...	OF	103	386	58	108	20	6	2	40	.280	34	56	21	225	5	8	.966
1997—Sarasota (Fla. St.)	OF	130	463	66	114	16	4	2	38	.246	41	80	24	*327	9	11	.968

RECORD AS PITCHER

Year Team (League)	W	L	Pct.	ERA	G	GS	CG	ShO	Sv.	IP	H	R	ER	BB	SO
1993—GC Red Sox (GCL)	0	1	.000	2.35	13	1	0	0	0	30²/₃	25	10	8	17	18
1994—GC Red Sox (GCL)	6	1	.857	2.99	15	12	0	0	1	72¹/₃	68	39	24	34	52
1995—Michigan (Midwest)	0	1	.000	6.48	4	1	0	0	0	8¹/₃	10	9	6	7	7
—Butte (Pioneer).................	2	7	.222	5.91	15	14	0	0	0	70	80	60	46	54	49

PAGNOZZI, TOM   C   CARDINALS

PERSONAL: Born July 30, 1962, in Tucson, Ariz. ... 6-1/195. ... Bats right, throws right. ... Full name: Thomas Alan Pagnozzi. ... Brother of Tim Pagnozzi, minor league shortstop (1976); and brother of Mike Pagnozzi, minor league pitcher (1975-78). ... Name pronounced pag-NAHZ-ee.
HIGH SCHOOL: Rincon (Tucson, Ariz.).
JUNIOR COLLEGE: Central Arizona College.
COLLEGE: Arkansas.
TRANSACTIONS/CAREER NOTES: Selected by Milwaukee Brewers organization in 24th round of free-agent draft (January 12, 1982); did not sign. ... Selected by St. Louis Cardinals organization in eighth round of free-agent draft (June 6, 1983). ... On St. Louis disabled list (May 8-June 17, 1993); included rehabilitation assignment to Louisville (June 2-17). ... On St. Louis disabled list (March 29-May 5, 1994); included rehabilitation assignment to Louisville (April 23-May 5). ... On St. Louis disabled list (July 18-August 26, 1995); included rehabilitation assignment to Louisville (August 17-26). ... On St. Louis disabled list (March 24-April 15, 1996); included rehabilitation assignment to Louisville (April 4-15). ... Granted free agency (October 31, 1996). ... Re-signed by Cardinals (December 6, 1996). ... On St. Louis disabled list (March 29-April 25 and April 30-August 11, 1997); included rehabilitation assignment to Arkansas (April 19-25).
HONORS: Won N.L. Gold Glove at catcher (1991-92 and 1994).
STATISTICAL NOTES: Led N.L. catchers with .998 fielding percentage in 1994. ... Career major league grand slams: 2.

Year Team (League)	Pos.	G	AB	R	H	2B	3B	HR	RBI	Avg.	BB	SO	SB	PO	A	E	Avg.
1983—Erie (N.Y.-Penn).........	C	45	168	28	52	9	1	6	22	.310	14	34	3	183	20	3	.985
—Macon (S. Atl.)........	C	18	57	7	14	2	1	0	6	.246	6	13	0	125	18	8	.947
1984—Springfield (Midw.)	C	114	396	57	112	20	4	10	68	.283	31	75	3	667	*90	12	.984
1985—Arkansas (Texas).......	C-1B	41	139	15	43	7	1	5	29	.309	13	21	0	243	27	1	.996
—Louisville (A.A.)..........	C	76	268	29	72	13	2	5	40	.269	21	47	0	266	25	4	.986
1986—Louisville (A.A.)..........	C	30	106	12	31	4	0	1	18	.292	6	21	0	160	19	3	.984
1987—Louisville (A.A.)..........	C-3B	84	320	53	100	20	2	14	71	.313	30	50	0	427	43	6	.987
—St. Louis (N.L.)..........	C-1B	27	48	8	9	1	0	2	9	.188	4	13	1	61	5	0	1.000
1988—St. Louis (N.L.)..........	1B-C-3B	81	195	17	55	9	0	0	15	.282	11	32	0	340	30	4	.989
1989—St. Louis (N.L.)..........	C-1B-3B	52	80	3	12	2	0	0	3	.150	6	19	0	100	9	2	.982
1990—St. Louis (N.L.)..........	C-1B	69	220	20	61	15	0	2	23	.277	14	37	1	345	39	4	.990
1991—St. Louis (N.L.)..........	C-1B	140	459	38	121	24	5	2	57	.264	36	63	9	682	81	7	.991
1992—St. Louis (N.L.)..........	C	139	485	33	121	26	3	7	44	.249	28	64	2	688	53	1	*.999
1993—St. Louis (N.L.)..........	C	92	330	31	85	15	1	7	41	.258	19	30	1	421	44	4	.991
—Louisville (A.A.)..........	C	12	43	5	12	3	0	1	1	.279	2	3	0	51	6	2	.966
1994—Louisville (A.A.)..........	C	10	25	4	6	3	0	0	3	.240	6	6	0	32	3	0	1.000
—St. Louis (N.L.)..........	C-1B	70	243	21	66	12	1	7	40	.272	21	39	0	370	41	1	†.998
1995—St. Louis (N.L.)..........	C	62	219	17	47	14	1	2	15	.215	11	31	0	336	38	2	.995
—Louisville (A.A.)..........	C	5	16	4	8	2	0	1	3	.500	1	0	0	19	0	0	1.000
1996—Louisville (A.A.)..........	C	8	26	5	4	0	0	2	3	.154	3	2	0	36	5	0	1.000
—St. Louis (N.L.)..........	C-1B	119	407	48	110	23	0	13	55	.270	24	78	4	717	48	8	.990
1997—Arkansas (Texas).......	C	21	63	8	20	0	0	5	17	.317	4	8	0	68	4	1	.986
—St. Louis (N.L.)..........	C-1B-3B	25	50	4	11	3	0	1	8	.220	1	7	0	63	2	0	1.000
—Louisville (A.A.)..........	C	3	5	0	0	0	0	0	0	.000	0	1	0	8	3	0	1.000
Major league totals (11 years)		876	2736	240	698	144	11	43	310	.255	175	413	18	4123	390	33	.993

DIVISION SERIES RECORD

Year Team (League)	Pos.	G	AB	R	H	2B	3B	HR	RBI	Avg.	BB	SO	SB	PO	A	E	Avg.
1996—St. Louis (N.L.)..........	C	3	11	0	3	0	0	0	2	.273	2	3	0	28	0	0	1.000

O
P

CHAMPIONSHIP SERIES RECORD

						BATTING									FIELDING		
Year Team (League)	Pos.	G	AB	R	H	2B	3B	HR	RBI	Avg.	BB	SO	SB	PO	A	E	Avg.
1987— St. Louis (N.L.).............	PH	1	1	0	0	0	0	0	0	.000	0	0	0	...	...	...	...
1996— St. Louis (N.L.).............	C	7	19	1	3	1	0	0	1	.158	1	4	0	49	1	0	1.000
Championship series totals (2 years)		8	20	1	3	1	0	0	1	.150	1	4	0	49	1	0	1.000

WORLD SERIES RECORD

						BATTING									FIELDING		
Year Team (League)	Pos.	G	AB	R	H	2B	3B	HR	RBI	Avg.	BB	SO	SB	PO	A	E	Avg.
1987— St. Louis (N.L.)...........	DH-PH	2	4	0	1	0	0	0	0	.250	0	0	0	...	...	...	...

ALL-STAR GAME RECORD

					BATTING									FIELDING		
Year League	Pos.	AB	R	H	2B	3B	HR	RBI	Avg.	BB	SO	SB	PO	A	E	Avg.
1992— National.....................	PH	1	0	0	0	0	0	0	.000	0	0	0	...	...	...	...

PAINTER, LANCE   P   CARDINALS

PERSONAL: Born July 21, 1967, in Bedford, England. ... 6-1/197. ... Throws left, bats left. ... Full name: Lance T. Painter.
HIGH SCHOOL: Nicolet (Glendale, Wis.).
COLLEGE: Wisconsin.
TRANSACTIONS/CAREER NOTES: Selected by San Diego Padres organization in 25th round of free-agent draft (June 4, 1990). ... Selected by Colorado Rockies in second round (34th pick overall) of expansion draft (November 17, 1992). ... On disabled list (April 17-May 6, 1995). ... On disabled list (August 6, 1996-remainder of season). ... Claimed on waivers by St. Louis Cardinals (December 2, 1996). ... On disabled list (April 5-May 12 and May 20-June 20, 1997); included rehabilitation assignment to Louisville (May 1-12).
STATISTICAL NOTES: Led Texas League with 10 hit batsmen in 1992.
MISCELLANEOUS: Received base on balls in only appearance as pinch-hitter with Colorado (1995). ... Struck out twice in two games as pinch-hitter (1996).

Year Team (League)	W	L	Pct.	ERA	G	GS	CG	ShO	Sv.	IP	H	R	ER	BB	SO
1990— Spokane (N'west)..........	7	3	.700	1.51	23	1	0	0	3	71²/₃	45	18	12	15	104
1991— Waterloo (Midw.)..........	14	8	.636	2.30	28	28	7	*4	0	200	162	64	51	57	201
1992— Wichita (Texas)	10	5	*.667	3.53	27	•27	1	1	0	163¹/₃	138	74	64	55	137
1993— Colo. Springs (PCL)■.....	9	7	.563	4.30	23	22	•4	1	0	138	165	90	66	44	91
— Colorado (N.L.)	2	2	.500	6.00	10	6	1	0	0	39	52	26	26	9	16
1994— Colo. Springs (PCL)	4	3	.571	4.79	13	13	1	0	0	71¹/₃	83	42	38	28	59
— Colorado (N.L.)	4	6	.400	6.11	15	14	0	0	0	73²/₃	91	51	50	26	41
1995— Colorado (N.L.)	3	0	1.000	4.37	33	1	0	0	1	45¹/₃	55	23	22	10	36
— Colo. Springs (PCL)	0	3	.000	5.96	11	4	0	0	0	25²/₃	32	20	17	11	12
1996— Colorado (N.L.)	4	2	.667	5.86	34	1	0	0	0	50²/₃	56	37	33	25	48
1997— St. Louis (N.L.)■..........	1	1	.500	4.76	14	0	0	0	0	17	13	9	9	8	11
— Louisville (A.A.)...............	1	0	1.000	5.23	18	2	0	0	0	20²/₃	18	14	12	4	22
Major league totals (5 years)......	14	11	.560	5.58	106	22	1	0	1	225²/₃	267	146	140	78	152

DIVISION SERIES RECORD

NOTES: Struck out in only appearance as pinch-hitter (1995).

Year Team (League)	W	L	Pct.	ERA	G	GS	CG	ShO	Sv.	IP	H	R	ER	BB	SO
1995— Colorado (N.L.)	0	0	...	5.40	1	1	0	0	0	5	5	3	3	2	4

PALL, DONN   P

PERSONAL: Born January 11, 1962, in Chicago. ... 6-1/179. ... Throws right, bats right. ... Full name: Donn Steven Pall.
HIGH SCHOOL: Evergreen Park (Ill.).
COLLEGE: Illinois (received degree, 1985).
TRANSACTIONS/CAREER NOTES: Selected by Chicago White Sox organization in 23rd round of free-agent draft (June 3, 1985). ... On Chicago disabled list (May 19-June 2, 1989); included rehabilitation assignment to South Bend (May 30-June 2). ... Traded by White Sox to Philadelphia Phillies for a player to be named later (September 1, 1993); White Sox acquired C Doug Lindsey to complete deal (September 8, 1993). ... Granted free agency (December 20, 1993). ... Signed by New York Yankees (January 16, 1994). ... Released by Yankees (July 29, 1994). ... Signed by Chicago Cubs (August 6, 1994). ... Granted free agency (October 21, 1994). ... Signed by Nashville, White Sox organization (March 27, 1995). ... Granted free agency (October 16, 1995). ... Signed by Charlotte, Florida Marlins organization (April 25, 1996). ... Granted free agency (October 15, 1996). ... Re-signed by Marlins (January 2, 1997). ... Granted free agency (October 15, 1997).

Year Team (League)	W	L	Pct.	ERA	G	GS	CG	ShO	Sv.	IP	H	R	ER	BB	SO
1985— GC White Sox (GCL)	•7	5	.583	1.67	13	13	•4	•2	0	*86	68	34	16	10	63
1986— Appleton (Midwest)..........	5	5	.500	2.31	11	11	3	1	0	78	71	29	20	14	51
— Birmingham (Southern)	3	4	.429	4.44	21	9	0	0	1	73	77	38	36	27	41
1987— Birmingham (Southern)	8	11	.421	4.27	30	23	3	0	0	158	173	100	75	63	139
1988— Vancouver (PCL)	5	2	.714	2.23	44	0	0	0	10	72²/₃	61	21	18	20	41
— Chicago (A.L.)	0	2	.000	3.45	17	0	0	0	0	28²/₃	39	11	11	8	16
1989— Chicago (A.L.)	4	5	.444	3.31	53	0	0	0	6	87	90	35	32	19	58
— South Bend (Mid.)...........	0	0	...	0.00	2	0	0	0	0	3¹/₃	1	0	0	0	4
1990— Chicago (A.L.)	3	5	.375	3.32	56	0	0	0	2	76	63	33	28	24	39
1991— Chicago (A.L.)	7	2	.778	2.41	51	0	0	0	0	71	59	22	19	20	40
1992— Chicago (A.L.)	5	2	.714	4.93	39	0	0	0	1	73	79	43	40	27	27
1993— Chicago (A.L.)	2	3	.400	3.22	39	0	0	0	0	58²/₃	62	25	21	11	29
— Philadelphia (N.L.)■.........	1	0	1.000	2.55	8	0	0	0	0	17²/₃	15	7	5	3	11
1994— New York (A.L.)■.............	1	2	.333	3.60	26	0	0	0	0	35	43	18	14	9	21
— Chicago (N.L.)	0	0	...	4.50	2	0	0	0	0	4	2	2	2	1	2
1995— Nashville (A.A.)■..............	4	3	.571	3.98	44	0	0	0	3	86	89	40	38	20	79
1996— Charlotte (Int'l)■..............	3	3	.500	2.96	38	0	0	0	17	51²/₃	42	21	17	12	53
— Florida (N.L.)	1	1	.500	5.79	12	0	0	0	0	18²/₃	16	15	12	9	9

P

Year— Team (League)	W	L	Pct.	ERA	G	GS	CG	ShO	Sv.	IP	H	R	ER	BB	SO
1997— Charlotte (Int'l)	4	7	.364	3.39	59	0	0	0	8	79²/₃	82	40	30	11	70
— Florida (N.L.)	0	0	...	3.86	2	0	0	0	0	2¹/₃	3	1	1	1	0
A.L. totals (7 years)	22	21	.512	3.46	281	0	0	0	10	429¹/₃	435	187	165	118	230
N.L. totals (4 years)	2	1	.667	4.22	24	0	0	0	0	42²/₃	42	25	20	14	22
Major league totals (9 years)	24	22	.522	3.53	305	0	0	0	10	472	477	212	185	132	252

PALMEIRO, ORLANDO   OF   ANGELS

PERSONAL: Born January 19, 1969, in Hoboken, N.J. ... 5-11/155. ... Bats left, throws right. ... Cousin of Rafael Palmeiro, first baseman, Baltimore Orioles. ... Name pronounced pal-MAIR-oh.
HIGH SCHOOL: Southridge (Miami).
JUNIOR COLLEGE: Miami-Dade (South) Community College.
COLLEGE: Miami (Fla.).
TRANSACTIONS/CAREER NOTES: Selected by California Angels organization in 33rd round of free-agent draft (June 3, 1991). ... On disabled list (September 1-26, 1994). ... Angels franchise renamed Anaheim Angels for 1997 season. ... On disabled list (August 23-September 7, 1997).
STATISTICAL NOTES: Tied for Northwest League lead in double plays by outfielder with two in 1991. ... Led Texas League with 18 sacrifice hits in 1993. ... Led Texas League outfielders with 328 total chances in 1993. ... Led Pacific Coast League in caught stealing with 16 in 1994. ... Led Pacific Coast League with 11 sacrifice hits in 1995.

Year— Team (League)	Pos.	G	AB	R	H	2B	3B	HR	RBI	Avg.	BB	SO	SB	PO	A	E	Avg.
1991— Boise (Northwest)	OF	70	277	56	77	11	2	1	24	.278	33	22	8	130	8	2	*.986
1992— Quad City (Midwest)	OF	127	451	83	143	22	4	0	41	*.317	56	41	31	211	9	6	.973
1993— Midland (Texas)	OF	131	*535	85	163	19	5	0	64	.305	42	35	18	*307	12	9	.973
1994— Vancouver (PCL)	OF	117	458	79	150	28	4	1	47	.328	58	46	21	254	6	1	.996
1995— Vancouver (PCL)	OF	107	398	66	122	21	4	0	47	.307	41	34	16	192	4	1	*.995
— California (A.L.)	OF-DH	15	20	3	7	0	0	0	1	.350	1	1	0	7	0	0	1.000
1996— Vancouver (PCL)	OF	62	245	40	75	13	4	0	33	.306	30	19	7	113	4	5	.959
— California (A.L.)	OF-DH	50	87	6	25	6	1	0	6	.287	8	13	0	33	0	0	1.000
1997— Anaheim (A.L.)	OF-DH	74	134	19	29	2	2	0	8	.216	17	11	2	78	1	2	.975
Major league totals (3 years)		139	241	28	61	8	3	0	15	.253	26	25	2	118	1	2	.983

PALMEIRO, RAFAEL   1B   ORIOLES

PERSONAL: Born September 24, 1964, in Havana, Cuba. ... 6-0/190. ... Bats left, throws left. ... Full name: Rafael Corrales Palmeiro. ... Cousin of Orlando Palmeiro, outfielder, Anaheim Angels. ... Name pronounced pal-MAIR-oh.
HIGH SCHOOL: Jackson (Miami).
COLLEGE: Mississippi State (degree in commercial art).
TRANSACTIONS/CAREER NOTES: Selected by New York Mets organization in eighth round of free-agent draft (June 7, 1982); did not sign. ... Selected by Chicago Cubs organization in first round (22nd pick overall) of free-agent draft (June 3, 1985); pick received as compensation for San Diego Padres signing Type A free-agent P Tim Stoddard. ... Traded by Cubs with P Jamie Moyer and P Drew Hall to Texas Rangers for P Mitch Williams, P Paul Kilgus, P Steve Wilson, IF Curtis Wilkerson, IF Luis Benitez and OF Pablo Delgado (December 5, 1988). ... Granted free agency (October 25, 1993). ... Signed by Baltimore Orioles (December 12, 1993).
HONORS: Named outfielder on THE SPORTING NEWS college All-America team (1985). ... Named Eastern League Most Valuable Player (1986). ... Won A.L. Gold Glove at first base (1997)
STATISTICAL NOTES: Led Eastern League with 225 total bases, 13 sacrifice flies and 13 intentional bases on balls received in 1986. ... Had 20-game hitting streak (July 18-August 11, 1988). ... Led A.L. first basemen in total chances with 1,540 in 1993 and 1,510 in 1996. ... Led A.L. first basemen in double plays with 133 in 1993 and 157 in 1996. ... Had 24-game hitting streak (April 23-May 22, 1994). ... Career major league grand slams: 4.

Year— Team (League)	Pos.	G	AB	R	H	2B	3B	HR	RBI	Avg.	BB	SO	SB	PO	A	E	Avg.
1985— Peoria (Midwest)	OF	73	279	34	83	22	4	5	51	.297	31	34	9	113	7	1	.992
1986— Pittsfield (Eastern)	OF	•140	509	66	*156	29	2	12	*95	.306	54	32	15	248	9	3	*.988
— Chicago (N.L.)	OF	22	73	9	18	4	0	3	12	.247	4	6	1	34	2	4	.900
1987— Iowa (Am. Assoc.)	OF-1B	57	214	36	64	14	3	11	41	.299	22	22	4	150	13	2	.988
— Chicago (N.L.)	OF-1B	84	221	32	61	15	1	14	30	.276	20	26	2	176	9	1	.995
1988— Chicago (N.L.)	OF-1B	152	580	75	178	41	5	8	53	.307	38	34	12	322	11	5	.985
1989— Texas (A.L.)■	1B-DH	156	559	76	154	23	4	8	64	.275	63	48	4	1167	*119	12	.991
1990— Texas (A.L.)	1B-DH	154	598	72	*191	35	6	14	89	.319	40	59	3	1215	91	7	.995
1991— Texas (A.L.)	1B-DH	159	631	115	203	*49	3	26	88	.322	68	72	4	1305	96	*12	.992
1992— Texas (A.L.)	1B-DH	159	608	84	163	27	4	22	85	.268	72	83	2	1251	*143	7	.995
1993— Texas (A.L.)	1B	160	597	*124	176	40	2	37	105	.295	73	85	22	*1388	*147	5	.997
1994— Baltimore (A.L.)■	1B	111	436	82	139	32	0	23	76	.319	54	63	7	959	66	4	.996
1995— Baltimore (A.L.)	1B	143	554	89	172	30	2	39	104	.310	62	65	3	1181	*119	4	.997
1996— Baltimore (A.L.)	1B-DH	162	626	110	181	40	2	39	142	.289	95	96	8	*1383	*119	8	.995
1997— Baltimore (A.L.)	1B-DH	158	614	95	156	24	2	38	110	.254	67	109	5	1305	112	10	.993
American League totals (9 years)		1362	5223	847	1535	300	25	246	863	.294	594	680	58	11154	1012	69	.994
National League totals (3 years)		258	874	116	257	60	6	25	95	.294	62	66	15	532	22	10	.982
Major league totals (12 years)		1620	6097	963	1792	360	31	271	958	.294	656	746	73	11686	1034	79	.994

DIVISION SERIES RECORD

Year— Team (League)	Pos.	G	AB	R	H	2B	3B	HR	RBI	Avg.	BB	SO	SB	PO	A	E	Avg.
1996— Baltimore (A.L.)	1B	4	17	4	3	1	0	1	2	.176	1	6	0	35	1	1	.973
1997— Baltimore (A.L.)	1B	4	12	2	3	2	0	0	0	.250	0	2	0	27	2	0	1.000
Division series totals (2 years)		8	29	6	6	3	0	1	2	.207	1	8	0	62	3	1	.985

P

NOTES: Hit home run in first at-bat (October 9, 1996).

Year Team (League)	Pos.	G	AB	R	H	2B	3B	HR	RBI	Avg.	BB	SO	SB	PO	A	E	Avg.
1996— Baltimore (A.L.)	1B	5	17	4	4	0	0	2	4	.235	4	4	0	44	3	0	1.000
1997— Baltimore (A.L.)	1B	6	25	3	7	2	0	1	2	.280	0	10	0	55	2	0	1.000
Championship series totals (2 years)		11	42	7	11	2	0	3	6	.262	4	14	0	99	5	0	1.000

ALL-STAR GAME RECORD

Year League	Pos.	AB	R	H	2B	3B	HR	RBI	Avg.	BB	SO	SB	PO	A	E	Avg.
1988— National	PH-OF	0	0	0	0	0	0	0	...	1	0	0	1	0	0	1.000
1991— American	1B	0	0	0	0	0	0	0	...	1	0	0	2	0	0	1.000
All-Star Game totals (2 years)		0	0	0	0	0	0	0	...	2	0	0	3	0	0	1.000

PALMER, DEAN   3B   ROYALS

PERSONAL: Born December 27, 1968, in Tallahassee, Fla. ... 6-1/210. ... Bats right, throws right. ... Full name: Dean William Palmer.
HIGH SCHOOL: Florida (Tallahassee, Fla.).
TRANSACTIONS/CAREER NOTES: Selected by Texas Rangers organization in third round of free-agent draft (June 2, 1986). ... On disabled list (July 19, 1988-remainder of season; April 28-May 13, 1994; and June 4-September 22, 1995). ... Traded by Rangers to Kansas City Royals for OF Tom Goodwin (July 25, 1997). ... Granted free agency (October 27, 1997). ... Re-signed by Royals (December 15, 1997).
RECORDS: Holds major league single-season record for fewest assists by third baseman (150 or more games)—220 (1996); and fewest total chances accepted by third baseman (150 or more games)—326 (1996). ... Shares A.L. single-season record for fewest double plays by third baseman (150 or more games)—17 (1996).
STATISTICAL NOTES: Led Texas League third basemen with 30 errors in 1989. ... Led A.L. third basemen with 29 errors in 1993. ... Career major league grand slams: 6.

Year Team (League)	Pos.	G	AB	R	H	2B	3B	HR	RBI	Avg.	BB	SO	SB	PO	A	E	Avg.
1986— GC Rangers (GCL)	3B	50	163	19	34	7	1	0	12	.209	22	34	6	25	75	13	.885
1987— Gastonia (S. Atl.)	3B	128	484	51	104	16	0	9	54	.215	36	126	5	58	209	*59	.819
1988— Charlotte (Fla. St.)	3B	74	305	38	81	12	1	4	35	.266	15	69	0	49	144	28	.873
1989— Tulsa (Texas)	3B-SS	133	498	82	125	32	5	*25	90	.251	41	*152	15	85	213	†31	.906
— Texas (A.L.)	3-DH-S-O	16	19	0	2	2	0	0	1	.105	0	12	0	3	4	2	.778
1990— Tulsa (Texas)	3B	7	24	4	7	0	1	3	9	.292	4	10	0	9	6	3	.833
— Oklahoma City (A.A.)	3B-1B	88	316	33	69	17	4	12	39	.218	20	106	1	206	110	21	.938
1991— Oklahoma City (A.A.)	3B-OF	60	234	45	70	11	2	*22	59	.299	20	61	4	49	105	11	.933
— Texas (A.L.)	3B-OF-DH	81	268	38	50	9	2	15	37	.187	32	98	0	69	75	9	.941
1992— Texas (A.L.)	3B	152	541	74	124	25	0	26	72	.229	62	*154	10	124	254	22	.945
1993— Texas (A.L.)	3B-SS	148	519	88	127	31	2	33	96	.245	53	154	11	86	258	†29	.922
1994— Texas (A.L.)	3B	93	342	50	84	14	2	19	59	.246	26	89	3	50	179	*22	.912
1995— Texas (A.L.)	3B	36	119	30	40	6	0	9	24	.336	21	21	1	19	72	5	.948
1996— Texas (A.L.)	3B-DH	154	582	98	163	26	2	38	107	.280	59	145	2	105	221	16	.953
1997— Texas (A.L.)	3B	94	355	47	87	21	0	14	55	.245	26	84	1	72	162	10	.959
— Kansas City (A.L.)■	3B-DH	49	187	23	52	10	1	9	31	.278	15	50	1	27	82	9	.924
Major league totals (8 years)		823	2932	448	729	144	9	163	482	.249	294	807	29	555	1307	124	.938

DIVISION SERIES RECORD

Year Team (League)	Pos.	G	AB	R	H	2B	3B	HR	RBI	Avg.	BB	SO	SB	PO	A	E	Avg.
1996— Texas (A.L.)	3B	4	19	3	4	1	0	1	2	.211	0	5	0	3	10	1	.929

PANIAGUA, JOSE   P   DEVIL RAYS

PERSONAL: Born August 20, 1973, in San Jose De Ocoa, Dominican Republic. ... 6-2/185. ... Throws right, bats right. ... Full name: Jose Luis Sanchez Paniagua.
HIGH SCHOOL: Liceo Nuestra Senora del Altagracia (Santo Domingo, Dominican Republic).
TRANSACTIONS/CAREER NOTES: Signed as non-drafted free agent by Montreal Expos organization (September 17, 1990). ... On Montreal disabled list (May 25-June 11, 1996). ... On Ottawa disabled list (July 16-August 2, 1996). ... Selected by Tampa Bay Devil Rays in second round (50th pick overall) of expansion draft (November 18, 1997).

Year Team (League)	W	L	Pct.	ERA	G	GS	CG	ShO	Sv.	IP	H	R	ER	BB	SO
1992— Dom. Expos (DSL)	3	7	.300	4.15	13	13	3	1	0	73 2/3	69	50	34	46	60
1993— GC Expos (GCL)	3	0	1.000	0.67	4	4	1	0	0	27	13	2	2	5	25
1994— W.P. Beach (FSL)	9	9	.500	3.64	26	26	1	0	0	141	131	82	57	54	110
1995— Harrisburg (Eastern)	7	•12	.368	5.34	25	25	2	1	0	126 1/3	140	84	75	62	89
1996— Ottawa (Int'l)	9	5	.643	3.18	15	14	2	1	0	85	72	39	30	23	61
— Montreal (N.L.)	2	4	.333	3.53	13	11	0	0	0	51	55	24	20	23	27
— Harrisburg (Eastern)	3	0	1.000	0.00	3	3	0	0	0	18	12	1	0	4	16
1997— W.P. Beach (FSL)	1	0	1.000	0.00	2	2	0	0	0	10	5	0	0	2	11
— Ottawa (Int'l)	8	10	.444	4.64	22	22	1	0	0	137 2/3	164	79	71	44	87
— Montreal (N.L.)	1	2	.333	12.00	9	3	0	0	0	18	29	24	24	16	8
Major league totals (2 years)	3	6	.333	5.74	22	14	0	0	0	69	84	48	44	39	35

P   PAQUETTE, CRAIG   3B   METS

PERSONAL: Born March 28, 1969, in Long Beach, Calif. ... 6-0/190. ... Bats right, throws right. ... Full name: Craig Howard Paquette.
HIGH SCHOOL: Ranchos Alamitos (Garden Grove, Calif.).
JUNIOR COLLEGE: Golden West College (Calif.).

TRANSACTIONS/CAREER NOTES: Selected by Minnesota Twins organization in 36th round of free-agent draft (June 2, 1987); did not sign. ... Selected by Oakland Athletics organization in eighth round of free-agent draft (June 5, 1989). ... On Modesto disabled list (April 10-May 5, 1991). ... On Huntsville disabled list (June 1-11, 1991). ... On Tacoma disabled list (July 18, 1994-remainder of season). ... Released by A's (March 26, 1996). ... Signed by Kansas City Royals organization (April 3, 1996). ... Granted free agency (October 15, 1997). ... Signed by New York Mets organization (December 23, 1997).

STATISTICAL NOTES: Tied for Northwest League lead with 163 total bases in 1989. ... Led Northwest League third basemen with .936 fielding percentage and 12 double plays in 1989. ... Led Southern League third basemen with 349 total chances in 1992. ... Career major league grand slams: 2.

								BATTING						FIELDING			
Year Team (League)	Pos.	G	AB	R	H	2B	3B	HR	RBI	Avg.	BB	SO	SB	PO	A	E	Avg.
1989— S. Oregon (N'west)	3B-SS-2B	71	277	53	93	*22	3	14	56	.336	30	46	9	61	155	15	†.935
1990— Modesto (California) ..	3B	130	495	65	118	23	4	15	59	.238	47	123	8	*88	218	26	*.922
1991— Huntsville (Southern) .	3B-1B	102	378	50	99	18	1	8	60	.262	28	87	0	51	132	16	.920
1992— Huntsville (Southern) .	3B	115	450	59	116	25	4	17	71	.258	29	118	13	69	*248	*32	.908
— Tacoma (PCL)	3B	17	66	10	18	7	0	2	11	.273	2	16	3	14	33	3	.940
1993— Tacoma (PCL)	3B-SS-2B	50	183	29	49	8	0	8	29	.268	14	54	3	32	116	15	.908
— Oakland (A.L.)	3B-DH-OF	105	393	35	86	20	4	12	46	.219	14	108	4	82	165	13	.950
1994— Tacoma (PCL)	3B	65	245	39	70	12	3	17	48	.286	14	48	3	40	166	14	.936
— Oakland (A.L.)	3B	14	49	0	7	2	0	0	0	.143	0	14	1	14	22	0	1.000
1995— Oakland (A.L.)	3-O-S-1	105	283	42	64	13	1	13	49	.226	12	88	5	72	92	8	.953
1996— Omaha (A.A.)■	3B-1B-OF	18	63	9	21	3	0	4	13	.333	8	14	1	24	9	3	.917
— Kansas City (A.L.) 3-O-1-S-DH		118	429	61	111	15	1	22	67	.259	23	101	5	261	102	14	.963
1997— Kansas City (A.L.)	3B-OF	77	252	26	58	15	1	8	33	.230	10	57	2	51	130	12	.938
— Omaha (A.A.)..............	3B	23	91	9	28	6	0	3	20	.308	6	26	0	12	29	2	.953
Major league totals (5 years)		419	1406	164	326	65	4	55	195	.232	59	368	17	480	511	47	.955

PARENT, MARK   C   PHILLIES

PERSONAL: Born September 16, 1961, in Ashland, Ore. ... 6-5/245. ... Bats right, throws right. ... Full name: Mark Alan Parent.

HIGH SCHOOL: Anderson (Calif.).

TRANSACTIONS/CAREER NOTES: Selected by San Diego Padres organization in fourth round of free-agent draft (June 5, 1979). ... On suspended list (August 27, 1983-remainder of season). ... On disabled list (September 4, 1984-remainder of season). ... Traded by Padres to Texas Rangers for 3B Scott Coolbaugh (December 12, 1990). ... On Texas disabled list (March 9-September 6, 1991); included rehabilitation assignment to Oklahoma City (August 31-September 5). ... Granted free agency (October 8, 1991). ... Signed by Baltimore Orioles organization (February 5, 1992). ... On Rochester disabled list (April 10-17, 1992). ... Released by Orioles (December 2, 1993). ... Signed by Chicago Cubs organization (December 14, 1993). ... Claimed on waivers by Pittsburgh Pirates (October 11, 1994). ... Traded by Pirates to Cubs for a player to be named later (August 31, 1995). ... Granted free agency (October 31, 1995). ... Signed by Detroit Tigers (December 13, 1995). ... Released by Tigers (August 21, 1996). ... Signed by Orioles (August 27, 1996). ... Granted free agency (November 18, 1996). ... Signed by Philadelphia Phillies (December 11, 1996).

STATISTICAL NOTES: Led Northwest League catchers with .979 fielding percentage in 1980. ... Led Carolina League catchers with 16 double plays in 1981. ... Led Pacific Coast League catchers with .988 fielding percentage in 1987. ... Led International League catchers with eight double plays in 1992. ... Tied for International League lead in double plays by catcher with 11 in 1993.

								BATTING						FIELDING			
Year Team (League)	Pos.	G	AB	R	H	2B	3B	HR	RBI	Avg.	BB	SO	SB	PO	A	E	Avg.
1979— Walla Walla (NWL)	C-OF	40	126	8	24	4	0	1	11	.190	8	31	8	229	34	6	.978
1980— Reno (California)	C	30	99	8	20	3	0	0	12	.202	16	12	0	128	23	2	.987
— Grays Har. (NWL).......	C-1B	66	230	29	55	11	2	7	32	.239	17	30	1	381	38	9	†.979
1981— Salem (Carolina)	C	123	438	44	103	16	3	6	47	.235	37	90	10	*694	87	*28	.965
1982— Amarillo (Texas)	C	26	89	12	17	3	1	1	13	.191	11	13	2	100	6	2	.981
— Salem (Carolina)	C-1B	99	360	39	81	15	2	6	41	.225	32	58	2	475	64	12	.978
1983— Beaumont (Texas)	C	81	282	38	71	22	1	7	33	.252	33	35	1	464	71	10	*.982
1984— Beaumont (Texas)	C-1B	111	380	52	109	24	3	7	60	.287	38	39	1	674	68	7	.991
1985— Las Vegas (PCL)	C-1B	105	361	36	87	23	3	7	45	.241	29	58	1	586	54	6	.991
1986— Las Vegas (PCL)	C-1B	86	267	29	77	10	4	5	40	.288	23	25	0	344	40	5	.987
— San Diego (N.L.)	C	8	14	1	2	0	0	0	0	.143	1	3	0	16	0	2	.889
1987— Las Vegas (PCL)	C-1-3-O	105	387	50	113	23	2	4	43	.292	38	53	2	556	58	8	†.987
— San Diego (N.L.)	C	12	25	0	2	0	0	0	2	.080	0	9	0	36	3	0	1.000
1988— San Diego (N.L.)	C	41	118	9	23	3	0	6	15	.195	6	23	0	203	15	3	.986
1989— San Diego (N.L.)	C-1B	52	141	12	27	4	0	7	21	.191	8	34	1	246	17	0	1.000
1990— San Diego (N.L.)	C	65	189	13	42	11	0	3	16	.222	16	29	1	324	31	3	.992
1991— Okla. City (A.A.)■.......	C	5	8	0	2	0	0	0	1	.250	0	1	0	4	0	0	1.000
— Texas (A.L.)	C	3	1	0	0	0	0	0	0	.000	0	1	0	5	0	0	1.000
1992— Rochester (Int'l)■.......	C	101	356	52	102	24	0	17	69	.287	35	64	4	588	49	4	.994
— Baltimore (A.L.).........	C	17	34	4	8	1	0	2	4	.235	3	7	0	73	7	1	.988
1993— Rochester (Int'l).........	C	92	332	47	82	15	0	14	56	.247	40	71	0	549	63	3	*.995
— Baltimore (A.L.).........	C-DH	22	54	7	14	2	0	4	12	.259	3	14	0	83	5	1	.989
1994— Chicago (N.L.)■.........	C	44	99	8	26	4	0	3	16	.263	13	24	0	184	21	5	.976
1995— Pittsburgh (N.L.)■.......	C	69	233	25	54	9	0	15	33	.232	23	62	0	365	39	4	.990
— Chicago (N.L.)■.........	C	12	32	5	8	2	0	3	5	.250	3	7	0	66	5	0	1.000
1996— Detroit (A.L.)■	C-1B	38	104	13	25	6	0	7	17	.240	3	27	0	159	14	1	.994
— Baltimore (A.L.)■.......	C	18	33	4	6	1	0	2	6	.182	2	10	0	73	3	1	.987
1997— Philadelphia (N.L.)■ ..	C	39	113	4	17	3	0	0	8	.150	7	39	0	225	21	1	.996
American League totals (4 years)		98	226	28	53	10	0	15	39	.235	11	59	0	393	29	4	.991
National League totals (8 years)		342	964	77	201	36	0	37	116	.209	77	230	2	1665	152	18	.990
Major league totals (12 years)		440	1190	105	254	46	0	52	155	.213	88	289	2	2058	181	22	.990

P

Year Team (League)	Pos.	G	AB	R	H	2B	3B	HR	RBI	Avg.	BB	SO	SB	PO	A	E	Avg.
						BATTING									FIELDING		
1996— Baltimore (A.L.).........	C	4	5	0	1	0	0	0	0	.200	0	2	0	19	0	0	1.000

CHAMPIONSHIP SERIES RECORD

Year Team (League)	Pos.	G	AB	R	H	2B	3B	HR	RBI	Avg.	BB	SO	SB	PO	A	E	Avg.
						BATTING									FIELDING		
1996— Baltimore (A.L.).........	C	2	6	0	1	0	0	0	0	.167	0	2	0	14	0	0	1.000

PARK, CHAN HO — P — DODGERS

PERSONAL: Born June 30, 1973, in Kong Ju City, Korea. ... 6-2/195. ... Throws right, bats right.
HIGH SCHOOL: Kong Ju (Kong Ju City, Korea).
COLLEGE: Han Yang University (Seoul, Korea).
TRANSACTIONS/CAREER NOTES: Signed as non-drafted free agent by Los Angeles Dodgers organization (January 14, 1994). ... On Albuquerque disabled list (July 16-29, 1995).

Year Team (League)	W	L	Pct.	ERA	G	GS	CG	ShO	Sv.	IP	H	R	ER	BB	SO
1994— Los Angeles (N.L.)	0	0	...	11.25	2	0	0	0	0	4	5	5	5	5	6
— San Antonio (Tex.)	5	7	.417	3.55	20	20	0	0	0	101 1/3	91	52	40	57	100
1995— Albuquerque (PCL)	6	7	.462	4.91	23	22	0	0	0	110	93	64	60	76	101
— Los Angeles (N.L.)	0	0	...	4.50	2	1	0	0	0	4	2	2	2	2	7
1996— Los Angeles (N.L.)	5	5	.500	3.64	48	10	0	0	0	108 2/3	82	48	44	71	119
1997— Los Angeles (N.L.)	14	8	.636	3.38	32	29	2	0	0	192	149	80	72	70	166
Major league totals (4 years)......	**19**	**13**	**.594**	**3.59**	**84**	**40**	**2**	**0**	**0**	**308 2/3**	**238**	**135**	**123**	**148**	**298**

PASQUALICCHIO, MICHAEL — P — BREWERS

PERSONAL: Born August 17, 1974, in Flushing, N.Y. ... 6-1/205. ... Throws left, bats right. ... Full name: Michael Anthony Pasqualicchio.
COLLEGE: Lamar.
TRANSACTIONS/CAREER NOTES: Selected by Milwaukee Brewers organization in second round of free-agent draft (June 1, 1995). ... On Stockton disabled list (April 3-June 1, 1997).

Year Team (League)	W	L	Pct.	ERA	G	GS	CG	ShO	Sv.	IP	H	R	ER	BB	SO
1995— Helena (Pioneer)	3	0	1.000	3.16	8	7	0	0	0	31 1/3	30	14	11	20	21
1996— Stockton (California)	3	3	.500	3.53	18	18	17	0	0	71 1/3	67	35	28	36	69
1997— Stockton (California)	1	10	.091	6.43	17	15	1	0	1	85 1/3	93	67	61	44	58

PATTERSON, BOB — P — CUBS

PERSONAL: Born May 16, 1959, in Jacksonville. ... 6-1/195. ... Throws left, bats right. ... Full name: Robert Chandler Patterson.
HIGH SCHOOL: Wade Hampton (Greenville, S.C.).
COLLEGE: East Carolina (degree in industrial technology).
TRANSACTIONS/CAREER NOTES: Selected by San Diego Padres organization in 21st round of free-agent draft (June 7, 1982). ... Traded by Padres to Pittsburgh Pirates for OF Marvell Wynne (April 3, 1986). ... On disabled list (April 28, 1988-remainder of season). ... Released by Pirates (November 20, 1992). ... Signed by Texas Rangers organization (December 8, 1992). ... Granted free agency (October 4, 1993). ... Signed by California Angels organization (January 18, 1994). ... Granted free agency (December 23, 1994). ... Re-signed by Angels organization (April 16, 1995). ... Granted free agency (November 2, 1995). ... Signed by Chicago Cubs (January 16, 1996).

Year Team (League)	W	L	Pct.	ERA	G	GS	CG	ShO	Sv.	IP	H	R	ER	BB	SO
1982— GC Padres (GCL)	4	3	.571	2.94	8	6	3	0	0	52	60	18	17	7	65
— Reno (California)	1	0	1.000	3.55	4	4	1	1	0	25 1/3	28	11	10	5	10
1983— Beaumont (Texas)	8	4	.667	4.01	43	9	2	0	11	116 2/3	107	61	52	36	97
1984— Las Vegas (PCL)	8	9	.471	3.27	*60	7	1	0	13	143 1/3	129	63	52	37	97
1985— Las Vegas (PCL)	10	11	.476	3.14	42	20	7	1	6	186 1/3	187	80	65	52	146
— San Diego (N.L.)	0	0	...	24.75	3	0	0	0	0	4	13	11	11	3	1
1986— Hawaii (Pac. Coast)■	9	6	.600	3.40	25	21	6	1	1	156	146	68	59	44	*137
— Pittsburgh (N.L.)	2	3	.400	4.95	11	5	0	0	0	36 1/3	49	20	20	5	20
1987— Pittsburgh (N.L.)	1	4	.200	6.70	15	7	0	0	0	43	49	34	32	22	27
— Vancouver (PCL)	5	2	.714	2.12	14	12	5	1	0	89	62	21	21	30	92
1988— Buffalo (A.A.)	2	0	1.000	2.32	4	4	1	0	0	31	26	12	8	4	20
1989— Buffalo (A.A.)	12	6	.667	3.35	31	25	4	1	1	177 1/3	177	69	66	35	103
— Pittsburgh (N.L.)	4	3	.571	4.05	12	3	0	0	1	26 2/3	23	13	12	8	20
1990— Pittsburgh (N.L.)	8	5	.615	2.95	55	5	0	0	5	94 2/3	88	33	31	21	70
1991— Pittsburgh (N.L.)	4	3	.571	4.11	54	1	0	0	2	65 2/3	67	32	30	15	57
1992— Pittsburgh (N.L.)	6	3	.667	2.92	60	0	0	0	9	64 2/3	59	22	21	23	43
1993— Texas (A.L.)■	2	4	.333	4.78	52	0	0	0	1	52 2/3	59	28	28	11	46
1994— California (A.L.)■	2	3	.400	4.07	47	0	0	0	0	42	35	21	19	15	30
1995— California (A.L.)	5	2	.714	3.04	62	0	0	0	0	53 1/3	48	18	18	13	41
1996— Chicago (N.L.)■	3	3	.500	3.13	79	0	0	0	8	54 2/3	46	19	19	22	53
1997— Chicago (N.L.)	1	6	.143	3.34	76	0	0	0	0	59 1/3	47	23	22	10	58
A.L. totals (3 years)	**9**	**9**	**.500**	**3.95**	**161**	**0**	**0**	**0**	**2**	**148**	**142**	**67**	**65**	**39**	**117**
N.L. totals (9 years)	**29**	**30**	**.492**	**3.97**	**365**	**21**	**0**	**0**	**25**	**449**	**441**	**207**	**198**	**129**	**349**
Major league totals (12 years)	**38**	**39**	**.494**	**3.96**	**526**	**21**	**0**	**0**	**27**	**597**	**583**	**274**	**263**	**168**	**466**

CHAMPIONSHIP SERIES RECORD

Year Team (League)	W	L	Pct.	ERA	G	GS	CG	ShO	Sv.	IP	H	R	ER	BB	SO
1990— Pittsburgh (N.L.)	0	0	...	0.00	2	0	0	0	1	1	1	0	0	2	0
1991— Pittsburgh (N.L.)	0	0	...	0.00	1	0	0	0	0	2	1	0	0	0	3
1992— Pittsburgh (N.L.)	0	0	...	5.40	2	0	0	0	0	1 2/3	3	1	1	1	1
Champ. series totals (3 years)	**0**	**0**	**...**	**1.93**	**5**	**0**	**0**	**0**	**1**	**4 2/3**	**5**	**1**	**1**	**3**	**4**

P

PATTERSON, DANNY — P — RANGERS

PERSONAL: Born February 17, 1971, in San Gabriel, Calif. ... 6-0/185. ... Throws right, bats right. ... Full name: Danny Shane Patterson.
HIGH SCHOOL: San Gabriel (Calif.).
JUNIOR COLLEGE: Cerritos College (Calif.).
TRANSACTIONS/CAREER NOTES: Selected by Texas Rangers organization in 47th round of free-agent draft (June 5, 1989). ... On Texas disabled list (May 22-June 14, 1997); included rehabilitation assignment to Tulsa (June 9-14).

Year Team (League)	W	L	Pct.	ERA	G	GS	CG	ShO	Sv.	IP	H	R	ER	BB	SO
1990— Butte (Pioneer)	0	3	.000	6.35	13	3	0	0	1	28 1/3	36	23	20	14	18
1991— GC Rangers (GCL)	5	3	.625	3.24	11	9	0	0	0	50	43	21	18	12	46
1992— Gastonia (S. Atl.)	4	6	.400	3.59	23	21	3	1	0	105 1/3	106	47	42	33	84
1993— Charlotte (Fla. St.)	5	6	.455	2.51	47	0	0	0	7	68	55	22	19	28	41
1994— Tulsa (Texas)	1	4	.200	1.64	30	1	0	0	6	44	35	13	8	17	33
—Charlotte (Fla. St.)	1	0	1.000	4.61	7	0	0	0	0	13 2/3	13	7	7	5	9
1995— Tulsa (Texas)	2	2	.500	6.19	26	0	0	0	5	36 1/3	45	27	25	13	24
—Oklahoma City (A.A.)	1	0	1.000	1.65	14	0	0	0	2	27 1/3	23	8	5	9	9
1996— Oklahoma City (A.A.)	6	2	.750	1.68	44	0	0	0	10	80 1/3	79	22	15	15	53
—Texas (A.L.)	0	0	...	0.00	7	0	0	0	0	8 2/3	10	4	0	3	5
1997— Texas (A.L.)	10	6	.625	3.42	54	0	0	0	1	71	70	29	27	23	69
—Tulsa (Texas)	0	0	...	4.50	2	2	0	0	0	2	5	4	1	0	0
Major league totals (2 years)	10	6	.625	3.05	61	0	0	0	1	79 2/3	80	33	27	26	74

DIVISION SERIES RECORD

Year Team (League)	W	L	Pct.	ERA	G	GS	CG	ShO	Sv.	IP	H	R	ER	BB	SO
1996— Texas (A.L.)	0	0	...	0.00	1	0	0	0	0	1/3	1	0	0	0	0

PATTERSON, JOHN — P — DIAMONDBACKS

PERSONAL: Born January 30, 1978, in Orange, Texas. ... 6-6/185. ... Throws right, bats right.
TRANSACTIONS/CAREER NOTES: Signed as non-drafted free agent by Arizona Diamondbacks organization (November 7, 1996).
HIGH SCHOOL: West Orange-Stark (Orange, Texas).

Year Team (League)	W	L	Pct.	ERA	G	GS	CG	ShO	Sv.	IP	H	R	ER	BB	SO
1996—								Did not play.							
1997— South Bend (Mid.)	1	9	.100	3.23	18	18	0	0	0	78	63	32	28	34	95

PATZKE, JEFF — 2B/3B — BLUE JAYS

PERSONAL: Born November 18, 1973, in Klamath Falls, Ore. ... 6-0/185. ... Bats both, throws right. ... Full name: Jeffrey James Patzke. ... Son of former professional boxer James Patzke.
HIGH SCHOOL: Klamath Union (Klamath Falls, Ore.).
TRANSACTIONS/CAREER NOTES: Selected by Toronto Blue Jays organization in fifth round of free-agent draft (June 1, 1992). ... Granted free agency (December 21, 1997). ... On disabled list (May 15-June 23, 1997). ... Re-signed by Blue Jays organization (January 5, 1998).
STATISTICAL NOTES: Led Pioneer League shortstops with 369 total chances and 37 double plays in 1993. ... Led Florida State League second basemen with 255 putouts and .977 fielding percentage in 1995. ... Led Florida State League with eight intentional bases on balls received in 1995.

Year Team (League)	Pos.	G	AB	R	H	2B	3B	HR	RBI	Avg.	BB	SO	SB	PO	A	E	Avg.
1992— GC Jays (GCL)	SS	6	21	3	2	0	0	0	1	.095	3	2	0	12	13	2	.926
—Medicine Hat (Pio.)	SS	59	193	19	42	4	0	2	17	.218	17	42	3	•117	180	24	.925
1993— Medicine Hat (Pio.)	SS	71	273	45	80	11	2	1	22	.293	34	31	5	*119	*223	27	.927
1994— Hagerstown (SAL)	SS-2B	80	271	43	55	10	1	4	22	.203	36	57	7	148	211	17	.955
1995— Dunedin (Fla. St.)	SS-2B	129	470	68	124	32	6	11	75	.264	*85	81	5	†274	329	16	†.974
1996— Knoxville (Southern)	2B	124	429	70	130	31	4	4	66	.303	80	103	6	223	343	16	.973
1997— Syracuse (Int'l)	2B-3B	96	316	38	90	25	2	2	29	.285	51	66	0	155	240	10	.975

PAVANO, CARL — P — EXPOS

PERSONAL: Born January 8, 1976, in New Britain, Conn. ... 6-5/228. ... Throws right, bats right. ... Full name: Carl Anthony Pavano.
HIGH SCHOOL: Southington (Conn.).
TRANSACTIONS/CAREER NOTES: Selected by Boston Red Sox organization in 13th round of free-agent draft (June 2, 1994). ... Traded by Red Sox with a player to be named later to Montreal Expos for P Pedro J. Martinez (November 18, 1997).
HONORS: Named Eastern League Pitcher of the Year (1996).

Year Team (League)	W	L	Pct.	ERA	G	GS	CG	ShO	Sv.	IP	H	R	ER	BB	SO
1994— GC Red Sox (GCL)	4	3	.571	1.84	9	7	0	0	0	44	31	14	9	7	47
1995— Michigan (Midwest)	6	6	.500	3.45	22	22	1	0	0	141	118	63	54	52	138
1996— Trenton (Eastern)	*16	5	.762	2.63	27	26	•6	2	0	185	154	66	54	47	146
1997— Pawtucket (Int'l)	11	6	.647	3.12	23	23	3	0	0	161 2/3	148	62	56	34	147

PAVLAS, DAVE — P — DIAMONDBACKS

PERSONAL: Born August 12, 1962, in Frankfurt, West Germany. ... 6-7/195. ... Throws right, bats right. ... Full name: David Lee Pavlas.
HIGH SCHOOL: Shiner (Texas).
COLLEGE: Rice.
TRANSACTIONS/CAREER NOTES: Signed as non-drafted free agent by Chicago Cubs organization (December 15, 1984). ... Traded by Cubs organization to Texas Rangers organization (June 6, 1987), completing deal in which Rangers traded P Mike Mason to Cubs for a player to be named later (May 15, 1987). ... Contract sold by Rangers organization to Cubs organization (January 3, 1990). ... Released by Cubs (September 5, 1991). ... Signed by Greenville, Atlanta Braves organization (February 9, 1992). ... Released by Greenville (March 31, 1992). ... Played in Mexican League (1992). ... Signed by Iowa, Cubs organization (July 26, 1992). ... Granted free agency (October 15, 1992). ...

P

Signed by Buffalo, Pittsburgh Pirates organization (June 1, 1993). ... Loaned by Buffalo to Mexico City Red Devils of Mexican League (June 1, 1993-remainder of season). ... Granted free agency (October 15, 1993). ... Played in Taiwan (1993). ... Played in Italy (1993). ... Signed by New York Yankees organization (February 8, 1995). ... On Columbus disabled list (April 21-28, 1995). ... Granted free agency (October 16, 1995). ... Re-signed by Yankees organization (January 19, 1996). ... Released by Yankees (October 31, 1996). ... Re-signed by Yankees (November 18, 1996). ... Contract sold to Yomiuri Giants of Japan Pacific League (June 5, 1997). ... Signed by Arizona Diamondbacks organization (December 18, 1997).

HONORS: Named Carolina League Pitcher of the Year (1986).
STATISTICAL NOTES: Led American Association with 10 hit batsmen in 1990.

Year Team (League)	W	L	Pct.	ERA	G	GS	CG	ShO	Sv.	IP	H	R	ER	BB	SO
1985— Peoria (Midwest)	8	3	.727	2.62	17	15	3	1	1	110	90	40	32	32	86
1986— Win.-Salem (Car.)	14	6	.700	3.84	28	26	5	2	0	$173\frac{1}{3}$	172	91	74	57	143
1987— Pittsfield (Eastern)	6	1	.857	3.80	7	7	0	0	0	45	49	25	19	17	27
— Tulsa (Texas)■	1	6	.143	7.69	13	12	0	0	0	$59\frac{2}{3}$	79	51	51	27	46
1988— Tulsa (Texas)	5	2	.714	1.98	26	5	1	0	2	$77\frac{1}{3}$	52	26	17	18	69
— Oklahoma City (A.A.)	3	1	.750	4.47	13	8	0	0	0	$52\frac{1}{3}$	59	29	26	28	40
1989— Oklahoma City (A.A.)	2	*14	.125	4.70	29	21	4	0	0	$143\frac{2}{3}$	175	89	75	67	94
1990— Iowa (Am. Assoc.)■	8	3	.727	3.26	53	3	0	0	8	$99\frac{1}{3}$	84	38	36	48	96
— Chicago (N.L.)	2	0	1.000	2.11	13	0	0	0	0	$21\frac{1}{3}$	23	7	5	6	12
1991— Iowa (Am. Assoc.)	5	6	.455	3.98	61	0	0	0	7	$97\frac{1}{3}$	92	49	43	43	54
— Chicago (N.L.)	0	0	...	18.00	1	0	0	0	0	1	3	2	2	0	0
1992— Jalisco (Mexican)■	1	4	.200	2.61	12	4	1	0	4	$41\frac{1}{3}$	35	16	12	10	25
— Iowa (Am. Assoc.)	3	3	.500	3.38	12	4	0	0	0	$37\frac{1}{3}$	43	20	14	8	34
1993— M.C. Red Devils (Mex.)■	5	3	.625	3.49	11	11	1	0	0	$56\frac{2}{3}$	59	24	22	19	32
1994—								Did not play.							
1995— Columbus (Int'l)■	3	3	.500	2.61	48	0	0	0	18	$58\frac{2}{3}$	43	19	17	20	51
— New York (A.L.)	0	0	...	3.18	4	0	0	0	0	$5\frac{2}{3}$	8	2	2	0	3
1996— Columbus (Int'l)	8	2	.800	1.99	57	0	0	0	26	77	64	20	17	13	65
— New York (A.L.)	0	0	...	2.35	16	0	0	0	1	23	23	7	6	7	18
1997— Columbus (Int'l)	1	3	.250	4.62	26	0	0	0	12	$25\frac{1}{3}$	33	14	13	4	34
— Yomiuri (Jp. Pac.)■	0	0	...	6.00	7	0	0	0	4	6	10	4	4	4	4
A.L. totals (2 years)	0	0	...	2.51	20	0	0	0	1	$28\frac{2}{3}$	31	9	8	7	21
N.L. totals (2 years)	2	0	1.000	2.82	14	0	0	0	0	$22\frac{1}{3}$	26	9	7	6	12
Major league totals (4 years)	2	0	1.000	2.65	34	0	0	0	1	51	57	18	15	13	33

PAVLIK, ROGER   P   RANGERS

PERSONAL: Born October 4, 1967, in Houston. ... 6-2/220. ... Throws right, bats right. ... Full name: Roger Allen Pavlik.
HIGH SCHOOL: Aldine (Houston).
TRANSACTIONS/CAREER NOTES: Selected by Texas Rangers organization in second round of free-agent draft (June 2, 1986). ... On disabled list (June 21, 1986-remainder of season; June 4-August 6, 1987; and April 29-May 6 and May 23-July 29, 1991). ... On Texas disabled list (March 25-May 15, 1994); included rehabilitation assignments to Charlotte (April 23-May 10) and Oklahoma City (May 10-15). ... On Texas disabled list (June 12-July 2, 1994); included rehabilitation assignment to Oklahoma City (June 27-July 2). ... On Texas disabled list (July 3-24, 1994); included rehabilitation assignment to Oklahoma City (July 7-27). ... On Texas disabled list (May 7-September 2, 1997); included rehabilitation assignments to Tulsa (August 23-28) and Oklahoma City (August 28-September 2). ... Granted free agency (December 21, 1997). ... Re-signed by Rangers (December 23, 1997).
STATISTICAL NOTES: Pitched $5\frac{1}{3}$ innings, combining with reliever Steve Peters ($2\frac{2}{3}$ innings) for eight no-hit innings in a 1-0 loss to Indianapolis (April 17, 1991). ... Pitched 3-1 one-hit, complete-game victory against Detroit (May 4, 1996).

Year Team (League)	W	L	Pct.	ERA	G	GS	CG	ShO	Sv.	IP	H	R	ER	BB	SO
1986—								Did not play.							
1987— Gastonia (S. Atl.)	2	7	.222	4.95	15	14	0	0	0	$67\frac{1}{3}$	66	46	37	42	55
1988— Gastonia (S. Atl.)	2	12	.143	4.59	18	16	0	0	0	$84\frac{1}{3}$	94	65	43	58	89
— Butte (Pioneer)	4	0	1.000	4.59	8	8	1	1	0	49	45	29	25	34	56
1989— Charlotte (Fla. St.)	3	8	.273	3.41	26	22	1	1	1	$118\frac{2}{3}$	92	60	45	72	98
1990— Charlotte (Fla. St.)	5	3	.625	2.44	11	11	1	0	0	$66\frac{1}{3}$	50	21	18	40	76
— Tulsa (Texas)	6	5	.545	2.33	16	16	2	1	0	$100\frac{1}{3}$	66	29	26	71	91
1991— Oklahoma City (A.A.)	0	5	.000	5.19	8	7	0	0	0	26	19	21	15	26	43
1992— Oklahoma City (A.A.)	7	5	.583	2.98	18	18	0	0	0	$117\frac{2}{3}$	90	44	39	51	104
— Texas (A.L.)	4	4	.500	4.21	13	12	1	0	0	62	66	32	29	34	45
1993— Oklahoma City (A.A.)	3	2	.600	1.70	6	6	0	0	0	37	26	12	7	14	32
— Texas (A.L.)	12	6	.667	3.41	26	26	2	0	0	$166\frac{1}{3}$	151	67	63	80	131
1994— Charlotte (Fla. St.)	2	1	.667	1.08	3	3	0	0	0	$16\frac{2}{3}$	13	2	2	7	15
— Oklahoma City (A.A.)	2	2	.500	3.10	5	5	0	0	0	29	26	11	10	7	34
— Texas (A.L.)	2	5	.286	7.69	11	11	0	0	0	$50\frac{1}{3}$	61	45	43	30	31
1995— Texas (A.L.)	10	10	.500	4.37	31	31	2	1	0	$191\frac{2}{3}$	174	96	93	90	149
1996— Texas (A.L.)	15	8	.652	5.19	34	34	7	0	0	201	216	120	116	81	127
1997— Texas (A.L.)	3	5	.375	4.37	11	11	0	0	0	$57\frac{2}{3}$	59	29	28	31	35
— GC Rangers (GCL)	0	0	...	1.29	2	2	0	0	0	7	8	1	1	0	5
— Tulsa (Texas)	0	0	...	3.60	1	1	0	0	0	5	3	2	2	2	4
— Oklahoma City (A.A.)	0	0	...	0.00	1	1	0	0	0	6	2	0	0	0	4
Major league totals (6 years)	46	38	.548	4.59	126	125	12	1	0	729	727	389	372	346	518

DIVISION SERIES RECORD

Year Team (League)	W	L	Pct.	ERA	G	GS	CG	ShO	Sv.	IP	H	R	ER	BB	SO
1996— Texas (A.L.)	0	1	.000	6.75	1	1	0	0	0	$2\frac{2}{3}$	4	2	2	0	1

ALL-STAR GAME RECORD

Year League	W	L	Pct.	ERA	GS	CG	ShO	Sv.	IP	H	R	ER	BB	SO
1996— American	0	0	...	9.00	0	0	0	0	2	3	2	2	0	2

PAYTON, JAY   OF   METS

PERSONAL: Born November 22, 1972, in Zanesville, Ohio. ... 5-10/185. ... Bats right, throws right. ... Full name: Jayson Lee Payton.
HIGH SCHOOL: Zanesville (Ohio).

COLLEGE: Georgia Tech.
TRANSACTIONS/CAREER NOTES: Selected by New York Mets organization in supplemental round ("sandwich pick" between first and second round, 29th pick overall) of free-agent draft (June 2, 1994); pick received as part of compensation for Baltimore Orioles signing Type A free-agent P Sid Fernandez. ... On Norfolk disabled list (April 29-July 3, 1996). ... On St. Lucie temporarily inactive list (July 11-16, 1996). ... On disabled list (April 3, 1997-entire season).

Year Team (League)	Pos.	G	AB	R	H	2B	3B	HR	RBI	Avg.	BB	SO	SB	PO	A	E	Avg.
1994— Pittsfield (NYP)	OF	58	219	47	80	16	2	3	37	.365	23	18	10	124	8	5	.964
— Binghamton (East.)	OF	8	25	3	7	1	0	0	1	.280	2	3	1	11	0	1	.917
1995— Binghamton (East.)	OF	85	357	59	123	20	3	14	54	.345	29	32	16	230	7	3	.988
— Norfolk (Int'l)	OF	50	196	33	47	11	4	4	30	.240	11	22	11	106	3	2	.982
1996— GC Mets (GCL)	DH	3	13	3	5	1	0	1	2	.385	0	1	1	...	...	...	...
— Norfolk (Int'l)	OF	55	153	30	47	6	3	6	26	.307	11	26	10	7	1	0	1.000
— St. Lucie (Fla. St.)	DH	9	26	4	8	2	0	0	1	.308	4	5	2	...	...	...	...
1997—							Did not play.										

PEEPLES, MIKE   2B   BLUE JAYS

PERSONAL: Born September 3, 1976, in Orange Park, Fla. ... 6-0/160. ... Bats right, throws right. ... Full name: Michael Eddie Peeples.
HIGH SCHOOL: Clay (Green Cove Springs, Fla.).
TRANSACTIONS/CAREER NOTES: Selected by Toronto Blue Jays organization in sixth round of free-agent draft (June 2, 1994).
STATISTICAL NOTES: Led Florida State League second basemen with 23 errors in 1997.

Year Team (League)	Pos.	G	AB	R	H	2B	3B	HR	RBI	Avg.	BB	SO	SB	PO	A	E	Avg.
1994— GC Jays (GCL)............	SS-2B	47	172	22	40	5	3	0	11	.233	13	25	17	49	81	5	.963
1995— Medicine Hat (Pio.)	2B-OF-SS	•72	285	55	89	14	4	3	50	.312	35	46	27	112	90	27	.882
1996— Hagerstown (SAL)........	DH	74	268	30	63	15	1	3	31	.235	37	55	15	...	...	...	...
1997— Dunedin (Fla. St.)	2B-OF	129	477	73	122	29	2	2	42	.256	54	83	26	219	341	†23	.961

PEMBERTON, RUDY   OF

PERSONAL: Born December 17, 1969, in San Pedro de Macoris, Dominican Republic. ... 6-1/185. ... Bats right, throws right. ... Full name: Rudy Hector Perez Pemberton.
TRANSACTIONS/CAREER NOTES: Signed as non-drafted free agent by Detroit Tigers organization (June 7, 1987). ... On disabled list (April 7-May 10, 1994). ... Granted free agency (October 3, 1995). ... Signed by Texas Rangers organization (December 19, 1995). ... On Oklahoma City suspended list (April 11-13, 1996). ... Traded by Rangers organization to Boston Red Sox organization (April 24, 1996); completing deal in which Red Sox traded P Bryan Eversgerd to Rangers for a player to be named later (April 18, 1996). ... Granted free agency (June 18, 1997). ... Signed by Seibu Lions of Japan Pacific League during 1997 season.
STATISTICAL NOTES: Tied for Florida State League lead in being hit by pitch with 13 in 1992. ... Led International League with .616 slugging percentage and tied for lead in being hit by pitch with 14 in 1996. ... Career major league grand slams: 1.

Year Team (League)	Pos.	G	AB	R	H	2B	3B	HR	RBI	Avg.	BB	SO	SB	PO	A	E	Avg.
1987—						Dominican Summer League statistics unavailable.											
1988— Bristol (Appal.)	OF	6	5	2	0	0	0	0	0	.000	1	3	0	0	0	0	...
1989— Bristol (Appal.)	OF	50	214	40	58	9	2	6	39	.271	14	43	19	84	4	5	.946
1990— Fayetteville (SAL)	OF	127	454	59	126	14	5	6	61	.278	42	91	12	192	12	10	.953
1991— Lakeland (Fla. St.)	OF	111	375	40	86	15	2	3	36	.229	25	52	25	184	9	9	.955
1992— Lakeland (Fla. St.)	OF	104	343	41	91	16	5	3	43	.265	21	37	25	147	17	3	.982
1993— London (Eastern)	OF	124	471	70	130	22	4	15	67	.276	24	80	14	215	11	8	.966
1994— Toledo (Int'l)	OF	99	360	49	109	13	3	12	58	.303	18	62	30	182	5	8	.959
1995— Detroit (A.L.)	OF-DH	12	30	3	9	3	1	0	3	.300	1	5	0	15	0	0	1.000
— Toledo (Int'l)	OF	67	224	31	77	15	3	7	23	.344	15	36	8	59	2	3	.953
1996— Okla. City (A.A.)■.......	OF	17	71	6	18	3	0	2	11	.254	1	10	1	29	2	2	.939
— Pawtucket (Int'l)■......	OF	102	396	77	129	28	3	27	92	.326	18	63	16	180	1	5	.973
— Boston (A.L.)..............	OF	13	41	11	21	8	0	1	10	.512	2	4	3	9	0	0	1.000
1997— Boston (A.L.)..............	OF	27	63	8	15	2	0	2	10	.238	4	13	0	35	2	2	.949
— Seibu (Jp. Pac.)■	...	25	63	3	11	5	0	1	5	.175	6	17	2	...	...	...	...
Major league totals (3 years)		52	134	22	45	13	1	3	23	.336	7	22	3	59	2	2	.968

PENA, ANGEL   C   DODGERS

PERSONAL: Born February 16, 1975, in San Pedro de Macoris, Dominican Republic. ... 5-10/225. ... Full name: Angel Maria Pena.
HIGH SCHOOL: Escuela Puerto Rico (San Pedro de Macoris, Dominican Republic).
TRANSACTIONS/CAREER NOTES: Signed as non-drafted free agent by Los Angeles Dodgers organization (July 24, 1992). ... On San Bernardino disabled list (July 26-September 17, 1997).
STATISTICAL NOTES: Led California League catchers with 31 passed balls in 1997.

Year Team (League)	Pos.	G	AB	R	H	2B	3B	HR	RBI	Avg.	BB	SO	SB	PO	A	E	Avg.
1993— Dom. Dodgers (DSL) .	C	50	168	27	47	3	2	1	24	.280	10	41	6	197	57	15	.944
1994—							Did not play.										
1995— Great Falls (Pio.)	C	49	138	24	40	11	1	4	15	.290	21	32	2	297	42	7	.980
1996— Savannah (S. Atl.)	C	36	127	13	26	4	0	6	16	.205	7	37	1	238	39	6	.979
— Dom. Dodgers (DSL) .	C	23	78	30	37	9	1	8	40	.474	24	12	1	86	11	1	.990
1997— San Bern. (Calif.)........	C	86	322	53	89	22	4	16	64	.276	32	84	3	661	83	10	.987

P

PERSONAL: Born June 4, 1957, in Monte Cristi, Dominican Republic. ... 6-0/190. ... Bats right, throws right. ... Full name: Antonio Francisco Padilla Pena. ... Brother of Ramon Pena, pitcher, Detroit Tigers (1989).
HIGH SCHOOL: Liceo Marti (Monte Cristi, Dominican Republic).
TRANSACTIONS/CAREER NOTES: Signed as non-drafted free agent by Pittsburgh Pirates organization (July 22, 1975). ... Traded by Pirates to St. Louis Cardinals for OF Andy Van Slyke, C Mike LaValliere and P Mike Dunne (April 1, 1987). ... On St. Louis disabled list (April 11-May 22, 1987); included rehabilitation assignment to Louisville (May 19-22). ... Granted free agency (November 13, 1989). ... Signed by Boston Red Sox (November 27, 1989). ... Granted free agency (October 29, 1993). ... Signed by Cleveland Indians organization (February 7, 1994). ... Granted free agency (October 25, 1994). ... Re-signed by Indians organization (December 13, 1994). ... Granted free agency (November 2, 1995). ... Re-signed by Indians (December 6, 1995). ... Granted free agency (November 18, 1996). ... Signed by Chicago White Sox organization (January 10, 1997). ... On Chicago disabled list (June 10-20, 1997). ... Traded by White Sox to Houston Astros for P Julien Tucker (August 15, 1997). ... Granted free agency (October 30, 1997).
HONORS: Named catcher on The Sporting News N.L. All-Star team (1983). ... Won N.L. Gold Glove at catcher (1983-85). ... Won A.L. Gold Glove at catcher (1991).
STATISTICAL NOTES: Led Carolina League catchers with nine double plays and tied for lead with 16 passed balls in 1977. ... Led Eastern League catchers with 14 double plays in 1979. ... Led N.L. catchers with 1,075 total chances in 1983, 999 in 1984 and 1,034 in 1985. ... Led N.L. catchers with 15 double plays in 1984 and 13 in 1989. ... Led N.L. catchers with 100 assists in 1985. ... Led N.L. catchers with 18 errors in 1986. ... Tied for N.L. lead in grounding into double plays with 21 in 1986. ... Led N.L. catchers with .994 fielding percentage in 1988 and .997 in 1989. ... Led A.L. catchers with 864 putouts and 943 total chances in 1990. ... Led A.L. catchers with 929 total chances and 15 double plays in 1991. ... Led A.L. catchers with 12 double plays in 1992. ... Career major league grand slams: 3.

Year Team (League)	Pos.	G	AB	R	H	2B	3B	HR	RBI	Avg.	BB	SO	SB	PO	A	E	Avg.
1976—GC Pirates (GCL)	O-1-C-3	33	110	10	23	2	2	1	11	.209	4	17	5	108	14	4	.968
—Char., S.C. (W. Car.)	C	14	49	4	11	2	0	1	8	.224	4	7	0	64	7	2	.973
1977—Char., S.C. (W. Car.)	C	29	101	10	24	4	0	3	16	.238	7	21	2	172	19	6	.970
—Salem (Carolina)	C	84	319	36	88	15	3	7	46	.276	14	60	3	*470	*66	*17	.969
1978—Shreveport (Texas)	C	104	348	34	80	14	0	8	42	.230	15	96	3	637	54	*25	.965
1979—Buffalo (Eastern)	C	134	515	89	161	16	4	34	97	.313	39	83	5	*768	*120	*26	.972
1980—Portland (PCL)	C	124	452	57	148	24	13	9	77	.327	29	75	5	*639	85	•23	.969
—Pittsburgh (N.L.)	C	8	21	1	9	1	1	0	1	.429	0	4	0	38	2	2	.952
1981—Pittsburgh (N.L.)	C	66	210	16	63	9	1	2	17	.300	8	23	1	286	41	5	.985
1982—Pittsburgh (N.L.)	C	138	497	53	147	28	4	11	63	.296	17	57	2	763	89	16	.982
1983—Pittsburgh (N.L.)	C	151	542	51	163	22	3	15	70	.301	31	73	6	*976	90	9	.992
1984—Pittsburgh (N.L.)	C	147	546	77	156	27	2	15	78	.286	36	79	12	*895	*95	9	.991
1985—Pittsburgh (N.L.)	C-1B	147	546	53	136	27	2	10	59	.249	29	67	12	925	†102	12	.988
1986—Pittsburgh (N.L.)	C-1B	144	510	56	147	26	2	10	52	.288	53	69	9	824	99	†18	.981
1987—St. Louis (N.L.)■	C-1B-OF	116	384	40	82	13	4	5	44	.214	36	54	6	624	51	8	.988
—Louisville (A.A.)	C	2	8	0	3	0	0	0	0	.375	0	2	0	7	1	0	1.000
1988—St. Louis (N.L.)	C-1B	149	505	55	133	23	1	10	51	.263	33	60	6	796	72	6	†.993
1989—St. Louis (N.L.)■	C-OF	141	424	36	110	17	2	4	37	.259	35	33	5	675	70	2	†.997
1990—Boston (A.L.)■	C-1B	143	491	62	129	19	1	7	56	.263	43	71	8	†866	74	5	.995
1991—Boston (A.L.)	C	141	464	45	107	23	2	5	48	.231	37	53	8	*864	60	5	.995
1992—Boston (A.L.)	C	133	410	39	99	21	1	1	38	.241	24	61	3	*786	57	6	.993
1993—Boston (A.L.)	C-DH	126	304	20	55	11	0	4	19	.181	25	46	1	698	53	4	.995
1994—Cleveland (A.L.)■	C	40	112	18	33	8	1	2	10	.295	9	11	0	209	17	1	.996
1995—Cleveland (A.L.)	C	91	263	25	69	15	0	5	28	.262	14	44	1	508	36	7	.987
1996—Cleveland (A.L.)	C	67	174	14	34	4	0	1	27	.195	15	25	0	336	27	3	.992
1997—Chicago (A.L.)■	C-3B	31	67	4	11	1	0	0	8	.164	8	13	0	143	8	0	1.000
—Houston (N.L.)■	C	9	19	2	4	3	0	0	2	.211	2	3	0	48	6	0	1.000
American League totals (8 years)		772	2285	227	537	102	5	25	234	.235	175	324	21	4410	332	31	.994
National League totals (11 years)		1216	4204	440	1150	196	22	82	474	.274	280	522	59	6850	717	87	.989
Major league totals (18 years)		1988	6489	667	1687	298	27	107	708	.260	455	846	80	11260	1049	118	.991

DIVISION SERIES RECORD

Year Team (League)	Pos.	G	AB	R	H	2B	3B	HR	RBI	Avg.	BB	SO	SB	PO	A	E	Avg.
1995—Cleveland (A.L.)	C	2	2	1	1	0	0	1	1	.500	0	0	0	5	0	0	1.000
1996—Cleveland (A.L.)	C	1	0	0	0	0	0	0	0	...	0	0	0	1	0	0	1.000
1997—Houston (N.L.)	C	2	0	0	0	0	0	0	0	...	0	0	0	2	0	0	1.000
Division series totals (3 years)		5	2	1	1	0	0	1	1	.500	0	0	0	8	0	0	1.000

CHAMPIONSHIP SERIES RECORD

Year Team (League)	Pos.	G	AB	R	H	2B	3B	HR	RBI	Avg.	BB	SO	SB	PO	A	E	Avg.
1987—St. Louis (N.L.)	C	7	21	5	8	0	1	0	0	.381	3	4	1	55	5	0	1.000
1990—Boston (A.L.)	C	4	14	0	3	0	0	0	0	.214	0	0	0	22	4	1	.963
1995—Cleveland (A.L.)	C	4	6	1	2	1	0	0	0	.333	1	0	0	15	1	0	1.000
Championship series totals (3 years)		15	41	6	13	1	1	0	0	.317	4	4	1	92	10	1	.990

WORLD SERIES RECORD

Year Team (League)	Pos.	G	AB	R	H	2B	3B	HR	RBI	Avg.	BB	SO	SB	PO	A	E	Avg.
1987—St. Louis (N.L.)	C-DH	7	22	2	9	1	0	0	4	.409	3	2	1	32	1	1	.971
1995—Cleveland (A.L.)	C	2	6	0	1	0	0	0	0	.167	0	0	0	7	1	0	1.000
World Series totals (2 years)		9	28	2	10	1	0	0	4	.357	3	2	1	39	2	1	.976

ALL-STAR GAME RECORD

Year League	Pos.	AB	R	H	2B	3B	HR	RBI	Avg.	BB	SO	SB	PO	A	E	Avg.
1982—National	PR-C	1	0	0	0	0	0	0	.000	0	0	1	3	0	0	1.000
1984—National	C	0	0	0	0	0	0	0	...	0	0	0	2	0	0	1.000
1985—National	C	0	0	0	0	0	0	0	...	0	0	1	4	1	0	1.000

P

		BATTING												FIELDING			
Year League	Pos.	AB	R	H	2B	3B	HR	RBI	Avg.	BB	SO	SB	PO	A	E	Avg.
1986— National	PR	0	0	0	0	0	0	0	...	0	0	0	...	...	...	
1989— National	PH-C	2	0	0	0	0	0	0	.000	0	0	0	2	0	0	1.000
All-Star Game totals (5 years)		3	0	0	0	0	0	0	.000	0	1	1	11	1	0	1.000

PENDLETON, TERRY   3B   ROYALS

PERSONAL: Born July 16, 1960, in Los Angeles. ... 5-9/195. ... Bats both, throws right. ... Full name: Terry Lee Pendleton.
HIGH SCHOOL: Channel Island (Oxnard, Calif.).
JUNIOR COLLEGE: Oxnard (Calif.) College.
COLLEGE: Fresno State.
TRANSACTIONS/CAREER NOTES: Selected by St. Louis Cardinals organization in seventh round of free-agent draft (June 7, 1982). ... On disabled list (April 8-May 23 and July 16-September 5, 1983; June 15-30, 1985; May 28-June 24, 1988; and April 24-May 9, 1990). ... Granted free agency (November 5, 1990). ... Signed by Atlanta Braves (December 3, 1990). ... On Atlanta disabled list (June 21-July 25, 1994); included rehabilitation assignment to Greenville (July 23-25). ... Granted free agency (October 24, 1994). ... Signed by Florida Marlins (April 7, 1995). ... On suspended list (June 17-21, 1995). ... Traded by Marlins to Braves for OF Roosevelt Brown (August 13, 1996). ... Granted free agency (October 29, 1996). ... Signed by Cincinnati Reds organization (January 27, 1997). ... On Cincinnati disabled list (March 18-April 29 and July 7-23, 1997); included rehabilitation assignment to Indianapolis (April 25-29). ... Released by Reds (July 24, 1997). ... Signed by Kansas City Royals organization (January 20, 1998).
RECORDS: Holds major league single-season record for fewest putouts by third baseman for leader—110 (1996).
HONORS: Won N.L. Gold Glove at third base (1987, 1989 and 1992). ... Named N.L. Comeback Player of the Year by THE SPORTING NEWS (1991). ... Named third baseman on THE SPORTING NEWS N.L. All-Star team (1991). ... Named N.L. Most Valuable Player by Baseball Writers' Association of America (1991).
STATISTICAL NOTES: Led American Association third basemen with .964 fielding percentage and 88 putouts in 1984. ... Led N.L. third basemen with 133 putouts and 371 assists in 1986. ... Led N.L. third basemen with 524 total chances in 1986, 512 in 1987, 520 in 1989, 481 in 1991 and 477 in 1992. ... Led N.L. third basemen with 36 double plays in 1986 and 31 in 1991. ... Tied for N.L. lead with 303 total bases in 1991. ... Led N.L. third basemen with 110 putouts in 1996. ... Career major league grand slams: 5.

					BATTING									FIELDING			
Year Team (League)	Pos.	G	AB	R	H	2B	3B	HR	RBI	Avg.	BB	SO	SB	PO	A	E	Avg.
1982— Johnson City (App.) ...	2B	43	181	38	58	14	•4	4	27	.320	12	28	13	79	105	17	.915
—St. Petersburg (FSL) ..	2B	20	69	4	18	2	1	1	7	.261	2	18	1	41	51	2	.979
1983— Arkansas (Texas)........	2B	48	185	29	51	10	3	4	20	.276	9	24	4	94	135	7	.970
1984— Louisville (A.A.)..........	3B-2B	91	330	52	98	23	5	4	44	.297	24	51	6	†91	157	10	†.961
—St. Louis (N.L.)........	3B	67	262	37	85	16	3	1	33	.324	16	32	20	59	155	13	.943
1985— St. Louis (N.L.)..........	3B	149	559	56	134	16	3	5	69	.240	37	75	17	129	361	18	.965
1986— St. Louis (N.L.)..........	3B-OF	159	578	56	138	26	5	1	59	.239	34	59	24	†133	†371	20	.962
1987— St. Louis (N.L.)..........	3B	159	583	82	167	29	4	12	96	.286	70	74	19	117	*369	26	.949
1988— St. Louis (N.L.)..........	3B	110	391	44	99	20	2	6	53	.253	21	51	3	75	239	12	.963
1989— St. Louis (N.L.)..........	3B	162	613	83	162	28	5	13	74	.264	44	81	9	113	*392	15	*.971
1990— St. Louis (N.L.)..........	3B	121	447	46	103	20	2	6	58	.230	30	58	7	91	248	19	.947
1991— Atlanta (N.L.)■...........	3B	153	586	94	*187	34	8	22	86	*.319	43	70	10	108	*349	24	.950
1992— Atlanta (N.L.).............	3B	160	640	98	•199	39	1	21	105	.311	37	67	5	*133	*325	19	.960
1993— Atlanta (N.L.).............	3B	161	633	81	172	33	1	17	84	.272	36	97	5	*128	319	19	.959
1994— Atlanta (N.L.).............	3B	77	309	25	78	18	3	7	30	.252	12	57	2	60	149	11	.950
—Greenville (Sou.)	3B	2	6	0	3	1	0	0	2	.500	0	1	0	1	1	1	.667
1995— Florida (N.L.)■...........	3B	133	513	70	149	32	1	14	78	.290	38	84	1	•104	250	18	.952
1996— Florida (N.L.).............	3B	111	406	30	102	20	1	6	58	.251	26	75	0	*83	214	12	.961
—Atlanta (N.L.).............	3B	42	162	21	33	6	0	4	17	.204	15	36	2	*27	80	7	.939
1997— Indianapolis (A.A.)■..	3B	4	12	2	2	0	0	0	2	.167	4	1	0	3	10	0	1.000
—Cincinnati (N.L.)	3B	50	113	11	28	9	0	1	17	.248	12	14	2	14	35	3	.942
Major league totals (14 years)		1814	6795	834	1836	346	39	137	917	.270	471	930	126	1374	3856	236	.957

DIVISION SERIES RECORD

					BATTING									FIELDING			
Year Team (League)	Pos.	G	AB	R	H	2B	3B	HR	RBI	Avg.	BB	SO	SB	PO	A	E	Avg.
1996— Atlanta (N.L.)..............	PH	1	1	0	0	0	0	0	0	.000	0	1	0	0	0	0	...

CHAMPIONSHIP SERIES RECORD

RECORDS: Shares record for most at-bats in one inning—2 (October 13, 1985, second inning). ... Holds N.L. career record for most games—38; and most at-bats—135.

					BATTING									FIELDING			
Year Team (League)	Pos.	G	AB	R	H	2B	3B	HR	RBI	Avg.	BB	SO	SB	PO	A	E	Avg.
1985— St. Louis (N.L.)..........	3B	6	24	2	5	1	0	0	4	.208	1	3	0	6	18	1	.960
1987— St. Louis (N.L.)..........	3B	6	19	3	4	0	1	0	1	.211	0	6	0	3	11	0	1.000
1991— Atlanta (N.L.).............	3B	7	30	1	5	1	1	0	1	.167	1	3	0	5	11	0	1.000
1992— Atlanta (N.L.).............	3B	7	30	2	7	2	0	0	3	.233	0	2	0	4	18	0	1.000
1993— Atlanta (N.L.).............	3B	6	26	4	9	1	0	1	5	.346	0	3	0	7	5	0	1.000
1996— Atlanta (N.L.).............	PH-3B	6	6	0	0	0	0	0	0	.000	2	3	0	0	1	0	1.000
Championship series totals (6 years)		38	135	12	30	5	2	1	14	.222	4	19	0	25	64	1	.989

WORLD SERIES RECORD

					BATTING									FIELDING			
Year Team (League)	Pos.	G	AB	R	H	2B	3B	HR	RBI	Avg.	BB	SO	SB	PO	A	E	Avg.
1985— St. Louis (N.L.)..........	3B	7	23	3	6	1	1	0	3	.261	3	2	0	6	14	1	.952
1987— St. Louis (N.L.)..........	DH-PH	3	7	2	3	0	0	0	1	.429	1	1	2	...	...	...	
1991— Atlanta (N.L.).............	3B	7	30	6	11	3	0	2	3	.367	3	1	0	3	20	2	.920
1992— Atlanta (N.L.).............	3B	6	25	2	6	2	0	0	2	.240	1	5	0	4	19	0	1.000
1996— Atlanta (N.L.).............	DH-PH-3B	4	9	1	2	1	0	0	0	.222	1	1	0	2	2	0	1.000
World Series totals (5 years)		27	94	14	28	7	1	2	9	.298	9	10	2	13	55	3	.958

P

Year League		Pos.	AB	R	H	2B	3B	HR	RBI	Avg.	BB	SO	SB	PO	A	E	Avg.
								BATTING								FIELDING	
1992— National		3B	2	0	1	0	0	0	0	.500	0	0	0	0	2	0	1.000

PERCIBAL, BILLY — P — ORIOLES

PERSONAL: Born February 2, 1974, in San Pedro de Macoris, Dominican Republic. ... 6-1/156. ... Throws right, bats right. ... Full name: William Percibal.

TRANSACTIONS/CAREER NOTES: Signed as non-drafted free agent by Baltimore Orioles organization (August 2, 1991). ... On disabled list (April 26, 1996-remainder of season). ... On Frederick disabled list (April 4-July 18, 1997).

Year Team (League)	W	L	Pct.	ERA	G	GS	CG	ShO	Sv.	IP	H	R	ER	BB	SO
1992—GC Orioles (GCL)	2	1	.667	8.10	16	0	0	0	0	26²/₃	42	26	24	7	25
1993—Bluefield (Appalachian)	6	0	1.000	3.81	13	13	0	0	0	82²/₃	71	48	35	33	81
1994—Albany (S. Atl.)	13	9	.591	3.56	28	•28	3	2	0	169¹/₃	160	80	67	90	132
1995—High Desert (Calif.)	7	6	.538	3.23	21	20	2	0	0	128	123	63	46	55	105
—Bowie (Eastern)	1	0	1.000	0.00	2	2	0	0	0	14	7	0	0	7	7
1996—								Did not play.							
1997—Frederick (Carolina)	1	3	.250	5.74	7	6	0	0	0	26²/₃	28	18	17	18	28
—Bowie (Eastern)	0	1	.000	3.00	1	1	1	0	0	6	5	2	2	1	5
—GC Orioles (GCL)	0	0	...	0.90	4	3	0	0	0	10	11	1	1	2	12

PERCIVAL, TROY — P — ANGELS

PERSONAL: Born August 9, 1969, in Fontana, Calif. ... 6-3/200. ... Throws right, bats right. ... Full name: Troy Eugene Percival. ... Name pronounced PER-sih-vol.

HIGH SCHOOL: Moreno Valley (Calif.).

COLLEGE: UC Riverside.

TRANSACTIONS/CAREER NOTES: Selected by California Angels organization in sixth round of free-agent draft (June 5, 1990). ... On Palm Springs disabled list (June 3-July 2, 1992). ... On disabled list (May 28, 1993-remainder of season). ... Angels franchise renamed Anaheim Angels for 1997 season. ... On disabled list (April 7-May 16, 1997); included rehabilitation assignment to Lake Elsinore (May 13-16).

MISCELLANEOUS: Struck out in only appearance as pinch-hitter (1996).

Year Team (League)	W	L	Pct.	ERA	G	GS	CG	ShO	Sv.	IP	H	R	ER	BB	SO
1991—Boise (Northwest)	2	0	1.000	1.41	28	0	0	0	*12	38¹/₃	23	7	6	18	63
1992—Palm Springs (California)	1	1	.500	5.06	11	0	0	0	2	10²/₃	6	7	6	8	16
—Midland (Texas)	3	0	1.000	2.37	20	0	0	0	5	19	18	5	5	11	21
1993—Vancouver (PCL)	0	1	.000	6.27	18	0	0	0	4	18²/₃	24	14	13	13	19
1994—Vancouver (PCL)	2	6	.250	4.13	49	0	0	0	15	61	63	31	28	29	73
1995—California (A.L.)	3	2	.600	1.95	62	0	0	0	3	74	37	19	16	26	94
1996—California (A.L.)	0	2	.000	2.31	62	0	0	0	36	74	38	20	19	31	100
1997—Anaheim (A.L.)	5	5	.500	3.46	55	0	0	0	27	52	40	20	20	22	72
—Lake Elsinore (Calif.)	0	0	...	0.00	2	1	0	0	0	2	1	0	0	0	3
Major league totals (3 years)	8	9	.471	2.48	179	0	0	0	66	200	115	59	55	79	266

Year League	W	L	Pct.	ERA	GS	CG	ShO	Sv.	IP	H	R	ER	BB	SO
1996— American	0	0	...	0.00	0	0	0	0	1	1	0	0	0	1

RECORD AS POSITION PLAYER

Year Team (League)		Pos.	G	AB	R	H	2B	3B	HR	RBI	Avg.	BB	SO	SB	PO	A	E	Avg.
									BATTING								FIELDING	
1990—Boise (Northwest)		C	29	79	12	16	0	0	0	5	.203	19	25	0	215	25	5	.980

PEREZ, CARLOS — P — EXPOS

PERSONAL: Born January 14, 1971, in Nigua, Dominican Republic. ... 6-3/195. ... Throws left, bats left. ... Full name: Carlos Gross Perez. ... Brother of Melido Perez, major league pitcher with Chicago White Sox (1988-91) and New York Yankees (1992-96); brother of Pascual Perez, major league pitcher with four teams (1980-85 and 1987-92); brother of Vladimir Perez, minor league pitcher (1986-94); brother of Dario Perez, minor league pitcher (1988-94); and brother of Valerio Perez, minor league pitcher (1983-84).

TRANSACTIONS/CAREER NOTES: Signed as non-drafted free agent by Montreal Expos organization (January 7, 1988). ... On disabled list (April 9-24 and May 18-July 7, 1992). ... On suspended list (July 7-October 22, 1992). ... On Montreal disabled list (March 31, 1996- entire season).

Year Team (League)	W	L	Pct.	ERA	G	GS	CG	ShO	Sv.	IP	H	R	ER	BB	SO
1989—DSL Expos (DSL)	3	3	.500	3.07	16	4	0	0	2	44	25	21	15	32	45
1990—GC Expos (GCL)	3	1	.750	2.52	13	2	0	0	2	35²/₃	24	14	10	15	38
1991—Sumter (S. Atl.)	2	2	.500	2.44	16	12	0	0	0	73²/₃	57	29	20	32	69
1992—Rockford (Midwest)	0	1	.000	5.79	7	1	0	0	1	9¹/₃	12	7	6	5	8
1993—Burlington (Midw.)	1	0	1.000	3.24	12	1	0	0	0	16²/₃	13	6	6	9	21
—San Bernardino (Calif.)	8	7	.533	3.44	20	18	0	0	0	131	120	57	50	44	98
1994—Harrisburg (Eastern)	7	2	.778	1.94	12	11	2	2	1	79	55	27	17	18	60
—Ottawa (Int'l)	7	5	.583	3.33	17	17	3	0	0	119	130	50	44	41	82
1995—Montreal (N.L.)	10	8	.556	3.69	28	23	2	1	0	141¹/₃	142	61	58	28	106
1996—								Did not play.							
1997—Montreal (N.L.)	12	13	.480	3.88	33	32	8	*5	0	206²/₃	206	109	89	48	110
Major league totals (2 years)	22	21	.512	3.80	61	55	10	6	0	348	348	170	147	76	216

Year League	W	L	Pct.	ERA	GS	CG	ShO	Sv.	IP	H	R	ER	BB	SO
1995— National	0	0	...	0.00	0	0	0	0	¹/₃	1	0	0	0	0

P

PEREZ, EDDIE — C/1B — BRAVES

PERSONAL: Born May 4, 1968, in Cuidad Ojeda, Venezuela. ... 6-1/175. ... Bats right, throws right. ... Full name: Eduardo Perez.
HIGH SCHOOL: Doctor Raul Cuenca (Cuidad Ojeda, Venezuela).
TRANSACTIONS/CAREER NOTES: Signed as non-drafted free agent by Atlanta Braves organization (September 27, 1986). ... On disabled list (August 30-September 14, 1996).
STATISTICAL NOTES: Led South Atlantic League catchers with 13 double plays in 1989. ... Tied for International League lead in errors by catcher with 11 in 1994. ... Led International League catchers with 539 putouts, 69 assists and 615 total chances in 1995. ... Tied for International League lead with seven double plays in 1995.

| | | | | | | | BATTING | | | | | | | FIELDING | | |
Year Team (League)	Pos.	G	AB	R	H	2B	3B	HR	RBI	Avg.	BB	SO	SB	PO	A	E	Avg.
1987—GC Braves (GCL)	C	31	89	8	18	1	0	1	5	.202	8	14	0	161	31	4	.980
1988—Burlington (Midw.)	C-1B	64	186	14	43	8	0	4	19	.231	10	33	1	245	42	11	.963
1989—Sumter (S. Atl.)	C-1B	114	401	39	93	21	0	5	44	.232	44	68	2	760	96	16	.982
1990—Sumter (S. Atl.)	C-1B	41	123	11	22	7	1	3	17	.179	14	18	0	315	32	3	.991
—Durham (Carolina)	C-1B	31	93	9	22	1	0	3	10	.237	1	12	0	197	17	3	.986
1991—Durham (Carolina)	C-1B	92	277	38	75	10	1	9	41	.271	17	33	0	497	55	8	.986
—Greenville (Southern)	1B	1	4	0	1	0	0	0	0	.250	0	1	0	9	0	0	1.000
1992—Greenville (Southern)	C-1B	91	275	28	63	16	0	6	41	.229	24	41	3	631	64	14	.980
1993—Greenville (Southern)	1B-C	28	84	15	28	6	0	6	17	.333	2	8	1	146	19	3	.982
1994—Richmond (Int'l)	C-1B	113	388	37	101	16	2	9	49	.260	18	47	1	718	80	‡12	.985
1995—Richmond (Int'l)	C-1B	92	324	31	86	19	0	5	40	.265	12	58	1	†540	†69	7	.989
—Atlanta (N.L.)	C-1B	7	13	1	4	1	0	1	4	.308	0	2	0	34	2	0	1.000
1996—Atlanta (N.L.)	C-1B	68	156	19	40	9	1	4	17	.256	8	19	0	281	22	3	.990
1997—Atlanta (N.L.)	C-1B	73	191	20	41	5	0	6	18	.215	10	35	0	417	24	5	.989
Major league totals (3 years)		148	360	40	85	15	1	11	39	.236	18	56	0	732	48	8	.990

DIVISION SERIES RECORD

| | | | | | | | BATTING | | | | | | | FIELDING | | |
Year Team (League)	Pos.	G	AB	R	H	2B	3B	HR	RBI	Avg.	BB	SO	SB	PO	A	E	Avg.
1995—Atlanta (N.L.)								Did not play.									
1996—Atlanta (N.L.)	C	1	3	0	1	0	0	0	0	.333	0	0	0	10	0	0	1.000
1997—Atlanta (N.L.)	C	1	3	0	0	0	0	0	0	.000	0	1	0	6	0	0	1.000
Division series totals (2 years)		2	6	0	1	0	0	0	0	.167	0	1	0	16	0	0	1.000

CHAMPIONSHIP SERIES RECORD

| | | | | | | | BATTING | | | | | | | FIELDING | | |
Year Team (League)	Pos.	G	AB	R	H	2B	3B	HR	RBI	Avg.	BB	SO	SB	PO	A	E	Avg.
1995—Atlanta (N.L.)								Did not play.									
1996—Atlanta (N.L.)	C-1B	4	1	0	0	0	0	0	0	.000	1	0	0	7	0	0	1.000
1997—Atlanta (N.L.)	C	2	3	0	0	0	0	0	0	.000	0	0	0	14	0	0	1.000
Championship series totals (2 years)		6	4	0	0	0	0	0	0	.000	1	0	0	21	0	0	1.000

WORLD SERIES RECORD

NOTES: Member of World Series championship team (1995).

| | | | | | | | BATTING | | | | | | | FIELDING | | |
Year Team (League)	Pos.	G	AB	R	H	2B	3B	HR	RBI	Avg.	BB	SO	SB	PO	A	E	Avg.
1995—Atlanta (N.L.)								Did not play.									
1996—Atlanta (N.L.)	C	2	1	0	0	0	0	0	0	.000	0	0	0	2	0	0	1.000
World Series totals (1 year)		2	1	0	0	0	0	0	0	.000	0	0	0	2	0	0	1.000

PEREZ, EDUARDO — 1B/OF/3B — REDS

PERSONAL: Born September 11, 1969, in Cincinnati. ... 6-4/215. ... Bats right, throws right. ... Full name: Eduardo Antanacio Perez. ... Son of Tony Perez, special assistant to general managaer, Florida Marlins; major league infielder with four teams (1964-86) and manager, Cincinnati Reds (1993); and brother of Victor Perez, minor league outfielder/first baseman (1990).
HIGH SCHOOL: Robinson (Santurce, Puerto Rico).
COLLEGE: Florida State.
TRANSACTIONS/CAREER NOTES: Selected by California Angels organization in first round (17th pick overall) of free-agent draft (June 3, 1991). ... On Palm Springs disabled list (May 9-19, 1992). ... On Vancouver disabled list (June 26-July 7, 1994). ... Traded by Angels to Cincinnati Reds for P Will Pennyfeather (April 5, 1996).
STATISTICAL NOTES: Career major league grand slams: 1.

| | | | | | | | BATTING | | | | | | | FIELDING | | |
Year Team (League)	Pos.	G	AB	R	H	2B	3B	HR	RBI	Avg.	BB	SO	SB	PO	A	E	Avg.
1991—Boise (Northwest)	OF-1B	46	160	35	46	13	0	1	22	.288	19	39	12	87	6	3	.969
1992—Palm Springs (Cal.)	3B-SS-OF	54	204	37	64	8	4	3	35	.314	23	33	14	30	90	16	.882
—Midland (Texas)	3B-OF-1B	62	235	27	54	8	1	3	23	.230	22	49	19	53	97	13	.920
1993—Vancouver (PCL)	3B-1B-OF	96	363	66	111	23	6	12	70	.306	28	83	21	98	174	23	.922
—California (A.L.)	3B-DH	52	180	16	45	6	2	4	30	.250	9	39	5	24	101	5	.962
1994—California (A.L.)	1B	38	129	10	27	7	0	5	16	.209	12	29	3	305	15	1	.997
—Vancouver (PCL)	3B	61	219	31	65	14	3	7	38	.297	34	53	1	35	116	12	.926
—Ariz. Angels (Ariz.)	3B	1	3	0	0	0	0	0	0	.000	1	1	0	0	3	0	1.000
1995—Vancouver (PCL)■	3B-1B	69	246	39	80	12	7	6	37	.325	25	34	6	94	90	6	.968
—California (A.L.)	3B-DH	29	71	9	12	4	1	1	7	.169	12	9	0	16	37	7	.883
1996—Indianapolis (A.A.)■	3B-1B	122	451	84	132	29	5	21	84	.293	51	69	11	110	215	21	.939
—Cincinnati (N.L.)	3B-1B	18	36	8	8	0	0	3	5	.222	5	9	0	59	11	0	1.000
1997—Cincinnati (N.L.)	1-O-3-DH	106	297	44	75	18	0	16	52	.253	29	76	5	506	49	2	.996
American League totals (3 years)		119	380	35	84	17	3	10	53	.221	33	77	8	345	153	13	.975
National League totals (2 years)		124	333	52	83	18	0	19	57	.249	34	85	5	565	60	2	.997
Major league totals (5 years)		243	713	87	167	35	3	29	110	.234	67	162	13	910	213	15	.987

P

PEREZ, MIKE — P

PERSONAL: Born October 19, 1964, in Yauco, Puerto Rico. ... 6-0/200. ... Throws right, bats right. ... Full name: Michael Irvin Perez.
HIGH SCHOOL: Yauco (Puerto Rico).
JUNIOR COLLEGE: San Jose (Calif.) City College.
COLLEGE: Troy (Ala.) State.
TRANSACTIONS/CAREER NOTES: Selected by St. Louis Cardinals organization in 12th round of free-agent draft (June 2, 1986). ... On Louisville disabled list (July 25-August 6, 1991). ... On St. Louis disabled list (July 6-August 15, 1993); included rehabilitation assignment to Arkansas (August 7-15). ... On St. Louis disabled list (April 25-May 25 and July 16, 1994-remainder of season). ... Granted free agency (December 23, 1994). ... Signed by Iowa, Chicago Cubs organization (April 11, 1995). ... Granted free agency (October 15, 1996). ... Signed by Omaha, Kansas City Royals organization (May 2, 1997). ... Released by Royals (August 22, 1997).

Year Team (League)	W	L	Pct.	ERA	G	GS	CG	ShO	Sv.	IP	H	R	ER	BB	SO
1986— Johnson City (App.)	3	5	.375	2.97	18	8	2	0	3	72 2/3	69	35	24	22	72
1987— Springfield (Mid.)	6	2	.750	0.85	58	0	0	0	*41	84 1/3	47	12	8	21	119
1988— Arkansas (Texas)	1	3	.250	11.30	11	0	0	0	0	14 1/3	18	18	18	13	17
— St. Petersburg (FSL)	2	2	.500	2.08	35	0	0	0	17	43 1/3	24	12	10	16	45
1989— Arkansas (Texas)	4	6	.400	3.64	57	0	0	0	*33	76 2/3	68	34	31	32	74
1990— Louisville (A.A.)	7	7	.500	4.28	•57	0	0	0	*31	67 1/3	64	34	32	33	69
— St. Louis (N.L.)	1	0	1.000	3.95	13	0	0	0	1	13 2/3	12	6	6	3	5
1991— St. Louis (N.L.)	0	2	.000	5.82	14	0	0	0	0	17	19	11	11	7	7
— Louisville (A.A.)	3	5	.375	6.13	37	0	0	0	4	47	54	38	32	25	39
1992— St. Louis (N.L.)	9	3	.750	1.84	77	0	0	0	0	93	70	23	19	32	46
1993— St. Louis (N.L.)	7	2	.778	2.48	65	0	0	0	7	72 2/3	65	24	20	20	58
— Arkansas (Texas)	0	0	. . .	7.36	4	0	0	0	0	3 2/3	7	3	3	0	4
1994— St. Louis (N.L.)	2	3	.400	8.71	36	0	0	0	12	31	52	32	30	10	20
1995— Chicago (N.L.)■	2	6	.250	3.66	68	0	0	0	2	71 1/3	72	30	29	27	49
1996— Chicago (N.L.)	1	0	1.000	4.67	24	0	0	0	0	27	29	14	14	13	22
— Iowa (Am. Assoc.)	0	4	.000	6.53	23	0	0	0	0	30 1/3	42	24	22	15	19
1997— Omaha (Am. Assoc.)■	4	1	.800	4.71	34	0	0	0	8	36 1/3	38	22	19	18	29
— Kansas City (A.L.)	2	0	1.000	3.54	16	0	0	0	0	20 1/3	15	8	8	8	17
A.L. totals (1 year)	2	0	1.000	3.54	16	0	0	0	0	20 1/3	15	8	8	8	17
N.L. totals (7 years)	22	16	.579	3.56	297	0	0	0	22	325 2/3	319	140	129	112	207
Major league totals (8 years)	24	16	.600	3.56	313	0	0	0	22	346	334	148	137	120	224

PEREZ, NEIFI — SS — ROCKIES

PERSONAL: Born February 2, 1975, in Villa Mella, Dominican Republic. ... 6-0/173. ... Bats left, throws right. ... Full name: Neifi Neftali Diaz Perez.
TRANSACTIONS/CAREER NOTES: Signed as non-drafted free agent by Colorado Rockies organization (November 9, 1992).
STATISTICAL NOTES: Led California League shortstops with 650 total chances and 86 double plays in 1994. ... Tied for Eastern League lead in double plays by shortstop with 80 in 1995. ... Led Pacific Coast League shortstops with 678 total chances and 91 double plays in 1996.

Year Team (League)	Pos.	G	AB	R	H	2B	3B	HR	RBI	Avg.	BB	SO	SB	PO	A	E	Avg.
1993— Bend (Northwest)	SS-2B	75	296	35	77	11	4	3	32	.260	19	43	19	127	244	25	.937
1994— Central Valley (Cal.) ...	SS	•134	506	64	121	16	7	1	35	.239	32	79	9	*223	388	*39	.940
1995— Colo. Springs (PCL) ...	SS	11	36	4	10	4	0	0	2	.278	0	5	1	16	28	3	.936
— New Haven (Eastern)..	SS	116	427	59	108	28	3	5	43	.253	24	52	5	175	358	18	*.967
1996— Colo. Springs (PCL) ...	SS	133	*570	77	180	28	12	7	72	.316	21	48	16	*244	*409	*25	.963
— Colorado (N.L.)	SS-2B	17	45	4	7	2	0	0	3	.156	0	8	2	21	28	2	.961
1997— Colo. Springs (PCL) ...	SS	68	303	68	110	24	3	8	46	.363	17	27	8	119	198	8	.975
— Colorado (N.L.)	SS-2B-3B	83	313	46	91	13	10	5	31	.291	21	43	4	185	287	9	.981
Major league totals (2 years)		100	358	50	98	15	10	5	34	.274	21	51	6	206	315	11	.979

PEREZ, ROBERT — OF — BLUE JAYS

PERSONAL: Born June 4, 1969, in Bolivar, Venezuela. ... 6-3/220. ... Bats right, throws right. ... Full name: Robert Alexander Jimenez Perez.
HIGH SCHOOL: Raul Leoni Otero (Bolivar, Venezuela).
TRANSACTIONS/CAREER NOTES: Signed as non-drafted free agent by Toronto Blue Jays organization (May 1, 1989).
STATISTICAL NOTES: Led International League outfielders with 303 total chances in 1993. ... Tied for International League lead in grounding into double plays with 19 in 1993. ... Led International League in grounding into double plays with 21 in 1994. ... Tied for International League lead with eight sacrifice flies in 1994. ... Led International League with 249 total bases in 1995.

Year Team (League)	Pos.	G	AB	R	H	2B	3B	HR	RBI	Avg.	BB	SO	SB	PO	A	E	Avg.
1989— Dom. Dodgers (DSL) .	OF	52	219	34	*79	*20	3	5	40	.361	21	23	5	. . .	. . .	. . .	. . .
1990— St. Catharines (NYP) ..	OF	52	207	21	54	10	2	5	25	.261	8	34	7	80	5	1	.988
— Myrtle Beach (SAL)	OF	21	72	8	21	2	0	1	10	.292	3	9	2	40	1	1	.976
1991— Dunedin (Fla. St.)	OF	127	480	50	*145	28	6	4	50	*.302	22	72	8	160	10	5	.971
— Syracuse (Int'l)	OF	4	20	2	4	1	0	0	1	.200	0	2	0	5	0	1	.833
1992— Knoxville (Southern) ..	OF	*139	•526	59	137	25	5	9	59	.260	13	87	11	241	13	7	.973
1993— Syracuse (Int'l)	OF	138	524	72	154	26	10	12	64	.294	24	65	13	278	•13	*12	.960
1994— Syracuse (Int'l)	OF	128	510	63	155	28	3	10	65	.304	27	76	4	231	8	9	.964
— Toronto (A.L.)	OF	4	8	0	1	0	0	0	0	.125	0	1	0	3	1	0	1.000
1995— Syracuse (Int'l)	OF	122	502	70	*172	*38	6	9	67	*.343	13	60	7	208	7	8	.964
— Toronto (A.L.)	OF	17	48	2	9	2	0	1	3	.188	0	5	0	30	0	0	1.000
1996— Toronto (A.L.)	OF-DH	86	202	30	66	10	0	2	21	.327	8	17	3	114	3	0	1.000
1997— Toronto (A.L.)	OF-DH	37	78	4	15	4	1	2	6	.192	0	16	0	35	0	2	.946
Major league totals (4 years)		144	336	36	91	16	1	5	30	.271	8	39	3	182	4	2	.989

P

PEREZ, SANTIAGO   SS   BREWERS

PERSONAL: Born December 30, 1975, in Santo Domingo, Dominican Republic. ... 6-2/150. ... Bats both, throws right. ... Full name: Santiago Alberto Perez.
HIGH SCHOOL: Liceo Victor Estrella (Santo Domingo, Dominican Republic).
TRANSACTIONS/CAREER NOTES: Signed as non-drafted free agent by Detroit Tigers organization (March 10, 1993).

							BATTING								FIELDING			
Year Team (League)	Pos.	G	AB	R	H	2B	3B	HR	RBI	Avg.	BB	SO	SB	PO	A	E	Avg.
1993— Dom. Tigers (DSL)	IF-OF	58	171	28	45	6	2	0	17	.263	20	22	17	59	47	16	.869
1994— Dom. Tigers (DSL)	SS	60	227	54	78	7	9	2	47	.344	32	43	20	106	183	39	.881
1995— Fayetteville (SAL)	SS	130	425	54	101	15	1	4	44	.238	30	98	10	176	327	46	.916
1996— Lakeland (Fla. St.)	SS	122	418	33	105	18	2	1	27	.251	16	88	6	192	310	41	.924
1997— Lakeland (Fla. St.)	SS	111	445	66	122	20	12	4	46	.274	20	98	21	148	322	34	.933

PEREZ, TOMAS   IF   BLUE JAYS

PERSONAL: Born December 29, 1973, in Barquisimeto, Venezuela. ... 5-11/172. ... Bats both, throws right. ... Full name: Tomas Orlando Perez.
TRANSACTIONS/CAREER NOTES: Signed as non-drafted free agent by Montreal Expos organization (July 11, 1991). ... Selected by California Angels from Expos organization in Rule 5 major league draft (December 5, 1994). ... Contract sold by Angels to Toronto Blue Jays (December 5, 1994). ... On Toronto disabled list (June 25-July 25, 1997); included rehabilitation assignment to Syracuse (July 12-24).
STATISTICAL NOTES: Led Midwest League shortstops with 217 putouts and 65 double plays in 1994. ... Led International League with 14 sacrifice hits in 1997.

							BATTING								FIELDING			
Year Team (League)	Pos.	G	AB	R	H	2B	3B	HR	RBI	Avg.	BB	SO	SB	PO	A	E	Avg.
1992— Dom. Expos (DSL)	IF	44	151	35	46	7	0	1	19	.305	27	20	12	112	138	12	.954
1993— GC Expos (GCL)	SS	52	189	27	46	3	1	2	21	.243	23	25	8	*121	*205	12	*.964
1994— Burl. (Midw.)	SS-2B	119	465	76	122	22	1	8	47	.262	48	78	8	†221	347	34	.944
1995— Toronto (A.L.)■..........	SS-2B-3B	41	98	12	24	3	1	1	8	.245	7	18	0	48	77	5	.962
1996— Syracuse (Int'l)..........	SS-2B	40	123	15	34	10	1	1	13	.276	7	19	8	80	97	7	.962
— Toronto (A.L.).............	2B-3B-SS	91	295	24	74	13	4	1	19	.251	25	29	1	151	250	15	.964
1997— Syracuse (Int'l)..........	SS	89	303	32	68	13	0	1	20	.224	37	67	3	158	274	12	.973
— Toronto (A.L.).............	SS-2B	40	123	9	24	3	2	0	9	.195	11	28	1	58	124	3	.984
Major league totals (3 years)		172	516	45	122	19	7	2	36	.236	43	75	2	257	451	23	.969

PEREZ, YORKIS   P

PERSONAL: Born September 30, 1967, in Bajos de Haina, Dominican Republic. ... 6-0/180. ... Throws left, bats left. ... Full name: Yorkis Miguel Perez.
TRANSACTIONS/CAREER NOTES: Signed as non-drafted free agent by Minnesota Twins organization (February 23, 1983). ... Traded by Twins organization with P Neal Heaton, P Al Cardwood and C Jeff Reed to Montreal Expos for P Jeff Reardon and C Tom Nieto (February 3, 1987). ... Granted free agency (October 15, 1990). ... Signed by Atlanta Braves organization (February 1, 1991). ... Traded by Braves with P Turk Wendell to Chicago Cubs for P Mike Bielecki and C Damon Berryhill (September 29, 1991). ... Released by Cubs (December 11, 1991). ... Signed by Yomiuri Giants of Japan Central League (1992). ... Released by Yomiuri (August 17, 1992). ... Signed as free agent by Jacksonville, Seattle Mariners organization (August 19, 1992). ... Released by Mariners organization (January 11, 1993). ... Signed by Montreal Expos organization (February 15, 1993). ... Granted free agency (October 15, 1993). ... Signed by Edmonton, Florida Marlins organization (December 15, 1993). ... On Florida disabled list (June 10-30, 1994); included rehabilitation assignment to Portland (June 25-30). ... Traded by Marlins to Braves for P Martin Sanchez (December 13, 1996). ... Claimed on waivers by New York Mets (March 31, 1997). ... On New York disabled list (April 5-June 5, 1997); included rehabilitation assignment to Norfolk (May 15-June 5). ... Granted free agency (October 15, 1997).

Year Team (League)	W	L	Pct.	ERA	G	GS	CG	ShO	Sv.	IP	H	R	ER	BB	SO
1983— Elizabethton (Appal.)	0	1	.000	20.25	3	1	0	0	0	4	5	9	9	9	6
1984— Elizabethton (Appal.)	0	0	. . .	0.00	1	0	0	0	0	1 1/3	1	0	0	1	1
1985— Santiago (DSL)	6	8	.429	3.17	21	16	7	2	1	122	104	58	43	63	69
1986— Kenosha (Midwest)	4	11	.267	5.15	31	18	3	0	0	131	120	81	75	88	144
1987— W.P. Beach (FSL)■..........	6	2	.750	2.34	15	15	3	0	0	100	78	36	26	46	111
— Jacksonville (Southern)......	2	7	.222	4.05	12	10	1	1	1	60	61	34	27	30	60
1988— Jacksonville (Southern)......	8	12	.400	5.82	27	25	2	1	0	130	142	96	84	94	105
1989— W.P. Beach (FSL).............	7	6	.538	2.76	18	12	0	0	1	94 2/3	62	34	29	54	85
— Jacksonville (Southern)......	4	3	.571	3.60	20	0	0	0	0	35	25	16	14	34	50
1990— Jacksonville (Southern)......	2	2	.500	6.00	28	2	0	0	1	42	36	34	28	34	39
— Indianapolis (A.A.).............	1	1	.500	2.31	9	0	0	0	0	11 2/3	8	5	3	6	8
1991— Richmond (Int'l)■.............	•12	3	•.800	3.79	36	10	0	0	1	107	99	47	45	53	102
— Chicago (N.L.)■.................	1	0	1.000	2.08	3	0	0	0	0	4 1/3	2	1	1	2	3
1992— Yomiuri (Jp. Cen.)■...........	0	0	.000	7.11	3	. . .	. . .	. . .	0	6 1/3	8	. . .	5	3	6
1993— Harrisburg (Eastern)■........	4	2	.667	3.45	34	0	0	0	3	44 1/3	49	26	17	20	58
— Ottawa (Int'l).....................	0	1	.000	3.60	20	0	0	0	5	20	14	12	8	7	17
1994— Florida (N.L.)■.................	3	0	1.000	3.54	44	0	0	0	0	40 2/3	33	18	16	14	41
— Portland (Eastern)	0	0	. . .	0.00	2	0	0	0	0	2	1	0	0	0	2
1995— Florida (N.L.)	2	6	.250	5.21	69	0	0	0	1	46 2/3	35	29	27	28	47
1996— Florida (N.L.)	3	4	.429	5.29	64	0	0	0	0	47 2/3	51	28	28	31	47
— Charlotte (Int'l)	3	0	1.000	4.22	9	0	0	0	0	10 2/3	6	5	5	3	13
1997— New York (N.L.)■.............	0	1	.000	8.31	9	0	0	0	0	8 2/3	15	8	8	4	7
— Norfolk (Int'l)	1	0	1.000	3.48	17	0	0	0	3	20 2/3	22	9	8	7	24
— Binghamton (Eastern)	2	1	.667	0.66	12	3	0	0	0	27 1/3	15	4	2	12	39
Major league totals (5 years)......	9	11	.450	4.86	189	0	0	0	1	148	136	84	80	79	145

P

PERSONAL: Born June 8, 1975, in Burlington, Iowa. ... 6-0/175. ... Throws left, bats left. ... Full name: Matthew Alan Perisho.
HIGH SCHOOL: McClintock (Tempe, Ariz.).
TRANSACTIONS/CAREER NOTES: Selected by California Angels organization in third round of free-agent draft (June 3, 1993). ... Angels franchise renamed Anaheim Angels for 1997 season. ... Traded by Angels to Texas Rangers for IF Mike Bell (October 31, 1997).

Year Team (League)	W	L	Pct.	ERA	G	GS	CG	ShO	Sv.	IP	H	R	ER	BB	SO
1993— Ariz. Angels (Ariz.)	7	3	.700	3.66	11	11	1	1	0	64	58	32	26	23	65
1994— Cedar Rapids (Midw.)	12	9	.571	4.33	27	27	0	0	0	147 2/3	165	90	71	88	107
1995— Lake Elsinore (Calif.)	8	9	.471	6.32	24	22	0	0	0	115 1/3	137	91	81	60	68
1996— Lake Elsinore (Calif.)	7	5	.583	4.20	21	18	1	1	0	128 2/3	131	72	60	58	97
— Midland (Texas)	3	2	.600	3.21	8	8	0	0	0	53 1/3	48	22	19	20	50
1997— Midland (Texas)	5	2	.714	2.96	10	10	3	•1	0	73	60	26	24	26	62
— Anaheim (A.L.)	0	2	.000	6.00	11	8	0	0	0	45	59	34	30	28	35
— Vancouver (PCL)	4	4	.500	5.33	9	9	1	0	0	52 1/3	68	42	31	29	47
Major league totals (1 year)	0	2	.000	6.00	11	8	0	0	0	45	59	34	30	28	35

PERSONAL: Born March 15, 1975, in Miami. ... 6-2/193. ... Throws right, bats right. ... Full name: Daniel Lee Perkins.
HIGH SCHOOL: Westminster Christian (Miami).
TRANSACTIONS/CAREER NOTES: Selected by Minnesota Twins organization in second round of free-agent draft (June 3, 1993).

Year Team (League)	W	L	Pct.	ERA	G	GS	CG	ShO	Sv.	IP	H	R	ER	BB	SO
1993— Elizabethton (Appal.)	3	3	.500	5.00	10	10	0	0	0	45	46	33	25	25	30
1994— Fort Wayne (Midw.)	1	8	.111	6.22	12	12	0	0	0	50 2/3	61	38	35	22	34
— Elizabethton (Appal.)	0	2	.000	3.67	10	9	1	0	0	54	51	31	22	14	34
1995— Fort Wayne (Midw.)	7	12	.368	5.49	29	22	0	0	0	121 1/3	133	86	74	69	82
1996— Fort Myers (Fla. St.)	13	7	.650	2.96	39	13	3	1	2	136 2/3	125	52	45	37	111
1997— New Britain (East.)	7	10	.412	4.91	24	24	2	0	0	144 2/3	158	94	79	53	114

PERSONAL: Born September 15, 1969, in Mayo, Fla. ... 6-2/215. ... Bats right, throws right. ... Full name: Herbert Edward Perry Jr. ... Brother of Chan Perry, outfielder, Cleveland Indians organization.
HIGH SCHOOL: Lafayette (Mayo, Fla.).
COLLEGE: Florida.
TRANSACTIONS/CAREER NOTES: Selected by Cleveland Indians organization in second round of free-agent draft (June 3, 1991). ... On disabled list (June 18-July 13, 1991 and July 23, 1993-remainder of season). ... On Buffalo disabled list (June 7-27, 1996). ... On Cleveland disabled list (September 11, 1996-remainder of season). ... On disabled list (March 26, 1997-enitre season). ... Selected by Tampa Bay Devil Rays in third round (68th pick overall) of expansion draft (November 18, 1997).
STATISTICAL NOTES: Led Eastern League in being hit by pitch with 15 in 1993.

Year Team (League)	Pos.	G	AB	R	H	2B	3B	HR	RBI	Avg.	BB	SO	SB	PO	A	E	Avg.
1991— Watertown (NYP)	DH	14	52	3	11	2	0	0	5	.212	8	7	0	...	...	...	...
1992— Kinston (Carolina)	1B-OF-3B	121	449	74	125	16	1	19	77	.278	46	89	12	297	39	5	.985
1993— Cant./Akr. (Eastern)	1B-3B-OF	89	327	52	88	21	1	9	55	.269	37	47	7	378	86	10	.979
1994— Charlotte (Int'l)	1B-3B-OF	102	376	67	123	20	4	13	70	.327	41	55	9	747	55	6	.993
— Cleveland (A.L.)	1B-3B	4	9	1	1	0	0	0	1	.111	3	1	0	25	5	1	.968
1995— Buffalo (A.A.)	1B	49	180	27	57	14	1	2	17	.317	15	18	1	419	44	3	.994
— Cleveland (A.L.)	1B-DH-3B	52	162	23	51	13	1	3	23	.315	13	28	1	391	30	0	1.000
1996— Buffalo (A.A.)	1B-3B-OF	40	151	21	51	7	1	5	30	.338	7	19	4	217	24	4	.984
— Cleveland (A.L.)	1B-3B	7	12	1	1	1	0	0	0	.083	1	2	1	29	2	0	1.000
1997—								Did not play.									
Major league totals (3 years)		63	183	25	53	14	1	3	24	.290	17	31	2	445	37	1	.998

DIVISION SERIES RECORD

Year Team (League)	Pos.	G	AB	R	H	2B	3B	HR	RBI	Avg.	BB	SO	SB	PO	A	E	Avg.
1995— Cleveland (A.L.)	PH	1	1	0	0	0	0	0	0	.000	0	0	0	...	...	...	...

CHAMPIONSHIP SERIES RECORD

Year Team (League)	Pos.	G	AB	R	H	2B	3B	HR	RBI	Avg.	BB	SO	SB	PO	A	E	Avg.
1995— Cleveland (A.L.)	1B	3	8	0	0	0	0	0	0	.000	1	3	0	30	0	0	1.000

WORLD SERIES RECORD

Year Team (League)	Pos.	G	AB	R	H	2B	3B	HR	RBI	Avg.	BB	SO	SB	PO	A	E	Avg.
1995— Cleveland (A.L.)	1B	3	5	0	00	0	0	0	0	.000	0	2	0	13	2	0	1.000

P

PERSONAL: Born October 6, 1969, in Lowell, Mass. ... 6-0/185. ... Throws right, bats right. ... Full name: Robert Alan Person.
HIGH SCHOOL: University City (Mo.).
JUNIOR COLLEGE: Seminole (Okla.).
TRANSACTIONS/CAREER NOTES: Selected by Cleveland Indians organization in 25th round of free-agent draft (June 5, 1989). ... Loaned by Indians organization to Bend, independent (June 12-25, 1991). ... Traded by Indians organization to Chicago White Sox organization for P Grady Hall (June 27, 1991). ... On disabled list (April 10-May 13, 1992). ... Selected by Florida Marlins in second round (47th pick overall) of

expansion draft (November 17, 1992). ... Granted free agency (December 19, 1992). ... Re-signed by Edmonton, Marlins organization (January 8, 1993). ... Traded by Marlins organization to New York Mets organization for P Steve Long (March 30, 1994). ... Traded by Mets to Toronto Blue Jays for 1B John Olerud and cash (December 20, 1996). ... On Toronto disabled list (May 8-26 and September 9-28, 1997).

MISCELLANEOUS: Appeared in two games as pinch-runner with New York (1996).

Year Team (League)	W	L	Pct.	ERA	G	GS	CG	ShO	Sv.	IP	H	R	ER	BB	SO
1989— Burlington (Appalachian)....	0	1	.000	3.18	10	5	0	0	1	34	23	13	12	17	19
1990— Watertown (NYP)	1	0	1.000	1.10	5	2	0	0	0	16 1/3	8	2	2	7	19
— Kinston (Carolina)	1	0	1.000	2.70	4	3	0	0	0	16 2/3	17	6	5	9	7
— GC Indians (GCL)	0	2	.000	7.36	8	0	0	0	2	7 1/3	10	7	6	4	8
1991— Kinston (Carolina)	3	5	.375	4.67	11	11	0	0	0	52	56	37	27	42	45
— Bend (Northwest)■	1	1	.500	3.60	2	2	0	0	0	10	6	6	4	5	6
— South Bend (Mid.)■	4	3	.571	3.30	13	13	0	0	0	76 1/3	50	35	28	56	66
1992— Sarasota (Florida State)......	5	7	.417	3.59	19	18	1	0	0	105 1/3	90	48	42	62	85
1993— High Desert (Calif.)■	12	10	.545	4.69	28	26	4	0	0	169	184	*115	88	48	107
1994— Binghamton (Eastern)■	9	6	.600	3.45	31	23	3	2	0	159	124	68	61	68	130
1995— Binghamton (Eastern)	5	4	.556	3.11	26	7	1	0	7	66 2/3	46	27	23	25	65
— Norfolk (Int'l)	2	1	.667	4.50	5	4	0	0	0	32	30	17	16	13	33
— New York (N.L.)..................	1	0	1.000	0.75	3	1	0	0	0	12	5	1	1	2	10
1996— New York (N.L.)	4	5	.444	4.52	27	13	0	0	0	89 2/3	86	50	45	35	76
— Norfolk (Int'l)	5	0	1.000	3.35	8	8	0	0	0	43	33	16	16	21	32
1997— Toronto (A.L.)■	5	10	.333	5.61	23	22	0	0	0	128 1/3	125	86	80	60	99
— Syracuse (Int'l)	1	0	1.000	0.00	1	1	0	0	0	7	4	1	0	4	5
A.L. totals (1 year)	5	10	.333	5.61	23	22	0	0	0	128 1/3	125	86	80	60	99
N.L. totals (2 years)	5	5	.500	4.07	30	14	0	0	0	101 2/3	91	51	46	37	86
Major league totals (3 years)	10	15	.400	4.93	53	36	0	0	0	230	216	137	126	97	185

RECORD AS POSITION PLAYER

					BATTING								FIELDING		
Year Team (League)	Pos.	G	AB	R	H	2B	3B	HR	RBI	Avg.	BB	SO	SB	PO	A	E	Avg.
1990— GC Indians (GCL)	OF	24	46	6	4	0	0	0	3	.087	10	12	1	10	2	0	1.000

PETAGINE, ROBERTO   1B   METS

PERSONAL: Born June 2, 1971, in Nueva Esparita, Venezuela. ... 6-1/170. ... Bats left, throws left. ... Full name: Roberto Antonio Petagine. ... Name pronounced PET-uh-GHEEN.

TRANSACTIONS/CAREER NOTES: Signed as non-drafted free agent by Houston Astros organization (February 13, 1990). ... On Tucson disabled list (April 30-June 11, 1994). ... Traded by Astros with 3B Ken Caminiti, OF Steve Finley, SS Andujar Cedeno, P Brian Williams and a player to be named later to San Diego Padres for OF Phil Plantier, OF Derek Bell, P Pedro Martinez, P Doug Brocail, IF Craig Shipley and SS Ricky Gutierrez (December 28, 1994); Padres acquired P Sean Fesh to complete deal (May 1, 1995). ... Traded by Padres with P Scott Adair to New York Mets for P Luis Arroyo and P Pete Walker (March 17, 1996).

HONORS: Named Texas League Player of the Year (1993). ... Named International League Most Valuable Player (1997).

STATISTICAL NOTES: Led Gulf Coast League first basemen with .990 fielding percentage and 46 double plays in 1990. ... Led Texas League with .442 on-base percentage and 14 intentional bases on balls received in 1993. ... Led International League with seven intentional bases on balls received in 1996. ... Led International League with .430 on-base percentage in 1997. ... Led International League first basemen with 117 double plays in 1997.

					BATTING								FIELDING		
Year Team (League)	Pos.	G	AB	R	H	2B	3B	HR	RBI	Avg.	BB	SO	SB	PO	A	E	Avg.
1990— GC Astros (GCL)	1B-OF	55	187	35	54	5	4	2	24	.289	26	23	9	474	36	5	†.990
1991— Burl. (Midw.)	1B	124	432	72	112	24	1	12	58	.259	71	74	7	940	60	22	.978
1992— Osceola (Fla. St.)........	1B	86	307	52	90	22	4	7	49	.293	47	47	3	701	74	10	.987
— Jackson (Texas)	1B	21	70	8	21	4	0	4	12	.300	6	15	1	151	15	0	1.000
1993— Jackson (Texas)	1B	128	437	73	146	*36	2	15	90	*.334	*84	89	6	1033	*110	14	.988
1994— Houston (N.L.)	1B	8	7	0	0	0	0	0	0	.000	1	3	0	3	0	0	1.000
— Tucson (PCL)	1B	65	247	53	78	19	0	10	44	.316	35	54	3	597	35	10	.984
1995— San Diego (N.L.)■	1B-OF	89	124	15	29	8	0	3	17	.234	26	41	0	263	22	1	.997
— Las Vegas (PCL)	1B	19	56	8	12	2	1	1	5	.214	13	17	1	110	7	3	.975
1996— Norfolk (Int'l)■	1B	95	314	49	100	24	3	12	65	.318	51	75	4	743	67	*15	.982
— New York (N.L.)..........	1B	50	99	10	23	3	0	4	17	.232	9	27	0	209	23	1	.996
1997— Norfolk (Int'l)	1B-OF	129	441	90	140	32	1	31	100	.317	*85	92	0	1023	68	11	.990
— New York (N.L.)..........	1B-OF	12	15	2	1	0	0	0	2	.067	3	6	0	10	3	0	1.000
Major league totals (4 years)		159	245	27	53	11	0	7	36	.216	39	77	0	485	48	2	.996

PETERS, CHRIS   P   PIRATES

PERSONAL: Born January 28, 1972, in Fort Thomas, Ky. ... 6-1/169. ... Throws left, bats left. ... Full name: Christopher Michael Peters.

HIGH SCHOOL: Peters Township (McMurray, Pa.).

COLLEGE: Indiana.

TRANSACTIONS/CAREER NOTES: Selected by Pittsburgh Pirates organization in 37th round of free-agent draft (June 3, 1993).

Year Team (League)	W	L	Pct.	ERA	G	GS	CG	ShO	Sv.	IP	H	R	ER	BB	SO
1993— Welland (N.Y.-Penn)	1	0	1.000	4.55	16	0	0	0	0	27 2/3	33	16	14	20	25
1994— Augusta (S. Atl.)................	4	5	.444	4.30	54	0	0	0	4	60 2/3	51	34	29	33	83
— Salem (Carolina)	1	0	1.000	13.50	3	0	0	0	0	3 1/3	5	5	5	1	2
1995— Lynchburg (Carolina)	11	5	.688	2.43	24	24	3	*3	0	144 2/3	126	57	39	35	132
— Carolina (Southern)...........	2	1	1.000	1.29	2	2	0	0	0	14	9	2	2	2	7
1996— Carolina (Southern)	7	3	.700	2.64	14	14	0	0	0	92	73	37	27	34	69
— Calgary (PCL)................	1	1	.500	0.98	4	4	0	0	0	27 2/3	18	3	3	8	16
— Pittsburgh (N.L.).............	2	4	.333	5.63	16	10	0	0	0	64	72	43	40	25	28
1997— Calgary (PCL)................	2	4	.333	4.38	14	9	0	0	1	51 1/3	52	32	25	30	55
— Pittsburgh (N.L.).............	2	2	.500	4.58	31	1	0	0	0	37 1/3	38	23	19	21	17
Major league totals (2 years)	4	6	.400	5.24	47	11	0	0	0	101 1/3	110	66	59	46	45

P

PETERSON, CHARLES — OF — PIRATES

PERSONAL: Born May 8, 1974, in Laurens, S.C. ... 6-3/203. ... Bats right, throws right. ... Full name: Charles Edward Peterson.
HIGH SCHOOL: Laurens (S.C.).
TRANSACTIONS/CAREER NOTES: Selected by Pittsburgh Pirates organization in first round (22nd pick overall) of free-agent draft (June 3, 1993). ... On disabled list (April 8-16, 1996).
STATISTICAL NOTES: Led Southern League in grounding into double plays with 15 in 1996. ... Led Southern League outfielders with five double plays in 1996. ... Led Southern League outfielders with six double plays in 1997.

Year Team (League)	Pos.	G	AB	R	H	2B	3B	HR	RBI	Avg.	BB	SO	SB	PO	A	E	Avg.
1993— GC Pirates (GCL)........	OF	49	188	28	57	11	3	1	23	.303	22	22	8	75	7	5	.943
1994— Augusta (S. Atl.).........	OF	108	415	55	106	14	6	4	40	.255	35	78	27	172	11	11	.943
1995— Lynchburg (Caro.)......	OF	107	391	61	107	9	4	7	51	.274	43	73	31	192	11	8	.962
— Carolina (Southern)....	OF	20	70	13	23	3	1	0	7	.329	9	15	2	40	2	1	.977
1996— Carolina (Southern)....	OF	125	462	71	127	24	2	7	63	.275	50	104	33	186	16	*11	.948
1997— Carolina (Southern)....	OF	126	442	59	111	26	4	7	68	.251	40	105	20	186	17	7	.967

PETKOVSEK, MARK — P — CARDINALS

PERSONAL: Born November 18, 1965, in Beaumont, Texas. ... 6-0/185. ... Throws right, bats right. ... Full name: Mark Joseph Petkovsek. ... Name pronounced PET-kie-zeck.
HIGH SCHOOL: Kelly (Beaumont, Texas).
COLLEGE: Texas.
TRANSACTIONS/CAREER NOTES: Selected by Texas Rangers organization in supplemental round ("sandwich pick" between first and second round, 29th pick overall) of free-agent draft (June 2, 1987); pick received as compensation for New York Yankees signing Type A free-agent OF Gary Ward. ... Granted free agency (October 16, 1991). ... Signed by Pittsburgh Pirates organization (January 22, 1992). ... Granted free agency (October 15, 1992). ... Re-signed by Pirates organization (November 9, 1992). ... On Buffalo disabled list (July 4-23, 1993). ... Granted free agency (October 12, 1993). ... Signed by Tucson, Houston Astros organization (March 4, 1994). ... On disabled list (July 20-August 12, 1994). ... Granted free agency (October 15, 1994). ... Signed by St. Louis Cardinals organization (November 10, 1994). ... On Louisville suspended list (May 12-17, 1995). ... On St. Louis disabled list (March 22-April 19, 1996); included rehabilitation assignments to St. Petersburg (April 5-12) and Louisville (April 12-19).
STATISTICAL NOTES: Pitched 5-0 no-hit victory against Colorado Springs (May 16, 1994).

Year Team (League)	W	L	Pct.	ERA	G	GS	CG	ShO	Sv.	IP	H	R	ER	BB	SO
1987— GC Rangers (GCL).............	0	0	...	3.18	3	1	0	0	0	5²/₃	4	2	2	2	7
— Charlotte (Fla. St.)...........	3	4	.429	4.02	11	10	0	0	0	56	67	36	25	17	23
1988— Charlotte (Fla. St.)...........	10	11	.476	2.97	28	28	7	•5	0	175²/₃	156	71	58	42	95
1989— Tulsa (Texas)	8	5	.615	3.47	21	21	1	0	0	140	144	63	54	35	66
— Oklahoma City (A.A.).........	0	4	.000	7.34	6	6	0	0	0	30²/₃	39	27	25	18	8
1990— Oklahoma City (A.A.).........	7	*14	.333	5.25	28	28	2	1	0	151	*187	*103	88	42	81
1991— Oklahoma City (A.A.).........	9	8	.529	4.93	25	24	3	1	0	149²/₃	162	89	82	38	67
— Texas (A.L.)	0	1	.000	14.46	4	1	0	0	0	9¹/₃	21	16	15	4	6
1992— Buffalo (A.A.)■	8	8	.500	3.53	32	22	1	0	1	150¹/₃	150	76	59	44	49
1993— Buffalo (A.A.)	3	4	.429	4.33	14	11	1	0	0	70²/₃	74	38	34	16	27
— Pittsburgh (N.L.)	3	0	1.000	6.96	26	0	0	0	0	32¹/₃	43	25	25	9	14
1994— Tucson (PCL)■	10	7	.588	4.62	25	23	1	1	0	138¹/₃	176	87	71	40	69
1995— Louisville (A.A.)■	4	1	.800	2.32	8	8	2	1	0	54¹/₃	38	16	14	8	30
— St. Louis (N.L.)	6	6	.500	4.00	26	21	1	1	0	137¹/₃	136	71	61	35	71
1996— St. Petersburg (FSL)	0	0	...	4.50	3	0	0	0	0	6	6	3	3	0	5
— Louisville (A.A.)	0	1	.000	9.00	2	1	0	0	0	3	5	4	3	1	4
— St. Louis (N.L.)	11	2	.846	3.55	48	6	0	0	0	88²/₃	83	37	35	35	45
1997— St. Louis (N.L.)..................	4	7	.364	5.06	55	2	0	0	2	96	109	61	54	31	51
A.L. totals (1 year)	0	1	.000	14.46	4	1	0	0	0	9¹/₃	21	16	15	4	6
N.L. totals (4 years)	24	15	.615	4.44	155	29	1	1	2	354¹/₃	371	194	175	110	181
Major league totals (5 years)......	24	16	.600	4.70	159	30	1	1	2	363²/₃	392	210	190	114	187

DIVISION SERIES RECORD

Year Team (League)	W	L	Pct.	ERA	G	GS	CG	ShO	Sv.	IP	H	R	ER	BB	SO
1996— St. Louis (N.L.)..................	0	0	...	0.00	1	0	0	0	0	2	0	0	0	0	1

CHAMPIONSHIP SERIES RECORD

RECORDS: Holds single-series record for most games pitched—6 (1996).

Year Team (League)	W	L	Pct.	ERA	G	GS	CG	ShO	Sv.	IP	H	R	ER	BB	SO
1996— St. Louis (N.L.)..................	0	1	.000	7.36	6	0	0	0	0	7¹/₃	11	6	6	4	7

PETRICK, BEN — C — ROCKIES

PERSONAL: Born April 7, 1977, in Hillsboro, Ore. ... 6-0/190. ... Bats right, throws right. ... Full name: Benjamin Wayne Petrick.
HIGH SCHOOL: Glencoe (Hillsboro, Ore.).
TRANSACTIONS/CAREER NOTES: Selected by Colorado Rockies organization in second round of free agent draft (June 3, 1995).

Year Team (League)	Pos.	G	AB	R	H	2B	3B	HR	RBI	Avg.	BB	SO	SB	PO	A	E	Avg.
1996— Asheville (S. Atl.)........	C	122	446	74	105	24	2	14	52	.235	75	98	19	766	95	12	.986
1997— Salem (Carolina)	C	121	412	68	102	23	3	15	56	.248	62	100	30	754	91	10	.988

P

PETT, JOSE — P — PIRATES

PERSONAL: Born January 8, 1976, in Sao Paulo, Brazil. ... 6-6/200. ... Throws right, bats right. ... Full name: Jose Augusto Pett.
TRANSACTIONS/CAREER NOTES: Signed as non-drafted free agent by Toronto Blue Jays organization (July 2, 1992). ... Traded by Blue Jays with P Jose Silva and SS Brandon Cromer and three players to be named later to Pittsburgh Pirates organization for OF Orlando Merced, IF

Carlos Garcia and P Don Plesac (November 14, 1996); Pirates acquired P Mike Halperin, IF Abraham Nunez and C/OF Craig Wilson to complete deal (December 11, 1996). ... On Carolina disabled list (April 3-May 11, 1997).

Year Team (League)	W	L	Pct.	ERA	G	GS	CG	ShO	Sv.	IP	H	R	ER	BB	SO
1993— GC Blue Jays (GCL)	1	1	.500	3.60	4	4	0	0	0	10	10	4	4	3	7
1994— Dunedin (Fla. St.)	4	8	.333	3.77	15	15	1	0	0	90 2/3	103	47	38	20	49
1995— Knoxville (Southern)	8	9	.471	4.26	26	25	1	1	0	141 2/3	132	87	67	48	89
1996— Knoxville (Southern)	4	2	.667	4.09	7	7	1	1	0	44	37	20	20	10	38
—Syracuse (Int'l)	2	9	.182	5.83	20	18	1	0	0	109 2/3	134	81	71	42	50
1997— Carolina (Southern)■	4	4	.500	3.51	14	14	0	0	0	74 1/3	76	37	29	25	39
—Calgary (PCL)	0	3	.000	9.64	3	3	0	0	0	14	25	15	15	8	8

PETTITTE, ANDY — P — YANKEES

PERSONAL: Born June 15, 1972, in Baton Rouge, La. ... 6-5/235. ... Throws left, bats left. ... Full name: Andrew Eugene Pettitte.
HIGH SCHOOL: Deer Park (Texas).
COLLEGE: San Jacinto College (Texas).
TRANSACTIONS/CAREER NOTES: Selected by New York Yankees organization in 22nd round of free-agent draft (June 4, 1990); did not sign. ... Signed as non-drafted free agent by Yankees organization (May 25, 1991). ... On Albany temporarily inactive list (June 5-10, 1994).
HONORS: Named lefthanded pitcher on THE SPORTING NEWS A.L. All-Star team (1996).

Year Team (League)	W	L	Pct.	ERA	G	GS	CG	ShO	Sv.	IP	H	R	ER	BB	SO
1991— GC Yankees (GCL)	4	1	.800	0.98	6	6	0	0	0	36 2/3	16	6	4	8	51
—Oneonta (N.Y.-Penn)	2	2	.500	2.18	6	6	1	0	0	33	33	18	8	16	32
1992— Greensboro (S. Atl.)	10	4	.714	2.20	27	27	2	1	0	168	141	53	41	55	130
1993— Prince William (Caro.)	11	9	.550	3.04	26	26	2	1	0	159 2/3	146	68	54	47	129
—Albany (S. Atl.)	1	0	1.000	3.60	1	1	0	0	0	5	5	4	2	2	6
1994— Alb./Colon. (Eastern)	7	2	.778	2.71	11	11	0	0	0	73	60	32	22	18	50
—Columbus (Int'l)	7	2	.778	2.98	16	16	3	0	0	96 2/3	101	40	32	21	61
1995— Columbus (Int'l)	0	0	...	0.00	2	2	0	0	0	11 2/3	7	0	0	0	8
—New York (A.L.)	12	9	.571	4.17	31	26	3	0	0	175	183	86	81	63	114
1996— New York (A.L.)	*21	8	.724	3.87	35	34	2	0	0	221	229	105	95	72	162
1997— New York (A.L.)	18	7	.720	2.88	35	•35	4	1	0	240 1/3	233	86	77	65	166
Major league totals (3 years)	51	24	.680	3.58	101	95	9	1	0	636 1/3	645	277	253	200	442

DIVISION SERIES RECORD

Year Team (League)	W	L	Pct.	ERA	G	GS	CG	ShO	Sv.	IP	H	R	ER	BB	SO
1995— New York (A.L.)	0	0	...	5.14	1	1	0	0	0	7	9	4	4	3	0
1996— New York (A.L.)	0	0	...	5.68	1	1	0	0	0	6 1/3	4	4	4	6	3
1997— New York (A.L.)	0	2	.000	8.49	2	2	0	0	0	11 2/3	15	11	11	1	5
Div. series totals (3 years)	0	2	.000	6.84	4	4	0	0	0	25	28	19	19	10	8

CHAMPIONSHIP SERIES RECORD

Year Team (League)	W	L	Pct.	ERA	G	GS	CG	ShO	Sv.	IP	H	R	ER	BB	SO
1996— New York (A.L.)	1	0	1.000	3.60	2	2	0	0	0	15	10	6	6	5	7

WORLD SERIES RECORD

RECORDS: Shares single-game record for most earned runs allowed—7 (October 20, 1996).
NOTES: Member of World Series championship team (1996).

Year Team (League)	W	L	Pct.	ERA	G	GS	CG	ShO	Sv.	IP	H	R	ER	BB	SO
1996— New York (A.L.)	1	1	.500	5.91	2	2	0	0	0	10 2/3	11	7	7	4	5

ALL-STAR GAME RECORD

Year League	W	L	Pct.	ERA	GS	CG	ShO	Sv.	IP	H	R	ER	BB	SO
1996— American							Did not play.							

PHELPS, TOMMY — P — EXPOS

PERSONAL: Born March 4, 1974, in Seoul, Korea. ... 6-4/205. ... Throws left, bats left. ... Full name: Thomas Allen Phelps.
HIGH SCHOOL: Robinson (Tampa, Fla.).
TRANSACTIONS/CAREER NOTES: Selected by Montreal Expos organization in eighth round of free-agent draft (June 1, 1992). ... On Harrisburg disabled list (June 24-July 13, 1997).

Year Team (League)	W	L	Pct.	ERA	G	GS	CG	ShO	Sv.	IP	H	R	ER	BB	SO
1993— Burlington (Midw.)	2	4	.333	3.73	8	8	0	0	0	41	36	18	17	13	33
—Jamestown (NYP)	3	•8	.273	4.58	16	15	1	0	0	92 1/3	102	62	47	37	74
1994— Burlington (Midw.)	8	8	.500	5.55	23	23	1	1	0	118 1/3	143	91	73	48	82
1995— W.P. Beach (FSL)	0	2	.000	16.20	2	2	0	0	0	5	10	10	9	11	5
—Albany (S. Atl.)	10	9	.526	3.33	24	24	1	0	0	135 1/3	142	76	50	45	119
1996— W.P. Beach (FSL)	10	2	.833	2.89	18	18	1	1	0	112	105	42	36	35	71
—Harrisburg (Eastern)	2	2	.500	2.47	8	8	2	2	0	47 1/3	43	16	13	19	23
1997— Harrisburg (Eastern)	10	6	.625	4.71	18	18	0	0	0	101 1/3	115	68	53	39	86

PHILLIPS, J.R. — 1B

PERSONAL: Born April 29, 1970, in West Covina, Calif. ... 6-1/185. ... Bats left, throws left. ... Full name: Charles Gene Phillips.
HIGH SCHOOL: Bishop Amat (La Puente, Calif.).
TRANSACTIONS/CAREER NOTES: Selected by California Angels organization in fourth round of free-agent draft (June 1, 1988). ... Claimed on waivers by San Francisco Giants (December 17, 1992). ... On Phoenix disabled list (August 14, 1994-remainder of season). ... Traded by Giants to Philadelphia Phillies for a player to be named later or cash (May 2, 1996); Phillies sent Giants an undisclosed amount of cash to complete deal (June 14, 1996). ... Granted free agency (October 10, 1996). ... Signed by Houston Astros organization (March 14, 1997). ... Granted free agency (October 15, 1997).

P

STATISTICAL NOTES: Led Northwest League first basemen with 641 putouts, 42 assists and 691 total chances in 1990. ... Led California League first basemen with 1,166 putouts, 1,272 total chances and 117 double plays in 1991. ... Led Texas League first basemen with 1,222 putouts, 100 assists, 17 errors, 1,339 total chances and 106 double plays in 1992. ... Led Pacific Coast League first basemen with 1,135 putouts, 93 assists, 28 errors and 1,256 total chances in 1993.

							BATTING							FIELDING			
Year Team (League)	Pos.	G	AB	R	H	2B	3B	HR	RBI	Avg.	BB	SO	SB	PO	A	E	Avg.
1988— Bend (Northwest).......	OF-1B	56	210	24	40	8	0	4	23	.190	21	70	3	197	9	3	.986
1989— Quad City (Midwest) ..	1B-OF	125	442	41	85	29	1	8	50	.192	49	146	3	954	46	20	.980
1990— Palm Springs (Cal.)..	1B	46	162	14	32	4	1	1	15	.198	10	58	3	436	26	16	.967
—Boise (Northwest)	1B-OF	70	237	30	46	6	0	10	34	.194	19	78	1	†642	†42	8	.988
1991— Palm Springs (Cal.)..	1B-P	130	471	64	117	22	2	20	70	.248	57	†144	15	†1166	94	12	.991
1992— Midland (Texas).........	1B-OF	127	497	58	118	32	4	14	77	.237	32	*165	5	†1223	†100	†17	.987
1993— Phoenix (PCL)■.........	1B-OF	134	506	80	133	35	2	*27	94	.263	53	127	7	†1138	†93	†29	.977
—San Francisco (N.L.) ..	1B	11	16	1	5	1	1	1	4	.313	0	5	0	32	2	1	.971
1994— Phoenix (PCL)..........	1B	95	360	69	108	28	5	27	79	.300	45	96	4	782	78	6	.993
—San Francisco (N.L.) ..	1B	15	38	1	5	0	0	1	3	.132	1	13	1	79	10	1	.989
1995— San Francisco (N.L.) ..	1B-OF	92	231	27	45	9	0	9	28	.195	19	69	1	536	37	4	.993
1996— San Francisco (N.L.) ..	1B	15	25	3	5	0	0	2	5	.200	1	13	0	49	2	1	.981
—Philadelphia (N.L.)■..	OF-1B	35	79	9	12	5	0	5	10	.152	10	38	1	113	4	2	.983
—Scran./W.B. (Int'l).........	OF-1B	53	200	33	57	14	2	13	42	.285	19	53	2	112	6	5	.959
1997— New Orleans (A.A.)■..	OF-1B	104	411	59	119	28	0	21	71	.290	39	112	0	411	36	7	.985
—Houston (N.L.).............	1B-OF	13	15	2	2	0	0	1	4	.133	0	7	0	9	0	0	1.000
Major league totals (5 years)		181	404	43	74	15	1	19	54	.183	31	145	2	818	55	9	.990

RECORD AS PITCHER

Year Team (League)	W	L	Pct.	ERA	G	GS	CG	ShO	Sv.	IP	H	R	ER	BB	SO
1991— Palm Springs (California)...	0	0	...	4.50	2	0	0	0	0	2	3	1	1	2	3

PHILLIPS, JASON   P   PIRATES

PERSONAL: Born March 22, 1974, in Williamsport, Pa. ... 6-5/220. ... Throws right, bats right. ... Full name: Jason Charles Phillips.
HIGH SCHOOL: Hughesville (Pa.).
TRANSACTIONS/CAREER NOTES: Selected by Pittsburgh Pirates organization in 14th round of free-agent draft (June 1, 1992).

Year Team (League)	W	L	Pct.	ERA	G	GS	CG	ShO	Sv.	IP	H	R	ER	BB	SO
1992— GC Pirates (GCL)................	1	2	.333	8.47	4	4	0	0	0	17	21	21	16	13	10
1993— Welland (N.Y.-Penn)..........	4	6	.400	3.53	14	14	0	0	0	71 1/3	60	44	28	36	66
1994— Augusta (S. Atl.)................	6	12	.333	6.73	23	1	0	0	0	108 1/3	118	97	81	88	108
1995— Augusta (S. Atl.)................	4	3	.571	3.60	30	6	0	0	0	80	76	46	32	53	65
1996— Augusta (S. Atl.)................	5	4	.556	2.41	14	14	1	1	0	89 2/3	79	35	24	29	75
—Lynchburg (Carolina)	5	6	.455	4.52	13	13	1	1	0	73 2/3	82	47	37	35	63
1997— Lynchburg (Carolina)	11	6	.647	3.76	23	23	2	1	0	138 2/3	129	66	58	35	140
—Carolina (Southern).............	1	2	.333	2.32	4	4	2	1	0	31	21	8	8	9	22

PHILLIPS, TONY   OF/2B

PERSONAL: Born April 25, 1959, in Atlanta. ... 5-10/175. ... Bats both, throws right. ... Full name: Keith Anthony Phillips.
HIGH SCHOOL: Roswell (Ga.).
JUNIOR COLLEGE: New Mexico Military Institute.
TRANSACTIONS/CAREER NOTES: Selected by Seattle Mariners organization in 16th round of free-agent draft (June 7, 1977); did not sign. ... Selected by Montreal Expos organization in secondary phase of free-agent draft (January 10, 1978). ... On West Palm Beach temporarily inactive list (April 11-May 4, 1978). ... Traded by Expos organization with cash to San Diego Padres for 1B Willie Montanez (August 31, 1980). ... Traded by Padres organization with P Eric Mustad and IF Kevin Bell to Oakland Athletics organization for P Bob Lacey and P Roy Moretti (March 27, 1981). ... On Oakland disabled list (March 26-August 22, 1985); included rehabilitation assignments to Tacoma (July 30-August 5 and August 7-20). ... On disabled list (August 14-October 3, 1986). ... On Oakland disabled list (July 12-August 28, 1987); included rehabilitation assignment to Tacoma (August 20-28). ... Released by A's (December 21, 1987). ... Re-signed by A's (March 9, 1988). ... On Oakland disabled list (May 18-July 8, 1988); included rehabilitation assignment to Tacoma (June 16-July 4). ... Granted free agency (November 13, 1989). ... Signed by Detroit Tigers (December 5, 1989). ... Traded by Tigers to California Angels for OF Chad Curtis (April 12, 1995). ... On suspended list (August 8-11, 1995). ... Granted free agency (October 31, 1995). ... Signed by Chicago White Sox (January 20, 1996). ... On suspended list (April 30-May 2, 1997). ... Traded by White Sox with C Chad Kreuter to Angels for P Chuck McElroy and C Jorge Fabregas (May 18, 1997). ... Granted free agency (December 21, 1997).
RECORDS: Shares major league single-game record (nine innings) for most assists by second baseman—12 (July 6, 1986).
STATISTICAL NOTES: Led Southern League shortstops with 42 errors in 1980. ... Led Eastern League in being hit by pitch with 10 in 1981. ... Hit for the cycle (May 16, 1986). ... Led A.L. third basemen with 19 errors in 1995. ... Career major league grand slams: 1.

							BATTING							FIELDING			
Year Team (League)	Pos.	G	AB	R	H	2B	3B	HR	RBI	Avg.	BB	SO	SB	PO	A	E	Avg.
1978— W.P. Beach (FSL)........	3B-SS-2B	32	54	8	9	0	0	0	3	.167	9	7	2	13	33	5	.902
—Jamestown (NYP)........	SS-2B-3B	52	152	24	29	5	2	1	17	.191	27	24	3	73	146	16	.932
1979— W.P. Beach (FSL)........	2B-SS	60	203	30	47	5	1	0	18	.232	36	26	7	120	156	21	.929
—Memphis (South.)■...	SS-2B	52	156	31	44	4	2	3	11	.282	19	13	3	68	134	18	.918
1980— Memphis (Southern)...	SS-2B	136	502	100	125	18	4	5	41	.249	*98	89	50	226	408	†42	.938
1981— West Haven (East.)■..	SS	131	461	79	114	25	3	9	64	.247	67	69	40	200	391	*33	.947
—Tacoma (PCL)	2B-SS	4	11	1	4	1	0	0	2	.364	0	0	0	8	10	0	1.000
1982— Tacoma (PCL)	SS	86	300	76	89	18	5	4	47	.297	73	63	29	138	236	30	.926
—Oakland (A.L.)	SS	40	81	11	17	2	2	0	8	.210	12	26	2	46	95	7	.953
1983— Oakland (A.L.)	S-2-3-DH	148	412	54	102	12	3	4	35	.248	48	70	16	218	383	30	.952
1984— Oakland (A.L.)	SS-2B-OF	154	451	62	120	24	3	4	37	.266	42	86	10	255	391	28	.958
1985— Tacoma (PCL)	3B-2B	20	69	9	9	1	0	0	5	.130	8	28	3	15	36	4	.927
—Oakland (A.L.)	2B	42	161	23	45	12	2	4	17	.280	13	34	3	54	103	3	.981
1986— Oakland (A.L.) 2-3-0-DH-S		118	441	76	113	14	5	5	52	.256	76	82	15	191	326	13	.975
1987— Oakland (A.L.) 2-3-S-O-DH		111	379	48	91	20	0	10	46	.240	57	76	7	179	299	14	.972
—Tacoma (PCL)	2B-3B	7	26	5	9	2	1	1	6	.346	4	3	1	8	10	0	1.000

P

Year	Team (League)	Pos.	G	AB	R	H	2B	3B	HR	RBI	Avg.	BB	SO	SB	PO	A	E	Avg.
1988—Tacoma (PCL)	S-0-2-3	16	59	10	16	0	0	2	8	.271	12	13	0	25	27	2	.963
—Oakland (A.L.)	3-0-2-S-1-DH	79	212	32	43	8	4	2	17	.203	36	50	0	84	80	10	.943
1989—Oakland (A.L.)	2-3-S-0-1	143	451	48	118	15	6	4	47	.262	58	66	3	184	321	15	.971
1990—Detroit (A.L.)■	3-2-S-0-DH	152	573	97	144	23	5	8	55	.251	99	85	19	180	368	23	.960
1991—Detroit (A.L.)	0-3-2-DH-S	146	564	87	160	28	4	17	72	.284	79	95	10	269	237	8	.984
1992—Detroit (A.L.)	0-2-DH-3-S	159	606	*114	167	32	3	10	64	.276	114	93	12	301	195	11	.978
1993—Detroit (A.L.)	0-2-DH-3	151	566	113	177	27	0	7	57	.313	*132	102	16	321	165	13	.974
1994—Detroit (A.L.)	OF-2B-DH	114	438	91	123	19	3	19	61	.281	95	105	13	254	42	6	.980
1995—California (A.L.)■	3B-OF-DH	139	525	119	137	21	1	27	61	.261	113	135	13	166	179	†20	.945
1996—Chicago (A.L.)■	OF-2B-DH	153	581	119	161	29	3	12	63	.277	*125	132	13	351	18	7	.981
1997—Chicago (A.L.)	OF-3B	36	129	23	40	6	0	2	9	.310	29	29	4	74	15	3	.967
—Anaheim (A.L.)■	2-0-DH-3	105	405	73	107	28	2	6	48	.264	73	89	9	137	103	8	.968
Major league totals (16 years)		1990	6975	1190	1865	320	46	141	749	.267	1201	1355	165	3264	3320	219	.968

CHAMPIONSHIP SERIES RECORD

Year	Team (League)	Pos.	G	AB	R	H	2B	3B	HR	RBI	Avg.	BB	SO	SB	PO	A	E	Avg.
1988—Oakland (A.L.)	OF-2B	2	7	0	2	1	0	0	0	.286	1	3	0	10	0	0	1.000
1989—Oakland (A.L.)	2B-3B	5	18	1	3	1	0	0	1	.167	2	4	2	4	14	0	1.000
Championship series totals (2 years)		7	25	1	5	2	0	0	1	.200	3	7	2	14	14	0	1.000

WORLD SERIES RECORD

NOTES: Member of World Series championship team (1989).

Year	Team (League)	Pos.	G	AB	R	H	2B	3B	HR	RBI	Avg.	BB	SO	SB	PO	A	E	Avg.
1988—Oakland (A.L.)	OF-2B	2	4	1	1	0	0	0	0	.250	1	2	2	3	5	0	1.000
1989—Oakland (A.L.)	2B-3B-OF	4	17	2	4	1	0	1	3	.235	0	3	0	8	15	0	1.000
World Series totals (2 years)		6	21	3	5	1	0	1	3	.238	1	5	2	11	20	0	1.000

PIAZZA, MIKE   C   DODGERS

PERSONAL: Born September 4, 1968, in Norristown, Pa. ... 6-3/215. ... Bats right, throws right. ... Full name: Michael Joseph Piazza. ... Name pronounced pee-AH-za.

HIGH SCHOOL: Phoenixville (Pa.) Area.

JUNIOR COLLEGE: Miami-Dade (North) Community College.

TRANSACTIONS/CAREER NOTES: Selected by Los Angeles Dodgers organization in 62nd round of free-agent draft (June 1, 1988). ... On disabled list (May 11-June 4, 1995).

RECORDS: Holds single-season record for highest batting average by a catcher (100 or more games)—.363 (1997).

HONORS: Named N.L. Rookie Player of the Year by THE SPORTING NEWS (1993). ... Named catcher on THE SPORTING NEWS N.L. All-Star team (1993-97). ... Named catcher on THE SPORTING NEWS N.L. Silver Slugger team (1993-97). ... Named N.L. Rookie of the Year by Baseball Writers' Association of America (1993).

STATISTICAL NOTES: Led California League with .540 slugging percentage and in grounding into double plays with 19 in 1991. ... Led N.L. catchers with 98 assists and tied for lead with 11 errors in 1993. ... Led N.L. catchers in total chances with 866 in 1995 and 1,055 in 1996. ... Led N.L. catchers in passed balls with 12 in 1995 and 12 in 1996. ... Hit three home runs in one game (June 29, 1996). ... Led N.L. catchers in total chances with 1,135 in 1997. ... Career major league grand slams: 5.

Year	Team (League)	Pos.	G	AB	R	H	2B	3B	HR	RBI	Avg.	BB	SO	SB	PO	A	E	Avg.
1989—Salem (Northwest)	C	57	198	22	53	11	0	8	25	.268	13	51	0	230	21	6	.977
1990—Vero Beach (FSL)	C-1B	88	272	27	68	20	0	6	45	.250	11	68	0	428	38	16	.967
1991—Bakersfield (Calif.)	C-1B	117	448	71	124	27	2	29	80	.277	47	83	0	723	69	15	.981
1992—San Antonio (Tex.)	C	31	114	18	43	11	0	7	21	.377	13	18	0	189	22	4	.981
—Albuquerque (PCL).....	C-1B	94	358	54	122	22	5	16	69	.341	37	57	1	550	50	9	.985
—Los Angeles (N.L.)	C	21	69	5	16	3	0	1	7	.232	4	12	0	94	7	1	.990
1993—Los Angeles (N.L.)	C-1B	149	547	81	174	24	2	35	112	.318	46	86	3	901	†98	‡11	.989
1994—Los Angeles (N.L.)	C	107	405	64	129	18	0	24	92	.319	33	65	1	640	38	*10	.985
1995—Los Angeles (N.L.)	C	112	434	82	150	17	0	32	93	.346	39	80	1	*805	52	9	.990
1996—Los Angeles (N.L.)	C	148	547	87	184	16	0	36	105	.336	81	93	0	*1055	70	9	.992
1997—Los Angeles (N.L.)	C-DH	152	556	104	201	32	1	40	124	.362	69	77	5	*1045	74	*16	.986
Major league totals (6 years)		689	2558	423	854	110	3	168	533	.334	272	413	10	4540	339	56	.989

DIVISION SERIES RECORD

Year	Team (League)	Pos.	G	AB	R	H	2B	3B	HR	RBI	Avg.	BB	SO	SB	PO	A	E	Avg.
1995—Los Angeles (N.L.)	C	3	14	1	3	1	0	1	1	.214	0	2	0	31	0	0	1.000
1996—Los Angeles (N.L.)	C	3	10	1	3	0	0	0	2	.300	1	2	0	25	4	0	1.000
Division series totals (2 years)		6	24	2	6	1	0	1	3	.250	1	4	0	56	4	0	1.000

ALL-STAR GAME RECORD

NOTES: Named Most Valuable Player (1996).

Year	League	Pos.	AB	R	H	2B	3B	HR	RBI	Avg.	BB	SO	SB	PO	A	E	Avg.
1993—National	C	1	0	0	0	0	0	0	.000	0	1	0	3	0	0	1.000
1994—National	C	4	0	1	0	0	0	1	.250	0	0	0	6	0	0	1.000
1995—National	C	3	1	1	0	0	1	1	.333	0	0	0	6	1	0	1.000
1996—National	C	3	1	2	1	0	1	2	.667	0	1	0	6	1	0	1.000
1997—National	C	1	0	0	0	0	0	0	.000	1	0	0	2	0	0	1.000
All-Star Game totals (5 years)		12	2	4	1	0	2	4	.333	1	2	0	23	2	0	1.000

P

PICHARDO, HIPOLITO   P   ROYALS

PERSONAL: Born August 22, 1969, in Jicome Esperanza, Dominican Republic. ... 6-1/185. ... Throws right, bats right. ... Full name: Hipolito Antonio Pichardo. ... Name pronounced ee-POL-uh-toe puh-CHAR-doh.
HIGH SCHOOL: Liceo Enriguillo (Jicome Esperanza, Dominican Republic).
TRANSACTIONS/CAREER NOTES: Signed as non-drafted free agent by Kansas City Royals organization (December 16, 1987). ... On disabled list (August 14-September 1, 1993 and August 15-September 1, 1995). ... On Kansas City disabled list (July 5-August 25, 1997); included rehabilitation assignment to Omaha (July 25-August 25). ... Granted free agency (October 31, 1997). ... Re-signed by Royals (December 4, 1997).
STATISTICAL NOTES: Pitched 8-0 one-hit, complete-game victory for Kansas City against Boston (July 21, 1992).

Year Team (League)	W	L	Pct.	ERA	G	GS	CG	ShO	Sv.	IP	H	R	ER	BB	SO
1988— GC Royals (GCL)	0	0	...	13.50	1	0	0	0	0	1 1/3	3	2	2	1	3
1989— Appleton (Midwest)	5	4	.556	2.97	12	12	2	0	0	75 2/3	58	29	25	18	50
1990— Baseball City (FSL)	1	6	.143	3.80	11	10	0	0	0	45	47	28	19	25	40
1991— Memphis (Southern)	3	11	.214	4.27	34	11	0	0	0	99	116	56	47	38	75
1992— Memphis (Southern)	0	0	...	0.64	2	2	0	0	0	14	13	2	1	1	10
— Kansas City (A.L.)	9	6	.600	3.95	31	24	1	1	0	143 2/3	148	71	63	49	59
1993— Kansas City (A.L.)	7	8	.467	4.04	30	25	2	0	0	165	183	85	74	53	70
1994— Kansas City (A.L.)	5	3	.625	4.92	45	0	0	0	3	67 2/3	82	42	37	24	36
1995— Kansas City (A.L.)	8	4	.667	4.36	44	0	0	0	3	64	66	34	31	30	43
1996— Kansas City (A.L.)	3	5	.375	5.43	57	0	0	0	3	68	74	41	41	26	43
1997— Kansas City (A.L.)	3	5	.375	4.22	47	0	0	0	11	49	51	24	23	24	34
— Omaha (Am. Assoc.)	0	0	...	5.79	5	1	0	0	1	4 2/3	5	3	3	3	3
Major league totals (6 years)	35	31	.530	4.34	254	49	3	1	18	557 1/3	604	297	269	206	285

PICKERING, CALVIN   1B   ORIOLES

PERSONAL: Born September 29, 1976, in St. Thomas, Virgin Islands. ... 6-5/283. ... Bats left, throws left. ... Full name: Calvin E. Pickering.
HIGH SCHOOL: King (Tampa).
TRANSACTIONS/CAREER NOTES: Selected by Baltimore Orioles organization in 35th round of free-agent draft (June 3, 1995).
STATISTICAL NOTES: Led Appalachian League with .675 slugging percentage, 135 totals bases and four intentional bases on balls received in 1996.

Year Team (League)	Pos.	G	AB	R	H	2B	3B	HR	RBI	Avg.	BB	SO	SB	PO	A	E	Avg.
1995— GC Orioles (GCL)	1B	15	60	8	30	10	0	1	22	.500	2	6	0	86	6	3	.968
1996— Bluefield (Appal.)	1B	60	200	45	65	14	1	*18	*66	.325	28	64	8	396	26	9	.979
1997— Delmarva (S. Atl.)	1B	122	444	88	138	31	1	25	79	.311	53	139	6	940	70	*27	.974

PICKETT, RICKY   P   GIANTS

PERSONAL: Born January 19, 1970, in Fort Worth, Texas ... 6-1/220. ... Throws left, bats left. ... Full name: Cecil Lee Pickett.
HIGH SCHOOL: Eastern Hills (Fort Worth, Texas).
JUNIOR COLLEGE: Northeastern Oklahoma A&M.
TRANSACTIONS/CAREER NOTES: Selected by Cincinnati Reds organization in 28th round of free-agent draft (June 1, 1992). ... Traded by Reds organization with OF Deion Sanders, P John Roper, P Scott Service and 1B Dave McCarty to San Francisco Giants organization for P Mark Portugal, P Dave Burba and OF Darren Lewis (July 21, 1995).

Year Team (League)	W	L	Pct.	ERA	G	GS	CG	ShO	Sv.	IP	H	R	ER	BB	SO
1992— Billings (Pioneer)	1	2	.333	2.35	20	4	0	0	2	53 2/3	35	21	14	28	41
1993— Char., W.Va. (S. Atl.)	1	2	.333	6.75	44	1	0	0	0	44	42	40	33	48	65
1994— Char., W.Va. (S. Atl.)	1	1	.500	1.98	28	0	0	0	13	27 1/3	14	8	6	20	48
— Win.-Salem (Car.)	2	1	.667	3.75	21	0	0	0	4	24	16	11	10	23	33
1995— Chattanooga (Southern)	4	5	.444	3.28	40	0	0	0	9	46 2/3	22	20	17	44	69
— Shreveport (Texas)■	2	1	1.000	1.71	14	0	0	0	3	21	9	5	4	9	23
1996— Phoenix (PCL)	0	3	.000	8.64	8	0	0	0	0	8 1/3	12	8	8	5	7
— Shreveport (Texas)	4	1	.800	2.77	29	0	0	0	2	48 2/3	35	21	15	35	51
1997— Phoenix (PCL)	3	3	.500	3.19	61	0	0	0	12	67 2/3	52	27	24	49	85

PIERZYNSKI, A.J.   C   TWINS

PERSONAL: Born December 30, 1976, in Bridgehampton, N.Y. ... 6-3/202. ... Bats left, throws right. ... Full name: Anthony John Pierzynski.
HIGH SCHOOL: Dr. Phillips (Orlando).
TRANSACTIONS/CAREER NOTES: Selected by Minnesota Twins organization in third round of free-agent draft (June 2, 1994).
STATISTICAL NOTES: Tied for Appalachian League lead in errors by catcher with 12 in 1995. ... Led Appalachian League catchers with 71 assists in 1995. ... Tied for Midwest League lead with 20 errors by catcher in 1996.

Year Team (League)	Pos.	G	AB	R	H	2B	3B	HR	RBI	Avg.	BB	SO	SB	PO	A	E	Avg.
1994— GC Twins (GCL)	C	43	152	21	44	8	1	1	19	.289	12	19	0	198	28	8	.966
1995— Fort Wayne (Midw.)	C	22	84	10	26	5	1	2	14	.310	2	10	0	119	34	10	.939
— Elizabethton (App.)	C-1B	56	205	29	68	13	1	7	45	.332	14	23	0	376	†72	‡12	.974
1996— Fort Wayne (Midw.)	C-OF	114	431	48	118	30	3	7	70	.274	22	53	0	658	80	†21	.972
1997— Fort Myers (FSL)	C-1B	118	412	49	115	23	1	9	64	.279	16	59	2	677	78	10	.987

P

PISCIOTTA, MARC   P   CUBS

PERSONAL: Born August 7, 1970, in Edison, N.J. ... 6-5/227. ... Throws right, bats right. ... Full name: Marc George Pisciotta. ... Name pronounced pih-SHO-tuh.
HIGH SCHOOL: George Walton Comprehensive (Marietta, Ga.).

COLLEGE: Georgia Tech.
TRANSACTIONS/CAREER NOTES: Selected by Pittsburgh Pirates organization in 19th round of free-agent draft (June 3, 1991). ... On disabled list (May 22-June 19, 1992). ... Selected by Colorado Rockies from Pirates organization in Rule 5 major league draft (December 13, 1993). ... Returned to Pirates organization (March 28, 1994). ... Claimed on waivers by Chicago Cubs (November 20, 1996).

Year Team (League)	W	L	Pct.	ERA	G	GS	CG	ShO	Sv.	IP	H	R	ER	BB	SO
1991— Welland (N.Y.-Penn)	1	1	.500	0.26	24	0	0	0	8	34	16	4	1	20	47
1992— Augusta (S. Atl.)	4	5	.444	4.54	20	12	1	0	1	79 1/3	91	51	40	43	54
1993— Augusta (S. Atl.)	5	2	.714	2.68	34	0	0	0	12	43 2/3	31	18	13	17	49
—Salem (Carolina)	0	0	...	2.95	20	0	0	0	12	18 1/3	23	13	6	13	13
1994— Salem (Carolina)	1	4	.200	1.53	31	0	0	0	19	29 1/3	24	14	5	13	23
—Carolina (Southern)	3	4	.429	5.61	26	0	0	0	5	25 2/3	32	21	16	15	21
1995— Carolina (Southern)	6	4	.600	4.15	56	0	0	0	9	69 1/3	60	37	32	45	57
1996— Calgary (PCL)	2	7	.222	4.11	57	0	0	0	1	65 2/3	71	38	30	46	46
1997— Iowa (Am. Assoc.)■	6	2	.750	2.36	42	0	0	0	22	45 2/3	29	12	12	23	48
—Chicago (N.L.)	3	1	.750	3.18	24	0	0	0	0	28 1/3	20	10	10	16	21
Major league totals (1 year)	3	1	.750	3.18	24	0	0	0	0	28 1/3	20	10	10	16	21

PITTSLEY, JIM   P   ROYALS

PERSONAL: Born April 3, 1974, in DuBois, Pa. ... 6-7/215. ... Throws right, bats right. ... Full name: James Michael Pittsley.
HIGH SCHOOL: DuBois (Pa.) High.
TRANSACTIONS/CAREER NOTES: Selected by Kansas City Royals organization in first round (17th pick overall) of free-agent draft (June 1, 1992); pick received as part of compensation for San Diego Padres signing Type A free-agent IF Kurt Stillwell. ... On disabled list (May 29-June 6 and July 29-September 13, 1993). ... On Kansas City disabled list (August 17, 1995-remainder of season). ... On Kansas City disabled list (March 30-July 6, 1996); included rehabilitation assignments to Wilmington (June 6-14), Wichita (June 14-28) and Omaha (June 28-July 5).

Year Team (League)	W	L	Pct.	ERA	G	GS	CG	ShO	Sv.	IP	H	R	ER	BB	SO
1992— GC Royals (GCL)	4	1	.800	3.32	9	9	0	0	0	43 1/3	27	16	16	15	47
—Baseball City (FSL)	0	0	...	0.00	1	1	0	0	0	3	2	0	0	1	4
1993— Rockford (Midwest)	5	5	.500	4.26	15	15	2	1	0	80 1/3	76	43	38	32	87
1994— Wilmington (Caro.)	11	5	.688	3.17	27	27	1	1	0	161 2/3	154	73	57	42	*171
1995— Omaha (Am. Assoc.)	4	1	.800	3.21	8	8	0	0	0	47 2/3	38	20	17	16	39
—Kansas City (A.L.)	0	0	...	13.50	1	1	0	0	0	3 1/3	7	5	5	1	0
1996— Wilmington (Caro.)	0	1	.000	11.00	2	2	0	0	0	9	13	12	11	5	10
—Wichita (Texas)	3	0	1.000	0.41	3	3	0	0	0	22	9	1	1	5	7
—Omaha (Am. Assoc.)	7	1	.875	3.97	13	13	0	0	0	70 1/3	74	34	31	39	53
1997— Omaha (Am. Assoc.)	1	2	.333	4.42	7	7	0	0	0	38 2/3	36	21	19	20	30
—Kansas City (A.L.)	5	8	.385	5.46	21	21	0	0	0	112	120	72	68	54	52
Major league totals (2 years)	5	8	.385	5.70	22	22	0	0	0	115 1/3	127	77	73	55	52

PLANTENBERG, ERIK   P   GIANTS

PERSONAL: Born October 30, 1968, in Renton, Wash. ... 6-1/180. ... Throws left, bats both. ... Full name: Erik John Plantenberg.
HIGH SCHOOL: Newport (Bellevue, Wash.).
COLLEGE: San Diego State.
TRANSACTIONS/CAREER NOTES: Selected by Kansas City Royals organization in 66th round of free-agent draft (June 2, 1987); did not sign. ... Selected by Boston Red Sox organization in 16th round of free-agent draft (June 4, 1990). ... On disabled list (May 13-June 11, 1991 and July 28, 1992-remainder of season). ... Selected by Jacksonville, Seattle Mariners organization, from Lynchburg, Red Sox organization, in Rule 5 minor league draft (December 7, 1992). ... On Jacksonville disabled list (May 25-June 10, 1993). ... Claimed on waivers by San Diego Padres (November 17, 1994). ... On Las Vegas disabled list (April 21-June 2, 1995). ... Signed by Philadelphia Phillies organization (October 31, 1996). ... Claimed on waivers by Cleveland Indians organization (April 30, 1996). ... Granted free agency (October 15, 1996). ... Granted free agency (October 15, 1997). ... Signed by San Francisco Giants organization (January 12, 1998).

Year Team (League)	W	L	Pct.	ERA	G	GS	CG	ShO	Sv.	IP	H	R	ER	BB	SO
1990— Elmira (N.Y.-Penn)	2	3	.400	4.02	16	5	0	0	0	40 1/3	44	26	18	19	36
1991— Lynchburg (Carolina)	11	5	.688	3.76	20	20	0	0	0	103	116	59	43	51	73
1992— Lynchburg (Carolina)	2	3	.400	5.18	21	12	0	0	0	81 2/3	112	69	47	36	62
1993— Jacksonville (Southern)■	2	1	.667	2.01	34	0	0	0	1	44 2/3	38	11	10	14	49
—Seattle (A.L.)	0	0	...	6.52	20	0	0	0	1	9 2/3	11	7	7	12	3
1994— Jacksonville (Southern)	0	1	.000	1.33	14	0	0	0	4	20 1/3	19	6	3	8	23
—Seattle (A.L.)	0	0	...	0.00	6	0	0	0	0	7	4	0	0	7	1
—Calgary (PCL)	6	7	.462	5.84	19	19	1	1	0	101 2/3	122	82	66	62	69
1995— Las Vegas (PCL)■	0	0	...	81.00	2	0	0	0	0	1/3	3	3	3	0	1
—Memphis (Southern)	2	0	1.000	1.66	20	0	0	0	2	21 2/3	19	4	4	2	16
1996— Cant./Akr. (Eastern)■	0	0	...	3.00	19	0	0	0	0	21	21	7	7	2	26
—Buffalo (A.A.)	2	2	.500	3.74	17	1	0	0	1	33 2/3	35	16	14	14	29
1997— Philadelphia (N.L.)■	0	0	...	4.91	35	0	0	0	0	25 2/3	25	14	14	12	12
—Scran./W.B. (Int'l)	0	2	.000	7.53	18	0	0	0	0	14 1/3	22	12	12	9	12
A.L. totals (2 years)	0	0	...	3.78	26	0	0	0	1	16 2/3	15	7	7	19	4
N.L. totals (1 year)	0	0	...	4.91	35	0	0	0	0	25 2/3	25	14	14	12	12
Major league totals (3 years)	0	0	...	4.46	61	0	0	0	1	42 1/3	40	21	21	31	16

PLANTIER, PHIL   OF   BLUE JAYS

PERSONAL: Born January 27, 1969, in Manchester, N.H. ... 5-11/195. ... Bats left, throws right. ... Full name: Phillip Alan Plantier. ... Name pronounced plan-TEER.
HIGH SCHOOL: Poway (Calif.).
TRANSACTIONS/CAREER NOTES: Selected by Boston Red Sox organization in 11th round of free-agent draft (June 2, 1987). ... On Pawtucket disabled list (August 28-September 4, 1992). ... Traded by Red Sox to San Diego Padres for P Jose Melendez (December 9, 1992). ... On disabled list (April 26-May 11, 1993). ... Traded by Padres with OF Derek Bell, P Pedro Martinez, P Doug Brocail, IF Craig Shipley and SS Ricky Gutierrez to Houston Astros for 3B Ken Caminiti, OF Steve Finley, SS Andujar Cedeno, 1B Robert Petagine, P Brian Williams and a player to

be named later (December 28, 1994); Padres acquired P Sean Fesh to complete deal (May 1, 1995). ... On Houston disabled list (May 17-July 7, 1995); included rehabilitation assignments to Tucson (June 1-5 and July 2-7). ... Traded by Astros to Padres for P Jeff Tabaka and P Rich Loiselle (July 19, 1995). ... Released by Padres (November 20, 1995). ... Signed by Detroit Tigers (December 7, 1995). ... Traded by Tigers to Oakland Athletics for P Ramon Fermin and IF Fausto Cruz (March 22, 1996). ... Granted free agency (October 15, 1996). ... Signed by Padres organization (January 17, 1997). ... On San Diego disabled list (May 8-June 13, 1997). ... Traded by Padres with P Fernando Valenzuela, 3B Scott Livingstone and OF Phil Plantier to St. Louis Cardinals for P Danny Jackson, P Rich Batchelor and OF Mark Sweeney (June 13, 1997). ... On St. Louis disabled list (June 13-July 13 and August 4-25, 1997); included rehabilitation assignments to Louisville (June 15-July 13 and August 22-25). ... Granted free agency (October 28, 1997). ... Signed by Toronto Blue Jays organization (January 20, 1998).

RECORDS: Shares major league single-game record (nine innings) for most strikeouts—5 (October 1, 1991).

HONORS: Named Carolina League Most Valuable Player (1989).

STATISTICAL NOTES: Led Carolina League with 242 total bases, .546 slugging percentage and tied for lead with seven intentional bases on balls received in 1989. ... Led International League with .549 slugging percentage in 1990. ... Career major league grand slams: 1.

Year Team (League)	Pos.	G	AB	R	H	2B	3B	HR	RBI	Avg.	BB	SO	SB	PO	A	E	Avg.
1987— Elmira (N.Y.-Penn)	3B	28	80	7	14	2	0	2	9	.175	9	9	0	12	34	12	.793
1988— Winter Haven (FSL)	OF-3B-2B	111	337	29	81	13	1	4	32	.240	51	62	0	106	72	18	.908
1989— Lynchburg (Caro.)	OF	131	443	73	133	26	1	*27	*105	.300	74	122	4	140	10	8	.949
1990— Pawtucket (Int'l)	OF	123	430	83	109	22	3	*33	79	.253	62	*148	1	245	8	*14	.948
— Boston (A.L.)	DH-OF	14	15	1	2	1	0	0	3	.133	4	6	0	0	0	0	...
1991— Pawtucket (Int'l)	OF-3B	84	298	69	91	19	4	16	61	.305	65	64	6	173	6	0	1.000
— Boston (A.L.)	OF-DH	53	148	27	49	7	1	11	35	.331	23	38	1	80	1	2	.976
1992— Boston (A.L.)	OF-DH	108	349	46	86	19	0	7	30	.246	44	83	2	148	6	4	.975
— Pawtucket (Int'l)	OF	12	40	7	17	0	0	5	14	.425	6	4	0	23	1	0	1.000
1993— San Diego (N.L.)■	OF	138	462	67	111	20	1	34	100	.240	61	124	4	272	14	3	.990
1994— San Diego (N.L.)	OF	96	341	44	75	21	0	18	41	.220	36	91	3	158	5	2	.988
1995— Houston (N.L.)■	OF	22	68	12	17	2	0	4	15	.250	11	19	0	25	0	1	.962
— San Diego (N.L.)■	OF	10	24	6	6	2	0	1	4	.250	5	4	0	9	0	0	1.000
— San Diego (N.L.)■	OF	54	148	21	38	4	0	5	19	.257	17	29	1	64	5	3	.958
1996— Oakland (A.L.)■	OF-DH	73	231	29	49	8	1	7	31	.212	28	56	2	138	8	4	.973
— Edmonton (PCL)	OF	34	122	25	43	7	1	9	45	.352	12	25	1	18	1	3	.864
1997— Las Vegas (PCL)■	OF	15	56	13	24	6	0	5	9	.429	4	8	1	17	2	0	1.000
— San Diego (N.L.)	OF	10	8	0	1	0	0	0	0	.125	2	3	0	3	0	0	1.000
— Rancho Cuca. (Cal.)	OF	4	17	1	4	1	1	0	3	.235	2	0	1	5	0	0	1.000
— Louisville (A.A.)■	OF	9	31	6	8	3	0	1	10	.258	6	3	0	7	0	0	1.000
— St. Louis (N.L.)	OF	42	113	13	29	8	0	5	18	.257	11	27	0	52	1	1	.981
American League totals (4 years)		248	743	103	186	35	2	25	99	.250	99	183	5	366	15	10	.974
National League totals (4 years)		362	1140	157	271	55	1	66	193	.238	138	293	8	574	25	10	.984
Major league totals (8 years)		610	1883	260	457	90	3	91	292	.243	237	476	13	940	40	20	.980

PLESAC, DAN   P   BLUE JAYS

PERSONAL: Born February 4, 1962, in Gary, Ind. ... 6-5/220. ... Throws left, bats left. ... Full name: Daniel Thomas Plesac. ... Name pronounced PLEE-sack.

HIGH SCHOOL: Crown Point (Ind.).

COLLEGE: North Carolina State.

TRANSACTIONS/CAREER NOTES: Selected by St. Louis Cardinals organization in second round of free-agent draft (June 3, 1980); did not sign. ... Selected by Milwaukee Brewers organization in first round (26th pick overall) of free-agent draft (June 6, 1983). ... Granted free agency (October 27, 1992). ... Signed by Chicago Cubs (December 8, 1992). ... Granted free agency (October 25, 1994). ... Signed by Pittsburgh Pirates (November 9, 1994). ... Traded by Pirates with OF Orlando Merced and IF Carlos Garcia to Toronto Blue Jays for P Jose Silva, P Jose Pett, IF Brandon Cromer and three players to be named later (November 14, 1996); Pirates acquired P Mike Halperin, IF Abraham Nunez and C/OF Craig Wilson to complete deal (December 11, 1996).

STATISTICAL NOTES: Led Appalachian League pitchers with three balks in 1983.

MISCELLANEOUS: Holds Milwaukee Brewers all-time records for lowest earned run average (3.21), most games pitched (365) and most saves (133).

Year Team (League)	W	L	Pct.	ERA	G	GS	CG	ShO	Sv.	IP	H	R	ER	BB	SO
1983— Paintsville (Appal.)	*9	1	.900	3.50	14	•14	2	0	0	82 1/3	76	44	32	57	*85
1984— Stockton (California)	6	6	.500	3.32	16	16	2	0	0	108 1/3	106	51	40	50	101
— El Paso (Texas)	2	2	.500	3.46	7	7	0	0	0	39	43	19	15	16	24
1985— El Paso (Texas)	12	5	.706	4.97	25	24	2	0	0	150 1/3	171	91	83	68	128
1986— Milwaukee (A.L.)	10	7	.588	2.97	51	0	0	0	14	91	81	34	30	29	75
1987— Milwaukee (A.L.)	5	6	.455	2.61	57	0	0	0	23	79 1/3	63	30	23	23	89
1988— Milwaukee (A.L.)	1	2	.333	2.41	50	0	0	0	30	52 1/3	46	14	14	12	52
1989— Milwaukee (A.L.)	3	4	.429	2.35	52	0	0	0	33	61 1/3	47	16	16	17	52
1990— Milwaukee (A.L.)	3	7	.300	4.43	66	0	0	0	24	69	67	36	34	31	65
1991— Milwaukee (A.L.)	2	7	.222	4.29	45	10	0	0	8	92 1/3	92	44	44	39	61
1992— Milwaukee (A.L.)	5	4	.556	2.96	44	4	0	0	1	79	64	28	26	35	54
1993— Chicago (N.L.)■	2	1	.667	4.74	57	0	0	0	0	62 2/3	74	37	33	21	47
1994— Chicago (N.L.)	2	3	.400	4.61	54	0	0	0	1	54 2/3	61	30	28	13	53
1995— Pittsburgh (N.L.)■	4	4	.500	3.58	58	0	0	0	3	60 1/3	53	26	24	27	57
1996— Pittsburgh (N.L.)	6	5	.545	4.09	73	0	0	0	11	70 1/3	67	35	32	24	76
1997— Toronto (A.L.)■	2	4	.333	3.58	73	0	0	0	1	50 1/3	47	22	20	19	61
A.L. totals (8 years)	31	41	.431	3.24	438	14	0	0	134	574 2/3	507	229	207	205	509
N.L. totals (4 years)	14	13	.519	4.25	242	0	0	0	15	248	255	128	117	85	233
Major league totals (12 years)	45	54	.455	3.54	680	14	0	0	149	822 2/3	762	357	324	290	742

ALL-STAR GAME RECORD

Year League	W	L	Pct.	ERA	GS	CG	ShO	Sv.	IP	H	R	ER	BB	SO
1987— American	0	0	...	0.00	0	0	0	0	1	0	0	0	0	1
1988— American	0	0	...	0.00	0	0	0	0	1/3	0	0	0	0	1
1989— American	0	0	...	...	0	0	0	0	0	1	0	0	0	0
All-Star totals (3 years)	0	0	...	0.00	0	0	0	0	1 1/3	1	0	0	0	2

P

PLUNK, ERIC   P   INDIANS

PERSONAL: Born September 3, 1963, in Wilmington, Calif. ... 6-6/220. ... Throws right, bats right. ... Full name: Eric Vaughn Plunk.
HIGH SCHOOL: Bellflower (Calif.).
COLLEGE: Cal State Dominguez Hills.
TRANSACTIONS/CAREER NOTES: Selected by New York Yankees organization in fourth round of free-agent draft (June 8, 1981). ... On disabled list (August 11-26, 1983). ... Traded by Yankees with OF Stan Javier, P Jay Howell, P Jose Rijo and P Tim Birtsas to Oakland Athletics for OF Rickey Henderson, P Bert Bradley and cash (December 5, 1984). ... On disabled list (July 2-17, 1988). ... Traded by A's with P Greg Cadaret and OF Luis Polonia to New York Yankees for OF Rickey Henderson (June 21, 1989). ... Released by Yankees (November 20, 1991). ... Signed by Syracuse, Toronto Blue Jays organization (December 12, 1991). ... Released by Syracuse, Blue Jays organization (March 27, 1992). ... Signed by Canton/Akron, Cleveland Indians organization (April 9, 1992). ... Granted free agency (October 27, 1992). ... Re-signed by Indians (November 12, 1992). ... Granted free agency (October 29, 1996). ... Re-signed by Indians (December 10, 1996).
STATISTICAL NOTES: Tied for Florida State League lead with seven balks in 1984. ... Led A.L. with six balks in 1986.

Year Team (League)	W	L	Pct.	ERA	G	GS	CG	ShO	Sv.	IP	H	R	ER	BB	SO
1981—GC Yankees (GCL)	3	4	.429	3.83	11	11	1	0	0	54	56	29	23	20	47
1982—Paintsville (Appal.)	6	3	.667	4.64	12	8	4	0	0	64	63	35	33	30	59
1983—Fort Lauderdale (FSL)	8	10	.444	2.74	20	20	5	•4	0	125	115	55	38	63	109
1984—Fort Lauderdale (FSL)	12	12	.500	2.86	28	28	7	1	0	176 1/3	153	85	56	*123	*152
1985—Huntsville (Southern)■	8	2	.800	3.40	13	13	2	1	0	79 1/3	61	36	30	56	68
—Tacoma (PCL)	0	5	.000	5.77	11	10	0	0	0	53	51	41	34	50	43
1986—Tacoma (PCL)	2	3	.400	4.68	6	6	0	0	0	32 2/3	25	18	17	33	31
—Oakland (A.L.)	4	7	.364	5.31	26	15	0	0	0	120 1/3	91	75	71	102	98
1987—Oakland (A.L.)	4	6	.400	4.74	32	11	0	0	2	95	91	53	50	62	90
—Tacoma (PCL)	1	1	.500	1.56	24	0	0	0	9	34 2/3	21	8	6	17	56
1988—Oakland (A.L.)	7	2	.778	3.00	49	0	0	0	5	78	62	27	26	39	79
1989—Oakland (A.L.)	1	1	.500	2.20	23	0	0	0	1	28 2/3	17	7	7	12	24
—New York (A.L.)■	7	5	.583	3.69	27	7	0	0	0	75 2/3	65	36	31	52	61
1990—New York (A.L.)	6	3	.667	2.72	47	0	0	0	0	72 2/3	58	27	22	43	67
1991—New York (A.L.)	2	5	.286	4.76	43	8	0	0	0	111 2/3	128	69	59	62	103
1992—Cant./Akr. (Eastern)■	1	2	.333	1.72	9	0	0	0	0	15 2/3	11	4	3	5	21
—Cleveland (A.L.)	9	6	.600	3.64	58	0	0	0	4	71 2/3	61	31	29	38	50
1993—Cleveland (A.L.)	4	5	.444	2.79	70	0	0	0	15	71	61	29	22	30	77
1994—Cleveland (A.L.)	7	2	.778	2.54	41	0	0	0	3	71	61	25	20	37	73
1995—Cleveland (A.L.)	6	2	.750	2.67	56	0	0	0	2	64	48	19	19	27	71
1996—Cleveland (A.L.)	3	2	.600	2.43	56	0	0	0	2	77 2/3	56	21	21	34	85
1997—Cleveland (A.L.)	4	5	.444	4.66	55	0	0	0	0	65 2/3	62	37	34	36	66
Major league totals (12 years)	**64**	**51**	**.557**	**3.69**	**583**	**41**	**0**	**0**	**34**	**1003**	**861**	**456**	**411**	**574**	**944**

DIVISION SERIES RECORD

Year Team (League)	W	L	Pct.	ERA	G	GS	CG	ShO	Sv.	IP	H	R	ER	BB	SO
1995—Cleveland (A.L.)	0	0	...	0.00	1	0	0	0	0	1 1/3	1	0	0	1	1
1996—Cleveland (A.L.)	0	1	.000	6.75	3	0	0	0	0	4	1	3	3	3	6
1997—Cleveland (A.L.)	0	1	.000	13.50	1	0	0	0	0	1 1/3	4	4	2	0	1
Div. series totals (3 years)	**0**	**2**	**.000**	**6.75**	**5**	**0**	**0**	**0**	**0**	**6 2/3**	**6**	**7**	**5**	**4**	**8**

CHAMPIONSHIP SERIES RECORD

Year Team (League)	W	L	Pct.	ERA	G	GS	CG	ShO	Sv.	IP	H	R	ER	BB	SO
1988—Oakland (A.L.)	0	0	...	0.00	1	0	0	0	0	1/3	1	0	0	0	1
1995—Cleveland (A.L.)	0	0	...	9.00	3	0	0	0	0	2	1	2	2	3	2
1997—Cleveland (A.L.)	1	0	1.000	0.00	1	0	0	0	0	2/3	1	0	0	0	0
Champ. series totals (3 years)	**1**	**0**	**1.000**	**6.00**	**5**	**0**	**0**	**0**	**0**	**3**	**3**	**2**	**2**	**3**	**3**

WORLD SERIES RECORD

Year Team (League)	W	L	Pct.	ERA	G	GS	CG	ShO	Sv.	IP	H	R	ER	BB	SO
1988—Oakland (A.L.)	0	0	...	0.00	2	0	0	0	0	1 2/3	0	0	0	0	3
1995— Cleveland (A.L.)							Did not play.								
1997—Cleveland (A.L.)	0	1	.000	9.00	3	0	0	0	0	3	3	4	3	4	3
World Series totals (2 years)	**0**	**1**	**.000**	**5.79**	**5**	**0**	**0**	**0**	**0**	**4 2/3**	**3**	**4**	**3**	**4**	**6**

POLANCO, PLACIDO   SS   CARDINALS

PERSONAL: Born October 10, 1975, in Santo Domingo, Dominican Republic. ... 5-10/170. ... Bats right, throws right. ... Full name: Placido E. Polanco.
HIGH SCHOOL: Santo Claro (Santo Domingo, Dominican Republic).
JUNIOR COLLEGE: Miami-Dade (Wolfson New World Center) Community College.
TRANSACTIONS/CAREER NOTES: Selected by St. Louis Cardinals in 19th round of free-agent draft (June 3, 1994).
STATISTICAL NOTES: Led Florida State League in grounding into double plays with 31 in 1996. ... Tied for Texas League lead in double plays by second baseman with 110 in 1997.

Year Team (League)	Pos.	G	AB	R	H	2B	3B	HR	RBI	Avg.	BB	SO	SB	PO	A	E	Avg.
1994—Ariz. Cardinals (Ariz.)	SS-2B	32	127	17	27	4	0	1	10	.213	7	15	4	47	89	10	.932
1995—Peoria (Midwest)	SS-2B	103	361	43	96	7	4	2	41	.266	18	30	7	114	285	21	.950
1996—St. Petersburg (FSL)	2B	*137	540	65	*157	29	5	0	51	.291	24	34	4	198	*383	4	*.993
1997—Arkansas (Texas)	2B	129	508	71	148	16	3	2	51	.291	29	51	19	240	*425	14	*.979

POLCOVICH, KEVIN   SS   PIRATES

PERSONAL: Born June 28, 1970, in Auburn, N.Y. ... 5-9/168. ... Bats right, throws right. ... Full name: Kevin Michael Polcovich.
COLLEGE: Florida.
TRANSACTIONS/CAREER NOTES: Selected by Pittsburgh Pirates organization in 30th round of free-agent draft (June 1, 1992).

Year—Team (League)	Pos.	G	AB	R	H	2B	3B	HR	RBI	Avg.	BB	SO	SB	PO	A	E	Avg.
								BATTING							FIELDING		
1992—Augusta (S. Atl.)	SS-2B-3B	46	153	24	40	6	2	0	10	.261	18	30	7	78	119	9	.956
—Carolina (Southern)	SS	13	35	1	6	0	0	0	1	.171	4	4	0	16	45	2	.968
1993—Augusta (S. Atl.)	SS-2B	14	48	9	13	2	0	0	4	.271	7	8	2	11	33	6	.880
—Salem (Carolina)	SS-2B-3B	94	282	44	72	10	3	1	25	.255	49	42	13	111	281	22	.947
—Carolina (Southern)	2B-SS	4	11	1	3	0	0	0	1	.273	1	1	0	...	...	...	...
1994—Carolina (Southern)	SS	125	406	46	95	14	2	2	33	.234	38	70	9	185	351	28	.950
1995—Carolina (Southern)	SS	64	221	27	70	8	0	3	18	.317	14	29	10	88	208	18	.943
—Calgary (PCL)	SS	62	213	31	60	8	1	3	27	.282	11	32	5	90	215	13	.959
1996—Calgary (PCL)	SS-2B	104	336	53	92	21	3	1	46	.274	18	49	7	165	292	18	.962
1997—Carolina (Southern)	3B-2B-SS	17	50	13	16	5	0	3	7	.320	10	4	4	12	33	5	.900
—Calgary (PCL)	SS	17	62	7	19	4	0	1	9	.306	1	7	0	27	53	6	.930
—Pittsburgh (N.L.)	SS-2B-3B	84	245	37	67	16	1	4	21	.273	21	45	2	121	246	12	.968
Major league totals (1 year)		84	245	37	67	16	1	4	21	.273	21	45	2	121	246	12	.968

PONSON, SIDNEY   P   ORIOLES

PERSONAL: Born November 2, 1976, in Aruba. ... 6-1/220. ... Throws right, bats right. ... Full name: Sidney Alton Ponson.
COLLEGE: Maria (Aruba).
TRANSACTIONS/CAREER NOTES: Signed as non-drafted free agent by Baltimore Orioles organization (August 17, 1993). ... On Bowie disabled list (June 13-July 15, 1997).

Year—Team (League)	W	L	Pct.	ERA	G	GS	CG	ShO	Sv.	IP	H	R	ER	BB	SO
1994—GC Orioles (GCL)	4	3	.571	2.96	12	10	1	0	0	73	68	30	24	17	53
1995—Bluefield (Appalachian)	6	3	.667	4.17	13	13	0	0	0	77²/₃	79	44	36	16	56
1996—Frederick (Carolina)	7	6	.538	3.45	18	16	3	0	0	107	98	56	41	28	110
1997—Bowie (Eastern)	2	7	.222	5.42	13	13	1	1	0	74²/₃	7	51	45	32	56
—GC Orioles (GCL)	1	0	1.000	0.00	1	0	0	0	0	2	0	0	0	0	1

POOLE, JIM   P   GIANTS

PERSONAL: Born April 28, 1966, in Rochester, N.Y. ... 6-2/195. ... Throws left, bats left. ... Full name: James Richard Poole.
HIGH SCHOOL: South College (Philadelphia).
COLLEGE: Georgia Tech.
TRANSACTIONS/CAREER NOTES: Selected by Los Angeles Dodgers organization in 34th round of free-agent draft (June 2, 1987); did not sign. ... Selected by Dodgers organization in ninth round of free-agent draft (June 1, 1988). ... Traded by Dodgers with cash to Texas Rangers for P Steve Allen and P David Lynch (December 30, 1990). ... Claimed on waivers by Baltimore Orioles (May 31, 1991). ... On Baltimore disabled list (April 3-June 23, 1992); included rehabilitation assignments to Hagerstown (May 25-June 12) and Rochester (June 12-23). ... Granted free agency (December 23, 1994). ... Signed by Buffalo, Cleveland Indians organization (March 18, 1995). ... Traded by Indians with a player to be named later or cash to San Francisco Giants for 1B/OF Mark Carreon (July 9, 1996).

Year—Team (League)	W	L	Pct.	ERA	G	GS	CG	ShO	Sv.	IP	H	R	ER	BB	SO
1988—Vero Beach (FSL)	1	1	.500	3.77	10	0	0	0	0	14¹/₃	13	7	6	9	12
1989—Vero Beach (FSL)	11	4	.733	1.61	*60	0	0	0	19	78¹/₃	57	16	14	24	93
—Bakersfield (California)	0	0	...	0.00	1	0	0	0	0	1²/₃	2	1	0	0	1
1990—San Antonio (Tex.)	6	7	.462	2.40	54	0	0	0	16	63²/₃	55	31	17	27	77
—Los Angeles (N.L.)	0	0	...	4.22	16	0	0	0	0	10²/₃	7	5	5	8	6
1991—Oklahoma City (A.A.)■	0	0	...	0.00	10	0	0	0	3	12¹/₃	4	0	0	1	14
—Texas (A.L.)	0	0	...	4.50	5	0	0	0	1	6	10	4	3	3	4
—Rochester (Int'l)■	3	2	.600	2.79	27	0	0	0	9	29	29	11	9	9	25
—Baltimore (A.L.)	3	2	.600	2.00	24	0	0	0	0	36	19	10	8	9	34
1992—Hagerstown (Eastern)	0	1	.000	2.77	7	3	0	0	0	13	14	4	4	1	4
—Rochester (Int'l)	1	6	.143	5.31	32	0	0	0	10	42¹/₃	40	26	25	18	30
—Baltimore (A.L.)	0	0	...	0.00	6	0	0	0	0	3¹/₃	3	3	0	1	3
1993—Baltimore (A.L.)	2	1	.667	2.15	55	0	0	0	2	50¹/₃	30	18	12	21	29
1994—Baltimore (A.L.)	1	0	1.000	6.64	38	0	0	0	0	20¹/₃	32	15	15	11	18
1995—Buffalo (A.A.)■	0	0	...	27.00	1	1	0	0	0	2²/₃	7	8	8	2	0
—Cleveland (A.L.)	3	3	.500	3.75	42	0	0	0	0	50¹/₃	40	22	21	17	41
1996—Cleveland (A.L.)	4	0	1.000	3.04	32	0	0	0	0	26²/₃	29	15	9	14	19
—San Francisco (N.L.)■	2	1	.667	2.66	35	0	0	0	0	23²/₃	15	7	7	13	19
1997—San Francisco (N.L.)	3	1	.750	7.11	63	0	0	0	0	49¹/₃	73	44	39	25	26
A.L. totals (6 years)	13	6	.684	3.17	202	0	0	0	3	193	163	87	68	76	148
N.L. totals (3 years)	5	2	.714	5.49	114	0	0	0	0	83²/₃	95	56	51	46	51
Major league totals (8 years)	18	8	.692	3.87	316	0	0	0	3	276²/₃	258	143	119	122	199

DIVISION SERIES RECORD

Year—Team (League)	W	L	Pct.	ERA	G	GS	CG	ShO	Sv.	IP	H	R	ER	BB	SO
1995—Cleveland (A.L.)	0	0	...	5.40	1	0	0	0	0	1²/₃	2	1	1	1	2

CHAMPIONSHIP SERIES RECORD

Year—Team (League)	W	L	Pct.	ERA	G	GS	CG	ShO	Sv.	IP	H	R	ER	BB	SO
1995—Cleveland (A.L.)	0	0	...	0.00	1	0	0	0	0	1	0	0	0	0	2

WORLD SERIES RECORD

Year—Team (League)	W	L	Pct.	ERA	G	GS	CG	ShO	Sv.	IP	H	R	ER	BB	SO
1995—Cleveland (A.L.)	0	1	.000	3.86	2	0	0	0	0	2¹/₃	1	1	1	0	1

P

PORTUGAL, MARK   P   PHILLIES

PERSONAL: Born October 30, 1962, in Los Angeles. ... 6-0/190. ... Throws right, bats right. ... Full name: Mark Steven Portugal.
HIGH SCHOOL: Norwalk (Calif.).

TRANSACTIONS/CAREER NOTES: Signed as non-drafted free agent by Minnesota Twins organization (October 23, 1980). ... On Toledo disabled list (July 22-August 2, 1985). ... On Minnesota disabled list (August 7-28, 1988). ... Traded by Twins to Houston Astros for a player to be named later (December 4, 1988); Twins organization acquired P Todd McClure to complete deal (December 7, 1988). ... On disabled list (July 18-August 13, 1991). ... On Houston disabled list (June 13-July 4 and July 10-September 23, 1992). ... Granted free agency (October 25, 1993). ... Signed by San Francisco Giants (November 21, 1993). ... On disabled list (June 17-July 3 and August 6, 1994-remainder of season). ... Traded by Giants with OF Darren Lewis and P Dave Burba to Cincinnati Reds for OF Deion Sanders, P John Roper, P Ricky Pickett, P Scott Service and IF Dave McCarty (July 21, 1995). ... On disabled list (August 28-September 15, 1996). ... Granted free agency (November 18, 1996). ... Signed by Philadelphia Phillies (December 12, 1996). ... On Philadelphia disabled list (March 24-April 20 and May 4, 1997-remainder of season).
HONORS: Named pitcher on THE SPORTING NEWS N.L. Silver Slugger team (1994).
STATISTICAL NOTES: Led Appalachian League with 12 wild pitches, 11 home runs allowed and tied for lead with five hit batsmen in 1981. ... Tied for N.L. lead in games started by pitcher with 31 in 1995.
MISCELLANEOUS: Appeared in one game as pinch-runner (1991). ... Had one sacrifice hit in only appearance as pinch-hitter (1996).

Year Team (League)	W	L	Pct.	ERA	G	GS	CG	ShO	Sv.	IP	H	R	ER	BB	SO
1981—Elizabethton (Appal.)	7	1	.875	3.71	14	13	2	0	1	85	65	41	35	39	65
1982—Wis. Rap. (Midw.)	9	8	.529	4.01	36	15	4	1	2	119	110	62	53	62	95
1983—Visalia (California)	10	5	.667	4.18	24	23	2	0	0	131⅓	142	77	61	84	132
1984—Orlando (South.)	14	7	.667	2.98	27	27	10	3	0	196	171	80	65	113	110
1985—Toledo (Int'l)	8	5	.615	3.78	19	19	5	1	0	128⅔	129	60	54	60	89
—Minnesota (A.L.)	1	3	.250	5.55	6	4	0	0	0	24⅓	24	16	15	14	12
1986—Toledo (Int'l)	5	1	.833	2.60	6	6	3	1	0	45	34	15	13	23	30
—Minnesota (A.L.)	6	10	.375	4.31	27	15	3	0	1	112⅔	112	56	54	50	67
1987—Minnesota (A.L.)	1	3	.250	7.77	13	7	0	0	0	44	58	40	38	24	28
—Portland (PCL)	1	10	.091	6.00	17	16	2	0	0	102	108	75	68	50	69
1988—Portland (PCL)	2	0	1.000	1.37	3	3	1	1	0	19⅔	15	3	3	8	9
—Minnesota (A.L.)	3	3	.500	4.53	26	0	0	0	3	57⅔	60	30	29	17	31
1989—Tucson (PCL)■	7	5	.583	3.78	17	17	5	0	0	116⅔	107	55	49	32	90
—Houston (N.L.)	7	1	.875	2.75	20	15	2	1	0	108	91	34	33	37	86
1990—Houston (N.L.)	11	10	.524	3.62	32	32	1	0	0	196⅔	187	90	79	67	136
1991—Houston (N.L.)	10	12	.455	4.49	32	27	1	0	1	168⅓	163	91	84	59	120
1992—Houston (N.L.)	6	3	.667	2.66	18	16	1	1	0	101⅓	76	32	30	41	62
1993—Houston (N.L.)	18	4	*.818	2.77	33	33	1	1	0	208	194	75	64	77	131
1994—San Francisco (N.L.)■	10	8	.556	3.93	21	21	1	0	0	137⅓	135	68	60	45	87
1995—San Francisco (N.L.)	5	5	.500	4.15	17	17	1	0	0	104	106	56	48	34	63
—Cincinnati (N.L.)■	6	5	.545	3.82	14	§14	0	0	0	77⅔	79	35	33	22	33
1996—Cincinnati (N.L.)	8	9	.471	3.98	27	26	1	1	0	156	146	77	69	42	93
1997—Philadelphia (N.L.)■	0	2	.000	4.61	3	3	0	0	0	13⅔	17	8	7	5	2
A.L. totals (4 years)	11	19	.367	5.13	72	26	3	0	4	238⅔	254	142	136	105	138
N.L. totals (9 years)	81	59	.579	3.59	217	204	9	4	1	1271	1194	566	507	429	813
Major league totals (13 years)	92	78	.541	3.83	289	230	12	4	5	1509⅔	1448	708	643	534	951

CHAMPIONSHIP SERIES RECORD

Year Team (League)	W	L	Pct.	ERA	G	GS	CG	ShO	Sv.	IP	H	R	ER	BB	SO
1995—Cincinnati (N.L.)	0	1	.000	36.00	1	0	0	0	0	1	3	4	4	1	0

POSADA, JORGE   C   YANKEES

PERSONAL: Born August 17, 1971, in Santurce, Puerto Rico. ... 6-2/205. ... Bats both, throws right. ... Full name: Jorge Rafael Posada.
HIGH SCHOOL: Colegio Alejandrino (Puerto Rico).
TRANSACTIONS/CAREER NOTES: Selected by New York Yankees organization in 24th round of free-agent draft (June 4, 1990). ... On disabled list (July 26-September 4, 1994). ... On Columbus disabled list (May 3-12, 1995).
STATISTICAL NOTES: Led New York-Pennsylvania League second basemen with 42 double plays in 1991. ... Led Carolina League with 38 passed balls in 1993. ... Tied for Carolina League lead in intentional bases on balls received with four in 1993. ... Tied for International League lead in errors by catcher with 11 in 1994. ... Tied for International League lead in double plays by catcher with seven in 1995. ... Led International League with 14 passed balls in 1995.

						BATTING								FIELDING		
Year Team (League)	Pos.	G	AB	R	H	2B	3B	HR	RBI	Avg.	BB	SO	SB	PO	A	E	Avg.
1991—Oneonta (NYP)	2B-C	71	217	34	51	5	5	4	33	.235	51	51	6	172	205	21	.947
1992—Greensboro (S. Atl.)	C-3B	101	339	60	94	22	4	12	58	.277	58	87	11	263	39	11	.965
1993—Prince William (Car.)	C-3B	118	410	71	106	27	2	17	61	.259	67	90	17	677	98	15	.981
—Albany (Eastern)	C	7	25	3	7	0	0	0	0	.280	2	7	0	39	7	2	.958
1994—Columbus (Int'l)	C-OF	92	313	46	75	13	3	11	48	.240	32	81	5	425	39	‡11	.977
1995—Columbus (Int'l)	C	108	368	60	94	32	5	8	51	.255	54	101	4	500	58	4	*.993
—New York (A.L.)	C	1	0	0	0	0	0	0	0	...	0	0	0	1	0	0	1.000
1996—Columbus (Int'l)	C-OF	106	354	76	96	22	6	11	62	.271	*79	86	3	598	51	10	.985
—New York (A.L.)	C-DH	8	14	1	1	0	0	0	0	.071	1	6	0	17	2	0	1.000
1997—New York (A.L.)	C	60	188	29	47	12	0	6	25	.250	30	33	1	367	23	3	.992
Major league totals (3 years)		69	202	30	48	12	0	6	25	.238	31	39	1	385	25	3	.993

DIVISION SERIES RECORD

						BATTING								FIELDING		
Year Team (League)	Pos.	G	AB	R	H	2B	3B	HR	RBI	Avg.	BB	SO	SB	PO	A	E	Avg.
1995—New York (A.L.)	PR	1	0	1	0	0	0	0	0	...	0	0	0	...	...	...	...
1997—New York (A.L.)	C-PH	2	2	0	0	0	0	0	0	.000	0	1	0	1	1	0	1.000
Division series totals (2 years)		3	2	1	0	0	0	0	0	.000	0	1	0	1	1	0	1.000

POSE, SCOTT   OF   P

PERSONAL: Born February 11, 1967, in Davenport, Iowa. ... 5-11/165. ... Bats left, throws right. ... Full name: Scott Vernon Pose.
HIGH SCHOOL: Dowling (West Des Moines, Iowa).
COLLEGE: Arkansas.

TRANSACTIONS/CAREER NOTES: Selected by Cincinnati Reds organization in 34th round of free-agent draft (June 5, 1989). ... Selected by Florida Marlins from Reds organization in Rule 5 major league draft (December 7, 1992). ... Granted free agency (March 23, 1994). ... Signed by New Orleans, Milwaukee Brewers organization (April 5, 1994). ... Contract sold by Brewers organization to Los Angeles Dodgers organization (February 9, 1995). ... Released by Dodgers organization (April 17, 1995). ... Signed by Salt Lake, Minnesota Twins organization (June 1, 1995). ... Granted free agency (October 16, 1995). ... Signed by Cleveland Indians organization (December 6, 1995). ... Traded by Indians to Toronto Blue Jays for IF Joe Lis (March 13, 1996). ... Granted free agency (October 15, 1996). ... Signed by New York Yankees organization (November 27, 1996). ... Granted free agency (October 15, 1997).

STATISTICAL NOTES: Tied for Pioneer League lead with three intentional bases on balls received in 1989. ... Led South Atlantic League with eight intentional bases on balls received and .435 on-base percentage in 1990. ... Led Southern League in on-base percentage with .414 and in caught stealing with 27 in 1992. ... Led International League in caught stealing with 16 in 1996. ... Led International League outfielders with .990 fielding percentage in 1996.

Year Team (League)	Pos.	G	AB	R	H	2B	3B	HR	RBI	Avg.	BB	SO	SB	PO	A	E	Avg.
1989— Billings (Pioneer)	OF-2B	60	210	52	74	7	2	0	25	.352	*54	31	26	94	19	7	.942
1990— Char., W.Va. (SAL)	OF	135	480	*106	143	13	5	0	46	.298	*114	56	49	210	*17	3	*.987
1991— Chattanooga (Sou.)	OF	117	402	61	110	8	5	1	31	.274	69	50	17	215	9	1	*.996
— Nashville (A.A.)	OF	15	52	7	10	0	0	0	3	.192	2	9	3	23	0	1	.958
1992— Chattanooga (Sou.)	OF	136	•526	*87	*180	22	8	2	45	*.342	63	66	21	216	10	1	*.996
1993— Florida (N.L.)■	OF	15	41	0	8	2	0	0	3	.195	2	4	0	14	0	1	1.000
— Edmonton (PCL)	OF	109	398	61	113	8	6	0	27	.284	42	36	19	192	4	6	.970
1994— New Orleans (A.A.)■	OF-P-2B	124	429	60	121	13	7	0	52	.282	47	52	20	196	9	1	.995
1995— Albuquerque (PCL)■	OF	7	16	5	3	1	0	0	1	.188	2	0	2	2	0	0	1.000
— Salt Lake (PCL)	OF-P	70	219	46	66	10	1	0	20	.301	31	28	15	92	8	2	.980
1996— Syracuse (Int'l)■	OF-P-1B	113	419	71	114	11	6	0	39	.272	58	71	30	195	9	2	†.990
1997— Columbus (Int'l)■	OF	57	227	50	70	10	7	2	32	.308	32	29	13	113	6	1	.992
— New York (A.L.)	OF-DH	54	87	19	19	2	1	0	5	.218	9	11	3	44	2	0	1.000
American League totals (1 year)		54	87	19	19	2	1	0	5	.218	9	11	3	44	2	0	1.000
National League totals (1 year)		15	41	0	8	2	0	0	3	.195	2	4	0	14	0	1	1.000
Major league totals (2 years)		69	128	19	27	4	1	0	8	.211	11	15	3	58	2	0	1.000

DIVISION SERIES RECORD

Year Team (League)	Pos.	G	AB	R	H	2B	3B	HR	RBI	Avg.	BB	SO	SB	PO	A	E	Avg.
1997— New York (A.L.)	PR	1	0	0	0	0	0	0	0	...	0	0	0	0	0	0	...

RECORD AS PITCHER

Year Team (League)	W	L	Pct.	ERA	G	GS	CG	ShO	Sv.	IP	H	R	ER	BB	SO
1994— New Orleans (A.A.)■	0	0	...	0.00	2	0	0	0	0	2	3	0	0	2	2
1995— Salt Lake (PCL)■	0	0	...	0.00	1	0	0	0	0	1	0	0	0	1	0
1996— Syracuse (Int'l)■	0	0	...	13.50	2	0	0	0	0	2	4	3	3	2	3

POWELL, BRIAN — P — TIGERS

PERSONAL: Born October 10, 1973, in Bainbridge, Ga. ... 6-2/205. ... Throws right, bats right. ... Full name: William Brian Powell.
HIGH SCHOOL: Bainbridge (Ga.).
COLLEGE: Georgia.
TRANSACTIONS/CAREER NOTES: Selected by Detroit Tigers organization in second round of free-agent draft (June 1, 1995).

Year Team (League)	W	L	Pct.	ERA	G	GS	CG	ShO	Sv.	IP	H	R	ER	BB	SO
1995— Jamestown (NYP)	2	1	.667	3.08	5	5	0	0	0	26 1/3	19	12	9	8	15
— Fayetteville (S. Atl.)	4	0	1.000	1.61	5	5	0	0	0	28	15	5	5	11	37
1996— Lakeland (Fla. St.)	8	13	.381	4.90	29	27	*5	0	0	*174 1/3	*195	106	*95	47	84
1997— Lakeland (Fla. St.)	13	9	.591	2.50	27	27	*8	2	0	*183 1/3	153	70	51	35	122

POWELL, DANTE — OF — GIANTS

PERSONAL: Born August 25, 1973, in Long Beach, Calif. ... 6-2/185. ... Bats right, throws right. ... Full name: LeJon Dante Powell.
HIGH SCHOOL: Millikan (Long Beach, Calif.).
COLLEGE: Cal State Fullerton.
TRANSACTIONS/CAREER NOTES: Selected by Toronto Blue Jays in supplemental round ("sandwich pick" between first and second round, 42nd pick overall) of free-agent draft (June 3, 1991); did not sign. ... Selected by San Francisco Giants organization in first round (22nd pick overall) of free-agent draft (June 2, 1994).
STATISTICAL NOTES: Led Texas League with 23 caught stealing in 1996. ... Led Texas League outfielders with 347 total chances in 1996.

Year Team (League)	Pos.	G	AB	R	H	2B	3B	HR	RBI	Avg.	BB	SO	SB	PO	A	E	Avg.
1994— Everett (N'west)	OF	41	165	31	51	15	1	5	25	.309	19	47	27	88	3	2	.978
— San Jose (Calif.)	OF	1	4	0	2	0	0	0	0	.500	0	1	0	1	0	0	1.000
1995— San Jose (Calif.)	OF	135	505	74	125	23	8	10	70	.248	46	131	43	*308	*18	11	.967
1996— Shreveport (Texas)	OF	135	508	*92	142	27	2	21	78	.280	72	92	*43	*331	8	8	.977
— Phoenix (PCL)	OF	2	8	0	2	0	1	0	0	.250	2	3	0	4	0	0	1.000
1997— Phoenix (PCL)	OF	108	452	91	109	24	4	11	42	.241	52	105	34	*266	7	4	.986
— San Francisco (N.L.)	OF	27	39	8	12	1	0	1	3	.308	4	11	1	27	0	0	1.000
Major league totals (1 year)		27	39	8	12	1	0	1	3	.308	4	11	1	27	0	0	1.000

DIVISION SERIES RECORD

Year Team (League)	Pos.	G	AB	R	H	2B	3B	HR	RBI	Avg.	BB	SO	SB	PO	A	E	Avg.
1997— San Francisco (N.L.)	OF	1	0	0	0	0	0	0	0	...	0	0	0	0	0	0	...

P

PERSONAL: Born January 19, 1972, in Meridian, Miss. ... 6-4/225. ... Throws right, bats right. ... Full name: James Willard Powell Jr. ... Brother-in-law of Bud Brown, defensive back, Miami Dolphins (1984-88).
HIGH SCHOOL: West Lauderdale (Collinsville, Miss.).
COLLEGE: Mississippi State.
TRANSACTIONS/CAREER NOTES: Selected by San Diego Padres organization in 11th round of free-agent draft (June 4, 1990); did not sign. ... Selected by Baltimore Orioles organization in first round (19th pick overall) of free-agent draft (June 3, 1993). ... On disabled list (April 7-26, 1994). ... Traded by Orioles organization to Florida Marlins organization for IF Bret Barberie (December 6, 1994). ... On Florida disabled list (April 20-May 10, 1996); included rehabilitation assignment to Brevard County (May 8-10).
MISCELLANEOUS: Struck out in only appearance as pinch-hitter with Florida (1996).

Year Team (League)	W	L	Pct.	ERA	G	GS	CG	ShO	Sv.	IP	H	R	ER	BB	SO
1993— Albany (S. Atl.)	0	2	.000	4.55	6	6	0	0	0	27 2/3	29	19	14	13	29
1994— Frederick (Carolina)	7	7	.500	4.96	26	20	0	0	1	123 1/3	132	79	68	54	87
1995— Portland (Eastern)■	5	4	.556	1.87	50	0	0	0	*24	53	42	12	11	15	53
— Florida (N.L.)	0	0	...	1.08	9	0	0	0	0	8 1/3	7	2	1	6	4
1996— Florida (N.L.)	4	3	.571	4.54	67	0	0	0	2	71 1/3	71	41	36	36	52
— Brevard County (FSL)	0	0	...	0.00	1	1	0	0	0	2	0	0	0	0	4
1997— Florida (N.L.)	7	2	.778	3.28	74	0	0	0	2	79 2/3	71	35	29	30	65
Major league totals (3 years)	11	5	.688	3.73	150	0	0	0	4	159 1/3	149	78	66	72	121

CHAMPIONSHIP SERIES RECORD

Year Team (League)	W	L	Pct.	ERA	G	GS	CG	ShO	Sv.	IP	H	R	ER	BB	SO
1997— Florida (N.L.)	0	0	...	0.00	1	0	0	0	0	2/3	0	0	0	0	1

WORLD SERIES RECORD

NOTES: Member of World Series championship team (1997).

Year Team (League)	W	L	Pct.	ERA	G	GS	CG	ShO	Sv.	IP	H	R	ER	BB	SO
1997— Florida (N.L.)	1	0	1.000	7.36	4	0	0	0	0	3 2/3	5	3	3	4	2

PERSONAL: Born June 18, 1976, in La Miranda, Calif. ... 6-6/225. ... Throws right, bats right. ... Full name: Jeremy Robert Powell.
HIGH SCHOOL: Highlands (North Highlands, Calif.).
TRANSACTIONS/CAREER NOTES: Selected by Montreal Expos organization in fourth round of free-agent draft (June 2, 1994).

Year Team (League)	W	L	Pct.	ERA	G	GS	CG	ShO	Sv.	IP	H	R	ER	BB	SO
1994— GC Expos (GCL)	2	2	.500	2.93	9	9	1	0	0	43	37	16	14	14	36
1995— Albany (S. Atl.)	1	0	1.000	1.59	1	1	0	0	0	5 2/3	4	1	1	1	6
— Vermont (NYP)	5	5	.500	4.34	15	•15	0	0	0	87	88	48	42	34	47
1996— Delmarva (S. Atl.)	12	9	.571	3.03	27	27	1	0	0	157 2/3	127	68	53	66	109
1997— W.P. Beach (FSL)	9	10	.474	3.02	26	26	1	0	0	155	162	75	52	62	121

PERSONAL: Born August 24, 1973, in Santo Domingo, Dominican Republic. ... 5-10/160. ... Bats right, throws right.
TRANSACTIONS/CAREER NOTES: Signed as non-drafted free agent by Seattle Mariners (August 26, 1990). ... Traded by Mariners to Boston Red Sox for IF Jeff Manto (July 23, 1996).
STATISTICAL NOTES: Career major league grand slams: 1.

Year Team (League)	Pos.	G	AB	R	H	2B	3B	HR	RBI	Avg.	BB	SO	SB	PO	A	E	Avg.
1991—						Dominican Summer League statistics unavailable.											
1992— San Bern. (Calif.)	2B	54	199	33	52	8	4	3	19	.261	20	41	13	105	157	15	.946
— Bellingham (N'west)	2B	39	149	37	48	12	0	7	21	.322	20	24	9	85	129	10	.955
1993— Riverside (Calif.)	2B	127	515	98	176	44	6	13	83	.342	56	56	10	249	*367	•24	.963
1994— Jacksonville (South.)	2B	119	447	70	129	31	1	14	54	.289	32	43	11	240	349	17	.972
1995— Tacoma (PCL)	2B-3B	122	450	57	135	19	6	10	62	.300	26	31	3	191	304	17	.967
— Seattle (A.L.)	2B	1	1	0	0	0	0	0	0	.000	0	0	0	0	1	0	1.000
1996— Tacoma (PCL)	2B	95	365	55	102	12	5	15	64	.279	39	40	3	73	177	13	.951
— Boston (A.L.)■	2B-3B-DH	21	58	4	10	3	1	1	11	.172	2	10	1	23	39	4	.939
— Pawtucket (Int'l)	3B	11	37	6	9	1	0	1	3	.243	3	6	0	11	20	4	.886
1997— Pawtucket (Int'l)	3B-2B	101	377	61	107	18	1	22	70	.284	37	55	4	66	170	10	.959
— Boston (A.L.)	3B	4	15	0	4	1	0	0	3	.267	0	5	0	4	14	1	.947
Major league totals (3 years)		26	74	4	14	4	1	1	14	.189	2	15	1	27	54	5	.942

PERSONAL: Born February 9, 1967, in Bellevue, Neb. ... 6-3/224. ... Bats right, throws right. ... Full name: Todd Alan Pratt.
HIGH SCHOOL: Hilltop (Chula Vista, Calif.).
TRANSACTIONS/CAREER NOTES: Selected by Boston Red Sox organization in sixth round of free-agent draft (June 3, 1985). ... Selected by Cleveland Indians organization from Red Sox organization in Rule 5 minor league draft (December 7, 1987). ... Returned to Red Sox organization (March 1988). ... Granted free agency (October 15, 1991). ... Signed by Baltimore Orioles organization (November 13, 1991). ... Selected by Philadelphia Phillies from Orioles organization in Rule 5 major league draft (December 9, 1991). ... On Philadelphia disabled list (April 28-May 27, 1993); included rehabilitation assignment to Scranton/Wilkes-Barre (May 23-27). ... Granted free agency (December 21, 1994). ... Signed by Iowa, Chicago Cubs organization (April 8, 1995). ... Granted free agency (October 16, 1995). ... Signed by Seattle Mariners organization (January 25, 1996). ... Released by Mariners organization (March 27, 1996). ... Signed by New York Mets organization (December 23, 1996).
STATISTICAL NOTES: Led South Atlantic League catchers with 660 putouts and nine double plays and tied for lead with 13 errors in 1986. ... Led Eastern League catchers with 11 errors in 1989.

P

Year Team (League)	Pos.	G	AB	R	H	2B	3B	HR	RBI	Avg.	BB	SO	SB	PO	A	E	Avg.
										BATTING					FIELDING		
1985— Elmira (N.Y.-Penn)......	C	39	119	7	16	1	1	0	5	.134	10	27	0	254	29	6	.979
1986— Greensboro (S. Atl.)...	C-1B	107	348	63	84	16	0	12	56	.241	75	114	0	†826	55	‡15	.983
1987— Winter Haven (FSL)....	C-1B-OF	118	407	57	105	22	0	12	65	.258	70	94	0	672	64	15	.980
1988— New Britain (Eastern).	C-1B	124	395	41	89	15	2	8	49	.225	41	110	1	540	46	15	.975
1989— New Britain (Eastern).	C-1B	109	338	30	77	17	1	2	35	.228	44	66	1	435	42	†11	.977
1990— New Britain (Eastern).	C-1B	70	195	15	45	14	1	2	22	.231	18	56	0	166	15	4	.978
1991— Pawtucket (Int'l)■	C-1B	68	219	68	64	16	0	11	41	.292	23	42	0	236	21	4	.985
1992— Reading (Eastern)■......	C	41	132	20	44	6	1	6	26	.333	24	28	2	90	6	3	.970
— Scran./W.B. (Int'l)......	C-1B	41	125	20	40	9	1	7	28	.320	30	14	1	152	16	4	.977
— Philadelphia (N.L.)......	C	16	46	6	13	1	0	2	10	.283	4	12	0	65	4	2	.972
1993— Philadelphia (N.L.)......	C	33	87	8	25	6	0	5	13	.287	5	19	0	169	7	2	.989
— Scran./W.B. (Int'l)......	C	3	9	1	2	1	0	0	1	.222	3	1	0	11	0	0	1.000
1994— Philadelphia (N.L.)......	C	28	102	10	20	6	1	2	9	.196	12	29	0	172	8	0	1.000
1995— Iowa (Am. Assoc.)■ ..	C-1B	23	58	3	19	1	0	0	5	.328	4	17	0	82	8	2	.978
— Chicago (N.L.)...........	C	25	60	3	8	2	0	0	4	.133	6	21	0	149	9	3	.981
1996—							Did not play.										
1997— Norfolk (Int'l)...........	C	59	206	42	62	8	3	9	34	.301	26	48	1	317	24	4	.988
— New York (N.L.)..........	C	39	106	12	30	6	0	2	19	.283	13	32	0	186	22	2	.990
Major league totals (5 years)		141	401	39	96	21	1	11	55	.239	40	113	0	741	50	9	.989

CHAMPIONSHIP SERIES RECORD

Year Team (League)	Pos.	G	AB	R	H	2B	3B	HR	RBI	Avg.	BB	SO	SB	PO	A	E	Avg.
										BATTING					FIELDING		
1993— Philadelphia (N.L.)......	C	1	1	0	0	0	0	0	0	.000	0	1	0	1	0	0	1.000

WORLD SERIES RECORD

Year Team (League)	Pos.	G	AB	R	H	2B	3B	HR	RBI	Avg.	BB	SO	SB	PO	A	E	Avg.
										BATTING					FIELDING		
1993— Philadelphia (N.L.)							Did not play.										

PRIDE, CURTIS — OF

PERSONAL: Born December 17, 1968, in Washington, D.C. ... 6-0/200. ... Bats left, throws right. ... Full name: Curtis John Pride.
HIGH SCHOOL: John F. Kennedy (Silver Spring, Md.).
COLLEGE: William & Mary (degree in finance).
TRANSACTIONS/CAREER NOTES: Selected by New York Mets organization in 10th round of free-agent draft (June 2, 1986). ... Granted free agency (October 15, 1992). ... Signed by Ottawa, Montreal Expos organization (December 8, 1992). ... On Ottawa disabled list (April 7-May 13, July 6-15 and August 7-14, 1994). ... Granted free agency (October 16, 1995). ... Signed by Detroit Tigers (March 31, 1996). ... On Detroit disabled list (April 13-May 10, 1996); included rehabilitation assignment to Toledo (April 30-May 10). ... Granted free agency (August 21, 1997). ... Signed by Boston Red Sox organization (August 30, 1997). ... Granted free agency (October 15, 1997).

Year Team (League)	Pos.	G	AB	R	H	2B	3B	HR	RBI	Avg.	BB	SO	SB	PO	A	E	Avg.
										BATTING					FIELDING		
1986— Kingsport (Appal.)......	OF	27	46	5	5	0	0	1	4	.109	6	24	5	17	1	0	1.000
1987— Kingsport (Appal.)......	OF	31	104	22	25	4	0	1	9	.240	16	34	14	39	3	5	.894
1988— Kingsport (Appal.)......	OF	70	268	*59	76	13	1	8	27	.284	50	48	23	118	6	5	.961
1989— Pittsfield (NYP)	OF	55	212	35	55	7	3	6	23	.259	25	47	9	105	3	4	.964
1990— Columbia (S. Atl.)......	OF	53	191	38	51	4	4	6	25	.267	21	45	11	72	4	11	.874
1991— St. Lucie (Fla. St.).....	OF	116	392	57	102	21	7	9	37	.260	43	94	24	199	5	4	.981
1992— Binghamton (East.)	OF	118	388	54	88	15	3	10	42	.227	47	110	14	214	3	8	.964
1993— Harrisburg (Eastern)■	OF	50	180	51	64	6	3	15	39	.356	12	36	21	69	0	2	.972
— Ottawa (Int'l)...........	OF	69	262	55	79	11	4	6	22	.302	34	61	29	136	3	2	.986
— Montreal (N.L.)..........	OF	10	9	3	4	1	1	1	5	.444	0	3	1	2	0	0	1.000
1994— W.P. Beach (FSL)......	OF	3	8	5	6	1	0	1	3	.750	4	2	2	11	0	0	1.000
— Ottawa (Int'l)...........	OF	82	300	56	77	16	4	9	32	.257	39	81	22	164	1	3	.982
1995— Ottawa (Int'l)...........	OF	42	154	25	43	8	3	4	24	.279	12	35	8	69	5	2	.974
— Montreal (N.L.)..........	OF	48	63	10	11	1	0	2	2	.175	5	16	3	23	0	2	.920
1996— Detroit (A.L.)■	OF-DH	95	267	52	80	17	5	10	31	.300	31	63	11	89	0	3	.967
— Toledo (Int'l)............	OF	9	26	4	6	1	0	1	2	.231	9	7	4	3	0	0	1.000
1997— Detroit (A.L.)..........	OF-DH	79	162	21	34	4	4	2	19	.210	24	45	6	49	0	1	.980
— Pawtucket (Int'l)■......	OF	1	3	0	0	0	0	0	0	.000	0	2	0	2	0	0	1.000
— Boston (A.L.).............	PH	2	2	1	1	0	0	0	1	.500	0	1	0	...	...	...	...
American League totals (2 years)		176	431	74	115	21	9	13	51	.267	55	109	17	138	0	4	.972
National League totals (2 years)		58	72	13	15	2	1	1	7	.208	5	19	4	25	0	2	.926
Major league totals (4 years)		234	503	87	130	23	10	14	58	.258	60	128	21	163	0	6	.964

PRIEST, EDDIE — P — REDS

PERSONAL: Born April 8, 1974, in Boaz, Ala. ... 6-1/195. ... Throws left, bats right. ... Full name: Eddie Lee Priest.
HIGH SCHOOL: Susan Moore (Blountsville, Ala.).
JUNIOR COLLEGE: Southern Union State.
TRANSACTIONS/CAREER NOTES: Selected by Cincinnati Reds organization in ninth round of free-agent draft (June 2, 1994). ... On disabled list (April 8-July 15 and August 27-September 13, 1996).

Year Team (League)	W	L	Pct.	ERA	G	GS	CG	ShO	Sv.	IP	H	R	ER	BB	SO
1994— Billings (Pioneer)...............	7	4	.636	2.54	13	13	2	0	0	85	74	31	24	14	82
1995— Win.-Salem (Car.)...............	5	5	.500	3.63	12	12	1	1	0	67	60	32	27	22	60
1996— Win.-Salem (Car.)...............	1	0	1.000	0.73	4	4	0	0	0	12 1/3	5	2	1	6	9
1997— Char., W.Va. (S. Atl.)	5	3	.625	3.62	14	14	0	0	0	77	79	38	31	10	70
— Chattanooga (Southern).....	4	6	.400	3.44	14	14	1	0	0	91 2/3	101	39	35	17	63

P

PRIETO, ARIEL P ATHLETICS

PERSONAL: Born October 22, 1969, in Havana, Cuba. ... 6-3/230. ... Throws right, bats right.
TRANSACTIONS/CAREER NOTES: Selected by Oakland Athletics organization in first round (fifth pick overall) of free-agent draft (June 1, 1995). ... On disabled list (August 19-September 3, 1995). ... On Oakland disabled list (May 19-July 28, 1996); included rehabilitation assignments to Modesto (July 1-11) and Edmonton (July 11-28). ... On Oakland disabled list (July 13-August 8 and August 23, 1997-remainder of season); included rehabilitation assignment to Edmonton (August 8-17).

Year Team (League)	W	L	Pct.	ERA	G	GS	CG	ShO	Sv.	IP	H	R	ER	BB	SO
1995— Oakland (A.L.)	2	6	.250	4.97	14	9	1	0	0	58	57	35	32	32	37
1996— Oakland (A.L.)	6	7	.462	4.15	21	21	2	0	0	125²/₃	130	66	58	54	75
—Modesto (California)	0	0	...	3.00	2	1	0	0	1	9	9	4	3	2	8
—Edmonton (PCL)	3	0	1.000	0.57	3	3	0	0	0	15²/₃	11	1	1	6	18
1997— Oakland (A.L.)	6	8	.429	5.04	22	22	0	0	0	125	155	84	70	70	90
—Edmonton (PCL)	0	0	...	1.50	2	2	0	0	0	6	4	1	1	1	7
Major league totals (3 years)	14	21	.400	4.67	57	52	3	0	0	308²/₃	342	185	160	156	202

PRINCE, TOM C DODGERS

PERSONAL: Born August 13, 1964, in Kankakee, Ill. ... 5-11/202. ... Bats right, throws right. ... Full name: Thomas Albert Prince.
HIGH SCHOOL: Bradley Bourbonnais (Kankakee, Ill.).
JUNIOR COLLEGE: Kankakee (Ill.) Community College.
TRANSACTIONS/CAREER NOTES: Selected by Atlanta Braves organization in eighth round of free-agent draft (January 11, 1983); did not sign. ... Selected by Braves organization in secondary phase of free-agent draft (June 6, 1983); did not sign. ... Selected by Pittsburgh Pirates organization in secondary phase of free-agent draft (January 17, 1984). ... On Pittsburgh disabled list (August 13-September 1, 1991); included rehabilitation assignment to Buffalo (August 28-September 1). ... Granted free agency (October 15, 1993). ... Signed by Albuquerque, Los Angeles Dodgers organization (November 12, 1993). ... On Albuquerque disabled list (April 30-May 7, 1994). ... Released by Dodgers (December 5, 1994). ... Re-signed by Dodgers organization (January 5, 1995). ... On Los Angeles disabled list (June 4-July 10, 1995); included rehabilitation assignment to Albuquerque (June 26-July 10). ... Granted free agency (October 15, 1995). ... Re-signed by Dodgers organization (November 1, 1995).
STATISTICAL NOTES: Led South Atlantic League catchers with 930 total chances, 10 double plays and 27 passed balls in 1985. ... Led Carolina League catchers with 954 total chances and 15 passed balls in 1986. ... Led Eastern League catchers with 721 total chances and nine double plays in 1987. ... Led American Association catchers with 12 double plays in 1992. ... Led Pacific Coast League catchers with 677 total chances and nine double plays in 1994.

Year Team (League)	Pos.	G	AB	R	H	2B	3B	HR	RBI	Avg.	BB	SO	SB	PO	A	E	Avg.
1984— Watertown (NYP)	C-3B	23	69	6	14	3	0	2	13	.203	9	13	0	155	26	2	.989
—GC Pirates (GCL)	C-1B	18	48	4	11	0	0	1	6	.229	8	10	1	75	16	4	.958
1985— Macon (S. Atl.)	C	124	360	60	75	20	1	10	42	.208	96	92	13	*810	*101	*19	.980
1986— Prince William (Car.)	C	121	395	59	100	34	1	10	47	.253	50	74	4	*821	•113	20	.979
1987— Harrisburg (Eastern)	C	113	365	41	112	23	2	6	54	.307	51	46	6	*622	*88	•11	.985
—Pittsburgh (N.L.)	C	4	9	1	2	1	0	1	2	.222	0	2	0	14	3	0	1.000
1988— Buffalo (A.A.)	C	86	304	35	79	16	0	14	42	.260	23	53	3	456	51	*12	.977
—Pittsburgh (N.L.)	C	29	74	3	13	2	0	0	6	.176	4	15	0	108	8	2	.983
1989— Buffalo (A.A.)	C	65	183	21	37	8	1	6	33	.202	22	30	2	312	22	5	.985
—Pittsburgh (N.L.)	C	21	52	1	7	4	0	0	5	.135	6	12	1	85	11	4	.960
1990— Pittsburgh (N.L.)	C	4	10	1	1	0	0	0	0	.100	1	2	0	16	1	0	1.000
—Buffalo (A.A.)	C-1B	94	284	38	64	13	0	7	37	.225	39	46	4	461	62	8	.985
1991— Pittsburgh (N.L.)	C-1B	26	34	4	9	3	0	1	2	.265	7	3	0	53	9	1	.984
—Buffalo (A.A.)	C	80	221	29	46	8	3	6	32	.208	37	31	3	379	61	5	.989
1992— Pittsburgh (N.L.)	C-3B	27	44	1	4	2	0	0	5	.091	6	9	1	76	8	2	.977
—Buffalo (A.A.)	C-OF	75	244	34	64	17	0	9	35	.262	20	35	3	307	50	8	.978
1993— Pittsburgh (N.L.)	C	66	179	14	35	14	0	2	24	.196	13	38	1	271	31	5	.984
1994— Albuquerque (PCL)■	C	103	330	61	94	31	2	20	54	.285	51	67	2	593	*75	9	.987
—Los Angeles (N.L.)	C	3	6	2	2	0	0	0	1	.333	1	3	0	11	1	0	1.000
1995— Los Angeles (N.L.)	C	18	40	3	8	2	1	1	4	.200	4	10	0	71	8	1	.988
—Albuquerque (PCL)	C	61	192	30	61	15	0	7	36	.318	27	41	0	310	34	4	.989
1996— Albuquerque (PCL)	C-3B-OF	32	95	24	39	5	1	7	22	.411	15	14	0	88	20	1	.991
—Los Angeles (N.L.)	C	40	64	6	19	6	0	1	11	.297	6	15	0	161	11	1	.994
1997— Los Angeles (N.L.)	C	47	100	17	22	5	0	3	14	.220	5	15	0	221	25	1	.996
Major league totals (11 years)		285	612	53	122	39	1	9	74	.199	53	124	3	1087	116	17	.986

PRITCHETT, CHRIS 1B ANGELS

PERSONAL: Born January 31, 1970, in Merced, Calif. ... 6-4/185. ... Bats left, throws right. ... Full name: Christopher Davis Pritchett.
HIGH SCHOOL: Central Catholic (Modesto, Calif.).
COLLEGE: UCLA.
TRANSACTIONS/CAREER NOTES: Selected by California Angels organization in second round of free-agent draft (June 3, 1991). ... Angels franchise renamed Anaheim Angels for 1997 season.
STATISTICAL NOTES: Tied for Midwest League lead with six intentional bases on balls received in 1992. ... Led Texas League first basemen with 1,075 putouts, 19 errors and 1,182 total chances in 1993. ... Led Texas League with .421 on-base percentage in 1994. ... Led Texas League first basemen with 100 double plays in 1994. ... Tied for Pacific Coast League lead with 11 intentional bases on balls received in 1996. ... Led Pacific Coast League first baseman with 1,107 putouts, 98 assists, 1,211 total chances, .995 fielding percentage and 107 double plays in 1996.

Year Team (League)	Pos.	G	AB	R	H	2B	3B	HR	RBI	Avg.	BB	SO	SB	PO	A	E	Avg.
1991— Boise (Northwest)	1B	70	255	41	68	10	3	9	50	.267	47	41	1	636	26	5	*.993
1992— Quad City (Midwest)	1B	128	448	79	130	19	1	13	72	.290	71	88	9	*1059	84	13	*.989

P

Year Team (League)	Pos.	G	AB	R	H	2B	3B	HR	RBI	Avg.	BB	SO	SB	PO	A	E	Avg.
1993— Midland (Texas)	1B-2B	127	464	61	143	30	6	2	66	.308	61	72	3	†1076	92	†19	.984
1994— Midland (Texas)	1B-OF-3B	127	460	86	142	25	4	6	91	.309	*92	87	5	1028	94	13	.989
1995— Vancouver (PCL)	1B-OF	123	434	66	120	27	4	8	53	.276	56	79	2	999	92	12	.989
1996— Vancouver (PCL)	1B-OF	130	485	78	143	39	1	16	73	.295	71	96	5	†1116	†98	6	†.995
— California (A.L.)	1B	5	13	1	2	0	0	0	1	.154	0	3	0	29	1	0	1.000
1997— Vancouver (PCL)	1B-OF	109	383	60	107	30	3	7	47	.279	42	72	5	621	51	7	.990
Major league totals (1 year)		5	13	1	2	0	0	0	1	.154	0	3	0	29	1	0	1.000

PUGH, TIM   P

PERSONAL: Born January 26, 1967, in Lake Tahoe, Calif. ... 6-6/225. ... Throws right, bats right. ... Full name: Timothy Dean Pugh.
HIGH SCHOOL: Bartlesville (Okla.).
COLLEGE: Oklahoma State.
TRANSACTIONS/CAREER NOTES: Selected by Toronto Blue Jays organization in eighth round of free-agent draft (June 1, 1988); did not sign. ... Selected by Cincinnati Reds organization in sixth round of free-agent draft (June 5, 1989). ... On Indianapolis disabled list (June 17-July 29, 1994). ... Claimed on waivers by Kansas City Royals (May 10, 1996). ... Released by Royals (July 8, 1996). ... Claimed on waivers by Reds (July 8, 1996). ... Claimed on waivers by Royals (July 12, 1996). ... Claimed on waivers by Reds (August 15, 1996). ... Granted free agency (October 15, 1996). ... Signed by Detroit Tigers organization (November 20, 1996). ... Granted free agency (October 15, 1997).
STATISTICAL NOTES: Pitched 8-0 one-hit, complete-game victory against San Diego (September 29, 1993).
MISCELLANEOUS: Struck out in only appearance as pinch-hitter with Cincinnati (1995).

Year Team (League)	W	L	Pct.	ERA	G	GS	CG	ShO	Sv.	IP	H	R	ER	BB	SO
1989— Billings (Pioneer)	2	6	.250	3.94	13	13	2	0	0	77 2/3	81	44	34	25	72
1990— Char., W.Va. (S. Atl.)	*15	6	.714	1.93	27	27	*8	2	0	177 1/3	142	58	38	56	153
1991— Chattanooga (Southern)	3	1	.750	1.64	5	5	0	0	0	38 1/3	20	7	7	11	24
— Nashville (A.A.)	7	11	.389	3.81	23	23	3	1	0	148 2/3	130	68	63	56	89
1992— Nashville (A.A.)	•12	9	.571	3.55	27	27	3	2	0	169 2/3	165	75	67	65	117
— Cincinnati (N.L.)	4	2	.667	2.58	7	7	0	0	0	45 1/3	47	15	13	13	18
1993— Cincinnati (N.L.)	10	15	.400	5.26	31	27	3	1	0	164 1/3	200	102	96	59	94
1994— Cincinnati (N.L.)	3	3	.500	6.04	10	9	1	0	0	47 2/3	60	37	32	26	24
— Indianapolis (A.A.)	2	3	.400	4.60	9	7	1	1	0	45	50	26	23	15	21
1995— Indianapolis (A.A.)	2	4	.333	4.68	6	6	1	1	0	42 1/3	42	24	22	14	20
— Cincinnati (N.L.)	6	5	.545	3.84	28	12	0	0	0	98 1/3	100	46	42	32	24
1996— Indianapolis (A.A.)	2	1	.667	2.45	4	4	1	1	0	25 2/3	19	7	7	4	18
— Kansas City (A.L.)■	0	1	.000	5.45	19	1	0	0	0	36 1/3	42	24	22	12	27
— Cincinnati (N.L.)	1	1	.500	11.49	10	0	0	0	0	15 2/3	24	20	20	11	9
1997— Toledo (Int'l)■	3	5	.375	4.29	19	17	0	0	0	109	115	60	52	28	97
— Detroit (A.L.)	1	1	.500	5.00	2	2	0	0	0	9	6	5	5	5	4
A.L. totals (2 years)	1	2	.333	5.36	21	3	0	0	0	45 1/3	48	29	27	17	31
N.L. totals (5 years)	24	26	.480	4.92	86	55	4	1	0	371 1/3	431	220	203	141	183
Major league totals (6 years)	25	28	.472	4.97	107	58	4	1	0	416 2/3	479	249	230	158	214

PULLIAM, HARVEY   OF

PERSONAL: Born October 20, 1967, in San Francisco. ... 6-0/218. ... Bats right, throws right. ... Full name: Harvey Jerome Pulliam Jr.
HIGH SCHOOL: McAteer (San Francisco).
TRANSACTIONS/CAREER NOTES: Selected by Kansas City Royals organization in third round of free-agent draft (June 2, 1986). ... Granted free agency (October 15, 1993). ... Signed by Las Vegas, San Diego Padres organization (March 1, 1994). ... On disabled list (June 16-28, 1994). ... Granted free agency (October 15, 1994). ... Signed by Colorado Springs, Colorado Rockies organization (January 31, 1995). ... On Colorado disabled list (April 22-June 4, 1996); included rehabilitation assignment to Colorado Springs (May 14-June 4). ... Granted free agency (October 15, 1996). ... Traded by Rockies to Arizona Diamondbacks for P Chuck McElroy (November 18, 1997). ... Contract sold by Diamondbacks to Orix of Japan Pacific League (December 17, 1997).
STATISTICAL NOTES: Led Pacific Coast League with .614 slugging percentage in 1995. ... Led Pacific Coast League with 10 intentional bases on balls received in 1995. ... Led Pacific Coast League outfielders with six double plays in 1995.

Year Team (League)	Pos.	G	AB	R	H	2B	3B	HR	RBI	Avg.	BB	SO	SB	PO	A	E	Avg.
1986— GC Royals (GCL)	OF	48	168	14	35	3	0	4	23	.208	8	33	3	62	5	4	.944
1987— Appleton (Midwest)	OF	110	395	54	109	20	1	9	55	.276	26	79	21	195	8	6	.971
1988— Baseball City (FSL)	OF	132	457	56	111	19	4	4	42	.243	34	87	21	289	9	6	.980
1989— Memphis (Southern)	OF	116	417	67	121	28	8	10	67	.290	44	65	5	157	8	5	.971
— Omaha (A.A.)	OF	7	22	3	4	2	0	0	2	.182	3	6	0	12	1	0	1.000
1990— Omaha (A.A.)	OF	123	436	72	117	18	5	16	72	.268	49	82	9	188	12	4	.980
1991— Omaha (A.A.)	OF	104	346	35	89	18	2	6	39	.257	31	62	2	162	12	3	.983
— Kansas City (A.L.)	OF	18	33	4	9	1	0	3	4	.273	3	9	0	21	1	2	.917
1992— Omaha (A.A.)	OF	100	359	55	97	12	2	16	60	.270	32	53	4	168	7	1	.994
— Kansas City (A.L.)	DH-OF	4	5	2	1	1	0	0	0	.200	1	3	0	3	0	0	1.000
1993— Kansas City (A.L.)	OF	27	62	7	16	5	0	1	6	.258	2	14	0	33	0	1	.971
— Omaha (A.A.)	OF	54	208	28	55	10	0	5	26	.264	17	36	1	102	7	6	.948
1994— Las Vegas (PCL)■	OF	95	314	48	72	10	0	20	53	.229	21	65	0	144	6	4	.974
1995— Colo. Springs (PCL)■	OF	115	407	90	133	30	6	*25	•91	.327	49	59	6	186	8	3	.985
— Colorado (N.L.)	OF	5	5	1	2	1	0	1	3	.400	0	2	0	0	0	0	...
1996— Colo. Springs (PCL)	OF	79	283	46	78	13	1	10	58	.276	32	49	2	124	6	9	.935
— Colorado (N.L.)	OF	10	15	2	2	0	0	0	0	.133	2	6	0	4	0	0	1.000
1997— Colo. Springs (PCL)	OF	40	137	44	55	10	2	12	43	.401	21	19	1	44	0	2	.957
— Colorado (N.L.)	OF	59	67	15	19	3	0	3	9	.284	5	15	0	23	2	1	.962
American League totals (3 years)		49	100	13	26	7	0	4	10	.260	6	26	0	57	1	3	.951
National League totals (3 years)		74	87	18	23	4	0	4	12	.264	7	23	0	27	2	1	.967
Major league totals (6 years)		123	187	31	49	11	0	8	22	.262	13	49	0	84	3	4	.956

P

PULSIPHER, BILL — P — METS

PERSONAL: Born October 9, 1973, in Fort Benning, Ga. ... 6-3/200. ... Throws left, bats left. ... Full name: William Thomas Pulsipher.
HIGH SCHOOL: Fairfax (Va.).
TRANSACTIONS/CAREER NOTES: Selected by New York Mets organization in second round of free-agent draft (June 3, 1991). ... On disabled list (March 22, 1996-entire season). ... On New York disabled list (March 24-May 3 and June 30-July 30, 1997); included rehabilitation assignment to Norfolk (April 4-May 3).
STATISTICAL NOTES: Tied for Eastern League lead with four balks in 1994.

Year Team (League)	W	L	Pct.	ERA	G	GS	CG	ShO	Sv.	IP	H	R	ER	BB	SO
1992—Pittsfield (NYP)	6	3	.667	2.84	14	14	0	0	0	95	88	40	30	56	83
1993—Capital City (S. Atl.)	2	3	.400	2.08	6	6	1	0	0	43 1/3	34	17	10	12	29
—St. Lucie (Fla. St.)	7	3	.700	2.24	13	13	3	1	0	96 1/3	63	27	24	39	102
1994—Binghamton (Eastern)	14	9	.609	3.22	28	28	5	1	0	*201	179	90	72	89	171
1995—Norfolk (Int'l)	6	4	.600	3.14	13	13	•4	2	0	91 2/3	84	36	32	33	63
—New York (N.L.)	5	7	.417	3.98	17	17	2	0	0	126 2/3	122	58	56	45	81
1996—							Did not play.								
1997—Norfolk (Int'l)	0	5	.000	7.81	8	5	0	0	0	27 2/3	23	29	24	38	18
—St. Lucie (Fla. St.)	1	4	.200	5.89	12	7	0	0	0	36 2/3	29	27	24	35	35
—Binghamton (Eastern)	0	0	. . .	1.42	10	0	0	0	0	12 2/3	11	3	2	7	12
—GC Mets (GCL)	0	0	. . .	1.80	2	2	0	0	0	5	3	1	1	1	4
Major league totals (1 year)	5	7	.417	3.98	17	17	2	0	0	126 2/3	122	58	56	45	81

QUANTRILL, PAUL — P — BLUE JAYS

PERSONAL: Born November 3, 1968, in London, Ont. ... 6-1/185. ... Throws right, bats left. ... Full name: Paul John Quantrill.
HIGH SCHOOL: Okemos (Mich.).
COLLEGE: Wisconsin.
TRANSACTIONS/CAREER NOTES: Selected by Los Angeles Dodgers organization in 26th round of free-agent draft (June 2, 1986); did not sign. ... Selected by Boston Red Sox organization in sixth round of free-agent draft (June 5, 1989). ... Traded by Red Sox with OF Billy Hatcher to Philadelphia Phillies for OF Wes Chamberlain and P Mike Sullivan (May 31, 1994). ... Traded by Phillies to Toronto Blue Jays for 3B Howard Battle and P Ricardo Jordan (December 6, 1995).

Year Team (League)	W	L	Pct.	ERA	G	GS	CG	ShO	Sv.	IP	H	R	ER	BB	SO
1989—GC Red Sox (GCL)	0	0	. . .	0.00	2	0	0	0	2	5	2	0	0	0	5
—Elmira (N.Y.-Penn)	5	4	.556	3.43	20	7	•5	0	2	76	90	37	29	12	57
1990—Winter Haven (FSL)	2	5	.286	4.14	7	7	1	0	0	45 2/3	46	24	21	6	14
—New Britain (East.)	7	11	.389	3.53	22	22	1	1	0	132 2/3	148	65	52	23	53
1991—New Britain (East.)	2	1	.667	2.06	5	5	1	0	0	35	32	14	8	8	18
—Pawtucket (Int'l)	10	7	.588	4.45	25	23	•6	2	0	155 2/3	169	81	77	30	75
1992—Pawtucket (Int'l)	6	8	.429	4.46	19	18	4	1	0	119	143	63	59	20	56
—Boston (A.L.)	2	3	.400	2.19	27	0	0	0	1	49 1/3	55	18	12	15	24
1993—Boston (A.L.)	6	12	.333	3.91	49	14	1	1	1	138	151	73	60	44	66
1994—Boston (A.L.)	1	1	.500	3.52	17	0	0	0	0	23	25	10	9	5	15
—Philadelphia (N.L.)■	2	2	.500	6.00	18	1	0	0	1	30	39	21	20	10	13
—Scran./W.B. (Int'l)	3	3	.500	3.47	8	8	1	1	0	57	55	25	22	6	36
1995—Philadelphia (N.L.)	11	12	.478	4.67	33	29	0	0	0	179 1/3	212	102	93	44	103
1996—Toronto (A.L.)■	5	14	.263	5.43	38	20	0	0	0	134 1/3	172	90	81	51	86
1997—Toronto (A.L.)	6	7	.462	1.94	77	0	0	0	5	88	103	25	19	17	56
A.L. totals (5 years)	20	37	.351	3.77	208	34	1	1	7	432 2/3	506	216	181	132	247
N.L. totals (2 years)	13	14	.481	4.86	51	30	0	0	1	209 1/3	251	123	113	54	116
Major league totals (6 years)	33	51	.393	4.12	259	64	1	1	8	642	757	339	294	186	363

QUINN, MARK — OF — ROYALS

PERSONAL: Born May 21, 1974, in La Miranda, Calif. ... 6-1/175. ... Bats right, throws right. ... Full name: Mark David Quinn.
HIGH SCHOOL: Clements (Sugar Land, Texas).
COLLEGE: Rice.
TRANSACTIONS/CAREER NOTES: Selected by Kansas City Royals organization in 11th round of free-agent draft (June 1, 1995).

					BATTING								FIELDING		
Year Team (League)	Pos.	G	AB	R	H	2B	3B	HR	RBI	Avg.	BB	SO	SB	PO	A	E	Avg.
1995—Spokane (N'west)	3B	44	162	28	46	12	2	6	36	.284	15	28	0	8	33	8	.837
1996—Lansing (Midwest)	OF	113	437	63	132	23	3	9	71	.302	43	54	14	143	15	7	.958
1997—Wilmington (Caro.)	OF	87	299	51	92	22	3	16	71	.308	42	47	3	75	7	6	.932
—Wichita (Texas)	OF	26	96	26	36	13	0	2	19	.375	15	19	1	35	0	1	.972

RAABE, BRIAN — 2B/3B

PERSONAL: Born November 5, 1967, in New Ulm, Minn. ... 5-9/176. ... Bats right, throws right. ... Full name: Brian Charles Raabe. ... Name pronounced ROB-ee.
HIGH SCHOOL: New Ulm (Minn.).
COLLEGE: Minnesota.
TRANSACTIONS/CAREER NOTES: Selected by Minnesota Twins organization in 41st round of free-agent draft (June 4, 1990). ... Released by Twins (December 4, 1996). ... Signed by Seattle Mariners organization (December 18, 1996). ... Traded by Mariners to Colorado Rockies for P Donnie Schmidt (September 8, 1997). ... Contract sold by Rockies to Seibu Lions of the Japan Pacific League (November 20, 1997).
STATISTICAL NOTES: Led Pacific Coast League in being hit by pitch with 16 and tied for league lead with nine sacrifice flies in 1997.

Year	Team (League)	Pos.	G	AB	R	H	2B	3B	HR	RBI	Avg.	BB	SO	SB	PO	A	E	Avg.
							BATTING								FIELDING			
1990—Visalia (California)	2B	42	138	11	34	3	2	0	17	.246	10	9	5	98	98	2	.990
1991—Visalia (California)	2B-3B-P	85	311	36	80	3	1	1	22	.257	40	14	15	120	198	2	.994
1992—Miracle (Florida State)	2B	102	361	52	104	16	2	2	32	.288	48	17	7	231	300	5	*.991
—Orlando (South.)	2B-P	32	108	12	30	6	0	2	6	.278	2	2	0	47	83	1	.992
1993—Nashville (Southern)	2-3-S-P	134	524	80	150	23	2	6	52	.286	56	28	18	139	308	16	.965
1994—Salt Lake (PCL)	2B-SS-3B	123	474	78	152	26	3	6	49	.321	50	11	9	185	300	7	.986
1995—Salt Lake (PCL)	2B-3B-SS	112	440	88	134	32	6	3	60	.305	45	14	15	120	249	6	.984
—Minnesota (A.L.)	2B-3B	6	14	4	3	0	0	0	1	.214	1	0	0	5	8	0	1.000
1996—Salt Lake (PCL)	2B-SS-3B	116	482	*103	169	39	4	18	69	*.351	47	19	8	180	295	4	.992
—Minnesota (A.L.)	3B-2B	7	9	0	2	0	0	0	1	.222	0	1	0	2	4	1	.857
1997—Tacoma (PCL)	2B-3B	*135	*543	*101	*191	35	4	14	80	.352	38	20	1	191	340	8	.985
—Seattle (A.L.)	3B-2B	2	3	0	0	0	0	0	0	.000	1	2	0	1	1	0	1.000
—Colorado (N.L.)■	2B	2	3	0	1	0	0	0	0	.333	0	1	0	0	4	0	1.000
American League totals (3 years)		15	26	4	5	0	0	0	2	.192	2	3	0	8	13	1	.955
National League totals (1 year)		2	3	0	1	0	0	0	0	.333	0	1	0	0	4	0	1.000
Major league totals (3 years)		17	29	4	6	0	0	0	2	.207	2	4	0	8	17	1	.962

RECORD AS PITCHER

Year	Team (League)	W	L	Pct.	ERA	G	GS	CG	ShO	Sv.	IP	H	R	ER	BB	SO
1991—Visalia (California)	0	0	...	0.00	1	0	0	0	0	1	0	0	0	0	0
1992—Orlando (South.)	0	0	...	0.00	1	0	0	0	0	2/3	1	0	0	0	0
1993—Nashville (Southern)■	0	0	...	54.00	1	0	0	0	0	1	8	6	6	0	0

RADINSKY, SCOTT   P   DODGERS

PERSONAL: Born March 3, 1968, in Glendale, Calif. ... 6-3/204. ... Throws left, bats left. ... Full name: Scott David Radinsky.
HIGH SCHOOL: Simi Valley (Calif.).
TRANSACTIONS/CAREER NOTES: Selected by Chicago White Sox organization in third round of free-agent draft (June 2, 1986). ... On Chicago disabled list (March 2, 1994-entire season). ... On Chicago disabled list (July 17-August 15, 1995); included rehabilitation assignment to South Bend (August 1-15). ... Granted free agency (December 21, 1995). ... Signed by Los Angeles Dodgers organization (January 16, 1996). ... On Los Angeles disabled list (March 28-April 12, 1996); included rehabilitation assignment to San Bernardino (April 4-12).

Year	Team (League)	W	L	Pct.	ERA	G	GS	CG	ShO	Sv.	IP	H	R	ER	BB	SO
1986—GC White Sox (GCL)	1	0	1.000	3.38	7	7	0	0	0	26 2/3	24	20	10	17	18
1987—Peninsula (Caro.)	1	7	.125	5.77	12	8	0	0	0	39	43	30	25	32	37
—GC White Sox (GCL)	3	3	.500	2.31	11	10	0	0	0	58 1/3	43	23	15	39	41
1988—GC White Sox (GCL)	0	0	...	5.40	5	0	0	0	0	3 1/3	2	2	2	4	7
1989—South Bend (Mid.)	7	5	.583	1.75	53	0	0	0	31	61 2/3	39	21	12	19	83
1990—Chicago (A.L.)	6	1	.857	4.82	62	0	0	0	4	52 1/3	47	29	28	36	46
1991—Chicago (A.L.)	5	5	.500	2.02	67	0	0	0	8	71 1/3	53	18	16	23	49
1992—Chicago (A.L.)	3	7	.300	2.73	68	0	0	0	15	59 1/3	54	21	18	34	48
1993—Chicago (A.L.)	8	2	.800	4.28	73	0	0	0	4	54 2/3	61	33	26	19	44
1994—Chicago (A.L.)						Did not play.									
1995—Chicago (A.L.)	2	1	.667	5.45	46	0	0	0	1	38	46	23	23	17	14
—South Bend (Mid.)	0	0	...	0.00	6	0	0	0	2	9 2/3	5	0	0	0	11
1996—San Bernardino (Calif.)■	0	0	...	2.08	3	0	0	0	0	4 1/3	2	1	1	2	4
—Los Angeles (N.L.)	5	1	.833	2.41	56	0	0	0	1	52 1/3	52	19	14	17	48
1997—Los Angeles (N.L.)	5	1	.833	2.89	75	0	0	0	3	62 1/3	54	22	20	21	44
A.L. totals (5 years)	24	16	.600	3.62	316	0	0	0	32	275 2/3	261	124	111	129	201
N.L. totals (2 years)	10	2	.833	2.67	131	0	0	0	4	114 2/3	106	41	34	38	92
Major league totals (7 years)	34	18	.654	3.34	447	0	0	0	36	390 1/3	367	165	145	167	293

DIVISION SERIES RECORD

Year	Team (League)	W	L	Pct.	ERA	G	GS	CG	ShO	Sv.	IP	H	R	ER	BB	SO
1996—Los Angeles (N.L.)	0	0	...	0.00	2	0	0	0	0	1 1/3	0	0	0	1	2

CHAMPIONSHIP SERIES RECORD

Year	Team (League)	W	L	Pct.	ERA	G	GS	CG	ShO	Sv.	IP	H	R	ER	BB	SO
1993—Chicago (A.L.)	0	0	...	10.80	4	0	0	0	0	1 2/3	3	4	2	1	1

RADKE, BRAD   P   TWINS

PERSONAL: Born October 27, 1972, in Eau Claire, Wis. ... 6-2/185. ... Throws right, bats right. ... Full name: Brad William Radke.
HIGH SCHOOL: Jesuit (Tampa).
TRANSACTIONS/CAREER NOTES: Selected by Minnesota Twins organization in eighth round of free-agent draft (June 3, 1991).
STATISTICAL NOTES: Led A.L. with 32 home runs allowed in 1995 and 40 in 1996.

Year	Team (League)	W	L	Pct.	ERA	G	GS	CG	ShO	Sv.	IP	H	R	ER	BB	SO
1991—GC Twins (GCL)	3	4	.429	3.08	10	9	1	0	1	49 2/3	41	21	17	14	46
1992—Kenosha (Midwest)	10	10	.500	2.93	26	25	4	1	0	165 2/3	149	70	54	47	127
1993—Fort Myers (Fla. St.)	3	5	.375	3.82	14	14	0	0	0	92	85	42	39	21	69
—Nashville (Southern)	2	6	.250	4.62	13	13	1	0	0	81	82	42	39	16	76
1994—Nashville (Southern)	12	9	.571	2.66	29	*28	5	1	0	186 1/3	167	66	55	34	123
1995—Minnesota (A.L.)	11	14	.440	5.32	29	28	2	1	0	181	195	112	107	47	75
1996—Minnesota (A.L.)	11	16	.407	4.46	35	35	3	0	0	232	231	125	115	57	148
1997—Minnesota (A.L.)	20	10	.667	3.87	35	•35	4	1	0	239 2/3	238	114	103	48	174
Major league totals (3 years)	42	40	.512	4.48	99	98	9	2	0	652 2/3	664	351	325	152	397

RADMANOVICH, RYAN   OF   TWINS

PERSONAL: Born August 9, 1971, in Calgary, Alta. ... 6-2/192. ... Bats left, throws right. ... Full name: Ryan Ashley Radmanovich.
HIGH SCHOOL: John Diefenbaker (Calgary, Alberta).

JUNIOR COLLEGE: Allan Hancock.
COLLEGE: Pepperdine.
TRANSACTIONS/CAREER NOTES: Selected by Minnesota Twins organization in 14th round of free-agent draft (June 3, 1993). ... On disabled list (April 21-May 12 and May 23-September 15, 1995).
STATISTICAL NOTES: Led Midwest League third basemen with 21 double plays in 1994.
MISCELLANEOUS: Member of 1992 Canadian Olympic baseball team.

			BATTING											FIELDING			
Year Team (League)	Pos.	G	AB	R	H	2B	3B	HR	RBI	Avg.	BB	SO	SB	PO	A	E	Avg.
1993— Fort Wayne (Midw.)....	OF	62	204	36	59	7	5	8	38	.289	30	60	8	84	6	3	.968
1994— Fort Myers (FSL)........	3B-OF	26	85	11	16	4	0	2	9	.188	7	19	3	12	47	12	.831
— Fort Wayne (Midw.)....	3B	101	383	64	105	20	6	19	69	.274	45	98	19	75	169	28	.897
1995— Fort Myers (FSL)........	3B	12	41	3	13	2	0	0	5	.317	2	8	0	7	22	7	.806
1996— New Britain (Eastern).	OF	125	453	77	127	31	2	25	86	.280	49	122	4	246	3	4	.984
1997— Salt Lake (PCL)..........	OF-3B	133	485	92	128	25	4	28	78	.264	67	*138	11	226	7	9	.963

RAGGIO, BRADY — P — CARDINALS

PERSONAL: Born September 17, 1972, in Los Angeles. ... 6-4/210. ... Throws right, bats right. ... Full name: Brady J. Raggio. ... Name pronounced RAZH-ee-oh.
HIGH SCHOOL: San Ramon (Danville, Calif.).
JUNIOR COLLEGE: Chabot College (Calif.).
TRANSACTIONS/CAREER NOTES: Selected by St. Louis Cardinals organization in 20th round of free-agent draft (June 1, 1992). ... Suffered non-baseball injury; missed entire 1993 season.

Year Team (League)	W	L	Pct.	ERA	G	GS	CG	ShO	Sv.	IP	H	R	ER	BB	SO
1992— Ariz. Cardinals (Ariz.)	4	3	.571	3.54	14	6	3	0	1	48 1/3	51	26	19	7	48
1993—							Did not play.								
1994— New Jersey (NYP).............	3	0	1.000	1.67	4	4	0	0	0	27	28	7	5	4	20
— Madison (Midwest)...........	4	3	.571	3.21	11	11	1	0	0	67 1/3	63	31	24	14	66
1995— Peoria (Midwest)................	3	0	1.000	1.85	8	8	3	0	0	48 2/3	42	13	10	2	34
— St. Petersburg (FSL).........	2	3	.400	3.80	20	3	0	0	0	47 1/3	43	24	20	13	25
1996— Arkansas (Texas)...............	9	10	.474	3.22	26	24	4	1	0	162 1/3	160	68	58	40	123
1997— Louisville (A.A.)..................	8	11	.421	4.17	22	22	2	0	0	138	145	68	64	32	91
— St. Louis (N.L.).................	1	2	.333	6.89	15	4	0	0	0	31 1/3	44	24	24	16	21
Major league totals (1 year)........	1	2	.333	6.89	15	4	0	0	0	31 1/3	44	24	24	16	21

RAIN, STEVE — P — CUBS

PERSONAL: Born June 2, 1975, in Los Angeles. ... 6-6/245. ... Throws right, bats right. ... Full name: Steven Nicholas Rain.
HIGH SCHOOL: Walnut (Calif.).
TRANSACTIONS/CAREER NOTES: Selected by Chicago Cubs organization in 11th round of free-agent draft (June 3, 1993).

Year Team (League)	W	L	Pct.	ERA	G	GS	CG	ShO	Sv.	IP	H	R	ER	BB	SO
1993— GC Cubs (GCL)....................	1	3	.250	3.89	10	6	0	0	0	37	37	20	16	17	29
1994— Huntington (Appal.)............	3	3	.500	2.65	14	10	1	1	0	68	55	26	20	19	55
1995— Rockford (Midwest)	5	2	.714	1.21	53	0	0	0	23	59 1/3	38	12	8	23	66
1996— Orlando (South.)	1	0	1.000	2.56	35	0	0	0	10	38 2/3	32	15	11	12	48
— Iowa (Am. Assoc.)..............	2	1	.667	3.12	26	0	0	0	10	26	17	9	9	8	23
1997— Iowa (Am. Assoc.)..............	7	1	.875	5.89	40	0	0	0	1	44 1/3	51	30	29	34	50
— Orlando (South.)	1	2	.333	3.07	14	0	0	0	4	14 2/3	16	7	5	8	11

RAINES, TIM — OF — YANKEES

PERSONAL: Born September 16, 1959, in Sanford, Fla. ... 5-8/186. ... Bats both, throws right. ... Full name: Timothy Raines. ... Brother of Ned Raines, minor league outfielder (1978-80).
HIGH SCHOOL: Seminole (Sanford, Fla.).
TRANSACTIONS/CAREER NOTES: Selected by Montreal Expos organization in fifth round of free-agent draft (June 7, 1977). ... On disabled list (May 23-June 5, 1978). ... Granted free agency (November 12, 1986). ... Re-signed by Expos (May 2, 1987). ... On disabled list (June 24-July 9, 1988 and June 25-July 10, 1990). ... Traded by Expos with P Jeff Carter and a player to be named later to Chicago White Sox for OF Ivan Calderon and P Barry Jones (December 23, 1990); White Sox acquired P Mario Brito to complete deal (February 15, 1991). ... On Chicago disabled list (April 10-May 22, 1993); included rehabilitation assignment to Nashville (May 19-22). ... Granted free agency (November 1, 1993). ... Re-signed by White Sox (December 22, 1993). ... Traded by White Sox to New York Yankees for a player to be named later (December 28, 1995); White Sox acquired 3B Blaise Kozeniewski to complete deal (February 6, 1996). ... On New York disabled list (March 21-April 16 and May 22-August 11, 1996); included rehabilitation assignments to Tampa (April 12-13 and July 25-August 2), Columbus (April 13-16 and June 23-24), Gulf Coast Yankees (June 22-23) and Norwich (August 2-10). ... On New York disabled list (March 27-April 11 and July 2-August 12, 1997); included rehabilitation assignments to Tampa (April 7-10, July 24-27 and August 5-7), Gulf Coast Yankees (July 24), Norwich (July 26-27) and Columbus (August 8-11). ... Granted free agency (October 29, 1997). ... Re-signed by Yankees (December 19, 1997).
RECORDS: Holds major league single-season record for most intentional bases on balls received by switch-hitter—26 (1987). ... Holds A.L. career record for most consecutive stolen bases without being caught stealing—40 (July 23, 1993 through August 4, 1995). ... Shares A.L. single-game record for most consecutive times reached base safely—7 (April 20, 1994, 12 innings).
HONORS: Named Minor League Player of the Year by The Sporting News (1980). ... Named N.L. Rookie Player of the Year by The Sporting News (1981). ... Named outfielder on The Sporting News N.L. All-Star team (1983 and 1986). ... Won The Sporting News Gold Shoe Award (1984). ... Named outfielder on The Sporting News N.L. Silver Slugger team (1986).
STATISTICAL NOTES: Led N.L. outfielders with 21 assists in 1983. ... Led N.L. with .413 on-base percentage in 1986. ... Hit for the cycle (August 16, 1987). ... Switch-hit home runs in one game (July 16, 1988 and August 31, 1993). ... Hit three home runs in one game (April 18, 1994). ... Career major league grand slams: 5.
MISCELLANEOUS: Holds Montreal Expos all-time records for most runs (934), most triples (81), highest career batting average (.301) and most stolen bases (634).

Year	Team (League)	Pos.	G	AB	R	H	2B	3B	HR	RBI	Avg.	BB	SO	SB	PO	A	E	Avg.
1977—	GC Expos (GCL)	2B-3B-OF	49	161	28	45	6	2	0	21	.280	27	16	29	79	72	13	.921
1978—	W.P. Beach (FSL)	2B-SS	100	359	67	103	10	0	0	23	.287	64	44	57	219	273	24	.953
1979—	Memphis (Southern)	2B	•145	552	*104	160	25	10	5	50	.290	90	51	59	*341	*413	*23	.970
—	Montreal (N.L.)	PR	6	0	3	0	0	0	0	0	...	0	0	2	...	...	...	...
1980—	Denver (A.A.)	2B	108	429	105	152	23	•11	6	64	*.354	61	42	*77	226	338	16	.972
—	Montreal (N.L.)	2B-OF	15	20	5	1	0	0	0	0	.050	6	3	5	15	16	0	1.000
1981—	Montreal (N.L.)	OF-2B	88	313	61	95	13	7	5	37	.304	45	31	*71	162	8	4	.977
1982—	Montreal (N.L.)	OF-2B	156	647	90	179	32	8	4	43	.277	75	83	*78	293	126	8	.981
1983—	Montreal (N.L.)	OF-2B	156	615	*133	183	32	8	11	71	.298	97	70	*90	314	†23	4	.988
1984—	Montreal (N.L.)	OF-2B	160	622	106	192	•38	9	8	60	.309	87	69	*75	420	8	6	.986
1985—	Montreal (N.L.)	OF	150	575	115	184	30	13	11	41	.320	81	60	70	284	8	2	.993
1986—	Montreal (N.L.)	OF	151	580	91	194	35	10	9	62	*.334	78	60	70	270	13	6	.979
1987—	Montreal (N.L.)	OF	139	530	*123	175	34	8	18	68	.330	90	52	50	297	9	4	.987
1988—	Montreal (N.L.)	OF	109	429	66	116	19	7	12	48	.270	53	44	33	235	5	3	.988
1989—	Montreal (N.L.)	OF	145	517	76	148	29	6	9	60	.286	93	48	41	253	7	1	.996
1990—	Montreal (N.L.)	OF	130	457	65	131	11	5	9	62	.287	70	43	49	239	3	6	.976
1991—	Chicago (A.L.)■	OF-DH	155	609	102	163	20	6	5	50	.268	83	68	51	273	12	3	.990
1992—	Chicago (A.L.)	OF-DH	144	551	102	162	22	9	7	54	.294	81	48	45	312	12	2	.994
1993—	Chicago (A.L.)	OF	115	415	75	127	16	4	16	54	.306	64	35	21	200	5	4	.981
—	Nashville (A.A.)	OF	3	11	3	5	1	0	0	2	.455	2	0	2	3	0	0	*1.000
1994—	Chicago (A.L.)	OF	101	384	80	102	15	5	10	52	.266	61	43	13	204	3	4	.981
1995—	Chicago (A.L.)	OF-DH	133	502	81	143	25	4	12	67	.285	70	52	13	193	7	4	.980
1996—	Tampa (Florida State)■	OF	9	36	9	13	2	0	2	11	.361	8	3	0	10	2	0	1.000
—	Columbus (Int'l)	OF	4	12	3	3	1	0	0	0	.250	1	3	1	2	0	0	1.000
—	New York (A.L.)	OF-DH	59	201	45	57	10	0	9	33	.284	34	29	10	79	3	1	.988
—	GC Yankees (GCL)	DH	1	5	2	3	2	0	0	3	.600	1	0	0	0	0	0	...
—	Norwich (Eastern)	OF	8	27	8	5	1	0	1	1	.185	9	2	2	4	0	0	1.000
1997—	Tampa (Florida State)	OF	11	35	8	12	0	0	2	5	.343	11	1	1	13	1	0	1.000
—	New York (A.L.)	OF-DH	74	271	56	87	20	2	4	38	.321	41	34	8	79	1	1	.988
—	GC Yankees (GCL)	OF	1	4	0	1	0	0	0	2	.250	1	1	0	2	0	0	1.000
—	Norwich (Eastern)	OF	2	7	0	2	1	0	0	2	.286	0	2	0	2	0	0	1.000
—	Columbus (Int'l)	OF	4	13	1	2	0	0	0	2	.154	3	2	0	4	0	0	1.000
American League totals (7 years)			781	2933	541	841	128	30	63	348	.287	434	309	161	1340	43	15	.989
National League totals (12 years)			1405	5305	934	1598	273	81	96	552	.301	775	563	634	2782	226	44	.986
Major league totals (19 years)			2186	8238	1475	2439	401	111	159	900	.296	1209	872	795	4122	269	59	.987

DIVISION SERIES RECORD

Year	Team (League)	Pos.	G	AB	R	H	2B	3B	HR	RBI	Avg.	BB	SO	SB	PO	A	E	Avg.
1996—	New York (A.L.)	OF	4	16	3	4	0	0	0	0	.250	3	1	0	5	0	0	1.000
1997—	New York (A.L.)	DH-OF	5	19	4	4	0	0	1	3	.211	3	1	2	7	00	0	1.000
Division series totals (2 years)			9	35	7	8	0	0	1	3	.229	6	2	2	12	0	0	1.000

CHAMPIONSHIP SERIES RECORD

RECORDS: Holds single-series record for most singles—10 (1993). ... Shares A.L. single-series record for most hits—12 (1993).

Year	Team (League)	Pos.	G	AB	R	H	2B	3B	HR	RBI	Avg.	BB	SO	SB	PO	A	E	Avg.
1981—	Montreal (N.L.)	OF	5	21	1	5	2	0	0	1	.238	0	3	0	9	0	0	1.000
1993—	Chicago (A.L.)	OF	6	27	5	12	2	0	0	1	.444	2	2	1	12	2	0	1.000
1996—	New York (A.L.)	OF	5	15	2	4	1	0	0	0	.267	1	1	0	5	0	0	1.000
Championship series totals (3 years)			16	63	8	21	5	0	0	2	.333	3	6	1	26	2	0	1.000

WORLD SERIES RECORD

NOTES: Member of World Series championship team (1996).

Year	Team (League)	Pos.	G	AB	R	H	2B	3B	HR	RBI	Avg.	BB	SO	SB	PO	A	E	Avg.
1996—	New York (A.L.)	OF	4	14	2	3	0	0	0	0	.214	2	1	0	5	0	1	.833

ALL-STAR GAME RECORD

NOTES: Named Most Valuable Player (1987).

Year	League	Pos.	AB	R	H	2B	3B	HR	RBI	Avg.	BB	SO	SB	PO	A	E	Avg.
1981—	National	PR-OF	0	0	0	0	0	0	0	...	0	0	0	1	0	0	1.000
1982—	National	OF	1	0	0	0	0	0	0	.000	1	1	1	0	0	0	...
1983—	National	OF	3	0	0	0	0	0	0	.000	0	1	1	2	0	0	1.000
1984—	National	OF	1	0	0	0	0	0	0	.000	0	1	0	4	0	0	1.000
1985—	National	PH-OF	0	1	0	0	0	0	0	...	1	0	0	0	0	0	...
1986—	National	PH-OF	2	0	0	0	0	0	0	.000	0	1	0	1	0	0	1.000
1987—	National	OF	3	0	3	0	1	0	2	1.000	0	0	1	1	0	0	1.000
All-Star Game totals (7 years)			10	1	3	0	1	0	2	.300	2	4	3	9	0	0	1.000

RAKERS, JASON   P   INDIANS

PERSONAL: Born June 29, 1973, in Pittsburgh. ... 6-2/200. ... Throws right, bats right. ... Full name: Jason P. Rakers.
COLLEGE: New Mexico State.
TRANSACTIONS/CAREER NOTES: Selected by Cleveland Indians organization in 25th round of free-agent draft (June 1, 1995). ... On disabled list (April 4-June 23, 1996).
STATISTICAL NOTES: Pitched 8-0 no-hit victory against Durham (June 4, 1997, first game).

Year— Team (League)	W	L	Pct.	ERA	G	GS	CG	ShO	Sv.	IP	H	R	ER	BB	SO
1995— Watertown (NYP)	4	3	.571	3.00	14	14	1	•1	0	75	72	27	25	24	73
1996— Columbus (S. Atl.)	5	4	.556	3.61	14	14	1	1	0	77 1/3	84	37	31	17	64
1997— Kinston (Carolina)	8	5	.615	3.07	17	17	2	2	0	102 2/3	93	41	35	18	105
— Buffalo (A.A.)	1	0	1.000	0.00	1	1	0	0	0	7	5	0	0	1	3
— Akron (Eastern)	1	4	.200	4.39	7	7	1	1	0	41	36	21	20	11	31

RAMIREZ, ALEX — OF — INDIANS

R

PERSONAL: Born October 3, 1974, in Caracas, Venezuela. ... 5-11/180. ... Bats right, throws right. ... Full name: Alexander Ramirez.
TRANSACTIONS/CAREER NOTES: Signed as non-drafted free agent by Cleveland Indians organization (July 1, 1991).
STATISTICAL NOTES: Led Appalachian League outfielders with three double plays in 1993.

							BATTING							FIELDING			
Year— Team (League)	Pos.	G	AB	R	H	2B	3B	HR	RBI	Avg.	BB	SO	SB	PO	A	E	Avg.
1992— Dom. Inds. (DSL)	OF	69	272	28	79	13	3	8	48	.290	13	34	17	136	9	8	.948
1993— Kinston (Carolina)	OF	3	12	0	2	0	0	0	1	.167	0	5	0	3	0	1	.750
— Burlington (Appal.)	OF	64	252	44	68	14	4	13	58	.270	13	52	13	85	8	7	.930
1994— Columbus (S. Atl.)	OF	125	458	64	115	23	3	18	57	.251	26	100	7	168	6	9	.951
1995— Bakersfield (California)	OF	98	406	56	131	25	2	10	52	.323	18	76	13	150	9	10	.941
— Cant./Akr. (Eastern)	OF	33	133	15	33	3	4	1	11	.248	5	24	3	72	5	2	.975
1996— Cant./Akr. (Eastern)	OF	131	513	79	*169	28	*12	14	85	.329	16	74	18	209	4	5	.977
1997— Buffalo (A.A.)	OF	119	416	59	119	19	*8	11	44	.286	24	95	10	167	8	*10	.946

RAMIREZ, ARAMIS — IF — PIRATES

PERSONAL: Born June 25, 1978, in Santo Domingo, Dominican Republic. ... 6-1/176. ... Bats right, throws right. ... Full name: Aramis Nin Ramirez.
TRANSACTIONS/CAREER NOTES: Signed as non-drafted free agent by Pittsburgh Pirates organization (November 7, 1994).
HONORS: Named Carolina League Most Valuable Player (1997).
STATISTICAL NOTES: Led Carolina League third basemen with 379 total chances in 1997.

							BATTING							FIELDING			
Year— Team (League)	Pos.	G	AB	R	H	2B	3B	HR	RBI	Avg.	BB	SO	SB	PO	A	E	Avg.
1995— Dom. Pirates (DSL)	3B	64	214	41	63	13	0	11	54	.294	42	26	2	65	82	19	.886
1996— Erie (N.Y.-Penn)	3B	61	223	37	68	14	4	9	42	.305	31	41	0	39	107	17	.896
— Augusta (S. Atl.)	3B	6	20	3	4	1	0	1	2	.200	1	7	0	3	7	2	.833
1997— Lynchburg (Caro.)	3B	137	482	85	134	24	2	29	*114	.278	80	103	5	75	*265	*39	.897

RAMIREZ, HECTOR — P — YANKEES

PERSONAL: Born December 15, 1971, in El Seybo, Dominican Republic. ... 6-3/218. ... Throws right, bats right. ... Full name: Hector Benvenido Ramirez.
HIGH SCHOOL: Liceo Local (El Seybo, Dominican Republic).
TRANSACTIONS/CAREER NOTES: Signed as non-drafted free agent by New York Mets organization (August 22, 1988). ... Traded by Mets to Baltimore Orioles for IF Manny Alexander and IF Scott McLain (March 22, 1997). ... Claimed on waivers by New York Yankees (January 20, 1998).
STATISTICAL NOTES: Tied for Florida State League lead with eight balks in 1994.

Year— Team (League)	W	L	Pct.	ERA	G	GS	CG	ShO	Sv.	IP	H	R	ER	BB	SO
1989— GC Mets (GCL)	0	5	.000	4.50	15	5	0	0	0	42	35	29	21	24	14
1990— GC Mets (GCL)	3	5	.375	4.26	11	8	1	0	0	50 2/3	54	34	24	21	43
1991— Kingsport (Appalachian)	8	2	.800	2.65	14	13	0	0	0	85	83	39	25	28	64
1992— Columbia (S. Atl.)	5	4	.556	3.61	17	17	1	0	0	94 2/3	93	50	38	33	53
1993— GC Mets (GCL)	1	0	1.000	0.00	1	1	0	0	0	7	5	1	0	1	6
— Capital City (S. Atl.)	4	6	.400	5.34	14	14	0	0	0	64	86	51	38	23	42
1994— St. Lucie (Fla. St.)	11	12	.478	3.43	27	27	•6	1	0	*194	*202	86	74	50	110
1995— Binghamton (Eastern)	4	•12	.250	4.60	20	20	2	0	0	123 1/3	127	69	63	48	63
1996— Binghamton (Eastern)	1	5	.167	5.14	38	0	0	0	6	56	51	34	32	23	49
— Norfolk (Int'l)	1	0	1.000	3.38	3	1	0	0	0	10 2/3	13	7	4	3	8
1997— Rochester (Int'l)■	8	7	.533	4.91	39	9	0	0	3	102 2/3	114	65	56	38	50

RAMIREZ, JULIO — OF — MARLINS

PERSONAL: Born August 10, 1977, in San Juan de la Maguana, Dominican Republic. ... 5-11/170. ... Bats right, throws right.
HIGH SCHOOL: Escuela Otilia Pelaez (Santo Domingo, Dominican Republic).
TRANSACTIONS/CAREER NOTES: Signed as non-drafted free agent by Florida Marlins organization (December 6, 1993).

							BATTING							FIELDING			
Year— Team (League)	Pos.	G	AB	R	H	2B	3B	HR	RBI	Avg.	BB	SO	SB	PO	A	E	Avg.
1994— Dom. Marlins (DSL)	OF	67	274	54	75	18	0	7	32	.274	28	41	29	136	11	10	.936
1995— GC Marlins (GCL)	OF	48	204	35	58	9	4	2	13	.284	13	42	17	109	7	2	.983
1996— Brevard Co. (Fla. St.)	OF	17	61	11	15	0	1	0	2	.246	4	18	2	12	2	1	.933
— GC Marlins (GCL)	OF	43	174	35	50	5	4	0	16	.287	15	34	26	95	2	2	.980
1997— Kane County (Midw.)	OF	99	376	70	96	18	7	14	53	.255	37	122	41	179	8	4	.979

RAMIREZ, MANNY — OF — INDIANS

PERSONAL: Born May 30, 1972, in Santo Domingo, Dominican Republic. ... 6-0/200. ... Bats right, throws right. ... Full name: Manuel Aristides Ramirez.
HIGH SCHOOL: George Washington (New York).

TRANSACTIONS/CAREER NOTES: Selected by Cleveland Indians organization in first round (13th pick overall) of free-agent draft (June 3, 1991). ... On disabled list (July 10, 1992-remainder of season).
HONORS: Named Appalachian League Most Valuable Player (1991). ... Named outfielder on THE SPORTING NEWS A.L. All-Star team (1995). ... Named outfielder on THE SPORTING NEWS A.L. Silver Slugger team (1995).
STATISTICAL NOTES: Led Appalachian League with 146 total bases and .679 slugging percentage in 1991. ... Career major league grand slams: 6.

Year Team (League)	Pos.	G	AB	R	H	2B	3B	HR	RBI	Avg.	BB	SO	SB	PO	A	E	Avg.
1991—Burlington (Appal.).....	OF	59	215	44	70	11	4	*19	*63	.326	34	41	7	83	2	3	.966
1992—Kinston (Carolina)......	OF	81	291	52	81	18	4	13	63	.278	45	74	1	128	3	6	.956
1993—Cant./Akr. (Eastern)....	OF	89	344	67	117	32	0	17	79	*.340	45	68	2	142	3	6	.967
—Charlotte (Int'l)..........	OF	40	145	38	46	12	0	14	36	.317	27	35	1	70	3	3	.961
—Cleveland (A.L.)..........	DH-OF	22	53	5	9	1	0	2	5	.170	2	8	0	3	0	0	1.000
1994—Cleveland (A.L.).......	OF-DH	91	290	51	78	22	0	17	60	.269	42	72	4	150	7	1	.994
1995—Cleveland (A.L.).......	OF-DH	137	484	85	149	26	1	31	107	.308	75	112	6	220	3	5	.978
1996—Cleveland (A.L.).......	OF-DH	152	550	94	170	45	3	33	112	.309	85	104	6	272	*19	9	.970
1997—Cleveland (A.L.).......	OF-DH	150	561	99	184	40	3	26	88	.328	79	115	2	259	10	7	.975
Major league totals (5 years)		552	1938	334	590	134	4	109	372	.304	283	411	20	904	39	22	.977

DIVISION SERIES RECORD

Year Team (League)	Pos.	G	AB	R	H	2B	3B	HR	RBI	Avg.	BB	SO	SB	PO	A	E	Avg.
1995—Cleveland (A.L.).........	OF	3	12	1	0	0	0	0	0	.000	1	2	0	3	0	0	1.000
1996—Cleveland (A.L.).........	OF	4	16	4	6	2	0	2	2	.375	1	4	0	8	2	0	1.000
1997—Cleveland (A.L.).........	OF	5	21	2	3	1	0	0	3	.143	0	3	0	3	0	1	.750
Division series totals (3 years)		12	49	7	9	3	0	2	5	.184	2	9	0	14	2	1	.941

CHAMPIONSHIP SERIES RECORD

Year Team (League)	Pos.	G	AB	R	H	2B	3B	HR	RBI	Avg.	BB	SO	SB	PO	A	E	Avg.
1995—Cleveland (A.L.)..........	OF	6	21	2	6	0	0	2	2	.286	2	5	0	9	0	0	1.000
1997—Cleveland (A.L.)..........	OF	6	21	3	6	1	0	2	3	.286	5	5	0	14	0	1	.933
Championship series totals (2 years)		12	42	5	12	1	0	4	5	.286	7	10	0	23	0	1	.958

WORLD SERIES RECORD

Year Team (League)	Pos.	G	AB	R	H	2B	3B	HR	RBI	Avg.	BB	SO	SB	PO	A	E	Avg.
1995—Cleveland (A.L.)..........	OF	6	18	2	4	0	0	1	2	.222	4	5	1	8	0	0	1.000
1997—Cleveland (A.L.)..........	OF	7	26	3	4	0	0	2	6	.154	6	5	0	16	1	1	.944
World Series totals (2 years)		13	44	5	8	0	0	3	8	.182	10	10	1	24	1	1	.962

ALL-STAR GAME RECORD

Year League	Pos.	AB	R	H	2B	3B	HR	RBI	Avg.	BB	SO	SB	PO	A	E	Avg.
1995—American...................	PH-OF	0	0	0	0	0	0	0	...	2	0	0	2	0	0	1.000

RAMOS, EDGAR — P — PHILLIES

PERSONAL: Born March 6, 1975, in Cuinana Edo Sucre, Venezuela. ... 6-5/190. ... Throws right, bats right.
TRANSACTIONS/CAREER NOTES: Signed as non-drafted free agent by Houston Astros organization (February 3, 1992). ... On Quad City disabled list (April 13-August 13, 1995). ... Selected by Philadelphia Phillies organization from Astros oganization in Rule 5 major league draft (December 9, 1996). ... On disabled list (March 23-May 16, 1997); included rehabilitation assignments to Clearwater (April 6-7 and May 13-16). ... Returned by Phillies to Astros (June 6, 1997).

Year Team (League)	W	L	Pct.	ERA	G	GS	CG	ShO	Sv.	IP	H	R	ER	BB	SO
1993—GC Astros (GCL)	5	2	.714	2.16	14	•12	0	0	0	75	59	23	18	13	70
1994—Quad City (Midwest)	2	8	.200	4.47	22	16	1	0	1	98 2/3	110	59	49	30	92
1995—GC Astros (GCL)	0	01	.000	1.84	5	5	0	0	0	14 2/3	14	6	3	6	16
—Quad City (Midwest)	0	1	.000	15.43	2	2	0	0	0	4 2/3	5	9	8	7	5
—Kissimmee (Florida State)..	4	0	1.000	0.41	4	4	0	0	0	22	11	1	1	1	16
1996—Kissimmee (Florida State)..	9	0	1.000	1.51	11	11	1	0	0	77 2/3	51	17	13	15	81
—Jackson (Texas)	4	5	.444	4.88	12	12	1	1	0	66 1/3	63	41	36	29	52
1997—Clearwater (Fla. St.)■	0	0	...	3.60	2	2	0	0	0	5	3	3	2	2	3
—Philadelphia (N.L.)	0	2	.000	5.14	4	2	0	0	0	14	15	9	8	6	4
—Jackson (Texas)■	0	2	.000	4.82	4	3	0	0	0	18 2/3	24	12	10	7	12
Major league totals (1 year)........	0	2	.000	5.14	4	2	0	0	0	14	15	9	8	6	4

RAMOS, KEN — OF

PERSONAL: Born June 8, 1967, in Sidney, Neb. ... 6-0/185. ... Bats left, throws left. ... Full name: Kenneth Cecil Ramos.
HIGH SCHOOL: East (Pueblo, Colo.).
JUNIOR COLLEGE: Otero Junior College (Colo.).
COLLEGE: Nebraska.
TRANSACTIONS/CAREER NOTES: Selected by Chicago Cubs organization in sixth round of free-agent draft (January 14, 1986); did not sign. ... Signed as non-drafted free agent by Cleveland Indians organization (June 22, 1989). ... On disabled list (April 10-17, 1991). ... Traded by Indians to Chicago White Sox for C Matt Merullo (March 30, 1994). ... Claimed on waivers by Houston Astros organization (April 6, 1994). ... Granted free agency (October 15, 1996).
STATISTICAL NOTES: Led Carolina League with .426 on-base percentage in 1990. ... Led Eastern League with .442 on-base percentage in 1992.

Year Team (League)	Pos.	G	AB	R	H	2B	3B	HR	RBI	Avg.	BB	SO	SB	PO	A	E	Avg.
1989—GC Indians (GCL)	OF	54	193	41	60	7	2	1	14	.311	*39	18	17	86	5	2	.978
—Kinston (Carolina)	OF	8	21	6	3	0	0	0	0	.143	5	2	2	6	0	0	1.000
1990—Kinston (Carolina)	OF	96	339	71	117	16	6	0	31	*.345	48	34	18	163	5	3	.982
—Cant./Akr. (Eastern)	OF	19	73	12	24	2	2	0	11	.329	8	10	2	53	0	1	.981
1991—Cant./Akr. (Eastern)	OF	74	257	41	62	6	3	2	13	.241	28	22	8	96	8	6	.945
1992—Cant./Akr. (Eastern)	OF	125	442	*93	150	23	5	5	42	*.339	82	37	14	158	6	7	.959
1993—Charlotte (Int'l)	OF	132	480	77	140	16	11	3	41	.292	47	41	12	205	11	2	.991
1994—Tucson (PCL)■	OF	121	393	81	118	19	7	1	32	.300	74	27	22	173	13	5	.974
1995—Tucson (PCL)	OF	112	327	57	103	24	8	3	47	.315	51	27	14	165	5	2	.988
1996—Tucson (PCL)	OF	104	385	54	104	22	3	4	34	.270	41	41	6	165	10	8	.956
1997—New Orleans (A.A.)	OF	92	253	32	73	9	1	0	22	.289	45	15	2	129	4	1	.993
—Houston (N.L.)	OF	14	12	0	0	0	0	0	1	.000	2	0	0	0	0	0	...
Major league totals (1 year)		14	12	0	0	0	0	0	1	.000	2	0	0	0	0	0	...

RANDA, JOE   3B   TIGERS

PERSONAL: Born December 18, 1969, in Milwaukee. ... 5-11/185. ... Bats right, throws right. ... Full name: Joseph Gregory Randa.
HIGH SCHOOL: Kettle Moraine Public (Wales, Wis.).
JUNIOR COLLEGE: Indian River Community College (Fla.).
COLLEGE: Tennessee.
TRANSACTIONS/CAREER NOTES: Selected by California Angels organization in 30th round of free-agent draft (June 5, 1989); did not sign. ... Selected by Kansas City Royals organization in 11th round of free-agent draft (June 3, 1991). ... On Kansas City disabled list (May 5-27, 1996); included rehabilitation assignment to Omaha (May 23-27). ... Traded by Royals with P Jeff Granger, P Jeff Martin and P Jeff Wallace to Pittsburgh Pirates for SS Jay Bell and 1B Jeff King (December 13, 1996). ... On Pittsburgh disabled list (June 28-July 27, 1997); included rehabilitation assignment to Calgary (July 25-27). ... Selected by Arizona Diamondbacks in third round (57th pick overall) of expansion draft (November 18, 1997). ... Traded by Diamondbacks with P Matt Drews and 3B Gabe Alvarez to Detroit Tigers for 3B Travis Fryman (November 18, 1997).
HONORS: Named Northwest League Most Valuable Player (1991).
STATISTICAL NOTES: Led Northwest League with 150 total bases and .438 on-base percentage in 1991. ... Led Northwest League third basemen with 182 total chances and 12 double plays in 1991. ... Led Southern League with 10 sacrifice flies in 1993. ... Led American Association third basemen with 433 total chances and 28 double plays in 1994.

Year Team (League)	Pos.	G	AB	R	H	2B	3B	HR	RBI	Avg.	BB	SO	SB	PO	A	E	Avg.
1991—Eugene (Northwest)	3B	72	275	53	*93	20	2	11	59	.338	46	29	6	*57	*111	14	*.923
1992—Appleton (Midwest)	3B	72	266	55	80	13	0	5	43	.301	34	37	6	53	137	12	.941
—Baseball City (FSL)	3B-SS	51	189	22	52	7	0	1	12	.275	12	21	4	43	105	6	.961
1993—Memphis (Southern)	3B	131	505	74	149	31	5	11	72	.295	39	64	8	*97	309	25	.942
1994—Omaha (A.A.)	3B	127	455	65	125	27	2	10	51	.275	30	49	5	*85	*324	*24	.945
1995—Omaha (A.A.)	3B	64	233	33	64	10	2	8	33	.275	22	33	2	42	96	6	.958
—Kansas City (A.L.)	3B-2B-DH	34	70	6	12	2	0	1	5	.171	6	17	0	15	44	3	.952
1996—Kansas City (A.L.)	3-2-1-DH	110	337	36	102	24	1	6	47	.303	26	47	13	80	160	10	.960
—Omaha (A.A.)	3B	3	9	1	1	0	1	0	0	.111	1	1	0	1	10	0	1.000
1997—Pittsburgh (N.L.)■	3B-2B	126	443	58	134	27	9	7	60	.302	41	64	4	91	288	21	.948
—Calgary (PCL)	3B	3	11	4	4	1	0	1	4	.364	3	4	0	2	7	1	.900
American League totals (2 years)		144	407	42	114	26	1	7	52	.280	32	64	13	95	204	13	.958
National League totals (1 year)		126	443	58	134	27	9	7	60	.302	41	64	4	91	288	21	.948
Major league totals (3 years)		270	850	100	248	53	10	14	112	.292	73	128	17	186	492	34	.952

RANDALL, SCOTT   P   ROCKIES

PERSONAL: Born October 29, 1975, in Fullerton, Calif. ... 6-3/180. ... Throws right, bats right.
HIGH SCHOOL: Dos Pueblos (Goleta, Calif.).
JUNIOR COLLEGE: Santa Barbara (Calif.) City.
TRANSACTIONS/CAREER NOTES: Selected by Colorado Rockies organization in 11th round of free-agent draft (June 1, 1995).

Year Team (League)	W	L	Pct.	ERA	G	GS	CG	ShO	Sv.	IP	H	R	ER	BB	SO
1995—Portland (Northwest)	7	3	.700	*1.99	15	•15	1	0	0	95	76	35	21	28	78
1996—Asheville (S. Atl.)	14	4	.778	2.74	24	24	1	1	0	154 1/3	121	53	47	50	136
1997—Salem (Carolina)	9	10	.474	3.84	27	26	2	1	0	176	167	93	75	66	128

RANDOLPH, STEPHEN   P   DIAMONDBACKS

PERSONAL: Born May 1, 1974, in Okinawa, Japan. ... 6-3/185. ... Throws left, bats left. ... Full name: Stephen LaCharles Randolph.
HIGH SCHOOL: James Bowie (Texas).
JUNIOR COLLEGE: Galveston (Texas) College.
COLLEGE: Texas.
TRANSACTIONS/CAREER NOTES: Selected by New York Yankees organization in 18th round of free-agent draft (June 1, 1995). ... Selected by Arizona Diamondbacks from Yankees organization in Rule 5 major league draft (December 15, 1997).

Year Team (League)	W	L	Pct.	ERA	G	GS	CG	ShO	Sv.	IP	H	R	ER	BB	SO
1995—Tampa (Florida State)	4	0	1.000	2.22	8	3	0	0	0	24 1/3	11	7	6	16	34
—Oneonta (NY-Penn)	0	3	.000	7.48	6	6	0	0	0	21 2/3	19	22	18	23	31
1996—Grensboro (S. Atl.)	4	7	.364	3.77	32	17	0	0	0	100 1/3	64	46	42	96	111
1997—Tampa (Florida State)	4	7	.364	3.87	34	13	1	0	1	95 1/3	74	55	41	63	108

RAPP, PAT — P — ROYALS

PERSONAL: Born July 13, 1967, in Jennings, La. ... 6-3/215. ... Throws right, bats right. ... Full name: Patrick Leland Rapp.
HIGH SCHOOL: Sulphur (La.).
JUNIOR COLLEGE: Hinds Community College (Miss.).
COLLEGE: Southern Mississippi.
TRANSACTIONS/CAREER NOTES: Selected by San Francisco Giants organization in 15th round of free-agent draft (June 5, 1989). ... Selected by Florida Marlins in first round (10th pick overall) of expansion draft (November 17, 1992). ... Traded by Marlins to Giants for P Brandon Leese and P Bobby Rector (July 18, 1997). ... On San Francisco disabled list (July 25-August 5, 1997). ... Granted free agency (December 21, 1997). ... Signed by Kansas City Royals organization (January 22, 1998).
STATISTICAL NOTES: Pitched 17-0 one-hit, complete-game victory against Colorado (September 17, 1995).
MISCELLANEOUS: Appeared in one game as pinch-runner (1994). ... Holds Florida Marlins all-time records for most wins (37), most strikeouts (384) and most innings pitched (665 ⅔).

Year Team (League)	W	L	Pct.	ERA	G	GS	CG	ShO	Sv.	IP	H	R	ER	BB	SO
1989— Pocatello (Pioneer)	4	6	.400	5.30	16	12	1	0	0	73	90	54	43	29	40
1990— Clinton (Midwest)	14	10	.583	2.64	27	26	4	0	0	167 ⅓	132	60	49	79	132
1991— San Jose (California)	7	5	.583	2.50	16	15	1	0	0	90	88	41	25	37	73
— Shreveport (Texas)	6	2	.750	2.69	10	10	1	1	0	60 ⅓	52	23	18	22	46
1992— Phoenix (PCL)	7	8	.467	3.05	39	12	2	1	3	121	115	54	41	40	79
— San Francisco (N.L.)	0	2	.000	7.20	3	2	0	0	0	10	8	8	8	6	3
1993— Edmonton (PCL)■	8	3	.727	3.43	17	17	•4	1	0	107 ⅔	89	45	41	34	93
— Florida (N.L.)	4	6	.400	4.02	16	16	1	0	0	94	101	49	42	39	57
1994— Florida (N.L.)	7	8	.467	3.85	24	23	2	1	0	133 ⅓	132	67	57	69	75
1995— Charlotte (Int'l)	0	1	.000	6.00	1	1	0	0	0	6	6	4	4	1	5
— Florida (N.L.)	14	7	.667	3.44	28	28	3	2	0	167 ⅓	158	72	64	76	102
1996— Florida (N.L.)	8	•16	.333	5.10	30	29	0	0	0	162 ⅓	184	95	92	91	86
— Charlotte (Int'l)	1	1	.500	8.18	2	2	0	0	0	11	18	12	10	4	9
1997— Florida (N.L.)	4	6	.400	4.47	19	19	1	1	0	108 ⅔	121	59	54	51	64
— San Francisco (N.L.)■	1	2	.333	6.00	8	6	0	0	0	33	37	24	22	21	28
— Phoenix (PCL)	2	0	1.000	3.60	3	3	0	0	0	15	16	6	6	9	6
Major league totals (6 years)	38	47	.447	4.31	128	123	7	4	0	708 ⅔	741	374	339	353	415

RATH, FRED — P — TWINS

PERSONAL: Born January 5, 1973, in Dallas. ... 6-3/205. ... Throws right, bats right. ... Full name: Frederick Helsher Rath.
HIGH SCHOOL: Thomas Jefferson (Tampa, Fla.).
COLLEGE: South Florida.
TRANSACTIONS/CAREER NOTES: Signed as non-drafted free agent by Minnesota Twins organization (June 6, 1995).

Year Team (League)	W	L	Pct.	ERA	G	GS	CG	ShO	Sv.	IP	H	R	ER	BB	SO
1995— Elizabethton (Appal.)	1	1	.500	1.35	27	0	0	0	12	33 ⅓	20	8	5	11	50
1996— Fort Wayne (Midw.)	1	2	.333	1.51	32	0	0	0	14	41 ⅔	26	12	7	10	63
— Fort Myers (Fla. St.)	2	5	.286	2.79	22	0	0	0	4	29	25	10	9	10	29
1997— Fort Myers (Fla. St.)	4	0	1.000	1.64	17	0	0	0	2	22	18	4	4	3	22
— New Britain (East.)	3	3	.500	2.68	33	0	0	0	12	50 ⅓	43	17	15	13	33
— Salt Lake (PCL)	0	1	.000	1.64	10	0	0	0	3	11	11	2	2	2	11

RATLIFF, JON — P — CUBS

PERSONAL: Born December 22, 1971, in Syracuse, N.Y. ... 6-5/200. ... Throws right, bats right. ... Full name: Jon Charles Ratliff.
HIGH SCHOOL: Liverpool (N.Y.).
COLLEGE: Lemoyne (N.Y.).
TRANSACTIONS/CAREER NOTES: Selected by San Diego Padres organization in 22nd round of free-agent draft (June 4, 1990); did not sign. ... Selected by Chicago Cubs organization in first round (24th pick overall) of free-agent draft (June 3, 1993); pick received as part of compensation for Atlanta Braves signing Type A free-agent P Greg Maddux. ... Selected by Detroit Tigers from Cubs organization in Rule 5 major league draft (December 4, 1995). ... Returned by Tigers to Cubs (March 13, 1996). ... On disabled list (April 26-May 17, 1996).

Year Team (League)	W	L	Pct.	ERA	G	GS	CG	ShO	Sv.	IP	H	R	ER	BB	SO
1993— Geneva (N.Y.-Penn)	1	1	.500	3.21	3	3	0	0	0	14	12	8	5	8	7
— Daytona (Fla. St.)	2	4	.333	3.95	8	8	0	0	0	41	50	29	18	23	15
1994— Daytona (Fla. St.)	3	2	.600	3.50	8	8	1	0	0	54	64	23	21	5	17
— Iowa (Am. Assoc.)	1	3	.250	5.40	5	4	0	0	0	28 ⅓	39	19	17	7	10
— Orlando (South.)	1	9	.100	5.63	12	12	1	0	0	62 ⅓	78	44	39	26	19
1995— Orlando (South.)	10	5	.667	3.47	26	25	1	1	0	140	143	67	54	42	94
1996— Iowa (Am. Assoc.)	4	8	.333	5.28	32	13	0	0	1	93 ⅔	107	63	55	31	59
1997— Iowa (Am. Assoc.)	1	3	.250	5.57	9	4	0	0	1	32 ⅓	30	20	20	7	25
— Orlando (South.)	6	4	.600	4.35	18	15	0	0	0	101 ⅓	112	59	49	32	68

RAY, KEN — P — ROYALS

PERSONAL: Born January 27, 1974, in Atlanta. ... 6-2/180. ... Throws right, bats right. ... Full name: Kenneth Alan Ray.
HIGH SCHOOL: Roswell (Ga.).
TRANSACTIONS/CAREER NOTES: Selected by Kansas City Royals organization in 18th round of free-agent draft (June 3, 1993). ... On disabled list (April 14-24, 1996).

Year Team (League)	W	L	Pct.	ERA	G	GS	CG	ShO	Sv.	IP	H	R	ER	BB	SO
1993— GC Royals (GCL)	2	3	.400	2.28	13	7	0	0	0	47 ⅓	44	21	12	17	45
1994— Rockford (Midwest)	10	4	.714	1.82	27	18	0	0	3	128 ⅔	94	34	26	56	128
1995— Wichita (Texas)	4	5	.444	5.97	14	14	0	0	0	75 ⅓	83	55	50	46	53
— Wilmington (Caro.)	6	4	.600	2.69	13	13	1	0	0	77	74	32	23	22	63
1996— Wichita (Texas)	4	12	.250	6.12	22	22	1	0	0	120 ⅔	151	94	82	57	79
1997— Omaha (Am. Assoc.)	5	12	.294	6.37	25	21	2	0	0	113	131	86	80	63	96

REBOULET, JEFF 2B ORIOLES

PERSONAL: Born April 30, 1964, in Dayton, Ohio. ... 6-0/174. ... Bats right, throws right. ... Full name: Jeffrey Allen Reboulet. ... Name pronounced REB-uh-lay.
HIGH SCHOOL: Alter (Kettering, Ohio).
COLLEGE: Louisiana State.
TRANSACTIONS/CAREER NOTES: Selected by Houston Astros organization in 26th round of free-agent draft (June 3, 1985); did not sign. ... Selected by Minnesota Twins organization in 10th round of free-agent draft (June 2, 1986). ... Granted free agency (October 4, 1996). ... Signed by Baltimore Orioles organization (January 30, 1997).
STATISTICAL NOTES: Led Southern League shortstops with 602 total chances in 1988. ... Led Pacific Coast League with 17 sacrifice hits in 1991. ... Led Pacific Coast League shortstops with 649 total chances and 99 double plays in 1991.

							BATTING								FIELDING		
Year Team (League)	Pos.	G	AB	R	H	2B	3B	HR	RBI	Avg.	BB	SO	SB	PO	A	E	Avg.
1986—Visalia (California)......	SS	72	254	54	73	13	1	0	29	.287	54	33	14	118	188	20	.939
1987—Orlando (South.)........	SS-2B-3B	129	422	52	108	15	1	1	35	.256	58	56	9	220	370	26	.958
1988—Orlando (South.)........	SS	125	439	57	112	24	2	4	41	.255	53	55	18	*225	347	30	.950
—Portland (PCL)..........	2B-SS	4	12	0	1	0	0	0	1	.083	3	2	0	8	13	1	.955
1989—Portland (PCL)..........	S-2-3-O	26	65	9	16	1	0	0	3	.246	12	11	2	38	62	7	.935
—Orlando (South.)........	SS-2B-OF	81	291	43	63	5	1	0	26	.216	49	33	11	129	228	22	.942
1990—Orlando (South.)........	2-3-S-O-1	97	287	43	66	12	2	2	28	.230	57	37	10	131	230	12	.968
1991—Portland (PCL)..........	SS	134	391	50	97	27	3	3	46	.248	57	52	5	*202	415	*32	.951
1992—Portland (PCL)..........	SS	48	161	21	46	11	1	2	21	.286	35	18	3	72	141	7	.968
—Minnesota (A.L.).......S-3-2-0-DH		73	137	15	26	7	1	1	16	.190	23	26	3	71	163	5	.979
1993—Minnesota (A.L.).....S-3-2-0-DH		109	240	33	62	8	0	1	15	.258	35	37	5	122	215	6	.983
1994—Minnesota (A.L.).....S-2-1-3-0-DH		74	189	28	49	11	1	3	23	.259	18	23	0	150	131	7	.976
1995—Minnesota (A.L.) . S-3-1-2-C		87	216	39	63	11	0	4	23	.292	27	34	1	164	160	4	.988
1996—Minnesota (A.L.).....S-3-2-1-0-DH		107	234	20	52	9	0	4	23	.222	25	34	4	138	114	2	.992
1997—Baltimore (A.L.).■....	2-S-3-O	99	228	26	54	9	0	4	27	.237	23	44	3	106	163	7	.975
Major league totals (6 years)		549	1244	161	306	55	2	13	127	.246	151	198	16	751	946	31	.982

DIVISION SERIES RECORD

							BATTING								FIELDING		
Year Team (League)	Pos.	G	AB	R	H	2B	3B	HR	RBI	Avg.	BB	SO	SB	PO	A	E	Avg.
1997—Baltimore (A.L.)..........	2B	2	5	1	1	0	0	1	1	.200	0	2	0	2	3	0	1.000

CHAMPIONSHIP SERIES RECORD

							BATTING								FIELDING		
Year Team (League)	Pos.	G	AB	R	H	2B	3B	HR	RBI	Avg.	BB	SO	SB	PO	A	E	Avg.
1997—Baltimore (A.L.)..........	SS-PR	1	2	1	0	0	0	0	0	.000	0	1	0	0	0	0	...

REDMAN, MARK P TWINS

PERSONAL: Born January 5, 1974, in San Diego. ... 6-5/220. ... Throws left, bats left. ... Full name: Mark Allen Redman.
HIGH SCHOOL: Escondido (Calif.).
COLLEGE: The Master's (Calif.), then Oklahoma.
TRANSACTIONS/CAREER NOTES: Selected by Detroit Tigers organization in 41st round of free-agent draft (June 1, 1992); did not sign. ... Selected by Minnesota Twins organization in first round (first pick overall) of free-agent draft (June 1, 1995).

Year Team (League)	W	L	Pct.	ERA	G	GS	CG	ShO	Sv.	IP	H	R	ER	BB	SO
1995—Fort Myers (Fla. St.)..........	2	1	.667	2.76	8	5	0	0	0	32 2/3	28	13	10	13	26
1996—Fort Myers (Fla. St.)..........	3	4	.429	1.85	13	13	0	0	0	82 2/3	63	24	17	34	75
—New Britain (East.).............	7	7	.500	3.81	16	16	3	0	0	106 1/3	101	51	45	50	96
—Salt Lake (PCL)..................	0	0	...	9.00	1	1	0	0	0	4	7	4	4	2	4
1997—Salt Lake (PCL).................	8	*15	.348	6.31	29	28	0	0	1	158 1/3	204	*123	111	80	125

REED, JEFF C ROCKIES

PERSONAL: Born November 12, 1962, in Joliet, Ill. ... 6-2/190. ... Bats left, throws right. ... Full name: Jeffrey Scott Reed. ... Brother of Curtis Reed, minor league outfielder (1977-84).
HIGH SCHOOL: West (Joliet, Ill.).
TRANSACTIONS/CAREER NOTES: Selected by Minnesota Twins organization in first round (12th pick overall) of free-agent draft (June 3, 1980). ... Traded by Twins organization with P Neal Heaton, P Al Cardwood and P Yorkis Perez to Montreal Expos for P Jeff Reardon and C Tom Nieto (February 3, 1987). ... On Montreal disabled list (April 20-May 25, 1987); included rehabilitation assignment to Indianapolis (May 19-25). ... Traded by Expos with OF Herm Winningham and P Randy St. Claire to Cincinnati Reds for OF Tracy Jones and P Pat Pacillo (July 13, 1988). ... On disabled list (July 1-19, 1991). ... On Cincinnati disabled list (April 26-September 1, 1992); included rehabilitation assignment to Nashville (August 17-September 1). ... Granted free agency (October 27, 1992). ... Signed by San Francisco Giants organization (January 15, 1993). ... On San Francisco disabled list (June 30-August 3, 1993); included rehabilitation assignment to San Jose (July 21-22 and July 30-August 3). ... Granted free agency (November 3, 1995). ... Signed by Colorado Rockies (December 18, 1995). ... Granted free agency (October 27, 1997). ... Re-signed by Rockies (November 18, 1997).
RECORDS: Holds modern N.L. record for most errors by catcher in one inning—3 (July 28, 1987, seventh inning).
STATISTICAL NOTES: Led California League catchers with 758 total chances and tied for lead with nine double plays in 1982. ... Led Southern League catchers with 714 total chances and 12 double plays in 1983. ... Led International League catchers with 720 total chances in 1985. ... Career major league grand slams: 1.

							BATTING								FIELDING		
Year Team (League)	Pos.	G	AB	R	H	2B	3B	HR	RBI	Avg.	BB	SO	SB	PO	A	E	Avg.
1980—Elizabethton (App.).....	C	65	225	39	64	15	1	1	20	.284	51	23	2	269	*41	9	.972
1981—Wis. Rap. (Mid.).........	C	106	312	63	73	12	1	4	34	.234	86	36	4	547	*93	7	.989
—Orlando (South.)	C	3	4	0	1	0	0	0	0	.250	1	0	0	4	1	0	1.000
1982—Visalia (California)......	C	125	395	69	130	19	2	5	54	.329	78	32	1	*642	•106	10	.987

R

Year Team (League)	Pos.	G	AB	R	H	2B	3B	HR	RBI	Avg.	BB	SO	SB	PO	A	E	Avg.
1983— Orlando (South.)	C	118	379	52	100	16	5	6	45	.264	76	40	2	*618	*88	8	*.989
—Toledo (Int'l)	C	14	41	5	7	1	1	0	3	.171	5	9	0	77	6	1	.988
1984— Minnesota (A.L.)	C	18	21	3	3	3	0	0	1	.143	2	6	0	41	2	1	.977
—Toledo (Int'l)	C	94	301	30	80	16	3	3	35	.266	37	35	1	546	43	5	*.992
1985— Toledo (Int'l)	C	122	404	53	100	15	3	5	36	.248	59	49	1	*627	*81	12	.983
—Minnesota (A.L.)	C	7	10	2	2	0	0	0	0	.200	0	3	0	9	3	0	1.000
1986— Minnesota (A.L.)	C	68	165	13	39	6	1	2	9	.236	16	19	1	332	19	2	.994
—Toledo (Int'l)	C	25	71	10	22	5	3	1	14	.310	17	9	0	108	22	2	.985
1987— Montreal (N.L.)■.....	C	75	207	15	44	11	0	1	21	.213	12	20	0	357	36	12	.970
—Indianapolis (A.A.)......	C	5	17	0	3	0	0	0	0	.176	1	2	0	27	2	0	1.000
1988— Montreal (N.L.)	C	43	123	10	27	3	2	0	9	.220	13	22	1	197	20	1	.995
—Indianapolis (A.A.)......	C	8	22	1	7	3	0	0	1	.318	2	2	0	30	11	0	1.000
—Cincinnati (N.L.)■...	C	49	142	10	33	6	0	1	7	.232	15	19	0	271	18	2	.993
1989— Cincinnati (N.L.)	C	102	287	16	64	11	0	3	23	.223	34	46	0	504	50	7	.988
1990— Cincinnati (N.L.)	C	72	175	12	44	8	1	3	16	.251	24	26	0	358	26	5	.987
1991— Cincinnati (N.L.)	C	91	270	20	72	15	2	3	31	.267	23	38	0	527	29	5	.991
1992— Nashville (A.A.)	C	14	25	1	6	1	0	1	2	.240	2	7	0	47	4	0	1.000
—Cincinnati (N.L.)	C	15	25	2	4	0	0	0	2	.160	1	4	0	29	2	0	1.000
1993— San Fran. (N.L.)■.....	C	66	119	10	31	3	0	6	12	.261	16	22	0	180	14	0	1.000
—San Jose (Calif.)	C	4	10	2	5	1	0	0	2	.500	1	0	0	19	2	0	1.000
1994— San Francisco (N.L.) ..	C	50	103	11	18	3	0	1	7	.175	11	21	0	138	9	1	.993
1995— San Francisco (N.L.) ..	C	66	113	12	30	2	0	0	9	.265	20	17	0	175	21	1	.995
1996— Colorado (N.L.)■.....	C	116	341	34	97	20	1	8	37	.284	43	65	2	546	51	11	.982
1997— Colorado (N.L.)	C	90	256	43	76	10	0	17	47	.297	35	55	2	428	37	6	.987
American League totals (3 years)		93	196	18	44	9	1	2	10	.224	18	28	1	382	24	3	.993
National League totals (11 years)		835	2161	195	540	92	6	43	221	.250	247	355	5	3710	313	51	.987
Major league totals (14 years)		928	2357	213	584	101	7	45	231	.248	265	383	6	4092	337	54	.988

CHAMPIONSHIP SERIES RECORD

Year Team (League)	Pos.	G	AB	R	H	2B	3B	HR	RBI	Avg.	BB	SO	SB	PO	A	E	Avg.
1990— Cincinnati (N.L.)	C	4	7	0	0	0	0	0	0	.000	2	0	0	24	1	0	1.000

WORLD SERIES RECORD

NOTES: Member of World Series championship team (1990).

Year Team (League)	Pos.	G	AB	R	H	2B	3B	HR	RBI	Avg.	BB	SO	SB	PO	A	E	Avg.
1990— Cincinnati (N.L.).........								Did not play.									

REED, JODY — 2B

PERSONAL: Born July 26, 1962, in Tampa. ... 5-9/165. ... Bats right, throws right. ... Full name: Jody Eric Reed.
HIGH SCHOOL: Brandon (Fla.).
JUNIOR COLLEGE: Manatee Junior College (Fla.).
COLLEGE: Florida State (degree in criminology, 1985).
TRANSACTIONS/CAREER NOTES: Selected by Texas Rangers organization in third round of free-agent draft (January 12, 1982); did not sign. ... Selected by San Francisco Giants organization in secondary phase of free-agent draft (June 7, 1982); did not sign. ... Selected by Rangers organization in secondary phase of free-agent draft (June 6, 1983); did not sign. ... Selected by Boston Red Sox organization in eighth round of free-agent draft (June 4, 1984). ... Selected by Colorado Rockies in first round (13th pick overall) of expansion draft (November 17, 1992). ... Traded by Rockies to Los Angeles Dodgers for P Rudy Seanez (November 17, 1992). ... On disabled list (June 16-July 15, 1993). ... Granted free agency (October 25, 1993). ... Signed by Milwaukee Brewers organization (February 3, 1994). ... Granted free agency (October 18, 1994). ... Signed by San Diego Padres (April 19, 1995). ... Granted free agency (November 11, 1995). ... Re-signed by Padres (December 19, 1995). ... Traded by Padres to Detroit Tigers for OF Mike Darr and P Matt Skrmetta (March 22, 1997). ... Granted free agency (September 12, 1997).
RECORDS: Shares major league record for most doubles in one inning—2 (September 8, 1991, third inning). ... Shares modern major league record for most long hits in one inning—2 (September 8, 1991, third inning).
STATISTICAL NOTES: Led Florida State League shortstops with 101 double plays in 1985. ... Led International League shortstops with 683 total chances and 86 double plays in 1987. ... Led A.L. second basemen with 587 total chances and 72 double plays in 1994.

Year Team (League)	Pos.	G	AB	R	H	2B	3B	HR	RBI	Avg.	BB	SO	SB	PO	A	E	Avg.
1984— Winter Haven (FSL)....	SS	77	273	46	74	14	1	0	20	.271	52	19	9	128	271	26	.939
1985— Winter Haven (FSL)....	SS	134	489	*95	157	25	1	0	45	*.321	*94	26	16	*256	*478	37	*.952
1986— New Britain (Eastern) .	SS	60	218	33	50	12	1	0	11	.229	52	9	10	114	190	14	.956
—Pawtucket (Int'l)	SS	69	227	27	64	11	0	1	30	.282	31	18	8	115	222	12	.966
1987— Pawtucket (Int'l)	SS	136	510	77	151	22	2	7	51	.296	69	23	9	*236	*427	20	.971
—Boston (A.L.).............	SS	9	30	4	9	1	1	0	8	.300	4	0	1	11	26	0	1.000
1988— Boston (A.L.)	S-2-3-DH	109	338	60	99	23	1	1	28	.293	45	21	1	147	282	11	.975
1989— Boston (A.L.).............	S-2-3-O-DH	146	524	76	151	42	2	3	40	.288	73	44	4	255	423	19	.973
1990— Boston (A.L.)	2B-SS-DH	155	598	70	173	*45	0	5	51	.289	75	65	4	278	478	16	.979
1991— Boston (A.L.).............	2B	153	618	87	175	42	2	5	60	.283	60	53	6	312	444	14	.982
1992— Boston (A.L.)	2B-DH	143	550	64	136	27	1	3	40	.247	62	44	7	304	472	14	.982
1993— Los Angeles (N.L.)■...	2B	132	445	48	123	21	2	2	31	.276	38	40	1	280	413	5	*.993
1994— Milwaukee (A.L.)■	2B	108	399	48	108	22	0	2	37	.271	57	34	5	*231	*353	3	*.995
1995— San Diego (N.L.)■	2B-SS	131	445	58	114	18	1	4	40	.256	59	38	6	304	366	4	.994
1996— San Diego (N.L.)	2B	146	495	45	121	20	0	2	49	.244	59	53	2	275	411	9	.987
1997— Detroit (A.L.)■...........	2B-DH	52	112	6	22	2	0	0	8	.196	10	15	3	49	107	2	.987
American League totals (8 years)		875	3169	415	873	204	7	19	272	.275	386	276	31	1587	2585	79	.981
National League totals (3 years)		409	1385	151	358	59	3	8	120	.258	156	131	9	859	1190	18	.991
Major league totals (11 years)		1284	4554	566	1231	263	10	27	392	.270	542	407	40	2446	3775	97	.985

DIVISION SERIES RECORD

						BATTING									FIELDING		
Year Team (League)	Pos.	G	AB	R	H	2B	3B	HR	RBI	Avg.	BB	SO	SB	PO	A	E	Avg.
1996—San Diego (N.L.)	2B	3	11	0	3	1	0	0	2	.273	0	1	0	6	6	0	1.000

CHAMPIONSHIP SERIES RECORD

						BATTING									FIELDING		
Year Team (League)	Pos.	G	AB	R	H	2B	3B	HR	RBI	Avg.	BB	SO	SB	PO	A	E	Avg.
1988—Boston (A.L.).............	SS	4	11	0	3	1	0	0	0	.273	2	1	0	3	10	0	1.000
1990—Boston (A.L.).............	2B-SS	4	15	0	2	0	0	0	1	.133	0	2	0	11	11	0	1.000
Championship series totals (2 years)		8	26	0	5	1	0	0	1	.192	2	3	0	14	21	0	1.000

REED, RICK   P   METS

R

PERSONAL: Born August 16, 1964, in Huntington, W.Va. ... 6-0/200. ... Throws right, bats right. ... Full name: Richard Allen Reed.
HIGH SCHOOL: Huntington (W.Va.).
COLLEGE: Marshall.
TRANSACTIONS/CAREER NOTES: Selected by Pittsburgh Pirates organization in 26th round of free-agent draft (June 2, 1986). ... On Buffalo disabled list (May 2-13, 1991). ... Granted free agency (April 3, 1992). ... Signed by Omaha, Kansas City Royals organization (April 4, 1992). ... Granted free agency (August 5, 1993). ... Signed by Oklahoma City, Texas Rangers organization (August 11, 1993). ... Claimed on waivers by Cincinnati Reds (May 13, 1994). ... On Indianapolis disabled list (May 29-June 9, 1995). ... Granted free agency (October 16, 1995). ... Signed by New York Mets organization (November 7, 1995).
HONORS: Named American Association Most Valuable Pitcher (1991).

Year Team (League)	W	L	Pct.	ERA	G	GS	CG	ShO	Sv.	IP	H	R	ER	BB	SO
1986—GC Pirates (GCL)................	0	2	.000	3.75	8	3	0	0	0	24	20	12	10	6	15
—Macon (S. Atl.)...................	0	0	...	2.84	1	1	0	0	0	6 1/3	5	3	2	2	1
1987—Macon (S. Atl.)................	8	4	.667	2.50	46	0	0	0	7	93 2/3	80	38	26	29	92
1988—Salem (Carolina)	6	2	.750	2.74	15	8	4	1	0	72 1/3	56	28	22	17	73
—Harrisburg (Eastern)	1	0	1.000	1.13	2	2	0	0	0	16	11	2	2	2	17
—Buffalo (A.A.)...................	5	2	.714	1.64	10	9	3	2	0	77	62	15	14	12	50
—Pittsburgh (N.L.)	1	0	1.000	3.00	2	2	0	0	0	12	10	4	4	2	6
1989—Buffalo (A.A.)...................	9	8	.529	3.72	20	20	3	0	0	125 2/3	130	58	52	28	75
—Pittsburgh (N.L.)	1	4	.200	5.60	15	7	0	0	0	54 2/3	62	35	34	11	34
1990—Buffalo (A.A.)...................	7	4	.636	3.46	15	15	2	2	0	91	82	37	35	21	63
—Pittsburgh (N.L.)	2	3	.400	4.36	13	8	1	1	1	53 2/3	62	32	26	12	27
1991—Buffalo (A.A.)...................	*14	4	*.778	*2.15	25	25	•5	2	0	167 2/3	151	45	40	26	102
—Pittsburgh (N.L.)	0	0	...	10.38	1	1	0	0	0	4 1/3	8	6	5	1	2
1992—Omaha (Am. Assoc.)■........	5	4	.556	4.35	11	10	3	0	1	62	67	33	30	12	35
—Kansas City (A.L.)	3	7	.300	3.68	19	18	1	1	0	100 1/3	105	47	41	20	49
1993—Omaha (Am. Assoc.)	11	4	.733	3.09	19	19	3	*2	0	128 1/3	116	48	44	14	58
—Kansas City (A.L.)	0	0	...	9.82	1	0	0	0	0	3 2/3	6	4	4	1	3
—Oklahoma City (A.A.)■........	1	3	.250	4.19	5	5	1	0	0	34 1/3	43	20	16	2	21
—Texas (A.L.)	1	0	1.000	2.25	2	0	0	0	0	4	6	1	1	1	2
1994—Oklahoma City (A.A.)........	1	1	.500	3.86	2	2	0	0	0	11 2/3	10	5	5	0	8
—Texas (A.L.)	1	1	.500	5.94	4	3	0	0	0	16 2/3	17	13	11	7	12
—Indianapolis (A.A.)■	9	5	.643	4.68	21	21	3	1	0	140 1/3	162	80	73	19	79
1995—Indianapolis (A.A.).............	11	4	.733	3.33	22	21	3	1	0	135	127	60	50	26	92
—Cincinnati (N.L.)	0	0	...	5.82	4	3	0	0	0	17	18	12	11	3	10
1996—Norfolk (Int'l)■	8	10	.444	3.16	28	28	1	0	0	182	164	72	64	33	128
1997—New York (N.L.)................	13	9	.591	2.89	33	31	2	0	0	208 1/3	186	76	67	31	113
A.L. totals (3 years)	5	8	.385	4.11	26	21	1	1	0	124 2/3	134	65	57	29	66
N.L. totals (6 years)	17	16	.515	3.78	68	52	3	1	1	350	346	165	147	60	192
Major league totals (9 years)......	22	24	.478	3.87	94	73	4	2	1	474 2/3	480	230	204	89	258

REED, STEVE   P   GIANTS

PERSONAL: Born March 11, 1966, in Los Angeles. ... 6-2/212. ... Throws right, bats right. ... Full name: Steven Vincent Reed.
HIGH SCHOOL: Chatsworth (Calif.).
COLLEGE: Lewis-Clark State College (Idaho).
TRANSACTIONS/CAREER NOTES: Signed as non-drafted free agent by San Francisco Giants organization (June 24, 1988). ... On disabled list (July 17-August 13, 1990). ... Selected by Colorado Rockies in third round (60th pick overall) of expansion draft (November 17, 1992). ... Granted free agency (December 21, 1997). ... Signed by San Francisco Giants (December 24, 1997).
RECORDS: Holds Colorado Rockies all-time record for most games pitched (329).

Year Team (League)	W	L	Pct.	ERA	G	GS	CG	ShO	Sv.	IP	H	R	ER	BB	SO
1988—Pocatello (Pioneer).............	4	1	.800	2.54	31	0	0	0	*13	46	42	20	13	8	49
1989—Clinton (Midwest).............	5	3	.625	1.05	60	0	0	0	26	94 2/3	54	16	11	38	104
—San Jose (California)..........	0	0	...	0.00	2	0	0	0	0	2	0	0	0	1	3
1990—Shreveport (Texas).............	3	1	.750	1.64	45	0	0	0	8	60 1/3	53	20	11	20	59
1991—Shreveport (Texas)..........	2	0	1.000	0.83	15	0	0	0	7	21 2/3	17	2	2	3	26
—Phoenix (PCL)...................	2	3	.400	4.31	41	0	0	0	6	56 1/3	62	33	27	12	46
1992—Shreveport (Texas).............	1	0	1.000	0.62	27	0	0	0	23	29	18	3	2	0	33
—Phoenix (PCL)...................	1	0	1.000	3.48	29	0	0	0	20	31	27	13	12	10	30
—San Francisco (N.L.)	1	0	1.000	2.30	18	0	0	0	0	15 2/3	13	5	4	3	11
1993—Colorado (N.L.)■.............	9	5	.643	4.48	64	0	0	0	3	84 1/3	80	47	42	30	51
—Colo. Springs (PCL)..........	0	0	...	0.00	11	0	0	0	7	12 1/3	8	1	0	3	10
1994—Colorado (N.L.)................	3	2	.600	3.94	*61	0	0	0	3	64	79	33	28	26	51
1995—Colorado (N.L.)................	5	2	.714	2.14	71	0	0	0	3	84	61	24	20	21	79
1996—Colorado (N.L.)................	4	3	.571	3.96	70	0	0	0	0	75	66	38	33	19	51
1997—Colorado (N.L.)	4	6	.400	4.04	63	0	0	0	6	62 1/3	49	28	28	27	43
Major league totals (6 years)......	26	18	.591	3.62	347	0	0	0	15	385 1/3	348	175	155	126	286

Year Team (League)	W	L	Pct.	ERA	G	GS	CG	ShO	Sv.	IP	H	R	ER	BB	SO
1995— Colorado (N.L.)	0	0	...	0.00	3	0	0	0	0	2 2/3	2	0	0	1	3

REESE, POKEY SS/2B REDS

PERSONAL: Born June 10, 1973, in Columbia, S.C. ... 5-11/180. ... Bats right, throws right. ... Full name: Calvin Reese Jr.
HIGH SCHOOL: Lower Richland (Hopkins, S.C.).
TRANSACTIONS/CAREER NOTES: Selected by Cincinnati Reds organization in first round (20th pick overall) of free-agent draft (June 3, 1991). ... On disabled list (June 23-July 22, 1995). ... On disabled list (September 17, 1996-remainder of season).

Year Team (League)	Pos.	G	AB	R	H	2B	3B	HR	RBI	Avg.	BB	SO	SB	PO	A	E	Avg.
1991— Princeton (Appal.)	SS	62	231	30	55	8	3	3	27	.238	23	44	10	93	146	*31	.885
1992— Char., W.Va. (SAL)......	SS	106	380	50	102	19	3	6	53	.268	24	75	19	181	287	34	.932
1993— Chattanooga (Sou.)....	SS	102	345	35	73	17	4	3	37	.212	23	77	8	181	300	25	.951
1994— Chattanooga (Sou.)....	SS	134	484	77	130	23	4	12	49	.269	43	75	21	*221	362	38	.939
1995— Indianapolis (A.A.)......	SS	89	343	51	82	21	1	10	46	.239	36	81	8	131	258	27	.935
1996— Indianapolis (A.A.)......	SS-3B	79	280	26	65	16	0	1	23	.232	21	46	5	131	239	22	.944
1997— Cincinnati (N.L.)	SS-2B-3B	128	397	48	87	15	0	4	26	.219	31	82	25	182	284	15	.969
— Indianapolis (A.A.)......	SS-2B	17	72	12	17	2	0	4	11	.236	9	12	4	43	42	3	.966
Major league totals (1 year)		128	397	48	87	15	0	4	26	.219	31	82	25	182	284	15	.969

REKAR, BRYAN P DEVIL RAYS

PERSONAL: Born June 3, 1972, in Oak Lawn, Ill. ... 6-3/210. ... Throws right, bats right.
HIGH SCHOOL: Providence Catholic (New Lenox, Ill.).
COLLEGE: Bradley.
TRANSACTIONS/CAREER NOTES: Selected by Colorado Rockies organization in second round of free-agent draft (June 3, 1993). ... Selected by Tampa Bay Devil Rays in second round (38th pick overall) of expansion draft (November 18, 1997).

Year Team (League)	W	L	Pct.	ERA	G	GS	CG	ShO	Sv.	IP	H	R	ER	BB	SO
1993— Bend (Northwest)...............	3	5	.375	4.08	13	13	1	0	0	75	81	36	34	18	59
1994— Central Valley (Cal.)...........	6	6	.500	3.48	22	19	0	0	0	111 1/3	120	52	43	31	91
1995— New Haven (Eastern)...........	6	3	.667	2.13	12	12	1	1	0	80 1/3	65	28	19	16	80
— Colo. Springs (PCL)..........	4	2	.667	1.49	7	7	2	1	0	48 1/3	29	10	8	13	39
— Colorado (N.L.)	4	6	.400	4.98	15	14	1	0	0	85	95	51	47	24	60
1996— Colo. Springs (PCL)..........	8	8	.500	4.46	19	19	0	0	0	123	138	68	61	36	75
— Colorado (N.L.)	2	4	.333	8.95	14	11	0	0	0	58 1/3	87	61	58	26	25
1997— Colo. Springs (PCL)..........	10	9	.526	5.46	28	25	0	0	0	145	169	96	88	39	116
— Colorado (N.L.)	1	0	1.000	5.79	2	2	0	0	0	9 1/3	11	7	6	6	4
Major league totals (3 years)......	7	10	.412	6.54	31	27	1	0	0	152 2/3	193	119	111	56	89

RELAFORD, DESI SS PHILLIES

PERSONAL: Born September 16, 1973, in Valdosta, Ga. ... 5-8/155. ... Bats both, throws right. ... Full name: Desmond Lamont Relaford.
HIGH SCHOOL: Sandalwood (Jacksonville).
TRANSACTIONS/CAREER NOTES: Selected by Seattle Mariners organization in fourth round of free-agent draft (June 3, 1991). ... Traded by Mariners to Philadelphia Phillies for P Terry Mulholland (July 31, 1996).
STATISTICAL NOTES: Led California League shortstops with 601 total chances in 1992. ... Led Southern League shortstops with 35 errors in 1993. ... Led International League shortstops with 587 total chances and 81 double plays in 1997.

Year Team (League)	Pos.	G	AB	R	H	2B	3B	HR	RBI	Avg.	BB	SO	SB	PO	A	E	Avg.
1991— Ariz. Mariners (Ariz.)..	SS-2B	46	163	36	44	7	3	0	18	.270	22	24	17	58	126	24	.885
1992— Peninsula (Caro.)	SS	130	445	53	96	18	1	3	34	.216	39	88	27	167	*382	*52	.913
1993— Jacksonville (South.)..	SS-2B-3B	133	472	49	115	16	4	8	47	.244	50	103	16	157	386	†38	.935
1994— Jacksonville (South.)...	SS	37	143	24	29	7	3	3	11	.203	22	28	10	71	119	4	.979
— Riverside (Calif.).........	SS	99	374	95	116	27	5	5	59	.310	78	78	27	125	296	36	.921
1995— Port City (Southern) ...	SS-2B	90	352	51	101	11	2	7	27	.287	41	58	25	134	276	31	.930
— Tacoma (PCL)	2B-SS	30	113	20	27	5	1	2	7	.239	13	24	6	52	93	6	.960
1996— Tacoma (PCL)	2B-SS	93	317	27	65	12	0	4	32	.205	23	58	10	174	306	20	.960
— Scran./W.B. (Int'l)■...	SS	21	85	12	20	4	1	1	11	.235	8	19	7	25	65	6	.938
— Philadelphia (N.L.)......	SS-2B	15	40	2	7	2	0	0	1	.175	3	9	1	21	26	2	.959
1997— Scran./W.B. (Int'l)......	SS	131	517	82	138	34	4	9	53	.267	43	77	29	180	*373	34	.942
— Philadelphia (N.L.)......	SS	15	38	3	7	1	2	0	6	.184	5	6	3	12	31	1	.977
Major league totals (2 years)		30	78	5	14	3	2	0	7	.179	8	15	4	33	57	3	.968

REMLINGER, MIKE P REDS

PERSONAL: Born March 26, 1966, in Middletown, N.Y. ... 6-0/195. ... Throws left, bats left. ... Full name: Michael John Remlinger. ... Name pronounced REM-lynn-jer.
HIGH SCHOOL: Carver (Plymouth, Mass.).
COLLEGE: Dartmouth.
TRANSACTIONS/CAREER NOTES: Selected by San Francisco Giants organization in first round (16th pick overall) of free-agent draft (June 2, 1987). ... On disabled list (April 30, 1988-remainder of season). ... Traded by Giants with OF Kevin Mitchell to Seattle Mariners for P Bill Swift, P Mike Jackson and P Dave Burba (December 11, 1991). ... On Jacksonville disabled list (July 30, 1992-remainder of season). ... Granted free agency (October 15, 1993). ... Signed by New York Mets organization (November 22, 1993). ... Traded by Mets to Cincinnati

Reds for OF Cobi Cradle (May 11, 1995). ... Granted free agency (October 6, 1995). ... Traded by Reds to Kansas City Royals as part of a three-team deal in which Reds sent SS Luis Ordaz to St. Louis Cardinals for OF Andre King. Royals then sent OF Miguel Mejia to Cardinals to complete deal (December 4, 1995). ... Claimed on waivers by Reds (April 4, 1996).
RECORDS: Shares major league record for pitching shutout in first major league game (June 15, 1991).
STATISTICAL NOTES: Led American Association with 18 wild pitches in 1996. ... Led N.L. with 12 wild pitches in 1997.
MISCELLANEOUS: Appeared in two games as pinch-runner (1997).

Year	Team (League)	W	L	Pct.	ERA	G	GS	CG	ShO	Sv.	IP	H	R	ER	BB	SO
1987—	Everett (Northwest)	0	0	. . .	3.60	2	1	0	0	0	5	1	2	2	5	11
	—Clinton (Midwest)	2	1	.667	3.30	6	5	0	0	0	30	21	12	11	14	43
	—Shreveport (Texas)	4	2	.667	2.36	6	6	0	0	0	34 1/3	14	11	9	22	51
1988—	Shreveport (Texas)	1	0	1.000	0.69	3	3	0	0	0	13	7	4	1	4	18
1989—	Shreveport (Texas)	4	6	.400	2.98	16	16	0	0	0	90 2/3	68	43	30	73	92
	—Phoenix (PCL)	1	6	.143	9.21	11	10	0	0	0	43	51	47	44	52	28
1990—	Shreveport (Texas)	9	11	.450	3.90	25	25	2	1	0	147 1/3	149	82	64	72	75
1991—	Phoenix (PCL)	5	5	.500	6.38	19	19	1	1	0	108 2/3	134	86	77	59	68
	—San Francisco (N.L.)	2	1	.667	4.37	8	6	1	1	0	35	36	17	17	20	19
1992—	Calgary (PCL)■	1	7	.125	6.65	21	11	0	0	0	70 1/3	97	65	52	48	24
	—Jacksonville (Southern)......	1	1	.500	3.46	5	5	0	0	0	26	25	15	10	11	21
1993—	Calgary (PCL)	4	3	.571	5.53	19	18	0	0	0	84 2/3	100	57	52	52	51
	—Jacksonville (Southern)......	1	3	.250	6.58	7	7	0	0	0	39 2/3	40	30	29	19	23
1994—	Norfolk (Int'l)■	2	4	.333	3.14	12	9	0	0	0	63	57	29	22	25	45
	—New York (N.L.)	1	5	.167	4.61	10	9	0	0	0	54 2/3	55	30	28	35	33
1995—	New York (N.L.)■	0	1	.000	6.35	5	0	0	0	0	5 2/3	7	5	4	2	6
	—Cincinnati (N.L.)■	0	0	. . .	9.00	2	0	0	0	0	1	2	1	1	3	1
	—Indianapolis (A.A.)	5	3	.625	4.05	41	1	0	0	0	46 2/3	40	24	21	32	58
1996—	Indianapolis (A.A.)	4	3	.571	2.52	28	13	0	0	0	89 1/3	64	29	25	44	97
	—Cincinnati (N.L.)	0	1	.000	5.60	19	4	0	0	0	27 1/3	24	17	17	19	19
1997—	Cincinnati (N.L.)	8	8	.500	4.14	69	12	2	0	2	124	100	61	57	60	145
Major league totals (5 years)		**11**	**16**	**.407**	**4.51**	**113**	**31**	**3**	**1**	**2**	**247 1/3**	**224**	**131**	**124**	**139**	**223**

RENTERIA, EDGAR · SS · MARLINS

PERSONAL: Born August 7, 1975, in Barranquilla, Colombia. ... 6-1/180. ... Bats right, throws right. ... Full name: Edgar Enrique Renteria. ... Brother of Edinson Renteria, infielder in Houston Astros and Florida Marlins organization (1985-1994).
HIGH SCHOOL: Instituto Los Alpes (Barranquilla, Colombia).
TRANSACTIONS/CAREER NOTES: Signed as non-drafted free agent by Florida Marlins organization (February 14, 1992). ... On Florida disabled list (June 24-July 11, 1996); included rehabilitation assignment to Charlotte (July 3-11).
STATISTICAL NOTES: Had 22-game hitting streak (July 25-August 16, 1996). ... Led N.L. in sacrifice hits with 19 in 1997.

Year	Team (League)	Pos.	G	AB	R	H	2B	3B	HR	RBI	Avg.	BB	SO	SB	PO	A	E	Avg.
1992—	GC Marlins (GCL)	SS	43	163	25	47	8	1	0	9	.288	8	29	10	56	152	*24	.897
1993—	Kane County (Midw.)..	SS	116	384	40	78	8	0	1	35	.203	35	94	7	•173	306	34	.934
1994—	Brevard Co. (Fla. St.)..	SS	128	439	46	111	15	1	0	36	.253	35	56	6	167	372	23	.959
1995—	Portland (Eastern)	SS	135	508	70	147	15	7	7	68	.289	32	85	30	179	379	33	.944
1996—	Charlotte (Int'l)	SS	35	132	17	37	8	0	2	16	.280	9	17	10	48	114	7	.959
	—Florida (N.L.)	SS	106	431	68	133	18	3	5	31	.309	33	68	16	163	344	11	.979
1997—	Florida (N.L.)	SS	154	617	90	171	21	3	4	52	.277	45	108	32	*242	415	17	.975
Major league totals (2 years)			**260**	**1048**	**158**	**304**	**39**	**6**	**9**	**83**	**.290**	**78**	**176**	**48**	**405**	**759**	**28**	**.977**

DIVISION SERIES RECORD

Year	Team (League)	Pos.	G	AB	R	H	2B	3B	HR	RBI	Avg.	BB	SO	SB	PO	A	E	Avg.
1997—	Florida (N.L.)	SS	3	13	1	2	0	0	0	1	.154	2	4	0	9	11	2	.909

CHAMPIONSHIP SERIES RECORD

Year	Team (League)	Pos.	G	AB	R	H	2B	3B	HR	RBI	Avg.	BB	SO	SB	PO	A	E	Avg.
1997—	Florida (N.L.)	SS	6	22	4	5	1	0	0	0	.227	3	6	1	14	15	0	1.000

WORLD SERIES RECORD

RECORDS: Holds record for most strikeouts in one inning—2 (October 23, 1997, sixth inning).
NOTES: Member of World Series championship team (1997).

Year	Team (League)	Pos.	G	AB	R	H	2B	3B	HR	RBI	Avg.	BB	SO	SB	PO	A	E	Avg.
1997—	Florida (N.L.)	SS	7	31	3	9	2	0	0	3	.290	3	5	0	12	26	1	.974

REYES, AL · P · BREWERS

PERSONAL: Born April 10, 1971, in San Cristobal, Dominican Republic. ... 6-1/193. ... Throws right, bats right. ... Full name: Rafael Alberto Reyes.
TRANSACTIONS/CAREER NOTES: Signed as non-drafted free agent by Montreal Expos organization (February 17, 1988). ... On disabled list (May 23, 1991-remainder of season). ... Selected by Milwaukee Brewers from Expos organization in Rule 5 major league draft (December 5, 1994). ... On disabled list (July 19, 1995-remainder of season). ... On New Orleans disabled list (April 4-August 2, 1996).

Year	Team (League)	W	L	Pct.	ERA	G	GS	CG	ShO	Sv.	IP	H	R	ER	BB	SO
1989—	DSL Expos (DSL)	3	4	.429	2.79	12	10	1	0	0	71	68	36	22	33	49
1990—	W.P. Beach (FSL)	5	4	.556	4.74	16	10	0	0	1	57	58	32	30	32	47
1991—	Rockford (Midwest)	0	1	.000	5.56	3	3	0	0	0	11 1/3	14	8	7	2	10
1992—	Albany (S. Atl.)	0	2	.000	3.95	27	0	0	0	4	27 1/3	24	14	12	13	29
1993—	Burlington (Midw.)	7	6	.538	2.68	53	0	0	0	11	74	52	33	22	26	80
1994—	Harrisburg (Eastern)	2	2	.500	3.25	60	0	0	0	*35	69 1/3	68	26	25	13	60

R

Year Team (League)	W	L	Pct.	ERA	G	GS	CG	ShO	Sv.	IP	H	R	ER	BB	SO
1995— Milwaukee (A.L.)■	1	1	.500	2.43	27	0	0	0	1	33⅓	19	9	9	18	29
1996— Beloit (Midwest)	1	0	1.000	1.83	13	0	0	0	0	19⅔	17	7	4	6	22
— Milwaukee (A.L.)	1	0	1.000	7.94	5	0	0	0	0	5⅔	8	5	5	2	2
1997— Tucson (PCL)	2	4	.333	5.02	38	0	0	0	7	57⅓	52	39	32	34	70
— Milwaukee (A.L.)	1	2	.333	5.46	19	0	0	0	1	29⅔	32	19	18	9	28
Major league totals (3 years)	3	3	.500	4.19	51	0	0	0	2	68⅔	59	33	32	29	59

REYES, CARLOS — P — PADRES

PERSONAL: Born April 4, 1969, in Miami. ... 6-1/190. ... Throws right, bats both. ... Full name: Carlos Alberto Reyes Jr.
HIGH SCHOOL: Tampa Catholic.
JUNIOR COLLEGE: Brevard Community College (Fla.).
COLLEGE: Florida Southern.
TRANSACTIONS/CAREER NOTES: Signed as non-drafted free agent by Atlanta Braves organization (June 21, 1991). ... Selected by Oakland Athletics from Braves organization in Rule 5 major league draft (December 13, 1993). ... On Oakland disabled list (July 18-August 4, 1994); included rehabilitation assignment to Modesto (July 25-30). ... Granted free agency (December 20, 1996). ... Signed by New York Yankees organization (February 6, 1997). ... Released by Yankees (April 8, 1997). ... Signed by Athletics (April 10, 1997). ...On Oakland disabled list (August 21-September 12, 1997); included rehabilitation assignment to Edmonton (September 3-12). ... Granted free agency (October 15, 1997). ... Signed by San Diego Padres (November 7, 1997).

Year Team (League)	W	L	Pct.	ERA	G	GS	CG	ShO	Sv.	IP	H	R	ER	BB	SO
1991— GC Braves (GCL)	3	2	.600	1.77	20	0	0	0	5	45⅔	44	15	9	9	37
1992— Macon (S. Atl.)	2	3	.400	2.10	23	0	0	0	2	60	57	16	14	11	57
— Durham (Carolina)	2	1	.667	2.43	21	0	0	0	5	40⅔	31	11	11	10	33
1993— Greenville (Southern)	8	1	.889	2.06	33	2	0	0	2	70	64	22	16	24	57
— Richmond (Int'l)	1	0	1.000	3.77	18	1	0	0	1	28⅔	30	12	12	11	30
1994— Oakland (A.L.)■	0	3	.000	4.15	27	9	0	0	1	78	71	38	36	44	57
— Modesto (California)	0	0	...	0.00	3	3	0	0	0	5	2	0	0	0	3
1995— Oakland (A.L.)	4	6	.400	5.09	40	1	0	0	0	69	71	43	39	28	48
1996— Oakland (A.L.)	7	10	.412	4.78	46	10	0	0	0	122⅓	134	71	65	61	78
1997— Columbus (Int'l)■	0	0	...	18.00	1	1	0	0	0	2	5	4	4	0	2
— Edmonton (PCL)■	2	0	1.000	3.48	5	4	1	0	0	31	30	14	12	3	23
— Oakland (A.L.)	3	4	.429	5.82	37	6	0	0	0	77⅓	101	52	50	25	43
Major league totals (4 years)	14	23	.378	4.93	150	26	0	0	1	346⅔	377	204	190	158	226

REYES, DENNIS — P — DODGERS

PERSONAL: Born April 19, 1977, in Higuera de Zaragoza, Mexico. ... 6-3/245. ... Throws left, bats left.
HIGH SCHOOL: Ignacio Zaragoza (Higuera de Zaragoza, Mexico).
TRANSACTIONS/CAREER NOTES: Signed as non-drafted free agent by Los Angeles Dodgers organization (July 5, 1993).

Year Team (League)	W	L	Pct.	ERA	G	GS	CG	ShO	Sv.	IP	H	R	ER	BB	SO
1994— Vero Beach (FSL)	2	4	.333	6.70	9	9	0	0	0	41⅔	58	37	31	18	25
— Great Falls (Pio.)	7	1	.875	3.78	14	9	0	0	0	66⅔	71	37	28	25	70
1995— Vero Beach (FSL)	1	0	1.000	1.80	3	2	0	0	0	10	8	2	2	6	9
— M.C. Red Devils (Mex.)	5	5	.500	6.60	17	15	1	0	0	58⅔	76	49	43	41	44
1996— San Bernardino (Calif.)	11	12	.478	4.17	29	•28	0	0	0	166	166	106	77	77	176
1997— San Antonio (Tex.)	8	1	.889	3.02	12	12	1	0	0	80⅓	79	33	27	28	66
— Albuquerque (PCL)	6	3	.667	5.65	10	10	1	0	0	57⅓	70	40	36	33	45
— Los Angeles (N.L.)	2	3	.400	3.83	14	5	0	0	0	47	51	21	20	18	36
Major league totals (1 year)	2	3	.400	3.83	14	5	0	0	0	47	51	21	20	18	36

REYNOLDS, SHANE — P — ASTROS

PERSONAL: Born March 26, 1968, in Bastrop, La. ... 6-3/210. ... Throws right, bats right. ... Full name: Richard Shane Reynolds.
HIGH SCHOOL: Ouachita Christian (Monroe, La.).
JUNIOR COLLEGE: Faulkner State Junior College (Ala.).
COLLEGE: Texas.
TRANSACTIONS/CAREER NOTES: Selected by Houston Astros organization in third round of free-agent draft (June 5, 1989). ... On Houston disabled list (June 10-July 14, 1997); included rehabilitation assignment to New Orleans (July 10-14).
MISCELLANEOUS: Appeared in one game as pinch-runner (1995).

Year Team (League)	W	L	Pct.	ERA	G	GS	CG	ShO	Sv.	IP	H	R	ER	BB	SO
1989— Auburn (N.Y.-Penn)	3	2	.600	2.31	6	6	1	0	0	35	36	16	9	14	23
— Asheville (S. Atl.)	5	3	.625	3.68	8	8	2	1	0	51⅓	53	25	21	21	33
1990— Columbus (Southern)	9	10	.474	4.81	29	27	2	1	0	155⅓	•181	104	83	70	92
1991— Jackson (Texas)	8	9	.471	4.47	27	•27	2	0	0	151	165	93	75	62	116
1992— Tucson (PCL)	9	8	.529	3.68	25	22	2	0	1	142	156	73	58	34	106
— Houston (N.L.)	1	3	.250	7.11	8	5	0	0	0	25⅓	42	22	20	6	10
1993— Tucson (PCL)	10	6	.625	3.62	25	20	2	0	1	139⅓	147	74	56	21	106
— Houston (N.L.)	0	0	...	0.82	5	1	0	0	0	11	11	4	1	6	10
1994— Houston (N.L.)	8	5	.615	3.05	33	14	1	1	0	124	128	46	42	21	110
1995— Houston (N.L.)	10	11	.476	3.47	30	30	3	2	0	189⅓	196	87	73	37	175
1996— Houston (N.L.)	16	10	.615	3.65	35	35	4	1	0	239	227	103	97	44	204
1997— Houston (N.L.)	9	10	.474	4.23	30	30	2	0	0	181	189	92	85	47	152
— New Orleans (A.A.)	1	0	1.000	0.00	1	1	0	0	0	5	3	0	0	1	6
Major league totals (6 years)	44	39	.530	3.72	141	115	10	4	0	769⅔	793	354	318	161	661

DIVISION SERIES RECORD

Year Team (League)	W	L	Pct.	ERA	G	GS	CG	ShO	Sv.	IP	H	R	ER	BB	SO
1997— Houston (N.L.)	0	1	.000	3.00	1	1	0	0	0	6	5	2	2	1	5

REYNOSO, ARMANDO   P   METS

PERSONAL: Born May 1, 1966, in San Luis Potosi, Mexico. ... 6-0/204. ... Throws right, bats right. ... Full name: Martin Armando Gutierrez Reynoso. ... Name pronounced ray-NO-so.
HIGH SCHOOL: Escuela Secandaria Mita del Estado (Jalisco, Mexico).
TRANSACTIONS/CAREER NOTES: Signed as free agent by Saltillo of Mexican League. ... Contract sold by Saltillo to Atlanta Braves organization (August 15, 1990). ... Selected by Colorado Rockies in third round (58th pick overall) of expansion draft (November 17, 1992). ... On disabled list (May 21, 1994-remainder of season). ... On Colorado disabled list (April 17-June 18, 1995); included rehabilitation assignments to Colorado Springs (May 9-20 and June 8-14). ... Traded by Rockies to New York Mets for P Jerry DiPoto (November 27, 1996). ... On New York disabled list (March 24-April 15, 1997); included rehabilitation assignment to St. Lucie (April 5-15). ... On disabled list (July 17, 1997-remainder of season).
STATISTICAL NOTES: Led International League with six balks in 1991 and five in 1992. ... Tied for International League lead with 10 hit batsmen in 1991.
MISCELLANEOUS: Shares Colorado Rockies all-time record for most complete games (5). ... Appeared in one game as pinch-runner with Colorado (1993).

Year — Team (League)	W	L	Pct.	ERA	G	GS	CG	ShO	Sv.	IP	H	R	ER	BB	SO
1988— Saltillo (Mexican)	11	11	.500	4.30	32	29	10	2	2	180	176	98	86	85	92
1989— Saltillo (Mexican)	13	9	.591	3.48	27	25	7	2	0	160⅓	155	78	62	64	107
1990— Saltillo (Mexican)	*20	3	.870	2.60	27	•27	12	5	0	200⅔	174	61	58	73	*170
— Richmond (Int'l)■............	3	1	.750	2.25	4	3	0	0	0	24	26	7	6	7	15
1991— Richmond (Int'l).............	10	6	.625	*2.61	22	19	3	•3	0	131	117	44	38	39	97
— Atlanta (N.L.).................	2	1	.667	6.17	6	5	0	0	0	23⅓	26	18	16	10	10
1992— Richmond (Int'l).............	12	9	.571	2.66	28	27	4	1	0	169⅓	156	65	50	52	108
— Atlanta (N.L.).................	1	0	1.000	4.70	3	1	0	0	1	7⅔	11	4	4	2	2
1993— Colo. Springs (PCL)■.....	2	1	.667	3.22	4	4	0	0	0	22⅓	19	10	8	8	22
— Colorado (N.L.)	12	11	.522	4.00	30	30	4	0	0	189	206	101	84	63	117
1994— Colorado (N.L.)	3	4	.429	4.82	9	9	1	0	0	52⅓	54	30	28	22	25
1995— Colo. Springs (PCL)	2	1	.667	1.57	5	5	0	0	0	23	14	4	4	6	17
— Colorado (N.L.)	7	7	.500	5.32	20	18	0	0	0	93	116	61	55	36	40
1996— Colorado (N.L.)	8	9	.471	4.96	30	30	0	0	0	168⅔	195	97	93	49	88
1997— St. Lucie (Fla. St.)■.......	1	1	.500	2.70	2	2	0	0	0	10	9	3	3	1	6
— New York (N.L.).............	6	3	.667	4.53	16	16	1	1	0	91⅓	95	47	46	29	47
Major league totals (7 years)......	39	35	.527	4.69	114	109	6	1	1	625⅓	703	358	326	211	329

DIVISION SERIES RECORD

Year — Team (League)	W	L	Pct.	ERA	G	GS	CG	ShO	Sv.	IP	H	R	ER	BB	SO
1995— Colorado (N.L.)	0	0	...	0.00	1	0	0	0	0	1	2	0	0	0	0

RHODES, ARTHUR   P   ORIOLES

PERSONAL: Born October 24, 1969, in Waco, Texas. ... 6-2/205. ... Throws left, bats left. ... Full name: Arthur Lee Rhodes Jr. ... Brother of Ricky Rhodes, minor league pitcher, New York Yankees organization (1988-92).
HIGH SCHOOL: LaVega (Waco, Texas).
TRANSACTIONS/CAREER NOTES: Selected by Baltimore Orioles organization in second round of free-agent draft (June 1, 1988). ... On Hagerstown disabled list (May 13-June 5, 1991). ... On Baltimore disabled list (May 16-August 2, 1993); included rehabilitation assignment to Rochester (July 4-August 2). ... On Baltimore disabled list (May 2-20, 1994); included rehabilitation assignment to Frederick (May 16-20). ... On Baltimore disabled list (August 25, 1995-remainder of season). ... On disabled list (July 14-August 2 and August 6-September 27, 1996).
HONORS: Named Eastern League Pitcher of the Year (1991).
MISCELLANEOUS: Appeared in one game as pinch-runner (1997).

Year — Team (League)	W	L	Pct.	ERA	G	GS	CG	ShO	Sv.	IP	H	R	ER	BB	SO
1988— Bluefield (Appalachian)	3	4	.429	3.31	11	7	0	0	0	35⅓	29	17	13	15	44
1989— Erie (N.Y.-Penn).................	2	0	1.000	1.16	5	5	1	0	0	31	13	7	4	10	45
— Frederick (Carolina)...........	2	2	.500	5.18	7	6	0	0	0	24⅓	19	16	14	19	28
1990— Frederick (Carolina)..........	4	6	.400	2.12	13	13	3	0	0	80⅔	62	25	19	21	103
— Hagerstown (Eastern)	3	4	.429	3.73	12	12	0	0	0	72⅓	62	32	30	39	60
1991— Hagerstown (Eastern)	7	4	.636	2.70	19	19	2	2	0	106⅔	73	37	32	47	115
— Baltimore (A.L.).................	0	3	.000	8.00	8	8	0	0	0	36	47	35	32	23	23
1992— Rochester (Int'l)	6	6	.500	3.72	17	17	1	0	0	101⅔	84	48	42	46	115
— Baltimore (A.L.).................	7	5	.583	3.63	15	15	2	1	0	94⅓	87	39	38	38	77
1993— Baltimore (A.L.)...............	5	6	.455	6.51	17	17	0	0	0	85⅔	91	62	62	49	49
— Rochester (Int'l)	1	1	.500	4.05	6	6	0	0	0	26⅔	26	12	12	15	33
1994— Baltimore (A.L.)...............	3	5	.375	5.81	10	10	3	2	0	52⅔	51	34	34	30	47
— Frederick (Carolina)...........	0	0	...	0.00	1	1	0	0	0	5	3	0	0	0	7
— Rochester (Int'l)	7	5	.583	2.79	15	15	3	0	0	90⅓	70	41	28	34	86
1995— Rochester (Int'l)	2	1	.667	2.70	4	4	1	0	0	30	27	12	9	8	33
— Baltimore (A.L.).................	2	5	.286	6.21	19	9	0	0	0	75⅓	68	53	52	48	77
1996— Baltimore (A.L.)...............	9	1	.900	4.08	28	2	0	0	1	53	48	28	24	23	62
1997— Baltimore (A.L.)...............	10	3	.769	3.02	53	0	0	0	0	95⅓	75	32	32	26	102
Major league totals (7 years)......	36	28	.563	5.01	150	61	5	3	2	492⅓	467	283	274	237	437

DIVISION SERIES RECORD

Year — Team (League)	W	L	Pct.	ERA	G	GS	CG	ShO	Sv.	IP	H	R	ER	BB	SO
1996— Baltimore (A.L.)...............	0	0	...	9.00	2	0	0	0	0	1	1	1	1	1	1
1997— Baltimore (A.L.)...............	0	0	...	0.00	1	0	0	0	0	2⅓	0	0	0	0	4
Div. series totals (2 years)	0	0	...	2.70	3	0	0	0	0	3⅓	1	1	1	1	5

CHAMPIONSHIP SERIES RECORD

Year — Team (League)	W	L	Pct.	ERA	G	GS	CG	ShO	Sv.	IP	H	R	ER	BB	SO
1996— Baltimore (A.L.)...............	0	0	...	0.00	3	0	0	0	0	2	2	0	0	0	2
1997— Baltimore (A.L.)...............	0	0	...	0.00	2	0	0	0	0	2⅓	2	0	0	3	2
Champ. series totals (2 years)	0	0	...	0.00	5	0	0	0	0	4⅓	4	0	0	3	4

R

RICHARD, CHRIS — 1B/OF — CARDINALS

PERSONAL: Born June 7, 1974, in San Diego. ... 6-2/190. ... Bats left, throws left. ... Full name: Christopher R. Richard.
HIGH SCHOOL: University City (San Diego).
JUNIOR COLLEGE: San Diego City College and San Diego Mesa College.
COLLEGE: Oklahoma State.
TRANSACTIONS/CAREER NOTES: Selected by St. Louis Cardinals organization in 19th round of free-agent draft (June 1, 1995).

Year Team (League)	Pos.	G	AB	R	H	2B	3B	HR	RBI	Avg.	BB	SO	SB	PO	A	E	Avg.
1995— New Jersey (NYP)......	1B	75	284	36	80	14	3	3	43	.282	47	31	6	620	43	11	.984
1996— St. Petersburg (FSL)..	1B-OF	129	460	65	130	28	6	14	82	.283	57	50	7	1138	58	7	.994
1997— Arkansas (Texas)........	1B-OF	113	390	62	105	24	3	11	58	.269	60	59	6	924	68	10	.990

RICHARDSON, BRIAN — 3B — DODGERS

PERSONAL: Born August 31, 1975, in Los Angeles. ... 6-2/198. ... Throws right, bats right. ... Full name: Brian Christian Richardson.
HIGH SCHOOL: Saint Bernard (Eureka, Calif.).
TRANSACTIONS/CAREER NOTES: Selected by Los Angeles Dodgers organization in seventh round of free-agent draft (June 3, 1991).
STATISTICAL NOTES: Led California League third basemen with 254 assists and 363 total chances and tied for lead with 82 putouts in 1995. ... Led Pacific Coast League third basemen with 25 errors in 1996. ... Led Texas League third basemen with .946 fielding percentage and 268 assists in 1997.

Year Team (League)	Pos.	G	AB	R	H	2B	3B	HR	RBI	Avg.	BB	SO	SB	PO	A	E	Avg.
1992— GC Dodgers (GCL)	3B	37	122	8	26	6	2	0	15	.213	11	27	3	25	54	15	.840
1993— Great Falls (Pio.).......	3B-1B	54	178	16	40	11	0	0	13	.225	14	47	1	29	107	26	.840
1994— Vero Beach (FSL)	3B-1B	19	52	3	12	0	1	0	3	.231	4	15	2	62	16	6	.929
— Yakima (N'west)	1B-3B	70	266	35	62	15	0	5	42	.233	35	82	12	384	93	14	.971
1995— San Bernardino (Calif.)	3B-1B	127	462	68	131	18	1	12	58	.284	35	122	17	‡123	†258	27	.934
1996— San Antonio (Texas)...	3B	19	62	10	20	1	1	0	7	.323	2	10	0	11	38	4	.925
— Albuquerque (PCL).....	3B-2B-SS	105	355	52	87	17	2	9	43	.245	32	89	4	66	186	25	.910
1997— San Antonio (Tex.)	3B-1B	133	484	73	144	23	*13	13	90	.298	42	97	3	94	†270	21	†.945

RIGBY, BRAD — P — ATHLETICS

PERSONAL: Born May 14, 1973, in Milwaukee. ... 6-6/195. ... Throws right, bats right. ... Full name: Bradley Kenneth Rigby.
HIGH SCHOOL: Lake Brantley (Altamonte Springs, Fla.).
COLLEGE: Georgia Tech.
TRANSACTIONS/CAREER NOTES: Selected by Oakland Athletics organization in second round of free-agent draft (June 2, 1994). ... On Oakland disabled list (August 8-23, 1997).

Year Team (League)	W	L	Pct.	ERA	G	GS	CG	ShO	Sv.	IP	H	R	ER	BB	SO
1994— Modesto (California)	2	1	.667	3.80	11	1	0	0	2	23²/₃	20	10	10	10	28
1995— Modesto (California)	11	4	.733	3.84	31	23	0	0	2	154²/₃	135	79	66	48	145
1996— Huntsville (Southern)	9	12	.429	3.95	26	26	3	0	0	159¹/₃	161	89	70	59	127
1997— Edmonton (PCL)	8	4	.667	4.37	15	15	0	0	0	82¹/₃	95	49	40	26	49
— Oakland (A.L.)	1	7	.125	4.87	14	14	0	0	0	77²/₃	92	44	42	22	34
Major league totals (1 year).......	**1**	**7**	**.125**	**4.87**	**14**	**14**	**0**	**0**	**0**	**77²/₃**	**92**	**44**	**42**	**22**	**34**

RIGGS, ADAM — 2B — DODGERS

PERSONAL: Born October 4, 1972, in Steubenville, Ohio. ... 6-0/194. ... Bats right, throws right.
HIGH SCHOOL: Lenape Valley (Stanhope, N.J.).
COLLEGE: South Carolina-Aiken.
TRANSACTIONS/CAREER NOTES: Selected by Los Angeles Dodgers organization in 22nd round of free-agent draft (June 2, 1994). ... On Albuquerque disabled list (April 4-June 9, 1997).
HONORS: Named California League Most Valuable Player (1995).
STATISTICAL NOTES: Led California League with 317 total bases and .431 on-base percentage in 1995. ... Led Texas League second basemen with 717 total chances and 91 double plays in 1996.

Year Team (League)	Pos.	G	AB	R	H	2B	3B	HR	RBI	Avg.	BB	SO	SB	PO	A	E	Avg.
1994— Yakima (N'west)	2B	4	7	1	2	1	0	0	0	.286	0	1	0				...
— Great Falls (Pio.)	2B	62	234	55	73	20	3	5	44	.312	31	38	19	93	133	23	.908
1995— San Bern. (Calif.)	2B	134	*542	*111	*196	*39	5	24	106	*.362	59	93	31	223	303	*41	.928
1996— San Antonio (Tex.)	2B	134	506	68	143	31	6	14	66	.283	37	82	16	*295	*395	27	.962
1997— Albuquerque (PCL).....	2B-3B-OF	57	227	59	69	8	3	13	28	.304	29	39	12	131	162	8	.973
— Los Angeles (N.L.)	2B	9	20	3	4	1	0	0	1	.200	4	3	1	6	19	0	1.000
Major league totals (1 year)		**9**	**20**	**3**	**4**	**1**	**0**	**0**	**1**	**.200**	**4**	**3**	**1**	**6**	**19**	**0**	**1.000**

RINCON, RICARDO — P — PIRATES

PERSONAL: Born April 13, 1970, in Veracruz, Mexico ... 6-0/190. ... Throws left, bats left. ... Full name: Ricardo Rincon Espinoza.
TRANSACTIONS/CAREER NOTES: Signed as non-drafted free agent by Pittsburgh Pirates organization (March 30, 1997).

Year Team (League)	W	L	Pct.	ERA	G	GS	CG	ShO	Sv.	IP	H	R	ER	BB	SO
1990— Union Laguna (Mex.)	3	0	1.000	3.78	19	4	0	0	0	47²/₃	53	22	20	32	29
1991— Union Laguna (Mex.)	2	8	.200	6.54	32	9	0	0	0	74¹/₃	99	60	54	48	66
1992— Union Laguna (Mex.)	6	5	.545	3.91	49	9	0	0	4	89²/₃	87	45	39	46	91
1993— Torreon (Mexican)■..........	7	3	.700	3.17	—	57	4	0	8	82¹/₃	80	33	29	36	81
1994— M.C. Red Devils (Mex.)■■..	2	4	.333	3.21	20	9	0	1	1	53¹/₃	57	23	19	20	38
1995— M.C. Red Devils (Mex.)	6	6	.500	5.16	27	11	0	0	3	75	86	45	43	41	41

Year Team (League)	W	L	Pct.	ERA	G	GS	CG	ShO	Sv.	IP	H	R	ER	BB	SO
1996— M.C. Red Devils (Mex.)	5	3	.625	2.97	50	0	0	0	10	78²/₃	58	28	26	27	60
1997— Pittsburgh (N.L.)■	4	8	.333	3.45	62	0	0	0	4	60	51	26	23	24	71
Major league totals (1 year)	4	8	.333	3.45	62	0	0	0	4	60	51	26	23	24	71

RIOS, ARMANDO — OF — GIANTS

PERSONAL: Born September 13, 1971, in Santurce, Puerto Rico. ... 5-9/185. ... Bats left, throws left.
HIGH SCHOOL: Villa Fontana (Carolina, Puerto Rico).
JUNIOR COLLEGE: North Carolina-Charlotte, then Louisiana State.
TRANSACTIONS/CAREER NOTES: Signed as non-drafted free agent by San Francisco Giants organization (January 6, 1994). ... On disabled list (May 15-29, 1996).

										BATTING				FIELDING		
Year Team (League)	Pos.	G	AB	R	H	2B	3B	HR	RBI	Avg.	BB	SO	SB	PO	A	E	Avg.
1994— Clinton (Midwest)	OF	119	407	67	120	23	4	8	60	.295	59	69	16	216	17	12	.951
1995— San Jose (Calif.)	OF	128	488	76	143	34	3	8	75	.293	74	75	51	220	16	9	.963
1996— Shreveport (Texas)	OF	92	329	62	93	22	2	12	49	.283	44	42	9	165	*15	7	.963
1997— Shreveport (Texas)	OF	127	461	86	133	30	6	14	79	.289	63	85	17	191	*17	6	.972

RIOS, DAN — P — YANKEES

PERSONAL: Born November 11, 1972, in Madrid, Spain. ... 6-2/190. ... Throws right, bats right. ... Full name: Daniel Rios.
JUNIOR COLLEGE: Seminole Community College (Fla.).
COLLEGE: Miami (Fla.).
TRANSACTIONS/CAREER NOTES: Signed as non-drafted free agent by New York Yankees organization (June 7, 1993).

Year Team (League)	W	L	Pct.	ERA	G	GS	CG	ShO	Sv.	IP	H	R	ER	BB	SO
1993— GC Yankees (GCL)	2	0	1.000	3.52	24	0	0	0	6	38¹/₃	34	18	15	16	29
1994— Greensboro (S. Atl.)	3	2	.600	0.87	37	0	0	0	17	41¹/₃	32	4	4	13	36
— Tampa (Florida State)	0	0	...	0.00	9	0	0	0	2	10¹/₃	6	2	0	4	11
1995— Tampa (Florida State)	0	4	.000	2.00	57	0	0	0	24	67¹/₃	67	24	15	20	72
1996— Norwich (Eastern)	3	1	.750	2.09	38	0	0	0	17	43	34	14	10	21	38
— Columbus (Int'l)	4	1	.800	1.95	24	0	0	0	0	27²/₃	22	7	6	6	22
1997— Columbus (Int'l)	7	4	.636	3.08	58	0	0	0	3	84²/₃	73	37	29	31	53
— New York (A.L.)	0	0	...	19.29	2	0	0	0	0	2¹/₃	9	5	5	2	1
Major league totals (1 year)	0	0	...	19.29	2	0	0	0	0	2¹/₃	9	5	5	2	1

RIPKEN, BILLY — IF — TIGERS

PERSONAL: Born December 16, 1964, in Havre de Grace, Md. ... 6-1/190. ... Bats right, throws right. ... Full name: William Oliver Ripken. ... Son of Cal Ripken Sr., minor league catcher (1957-62 and 1964), manager, Baltimore Orioles (1987-88), and coach, Orioles (1976-86 and 1989-92); and brother of Cal Ripken Jr., shortstop, Orioles.
HIGH SCHOOL: Aberdeen (Md.).
TRANSACTIONS/CAREER NOTES: Selected by Baltimore Orioles organization in 11th round of free-agent draft (June 7, 1982). ... On disabled list (April 20-May 3, 1984; June 23-July 6, 1985; March 27-April 14 and August 23-September 7, 1989; and August 5-20, 1990). ... On Baltimore disabled list (July 15-August 15, 1991; included rehabilitation assignments to Frederick (August 12-13) and Hagerstown (August 13-15). ... Released by Orioles (December 11, 1992). ... Signed by Texas Rangers organization (February 1, 1993). ... On Texas disabled list (May 13-28 and June 21-September 1, 1993). ... Granted free agency (October 4, 1993). ... Re-signed by Rangers organization (December 18, 1993). ... On disabled list (May 10-25 and July 16, 1994-remainder of season). ... Granted free agency (October 14, 1994). ... Signed by Buffalo, Cleveland Indians organization (March 25, 1995). ... Granted free agency (November 2, 1995). ... Signed by Orioles organization (December 23, 1995). ... Granted free agency (October 29, 1996). ... Signed by Texas Rangers (December 10, 1996). ... On disabled list (June 18-July 6 and July 25-August 8, 1997). ... Granted free agency (October 30, 1997). ... Signed by Detroit Tigers organization (December 16, 1997).
STATISTICAL NOTES: Led Southern League second basemen with 723 total chances and 79 double plays in 1986. ... Tied for Southern League lead in grounding into double plays with 21 in 1986. ... Tied for A.L. lead with 17 sacrifice hits in 1990. ... Tied for American Association lead with eight sacrifice flies in 1995. ... Led American Association shortstops with .978 fielding percentage, 389 assists and 80 double plays in 1995.

										BATTING				FIELDING		
Year Team (League)	Pos.	G	AB	R	H	2B	3B	HR	RBI	Avg.	BB	SO	SB	PO	A	E	Avg.
1982— Bluefield (Appal.)	SS-3B-2B	27	45	8	11	1	0	0	4	.244	8	6	0	15	17	3	.914
1983— Bluefield (Appal.)	SS-3B	48	152	24	33	6	0	0	13	.217	12	13	7	82	145	23	.908
1984— Hagerstown (Car.)	SS-2B	115	409	48	94	15	3	2	40	.230	36	64	3	187	358	28	.951
1985— Charlotte (Southern) ...	SS	18	51	2	7	1	0	0	3	.137	6	4	0	18	52	4	.946
— Daytona Beach (FSL)..	SS-3B-2B	67	222	23	51	11	0	0	18	.230	22	24	7	90	198	8	.973
1986— Charlotte (Southern) ..	2B	141	530	58	142	20	3	5	62	.268	24	47	9	*305	*395	*23	.968
1987— Rochester (Int'l)	2B-SS	74	238	32	68	15	0	0	11	.286	21	24	7	154	200	9	.975
— Baltimore (A.L.)	2B	58	234	27	72	9	0	2	20	.308	21	23	4	133	162	3	.990
1988— Baltimore (A.L.)	2B-3B-DH	150	512	52	106	18	1	2	34	.207	33	63	8	310	440	12	.984
1989— Baltimore (A.L.)	2B	115	318	31	76	11	2	2	26	.239	22	53	1	255	335	9	.985
1990— Baltimore (A.L.)	2B	129	406	48	118	28	1	3	38	.291	28	43	5	250	366	8	.987
1991— Baltimore (A.L.)	2B	104	287	24	62	11	1	0	14	.216	15	31	0	201	284	7	.986
— Frederick (Carolina)....	DH	1	4	2	1	0	0	0	1	.250	0	1	0	...	...	...	...
— Hagerstown (Eastern)	2B	1	5	1	3	0	0	0	0	.600	0	0	1	2	1	0	1.000
1992— Baltimore (A.L.)	2B-DH	111	330	35	76	15	0	4	36	.230	18	26	2	217	317	4	*.993
1993— Texas (A.L.)■	2B-SS-3B	50	132	12	25	4	0	0	11	.189	11	19	0	80	123	2	.990
1994— Texas (A.L.)	3-2-S-1	32	81	9	25	5	0	0	6	.309	3	11	2	29	50	2	.975
1995— Buffalo (A.A.)■	SS-2B	130	448	51	131	34	1	4	56	.292	28	38	6	163	†401	12	†.979
— Cleveland (A.L.)	2B-3B	8	17	4	7	0	0	2	3	.412	0	3	0	7	6	0	1.000
1996— Baltimore (A.L.)■........	2B-3B-1B	57	135	19	31	8	0	2	12	.230	9	18	0	40	95	3	.978
1997— Texas (A.L.)■	S-2-3-1	71	203	18	56	9	1	3	24	.276	9	32	0	116	158	5	.982
Major league totals (11 years)		885	2655	279	654	118	6	20	224	.246	169	322	22	1638	2336	55	.986

R

PERSONAL: Born August 24, 1960, in Havre de Grace, Md. ... 6-4/220. ... Bats right, throws right. ... Full name: Calvin Edwin Ripken Jr. ... Son of Cal Ripken Sr., minor league catcher (1957-62 and 1964), manager, Baltimore Orioles (1987-88), and coach, Orioles (1976-86 and 1989-92); and brother of Bill Ripken, infielder, Detroit Tigers.

HIGH SCHOOL: Aberdeen (Md.).

TRANSACTIONS/CAREER NOTES: Selected by Baltimore Orioles organization in second round of free-agent draft (June 6, 1978).

RECORDS: Holds major league career records for most consecutive games played—2,478 (May 30, 1982 to present); most consecutive years leading league in games played—9; most consecutive years played all club's games—15 (1983 to present); most years played all club's games—15; most home runs by shortstop—345; most years leading league in games by shortstop—12; most consecutive games by shortstop—2,216; and most years leading league in double plays by shortstop—8. ... Holds major league single-season records for most at-bats without a triple—646 (1989); highest fielding percentage by shortstop—.996 (1990); fewest errors by shortstop (150 or more games)—3 (1990); most consecutive errorless games by shortstop—95 (April 14 through July 27, 1990); and most consecutive chances accepted by shortstop without an error—431 (April 14-July 28, 1990, first game). ... Holds A.L. career records for most double plays by shortstop—1,565; most years leading league in putouts by shortstop—6; and most years with 600 or more at-bats—12. ... Holds A.L. single-season record for most assists by shortstop—583 (1984). ... Shares A.L. career records for most years leading league in assists by shortstop—7; and most years with 150 or more games played—14.

HONORS: Named A.L. Rookie Player of the Year by The Sporting News (1982). ... Named A.L. Rookie of the Year by Baseball Writers' Association of America (1982). ... Named Major League Player of the Year by The Sporting News (1983 and 1991). ... Named A.L. Player of the Year by The Sporting News (1983 and 1991). ... Named shortstop on The Sporting News A.L. All-Star team (1983-85, 1989, 1991 and 1993-95). ... Named shortstop on The Sporting News A.L. Silver Slugger team (1983-86, 1989, 1991 and 1993-94). ... Named A.L. Most Valuable Player by Baseball Writers' Association of America (1983 and 1991). ... Won A.L. Gold Glove at shortstop (1991-92). ... Named Sportsman of the Year by The Sporting News (1995).

STATISTICAL NOTES: Tied for Appalachian League lead in double plays by shortstop with 31 in 1978. ... Led Southern League third basemen with .933 fielding percentage, 119 putouts, 268 assists, 415 total chances and 34 double plays in 1980. ... Tied for Southern League lead with nine sacrifice flies in 1980. ... Led A.L. shortstops with 831 total chances in 1983, 906 in 1984, 815 in 1989, 806 in 1991 and 738 in 1993. ... Led A.L. shortstops with 113 double plays in 1983, 122 in 1984, 123 in 1985, 119 in 1989, 114 in 1991, 119 in 1992, 72 in 1994 and 100 in 1995. ... Hit for the cycle (May 6, 1984). ... Tied for A.L. lead with 15 game-winning RBIs in 1986. ... Tied for A.L. lead with 10 sacrifice flies in 1988. ... Led A.L. with 368 total bases in 1991. ... Hit three home runs in one game (May 28, 1996). ... Led A.L. in grounding into double plays with 28 in 1996. ... Career major league grand slams: 7.

MISCELLANEOUS: Holds Baltimore Orioles all-time records for most runs (1,445), most doubles (517), most home runs (370) and most runs batted in (1,453).

Year	Team (League)	Pos.	G	AB	R	H	2B	3B	HR	RBI	Avg.	BB	SO	SB	PO	A	E	Avg.
									BATTING						FIELDING			
1978—Bluefield (Appal.)		SS	63	239	27	63	7	1	0	24	.264	24	46	1	*92	204	*33	.900
1979—Miami (Fla. St.)		3B-SS-2B	105	393	51	119	*28	1	5	54	.303	31	64	4	149	260	30	.932
—Charlotte (Southern)		3B	17	61	6	11	0	1	3	8	.180	3	13	1	13	26	3	.929
1980—Charlotte (Southern)		3B-SS	•144	522	91	144	28	5	25	78	.276	77	81	4	†151	†341	35	†.934
1981—Rochester (Int'l)		3B-SS	114	437	74	126	31	4	23	75	.288	66	85	0	128	320	21	.955
—Baltimore		SS-3B	23	39	1	5	0	0	0	0	.128	1	8	0	13	30	3	.935
1982—Baltimore (A.L.)		SS-3B	160	598	90	158	32	5	28	93	.264	46	95	3	221	440	19	.972
1983—Baltimore (A.L.)		SS	•162	*663	*121	211	*47	2	27	102	.318	58	97	0	272	*534	25	.970
1984—Baltimore (A.L.)		SS	•162	641	103	195	37	7	27	86	.304	71	89	2	*297	*583	26	.971
1985—Baltimore (A.L.)		SS	161	642	116	181	32	5	26	110	.282	67	68	2	*286	474	26	.967
1986—Baltimore (A.L.)		SS	162	627	98	177	35	1	25	81	.282	70	60	4	240	*482	13	.982
1987—Baltimore (A.L.)		SS	*162	624	97	157	28	3	27	98	.252	81	77	3	240	*480	20	.973
1988—Baltimore (A.L.)		SS	161	575	87	152	25	1	23	81	.264	102	69	2	*284	480	21	.973
1989—Baltimore (A.L.)		SS	•162	646	80	166	30	0	21	93	.257	57	72	3	*276	*531	8	.990
1990—Baltimore (A.L.)		SS	161	600	78	150	28	4	21	84	.250	82	66	3	242	435	3	*.996
1991—Baltimore (A.L.)		SS	•162	650	99	210	46	5	34	114	.323	53	46	6	*267	*528	11	*.986
1992—Baltimore (A.L.)		SS	*162	637	73	160	29	1	14	72	.251	64	50	4	*287	445	12	.984
1993—Baltimore (A.L.)		SS	*162	*641	87	165	26	3	24	90	.257	65	58	1	226	*495	17	.977
1994—Baltimore (A.L.)		SS	112	444	71	140	19	3	13	75	.315	32	41	1	132	321	7	*.985
1995—Baltimore (A.L.)		SS	144	550	71	144	33	2	17	88	.262	52	59	0	206	409	7	*.989
1996—Baltimore (A.L.)		SS-3B	*163	640	94	178	40	1	26	102	.278	59	78	1	233	483	14	.981
1997—Baltimore (A.L.)		3B-SS	•162	615	79	166	30	0	17	84	.270	56	73	1	100	313	22	.949
Major league totals (17 years)			2543	9832	1445	2715	517	43	370	1453	.276	1016	1106	36	3822	7463	254	.978

DIVISION SERIES RECORD

RECORDS: Holds career records for highest batting average (20 or more at-bats)—.441; and most doubles—5.

Year	Team (League)	Pos.	G	AB	R	H	2B	3B	HR	RBI	Avg.	BB	SO	SB	PO	A	E	Avg.
									BATTING						FIELDING			
1996—Baltimore (A.L.)		SS	4	18	2	8	3	0	0	2	.444	0	3	0	7	15	0	1.000
1997—Baltimore (A.L.)		3B	4	16	1	7	2	0	0	1	.438	2	2	0	4	4	0	1.000
Division series totals (2 years)			8	34	3	15	5	0	0	3	.441	2	5	0	11	19	0	1.000

CHAMPIONSHIP SERIES RECORD

Year	Team (League)	Pos.	G	AB	R	H	2B	3B	HR	RBI	Avg.	BB	SO	SB	PO	A	E	Avg.
									BATTING						FIELDING			
1983—Baltimore (A.L.)		SS	4	15	5	6	2	0	0	1	.400	2	3	0	7	11	0	1.000
1996—Baltimore (A.L.)		SS	5	20	1	5	1	0	0	0	.250	1	4	0	4	14	1	.947
1997—Baltimore (A.L.)		3B	6	23	3	8	2	0	1	3	.348	4	6	0	1	14	0	1.000
Championship series totals (3 years)			15	58	9	19	5	0	1	4	.328	7	13	0	12	39	1	.981

WORLD SERIES RECORD

NOTES: Member of World Series championship team (1983).

Year	Team (League)	Pos.	G	AB	R	H	2B	3B	HR	RBI	Avg.	BB	SO	SB	PO	A	E	Avg.
									BATTING						FIELDING			
1983—Baltimore (A.L.)		SS	5	18	2	3	0	0	0	1	.167	3	4	0	6	14	0	1.000

ALL-STAR GAME RECORD

RECORDS: Shares single-game record for most at-bats in nine-inning game—5 (July 12, 1994).

NOTES: Named Most Valuable Player (1991).

Year	League	Pos.	AB	R	H	2B	3B	HR	RBI	Avg.	BB	SO	SB	PO	A	E	Avg.
1983—American		SS	0	0	0	0	0	0	0	...	1	0	0	1	0	0	1.000
1984—American		SS	3	0	0	0	0	0	0	.000	0	0	0	0	0	0	...
1985—American		SS	3	0	1	0	0	0	0	.333	0	0	0	2	1	0	1.000
1986—American		SS	4	0	0	0	0	0	0	.000	0	0	0	0	1	0	1.000
1987—American		SS	2	0	1	0	0	0	0	.500	0	0	0	0	5	0	1.000
1988—American		SS	3	0	0	0	0	0	0	.000	1	0	0	1	4	0	1.000
1989—American		SS	3	0	1	1	0	0	0	.333	0	0	0	0	0	0	...
1990—American		SS	2	0	0	0	0	0	0	.000	0	0	0	1	1	0	1.000
1991—American		SS	3	1	2	0	0	1	3	.667	0	0	0	2	1	0	1.000
1992—American		SS	3	0	1	0	0	0	0	.333	0	0	0	1	1	0	1.000
1993—American		SS	3	0	0	0	0	0	0	.000	0	1	0	1	2	0	1.000
1994—American		SS	5	0	1	1	0	0	0	.200	0	2	0	1	2	0	1.000
1995—American		SS	3	0	2	0	0	0	0	.667	0	0	0	2	1	0	1.000
1996—American		SS	3	0	0	0	0	0	0	.000	0	0	0	1	1	0	1.000
1997—American		3B	2	0	1	0	0	0	0	.500	0	0	0	0	4	0	1.000
All-Star Game totals (15 years)			42	1	10	2	0	1	4	.238	2	3	0	13	24	0	1.000

RISLEY, BILL   P   BLUE JAYS

PERSONAL: Born May 29, 1967, in Chicago. ... 6-2/220. ... Throws right, bats right. ... Full name: William Charles Risley. ... Name pronounced RIZZ-lee.

HIGH SCHOOL: Marist (Chicago).

TRANSACTIONS/CAREER NOTES: Selected by Cincinnati Reds organization in 14th round of free-agent draft (June 2, 1987). ... Traded by Reds with P John Wetteland to Montreal Expos for OF Dave Martinez, P Scott Ruskin and SS Willie Greene (December 11, 1991). ... On Indianapolis disabled list (April 9-20 and May 16-June 3, 1992). ... On Ottawa disabled list (April 8-23 and June 30-July 10, 1993). ... Claimed on waivers by Seattle Mariners (March 17, 1994). ... On Seattle disabled list (May 29-June 13, 1995); included rehabilitation assignment to Tacoma (June 12-13). ... Traded by Mariners with 2B Miguel Cairo to Toronto Blue Jays for P Edwin Hurtado and P Paul Menhart (December 18, 1995). ... On Toronto disabled list (May 10-June 11 and June 26-July 31, 1996); included rehabilitation assignments to Syracuse (June 6-9) and St. Catharines (July 19-31). ... On Toronto disabled list (March 12-September 12, 1997); included rehabiliation assignment to Dunedin (May 22-September 1).

STATISTICAL NOTES: Tied for Southern League lead with five balks in 1991.

Year	Team (League)	W	L	Pct.	ERA	G	GS	CG	ShO	Sv.	IP	H	R	ER	BB	SO
1987—GC Reds (GCL)		1	4	.200	1.89	11	11	0	0	0	52 1/3	38	24	11	26	50
1988—Greensboro (S. Atl.)		8	4	.667	4.11	23	23	3	3	0	120 1/3	82	60	55	84	135
1989—Cedar Rapids (Midw.)		9	10	.474	3.90	27	27	2	0	0	140 2/3	87	72	61	81	128
1990—Cedar Rapids (Midw.)		8	9	.471	2.81	22	22	•7	1	0	137 2/3	99	51	43	68	123
1991—Chattanooga (Southern)		5	7	.417	3.16	19	19	3	0	0	108 1/3	81	48	38	60	77
—Nashville (A.A.)		3	5	.375	4.91	8	8	1	0	0	44	45	27	24	26	32
1992—Indianapolis (A.A.)■		5	8	.385	6.40	25	15	0	0	0	95 2/3	105	69	68	47	64
—Montreal (N.L.)		1	0	1.000	1.80	1	1	0	0	0	5	4	1	1	1	2
1993—Ottawa (Int'l)		2	4	.333	2.69	41	0	0	0	1	63 2/3	51	26	19	34	74
—Montreal (N.L.)		0	0	...	6.00	2	0	0	0	0	3	2	3	2	2	2
1994—Calgary (PCL)■		0	0	...	3.00	6	1	0	0	1	12	13	5	4	4	15
—Seattle (A.L.)		9	6	.600	3.44	37	0	0	0	0	52 1/3	31	20	20	19	61
1995—Tacoma (PCL)		0	0	...	0.00	1	0	0	0	0	1	0	0	0	1	2
—Seattle (A.L.)		2	1	.667	3.13	45	0	0	0	1	60 1/3	55	21	21	18	65
1996—Toronto (A.L.)■		0	1	.000	3.89	25	0	0	0	0	41 2/3	33	20	18	25	29
—Syracuse (Int'l)		0	0	...	0.00	2	0	0	0	0	1	0	1	0	1	0
—St. Catharines (NYP)		0	0	...	1.29	3	1	0	0	0	7	3	1	1	2	10
1997—Dunedin (Fla. St.)		0	2	.000	4.50	8	6	0	0	0	12	9	9	6	3	11
—Syracuse (Int'l)		1	2	.333	8.22	11	1	0	0	0	15 1/3	19	15	14	10	20
—Toronto (A.L.)		0	1	.000	8.31	3	0	0	0	0	4 1/3	3	4	4	2	2
A.L. totals (4 years)		11	9	.550	3.57	110	0	0	0	1	158 2/3	122	65	63	64	157
N.L. totals (2 years)		1	0	1.000	3.38	3	1	0	0	0	8	6	4	3	3	4
Major league totals (6 years)		12	9	.571	3.56	113	1	0	0	1	166 2/3	128	69	66	67	161

DIVISION SERIES RECORD

Year	Team (League)	W	L	Pct.	ERA	G	GS	CG	ShO	Sv.	IP	H	R	ER	BB	SO
1995—Seattle (A.L.)		0	0	...	6.00	4	0	0	0	1	3	2	2	2	0	1

CHAMPIONSHIP SERIES RECORD

Year	Team (League)	W	L	Pct.	ERA	G	GS	CG	ShO	Sv.	IP	H	R	ER	BB	SO
1995—Seattle (A.L.)		0	0	...	0.00	3	0	0	0	0	2 2/3	2	0	0	1	2

RITCHIE, TODD   P   TWINS

PERSONAL: Born November 7, 1971, in Portsmouth, Va. ... 6-3/205. ... Throws right, bats right. ... Full name: Todd Everett Ritchie.

HIGH SCHOOL: Duncanville (Texas).

TRANSACTIONS/CAREER NOTES: Selected by Minnesota Twins organization in first round (12th pick overall) of free-agent draft (June 4, 1990). ... On disabled list (August 19, 1991-remainder of season; June 24-July 9, 1993; and April 28, 1994-remainder of season).

Year	Team (League)	W	L	Pct.	ERA	G	GS	CG	ShO	Sv.	IP	H	R	ER	BB	SO
1990—Elizabethton (Appal.)		5	2	.714	1.94	11	11	1	0	0	65	45	22	14	24	49
1991—Kenosha (Midwest)		7	6	.538	3.55	21	21	0	0	0	116 2/3	113	53	46	50	101
1992—Visalia (California)		11	9	.550	5.06	28	•28	3	1	0	172 2/3	193	113	97	65	129
1993—Nashville (Southern)		3	2	.600	3.66	12	10	0	0	0	46 2/3	46	21	19	15	41
1994—Nashville (Southern)		0	2	.000	4.24	4	4	0	0	0	17	24	10	8	7	9
1995—New Britain (East.)		4	9	.308	5.73	24	21	0	0	0	113	135	78	72	54	60
1996—New Britain (East.)		3	7	.300	5.44	29	11	0	0	4	82 2/3	101	55	50	30	53
—Salt Lake (PCL)		0	4	.000	5.47	16	0	0	0	0	24 2/3	27	15	15	11	19
1997—Minnesota (A.L.)		2	3	.400	4.58	42	0	0	0	0	74 2/3	87	41	38	28	44
Major league totals (1 year)		2	3	.400	4.58	42	0	0	0	0	74 2/3	87	41	38	28	44

RITZ, KEVIN　　　　　　　　P　　　　　　　　ROCKIES

PERSONAL: Born June 8, 1965, in Eatonstown, N.J. ... 6-4/222. ... Throws right, bats right. ... Full name: Kevin D. Ritz.
HIGH SCHOOL: Davis County (Iowa).
JUNIOR COLLEGE: Indian Hills Community College (Ia.).
COLLEGE: William Penn (Ia.).
TRANSACTIONS/CAREER NOTES: Selected by San Francisco Giants organization in fourth round of free-agent draft (January 9, 1985); did not sign. ... Selected by Detroit Tigers organization in secondary phase of free-agent draft (June 3, 1985). ... On Detroit disabled list (August 4, 1992-remainder of season). ... Selected by Colorado Rockies in second round (46th pick overall) of expansion draft (November 17, 1992). ... On disabled list (April 4, 1993-entire season). ... Released by Rockies (October 12, 1993). ... Re-signed by Rockies organization (December 1, 1993). ... On disabled list (July 11, 1997-remainder of season).
MISCELLANEOUS: Holds Colorado Rockies all-time records for most wins (39), most strikeouts (334) and most innings pitched (567.1).

Year　Team (League)	W	L	Pct.	ERA	G	GS	CG	ShO	Sv.	IP	H	R	ER	BB	SO
1986— Gastonia (S. Atl.)	1	2	.333	4.21	7	7	0	0	0	36 1/3	29	19	17	21	34
— Lakeland (Fla. St.)	3	9	.250	5.57	18	15	0	0	1	85 2/3	114	60	53	45	39
1987— Glens Falls (Eastern)	8	8	.500	4.89	25	25	1	0	0	152 2/3	171	95	83	71	78
1988— Glens Falls (Eastern)	8	10	.444	3.82	26	26	4	2	0	136 2/3	115	68	58	70	75
1989— Toledo (Int'l)	7	8	.467	3.16	16	16	1	0	0	102 2/3	95	48	36	60	74
— Detroit (A.L.)	4	6	.400	4.38	12	12	1	0	0	74	75	41	36	44	56
1990— Toledo (Int'l)	3	6	.333	5.22	20	18	0	0	0	89 2/3	93	68	52	59	57
— Detroit (A.L.)	0	4	.000	11.05	4	4	0	0	0	7 1/3	14	12	9	14	3
1991— Toledo (Int'l)	8	7	.533	3.28	20	19	3	0	0	126 1/3	116	50	46	60	105
— Detroit (A.L.)	0	3	.000	11.74	11	5	0	0	0	15 1/3	17	22	20	22	9
1992— Detroit (A.L.)	2	5	.286	5.60	23	11	0	0	0	80 1/3	88	52	50	44	57
1993—							Did not play.								
1994— Colo. Springs (PCL)■	5	0	1.000	1.29	9	3	1	0	1	35	26	6	5	6	27
— Colorado (N.L.)■	5	6	.455	5.62	15	15	0	0	0	73 2/3	88	49	46	35	53
1995— Colorado (N.L.)	11	11	.500	4.21	31	28	0	0	2	173 1/3	171	91	81	65	120
1996— Colorado (N.L.)	17	11	.607	5.28	35	35	2	0	0	213	236	*135	*125	105	105
1997— Colorado (N.L.)	6	8	.429	5.87	18	18	1	0	0	107 1/3	142	72	70	46	56
A.L. totals (4 years)	6	18	.250	5.85	50	32	1	0	0	177	194	127	115	124	125
N.L. totals (4 years)	39	36	.520	5.11	99	96	3	0	2	567 1/3	637	347	322	251	334
Major league totals (8 years)	45	54	.455	5.28	149	128	4	0	2	744 1/3	831	474	437	375	459

DIVISION SERIES RECORD

Year　Team (League)	W	L	Pct.	ERA	G	GS	CG	ShO	Sv.	IP	H	R	ER	BB	SO
1995— Colorado (N.L.)	0	0	...	7.71	2	1	0	0	0	7	12	7	6	3	5

RIVERA, LUIS　　　　　　　　SS/2B

PERSONAL: Born January 3, 1964, in Cidra, Puerto Rico. ... 5-9/175. ... Bats right, throws right. ... Full name: Luis Antonio Rivera.
HIGH SCHOOL: Luis Munoz Iglesias (Cidra, Puerto Rico).
TRANSACTIONS/CAREER NOTES: Signed as non-drafted free agent by Montreal Expos organization (September 22, 1981). ... Traded by Expos with P John Dopson to Boston Red Sox for SS Spike Owen and P Dan Gakeler (December 8, 1988). ... On disabled list (June 21-July 18 and August 21-September 5, 1993). ... Granted free agency (October 25, 1993). ... Signed by New York Mets (January 19, 1994). ... Granted free agency (October 24, 1994). ... Signed by St. Louis Cardinals organization (April 18, 1995). ... Released by St. Louis Cardinals (April 24, 1995). ... Signed by Texas Rangers organization (May 3, 1995). ... On disabled list (May 27-June 4, 1995). ... Released by Rangers organization (June 10, 1995). ... Signed by New York Mets organization (November 15, 1995). ... Granted free agency (October 15, 1996). ... Signed by Houston Astros organization (January 25, 1997). ...Granted free agency (October 27, 1997).
STATISTICAL NOTES: Led Florida State League shortstops with 704 total chances and 95 double plays in 1983. ... Tied for Florida State League lead in total chances by shortstop with 626 in 1984. ... Led Southern League shortstops with 643 total chances and 107 double plays in 1985. ... Led American Association shortstops with 84 double plays in 1987. ... Career major league grand slams: 1.

Year　Team (League)	Pos.	G	AB	R	H	2B	3B	HR	RBI	Avg.	BB	SO	SB	PO	A	E	Avg.
1982— San Jose (Calif.)	SS	130	476	53	123	20	3	3	49	.258	27	94	12	226	389	55	.918
1983— W.P. Beach (FSL)	SS	129	419	63	95	18	5	5	53	.227	58	88	6	217	*436	*51	.928
1984— W.P. Beach (FSL)	SS	124	439	54	100	23	0	6	43	.228	50	79	14	*198	*389	39	.938
1985— Jacksonville (South.)	SS	138	*538	74	129	20	2	16	72	.240	44	69	18	*198	*412	33	.949
1986— Indianapolis (A.A.)	SS	108	407	60	100	17	5	7	43	.246	29	68	18	178	330	24	.955
— Montreal (N.L.)	SS	55	166	20	34	11	1	0	13	.205	17	33	1	64	119	9	.953
1987— Indianapolis (A.A.)	SS	108	433	73	135	26	3	8	53	.312	32	73	24	190	291	18	.964
— Montreal (N.L.)	SS	18	32	0	5	2	0	0	1	.156	1	8	0	9	27	3	.923
1988— Montreal (N.L.)	SS	123	371	35	83	17	3	4	30	.224	24	69	3	160	301	18	.962
1989— Pawtucket (Int'l)■	SS-3B	43	175	22	44	9	0	1	13	.251	11	23	5	53	106	9	.946
— Boston (A.L.)	SS-2B-DH	93	323	35	83	17	1	5	29	.257	20	60	2	127	290	16	.958
1990— Boston (A.L.)	SS-2B-3B	118	346	38	78	20	0	7	45	.225	25	58	4	187	310	18	.965
1991— Boston (A.L.)	SS	129	414	64	107	22	3	8	40	.258	35	86	4	180	386	*24	.959
1992— Boston (A.L.)	S-DH-O-3-2	102	288	17	62	11	1	0	29	.215	26	56	4	120	287	14	.967
1993— Boston (A.L.)	S-2-DH-3	62	130	13	27	8	1	1	7	.208	11	36	1	65	111	6	.967
1994— New York (N.L.)■	SS-2B	43	43	11	12	2	1	3	5	.279	4	14	0	19	29	2	.960
1995— Okla. City (A.A.)■	SS	19	58	3	8	4	0	1	3	.138	1	6	0	24	51	3	.962
1996— Norfolk (Int'l)	SS-3B	114	356	34	80	23	3	6	39	.225	31	58	1	126	330	21	.956
1997— New Orleans (A.A.)■	SS-3B-2B	124	382	46	91	23	4	3	45	.238	34	51	5	148	366	17	.968
— Houston (N.L.)	SS-2B	7	13	2	3	0	1	0	3	.231	1	6	0	9	9	2	.900
American League totals (5 years)		504	1501	167	357	78	6	21	150	.238	117	296	15	679	1334	78	.963
National League totals (5 years)		235	625	68	137	32	6	7	52	.219	47	130	4	261	485	34	.956
Major league totals (10 years)		739	2126	235	494	110	12	28	202	.232	164	426	19	940	1819	112	.961

CHAMPIONSHIP SERIES RECORD

Year　Team (League)	Pos.	G	AB	R	H	2B	3B	HR	RBI	Avg.	BB	SO	SB	PO	A	E	Avg.
1990— Boston (A.L.)	SS	4	9	1	2	1	0	0	0	.222	0	2	0	6	16	1	.957

RIVERA, MARIANO   P   YANKEES

PERSONAL: Born November 29, 1969, in Panama City, Panama. ... 6-2/168. ... Throws right, bats right. ... Cousin of Ruben Rivera, outfielder, San Diego Padres.

TRANSACTIONS/CAREER NOTES: Signed as non-drafted free agent by New York Yankees organization (February 17, 1990). ... On disabled list (April 10-May 19, July 11-28 and August 12-September 8, 1992). ... On Albany/Colonie disabled list (April 9-June 28, 1993). ... On Greensboro disabled list (September 6, 1993-remainder of season). ... On Tampa disabled list (April 23-May 9, 1994). ... On Columbus disabled list (August 4-14, 1994).

HONORS: Named A.L. Fireman of the Year by THE SPORTING NEWS (1997).

STATISTICAL NOTES: Pitched seven-inning, 3-0 no-hit victory against Gulf Coast Pirates (August 31, 1990). ... Pitched five-inning, 3-0 no-hit victory for Columbus against Rochester (June 26, 1995).

Year Team (League)	W	L	Pct.	ERA	G	GS	CG	ShO	Sv.	IP	H	R	ER	BB	SO
1990—GC Yankees (GCL)	5	1	.833	*0.17	22	1	1	1	1	52	17	3	1	7	58
1991—Greensboro (S. Atl.)	4	9	.308	2.75	29	15	1	0	0	114 2/3	103	48	35	36	123
1992—Fort Lauderdale (FSL)	5	3	.625	2.28	10	10	3	1	0	59 1/3	40	17	15	5	42
1993—Greensboro (S. Atl.)	1	0	1.000	2.06	10	10	0	0	0	39 1/3	31	12	9	15	32
—GC Yankees (GCL)	0	1	.000	2.25	2	2	0	0	0	4	2	1	1	1	6
1994—Tampa (Florida State)	3	0	1.000	2.21	7	7	0	0	0	36 2/3	34	12	9	12	27
—Alb./Colon. (Eastern)	3	0	1.000	2.27	9	9	0	0	0	63 1/3	58	20	16	8	39
—Columbus (Int'l)	4	2	.667	5.81	6	6	1	0	0	31	34	22	20	10	23
1995—Columbus (Int'l)	2	2	.500	2.10	7	7	1	1	0	30	25	10	7	3	30
—New York (A.L.)	5	3	.625	5.51	19	10	0	0	0	67	71	43	41	30	51
1996—New York (A.L.)	8	3	.727	2.09	61	0	0	0	5	107 2/3	73	25	25	34	130
1997—New York (A.L.)	6	4	.600	1.88	66	0	0	0	43	71 2/3	65	17	15	20	68
Major league totals (3 years)	19	10	.655	2.96	146	10	0	0	48	246 1/3	209	85	81	84	249

DIVISION SERIES RECORD

Year Team (League)	W	L	Pct.	ERA	G	GS	CG	ShO	Sv.	IP	H	R	ER	BB	SO
1995—New York (A.L.)	1	0	1.000	0.00	3	0	0	0	0	5 1/3	3	0	0	1	8
1996—New York (A.L.)	0	0	. . .	0.00	2	0	0	0	0	4 2/3	0	0	0	1	1
1997—New York (A.L.)	0	0	. . .	4.50	2	0	0	0	1	2	2	1	1	0	1
Div. series totals (3 years)	1	0	1.000	0.75	7	0	0	0	1	12	5	1	1	2	10

CHAMPIONSHIP SERIES RECORD

Year Team (League)	W	L	Pct.	ERA	G	GS	CG	ShO	Sv.	IP	H	R	ER	BB	SO
1996—New York (A.L.)	1	0	1.000	0.00	2	0	0	0	0	4	6	0	0	1	5

WORLD SERIES RECORD

NOTES: Member of World Series championship team (1996).

Year Team (League)	W	L	Pct.	ERA	G	GS	CG	ShO	Sv.	IP	H	R	ER	BB	SO
1996—New York (A.L.)	0	0	. . .	1.59	4	0	0	0	0	5 2/3	4	1	1	3	4

ALL-STAR GAME RECORD

Year League	W	L	Pct.	ERA	GS	CG	ShO	Sv.	IP	H	R	ER	BB	SO
1997—American	0	0	. . .	0.00	0	0	0	1	1	0	0	0	0	1

RIVERA, RUBEN   OF   PADRES

PERSONAL: Born November 14, 1973, in Chorrera, Panama. ... 6-3/200. ... Bats right, throws right. ... Full name: Ruben Moreno Rivera. ... Cousin of Mariano Rivera, pitcher, New York Yankees.

TRANSACTIONS/CAREER NOTES: Signed as non-drafted free agent by New York Yankees organization (November 21, 1990). ... On New York disabled list (March 27-May 30, 1997). ... Traded by Yankees with P Rafael Medina and $3 million to San Diego Padres for the rights to P Hideki Irabu, 2B Homer Bush, OF Gordon Amerson and a player to be named later (April 22, 1997); Padres traded OF Vernon Maxwell to Yankees to complete deal (June 9). ... On San Diego disabled list (May 30-August 13, 1997); included rehabilitation assignments to Rancho Cucamonga (May 30-July 22) and Las Vegas (July 23-August 4).

HONORS: Named New York-Pennsylvania League Most Valuable Player (1993). ... Named South Atlantic League Most Valuable Player (1994).

STATISTICAL NOTES: Led New York-Pennsylvania League outfielders with three double plays in 1993. ... Led South Atlantic League with .573 slugging percentage in 1994.

Year Team (League)	Pos.	G	AB	R	H	2B	3B	HR	RBI	Avg.	BB	SO	SB	PO	A	E	Avg.
1991—Dom. Dodgers (DSL)	. . .	51	170	27	34	3	2	2	16	.200	23	37	14	. . .	. . .	. . .	. . .
1992—GC Yankees (GCL)	OF	53	194	37	53	10	3	1	20	.273	42	49	21	67	10	4	.951
1993—Oneonta (NYP)	OF	55	199	45	55	7	6	13	47	.276	32	66	12	111	9	3	.976
1994—Greensboro (S. Atl.)	OF	105	400	83	115	24	3	•28	81	.288	47	125	36	217	14	5	.979
—Tampa (Florida State)	OF	34	134	18	35	4	3	5	20	.261	8	38	12	76	6	2	.976
1995—Norwich (Eastern)	OF	71	256	49	75	16	8	9	39	.293	37	77	16	176	7	3	.984
—Columbus (Int'l)	OF	48	174	37	47	8	2	15	35	.270	26	62	8	113	6	3	.975
—New York (A.L.)	OF	5	1	0	0	0	0	0	0	.000	0	1	0	2	0	0	1.000
1996—Columbus (Int'l)	OF	101	362	59	85	20	4	10	46	.235	40	96	15	239	6	7	.972
—New York (A.L.)	OF	46	88	17	25	6	1	2	16	.284	13	26	6	77	2	0	1.000
1997—Rancho Cuca. (Cal.)■	DH	6	23	6	4	1	0	1	3	.174	3	9	1	. . .	. . .	. . .	. . .
—Las Vegas (PCL)	1B	12	48	6	12	5	1	1	6	.250	1	20	1	1	0	0	1.000
—San Diego (NL)	OF	17	20	2	5	1	0	0	1	.250	2	9	2	13	0	0	1.000
American League totals (2 years)		51	89	17	25	6	1	2	16	.281	13	27	6	79	2	0	1.000
National League totals (1 year)		17	20	2	5	1	0	0	1	.250	2	9	2	13	0	0	1.000
Major league totals (3 years)		68	109	19	30	7	1	2	17	.275	15	36	8	92	2	0	1.000

DIVISION SERIES RECORD

Year Team (League)	Pos.	G	AB	R	H	2B	3B	HR	RBI	Avg.	BB	SO	SB	PO	A	E	Avg.
1996—New York (A.L.)	OF-PH	2	1	0	0	0	0	00	0	.000	0	1	0	0	0	0	. . .

NOTES: Member of World Series championship team (1996); inactive due to injury.

Year	Team (League)	Pos.	G	AB	R	H	2B	3B	HR	RBI	Avg.	BB	SO	SB	PO	A	E	Avg.
							BATTING									FIELDING		
1996— New York (A.L.)									Did not play.									

R

RIZZO, TODD — P — WHITE SOX

PERSONAL: Born May 24, 1971, in Clifton Heights, Pa. ... 6-2/220. ... Throws left, bats right.
HIGH SCHOOL: Garnet Valley (Concordville, Pa.).
TRANSACTIONS/CAREER NOTES: Signed as non-drafted free agent by Los Angeles Dodgers organization (May 6, 1992). ... Released by Dodgers organization (April 1993). ... Signed by Chicago White Sox organization (March 4, 1995).

Year Team (League)	W	L	Pct.	ERA	G	GS	CG	ShO	Sv.	IP	H	R	ER	BB	SO
1992— GC Dodgers (GCL)	0	1	.000	3.86	3	1	0	0	0	7	4	4	3	8	7
— Yakima (N'west)	2	0	1.000	4.50	15	0	0	0	0	26	21	13	13	24	26
1993—							Did not play.								
1994— Tyler (Texas-Louisiana)	0	0	...	8.35	14	1	0	0	0	18 1/3	24	23	17	21	13
— San Antonio (Tex.)	0	2	.000	7.53	17	0	0	0	1	28 2/3	30	32	24	41	20
1995— Prince William (Caro.)■	3	5	.375	2.78	36	0	0	0	1	68	68	30	21	39	59
1996— Birmingham (Southern)	4	4	.500	2.75	46	0	0	0	8	68 2/3	61	28	21	40	48
1997— Nashville (A.A.)	4	5	.444	3.57	54	0	0	0	6	70 2/3	63	39	28	33	60

ROA, JOE — P — GIANTS

PERSONAL: Born October 11, 1971, in Southfield, Mich. ... 6-1/195. ... Throws right, bats right. ... Full name: Joe Rodger Roa. ... Name pronounced ROE-ah.
HIGH SCHOOL: Hazel Park (Mich.).
TRANSACTIONS/CAREER NOTES: Selected by Atlanta Braves organization in 18th round of free-agent draft (June 5, 1989). ... Traded by Braves to New York Mets organization (August 29, 1991), completing deal in which Mets traded P Alejandro Pena to Braves for P Tony Castillo and a player to be named (August 28, 1991). ... On Norfolk suspended list (July 31-August 2, 1994). ... Traded by Mets organization with OF Jeromy Burnitz to Cleveland Indians organization for P Dave Mlicki, P Paul Byrd, P Jerry DiPoto and a player to be named (November 18, 1994); Mets acquired 2B Jesus Azuaje to complete deal (December 6, 1994). ... Traded by Indians to San Francisco Giants for OF Trenidad Hubbard (December 16, 1996), completing deal in which Giants traded 3B Matt Williams and a player to be named later to Indians for IF Jeff Kent, IF Jose Vizcaino, P Julian Tavarez and a player to be named later (November 13, 1996).

Year Team (League)	W	L	Pct.	ERA	G	GS	CG	ShO	Sv.	IP	H	R	ER	BB	SO
1989— GC Braves (GCL)	2	2	.500	2.89	13	4	0	0	0	37 1/3	40	18	12	10	21
1990— Pulaski (Appalachian)........	4	2	.667	2.97	14	11	3	1	0	75 2/3	55	29	25	26	49
1991— Macon (S. Atl.)	13	3	.813	2.17	30	18	4	2	1	141	106	46	34	33	96
1992— St. Lucie (Fla. St.)■	9	7	.563	3.63	26	24	2	1	0	156 1/3	176	80	63	15	61
1993— Binghamton (Eastern)	12	7	.632	3.87	32	23	2	1	0	167 1/3	190	80	72	24	73
1994— Binghamton (Eastern)	2	1	.667	1.80	3	3	0	0	0	20	18	6	4	1	11
— Norfolk (Int'l)	8	8	.500	3.49	25	25	5	0	0	167 2/3	184	82	65	34	74
1995— Buffalo (A.A.)■	*17	3	.850	3.50	25	24	3	0	0	164 2/3	168	71	64	28	93
— Cleveland (A.L.)................	0	1	.000	6.00	1	1	0	0	0	6	9	4	4	2	0
1996— Buffalo (A.A.).................	11	8	.579	3.27	26	24	5	0	0	165 1/3	161	66	60	36	82
— Cleveland (A.L.)................	0	0	...	10.80	1	0	0	0	0	1 2/3	4	2	2	3	0
1997— San Francisco (N.L.)■	2	5	.286	5.21	28	3	0	0	0	65 2/3	86	40	38	20	34
— Phoenix (PCL)	3	1	.750	4.75	6	5	0	0	0	36	43	21	19	11	16
A.L. totals (2 years)	0	1	.000	7.04	2	1	0	0	0	7 2/3	13	6	6	5	0
N.L. totals (1 year)	2	5	.286	5.21	28	3	0	0	0	65 2/3	86	40	38	20	34
Major league totals (3 years)......	2	6	.250	5.40	30	4	0	0	0	73 1/3	99	46	44	25	34

ROBERTS, BIP — 2B/OF — TIGERS

PERSONAL: Born October 27, 1963, in Berkeley, Calif. ... 5-7/165. ... Bats both, throws right. ... Full name: Leon Joseph Roberts III.
HIGH SCHOOL: Skyline (Oakland).
JUNIOR COLLEGE: Chabot College (Calif.).
COLLEGE: UNLV.
TRANSACTIONS/CAREER NOTES: Selected by Pittsburgh Pirates organization in fifth round of free-agent draft (June 8, 1981); did not sign. ... Selected by Pirates organization in secondary phase of free-agent draft (June 7, 1982). ... On suspended list (June 30-July 3, 1985). ... Selected by San Diego Padres from Pirates organization in Rule 5 major league draft (December 10, 1985). ... On disabled list (May 21-June 5, 1986 and August 17-September 9, 1991). ... Traded by Padres with a player to be named later to Cincinnati Reds for P Randy Myers (December 8, 1991); Reds acquired OF Craig Pueschner to complete deal (December 9, 1991). ... On disabled list (July 2-17 and August 4, 1993-remainder of season). ... Granted free agency (October 26, 1993). ... Signed by Padres (January 10, 1994). ... Granted free agency (October 20, 1994). ... Re-signed by Padres (December 23, 1994). ... On San Diego disabled list (June 28-July 13 and July 14-August 22, 1995); included rehabilitation assignments to Rancho Cucamonga (August 18-19) and Las Vegas (August 19-22). ... Traded by Padres with P Bryan Wolff to Kansas City Royals for 1B Wally Joyner and P Aaron Dorlarque (December 21, 1995). ... On disabled list (June 10-July 19 and August 7-September 1, 1996). ... On Kansas City disabled list (June 17-July 10, 1997). ... Traded by Royals to Cleveland Indians for P Roland de la Maza (August 31, 1997). ... Granted free agency (November 7, 1997). ... Signed by Detroit Tigers (December 12, 1997).
RECORDS: Shares N.L. single-season record for most consecutive hits—10 (September 19, 20, 22 [second game] and 23, 1992; one base on balls).
STATISTICAL NOTES: Led South Atlantic League second basemen with .962 fielding percentage and tied for lead with 76 double plays in 1983. ... Led Carolina League second basemen with 654 total chances and 91 double plays in 1984. ... Had 23-game hitting streak (May 26-June 20, 1994). ... Career major league grand slams: 1.

			BATTING										FIELDING			
Year Team (League)	Pos.	G	AB	R	H	2B	3B	HR	RBI	Avg.	BB	SO	SB	PO	A	E	Avg.
1982— GC Pirates (GCL).......	2B	6	23	4	7	1	0	0	1	.304	2	4	4	14	15	0	1.000
— Greenwood (SAL).......	2B	33	107	15	23	3	1	0	6	.215	15	18	10	52	82	7	.950
1983— Greenwood (SAL)......	2B-SS	122	438	78	140	20	5	6	63	.320	69	43	27	273	311	24	†.961
1984— Prince William (Car.)..	2B	134	498	81	*150	25	5	8	77	.301	44	63	50	*282	352	20	*.969
1985— Nashua (Eastern).....	2B	105	401	64	109	19	5	1	23	.272	29	43	•40	217	249	•29	.941
1986— San Diego (N.L.)■.....	2B	101	241	34	61	5	2	1	12	.253	14	29	14	166	172	10	.971
1987— Las Vegas (PCL).......	2B-OF-3B	98	359	66	110	18	10	1	38	.306	37	39	27	147	150	8	.974
1988— Las Vegas (PCL)......	3B-OF-2B	100	343	73	121	21	8	7	51	.353	32	45	29	103	130	17	.932
— San Diego (N.L.).......	2B-3B	5	9	1	3	0	0	0	0	.333	1	2	0	2	3	1	.833
1989— San Diego (N.L.)......	O-3-S-2	117	329	81	99	15	8	3	25	.301	49	45	21	134	113	9	.965
1990— San Diego (N.L.)......	O-3-S-2	149	556	104	172	36	3	9	44	.309	55	65	46	227	160	13	.968
1991— San Diego (N.L.)......	2B-OF	117	424	66	119	13	3	3	32	.281	37	71	26	239	185	10	.977
1992— Cincinnati (N.L.)■.....	OF-2B-3B	147	532	92	172	34	6	4	45	.323	62	54	44	209	152	7	.981
1993— Cincinnati (N.L.)......	2-0-3-S	83	292	46	70	13	0	1	18	.240	38	46	26	152	176	6	.982
1994— San Diego (N.L.)■.....	2B-OF	105	403	52	129	15	5	2	31	.320	39	57	21	178	221	9	.978
1995— San Diego (N.L.)......	OF-2B-SS	73	296	40	90	14	0	2	25	.304	17	36	20	135	88	4	.982
— Rancho Cuca. (Cal.)......	DH	1	3	1	0	0	0	0	0	.000	1	1	1	0	0	0	...
— Las Vegas (PCL)........	SS-2B	3	12	1	4	0	0	0	2	.333	0	3	1	2	15	1	.944
1996— Kansas City (A.L.)■.....	2B-DH-OF	90	339	39	96	21	2	0	52	.283	25	38	12	115	190	4	.987
1997— Kansas City (A.L.)......	OF-3B	97	346	44	107	17	2	1	36	.309	21	53	15	149	17	3	.982
— Cleveland (A.L.)■......	2B-OF	23	85	19	23	3	0	3	8	.271	7	14	3	37	33	4	.946
American League totals (2 years)		210	770	102	226	41	4	4	96	.294	53	105	30	301	240	11	.980
National League totals (9 years)		897	3082	516	915	145	27	25	232	.297	312	405	218	1442	1270	69	.975
Major league totals (11 years)		1107	3852	618	1141	186	31	29	328	.296	365	510	248	1743	1510	80	.976

R

DIVISION SERIES RECORD

			BATTING										FIELDING			
Year Team (League)	Pos.	G	AB	R	H	2B	3B	HR	RBI	Avg.	BB	SO	SB	PO	A	E	Avg.
1997— Cleveland (A.L.).........	2B-OF	5	19	1	6	0	0	0	1	.316	2	2	2	5	8	0	1.000

CHAMPIONSHIP SERIES RECORD

			BATTING										FIELDING			
Year Team (League)	Pos.	G	AB	R	H	2B	3B	HR	RBI	Avg.	BB	SO	SB	PO	A	E	Avg.
1997— Cleveland (A.L.).........	2B-OF	5	20	0	3	1	0	0	0	.150	0	0	1	11	7	1	.947

WORLD SERIES RECORD

			BATTING										FIELDING			
Year Team (League)	Pos.	G	AB	R	H	2B	3B	HR	RBI	Avg.	BB	SO	SB	PO	A	E	Avg.
1997— Cleveland (A.L.).........	2B-OF	6	22	3	6	4	0	0	4	.273	3	5	0	8	8	0	1.000

ALL-STAR GAME RECORD

			BATTING									FIELDING			
Year League	Pos.	AB	R	H	2B	3B	HR	RBI	Avg.	BB	SO	SB	PO	A	E	Avg.
1992— National	OF	2	1	2	0	0	0	2	1.000	0	0	0	0	0	0	...

ROBERTS, WILLIS P TIGERS

PERSONAL: Born June 19, 1975, in San Cristobal, Dominican Republic. ... 6-3/175. ... Throws right, bats right. ... Full name: Willis Augusto Roberts.
TRANSACTIONS/CAREER NOTES: Signed as non-drafted free agent by Detroit Tigers organization (February 18, 1992). ... On disabled list (July 14-August 1 and August 1-September 13, 1994).

Year Team (League)	W	L	Pct.	ERA	G	GS	CG	ShO	Sv.	IP	H	R	ER	BB	SO
1992— Dom. Tigers (DSL).............	0	6	.000	8.23	12	7	1	0	0	35	43	49	32	46	17
1993— Bristol (Appalachian).........	2	3	.400	1.38	10	2	0	0	1	26	24	16	4	11	23
1994— Bristol (Appalachian).........	1	2	.333	3.92	4	4	0	0	0	20 2/3	9	9	9	8	17
1995— Fayetteville (S. Atl.)............	6	3	.667	2.70	17	15	0	0	0	80	72	33	24	40	52
1996— Lakeland (Fla. St.)..............	9	7	.563	2.89	23	22	2	00	0	149 1/3	133	60	48	69	105
1997— Jacksonville (Southern)......	6	*15	.286	6.28	26	26	2	0	0	149	181	*120	*104	64	86

ROBERTSON, MIKE 1B PHILLIES

PERSONAL: Born October 9, 1970, in Norwich, Conn. ... 6-0/180. ... Bats left, throws left. ... Full name: Michael Francis Robertson..
HIGH SCHOOL: Servite (Anaheim, Calif.).
TRANSACTIONS/CAREER NOTES: Selected by California Angels organization in 13th round of free-agent draft (June 1, 1988); did not sign. ... Selected by Chicago White Sox organization in third round of free-agent draft (June 3, 1991). ... Traded by White Sox to Philadelphia Phillies for 1B Gene Schall (January 31, 1997).
STATISTICAL NOTES: Led American Association first basemen with 1,172 putouts, 75 assists, .992 fielding percentage, 1,257 total chances and 111 double plays in 1995. ... Led International League first basemen with 97 assists and tied for league lead with 14 errors in 1997.

			BATTING										FIELDING			
Year Team (League)	Pos.	G	AB	R	H	2B	3B	HR	RBI	Avg.	BB	SO	SB	PO	A	E	Avg.
1991— Utica (N.Y.-Penn)........	1B	13	54	6	9	2	1	0	8	.167	5	11	1	116	13	3	.977
— South Bend (Mid.)......	1B	54	210	30	69	16	2	1	26	.329	18	24	7	403	40	3	.993
1992— Sarasota (Fla. St.)......	1B	106	395	50	99	21	3	10	59	.251	50	55	5	870	112	9	.991
— Birmingham (Sou.)......	1B	27	90	6	17	8	1	1	9	.189	10	19	0	213	21	3	.987
1993— Birmingham (Sou.).....	1B-OF	138	511	73	138	31	3	11	73	.270	59	97	10	1065	108	13	.989
1994— Birmingham (Sou.).....	OF-1B	53	196	32	62	20	2	3	30	.316	31	34	6	206	13	3	.986

Year Team (League)	Pos.	G	AB	R	H	2B	3B	HR	RBI	Avg.	BB	SO	SB	PO	A	E	Avg.
—Nashville (A.A.)	OF-1B	67	213	21	48	8	1	8	21	.225	15	27	0	193	12	1	.995
1995—Nashville (A.A.)	1B-OF	139	499	55	124	17	4	19	52	.248	50	72	2	†1180	†75	11	†.991
1996—Nashville (A.A.)	1B	•138	450	64	116	16	4	21	74	.258	38	83	1	1074	54	4	*.996
—Chicago (A.L.)	1B-DH	6	7	0	1	0	0	0	0	.143	0	1	0	11	1	0	1.000
1997—Scran./W.B. (Int'l)■....	1B-OF	121	416	61	124	17	3	12	72	.298	58	67	0	951	†97	‡14	.987
—Philadelphia (N.L.)......	1B-OF-DH	22	38	3	8	2	1	0	4	.211	0	6	1	28	1	0	1.000
American League totals (1 year)		6	7	0	1	1	0	0	0	.143	0	1	0	11	1	0	1.000
National League totals (1 year)		22	38	3	8	2	1	0	4	.211	0	6	1	28	1	0	1.000
Major league totals (2 years)		28	45	3	9	3	1	0	4	.200	0	7	1	39	2	0	1.000

ROBERTSON, RICH   P   ANGELS

PERSONAL: Born September 15, 1968, in Nacogdoches, Texas. ... 6-4/180. ... Throws left, bats left. ... Full name: Richard Wayne Robertson.
HIGH SCHOOL: Waller (Texas).
JUNIOR COLLEGE: San Jacinto College (Texas).
COLLEGE: Texas A&M.
TRANSACTIONS/CAREER NOTES: Selected by San Diego Padres organization in 32nd round of free-agent draft (June 5, 1989); did not sign. ... Selected by Pittsburgh Pirates organization in ninth round of free-agent draft (June 4, 1990). ... On Buffalo disabled list (June 10-19, 1993). ... Claimed on waivers by Minnesota Twins (November 4, 1994). ... Released by Twins (December 12, 1997). ... Signed by Anaheim Angels organization (January 19, 1998).

Year Team (League)	W	L	Pct.	ERA	G	GS	CG	ShO	Sv.	IP	H	R	ER	BB	SO
1990—Welland (N.Y.-Penn)..........	3	4	.429	3.08	16	13	0	0	0	64 1/3	51	34	22	55	80
1991—Augusta (S. Atl.)........	4	7	.364	4.99	13	12	1	0	0	74	73	52	41	51	62
—Salem (Carolina)	2	4	.333	4.93	12	11	0	0	0	45 2/3	34	32	25	42	32
1992—Salem (Carolina)	3	0	1.000	3.41	6	6	0	0	0	37	29	18	14	10	27
—Carolina (Southern)	6	7	.462	3.03	20	20	1	1	0	124 2/3	127	51	42	41	107
1993—Buffalo (A.A.)	9	8	.529	4.28	23	23	2	0	0	132 1/3	141	67	63	52	71
—Pittsburgh (N.L.)	0	1	.000	6.00	9	0	0	0	0	9	15	6	6	4	5
1994—Buffalo (A.A.)	5	10	.333	3.11	18	17	0	0	0	118 2/3	112	47	41	36	71
—Pittsburgh (N.L.)	0	0	...	6.89	8	0	0	0	0	15 2/3	20	12	12	10	8
1995—Salt Lake (PCL)■..........	5	0	1.000	2.44	7	7	1	0	0	44 1/3	31	13	12	12	40
—Minnesota (A.L.)	2	0	1.000	3.83	25	4	1	0	0	51 2/3	48	28	22	31	33
1996—Minnesota (A.L.)	7	17	.292	5.12	36	31	5	•3	0	186 1/3	197	113	106	*116	114
1997—Minnesota (A.L.)	8	12	.400	5.69	31	26	0	0	0	147	169	105	93	70	69
A.L. totals (3 years)	17	29	.370	5.17	92	61	6	3	0	385	414	246	221	217	221
N.L. totals (2 years)	0	1	.000	6.57	17	0	0	0	0	24 2/3	35	18	18	14	13
Major league totals (5 years)......	17	30	.362	5.25	109	61	6	3	0	409 2/3	449	264	239	231	234

ROBINSON, KEN   P   BLUE JAYS

PERSONAL: Born November 3, 1969, in Barberton, Ohio. ... 5-9/170. ... Throws right, bats right. ... Full name: Kenneth Neal Robinson.
COLLEGE: Florida State.
TRANSACTIONS/CAREER NOTES: Selected by Toronto Blue Jays organization in 10th round of free-agent draft (June 3, 1991). ... Claimed on waivers by Kansas City Royals organization (March 29, 1996). ... Claimed on waivers by Blue Jays organization (May 7, 1996).

Year Team (League)	W	L	Pct.	ERA	G	GS	CG	ShO	Sv.	IP	H	R	ER	BB	SO
1991—Medicine Hat (Pio.)	0	1	.000	3.86	6	2	0	0	0	11 2/3	12	8	5	5	18
1992—Myrtle Beach (SAL)..........	1	0	1.000	2.82	20	0	0	0	1	38 1/3	25	12	12	30	45
1993—Hagerstown (S. Atl.)..........	4	7	.364	4.65	40	0	0	0	7	71 2/3	74	43	37	31	65
1994—Hagerstown (S. Atl.)..........	4	1	.800	3.20	10	0	0	0	1	19 2/3	15	8	7	4	27
—Dunedin (Fla. St.)	1	1	.500	1.80	5	0	0	0	0	10	6	2	2	4	16
—Syracuse (Int'l)	4	2	.667	3.74	30	3	0	0	0	55 1/3	46	27	23	25	48
1995—Syracuse (Int'l)	5	3	.625	3.22	38	0	0	0	2	50 1/3	37	18	18	12	61
—Toronto (A.L.)....................	1	2	.333	3.69	21	0	0	0	0	39	25	21	16	22	31
1996—Omaha (Am. Assoc.)■..........	2	0	1.000	0.79	6	0	0	0	0	11 1/3	7	1	1	4	9
—Kansas City (A.L.)	1	0	1.000	6.00	5	0	0	0	0	6	9	4	4	3	5
—Syracuse (Int'l)■..................	3	7	.300	4.64	47	0	0	0	1	64	52	37	33	39	78
1997—Syracuse (Int'l)..................	7	7	.500	2.56	56	0	0	0	17	81	44	24	23	36	96
—Toronto (A.L.)....................	0	0	...	2.70	3	0	0	0	0	3 1/3	1	1	1	1	4
Major league totals (3 years)......	2	2	.500	3.91	29	0	0	0	0	48 1/3	35	26	21	26	40

ROBINSON, KERRY   OF   DEVIL RAYS

PERSONAL: Born October 3, 1973, in St. Louis. ... 6-0/170. ... Bats left, throws left. ... Full name: Kerry K. Robinson. ... Son of Rogers Robinson, outfielder, in St. Louis Cardinals organization (1957-69).
HIGH SCHOOL: Hazelwood East (St. Louis County, Mo.).
COLLEGE: Southeast Missouri State.
TRANSACTIONS/CAREER NOTES: Selected by St. Louis Cardinals organization in 34th round of free-agent draft (June 1, 1995). ... Selected by Tampa Bay Devil Rays in second round (44th pick overall) of expansion draft (November 18, 1997).
STATISTICAL NOTES: Led Midwest League in caught stealing with 27 in 1996. ... Led Texas League in caught stealing with 23 in 1997

Year Team (League)	Pos.	G	AB	R	H	2B	3B	HR	RBI	Avg.	BB	SO	SB	PO	A	E	Avg.
1995—Johnson City (App.) ...	OF	60	250	44	74	12	8	1	26	.296	16	30	14	86	5	6	.938
1996—Peoria (Midwest)........	OF	123	440	98	158	17	4	2	47	.359	51	51	•50	168	7	7	.962
1997—Arkansas (Texas)........	OF	135	*523	80	168	16	3	2	62	.321	54	64	40	193	6	7	.966
—Louisville (A.A.)	OF	2	9	0	1	0	0	0	0	.111	0	1	0	3	0	0	1.000

ROCKER, JOHN — P — BRAVES

PERSONAL: Born October 17, 1974, in Statesboro, Ga. ... 6-4/210. ... Throws left, bats right. ... Full name: John Loy Rocker.
HIGH SCHOOL: First Presbyterian Day School (Macon, Ga.).
TRANSACTIONS/CAREER NOTES: Selected by Atlanta Braves organization in 18th round of free-agent draft (June 3, 1993).
STATISTICAL NOTES: Pitched 2-0 no-hit victory against Charleston, S.C. (June 9, 1996). ... Led Southern League with 17 wild pitches in 1997.

Year	Team (League)	W	L	Pct.	ERA	G	GS	CG	ShO	Sv.	IP	H	R	ER	BB	SO
1994—	Danville (Appalachian)	1	5	.167	3.53	12	12	1	0	0	63 2/3	50	36	25	38	72
1995—	Eugene (Northwest)	1	5	.167	5.16	12	12	0	0	0	59 1/3	45	40	34	36	74
	— Macon (S. Atl.)	4	4	.500	4.50	16	16	0	0	0	86	86	50	43	52	61
1996—	Macon (S. Atl.)	5	3	.625	3.89	20	19	2	2	0	106 1/3	85	60	46	63	107
	— Durham (Carolina)	4	3	.571	3.39	9	9	0	0	0	58 1/3	63	24	22	25	43
1997—	Durham (Carolina)	1	1	.500	4.33	11	1	0	0	0	35 1/3	33	21	17	22	39
	— Greenville (Southern)	5	6	.455	4.86	22	18	0	0	0	113	119	69	61	61	96

RODRIGUEZ, ALEX — SS — MARINERS

PERSONAL: Born July 27, 1975, in New York. ... 6-3/190. ... Bats right, throws right. ... Full name: Alexander Emmanuel Rodriguez.
HIGH SCHOOL: Westminster Christian (Miami).
TRANSACTIONS/CAREER NOTES: Selected by Seattle Mariners organization in first round (first pick overall) of free-agent draft (June 3, 1993). ... On Seattle disabled list (April 22-May 7, 1996); included rehabilitation assignment to Tacoma (May 5-7). ... On disabled list (June 12-27, 1997).
HONORS: Named Major League Player of the Year by THE SPORTING NEWS (1996). ... Named shortstop on THE SPORTING NEWS A.L. All-Star team (1996). ... Named shortstop on THE SPORTING NEWS A.L. Silver Slugger team (1996).
STATISTICAL NOTES: Had 20-game hitting streak (August 16-September 4, 1996). ... Led A.L. with 379 total bases in 1996. ... Hit for the cycle (June 5, 1997). ... Career major league grand slams: 3.

Year	Team (League)	Pos.	G	AB	R	H	2B	3B	HR	RBI	Avg.	BB	SO	SB	PO	A	E	Avg.
1993—									Did not play.									
1994—	Appleton (Midwest)	SS	65	248	49	79	17	6	14	55	.319	24	44	16	86	185	19	.934
	— Jacksonville (South.)	SS	17	59	7	17	4	1	1	8	.288	10	13	2	17	63	3	.964
	— Seattle (A.L.)	SS	17	54	4	11	0	0	0	2	.204	3	20	3	20	45	6	.915
	— Calgary (PCL)	SS	32	119	22	37	7	4	6	21	.311	8	25	2	45	104	3	.980
1995—	Tacoma (PCL)	SS	54	214	37	77	12	3	15	45	.360	18	44	2	90	157	10	.961
	— Seattle (A.L.)	SS-DH	48	142	15	33	6	2	5	19	.232	6	42	4	56	106	8	.953
1996—	Seattle (A.L.)	SS	146	601	*141	215	*54	1	36	123	*.358	59	104	15	238	404	15	.977
	— Tacoma (PCL)	SS	2	5	0	1	0	0	0	0	.200	2	1	0	1	4	1	.833
1997—	Seattle (A.L.)	SS-DH	141	587	100	176	40	3	23	84	.300	41	99	29	209	394	*24	.962
	Major league totals (4 years)		352	1384	260	435	100	6	64	228	.314	109	265	51	523	949	53	.965

DIVISION SERIES RECORD

Year	Team (League)	Pos.	G	AB	R	H	2B	3B	HR	RBI	Avg.	BB	SO	SB	PO	A	E	Avg.
1995—	Seattle (A.L.)	SS-PR	1	1	1	0	0	0	0	0	.000	0	0	0	0	0	0	...
1997—	Seattle (A.L.)	SS	4	16	1	5	1	0	1	1	.313	0	5	0	5	10	0	1.000
	Division series totals (2 years)		5	17	2	5	1	0	1	1	.294	0	5	0	5	10	0	1.000

CHAMPIONSHIP SERIES RECORD

Year	Team (League)	Pos.	G	AB	R	H	2B	3B	HR	RBI	Avg.	BB	SO	SB	PO	A	E	Avg.
1995—	Seattle (A.L.)	PH	1	1	0	0	0	0	0	0	.000	0	1	0	...	...		...

ALL-STAR GAME RECORD

Year	League	Pos.	AB	R	H	2B	3B	HR	RBI	Avg.	BB	SO	SB	PO	A	E	Avg.
1996—	American	SS	1	0	0	0	0	0	0	.000	0	0	0	0	0	0	...
1997—	American	SS	3	0	1	0	0	0	0	.333	0	2	0	0	1	0	1.000
	All-Star Game totals (2 years)		4	0	1	0	0	0	0	.250	0	2	0	0	1	0	1.000

RODRIGUEZ, FELIX — P — DIAMONDBACKS

PERSONAL: Born December 5, 1972, in Montecristi, Dominican Republic. ... 6-1/180. ... Throws right, bats right. ... Full name: Felix Antonio Rodriguez.
HIGH SCHOOL: Liceo Bijiador (Montecristi, Dominican Republic).
TRANSACTIONS/CAREER NOTES: Signed as non-drafted free agent by Los Angeles Dodgers organization (October 17, 1989). ... On disabled list (August 11, 1992-remainder of season). ... On Albuquerque disabled list (July 5-18, 1995). ... On disabled list (April 20-May 2 and May 12-27, 1996). ... Claimed on waivers by Cincinnati Reds (December 18, 1996). ... Traded by Reds to Arizona Diamondbacks for a player to be named later (November 11, 1997); Reds acquired P Scott Winchester to complete deal (November 18, 1997).
STATISTICAL NOTES: Pitched 11-0 no-hit victory against Sarasota (August 28, 1993).

Year	Team (League)	W	L	Pct.	ERA	G	GS	CG	ShO	Sv.	IP	H	R	ER	BB	SO
1993—	Vero Beach (FSL)	8	8	.500	3.75	32	20	2	1	0	132	109	71	55	71	80
1994—	San Antonio (Tex.)	6	8	.429	4.03	26	26	0	0	0	136 1/3	106	70	61	*88	126
1995—	Albuquerque (PCL)	3	2	.600	4.24	14	11	0	0	0	51	52	29	24	26	46
	— Los Angeles (N.L.)	1	1	.500	2.53	11	0	0	0	0	10 2/3	11	3	3	5	5
1996—	Albuquerque (PCL)	3	9	.250	5.53	27	19	0	0	0	107 1/3	111	70	66	60	65
1997—	Indianapolis (A.A.)■	3	3	.500	1.01	23	0	0	0	1	26 2/3	22	10	3	16	26
	— Cincinnati (N.L.)	0	0	...	4.30	26	0	0	0	0	46	48	23	22	28	34
	Major league totals (2 years)	1	1	.500	3.97	37	0	0	0	0	56 2/3	59	26	25	33	39

Year Team (League)	Pos.	G	AB	R	H	2B	3B	HR	RBI	Avg.	BB	SO	SB	PO	A	E	Avg.
1990— Dom. Dodgers (DSL) .	...	63	241	23	55	10	0	2	33	.228	15	52	4	...	...	...	...
1991— GC Dodgers (GCL)	C	45	139	15	37	8	1	2	21	.266	6	32	1	161	18	5	.973
1992— Great Falls (Pio.)	C-OF	32	110	20	32	8	0	2	20	.291	1	16	2	221	33	2	.992

RODRIGUEZ, FRANK   P   TWINS

PERSONAL: Born December 11, 1972, in Brooklyn, N.Y. ... 6-0/197. ... Throws right, bats right. ... Full name: Francisco Rodriguez.
HIGH SCHOOL: Eastern District (Brooklyn, N.Y.).
JUNIOR COLLEGE: Howard College (Texas).
TRANSACTIONS/CAREER NOTES: Selected by Boston Red Sox in second round of free-agent draft (June 4, 1990); pick received as compensation for Atlanta Braves signing of Type B free-agent 1B Nick Esasky. ... Traded by Red Sox with a player to be named later to Minnesota Twins for P Rick Aguilera (July 6, 1995); Twins acquired OF J.J. Johnson to complete deal (October 11, 1995).

Year Team (League)	W	L	Pct.	ERA	G	GS	CG	ShO	Sv.	IP	H	R	ER	BB	SO
1992— Lynchburg (Caroline)	12	7	.632	3.09	25	25	1	0	0	148 2/3	125	56	51	65	129
1993— New Britain (East.)	7	11	.389	3.74	28	26	•4	1	0	170 2/3	147	79	71	78	151
1994— Pawtucket (Int'l)	8	13	.381	3.92	28	28	*8	1	0	*186	182	95	81	60	*160
1995— Boston (A.L.).....................	0	2	.000	10.57	9	2	0	0	0	15 1/3	21	19	18	10	14
— Pawtucket (Int'l)	1	1	.500	4.00	13	2	0	0	2	27	19	12	12	8	18
— Minnesota (A.L.)■............	5	6	.455	5.38	16	16	0	0	0	90 1/3	93	64	54	47	45
1996— Minnesota (A.L.)	13	14	.481	5.05	38	33	3	0	2	206 2/3	218	129	116	78	110
1997— Minnesota (A.L.)	3	6	.333	4.62	43	15	0	0	0	142 1/3	147	82	73	60	65
Major league totals (3 years)......	21	28	.429	5.17	106	66	3	0	2	454 2/3	479	294	261	195	234

RECORD AS POSITION PLAYER

Year Team (League)	Pos.	G	AB	R	H	2B	3B	HR	RBI	Avg.	BB	SO	SB	PO	A	E	Avg.
1991— GC Red Sox (GCL)	SS	3	14	3	7	0	1	0	3	.500	0	1	0	9	10	1	.950
— Elmira (N.Y.-Penn)......	SS	67	255	36	69	5	3	6	31	.271	13	38	3	95	209	24	.927

RODRIGUEZ, HENRY   OF   CUBS

PERSONAL: Born November 8, 1967, in Santo Domingo, Dominican Republic. ... 6-1/205. ... Bats left, throws left. ... Full name: Henry Anderson Lorenzo Rodriguez.
HIGH SCHOOL: Liceo Republica de Paraguay.
TRANSACTIONS/CAREER NOTES: Signed as non-drafted free agent by Los Angeles Dodgers organization (July 14, 1985). ... Traded by Dodgers with IF Jeff Treadway to Montreal Expos for OF Roberto Kelly and P Joey Eischen (May 23, 1995). ... On Montreal disabled list (June 2-September 1, 1995); included rehabilitation assignment to Ottawa (August 7-16). ... On suspended list (August 16-19, 1996). ... Traded by Expos to Chicago Cubs for P Miguel Batista (December 12, 1997).
RECORDS: Holds N.L. single-season record for most strikeouts by lefthander—160 (1996).
HONORS: Named Texas League Most Valuable Player (1990).
STATISTICAL NOTES: Tied for Gulf Coast League lead with seven intentional bases on balls received in 1987. ... Led Texas League with 14 sacrifice flies in 1990. ... Tied for Pacific Coast League lead with 10 sacrifice flies in 1992. ... Career major league grand slams: 3.

Year Team (League)	Pos.	G	AB	R	H	2B	3B	HR	RBI	Avg.	BB	SO	SB	PO	A	E	Avg.
1987— GC Dodgers (GCL)	1B-SS	49	148	23	49	7	3	0	15	*.331	16	15	3	309	23	6	.982
1988— Dom. Dodgers (DSL) .	...	19	21	9	8	2	0	0	10	.381	10	6	4	...	...	...	...
— Salem (Northwest)	1B	72	291	47	84	14	4	2	39	.289	21	42	14	585	*38	7	.989
1989— Vero Beach (FSL)	1B-OF	126	433	53	123	*33	1	10	73	.284	48	58	7	1072	66	12	.990
— Bakersfield (California)	1B	3	9	2	2	0	0	1	2	.222	0	3	0	8	0	0	1.000
1990— San Antonio (Tex.)	OF	129	495	82	144	22	9	*28	*109	.291	61	66	5	223	5	10	.958
1991— Albuquerque (PCL).....	OF-1B	121	446	61	121	22	5	10	67	.271	25	62	4	234	12	5	.980
1992— Albuquerque (PCL).....	1B-OF	94	365	59	111	21	5	14	72	.304	31	57	1	484	41	10	.981
— Los Angeles (N.L.).....	OF-1B	53	146	11	32	7	0	3	14	.219	8	30	0	68	8	3	.962
1993— Albuquerque (PCL).....	1B-OF	46	179	26	53	13	5	4	30	.296	14	37	1	277	18	5	.983
— Los Angeles (N.L.).....	OF-1B	76	176	20	39	10	0	8	23	.222	11	39	1	127	9	1	.993
1994— Los Angeles (N.L.)	OF-1B	104	306	33	82	14	2	8	49	.268	17	58	0	198	9	2	.990
1995— Los Angeles (N.L.)	OF-1B	21	80	6	21	4	1	1	10	.263	5	17	0	37	0	0	1.000
— Montreal (N.L.)■.........	1B-OF	24	58	7	12	0	0	1	5	.207	6	11	0	88	7	1	.990
— Ottawa (Int'l)	DH	4	15	0	3	1	0	0	2	.200	1	4	0	...	...	...	...
1996— Montreal (N.L.)..........	OF-1B	145	532	81	147	42	1	36	103	.276	37	*160	2	528	33	11	.981
1997— Montreal (N.L.)..........	OF-1B	132	476	55	116	28	3	26	83	.244	42	149	3	220	6	3	.987
Major league totals (6 years)		555	1774	213	449	105	7	83	287	.253	126	464	6	1266	72	21	.985

ALL-STAR GAME RECORD

Year League	Pos.	AB	R	H	2B	3B	HR	RBI	Avg.	BB	SO	SB	PO	A	E	Avg.
1996— National	PH	1	0	1	0	0	0	1	1.000	0	0	0	0	0	0	...

RODRIGUEZ, IVAN   C   RANGERS

PERSONAL: Born November 30, 1971, in Vega Baja, Puerto Rico. ... 5-9/205. ... Bats right, throws right.
HIGH SCHOOL: Lina Padron Rivera (Vega Baja, Puerto Rico).
TRANSACTIONS/CAREER NOTES: Signed as non-drafted free agent by Texas Rangers organization (July 27, 1988). ... On disabled list (June 6-27, 1992).

HONORS: Won A.L. Gold Glove at catcher (1992-97). ... Named catcher on THE SPORTING NEWS A.L. All-Star team (1994-97). ... Named catcher on THE SPORTING NEWS A.L. Silver Slugger team (1994-97).

STATISTICAL NOTES: Led South Atlantic League catchers with 34 double plays in 1989. ... Led Florida State League catchers with 842 total chances in 1990. ... Led A.L. catchers with 941 total chances and 11 double plays in 1996. ... Hit three home runs in one game (September 11, 1997).

Year Team (League)	Pos.	G	AB	R	H	2B	3B	HR	RBI	Avg.	BB	SO	SB	PO	A	E	Avg.
1989—Gastonia (S. Atl.)........	C	112	386	38	92	22	1	7	42	.238	21	58	2	691	*96	11	.986
1990—Charlotte (Fla. St.)......	C	109	408	48	117	17	7	2	55	.287	12	50	1	*727	101	14	.983
1991—Tulsa (Texas)	C	50	175	16	48	7	2	3	28	.274	6	27	1	210	33	3	.988
—Texas (A.L.)	C	88	280	24	74	16	0	3	27	.264	5	42	0	517	62	10	.983
1992—Texas (A.L.)	C-DH	123	420	39	109	16	1	8	37	.260	24	73	0	763	85	*15	.983
1993—Texas (A.L.)	C-DH	137	473	56	129	28	4	10	66	.273	29	70	8	801	76	8	.991
1994—Texas (A.L.)	C	99	363	56	108	19	1	16	57	.298	31	42	6	600	44	5	.992
1995—Texas (A.L.)	C-DH	130	492	56	149	32	2	12	67	.303	16	48	0	707	*67	3	.990
1996—Texas (A.L.)	C-DH	153	639	116	192	47	3	19	86	.300	38	55	5	*850	*81	•10	.989
1997—Texas (A.L.)	C-DH	150	597	98	187	34	4	20	77	.313	38	89	7	821	*75	7	.992
Major league totals (7 years)		880	3264	445	948	192	15	88	417	.290	181	419	26	5059	490	63	.989

DIVISION SERIES RECORD

Year Team (League)	Pos.	G	AB	R	H	2B	3B	HR	RBI	Avg.	BB	SO	SB	PO	A	E	Avg.
1996—Texas (A.L.)	C	4	16	1	6	1	0	0	2	.375	2	3	0	21	3	0	1.000

ALL-STAR GAME RECORD

RECORDS: Shares single-game record for most at-bats in nine-inning game—5 (July 12, 1994).

Year League	Pos.	AB	R	H	2B	3B	HR	RBI	Avg.	BB	SO	SB	PO	A	E	Avg.
1992—American	C	2	0	0	0	0	0	0	.000	0	1	0	4	0	0	1.000
1993—American	C	2	1	1	1	0	0	0	.500	0	0	0	3	0	0	1.000
1994—American	C	5	1	2	0	0	0	0	.400	0	1	0	5	0	0	1.000
1995—American	C	3	0	0	0	0	0	0	.000	0	1	0	6	1	0	1.000
1996—American	C	2	0	0	0	0	0	0	.000	0	1	0	6	2	0	1.000
1997—American	C	2	0	0	0	0	0	0	.000	0	0	0	3	1	0	1.000
All-Star Game totals (6 years)		16	2	3	1	0	0	0	.188	0	4	0	27	4	0	1.000

RODRIGUEZ, NERIO   P   ORIOLES

PERSONAL: Born March 22, 1973, in San Pedro de Macoris, Dominican Republic. ... 6-1/195. ... Throws right, bats right.

TRANSACTIONS/CAREER NOTES: Signed as non-drafted free agent by Chicago White Sox organization (February 2, 1990). ... Selected by Baltimore Orioles organization from White Sox organization in Rule 5 minor league draft (December 5, 1994). ... On Frederick disabled list (April 5-August 11, 1996).

STATISTICAL NOTES: Led Gulf Coast League catchers with 312 total chances in 1992.

Year Team (League)	W	L	Pct.	ERA	G	GS	CG	ShO	Sv.	IP	H	R	ER	BB	SO
1995—High Desert (Calif.)............	0	0	. . .	1.80	7	0	0	0	0	10	8	2	2	7	10
1996—Frederick (Carolina)............	8	7	.533	2.26	24	17	1	0	2	111 1/3	83	42	28	40	114
—Baltimore (A.L.).................	0	1	.000	4.32	8	1	0	0	0	16 2/3	18	11	8	7	12
—Rochester (Int'l)	1	0	1.000	1.80	2	2	0	0	0	15	10	3	3	2	6
1997—Rochester (Int'l)	11	10	.524	3.90	27	27	1	1	0	168 1/3	124	82	73	62	*160
—Baltimore (A.L.).................	2	1	.667	4.91	6	2	0	0	0	22	21	15	12	8	11
Major league totals (2 years)......	2	2	.500	4.66	14	3	0	0	0	38 2/3	39	26	20	15	23

RECORD AS POSITION PLAYER

Year Team (League)	Pos.	G	AB	R	H	2B	3B	HR	RBI	Avg.	BB	SO	SB	PO	A	E	Avg.
1991—GC Whi. Sox (GCL)	C	26	89	4	20	1	0	0	8	.225	2	24	3	153	23	5	.972
1992—GC Whi. Sox (GCL)	C	41	122	18	33	8	1	2	13	.270	10	31	1	*257	43	*12	.962
1993—Hickory (S. Atl.)	C	82	262	31	54	9	2	4	32	.206	27	70	4	476	45	13	.976
1994—South Bend (Mid.)......	C	18	59	4	13	4	0	0	8	.220	2	14	0	95	19	0	1.000
—Prince William (Car.) ..	C	6	19	2	4	1	1	0	1	.211	1	9	0	34	6	0	1.000
1995—Bowie (Eastern)■.......	C	3	4	0	0	0	0	0	0	.000	2	2	0	13	1	0	1.000
—High Desert (Calif.).....	C-P	58	144	20	34	7	0	4	12	.236	18	50	5	325	34	8	.978

RODRIGUEZ, RICH   P   GIANTS

PERSONAL: Born March 1, 1963, in Downey, Calif. ... 6-0/200. ... Throws left, bats left. ... Full name: Richard Anthony Rodriguez.

HIGH SCHOOL: Mountain View (El Monte, Calif.).

COLLEGE: Tennessee.

TRANSACTIONS/CAREER NOTES: Selected by Kansas City Royals organization in 17th round of free-agent draft (June 8, 1981); did not sign. ... Selected by New York Mets organization in ninth round of free-agent draft (June 4, 1984). ... Traded by Mets organization to Wichita, San Diego Padres organization, for 1B Brad Pounders and 1B Bill Stevenson (January 13, 1989). ... Traded by Padres with 3B Gary Sheffield to Florida Marlins for P Trevor Hoffman, P Jose Martinez and P Andres Berumen (June 24, 1993). ... Released by Marlins (March 29, 1994). ... Signed by St. Louis Cardinals (April 1, 1994). ... On disabled list (April 27, 1995-remainder of season). ... Released by Cardinals (November 20, 1995). ... Signed by Cincinnati Reds organization (January 2, 1996). ... Released by Reds (March 24, 1996). ... Signed by Omaha, Kansas City Royals organization (April 9, 1996). ... On disabled list (May 18-29, 1996). ... Granted free agency (October 15, 1996). ... Signed by San Francisco Giants organization (November 25, 1996). ... Granted free agency (October 30, 1997). ... Re-signed by Giants (December 7, 1997).

MISCELLANEOUS: Appeared in one game as pinch-runner (1991). ... Had sacrifice hit in only appearance as pinch-hitter (1992).

R

Year—Team (League)	W	L	Pct.	ERA	G	GS	CG	ShO	Sv.	IP	H	R	ER	BB	SO
1984— Little Falls (NYP)	2	1	.667	2.80	25	1	0	0	0	35 1/3	28	21	11	36	27
1985— Columbia (S. Atl.)	6	3	.667	4.03	49	3	0	0	6	80 1/3	89	41	36	36	71
1986— Lynchburg (Caroline)	2	1	.667	3.57	36	0	0	0	3	45 1/3	37	20	18	19	38
— Jackson (Texas)	3	4	.429	9.00	13	5	1	0	0	33	51	35	33	15	15
1987— Lynchburg (Caroline)	3	1	.750	2.78	*69	0	0	0	5	68	69	23	21	26	59
1988— Jackson (Texas)	2	7	.222	2.87	47	1	0	0	6	78 1/3	66	35	25	42	68
1989— Wichita (Texas)■	8	3	.727	3.63	54	0	0	0	8	74 1/3	74	30	30	37	40
1990— Las Vegas (PCL)	3	4	.429	3.51	27	2	0	0	8	59	50	24	23	22	46
— San Diego (N.L.)	1	1	.500	2.83	32	0	0	0	1	47 2/3	52	17	15	16	22
1991— San Diego (N.L.)	3	1	.750	3.26	64	1	0	0	0	80	66	31	29	44	40
1992— San Diego (N.L.)	6	3	.667	2.37	61	1	0	0	0	91	77	28	24	29	64
1993— San Diego (N.L.)	2	3	.400	3.30	34	0	0	0	2	30	34	15	11	9	22
— Florida (N.L.)■	0	1	.000	4.11	36	0	0	0	1	46	39	23	21	24	21
1994— St. Louis (N.L.)■	3	5	.375	4.03	56	0	0	0	0	60 1/3	62	30	27	26	43
1995— St. Louis (N.L.)	0	0	. . .	0.00	1	0	0	0	0	1 2/3	0	0	0	0	0
1996— Omaha (Am. Assoc.)■	2	3	.400	3.99	47	0	0	0	3	70	75	40	31	20	68
1997— San Francisco (N.L.)■	4	3	.571	3.17	71	0	0	0	1	65 1/3	65	24	23	21	32
Major league totals (7 years)	19	17	.528	3.20	355	2	0	0	5	422	395	168	150	169	244

DIVISION SERIES RECORD

Year—Team (League)	W	L	Pct.	ERA	G	GS	CG	ShO	Sv.	IP	H	R	ER	BB	SO
1997— San Francisco (N.L.)	0	0	. . .	0.00	2	0	0	0	0	1	1	0	0	0	0

ROGERS, KENNY   P   ATHLETICS

PERSONAL: Born November 10, 1964, in Savannah, Ga. ... 6-1/205. ... Throws left, bats left. ... Full name: Kenneth Scott Rogers.
HIGH SCHOOL: Plant City (Fla.).
TRANSACTIONS/CAREER NOTES: Selected by Texas Rangers organization in 39th round of free-agent draft (June 7, 1982). ... On Tulsa disabled list (April 12-30, 1986). ... Granted free agency (October 31, 1995). ... Signed by New York Yankees (December 30, 1995). ... Traded by Yankees with IF Mariano Duncan and P Kevin Henthorne to San Diego Padres for OF Greg Vaughn, P Kerry Taylor and P Chris Clark (July 4, 1997) ; trade later voided because Vaughn failed physical (July 6, 1997). ... Traded by Yankees with cash to Oakland Athletics for a player to be named later (November 7, 1997); Yankees acquired 3B Scott Brosius to complete deal (November 18, 1997).
STATISTICAL NOTES: Tied for A.L. lead with five balks in 1993. ... Pitched 4-0 perfect game against California (July 28, 1994).
MISCELLANEOUS: Holds Texas Rangers all-time record for highest winning percentage (.579).

Year—Team (League)	W	L	Pct.	ERA	G	GS	CG	ShO	Sv.	IP	H	R	ER	BB	SO
1982— GC Rangers (GCL)	0	0	. . .	0.00	2	0	0	0	0	3	0	0	0	0	4
1983— GC Rangers (GCL)	4	1	.800	2.36	15	6	0	0	1	53 1/3	40	21	14	20	36
1984— Burlington (Midw.)	4	7	.364	3.98	39	4	1	0	3	92 2/3	87	52	41	33	93
1985— Daytona Beach (FSL)	0	1	.000	7.20	6	0	0	0	0	10	12	9	8	11	9
— Burlington (Midw.)	2	5	.286	2.84	33	4	2	1	4	95	67	34	30	62	96
1986— Tulsa (Texas)	0	3	.000	9.91	10	4	0	0	0	26 1/3	39	30	29	18	23
— Salem (Carolina)	2	7	.222	6.27	12	12	0	0	0	66	75	54	46	26	46
1987— Charlotte (Fla. St.)	0	3	.000	4.76	5	3	0	0	0	17	17	13	9	8	14
— Tulsa (Texas)	1	5	.167	5.35	28	6	0	0	2	69	80	51	41	35	59
1988— Tulsa (Texas)	4	6	.400	4.00	13	13	2	0	0	83 1/3	73	43	37	34	76
— Charlotte (Fla. St.)	2	0	1.000	1.27	8	6	0	0	1	35 1/3	22	8	5	11	26
1989— Texas (A.L.)	3	4	.429	2.93	73	0	0	0	2	73 2/3	60	28	24	42	63
1990— Texas (A.L.)	10	6	.625	3.13	69	3	0	0	15	97 2/3	93	40	34	42	74
1991— Texas (A.L.)	10	10	.500	5.42	63	9	0	0	5	109 2/3	121	80	66	61	73
1992— Texas (A.L.)	3	6	.333	3.09	*81	0	0	0	6	78 2/3	80	32	27	26	70
1993— Texas (A.L.)	16	10	.615	4.10	35	33	5	0	0	208 1/3	210	108	95	71	140
1994— Texas (A.L.)	11	8	.579	4.46	24	24	6	2	0	167 1/3	169	93	83	52	120
1995— Texas (A.L.)	17	7	.708	3.38	31	31	3	1	0	208	192	87	78	76	140
1996— New York (A.L.)■	12	8	.600	4.68	30	30	2	1	0	179	179	97	93	83	92
1997— New York (A.L.)	6	7	.462	5.65	31	22	1	0	0	145	161	100	91	62	78
Major league totals (9 years)	88	66	.571	4.20	437	152	17	4	28	1267 1/3	1265	665	591	515	850

DIVISION SERIES RECORD

Year—Team (League)	W	L	Pct.	ERA	G	GS	CG	ShO	Sv.	IP	H	R	ER	BB	SO
1996— New York (A.L.)	0	0	. . .	9.00	2	1	0	0	0	2	5	2	2	2	1

CHAMPIONSHIP SERIES RECORD

Year—Team (League)	W	L	Pct.	ERA	G	GS	CG	ShO	Sv.	IP	H	R	ER	BB	SO
1996— New York (A.L.)	0	0	. . .	12.00	1	1	0	0	0	3	5	4	4	2	3

WORLD SERIES RECORD

NOTES: Member of World Series championship team (1996).

Year—Team (League)	W	L	Pct.	ERA	G	GS	CG	ShO	Sv.	IP	H	R	ER	BB	SO
1996— New York (A.L.)	0	0	. . .	22.50	1	1	0	0	0	2	5	5	5	2	0

ALL-STAR GAME RECORD

Year—League	W	L	Pct.	ERA	GS	CG	ShO	Sv.	IP	H	R	ER	BB	SO
1995— American	0	0	. . .	9.00	0	0	0	0	1	1	1	1	0	2

ROHRMEIER, DAN   1B/OF   MARINERS

PERSONAL: Born January 27, 1965, in Cincinnati. ... 6-0/195. ... Bats right, throws right. ... Full name: Daniel Rohrmeier.
HIGH SCHOOL: Elder (Cincinnati).
JUNIOR COLLEGE: Miami-Dade (North) Community College.
COLLEGE: St. Thomas (Fla.).

TRANSACTIONS/CAREER NOTES: Selected by Chicago White Sox organization in fifth round of free-agent draft (June 2, 1987). ... Traded by White Sox organization to Texas Rangers organization (June 3, 1989). ... Released by Rangers organization following 1991 season. ... Signed by Kansas City Royals organization (February 23, 1992). ... Released by Memphis, Royals organization (August 10, 1994). ... Signed by Chattanooga, Cincinnati Reds organization (August 12, 1994). ... Granted free agency (October 15, 1995). ... Signed by San Diego Padres organization (November 11, 1995). ... Granted free agency (October 15, 1996). ... Signed by Seattle Mariners organization (December 12, 1996).
STATISTICAL NOTES: Tied for Southern League lead with 10 intentional bases on balls received in 1996.

							BATTING								FIELDING		
Year Team (League)	Pos.	G	AB	R	H	2B	3B	HR	RBI	Avg.	BB	SO	SB	PO	A	E	Avg.
1987—Peninsula (Caro.)	3B	68	243	43	80	13	2	5	34	.329	29	37	2	47	124	21	.891
1988—Tampa (Florida State)	OF	114	421	53	109	•28	8	5	50	.259	27	58	11	207	12	7	.969
1989—Sarasota (Fla. St.)	OF	25	74	11	16	2	0	1	4	.216	12	15	1		1		.000
—Charlotte (Fla. St.)■	OF	18	65	9	20	3	1	1	11	.308	7	8	0				...
—Tulsa (Texas)	OF	57	210	24	67	3	4	5	27	.319	11	20	5	91	3	6	.940
1990—Tulsa (Texas)	OF-1B	119	453	76	138	24	7	10	62	.305	37	51	14	93	4	2	.980
1991—Tulsa (Texas)	OF	121	418	67	122	20	2	5	62	.292	60	57	3	168	12	3	.984
1992—Memphis (Southern)■	OF-1B	123	433	54	140	33	2	6	69	.323	26	46	3	203	11	3	.986
—Omaha (A.A.)	OF	8	29	4	7	1	0	1	5	.241	3	4	0	17	0	1	.944
1993—Omaha (A.A.)	OF-1B	118	432	51	107	23	3	17	70	.248	23	59	2	71	3	0	1.000
1994—Memphis (Southern)	1B-OF	112	436	64	118	34	0	18	72	.271	31	80	2	274	16	1	.997
—Chattanooga (Sou.)■	OF-1B	17	66	9	22	7	0	0	10	.333	5	5	0	48	2	2	.962
1995—Indianapolis (A.A.)	OF	10	34	5	6	3	1	0	3	.176	0	4	0	10	0	0	1.000
—Chattanooga (Sou.)	OF-3B-1B	118	426	77	139	31	0	17	76	.326	41	63	0	146	19	4	.976
1996—Memphis (Southern)	OF-1B-3B	134	471	98	*162	29	2	28	95	*.344	77	76	2	107	9	1	.991
1997—Tacoma (PCL)	OF-1B-P	1	471	86	140	43	4	33	120	.297	45	81	1	405	31	5	.989
—Seattle (A.L.)■	DH-1B	7	9	4	3	0	0	0	2	.333	2	4	0	6	1	0	1.000
Major league totals (1 year)		7	9	4	3	0	0	0	2	.333	2	4	0	6	1	0	1.000

RECORD AS PITCHER

Year Team (League)	W	L	Pct.	ERA	G	GS	CG	ShO	Sv.	IP	H	R	ER	BB	SO
1997—Tacoma (PCL)	0	0	...	0.00	1	0	0	0	0	1	2	1	0	0	0

ROJAS, MEL P METS

PERSONAL: Born December 10, 1966, in Haina, Dominican Republic. ... 5-11/195. ... Throws right, bats right. ... Full name: Melquiades Rojas. ... Nephew of Felipe Alou, manager, Montreal Expos, and major league outfielder/first baseman with six teams (1958-74); nephew of Matty Alou, major league outfielder with six teams (1960-74); nephew of Jesus Alou, major league outfielder with four teams (1963-75 and 1978-79); brother of Francisco Rojas, minor league outfielder (1978-79); and cousin of Moises Alou, outfielder, Houston Astros. ... Name pronounced RO-hoss.
HIGH SCHOOL: Liceo Manresa (Santo Domingo, Dominican Republic).
TRANSACTIONS/CAREER NOTES: Signed as non-drafted free agent by Montreal Expos organization (November 7, 1985). ... On Rockford disabled list (May 7-June 14, 1988). ... On West Palm Beach disabled list (August 8, 1988-remainder of season). ... On Indianapolis disabled list (June 26-July 5, 1991). ... On disabled list (July 4-19, 1993). ... Granted free agency (December 7, 1996). ... Signed by Chicago Cubs (December 11, 1996). ... Traded by Cubs with OF Brian McRae and P Turk Wendell to New York Mets for OF Lance Johnson and two players to be named later (August 8, 1997); Mets traded P Mark Clark (August 11) and IF Manny Alexander (August 14) to Cubs to complete deal.
RECORDS: Shares major league record for striking out side on nine pitches (May 11, 1994, ninth inning).

Year Team (League)	W	L	Pct.	ERA	G	GS	CG	ShO	Sv.	IP	H	R	ER	BB	SO
1986—GC Expos (GCL)	4	5	.444	4.88	13	12	1	0	0	55 1/3	63	39	30	37	34
1987—Burlington (Midw.)	8	9	.471	3.80	25	25	4	1	0	158 2/3	146	84	67	67	100
1988—Rockford (Midwest)	6	4	.600	2.45	12	12	0	0	0	73 1/3	52	30	20	29	72
—W.P. Beach (FSL)	1	0	1.000	3.60	2	2	0	0	0	5	4	2	2	1	4
1989—Jacksonville (Southern)	10	7	.588	2.49	34	12	1	1	5	112	62	39	31	57	104
1990—Indianapolis (A.A.)	2	4	.333	3.13	17	17	0	0	0	97 2/3	84	42	34	47	64
—Montreal (N.L.)	3	1	.750	3.60	23	0	0	0	1	40	34	17	16	24	26
1991—Montreal (N.L.)	3	3	.500	3.75	37	0	0	0	6	48	42	21	20	13	37
—Indianapolis (A.A.)	4	2	.667	4.10	14	10	0	0	1	52 2/3	50	29	24	14	55
1992—Indianapolis (A.A.)	2	1	.667	5.40	4	0	0	0	0	8 1/3	10	5	5	3	7
—Montreal (N.L.)	7	1	.875	1.43	68	0	0	0	10	100 2/3	71	17	16	34	70
1993—Montreal (N.L.)	5	8	.385	2.95	66	0	0	0	10	88 1/3	80	39	29	30	48
1994—Montreal (N.L.)	3	2	.600	3.32	58	0	0	0	16	84	71	35	31	21	84
1995—Montreal (N.L.)	1	4	.200	4.12	59	0	0	0	30	67 2/3	69	32	31	29	61
1996—Montreal (N.L.)	7	4	.636	3.22	74	0	0	0	36	81	56	30	29	28	92
1997—Chicago (N.L.)■	0	4	.000	4.42	54	0	0	0	13	59	54	30	29	30	61
—New York (N.L.)■	0	2	.000	5.13	23	0	0	0	2	26 1/3	24	17	15	6	32
Major league totals (8 years)	29	29	.500	3.27	462	0	0	0	124	595	501	238	216	215	511

ROLEN, SCOTT 3B PHILLIES

PERSONAL: Born April 4, 1975, in Evansville, Ind. ... 6-4/195. ... Bats right, throws right. ... Full name: Scott Bruce Rolen.
HIGH SCHOOL: Jasper (Ind.).
TRANSACTIONS/CAREER NOTES: Selected by Philadelphia Phillies organization in second round of free-agent draft (June 3, 1993).
HONORS: Named N.L. Rookie Player of the Year by THE SPORTING NEWS (1997). ... Named N.L. Rookie of the Year by Baseball Writers' Association of America (1997).
STATISTICAL NOTES: Led South Atlantic League third basemen with 457 total chances and 36 double plays in 1994. ... Led N.L. third basemen in total chances with 459 in 1997.

							BATTING								FIELDING		
Year Team (League)	Pos.	G	AB	R	H	2B	3B	HR	RBI	Avg.	BB	SO	SB	PO	A	E	Avg.
1993—Martinsville (App.)	3B	25	80	8	25	5	0	0	12	.313	10	15	3	23	57	10	.889
1994—Spartanburg (SAL)	3B	138	513	83	151	34	5	14	72	.294	55	90	6	96	323	38	.917

Year Team (League)	Pos.	G	AB	R	H	2B	3B	HR	RBI	Avg.	BB	SO	SB	PO	A	E	Avg.
1995— Clearwater (FSL)	3B	66	238	45	69	13	2	10	39	.290	37	46	4	43	135	20	.899
—Reading (Eastern)	3B	20	76	16	22	3	0	3	15	.289	7	14	1	10	47	4	.934
1996—Reading (Eastern)	3B	61	230	44	83	22	2	9	42	.361	34	32	8	41	125	9	.949
—Scran./W.B. (Int'l)......	3B	45	168	23	46	17	0	2	19	.274	28	28	4	32	88	6	.952
—Philadelphia (N.L.)......	3B	37	130	10	33	7	0	4	18	.254	13	27	0	29	54	4	.954
1997—Philadelphia (N.L.)......	3B	156	561	93	159	35	3	21	92	.283	76	138	16	*144	291	24	.948
Major league totals (2 years)		193	691	103	192	42	3	25	110	.278	89	165	16	173	345	28	.949

ROMERO, MANDY C PADRES

PERSONAL: Born October 19, 1967, in Miami. ... 5-11/196. ... Bats both, throws right. ... Full name: Armando Romero. ... Brother of Andy Romero, minor league first baseman/outfielder (1977-80).
HIGH SCHOOL: Miami Jackson.
JUNIOR COLLEGE: Brevard Community College (Fla.).
TRANSACTIONS/CAREER NOTES: Selected by Pittsburgh Pirates in 19th round of free-agent draft (June 1, 1988). ... On disabled list (April 11-29 and June 20-28, 1991; July 13-August 7, 1992; and June 28-July 8 and August 23, 1993-remainder of season). ... Released by Pirates organization (May 6, 1994). ... Signed by Kansas City Royals organization (January 30, 1995). ... Granted free agency (October 16, 1995). ... Signed by San Diego Padres organization (November 25, 1995). ... Granted free agency (October 15, 1996). ... Re-signed by Padres (October 27, 1996).
STATISTICAL NOTES: Led South Atlantic League catchers with .989 fielding percentage in 1989. ... Led Carolina League with 222 total bases and .483 slugging percentage in 1990. ... Tied for Southern League lead with 14 passed balls in 1991. ... Tied for Southern League lead in errors by catcher with 14 in 1992.

Year Team (League)	Pos.	G	AB	R	H	2B	3B	HR	RBI	Avg.	BB	SO	SB	PO	A	E	Avg.
1988— Princeton (Appal.)	C	30	71	7	22	6	0	2	11	.310	13	15	1	143	14	2	.987
1989— Augusta (S. Atl.).........	C-3B	121	388	58	87	26	3	4	55	.224	67	74	8	629	74	9	†.987
1990— Salem (Carolina)	C	124	460	62	134	31	3	17	*90	.291	55	68	0	565	60	7	.989
1991— Carolina (Southern)....	C	98	323	29	70	12	0	3	31	.217	45	53	1	552	63	4	*.994
1992— Carolina (Southern)....	C-3B	80	269	28	58	16	0	3	27	.216	29	39	0	523	43	‡14	.976
1993— Buffalo (A.A.).............	C	42	136	11	31	6	1	2	14	.228	6	12	1	168	13	5	.973
1994— Buffalo (A.A.).............	C	7	23	3	3	0	0	0	1	.130	2	1	0	34	5	0	1.000
1995— Wichita (Texas)■.........	C-1B	121	440	73	133	32	1	21	82	.302	69	60	1	159	18	4	.978
1996— Memphis (South.)■......	C	88	297	40	80	15	0	10	46	.269	41	52	3	657	52	12	.983
1997— Mobile (Southern).......	C	61	222	50	71	22	0	13	52	.320	38	31	0	436	33	6	.987
—Las Vegas (PCL)	C-3B-1B	33	91	19	28	4	1	3	13	.308	11	19	0	145	8	3	.981
—San Diego (N.L.)	C	21	48	7	10	0	0	2	4	.208	2	18	1	96	8	0	1.000
Major league totals (1 year)		21	48	7	10	0	0	2	4	.208	2	18	1	96	8	0	1.000

ROSADO, JOSE P ROYALS

PERSONAL: Born November 9, 1974, in Jersey City, N.J. ... 6-0/175. ... Throws left, bats left. ... Full name: Jose Antonio Rosado.
HIGH SCHOOL: Jose Salegria (Dorado, Puerto Rico).
JUNIOR COLLEGE: Galveston College (Texas).
TRANSACTIONS/CAREER NOTES: Selected by Kansas City Royals organization in 12th round of free-agent draft (June 2, 1994).
MISCELLANEOUS: Appeared in one game as pinch-runner (1997).

Year Team (League)	W	L	Pct.	ERA	G	GS	CG	ShO	Sv.	IP	H	R	ER	BB	SO
1994— GC Royals (GCL)	6	2	.750	*1.25	14	12	0	0	0	64²/₃	45	14	9	7	56
1995— Wilmington (Caro.).............	10	7	.588	3.13	25	25	0	0	0	138	128	53	48	30	117
1996— Wichita (Texas)	2	0	1.000	0.00	2	2	0	0	0	13	10	0	0	1	12
—Omaha (Am. Assoc.)..........	8	3	.727	3.17	15	15	1	0	0	96²/₃	80	38	34	38	82
—Kansas City (A.L.)	8	6	.571	3.21	16	16	2	1	0	106²/₃	101	39	38	26	64
1997— Kansas City (A.L.)	9	12	.429	4.69	33	33	2	0	0	203¹/₃	208	117	106	73	129
Major league totals (2 years)......	17	18	.486	4.18	49	49	4	1	0	310	309	156	144	99	193

ALL-STAR GAME RECORD

Year League	W	L	Pct.	ERA	GS	CG	ShO	Sv.	IP	H	R	ER	BB	SO
1997— American	1	0	1.000	9.00	0	0	0	0	1	2	1	1	1	1

ROSARIO, MELVIN C ORIOLES

PERSONAL: Born May 25, 1973, in Santo Domingo, Dominican Republic. ... 6-0/200. ... Bats both, throws right. ... Full name: Melvin Gregario Rosario.
HIGH SCHOOL: Sonador Bonao (Santo Domingo, Dominican Republic).
COLLEGE: Utesa-Santo Domingo.
TRANSACTIONS/CAREER NOTES: Signed as non-drafted free agent by San Diego Padres organization (April 6, 1991). ... Released by Padres organization (January 7, 1994). ... Signed by Chicago White Sox organization (January 10, 1995). ... Selected by Padres organization from White Sox organization in Rule 5 minor league draft (December 5, 1995). ... Traded by Padres organization to Baltimore Orioles organization for OF Keith Eaddy (April 23, 1996).
STATISTICAL NOTES: Led Northwest League catchers with six double plays in 1992.

Year Team (League)	Pos.	G	AB	R	H	2B	3B	HR	RBI	Avg.	BB	SO	SB	PO	A	E	Avg.
1992— Spokane (N'west).......	C	66	237	38	54	13	1	10	40	.228	20	62	5	313	*67	*18	.955
1993— Waterloo (Midw.)	C	32	105	15	22	6	2	5	15	.210	7	37	5	62	11	1	.986
—Spokane (N'west).......	C	41	140	17	32	5	0	4	19	.229	8	36	2	132	16	5	.967
1994—								Did not play.									

— 488 —

Year Team (League)	Pos.	G	AB	R	H	2B	3B	HR	RBI	Avg.	BB	SO	SB	PO	A	E	Avg.
1995— South Bend (Mid.)■...	C	118	450	58	123	30	6	15	57	.273	30	109	1	271	58	13	.962
1996— Rancho Cuca. (Cal.) ...	C	10	33	7	9	3	0	3	10	.273	3	8	1	37	10	0	1.000
— High Desert (Cal.)■ ...	C	42	163	35	52	9	1	10	34	.319	21	45	4	223	31	5	.981
— Bowie (Eastern)...	C	47	162	14	34	10	0	2	17	.210	6	43	3	219	38	7	.973
— Rochester (Int'l)	C	3	2	0	0	0	0	0	0	.000	0	1	0	7	0	1	.875
1997— Bowie (Eastern)	C	123	430	68	113	26	1	12	60	.263	27	106	4	621	*87	10	.986
— Baltimore (A.L.)..........	C	4	3	0	0	0	0	0	0	.000	0	1	0	7	0	1	.875
Major league totals (1 year)		4	3	0	0	0	0	0	0	.000	0	1	0	7	0	1	.875

ROSE, BRIAN   P   RED SOX

PERSONAL: Born February 13, 1976, in New Bedford, Mass. ... 6-3/210. ... Throws right, bats right. ... Full name: Brian Leonard Rose.
HIGH SCHOOL: Dartmouth (North Dartmouth, Mass.).
TRANSACTIONS/CAREER NOTES: Selected by Boston Red Sox organization in third round of free-agent draft (June 2, 1994).
HONORS: Named International League Most Valuable Pitcher (1997).

Year Team (League)	W	L	Pct.	ERA	G	GS	CG	ShO	Sv.	IP	H	R	ER	BB	SO
1995— Michigan (Midwest)	8	5	.615	3.44	21	20	2	0	0	136	127	63	52	31	105
1996— Trenton (Eastern)	12	7	.632	4.01	27	27	4	2	0	163 2/3	157	82	73	45	115
1997— Pawtucket (Int'l)	*17	5	.773	*3.02	27	26	3	0	0	*190 2/3	188	74	64	46	116
— Boston (A.L.).......................	0	0	. . .	12.00	1	1	0	0	0	3	5	4	4	2	3
Major league totals (1 year)........	0	0	. . .	12.00	1	1	0	0	0	3	5	4	4	2	3

ROSE, PETE   3B   REDS

PERSONAL: Born November 16, 1969, in Cincinnati. ... 6-1/180. ... Bats left, throws right. ... Full name: Peter Edward Rose Jr. ... Son of Pete Rose, former major league infielder/outfielder with Cincinnati Reds, Philadelphia Phillies and Montreal Expos (1963-86) and former manager of Reds (1984-89).
HIGH SCHOOL: Oak Hills (Cincinnati).
TRANSACTIONS/CAREER NOTES: Selected by Baltimore Orioles organization in 13th round of free-agent draft (June 1, 1988). ... Traded by Orioles organization to Chicago White Sox organization (March 31, 1991). ... Selected by Cleveland Indians organization from White Sox organization in Rule 5 minor league draft (December 9, 1991). ... On disabled list (July 9, 1993-remainder of season). ... Released by Indians organization (March 30, 1994). ... Signed by White Sox organization (April 4, 1994). ... Granted free agency (October 15, 1996). ... Signed by Chattanooga, Cincinnati Reds organization (December 13, 1996). ... Granted free agency (October 15, 1997). ... Re-signed by Reds organization (January 12, 1998).
STATISTICAL NOTES: Led Midwest League third basemen with 124 putouts and 405 total chances in 1995. ... Led Southern League third basemen with .943 fielding percentage in 1996.

Year Team (League)	Pos.	G	AB	R	H	2B	3B	HR	RBI	Avg.	BB	SO	SB	PO	A	E	Avg.
1989— Frederick (Carolina)....	3B	24	67	3	12	3	0	0	7	.179	0	15	1	15	39	8	.871
— Erie (N.Y.-Penn).........	3B	58	228	30	63	13	5	2	26	.276	12	34	1	46	96	13	.916
1990— Frederick (Carolina)...	3B	97	323	32	75	14	2	1	41	.232	26	33	0	51	120	12	.934
1991— Sarasota (Fla. St.)■...	3B-2B	99	323	31	70	12	2	0	35	.217	36	35	5	69	175	21	.921
1992— Columbus (S. Atl.)■ ..	3B	131	510	67	129	24	6	9	54	.253	48	53	2	90	*282	20	.949
1993— Kinston (Carolina)	3D	74	204	33	62	10	1	7	30	.218	25	34	1	40	140	23	.892
1994— Hickory (S. Atl.)■	3B	32	114	14	25	4	1	0	12	.219	13	18	0	23	81	9	.920
— Prince William (Car.) ..	3B	45	146	18	41	3	1	4	22	.281	18	15	0	23	123	9	.942
— GC Whi. Sox (GCL)	3B	2	4	1	2	0	0	0	1	.500	0	0	0	1	1	1	.667
1995— Birmingham (Sou.)......	3B	5	13	1	5	1	0	0	2	.385	3	3	0	4	8	0	1.000
— South Bend (Mid.)......	3B-1B	116	423	56	117	24	6	4	65	.277	54	45	2	•127	249	32	.922
1996— Birmingham (Sou.).....	3-1-2-S	108	399	40	97	13	1	3	44	.243	32	54	1	133	208	20	†.945
1997— Chattanooga (Sou.).....	3B	112	445	75	137	31	0	25	98	.308	34	63	0	81	217	27	.917
— Indianapolis (A.A.)......	3B	12	40	2	9	2	0	0	1	.225	2	11	0	3	19	1	.957
— Cincinnati (N.L.)■......	3B-1B	11	14	2	2	0	0	0	0	.143	2	9	0	6	3	2	.818
Major league totals (1 year)		11	14	2	2	0	0	0	0	.143	2	9	0	6	3	2	.818

ROSENGREN, JOHN   P   TIGERS

PERSONAL: Born August 10, 1972, in Bronxville, N.Y. ... 6-4/190. ... Throws left, bats left. ... Full name: John Eric Rosengren.
COLLEGE: North Carolina.
TRANSACTIONS/CAREER NOTES: Selected by Detroit Tigers organization in 23rd round of free-agent draft (June 1, 1992).

Year Team (League)	W	L	Pct.	ERA	G	GS	CG	ShO	Sv.	IP	H	R	ER	BB	SO
1992— Bristol (Appalachian)..........	0	3	.000	7.83	14	3	0	0	0	23	16	21	20	30	28
1993— Niagara Falls (NYP)............	7	3	.700	2.41	15	15	0	0	0	82	52	32	22	38	91
1994— Lakeland (Fla. St.)	9	6	.600	2.52	22	22	4	•3	0	135 2/3	113	51	38	56	101
— Trenton (Eastern)	0	2	.000	7.27	3	3	0	0	0	17 1/3	21	15	14	11	7
1995— Jacksonville (Southern)......	2	7	.222	4.52	14	13	0	0	0	67 2/3	73	39	34	40	59
— Lakeland (Fla. St.)	3	3	.500	3.99	13	8	0	0	0	56 1/3	46	33	25	36	35
1996— Jacksonville (Southern)......	5	1	.833	4.55	60	0	0	0	1	55 1/3	48	36	28	37	47
1997— Toledo (Int'l)......................	1	3	.250	3.99	54	0	0	0	2	56 1/3	44	29	25	49	53

ROSKOS, JOHN   C/1B   MARLINS

PERSONAL: Born November 19, 1974, in Victorville, Calif. ... 5-11/195. ... Bats right, throws right. ... Full name: John Edward Roskos.
HIGH SCHOOL: Cibola (Albuquerque, N.M.).

TRANSACTIONS/CAREER NOTES: Selected by Florida Marlins organization in second round of free-agent draft (June 3, 1993). ... On Elmira disabled list (August 9-September 19, 1994). ... On Kane County disabled list (August 28-September 7, 1995). ... Granted free agency (December 21, 1997). ... Re-signed by Marlins organization (December 21, 1997).

Year Team (League)	Pos.	G	AB	R	H	2B	3B	HR	RBI	Avg.	BB	SO	SB	PO	A	E	Avg.
1993— GC Marlins (GCL)	C	11	40	6	7	1	0	1	3	.175	5	11	1	18	2	2	.909
1994— Elmira (N.Y.-Penn)	C	39	136	11	38	7	0	4	23	.279	27	37	0	143	13	4	.975
1995— Kane County (Midw.)	C	114	418	74	124	36	3	12	88	.297	42	86	2	431	47	7	.986
1996— Portland (Eastern)	1B-C	121	396	53	109	26	3	9	58	.275	67	102	3	719	50	10	.987
1997— Portland (Eastern)	C-1B	123	451	66	139	31	1	24	84	.308	50	81	4	630	37	8	.988

RUEBEL, MATT — P

PERSONAL: Born October 16, 1969, in Cincinnati. ... 6-2/180. ... Throws left, bats left. ... Full name: Matthew Alexander Ruebel.
HIGH SCHOOL: Ames (Iowa).
COLLEGE: Oklahoma.
TRANSACTIONS/CAREER NOTES: Selected by Pittsburgh Pirates organization in third round of free-agent draft (June 3, 1991). ... On Calgary disabled list (July 1-15, 1996). ... On disabled list (May 5-21, 1997). ... Granted free agency (October 15, 1997).

Year Team (League)	W	L	Pct.	ERA	G	GS	CG	ShO	Sv.	IP	H	R	ER	BB	SO
1991— Welland (N.Y.-Penn)	1	1	.500	1.95	6	6	0	0	0	27 2/3	16	9	6	11	27
—Augusta (S. Atl.)	3	4	.429	3.83	8	8	2	1	0	47	43	26	20	25	35
1992— Augusta (S. Atl.)	5	2	.714	2.78	12	10	1	0	0	64 2/3	53	26	20	19	65
—Salem (Carolina)	1	6	.143	4.71	13	13	1	0	0	78 1/3	77	49	41	43	46
1993— Salem (Carolina)	1	4	.200	5.94	19	1	0	0	0	33 1/3	34	31	22	32	29
—Augusta (S. Atl.)	5	5	.500	2.42	23	7	1	1	0	63 1/3	51	28	17	34	50
1994— Salem (Carolina)	6	6	.500	3.44	21	13	0	0	0	86 1/3	87	49	33	27	72
—Carolina (Southern)	1	1	.500	6.61	6	3	0	0	0	16 1/3	28	15	12	3	14
1995— Carolina (Southern)	13	5	.722	2.76	27	27	4	*3	0	169 1/3	150	68	52	45	136
1996— Calgary (PCL)	5	3	.625	4.60	13	13	1	0	0	76 1/3	89	43	39	28	48
—Pittsburgh (N.L.)	1	1	.500	4.60	26	7	0	0	1	58 2/3	64	38	30	25	22
1997— Pittsburgh (N.L.)	3	2	.600	6.32	44	0	0	0	0	62 2/3	77	50	44	27	50
Major league totals (2 years)	4	3	.571	5.49	70	7	0	0	1	121 1/3	141	88	74	52	72

RUETER, KIRK — P — GIANTS

PERSONAL: Born December 1, 1970, in Centralia, Ill. ... 6-3/207. ... Throws left, bats left. ... Full name: Kirk Wesley Rueter. ... Name pronounced REE-ter.
HIGH SCHOOL: Nashville (Ill.) Community.
COLLEGE: Murray State.
TRANSACTIONS/CAREER NOTES: Selected by Montreal Expos organization in 19th round of free-agent draft (June 3, 1991). ... On Montreal disabled list (May 10-26, 1996); included rehabilitation assignment to Ottawa (May 20-24). ... Traded by Expos with P Tim Scott to San Francisco Giants for P Mark Leiter (July 30, 1996).
HONORS: Named N.L. Rookie Pitcher of the Year by THE SPORTING NEWS (1993).
STATISTICAL NOTES: Pitched 1-0 one-hit, complete-game victory for Montreal against San Francisco (August 27, 1995).

Year Team (League)	W	L	Pct.	ERA	G	GS	CG	ShO	Sv.	IP	H	R	ER	BB	SO
1991— GC Expos (GCL)	1	1	.500	0.95	5	4	0	0	0	19	16	5	2	4	19
—Sumter (S. Atl.)	3	1	.750	1.33	8	5	0	0	0	40 2/3	32	8	6	10	27
1992— Rockford (Midwest)	11	9	.550	2.58	26	26	6	•2	0	174 1/3	150	68	50	36	153
1993— Harrisburg (Eastern)	5	0	1.000	1.36	9	8	1	1	0	59 2/3	47	10	9	7	36
—Ottawa (Int'l)	4	2	.667	2.70	7	7	1	0	0	43 1/3	46	20	13	3	27
—Montreal (N.L.)	8	0	1.000	2.73	14	14	1	0	0	85 2/3	85	33	26	18	31
1994— Montreal (N.L.)	7	3	.700	5.17	20	20	0	0	0	92 1/3	106	60	53	23	50
—Ottawa (Int'l)	0	0	...	4.50	1	1	0	0	0	2	1	1	1	0	1
1995— Montreal (N.L.)	5	3	.625	3.23	9	9	1	1	0	47 1/3	38	17	17	9	28
—Ottawa (Int'l)	9	7	.563	3.06	20	20	3	1	0	120 2/3	120	50	41	25	67
1996— Ottawa (Int'l)	1	2	.333	4.20	3	3	1	0	0	15	21	7	7	3	3
—Montreal (N.L.)	5	6	.455	4.58	16	16	0	0	0	78 2/3	91	44	40	22	30
—San Francisco (N.L.)■	1	2	.333	1.93	4	3	0	0	0	23 1/3	18	6	5	5	16
—Phoenix (PCL)	1	2	.333	3.51	5	5	0	0	0	25 2/3	25	12	10	12	15
1997— San Francisco (N.L.)	13	6	.684	3.45	32	32	0	0	0	190 2/3	194	83	73	51	115
Major league totals (5 years)	39	20	.661	3.72	95	94	2	1	0	518	532	243	214	128	270

DIVISION SERIES RECORD

Year Team (League)	W	L	Pct.	ERA	G	GS	CG	ShO	Sv.	IP	H	R	ER	BB	SO
1997— San Francisco (N.L.)	0	0	...	1.29	1	1	0	0	0	7	4	1	1	3	5

RUFFCORN, SCOTT — P

PERSONAL: Born December 29, 1969, in New Braunfels, Texas. ... 6-4/210. ... Throws right, bats right. ... Full name: Scott Patrick Ruffcorn.
HIGH SCHOOL: S.F. Austin (Austin, Texas).
COLLEGE: Baylor.
TRANSACTIONS/CAREER NOTES: Selected by Atlanta Braves organization in 39th round of free-agent draft (June 1, 1988); did not sign. Selected by Chicago White Sox organization in first round (25th pick overall) of free-agent draft (June 3, 1991). ... On Nashville disabled list (May 28-August 17, 1995). ... Traded by White Sox to Philadelphia Phillies for cash (January 10, 1997). ... On Philadelphia disabled list (August 18, 1997-remainder of season). ... Released by Phillies (October 10, 1997).

Year	Team (League)	W	L	Pct.	ERA	G	GS	CG	ShO	Sv.	IP	H	R	ER	BB	SO
1991—	GC White Sox (GCL)	0	0	...	3.18	4	2	0	0	0	11 1/3	8	7	4	5	15
—	South Bend (Mid.)	1	3	.250	3.92	9	9	0	0	0	43 2/3	35	26	19	25	45
1992—	Sarasota (Florida State)......	14	5	.737	2.19	25	24	2	0	0	160 1/3	122	53	39	39	140
1993—	Birmingham (Southern)	9	4	.692	2.73	20	20	3	*3	0	135	108	47	41	52	*141
—	Chicago (A.L.)	0	2	.000	8.10	3	2	0	0	0	10	9	11	9	10	2
—	Nashville (A.A.)	2	2	.500	2.80	7	6	1	0	0	45	30	16	14	8	44
1994—	Chicago (A.L.)	0	2	.000	12.79	2	2	0	0	0	6 1/3	15	11	9	5	3
—	Nashville (A.A.)	*15	3	•.833	2.72	24	24	3	•3	0	165 2/3	139	57	50	40	144
1995—	Nashville (A.A.)	0	0	...	108.00	2	2	0	0	0	1/3	3	4	4	3	0
—	Birmingham (Southern)	0	2	.000	5.63	3	3	0	0	0	16	17	11	10	10	13
—	GC White Sox (GCL)	0	0	...	0.90	3	3	0	0	0	10	7	4	1	5	7
—	Chicago (A.L.)	0	0	...	7.88	4	0	0	0	0	8	10	7	7	13	5
1996—	Nashville (A.A.)	13	4	.765	3.87	24	24	2	1	0	149	142	71	64	61	129
—	Chicago (A.L.)	0	1	.000	11.37	3	1	0	0	0	6 1/3	10	8	8	6	3
1997—	Philadelphia (N.L.)■	0	3	.000	7.71	18	4	0	0	0	39 2/3	42	40	34	36	33
—	Scran./W.B. (Int'l).............	2	0	1.000	1.16	5	5	2	2	0	31	22	6	4	10	20
A.L. totals (4 years)		0	5	.000	9.68	12	5	0	0	0	30 2/3	44	37	33	34	13
N.L. totals (1 year)		0	3	.000	7.71	18	4	0	0	0	39 2/3	42	40	34	36	33
Major league totals (5 years)......		0	8	.000	8.57	30	9	0	0	0	70 1/3	86	77	67	70	46

R

RUFFIN, BRUCE — P — ROCKIES

PERSONAL: Born October 4, 1963, in Lubbock, Texas. ... 6-2/215. ... Throws left, bats both. ... Full name: Bruce Wayne Ruffin.
HIGH SCHOOL: J.M. Hanks (El Paso, Texas).
COLLEGE: Texas.
TRANSACTIONS/CAREER NOTES: Selected by Philadelphia Phillies organization in 31st round of free-agent draft (June 7, 1982); did not sign. ... Selected by Phillies organization in second round of free-agent draft (June 3, 1985); pick received as compensation for Pittsburgh Pirates signing free-agent OF Sixto Lezcano. ... Traded by Phillies to Milwaukee Brewers for SS/3B Dale Sveum (December 11, 1991). ... Granted free agency (November 5, 1992). ... Signed by Colorado Rockies (December 7, 1992). ... On Colorado disabled list (May 29-June 17 and June 26-August 22, 1995); included rehabilitation assignment to New Haven (August 16-20). ... On Colorado disabled list (May 19-June 17 and June 27, 1997-remainder of season); included rehabilitation assignment to Colorado Springs (June 12-17). ... Granted free agency (October 31, 1997). ... Re-signed by Rockies organization (January 3, 1998).
RECORDS: Shares major league record for most strikeouts in one inning—4 (July 25, 1996, ninth inning). ... Holds Colorado Rockies all-time records for most saves (53) and most strikeouts (288).
MISCELLANEOUS: Struck out in only appearance as pinch-hitter (1990). ... Holds Colorado Rockies all-time record for most saves (60).

Year	Team (League)	W	L	Pct.	ERA	G	GS	CG	ShO	Sv.	IP	H	R	ER	BB	SO
1985—	Clearwater (Fla. St.)	5	5	.500	2.88	14	14	3	1	0	97	87	33	31	34	74
1986—	Reading (Eastern)	8	4	.667	3.29	16	13	4	2	0	90 1/3	89	41	33	26	68
—	Philadelphia (N.L.).............	9	4	.692	2.46	21	21	6	0	0	146 1/3	138	53	40	44	70
1987—	Philadelphia (N.L.).............	11	14	.440	4.35	35	35	3	1	0	204 2/3	236	118	99	73	93
1988—	Philadelphia (N.L.).............	6	10	.375	4.43	55	15	3	0	3	144 1/3	151	86	71	80	82
1989—	Philadelphia (N.L.).............	6	10	.375	4.44	24	23	1	0	0	125 2/3	152	69	62	62	70
—	Scran./W.B. (Int'l).............	5	1	.833	4.68	9	9	0	0	0	50	44	28	26	39	44
1990—	Philadelphia (N.L.).............	6	13	.316	5.38	32	25	2	1	0	149	178	99	89	62	79
1991—	Scran./W.B. (Int'l).............	4	5	.444	4.66	13	13	1	0	0	75 1/3	82	43	39	41	50
—	Philadelphia (N.L.).............	4	7	.364	3.78	31	15	1	1	0	119	125	52	50	38	85
1992—	Milwaukee (A.L.)■	1	6	.143	6.67	25	6	1	0	0	58	66	43	43	41	45
—	Denver (Am. Assoc.)	3	0	1.000	0.94	4	4	1	0	0	28 2/3	28	12	3	8	17
1993—	Colorado (N.L.)■	6	5	.545	3.87	59	12	0	0	2	139 2/3	145	71	60	69	126
1994—	Colorado (N.L.).................	4	5	.444	4.04	56	0	0	0	16	55 2/3	55	28	25	30	65
1995—	Colorado (N.L.).................	0	1	.000	2.12	37	0	0	0	11	34	26	8	8	19	23
—	New Haven (Eastern)..........	0	0	...	0.00	2	2	0	0	0	2	1	0	0	0	2
1996—	Colorado (N.L.).................	7	5	.583	4.00	71	0	0	0	24	69 2/3	55	35	31	29	74
1997—	Colorado (N.L.).................	0	2	.000	5.32	23	0	0	0	7	22	18	15	13	18	31
—	Colo. Springs (PCL)	0	0	...	3.38	2	0	0	0	0	2 2/3	1	1	1	0	2
A.L. totals (1 year)		1	6	.143	6.67	25	6	1	0	0	58	66	43	43	41	45
N.L. totals (11 years)		59	76	.437	4.08	444	146	16	3	63	1210	1279	634	548	524	798
Major league totals (12 years)....		60	82	.423	4.19	469	152	17	3	63	1268	1345	677	591	565	843

DIVISION SERIES RECORD

Year	Team (League)	W	L	Pct.	ERA	G	GS	CG	ShO	Sv.	IP	H	R	ER	BB	SO
1995—	Colorado (N.L.)	0	0	...	2.70	4	0	0	0	0	3 1/3	3	1	1	2	2

RUNYAN, SEAN — P — TIGERS

PERSONAL: Born June 21, 1974, in Fort Smith, Ark. ... 6-3/200. ... Throws left, bats left. ... Full name: Sean David Runyan.
HIGH SCHOOL: Urbandale (Iowa).
TRANSACTIONS/CAREER NOTES: Selected by Houston Astros organization in fifth round of free-agent draft (June 1, 1992). ... Traded by Astros to San Diego Padres for IF Luis Lopez (March 16, 1997). ... Selected by Detroit Tigers from Padres organization in Rule 5 major league draft (December 15, 1997).

Year	Team (League)	W	L	Pct.	ERA	G	GS	CG	ShO	Sv.	IP	H	R	ER	BB	SO
1992—	GC Astros (GCL)	3	3	.500	3.20	10	10	0	0	0	45	54	19	16	16	30
1993—	GC Astros (GCL)	4	3	.571	2.98	12	12	0	0	0	66 1/3	66	35	22	24	52
1994—	Auburn (N.Y.-Penn)	7	5	.583	3.49	14	14	2	1	0	95 1/3	90	49	37	19	66
1995—	Quad City (Midwest)	4	6	.400	3.66	22	11	0	0	0	76 1/3	67	37	31	29	65
1996—	Quad City (Midwest)	9	4	.692	3.88	29	17	0	0	0	132 1/3	128	61	57	30	104
1997—	Mobile (Southern)■	5	2	.714	2.34	40	1	0	0	1	61 2/3	54	25	16	18	52

RUSCH, GLENDON   P   ROYALS

PERSONAL: Born November 7, 1974, in Seattle. ... 6-2/170. ... Throws left, bats left. ... Full name: Glendon James Rusch.
HIGH SCHOOL: Shorecrest (Seattle).
TRANSACTIONS/CAREER NOTES: Selected by Kansas City Royals organization in 17th round of free-agent draft (June 3, 1993). ... On Kansas City disabled list (June 16-July 1, 1997); included rehabilitation assignment to Omaha (June 26-July 1).
STATISTICAL NOTES: Pitched 9-0 no-hit victory against Kane County (August 7, 1994).

Year — Team (League)	W	L	Pct.	ERA	G	GS	CG	ShO	Sv.	IP	H	R	ER	BB	SO
1993— GC Royals (GCL)	4	2	.667	1.60	11	10	0	0	0	62	43	14	11	11	48
— Rockford (Midwest)	0	1	.000	3.38	2	2	0	0	0	8	10	6	3	7	8
1994— Rockford (Midwest)	8	5	.615	4.66	28	17	1	1	1	114	111	61	59	34	122
1995— Wilmington (Caro.)	*14	6	.700	*1.74	26	26	1	1	0	165²/₃	110	41	32	34	147
1996— Omaha (Am. Assoc.)	11	9	.550	3.98	28	28	1	0	0	169²/₃	177	88	75	40	117
1997— Kansas City (A.L.)	6	9	.400	5.50	30	27	1	0	0	170¹/₃	206	111	104	52	116
— Omaha (Am. Assoc.)	0	1	.000	4.50	1	1	0	0	0	6	7	3	3	1	2
Major league totals (1 year)	**6**	**9**	**.400**	**5.50**	**30**	**27**	**1**	**0**	**0**	**170¹/₃**	**206**	**111**	**104**	**52**	**116**

RYAN, JASON   P   CUBS

PERSONAL: Born January 23, 1976, in Long Branch, N.J. ... 6-3/185. ... Throws right, bats both. ... Full name: Jason Paul Ryan. ... Nephew of Ed Madjeski, catcher, Philadelphia Athletics, Chicago White Sox and New York Giants (1932-34 and 1937).
HIGH SCHOOL: Immaculata (Somerville, N.J.).
TRANSACTIONS/CAREER NOTES: Selected by Chicago Cubs organization in ninth round of free-agent draft (June 2, 1994).

Year — Team (League)	W	L	Pct.	ERA	G	GS	CG	ShO	Sv.	IP	H	R	ER	BB	SO
1994— GC Cubs (GCL)	1	2	.333	4.09	7	7	0	0	0	33	32	19	15	4	30
— Huntington (Appal.)	2	0	1.000	0.35	4	4	1	1	0	26	7	1	1	8	32
— Orlando (South.)	2	0	1.000	2.45	2	2	0	0	0	11	6	3	3	6	12
1995— Daytona (Fla. St.)	11	5	.688	3.48	26	26	0	0	0	134²/₃	128	61	52	54	98
1996— Orlando (South.)	2	5	.286	5.71	7	7	0	0	0	34²/₃	39	30	22	24	25
— Daytona (Fla. St.)	1	8	.111	5.24	17	10	0	0	1	67	72	42	39	33	49
1997— Daytona (Fla. St.)	9	8	.529	4.44	27	27	5	0	0	170¹/₃	168	105	84	55	140

RYAN, KEN   P   PHILLIES

PERSONAL: Born October 24, 1968, in Pawtucket, R.I. ... 6-3/230. ... Throws right, bats right. ... Full name: Kenneth Frederick Ryan Jr.
HIGH SCHOOL: Seekonk (Mass.).
TRANSACTIONS/CAREER NOTES: Signed as non-drafted free agent by Boston Red Sox organization (June 16, 1986). ... Traded by Red Sox with OF Lee Tinsley and OF Glenn Murray to Philadelphia Phillies for P Heathcliff Slocumb, P Larry Wimberly and OF Rick Holifield (January 29, 1996). ... On Philadelphia disabled list (March 25-May 9 and June 13-September 1, 1997); included rehabilitation assignment to Reading (May 6-9).

Year — Team (League)	W	L	Pct.	ERA	G	GS	CG	ShO	Sv.	IP	H	R	ER	BB	SO
1986— Elmira (N.Y.-Penn)	2	2	.500	5.82	13	1	0	0	0	21²/₃	20	14	14	21	12
1987— Greensboro (S. Atl.)	3	12	.200	5.49	28	19	2	0	0	121¹/₃	139	88	74	63	75
1988— Lynchburg (Caroline)	2	7	.222	6.18	19	14	0	0	0	71¹/₃	79	51	49	45	49
1989— Winter Haven (FSL)	8	8	.500	3.15	24	22	3	0	0	137	114	58	48	81	78
1990— Lynchburg (Caroline)	6	•14	.300	5.13	28	•28	3	1	0	161¹/₃	182	104	92	82	109
1991— Winter Haven (FSL)	1	3	.250	2.05	21	1	0	0	1	52²/₃	40	15	12	19	53
— New Britain (East.)	1	2	.333	1.73	14	0	0	0	0	26	23	7	5	12	26
— Pawtucket (Int'l)	1	0	1.000	4.91	9	0	0	0	1	18¹/₃	15	11	10	11	14
1992— New Britain (East.)	1	4	.200	1.95	44	0	0	0	22	50²/₃	44	17	11	24	51
— Pawtucket (Int'l)	2	0	1.000	2.08	9	0	0	0	7	8²/₃	6	2	2	4	6
— Boston (A.L.)	0	0	...	6.43	7	0	0	0	1	7	4	5	5	5	5
1993— Boston (A.L.)	7	2	.778	3.60	47	0	0	0	1	50	43	23	20	29	49
— Pawtucket (Int'l)	0	2	.000	2.49	18	0	0	0	8	25¹/₃	18	9	7	17	22
1994— Sarasota (Florida State)	0	0	...	3.68	8	0	0	0	1	7¹/₃	6	3	3	2	11
— Boston (A.L.)	2	3	.400	2.44	42	0	0	0	13	48	46	14	13	17	32
1995— Boston (A.L.)	0	4	.000	4.96	28	0	0	0	7	32²/₃	34	20	18	24	34
— Trenton (Eastern)	0	2	.000	5.82	11	0	0	0	2	17	23	13	11	5	16
— Pawtucket (Int'l)	1	0	1.000	6.30	9	0	0	0	0	10	12	7	7	4	6
1996— Philadelphia (N.L.)■	3	5	.375	2.43	62	0	0	0	8	89	71	32	24	45	70
1997— Reading (Eastern)	0	0	...	0.00	2	2	0	0	0	2	1	0	0	1	0
— Philadelphia (N.L.)	1	0	1.000	9.58	22	0	0	0	0	20²/₃	31	23	22	13	10
— Scran./W.B. (Int'l)	1	0	1.000	4.50	3	0	0	0	1	4	5	2	2	3	3
A.L. totals (4 years)	**9**	**9**	**.500**	**3.66**	**124**	**0**	**0**	**0**	**22**	**137²/₃**	**127**	**62**	**56**	**75**	**120**
N.L. totals (2 years)	**4**	**5**	**.444**	**3.78**	**84**	**0**	**0**	**0**	**8**	**109²/₃**	**102**	**55**	**46**	**58**	**80**
Major league totals (6 years)	**13**	**14**	**.481**	**3.71**	**208**	**0**	**0**	**0**	**30**	**247¹/₃**	**229**	**117**	**102**	**133**	**200**

RYAN, MATT   P   PIRATES

PERSONAL: Born March 20, 1972, in Chattanooga, Tenn. ... 6-5/187. ... Throws right, bats right. ... Full name: William Mathew Ryan.
HIGH SCHOOL: Kirby (Memphis).
COLLEGE: Mississippi.
TRANSACTIONS/CAREER NOTES: Selected by Pittsburgh Pirates organization in 25th round of free-agent draft (June 3, 1993). ... On Calgary disabled list (July 18-August 11, 1995).

Year Team (League)	W	L	Pct.	ERA	G	GS	CG	ShO	Sv.	IP	H	R	ER	BB	SO
1993—GC Pirates (GCL)...............	1	1	.500	2.33	9	0	0	0	2	19⅓	17	8	5	9	20
—Welland (N.Y.-Penn)..........	0	1	.000	2.08	16	0	0	0	5	17⅓	11	10	4	12	25
1994—Augusta (S. Atl.).................	2	1	.667	1.14	33	0	0	0	13	39⅓	29	12	5	7	49
—Salem (Carolina)................	2	2	.500	1.91	25	0	0	0	7	28⅓	27	12	6	8	13
1995—Carolina (Southern)...........	2	1	.667	1.57	44	0	0	0	26	46	33	10	8	19	23
—Calgary (PCL)...................	0	0	...	1.93	5	0	0	0	1	4⅔	5	1	1	1	2
1996—Calgary (PCL)...................	2	6	.250	5.30	51	0	0	0	20	52⅔	70	39	31	28	35
1997—Carolina (Southern)...........	4	3	.571	2.22	48	0	0	0	14	52⅔	32	18	13	21	43

SABERHAGEN, BRET   P   RED SOX

PERSONAL: Born April 11, 1964, in Chicago Heights, Ill. ... 6-1/200. ... Throws right, bats right. ... Full name: Bret William Saberhagen. ... Name pronounced SAY-ber-HAY-gun.
HIGH SCHOOL: Cleveland (Reseda, Calif.).
TRANSACTIONS/CAREER NOTES: Selected by Kansas City Royals organization in 19th round of free-agent draft (June 7, 1982). ... On disabled list (August 10-September 1, 1986; July 16-September 10, 1990; and June 15-July 13, 1991). ... Traded by Royals with IF Bill Pecota to New York Mets for OF Kevin McReynolds, IF Gregg Jefferies and 2B Keith Miller (December 11, 1991). ... On disabled list (May 16-July 18 and August 2-September 7, 1992 and August 3, 1993-remainder of season). ... On suspended list (April 3-8, 1994). ... Traded by Mets with a player to be named later to Colorado Rockies for P Juan Acevedo and P Arnold Gooch (July 31, 1995). ... Rockies acquired P David Swanson to complete deal (August 4, 1995). ... On disabled list (March 22, 1996-entire season). ... Granted free agency (October 29, 1996). ... Signed by Boston Red Sox organization (December 9, 1996). ... On Boston disabled list (March 31-August 22, 1997); included rehabilitation assignments to Lowell (July 27-August 1), Trenton (August 1-12) and Pawtucket (August 12-22). ... Granted free agency (October 31, 1997). ... Re-signed by Red Sox (November 17, 1997).
HONORS: Named A.L. Pitcher of the Year by THE SPORTING NEWS (1985 and 1989). ... Named righthanded pitcher on THE SPORTING NEWS A.L. All-Star team (1985 and 1989). ... Named A.L. Cy Young Award winner by Baseball Writers' Association of America (1985 and 1989). ... Named A.L. Comeback Player of the Year by THE SPORTING NEWS (1987). ... Won A.L. Gold Glove at pitcher (1989).
STATISTICAL NOTES: Pitched 7-0 no-hit victory against Chicago (August 26, 1991).
MISCELLANEOUS: Appeared in one game as pinch-runner (1984). ... Appeared in three games as pinch-runner (1989).

Year Team (League)	W	L	Pct.	ERA	G	GS	CG	ShO	Sv.	IP	H	R	ER	BB	SO
1983—Fort Myers (Fla. St.)	10	5	.667	2.30	16	16	3	1	0	109⅔	98	34	28	19	82
—Jacksonville (Southern)......	6	2	.750	2.91	11	11	2	1	0	77⅓	66	31	25	29	48
1984—Kansas City (A.L.)	10	11	.476	3.48	38	18	2	1	1	157⅔	138	71	61	36	73
1985—Kansas City (A.L.)	20	6	.769	2.87	32	32	10	1	0	235⅓	211	79	75	38	158
1986—Kansas City (A.L.)	7	12	.368	4.15	30	25	4	2	0	156	165	77	72	29	112
1987—Kansas City (A.L.)	18	10	.643	3.36	33	33	15	4	0	257	246	99	96	53	163
1988—Kansas City (A.L.)	14	16	.467	3.80	35	35	9	0	0	260⅔	*271	122	110	59	171
1989—Kansas City (A.L.)	*23	6	.793	*2.16	36	35	*12	4	0	*262⅓	209	74	63	43	193
1990—Kansas City (A.L.)	5	9	.357	3.27	20	20	5	0	0	135	146	52	49	28	87
1991—Kansas City (A.L.)	13	8	.619	3.07	28	28	7	2	0	196⅓	165	76	67	45	136
1992—New York (N.L.)■	3	5	.375	3.50	17	15	1	1	0	97⅔	84	39	38	27	81
1993—New York (N.L.).............	7	7	.500	3.29	19	19	4	1	0	139⅓	131	55	51	17	93
1994—New York (N.L.).............	14	4	.778	2.74	24	24	4	0	0	177⅓	169	58	54	13	143
1995—New York (N.L.).............	5	5	.500	3.35	16	16	3	0	0	110	105	45	41	20	71
—Colorado (N.L.)■	2	1	.667	6.28	9	9	0	0	0	43	60	33	30	13	29
1996—							Did not play.								
1997—Lowell (New York-Penn.)■	0	0	...	0.00	1	1	0	0	0	3	1	0	0	0	2
—Trenton (Eastern)	0	0	...	0.00	2	2	0	0	0	8	2	0	0	1	9
—Pawtucket (Int'l)	0	1	.000	3.27	2	2	0	0	0	11	11	4	4	1	9
—Boston (A.L.).....................	0	1	.000	6.58	6	6	0	0	0	26	30	20	19	10	14
A.L. totals (9 years)	110	79	.582	3.27	258	232	64	14	1	1686⅓	1581	670	612	341	1107
N.L. totals (4 years)	31	22	.585	3.39	85	83	12	2	0	567⅓	549	230	214	90	417
Major league totals (13 years)....	141	101	.583	3.30	343	315	76	16	1	2253⅔	2130	900	826	431	1524

DIVISION SERIES RECORD

Year Team (League)	W	L	Pct.	ERA	G	GS	CG	ShO	Sv.	IP	H	R	ER	BB	SO
1995—Colorado (N.L.)	0	1	.000	11.25	1	1	0	0	0	4	7	6	5	1	3

CHAMPIONSHIP SERIES RECORD

Year Team (League)	W	L	Pct.	ERA	G	GS	CG	ShO	Sv.	IP	H	R	ER	BB	SO
1984—Kansas City (A.L.)	0	0	...	2.25	1	1	0	0	0	8	6	3	2	1	5
1985—Kansas City (A.L.)	0	0	...	6.14	2	2	0	0	0	7⅓	12	5	5	2	6
Champ. series totals (2 years)	0	0	...	4.11	3	3	0	0	0	15⅓	18	8	7	3	11

WORLD SERIES RECORD

NOTES: Named Most Valuable Player (1985). ... Member of World Series championship team (1985).

Year Team (League)	W	L	Pct.	ERA	G	GS	CG	ShO	Sv.	IP	H	R	ER	BB	SO
1985—Kansas City (A.L.)	2	0	1.000	0.50	2	2	1	0	0	18	11	1	1	1	10

ALL-STAR GAME RECORD

Year League	W	L	Pct.	ERA	GS	CG	ShO	Sv.	IP	H	R	ER	BB	SO
1987—American	0	0	...	0.00	1	0	0	0	3	1	0	0	0	0
1990—American	1	0	1.000	0.00	0	0	0	0	2	0	0	0	0	1
1994—National.............................							Did not play.							
All-Star totals (2 years)	1	0	1.000	0.00	1	0	0	0	5	1	0	0	0	1

SADLER, DONNIE   2B/SS   RED SOX

PERSONAL: Born June 17, 1975, in Gohlson, Texas. ... 5-6/165. ... Bats right, throws right. ... Full name: Donnie Lamont Sadler.
HIGH SCHOOL: Valley Mills (Texas).

TRANSACTIONS/CAREER NOTES: Selected by Boston Red Sox organization in 10th round of free-agent draft (June 2, 1994).
STATISTICAL NOTES: Tied for International League lead in errors by second baseman with 12 in 1997. ... Tied for International League lead in caught stealing with 14 in 1997.

Year Team (League)	Pos.	G	AB	R	H	2B	3B	HR	RBI	Avg.	BB	SO	SB	PO	A	E	Avg.
1994—Fort Myers (GCL)	SS	53	206	52	56	8	6	1	16	.272	23	27	32				...
1995—Michigan (Midwest) ...	SS	118	438	*103	124	25	8	9	55	.283	79	85	41	168	307	28	.944
1996—Trenton (Eastern)	SS-OF	115	454	68	121	20	8	6	46	.267	38	75	34	185	237	27	.940
1997—Pawtucket (Int'l)	2B-SS-OF	125	481	74	102	18	2	11	36	.212	57	121	20	252	354	‡15	.976

SAGER, A.J.　　　　P　　　　TIGERS

PERSONAL: Born March 3, 1965, in Columbus, Ohio. ... 6-4/220. ... Throws right, bats right. ... Full name: Anthony Joseph Sager.
HIGH SCHOOL: Watkins Memorial (Kirkersville, Ohio).
COLLEGE: Toledo (received degree).
TRANSACTIONS/CAREER NOTES: Selected by San Diego Padres organization in 10th round of free-agent draft (June 1, 1988). ... Granted free agency (October 15, 1994). ... Signed by Colorado Springs, Colorado Rockies organization (December 7, 1994). ... Granted free agency (October 16, 1995). ... Signed by Toledo, Detroit Tigers organization (December 8, 1995).

Year Team (League)	W	L	Pct.	ERA	G	GS	CG	ShO	Sv.	IP	H	R	ER	BB	SO
1988—Spokane (N'west)	8	3	.727	5.11	15	15	2	0	0	98 2/3	*123	*67	*56	27	74
1989—Charleston, S.C. (S. Atl.)	•14	9	.609	3.38	26	25	6	2	0	167 2/3	166	77	63	40	105
1990—Wichita (Texas)	11	•12	.478	5.48	26	26	2	1	0	154 1/3	*200	*105	*94	29	79
1991—Las Vegas (PCL)	7	5	.583	4.71	18	18	3	2	0	109	127	63	57	20	61
—Wichita (Texas)	4	3	.571	4.13	10	10	1	0	0	65 1/3	69	35	30	16	31
1992—Las Vegas (PCL)	1	7	.125	7.95	30	3	0	0	1	60	89	57	53	17	40
1993—Wichita (Texas)	5	3	.625	3.19	11	11	2	1	0	73 1/3	69	30	26	16	49
—Las Vegas (PCL)	6	5	.545	3.70	21	11	2	1	1	90	91	49	37	18	58
1994—San Diego (N.L.)	1	4	.200	5.98	22	3	0	0	0	46 2/3	62	34	31	16	26
—Las Vegas (PCL)	1	4	.200	4.43	23	2	0	0	5	40 2/3	57	24	20	8	23
1995—Colo. Springs (PCL)■	8	5	.615	3.50	23	22	1	1	0	133 2/3	153	61	52	23	80
—Colorado (N.L.)	0	0	...	7.36	10	0	0	0	0	14 2/3	19	16	12	7	10
1996—Toledo (Int'l)■	1	0	1.000	2.63	18	2	0	0	0	37 2/3	38	14	11	3	24
—Detroit (A.L.)	4	5	.444	5.01	22	9	0	0	0	79	91	46	44	29	52
1997—Detroit (A.L.)	3	4	.429	4.18	38	1	0	0	0	84	81	43	39	24	53
A.L. totals (2 years)	7	9	.438	4.58	60	10	0	0	0	163	172	89	83	53	105
N.L. totals (2 years)	1	4	.200	6.31	32	3	0	0	0	61 1/3	81	50	43	23	36
Major league totals (4 years)......	8	13	.381	5.05	92	13	0	0	3	224 1/3	253	139	126	76	141

SAGMOEN, MARC　　　　OF　　　　RANGERS

PERSONAL: Born April 16, 1971, in Seattle. ... 5-11/185. ... Bats left, throws left. ... Full name: Marc R. Sagmoen.
HIGH SCHOOL: Kennedy (Seattle).
COLLEGE: Nebraska.
TRANSACTIONS/CAREER NOTES: Selected by Texas Rangers organization in 13th round of free-agent draft (June 3, 1993). ... On Oklahoma City disabled list (April 14-26, 1995).

Year Team (League)	Pos.	G	AB	R	H	2B	3B	HR	RBI	Avg.	BB	SO	SB	PO	A	E	Avg.
1993—Erie (N.Y.-Penn)..........	OF	6	23	6	7	1	1	0	2	.304	3	7	0	15	1	0	1.000
—Char., S.C. (S. Atl.)	OF	63	234	44	69	13	4	6	34	.295	23	39	16	118	4	1	.992
1994—Charlotte (Fla. St.)	OF	122	475	74	139	25	10	3	47	.293	37	56	15	275	13	6	.980
1995—Oklahoma City (A.A.)..	OF	56	188	20	42	11	3	3	25	.223	16	31	5	97	3	2	.980
—Tulsa (Texas)	OF	63	242	36	56	8	5	5	22	.231	23	23	5	135	7	1	.993
1996—Tulsa (Texas)	OF	96	387	58	109	21	6	10	62	.282	33	58	5	198	7	4	.981
—Oklahoma City (A.A.)..	OF	32	116	16	34	6	0	5	16	.293	4	20	1	52	2	2	.964
1997—Oklahoma City (A.A.)..	OF-1B	111	418	47	110	32	6	5	44	.263	26	95	4	297	21	7	.978
—Texas (A.L.)	OF-1B-DH	21	43	2	6	2	0	1	4	.140	2	13	0	25	0	0	1.000
Major league totals (1 year)		21	43	2	6	2	0	1	4	.140	2	13	0	25	0	0	1.000

SAIPE, MIKE　　　　P　　　　ROCKIES

PERSONAL: Born September 10, 1973, in San Diego. ... 6-1/190. ... Throws right, bats right. ... Full name: Michael Eric Saipe.
HIGH SCHOOL: University City (San Diego).
COLLEGE: San Diego.
TRANSACTIONS/CAREER NOTES: Selected by Colorado Rockies organization in 12th round of free-agent draft (June 2, 1994).
STATISTICAL NOTES: Tied for Eastern League lead in balks with four in 1996.

Year Team (League)	W	L	Pct.	ERA	G	GS	CG	ShO	Sv.	IP	H	R	ER	BB	SO
1994—Bend (Northwest)	3	•7	.300	4.16	16	•16	0	0	0	84 1/3	73	52	39	34	74
1995—Salem (Carolina)	4	5	.444	3.48	21	9	0	0	3	85 1/3	68	35	33	32	90
1996—New Haven (Eastern)........	10	7	.588	3.07	32	19	1	1	3	138	114	53	47	42	126
1997—Nashville (Eastern)	8	5	.615	3.10	19	19	4	•2	0	136 2/3	127	57	47	29	123
—Colo. Springs (PCL)	4	3	.571	5.52	10	10	1	0	0	60 1/3	74	42	37	24	40

SAK, JIM　　　　P　　　　PADRES

PERSONAL: Born August 18, 1973, in Chicago. ... 6-1/195. ... Throws right, bats right. ... Full name: James Kenneth Sak Jr.
HIGH SCHOOL: St. Patrick (Chicago).
COLLEGE: Illinois Benedictine.
TRANSACTIONS/CAREER NOTES: Selected by San Diego Padres organization in 10th round of free-agent draft (June 1, 1995).

S

Year	Team (League)	W	L	Pct.	ERA	G	GS	CG	ShO	Sv.	IP	H	R	ER	BB	SO
1995—	Idaho Falls (Pioneer)	3	1	.750	1.65	13	0	0	0	1	32 2/3	15	9	6	12	55
	—Clinton (Midwest)...............	6	1	.857	1.98	7	7	3	0	0	50	42	12	11	14	37
1996—	Clinton (Midwest)...............	3	4	.429	3.56	21	7	0	0	0	65 2/3	46	31	26	45	72
	—Rancho Cucamonga (Cal.) .	0	3	.000	6.32	4	4	0	0	0	15 2/3	21	13	11	12	14
1997—	Rancho Cucamonga (Cal.) .	6	3	.667	2.93	57	3	0	0	27	70 2/3	42	28	23	30	113

SALKELD, ROGER   P   ASTROS

PERSONAL: Born March 6, 1971, in Burbank, Calif. ... 6-5/215. ... Throws right, bats right. ... Full name: Roger W. Salkeld. ... Grandson of Bill Salkeld, catcher with Pittsburgh Pirates, Boston Braves and Chicago White Sox (1945-50).

HIGH SCHOOL: Saugus (Calif.).

TRANSACTIONS/CAREER NOTES: Selected by Seattle Mariners organization in first round (third pick overall) of free-agent draft (June 5, 1989). ... On disabled list (April 6-21, 1990). ... On Calgary disabled list (April 9, 1992-entire season and April 8-June 22, 1993). ... Traded by Mariners organization to Cincinnati Reds organization for P Tim Belcher (May 15, 1995). ... Granted free agency (October 15, 1997). ... Signed by Houston Astros organization (December 29, 1997).

Year	Team (League)	W	L	Pct.	ERA	G	GS	CG	ShO	Sv.	IP	H	R	ER	BB	SO
1989—	Bellingham (N'west)...........	2	2	.500	1.29	8	6	0	0	0	42	27	17	6	10	55
1990—	San Bernardino (Calif.).......	11	5	.688	3.40	25	25	2	0	0	153 1/3	140	77	58	83	167
1991—	Jacksonville (Southern).......	8	8	.500	3.05	23	23	5	0	0	153 2/3	131	56	52	55	159
	—Calgary (PCL).....................	2	1	.667	5.12	4	4	0	0	0	19 1/3	18	16	11	13	21
1992—	....							Did not play.								
1993—	Jacksonville (Southern)......	4	3	.571	3.27	14	14	0	0	0	77	71	39	28	29	56
	—Seattle (A.L.)....................	0	0	...	2.51	3	2	0	0	0	14 1/3	13	4	4	4	13
1994—	Calgary (PCL).....................	3	7	.300	6.15	13	13	0	0	0	67 1/3	74	54	46	39	54
	—Seattle (A.L.)....................	2	5	.286	7.17	13	13	0	0	0	59	76	47	47	45	46
1995—	Tacoma (PCL).....................	1	0	1.000	1.80	4	3	0	0	1	15	8	4	3	7	11
	—Indianapolis (A.A.)■..........	12	2	*.857	4.22	20	20	1	0	0	119 1/3	96	60	56	57	86
1996—	Cincinnati (N.L.).................	8	5	.615	5.20	29	19	1	1	0	116	114	69	67	54	82
1997—	Indianapolis (A.A.).............	4	8	.333	6.75	36	11	0	0	1	88	91	75	66	60	88
A.L. totals (2 years)		2	5	.286	6.26	16	15	0	0	0	73 1/3	89	51	51	49	59
N.L. totals (1 year)		8	5	.615	5.20	29	19	1	1	0	116	114	69	67	54	82
Major league totals (3 years)		10	10	.500	5.61	45	34	1	1	0	189 1/3	203	120	118	103	141

SALMON, TIM   OF   ANGELS

PERSONAL: Born August 24, 1968, in Long Beach, Calif. ... 6-3/220. ... Bats right, throws right. ... Full name: Timothy James Salmon. ... Name pronounced SA-mon.

HIGH SCHOOL: Greenway (Phoenix).

COLLEGE: Grand Canyon (Ariz.).

TRANSACTIONS/CAREER NOTES: Selected by Atlanta Braves organization in 18th round of free-agent draft (June 2, 1986); did not sign. ... Selected by California Angels organization in third round of free-agent draft (June 5, 1989). ... On disabled list (May 12-23 and May 27-August 7, 1990; and July 18-August 3, 1994). ... Angels franchise renamed Anaheim Angels for 1997 season.

RECORDS: Shares major league record for fewest double plays by outfielder (150 or more games)—0 (1996). ... Shares A.L. record for most hits in three consecutive games—13 (May 10 [4], 11 [4]and 13 [5], 1994).

HONORS: Named Minor League Player of the Year by THE SPORTING NEWS (1992). ... Named Pacific Coast League Most Valuable Player (1992). ... Named A.L. Rookie Player of the Year by THE SPORTING NEWS (1993). ... Named A.L. Rookie of the Year by Baseball Writers' Association of America (1993). ... Named outfielder on THE SPORTING NEWS A.L. All-Star team (1995 and 1997). ... Named outfielder on THE SPORTING NEWS Silver Slugger team (1995).

STATISTICAL NOTES: Led Pacific Coast League with 275 total bases, .672 slugging percentage and .469 on-base percentage in 1992. ... Led A.L. outfielders with four double plays in 1994. ... Tied for A.L. lead in double plays by outfielder with five in 1997. ... Career major league grand slams: 3.

							BATTING								FIELDING		
Year	Team (League)	Pos.	G	AB	R	H	2B	3B	HR	RBI	Avg.	BB	SO	SB	PO	A	E	Avg.
1989—	Bend (Northwest).......	OF	55	196	37	48	6	5	6	31	.245	33	60	2	84	7	4	.958
1990—	Palm Springs (Cal.)....	OF	36	118	19	34	6	0	2	21	.288	21	44	11	63	3	1	.985
	—Midland (Texas)..........	OF	27	97	17	26	3	1	3	16	.268	18	38	1	51	6	3	.950
1991—	Midland (Texas)..........	OF	131	465	100	114	26	4	23	94	.245	*89	*166	12	265	16	10	.966
1992—	Edmonton (PCL)........	OF	118	409	•101	142	38	4	*29	*105	.347	91	103	9	231	14	3	.988
	—California (A.L.).........	OF	23	79	8	14	1	0	2	6	.177	11	23	1	40	1	2	.953
1993—	California (A.L.)..........	OF-DH	142	515	93	146	35	1	31	95	.283	82	135	5	335	12	7	.980
1994—	California (A.L.)..........	OF	100	373	67	107	18	2	23	70	.287	54	102	1	219	9	8	.966
1995—	California (A.L.)..........	OF-DH	143	537	111	177	34	3	34	105	.330	91	111	5	320	7	4	.988
1996—	California (A.L.)..........	OF-DH	156	581	90	166	27	4	30	98	.286	93	125	4	299	13	8	.975
1997—	Anaheim (A.L.)..........	OF-DH	157	582	95	172	28	1	33	129	.296	95	142	9	352	15	11	.971
Major league totals (6 years)			721	2667	464	782	143	11	153	503	.293	426	638	25	1565	57	40	.976

SAMPSON, BENJ   P   TWINS

PERSONAL: Born April 27, 1975, in Des Moines, Iowa. ... 6-1/205. ... Throws left, bats left. ... Full name: Benjamin Damon Sampson.

HIGH SCHOOL: Ankeny (Iowa).

TRANSACTIONS/CAREER NOTES: Selected by Minnesota Twins organization in sixth round of free-agent draft (June 3, 1993). ... On disabled list (May 14-23, 1997).

Year	Team (League)	W	L	Pct.	ERA	G	GS	CG	ShO	Sv.	IP	H	R	ER	BB	SO
1993—	Elizabethton (Appal.)	4	1	.800	1.91	11	6	0	0	1	42 1/3	33	12	9	15	34
1994—	Fort Wayne (Midw.).............	6	9	.400	3.80	25	25	0	0	0	139 2/3	149	72	59	60	111
1995—	Fort Myers (Fla. St.)	11	9	.550	3.49	28	27	3	2	0	160	148	71	62	52	95
1996—	Fort Myers (Fla. St.)	7	1	.875	3.47	11	11	2	0	0	70	55	28	27	26	65
	—New Britain (East.)	5	7	.417	5.73	16	16	1	0	0	75 1/3	108	54	48	25	51
1997—	New Britain (East.)	10	6	.625	4.19	25	20	0	0	0	118	112	56	55	49	92

PERSONAL: Born December 9, 1960, in San Pedro de Macoris, Dominican Republic. ... 5-11/185. ... Bats right, throws right. ... Full name: Juan Milton Samuel. ... Name pronounced sam-WELL.

HIGH SCHOOL: Licey Puerto Rico.

TRANSACTIONS/CAREER NOTES: Signed as non-drafted free agent by Philadelphia Phillies organization (April 29, 1980). ... On Philadelphia disabled list (April 13-May 2, 1986 and April 1-19, 1989). ... Traded by Phillies to New York Mets for OF Lenny Dykstra, P Roger McDowell and a player to be named later (June 18, 1989); Phillies organization acquired P Tom Edens to complete deal (July 27, 1989). ... Traded by Mets to Los Angeles Dodgers for P Alejandro Pena and OF Mike Marshall (December 20, 1989). ... Granted free agency (November 5, 1990). ... Re-signed by Dodgers (December 16, 1990). ... Granted free agency (October 28, 1991). ... Re-signed by Dodgers (February 27, 1992). ... On Los Angeles disabled list (April 28-June 11, 1992). ... Released by Dodgers (July 30, 1992). ... Signed by Kansas City Royals (August 6, 1992). ... Granted free agency (October 21, 1992). ... Signed by Cincinnati Reds organization (December 11, 1992). ... Granted free agency (October 25, 1993). ... Signed by Detroit Tigers organization (February 14, 1994). ... Granted free agency (October 25, 1994). ... Re-signed by Tigers organization (April 17, 1995). ... Traded by Tigers to Royals for a player to be named later (September 8, 1995); Tigers acquired OF Phil Hiatt to complete deal (September 14, 1995). ... Granted free agency (November 2, 1995). ... Signed by Toronto Blue Jays organization (January 16, 1996). ... On disabled list (June 26-July 11, 1996). ... Granted free agency (November 18, 1996). ... Re-signed by Blue Jays organization (December 18, 1996). ... Granted free agency (October 28, 1997). ... Re-signed by Blue Jays organization (December 6, 1997).

RECORDS: Holds major league single-season records for most at-bats by righthander—701 (1984); and fewest sacrifice hits with most at-bats—0 (1984). ... Holds N.L. single-season record for most at-bats—701 (1984). ... Shares major league record for most consecutive seasons leading league in strikeouts—4 (1984-1987). ... Shares major league single-game record (nine innings) for most assists by second baseman—12 (April 20, 1985).

HONORS: Named Carolina League Most Valuable Player (1982). ... Named N.L. Rookie Player of the Year by THE SPORTING NEWS (1984). ... Named second baseman on THE SPORTING NEWS N.L. All-Star team (1987). ... Named second baseman on THE SPORTING NEWS N.L. Silver Slugger team (1987).

STATISTICAL NOTES: Led Northwest League in caught stealing with 10 in 1980. ... Led South Atlantic League second basemen with 739 total chances and 82 double plays in 1981. ... Led Carolina League second basemen with 721 total chances and 82 double plays in 1982. ... Led Carolina League with 283 total bases and tied for lead in being hit by pitch with 15 in 1982. ... Led N.L. second basemen with 826 total chances in 1987. ... Led N.L. second basemen with 343 putouts and 92 double plays in 1988. ... Career major league grand slams: 2.

Year	Team (League)	Pos.	G	AB	R	H	2B	3B	HR	RBI	Avg.	BB	SO	SB	PO	A	E	Avg.
1980—Cen. Oregon (NWL)....		2B	69	*298	66	84	11	2	17	44	.282	17	*87	25	162	188	*30	.921
1981—Spartanburg (SAL).....		2B	135	512	88	127	22	8	11	74	.248	36	132	53	*280	*409	*50	.932
1982—Peninsula (Caro.)......		2B	135	494	*111	158	29	6	28	94	.320	31	124	64	*244	*442	*35	.951
1983—Reading (Eastern)		2B	47	184	36	43	10	0	11	39	.234	8	50	19	121	127	14	.947
—Portland (PCL)		2B	65	261	59	86	14	8	15	52	.330	22	46	33	110	168	15	.949
—Philadelphia (N.L.).......		2B	18	65	14	18	1	2	2	5	.277	4	16	3	44	54	9	.916
1984—Philadelphia (N.L.).....		2B	160	*701	105	191	36	•19	15	69	.272	28	*168	72	388	438	*33	.962
1985—Philadelphia (N.L.).....		2B	161	*663	101	175	31	13	19	74	.264	33	•141	53	*389	463	15	.983
1986—Philadelphia (N.L.).....		2B	145	591	90	157	36	12	16	78	.266	26	*142	42	290	440	*25	.967
1987—Philadelphia (N.L.).....		2B	160	*655	113	178	37	*15	28	100	.272	60	*162	35	*374	434	*18	.978
1988—Philadelphia (N.L.).....	2B-OF-3B	157	629	68	153	32	9	12	67	.243	39	151	33	†351	387	16	.979
1989—Philadelphia (N.L.).....	OF	51	199	32	49	3	1	8	20	.246	18	45	11	133	2	1	.993
—New York (N.L.)■......	OF	86	333	37	76	11	3	3	28	.228	24	75	31	206	4	3	.986
1990—Los Angeles (N.L.)■...	2B-OF	143	492	62	119	24	3	13	52	.242	51	126	38	273	262	16	.971
1991—Los Angeles (N.L.).....	2B	153	594	74	161	22	6	12	58	.271	49	133	23	300	442	17	.978
1992—Los Angeles (N.L.).....	2B-OF	47	122	7	32	3	1	0	15	.262	7	22	2	76	77	5	.968
—Kansas City (A.L.)■...	OF-2B	29	102	15	29	5	3	0	8	.284	7	27	6	45	29	6	.925
1993—Cincinnati (N.L.).......	2-1-3-O	103	261	31	60	10	4	4	26	.230	23	53	9	151	172	10	.970
1994—Detroit (A.L.)■.......	O-DH-2-1	59	136	32	42	9	5	5	21	.309	10	26	5	82	28	1	.991
1995—Detroit (A.L.).........	1-DH-O-2	76	171	28	48	10	1	10	34	.281	24	38	5	289	35	9	.973
—Kansas City (A.L.)■...	DH-OF-1B	15	34	3	6	0	0	2	5	.176	5	11	1	11	0	0	1.000
1996—Toronto (A.L.)■.......	DH-OF-1B	69	188	34	48	8	3	8	26	.255	15	65	9	117	3	2	.984
1997—Toronto (A.L.).......DH-3-1-2-O		45	95	13	27	5	4	3	15	.284	10	28	5	34	13	0	1.000
American League totals (5 years)			293	726	125	200	37	16	28	109	.275	71	195	31	578	108	18	.974
National League totals (11 years)			1384	5305	734	1369	248	86	132	592	.258	362	1234	352	2975	3175	168	.973
Major league totals (15 years)			1677	6031	859	1569	285	102	160	701	.260	433	1429	383	3553	3283	186	.974

CHAMPIONSHIP SERIES RECORD

Year	Team (League)	Pos.	G	AB	R	H	2B	3B	HR	RBI	Avg.	BB	SO	SB	PO	A	E	Avg.
1983—Philadelphia (N.L.)......		PR	1	0	0	0	0	0	0	0	...	0	0	0	...	...	...	...

WORLD SERIES RECORD

Year	Team (League)	Pos.	G	AB	R	H	2B	3B	HR	RBI	Avg.	BB	SO	SB	PO	A	E	Avg.
1983—Philadelphia (N.L.)......		PR-PH	3	1	0	0	0	0	0	0	.000	0	0	0	...	...	...	...

ALL-STAR GAME RECORD

RECORDS: Holds single-game record for most putouts by second baseman—7 (July 14, 1987). ... Shares single-game record for most chances accepted by second baseman—9 (July 14, 1987).

Year	League	Pos.	AB	R	H	2B	3B	HR	RBI	Avg.	BB	SO	SB	PO	A	E	Avg.
1984—National.....................								Did not play.									
1987—National.....................	2B	4	0	0	0	0	0	0	.000	0	1	0	7	2	0	1.000
1991—National.....................	2B	1	0	1	0	0	0	0	1.000	0	0	0	2	1	0	1.000
All-Star Game totals (2 years)		5	0	1	0	0	0	0	.200	0	1	0	9	3	0	1.000

PERSONAL: Born October 11, 1974, in Nizao Bani, Dominican Republic. ... 5-10/153. ... Throws left, bats left. ... Full name: Jesus P. Sanchez.

TRANSACTIONS/CAREER NOTES: Signed as non-drafted free agent by New York Mets organization (June 7, 1992). ... On disabled list (April 4-May 28, 1996).

STATISTICAL NOTES: Led Dominican Summer League in home runs allowed with 14 in 1992.

Year Team (League)	W	L	Pct.	ERA	G	GS	CG	ShO	Sv.	IP	H	R	ER	BB	SO
1992—Dominican Mets (DSL)	5	5	.500	4.19	15	15	1	0	0	81 2/3	86	52	38	38	72
1993—Dominican Mets (DSL)	7	3	.700	2.40	16	13	2	•2	0	82 1/3	63	30	22	36	94
1994—Kingsport (Appalachian)	7	4	.636	1.96	13	12	•3	0	0	87 1/3	61	27	19	27	71
1995—Capital City (S. Atl.)	9	7	.563	3.13	27	4	0	0	0	169 2/3	154	76	59	58	•177
1996—St. Lucie (Fla. St.)	9	3	.750	1.96	16	16	2	1	0	92	53	22	20	24	81
1997—Binghamton (Eastern)	*13	10	.565	4.30	26	26	3	0	0	165 1/3	146	87	79	61	*176

SANCHEZ, MARTIN — P — DIAMONDBACKS

PERSONAL: Born January 19, 1977, in Santo Domingo, Dominican Republic. ... 6-2/175. ... Throws right, bats right.

TRANSACTIONS/CAREER NOTES: Signed as non-drafted free agent by Atlanta Braves organization (September 26, 1993). ... Traded by Braves to Florida Marlins organization for P Yorkis Perez (December 13, 1996). ... Selected by Arizona Diamondbacks from Marlins organization in Rule 5 major league draft (December 15, 1997).

Year Team (League)	W	L	Pct.	ERA	G	GS	CG	ShO	Sv.	IP	H	R	ER	BB	SO
1994—Dominican Braves (DSL)	7	6	.538	2.73	16	16	0	0	0	99	94	54	30	52	89
1995—Dominican Braves (DSL)	4	4	.500	4.13	16	16	2	0	0	102 1/3	88	58	44	41	110
1996—Macon (South Atlantic)	5	5	.500	3.97	31	13	0	0	1	106 2/3	109	60	47	53	92
1997—Kane County (Midwest)■	3	5	.375	4.50	51	0	0	0	22	54	40	31	27	32	57

SANCHEZ, REY — 2B/SS — GIANTS

S

PERSONAL: Born October 5, 1967, in Rio Piedras, Puerto Rico. ... 5-9/170. ... Bats right, throws right. ... Full name: Rey Francisco Guadalupe Sanchez.

HIGH SCHOOL: Live Oak (Morgan Hill, Calif.).

TRANSACTIONS/CAREER NOTES: Selected by Texas Rangers organization in 13th round of free-agent draft (June 2, 1986). ... Traded by Rangers organization to Chicago Cubs organization for IF Bryan House (January 3, 1990). ... On disabled list (April 6, 1990-entire season). ... On Chicago disabled list (May 6-21, 1992; included rehabilitation assignment to Iowa (May 13-21). ... On disabled list (July 24-August 9, 1995). ... On Chicago disabled list (June 5-July 20 and August 11-September 1, 1996); included rehabilitation assignment to Iowa (July 16-20). ... Traded by Cubs to New York Yankees for P Frisco Parotte (August 16, 1997). ... Granted free agency (November 3, 1997). ... Signed by San Francisco Giants (January 22, 1998).

STATISTICAL NOTES: Led Gulf Coast League shortstops with .932 fielding percentage in 1986. ... Led American Association shortstops with 104 double plays in 1989. ... Led American Association shortstops with 596 total chances and 81 double plays in 1992.

						BATTING								FIELDING		
Year Team (League)	Pos.	G	AB	R	H	2B	3B	HR	RBI	Avg.	BB	SO	SB	PO	A	E	Avg.
1986—GC Rangers (GCL)	SS-2B	52	169	27	49	3	1	0	23	.290	41	18	10	69	158	15	†.938
1987—Gastonia (S. Atl.)	SS	50	160	19	35	1	2	1	10	.219	22	17	6	88	162	18	.933
—Butte (Pioneer)	SS	49	189	36	69	10	6	0	25	.365	21	12	22	84	162	12	.953
1988—Charlotte (Fla. St.)	SS	128	418	60	128	6	5	0	38	.306	35	24	29	226	*415	35	.948
1989—Oklahoma City (A.A.)	SS	134	464	38	104	10	4	1	39	.224	21	50	4	*237	*418	29	*.958
1990—							Did not play.										
1991—Iowa (Am. Assoc.)■	SS	126	417	60	121	16	5	2	46	.290	37	27	13	204	*375	17	*.971
—Chicago (N.L.)	SS-2B	13	23	1	6	0	0	0	2	.261	4	3	0	11	25	0	1.000
1992—Chicago (N.L.)	SS-2B	74	255	24	64	14	3	1	19	.251	10	17	2	148	202	9	.975
—Iowa (Am. Assoc.)	SS-2B	20	76	12	26	3	0	0	3	.342	4	1	6	31	77	5	.956
1993—Chicago (N.L.)	SS	105	344	35	97	11	2	0	28	.282	15	22	1	158	316	15	.969
1994—Chicago (N.L.)	2B-SS-3B	96	291	26	83	13	1	0	24	.285	20	29	2	152	278	9	.979
1995—Chicago (N.L.)	2B-SS	114	428	57	119	22	2	3	27	.278	14	48	6	195	351	7	.987
1996—Chicago (N.L.)	SS	95	289	28	61	9	0	1	12	.211	22	42	7	151	307	11	.977
—Iowa (Am. Assoc.)■	SS	3	12	2	2	0	0	0	1	.167	1	2	4	2	10	1	.933
1997—Chicago (N.L.)	SS-2B-3B	97	205	14	51	9	0	1	12	.249	11	26	4	100	157	6	.977
—New York (A.L.)■	2B-SS	38	138	21	43	12	0	1	15	.312	5	21	0	66	110	4	.978
American League totals (1 year)		38	138	21	43	12	0	1	15	.312	5	21	0	66	110	4	.978
National League totals (7 years)		594	1835	185	481	78	8	6	124	.262	96	187	22	915	1636	57	.978
Major league totals (7 years)		632	1973	206	524	90	8	7	139	.266	101	208	22	981	1746	61	.978

DIVISION SERIES RECORD

						BATTING								FIELDING		
Year Team (League)	Pos.	G	AB	R	H	2B	3B	HR	RBI	Avg.	BB	SO	SB	PO	A	E	Avg.
1997—New York (A.L.)	2B	5	15	1	3	1	0	0	1	.200	0	2	0	15	14	0	1.000

SANDBERG, RYNE — 2B

PERSONAL: Born September 18, 1959, in Spokane, Wash. ... 6-2/190. ... Bats right, throws right. ... Full name: Ryne Dee Sandberg.

HIGH SCHOOL: North Central (Spokane, Wash.).

TRANSACTIONS/CAREER NOTES: Selected by Philadelphia Phillies organization in 20th round of free-agent draft (June 6, 1978). ... Traded by Phillies with SS Larry Bowa to Chicago Cubs for SS Ivan DeJesus (January 27, 1982). ... On disabled list (June 14-July 11, 1987). ... On Chicago disabled list (March 27-April 30, 1993); included rehabilitation assignments to Daytona (April 25-27) and Orlando (April 27-29). ... On voluntarily retired list (June 13, 1994-October 31, 1995). ... Signed by Cubs (October 31, 1995). ... Granted free agency (November 5, 1996). ... Re-signed by Cubs (December 4, 1996). ... Announced retirement (September 29, 1997).

RECORDS: Holds major league career records for most home runs by second baseman—277; and most consecutive errorless games by second baseman—123 (June 21, 1989 through May 17, 1990). ... Holds major league single-season record for most consecutive errorless games by second baseman—90 (June 21 through October 1, 1989). ... Shares major league career record for highest fielding percentage by second baseman—.989; and most years with 500 or more assists by second baseman—6. ... Shares major league single-game record for most assists by second baseman—12 (June 12, 1983).

HONORS: Won N.L. Gold Glove at second base (1983-91). ... Named Major League Player of the Year by The Sporting News (1984). ... Named N.L. Player of the Year by The Sporting News (1984). ... Named second baseman on The Sporting News N.L. All-Star team (1984 and 1988-92). ... Named second baseman on The Sporting News N.L. Silver Slugger team (1984-85 and 1988-92). ... Named N.L. Most Valuable Player by Baseball Writers' Association of America (1984).

STATISTICAL NOTES: Led Pioneer League shortstops with 39 double plays in 1978. ... Led Western Carolinas League shortstops with 80 double plays in 1979. ... Led Eastern League shortstops with .964 fielding percentage, 386 assists and 81 double plays in 1980. ... Led N.L. second basemen with .986 fielding percentage, 571 assists and 126 double plays in 1983. ... Led N.L. second basemen with 914 total chances in 1983, 870 in 1984, 824 in 1988 and 830 in 1992. ... Led N.L. with 344 total bases in 1990. ... Career major league grand slams: 5.

Year Team (League)	Pos.	G	AB	R	H	2B	3B	HR	RBI	Avg.	BB	SO	SB	PO	A	E	Avg.
1978— Helena (Pioneer)	SS	56	190	34	59	6	6	1	23	.311	26	42	15	92	*200	24	.924
1979— Spartan. (W. Car.)	SS	•138	*539	83	133	21	7	4	47	.247	64	95	21	134	*467	35	*.945
1980— Reading (Eastern)	SS-3B	129	490	95	152	21	12	11	79	.310	73	72	32	156	†388	20	†.965
1981— Oklahoma City (A.A.)	SS-2B	133	519	78	152	17	5	9	62	.293	48	94	12	229	396	21	.967
—Philadelphia (N.L.)	SS-2B	13	6	2	1	0	0	0	0	.167	0	1	0	7	7	0	1.000
1982— Chicago (N.L.)■	3B-2B	156	635	103	172	33	5	7	54	.271	36	90	32	136	373	12	.977
1983— Chicago (N.L.)	2B-SS	158	633	94	165	25	4	8	48	.261	51	79	37	330	†572	13	†.986
1984— Chicago (N.L.)	2B	156	636	*114	200	36	•19	19	84	.314	52	101	32	314	*550	6	*.993
1985— Chicago (N.L.)	2B-SS	153	609	113	186	31	6	26	83	.305	57	97	54	353	501	12	.986
1986— Chicago (N.L.)	2B	154	627	68	178	28	5	14	76	.284	46	79	34	309	*492	5	*.994
1987— Chicago (N.L.)	2B	132	523	81	154	25	2	16	59	.294	59	79	21	294	375	10	.985
1988— Chicago (N.L.)	2B	155	618	77	163	23	8	19	69	.264	54	91	25	291	*522	11	.987
1989— Chicago (N.L.)	2B	157	606	•104	176	25	5	30	76	.290	59	85	15	294	466	6	.992
1990— Chicago (N.L.)	2B	155	615	*116	188	30	3	*40	100	.306	50	84	25	278	*469	8	.989
1991— Chicago (N.L.)	2B	158	585	104	170	32	2	26	100	.291	87	89	22	267	*515	4	*.995
1992— Chicago (N.L.)	2B	158	612	100	186	32	8	26	87	.304	68	73	17	283	*539	8	.990
1993— Daytona (Fla. St.)	2B	2	5	2	1	0	0	1	2	.200	1	0	0	3	4	0	1.000
—Orlando (South.)	2B	4	9	0	2	0	0	0	1	.222	3	1	0	3	8	0	1.000
—Chicago (N.L.)	2B	117	456	67	141	20	0	9	45	.309	37	62	9	209	347	7	.988
1994— Chicago (N.L.)	2B	57	223	36	53	9	5	5	24	.238	23	40	2	96	202	4	.987
1995—									Did not play.								
1996— Chicago (N.L.)	2B	150	554	85	135	28	4	25	92	.244	54	116	12	228	421	6	.991
1997— Chicago (N.L.)	2B-DH	135	447	54	118	26	0	12	64	.264	28	94	7	204	297	8	.984
Major league totals (16 years)		2164	8385	1318	2386	403	76	282	1061	.285	761	1260	344	3893	6648	120	.989

CHAMPIONSHIP SERIES RECORD

Year Team (League)	Pos.	G	AB	R	H	2B	3B	HR	RBI	Avg.	BB	SO	SB	PO	A	E	Avg.
1984— Chicago (N.L.)	2B	5	19	3	7	2	0	0	2	.368	3	2	3	13	18	1	.969
1989— Chicago (N.L.)	2B	5	20	6	8	3	1	1	4	.400	3	4	0	7	11	0	1.000
Championship series totals (2 years)		10	39	9	15	5	1	1	6	.385	6	6	3	20	29	1	.980

ALL-STAR GAME RECORD

Year League	Pos.	AB	R	H	2B	3B	HR	RBI	Avg.	BB	SO	SB	PO	A	E	Avg.
1984— National	2B	4	0	1	0	0	0	0	.250	0	0	1	0	0	0	...
1985— National	2B	1	1	0	0	0	0	0	.000	1	0	0	0	0	0	...
1986— National	2B	3	0	0	0	0	0	0	.000	0	0	0	0	2	0	1.000
1987— National	2B	2	0	0	0	0	0	0	.000	0	0	0	0	2	1	.667
1988— National	2B	4	0	1	0	0	0	0	.250	0	2	0	0	2	0	1.000
1989— National	2B	3	0	0	0	0	0	0	.000	0	2	0	2	4	0	1.000
1990— National	2B	3	0	0	0	0	0	0	.000	0	0	0	1	2	0	1.000
1991— National	2B	3	0	1	1	0	0	0	.333	0	0	0	2	1	0	1.000
1992— National	2B	2	0	0	0	0	0	0	.000	0	1	0	2	3	0	1.000
1993— National	2B	1	0	0	0	0	0	0	.000	1	0	0	2	2	0	1.000
All-Star Game totals (10 years)		26	1	3	1	0	0	0	.115	2	5	1	9	21	1	.968

SANDERS, ANTHONY OF BLUE JAYS

PERSONAL: Born March 2, 1974, in Tucson, Ariz. ... 6-2/190. ... Bats right, throws right. ... Full name: Anthony Marcus Sanders.
HIGH SCHOOL: Santa Rita (Tucson, Ariz.).
TRANSACTIONS/CAREER NOTES: Selected by Toronto Blue Jays organization in seventh round of free-agent draft (June 1, 1992).

Year Team (League)	Pos.	G	AB	R	H	2B	3B	HR	RBI	Avg.	BB	SO	SB	PO	A	E	Avg.
1993— Medicine Hat (Pio.)	OF	63	225	44	59	9	3	4	33	.262	20	49	6	88	8	2	.980
1994— St. Catharines (NYP)	OF	74	258	36	66	17	3	6	45	.256	27	53	8	120	9	3	.977
1995— Hagerstown (SAL)	OF	133	512	72	119	28	1	8	48	.232	52	103	26	274	15	3	.990
1996— Dunedin (Fla. St.)	OF	102	417	75	108	25	0	17	50	.259	34	93	16	209	8	4	.982
—Knoxville (Southern)	OF	38	133	16	36	8	0	1	18	.271	7	33	1	66	1	3	.957
1997— Dunedin (Fla. St.)	OF	1	5	0	1	1	0	0	1	.200	1	1	0	1	0	0	1.000
—Knoxville (Southern)	OF	111	429	68	114	20	4	26	69	.266	44	121	20	224	7	4	.983

SANDERS, DEION OF REDS

PERSONAL: Born August 9, 1967, in Fort Myers, Fla. ... 6-1/195. ... Bats left, throws left. ... Full name: Deion Luwynn Sanders.
HIGH SCHOOL: North Fort Myers (Fla.).
COLLEGE: Florida State.
TRANSACTIONS/CAREER NOTES: Selected by Kansas City Royals organization in sixth round of free-agent draft (June 3, 1985); did not sign. ... Selected by New York Yankees organization in 30th round of free-agent draft (June 1, 1988). ... On disqualified list (August 1-September 24, 1990). ... Released by Yankees organization (September 24, 1990). ... Signed by Atlanta Braves (January 29, 1991). ... Placed on Richmond temporarily inactive list (August 1, 1991). ... On disqualified list (April 29-May 21, 1993). ... On disabled list (August 22-September 6, 1993). ... Traded by Braves to Cincinnati Reds for OF Roberto Kelly and P Roger Etheridge (May 29, 1994). ... On Cincinnati disabled list (June 1-July 16, 1995); included rehabilitation assignment to Chattanooga (July 12-14). ... Traded by Reds with P John Roper, P Ricky

Pickett, P Scott Service and IF Dave McCarty to San Francisco Giants for OF Darren Lewis, P Mark Portugal and P Dave Burba (July 21, 1995). ... Granted free agency (December 21, 1995). ... Did not play baseball during 1996 season. ... Granted free agency (November 5, 1997). ... Re-signed by Reds (February 17, 1997). ... Re-signed by Reds organization (January 8, 1998).

STATISTICAL NOTES: Led N.L. in caught stealing with 16 in 1994.

MISCELLANEOUS: Only person in history to play in both the World Series (1992) and Super Bowl (1994 and 1995 seasons).

Year Team (League)	Pos.	G	AB	R	H	2B	3B	HR	RBI	Avg.	BB	SO	SB	PO	A	E	Avg.
1988— GC Yankees (GCL)......	OF	17	75	7	21	4	2	0	6	.280	2	10	11	33	1	2	.944
— Fort Lauderdale (FSL)	OF	6	21	5	9	2	0	0	2	.429	1	3	2	22	2	0	1.000
— Columbus (Int'l)	OF	5	20	3	3	1	0	0	0	.150	1	4	1	13	0	0	1.000
1989— Alb./Colon. (Eastern)..	OF	33	119	28	34	2	2	1	6	.286	11	20	17	79	3	0	1.000
— New York (A.L.).........	OF	14	47	7	11	2	0	2	7	.234	3	8	1	30	1	1	.969
— Columbus (Int'l)	OF	70	259	38	72	12	7	5	30	.278	22	46	16	165	0	4	.976
1990— New York (A.L.).........	OF-DH	57	133	24	21	2	2	3	9	.158	13	27	8	69	2	2	.973
— Columbus (Int'l)	OF	22	84	21	27	7	1	2	10	.321	17	15	9	49	1	0	1.000
1991— Atlanta (N.L.)■..........	OF	54	110	16	21	1	2	4	13	.191	12	23	11	57	3	3	.952
— Richmond (Int'l)........	OF	29	130	20	34	6	3	5	16	.262	10	28	12	73	1	1	.987
1992— Atlanta (N.L.)..............	OF	97	303	54	92	6	*14	8	28	.304	18	52	26	174	4	3	.983
1993— Atlanta (N.L.)..............	OF	95	272	42	75	18	6	6	28	.276	16	42	19	137	1	2	.986
1994— Atlanta (N.L.)..............	OF	46	191	32	55	10	0	4	21	.288	16	28	19	99	0	2	.980
— Cincinnati (N.L.)■......	OF	46	184	26	51	7	4	0	7	.277	16	35	19	110	2	0	1.000
1995— Cincinnati (N.L.).........	OF	33	129	19	31	2	3	1	10	.240	9	18	16	88	2	3	.968
— Chattanooga (Sou.)....	OF	2	7	1	4	0	0	1	2	.571	0	1	1	3	1	0	1.000
— San Fran. (N.L.)■......	OF	52	214	29	61	9	5	5	18	.285	18	42	8	127	0	2	.984
1996—								Did not play.									
1997— Cincinnati (N.L.)■......	OF	115	465	53	127	13	7	5	23	.273	34	67	56	236	3	4	.984
American League totals (2 years)		71	180	31	32	4	2	5	16	.178	16	35	9	99	3	3	.971
National League totals (6 years)		538	1868	271	513	66	41	33	148	.275	139	307	174	1028	15	19	.982
Major league totals (8 years)		609	2048	302	545	70	43	38	164	.266	155	342	183	1127	18	22	.981

CHAMPIONSHIP SERIES RECORD

Year Team (League)	Pos.	G	AB	R	H	2B	3B	HR	RBI	Avg.	BB	SO	SB	PO	A	E	Avg.
1992— Atlanta (N.L.)..............	OF-PH	4	5	0	0	0	0	0	0	.000	0	3	0	1	0	0	1.000
1993— Atlanta (N.L.)..............	PH-OF-PR	5	3	0	0	0	0	0	0	.000	0	1	0	0	0	0	...
Championship series totals (2 years)		9	8	0	0	0	0	0	0	.000	0	4	0	1	0	0	1.000

WORLD SERIES RECORD

Year Team (League)	Pos.	G	AB	R	H	2B	3B	HR	RBI	Avg.	BB	SO	SB	PO	A	E	Avg.
1992— Atlanta (N.L.)..............	OF	4	15	4	8	2	0	0	1	.533	2	1	5	5	1	0	1.000

RECORD AS FOOTBALL PLAYER

TRANSACTIONS/CAREER NOTES: Selected by Atlanta Falcons in first round (fifth pick overall) of 1989 NFL draft. ... Signed by Falcons (September 7, 1989). ... On reserve/did not report list (July 27-August 13, 1990). ... Granted roster exemption for one game (September 1992). ... On reserve/did not report list (July 23-October 14, 1993). ... Designated by Falcons as transition player (February 15, 1994). ... Free agency status changed by Falcons from transitional to unconditional (April 28, 1994). ... Signed by San Francisco 49ers (September 15, 1994). ... Granted unconditional free agency (February 17, 1995). ... Signed by Dallas Cowboys (September 9, 1995).

CHAMPIONSHIP GAME EXPERIENCE: Played in NFC championship game (1994 and 1995 seasons). ... Member of Super Bowl championship team (1994 and 1995 seasons).

HONORS: Named defensive back on THE SPORTING NEWS college All-America first team (1986-1988). ... Jim Thorpe Award winner (1988). ... Named cornerback on THE SPORTING NEWS NFL All-Pro team (1991-1997). ... Played in Pro Bowl (1991-1994 and 1997 seasons). ... Named kick returner on THE SPORTING NEWS NFL All-Pro team (1992). ... Named to play in Pro Bowl (1996 season); replaced by Darrell Green due to injury.

PRO STATISTICS: 1989—Fumbled twice and recovered one fumble. 1990—Fumbled four times and recovered two fumbles. 1991—Credited with a sack, fumbled once and recovered one fumble. 1992—Rushed once for minus four yards, fumbled three times and recovered two fumbles. 1993—Attempted one pass without a completion. 1994—Recovered one fumble. 1995—Rushed twice for nine yards. 1996—Rushed three times for two yards, fumbled twice and recovered three fumbles for 15 yards and a touchdown. 1997—Rushed once for minus 11 yards.

Year Team	G	GS	INTERCEPTIONS No.	Yds.	Avg.	TD	RECEIVING No.	Yds.	Avg.	TD	PUNT RETURNS No.	Yds.	Avg.	TD	KICKOFF RETURNS No.	Yds.	Avg.	TD	TOTALS TD	2pt.	Pts.
1989—Atlanta NFL	15	10	5	52	10.4	0	1	-8	-8.0	0	28	307	11.0	†1	35	725	20.7	0	1	...	6
1990—Atlanta NFL	16	16	∞3	153	51.0	2	0	0	...	0	29	250	8.6	†1	39	851	21.8	0	3	...	18
1991—Atlanta NFL	15	15	6	119	19.8	∞1	1	17	17.0	0	21	170	8.1	0	26	576	22.2	†1	2	...	12
1992—Atlanta NFL	13	12	3	105	35.0	0	3	45	15.0	1	13	41	3.2	0	40	*1067	‡26.7	*2	3	...	18
1993—Atlanta NFL	11	10	‡7	91	13.0	0	6	106	17.7	1	2	21	10.5	0	7	169	24.1	0	1	...	6
1994—San Fran. NFL	14	12	6	*303	50.5	†3	0	0	...	0	0	0	...	0	0	0	...	0	3	0	18
1995—Dallas NFL...........	9	9	2	34	17.0	0	2	25	12.5	0	1	54	54.0	0	1	15	15.0	0	0	0	0
1996—Dallas NFL...........	16	15	2	3	1.5	0	36	475	13.2	1	1	4	4.0	0	0	0	...	0	2	0	12
1997—Dallas NFL...........	12	12	2	81	40.5	1	0	0	...	0	33	407	12.3	1	1	18	18.0	0	2	0	12
Pro totals (9 years)	121	111	36	941	26.1	7	49	660	13.5	3	128	1254	9.8	3	149	3421	23.0	3	17	0	102

SANDERS, REGGIE   OF   REDS

PERSONAL: Born December 1, 1967, in Florence, S.C. ... 6-1/185. ... Bats right, throws right. ... Full name: Reginald Laverne Sanders.

HIGH SCHOOL: Wilson (Florence, S.C.).

COLLEGE: Spartanburg (S.C.) Methodist.

TRANSACTIONS/CAREER NOTES: Selected by Cincinnati Reds organization in seventh round of free-agent draft (June 2, 1987). ... On disabled list (July 11-September 15, 1988 and July 15-September 5, 1989). ... On Chattanooga disabled list (June 30-July 26, 1991). ... On Cincinnati disabled list (August 24-September 20, 1991; and May 13-29 and July 17-August 2, 1992). ... On suspended list (June 3-9, 1994).

... On Cincinnati disabled list (April 20-May 22, May 31-June 15 and September 17, 1996-remainder of season); included rehabilitation assignment to Indianapolis (May 17-22). ... On Cincinnati disabled list (April 19-May 6 and May 24-July 23, 1997); included rehabilitation assignments to Chattanooga (May 3-5) and Indianapolis (July 15-22).

HONORS: Named Midwest League Most Valuable Player (1990). ... Named outfielder on THE SPORTING NEWS N.L. All-Star team (1995).

STATISTICAL NOTES: Hit three home runs in one game (August 15, 1995).

Year	Team (League)	Pos.	G	AB	R	H	2B	3B	HR	RBI	Avg.	BB	SO	SB	PO	A	E	Avg.
1988—	Billings (Pioneer)	SS	17	64	11	15	1	1	0	3	.234	6	4	10	18	33	3	.944
1989—	Greensboro (S. Atl.)	SS	81	315	53	91	18	5	9	53	.289	29	63	21	125	169	42	.875
1990—	Cedar Rap. (Midw.)	OF	127	466	89	133	21	4	17	63	.285	59	97	40	241	10	10	.962
1991—	Chattanooga (Sou.)	OF	86	302	50	95	15	•8	8	49	.315	41	67	15	158	2	3	.982
—	Cincinnati (N.L.)	OF	9	40	6	8	0	0	1	3	.200	0	9	1	22	0	0	1.000
1992—	Cincinnati (N.L.)	OF	116	385	62	104	26	6	12	36	.270	48	98	16	262	11	6	.978
1993—	Cincinnati (N.L.)	OF	138	496	90	136	16	4	20	83	.274	51	118	27	312	3	8	.975
1994—	Cincinnati (N.L.)	OF	107	400	66	105	20	8	17	62	.263	41	*114	21	218	12	6	.975
1995—	Cincinnati (N.L.)	OF	133	484	91	148	36	6	28	99	.306	69	122	36	268	12	5	.982
1996—	Cincinnati (N.L.)	OF	81	287	49	72	17	1	14	33	.251	44	86	24	160	7	2	.988
—	Indianapolis (A.A.)	OF	4	12	3	5	2	0	1	4	.417	1	4	0	4	1	0	1.000
1997—	Cincinnati (N.L.)	OF	86	312	52	79	19	2	19	56	.253	42	93	13	183	4	5	.974
—	Chattanooga (Sou.)	OF	3	11	3	6	1	1	1	3	.545	1	2	0	11	0	0	1.000
—	Indianapolis (A.A.)	OF	5	19	1	4	0	0	0	1	.211	1	6	0	6	0	2	.750
Major league totals (7 years)			**670**	**2404**	**416**	**652**	**134**	**27**	**111**	**372**	**.271**	**295**	**640**	**138**	**1425**	**49**	**32**	**.979**

RECORDS: Shares N.L. career record for most strikeouts—9.

DIVISION SERIES RECORD

Year	Team (League)	Pos.	G	AB	R	H	2B	3B	HR	RBI	Avg.	BB	SO	SB	PO	A	E	Avg.
1995—	Cincinnati (N.L.)	OF	3	13	3	2	1	0	1	2	.154	1	9	2	7	0	1	.875

CHAMPIONSHIP SERIES RECORD

Year	Team (League)	Pos.	G	AB	R	H	2B	3B	HR	RBI	Avg.	BB	SO	SB	PO	A	E	Avg.
1995—	Cincinnati (N.L.)	OF	4	16	0	2	0	0	0	0	.125	2	10	0	7	0	1	.875

ALL-STAR GAME RECORD

Year	League	Pos.	AB	R	H	2B	3B	HR	RBI	Avg.	BB	SO	SB	PO	A	E	Avg.
1995—	National	OF	1	0	0	0	0	0	0	.000	0	1	0	0	0	0	...

SANDERS, SCOTT — P — TIGERS

PERSONAL: Born March 25, 1969, in Hannibal, Mo. ... 6-4/220. ... Throws right, bats right. ... Full name: Scott Gerald Sanders.

HIGH SCHOOL: Thibodaux (La.).

COLLEGE: Nicholls State (La.).

TRANSACTIONS/CAREER NOTES: Selected by San Diego Padres organization in supplemental round ("sandwich pick" between first and second round, 32nd pick overall) of free-agent draft (June 4, 1990); pick received as part of compensation for Kansas City Royals signing Type A free-agent P Mark Davis. ... On disabled list (May 1-17, 1994). ... On San Diego disabled list (July 18, 1995-remainder of season); included rehabilitation assignment to Las Vegas (August 28-September 1). ... Traded by Padres to Seattle Mariners for P Sterling Hitchcock (December 6, 1996). ... Traded by Mariners with P Dean Crow and 3B Carlos Villalobos to Detroit Tigers for P Omar Olivares and P Felipe Lira (July 18, 1997).

STATISTICAL NOTES: Tied for N.L. lead with 10 wild pitches in 1994. ... Pitched 4-0 one-hit, complete-game victory for Detroit against Texas (September 9, 1997).

MISCELLANEOUS: Appeared in one game as pinch-runner for Detroit (1997).

Year	Team (League)	W	L	Pct.	ERA	G	GS	CG	ShO	Sv.	IP	H	R	ER	BB	SO
1990—	Waterloo (Midw.)	2	2	.500	4.86	7	7	0	0	0	37	43	21	20	21	29
—	Spokane (N'west)	2	1	.667	0.95	3	3	0	0	0	19	12	3	2	5	21
1991—	Waterloo (Midw.)	3	0	1.000	0.68	4	4	0	0	0	26 1/3	17	2	2	6	18
—	High Desert (Calif.)	9	6	.600	3.66	21	21	4	2	0	132 2/3	114	72	54	72	93
1992—	Wichita (Texas)	7	5	.583	3.49	14	14	0	0	0	87 2/3	85	35	34	37	95
—	Las Vegas (PCL)	3	6	.333	5.50	14	12	1	1	0	72	97	49	44	31	51
1993—	Las Vegas (PCL)	5	10	.333	4.96	24	24	•4	0	0	152 1/3	170	101	84	62	*161
—	San Diego (N.L.)	3	3	.500	4.13	9	9	0	0	0	52 1/3	54	32	24	23	37
1994—	San Diego (N.L.)	4	8	.333	4.78	23	20	0	0	1	111	103	63	59	48	109
1995—	San Diego (N.L.)	5	5	.500	4.30	17	15	1	0	0	90	79	46	43	31	88
—	Las Vegas (PCL)	0	0	...	0.00	1	1	0	0	0	3	3	0	0	1	2
1996—	San Diego (N.L.)	9	5	.643	3.38	46	16	0	0	0	144	117	58	54	48	157
1997—	Seattle (A.L.)■	3	6	.333	6.47	33	6	0	0	2	65 1/3	73	48	47	38	62
—	Detroit (A.L.)■	3	8	.273	5.33	14	14	1	1	0	74 1/3	79	44	44	24	58
A.L. totals (1 year)		6	14	.300	5.86	47	20	1	1	2	139 2/3	152	92	91	62	120
N.L. totals (4 years)		21	21	.500	4.08	95	60	1	0	1	397 1/3	353	199	180	150	391
Major league totals (5 years)		27	35	.435	4.54	142	80	2	1	3	537	505	291	271	212	511

DIVISION SERIES RECORD

Year	Team (League)	W	L	Pct.	ERA	G	GS	CG	ShO	Sv.	IP	H	R	ER	BB	SO
1996—	San Diego (N.L.)	0	0	...	8.31	1	1	0	0	0	4 1/3	3	4	4	4	4

SANTANA, JULIO — P — RANGERS

PERSONAL: Born January 20, 1974, in San Pedro de Macoris, Dominican Republic. ... 6-0/185. ... Throws right, bats right. ... Full name: Julio Franklin Santana. ... Nephew of Rico Carty, major league outfielder with seven teams (1963-79).

TRANSACTIONS/CAREER NOTES: Signed as non-drafted free agent by Texas Rangers organization (February 18, 1990). ... On Texas disabled list (July 15-August 10, 1997).

Year Team (League)	W	L	Pct.	ERA	G	GS	CG	ShO	Sv.	IP	H	R	ER	BB	SO
1992— San Pedro (DSL)	0	1	.000	3.24	4	1	0	0	0	8 1/3	8	5	3	7	5
1993— GC Rangers (GCL)	4	1	.800	1.38	*26	0	0	0	7	39	31	9	6	7	50
1994— Char., W.Va. (S. Atl.)	6	7	.462	2.46	16	16	0	0	0	91 1/3	65	38	25	44	103
— Tulsa (Texas)	7	2	.778	2.90	11	11	2	0	0	71 1/3	50	26	23	41	45
1995— Oklahoma City (A.A.)	0	2	.000	39.00	2	2	0	0	0	3	9	14	13	7	6
— Charlotte (Fla. St.)	0	3	.000	3.73	5	5	1	0	0	31 1/3	32	16	13	16	27
— Tulsa (Texas)	6	4	.600	3.23	15	15	3	0	0	103	91	40	37	52	71
1996— Oklahoma City (A.A.)	11	12	.478	4.02	29	29	4	1	0	185 2/3	171	102	83	66	113
1997— Texas (A.L.)	4	6	.400	6.75	30	14	0	0	0	104	141	86	78	49	64
— Oklahoma City (A.A.)	0	0	. . .	15.00	1	1	0	0	0	3	9	6	5	2	1
Major league totals (1 year)	4	6	.400	6.75	30	14	0	0	0	104	141	86	78	49	64

RECORD AS POSITION PLAYER

							BATTING							FIELDING		
Year Team (League)	Pos.	G	AB	R	H	2B	3B	HR	RBI	Avg.	BB	SO	SB	PO	A	E	Avg.
1990— San Pedro (DSL)	. . .	11	34	4	7	0	0	1	3	.206	5	7	0	. . .	. . .	. . .	. . .
1991— San Pedro (DSL)	. . .	55	161	27	42	7	0	2	12	.261	27	37	5	. . .	. . .	. . .	. . .
1992— San Pedro (DSL)	OF-IF	17	48	7	11	2	0	2	2	.229	11	8	0	50	2	4	.929

SANTANGELO, F.P.   OF/IF   EXPOS

PERSONAL: Born October 24, 1967, in Livonia, Mich. ... 5-10/170. ... Bats both, throws right. ... Full name: Frank Paul Santangelo.
HIGH SCHOOL: Valley (Sacramento).
JUNIOR COLLEGE: Sacramento City College.
COLLEGE: Miami (Fla.).
TRANSACTIONS/CAREER NOTES: Selected by Montreal Expos organization in 20th round of free-agent draft (June 5, 1989). ... On disabled list (April 21-May 2, 1994).
STATISTICAL NOTES: Led Eastern League with 13 sacrifice hits in 1991. ... Switch-hit home runs in one game (June 7, 1997).

							BATTING							FIELDING		
Year Team (League)	Pos.	G	AB	R	H	2B	3B	HR	RBI	Avg.	BB	SO	SB	PO	A	E	Avg.
1989— Jamestown (NYP)	2B	2	6	0	3	1	0	0	0	.500	1	0	1	5	5	2	.833
— W.P. Beach (FSL)	SS-2B-OF	57	173	18	37	4	0	0	14	.214	23	12	3	32	67	8	.925
1990— W.P. Beach (FSL)	S-O-2-3	116	394	63	109	19	2	0	38	.277	51	49	22	151	202	22	.941
1991— Harrisburg (Eastern) ..	2-O-S-3	132	462	78	113	12	7	5	42	.245	74	45	21	234	253	16	.968
1992— Indianapolis (A.A.)	O-2-S-3	137	462	83	123	25	0	5	34	.266	62	58	12	291	119	4	.990
1993— Ottawa (Int'l)	O-S-3-2	131	453	86	124	21	2	4	45	.274	59	52	18	246	186	14	.969
1994— Ottawa (Int'l)	2-O-S-3	113	419	62	104	28	1	5	41	.252	59	64	7	235	140	12	.969
1995— Ottawa (Int'l)	3-2-O-S-C	95	267	37	68	15	3	2	25	.255	32	22	7	89	185	10	.965
— Montreal (N.L.)	OF-2B	35	98	11	29	5	1	1	9	.296	12	9	1	47	0	1	.979
1996— Montreal (N.L.)	0-3-2-S	152	393	54	109	20	5	7	56	.277	49	61	5	251	45	6	.980
1997— Montreal (N.L.)	0-3-2-S	130	350	56	87	19	5	5	31	.249	50	73	8	175	56	3	.987
Major league totals (3 years)		317	841	121	225	44	11	13	96	.268	111	143	14	473	101	10	.983

SANTIAGO, BENITO   C   BLUE JAYS

PERSONAL: Born March 9, 1965, in Ponce, Puerto Rico. ... 6-1/185. ... Bats right, throws right. ... Full name: Benito Rivera Santiago. ... Name pronounced SAHN-tee-AH-go.
HIGH SCHOOL: John F. Kennedy (Ponce, Puerto Rico).
TRANSACTIONS/CAREER NOTES: Signed as non-drafted free agent by San Diego Padres organization (September 1, 1982). ... On disabled list (June 21-July 2, 1985). ... On San Diego disabled list (June 15-August 10, 1990); included rehabilitation assignment to Las Vegas (August 2-9). ... On San Diego disabled list (May 31-July 11, 1992); included rehabilitation assignment to Las Vegas (July 7-11). ... Granted free agency (October 26, 1992). ... Signed by Florida Marlins (December 16, 1992). ... On suspended list (May 5-9, 1994). ... Granted free agency (October 20, 1994). ... Signed by Cincinnati Reds (April 17, 1995). ... On disabled list (May 8-July 4, 1995). ... Granted free agency (October 31, 1995). ... Signed by Philadelphia Phillies (January 30, 1996). ... Granted free agency (November 18, 1996). ... Signed by Toronto Blue Jays (December 9, 1996). ... On disabled list (April 14-28, 1997).
RECORDS: Holds major league rookie-season record for most consecutive games batted safely—34 (August 25-October 2, 1987). ... Shares major league single-season record for fewest passed balls (100 or more games)—0 (1992). ... Shares major league record for most consecutive home runs—4 (September 14 [1] and 15 [3], 1996).
HONORS: Named N.L. Rookie Player of the Year by THE SPORTING NEWS (1987). ... Named catcher on THE SPORTING NEWS N.L. All-Star team (1987, 1989 and 1991). ... Named catcher on THE SPORTING NEWS N.L. Silver Slugger team (1987-88 and 1990-91). ... Named N.L. Rookie of the Year by Baseball Writers' Association of America (1987). ... Won N.L. Gold Glove at catcher (1988-90).
STATISTICAL NOTES: Led Florida State League catchers with 26 passed balls and 12 double plays in 1983. ... Led Texas League catchers with 78 assists and 16 passed balls in 1985. ... Led Pacific Coast League catchers with 655 total chances in 1986. ... Had 34-game hitting streak (August 25-October 2, 1987). ... Led N.L. with 22 passed balls in 1987, 14 in 1989 and 23 in 1993. ... Led N.L. in grounding into double plays with 21 in 1991. ... Tied for N.L. lead in double plays by catcher with 11 in 1988 and 14 in 1991. ... Led N.L. catchers with 100 assists and 14 errors in 1991. ... Led N.L. catchers with .996 fielding percentage in 1995. ... Hit three home runs in one game (September 15, 1996). ... Career major league grand slams: 6.

							BATTING							FIELDING		
Year Team (League)	Pos.	G	AB	R	H	2B	3B	HR	RBI	Avg.	BB	SO	SB	PO	A	E	Avg.
1983— Miami (Fla. St.)	C	122	429	34	106	25	3	5	56	.247	11	79	3	471	*69	*21	.963
1984— Reno (California)	C	114	416	64	116	20	6	16	83	.279	36	75	5	692	96	25	.969
1985— Beaumont (Texas)	C-1B-3B	101	372	55	111	16	6	5	52	.298	16	59	12	525	†78	15	.976
1986— Las Vegas (PCL)	C	117	437	55	125	26	3	17	71	.286	17	81	19	*563	71	*21	.968
— San Diego (N.L.)	C	17	62	10	18	2	0	3	6	.290	2	12	0	80	7	5	.946
1987— San Diego (N.L.)	C	146	546	64	164	33	2	18	79	.300	16	112	21	817	80	*22	.976
1988— San Diego (N.L.)	C	139	492	49	122	22	2	10	46	.248	24	82	15	725	*75	*12	.985
1989— San Diego (N.L.)	C	129	462	50	109	16	3	16	62	.236	26	89	11	685	81	*20	.975
1990— San Diego (N.L.)	C	100	344	42	93	8	5	11	53	.270	27	55	5	538	51	12	.980
— Las Vegas (PCL)	C	6	20	5	6	2	0	1	8	.300	3	1	0	25	5	0	1.000

Year Team (League)	Pos.	G	AB	R	H	2B	3B	HR	RBI	Avg.	BB	SO	SB	PO	A	E	Avg.
1991—San Diego (N.L.)	C-OF	152	580	60	155	22	3	17	87	.267	23	114	8	830	†100	†14	.985
1992—San Diego (N.L.)	C	106	386	37	97	21	0	10	42	.251	21	52	2	584	53	*12	.982
—Las Vegas (PCL)	C	4	13	3	4	0	0	1	2	.308	1	1	0	13	2	0	1.000
1993—Florida (N.L.)■	C-OF	139	469	49	108	19	6	13	50	.230	37	88	10	740	64	11	.987
1994—Florida (N.L.)	C	101	337	35	92	14	2	11	41	.273	25	57	1	511	*66	5	.991
1995—Cincinnati (N.L.)■	C-1B	81	266	40	76	20	0	11	44	.286	24	48	2	480	35	2	†.996
1996—Philadelphia (N.L.)■ ..	C-1B	136	481	71	127	21	2	30	85	.264	49	104	2	834	67	11	.988
1997—Toronto (A.L.)■	C-DH	97	341	31	83	10	0	13	42	.243	17	80	1	621	40	2	.997
American League totals (1 year)		97	341	31	83	10	0	13	42	.243	17	80	1	621	40	2	.997
National League totals (11 years)		1246	4425	507	1161	198	25	150	595	.262	274	813	77	6824	679	126	.983
Major league totals (12 years)		1343	4766	538	1244	208	25	163	637	.261	291	893	78	7445	719	128	.985

DIVISION SERIES RECORD

NOTES: Hit home run in first at-bat (October 3, 1995).

Year Team (League)	Pos.	G	AB	R	H	2B	3B	HR	RBI	Avg.	BB	SO	SB	PO	A	E	Avg.
1995—Cincinnati (N.L.)	C	3	9	2	3	0	0	1	3	.333	3	3	0	20	0	0	1.000

CHAMPIONSHIP SERIES RECORD

Year Team (League)	Pos.	G	AB	R	H	2B	3B	HR	RBI	Avg.	BB	SO	SB	PO	A	E	Avg.
1995—Cincinnati (N.L.)	C	4	13	0	3	0	0	0	0	.231	2	3	0	23	1	0	1.000

ALL-STAR GAME RECORD

Year League	Pos.	AB	R	H	2B	3B	HR	RBI	Avg.	BB	SO	SB	PO	A	E	Avg.
1989—National	C	1	0	0	0	0	0	0	.000	0	1	0	0	0	1	.000
1990—National						Selected, did not play—injured.										
1991—National	C	3	0	0	0	0	0	0	.000	0	1	0	4	0	0	1.000
1992—National	C	1	0	0	0	0	0	0	.000	0	1	0	3	0	0	1.000
All-Star Game totals (3 years)		5	0	0	0	0	0	0	.000	0	3	0	7	0	1	.875

SANTIAGO, JOSE   P   ROYALS

PERSONAL: Born November 5, 1974, in Fajardo, Puerto Rico. ... 6-3/215. ... Throws right, bats right. ... Full name: Jose Rafael Santiago.
HIGH SCHOOL: Carlos Escobar Lopez (Loiza, Puerto Rico).
TRANSACTIONS/CAREER NOTES: Selected by Kansas City Royals organization in 70th round of free agent draft (June 3, 1994). ... On Kansas City disabled list (June 26-July 9, 1997).

Year Team (League)	W	L	Pct.	ERA	G	GS	CG	ShO	Sv.	IP	H	R	ER	BB	SO
1994—GC Royals (GCL)	1	0	1.000	2.37	10	1	0	0	2	19	17	7	5	7	10
1995—Spokane (N'west)	2	4	.333	3.14	22	0	0	0	1	48²/₃	60	26	17	20	32
1996—Lansing (Midwest)	7	6	.538	3.74	54	0	0	0	19	77	78	34	32	21	55
1997—Wilmington (Caro.)..........	1	1	.500	4.91	4	0	0	0	2	3²/₃	3	3	2	1	1
—Lansing (Midwest)	1	0	1.000	2.08	9	0	0	0	1	13	10	6	3	6	8
—Kansas City (A.L.)	0	0	...	1.93	4	0	0	0	0	4²/₃	7	2	1	2	1
—Wichita (Texas)	2	1	.667	4.00	22	0	0	0	3	27	32	13	12	8	12
Major league totals (1 year)........	0	0	...	1.93	4	0	0	0	0	4²/₃	7	2	1	2	1

SASSER, ROB   3B   RANGERS

PERSONAL: Born March 9, 1975, in Philadelphia. ... 6-4/190. ... Bats right, throws right. ... Full name: Robert Dofell Sasser.
HIGH SCHOOL: Oakland.
TRANSACTIONS/CAREER NOTES: Selected by Atlanta Braves organization in 10th round of free-agent draft (June 10, 1993). ... Selected by California Angels organization from Braves organization in Rule 5 minor league draft (December 9, 1996). ... Angels franchise renamed Anaheim Angels for 1997 season. ... Traded by Angels to Texas Rangers (October 31, 1997), completing deal in which Rangers traded P Ken Hill to Angels for C Jim Leyritz (July 29, 1997).
STATISTICAL NOTES: Led South Atlantic League third basemen with 45 errors in 1996. ... Led Midwest League third basemen with 435 total chances in 1997.

Year Team (League)	Pos.	G	AB	R	H	2B	3B	HR	RBI	Avg.	BB	SO	SB	PO	A	E	Avg.
1993—GC Braves (GCL)	3B	33	113	19	27	4	0	0	7	.239	6	25	2	15	61	10	.884
1994—Idaho Falls (Pio.)........	3B-SS	58	219	32	50	9	6	2	26	.228	19	58	13	35	122	20	.887
1995—Danville (Appal.).........	3B	12	47	8	15	2	1	0	7	.319	4	7	5	7	16	4	.852
1996—Macon (S. Atl.)..........	3-1-S-2	135	465	64	122	35	3	8	64	.262	65	108	38	247	262	†51	.909
1997—Cedar Rap. (Midw.)	3B-SS	134	497	103	135	26	5	17	77	.272	69	92	37	104	303	28	.936

SATURRIA, LUIS   OF   BLUE JAYS

PERSONAL: Born July 21, 1976, in San Pedro de Macoris, Dominican Republic. ... 6-2/165. ... Bats right, throws right. ... Full name: Luis A. Saturria.
TRANSACTIONS/CAREER NOTES: Signed as non-drafted free agent by St. Louis Cardinals organization (March 5, 1994). ... Selected by Toronto Blue Jays from Cardinals organization in Rule 5 major league draft (December 15, 1997).

Year Team (League)	Pos.	G	AB	R	H	2B	3B	HR	RBI	Avg.	BB	SO	SB	PO	A	E	Avg.
1994—Dm. Cardinals (DSL) ..	OF	61	227	29	63	2	6	1	23	.278	25	49	16	118	13	8	.942
1995—Dm. Cardinals (DSL) ..	OF	66	245	48	78	16	7	2	33	.318	34	26	12	126	14	22	.864
1996—Johnson City (App.) ...	OF	57	227	43	58	7	1	5	40	.256	24	61	12	68	5	3	.961
1997—Peoria (Midwest)........	OF	122	445	81	122	19	5	11	51	.274	44	95	23	196	*24	9	.961

SAUNDERS, TONY   P   DEVIL RAYS

PERSONAL: Born April 29, 1974, in Baltimore. ... 6-2/205. ... Throws left, bats left. ... Full name: Anthony S. Saunders.
HIGH SCHOOL: Glen Burnie (Md.).
TRANSACTIONS/CAREER NOTES: Signed as non-drafted free agent by Florida Marlins organization (June 9, 1992). ... On Florida disabled list (May 19-July 10, 1997). ... Selected by Tampa Bay Devil Rays in first round (first pick overall) of expansion draft (November 18, 1997).

Year Team (League)	W	L	Pct.	ERA	G	GS	CG	ShO	Sv.	IP	H	R	ER	BB	SO
1992— GC Marlins (GCL)	4	1	.800	1.18	24	0	0	0	7	45 2/3	29	10	6	13	37
1993— Kane County (Midwest)	6	1	.857	2.27	23	10	2	0	1	83 1/3	72	23	21	32	87
1994— Brevard County (FSL)	5	5	.500	3.15	10	10	1	0	0	60	54	24	21	9	46
1995— Brevard County (FSL)	6	5	.545	3.04	13	13	0	0	0	71	60	29	24	15	54
1996— Portland (Eastern)	13	4	.765	2.63	26	26	2	0	0	167 2/3	121	51	49	62	*156
1997— Florida (N.L.)	4	6	.400	4.61	22	21	0	0	0	111 1/3	99	62	57	64	102
— Portland (Eastern)	0	0	...	9.00	1	1	0	0	0	2	3	2	2	1	3
— Charlotte (Int'l)	1	0	1.000	2.77	3	3	0	0	0	13	9	4	4	6	9
Major league totals (1 year)	4	6	.400	4.61	22	21	0	0	0	111 1/3	99	62	57	64	102

CHAMPIONSHIP SERIES RECORD

Year Team (League)	W	L	Pct.	ERA	G	GS	CG	ShO	Sv.	IP	H	R	ER	BB	SO
1997— Florida (N.L.)	0	0	...	3.38	1	1	0	0	0	5 1/3	4	2	2	3	3

WORLD SERIES RECORD

NOTES: Member of World Series championship team (1997).

Year Team (League)	W	L	Pct.	ERA	G	GS	CG	ShO	Sv.	IP	H	R	ER	BB	SO
1997— Florida (N.L.)	0	1	.000	27.00	1	1	0	0	0	2	7	6	6	3	2

SCANLAN, BOB   P   ASTROS

PERSONAL: Born August 9, 1966, in Los Angeles. ... 6-4/220. ... Throws right, bats right. ... Full name: Robert Guy Scanlan Jr.
HIGH SCHOOL: Harvard (North Hollywood, Calif.).
TRANSACTIONS/CAREER NOTES: Selected by Philadelphia Phillies organization in 25th round of free-agent draft (June 4, 1984). ... Traded by Phillies with P Chuck McElroy to Chicago Cubs organization for P Mitch Williams (April 7, 1991). ... On suspended list (September 30-October 4, 1992 and September 17-20, 1993). ... Traded by Cubs to Milwaukee Brewers for P Rafael Novoa and OF Mike Carter (December 19, 1993). ... On Milwaukee disabled list (June 12-August 21, 1995); included rehabilitation assignment to New Orleans (August 4-21). ... Released by Brewers (December 18, 1995). ... Signed by Toledo, Detroit Tigers organization (January 15, 1996). ... Claimed on waivers by Kansas City Royals organization (August 8, 1996). ... Released by Royals (March 26, 1997). ... Signed by San Diego Padres organization (May 29, 1997). ... Granted free agency (October 15, 1997). ... Signed by Houston Astros organization (December 22, 1997).
STATISTICAL NOTES: Led International League with 17 wild pitches in 1988.

Year Team (League)	W	L	Pct.	ERA	G	GS	CG	ShO	Sv.	IP	H	R	ER	BB	SO
1984— GC Phillies (GCL)	0	2	.000	6.48	13	6	0	0	0	33 1/3	43	31	24	30	17
1985— Spartanburg (SAL)	8	12	.400	4.14	26	25	4	0	0	152 1/3	160	95	70	53	108
1986— Clearwater (Fla. St.)	8	12	.400	4.15	24	22	5	0	0	125 2/3	146	73	58	45	51
1987— Reading (Eastern)	*15	5	.750	5.10	27	26	3	1	0	164	187	98	93	55	91
1988— Maine (International)	5	*18	.217	5.59	28	27	4	1	0	161	181	*110	*100	50	79
1989— Reading (Eastern)	6	10	.375	5.78	31	17	4	1	0	118 1/3	124	88	•76	58	63
1990— Scran./W.B. (Int'l)	8	1	.889	4.85	23	23	0	0	0	130	128	79	70	59	74
1991— Iowa (Am. Assoc.)■	2	0	1.000	2.95	4	3	0	0	1	18 1/3	14	8	6	10	15
— Chicago (N.L.)	7	8	.467	3.89	40	13	0	0	0	111	114	60	48	40	44
1992— Chicago (N.L.)	3	6	.333	2.89	69	0	0	0	14	87 1/3	76	32	28	30	42
1993— Chicago (N.L.)	4	5	.444	4.54	70	0	0	0	0	75 1/3	79	41	38	28	44
1994— Milwaukee (A.L.)■	2	6	.250	4.11	30	12	0	0	2	103	117	53	47	28	65
1995— Milwaukee (A.L.)	4	7	.364	6.59	17	14	0	0	0	83 1/3	101	66	61	44	29
— New Orleans (A.A.)	0	1	.000	5.40	3	3	0	0	0	11 2/3	17	7	7	3	5
1996— Lakeland (Fla. St.)■	0	1	.000	5.00	2	2	0	0	0	9	9	6	5	3	4
— Toledo (Int'l)	1	3	.250	7.50	14	5	0	0	0	36	46	35	30	15	18
— Detroit (A.L.)	0	0	...	10.64	8	0	0	0	0	11	16	15	13	9	3
— Omaha (Am. Assoc.)■	0	0	...	0.73	12	0	0	0	5	12 1/3	10	2	1	3	9
— Kansas City (A.L.)	0	1	.000	3.18	9	0	0	0	0	11 1/3	13	4	4	3	3
1997— Las Vegas (PCL)■	3	1	.750	3.53	36	1	0	0	1	51	51	24	20	17	20
A.L. totals (3 years)	6	14	.300	5.39	64	26	0	0	2	208 2/3	247	138	125	84	100
N.L. totals (3 years)	14	19	.424	3.75	179	13	0	0	15	273 2/3	269	133	114	98	130
Major league totals (6 years)	20	33	.377	4.46	243	39	0	0	17	482 1/3	516	271	239	182	230

SCARSONE, STEVE   IF   ANGELS

PERSONAL: Born April 11, 1966, in Anaheim, Calif. ... 6-2/195. ... Bats right, throws right. ... Full name: Steven Wayne Scarsone. ... Name pronounced scar-SONE-ee.
HIGH SCHOOL: Canyon (Anaheim, Calif.).
COLLEGE: Santa Ana (Calif.) College.
TRANSACTIONS/CAREER NOTES: Selected by Philadelphia Phillies organization in second round of free-agent draft (January 14, 1986). ... Traded by Phillies to Baltimore Orioles for SS Juan Bell (August 11, 1992). ... Traded by Orioles to San Francisco Giants for OF Mark Leonard (March 20, 1993). ... On San Francisco disabled list (March 31-June 1, 1993). ... On Phoenix disabled list (June 22-29, 1993). ... Granted free agency (October 4, 1996). ... Signed by St. Louis Cardinals organization (January 13, 1997). ... Released by Cardinals (May 14, 1997). ... Granted free agency (October 15, 1997). ... Signed by Anaheim Angels organization (December 5, 1997).
STATISTICAL NOTES: Led Northwest League second basemen with 147 putouts, 29 errors and 45 double plays in 1986. ... Led International League second basemen with 20 errors in 1991. ... Led International League second basemen with 304 assists, 26 errors and 77 double plays in 1992.

Year	Team (League)	Pos.	G	AB	R	H	2B	3B	HR	RBI	Avg.	BB	SO	SB	PO	A	E	Avg.
											BATTING				FIELDING			
1986—	Bend (Northwest)	2B-SS	65	219	42	48	10	•4	4	21	.219	30	51	11	†149	188	†30	.918
1987—	Char., W.Va. (SAL)	SS-2B-3B	95	259	35	56	11	1	1	17	.216	31	64	8	127	212	25	.931
1988—	Clearwater (FSL)	SS-3B-2B	125	456	51	120	21	4	8	46	.263	18	93	14	179	326	33	.939
1989—	Reading (Eastern)	2B-SS	75	240	30	43	5	0	4	22	.179	15	67	2	171	200	11	.971
1990—	Clearwater (FSL)	2B	59	211	20	58	9	5	3	23	.275	19	57	3	116	147	13	.953
—	Reading (Eastern)	2B-SS	74	245	26	65	12	1	3	23	.265	14	63	0	141	206	8	.977
1991—	Reading (Eastern)	2B	15	49	6	15	0	0	3	3	.306	4	15	2	43	54	3	.970
—	Scran./W.B. (Int'l)	2B-SS	111	405	52	111	20	6	6	38	.274	19	81	10	222	343	†21	.964
1992—	Scran./W.B. (Int'l)	2B	89	325	43	89	23	4	11	48	.274	24	74	10	174	†253	†19	.957
—	Philadelphia (N.L.)	2B	7	13	1	2	0	0	0	0	.154	1	6	0	3	3	0	1.000
—	Rochester (Int'l)■	2B-3B	23	82	13	21	3	0	1	12	.256	6	12	3	36	†57	†7	.930
—	Baltimore (A.L.)	2B-3B-SS	11	17	2	3	0	0	0	0	.176	1	6	0	6	8	2	.875
1993—	Phoenix (PCL)■	2-3-S-1	19	70	13	18	1	2	3	9	.257	8	21	2	36	48	3	.966
—	San Francisco (N.L.)	2B-3B-1B	44	103	16	26	9	0	2	15	.252	4	32	0	53	44	1	.990
1994—	San Francisco (N.L.)	2-3-1-S	52	103	21	28	8	0	2	13	.272	10	20	0	66	80	2	.986
1995—	San Francisco (N.L.)	3B-2B-1B	80	233	33	62	10	3	11	29	.266	18	82	3	135	113	11	.958
1996—	San Francisco (N.L.)	2-3-1-S	105	283	28	62	12	1	5	23	.219	25	91	2	167	177	11	.969
1997—	Louisville (A.A.)■	2B-3B	10	26	5	4	0	0	1	3	.154	7	10	0	13	20	1	.971
—	St. Louis (N.L.)	2B-OF-3B	5	10	0	1	0	0	0	0	.100	2	5	1	4	2	0	1.000
—	Las Vegas (PCL)■	2-3-S-1-O	82	251	37	58	13	1	11	35	.231	38	78	2	126	209	13	.963
American League totals (1 year)			11	17	2	3	0	0	0	0	.176	1	6	0	6	8	2	.875
National League totals (6 years)			293	745	99	181	39	4	20	80	.243	60	236	6	428	419	25	.971
Major league totals (6 years)			304	762	101	184	39	4	20	80	.241	61	242	6	434	427	27	.970

SCHILLING, CURT P PHILLIES

PERSONAL: Born November 14, 1966, in Anchorage, Alaska. ... 6-4/226. ... Throws right, bats right. ... Full name: Curtis Montague Schilling.
HIGH SCHOOL: Shadow Mountain (Phoenix).
COLLEGE: Yavapai College (Ariz.).
TRANSACTIONS/CAREER NOTES: Selected by Boston Red Sox organization in second round of free-agent draft (January 14, 1986). ... Traded by Red Sox organization with OF Brady Anderson to Baltimore Orioles for P Mike Boddicker (July 29, 1988). ... Traded by Orioles with P Pete Harnisch and OF Steve Finley to Houston Astros for 1B Glenn Davis (January 10, 1991). ... Traded by Astros to Philadelphia Phillies for P Jason Grimsley (April 2, 1992). ... On Philadelphia disabled list (May 17-July 25, 1994); included rehabilitation assignments to Scranton/Wilkes-Barre (July 10-15) and Reading (July 15-20). ... On disabled list (July 19, 1995-remainder of season). ... On Philadelphia disabled list (March 23-May 14, 1996); included rehabilitation assignments to Clearwater (April 23-May 3) and Scranton/Wilkes-Barre (May 3-14).
RECORDS: Holds N.L. single-season record for most strikeouts by righthander—319 (1997).
STATISTICAL NOTES: Tied for International League lead with six balks in 1989. ... Pitched 2-1 one-hit, complete-game victory against New York (September 9, 1992). ... Struck out 15 batters in one game (July 21, 1997). ... Struck out 16 batters in one game (September 1, 1997).
MISCELLANEOUS: Struck out once in two games as pinch-hitter with Philadelphia (1996).

Year	Team (League)	W	L	Pct.	ERA	G	GS	CG	ShO	Sv.	IP	H	R	ER	BB	SO
1986—	Elmira (N.Y.-Penn)	7	3	.700	2.59	16	15	2	1	0	93 2/3	92	34	27	30	75
1987—	Greensboro (S. Atl.)	8	*15	.348	3.82	29	28	7	3	0	184	179	96	78	65	*189
1988—	New Britain (East.)	8	5	.615	2.97	21	17	4	1	0	106	91	44	35	40	62
—	Charlotte (Southern)■	5	2	.714	3.18	7	7	2	1	0	45 1/3	36	19	16	23	32
—	Baltimore (A.L.)	0	3	.000	9.82	4	4	0	0	0	14 2/3	22	19	16	10	4
1989—	Rochester (Int'l)	•13	11	.542	3.21	27	•27	•9	•3	0	•185 1/3	176	76	66	59	109
—	Baltimore (A.L.)	0	1	.000	6.23	5	1	0	0	0	8 2/3	10	6	6	3	6
1990—	Rochester (Int'l)	4	4	.500	3.92	15	14	1	0	0	87 1/3	95	46	38	25	83
—	Baltimore (A.L.)	1	2	.333	2.54	35	0	0	0	3	46	38	13	13	19	32
1991—	Houston (N.L.)■	3	5	.375	3.81	56	0	0	0	8	75 2/3	79	35	32	39	71
—	Tucson (PCL)	0	1	.000	3.42	13	0	0	0	3	23 2/3	16	9	9	12	21
1992—	Philadelphia (N.L.)■	14	11	.560	2.35	42	26	10	4	2	226 1/3	165	67	59	59	147
1993—	Philadelphia (N.L.)	16	7	.696	4.02	34	34	7	2	0	235 1/3	234	114	105	57	186
1994—	Philadelphia (N.L.)	2	8	.200	4.48	13	13	1	0	0	82 1/3	87	42	41	28	58
—	Scran./W.B. (Int'l)	0	0	...	1.80	2	2	0	0	0	10	6	2	2	5	6
—	Reading (Eastern)	0	0	...	0.00	1	1	0	0	0	4	6	0	0	1	4
1995—	Philadelphia (N.L.)	7	5	.583	3.57	17	17	1	0	0	116	96	52	46	26	114
1996—	Clearwater (Fla. St.)	2	0	1.000	1.29	2	2	0	0	0	14	9	2	2	2	17
—	Scran./W.B. (Int'l)	1	0	1.000	1.38	2	2	0	0	0	13	9	2	2	5	10
—	Philadelphia (N.L.)	9	10	.474	3.19	26	26	*8	2	0	183 1/3	149	69	65	50	182
1997—	Philadelphia (N.L.)	17	11	.607	2.97	35	•35	7	2	0	254 1/3	208	96	84	58	*319
A.L. totals (3 years)		1	6	.143	4.54	44	5	0	0	3	69 1/3	70	38	35	32	42
N.L. totals (7 years)		68	57	.544	3.31	223	151	34	10	10	1173 1/3	1018	475	432	317	1077
Major league totals (10 years)		69	63	.523	3.38	267	156	34	10	13	1242 2/3	1088	513	467	349	1119

CHAMPIONSHIP SERIES RECORD

RECORDS: Holds single-game records for most consecutive strikeouts—5; and most consecutive strikeouts from start of the game—5 (October 6, 1993).
NOTES: Named N.L. Championship Series Most Valuable Player (1993).

Year	Team (League)	W	L	Pct.	ERA	G	GS	CG	ShO	Sv.	IP	H	R	ER	BB	SO
1993—	Philadelphia (N.L.)	0	0	...	1.69	2	2	0	0	0	16	11	4	3	5	19

WORLD SERIES RECORD

Year	Team (League)	W	L	Pct.	ERA	G	GS	CG	ShO	Sv.	IP	H	R	ER	BB	SO
1993—	Philadelphia (N.L.)	1	1	.500	3.52	2	2	1	1	0	15 1/3	13	7	6	5	9

ALL-STAR GAME RECORD

Year	League	W	L	Pct.	ERA	GS	CG	ShO	Sv.	IP	H	R	ER	BB	SO
1997—	National	0	0	...	0.00	0	0	0	0	2	2	0	0	0	3

SCHMIDT, JASON   P   PIRATES

PERSONAL: Born January 29, 1973, in Kelso, Wash. ... 6-5/207. ... Throws right, bats right. ... Full name: Jason David Schmidt.
HIGH SCHOOL: Kelso (Wash.).
TRANSACTIONS/CAREER NOTES: Selected by Atlanta Braves organization in eighth round of free-agent draft (June 3, 1991). ... On Atlanta disabled list (July 15-August 30, 1996); included rehabilitation assignment to Greenville (August 11-30). ... Claimed on waivers by Pittsburgh Pirates (August 30, 1996), completing deal in which Pirates traded P Denny Neagle to Braves for a player to be named later (August 28, 1996).
MISCELLANEOUS: Received bases on balls in only appearance as pinch-hitter with Atlanta (1995).

Year — Team (League)	W	L	Pct.	ERA	G	GS	CG	ShO	Sv.	IP	H	R	ER	BB	SO
1991— GC Braves (GCL)	3	4	.429	2.38	11	11	0	0	0	45 1/3	32	21	12	23	44
1992— Pulaski (Appalachian)	3	4	.429	4.01	11	11	0	0	0	58 1/3	38	36	26	31	56
— Macon (S. Atl.)	0	3	.000	4.01	7	7	0	0	0	24 2/3	31	18	11	19	33
1993— Durham (Carolina)	7	11	.389	4.94	22	22	0	0	0	116 2/3	128	69	64	47	110
1994— Greenville (Southern)	8	7	.533	3.65	24	24	1	0	0	140 1/3	135	64	57	54	131
1995— Atlanta (N.L.)	2	2	.500	5.76	9	2	0	0	0	25	27	17	16	18	19
— Richmond (Int'l)	8	6	.571	*2.25	19	19	0	0	0	116	97	40	29	48	95
1996— Atlanta (N.L.)	3	4	.429	6.75	13	11	0	0	0	58 2/3	69	48	44	32	48
— Richmond (Int'l)	3	0	1.000	2.56	7	7	0	0	0	45 2/3	36	17	13	19	41
— Greenville (Southern)	0	0	...	9.00	1	1	0	0	0	2	4	2	2	0	2
— Pittsburgh (N.L.)■	2	2	.500	4.06	6	6	1	0	0	37 2/3	39	19	17	21	26
1997— Pittsburgh (N.L.)	10	9	.526	4.60	32	32	2	0	0	187 2/3	193	106	96	76	136
Major league totals (3 years)	17	17	.500	5.04	60	51	3	0	0	309	328	190	173	147	229

SCHMIDT, JEFF   P   ANGELS

PERSONAL: Born February 21, 1971, in Northfield, Minn. ... 6-5/190. ... Throws right, bats right. ... Full name: Jeffrey Thomas Schmidt.
HIGH SCHOOL: La Crosse (Wis.) Central.
COLLEGE: Minnesota.
TRANSACTIONS/CAREER NOTES: Selected by California Angels organization in supplemental round ("sandwich pick" between first and second round, 39th pick overall) of free-agent draft (June 1, 1992); pick received as part of compensation for Kansas City Royals signing Type A free-agent 1B Wally Joyner. ... Angels franchise renamed Anaheim Angels for 1997 season. ... On disabled list (April 3-13, July 8-August 15 and August 29, 1997-remainder of season).
STATISTICAL NOTES: Led Texas League with 18 wild pitches in 1995.

Year — Team (League)	W	L	Pct.	ERA	G	GS	CG	ShO	Sv.	IP	H	R	ER	BB	SO
1992— Boise (Northwest)	1	6	.143	4.47	11	11	00	0	0	52 1/3	55	41	26	18	41
1993— Cedar Rapids (Midw.)	3	•14	.176	4.90	26	25	3	0	0	152 1/3	166	*105	83	58	107
1994— Lake Elsinore (Calif.)	1	5	.167	4.11	39	11	0	0	12	92	94	54	42	28	70
1995— Midland (Texas)	4	12	.250	5.83	20	20	0	0	0	100 1/3	127	75	65	48	46
1996— Vancouver (PCL)	0	1	.000	2.87	35	0	0	0	19	37 2/3	29	12	12	25	19
— California (A.L.)	2	0	1.000	7.88	9	0	0	0	0	8	13	9	7	8	2
1997— Vancouver (PCL)	1	2	.333	5.32	27	0	0	0	10	22	22	14	13	20	14
Major league totals (1 year)	2	0	1.000	7.88	9	0	0	0	0	8	13	9	7	8	2

SCHOUREK, PETE   P   ASTROS

PERSONAL: Born May 10, 1969, in Austin, Texas. ... 6-5/205. ... Throws left, bats left. ... Full name: Peter Alan Schourek. ... Name pronounced SHUR-ek.
HIGH SCHOOL: George C. Marshall (Falls Church, Va.).
TRANSACTIONS/CAREER NOTES: Selected by New York Mets organization in second round of free-agent draft (June 2, 1987). ... On disabled list (June 17, 1988-remainder of season). ... Claimed on waivers by Cincinnati Reds (April 7, 1994). ... On disabled list (June 1-22 and July 2, 1996-remainder of season). ... On disabled list (June 14-July 18 and July 31-September 2, 1997). ... Released by Reds (October 10, 1997). ... Signed by Houston Astros organization (Janaury 9, 1998).
HONORS: Named lefthanded pitcher on THE SPORTING NEWS N.L. All-Star team (1995).
STATISTICAL NOTES: Pitched 9-0 one-hit, complete-game victory for New York against Montreal (September 10, 1991).
MISCELLANEOUS: Appeared in one game as pinch-runner with New York (1992). ... Struck out in only appearance as pinch-hitter (1996). ... Appeared in one game as pinch-runner (1997).

Year — Team (League)	W	L	Pct.	ERA	G	GS	CG	ShO	Sv.	IP	H	R	ER	BB	SO
1987— Kingsport (Appalachian)	4	5	.444	3.68	12	12	2	0	0	78 1/3	70	37	32	34	57
1988—						Did not play.									
1989— Columbia (S. Atl.)	5	9	.357	2.85	27	19	5	1	1	136	120	66	43	66	131
— St. Lucie (Fla. St.)	0	0	...	2.25	2	1	0	0	0	4	3	1	1	2	4
1990— St. Lucie (Fla. St.)	4	1	.800	0.97	5	5	2	2	0	37	29	4	4	8	28
— Tidewater (Int'l)	1	0	1.000	2.57	2	2	1	1	0	14	9	4	4	5	14
— Jackson (Texas)	11	4	.733	3.04	19	19	1	0	0	124 1/3	109	53	42	39	94
1991— Tidewater (Int'l)	1	1	.500	2.52	4	4	0	0	0	25	18	7	7	10	17
— New York (N.L.)	5	4	.556	4.27	35	8	1	1	2	86 1/3	82	49	41	43	67
1992— Tidewater (Int'l)	2	5	.286	2.73	8	8	2	1	0	52 2/3	46	20	16	23	42
— New York (N.L.)	6	8	.429	3.64	22	21	0	0	0	136	137	60	55	44	60
1993— New York (N.L.)	5	12	.294	5.96	41	18	0	0	0	128 1/3	168	90	85	45	72
1994— Cincinnati (N.L.)■	7	2	.778	4.09	22	10	0	0	0	81 1/3	90	39	37	29	69
1995— Cincinnati (N.L.)	18	7	.720	3.22	29	29	2	0	0	190 1/3	158	72	68	45	160
1996— Cincinnati (N.L.)	4	5	.444	6.01	12	12	0	0	0	67 1/3	79	48	45	24	54
1997— Cincinnati (N.L.)	5	8	.385	5.42	18	17	0	0	0	84 2/3	78	59	51	38	59
Major league totals (7 years)	50	46	.521	4.44	179	115	3	1	2	774 1/3	792	417	382	268	541

DIVISION SERIES RECORD

Year — Team (League)	W	L	Pct.	ERA	G	GS	CG	ShO	Sv.	IP	H	R	ER	BB	SO
1995— Cincinnati (N.L.)	1	0	1.000	2.57	1	1	0	0	0	7	5	2	2	3	5

CHAMPIONSHIP SERIES RECORD

Year — Team (League)	W	L	Pct.	ERA	G	GS	CG	ShO	Sv.	IP	H	R	ER	BB	SO
1995— Cincinnati (N.L.)	0	1	.000	1.26	2	2	0	0	0	14 1/3	14	2	2	3	13

S

SCHUTZ, CARL   P   BRAVES

PERSONAL: Born August 22, 1971, in Hammond, La. ... 5-11/200. ... Throws left, bats left. ... Full name: Carl James Schutz.
HIGH SCHOOL: Riverside Academy (Reserve, La.).
COLLEGE: Southeastern Louisiana.
TRANSACTIONS/CAREER NOTES: Selected by Atlanta Braves organization in third round of free-agent draft (June 3, 1993).

Year Team (League)	W	L	Pct.	ERA	G	GS	CG	ShO	Sv.	IP	H	R	ER	BB	SO
1993— Danville (Appalachian)........	1	0	1.000	0.61	13	0	0	0	4	14 2/3	6	1	1	6	25
— Greenville (S. Atl.)...........	2	1	.667	5.06	22	0	0	0	3	21 1/3	17	17	12	22	19
1994— Durham (Carolina)............	3	3	.500	4.89	53	0	0	0	20	53 1/3	35	30	29	46	81
1995— Greenville (Southern)	3	7	.300	4.94	51	0	0	0	26	58 1/3	53	36	32	36	56
1996— Richmond (Int'l).................	4	3	.571	5.30	41	7	0	0	3	69 2/3	86	46	41	26	52
— Atlanta (N.L.).................	0	0	...	2.70	3	0	0	0	0	3 1/3	3	1	1	2	5
1997— Richmond (Int'l).................	4	6	.400	5.33	27	10	0	0	0	79 1/3	83	56	47	51	66
Major league totals (1 year)........	0	0	...	2.70	3	0	0	0	0	3 1/3	3	1	1	2	5

SCOTT, TIM   P   DODGERS

PERSONAL: Born November 16, 1966, in Hanford, Calif. ... 6-2/205. ... Throws right, bats right. ... Full name: Timothy Dale Scott.
HIGH SCHOOL: Hanford (Calif.).
TRANSACTIONS/CAREER NOTES: Selected by Los Angeles Dodgers organization in second round of free-agent draft (June 4, 1984). ... On disabled list (July 23, 1985-remainder of season and April 11-May 15, 1986). ... Granted free agency (October 15, 1990). ... Signed by San Diego Padres organization (November 1, 1990). ... Traded by Padres to Montreal Expos for IF/OF Archi Cianfrocco (June 23, 1993). ... On disabled list (June 6-21, 1994). ... Traded by Expos with P Kirk Rueter to San Francisco Giants for P Mark Leiter (July 30, 1996). ... Claimed on waivers by Cincinnati Reds (October 14, 1996). ... Granted free agency (December 20, 1996). ... Signed by Padres organization (January 30, 1997). ... Released by Padres (May 18, 1997). ... Signed by Colorado Rockies (May 27, 1997). ... On Colorado disabled list (July 4-August 29, 1997). ... Claimed on waivers by Seattle Mariners (July 10, 1997). ... Waiver claim by Mariners voided (September 26, 1997). ... Signed by Dodgers organization (December 17, 1997).

Year Team (League)	W	L	Pct.	ERA	G	GS	CG	ShO	Sv.	IP	H	R	ER	BB	SO
1984— Great Falls (Pio.)	5	4	.556	4.38	13	13	3	•2	0	78	90	58	38	44	38
1985— Bakersfield (California).......	3	4	.429	5.80	12	10	2	0	0	63 2/3	84	46	41	28	31
1986— Vero Beach (FSL)	5	4	.556	3.40	20	13	3	1	0	95 1/3	113	44	36	24	37
1987— Bakersfield (California)	2	3	.400	4.45	7	5	1	0	0	32 1/3	33	19	16	10	29
— San Antonio (Tex.)	0	1	.000	16.88	2	2	0	0	0	5 1/3	14	10	10	2	6
1988— Bakersfield (California)	4	7	.364	3.64	36	2	0	0	7	64 1/3	52	34	26	26	59
1989— San Antonio (Tex.)	4	2	.667	3.71	48	0	0	0	4	68	71	30	28	36	64
1990— San Antonio (Tex.)	3	3	.500	2.85	30	0	0	0	7	47 1/3	35	17	15	14	52
— Albuquerque (PCL)	2	1	.667	4.20	17	0	0	0	3	15	14	9	7	14	15
1991— Las Vegas (PCL)■..............	8	8	.500	5.19	41	11	0	0	0	111	133	78	64	39	74
— San Diego (N.L.)	0	0	...	9.00	2	0	0	0	0	1	2	2	1	0	1
1992— Las Vegas (PCL)	1	2	.333	2.25	24	0	0	0	15	28	20	8	7	3	28
— San Diego (N.L.)	4	1	.800	5.26	34	0	0	0	0	37 2/3	39	24	22	21	30
1993— San Diego (N.L.)	2	0	1.000	2.39	24	0	0	0	0	37 2/3	38	13	10	15	30
— Montreal (N.L.)■..............	5	2	.714	3.71	32	0	0	0	1	34	31	15	14	19	35
1994— Montreal (N.L.).................	5	2	.714	2.70	40	0	0	0	1	53 1/3	51	17	16	18	37
1995— Montreal (N.L.).................	2	0	1.000	3.98	62	0	0	0	2	63 1/3	52	30	28	23	57
1996— Montreal (N.L.).................	3	5	.375	3.11	45	0	0	0	1	46 1/3	41	18	16	21	37
— San Francisco (N.L.)■........	2	2	.500	8.24	20	0	0	0	0	19 2/3	24	18	18	9	10
1997— San Diego (N.L.)■.............	1	1	.500	7.85	14	0	0	0	0	18 1/3	25	17	16	5	14
— Colo. Springs (PCL)■........	0	0	...	1.23	12	0	0	0	3	14 2/3	7	2	2	3	18
— Colorado (N.L.)	0	0	...	10.13	3	0	0	0	0	2 2/3	5	3	3	2	2
Major league totals (7 years)......	24	13	.649	4.13	276	0	0	0	5	314	308	157	144	133	253

SEFCIK, KEVIN   IF   PHILLIES

PERSONAL: Born February 10, 1971, in Oak Lawn, Ill. ... 5-10/175. ... Bats right, throws right. ... Full name: Kevin John Sefcik.
HIGH SCHOOL: Victor Andrews (Tinley Park, Ill.).
COLLEGE: St. Xavier (Ill.).
TRANSACTIONS/CAREER NOTES: Selected by Philadelphia Phillies organization in 33rd round of free-agent draft (June 3, 1993).
STATISTICAL NOTES: Led New York-Pennsylvania League second basemen with 212 assists and 359 total chances in 1993.

						BATTING								FIELDING		
Year Team (League)	Pos.	G	AB	R	H	2B	3B	HR	RBI	Avg.	BB	SO	SB	PO	A	E	Avg.
1993— Batavia (NY-Penn)	2B-3B	74	281	49	84	24	4	2	28	.299	27	22	20	136	†216	16	.957
1994— Clearwater (FSL)	3B-2B	130	516	83	147	29	8	2	46	.285	49	43	30	91	293	21	.948
1995— Scran./W.B. (Int'l)	2B	7	26	5	9	6	1	0	6	.346	3	1	0	13	16	0	1.000
— Reading (Eastern)	SS-3B	128	508	68	138	18	4	4	46	.272	38	48	14	166	349	18	.966
— Philadelphia (N.L.)	3B	5	4	1	0	0	0	0	0	.000	0	2	0	0	1	0	1.000
1996— Philadelphia (N.L.)......	SS-3B-2B	44	116	10	33	5	3	0	9	.284	9	16	3	30	83	7	.942
— Scran./W.B. (Int'l)	SS-2B-3B	45	180	34	60	7	5	0	19	.333	15	20	11	63	143	10	.954
1997— Philadelphia (N.L.)......	2B-SS-3B	61	119	11	32	3	0	2	6	.269	4	9	1	39	62	4	.962
— Scran./W.B. (Int'l)	2B-3B-OF	29	123	19	41	11	2	1	7	.333	9	11	5	51	56	6	.947
Major league totals (3 years)		110	239	22	65	8	3	2	15	.272	13	27	4	69	146	11	.951

SEGUI, DAVID   1B   MARINERS

PERSONAL: Born July 19, 1966, in Kansas City, Kan. ... 6-1/202. ... Bats both, throws left. ... Full name: David Vincent Segui. ... Son of Diego Segui, major league pitcher with five teams (1962-75 and 1977); and brother of Dan Segui, minor league infielder (1987-90). ... Name pronounced seh-GHEE.

HIGH SCHOOL: Bishop Ward (Kansas City, Kan.).
JUNIOR COLLEGE: Kansas City Kansas Community College.
COLLEGE: Louisiana Tech.
TRANSACTIONS/CAREER NOTES: Selected by Baltimore Orioles organization in 18th round of free-agent draft (June 2, 1987). ... On Rochester disabled list (April 19-26, 1991). ... On suspended list (August 16-19, 1993). ... Traded by Orioles to New York Mets for SS Kevin Baez and P Tom Wegmann (March 27, 1994). ... On disabled list (June 20-July 5, 1994). ... Traded by Mets to Montreal Expos for P Reid Cornelius (June 8, 1995). ... On disabled list (July 4-August 16, 1996). ... On disabled list (June 4-21, 1997). ... On suspended list (July 26, 1997). ... Granted free agency (October 28, 1997). ... Signed by Seattle Mariners (December 12, 1997).
STATISTICAL NOTES: Led N.L. first basemen with .996 fielding percentage in 1994. ... Career major league grand slams: 3.

Year	Team (League)	Pos.	G	AB	R	H	2B	3B	HR	RBI	Avg.	BB	SO	SB	PO	A	E	Avg.
1988—	Hagerstown (Car.)	1B-OF	60	190	35	51	12	4	3	31	.268	22	23	0	342	25	9	.976
1989—	Frederick (Carolina)	1B	83	284	43	90	19	0	10	50	.317	41	32	2	707	47	4	.995
	—Hagerstown (Eastern)	1B	44	173	22	56	14	1	1	27	.324	16	16	0	381	30	1	.998
1990—	Rochester (Int'l)	1B-OF	86	307	55	103	28	0	2	51	.336	45	28	5	704	62	3	.996
	—Baltimore (A.L.)	1B-DH	40	123	14	30	7	0	2	15	.244	11	15	0	283	26	3	.990
1991—	Rochester (Int'l)	1B-OF	28	96	9	26	2	0	1	10	.271	15	6	1	165	15	0	1.000
	—Baltimore (A.L.)	OF-1B-DH	86	212	15	59	7	0	2	22	.278	12	19	1	264	23	3	.990
1992—	Baltimore (A.L.)	1B-OF	115	189	21	44	9	0	1	17	.233	20	23	1	406	35	1	.998
1993—	Baltimore (A.L.)	1B-DH	146	450	54	123	27	0	10	60	.273	58	53	2	1152	98	5	.996
1994—	New York (N.L.)■	1B-OF	92	336	46	81	17	1	10	43	.241	33	43	0	695	52	5	†.993
1995—	New York (N.L.)	OF-1B	33	73	9	24	3	1	2	11	.329	12	9	1	56	5	0	1.000
	—Montreal (N.L.)■	1B-OF	97	383	59	117	22	3	10	57	.305	28	38	1	840	70	3	.997
1996—	Montreal (N.L.)	1B	115	416	69	119	30	1	11	58	.286	60	54	4	944	90	7	.993
1997—	Montreal (N.L.)	1B	125	459	75	141	22	3	21	68	.307	57	66	1	1035	88	6	.995
American League totals (4 years)			387	974	104	256	50	0	15	114	.263	101	110	4	2105	182	12	.995
National League totals (4 years)			462	1667	258	482	94	9	54	237	.289	190	210	7	3570	305	21	.995
Major league totals (8 years)			849	2641	362	738	144	9	69	351	.279	291	320	11	5675	487	33	.995

SEGUIGNOL, FERNANDO — 1B — EXPOS

PERSONAL: Born January 17, 1975, in Bocas del Toro, Panama. ... 6-5/190. ... Bats both, throws right. ... Full name: Fernando Alfredo Seguignol.
HIGH SCHOOL: Bocas del Toro (Bocas del Toro, Panama).
TRANSACTIONS/CAREER NOTES: Signed as non-drafted free agent by New York Yankees organization (January 29, 1993). ... Traded by Yankees with a player to be named later and cash to Montreal Expos for P John Wetteland (April 5, 1995).
STATISTICAL NOTES: Led Florida State League with 14 sacrifice flies in 1997. ... Tied for Florida State League lead in assists by first basemen with 91 in 1997.

Year	Team (League)	Pos.	G	AB	R	H	2B	3B	HR	RBI	Avg.	BB	SO	SB	PO	A	E	Avg.
1993—	GC Yankees (GCL)	OF-1B	45	161	16	35	3	3	2	20	.217	9	37	2	86	8	2	.979
1994—	Oneonta (NYP)	OF	73	266	36	77	14	*9	2	32	.289	16	61	4	77	3	4	.952
1995—	Albany (S. Atl.)■	OF	121	457	59	95	22	2	12	66	.208	28	141	12	205	7	8	.964
1996—	Delmarva (S. Atl.)	OF	118	410	59	98	14	5	8	55	.239	48	126	12	173	4	4	.978
1997—	W.P. Beach (FSL)	1B-OF	124	456	70	116	27	5	18	83	.254	30	129	5	967	‡91	15	.986

SEITZER, KEVIN — DH/1B

PERSONAL: Born March 26, 1962, in Springfield, Ill. ... 5-11/190. ... Bats right, throws right. ... Full name: Kevin Lee Seitzer. ... Brother of Brad Seitzer, infielder, Milwaukee Brewers organization. ... Name pronounced SITE-ser.
HIGH SCHOOL: Lincoln (Ill.).
COLLEGE: Eastern Illinois (bachelor of science degree in industrial electronics).
TRANSACTIONS/CAREER NOTES: Selected by Kansas City Royals organization in 11th round of free-agent draft (June 6, 1983). ... On disabled list (April 27-May 31, 1991). ... Released by Royals (March 26, 1992). ... Signed by Milwaukee Brewers (April 5, 1992). ... Granted free agency (October 27, 1992). ... Signed by Oakland Athletics (February 1, 1993). ... Released by A's (July 26, 1993). ... Signed by Brewers (July 29, 1993). ... Granted free agency (October 29, 1993). ... Re-signed by Brewers (February 11, 1994). ... On Milwaukee disabled list (May 10-June 14, 1994); included rehabilitation assignment to Beloit (June 11-14). ... Granted free agency (November 1, 1995). ... Re-signed by Brewers (December 7, 1995). ... Traded by Brewers to Cleveland Indians for OF Jeromy Burnitz (August 31, 1996). ... Granted free agency (October 29, 1997).
HONORS: Named South Atlantic League Most Valuable Player (1984).
STATISTICAL NOTES: Led Pioneer League third basemen with 122 assists and 172 total chances in 1983. ... Led South Atlantic League third basemen with 409 total chances in 1984. ... Tied for American Association lead in being hit by pitch with nine in 1986. ... Collected six hits in one game (August 2, 1987). ... Tied for A.L. lead in errors by third baseman with 22 in 1987. ... Led A.L. third basemen with 26 errors in 1988. ... Led A.L. third basemen with .969 fielding percentage in 1992. ... Career major league grand slams: 4.

Year	Team (League)	Pos.	G	AB	R	H	2B	3B	HR	RBI	Avg.	BB	SO	SB	PO	A	E	Avg.
1983—	Butte (Pioneer)	3B-SS	68	238	60	82	14	1	2	45	.345	46	36	11	52	†124	21	.893
1984—	Char., S.C. (S. Atl.)	3B	•141	489	*96	*145	26	5	8	79	.297	*118	70	23	80	*279	*50	.878
1985—	Fort Myers (FSL)	1B-3B	90	290	61	91	10	5	3	46	.314	85	30	28	569	88	9	.986
	—Memphis (Southern)	3B-1B-OF	52	187	26	65	6	2	1	20	.348	25	21	9	79	51	10	.929
1986—	Memphis (Southern)	1B	4	11	4	3	0	0	0	1	.273	7	1	2	28	3	1	.969
	—Omaha (A.A.)	OF-1B-3B	129	432	86	138	20	11	13	74	.319	89	57	20	338	39	9	.977
	—Kansas City (A.L.)	1B-OF-3B	28	96	16	31	4	1	2	11	.323	19	14	0	224	19	3	.988
1987—	Kansas City (A.L.)	3-1-O-DH	161	641	105	•207	33	8	15	83	.323	80	85	12	290	315	‡24	.962
1988—	Kansas City (A.L.)	3B-OF-DH	149	559	90	170	32	5	5	60	.304	72	64	10	93	297	†26	.938
1989—	Kansas City (A.L.)	3-S-O-1	160	597	78	168	17	2	4	48	.281	102	76	17	118	277	20	.952
1990—	Kansas City (A.L.)	3B-2B	158	622	91	171	31	5	6	38	.275	67	66	7	118	281	19	.955
1991—	Kansas City (A.L.)	3B-DH	85	234	28	62	11	3	1	25	.265	29	21	4	45	127	11	.940

Year Team (League)	Pos.	G	AB	R	H	2B	3B	HR	RBI	Avg.	BB	SO	SB	PO	A	E	Avg.
						BATTING									**FIELDING**		
1992— Milwaukee (A.L.)■.....	3B-2B-1B	148	540	74	146	35	1	5	71	.270	57	44	13	102	277	12	†.969
1993— Oakland (A.L.).........3-1-DH-O-2-P		73	255	24	65	10	2	4	27	.255	27	33	4	205	89	7	.977
— Milw. (A.L.)■.........3-1-DH-O-2-S		47	162	21	47	6	0	7	30	.290	17	15	3	70	61	5	.963
1994— Milwaukee (A.L.)	3B-1B-DH	80	309	44	97	24	2	5	49	.314	30	38	2	329	104	11	.975
— Beloit (Midwest)........	3B	3	12	3	4	3	0	0	3	.333	0	0	2	1	6	0	1.000
1995— Milwaukee (A.L.)	3B-1B-DH	132	492	56	153	33	3	5	69	.311	64	57	2	340	181	10	.981
1996— Milwaukee (A.L.)	1B-DH-3B	132	490	74	155	25	3	12	62	.316	73	68	6	498	66	5	.991
— Cleveland (A.L.)■.........	DH-1B	22	83	11	32	10	0	1	16	.386	14	11	0	31	9	0	1.000
1997— Cleveland (A.L.).........	DH-1B-3B	64	198	27	53	14	0	2	24	.268	18	25	0	149	33	3	.984
Major league totals (12 years)		1439	5278	739	1557	285	35	74	613	.295	669	617	80	2612	2136	156	.968

DIVISION SERIES RECORD

Year Team (League)	Pos.	G	AB	R	H	2B	3B	HR	RBI	Avg.	BB	SO	SB	PO	A	E	Avg.
						BATTING									**FIELDING**		
1996— Cleveland (A.L.).........	DH-1B	4	17	1	5	1	0	0	4	.294	2	4	1	7	1	1	.889
1997— Cleveland (A.L.).........	1B	1	4	0	0	0	0	0	0	.000	0	0	0	9	0	0	1.000
Division series totals (2 years)		5	21	1	5	1	0	0	4	.238	2	4	1	16	1	1	.944

CHAMPIONSHIP SERIES RECORD

Year Team (League)	Pos.	G	AB	R	H	2B	3B	HR	RBI	Avg.	BB	SO	SB	PO	A	E	Avg.
						BATTING									**FIELDING**		
1997— Cleveland (A.L.).........	1B-PH	4	4	0	0	0	0	0	0	.000	1	2	0	11	1	0	1.000

WORLD SERIES RECORD

Year Team (League)	Pos.	G	AB	R	H	2B	3B	HR	RBI	Avg.	BB	SO	SB	PO	A	E	Avg.
						BATTING									**FIELDING**		
1997— Florida (N.L.)..............	PH	1	1	0	0	0	0	0	0	.000	0	0	0	...	...	...	...

ALL-STAR GAME RECORD

Year League	Pos.	AB	R	H	2B	3B	HR	RBI	Avg.	BB	SO	SB	PO	A	E	Avg.
					BATTING									**FIELDING**		
1987— American	3B	2	0	0	0	0	0	0	.000	1	0	0	0	0	0	...
1995— American	PH-3B	2	0	0	0	0	0	0	.000	0	0	0	0	0	0	...
All-Star Game totals (2 years)		4	0	0	0	0	0	0	.000	1	0	0	0	0	0	...

RECORD AS PITCHER

Year Team (League)	W	L	Pct.	ERA	G	GS	CG	ShO	Sv.	IP	H	R	ER	BB	SO
1993— Oakland (A.L.)	0	0	...	0.00	1	0	0	0	0	1/3	0	0	0	0	1

SELE, AARON   P   RANGERS

PERSONAL: Born June 25, 1970, in Golden Valley, Minn. ... 6-5/215. ... Throws right, bats right. ... Full name: Aaron Helmer Sele. ... Name pronounced SEE-lee.
HIGH SCHOOL: North Kitsap (Poulsbo, Wash.).
COLLEGE: Washington State.
TRANSACTIONS/CAREER NOTES: Selected by Minnesota Twins organization in 37th round of free-agent draft (June 1, 1988); did not sign. ... Selected by Boston Red Sox organization in first round (23rd pick overall) of free-agent draft (June 3, 1991). ... On Boston disabled list (May 24, 1995-remainder of season); included rehabilitation assignments to Trenton (June 19-22), Sarasota (July 10-21 and August 7-16) and Pawtucket (August 16-23). ... On Boston disabled list (August 14-September 1, 1996); included rehabilitation assignment to Pawtucket (August 26-27). ... Traded by Red Sox with P Mark Brandenburg and C Bill Haselman to Texas Rangers for C Jim Leyritz and OF Damon Buford (November 6, 1997).
HONORS: Named A.L. Rookie Pitcher of the Year by THE SPORTING NEWS (1993). ... Named International League Most Valuable Pitcher (1993).
STATISTICAL NOTES: Led Carolina League with 14 hit batsmen in 1992. ... Tied for A.L. lead with nine hit batsmen in 1994.

Year Team (League)	W	L	Pct.	ERA	G	GS	CG	ShO	Sv.	IP	H	R	ER	BB	SO
1991— Winter Haven (FSL)...........	3	6	.333	4.96	13	11	4	0	1	69	65	42	38	32	51
1992— Lynchburg (Carolina)	13	5	.722	2.91	20	19	2	1	0	127	104	51	41	46	112
— New Britain (East.)	2	1	.667	6.27	7	6	1	0	0	33	43	24	23	15	29
1993— Pawtucket (Int'l)	8	2	.800	2.19	14	14	2	1	0	94 1/3	74	30	23	23	87
— Boston (A.L.)	7	2	.778	2.74	18	18	0	0	0	111 2/3	100	42	34	48	93
1994— Boston (A.L.)	8	7	.533	3.83	22	22	2	0	0	143 1/3	140	68	61	60	105
1995— Boston (A.L.)	3	1	.750	3.06	6	6	0	0	0	32 1/3	32	14	11	14	21
— Trenton (Eastern)	0	1	.000	3.38	2	2	0	0	0	8	8	3	3	2	9
— Sarasota (Florida State)......	0	0	...	0.00	2	2	0	0	0	7	6	0	0	1	8
— Pawtucket (Int'l)	0	0	...	9.00	2	2	0	0	0	5	9	5	5	2	1
1996— Boston (A.L.)	7	11	.389	5.32	29	29	1	0	0	157 1/3	192	110	93	67	137
— Pawtucket (Int'l)	0	0	...	6.00	1	1	0	0	0	3	3	2	2	1	4
1997— Boston (A.L.)	13	12	.520	5.38	33	33	1	0	0	177 1/3	196	115	106	80	122
Major league totals (5 years)......	38	33	.535	4.41	108	108	4	0	0	622	660	349	305	269	478

SERAFINI, DAN   P   TWINS

PERSONAL: Born January 25, 1974, in San Francisco. ... 6-1/191. ... Throws left, bats both.
HIGH SCHOOL: Serra (San Mateo, Calif.).
TRANSACTIONS/CAREER NOTES: Selected by Minnesota Twins organization in first round (26th pick overall) of free-agent draft (June 1, 1992). ... On Salt Lake disabled list (May 11-31, 1996).

Year Team (League)	W	L	Pct.	ERA	G	GS	CG	ShO	Sv.	IP	H	R	ER	BB	SO
1992— GC Twins (GCL).................	1	0	1.000	3.64	8	6	0	0	0	29 2/3	27	16	12	15	33
1993— Fort Wayne (Midw.)...........	10	8	.556	3.65	27	27	1	1	0	140 2/3	117	72	57	83	147

Year Team (League)	W	L	Pct.	ERA	G	GS	CG	ShO	Sv.	IP	H	R	ER	BB	SO
1994—Fort Myers (Fla. St.)	9	9	.500	4.61	23	23	2	1	0	136 2/3	149	84	70	57	130
1995—New Britain (East.)	12	9	.571	3.38	27	27	1	1	0	162 2/3	155	74	61	72	123
—Salt Lake (PCL)	0	0	. . .	6.75	1	0	0	0	1	4	4	3	3	1	4
1996—Salt Lake (PCL)	7	7	.500	5.58	25	23	1	0	0	130 2/3	164	84	81	58	109
—Minnesota (A.L.)	0	1	.000	10.38	1	1	0	0	0	4 1/3	7	5	5	2	1
1997—Salt Lake (PCL)	9	7	.563	4.97	28	24	2	0	0	152	166	87	84	55	118
—Minnesota (A.L.)	2	1	.667	3.42	6	4	1	0	0	26 1/3	27	11	10	11	15
Major league totals (2 years)......	2	2	.500	4.40	7	5	1	0	0	30 2/3	34	16	15	13	16

SERVAIS, SCOTT   C   CUBS

PERSONAL: Born June 4, 1967, in LaCrosse, Wis. ... 6-2/205. ... Bats right, throws right. ... Full name: Scott Daniel Servais. ... Name pronounced SER-viss.

HIGH SCHOOL: Westby (Wis.).

COLLEGE: Creighton.

TRANSACTIONS/CAREER NOTES: Selected by New York Mets organization in second round of free-agent draft (June 3, 1985); did not sign. ... Selected by Houston Astros organization in third round of free-agent draft (June 1, 1988). ... On Tucson disabled list (June 29-July 1, 1991). ... On Houston disabled list (August 4-September 7, 1991). ... Traded by Astros with OF Luis Gonzalez to Chicago Cubs for C Rick Wilkins (June 28, 1995). ... On Chicago disabled list (July 10-August 3, 1995).

STATISTICAL NOTES: Tied for Pacific Coast League lead in double plays by catcher with nine in 1990. ... Led N.L. catchers with 12 errors in 1995.

MISCELLANEOUS: Member of 1988 U.S. Olympic baseball team.

| | | | | | | | BATTING | | | | | | | FIELDING | | | |
Year Team (League)	Pos.	G	AB	R	H	2B	3B	HR	RBI	Avg.	BB	SO	SB	PO	A	E	Avg.
1989—Osceola (Fla. St.)........	C-1B	46	153	16	41	9	0	2	23	.268	16	35	0	168	24	4	.980
—Columbus (Southern).	C	63	199	20	47	5	0	1	22	.236	19	42	0	330	45	3	.992
1990—Tucson (PCL)	C	89	303	37	66	11	3	5	37	.218	18	61	0	453	63	9	.983
1991—Tucson (PCL)	C	60	219	34	71	12	0	2	27	.324	13	19	0	350	33	6	.985
—Houston (N.L.)	C	16	37	0	6	3	0	0	6	.162	4	8	0	77	4	1	.988
1992—Houston (N.L.)	C	77	205	12	49	9	0	0	15	.239	11	25	0	386	27	2	.995
1993—Houston (N.L.)	C	85	258	24	63	11	0	11	32	.244	22	45	0	493	40	2	.996
1994—Houston (N.L.)	C	78	251	27	49	15	1	9	41	.195	10	44	0	481	29	2	.996
1995—Houston (N.L.)	C	28	89	7	20	10	0	1	12	.225	9	15	0	198	17	5	.977
—Chicago (N.L.)■........	C	52	175	31	50	12	0	12	35	.286	23	37	2	328	33	§7	.981
1996—Chicago (N.L.)	C-1B	129	445	42	118	20	0	11	63	.265	30	75	0	798	73	11	.988
1997—Chicago (N.L.)	C-DH-1B	122	385	36	100	21	0	6	45	.260	24	56	0	736	73	8	.990
Major league totals (7 years)		587	1845	179	455	101	1	50	249	.247	133	305	2	3497	296	38	.990

SERVICE, SCOTT   P   ROYALS

PERSONAL: Born February 26, 1967, in Cincinnati. ... 6-6/226. ... Throws right, bats right. ... Full name: David Scott Service.

HIGH SCHOOL: Aiken (Cincinnati).

TRANSACTIONS/CAREER NOTES: Signed as non-drafted free agent by Philadelphia Phillies organization (August 24, 1985). ... Granted free agency (October 11, 1990). ... Signed by Montreal Expos organization (November 15, 1990). ... Released by Expos organization (July 19, 1991). ... Played with Chunichi Dragons of Japan Central League (August 1991). ... Signed by Expos organization (January 10, 1992). ... Granted free agency (June 8, 1992). ... Signed by Nashville, Cincinnati Reds organization (June 9, 1992). ... On Indianapolis disabled list (May 15-22, 1993). ... Claimed on waivers by Colorado Rockies (June 28, 1993). ... Claimed on waivers by Reds (July 7, 1993). ... On Indianapolis disabled list (April 17-24, 1994). ... Released by Reds (November 17, 1994). ... Re-signed by Indianapolis, Reds organization (February 24, 1995). ... Traded by Reds organization with OF Deion Sanders, P John Roper, P Ricky Pickett and IF Dave McCarty to San Francisco Giants for OF Darren Lewis, P Mark Portugal and P Dave Burba (July 21, 1995). ... Released by Giants (March 26, 1996). ... Signed by Indianapolis, Reds organization (April 2, 1996). ... Claimed on waivers by Oakland Athletics (March 27, 1997). ... Claimed on waivers by Reds (April 4, 1997). ... Traded by Reds with P Hector Carrasco to Kansas City Royals for OF Jon Nunnally and IF/OF Chris Stynes (July 15, 1997).

STATISTICAL NOTES: Led American Association with .800 winning percentage in 1992. ... Led American Association with 24 saves in 1997.

MISCELLANEOUS: Made an out in only appearance as pinch-hitter with Cincinnati (1993).

Year Team (League)	W	L	Pct.	ERA	G	GS	CG	ShO	Sv.	IP	H	R	ER	BB	SO
1986—Spartanburg (SAL)	1	6	.143	5.83	14	9	1	0	0	58 2/3	68	44	38	34	49
—Utica (N.Y.-Penn)...............	5	4	.556	2.67	10	10	2	0	0	70 2/3	65	30	21	18	43
—Clearwater (Fla. St.)	1	2	.333	3.20	4	4	1	1	0	25 1/3	20	10	9	15	19
1987—Reading (Eastern)	0	3	.000	7.78	5	4	0	0	0	19 2/3	22	19	17	16	12
—Clearwater (Fla. St.)	13	4	.765	2.48	21	21	5	2	0	137 2/3	127	46	38	32	73
1988—Reading (Eastern)	3	4	.429	2.86	10	9	1	1	0	56 2/3	52	25	18	22	39
—Maine (International)..........	8	8	.500	3.67	19	18	1	0	0	110 1/3	109	51	45	31	87
—Philadelphia (N.L.)	0	0	. . .	1.69	5	0	0	0	0	5 1/3	7	1	1	1	6
1989—Scran./W.B. (Int'l)	3	1	.750	2.16	23	0	0	0	6	33 1/3	27	8	8	23	23
—Reading (Eastern)	6	6	.500	3.26	23	10	1	1	1	85 2/3	71	36	31	23	82
1990—Scran./W.B. (Int'l)	5	4	.556	4.76	45	9	0	0	2	96 1/3	96	56	51	44	94
1991—Indianapolis (A.A.)■.........	6	7	.462	2.97	18	17	3	1	0	121 1/3	83	42	40	39	91
—Chunichi (Jp. Cn.)■..........	0	0	. . .	9.00	1	. . .	. . .	. . .	0	1	. . .	. . .	1	0	0
1992—Indianapolis (A.A.)■.........	2	0	1.000	0.74	13	0	0	0	2	24 1/3	12	3	2	9	25
—Montreal (N.L.)................	0	0	. . .	14.14	5	0	0	0	0	7	15	11	11	5	11
—Nashville (A.A.)■.............	6	2	§.750	2.29	39	2	0	0	4	70 2/3	54	22	18	35	87
1993—Indianapolis (A.A.)...........	4	2	.667	4.45	21	1	0	0	2	30 1/3	25	16	15	17	28
—Colorado (N.L.)■..............	0	0	. . .	9.64	3	0	0	0	0	4 2/3	8	5	5	1	3
—Cincinnati (N.L.)■.............	2	2	.500	3.70	26	0	0	0	0	41 1/3	36	19	17	15	40
1994—Indianapolis (A.A.)...........	5	5	.500	2.31	40	0	0	0	13	58 1/3	35	16	15	27	67
—Cincinnati (N.L.)	1	2	.333	7.36	6	0	0	0	0	7 1/3	8	9	6	3	5
1995—Indianapolis (A.A.)..........	4	1	.800	2.18	36	0	0	0	18	41 1/3	33	13	10	15	48
—San Francisco (N.L.)■.......	3	1	.750	3.19	28	0	0	0	0	31	18	11	11	20	30

Year Team (League)	W	L	Pct.	ERA	G	GS	CG	ShO	Sv.	IP	H	R	ER	BB	SO
1996— Indianapolis (A.A.)■	1	4	.200	3.00	35	1	0	0	15	48	34	18	16	10	58
—Cincinnati (N.L.)	1	0	1.000	3.94	34	1	0	0	0	48	51	21	21	18	46
1997— Cincinnati (N.L.)	0	0	. . .	11.81	4	0	0	0	0	5⅓	11	7	7	1	3
—Indianapolis (A.A.).............	3	2	.600	3.71	33	0	0	0	15	34	30	15	14	12	53
—Omaha (Am. Assoc.)■........	0	0	. . .	0.00	16	0	0	0	§9	14⅔	9	0	0	4	16
—Kansas City (A.L.)	0	3	.000	4.76	12	0	0	0	0	17	17	9	9	5	19
A.L. totals (1 year)	0	3	.000	4.76	12	0	0	0	0	17	17	9	9	5	19
N.L. totals (7 years)	7	5	.583	4.74	111	1	0	0	2	150	154	84	79	64	144
Major league totals (7 years)......	7	8	.467	4.74	123	1	0	0	2	167	171	93	88	69	163

SEXSON, RICHIE — 1B — INDIANS

PERSONAL: Born December 29, 1974, in Portland. ... 6-6/205. ... Bats right, throws right. ... Full name: Richmond Lockwood Sexson.
HIGH SCHOOL: Prairie (Brush Praire, Wash.).
TRANSACTIONS/CAREER NOTES: Selected by Cleveland Indians organization in 24th round of free-agent draft (June 2, 1993).
STATISTICAL NOTES: Led Carolina League with 251 total bases in 1995. ... Led Carolina League first basemen with 1,226 total chances and 109 double plays in 1995. ... Led American Association first basemen with .996 fielding percentage, 1,003 total chances and 105 double plays in 1997.

						BATTING								FIELDING		
Year Team (League)	Pos.	G	AB	R	H	2B	3B	HR	RBI	Avg.	BB	SO	SB	PO	A	E	Avg.
1993— Burlington (Appal.).....	1B	40	97	11	18	3	0	1	5	.186	18	21	1	309	15	4	.988
1994— Columbus (S. Atl.)......	1B	130	488	88	133	25	2	14	77	.273	37	87	7	*933	*63	10	*.990
1995— Kinston (Carolina)......	1B	131	494	80	*151	*34	0	22	*85	.306	43	115	4	*1135	*79	12	.990
1996— Cant./Akr. (Eastern)	1B	133	518	85	143	33	3	16	76	.276	39	118	2	892	76	11	.989
1997— Buffalo (A.A.).............	1B	115	434	57	113	20	2	*31	88	.260	27	87	5	*922	*77	4	*.996
—Cleveland (A.L.)...........	1B-DH	5	11	1	3	0	0	0	0	.273	0	2	0	11	1	0	1.000
Major league totals (1 year)		5	11	1	3	0	0	0	0	.273	0	2	0	11	1	0	1.000

SEXTON, CHRISTOPHER — SS/OF — ROCKIES

PERSONAL: Born August 3, 1971, in Cincinnati. ... 5-11/175. ... Bats right, throws right. ... Full name: Christopher Philip Sexton.
HIGH SCHOOL: St. Xavier (Cincinnati).
COLLEGE: Miami of Ohio (degree in business).
TRANSACTIONS/CAREER NOTES: Selected by Cinciannti Reds organization in 10th round of free-agent draft (June 3, 1993). ... Traded by Reds to Colorado Rockies organization for P Marcus Moore (April 10, 1995).
STATISTICAL NOTES: Led South Atlantic League with .412 on-base percentage in 1994. ... Led South Atlantic League shortstops with 71 double plays in 1994. ... Led Carolina League with 84 runs and 97 bases on balls received in 1995. ... Led Carolina League shortstops with .966 fielding percentage, 201 putouts, 423 assists, 646 total chances and 73 double plays in 1995.

						BATTING								FIELDING		
Year Team (League)	Pos.	G	AB	R	H	2B	3B	HR	RBI	Avg.	BB	SO	SB	PO	A	E	Avg.
1993— Billings (Pioneer)........	S-3-2-O	72	273	*63	91	14	4	4	46	.333	35	27	13	94	174	23	.921
1994— Charl., S.C. (S. Atl.)......	SS-OF	133	467	82	140	21	4	5	59	.300	91	67	18	189	326	36	.935
1995— Win.-Salem (Car.)........	SS	4	15	3	6	0	0	1	5	.400	4	0	0	6	17	0	1.000
—Salem (Carolina)■	SS	123	461	§81	123	16	6	4	32	.267	§93	55	14	195	406	22	.965
—New Haven (Eastern)..	SS	1	3	0	0	0	0	0	0	.000	0	0	0	0	3	0	1.000
1996— New Haven (Eastern)..	SS-OF	127	444	50	96	12	2	0	28	.216	71	68	8	190	294	23	.955
1997— Nashville (Eastern)	SS-OF	98	360	65	107	22	4	1	38	.297	62	37	8	178	200	14	.964
—Colo. Springs (PCL) ...	SS	33	112	18	30	3	1	1	8	.268	16	21	1	57	87	5	.966

SHAW, JEFF — P — REDS

PERSONAL: Born July 7, 1966, in Washington Court House, Ohio. ... 6-2/200. ... Throws right, bats right. ... Full name: Jeffrey Lee Shaw.
HIGH SCHOOL: Washington Senior (Washington Court House, Ohio).
JUNIOR COLLEGE: Cuyahoga Community College-Western Campus (Ohio).
COLLEGE: Rio Grande (Ohio) College.
TRANSACTIONS/CAREER NOTES: Selected by Cleveland Indians organization in first round (first pick overall) of free-agent draft (January 14, 1986). ... Granted free agency (October 16, 1992). ... Signed by Omaha, Kansas City Royals organization (November 9, 1992). ... Traded by Royals organization with C Tim Spehr to Montreal Expos organization for P Mark Gardner and P Doug Piatt (December 9, 1992). ... Granted free agency (February 17, 1995). ... Re-signed by Expos organization (April 9, 1995). ... Traded by Expos to Chicago White Sox for P Jose DeLeon (August 28, 1995). ... Granted free agency (December 21, 1995). ... Signed by Cincinnati Reds organization (January 2, 1996).
HONORS: Named N.L. Fireman of the Year by THE SPORTING NEWS (1997).
STATISTICAL NOTES: Led Eastern League with 14 hit batsmen in 1989. ... Tied for Pacific Coast League lead with 10 hit batsmen in 1992.

Year Team (League)	W	L	Pct.	ERA	G	GS	CG	ShO	Sv.	IP	H	R	ER	BB	SO
1986— Batavia (N.Y.-Penn)	8	4	.667	2.44	14	12	3	1	0	88⅔	79	32	24	35	71
1987— Waterloo (Midw.)	11	11	.500	3.52	28	*28	6	*4	0	184⅓	192	89	72	56	117
1988— Williamsport (Eastern)	5	*19	.208	3.63	27	•27	6	1	0	163⅔	•173	*94	66	75	61
1989— Cant./Akr. (Eastern)	7	10	.412	3.62	30	22	6	3	0	154⅓	134	84	62	67	95
1990— Colo. Springs (PCL)	10	3	.769	4.29	17	16	4	0	0	98⅔	98	54	47	52	55
—Cleveland (A.L.).............	3	4	.429	6.66	12	9	0	0	0	48⅔	73	38	36	20	25
1991— Colo. Springs (PCL)	6	3	.667	4.64	12	12	1	0	0	75⅔	77	47	39	25	55
—Cleveland (A.L.).............	0	5	.000	3.36	29	1	0	0	1	72⅓	72	34	27	27	31
1992— Colo. Springs (PCL)	10	5	.667	4.76	25	24	1	0	0	155	174	88	82	45	55
—Cleveland (A.L.).............	0	1	.000	8.22	2	1	0	0	0	7⅔	7	7	7	4	3
1993— Ottawa (Int'l)■	0	0	. . .	0.00	2	1	0	0	0	4	5	0	0	2	1
—Montreal (N.L.)..................	2	7	.222	4.14	55	8	0	0	0	95⅔	91	47	44	32	50

Year Team (League)	W	L	Pct.	ERA	G	GS	CG	ShO	Sv.	IP	H	R	ER	BB	SO
1994— Montreal (N.L.)	5	2	.714	3.88	46	0	0	0	1	67 $^{1}/_{3}$	67	32	29	15	47
1995— Montreal (N.L.)	1	6	.143	4.62	50	0	0	0	3	62 $^{1}/_{3}$	58	35	32	26	45
— Chicago (A.L.)■	0	0	...	6.52	9	0	0	0	0	9 $^{2}/_{3}$	12	7	7	1	6
1996— Cincinnati (N.L.)■	8	6	.571	2.49	78	0	0	0	4	104 $^{2}/_{3}$	99	34	29	29	69
1997— Cincinnati (N.L.)	4	2	.667	2.38	78	0	0	0	*42	94 $^{2}/_{3}$	79	26	25	12	74
A.L. totals (4 years)	3	10	.231	5.01	52	11	0	0	1	138 $^{1}/_{3}$	164	86	77	52	65
N.L. totals (5 years)	20	23	.465	3.37	307	8	0	0	50	424 $^{2}/_{3}$	394	174	159	114	285
Major league totals (8 years)	23	33	.411	3.77	359	19	0	0	51	563	558	260	236	166	350

SHEAFFER, DANNY   C   CARDINALS

PERSONAL: Born August 2, 1961, in Jacksonville. ... 6-0/195. ... Bats right, throws right. ... Full name: Danny Todd Sheaffer.
HIGH SCHOOL: Red Land (Lewisberry, Pa.).
JUNIOR COLLEGE: Harrisburg (Pa.) Junior College.
COLLEGE: Clemson.
TRANSACTIONS/CAREER NOTES: Selected by Boston Red Sox organization in first round (20th pick overall) of free-agent draft (January 13, 1981). ... On disabled list (May 3-14, 1982). ... Granted free agency (October 15, 1988). ... Signed by Colorado Springs, Cleveland Indians organization (November 15, 1988). ... Granted free agency (October 15, 1989). ... Signed by Buffalo, Pittsburgh Pirates organization (November 25, 1989). ... Granted free agency (October 15, 1990). ... Signed by Minnesota Twins organization (December 20, 1990). ... Granted free agency (October 15, 1992). ... Signed by Colorado Rockies organization (October 29, 1992). ... Granted free agency (October 15, 1994). ... Signed by Louisville, St. Louis Cardinals organization (December 19, 1994).
STATISTICAL NOTES: Led Florida State League with 14 errors in 1982. ... Led Pacific Coast League catchers with .994 fielding percentage in 1992. ... Career major league grand slams: 1.

							BATTING								FIELDING		
Year Team (League)	Pos.	G	AB	R	H	2B	3B	HR	RBI	Avg.	BB	SO	SB	PO	A	E	Avg.
1981— Elmira (N.Y.-Penn)	C	62	198	39	57	9	0	8	29	.288	23	38	2	220	35	5	.981
— Bristol (Eastern)	C-2B	8	12	0	0	0	0	0	1	.000	0	3	0	16	3	0	1.000
1982— Winter Haven (FSL)	C-3B	82	260	20	65	4	0	5	25	.250	18	37	2	316	51	†16	.958
1983— Win.-Salem (Car.)	C-1B-OF	112	380	48	105	14	2	15	63	.276	36	50	1	427	44	6	.987
1984— New Britain (Eastern)	C-OF	93	303	33	73	10	0	1	27	.241	29	31	2	438	47	6	.988
1985— Pawtucket (Int'l)	C	77	243	24	63	9	0	8	33	.259	17	35	0	289	18	6	.981
1986— Pawtucket (Int'l)	C-OF	79	265	34	90	16	1	2	36	.340	10	24	9	380	39	5	.988
1987— Boston (A.L.)	C	25	66	5	8	1	0	1	5	.121	0	14	0	121	5	3	.977
— Pawtucket (Int'l)	C-1B-OF	69	242	32	62	13	2	2	25	.256	6	29	6	346	32	5	.987
1988— Pawtucket (Int'l)	C-1-3-O	98	299	30	82	17	1	1	28	.274	18	32	20	509	58	6	.990
1989— Colo. Springs (PCL)■	OF-3B	107	401	62	113	26	2	3	47	.282	24	39	6	136	11	10	.936
— Cleveland (A.L.)	DH-3B-OF	7	16	1	1	0	0	0	0	.063	2	2	0	4	0	0	1.000
1990— Buffalo (A.A.)■	C-OF-1B	55	144	23	35	7	0	2	19	.243	11	14	4	163	10	5	.972
1991— Portland (PCL)■	C-1-O-2	93	330	46	100	14	2	1	43	.303	26	35	2	448	39	11	.978
1992— Portland (PCL)	C-OF-3B	116	442	54	122	23	4	5	56	.276	21	36	3	605	66	4	†.994
1993— Colorado (N.L.)■	C-1-O-3	82	216	26	60	9	1	4	32	.278	8	15	2	337	32	2	.995
1994— Colorado (N.L.)	C-1B-OF	44	110	11	24	4	0	1	12	.218	10	11	0	182	16	1	.995
1995— St. Louis (N.L.)■	C-1B-3B	76	208	24	48	10	1	5	30	.231	23	38	0	391	43	3	.993
1996— St. Louis (N.L.)	C-3-1-O	79	198	10	45	9	3	2	20	.227	9	25	3	277	44	6	.982
1997— St. Louis (N.L.)	3-O-C-2	76	132	10	33	5	0	0	11	.250	8	17	1	43	40	2	.976
American League totals (2 years)		32	82	6	9	1	0	1	5	.110	2	16	0	125	5	3	.977
National League totals (5 years)		357	864	81	210	37	5	12	105	.243	58	106	6	1230	175	14	.990
Major league totals (7 years)		389	946	87	219	38	5	13	110	.232	60	122	6	1355	180	17	.989

CHAMPIONSHIP SERIES RECORD

							BATTING								FIELDING		
Year Team (League)	Pos.	G	AB	R	H	2B	3B	HR	RBI	Avg.	BB	SO	SB	PO	A	E	Avg.
1996— St. Louis (N.L.)	C-PH	2	3	0	0	0	0	0	0	.000	0	1	0	3	0	0	1.000

SHEETS, ANDY   IF   PADRES

PERSONAL: Born November 19, 1971, in Baton Rouge, La. ... 6-2/180. ... Bats right, throws right.
HIGH SCHOOL: St. Amant (La.).
COLLEGE: Tulane, then Louisiana State.
TRANSACTIONS/CAREER NOTES: Selected by Seattle Mariners organization in fourth round of free-agent draft (June 1, 1992). ... Selected by Tampa Bay Devil Rays in first round (24th pick overall) of expansion draft (November 18, 1997). ... Traded by Devil Rays with P Brian Boehringer to San Diego Padres for C John Flaherty (November 18, 1997).
STATISTICAL NOTES: Led Pacific Coast League shortstops with .973 fielding percentage in 1997.

							BATTING								FIELDING		
Year Team (League)	Pos.	G	AB	R	H	2B	3B	HR	RBI	Avg.	BB	SO	SB	PO	A	E	Avg.
1993— Riverside (Calif.)	SS	52	176	23	34	9	1	1	12	.193	17	51	2	80	159	17	.934
— Appleton (Midwest)	SS-2B-OF	69	259	32	68	10	4	1	25	.263	20	59	7	98	194	11	.964
1994— Riverside (Calif.)	SS	31	100	17	27	5	1	2	10	.270	16	22	6	39	95	14	.905
— Jacksonville (South.)	SS	70	232	26	51	12	0	0	17	.220	20	54	3	105	205	17	.948
— Calgary (PCL)	SS	26	93	22	32	8	1	2	16	.344	11	20	1	32	80	2	.982
1995— Tacoma (PCL)	SS	132	437	57	128	29	9	2	47	.293	32	83	8	157	382	27	.952
1996— Tacoma (PCL)	SS-2B-3B	62	232	44	83	16	5	5	33	.358	25	56	6	95	176	14	.951
— Seattle (A.L.)	3B-2B-SS	47	110	18	21	8	0	0	9	.191	10	41	2	40	77	5	.959
1997— Tacoma (PCL)	SS-2B-3B	113	401	57	104	23	0	14	53	.259	46	97	7	174	314	13	.974
— Seattle (A.L.)	3B-SS-2B	32	89	18	22	3	0	4	9	.247	7	34	2	14	62	8	.905
Major league totals (2 years)		79	199	36	43	11	0	4	18	.216	17	75	4	54	139	13	.937

Year Team (League)	Pos.	G	AB	R	H	2B	3B	HR	RBI	Avg.	BB	SO	SB	PO	A	E	Avg.
1997—Seattle (A.L.)	3B	2	3	0	1	0	0	0	0	.333	0	2	0	0	0	0	...

SHEFFIELD, GARY   OF   MARLINS

PERSONAL: Born November 18, 1968, in Tampa. ... 5-11/205. ... Bats right, throws right. ... Full name: Gary Antonian Sheffield. ... Nephew of Dwight Gooden, pitcher, Cleveland Indians.
HIGH SCHOOL: Hillsborough (Tampa).
TRANSACTIONS/CAREER NOTES: Selected by Milwaukee Brewers organization in first round (sixth pick overall) of free-agent draft (June 2, 1986). ... On Milwaukee disabled list (July 14-September 9, 1989). ... On suspended list (August 31-September 3, 1990). ... On disabled list (June 15-July 3 and July 25, 1991-remainder of season). ... Traded by Brewers with P Geoff Kellogg to San Diego Padres for P Ricky Bones, SS Jose Valentin and OF Matt Mieske (March 27, 1992). ... Traded by Padres with P Rich Rodriguez to Florida Marlins for P Trevor Hoffman, P Jose Martinez and P Andres Berumen (June 24, 1993). ... On Florida suspended list (July 9-12, 1993). ... On Florida disabled list (May 10-25 and May 28-June 12, 1994); included rehabilitation assignment to Portland (June 10-12). ... On disabled list (June 11-September 1, 1995). ... On disabled list (May 14-29, 1997).
RECORDS: Shares major league record for fewest double plays by outfielder (150 or more games)—0 (1996).
HONORS: Named Minor League co-Player of the Year by THE SPORTING NEWS (1988). ... Named Major League Player of the Year by THE SPORTING NEWS (1992). ... Named N.L. Comeback Player of the Year by THE SPORTING NEWS (1992). ... Named third baseman on THE SPORTING NEWS N.L. All-Star team (1992). ... Named third baseman on THE SPORTING NEWS N.L. Silver Slugger team (1992). ... Named outfielder on THE SPORTING NEWS N.L. All-Star team (1996). ... Named outfielder on THE SPORTING NEWS N.L. Silver Slugger team (1996).
STATISTICAL NOTES: Led Pioneer League shortstops with 34 double plays in 1986. ... Led California League shortstops with 77 double plays in 1987. ... Led N.L. with 323 total bases in 1992. ... Led N.L. with .465 on-base percentage in 1996. ... Career major league grand slams: 5.
MISCELLANEOUS: Holds Florida Marlins all-time record for most home runs (116) and most runs (344).

							BATTING								FIELDING		
Year Team (League)	Pos.	G	AB	R	H	2B	3B	HR	RBI	Avg.	BB	SO	SB	PO	A	E	Avg.
1986—Helena (Pioneer)	SS	57	222	53	81	12	2	15	*71	.365	20	14	14	97	149	24	.911
1987—Stockton (California) ..	SS	129	469	84	130	23	3	17	*103	.277	81	49	25	235	345	39	.937
1988—El Paso (Texas)..........	SS-3B-OF	77	296	70	93	19	3	19	65	.314	35	41	5	130	206	23	.936
—Denver (A.A.).............	3B-SS	57	212	42	73	9	5	9	54	.344	21	22	8	54	97	8	.950
—Milwaukee (A.L.)	SS-3B	24	80	12	19	1	0	4	12	.238	7	7	3	39	48	3	.967
1989—Milwaukee (A.L.)	SS-3B-DH	95	368	34	91	18	0	5	32	.247	27	33	10	100	238	16	.955
—Denver (A.A.).............	SS	7	29	3	4	1	1	0	2	.138	2	0	0	2	6	0	1.000
1990—Milwaukee (A.L.)	3B	125	487	67	143	30	1	10	67	.294	44	41	25	98	254	25	.934
1991—Milwaukee (A.L.)	3B-DH	50	175	25	34	12	2	2	22	.194	19	15	5	29	65	8	.922
1992—San Diego (N.L.)■	3B	146	557	87	184	34	3	33	100	*.330	48	40	5	99	299	16	.961
1993—San Diego (N.L.)	3B	68	258	34	76	12	2	10	36	.295	18	30	5	41	102	15	.905
—Florida (N.L.)■...........	3B	72	236	33	69	8	3	10	37	.292	29	34	12	38	123	19	.894
1994—Florida (N.L.)	OF	87	322	61	89	16	1	27	78	.276	51	50	12	154	7	5	.970
—Portland (Eastern)......	OF	2	7	1	2	1	0	0	0	.286	1	3	0	3	0	0	1.000
1995—Florida (N.L.)	OF	63	213	46	69	8	0	16	46	.324	55	45	19	109	5	7	.942
1996—Florida (N.L.)	OF	161	519	118	163	33	1	42	120	.314	142	66	16	238	8	6	.976
1997—Florida (N.L.)	OF-DH	135	444	86	111	22	1	21	71	.250	121	79	11	226	14	5	.980
American League totals (4 years)		294	1110	138	287	61	3	21	133	.259	97	96	43	266	605	52	.944
National League totals (6 years)		732	2549	465	761	133	11	159	488	.299	464	344	80	905	558	73	.952
Major league totals (10 years)		1026	3659	603	1048	194	14	180	621	.286	561	440	123	1171	1163	125	.949

DIVISION SERIES RECORD

							BATTING								FIELDING		
Year Team (League)	Pos.	G	AB	R	H	2B	3B	HR	RBI	Avg.	BB	SO	SB	PO	A	E	Avg.
1997—Florida (N.L.)	OF	3	9	3	5	1	0	1	1	.556	5	0	1	6	0	0	1.000

CHAMPIONSHIP SERIES RECORD

							BATTING								FIELDING		
Year Team (League)	Pos.	G	AB	R	H	2B	3B	HR	RBI	Avg.	BB	SO	SB	PO	A	E	Avg.
1997—Florida (N.L.)	OF	6	17	6	4	0	0	1	1	.235	7	3	0	5	2	0	1.000

WORLD SERIES RECORD

NOTES: Member of World Series championship team (1997).

							BATTING								FIELDING		
Year Team (League)	Pos.	G	AB	R	H	2B	3B	HR	RBI	Avg.	BB	SO	SB	PO	A	E	Avg.
1997—Florida (N.L.)	OF	7	24	4	7	1	0	1	5	.292	8	5	0	16	0	1	.941

ALL-STAR GAME RECORD

						BATTING								FIELDING		
Year League	Pos.	AB	R	H	2B	3B	HR	RBI	Avg.	BB	SO	SB	PO	A	E	Avg.
1992—National	3B	2	0	0	0	0	0	0	.000	0	0	0	0	0	0	...
1993—National	3B	3	1	2	0	0	1	2	.667	0	0	0	0	2	0	1.000
1996—National	OF	1	0	0	0	0	0	0	.000	0	0	0	2	0	0	1.000
All-Star Game totals (3 years)		6	1	2	0	0	1	2	.333	0	0	0	2	2	0	1.000

SHIPLEY, CRAIG   SS/IF

PERSONAL: Born January 7, 1963, in Sydney, Australia. ... 6-1/190. ... Bats right, throws right. ... Full name: Craig Barry Shipley.
HIGH SCHOOL: Epping (Sydney, Australia).
COLLEGE: Alabama.

TRANSACTIONS/CAREER NOTES: Signed as non-drafted free agent by Los Angeles Dodgers organization (May 28, 1984). ... On Albuquerque disabled list (May 5-June 6, 1986). ... Traded by Dodgers to New York Mets organization for C John Gibbons (April 1, 1988). ... On disabled list (beginning of season-August 20, 1990). ... Selected by San Diego Padres organization from Mets organization in Rule 5 minor league draft (December 2, 1990). ... On Las Vegas disabled list (April 11-May 2, 1991). ... On disabled list (May 6-23, 1993 and April 25-May 20, 1994). ... Traded by Padres with OF Phil Plantier, OF Derek Bell, P Pedro Martinez, P Doug Brocail and SS Ricky Gutierrez to Houston Astros for 3B Ken Caminiti, OF Steve Finley, SS Andujar Cedeno, 1B Robert Petagine, P Brian Williams and a player to be named later (December 28, 1994); Padres acquired P Sean Fesh to complete deal (May 1, 1995). ... Granted free agency (December 21, 1995). ... Signed by Padres (January 5, 1996). ... On San Diego disabled list (April 23-May 8 and May 17-July 31, 1996); included rehabilitation assignments to Las Vegas (July 1-4) and Peoria Padres (July 29-31). ... Granted free agency (December 7, 1996). ... Re-signed by Padres (December 23, 1996). ... On San Diego disabled list (March 18-May 13 and June 8-July 2, 1997); included rehabilitation assignment to Las Vegas (May 4-12). ... Granted free agency (November 6, 1997).

STATISTICAL NOTES: Career major league grand slams: 1.

							BATTING							FIELDING			
Year Team (League)	Pos.	G	AB	R	H	2B	3B	HR	RBI	Avg.	BB	SO	SB	PO	A	E	Avg.
1984— Vero Beach (FSL)	SS	85	293	56	82	11	2	0	28	.280	52	44	18	137	216	17	.954
1985— Albuquerque (PCL).....	SS	124	414	50	100	9	2	0	30	.242	22	43	24	202	367	21	.964
1986— Albuquerque (PCL).....	SS	61	203	33	59	8	2	0	16	.291	11	23	6	99	173	18	.938
—Los Angeles (N.L.)	SS-2B-3B	12	27	3	3	1	0	0	4	.111	2	5	0	16	18	3	.919
1987— Albuquerque (PCL).....	SS	49	139	17	31	6	1	1	15	.223	13	19	6	70	101	9	.950
—San Antonio (Tex.)	3B	33	127	14	30	5	3	2	9	.236	5	17	2	19	56	3	.962
—Los Angeles (N.L.)	SS-3B	26	35	3	9	1	0	0	2	.257	0	6	0	15	28	3	.935
1988— Jackson (Texas)■......	SS	89	335	41	88	14	3	6	41	.263	24	40	6	141	266	16	.962
—Tidewater (Int'l)	2B-SS-3B	40	151	12	41	5	0	1	13	.272	4	15	0	54	110	2	.988
1989— Tidewater (Int'l)	SS-3B-2B	44	131	6	27	1	0	2	9	.206	7	22	0	48	110	6	.963
—New York (N.L.)	SS-3B	4	7	3	1	0	0	0	0	.143	0	1	0	0	4	0	1.000
1990— Tidewater (Int'l)	PH-PR	4	3	1	0	0	0	0	0	.000	0	1	0	...	...	...	...
1991— Las Vegas (PCL)■......	SS-2B	65	230	27	69	9	5	5	34	.300	10	32	2	83	177	6	.977
—San Diego (N.L.)	SS-2B	37	91	6	25	3	0	1	6	.275	2	14	0	39	70	7	.940
1992— San Diego (N.L.)	SS-2B-3B	52	105	7	26	6	0	0	7	.248	2	21	1	52	74	1	.992
1993— San Diego (N.L.)	S-3-2-O	105	230	25	54	9	0	4	22	.235	10	31	12	84	121	7	.967
1994— San Diego (N.L.)	3-S-2-O-1	81	240	32	80	14	4	4	30	.333	9	28	6	65	108	9	.951
1995— Houston (N.L.)■........	3-S-2-1	92	232	23	61	8	1	3	24	.263	8	28	6	43	116	3	.981
1996— San Diego (N.L.)■......	2-S-3-O	33	92	13	29	5	0	1	7	.315	2	15	7	35	64	1	.990
—Las Vegas (PCL)	SS	1	2	1	0	0	0	0	0	.000	0	1	0	0	2	0	1.000
—Ariz. Padres (Ariz.)	SS-3B	3	7	4	5	1	0	0	1	.714	0	0	0	0	2	0	1.000
1997— Las Vegas (PCL)	S-2-3-O	6	19	0	6	3	0	0	1	.316	0	5	0	4	5	0	1.000
—San Diego (N.L.)	S-2-1-3	63	139	22	38	9	0	5	19	.273	7	20	1	69	73	6	.959
Major league totals (10 years)		505	1198	137	326	56	5	18	121	.272	42	169	33	418	676	40	.965

SHOEMAKER, STEVE   P   ROCKIES

PERSONAL: Born February 3, 1973, in Phoenixville, Pa. ... 6-1/195. ... Throws right, bats left. ... Full name: Stephen Patrick Shoemaker.
HIGH SCHOOL: Phoenixville (Pa.).
COLLEGE: Alabama.
TRANSACTIONS/CAREER NOTES: Selected by New York Yankees organization in fourth round of free-agent draft (June 3, 1994). ... Traded by Yankees organization to Colorado Rockies organization (December 6, 1995), completing deal in which Rockies traded C Joe Girardi to Yankees for P Mike DeJean and a player to be named later (November 30, 1995).

Year Team (League)	W	L	Pct.	ERA	G	GS	CG	ShO	Sv.	IP	H	R	ER	BB	SO
1994— Oneonta (N.Y.-Penn)	3	5	.375	4.30	12	12	0	0	0	58 2/3	62	32	28	28	46
1995— Greensboro (S. Atl.)	4	4	.500	3.11	17	17	0	0	0	81	62	33	28	52	82
—Tampa (Florida State)........	0	1	1.000	1.08	3	2	0	0	0	16 2/3	9	5	2	13	12
1996— Salem (Carolina)■	2	7	.222	4.69	25	13	0	0	1	86 1/3	63	49	45	63	105
1997— Salem (Carolina)	3	3	.500	2.77	9	9	1	0	0	52	31	21	16	25	76
—Nashville (Eastern)	6	4	.600	3.02	14	14	1	0	0	95 1/3	64	36	32	53	111
—Colo. Springs (PCL)	1	1	.500	8.41	5	4	0	0	0	20 1/3	23	19	19	17	27

SHOUSE, BRIAN   P   RED SOX

PERSONAL: Born September 26, 1968, in Effingham, Ill. ... 5-11/180. ... Throws left, bats left. ... Full name: Brian Douglas Shouse.
HIGH SCHOOL: Effingham (Ill.).
COLLEGE: Bradley.
TRANSACTIONS/CAREER NOTES: Selected by Pittsburgh Pirates organization in 13th round of free-agent draft (June 4, 1990). ... Released by Pirates (May 16, 1996). ... Signed by Baltimore Orioles organization (May 22, 1996). ... Granted free agency (October 15, 1997). ... Signed by Boston Red Sox (October 28, 1997).

Year Team (League)	W	L	Pct.	ERA	G	GS	CG	ShO	Sv.	IP	H	R	ER	BB	SO
1990— Welland (N.Y.-Penn)...........	4	3	.571	5.22	17	1	0	0	2	39 2/3	50	27	23	7	39
1991— Augusta (S. Atl.).................	2	3	.400	3.19	26	0	0	0	8	31	22	13	11	9	32
—Salem (Carolina)	2	1	.667	2.94	17	0	0	0	3	33 2/3	35	12	11	15	25
1992— Carolina (Southern)...........	5	6	.455	2.44	59	0	0	0	4	77 1/3	71	31	21	28	79
1993— Buffalo (A.A.)......................	1	0	1.000	3.83	48	0	0	0	2	51 2/3	54	24	22	17	25
—Pittsburgh (N.L.)................	0	0	...	9.00	6	0	0	0	0	4	7	4	4	2	3
1994— Buffalo (A.A.)......................	3	4	.429	3.63	43	0	0	0	0	52	44	22	21	15	31
1995— Carolina (Southern)...........	7	6	.538	4.47	21	20	0	0	0	114 2/3	126	64	57	19	76
—Calgary (PCL).....................	4	4	.500	6.18	8	8	1	0	0	39 1/3	62	35	27	7	17
1996— Calgary (PCL).....................	1	0	1.000	10.66	12	1	0	0	0	12 2/3	22	15	15	4	12
—Rochester (Int'l)■...............	1	2	.333	4.50	32	0	0	0	2	50	53	27	25	16	45
1997— Rochester (Int'l)................	6	2	.750	2.27	54	0	0	0	9	71 1/3	48	21	18	21	81
Major league totals (1 year)........	0	0	...	9.00	6	0	0	0	0	4	7	4	4	2	3

SHUEY, PAUL   P   INDIANS

PERSONAL: Born September 16, 1970, in Lima, Ohio. ... 6-3/215. ... Throws right, bats right. ... Full name: Paul Kenneth Shuey.
HIGH SCHOOL: Millbrook (Raleigh, N.C.).
COLLEGE: North Carolina.
TRANSACTIONS/CAREER NOTES: Selected by Cleveland Indians organization in first round (second pick overall) of free-agent draft (June 1, 1992). ... On Cleveland disabled list (June 27-July 21, 1994); included rehabilitation assignment to Charlotte (July 5-21). ... On Cleveland disabled list (May 4-22, 1995). ... On Buffalo disabled list (June 2-July 10, 1995). ... On disabled list (April 25-May 18, June 19-July 4 and July 11-August 1, 1997); included rehabilitation assignment to Buffalo (May 5-16).
RECORDS: Shares major league record for most strikeouts in one inning—4 (May 14, 1994, ninth inning).

Year Team (League)	W	L	Pct.	ERA	G	GS	CG	ShO	Sv.	IP	H	R	ER	BB	SO
1992— Columbus (S. Atl.)	5	5	.500	3.35	14	14	0	0	0	78	62	35	29	47	73
1993— Cant./Akr. (Eastern)	4	8	.333	7.30	27	7	0	0	0	61²/₃	76	50	50	36	41
— Kinston (Carolina)	1	0	1.000	4.84	15	0	0	0	0	22¹/₃	29	12	12	8	27
1994— Kinston (Carolina)	1	0	1.000	3.75	13	0	0	0	8	12	10	5	5	3	16
— Cleveland (A.L.)	0	1	.000	8.49	14	0	0	0	5	11²/₃	14	11	11	12	16
— Charlotte (Int'l)	2	1	.667	1.93	20	0	0	0	10	23¹/₃	15	9	5	10	25
1995— Cleveland (A.L.)	0	2	.000	4.26	7	0	0	0	0	6¹/₃	5	4	3	5	5
— Buffalo (A.A.)	1	2	.333	2.63	25	0	0	0	11	27¹/₃	21	9	8	7	27
1996— Buffalo (A.A.)	3	2	.600	0.81	19	0	0	0	4	33¹/₃	14	4	3	9	57
— Cleveland (A.L.)	5	2	.714	2.85	42	0	0	0	4	53²/₃	45	19	17	26	44
1997— Cleveland (A.L.)	4	2	.667	6.20	40	0	0	0	2	45	52	31	31	28	46
— Buffalo (A.A.)	0	0	...	3.60	2	0	0	0	0	5	4	2	2	4	6
— Akron (Eastern)	0	0	...	3.38	3	0	0	0	0	8	10	3	3	0	9
Major league totals (4 years)	9	7	.563	4.78	103	0	0	0	11	116²/₃	116	65	62	71	111

DIVISION SERIES RECORD

Year Team (League)	W	L	Pct.	ERA	G	GS	CG	ShO	Sv.	IP	H	R	ER	BB	SO
1996— Cleveland (A.L.)	0	0	...	9.00	3	0	0	0	0	2	5	2	2	2	2

SHUMPERT, TERRY   2B   ROCKIES

PERSONAL: Born August 16, 1966, in Paducah, Ky. ... 6-0/190. ... Bats right, throws right. ... Full name: Terrance Darnell Shumpert.
HIGH SCHOOL: Paducah (Ky.) Tilghman.
COLLEGE: Kentucky.
TRANSACTIONS/CAREER NOTES: Selected by Kansas City Royals organization in second round of free-agent draft (June 2, 1987). ... On disabled list (July 19-August 13, 1989). ... On Kansas City disabled list (June 3-September 10, 1990); included rehabilitation assignment to Omaha (August 7-25). ... On Kansas City disabled list (August 7-September 7, 1992). ... Traded by Royals to Boston Red Sox for a player to be named later (December 13, 1994). ... Granted free agency (October 6, 1995). ... Signed by Iowa, Chicago Cubs organization (March 12, 1996). ... On Chicago disabled list (August 19-September 3, 1996). ... Granted free agency (October 15, 1996). ... Signed by San Diego Padres (November 4, 1996). ... On San Diego disabled list (May 27-August 5, 1997). ... Released by Padres (August 5, 1997). ... Signed by Colorado Rockies organization (August 13, 1997).
STATISTICAL NOTES: Led American Association with 21 sacrifice hits in 1993. ... Career major league grand slams: 1.

Year Team (League)	Pos.	G	AB	R	H	2B	3B	HR	RBI	Avg.	BB	SO	SB	PO	A	E	Avg.
1987— Eugene (Northwest)	2B	48	186	38	54	16	1	4	22	.290	27	41	16	81	107	11	.945
1988— Appleton (Midwest)	2B-OF	114	422	64	102	*37	2	7	38	.242	56	90	36	235	266	20	.962
1989— Omaha (A.A.)	2B	113	355	54	88	29	2	4	22	.248	25	63	23	218	295	*22	.959
1990— Omaha (A.A.)	2B	39	153	24	39	6	4	2	12	.255	14	28	18	72	95	7	.960
— Kansas City (A.L.)	2B-DH	32	91	7	25	6	1	0	8	.275	2	17	3	56	74	3	.977
1991— Kansas City (A.L.)	2B	144	369	45	80	16	4	5	34	.217	30	75	17	249	368	16	.975
1992— Kansas City (A.L.)	2B-DH-SS	36	94	6	14	5	1	1	11	.149	3	17	2	50	77	4	.969
— Omaha (A.A.)	2B-SS	56	210	23	42	12	0	1	14	.200	13	33	3	113	154	9	.967
1993— Omaha (A.A.)	2B	111	413	70	124	29	1	14	59	.300	41	62	*36	190	303	14	.972
— Kansas City (A.L.)	2B	8	10	0	1	0	0	0	0	.100	2	2	1	11	11	0	1.000
1994— Kansas City (A.L.)	2-3-DH-S	64	183	28	44	6	2	8	24	.240	13	39	18	70	129	8	.961
1995— Boston (A.L.)■	2-3-S-DH	21	47	6	11	3	0	0	3	.234	4	13	3	21	35	2	.966
— Pawtucket (Int'l)	3B-2B-OF	37	133	17	36	7	0	2	11	.271	14	27	10	29	69	11	.899
1996— Iowa (Am. Assoc.)■	2-3-1-S	72	246	45	68	13	4	5	32	.276	24	44	13	119	165	7	.976
— Chicago (N.L.)	3B-2B-SS	27	31	5	7	1	0	2	6	.226	2	11	0	11	9	1	.952
1997— Las Vegas (PCL)■	3B-2B-SS	32	109	18	31	8	1	1	16	.284	9	20	3	37	58	4	.960
— San Diego (N.L.)	2B-OF-3B	13	33	4	9	3	0	1	6	.273	3	4	0	23	17	2	.952
— New Haven (East.)■	2B	5	17	2	4	0	0	1	1	.235	0	2	0	8	17	0	1.000
— Colo. Springs (PCL)	S-2-3-O	10	37	8	11	3	0	1	2	.297	2	7	0	8	20	5	.848
American League totals (6 years)		305	794	92	175	36	8	14	80	.220	54	163	44	457	694	33	.972
National League totals (2 years)		40	64	9	16	4	0	3	12	.250	5	15	0	34	26	3	.952
Major league totals (8 years)		345	858	101	191	40	8	17	92	.223	59	178	44	491	720	36	.971

SIERRA, RUBEN   OF   WHITE SOX

PERSONAL: Born October 6, 1965, in Rio Piedras, Puerto Rico. ... 6-1/200. ... Bats both, throws right. ... Full name: Ruben Angel Garcia Sierra.
HIGH SCHOOL: Dr. Secario Rosario (Rio Piedras, Puerto Rico).
TRANSACTIONS/CAREER NOTES: Signed as non-drafted free agent by Texas Rangers organization (November 21, 1982). ... Traded by Rangers with P Jeff Russell, P Bobby Witt and cash to Oakland Athletics for OF Jose Canseco (August 31, 1992). ... Granted free agency (October 26, 1992). ... Re-signed by A's (December 21, 1992). ... On Oakland disabled list (July 7-22, 1995). ... Traded by A's with P Jason Beverlin to New York Yankees for OF/DH Danny Tartabull (July 28, 1995). ... Traded by Yankees with P Matt Drews to Detroit Tigers for 1B/DH Cecil Fielder (July 31, 1996). ... Traded by Tigers to Cincinnati Reds for OF Decomba Conner and P Ben Bailey (October 28, 1996). ... Released

S

by Reds (May 9, 1997). ... Signed by Toronto Blue Jays organization (May 11, 1997). ... Released by Blue Jays (June 16, 1997). ... Signed by Chicago White Sox organization (January 9, 1998).

HONORS: Named A.L. Player of the Year by THE SPORTING NEWS (1989). ... Named outfielder on THE SPORTING NEWS A.L. All-Star team (1989). ... Named outfielder on THE SPORTING NEWS A.L. Silver Slugger team (1989).

STATISTICAL NOTES: Switch-hit home runs in one game five times (September 13, 1986; August 27, 1988; June 8, 1989; June 7, 1994; and June 22, 1996). ... Led A.L. with 12 sacrifice flies in 1987. ... Led A.L. outfielders with six double plays in 1987. ... Led A.L. with 344 total bases and .543 slugging percentage in 1989. ... Career major league grand slams: 3.

MISCELLANEOUS: Holds Texas Rangers all-time record for most doubles (226) and most triples (43). ... Batted righthanded only (1983).

							BATTING								FIELDING		
Year Team (League)	Pos.	G	AB	R	H	2B	3B	HR	RBI	Avg.	BB	SO	SB	PO	A	E	Avg.
1983— GC Rangers (GCL)......	OF	48	182	26	44	7	3	1	26	.242	16	38	3	67	6	4	.948
1984— Burl. (Midw.)	OF	•138	482	55	127	33	5	6	75	.263	49	97	13	239	18	*20	.928
1985— Tulsa (Texas)	OF	*137	*545	63	138	34	*8	13	74	.253	35	111	22	234	12	*15	.943
1986— Oklahoma City (A.A.)..	OF	46	189	31	56	11	2	9	41	.296	15	27	8	114	4	2	.983
— Texas (A.L.)	OF-DH	113	382	50	101	13	10	16	55	.264	22	65	7	200	7	6	.972
1987— Texas (A.L.)	OF	158	*643	97	169	35	4	30	109	.263	39	114	16	272	•17	11	.963
1988— Texas (A.L.)	OF-DH	156	615	77	156	32	2	23	91	.254	44	91	18	310	11	7	.979
1989— Texas (A.L.)	OF	•162	634	101	194	35	*14	29	*119	.306	43	82	8	313	13	9	.973
1990— Texas (A.L.)	OF-DH	159	608	70	170	37	2	16	96	.280	49	86	9	283	7	10	.967
1991— Texas (A.L.)	OF	161	661	110	203	44	5	25	116	.307	56	91	16	305	15	7	.979
1992— Texas (A.L.)	OF-DH	124	500	66	139	30	6	14	70	.278	31	59	12	224	6	7	.970
— Oakland (A.L.)■	OF-DH	27	101	17	28	4	1	3	17	.277	14	9	2	59	0	0	1.000
1993— Oakland (A.L.)	OF-DH	158	630	77	147	23	5	22	101	.233	52	97	25	291	9	7	.977
1994— Oakland (A.L.)	OF-DH	110	426	71	114	21	1	23	92	.268	23	64	8	155	8	*9	.948
1995— Oakland (A.L.)	OF-DH	70	264	40	70	17	0	12	42	.265	24	42	4	89	1	4	.957
— New York (A.L.)■......	DH-OF	56	215	33	56	15	0	7	44	.260	22	34	1	18	1	1	.950
1996— Campeche (Mex.)■...	...	1	1	1	0	0	0	0	0	.000	0	0	0	0	0	0	...
— New York (A.L.)■......	DH-OF	96	360	39	93	17	1	11	52	.258	40	58	1	56	5	1	.984
— Detroit (A.L.)■	OF-DH	46	158	22	35	9	1	1	20	.222	20	25	3	52	1	5	.914
1997— Cincinnati (N.L.)■......	OF	25	90	6	22	5	1	2	7	.244	6	21	0	34	3	0	1.000
— Syracuse (Int'l)■.......	OF	8	32	5	7	2	0	1	5	.219	2	6	0	10	2	1	.923
— Toronto (A.L.)	OF-DH	14	48	4	10	0	2	1	5	.208	3	13	0	13	0	1	.929
American League totals (12 years)		1610	6245	874	1685	332	54	233	1029	.270	482	930	130	2640	101	85	.970
National League totals (1 year)		25	90	6	22	5	1	2	7	.244	6	21	0	34	3	0	1.000
Major league totals (12 years)		1635	6335	880	1707	337	55	235	1036	.269	488	951	130	2674	104	85	.970

DIVISION SERIES RECORD

							BATTING								FIELDING		
Year Team (League)	Pos.	G	AB	R	H	2B	3B	HR	RBI	Avg.	BB	SO	SB	PO	A	E	Avg.
1995— New York (A.L.)..........	DH	5	23	2	4	2	0	2	5	.174	2	7	0	...	...	...	...

CHAMPIONSHIP SERIES RECORD

							BATTING								FIELDING		
Year Team (League)	Pos.	G	AB	R	H	2B	3B	HR	RBI	Avg.	BB	SO	SB	PO	A	E	Avg.
1992— Oakland (A.L.)	OF	6	24	4	8	2	1	1	7	.333	2	1	1	12	0	0	1.000

ALL-STAR GAME RECORD

						BATTING							FIELDING		
Year League	Pos.	AB	R	H	2B	3B	HR	RBI	Avg.	BB	SO	SB	PO	A	E	Avg.
1989— American	OF	3	1	2	0	0	0	1	.667	0	0	0	1	0	0	1.000
1991— American	OF	2	0	0	0	0	0	0	.000	0	2	0	0	0	0	...
1992— American	OF	2	2	1	0	0	1	2	.500	0	0	0	1	0	0	1.000
1994— American	OF	2	0	1	0	0	0	0	.500	0	0	0	1	0	0	1.000
All-Star Game totals (4 years)		9	3	4	0	0	1	3	.444	0	2	0	3	0	0	1.000

SIKORSKI, BRIAN   P   ASTROS

PERSONAL: Born July 27, 1973, in Detroit. ... 6-1/190. ... Throws right, bats right. ... Full name: Brian Patrick Sikorski.
HIGH SCHOOL: Roseville (Mich.).
COLLEGE: Western Michigan.
TRANSACTIONS/CAREER NOTES: Selected by Houston Astros organization in fourth round of free-agent draft (June 1, 1995).
STATISTICAL NOTES: Led Midwest League with 12 balks in 1996.

Year Team (League)	W	L	Pct.	ERA	G	GS	CG	ShO	Sv.	IP	H	R	ER	BB	SO
1995— Auburn (N.Y.-Penn)	1	2	.333	2.10	23	0	0	0	12	34 1/3	22	8	8	14	35
— Quad City (Midwest)	1	0	1.000	0.00	2	0	0	0	0	3	1	1	0	0	4
1996— Quad City (Midwest)	11	8	.579	3.13	26	25	1	0	0	166 2/3	140	79	58	70	150
1997— Kissimmee (Florida State)..	8	2	.800	3.06	11	11	0	0	0	67 2/3	64	29	23	16	46
— Jackson (Texas)	5	5	.500	4.63	17	17	0	0	0	93 1/3	91	55	48	31	74

SILVA, JOSE   P   PIRATES

PERSONAL: Born December 19, 1973, in Tijuana, Mexico. ... 6-5/210. ... Throws right, bats right. ... Full name: Jose Leonel Silva.
HIGH SCHOOL: Hilltop (Chula Vista, Calif.).
TRANSACTIONS/CAREER NOTES: Selected by Toronto Blue Jays organization in sixth round of free-agent draft (June 3, 1991). ... On disabled list (April 6-August 17, 1995). ... On Knoxville disabled list (April 4-June 5, 1996). ... Traded by Blue Jays with IF Jose Pett, IF Brandon Cromer and three players to be named later to Pittsburgh Pirates for OF Orlando Merced, IF Carlos Garcia and P Dan Plesac (November 14, 1996); Pirates acquired P Mike Halperin, IF Abraham Nunez and C/OF Craig Wilson to complete deal (December 11, 1996). ... On Calgary disabled list (April 29-June 2, 1997).

Year Team (League)	W	L	Pct.	ERA	G	GS	CG	ShO	Sv.	IP	H	R	ER	BB	SO
1992— GC Blue Jays (GCL)...........	6	4	.600	2.28	12	•12	0	0	0	59 1/3	42	23	15	18	78
1993— Hagerstown (S. Atl.)..........	12	5	.706	2.52	24	24	0	0	0	142 2/3	103	50	40	62	161
1994— Dunedin (Fla. St.)...............	0	2	.000	3.77	8	7	0	0	0	43	41	32	18	24	41
— Knoxville (Southern)	4	8	.333	4.14	16	16	1	1	0	91 1/3	89	47	42	31	71
1995— Knoxville (Southern)	0	0	...	9.00	3	0	0	0	0	2	3	2	2	6	2
1996— Knoxville (Southern)	2	3	.400	4.91	22	6	0	0	0	44	45	27	24	22	26
— Toronto (A.L.)...................	0	0	...	13.50	2	0	0	0	0	2	5	3	3	0	0
1997— Calgary (PCL)■...............	5	1	.833	3.41	17	11	0	0	0	66	74	27	25	22	54
— Pittsburgh (N.L.)............	2	1	.667	5.94	11	4	0	0	0	36 1/3	52	26	24	16	30
A.L. totals (1 year)	0	0	...	13.50	2	0	0	0	0	2	5	3	3	0	0
N.L. totals (1 year)	2	1	.667	5.94	11	4	0	0	0	36 1/3	52	26	24	16	30
Major league totals (2 years)......	2	1	.667	6.34	13	4	0	0	0	38 1/3	57	29	27	16	30

SILVESTRI, DAVE   SS

PERSONAL: Born September 29, 1967, in St. Louis. ... 6-0/196. ... Bats right, throws right. ... Full name: David Joseph Silvestri.
HIGH SCHOOL: Parkway Central (Chesterfield, Mo.).
COLLEGE: Missouri.
TRANSACTIONS/CAREER NOTES: Selected by Houston Astros in second round of free-agent draft (June 1, 1988); pick received as compensation for New York Yankees signing Type B free-agent OF Jose Cruz. ... Traded by Astros organization with a player to be named later to Yankees organization for IF Orlando Miller (March 13, 1990); Yankees acquired P Daven Bond to complete deal (June 11, 1990). ... On New York disabled list (May 13-30, 1995). ... Traded by Yankees to Montreal Expos for OF Tyrone Horne (July 16, 1995). ... Claimed on waivers by Seattle Mariners (November 15, 1996). ... Calimed on waivers by Texas Rangers (March 27, 1997). ... Released by Rangers (April 1, 1997).
STATISTICAL NOTES: Led Florida State League shortstops with 221 putouts, 473 assists, 726 total chances and 93 double plays in 1989. ... Led Carolina League shortstops with 622 total chances and 96 double plays in 1990. ... Led Eastern League shortstops with 84 double plays in 1991.
MISCELLANEOUS: Member of 1988 U.S. Olympic baseball team.

Year Team (League)	Pos.	G	AB	R	H	2B	3B	HR	RBI	Avg.	BB	SO	SB	PO	A	E	Avg.
1989— Osceola (Fla. St.)........	SS-1B	129	437	67	111	20	1	2	50	.254	68	72	28	†238	†475	32	.957
1990— Prince Will. (Car.)■....	SS	131	465	74	120	30	7	5	56	.258	77	90	37	218	*382	22	*.965
— Alb./Colon. (Eastern)..	SS	2	7	0	2	0	0	0	2	.286	0	1	0	3	5	1	.889
1991— Alb./Colon. (Eastern)..	SS	*140	512	*97	134	31	8	19	83	.262	83	126	20	218	*362	*32	.948
1992— Columbus (Int'l)	SS	118	420	83	117	25	5	13	73	.279	58	110	19	*195	265	11	*.977
— New York (A.L.).........	SS	7	13	3	4	0	2	0	1	.308	0	3	0	4	12	2	.889
1993— Columbus (Int'l)	SS-3B-OF	120	428	76	115	26	4	20	65	.269	68	127	6	183	299	16	.968
— New York (A.L.).........	SS-3B	7	21	4	6	1	0	1	4	.286	4	3	0	9	20	3	.906
1994— Columbus (Int'l)	2-S-3-O-1	114	394	72	99	19	2	25	83	.251	*83	129	18	174	235	19	.956
— New York (A.L.).........	2B-3B-SS	12	18	3	2	0	1	1	2	.111	4	9	0	14	16	1	.968
1995— New York (A.L.).........	S-2-DH-1-S	17	21	4	2	0	0	1	4	.095	4	9	0	28	13	0	1.000
— Montreal (N.L.)■........	S-3-1-2-0	39	72	12	19	6	0	2	7	.264	9	27	2	34	36	1	.986
1996— Montreal (N.L.)...........	3-S-O-1-2	86	162	16	33	4	0	1	17	.204	34	41	2	23	92	10	.920
1997— Okla. City (A.A.)■......	3-1-2-S-O	124	467	54	112	25	3	17	68	.240	55	104	4	215	263	22	.956
— Texas (A.L.)...............	3B-SS	2	4	0	0	0	0	0	0	.000	0	1	0	0	2	0	1.000
American League totals (5 years)		45	77	14	14	1	3	3	11	.182	13	25	0	55	63	6	.952
National League totals (2 years)		125	234	28	52	10	0	3	24	.222	43	68	4	57	128	11	.944
Major league totals (6 years)		170	311	42	66	11	3	6	35	.212	56	93	4	112	191	17	.947

SIMAS, BILL   P   WHITE SOX

PERSONAL: Born November 28, 1971, in Hanford, Calif. ... 6-3/220. ... Throws right, bats left. ... Full name: William Anthony Simas Jr.
HIGH SCHOOL: St. Joseph (Calif.).
COLLEGE: Fresno (Calif.) City College.
TRANSACTIONS/CAREER NOTES: Selected by California Angels organization in sixth round of free-agent draft (June 1, 1992). ... Traded by Angels with P Andrew Lorraine, P John Snyder and OF McKay Christensen to Chicago White Sox for P Jim Abbott and P Tim Fortugno (July 27, 1995). ... On disabled list (July 23-August 5 and August 17, 1997-remainder of season).

Year Team (League)	W	L	Pct.	ERA	G	GS	CG	ShO	Sv.	IP	H	R	ER	BB	SO
1992— Boise (Northwest)	6	5	.545	3.95	14	12	0	0	1	70 2/3	82	44	31	29	39
1993— Cedar Rapids (Midw.)	5	8	.385	4.95	35	6	0	0	6	80	93	60	44	36	62
1994— Lake Elsinore (Calif.)	5	2	.714	2.11	37	0	0	0	13	47	44	17	11	10	44
— Midland (Texas).................	2	0	1.000	0.59	13	0	0	0	6	15 1/3	5	1	1	2	12
1995— Vancouver (PCL)	6	3	.667	3.55	30	0	0	0	6	38	44	19	15	14	44
— Nashville (A.A.)■.............	1	1	.500	3.86	7	0	0	0	0	11 2/3	12	5	5	3	12
— Chicago (A.L.)	1	1	.500	2.57	14	0	0	0	0	14	15	5	4	10	16
1996— Chicago (A.L.)	2	8	.200	4.58	64	0	0	0	2	72 2/3	75	39	37	39	65
1997— Chicago (A.L.)	3	1	.750	4.14	40	0	0	0	1	41 1/3	46	23	19	24	38
Major league totals (3 years)......	6	10	.375	4.22	118	0	0	0	3	128	136	67	60	73	119

SIMMONS, BRIAN   OF   WHITE SOX

PERSONAL: Born September 4, 1973, in Lebanon, Pa. ... 6-2/185. ... Bats both, throws right. ... Full name: Brian Lee Simmons.
HIGH SCHOOL: Peters Township (McMurray, Pa.).
COLLEGE: Michigan.
TRANSACTIONS/CAREER NOTES: Selected by Baltimore Orioles organization in 35th round of free-agent draft (June 1, 1992); did not sign. ... Selected by Chicago White Sox organization in second round of free-agent draft (June 1, 1995). ... On South Bend disabled list (April 5-17, 1996).
STATISTICAL NOTES: Led Southern League outfielders with 334 total chances in 1997.

Year Team (League)	Pos.	G	AB	R	H	2B	3B	HR	RBI	Avg.	BB	SO	SB	PO	A	E	Avg.
1995— Sarasota (Gulf Coast).	OF	5	17	5	3	1	0	1	5	.176	6	1	0	13	1	0	1.000
— Hickory (S. Atl.)	OF	41	163	13	31	6	1	2	11	.190	19	44	4	77	2	1	.988
1996— South Bend (Mid.)......	OF	92	356	73	106	29	6	17	58	.298	48	69	14	204	10	7	.968
— Prince William (Car.) ..	OF	33	131	17	26	4	3	4	14	.198	9	39	2	70	2	2	.973
1997— Birmingham (Sou.).....	OF	138	546	108	143	28	*12	15	72	.262	*88	124	15	*322	7	5	.985

SIMMS, MIKE — OF — RANGERS

PERSONAL: Born January 12, 1967, in Orange, Calif. ... 6-4/185. ... Bats right, throws right. ... Full name: Michael Howard Simms.
HIGH SCHOOL: Esperanza (Calif.).
TRANSACTIONS/CAREER NOTES: Selected by Houston Astros organization in sixth round of free-agent draft (June 3, 1985). ... On disabled list (May 11-28, 1989). ... On Tucson disabled list (July 31-August 16, 1992). ... Granted free agency (March 30, 1993). ... Signed by San Diego Padres organization (April 7, 1993). ... Granted free agency (October 15, 1993). ... Signed by Pittsburgh Pirates (December 15, 1993). ... Released by Buffalo, Pirates organization (April 28, 1994). ... Signed by Tucson, Astros organization (May 2, 1994). ... Granted free agency (October 15, 1994). ... Re-signed by Tucson (November 18, 1994). ... Granted free agency (October 15, 1996). ... Signed by Texas Rangers organization (December 19, 1996). ... Granted free agency (October 27, 1997). ... Re-signed by Rangers organization (December 17, 1997).
STATISTICAL NOTES: Led South Atlantic League with 264 total bases in 1987. ... Led South Atlantic League first basemen with 1,089 putouts, 19 errors and 1,158 total chances in 1987. ... Led Pacific Coast League first basemen with 19 errors in 1990. ... Career major league grand slams: 1.

Year Team (League)	Pos.	G	AB	R	H	2B	3B	HR	RBI	Avg.	BB	SO	SB	PO	A	E	Avg.
1985— GC Astros (GCL)	1B	21	70	10	19	2	1	3	18	.271	6	26	0	186	7	5	.975
1986— GC Astros (GCL)	1B	54	181	33	47	14	1	4	37	.260	22	48	2	433	28	7	.985
1987— Asheville (S. Atl.)........	1B-3B	133	469	93	128	19	0	*39	100	.273	73	*167	7	†1089	52	†19	.984
1988— Osceola (Fla. St.)........	1B	123	428	63	104	19	1	16	73	.243	76	130	9	1143	41	22	.982
1989— Columbus (Southern).	1B	109	378	64	97	21	3	20	81	.257	66	110	12	938	44	10	.990
1990— Tucson (PCL)	1B-3B-OF	124	421	75	115	34	5	13	72	.273	74	*135	3	1013	75	†19	.983
— Houston (N.L.)	1B	12	13	3	4	1	0	1	2	.308	0	4	0	20	1	0	1.000
1991— Tucson (PCL)	OF-1B	85	297	53	73	20	2	15	59	.246	36	94	2	325	25	8	.978
— Houston (N.L.)	OF	49	123	18	25	5	0	3	16	.203	18	38	1	44	4	6	.889
1992— Tucson (PCL)	OF-1B	116	404	73	114	22	6	11	75	.282	61	107	7	476	29	11	.979
— Houston (N.L.)	OF-1B	15	24	1	6	1	0	1	3	.250	2	9	0	10	2	0	1.000
1993— Las Vegas (PCL)	1-O-3-P	129	414	74	111	25	2	24	80	.268	67	114	1	774	46	13	.984
1994— Buffalo (A.A.)■	OF	18	55	10	13	5	0	4	8	.236	4	13	0	26	0	0	1.000
— Tucson (PCL)■	1B-O-3B	100	373	76	107	34	6	20	85	.287	51	79	9	555	32	9	.985
— Houston (N.L.)	OF	6	12	1	1	1	0	0	0	.083	0	5	1	6	0	1	.857
1995— Houston (N.L.)	1B-OF	50	121	14	31	4	0	9	24	.256	13	28	1	221	17	1	.996
— Tucson (PCL)	1B-OF	85	319	56	94	26	8	13	66	.295	35	65	10	424	30	8	.983
1996— Tucson (PCL)	1B	17	64	11	19	3	0	7	19	.297	9	17	0	138	9	5	.967
— Houston (N.L.)	OF-1B	49	68	6	12	2	1	1	8	.176	4	16	1	24	1	0	1.000
1997— Okla. City (A.A.)■......	OF	10	39	7	15	4	0	3	8	.385	6	8	0	17	1	0	1.000
— Texas (A.L.)	DH-OF-1B	59	111	13	28	8	0	5	22	.252	8	27	0	36	1	2	.949
American League totals (1 year)		59	111	13	28	8	0	5	22	.252	8	27	0	36	1	2	.949
National League totals (6 years)		181	361	43	79	14	1	15	53	.219	37	100	4	325	25	8	.978
Major league totals (7 years)		240	472	56	107	22	1	20	75	.227	45	127	4	361	26	10	.975

RECORD AS PITCHER

Year Team (League)	W	L	Pct.	ERA	G	GS	CG	ShO	Sv.	IP	H	R	ER	BB	SO
1993— Las Vegas (PCL)	0	0	...	0.00	1	0	0	0	0	2/3	1	0	0	0	0

SIMON, RANDALL — 1B — BRAVES

PERSONAL: Born May 26, 1975, in Willemstad, The Netherlands. ... 6-0/180. ... Bats left, throws left. ... Full name: Randall Carlito Simon.
HIGH SCHOOL: Juan Pablo Duarte Tech (Willemstad, Curacao).
TRANSACTIONS/CAREER NOTES: Signed as non-drafted free agent by Atlanta Braves organization (July 17, 1992).
STATISTICAL NOTES: Led International League in grounding into double plays with 18 in 1997.

Year Team (League)	Pos.	G	AB	R	H	2B	3B	HR	RBI	Avg.	BB	SO	SB	PO	A	E	Avg.
1993— Danville (Appal.).........	1B	61	232	28	59	17	1	3	31	.254	10	34	1	463	37	10	.980
1994— Macon (S. Atl.)...........	1B	106	358	48	105	23	1	10	54	.293	6	56	7	582	49	9	.986
1995— Durham (Carolina).....	1B	122	420	56	111	18	1	18	79	.264	36	63	6	864	51	10	.989
1996— Greenville (Southern) .	1B-OF	134	498	74	139	26	2	18	77	.279	37	61	4	723	55	16	.980
1997— Richmond (Int'l).........	1B	133	519	62	160	*45	1	14	*102	.308	17	76	1	*1063	72	•14	.988
— Atlanta (N.L.).............	1B	13	14	2	6	1	0	0	1	.429	1	2	0	16	2	0	1.000
Major league totals (1 year)		13	14	2	6	1	0	0	1	.429	1	2	0	16	2	0	1.000

SIMONTON, BENJI — OF — GIANTS

PERSONAL: Born May 5, 1972, in Walnut Creek, Calif. ... 6-1/225. ... Bats right, throws right. ... Full name: Benji K. Simonton.
HIGH SCHOOL: Pittsburg (Calif.).
COLLEGE: Diablo Valley (Calif.).
TRANSACTIONS/CAREER NOTES: Selected by San Francisco Giants organization in third round of free-agent draft (June 1, 1992). ... Selected by Boston Red Sox from Giants organization in Rule 5 major league draft (December 5, 1994). ... Returned to Giants organization (April 22, 1995).
STATISTICAL NOTES: Led Texas League with 110 double plays in 1997.

S

Year Team (League)	Pos.	G	AB	R	H	2B	3B	HR	RBI	Avg.	BB	SO	SB	PO	A	E	Avg.
1992—Everett (N'west)..........	OF	68	225	37	55	10	0	6	34	.244	39	78	9	89	3	5	.948
1993—Clinton (Midwest).......	OF	100	310	52	79	18	4	12	49	.255	40	112	8	89	3	5	.948
1994—Clinton (Midwest).......	OF	67	237	47	64	16	4	14	57	.270	52	73	10	91	3	2	.979
—San Jose (Calif.)..........	OF-1B	68	259	41	77	20	0	14	51	.297	32	86	0	130	8	5	.965
1995—San Jose (Calif.)......	1B	61	225	38	65	9	6	8	37	.289	40	78	7	309	19	3	.991
—Shreveport (Texas).....	OF-1B	38	108	18	33	9	3	4	30	.306	11	32	3	110	6	2	.983
1996—Shreveport (Texas).....	1B	*137	469	86	117	25	1	23	76	.249	*101	144	6	1171	79	15	.988
—Phoenix (PCL)...........	1B	1	4	1	3	0	0	1	2	.750	1	0	0	9	0	0	1.000
1997—Shreveport (Texas).....	1B	116	387	73	99	15	2	20	79	.256	*81	120	7	1079	77	11	.991

SINCLAIR, STEVE — P — BLUE JAYS

PERSONAL: Born August 2, 1971, in Victoria, B.C. ... 6-2/175. ... Throws left, bats left. ... Full name: Steven Scitt Sinclair.
HIGH SCHOOL: Oak Bay (Victoria, B.C.).
COLLEGE: Kwantlen (Vancouver, B.C.).
TRANSACTIONS/CAREER NOTES: Selected by Toronto Blue Jays organization in 28th round of free-agent draft (June 3, 1991).

Year Team (League)	W	L	Pct.	ERA	G	GS	CG	ShO	Sv.	IP	H	R	ER	BB	SO
1991—Medicine Hat (Pio.)...........	0	1	.000	6.75	12	0	0	0	0	$14\frac{2}{3}$	17	15	11	11	14
1992—GC Blue Jays (GCL)...........	1	2	.333	2.74	5	4	0	0	0	23	23	10	7	5	18
—Medicine Hat (Pio.)..........	2	3	.400	4.60	9	7	0	0	0	43	54	25	22	12	28
1993—Medicine Hat (Pio.)..........	5	2	.714	3.33	15	12	0	0	0	$78\frac{1}{3}$	87	41	29	16	45
1994—Hagerstown (S. Atl.).........	9	2	.818	3.77	38	1	0	0	3	105	127	53	44	25	75
1995—Dunedin (Fla. St.)............	5	3	.625	2.59	46	0	0	0	2	73	69	26	21	17	52
1996—Dunedin (Fla. St.)............	0	1	.000	3.38	3	0	0	0	0	$2\frac{2}{3}$	4	2	1	0	1
1997—Dunedin (Fla. St.)............	2	5	.286	2.90	43	0	0	0	3	$68\frac{1}{3}$	63	36	22	26	66
—Syracuse (Int'l)............	0	0	...	6.00	6	0	0	0	0	9	11	6	6	3	9

SINGLETON, CHRIS — OF — YANKEES

PERSONAL: Born August 15, 1972, in Martinez, Calif. ... 6-2/195. ... Bats left, throws left. ... Full name: Christopher V. Singleton.
HIGH SCHOOL: Pinole (Calif.) Valley.
COLLEGE: Nevada.
TRANSACTIONS/CAREER NOTES: Selected by San Francisco Giants organization in second round of free-agent draft (June 3, 1993). ... Traded by Giants with P Alberto Castillo to New York Yankees for 3B Charlie Hayes (November 11, 1997).
STATISTICAL NOTES: Led Texas League with nine sacrifice flies in 1997. ... Led Texas League outfielders with 271 total chances and tied for league lead with four double plays in 1997. ... Tied for Texas League lead with four intentional bases on balls in 1997.

Year Team (League)	Pos.	G	AB	R	H	2B	3B	HR	RBI	Avg.	BB	SO	SB	PO	A	E	Avg.
1993—Everett (N'west).........	OF	58	219	39	58	14	4	3	18	.265	18	46	14	106	6	3	.974
1994—San Jose (Calif.)........	OF	113	425	51	106	17	5	2	49	.249	27	62	19	248	10	13	.952
1995—San Jose (Calif.)........	OF	94	405	55	112	13	5	2	31	.277	17	49	33	142	6	7	.955
1996—Shreveport (Texas).....	OF	129	500	68	149	31	9	5	72	.298	24	58	27	262	10	4	.986
—Phoenix (PCL)..........	OF	9	32	3	4	0	0	0	0	.125	1	2	0	18	1	0	1.000
1997—Shreveport (Texas).....	OF	126	464	85	147	26	10	9	61	.317	22	50	27	*253	11	7	.974

SIROTKA, MIKE — P — WHITE SOX

PERSONAL: Born May 13, 1971, in Chicago. ... 6-1/200. ... Throws left, bats left. ... Full name: Michael R. Sirotka.
HIGH SCHOOL: Westfield (Houston).
COLLEGE: Louisiana State.
TRANSACTIONS/CAREER NOTES: Selected by Chicago White Sox organization in 15th round of free-agent draft (June 3, 1993). ... On Hickory disabled list (July 1-28, 1993). ... On South Bend temporarily inactive list (August 27-October 4, 1993).

Year Team (League)	W	L	Pct.	ERA	G	GS	CG	ShO	Sv.	IP	H	R	ER	BB	SO
1993—GC White Sox (GCL)	0	0	...	0.00	3	0	0	0	0	5	4	1	0	2	8
—South Bend (Mid.).............	0	1	.000	6.10	7	1	0	0	0	$10\frac{1}{3}$	12	8	7	6	12
1994—South Bend (Mid.)............	12	9	.571	3.07	27	27	8	2	0	$196\frac{2}{3}$	183	99	67	56	173
1995—Birmingham (Southern)	7	6	.538	3.20	16	16	1	0	0	$101\frac{1}{3}$	95	42	36	22	79
—Chicago (A.L.)................	1	2	.333	4.19	6	6	0	0	0	$34\frac{1}{3}$	39	16	16	17	19
—Nashville (A.A.)................	1	5	.167	2.83	8	8	0	0	0	54	51	21	17	13	34
1996—Nashville (A.A.)...............	7	5	.583	3.60	15	15	1	1	0	90	90	44	36	24	58
—Chicago (A.L.)................	1	2	.333	7.18	15	4	0	0	0	$26\frac{1}{3}$	34	27	21	12	11
1997—Nashville (A.A.)...............	7	5	.583	3.28	19	19	1	0	0	$112\frac{1}{3}$	115	49	41	22	92
—Chicago (A.L.)................	3	0	1.000	2.25	7	4	0	0	0	32	36	9	8	5	24
Major league totals (3 years)......	5	4	.556	4.37	28	14	0	0	0	$92\frac{2}{3}$	109	52	45	34	54

SLAUGHT, DON — C

PERSONAL: Born September 11, 1958, in Long Beach, Calif. ... 6-1/185. ... Bats right, throws right. ... Full name: Donald Martin Slaught.
HIGH SCHOOL: Rolling Hills (Palos Verdes, Calif.).
JUNIOR COLLEGE: El Camino College (Calif.).
COLLEGE: UCLA (bachelor of science degree in economics, 1983).
TRANSACTIONS/CAREER NOTES: Selected by Milwaukee Brewers organization in 19th round of free-agent draft (June 5, 1979); did not sign. ... Selected by Kansas City Royals organization in seventh round of free-agent draft (June 3, 1980). ... On Omaha disabled list (August 16-

S

September 29, 1981 and April 21-May 15, 1982). ... On disabled list (May 16-June 1, 1983). ... Traded by Royals to Texas Rangers as part of a six-player, four-team deal in which Royals acquired C Jim Sundberg from Brewers, Mets organization acquired P Frank Wills from Royals, Brewers acquired P Danny Darwin and a player to be named later from Rangers and P Tim Leary from Mets (January 18, 1985); Brewers organization acquired C Bill Hance from Rangers to complete deal (January 30, 1985). ... On disabled list (August 9-26, 1985). ... On Texas disabled list (May 18-July 4, 1986); included rehabilitation assignment to Oklahoma City (July 1-4). ... Traded by Rangers to New York Yankees for a player to be named later (November 2, 1987); Rangers acquired P Brad Arnsberg to complete deal (November 10, 1987). ... On disabled list (May 15-June 20, 1988). ... Traded by Yankees to Pittsburgh Pirates for P Jeff D. Robinson and P Willie Smith (December 4, 1989). ... On disabled list (June 30-July 16, 1990). ... Granted free agency (November 5, 1990). ... Re-signed by Pirates (December 19, 1990). ... On disabled list (July 22-August 13, 1991). ... On Pittsburgh disabled list (March 28-April 23, 1992); included rehabilitation assignment to Buffalo (April 17-20). ... On Pittsburgh disabled list (May 2-June 19 and July 21-August 31, 1995); included rehabilitation assignments to Gulf Coast Pirates (May 31-June 8) and Carolina (June 15-18). ... Granted free agency (November 1, 1995). ... Signed by Cincinnati Reds organization (January 2, 1996). ... Contract sold by Cincinnati Reds to California Angels (February 29, 1996). ... On California disabled list (July 12-27, 1996). ... Traded by Angels to Chicago White Sox for a player to be named later (August 31, 1996); Angels acquired C Scott Vollmer to complete deal (November 14, 1996). ... Granted free agency (November 18, 1996). ... Signed by San Diego Padres organization (December 23, 1996). ... Released by Padres (May 27, 1997).

STATISTICAL NOTES: Career major league grand slams: 1.

Year	Team (League)	Pos.	G	AB	R	H	2B	3B	HR	RBI	Avg.	BB	SO	SB	PO	A	E	Avg.
1980—Fort Myers (FSL)	C	50	176	13	46	9	0	2	16	.261	16	11	3	175	34	4	.981
1981—Jacksonville (South.)	C-1B	96	379	45	127	21	2	6	44	.335	32	44	13	482	61	9	.984
—Omaha (A.A.)	C	22	71	10	21	4	0	2	8	.296	4	7	3	91	7	3	.970
1982—Omaha (A.A.)	C	53	206	29	55	10	1	4	16	.267	7	20	6	216	25	5	.980
—Kansas City (A.L.)	C	43	115	14	32	6	0	3	8	.278	9	12	0	156	7	1	.994
1983—Kansas City (A.L.)	C-DH	83	276	21	86	13	4	0	28	.312	11	27	3	299	18	12	.964
1984—Kansas City (A.L.)	C-DH	124	409	48	108	27	4	4	42	.264	20	55	0	547	44	11	.982
1985—Texas (A.L.)■	C	102	343	34	96	17	4	8	35	.280	20	41	5	550	33	6	.990
1986—Texas (A.L.)	C-DH	95	314	39	83	17	1	13	46	.264	16	59	3	533	40	4	.993
—Oklahoma City (A.A.)	C	3	12	2	4	1	0	0	1	.333	0	3	0	6	1	0	1.000
1987—Texas (A.L.)	C-DH	95	237	25	53	15	2	8	16	.224	24	51	0	429	39	7	.985
1988—New York (A.L.)■	C-DH	97	322	33	91	25	1	9	43	.283	24	54	1	496	24	•11	.979
1989—New York (A.L.)	C-DH	117	350	34	88	21	3	5	38	.251	30	57	1	493	44	5	.991
1990—Pittsburgh (N.L.)■	C	84	230	27	69	18	3	4	29	.300	27	27	0	345	36	8	.979
1991—Pittsburgh (N.L.)	C-3B	77	220	19	65	17	1	1	29	.295	21	32	1	338	31	5	.987
1992—Buffalo (A.A.)	C	2	6	1	2	0	0	0	1	.333	0	0	0	15	3	0	1.000
—Pittsburgh (N.L.)	C	87	255	26	88	17	3	4	37	.345	17	23	2	365	35	5	.988
1993—Pittsburgh (N.L.)	C	116	377	34	113	19	2	10	55	.300	29	56	2	539	51	4	.993
1994—Pittsburgh (N.L.)	C	76	240	21	69	7	0	2	21	.288	34	31	0	425	36	3	.994
1995—Pittsburgh (N.L.)	C	35	112	13	34	6	0	0	13	.304	9	8	0	220	9	1	.996
—Carolina (Southern)	C	3	12	1	3	1	0	0	1	.250	0	3	0	24	1	0	1.000
1996—California (A.L.)■	C-DH	62	207	23	67	9	0	6	32	.324	13	20	0	338	27	3	.992
—Chicago (A.L.)■	C-DH	14	36	2	9	1	0	0	4	.250	2	2	0	70	0	1	.986
1997—San Diego (N.L.)■	C	20	20	2	0	0	0	0	0	.000	5	4	0	15	3	0	1.000
American League totals (9 years)		832	2609	273	713	151	19	56	292	.273	169	378	13	3911	276	61	.986
National League totals (7 years)		495	1454	142	438	84	9	21	184	.301	142	181	5	2247	201	26	.989
Major league totals (16 years)		1327	4063	415	1151	235	28	77	476	.283	311	559	18	6158	477	87	.987

CHAMPIONSHIP SERIES RECORD

Year	Team (League)	Pos.	G	AB	R	H	2B	3B	HR	RBI	Avg.	BB	SO	SB	PO	A	E	Avg.
1984—Kansas City (A.L.)	C	3	11	0	4	0	0	0	0	.364	0	0	0	17	0	3	.850
1990—Pittsburgh (N.L.)	C	4	11	0	1	1	0	0	1	.091	2	3	0	22	1	1	.958
1991—Pittsburgh (N.L.)	C-PH	6	17	0	4	0	0	0	1	.235	1	4	0	30	5	0	1.000
1992—Pittsburgh (N.L.)	C-PH	5	12	5	4	1	0	1	5	.333	6	3	0	17	1	0	1.000
Championship series totals (4 years)		18	51	5	13	2	0	1	7	.255	9	10	0	86	7	4	.959

SLOCUMB, HEATHCLIFF   P   MARINERS

PERSONAL: Born June 7, 1966, in Jamaica, N.Y. ... 6-3/220. ... Throws right, bats right.

HIGH SCHOOL: John Bowne (Flushing, N.Y.).

TRANSACTIONS/CAREER NOTES: Signed as non-drafted free agent by New York Mets organization (July 10, 1984). ... Selected by Chicago Cubs organization from Mets organization in Rule 5 minor league draft (December 9, 1986). ... Traded by Cubs to Cleveland Indians for SS Jose Hernandez (June 1, 1993). ... Traded by Indians to Philadelphia Phillies for OF Ruben Amaro (November 2, 1993). ... Traded by Phillies with P Larry Wimberly and OF Rick Holifield to Boston Red Sox for P Ken Ryan, OF Lee Tinsley and OF Glenn Murray (January 29, 1996). ... Traded by Red Sox to Seattle Mariners for C Jason Varitek and P Derek Lowe (July 31, 1997).

STATISTICAL NOTES: Led Carolina League with 19 wild pitches in 1988.

Year	Team (League)	W	L	Pct.	ERA	G	GS	CG	ShO	Sv.	IP	H	R	ER	BB	SO
1984—Kingsport (Appalachian)	0	0	. . .	0.00	1	0	0	0	0	1/3	0	1	0	1	0
—Little Falls (NYP)	0	0	. . .	11.00	4	1	0	0	0	9	8	11	11	16	10
1985—Kingsport (Appalachian)	3	2	.600	3.78	11	9	1	0	0	52 1/3	47	32	22	31	29
1986—Little Falls (NYP)	3	1	.750	1.65	25	0	0	0	1	43 2/3	24	17	8	36	41
1987—Win.-Salem (Car.)■	1	2	.333	6.26	9	4	0	0	0	27 1/3	26	25	19	26	27
—Peoria (Midwest)	10	4	.714	2.60	16	16	3	1	0	103 2/3	97	44	30	42	81
1988—Win.-Salem (Car.)	6	6	.500	4.96	25	19	2	1	1	119 2/3	122	75	66	90	78
1989—Peoria (Midwest)	5	3	.625	1.78	49	0	0	0	22	55 2/3	31	16	11	33	52
1990—Charlotte (Southern)	3	1	.750	2.15	43	0	0	0	12	50 1/3	50	20	12	32	37
—Iowa (Am. Assoc.)	3	2	.600	2.00	20	0	0	0	1	27	16	10	6	18	21
1991—Chicago (N.L.)	2	1	.667	3.45	52	0	0	0	1	62 2/3	53	29	24	30	34
—Iowa (Am. Assoc.)	1	0	1.000	4.05	12	0	0	0	1	13 1/3	10	8	6	6	9
1992—Chicago (N.L.)	0	3	.000	6.50	30	0	0	0	1	36	52	27	26	21	27
—Iowa (Am. Assoc.)	1	3	.250	2.59	36	1	0	0	7	41 2/3	36	13	12	16	47

Year— Team (League)	W	L	Pct.	ERA	G	GS	CG	ShO	Sv.	IP	H	R	ER	BB	SO
1993— Iowa (Am. Assoc.)	1	0	1.000	1.50	10	0	0	0	7	12	7	2	2	8	10
— Chicago (N.L.)	1	0	1.000	3.38	10	0	0	0	0	10 2/3	7	5	4	4	4
— Cleveland (A.L.)■	3	1	.750	4.28	20	0	0	0	0	27 1/3	28	14	13	16	18
— Charlotte (Int'l)	3	2	.600	3.56	23	0	0	0	1	30 1/3	25	14	12	11	25
1994— Philadelphia (N.L.)■	5	1	.833	2.86	52	0	0	0	0	72 1/3	75	32	23	28	58
1995— Philadelphia (N.L.)	5	6	.455	2.89	61	0	0	0	32	65 1/3	64	26	21	35	63
1996— Boston (A.L.)■	5	5	.500	3.02	75	0	0	0	31	83 1/3	68	31	28	55	88
1997— Boston (A.L.)	0	5	.000	5.79	49	0	0	0	17	46 2/3	58	32	30	34	36
— Seattle (A.L.)■	0	4	.000	4.13	27	0	0	0	10	28 1/3	26	13	13	15	28
A.L. totals (3 years)	8	15	.348	4.07	171	0	0	0	58	185 2/3	180	90	84	120	170
N.L. totals (5 years)	13	11	.542	3.57	205	0	0	0	34	247	251	119	98	118	186
Major league totals (7 years)	21	26	.447	3.79	376	0	0	0	92	432 2/3	431	209	182	238	356

DIVISION SERIES RECORD

Year— Team (League)	W	L	Pct.	ERA	G	GS	CG	ShO	Sv.	IP	H	R	ER	BB	SO
1997— Seattle (A.L.)	0	0	...	4.50	2	0	0	0	0	2	3	1	1	1	0

ALL-STAR GAME RECORD

Year— League	W	L	Pct.	ERA	GS	CG	ShO	Sv.	IP	H	R	ER	BB	SO
1995— National	1	0	1.000	0.00	0	0	0	0	1	1	0	0	0	2

SMALL, AARON — P — ATHLETICS

PERSONAL: Born November 23, 1971, in Oxnard, Calif. ... 6-5/214. ... Throws right, bats right. ... Full name: Aaron James Small.
HIGH SCHOOL: South Hills (Covina, Calif.).
TRANSACTIONS/CAREER NOTES: Selected by Toronto Blue Jays organization in 22nd round of free-agent draft (June 5, 1989). ... Traded by Blue Jays to Florida Marlins for a player to be named later (April 26, 1995); Blue Jays acquired P Ernie Delgado to complete deal (September 19, 1995). ... On Charlotte disabled list (May 3-June 14, 1995). ... Claimed on waivers by Seattle Mariners (January 23, 1996). ... Claimed on waivers by Oakland Athletics (January 29, 1996).
STATISTICAL NOTES: Pitched 6-0 no-hit victory for Edmonton against Vancouver (August 8, 1996).

Year— Team (League)	W	L	Pct.	ERA	G	GS	CG	ShO	Sv.	IP	H	R	ER	BB	SO
1989— Medicine Hat (Pio.)	1	7	.125	5.86	15	14	0	0	0	70 2/3	80	55	46	31	40
1990— Myrtle Beach (SAL)	9	9	.500	2.80	27	27	1	0	0	147 1/3	150	72	46	56	96
1991— Dunedin (Fla. St.)	8	7	.533	2.73	24	23	1	0	0	148 1/3	129	51	45	42	92
1992— Knoxville (Southern)	5	12	.294	5.27	27	24	2	1	0	135	152	94	79	61	79
1993— Knoxville (Southern)	4	4	.500	3.39	48	9	0	0	16	93	99	44	35	40	44
1994— Knoxville (Southern)	5	5	.500	2.99	29	11	1	1	5	96 1/3	92	37	32	38	75
— Syracuse (Int'l)	3	2	.600	2.22	13	0	0	0	0	24 1/3	19	8	6	9	15
— Toronto (A.L.)	0	0	...	9.00	1	0	0	0	0	2	5	2	2	2	0
1995— Syracuse (Int'l)	0	0	...	5.40	1	0	0	0	0	1 2/3	3	1	1	1	2
— Charlotte (Int'l)■	2	1	.667	2.88	33	0	0	0	10	40 2/3	36	15	13	10	31
— Florida (N.L.)	1	0	1.000	1.42	7	0	0	0	0	6 1/3	7	2	1	6	5
1996— Oakland (A.L.)■	1	3	.250	8.16	12	3	0	0	0	28 2/3	37	28	26	22	17
— Edmonton (PCL)	8	6	.571	4.29	25	19	1	1	1	119 2/3	111	65	57	28	83
1997— Edmonton (PCL)	1	0	1.000	0.00	1	1	0	0	0	5	1	0	0	0	4
— Oakland (A.L.)	9	5	.643	4.28	71	0	0	0	4	96 2/3	109	50	46	40	57
A.L. totals (3 years)	10	8	.556	5.23	84	3	0	0	4	127 1/3	151	80	74	64	74
N.L. totals (1 year)	1	0	1.000	1.42	7	0	0	0	0	6 1/3	7	2	1	6	5
Major league totals (4 years)	11	8	.579	5.05	91	3	0	0	4	133 2/3	158	82	75	70	79

SMILEY, JOHN — P — INDIANS

PERSONAL: Born March 17, 1965, in Phoenixville, Pa. ... 6-4/210. ... Throws left, bats left. ... Full name: John Patrick Smiley.
HIGH SCHOOL: Perkiomen Valley (Graterford, Pa.).
TRANSACTIONS/CAREER NOTES: Selected by Pittsburgh Pirates organization in 12th round of free-agent draft (June 6, 1983). ... On disabled list (April 27-May 27, 1984 and May 19-July 1, 1990). ... Traded by Pirates to Minnesota Twins for P Denny Neagle and OF Midre Cummings (March 17, 1992). ... Granted free agency (October 26, 1992). ... Signed by Cincinnati Reds (December 1, 1992). ... On disabled list (July 3, 1993-remainder of season and August 22-September 6, 1995). ... On Cincinnati disabled list (June 2-17, 1997). ... Traded by Reds with IF Jeff Branson to Cleveland Indians for P Danny Graves, P Jim Crowell, P Scott Winchester and IF Damian Jackson (July 31, 1997).
STATISTICAL NOTES: Tied for Gulf Coast League lead with five home runs allowed in 1983. ... Pitched 2-1 one-hit, complete-game victory against Montreal (June 3, 1988). ... Pitched 4-0 one-hit, complete-game victory against New York (April 17, 1991). ... Pitched 6-0 one-hit, complete-game victory against St. Louis (September 22, 1996).

Year— Team (League)	W	L	Pct.	ERA	G	GS	CG	ShO	Sv.	IP	H	R	ER	BB	SO
1983— GC Pirates (GCL)	3	4	.429	5.92	12	12	0	0	0	65 1/3	69	45	*43	27	42
1984— Macon (S. Atl.)	5	11	.313	3.95	21	19	2	0	1	130	119	73	57	41	73
1985— Prince William (Caro.)	2	2	.500	5.14	10	10	0	0	0	56	64	36	32	27	45
— Macon (S. Atl.)	3	8	.273	4.67	16	16	1	1	0	88 2/3	84	55	46	37	70
1986— Prince William (Caro.)	2	4	.333	3.10	48	2	0	0	14	90	64	35	31	40	93
— Pittsburgh (N.L.)	1	0	1.000	3.86	12	0	0	0	0	11 2/3	4	6	5	4	9
1987— Pittsburgh (N.L.)	5	5	.500	5.76	63	0	0	0	4	75	69	49	48	50	58
1988— Pittsburgh (N.L.)	13	11	.542	3.25	34	32	5	1	0	205	185	81	74	46	129
1989— Pittsburgh (N.L.)	12	8	.600	2.81	28	28	8	1	0	205 1/3	174	78	64	49	123
1990— Pittsburgh (N.L.)	9	10	.474	4.64	26	25	2	0	0	149 1/3	161	83	77	36	86
1991— Pittsburgh (N.L.)	•20	8	•.714	3.08	33	32	2	1	0	207 2/3	194	78	71	44	129
1992— Minnesota (A.L.)■	16	9	.640	3.21	34	34	5	2	0	241	205	93	86	65	163
1993— Cincinnati (N.L.)■	3	9	.250	5.62	18	18	2	0	0	105 2/3	117	69	66	31	60
1994— Cincinnati (N.L.)	11	10	.524	3.86	24	24	1	1	0	158 2/3	169	80	68	37	112
1995— Cincinnati (N.L.)	12	5	.706	3.46	28	27	1	0	0	176 2/3	173	72	68	39	124
1996— Cincinnati (N.L.)	13	14	.481	3.64	35	34	2	2	0	217 1/3	207	100	88	54	171

Year — Team (League)	W	L	Pct.	ERA	G	GS	CG	ShO	Sv.	IP	H	R	ER	BB	SO
1997— Cincinnati (N.L.)	9	10	.474	5.23	20	20	0	0	0	117	139	76	68	31	94
— Cleveland (A.L.)■	2	4	.333	5.54	6	6	0	0	0	37 1/3	45	23	23	10	26
A.L. totals (2 years)	18	13	.581	3.52	40	40	5	2	0	278 1/3	250	116	109	75	189
N.L. totals (11 years)	108	90	.545	3.85	321	240	23	6	4	1629 1/3	1592	772	697	421	1095
Major league totals (12 years)	126	103	.550	3.80	361	280	28	8	4	1907 2/3	1842	888	806	496	1284

DIVISION SERIES RECORD

Year — Team (League)	W	L	Pct.	ERA	G	GS	CG	ShO	Sv.	IP	H	R	ER	BB	SO
1995— Cincinnati (N.L.)	0	0	...	3.00	1	1	0	0	0	6	9	2	2	0	1

CHAMPIONSHIP SERIES RECORD

Year — Team (League)	W	L	Pct.	ERA	G	GS	CG	ShO	Sv.	IP	H	R	ER	BB	SO
1990— Pittsburgh (N.L.)	0	0	...	0.00	1	0	0	0	0	2	2	0	0	0	0
1991— Pittsburgh (N.L.)	0	2	.000	23.63	2	2	0	0	0	2 2/3	8	8	7	1	3
1995— Cincinnati (N.L.)	0	0	...	3.60	1	1	0	0	0	5	5	2	2	0	1
Champ. series totals (3 years)	0	2	.000	8.38	4	3	0	0	0	9 2/3	15	10	9	1	4

ALL-STAR GAME RECORD

Year — League	W	L	Pct.	ERA	GS	CG	ShO	Sv.	IP	H	R	ER	BB	SO
1991— National	0	0	...	...	0	0	0	0	0	1	1	1	0	0
1995— National	0	0	...	9.00	0	0	0	0	2	2	2	2	0	0
All-Star totals (2 years)	0	0	...	13.50	0	0	0	0	2	3	3	3	0	0

SMITH, BOBBY   SS   DEVIL RAYS

PERSONAL: Born May 10, 1974, in Oakland. ... 6-3/190. ... Bats right, throws right. ... Full name: Robert Eugene Smith.
HIGH SCHOOL: Fremont (Oakland).
TRANSACTIONS/CAREER NOTES: Selected by Atlanta Braves organization in 11th round of free-agent draft (June 1, 1992). ... Selected by Tampa Bay Devil Rays in first round (12th pick overall) of expansion draft (November 18, 1997).
STATISTICAL NOTES: Tied for Carolina League lead in grounding into double plays with 19 in 1994. ... Led Carolina League third basemen with 388 total chances and 27 double plays in 1994.

Year — Team (League)	Pos.	G	AB	R	H	2B	3B	HR	RBI	Avg.	BB	SO	SB	PO	A	E	Avg.
1992— GC Braves (GCL)	3B	57	217	31	51	9	1	3	28	.235	17	55	5	37	115	15	.910
1993— Macon (S. Atl.)	3B	108	384	53	94	16	7	4	38	.245	23	81	12	65	167	30	.885
1994— Durham (Carolina)	3B	127	478	49	127	27	2	12	71	.266	41	112	18	104	253	31	*.920
1995— Greenville (Southern)	3B	127	444	75	116	27	3	14	58	.261	40	109	12	*120	265	26	.937
1996— Richmond (Int'l)	3B-SS	124	445	49	114	27	0	8	58	.256	32	114	15	116	228	24	.935
1997— Richmond (Int'l)	SS	100	357	47	88	10	2	12	47	.246	44	109	6	161	297	*23	.952

SMITH, CAM   P   MARINERS

PERSONAL: Born September 20, 1973, in Brooklyn, N.Y. ... 6-3/190. ... Throws right, bats right. ... Full name: Cameron Smith.
COLLEGE: Ithaca (N.Y.) College.
TRANSACTIONS/CAREER NOTES: Selected by Detroit Tigers organization in third round of free-agent draft (June 3, 1993). ... On disabled list (May 31-June 14, 1996). ... Traded by Tigers with P Joey Eischen to San Diego Padres for C Brian Johnson and P Willie Blair (December 17, 1996). ... On disabled list (June 2-12, 1997). ... Claimed on waivers by Seattle Mariners (November 26, 1997).
STATISTICAL NOTES: Led South Atlantic League with 21 wild pitches and 18 hit batsmen in 1995.

Year — Team (League)	W	L	Pct.	ERA	G	GS	CG	ShO	Sv.	IP	H	R	ER	BB	SO
1993— Bristol (Appalachian)	3	1	.750	3.58	9	7	1	0	0	37 2/3	25	22	15	22	33
— Niagara Falls (NYP)	0	0	...	18.00	2	2	0	0	0	5	12	11	10	6	0
1994— Fayetteville (S. Atl.)	5	13	.278	6.06	26	26	1	0	0	133 2/3	133	100	90	86	128
1995— Fayetteville (S. Atl.)	13	8	.619	3.81	29	*29	2	2	0	149	110	75	63	87	166
1996— Lakeland (Fla. St.)	5	8	.385	4.59	22	21	0	0	0	113 2/3	93	64	58	71	114
1997— Mobile (Southern)■	3	5	.375	7.03	26	15	0	0	1	79 1/3	85	70	62	73	88

SMITH, DANNY   P   RANGERS

PERSONAL: Born April 20, 1969, in St. Paul, Minn. ... 6-5/195. ... Throws left, bats left. ... Full name: Daniel Scott Smith.
HIGH SCHOOL: Apple Valley (Minn.).
COLLEGE: Creighton.
TRANSACTIONS/CAREER NOTES: Selected by Minnesota Twins organization in 22nd round of free-agent draft (June 2, 1987); did not sign. ... Selected by Texas Rangers organization in first round (16th pick overall) of free-agent draft (June 4, 1990). ... On Tulsa disabled list (August 5-20, 1992). ... On Texas disabled list (March 27-May 18, 1993); included rehabilitation assignment to Charlotte (May 17-18). ... On Oklahoma City disabled list (June 23-September 1, 1993). ... On Texas disabled list (September 1, 1993-remainder of season). ... On Texas disabled list (March 26-June 2, 1994); included rehabilitation assignment to Charlotte (May 28-June 2). ... On disabled list (April 16, 1995-entire season). ... On Oklahoma City disabled list (April 12-May 26, 1996). ... Granted free agency (October 15, 1997). ... Re-signed by Rangers (January 8, 1998).
HONORS: Named Texas League Pitcher of the Year (1992).

Year — Team (League)	W	L	Pct.	ERA	G	GS	CG	ShO	Sv.	IP	H	R	ER	BB	SO
1990— Butte (Pioneer)	2	0	1.000	3.65	5	5	0	0	0	24 2/3	23	10	10	6	27
— Tulsa (Texas)	3	2	.600	3.76	7	7	0	0	0	38 1/3	27	16	16	16	32
1991— Oklahoma City (A.A.)	4	*17	.190	5.52	28	27	3	0	0	151 2/3	*195	*114	*93	75	85
1992— Tulsa (Texas)	11	7	.611	*2.52	24	23	4	*3	0	146 1/3	110	48	41	34	122
— Texas (A.L.)	0	3	.000	5.02	4	2	0	0	0	14 1/3	18	8	8	8	5
1993— Charlotte (Fla. St.)	1	0	1.000	0.00	1	1	0	0	0	7	3	0	0	0	5
— Oklahoma City (A.A.)	1	2	.333	4.70	3	3	0	0	0	15 1/3	16	11	8	5	12
1994— Charlotte (Fla. St.)	0	0	...	0.00	2	0	0	0	0	3 2/3	2	0	0	2	3
— Oklahoma City (A.A.)	2	1	.667	2.84	10	2	0	0	2	25 1/3	27	9	8	9	15
— Texas (A.L.)	1	2	.333	4.30	13	0	0	0	0	14 2/3	18	11	7	12	9
1995—								Did not play.							

Year Team (League)	W	L	Pct.	ERA	G	GS	CG	ShO	Sv.	IP	H	R	ER	BB	SO
1996—Oklahoma City (A.A.)	0	2	.000	9.00	5	5	0	0	0	15	27	19	15	7	12
—Charlotte (Fla. St.)	0	1	.000	2.74	5	5	0	0	0	23	21	7	7	8	16
—Tulsa (Texas)	2	3	.400	4.29	9	9	0	0	0	50 1/3	53	27	24	21	29
1997—Tulsa (Texas)	1	1	.500	3.64	5	5	0	0	0	29 2/3	25	18	12	15	27
—Oklahoma City (A.A.)	3	*14	.176	5.64	23	23	3	1	0	129 1/3	154	88	81	42	67
Major league totals (2 years)	1	5	.167	4.66	17	2	0	0	0	29	36	19	15	20	14

SMITH, LEE　　　　　　　　　　P　　　　　　　　　　ROYALS

PERSONAL: Born December 4, 1957, in Jamestown, La. ... 6-6/269. ... Throws right, bats right. ... Full name: Lee Arthur Smith.
HIGH SCHOOL: Castor (La.).
COLLEGE: Northwestern (La.) State.
TRANSACTIONS/CAREER NOTES: Selected by Chicago Cubs organization in second round of free-agent draft (June 4, 1975). ... On disabled list (April 21-May 6, 1986). ... Traded by Cubs to Boston Red Sox for P Al Nipper and P Calvin Schiraldi (December 8, 1987). ... Traded by Red Sox to St. Louis Cardinals for OF Tom Brunansky (May 4, 1990). ... Traded by Cardinals to New York Yankees for P Richard Batchelor (August 31, 1993). ... Granted free agency (October 25, 1993). ... Signed by Baltimore Orioles (January 29, 1994). ... Granted free agency (October 24, 1994). ... Signed by California Angels (December 14, 1994). ... On California disabled list (April 4-23, 1996); included rehabilitation assignment to Lake Elsinore (April 19-23). ... Traded by Angels to Cincinnati Reds for P Chuck McElroy (May 27, 1996). ... Granted free agency (October 29, 1996). ... Signed by Montreal Expos organization (January 21, 1997). ... Announced retirement (July 15, 1997). ... Signed by Kansas City Royals organization (January 20, 1998).
RECORDS: Holds major league career records for most saves—478; and most consecutive errorless games by pitcher—546 (July 5, 1982 through September 22, 1992). ... Holds N.L. career record for most saves—347.
HONORS: Named N.L. co-Fireman of the Year by THE SPORTING NEWS (1983 and 1992). ... Named N.L. Fireman of the Year by THE SPORTING NEWS (1991). ... Named A.L. Fireman of the Year by THE SPORTING NEWS (1994).
STATISTICAL NOTES: Tied for American Association lead with 16 wild pitches in 1980.
MISCELLANEOUS: Holds Chicago Cubs all-time record for most saves (180). ... Holds St. Louis Cardinals all-time record for most saves (160).

Year Team (League)	W	L	Pct.	ERA	G	GS	CG	ShO	Sv.	IP	H	R	ER	BB	SO
1975—GC Cubs (GCL)	3	5	.375	2.32	10	10	2	1	0	62	35	23	16	*49	35
1976—Pomp. Beach (FSL)	4	8	.333	5.35	26	18	2	1	0	101	120	76	60	74	52
1977—Pomp. Beach (FSL)	10	4	.714	4.29	26	18	4	0	0	130	131	67	62	85	82
1978—Midland (Texas)	8	10	.444	5.98	30	25	3	0	0	155	161	122	103	*128	71
1979—Midland (Texas)	9	5	.643	4.93	35	9	0	0	1	104	122	65	57	85	46
1980—Wichita (Am. Assoc.)	4	7	.364	3.70	50	2	0	0	15	90	70	49	37	56	63
—Chicago (N.L.)	2	0	1.000	2.86	18	0	0	0	0	22	21	9	7	14	17
1981—Chicago (N.L.)	3	6	.333	3.49	40	1	0	0	1	67	57	31	26	31	50
1982—Chicago (N.L.)	2	5	.286	2.69	72	5	0	0	17	117	105	38	35	37	99
1983—Chicago (N.L.)	4	10	.286	1.65	66	0	0	0	*29	103 1/3	70	23	19	41	91
1984—Chicago (N.L.)	9	7	.563	3.65	69	0	0	0	33	101	98	42	41	35	86
1985—Chicago (N.L.)	7	4	.636	3.04	65	0	0	0	33	97 2/3	87	35	33	32	112
1986—Chicago (N.L.)	9	9	.500	3.09	66	0	0	0	31	90 1/3	69	32	31	42	93
1987—Chicago (N.L.)	4	10	.286	3.12	62	0	0	0	36	83 2/3	84	30	29	32	96
1988—Boston (A.L.)■	4	5	.444	2.80	64	0	0	0	29	83 2/3	72	34	26	37	96
1989—Boston (A.L.)	6	1	.857	3.57	64	0	0	0	25	70 2/3	53	30	28	33	96
1990—Boston (A.L.)	2	1	.667	1.88	11	0	0	0	4	14 1/3	13	4	3	9	17
—St. Louis (N.L.)■	3	4	.429	2.10	53	0	0	0	27	68 2/3	58	20	16	20	70
1991—St. Louis (N.L.)	6	3	.667	2.34	67	0	0	0	*47	73	70	19	19	13	67
1992—St. Louis (N.L.)	4	9	.308	3.12	70	0	0	0	*43	75	62	28	26	26	60
1993—St. Louis (N.L.)	2	4	.333	4.50	55	0	0	0	43	50	49	25	25	9	49
—New York (A.L.)■	0	0	...	0.00	8	0	0	0	3	8	4	0	0	5	11
1994—Baltimore (A.L.)■	1	4	.200	3.29	41	0	0	0	*33	38 1/3	34	16	14	11	42
1995—California (A.L.)	0	5	.000	3.47	52	0	0	0	37	49 1/3	42	19	19	25	43
1996—Lake Elsinore (Calif.)	0	0	...	9.00	1	1	0	0	0	1	1	2	1	1	1
—California (A.L.)	0	0	...	2.45	11	0	0	0	0	11	8	4	3	3	6
—Cincinnati (N.L.)■	3	4	.429	4.06	43	0	0	0	2	44 1/3	49	20	20	23	35
1997—Montreal (N.L.)■	0	1	.000	5.82	25	0	0	0	5	21 2/3	28	16	14	8	15
A.L. totals (7 years)	13	16	.448	3.04	251	0	0	0	131	275 1/3	226	107	93	123	311
N.L. totals (14 years)	58	76	.433	3.02	771	6	0	0	347	1014 2/3	907	368	341	363	940
Major league totals (18 years)	71	92	.436	3.03	1022	6	0	0	478	1290	1133	475	434	486	1251

CHAMPIONSHIP SERIES RECORD

Year Team (League)	W	L	Pct.	ERA	G	GS	CG	ShO	Sv.	IP	H	R	ER	BB	SO
1984—Chicago (N.L.)	0	1	.000	9.00	2	0	0	0	1	2	3	2	2	0	3
1988—Boston (A.L.)	0	1	.000	8.10	2	0	0	0	0	3 1/3	6	3	3	1	4
Champ. series totals (2 years)	0	2	.000	8.44	4	0	0	0	1	5 1/3	9	5	5	1	7

ALL-STAR GAME RECORD

Year League	W	L	Pct.	ERA	GS	CG	ShO	Sv.	IP	H	R	ER	BB	SO
1983—National	0	0	...	9.00	0	0	0	0	1	2	2	1	0	1
1987—National	1	0	1.000	0.00	0	0	0	0	3	2	0	0	0	4
1991—National						Did not play.								
1992—National						Did not play.								
1993—National						Did not play.								
1994—American	0	0	...	18.00	0	0	0	0	1	1	2	2	1	0
1995—American						Did not play.								
All-Star totals (3 years)	1	0	1.000	5.40	0	0	0	0	5	5	4	3	1	5

SMITH, MARK　　　　　　　　　　OF　　　　　　　　　　PIRATES

PERSONAL: Born May 7, 1970, in Pasadena, Calif. ... 6-4/195. ... Bats right, throws right. ... Full name: Mark Edward Smith.
HIGH SCHOOL: Arcadia (Calif.).
COLLEGE: Southern California.

TRANSACTIONS/CAREER NOTES: Selected by Baltimore Orioles organization in first round (ninth pick overall) of free-agent draft (June 3, 1991). ... On Baltimore disabled list (July 23, 1996-remainder of season); included rehabilitation assignments to Frederick (August 12-13), Bowie (August 21-23) and Rochester (September 3-13). ... Traded by Orioles to San Diego Padres for C Leroy McKinnis (January 9, 1997). ... Traded by Padres with P Hal Garrett to Pittsburgh Pirates for OF Trey Beamon and OF Angelo Encarnacion (March 29, 1997). ... On Pittsburgh disabled list (May 23-June 14, 1997); included rehabilitation assignment to Carolina (June 12-14).

Year Team (League)	Pos.	G	AB	R	H	2B	3B	HR	RBI	Avg.	BB	SO	SB	PO	A	E	Avg.
1991— Frederick (Carolina)....	OF	38	148	20	37	5	1	4	29	.250	9	24	1	49	1	1	.980
1992— Hagerstown (Eastern)	OF	128	472	51	136	*32	6	4	62	.288	45	55	15	226	9	4	.983
1993— Rochester (Int'l)	OF	129	485	69	136	27	1	12	68	.280	37	90	4	261	9	7	.975
1994— Rochester (Int'l)	OF	114	437	69	108	27	1	19	66	.247	35	88	4	207	9	5	.977
— Baltimore (A.L.)..........	OF	3	7	0	1	0	0	0	2	.143	0	2	0	8	0	0	1.000
1995— Rochester (Int'l)	OF	96	364	55	101	25	3	12	66	.277	24	69	7	167	4	7	.961
— Baltimore (A.L.)..........	OF-DH	37	104	11	24	5	0	3	15	.231	12	22	3	60	2	0	1.000
1996— Rochester (Int'l)	OF	39	132	24	46	14	1	8	32	.348	14	22	10	55	1	2	.966
— Baltimore (A.L.)..........	OF-DH	27	78	9	19	2	0	4	10	.244	3	20	0	50	0	1	.980
— Frederick (Carolina)....	DH	1	1	0	0	0	0	0	0	.000	0	0	0	0	0	0	...
— Bowie (Eastern)........	DH	6	22	1	2	0	0	1	2	.091	1	6	0	0	0	0	...
1997— Calgary (PCL)■........	OF	39	137	37	51	14	1	14	42	.372	21	15	2	55	1	1	.982
— Pittsburgh (N.L.)	OF-1B-DH	71	193	29	55	13	1	9	35	.285	28	36	3	111	9	0	1.000
— Carolina (Southern)...	OF	3	12	5	5	1	0	3	4	.417	0	1	0	4	0	1	.800
American League totals (3 years)		67	189	20	44	7	0	7	27	.233	15	44	3	118	2	1	.992
National League totals (1 year)		71	193	29	55	13	1	9	35	.285	28	36	3	111	9	0	1.000
Major league totals (4 years)		138	382	49	99	20	1	16	62	.259	43	80	6	229	11	1	.996

SMITH, PETE — P — PADRES

PERSONAL: Born February 27, 1966, in Weymouth, Mass. ... 6-2/200. ... Throws right, bats right. ... Full name: Peter John Smith.
HIGH SCHOOL: Burlington (Mass.).
TRANSACTIONS/CAREER NOTES: Selected by Philadelphia Phillies organization in first round (21st pick overall) of free-agent draft (June 4, 1984). ... Traded by Phillies organization with C Ozzie Virgil to Atlanta Braves for P Steve Bedrosian and OF Milt Thompson (December 10, 1985). ... On Atlanta disabled list (June 25-September 3, 1990); included rehabilitation assignment to Greenville (August 26-September 2). ... On Atlanta disabled list (April 4-May 23, 1991); included rehabilitation assignments to Macon (April 12-24) and Richmond (April 24-May 9 and May 13-14). ... On disabled list (July 25-September 1, 1993). ... Traded by Braves to New York Mets for OF Dave Gallagher (November 24, 1993). ... On disabled list (July 18-August 7, 1994). ... Granted free agency (October 25, 1994). ... Signed by Cincinnati Reds (December 1, 1994). ... Released by Reds (June 27, 1995). ... Signed by Charlotte, Florida Marlins organization (July 1, 1995). ... Granted free agency (October 16, 1995). ... Signed by Las Vegas, San Diego Padres organization (December 23, 1995). ... Granted free agency (October 15, 1996). ... Granted free agency (October 30, 1997). ... Re-signed by Padres (December 16, 1997).
STATISTICAL NOTES: Led N.L. with seven balks in 1989. ... Pitched seven-inning, 1-0 no-hit victory for Richmond against Rochester (May 3, 1992). ... Led N.L. with 25 home runs allowed in 1997.
MISCELLANEOUS: Appeared in one game as pinch-runner (1989). ... Appeared in one game as pinch-runner (1997).

Year Team (League)	W	L	Pct.	ERA	G	GS	CG	ShO	Sv.	IP	H	R	ER	BB	SO
1984— GC Phillies (GCL)	1	2	.333	1.46	8	8	0	0	0	37	28	11	6	16	35
1985— Clearwater (Fla. St.)	12	10	.545	3.29	26	25	4	1	0	153	135	68	56	80	86
1986— Greenville (Southern)■	1	8	.111	5.85	24	19	0	0	0	104 2/3	117	88	68	78	64
1987— Greenville (Southern)	9	9	.500	3.35	29	25	5	1	1	177 1/3	162	76	66	67	119
— Atlanta (N.L.).....................	1	2	.333	4.83	6	6	0	0	0	31 2/3	39	21	17	14	11
1988— Atlanta (N.L.)...............	7	15	.318	3.69	32	32	5	3	0	195 1/3	183	89	80	88	124
1989— Atlanta (N.L.)...............	5	14	.263	4.75	28	27	1	0	0	142	144	83	75	57	115
1990— Atlanta (N.L.)...............	5	6	.455	4.79	13	13	3	0	0	77	77	45	41	24	56
— Greenville (Southern)	0	0	...	0.00	2	2	0	0	0	3 1/3	1	0	0	0	2
1991— Macon (S. Atl.).............	0	0	...	8.38	3	3	0	0	0	9 2/3	15	11	9	2	14
— Richmond (Int'l)...............	3	3	.500	7.24	10	10	1	0	0	51	66	44	41	24	41
— Atlanta (N.L.)...............	1	3	.250	5.06	14	6	0	0	0	48	48	33	27	22	29
1992— Richmond (Int'l)...............	7	4	.636	2.14	15	15	4	1	0	109 1/3	75	27	26	24	93
— Atlanta (N.L.)...............	7	0	1.000	2.05	12	11	2	1	0	79	63	19	18	28	43
1993— Atlanta (N.L.)...............	4	8	.333	4.37	20	14	0	0	0	90 2/3	92	45	44	36	53
1994— New York (N.L.)■.........	4	10	.286	5.55	21	21	1	0	0	131 1/3	145	83	81	42	62
1995— Cincinnati (N.L.).............	1	2	.333	6.66	11	2	0	0	0	24 1/3	30	19	18	7	14
— Charlotte (Int'l)■.............	2	1	.667	3.86	10	8	0	0	0	49	51	21	21	20	20
1996— Las Vegas (PCL)■.............	11	9	.550	4.95	26	26	2	1	0	169	192	106	93	42	95
1997— Las Vegas (PCL)	3	2	.600	4.28	6	6	0	0	0	33 2/3	38	16	16	6	24
— San Diego (N.L.)	7	6	.538	4.81	37	15	0	0	1	118	120	66	63	52	68
Major league totals (10 years)....	42	66	.389	4.46	194	151	12	4	1	937 1/3	941	503	464	370	575

CHAMPIONSHIP SERIES RECORD

Year Team (League)	W	L	Pct.	ERA	G	GS	CG	ShO	Sv.	IP	H	R	ER	BB	SO
1992— Atlanta (N.L.).....................	0	0	...	2.45	2	0	0	0	0	3 2/3	2	1	1	3	3

WORLD SERIES RECORD

Year Team (League)	W	L	Pct.	ERA	G	GS	CG	ShO	Sv.	IP	H	R	ER	BB	SO
1992— Atlanta (N.L.).....................	0	0	...	0.00	1	0	0	0	0	3	3	0	0	0	0

SMOLTZ, JOHN — P — BRAVES

PERSONAL: Born May 15, 1967, in Warren, Mich. ... 6-3/185. ... Throws right, bats right. ... Full name: John Andrew Smoltz.
HIGH SCHOOL: Waverly (Lansing, Mich.).
TRANSACTIONS/CAREER NOTES: Selected by Detroit Tigers organization in 22nd round of free-agent draft (June 3, 1985). ... Traded by Tigers organization to Atlanta Braves for P Doyle Alexander (August 12, 1987). ... On suspended list (June 20-29, 1994). ... Granted free agency (October 31, 1996). ... Re-signed by Braves (November 20, 1996).

RECORDS: Shares major league record for most home runs allowed in one inning—4 (June 19, 1994, first inning).
HONORS: Named N.L. Pitcher of the Year by THE SPORTING NEWS (1996). ... Named righthanded pitcher on THE SPORTING NEWS N.L. All-Star team (1996). ... Named N.L. Cy Young Award winner by Baseball Writers' Association of America (1996). ... Named pitcher on THE SPORTING NEWS N.L. Silver Slugger team (1997).
STATISTICAL NOTES: Tied for Florida State League lead with six balks in 1986. ... Led N.L. with 14 wild pitches in 1990, 20 in 1991 and 17 in 1992. ... Struck out 15 batters in one game (May 24, 1992).
MISCELLANEOUS: Appeared in three games as pinch-runner and struck out in only appearance in pinch-hitter (1989). ... Appeared in four games as pinch-runner (1990). ... Appeared in two games as pinch-runner (1991). ... Struck out in only appearance as pinch-hitter (1992). ... Appeared in one game as pinch-runner (1997).

Year Team (League)	W	L	Pct.	ERA	G	GS	CG	ShO	Sv.	IP	H	R	ER	BB	SO
1986— Lakeland (Fla. St.)	7	8	.467	3.56	17	14	2	1	0	96	86	44	38	31	47
1987— Glens Falls (Eastern)	4	10	.286	5.68	21	21	0	0	0	130	131	89	82	81	86
— Richmond (Int'l)■	0	1	.000	6.19	3	3	0	0	0	16	17	11	11	11	5
1988— Richmond (Int'l)	10	5	.667	2.79	20	20	3	0	0	135 1/3	118	49	42	37	115
— Atlanta (N.L.)	2	7	.222	5.48	12	12	0	0	0	64	74	40	39	33	37
1989— Atlanta (N.L.)	12	11	.522	2.94	29	29	5	0	0	208	160	79	68	72	168
1990— Atlanta (N.L.)	14	11	.560	3.85	34	34	6	2	0	231 1/3	206	109	99	*90	170
1991— Atlanta (N.L.)	14	13	.519	3.80	36	36	5	0	0	229 2/3	206	101	97	77	148
1992— Atlanta (N.L.)	15	12	.556	2.85	35	•35	9	3	0	246 2/3	206	90	78	80	*215
1993— Atlanta (N.L.)	15	11	.577	3.62	35	35	3	1	0	243 2/3	208	104	98	100	208
1994— Atlanta (N.L.)	6	10	.375	4.14	21	21	1	0	0	134 2/3	120	69	62	48	113
1995— Atlanta (N.L.)	12	7	.632	3.18	29	29	2	1	0	192 2/3	166	76	68	72	193
1996— Atlanta (N.L.)	*24	8	*.750	2.94	35	35	6	2	0	*253 2/3	199	93	83	55	*276
1997— Atlanta (N.L.)	15	12	.556	3.02	35	•35	7	2	0	*256	*234	97	86	63	241
Major league totals (10 years)	129	102	.558	3.40	301	301	44	11	0	2060 1/3	1779	858	778	690	1769

DIVISION SERIES RECORD

RECORDS: Holds N.L. single-game record for most strikeouts—11 (October 3, 1997). ... Holds N.L. career record for most strikeouts—24.

Year Team (League)	W	L	Pct.	ERA	G	GS	CG	ShO	Sv.	IP	H	R	ER	BB	SO
1995— Atlanta (N.L.)	0	0	...	7.94	1	1	0	0	0	5 2/3	5	5	5	1	6
1996— Atlanta (N.L.)	1	0	1.000	1.00	1	1	0	0	0	9	4	1	1	2	7
1997— Atlanta (N.L.)	1	0	1.000	1.00	1	1	1	0	0	9	3	1	1	1	11
Div. series totals (3 years)	2	0	1.000	2.66	3	3	1	0	0	23 2/3	12	7	7	4	24

CHAMPIONSHIP SERIES RECORD

RECORDS: Shares N.L. single-series record for most bases on balls allowed—10 (1992). ... Holds career record for most strikeouts—67; and most games started—9. ... Shares career record for most bases on balls allowed—28. ... Holds N.L. career record for most innings pitched—70; and most wins—6. ... Shares N.L. career record most series with one team—6 (Atlanta, 1991-93 and 1995-97).
NOTES: Named N.L. Championship Series Most Valuable Player (1992).

Year Team (League)	W	L	Pct.	ERA	G	GS	CG	ShO	Sv.	IP	H	R	ER	BB	SO
1991— Atlanta (N.L.)	2	0	1.000	1.76	2	2	1	1	0	15 1/3	14	3	3	3	15
1992— Atlanta (N.L.)	2	0	1.000	2.66	3	3	0	0	0	20 1/3	14	7	6	10	19
1993— Atlanta (N.L.)	0	1	.000	0.00	1	1	0	0	0	6 1/3	8	2	0	5	10
1995— Atlanta (N.L.)	0	0	...	2.57	1	1	0	0	0	7	7	2	2	2	2
1996— Atlanta (N.L.)	2	0	1.000	1.20	2	2	0	0	0	15	12	2	2	3	12
1997— Atlanta (N.L.)	0	1	.000	7.50	1	1	0	0	0	6.	5	5	5	5	9
Champ. series totals (6 years)	6	2	.750	2.31	10	10	1	1	0	70	60	21	18	28	67

WORLD SERIES RECORD

NOTES: Appeared in one game as pinch-runner (1992). ... Member of World Series championship team (1995).

Year Team (League)	W	L	Pct.	ERA	G	GS	CG	ShO	Sv.	IP	H	R	ER	BB	SO
1991— Atlanta (N.L.)	0	0	...	1.26	2	2	0	0	0	14 1/3	13	2	2	1	11
1992— Atlanta (N.L.)	1	0	1.000	2.70	2	2	0	0	0	13 1/3	13	5	4	7	12
1995— Atlanta (N.L.)	0	0	...	15.43	1	1	0	0	0	2 1/3	6	4	4	2	4
1996— Atlanta (N.L.)	1	1	.500	0.64	2	2	0	0	0	14	6	2	1	8	14
World Series totals (4 years)	2	1	.667	2.25	7	7	0	0	0	44	38	13	11	18	41

ALL-STAR GAME RECORD

RECORDS: Shares single-game record for most wild pitches—2 (July 13, 1993). ... Shares record for most wild pitches in one inning—2 (July 13, 1993, sixth inning).

Year League	W	L	Pct.	ERA	GS	CG	ShO	Sv.	IP	H	R	ER	BB	SO
1989— National	0	1	.000	9.00	0	0	0	0	1	2	1	1	0	0
1992— National	0	0	...	0.00	0	0	0	0	1/3	1	0	0	0	0
1993— National	0	0	...	0.00	0	0	0	0	1/3	1	0	0	1	0
1996— National	1	0	1.000	0.00	1	0	0	0	2	2	0	0	0	1
All-Star totals (4 years)	1	1	.500	2.45	1	0	0	0	3 2/3	5	1	1	1	1

SNOPEK, CHRIS   3B/SS   WHITE SOX

PERSONAL: Born September 20, 1970, in Cynthiana, Ky. ... 6-1/185. ... Bats right, throws right. ... Full name: Christopher Charles Snopek.
HIGH SCHOOL: Harrison County (Cynthiana, Ky.).
COLLEGE: Mississippi.
TRANSACTIONS/CAREER NOTES: Selected by Texas Rangers organization in 11th round of free-agent draft (June 5, 1989); did not sign. ... Selected by Chicago White Sox organization in sixth round of free-agent draft (June 1, 1992).
STATISTICAL NOTES: Led New York-Pennsylvania League third baseman with 18 double plays in 1992. ... Led Southern League third basemen with 29 double plays in 1994.

Year Team (League)	Pos.	G	AB	R	H	2B	3B	HR	RBI	Avg.	BB	SO	SB	PO	A	E	Avg.
1992— Utica (N.Y.-Penn)	3B-SS	73	245	49	69	15	1	2	29	.282	*52	44	14	48	151	11	.948
1993— South Bend (Mid.)	3B	22	72	20	28	8	1	5	18	.389	15	13	1	19	51	3	.959
— Sarasota (Fla. St.)	3B-SS	107	371	61	91	21	4	10	50	.245	65	67	3	94	240	24	.933

Year Team (League)	Pos.	G	AB	R	H	2B	3B	HR	RBI	Avg.	BB	SO	SB	PO	A	E	Avg.
1994— Birmingham (Sou.).....	3B-SS	106	365	58	96	25	3	6	54	.263	58	49	9	89	312	25	.941
1995— Nashville (A.A.)	SS-3B	113	393	56	127	23	4	12	55	.323	50	72	2	133	358	32	.939
— Chicago (A.L.)	SS-3B	22	68	12	22	4	0	1	7	.324	9	12	1	25	31	2	.966
1996— Chicago (A.L.)	3B-SS-DH	46	104	18	27	6	1	6	18	.260	6	16	0	25	65	5	.947
— Nashville (A.A.)	SS-3B	40	153	18	38	8	0	2	12	.248	21	24	2	38	107	6	.960
1997— Chicago (A.L.)	3B-SS	86	298	27	65	15	0	5	35	.218	18	51	3	61	125	16	.921
— Nashville (A.A.)	SS-3B	20	73	8	17	4	0	3	8	.233	7	13	0	29	52	3	.964
Major league totals (3 years)		154	470	57	114	25	1	12	60	.243	33	79	4	111	221	23	.935

SNOW, J.T.   1B   GIANTS

PERSONAL: Born February 26, 1968, in Long Beach, Calif. ... 6-2/202. ... Bats both, throws left. ... Full name: Jack Thomas Snow Jr. ... Son of Jack Snow, wide receiver, Los Angeles Rams (1965-75).
HIGH SCHOOL: Los Alamitos (Calif.).
COLLEGE: Arizona.
TRANSACTIONS/CAREER NOTES: Selected by New York Yankees organization in fifth round of free-agent draft (June 5, 1989). ... Traded by Yankees with P Jerry Nielsen and P Russ Springer to California Angels for P Jim Abbott (December 6, 1992). ... Traded by Angels to San Francisco Giants for P Allen Watson and P Fausto Macey (November 27, 1996).
HONORS: Named International League Most Valuable Player (1992). ... Won A.L. Gold Glove at first base (1995-96). ... Won N.L. Gold Glove at first base (1997).
STATISTICAL NOTES: Led New York-Pennsylvania League first basemen with 649 total chances in 1989. ... Led Carolina League in grounding into double plays with 20 in 1990. ... Led Carolina League first basemen with 1,298 total chances and 120 double plays in 1990. ... Tied for Eastern League lead with 10 sacrifice flies in 1991. ... Led Eastern League first basemen with 1,200 total chances in 1991. ... Led International League with 11 intentional bases on balls received in 1992. ... Led International League first basemen with .995 fielding percentage, 1,097 putouts, 93 assists, 1,196 total chances and 107 double plays in 1992. ... Switch-hit home runs in one game (June 9, 1996). ... Career major league grand slams: 3.

Year Team (League)	Pos.	G	AB	R	H	2B	3B	HR	RBI	Avg.	BB	SO	SB	PO	A	E	Avg.
1989— Oneonta (NYP)..........	1B	73	274	41	80	18	2	8	51	.292	29	35	4	*590	53	6	*.991
1990— Prince William (Car.) ..	1B	*138	520	57	133	25	1	8	72	.256	46	65	2	*1208	*78	12	.991
1991— Alb./Colon. (Eastern)..	1B	132	477	78	133	33	3	13	76	.279	67	78	5	*1102	90	8	*.993
1992— Columbus (Int'l)........	1B-OF	135	492	81	154	26	4	15	78	•.313	70	65	3	†1103	†93	2	†.993
— New York (A.L.)	1B-DH	7	14	1	2	1	0	0	2	.143	5	5	0	43	2	0	1.000
1993— California (A.L.)■......	1B	129	419	60	101	18	2	16	57	.241	55	88	3	1010	81	6	.995
— Vancouver (PCL)	1B	23	94	19	32	9	1	5	24	.340	10	13	0	200	13	2	.991
1994— Vancouver (PCL)	1B	53	189	35	56	13	2	8	43	.296	22	32	1	413	42	1	.998
— California (A.L.)	1B	61	223	22	49	4	0	8	30	.220	19	48	0	489	37	2	.996
1995— California (A.L.)	1B	143	544	80	157	22	1	24	102	.289	52	91	2	1161	57	4	.997
1996— California (A.L.)	1B	155	575	69	148	20	1	17	67	.257	56	96	1	1274	103	10	.993
1997— San Fran. (N.L.)■......	1B	157	531	81	149	36	1	28	104	.281	96	124	6	1308	108	7	.995
American League totals (5 years)		495	1775	232	457	65	4	65	258	.257	187	328	6	3977	280	22	.995
National League totals (1 year)		157	531	81	149	36	1	28	104	.281	96	124	6	1308	108	7	.995
Major league totals (6 years)		652	2306	313	606	101	5	93	362	.263	283	452	12	5285	388	29	.995

DIVISION SERIES RECORD

Year Team (League)	Pos.	G	AB	R	H	2B	3B	HR	RBI	Avg.	BB	SO	SB	PO	A	E	Avg.
1997— San Francisco (N.L.) ..	1B	3	6	0	1	0	0	0	0	.167	1	1	0	12	0	0	1.000

SNYDER, JOHN   P   WHITE SOX

PERSONAL: Born August 16, 1974, in Southfield, Mich. ... 6-3/185. ... Throws right, bats right. ... Full name: John Michael Snyder.
HIGH SCHOOL: Westlake (Westlake Village, Calif.).
TRANSACTIONS/CAREER NOTES: Selected by California Angels organization in 13th round of free-agent draft (June 1, 1992). ... Traded by Angels with P Andrew Lorraine, P Bill Simas and OF McKay Christensen to Chicago White Sox for P Jim Abbott and P Tim Fortugno (July 27, 1995). ... On Gulf Coast disabled list (July 21, 1996-remainder of season). ... On disabled list (April 3-May 4, 1997).

Year Team (League)	W	L	Pct.	ERA	G	GS	CG	ShO	Sv.	IP	H	R	ER	BB	SO
1992— Ariz. Angels (Ariz.)	2	4	.333	3.27	15	0	0	0	3	44	40	27	16	16	38
1993— Cedar Rapids (Midw.)	5	6	.455	5.91	21	16	1	1	0	99	125	88	65	39	79
1994— Lake Elsinore (Calif.)	10	11	.476	4.47	26	26	2	0	0	159	181	101	79	56	108
1995— Midland (Texas)	8	9	.471	5.74	21	21	0	0	0	133 1/3	158	93	85	48	81
— Birmingham (Southern)■ ..	1	0	1.000	6.64	5	4	0	0	0	20 1/3	24	16	15	6	13
1996— Birmingham (Southern)	3	5	.375	4.83	9	9	0	0	0	54	59	35	29	16	58
— GC White Sox (GCL)	1	0	1.000	1.65	4	4	0	0	0	16 1/3	5	3	3	4	23
1997— Birmingham (Southern)	7	8	.467	4.64	20	20	2	1	0	114 1/3	130	76	59	43	90

SODERSTROM, STEVE   P   GIANTS

PERSONAL: Born April 3, 1972, in Turlock, Calif. ... 6-3/215. ... Throws right, bats right. ... Full name: Stephen Andrew Soderstrom.
HIGH SCHOOL: Turlock (Calif.).
COLLEGE: Fresno State.
TRANSACTIONS/CAREER NOTES: Selected by New York Mets organization in 15th round of free-agent draft (June 4, 1990); did not sign. ... Selected by San Francisco Giants organization in first round (sixth pick overall) of free-agent draft (June 3, 1993). ... On disabled list (June 25-July 12, 1997).
STATISTICAL NOTES: Tied for Texas League lead with 10 hit batsmen in 1995.

Year Team (League)	W	L	Pct.	ERA	G	GS	CG	ShO	Sv.	IP	H	R	ER	BB	SO
1994—San Jose (California)	2	3	.400	4.20	8	8	0	0	0	40 2/3	34	20	19	26	40
1995—Shreveport (Texas)	9	5	.643	3.41	22	22	0	0	0	116	106	53	44	51	91
1996—Phoenix (PCL)	7	8	.467	4.41	29	29	0	0	0	171 1/3	178	94	84	58	80
—San Francisco (N.L.)	2	0	1.000	5.27	3	3	0	0	0	13 2/3	16	11	8	6	9
1997—Phoenix (PCL)	4	8	.333	6.47	31	15	0	0	1	105 2/3	141	81	76	52	78
Major league totals (1 year)	2	0	1.000	5.27	3	3	0	0	0	13 2/3	16	11	8	6	9

SODOWSKY, CLINT — P — DIAMONDBACKS

PERSONAL: Born July 13, 1972, in Ponca City, Okla. ... 6-4/200. ... Throws right, bats left. ... Full name: Clint Rea Sodowsky.
JUNIOR COLLEGE: Connors State (Okla.).
TRANSACTIONS/CAREER NOTES: Selected by Detroit Tigers organization in ninth round of free-agent draft (June 3, 1991). ... On disabled list (August 29-September 13, 1994). ... On Jacksonville suspended list (May 15-16, 1995). ... Traded by Tigers to Pittsburgh Pirates for P Dan Miceli (November 1, 1996). ... On disabled list (August 27-September 10, 1997). ... Selected by Arizona Diamondbacks in second round (35th pick overall) of expansion draft (November 18, 1997).

Year Team (League)	W	L	Pct.	ERA	G	GS	CG	ShO	Sv.	IP	H	R	ER	BB	SO
1991—Bristol (Appalachian)	0	5	.000	3.76	14	8	0	0	0	55	49	34	23	34	44
1992—Bristol (Appalachian)	2	2	.500	3.54	15	6	0	0	0	56	46	35	22	29	48
1993—Fayetteville (S. Atl.)	14	10	.583	5.09	27	27	1	0	0	155 2/3	177	101	88	51	80
1994—Lakeland (Fla. St.)	6	3	.667	3.83	19	18	1	1	0	110 1/3	111	58	47	34	73
1995—Jacksonville (Southern)	5	5	.500	2.55	19	19	5	•3	0	123 2/3	102	46	35	50	77
—Toledo (Int'l)	5	1	.833	2.85	9	9	1	0	0	60	47	21	19	30	32
—Detroit (A.L.)	2	2	.500	5.01	6	6	0	0	0	23 1/3	24	15	13	18	14
1996—Detroit (A.L.)	1	3	.250	11.84	7	7	0	0	0	24 1/3	40	34	32	20	9
—Toledo (Int'l)	6	8	.429	3.94	19	19	1	0	0	118 2/3	128	67	52	51	59
1997—Calgary (PCL)■	0	1	.000	6.59	8	0	0	0	1	13 2/3	19	10	10	6	9
—Pittsburgh (N.L.)	2	2	.500	3.63	45	0	0	0	0	52	49	22	21	34	51
A.L. totals (2 years)	3	5	.375	8.50	13	13	0	0	0	47 2/3	64	49	45	38	23
N.L. totals (1 year)	2	2	.500	3.63	45	0	0	0	0	52	49	22	21	34	51
Major league totals (3 years)	5	7	.417	5.96	58	13	0	0	0	99 2/3	113	71	66	72	74

SOJO, LUIS — 2B/SS — YANKEES

PERSONAL: Born January 3, 1966, in Barquisimeto, Venezuela. ... 5-11/175. ... Bats right, throws right. ... Name pronounced SO-ho.
TRANSACTIONS/CAREER NOTES: Signed as non-drafted free agent by Toronto Blue Jays organization (January 3, 1986). ... Traded by Blue Jays with OF Junior Felix and a player to be named later to California Angels for OF Devon White, P Willie Fraser and a player to be named later (December 2, 1990); Blue Jays acquired P Marcus Moore and Angels acquired C Ken Rivers to complete deal (December 4, 1990). ... Traded by Angels to Blue Jays for 3B Kelly Gruber and cash (December 8, 1992). ... On Toronto disabled list (May 10-30, 1993). ... Granted free agency (October 15, 1993). ... Signed by Seattle Mariners organization (January 10, 1994). ... On Seattle disabled list (June 7-23, 1995); included rehabilitation assignment to Tacoma (June 19-23). ... Claimed on waivers by New York Yankees (August 22, 1996). ... Granted free agency (December 20, 1996). ... Re-signed by Yankees (January 9, 1997). ... On disabled list (August 15-remainder of season, 1997). ... Granted free agency (October 31, 1997). ... Re-signed by Yankees (November 12, 1997).
STATISTICAL NOTES: Led International League shortstops with .957 fielding percentage in 1989. ... Led International League with nine sacrifice flies in 1990. ... Led A.L. with 19 sacrifice hits in 1991. ... Career major league grand slams: 1.

Year Team (League)	Pos.	G	AB	R	H	2B	3B	HR	RBI	Avg.	BB	SO	SB	PO	A	E	Avg.
1986—						Dominican Summer League statistics unavailable.											
1987—Myrtle Beach (SAL)	S-2-3-O	72	223	23	47	5	4	2	15	.211	17	18	5	104	123	14	.942
1988—Myrtle Beach (SAL)	SS	135	*536	83	*155	22	5	5	56	.289	35	35	14	191	407	28	.955
1989—Syracuse (Int'l)	SS-2B	121	482	54	133	20	5	3	54	.276	21	42	9	170	348	23	†.957
1990—Syracuse (Int'l)	2B-SS	75	297	39	88	12	3	6	25	.296	14	23	10	138	212	10	.972
—Toronto (A.L.)	2-S-O-3-DH	33	80	14	18	3	0	1	9	.225	5	5	1	34	31	5	.929
1991—California (A.L.)■	2-S-3-O-DH	113	364	38	94	14	1	3	20	.258	14	26	4	233	335	11	.981
1992—Edmonton (PCL)	3B-2B-SS	37	145	22	43	9	1	1	24	.297	9	17	4	32	106	4	.972
—California (A.L.)	2B-3B-SS	106	368	37	100	12	3	7	43	.272	14	24	7	196	293	9	.982
1993—Toronto (A.L.)■	SS-2B-3B	19	47	5	8	2	0	0	6	.170	4	2	0	24	35	2	.967
—Syracuse (Int'l)	2-0-3-S-1	43	142	17	31	7	2	1	12	.218	8	12	2	46	60	4	.964
1994—Calgary (PCL)■	SS-2B	24	102	19	33	9	3	1	18	.324	10	7	5	36	81	2	.983
—Seattle (A.L.)	2-S-DH-3	63	213	32	59	9	2	6	22	.277	8	25	2	97	186	7	.976
1995—Seattle (A.L.)	SS-2B-OF	102	339	50	98	18	2	7	39	.289	23	19	4	141	221	9	.976
—Tacoma (PCL)	2B-SS	4	17	1	3	0	0	1	1	.176	0	2	0	4	9	0	1.000
1996—Seattle (A.L.)	3B-2B-SS	77	247	20	52	8	1	1	16	.211	10	13	2	97	158	8	.970
—New York (A.L.)■	2B-SS-3B	18	40	3	11	2	0	0	5	.275	1	4	0	16	37	0	1.000
1997—New York (A.L.)	2-S-3-1	77	215	27	66	6	1	2	25	.307	16	14	3	131	153	5	.983
Major league totals (8 years)		608	1913	226	506	74	10	27	185	.265	95	132	23	969	1449	56	.977

DIVISION SERIES RECORD

Year Team (League)	Pos.	G	AB	R	H	2B	3B	HR	RBI	Avg.	BB	SO	SB	PO	A	E	Avg.
1995—Seattle (A.L.)	SS	5	20	0	5	0	0	0	3	.250	0	3	0	9	15	1	.960
1996—New York (A.L.)	2B	2	0	0	0	0	0	0	0	...	0	0	0	1	1	0	1.000
Division series totals (2 years)		7	20	0	5	0	0	0	3	.250	0	3	0	10	16	1	.963

CHAMPIONSHIP SERIES RECORD

Year Team (League)	Pos.	G	AB	R	H	2B	3B	HR	RBI	Avg.	BB	SO	SB	PO	A	E	Avg.
1995—Seattle (A.L.)	SS	6	20	0	5	2	0	0	1	.250	0	2	0	9	18	1	.964
1996—New York (A.L.)	2B	3	5	0	1	0	0	0	0	.200	0	1	0	4	4	0	1.000
Championship series totals (2 years)		9	25	0	6	2	0	0	1	.240	0	3	0	13	22	1	.972

NOTES: Member of World Series championship team (1996).

Year Team (League)	Pos.	G	AB	R	H	2B	3B	HR	RBI	Avg.	BB	SO	SB	PO	A	E	Avg.
							BATTING							FIELDING			
1996— New York (A.L.)..........	PH-2B	5	5	0	3	1	0	0	1	.600	0	0	0	5	2	0	1.000

SORRENTO, PAUL · 1B · DEVIL RAYS

PERSONAL: Born November 17, 1965, in Somerville, Mass. ... 6-2/220. ... Bats left, throws right. ... Full name: Paul Anthony Sorrento.
HIGH SCHOOL: St. John's Preparatory (Danvers, Mass.).
COLLEGE: Florida State.
TRANSACTIONS/CAREER NOTES: Selected by California Angels organization in fourth round of free-agent draft (June 2, 1986). ... Traded by Angels organization with P Mike Cook and P Rob Wassenaar to Minnesota Twins for P Bert Blyleven and P Kevin Trudeau (November 3, 1988). ... Traded by Twins to Cleveland Indians for P Oscar Munoz and P Curt Leskanic (March 28, 1992). ... Granted free agency (December 21, 1995). ... Signed by Seattle Mariners (January 3, 1996). ... Granted free agency (October 27, 1997). ... Signed by Tampa Bay Devil Rays (December 8, 1997).
STATISTICAL NOTES: Led Southern League first basemen with 103 double plays in 1989. ... Led Pacific Coast League first basemen with 14 errors in 1991. ... Career major league grand slams: 7.

Year Team (League)	Pos.	G	AB	R	H	2B	3B	HR	RBI	Avg.	BB	SO	SB	PO	A	E	Avg.
							BATTING							FIELDING			
1986— Quad Cities (Mid.)	OF	53	177	33	63	11	2	6	34	.356	24	40	0	83	7	1	.989
—Palm Springs (Cal.)....	OF	16	62	5	15	3	0	1	7	.242	4	15	0	16	1	1	.944
1987— Palm Springs (Cal.)....	OF	114	370	66	83	14	2	8	45	.224	78	95	1	123	10	4	.971
1988— Palm Springs (Cal.)....	1B-OF	133	465	91	133	30	6	14	99	.286	110	101	3	719	55	18	.977
1989— Orlando (South.)■......	1B	140	509	81	130	*35	2	27	*112	.255	84	119	1	1070	41	*24	.979
—Minnesota (A.L.)	1B-DH	14	21	2	5	0	0	0	1	.238	5	4	0	13	0	0	1.000
1990— Portland (PCL)	1B-OF	102	354	59	107	27	1	19	72	.302	64	95	3	695	52	13	.983
—Minnesota (A.L.)	DH-1B	41	121	11	25	4	1	5	13	.207	12	31	1	118	7	1	.992
1991— Portland (PCL)	1B-OF	113	409	59	126	30	2	13	79	.308	62	65	1	933	58	†14	.986
—Minnesota (A.L.)	1B-DH	26	47	6	12	2	0	4	13	.255	4	11	0	70	7	0	1.000
1992— Cleveland (A.L.)■........	1B-DH	140	458	52	123	24	1	18	60	.269	51	89	0	996	78	8	.993
1993— Cleveland (A.L.).........	1B-OF-DH	148	463	75	119	26	1	18	65	.257	58	121	3	1015	86	6	.995
1994— Cleveland (A.L.).........	1B-DH	95	322	43	90	14	0	14	62	.280	34	68	0	798	59	4	.995
1995— Cleveland (A.L.).........	1B-DH	104	323	50	76	14	0	25	79	.235	51	71	1	816	58	7	.992
1996— Seattle (A.L.)■..........	1B	143	471	67	136	32	1	23	93	.289	57	103	0	957	81	11	.990
1997— Seattle (A.L.)	1B-DH	146	457	68	123	19	0	31	80	.269	51	112	0	929	86	4	.996
Major league totals (9 years)		857	2683	374	709	135	4	138	466	.264	323	610	5	5712	462	41	.993

DIVISION SERIES RECORD

Year Team (League)	Pos.	G	AB	R	H	2B	3B	HR	RBI	Avg.	BB	SO	SB	PO	A	E	Avg.
							BATTING							FIELDING			
1995— Cleveland (A.L.)..........	1B	3	10	2	3	0	0	0	1	.300	2	3	0	27	5	2	.941
1997— Seattle (A.L.)	1B-PH	4	10	2	3	1	0	1	1	.300	2	3	0	27	4	1	.969
Division series totals (2 years)		7	20	4	6	1	0	1	2	.300	4	6	0	54	9	3	.955

CHAMPIONSHIP SERIES RECORD

Year Team (League)	Pos.	G	AB	R	H	2B	3B	HR	RBI	Avg.	BB	SO	SB	PO	A	E	Avg.
							BATTING							FIELDING			
1991— Minnesota (A.L.)	PH	1	1	0	0	0	0	0	0	.000	0	1	0	...	...	...	...
1995— Cleveland (A.L.)..........	1B	4	13	2	2	1	0	0	0	.154	2	3	0	34	1	2	.946
Championship series totals (2 years)		5	14	2	2	1	0	0	0	.143	2	4	0	34	1	2	.946

WORLD SERIES RECORD

NOTES: Member of World Series championship team (1991).

Year Team (League)	Pos.	G	AB	R	H	2B	3B	HR	RBI	Avg.	BB	SO	SB	PO	A	E	Avg.
							BATTING							FIELDING			
1991— Minnesota (A.L.)	PH-1B	3	2	0	0	0	0	0	0	.000	1	2	0	1	1	0	1.000
1995— Cleveland (A.L.)..........	1B-PH	6	11	0	2	1	0	0	0	.182	0	4	0	19	2	1	.955
World Series totals (2 years)		9	13	0	2	1	0	0	0	.154	1	6	0	20	3	1	.958

SOSA, SAMMY · OF · CUBS

PERSONAL: Born November 12, 1968, in San Pedro de Macoris, Dominican Republic. ... 6-0/200. ... Bats right, throws right. ... Full name: Samuel Sosa.
TRANSACTIONS/CAREER NOTES: Signed as non-drafted free agent by Texas Rangers organization (July 30, 1985). ... Traded by Rangers with SS Scott Fletcher and P Wilson Alvarez to Chicago White Sox for OF Harold Baines and IF Fred Manrique (July 29, 1989). ... Traded by White Sox with P Ken Patterson to Chicago Cubs for OF George Bell (March 30, 1992). ... On Chicago disabled list (June 13-July 27, 1992); included rehabilitation assignment to Iowa (July 21-27). ... On Chicago disabled list (August 7-September 16, 1992). ... On disabled list (August 21, 1996-remainder of season).
RECORDS: Shares major league record for most home runs in one inning—2 (May 16, 1996, seventh inning).
HONORS: Named outfielder on THE SPORTING NEWS N.L. All-Star team (1995). ... Named outfielder on THE SPORTING NEWS N.L. Silver Slugger team (1995).
STATISTICAL NOTES: Led Gulf Coast League with 96 total bases in 1986. ... Tied for South Atlantic League lead in double plays by outfielder with four in 1987. ... Collected six hits in one game (July 2, 1993). ... Tied for N.L. lead in double plays by outfielder with four in 1995. ... Hit three home runs in one game (June 5, 1996).

Year Team (League)	Pos.	G	AB	R	H	2B	3B	HR	RBI	Avg.	BB	SO	SB	PO	A	E	Avg.
1986—GC Rangers (GCL).....	OF	61	229	38	63	*19	1	4	28	.275	22	51	11	92	9	*6	.944
1987—Gastonia (S. Atl.)........	OF	129	519	73	145	27	4	11	59	.279	21	123	22	183	12	17	.920
1988—Charlotte (Fla. St.)......	OF	131	507	70	116	13	*12	9	51	.229	35	106	42	227	11	7	.971
1989—Texas (A.L.)..............	OF-DH	25	84	8	20	3	0	1	3	.238	0	20	0	33	1	2	.944
—Chicago (A.L.)■.....	OF	33	99	19	27	5	0	3	10	.273	11	27	7	61	1	2	.969
—Oklahoma City (A.A.)..	OF	10	39	2	4	2	0	0	3	.103	2	8	4	22	0	2	.917
—Vancouver (PCL).......	OF	13	49	7	18	3	0	1	5	.367	0	20	0	43	1	0	1.000
1990—Chicago (A.L.)..........	OF	153	532	72	124	26	10	15	70	.233	33	150	32	315	14	*13	.962
1991—Chicago (A.L.).........	OF-DH	116	316	39	64	10	1	10	33	.203	14	98	13	214	6	6	.973
—Vancouver (PCL).......	OF	32	116	19	31	7	2	3	19	.267	17	32	9	95	2	3	.970
1992—Chicago (N.L.)■......	OF	67	262	41	68	7	2	8	25	.260	19	63	15	145	4	6	.961
—Iowa (Am. Assoc.)......	OF	5	19	3	6	2	0	0	1	.316	1	2	5	14	0	0	1.000
1993—Chicago (N.L.).........	OF	159	598	92	156	25	5	33	93	.261	38	135	36	344	17	9	.976
1994—Chicago (N.L.).........	OF	105	426	59	128	17	6	25	70	.300	25	92	22	248	5	7	.973
1995—Chicago (N.L.).........	OF	•144	564	89	151	17	3	36	119	.268	58	134	34	320	13	*13	.962
1996—Chicago (N.L.)■.......	OF	124	498	84	136	21	2	40	100	.273	34	134	18	253	15	10	.964
1997—Chicago (N.L.)..........	OF	•162	642	90	161	31	4	36	119	.251	45	*174	22	325	16	8	.977
American League totals (3 years)		327	1031	138	235	44	11	29	116	.228	58	295	52	623	22	23	.966
National League totals (6 years)		761	2990	455	800	118	22	178	526	.268	219	732	147	1635	70	53	.970
Major league totals (9 years)		1088	4021	593	1035	162	33	207	642	.257	277	1027	199	2258	92	76	.969

ALL-STAR GAME RECORD

Year League	Pos.	AB	R	H	2B	3B	HR	RBI	Avg.	BB	SO	SB	PO	A	E	Avg.
1995—National....................	OF	1	0	0	0	0	0	0	.000	0	0	0	2	0	0	1.000

SPEHR, TIM   C   METS

PERSONAL: Born July 2, 1966, in Excelsior Springs, Mo. ... 6-2/200. ... Bats right, throws right. ... Full name: Timothy Joseph Spehr. ... Name pronounced SPEAR.

HIGH SCHOOL: Richfield (Waco, Texas).

COLLEGE: Arizona State.

TRANSACTIONS/CAREER NOTES: Selected by Kansas City Royals organization in fifth round of free-agent draft (June 1, 1988). ... On disabled list (June 25-July 27, 1988). ... On Baseball City disabled list (April 7-May 21, 1989). ... Traded by Royals organization with P Jeff Shaw to Montreal Expos organization for P Mark Gardner and P Doug Piatt (December 9, 1992). ... On disabled list (July 31, 1995-remainder of season and August 18-September 6, 1996). ... Granted free agency (October 21, 1996). ... Signed by Pawtucket, Boston Red Sox organization (March 6, 1997). ... Traded to Red Sox to Royals for cash (March 26, 1997). ... Released by Royals (May 27, 1997). ... Signed by Atlanta Braves (June 10, 1997). ... Granted free agency (December 21, 1997). ... Signed by New York Mets organization (January 8, 1998). ... Signed by New York Mets organization (January 8, 1998).

STATISTICAL NOTES: Led American Association catchers with 730 total chances and 14 double plays in 1990. ... Tied for American Association lead in being hit by pitch with 11 in 1992. ... Career major league grand slams: 2.

Year Team (League)	Pos.	G	AB	R	H	2B	3B	HR	RBI	Avg.	BB	SO	SB	PO	A	E	Avg.
1988—Appleton (Midwest)....	C	31	110	15	29	3	0	5	22	.264	10	28	3	146	14	7	.958
1989—Baseball City (FSL)...	C	18	64	8	16	5	0	1	7	.250	5	17	1	63	7	1	.986
—Memphis (Southern)..	C	61	216	22	42	9	0	8	23	.194	16	59	1	274	36	5	.984
1990—Omaha (A.A.)...........	C	102	307	42	69	10	2	6	34	.225	41	88	5	*658	67	5	*.993
1991—Omaha (A.A.)...........	C	72	215	27	59	14	2	6	26	.274	25	48	3	402	53	8	.983
—Kansas City (A.L.)......	C	37	74	7	14	5	0	3	14	.189	9	18	1	190	19	3	.986
1992—Omaha (A.A.)...........	C	109	336	48	85	22	0	15	42	.253	61	89	4	577	65	7	.989
1993—Montreal (N.L.)■.......	C	53	87	14	20	6	0	2	10	.230	6	20	2	166	22	9	.954
—Ottawa (Int'l)............	C	46	141	15	28	6	1	4	13	.199	14	35	2	248	24	6	.978
1994—Montreal (N.L.).........	C-OF	52	36	8	9	3	1	0	5	.250	4	11	2	104	6	0	1.000
1995—Montreal (N.L.).........	C	41	35	4	9	5	0	1	3	.257	6	7	0	92	12	1	.990
1996—Montreal (N.L.).........	C	63	44	4	4	1	0	1	3	.091	3	15	1	121	7	2	.985
1997—Kansas City (A.L.)■...	C	17	35	3	6	0	0	1	2	.171	2	12	0	78	7	0	1.000
—Richmond (Int'l)■......	C	36	120	13	23	5	0	3	14	.192	12	37	0	262	36	5	.983
—Atlanta (N.L.)...........	C	8	14	2	3	1	0	1	4	.214	0	4	1	32	4	2	.947
American League totals (2 years)		54	109	10	20	5	0	4	16	.183	11	30	1	268	26	3	.990
National League totals (5 years)		217	216	32	45	16	1	5	25	.208	19	57	6	515	51	14	.976
Major league totals (6 years)		271	325	42	65	21	1	9	41	.200	30	87	7	783	77	17	.981

SPEIER, JUSTIN   P   CUBS

PERSONAL: Born November 6, 1973, in Daly City, Calif. ... 6-4/200. ... Throws right, bats right. ... Full name: Justin James Speier. ... Son of Chris Speier, infielder with San Francisco Giants, Montreal Expos, St. Louis Cardinals, Minnesota Twins and Chicago Cubs (1971-89).

HIGH SCHOOL: Brophy College Prep (Phoenix).

COLLEGE: San Francisco, then Nicholls State.

TRANSACTIONS/CAREER NOTES: Selected by Chicago Cubs organization in 55th round of free-agent draft (June 1, 1995).

Year Team (League)	W	L	Pct.	ERA	G	GS	CG	ShO	Sv.	IP	H	R	ER	BB	SO
1995—Williamsport (NYP)...........	2	1	.667	1.49	30	0	0	0	12	36 1/3	27	6	6	4	39
1996—Daytona (Fla. St.).............	2	4	.333	3.76	33	0	0	0	13	38 1/3	32	19	16	19	34
—Orlando (South.).............	4	1	.800	2.05	24	0	0	0	6	26 1/3	23	7	6	5	14
1997—Orlando (South.).............	6	5	.545	4.48	50	0	0	0	6	78 1/3	77	46	39	23	63
—Iowa (Am. Assoc.).............	2	0	1.000	0.00	8	0	0	0	1	12 1/3	5	0	0	1	9

SPENCER, SHANE — OF — YANKEES

PERSONAL: Born February 20, 1972, in Key West, Fla. ... 5-11/210. ... Bats right, throws right. ... Full name: Michael Shane Spencer.
HIGH SCHOOL: Granite Hills (El Cajon, Calif.).
TRANSACTIONS/CAREER NOTES: Selected by New York Yankees organization in 28th round of free-agent draft (June 4, 1990). ... On disabled list (April 10-May 9, 1994).
HONORS: Named Florida State League Most Valuable Player (1995).
STATISTICAL NOTES: Led Florida State League with 235 total bases in 1995.

						BATTING								FIELDING			
Year Team (League)	Pos.	G	AB	R	H	2B	3B	HR	RBI	Avg.	BB	SO	SB	PO	A	E	Avg.
1990—GC Yankees (GCL)	OF	42	147	20	27	4	0	0	7	.184	20	23	11	79	3	3	.965
1991—GC Yankees (GCL)	OF	44	160	25	49	7	0	0	30	.306	14	19	9	64	6	3	.959
—Oneonta (NYP)	OF	18	53	10	13	2	1	0	3	.245	10	9	2	11	0	1	.917
1992—Greensboro (S. Atl.)	OF-P	83	258	43	74	10	2	3	27	.287	33	37	8	135	6	0	1.000
1993—Greensboro (S. Atl.)	OF-P	122	431	89	116	35	2	12	80	.269	52	62	14	138	10	5	.967
1994—Tampa (Florida State)	OF	90	334	44	97	22	3	8	53	.290	30	53	5	90	10	4	.962
1995—Tampa (Florida State)	OF	•134	500	87	*150	31	3	16	*88	.300	61	60	14	166	6	6	.966
1996—Norwich (Eastern)	OF-1B-3B	126	450	70	114	19	0	29	89	.253	68	99	4	218	24	3	.988
—Columbus (Int'l)	OF	9	31	7	11	4	0	3	6	.355	5	5	0	25	1	1	.963
1997—Columbus (Int'l)	OF-3B	125	452	78	109	34	4	30	86	.241	71	105	0	189	7	4	.980

RECORD AS PITCHER

Year Team (League)	W	L	Pct.	ERA	G	GS	CG	ShO	Sv.	IP	H	R	ER	BB	SO
1992—Greensboro (S. Atl.)	0	0	...	0.00	1	0	0	0	0	1	2	0	0	1	1
1993—Greensboro (S. Atl.)	0	0	...	4.50	2	0	0	0	0	4	5	2	2	2	5

SPIERS, BILL — 3B — ASTROS

PERSONAL: Born June 5, 1966, in Orangeburg, S.C. ... 6-2/190. ... Bats left, throws right. ... Full name: William James Spiers III. ... Name pronounced SPY-ers.
HIGH SCHOOL: Wade Hampton Academy (Orangeburg, S.C.).
COLLEGE: Clemson.
TRANSACTIONS/CAREER NOTES: Selected by Milwaukee Brewers organization in first round (13th pick overall) of free-agent draft (June 2, 1987). ... On Milwaukee disabled list (April 6-May 15, 1990); included rehabilitation assignment to Denver (April 27-May 14). ... On Milwaukee disabled list (April 5-September 2, 1992); included rehabilitation assignments to Beloit (May 6-15 and August 20-September 2). ... Granted free agency (December 20, 1993). ... Re-signed by Brewers (December 21, 1993). ... Claimed on waivers by New York Mets (October 25, 1994). ... On New York disabled list (May 15-June 5 and June 26-July 16, 1995); included rehabilitation assignment to Norfolk (May 22-June 5). ... Granted free agency (November 3, 1995). ... Signed by Houston Astros organization (January 10, 1996). ... Granted free agency (November 14, 1996). ... Re-signed by Astros (December 2, 1996). ... Granted free agency (November 3, 1997). ... Re-signed by Astros (November 25, 1997).
HONORS: Named shortstop on THE SPORTING NEWS college All-America team (1987).
STATISTICAL NOTES: Career major league grand slams: 2.

						BATTING								FIELDING			
Year Team (League)	Pos.	G	AB	R	H	2B	3B	HR	RBI	Avg.	BB	SO	SB	PO	A	E	Avg.
1987—Helena (Pioneer)	SS	6	22	4	9	1	0	0	3	.409	3	3	2	8	6	6	.700
—Beloit (Midwest)	SS	64	258	43	77	10	1	3	26	.298	15	38	11	111	160	20	.931
1988—Stockton (California)	SS	84	353	68	95	17	3	5	52	.269	42	41	27	140	240	19	.952
—El Paso (Texas)	SS	47	168	22	47	5	2	3	21	.280	15	20	4	73	141	13	.943
1989—Milwaukee (A.L.)	S-3-2-DH-1	114	345	44	88	9	3	4	33	.255	21	63	10	164	295	21	.956
—Denver (A.A.)	SS	14	47	9	17	2	1	2	8	.362	5	6	1	32	33	2	.970
1990—Denver (A.A.)	SS	11	38	6	12	0	0	1	7	.316	10	8	1	22	23	2	.957
—Milwaukee (A.L.)	SS	112	363	44	88	15	3	2	36	.242	16	46	11	159	326	12	.976
1991—Milwaukee (A.L.)	SS-DH-OF	133	414	71	117	13	6	8	54	.283	34	55	14	201	345	17	.970
1992—Beloit (Midwest)	SS	16	55	9	13	3	0	0	7	.236	7	7	4	12	28	3	.930
—Milwaukee (A.L.)	S-2-DH-3	12	16	2	5	2	0	0	2	.313	1	4	1	6	6	0	1.000
1993—Milwaukee (A.L.)	2-0-S-DH	113	340	43	81	8	4	2	36	.238	29	51	9	213	231	13	.972
1994—Milwaukee (A.L.)	3-S-DH-O-1	73	214	27	54	10	1	0	17	.252	19	42	7	70	129	8	.961
1995—New York (N.L.)■	3B-2B	63	72	5	15	2	1	0	11	.208	12	15	0	13	30	7	.860
—Norfolk (Int'l)	2B-3B	12	41	4	9	2	0	0	4	.220	8	6	0	23	29	4	.929
1996—Houston (N.L.)■	3-2-S-1-O	122	218	27	55	10	1	6	26	.252	20	34	7	44	108	5	.968
1997—Houston (N.L.)	3-S-1-2	132	291	51	93	27	4	4	48	.320	61	42	10	104	200	18	.944
American League totals (6 years)		557	1692	231	433	57	17	16	178	.256	120	261	52	813	1332	71	.968
National League totals (3 years)		317	581	83	163	39	6	10	85	.281	93	91	17	161	338	30	.943
Major league totals (9 years)		874	2273	314	596	96	23	26	263	.262	213	352	69	974	1670	101	.963

DIVISION SERIES RECORD

						BATTING								FIELDING			
Year Team (League)	Pos.	G	AB	R	H	2B	3B	HR	RBI	Avg.	BB	SO	SB	PO	A	E	Avg.
1997—Houston (N.L.)	3B	3	11	1	0	0	0	0	0	.000	1	2	0	1	3	0	1.000

SPIEZIO, SCOTT — 2B — ATHLETICS

PERSONAL: Born September 21, 1972, in Joliet, Ill. ... 6-2/205. ... Bats both, throws right. ... Full name: Scott Edward Spiezio. ... Son of Ed Spiezio, third baseman, St. Louis Cardinals, San Diego Padres and Chicago White Sox (1964-72).
HIGH SCHOOL: Morris (Ill.).
COLLEGE: Illinois.
TRANSACTIONS/CAREER NOTES: Selected by Oakland Athletics organization in sixth round of free-agent draft (June 3, 1993). ... On Oakland disabled list (June 8-25, 1997); included rehabilitation assignment to Southern Oregon (June 23-25).

Year Team (League)	Pos.	G	AB	R	H	2B	3B	HR	RBI	Avg.	BB	SO	SB	PO	A	E	Avg.
1993— S. Oregon (N'west).....	3B-1B	31	125	32	41	10	2	3	19	.328	16	18	0	76	40	9	.928
— Modesto (California) ..	3B-1B	32	110	12	28	9	1	1	13	.255	23	19	1	42	51	5	.949
1994— Modesto (California) ..	3B-1B-SS	127	453	84	127	32	5	14	68	.280	88	72	5	66	281	18	†.951
1995— Huntsville (Southern) .	3B-1B-2B	141	528	78	149	33	8	13	86	.282	67	78	10	122	†295	†29	.935
1996— Edmonton (PCL)	3B-1B	*140	523	87	137	30	4	20	91	.262	56	66	6	†174	†304	15	†.970
— Oakland (A.L.)	3B-DH	9	29	6	9	2	0	2	8	.310	4	4	0	6	5	2	.846
1997— Oakland (A.L.)	2B-3B	147	538	58	131	28	4	14	65	.243	44	75	9	280	415	7	†.990
— S. Oregon (N'west).....	2B	2	9	1	5	0	0	0	2	.556	2	1	0	3	4	1	.875
Major league totals (2 years)		156	567	64	140	30	4	16	73	.247	48	79	9	286	420	9	.987

SPOLJARIC, PAUL   P   MARINERS

PERSONAL: Born September 24, 1970, in Kelowna, B.C. ... 6-3/210. ... Throws left, bats right. ... Full name: Paul Nikola Spoljaric. ... Name pronounced spole-JAIR-ick.

HIGH SCHOOL: Springvalley Secondary (Kelowna, B.C.).

COLLEGE: Douglas College (B.C.).

TRANSACTIONS/CAREER NOTES: Signed as non-drafted free agent by Toronto Blue Jays organization (August 26, 1989). ... On Toronto disabled list (July 25-August 18, 1996); included rehabilitation assignment to St. Catharines (August 10-18). ... On Toronto disabled list (March 23-April 18, 1997); included rehabilitation assignment to Dunedin (April 4-17). ... Traded by Blue Jays with P Mike Timlin to Seattle Mariners for OF Jose Cruz Jr. (July 31, 1997).

HONORS: Named South Atlantic League Most Outstanding Pitcher (1992).

STATISTICAL NOTES: Tied for A.L. lead with three balks in 1997.

Year Team (League)	W	L	Pct.	ERA	G	GS	CG	ShO	Sv.	IP	H	R	ER	BB	SO
1990— Medicine Hat (Pio.)	3	7	.300	4.34	15	13	0	0	1	66 1/3	57	43	32	35	62
1991— St. Catharines (NYP)	0	2	.000	4.82	4	4	0	0	0	18 2/3	21	14	10	9	21
1992— Myrtle Beach (SAL)	10	8	.556	2.82	26	26	1	0	0	162 2/3	111	68	51	58	161
1993— Dunedin (Fla. St.)	3	0	1.000	1.38	4	4	0	0	0	26	16	5	4	12	29
— Knoxville (Southern)	4	1	.800	2.28	7	7	0	0	0	43 1/3	30	12	11	22	51
— Syracuse (Int'l)..................	8	7	.533	5.29	18	18	1	1	0	95 1/3	97	63	56	52	88
1994— Toronto (A.L.)...................	0	1	.000	38.57	2	1	0	0	0	2 1/3	5	10	10	9	2
— Syracuse (Int'l)..................	1	5	.167	5.70	8	8	0	0	0	47 1/3	47	37	30	28	38
— Knoxville (Southern)	6	5	.545	3.62	17	16	0	0	0	102	88	50	41	48	79
1995— Syracuse (Int'l)..................	2	10	.167	4.93	43	9	0	0	10	87 2/3	69	51	48	54	108
1996— Syracuse (Int'l)..................	3	0	1.000	3.27	17	0	0	0	4	22	20	9	8	6	24
— Toronto (A.L.)...................	2	2	.500	3.08	28	0	0	0	1	38	30	17	13	19	38
— St. Catharines (NYP)	0	0	. . .	0.00	2	2	0	0	0	5	3	0	0	0	7
1997— Dunedin (Fla. St.)	0	0	. . .	1.69	4	3	0	0	0	10 2/3	10	3	2	2	10
— Toronto (A.L.)...................	0	3	.000	3.19	37	0	0	0	3	48	37	17	17	21	43
— Seattle (A.L.)■................	0	0	. . .	4.76	20	0	0	0	0	22 2/3	24	13	12	15	27
Major league totals (3 years)......	2	6	.250	4.22	87	1	0	0	4	111	96	57	52	64	110

DIVISION SERIES RECORD

Year Team (League)	W	L	Pct.	ERA	G	GS	CG	ShO	Sv.	IP	H	R	ER	BB	SO
1997— Seattle (A.L.)	0	0	. . .	0.00	2	0	0	0	0	1 2/3	4	0	0	0	1

SPRADLIN, JERRY   P   PHILLIES

PERSONAL: Born June 14, 1967, in Fullerton, Calif. ... 6-7/240. ... Throws right, bats both. ... Full name: Jerry Carl Spradlin.

HIGH SCHOOL: Katella (Anaheim, Calif.).

COLLEGE: Fullerton (Calif.) College.

TRANSACTIONS/CAREER NOTES: Selected by Cincinnati Reds organization in 19th round of free-agent draft (June 1, 1988). ... Claimed on waivers by Florida Marlins (August 4, 1994). ... Granted free agency (October 16, 1995). ... Signed by Indianapolis, Reds orgnization (February 11, 1996). ... On Indianapolis disabled list (May 24-June 1, 1996). ... Released by Reds (October 30, 1996). ... Signed by Philadelphia Phillies (December 9, 1996).

HONORS: Named Southern League co-Most Valuable Pitcher (1992).

Year Team (League)	W	L	Pct.	ERA	G	GS	CG	ShO	Sv.	IP	H	R	ER	BB	SO
1988— Billings (Pioneer)..............	4	1	.800	3.21	17	5	0	0	0	47 2/3	45	25	17	14	23
1989— Greensboro (S. Atl.)..........	7	2	.778	2.76	42	1	0	0	2	94 2/3	88	35	29	23	56
1990— Cedar Rapids (Midw.)	0	1	.000	3.00	5	0	0	0	0	12	13	8	4	5	6
— Char., W.Va. (S. Atl.)	3	4	.429	2.54	43	1	1	0	17	74 1/3	74	23	21	17	39
1991— Chattanooga (Southern).....	7	3	.700	3.09	48	1	0	0	4	96	95	38	33	32	73
1992— Chattanooga (Southern)	3	3	.500	1.38	59	0	0	0	*34	65 1/3	52	11	10	13	35
— Cedar Rapids (Midw.)	1	0	1.000	7.71	1	0	0	0	0	2 1/3	5	2	2	0	2
1993— Indianapolis (A.A.).............	3	2	.600	3.49	34	0	0	0	1	56 2/3	58	24	22	12	46
— Cincinnati (N.L.)................	2	1	.667	3.49	37	0	0	0	2	49	44	20	19	9	24
1994— Indianapolis (A.A.).............	3	3	.500	3.68	28	5	0	0	3	73 1/3	87	36	30	16	49
— Cincinnati (N.L.)................	0	0	. . .	10.13	6	0	0	0	0	8	12	11	9	2	4
— Edmonton (PCL)■............	1	0	1.000	2.53	6	0	0	0	1	10 2/3	12	3	3	4	3
1995— Charlotte (Int'l).................	3	3	.500	3.03	41	0	0	0	1	59 1/3	59	26	20	15	38
1996— Indianapolis (A.A.)■.........	6	8	.429	3.33	49	8	0	0	15	100	94	49	37	23	79
— Cincinnati (N.L.)................	0	0	. . .	0.00	1	0	0	0	0	1/3	0	0	0	0	0
1997— Philadelphia (N.L.)■	4	8	.333	4.74	76	0	0	0	1	81 2/3	86	45	43	27	67
Major league totals (4 years)......	6	9	.400	4.60	120	0	0	0	3	139	142	76	71	38	95

S

PERSONAL: Born July 25, 1967, in Castro Valley, Calif. ... 6-2/205. ... Bats right, throws right. ... Full name: Edward Nelson Sprague. ... Son of Ed Sprague, major league pitcher with four teams (1968-69 and 1971-76); and husband of Kristen Babb, Olympic gold-medal synchronized swimmer (1992). ... Name pronounced SPRAYGH.

HIGH SCHOOL: St. Mary's (Stockton, Calif.).

COLLEGE: Stanford.

TRANSACTIONS/CAREER NOTES: Selected by Boston Red Sox organization in 26th round of free-agent draft (June 3, 1985); did not sign. ... Selected by Toronto Blue Jays organization in first round (25th pick overall) of free-agent draft (June 1, 1988). ... On suspended list (August 8-10, 1993). ... On disabled list (September 4-28, 1997).

STATISTICAL NOTES: Led International League third basemen with 31 errors and 364 total chances and tied for lead with 240 assists in 1990. ... Led A.L. in grounding into double plays with 23 in 1993. ... Led A.L. third basemen with 98 putouts in 1994 and 133 in 1995. ... Led A.L. in being hit by pitch with 15 in 1995. ... Career major league grand slams: 3.

MISCELLANEOUS: Member of 1988 U.S. Olympic baseball team.

Year Team (League)	Pos.	G	AB	R	H	2B	3B	HR	RBI	Avg.	BB	SO	SB	PO	A	E	Avg.
1989— Dunedin (Fla. St.)	3B	52	192	21	42	9	2	7	23	.219	16	40	1	33	86	14	.895
—Syracuse (Int'l)	3B	86	288	23	60	14	1	5	33	.208	18	73	0	51	149	*25	.889
1990—Syracuse (Int'l)	3B-1B-C	142	*519	60	124	23	5	20	75	.239	31	100	4	171	‡246	†35	.923
1991—Syracuse (Int'l)	C-3B	23	88	24	32	8	0	5	25	.364	10	21	2	111	17	6	.955
—Toronto (A.L.)	3-1-C-DH	61	160	17	44	7	0	4	20	.275	19	43	0	167	72	14	.945
1992—Syracuse (Int'l)	C-1B-3B	100	369	49	102	18	2	16	50	.276	44	73	0	438	44	12	.976
—Toronto (A.L.)	C-1-DH-3	22	47	6	11	2	0	1	7	.234	3	7	0	82	5	1	.989
1993—Toronto (A.L.)	3B	150	546	50	142	31	1	12	73	.260	32	85	1	*127	232	17	.955
1994—Toronto (A.L.)	3B-1B	109	405	38	97	19	1	11	44	.240	23	95	1	†117	147	14	.950
1995—Toronto (A.L.)	3B-1B-DH	144	521	77	127	27	4	18	74	.244	58	96	0	†167	234	17	.959
1996—Toronto (A.L.)	3B-DH	159	591	88	146	35	2	36	101	.247	60	146	0	108	218	15	.956
1997—Toronto (A.L.)	3B-DH	138	504	63	115	29	4	14	48	.228	51	102	0	106	202	18	.945
Major league totals (7 years)		783	2774	339	682	150	10	96	367	.246	246	574	2	874	1110	96	.954

CHAMPIONSHIP SERIES RECORD

Year Team (League)	Pos.	G	AB	R	H	2B	3B	HR	RBI	Avg.	BB	SO	SB	PO	A	E	Avg.
1991— Toronto (A.L.)							Did not play.										
1992—Toronto (A.L.)	PH	2	2	0	1	0	0	0	0	.500	0	1	0	...	...	...	...
1993— Toronto (A.L.)	3B	6	21	0	6	0	1	0	4	.286	2	4	0	5	9	0	1.000
Championship series totals (2 years)		8	23	0	7	0	1	0	4	.304	2	5	0	5	9	0	1.000

WORLD SERIES RECORD

NOTES: Hit home run in first at-bat (October 18, 1992). ... Member of World Series championship teams (1992 and 1993).

Year Team (League)	Pos.	G	AB	R	H	2B	3B	HR	RBI	Avg.	BB	SO	SB	PO	A	E	Avg.
1992—Toronto (A.L.)	PH-1B	3	2	1	1	0	0	1	2	.500	1	0	0	0	0	0	...
1993—Toronto (A.L.)	3B-PH-1B	5	15	0	1	0	0	0	2	.067	1	6	0	4	9	2	.867
World Series totals (2 years)		8	17	1	2	0	0	1	4	.118	2	6	0	4	9	2	.867

PERSONAL: Born November 7, 1968, in Alexandria, La. ... 6-4/205. ... Throws right, bats right. ... Full name: Russell Paul Springer.

HIGH SCHOOL: Grant (Dry Prong, La.).

COLLEGE: Louisiana State.

TRANSACTIONS/CAREER NOTES: Selected by New York Yankees organization in seventh round of free-agent draft (June 5, 1989). ... Traded by Yankees with 1B J.T. Snow and P Jerry Nielsen to California Angels for P Jim Abbott (December 6, 1992). ... On California disabled list (August 2, 1993-remainder of season). ... Traded by Angels to Philadelphia Phillies (August 15, 1995), completing deal in which Angels acquired OF Dave Gallagher from Phillies for 2B Kevin Flora and a player to be named later (August 9, 1995). ... Released by Phillies (December 20, 1996). ... Signed by Houston Astros organization (December 30, 1996). ... On Houston disabled list (June 17-July 10, 1997); included rehabilitation assignment to Jackson (July 8-10). ... Selected by Arizona Diamondbacks in third round (61st pick overall) of expansion draft (November 18, 1997).

Year Team (League)	W	L	Pct.	ERA	G	GS	CG	ShO	Sv.	IP	H	R	ER	BB	SO
1989— GC Yankees (GCL)	3	0	1.000	1.50	6	6	0	0	0	24	14	8	4	10	34
1990— GC Yankees (GCL)	0	2	.000	1.20	4	4	0	0	0	15	10	6	2	4	17
—Greensboro (S. Atl.)	2	3	.400	3.67	10	10	0	0	0	56 1/3	51	33	23	31	51
1991—Fort Lauderdale (FSL)	5	9	.357	3.49	25	25	2	0	0	152 1/3	118	68	59	62	139
—Alb./Colon. (Eastern)	1	0	1.000	1.80	2	2	0	0	0	15	9	4	3	6	16
1992—Columbus (Int'l)	8	5	.615	2.69	20	20	1	0	0	123 2/3	89	46	37	54	95
—New York (A.L.)	0	0	...	6.19	14	0	0	0	0	16	18	11	11	10	12
1993—Vancouver (PCL)■	5	4	.556	4.27	11	9	1	0	0	59	58	37	28	33	40
—California (A.L.)	1	6	.143	7.20	14	9	1	0	0	60	73	48	48	32	31
1994—Vancouver (PCL)	7	4	.636	3.04	12	12	•4	0	0	83	77	35	28	19	58
—California (A.L.)	2	2	.500	5.52	18	5	0	0	2	45 2/3	53	28	28	14	28
1995—Vancouver (PCL)	2	0	1.000	3.44	6	6	0	0	0	34	28	16	13	23	23
—California (A.L.)	1	2	.333	6.10	19	6	0	0	1	51 2/3	60	37	35	25	38
—Philadelphia (N.L.)■	0	0	...	3.71	14	0	0	0	0	26 2/3	22	11	11	10	32
1996—Philadelphia (N.L.)	3	10	.231	4.66	51	7	0	0	0	96 2/3	106	60	50	38	94
1997—Houston (N.L.)■	3	3	.500	4.23	54	0	0	0	3	55 1/3	48	28	26	27	74
—Jackson (Texas)	0	0	...	9.00	1	0	0	0	0	1	2	1	1	0	2
A.L. totals (4 years)	4	10	.286	6.33	65	20	1	0	3	173 1/3	204	124	122	81	109
N.L. totals (3 years)	6	13	.316	4.38	119	7	0	0	3	178 2/3	176	99	87	75	200
Major league totals (6 years)	10	23	.303	5.34	184	27	1	0	6	352	380	223	209	156	309

DIVISION SERIES RECORD

Year Team (League)	W	L	Pct.	ERA	G	GS	CG	ShO	Sv.	IP	H	R	ER	BB	SO
1997—Houston (N.L.)	0	0	...	5.40	2	0	0	0	0	1 2/3	2	1	1	1	3

SPRINGER, DENNIS   P   DEVIL RAYS

PERSONAL: Born February 12, 1965, in Fresno, Calif. ... 5-10/190. ... Throws right, bats right. ... Full name: Dennis LeRoy Springer.
HIGH SCHOOL: Washington (Fresno, Calif.).
COLLEGE: Fresno State.
TRANSACTIONS/CAREER NOTES: Selected by Los Angeles Dodgers organization in 21st round of free-agent draft (June 2, 1987). ... On San Antonio disabled list (April 19-27, 1992). ... On disabled list (August 24-September 6, 1993). ... Granted free agency (October 15, 1993). ... Signed by Philadelphia Phillies organization (May 19, 1994). ... Granted free agency (December 21, 1995). ... Signed by California Angels organization (January 5, 1996). ... Angels franchise renamed Anaheim Angels for 1997 season. ... Selected by Tampa Bay Devil Rays in first round (26th pick overall) of expansion draft (November 18, 1997).

Year Team (League)	W	L	Pct.	ERA	G	GS	CG	ShO	Sv.	IP	H	R	ER	BB	SO
1987—Great Falls (Pio.)	4	3	.571	2.88	23	5	1	0	6	65 2/3	70	38	21	16	54
1988—Bakersfield (California)	13	7	.650	3.27	32	20	6	•4	2	154	135	75	56	62	108
1989—San Antonio (Tex.)	6	8	.429	3.15	19	19	4	1	0	140	128	58	49	46	89
—Albuquerque (PCL)	4	1	.800	4.83	8	7	0	0	0	41	58	28	22	14	18
1990—San Antonio (Tex.)	8	6	.571	3.31	24	24	3	0	0	*163 1/3	147	76	60	73	77
1991—San Antonio (Tex.)	10	10	.500	4.43	30	24	2	0	0	164 2/3	153	96	81	91	*138
1992—San Antonio (Tex.)	6	7	.462	4.35	18	18	4	0	0	122	114	61	59	49	73
—Albuquerque (PCL)	2	7	.222	5.66	11	11	1	0	0	62	70	45	39	22	36
1993—Albuquerque (PCL)	3	8	.273	5.99	35	18	0	0	0	130 2/3	173	104	87	39	69
1994—Reading (Eastern)■	5	8	.385	3.40	24	19	2	0	2	135	125	74	51	44	118
1995—Scran./W.B. (Int'l)	10	11	.476	4.68	30	23	4	0	0	171	163	*101	89	47	115
—Philadelphia (N.L.)	0	0	.000	4.84	4	4	0	0	0	22 1/3	21	15	12	9	15
1996—California (A.L.)■	5	6	.455	5.51	20	15	2	1	0	94 2/3	91	65	58	43	64
—Vancouver (PCL)	10	3	.769	2.72	16	12	6	0	0	109 1/3	89	35	33	36	78
1997—Anaheim (A.L.)	9	9	.500	5.18	32	28	3	1	0	194 2/3	199	118	112	73	75
—Vancouver (PCL)	1	1	.500	3.00	2	2	2	0	0	15	12	6	5	6	7
A.L. totals (2 years)	14	15	.483	5.29	52	43	5	2	0	289 1/3	290	183	170	116	139
N.L. totals (1 year)	0	3	.000	4.84	4	4	0	0	0	22 1/3	21	15	12	9	15
Major league totals (3 years)	14	18	.438	5.26	56	47	5	2	0	311 2/3	311	198	182	125	154

STAHOVIAK, SCOTT   1B   TWINS

PERSONAL: Born March 6, 1970, in Waukegan, Ill. ... 6-5/230. ... Bats left, throws right. ... Full name: Scott Edmund Stahoviak. ... Name pronounced stuh-HO-vee-ak.
HIGH SCHOOL: Carmel (Mundelein, Ill.).
COLLEGE: Creighton.
TRANSACTIONS/CAREER NOTES: Selected by Minnesota Twins organization in 27th round of free-agent draft (June 1, 1988); did not sign. ... Selected by Twins organization in supplemental round ("sandwich pick" between first and second round, 27th pick overall) of free-agent draft (June 3, 1991); pick received as compensation for California Angels signing Type A free-agent 3B Gary Gaetti. ... On Nashville disabled list (May 12-June 24, 1993). ... On Minnesota disabled list (April 2-May 16, 1997); included rehabilitation assignments to Gulf Coast Twins (May 2-7) and Salt Lake (May 8-16).

Year Team (League)	Pos.	G	AB	R	H	2B	3B	HR	RBI	Avg.	BB	SO	SB	PO	A	E	Avg.
1991—Visalia (California)	3B		158	29	44	9	1	1	25	.278	22	28	9	31	89	12	.909
1992—Visalia (California)	3B	110	409	62	126	26	3	5	68	.308	82	66	17	92	181	*40	.872
1993—Nashville (Southern)	3-1-S-O	93	331	40	90	25	1	12	56	.272	56	95	10	89	150	24	.909
—Minnesota (A.L.)	3B	20	57	1	11	4	0	0	1	.193	3	22	0	9	38	4	.922
1994—Salt Lake (PCL)	3B-1B	123	437	96	139	41	6	13	94	.318	70	90	6	303	204	31	.942
1995—Salt Lake (PCL)	3B-1B	9	33	6	10	1	0	0	5	.303	6	3	2	36	16	0	1.000
—Minnesota (A.L.)	1B-3B-DH	94	263	28	70	19	0	3	23	.266	30	61	5	503	91	5	.992
1996—Minnesota (A.L.)	1B-DH	130	405	72	115	30	3	13	61	.284	59	114	3	801	92	5	.994
1997—Minnesota (A.L.)	1B-DH	91	275	33	63	17	0	10	33	.229	24	73	5	607	58	7	.990
—Salt Lake (PCL)	1B	8	28	5	6	0	0	2	10	.214	5	8	0	72	7	0	1.000
Major league totals (4 years)		335	1000	134	259	70	3	26	118	.259	116	270	13	1920	279	21	.991

STAIRS, MATT   OF   ATHLETICS

PERSONAL: Born February 27, 1968, in Fredericton, New Brunswick, Canada. ... 5-9/212. ... Bats left, throws right. ... Full name: Matthew Wade Stairs.
HIGH SCHOOL: Fredericton (New Brunswick).
TRANSACTIONS/CAREER NOTES: Signed as non-drafted free agent by Montreal Expos organization (January 17, 1989). ... On disabled list (May 16-23, 1991). ... On Ottawa disabled list (May 7-18, 1993). ... Released by Expos (June 8, 1993). ... Signed by Chunichi Dragons of Japan Central League (June 1993). ... Signed as free agent by Expos organization (December 15, 1993). ... Traded by Expos with P Pete Young to Boston Red Sox for a player to be named later and cash (February 18, 1994). ... Granted free agency (October 14, 1995). ... Signed by Oakland Athletics organization (December 1, 1995).
HONORS: Named Eastern League Most Valuable Player (1991).
STATISTICAL NOTES: Led Eastern League with .509 slugging percentage, 257 total bases and tied for lead with eight intentional bases on balls received in 1991. ... Career major league grand slams: 2.
MISCELLANEOUS: Member of 1988 Canadian Olympic baseball team.

Year Team (League)	Pos.	G	AB	R	H	2B	3B	HR	RBI	Avg.	BB	SO	SB	PO	A	E	Avg.
1989—W.P. Beach (FSL)	3B-SS-2B	36	111	12	21	3	1	1	9	.189	9	18	0	21	66	4	.956
—Jamestown (NYP)	2B-3B	14	43	8	11	1	0	1	5	.256	3	5	1	15	35	6	.893
—Rockford (Midwest)	3B	44	141	20	40	9	2	2	14	.284	15	29	5	30	62	7	.929
1990—W.P. Beach (FSL)	3B-2B	55	183	30	62	9	3	3	30	.339	41	19	15	40	112	17	.899
—Jacksonville (South.)	3-0-2-S	79	280	26	71	17	0	3	34	.254	22	43	5	76	107	22	.893

					BATTING									FIELDING			
Year — Team (League)	Pos.	G	AB	R	H	2B	3B	HR	RBI	Avg.	BB	SO	SB	PO	A	E	Avg.
1991— Harrisburg (Eastern) ..	2B-3B-OF	129	505	87	*168	30	•10	13	78	*.333	66	47	23	193	314	22	.958
1992— Indianapolis (A.A.)......	OF	110	401	57	107	23	4	11	56	.267	49	61	11	188	11	3	.985
— Montreal (N.L.)...........	OF	13	30	2	5	2	0	0	5	.167	7	7	0	14	0	1	.933
1993— Ottawa (Int'l)	OF	34	125	18	35	4	2	3	20	.280	11	15	4	49	4	0	1.000
— Montreal (N.L.)...........	OF	6	8	1	3	1	0	0	2	.375	0	1	0	1	0	0	1.000
— Chunichi (Jp. Cn.)■...		60	132	10	33	6	0	6	23	.250	7	34	1	...	...	...	...
1994— New Britain (East.)■..	OF-1B	93	317	44	98	25	2	9	61	.309	53	38	10	106	12	3	.975
1995— Pawtucket (Int'l)........	OF	75	271	40	77	17	0	13	56	.284	29	41	3	79	13	0	1.000
— Boston (A.L.)..........	OF-DH	39	88	8	23	7	1	1	17	.261	4	14	0	19	2	2	.913
1996— Oakland (A.L.)■......	OF-DH-1B	61	137	21	38	5	1	10	23	.277	19	23	1	65	11	1	.987
— Edmonton (PCL)	OF-1B	51	180	35	62	16	1	8	41	.344	21	34	0	49	2	3	.944
1997— Oakland (A.L.)	OF-DH-1B	133	352	62	105	19	0	27	73	.298	50	60	3	142	9	4	.974
American League totals (3 years)		233	577	91	166	31	2	38	113	.288	73	97	4	226	22	7	.973
National League totals (2 years)		19	38	3	8	3	0	0	7	.211	7	8	0	15	0	1	.938
Major league totals (5 years)		252	615	94	174	34	2	38	120	.283	80	105	4	241	22	8	.970

DIVISION SERIES RECORD

					BATTING									FIELDING			
Year — Team (League)	Pos.	G	AB	R	H	2B	3B	HR	RBI	Avg.	BB	SO	SB	PO	A	E	Avg.
1995— Boston (A.L.).............	PH	1	1	0	0	0	0	0	0	.000	0	1	0	...	...	...	...

STANIFER, ROB   P   MARLINS

PERSONAL: Born March 10, 1972, in Easley, S.C. ... 6-3/205. ... Throws right, bats right.
HIGH SCHOOL: Easley (S.C.).
COLLEGE: Anderson (S.C.); degree in sports administration, 1994.
TRANSACTIONS/CAREER NOTES: Selected by Florida Marlins organization in 12th round of free-agent draft (June 2, 1994).

Year — Team (League)	W	L	Pct.	ERA	G	GS	CG	ShO	Sv.	IP	H	R	ER	BB	SO
1994— Elmira (N.Y.-Penn).............	2	1	.667	2.57	9	8	1	0	0	49	54	17	14	12	38
— Brevard County (FSL)........	1	2	.333	6.29	5	5	0	0	0	24 1/3	32	20	17	10	12
1995— Brevard County (FSL)........	3	6	.333	4.14	18	13	0	0	0	82 2/3	97	47	38	15	45
1996— Brevard County (FSL)........	4	2	.667	2.39	22	0	0	0	0	49	54	17	13	9	32
— Portland (Eastern)	3	1	.750	1.57	18	0	0	0	2	34 1/3	27	15	6	9	33
1997— Charlotte (Int'l)	4	0	1.000	4.88	22	0	0	0	5	27 2/3	34	16	15	7	25
— Florida (N.L.)....................	1	2	.333	4.60	36	0	0	0	1	45	43	23	23	16	28
Major league totals (1 year)........	1	2	.333	4.60	36	0	0	0	1	45	43	23	23	16	28

STANKIEWICZ, ANDY   IF   DIAMONDBACKS

PERSONAL: Born August 10, 1964, In Inglewood, Calif. ... 5-9/165. ... Bats right, throws right. ... Full name: Andrew Neal Stankiewicz.
HIGH SCHOOL: St. Paul (Sante Fe Springs, Calif.).
COLLEGE: Pepperdine.
TRANSACTIONS/CAREER NOTES: Selected by Kansas City Royals organization in 26th round of free-agent draft (June 7, 1982); did not sign. ... Selected by Detroit Tigers organization in 18th round of free-agent draft (June 3, 1985); did not sign. ... Selected by New York Yankees organization in 12th round of free-agent draft (June 2, 1986). ... On disabled list (May 16-31, 1992). ... On Columbus disabled list (August 18-26, 1993). ... Traded by Yankees with P Domingo Jean to Houston Astros for P Xavier Hernandez (November 27, 1993). ... On Houston disabled list (July 6-August 7, 1994); included rehabilitation assignment to Jackson (August 1-7). ... On Houston disabled list (May 29-June 26, 1995); included rehabilitation assignment to Tucson (June 18-26). ... Granted free agency (October 16, 1995). ... Signed by Montreal Expos organization (December 20, 1995). ... On disabled list (August 12-September 1, 1996). ... Granted free agency (December 21, 1997). ... Signed by Arizona Diamondbacks (January 8, 1998).
STATISTICAL NOTES: Led Eastern League with 11 sacrifice flies in 1989. ... Led Eastern League second basemen with 615 total chances and 85 double plays in 1989.

					BATTING									FIELDING			
Year — Team (League)	Pos.	G	AB	R	H	2B	3B	HR	RBI	Avg.	BB	SO	SB	PO	A	E	Avg.
1986— Oneonta (NYP)	2B-SS	59	216	51	64	8	3	0	17	.296	38	41	14	107	152	12	.956
1987— Fort Lauderdale (FSL)	2B	119	456	80	140	18	7	2	47	.307	62	84	26	233	347	16	.973
1988— Alb./Colon. (Eastern) ..	2B	109	414	63	111	20	2	1	33	.268	39	53	15	230	325	*16	.972
— Columbus (Int'l)	2B	29	114	4	25	0	0	0	4	.219	6	25	2	56	97	3	.981
1989— Alb./Colon. (Eastern) ..	2B	133	498	*74	133	26	2	4	49	.267	57	59	*41	*242	*369	4	*.993
1990— Columbus (Int'l)	2B-SS-3B	135	446	68	102	14	4	1	48	.229	71	63	25	237	399	10	.985
1991— Columbus (Int'l)	2-S-3-P	125	372	47	101	12	4	1	41	.272	29	45	29	220	324	15	.973
1992— New York (A.L.)..........	SS-2B-DH	116	400	52	107	22	2	2	25	.268	38	42	9	185	346	12	.978
1993— Columbus (Int'l)	2B-3B-SS	90	331	45	80	12	5	0	32	.242	29	46	12	138	265	6	.985
— New York (A.L.)..........	2-3-DH-S	16	9	5	0	0	0	0	0	.000	1	1	0	7	15	0	1.000
1994— Houston (N.L.)■..........	SS-2B-3B	37	54	10	14	3	0	1	5	.259	12	12	1	12	45	0	1.000
— Jackson (Texas)	2B-SS	5	12	1	5	0	0	0	3	.417	0	0	0	8	7	1	.938
1995— Houston (N.L.)..........	SS-2B-3B	43	52	6	6	1	0	0	7	.115	12	19	4	20	59	1	.988
— Tucson (PCL)	SS-2B-3B	25	87	16	24	4	0	1	15	.276	14	8	3	36	81	3	.975
1996— Montreal (N.L.)■.........	2B-SS-3B	64	77	12	22	5	1	0	9	.286	6	12	1	16	43	3	.952
1997— Montreal (N.L.)..........	2-S-3-DH	76	107	11	24	9	0	1	5	.224	4	22	1	33	68	3	.971
American League totals (2 years)		132	409	57	107	22	2	2	25	.262	39	43	9	192	361	12	.979
National League totals (4 years)		220	290	39	66	18	1	2	26	.228	34	65	7	81	215	7	.977
Major league totals (6 years)		352	699	96	173	40	3	4	51	.247	73	108	16	273	576	19	.978

RECORD AS PITCHER

Year — Team (League)	W	L	Pct.	ERA	G	GS	CG	ShO	Sv.	IP	H	R	ER	BB	SO
1991— Columbus (Int'l)	0	0	...	0.00	1	0	0	0	0	1/3	1	0	0	1	0

PERSONAL: Born June 25, 1963, in Fort Lauderdale. ... 6-0/190. ... Bats right, throws right. ... Full name: Robert Michael Stanley.
HIGH SCHOOL: St. Thomas Aquinas (Fort Lauderdale).
COLLEGE: Florida.
TRANSACTIONS/CAREER NOTES: Selected by Texas Rangers organization in 16th round of free-agent draft (June 3, 1985). ... On disabled list (July 24-August 14, 1988 and August 18-September 2, 1989). ... Granted free agency (November 15, 1990). ... Re-signed by Rangers organization (February 4, 1991). ... Granted free agency (October 14, 1991). ... Signed by Columbus, New York Yankees organization (January 21, 1992). ... On disabled list (May 14-29, 1994). ... Granted free agency (November 1, 1995). ... Signed by Boston Red Sox (December 14, 1995). ... Traded by Red Sox with IF Randy Brown to Yankees for P Tony Armas and a player to be named later (August 13, 1997). ... Granted free agency (October 27, 1997). ... Signed by Toronto Blue Jays (December 8, 1997).
HONORS: Named catcher on THE SPORTING NEWS A.L. All-Star team (1993). ... Named catcher on THE SPORTING NEWS A.L. Silver Slugger team (1993).
STATISTICAL NOTES: Hit three home runs in one game (August 10, 1995, first game). ... Led A.L. catchers with 18 passed balls in 1996. ... Career major league grand slams: 8.

							BATTING								FIELDING		
Year Team (League)	Pos.	G	AB	R	H	2B	3B	HR	RBI	Avg.	BB	SO	SB	PO	A	E	Avg.
1985— Salem (Carolina)	1B-C	4	9	2	5	0	0	0	3	.556	1	1	0	19	1	1	.952
— Burl. (Midw.)	C-1B-OF	13	42	8	13	2	0	1	6	.310	6	5	0	45	2	0	1.000
— Tulsa (Texas)	C-1-0-2	46	165	24	51	10	0	3	17	.309	24	18	6	289	18	6	.981
1986— Tulsa (Texas)	C-1B-3B	67	235	41	69	16	2	6	35	.294	34	26	5	379	45	2	.995
— Texas (A.L.)	3-C-DH-O	15	30	4	10	3	0	1	1	.333	3	7	1	14	8	1	.957
— Oklahoma City (A.A.)	C-3B-1B	56	202	37	74	13	3	5	49	.366	44	42	1	206	55	9	.967
1987— Oklahoma City (A.A.)	C-1B	46	182	43	61	8	3	13	54	.335	29	36	2	277	32	2	.994
— Texas (A.L.)	C-1-DH-O	78	216	34	59	8	1	6	37	.273	31	48	3	389	26	7	.983
1988— Texas (A.L.)	C-DH-1-3	94	249	21	57	8	0	3	27	.229	37	62	0	342	17	4	.989
1989— Texas (A.L.)	C-DH-1-3	67	122	9	30	3	1	1	11	.246	12	29	1	117	8	3	.977
1990— Texas (A.L.)	C-DH-3-1	103	189	21	47	8	1	2	19	.249	30	25	1	261	25	4	.986
1991— Texas (A.L.)	C-1-3-DH-O	95	181	25	45	13	1	3	25	.249	34	44	0	288	20	6	.981
1992— New York (A.L.)■	C-DH-1B	68	173	24	43	7	0	8	27	.249	33	45	0	287	30	6	.981
1993— New York (A.L.)	C-DH	130	423	70	129	17	1	26	84	.305	57	85	1	652	46	3	*.996
1994— New York (A.L.)	C-1B-DH	82	290	54	87	20	0	17	57	.300	39	56	0	442	35	5	.990
1995— New York (A.L.)	C-DH	118	399	63	107	29	1	18	83	.268	57	106	1	651	35	5	.993
1996— Boston (A.L.)■	C-DH	121	397	73	107	20	1	24	69	.270	69	62	2	654	19	•10	.985
1997— Boston (A.L.)	DH-1B-C	97	260	45	78	17	0	13	53	.300	39	50	0	284	21	2	.993
— New York (A.L.)■	DH-1B	28	87	16	25	8	0	3	12	.287	15	22	0	71	3	0	1.000
Major league totals (12 years)		1096	3016	459	824	161	7	125	505	.273	456	641	10	4452	293	56	.988

DIVISION SERIES RECORD

							BATTING								FIELDING		
Year Team (League)	Pos.	G	AB	R	H	2B	3B	HR	RBI	Avg.	BB	SO	SB	PO	A	E	Avg.
1995— New York (A.L.)	C	4	16	2	5	0	0	1	3	.313	2	1	0	30	0	1	.968
1997— New York (A.L.)	PH-DH	2	4	1	3	1	0	0	1	.750	0	1	0	...	...	...	...
Division series totals (2 years)		6	20	3	8	1	0	1	4	.400	2	2	0	30	0	1	.968

ALL-STAR GAME RECORD

						BATTING								FIELDING		
Year League	Pos.	AB	R	H	2B	3B	HR	RBI	Avg.	BB	SO	SB	PO	A	E	Avg.
1995— American	C	1	0	0	0	0	0	0	.000	0	0	0	3	0	0	1.000

PERSONAL: Born June 2, 1967, in Houston. ... 6-1/215. ... Throws left, bats left. ... Full name: William Michael Stanton.
HIGH SCHOOL: Midland (Texas).
JUNIOR COLLEGE: Alvin (Texas) Community College.
TRANSACTIONS/CAREER NOTES: Selected by Atlanta Braves organization in 13th round of free-agent draft (June 2, 1987). ... On Atlanta disabled list (April 27, 1990-remainder of season); included rehabilitation assignments to Greenville (May 31-June 5 and August 21-29). ... Granted free agency (December 23, 1994). ... Re-signed by Braves (April 12, 1995). ... Traded by Braves with a player to be named later to Boston Red Sox for two players to be named later (July 31, 1995); Red Sox acquired P Matt Murray and Braves acquired OF Marc Lewis and P Mike Jacobs to complete deal (August 31, 1995). ... Traded by Red Sox to Texas Rangers for P Mark Brandenburg and P Kerry Lacy (July 31, 1996). ... Granted free agency (October 27, 1996). ... Signed by New York Yankees (December 11, 1996).

Year Team (League)	W	L	Pct.	ERA	G	GS	CG	ShO	Sv.	IP	H	R	ER	BB	SO
1987— Pulaski (Appalachian)	4	8	.333	3.24	15	13	3	2	0	83 1/3	64	37	30	42	82
1988— Burlington (Midw.)	11	5	.688	3.62	30	23	1	1	0	154	154	86	62	69	160
— Durham (Carolina)	1	0	1.000	1.46	2	2	1	1	0	12 1/3	14	3	2	5	14
1989— Greenville (Southern)	4	1	.800	1.58	47	0	0	0	19	51 1/3	32	10	9	31	58
— Richmond (Int'l)	2	0	1.000	0.00	13	0	0	0	8	20	6	0	0	13	20
— Atlanta (N.L.)	0	1	.000	1.50	20	0	0	0	7	24	17	4	4	8	27
1990— Atlanta (N.L.)	0	3	.000	18.00	7	0	0	0	2	7	16	16	14	4	7
— Greenville (Southern)	0	1	.000	1.59	4	4	0	0	0	5 2/3	7	1	1	3	4
1991— Atlanta (N.L.)	5	5	.500	2.88	74	0	0	0	7	78	62	27	25	21	54
1992— Atlanta (N.L.)	5	4	.556	4.10	65	0	0	0	8	63 2/3	59	32	29	20	44
1993— Atlanta (N.L.)	4	6	.400	4.67	63	0	0	0	27	52	51	35	27	29	43
1994— Atlanta (N.L.)	3	1	.750	3.55	49	0	0	0	3	45 2/3	41	18	18	26	35
1995— Atlanta (N.L.)	1	1	.500	5.59	26	0	0	0	1	19 1/3	31	14	12	6	13
— Boston (A.L.)■	1	0	1.000	3.00	22	0	0	0	0	21	17	9	7	8	10
— Texas (A.L.)■	0	1	.000	3.22	22	0	0	0	0	22 1/3	20	8	8	4	14
1996— Boston (A.L.)	4	3	.571	3.83	59	0	0	0	1	56 1/3	58	28	24	23	46
1997— New York (A.L.)■	6	1	.857	2.57	64	0	0	0	3	66 2/3	50	19	19	34	70
A.L. totals (3 years)	11	5	.688	3.14	167	0	0	0	4	166 1/3	145	60	58	69	140
N.L. totals (7 years)	18	21	.462	4.01	304	0	0	0	55	289 2/3	277	146	129	114	223
Major league totals (9 years)	29	26	.527	3.69	471	0	0	0	59	456	422	206	187	183	363

DIVISION SERIES RECORD

Year Team (League)	W	L	Pct.	ERA	G	GS	CG	ShO	Sv.	IP	H	R	ER	BB	SO
1995— Boston (A.L.)	0	0	...	0.00	1	0	0	0	0	2 1/3	1	0	0	0	4
1996— Texas (A.L.)	0	1	.000	2.70	3	0	0	0	0	3 1/3	2	2	1	3	3
1997— New York (A.L.)	0	0	...	0.00	3	0	0	0	0	1	1	0	0	1	3
Div. series totals (3 years)	0	1	.000	1.35	7	0	0	0	0	6 2/3	4	2	1	4	10

CHAMPIONSHIP SERIES RECORD

Year Team (League)	W	L	Pct.	ERA	G	GS	CG	ShO	Sv.	IP	H	R	ER	BB	SO
1991— Atlanta (N.L.)	0	0	...	2.45	3	0	0	0	0	3 2/3	4	1	1	3	3
1992— Atlanta (N.L.)	0	0	...	0.00	5	0	0	0	0	4 1/3	2	1	0	2	5
1993— Atlanta (N.L.)	0	0	...	0.00	1	0	0	0	0	1	1	0	0	1	0
Champ. series totals (3 years)	0	0	...	1.00	9	0	0	0	0	9	7	2	1	6	8

WORLD SERIES RECORD

Year Team (League)	W	L	Pct.	ERA	G	GS	CG	ShO	Sv.	IP	H	R	ER	BB	SO
1991— Atlanta (N.L.)	1	0	1.000	0.00	5	0	0	0	0	7 1/3	5	0	0	2	7
1992— Atlanta (N.L.)	0	0	...	0.00	4	0	0	0	1	5	3	0	0	2	1
World Series totals (2 years)	1	0	1.000	0.00	9	0	0	0	1	12 1/3	8	0	0	4	8

STATON, T.J.   OF   PIRATES

PERSONAL: Born February 17, 1975, in Norfolk, Va. ... 6-3/210. ... Bats left, throws left. ... Full name: Tarrence Jervon Staton.
HIGH SCHOOL: Elyria West (Elyria, Ohio).
TRANSACTIONS/CAREER NOTES: Selected by Pittsburgh Pirates organization in 10th round of free-agent draft (June 3, 1993).

							BATTING						FIELDING			
Year Team (League)	Pos.	G	AB	R	H	2B	3B	HR	RBI	Avg.	BB	SO	SB	PO	A	E	Avg.
1993— GC Pirates (GCL)	OF	32	115	23	41	9	2	1	18	.357	8	14	10	44	4	5	.906
1994— GC Pirates (GCL)	OF	11	39	3	10	3	0	1	5	.256	1	8	0	23	1	1	.960
— Welland (NYP)	OF	12	45	4	8	3	0	0	5	.178	0	7	5	18	1	0	1.000
— Augusta (S. Atl.)	OF	37	125	9	27	6	1	0	5	.216	10	38	6	66	2	7	.907
1995— Augusta (S. Atl.)	OF	112	391	43	114	21	5	5	53	.292	27	97	27	153	10	9	.948
1996— Carolina (Southern)	OF	112	386	72	119	24	3	15	57	.308	58	99	17	178	7	4	.979
1997— Calgary (PCL)	OF	65	199	30	47	14	0	2	22	.236	22	51	3	78	3	1	.988
— Carolina (Southern)	OF	58	207	33	60	11	2	6	33	.290	12	60	8	79	4	3	.965

STEIN, BLAKE   P   ATHLETICS

PERSONAL: Born August 3, 1973, in McComb, Miss. ... 6-7/210. ... Throws right, bats right. ... Full name: William Blake Stein.
HIGH SCHOOL: Covington (La.).
COLLEGE: Spring Hill College (Ala.).
TRANSACTIONS/CAREER NOTES: Selected by St. Louis Cardinals organization in sixth round of free-agent draft (June 2, 1994). ... Traded by Cardinals with P T.J. Mathews and P Eric Ludwick to Oakland Athletics for 1B Mark McGwire (July 31, 1997).

Year Team (League)	W	L	Pct.	ERA	G	GS	CG	ShO	Sv.	IP	H	R	ER	BB	SO
1994— Johnson City (App.)	4	1	.800	2.87	13	13	1	0	0	59 2/3	44	21	19	24	69
1995— Peoria (Midwest)	10	6	.625	3.80	27	•27	1	0	0	139 2/3	122	69	59	61	133
1996— St. Petersburg (FSL)	•16	5	.762	*2.15	28	27	2	1	1	172	122	48	41	54	*159
1997— Arkansas (Texas)	8	7	.533	4.24	22	22	1	0	0	133 2/3	128	67	63	49	114
— Huntsville (Southern)■	3	2	.600	5.71	7	7	0	0	0	34 2/3	36	24	22	20	25

STEINBACH, TERRY   C   TWINS

PERSONAL: Born March 2, 1962, in New Ulm, Minn. ... 6-1/195. ... Bats right, throws right. ... Full name: Terry Lee Steinbach. ... Brother of Tom Steinbach, minor league outfielder (1983).
HIGH SCHOOL: New Ulm (Minn.).
COLLEGE: Minnesota.
TRANSACTIONS/CAREER NOTES: Selected by Cleveland Indians organization in 16th round of free-agent draft (June 3, 1980); did not sign. ... Selected by Oakland Athletics organization in ninth round of free-agent draft (June 6, 1983). ... On disabled list (May 6-June 1, 1988; July 3-28, 1990; and April 10-25, 1992). ... Granted free agency (October 26, 1992). ... Re-signed by A's (December 14, 1992). ... On disabled list (August 16, 1993-remainder of season and August 13-29, 1995). ... Granted free agency (November 17, 1996). ... Signed by Minnesota Twins (December 5, 1996).
RECORDS: Holds A.L. single-season record for most home runs by catcher—34 (1996; also hit one home run as pinch hitter).
HONORS: Named Southern League Most Valuable Player (1986).
STATISTICAL NOTES: Led Northwest League third basemen with 122 assists and tied for lead with 17 errors in 1983. ... Led Midwest League third basemen with 31 double plays in 1984. ... Led Southern League with 22 passed balls in 1986. ... Hit home run in first major league at-bat (September 12, 1986). ... Led A.L. catchers with 15 errors in 1991. ... Led A.L. catchers with .998 fielding percentage in 1994. ... Career major league grand slams: 8.

							BATTING						FIELDING			
Year Team (League)	Pos.	G	AB	R	H	2B	3B	HR	RBI	Avg.	BB	SO	SB	PO	A	E	Avg.
1983— Medford (N'west)	3B-OF-1B	62	219	42	69	16	0	6	38	.315	28	22	8	105	†124	‡21	.916
1984— Madison (Midwest)	3B-1B-P	135	474	57	140	24	6	11	79	.295	49	59	5	107	257	27	.931
1985— Huntsville (Southern)	C-3-1-O-P	128	456	64	124	31	3	9	72	.272	45	36	4	187	43	6	.975
1986— Huntsville (Southern)	C-1B-3B	138	505	113	164	33	2	24	*132	.325	94	74	10	620	73	14	.980
— Oakland (A.L.)	C	6	15	3	5	0	0	2	4	.333	1	0	0	21	4	1	.962
1987— Oakland (A.L.)	C-3-DH-1	122	391	66	111	16	3	16	56	.284	32	66	1	642	44	10	.986
1988— Oakland (A.L.)	C-3-1-DH-O	104	351	42	93	19	1	9	51	.265	33	47	3	536	58	9	.985
1989— Oakland (A.L.)	C-O-1-DH-3	130	454	37	124	13	1	7	42	.273	30	66	1	612	47	11	.984
1990— Oakland (A.L.)	C-DH-1B	114	379	32	95	15	2	9	57	.251	19	66	0	401	31	5	.989

Year Team (League)	Pos.	G	AB	R	H	2B	3B	HR	RBI	Avg.	BB	SO	SB	PO	A	E	Avg.
1991—Oakland (A.L.)............	C-1B-DH	129	456	50	125	31	1	6	67	.274	22	70	2	639	53	†15	.979
1992—Oakland (A.L.)............	C-1B-DH	128	438	48	122	20	1	12	53	.279	45	58	2	598	72	10	.985
1993—Oakland (A.L.)............	C-1B-DH	104	389	47	111	19	1	10	43	.285	25	65	3	524	47	7	.988
1994—Oakland (A.L.)............	C-DH-1B	103	369	51	105	21	2	11	57	.285	26	62	2	597	59	1	†.998
1995—Oakland (A.L.)............	C-1B	114	406	43	113	26	1	15	65	.278	25	74	1	686	57	6	.992
1996—Oakland (A.L.)............	C-DH-1B	145	514	79	140	25	1	35	100	.272	49	115	0	732	46	7	.991
1997—Minnesota (A.L.)■	C-1B-DH	122	447	60	111	27	1	12	54	.248	35	106	6	657	51	6	.992
Major league totals (12 years)		1321	4609	558	1255	232	15	144	649	.272	342	795	21	6645	569	88	.988

CHAMPIONSHIP SERIES RECORD

Year Team (League)	Pos.	G	AB	R	H	2B	3B	HR	RBI	Avg.	BB	SO	SB	PO	A	E	Avg.
1988—Oakland (A.L.)...........	C	2	4	0	1	0	0	0	0	.250	2	0	0	12	0	0	1.000
1989—Oakland (A.L.)...........	C-DH	4	15	0	3	0	0	0	1	.200	1	5	0	17	0	0	1.000
1990—Oakland (A.L.)...........	C	3	11	2	5	0	0	0	1	.455	1	2	0	11	0	0	1.000
1992—Oakland (A.L.)...........	C	6	24	1	7	0	0	1	5	.292	2	7	0	30	7	0	1.000
Championship series totals (4 years)		15	54	3	16	0	0	1	7	.296	6	14	0	70	7	0	1.000

WORLD SERIES RECORD

NOTES: Member of World Series championship team (1989).

Year Team (League)	Pos.	G	AB	R	H	2B	3B	HR	RBI	Avg.	BB	SO	SB	PO	A	E	Avg.
1988—Oakland (A.L.)...........	C-DH	3	11	0	4	1	0	0	0	.364	0	2	0	11	3	0	1.000
1989—Oakland (A.L.)...........	C	4	16	3	4	0	1	1	7	.250	2	1	0	27	2	0	1.000
1990—Oakland (A.L.)...........	C	3	8	0	1	0	0	0	0	.125	0	1	0	8	1	0	1.000
World Series totals (3 years)		10	35	3	9	1	1	1	7	.257	2	4	0	46	6	0	1.000

ALL-STAR GAME RECORD

NOTES: Named Most Valuable Player (1988). ... Hit home run in first at-bat (July 12, 1988).

Year League	Pos.	AB	R	H	2B	3B	HR	RBI	Avg.	BB	SO	SB	PO	A	E	Avg.
1988—American..................	C	1	1	1	0	0	1	2	1.000	0	0	0	3	1	1	.800
1989—American..................	C	3	0	1	0	0	0	0	.333	0	0	0	6	1	0	1.000
1993—American..................	C	2	0	1	1	0	0	1	.500	0	1	0	6	0	0	1.000
All-Star Game totals (3 years)		6	1	3	1	0	1	3	.500	0	1	0	15	2	1	.944

RECORD AS PITCHER

Year Team (League)	W	L	Pct.	ERA	G	GS	CG	ShO	Sv.	IP	H	R	ER	BB	SO
1984—Madison (Midwest)...........	0	0	...	9.00	2	0	0	0	0	3	2	4	3	4	0
1985—Huntsville (Southern).........	0	0	...	0.00	1	0	0	0	0	1	0	0	0	0	0

STEPHENSON, GARRETT   P   PHILLIES

PERSONAL: Born January 2, 1972, in Takoma Park, Md. ... 6-4/195. ... Throws right, bats right. ... Full name: Garrett Charles Stephenson.
HIGH SCHOOL: Linganore (Frederick, Md.), then Boonsboro (Md.).
JUNIOR COLLEGE: Ricks (Idaho).
COLLEGE: Idaho State.
TRANSACTIONS/CAREER NOTES: Selected by Baltimore Orioles organization in 18th round of free-agent draft (June 1, 1992). ... Traded by Orioles with P Calvin Maduro to Philadelphia Phillies (September 4, 1996), completing deal in which Phillies traded 3B Todd Zeile and OF Pete Incaviglia to Orioles for two players to be named later (August 29, 1996). ... On Philadelphia disabled list (June 5-22 and August 18-September 2, 1997).
STATISTICAL NOTES: Led Eastern League with 23 home runs allowed and 18 hit batsmen in 1995.

Year Team (League)	W	L	Pct.	ERA	G	GS	CG	ShO	Sv.	IP	H	R	ER	BB	SO
1992—Bluefield (Appalachian)	3	1	.750	4.73	12	3	0	0	0	32 1/3	35	22	17	7	30
1993—Albany (S. Atl.)..................	16	7	.696	2.84	30	24	3	•2	1	171 1/3	142	65	54	44	147
1994—Frederick (Carolina)...........	7	5	.583	4.02	18	17	1	0	0	107 1/3	91	62	48	36	133
—Bowie (Eastern).................	3	2	.600	5.15	7	7	1	1	0	36 2/3	47	22	21	11	32
1995—Bowie (Eastern).................	7	10	.412	3.64	29	*29	1	0	0	175 1/3	154	87	71	47	139
1996—Rochester (Int'l).................	7	6	.538	4.81	23	21	3	1	0	121 2/3	123	66	65	44	86
—Baltimore (A.L.)................	0	1	.000	12.79	3	0	0	0	0	6 1/3	13	9	9	3	3
1997—Scran./W.B. (Int'l)■	3	1	.750	5.90	7	3	0	0	0	29	27	19	19	12	27
—Philadelphia (N.L.).........	8	6	.571	3.15	20	18	2	0	0	117	104	45	41	38	81
A.L. totals (1 year)	0	1	.000	12.79	3	0	0	0	0	6 1/3	13	9	9	3	3
N.L. totals (1 year)	8	6	.571	3.15	20	18	2	0	0	117	104	45	41	38	81
Major league totals (2 years)......	8	7	.533	3.65	23	18	2	0	0	123 1/3	117	54	50	41	84

STEVENS, DAVE   P   CUBS

PERSONAL: Born March 4, 1970, in Fullerton, Calif. ... 6-3/195. ... Throws right, bats right. ... Full name: David James Stevens.
HIGH SCHOOL: La Habra (Calif.).
COLLEGE: Fullerton (Calif.) College.
TRANSACTIONS/CAREER NOTES: Selected by Chicago Cubs organization in 20th round of free-agent draft (June 5, 1989). ... On disabled list (June 17-July 4, 1991). ... On Iowa disabled list (April 8-May 20, 1993). ... Traded by Cubs with C Matt Walbeck to Minnesota Twins for P Willie Banks (November 24, 1993). ... On disabled list (May 30-June 21 and July 21-August 9, 1996). ... Claimed on waivers by Cubs organization (July 31, 1997).

Year Team (League)	W	L	Pct.	ERA	G	GS	CG	ShO	Sv.	IP	H	R	ER	BB	SO
1990—Huntington (Appal.)..........	2	4	.333	4.61	13	11	0	0	0	56 2/3	48	44	29	47	55
1991—Geneva (N.Y.-Penn)...........	2	3	.400	2.85	9	9	1	0	0	47 1/3	49	20	15	14	44
1992—Charlotte (Southern)	9	13	.409	3.91	26	26	2	0	0	149 2/3	147	79	65	53	89

S

Year Team (League)	W	L	Pct.	ERA	G	GS	CG	ShO	Sv.	IP	H	R	ER	BB	SO
1993— Iowa (Am. Assoc.)	4	0	1.000	4.19	24	0	0	0	4	34 1/3	24	16	16	14	29
— Orlando (South.)	6	1	.857	4.22	11	11	1	1	0	70 1/3	69	36	33	35	49
1994— Salt Lake (PCL)■	6	2	.750	1.67	23	0	0	0	3	43	41	13	8	16	30
— Minnesota (A.L.)	5	2	.714	6.80	24	0	0	0	0	45	55	35	34	23	24
1995— Minnesota (A.L.)	5	4	.556	5.07	56	0	0	0	10	65 2/3	74	40	37	32	47
1996— Minnesota (A.L.)	3	3	.500	4.66	49	0	0	0	11	58	58	31	30	25	29
1997— Salt Lake (PCL)	9	3	.750	4.30	16	14	0	0	0	90	93	52	43	31	71
— Minnesota (A.L.)	1	3	.250	9.00	6	6	0	0	0	23	41	23	23	17	16
— Iowa (Am. Assoc.)■	1	1	.500	4.70	6	0	0	0	1	7 2/3	8	4	4	5	8
— Chicago (N.L.)	0	2	.000	9.64	10	0	0	0	0	9 1/3	13	11	10	9	13
A.L. totals (4 years)	14	12	.538	5.82	135	6	0	0	21	191 2/3	228	129	124	97	116
N.L. totals (1 year)	0	2	.000	9.64	10	0	0	0	0	9 1/3	13	11	10	9	13
Major league totals (4 years)	14	14	.500	6.00	145	6	0	0	21	201	241	140	134	106	129

STEVENS, LEE — 1B/OF — RANGERS

PERSONAL: Born July 10, 1967, in Kansas City, Mo. ... 6-4/219. ... Bats left, throws left. ... Full name: DeWain Lee Stevens.
HIGH SCHOOL: Lawrence (Kan.).
TRANSACTIONS/CAREER NOTES: Selected by California Angels organization in first round (22nd pick overall) of free-agent draft (June 2, 1986). ... Traded by Angels to Montreal Expos for P Jeff Tuss (January 15, 1993); Tuss announced his retirement and Expos sent P Keith Morrison to Angels to complete deal (January 21, 1993). ... Released by Expos (March 30, 1993). ... Signed by Toronto Blue Jays organization (April 8, 1993). ... Granted free agency (October 15, 1993). ... Signed by Vancouver, Angels organization (October 25, 1993). ... Released by Vancouver (November 16, 1993). ... Played in Japan (1994-95). ... Signed by Texas Rangers organization (April 3, 1996). ... On Texas disabled list (August 4-September 1, 1996); included rehabilitation assignment to Oklahoma City (August 13-September 1, 1996).
HONORS: Named American Association Most Valuable Player (1996).
STATISTICAL NOTES: Led California League first basemen with .986 fielding percentage, 1,028 putouts and 66 assists in 1987. ... Led Texas League outfielders with 12 errors in 1988. ... Tied for Pacific Coast League lead with 11 intentional bases on balls received in 1990. ... Led American Association with 277 total bases, .643 slugging percentage and .404 on-base percentage in 1996. ... Tied for American Association lead with eight intentional bases on balls received in 1996. ... Career major league grand slams: 2.

						BATTING								FIELDING			
Year Team (League)	Pos.	G	AB	R	H	2B	3B	HR	RBI	Avg.	BB	SO	SB	PO	A	E	Avg.
1986— Salem (Northwest)	OF-1B	72	267	45	75	18	2	6	47	.281	45	49	13	231	18	5	.980
1987— Palm Springs (Cal.)	1B-OF	140	532	82	130	29	2	19	97	.244	61	117	1	†1031	†68	18	†.984
1988— Midland (Texas)	OF-1B	116	414	79	123	26	2	23	76	.297	58	108	0	217	16	†14	.943
1989— Edmonton (PCL)	1B-OF	127	446	72	110	29	9	14	74	.247	61	115	5	635	40	7	.990
1990— Edmonton (PCL)	OF-1B	90	338	57	99	31	2	16	66	.293	55	83	1	284	10	6	.980
— California (A.L.)	1B	67	248	28	53	10	0	7	32	.214	22	75	1	597	36	4	.994
1991— Edmonton (PCL)	OF-1B	123	481	75	151	29	3	19	96	.314	37	79	3	519	33	7	.987
— California (A.L.)	OF-1B	18	58	8	17	7	0	0	9	.293	6	12	1	100	6	1	.991
1992— California (A.L.)	1B-DH	106	312	25	69	19	0	7	37	.221	29	64	1	764	49	4	.995
1993— Syracuse (Int'l)■	OF-1B	116	401	61	106	30	1	14	66	.264	39	85	2	201	12	3	.986
1994— Kintetsu (Jp. Pac.)■	OF	93	302	...	87	...	...	20	66	.288	...	...	...	...	...	...	...
1995— Kintetsu (Jp. Pac.)	OF	129	476	54	117	...	...	23	70	.246	46	129	0	...	...	...	...
1996— Okla. City (A.A.)■	1B-OF	117	431	84	140	*37	2	*32	94	.325	58	90	3	348	24	3	.992
— Texas (A.L.)	1B-OF	27	78	6	18	2	3	3	12	.231	6	22	0	157	14	1	.994
1997— Texas (A.L.)	1B-DH-OF	137	426	58	128	24	2	21	74	.300	23	83	1	486	33	3	.994
Major league totals (5 years)		355	1122	125	285	62	5	38	164	.254	86	256	4	2104	138	13	.994

STEVENSON, JASON — P — BLUE JAYS

PERSONAL: Born August 11, 1974, in Phenix City, Ala. ... 6-3/180. ... Throws right, bats right. ... Full name: Jason Keith Stevenson.
HIGH SCHOOL: Central (Phenix, Ala.).
JUNIOR COLLEGE: Chattahoochee Valley Community College (Ala.).
TRANSACTIONS/CAREER NOTES: Selected by Chicago Cubs organization in 17th round of free-agent draft (June 2, 1994). ... Traded by Cubs organization to Toronto Blue Jays organization for IF Miguel Cairo (November 21, 1996).

Year Team (League)	W	L	Pct.	ERA	G	GS	CG	ShO	Sv.	IP	H	R	ER	BB	SO
1994— Huntington (Appal.)	1	1	.500	4.22	5	1	0	0	1	10 2/3	12	5	5	6	5
— GC Cubs (GCL)	1	1	.500	2.52	5	5	0	0	0	25	31	12	7	4	19
1995— Rockford (Midwest)	4	3	.571	5.59	33	5	0	0	2	77 1/3	85	50	48	31	54
— Daytona (Fla. St.)	2	0	1.000	2.95	8	0	0	0	1	18 1/3	11	6	6	6	15
1996— Daytona (Fla. St.)	8	5	.615	3.54	27	17	2	1	2	122	136	56	48	22	86
1997— Knoxville (Southern)■	12	9	.571	4.27	26	26	2	•2	0	149 2/3	166	88	71	43	101

STEWART, ANDY — C/1B — ROYALS

PERSONAL: Born December 5, 1970, in Oshawa, Ont. ... 5-11/205. ... Bats right, throws right. ... Full name: Andrew David Stewart.
HIGH SCHOOL: East Dale Collegiate (Oshawa, Ont.).
TRANSACTIONS/CAREER NOTES: Signed as non-drafted free agent by Kansas City Royals organization (September 1, 1989).

						BATTING								FIELDING			
Year Team (League)	Pos.	G	AB	R	H	2B	3B	HR	RBI	Avg.	BB	SO	SB	PO	A	E	Avg.
1990— GC Royals (GCL)	3B-C	21	52	5	10	4	0	0	1	.192	9	13	3	16	24	0	1.000
1991— Baseball City (FSL)	C-1B-OF	77	268	27	62	15	1	3	35	.231	7	56	6	232	41	1	.996
1992— Baseball City (FSL)	C-1B	94	283	31	73	13	1	4	38	.258	21	45	3	445	60	10	.981
1993— Wilmington (Caro.)	1B-C-3B	110	361	54	100	20	3	8	42	.277	26	88	7	172	36	5	.977
1994— Wilmington (Caro.)	C-OF-1B	94	360	53	114	24	3	17	66	.317	30	56	0	293	44	1	.997
— Memphis (Southern)	1B-C	20	72	10	17	1	0	0	5	.236	3	5	0	79	10	0	1.000
1995— Wichita (Texas)	C-OF-1B	58	202	29	61	17	3	3	32	.302	14	25	3	217	35	6	.977
— Omaha (A.A.)	C	50	181	23	39	10	2	2	13	.215	15	25	0	83	6	0	1.000

Year Team (League)	Pos.	G	AB	R	H	2B	3B	HR	RBI	Avg.	BB	SO	SB	PO	A	E	Avg.
1996— Omaha (A.A.)	1B-C	50	181	23	39	10	2	2	13	.215	15	25	0	323	26	1	.997
—Wichita (Texas)	C-OF	58	202	29	61	17	3	3	32	.302	14	25	3	217	35	6	.977
1997— Omaha (A.A.)	C-1B-OF	86	288	38	79	10	1	6	24	.274	18	43	1	477	58	4	.993
—Kansas City (A.L.)	C	5	8	1	2	1	0	0	0	.250	0	0	0	10	1	0	1.000
Major league totals (1 year)		5	8	1	2	1	0	0	0	.250	0	0	0	10	1	0	1.000

STEWART, SHANNON — OF — BLUE JAYS

PERSONAL: Born February 25, 1974, in Cincinnati. ... 6-1/194. ... Bats right, throws right. ... Full name: Shannon Harold Stewart.
HIGH SCHOOL: Southridge (Miami).
TRANSACTIONS/CAREER NOTES: Selected by Toronto Blue Jays organization in first round (19th pick overall) of free-agent draft (June 1, 1992); pick received as part of compensation for Los Angeles Dodgers signing Type A free-agent P Tom Candiotti. ... On disabled list (June 13-September 13, 1994). ... On Syracuse disabled list (May 13-31, 1996).
STATISTICAL NOTES: Led International League outfielders with 286 total chances in 1996.

Year Team (League)	Pos.	G	AB	R	H	2B	3B	HR	RBI	Avg.	BB	SO	SB	PO	A	E	Avg.
1992— GC Jays (GCL)	OF	50	172	44	40	1	0	1	11	.233	24	27	*32	81	1	1	.988
1993— St. Catharines (NYP)	OF	75	*301	•53	84	15	2	3	29	.279	33	43	25	81	0	0	1.000
1994— Hagerstown (SAL)	OF	56	225	39	73	10	5	4	25	.324	23	39	15	92	4	1	.990
1995— Knoxville (Southern)	OF	138	498	89	143	24	6	5	55	.287	*89	61	42	283	6	6	.980
—Toronto (A.L.)	OF	12	38	2	8	0	0	0	1	.211	5	5	2	20	1	1	.955
1996— Syracuse (Int'l)	OF	112	420	77	125	26	8	6	42	.298	54	61	*35	*274	7	5	.983
—Toronto (A.L.)	OF	7	17	2	3	1	0	0	2	.176	1	4	1	4	0	1	.800
1997— Toronto (A.L.)	OF-DH	44	168	25	48	13	7	0	22	.286	19	24	10	97	1	2	.980
—Syracuse (Int'l)	OF	58	208	41	72	13	1	5	24	.346	36	26	9	115	1	2	.983
Major league totals (3 years)		63	223	29	59	14	7	0	25	.265	25	33	13	121	2	4	.969

STINNETT, KELLY — C — DIAMONDBACKS

PERSONAL: Born February 14, 1970, in Lawton, Okla. ... 5-11/195. ... Bats right, throws right. ... Full name: Kelly Lee Stinnett. ... Name pronounced stih-NET.
HIGH SCHOOL: Lawton (Okla.).
JUNIOR COLLEGE: Seminole (Okla.) Junior College.
TRANSACTIONS/CAREER NOTES: Selected by Cleveland Indians organization in 11th round of free-agent draft (June 5, 1989). ... Selected by New York Mets from Indians organization in Rule 5 major league draft (December 13, 1993). ... Traded by Mets to Milwaukee Brewers for P Cory Lidle (January 17, 1996). ... On Milwaukee disabled list (July 27-September 2, 1997). ... Selected by Arizona Diamondbacks in third round (65th pick overall) of expansion draft (November 18, 1997).
STATISTICAL NOTES: Led New York-Pennsylvania League catchers with 18 errors in 1990. ... Led South Atlantic League catchers with 27 errors in 1991. ... Tied for American Association lead in being hit by pitch with 13 in 1996. ... Led American Association catchers with 10 errors and tied for lead with nine double plays in 1996.

Year Team (League)	Pos.	G	AB	R	H	2B	3B	HR	RBI	Avg.	BB	SO	SB	PO	A	E	Avg.
1990— Watertown (NYP)	C-1B	60	192	29	46	10	2	2	21	.240	40	43	3	348	48	†18	.957
1991— Columbus (S. Atl.)	C-1B	102	384	49	101	15	1	14	74	.263	26	70	4	685	100	†28	.966
1992— Cant./Akr. (Eastern)	C	91	296	37	84	10	0	6	32	.284	16	43	7	560	57	*13	.979
1993— Charlotte (Int'l)	C	98	288	42	79	10	3	6	33	.274	17	52	0	495	48	8	.985
1994— New York (N.L.)	C	47	150	20	38	6	2	2	14	.253	11	28	2	211	20	5	.979
1995— New York (N.L.)	C	77	196	23	43	8	1	4	18	.219	29	65	2	380	22	7	.983
1996— Milwaukee (A.L.)	C-DH	14	26	1	2	0	0	0	0	.077	2	11	0	46	2	2	.960
—New Orleans (A.A.)	C-3B	95	334	63	96	21	1	27	70	.287	31	83	3	485	52	†11	.980
1997— Tucson (PCL)	C-1B	64	209	50	67	15	3	10	43	.321	42	46	1	256	34	2	.993
—Milwaukee (A.L.)	C-DH	30	36	2	9	4	0	0	3	.250	3	9	0	81	5	1	.989
American League totals (2 years)		44	62	3	11	4	0	0	3	.177	5	20	0	127	7	3	.978
National League totals (2 years)		124	346	43	81	14	3	6	32	.234	40	93	4	591	42	12	.981
Major league totals (4 years)		168	408	46	92	18	3	6	35	.225	45	113	4	718	49	15	.981

STOCKER, KEVIN — SS — DEVIL RAYS

PERSONAL: Born February 13, 1970, in Spokane, Wash. ... 6-1/175. ... Bats both, throws right. ... Full name: Kevin Douglas Stocker.
HIGH SCHOOL: Central Valley (Veradale, Wash.).
COLLEGE: Washington.
TRANSACTIONS/CAREER NOTES: Selected by Philadelphia Phillies organization in second round of free-agent draft (June 3, 1991). ... On Philadelphia disabled list (April 28-June 1, 1994); included rehabilitation assignment to Scranton Wilkes-Barre (May 28-June 1). ... Traded by Phillies to Tampa Bay Devil Rays for OF Bob Abreu (November 18, 1997).

Year Team (League)	Pos.	G	AB	R	H	2B	3B	HR	RBI	Avg.	BB	SO	SB	PO	A	E	Avg.
1991— Spartanburg (SAL)	SS	70	250	26	55	11	1	0	20	.220	31	37	15	83	176	18	.935
1992— Clearwater (FSL)	SS	63	244	43	69	13	4	1	33	.283	27	31	15	102	220	16	.953
—Reading (Eastern)	SS	62	240	31	60	9	2	1	13	.250	22	30	17	100	172	14	.951
1993— Scran./W.B. (Int'l)	SS	83	313	54	73	14	1	3	17	.233	29	56	17	122	248	15	.961
—Philadelphia (N.L.)	SS	70	259	46	84	12	3	2	31	.324	30	43	5	118	202	14	.958
1994— Philadelphia (N.L.)	SS	82	271	38	74	11	2	2	28	.273	44	41	2	118	253	16	.959
—Scran./W.B. (Int'l)	SS	4	13	1	4	1	0	0	2	.308	1	0	0	5	11	0	1.000
1995— Philadelphia (N.L.)	SS	125	412	42	90	14	3	1	32	.218	43	75	6	147	383	17	.969
1996— Philadelphia (N.L.)	SS	119	394	46	100	22	6	5	41	.254	43	89	6	165	352	13	.975
—Scran./W.B. (Int'l)	SS	12	44	5	10	3	0	2	6	.227	0	4	1	17	39	1	.982
1997— Philadelphia (N.L.)	SS	149	504	51	134	23	5	4	40	.266	51	91	11	190	376	11	.981
Major league totals (5 years)		545	1840	223	482	82	19	14	172	.262	211	339	30	738	1566	71	.970

Year Team (League)	Pos.	G	AB	R	H	2B	3B	HR	RBI	Avg.	BB	SO	SB	PO	A	E	Avg.
					BATTING										FIELDING		
1993— Philadelphia (N.L.)......	SS	6	22	0	4	1	0	0	1	.182	2	5	0	10	13	1	.958

WORLD SERIES RECORD

Year Team (League)	Pos.	G	AB	R	H	2B	3B	HR	RBI	Avg.	BB	SO	SB	PO	A	E	Avg.
					BATTING										FIELDING		
1993— Philadelphia (N.L.)......	SS	6	19	1	4	1	0	0	1	.211	5	5	0	8	13	0	1.000

STONER, MIKE — OF — DIAMONDBACKS

PERSONAL: Born May 23, 1973, in Shelbyville, Ky. ... 6-0/200. ... Bats right, throws right. ... Full name: Michael Andre Stoner.
HIGH SCHOOL: Shelbyville (Ky.).
JUNIOR COLLEGE: North Florida Junior College.
COLLEGE: North Carolina.
TRANSACTIONS/CAREER NOTES: Signed as non-drafted free agent by Arizona Diamondbacks organization (May 17, 1996).
STATISTICAL NOTES: Led California League with .628 slugging percentage and 11 sacrifice flies in 1997.

Year Team (League)	Pos.	G	AB	R	H	2B	3B	HR	RBI	Avg.	BB	SO	SB	PO	A	E	Avg.
					BATTING										FIELDING		
1996— Lethbridge (Pioneer) ..	1B	24	78	13	25	1	2	1	13	.321	12	13	1	69	5	3	.961
— Bakersfield (Calif.)......	1B-OF	36	147	25	43	6	1	6	22	.293	8	18	1	277	25	4	.987
1997— High Desert (Calif.)....	OF	136	567	*115	*203	*44	5	•33	*142	.358	36	91	6	201	6	6	.972

STOTTLEMYRE, TODD — P — CARDINALS

S

PERSONAL: Born May 20, 1965, in Yakima, Wash. ... 6-3/200. ... Throws right, bats left. ... Full name: Todd Vernon Stottlemyre. ... Son of Mel Stottlemyre Sr., pitching coach, New York Yankees; pitcher, New York Yankees (1964-74) and pitching coach, New York Mets (1984-93); and brother of Mel Stottlemyre Jr., pitcher, Kansas City Royals (1990).
HIGH SCHOOL: A.C. Davis (Yakima, Wash.).
COLLEGE: Yakima (Wash.) Valley College.
TRANSACTIONS/CAREER NOTES: Selected by New York Yankees organization in fifth round of free-agent draft (June 6, 1983); did not sign. ... Selected by St. Louis Cardinals organization in secondary phase of free-agent draft (January 9, 1985); did not sign. ... Selected by Toronto Blue Jays organization in secondary phase of free-agent draft (June 3, 1985). ... On disabled list (June 20-July 13, 1992). ... On suspended list (September 23-28, 1992). ... On disabled list (May 23-June 13, 1993). ... Granted free agency (October 18, 1994). ... Signed by Oakland Athletics (April 11, 1995). ... Traded by A's to St. Louis Cardinals for P Bret Wagner, P Jay Witasick and P Carl Dale (January 9, 1996).
STATISTICAL NOTES: Pitched 9-0 one-hit, complete-game victory against Chicago (August 26, 1992). ... Struck out 15 batters in one game (June 16, 1995).
MISCELLANEOUS: Struck out in only appearance as pinch-hitter (1997).

Year Team (League)	W	L	Pct.	ERA	G	GS	CG	ShO	Sv.	IP	H	R	ER	BB	SO
1986— Vent. County (Cal.)............	9	4	.692	2.43	17	17	2	0	0	103²/₃	76	39	28	36	104
— Knoxville (Southern)	8	7	.533	4.18	18	18	1	0	0	99	93	56	46	49	81
1987— Syracuse (Int'l).................	11	•13	.458	4.44	34	*34	1	0	0	186²/₃	189	•103	*92	*87	143
1988— Toronto (A.L.)...................	4	8	.333	5.69	28	16	0	0	0	98	109	70	62	46	67
— Syracuse (Int'l).................	5	0	1.000	2.05	7	7	1	0	0	48¹/₃	36	12	11	8	51
1989— Toronto (A.L.)...................	7	7	.500	3.88	27	18	0	0	0	127²/₃	137	56	55	44	63
— Syracuse (Int'l).................	3	2	.600	3.23	10	9	2	0	0	55²/₃	46	23	20	15	45
1990— Toronto (A.L.)...................	13	17	.433	4.34	33	33	4	0	0	203	214	101	98	69	115
1991— Toronto (A.L.)...................	15	8	.652	3.78	34	34	1	0	0	219	194	97	92	75	116
1992— Toronto (A.L.)...................	12	11	.522	4.50	28	27	6	2	0	174	175	99	87	63	98
1993— Toronto (A.L.)...................	11	12	.478	4.84	30	28	1	1	0	176²/₃	204	107	95	69	98
1994— Toronto (A.L.)...................	7	7	.500	4.22	26	19	3	1	1	140²/₃	149	67	66	48	105
1995— Oakland (A.L.)■...............	14	7	.667	4.55	31	31	2	0	0	209²/₃	228	117	106	80	205
1996— St. Louis (N.L.)■.............	14	11	.560	3.87	34	33	5	2	0	223¹/₃	191	100	96	93	194
1997— St. Louis (N.L.).................	12	9	.571	3.88	28	28	0	0	0	181	155	86	78	65	160
A.L. totals (8 years)	83	77	.519	4.41	237	206	17	4	1	1348²/₃	1410	714	661	494	867
N.L. totals (2 years)	26	20	.565	3.87	62	61	5	2	0	404¹/₃	346	186	174	158	354
Major league totals (10 years)....	109	97	.529	4.29	299	267	22	6	1	1753	1756	900	835	652	1221

DIVISION SERIES RECORD

Year Team (League)	W	L	Pct.	ERA	G	GS	CG	ShO	Sv.	IP	H	R	ER	BB	SO
1996— St. Louis (N.L.).................	1	0	1.000	1.35	1	1	0	0	0	6²/₃	5	1	1	2	7

CHAMPIONSHIP SERIES RECORD

RECORDS: Shares single-series record for most earned runs allowed—11 (1996). ... Shares single-game record for most earned runs allowed—7 (1996). ... Shares record for most hits allowed in one inning—6 (October 14, 1996, first inning).

Year Team (League)	W	L	Pct.	ERA	G	GS	CG	ShO	Sv.	IP	H	R	ER	BB	SO
1989— Toronto (A.L.)...................	0	1	.000	7.20	1	1	0	0	0	5	7	4	4	2	3
1991— Toronto (A.L.)...................	0	1	.000	9.82	1	1	0	0	0	3²/₃	7	4	4	1	3
1992— Toronto (A.L.)...................	0	0	...	2.45	1	1	0	0	0	3²/₃	3	1	1	0	1
1993— Toronto (A.L.)...................	0	1	.000	7.50	1	1	0	0	0	6	6	5	5	4	4
1996— St. Louis (N.L.).................	1	1	.500	12.38	3	2	0	0	0	8	15	11	11	3	11
Champ. series totals (5 years)	1	4	.200	8.54	7	5	0	0	0	26¹/₃	38	25	25	10	22

WORLD SERIES RECORD

RECORDS: Shares records for most bases on balls allowed in one inning—4 (October 20, 1993, first inning); and most consecutive bases on balls allowed in one inning—3 (October 20, 1993, first inning).
NOTES: Member of World Series championship teams (1992 and 1993).

Year Team (League)	W	L	Pct.	ERA	G	GS	CG	ShO	Sv.	IP	H	R	ER	BB	SO
1992— Toronto (A.L.)...................	0	0	...	0.00	4	0	0	0	0	3²/₃	4	0	0	0	4
1993— Toronto (A.L.)...................	0	0	...	27.00	1	1	0	0	0	2	3	6	6	4	1
World Series totals (2 years)	0	0	...	9.53	5	1	0	0	0	5²/₃	7	6	6	4	5

STOVALL, DAROND   OF   EXPOS

PERSONAL: Born January 3, 1973, in St. Louis. ... 6-1/185. ... Bats both, throws left. ... Full name: DaRond T. Stovall.
HIGH SCHOOL: Althoff Catholic (Belleville, Ill.).
TRANSACTIONS/CAREER NOTES: Selected by St. Louis Cardinals organization in fifth round of free-agent draft (June 3, 1991). ... Traded by Cardinals organization with P Bryan Eversgerd and P Kirk Bullinger to Montreal Expos organization for P Ken Hill (April 5, 1995). ... On Harrisburg disabled list (May 16-July 9, 1996).
STATISTICAL NOTES: Led Florida State League outfielders with 339 total chances in 1994.

| | | | | | | | | BATTING | | | | | | | FIELDING | | |
Year Team (League)	Pos.	G	AB	R	H	2B	3B	HR	RBI	Avg.	BB	SO	SB	PO	A	E	Avg.
1991— Johnson City (App.) ...	OF	48	134	16	19	2	2	0	5	.142	23	63	9	69	2	5	.934
1992— Savannah (S. Atl.)	OF	135	450	51	92	13	7	7	40	.204	63	138	20	250	8	12	.956
1993— Springfield (Midw.)	OF	*135	460	73	118	19	4	20	81	.257	53	143	18	247	6	11	.958
1994— St. Petersburg (FSL) ..	OF	134	507	68	113	20	6	15	69	.223	62	*154	24	*328	7	4	.988
1995— W.P. Beach (FSL)■.....	OF	121	461	52	107	22	2	4	51	.232	44	117	18	283	13	3	.990
1996— Harrisburg (Eastern) ..	OF	74	272	38	60	7	1	10	36	.221	32	86	10	171	4	3	.983
— G.C. Expos (GCL) ...	OF	9	34	5	15	3	2	0	7	.441	3	6	3	10	0	0	1.000
— W.P. Beach (FSL)........	OF	8	31	8	14	4	0	1	8	.452	6	7	2	19	0	1	.950
1997— Harrisburg (Eastern) ..	OF	45	169	29	48	4	1	9	39	.284	23	30	4	93	3	1	.990
— Ottawa (Int'l)	OF	98	342	40	83	23	2	4	48	.243	31	114	10	181	10	7	.965

STRANGE, DOUG   3B   PIRATES

PERSONAL: Born April 13, 1964, in Greenville, S.C. ... 6-1/185. ... Bats both, throws right. ... Full name: Joseph Douglas Strange.
HIGH SCHOOL: Wade Hampton (Greenville, S.C.).
COLLEGE: North Carolina State.
TRANSACTIONS/CAREER NOTES: Selected by Detroit Tigers organization in seventh round of free-agent draft (June 3, 1985). ... Traded by Tigers to Houston Astros organization for IF/OF Lou Frazier (March 30, 1990). ... Released by Astros organization (May 25, 1990). ... Signed by Chicago Cubs organization (June 11, 1990). ... Granted free agency (December 19, 1992). ... Signed by Texas Rangers organization (January 11, 1993). ... On disabled list (July 2-17, 1994). ... Granted free agency (December 23, 1994). ... Signed by Tacoma, Seattle Mariners organization (April 5, 1995). ... Granted free agency (October 8, 1996). ... Signed by Montreal Expos organization (February 4, 1997). ... On Montreal disabled list (June 17-July 2, 1997). ... Granted free agency (November 5, 1997). ... Signed by Pittsburgh Pirates (December 2, 1997).
STATISTICAL NOTES: Led Florida State League third basemen with 116 putouts and tied for lead with 20 double plays in 1986. ... Led American Association third basemen with 16 double plays in 1990. ... Led American Association with 10 intentional bases on balls received in 1991. ... Career major league grand slams: 1.
MISCELLANEOUS: Batted righthanded only (Glens Falls, 1987).

| | | | | | | | | BATTING | | | | | | | FIELDING | | |
Year Team (League)	Pos.	G	AB	R	H	2B	3B	HR	RBI	Avg.	BB	SO	SB	PO	A	E	Avg.
1985— Bristol (Appal.)	OF-2B-3B	65	226	43	69	16	1	6	45	.305	22	30	6	84	59	11	.929
1986— Lakeland (Fla. St.)	3B-1B	126	466	59	119	29	4	2	63	.255	65	59	18	†202	215	37	.919
1987— Glens Falls (Eastern) ..	3-2-0-S	115	431	63	130	31	1	13	70	.302	31	53	5	110	214	20	.942
— Toledo (Int'l)	3B	16	45	7	11	2	0	1	5	.244	4	7	3	14	28	3	.933
1988— Toledo (Int'l)	3B-SS-1B	82	278	23	56	8	2	6	19	.201	8	38	9	52	126	13	.932
— Glens Falls (Eastern) ..	3B	57	218	32	61	11	1	1	36	.280	16	28	11	45	112	12	.929
1989— Toledo (Int'l)	3B-SS	83	304	38	75	15	2	8	42	.247	34	49	8	108	197	17	.947
— Detroit (A.L.)	3B-2B-SS	64	196	16	42	4	1	1	14	.214	17	36	3	53	118	19	.900
1990— Tucson (PCL)■	3B-SS	37	98	7	22	3	0	0	7	.224	8	23	0	9	47	9	.862
— Iowa (Am. Assoc.)■ ..	3B-2B-SS	82	269	31	82	17	1	5	35	.305	28	42	6	58	149	16	.928
1991— Iowa (Am. Assoc.)..	3-2-1-S-O	131	509	76	149	35	5	8	56	.293	49	75	10	263	273	21	.962
— Chicago (N.L.)	3B	3	9	0	4	1	0	0	1	.444	0	1	1	1	3	1	.800
1992— Iowa (Am. Assoc.)..	2B-3B	55	212	32	65	16	1	4	26	.307	9	32	3	84	126	16	.929
— Chicago (N.L.)	3B-2B	52	94	7	15	1	0	1	5	.160	10	15	1	24	51	6	.926
1993— Texas (A.L.)■	2B-3B-SS	145	484	58	124	29	0	7	60	.256	43	69	6	276	374	13	.980
1994— Texas (A.L.)	2B-3B-OF	73	226	26	48	12	1	5	26	.212	15	38	1	88	175	11	.960
1995— Seattle (A.L.)■	3-2-0-DH	74	155	19	42	9	2	2	21	.271	10	25	0	39	69	5	.956
1996— Seattle (A.L.)..	3-0-DH-1-2	88	183	19	43	7	1	3	23	.235	14	31	1	26	39	2	.970
1997— Montreal (N.L.)■...	3-2-0-1	118	327	40	84	16	2	12	47	.257	36	76	0	70	176	13	.950
— Ottawa (Int'l)	3B	2	7	3	3	1	0	0	0	.429	1	1	0	2	3	0	1.000
American League totals (5 years)		444	1244	138	299	61	5	18	144	.240	99	199	11	482	775	50	.962
National League totals (3 years)		173	430	47	103	18	2	13	53	.240	46	92	2	95	230	20	.942
Major league totals (8 years)		617	1674	185	402	79	7	31	197	.240	145	291	13	577	1005	70	.958

DIVISION SERIES RECORD

| | | | | | | | | BATTING | | | | | | | FIELDING | | |
Year Team (League)	Pos.	G	AB	R	H	2B	3B	HR	RBI	Avg.	BB	SO	SB	PO	A	E	Avg.
1995— Seattle (A.L.)	3B-PH	2	4	0	0	0	0	0	1	.000	1	1	0	0	0	0	...

CHAMPIONSHIP SERIES RECORD

| | | | | | | | | BATTING | | | | | | | FIELDING | | |
Year Team (League)	Pos.	G	AB	R	H	2B	3B	HR	RBI	Avg.	BB	SO	SB	PO	A	E	Avg.
1995— Seattle (A.L.)	PH-3B	4	4	0	0	0	0	0	0	.000	0	2	0	2	3	0	1.000

STRAWBERRY, DARRYL   OF   YANKEES

PERSONAL: Born March 12, 1962, in Los Angeles. ... 6-6/215. ... Bats left, throws left. ... Full name: Darryl Eugene Strawberry. ... Brother of Michael Strawberry, minor league outfielder (1980-81).
HIGH SCHOOL: Crenshaw (Los Angeles).

S

TRANSACTIONS/CAREER NOTES: Selected by New York Mets organization in first round (first pick overall) of free-agent draft (June 3, 1980). ... On disabled list (May 12-June 28, 1985). ... Granted free agency (November 5, 1990). ... Signed by Los Angeles Dodgers (November 8, 1990). ... On disabled list (June 18-July 3, 1991; May 14-July 6 and July 21-September 1, 1992). ... On Los Angeles disabled list (May 13-June 5, 1993); included rehabilitation assignment to Albuquerque (May 28-June 5). ... On Los Angeles disabled list (June 17, 1993-remainder of season and April 4-May 26, 1994). ... Released by Dodgers (May 26, 1994). ... Signed by San Francisco Giants organization (June 19, 1994). ... On San Francisco suspended list (February 6-June 19, 1995). ... Released by Giants (February 8, 1995). ... Signed by New York Yankees organization (June 19, 1995). ... On Columbus disabled list (June 22-July 4, 1995). ... Granted free agency (November 30, 1995). ... Re-signed by Yankees. ... Signed by St. Paul of Northern League (May 3, 1996). ... Contract purchased by Yankees orgnization (July 4, 1996). ... On New York disabled list (April 7-August 15, 1997); included rehabilitation assignments to Norwich (May 19), Columbus (June 9-13 and August 8-15) and Tampa (August 4-7). ... Granted free agency (October 30, 1997). ... Re-signed by Yankees (January 8, 1998).

RECORDS: Shares major league single-game record (nine innings) for most strikeouts—5 (May 1, 1991).

HONORS: Named Texas League Most Valuable Player (1982). ... Named N.L. Rookie Player of the Year by The Sporting News (1983). ... Named N.L. Rookie of the Year by Baseball Writers' Association of America (1983). ... Named outfielder on The Sporting News N.L. All-Star team (1988 and 1990). ... Named outfielder on The Sporting News N.L. Silver Slugger team (1988 and 1990).

STATISTICAL NOTES: Led Texas League in slugging percentage with .602 and in caught stealing with 22 in 1982. ... Hit three home runs in one game (August 5, 1985 and August 6, 1996). ... Led N.L. with .545 slugging percentage in 1988. ... Led Gulf Coast League with five intentional bases on balls received in 1995. ... Career major league grand slams: 6.

MISCELLANEOUS: Holds New York Mets all-time records for most runs (662), most home runs (252) and most runs batted in (733).

Year Team (League)	Pos.	G	AB	R	H	2B	3B	HR	RBI	Avg.	BB	SO	SB	PO	A	E	Avg.
1980—Kingsport (Appal.)......	OF	44	157	27	42	5	2	5	20	.268	20	39	5	55	4	3	.952
1981—Lynchburg (Caro.)......	OF	123	420	84	107	22	6	13	78	.255	82	105	31	173	8	13	.933
1982—Jackson (Texas)	OF	129	435	93	123	19	9	*34	97	.283	*100	145	45	211	8	9	.961
1983—Tidewater (Int'l)..........	OF	16	57	12	19	4	1	3	13	.333	14	18	7	22	0	4	.846
—New York (N.L.)..........	OF	122	420	63	108	15	7	26	74	.257	47	128	19	232	8	4	.984
1984—New York (N.L.).........	OF	147	522	75	131	27	4	26	97	.251	75	131	27	276	11	6	.980
1985—New York (N.L.).........	OF	111	393	78	109	15	4	29	79	.277	73	96	26	211	5	2	.991
1986—New York (N.L.).........	OF	136	475	76	123	27	5	27	93	.259	72	141	28	226	10	6	.975
1987—New York (N.L.).........	OF	154	532	108	151	32	5	39	104	.284	97	122	36	272	6	8	.972
1988—New York (N.L.).........	OF	153	543	101	146	27	3	*39	101	.269	85	127	29	297	4	9	.971
1989—New York (N.L.).........	OF	134	476	69	107	26	1	29	77	.225	61	105	11	272	4	8	.972
1990—New York (N.L.).........	OF	152	542	92	150	18	1	37	108	.277	70	110	15	268	10	3	.989
1991—Los Angeles (N.L.)■...	OF	139	505	86	134	22	4	28	99	.265	75	125	10	209	11	5	.978
1992—Los Angeles (N.L.)	OF	43	156	20	37	8	0	5	25	.237	19	34	3	67	2	1	.986
1993—Los Angeles (N.L.)	OF	32	100	12	14	2	0	5	12	.140	16	19	1	37	1	4	.905
—Albuquerque (PCL)......	OF	5	19	3	6	2	0	1	2	.316	2	5	1	7	0	0	1.000
1994—Phoenix (PCL)■........	OF	3	10	3	3	0	0	2	3	.300	0	4	0	4	0	0	1.000
—San Francisco (N.L.) ..	OF	29	92	13	22	3	1	4	17	.239	19	22	0	61	1	2	.969
1995—GC Yankees (GCL)■....	OF	7	20	3	5	2	0	0	4	.250	9	5	2	3	1	0	1.000
—Tampa (Florida State).	DH	2	9	1	2	1	0	1	2	.222	1	2	0	...	...	...	...
—Columbus (Int'l).........	OF	22	83	20	25	3	1	7	29	.301	15	17	1	9	0	0	1.000
—New York (A.L.).........	DH-OF	32	87	15	24	4	1	3	13	.276	10	22	0	18	2	2	.909
1996—St. Paul (Northern)■..	OF	29	108	31	47	7	0	18	39	.435	22	16	4	...	...	...	...
—Columbus (Int'l)■........	DH	2	8	3	3	0	0	3	5	.375	0	3	0	...	...	...	...
—New York (A.L.)..........	OF-DH	63	202	35	53	13	0	11	36	.262	31	55	6	45	1	0	1.000
1997—New York (A.L.)..........	DH-OF	11	29	1	3	1	0	0	2	.103	3	9	0	5	0	0	1.000
—Norwich (Eastern)	OF	1	2	0	0	0	0	0	0	.000	0	1	0	0	0	0	...
—Columbus (Int'l)	DH	11	38	8	11	3	0	6	19	.289	8	10	0	...	...	...	...
—Tampa (Florida State).	DH	4	16	2	7	1	0	0	4	.438	1	3	0	...	...	...	...
American League totals (3 years)		106	318	51	80	18	1	14	51	.252	44	86	6	68	3	2	.973
National League totals (12 years)		1352	4756	793	1232	222	35	294	886	.259	709	1160	205	2428	73	58	.977
Major league totals (15 years)		1458	5074	844	1312	240	36	308	937	.259	753	1246	211	2496	76	60	.977

DIVISION SERIES RECORD

Year Team (League)	Pos.	G	AB	R	H	2B	3B	HR	RBI	Avg.	BB	SO	SB	PO	A	E	Avg.
1995—New York (A.L.)..........	PH	2	2	0	0	0	0	0	0	.000	0	1	0	0	0	0	...
1996—New York (A.L.)..........	DH	2	5	0	0	0	0	0	0	.000	0	2	0	0	0	0	...
Division series totals (2 years)		4	7	0	0	0	0	0	0	.000	0	3	0	0	0	0	...

CHAMPIONSHIP SERIES RECORD

RECORDS: Shares single-series record for most strikeouts—12 (1986).

Year Team (League)	Pos.	G	AB	R	H	2B	3B	HR	RBI	Avg.	BB	SO	SB	PO	A	E	Avg.
1986—New York (N.L.)..........	OF	6	22	4	5	1	0	2	5	.227	3	12	1	9	0	0	1.000
1988—New York (N.L.)..........	OF	7	30	5	9	2	0	1	6	.300	2	5	0	11	0	0	1.000
1996—New York (A.L.)..........	OF-PH	4	12	4	5	0	0	3	5	.417	2	2	0	5	0	0	1.000
Championship series totals (3 years)		17	64	13	19	3	0	6	16	.297	7	19	1	25	0	0	1.000

WORLD SERIES RECORD

NOTES: Member of World Series championship team (1986 and 1996).

Year Team (League)	Pos.	G	AB	R	H	2B	3B	HR	RBI	Avg.	BB	SO	SB	PO	A	E	Avg.
1986—New York (N.L.)..........	OF	7	24	4	5	1	0	1	1	.208	4	6	3	19	0	0	1.000
1996—New York (A.L.)..........	OF	5	16	0	3	0	0	0	1	.188	5	6	0	11	0	0	1.000
World Series totals (2 years)		12	40	4	8	1	0	1	2	.200	9	12	3	30	0	0	1.000

ALL-STAR GAME RECORD

Year League	Pos.	AB	R	H	2B	3B	HR	RBI	Avg.	BB	SO	SB	PO	A	E	Avg.
1984—National......................	OF	2	0	1	0	0	0	0	.500	0	1	0	0	0	0	...
1985—National......................	OF	1	2	1	0	0	0	0	1.000	1	0	1	3	0	0	1.000
1986—National......................	OF	2	0	1	0	0	0	0	.500	0	1	0	1	0	0	1.000

Year	League	Pos.	AB	R	H	2B	3B	BATTING HR	RBI	Avg.	BB	SO	SB	FIELDING PO	A	E	Avg.
1987— National		OF	2	0	0	0	0	0	0	.000	0	0	0	0	0	0	...
1988— National		OF	4	0	1	0	0	0	0	.250	0	1	0	4	0	0	1.000
1989— National								Selected, did not play—injured.									
1990— National		OF	1	0	0	0	0	0	0	.000	0	1	0	3	1	1	.800
1991— National								Selected, did not play—injured.									
All-Star Game totals (6 years)			12	2	4	0	0	0	0	.333	1	4	1	11	1	1	.923

STULL, EVERETT   P   ORIOLES

PERSONAL: Born August 24, 1971, in Fort Riley, Kan. ... 6-3/200. ... Throws right, bats right. ... Full name: Everett James Stull.
HIGH SCHOOL: Redan (Stone Mountain, Ga.).
COLLEGE: Tennessee State.
TRANSACTIONS/CAREER NOTES: Selected by Montreal Expos organization in third round of free-agent draft (June 1, 1992). ... Traded by Expos to Baltimore Orioles (October 31, 1997), completing deal in which Orioles traded P Mike Johnson to Expos for a player to be named later (July 31, 1997).
STATISTICAL NOTES: Led New York-Pennsylvania League with 18 wild pitches in 1992.

Year	Team (League)	W	L	Pct.	ERA	G	GS	CG	ShO	Sv.	IP	H	R	ER	BB	SO
1992— Jamestown (NYP)		3	5	.375	5.40	14	14	0	0	0	63 1/3	52	49	38	*61	64
1993— Burlington (Midw.)		4	9	.308	3.83	15	15	0	0	0	82 1/3	68	44	35	59	85
1994— W.P. Beach (FSL)		10	10	.500	3.31	27	26	3	1	0	147	116	60	54	78	165
1995— Harrisburg (Eastern)		3	•12	.200	5.54	24	24	0	0	0	126 2/3	114	88	78	79	132
1996— Harrisburg (Eastern)		6	3	.667	3.15	14	14	0	0	0	80	64	31	28	52	81
— Ottawa (Int'l)		2	6	.250	6.33	13	13	1	0	0	69 2/3	87	57	49	39	69
1997— Ottawa (Int'l)		8	10	.444	5.82	27	27	1	0	0	159 1/3	166	110	*103	86	130
— Montreal (N.L.)		0	1	.000	16.20	3	0	0	0	0	3 1/3	7	7	6	4	2
Major league totals (1 year)		0	1	.000	16.20	3	0	0	0	0	3 1/3	7	7	6	4	2

STURTZE, TANYON   P   RANGERS

PERSONAL: Born October 12, 1970, in Worcester, Mass. ... 6-5/205. ... Throws right, bats right. ... Full name: Tanyon James Sturtze. ... Name pronounced STURTS.
HIGH SCHOOL: St. Peter-Marian (Worcester, Mass.).
JUNIOR COLLEGE: Quinsigamond Community College (Mass.).
TRANSACTIONS/CAREER NOTES: Selected by Oakland Athletics organization in 23rd round of free-agent draft (June 4, 1990). ... On Huntsville disabled list (April 7-16, 1994). ... Selected by Chicago Cubs from A's organization in Rule 5 major league draft (December 5, 1994). ... Granted free agency (October 15, 1996). ... Signed by Texas Rangers (November 20, 1996).
STATISTICAL NOTES: Pitched 5-0 no-hit victory against Chattanooga (June 13, 1993).

Year	Team (League)	W	L	Pct.	ERA	G	GS	CG	ShO	Sv.	IP	H	R	ER	BB	SO
1990— Arizona A's (Arizona)		2	5	.286	5.44	12	10	0	0	0	48	55	41	29	27	30
1991— Madison (Midwest)		10	5	.667	3.09	27	27	0	0	0	163	136	77	56	58	88
1992— Modesto (California)		7	11	.389	3.75	25	25	1	0	0	151	143	72	63	78	126
1993— Huntsville (Southern)		5	12	.294	4.78	28	•28	1	1	0	165 2/3	169	102	*88	85	112
1994— Huntsville (Southern)		6	3	.667	3.22	17	17	1	0	0	103 1/3	100	40	37	39	63
— Tacoma (PCL)		4	5	.444	4.04	11	9	0	0	0	64 2/3	73	36	29	34	28
1995— Chicago (N.L.)■		0	0	...	9.00	2	0	0	0	0	2	2	2	2	1	0
— Iowa (Am. Assoc.)		4	7	.364	6.80	23	17	1	1	0	86	108	66	65	42	48
1996— Iowa (Am. Assoc.)		6	4	.600	4.85	51	1	0	0	4	72 1/3	80	42	39	33	51
— Chicago (N.L.)		1	0	1.000	9.00	6	0	0	0	0	11	16	11	11	5	7
1997— Oklahoma City (A.A.)■		8	6	.571	5.10	25	19	1	0	0	114 2/3	133	76	65	47	79
— Texas (A.L.)		1	1	.500	8.27	9	5	0	0	0	32 2/3	45	30	30	18	18
A.L. totals (1 year)		1	1	.500	8.27	9	5	0	0	0	32 2/3	45	30	30	18	18
N.L. totals (2 years)		1	0	1.000	9.00	8	0	0	0	0	13	18	13	13	6	7
Major league totals (3 years)		2	1	.667	8.47	17	5	0	0	0	45 2/3	63	43	43	24	25

STYNES, CHRIS   OF/2B   REDS

PERSONAL: Born January 19, 1973, in Queens, N.Y. ... 5-9/175. ... Bats right, throws right. ... Full name: Christopher Desmond Stynes.
HIGH SCHOOL: Boca Raton (Fla.).
TRANSACTIONS/CAREER NOTES: Selected by Toronto Blue Jays in third round of free-agent draft (June 3, 1991). ... Traded by Blue Jays with P David Sinnes and IF Tony Medrano to Kansas City Royals for P David Cone (April 6, 1995). ... Traded by Royals with OF Jon Nunnally to Cincinnati Reds for P Hector Carrasco and P Scott Service (July 15, 1997).
STATISTICAL NOTES: Tied for Florida State League lead in double plays by third basemen with 22 in 1993. ... Led Southern League with 237 total bases in 1994.

Year	Team (League)	Pos.	G	AB	R	H	2B	3B	BATTING HR	RBI	Avg.	BB	SO	SB	FIELDING PO	A	E	Avg.
1991— GC Jays (GCL)		3B	57	219	29	67	15	1	4	39	.306	9	39	10	42	*138	8	*.957
1992— Myrtle Beach (SAL)		3B	127	489	67	139	36	0	7	46	.284	16	43	28	86	208	26	.919
1993— Dunedin (Fla. St.)		3B	123	496	72	151	28	5	7	48	.304	25	40	19	83	234	21	*.938
1994— Knoxville (Southern)		2B	136	*545	79	*173	32	4	8	79	.317	23	36	28	247	•366	20	.968
1995— Omaha (A.A.)■		2B-3B	83	306	51	84	12	5	9	42	.275	27	24	4	144	204	13	.964
— Kansas City (A.L.)		2B-DH	22	35	7	6	1	0	0	2	.171	4	3	0	21	35	1	.982
1996— Omaha (A.A.)		OF-3B-2B	72	284	50	101	22	2	10	40	.356	18	17	7	98	77	9	.951
— Kansas City (A.L.)		O-2-DH-3	36	92	8	27	6	0	0	6	.293	2	5	5	38	8	3	.939
1997— Omaha (A.A.)		2B-OF-3B	82	332	53	88	18	1	8	44	.265	19	25	3	101	80	10	.948
— Indianapolis (A.A.)■		2B	21	86	14	31	8	0	1	17	.360	2	5	4	47	61	2	.982
— Cincinnati (N.L.)		OF-2B-3B	49	198	31	69	7	1	6	28	.348	11	13	11	87	33	2	.984
American League totals (2 years)			58	127	15	33	7	0	0	8	.260	6	8	5	59	43	4	.962
National League totals (1 year)			49	198	31	69	7	1	6	28	.348	11	13	11	87	33	2	.984
Major league totals (3 years)			107	325	46	102	14	1	6	36	.314	17	21	16	146	76	6	.974

SULLIVAN, SCOTT   P   REDS

PERSONAL: Born March 13, 1971, in Tuscaloosa, Ala. ... 6-4/210. ... Throws right, bats right. ... Full name: William Scott Sullivan.
HIGH SCHOOL: Pickens Academy (Carrollton, Ala.).
COLLEGE: Auburn.
TRANSACTIONS/CAREER NOTES: Selected by Cincinnati Reds organization in second round of free-agent draft (June 3, 1993). ... On Indianapolis disabled list (August 21, 1995-remainder of season).

Year Team (League)	W	L	Pct.	ERA	G	GS	CG	ShO	Sv.	IP	H	R	ER	BB	SO
1993— Billings (Pioneer)	5	0	1.000	1.67	18	7	2	2	3	54	33	13	10	25	79
1994— Chattanooga (Southern)	11	7	.611	3.41	34	13	2	0	7	121 1/3	101	60	46	40	111
1995— Indianapolis (A.A.)	4	3	.571	3.53	44	0	0	0	1	58 2/3	51	31	23	24	54
— Cincinnati (N.L.)	0	0	...	4.91	3	0	0	0	0	3 2/3	4	2	2	2	2
1996— Indianapolis (A.A.)	5	2	.714	2.73	53	3	0	0	1	108 2/3	95	38	33	37	77
— Cincinnati (N.L.)	0	0	...	2.25	7	0	0	0	0	8	7	2	2	5	3
1997— Cincinnati (N.L.)	5	3	.625	3.24	59	0	0	0	1	97 1/3	79	36	35	30	96
— Indianapolis (A.A.)	3	1	.750	1.30	19	0	0	0	2	27 2/3	16	4	4	4	23
Major league totals (3 years)	**5**	**3**	**.625**	**3.22**	**69**	**0**	**0**	**0**	**1**	**109**	**90**	**40**	**39**	**37**	**101**

SUPPAN, JEFF   P   DIAMONDBACKS

PERSONAL: Born January 2, 1975, in Oklahoma City. ... 6-2/210. ... Throws right, bats right. ... Full name: Jeffrey Scot Suppan.
HIGH SCHOOL: Crespi (Encino, Calif.).
TRANSACTIONS/CAREER NOTES: Selected by Boston Red Sox organization in second round of free-agent draft (June 3, 1993). ... On Trenton disabled list (April 9-29, 1995). ... On Boston disabled list (August 25, 1996-remainder of season). ... Selected by Arizona Diamondbacks in first round (third pick overall) of expansion draft (November 18, 1997).

Year Team (League)	W	L	Pct.	ERA	G	GS	CG	ShO	Sv.	IP	H	R	ER	BB	SO
1993— GC Red Sox (GCL)	4	3	.571	2.18	10	9	2	1	0	57 2/3	52	20	14	16	64
1994— Sarasota (Florida State)	•13	7	.650	3.26	27	27	4	2	0	174	153	74	63	50	*173
1995— Trenton (Eastern)	6	2	.750	2.36	15	15	1	1	0	99	86	35	26	26	88
— Boston (A.L.)	1	2	.333	5.96	8	3	0	0	0	22 2/3	29	15	15	5	19
— Pawtucket (Int'l)	2	3	.400	5.32	7	7	0	0	0	45 2/3	50	29	27	9	32
1996— Boston (A.L.)	1	1	.500	7.54	8	4	0	0	0	22 2/3	29	19	19	13	13
— Pawtucket (Int'l)	10	6	.625	3.22	22	22	7	1	0	145 1/3	130	66	52	25	142
1997— Pawtucket (Int'l)	5	1	.833	3.71	9	9	2	1	0	60 2/3	51	26	25	15	40
— Boston (A.L.)	7	3	.700	5.69	23	22	0	0	0	112 1/3	140	75	71	36	67
Major league totals (3 years)	**9**	**6**	**.600**	**5.99**	**39**	**29**	**0**	**0**	**0**	**157 2/3**	**198**	**109**	**105**	**54**	**99**

SURHOFF, B.J.   OF   ORIOLES

PERSONAL: Born August 4, 1964, in Bronx, N.Y. ... 6-1/200. ... Bats left, throws right. ... Full name: William James Surhoff. ... Son of Dick Surhoff, forward, New York Knicks and Milwaukee Hawks of National Basketball Association (1952-53 and 1953-54); and brother of Rich Surhoff, pitcher, Philadelphia Phillies and Texas Rangers (1985).
HIGH SCHOOL: Rye (N.Y.).
COLLEGE: North Carolina.
TRANSACTIONS/CAREER NOTES: Selected by New York Yankees organization in fifth round of free-agent draft (June 7, 1982); did not sign. ... Selected by Milwaukee Brewers organization in first round (first pick overall) of free-agent draft (June 3, 1985). ... On suspended list (August 23-25, 1990). ... On Milwaukee disabled list (March 25-April 16, April 20-May 23 and July 7, 1994-remainder of season); included rehabilitation assignments to El Paso (April 12-16) and New Orleans (May 17-23). ... Granted free agency (October 20, 1994). ... Re-signed by New Orleans, Brewers organization (April 7, 1995). ... Granted free agency (November 6, 1995). ... Signed by Baltimore Orioles (December 20, 1995). ... On disabled list (May 18-June 2, 1996).
HONORS: Named College Player of the Year by THE SPORTING NEWS (1985). ... Named catcher on THE SPORTING NEWS college All-America team (1985).
STATISTICAL NOTES: Tied for Pacific Coast League lead in double plays by catcher with 10 in 1986. ... Led A.L. catchers with 68 assists in 1991. ... Career major league grand slams: 4.
MISCELLANEOUS: Member of 1984 U.S. Olympic baseball team.

Year Team (League)	Pos.	G	AB	R	H	2B	3B	HR	RBI	Avg.	BB	SO	SB	PO	A	E	Avg.
1985— Beloit (Midwest)	C	76	289	39	96	13	4	7	58	.332	22	35	10	475	44	3	.994
1986— Vancouver (PCL)	C	116	458	71	141	19	3	5	59	.308	29	30	21	539	70	7	*.989
1987— Milwaukee (A.L.)	C-3-DH-1	115	395	50	118	22	3	7	68	.299	36	30	11	648	56	11	.985
1988— Milwaukee (A.L.)	C-3-1-S-O	139	493	47	121	21	0	5	38	.245	31	49	21	550	94	8	.988
1989— Milwaukee (A.L.)	C-DH-3B	126	436	42	108	17	4	5	55	.248	25	29	14	530	58	10	.983
1990— Milwaukee (A.L.)	C-3B	135	474	55	131	21	4	6	59	.276	41	37	18	619	62	12	.983
1991— Milwaukee (A.L.)	C-DH-3-0-2	143	505	57	146	19	4	5	68	.289	26	33	5	665	†71	4	.995
1992— Milwaukee (A.L.)	C-1-DH-0-3	139	480	63	121	19	1	4	62	.252	46	41	14	699	74	6	.992
1993— Milwaukee (A.L.)	3-0-1-C-DH	148	552	66	151	38	3	7	79	.274	36	47	12	175	220	18	.956
1994— El Paso (Texas)	OF	3	12	2	3	1	0	0	0	.250	0	2	0	3	0	0	1.000
— Milwaukee (A.L.)	3-0-C-1-0-DH	40	134	20	35	11	2	5	22	.261	16	14	0	121	29	4	.974
— New Orleans (A.A.)	3-0-C-1	5	19	3	6	2	0	0	1	.316	1	2	0	21	3	0	1.000
1995— Milwaukee (A.L.)	0-1-C-DH	117	415	72	133	26	3	13	73	.320	37	43	7	530	44	5	.991
1996— Baltimore (A.L.)■	3-0-DH-1	143	537	74	157	27	6	21	82	.292	47	79	0	137	178	15	.955
1997— Baltimore (A.L.)	0-DH-1-3	147	528	80	150	30	4	18	88	.284	49	60	1	268	16	2	.993
Major league totals (11 years)		**1392**	**4949**	**626**	**1371**	**251**	**34**	**96**	**694**	**.277**	**390**	**462**	**103**	**4942**	**902**	**95**	**.984**

DIVISION SERIES RECORD

NOTES: Shares single-game record for most home runs—2 (October 1, 1996).

Year	Team (League)	Pos.	G	AB	R	H	2B	3B	HR	RBI	Avg.	BB	SO	SB	PO	A	E	Avg.
							BATTING								FIELDING			
1996—Baltimore (A.L.).........		OF-PH	4	13	3	5	0	0	3	5	.385	0	1	0	6	0	0	1.000
1997—Baltimore (A.L.).........		OF-PH	3	11	0	3	1	0	0	2	.273	0	2	0	1	1	0	1.000
Division series totals (2 years)			7	24	3	8	1	0	3	7	.333	0	3	0	7	1	0	1.000

CHAMPIONSHIP SERIES RECORD

Year	Team (League)	Pos.	G	AB	R	H	2B	3B	HR	RBI	Avg.	BB	SO	SB	PO	A	E	Avg.
							BATTING								FIELDING			
1996—Baltimore (A.L.).........		OF-PH	5	15	0	4	0	0	0	2	.267	1	2	0	11	1	0	1.000
1997—Baltimore (A.L.).........		OF-1B	6	25	1	5	2	0	0	1	.200	2	2	0	13	0	0	1.000
Championship series totals (2 years)			11	40	1	9	2	0	0	3	.225	3	4	0	24	1	0	1.000

SUTTON, LARRY — 1B — ROYALS

PERSONAL: Born May 14, 1970, in West Covina, Calif. ... 5-11/175. ... Bats left, throws left. ... Full name: Larry James Sutton.
HIGH SCHOOL: Mater Dei (Santa Ana, Calif.).
COLLEGE: Illinois.
TRANSACTIONS/CAREER NOTES: Selected by Kansas City organization in 21st round of free-agent draft (June 1, 1992).
HONORS: Named Northwest League Most Valuable Player (1992). ... Named Carolina League Most Valuable Player (1994).
STATISTICAL NOTES: Led Northwest League with 142 total bases in 1992. ... Led Midwest League first basemen with 92 double plays in 1993. ... Led Carolina League with .542 slugging percentage, 10 intentional bases on balls received and nine sacrifice flies in 1994. ... Led Texas League first basemen with .989 fielding percentage in 1996.

Year	Team (League)	Pos.	G	AB	R	H	2B	3B	HR	RBI	Avg.	BB	SO	SB	PO	A	E	Avg.
							BATTING								FIELDING			
1992—Eugene (Northwest) ...		1B	70	238	45	74	17	3	*15	*58	.311	48	33	3	517	29	14	.975
—Appleton (Midwest)....		DH	1	2	1	0	0	0	0	0	.000	2	1	0	...	...	...	...
1993—Rockford (Midwest).....		1B	113	361	67	97	24	1	7	50	.269	*95	65	3	911	76	11	.989
1994—Wilmington (Caro.).....		1B	129	480	91	147	33	1	26	94	.306	*81	71	2	1086	71	12	*.990
1995—Wichita (Texas)		1B	53	197	31	53	11	1	5	32	.269	26	33	1	452	25	7	.986
1996—Wichita (Texas)		1B-OF	125	463	84	137	22	2	22	84	.296	77	66	4	1105	76	13	*.989
1997—Omaha (A.A.)..............		1B	106	380	61	114	27	1	19	72	.300	61	57	0	839	54	5	.994
—Kansas City (A.L.)		1B-DH-OF	27	69	9	20	2	0	2	8	.290	5	12	0	92	8	0	1.000
Major league totals (1 year)			27	69	9	20	2	0	2	8	.290	5	12	0	92	8	0	1.000

SUZUKI, MAKOTO — P — MARINERS

PERSONAL: Born May 31, 1975, in Kobe, Japan. ... 6-3/195. ... Throws right, bats right.
HIGH SCHOOL: Takigawa Daini (Kobe, Japan).
TRANSACTIONS/CAREER NOTES: Played with Salinas, independent (August 30, 1992). ... Signed as non-drafted free agent by Seattle Mariners organization (September 5, 1993). ... On disabled list (April 19-June 15 and July 10, 1994-remainder of season). ... On Riverside temporarily inactive list (April 22-August 3, 1995). ... On Riverside disabled list (August 3-18, 1995). ... On Port City disabled list (May 8-17, 1996).

Year	Team (League)	W	L	Pct.	ERA	G	GS	CG	ShO	Sv.	IP	H	R	ER	BB	SO
1992—Salinas (Calif.)	0	0	...	0.00	1	0	0	0	0	1	0	0	0	0	1
1993—San Bernardino (Calif.)■....	4	4	.500	3.68	48	1	0	0	12	80 2/3	59	37	33	56	87
1994—Jacksonville (Southern).......	1	0	1.000	2.84	8	0	0	0	1	12 2/3	15	4	4	6	10
1995—Riverside (California)..........	0	1	.000	4.70	6	0	0	0	0	7 2/3	10	4	4	6	6
—Ariz. Mariners (Ariz.)	1	0	1.000	6.75	4	3	0	0	0	4	5	4	3	0	3
1996—Tacoma (PCL)	0	3	.000	7.25	13	2	0	0	0	22 1/3	31	19	18	12	14
—Port City (Southern)..........	3	6	.333	4.72	16	16	0	0	0	74 1/3	69	41	39	32	66
—Seattle (A.L.)	0	0	...	20.25	1	0	0	0	0	1 1/3	2	3	3	2	1
1997—Tacoma (PCL)	4	9	.308	5.94	32	10	0	0	0	83 1/3	79	60	55	64	63
Major league totals (1 year)........	0	0	...	20.25	1	0	0	0	0	1 1/3	2	3	3	2	1

SVEUM, DALE — IF — YANKEES

PERSONAL: Born November 23, 1963, in Richmond, Calif. ... 6-3/185. ... Bats both, throws right. ... Full name: Dale Curtis Sveum. ... Name pronounced SWAIM.
HIGH SCHOOL: Pinole Valley (Calif.).
TRANSACTIONS/CAREER NOTES: Selected by Milwaukee Brewers organization in first round (25th pick overall) of free-agent draft (June 7, 1982). ... On Milwaukee disabled list (July 23-August 9, 1986). ... On Milwaukee disabled list (March 19, 1989-entire season); included rehabilitation assignments to Beloit (June 30-July 5) and Stockton (July 6-18). ... Traded by Brewers to Philadelphia Phillies for P Bruce Ruffin (December 11, 1991). ... On disabled list (April 9-24, 1992). ... Traded by Phillies to Chicago White Sox for P Keith Shepherd (August 10, 1992). ... Granted free agency (October 26, 1992). ... Signed by Oakland Athletics organization (January 21, 1993). ... Released by A's (June 17, 1993). ... Signed by Calgary, Seattle Mariners organization (June 27, 1993). ... On Calgary disabled list (August 3-13 and August 18, 1993-remainder of season and June 14-21, 1994). ... Granted free agency (October 7, 1994). ... Signed by Buffalo, Pittsburgh Pirates organization (November 10, 1994). ... Granted free agency (October 16, 1995). ... Re-signed by Carolina, Pirates organization (February 2, 1996). ... On Calgary disabled list (May 17-June 18, 1996). ... Granted free agency (October 28, 1997). ... Signed by New York Yankees (November 25, 1997).
STATISTICAL NOTES: Led California League third basemen with 261 assists in 1983. ... Led Texas League with 256 total bases in 1984. ... Led Texas League third basemen with 111 putouts and 30 errors in 1984. ... Led American League third basemen with 26 errors in 1986. ... Hit three home runs in one game (July 17, 1987). ... Switch-hit home runs in one game (July 17, 1987 and June 12, 1988). ... Led American League shortstops with 27 errors in 1988. ... Led Pacific Coast League third basemen with 20 double plays in 1995.

Year	Team (League)	Pos.	G	AB	R	H	2B	3B	HR	RBI	Avg.	BB	SO	SB	PO	A	E	Avg.
							BATTING								FIELDING			
1982—Pikeville (Appal.)		SS-3B	58	223	29	52	13	1	2	21	.233	20	50	6	84	158	36	.871
1983—Stockton (California) ..		3B-SS	135	533	70	139	26	5	5	70	.261	29	73	15	105	†281	40	.906
1984—El Paso (Texas)..........		3B-SS	131	523	92	*172	*41	8	9	84	.329	43	72	6	†113	259	†30	.925
1985—Vancouver (PCL)		3B-SS	122	415	42	98	17	3	6	48	.236	48	79	4	81	200	26	.915

Year	Team (League)	Pos.	G	AB	R	H	2B	3B	HR	RBI	Avg.	BB	SO	SB	PO	A	E	Avg.
1986—	Vancouver (PCL).......	3B	28	105	16	31	3	2	1	23	.295	13	22	0	22	54	4	.950
	—Milwaukee (A.L.)........	3B-SS-2B	91	317	35	78	13	2	7	35	.246	32	63	4	92	179	†30	.900
1987—	Milwaukee (A.L.)........	SS-2B	153	535	86	135	27	3	25	95	.252	40	133	2	242	396	23	.965
1988—	Milwaukee (A.L.)........	SS-2B-DH	129	467	41	113	14	4	9	51	.242	21	122	1	209	375	†27	.956
1989—	Beloit (Midwest).........	DH	6	15	0	2	1	0	0	2	.133	5	6	0	...	...	...	...
	—Stockton (California)..	DH	11	43	5	8	0	0	1	5	.186	6	14	0	...	...	...	...
1990—	Milwaukee (A.L.)........	3-2-1-S	48	117	15	23	7	0	1	12	.197	12	30	0	59	63	6	.953
	—Denver (A.A.)........	3-S-1-2	57	218	25	63	17	2	2	26	.289	20	49	1	134	102	12	.952
1991—	Milwaukee (A.L.)........	S-3-DH-2	90	266	33	64	19	1	4	43	.241	32	78	2	85	189	10	.965
1992—	Philadelphia (N.L.)■ ..	SS-3B-1B	54	135	13	24	4	0	2	16	.178	16	39	0	78	100	8	.957
	—Chicago (A.L.)■........	SS-3B-1B	40	114	15	25	9	0	2	12	.219	12	29	1	43	98	8	.946
1993—	Tacoma (PCL)■	2B-1B-SS	12	43	10	15	1	0	2	6	.349	6	7	2	29	21	0	1.000
	—Oakland (A.L.).....1-3-2-DH-O-S		30	79	12	14	2	1	2	6	.177	16	21	0	128	17	3	.980
	—Calgary (PCL)■........	3B-1B	33	120	31	36	11	1	6	26	.300	24	32	0	62	29	3	.968
1994—	Calgary (PCL).............	3B-1B-OF	102	393	71	111	21	3	22	78	.282	49	98	1	100	185	30	.905
	—Seattle (A.L.)........	DH-3B	10	27	3	5	0	0	1	2	.185	2	10	0	2	8	1	.909
1995—	Calgary (PCL).............	3-1-P-S	118	408	71	116	34	1	12	70	.284	48	78	2	356	240	16	.974
1996—	Calgary (PCL).............	3B-1B-2B	101	343	62	103	28	2	23	84	.300	33	71	2	226	161	8	.980
	—Pittsburgh (N.L.)........	3B	12	34	9	12	5	0	1	5	.353	6	6	0	4	17	2	.913
1997—	Pittsburgh (N.L.)........	3-S-1-2	126	306	30	80	20	1	12	47	.261	27	81	0	154	142	8	.974
American League totals (8 years)			591	1922	240	457	91	11	51	256	.238	167	486	10	860	1325	108	.953
National League totals (3 years)			192	475	52	116	29	1	15	68	.244	49	126	0	236	259	18	.965
Major league totals (10 years)			783	2397	292	573	120	12	66	324	.239	216	612	10	1096	1584	126	.955

RECORD AS PITCHER

Year	Team (League)	W	L	Pct.	ERA	G	GS	CG	ShO	Sv.	IP	H	R	ER	BB	SO
1995—	Calgary (PCL)..................	0	0	...	0.00	2	0	0	0	0	2	1	0	0	0	2

SWARTZBAUGH, DAVE — P — CUBS

PERSONAL: Born February 11, 1968, in Middletown, Ohio. ... 6-2/205. ... Throws right, bats right. ... Full name: David Theodore Swartzbaugh.
HIGH SCHOOL: Middletown (Ohio).
COLLEGE: Miami of Ohio.
TRANSACTIONS/CAREER NOTES: Selected by Chicago Cubs organization in ninth round of free-agent draft (June 5, 1989). ... On Iowa disabled list (April 6-13, 1995).

Year	Team (League)	W	L	Pct.	ERA	G	GS	CG	ShO	Sv.	IP	H	R	ER	BB	SO
1989—	Geneva (N.Y.-Penn)...........	2	3	.400	4.92	18	10	0	0	0	75	81	59	41	35	77
1990—	Peoria (Midwest)...............	8	11	.421	3.82	29	•29	5	2	0	169 2/3	147	88	72	89	128
1991—	Peoria (Midwest)...............	0	5	.000	1.83	5	5	1	0	0	34 1/3	21	16	7	15	31
	—Win.-Salem (Car.)...........	10	4	.714	1.83	15	15	2	1	0	93 2/3	71	22	19	42	73
	—Charlotte (Southern).........	0	1	.000	10.13	1	1	0	0	0	5 1/3	6	7	6	3	5
1992—	Charlotte (Southern)...........	7	10	.412	3.65	27	27	5	2	0	165	134	78	67	62	111
1993—	Iowa (Am. Assoc.).............	4	6	.400	5.30	26	9	0	0	1	86 2/3	90	57	51	44	69
	—Orlando (South.).............	1	3	.250	4.23	10	9	1	0	0	66	52	33	31	18	59
1994—	Orlando (South.).............	2	4	.333	3.30	42	1	0	0	2	79	70	36	29	19	70
	—Iowa (Am. Assoc.).............	1	0	1.000	8.38	10	0	0	0	0	19 1/3	24	18	18	15	14
1995—	Iowa (Am. Assoc.).............	3	0	1.000	1.53	30	0	0	0	0	47	33	10	8	18	38
	—Orlando (South.).............	4	0	1.000	2.48	16	0	0	0	0	29	18	10	8	7	37
	—Chicago (N.L.).............	0	0	...	0.00	7	0	0	0	0	7 1/3	5	2	0	3	5
1996—	Iowa (Am. Assoc.).............	8	11	.421	3.88	44	13	0	0	0	118 1/3	106	61	51	33	103
	—Chicago (N.L.).............	0	2	.000	6.38	6	5	0	0	0	24	26	17	17	14	13
1997—	Chicago (N.L.).............	0	1	.000	9.00	2	2	0	0	0	8	12	8	8	7	4
	—Iowa (Am. Assoc.).............	8	7	.533	2.82	24	20	1	1	1	134	129	55	42	48	97
Major league totals (3 years)......		0	3	.000	5.72	15	7	0	0	0	39 1/3	43	27	25	24	22

SWEENEY, MARK — OF — PADRES

PERSONAL: Born October 26, 1969, in Framingham, Mass. ... 6-1/195. ... Bats left, throws left. ... Full name: Mark Patrick Sweeney.
HIGH SCHOOL: Holliston (Mass.).
COLLEGE: Maine.
TRANSACTIONS/CAREER NOTES: Selected by Los Angeles Dodgers organization in 39th round of free-agent draft (June 4, 1990); did not sign. ... Selected by California Angels organization in ninth round of free-agent draft (June 3, 1991). ... Traded by Angels organization with a player to be named later to St. Louis Cardinals for P John Habyan (July 8, 1995); Cardinals acquired IF Rod Correia to complete deal (January 31, 1996). ... Traded by Cardinals with P Danny Jackson and P Rich Batchelor to San Diego Padres for P Fernando Valenzuela, 3B Scott Livingstone and OF Phil Plantier (June 13, 1997).

Year	Team (League)	Pos.	G	AB	R	H	2B	3B	HR	RBI	Avg.	BB	SO	SB	PO	A	E	Avg.
1991—	Boise (Northwest)......	OF	70	234	45	66	10	3	4	34	.282	*51	42	9	81	2	4	.954
1992—	Quad City (Midwest)...	OF	120	424	65	115	20	5	14	76	.271	47	85	15	205	5	4	.981
1993—	Palm Springs (Cal.).....	OF-1B	66	245	41	87	18	3	3	47	.355	42	29	9	145	2	7	.955
	—Midland (Texas).........	OF	51	188	41	67	13	2	9	32	.356	27	22	1	85	3	1	.989
1994—	Vancouver (PCL).......	1B-OF	103	344	59	98	12	3	8	49	.285	59	50	3	330	12	2	.994
	—Midland (Texas).........	OF-1B	14	50	13	15	3	0	3	18	.300	10	10	1	66	5	2	.973
1995—	Vancouver (PCL).......	OF-1B	69	226	48	78	14	2	7	59	.345	43	33	3	102	2	2	.981
	—Louisville (A.A.)■......	1B	22	76	15	28	8	0	2	22	.368	14	8	2	176	19	2	.990
	—St. Louis (N.L.)...........	1B-OF	37	77	5	21	2	0	2	13	.273	10	15	1	153	11	2	.988
1996—	St. Louis (N.L.)...........	OF-1B	98	170	32	45	9	0	3	22	.265	33	29	3	126	3	3	.977
1997—	St. Louis (N.L.)...........	OF-1B	44	61	5	13	3	0	0	4	.213	9	14	0	31	1	0	1.000
	—San Diego (N.L.)■.....	OF-1B	71	103	11	33	4	0	2	19	.320	11	18	2	41	3	2	.957
Major league totals (3 years)			250	411	53	112	18	0	7	58	.273	63	76	6	351	18	7	.981

Year Team (League)	Pos.	G	AB	R	H	2B	3B	HR	RBI	Avg.	BB	SO	SB	PO	A	E	Avg.
1996— St. Louis (N.L.)..........	PH	1	1	0	1	0	0	0	0	1.000	0	0	0	...	...	...	...

CHAMPIONSHIP SERIES RECORD

Year Team (League)	Pos.	G	AB	R	H	2B	3B	HR	RBI	Avg.	BB	SO	SB	PO	A	E	Avg.
1996— St. Louis (N.L.)..........	PH-OF	5	4	1	0	0	0	0	0	.000	0	2	0	2	0	0	1.000

SWEENEY, MIKE — C — ROYALS

PERSONAL: Born July 22, 1973, in Orange, Calif. ... 6-2/215. ... Bats right, throws right. ... Full name: Michael John Sweeney.
HIGH SCHOOL: Ontario (Calif.).
TRANSACTIONS/CAREER NOTES: Selected by Kansas City Royals organization in 10th round of free-agent draft (June 3, 1991). ... On disabled list (May 24-July 5, 1994).
STATISTICAL NOTES: Led Carolina League with .548 slugging percentage in 1995. ... Tied for A.L. lead in double plays by catcher with 13 in 1997.

							BATTING								FIELDING		
Year Team (League)	Pos.	G	AB	R	H	2B	3B	HR	RBI	Avg.	BB	SO	SB	PO	A	E	Avg.
1991— GC Royals (GCL)	C-1B	38	102	8	22	3	0	1	11	.216	11	9	1	124	16	4	.972
1992— Eugene (Northwest) ...	C	59	199	17	44	12	1	4	28	.221	13	54	3	367	42	14	.967
1993— Eugene (Northwest) ...	C	53	175	32	42	10	2	6	29	.240	30	41	1	364	46	7	.983
1994— Rockford (Midwest)...	C	86	276	47	83	20	3	10	52	.301	55	43	0	453	54	6	.988
1995— Wilmington (Caro.)....	C-3B	99	332	61	103	23	1	18	53	*.310	60	39	6	575	45	7	.989
— Kansas City (A.L.)......	C	4	4	1	1	0	0	0	0	.250	0	0	0	7	0	1	.875
1996— Wichita (Texas)..........	C	66	235	45	75	18	1	14	51	.319	32	29	3	201	13	1	.995
— Omaha (A.A.)............	C	25	101	14	26	9	0	3	16	.257	6	13	0	167	8	0	1.000
— Kansas City (A.L.)......	C-DH	50	165	23	46	10	0	4	24	.279	18	21	1	158	7	1	.994
1997— Kansas City (A.L.)......	C-DH	84	240	30	58	8	0	7	31	.242	17	33	3	425	31	3	.993
— Omaha (A.A.)..........	C	40	144	22	34	8	1	10	29	.236	18	20	0	229	15	1	.996
Major league totals (3 years)		138	409	54	105	18	0	11	55	.257	35	54	4	590	38	5	.992

SWIFT, BILL — P — ORIOLES

PERSONAL: Born October 27, 1961, in South Portland, Maine. ... 6-0/197. ... Throws right, bats right. ... Full name: William Charles Swift.
HIGH SCHOOL: South Portland (Portland, Maine).
COLLEGE: Maine.
TRANSACTIONS/CAREER NOTES: Selected by Minnesota Twins organization in second round of free-agent draft (June 6, 1983); did not sign. ... Selected by Seattle Mariners organization in first round (second pick overall) of free-agent draft (June 4, 1984). ... On disabled list (May 6-21, 1985 and April 22, 1987-remainder of season). ... On Seattle disabled list (March 28-April 27, 1989); included rehabilitation assignment to San Bernardino (April 18-27). ... On disabled list (April 11-26, 1991). ... Traded to Mariners with P Mike Jackson and P Dave Burba to San Francisco Giants for OF Kevin Mitchell and P Mike Remlinger (December 11, 1991). ... On disabled list (May 23-June 21 and August 25-September 9, 1992; May 18-June 6 and June 24-July 21, 1994). ... Granted free agency (October 15, 1994). ... Signed by Colorado Rockies (April 8, 1995). ... On disabled list (May 28-June 16 and July 26-September 1, 1995). ... On Colorado disabled list (March 22-June 3 and June 4-August 26, 1996); included rehabilitation assignment to Salem (August 16-26). ... On Colorado disabled list (May 13-July 11, 1997); included rehabilitation assignment to Salem (June 29-July 4) and Colorado Springs (July 4-July 11). ... Released by Rockies (August 20, 1997). ... Signed by Baltimore Orioles (August 26, 1997).
MISCELLANEOUS: Member of 1984 U.S. Olympic baseball team. ... Appeared in five games as pinch-runner (1992). ... Appeared in one game as pinch-runner (1994). ... Appeared in one game as pinch-runner (1997). ... Had sacrifice hit in only appearance as pinch-hitter (1997).

Year Team (League)	W	L	Pct.	ERA	G	GS	CG	ShO	Sv.	IP	H	R	ER	BB	SO
1985— Chattanooga (Southern).....	2	1	.667	3.69	7	7	0	0	0	39	34	16	16	21	21
— Seattle (A.L.)	6	10	.375	4.77	23	21	0	0	0	120²/₃	131	71	64	48	55
1986— Seattle (A.L.)	2	9	.182	5.46	29	17	1	0	0	115¹/₃	148	85	70	55	55
— Calgary (PCL)	4	4	.500	3.95	10	8	3	1	1	57	57	33	25	22	29
1987— Calgary (PCL)	0	0	...	8.84	5	5	0	0	0	18¹/₃	32	22	18	13	5
1988— Seattle (A.L.)	8	12	.400	4.59	38	24	6	1	0	174²/₃	199	99	89	65	47
1989— San Bernardino (Calif.)......	1	0	1.000	0.00	2	2	0	0	0	10	8	0	0	2	4
— Seattle (A.L.)	7	3	.700	4.43	37	16	0	0	1	130	140	72	64	38	45
1990— Seattle (A.L.)	6	4	.600	2.39	55	8	0	0	6	128	135	46	34	21	42
1991— Seattle (A.L.)	1	2	.333	1.99	71	0	0	0	17	90¹/₃	74	22	20	26	48
1992— San Francisco (N.L.)■	10	4	.714	*2.08	30	22	3	2	1	164²/₃	144	41	38	43	77
1993— San Francisco (N.L.)	21	8	.724	2.82	34	34	1	1	0	232²/₃	195	82	73	55	157
1994— San Francisco (N.L.)	8	7	.533	3.38	17	17	0	0	0	109¹/₃	109	49	41	31	62
1995— Colorado (N.L.)■	9	3	.750	4.94	19	19	0	0	0	105²/₃	122	62	58	43	68
1996— Salem (Carolina)	0	0	...	4.50	2	2	0	0	0	6	9	4	3	1	4
— Colorado (N.L.)	1	1	.500	5.40	7	3	0	0	2	18¹/₃	23	12	11	5	5
1997— Colorado (N.L.)	4	6	.400	6.34	14	13	0	0	0	65¹/₃	85	57	46	26	29
— Salem (Carolina)	0	1	.000	6.75	1	1	0	0	0	4	4	3	3	0	1
— Colo. Springs (PCL)	0	1	.000	12.00	1	1	0	0	0	3	4	4	4	3	4
— Rochester (Int'l)■	0	1	.000	4.91	2	0	0	0	0	3²/₃	2	2	2	3	2
A.L. totals (6 years)	30	40	.429	4.04	253	86	7	1	24	759	827	395	341	253	292
N.L. totals (6 years)	53	29	.646	3.45	121	108	4	3	3	696	678	303	267	203	398
Major league totals (12 years)....	83	69	.546	3.76	374	194	11	4	27	1455	1505	698	608	456	690

DIVISION SERIES RECORD

Year Team (League)	W	L	Pct.	ERA	G	GS	CG	ShO	Sv.	IP	H	R	ER	BB	SO
1995— Colorado (N.L.)	0	0	...	6.00	1	1	0	0	0	6	7	4	4	2	3

PERSONAL: Born January 2, 1965, in Fort Worth, Texas. ... 6-3/225. ... Throws left, bats right. ... Full name: Forest Gregory Swindell. ... Name pronounced swin-DELL.

HIGH SCHOOL: Sharpstown (Texas).

COLLEGE: Texas.

TRANSACTIONS/CAREER NOTES: Selected by Cleveland Indians organization in first round (second pick overall) of free-agent draft (June 2, 1986). ... On disabled list (June 30, 1987-remainder of season and July 26-August 30, 1989). ... Traded by Indians to Cincinnati Reds for P Jack Armstrong, P Scott Scudder and P Joe Turek (November 15, 1991). ... On disabled list (August 23-September 7, 1992). ... Granted free agency (October 26, 1992). ... Signed by Houston Astros (December 4, 1992). ... On disabled list (July 6-26, 1993). ... On Houston disabled list (April 20-May 22, 1996). ... Released by Astros (June 3, 1996). ... Signed by Indians (June 15, 1996). ... On Cleveland disabled list (July 4-21, 1996). ... Granted free agency (October 3, 1996). ... Signed by Minnesota Twins organization (December 18, 1996).

HONORS: Named lefthanded pitcher on THE SPORTING NEWS college All-America team (1985-86).

STATISTICAL NOTES: Struck out 15 batters in one game (May 10, 1987).

MISCELLANEOUS: Struck out in only appearance as pinch-hitter (1995).

Year	Team (League)	W	L	Pct.	ERA	G	GS	CG	ShO	Sv.	IP	H	R	ER	BB	SO
1986—	Waterloo (Midw.)	2	1	.667	1.00	3	3	0	0	0	18	12	2	2	3	25
	—Cleveland (A.L.)	5	2	.714	4.23	9	9	1	0	0	61 2/3	57	35	29	15	46
1987—	Cleveland (A.L.)	3	8	.273	5.10	16	15	4	1	0	102 1/3	112	62	58	37	97
1988—	Cleveland (A.L.)	18	14	.563	3.20	33	33	12	4	0	242	234	97	86	45	180
1989—	Cleveland (A.L.)	13	6	.684	3.37	28	28	5	2	0	184 1/3	170	71	69	51	129
1990—	Cleveland (A.L.)	12	9	.571	4.40	34	34	3	0	0	214 2/3	245	110	105	47	135
1991—	Cleveland (A.L.)	9	16	.360	3.48	33	33	7	0	0	238	241	112	92	31	169
1992—	Cincinnati (N.L.)■	12	8	.600	2.70	31	30	5	3	0	213 2/3	210	72	64	41	138
1993—	Houston (N.L.)■	12	13	.480	4.16	31	30	1	1	0	190 1/3	215	98	88	40	124
1994—	Houston (N.L.)	8	9	.471	4.37	24	24	1	0	0	148 1/3	175	80	72	26	74
1995—	Houston (N.L.)	10	9	.526	4.47	33	26	1	1	0	153	180	86	76	39	96
1996—	Houston (N.L.)	0	3	.000	7.83	8	4	0	0	0	23	35	25	20	11	15
	—Cleveland (A.L.)	1	1	.500	6.59	13	2	0	0	0	28 2/3	31	21	21	8	21
1997—	Minnesota (A.L.)■	7	4	.636	3.58	65	1	0	0	1	115 2/3	102	46	46	25	75
A.L. totals (8 years)		68	60	.531	3.84	231	155	32	7	1	1187 1/3	1192	554	506	259	852
N.L. totals (5 years)		42	42	.500	3.95	127	114	8	5	0	728 1/3	815	361	320	157	447
Major league totals (12 years)		110	102	.519	3.88	358	269	40	12	1	1915 2/3	2007	915	826	416	1299

ALL-STAR GAME RECORD

Year	League	W	L	Pct.	ERA	GS	CG	ShO	Sv.	IP	H	R	ER	BB	SO
1989—	American	0	0	...	0.00	0	0	0	0	1 2/3	2	0	0	0	3

PERSONAL: Born January 17, 1964, in Barberton, Ohio. ... 6-2/195. ... Throws left, bats right. ... Full name: Jeffrey Jon Tabaka. ... Name pronounced tuh-BAW-kuh.

HIGH SCHOOL: Copley (Ohio) Senior.

COLLEGE: Kent.

TRANSACTIONS/CAREER NOTES: Selected by Montreal Expos organization in free-agent draft (June 2, 1986). ... On West Palm Beach disabled list (May 2-June 23, 1988). ... Selected by Philadelphia Phillies from Expos organization in Rule 5 major league draft (December 5, 1988); Expos waived right to reclaim him as part of deal in which Expos traded P Floyd Youmans and P Jeff Parrett to Phillies for P Kevin Gross (December 6, 1988). ... Released by Reading, Phillies organization (July 26, 1991). ... Signed by Milwaukee Brewers organization (August 8, 1991). ... On disabled list (June 18-July 4, 1992). ... Granted free agency (October 15, 1992). ... Re-signed by Brewers (October 30, 1992). ... Selected by Florida Marlins in third round (71st pick overall) of expansion draft (November 17, 1992). ... Granted free agency (March 21, 1993). ... Signed by New Orleans, Brewers organization (March 26, 1993). ... Granted free agency (October 15, 1993). ... Re-signed by Brewers organization (January 6, 1994). ... Released by New Orleans (April 2, 1994). ... Signed by Pittsburgh Pirates organization (April 3, 1994). ... Claimed on waivers by San Diego Padres (May 12, 1994). ... Traded by Padres with P Rich Loiselle to Houston Astros for OF Phil Plantier (July 19, 1995). ... Granted free agency (December 20, 1996). ... Granted free agency (October 15, 1997). ... Signed by Pirates (December 10, 1997).

MISCELLANEOUS: Made two outs in one game as designated hitter with New Orleans (1993).

Year	Team (League)	W	L	Pct.	ERA	G	GS	CG	ShO	Sv.	IP	H	R	ER	BB	SO
1986—	Jamestown (NYP)	2	4	.333	4.30	13	9	0	0	0	52 1/3	51	31	25	34	57
1987—	W.P. Beach (FSL)	8	6	.571	4.17	28	15	0	0	5	95	90	46	44	58	71
1988—	W.P. Beach (FSL)	7	5	.583	1.71	16	16	2	2	0	95	71	38	18	34	52
	—Jacksonville (Southern)	1	0	1.000	6.55	2	2	0	0	0	11	14	8	8	5	7
1989—	Reading (Eastern)■	8	7	.533	4.65	21	17	6	1	0	100 2/3	109	59	52	54	80
	—Scran./W.B. (Int'l)	0	4	.000	6.32	6	6	0	0	0	31 1/3	32	26	22	23	15
1990—	Clearwater (Fla. St.)	5	2	.714	3.03	8	5	0	0	0	35 2/3	39	17	12	18	23
1991—	Reading (Eastern)■	4	8	.333	5.07	21	20	1	1	0	108 1/3	117	65	61	78	68
	—Stockton (California)■	0	2	.000	5.19	4	4	0	0	0	17 1/3	19	11	10	16	19
1992—	El Paso (Texas)■	9	5	.643	2.52	50	0	0	0	10	82	67	23	23	38	75
1993—	New Orleans (A.A.)	6	6	.500	3.24	53	0	0	0	1	58 1/3	50	26	21	30	63
1994—	Buffalo (A.A.)	1	0	1.000	3.38	9	0	0	0	1	5 1/3	3	2	2	4	4
	—Pittsburgh (N.L.)	0	0	...	18.00	5	0	0	0	0	4	4	8	8	8	2
	—San Diego (N.L.)■	3	1	.750	3.89	34	0	0	0	1	37	28	21	16	19	30
1995—	Las Vegas (PCL)	0	1	.000	1.99	19	0	0	0	6	22 2/3	16	6	5	14	27
	—San Diego (N.L.)	0	0	...	7.11	10	0	0	0	0	6 1/3	10	5	5	5	6
	—Houston (N.L.)■	1	0	1.000	2.22	24	0	0	0	0	24 1/3	17	6	6	12	19
1996—	Houston (N.L.)	0	2	.000	6.64	18	0	0	0	1	20 1/3	28	18	15	14	18
	—Tucson (PCL)	6	2	.750	2.93	41	0	0	0	4	43	40	16	14	21	51
1997—	Indianapolis (A.A.)■	3	2	.600	2.65	58	0	0	0	3	57 2/3	44	19	17	19	68
	—Cincinnati (N.L.)	0	0	...	4.50	3	0	0	0	0	2	1	1	1	1	1
Major league totals (4 years)		4	3	.571	4.88	94	0	0	0	2	94	88	59	51	59	76

TAPANI, KEVIN — P — CUBS

PERSONAL: Born February 18, 1964, in Des Moines, Iowa. ... 6-0/189. ... Throws right, bats right. ... Full name: Kevin Ray Tapani. ... Name pronounced TAP-uh-nee.
HIGH SCHOOL: Escanaba (Mich.).
COLLEGE: Central Michigan (degree in finance, 1987).
TRANSACTIONS/CAREER NOTES: Selected by Chicago Cubs organization in ninth round of free-agent draft (June 3, 1985); did not sign. ... Selected by Oakland Athletics organization in second round of free-agent draft (June 2, 1986). ... Traded by A's as part of an eight-player, three-team deal in which New York Mets traded P Jesse Orosco to A's (December 11, 1987). A's traded Orosco, SS Alfredo Griffin and P Jay Howell to Los Angeles Dodgers for P Bob Welch, P Matt Young and P Jack Savage. A's then traded Savage, P Wally Whitehurst and Tapani to Mets. ... Traded by Mets with P Tim Drummond to Portland, Minnesota Twins organization (August 1, 1989), as partial completion of deal in which Twins traded P Frank Viola to Mets for P Rick Aguilera, P David West and three players to be named later (July 31, 1989); Twins acquired P Jack Savage to complete deal (October 16, 1989). ... On disabled list (August 17-September 10, 1990). ... Traded by Twins with P Mark Guthrie to Los Angeles Dodgers for 1B/3B Ron Coomer, P Greg Hansell, P Jose Parra and a player to be named later (July 31, 1995); Twins acquired OF Chris Latham to complete deal (October 30, 1995). ... Granted free agency (December 21, 1995). ... Signed by Chicago White Sox (February 3, 1996). ... Granted free agency (October 29, 1996). ... Signed by Cubs (December 16, 1996). ... On disabled list (March 27-July 23, 1997); included rehabilitation assignments to Rockford (June 25-26 and July 12-13), Orlando (July 1-7), Daytona (July 7-8) and Iowa (July 18-19).
STATISTICAL NOTES: Pitched 5-0 one-hit, complete-game victory for Chicago against Cincinnati (September 16, 1997).

Year Team (League)	W	L	Pct.	ERA	G	GS	CG	ShO	Sv.	IP	H	R	ER	BB	SO
1986— Medford (N'west)	1	0	1.000	0.00	2	2	0	0	0	8 1/3	6	3	0	3	9
— Modesto (California)	6	1	.857	2.48	11	11	1	0	0	69	74	26	19	22	44
— Huntsville (Southern)	1	0	1.000	6.00	1	1	0	0	0	6	8	4	4	1	2
— Tacoma (PCL)	0	1	.000	15.43	1	1	0	0	0	2 1/3	5	6	4	1	1
1987— Modesto (California)	10	7	.588	3.76	24	24	6	1	0	148 1/3	122	74	62	60	121
1988— St. Lucie (Fla. St.)■	1	0	1.000	1.42	3	3	0	0	0	19	17	5	3	4	11
— Jackson (Texas)	5	1	.833	2.74	24	5	0	0	3	62 1/3	46	23	19	19	35
1989— Tidewater (Int'l)	7	5	.583	3.47	17	17	2	1	0	109	113	49	42	25	63
— New York (N.L.)	0	0	...	3.68	3	0	0	0	0	7 1/3	5	3	3	4	2
— Portland (PCL)■	4	2	.667	2.20	6	6	1	0	0	41	38	15	10	12	30
— Minnesota (A.L.)	2	2	.500	3.86	5	5	0	0	0	32 2/3	34	15	14	8	21
1990— Minnesota (A.L.)	12	8	.600	4.07	28	28	1	1	0	159 1/3	164	75	72	29	101
1991— Minnesota (A.L.)	16	9	.640	2.99	34	34	4	1	0	244	225	84	81	40	135
1992— Minnesota (A.L.)	16	11	.593	3.97	34	34	4	1	0	220	226	103	97	48	138
1993— Minnesota (A.L.)	12	15	.444	4.43	36	35	3	1	0	225 2/3	243	123	111	57	150
1994— Minnesota (A.L.)	11	7	.611	4.62	24	24	4	1	0	156	181	86	80	39	91
1995— Minnesota (A.L.)	6	11	.353	4.92	20	20	3	1	0	133 2/3	155	79	73	34	88
— Los Angeles (N.L.)■	4	2	.667	5.05	13	11	0	0	0	57	72	37	32	14	43
1996— Chicago (A.L.)■	13	10	.565	4.59	34	34	1	0	0	225 1/3	236	123	115	76	150
1997— Rockford (Midwest)■	1	0	1.000	0.82	2	2	0	0	0	11	5	1	1	0	7
— Orlando (South.)	0	0	...	4.50	1	1	0	0	0	4	3	2	2	2	2
— Daytona (Fla. St.)	0	0	...	3.86	1	1	0	0	0	4 2/3	5	2	2	2	4
— Iowa (Am. Assoc.)	0	1	.000	4.00	1	1	1	0	0	9	5	4	4	1	4
— Chicago (N.L.)	9	3	.750	3.39	13	13	1	1	0	85	77	33	32	23	55
A.L. totals (8 years)	88	73	.547	4.14	215	214	20	6	0	1396 2/3	1464	688	643	331	874
N.L. totals (3 years)	13	5	.722	4.04	29	24	1	1	0	149 1/3	154	73	67	41	100
Major league totals (9 years)	101	78	.564	4.13	244	238	21	7	0	1546	1618	761	710	372	974

DIVISION SERIES RECORD

Year Team (League)	W	L	Pct.	ERA	G	GS	CG	ShO	Sv.	IP	H	R	ER	BB	SO
1995— Los Angeles (N.L.)	0	0	...	81.00	2	0	0	0	0	1/3	0	3	3	4	1

CHAMPIONSHIP SERIES RECORD

Year Team (League)	W	L	Pct.	ERA	G	GS	CG	ShO	Sv.	IP	H	R	ER	BB	SO
1991— Minnesota (A.L.)	0	1	.000	7.84	2	2	0	0	0	10 1/3	16	9	9	3	9

WORLD SERIES RECORD

NOTES: Member of World Series championship team (1991).

Year Team (League)	W	L	Pct.	ERA	G	GS	CG	ShO	Sv.	IP	H	R	ER	BB	SO
1991— Minnesota (A.L.)	1	1	.500	4.50	2	2	0	0	0	12	13	6	6	2	7

TARASCO, TONY — OF — ORIOLES

PERSONAL: Born December 9, 1970, in New York. ... 6-1/205. ... Bats left, throws right. ... Full name: Anthony Giacinto Tarasco.
HIGH SCHOOL: Santa Monica (Calif.).
TRANSACTIONS/CAREER NOTES: Selected by Atlanta Braves organization in 15th round of free-agent draft (June 1, 1988). ... On disabled list (August 4-September 12, 1991). ... Traded by Braves with OF Roberto Kelly and P Esteban Yan to Montreal Expos for OF Marquis Grissom (April 6, 1995). ... Traded by Expos to Baltimore Orioles for OF Sherman Obando (March 13, 1996). ... On Rochester disabled list (June 16-August 25, 1996). ... On Baltimore disabled list (August 25-September 13, 1996); included rehabilitation assignments to Frederick (August 25-September 8) and Rochester (September 9-13).

Year Team (League)	Pos.	G	AB	R	H	2B	3B	HR	RBI	Avg.	BB	SO	SB	PO	A	E	Avg.
1988— Idaho Falls (Pio.)	OF	7	10	1	0	0	0	0	1	.000	5	2	1	2	0	1	.667
— GC Braves (GCL)	OF	21	64	10	15	6	1	0	4	.234	7	7	3	25	1	1	.963
1989— Pulaski (Appalachian)	OF	49	156	22	53	8	2	2	22	.340	21	20	7	45	4	3	.942
1990— Sumter (S. Atl.)	OF	107	355	42	94	13	3	3	37	.265	37	57	9	173	14	9	.954
1991— Durham (Carolina)	OF	78	248	31	62	8	2	12	38	.250	21	64	11	119	6	3	.977
1992— Greenville (Southern)	OF-2B	133	489	73	140	22	2	15	54	.286	27	84	33	209	17	5	.978
1993— Richmond (Int'l)	OF	93	370	73	122	15	7	15	53	.330	36	54	19	143	8	2	.987
— Atlanta (N.L.)	OF	24	35	6	8	0	0	0	2	.229	0	5	0	11	0	0	1.000

Year	Team (League)	Pos.	G	AB	R	H	2B	3B	HR	RBI	Avg.	BB	SO	SB	PO	A	E	Avg.
1994— Atlanta (N.L.)	OF	87	132	16	36	6	0	5	19	.273	9	17	5	42	1	0	1.000
1995— Montreal (N.L.)■	OF	126	438	64	109	18	4	14	40	.249	51	78	24	230	7	5	.979
1996— Baltimore (A.L.)■	OF-DH	31	84	14	20	3	0	1	9	.238	7	15	5	50	1	0	1.000
— Rochester (Int'l)	OF	29	103	18	27	6	0	2	9	.262	17	20	4	4	0	0	1.000
— Frederick (Carolina)	DH	9	35	6	8	3	0	1	5	.229	4	4	0	0	0	0	...
— GC Orioles (GCL)	DH	3	8	2	3	1	0	0	3	.375	2	1	0	0	0	0	...
1997— Baltimore (A.L.)	OF-DH	100	166	26	34	8	1	7	26	.205	25	33	2	104	4	1	.991
— Rochester (Int'l)	OF	10	35	4	7	0	0	2	6	.200	7	7	0	19	1	0	1.000
American League totals (2 years)		131	250	40	54	11	1	8	35	.216	32	48	7	154	5	1	.994
National League totals (3 years)		237	605	86	153	26	4	19	61	.253	60	100	29	283	8	5	.983
Major league totals (5 years)		368	855	126	207	37	5	27	96	.242	92	148	36	437	13	6	.987

DIVISION SERIES RECORD

Year	Team (League)	Pos.	G	AB	R	H	2B	3B	HR	RBI	Avg.	BB	SO	SB	PO	A	E	Avg.
1996— Baltimore (A.L.)								Did not play.									

CHAMPIONSHIP SERIES RECORD

Year	Team (League)	Pos.	G	AB	R	H	2B	3B	HR	RBI	Avg.	BB	SO	SB	PO	A	E	Avg.
1993— Atlanta (N.L.)	OF-PR	2	1	0	0	0	0	0	0	.000	0	1	0	0	0	0	...
1996— Baltimore (A.L.)	OF	2	1	0	0	0	0	0	0	.000	0	1	0	2	0	0	1.000
Championship series totals (2 years)		4	2	0	0	0	0	0	0	.000	0	2	0	2	0	0	1.000

TARTABULL, DANNY   OF

PERSONAL: Born October 30, 1962, in Miami. ... 6-1/204. ... Bats right, throws right. ... Full name: Danilo Mora Tartabull. ... Son of Jose Tartabull, outfielder, Kansas City A's, Boston Red Sox and Oakland A's (1962-70); and brother of Jose Tartabull Jr., minor league outfielder (1986-88).

HIGH SCHOOL: Carol City (Miami).

TRANSACTIONS/CAREER NOTES: Selected by Cincinnati Reds organization in third round of free-agent draft (June 3, 1980). ... Selected by Seattle Mariners organization in player compensation pool draft (January 20, 1983); pick received as compensation for Chicago White Sox signing free-agent P Floyd Bannister (December 13, 1982). ... On disabled list (May 15-30, 1986). ... Traded by Mariners with P Rick Luecken to Kansas City Royals for P Scott Bankhead, P Steve Shields and OF Mike Kingery (December 10, 1986). ... On disabled list (June 15-30, 1989; April 11-May 18 and July 14-31, 1990). ... Granted free agency (October 28, 1991). ... Signed by New York Yankees (January 6, 1992). ... On disabled list (April 21-May 8 and July 27-August 14, 1992; and May 25-June 15, 1993). ... Traded by Yankees to Oakland Athletics for OF Ruben Sierra and P Jason Beverlin (July 28, 1995). ... On Oakland disabled list (August 3-September 1, 1995). ... Traded by A's to Chicago White Sox for P Andrew Lorraine and OF Charles Poe (January 22, 1996). ... Granted free agency (November 18, 1996). ... Signed by Philadelphia Phillies (February 25, 1997). ... On disabled list (April 8, 1997-remainder of season). ... Granted free agency (October 10, 1997).

HONORS: Named Florida State League Most Valuable Player (1981). ... Named Pacific Coast League Player of the Year (1985).

STATISTICAL NOTES: Led Florida State League third basemen with 29 errors in 1981. ... Led Pacific Coast League shortstops with 68 double plays in 1984. ... Led Pacific Coast League with .615 slugging percentage and 291 total bases in 1985. ... Led Pacific Coast League shortstops with 35 errors in 1985. ... Led A.L. with 21 game-winning RBIs in 1987. ... Hit three home runs in one game (July 6, 1991). ... Led A.L. with .593 slugging percentage in 1991. ... Career major league grand slams: 11.

Year	Team (League)	Pos.	G	AB	R	H	2B	3B	HR	RBI	Avg.	BB	SO	SB	PO	A	E	Avg.
1980— Billings (Pioneer)	3B-OF-2B	59	157	33	47	10	0	2	27	.299	37	24	7	34	54	14	.863
1981— Tampa (Florida State)	3B-2B	127	422	86	131	*28	10	14	81	*.310	90	77	11	150	248	†39	.911
1982— Waterbury (Eastern)	2B	126	409	64	93	17	3	17	63	.227	89	120	12	237	306	*32	.944
1983— Chattanooga (Sou.)■	2B	128	481	95	145	32	7	13	66	.301	47	63	25	252	405	23	.966
1984— Salt Lake (PCL)	SS	116	418	69	127	22	9	13	73	.304	57	69	11	181	333	24	.955
— Seattle (A.L.)	SS-2B	10	20	3	6	1	0	2	7	.300	2	3	0	8	21	2	.935
1985— Calgary (PCL)	SS-3B	125	473	102	142	14	3	*43	*109	.300	67	123	17	181	399	†36	.942
— Seattle (A.L.)	SS-3B	19	61	8	20	7	1	1	7	.328	8	14	1	28	43	4	.947
1986— Seattle (A.L.)	O-2-DH-3	137	511	76	138	25	6	25	96	.270	61	157	4	233	111	18	.950
1987— Kansas City (A.L.)■	OF-DH	158	582	95	180	27	3	34	101	.309	79	136	9	228	11	6	.976
1988— Kansas City (A.L.)	OF-DH	146	507	80	139	38	3	26	102	.274	76	119	8	227	8	9	.963
1989— Kansas City (A.L.)	OF-DH	133	441	54	118	22	0	18	62	.268	69	123	4	108	3	2	.982
1990— Kansas City (A.L.)	OF-DH	88	313	41	84	19	0	15	60	.268	36	93	1	81	1	3	.965
1991— Kansas City (A.L.)	OF-DH	132	484	78	153	35	3	31	100	.316	65	121	6	190	4	7	.965
1992— New York (A.L.)■	OF-DH	123	421	72	112	19	0	25	85	.266	103	115	2	143	3	3	.980
1993— New York (A.L.)	DH-OF	138	513	87	128	33	2	31	102	.250	92	156	0	88	3	2	.978
1994— New York (A.L.)	DH-OF	104	399	68	102	24	1	19	67	.256	66	111	1	43	1	0	1.000
1995— New York (A.L.)	DH-OF	59	192	25	43	12	0	6	28	.224	33	54	0	27	1	0	1.000
— Oakland (A.L.)■	DH-OF	24	88	9	23	4	0	2	7	.261	10	28	0	1	0	0	1.000
1996— Chicago (A.L.)■	OF-DH	132	472	58	120	23	3	27	101	.254	64	128	1	253	4	7	.973
1997— Philadelphia (N.L.)■	OF	3	7	2	0	0	0	0	0	.000	4	4	0	2	0	0	1.000
American League totals (13 years)		1403	5004	754	1366	289	22	262	925	.273	764	1358	37	1658	214	63	.967
National League totals (1 year)		3	7	2	0	0	0	0	0	.000	4	4	0	2	0	0	1.000
Major league totals (14 years)		1406	5011	756	1366	289	22	262	925	.273	768	1362	37	1660	214	63	.967

ALL-STAR GAME RECORD

Year	League	Pos.	AB	R	H	2B	3B	HR	RBI	Avg.	BB	SO	SB	PO	A	E	Avg.
1991— American	DH	2	0	0	0	0	0	0	.000	0	1	0	...	...	...	...

TATIS, FERNANDO   3B   RANGERS

PERSONAL: Born January 1, 1975, in San Pedro De Macoris, Dominican Republic. ... 6-1/175. ... Bats left, throws right.
TRANSACTIONS/CAREER NOTES: Signed as non-drafted free agent by Texas Rangers organization (August 25, 1992).
STATISTICAL NOTES: Tied for Gulf Coast League lead in intentional bases on balls received with four in 1994. ... Led Gulf Coast League third basemen with 165 assists and 227 total chances in 1994. ... Tied for Texas League lead with four intentional bases on balls in 1997.

										BATTING					FIELDING		
Year Team (League)	Pos.	G	AB	R	H	2B	3B	HR	RBI	Avg.	BB	SO	SB	PO	A	E	Avg.
1993— Dom. Rangers (DSL)..	IF	59	198	22	54	5	1	4	34	.273	27	12	7	135	37	11	.940
1994— GC Rangers (GCL)......	3B-2B	•60	212	34	70	10	2	6	32	.330	25	33	21	47	†168	17	.927
1995— Char., S.C. (S. Atl.)...	3B	131	499	74	•151	*43	4	15	84	.303	45	94	22	*98	235	37	.900
1996— Charlotte (Fla. St.)......	3B	85	325	46	93	25	0	12	53	.286	30	48	9	53	148	24	.893
—Oklahoma City (A.A.)..	3B	2	4	0	2	1	0	0	0	.500	0	1	0	0	1	0	1.000
1997— Tulsa (Texas)	3B	102	382	73	120	26	1	24	61	.314	46	72	17	53	193	21	.921
—Texas (A.L.)................	3B	60	223	29	57	9	0	8	29	.256	14	42	3	45	90	7	.951
Major league totals (1 year)		60	223	29	57	9	0	8	29	.256	14	42	3	45	90	7	.951

TATIS, RAMON   P   DEVIL RAYS

PERSONAL: Born January 5, 1973, in Guayabin, Dominican Republic. ... 6-2/185. ... Throws left, bats left. ... Full name: Ramon Francisco Tatis.
TRANSACTIONS/CAREER NOTES: Signed as non-drafted free agent by New York Mets organization (September 6, 1990). ... Selected by Chicago Cubs organization from Mets organization in Rule 5 major league draft (December 9, 1996). ... Selected by Tampa Bay Devil Rays in second round (42nd pick overall) of expansion draft (November 18, 1997).

Year Team (League)	W	L	Pct.	ERA	G	GS	CG	ShO	Sv.	IP	H	R	ER	BB	SO
1991— Dominican Mets (DSL).......	2	6	.250	4.26	12	12	0	0	0	57	59	41	27	34	43
1992— GC Mets (GCL).................	1	3	.250	8.50	11	5	0	0	0	36	56	40	34	15	25
1993— Kingsport (Appalachian).....	0	2	.000	6.12	13	3	0	0	1	42²/₃	51	42	29	23	25
1994— Kingsport (Appalachian).....	1	3	.250	3.32	13	4	0	0	0	40²/₃	35	25	15	31	36
1995— Columbia (South Atlantic)..	2	3	.400	5.63	16	2	0	0	0	32	34	27	20	14	27
—Pittsfield (NYP)	4	5	.444	3.63	13	13	1	•1	0	79¹/₃	88	40	32	27	69
1996— St. Lucie (Fla. St.)	4	2	.667	3.39	46	1	0	0	6	74¹/₃	71	35	28	38	46
1997— Chicago (N.L.)■..................	1	1	.500	5.34	56	0	0	0	0	55²/₃	66	36	33	29	33
Major league totals (1 year)........	1	1	.500	5.34	56	0	0	0	0	55²/₃	66	36	33	29	33

TAUBENSEE, EDDIE   C   REDS

PERSONAL: Born October 31, 1968, in Beeville, Texas. ... 6-4/205. ... Bats left, throws right. ... Full name: Edward Kenneth Taubensee. ... Name pronounced TAW-ben-see.
HIGH SCHOOL: Lake Howell (Casselberry, Fla.).
TRANSACTIONS/CAREER NOTES: Selected by Cincinnati Reds organization in sixth round of free-agent draft (June 2, 1986). ... Selected by Oakland Athletics from Reds organization in Rule 5 major league draft (December 3, 1990). ... Claimed on waivers by Cleveland Indians (April 4, 1991). ... Traded by Indians with P Willie Blair to Houston Astros for OF Kenny Lofton and IF Dave Rohde (December 10, 1991). ... Traded by Astros to Reds for P Ross Powell and P Marty Lister (April 19, 1994).
STATISTICAL NOTES: Led Pioneer League with 19 passed balls in 1987. ... Tied for South Atlantic League lead in double plays by catcher with seven in 1988.

										BATTING					FIELDING		
Year Team (League)	Pos.	G	AB	R	H	2B	3B	HR	RBI	Avg.	BB	SO	SB	PO	A	E	Avg.
1986— GC Reds (GCL)..........	C-1B	35	107	8	21	3	0	1	11	.196	11	33	0	208	27	8	.967
1987— Billings (Pioneer)........	C	55	162	24	43	7	0	5	28	.265	25	47	2	344	29	6	.984
1988— Greensboro (S. Atl.) ...	C	103	330	36	85	16	1	10	41	.258	44	93	8	640	70	15	.979
—Chattanooga (Sou.)	C	5	12	2	2	0	0	1	1	.167	3	4	0	17	5	1	.957
1989— Cedar Rap. (Midw.)	C	59	196	25	39	5	0	8	22	.199	25	55	4	400	9	1	.998
—Chattanooga (Sou.)	C	45	127	11	24	2	0	3	13	.189	11	28	0	213	31	6	.976
1990— Cedar Rap. (Midw.)	C	122	417	57	108	21	1	16	62	.259	51	98	11	795	94	16	.982
1991— Cleveland (A.L.)■.......	C	26	66	5	16	2	1	0	8	.242	5	16	0	89	6	2	.979
—Colo. Springs (PCL).....	C	91	287	53	89	23	3	13	39	.310	31	61	0	412	47	12	.975
1992— Houston (N.L.)■........	C	104	297	23	66	15	0	5	28	.222	31	78	2	557	66	5	.992
—Tucson (PCL)	C	20	74	13	25	8	1	1	10	.338	8	17	0	127	10	4	.972
1993— Houston (N.L.)	C	94	288	26	72	11	1	9	42	.250	21	44	1	551	41	5	.992
1994— Houston (N.L.)	C	5	10	0	1	0	0	0	0	.100	0	3	0	19	2	0	1.000
—Cincinnati (N.L.)■.......	C	61	177	29	52	8	2	8	21	.294	15	28	2	362	17	4	.990
1995— Cincinnati (N.L.)	C-1B	80	218	32	62	14	2	9	44	.284	22	52	2	338	22	6	.984
1996— Cincinnati (N.L.)	C	108	327	46	95	20	0	12	48	.291	26	64	3	538	42	11	.981
1997— Cincinnati (N.L.)	C-O-1-DH	108	254	26	68	18	0	10	34	.268	22	66	0	408	26	5	.989
American League totals (1 year)		26	66	5	16	2	1	0	8	.242	5	16	0	89	6	2	.979
National League totals (6 years)		560	1571	182	416	86	5	53	217	.265	137	335	10	2773	216	36	.988
Major league totals (7 years)		586	1637	187	432	88	6	53	225	.264	142	351	10	2862	222	38	.988

CHAMPIONSHIP SERIES RECORD

										BATTING					FIELDING		
Year Team (League)	Pos.	G	AB	R	H	2B	3B	HR	RBI	Avg.	BB	SO	SB	PO	A	E	Avg.
1995— Cincinnati (N.L.)	PH-C	2	2	0	1	0	0	0	0	.500	0	0	0	0	0	0	...

TAVAREZ, JESUS   OF

PERSONAL: Born March 26, 1971, in Santo Domingo, Dominican Republic. ... 6-0/170. ... Bats both, throws right. ... Full name: Jesus Rafael Tavarez. ... Name pronounced tuh-VARE-ez.

TRANSACTIONS/CAREER NOTES: Signed as non-drafted free agent by Seattle Mariners organization (June 8, 1989). ... On disabled list (April 20-May 20, 1992). ... Selected by Florida Marlins in first round (26th pick overall) of expansion draft (November 17, 1992). ... On disabled list (May 18-June 4, 1993). ... On Florida disabled list (June 11-27, 1995). ... Traded by Marlins to Boston Red Sox for a player to be named later (November 25, 1996); Marlins acquired P Robert Rodgers to complete deal (December 10, 1996). ... Granted free agency (October 7, 1997).

STATISTICAL NOTES: Tied for Carolina League lead in double plays by outfielder with four in 1990.

MISCELLANEOUS: Batted righthanded only (1990-92).

Year	Team (League)	Pos.	G	AB	R	H	2B	3B	HR	RBI	Avg.	BB	SO	SB	PO	A	E	Avg.
								BATTING								FIELDING		
1989—	....						Dominican Summer League statistics unavailable.											
1990—	Peninsula (Caro.)	OF	108	379	39	90	10	1	0	32	.237	20	79	40	228	•12	9	.964
1991—	San Bernardino (Calif.)	OF	124	466	80	132	11	3	5	41	.283	39	78	69	231	9	9	.964
1992—	Jacksonville (South.)..	OF	105	392	38	101	9	2	3	25	.258	23	54	29	208	7	5	.977
1993—	High Desert (Calif.)■ .	OF	109	444	104	130	21	8	7	71	.293	57	66	47	194	10	9	.958
1994—	Portland (Eastern)	OF	89	353	60	101	11	8	2	32	.286	35	63	20	171	3	6	.967
	— Florida (N.L.)	OF	17	39	4	7	0	0	0	4	.179	1	5	1	28	1	0	1.000
1995—	Charlotte (Int'l)	OF	39	140	15	42	6	2	1	8	.300	9	19	7	92	2	2	.979
	— Florida (N.L.)	OF	63	190	31	55	6	2	2	13	.289	16	27	7	118	1	0	1.000
1996—	Florida (N.L.)	OF	98	114	14	25	3	0	0	6	.219	7	18	5	58	0	0	1.000
1997—	Pawtucket (Int'l)■......	OF	59	229	43	61	6	3	3	20	.266	27	31	22	127	7	3	.978
	— Boston (A.L.)	OF-DH	42	69	12	12	3	1	0	9	.174	4	9	0	49	1	1	.980
	American League totals (1 year)		42	69	12	12	3	1	0	9	.174	4	9	0	49	1	1	.980
	National League totals (3 years)		178	343	49	87	9	2	2	23	.254	24	50	13	204	2	0	1.000
	Major league totals (4 years)		220	412	61	99	12	3	2	32	.240	28	59	13	253	3	1	.996

TAVAREZ, JULIAN   P   GIANTS

PERSONAL: Born May 22, 1973, in Santiago, Dominican Republic. ... 6-2/190. ... Throws right, bats right.

HIGH SCHOOL: Santiago (Dominican Republic) Public School.

TRANSACTIONS/CAREER NOTES: Signed as non-drafted free agent by Cleveland Indians organization (March 16, 1990). ... On Cleveland suspended list (June 18-21, 1996). ... Traded by Indians with IF Jeff Kent, IF Jose Vizcaino and a player to be named later to San Francisco Giants for 3B Matt Williams and a player to be named later (November 13, 1996); Indians traded P Joe Roa to Giants for OF Trenidad Hubbard to complete deal (December 16, 1996).

HONORS: Named A.L. Rookie Pitcher of the Year by THE SPORTING NEWS (1995).

STATISTICAL NOTES: Led Appalachian League with 10 hit batsmen in 1993.

Year	Team (League)	W	L	Pct.	ERA	G	GS	CG	ShO	Sv.	IP	H	R	ER	BB	SO
1990—	DSL Indians (DSL)	5	5	.500	3.29	14	12	3	0	0	82	85	53	30	48	33
1991—	DSL Indians (DSL)	8	2	.800	2.67	19	18	1	0	0	121 1/3	95	41	36	28	75
1992—	Burlington (Appalachian)....	6	3	.667	2.68	14	*14	2	•2	0	87 1/3	86	41	26	12	69
1993—	Kinston (Carolina)	11	5	.688	2.42	18	18	2	0	0	119	102	48	32	28	107
	— Cant./Akr. (Eastern)	2	1	.667	0.95	3	2	1	1	0	19	14	2	2	1	11
	— Cleveland (A.L.)	2	2	.500	6.57	8	7	0	0	0	37	53	29	27	13	19
1994—	Charlotte (Int'l)	•15	6	.714	3.48	26	26	2	2	0	176	167	79	68	43	102
	— Cleveland (A.L.)	0	1	.000	21.60	1	1	0	0	0	1 2/3	6	8	4	1	0
1995—	Cleveland (A.L.)	10	2	.833	2.44	57	0	0	0	0	85	76	36	23	21	68
1996—	Cleveland (A.L.)	4	7	.364	5.36	51	4	0	0	0	80 2/3	101	49	48	22	46
	— Buffalo (A.A.)	1	0	1.000	1.29	2	2	0	0	0	14	10	2	2	3	10
1997—	San Francisco (N.L.)■	6	4	.600	3.87	*89	0	0	0	0	88 1/3	91	43	38	34	38
	A.L. totals (4 years)	16	12	.571	4.49	117	12	0	0	0	204 1/3	236	122	102	57	133
	N.L. totals (1 year)	6	4	.600	3.87	89	0	0	0	0	88 1/3	91	43	38	34	38
	Major league totals (5 years)......	22	16	.579	4.31	206	12	0	0	0	292 2/3	327	165	140	91	171

DIVISION SERIES RECORD

Year	Team (League)	W	L	Pct.	ERA	G	GS	CG	ShO	Sv.	IP	H	R	ER	BB	SO
1995—	Cleveland (A.L.)	0	0	...	6.75	3	0	0	0	0	2 2/3	5	2	2	0	3
1996—	Cleveland (A.L.)	0	0	...	0.00	2	0	0	0	0	1 1/3	1	0	0	2	1
1997—	San Francisco (N.L.)	0	1	.000	4.50	3	0	0	0	0	4	4	2	2	2	0
	Div. series totals (3 years)	0	1	.000	4.50	8	0	0	0	0	8	10	4	4	4	4

CHAMPIONSHIP SERIES RECORD

Year	Team (League)	W	L	Pct.	ERA	G	GS	CG	ShO	Sv.	IP	H	R	ER	BB	SO
1995—	Cleveland (A.L.).................	0	1	.000	2.70	4	0	0	0	0	3 1/3	3	1	1	1	2

WORLD SERIES RECORD

Year	Team (League)	W	L	Pct.	ERA	G	GS	CG	ShO	Sv.	IP	H	R	ER	BB	SO
1995—	Cleveland (A.L.).................	0	0	...	0.00	5	0	0	0	0	4 1/3	3	0	0	2	1

TAYLOR, BILL   P   ATHLETICS

PERSONAL: Born October 16, 1961, in Monticello, Fla. ... 6-8/232. ... Throws right, bats right. ... Full name: William Howell Taylor.

HIGH SCHOOL: Central (Thomasville, Ga.).

COLLEGE: Abraham Baldwin Agricultural College (Ga.).

TRANSACTIONS/CAREER NOTES: Selected by Texas Rangers organization in second round of free-agent draft (January 8, 1980). ... Loaned by Rangers organization to Wausau, Seattle Mariners organization (April 5-June 23, 1982). ... Granted free agency (October 22, 1988). ... Signed by Las Vegas, San Diego Padres organization (March 30, 1989). ... Granted free agency (October 22, 1989). ... Signed by Atlanta Braves organization (August 16, 1990). ... Selected by Toronto Blue Jays from Braves organization in Rule 5 major league draft (December 7, 1992). ... Returned to Braves organization (April 3, 1993). ... Granted free agency (October 15, 1993). ... Signed by Oakland Athletics organization (December 13, 1993). ... On disabled list (July 27, 1994-remainder of season and April 12, 1995-entire season). ... On Oakland disabled list (August 15-September 13, 1996).

Year Team (League)	W	L	Pct.	ERA	G	GS	CG	ShO	Sv.	IP	H	R	ER	BB	SO
1980—Asheville (S. Atl.)...............	0	2	.000	10.93	6	2	0	0	0	14	24	24	17	9	12
—GC Rangers (GCL).............	0	0	...	2.31	14	2	0	0	0	35	36	14	9	16	22
1981—Asheville (S. Atl.)...............	1	7	.125	4.64	14	12	1	0	0	64	76	43	33	35	44
—GC Rangers (GCL).............	4	2	.667	2.72	12	11	0	0	0	53	42	23	16	29	35
1982—Wausau (Midwest)■........	2	5	.286	5.03	19	1	0	0	2	39 1/3	36	27	22	27	34
—Burlington (Midw.)■........	5	4	.556	3.72	18	8	2	0	1	72 2/3	64	37	30	36	61
1983—Salem (Carolina)	1	1	.500	6.26	7	7	1	0	0	41 2/3	30	34	29	42	42
—Tulsa (Texas)	5	8	.385	6.87	21	12	0	0	0	76	86	65	58	51	75
1984—Tulsa (Texas)	5	3	.625	3.83	42	2	0	0	7	80	65	38	34	51	80
1985—Tulsa (Texas)	3	9	.250	3.47	20	17	2	0	0	103 2/3	84	55	40	48	87
1986—Tulsa (Texas)	3	7	.300	3.95	11	11	2	1	0	68 1/3	65	40	30	37	64
—Oklahoma City (A.A.).........	5	5	.500	4.60	16	16	1	0	0	101 2/3	94	56	52	57	68
1987—Oklahoma City (A.A.).........	*12	9	.571	5.61	28	•28	0	0	0	168 1/3	198	122	105	91	100
1988—Oklahoma City (A.A.).........	4	8	.333	5.49	20	12	1	1	1	82	98	55	50	35	42
1989—Las Vegas (PCL)■............	7	4	.636	5.13	47	0	0	0	1	79	93	48	45	27	71
1990—Durham (Carolina) ■..........	0	0	...	3.24	5	0	0	0	0	8 1/3	8	3	3	1	10
—Richmond (Int'l)	0	0	...	0.00	2	0	0	0	0	2 1/3	4	0	0	0	0
1991—Greenville (Southern)	6	2	.750	1.51	•59	0	0	0	22	77 1/3	49	16	13	15	65
1992—Richmond (Int'l)	2	3	.400	2.28	47	0	0	0	12	79	72	27	20	27	82
1993—Richmond (Int'l)	2	4	.333	1.98	59	0	0	0	*26	68 1/3	56	19	15	26	81
1994—Oakland (A.L.)■...............	1	3	.250	3.50	41	0	0	0	1	46 1/3	38	24	18	18	48
1996—Edmonton (PCL)	0	0	...	0.79	7	0	0	0	4	11 1/3	10	1	1	3	13
—Oakland (A.L.)	6	3	.667	4.33	55	0	0	0	17	60 1/3	52	30	29	25	67
1997—Oakland (A.L.)	3	4	.429	3.82	72	0	0	0	23	73	70	32	31	36	66
Major league totals (3 years)......	10	10	.500	3.91	168	0	0	0	41	179 2/3	160	86	78	79	181

TEJADA, MIGUEL   SS   ATHLETICS

PERSONAL: Born May 25, 1976, in Bani, Dominican Republic. ... 5-10/170. ... Bats right, throws right. ... Full name: Miguel Odalis Martinez Tejada.

TRANSACTIONS/CAREER NOTES: Signed as non-drafted free agent by Oakland Athletics organization (July 17, 1993). ... On suspended list (July 4-7, 1996. ... On disabled list (July 20-August 10, 1996).

STATISTICAL NOTES: Led California League shortstops with 44 errors in 1996. ... Led Southern League shortstops with 688 total chances and 97 double plays in 1997.

							BATTING						FIELDING			
Year Team (League)	Pos.	G	AB	R	H	2B	3B	HR	RBI	Avg.	BB	SO	SB	PO	A	E	Avg.
1993—							Dominican League statistics unavailable.										
1994—Dominican Athletics (DSL)	2B	74	218	51	64	9	1	18	62	.294	37	36	13	76	126	16	.927
1995—S. Oregon (N'west).....	SS	74	269	45	66	15	5	8	44	.245	41	54	19	*129	*214	26	.930
1996—Modesto (California) ..	SS-3B	114	458	97	128	12	5	20	72	.279	51	93	27	194	358	†45	.925
1997—Huntsville (Southern)..	SS	128	502	85	138	20	3	22	97	.275	50	99	15	*229	*423	*36	.948
—Oakland (A.L.)	SS	26	99	10	20	3	2	2	10	.202	2	22	2	54	69	4	.969
Major league totals (1 year)		26	99	10	20	3	2	2	10	.202	2	22	2	54	69	4	.969

TELEMACO, AMAURY   P   CUBS

PERSONAL: Born January 19, 1974, in Higuey, Dominican Republic. ... 6-3/215. ... Throws right, bats right. ... Full name: Amaury Regalado Telemaco. ... Name pronounced AH-mer-ee tel-ah-MAH-ko.

TRANSACTIONS/CAREER NOTES: Signed as non-drafted free agent by Chicago Cubs organization (May 23, 1991). ... On temporarily inactive list (August 17, 1993-remainder of season). ... On Orlando disabled list (August 23-September 8, 1994). ... On Chicago disabled list (August 20-September 4, 1996); included rehabilitation assignment to Iowa (September 2-4).

Year Team (League)	W	L	Pct.	ERA	G	GS	CG	ShO	Sv.	IP	H	R	ER	BB	SO
1991—Puerta Plata (DSL)	3	3	.500	3.55	15	13	0	0	0	66	81	43	26	32	43
1992—Huntington (Appal.)............	3	5	.375	4.01	12	12	2	0	0	76 1/3	71	45	34	17	*93
—Peoria (Midwest)...............	0	1	.000	7.94	2	1	0	0	0	5 2/3	9	5	5	5	5
1993—Peoria (Midwest)...............	8	11	.421	3.45	23	23	3	0	0	143 2/3	129	69	55	54	133
1994—Daytona (Fla. St.).............	7	3	.700	3.40	11	11	2	0	0	76 2/3	62	35	29	23	59
—Orlando (South.)	3	5	.375	3.45	12	12	2	0	0	62 2/3	56	29	24	20	42
1995—Orlando (South.)	8	8	.500	3.29	22	22	3	1	0	147 2/3	112	60	54	42	151
1996—Iowa (Am. Assoc.).............	3	1	.750	3.06	8	8	1	0	0	50	38	19	17	18	42
—Chicago (N.L.).................	5	7	.417	5.46	25	17	0	0	0	97 1/3	108	67	59	31	64
1997—Iowa (Am. Assoc.).............	5	9	.357	4.51	18	18	3	•2	0	113 2/3	121	70	57	38	75
—Chicago (N.L.).................	0	3	.000	6.16	10	5	0	0	0	38	47	26	26	11	29
—Orlando (South.)	1	0	1.000	2.25	1	1	0	0	0	8	9	2	2	2	6
Major league totals (2 years)......	5	10	.333	5.65	35	22	0	0	0	135 1/3	155	93	85	42	93

TELFORD, ANTHONY   P   EXPOS

PERSONAL: Born March 6, 1966, in San Jose, Calif. ... 6-0/189. ... Throws right, bats right. ... Full name: Anthony Charles Telford.

HIGH SCHOOL: Silver Creek (Calif.).

COLLEGE: San Jose State.

TRANSACTIONS/CAREER NOTES: Selected by Baltimore Orioles organization in third round of free-agent draft (June 2, 1987). ... On disabled list (April 20, 1988-remainder of season). ... On Frederick disabled list (April 7-18, 1989). ... On Erie disabled list (June 16-30, 1989). ... Granted free agency (October 15, 1993). ... Signed by Atlanta Braves organization (November 23, 1993). ... Granted free agency (October 15, 1994). ... Signed by Edmonton, Oakland Athletics organization (January 20, 1995). ... Released by Edmonton (May 16, 1995). ... Signed by Cleveland Indians organization (June 15, 1995). ... Granted free agency (October 16, 1995). ... Granted free agency (October 15, 1996). ... Signed by Montreal Expos organization (February 9, 1996).

Year	Team (League)	W	L	Pct.	ERA	G	GS	CG	ShO	Sv.	IP	H	R	ER	BB	SO
1987—	Newark (N.Y.-Penn)	1	0	1.000	1.02	6	2	0	0	0	17 2/3	16	2	2	3	27
	—Hagerstown (Caro.)	1	0	1.000	1.59	2	2	0	0	0	11 1/3	9	2	2	5	10
	—Rochester (Int'l)	0	0	...	0.00	1	0	0	0	0	2	0	0	0	3	3
1988—	Hagerstown (Caro.)	1	0	1.000	0.00	1	1	0	0	0	7	3	0	0	0	10
1989—	Frederick (Carolina)	2	1	.667	4.21	9	5	0	0	1	25 2/3	25	15	12	12	19
1990—	Frederick (Carolina)	4	2	.667	1.68	8	8	1	0	0	53 2/3	35	15	10	11	49
	—Hagerstown (Eastern)	10	2	.833	1.97	14	13	3	1	0	96	80	26	21	25	73
	—Baltimore (A.L.)	3	3	.500	4.95	8	8	0	0	0	36 1/3	43	22	20	19	20
1991—	Rochester (Int'l)	•12	9	.571	3.95	27	25	3	0	0	157 1/3	166	82	69	48	115
	—Baltimore (A.L.)	0	0	...	4.05	9	1	0	0	0	26 2/3	27	12	12	6	24
1992—	Rochester (Int'l)	12	7	.632	4.18	27	26	3	0	0	*181	*183	89	84	64	129
1993—	Rochester (Int'l)	7	7	.500	4.27	38	6	0	0	2	90 2/3	98	51	43	33	66
	—Baltimore (A.L.)	0	0	...	9.82	3	0	0	0	0	7 1/3	11	8	8	1	6
1994—	Richmond (Int'l)■	10	6	.625	4.23	38	20	3	1	0	142 2/3	148	82	67	41	111
1995—	Edmonton (PCL)■	3	2	.600	7.18	8	6	0	0	0	36 1/3	47	32	29	16	17
	—Cant./Akr. (Eastern)■	2	0	1.000	0.82	2	2	0	0	0	11	6	2	1	4	4
	—Buffalo (A.A.)	4	1	.800	3.46	16	2	0	0	0	39	35	15	15	10	24
1996—	Ottawa (Int'l)■	7	2	.778	4.11	30	15	1	1	0	118 1/3	128	62	54	34	69
1997—	Montreal (N.L.)	4	6	.400	3.24	65	0	0	0	1	89	77	34	32	33	61
A.L. totals (3 years)		3	3	.500	5.12	20	9	0	0	0	70 1/3	81	42	40	26	50
N.L. totals (1 year)		4	6	.400	3.24	65	0	0	0	1	89	77	34	32	33	61
Major league totals (4 years)		7	9	.438	4.07	85	9	0	0	1	159 1/3	158	76	72	59	111

TELGHEDER, DAVID   P   ATHLETICS

PERSONAL: Born November 11, 1966, in Middletown, N.Y. ... 6-3/213. ... Throws right, bats right. ... Full name: David William Telgheder. ... Name pronounced tell-GATOR.
HIGH SCHOOL: Minisink Valley (Slate Hill, N.Y.).
COLLEGE: Massachusetts (received degree, 1989).
TRANSACTIONS/CAREER NOTES: Selected by New York Mets organization in 31st round of free-agent draft (June 5, 1989). ... On Norfolk disabled list (September 1-8, 1994). ... Granted free agency (October 16, 1995). ... Signed by Oakland Athletics organization (November 21, 1995). ... On Oakland disabled list (June 24-September 8, 1997); included rehabilitation assignments to Modesto (August 28-September 3) and Edmonton (September 3-8).
RECORDS: Shares major league record for most home runs allowed in one inning—4 (September 21, 1996, third inning).
STATISTICAL NOTES: Pitched 1-0 no-hit victory against Pawtucket (May 15, 1992).

Year	Team (League)	W	L	Pct.	ERA	G	GS	CG	ShO	Sv.	IP	H	R	ER	BB	SO
1989—	Pittsfield (NYP)	5	3	.625	2.45	13	7	4	1	2	58 2/3	43	18	16	9	65
1990—	Columbia (S. Atl.)	9	3	.750	1.54	14	13	5	1	0	99 1/3	79	22	17	10	81
	—St. Lucie (Fla. St.)	9	4	.692	3.00	14	14	3	0	0	96	84	38	32	14	77
1991—	Williamsport (Eastern)	•13	11	.542	3.60	28	26	1	0	0	167 2/3	185	81	67	33	90
1992—	Tidewater (Int'l)	6	*14	.300	4.21	28	27	3	2	0	169	173	87	79	36	118
1993—	Norfolk (Int'l)	7	3	.700	2.95	13	12	0	0	1	76 1/3	81	29	25	19	52
	—New York (N.L.)	6	2	.750	4.76	24	7	0	0	0	75 2/3	82	40	40	21	35
1994—	New York (N.L.)	0	1	.000	7.20	6	0	0	0	0	10	11	8	8	8	4
	—Norfolk (Int'l)	8	10	.444	3.40	23	23	3	2	0	158 2/3	156	65	60	26	83
1995—	Norfolk (Int'l)	5	4	.556	2.24	29	11	0	0	3	92 1/3	77	34	23	8	75
	—New York (N.L.)■	1	2	.333	5.61	7	4	0	0	0	25 2/3	34	18	16	7	16
1996—	Edmonton (PCL)■	8	6	.571	4.17	17	17	1	0	0	101 1/3	102	53	47	23	59
	—Modesto (California)	1	0	1.000	1.50	1	1	0	0	0	6	4	3	1	1	3
	—Oakland (A.L.)	4	7	.364	4.65	16	14	1	1	0	79 1/3	92	42	41	26	43
1997—	Modesto (California)	0	0	...	3.38	2	2	0	0	0	5 1/3	3	2	2	2	4
	—Oakland (A.L.)	4	6	.400	6.06	20	19	0	0	0	101	134	71	68	35	55
A.L. totals (2 years)		8	13	.381	5.44	36	33	1	1	0	180 1/3	226	113	109	61	98
N.L. totals (3 years)		7	5	.583	5.17	37	11	0	0	0	111 1/3	127	66	64	36	55
Major league totals (5 years)		15	18	.455	5.34	73	44	1	1	0	291 2/3	353	179	173	97	153

TESSMER, JAY   P   YANKEES

PERSONAL: Born December 26, 1971, in Meadville, Pa. ... 6-3/190. ... Throws right, bats right. ... Full name: Jay W. Tessmer.
HIGH SCHOOL: Cochranton (Pa.).
COLLEGE: Miami (Fla.).
TRANSACTIONS/CAREER NOTES: Selected by New York Yankees organization in 19th round of free-agent draft (June 1, 1995).
HONORS: Name Florida State League Most Valuable Player (1996).

Year	Team (League)	W	L	Pct.	ERA	G	GS	CG	ShO	Sv.	IP	H	R	ER	BB	SO
1995—	Oneonta (N.Y.-Penn)	2	0	1.000	0.95	34	0	0	0	20	38	27	8	4	12	52
1996—	Tampa (Florida State)	12	4	.750	1.48	*68	0	0	0	*35	97 1/3	68	18	16	19	104
1997—	Norwich (Eastern)	3	6	.333	5.31	55	0	0	0	17	62 2/3	78	41	37	24	51

TETTLETON, MICKEY   DH

PERSONAL: Born September 16, 1960, in Oklahoma City. ... 6-2/212. ... Bats both, throws right. ... Full name: Mickey Lee Tettleton.
HIGH SCHOOL: Southeast (Oklahoma City).
COLLEGE: Oklahoma State.
TRANSACTIONS/CAREER NOTES: Selected by Oakland Athletics organization in fifth round of free-agent draft (June 8, 1981). ... On disabled list (August 4-25, 1985); included rehabilitation assignment to Modesto (August 21-25). ... On Oakland disabled list (May 9-June 16, 1986); included rehabilitation assignment to Modesto (May 23-June 13). ... On Oakland disabled list (July 22-August 6, 1987); included rehabilitation assignment to Modesto (August 2-6). ... Released by A's (March 28, 1988). ... Signed by Rochester, Baltimore Orioles organization (April 5, 1988). ... On disabled list (August 5-September 2, 1989). ... Granted free agency

(November 5, 1990). ... Re-signed by Orioles (December 19, 1990). ... Traded by Orioles to Detroit Tigers for P Jeff M. Robinson (January 11, 1991). ... Granted free agency (October 18, 1994). ... Signed by Texas Rangers (April 13, 1995). ... Granted free agency (November 3, 1995). ... Re-signed by Rangers (December 9, 1995). ... On disabled list (April 19-June 23, 1997); included rehabilitation assignments to Oklahoma City (June 13-17) and Tulsa (June 18-23). ... Announced retirement (July 6, 1997).

RECORDS: Holds major league single-season record for most strikeouts by switch-hitter—160 (1990).

HONORS: Named catcher on THE SPORTING NEWS A.L. All-Star team (1989 and 1991-92). ... Named catcher on THE SPORTING NEWS A.L. Silver Slugger team (1989 and 1991-92).

STATISTICAL NOTES: Tied for Eastern League lead with eight intentional bases on balls received in 1984. ... Led Eastern League catchers with .993 fielding percentage in 1984. ... Switch-hit home runs in one game three times (June 13, 1988; May 7, 1993, 12 innings; and April 28, 1995). ... Led A.L. catchers with .996 fielding percentage in 1992. ... Career major league grand slams: 6.

Year Team (League)	Pos.	G	AB	R	H	2B	3B	HR	RBI	Avg.	BB	SO	SB	PO	A	E	Avg.
1981— Modesto (California) ..	C-OF-1B	48	138	28	34	3	0	5	19	.246	46	33	2	235	31	14	.950
1982— Modesto (California) ..	C-OF	88	253	44	63	18	0	8	37	.249	63	46	4	424	36	8	.983
1983— Modesto (California) ..	C-OF	124	378	55	92	18	2	7	62	.243	82	71	1	582	46	11	.983
1984— Alb./Colon. (Eastern) ..	C-O-1-3-S	86	281	32	65	18	0	5	47	.231	52	52	2	368	42	3	†.993
— Oakland (A.L.)	C	33	76	10	20	2	1	1	5	.263	11	21	0	112	10	1	.992
1985— Oakland (A.L.)	C-DH	78	211	23	53	12	0	3	15	.251	28	59	2	344	24	4	.989
— Modesto (California) ..	C	4	14	1	3	3	0	0	2	.214	0	4	0	20	1	0	1.000
1986— Oakland (A.L.)	C	90	211	26	43	9	0	10	35	.204	39	51	7	463	32	8	.984
— Modesto (California) ..	C	15	42	14	10	1	0	2	8	.238	19	9	2	40	3	2	.956
1987— Oakland (A.L.)	C-1B-DH	82	211	19	41	3	0	8	26	.194	30	65	1	435	29	6	.987
— Modesto (California) ..	C	3	11	4	4	1	0	2	2	.364	1	4	0	5	0	1	1.000
1988— Rochester (Int'l)■.....	C-OF	19	41	9	10	3	1	1	4	.244	9	15	0	71	7	3	.963
— Baltimore (A.L.)........	C	86	283	31	74	11	1	11	37	.261	28	70	0	361	31	3	.992
1989— Baltimore (A.L.)	C-DH	117	411	72	106	21	2	26	65	.258	73	117	3	297	42	2	.994
1990— Baltimore (A.L.)	C-DH-1-O	135	444	68	99	21	2	15	51	.223	106	160	2	458	39	5	.990
1991— Detroit (A.L.)■..........	C-DH-O-1	154	501	85	132	17	2	31	89	.263	101	131	3	562	55	6	.990
1992— Detroit (A.L.)	C-DH-1-O	157	525	82	125	25	0	32	83	.238	•122	137	0	481	47	2	†.996
1993— Detroit (A.L.)	1-C-O-DH	152	522	79	128	25	4	32	110	.245	109	139	3	724	47	6	.992
1994— Detroit (A.L.)	C-1-DH-O	107	339	57	84	18	2	17	51	.248	97	98	0	368	31	5	.988
1995— Texas (A.L.)■..........	O-DH-1-C	134	429	76	102	19	1	32	78	.238	107	110	0	185	10	3	.985
1996— Texas (A.L.)	DH-1B	143	491	78	121	26	1	24	83	.246	95	137	2	161	11	4	.977
1997— Texas (A.L.)	DH	17	44	5	4	1	0	3	4	.091	3	12	0	0	0	0	...
— Oklahoma City (A.A.)..	DH	4	9	4	4	1	0	0	0	.444	6	1	0	0	0	0	...
— Tulsa (Texas)	DH	3	11	4	2	0	0	1	2	.182	4	2	0	0	0	0	...
Major league totals (14 years)		1485	4698	711	1132	210	16	245	732	.241	949	1307	23	4951	408	55	.990

DIVISION SERIES RECORD

Year Team (League)	Pos.	G	AB	R	H	2B	3B	HR	RBI	Avg.	BB	SO	SB	PO	A	E	Avg.
1996— Texas (A.L.)	DH	4	12	1	1	0	0	0	1	.083	5	7	0	...	...	...	...

ALL-STAR GAME RECORD

Year League	Pos.	AB	R	H	2B	3B	HR	RBI	Avg.	BB	SO	SB	PO	A	E	Avg.
1989— American	C	1	0	0	0	0	0	0	.000	0	0	0	2	0	0	1.000
1994— American	PH	0	0	0	0	0	0	0	...	1	0	0	...	...	...	...
All-Star Game totals (2 years)		1	0	0	0	0	0	0	.000	1	0	0	2	0	0	1.000

TEWKSBURY, BOB   P   TWINS

PERSONAL: Born November 30, 1960, in Concord, N.H. ... 6-4/205. ... Throws right, bats right. ... Full name: Robert Alan Tewksbury.

HIGH SCHOOL: Merrimack (Penacook, N.H.).

COLLEGE: Rutgers, then St. Leo College (Fla.).

TRANSACTIONS/CAREER NOTES: Selected by New York Yankees organization in 19th round of free-agent draft (June 8, 1981). ... On Fort Lauderdale disabled list (April 8-June 7, 1983). ... On disabled list (April 9-27, 1984). ... On Albany/Colonie disabled list (June 10-25, 1985). ... Traded by Yankees with P Rich Scheid and P Dean Wilkins to Chicago Cubs for P Steve Trout (July 13, 1987). ... On Chicago disabled list (August 13, 1987-remainder of season and May 22-June 12, 1988). ... Granted free agency (October 15, 1988). ... Signed by St. Louis Cardinals (December 16, 1988). ... Granted free agency (October 17, 1994). ... Signed by Texas Rangers (April 10, 1995). ... On Texas disabled list (July 23-August 26, 1995); included rehabilitation assignment to Charlotte (August 22-26). ... Granted free agency (November 3, 1995). ... Signed by San Diego Padres (December 18, 1995). ... Granted free agency (October 31, 1996). ... Signed by Minnesota Twins (December 12, 1996). ... On disabled list (May 5-25 and July 18-August 18, 1997).

STATISTICAL NOTES: Pitched 5-0 one-hit, complete-game victory for St. Louis against Houston (August 17, 1990).

MISCELLANEOUS: Struck out in only appearance as pinch-hitter with Texas (1995).

Year Team (League)	W	L	Pct.	ERA	G	GS	CG	ShO	Sv.	IP	H	R	ER	BB	SO
1981— Oneonta (N.Y.-Penn)	7	3	.700	3.60	14	14	6	1	0	85	85	43	34	37	62
1982— Fort Lauderdale (FSL)	*15	4	.789	*1.88	24	23	•13	*5	1	182 1/3	146	46	38	47	92
1983— Fort Lauderdale (FSL)	2	0	1.000	0.00	2	2	1	0	0	16	6	1	0	1	5
— Nashville (Southern)	5	1	.833	2.82	7	7	3	0	0	51	49	20	16	10	15
1984— Nashville (Southern)	11	9	.550	2.83	26	26	6	0	0	172	185	69	54	42	78
1985— Alb./Colon. (Eastern)	6	5	.545	3.54	17	17	4	2	0	106 2/3	101	48	42	19	63
— Columbus (Int'l)	3	0	1.000	1.02	6	6	1	1	0	44	27	5	5	5	21
1986— New York (A.L.)	9	5	.643	3.31	23	20	2	0	0	130 1/3	144	58	48	31	49
— Columbus (Int'l)	1	0	1.000	2.70	2	2	0	0	0	10	6	3	3	2	4
1987— New York (A.L.)	1	4	.200	6.75	8	6	0	0	0	33 1/3	47	26	25	7	12
— Columbus (Int'l)	6	1	.857	2.53	11	11	3	0	0	74 2/3	68	23	21	11	32
— Chicago (N.L.)■.........	0	4	.000	6.50	7	3	0	0	0	18	32	15	13	13	10
1988— Iowa (Am. Assoc.).........	4	2	.667	3.76	10	10	2	2	0	67	73	28	28	10	43
— Chicago (N.L.)	0	0	...	8.10	1	1	0	0	0	3 1/3	6	5	3	2	1
1989— Louisville (A.A.)■.........	•13	5	.722	2.43	28	28	2	1	0	*189	170	63	51	34	72
— St. Louis (N.L.)	1	0	1.000	3.30	7	4	1	1	0	30	25	12	11	10	17

Year	Team (League)	W	L	Pct.	ERA	G	GS	CG	ShO	Sv.	IP	H	R	ER	BB	SO
1990—	St. Louis (N.L.)	10	9	.526	3.47	28	20	3	2	1	145 1/3	151	67	56	15	50
	—Louisville (A.A.)	3	2	.600	2.43	6	6	0	0	0	40 2/3	41	15	11	3	22
1991—	St. Louis (N.L.)	11	12	.478	3.25	30	30	3	0	0	191	206	86	69	38	75
1992—	St. Louis (N.L.)	16	5	*.762	2.16	33	32	5	0	0	233	217	63	56	20	91
1993—	St. Louis (N.L.)	17	10	.630	3.83	32	32	2	0	0	213 2/3	*258	99	91	20	97
1994—	St. Louis (N.L.)	12	10	.545	5.32	24	24	4	1	0	155 2/3	*190	97	92	22	79
1995—	Texas (A.L.)■	8	7	.533	4.58	21	21	4	1	0	129 2/3	169	75	66	20	53
	—Charlotte (Fla. St.)	1	0	1.000	0.00	1	1	0	0	0	6	3	0	0	0	4
1996—	San Diego (N.L.)■	10	10	.500	4.32	36	33	1	0	0	206 1/3	224	116	99	43	126
1997—	Minnesota (A.L.)■	8	13	.381	4.22	26	26	5	2	0	168 2/3	200	83	79	31	92
A.L. totals (4 years)		26	29	.473	4.25	78	73	11	3	0	462	560	242	218	89	206
N.L. totals (9 years)		77	60	.562	3.69	198	179	19	4	1	1196 1/3	1309	560	490	183	546
Major league totals (12 years)		103	89	.536	3.84	276	252	30	7	1	1658 1/3	1869	802	708	272	752

DIVISION SERIES RECORD

Year	Team (League)	W	L	Pct.	ERA	G	GS	CG	ShO	Sv.	IP	H	R	ER	BB	SO
1996—	San Diego (N.L.)						Did not play									

ALL-STAR GAME RECORD

Year	League	W	L	Pct.	ERA	GS	CG	ShO	Sv.	IP	H	R	ER	BB	SO
1992—	National	0	0	...	21.60	0	0	0	0	1 2/3	4	4	4	1	0

THOBE, TOM   P   BRAVES

PERSONAL: Born September 3, 1969, in Covington, Ky. ... 6-6/195. ... Throws left, bats left. ... Full name: Thomas Neal Thobe. ... Brother of J.J. Thobe, pitcher with Montreal Expos (1995).
HIGH SCHOOL: Edison (Huntington Beach, Calif.).
JUNIOR COLLEGE: Golden West (Huntington Beach, Calif.).
TRANSACTIONS/CAREER NOTES: Selected by Chicago Cubs organization in 38th round of free-agent draft (June 2, 1987). ... Released by Cubs organization (1988). ... Signed by Atlanta Braves organization (June 6, 1988). ... On disabled list (April 7-May 6 and June 19-July 12, 1997).

Year	Team (League)	W	L	Pct.	ERA	G	GS	CG	ShO	Sv.	IP	H	R	ER	BB	SO
1988—	Wytheville (Appal.)	3	3	.500	8.95	18	5	0	0	0	57 1/3	90	66	57	30	31
1989—							Out of organized baseball.									
1990—							Out of organized baseball.									
1991—							Out of organized baseball.									
1992—							Out of organized baseball.									
1993—	Macon (S. Atl.)■	7	5	.583	2.69	43	0	0	0	5	70 1/3	70	25	21	16	55
1994—	Greenville (Southern)	7	6	.538	2.54	51	0	0	0	9	63 2/3	65	21	18	26	52
1995—	Richmond (Int'l)	7	0	1.000	1.84	48	2	1	1	5	88	65	27	18	26	57
	—Atlanta (N.L.)	0	0	...	10.80	3	0	0	0	0	3 1/3	7	4	4	0	2
1996—	Richmond (Int'l)	1	8	.111	6.13	31	6	1	0	3	72	89	60	49	37	40
	—Atlanta (N.L.)	0	1	.000	1.50	4	0	0	0	0	6	5	2	1	0	1
1997—	Richmond (Int'l)	5	2	.714	4.14	19	10	0	0	0	71 2/3	70	37	33	22	36
Major league totals (2 years)		0	1	.000	4.82	7	0	0	0	0	9 1/3	12	6	5	0	3

THOMAS, FRANK   1B   WHITE SOX

PERSONAL: Born May 27, 1968, in Columbus, Ga. ... 6-5/257. ... Bats right, throws right. ... Full name: Frank Edward Thomas.
HIGH SCHOOL: Columbus (Ga.).
COLLEGE: Auburn.
TRANSACTIONS/CAREER NOTES: Selected by Chicago White Sox organization in first round (seventh pick overall) of free-agent draft (June 5, 1989). ... On disabled list (July 11-30, 1996). ... On disabled list (June 15-22, 1997).
RECORDS: Shares A.L. single-season record for most intentional bases on balls received by righthanded batter—29 (1995).
HONORS: Named first baseman on The Sporting News college All-America team (1989). ... Named designated hitter on The Sporting News A.L. All-Star team (1991). ... Named designated hitter on The Sporting News A.L. Silver Slugger team (1991). ... Named Major League Player of the Year by The Sporting News (1993). ... Named first baseman on The Sporting News A.L. All-Star team (1993-94). ... Named first baseman on The Sporting News A.L. Silver Slugger team (1993-94). ... Named A.L. Most Valuable Player by Baseball Writers' Association of America (1993-94).
STATISTICAL NOTES: Led Southern League with .581 slugging percentage and .487 on-base percentage in 1990. ... Led A.L. with .453 on-base percentage in 1991, .439 in 1992, .487 in 1994 and .456 in 1997. ... Led A.L. first basemen with 1,533 total chances in 1992. ... Led A.L. with .729 slugging percentage in 1994. ... Led A.L. with 12 sacrifice flies in 1995. ... Led A.L. with 29 intentional bases on balls received in 1995 and 26 in 1996. ... Hit three home runs in one game (September 15, 1996). ... Career major league grand slams: 4.
MISCELLANEOUS: Holds Chicago White Sox all-time record for most home runs (257).

| | | | | | | BATTING | | | | | | | | FIELDING | | | |
Year	Team (League)	Pos.	G	AB	R	H	2B	3B	HR	RBI	Avg.	BB	SO	SB	PO	A	E	Avg.
1989—	GC Whi. Sox (GCL)	1B	17	52	8	19	5	0	1	11	.365	10	24	4	130	8	2	.986
	—Sarasota (Fla. St.)	1B	55	188	27	52	9	1	4	30	.277	31	33	0	420	31	7	.985
1990—	Birmingham (Sou.)	1B	109	353	85	114	27	5	18	71	.323	*112	74	7	954	77	14	.987
	—Chicago (A.L.)	1B-DH	60	191	39	63	11	3	7	31	.330	44	54	0	428	26	5	.989
1991—	Chicago (A.L.)	DH-1B	158	559	104	178	31	2	32	109	.318	*138	112	1	459	27	2	.996
1992—	Chicago (A.L.)	1B-DH	160	573	108	185	•46	2	24	115	.323	*122	88	6	*1428	92	13	.992
1993—	Chicago (A.L.)	1B-DH	153	549	106	174	36	0	41	128	.317	112	54	4	1222	83	15	.989
1994—	Chicago (A.L.)	1B-DH	113	399	*106	141	34	1	38	101	.353	*109	61	2	735	45	7	.991
1995—	Chicago (A.L.)	1B-DH	•145	493	102	152	27	0	40	111	.308	*136	74	3	738	34	7	.991
1996—	Chicago (A.L.)	1B	141	527	110	184	26	0	40	134	.349	109	70	1	1098	85	9	.992
1997—	Chicago (A.L.)	1B-DH	146	530	110	184	35	0	35	125	*.347	109	69	1	739	49	11	.986
Major league totals (8 years)			1076	3821	785	1261	246	8	257	854	.330	879	582	18	6847	441	69	.991

RECORDS: Holds single-series record for most bases on balls received—10 (1993). ... Shares single-game record for most bases on balls received—4 (October 5, 1993).

							BATTING								FIELDING			
Year	Team (League)	Pos.	G	AB	R	H	2B	3B	HR	RBI	Avg.	BB	SO	SB	PO	A	E	Avg.
1993— Chicago (A.L.)		1B-DH	6	17	2	6	0	0	1	3	.353	10	5	0	24	3	0	1.000

ALL-STAR GAME RECORD

					BATTING									FIELDING			
Year	League	Pos.	AB	R	H	2B	3B	HR	RBI	Avg.	BB	SO	SB	PO	A	E	Avg.
1993— American		PH-DH	1	0	1	0	0	0	0	1.000	0	0	0	...	...	...	...
1994— American		1B	2	1	2	0	0	0	1	1.000	1	0	0	6	0	0	1.000
1995— American		1B	2	1	1	0	0	1	2	.500	0	0	0	5	1	0	1.000
1996— American						Selected, did not play—injured.											
1997— American						Selected, did not play—injured.											
All-Star Game totals (3 years)			5	2	4	0	0	1	3	.800	1	0	0	11	1	0	1.000

THOMAS, LARRY   P   RANGERS

PERSONAL: Born October 25, 1969, in Miami. ... 6-1/195. ... Throws left, bats right. ... Full name: Larry Wayne Thomas Jr.
HIGH SCHOOL: Winthrop (Mass.).
COLLEGE: Maine.
TRANSACTIONS/CAREER NOTES: Selected by Chicago White Sox organization in second round of free-agent draft (June 3, 1991). ... On disabled list (July 3-14, 1994) ... On disabled list (August 17-September 6, 1996). ... Traded by White Sox with P Al Levine to Texas Rangers for SS Benji Gil (December 19, 1997).

Year	Team (League)	W	L	Pct.	ERA	G	GS	CG	ShO	Sv.	IP	H	R	ER	BB	SO
1991— Utica (N.Y.-Penn)...............		1	3	.250	1.47	11	10	0	0	0	73 1/3	55	22	12	25	61
— Birmingham (Southern)......		0	0	...	3.00	2	0	0	0	0	6	6	3	2	4	2
1992— Sarasota (Florida State)......		5	0	1.000	1.62	8	8	0	0	0	55 2/3	44	14	10	7	50
— Birmingham (Southern)......		8	6	.571	*1.94	17	17	3	0	0	120 2/3	102	32	26	30	72
1993— Nashville (A.A.)		4	6	.400	5.99	18	18	1	0	0	100 2/3	114	73	67	32	67
— Sarasota (Florida State)......		4	2	.667	2.48	8	8	3	2	0	61 2/3	52	19	17	15	27
— Birmingham (Southern)......		0	1	.000	5.14	1	1	0	0	0	7	9	5	4	1	5
1994— Birmingham (Southern)......		5	10	.333	4.63	24	24	1	0	0	144	159	96	74	53	77
1995— Birmingham (Southern)......		4	1	.800	1.34	35	0	0	0	2	40 1/3	24	9	6	15	47
— Chicago (A.L.)		0	0	...	1.32	17	0	0	0	0	13 2/3	8	2	2	6	12
1996— Chicago (A.L.)		2	3	.400	3.23	57	0	0	0	0	30 2/3	32	11	11	14	20
1997— Nashville (A.A.)		3	2	.600	3.94	44	1	0	0	2	48	47	21	21	18	53
— Chicago (A.L.)		0	0	...	8.10	5	0	0	0	0	3 1/3	3	3	3	2	0
Major league totals (3 years)......		2	3	.400	3.02	79	0	0	0	0	47 2/3	43	16	16	22	32

THOME, JIM   1B   INDIANS

PERSONAL: Born August 27, 1970, in Peoria, Ill. ... 6-4/225. ... Bats left, throws right. ... Full name: James Howard Thome. ... Name pronounced TOE-me.
HIGH SCHOOL: Limestone (Bartonville, Ill.).
JUNIOR COLLEGE: Illinois Central College.
TRANSACTIONS/CAREER NOTES: Selected by Cleveland Indians organization in 13th round of free-agent draft (June 5, 1989). ... On Cleveland disabled list (March 28-May 18, 1992); included rehabilitation assignment to Canton/Akron (May 9-18). ... On Cleveland disabled list (May 20-June 15, 1992); included rehabilitation assignment to Canton/Akron (June 1-15).
HONORS: Named International League Most Valuable Player (1993). ... Named third baseman on THE SPORTING NEWS A.L. All-Star team (1995 and 1996). ... Named third baseman on THE SPORTING NEWS A.L. Silver Slugger team (1996).
STATISTICAL NOTES: Led International League with .441 on-base percentage in 1993. ... Hit three home runs in one game (July 22, 1994). ... Career major league grand slams: 2.

							BATTING								FIELDING			
Year	Team (League)	Pos.	G	AB	R	H	2B	3B	HR	RBI	Avg.	BB	SO	SB	PO	A	E	Avg.
1989— GC Indians (GCL)		SS-3B	55	186	22	44	5	3	0	22	.237	21	33	6	65	144	21	.909
1990— Burlington (Appal.).....		3B	34	118	31	44	7	1	12	34	.373	27	18	6	28	79	11	.907
— Kinston (Carolina)		3B	33	117	19	36	4	1	4	16	.308	24	26	4	10	66	8	.905
1991— Cant./Akr. (Eastern) ...		3B	84	294	47	99	20	2	5	45	.337	44	58	8	41	167	17	.924
— Colo. Springs (PCL) ...		3B	41	151	20	43	7	3	2	28	.285	12	29	0	28	84	6	.949
— Cleveland (A.L.)		3B	27	98	7	25	4	2	1	9	.255	5	16	1	12	60	8	.900
1992— Colo. Springs (PCL) ...		3B	12	48	11	15	4	1	2	14	.313	6	16	0	9	20	8	.784
— Cleveland (A.L.)		3B	40	117	8	24	3	1	2	12	.205	10	34	2	21	61	11	.882
— Cant./Akr. (Eastern) ...		3B	30	107	16	36	9	2	1	14	.336	24	30	0	11	35	4	.920
1993— Charlotte (Int'l)..........		3B	115	410	85	136	21	4	25	*102	*.332	76	94	1	67	226	15	.951
— Cleveland (A.L.)		3B	47	154	28	41	11	0	7	22	.266	29	36	2	29	86	6	.950
1994— Cleveland (A.L.)		3B	98	321	58	86	20	1	20	52	.268	46	84	3	62	173	15	.940
1995— Cleveland (A.L.)		3B-DH	137	452	92	142	29	3	25	73	.314	97	113	4	75	214	16	.948
1996— Cleveland (A.L.)		3B-DH	151	505	122	157	28	5	38	116	.311	123	141	2	86	262	17	.953
1997— Cleveland (A.L.)		1B	147	496	104	142	25	0	40	102	.286	*120	146	1	1233	95	10	.993
Major league totals (7 years)			647	2143	419	617	120	12	133	386	.288	430	570	15	1518	951	83	.967

DIVISION SERIES RECORD

RECORDS: Holds career record for most strikeouts—16.

							BATTING								FIELDING			
Year	Team (League)	Pos.	G	AB	R	H	2B	3B	HR	RBI	Avg.	BB	SO	SB	PO	A	E	Avg.
1995— Cleveland (A.L.)..........		3B	3	13	1	2	0	0	1	3	.154	1	6	0	6	6	0	1.000
1996— Cleveland (A.L.)..........		3B	4	10	1	3	0	0	0	0	.300	1	5	0	1	1	0	1.000
1997— Cleveland (A.L.)..........		1B	4	15	1	3	0	0	0	1	.200	0	5	0	44	3	0	1.000
Division series totals (3 years)			11	38	3	8	0	0	1	4	.211	2	16	0	51	10	0	1.000

CHAMPIONSHIP SERIES RECORD

							BATTING								FIELDING		
Year	Team (League)	Pos.	G	AB	R	H	2B	3B	HR	RBI	Avg.	BB	SO	SB	PO	A	E	Avg.
1995— Cleveland (A.L.).........	3B	5	15	2	4	0	0	2	5	.267	2	3	0	1	5	1	.857
1997— Cleveland (A.L.).........	1B-PH	6	14	3	1	0	0	0	0	.071	5	4	0	35	2	0	1.000
Championship series totals (2 years)		11	29	5	5	0	0	2	5	.172	7	7	0	36	7	1	.977

WORLD SERIES RECORD

							BATTING								FIELDING		
Year	Team (League)	Pos.	G	AB	R	H	2B	3B	HR	RBI	Avg.	BB	SO	SB	PO	A	E	Avg.
1995— Cleveland (A.L.).........	3B-PH	6	19	1	4	1	0	1	2	.211	2	5	0	3	5	1	.889
1997— Cleveland (A.L.).........	1B	7	28	8	8	0	1	2	4	.286	5	7	0	57	5	1	.984
World Series totals (2 years)		13	47	9	12	1	1	3	6	.255	7	12	0	60	10	2	.972

ALL-STAR GAME RECORD

					BATTING								FIELDING		
Year	League	Pos.	AB	R	H	2B	3B	HR	RBI	Avg.	BB	SO	SB	PO	A	E	Avg.
1997— American....................	PH-DH	1	0	0	0	0	0	0	.000	0	0	0				...

THOMPSON, JUSTIN   P   TIGERS

PERSONAL: Born March 8, 1973, in San Antonio, Texas. ... 6-3/175. ... Throws left, bats left. ... Full name: Justin Willard Thompson.
HIGH SCHOOL: Klein Oak (Spring, Texas).
TRANSACTIONS/CAREER NOTES: Selected by Detroit Tigers organization in supplemental round ("sandwich pick" between first and second round, 32nd pick overall) of free-agent draft (June 3, 1991); pick received as part of compensation for Minnesota Twins signing Type A free agent P Jack Morris. ... On Trenton disabled list (April 8, 1994-entire season). ... On Detroit disabled list (June 3-August 17, 1996); included rehabilitation assignments to Fayetteville (July 19-23), Visalia (July 23-26) and Toledo (July 26-August 11). ... On disabled list (July 6-21, 1997).

Year	Team (League)	W	L	Pct.	ERA	G	GS	CG	ShO	Sv.	IP	H	R	ER	BB	SO
1991— Bristol (Appalachian).........	2	5	.286	3.60	10	10	0	0	0	50	45	29	20	24	60
1992— Fayetteville (S. Atl.)	4	4	.500	2.18	20	19	0	0	0	95	79	32	23	40	88
1993— Lakeland (Fla. St.)	4	4	.500	3.56	11	11	0	0	0	55 2/3	65	25	22	16	46
—London (Eastern)	3	6	.333	4.09	14	14	1	0	0	83 2/3	96	51	38	37	72
1994—							Did not play.									
1995— Lakeland (Fla. St.)	2	1	.667	4.88	6	6	0	0	0	24	30	13	13	8	20
—Jacksonville (Southern)......	6	7	.462	3.73	18	18	3	0	0	123	110	55	51	38	98
1996— Toledo (Int'l).......................	6	3	.667	3.42	13	13	3	1	0	84 1/3	74	36	32	26	69
—Detroit (A.L.)	1	6	.143	4.58	11	11	0	0	0	59	62	35	30	31	44
—Fayetteville (S. Atl.)	0	0	...	3.00	1	1	0	0	0	3	1	1	1	0	5
—Visalia (California)	0	0	...	0.00	1	1	0	0	0	3	2	0	0	2	7
1997— Detroit (A.L.)......................	15	11	.577	3.02	32	32	4	0	0	223 1/3	188	82	75	66	151
Major league totals (2 years)......	16	17	.485	3.35	43	43	4	0	0	282 1/3	250	117	105	97	195

ALL-STAR GAME RECORD

Year	League	W	L	Pct.	ERA	GS	CG	ShO	Sv.	IP	H	R	ER	BB	SO
1997— American	0	0	...	0.00	0	0	0	0	1	0	0	0	0	1

THOMPSON, MARK   P   ROCKIES

PERSONAL: Born April 7, 1971, in Russellville, Ky. ... 6-2/205. ... Throws right, bats right. ... Full name: Mark Radford Thompson.
HIGH SCHOOL: Logan County (Russellville, Ky.).
COLLEGE: Kentucky.
TRANSACTIONS/CAREER NOTES: Selected by Colorado Rockies organization in second round of free-agent draft (June 1, 1992). ... On Colorado Springs disabled list (June 30-September 7, 1993; August 9-18 and August 27-September 5, 1994). ... On Colorado disabled list (May 8, 1997-remainder of season); included rehabilitation assignments to Asheville (June 29-July 15) and Colorado Springs (July 15-July 20).
RECORDS: Shares N.L. record for most consecutive home runs allowed in one inning—3 (June 30, 1996, third inning).

Year	Team (League)	W	L	Pct.	ERA	G	GS	CG	ShO	Sv.	IP	H	R	ER	BB	SO
1992— Bend (Northwest)...............	8	4	.667	1.95	16	•16	*4	0	0	*106 1/3	81	32	23	31	*102
1993— Central Valley (Cal.)............	3	2	.600	2.20	11	11	0	0	0	69 2/3	46	19	17	18	72
—Colo. Springs (PCL)	3	0	1.000	2.70	4	4	2	0	0	33 1/3	31	13	10	11	22
1994— Colo. Springs (PCL)	8	9	.471	4.49	23	23	•4	1	0	140 1/3	169	83	70	57	82
—Colorado (N.L.)	1	1	.500	9.00	2	2	0	0	0	9	16	9	9	8	5
1995— Colorado (N.L.)	2	3	.400	6.53	21	5	0	0	0	51	73	42	37	22	30
—Colo. Springs (PCL)	5	3	.625	6.10	11	10	0	0	0	62	73	43	42	25	38
1996— Colorado (N.L.)	9	11	.450	5.30	34	28	3	1	0	169 2/3	189	109	100	74	99
1997— Colorado (N.L.)	3	3	.500	7.89	6	6	0	0	0	29 2/3	40	27	26	13	9
—Asheville (S. Atl.)............	0	2	.000	2.70	4	4	0	0	0	13 1/3	11	5	4	5	9
—Colo. Springs (PCL)	0	0	...	12.00	1	1	0	0	0	3	6	4	4	1	1
Major league totals (4 years)......	15	18	.455	5.97	63	41	3	1	0	259 1/3	318	187	172	117	143

DIVISION SERIES RECORD

Year	Team (League)	W	L	Pct.	ERA	G	GS	CG	ShO	Sv.	IP	H	R	ER	BB	SO
1995— Colorado (N.L.)	0	0	...	0.00	1	0	0	0	1	1	0	0	0	0	0

THOMSON, JOHN   P   ROCKIES

PERSONAL: Born October 1, 1973, in Vicksburg, Miss. ... 6-3/175. ... Throws right, bats right.
HIGH SCHOOL: Sulphur (La.).
JUNIOR COLLEGE: Blinn College (Texas).
COLLEGE: McNeese State.
TRANSACTIONS/CAREER NOTES: Selected by Colorado Rockies organization in seventh round of free-agent draft (June 3, 1993).
STATISTICAL NOTES: Tied for Arizona League lead with 14 wild pitches in 1993.

Year—Team (League)	W	L	Pct.	ERA	G	GS	CG	ShO	Sv.	IP	H	R	ER	BB	SO
1993—Ariz. Rockies (Ariz.)	3	5	.375	4.62	11	11	0	0	0	50 2/3	43	40	26	31	36
1994—Asheville (S. Atl.)	6	6	.500	2.85	19	15	1	1	0	88 1/3	70	34	28	33	79
—Central Valley (Cal.)	3	1	.750	3.28	9	8	0	0	0	49 1/3	43	20	18	18	41
1995—New Haven (Eastern)	7	8	.467	4.18	26	24	0	0	0	131 1/3	132	69	61	56	82
1996—New Haven (Eastern)	9	4	.692	2.86	16	16	1	0	0	97 2/3	82	35	31	27	86
—Colo. Springs (PCL)	4	7	.364	5.04	11	11	0	0	0	69 2/3	76	45	39	26	62
1997—Colo. Springs (PCL)	4	2	.667	3.43	7	7	0	0	0	42	36	18	16	14	49
—Colorado (N.L.)	7	9	.438	4.71	27	27	2	1	0	166 1/3	193	94	87	51	106
Major league totals (1 year)	7	9	.438	4.71	27	27	2	1	0	166 1/3	193	94	87	51	106

THURMAN, GARY — OF — ANGELS

PERSONAL: Born November 12, 1964, in Indianapolis. ... 5-10/180. ... Bats right, throws right. ... Full name: Gary Montez Thurman Jr.
HIGH SCHOOL: Indianapolis North Central.
TRANSACTIONS/CAREER NOTES: Selected by Kansas City Royals organization in first round (21st pick overall) of free-agent draft (June 6, 1983). ... On Kansas City disabled list (March 26-April 13, 1989). ... On Kansas City disabled list (May 10-July 26, 1989); included rehabilitation assignment to Omaha (June 15-July 26). ... On disabled list (August 6-September 9, 1991). ... Claimed on waivers by Detroit Tigers (March 26, 1993). ... Granted free agency (December 20, 1993). ... Signed by Chicago White Sox organization (February 10, 1994). ... Granted free agency (October 15, 1994). ... Signed by Tacoma, Seattle Mariners organization (December 12, 1994). ... Granted free agency (October 16, 1995). ... Signed by New York Mets organization (December 20, 1995). ... Granted free agency (October 15, 1996). ... Re-signed by Mets organization (November 25, 1996). ... Released by Mets (June 2, 1997). ... Signed by Montreal Expos organization (June 23, 1997). ... On Ottawa suspended list (June 23-28, 1997). ... Granted free agency (October 15, 1997). ... Signed by Anaheim Angels organization (January 22, 1998).
STATISTICAL NOTES: Led Gulf Coast League outfielders with 143 total chances in 1983. ... Tied for South Atlantic League lead in caught stealing with 17 in 1984. ... Led South Atlantic League outfielders with 329 total chances in 1984. ... Led Florida State League outfielders with 396 total chances in 1985. ... Tied for American Association lead in double plays by outfielder with six in 1987.

Year—Team (League)	Pos.	G	AB	R	H	2B	3B	HR	RBI	Avg.	BB	SO	SB	PO	A	E	Avg.
1983—GC Royals (GCL)	OF	59	203	32	52	8	2	0	19	.256	34	*58	31	*127	*13	3	.979
1984—Char., S.C. (S. Atl.)	OF	129	478	71	109	6	8	6	51	.228	81	127	44	*311	5	13	.960
1985—Fort Myers (FSL)	OF	134	453	68	137	9	9	0	45	.302	68	93	*70	*368	18	10	.975
1986—Memphis (Southern)	OF	131	525	88	164	24	12	7	62	.312	56	81	53	277	5	11	.962
—Omaha (A.A.)	OF	3	2	1	1	0	0	0	0	.500	2	0	2	2	0	0	1.000
1987—Omaha (A.A.)	OF	115	450	88	132	14	9	8	39	.293	48	84	*58	283	11	•8	.974
—Kansas City (A.L.)	OF	27	81	12	24	2	0	0	5	.296	8	20	7	61	5	2	.971
1988—Omaha (A.A.)	OF	106	422	77	106	12	6	3	40	.251	38	80	35	195	16	6	.972
—Kansas City (A.L.)	OF-DH	35	66	6	11	1	0	0	2	.167	4	20	5	36	1	2	.949
1989—Kansas City (A.L.)	OF-DH	72	87	24	17	2	1	0	5	.195	15	26	16	54	2	3	.949
—Omaha (A.A.)	OF	17	64	5	14	3	2	0	3	.219	7	18	5	34	1	2	.946
1990—Kansas City (A.L.)	OF	23	60	5	14	3	0	0	3	.233	2	12	1	32	0	0	1.000
—Omaha (A.A.)	OF	98	381	65	126	14	8	0	26	.331	31	68	39	163	6	6	.966
1991—Kansas City (A.L.)	OF	80	184	24	51	9	0	2	13	.277	11	42	15	129	2	4	.970
1992—Kansas City (A.L.)	OF-DH	88	200	25	49	6	3	0	20	.245	9	34	9	138	5	2	.986
1993—Detroit (A.L.)■	OF-DH	75	89	22	19	2	2	0	13	.213	11	30	7	54	3	3	.950
1994—Nashville (A.A.)■	OF	130	470	76	124	17	•12	5	60	.264	35	85	20	264	11	4	.986
1995—Tacoma (PCL)■	OF	93	363	65	109	10	12	5	46	.300	20	62	22	180	13	7	.965
—Seattle (A.L.)■	OF	13	25	3	8	2	0	0	3	.320	1	3	5	15	0	0	1.000
1996—Norfolk (Int'l)	OF	127	449	81	120	24	6	9	39	.267	40	108	25	262	7	5	.982
1997—Norfolk (Int'l)	OF	23	80	7	20	4	0	0	12	.250	11	16	4	51	2	1	.981
—New York (N.L.)	OF	11	6	0	1	0	0	0	0	.167	0	0	0	4	0	0	1.000
—Ottawa (Int'l)■	OF	43	104	16	22	4	1	0	5	.212	18	28	8	57	1	1	.983
American League totals (8 years)		413	792	121	193	27	6	2	64	.244	61	187	65	519	18	16	.971
National League totals (1 year)		11	6	0	1	0	0	0	0	.167	0	0	0	4	0	0	1.000
Major league totals (9 years)		424	798	121	194	27	6	2	64	.243	61	187	65	523	18	16	.971

THURMAN, MIKE — P — EXPOS

PERSONAL: Born July 22, 1973, in Corvallis, Ore. ... 6-4/210. ... Throws right, bats right. ... Full name: Michael R. Thurman.
HIGH SCHOOL: Philomath (Ore.).
COLLEGE: Oregon State.
TRANSACTIONS/CAREER NOTES: Selected by Montreal Expos organization in supplemental round ("sandwich pick" between first and second round, 31st pick overall) of free-agent draft (June 2, 1994); pick received as compensation for Cleveland Indians signing type A free-agent P Dennis Martinez. ... On Harrisburg disabled list (June 17-July 5, 1997).

Year—Team (League)	W	L	Pct.	ERA	G	GS	CG	ShO	Sv.	IP	H	R	ER	BB	SO
1994—Vermont (NYP)	0	1	.000	5.40	3	2	0	0	0	6 2/3	6	4	4	2	3
1995—Albany (S. Atl.)	3	8	.273	5.47	22	22	2	0	0	110 1/3	133	79	67	32	77
1996—W.P. Beach (FSL)	6	8	.429	3.33	19	19	0	0	0	113 2/3	122	53	42	23	68
—Harrisburg (Eastern)	3	1	.750	5.11	4	4	1	0	0	24 2/3	25	14	14	5	14
1997—Harrisburg (Eastern)	9	6	.600	3.81	20	20	1	0	0	115 2/3	102	54	49	30	85
—Ottawa (Int'l)	1	3	.250	5.49	4	4	0	0	0	19 2/3	17	13	12	9	15
—Montreal (N.L.)	1	0	1.000	5.40	5	2	0	0	0	11 2/3	8	9	7	4	8
Major league totals (1 year)	1	0	1.000	5.40	5	2	0	0	0	11 2/3	8	9	7	4	8

TIMLIN, MIKE — P — MARINERS

PERSONAL: Born March 10, 1966, in Midland, Texas. ... 6-4/210. ... Throws right, bats right. ... Full name: Michael August Timlin.
HIGH SCHOOL: Midland (Texas).
COLLEGE: Southwestern University (Texas).

TRANSACTIONS/CAREER NOTES: Selected by Toronto Blue Jays organization in fifth round of free-agent draft (June 2, 1987). ... On disabled list (April 4-May 2, 1989 and August 2-17, 1991). ... On Toronto disabled list (March 27-June 12, 1992); included rehabilitation assignments to Dunedin (April 11-15 and May 24-June 5) and Syracuse (June 5-12). ... On disabled list (May 25-June 9, 1994). ... On Toronto disabled list (June 22-August 18, 1995); included rehabilitation assignment to Syracuse (July 31-August 18). ... Traded by Blue Jays with P Paul Spoljaric to Seattle Mariners for OF Jose Cruz Jr. (July 31, 1997).

STATISTICAL NOTES: Led South Atlantic League with 19 hit batsmen in 1988.

Year—Team (League)	W	L	Pct.	ERA	G	GS	CG	ShO	Sv.	IP	H	R	ER	BB	SO
1987— Medicine Hat (Pio.)	4	8	.333	5.14	13	12	2	0	0	75 1/3	79	50	43	26	66
1988— Myrtle Beach (SAL)	10	6	.625	2.86	35	22	0	0	0	151	119	68	48	77	106
1989— Dunedin (Fla. St.)	5	8	.385	3.25	33	7	1	0	7	88 2/3	90	44	32	36	64
1990— Dunedin (Fla. St.)	7	2	.778	1.43	42	0	0	0	22	50 1/3	36	11	8	16	46
— Knoxville (Southern)	1	2	.333	1.73	17	0	0	0	8	26	20	6	5	7	21
1991— Toronto (A.L.)	11	6	.647	3.16	63	3	0	0	3	108 1/3	94	43	38	50	85
1992— Dunedin (Fla. St.)	0	0	...	0.90	6	1	0	0	1	10	9	2	1	2	7
— Syracuse (Int'l)	0	1	.000	8.74	7	1	0	0	3	11 1/3	15	11	11	5	7
— Toronto (A.L.)	0	2	.000	4.12	26	0	0	0	1	43 2/3	45	23	20	20	35
1993— Toronto (A.L.)	4	2	.667	4.69	54	0	0	0	1	55 2/3	63	32	29	27	49
— Dunedin (Fla. St.)	0	0	...	1.00	4	0	0	0	1	9	4	1	1	0	8
1994— Toronto (A.L.)	0	1	.000	5.18	34	0	0	0	2	40	41	25	23	20	38
1995— Toronto (A.L.)	4	3	.571	2.14	31	0	0	0	0	42	38	13	10	17	36
— Syracuse (Int'l)	1	1	.500	1.04	8	0	0	0	0	17 1/3	13	6	2	4	13
1996— Toronto (A.L.)	1	6	.143	3.65	59	0	0	0	31	56 2/3	47	25	23	18	52
1997— Toronto (A.L.)	3	2	.600	2.87	38	0	0	0	9	47	41	17	15	15	36
— Seattle (A.L.)■	3	2	.600	3.86	26	0	0	0	1	25 2/3	28	13	11	5	9
Major league totals (7 years)	26	24	.520	3.63	331	3	0	0	53	419	397	191	169	172	340

DIVISION SERIES RECORD

Year—Team (League)	W	L	Pct.	ERA	G	GS	CG	ShO	Sv.	IP	H	R	ER	BB	SO
1997— Seattle (A.L.)	0	0	...	54.00	1	0	0	0	0	2/3	3	4	4	1	1

CHAMPIONSHIP SERIES RECORD

Year—Team (League)	W	L	Pct.	ERA	G	GS	CG	ShO	Sv.	IP	H	R	ER	BB	SO
1991— Toronto (A.L.)	0	1	.000	3.18	4	0	0	0	0	5 2/3	5	4	2	2	5
1992— Toronto (A.L.)	0	0	...	6.75	2	0	0	0	0	1 1/3	4	1	1	0	1
1993— Toronto (A.L.)	0	0	...	3.86	1	0	0	0	0	2 1/3	3	1	1	0	2
Champ. series totals (3 years)	0	1	.000	3.86	7	0	0	0	0	9 1/3	12	6	4	2	8

WORLD SERIES RECORD

NOTES: Member of World Series championship teams (1992 and 1993).

Year—Team (League)	W	L	Pct.	ERA	G	GS	CG	ShO	Sv.	IP	H	R	ER	BB	SO
1992— Toronto (A.L.)	0	0	...	0.00	2	0	0	0	1	1 1/3	0	0	0	0	0
1993— Toronto (A.L.)	0	0	...	0.00	2	0	0	0	0	2 1/3	2	0	0	0	4
World Series totals (2 years)	0	0	...	0.00	4	0	0	0	1	3 2/3	2	0	0	0	4

TIMMONS, OZZIE — OF — REDS

PERSONAL: Born September 18, 1970, in Tampa. ... 6-2/225. ... Bats right, throws right. ... Full name: Osborne Llewellyn Timmons.
HIGH SCHOOL: Brandon (Fla.).
COLLEGE: University of Tampa (Fla.).
TRANSACTIONS/CAREER NOTES: Selected by Chicago White Sox organization in 44th round of free-agent draft (June 1, 1988); did not sign. ... Selected by Chicago Cubs organization in fifth round of free-agent draft (June 3, 1991). ... On disabled list (August 9, 1993-remainder of season). ... Traded by Cubs with P Jayson Peterson to Cincinnati Reds for P Curt Lyons (March 31, 1997).

						BATTING							FIELDING		
Year—Team (League)	Pos.	G	AB	R	H	2B	3B	HR	RBI	Avg.	BB	SO	SB	PO	A	E	Avg.
1991— Geneva (NY-Penn)	OF	73	294	35	65	10	1	•12	47	.221	18	39	4	118	3	4	.968
1992— Win.-Salem (Car.)	OF	86	305	64	86	18	0	18	56	.282	58	46	11	90	7	1	.990
— Charlotte (Southern)	OF	36	122	13	26	7	0	3	13	.213	12	26	2	41	3	1	.978
1993— Orlando (Sou.)	OF	107	359	65	102	22	2	18	58	.284	62	80	5	169	14	6	.968
1994— Iowa (Am. Assoc.)	OF	126	440	63	116	30	2	22	66	.264	36	93	0	228	14	6	.976
1995— Chicago (N.L.)	OF	77	171	30	45	10	1	8	28	.263	13	32	3	63	1	2	.970
1996— Chicago (N.L.)	OF	65	140	18	28	4	0	7	16	.200	15	30	1	65	1	1	.985
— Iowa (Am. Assoc.)	OF	59	213	32	53	7	0	17	40	.249	28	42	1	98	1	3	.971
1997— Cincinnati (N.L.)■	OF	6	9	1	3	1	0	0	0	.333	0	1	0	0	0	1	.000
— Indianapolis (A.A.)	OF	125	407	46	103	14	1	14	55	.253	60	100	1	172	3	3	.983
Major league totals (3 years)		148	320	49	76	15	1	15	44	.238	28	63	4	128	2	4	.970

TINSLEY, LEE — OF

PERSONAL: Born March 4, 1969, in Shelbyville, Ky. ... 5-10/198. ... Bats both, throws right. ... Full name: Lee Owen Tinsley.
HIGH SCHOOL: Shelby County (Ky.).
TRANSACTIONS/CAREER NOTES: Selected by Oakland Athletics organization in first round (11th pick overall) of free-agent draft (June 2, 1987). ... Traded by A's with P Apolinar Garcia to Cleveland Indians for 3B Brook Jacoby (July 26, 1991). ... Claimed on waivers by Seattle Mariners (September 21, 1992). ... Traded by Mariners to Boston Red Sox for a player to be named later (March 22, 1994); Mariners acquired P Jim Smith to complete deal (September 15, 1994). ... On Boston disabled list (May 19-June 8 and August 23-September 8, 1995); included rehabilitation assignment to Trenton (June 4-8). ... Traded by Red Sox with P Ken Ryan and OF Glenn Murray to Philadelphia Phillies for P Heathcliff Slocumb, P Larry Wimberly and OF Rick Holifield (January 29, 1996). ... On Philadelphia disabled list (May 5-21, 1996); included rehabilitation assignment to Clearwater (May 16-21). ... Traded by Phillies to Red Sox for P Scott Bakkum (June 9, 1996). ... Traded by Red Sox to Mariners for a player to be named later (November 25, 1996). ... On Seattle disabled list (May 3-August 2 and August 18-September 3, 1997); included rehabilitation assignments to Tacoma (June 8-12 and June 26-August 1). ... Released by Mariners (December 15, 1997).
STATISTICAL NOTES: Tied for Northwest League lead in caught stealing with 10 in 1988. ... Led Midwest League outfielders with 320 total chances in 1990.

Year Team (League)	Pos.	G	AB	R	H	2B	3B	HR	RBI	Avg.	BB	SO	SB	PO	A	E	Avg.
1987— Medford (N'west)	OF	45	132	22	23	3	2	0	13	.174	35	57	9	77	2	4	.952
1988— S. Oregon (N'west)	OF	73	256	56	64	8	2	3	28	.250	*66	*106	*42	127	6	6	.957
1989— Madison (Midwest)	OF	123	397	51	72	10	2	6	31	.181	67	*177	19	274	7	8	.972
1990— Madison (Midwest)	OF	132	482	88	121	14	12	12	59	.251	78	*175	44	*302	7	11	.966
1991— Huntsville (Southern)	OF	92	303	47	68	7	6	2	24	.224	52	97	36	175	3	7	.962
— Cant./Akr. (Eastern)■	OF	38	139	26	41	7	2	3	8	.295	18	37	18	56	1	2	.966
1992— Colo. Springs (PCL)	OF	27	81	19	19	2	1	0	4	.235	16	19	3	42	1	1	.977
— Cant./Akr. (Eastern)	OF	96	349	65	100	9	8	5	38	.287	42	82	18	226	5	5	.979
1993— Seattle (A.L.)■	OF-DH	11	19	2	3	1	0	1	2	.158	2	9	0	9	0	1	.900
— Calgary (PCL)	OF	111	450	95	136	25	*18	10	63	.302	50	98	34	241	4	3	.988
1994— Boston (A.L.)■	OF-DH	78	144	27	32	4	0	2	14	.222	19	36	13	113	1	1	.991
1995— Boston (A.L.)	OF	100	341	61	97	17	1	7	41	.284	39	74	18	228	4	5	.979
— Trenton (Eastern)	OF	4	18	3	7	1	0	0	3	.389	1	5	1	4	0	0	1.000
1996— Philadelphia (N.L.)■	OF	31	52	1	7	0	0	0	2	.135	4	22	2	24	0	1	.960
— Clearwater (FSL)	OF	4	17	4	5	0	1	0	3	.294	2	4	2	12	0	0	1.000
— Boston (A.L.)	OF	92	192	28	47	6	1	3	14	.245	13	56	6	132	8	1	.993
1997— Seattle (A.L.)■	OF-DH	49	122	12	24	6	2	0	6	.197	11	34	2	68	2	0	1.000
— Tacoma (PCL)	OF	31	105	15	19	2	1	2	7	.181	12	34	1	32	1	3	.917
American League totals (5 years)		330	818	130	203	34	4	13	77	.248	84	209	39	550	15	8	.986
National League totals (1 year)		31	52	1	7	0	0	0	2	.135	4	22	2	24	0	1	.960
Major league totals (5 years)		361	870	131	210	34	4	13	79	.241	88	231	41	574	15	9	.985

DIVISION SERIES RECORD

Year Team (League)	Pos.	G	AB	R	H	2B	3B	HR	RBI	Avg.	BB	SO	SB	PO	A	E	Avg.
1995— Boston (A.L.)	OF	1	5	0	0	0	0	0	0	.000	1	2	0	1	0	0	1.000

TOMBERLIN, ANDY — OF

PERSONAL: Born November 7, 1966, in Monroe, N.C. ... 5-11/160. ... Bats left, throws left. ... Full name: Andy Lee Tomberlin.

HIGH SCHOOL: Piedmont (Monroe, N.C.).

TRANSACTIONS/CAREER NOTES: Signed as non-drafted free agent by Atlanta Braves organization (August 16, 1985). ... On disabled list (April 10-May 28, 1991). ... Granted free agency (October 15, 1992). ... Signed by Buffalo, Pittsburgh Pirates organization (November 24, 1992). ... On Buffalo disabled list (May 22-June 5 and June 30-July 27, 1993). ... Granted free agency (October 13, 1993). ... Signed by Pawtucket, Boston Red Sox organization (February 4, 1994). ... On Boston disabled list (June 9-July 26, 1994). ... Granted free agency (October 6, 1994). ... Signed by Oakland Athletics organization (December 11, 1994). ... On Edmonton disabled list (August 2-September 12, 1995). ... Granted free agency (October 16, 1995). ... Re-signed by A's organization (January 12, 1996). ... On Edmonton temporarily inactive list (April 26-May 1, 1996). ... Traded by A's organization to New York Mets organization for a player to be named later (May 1, 1996). ... Granted free agency (October 15, 1996). ... Re-signed by Mets organization (November 21, 1996). ... On New York disabled list (April 9, 1997-remainder of season); included rehabilitation assignments to Gulf Coast Mets (August 13-20) and St. Lucie (August 21-28). ... Granted free agency (October 15, 1997).

STATISTICAL NOTES: Tied for Carolina League lead with seven intentional bases on balls received in 1989.

Year Team (League)	Pos.	G	AB	R	H	2B	3B	HR	RBI	Avg.	BB	SO	SB	PO	A	E	Avg.
1986— Sumter (S. Atl.)	P	13	1	0	0	0	0	0	0	.000	1	1	0	2	2	2	.667
— Pulaski (Appalachian)	P	3	4	2	1	0	0	0	0	.250	2	1	0	0	5	0	1.000
1987— Pulaski (Appalachian)	P	14	7	1	2	0	0	0	1	.286	0	0	0	1	9	1	.909
1988— Burl. (Midw.)	OF	43	134	24	46	7	3	3	18	.343	22	33	7	62	6	3	.958
— Durham (Carolina)	OF-P	83	256	43	77	16	3	6	35	.301	49	42	16	152	2	3	.981
1989— Durham (Carolina)	OF-1B-P	119	363	63	102	13	2	16	61	.281	54	82	35	442	16	1	.998
1990— Greenville (Southern)	OF-P	60	196	31	61	9	1	4	25	.311	20	35	9	95	4	3	.971
— Richmond (Int'l)	OF-1B	80	283	36	86	19	3	4	31	.304	39	43	11	180	9	4	.979
1991— Richmond (Int'l)	OF	93	329	47	77	13	2	2	24	.234	41	85	10	192	1	1	.995
1992— Richmond (Int'l)	OF	118	406	69	110	16	5	9	47	.271	41	102	12	184	9	3	.985
1993— Buffalo (A.A.)	OF-P	68	221	41	63	11	6	12	45	.285	18	48	3	104	7	5	.957
— Pittsburgh (N.L.)	OF	27	42	4	12	0	1	1	5	.286	2	14	0	9	1	0	1.000
1994— Pawtucket (Int'l)■	OF	54	189	38	63	12	2	13	39	.333	22	60	11	90	4	2	.979
— Boston (A.L.)	OF-DH-P	18	36	1	7	0	1	1	1	.194	6	12	1	12	2	0	1.000
1995— Edmonton (PCL)■	OF	14	52	9	13	3	0	2	7	.250	5	15	0	25	1	2	.929
— Oakland (A.L.)	OF-DH	46	85	15	18	0	0	4	10	.212	5	22	4	45	1	1	.979
1996— Edmonton (PCL)	OF	17	60	12	17	2	1	0	5	.283	8	15	1	25	1	1	.963
— Norfolk (Int'l)■	OF	38	129	17	42	6	1	8	18	.326	9	27	0	66	1	1	.985
— New York (N.L.)	OF-1B	63	66	12	17	4	0	3	10	.258	9	27	0	8	1	0	1.000
1997— New York (N.L.)	OF	6	7	0	2	0	0	0	0	.286	1	3	0	2	0	0	1.000
— GC Mets (GCL)	OF	7	22	6	7	0	0	2	7	.318	3	7	1	5	1	0	1.000
— St. Lucie (Fla. St.)	DH	1	3	0	0	0	0	0	1	.000	1	2	0	0	0	0	...
American League totals (2 years)		64	121	16	25	0	1	5	11	.207	11	34	5	57	3	1	.984
National League totals (3 years)		96	115	16	31	4	1	4	15	.270	12	44	0	19	2	0	1.000
Major league totals (5 years)		160	236	32	56	4	2	9	26	.237	23	78	5	76	5	1	.988

RECORD AS PITCHER

Year Team (League)	W	L	Pct.	ERA	G	GS	CG	ShO	Sv.	IP	H	R	ER	BB	SO
1986— Sumter (S. Atl.)	1	0	1.000	4.62	13	0	0	0	0	25 1/3	18	17	13	27	22
— Pulaski (Appalachian)	2	0	1.000	2.12	3	3	0	0	0	17	13	4	4	9	15
1987— Pulaski (Appalachian)	4	2	.667	4.43	12	6	0	0	0	44 2/3	35	23	22	29	51
1988— Durham (Carolina)	0	0	...	0.00	1	0	0	0	0	1	0	0	0	0	0
1989— Durham (Carolina)	0	0	...	18.00	1	0	0	0	0	1	2	2	2	2	2
1990— Greenville (Southern)	0	0	...	0.00	1	0	0	0	0	1	1	0	0	1	1
1993— Buffalo (A.A.)	0	0	...	0.00	2	0	0	0	0	2	0	0	0	3	1
1994— Boston (A.L.)	0	0	...	0.00	1	0	0	0	0	2	1	0	0	1	1
Major league totals (1 year)	0	0	...	0.00	1	0	0	0	0	2	1	0	0	1	1

TOMKO, BRETT   P   REDS

PERSONAL: Born April 7, 1973, in Cleveland. ... 6-4/205. ... Throws right, bats right. ... Full name: Brett Daniel Tomko.
HIGH SCHOOL: El Dorado (Placentia, Calif.).
JUNIOR COLLEGE: Mt. San Antonio College (Calif.).
COLLEGE: Florida Southern.
TRANSACTIONS/CAREER NOTES: Selected by Cincinnati Reds organization in second round of free-agent draft (June 1, 1995).
MISCELLANEOUS: Appeared in two games as pinch-runner (1997).

Year Team (League)	W	L	Pct.	ERA	G	GS	CG	ShO	Sv.	IP	H	R	ER	BB	SO
1995—Char., W.Va. (S. Atl.)	4	2	.667	1.84	9	7	0	0	0	49	41	12	10	9	46
1996—Chattanooga (Southern).....	11	7	.611	3.88	27	27	0	0	0	157 2/3	131	73	68	54	164
1997—Indianapolis (A.A.)..............	6	3	.667	2.95	10	10	0	0	0	61	53	21	20	9	60
— Cincinnati (N.L.)................	11	7	.611	3.43	22	19	0	0	0	126	106	50	48	47	95
Major league totals (1 year)........	**11**	**7**	**.611**	**3.43**	**22**	**19**	**0**	**0**	**0**	**126**	**106**	**50**	**48**	**47**	**95**

TORRES, SALOMON   P   EXPOS

PERSONAL: Born March 11, 1972, in San Pedro de Macoris, Dominican Republic. ... 5-11/165. ... Throws right, bats right. ... Full name: Salomon Ramirez Torres.
HIGH SCHOOL: Centro Academico Rogus (San Pedro de Macoris, Dominican Republic).
TRANSACTIONS/CAREER NOTES: Signed as non-drafted free agent by San Francisco Giants organization (September 15, 1989). ... Traded by Giants to Seattle Mariners for P Shawn Estes and IF Wilson Delgado (May 21, 1995). ... Claimed on waivers by Montreal Expos (April 18, 1997).
HONORS: Named Midwest League Most Valuable Player (1991).

Year Team (League)	W	L	Pct.	ERA	G	GS	CG	ShO	Sv.	IP	H	R	ER	BB	SO
1990—San Pedro (DSL)	11	1	.917	0.50	13	13	6	0	0	90	44	15	5	30	101
1991—Clinton (Midwest)...............	•16	5	.762	*1.41	28	28	*8	3	0	*210 1/3	148	48	33	47	*214
1992—Shreveport (Texas)..........	6	10	.375	4.21	25	25	4	2	0	162 1/3	167	93	76	34	151
1993—Shreveport (Texas)..........	7	4	.636	2.70	12	12	2	1	0	83 1/3	67	27	25	12	67
— Phoenix (PCL)..................	7	4	.636	3.50	14	14	•4	1	0	105 1/3	105	43	41	27	99
— San Francisco (N.L.)	3	5	.375	4.03	8	8	0	0	0	44 2/3	37	21	20	27	23
1994—San Francisco (N.L.)	2	8	.200	5.44	16	14	1	0	0	84 1/3	95	55	51	34	42
— Phoenix (PCL)..................	5	6	.455	4.22	13	13	0	0	0	79	85	49	37	31	64
1995—San Francisco (N.L.)	0	1	.000	9.00	4	1	0	0	0	8	13	8	8	7	2
— Phoenix (PCL)..................	0	0	...	0.00	1	0	0	0	0	2	2	0	0	0	5
— Tacoma (PCL)■...............	1	1	.500	3.21	5	4	0	0	0	28	20	10	10	13	19
— Seattle (A.L.)...................	3	8	.273	6.00	16	13	1	0	0	72	87	53	48	42	45
1996—Tacoma (PCL).................	7	10	.412	5.29	22	21	3	1	0	134 1/3	150	87	79	52	121
— Seattle (A.L.)...................	3	3	.500	4.59	10	7	1	1	0	49	44	27	25	23	36
1997—Seattle (A.L.)..................	0	0	...	27.00	2	0	0	0	0	3 1/3	7	10	10	3	0
— Ottawa (Int'l)■................	0	0	...	5.40	2	1	0	0	0	5	7	5	3	2	2
— Montreal (N.L.)................	0	0	...	7.25	12	0	0	0	0	22 1/3	25	19	18	12	11
A.L. totals (3 years)	6	11	.353	6.01	28	20	2	1	0	124 1/3	138	90	83	68	81
N.L. totals (4 years)	5	14	.263	5.48	40	23	1	0	0	159 1/3	170	103	97	80	78
Major league totals (5 years)......	11	25	.306	5.71	68	43	3	1	0	283 2/3	308	193	180	148	159

TOWLE, JUSTIN   C   REDS

PERSONAL: Born February 21, 1974, in Seattle. ... 6-2/210. ... Bats right, throws right. ... Full name: Justin Ellison Towle.
HIGH SCHOOL: Inglemoor (Bothell, Wash.).
TRANSACTIONS/CAREER NOTES: Selected by Cincinnati Reds organization in 12th round of free-agent draft (June 1, 1992).
STATISTICAL NOTES: Led Carolina League catchers with 100 assists and 20 passed balls in 1996. ... Led Southern League catchers with 68 assists and 18 passed balls and tied for league lead with 10 errors in 1997.

						BATTING								FIELDING		
Year Team (League)	Pos.	G	AB	R	H	2B	3B	HR	RBI	Avg.	BB	SO	SB	PO	A	E	Avg.
1992— Princeton (Appal.)	C	19	42	5	3	1	1	0	2	.071	9	16	1	93	14	4	.964
— Billings (Pioneer)........	C	7	11	1	4	1	0	0	1	.364	3	4	0	25	4	0	1.000
1993— Billings (Pioneer)........	C	47	137	29	36	6	0	7	23	.263	27	37	4	272	*48	8	.976
1994— Char., W.Va. (SAL)......	C	83	221	27	49	9	0	2	19	.222	26	59	2	477	67	5	*.991
— Win.-Salem (Car.)......	C	2	7	1	1	0	0	0	0	.143	0	2	0	12	2	0	1.000
1995— Char., W.Va. (SAL)......	C-1B	107	343	54	92	22	2	8	60	.268	44	95	3	622	103	12	.984
1996— Win.-Salem (Car.)......	C-1B	116	351	60	90	19	1	16	47	.256	93	96	17	605	†100	13	.982
1997— Chattanooga (Sou.)...	C-1B-OF	119	418	62	129	37	5	11	70	.309	55	77	5	574	†71	‡10	.985

TRACHSEL, STEVE   P   CUBS

PERSONAL: Born October 31, 1970, in Oxnard, Calif. ... 6-4/200. ... Throws right, bats right. ... Full name: Stephen Christopher Trachsel. ... Name pronounced TRACK-sul.
HIGH SCHOOL: Troy (Fullerton, Calif.).
JUNIOR COLLEGE: Fullerton (Calif.) College.
COLLEGE: Long Beach State.
TRANSACTIONS/CAREER NOTES: Selected by Chicago Cubs organization in eighth round of free-agent draft (June 3, 1991). ... On Chicago disabled list (July 20-August 4, 1994).
HONORS: Named N.L. Rookie Pitcher of the Year by THE SPORTING NEWS (1994).
STATISTICAL NOTES: Pitched 4-2 no-hit victory for Winston-Salem against Peninsula (July 12, 1991, second game). ... Pitched 6-0 one-hit, complete-game victory against Houston (May 13, 1996). ... Led N.L. with 32 home runs allowed in 1997.

Year	Team (League)	W	L	Pct.	ERA	G	GS	CG	ShO	Sv.	IP	H	R	ER	BB	SO
1991—	Geneva (N.Y.-Penn)	1	0	1.000	1.26	2	2	0	0	0	14 1/3	10	2	2	6	7
	—Win.-Salem (Car.)	4	4	.500	3.67	12	12	1	0	0	73 2/3	70	38	30	19	69
1992—	Charlotte (Southern)	•13	8	.619	3.06	29	•29	5	2	0	*191	180	76	65	35	135
1993—	Iowa (Am. Assoc.)	13	6	.684	3.96	27	26	1	1	0	170 2/3	170	78	75	45	135
	—Chicago (N.L.)	0	2	.000	4.58	3	3	0	0	0	19 2/3	16	10	10	3	14
1994—	Chicago (N.L.)	9	7	.563	3.21	22	22	1	0	0	146	133	57	52	54	108
	—Iowa (Am. Assoc.)	0	2	.000	10.00	2	2	0	0	0	9	11	10	10	7	8
1995—	Chicago (N.L.)	7	13	.350	5.15	30	29	2	0	0	160 2/3	174	104	92	76	117
1996—	Orlando (South.)	0	1	.000	2.77	2	2	0	0	0	13	11	6	4	0	12
	—Chicago (N.L.)	13	9	.591	3.03	31	31	3	2	0	205	181	82	69	62	132
1997—	Chicago (N.L.)	8	12	.400	4.51	34	34	0	0	0	201 1/3	225	110	101	69	160
Major league totals (5 years)		37	43	.463	3.98	120	119	6	2	0	732 2/3	729	363	324	264	531

ALL-STAR GAME RECORD

Year	League	W	L	Pct.	ERA	GS	CG	ShO	Sv.	IP	H	R	ER	BB	SO
1996—	National	0	0	...	0.00	0	0	0	0	1	0	0	0	0	3

TRAMMELL, BUBBA — OF — DEVIL RAYS

PERSONAL: Born November 6, 1971, in Knoxville, Tenn. ... 6-3/205. ... Bats right, throws right. ... Full name: Thomas Bubba Trammell.
HIGH SCHOOL: Knoxville (Tenn.) Central.
JUNIOR COLLEGE: Cleveland (Tenn.) State Community College.
COLLEGE: Tennessee.
TRANSACTIONS/CAREER NOTES: Selected by Detroit Tigers organization in 11th round of free-agent draft (June 2, 1994). ... Selected by Tampa Bay Devil Rays in first round (22nd pick overall) of expansion draft (November 18, 1997).

			BATTING												FIELDING			
Year	Team (League)	Pos.	G	AB	R	H	2B	3B	HR	RBI	Avg.	BB	SO	SB	PO	A	E	Avg.
1994—	Jamestown (NYP)	OF	65	235	37	70	18	6	5	41	.298	23	32	9	77	3	5	.941
1995—	Lakeland (Fla. St.)	OF	122	454	61	129	32	6	16	72	.284	48	80	13	176	7	5	.973
1996—	Jacksonville (South.)	OF	83	311	63	102	23	2	27	75	.328	32	61	3	100	6	5	.955
	—Toledo (Int'l)	OF	51	180	32	53	14	1	6	24	.294	22	44	5	72	5	1	.987
1997—	Detroit (A.L.)	OF-DH	44	123	14	28	5	0	4	13	.228	15	35	3	52	1	0	1.000
	—Toledo (Int'l)	OF	90	319	56	80	15	1	28	75	.251	38	91	2	103	3	3	.972
Major league totals (1 year)			44	123	14	28	5	0	4	13	.228	15	35	3	52	1	0	1.000

T

TRLICEK, RICK — P — METS

PERSONAL: Born April 26, 1969, in Houston. ... 6-2/200. ... Throws right, bats right. ... Full name: Richard Alan Trlicek. ... Name pronounced TRILL-a-CHECK.
HIGH SCHOOL: LaGrange (Texas).
TRANSACTIONS/CAREER NOTES: Selected by Philadelphia Phillies organization in fourth round of free-agent draft (June 2, 1987). ... Released by Phillies organization (March 23, 1989). ... Signed by Atlanta Braves organization (April 2, 1989). ... Traded by Braves organization to Toronto Blue Jays for C Ernie Whitt and OF Kevin Batiste (December 17, 1989). ... On disabled list (August 4, 1991-remainder of season). ... On Syracuse disabled list (July 31-September 8, 1992). ... Claimed on waivers by Los Angeles Dodgers (March 16, 1993). ... On suspended list (June 29-July 2, 1993). ... Claimed on waivers by Boston Red Sox (April 1, 1994). ... Released by Red Sox (December 5, 1994). ... Signed by Phoenix, San Francisco Giants organization (January 27, 1995). ... Released by Phoenix (July 18, 1995). ... Signed by Canton/Akron, Cleveland Indians organization (July 28, 1995). ... Granted free agency (October 16, 1995). ... Signed by Detroit Tigers organization (November 30, 1995). ... Released by Tigers organization (March 27, 1996). ... Signed by Norfolk, New York Mets organization (March 28, 1996). ... Claimed on waivers by Boston Red Sox (October 14, 1996). ... Traded by Red Sox to Mets for P Toby Borland (May 12, 1997). ... On disabled list (June 13, 1997-remainder of season). ... Granted free agency (October 15, 1997). ... Re-signed by Mets organization (December 19, 1997).

Year	Team (League)	W	L	Pct.	ERA	G	GS	CG	ShO	Sv.	IP	H	R	ER	BB	SO
1987—	Utica (N.Y.-Penn)	2	5	.286	4.10	10	8	1	1	0	37 1/3	43	28	17	31	22
1988—	Batavia (N.Y.-Penn)	2	3	.400	7.39	8	8	0	0	0	31 2/3	27	32	26	31	26
1989—	Sumter (S. Atl.)■	6	5	.545	2.59	15	15	0	0	0	93 2/3	73	40	27	40	72
	—Durham (Carolina)	0	0	...	1.13	1	1	0	0	0	8	3	2	1	1	4
1990—	Dunedin (Fla. St.)■	5	8	.385	3.73	26	26	0	0	0	154 1/3	128	74	64	72	125
1991—	Knoxville (Southern)	2	5	.286	2.45	41	0	0	0	16	51 1/3	36	26	14	22	55
1992—	Toronto (A.L.)	0	0	...	10.80	2	0	0	0	0	1 2/3	2	2	2	2	1
	—Syracuse (Int'l)	1	1	.500	4.36	35	0	0	0	10	43 1/3	37	22	21	31	35
1993—	Los Angeles (N.L.)■	1	2	.333	4.08	41	0	0	0	1	64	59	32	29	21	41
1994—	Boston (A.L.)■	1	1	.500	8.06	12	1	0	0	0	22 1/3	32	21	20	16	7
	—New Britain (East.)	0	1	.000	0.73	6	6	0	0	0	24 2/3	12	3	2	6	13
	—Pawtucket (Int'l)	2	1	.667	2.63	11	3	0	0	0	27 1/3	19	11	8	13	19
1995—	Phoenix (PCL)■	5	4	.556	5.29	38	0	0	0	0	63	72	44	37	21	43
	—Cant./Akr. (Eastern)■	5	3	.625	3.05	24	0	0	0	3	38 1/3	33	16	13	16	27
1996—	Norfolk (Int'l)■	4	5	.444	1.87	62	0	0	0	10	77	52	18	16	16	54
	—New York (N.L.)	0	1	.000	3.38	5	0	0	0	0	5 1/3	3	2	2	3	3
1997—	Boston (A.L.)■	3	4	.429	4.63	18	0	0	0	0	23 1/3	26	14	12	18	10
	—New York (N.L.)■	0	0	...	8.00	9	0	0	0	0	9	10	9	8	5	4
A.L. totals (3 years)		4	5	.444	6.46	32	1	0	0	0	47 1/3	60	37	34	36	18
N.L. totals (3 years)		1	3	.250	4.48	55	0	0	0	1	78 1/3	72	43	39	29	48
Major league totals (5 years)		5	8	.385	5.23	87	1	0	0	1	125 2/3	132	80	73	65	66

TROMBLEY, MIKE — P — TWINS

PERSONAL: Born April 14, 1967, in Springfield, Mass. ... 6-2/203. ... Throws right, bats right. ... Full name: Michael Scott Trombley.
HIGH SCHOOL: Minnechaug Regional (Wilbraham, Mass.).
COLLEGE: Duke.

TRANSACTIONS/CAREER NOTES: Selected by Minnesota Twins organization in 14th round of free-agent draft (June 5, 1989).
STATISTICAL NOTES: Pitched 3-0 no-hit victory against Knoxville (August 8, 1991). ... Led Pacific Coast League with 18 home runs allowed in 1992.

Year Team (League)	W	L	Pct.	ERA	G	GS	CG	ShO	Sv.	IP	H	R	ER	BB	SO
1989— Kenosha (Midwest)	5	1	.833	3.12	12	3	0	0	2	49	45	23	17	13	41
— Visalia (California)	2	2	.500	2.14	6	6	2	1	0	42	31	12	10	11	36
1990— Visalia (California)	14	6	.700	3.43	27	25	3	1	0	176	163	79	67	50	164
1991— Orlando (South.)	12	7	.632	2.54	27	27	7	2	0	*191	153	65	54	57	*175
1992— Portland (PCL)	10	8	.556	3.65	25	25	2	0	0	165	149	70	67	58	*138
— Minnesota (A.L.)	3	2	.600	3.30	10	7	0	0	0	46 1/3	43	20	17	17	38
1993— Minnesota (A.L.)	6	6	.500	4.88	44	10	0	0	2	114 1/3	131	72	62	41	85
1994— Minnesota (A.L.)	2	0	1.000	6.33	24	0	0	0	0	48 1/3	56	36	34	18	32
— Salt Lake (PCL)	4	4	.500	5.04	11	10	0	0	0	60 2/3	75	37	34	20	63
1995— Salt Lake (PCL)	5	3	.625	3.62	12	12	0	0	0	69 2/3	71	32	28	26	59
— Minnesota (A.L.)	4	8	.333	5.62	20	18	0	0	0	97 2/3	107	68	61	42	68
1996— Salt Lake (PCL)	2	2	.500	2.45	24	0	0	0	10	36 2/3	24	12	10	10	38
— Minnesota (A.L.)	5	1	.833	3.01	40	0	0	0	6	68 2/3	61	24	23	25	57
1997— Minnesota (A.L.)	2	3	.400	4.37	67	0	0	0	1	82 1/3	77	43	40	31	74
Major league totals (6 years)	22	20	.524	4.66	208	35	0	0	9	457 2/3	475	263	237	174	354

TUCKER, MICHAEL   OF   BRAVES

PERSONAL: Born June 25, 1971, in South Boston, Va. ... 6-2/185. ... Bats left, throws right. ... Full name: Michael Anthony Tucker.
HIGH SCHOOL: Bluestone (Skipwith, Va.).
COLLEGE: Longwood (Va.).
TRANSACTIONS/CAREER NOTES: Selected by Kansas City Royals organization in first round (10th pick overall) of free-agent draft (June 1, 1992). ... On Kansas City disabled list (June 4-21 and August 28, 1996-remainder of season); included rehabilitation assignment to Wichita (June 15-21). ... Traded by Royals with IF Keith Lockhart to Atlanta Braves for OF Jermaine Dye and P Jamie Walker (March 27, 1997).

						BATTING								FIELDING			
Year Team (League)	Pos.	G	AB	R	H	2B	3B	HR	RBI	Avg.	BB	SO	SB	PO	A	E	Avg.
1993— Wilmington (Caro.)	2B	61	239	42	73	14	2	6	44	.305	34	49	12	120	157	10	.965
— Memphis (Southern)	2B	72	244	38	68	7	4	9	35	.279	42	51	12	153	176	13	.962
1994— Omaha (A.A.)	OF	132	485	75	134	16	7	21	77	.276	69	111	11	196	11	•7	.967
1995— Kansas City (A.L.)	OF-DH	62	177	23	46	10	0	4	17	.260	18	51	2	67	3	1	.986
— Omaha (A.A.)	OF	71	275	37	84	18	4	4	28	.305	24	39	11	133	11	2	.986
1996— Kansas City (A.L.)	OF-1B-DH	108	339	55	88	18	4	12	53	.260	40	69	10	235	8	2	.992
— Wichita (Texas)	OF-1B	6	20	4	9	1	3	0	7	.450	5	4	0	17	1	0	1.000
1997— Atlanta (N.L.)■	OF	138	499	80	141	25	7	14	56	.283	44	116	12	237	6	5	.980
American League totals (2 years)		170	516	78	134	28	4	16	70	.260	58	120	12	302	11	3	.991
National League totals (1 year)		138	499	80	141	25	7	14	56	.283	44	116	12	237	6	5	.980
Major league totals (3 years)		308	1015	158	275	53	11	30	126	.271	102	236	24	539	17	8	.986

DIVISION SERIES RECORD

						BATTING								FIELDING			
Year Team (League)	Pos.	G	AB	R	H	2B	3B	HR	RBI	Avg.	BB	SO	SB	PO	A	E	Avg.
1997— Atlanta (N.L.)	OF	2	6	0	1	0	0	0	1	.167	0	1	0	3	0	0	1.000

CHAMPIONSHIP SERIES RECORD

						BATTING								FIELDING			
Year Team (League)	Pos.	G	AB	R	H	2B	3B	HR	RBI	Avg.	BB	SO	SB	PO	A	E	Avg.
1997— Atlanta (N.L.)	OF-PH	5	10	1	1	0	0	1	1	.100	3	4	0	5	1	0	1.000

TURNER, CHRIS   C   TWINS

PERSONAL: Born March 23, 1969, in Bowling Green, Ky. ... 6-1/190. ... Bats right, throws right. ... Full name: Christopher Wan Turner.
HIGH SCHOOL: Warren Central (Bowling Green, Ky.).
COLLEGE: Western Kentucky (degree in psychology, 1991).
TRANSACTIONS/CAREER NOTES: Selected by California Angels organization in seventh round of free-agent draft (June 3, 1991). ... Angels franchise renamed Anaheim Angels for 1997 season. ... On Anaheim disabled list (March 31-July 4, 1997); included rehabilitation assignment to Lake Elsinore (July 2-4). ... Granted free agency (October 10, 1997). ... Signed by Minnesota Twins organization (December 5, 1997).
STATISTICAL NOTES: Led Northwest League catchers with .997 fielding percentage in 1991. ... Led Pacific Coast League with 17 passed balls in 1993.

						BATTING								FIELDING			
Year Team (League)	Pos.	G	AB	R	H	2B	3B	HR	RBI	Avg.	BB	SO	SB	PO	A	E	Avg.
1991— Boise (Northwest)	C-OF	52	163	26	37	5	0	2	29	.227	32	32	10	360	39	2	†.995
1992— Quad City (Midwest)	C-1B	109	330	66	83	18	1	9	53	.252	85	65	8	727	98	9	.989
1993— Vancouver (PCL)	C-1B	90	283	50	78	12	1	4	57	.276	49	44	6	524	56	6	.990
— California (A.L.)	C	25	75	9	21	5	0	1	13	.280	9	16	1	116	14	1	.992
1994— California (A.L.)	C	58	149	23	36	7	1	1	12	.242	10	29	3	268	29	1	.997
— Vancouver (PCL)	C	3	10	1	2	1	0	0	1	.200	0	2	0	10	1	1	.917
1995— Vancouver (PCL)	C-3-1-0	80	282	44	75	20	2	3	48	.266	34	54	3	345	49	6	.983
— California (A.L.)	C	5	10	0	1	0	0	0	1	.100	0	3	0	17	2	0	1.000
1996— Vancouver (PCL)	C-0-3-1	113	390	51	100	19	1	2	47	.256	61	85	1	396	57	8	.983
— California (A.L.)	C-OF	4	3	1	1	0	0	0	1	.333	1	0	0	3	2	0	1.000
1997— Lake Elsinore (Calif.)	C	3	12	0	1	0	1	0	1	.083	0	3	0	25	1	1	.963
— Vancouver (PCL)	1B-C-OF	37	135	26	50	10	0	4	22	.370	14	22	0	291	15	5	.984
— Anaheim (A.L.)	C-1-DH-O	13	23	4	6	1	1	1	2	.261	5	8	0	34	2	0	1.000
Major league totals (5 years)		105	260	37	65	13	2	3	29	.250	25	56	4	438	49	2	.996

UNROE, TIM — 1B/3B — BREWERS

PERSONAL: Born October 7, 1970, in Round Lake, Ill. ... 6-3/200. ... Bats right, throws right. ... Full name: Timothy Brian Unroe.
HIGH SCHOOL: Round Lake (Ill.).
JUNIOR COLLEGE: Lake County (Ill.).
COLLEGE: Lewis (Ill.).
TRANSACTIONS/CAREER NOTES: Selected by Milwaukee Brewers organization in 28th round of free-agent draft (June 1, 1992).
HONORS: Named Texas League Player of the Year (1994).
STATISTICAL NOTES: Led Pioneer League third basemen with 62 putouts, 155 assists, 16 double plays and 236 total chances in 1992. ... Led California League third basemen with .936 fielding percentage, 78 putouts, 244 assists and 344 total chances in 1993. ... Led Texas League with 242 total bases and nine sacrifice flies in 1994. ... Career major league grand slams: 1.

												BATTING					FIELDING		
Year	Team (League)	Pos.	G	AB	R	H	2B	3B	HR	RBI	Avg.	BB	SO	SB	PO	A	E	Avg.
1992—Helena (Pioneer)		3B-1B	74	266	61	74	13	2	*16	58	.278	47	91	3	†70	†155	20	.918
1993—Stockton (California) ..		3B-OF	108	382	57	96	21	6	12	63	.251	36	96	9	†81	†244	23	†.934
1994—El Paso (Texas).........		3B-1B-OF	126	474	*97	*147	36	7	15	*103	.310	42	107	14	383	203	19	.969
1995—New Orleans (A.A.)....		3B-1B-OF	102	371	43	97	21	2	6	45	.261	18	94	4	373	160	12	.978
— Milwaukee (A.L.)........		1B	2	4	0	1	0	0	0	0	.250	0	0	0	11	0	0	1.000
1996—New Orleans (A.A.)....		3-1-S-O	109	404	72	109	26	4	25	67	.270	36	121	8	175	231	25	.942
— Milwaukee (A.L.)........		1-3-DH-O	14	16	5	3	0	0	0	0	.188	4	5	0	41	10	1	.981
1997—Tucson (PCL)...........		3-0-2-S	63	234	45	68	17	1	9	46	.291	9	62	3	65	92	7	.957
— Milwaukee (A.L.)........		1-3-0-2	32	16	3	4	1	0	2	5	.250	2	9	2	59	9	2	.971
Major league totals (3 years)			**48**	**36**	**8**	**8**	**1**	**0**	**2**	**5**	**.222**	**6**	**14**	**2**	**111**	**19**	**3**	**.977**

URBINA, UGUETH — P — EXPOS

PERSONAL: Born February 15, 1974, in Caracas, Venezuela. ... 6-2/185. ... Throws right, bats right. ... Full name: Ugueth Urtain Urbina. ... Name pronounced OOO-get.
HIGH SCHOOL: Liceo Peres Bonalde (Miranda, Venezuala).
TRANSACTIONS/CAREER NOTES: Signed as non-drafted free agent by Montreal Expos organization (July 2, 1990). ... On disabled list (April 8-17, 1994). ... On temporarily inactive list (May 9-June 6, 1994). ... On Ottawa disabled list (August 10-September 14, 1995).

Year	Team (League)	W	L	Pct.	ERA	G	GS	CG	ShO	Sv.	IP	H	R	ER	BB	SO
1991—GC Expos (GCL)		3	3	.500	2.29	10	10	3	•1	0	63	58	24	16	10	51
1992—Albany (S. Atl.)..................		7	•13	.350	3.22	24	24	5	2	0	142 1/3	111	68	51	54	100
1993—Burlington (Midw.).............		2	3	.400	4.50	10	8	0	0	0	46	41	31	23	22	30
— Harrisburg (Eastern)		4	5	.444	3.99	11	11	3	1	0	70	66	32	31	32	45
1994—Harrisburg (Eastern)		9	3	.750	3.28	21	21	0	0	0	120 2/3	95	49	44	43	86
1995—W.P. Beach (FSL).............		1	0	1.000	0.00	2	2	0	0	0	9	4	0	0	1	11
— Ottawa (Int'l)		6	2	.750	3.04	13	11	2	1	0	68	46	26	23	26	55
— Montreal (N.L.)..................		2	2	.500	6.17	7	4	0	0	0	23 1/3	26	17	16	14	15
1996—W.P. Beach (FSL).............		1	1	.500	1.29	3	3	0	0	0	14	13	3	2	3	21
— Ottawa (Int'l)		2	0	1.000	2.66	5	5	0	0	0	23 2/3	17	9	7	6	28
— Montreal (N.L.)..................		10	5	.667	3.71	33	17	0	0	0	114	102	54	47	44	108
1997—Montreal (N.L.)..................		5	8	.385	3.78	63	0	0	0	27	64 1/3	52	29	27	29	84
Major league totals (3 years)......		**17**	**15**	**.531**	**4.02**	**103**	**21**	**0**	**0**	**27**	**201 2/3**	**180**	**100**	**90**	**87**	**207**

VALDES, ISMAEL — P — DODGERS

PERSONAL: Born August 21, 1973, in Victoria, Mexico. ... 6-3/207. ... Throws right, bats right.
HIGH SCHOOL: CBTIS #119 (Victoria, Mexico).
TRANSACTIONS/CAREER NOTES: Signed as non-drafted free agent by Los Angeles Dodgers (June 14, 1991). ... Loaned by Dodgers organization to Mexico City Tigers of Mexican League (April 21-June 26, 1992 and March 17-August 19, 1993). ... On disabled list (July 6-28, 1997).
STATISTICAL NOTES: Led N.L. with five balks in 1996.

Year	Team (League)	W	L	Pct.	ERA	G	GS	CG	ShO	Sv.	IP	H	R	ER	BB	SO
1991—GC Dodgers (GCL)		2	2	.500	2.32	10	10	0	0	0	50 1/3	44	15	13	13	44
1992—La Vega (DSL)		3	0	1.000	1.42	6	0	0	0	0	38	27	9	6	17	34
— M.C. Tigers (Mex.)■...........		0	0	....	19.64	5	0	0	0	0	3 2/3	15	9	8	1	2
1993—San Antonio (Tex.)■..........		1	0	1.000	1.38	3	2	0	0	0	13	12	2	2	0	11
— M.C. Tigers (Mex.)■...........		16	7	.696	3.94	26	25	11	1	0	173 2/3	192	87	76	55	113
1994—San Antonio (Tex.)..........		2	3	.400	3.38	8	8	0	0	0	53 1/3	54	22	20	9	55
— Albuquerque (PCL)............		4	1	.800	3.40	8	8	0	0	0	45	44	21	17	13	39
— Los Angeles (N.L.)............		3	1	.750	3.18	21	1	0	0	0	28 1/3	21	10	10	10	28
1995—Los Angeles (N.L.)		13	11	.542	3.05	33	27	6	2	1	197 2/3	168	76	67	51	150
1996—Los Angeles (N.L.)		15	7	.682	3.32	33	33	0	0	0	225	219	94	83	54	173
1997—Los Angeles (N.L.)		10	11	.476	2.65	30	30	0	0	0	196 2/3	171	68	58	47	140
Major league totals (4 years)......		**41**	**30**	**.577**	**3.03**	**117**	**91**	**6**	**2**	**1**	**647 2/3**	**579**	**248**	**218**	**162**	**491**

DIVISION SERIES RECORD

Year	Team (League)	W	L	Pct.	ERA	G	GS	CG	ShO	Sv.	IP	H	R	ER	BB	SO
1995—Los Angeles (N.L.)		0	0	...	0.00	1	1	0	0	0	7	3	2	0	1	6
1996—Los Angeles (N.L.)		0	1	.000	4.26	1	1	0	0	0	6 1/3	5	3	3	0	5
Div. series totals (2 years)		**0**	**1**	**.000**	**2.03**	**2**	**2**	**0**	**0**	**0**	**13 1/3**	**8**	**5**	**3**	**1**	**11**

VALDES, MARC — P — EXPOS

PERSONAL: Born December 20, 1971, in Dayton, Ohio. ... 6-0/187. ... Throws right, bats right. ... Full name: Marc Christopher Valdes.
HIGH SCHOOL: Jesuit (Tampa).
COLLEGE: Florida.

U
V

TRANSACTIONS/CAREER NOTES: Selected by Cincinnati Reds organization in 20th round of free-agent draft (June 4, 1990); did not sign. ... Selected by Florida Marlins organization in first round (27th pick overall) of free-agent draft (June 3, 1993). ... Claimed on waivers by Montreal Expos (December 12, 1996).

Year Team (League)	W	L	Pct.	ERA	G	GS	CG	ShO	Sv.	IP	H	R	ER	BB	SO
1993—Elmira (N.Y.-Penn).............	0	2	.000	5.59	3	3	0	0	0	9 2/3	8	9	6	7	15
1994—Kane County (Midwest)......	7	4	.636	2.95	11	11	2	0	0	76 1/3	62	30	25	21	68
—Portland (Eastern).............	8	4	.667	2.55	15	15	0	0	0	99	77	31	28	39	70
1995—Charlotte (Int'l)...............	9	•13	.409	4.86	27	27	3	2	0	170 1/3	189	98	•92	59	104
—Florida (N.L.)......................	0	0	...	14.14	3	3	0	0	0	7	17	13	11	9	2
1996—Charlotte (Int'l)...............	2	4	.333	5.12	8	8	1	0	0	51	66	32	29	15	24
—Portland (Eastern).............	6	2	.750	2.66	10	10	1	0	0	64 1/3	60	25	19	12	49
—Florida (N.L.).....................	1	3	.250	4.81	11	8	0	0	0	48 2/3	63	32	26	23	13
1997—Montreal (N.L.)■..............	4	4	.500	3.13	48	7	0	0	2	95	84	36	33	39	54
Major league totals (3 years)......	5	7	.417	4.18	62	18	0	0	2	150 2/3	164	81	70	71	69

VALDES, PEDRO — OF/1B — CUBS

PERSONAL: Born June 29, 1973, in Fajardo, Peurto Rico. ... 6-1/180. ... Bats left, throws left. ... Full name: Pedro Jose Manzo Valdes.
HIGH SCHOOL: Carlos Escobar (Loiza, Puerto Rico).
TRANSACTIONS/CAREER NOTES: Selected by Chicago Cubs organization in 12th round of free-agent draft (June 4, 1990). ... On Iowa disabled list (August 4-11, 1996).
STATISTICAL NOTES: Led Southern League outfielders with six double plays in 1995.

Year Team (League)	Pos.	G	AB	R	H	2B	3B	HR	RBI	Avg.	BB	SO	SB	PO	A	E	Avg.
1991—Hunting. (Appal.)........	OF	49	152	17	44	11	1	0	16	.289	17	30	5	66	4	6	.921
1992—Peoria (Midwest).......	OF	33	112	8	26	7	0	0	20	.232	7	32	0	32	1	1	.971
—Geneva (NY-Penn)......	OF-1B	66	254	27	69	10	0	5	24	.272	3	33	4	210	18	9	.962
1993—Peoria (Midwest).......	OF-1B	65	234	33	74	11	1	7	36	.316	10	40	2	51	2	1	.981
—Daytona (Fla. St.)......	OF-1B	60	230	27	66	16	1	8	49	.287	9	30	3	176	7	3	.984
1994—Orlando (South.).......	OF	116	365	39	103	14	4	1	37	.282	20	45	2	177	12	7	.964
1995—Orlando (South.)	OF	114	426	57	128	28	3	7	68	.300	37	77	3	172	11	4	.979
1996—Iowa (Am. Assoc.)......	OF	103	397	61	117	23	0	15	60	.295	31	57	2	183	7	5	.974
—Chicago (N.L.)...........	OF	9	8	2	1	1	0	0	1	.125	1	5	0	1	0	0	1.000
1997—Iowa (Am. Assoc.)......	OF	125	464	65	132	30	1	14	60	.284	48	67	9	256	13	3	.989
Major league totals (1 year)		9	8	2	1	1	0	0	1	.125	1	5	0	1	0	0	1.000

VALDEZ, MARIO — 1B — WHITE SOX

PERSONAL: Born November 19, 1974, in Obregon, Mexico ... 6-2/190. ... Bats left, throws left. ... Full name: Mario A. Valdez.
HIGH SCHOOL: Miami Senior (Miami).
JUNIOR COLLEGE: Miami-Dade North
TRANSACTIONS/CAREER NOTES: Selected by Chicago White Sox organization in 48th round of free-agent draft (June 3, 1993).

Year Team (League)	Pos.	G	AB	R	H	2B	3B	HR	RBI	Avg.	BB	SO	SB	PO	A	E	Avg.
1994—GC Whi. Sox (GCL)	1B-OF	53	157	20	37	11	2	2	25	.236	30	28	0	351	28	8	.979
1995—Hickory (S. Atl.)	1B	130	441	65	120	30	5	11	56	.272	67	107	9	1040	67	12	.989
1996—South Bend (Mid.)......	1B	61	202	46	76	19	0	10	43	.376	36	42	2	438	41	8	.984
—Birmingham (Sou.).....	1B-OF	50	168	22	46	10	2	3	28	.274	32	34	0	284	26	2	.994
1997—Nashville (A.A.)	1B	81	282	44	79	20	1	15	61	.280	43	77	1	616	44	6	.991
—Chicago (A.L.)	1B-DH-3B	54	115	11	28	7	0	1	13	.243	17	39	1	256	12	0	1.000
Major league totals (1 year)		54	115	11	28	7	0	1	13	.243	17	39	1	256	12	0	1.000

VALENTIN, JAVIER — C — TWINS

PERSONAL: Born September 19, 1975, in Manati, Puerto Rico. ... 5-10/191. ... Bats both, throws right. ... Full name: Jose Javier Valentin. ... Brother of Jose Valentin, shortstop, Milwaukee Brewers. ... Name pronounced VAL-un-TEEN..
HIGH SCHOOL: Fernando Callejo (Manati, Puerto Rico).
TRANSACTIONS/CAREER NOTES: Selected by Minnesota Twins organization in third round of free-agent draft (June 3, 1993).
STATISTICAL NOTES: Led Appalachian League catchers with 48 assists and 348 total chances in 1993. ... Led Midwest League with 730 putouts, 108 assists, 861 total chances, 23 errors and 11 double plays by catcher in 1995.

Year Team (League)	Pos.	G	AB	R	H	2B	3B	HR	RBI	Avg.	BB	SO	SB	PO	A	E	Avg.
1993—GC Twins (GCL)........	C-3B	32	103	18	27	6	1	1	19	.262	14	19	0	120	23	5	.966
—Elizabethton (App.).....	C	9	24	3	5	1	0	0	3	.208	4	2	0	81	3	2	.977
1994—Elizabethton (App.).....	C-3B	54	210	23	44	5	0	9	27	.210	15	44	0	288	†50	12	.966
1995—Fort Wayne (Midw.).....	C-3B	112	383	59	124	26	5	19	65	.324	47	75	0	†736	†122	†23	.974
1996—Fort Myers (FSL)........	C-3B	87	338	34	89	26	1	7	54	.263	32	65	1	360	71	4	.991
—New Britain (Eastern) .	C-3B	48	165	22	39	8	0	3	14	.236	16	35	0	188	36	5	.978
1997—New Britain (Eastern) .	C-3B	102	370	41	90	17	0	8	50	.243	30	61	2	516	65	6	.990
—Minnesota (A.L.)	C	4	7	1	2	0	0	0	0	.286	0	3	0	11	2	0	1.000
Major league totals (1 year)		4	7	1	2	0	0	0	0	.286	0	3	0	11	2	0	1.000

VALENTIN, JOHN — IF — RED SOX

PERSONAL: Born February 18, 1967, in Mineola, N.Y. ... 6-0/180. ... Bats right, throws right. ... Full name: John William Valentin. ... Name pronounced VAL-en-tin.
HIGH SCHOOL: St. Anthony (Jersey City, N.J.).
COLLEGE: Seton Hall.

V

TRANSACTIONS/CAREER NOTES: Selected by Boston Red Sox organization in fifth round of free-agent draft (June 1, 1988). ... On Boston disabled list (April 1-20, 1993); included rehabilitation assignment to Pawtucket (April 16-20). ... On Boston disabled list (May 4-June 6, 1994); included rehabilitation assignment to Pawtucket (May 31-June 6). ... On disabled list (August 3-18, 1996).
HONORS: Named shortstop on THE SPORTING NEWS A.L. Silver Slugger team (1995).
STATISTICAL NOTES: Led New York-Pennsylvania League shortstops with .949 fielding percentage in 1988. ... Hit three home runs in one game (June 2, 1995). ... Led A.L. shortstops with 659 total chances in 1995. ... Hit for the cycle (June 6, 1996). ... Career major league grand slams: 2.
MISCELLANEOUS: Turned unassisted triple play while playing shortstop (July 8, 1994, sixth inning); 10th player ever to accomplish feat.

Year Team (League)	Pos.	G	AB	R	H	2B	3B	HR	RBI	Avg.	BB	SO	SB	PO	A	E	Avg.
1988—Elmira (N.Y.-Penn)	SS-3B	60	207	18	45	5	1	2	16	.217	36	35	5	96	175	14	†.951
1989—Winter Haven (FSL)	SS-3B	55	215	27	58	13	1	3	18	.270	13	29	4	99	177	12	.958
—Lynchburg (Caro.)	SS	75	264	47	65	7	2	8	34	.246	41	40	5	105	220	16	.953
1990—New Britain (Eastern)	SS	94	312	20	68	18	1	2	31	.218	25	46	1	139	266	21	.951
1991—New Britain (Eastern)	SS	23	81	8	16	3	0	0	5	.198	9	14	1	50	65	3	.975
—Pawtucket (Int'l)	SS	100	329	52	87	22	4	9	49	.264	60	42	0	184	300	25	.951
1992—Pawtucket (Int'l)	SS	97	331	47	86	18	1	9	29	.260	48	50	1	148	*358	20	.962
—Boston (A.L.)	SS	58	185	21	51	13	0	5	25	.276	20	17	1	79	182	10	.963
1993—Pawtucket (Int'l)	SS	2	9	3	3	0	0	1	1	.333	0	1	0	8	9	0	1.000
—Boston (A.L.)	SS	144	468	50	130	40	3	11	66	.278	49	77	3	238	432	20	.971
1994—Boston (A.L.)	SS-DH	84	301	53	95	26	2	9	49	.316	42	38	3	134	242	8	.979
—Pawtucket (Int'l)	SS	5	18	2	6	0	0	1	2	.333	3	4	0	7	16	3	.885
1995—Boston (A.L.)	SS	135	520	108	155	37	2	27	102	.298	81	67	20	227	*414	*18	.973
1996—Boston (A.L.)	SS-3B-DH	131	527	84	156	29	3	13	59	.296	63	59	9	202	357	17	.970
1997—Boston (A.L.)	2B-3B	143	575	95	176	*47	5	18	77	.306	58	66	7	239	380	22	.966
Major league totals (6 years)		695	2576	411	763	192	15	83	378	.296	313	324	43	1119	2007	95	.971

DIVISION SERIES RECORD

Year Team (League)	Pos.	G	AB	R	H	2B	3B	HR	RBI	Avg.	BB	SO	SB	PO	A	E	Avg.
1995—Boston (A.L.)	SS	3	12	1	3	1	0	1	2	.250	3	1	0	5	5	1	.909

VALENTIN, JOSE   SS   BREWERS

PERSONAL: Born October 12, 1969, in Manati, Puerto Rico. ... 5-10/166. ... Bats both, throws right. ... Full name: Jose Antonio Valentin. ... Brother of Javier Valentin, catcher, Minnesota Twins organization. ... Name pronounced VAL-un-TEEN.
TRANSACTIONS/CAREER NOTES: Signed as non-drafted free agent by San Diego Padres organization (October 12, 1986). ... On disabled list (April 16-May 1 and May 18-July 11, 1990). ... Traded by Padres with P Ricky Bones and OF Matt Mieske to Milwaukee Brewers for 3B Gary Sheffield and P Geoff Kellogg (March 27, 1992). ... On Milwaukee disabled list (April 14-May 5, 1997); included rehabilitation assignment to Beloit (May 3-5).
STATISTICAL NOTES: Led Texas League shortstops with 658 total chances in 1991. ... Led American Association shortstops with 639 total chances and 70 double plays in 1992. ... Led American Association shortstops with 211 putouts and 80 double plays in 1993. ... Led A.L. shortstops with 20 errors in 1994. ... Career major league grand slams: 3.

Year Team (League)	Pos.	G	AB	R	H	2B	3B	HR	RBI	Avg.	BB	SO	SB	PO	A	E	Avg.
1987—Spokane (N'west)	SS	70	244	52	61	8	2	2	24	.250	35	38	8	101	175	26	.914
1988—Char., S.C. (S. Atl.)	SS	133	444	56	103	20	1	6	44	.232	45	83	11	204	412	60	.911
1989—Riverside (Calif.)	SS	114	381	40	74	10	5	10	41	.194	37	93	8	*227	333	*46	.924
—Wichita (Texas)	SS-3B	18	49	8	12	1	0	2	5	.245	5	12	1	26	45	8	.899
1990—Wichita (Texas)	SS	11	36	4	10	2	0	0	2	.278	5	7	2	14	33	2	.959
1991—Wichita (Texas)	SS	129	447	73	112	22	5	17	68	.251	55	115	8	176	*442	40	.939
1992—Denver (A.A.)■	SS	*139	492	78	118	19	11	3	45	.240	53	99	9	*187	*414	*38	.941
—Milwaukee (A.L.)	SS-2B	3	3	1	0	0	0	0	1	.000	0	0	0	1	1	1	.667
1993—New Orleans (A.A.)	SS-1B	122	389	56	96	22	5	9	53	.247	47	87	9	†212	351	29	.951
—Milwaukee (A.L.)	SS	19	53	10	13	1	2	1	7	.245	7	16	1	20	51	6	.922
1994—Milwaukee (A.L.)	S-2-DH-3	97	285	47	68	19	0	11	46	.239	38	75	12	151	336	†20	.961
1995—Milwaukee (A.L.)	SS-DH-3B	112	338	62	74	23	3	11	49	.219	37	83	16	164	335	15	.971
1996—Milwaukee (A.L.)	SS	154	552	90	143	33	7	24	95	.259	66	145	17	243	460	*37	.950
1997—Milwaukee (A.L.)	SS-DH	136	494	58	125	23	1	17	58	.253	39	109	19	208	383	20	.967
—Beloit (Midwest)	SS	2	6	3	3	1	0	0	1	.500	2	1	0	1	8	0	1.000
Major league totals (6 years)		522	1725	268	423	99	13	64	256	.245	187	428	65	787	1566	99	.960

VALENZUELA, FERNANDO   P

PERSONAL: Born November 1, 1960, in Navojoa, Sonora, Mexico. ... 5-11/200. ... Throws left, bats left. ... Full name: Fernando Anguamea Valenzuela. ... Name pronounced VAL-en-ZWAY-luh.
TRANSACTIONS/CAREER NOTES: Contract sold by Puebla of Mexican League to Los Angeles Dodgers organization (July 6, 1979). ... On disabled list (July 31-September 26, 1988). ... Granted free agency (November 5, 1989). ... Re-signed by Dodgers (December 15, 1989). ... Granted free agency (November 5, 1990). ... Re-signed by Dodgers (December 19, 1990). ... Released by Dodgers (March 28, 1991). ... Signed by California Angels organization (May 20, 1991). ... On California disabled list (June 13-July 5, 1991). ... Released by Angels (July 5, 1991). ... Re-signed by Angels organization (July 10, 1991). ... Released by Angels organization (September 10, 1991). ... Signed by Toledo, Detroit Tigers organization (March 20, 1992). ... Loaned by Toledo to Jalisco of Mexican League (March 20-June 3, 1992). ... Contract acquired by Jalisco from Tigers organization (June 3, 1992). ... Signed as free agent by Baltimore Orioles organization (February 27, 1993). ... Granted free agency (October 29, 1993). ... Signed by Jalisco (1994). ... Signed as free agent by Philadelphia Phillies (June 24, 1994). ... Granted free agency (October 1994). ... Signed by Las Vegas, San Diego Padres organization (April 5, 1995). ... Granted free agency (November 11, 1995). ... Re-signed by Padres (December 7, 1995). ... Granted free agency (November 5, 1996). ... Re-signed by Padres (January 7, 1997). ... Traded by Padres with 3B Scott Livingstone and OF Phil Plantier to St. Louis Cardinals for P Danny Jackson, P Rich Batchelor and OF Mark Sweeney (June 13, 1997). ... Released by Cardinals (July 15, 1997).
RECORDS: Shares modern major league rookie-season record for most shutout games won or tied—8 (1981). ... Shares N.L. single-season record for fewest assists by pitcher who led league in assists—47 (1986).

HONORS: Named Major League Player of the Year by THE SPORTING NEWS (1981). ... Named N.L. Pitcher of the Year by THE SPORTING NEWS (1981). ... Named N.L. Rookie Pitcher of the Year by THE SPORTING NEWS (1981). ... Named lefthanded pitcher on THE SPORTING NEWS N.L. All-Star team (1981 and 1986). ... Named pitcher on THE SPORTING NEWS N.L. Silver Slugger team (1981 and 1983). ... Named N.L. Cy Young Award winner by Baseball Writers' Association of America (1981). ... Named N.L. Rookie of the Year by Baseball Writers' Association of America (1981). ... Won N.L. Gold Glove at pitcher (1986).

STATISTICAL NOTES: Led Mexican Center League with 13 wild pitches in 1978. ... Struck out 15 batters in one game (May 23, 1984). ... Led N.L. with 14 wild pitches in 1987. ... Pitched 6-0 no-hit victory against St. Louis (June 29, 1990).

MISCELLANEOUS: Appeared in one game as outfielder with no chances (1982). ... Struck out twice in two appearances as pinch-hitter (1989). ... Doubled and singled in two appearances as pinch-hitter (1990). ... Appeared in one game as first baseman with two putouts (1989). ... Singled and struck out twice in three games as pinch-hitter (1996). ... Singled in only appearance as pinch-hitter (1997).

Year Team (League)	W	L	Pct.	ERA	G	GS	CG	ShO	Sv.	IP	H	R	ER	BB	SO
1978— Guana. (Mex. Cen.)	5	6	.455	2.23	16	13	6	0	1	93	88	46	23	46	*91
1979— Yucatan (Mexican)	10	12	.455	2.49	26	26	12	2	0	181	157	68	50	70	141
— Lodi (California)■	1	2	.333	1.13	3	3	0	0	0	24	21	10	3	3	18
1980— San Antonio (Tex.)	13	9	.591	3.10	27	25	11	4	0	174	156	70	60	70	*162
— Los Angeles (N.L.)	2	0	1.000	0.00	10	0	0	0	1	18	8	2	0	5	16
1981— Los Angeles (N.L.)	13	7	.650	2.48	25	*25	*11	*8	0	*192	140	55	53	61	*180
1982— Los Angeles (N.L.)	19	13	.594	2.87	37	37	18	4	0	285	247	105	91	83	199
1983— Los Angeles (N.L.)	15	10	.600	3.75	35	35	9	4	0	257	245	*122	107	99	189
1984— Los Angeles (N.L.)	12	17	.414	3.03	34	34	12	2	0	261	218	109	88	*106	240
1985— Los Angeles (N.L.)	17	10	.630	2.45	35	35	14	5	0	272 1/3	211	92	74	101	208
1986— Los Angeles (N.L.)	*21	11	.656	3.14	34	34	*20	3	0	269 1/3	226	104	94	85	242
1987— Los Angeles (N.L.)	14	14	.500	3.98	34	34	•12	1	0	251	*254	120	111	*124	190
1988— Los Angeles (N.L.)	5	8	.385	4.24	23	22	3	0	1	142 1/3	142	71	67	76	64
1989— Los Angeles (N.L.)	10	13	.435	3.43	31	31	3	0	0	196 2/3	185	89	75	98	116
1990— Los Angeles (N.L.)	13	13	.500	4.59	33	33	5	2	0	204	223	112	*104	77	115
1991— Palm Springs (Calif.)■	0	0	...	0.00	1	1	0	0	0	4	4	1	0	3	2
— Midland (Texas)	3	1	.750	1.96	4	4	1	1	0	23	18	5	5	6	17
— California (A.L.)	0	2	.000	12.15	2	2	0	0	0	6 2/3	14	10	9	3	5
— Edmonton (PCL)	3	3	.500	7.12	7	7	0	0	0	36 2/3	48	34	29	17	36
1992— Jalisco (Mexican)■	10	9	.526	3.86	22	22	•13	0	0	156 1/3	154	81	67	51	98
1993— Baltimore (A.L.)■	8	10	.444	4.94	32	31	5	2	0	178 2/3	179	104	98	79	78
— Rochester (Int'l)	0	1	.000	10.80	1	1	0	0	0	3 1/3	6	4	4	3	1
— Bowie (Eastern)	0	0	...	1.50	1	1	0	0	0	6	4	1	1	0	4
1994— Jalisco (Mexican)■	10	3	.769	2.67	17	17	8	0	0	118	133	56	35	39	73
— Philadelphia (N.L.)■	1	2	.333	3.00	8	7	0	0	0	45	42	16	15	7	19
1995— San Diego (N.L.)■	8	3	.727	4.98	29	15	0	0	0	90 1/3	101	53	50	34	57
1996— San Diego (N.L.)	13	8	.619	3.62	33	31	0	0	0	171 2/3	177	78	69	67	95
1997— San Diego (N.L.)	2	8	.200	4.75	13	13	1	0	0	66 1/3	84	42	35	32	51
— St. Louis (N.L.)■	0	4	.000	5.56	5	5	0	0	0	22 2/3	22	19	14	14	10
A.L. totals (2 years)	8	12	.400	5.20	34	33	5	2	0	185 1/3	193	114	107	82	83
N.L. totals (15 years)	165	141	.539	3.43	419	391	108	29	2	2744 2/3	2525	1189	1047	1069	1991
Major league totals (17 years)	173	153	.531	3.54	453	424	113	31	2	2930	2718	1303	1154	1151	2074

DIVISION SERIES RECORD

Year Team (League)	W	L	Pct.	ERA	G	GS	CG	ShO	Sv.	IP	H	R	ER	BB	SO
1981— Los Angeles (N.L.)	1	0	1.000	1.06	2	2	1	0	0	17	10	2	2	3	10
1996— San Diego (N.L.)	0	0	...	0.00	1	0	0	0	0	2/3	0	0	0	2	1
Div. series totals (2 years)	1	0	1.000	1.02	3	2	1	0	0	17 2/3	10	2	2	5	11

CHAMPIONSHIP SERIES RECORD

RECORDS: Holds N.L. single-game record for most bases on balls allowed—8 (October 14, 1985). ... Shares N.L. single-series record for most bases on balls allowed—10 (1985).

Year Team (League)	W	L	Pct.	ERA	G	GS	CG	ShO	Sv.	IP	H	R	ER	BB	SO
1981— Los Angeles (N.L.)	1	1	.500	2.45	2	2	0	0	0	14 2/3	10	4	4	5	10
1983— Los Angeles (N.L.)	1	0	1.000	1.13	1	1	0	0	0	8	7	1	1	4	5
1985— Los Angeles (N.L.)	1	0	1.000	1.88	2	2	0	0	0	14 1/3	11	3	3	10	13
1988— Los Angeles (N.L.)							Did not play.								
Champ. series totals (3 years)	3	1	.750	1.95	5	5	0	0	0	37	28	8	8	19	28

WORLD SERIES RECORD

NOTES: Member of World Series championship team (1981 and 1988).

Year Team (League)	W	L	Pct.	ERA	G	GS	CG	ShO	Sv.	IP	H	R	ER	BB	SO
1981— Los Angeles (N.L.)	1	0	1.000	4.00	1	1	1	0	0	9	9	4	4	7	6
1988— Los Angeles (N.L.)							Did not play.								
World Series totals (1 years)	1	0	1.000	4.00	1	1	1	0	0	9	9	4	4	7	6

ALL-STAR GAME RECORD

RECORDS: Shares single-game record for most consecutive strikeouts—5 (July 15, 1986).

Year League	W	L	Pct.	ERA	GS	CG	ShO	Sv.	IP	H	R	ER	BB	SO
1981— National	0	0	...	0.00	1	0	0	0	1	2	0	0	0	0
1982— National	0	0	...	0.00	0	0	0	0	2/3	0	0	0	2	0
1983— National						Did not play.								
1984— National	0	0	...	0.00	0	0	0	0	2	2	0	0	0	3
1985— National	0	0	...	0.00	0	0	0	0	0	1	0	0	1	1
1986— National	0	0	...	0.00	0	0	0	0	3	1	0	0	0	5
All-Star totals (5 years)	0	0	...	0.00	1	0	0	0	7 2/3	5	0	0	3	9

V

VANDER WAL, JOHN   OF   ROCKIES

PERSONAL: Born April 29, 1966, in Grand Rapids, Mich. ... 6-2/198. ... Bats left, throws left. ... Full name: John Henry Vander Wal.
HIGH SCHOOL: Hudsonville (Mich.).
COLLEGE: Western Michigan.

TRANSACTIONS/CAREER NOTES: Selected by Houston Astros organization in eighth round of free-agent draft (June 4, 1984); did not sign. ... Selected by Montreal Expos organization in third round of free-agent draft (June 2, 1987). ... Contract sold by Expos with OF Ronnie Hall to Colorado Rockies (March 31, 1994).

RECORDS: Holds major league single-season record for most hits by pinch-hitter—28 (1995).

Year Team (League)	Pos.	G	AB	R	H	2B	3B	HR	RBI	Avg.	BB	SO	SB	PO	A	E	Avg.
1987—Jamestown (NYP)	OF	18	69	24	33	12	3	3	15	.478	3	14	3	20	0	0	1.000
—W.P. Beach (FSL)	OF	50	189	29	54	11	2	2	22	.286	30	25	8	103	1	3	.972
1988—W.P. Beach (FSL)	OF	62	231	50	64	15	2	10	33	.277	32	40	11	109	3	1	.991
—Jacksonville (South.)	OF	58	208	22	54	14	0	3	14	.260	17	49	3	99	0	0	1.000
1989—Jacksonville (South.)	OF	71	217	30	55	9	2	6	24	.253	22	51	2	72	3	1	.987
1990—Indianapolis (A.A.)	OF	51	135	16	40	6	0	2	14	.296	13	28	0	48	4	2	.963
—Jacksonville (South.)	OF	77	277	45	84	25	3	8	40	.303	39	46	6	106	4	1	.991
1991—Indianapolis (A.A.)	OF	133	478	84	140	36	8	15	71	.293	79	118	8	197	7	1	*.995
—Montreal (N.L.)	OF	21	61	4	13	4	1	1	8	.213	1	18	0	29	0	0	1.000
1992—Montreal (N.L.)	OF-1B	105	213	21	51	8	2	4	20	.239	24	36	3	122	6	2	.985
1993—Montreal (N.L.)	1B-OF	106	215	34	50	7	4	5	30	.233	27	30	6	271	14	4	.986
1994—Colorado (N.L.)■	1B-OF	91	110	12	27	3	1	5	15	.245	16	31	2	106	3	0	1.000
1995—Colorado (N.L.)	1B-OF	105	101	15	35	8	1	5	21	.347	16	23	1	51	4	2	.965
1996—Colorado (N.L.)	OF-1B	104	151	20	38	6	2	5	31	.252	19	38	2	72	2	1	.987
1997—Colorado (N.L.)	OF-1B-DH	76	92	7	16	2	0	1	11	.174	10	33	1	38	0	1	.974
—Colo. Springs (PCL)	1B-OF	25	103	29	42	12	1	3	19	.408	11	28	1	158	10	4	.977
Major league totals (7 years)		608	943	113	230	38	11	26	136	.244	113	209	15	689	29	10	.986

DIVISION SERIES RECORD

Year Team (League)	Pos.	G	AB	R	H	2B	3B	HR	RBI	Avg.	BB	SO	SB	PO	A	E	Avg.
1995—Colorado (N.L.)	PH	4	4	0	0	0	0	0	0	.000	0	2	0	...	...	...	...

VanLANDINGHAM, WILLIAM   P   ANGELS

PERSONAL: Born July 16, 1970, in Columbia, Tenn. ... 6-2/208. ... Throws right, bats right. ... Full name: William Joseph VanLandingham.
HIGH SCHOOL: Battle Ground Academy (Franklin, Tenn.).
COLLEGE: Kentucky.
TRANSACTIONS/CAREER NOTES: Selected by San Francisco Giants organization in fifth round of free-agent draft (June 3, 1991). ... On San Jose disabled list (May 30-July 14, 1992). ... On San Francisco disabled list (April 24-June 6, 1995); included rehabilitation assignment to San Jose (May 30-June 6). ... Released by Giants (August 8, 1997). ... Re-signed by Giants organization (August 19, 1997). ... Granted free agency (December 21, 1997). ... Signed by Anaheim Angels (January 10, 1998).
STATISTICAL NOTES: Led Northwest League with 25 wild pitches in 1991.

Year Team (League)	W	L	Pct.	ERA	G	GS	CG	ShO	Sv.	IP	H	R	ER	BB	SO
1991—Everett (Northwest)	•8	4	.667	4.09	15	15	0	0	0	77	58	43	35	*79	86
1992—San Jose (California)	1	3	.250	5.57	6	6	0	0	0	21	22	18	13	13	18
—Clinton (Midwest)	0	4	.000	5.67	10	10	0	0	0	54	49	40	34	29	59
1993—San Jose (California)	•14	8	.636	5.12	27	•27	1	0	0	163 1/3	167	103	*93	87	*171
—Phoenix (PCL)	0	1	.000	6.43	1	1	0	0	0	7	8	6	5	0	2
1994—Shreveport (Texas)	4	3	.571	2.81	8	8	1	0	0	51 1/3	41	21	16	11	45
—San Francisco (N.L.)	8	2	.800	3.54	16	14	0	0	0	84	70	37	33	43	56
—Phoenix (PCL)	1	1	.500	2.48	5	5	0	0	0	29	21	15	8	14	29
1995—San Jose (California)	1	0	1.000	0.00	1	1	0	0	0	6 2/3	4	0	0	2	5
—San Francisco (N.L.)	6	3	.667	3.67	18	18	1	0	0	122 2/3	124	58	50	40	95
1996—San Francisco (N.L.)	9	14	.391	5.40	32	32	0	0	0	181 2/3	196	123	109	78	97
1997—San Francisco (N.L.)	4	7	.364	4.96	18	17	0	0	0	89	80	56	49	59	52
—Phoenix (PCL)	1	1	.500	9.00	4	4	0	0	0	17	20	19	17	21	7
Major league totals (4 years)	27	26	.509	4.54	84	81	1	0	0	477 1/3	470	274	241	220	300

VARITEK, JASON   C   RED SOX

PERSONAL: Born April 11, 1972, in Rochester, Minn. ... 6-2/210. ... Bats both, throws right. ... Full name: Jason A. Varitek.
HIGH SCHOOL: Lake Brantley (Longwood, Fla.).
COLLEGE: Georgia Tech.
TRANSACTIONS/CAREER NOTES: Selected by Minnesota Twins organization first round (21st pick overall) of free-agent draft (June 3, 1993). ... Selected by Seattle Mariners organization in first round (14th pick overall) of free-agent draft (June 2, 1994). ... Traded by Mariners with P Derek Lowe to Boston Red Sox for P Heathcliff Slocumb (July 31, 1997).
STATISTICAL NOTES: Tied for Southern League lead in double plays by catcher with 10 in 1996. ... Led Southern League catchers with .993 fielding percentage and tied for lead with 10 double plays in 1996.

Year Team (League)	Pos.	G	AB	R	H	2B	3B	HR	RBI	Avg.	BB	SO	SB	PO	A	E	Avg.
1995—Port City (Southern)	C	104	352	42	79	14	3	10	44	.224	61	126	0	589	59	8	.988
1996—Port City (Southern)	C-3B-OF	134	503	63	132	34	1	12	67	.262	66	93	7	663	79	5	*.993
1997—Tacoma (PCL)	C	87	307	54	78	13	0	15	48	.254	34	71	0	613	49	3	*.995
—Pawtucket (Int'l)■	C	20	66	6	13	5	0	1	5	.197	8	12	0	123	10	1	.993
—Boston (A.L.)	C	1	1	0	1	0	0	0	0	1.000	0	0	0	1	0	0	1.000
Major league totals (1 year)		1	1	0	1	0	0	0	0	1.000	0	0	0	1	0	0	1.000

VAUGHN, GREG   OF   PADRES

PERSONAL: Born July 3, 1965, in Sacramento. ... 6-0/202. ... Bats right, throws right. ... Full name: Gregory Lamont Vaughn.
HIGH SCHOOL: John F. Kennedy (Sacramento).
JUNIOR COLLEGE: Sacramento City College.
COLLEGE: Miami (Fla.).

TRANSACTIONS/CAREER NOTES: Selected by St. Louis Cardinals organization in fifth round of free-agent draft (January 17, 1984); did not sign. ... Selected by Milwaukee Brewers organization in secondary phase of free-agent draft (June 4, 1984); did not sign. ... Selected by Pittsburgh Pirates organization in secondary phase of free-agent draft (January 9, 1985); did not sign. ... Selected by California Angels organization in secondary phase of free-agent draft (June 3, 1985); did not sign. ... Selected by Brewers organization in secondary phase of free-agent draft (June 2, 1986). ... On disabled list (May 26-June 10, 1990). ... On Milwaukee disabled list (April 8-27, 1994); included rehabilitation assignment to Beloit (April 25-27). ... Traded by Brewers with a player to be named later to San Diego Padres for P Bryce Florie, P Ron Villone and OF Marc Newfield (July 31, 1996); Padres acquired OF Gerald Parent to complete deal (September 16, 1996). ... Granted free agency (October 28, 1996). ... Re-signed by Padres (December 19, 1996). ... Traded by Padres with P Kerry Taylor and P Chris Clark to New York Yankees for P Kenny Rogers, IF Mariano Duncan and P Kevin Henthorne (July 4, 1997); trade later voided because Vaughn failed physical (July 6, 1997).

HONORS: Named Midwest League co-Most Valuable Player (1987). ... Named American Association Most Valuable Player (1989).

STATISTICAL NOTES: Led Midwest League with 292 total bases in 1987. ... Led Texas League with 279 total bases in 1988. ... Led American Association with .548 slugging percentage in 1989. ... Career major league grand slams: 3.

							BATTING								FIELDING		
Year Team (League)	Pos.	G	AB	R	H	2B	3B	HR	RBI	Avg.	BB	SO	SB	PO	A	E	Avg.
1986— Helena (Pioneer)	OF	66	258	64	75	13	2	16	54	.291	30	69	23	99	5	3	.972
1987— Beloit (Midwest)	OF	139	492	*120	150	31	6	*33	105	.305	102	115	36	247	11	10	.963
1988— El Paso (Texas)	OF	131	505	*104	152	*39	2	*28	*105	.301	63	120	22	216	12	7	.970
1989— Denver (A.A.)	OF	110	387	74	107	17	5	*26	*92	.276	62	94	20	140	4	3	.980
— Milwaukee (A.L.)	OF-DH	38	113	18	30	3	0	5	23	.265	13	23	4	32	1	2	.943
1990— Milwaukee (A.L.)	OF-DH	120	382	51	84	26	2	17	61	.220	33	91	7	195	8	7	.967
1991— Milwaukee (A.L.)	OF-DH	145	542	81	132	24	5	27	98	.244	62	125	2	315	5	2	.994
1992— Milwaukee (A.L.)	OF-DH	141	501	77	114	18	2	23	78	.228	60	123	15	288	6	3	.990
1993— Milwaukee (A.L.)	OF-DH	154	569	97	152	28	2	30	97	.267	89	118	10	214	1	3	.986
1994— Milwaukee (A.L.)	OF-DH	95	370	59	94	24	1	19	55	.254	51	93	9	162	5	3	.982
— Beloit (Midwest)	DH	2	6	1	1	0	0	0	0	.167	4	1	0	...	...	...	...
1995— Milwaukee (A.L.)	DH	108	392	67	88	19	1	17	59	.224	55	89	10	...	...	...	...
1996— Milwaukee (A.L.)	OF-DH	102	375	78	105	16	0	31	95	.280	58	99	5	192	5	4	.980
— San Diego (N.L.)■	OF	43	141	20	29	3	1	10	22	.206	24	31	4	74	2	2	.974
1997— San Diego (N.L.)	OF-DH	120	361	60	78	10	0	18	57	.216	56	110	7	153	7	1	.994
American League totals (8 years)		903	3244	528	799	158	13	169	566	.246	421	761	62	1398	31	24	.983
National League totals (2 years)		163	502	80	107	13	1	28	79	.213	80	141	11	227	9	3	.987
Major league totals (9 years)		1066	3746	608	906	171	14	197	645	.242	501	902	73	1625	40	27	.984

DIVISION SERIES RECORD

							BATTING								FIELDING		
Year Team (League)	Pos.	G	AB	R	H	2B	3B	HR	RBI	Avg.	BB	SO	SB	PO	A	E	Avg.
1996— San Diego (N.L.)	PH	3	3	0	0	0	0	0	0	.000	0	1	0	0	0	0	...

ALL-STAR GAME RECORD

					BATTING							FIELDING		
Year League	Pos.	AB	R	H	2B	3B	HR	RBI	Avg.	BB	SO	SB	PO	A	E	Avg.
1993— American	OF	1	1	1	0	0	0	0	1.000	0	0	0	0	0	0	...

VAUGHN, MO   1B   RED SOX

PERSONAL: Born December 15, 1967, in Norwalk, Conn. ... 6-1/240. ... Bats left, throws right. ... Full name: Maurice Samuel Vaughn.

HIGH SCHOOL: Trinity Pawling Prep (Pawling, N.Y.).

COLLEGE: Seton Hall.

TRANSACTIONS/CAREER NOTES: Selected by Boston Red Sox organization in first round (23rd pick overall) of free-agent draft (June 9, 1989). ... On disabled list (June 17-July 10, 1997).

HONORS: Named first baseman on THE SPORTING NEWS A.L. All-Star team (1995). ... Named first baseman on THE SPORTING NEWS A.L. Silver Slugger team (1995). ... Named A.L. Most Valuable Player by Baseball Writers' Association of America (1995).

STATISTICAL NOTES: Led A.L. with 20 intentional bases on balls received in 1994. ... Led A.L. first basemen with 103 double plays in 1994. ... Led A.L. first basemen with 1,368 total chances and 128 double plays in 1995. ... Hit three home runs in one game (September 24, 1996 and May 30, 1997). ... Career major league grand slams: 6.

V

							BATTING								FIELDING		
Year Team (League)	Pos.	G	AB	R	H	2B	3B	HR	RBI	Avg.	BB	SO	SB	PO	A	E	Avg.
1989— New Britain (Eastern)	1B	73	245	28	68	15	0	8	38	.278	25	47	1	541	45	•10	.983
1990— Pawtucket (Int'l)	1B	108	386	62	114	26	1	22	72	.295	44	87	3	828	60	11	.988
1991— Pawtucket (Int'l)	1B	69	234	35	64	10	0	14	50	.274	60	44	2	432	24	3	.993
— Boston (A.L.)	1B-DH	74	219	21	57	12	0	4	32	.260	26	43	2	378	26	6	.985
1992— Boston (A.L.)	1B-DH	113	355	42	83	16	2	13	57	.234	47	67	3	741	57	*15	.982
— Pawtucket (Int'l)	1B	39	149	15	42	6	0	6	28	.282	18	35	1	368	15	8	.980
1993— Boston (A.L.)	1B-DH	152	539	86	160	34	1	29	101	.297	79	130	4	1110	70	*16	.987
1994— Boston (A.L.)	1B-DH	111	394	65	122	25	1	26	82	.310	57	112	4	880	57	10	.989
1995— Boston (A.L.)	1B-DH	140	550	98	165	28	3	39	•126	.300	68	*150	11	*1262	95	11	.992
1996— Boston (A.L.)	1B-DH	161	635	118	207	29	1	44	143	.326	95	154	2	1207	74	*15	.988
1997— Boston (A.L.)	1B-DH	141	527	91	166	24	0	35	96	.315	86	154	2	1088	75	*14	.988
Major league totals (7 years)		892	3219	521	960	168	8	190	637	.298	458	810	28	6666	454	87	.988

DIVISION SERIES RECORD

							BATTING								FIELDING		
Year Team (League)	Pos.	G	AB	R	H	2B	3B	HR	RBI	Avg.	BB	SO	SB	PO	A	E	Avg.
1995— Boston (A.L.)	1B	3	14	0	0	0	0	0	0	.000	1	7	0	27	2	0	1.000

ALL-STAR GAME RECORD

					BATTING							FIELDING		
Year League	Pos.	AB	R	H	2B	3B	HR	RBI	Avg.	BB	SO	SB	PO	A	E	Avg.
1995— American	1B	2	0	0	0	0	0	0	.000	0	2	0	4	0	0	1.000

VAVREK, MIKE   P   ROCKIES

PERSONAL: Born April 23, 1974, in Winfield, Ill. ... 6-2/185. ... Throws left, bats left. ... Full name: Michael Vavrek.
HIGH SCHOOL: Driscoll Catholic (Addison, Ill.).
COLLEGE: Lewis (Ill.).
TRANSACTIONS/CAREER NOTES: Selected by Colorado Rockies organization in fifth round of free-agent draft (June 1, 1995).
HONORS: Named Eastern League Player of the Year (1997).

Year Team (League)	W	L	Pct.	ERA	G	GS	CG	ShO	Sv.	IP	H	R	ER	BB	SO
1995— Portland (Northwest)..........	0	0	...	0.00	3	3	0	0	0	14	8	0	0	3	14
—Asheville (S. Atl.).............	5	4	.556	2.00	12	12	1	0	0	76²/₃	64	24	17	25	54
1996— Salem (Carolina)	10	8	.556	4.87	26	25	2	1	0	149²/₃	167	92	81	59	103
1997— Salem (Carolina)	2	2	.500	2.15	10	9	0	0	0	62²/₃	55	21	15	18	48
—Nashville (Eastern).............	12	3	*.800	*2.57	17	17	2	0	0	122²/₃	94	38	35	34	101

VAZQUEZ, JAVIER   P   EXPOS

PERSONAL: Born July 25, 1976, in Ponce, Puerto Rico. ... 6-2/180. ... Throws right, bats right. ... Full name: Javier Carlos Vazquez.
HIGH SCHOOL: Colegio Ponceno (Ponce, Puerto Rico).
TRANSACTIONS/CAREER NOTES: Selected by Montreal Expos organization in fifth round of free-agent draft (June 2, 1994).

Year Team (League)	W	L	Pct.	ERA	G	GS	CG	ShO	Sv.	IP	H	R	ER	BB	SO
1994— G.C. Expos (GCL)	5	2	.714	2.53	15	11	1	1	0	67²/₃	37	25	19	15	56
1995— Albany (S. Atl.).................	6	6	.500	5.08	21	21	1	0	0	102²/₃	109	67	58	47	87
1996— Delmarva (S. Atl.)..............	14	3	*.824	2.68	27	27	1	0	0	164¹/₃	138	64	49	57	173
1997— Harrisburg (Eastern)	4	0	1.000	1.07	6	6	1	0	0	42	15	5	5	12	47
—W.P. Beach (FSL).................	6	3	.667	2.16	19	19	1	0	0	112²/₃	98	40	27	28	100

VELANDIA, JORGE   SS   ATHLETICS

PERSONAL: Born January 12, 1975, in Miranda, Venezuela. ... 5-9/160. ... Bats right, throws right. ... Full name: Jorge Macias Velandia.
TRANSACTIONS/CAREER NOTES: Signed as non-drafted free agent by Detroit Tigers organization (January 15, 1992). ... Traded by Tigers organization with 3B Scott Livingstone to San Diego Padres organization for P Gene Harris (May 11, 1994). ... Traded by Padres with P Doug Bochtler to Oakland Athletics for P Don Wengert and IF David Newhan (November 26, 1997).

Year Team (League)	Pos.	G	AB	R	H	2B	3B	HR	RBI	Avg.	BB	SO	SB	PO	A	E	Avg.
1992— Bristol (Appal.)	SS-2B	45	119	20	24	6	1	0	9	.202	15	16	3	54	88	12	.922
1993— Niag. Falls (NYP)	SS	72	212	30	41	11	0	1	22	.193	19	48	22	82	186	24	.918
—Fayetteville (SAL)	SS-2B-3B	37	106	15	17	4	0	0	11	.160	13	21	5	47	94	9	.940
1994— Lakeland (Fla. St.)	SS-2B-3B	22	60	8	14	4	0	0	3	.233	6	14	0	40	56	4	.960
—Springfield (Midw.)■ .	SS-2B	98	290	42	71	14	0	4	36	.245	21	46	5	118	303	26	.942
1995— Memphis (Southern)..	SS	63	186	23	38	10	2	0	17	.204	14	37	0	88	152	12	.952
—Las Vegas (PCL)	SS	66	206	25	54	12	3	0	25	.262	13	37	0	97	190	*31	.903
1996— Memphis (Southern)..	SS	122	392	42	94	19	0	9	48	.240	31	65	3	173	368	33	.943
1997— Las Vegas (PCL)	SS	114	405	46	110	15	2	3	35	.272	29	62	13	170	*347	21	.961
—San Diego (N.L.)	SS-2B-3B	14	29	0	3	2	0	0	0	.103	1	7	0	11	23	3	.919
Major league totals (1 year)		14	29	0	3	2	0	0	0	.103	1	7	0	11	23	3	.919

VELARDE, RANDY   IF   ANGELS

PERSONAL: Born November 24, 1962, in Midland, Texas. ... 6-0/192. ... Bats right, throws right. ... Full name: Randy Lee Velarde. ... Name pronounced vel-ARE-dee.
HIGH SCHOOL: Robert E. Lee (Midland, Texas).
COLLEGE: Lubbock (Texas) Christian College.
TRANSACTIONS/CAREER NOTES: Selected by Chicago White Sox organization in 19th round of free-agent draft (June 3, 1985). ... Traded by White Sox organization with P Pete Filson to New York Yankees for P Scott Nielsen and IF Mike Soper (January 5, 1987). ... On New York disabled list (August 9-29, 1989). ... On New York disabled list (June 6-July 30, 1993); included rehabilitation assignment to Albany/Colonie (July 24-30). ... Granted free agency (December 23, 1994). ... Re-signed by Oneonta, Yankees organization (April 12, 1995). ... Granted free agency (November 2, 1995). ... Signed by California Angels (November 11, 1995). ... Angels franchise renamed Anaheim Angels for 1997 season. ... On disabled list (March 23-September 1 and September 2, 1997-remainder of season).
STATISTICAL NOTES: Led Midwest League shortstops with 52 errors in 1986. ... Had 21-game hitting streak (June 9-July 4, 1996). ... Career major league grand slams: 1.

Year Team (League)	Pos.	G	AB	R	H	2B	3B	HR	RBI	Avg.	BB	SO	SB	PO	A	E	Avg.
1985— Niag. Falls (NYP)........	O-S-2-3	67	218	28	48	7	3	1	16	.220	35	72	8	124	117	15	.941
1986— Appleton (Midwest)....	SS-3B-OF	124	417	55	105	31	4	11	50	.252	58	96	13	205	300	†54	.903
—Buffalo (A.A.).............	SS	9	20	2	4	1	0	0	2	.200	2	4	1	9	28	3	.925
1987— Alb./Colon. (East.)■...	SS-OF	71	263	40	83	20	2	7	32	.316	25	47	8	128	254	17	.957
—Columbus (Int'l)........	SS	49	185	21	59	10	6	5	33	.319	15	36	8	100	164	16	.943
—New York (A.L.)..........	SS	8	22	1	4	0	0	0	1	.182	0	6	0	8	20	2	.933
1988— Columbus (Int'l)	SS-2B-3B	78	293	39	79	23	4	5	37	.270	25	71	7	123	271	25	.940
—New York (A.L.)..........	2B-SS-3B	48	115	18	20	6	0	5	12	.174	8	24	1	72	98	8	.955
1989— Columbus (Int'l)	SS-3B	103	387	59	103	26	3	11	53	.266	38	105	3	150	295	22	.953
—New York (A.L.)..........	3B-SS	33	100	12	34	4	2	2	11	.340	7	14	0	26	61	4	.956
1990— New York (A.L.).........3-S-O-2-DH		95	229	21	48	6	2	5	19	.210	20	53	0	70	159	12	.950
1991— New York (A.L.)..........	3B-SS-OF	80	184	19	45	11	1	1	15	.245	18	43	3	64	148	15	.934
1992— New York (A.L.).........	S-3-O-2	121	412	57	112	24	1	7	46	.272	38	78	7	179	257	15	.945
1993— New York (A.L.).........	O-S-3-DH	85	226	28	68	13	2	7	24	.301	18	39	2	102	92	9	.956
—Alb./Colon. (Eastern)..	SS-OF	5	17	2	4	0	0	1	2	.235	2	2	0	6	12	2	.900

V

Year Team (League)	Pos.	G	AB	R	H	2B	3B	HR	RBI	Avg.	BB	SO	SB	PO	A	E	Avg.
1994— New York (A.L.).........	S-3-0-2	77	280	47	78	16	1	9	34	.279	22	61	4	92	188	19	.936
1995— New York (A.L.).........	2-S-0-3	111	367	60	102	19	1	7	46	.278	55	64	5	168	258	10	.977
1996— California (A.L.)■...	2B-3B-SS	136	530	82	151	27	3	14	54	.285	70	118	7	255	306	16	.972
1997— Anaheim (A.L.)..........	PR	1	0	0	0	0	0	0	0	...	0	0	0	...	...	...	...
Major league totals (11 years)		795	2465	345	662	126	13	57	262	.269	256	500	29	1036	1587	110	.960

DIVISION SERIES RECORD

Year Team (League)	Pos.	G	AB	R	H	2B	3B	HR	RBI	Avg.	BB	SO	SB	PO	A	E	Avg.
1995— New York (A.L.)..........	2B-3B-OF	5	17	3	3	0	0	0	1	.176	6	4	0	15	11	1	.963

VELAZQUEZ, EDGARD   OF   ROCKIES

PERSONAL: Born December 15, 1975, in Santurce, Puerto Rico. ... 5-11/170. ... Bats right, throws right. ... Nephew of Roberto Clemente, outfielder with Pittsburgh Pirates (1955-72) and member of Baseball Hall of Fame.
HIGH SCHOOL: Colegio Hostos (Guaynabo, Puerto Rico).
TRANSACTIONS/CAREER NOTES: Selected by Colorado Rockies organization in 10th round of free-agent draft (June 3, 1993).
STATISTICAL NOTES: Tied for South Atlantic League record in double plays by outfielder with five in 1994. ... Led Carolina League outfielders with 296 total chances in 1995. ... Led Pacific Coast League with 5 double plays in 1997.

Year Team (League)	Pos.	G	AB	R	H	2B	3B	HR	RBI	Avg.	BB	SO	SB	PO	A	E	Avg.
1993— Ariz. Rockies (Ariz.)....	OF	39	147	20	36	4	2	2	20	.245	16	35	7	70	3	6	.924
1994— Asheville (S. Atl.)........	OF	119	447	50	106	22	3	11	39	.237	23	120	9	219	15	•12	.951
1995— Salem (Carolina)........	OF	131	497	74	149	25	6	13	69	.300	40	102	7	273	•16	7	.976
1996— New Haven (Eastern)..	OF	132	486	72	141	29	4	19	62	.290	53	114	6	215	9	5	.978
1997— Colo. Springs (PCL) ...	OF	120	438	70	123	24	10	17	73	.281	34	119	6	208	13	6	.974

VENTURA, ROBIN   3B   WHITE SOX

PERSONAL: Born July 14, 1967, in Santa Maria, Calif. ... 6-1/198. ... Bats left, throws right. ... Full name: Robin Mark Ventura.
HIGH SCHOOL: Righetti (Santa Maria, Calif.).
COLLEGE: Oklahoma State.
TRANSACTIONS/CAREER NOTES: Selected by Chicago White Sox organization in first round (10th pick overall) of free-agent draft (June 1, 1988). ... On suspended list (August 23-25, 1993). ... On disabled list (March 31-July 24, 1997); included rehabilitation assignments to Nashville (July 13-17) and Birmingham (July 18-22).
RECORDS: Holds A.L. single-season record for fewest chances accepted by third baseman for leader—372 (1996). ... Shares major league single-game record for most grand slams—2 (September 4, 1995).
HONORS: Named College Player of the Year by THE SPORTING NEWS (1987-88). ... Named third baseman on THE SPORTING NEWS college All-America team (1987-88). ... Named Golden Spikes Award winner by USA Baseball (1988). ... Won A.L. Gold Glove at third base (1991-93 and 1996).
STATISTICAL NOTES: Led Southern League with 12 intentional bases on balls received in 1989. ... Led Southern League third basemen with .930 fielding percentage and tied for lead with 21 double plays in 1989. ... Led A.L. third basemen with 18 errors in 1991. ... Led A.L. third basemen in putouts with 134 in 1991, 141 in 1992 and 133 in 1996. ... Led A.L. third basemen in total chances with 536 in 1992, 404 in 1993 and 382 in 1996. ... Led A.L. third basemen with 372 assists and tied for lead in double plays with 29 in 1992. ... Led A.L. third basemen in double plays with 22 in 1994 and 34 in 1996 and tied for lead with 29 in 1992. ... Career major league grand slams: 9.
MISCELLANEOUS: Member of 1988 U.S. Olympic baseball team.

Year Team (League)	Pos.	G	AB	R	H	2B	3B	HR	RBI	Avg.	BB	SO	SB	PO	A	E	Avg.
1989— Birmingham (Sou.).....	3B-1B-2B	129	454	75	126	25	2	3	67	.278	93	51	9	108	249	27	†.930
— Chicago (A.L.)............	3B	16	45	5	8	3	0	0	7	.178	8	6	0	17	33	2	.962
1990— Chicago (A.L.)............	3B-1B	150	493	48	123	17	1	5	54	.249	55	53	1	116	268	25	.939
1991— Chicago (A.L.)............	3B-1B	157	606	92	172	25	1	23	100	.284	80	67	2	†225	291	†18	.966
1992— Chicago (A.L.)............	3B-1B	157	592	85	167	38	1	16	93	.282	93	71	2	†141	†375	23	.957
1993— Chicago (A.L.)............	3B-1B	157	554	85	145	27	1	22	94	.262	105	82	1	119	278	14	.966
1994— Chicago (A.L.)............	3B-1B-SS	109	401	57	113	15	1	18	78	.282	61	69	3	89	180	20	.931
1995— Chicago (A.L.)............	3B-1B-DH	135	492	79	145	22	0	26	93	.295	75	98	4	201	216	19	.956
1996— Chicago (A.L.)............	3B-1B	158	586	96	168	31	2	34	105	.287	78	81	1	†189	247	11	.975
1997— Nashville (A.A.).........	3B	5	15	3	6	1	0	2	5	.400	2	1	0	1	12	0	1.000
— Birmingham (Sou.).....	3B	4	17	3	5	1	0	1	2	.294	1	1	0	2	3	2	.714
— Chicago (A.L.)............	3B	54	183	27	48	10	1	6	26	.262	34	21	0	53	99	7	.956
Major league totals (9 years)		1093	3952	574	1089	188	8	150	650	.276	589	548	14	1150	1987	139	.958

CHAMPIONSHIP SERIES RECORD

Year Team (League)	Pos.	G	AB	R	H	2B	3B	HR	RBI	Avg.	BB	SO	SB	PO	A	E	Avg.
1993— Chicago (A.L.)............	3B-1B	6	20	2	4	0	0	1	5	.200	6	6	0	9	6	1	.938

ALL-STAR GAME RECORD

Year League	Pos.	AB	R	H	2B	3B	HR	RBI	Avg.	BB	SO	SB	PO	A	E	Avg.
1992— American..................	3B	2	1	2	1	0	0	1	1.000	0	0	0	1	1	0	1.000

VERAS, DARIO   P   PADRES

PERSONAL: Born March 13, 1973, in Santiago, Dominican Republic. ... 6-1/155. ... Throws right, bats right. ... Full name: Dario Antonio Veras.
HIGH SCHOOL: Juan De Jesus (Pimental, Dominican Republic).

V

TRANSACTIONS/CAREER NOTES: Signed as non-drafted free agent by Los Angeles Dodgers organization (May 19, 1990). ... Selected by San Diego Padres organization in Rule 5 Minor League draft (December 12, 1993). ... On San Diego disabled list (April 23-May 9, 1997). ... On San Diego disabled list (May 17-July 28, 1997); included rehabilitation assignments to Mobile (June 8-16), Rancho Cucamonga (July 7-9) and Las Vegas (July 11-28).

Year— Team (League)	W	L	Pct.	ERA	G	GS	CG	ShO	Sv.	IP	H	R	ER	BB	SO
1991— Dom. Dodgers (DSL)	4	1	.800	2.53	20	0	0	0	6	32	28	11	9	4	22
1992— La Vega (DSL)	7	1	.875	*0.89	26	0	0	0	7	61	34	11	6	15	54
1993— Bakersfield (California)	1	0	1.000	7.43	7	0	0	0	0	13 1/3	13	11	11	8	11
— Vero Beach (FSL)	2	2	.500	2.80	24	0	0	0	02	54 2/3	59	23	17	14	31
1994— Rancho Cuca. (Calif.)■ ...	9	2	.818	2.05	*59	0	0	0	3	79	66	28	18	25	56
1995— Memphis (Southern)	7	3	.700	3.81	58	0	0	0	1	82 2/3	81	38	35	27	70
1996— Memphis (Southern)	3	1	.750	2.32	29	0	0	0	1	42 2/3	38	14	11	9	47
— Las Vegas (PCL)	6	2	.750	2.90	19	1	0	0	1	40 1/3	41	17	13	6	30
— San Diego (N.L.)	3	1	.750	2.79	23	0	0	0	0	29	24	10	9	10	23
1997— San Diego (N.L.)	2	1	.667	5.11	23	0	0	0	0	24 2/3	28	18	14	12	21
— Las Vegas (PCL)	0	2	.000	5.02	12	0	0	0	2	14 1/3	14	8	8	6	13
— Mobile (Southern)	0	0	...	9.00	5	2	0	0	0	5	8	5	5	3	5
— Rancho Cuca. (Cal.)	0	0	...	6.00	2	0	0	0	1	3	3	3	2	1	3
Major league totals (2 years)	5	2	.714	3.86	46	0	0	0	0	53 2/3	52	28	23	22	44

DIVISION SERIES RECORD

Year— Team (League)	W	L	Pct.	ERA	G	GS	CG	ShO	Sv.	IP	H	R	ER	BB	SO
1996— San Diego (N.L.)	0	0	...	0.00	2	0	0	0	0	1	1	0	0	0	1

VERAS, QUILVIO — 2B — PADRES

PERSONAL: Born April 3, 1971, in Santo Domingo, Dominican Republic. ... 5-9/166. ... Bats both, throws right. ... Full name: Quilvio Alberto Perez Veras.

HIGH SCHOOL: Victor E. Liz (Santo Domingo, Dominican Republic).

TRANSACTIONS/CAREER NOTES: Signed as non-drafted free agent by New York Mets organization (November 22, 1989). ... On suspended list (July 31-August 2, 1994). ... On disabled list (August 7-15, 1994). ... Traded by Mets to Florida Marlins for OF Carl Everett (November 29, 1994). ... On Florida disabled list (May 10-June 21, 1996); included rehabilitation assignment to Charlotte (June 13-21). ... Traded by Marlins to San Diego Padres for P Dustin Hermanson (November 21, 1996).

STATISTICAL NOTES: Tied for Appalachian League lead in double plays by second baseman with 30 in 1991. ... Led Appalachian League second basemen with 282 total chances in 1991. ... Led South Atlantic League in on-base percentage with .441 and in caught stealing with 35 in 1992. ... Led Eastern League in on-base percentage with .430 and in caught stealing with 19 in 1993. ... Led Eastern League second basemen with 669 total chances in 1993. ... Led International League in caught stealing with 18 in 1994. ... Led International League second basemen with 589 total chances and 84 double plays in 1994. ... Led N.L. in caught stealing with 21 in 1995. ... Career major league grand slams: 1.

Year— Team (League)	Pos.	G	AB	R	H	2B	3B	HR	RBI	Avg.	BB	SO	SB	PO	A	E	Avg.
1990— GC Mets (GCL)	2B	30	98	26	29	3	3	1	5	.296	19	16	16	45	76	3	.976
— Kingsport (Appal.)......	2B	24	94	21	36	6	0	1	14	.383	13	14	9	55	79	8	.944
1991— Kingsport (Appal.)......	2B	64	226	*54	76	11	4	1	16	.336	36	28	38	*113	*161	8	.972
— Pittsfield (NYP)	2B-SS	5	15	3	4	0	1	0	2	.267	5	1	2	16	16	1	.970
1992— Columbia (S. Atl.)......	2B	117	414	97	132	24	10	2	40	*.319	84	52	*66	208	313	20	.963
1993— Binghamton (East.)	2B	128	444	87	136	19	7	2	51	.306	*91	62	52	*274	*372	23	.966
1994— Norfolk (Int'l)	2B	123	457	71	114	22	4	0	43	.249	59	56	40	*267	*308	*14	.976
1995— Florida (N.L.)■	2B-OF	124	440	86	115	20	7	5	32	.261	80	68	*56	299	315	9	.986
1996— Florida (N.L.)	2B	73	253	40	64	8	1	4	14	.253	51	42	8	174	191	5	.986
— Charlotte (Int'l)..........	2B	28	104	22	34	5	2	2	8	.327	13	14	8	44	66	3	.973
1997— San Diego (N.L.)■	2B	145	539	74	143	23	1	3	45	.265	72	84	33	276	407	11	.984
Major league totals (3 years)		342	1232	200	322	51	9	12	91	.261	203	194	97	749	913	25	.985

V

VERES, DAVE — P — ROCKIES

PERSONAL: Born October 19, 1966, in Montgomery, Ala. ... 6-2/195. ... Throws right, bats right. ... Full name: David Scott Veres. ... Name pronounced VER-es.

HIGH SCHOOL: Gresham (Ore.).

JUNIOR COLLEGE: Mount Hood Community College (Ore.).

TRANSACTIONS/CAREER NOTES: Selected by Oakland Athletics organization in fourth round of free-agent draft (January 14, 1986). ... Traded by A's organization to Los Angeles Dodgers organization for P Kevin Campbell (January 15, 1991). ... Loaned by Dodgers organization to Mexico City Tigers of Mexican League (April 3-May 15, 1992). ... Released by Albuquerque, Dodgers organization (May 15, 1992). ... Signed by Houston Astros organization (May 28, 1992). ... Traded by Astros with C Raul Chavez to Montreal Expos for 3B Sean Berry (December 20, 1995). ... On disabled list (August 21-September 17, 1997). ... Traded by Expos with a player to be named later to Colorado Rockies for OF Terry Jones and a player to be named later (December 10, 1997).

STATISTICAL NOTES: Tied for California League lead with 29 wild pitches in 1987. ... Led Southern League with 16 wild pitches in 1989.

Year— Team (League)	W	L	Pct.	ERA	G	GS	CG	ShO	Sv.	IP	H	R	ER	BB	SO
1986— Medford (N'west)	5	2	.714	3.26	15	•15	0	0	0	77 1/3	58	38	28	57	60
1987— Modesto (California)	8	9	.471	4.79	26	26	2	0	0	148 1/3	124	90	79	108	124
1988— Modesto (California)	4	11	.267	3.31	19	19	3	0	0	125	100	61	46	78	91
— Huntsville (Southern)	3	4	.429	4.15	8	8	0	0	0	39	50	20	18	15	17
1989— Huntsville (Southern)	8	11	.421	4.86	29	28	2	1	0	159 1/3	160	93	86	83	105
1990— Tacoma (PCL)	11	8	.579	4.69	32	23	2	0	1	151 2/3	136	90	79	88	88
1991— Albuquerque (PCL)■	7	6	.538	4.47	57	3	0	0	5	100 2/3	89	52	50	52	81
1992— M.C. Tigers (Mex.)■	1	5	.167	8.10	14	1	0	0	1	23 1/3	29	21	21	12	12
— Tucson (PCL)■	2	3	.400	5.30	29	1	0	0	0	52 2/3	60	36	31	17	46
1993— Tucson (PCL)	6	10	.375	4.90	43	15	1	0	5	130 1/3	156	88	71	32	122
1994— Tucson (PCL)	1	1	.500	1.88	16	0	0	0	1	24	17	8	5	10	19
— Houston (N.L.)	3	3	.500	2.41	32	0	0	0	1	41	39	13	11	7	28

Year	Team (League)	W	L	Pct.	ERA	G	GS	CG	ShO	Sv.	IP	H	R	ER	BB	SO
1995—	Houston (N.L.)	5	1	.833	2.26	72	0	0	0	1	103 1/3	89	29	26	30	94
1996—	Montreal (N.L.)■	6	3	.667	4.17	68	0	0	0	4	77 2/3	85	39	36	32	81
1997—	Montreal (N.L.)	2	3	.400	3.48	53	0	0	0	1	62	68	28	24	27	47
	Major league totals (4 years)	16	10	.615	3.07	225	0	0	0	7	284	281	109	97	96	250

VERES, RANDY   P

PERSONAL: Born November 25, 1965, in San Francisco. ... 6-3/210. ... Throws right, bats right. ... Full name: Randolph Ruhland Veres. ... Name pronounced VER-es.

HIGH SCHOOL: Cordova (Rancho Cordova, Calif.).

COLLEGE: Sacramento City College.

TRANSACTIONS/CAREER NOTES: Selected by New York Mets organization in 32nd round of free-agent draft (June 4, 1984); did not sign. ... Selected by Milwaukee Brewers organization in secondary phase of free-agent draft (January 9, 1985). ... On disabled list (August 17, 1986-remainder of season). ... Signed as free agent by Richmond, Atlanta Braves organization (May 3, 1991). ... Released by Richmond (June 12, 1991). ... Signed by Phoenix, San Francisco Giants organization (June 19, 1991). ... Granted free agency (September 15, 1991). ... Re-signed by Giants organization (October 11, 1991). ... On disabled list (May 16-September 8, 1992). ... Granted free agency (October 15, 1992). ... Signed by Canton/Akron, Cleveland Indians organization (June 15, 1993). ... On disabled list (July 9-16, 1993). ... Granted free agency (October 15, 1993). ... Signed by Chicago Cubs organization (December 3, 1993). ... Released by Cubs (November 15, 1994). ... Signed by Charlotte, Florida Marlins organization (March 12, 1995). ... On Charlotte disabled list (April 6-25, 1995). ... On Florida disabled list (September 4, 1995-remainder of season). ... Traded by Marlins to Detroit Tigers for SS Matt Brunson (March 11, 1996). ... Granted free agency (October 15, 1996). ... Signed by Kansas City Royals organization (March 2, 1997). ... On Kansas City disabled list (June 24-August 25, 1997); included rehabilitation assignment to Omaha (July 26-August 25). ... Released by Royals (August 25, 1997).

Year	Team (League)	W	L	Pct.	ERA	G	GS	CG	ShO	Sv.	IP	H	R	ER	BB	SO
1985—	Helena (Pioneer)	7	4	.636	3.84	13	13	3	2	0	77 1/3	66	43	33	36	67
1986—	Beloit (Midwest)	4	12	.250	3.89	23	22	3	1	0	113 1/3	132	78	49	52	87
1987—	Beloit (Midwest)	10	6	.625	3.12	21	21	6	0	0	127	132	63	44	52	98
1988—	Stockton (California)	8	4	.667	3.35	20	14	1	1	0	110	94	54	41	77	96
	El Paso (Texas)	3	2	.600	3.66	6	6	0	0	0	39 1/3	35	18	16	12	31
1989—	El Paso (Texas)	2	3	.400	4.78	8	8	0	0	0	43 1/3	43	29	23	25	41
	Denver (Am. Assoc.)	6	7	.462	3.95	17	17	2	1	0	107	108	57	47	38	80
	Milwaukee (A.L.)	0	1	.000	4.32	3	1	0	0	0	8 1/3	9	5	4	4	8
1990—	Denver (Am. Assoc.)	1	6	.143	5.19	16	7	0	0	2	50 1/3	60	36	29	27	36
	Milwaukee (A.L.)	0	3	.000	3.67	26	0	0	0	1	41 2/3	38	17	17	16	16
1991—	Richmond (Int'l)■	0	2	.000	5.04	9	3	0	0	0	25	32	14	14	10	12
	Phoenix (PCL)■	3	0	1.000	3.56	19	1	0	0	1	43	42	26	17	14	41
1992—	Phoenix (PCL)	0	2	.000	8.10	12	0	0	0	0	13 1/3	12	12	12	13	13
1993—	Cant./Akr. (Eastern)■	1	5	.167	4.89	13	12	0	0	0	57	59	33	31	19	49
1994—	Iowa (Am. Assoc.)■	5	6	.455	2.93	33	3	0	0	5	55 1/3	43	25	18	11	42
	Chicago (N.L.)	1	1	.500	5.59	10	0	0	0	0	9 2/3	12	6	6	2	5
1995—	Charlotte (Int'l)■	1	0	1.000	2.70	6	0	0	0	1	6 2/3	3	2	2	5	5
	Florida (N.L.)	4	4	.500	3.88	47	0	0	0	1	48 2/3	46	25	21	22	31
1996—	Detroit (A.L.)■	0	4	.000	8.31	25	0	0	0	0	30 1/3	38	29	28	23	28
1997—	Kansas City (A.L.)■	4	0	1.000	3.31	24	0	0	0	1	35 1/3	36	17	13	7	28
	Omaha (Am. Assoc.)	1	1	.500	6.60	11	1	0	0	0	15	15	11	11	5	19
	A.L. totals (4 years)	4	8	.333	4.82	78	1	0	0	2	115 2/3	121	68	62	50	80
	N.L. totals (2 years)	5	5	.500	4.17	57	0	0	0	1	58 1/3	58	31	27	24	36
	Major league totals (6 years)	9	13	.409	4.60	135	1	0	0	3	174	179	99	89	74	116

VESSEL, ANDREW   OF   RANGERS

PERSONAL: Born March 11, 1975, in San Leandro, Calif. ... 6-3/225. ... Throws right, bats right.

HIGH SCHOOL: John F. Kennedy (Richmond, Calif.).

TRANSACTIONS/CAREER NOTES: Selected by Texas Rangers organization in third round of free-agent draft (June 3, 1993).

STATISTICAL NOTES: Led Gulf Coast League outfielders with four double plays in 1993.

							BATTING							FIELDING		
Year	Team (League)	Pos.	G	AB	R	H	2B	3B	HR	RBI	Avg.	BB	SO	SB	PO	A	E	Avg.
1993—	GC Rangers (GCL)	OF	51	192	23	42	10	2	1	31	.219	8	26	6	81	*12	0	*1.000
1994—	Char., S.C. (S. Atl.)	OF	114	411	40	99	23	2	8	55	.241	29	102	7	181	13	1	.995
1995—	Charlotte (Fla. St.)	OF	129	498	67	132	26	2	9	78	.265	32	75	3	218	9	6	.974
1996—	Charlotte (Fla. St.)	OF	126	484	63	111	25	6	3	67	.229	45	94	1	241	14	3	.988
1997—	Tulsa (Texas)	OF	*138	517	78	135	35	1	12	75	.261	41	87	3	225	9	8	.967

VIANO, JAKE   P   ROCKIES

PERSONAL: Born September 4, 1973, in Los Altos, Calif. ... 5-10/177. ... Throws right, bats right. ... Full name: Jacob Viano.

JUNIOR COLLEGE: Long Beach (Calif.) City College.

TRANSACTIONS/CAREER NOTES: Selected by Colorado Rockies organization in 11th round of free-agent draft (June 3, 1993). ... On New Haven disabled list (May 20-June 9, 1996).

Year	Team (League)	W	L	Pct.	ERA	G	GS	CG	ShO	Sv.	IP	H	R	ER	BB	SO
1993—	Ariz. Rockies (Ariz.)	2	2	.500	3.27	22	1	0	0	1	33	24	15	12	6	32
1994—	Asheville (S. Atl.)	4	1	.800	1.35	41	0	0	0	23	53 1/3	36	11	8	24	58
	New Haven (Eastern)	0	3	.000	2.38	8	0	0	0	0	11 1/3	7	7	3	8	14
1995—	New Haven (Eastern)	3	6	.333	3.38	57	0	0	0	19	72	51	31	27	38	85
1996—	Colo. Springs (PCL)	0	2	.000	10.89	7	3	0	0	0	20 2/3	33	25	25	13	12
	New Haven (Eastern)	4	3	.571	4.84	23	5	0	0	0	44 2/3	39	28	24	24	32
1997—	St. Petersburg (FSL)	3	4	.429	3.15	31	2	0	0	1	60	62	23	21	18	68

VIDRO, JOSE   3B   EXPOS

PERSONAL: Born August 27, 1974, in Mayaguez, Puerto Rico. ... 6-0/185. ... Bats both, throws right. ... Full name: Jose Angel Cetty Vidro.
HIGH SCHOOL: Blanca Morales (Sabana Grande, Puerto Rico).
TRANSACTIONS/CAREER NOTES: Selected by Montreal Expos organization in sixth round of free agent draft (June 1, 1992). ... On disabled list (June 1-June 15, 1993). ... On disabled list (July 26, 1993-remainder of season).

Year Team (League)	Pos.	G	AB	R	H	2B	3B	HR	RBI	Avg.	BB	SO	SB	PO	A	E	Avg.
1992—G.C. Expos (GCL)	2B	54	200	29	66	6	2	4	31	.330	16	31	10	114	107	4	*.982
1993—Burl. (Midw.)	2B	76	287	39	69	19	0	2	34	.240	28	54	3	107	153	7	.974
1994—W.P. Beach (FSL)	2B	125	465	57	124	30	2	4	49	.267	51	56	8	204	328	20	.964
1995—W.P. Beach (FSL)	IF	44	163	20	53	15	2	3	24	.325	8	21	0	101	110	4	.981
—Harrisburg (Eastern)	IF	64	246	33	64	16	2	4	38	.260	20	37	7	97	162	9	.966
1996—Harrisburg (Eastern)	IF	126	452	57	117	25	3	18	82	.259	29	71	3	135	271	15	.964
1997—Ottawa (Int'l)	3B-2B	73	279	40	90	17	0	13	47	.323	22	40	2	70	161	8	.967
—Montreal (N.L.)	3B-DH-2B	67	169	19	42	12	1	2	17	.249	11	20	1	25	59	4	.955
Major league totals (1 year)		67	169	19	42	12	1	2	17	.249	11	20	1	25	59	4	.955

VILLANO, MIKE   P   MARLINS

PERSONAL: Born August 10, 1971, in Bay City, Mich. ... 6-0/200. ... Throws right, bats right. ... Full name: Michael John Villano.
HIGH SCHOOL: Handy (Bay City, Mich.).
COLLEGE: Saginaw Valley State (Mich.).
TRANSACTIONS/CAREER NOTES: Selected by San Francisco Giants organization in 25th round of free-agent draft (June 2, 1994). ... Traded by Giants with P Joe Fontenot and P Mick Pageler to Florida Marlins for P Robb Nen (November 18, 1997).

Year Team (League)	W	L	Pct.	ERA	G	GS	CG	ShO	Sv.	IP	H	R	ER	BB	SO
1995—Burlington (Midw.)	3	1	.750	2.84	16	0	0	0	1	25 1/3	20	12	8	21	29
—San Jose (California)	0	1	.000	1.65	21	0	0	0	1	32 2/3	27	7	6	11	42
1996—San Jose (California)	7	1	.875	0.72	39	2	0	0	8	88	48	12	7	33	133
—Shreveport (Texas)	2	0	1.000	3.00	2	2	0	0	0	12	6	4	4	8	7
1997—Shreveport (Texas)	3	1	.750	6.29	30	0	0	0	2	34 1/3	41	25	24	20	26
—Phoenix (PCL)	5	3	.625	4.16	13	11	0	0	0	71 1/3	75	36	33	27	41

VILLONE, RON   P   INDIANS

PERSONAL: Born January 16, 1970, in Englewood, N.J. ... 6-3/235. ... Throws left, bats left. ... Full name: Ronald Thomas Villone Jr.
COLLEGE: Massachusetts.
TRANSACTIONS/CAREER NOTES: Selected by Seattle Mariners in first round (14th pick overall) of free-agent draft (June 1, 1992). ... On disabled list (April 19-26, 1994). ... Traded by Mariners with OF Marc Newfield to San Diego Padres for P Andy Benes and a player to be named later (July 31, 1995); Mariners acquired P Greg Keagle to complete deal (September 16, 1995). ... Traded by Padres with P Bryce Florie and OF Marc Newfield to Milwaukee Brewers for OF Greg Vaughn and a player to be named later (July 31, 1996); Padres acquired OF Gerald Parent to complete deal (September 16, 1996). ... Traded by Brewers with P Ben McDonald and P Mike Fetters to Cleveland Indians for OF Marquis Grissom and P Jeff Juden (December 8, 1997).
MISCELLANEOUS: Member of 1992 U.S. Olympic baseball team.

Year Team (League)	W	L	Pct.	ERA	G	GS	CG	ShO	Sv.	IP	H	R	ER	BB	SO
1993—Riverside (California)	7	4	.636	4.21	16	16	0	0	0	83 1/3	74	47	39	62	82
—Jacksonville (Southern)	3	4	.429	4.38	11	11	0	0	0	63 2/3	49	34	31	41	66
1994—Jacksonville (Southern)	6	7	.462	3.86	41	5	0	0	8	79 1/3	56	37	34	68	94
1995—Seattle (A.L.)	0	2	.000	7.91	19	0	0	0	0	19 1/3	20	19	17	23	26
—Tacoma (PCL)	1	0	1.000	0.61	22	0	0	0	13	29 2/3	9	6	2	19	43
—San Diego (N.L.)■	2	1	.667	4.21	19	0	0	0	1	25 2/3	24	12	12	19	37
1996—Las Vegas (PCL)	2	1	.667	1.64	23	0	0	0	3	22	13	5	4	9	29
—San Diego (N.L.)	1	1	.500	2.95	21	0	0	0	0	18 1/3	17	6	6	7	19
—Milwaukee (A.L.)■	0	0	...	3.28	23	0	0	0	2	24 2/3	14	9	9	18	19
1997—Milwaukee (A.L.)	1	0	1.000	3.42	50	0	0	0	0	52 2/3	54	23	20	36	40
A.L. totals (3 years)	1	2	.333	4.28	92	0	0	0	2	96 2/3	88	51	46	77	85
N.L. totals (2 years)	3	2	.600	3.68	40	0	0	0	1	44	41	18	18	18	56
Major league totals (3 years)	4	4	.500	4.09	132	0	0	0	3	140 2/3	129	69	64	95	141

VINA, FERNANDO   2B   BREWERS

PERSONAL: Born April 16, 1969, in Sacramento. ... 5-9/170. ... Bats left, throws right. ... Name pronounced VEEN-ya.
HIGH SCHOOL: Valley (Sacramento).
JUNIOR COLLEGE: Cosumnes River College (Calif.), then Sacramento City College.
COLLEGE: Arizona State.
TRANSACTIONS/CAREER NOTES: Selected by New York Yankees organization in 51st round of free-agent draft (June 1, 1988); did not sign. ... Selected by New York Mets organization in ninth round of free-agent draft (June 4, 1990). ... Selected by Seattle Mariners from Mets organization in Rule 5 major league draft (December 7, 1992). ... Returned to Mets organization (June 15, 1993). ... On New York disabled list (May 22-June 6, 1994). ... On Norfolk disabled list (August 30-September 6, 1994). ... Traded by Mets to Milwaukee Brewers (December 22, 1994), completing deal in which Brewers traded P Doug Henry for two players to be named later (November 30, 1994); Brewers acquired C Javier Gonzalez as partial completion of deal (December 6, 1994). ... Re-signed by Brewers (November 25, 1996). ... On Milwaukee disabled list (April 20-July 17, 1997); included rehabilitation assignments to Stockton (July 9-11) and Tucson (July 12-17).
STATISTICAL NOTES: Tied for South Atlantic League lead in caught stealing with 22 in 1991. ... Led South Atlantic League second basemen with 600 total chances and 61 double plays in 1991. ... Led Florida State League second basemen with 85 double plays in 1992. ... Led N.L. in being hit by pitch with 12 in 1994. ... Led A.L. second basemen with 116 double plays in 1996. ... Career major league grand slams: 1.

Year	Team (League)	Pos.	G	AB	R	H	2B	3B	HR	RBI	Avg.	BB	SO	SB	PO	A	E	Avg.
1991—	Columbia (S. Atl.)......	2B	129	498	77	135	23	6	6	50	.271	46	27	42	194	*385	21	*.965
1992—	St. Lucie (Fla. St.)	2B	111	421	61	124	15	5	1	42	.295	32	26	36	219	*360	17	.971
	—Tidewater (Int'l)	2B	11	30	3	6	0	0	0	2	.200	0	2	0	16	28	1	.978
1993—	Seattle (A.L.)■	2B-SS-DH	24	45	5	10	2	0	0	2	.222	4	3	6	28	40	0	1.000
	—Norfolk (Int'l)■	SS-2B-OF	73	287	24	66	6	4	4	27	.230	7	17	16	146	232	14	.964
1994—	New York (N.L.)......	2-3-S-O	79	124	20	31	6	0	0	6	.250	12	11	3	46	59	4	.963
	—Norfolk (Int'l)	SS-2B	6	17	2	3	0	0	0	1	.176	1	1	1	9	11	1	.952
1995—	Milwaukee (A.L.)■...	2B-SS-3B	113	288	46	74	7	7	3	29	.257	22	28	6	194	245	8	.982
1996—	Milwaukee (A.L.).......	2B	140	554	94	157	19	10	7	46	.283	38	35	16	*333	412	*16	.979
1997—	Milwaukee (A.L.)	2B-DH	79	324	37	89	12	2	4	28	.275	12	23	8	149	227	7	.982
	—Stockton (California) ..	2B	3	9	2	4	0	1	0	3	.444	0	0	0	2	7	0	1.000
	—Tucson (PCL)	2B	6	19	3	9	3	0	1	5	.474	3	1	0	8	16	2	.923
American League totals (4 years)			356	1211	182	330	40	19	14	105	.273	76	89	36	704	924	31	.981
National League totals (1 year)			79	124	20	31	6	0	0	6	.250	12	11	3	46	59	4	.963
Major league totals (5 years)			435	1335	202	361	46	19	14	111	.270	88	100	39	750	983	35	.980

VINAS, JULIO   C   PIRATES

PERSONAL: Born February 14, 1973, in Miami. ... 6-1/205. ... Bats right, throws right. ... Full name: Julio C. Vinas.
HIGH SCHOOL: American (Hialeah, Fla.).
TRANSACTIONS/CAREER NOTES: Selected by Chicago White Sox organization in 33rd round of free-agent draft (June 3, 1991). ... Granted free agency (October 15, 1997). ... Signed by Pittsburgh Pirates organization (December 18, 1997).

Year	Team (League)	Pos.	G	AB	R	H	2B	3B	HR	RBI	Avg.	BB	SO	SB	PO	A	E	Avg.
1991—	GC Whi. Sox (GCL)	1B-C-OF	50	187	21	42	9	0	3	29	.225	19	40	2	381	31	13	.969
1992—	Utica (N.Y.-Penn)......	C-1B	47	151	22	37	6	4	0	24	.245	11	29	1	320	37	9	.975
	—South Bend (Mid.)......	C-1B	33	94	7	16	3	0	0	10	.170	9	17	1	220	20	5	.980
1993—	South Bend (Mid.)......	C	55	188	24	60	15	1	9	37	.319	12	29	1	333	30	12	.968
	—Sarasota (Fla. St.)......	C	18	65	5	16	2	1	1	7	.246	5	13	0	93	14	2	.982
1994—	South Bend (Mid.)......	C	121	466	68	118	31	1	9	75	.253	43	75	0	697	90	8	.990
1995—	Birmingham (Sou.)......	C-1B	102	372	47	100	16	2	6	61	.269	37	80	3	425	53	10	.980
1996—	Nashville (A.A.)	C-1B-3B	104	338	48	80	18	2	11	52	.237	36	63	1	584	61	6	.991
1997—	Nashville (A.A.)	C-1B-3B	91	314	39	73	12	2	11	41	.232	25	72	4	331	32	8	.978

VITIELLO, JOE   OF   ROYALS

PERSONAL: Born April 11, 1970, in Cambridge, Mass. ... 6-3/230. ... Bats right, throws right. ... Full name: Joseph David Vitiello. ... Name pronounced VIT-ee-ELL-oh.
HIGH SCHOOL: Stoneham (Mass.).
COLLEGE: Alabama.
TRANSACTIONS/CAREER NOTES: Selected by New York Yankees organization in 31st round of free-agent draft (June 1, 1988); did not sign. ... Selected by Kansas City Royals organization in first round (seventh pick overall) of free-agent draft (June 3, 1991). ... On disabled list (April 12-23, 1992; June 2-11, 1993; and May 23-June 16, 1994). ... On Kansas City disabled list (June 17-July 28 and August 13, 1997-remainder of season); included rehabilitation assignment to Omaha (July 15-28).
STATISTICAL NOTES: Led American Association with .440 on-base percentage in 1994.

Year	Team (League)	Pos.	G	AB	R	H	2B	3B	HR	RBI	Avg.	BB	SO	SB	PO	A	E	Avg.
1991—	Eugene (Northwest) ...	OF-1B	19	64	16	21	2	0	6	21	.328	11	18	1	49	4	1	.981
	—Memphis (Southern)..	OF-1B	36	128	15	28	4	1	0	18	.219	23	36	0	77	4	1	.988
1992—	Baseball City (FSL).....	1B	115	400	52	113	16	1	8	65	.283	46	101	0	879	44	13	.986
1993—	Memphis (Southern)..	1B	117	413	62	119	25	2	15	66	.288	57	95	2	830	53	•17	.981
1994—	Omaha (A.A.)..............	1B	98	352	46	121	28	3	10	61	*.344	56	63	3	605	46	8	.988
1995—	Kansas City (A.L.)	DH-1B	53	130	13	33	4	0	7	21	.254	8	25	0	51	3	1	.982
	—Omaha (A.A.)..............	1B-OF	59	229	33	64	14	2	12	42	.279	12	50	0	225	21	4	.984
1996—	Kansas City (A.L.)	DH-1B-OF	85	257	29	62	15	1	8	40	.241	38	69	2	40	5	0	1.000
	—Omaha (A.A.)..............	1B	36	132	26	37	7	0	9	31	.280	16	32	1	281	20	3	.990
1997—	Kansas City (A.L.)	OF-DH-1B	51	130	11	31	6	0	5	18	.238	14	37	0	56	0	1	.982
	—Omaha (A.A.)..............	OF	13	42	5	9	1	0	3	9	.214	5	16	0	1	0	0	1.000
Major league totals (3 years)			189	517	53	126	25	1	20	79	.244	60	131	2	147	8	2	.987

V

VIZCAINO, JOSE   SS   DODGERS

PERSONAL: Born March 26, 1968, in San Cristobal, Dominican Republic. ... 6-1/180. ... Bats both, throws right. ... Full name: Jose Luis Pimental Vizcaino. ... Name pronounced VIS-ky-EE-no.
HIGH SCHOOL: Americo Tolentino (Palenque de San Cristobal, Dominican Republic).
TRANSACTIONS/CAREER NOTES: Signed as non-drafted free agent by Los Angeles Dodgers organization (February 18, 1986). ... Traded by Dodgers to Chicago Cubs for IF Greg Smith (December 14, 1990). ... On disabled list (April 20-May 6 and August 26-September 16, 1992). ... Traded by Cubs to New York Mets for P Anthony Young and P Ottis Smith (March 30, 1994). ... Traded by Mets with IF Jeff Kent to Cleveland Indians for 2B Carlos Baerga and IF Alvaro Espinoza (July 29, 1996). ... Traded by Indians with IF Jeff Kent, P Julian Tavarez and a player to be named later to San Francisco Giants for 3B Matt Williams and a player to be named later (November 13, 1996); Indians traded P Joe Roa to Giants for OF Trenidad Hubbard to complete deal (December 16, 1996). ... Granted free agency (October 29, 1997). ... Signed by Dodgers (December 8, 1997).
STATISTICAL NOTES: Led Gulf Coast League shortstops with 23 double plays in 1987. ... Led Pacific Coast League shortstops with 611 total chances and 82 double plays in 1989. ... Tied for N.L. lead in fielding percentage by shortstop with .984 and assists by shortstop with 411 in 1995.

Year	Team (League)	Pos.	G	AB	R	H	2B	3B	HR	RBI	Avg.	BB	SO	SB	PO	A	E	Avg.
1987—GC Dodgers (GCL)	SS-1B	49	150	26	38	5	1	0	12	.253	22	24	8	73	107	13	.933	
1988—Bakersfield (Calif.)	SS	122	433	77	126	11	4	0	38	.291	50	54	13	185	340	30	.946	
1989—Albuquerque (PCL)	SS	129	434	60	123	10	4	1	44	.283	33	41	16	*191	*390	*30	.951	
—Los Angeles (N.L.)	SS	7	10	2	2	0	0	0	0	.200	0	1	0	6	9	2	.882	
1990—Albuquerque (PCL)	2B-SS	81	276	46	77	10	2	2	38	.279	30	33	13	141	229	14	.964	
—Los Angeles (N.L.)	SS-2B	37	51	3	14	1	1	0	2	.275	4	8	1	23	27	2	.962	
1991—Chicago (N.L.)■	3B-SS-2B	93	145	7	38	5	0	0	10	.262	5	18	2	49	118	7	.960	
1992—Chicago (N.L.)	SS-3B-2B	86	285	25	64	10	4	1	17	.225	14	35	3	93	195	9	.970	
1993—Chicago (N.L.)	SS-3B-2B	151	551	74	158	19	4	4	54	.287	46	71	12	217	410	17	.974	
1994—New York (N.L.)■	SS	103	410	47	105	13	3	3	33	.256	33	62	1	136	291	13	.970	
1995—New York (N.L.)	SS-2B	135	509	66	146	21	5	3	56	.287	35	76	8	189	‡411	10	‡.984	
1996—New York (N.L.)	2B	96	363	47	110	12	6	1	32	.303	28	58	9	179	259	6	.986	
—Cleveland (A.L.)	2B-SS-DH	48	179	23	51	5	2	0	13	.285	7	24	6	82	135	4	.982	
1997—San Fran. (N.L.)■	SS-2B	151	568	77	151	19	7	5	50	.266	48	87	8	206	450	16	.976	
American League totals (1 year)		48	179	23	51	5	2	0	13	.285	7	24	6	82	135	4	.982	
National League totals (9 years)		859	2892	348	788	100	30	17	254	.272	213	416	44	1098	2170	82	.976	
Major league totals (9 years)		907	3071	371	839	105	32	17	267	.273	220	440	50	1180	2305	86	.976	

DIVISION SERIES RECORD

Year	Team (League)	Pos.	G	AB	R	H	2B	3B	HR	RBI	Avg.	BB	SO	SB	PO	A	E	Avg.
1996—Cleveland (A.L.)	2B	3	12	1	4	2	0	0	1	.333	1	1	0	4	3	1	.875	
1997—San Francisco (N.L.)	SS	3	11	1	2	1	0	0	0	.182	0	5	0	3	10	0	1.000	
Division series totals (2 years)		6	23	2	6	3	0	0	1	.261	1	6	0	7	13	1	.952	

VIZQUEL, OMAR   SS   INDIANS

PERSONAL: Born April 24, 1967, in Caracas, Venezuela. ... 5-9/170. ... Bats both, throws right. ... Full name: Omar Enrique Vizquel. ... Name pronounced vis-KEL.

HIGH SCHOOL: Francisco Espejo (Caracas, Venezuela).

TRANSACTIONS/CAREER NOTES: Signed as non-drafted free agent by Seattle Mariners organization (April 1, 1984). ... On Seattle disabled list (April 7-May 13, 1990); included rehabilitation assignments to Calgary (May 3-7) and San Bernardino (May 8-12). ... On Seattle disabled list (April 13-May 11, 1992); included rehabilitation assignment to Calgary (May 5-11). ... Traded by Mariners to Cleveland Indians for SS Felix Fermin, 1B Reggie Jefferson and cash (December 20, 1993). ... On Cleveland disabled list (April 23-June 13, 1994); included rehabilitation assignment to Charlotte (June 6-13).

RECORDS: Shares major league career record for highest fielding percentage by shortstop (1,000 or more games)—.980.

HONORS: Won A.L. Gold Glove at shortstop (1993-97).

STATISTICAL NOTES: Led Midwest League shortstops with .969 fielding percentage in 1986. ... Tied for A.L. lead in double plays by shortstop with 108 in 1993. ... Led A.L. in sacrifice hits with 16 in 1997. ... Career major league grand slams: 2.

MISCELLANEOUS: Batted righthanded only (1984-88).

Year	Team (League)	Pos.	G	AB	R	H	2B	3B	HR	RBI	Avg.	BB	SO	SB	PO	A	E	Avg.
1984—Butte (Pioneer)	SS-2B	15	45	7	14	2	0	0	4	.311	3	8	2	13	29	5	.894	
1985—Bellingham (N'west)	SS-2B	50	187	24	42	9	0	5	17	.225	12	27	4	85	175	19	.932	
1986—Wausau (Midwest)	SS-2B	105	352	60	75	13	2	4	28	.213	64	56	19	153	328	16	†.968	
1987—Salinas (Calif.)	SS-2B	114	407	61	107	12	8	0	38	.263	57	55	25	81	295	25	.938	
1988—Vermont (Eastern)	SS	103	374	54	95	18	2	2	35	.254	42	44	30	173	268	19	*.959	
—Calgary (PCL)	SS	33	107	10	24	2	3	1	12	.224	5	14	2	43	92	6	.957	
1989—Calgary (PCL)	SS	7	28	3	6	2	0	0	3	.214	3	4	0	15	14	0	1.000	
—Seattle (A.L.)	SS	143	387	45	85	7	3	1	20	.220	28	40	1	208	388	18	.971	
1990—Calgary (PCL)	SS	48	150	18	35	6	2	0	8	.233	13	10	4	70	142	6	.972	
—San Bern. (Calif.)	SS	2	8	5	7	0	0	0	3	.250	3	1	1	11	21	3	.914	
—Seattle (A.L.)	SS	81	255	19	63	3	2	2	18	.247	18	22	4	103	239	7	.980	
1991—Seattle (A.L.)	SS-2B	142	426	42	98	16	4	1	41	.230	45	37	7	224	422	13	.980	
1992—Seattle (A.L.)	SS	136	483	49	142	20	4	0	21	.294	32	38	15	223	403	7	*.989	
—Calgary (PCL)	SS	6	22	0	6	1	0	0	2	.273	1	3	0	14	21	1	.972	
1993—Seattle (A.L.)	SS-DH	158	560	68	143	14	2	2	31	.255	50	71	12	245	475	15	.980	
1994—Cleveland (A.L.)■	SS	69	286	39	78	10	1	1	33	.273	23	23	13	113	204	6	.981	
—Charlotte (Int'l)	SS	7	26	3	7	1	0	0	1	.269	2	1	1	11	18	1	.967	
1995—Cleveland (A.L.)	SS	136	542	87	144	28	0	6	56	.266	59	59	29	210	405	9	.980	
1996—Cleveland (A.L.)	SS	151	542	98	161	36	1	9	64	.297	56	42	35	226	447	20	.971	
1997—Cleveland (A.L.)	SS	153	565	89	158	23	6	5	49	.280	57	58	43	245	428	10	.985	
Major league totals (9 years)		1169	4046	536	1072	157	23	27	333	.265	368	390	159	1797	3411	105	.980	

DIVISION SERIES RECORD

Year	Team (League)	Pos.	G	AB	R	H	2B	3B	HR	RBI	Avg.	BB	SO	SB	PO	A	E	Avg.
1995—Cleveland (A.L.)	SS	3	12	2	2	1	0	0	4	.167	2	2	1	4	11	0	1.000	
1996—Cleveland (A.L.)	SS	4	14	4	6	1	0	0	2	.429	3	4	4	6	10	0	1.000	
1997—Cleveland (A.L.)	SS	5	18	3	9	0	0	0	1	.500	2	1	4	12	14	0	1.000	
Division series totals (3 years)		12	44	9	17	2	0	0	7	.386	7	7	9	22	35	0	1.000	

CHAMPIONSHIP SERIES RECORD

Year	Team (League)	Pos.	G	AB	R	H	2B	3B	HR	RBI	Avg.	BB	SO	SB	PO	A	E	Avg.
1995—Cleveland (A.L.)	SS	6	23	2	2	1	0	0	2	.087	5	2	3	9	21	0	1.000	
1997—Cleveland (A.L.)	SS	6	25	1	1	0	0	0	0	.040	2	10	0	16	15	0	1.000	
Championship series totals (2 years)		12	48	3	3	1	0	0	2	.063	7	12	3	25	36	0	1.000	

V

RECORDS: Shares single-inning record for most stolen bases—2 (October 26, 1997).

Year	Team (League)	Pos.	G	AB	R	H	2B	3B	HR	RBI	Avg.	BB	SO	SB	PO	A	E	Avg.
1995—	Cleveland (A.L.).........	SS	6	23	3	4	0	1	0	1	.174	3	5	1	12	22	0	1.000
1997—	Cleveland (A.L.).........	SS	7	30	5	7	2	0	0	1	.233	3	5	5	12	17	0	1.000
	World Series totals (2 years)		13	53	8	11	2	1	0	2	.208	6	10	6	24	39	0	1.000

VOIGT, JACK   ·   OF   ATHLETICS

PERSONAL: Born May 17, 1966, in Sarasota, Fla. ... 6-1/175. ... Bats right, throws right. ... Full name: John David Voigt.
HIGH SCHOOL: Venice (Fla.).
COLLEGE: Louisiana State.
TRANSACTIONS/CAREER NOTES: Selected by Baltimore Orioles organization in ninth round of free-agent draft (June 2, 1987). ... Traded by Orioles to Texas Rangers for P John Dettmer (May 16, 1995). ... Traded by Rangers organization to Boston Red Sox organization for P Chris Howard (August 31, 1995). ... Granted free agency (October 16, 1995). ... Signed by Charlotte, Rangers organization (April 13, 1996). ... Granted free agency (October 9, 1996). ... Signed by Milwaukee Brewers organization (January 30, 1997). ... Released by Brewers (December 1, 1997). ... Signed by Oakland Athletics organization (December 5, 1997).
STATISTICAL NOTES: Led New York-Pennsylvania League third basemen with .941 fielding percentage and 16 double plays in 1987. ... Led Carolina League third basemen with .990 fielding percentage in 1989. ... Led Eastern League with 11 sacrifice flies in 1990.

Year	Team (League)	Pos.	G	AB	R	H	2B	3B	HR	RBI	Avg.	BB	SO	SB	PO	A	E	Avg.
1987—	Newark (NY-Penn)......	3B-1B	63	219	41	70	10	1	11	52	*.320	33	45	1	63	141	11	†.949
	— Hagerstown (Car.)......	1B	2	9	0	1	0	0	0	1	.111	1	4	0	9	0	2	.818
1988—	Hagerstown (Car.)	OF-1B	115	367	62	83	18	2	12	42	.226	66	92	5	213	11	6	.974
1989—	Frederick (Carolina)....	OF-1B	127	406	61	107	26	5	10	77	.264	62	106	17	189	16	2	†.990
1990—	Hagerstown (Eastern)...	OF	126	418	55	107	26	2	12	70	.256	59	97	5	249	12	6	.978
1991—	Hagerstown (Eastern)...	OF	29	90	15	22	3	0	0	6	.244	15	19	6	8	0	0	1.000
	— Rochester (Int'l).........	OF-1B-3B	83	267	46	72	12	4	6	35	.270	40	53	9	198	32	3	.987
1992—	Rochester (Int'l).........	OF-1B-3B	129	443	74	126	23	4	16	64	.284	58	102	9	330	36	10	.973
	— Baltimore (A.L.).........	PR	1	0	0	0	0	0	0	0	...	0	0	0	...	...	...	...
1993—	Rochester (Int'l).........	OF-3B-1B	18	61	16	22	6	1	3	11	.361	9	14	0	38	5	1	.977
	— Baltimore (A.L.).........	O-DH-1-3	64	152	32	45	11	1	6	23	.296	25	33	1	101	6	1	.991
1994—	Baltimore (A.L.).........	OF-1B-DH	59	141	15	34	5	0	3	20	.241	18	25	0	114	5	2	.983
	— Bowie (Eastern).........	1B-3B-OF	41	154	26	48	9	1	6	35	.312	26	26	5	222	36	1	.996
1995—	Baltimore (A.L.)■.........	DH-1B	3	1	1	1	0	0	0	0	1.000	0	0	0	1	1	0	1.000
	— Texas (A.L.)■............	OF-1B-DH	33	62	8	10	3	0	2	8	.161	10	14	0	55	2	1	.983
	— Tulsa (Texas)	OF-1B	4	16	1	3	0	0	1	3	.188	2	5	1	8	1	0	1.000
1996	Charlotte (Fla. St.)......	1B-OF	7	27	7	11	3	0	1	8	.407	3	3	0	46	7	0	1.000
	— Oklahoma City (A.A.)..	OF-3B-1B	127	445	77	132	26	1	21	80	.297	*76	103	5	149	113	16	.942
	— Texas (A.L.)	OF-3B	5	9	1	1	0	0	0	0	.111	0	2	0	5	1	0	1.000
1997—	Tucson (PCL)■............	O-1-3-2	66	235	36	64	20	0	5	40	.272	43	57	4	112	10	2	.984
	— Milwaukee (A.L.)	O-1-3-DH	72	151	20	37	9	2	8	22	.245	19	36	1	144	10	1	.994
	Major league totals (6 years)		237	516	77	128	28	3	19	73	.248	72	110	2	420	25	5	.989

VOSBERG, ED   P   PADRES

PERSONAL: Born September 28, 1961, in Tucson, Ariz. ... 6-1/190. ... Throws left, bats left. ... Full name: Edward John Vosberg.
HIGH SCHOOL: Salpointe (Tucson, Ariz.).
COLLEGE: Arizona.
TRANSACTIONS/CAREER NOTES: Selected by St. Louis Cardinals organization in third round of free-agent draft (June 5, 1979); did not sign. ... Selected by Toronto Blue Jays organization in 11th round of free-agent draft (June 7, 1982); did not sign. ... Selected by San Diego Padres organization in third round of free-agent draft (June 6, 1983). ... Traded by Padres organization to Houston Astros organization for C Dan Walters (December 13, 1988). ... Traded by Astros organization to Los Angeles Dodgers organization (August 1, 1989), completing deal in which Dodgers organization traded OF Javier Ortiz to Astros organization for a player to be named later (July 22, 1989). ... Granted free agency (October 15, 1989). ... Signed by Phoenix, San Francisco Giants organization (March 13, 1990). ... Granted free agency (October 15, 1990). ... Signed by California Angels organization (December 4, 1990). ... Released by Angels organization (May 11, 1991). ... Signed by Calgary, Seattle Mariners organization (May 20, 1991). ... Released by Mariners organization (July 10, 1991). ... Pitched in Italy (1992). ... Signed by Iowa, Chicago Cubs organization (March 17, 1993). ... Granted free agency (October 15, 1993). ... Signed by Oakland Athletics organization (December 3, 1993). ... Granted free agency (October 15, 1994). ... Re-signed by A's organization (November 11, 1994). ... Selected by Los Angeles Dodgers from A's organization in Rule 5 major league draft (December 5, 1994). ... Granted free agency (April 24, 1995). ... Signed by Texas Rangers organization (April 26, 1995). ... Traded by Rangers to Florida Marlins for P Rick Helling (August 12, 1997). ... Traded by Marlins to Padres for P Chris Clark (November 20, 1997).
STATISTICAL NOTES: Led Pacific Coast League with 11 balks in 1987.

Year	Team (League)	W	L	Pct.	ERA	G	GS	CG	ShO	Sv.	IP	H	R	ER	BB	SO
1983—	Reno (California)	6	6	.500	3.87	15	15	3	0	0	97²/₃	111	61	42	39	70
	— Beaumont (Texas)	1	0	1.000	0.00	1	1	1	1	0	7	2	0	0	2	1
1984—	Beaumont (Texas)	13	•11	.542	3.43	27	•27	5	2	0	183²/₃	196	87	70	74	100
1985—	Beaumont (Texas)	9	11	.450	3.91	27	•27	2	1	0	175	178	92	76	69	124
1986—	Las Vegas (PCL)	7	8	.467	4.72	25	24	2	1	0	129²/₃	136	80	68	64	93
	— San Diego (N.L.)	0	1	.000	6.59	5	3	0	0	0	13²/₃	17	11	10	9	8
1987—	Las Vegas (PCL)	9	8	.529	3.92	34	24	3	0	0	167²/₃	154	88	73	97	98
1988—	Las Vegas (PCL)	11	7	.611	4.15	45	11	1	0	2	128	137	67	59	56	75
1989—	Tucson (PCL)■	4	7	.364	6.78	23	14	0	0	1	87²/₃	122	70	66	49	68
	— Albuquerque (PCL)■.........	2	1	.667	2.70	12	0	0	0	0	20	17	8	6	5	18
1990—	Phoenix (PCL)■	1	3	.250	2.65	24	0	0	0	3	34	36	14	10	16	28
	— San Francisco (N.L.)	1	1	.500	5.55	18	0	0	0	0	24¹/₃	21	16	15	12	12

Year—Team (League)	W	L	Pct.	ERA	G	GS	CG	ShO	Sv.	IP	H	R	ER	BB	SO
1991— Ed monton (PCL)■	0	1	.000	6.28	12	0	0	0	0	14 1/3	19	10	10	5	14
—Calgary (PCL)■	0	2	.000	7.23	16	0	0	0	2	23 2/3	38	26	19	12	15
1992—							Italian statistics unavailable.								
1993— Iowa (Am. Assoc.)■	5	1	.833	3.57	52	0	0	0	3	63	67	32	25	22	64
1994— Tacoma (PCL)■	4	2	.667	3.35	26	1	0	0	3	53 2/3	39	21	20	19	54
—Oakland (A.L.)	0	2	.000	3.95	16	0	0	0	0	13 2/3	16	7	6	5	12
1995— Oklahoma City (A.A.)■	1	0	1.000	0.00	1	0	0	0	0	1 2/3	1	0	0	1	2
—Texas (A.L.)	5	5	.500	3.00	44	0	0	0	4	36	32	15	12	16	36
1996— Texas (A.L.)	1	1	.500	3.27	52	0	0	0	8	44	51	17	16	21	32
1997— Texas (A.L.)	1	2	.333	4.61	42	0	0	0	0	41	44	23	21	15	29
—Florida (N.L.)■	1	1	.500	3.75	17	0	0	0	1	12	15	7	5	6	8
A.L. totals (4 years)	7	10	.412	3.68	154	0	0	0	12	134 2/3	143	62	55	57	109
N.L. totals (3 years)	2	3	.400	5.40	40	3	0	0	1	50	53	34	30	27	28
Major league totals (6 years)......	9	13	.409	4.14	194	3	0	0	13	184 2/3	196	96	85	84	137

DIVISION SERIES RECORD

Year—Team (League)	W	L	Pct.	ERA	G	GS	CG	ShO	Sv.	IP	H	R	ER	BB	SO
1996— Texas (A.L.)	0	0	...	...	1	0	0	0	0	0	1	0	0	0	0

CHAMPIONSHIP SERIES RECORD

Year—Team (League)	W	L	Pct.	ERA	G	GS	CG	ShO	Sv.	IP	H	R	ER	BB	SO
1997— Florida (N.L.)	0	0	...	0.00	2	0	0	0	0	2 2/3	2	0	0	1	3

WORLD SERIES RECORD

NOTES: Member of World Series championship team (1997).

Year—Team (League)	W	L	Pct.	ERA	G	GS	CG	ShO	Sv.	IP	H	R	ER	BB	SO
1997— Florida (N.L.)	0	0	...	6.00	2	0	0	0	0	3	3	2	2	3	2

WADE, TERRELL   P   DEVIL RAYS

PERSONAL: Born January 25, 1973, in Rembert, S.C. ... 6-3/205. ... Throws left, bats left. ... Full name: Hawatha Terrell Wade.
HIGH SCHOOL: Hillcrest (S.C.).
TRANSACTIONS/CAREER NOTES: Signed as non-drafted free agent by Atlanta Braves organization (June 17, 1991). ... On Greenville disabled list (April 7-August 9, 1994). ... On Atlanta disabled list (June 7, 1997-remainder of season); included rehabilitation assignment to Greenville (July 22-August 15). ... Selected by Tampa Bay Devil Rays in third round (60th pick overall) of expansion draft (November 18, 1997).

Year—Team (League)	W	L	Pct.	ERA	G	GS	CG	ShO	Sv.	IP	H	R	ER	BB	SO
1991— GC Braves (GCL)	2	0	1.000	6.26	10	2	0	0	0	23	29	17	16	15	22
1992— Idaho Falls (Pioneer)	1	4	.200	6.44	13	11	0	0	0	50 1/3	59	46	36	42	54
1993— Macon (S. Atl.)	8	2	.800	1.73	14	14	0	0	0	83 1/3	57	16	16	36	121
—Durham (Carolina)	2	1	.667	3.27	5	5	0	0	0	33	26	13	12	18	47
—Greenville (Southern)	2	1	.667	3.21	8	8	1	1	0	42	32	16	15	29	40
1994— Greenville (Southern)	9	3	.750	3.83	21	21	0	0	0	105 2/3	87	49	45	58	105
—Richmond (Int'l)	2	2	.500	2.63	4	4	0	0	0	24	23	9	7	15	26
1995— Richmond (Int'l)	10	9	.526	4.56	24	23	1	0	0	142	137	76	72	63	124
—Atlanta (N.L.)	0	1	.000	4.50	3	0	0	0	0	4	3	2	2	4	3
1996— Atlanta (N.L.)	5	0	1.000	2.97	44	8	0	0	1	69 2/3	57	28	23	47	79
1997— Atlanta (N.L.)	2	3	.400	5.36	12	9	0	0	0	42	60	31	25	16	35
—Greenville (Southern)	0	2	.000	4.97	8	6	0	0	0	12 2/3	15	10	7	8	14
Major league totals (3 years)......	7	4	.636	3.89	59	17	0	0	1	115 2/3	120	61	50	67	117

CHAMPIONSHIP SERIES RECORD

Year—Team (League)	W	L	Pct.	ERA	G	GS	CG	ShO	Sv.	IP	H	R	ER	BB	SO
1996— Atlanta (N.L.)	0	0	...	0.00	1	0	0	0	0	1/3	0	0	0	0	1

WORLD SERIES RECORD

Year—Team (League)	W	L	Pct.	ERA	G	GS	CG	ShO	Sv.	IP	H	R	ER	BB	SO
1996— Atlanta (N.L.)	0	0	...	0.00	2	0	0	0	0	2/3	0	0	0	1	0

WAGNER, BILLY   P   ASTROS

W

PERSONAL: Born June 25, 1971, in Tannersville, Va. ... 5-11/180. ... Throws left, bats left. ... Full name: William Edward Wagner.
HIGH SCHOOL: Tazewell (Va.).
COLLEGE: Ferrum (Va.).
TRANSACTIONS/CAREER NOTES: Selected by Houston Astros organization in first round (12th pick overall) of free-agent draft (June 3, 1993). ... On Houston disabled list (August 23-September 7, 1996).

Year—Team (League)	W	L	Pct.	ERA	G	GS	CG	ShO	Sv.	IP	H	R	ER	BB	SO
1993— Auburn (N.Y.-Penn)	1	3	.250	4.08	7	7	0	0	0	28 2/3	25	19	13	25	31
1994— Quad City (Midwest)	8	9	.471	3.29	26	26	2	0	0	153	99	71	56	*91	*204
1995— Jackson (Texas)	2	2	.500	2.57	12	12	0	0	0	70	49	25	20	36	77
—Tucson (PCL)	5	3	.625	3.18	13	13	0	0	0	76 1/3	70	28	27	32	80
—Houston (N.L.)	0	0	...	0.00	1	0	0	0	0	1/3	0	0	0	0	0
1996— Tucson (PCL)	6	2	.750	3.28	12	12	1	1	0	74	62	32	27	33	86
—Houston (N.L.)	2	2	.500	2.44	37	0	0	0	9	51 2/3	28	16	14	30	67
1997— Houston (N.L.)	7	8	.467	2.85	62	0	0	0	23	66 1/3	49	23	21	30	106
Major league totals (3 years)......	9	10	.474	2.66	100	0	0	0	32	118 1/3	77	39	35	60	173

DIVISION SERIES RECORD

Year—Team (League)	W	L	Pct.	ERA	G	GS	CG	ShO	Sv.	IP	H	R	ER	BB	SO
1997— Houston (N.L.)	0	0	...	18.00	1	0	0	0	0	1	3	2	2	0	2

WAGNER, MATT — P — EXPOS

PERSONAL: Born April 4, 1972, in Cedar Falls, Iowa. ... 6-5/215. ... Throws right, bats right. ... Full name: Matthew William Wagner.
HIGH SCHOOL: Cedar Falls (Iowa).
COLLEGE: Arkansas, then Iowa State.
TRANSACTIONS/CAREER NOTES: Selected by Seattle Mariners organization in third round of free-agent draft (June 2, 1994). ... Traded by Mariners with C Chris Widger and P Trey Moore to Montreal Expos for P Jeff Fassero and P Alex Pacheco (October 29, 1996). ... On Montreal disabled list (March 27, 1997-remainder of season); included rehabilitation assignment to West Palm Beach (April 13-14).

Year Team (League)	W	L	Pct.	ERA	G	GS	CG	ShO	Sv.	IP	H	R	ER	BB	SO
1994— Appleton (Midwest)	4	2	.667	0.83	15	1	0	0	1	32²/₃	23	8	3	8	48
1995— Port City (Southern)	5	8	.385	2.82	23	23	23	0	0	137	121	57	43	33	111
1996— Tacoma (PCL)	9	2	.818	2.31	15	15	0	0	0	93¹/₃	89	30	24	30	82
— Seattle (A.L.)	3	5	.375	6.98	15	14	1	0	0	80	91	63	62	38	41
1997— W.P. Beach (FSL)	0	0	...	54.00	1	1	0	0	0	²/₃	4	4	4	1	0
Major league totals (1 year)	3	5	.375	6.98	15	14	1	0	0	80	91	63	62	38	41

WAGNER, PAUL — P — BREWERS

PERSONAL: Born November 14, 1967, in Milwaukee. ... 6-1/210. ... Throws right, bats right. ... Full name: Paul Alan Wagner.
HIGH SCHOOL: Washington (Germantown, Wis.).
COLLEGE: Illinois State.
TRANSACTIONS/CAREER NOTES: Selected by Pittsburgh Pirates organization in 12th round of free-agent draft (June 5, 1989). ... On disabled list (August 3-19, 1993 and July 3-21, 1995). ... On Pittsburgh disabled list (June 7-July 2 and July 20, 1996-remainder of season); included rehabilitation assignment to Gulf Coast Pirates (June 24-28). ... On Pittsburgh disabled list (March 31-May 28, 1997); included rehabilitation assignment to Carolina (May 9-28). ... Signed by Milwaukee Brewers (September 2, 1997).
STATISTICAL NOTES: Pitched 4-0 one-hit, complete-game victory against Colorado (August 29, 1995).
MISCELLANEOUS: Made an out in only appearance as pinch-hitter (1995). ... Walked in one game as pinch-hitter with Pittsburgh (1996).

Year Team (League)	W	L	Pct.	ERA	G	GS	CG	ShO	Sv.	IP	H	R	ER	BB	SO
1989— Welland (N.Y.-Penn)	4	5	.444	4.47	13	10	0	0	0	50¹/₃	54	34	25	15	30
1990— Augusta (S. Atl.)	7	7	.500	2.75	35	1	0	0	4	72	71	30	22	30	71
— Salem (Carolina)	0	1	.000	5.00	11	4	0	0	2	36	39	22	20	17	28
1991— Salem (Carolina)	11	6	.647	3.12	25	25	5	•2	0	158²/₃	124	70	55	60	113
1992— Carolina (Southern)	6	6	.500	3.03	19	19	2	1	0	121²/₃	104	52	41	47	101
— Pittsburgh (N.L.)	2	0	1.000	0.69	6	1	0	0	0	13	9	1	1	5	5
— Buffalo (A.A.)	3	3	.500	5.49	8	8	0	0	0	39¹/₃	51	27	24	14	19
1993— Pittsburgh (N.L.)	8	8	.500	4.27	44	17	1	1	2	141¹/₃	143	72	67	42	114
1994— Pittsburgh (N.L.)	7	8	.467	4.59	29	17	1	0	0	119²/₃	136	69	61	50	86
1995— Pittsburgh (N.L.)	5	*16	.238	4.80	33	25	3	1	1	165	174	96	88	72	120
1996— Pittsburgh (N.L.)	4	8	.333	5.40	16	15	1	0	0	81²/₃	86	49	49	39	81
— GC Pirates (GCL)	0	0	...	0.00	1	1	0	0	0	3	2	0	0	0	4
1997— Carolina (Southern)	0	1	.000	10.13	12	3	0	0	0	16	25	20	18	16	20
— Pittsburgh (N.L.)	0	0	...	3.94	14	0	0	0	0	16	17	7	7	13	9
— Milwaukee (A.L.)■	1	0	1.000	9.00	2	0	0	0	0	2	3	2	2	0	0
A.L. totals (1 year)	1	0	1.000	9.00	2	0	0	0	0	2	3	2	2	0	0
N.L. totals (6 years)	26	40	.394	4.58	142	75	6	2	3	536²/₃	565	294	273	221	415
Major league totals (6 years)	27	40	.403	4.59	144	75	6	2	3	538²/₃	568	296	275	221	415

WAINHOUSE, DAVE — P — ROCKIES

PERSONAL: Born November 7, 1967, in Toronto. ... 6-2/185. ... Throws right, bats left. ... Full name: David Paul Wainhouse.
HIGH SCHOOL: Mercer Island (Wash.).
COLLEGE: Washington State.
TRANSACTIONS/CAREER NOTES: Selected by Montreal Expos organization in first round (19th pick overall) of free-agent draft (June 1, 1988). ... On Harrisburg disabled list (April 25-May 3, 1991). ... On disabled list (August 13-September 8, 1992). ... Traded by Expos with P Kevin Foster to Seattle Mariners for IF Frank Bolick and a player to be named later (November 20, 1992); Expos organization acquired C Miah Bradbury to complete deal (December 8, 1992). ... On Calgary disabled list (April 23-August 3, 1993). ... Released by Mariners (March 29, 1994). ... Signed by Syracuse, Toronto Blue Jays organization (December 20, 1994). ... Released by Syracuse (June 5, 1995). ... Signed by Charlotte, Florida Marlins organization (June 8, 1995). ... Granted free agency (October 16, 1995). ... Signed by Carolina, Pittsburgh Pirates organization (January 28, 1996). ... Granted free agency (October 15, 1997). ... Signed by Colorado Rockies organization (January 7, 1998).
MISCELLANEOUS: Member of 1988 Canadian Olympic baseball team.

Year Team (League)	W	L	Pct.	ERA	G	GS	CG	ShO	Sv.	IP	H	R	ER	BB	SO
1989— W.P. Beach (FSL)	1	5	.167	4.07	13	13	0	0	0	66¹/₃	75	35	30	19	26
1990— W.P. Beach (FSL)	6	3	.667	2.11	12	12	2	1	0	76²/₃	68	28	18	34	58
— Jacksonville (Southern)	7	7	.500	4.33	17	16	2	0	0	95²/₃	97	59	46	47	59
1991— Harrisburg (Eastern)	2	2	.500	2.60	33	0	0	0	11	52	49	17	15	17	46
— Indianapolis (A.A.)	2	0	1.000	4.08	14	0	0	0	1	28²/₃	28	14	13	15	13
— Montreal (N.L.)	0	1	.000	6.75	2	0	0	0	0	2²/₃	2	2	2	4	1
1992— Indianapolis (A.A.)	5	4	.556	4.11	44	0	0	0	21	46	48	22	21	24	37
1993— Seattle (A.L.)■	0	0	...	27.00	3	0	0	0	0	2¹/₃	7	7	7	5	2
— Calgary (PCL)	0	1	.000	4.02	13	0	0	0	0	15²/₃	10	7	7	7	7
1994—							Did not play.								
1995— Syracuse (Int'l)■	3	2	.600	3.70	26	0	0	0	5	24¹/₃	29	13	10	11	18
— Portland (Eastern)■	2	1	.667	7.20	17	0	0	0	0	25	39	22	20	8	16
— Charlotte (Int'l)	0	0	...	9.82	4	0	0	0	0	3²/₃	6	6	4	4	2
1996— Carolina (Southern)■	5	3	.625	3.16	45	0	0	0	25	51¹/₃	43	22	18	31	34
— Pittsburgh (N.L.)	1	0	1.000	5.70	17	0	0	0	0	23²/₃	22	16	15	10	16
1997— Pittsburgh (N.L.)	0	1	.000	8.04	25	0	0	0	0	28	34	28	25	17	21
— Calgary (PCL)	2	0	1.000	5.92	25	0	0	0	1	38	46	25	25	13	24
A.L. totals (1 year)	0	0	...	27.00	3	0	0	0	0	2¹/₃	7	7	7	5	2
N.L. totals (3 years)	1	2	.333	6.96	44	0	0	0	0	54¹/₃	58	46	42	31	38
Major league totals (4 years)	1	2	.333	7.78	47	0	0	0	0	56²/₃	65	53	49	36	40

W

WAKEFIELD, TIM P RED SOX

PERSONAL: Born August 2, 1966, in Melbourne, Fla. ... 6-2/206. ... Throws right, bats right. ... Full name: Timothy Stephen Wakefield.
HIGH SCHOOL: Eau Gallie (Melbourne, Fla.).
COLLEGE: Florida Tech.
TRANSACTIONS/CAREER NOTES: Selected by Pittsburgh Pirates organization in eighth round of free-agent draft (June 1, 1988). ... Released by Pirates (April 20, 1995). ... Signed by Boston Red Sox organization (April 26, 1995). ... On disabled list (April 15-May 6, 1997).
HONORS: Named N.L. Rookie Pitcher of the Year by THE SPORTING NEWS (1992). ... Named A.L. Comeback Player of the Year by THE SPORTING NEWS (1995).
STATISTICAL NOTES: Led Carolina League with 24 home runs allowed in 1990. ... Led American Association with 27 home runs allowed and 23 hit batsmen in 1994. ... Led A.L. with 16 hit batsmen in 1997.
MISCELLANEOUS: Appeared in one game as pinch-runner with Pittsburgh (1992).

Year Team (League)	W	L	Pct.	ERA	G	GS	CG	ShO	Sv.	IP	H	R	ER	BB	SO
1989— Welland (N.Y.-Penn)	1	1	.500	3.40	18	1	0	0	2	39 2/3	30	17	15	21	42
1990— Salem (Carolina)	10	•14	.417	4.73	28	•28	2	0	0	*190 1/3	*187	109	*100	*85	127
1991— Carolina (Southern)	15	8	.652	2.90	26	25	•8	1	0	183	155	68	59	51	120
— Buffalo (A.A.)	0	1	.000	11.57	1	1	0	0	0	4 2/3	8	6	6	1	4
1992— Buffalo (A.A.)	10	3	.769	3.06	20	20	*6	1	0	135 1/3	122	52	46	51	71
— Pittsburgh (N.L.)	8	1	.889	2.15	13	13	4	1	0	92	76	26	22	35	51
1993— Pittsburgh (N.L.)	6	11	.353	5.61	24	20	3	2	0	128 1/3	145	83	80	75	59
— Carolina (Southern)	3	5	.375	6.99	9	9	1	0	0	56 2/3	68	48	44	22	36
1994— Buffalo (A.A.)	5	*15	.250	5.84	30	•29	4	1	0	175 2/3	*197	*127	*114	*98	83
1995— Pawtucket (Int'l)■	2	1	.667	2.52	4	4	0	0	0	25	23	10	7	9	14
— Boston (A.L.)	16	8	.667	2.95	27	27	6	1	0	195 1/3	163	76	64	68	119
1996— Boston (A.L.)	14	13	.519	5.14	32	32	6	0	0	211 2/3	238	*151	121	90	140
1997— Boston (A.L.)	12	•15	.444	4.25	35	29	4	2	0	201 1/3	193	109	95	87	151
A.L. totals (3 years)	42	36	.538	4.14	94	88	16	3	0	608 1/3	594	336	280	245	410
N.L. totals (2 years)	14	12	.538	4.17	37	33	7	3	0	220 1/3	221	109	102	110	110
Major league totals (5 years)	56	48	.538	4.15	131	121	23	6	0	828 2/3	815	445	382	355	520

DIVISION SERIES RECORD

Year Team (League)	W	L	Pct.	ERA	G	GS	CG	ShO	Sv.	IP	H	R	ER	BB	SO
1995— Boston (A.L.)	0	1	.000	11.81	1	1	0	0	0	5 1/3	5	7	7	5	4

CHAMPIONSHIP SERIES RECORD

Year Team (League)	W	L	Pct.	ERA	G	GS	CG	ShO	Sv.	IP	H	R	ER	BB	SO
1992— Pittsburgh (N.L.)	2	0	1.000	3.00	2	2	2	0	0	18	14	6	6	5	7

RECORD AS POSITION PLAYER

Year Team (League)	Pos.	G	AB	R	H	2B	3B	HR	RBI	Avg.	BB	SO	SB	PO	A	E	Avg.
1988— Watertown (NYP)	1B	54	159	24	30	6	2	3	20	.189	25	57	3	377	25	8	.980
1989— Augusta (S. Atl.)	3B-1B	11	34	5	8	2	1	0	5	.235	1	14	1	27	6	3	.917
— Welland (NYP)	3B-2B-1B	36	63	7	13	4	0	1	3	.206	3	21	1	26	31	4	.877

WALBECK, MATT C ANGELS

PERSONAL: Born October 2, 1969, in Sacramento. ... 5-11/191. ... Bats both, throws right. ... Full name: Matthew Lovick Walbeck.
HIGH SCHOOL: Sacramento.
TRANSACTIONS/CAREER NOTES: Selected by Chicago Cubs organization in eighth round of free-agent draft (June 2, 1987). ... On Winston-Salem disabled list (April 12-July 11, 1990). ... On Charleston, W.Va. disabled list (September 5, 1992-remainder of season). ... Traded by Cubs with P Dave Stevens to Minnesota Twins for P Willie Banks (November 24, 1993). ... On Minnesota disabled list (March 31-June 17, 1996); included rehabilitation assignments to Fort Myers (May 31-June 11) and New Britain (June 11-17). ... Traded by Twins to Detroit Tigers for P Brent Stentz (December 11, 1996). ... On Detroit disabled list (April 19-July 9, 1997); included rehabilitation assignments to Lakeland (June 12-15) and Toledo (June 16-July 9). ... Traded by Tigers with 3B Phil Nevin to Anaheim Angels for P Nick Skuse (November 20, 1997).
STATISTICAL NOTES: Tied for Carolina League lead with 10 sacrifice flies in 1991. ... Led American Association catchers with 561 total chances and tied for lead with nine double plays in 1993. ... Career major league grand slams: 1.
MISCELLANEOUS: Batted righthanded only (1987-89).

Year Team (League)	Pos.	G	AB	R	H	2B	3B	HR	RBI	Avg.	BB	SO	SB	PO	A	E	Avg.
1987— Wytheville (App.)	C	51	169	24	53	9	3	1	28	.314	22	39	0	293	22	1	*.997
1988— Char., W.Va. (SAL)	C	104	312	28	68	9	0	2	24	.218	30	44	7	549	68	14	.978
1989— Peoria (Midwest)	C	94	341	38	86	19	0	4	47	.252	20	47	5	605	72	11	.984
1990— Peoria (Midwest)	C	25	66	2	15	1	0	0	5	.227	5	7	1	137	16	2	.987
1991— Win.-Salem (Car.)	C	91	260	25	70	11	0	3	41	.269	20	23	3	473	64	12	.978
1992— Charlotte (Southern)	C-1B	105	385	48	116	22	1	7	42	.301	33	56	0	552	80	10	.984
1993— Chicago (N.L.)	C	11	30	2	6	2	0	1	6	.200	1	6	0	49	2	0	1.000
— Iowa (Am. Assoc.)	C	87	331	31	93	18	2	6	43	.281	18	47	1	496	*64	1	*.998
1994— Minnesota (A.L.)■	C-DH	97	338	31	69	12	0	5	35	.204	17	37	1	496	45	4	.993
1995— Minnesota (A.L.)	C	115	393	40	101	18	1	1	44	.257	25	71	3	604	35	6	.991
1996— Fort Myers (FSL)	C	9	33	4	9	1	0	0	9	.273	4	2	0	46	6	0	1.000
— New Britain (Eastern)	C	7	24	1	5	0	0	0	0	.208	1	1	0	11	2	0	1.000
— Minnesota (A.L.)	C	63	215	25	48	10	0	2	24	.223	9	34	3	326	19	2	.994
1997— Detroit (A.L.)■	C	47	137	18	38	3	0	3	10	.277	12	19	3	240	15	3	.988
— Lakeland (Fla. St.)	C	4	10	4	5	1	0	0	3	.500	4	1	0	14	0	1	.933
— Toledo (Int'l)	C	17	59	6	18	2	1	1	8	.305	4	15	0	55	9	3	.955
American League totals (4 years)		322	1083	114	256	43	1	11	113	.236	63	161	10	1666	114	15	.992
National League totals (1 year)		11	30	2	6	2	0	1	6	.200	1	6	0	49	2	0	1.000
Major league totals (5 years)		333	1113	116	262	45	1	12	119	.235	64	167	10	1715	116	15	.992

W

WALKER, JAMIE P ROYALS

PERSONAL: Born July 1, 1971, in McMinnville, Tenn. ... 6-2/190. ... Throws left, bats left. ... Full name: Jamie Ross Walker.
HIGH SCHOOL: Warren County (McMinnville, Tenn.).
COLLEGE: Austin Peay.
TRANSACTIONS/CAREER NOTES: Selected by Houston Astros organization in 10th round of free-agent draft (June 1, 1992). ... Selected by Atlanta Braves organization from Astros organization in Rule 5 major league draft (December 9, 1996). ... Traded by Braves with OF Jermaine Dye to Kansas City Royals for OF Michael Tucker and IF Keith Lockhart (March 27, 1997). ... On Kansas City disabled list (June 5-24, 1997); included rehabilitation assignment to Wichita (June 11-24).

Year Team (League)	W	L	Pct.	ERA	G	GS	CG	ShO	Sv.	IP	H	R	ER	BB	SO
1992—Auburn (N.Y.-Penn)	4	6	.400	3.13	15	14	0	0	0	83⅓	75	35	29	21	67
1993—Quad City (Midwest)	3	11	.214	5.13	25	24	1	1	0	131⅔	140	92	75	48	121
1994—Quad City (Midwest)	8	10	.444	4.18	32	18	0	0	1	125	133	80	58	42	104
1995—Jackson (Texas)	4	2	.667	4.50	50	0	0	0	2	58	59	29	29	24	38
1996—Jackson (Texas)	5	1	.833	2.50	45	7	0	0	2	101	94	34	28	35	79
1997—Kansas City (A.L.)■	3	3	.500	5.44	50	0	0	0	0	43	46	28	26	20	24
—Wichita (Texas)	0	1	.000	9.45	5	0	0	0	0	6⅔	6	8	7	5	6
Major league totals (1 year)	3	3	.500	5.44	50	0	0	0	0	43	46	28	26	20	24

WALKER, LARRY OF ROCKIES

PERSONAL: Born December 1, 1966, in Maple Ridge, B.C. ... 6-3/225. ... Bats left, throws right. ... Full name: Larry Kenneth Robert Walker.
HIGH SCHOOL: Maple Ridge (B.C.) Senior Secondary School.
TRANSACTIONS/CAREER NOTES: Signed as non-drafted free agent by Montreal Expos organization (November 14, 1984). ... On disabled list (April 4, 1988-entire season; June 28-July 13, 1991; and May 26-June 10, 1993). ... On suspended list (June 24-28, 1994). ... Granted free agency (October 24, 1994). ... Signed by Colorado Rockies (April 8, 1995). ... On Colorado disabled list (June 10-August 15, 1996); included rehabilitation assignments to Salem (August 6-9) and Colorado Springs (August 9-15).
RECORDS: Shares major league record for most long hits in two consecutive games (May 21-22, 1996; 2 doubles, 3 triples and 1 home run). ... Holds N.L. single-season records for most consecutive long hits—6 (May 21-22, 1996; 2 doubles, 3 triples and 1 home run); and highest slugging average—.720 (1997).
HONORS: Named outfielder on The Sporting News N.L. All-Star team (1992 and 1997). ... Won N.L. Gold Glove as outfielder (1992-93 and 1997). ... Named outfielder on The Sporting News N.L. Silver Slugger team (1992 and 1997). ... Named N.L. Most Valuable Player by Baseball Writers' Association of America (1997).
STATISTICAL NOTES: Hit three home runs in one game (April 5, 1997). ... Led N.L. with 409 total bases in 1997. ... Led N.L. with .452 on-base percentage in 1997. ... Led N.L. in slugging percentage with .720 in 1997. ... Led N.L. outfielders in double plays with four in 1997. ... Career major league grand slams: 1.

							BATTING								FIELDING		
Year Team (League)	Pos.	G	AB	R	H	2B	3B	HR	RBI	Avg.	BB	SO	SB	PO	A	E	Avg.
1985—Utica (N.Y.-Penn)	1B-3B	62	215	24	48	8	2	2	26	.223	18	57	12	354	62	8	.981
1986—Burl. (Midw.)	OF-3B	95	332	67	96	12	6	29	74	.289	46	112	16	106	51	10	.940
—W.P. Beach (FSL)	OF	38	113	20	32	7	5	4	16	.283	26	32	2	44	5	0	1.000
1987—Jacksonville (South.)	OF	128	474	91	136	25	7	26	83	.287	67	120	24	263	9	9	.968
1988—								Did not play.									
1989—Indianapolis (A.A.)	OF	114	385	68	104	18	2	12	59	.270	50	87	36	241	*18	*11	.959
—Montreal (N.L.)	OF	20	47	4	8	0	0	0	4	.170	5	13	1	19	2	0	1.000
1990—Montreal (N.L.)	OF	133	419	59	101	18	3	19	51	.241	49	112	21	249	12	4	.985
1991—Montreal (N.L.)	OF-1B	137	487	59	141	30	2	16	64	.290	42	102	14	536	36	6	.990
1992—Montreal (N.L.)	OF	143	528	85	159	31	4	23	93	.301	41	97	18	269	16	2	.993
1993—Montreal (N.L.)	OF-1B	138	490	85	130	24	5	22	86	.265	80	76	29	316	16	6	.982
1994—Montreal (N.L.)	OF-1B	103	395	76	127	44	2	19	86	.322	47	74	15	423	29	9	.980
1995—Colorado (N.L.)■	OF	131	494	96	151	31	5	36	101	.306	49	72	16	225	13	3	.988
1996—Colorado (N.L.)	OF	83	272	58	75	18	4	18	58	.276	20	58	18	153	4	1	.994
—Salem (Carolina)	DH	2	8	3	4	3	0	1	1	.500	0	1	0	...	...	...	...
—Colo. Springs (PCL)	OF	3	11	2	4	0	0	2	8	.364	1	4	0	6	2	0	1.000
1997—Colorado (N.L.)	OF-1B-DH	153	568	143	208	46	4	*49	130	.366	78	90	33	254	14	2	.993
Major league totals (9 years)		1041	3700	665	1100	242	29	202	673	.297	411	694	165	2444	142	33	.987

DIVISION SERIES RECORD

							BATTING								FIELDING		
Year Team (League)	Pos.	G	AB	R	H	2B	3B	HR	RBI	Avg.	BB	SO	SB	PO	A	E	Avg.
1995—Colorado (N.L.)	OF	4	14	3	3	0	0	1	3	.214	3	4	1	3	0	0	1.000

ALL-STAR GAME RECORD

						BATTING							FIELDING		
Year League	Pos.	AB	R	H	2B	3B	HR	RBI	Avg.	BB	SO	SB	PO	A	E	Avg.
1992—National	PH	1	0	1	0	0	0	0	1.000	0	0	0	...	...	...	...
1997—National	OF	1	0	0	0	0	0	0	.000	1	0	0	0	0	0	...
All-Star Game totals (2 years)		2	0	1	0	0	0	0	.500	1	0	0	0	0	0	...

W

WALKER, TODD 3B TWINS

PERSONAL: Born May 25, 1973, in Bakersfield, Calif. ... 6-0/177. ... Bats left, throws right. ... Full name: Todd Arthur Walker.
HIGH SCHOOL: Airline (Bossier City, La.).
COLLEGE: Louisiana State.
TRANSACTIONS/CAREER NOTES: Selected by Texas Rangers organization in 51st round of free-agent draft (June 3, 1991); did not sign. ... Selected by Minnesota Twins organization in first round (eighth pick overall) of free-agent draft (June 2, 1994).
HONORS: Named Most Outstanding Player of College World Series (1993).
STATISTICAL NOTES: Led Pacific Coast League with 330 total bases and .599 slugging percentage and tied for lead in intentional bases on balls received with 11 in 1996.

Year Team (League)	Pos.	G	AB	R	H	2B	3B	HR	RBI	Avg.	BB	SO	SB	PO	A	E	Avg.
1994—Fort Myers (FSL)	2B	46	171	29	52	5	2	10	34	.304	32	15	6	98	112	9	.959
1995—New Britain (Eastern)	2B-3B	137	513	83	149	27	3	21	85	.290	63	101	23	215	355	27	.955
1996—Salt Lake (PCL)	3B-2B	135	551	94	*187	*41	9	*28	*111	.339	57	91	13	129	276	19	.955
—Minnesota (A.L.)	3B-2B-DH	25	82	8	21	6	0	0	6	.256	4	13	2	16	39	2	.965
1997—Minnesota (A.L.)	3B-2B-DH	52	156	15	37	7	1	3	16	.237	11	30	7	35	86	4	.968
—Salt Lake (PCL)	3B	83	322	69	111	20	1	11	53	.345	46	49	5	44	174	*24	.901
Major league totals (2 years)		77	238	23	58	13	1	3	22	.244	15	43	9	51	125	6	.967

WALL, DONNE — P — PADRES

PERSONAL: Born July 11, 1967, in Potosi, Mo. ... 6-1/180. ... Throws right, bats right. ... Full name: Donnell Lee Wall. ... Name pronounced DON-ee.

HIGH SCHOOL: Festus (Mo.).

JUNIOR COLLEGE: Jefferson College (Mo.), then Meramec Community College (Mo.).

COLLEGE: Southwestern Louisiana.

TRANSACTIONS/CAREER NOTES: Selected by Houston Astros organization in 18th round of free-agent draft (June 5, 1989). ... On disabled list (May 27-June 16, 1994). ... Claimed on waivers by Cincinnati Reds (October 7, 1997). ... Traded by Reds with C Paul Bako to Detroit Tigers for OF Mel Nieves (November 11, 1997). ... Traded by Tigers with P Dan Miceli and 3B Ryan Balfe to San Diego Padres for P Tim Worrell and OF Trey Beamon (November 19, 1997).

HONORS: Named Pacific Coast League Most Valuable Player (1995).

STATISTICAL NOTES: Led South Atlantic League with 18 home runs allowed in 1990.

Year Team (League)	W	L	Pct.	ERA	G	GS	CG	ShO	Sv.	IP	H	R	ER	BB	SO
1989—Auburn (N.Y.-Penn)	7	0	*1.000	1.79	12	8	3	1	1	65 1/3	45	17	13	12	69
1990—Asheville (S. Atl.)	6	8	.429	5.18	28	22	1	0	1	132	149	87	76	47	111
1991—Burlington (Midw.)	7	5	.583	2.03	16	16	3	1	0	106 2/3	73	30	24	21	102
—Osceola (Florida St.)	6	3	.667	2.09	12	12	4	2	0	77 1/3	55	22	18	11	62
1992—Osceola (Florida St.)	3	1	.750	2.63	7	7	0	0	0	41	37	13	12	8	30
—Jackson (Texas)	9	6	.600	3.54	18	18	2	0	0	114 1/3	114	51	45	26	99
1993—Tucson (PCL)	6	4	.600	3.83	25	22	2	0	0	131 2/3	147	73	56	25	89
1994—Tucson (PCL)	11	8	.579	4.43	26	24	2	2	0	148 1/3	171	87	73	35	84
1995—Tucson (PCL)	*17	6	.739	*3.30	28	•28	0	0	0	*177 1/3	190	72	65	32	*119
—Houston (N.L.)	3	1	.750	5.55	6	5	0	0	0	24 1/3	33	19	15	5	16
1996—Tucson (PCL)	3	3	.500	4.13	8	8	0	0	0	52 1/3	67	30	24	6	36
—Houston (N.L.)	9	8	.529	4.56	26	23	2	1	0	150	170	84	76	34	99
1997—New Orleans (A.A.)	8	7	.533	3.85	17	17	1	0	0	110	109	49	47	24	84
—Houston (N.L.)	2	5	.286	6.26	8	8	0	0	0	41 2/3	53	31	29	16	25
Major league totals (3 years)	14	14	.500	5.00	40	36	2	1	0	216	256	134	120	55	140

WALLACE, DEREK — P — METS

PERSONAL: Born September 1, 1971, in Van Nuys, Calif. ... 6-3/215. ... Throws right, bats right. ... Full name: Derek Robert Wallace.

HIGH SCHOOL: Chatsworth (Calif.).

COLLEGE: Pepperdine.

TRANSACTIONS/CAREER NOTES: Selected by Pittsburgh Pirates organization in 36th round of free-agent draft (June 5, 1989); did not sign. ... Selected by Chicago Cubs organization in first round (11th pick overall) of free-agent draft (June 1, 1992). ... Traded by Cubs with P Geno Morones to Kansas City Royals for OF Brian McRae (April 5, 1995). ... Traded by Royals organization with a player to be named later to New York Mets organization for P Jason Jacome and P Allen McDill (July 21, 1995); Mets acquired P John Carter to complete deal (November 16, 1995). ... On New York disabled list (March 27, 1997-remainder of season).

RECORDS: Shares major league record for most strikeouts in one inning—4 (September 13, 1996, ninth inning).

STATISTICAL NOTES: Led Florida State League with 11 balks in 1993.

Year Team (League)	W	L	Pct.	ERA	G	GS	CG	ShO	Sv.	IP	H	R	ER	BB	SO
1992—Peoria (Midwest)	0	1	.000	4.91	2	0	0	0	0	3 2/3	3	2	2	1	2
1993—Daytona (Fla. St.)	5	6	.455	4.20	14	12	0	0	1	79 1/3	85	50	37	23	34
—Iowa (Am. Assoc.)	0	0	...	11.25	1	1	0	0	0	4	8	5	5	1	2
—Orlando (South.)	5	7	.417	5.03	15	15	2	0	0	96 2/3	105	59	54	28	69
1994—Orlando (South.)	2	9	.182	5.74	33	12	1	0	8	89 1/3	95	61	57	31	49
—Iowa (Am. Assoc.)	0	1	.000	4.15	5	0	0	0	1	4 1/3	4	4	2	4	3
1995—Wichita (Texas)■	4	3	.571	4.40	26	0	0	0	6	43	51	23	21	13	24
—Binghamton (Eastern)■	0	1	.000	5.28	15	0	0	0	2	15 1/3	11	9	9	9	8
1996—Norfolk (Int'l)	5	2	.714	1.72	49	0	0	0	26	57 2/3	37	20	11	17	52
—New York (N.L.)	2	3	.400	4.01	19	0	0	0	3	24 2/3	29	12	11	14	15
1997—Norfolk (Int'l)	0	1	.000	9.00	1	0	0	0	0	1	2	2	1	1	0
—St. Lucie (Fla. St.)	0	0	...	6.43	5	0	0	0	0	7	7	6	5	2	8
—GC Mets (GCL)	0	1	.000	3.38	8	5	0	0	0	8	6	3	3	1	9
Major league totals (1 year)	2	3	.400	4.01	19	0	0	0	3	24 2/3	29	12	11	14	15

WALLACE, JEFF — P — PIRATES

PERSONAL: Born April 12, 1976, in Wheeling, W.Va. ... 6-2/235. ... Throws left, bats left. ... Full name: Jeffrey Allen Wallace.

HIGH SCHOOL: Minerva (Ohio).

TRANSACTIONS/CAREER NOTES: Selected by Kansas City Royals organization in 25th round of free-agent draft (June 1, 1995). ... Traded by Royals with P Jeff Granger, P Jeff Martin and 3B Joe Randa to Pittsburgh Pirates for SS Jay Bell and 1B Jeff King (December 13, 1996).

Year Team (League)	W	L	Pct.	ERA	G	GS	CG	ShO	Sv.	IP	H	R	ER	BB	SO
1995—Sara. Royals (GCL)	5	3	.625	1.22	12	7	0	0	1	44 1/3	28	20	6	15	51
1996—Lansing (Midwest)	4	9	.308	5.30	30	21	0	0	0	122 1/3	140	79	72	66	84

W

Year Team (League)	W	L	Pct.	ERA	G	GS	CG	ShO	Sv.	IP	H	R	ER	BB	SO
1997— Lynchburg (Carolina)	5	0	1.000	1.65	9	0	0	0	1	16 1/3	9	3	3	10	13
— Carolina (Southern)............	4	8	.333	5.40	38	0	0	0	3	43 1/3	43	37	26	36	39
— Pittsburgh (N.L.)	0	0	...	0.75	11	0	0	0	0	12	8	2	1	8	14
Major league totals (1 year).......	0	0	...	0.75	11	0	0	0	0	12	8	2	1	8	14

WALTER, MIKE   P   ASTROS

PERSONAL: Born October 23, 1974, in San Diego. ... 6-1/190. ... Throws right, bats right. ... Full name: Michael John Walter.
JUNIOR COLLEGE: Palomar College (Calif.).
TRANSACTIONS/CAREER NOTES: Selected by Houston Astros organization in 25th round of free-agent draft (June 3, 1993).

Year Team (League)	W	L	Pct.	ERA	G	GS	CG	ShO	Sv.	IP	H	R	ER	BB	SO
1993— GC Astros (GCL)	0	1	.000	2.79	17	0	0	0	8	19 1/3	15	10	6	12	16
1994— Quad City (Midwest)	2	2	.500	4.13	23	0	0	0	3	28 1/3	27	18	13	20	28
1995— Kissimmee (Florida State)..	4	3	.571	5.55	41	0	0	0	0	71 1/3	78	58	44	42	42
1996— Quad City (Midwest)	3	6	.333	2.04	52	0	0	0	21	61 2/3	37	20	14	34	85
1997— Jackson (Texas)	2	3	.400	3.63	34	0	0	0	7	44 2/3	38	20	18	30	41

WALTON, JEROME   OF

PERSONAL: Born July 8, 1965, in Newnan, Ga. ... 6-1/185. ... Bats right, throws right. ... Full name: Jerome O'Terrell Walton.
HIGH SCHOOL: Enterprise (Ala.).
JUNIOR COLLEGE: Enterprise (Ala.) State Junior College.
TRANSACTIONS/CAREER NOTES: Selected by Chicago Cubs organization in second round of free-agent draft (January 14, 1986). ... On Chicago disabled list (May 11-June 11, 1989); included rehabilitation assignment to Iowa (June 6-11). ... On Chicago disabled list (June 18-August 2, 1990); included rehabilitation assignment to Iowa (July 29-August 1). ... On Chicago disabled list (March 28-April 24, 1992); included rehabilitation assignment to Iowa (April 17-24). ... On Iowa disabled list (July 1-September 14, 1992). ... Granted free agency (December 19, 1992). ... Signed by California Angels organization (January 29, 1993). ... On Vancouver disabled list (July 19-August 20, 1993). ... Released by Angels organization (August 20, 1993). ... Signed by Cincinnati Reds organization (November 4, 1993). ... On disabled list (July 1-23 and July 27, 1994-remainder of season). ... Granted free agency (December 21, 1995). ... Signed by Atlanta Braves (January 3, 1996). ... On Atlanta disabled list (May 30, 1996-remainder of season); included rehabilitation assignments to Greenville (June 20-23) and Richmond (July 15-21). ... Granted free agency (October 29, 1996). ... Signed by Baltimore Orioles organization (December 18, 1996). ... On Baltimore disabled list (April 25-September 1, 1997); included rehabilitation assignment to Frederick (August 22-September 1). ... Granted free agency (October 30, 1997).
HONORS: Named N.L. Rookie Player of the Year by THE SPORTING NEWS (1989). ... Named N.L. Rookie of the Year by Baseball Writers' Association of America (1989).
STATISTICAL NOTES: Led Appalachian League outfielders with 128 putouts and 131 total chances and tied for lead with two double plays in 1986. ... Led Midwest League in caught stealing with 25 in 1987. ... Had 30-game hitting streak (July 21-August 20, 1989).

Year Team (League)	Pos.	G	AB	R	H	2B	3B	HR	RBI	Avg.	BB	SO	SB	PO	A	E	Avg.
1986— Wytheville (App.)........	OF-3B	62	229	48	66	7	4	5	34	.288	28	40	21	†130	7	3	.979
1987— Peoria (Midwest)........	OF	128	472	102	158	24	11	6	38	.335	91	91	49	255	9	7	.974
1988— Pittsfield (Eastern)......	OF	120	414	64	137	26	2	3	49	*.331	41	69	42	270	11	2	*.993
1989— Chicago (N.L.)............	OF	116	475	64	139	23	3	5	46	.293	27	77	24	289	2	3	.990
— Iowa (Am. Assoc.)......	OF	4	18	4	6	1	0	1	3	.333	1	5	2	8	0	0	1.000
1990— Chicago (N.L.)............	OF	101	392	63	103	16	2	2	21	.263	50	70	14	247	3	6	.977
— Iowa (Am. Assoc.)......	OF	4	16	3	3	0	0	1	1	.188	2	4	0	6	1	0	1.000
1991— Chicago (N.L.)............	OF	123	270	42	59	13	1	5	17	.219	19	55	7	170	2	3	.983
1992— Iowa (Am. Assoc.)......	OF	7	27	8	8	2	1	0	3	.296	4	6	1	10	0	0	1.000
— Chicago (N.L.)............	OF	30	55	7	7	0	1	0	1	.127	9	13	1	34	0	2	.944
1993— California (A.L.)■......	DH-OF	5	2	2	0	0	0	0	0	.000	1	2	1	2	0	0	1.000
— Vancouver (PCL)	OF	54	176	34	55	11	1	2	20	.313	16	24	5	82	3	0	1.000
1994— Cincinnati (N.L.)■......	OF-1B	46	68	10	21	4	0	1	9	.309	4	12	1	57	1	1	.983
1995— Cincinnati (N.L.)........	OF-1B	102	162	32	47	12	1	8	22	.290	17	25	10	110	2	2	.982
1996— Atlanta (N.L.)■..........	OF	37	47	9	16	5	0	1	4	.340	5	10	0	34	0	0	1.000
— Greenville (Southern) .	OF	3	5	0	1	0	1	0	0	.200	3	1	0	2	0	0	1.000
— Richmond (Int'l)........	OF	6	18	3	8	2	1	1	5	.444	1	5	0	12	0	0	1.000
1997— Baltimore (A.L.)■......	OF-1B-DH	26	68	8	20	1	0	3	9	.294	4	10	0	52	1	0	1.000
— Frederick (Carolina)....	OF-1B	7	19	1	4	0	0	1	2	.211	5	0	1	15	0	0	1.000
American League totals (2 years)		31	70	10	20	1	0	3	9	.286	5	12	1	54	1	0	1.000
National League totals (7 years)		555	1469	227	392	73	8	22	120	.267	131	262	57	941	10	17	.982
Major league totals (9 years)		586	1539	237	412	74	8	25	129	.268	136	274	58	995	11	17	.983

DIVISION SERIES RECORD

Year Team (League)	Pos.	G	AB	R	H	2B	3B	HR	RBI	Avg.	BB	SO	SB	PO	A	E	Avg.
1995— Cincinnati (N.L.)	OF-PH	3	3	0	0	0	0	0	0	.000	1	1	0	3	0	0	1.000
1997— Baltimore (A.L.)	1B	2	4	0	0	0	0	0	0	.000	0	2	0	5	1	0	1.000
Division series totals (2 years)		5	7	0	0	0	0	0	0	.000	1	3	0	8	1	0	1.000

CHAMPIONSHIP SERIES RECORD

RECORDS: Shares records for most at-bats—2; most hits—2; and most singles—2, in one inning (October 5, 1989, first inning).

Year Team (League)	Pos.	G	AB	R	H	2B	3B	HR	RBI	Avg.	BB	SO	SB	PO	A	E	Avg.
1989— Chicago (N.L.)............	OF	5	22	4	8	0	0	0	2	.364	2	2	0	11	0	0	1.000
1995— Cincinnati (N.L.)	OF	2	7	0	0	0	0	0	0	.000	0	2	0	6	0	0	1.000
1997— Baltimore (A.L.)	OF	1	0	0	0	0	0	0	0	...	0	0	0	0	0	0	...
Championship series totals (3 years)		8	29	4	8	0	0	0	2	.276	2	4	0	17	0	0	1.000

W

WARD, BRYAN — P — WHITE SOX

PERSONAL: Born January 28, 1972, in Bristol, Pa. ... 6-2/210. ... Throws left, bats left.
HIGH SCHOOL: Rancoccas Valley Regional (Mount Holly, N.J.).
JUNIOR COLLEGE: County College of Morris (N.J.).
COLLEGE: South Carolina-Aiken.
TRANSACTIONS/CAREER NOTES: Selected by Florida Marlins organization in 20th round of free-agent draft (June 3, 1993). ... On Portland disabled list (April 23-May 1, 1997). ... Claimed on waivers by Chicago White Sox (October 14, 1997).

Year Team (League)	W	L	Pct.	ERA	G	GS	CG	ShO	Sv.	IP	H	R	ER	BB	SO
1993— Elmira (N.Y.-Penn)	2	5	.286	4.99	14	11	0	0	0	61 1/3	82	41	34	26	63
1994— Kane County (Midwest)	3	4	.429	3.40	47	0	0	0	11	55 2/3	46	27	21	21	62
1995— Brevard County (FSL)	5	1	.833	2.88	11	11	0	0	0	72	68	27	23	17	65
— Portland (Eastern)	7	3	.700	4.50	20	11	1	1	2	72	70	42	36	31	71
1996— Portland (Eastern)	9	9	.500	4.91	28	25	2	0	0	146 2/3	170	97	80	32	124
1997— Portland (Eastern)	6	3	.667	3.91	12	12	0	0	0	76	71	39	33	19	69
— Charlotte (Int'l)	2	9	.182	6.93	15	14	2	0	0	75 1/3	102	62	58	30	48

WARD, DARYLE — 1B — ASTROS

PERSONAL: Born June 27, 1975, in Lynwood, Calif. ... 6-2/240. ... Bats left, throws left. ... Full name: Daryle Lamar Ward. ... Son of Gary Ward, major league outfielder with four teams (1979-90).
JUNIOR COLLEGE: Rancho Santiago College (Calif.).
TRANSACTIONS/CAREER NOTES: Selected by Detroit Tigers organization in 15th round of free-agent draft (June 2, 1994). ... Traded by Tigers with C Brad Ausmus, P Jose Lima, P C.J. Nitkowski and P Trever Miller to Houston Astros for OF Brian Hunter, IF Orlando Miller, P Doug Brocail, P Todd Jones and a player to be named later (December 10, 1996).
STATISTICAL NOTES: Tied for Texas League lead with four intentional bases on balls in 1997.

Year Team (League)	Pos.	G	AB	R	H	2B	3B	HR	RBI	Avg.	BB	SO	SB	PO	A	E	Avg.
1994— Bristol (Appal.)	1B	48	161	17	43	6	0	5	30	.267	19	33	5	308	23	11	.968
1995— Fayetteville (SAL)	1B	137	524	75	149	32	0	14	106	.284	46	111	1	1009	77	14	.987
1996— Lakeland (Fla. St.)	1B	128	464	65	135	29	4	10	68	.291	57	77	1	1058	103	8	.993
— Toledo (Int'l)	1B	6	23	1	4	0	0	0	1	.174	0	3	0	42	5	1	.979
1997— Jackson (Texas)■	1B	114	422	72	139	25	0	19	90	.329	46	68	4	951	76	12	.988
— New Orleans (A.A.)	1B	14	48	4	18	1	0	2	8	.375	7	7	0	75	6	2	.976

WARD, TURNER — OF — PIRATES

PERSONAL: Born April 11, 1965, in Orlando. ... 6-2/198. ... Bats both, throws right. ... Full name: Turner Max Ward.
HIGH SCHOOL: Satsuma (Ala.).
COLLEGE: South Alabama.
TRANSACTIONS/CAREER NOTES: Selected by New York Yankees organization in 18th round of free-agent draft (June 2, 1986). ... Traded by Yankees organization with C Joel Skinner to Cleveland Indians organization for OF Mel Hall (March 19, 1989). ... On Gulf Coast Indians disabled list (April 7-July 24, 1989). ... Traded by Indians with P Tom Candiotti to Toronto Blue Jays for P Denis Boucher, OF Glenallen Hill, OF Mark Whiten and a player to be named later (June 27, 1991); Indians acquired cash to complete deal (October 15, 1991). ... On Toronto disabled list (August 2-September 1, 1993); included rehabilitation assignment to Knoxville (August 21-September 1). ... Claimed on waivers by Milwaukee Brewers (November 24, 1993). ... On Milwaukee disabled list (June 7-22, July 2-19 and July 24, 1995-remainder of season); included rehabilitation assignments to Beloit (July 17-19) and New Orleans (August 10-17 and August 31-September 5). ... On Milwaukee disabled list (May 25-September 1, 1996). ... Released by Brewers (November 1, 1996). ... Signed by Calgary, Pittsburgh Pirates organization (April 22, 1997).
STATISTICAL NOTES: Led Pacific Coast League outfielders with 292 putouts and 308 total chances in 1990.

Year Team (League)	Pos.	G	AB	R	H	2B	3B	HR	RBI	Avg.	BB	SO	SB	PO	A	E	Avg.
1986— Oneonta (NYP)	OF-1B-3B	63	221	42	62	4	1	1	19	.281	31	39	6	97	6	5	.954
1987— Fort Laud. (FSL)	OF-3B	130	493	83	145	15	2	7	55	.294	64	83	25	332	11	8	.977
1988— Columbus (Int'l)	OF	134	490	55	123	24	1	7	50	.251	48	100	28	223	5	1	*.996
1989— GC Indians (GCL)■	DH	4	15	2	3	0	0	0	1	.200	2	2	1	...	...	...	...
— Cant./Akr. (Eastern)	OF	30	93	19	28	5	1	0	3	.301	15	16	1	2	0	0	1.000
1990— Colo. Springs (PCL)	OF-2B	133	495	89	148	24	9	6	65	.299	72	70	22	†292	7	9	.971
— Cleveland (A.L.)	OF-DH	14	46	10	16	2	1	1	10	.348	3	8	3	20	2	1	.957
1991— Cleveland (A.L.)	OF	40	100	11	23	7	0	0	5	.230	10	16	0	65	1	0	1.000
— Colo. Springs (PCL)	OF	14	51	5	10	1	1	1	3	.196	6	9	2	30	0	1	.968
— Toronto (A.L.)■	OF	8	13	1	4	0	0	2	.308	1	2	1	5	0	0	1.000
— Syracuse (Int'l)	OF	59	218	40	72	11	3	7	32	.330	47	22	9	136	5	0	1.000
1992— Toronto (A.L.)	OF	18	29	7	10	3	0	1	3	.345	4	4	0	18	1	0	1.000
— Syracuse (Int'l)	OF	81	280	41	67	10	2	10	29	.239	44	43	7	143	3	5	.967
1993— Toronto (A.L.)	OF-1B	72	167	20	32	4	2	4	28	.192	23	26	3	97	2	1	.990
— Knoxville (Southern)	OF	7	23	6	6	2	0	0	2	.261	7	3	3	20	0	0	1.000
1994— Milwaukee (A.L.)■	OF-3B	102	367	55	85	15	2	9	45	.232	52	68	6	260	9	4	.985
1995— Milwaukee (A.L.)	OF-DH	44	129	19	34	3	1	4	16	.264	14	21	6	81	5	1	.989
— Beloit (Midwest)	OF	2	5	0	0	0	0	0	0	.000	3	1	0	1	0	0	1.000
— New Orleans (A.A.)	OF	11	33	3	8	1	0	0	3	.242	4	10	0	9	0	1	.900
1996— Milwaukee (A.L.)	OF-DH	43	67	7	12	2	1	2	10	.179	13	17	3	54	1	0	1.000
— New Orleans (A.A.)	DH	9	23	4	8	1	0	1	1	.348	7	4	0	...	...	...	...
1997— Calgary (PCL)■	OF-1B	59	209	44	71	18	3	9	44	.340	24	26	7	87	6	3	.969
— Pittsburgh (N.L.)	OF	71	167	33	59	16	1	7	33	.353	18	17	4	71	2	0	1.000
American League totals (7 years)		341	918	130	216	36	7	21	119	.235	120	162	21	600	21	7	.989
National League totals (1 year)		71	167	33	59	16	1	7	33	.353	18	17	4	71	2	0	1.000
Major league totals (8 years)		412	1085	163	275	52	8	28	152	.253	138	179	25	671	23	7	.990

W

WASDIN, JOHN   P   RED SOX

PERSONAL: Born August 5, 1972, in Fort Belvoir, Va. ... 6-2/193. ... Throws right, bats right. ... Full name: John Truman Wasdin.
HIGH SCHOOL: Amos P. Godby (Tallahassee, Fla.).
COLLEGE: Florida State.
TRANSACTIONS/CAREER NOTES: Selected by New York Yankees organization in 41st round of free-agent draft (June 4, 1990); did not sign. ... Selected by Oakland Athletics organization in first round (25th pick overall) of free-agent draft (June 3, 1993). ... Traded by A's with cash to Boston Red Sox for OF Jose Canseco (January 27, 1997).
STATISTICAL NOTES: Led Pacific Coast League with 26 home runs allowed in 1995.

Year Team (League)	W	L	Pct.	ERA	G	GS	CG	ShO	Sv.	IP	H	R	ER	BB	SO
1993— Arizona A's (Arizona)	0	0	...	3.00	1	1	0	0	0	3	3	1	1	0	1
— Madison (Midwest)	2	3	.400	1.86	9	9	0	0	0	48 1/3	32	11	10	9	40
— Modesto (California)	0	3	.000	3.86	3	3	0	0	0	16 1/3	17	9	7	4	11
1994— Modesto (California)	3	1	.750	1.69	6	4	0	0	0	26 2/3	17	6	5	5	30
— Huntsville (Southern)	12	3	.800	3.43	21	21	0	0	0	141 2/3	126	61	54	29	108
1995— Edmonton (PCL)	12	8	.600	5.52	29	•28	2	1	0	174 1/3	193	117	107	38	111
— Oakland (A.L.)	1	1	.500	4.67	5	2	0	0	0	17 1/3	14	9	9	3	6
1996— Edmonton (PCL)	2	1	.667	4.14	9	9	0	0	0	50	52	23	23	17	30
— Oakland (A.L.)	8	7	.533	5.96	25	21	1	0	0	131 1/3	145	96	87	50	75
1997— Boston (A.L.)■	4	6	.400	4.40	53	7	0	0	0	124 2/3	121	68	61	38	84
Major league totals (3 years)	13	14	.481	5.17	83	30	1	0	0	273 1/3	280	173	157	91	165

WASHBURN, JARROD   P   ANGELS

PERSONAL: Born August 13, 1974, in LaCrosse, Wis. ... 6-1/190. ... Throws left, bats left. ... Full name: Jarrod M. Washburn.
HIGH SCHOOL: Webster (Wis.).
COLLEGE: Wisconsin-Oshkosh.
TRANSACTIONS/CAREER NOTES: Selected by California Angels organization in second round of free-agent draft (June 1, 1995).

Year Team (League)	W	L	Pct.	ERA	G	GS	CG	ShO	Sv.	IP	H	R	ER	BB	SO
1995— Cedar Rapids (Midw.)	0	1	.000	3.44	3	3	0	0	0	18 1/3	7	7	7	7	20
— Boise (Northwest)	3	2	.600	3.33	8	8	0	0	0	46	35	17	17	14	54
1996— Lake Elsinore (Calif.)	6	3	.667	3.30	14	14	3	0	0	92 2/3	79	38	34	33	93
— Midland (Texas)	5	6	.455	4.40	13	13	1	0	0	88	77	44	43	25	58
1997— Midland (Texas)	15	•12	.556	4.80	29	*29	29	•1	0	*189 1/3	*211	*115	*101	65	*146
— Vancouver (PCL)	0	0	...	3.60	1	1	0	0	0	5	4	2	2	2	6

WATKINS, PAT   OF   REDS

PERSONAL: Born September 2, 1972, in Raleigh, N.C. ... 6-2/185. ... Bats right, throws right. ... Full name: William Patrick Watkins.
HIGH SCHOOL: Garner (N.C.).
COLLEGE: East Carolina.
TRANSACTIONS/CAREER NOTES: Selected by Cincinnati Reds organization in supplemental round ("sandwich pick" between first and second round, 32nd pick overall) of free-agent draft (June 3, 1993); pick recieved as part of compensation for Houston Astros signing Type A free-agent P Greg Swindell.
STATISTICAL NOTES: Led Carolina League with 267 total bases in 1994. ... Tied for Carolina League lead in double plays by outfielder with four in 1994.

Year Team (League)	Pos.	G	AB	R	H	2B	3B	HR	RBI	Avg.	BB	SO	SB	PO	A	E	Avg.
1993— Billings (Pioneer)	OF	66	235	46	63	10	3	6	30	.268	22	44	15	123	5	2	.985
1994— Win.-Salem (Car.)	OF	132	*524	*107	*152	24	5	27	83	.290	62	84	31	262	13	7	.975
1995— Win.-Salem (Car.)	OF	27	107	14	22	3	1	4	13	.206	10	24	1	51	5	1	.982
— Chattanooga (Sou.)	OF	105	358	57	104	26	2	12	57	.291	33	53	5	185	8	8	.960
1996— Chattanooga (Sou.)	OF	127	492	63	136	31	2	8	59	.276	30	64	15	220	*21	4	.984
1997— Chattanooga (Sou.)	OF	46	177	35	62	15	1	7	30	.350	15	16	9	78	3	0	1.000
— Indianapolis (A.A.)	OF	84	325	46	91	14	7	9	35	.280	24	55	13	170	5	2	.989
— Cincinnati (N.L.)	OF	17	29	2	6	2	0	0	0	.207	0	5	1	12	1	0	1.000
Major league totals (1 year)		17	29	2	6	2	0	0	0	.207	0	5	1	12	1	0	1.000

WATKINS, SCOTT   P   RANGERS

PERSONAL: Born May 15, 1970, in Tulsa, Okla. ... 6-3/180. ... Throws left, bats left. ... Full name: Scott Allen Watkins.
HIGH SCHOOL: Charles Page (Sand Springs, Calif.).
JUNIOR COLLEGE: Seminole (Okla.).
COLLEGE: Oklahoma State.
TRANSACTIONS/CAREER NOTES: Selected by Minnesota Twins organization in 23rd round of free-agent draft (June 1, 1992). ... Released by Twins following 1996 season. ... Signed by Wilmington, Kansas City Royals organization (May 12, 1997). ... Released by Royals organization (June 13, 1997). ... Signed by New Haven, Colorado Rockies organization (July 16, 1997). ...Granted free agency (October 15, 1997). ... Signed by Texas Rangers organization (December 16, 1997).

Year Team (League)	W	L	Pct.	ERA	G	GS	CG	ShO	Sv.	IP	H	R	ER	BB	SO
1992— Kenosha (Midwest)	2	5	.286	3.69	27	0	0	0	1	46 1/3	43	21	19	14	58
1993— Fort Wayne (Midw.)	2	0	1.000	3.26	15	0	0	0	1	30 1/3	26	13	11	9	31
— Fort Myers (Fla. St.)	2	2	.500	2.93	20	0	0	0	3	27 2/3	27	14	9	12	41
— Nashville (Southern)	0	1	1.000	5.94	13	0	0	0	0	16 2/3	19	15	11	7	17
1994— Nashville (Southern)	1	0	1.000	4.61	11	0	0	0	3	13 2/3	13	9	7	4	11
— Salt Lake (PCL)	2	6	.250	6.75	46	0	0	0	3	57 1/3	73	46	43	28	47

W

Year Team (League)	W	L	Pct.	ERA	G	GS	CG	ShO	Sv.	IP	H	R	ER	BB	SO
1995— Salt Lake (PCL)	4	2	.667	2.80	45	0	0	0	*20	54²/₃	45	18	17	13	57
— Minnesota (A.L.)	0	0	...	5.40	27	0	0	0	0	21²/₃	22	14	13	11	11
1996— Salt Lake (PCL)	4	6	.400	7.69	47	0	0	0	1	50¹/₃	60	46	43	34	43
1997— Omaha (Am. Assoc.)■	0	0	...	6.46	9	0	0	0	0	15¹/₃	19	13	11	6	15
— New Haven (Eastern)■	2	0	1.000	3.52	13	0	0	0	0	15¹/₃	9	6	6	3	8
Major league totals (1 year)	0	0	...	5.40	27	0	0	0	0	21²/₃	22	14	13	11	11

WATSON, ALLEN   P   ANGELS

PERSONAL: Born November 18, 1970, in Jamaica, N.Y. ... 6-3/190. ... Throws left, bats left. ... Full name: Allen Kenneth Watson.
HIGH SCHOOL: Christ the King (Queens, N.Y.).
COLLEGE: New York State Institute of Technology.
TRANSACTIONS/CAREER NOTES: Selected by St. Louis Cardinals organization in first round (21st pick overall) of free-agent draft (June 3, 1991); pick received as part of compensation for Toronto Blue Jays signing Type A free-agent P Ken Dayley. ... On Savannah disabled list (August 19, 1991-remainder of season). ... On suspended list (June 25-July 3, 1994). ... On St. Louis disabled list (June 7-July 8, 1995); included rehabilitation assignments to Arkansas (June 21-26) and Louisville (June 26-July 8). ... Traded by Cardinals with P Rich DeLucia and P Doug Creek to San Francisco Giants for SS Royce Clayton and a player to be named later (December 14, 1995); Cardinals acquired 2B Chris Wimmer to complete deal (January 16, 1996). ... On San Francisco disabled list (July 2-25, 1996); included rehabilitation assignment to San Jose (July 15-25). ... Traded by Giants with P Fausto Macey to Anaheim Angels for 1B J.T. Snow (November 27, 1996).
STATISTICAL NOTES: Led A.L. with 37 home runs allowed in 1997.
MISCELLANEOUS: Singled in three games as pinch-hitter with San Francisco (1996).

Year Team (League)	W	L	Pct.	ERA	G	GS	CG	ShO	Sv.	IP	H	R	ER	BB	SO
1991— Hamilton (NYP)	1	1	.500	2.52	8	8	0	0	0	39¹/₃	22	15	11	17	46
— Savannah (S. Atl.)	1	1	.500	3.95	3	3	0	0	0	13²/₃	16	7	6	8	12
1992— St. Petersburg (FSL)	5	4	.556	1.91	14	14	2	0	0	89²/₃	81	31	19	18	80
— Arkansas (Texas)	8	5	.615	2.15	14	14	3	1	0	96¹/₃	77	24	23	23	93
— Louisville (A.A.)	1	0	1.000	1.46	2	2	0	0	0	12¹/₃	8	4	2	5	9
1993— Louisville (A.A.)	5	4	.556	2.91	17	17	2	0	0	120²/₃	101	46	39	31	86
— St. Louis (N.L.)	6	7	.462	4.60	16	15	0	0	0	86	90	53	44	28	49
1994— St. Louis (N.L.)	6	5	.545	5.52	22	22	0	0	0	115²/₃	130	73	71	53	74
1995— St. Louis (N.L.)	7	9	.438	4.96	21	19	0	0	0	114¹/₃	126	68	63	41	49
— Louisville (A.A.)	2	2	.500	2.63	4	4	1	0	0	24	20	10	7	6	19
— Arkansas (Texas)	1	0	1.000	0.00	1	1	0	0	0	5	4	1	0	0	7
1996— San Francisco (N.L.)■	8	12	.400	4.61	29	29	2	0	0	185²/₃	189	105	95	69	128
— San Jose (California)	0	0	...	1.42	2	2	0	0	0	6¹/₃	7	1	1	0	12
1997— Anaheim (A.L.)■	12	12	.500	4.93	35	34	0	0	0	199	220	121	109	73	141
A.L. totals (1 year)	12	12	.500	4.93	35	34	0	0	0	199	220	121	109	73	141
N.L. totals (4 years)	27	33	.450	4.90	88	85	2	0	0	501²/₃	535	299	273	191	300
Major league totals (5 years)	39	45	.464	4.91	123	119	2	0	0	700²/₃	755	420	382	264	441

WEATHERS, DAVE   P   REDS

PERSONAL: Born September 25, 1969, in Lawrenceburg, Tenn. ... 6-3/220. ... Throws right, bats right. ... Full name: John David Weathers.
HIGH SCHOOL: Loretto (Tenn.).
JUNIOR COLLEGE: Motlow State Community College (Tenn.).
TRANSACTIONS/CAREER NOTES: Selected by Toronto Blue Jays organization in third round of free-agent draft (June 1, 1988). ... On Syracuse disabled list (May 11-July 31, 1992). ... Selected by Florida Marlins in second round (29th pick overall) of expansion draft (November 17, 1992). ... On Florida disabled list (June 26-July 13, 1995); included rehabilitation assignment to Brevard County (July 4-10). ... Traded by Marlins to New York Yankees for P Mark Hutton (July 31, 1996). ... Traded by Yankees to Cleveland Indians for OF Chad Curtis (June 9, 1997). ... Claimed on waivers by Cincinnati Reds (December 20, 1997).
MISCELLANEOUS: Appeared in two games as pinch-runner (1994). ... Appeared in one game as pinch-runner with Florida (1996).

Year Team (League)	W	L	Pct.	ERA	G	GS	CG	ShO	Sv.	IP	H	R	ER	BB	SO
1988— St. Catharines (NYP)	4	4	.500	3.02	15	12	0	0	0	62²/₃	58	30	21	26	36
1989— Myrtle Beach (SAL)	11	•13	.458	3.86	31	*31	2	0	0	172²/₃	163	99	74	86	111
1990— Dunedin (Fla. St.)	10	7	.588	3.70	27	•27	2	0	0	158	158	82	65	59	96
1991— Knoxville (Southern)	10	7	.588	2.45	24	22	5	2	0	139¹/₃	121	51	38	49	114
— Toronto (A.L.)	1	0	1.000	4.91	15	0	0	0	0	14²/₃	15	9	8	17	13
1992— Syracuse (Int'l)	1	4	.200	4.66	12	10	0	0	0	48¹/₃	48	29	25	21	30
— Toronto (A.L.)	0	0	...	8.10	2	0	0	0	0	3¹/₃	5	3	3	2	3
1993— Edmonton (PCL)■	11	4	•.733	3.83	22	22	3	1	0	141	150	77	60	47	117
— Florida (N.L.)	2	3	.400	5.12	14	6	0	0	0	45²/₃	57	26	26	13	34
1994— Florida (N.L.)	8	12	.400	5.27	24	24	0	0	0	135	166	87	79	59	72
1995— Florida (N.L.)	4	5	.444	5.98	28	15	0	0	0	90¹/₃	104	68	60	52	60
— Brevard County (FSL)	0	0	...	0.00	1	1	0	0	0	4	4	0	0	1	3
— Charlotte (Int'l)	0	1	.000	9.00	1	1	0	0	0	5	10	5	5	5	0
1996— Florida (N.L.)	2	2	.500	4.54	31	8	0	0	0	71¹/₃	85	41	36	28	40
— Charlotte (Int'l)	0	0	...	7.71	1	1	0	0	0	2¹/₃	5	2	2	3	0
— New York (A.L.)■	0	2	.000	9.35	11	4	0	0	0	17¹/₃	23	19	18	14	13
— Columbus (Int'l)	0	2	.000	5.40	3	3	0	0	0	16²/₃	20	13	10	5	7
1997— New York (A.L.)	0	1	.000	10.00	10	0	0	0	0	9	15	10	10	7	4
— Columbus (Int'l)	2	2	.500	3.19	5	5	1	0	0	36²/₃	35	18	13	7	35
— Buffalo (A.A.)■	4	3	.571	3.15	11	11	2	1	0	68²/₃	71	37	24	17	51
— Cleveland (A.L.)	1	2	.333	7.56	9	1	0	0	0	16²/₃	23	14	14	8	14
A.L. totals (4 years)	2	5	.286	7.82	47	5	0	0	0	61	81	55	53	48	47
N.L. totals (4 years)	16	22	.421	5.28	97	53	0	0	0	342¹/₃	412	222	201	152	206
Major league totals (7 years)	18	27	.400	5.67	144	58	0	0	0	403¹/₃	493	277	254	200	253

DIVISION SERIES RECORD

Year Team (League)	W	L	Pct.	ERA	G	GS	CG	ShO	Sv.	IP	H	R	ER	BB	SO
1996— New York (A.L.)	1	0	1.000	0.00	2	0	0	0	0	5	1	0	0	0	5

Year	Team (League)	W	L	Pct.	ERA	G	GS	CG	ShO	Sv.	IP	H	R	ER	BB	SO
1996— New York (A.L.).................		1	0	1.000	0.00	2	0	0	0	0	3	3	0	0	0	0

WORLD SERIES RECORD

NOTES: Member of World Series championship team (1996).

Year	Team (League)	W	L	Pct.	ERA	G	GS	CG	ShO	Sv.	IP	H	R	ER	BB	SO
1996— New York (A.L.).................		0	0	...	3.00	3	0	0	0	0	3	2	1	1	4	3

WEBER, NEIL — P — DIAMONDBACKS

PERSONAL: Born December 6, 1972, in Newport Beach, Calif. ... 6-5/215. ... Throws left, bats left. ... Full name: Neil Aaron Weber.

HIGH SCHOOL: Corona Del Mar (Newport Beach, Calif.).

JUNIOR COLLEGE: Cuesta College (Calif.).

TRANSACTIONS/CAREER NOTES: Selected by Montreal Expos organization in eighth round of free-agent draft (June 3, 1993). ... On disabled list (July 12-September 12, 1996). ... Selected by Arizona Diamondbacks in first round (21st pick overall) of expansion draft (November 18, 1997).

Year	Team (League)	W	L	Pct.	ERA	G	GS	CG	ShO	Sv.	IP	H	R	ER	BB	SO
1993— Jamestown (NYP)		6	5	.545	2.77	16	•16	2	•1	0	94 1/3	84	46	29	36	80
1994— W.P. Beach (FSL)................		9	7	.563	3.20	25	24	1	0	0	135	113	58	48	62	134
1995— Harrisburg (Eastern)		6	11	.353	5.01	28	28	0	0	0	152 2/3	157	98	*85	*90	119
1996— Harrisburg (Eastern)		7	4	.636	3.03	18	18	1	0	0	107	90	37	36	44	74
1997— Ottawa (Int'l)		2	5	.286	7.94	9	9	0	0	0	39 2/3	46	46	35	40	27
— Harrisburg (Eastern)		7	6	.538	3.83	18	18	1	1	0	112 2/3	93	56	48	51	121

WEBSTER, LENNY — C — ORIOLES

PERSONAL: Born February 10, 1965, in New Orleans. ... 5-9/202. ... Bats right, throws right. ... Full name: Leonard Irell Webster.

HIGH SCHOOL: Lutcher (La.).

COLLEGE: Grambling State.

TRANSACTIONS/CAREER NOTES: Selected by Minnesota Twins organization in 16th round of free-agent draft (June 7, 1982); did not sign. ... Selected by Twins organization in 21st round of free-agent draft (June 3, 1985). ... Traded by Twins to Montreal Expos organization for a player to be named later (March 14, 1994). ... Granted free agency (December 23, 1994). ... Signed by Scranton Wilkes/Barre, Philadelphia Phillies organization (April 7, 1995). ... Claimed on waivers by Expos (March 29, 1996). ... Granted free agency (October 16, 1996). ... Signed by Baltimore Orioles organization (December 18, 1996). ... Granted free agency (October 30, 1997). ... Re-signed by Orioles (November 24, 1997).

HONORS: Named Midwest League Most Valuable Player (1988).

Year	Team (League)	Pos.	G	AB	R	H	2B	3B	HR	RBI	Avg.	BB	SO	SB	PO	A	E	Avg.
1986— Kenosha (Midwest)	C	22	65	2	10	2	0	0	8	.154	10	12	0	87	9	0	1.000
— Elizabethton (App.).....	C	48	152	29	35	4	0	3	14	.230	22	21	1	88	11	3	.971
1987— Kenosha (Midwest)	C	52	140	17	35	7	0	3	17	.250	17	20	2	228	29	5	.981
1988— Kenosha (Midwest)	C	129	465	82	134	23	2	11	87	.288	71	47	3	606	96	14	.980
1989— Visalia (California)	C	63	231	36	62	7	0	5	39	.268	27	27	2	352	57	4	.990
— Orlando (South.)	C	59	191	29	45	7	0	2	17	.236	44	20	2	293	46	4	.988
— Minnesota (A.L.)	C	14	20	3	6	2	0	0	1	.300	3	2	0	32	0	0	1.000
1990— Orlando (South.)	C	126	455	69	119	31	0	8	71	.262	68	57	0	629	70	9	.987
— Minnesota (A.L.)	C	2	6	1	2	1	0	0	0	.333	1	1	0	9	0	0	1.000
1991— Portland (PCL)	C	87	325	43	82	18	0	7	34	.252	24	32	1	477	65	6	*.989
— Minnesota (A.L.)	C	18	34	7	10	1	0	3	8	.294	6	10	0	61	10	1	.986
1992— Minnesota (A.L.)	C-DH	53	118	10	33	10	1	1	13	.280	9	11	0	190	11	1	.995
1993— Minnesota (A.L.)	C-DH	49	106	14	21	2	0	1	8	.198	11	8	1	177	13	0	1.000
1994— Montreal (N.L.)■.......	C	57	143	13	39	10	0	5	23	.273	16	24	0	237	19	1	.996
1995— Philadelphia (N.L.)■ ..	C	49	150	18	40	9	0	4	14	.267	16	27	0	274	18	3	.990
1996— Montreal (N.L.)■.......	C	78	174	18	40	10	0	2	17	.230	25	21	1	390	25	1	.998
1997— Baltimore (A.L.)■.......	C-DH	98	259	29	66	8	1	7	37	.255	22	46	0	532	36	3	.995
American League totals (6 years)		234	543	64	138	24	2	12	67	.254	52	78	1	1001	70	5	.995
National League totals (3 years)		184	467	49	119	29	0	11	54	.255	57	72	0	901	62	5	.995
Major league totals (9 years)		418	1010	113	257	53	2	23	121	.254	109	150	1	1902	132	10	.995

DIVISION SERIES RECORD

Year	Team (League)	Pos.	G	AB	R	H	2B	3B	HR	RBI	Avg.	BB	SO	SB	PO	A	E	Avg.
1997— Baltimore (A.L.).........	C	3	6	1	1	0	0	0	1	.167	1	0	0	20	0	0	1.000

CHAMPIONSHIP SERIES RECORD

Year	Team (League)	Pos.	G	AB	R	H	2B	3B	HR	RBI	Avg.	BB	SO	SB	PO	A	E	Avg.
1997— Baltimore (A.L.).........	C-PH	4	9	0	2	0	0	0	0	.222	0	1	0	14	0	2	.875

W

WEHNER, JOHN — 3B/OF

PERSONAL: Born June 29, 1967, in Pittsburgh. ... 6-3/206. ... Bats right, throws right. ... Full name: John Paul Wehner. ... Name pronounced WAY-ner.

HIGH SCHOOL: Carrick (Pittsburgh).

COLLEGE: Indiana.

TRANSACTIONS/CAREER NOTES: Selected by Pittsburgh Pirates organization in seventh round of free-agent draft (June 1, 1988). ... On Pittsburgh disabled list (August 29-October 7, 1991 and July 20, 1994-remainder of season). ... Claimed on waivers by Los Angeles Dodgers (October 15, 1996). ... Released by Dodgers (March 17, 1997). ... Signed by Florida Marlins organization (March 21, 1997). ... On Florida disabled list (June 26-September 1, 1997). ... Released by Marlins (November 20, 1997).

STATISTICAL NOTES: Led New York-Pennsylvania League third basemen with 219 total chances and 14 double plays in 1988. ... Led Carolina League third basemen with 403 total chances and tied for lead with 24 double plays in 1989. ... Led Eastern League third basemen with 476 total chances and 40 double plays in 1990.

Year	Team (League)	Pos.	G	AB	R	H	2B	3B	HR	RBI	Avg.	BB	SO	SB	PO	A	E	Avg.
1988—Watertown (NYP)		3B	70	265	41	73	6	0	3	31	.275	21	39	18	*65	137	17	.922
1989—Salem (Carolina)		3B	*137	*515	69	*155	32	6	14	73	.301	42	81	21	*89	*278	36	.911
1990—Harrisburg (Eastern)		3B	•138	*511	71	147	27	1	4	62	.288	40	51	24	*109	*317	*50	.895
1991—Carolina (Southern)		3B-1B	61	234	30	62	5	1	3	21	.265	24	32	17	182	134	10	.969
— Buffalo (A.A.)		3B	31	112	18	34	9	2	1	15	.304	14	12	6	30	69	8	.925
— Pittsburgh (N.L.)		3B	37	106	15	36	7	0	0	7	.340	7	17	3	23	65	6	.936
1992—Buffalo (A.A.)		2B-1B-3B	60	223	37	60	13	2	7	27	.269	29	30	10	226	122	7	.980
— Pittsburgh (N.L.)		3B-1B-2B	55	123	11	22	6	0	0	4	.179	12	22	3	96	64	4	.976
1993—Pittsburgh (N.L.)		OF-3B-2B	29	35	3	5	0	0	0	0	.143	6	10	0	17	8	0	1.000
— Buffalo (A.A.)		3B-2B-OF	89	330	61	83	22	2	7	34	.252	40	53	17	133	256	17	.958
1994—Buffalo (A.A.)		OF-3B-2B	88	330	52	100	19	3	7	44	.303	32	36	21	131	113	11	.957
— Pittsburgh (N.L.)		3B	2	4	1	1	1	0	0	3	.250	0	1	0	0	2	0	1.000
1995—Calgary (PCL)		3B-2B-OF	40	158	30	52	12	2	4	24	.329	12	16	8	36	98	12	.918
— Pittsburgh (N.L.)		O-3-C-S	52	107	13	33	0	3	0	5	.308	10	17	3	35	29	0	1.000
1996—Pittsburgh (N.L.)		O-3-2-C	86	139	19	36	9	1	2	13	.259	8	22	1	60	43	2	.981
1997—Charlotte (Int'l)■		3-0-1-2	31	93	16	26	5	0	3	11	.280	6	18	3	32	33	2	.970
— Florida (N.L.)		OF-3B	44	36	8	10	2	0	0	2	.278	2	5	1	14	3	0	1.000
Major league totals (7 years)			305	550	70	143	25	4	2	34	.260	45	94	11	245	214	12	.975

DIVISION SERIES RECORD

Year	Team (League)	Pos.	G	AB	R	H	2B	3B	HR	RBI	Avg.	BB	SO	SB	PO	A	E	Avg.
1997—Florida (N.L.)		PR-OF	1	0	0	0	0	0	0	0	...	0	0	0	0	0	0	...

CHAMPIONSHIP SERIES RECORD

Year	Team (League)	Pos.	G	AB	R	H	2B	3B	HR	RBI	Avg.	BB	SO	SB	PO	A	E	Avg.
1992—Pittsburgh (N.L.)		PH	2	2	0	0	0	0	0	0	.000	0	2	0	...	...	...	...

WEISS, WALT   SS   BRAVES

PERSONAL: Born November 28, 1963, in Tuxedo, N.Y. ... 6-0/175. ... Bats both, throws right. ... Full name: Walter William Weiss Jr.
HIGH SCHOOL: Suffern (N.Y.).
COLLEGE: North Carolina.
TRANSACTIONS/CAREER NOTES: Selected by Baltimore Orioles organization in 10th round of free-agent draft (June 7, 1982); did not sign. ... Selected by Oakland Athletics organization in first round (11th pick overall) of free-agent draft (June 3, 1985). ... On Oakland disabled list (May 18-July 31, 1989); included rehabilitation assignments to Tacoma (July 18-25) and Modesto (July 26-31). ... On disabled list (August 23-September 7, 1990; April 15-30 and June 7, 1991-remainder of season). ... On Oakland disabled list (March 30-June 3, 1992); included rehabilitation assignment to Tacoma (May 26-June 3). ... Traded by A's to Florida Marlins for C Eric Helfand and a player to be named later (November 17, 1992); A's acquired P Scott Baker from Marlins to complete deal (November 20, 1992). ... Granted free agency (October 25, 1993). ... Signed by Colorado Rockies (January 7, 1994). ... Granted free agency (November 3, 1995). ... Re-signed by Rockies (December 6, 1995). ... On disabled list (July 22-August 8, 1997). ... Granted free agency (October 27, 1997). ... Signed by Atlanta Braves (November 17, 1997).
HONORS: Named A.L. Rookie Player of the Year by THE SPORTING NEWS (1988). ... Named A.L. Rookie of the Year by Baseball Writers' Association of America (1988).
STATISTICAL NOTES: Led N.L. shortstops with 99 double plays in 1995. ... Career major league grand slams: 1.

Year	Team (League)	Pos.	G	AB	R	H	2B	3B	HR	RBI	Avg.	BB	SO	SB	PO	A	E	Avg.
1985—Pocatello (Pioneer)		SS	40	158	19	49	9	3	0	21	.310	12	18	6	51	126	11	.941
— Modesto (California)		SS	30	122	17	24	4	1	0	7	.197	12	20	3	36	97	7	.950
1986—Madison (Midwest)		SS	84	322	50	97	15	5	2	54	.301	33	66	12	143	251	20	.952
— Huntsville (Southern)		SS	46	160	19	40	2	1	0	13	.250	11	39	5	72	142	11	.951
1987—Huntsville (Southern)		SS	91	337	43	96	16	2	1	32	.285	47	67	23	152	259	17	.960
— Oakland (A.L.)		SS-DH	16	26	3	12	4	0	1	1	.462	2	2	1	8	30	1	.974
— Tacoma (PCL)		SS	46	179	35	47	4	3	0	17	.263	28	31	8	76	140	11	.952
1988—Oakland (A.L.)		SS	147	452	44	113	17	3	3	39	.250	35	56	4	254	431	15	.979
1989—Oakland (A.L.)		SS	84	236	30	55	11	0	3	21	.233	21	39	6	106	195	15	.953
— Tacoma (PCL)		SS	2	9	1	1	1	0	0	1	.111	0	0	0	0	3	1	.750
— Modesto (California)		SS	5	8	1	3	0	0	0	1	.375	4	1	0	6	9	0	1.000
1990—Oakland (A.L.)		SS	138	445	50	118	17	1	2	35	.265	46	53	9	194	373	12	.979
1991—Oakland (A.L.)		SS	40	133	15	30	6	1	0	13	.226	12	14	6	64	99	5	.970
1992—Tacoma (PCL)		SS	4	13	2	3	1	0	0	3	.231	2	1	0	8	14	1	.957
— Oakland (A.L.)		SS	103	316	36	67	5	2	0	21	.212	43	39	6	144	270	19	.956
1993—Florida (N.L.)■		SS	158	500	50	133	14	2	1	39	.266	79	73	7	229	406	15	.977
1994—Colorado (N.L.)■		SS	110	423	58	106	11	4	1	32	.251	56	58	12	157	318	13	.973
1995—Colorado (N.L.)		SS	137	427	65	111	17	3	1	25	.260	98	57	15	201	406	16	.974
1996—Colorado (N.L.)		SS	155	517	89	146	20	2	8	48	.282	80	78	10	220	450	*30	.957
1997—Colorado (N.L.)		SS	121	393	52	106	23	5	4	38	.270	66	56	5	191	372	10	.983
American League totals (6 years)			528	1608	178	395	60	7	8	130	.246	159	203	32	770	1398	67	.970
National League totals (5 years)			681	2260	314	602	85	16	15	182	.266	379	322	49	998	1952	84	.972
Major league totals (11 years)			1209	3868	492	997	145	23	23	312	.258	538	525	81	1768	3350	151	.971

DIVISION SERIES RECORD

Year	Team (League)	Pos.	G	AB	R	H	2B	3B	HR	RBI	Avg.	BB	SO	SB	PO	A	E	Avg.
1995—Colorado (N.L.)		SS	4	12	1	2	0	0	0	0	.167	3	3	1	6	12	0	1.000

W

Year	Team (League)	Pos.	G	AB	R	H	2B	3B	HR	RBI	Avg.	BB	SO	SB	PO	A	E	Avg.
							BATTING									FIELDING		
1988—Oakland (A.L.)		SS	4	15	2	5	2	0	0	2	.333	0	4	0	7	10	0	1.000
1989—Oakland (A.L.)		SS-PR	4	9	2	1	1	0	0	0	.111	1	1	1	5	9	0	1.000
1990—Oakland (A.L.)		SS	2	7	2	0	0	0	0	0	.000	2	2	0	2	7	1	.900
1992—Oakland (A.L.)		SS	3	6	1	1	0	0	0	0	.167	2	1	2	5	6	0	1.000
Championship series totals (4 years)			13	37	7	7	3	0	0	2	.189	5	8	3	19	32	1	.981

WORLD SERIES RECORD

NOTES: Member of World Series championship team (1989).

Year	Team (League)	Pos.	G	AB	R	H	2B	3B	HR	RBI	Avg.	BB	SO	SB	PO	A	E	Avg.
							BATTING									FIELDING		
1988—Oakland (A.L.)		SS	5	16	1	1	0	0	0	0	.063	0	1	0	5	11	1	.941
1989—Oakland (A.L.)		SS	4	15	3	2	0	0	1	1	.133	2	2	0	7	8	0	1.000
World Series totals (2 years)			9	31	4	3	0	0	1	1	.097	2	3	0	12	19	1	.969

WELCH, MIKE — P — PHILLIES

PERSONAL: Born August 25, 1972, in Haverhill, Mass. ... 6-2/210. ... Throws right, bats left. ... Full name: Michael P. Welch.
HIGH SCHOOL: Nashua (N.H.).
COLLEGE: Southern Maine.
TRANSACTIONS/CAREER NOTES: Selected by New York Mets organization in third round of free-agent draft (June 3, 1993). ... Traded by Mets to Philadelphia Phillies for P Hector Mercado (December 15, 1997).

Year	Team (League)	W	L	Pct.	ERA	G	GS	CG	ShO	Sv.	IP	H	R	ER	BB	SO
1993—Pittsfield (NYP)		3	1	.750	1.45	17	0	0	0	9	31	23	9	5	6	31
1994—Capital City (S. Atl.)...........		7	11	.389	3.61	24	24	5	2	0	159²/₃	151	81	64	33	127
1995—St. Lucie (Fla. St.).............		4	4	.500	5.40	44	6	0	0	15	70	96	50	42	18	51
—Binghamton (Eastern)		0	0	. . .	0.00	1	0	0	0	0	1	0	0	0	0	2
1996—Binghamton (Eastern)		4	2	.667	4.59	46	0	0	0	27	51	55	29	26	10	53
—Norfolk (Int'l)		0	1	.000	4.15	10	0	0	0	2	8²/₃	8	4	4	2	6
1997—Norfolk (Int'l)		2	2	.500	3.66	46	0	0	0	20	51²/₃	53	21	21	16	35

WELLS, BOB — P — MARINERS

PERSONAL: Born November 1, 1966, in Yakima, Wash. ... 6-0/180. ... Throws right, bats right. ... Full name: Robert Lee Wells.
HIGH SCHOOL: Elsenhower (Yakima, Wash.).
JUNIOR COLLEGE: Spokane Falls Community College (Wash.).
TRANSACTIONS/CAREER NOTES: Signed as non-drafted free agent by Philadelphia Phillies organization (August 18, 1988). ... On Reading disabled list (July 21, 1991-remainder of season). ... On Scranton/Wilkes-Barre disabled list (April 9-28, 1992). ... On Reading disabled list (June 9, 1992-remainder of season and April 8-June 13, 1993). ... Claimed on waivers by Seattle Mariners (June 30, 1994).

Year	Team (League)	W	L	Pct.	ERA	G	GS	CG	ShO	Sv.	IP	H	R	ER	BB	SO
1989—Martinsville (App.)............		0	0	. . .	4.50	4	0	0	0	0	6	8	5	3	2	3
1990—Spartanburg (SAL)............		5	8	.385	2.87	20	19	2	0	0	113	94	47	36	40	73
—Clearwater (Fla. St.)		0	2	.000	4.91	6	1	0	0	1	14²/₃	17	9	8	6	11
1991—Clearwater (Fla. St.)		7	2	.778	3.11	24	9	1	0	0	75¹/₃	63	27	26	19	66
—Reading (Eastern)		1	0	1.000	3.60	1	1	0	0	0	5	4	2	2	1	3
1992—Clearwater (Fla. St.)		1	0	1.000	3.86	9	0	0	0	5	9¹/₃	10	4	4	3	9
—Reading (Eastern)		0	1	.000	1.17	3	3	0	0	0	15¹/₃	12	2	2	5	11
1993—Clearwater (Fla. St.)		1	0	1.000	0.98	12	1	0	0	2	27²/₃	23	5	3	6	24
—Scran./W.B. (Int'l).............		1	1	.500	2.79	11	0	0	0	0	19¹/₃	19	7	6	5	8
1994—Reading (Eastern)		1	3	.250	2.79	14	0	0	0	4	19¹/₃	18	6	6	3	19
—Philadelphia (N.L.)..............		1	0	1.000	1.80	6	0	0	0	0	5	4	1	1	3	3
—Scran./W.B. (Int'l)..............		0	2	.000	2.45	11	0	0	0	0	14²/₃	18	6	4	6	13
—Calgary (PCL)■..................		3	2	.600	6.54	6	6	0	0	0	31²/₃	43	27	23	9	17
—Seattle (A.L.)		1	0	1.000	2.25	1	0	0	0	0	4	4	1	1	1	3
1995—Seattle (A.L.)		4	3	.571	5.75	30	4	0	0	0	76²/₃	88	51	49	39	38
1996—Seattle (A.L.)		12	7	.632	5.30	36	16	1	1	0	130²/₃	141	78	77	46	94
1997—Seattle (A.L.)		2	0	1.000	5.75	46	1	0	0	2	67¹/₃	88	49	43	18	51
A.L. totals (4 years)		19	10	.655	5.49	113	21	1	1	2	278²/₃	321	179	170	104	186
N.L. totals (1 year)		1	0	1.000	1.80	6	0	0	0	0	5	4	1	1	3	3
Major league totals (4 years)......		20	10	.667	5.43	119	21	1	1	2	283²/₃	325	180	171	107	189

DIVISION SERIES RECORD

Year	Team (League)	W	L	Pct.	ERA	G	GS	CG	ShO	Sv.	IP	H	R	ER	BB	SO
1995—Seattle (A.L.)		0	0	. . .	9.00	1	0	0	0	0	1	2	1	1	1	0
1997—Seattle (A.L.)		0	0	. . .	0.00	1	0	0	0	0	1¹/₃	1	0	0	1	1
Div. series totals (2 years)		0	0	. . .	3.86	2	0	0	0	0	2¹/₃	3	1	1	1	1

CHAMPIONSHIP SERIES RECORD

Year	Team (League)	W	L	Pct.	ERA	G	GS	CG	ShO	Sv.	IP	H	R	ER	BB	SO
1995—Seattle (A.L.)		0	0	. . .	3.00	1	0	0	0	0	3	2	1	1	2	2

WELLS, DAVID — P — YANKEES

PERSONAL: Born May 20, 1963, in Torrance, Calif. ... 6-4/225. ... Throws left, bats left. ... Full name: David Lee Wells.
HIGH SCHOOL: Point Loma (San Diego).

W

TRANSACTIONS/CAREER NOTES: Selected by Toronto Blue Jays organization in second round of free-agent draft (June 7, 1982). ... On Knoxville disabled list (June 28, 1984-remainder of season). ... On disabled list (April 10, 1985-entire season). ... On Knoxville disabled list (July 7-August 20, 1986). ... Released by Blue Jays (March 30, 1993). ... Signed by Detroit Tigers (April 3, 1993). ... On disabled list (August 1-20, 1993). ... Granted free agency (October 28, 1993). ... Re-signed by Tigers (December 13, 1993). ... On Detroit disabled list (April 19-June 6, 1994); included rehabilitation assignment to Lakeland (May 27-June 6). ... Traded by Tigers to Cincinnati Reds for P C.J. Nitkowski, P David Tuttle and a player to be named later (July 31, 1995); Tigers acquired IF Mark Lewis to complete deal (November 16, 1995). ... Traded by Reds to Baltimore Orioles for OF Curtis Goodwin and OF Trovin Valdez (December 26, 1995). ... Granted free agency (October 29, 1996). ... Signed by New York Yankees (December 24, 1996).

STATISTICAL NOTES: Struck out 16 batters in one game (July 30, 1997).

Year Team (League)	W	L	Pct.	ERA	G	GS	CG	ShO	Sv.	IP	H	R	ER	BB	SO
1982—Medicine Hat (Pio.)	4	3	.571	5.18	12	12	1	0	0	64 1/3	71	42	37	32	53
1983—Kinston (Carolina)	6	5	.545	3.73	25	25	5	0	0	157	141	81	65	71	115
1984—Kinston (Carolina)	1	6	.143	4.71	7	7	0	0	0	42	51	29	22	19	44
—Knoxville (Southern)	3	2	.600	2.59	8	8	3	1	0	59	58	22	17	17	34
1985—						Did not play.									
1986—Florence (S. Atl.)	0	0	...	3.55	4	1	0	0	0	12 2/3	7	6	5	9	14
—Ventura (Calif.)	2	1	.667	1.89	5	2	0	0	0	19	13	5	4	4	26
—Knoxville (Southern)	1	3	.250	4.05	10	7	1	0	0	40	42	24	18	18	32
—Syracuse (Int'l)	0	1	.000	9.82	3	0	0	0	0	3 2/3	6	4	4	1	2
1987—Syracuse (Int'l)	4	6	.400	3.87	43	12	0	0	6	109 1/3	102	49	47	32	106
—Toronto (A.L.)	4	3	.571	3.99	18	2	0	0	1	29 1/3	37	14	13	12	32
1988—Toronto (A.L.)	3	5	.375	4.62	41	0	0	0	4	64 1/3	65	36	33	31	56
—Syracuse (Int'l)	0	0	...	0.00	6	0	0	0	3	5 2/3	7	1	0	2	8
1989—Toronto (A.L.)	7	4	.636	2.40	54	0	0	0	2	86 1/3	66	25	23	28	78
1990—Toronto (A.L.)	11	6	.647	3.14	43	25	0	0	3	189	165	72	66	45	115
1991—Toronto (A.L.)	15	10	.600	3.72	40	28	2	0	1	198 1/3	188	88	82	49	106
1992—Toronto (A.L.)	7	9	.438	5.40	41	14	0	0	2	120	138	84	72	36	62
1993—Detroit (A.L.)■	11	9	.550	4.19	32	30	0	0	0	187	183	93	87	42	139
1994—Lakeland (Fla. St.)	0	0	...	0.00	2	2	0	0	0	6	5	1	0	0	3
—Detroit (A.L.)	5	7	.417	3.96	16	16	5	1	0	111 1/3	113	54	49	24	71
1995—Detroit (A.L.)	10	3	.769	3.04	18	18	3	0	0	130 1/3	120	54	44	37	83
—Cincinnati (N.L.)■	6	5	.545	3.59	11	11	3	0	0	72 2/3	74	34	29	16	50
1996—Baltimore (A.L.)■	11	14	.440	5.14	34	34	3	0	0	224 1/3	247	132	128	51	130
1997—New York (A.L.)■	16	10	.615	4.21	32	32	5	2	0	218	239	109	102	45	156
A.L. totals (11 years)	100	80	.556	4.04	369	199	18	3	13	1558 1/3	1561	761	699	400	1028
N.L. totals (1 year)	6	5	.545	3.59	11	11	3	0	0	72 2/3	74	34	29	16	50
Major league totals (11 years)	106	85	.555	4.02	380	210	21	3	13	1631	1635	795	728	416	1078

DIVISION SERIES RECORD

Year Team (League)	W	L	Pct.	ERA	G	GS	CG	ShO	Sv.	IP	H	R	ER	BB	SO
1995—Cincinnati (N.L.)	1	0	1.000	0.00	1	1	0	0	0	6 1/3	6	1	0	1	8
1996—Baltimore (A.L.)	1	0	1.000	4.61	2	2	0	0	0	13 2/3	15	7	7	5	6
1997—New York (A.L.)	1	0	1.000	1.00	1	1	1	0	0	9	5	1	1	0	1
Div. series totals (3 years)	3	0	1.000	2.48	4	4	1	0	0	29	26	9	8	6	15

CHAMPIONSHIP SERIES RECORD

Year Team (League)	W	L	Pct.	ERA	G	GS	CG	ShO	Sv.	IP	H	R	ER	BB	SO
1989—Toronto (A.L.)	0	0	...	0.00	1	0	0	0	0	1	0	1	0	2	1
1991—Toronto (A.L.)	0	0	...	2.35	4	0	0	0	0	7 2/3	6	2	2	2	9
1992—Toronto (A.L.)						Did not play.									
1995—Cincinnati (N.L.)	0	1	.000	4.50	1	1	0	0	0	6	8	3	3	2	3
1996—Baltimore (A.L.)	1	0	1.000	4.05	1	1	0	0	0	6 2/3	8	3	3	3	6
Champ. series totals (4 years)	1	1	.500	3.38	7	2	0	0	0	21 1/3	22	9	8	9	19

WORLD SERIES RECORD

NOTES: Member of World Series championship team (1992).

Year Team (League)	W	L	Pct.	ERA	G	GS	CG	ShO	Sv.	IP	H	R	ER	BB	SO
1992—Toronto (A.L.)	0	0	...	0.00	4	0	0	0	0	4 1/3	1	0	0	2	3

ALL-STAR GAME RECORD

Year League	W	L	Pct.	ERA	GS	CG	ShO	Sv.	IP	H	R	ER	BB	SO
1995—American	0	0	...	0.00	0	0	0	0	1/3	0	0	0	0	1

W

WENDELL, TURK   P   METS

PERSONAL: Born May 19, 1967, in Pittsfield, Mass. ... 6-2/205. ... Throws right, bats left. ... Full name: Steven John Wendell.
HIGH SCHOOL: Wahconah Regional (Dalton, Mass.).
COLLEGE: Quinnipiac College (Conn.).
TRANSACTIONS/CAREER NOTES: Selected by Atlanta Braves organization in fifth round of free-agent draft (June 1, 1988). ... Traded by Braves with P Yorkis Perez to Chicago Cubs for P Mike Bielecki and C Damon Berryhill (September 29, 1991). ... On disabled list (May 4, 1992-remainder of season). ... On Chicago disabled list (April 16-May 27, 1995); included rehabilitation assignments to Daytona (May 5-15) and Orlando (May 15-27). ... Traded by Cubs with OF Brian McRae and P Mel Rojas to New York Mets for OF Lance Johnson and two players to be named later (August 8, 1997); Mets traded P Mark Clark (August 11) and IF Manny Alexander (August 14) to Cubs to complete deal.

Year Team (League)	W	L	Pct.	ERA	G	GS	CG	ShO	Sv.	IP	H	R	ER	BB	SO
1988—Pulaski (Appalachian)	3	•8	.273	3.83	14	14	*6	1	0	*101	85	50	43	30	87
1989—Burlington (Midw.)	9	11	.450	2.21	22	22	•9	*5	0	159	127	63	39	41	153
—Greenville (Southern)	0	0	...	9.82	1	1	0	0	0	3 2/3	7	5	4	1	3
—Durham (Carolina)	2	0	1.000	1.13	3	3	1	0	0	24	13	4	3	6	27
1990—Durham (Carolina)	1	3	.250	1.86	6	5	1	0	0	38 2/3	24	10	8	15	26
—Greenville (Southern)	4	9	.308	5.74	36	13	1	1	2	91	105	70	58	48	85

Year Team (League)	W	L	Pct.	ERA	G	GS	CG	ShO	Sv.	IP	H	R	ER	BB	SO
1991— Greenville (Southern)	11	3	*.786	2.56	25	20	1	1	0	147 2/3	130	47	42	51	122
— Richmond (Int'l)	0	2	.000	3.43	3	3	1	0	0	21	20	9	8	16	18
1992— Iowa (Am. Assoc.)■	2	0	1.000	1.44	4	4	0	0	0	25	17	7	4	15	12
1993— Iowa (Am. Assoc.)	10	8	.556	4.60	25	25	3	0	0	148 2/3	148	88	76	47	110
— Chicago (N.L.)	1	2	.333	4.37	7	4	0	0	0	22 2/3	24	13	11	8	15
1994— Iowa (Am. Assoc.)	11	6	.647	2.95	23	23	6	•3	0	168	141	58	55	28	118
— Chicago (N.L.)	0	1	.000	11.93	6	2	0	0	0	14 1/3	22	20	19	10	9
1995— Daytona (Fla. St.)	0	0	...	1.17	4	2	0	0	0	7 2/3	5	2	1	1	8
— Orlando (South.)	1	0	1.000	3.86	5	0	0	0	1	7	6	3	3	4	7
— Chicago (N.L.)	3	1	.750	4.92	43	0	0	0	0	60 1/3	71	35	33	24	50
1996— Chicago (N.L.)	4	5	.444	2.84	70	0	0	0	18	79 1/3	58	26	25	44	75
1997— Chicago (N.L.)	3	5	.375	4.20	52	0	0	0	4	60	53	32	28	39	54
— New York (N.L.)■	0	0	...	4.96	13	0	0	0	1	16 1/3	15	10	9	14	10
Major league totals (5 years)	11	14	.440	4.45	191	6	0	0	23	253	243	136	125	139	213

WENGERT, DON   P   PADRES

PERSONAL: Born November 6, 1969, in Sioux City, Iowa. ... 6-2/212. ... Throws right, bats right. ... Full name: Donald Paul Wengert. ... Brother of Bill Wengert, pitcher, Los Angeles Dodgers, San Diego Padres and Boston Red Sox organizations (1988-95).
HIGH SCHOOL: Heelan Catholic (Sioux City, Iowa).
COLLEGE: Iowa State.
TRANSACTIONS/CAREER NOTES: Selected by Cincinnati Reds organization in 60th round of free-agent draft (June 1, 1988); did not sign. ... Selected by Oakland Athletics organization in fourth round of free-agent draft (June 1, 1992). ... On Oakland disabled list (July 30-August 18, 1995); included rehabilitation assignment to Edmonton (August 7-18). ... On disabled list (July 24-August 8, 1996). ... Traded by Athletics with IF David Newhan to San Diego Padres for P Doug Bochtler and IF Jorge Velandia (November 26, 1997).

Year Team (League)	W	L	Pct.	ERA	G	GS	CG	ShO	Sv.	IP	H	R	ER	BB	SO
1992— S. Oregon (N'west)	2	0	1.000	1.46	6	5	1	0	0	37	32	6	6	7	29
— Madison (Midwest)	3	4	.429	3.38	7	7	0	0	0	40	42	20	15	17	29
1993— Madison (Midwest)	6	5	.545	3.32	13	13	2	0	0	78 2/3	79	30	29	18	46
— Modesto (California)	3	6	.333	4.73	12	12	0	0	0	70 1/3	75	42	37	29	43
1994— Modesto (California)	4	1	.800	2.95	10	7	0	0	2	42 2/3	40	15	14	11	52
— Huntsville (Southern)	6	4	.600	3.26	17	17	1	0	0	99 1/3	86	43	36	33	92
1995— Oakland (A.L.)	1	1	.500	3.34	19	0	0	0	0	29 2/3	30	14	11	12	16
— Edmonton (PCL)	1	1	.500	7.38	16	6	0	0	1	39	55	32	32	16	20
1996— Oakland (A.L.)	7	11	.389	5.58	36	25	1	1	0	161 1/3	200	102	100	60	75
1997— Oakland (A.L.)	5	11	.313	6.04	49	12	1	0	2	134	177	96	90	41	68
Major league totals (3 years)	13	23	.361	5.57	104	37	2	1	2	325	407	212	201	113	159

WETTELAND, JOHN   P   RANGERS

PERSONAL: Born August 21, 1966, in San Mateo, Calif. ... 6-2/215. ... Throws right, bats right. ... Full name: John Karl Wetteland.
HIGH SCHOOL: Cardinal Newman (Santa Rosa, Calif.).
COLLEGE: College of San Mateo (Calif.).
TRANSACTIONS/CAREER NOTES: Selected by New York Mets organization in 12th round of free-agent draft (June 4, 1984); did not sign. ... Selected by Los Angeles Dodgers organization in secondary phase of free-agent draft (January 9, 1985). ... Selected by Detroit Tigers from Dodgers organization in Rule 5 major league draft (December 7, 1987). ... Returned to Dodgers organization (March 29, 1988). ... On Albuquerque disabled list (May 1-8 and June 3-29, 1991). ... Traded by Dodgers with P Tim Belcher to Cincinnati Reds for OF Eric Davis and P Kip Gross (November 25, 1991). ... Traded by Reds with P Bill Risley to Montreal Expos for OF Dave Martinez, P Scott Ruskin and SS Willie Greene (December 11, 1991). ... On Montreal disabled list (March 23-April 23, 1993); included rehabilitation assignment to West Palm Beach (April 18-23). ... On disabled list (April 18-May 4, 1994). ... Traded by Expos to New York Yankees for OF Fernando Seguignol, a player to be named later and cash (April 5, 1995). ... On disabled list (August 13-September 6, 1996). ... Granted free agency (November 5, 1996). ... Signed by Texas Rangers (December 17, 1996).
HONORS: Named A.L. Fireman of the Year by THE SPORTING NEWS (1996).
STATISTICAL NOTES: Tied for Florida State League lead with 11 home runs allowed and 17 wild pitches in 1987. ... Led Texas League with 22 wild pitches in 1988.

Year Team (League)	W	L	Pct.	ERA	G	GS	CG	ShO	Sv.	IP	H	R	ER	BB	SO
1985— Great Falls (Pio.)	1	1	.500	3.92	11	2	0	0	0	20 2/3	17	10	9	15	23
1986— Bakersfield (California)	0	7	.000	5.78	15	12	4	0	0	67	71	50	43	46	38
— Great Falls (Pio.)	4	3	.571	5.45	12	12	1	0	0	69 1/3	70	51	42	40	59
1987— Vero Beach (FSL)	12	7	.632	3.13	27	27	7	2	0	175 2/3	150	81	61	92	144
1988— San Antonio (Tex.)	10	8	.556	3.88	25	25	3	1	0	162 1/3	141	74	70	•77	140
1989— Albuquerque (PCL)	5	3	.625	3.65	10	10	1	0	0	69	61	28	28	20	73
— Los Angeles (N.L.)	5	8	.385	3.77	31	12	0	0	1	102 2/3	81	46	43	34	96
1990— Los Angeles (N.L.)	2	4	.333	4.81	22	5	0	0	0	43	44	28	23	17	36
— Albuquerque (PCL)	2	2	.500	5.59	8	5	1	0	0	29	27	19	18	13	26
1991— Albuquerque (PCL)	4	3	.571	2.79	41	4	0	0	20	61 1/3	48	22	19	26	55
— Los Angeles (N.L.)	1	0	1.000	0.00	6	0	0	0	0	9	5	2	0	3	9
1992— Montreal (N.L.)■	4	4	.500	2.92	67	0	0	0	37	83 1/3	64	27	27	36	99
1993— W.P. Beach (FSL)	0	0	...	0.00	2	2	0	0	0	3	0	0	0	0	6
— Montreal (N.L.)	9	3	.750	1.37	70	0	0	0	43	85 1/3	58	17	13	28	113
1994— Montreal (N.L.)	4	6	.400	2.83	52	0	0	0	25	63 2/3	46	22	20	21	68
1995— New York (A.L.)■	1	5	.167	2.93	60	0	0	0	31	61 1/3	40	22	20	14	66
1996— New York (A.L.)	2	3	.400	2.83	62	0	0	0	*43	63 2/3	54	23	20	21	69
1997— Texas (A.L.)■	7	5	.778	1.94	61	0	0	0	31	65	43	18	14	21	63
A.L. totals (3 years)	10	10	.500	2.56	183	0	0	0	105	190	137	63	54	56	198
N.L. totals (6 years)	25	25	.500	2.93	248	17	0	0	106	387	298	142	126	139	421
Major league totals (9 years)	35	35	.500	2.81	431	17	0	0	211	577	435	205	180	195	619

W

DIVISION SERIES RECORD

Year — Team (League)	W	L	Pct.	ERA	G	GS	CG	ShO	Sv.	IP	H	R	ER	BB	SO
1995— New York (A.L.)	0	1	.000	14.54	3	0	0	0	0	4 1/3	8	7	7	2	5
1996— New York (A.L.)	0	0	...	0.00	3	0	0	0	2	4	2	0	0	5	4
Div. series totals (2 years)	0	1	.000	7.56	6	0	0	0	2	8 1/3	10	7	7	7	9

CHAMPIONSHIP SERIES RECORD

Year — Team (League)	W	L	Pct.	ERA	G	GS	CG	ShO	Sv.	IP	H	R	ER	BB	SO
1996— New York (A.L.)	0	0	...	4.50	4	0	0	0	1	4	2	2	2	1	5

WORLD SERIES RECORD

RECORDS: Holds single-series record for most saves—4 (1996).
NOTES: Named Most Valuable Player (1996). ... Member of World Series championship team (1996).

Year — Team (League)	W	L	Pct.	ERA	G	GS	CG	ShO	Sv.	IP	H	R	ER	BB	SO
1996— New York (A.L.)	0	0	...	2.08	5	0	0	0	4	4 1/3	4	1	1	1	6

ALL-STAR GAME RECORD

Year — League	W	L	Pct.	ERA	GS	CG	ShO	Sv.	IP	H	R	ER	BB	SO
1996— American				Did not play.										

WHISENANT, MATT   P   ROYALS

PERSONAL: Born June 8, 1971, in Los Angeles. ... 6-3/215. ... Throws left, bats right. ... Full name: Matthew Michael Whisenant.
HIGH SCHOOL: La Canada (Calif.).
JUNIOR COLLEGE: Glendale (Ariz.) Community College.
TRANSACTIONS/CAREER NOTES: Selected by Philadelphia Phillies organization in 18th round of free-agent draft (June 5, 1989). ... Traded by Phillies organization with P Joel Adamson to Florida Marlins organization for P Danny Jackson (November 17, 1992). ... On disabled list (July 13, 1993-remainder of season). ... On Florida disabled list (March 28-July 4, 1997); included rehabilitation assignment to Brevard County (April 18-21) and Charlotte (May 5-July 4). ... Traded by Marlins to Kansas City Royals for C Matt Treanor (July 29, 1997).
STATISTICAL NOTES: Led International League with 30 wild pitches in 1996.
MISCELLANEOUS: Appeared in one game as pinch-runner (1997).

Year — Team (League)	W	L	Pct.	ERA	G	GS	CG	ShO	Sv.	IP	H	R	ER	BB	SO
1990— Princeton (Appalachian)	0	0	...	11.40	9	2	0	0	0	15	16	27	19	20	25
1991— Batavia (N.Y.-Penn)	2	1	.667	2.45	11	10	0	0	0	47 2/3	31	19	13	42	55
1992— Spartanburg (SAL)	11	7	.611	3.23	27	27	2	0	0	150 2/3	117	69	54	85	151
1993— Kane County (Midwest)■	2	6	.250	4.69	15	15	0	0	0	71	68	45	37	56	74
1994— Brevard County (FSL)	6	9	.400	3.38	28	26	5	1	0	160	125	71	60	82	103
1995— Portland (Eastern)	10	6	.625	3.50	23	22	2	0	0	128 2/3	103	57	50	65	107
1996— Charlotte (Int'l)	8	10	.444	6.92	28	22	1	0	0	121	149	107	93	101	97
1997— Brevard County (FSL)	0	0	...	8.10	2	1	0	0	0	3 1/3	3	3	3	3	4
— Charlotte (Int'l)	2	1	.667	7.20	16	0	0	0	0	15	16	12	12	12	19
— Florida (N.L.)	0	0	...	16.88	4	0	0	0	0	2 2/3	4	6	5	6	4
— Kansas City (A.L.)■	1	0	1.000	2.84	24	0	0	0	0	19	15	7	6	12	16
A.L. totals (1 year)	1	0	1.000	2.84	24	0	0	0	0	19	15	7	6	12	16
N.L. totals (1 year)	0	0	...	16.88	4	0	0	0	0	2 2/3	4	6	5	6	4
Major league totals (1 year)	1	0	1.000	4.57	28	0	0	0	0	21 2/3	19	13	11	18	20

WHITE, DEVON   OF   DIAMONDBACKS

PERSONAL: Born December 29, 1962, in Kingston, Jamaica. ... 6-2/195. ... Bats both, throws right. ... Full name: Devon Markes White. ... Name pronounced de-VON.
HIGH SCHOOL: Park West (New York).
TRANSACTIONS/CAREER NOTES: Selected by California Angels organization in sixth round of free-agent draft (June 8, 1981). ... On suspended list (June 11-12 and July 19, 1982-remainder of season). ... On Edmonton disabled list (May 12-22, 1986). ... On disabled list (May 7-June 10, 1988). ... Traded by Angels organization with P Willie Fraser and a player to be named later to Toronto Blue Jays for OF Junior Felix, IF Luis Sojo and a player to be named later (December 2, 1990); Blue Jays acquired P Marcus Moore and Angels acquired C Ken Rivers to complete deal (December 4, 1990). ... Granted free agency (November 1, 1995). ... Signed by Florida Marlins (November 21, 1995). ... On disabled list (April 25-May 30 and June 8-July 28, 1997). ... Traded by Marlins to Arizona Diamondbacks for P Jesus Martinez (November 18, 1997).
RECORDS: Shares major league record for most stolen bases in one inning—3 (September 9, 1989, sixth inning).
HONORS: Won A.L. Gold Glove as outfielder (1988-89 and 1991-95).
STATISTICAL NOTES: Led Midwest League outfielders with 286 total chances in 1983. ... Led California League outfielders with 351 total chances in 1984. ... Led Pacific Coast League outfielders with 339 total chances in 1986. ... Switch-hit home runs in one game three times (June 23, 1987; June 29, 1990; and June 1, 1992). ... Led A.L. outfielders with 449 total chances in 1987, 448 in 1991 and 458 in 1992. ... Career major league grand slams: 6.

Year — Team (League)	Pos.	G	AB	R	H	2B	3B	HR	RBI	Avg.	BB	SO	SB	PO	A	E	Avg.
1981— Idaho Falls (Pio.)	OF-3B-1B	30	106	10	19	2	0	0	10	.179	12	34	4	33	10	3	.935
1982— Danville (Midwest)	OF	57	186	21	40	6	1	1	11	.215	11	41	11	89	3	8	.920
1983— Peoria (Midwest)	OF	117	430	69	109	17	6	13	66	.253	36	124	32	267	8	11	.962
— Nashua (Eastern)	OF	17	70	11	18	7	2	0	2	.257	7	22	5	37	0	3	.925
1984— Redwood (Calif.)	OF	138	520	101	147	25	5	7	45	.283	56	118	36	*322	16	13	.963
1985— Midland (Texas)	OF	70	260	52	77	10	4	4	35	.296	35	46	38	176	10	4	.979
— Edmonton (PCL)	OF	66	277	53	70	16	5	4	39	.253	24	77	21	205	6	2	.991
— California (A.L.)	OF	21	7	7	1	0	0	0	0	.143	1	3	3	10	1	0	1.000
1986— Edmonton (PCL)	OF	112	461	84	134	25	10	14	60	.291	31	90	*42	317	•16	6	.982
— California (A.L.)	OF	29	51	8	12	1	1	1	3	.235	6	8	6	49	0	2	.961
1987— California (A.L.)	OF	159	639	103	168	33	5	24	87	.263	39	135	32	*424	16	9	.980
1988— California (A.L.)	OF	122	455	76	118	22	2	11	51	.259	23	84	17	364	7	9	.976
1989— California (A.L.)	OF-DH	156	636	86	156	18	13	12	56	.245	31	129	44	430	10	5	.989

Year Team (League)	Pos.	BATTING												FIELDING			
		G	AB	R	H	2B	3B	HR	RBI	Avg.	BB	SO	SB	PO	A	E	Avg.
1990— California (A.L.)	OF	125	443	57	96	17	3	11	44	.217	44	116	21	302	11	9	.972
—Edmonton (PCL)	OF	14	55	9	20	4	4	0	6	.364	7	12	4	31	1	3	.914
1991— Toronto (A.L.)■	OF	156	642	110	181	40	10	17	60	.282	55	135	33	*439	8	1	*.998
1992— Toronto (A.L.)	OF-DH	153	641	98	159	26	7	17	60	.248	47	133	37	*443	8	7	.985
1993— Toronto (A.L.)	OF	146	598	116	163	42	6	15	52	.273	57	127	34	399	6	3	.993
1994— Toronto (A.L.)	OF	100	403	67	109	24	6	13	49	.270	21	80	11	268	3	6	.978
1995— Toronto (A.L.)	OF	101	427	61	121	23	5	10	53	.283	29	97	11	261	7	3	.989
1996— Florida (N.L.)■	OF	146	552	77	151	37	6	17	84	.274	38	99	22	296	5	4	.987
1997— Florida (N.L.)	OF	74	265	37	65	13	1	6	34	.245	32	65	13	152	4	2	.987
American League totals (11 years)		1268	4942	789	1284	246	58	131	515	.260	353	1047	249	3389	77	54	.985
National League totals (2 years)		220	817	114	216	50	7	23	118	.264	70	164	35	448	9	6	.987
Major league totals (13 years)		1488	5759	903	1500	296	65	154	633	.260	423	1211	284	3837	86	60	.985

DIVISION SERIES RECORD

Year Team (League)	Pos.	BATTING												FIELDING			
		G	AB	R	H	2B	3B	HR	RBI	Avg.	BB	SO	SB	PO	A	E	Avg.
1997— Florida (N.L.)	OF	3	11	1	2	0	0	1	4	.182	2	3	0	3	0	0	1.000

CHAMPIONSHIP SERIES RECORD

RECORDS: Holds A.L. career record for highest batting average (50 or more at-bats)—.392. ... Holds single-series record for most times caught stealing—4 (1992). ... Shares A.L. single-series record for most hits—12 (1993). ... Shares A.L. single-game record for most at-bats—6 (October 11, 1992, 11 innings).

Year Team (League)	Pos.	BATTING												FIELDING			
		G	AB	R	H	2B	3B	HR	RBI	Avg.	BB	SO	SB	PO	A	E	Avg.
1986— California (A.L.)	OF-PR	4	2	2	1	0	0	0	0	.500	0	1	0	3	0	0	1.000
1991— Toronto (A.L.)	OF	5	22	5	8	1	0	0	0	.364	2	3	3	16	0	0	1.000
1992— Toronto (A.L.)	OF	6	23	2	8	2	0	0	2	.348	1	5	6	16	0	1	.941
1993— Toronto (A.L.)	OF	6	27	3	12	1	1	1	2	.444	1	5	0	15	0	0	1.000
1997— Florida (N.L.)	OF	6	21	4	4	1	0	0	1	.190	2	7	1	16	0	0	1.000
Championship series totals (5 years)		27	95	16	33	5	1	1	5	.347	10	22	4	66	0	1	.985

WORLD SERIES RECORD

RECORDS: Shares record for most consecutive strikeouts in one series—5 (October 21 [1] and 22 [4], 1997).

NOTES: Member of World Series championship teams (1992, 1993 and 1997).

Year Team (League)	Pos.	BATTING												FIELDING			
		G	AB	R	H	2B	3B	HR	RBI	Avg.	BB	SO	SB	PO	A	E	Avg.
1992— Toronto (A.L.)	OF	6	26	2	6	1	0	0	2	.231	0	6	1	22	0	0	1.000
1993— Toronto (A.L.)	OF	6	24	8	7	3	2	1	7	.292	4	7	1	16	0	0	1.000
1997— Florida (N.L.)	OF	7	33	0	8	3	1	0	2	.242	3	10	1	16	0	0	1.000
World Series totals (3 years)		19	83	10	21	7	3	1	11	.253	7	23	3	54	0	0	1.000

ALL-STAR GAME RECORD

Year League	Pos.	BATTING											FIELDING			
		AB	R	H	2B	3B	HR	RBI	Avg.	BB	SO	SB	PO	A	E	Avg.
1989— American	OF	1	0	0	0	0	0	0	.000	0	0	0	0	0	0	...
1993— American	OF	2	1	1	1	0	0	1	.500	0	0	1	1	0	0	1.000
All-Star Game totals (2 years)		3	1	1	1	0	0	1	.333	0	0	1	1	0	0	1.000

WHITE, GABE · P · REDS

PERSONAL: Born November 20, 1971, in Sebring, Fla. ... 6-2/200. ... Throws left, bats left. ... Full name: Gabriel Allen White.

HIGH SCHOOL: Sebring (Fla.).

TRANSACTIONS/CAREER NOTES: Selected by Montreal Expos organization in supplemental round ("sandwich pick" between first and second round, 28th pick overall) of free-agent draft (June 4, 1990); pick received as part of compensation for California Angels signing Type A free-agent P Mark Langston. ... On Harrisburg disabled list (July 2-27, 1993). ... On Ottawa disabled list (April 7-May 6, 1994). ... Traded by Expos to Cincinnati Reds for 2B Jhonny Carvajal (December 15, 1995). ... On disabled list (September 17, 1996-remainder of season).

RECORDS: Shares N.L. record for most consecutive home runs allowed in one inning—3 (July 7, 1995, second inning).

Year Team (League)	W	L	Pct.	ERA	G	GS	CG	ShO	Sv.	IP	H	R	ER	BB	SO
1990— GC Expos (GCL)	4	2	.667	3.14	11	11	1	0	0	57 1/3	50	21	20	12	41
1991— Sumter (S. Atl.)	6	9	.400	3.26	24	24	5	0	0	149	127	73	54	53	140
1992— Rockford (Midwest)	14	8	.636	2.84	27	27	7	0	0	187	148	73	59	61	*176
1993— Harrisburg (Eastern)	7	2	.778	2.16	16	16	2	1	0	100	80	30	24	28	80
—Ottawa (Int'l)	2	1	.667	3.12	6	6	1	1	0	40 1/3	38	15	14	6	28
1994— W.P. Beach (FSL)	1	0	1.000	1.50	1	1	0	0	0	6	2	2	1	1	4
—Ottawa (Int'l)	8	3	.727	5.05	14	14	0	0	0	73	77	49	41	28	63
—Montreal (N.L.)	1	1	.500	6.08	7	5	0	0	1	23 2/3	24	16	16	11	17
1995— Ottawa (Int'l)	2	3	.400	3.90	12	12	0	0	0	62 1/3	58	31	27	17	37
—Montreal (N.L.)	1	2	.333	7.01	19	1	0	0	0	25 2/3	26	21	20	9	25
1996— Indianapolis (A.A.)■	6	3	.667	2.77	11	11	0	0	0	68 1/3	69	25	21	9	51
1997— Indianapolis (A.A.)	7	4	.636	2.82	20	19	0	0	0	118	119	46	37	18	62
—Cincinnati (N.L.)	2	2	.500	4.39	12	6	0	0	0	41	39	20	20	8	25
Major league totals (3 years)	4	5	.444	5.58	38	12	0	0	2	90 1/3	89	57	56	28	67

WHITE, RONDELL · OF · EXPOS

PERSONAL: Born February 23, 1972, in Milledgeville, Ga. ... 6-1/205. ... Bats right, throws right. ... Full name: Rondell Bernard White.

HIGH SCHOOL: Jones County (Gray, Ga.).

TRANSACTIONS/CAREER NOTES: Selected by Montreal Expos organization in first round (24th pick overall) of free-agent draft (June 4, 1990); pick received as part of compensation for California Angels signing Type A free-agent P Mark Langston. ... On Montreal disabled list (April 28-July 16, 1996); included rehabilitation assignments to West Palm Beach (July 5-10) and Harrisburg (July 10-16).

STATISTICAL NOTES: Led Gulf Coast League with 96 total bases in 1990. ... Hit for the cycle (June 11, 1995, 13 innings). ... Collected six hits in one game (June 11, 1995). ... Led N.L. outfielders in total chances with 385 in 1997. ... Career major league grand slams: 2.

Year Team (League)	Pos.	G	AB	R	H	2B	3B	HR	RBI	Avg.	BB	SO	SB	PO	A	E	Avg.
1990—GC Expos (GCL)	OF	57	221	33	66	7	4	5	34	.299	17	33	10	71	1	2	.973
1991—Sumter (S. Atl.)	OF	123	465	80	122	23	6	13	68	.262	57	109	50	215	6	3	*.987
1992—W.P. Beach (FSL)	OF	111	450	80	142	10	*12	4	41	.316	46	78	42	187	2	3	.984
—Harrisburg (Eastern)	OF	21	89	22	27	7	1	2	7	.303	6	14	6	29	1	2	.938
1993—Harrisburg (Eastern)	OF	90	372	72	122	16	10	12	52	.328	22	72	21	179	4	1	.995
—Ottawa (Int'l)	OF	37	150	28	57	8	2	7	32	.380	12	20	10	79	0	1	.988
—Montreal (N.L.)	OF	23	73	9	19	3	1	2	15	.260	7	16	1	33	0	0	1.000
1994—Montreal (N.L.)	OF	40	97	16	27	10	1	2	13	.278	9	18	1	34	1	2	.946
—Ottawa (Int'l)	OF	42	169	23	46	7	0	7	18	.272	15	17	9	91	4	2	.979
1995—Montreal (N.L.)	OF	130	474	87	140	33	4	13	57	.295	41	87	25	270	5	4	.986
1996—Montreal (N.L.)	OF	88	334	35	98	19	4	6	41	.293	22	53	14	185	5	2	.990
—W.P. Beach (FSL)	OF	3	10	0	2	1	0	0	2	.200	0	4	0	2	0	0	1.000
—G.C. Expos (GCL)	OF	3	12	3	3	0	0	2	4	.250	0	1	1	4	0	1	1.000
—Harrisburg (Eastern)	OF	3	20	5	7	1	0	3	6	.350	1	1	1	12	0	0	1.000
1997—Montreal (N.L.)	OF	151	592	84	160	29	5	28	82	.270	31	111	16	*376	6	3	.992
Major league totals (5 years)		432	1570	231	444	94	15	51	208	.283	110	285	57	898	17	11	.988

WHITEMAN, GREG — P — PHILLIES

PERSONAL: Born June 12, 1973, in Cumberland, Md. ... 6-2/180. ... Throws left, bats left. ... Full name: Gregory Alan Whiteman.
HIGH SCHOOL: Frankfurt (Md.).
COLLEGE: James Madison.
TRANSACTIONS/CAREER NOTES: Selected by Detroit Tigers organization in third round of free-agent draft (June 2, 1994). ... Claimed on waivers by Boston Red Sox (April 18, 1997); waiver claim denied and granted free agency (April 21, 1997). ... Signed by Philadelphia Phillies (May 9, 1997).

Year Team (League)	W	L	Pct.	ERA	G	GS	CG	ShO	Sv.	IP	H	R	ER	BB	SO
1994—Jamestown (NYP)	6	5	.545	4.04	15	•15	1	1	0	75 2/3	72	39	34	35	67
1995—Fayetteville (S. Atl.)	6	8	.429	4.23	23	23	1	1	0	125 2/3	108	68	59	58	145
1996—Lakeland (Fla. St.)	11	10	.524	3.71	27	27	1	0	0	150 1/3	134	66	62	89	122
1997—Clearwater (Fla. St.)■	3	3	.500	4.59	11	11	0	0	0	51	57	30	26	26	32
—Reading (Eastern)	4	4	.500	4.05	9	9	0	0	0	53 1/3	57	27	24	21	31

WHITEN, MARK — OF

PERSONAL: Born November 25, 1966, in Pensacola, Fla. ... 6-3/235. ... Bats both, throws right. ... Full name: Mark Anthony Whiten. ... Name pronounced WHITT-en.
HIGH SCHOOL: Pensacola (Fla.).
JUNIOR COLLEGE: Pensacola (Fla.) Junior College.
TRANSACTIONS/CAREER NOTES: Selected by Toronto Blue Jays organization in fifth round of free-agent draft (January 14, 1986). ... On Toronto suspended list (May 23-25, 1991). ... Traded by Blue Jays with P Denis Boucher, OF Glenallen Hill and a player to be named later to Cleveland Indians for P Tom Candiotti and OF Turner Ward (June 27, 1991); Indians acquired cash to complete deal (October 15, 1991). ... Traded by Indians to St. Louis Cardinals for P Mark Clark and SS Juan Andujar (March 31, 1993). ... On St. Louis disabled list (April 18-May 5, 1994); included rehabilitation assignment to Louisville (May 2-5). ... Traded by Cardinals with P Rheal Cormier to Boston Red Sox for 3B Scott Cooper, P Cory Bailey and a player to be named later (April 8, 1995). ... On Boston disabled list (May 22-June 9, 1995); included rehabilitation assignment to Pawtucket (June 2-9). ... Traded by Red Sox to Philadelphia Phillies for 1B Dave Hollins (July 24, 1995). ... Released by Phillies (June 17, 1996). ... Signed by Atlanta Braves (June 24, 1996). ... Traded by Braves to Seattle Mariners for P Roger Blanco (August 14, 1996). ... Granted free agency (December 7, 1996). ... Signed by New York Yankees (January 9, 1997). ... Released by Yankees (August 15, 1997).

RECORDS: Shares major league single-game records for most home runs—4 (September 7, 1993, second game); and most runs batted in—12 (September 7, 1993, second game). ... Shares major league record for most runs batted in during doubleheader—13 (September 7, 1993). ... Shares N.L. record for most runs batted in during two consecutive games—13 (September 7, 1993, first and second games).

STATISTICAL NOTES: Tied for Pioneer League lead in being hit by pitch with six in 1986. ... Led South Atlantic League outfielders with 322 total chances and tied for lead with four double plays in 1987. ... Led South Atlantic League in being hit by pitch with 16 and tied for lead in intentional bases on balls received with 10 in 1987. ... Led Southern League in being hit by pitch with 11 in 1989. ... Hit four home runs in one game (September 7, 1993, second game). ... Switch-hit home runs in one game (September 14, 1993). ... Career major league grand slams: 4.

MISCELLANEOUS: Batted righthanded only (1988-89).

Year Team (League)	Pos.	G	AB	R	H	2B	3B	HR	RBI	Avg.	BB	SO	SB	PO	A	E	Avg.
1986—Medicine Hat (Pio.)	OF	•70	270	53	81	16	3	10	44	.300	29	56	22	111	9	*10	.923
1987—Myrtle Beach (SAL)	OF	*139	494	90	125	22	5	15	64	.253	76	149	49	*292	*18	12	.963
1988—Dunedin (Fla. St.)	OF	99	385	61	97	8	5	7	37	.252	41	69	17	200	*21	9	.961
—Knoxville (Southern)	OF	28	108	20	28	3	1	2	9	.259	12	20	6	62	3	4	.942
1989—Knoxville (Southern)	OF	129	423	75	109	13	6	12	47	.258	60	114	11	223	17	8	.968
1990—Syracuse (Int'l)	OF	104	390	65	113	19	4	14	48	.290	37	72	14	158	14	6	.966
—Toronto (A.L.)	OF-DH	33	88	12	24	1	1	2	7	.273	7	14	2	60	3	0	1.000
1991—Toronto (A.L.)	OF	46	149	12	33	4	3	2	19	.221	11	35	0	90	2	0	1.000
—Cleveland (A.L.)■	OF-DH	70	258	34	66	14	4	7	26	.256	19	50	4	166	11	7	.962
1992—Cleveland (A.L.)	OF-DH	148	508	73	129	19	4	9	43	.254	72	102	16	321	14	7	.980
1993—St. Louis (N.L.)■	OF	152	562	81	142	13	4	25	99	.253	58	110	15	329	9	10	.971
1994—St. Louis (N.L.)	OF	92	334	57	98	18	2	14	53	.293	37	75	10	234	9	9	.964
—Louisville (A.A.)	OF	3	10	2	3	1	0	1	3	.300	1	1	0	3	0	0	1.000

Year Team (League)	Pos.	G	AB	R	H	2B	3B	HR	RBI	Avg.	BB	SO	SB	PO	A	E	Avg.
1995—Boston (A.L.)■	OF-DH	32	108	13	20	3	0	1	10	.185	8	23	1	52	4	0	1.000
—Pawtucket (Int'l)	OF	28	102	19	29	3	1	4	13	.284	19	30	4	43	4	3	.940
—Philadelphia (N.L.)■ ..	OF	60	212	38	57	10	1	11	37	.269	31	63	7	105	4	4	.965
1996—Philadelphia (N.L.)	OF	60	182	33	43	8	0	7	21	.236	33	62	13	97	6	6	.945
—Atlanta (N.L.)■	OF	36	90	12	23	5	1	3	17	.256	16	25	2	41	1	3	.933
—Seattle (N.L.)■	OF	40	140	31	42	7	0	12	33	.300	21	40	2	90	4	3	.969
1997—New York (A.L.)■	OF-DH	69	215	34	57	11	0	5	24	.265	30	47	4	102	2	5	.954
American League totals (6 years)		438	1466	209	371	59	12	38	162	.253	168	311	29	881	40	22	.977
National League totals (4 years)		400	1380	221	363	54	8	60	227	.263	175	335	47	806	29	32	.963
Major league totals (8 years)		838	2846	430	734	113	20	98	389	.258	343	646	76	1687	69	54	.970

WHITESIDE, MATT — P — RANGERS

PERSONAL: Born August 8, 1967, in Charleston, Mo. ... 6-0/205. ... Throws right, bats right. ... Full name: Matthew Christopher Whiteside.
HIGH SCHOOL: Charleston (Mo.).
COLLEGE: Arkansas State (degree in physical education).
TRANSACTIONS/CAREER NOTES: Selected by Texas Rangers organization in 25th round of free-agent draft (June 4, 1990). ... On disabled list (May 9-25, 1995). ... Granted free agency (October 30, 1996). ... Re-signed by Rangers (November 22, 1996).
STATISTICAL NOTES: Tied for American Association lead with three balks in 1996.

Year Team (League)	W	L	Pct.	ERA	G	GS	CG	ShO	Sv.	IP	H	R	ER	BB	SO
1990—Butte (Pioneer)	4	4	.500	3.45	18	5	0	0	2	57 1/3	57	33	22	25	45
1991—Gastonia (S. Atl.)	3	1	.750	2.15	48	0	0	0	29	62 2/3	44	19	15	21	71
1992—Tulsa (Texas)	0	1	.000	2.41	33	0	0	0	21	33 2/3	31	9	9	3	30
—Oklahoma City (A.A.)	1	0	1.000	0.79	12	0	0	0	8	11 1/3	7	1	1	3	13
—Texas (A.L.)	1	1	.500	1.93	20	0	0	0	4	28	26	8	6	11	13
1993—Texas (A.L.)	2	1	.667	4.32	60	0	0	0	1	73	78	37	35	23	39
—Oklahoma City (A.A.)	2	1	.667	5.56	8	0	0	0	1	11 1/3	17	7	7	8	10
1994—Texas (A.L.)	2	2	.500	5.02	47	0	0	0	1	61	68	40	34	28	37
1995—Texas (A.L.)	5	4	.556	4.08	40	0	0	0	3	53	48	24	24	19	46
1996—Texas (A.L.)	0	1	.000	6.68	14	0	0	0	0	32 1/3	43	24	24	11	15
—Oklahoma City (A.A.)	9	6	.600	3.45	36	7	0	0	0	94	95	41	36	24	52
1997—Oklahoma City (A.A.)	1	1	.500	3.54	10	1	0	0	1	28	30	14	11	13	11
—Texas (A.L.)	4	1	.800	5.08	42	1	0	0	0	72 2/3	85	45	41	26	44
Major league totals (6 years)	14	10	.583	4.61	223	1	0	0	9	320	348	178	164	118	194

WICKMAN, BOB — P — BREWERS

PERSONAL: Born February 6, 1969, in Green Bay. ... 6-1/212. ... Throws right, bats right. ... Full name: Robert Joe Wickman.
HIGH SCHOOL: Oconto Falls (Wis.).
COLLEGE: Wisconsin-Whitewater.
TRANSACTIONS/CAREER NOTES: Selected by Chicago White Sox organization in second round of free-agent draft (June 4, 1990). ... Traded by White Sox organization with P Melido Perez and P Domingo Jean to New York Yankees organization for 2B Steve Sax and cash (January 10, 1992). ... Traded by Yankees with OF Gerald Williams to Milwaukee Brewers for P Graeme Lloyd and OF Pat Listach (August 23, 1996).

Year Team (League)	W	L	Pct.	ERA	G	GS	CG	ShO	Sv.	IP	H	R	ER	BB	SO
1990—GC White Sox (GCL)	2	0	1.000	2.45	2	2	0	0	0	11	7	4	3	1	15
—Sarasota (Florida State)	0	1	.000	1.98	2	2	0	0	0	13 2/3	17	7	3	4	8
—South Bend (Mid.)	7	2	.778	1.38	9	9	3	0	0	65 1/3	50	16	10	16	50
1991—Sarasota (Florida State)	5	1	.833	2.05	7	7	1	1	0	44	43	16	10	11	32
—Birmingham (Southern)	6	10	.375	3.56	20	20	4	1	0	131 1/3	127	68	52	50	81
1992—Columbus (Int'l)■	12	5	.706	2.92	23	23	2	1	0	157	131	61	51	55	108
—New York (A.L.)	6	1	.857	4.11	8	8	0	0	0	50 1/3	51	25	23	20	21
1993—New York (A.L.)	14	4	.778	4.63	41	19	1	1	4	140	156	82	72	69	70
1994—New York (A.L.)	5	4	.556	3.09	*53	0	0	0	6	70	54	26	24	27	56
1995—New York (A.L.)	2	4	.333	4.05	63	1	0	0	0	80	77	38	36	33	51
1996—New York (A.L.)	4	1	.800	4.67	58	0	0	0	0	79	94	41	41	34	61
—Milwaukee (A.L.)■	3	0	1.000	3.24	12	0	0	0	0	16 2/3	12	9	6	10	14
1997—Milwaukee (A.L.)	7	6	.538	2.73	74	0	0	0	1	95 2/3	89	32	29	41	78
Major league totals (6 years)	41	20	.672	3.91	309	28	1	1	12	531 2/3	533	253	231	234	351

DIVISION SERIES RECORD

Year Team (League)	W	L	Pct.	ERA	G	GS	CG	ShO	Sv.	IP	H	R	ER	BB	SO
1995—New York (A.L.)	0	0	...	0.00	3	0	0	0	0	3	5	0	0	0	3

W

WIDGER, CHRIS — C — EXPOS

PERSONAL: Born May 21, 1971, in Wilmington, Del. ... 6-3/195. ... Bats right, throws right. ... Full name: Christopher Jon Widger. ... Nephew of Mike Widger, linebacker, Montreal Alouettes and Ottawa Rough Riders of Canadian Football League (1970-78).
HIGH SCHOOL: Pennsville (N.J.).
COLLEGE: George Mason.
TRANSACTIONS/CAREER NOTES: Selected by Seattle Mariners organization in third round of free-agent draft (June 1, 1992). ... On disabled list (June 6-16, 1993). ... Traded by Mariners with P Trey Moore and P Matt Wagner to Montreal Expos for P Jeff Fassero and P Alex Pacheco (October 29, 1996).

Year Team (League)	Pos.	G	AB	R	H	2B	3B	HR	RBI	Avg.	BB	SO	SB	PO	A	E	Avg.
1992—Bellingham (N'west)	C	51	166	28	43	7	2	5	30	.259	22	36	8	266	39	4	*.987
1993—Riverside (Calif.)	C-OF	97	360	44	95	28	2	9	58	.264	19	64	5	472	63	14	.974

Year Team (League)	Pos.	G	AB	R	H	2B	3B	HR	RBI	Avg.	BB	SO	SB	PO	A	E	Avg.
1994—Jacksonville (South.)..	C-OF-1B	116	388	58	101	15	3	16	59	.260	39	69	8	564	73	13	.980
1995—Tacoma (PCL)	C-OF	50	174	29	48	11	1	9	21	.276	9	29	0	189	22	4	.981
—Seattle (A.L.)	C-OF-DH	23	45	2	9	0	0	1	2	.200	3	11	0	64	1	0	1.000
1996—Tacoma (PCL)	C	97	352	42	107	20	2	13	48	.304	27	62	7	622	41	8	.988
—Seattle (A.L.)	C	8	11	1	2	0	0	0	0	.182	0	5	0	18	1	2	.905
1997—Montreal (N.L.).■..	C	91	278	30	65	20	3	7	37	.234	22	59	2	516	40	11	.981
American League totals (2 years)		31	56	3	11	0	0	1	2	.196	3	16	0	82	2	2	.977
National League totals (1 year)		91	278	30	65	20	3	7	37	.234	22	59	2	516	40	11	.981
Major league totals (3 years)		122	334	33	76	20	3	8	39	.228	25	75	2	598	42	13	.980

DIVISION SERIES RECORD

Year Team (League)	Pos.	G	AB	R	H	2B	3B	HR	RBI	Avg.	BB	SO	SB	PO	A	E	Avg.
1995—Seattle (A.L.)	C	2	3	0	0	0	0	0	0	.000	0	3	0	14	0	0	1.000

CHAMPIONSHIP SERIES RECORD

Year Team (League)	Pos.	G	AB	R	H	2B	3B	HR	RBI	Avg.	BB	SO	SB	PO	A	E	Avg.
1995—Seattle (A.L.)	C	3	1	0	0	0	0	0	0	.000	0	1	0	7	0	0	1.000

WILCOX, LUKE — OF — DEVIL RAYS

PERSONAL: Born November 15, 1973, in Lansing, Mich. ... 6-4/195. ... Bats left, throws right. ... Full name: Christopher Luke Wilcox.
HIGH SCHOOL: St. John's (Mich.).
TRANSACTIONS/CAREER NOTES: Selected by New York Yankees organization in third round of free-agent draft (June 1, 1995). ... On Norwich disabled list (April 6-June 3, 1997). ... Selected by Tampa Bay Devil Rays in third round (66th pick overall) of expansion draft (November 18, 1997).

Year Team (League)	Pos.	G	AB	R	H	2B	3B	HR	RBI	Avg.	BB	SO	SB	PO	A	E	Avg.
1995—Oneonta (NYP)	OF	59	223	25	73	16	7	1	28	.327	20	28	9	84	6	5	.947
1996—Tampa (Florida State)	OF	119	470	72	133	32	5	11	76	.283	40	71	14	209	10	3	.986
1997—Norwich (Eastern)	OF	74	300	45	83	13	1	6	34	.277	18	36	13	141	6	3	.980
—Tampa (Florida State)	OF	12	40	7	12	4	0	0	4	.300	7	6	1	10	0	0	1.000

WILKINS, MARC — P — PIRATES

PERSONAL: Born October 21, 1970, in Mansfield, Ohio ... 5-10/210. ... Throws right, bats right. ... Full name: Marc Allen Wilkins.
HIGH SCHOOL: Ontario (Ohio).
COLLEGE: Toledo.
TRANSACTIONS/CAREER NOTES: Selected by Pittsburgh Pirates organization in 47th round of free-agent draft (June 1, 1992).
STATISTICAL NOTES: Led Carolina League with 22 hit batsmen in 1994.

Year Team (League)	W	L	Pct.	ERA	G	GS	CG	ShO	Sv.	IP	H	R	ER	BB	SO
1992—Welland (N.Y.-Penn)	4	2	.667	7.29	28	1	0	0	1	42	49	36	34	24	42
1993—Augusta (S. Atl.)	5	6	.455	4.21	48	5	0	0	1	77	83	52	36	31	73
1994—Salem (Carolina)	8	5	.615	3.70	28	•28	0	0	0	151	155	84	62	45	90
1995—Carolina (Southern)	5	3	.625	3.99	37	12	0	0	0	99 1/3	91	47	44	44	80
1996—Carolina (Southern)	2	3	.400	4.01	11	3	0	0	0	24 2/3	19	12	11	11	19
—Pittsburgh (N.L.)	4	3	.571	3.84	47	2	0	0	1	75	75	36	32	36	62
1997—Pittsburgh (N.L.)	9	5	.643	3.69	70	0	0	0	2	75 2/3	65	33	31	33	47
Major league totals (2 years)	13	8	.619	3.76	117	2	0	0	3	150 2/3	140	69	63	69	109

WILKINS, RICK — C — MARINERS

PERSONAL: Born June 4, 1967, in Jacksonville. ... 6-2/215. ... Bats left, throws right. ... Full name: Richard David Wilkins.
HIGH SCHOOL: The Bolles School (Jacksonville).
JUNIOR COLLEGE: Florida Community College-Jacksonville.
COLLEGE: Furman.
TRANSACTIONS/CAREER NOTES: Selected by Chicago Cubs organization in 23rd round of free-agent draft (June 2, 1986). ... On Chicago disabled list (June 2-28, 1995). ... Traded by Cubs to Houston Astros for OF Luis Gonzalez and C Scott Servais (June 28, 1995). ... On Houston disabled list (July 2-September 5, 1995); included rehabilitation assignments to Jackson (August 28-September 1) and Tucson (September 1-5). ... Traded by Astros with cash to San Francisco Giants for C Kirt Manwaring (July 27, 1996). ... Released by Giants (August 1, 1997). ... Signed by Seattle Mariners (August 15, 1997). ... On Seattle disabled list (August 15-September 1, 1997); included rehabilitation assignment to Tacoma (August 15-September 1). ... Granted free agency (October 16, 1997). ... Re-signed by Mariners (December 15, 1997).
STATISTICAL NOTES: Led Appalachian League with eight intentional bases on balls received in 1987. ... Led Appalachian League catchers with .989 fielding percentage, 483 putouts and 540 total chances and tied for lead with six double plays in 1987. ... Led Midwest League catchers with 984 total chances in 1988. ... Led Carolina League catchers with 860 total chances and tied for lead with eight double plays in 1989. ... Led Southern League catchers with 857 total chances, 11 double plays and 15 passed balls in 1990. ... Tied for N.L. lead with 10 sacrifice flies in 1996. ... Career major league grand slams: 2.

Year Team (League)	Pos.	G	AB	R	H	2B	3B	HR	RBI	Avg.	BB	SO	SB	PO	A	E	Avg.
1987—Geneva (NY-Penn)	C-1B	75	243	35	61	8	2	8	43	.251	58	40	7	†503	51	7	†.988
1988—Peoria (Midwest)	C	137	490	54	119	30	1	8	63	.243	67	110	4	*864	*101	*19	.981
1989—Win.-Salem (Car.)	C	132	445	61	111	24	1	12	54	.249	50	87	6	*764	*78	*18	.979
1990—Charlotte (Southern)	C	127	449	48	102	18	1	17	71	.227	43	95	4	*740	*103	14	.984
1991—Iowa (Am. Assoc.)	C-OF	38	107	12	29	3	1	5	14	.271	11	17	1	204	24	3	.987
—Chicago (N.L.)	C	86	203	21	45	9	0	6	22	.222	19	56	3	373	42	3	.993

W

Year Team (League)	Pos.	G	AB	R	H	2B	3B	HR	RBI	Avg.	BB	SO	SB	PO	A	E	Avg.
1992—Chicago (N.L.)	C	83	244	20	66	9	1	8	22	.270	28	53	0	408	47	3	.993
—Iowa (Am. Assoc.)	C	47	155	20	43	11	2	5	28	.277	19	42	0	177	18	2	.990
1993—Chicago (N.L.)	C	136	446	78	135	23	1	30	73	.303	50	99	2	717	89	3	.996
1994—Chicago (N.L.)	C-1B	100	313	44	71	25	2	7	39	.227	40	86	4	550	51	4	.993
1995—Chicago (N.L.)	C-1B	50	162	24	31	2	0	6	14	.191	36	51	0	294	31	4	.988
—Houston (N.L.)■	C	15	40	6	10	1	0	1	5	.250	10	10	0	87	4	0	1.000
—Jackson (Texas)	C	4	11	0	0	0	0	0	0	.000	3	2	0	23	1	0	1.000
—Tucson (PCL)	C	4	12	0	4	0	0	0	4	.333	2	0	0	27	4	0	1.000
1996—Houston (N.L.)	C	84	254	34	54	8	2	6	23	.213	46	81	0	550	39	6	.990
—San Francisco (N.L.)■	C-1B	52	157	19	46	10	0	8	36	.293	21	40	0	240	34	2	.993
1997—San Francisco (N.L.)	C-1B	66	190	18	37	5	0	6	23	.195	17	65	0	326	37	5	.986
—Tacoma (PCL)■	C-1B	17	68	16	23	8	0	1	14	.338	8	12	0	82	4	1	.989
—Seattle (A.L.)	C-DH	5	12	2	3	1	0	1	4	.250	1	2	0	9	1	0	1.000
American League totals (1 year)		5	12	2	3	1	0	1	4	.250	1	2	0	9	1	0	1.000
National League totals (7 years)		672	2009	264	495	92	6	78	257	.246	267	541	9	3545	374	30	.992
Major league totals (7 years)		677	2021	266	498	93	6	79	261	.246	268	543	9	3554	375	30	.992

DIVISION SERIES RECORD

Year Team (League)	Pos.	G	AB	R	H	2B	3B	HR	RBI	Avg.	BB	SO	SB	PO	A	E	Avg.
1997—Seattle (A.L.)	C-PH	1	1	0	0	0	0	0	0	.000	1	0	0	2	0	0	1.000

WILLIAMS, BERNIE   OF   YANKEES

PERSONAL: Born September 13, 1968, in San Juan, Puerto Rico. ... 6-2/205. ... Bats both, throws right. ... Full name: Bernabe Figueroa Williams.

TRANSACTIONS/CAREER NOTES: Signed as non-drafted free agent by New York Yankees organization (September 13, 1985). ... On disabled list (July 15, 1988-remainder of season and May 13-June 7, 1993). ... On disabled list (May 11-26, 1996). ... On disabled list (June 16-July 2 and July 15-August 1, 1997).

RECORDS: Shares major league single-game record (nine innings) for most strikeouts—5 (August 21, 1991). ... Shares major league record for most doubles in one inning—2 (June 22, 1994, seventh inning). ... Shares modern major league record for most long hits in one inning—2 (June 22, 1994, seventh inning).

HONORS: Won A.L. Gold Glove as outfielder (1997).

STATISTICAL NOTES: Led Gulf Coast League outfielders with 123 total chances in 1986. ... Tied for Gulf Coast League lead in caught stealing with 12 in 1986. ... Led Eastern League in caught stealing with 18 in 1990. ... Led Eastern League outfielders with 307 total chances and tied for lead with four double plays in 1990. ... Had 21-game hitting streak (August 1-23, 1993). ... Switch-hit home runs in one game two times (June 6, 1994 and September 12, 1996). ... Led A.L. outfielders with 441 total chances in 1995. ... Career major league grand slams: 4.

MISCELLANEOUS: Batted righthanded only (1986-88).

Year Team (League)	Pos.	G	AB	R	H	2B	3B	HR	RBI	Avg.	BB	SO	SB	PO	A	E	Avg.
1986—GC Yankees (GCL)	OF	61	230	*45	62	5	3	2	25	.270	39	40	33	*117	3	3	.976
1987—Fort Lauderdale (FSL)	OF	25	71	11	11	3	0	0	4	.155	18	22	9	49	1	0	1.000
—Oneonta (NYP)	OF	25	93	13	32	4	0	0	15	.344	10	14	9	40	0	2	.952
1988—Prince William (Car.)	OF	92	337	72	113	16	7	7	45	*.335	65	65	29	186	8	5	.975
1989—Columbus (Int'l)	OF	50	162	21	35	8	1	2	16	.216	25	38	11	112	2	1	.991
—Alb./Colon. (Eastern)	OF	91	314	63	79	11	8	11	42	.252	60	72	26	180	5	5	.974
1990—Alb./Colon. (Eastern)	OF	134	466	*91	131	28	5	8	54	.281	*98	97	*39	*288	15	4	.987
1991—Columbus (Int'l)	OF	78	306	52	90	14	6	8	37	.294	38	43	9	164	2	1	.994
—New York (A.L.)	OF	85	320	43	76	19	4	3	34	.238	48	57	10	230	3	5	.979
1992—New York (A.L.)	OF	62	261	39	73	14	2	5	26	.280	29	36	7	187	5	1	.995
—Columbus (Int'l)	OF	95	363	68	111	23	•9	8	50	.306	52	61	20	205	2	2	.990
1993—New York (A.L.)	OF	139	567	67	152	31	4	12	68	.268	53	106	9	366	5	4	.989
1994—New York (A.L.)	OF	108	408	80	118	29	1	12	57	.289	61	54	16	277	7	3	.990
1995—New York (A.L.)	OF	144	563	93	173	29	9	18	82	.307	75	98	8	*432	1	•8	.982
1996—New York (A.L.)	OF-DH	143	551	108	168	26	7	29	102	.305	82	72	17	334	10	5	.986
1997—New York (A.L.)	OF	129	509	107	167	35	6	21	100	.328	73	80	15	270	2	2	.993
Major league totals (7 years)		810	3179	537	927	183	33	100	469	.292	421	503	82	2096	33	28	.987

DIVISION SERIES RECORD

RECORDS: Shares single-game record for most home runs—2 (October 6, 1995 and October 5, 1996). ... Holds career records for most runs—16; most hits—18; and bases on balls—13. ... Shares career records for most games—14; and home runs—5.

Year Team (League)	Pos.	G	AB	R	H	2B	3B	HR	RBI	Avg.	BB	SO	SB	PO	A	E	Avg.
1995—New York (A.L.)	OF	5	21	8	9	2	0	2	5	.429	7	3	1	13	0	0	1.000
1996—New York (A.L.)	OF	4	15	5	7	0	0	3	5	.467	2	1	1	10	0	0	1.000
1997—New York (A.L.)	OF	5	17	3	2	1	0	0	1	.118	4	3	0	7	0	0	1.000
Division series totals (3 years)		14	53	16	18	3	0	5	11	.340	13	7	2	30	0	0	1.000

CHAMPIONSHIP SERIES RECORD

NOTES: Named A.L. Championship Series Most Valuable Player (1996).

Year Team (League)	Pos.	G	AB	R	H	2B	3B	HR	RBI	Avg.	BB	SO	SB	PO	A	E	Avg.
1996—New York (A.L.)	OF	5	19	6	9	3	0	2	6	.474	6	4	1	20	0	0	1.000

WORLD SERIES RECORD

NOTES: Member of World Series championship team (1996).

Year Team (League)	Pos.	G	AB	R	H	2B	3B	HR	RBI	Avg.	BB	SO	SB	PO	A	E	Avg.
1996—New York (A.L.)	OF	6	24	3	4	0	0	1	4	.167	4	6	1	15	0	0	1.000

W

Year League	Pos.	AB	R	H	2B	3B	BATTING HR	RBI	Avg.	BB	SO	SB	FIELDING PO	A	E	Avg.
1997— American	OF	0	1	0	0	0	0	0	...	1	0	1	1	0	0	1.000

WILLIAMS, BRIAN   P

PERSONAL: Born February 15, 1969, in Lancaster, S.C. ... 6-2/225. ... Throws right, bats right. ... Full name: Brian O'Neal Williams.
HIGH SCHOOL: Lewisville (Fort Lawn, S.C.).
COLLEGE: South Carolina.
TRANSACTIONS/CAREER NOTES: Selected by Pittsburgh Pirates organization in third round of free-agent draft (June 2, 1987); did not sign. ... Selected by Houston Astros organization in supplemental round ("sandwich pick" between first and second round, 31st pick overall) of free-agent draft (June 4, 1990); pick received as part of compensation for San Francisco Giants signing Type A free-agent OF Kevin Bass. ... On Tucson disabled list (May 25-June 1, 1992). ... On Houston disabled list (August 5-20, 1993); included rehabilitation assignment to Tucson (August 15-20). ... On Houston disabled list (August 1-September 19, 1994). ... Traded by Astros with 3B Ken Caminiti, SS Andujar Cedeno, 1B Robert Petagine and a player to be named later to San Diego Padres for OF Phil Plantier, OF Derek Bell, P Pedro Martinez, P Doug Brocail, IF Craig Shipley and SS Ricky Gutierrez (December 28, 1994); Padres acquired P Sean Fesh to complete deal (May 1, 1995). ... Granted free agency (December 21, 1995). ... Signed by Detroit Tigers (January 10, 1996). ... Released by Tigers following 1996 season. ... Signed by Baltimore Orioles organization (January 21, 1997). ... Released by Orioles (December 11, 1997).
MISCELLANEOUS: Appeared in four games as pinch-runner with Houston (1992).

Year Team (League)	W	L	Pct.	ERA	G	GS	CG	ShO	Sv.	IP	H	R	ER	BB	SO
1990— Auburn (N.Y.-Penn)	0	0	...	4.05	3	3	0	0	0	6 2/3	6	5	3	6	7
1991— Osceola (Florida St.)...........	6	4	.600	2.91	15	15	0	0	0	89 2/3	72	41	29	40	67
— Jackson (Texas)	2	1	.667	4.20	3	3	0	0	0	15	17	8	7	7	15
— Tucson (PCL)	0	1	.000	4.93	7	7	0	0	0	38 1/3	39	25	21	22	29
— Houston (N.L.)	0	1	.000	3.75	2	2	0	0	0	12	11	5	5	4	4
1992— Tucson (PCL)	6	1	.857	4.50	12	12	0	0	0	70	78	37	35	26	58
— Houston (N.L.)	7	6	.538	3.92	16	16	0	0	0	96 1/3	92	44	42	42	54
1993— Houston (N.L.)	4	4	.500	4.83	42	5	0	0	0	82	76	48	44	38	56
— Tucson (PCL)	1	0	1.000	0.00	2	0	0	0	3	3	1	0	0	0	3
1994— Houston (N.L.)■...............	6	5	.545	5.74	20	13	0	0	0	78 1/3	112	64	50	41	75
— Tucson (PCL)	2	0	1.000	2.21	3	3	0	0	0	20 1/3	22	6	5	9	17
1995— San Diego (N.L.)■■	3	10	.231	6.00	44	6	0	0	0	72	79	54	48	38	75
1996— Detroit (A.L.)■...............	3	10	.231	6.77	40	17	2	1	2	121	145	107	91	85	72
— Toledo (Int'l)	1	2	.333	5.49	3	3	1	0	0	19 2/3	22	13	12	9	21
1997— Rochester (Int'l)■...........	4	3	.571	3.89	22	9	0	0	8	69 1/3	68	33	30	23	78
— Baltimore (A.L.)	0	0	...	3.00	13	0	0	0	0	24	20	8	8	18	14
A.L. totals (2 years)	3	10	.231	6.14	53	17	2	1	2	145	165	115	99	103	86
N.L. totals (5 years)	20	26	.435	4.99	124	42	0	0	3	340 2/3	370	215	189	163	238
Major league totals (7 years)......	23	36	.390	5.34	177	59	2	1	5	485 2/3	535	330	288	266	324

WILLIAMS, EDDIE   1B   PADRES

PERSONAL: Born November 1, 1964, in Shreveport, La. ... 6-0/210. ... Bats right, throws right. ... Full name: Edward Laquan Williams.
HIGH SCHOOL: Hoover (San Diego).
TRANSACTIONS/CAREER NOTES: Selected by New York Mets organization in first round (fourth pick overall) of free-agent draft (June 6, 1983). ... Traded by Mets organization with P Matt Bullinger and P Jay Tibbs to Cincinnati Reds for P Bruce Berenyi (June 15, 1984). ... Selected by Cleveland Indians from Reds organization in Rule 5 major league draft (December 10, 1985). ... Traded by Indians to Chicago White Sox for P Joel Davis and P Ed Wojna (January 23, 1989). ... Granted free agency (October 15, 1989). ... Signed by Las Vegas, San Diego Padres organization (December 21, 1989). ... Contract sold by Padres to Fukuoka Daiei Hawks of Japan Pacific League (December 2, 1990). ... Released by Fukuoka (September 1991). ... Signed by Greenville, Atlanta Braves organization (February 16, 1992). ... Released by Richmond, Braves organization (May 14, 1992). ... Signed by Denver, Milwaukee Brewers organization (November 30, 1992). ... Released by New Orleans, Brewers organization (April 19, 1993). ... Signed by Las Vegas, Padres organization (December 17, 1993). ... Granted free agency (December 21, 1995). ... Signed by Detroit Tigers (January 2, 1996). ... Granted free agency (October 15, 1996). ... Traded by Dodgers to Pittsburgh Pirates for P Hal Garrett (August 9, 1997). ... Released by Pirates (October 15, 1997). ... Signed by San Diego Padres organization (January 13, 1998).
HONORS: Named Midwest League Most Valuable Player (1985).
STATISTICAL NOTES: Led Midwest League in being hit by pitch with 15 in 1985. ... Led American Association third basemen with 352 total chances, 24 double plays, 237 assists, and 27 errors in 1987. ... Led American Association in being hit by pitch with 15 in 1987. ... Led Pacific Coast League in being hit by pitch with 12 in 1988. ... Career major league grand slams: 2.

Year Team (League)	Pos.	G	AB	R	H	2B	3B	BATTING HR	RBI	Avg.	BB	SO	SB	FIELDING PO	A	E	Avg.
1983— Little Falls (NYP)	3B	50	190	30	50	6	2	6	28	.263	19	41	3	50	53	13	.888
1984— Columbia (S. Atl.)........	3B	43	152	17	28	4	2	3	24	.184	15	31	1	24	76	16	.862
— Tampa (Florida State)■	3B	50	138	20	35	8	0	2	16	.254	25	23	0	25	43	11	.861
1985— Cedar Rap. (Midw.)	3B	119	406	71	106	13	3	20	83	.261	62	101	5	83	204	33	.897
1986— Cleveland (A.L.)■.......	OF	5	7	2	1	0	0	0	1	.143	0	3	0	0	0	0	...
— Waterbury (Eastern)...	3B	62	214	24	51	10	0	7	30	.238	28	41	3	39	100	15	.903
1987— Buffalo (A.A.)..........	3B-SS	131	488	90	142	29	2	22	85	.291	55	117	6	88	†237	†27	.923
— Cleveland (A.L.)..........	3B	22	64	9	11	4	0	1	4	.172	9	19	0	17	37	1	.982
1988— Colo. Springs (PCL)...	3B-SS-1B	101	365	53	110	24	3	12	58	.301	18	51	0	93	177	29	.903
— Cleveland (A.L.)..........	3B	10	21	3	4	0	0	1	1	.190	0	3	0	3	18	0	1.000
1989— Chicago (A.L.)■........	3B	66	201	25	55	8	0	3	10	.274	18	31	1	37	123	16	.909
— Vancouver (PCL)	3B-1B	35	114	12	28	8	0	1	13	.246	15	18	1	8	10	4	.818
1990— Las Vegas (PCL)■......	3B-1B	93	348	59	110	29	2	17	75	.316	42	47	0	106	121	17	.930
— San Diego (N.L.)	3B	14	42	5	12	3	0	3	4	.286	5	6	0	5	21	3	.897
1991— Fukuoka (Jp. Pac.)■..	3B	49	163	20	41	...	...	5	16	.252	21	32	2	...	...	...	...
1992— Richmond (Int'l)■......	3B	24	74	8	15	3	0	1	5	.203	3	9	0	7	26	5	.868

						BATTING										FIELDING			
Year	Team (League)	Pos.	G	AB	R	H	2B	3B	HR	RBI	Avg.	BB	SO	SB	PO	A	E	Avg.
1993—	Monter. Sul. (Mx.)■..	OF-3B-1B	59	210	40	74	17	0	12	34	.352	21	29	0	71	14	1	.988
	— New Orleans (A.A.)■..	3B-1B	8	27	2	7	0	1	1	4	.259	7	4	0	14	13	1	.964
1994—	Las Vegas (PCL)■	1B-3B	59	219	48	77	12	1	20	54	.352	24	34	0	276	49	4	.988
	— San Diego (N.L.)	1B-3B	49	175	32	58	11	1	11	42	.331	15	26	0	383	29	5	.988
1995—	San Diego (N.L.)	1B	97	296	35	77	11	1	12	47	.260	23	47	0	571	49	7	.989
1996—	Detroit (A.L.)■.........	DH-1-3-O	77	215	22	43	5	0	6	26	.200	18	50	0	25	2	0	1.000
1997—	Albuquerque (PCL)■..	1B-3B	76	279	73	102	17	0	29	76	.366	37	45	0	232	15	1	.996
	— Los Angeles (N.L.)	PH	8	7	0	1	0	0	0	1	.143	1	1	0	...	...	...	...
	— Pittsburgh (N.L.)■	1B	30	89	12	22	5	0	3	11	.247	10	24	1	202	8	2	.991
American League totals (5 years)			180	508	61	114	17	0	10	42	.224	45	106	1	82	180	17	.939
National League totals (4 years)			198	609	84	170	30	2	29	105	.279	54	104	1	1161	107	17	.987
Major league totals (9 years)			378	1117	145	284	47	2	39	147	.254	99	210	2	1243	287	34	.978

WILLIAMS, GEORGE — C — ATHLETICS

PERSONAL: Born April 22, 1969, in La Crosse, Wis. ... 5-10/190. ... Bats both, throws right. ... Full name: George Erik Williams.
HIGH SCHOOL: La Crosse (Wis.) Central.
COLLEGE: Texas-Pan American.
TRANSACTIONS/CAREER NOTES: Selected by Oakland Athletics organization in 24th round of free-agent draft (June 3, 1991). ... On disabled list (April 7-June 23, 1994). ... On Oakland disabled list (April 14-May 5 and July 20-August 21, 1997); included rehabilitation assignments to Modesto (April 29-May 5 and August 13-21) and Edmonton (August 10-12).
STATISTICAL NOTES: Tied for Midwest League lead with six intentional bases on balls received in 1992. ... Career major league grand slams: 2.

						BATTING										FIELDING			
Year	Team (League)	Pos.	G	AB	R	H	2B	3B	HR	RBI	Avg.	BB	SO	SB	PO	A	E	Avg.
1991—	S. Oregon (N'west).....	C-3B	55	174	24	41	10	0	2	24	.236	38	36	9	126	44	6	.966
1992—	Madison (Midwest)	C-OF	115	349	56	106	18	2	5	42	.304	76	53	9	455	57	18	.966
1993—	Huntsville (Southern) .	C-OF-3B	124	434	80	128	26	2	14	77	.295	67	66	6	430	63	11	.978
1994—	W. Mich. (Mid.)	C	63	221	40	67	20	1	8	48	.303	44	47	6	21	3	0	1.000
1995—	Edmonton (PCL)	C-OF	81	290	53	90	20	0	13	55	.310	50	52	0	310	44	7	.981
	— Oakland (A.L.)	C-DH	29	79	13	23	5	1	3	14	.291	11	21	0	58	7	3	.956
1996—	Oakland (A.L.)	C-DH	56	132	17	20	5	0	3	10	.152	28	32	0	154	12	3	.982
	— Edmonton (PCL)	C-OF	14	57	10	23	5	0	5	18	.404	6	11	0	76	0	0	1.000
1997—	Oakland (A.L.)	C-DH	76	201	30	58	9	1	3	22	.289	35	46	0	337	27	6	.984
	— Modesto (California) ..	C	13	44	8	14	4	0	1	6	.318	7	14	0	53	9	0	1.000
	— Edmonton (PCL)	C	3	7	0	0	0	0	0	0	.000	1	1	0	8	1	0	1.000
Major league totals (3 years)			161	412	60	101	19	2	9	46	.245	74	99	0	549	46	12	.980

WILLIAMS, GERALD — OF — BRAVES

PERSONAL: Born August 10, 1966, in New Orleans. ... 6-2/190. ... Bats right, throws right. ... Full name: Gerald Floyd Williams.
HIGH SCHOOL: East St. John (Reserve, La.).
COLLEGE: Grambling State.
TRANSACTIONS/CAREER NOTES: Selected by New York Yankees organization in 14th round of free-agent draft (June 2, 1987). ... Traded by Yankees with P Bob Wickman to Milwaukee Brewers for P Graeme Lloyd and OF Pat Listach (August 23, 1996). ... Traded by Brewers to Atlanta Braves for P Chad Fox (December 11, 1997).
STATISTICAL NOTES: Led Carolina League outfielders with 307 total chances in 1989. ... Led International League outfielders with 354 total chances in 1992. ... Tied for International League lead in double plays by outfielder with five in 1992. ... Collected six hits in one game (May 1, 1996). ... Career major league grand slams: 1.

						BATTING										FIELDING			
Year	Team (League)	Pos.	G	AB	R	H	2B	3B	HR	RBI	Avg.	BB	SO	SB	PO	A	E	Avg.
1987—	Oneonta (NYP)	OF	29	115	26	42	6	2	2	29	.365	16	18	6	68	3	3	.959
1988—	Prince William (Car.) ..	OF	54	159	20	29	3	0	2	18	.182	15	47	6	71	2	3	.961
	— Fort Lauderdale (FSL)	OF	63	212	21	40	7	2	2	17	.189	16	56	4	163	2	6	.965
1989—	Prince William (Car.) ..	OF	134	454	63	104	19	6	13	69	.229	51	120	15	*292	7	8	.974
1990—	Fort Lauderdale (FSL)	OF	50	204	25	59	4	5	7	43	.289	16	52	19	115	1	3	.975
	— Alb./Colon. (Eastern) ..	OF	96	324	54	81	17	2	13	58	.250	35	74	18	210	6	7	.969
1991—	Alb./Colon. (Eastern) ..	OF	45	175	28	50	15	0	5	32	.286	18	26	18	109	4	3	.974
	— Columbus (Int'l)	OF	61	198	20	51	8	3	2	27	.258	16	39	9	124	1	3	.977
1992—	Columbus (Int'l)	OF	*142	547	92	*156	31	6	16	86	.285	38	98	36	*332	*14	8	.977
	— New York (A.L.)	OF	15	27	7	8	2	0	3	6	.296	0	3	2	20	1	2	.913
1993—	Columbus (Int'l)	OF	87	336	53	95	19	6	8	38	.283	20	66	29	191	6	3	.985
	— New York (A.L.)	OF-DH	42	67	11	10	2	3	0	6	.149	1	14	2	41	2	2	.956
1994—	New York (A.L.)	OF-DH	57	86	19	25	8	0	4	13	.291	4	17	1	43	2	2	.957
1995—	New York (A.L.)	OF-DH	100	182	33	45	18	2	6	28	.247	22	34	4	138	6	1	.993
1996—	New York (A.L.)	OF-DH	99	233	37	63	15	4	5	30	.270	15	39	7	132	1	3	.978
	— Milwaukee (A.L.)■.....	OF	26	92	6	19	4	0	0	4	.207	4	18	3	75	3	1	.987
1997—	Milwaukee (A.L.)	OF-DH	155	566	73	143	32	2	10	41	.253	19	90	23	357	11	3	.992
Major league totals (6 years)			494	1253	186	313	81	11	28	128	.250	65	215	42	806	26	14	.983

DIVISION SERIES RECORD

						BATTING										FIELDING			
Year	Team (League)	Pos.	G	AB	R	H	2B	3B	HR	RBI	Avg.	BB	SO	SB	PO	A	E	Avg.
1995—	New York (A.L.)	OF-PR	5	5	1	0	0	0	0	0	.000	2	3	0	7	1	0	1.000

W

WILLIAMS, GLENN   2B   BRAVES

PERSONAL: Born July 18, 1977, in Gosford, Australia. ... 6-2/170. ... Bats both, throws right. ... Full name: Glenn David Williams.
TRANSACTIONS/CAREER NOTES: Signed as non-drafted free agent by Atlanta Braves organization (July 2, 1993). ... On disabled list (May 2-20, June 2-19 and July 5-September 25, 1996). ... On disabled list (April 22-June 5, 1997).

Year Team (League)	Pos.	G	AB	R	H	2B	3B	HR	RBI	Avg.	BB	SO	SB	PO	A	E	Avg.
1994— GC Braves (GCL)	SS	24	89	8	18	2	0	2	7	.202	9	32	4	29	67	10	.906
— Danville (Appal.)	SS	24	79	11	20	2	0	1	9	.253	8	20	2	29	50	10	.888
1995— Eugene (Northwest)	SS	71	268	39	60	11	4	7	36	.224	21	71	7	15	23	4	.905
— Macon (S. Atl.)	SS	38	120	13	21	4	0	0	14	.175	16	42	2	37	87	19	.867
1996— Macon (S. Atl.)	SS	51	181	14	35	7	3	3	18	.193	18	47	4	73	129	15	.931
1997— Macon (S. Atl.)	SS	77	297	52	79	18	2	14	52	.266	24	105	9	113	171	17	.944

WILLIAMS, KEITH   OF   GIANTS

PERSONAL: Born April 21, 1972, in Bedford, Pa. ... 6-0/190. ... Bats right, throws right. ... Full name: David Keith Williams.
HIGH SCHOOL: Bedford (Pa.).
COLLEGE: Clemson.
TRANSACTIONS/CAREER NOTES: Selected by San Francisco Giants organization in seventh round of free-agent draft (June 3, 1993).
STATISTICAL NOTES: Led Northwest League with 154 total bases in 1993.

Year Team (League)	Pos.	G	AB	R	H	2B	3B	HR	RBI	Avg.	BB	SO	SB	PO	A	E	Avg.
1993— Everett (N'west)	OF	75	288	57	*87	21	5	12	49	.302	48	73	21	106	3	3	.973
1994— San Jose (Calif.)	OF	128	504	91	151	30	8	21	97	.300	60	102	4	197	6	3	*.985
1995— Shreveport (Texas)	OF	75	275	39	84	20	1	9	55	.305	23	39	5	109	4	4	.966
— Phoenix (PCL)	OF	24	83	7	25	4	1	2	14	.301	5	11	5	38	1	0	1.000
1996— Phoenix (PCL)	OF	108	398	63	109	25	3	13	63	.274	52	96	2	160	6	2	.988
— San Francisco (N.L.)	OF	9	20	0	5	0	0	0	0	.250	0	6	0	8	0	0	1.000
1997— Phoenix (PCL)	OF	3	5	0	1	0	0	0	0	.200	0	2	0	0	0	0	...
— Shreveport (Texas)	OF-1B	131	493	83	158	37	7	22	106	.320	46	94	3	244	14	6	.977
Major league totals (1 year)		9	20	0	5	0	0	0	0	.250	0	6	0	8	0	0	1.000

WILLIAMS, MATT   3B   DIAMONDBACKS

PERSONAL: Born November 28, 1965, in Bishop, Calif. ... 6-2/216. ... Bats right, throws right. ... Full name: Matthew Derrick Williams. ... Grandson of Bartholomew (Bart) Griffith, outfielder/first baseman, Brooklyn Dodgers and Washington Senators (1922-24).
HIGH SCHOOL: Carson (Nev.).
COLLEGE: UNLV.
TRANSACTIONS/CAREER NOTES: Selected by New York Mets organization in 27th round of free-agent draft (June 6, 1983); did not sign. ... Selected by San Francisco Giants organization in first round (third pick overall) of free-agent draft (June 2, 1986). ... On disabled list (June 28-July 14, 1993). ... On San Francisco disabled list (June 4-August 19, 1995); included rehabilitation assignments to San Jose (July 24-25 and August 13-19). ... On disabled list (August 5, 1996-remainder of season). ... Traded by Giants with a player to be named later to Cleveland Indians for IF Jeff Kent, IF Jose Vizcaino, P Julian Tavarez and a player to be named later (November 13, 1996); Giants traded OF Trenidad Hubbard to Indians for P Joe Roa to complete deal (December 16, 1996). ... Traded by Indians to Arizona Diamondbacks for 3B Travis Fryman, P Tom Martin and cash (December 1, 1997).
RECORDS: Shares major league record for most home runs in two consecutive games—5 (April 25 [3] and 26 [2], 1997).
HONORS: Named shortstop on THE SPORTING NEWS college All-America team (1986). ... Named third baseman on THE SPORTING NEWS N.L. All-Star team (1990 and 1993-94). ... Named third baseman on THE SPORTING NEWS N.L. Silver Slugger team (1990 and 1993-94). ... Won N.L. Gold Glove at third base (1991 and 1993-94). ... Named third baseman on THE SPORTING NEWS A.L. All-Star team (1997). ... Won A.L. Gold Glove at third base (1997). ... Named third baseman on THE SPORTING NEWS A.L. Silver Slugger team (1997).
STATISTICAL NOTES: Led N.L. third basemen with 33 double plays in 1990 and 1992 and 34 in 1993. ... Tied for N.L. lead in total chances by third baseman with 465 in 1990. ... Led N.L. third basemen with 131 putouts in 1991. ... Led N.L. third basemen with 326 total chances in 1994. ... Hit three home runs in one game (April 25, 1997). ... Had 24-game hitting streak (August 13-September 8, 1997). ... Career major league grand slams: 5.

Year Team (League)	Pos.	G	AB	R	H	2B	3B	HR	RBI	Avg.	BB	SO	SB	PO	A	E	Avg.
1986— Everett (N'west)	SS	4	17	3	4	0	1	1	10	.235	1	4	0	5	10	2	.882
— Clinton (Midwest)	SS	68	250	32	60	14	3	7	29	.240	23	62	3	89	150	10	.960
1987— Phoenix (PCL)	3B-2B-SS	56	211	36	61	15	2	6	37	.289	19	53	6	53	136	14	.931
— San Francisco (N.L.)	SS-3B	84	245	28	46	9	2	8	21	.188	16	68	4	110	234	9	.975
1988— Phoenix (PCL)	3-S-2-O	82	306	45	83	19	1	12	51	.271	13	56	6	56	173	13	.946
— San Francisco (N.L.)	3B-SS	52	156	17	32	6	1	8	19	.205	8	41	0	48	108	7	.957
1989— San Francisco (N.L.)	3B-SS	84	292	31	59	18	1	18	50	.202	14	72	1	90	168	10	.963
— Phoenix (PCL)	3B-SS-OF	76	284	61	91	20	2	26	61	.320	32	51	9	57	197	11	.958
1990— San Francisco (N.L.)	3B	159	617	87	171	27	2	33	*122	.277	33	138	7	*140	306	19	.959
1991— San Francisco (N.L.)	3B-SS	157	589	72	158	24	5	34	98	.268	33	128	5	†134	295	16	.953
1992— San Francisco (N.L.)	3B	146	529	58	120	13	5	20	66	.227	39	109	7	105	289	*23	.945
1993— San Francisco (N.L.)	3B	145	579	105	170	33	4	38	110	.294	27	80	1	117	266	12	.970
1994— San Francisco (N.L.)	3B	112	445	74	119	16	3	*43	96	.267	33	87	1	79	*235	12	.963
1995— San Francisco (N.L.)	3B	76	283	53	95	17	1	23	65	.336	30	58	2	49	178	10	.958
— San Jose (Calif.)	3B	4	11	2	2	0	0	1	2	.182	0	3	0	0	4	0	1.000
1996— San Francisco (N.L.)	3B-1B-SS	105	404	69	122	16	1	22	85	.302	39	91	1	164	191	14	.962
1997— Cleveland (A.L.)■...	3B	151	596	86	157	32	3	32	105	.263	34	108	12	89	301	12	.970
American League totals (1 year)		151	596	86	157	32	3	32	105	.263	34	108	12	89	301	12	.970
National League totals (10 years)		1120	4139	594	1092	179	26	247	732	.264	272	872	29	1036	2270	132	.962
Major league totals (11 years)		1271	4735	680	1249	211	28	279	837	.264	306	980	41	1125	2571	144	.963

W

DIVISION SERIES RECORD

Year Team (League)	Pos.	G	AB	R	H	2B	3B	HR	RBI	Avg.	BB	SO	SB	PO	A	E	Avg.
1997— Cleveland (A.L.).........	3B	5	17	4	4	1	0	1	3	.235	3	3	0	2	10	0	1.000

CHAMPIONSHIP SERIES RECORD

RECORDS: Holds N.L. single-series record for most runs batted in—9 (1989).

Year Team (League)	Pos.	G	AB	R	H	2B	3B	HR	RBI	Avg.	BB	SO	SB	PO	A	E	Avg.
1987— San Francisco (N.L.) ..								Did not play.									
1989— San Francisco (N.L.) ..	3B-SS	5	20	2	6	1	0	2	9	.300	0	2	0	5	12	0	1.000
1997— Cleveland (A.L.).........	3B	6	23	1	5	1	0	0	2	.217	3	7	1	6	18	2	.923
Championship series totals (2 years)		11	43	3	11	2	0	2	11	.256	3	9	1	11	30	2	.953

WORLD SERIES RECORD

Year Team (League)	Pos.	G	AB	R	H	2B	3B	HR	RBI	Avg.	BB	SO	SB	PO	A	E	Avg.
1989— San Francisco (N.L.) ..	SS-3B	4	16	1	2	0	0	1	1	.125	0	6	0	4	12	0	1.000
1997— Cleveland (A.L.).........	3B	7	26	8	10	1	0	1	3	.385	7	6	0	5	9	0	1.000
World Series totals (2 years)		11	42	9	12	1	0	2	4	.286	7	12	0	9	21	0	1.000

ALL-STAR GAME RECORD

NOTES: Named to N.L. All-Star team for 1996 game; replaced by Ken Caminiti due to injury.

Year League	Pos.	AB	R	H	2B	3B	HR	RBI	Avg.	BB	SO	SB	PO	A	E	Avg.
1990— National.....................	PH	1	0	0	0	0	0	0	.000	0	1	0	...	...	...	...
1994— National.....................	3B	3	0	0	0	0	0	0	.000	0	2	0	0	1	1	.500
1995— National.....................					Selected, did not play—injured.											
All-Star Game totals (2 years)		4	0	0	0	0	0	0	.000	0	3	0	0	1	1	.500

WILLIAMS, MIKE   P   PIRATES

PERSONAL: Born July 29, 1968, in Radford, Va. ... 6-3/195. ... Throws right, bats right. ... Full name: Michael Darren Williams.
HIGH SCHOOL: Giles (Pearisburg, Va.).
COLLEGE: Virginia Tech.
TRANSACTIONS/CAREER NOTES: Selected by Philadelphia Phillies organization in 14th round of free-agent draft (June 4, 1990). ... On suspended list (September 26, 1996-remainder of season). ... Released by Phillies following 1996 season. ... Signed by Boston Red Sox organization (February 15, 1997). ... Released by Red Sox (March 14, 1997). ... Signed by Omaha, Kansas City Royals organization (April 30, 1997). ... On suspended list (May 16-18, 1997). ... Granted free agency (October 15, 1997). ... Signed by Pittsburgh Pirates organization (December 18, 1997).
STATISTICAL NOTES: Led N.L. with 16 wild pitches in 1996.
MISCELLANEOUS: Appeared in one game as pinch-runner (1996).

Year Team (League)	W	L	Pct.	ERA	G	GS	CG	ShO	Sv.	IP	H	R	ER	BB	SO
1990— Batavia (N.Y.-Penn)	2	3	.400	2.30	27	0	0	0	11	47	39	17	12	13	42
1991— Clearwater (Fla. St.)	7	3	.700	1.74	14	14	2	1	0	93 1/3	65	23	18	14	76
—Reading (Eastern)	7	5	.583	3.69	16	15	2	1	0	102 1/3	93	44	42	36	51
1992— Reading (Eastern)	1	2	.333	5.17	3	3	0	0	0	15 2/3	17	10	9	7	12
—Scran./W.B. (Int'l)	9	1	*.900	2.43	16	16	3	1	0	92 2/3	84	26	25	30	59
—Philadelphia (N.L.)	1	1	.500	5.34	5	5	1	0	0	28 2/3	29	20	17	7	5
1993— Scran./W.B. (Int'l)	9	2	*.818	2.87	14	13	1	1	0	97 1/3	93	34	31	16	53
—Philadelphia (N.L.)	1	3	.250	5.29	17	4	0	0	0	51	50	32	30	22	33
1994— Scran./W.B. (Int'l)	2	4	.333	5.01	12	8	0	0	0	50 1/3	61	31	28	20	29
—Philadelphia (N.L.)	2	7	.222	5.79	14	14	1	0	0	84	91	55	54	36	53
1995— Philadelphia (N.L.)	3	3	.500	3.29	33	8	0	0	0	87 2/3	78	37	32	29	57
—Scran./W.B. (Int'l)	0	1	.000	4.66	3	3	1	0	0	9 2/3	8	5	5	2	8
1996— Philadelphia (N.L.)	6	14	.300	5.44	32	29	0	0	0	167	188	107	101	67	103
1997— Omaha (Am. Assoc.)■............	3	6	.333	4.22	20	11	1	0	5	79	71	41	37	38	68
—Kansas City (A.L.)	0	2	.000	6.43	10	0	0	0	1	14	20	11	10	8	10
A.L. totals (1 year)	0	2	.000	6.43	10	0	0	0	1	14	20	11	10	8	10
N.L. totals (5 years)	13	25	.342	4.87	99	54	1	0	0	384 2/3	406	227	208	145	227
Major league totals (6 years)	13	27	.325	4.92	109	54	1	0	1	398 2/3	426	238	218	153	237

WILLIAMS, MITCH   P

PERSONAL: Born November 17, 1964, in Santa Ana, Calif. ... 6-4/205. ... Throws left, bats left. ... Full name: Mitchell Steven Williams. ... Brother of Bruce Williams, minor league pitcher (1981-85).
HIGH SCHOOL: West Linn (Ore.).
TRANSACTIONS/CAREER NOTES: Selected by San Diego Padres organization in eighth round of free-agent draft (June 7, 1982). ... Selected by Texas Rangers from Padres organization in Rule 5 major league draft (December 3, 1984). ... Returned to Padres organization (April 6, 1985). ... Traded by Padres organization to Rangers for 3B Randy Asadoor (April 6, 1985). ... On suspended list (May 2-4, 1988). ... Traded by Rangers with P Paul Kilgus, P Steve Wilson, IF Curtis Wilkerson, IF Luis Benitez and OF Pablo Delgado to Chicago Cubs for OF Rafael Palmeiro, P Jamie Moyer and P Drew Hall (December 5, 1988). ... On disabled list (June 12-July 12, 1990). ... Traded by Cubs to Philadelphia Phillies for P Chuck McElroy and P Bob Scanlan (April 7, 1991). ... Granted free agency (October 31, 1991). ... Re-signed by Phillies (December 18, 1991). ... Traded by Phillies to Houston Astros for P Doug Jones and P Jeff Juden (December 2, 1993). ... Released by Astros (May 31, 1994). ... Signed by California Angels (November 30, 1994). ... Released by Angels (June 19, 1995). ... Signed by Clearwater, Phillies organization (July 6, 1996). ... On Clearwater suspended list (July 6-15, 1996). ... Released by Phillies (August 19, 1996). ... Signed by Kansas City Royals organization (January 14, 1997). ... Released by Royals (May 12, 1997).
RECORDS: Holds major league rookie-season record for most games pitched—80 (1986).
STATISTICAL NOTES: Led Northwest League pitchers with 14 wild pitches and tied for lead with two balks in 1983.

W

Year	Team (League)	W	L	Pct.	ERA	G	GS	CG	ShO	Sv.	IP	H	R	ER	BB	SO
1982—	Walla Walla (N'west)	3	4	.429	4.78	12	12	0	0	0	58⅓	37	37	31	*72	66
1983—	Reno (California)	1	7	.125	7.14	11	11	0	0	0	58	58	56	46	60	44
	—Spokane (N'west)	7	6	.538	4.48	14	•14	3	1	0	92⅓	84	51	•46	55	87
1984—	Reno (California)	9	8	.529	4.99	26	26	3	1	0	164	163	113	91	127	165
1985—	Salem (Carolina)■	6	9	.400	5.45	22	21	1	0	0	99	57	64	60	*117	138
	—Tulsa (Texas)	2	2	.500	4.64	6	6	0	0	0	33	17	24	17	48	37
1986—	Texas (A.L.)	8	6	.571	3.58	*80	0	0	0	8	98	69	39	39	79	90
1987—	Texas (A.L.)	8	6	.571	3.23	85	1	0	0	6	108⅔	63	47	39	94	129
1988—	Texas (A.L.)	2	7	.222	4.63	67	0	0	0	18	68	48	38	35	47	61
1989—	Chicago (N.L.)■	4	4	.500	2.64	*76	0	0	0	36	81⅔	71	27	24	52	67
1990—	Chicago (N.L.)	1	8	.111	3.93	59	2	0	0	16	66⅓	60	38	29	50	55
1991—	Philadelphia (N.L.)■	12	5	.706	2.34	69	0	0	0	30	88⅓	56	24	23	62	84
1992—	Philadelphia (N.L.)	5	8	.385	3.78	66	0	0	0	29	81	69	39	34	64	74
1993—	Philadelphia (N.L.)	3	7	.300	3.34	65	0	0	0	43	62	56	30	23	44	60
1994—	Houston (N.L.)■	1	4	.200	7.65	25	0	0	0	6	20	21	17	17	24	21
1995—	California (A.L.)■	1	2	.333	6.75	20	0	0	0	0	10⅔	13	10	8	21	9
1996—	Clearwater (Fla. St.)■	0	0	...	2.25	6	0	0	0	0	8	10	3	2	1	6
	—Scran./W.B. (Int'l)	2	2	.500	10.20	9	0	0	0	0	15	25	20	17	11	15
1997—	Omaha (Am. Assoc.)■	0	0	...	2.08	3	0	0	0	0	8⅔	6	2	2	5	8
	—Kansas City (A.L.)	0	1	.000	10.80	7	0	0	0	0	6⅔	11	8	8	7	10
A.L. totals (5 years)		19	22	.463	3.98	259	1	0	0	32	292	204	142	129	248	299
N.L. totals (6 years)		26	36	.419	3.38	360	2	0	0	160	399⅓	333	175	150	296	361
Major league totals (11 years)		45	58	.437	3.63	619	3	0	0	192	691⅓	537	317	279	544	660

CHAMPIONSHIP SERIES RECORD

Year	Team (League)	W	L	Pct.	ERA	G	GS	CG	ShO	Sv.	IP	H	R	ER	BB	SO
1989—	Chicago (N.L.)	0	0	...	0.00	2	0	0	0	0	1	1	0	0	0	2
1993—	Philadelphia (N.L.)	2	0	1.000	1.69	4	0	0	0	2	5⅓	6	2	1	2	5
Champ. series totals (2 years)		2	0	1.000	1.42	6	0	0	0	2	6⅓	7	2	1	2	7

WORLD SERIES RECORD

Year	Team (League)	W	L	Pct.	ERA	G	GS	CG	ShO	Sv.	IP	H	R	ER	BB	SO
1993—	Philadelphia (N.L.)	0	2	.000	20.25	3	0	0	0	1	2⅔	5	6	6	4	1

ALL-STAR GAME RECORD

Year	League	W	L	Pct.	ERA	GS	CG	ShO	Sv.	IP	H	R	ER	BB	SO
1989—	National	0	0	...	0.00	0	0	0	0	1	0	0	0	1	1

WILLIAMS, SHAD   P

PERSONAL: Born March 10, 1971, in Fresno, Calif. ... 6-0/185. ... Throws right, bats right. ... Full name: Shad Clayton Williams.
HIGH SCHOOL: San Joaquin Memorial (Fresno, Calif.).
COLLEGE: Fresno (Calif.) City College.
TRANSACTIONS/CAREER NOTES: Selected by California Angels organization in 17th round of free-agent draft (June 3, 1991). ... On Midland disabled list (April 19-May 24, 1994). ... Angels franchise renamed Anaheim Angels for 1997 season. ... Granted free agency (October 15, 1997).
STATISTICAL NOTES: Pitched 7-0 no-hit victory for Midland against Arkansas (May 28, 1994, second game).

Year	Team (League)	W	L	Pct.	ERA	G	GS	CG	ShO	Sv.	IP	H	R	ER	BB	SO
1992—	Quad City (Midwest)	13	11	.542	3.26	27	26	7	0	0	179⅓	161	81	65	55	152
1993—	Midland (Texas)	7	10	.412	4.71	27	•27	2	0	0	175⅔	192	100	92	65	91
1994—	Midland (Texas)	3	0	1.000	1.11	5	5	1	1	0	32⅓	13	4	4	4	29
	—Vancouver (PCL)	4	6	.400	4.60	16	16	1	1	0	86	100	61	44	30	42
1995—	Vancouver (PCL)	9	7	.563	3.37	25	25	3	1	0	149⅔	142	65	56	48	114
1996—	Vancouver (PCL)	6	2	.750	3.96	15	13	1	1	0	75	73	36	33	28	57
	—California (A.L.)	0	2	.000	8.89	13	2	0	0	0	28⅓	42	34	28	21	26
1997—	Vancouver (PCL)	6	2	.750	3.82	40	10	0	0	0	99	98	52	42	41	52
	—Anaheim (A.L.)	0	0	...	0.00	1	0	0	0	0	1	1	0	0	1	0
Major league totals (2 years)		0	2	.000	8.59	14	2	0	0	0	29⅓	43	34	28	22	26

WILLIAMS, TODD   P   REDS

PERSONAL: Born February 13, 1971, in Syracuse, N.Y. ... 6-3/185. ... Throws right, bats right. ... Full name: Todd Michael Williams.
HIGH SCHOOL: East Syracuse (N.Y.) Minoa.
JUNIOR COLLEGE: Onondaga Community College (N.Y.).
TRANSACTIONS/CAREER NOTES: Selected by Los Angeles Dodgers organization in 54th round of free-agent draft (June 4, 1990). ... On disabled list (April 7-16, 1994). ... Traded by Dodgers to Oakland Athletics for P Matt McDonald (September 8, 1995). ...Signed by Reds organization (February 3, 1997).

Year	Team (League)	W	L	Pct.	ERA	G	GS	CG	ShO	Sv.	IP	H	R	ER	BB	SO
1991—	Great Falls (Pio.)	5	2	.714	2.72	28	0	0	0	8	53	50	26	16	24	59
1992—	Bakersfield (California)	0	0	...	2.30	13	0	0	0	9	15⅓	11	4	4	7	11
	—San Antonio (Tex.)	7	4	.636	3.27	39	0	0	0	13	44	47	17	16	23	35
1993—	Albuquerque (PCL)	5	5	.500	4.99	*65	0	0	0	*21	70⅓	87	44	39	31	56
1994—	Albuquerque (PCL)	4	2	.667	3.11	59	0	0	0	13	72⅓	78	29	25	17	30
1995—	Los Angeles (N.L.)	2	2	.500	5.12	16	0	0	0	0	19⅓	19	11	11	7	8
	—Albuquerque (PCL)	4	1	.800	3.38	25	0	0	0	0	45⅓	59	21	17	15	23
1996—	Edmonton (PCL)■	5	3	.625	5.50	35	10	0	0	0	91⅔	125	71	56	37	33
1997—	Chattanooga (Southern)■..	3	3	.500	2.10	48	0	0	0	*31	55⅔	38	16	13	25	45
	—Indianapolis (A.A.)	2	0	1.000	2.13	12	0	0	0	2	12⅔	11	4	3	6	11
Major league totals (1 year)		2	2	.500	5.12	16	0	0	0	0	19⅓	19	11	11	7	8

W

WILLIAMS, WOODY   P   BLUE JAYS

PERSONAL: Born August 19, 1966, in Houston. ... 6-0/190. ... Throws right, bats right. ... Full name: Gregory Scott Williams.
HIGH SCHOOL: Cy-Fair (Houston).
COLLEGE: Houston.
TRANSACTIONS/CAREER NOTES: Selected by Toronto Blue Jays organization in 28th round of free-agent draft (June 1, 1988). ... On disabled list (April 9-May 17, 1992). ... On Toronto disabled list (July 17, 1995-remainder of season); included rehabilitation assignment to Syracuse (August 15-25). ... On Toronto disabled list (March 22-May 31 and June 11-July 26, 1996); included rehabilitation assignments to Dunedin (May 2-10), Syracuse (May 10-28 and July 13-20) and St. Catharines (July 20-26).

Year Team (League)	W	L	Pct.	ERA	G	GS	CG	ShO	Sv.	IP	H	R	ER	BB	SO
1988— St. Catharines (NYP)	8	2	.800	1.54	12	12	2	0	0	76	48	22	13	21	58
— Knoxville (Southern)	2	2	.500	3.81	6	4	0	0	0	28 1/3	27	13	12	12	25
1989— Dunedin (Fla. St.)	3	5	.375	2.32	20	9	0	0	3	81 1/3	63	26	21	27	60
— Knoxville (Southern)	3	5	.375	3.55	14	12	2	•2	1	71	61	32	28	33	51
1990— Knoxville (Southern)	7	9	.438	3.14	42	12	0	0	5	126	111	55	44	39	74
— Syracuse (Int'l)	0	1	.000	10.00	3	0	0	0	0	9	15	10	10	4	8
1991— Knoxville (Southern)	3	2	.600	3.59	18	1	0	0	3	42 2/3	42	18	17	14	37
— Syracuse (Int'l)	3	4	.429	4.12	31	0	0	0	6	54 2/3	52	27	25	27	37
1992— Syracuse (Int'l)	6	8	.429	3.13	25	16	1	0	1	120 2/3	115	46	42	41	81
1993— Syracuse (Int'l)	1	1	.500	2.20	12	0	0	0	3	16 1/3	15	5	4	5	16
— Toronto (A.L.)	3	1	.750	4.38	30	0	0	0	0	37	40	18	18	22	24
— Dunedin (Fla. St.)	0	0	...	0.00	2	0	0	0	0	4	0	0	0	2	2
1994— Toronto (A.L.)	1	3	.250	3.64	38	0	0	0	0	59 1/3	44	24	24	33	56
— Syracuse (Int'l)	0	0	...	0.00	1	0	0	0	1	1 2/3	0	0	0	0	1
1995— Toronto (A.L.)	1	2	.333	3.69	23	3	0	0	0	53 2/3	44	23	22	28	41
— Syracuse (Int'l)	0	0	...	3.52	5	1	0	0	1	7 2/3	5	3	3	5	13
1996— Dunedin (Fla. St.)	0	2	.000	8.22	2	2	0	0	0	7 2/3	9	7	7	2	11
— Syracuse (Int'l)	3	1	.750	1.41	7	7	1	1	0	32	22	5	5	7	33
— Toronto (A.L.)	4	5	.444	4.73	12	10	1	0	0	59	64	33	31	21	43
— St. Catharines (NYP)	0	0	...	3.68	2	2	0	0	0	7 1/3	7	3	3	4	12
1997— Toronto (A.L.)	9	14	.391	4.35	31	31	0	0	0	194 2/3	201	98	94	66	124
Major league totals (5 years)	**18**	**25**	**.419**	**4.21**	**134**	**44**	**1**	**0**	**0**	**403 2/3**	**393**	**196**	**189**	**170**	**288**

WILLIAMSON, ANTONE   1B/3B   BREWERS

PERSONAL: Born July 18, 1973, in Harbor City, Calif. ... 6-1/195. ... Bats left, throws right. ... Full name: Anthony Joseph Williamson. ... Cousin of Kevin Higgins, infielder with San Diego Padres (1993).
HIGH SCHOOL: Torrance (Calif.).
COLLEGE: Arizona State.
TRANSACTIONS/CAREER NOTES: Selected by Milwaukee Brewers organization in first round (fourth pick overall) of free-agent draft (June 2, 1994). ... On disabled list (May 15-23, 1995). ... On suspended list (June 21-25, 1995). ... On disabled list (April 4-June 20, 1996).

Year Team (League)	Pos.	G	AB	R	H	2B	3B	HR	RBI	Avg.	BB	SO	SB	PO	A	E	Avg.
1994— Helena (Pioneer)	3B	6	26	5	11	2	1	0	4	.423	2	4	0	2	5	0	1.000
— Stockton (California)	3B	23	85	6	19	4	0	3	13	.224	7	19	0	14	31	4	.918
— El Paso (Texas)	3B	14	48	8	12	3	0	1	9	.250	7	8	0	6	31	4	.902
1995— El Paso (Texas)	3B-1B	104	392	62	121	30	6	7	90	.309	47	57	3	79	135	29	.881
1996— New Orleans (A.A.)	1B-3B	55	199	23	52	10	1	5	23	.261	19	40	1	271	20	8	.973
1997— Tucson (PCL)	1B-3B	83	304	53	87	20	5	5	41	.286	49	41	3	550	61	14	.978
— Milwaukee (A.L.)	1B-DH	24	54	2	11	3	0	0	6	.204	4	8	0	82	4	2	.977
Major league totals (1 year)		**24**	**54**	**2**	**11**	**3**	**0**	**0**	**6**	**.204**	**4**	**8**	**0**	**82**	**4**	**2**	**.977**

WILSON, DAN   C   MARINERS

PERSONAL: Born March 25, 1969, in Arlington Heights, Ill. ... 6-3/190. ... Bats right, throws right. ... Full name: Daniel Allen Wilson.
HIGH SCHOOL: Barrington (Ill.).
COLLEGE: Minnesota.
TRANSACTIONS/CAREER NOTES: Selected by New York Mets organization in 26th round of free-agent draft (June 2, 1987); did not sign. ... Selected by Cincinnati Reds organization in first round (seventh pick overall) of free-agent draft (June 4, 1990). ... Traded by Reds with P Bobby Ayala to Seattle Mariners for P Erik Hanson and 2B Bret Boone (November 2, 1993).
STATISTICAL NOTES: Led American Association catchers with 810 total chances in 1992. ... Led A.L. catchers with 952 total chances in 1995 and 1,129 in 1997. ... Hit three home runs in one game (April 11, 1996). ... Tied for A.L. lead in double plays by catcher with 13 in 1997. ... Career major league grand slams: 1.

Year Team (League)	Pos.	G	AB	R	H	2B	3B	HR	RBI	Avg.	BB	SO	SB	PO	A	E	Avg.
1990— Char., W.Va. (SAL)	C	32	113	16	28	9	1	2	17	.248	13	17	0	190	24	1	.995
1991— Char., W.Va. (SAL)	C	52	197	25	62	11	1	3	29	.315	25	21	1	355	41	3	.992
— Chattanooga (Sou.)	C	81	292	32	75	19	2	2	38	.257	21	39	2	486	49	4	.993
1992— Nashville (A.A.)	C	106	366	27	92	16	1	4	34	.251	31	58	1	*733	*69	*8	.990
— Cincinnati (N.L.)	C	12	25	2	9	1	0	0	3	.360	3	8	0	42	4	0	1.000
1993— Cincinnati (N.L.)	C	36	76	6	17	3	0	0	8	.224	9	16	0	146	9	1	.994
— Indianapolis (A.A.)	C	51	191	18	50	11	1	1	17	.262	19	31	1	314	24	2	.994
1994— Seattle (A.L.)■	C	91	282	24	61	14	2	3	27	.216	10	57	1	602	45	*9	.986
1995— Seattle (A.L.)	C	119	399	40	111	22	3	9	51	.278	33	63	2	*895	52	5	.995
1996— Seattle (A.L.)	C	138	491	51	140	24	0	18	83	.285	32	88	1	834	58	4	.996
1997— Seattle (A.L.)	C	146	508	66	137	31	1	15	74	.270	39	72	7	*1051	72	6	.995
American League totals (4 years)		**494**	**1680**	**181**	**449**	**91**	**6**	**45**	**235**	**.267**	**114**	**280**	**11**	**3382**	**227**	**24**	**.993**
National League totals (2 years)		**48**	**101**	**8**	**26**	**4**	**0**	**0**	**11**	**.257**	**12**	**24**	**0**	**188**	**13**	**1**	**.995**
Major league totals (6 years)		**542**	**1781**	**189**	**475**	**95**	**6**	**45**	**246**	**.267**	**126**	**304**	**11**	**3570**	**240**	**25**	**.993**

W

DIVISION SERIES RECORD

Year Team (League)	Pos.	G	AB	R	H	2B	3B	HR	RBI	Avg.	BB	SO	SB	PO	A	E	Avg.
								BATTING							FIELDING		
1995— Seattle (A.L.)	C	5	17	0	2	0	0	0	1	.118	2	6	0	34	1	0	1.000
1997— Seattle (A.L.)	C	4	13	0	0	0	0	0	0	.000	0	9	0	29	1	0	1.000
Division series totals (2 years)		9	30	0	2	0	0	0	1	.067	2	15	0	63	2	0	1.000

CHAMPIONSHIP SERIES RECORD

Year Team (League)	Pos.	G	AB	R	H	2B	3B	HR	RBI	Avg.	BB	SO	SB	PO	A	E	Avg.
								BATTING							FIELDING		
1995— Seattle (A.L.)	C	6	16	0	0	0	0	0	0	.000	0	4	0	35	3	1	.974

ALL-STAR GAME RECORD

Year League	Pos.	AB	R	H	2B	3B	HR	RBI	Avg.	BB	SO	SB	PO	A	E	Avg.
							BATTING							FIELDING		
1996— American	PH	0	0	0	0	0	0	0	...	0	0	0	...	...	...	...

WILSON, DESI — 1B/OF

PERSONAL: Born May 9, 1969, in Glen Cove, N.Y. ... 6-7/230. ... Bats left, throws left. ... Full name: Desi Bernard Wilson.
HIGH SCHOOL: Glen Cove (N.Y.).
COLLEGE: Fairleigh Dickinson.
TRANSACTIONS/CAREER NOTES: Selected by Boston Red Sox organization in 15th round of free-agent draft (June 2, 1987); did not sign. ... Selected by Houston Astros organization in 87th round of free-agent draft (June 5, 1989); did not sign. ... Selected by Texas Rangers organization in 30th round of free-agent draft (June 3, 1991). ... Traded by Rangers with IF Rich Aurilia to San Francisco Giants for P John Burkett (December 22, 1994). ... On disabled list (March 23-April 6, 1997). ... Released by Giants (September 26, 1997).

Year Team (League)	Pos.	G	AB	R	H	2B	3B	HR	RBI	Avg.	BB	SO	SB	PO	A	E	Avg.
								BATTING							FIELDING		
1991— GC Rangers (GCL)......	OF	8	25	1	4	2	0	0	7	.160	3	2	0	2	0	0	1.000
1992— Butte (Pioneer)...........	OF	72	253	45	81	9	4	5	42	.320	31	45	13	90	8	9	.916
1993— Charlotte (Fla. St.)......	1B-OF	131	511	83	•156	21	7	3	70	.305	50	90	29	859	57	15	.984
1994— Tulsa (Texas)............	OF-1B	129	493	69	142	27	0	6	55	.288	40	115	16	410	34	13	.972
1995— Shreveport (Texas)■..	1B	122	482	77	138	27	3	5	72	.286	40	68	11	*1113	72	9	.992
1996— Phoenix (PCL)...........	1B-OF	113	407	56	138	26	7	5	59	.339	18	80	15	847	52	8	.991
— San Francisco (N.L.) ..	1B	41	118	10	32	2	0	2	12	.271	12	27	0	236	18	4	.984
1997— Phoenix (PCL)...........	1B-OF	121	451	76	155	27	6	7	53	.344	44	73	16	658	49	9	.987
Major league totals (1 year)		41	118	10	32	2	0	2	12	.271	12	27	0	236	18	4	.984

WILSON, ENRIQUE — SS/2B — INDIANS

PERSONAL: Born July 27, 1975, in Santo Domingo, Dominican Republic. ... 5-11/160. ... Bats both, throws right. ... Full name: Enrique Martes Wilson.
HIGH SCHOOL: Liceo Ramon Amelio Jiminez (Santo Domingo, Dominican Republic).
TRANSACTIONS/CAREER NOTES: Signed as non-drafted free agent by Minnesota Twins organization (April 15, 1992). ... Traded by Twins organization to Cleveland Indians organization (February 21, 1994), completing deal in which Twins acquired P Shawn Bryant for a player to be named later (February 21, 1994).
STATISTICAL NOTES: Led South Atlantic League shortstops with 625 total chances and 66 double plays in 1994. ... Led Carolina League with 10 sacrifice flies in 1995. ... Led Eastern League shortstops with 74 double plays in 1996.

Year Team (League)	Pos.	G	AB	R	H	2B	3B	HR	RBI	Avg.	BB	SO	SB	PO	A	E	Avg.
								BATTING							FIELDING		
1992— GC Twins (GCL).........	SS	13	44	12	15	1	0	0	8	.341	4	4	3	9	26	4	.897
1993— Elizabethton (App.)....	SS-3B	58	197	42	57	8	4	13	50	.289	14	18	5	50	139	19	.909
1994— Columbus (S. Atl.)■..	SS	133	512	82	143	28	12	10	72	.279	44	34	21	*185	*407	33	.947
1995— Kinston (Carolina)	SS-2B	117	464	55	124	24	•7	6	52	.267	25	38	18	181	375	21	.964
1996— Cant./Akr. (Eastern)	SS-2B	117	484	70	147	17	5	5	50	.304	31	46	23	179	344	28	.949
— Buffalo (A.A.)..............	3B-SS	3	8	1	4	1	0	0	0	.500	1	1	0	1	2	1	.750
1997— Buffalo (A.A.)..............	SS-2B-3B	118	451	78	138	20	3	11	39	.306	42	41	9	218	332	20	.965
— Cleveland (A.L.).........	SS-2B	5	15	2	5	0	0	0	1	.333	0	2	0	7	13	1	.952
Major league totals (1 year)		5	15	2	5	0	0	0	1	.333	0	2	0	7	13	1	.952

DIVISION SERIES RECORD

Year Team (League)	Pos.	G	AB	R	H	2B	3B	HR	RBI	Avg.	BB	SO	SB	PO	A	E	Avg.
								BATTING							FIELDING		
1996— Cleveland (A.L.).........	PH	1	1	0	0	0	00	0	0	.000	0	0	0	0	0	0	...

WILSON, GARY — P — PIRATES

PERSONAL: Born January 1, 1970, in Arcata, Calif. ... 6-3/190. ... Throws right, bats right. ... Full name: Gary Morris Wilson.
HIGH SCHOOL: Arcata (Calif.).
COLLEGE: Cal State Sacramento.
TRANSACTIONS/CAREER NOTES: Selected by Pittsburgh Pirates organization in 18th round of free-agent draft (June 1, 1992). ... On Calgary disabled list (June 25-July 5 and July 6-August 15, 1995). ... On Calgary disabled list (July 8-24 and July 30-August 6, 1997).

Year Team (League)	W	L	Pct.	ERA	G	GS	CG	ShO	Sv.	IP	H	R	ER	BB	SO
1992— Welland (N.Y.-Penn)..........	3	2	.600	1.06	13	4	0	0	0	42 1/3	27	9	5	13	40
— Augusta (S. Atl.)................	2	3	.400	3.67	7	7	0	0	0	41 2/3	43	22	17	7	27
1993— Augusta (S. Atl.)................	3	7	.300	5.47	20	6	0	0	0	51	66	35	31	11	42
— Salem (Carolina)	5	5	.500	5.74	15	15	0	0	0	78 1/3	102	58	50	25	54

W

Year Team (League)	W	L	Pct.	ERA	G	GS	CG	ShO	Sv.	IP	H	R	ER	BB	SO
1994—Salem (Carolina)	3	1	.750	2.31	6	6	1	1	0	35	41	12	9	4	26
—Carolina (Southern)	8	5	.615	2.56	22	22	*7	2	0	161 2/3	144	55	46	37	97
1995—Pittsburgh (N.L.)	0	1	.000	5.02	10	0	0	0	0	14 1/3	13	8	8	5	8
—Calgary (PCL)	1	2	.333	5.51	6	4	0	0	0	16 1/3	19	16	10	9	12
—Carolina (Southern)	0	0	...	0.00	1	1	0	0	0	4 2/3	0	0	0	3	5
1996—Calgary (PCL)	6	9	.400	5.08	27	27	1	0	0	161 1/3	209	105	91	44	88
1997—Carolina (Southern)	1	2	.333	5.65	7	4	0	0	1	28 2/3	34	19	18	5	19
—Calgary (PCL)	6	3	.667	5.87	21	11	0	0	0	84 1/3	115	59	55	22	54
Major league totals (1 year)	0	1	.000	5.02	10	0	0	0	0	14 1/3	13	8	8	5	8

WILSON, PAUL — P — METS

PERSONAL: Born March 28, 1973, in Orlando. ... 6-5/235. ... Throws right, bats right. ... Full name: Paul Anthony Wilson.
HIGH SCHOOL: William R. Boone (Orlando).
COLLEGE: Florida State.
TRANSACTIONS/CAREER NOTES: Selected by New York Mets organization in first round (first pick overall) of free-agent draft (June 2, 1994). ... On New York disabled list (June 5-July 15, 1996); included rehabilitation assignments to St. Lucie (June 28-July 10) and Binghamton (July 10-15). ... On New York disabled list (March 27, 1997-entire season); included rehabilitation assignment, to Gulf Coast Mets (August 2-23) and St. Lucie (August 28-September 8).
STATISTICAL NOTES: Named Eastern League Pitcher of the Year (1995).

Year Team (League)	W	L	Pct.	ERA	G	GS	CG	ShO	Sv.	IP	H	R	ER	BB	SO
1994—GC Mets (GCL)	0	2	.000	3.00	3	3	0	0	0	12	8	4	4	4	13
—St. Lucie (Fla. St.)	0	5	.000	5.06	8	8	0	0	0	37 1/3	32	23	21	17	37
1995—Binghamton (Eastern)	6	3	.667	*2.17	16	16	4	1	0	120 1/3	89	34	29	24	127
—Norfolk (Int'l)	5	3	.625	2.85	10	10	*4	2	0	66 1/3	59	25	21	20	67
1996—New York (N.L.)	5	12	.294	5.38	26	26	1	0	0	149	157	102	89	71	109
—St. Lucie (Fla. St.)	0	1	.000	3.38	2	2	0	0	0	8	6	5	3	4	5
—Binghamton (Eastern)	0	1	.000	7.20	1	1	0	0	0	5	6	4	4	5	5
1997—GC Mets (GCL)	1	0	1.000	1.45	4	3	0	0	1	18 2/3	14	7	3	4	18
—St. Lucie (Fla. St.)	0	0	...	2.57	1	1	0	0	0	7	6	2	2	0	6
Major league totals (1 year)	5	12	.294	5.38	26	26	1	0	0	149	157	102	89	71	109

WILSON, PRESTON — OF — METS

PERSONAL: Born July 19, 1974, in Bamberg, S.C. ... 6-2/193. ... Bats right, throws right. ... Full name: Preston James David Wilson. ... Son of Mookie Wilson, first base/outfield coach, New York Mets and outfielder with Mets (1980-89) and Toronto Blue Jays (1989-91).
HIGH SCHOOL: Bamberg-Ehrhardt (Bamberg, S.C.).
TRANSACTIONS/CAREER NOTES: Selected by New York Mets organization in first round (ninth pick overall) of free-agent draft (June 1, 1992). ... On disabled list (April 4-29, May 21-July 13 and July 29-September 8, 1996).
STATISTICAL NOTES: Led Appalachian League third basemen with 197 total chances in 1993.

Year Team (League)	Pos.	G	AB	R	H	2B	3B	HR	RBI	Avg.	BB	SO	SB	PO	A	E	Avg.
1993—Kingsport (Appal.)	3B	66	259	44	60	10	0	*16	48	.232	24	75	6	*45	*127	*25	.873
—Pittsfield (NYP)	3B	8	29	6	16	5	1	1	12	.552	2	7	1	5	9	6	.700
1994—Capital City (SAL)	3B	131	474	55	108	17	4	14	58	.228	20	135	10	78	281	47	.884
1995—Capital City (SAL)	OF	111	442	70	119	26	5	20	61	.269	19	114	20	189	10	8	.961
1996—St. Lucie (Fla. St.)	OF	23	85	6	15	3	0	1	7	.176	8	21	1	39	4	2	.956
1997—St. Lucie (Fla. St.)	OF	63	245	32	60	12	1	11	48	.245	8	66	3	116	5	3	.973
—Binghamton (East.)	OF-3B	70	259	37	74	12	1	19	47	.286	21	71	7	116	3	6	.952

WILSON, VANCE — C — METS

PERSONAL: Born March 17, 1973, in Mesa, Ariz. ... 5-11/190. ... Bats right, throws right. ... Full name: Vance Allen Wilson.
HIGH SCHOOL: Red Mountain (Mesa, Ariz.).
JUNIOR COLLEGE: Mesa (Ariz.) Community College.
TRANSACTIONS/CAREER NOTES: Selected by New York Mets organization in 44th round of free-agent draft (June 3, 1993).

Year Team (League)	Pos.	G	AB	R	H	2B	3B	HR	RBI	Avg.	BB	SO	SB	PO	A	E	Avg.
1994—Pittsfield (NYP)	C	44	166	22	51	12	0	2	20	.307	5	27	4	190	25	5	.977
1995—Columbia (South Atlantic)	C	91	324	34	81	11	0	6	32	.250	19	45	4	605	99	*14	.981
1996—St. Lucie (Fla. St.)	C	93	311	29	76	14	2	6	44	.244	31	41	2	502	87	8	.987
1997—Binghamton (East.)	C	92	322	46	89	17	0	15	40	.276	20	46	2	604	69	11	.984

W

WINCHESTER, SCOTT — P — REDS

PERSONAL: Born April 20, 1973, in Midland, Mich. ... 6-2/210. ... Throws right, bats right. ... Full name: Scott J. Winchester.
HIGH SCHOOL: H.H. Dow (Midland, Mich.).
COLLEGE: Clemson.
TRANSACTIONS/CAREER NOTES: Selected by Cleveland Indians organization in 14th round of free-agent draft (June 1, 1995). ... Traded by Indians with P Jim Crowell, P Danny Graves and IF Damian Jackson to Cincinnati Reds for P John Smiley and IF Jeff Branson (July 31, 1997). ... Selected by Arizona Diamondbacks in second round (33rd pick overall) of expansion draft (November 18, 1997). ... Traded by Diamondbacks to Reds (November 18, 1997), completing trade in which Reds traded P Felix Rodriguez to Diamondbacks for a player to be named later (November 11, 1997).

Year Team (League)	W	L	Pct.	ERA	G	GS	CG	ShO	Sv.	IP	H	R	ER	BB	SO
1995— Watertown (NYP)	3	1	.750	2.83	23	0	0	0	11	28⅔	24	10	9	6	27
1996— Columbus (S. Atl.)	7	3	.700	3.23	52	0	0	0	26	61⅓	50	27	22	16	60
1997— Kinston (Carolina)	2	1	.667	1.47	34	0	0	0	29	36⅔	21	6	6	11	45
—Akron (Eastern)	0	0	...	3.86	6	0	0	0	1	7	8	3	3	2	8
—Chattanooga (Southern)■	2	1	.667	1.69	9	0	0	0	3	10⅔	9	4	2	3	3
—Indianapolis (A.A.)	0	0	...	0.00	4	0	0	0	0	5⅔	2	0	0	2	2
—Cincinnati (N.L.)	0	0	...	6.00	5	0	0	0	0	6	9	5	4	2	3
Major league totals (1 year)	0	0	...	6.00	5	0	0	0	0	6	9	5	4	2	3

WINN, RANDY OF DEVIL RAYS

PERSONAL: Born June 9, 1974, in Los Angeles. ... 6-2/175. ... Bats both, throws right. ... Full name: Randolph Winn.
HIGH SCHOOL: San Ramon Valley (Danville, Calif.).
COLLEGE: Santa Clara.
TRANSACTIONS/CAREER NOTES: Selected by Florida Marlins organization in third round of free-agent draft (June 1, 1995). ... On disabled list (August 22-September 11, 1995). ... Selected by Tampa Bay Devil Rays in third round (58th pick overall) of expansion draft (November 18, 1997).
STATISTICAL NOTES: Led Eastern League in caught stealing with 20 in 1997.

Year Team (League)	Pos.	G	AB	R	H	2B	3B	HR	RBI	Avg.	BB	SO	SB	PO	A	E	Avg.
1995— Elmira (N.Y.-Penn)	OF	51	213	38	67	7	4	0	22	.315	15	31	19	103	1	5	.954
1996— Kane County (Midw.)	OF	130	514	90	139	16	3	0	35	.270	47	115	30	260	2	8	.970
1997— Brevard Co. (Fla. St.)	OF	36	143	26	45	8	2	0	15	.315	16	28	16	95	0	0	1.000
—Portland (Eastern)	OF	96	384	66	112	15	6	8	36	.292	42	92	35	182	6	4	.979

WINSTON, DARRIN P PHILLIES

PERSONAL: Born July 6, 1966, in Passaic, N.J. ... 6-0/195. ... Throws left, bats right. ... Full name: Darrin Alexander Winston.
HIGH SCHOOL: Bishop Ahr (Edison, N.J.).
COLLEGE: Rutgers.
TRANSACTIONS/CAREER NOTES: Selected by Montreal Expos in 18th round of free-agent draft (June 1, 1988). ... On disabled list (July 1, 1991 through 1992 season). ... Granted free agency (October 15, 1994). ... Signed by Pittsburgh Pirates organization (December 8, 1994). ... Granted free agency (October 15, 1995). ... Signed by New York Mets organization (December 20, 1996). ... Released by Mets organization (March 31, 1997). ... Signed by Scranton/Wilkes-Barre, Philadelphia Phillies organization (April 7, 1997).

Year Team (League)	W	L	Pct.	ERA	G	GS	CG	ShO	Sv.	IP	H	R	ER	BB	SO
1988— Jamestown (NYP)	2	4	.333	4.91	14	7	0	0	2	44	47	28	24	19	29
1989— Rockford (Midwest)	7	1	.875	1.52	47	0	0	0	16	65	52	16	11	11	70
1990— Jacksonville (Southern)	6	2	.750	2.14	47	0	0	0	7	63	38	16	15	28	45
1991— Indianapolis (A.A.)	1	0	1.000	1.45	27	0	0	0	0	31	26	10	5	21	23
1992—								Did not play.							
1993— Harrisburg (Eastern)	1	0	1.000	4.63	24	0	0	0	1	44⅔	53	30	23	19	36
—W.P. Beach (FSL)	2	0	1.000	1.46	8	2	1	0	0	24⅔	18	6	4	3	21
1994— Harrisburg (Eastern)	4	2	.667	1.53	25	0	0	0	0	35⅓	32	12	6	9	27
—Ottawa (Int'l)	2	0	1.000	3.81	23	0	0	0	0	28⅓	27	15	12	10	17
1995— Calgary (PCL)■	4	6	.400	4.80	53	0	0	0	2	50⅔	59	33	27	17	40
1996—								Did not play.							
1997— Scran./W.B. (Int'l)■	7	4	.636	3.43	39	9	1	0	0	89⅓	74	38	34	36	66
—Philadelphia (N.L.)	2	0	1.000	5.25	7	1	0	0	0	12	8	8	7	3	8
Major league totals (1 year)	2	0	1.000	5.25	7	1	0	0	0	12	8	8	7	3	8

WITASICK, JAY P ATHLETICS

PERSONAL: Born August 28, 1972, in Baltimore. ... 6-4/234. ... Throws right, bats right. ... Full name: Gerald A. Witasick.
HIGH SCHOOL: C. Milton Wright (Bel Air, Md.).
JUNIOR COLLEGE: Brevard Community College (Fla.).
COLLEGE: Maryland-Baltimore County.
TRANSACTIONS/CAREER NOTES: Selected by St. Louis Cardinals organization in second round of free-agent draft (June 3, 1993). ... On disabled list (July 17, 1995-remainder of season). ... Traded by Cardinals with OF Allen Battle, P Bret Wagner and P Carl Dale to Oakland Athletics for P Todd Stottlemyre (January 9, 1996). ... On Oakland disabled list (March 31-June 14, 1997); included rehabilitation assignment to Modesto (June 11-14).

Year Team (League)	W	L	Pct.	ERA	G	GS	CG	ShO	Sv.	IP	H	R	ER	BB	SO
1993— Johnson City (App.)	4	3	.571	4.12	12	12	0	0	0	67⅔	65	42	31	19	74
—Savannah (S. Atl.)	1	0	1.000	4.50	1	1	0	0	0	6	7	3	3	2	8
1994— Madison (Midwest)	10	4	.714	2.32	18	18	2	0	0	112⅓	74	36	29	42	141
1995— St. Petersburg (FSL)	7	7	.500	2.74	18	18	1	1	0	105	80	39	32	36	109
—Arkansas (Texas)	2	4	.333	6.88	7	7	0	0	0	34	46	29	26	16	26
1996— Huntsville (Southern)■	0	3	.000	2.30	25	6	0	0	4	66⅔	47	21	17	26	63
—Oakland (A.L.)	1	1	.500	6.23	12	0	0	0	0	13	12	9	9	5	12
—Edmonton (PCL)	0	0	...	4.15	6	0	0	0	2	8⅔	9	4	4	6	9
1997— Modesto (California)■	0	1	.000	4.15	9	2	0	0	1	17⅓	16	9	8	5	17
—Edmonton (PCL)■	3	2	.600	4.28	13	1	0	0	0	27⅓	25	13	13	15	17
—Oakland (A.L.)	0	0	...	5.73	8	0	0	0	0	11	14	7	7	6	8
Major league totals (2 years)	1	1	.500	6.00	20	0	0	0	0	24	26	16	16	11	20

W

WITT, BOBBY   P

PERSONAL: Born May 11, 1964, in Arlington, Va. ... 6-2/205. ... Throws right, bats right. ... Full name: Robert Andrew Witt.
HIGH SCHOOL: Canton (Mass.).
COLLEGE: Oklahoma.
TRANSACTIONS/CAREER NOTES: Selected by Cincinnati Reds organization in seventh round of free-agent draft (June 7, 1982); did not sign. ... Selected by Texas Rangers organization in first round (third pick overall) of free-agent draft (June 3, 1985). ... On Texas disabled list (May 21-June 20, 1987); included rehabilitation assignments to Oklahoma City (June 7-12) and Tulsa (June 13). ... On Texas disabled list (May 27-July 31, 1991); included rehabilitation assignment to Oklahoma City (July 22-29). ... Traded by Rangers with OF Ruben Sierra, P Jeff Russell and cash to Oakland Athletics for OF Jose Canseco (August 31, 1992). ... Granted free agency (October 26, 1994). ... Signed by Florida Marlins (April 9, 1995). ... Traded by Marlins to Rangers for two players to be named later (August 8, 1995); Marlins acquired P Wilson Heredia (August 11, 1995) and OF Scott Podsednik (October 2, 1995) to complete deal. ... Granted free agency (November 3, 1995). ... Re-signed by Rangers (December 24, 1995). ... Granted free agency (October 27, 1997).
RECORDS: Shares major league record for most strikeouts in one inning—4 (August 2, 1987, second inning).
HONORS: Named righthanded pitcher on THE SPORTING NEWS college All-America team (1985).
STATISTICAL NOTES: Led A.L. with 22 wild pitches in 1986 and tied for lead with 16 in 1988. ... Pitched 4-0 one-hit, complete-game victory against Kansas City (June 23, 1994).
MISCELLANEOUS: Member of 1984 U.S. Olympic baseball team. ... Struck out in only appearance as pinch-hitter with Texas (1987). ... Appeared in two games as pinch-runner (1990). ... Appeared in one game as pinch-runner (1994). ... Appeared in two games as pinch-runner with Florida (1995).

Year Team (League)	W	L	Pct.	ERA	G	GS	CG	ShO	Sv.	IP	H	R	ER	BB	SO
1985—Tulsa (Texas)	0	6	.000	6.43	11	8	0	0	0	35	26	26	25	44	39
1986—Texas (A.L.)	11	9	.550	5.48	31	31	0	0	0	157²/₃	130	104	96	*143	174
1987—Texas (A.L.)	8	10	.444	4.91	26	25	1	0	0	143	114	82	78	*140	160
—Oklahoma City (A.A.)	1	0	1.000	9.00	1	1	0	0	0	5	5	5	5	3	2
—Tulsa (Texas)	0	1	.000	5.40	1	1	0	0	0	5	5	9	3	6	2
1988—Texas (A.L.)	8	10	.444	3.92	22	22	13	2	0	174¹/₃	134	83	76	101	148
—Oklahoma City (A.A.)	4	6	.400	4.34	11	11	3	0	0	76²/₃	69	42	37	47	70
1989—Texas (A.L.)	12	13	.480	5.14	31	31	5	1	0	194¹/₃	182	123	•111	*114	166
1990—Texas (A.L.)	17	10	.630	3.36	33	32	7	1	0	222	197	98	83	110	221
1991—Texas (A.L.)	3	7	.300	6.09	17	16	1	1	0	88²/₃	84	66	60	74	82
—Oklahoma City (A.A.)	1	1	.500	1.13	2	2	0	0	0	8	3	1	1	8	12
1992—Texas (A.L.)■	9	13	.409	4.46	25	25	0	0	0	161¹/₃	152	87	80	95	100
—Oakland (A.L.)■	1	1	.500	3.41	6	6	0	0	0	31²/₃	31	12	12	19	25
1993—Oakland (A.L.)	14	13	.519	4.21	35	33	5	1	0	220	226	112	103	91	131
1994—Oakland (A.L.)	8	10	.444	5.04	24	24	5	3	0	135²/₃	151	88	76	70	111
1995—Florida (N.L.)■	2	7	.222	3.90	19	19	1	0	0	110²/₃	104	52	48	47	95
—Texas (A.L.)■	3	4	.429	4.55	10	10	1	0	0	61¹/₃	81	35	31	21	46
1996—Texas (A.L.)	16	12	.571	5.41	33	32	2	0	0	199²/₃	235	129	120	96	157
1997—Texas (A.L.)	12	12	.500	4.82	34	32	3	0	0	209	245	118	112	74	121
A.L. totals (12 years)	122	124	.496	4.67	327	319	43	9	0	1998²/₃	1962	1137	1038	1148	1642
N.L. totals (1 year)	2	7	.222	3.90	19	19	1	0	0	110²/₃	104	52	48	47	95
Major league totals (12 years)	124	131	.486	4.63	346	338	44	9	0	2109¹/₃	2066	1189	1086	1195	1737

DIVISION SERIES RECORD

Year Team (League)	W	L	Pct.	ERA	G	GS	CG	ShO	Sv.	IP	H	R	ER	BB	SO
1996—Texas (A.L.)	0	0	...	8.10	1	1	0	0	0	3¹/₃	4	3	3	2	3

CHAMPIONSHIP SERIES RECORD

Year Team (League)	W	L	Pct.	ERA	G	GS	CG	ShO	Sv.	IP	H	R	ER	BB	SO
1992—Oakland (A.L.)	0	0	...	18.00	1	0	0	0	0	1	2	2	2	1	1

WITT, KEVIN   SS   BLUE JAYS

PERSONAL: Born January 5, 1976, in High Point, N.C. ... 6-4/185. ... Bats left, throws right. ... Full name: Kevin Joseph Witt.
TRANSACTIONS/CAREER NOTES: Selected by Toronto Blue Jays organization in first round (28th pick overall) of free-agent draft (June 2, 1994).
STATISTICAL NOTES: Tied for Southern League lead with seven intentional bases on balls in 1997.

Year Team (League)	Pos.	G	AB	R	H	2B	3B	HR	RBI	Avg.	BB	SO	SB	PO	A	E	Avg.
							BATTING								FIELDING		
1994—Medicine Hat (Pio.	SS	60	243	37	62	10	4	7	36	.255	15	52	4	*99	167	25	.914
1995—Hagerstown (SAL)	SS	119	479	58	111	35	1	14	50	.232	28	148	1	203	338	48	.919
1996—Dunedin (Fla. State)	SS	124	446	63	121	18	6	13	70	.271	39	96	9	161	369	48	.917
1997—Knoxville (Southern)	1-3-D-O-S	127	501	76	145	27	4	•30	91	.289	44	109	1	553	118	15	.978

WOHLERS, MARK   P   BRAVES

PERSONAL: Born January 23, 1970, in Holyoke, Mass. ... 6-4/207. ... Throws right, bats right. ... Full name: Mark Edward Wohlers.
HIGH SCHOOL: Holyoke (Mass.).
TRANSACTIONS/CAREER NOTES: Selected by Atlanta Braves organization in eighth round of free-agent draft (June 1, 1988).
RECORDS: Shares major league record for most strikeouts in one inning—4 (June 7, 1995, ninth inning).
HONORS: Named Southern League Outstanding Pitcher (1991).
STATISTICAL NOTES: Pitched two innings, combining with starter Kent Mercker (six innings) and Alejandro Pena (one inning) in 1-0 no-hit victory for Atlanta against San Diego (September 11, 1991).

Year Team (League)	W	L	Pct.	ERA	G	GS	CG	ShO	Sv.	IP	H	R	ER	BB	SO
1988—Pulaski (Appalachian)	5	3	.625	3.32	13	9	1	0	0	59²/₃	47	37	22	50	49
1989—Sumter (S. Atl.)	2	7	.222	6.49	14	14	0	0	0	68	74	55	49	59	51
—Pulaski (Appalachian)	1	1	.500	5.48	14	8	0	0	0	46	48	36	28	28	50

W

Year	Team (League)	W	L	Pct.	ERA	G	GS	CG	ShO	Sv.	IP	H	R	ER	BB	SO
1990—	Greenville (Southern)	0	1	.000	4.02	14	0	0	0	6	15 2/3	14	7	7	14	20
—	Sumter (S. Atl.)	5	4	.556	1.88	37	2	0	0	5	52 2/3	27	13	11	20	85
1991—	Greenville (Southern)	0	0	...	0.57	28	0	0	0	21	31 1/3	9	4	2	13	44
—	Richmond (Int'l)	1	0	1.000	1.03	23	0	0	0	11	26 1/3	23	4	3	12	22
—	Atlanta (N.L.)	3	1	.750	3.20	17	0	0	0	2	19 2/3	17	7	7	13	13
1992—	Richmond (Int'l)	0	2	.000	3.93	27	2	0	0	9	34 1/3	32	16	15	17	33
—	Atlanta (N.L.)	1	2	.333	2.55	32	0	0	0	4	35 1/3	28	11	10	14	17
1993—	Richmond (Int'l)	1	3	.250	1.84	25	0	0	0	4	29 1/3	21	7	6	11	39
—	Atlanta (N.L.)	6	2	.750	4.50	46	0	0	0	0	48	37	25	24	22	45
1994—	Atlanta (N.L.)	7	2	.778	4.59	51	0	0	0	1	51	51	35	26	33	58
1995—	Atlanta (N.L.)	7	3	.700	2.09	65	0	0	0	25	64 2/3	51	16	15	24	90
1996—	Atlanta (N.L.)	2	4	.333	3.03	77	0	0	0	39	77 1/3	71	30	26	21	100
1997—	Atlanta (N.L.)	5	7	.417	3.50	71	0	0	0	33	69 1/3	57	29	27	38	92
Major league totals (7 years)		31	21	.596	3.33	359	0	0	0	104	365 1/3	312	153	135	165	415

DIVISION SERIES RECORD

RECORDS: Holds career record for most saves—5. ... Holds N.L. career record for most games pitched—7.

Year	Team (League)	W	L	Pct.	ERA	G	GS	CG	ShO	Sv.	IP	H	R	ER	BB	SO
1995—	Atlanta (N.L.)	0	1	.000	6.75	3	0	0	0	2	2 2/3	6	2	2	2	4
1996—	Atlanta (N.L.)	0	0	...	0.00	3	0	0	0	3	3 1/3	1	0	0	0	4
1997—	Atlanta (N.L.)	0	0	...	0.00	1	0	0	0	0	1	1	0	0	0	1
Div. series totals (3 years)		0	1	.000	2.57	7	0	0	0	5	7	8	2	2	2	9

CHAMPIONSHIP SERIES RECORD

RECORDS: Holds N.L. career records for most games pitched—18; and most games as relief pitcher—18. ... Shares N.L. career record for most series with one team—6 (Atlanta, 1991-93 and 1995-97).

Year	Team (League)	W	L	Pct.	ERA	G	GS	CG	ShO	Sv.	IP	H	R	ER	BB	SO
1991—	Atlanta (N.L.)	0	0	...	0.00	3	0	0	0	0	1 2/3	3	0	0	1	1
1992—	Atlanta (N.L.)	0	0	...	0.00	3	0	0	0	0	3	2	0	0	1	2
1993—	Atlanta (N.L.)	0	1	.000	3.38	4	0	0	0	0	5 1/3	2	2	2	3	10
1995—	Atlanta (N.L.)	1	0	1.000	1.80	4	0	0	0	0	5	2	1	1	0	8
1996—	Atlanta (N.L.)	0	0	...	0.00	3	0	0	0	2	3	0	0	0	0	4
1997—	Atlanta (N.L.)	0	0	...	0.00	1	0	0	0	0	1	0	0	0	1	1
Champ. series totals (6 years)		1	1	.500	1.42	18	0	0	0	2	19	9	3	3	6	26

WORLD SERIES RECORD

NOTES: Member of World Series championship team (1995).

Year	Team (League)	W	L	Pct.	ERA	G	GS	CG	ShO	Sv.	IP	H	R	ER	BB	SO
1991—	Atlanta (N.L.)	0	0	...	0.00	3	0	0	0	0	1 2/3	2	0	0	2	1
1992—	Atlanta (N.L.)	0	0	...	0.00	2	0	0	0	0	2/3	0	0	0	1	0
1995—	Atlanta (N.L.)	0	0	...	1.80	4	0	0	0	0	5	4	1	1	3	3
1996—	Atlanta (N.L.)	0	0	...	6.23	4	0	0	0	0	4 1/3	7	3	3	3	4
World Series totals (4 years)		0	0	...	3.09	13	0	0	0	0	11 2/3	13	4	4	9	8

WOJCIECHOWSKI, STEVE   P

PERSONAL: Born July 29, 1970, in Blue Island, Ill. ... 6-2/195. ... Throws left, bats left. ... Full name: Steven Joseph Wojciechowski. ... Name pronounced wo-jo-KOW-ski.

HIGH SCHOOL: Thornton Fractional North (Calumet City, Ill.).

COLLEGE: St. Xavier (Ill.).

TRANSACTIONS/CAREER NOTES: Selected by Oakland Athletics organization in fourth round of free-agent draft (June 3, 1991). ... On disabled list (June 16-August 6, 1992). ... On Oakland disabled list (July 19, 1997-remainder of season). ... Granted free agency (October 15, 1997).

MISCELLANEOUS: Appeared in two games as pinch-runner with Oakland (1996).

Year	Team (League)	W	L	Pct.	ERA	G	GS	CG	ShO	Sv.	IP	H	R	ER	BB	SO
1991—	S. Oregon (N'west)	2	5	.286	3.76	16	11	0	0	0	67	74	45	28	29	50
1992—	Modesto (California)	6	3	.667	3.53	14	14	0	0	0	66 1/3	60	32	26	27	53
1993—	Modesto (California)	8	2	.800	2.55	14	14	1	1	0	84 2/3	64	29	24	36	52
—	Huntsville (Southern)	4	6	.400	5.32	13	13	1	1	0	67 2/3	91	50	40	30	52
1994—	Huntsville (Southern)	10	5	.667	3.10	27	26	1	0	0	177	148	72	61	62	114
1995—	Edmonton (PCL)	6	3	.667	3.69	14	12	2	1	0	78	75	37	32	21	39
—	Oakland (A.L.)	2	3	.400	5.18	14	7	0	0	0	48 2/3	51	28	28	28	13
1996—	Edmonton (PCL)	4	3	.571	3.73	11	11	1	1	0	60 1/3	56	32	25	21	46
—	Oakland (A.L.)	5	5	.500	5.65	16	15	0	0	0	79 2/3	97	57	50	28	30
1997—	Edmonton (PCL)	8	2	.800	3.84	26	7	0	0	1	65 2/3	68	33	28	23	49
—	Oakland (A.L.)	0	2	.000	7.84	2	2	0	0	0	10 1/3	17	9	9	1	5
Major league totals (3 years)		7	10	.412	5.65	32	24	0	0	0	138 2/3	165	94	87	57	48

WOLCOTT, BOB   P   DIAMONDBACKS

PERSONAL: Born September 8, 1973, in Huntington Beach, Calif. ... 6-0/195. ... Throws right, bats right. ... Full name: Robert William Wolcott.

HIGH SCHOOL: North (Medford, Ore.).

TRANSACTIONS/CAREER NOTES: Selected by Seattle Mariners organization in second round of free-agent draft (June 1, 1992). ... Selected by Arizona Diamondbacks in second round (53rd pick overall) of expansion draft (November 18, 1997).

Year	Team (League)	W	L	Pct.	ERA	G	GS	CG	ShO	Sv.	IP	H	R	ER	BB	SO
1992—	Bellingham (N'west)	0	1	.000	6.85	9	7	0	0	0	22 1/3	25	18	17	19	17
1993—	Bellingham (N'west)	8	4	.667	2.64	15	15	1	0	0	95 1/3	70	31	28	26	79
1994—	Riverside (California)	14	8	.636	2.84	26	26	•5	1	0	*180 2/3	173	75	57	50	142
—	Calgary (PCL)	0	1	.000	3.00	1	1	0	0	0	6	6	2	2	3	5

W

Year Team (League)	W	L	Pct.	ERA	G	GS	CG	ShO	Sv.	IP	H	R	ER	BB	SO
1995— Port City (Southern)	7	3	.700	2.20	12	12	2	1	0	86	60	26	21	13	53
—Tacoma (PCL)	6	3	.667	4.08	13	13	2	1	0	79 1/3	94	49	36	16	43
—Seattle (A.L.)	3	2	.600	4.42	7	6	0	0	0	36 2/3	43	18	18	14	19
1996—Seattle (A.L.)	7	10	.412	5.73	30	28	1	0	0	149 1/3	179	101	95	54	78
—Lancaster (Calif.)	0	1	.000	10.50	1	1	0	0	0	6	9	7	7	0	6
—Tacoma (PCL)	0	2	.000	7.30	3	3	0	0	0	12 1/3	17	13	10	3	16
1997—Seattle (A.L.)	5	6	.455	6.03	19	18	0	0	0	100	129	71	67	29	58
—Tacoma (PCL)	1	3	.250	5.11	7	7	0	0	0	37	40	23	21	7	29
Major league totals (3 years)	15	18	.455	5.66	56	52	1	0	0	286	351	190	180	97	155

CHAMPIONSHIP SERIES RECORD

Year Team (League)	W	L	Pct.	ERA	G	GS	CG	ShO	Sv.	IP	H	R	ER	BB	SO
1995—Seattle (A.L.)	1	0	1.000	2.57	1	1	0	0	0	7	8	2	2	5	2

WOMACK, TONY — 2B — PIRATES

PERSONAL: Born June 25, 1969, in Danville, Va. ... 5-9/155. ... Bats left, throws right. ... Full name: Anthony Darrell Womack.
HIGH SCHOOL: Gretna (Va.).
COLLEGE: Guilford (N.C.); degree in sports management, then UNC Greensboro (did not play); master's degree in sports management.
TRANSACTIONS/CAREER NOTES: Selected by Pittsburgh Pirates organization in seventh round of free-agent draft (June 3, 1991). ... On disabled list (April 17-26 and August 28, 1992-remainder of season).
STATISTICAL NOTES: Tied for American Association lead with 12 sacrifice hits in 1994. ... Led Pacific Coast League with 14 sacrifice hits in 1996. ... Led N.L. second basemen with 20 errors in 1997.

Year Team (League)	Pos.	G	AB	R	H	2B	3B	HR	RBI	Avg.	BB	SO	SB	PO	A	E	Avg.
1991—Welland (NYP)	SS-2B	45	166	30	46	3	0	1	8	.277	17	39	26	78	109	16	.921
1992—Augusta (S. Atl.)	SS-2B	102	380	62	93	8	3	0	18	.245	41	59	50	186	291	40	.923
1993—Salem (Carolina)	SS	72	304	41	91	11	3	2	18	.299	13	34	28	130	223	28	.927
—Carolina (Southern)	SS	60	247	41	75	7	2	0	23	.304	17	34	21	102	169	11	.961
—Pittsburgh (N.L.)	SS	15	24	5	2	0	0	0	0	.083	3	3	2	11	22	1	.971
1994—Buffalo (A.A.)	SS-2B	106	421	40	93	9	2	0	18	.221	19	76	41	211	283	22	.957
—Pittsburgh (N.L.)	2B-SS	5	12	4	4	0	0	0	1	.333	2	3	0	3	6	2	.818
1995—Calgary (PCL)	2B-SS	30	107	12	30	3	1	0	6	.280	12	11	7	37	94	5	.963
—Carolina (Southern)	2B-SS	82	332	52	85	9	4	1	19	.256	19	36	27	126	241	18	.953
1996—Calgary (PCL)	SS-2B-OF	131	506	75	151	19	11	1	47	.298	31	79	37	258	335	24	.961
—Pittsburgh (N.L.)	OF-2B	17	30	11	10	3	1	0	7	.333	6	1	2	11	8	2	.905
1997—Pittsburgh (N.L.)	2B-SS	155	641	85	178	26	9	6	50	.278	43	109	*60	335	430	†20	.975
Major league totals (4 years)		192	707	105	194	29	10	6	58	.274	54	116	64	360	466	25	.971

ALL-STAR GAME RECORD

Year League	Pos.	AB	R	H	2B	3B	HR	RBI	Avg.	BB	SO	SB	PO	A	E	Avg.
1997—National	2B	1	0	0	0	0	0	0	.000	0	0	0	1	0	0	1.000

WOOD, KERRY — P — CUBS

PERSONAL: Born June 16, 1977, in Irving, Texas. ... 6-5/195. ... Throws right, bats right. ... Full name: Kerry Lee Wood.
HIGH SCHOOL: Grand Praire (Texas).
TRANSACTIONS/CAREER NOTES: Selected by Chicago Cubs organization in first round (fourth pick overall) of free-agent draft (June 1, 1995). ... On disabled list (May 24-June 19, 1996).
STATISTICAL NOTES: Led Florida State League with 14 hit batsmen and seven balks in 1996.

Year Team (League)	W	L	Pct.	ERA	G	GS	CG	ShO	Sv.	IP	H	R	ER	BB	SO
1995—Fort Myers (Fla. St.)	0	0	...	0.00	1	1	0	0	0	3	0	0	0	1	2
—Williamsport (NYP)	0	0	...	10.38	2	2	0	0	0	4 1/3	5	8	5	5	5
1996—Daytona (Fla. St.)	10	2	•.833	2.91	22	22	0	0	0	114 1/3	72	51	37	70	136
1997—Orlando (South.)	6	7	.462	4.50	19	19	0	0	0	94	58	49	47	79	106
—Iowa (Am. Assoc.)	4	2	.667	4.68	10	10	0	0	0	57 2/3	35	35	30	52	80

WOODARD, STEVE — P — BREWERS

PERSONAL: Born May 15, 1975, in Hartselle, Ala. ... 6-4/225. ... Throws right, bats left. ... Full name: Steve Larry Woodard Jr.
HIGH SCHOOL: Hartselle (Ala.).
TRANSACTIONS/CAREER NOTES: Selected by Milwaukee Brewers organization in fifth round of free-agent draft (June 2, 1994).
RECORDS: Shares A.L. record for most strikeouts in first major league game—12 (July 28, 1997).
HONORS: Named Texas League Pitcher of the Year (1997).

Year Team (League)	W	L	Pct.	ERA	G	GS	CG	ShO	Sv.	IP	H	R	ER	BB	SO
1994—Stockton (California)	8	0	1.000	2.40	15	12	2	0	0	82 2/3	68	29	22	13	85
1995—Beloit (Midwest)	7	4	.636	4.54	21	21	0	0	0	115	113	68	58	31	94
1996—Stockton (California)	12	9	.571	4.02	28	•28	0	0	0	181 1/3	201	89	81	33	142
1997—El Paso (Texas)	14	3	.824	3.17	19	19	*6	•1	0	136 1/3	136	56	48	25	97
—Tucson (PCL)	1	0	1.000	0.00	1	1	0	0	0	7	3	0	0	1	6
—Milwaukee (A.L.)	3	3	.500	5.15	7	7	0	0	0	36 2/3	39	25	21	6	32
Major league totals (1 year)	3	3	.500	5.15	7	7	0	0	0	36 2/3	39	25	21	6	32

W

WORRELL, TIM   P   TIGERS

PERSONAL: Born July 5, 1967, in Pasadena, Calif. ... 6-4/220. ... Throws right, bats right. ... Full name: Timothy Howard Worrell. ... Brother of Todd Worrell, pitcher with St. Louis Cardinals (1985-92) and Los Angeles Dodgers (1993-97). ... Name pronounced wor-RELL.
HIGH SCHOOL: Maranatha (Sierra Madre, Calif.).
COLLEGE: Biola (Calif.).
TRANSACTIONS/CAREER NOTES: Selected by San Diego Padres organization in 20th round of free-agent draft (June 5, 1989). ... On disabled list (April 19, 1994-remainder of season). ... On San Diego disabled list (April 24-September 1, 1995); included rehabilitation assignments to Rancho Cucamonga (May 3-17 and August 1-10) and Las Vegas (May 17-June 1 and August 10-30). ... Traded by Padres with OF Trey Beamon to Detroit Tigers for P Dan Miceli, P Donne Wall and 3B Ryan Balfe (November 19, 1997).
STATISTICAL NOTES: Pitched 2-0 no-hit victory for Las Vegas against Phoenix (September 5, 1992).

Year	Team (League)	W	L	Pct.	ERA	G	GS	CG	ShO	Sv.	IP	H	R	ER	BB	SO
1989—	....							Did not play.								
1990—	Charleston, S.C. (S. Atl.) ...	5	8	.385	4.64	20	19	3	0	0	110 2/3	120	65	57	28	68
1991—	Waterloo (Midw.)	8	4	.667	3.34	14	14	3	2	0	86 1/3	70	36	32	33	83
	— High Desert (Calif.)...........	5	2	.714	4.24	11	11	2	0	0	63 2/3	65	32	30	33	70
1992—	Wichita (Texas)	8	6	.571	2.86	19	19	1	1	0	125 2/3	115	46	40	32	109
	— Las Vegas (PCL)	4	2	.667	4.26	10	10	1	1	0	63 1/3	61	32	30	19	32
1993—	Las Vegas (PCL)	5	6	.455	5.48	15	14	2	0	0	87	102	61	53	26	89
	— San Diego (N.L.)	2	7	.222	4.92	21	16	0	0	0	100 2/3	104	63	55	43	52
1994—	San Diego (N.L.)	0	1	.000	3.68	3	3	0	0	0	14 2/3	9	7	6	5	14
1995—	Rancho Cucamonga (Cal.) .	0	2	.000	5.16	9	3	0	0	1	22 2/3	25	17	13	6	17
	— Las Vegas (PCL)	0	2	.000	6.00	10	3	0	0	0	24	27	21	16	17	18
	— San Diego (N.L.)	1	0	1.000	4.73	9	0	0	0	0	13 1/3	16	7	7	6	13
1996—	San Diego (N.L.)	9	7	.563	3.05	50	11	0	0	1	121	109	45	41	39	99
1997—	San Diego (N.L.)	4	8	.333	5.16	60	10	0	0	3	106 1/3	116	67	61	50	81
Major league totals (5 years)......		**16**	**23**	**.410**	**4.30**	**143**	**40**	**0**	**0**	**4**	**356**	**354**	**189**	**170**	**143**	**259**

					DIVISION SERIES RECORD											
Year	Team (League)	W	L	Pct.	ERA	G	GS	CG	ShO	Sv.	IP	H	R	ER	BB	SO
1996—	San Diego (N.L.)	0	0	...	2.45	2	0	0	0	0	3 2/3	4	1	1	1	2

WORRELL, TODD   P

PERSONAL: Born September 28, 1959, in Arcadia, Calif. ... 6-5/227. ... Throws right, bats right. ... Full name: Todd Roland Worrell. ... Brother of Tim Worrell, pitcher, Detroit Tigers. ... Name pronounced wor-RELL.
HIGH SCHOOL: Maranatha (Sierra Madre, Calif.).
COLLEGE: Biola Calif. (degree in Christian education).
TRANSACTIONS/CAREER NOTES: Selected by St. Louis Cardinals organization in first round (21st pick overall) of free-agent draft (June 7, 1982). ... On St. Louis disabled list (May 14-June 7, 1989); included rehabilitation assignment to Louisville (June 6-7). ... On St. Louis disabled list (March 31, 1990-entire season). ... On St. Louis disabled list (April 4, 1991-entire season); included rehabilitation assignment to Louisville (May 4-10). ... Granted free agency (October 26, 1992). ... Signed by Los Angeles Dodgers (December 9, 1992). ... On Los Angeles disabled list (April 8-May 27, 1993); included rehabilitation assignment to Bakersfield (May 23-27). ... On Los Angeles disabled list (June 11-July 15, 1993); included rehabilitation assignment to Albuquerque (June 30-July 15). ... On disabled list (May 5-23, 1994). ... Granted free agency (October 28, 1997). ... Announced retirement (December 4, 1997).
RECORDS: Holds major league rookie-season record for most saves—36 (1986).
HONORS: Named righthanded pitcher on THE SPORTING NEWS college All-America team (1982). ... Named N.L. Rookie Pitcher of the Year by THE SPORTING NEWS (1986). ... Named N.L. Fireman of the Year by THE SPORTING NEWS (1986). ... Named N.L. Rookie of the Year by Baseball Writers' Association of America (1986).
MISCELLANEOUS: Appeared in two games as outfielder with no chances (1986). ... Appeared in one game as outfielder with no chances (1987 and 1989 with St. Louis).

Year	Team (League)	W	L	Pct.	ERA	G	GS	CG	ShO	Sv.	IP	H	R	ER	BB	SO
1982—	Erie (N.Y.-Penn).................	4	1	.800	3.31	9	8	0	0	0	51 2/3	52	23	19	15	57
1983—	Louisville (A.A.)	4	2	.667	4.74	15	14	1	0	0	79 2/3	76	49	42	42	46
	— Arkansas (Texas)...............	5	2	.714	3.07	10	10	4	0	0	70 1/3	57	33	24	37	74
1984—	Arkansas (Texas).................	3	10	.231	4.49	18	18	5	0	0	100 1/3	109	72	50	67	88
	— St. Petersburg (FSL)	3	2	.600	2.09	8	7	2	0	0	47 1/3	41	22	11	24	33
1985—	Louisville (A.A.)	8	6	.571	3.60	34	17	2	1	11	127 2/3	114	59	51	47	*126
	— St. Louis (N.L.)	3	0	1.000	2.91	17	0	0	0	5	21 2/3	17	7	7	7	17
1986—	St. Louis (N.L.)	9	10	.474	2.08	74	0	0	0	*36	103 2/3	86	29	24	41	73
1987—	St. Louis (N.L.)	8	6	.571	2.66	75	0	0	0	33	94 2/3	86	29	28	34	92
1988—	St. Louis (N.L.)	5	9	.357	3.00	68	0	0	0	32	90	69	32	30	34	78
1989—	St. Louis (N.L.)	3	5	.375	2.96	47	0	0	0	20	51 2/3	42	21	17	26	41
	— Louisville (A.A.)	0	0	...	0.00	1	1	0	0	0	1	0	0	0	0	1
1990—					0.00				Did not play.								
1991—	Louisville (A.A.)	0	0	...	18.00	3	3	0	0	0	3	4	6	6	3	4
1992—	St. Louis (N.L.)	5	3	.625	2.11	67	0	0	0	3	64	45	15	15	25	64
1993—	Los Angeles (N.L.)■	1	1	.500	6.05	35	0	0	0	5	38 2/3	46	28	26	11	31
	— Bakersfield (California).......	0	0	...	0.00	2	2	0	0	0	2	1	0	0	0	5
	— Albuquerque (PCL)	1	0	1.000	1.04	7	2	0	0	0	8 2/3	7	2	1	2	13
1994—	Los Angeles (N.L.)	6	5	.545	4.29	38	0	0	0	11	42	37	21	20	12	44
1995—	Los Angeles (N.L.)	4	1	.800	2.02	59	0	0	0	32	62 1/3	50	15	14	19	61
1996—	Los Angeles (N.L.)	4	6	.400	3.03	72	0	0	0	•44	65 1/3	70	29	22	15	66
1997—	Los Angeles (N.L.)	2	6	.250	5.28	65	0	0	0	35	59 2/3	60	38	35	23	61
Major league totals (11 years)....		**50**	**52**	**.490**	**3.09**	**617**	**0**	**0**	**0**	**256**	**693 2/3**	**608**	**264**	**238**	**247**	**628**

					DIVISION SERIES RECORD											
Year	Team (League)	W	L	Pct.	ERA	G	GS	CG	ShO	Sv.	IP	H	R	ER	BB	SO
1996—	Los Angeles (N.L.)	0	0	...	0.00	1	0	0	0	0	1	0	0	0	1	1

CHAMPIONSHIP SERIES RECORD

NOTES: Appeared in one game as outfielder (1987).

W

Year	Team (League)	W	L	Pct.	ERA	G	GS	CG	ShO	Sv.	IP	H	R	ER	BB	SO
1985—	St. Louis (N.L.)	1	0	1.000	1.42	4	0	0	0	0	6⅓	4	1	1	2	3
1987—	St. Louis (N.L.)	0	0	...	2.08	3	0	0	0	1	4⅓	4	1	1	1	6
Champ. series totals (2 years)		1	0	1.000	1.69	7	0	0	0	1	10⅔	8	2	2	3	9

WORLD SERIES RECORD

RECORDS: Shares single-game record for most consecutive strikeouts—6 (October 24, 1985).

Year	Team (League)	W	L	Pct.	ERA	G	GS	CG	ShO	Sv.	IP	H	R	ER	BB	SO
1985—	St. Louis (N.L.)	0	1	.000	3.86	3	0	0	0	1	4⅔	4	2	2	2	6
1987—	St. Louis (N.L.)	0	0	...	1.29	4	0	0	0	2	7	6	1	1	4	3
World Series totals (2 years)		0	1	.000	2.31	7	0	0	0	3	11⅔	10	3	3	6	9

ALL-STAR GAME RECORD

Year	League	W	L	Pct.	ERA	GS	CG	ShO	Sv.	IP	H	R	ER	BB	SO
1988—	National	0	0	...	0.00	0	0	0	0	1	0	0	0	0	0
1995—	National					Did not play.									
1996—	National	0	0	...	0.00	0	0	0	0	1	2	0	0	0	1
All-Star totals (2 years)		0	0	...	0.00	0	0	0	0	2	2	0	0	0	1

WRIGHT, JAMEY   P   ROCKIES

PERSONAL: Born December 24, 1974, in Oklahoma City. ... 6-5/203. ... Throws right, bats right. ... Full name: Jamey Alan Wright.
HIGH SCHOOL: Westmoore (Oklahoma City).
TRANSACTIONS/CAREER NOTES: Selected by Colorado Rockies organization in first round (28th pick overall) of free-agent draft (June 3, 1993). ... On Colorado disabled list (May 15-June 8, 1997); included rehabilitation assignment to Salem (June 1-8).

Year	Team (League)	W	L	Pct.	ERA	G	GS	CG	ShO	Sv.	IP	H	R	ER	BB	SO
1993—	Ariz. Rockies (Ariz.)	1	3	.250	4.00	8	8	8	0	0	36	35	19	16	9	26
1994—	Asheville (S. Atl.)	7	•14	.333	5.97	28	27	2	0	0	143⅓	*188	107	*95	59	103
1995—	Salem (Carolina)	10	8	.556	2.47	26	26	2	1	0	*171	160	74	47	72	95
—	New Haven (Eastern)	0	1	.000	9.00	1	1	0	0	0	3	6	6	3	3	0
1996—	New Haven (Eastern)	5	1	.833	0.81	7	7	1	1	0	44⅔	27	7	4	12	54
—	Colo. Springs (PCL)	4	2	.667	2.72	9	9	0	0	0	59⅔	53	20	18	22	40
—	Colorado (N.L.)	4	4	.500	4.93	16	15	0	0	0	91⅓	105	60	50	41	45
1997—	Colorado (N.L.)	8	12	.400	6.25	26	26	1	0	0	149⅔	198	113	104	71	59
—	Salem (Carolina)	0	1	.000	9.00	1	1	0	0	0	1	1	1	1	1	1
—	Colo. Springs (PCL)	1	0	1.000	1.64	2	2	0	0	0	11	9	3	2	5	11
Major league totals (2 years)		12	16	.429	5.75	42	41	1	0	0	241	303	173	154	112	104

WRIGHT, JARET   P   INDIANS

PERSONAL: Born December 29, 1975, In Anaheim, Calif. ... 6-2/220. ... Throws right, bats right. ... Full name: Jaret S. Wright. ... Son of Clyde Wright, major league pitcher with California Angels, Milwaukee Brewers and Texas Rangers (1966-75).
HIGH SCHOOL: Katella (Anaheim, Calif.).
TRANSACTIONS/CAREER NOTES: Selected by Cleveland Indians organization in first round (10th pick overall) of free-agent draft (June 2, 1994). ... On disabled list (June 19-September 23, 1996).

Year	Team (League)	W	L	Pct.	ERA	G	GS	CG	ShO	Sv.	IP	H	R	ER	BB	SO
1994—	Burlington (Appalachian)	0	1	.000	5.40	4	4	0	0	0	13⅓	13	10	8	9	16
1995—	Columbus (S. Atl.)	5	6	.455	3.00	24	24	0	0	0	129	93	55	43	79	113
1996—	Kinston (Carolina)	7	4	.636	2.50	19	19	0	0	0	101	65	32	28	55	109
1997—	Akron (Eastern)	3	3	.500	3.67	8	8	1	0	0	54	43	26	22	23	59
—	Buffalo (A.A.)	4	1	.800	1.80	7	7	1	1	0	45	30	16	9	19	47
—	Cleveland (A.L.)	8	3	.727	4.38	16	16	0	0	0	90⅓	81	45	44	35	63
Major league totals (1 year)		8	3	.727	4.38	16	16	0	0	0	90⅓	81	45	44	35	63

DIVISION SERIES RECORD

Year	Team (League)	W	L	Pct.	ERA	G	GS	CG	ShO	Sv.	IP	H	R	ER	BB	SO
1997—	Cleveland (A.L.)	2	0	1.000	3.97	2	2	0	0	0	11⅓	11	6	5	7	10

CHAMPIONSHIP SERIES RECORD

RECORDS: Shares single-game record for most home runs allowed—3 (October 12, 1997).

Year	Team (League)	W	L	Pct.	ERA	G	GS	CG	ShO	Sv.	IP	H	R	ER	BB	SO
1997—	Cleveland (A.L.)	0	0	...	15.00	1	1	0	0	0	3	6	5	5	2	3

WORLD SERIES RECORD

Year	Team (League)	W	L	Pct.	ERA	G	GS	CG	ShO	Sv.	IP	H	R	ER	BB	SO
1997—	Cleveland (A.L.)	1	0	1.000	2.92	2	2	0	0	0	12⅓	7	4	4	10	12

WRIGHT, RON   1B   PIRATES

PERSONAL: Born January 21, 1976, in Delta, Utah. ... 6-0/210. ... Bats right, throws right. ... Full name: Ronald Wade Wright.
HIGH SCHOOL: Kamiakin (Kennewick, Wash.).
TRANSACTIONS/CAREER NOTES: Selected by Atlanta Braves organization in seventh round of free-agent draft (June 2, 1994). ... Traded by Braves with OF Corey Pointer and a player to be named later to Pittsburgh Pirates for P Denny Neagle (August 28, 1996); Pirates acquired P Jason Schmidt to complete deal (August 30, 1996). ... On Calgary disabled list (July 24-September 2, 1997).
STATISTICAL NOTES: Led South Atlantic League first baseman with 1,152 total chances in 1995.

Year	Team (League)	Pos.	G	AB	R	H	2B	3B	HR	RBI	Avg.	BB	SO	SB	PO	A	E	Avg.
1994—	GC Braves (GCL)	1B	45	169	10	29	9	0	1	16	.172	10	21	1	382	31	6	.986
1995—	Macon (S. Atl.)	1B	135	537	93	143	23	1	•32	104	.266	62	118	2	1035	*99	18	.984
1996—	Durham (Carolina)	1B	66	240	47	66	15	2	20	62	.275	37	71	1	494	34	7	.987
—	Greenville (Southern)	1B	63	232	39	59	11	1	16	52	.254	38	73	1	434	45	6	.988
—	Carolina (Southern)■	1B	4	14	1	2	0	0	0	0	.143	2	7	0	32	0	2	.941
1997—	Calgary (PCL)	1B	91	336	50	102	31	0	16	63	.304	24	81	0	610	44	3	.995

W

YAN, ESTEBAN   P   DEVIL RAYS

PERSONAL: Born June 22, 1974, in Campha Deleseybo, Dominican Republic. ... 6-4/230. ... Throws right, bats right.
TRANSACTIONS/CAREER NOTES: Signed as non-drafted free agent by Atlanta Braves organization (November 21, 1990). ... Traded by Braves with OF Roberto Kelly and OF Tony Tarasco to Montreal Expos for OF Marquis Grissom (April 6, 1995). ... Contract sold by Expos organization to Baltimore Orioles organization (April 6, 1996). ... Selected by Tampa Bay Devil Rays in first round (18th pick overall) of expansion draft (November 18, 1997).
STATISTICAL NOTES: Led South Atlantic League with six balks in 1994.

Year — Team (League)	W	L	Pct.	ERA	G	GS	CG	ShO	Sv.	IP	H	R	ER	BB	SO
1991— San Pedro (DSL)	4	1	.800	3.63	18	11	0	0	0	72	61	36	29	26	34
1992— San Pedro (DSL)	12	3	.800	1.32	16	16	7	4	0	115 2/3	85	37	17	23	86
1993— Danville (Appalachian)	4	7	.364	3.03	14	14	0	0	0	71 1/3	73	46	24	24	50
1994— Macon (S. Atl.)	11	12	.478	3.27	28	•28	4	•3	0	170 2/3	155	85	62	34	121
1995— W.P. Beach (FSL)■	6	8	.429	3.07	24	21	1	0	1	137 2/3	139	63	47	33	89
1996— Bowie (Eastern)■	0	2	.000	5.63	9	1	0	0	0	16	18	12	10	8	15
— Rochester (Int'l)	5	4	.556	4.27	22	10	0	0	1	71 2/3	75	37	34	18	61
— Baltimore (A.L.)	0	0	...	5.79	4	0	0	0	0	9 1/3	13	7	6	3	7
1997— Rochester (Int'l)	11	5	.688	3.10	34	12	0	0	2	119	107	54	41	37	131
— Baltimore (A.L.)	0	1	.000	15.83	3	2	0	0	0	9 2/3	20	18	17	7	4
Major league totals (2 years)	0	1	.000	10.89	7	2	0	0	0	19	33	25	23	10	11

YOSHII, MASATO   P   METS

PERSONAL: Born April 20, 1965, in Osaka, Japan. ... 6-2/210. ... Throws right, bats right.
TRANSACTIONS/CAREER NOTES: Played for Kintetsu Buffaloes of Japan Pacific League (1985-94). ... Played for Yakult Swallows of Japan Central League (1995-97). ... Signed by New York Mets (January 18, 1998).

Year — Team (League)	W	L	Pct.	ERA	G	GS	CG	ShO	Sv.	IP	H	R	ER	BB	SO
1985— Kintetsu (Jap. Pac.)	0	1	.000	21.00	2	...	...	...	0	3	...	...	7	...	1
1986— Kintetsu (Jap. Pac.)	0	0	...	23.14	2	...	...	...	0	2 1/3	...	...	6	...	2
1987— Kintetsu (Jap. Pac.)	2	1	.667	4.75	13	...	...	...	0	36	...	...	19	...	23
1988— Kintetsu (Jap. Pac.)	10	2	.833	2.69	50	...	...	...	24	80 1/3	...	...	24	...	44
1989— Kintetsu (Jap. Pac.)	5	5	.500	2.99	47	...	...	...	20	84 1/3	...	...	28	...	44
1990— Kintetsu (Jap. Pac.)	8	9	.471	3.39	45	...	...	...	15	74 1/3	...	...	28	...	55
1991— Kintetsu (Jap. Pac.)	2	1	.667	3.42	21	...	...	...	2	26 1/3	...	...	10	...	13
1992— Kintetsu (Jap. Pac.)	1	0	1.000	2.31	9	...	...	...	0	11 2/3	...	...	3	...	4
1993— Kintetsu (Jap. Pac.)	5	5	.500	2.67	22	...	...	...	0	104 2/3	...	...	31	...	66
1994— Kintetsu (Jap. Pac.)	7	7	.500	5.47	21	...	...	...	0	97	...	...	59	...	42
1995— Yakult (Jp. Cen.)■	10	7	.588	3.12	25	...	...	...	0	147 1/3	...	...	51	...	91
1996— Yakult (Jp. Cen.)	10	7	.588	3.24	25	9	...	...	0	180 1/3	...	...	65	...	145
1997— Yakult (Jp. Cen.)	13	6	.684	2.99	28	26	6	2	0	174 1/3	149	61	58	48	104

YOUNG, DMITRI   1B/OF   REDS

PERSONAL: Born October 11, 1973, in Vicksburg, Miss. ... 6-2/210. ... Bats both, throws right. ... Full name: Dmitri Dell Young. ... Name pronounced duh-MEE-tree.
HIGH SCHOOL: Rio Mesa (Oxnard, Calif.).
TRANSACTIONS/CAREER NOTES: Selected by St. Louis Cardinals organization in first round (fourth pick overall) of free-agent draft (June 3, 1991). ... On disabled list (June 2-9, 1994). ... On Arkansas suspended list (August 1-11 and August 17-27, 1995). ... On Louisville disabled list (July 14-24, 1996). ... On St. Louis disabled list (May 11-29, 1997); included rehabilitation assignment to Louisville (May 25-29). ... Traded by Cardinals to Cincinnati Reds for P Jeff Brantley (November 10, 1997). ... Selected by Tampa Bay Devil Rays in first round (16th pick overall) of expansion draft (November 18, 1997). ... Traded by Devil Rays to Reds (November 18, 1997), completing deal in which Reds traded OF Mike Kelly to Devil Rays for a player to be named later (November 11).
STATISTICAL NOTES: Led Texas League with 14 intentional bases on balls received in 1994. ... Led Texas League first basemen with 15 errors in 1994. ... Tied for American Association lead with eight bases on balls received in 1996. ... Led American Association first basemen with 1,182 total chances and 102 double plays in 1996.

Year — Team (League)	Pos.	G	AB	R	H	2B	3B	HR	RBI	Avg.	BB	SO	SB	PO	A	E	Avg.
1991— Johnson City (App.)	3B	37	129	22	33	10	0	2	22	.256	21	28	2	19	49	5	.932
1992— Springfield (Midw.)	3B	135	493	74	153	*36	6	14	72	.310	51	94	14	66	239	42	.879
1993— St. Petersburg (FSL)	3B-1B	69	270	31	85	13	3	5	43	.315	24	28	3	260	90	10	.972
— Arkansas (Texas)	1B-3B	45	166	13	41	11	2	3	21	.247	9	29	4	348	29	7	.982
1994— Arkansas (Texas)	OF-1B	125	453	53	123	33	2	8	54	.272	36	60	0	485	44	†16	.971
1995— Arkansas (Texas)	OF	97	367	54	107	18	6	10	62	.292	30	46	2	116	5	9	.931
— Louisville (A.A.)	OF	2	7	3	2	0	0	0	0	.286	1	1	0	3	0	1	.750
1996— Louisville (A.A.)	1B	122	459	*90	153	31	6	15	64	*.333	34	67	16	*1091	83	8	.993
— St. Louis (N.L.)	1B	16	29	3	7	0	0	0	2	.241	4	5	0	39	1	1	.976
1997— St. Louis (N.L.)	1B-OF-DH	110	333	38	86	14	3	5	34	.258	38	63	6	641	47	13	.981
— Louisville (A.A.)	OF-1B	24	84	10	23	7	0	4	14	.274	13	15	1	64	2	1	.985
Major league totals (2 years)		126	362	41	93	14	3	5	36	.257	42	68	6	680	48	14	.981

CHAMPIONSHIP SERIES RECORD

Year — Team (League)	Pos.	G	AB	R	H	2B	3B	HR	RBI	Avg.	BB	SO	SB	PO	A	E	Avg.
1996— St. Louis (N.L.)	PH-1B	4	7	1	2	0	1	0	2	.286	0	2	0	11	1	0	1.000

YOUNG, ERIC   2B   DODGERS

PERSONAL: Born May 18, 1967, in New Brunswick, N.J. ... 5-9/170. ... Bats right, throws right. ... Full name: Eric Orlando Young.
HIGH SCHOOL: New Brunswick (N.J.).

Y

COLLEGE: Rutgers.

TRANSACTIONS/CAREER NOTES: Selected by Los Angeles Dodgers organization in 43rd round of free-agent draft (June 5, 1989). ... Selected by Colorado Rockies in first round (11th pick overall) of expansion draft (November 17, 1992). ... On Colorado disabled list (March 22-April 22, 1996); included rehabilitation assignments to New Haven (April 5-10), Salem (April 10-13) and Colorado Springs (April 13-22). ... Traded by Rockies to Dodgers for P Pedro Astacio (August 19, 1997).

RECORDS: Shares major league record for most stolen bases in one inning—3 (June 30, 1996, third inning).

HONORS: Named second baseman on THE SPORTING NEWS N.L. All-Star team (1996). ... Named second baseman on THE SPORTING NEWS N.L. Silver Slugger team (1996).

STATISTICAL NOTES: Led Florida State League second basemen with 24 errors in 1990. ... Led Texas League in caught stealing with 26 in 1991. ... Led Texas League second basemen with .974 fielding percentage in 1991. ... Tied for N.L. lead in errors by second baseman with 11 in 1995. ... Hit three home runs in one game (May 10, 1996). ... Led N.L. in caught stealing with 19 in 1996. ... Led N.L. second basemen with 109 double plays in 1996 and 111 in 1997.

MISCELLANEOUS: Holds Colorado Rockies all-time records for most triples (28) and most stolen bases (180).

| | | | | | | | | | | | BATTING | | | | FIELDING | | |
Year	Team (League)	Pos.	G	AB	R	H	2B	3B	HR	RBI	Avg.	BB	SO	SB	PO	A	E	Avg.
1989—GC Dodgers (GCL)		2B	56	197	53	65	11	5	2	22	.330	33	16	*41	104	128	*15	.939
1990—Vero Beach (FSL)		2B-OF	127	460	*101	132	23	7	2	50	.287	69	35	*76	156	218	†25	.937
1991—San Antonio (Tex.)		2B-OF	127	461	82	129	17	4	3	35	.280	67	36	*70	206	282	13	†.974
—Albuquerque (PCL).....		2B	1	5	0	2	0	0	0	0	.400	0	0	0	1	2	0	1.000
1992—Albuquerque (PCL).....		2B	94	350	61	118	16	5	3	49	.337	33	18	28	210	287	•20	.961
—Los Angeles (N.L.).....		2B	49	132	9	34	1	0	1	11	.258	8	9	6	85	114	9	.957
1993—Colorado (N.L.)■		2B-OF	144	490	82	132	16	8	3	42	.269	63	41	42	254	230	18	.964
1994—Colorado (N.L.)		OF-2B	90	228	37	62	13	1	7	30	.272	38	17	18	97	4	2	.981
1995—Colorado (N.L.)		2B-OF	120	366	68	116	21	•9	6	36	.317	49	29	35	180	230	11	.974
1996—All Star National (N.L.).		PR-2B	1	1	0	0	0	0	0	0	.000	0	0	0	2	1	0	1.000
—New Haven (Eastern)..		2B	3	15	0	1	0	0	0	0	.067	0	3	0	9	5	0	1.000
—Salem (Carolina)		2B	3	10	2	3	3	0	0	0	.300	3	1	2	8	6	2	.875
—Colo. Springs (PCL)		2B	7	23	4	6	1	1	0	3	.261	5	1	0	15	18	3	.917
—Colorado (N.L.)		2B	141	568	113	184	23	4	8	74	.324	47	31	*53	340	431	12	.985
1997—Colorado (N.L.)		2B	118	468	78	132	29	6	6	45	.282	57	37	32	258	414	15	.978
—Los Angeles (N.L.)■..		2B	37	154	28	42	4	2	2	16	.273	14	17	13	60	79	3	.979
Major league totals (6 years)			700	2407	415	702	107	30	33	254	.292	276	181	199	1276	1503	70	.975

DIVISION SERIES RECORD

| | | | | | | | | | | | BATTING | | | | FIELDING | | |
Year	Team (League)	Pos.	G	AB	R	H	2B	3B	HR	RBI	Avg.	BB	SO	SB	PO	A	E	Avg.
1995—Colorado (N.L.)		2B	4	16	3	7	1	0	1	2	.438	2	2	1	8	13	3	.875

YOUNG ERNIE   OF   ATHLETICS

PERSONAL: Born July 8, 1969, in Chicago. ... 6-1/214. ... Bats right, throws right. ... Full name: Ernest Wesley Young.

HIGH SCHOOL: Mendel Catholic (Chicago).

COLLEGE: Lewis (Ill.).

TRANSACTIONS/CAREER NOTES: Selected by Oakland Athletics organization in 10th round of free-agent draft (June 4, 1990). ... On disabled list (July 11, 1992-remainder of season).

STATISTICAL NOTES: Led California League with .635 slugging percentage in 1993.

| | | | | | | | | | | | BATTING | | | | FIELDING | | |
Year	Team (League)	Pos.	G	AB	R	H	2B	3B	HR	RBI	Avg.	BB	SO	SB	PO	A	E	Avg.
1990—S. Oregon (N'west).....		OF	50	168	34	47	6	2	6	23	.280	29	53	4	62	5	2	.971
1991—Madison (Midwest)......		OF	114	362	75	92	19	2	15	71	.254	58	115	20	204	9	7	.968
1992—Modesto (California) ..		OF	74	253	55	63	12	4	11	33	.249	47	74	11	126	11	6	.958
1993—Modesto (California) ..		OF	85	301	83	92	18	6	23	71	.306	72	92	23	178	8	3	.984
—Huntsville (Southern).		OF	45	120	26	25	5	0	5	15	.208	24	36	8	97	8	4	.963
1994—Huntsville (Southern).		OF	72	257	45	89	19	4	14	55	.346	37	45	5	98	13	2	.982
—Oakland (A.L.)		OF-DH	11	30	2	2	1	0	0	3	.067	1	8	0	22	1	1	.958
—Tacoma (PCL)		OF	29	102	19	29	4	0	6	16	.284	13	27	0	53	2	2	.965
1995—Edmonton (PCL)		OF	95	347	70	96	21	4	15	72	.277	49	73	2	194	7	6	.971
—Oakland (A.L.)		OF	26	50	9	10	3	0	2	5	.200	8	12	0	35	0	2	.946
1996—Oakland (A.L.)		OF	141	462	72	112	19	4	19	64	.242	52	118	7	353	8	1	.997
1997—Oakland (A.L.)		OF	71	175	22	39	7	0	5	15	.223	19	57	1	135	4	4	.972
—Edmonton (PCL)		OF	54	195	39	63	10	0	9	45	.323	37	46	5	100	5	1	.991
Major league totals (4 years)			249	717	105	163	30	4	26	87	.227	80	195	8	545	13	8	.986

YOUNG JOE   P   BLUE JAYS

PERSONAL: Born April 28, 1975, in Ft. McMurray, Alta. ... 6-4/205. ... Throws right, bats right. ... Full name: Reginald Quentin Young.

HIGH SCHOOL: Harry Ainlay (Ft. McMurray, Alta.).

TRANSACTIONS/CAREER NOTES: Selected by Toronto Blue Jays organization in third round of free-agent draft (June 3, 1993).

Year	Team (League)	W	L	Pct.	ERA	G	GS	CG	ShO	Sv.	IP	H	R	ER	BB	SO
1993—GC Blue Jays (GCL)...........	4	5	.444	3.90	14	•12	0	0	0	62 1/3	59	30	27	31	61
—Medicine Hat (Pio.)	0	1	.000	2.38	2	2	0	0	0	11 1/3	6	3	3	6	7
1994—Medicine Hat (Pio.)	3	5	.375	5.35	15	15	0	0	0	70 2/3	86	55	42	46	59
1995—St. Catharines (NYP)	6	5	.545	2.04	15	•15	0	0	0	83 2/3	72	29	19	35	73
1996—Hagerstown (S. Atl.)...........	9	9	.500	3.84	21	21	3	1	0	122	101	64	52	63	157
—Dunedin (Fla. St.)...........	1	3	.250	5.88	6	6	0	0	0	33 2/3	30	24	22	17	36
1997—Knoxville (Southern)	5	4	.556	4.42	19	11	0	0	0	59	52	38	29	40	62

Y

YOUNG, KEVIN   1B   PIRATES

PERSONAL: Born June 16, 1969, in Alpena, Mich. ... 6-3/221. ... Bats right, throws right. ... Full name: Kevin Stacey Young.
HIGH SCHOOL: Washington (Kansas City, Kan.).
JUNIOR COLLEGE: Kansas City Kansas Community College.
COLLEGE: Southern Mississippi.
TRANSACTIONS/CAREER NOTES: Selected by Pittsburgh Pirates organization in seventh round of free-agent draft (June 4, 1990). ... On Pittsburgh disabled list (July 24-August 8, 1995). ... Released by Pirates (March 26, 1996). ... Signed by Kansas City Royals organization (April 1, 1996). ... Released by Royals (December 5, 1996). ... Signed by Pirates (March 31, 1997).
STATISTICAL NOTES: Tied for Southern League lead in errors by third baseman with 26 in 1991. ... Tied for American Association lead in being hit by pitch with 11 in 1992. ... Led American Association third basemen with 300 assists, 32 errors, 436 total chances and 41 double plays in 1992. ... Led N.L. first basemen with .998 fielding percentage in 1993. ... Career major league grand slams: 1.

									BATTING						FIELDING		
Year	Team (League)	Pos.	G	AB	R	H	2B	3B	HR	RBI	Avg.	BB	SO	SB	PO	A	E	Avg.
1990—	Welland (NYP)	SS	72	238	46	58	16	2	5	30	.244	31	36	10	*79	118	26	.883
1991—	Salem (Carolina)	3B	56	201	38	63	12	4	6	28	.313	20	34	3	54	93	12	.925
	—Carolina (Southern)	3B-1B	75	263	36	90	19	6	3	33	.342	15	38	9	157	116	‡28	.907
	—Buffalo (A.A.)	3B-1B	4	9	1	2	1	0	0	2	.222	0	0	1	6	6	2	.857
1992—	Buffalo (A.A.)	3B-1B	137	490	*91	154	29	6	8	65	.314	67	67	18	129	†313	†32	.932
	—Pittsburgh (N.L.)	3B-1B	10	7	2	4	0	0	0	4	.571	2	0	1	3	1	1	.800
1993—	Pittsburgh (N.L.)	1B-3B	141	449	38	106	24	3	6	47	.236	36	82	2	1122	112	3	†.998
1994—	Pittsburgh (N.L.)	1B-3B-OF	59	122	15	25	7	2	1	11	.205	8	34	0	179	45	3	.987
	—Buffalo (A.A.)	3B-1B	60	228	26	63	14	5	5	27	.276	15	45	6	59	162	4	.982
1995—	Calgary (PCL)	3B-1B	45	163	24	58	23	1	8	34	.356	15	21	6	144	85	12	.950
	—Pittsburgh (N.L.)	1B-3B	56	181	13	42	9	0	6	22	.232	8	53	1	58	110	12	.933
1996—	Omaha (A.A.)■	1B-3B	50	186	29	57	11	1	13	46	.306	12	41	3	280	45	5	.985
	—Kansas City (A.L.)	1-0-3-DH	55	132	20	32	6	0	8	23	.242	11	32	3	199	19	1	.995
1997—	Pittsburgh (N.L.)	1B-3B-OF	97	333	59	100	18	3	18	74	.300	16	89	11	644	66	5	.993
American League totals (1 year)			55	132	20	32	6	0	8	23	.242	11	32	3	199	19	1	.995
National League totals (5 years)			363	1092	127	277	58	8	31	158	.254	70	258	15	2006	334	24	.990
Major league totals (6 years)			418	1224	147	309	64	8	39	181	.252	81	290	18	2205	353	25	.990

ZAUN, GREGG   C   MARLINS

PERSONAL: Born April 14, 1971, in Glendale, Calif. ... 5-10/180. ... Bats both, throws right. ... Full name: Gregory Owen Zaun. ... Nephew of Rick Dempsey, manager, Norfolk Tides and major league catcher with six teams (1969-92).
HIGH SCHOOL: St. Francis (La Canada, Calif.).
TRANSACTIONS/CAREER NOTES: Selected by Baltimore Orioles organization in 17th round of free-agent draft (June 5, 1989). ... On Bowie disabled list (June 17-July 15, 1993). ... Traded by Orioles to Florida Marlins (August 23, 1996), completing deal in which Marlins traded P Terry Mathews to Orioles for a player to be named later (August 21, 1996).
STATISTICAL NOTES: Led Appalachian League catchers with 460 putouts and 501 total chances in 1990. ... Led Midwest League catchers with 796 total chances in 1991. ... Led Carolina League catchers with 746 putouts, 91 assists, 18 errors, 855 total chances and 10 double plays in 1992. ... Led International League catchers with 841 total chances and 11 double plays in 1994.

									BATTING						FIELDING		
Year	Team (League)	Pos.	G	AB	R	H	2B	3B	HR	RBI	Avg.	BB	SO	SB	PO	A	E	Avg.
1990—	Wausau (Midwest)	C	37	100	3	13	0	1	1	7	.130	7	17	0	270	26	3	.990
	—Bluefield (Appal.)	C-3-S-P	61	184	29	55	5	2	2	21	.299	23	15	5	†462	34	10	.980
1991—	Kane County (Midw.)	C	113	409	67	112	17	5	4	51	.274	50	41	4	*697	83	16	.980
1992—	Frederick (Carolina)	C-2B	108	383	54	96	18	6	6	52	.251	42	45	3	†746	†91	†18	.979
1993—	Bowie (Eastern)	C-2-3-P	79	258	25	79	10	0	3	38	.306	27	26	4	423	51	10	.979
	—Rochester (Int'l)	C	21	78	10	20	4	2	1	11	.256	6	11	0	141	18	4	.975
1994—	Rochester (Int'l)	C	123	388	61	92	16	4	7	43	.237	56	72	4	*750	82	9	*.989
1995—	Rochester (Int'l)	C	42	140	26	41	13	1	6	18	.293	14	21	0	243	18	3	.989
	—Baltimore (A.L.)	C	40	104	18	27	5	0	3	14	.260	16	14	1	216	13	3	.987
1996—	Baltimore (A.L.)	C	50	108	16	25	8	1	1	13	.231	11	15	0	215	10	3	.987
	—Rochester (Int'l)	C	14	47	11	15	2	0	0	4	.319	11	6	0	52	3	2	.965
	—Florida (N.L.)■	C	10	31	4	9	1	0	1	2	.290	3	5	1	60	6	0	1.000
1997—	Florida (N.L.)	C-1B	58	143	21	43	10	2	2	20	.301	26	18	1	329	25	8	.978
American League totals (2 years)			90	212	34	52	13	1	4	27	.245	27	29	1	431	23	6	.987
National League totals (2 years)			68	174	25	52	11	2	3	22	.299	29	23	2	389	31	8	.981
Major league totals (3 years)			158	386	59	104	24	3	7	49	.269	56	52	3	820	54	14	.984

CHAMPIONSHIP SERIES RECORD

									BATTING						FIELDING		
Year	Team (League)	Pos.	G	AB	R	H	2B	3B	HR	RBI	Avg.	BB	SO	SB	PO	A	E	Avg.
1997—	Florida (N.L.)	C	1	0	0	0	0	0	0	0	...	0	0	0	2	0	0	1.000

WORLD SERIES RECORD

NOTES: Member of World Series championship team (1997).

									BATTING						FIELDING		
Year	Team (League)	Pos.	G	AB	R	H	2B	3B	HR	RBI	Avg.	BB	SO	SB	PO	A	E	Avg.
1997—	Florida (N.L.)	PH-C-PR	2	2	0	0	0	0	0	0	.000	0	0	0	3	0	0	1.000

RECORD AS PITCHER

Year	Team (League)	W	L	Pct.	ERA	G	GS	CG	ShO	Sv.	IP	H	R	ER	BB	SO
1990—	Bluefield (Appalachian)	0	0	...	0.00	1	0	0	0	0	1	1	0	0	1	1
1993—	Bowie (Eastern)	0	0	...	0.00	1	0	0	0	0	2 1/3	1	0	0	0	0

ZEILE, TODD   3B   DODGERS

PERSONAL: Born September 9, 1965, in Van Nuys, Calif. ... 6-1/200. ... Bats right, throws right. ... Full name: Todd Edward Zeile. ... Husband of Julianne McNamara, Olympic gold-medal gymnast (1984). ... Name pronounced ZEEL.
HIGH SCHOOL: Hart (Newhall, Calif.).
COLLEGE: UCLA.
TRANSACTIONS/CAREER NOTES: Selected by Kansas City Royals organization in 30th round of free-agent draft (June 6, 1983); did not sign. ... Selected by St. Louis Cardinals organization in supplemental round ("sandwich pick" between second and third round 55th pick overall) of free-agent draft (June 2, 1986); pick received as compensation for New York Yankees signing Type C free-agent IF Ivan DeJesus. ... On St. Louis disabled list (April 23-May 9, 1995); included rehabilitation assignment to Louisville (May 6-9). ... Traded by Cardinals with cash to Chicago Cubs for P Mike Morgan, 3B/OF Paul Torres and C Francisco Morales (June 16, 1995). ... Granted free agency (December 21, 1995). ... Signed by Philadelphia Phillies (December 22, 1995). ... Traded by Phillies with OF Pete Incaviglia to Baltimore Orioles for two players to be named later (August 29, 1996); Phillies acquired P Calvin Maduro and P Garrett Stephenson to complete deal (September 4, 1996). ... Granted free agency (October 27, 1996). ... Signed by Los Angeles Dodgers (December 8, 1996).
RECORDS: Holds N.L. single-season record for fewest putouts by third baseman (150 or more games)—83 (1993). ... Shares A.L. single-game record for most errors by third baseman—4 (August 7, 1996).
HONORS: Named Midwest League co-Most Valuable Player (1987).
STATISTICAL NOTES: Led New York-Pennsylvania League with six sacrifice flies in 1986. ... Tied for New York-Pennsylvania League lead in double plays by catcher with seven in 1986. ... Led Texas League catchers with 687 putouts and 761 total chances in 1988. ... Led American Association catchers with .992 fielding percentage and 17 passed balls in 1989. ... Career major league grand slams: 5.

							BATTING							FIELDING		
Year Team (League)	Pos.	G	AB	R	H	2B	3B	HR	RBI	Avg.	BB	SO	SB	PO	A	E	Avg.
1986—Erie (N.Y.-Penn)	C	70	248	40	64	14	1	14	*63	.258	37	52	5	407	*66	8	.983
1987—Springfield (Midw.)	C-3B	130	487	94	142	24	4	25	*106	.292	70	85	1	867	79	14	.985
1988—Arkansas (Texas)	C-OF-1B	129	430	95	117	33	2	19	75	.272	83	64	6	†697	66	10	.987
1989—Louisville (A.A.)	C-3B-1B	118	453	71	131	26	3	19	85	.289	45	78	0	583	71	6	†.991
—St. Louis (N.L.)	C	28	82	7	21	3	1	1	8	.256	9	14	0	125	10	4	.971
1990—St. Louis (N.L.)	C-3-1-O	144	495	62	121	25	3	15	57	.244	67	77	2	648	106	15	.980
1991—St. Louis (N.L.)	3B	155	565	76	158	36	3	11	81	.280	62	94	17	124	290	*25	.943
1992—St. Louis (N.L.)	3B	126	439	51	113	18	4	7	48	.257	68	70	7	81	235	13	.960
—Louisville (A.A.)	3B	21	74	11	23	4	1	5	13	.311	9	13	0	15	41	5	.918
1993—St. Louis (N.L.)	3B	157	571	82	158	36	1	17	103	.277	70	76	5	83	310	33	.923
1994—St. Louis (N.L.)	3B	113	415	62	111	25	1	19	75	.267	52	56	1	66	224	12	.960
1995—Louisville (A.A.)	1B	2	8	0	1	0	0	0	0	.125	0	2	0	11	1	1	.923
—St. Louis (N.L.)	1B	34	127	16	37	6	0	5	22	.291	18	23	1	310	30	7	.980
—Chicago (N.L.)	3B-OF-1B	79	299	34	68	16	0	9	30	.227	16	53	0	52	134	12	.939
1996—Philadelphia (N.L.)■	3B-1B	134	500	61	134	24	0	20	80	.268	67	88	1	295	195	14	.972
—Baltimore (A.L.)■	3B	29	117	17	28	8	0	5	19	.239	15	16	0	24	56	3	.964
1997—Los Angeles (N.L.)■	3B	160	575	89	154	17	0	31	90	.268	85	112	8	105	248	*26	.931
American League totals (1 year)		29	117	17	28	8	0	5	19	.239	15	16	0	24	56	3	.964
National League totals (9 years)		1130	4068	540	1075	206	13	135	594	.264	514	663	42	1889	1782	161	.958
Major league totals (9 years)		1159	4185	557	1103	214	13	140	613	.264	529	679	42	1913	1838	164	.958

DIVISION SERIES RECORD

							BATTING							FIELDING		
Year Team (League)	Pos.	G	AB	R	H	2B	3B	HR	RBI	Avg.	BB	SO	SB	PO	A	E	Avg.
1996—Baltimore (A.L.)	3B	4	19	2	5	1	00	0	0	.263	2	5	0	4	9	2	.867

CHAMPIONSHIP SERIES RECORD

							BATTING							FIELDING		
Year Team (League)	Pos.	G	AB	R	H	2B	3B	HR	RBI	Avg.	BB	SO	SB	PO	A	E	Avg.
1996—Baltimore (A.L.)	3B	5	22	3	8	17	0	0	3	.364	5	2	1	3	7	1	.909

ZIMMERMAN, JORDAN   P   MARINERS

PERSONAL: Born April 28, 1975, in Kelowna, B.C. ... 6-0/200. ... Throws left, bats right. ... Full name: Jordan William Zimmerman.
HIGH SCHOOL: Brenham (Texas).
JUNIOR COLLEGE: Blinn College (Texas).
TRANSACTIONS/CAREER NOTES: Selected by Seattle Mariners organization in 32nd round of free-agent draft (June 2, 1994). ... On disabled list (July 7-September 15, 1995). ... On disabled list (June 18-September 6, 1996).

Year Team (League)	W	L	Pct.	ERA	G	GS	CG	ShO	Sv.	IP	H	R	ER	BB	SO
1995—					Did not play.										
1996—					Did not play.										
1997—Everett (Northwest)	2	3	.400	4.15	11	9	0	0	0	39	37	27	18	23	54
—Wisconsin (Midwest)	0	1	.000	5.82	3	3	0	0	0	17	18	11	11	10	18

ZIMMERMAN, MIKE   P

PERSONAL: Born February 6, 1969, in Brooklyn, N.Y. ... 6-0/185. ... Throws right, bats right. ... Full name: Michael Alan Zimmerman.
HIGH SCHOOL: Lincoln (Brooklyn, N.Y.).
COLLEGE: South Alabama.
TRANSACTIONS/CAREER NOTES: Selected by Pittsburgh Pirates organization in supplemental round ("sandwich pick" between first and second round, 27th pick overall) of free-agent draft (June 4, 1990); pick received as part of compensation for Los Angeles Dodgers signing Type A free-agent P Jim Gott. ... On Buffalo disabled list (June 22-30, 1994). ... Claimed on waivers by Florida Marlins (July 15, 1994). ... On disabled list (May 7-17, 1995). ... On Port City suspended list (July 16-19, 1996). ... Granted free agency (October 15, 1996). ... Played for Rio Grande Valley, independent, during 1997 season. ... Signed by Kansas City Royals organization (June 4, 1997). ... Granted free agency (October 15, 1997).

STATISTICAL NOTES: Led Carolina League with 14 hit batsmen and 20 wild pitches in 1991. ... Pitched seven innings, combining with Dennis Tafoya (one inning) in eight-inning, 1-0 no-hit victory against Chattanooga (May 8, 1992).

Year	Team (League)	W	L	Pct.	ERA	G	GS	CG	ShO	Sv.	IP	H	R	ER	BB	SO
1990—	Welland (N.Y.-Penn)	2	0	1.000	0.68	9	0	0	0	2	13 1/3	7	4	1	9	22
—	Salem (Carolina)	1	1	.500	5.96	19	0	0	0	8	25 2/3	28	19	17	16	24
1991—	Salem (Carolina)	4	2	.667	4.37	49	1	0	0	9	70	51	47	34	72	63
1992—	Carolina (Southern)	4	•15	.211	3.82	27	27	1	0	0	153	141	82	65	75	107
1993—	Buffalo (A.A.)	3	1	.750	4.08	33	0	0	0	1	46 1/3	45	23	21	28	32
—	Carolina (Southern)	2	3	.400	3.60	33	0	0	0	9	45	40	26	18	21	30
1994—	Carolina (Southern)	2	2	.500	2.76	16	0	0	0	9	16 1/3	13	6	5	8	9
—	Buffalo (A.A.)	0	1	.000	3.47	19	0	0	0	0	23 1/3	25	10	9	13	14
—	Edmonton (PCL)■	5	1	.833	3.49	9	7	0	0	1	38 2/3	33	19	15	29	23

Year	Team (League)	W	L	Pct.	ERA	G	GS	CG	ShO	Sv.	IP	H	R	ER	BB	SO
1995—	Charlotte (Int'l)■	2	2	.500	5.30	31	7	0	0	0	69 2/3	84	46	41	41	30
1996—	Tacoma (PCL)■	1	1	.500	9.17	13	0	0	0	0	17 2/3	23	19	18	13	13
—	Port City (Southern)	4	4	.500	6.94	14	8	0	0	0	48	56	40	37	33	25
1997—	R. G. Valley.(Tex.-Louis.)■	1	1	.500	1.69	3	3	0	0	0	16	13	11	3	5	9
—	Omaha (Am. Assoc.)■	1	3	.250	10.59	7	6	0	0	0	26 1/3	41	32	31	20	17
—	Wichita (Texas)	1	2	.333	3.67	11	4	0	0	0	27	21	14	11	17	11

ZUBER, JON — 1B — PHILLIES

PERSONAL: Born December 10, 1969, in Encino, Calif. ... 6-0/190. ... Bats left, throws left. ... Full name: Jon Edward Zuber.
HIGH SCHOOL: Campolindo (Moraga, Calif.).
COLLEGE: California.
TRANSACTIONS/CAREER NOTES: Selected by Philadelphia Phillies organization in 12th round of free-agent draft (June 1, 1992).
STATISTICAL NOTES: Tied for Florida State League lead with 214 total bases in 1993. ... Led Florida State League first basemen in fielding with .996 in 1993. ... Led Eastern League first basemen with 1,070 putouts and 1,180 total chances in 1994.

Year	Team (League)	Pos.	G	AB	R	H	2B	3B	HR	RBI	Avg.	BB	SO	SB	PO	A	E	Avg.
							BATTING									FIELDING		
1992—	Batavia (NY-Penn)	1B	22	88	14	30	6	3	1	21	.341	9	11	1	132	16	3	.980
—	Spartanburg (SAL)	OF-1B	54	206	24	59	13	1	3	36	.286	33	31	3	54	1	1	.982
1993—	Clearwater (FSL)	1B-OF-3B	129	494	70	152	*37	5	5	69	.308	49	47	6	1080	90	6	†.995
1994—	Reading (Eastern)	1B-OF	138	498	81	146	29	5	9	70	.293	71	71	2	†1078	99	13	.989
1995—	Scran./W.B. (Int'l)	1B	119	418	53	120	19	5	3	50	.287	49	68	1	825	63	4	.996
1996—	Scran./W.B. (Int'l)	1B-OF	118	412	62	128	22	5	4	59	.311	58	50	4	522	46	6	.990
—	Philadelphia (N.L.)	1B	30	91	7	23	4	0	1	10	.253	6	11	1	145	11	2	.987
1997—	Scran./W.B. (Int'l)	OF-1B	126	435	85	137	37	2	6	64	.315	79	53	3	300	18	1	.997
	Major league totals (1 year)		30	91	7	23	4	0	1	10	.253	6	11	1	145	11	2	.987

ALOU, FELIPE   EXPOS

PERSONAL: Born May 12, 1935, in Haina, Dominican Republic. ... 6-1/195. ... Batted right, threw right. ... Full name: Felipe Rojas Alou. ... Father of Moises Alou, outfielder, Houston Astros; brother of Jesus Alou, major league outfielder with four teams (1965-75 and 1978-79); brother of Matty Alou, major league outfielder with six teams (1960-74); and uncle of Mel Rojas, pitcher, New York Mets.

COLLEGE: University of Santo Domingo (Dominican Republic).

TRANSACTIONS/CAREER NOTES: Signed as free agent by New York Giants organization (November 14, 1955). ... Giants franchise moved from New York to San Francisco (1958). ... Traded by Giants with P Billy Hoeft, C Ed Bailey and a player to be named later to Milwaukee Braves for P Bob Hendley, P Bob Shaw and C Del Crandall (December 3, 1963); Braves acquired IF Ernie Bowman to complete deal (January 8, 1964). ... On disabled list (June 24-July 25, 1964). ... Braves franchise moved from Milwaukee to Atlanta (1966). ... Traded by Braves to Oakland Athletics for P Jim Nash (December 3, 1969). ... Traded by A's to New York Yankees for P Rob Gardner and P Ron Klimkowski (April 9, 1971). ... Contract sold by Yankees to Montreal Expos (September 5, 1973). ... Contract sold by Expos to Milwaukee Brewers (December 7, 1973). ... Released by Brewers (April 29, 1974).

HONORS: Named first baseman on THE SPORTING NEWS N.L. All-Star team (1966).

STATISTICAL NOTES: Led N.L. with 355 total bases in 1966. ... Career major league grand slams: 2.

								BATTING							FIELDING			
Year	Team (League)	Pos.	G	AB	R	H	2B	3B	HR	RBI	Avg.	BB	SO	SB	PO	A	E	Avg.
1956—	Lake Charles (Evan.) ..	OF	5	9	1	2	0	0	0	1	.222	...	...	0	6	1	0	1.000
	—Cocoa (Fla. St.)	OF-3B	119	445	111	169	15	6	21	99	*.380	68	40	*48	199	60	23	.918
1957—	Minneapolis (A.A.)......	OF	24	57	7	12	2	0	0	3	.211	5	8	1	32	1	1	.971
	—Springfield (Eastern) ..	OF-3B	106	359	45	110	14	3	12	71	.306	27	29	18	215	26	9	.964
1958—	Phoenix (PCL)	OF	55	216	61	69	16	2	13	42	.319	17	24	10	150	3	3	.981
	—San Francisco (N.L.) ..	OF	75	182	21	46	9	2	4	16	.253	19	34	4	126	2	2	.985
1959—	San Francisco (N.L.) ..	OF	95	247	38	68	13	2	10	33	.275	17	38	5	111	2	3	.974
1960—	San Francisco (N.L.) ..	OF	106	322	48	85	17	3	8	44	.264	16	42	10	156	5	7	.958
1961—	San Francisco (N.L.) ..	OF	132	415	59	120	19	0	18	52	.289	26	41	11	196	10	2	.990
1962—	San Francisco (N.L.) ..	OF	154	561	96	177	30	3	25	98	.316	33	66	10	262	7	8	.971
1963—	San Francisco (N.L.) ..	OF	157	565	75	159	31	9	20	82	.281	27	87	11	279	9	4	.986
1964—	Milwaukee (N.L.)■....	OF-1B	121	415	60	105	26	3	9	51	.253	30	41	5	329	12	5	.986
1965—	Milwaukee (N.L.)......	0-1-3-S	143	555	80	165	29	2	23	78	.297	31	63	8	626	43	6	.991
1966—	Atlanta (N.L.)...........	1-0-3-S	154	*666	*122	*218	32	6	31	74	.327	24	51	5	935	64	13	.987
1967—	Atlanta (N.L.)...........	1B-OF	140	574	76	157	26	3	15	43	.274	32	50	6	864	34	9	.990
1968—	Atlanta (N.L.)...........	OF	160	*662	72	•210	37	5	11	57	.317	48	56	12	379	8	8	.980
1969—	Atlanta (N.L.)...........	OF	123	476	54	134	13	1	5	32	.282	23	23	4	260	4	3	.989
1970—	Oakland (A.L.)■.......	OF-1B	154	575	70	156	25	3	8	55	.271	32	31	10	290	11	7	.977
1971—	Oakland (A.L.)	OF	2	8	0	2	1	0	0	0	.250	0	1	0	7	0	0	1.000
	—New York (A.L.)■.....	OF-1B	131	461	52	133	20	6	8	69	.289	32	24	5	506	23	4	.992
1972—	New York (A.L.)	1B-OF	120	324	33	90	18	1	6	37	.278	22	27	1	669	54	7	.990
1973—	New York (A.L.)	1B-OF	93	280	25	66	12	0	4	27	.236	9	25	0	512	31	7	.987
	—Montreal (N.L.)■......	OF-1B	19	48	4	10	1	0	1	4	.208	2	4	0	30	3	0	1.000
1974—	Milwaukee (A.L.)■.....	OF	3	3	0	0	0	0	0	0	.000	0	2	0	0	0	1	.000
	American League totals (5 years)		503	1651	180	447	76	10	26	188	.271	95	110	16	1984	119	26	.988
	National League totals (13 years)		1579	5688	805	1654	283	39	180	664	.291	328	596	91	4553	203	70	.985
	Major league totals (17 years)		2082	7339	985	2101	359	49	206	852	.286	423	706	107	6537	322	96	.986

CHAMPIONSHIP SERIES RECORD

							BATTING							FIELDING			
Year	Team (League)	Pos.	G	AB	R	H	2B	3B	HR	RBI	Avg.	BB	SO	SB	PO	A	E	Avg.
1969—	Atlanta (N.L.)...........	PH	1	1	0	0	0	0	0	0	.000	0	0	0	...	...	...	...

WORLD SERIES RECORD

							BATTING							FIELDING			
Year	Team (League)	Pos.	G	AB	R	H	2B	3B	HR	RBI	Avg.	BB	SO	SB	PO	A	E	Avg.
1962—	San Francisco (N.L.) ..	OF	7	26	2	7	1	1	0	1	.269	1	4	0	8	0	1	.889

ALL-STAR GAME RECORD

					BATTING								FIELDING			
Year	League	Pos.	AB	R	H	2B	3B	HR	RBI	Avg.	BB	SO	SB	PO	A	E	Avg.
1962—	National	OF	0	0	0	0	0	0	1	...	0	0	0	0	0	0	...
1966—	National							Did not play.									
1968—	National	OF	0	0	0	0	0	0	0	...	0	0	0	0	0	0	...
	All-Star Game totals (2 years)		0	0	0	0	0	0	1	...	0	0	0	0	0	0	...

RECORD AS MANAGER

BACKGROUND: Spring training instructor, Montreal Expos (1976). ... Coach, Expos (1979-80, 1984 and October 8, 1991-May 22, 1992).

HONORS: Named Florida State League Manager of the Year (1990). ... Named N.L. Manager of the Year by THE SPORTING NEWS (1994). ... Named N.L. Manager of the Year by Baseball Writers' Association of America (1994).

		REGULAR SEASON				POSTSEASON							
						Playoff		Champ. Series		World Series		All-Star Game	
Year	Team (League)	W	L	Pct.	Pos.	W	L	W	L	W	L	W	L
1977—	West Palm Beach (Florida State)	77	55	.583	1st (S)	1	2	—	—	—	—	—	—
1978—	Memphis (Southern)................................	71	73	.493	2nd (W)	—	—	—	—	—	—	—	—
1981—	Denver (American Association)	76	60	.559	2nd (W)	4	0	—	—	—	—	—	—
1982—	Wichita (American Association)...............	70	67	.511	2nd (W)	—	—	—	—	—	—	—	—
1983—	Wichita (American Association)...............	65	71	.478	3rd (W)	—	—	—	—	—	—	—	—
1985—	Indianapolis (American Association)	61	81	.430	4th (E)	—	—	—	—	—	—	—	—
1986—	West Palm Beach (Florida State)	80	55	.593	1st (S)	3	3	—	—	—	—	—	—

		— REGULAR SEASON —				Playoff		Champ. Series		World Series		All-Star Game	
Year	Team (League)	W	L	Pct.	Pos.	W	L	W	L	W	L	W	L
1987—	West Palm Beach (Florida State)	75	63	.543	2nd (S)	—	—	—	—	—	—	—	—
1988—	West Palm Beach (Florida State)	41	27	.603	2nd (E)	—	—	—	—	—	—	—	—
	—(Second half)	30	36	.455	3rd (E)	2	2	—	—	—	—	—	—
1989—	West Palm Beach (Florida State)	39	31	.557	T2nd (E)	—	—	—	—	—	—	—	—
	—(Second half)	35	33	.515	2nd (E)	—	—	—	—	—	—	—	—
1990—	West Palm Beach (Florida State)	49	19	.721	1st (E)	—	—	—	—	—	—	—	—
	—(Second half)	43	21	.672	1st (E)	3	3	—	—	—	—	—	—
1991—	West Palm Beach (Florida State)	33	31	.516	4th (E)	—	—	—	—	—	—	—	—
	—(Second half)	39	28	.582	2nd (E)	6	1	—	—	—	—	—	—
1992—	Montreal (N.L.)	70	55	.560	2nd (E)	—	—	—	—	—	—	—	—
1993—	Montreal (N.L.)	94	68	.580	2nd (E)	—	—	—	—	—	—	—	—
1994—	Montreal (N.L.)	74	40	.649		—	—	—	—	—	—	—	—
1995—	Montreal (N.L.)	66	78	.458	5th (E)	—	—	—	—	—	—	—	—
1996—	Montreal (N.L.)	88	74	.543	2nd (E)	—	—	—	—	—	—	1	0
1997—	Montreal (N.L.)	78	84	.481	4th (E)	—	—	—	—	—	—	—	—
	Major league totals (6 years)	470	399	.541		—	—	—	—	—	—	1	0

NOTES:
1977—Lost to St. Petersburg in semifinals.
1978—Memphis tied one game.
1981—Defeated Omaha in league championship.
1986—Defeated Winter Haven, two games to none, in semifinals; lost to St. Petersburg, three games to one, in league championship.
1988—Defeated Vero Beach, two games to none, in first round; lost to Osceola, two games to none, in semifinals.
1990—Defeated Lakeland, two games to one, in semifinals; lost to Vero Beach, two games to one, in league championship.
1991—Defeated Vero Beach, two games to one, in first round; defeated Lakeland, two games to none, in semifinals; defeated Clearwater, two games to none, in league championship.
1992—Replaced Montreal manager Tom Runnells with club in fourth place and record of 17-20 (May 22).
1994—Montreal was in first place in N.L. East at time of season-ending strike (August 12).

BAKER, DUSTY — GIANTS

PERSONAL: Born June 15, 1949, in Riverside, Calif. ... 6-2/200. ... Batted right, threw right. ... Full name: Johnnie B. Baker Jr.
HIGH SCHOOL: Del Campo (Fair Oaks, Calif.).
COLLEGE: American River College (Calif.).
TRANSACTIONS/CAREER NOTES: Selected by Atlanta Braves organization in 26th round of free-agent draft (June 6, 1967). ... On West Palm Beach restricted list (April 5-June 13, 1968). ... On Atlanta military list (January 24-April 3, 1969 and June 17-July 3, 1972). ... Traded by Braves with 1B/3B Ed Goodson to Los Angeles Dodgers for OF Jimmy Wynn, 2B Lee Lacy, 1B/OF Tom Paciorek and IF Jerry Royster (November 17, 1975). ... Released on waivers by Dodgers (February 10, 1984); San Francisco Giants claim rejected (February 16, 1984). ... Granted free agency (February 21, 1984). ... Signed by Giants (April 1, 1984). ... On restricted list (April 2-11, 1984). ... Traded by Giants to Oakland Athletics for P Ed Puikunas and C Dan Winters (March 24, 1985). ... Granted free agency (November 10, 1986).
RECORDS: Shares major league records for most plate appearances, most at-bats and most times faced pitcher as batsman in one inning— 3 (September 20, 1972, second inning); and most stolen bases in one inning—3 (June 27, 1984, third inning).
HONORS: Named outfielder on THE SPORTING NEWS N.L. All-Star team (1980). ... Named outfielder on THE SPORTING NEWS N.L. Silver Slugger team (1980-81). ... Won N.L. Gold Glove as outfielder (1981).
STATISTICAL NOTES: Led N.L. outfielders with 407 total chances in 1973. ... Career major league grand slams: 4.

							BATTING								FIELDING			
Year	Team (League)	Pos.	G	AB	R	H	2B	3B	HR	RBI	Avg.	BB	SO	SB	PO	A	E	Avg.
1967—	Austin (Texas)	OF	9	39	6	9	1	0	0	1	.231	2	7	0	17	0	1	.944
1968—	W.Palm Beach (FSL) ..	OF	6	21	2	4	0	0	0	2	.190	1	4	0	6	2	0	1.000
	—Greenwood (W. Car.)..	OF	52	199	45	68	11	3	6	39	.342	23	39	6	82	1	3	.965
	—Atlanta (N.L.)	OF	6	5	0	2	0	0	0	0	.400	0	1	0	0	0	0	...
1969—	Shreveport (Texas)	OF	73	265	40	68	5	1	9	31	.257	36	41	2	135	10	3	.980
	—Richmond (Int'l)	OF-3B	25	89	7	22	4	0	0	8	.247	11	22	3	40	9	4	.925
	—Atlanta (N.L.)	OF	3	7	0	0	0	0	0	0	.000	0	3	0	2	0	0	1.000
1970—	Richmond (Int'l)	OF	118	461	97	150	29	3	11	51	.325	53	45	10	236	10	7	.972
	—Atlanta (N.L.)	OF	13	24	3	7	0	0	0	4	.292	2	4	0	11	1	3	.800
1971—	Richmond (Int'l)	OF-3B	80	341	62	106	23	2	11	41	.311	25	37	10	136	13	4	.974
	—Atlanta (N.L.)	OF	29	62	2	14	2	0	0	4	.226	1	14	0	29	1	0	1.000
1972—	Atlanta (N.L.)	OF	127	446	62	143	27	2	17	76	.321	45	68	4	344	8	4	.989
1973—	Atlanta (N.L.)	OF	159	604	101	174	29	4	21	99	.288	67	72	24	*390	10	7	.983
1974—	Atlanta (N.L.)	OF	149	574	80	147	35	0	20	69	.256	71	87	18	359	10	7	.981
1975—	Atlanta (N.L.)	OF	142	494	63	129	18	2	19	72	.261	67	57	12	287	10	3	.990
1976—	Los Angeles (N.L.)■ ..	OF	112	384	36	93	13	0	4	39	.242	31	54	2	254	3	1	.996
1977—	Los Angeles (N.L.)	OF	153	533	86	155	26	1	30	86	.291	58	89	2	227	8	3	.987
1978—	Los Angeles (N.L.)	OF	149	522	62	137	24	1	11	66	.262	47	66	12	250	13	4	.985
1979—	Los Angeles (N.L.)	OF	151	554	86	152	29	1	23	88	.274	56	70	11	289	14	3	.990
1980—	Los Angeles (N.L.)	OF	153	579	80	170	26	4	29	97	.294	43	66	12	308	5	3	.991
1981—	Los Angeles (N.L.)	OF	103	400	48	128	17	3	9	49	.320	29	43	10	181	8	2	.990
1982—	Los Angeles (N.L.)	OF	147	570	80	171	19	1	23	88	.300	56	62	17	226	7	6	.975
1983—	Los Angeles (N.L.)	OF	149	531	71	138	25	1	15	73	.260	72	59	7	249	4	5	.981
1984—	San Fran. (N.L.)■......	OF	100	243	31	71	7	2	3	32	.292	40	27	4	112	1	3	.974
1985—	Oakland (A.L.)■	1B-OF-DH	111	343	48	92	15	1	14	52	.268	50	47	2	465	29	5	.990
1986—	Oakland (A.L.)	OF-DH-1B	83	242	25	58	8	0	4	19	.240	27	37	0	90	4	0	1.000
	American League totals (2 years)		194	585	73	150	23	1	18	71	.256	77	84	2	555	33	5	.992
	National League totals (17 years)		1845	6532	891	1831	297	22	224	942	.280	685	842	135	3518	103	54	.985
	Major league totals (19 years)		2039	7117	964	1981	320	23	242	1013	.278	762	926	137	4073	136	59	.986

DIVISION SERIES RECORD

					BATTING										FIELDING			
Year	Team (League)	Pos.	G	AB	R	H	2B	3B	HR	RBI	Avg.	BB	SO	SB	PO	A	E	Avg.
1981— Los Angeles (N.L.)		OF	5	18	2	3	1	0	0	1	.167	2	0	0	12	0	0	1.000

CHAMPIONSHIP SERIES RECORD

RECORDS: Shares single-game record for most grand slams—1 (October 5, 1977). ... Shares record for most runs batted in in one inning—4 (October 5, 1977, fourth inning). ... Shares N.L. single-game record for most hits—4 (October 7, 1978).
NOTES: Named N.L. Championship Series Most Valuable Player (1977).

					BATTING										FIELDING			
Year	Team (League)	Pos.	G	AB	R	H	2B	3B	HR	RBI	Avg.	BB	SO	SB	PO	A	E	Avg.
1977— Los Angeles (N.L.)		OF	4	14	4	5	1	0	2	8	.357	2	3	0	3	0	0	1.000
1978— Los Angeles (N.L.)		OF	4	15	1	7	2	0	0	1	.467	3	0	0	5	0	0	1.000
1981— Los Angeles (N.L.)		OF	5	19	3	6	1	0	0	3	.316	1	0	0	10	0	1	.909
1983— Los Angeles (N.L.)		OF	4	14	4	5	1	0	1	1	.357	2	0	0	9	0	0	1.000
Championship series totals (4 years)			17	62	12	23	5	0	3	13	.371	8	3	0	27	0	1	.964

WORLD SERIES RECORD

NOTES: Member of World Series championship team (1981).

					BATTING										FIELDING			
Year	Team (League)	Pos.	G	AB	R	H	2B	3B	HR	RBI	Avg.	BB	SO	SB	PO	A	E	Avg.
1977— Los Angeles (N.L.)		OF	6	24	4	7	0	0	1	5	.292	0	2	0	11	0	1	.917
1978— Los Angeles (N.L.)		OF	6	21	2	5	0	0	1	1	.238	1	3	0	12	0	0	1.000
1981— Los Angeles (N.L.)		OF	6	24	3	4	0	0	0	1	.167	1	6	0	13	0	0	1.000
World Series totals (3 years)			18	69	9	16	0	0	2	7	.232	2	11	0	36	0	1	.973

ALL-STAR GAME RECORD

				BATTING									FIELDING			
Year	League	Pos.	AB	R	H	2B	3B	HR	RBI	Avg.	BB	SO	SB	PO	A	E	Avg.
1981— National		OF	2	0	1	0	0	0	0	.500	0	0	0	2	0	0	1.000
1982— National		OF	2	0	0	0	0	0	0	.000	0	0	0	0	0	0	...
All-Star Game totals (2 years)			4	0	1	0	0	0	0	.250	0	0	0	2	0	0	1.000

RECORD AS MANAGER

BACKGROUND: Coach, San Francisco Giants (1988-92). ... Manager, Scottsdale Scorpions, Arizona Fall League (1992, record: 20-22, second place/Northern Division).
HONORS: Named N.L. Manager of the Year by the Baseball Writers' Association of America (1993). ... Coach, N.L. All-Star team (1994 and 1997). ... Named N.L. Manager of the Year by THE SPORTING NEWS (1997).

		REGULAR SEASON				POSTSEASON						
						Playoff		Champ. Series		World Series		All-Star Game	
Year	Team (League)	W	L	Pct.	Pos.	W	L	W	L	W	L	W	L
1993— San Francisco (N.L.)		103	59	.636	2nd (W)	—	—	—	—	—	—	—	—
1994— San Francisco (N.L.)		55	60	.478		—	—	—	—	—	—	—	—
1995— San Francisco (N.L.)		67	77	.465	4th (W)	—	—	—	—	—	—	—	—
1996— San Francisco (N.L.)		68	94	.420	4th (W)	—	—	—	—	—	—	—	—
1997— San Francisco (N.L.)		90	72	.556	1st (W)	0	3	—	—	—	—	—	—
Major league totals (5 years)		383	362	.514		0	3	—	—	—	—	—	—

NOTES:
1994—San Francisco was in second place in N.L. West at time of season-ending strike (August 12).
1997—Lost to Florida in N.L. divisional playoff.

BAYLOR, DON — ROCKIES

PERSONAL: Born June 28, 1949, in Austin, Texas. ... 6-1/220. ... Batted right, threw right. ... Full name: Donald Edward Baylor. ... Cousin of Pat Ballage, safety, Indianapolis Colts (1986-87).
HIGH SCHOOL: Stephen F. Austin (Austin, Texas).
JUNIOR COLLEGE: Miami-Dade Junior College and Blinn College (Texas).
TRANSACTIONS/CAREER NOTES: Selected by Baltimore Orioles organization in second round of free-agent draft (June 6, 1967). ... Traded by Orioles with P Mike Torrez and P Paul Mitchell to Oakland Athletics for OF Reggie Jackson, P Ken Holtzman and P Bill Van Bommel (April 2, 1976). ... Granted free agency (November 1, 1976). ... Signed by California Angels (November 16, 1976). ... On disabled list (May 11-June 26, 1980). ... Granted free agency (November 10, 1982). ... Signed by New York Yankees (December 1, 1982). ... Traded by Yankees to Boston Red Sox for DH Mike Easler (March 28, 1986). ... Traded by Red Sox to Minnesota Twins for a player to be named later (August 31, 1987); Red Sox acquired P Enrique Rios to complete deal (December 18, 1987). ... Released by Twins (December 21, 1987). ... Signed by A's (February 9, 1988). ... Granted free agency (November 4, 1988).
RECORDS: Holds major league career record for most times hit by pitch—267. ... Shares major league records for most consecutive home runs in two consecutive games—4 (July 1 [1] and 2 [3], 1975, bases on balls included); and most long hits in opening game of season—4 (2 doubles, 1 triple, 1 home run, April 6, 1973). ... Shares major league record for most times caught stealing in one inning—2 (June 15, 1974, ninth inning). ... Shares modern major league single-game record for most at-bats (nine-inning game)—7 (August 25, 1979). ... Holds A.L. single-season record for most times hit by pitch—35 (1986).
HONORS: Named Appalachian League Player of the Year (1967). ... Named Minor League Player of the Year by THE SPORTING NEWS (1970). ... Named A.L. Player of the Year by THE SPORTING NEWS (1979). ... Named A.L. Most Valuable Player by Baseball Writers' Association of America (1979). ... Named designated hitter on THE SPORTING NEWS A.L. All-Star team (1979, 1985-86). ... Named designated hitter on THE SPORTING NEWS A.L. Silver Slugger team (1983 and 1985-86).
STATISTICAL NOTES: Led Appalachian League with 135 total bases and tied for lead in caught stealing with 6 in 1967. ... Led Texas League in being hit by pitch with 13 in 1969. ... Led International League with 296 total bases in 1970. ... Led International League in being hit by pitch with 19 in 1970 and 16 in 1971. ... Led A.L. in being hit by pitch with 13 in 1973, 20 in 1976, 18 in 1978, 23 in 1984, 24 in 1985, 35 in 1986, 28 in 1987 and tied for lead with 13 in 1975. ... Hit three home runs in one game (July 2, 1975). ... Led A.L. with 12 sacrifice flies in 1978. ... Led A.L. with 21 game-winning RBIs in 1982. ... Career major league grand slams: 12.

Year Team (League)	Pos.	G	AB	R	H	2B	3B	HR	RBI	Avg.	BB	SO	SB	PO	A	E	Avg.
1967— Bluefield (Appal.)........	OF	•67	246	50	*85	10	*8	8	47	*.346	35	52	*26	106	5	5	.957
1968— Stockton (California) ..	OF	68	244	52	90	6	3	7	40	.369	35	65	14	135	3	7	.952
—Elmira (Eastern)	OF	6	24	4	8	1	1	1	3	.333	3	4	1	10	1	0	1.000
—Rochester (Int'l)	OF	15	46	4	10	2	0	0	4	.217	3	17	1	29	1	4	.882
1969— Miami (Fla. St.)	OF	17	56	13	21	5	4	3	24	.375	7	8	3	30	2	3	.914
—Dall./Fort Worth (Tex.)	OF	109	406	71	122	17	•10	11	57	.300	48	77	19	241	7	*13	.950
1970— Rochester (Int'l)	OF	•140	508	*127	166	*34	*15	22	107	.327	76	99	26	286	5	7	.977
—Baltimore (A.L.)	OF	8	17	4	4	0	0	0	4	.235	2	3	1	15	0	0	1.000
1971— Rochester (Int'l)	OF	136	492	104	154	•31	10	20	95	.313	79	73	25	210	4	9	.960
—Baltimore (A.L.)	OF	1	2	0	0	0	0	0	1	.000	2	1	0	4	0	0	1.000
1972— Baltimore (A.L.)........	OF-1B	102	320	33	81	13	3	11	38	.253	29	50	24	206	4	5	.977
1973— Baltimore (A.L.)	OF-1B-DH	118	405	64	116	20	4	11	51	.286	35	48	32	228	10	6	.975
1974— Baltimore (A.L.)	OF-1B	137	489	66	133	22	1	10	59	.272	43	56	29	260	2	5	.981
1975— Baltimore (A.L.)	OF-DH-1B	145	524	79	148	21	6	25	76	.282	53	64	32	286	8	5	.983
1976— Oakland (A.L.)■........	OF-1B-DH	157	595	85	147	25	1	15	68	.247	58	72	52	781	45	12	.986
1977— California (A.L.)■■.....	OF-DH-1B	154	561	87	141	27	0	25	75	.251	62	76	26	280	16	7	.977
1978— California (A.L.)	DH-OF-1B	158	591	103	151	26	0	34	99	.255	56	71	22	194	9	6	.971
1979— California (A.L.)	OF-DH-1B	•162	628	*120	186	33	3	36	*139	.296	71	51	22	203	3	5	.976
1980— California (A.L.)	OF-DH	90	340	39	85	12	2	5	51	.250	24	32	6	119	4	4	.969
1981— California (A.L.)	DH-1B-OF	103	377	52	90	18	1	17	66	.239	42	51	3	38	3	0	1.000
1982— California (A.L.)	DH	157	608	80	160	24	1	24	93	.263	57	69	10	...	...	...	...
1983— New York (A.L.)■.......	DH-OF-1B	144	534	82	162	33	3	21	85	.303	40	53	17	23	2	1	.962
1984— New York (A.L.)	DH-OF	134	493	84	129	29	1	27	89	.262	38	68	1	8	0	1	.889
1985— New York (A.L.)	DH	142	477	70	110	24	1	23	91	.231	52	90	0	...	...	...	...
1986— Boston (A.L.)■........	DH-1B-OF	160	585	93	139	23	1	31	94	.238	62	111	3	71	4	1	.987
1987— Boston (A.L.)	DH	108	339	64	81	8	0	16	57	.239	40	47	5	...	...	...	...
—Minnesota (A.L.)■	DH	20	49	3	14	1	0	0	6	.286	5	12	0	...	...	...	...
1988— Oakland (A.L.)■........	DH	92	264	28	58	7	0	7	34	.220	34	44	0	...	...	...	...
Major league totals (19 years)		2292	8198	1236	2135	366	28	338	1276	.260	805	1069	285	2716	110	58	.980

CHAMPIONSHIP SERIES RECORD

RECORDS: Holds career record for most clubs played with—5. ... Holds single-series record for most runs batted in—10 (1982). ... Shares single-game records for most times reached base safely—5 (October 8, 1986); and most grand slams—1 (October 9, 1982). ... Shares record for most runs batted in in one inning—4 (October 9, 1982, eighth inning). ... Holds A.L. record for most consecutive games with one or more hits—12 (1982 [last three games], 1986-87). ... Shares A.L. single-game record for most runs batted in—5 (October 5, 1982).

Year Team (League)	Pos.	G	AB	R	H	2B	3B	HR	RBI	Avg.	BB	SO	SB	PO	A	E	Avg.
1973— Baltimore (A.L.).........	OF-PH	4	11	3	3	0	0	0	1	.273	3	5	0	7	0	0	1.000
1974— Baltimore (A.L.).........	OF-DH	4	15	0	4	0	0	0	0	.267	0	2	0	9	0	0	1.000
1979— California (A.L.)	DH-OF	4	16	2	3	0	0	1	2	.188	1	2	0	4	0	0	1.000
1982— California (A.L.)	DH	5	17	2	5	1	1	1	10	.294	2	0	0	...	...	...	...
1986— Boston (A.L.)	DH	7	26	6	9	3	0	1	2	.346	4	5	0	...	...	...	...
1987— Minnesota (A.L.)	PH-DH	2	5	0	2	0	0	0	1	.400	0	0	0	...	...	...	...
1988— Oakland (A.L.)	DH	2	6	0	0	0	0	0	1	.000	1	2	0	...	...	...	...
Championship series totals (7 years)		28	96	13	26	4	1	3	17	.271	11	16	0	20	0	0	1.000

WORLD SERIES RECORD

RECORDS: Shares record for most at-bats in one inning—2 (October 17, 1987, fourth inning).
NOTES: Member of World Series championship team (1987).

Year Team (League)	Pos.	G	AB	R	H	2B	3B	HR	RBI	Avg.	BB	SO	SB	PO	A	E	Avg.
1986— Boston (A.L.)..............	DH-PH	4	11	1	2	1	0	0	1	.182	1	3	0	...	...	...	...
1987— Minnesota (A.L.)	DH-PH	5	13	3	5	0	0	1	3	.385	1	1	0	...	...	...	...
1988— Oakland (A.L.)	PH	1	1	0	0	0	0	0	0	.000	0	1	0	...	...	...	...
World Series totals (3 years)		10	25	4	7	1	0	1	4	.280	2	5	0	...	...	...	...

ALL-STAR GAME RECORD

Year League	Pos.	AB	R	H	2B	3B	HR	RBI	Avg.	BB	SO	SB	PO	A	E	Avg.
1979— American	OF	4	2	2	1	0	0	1	.500	0	0	0	1	0	0	1.000

RECORD AS MANAGER

BACKGROUND: Special assistant to general manager, Milwaukee Brewers (September 5-December 4, 1989). ... Coach, Brewers (December 4, 1989-91). ... Coach, St. Louis Cardinals (1992).
HONORS: Coach, N.L. All-Star team (1994). ... Named N.L. Manager of the Year by THE SPORTING NEWS (1995). ... Named N.L. Manager of the Year by Baseball Writers' Association of America (1995).

Year Team (League)	REGULAR SEASON				POSTSEASON								
					Playoff		Champ. Series		World Series		All-Star Game		
	W	L	Pct.	Pos.	W	L	W	L	W	L	W	L	
1993— Colorado (N.L.)	67	95	.414	6th (W)	—	—	—	—	—	—	—	—	
1994— Colorado (N.L.)	53	64	.453	—	—	—	—	—	—	—	—	—	
1995— Colorado (N.L.)	77	67	.535	2nd (W)	1	3	—	—	—	—	—	—	
1996— Colorado (N.L.)	83	79	.512	3rd (W)	—	—	—	—	—	—	—	—	
1997— Colorado (N.L.)	83	79	.512	3rd (W)	—	—	—	—	—	—	—	—	
Major league totals (5 years)	363	384	.486		1	3	—	—	—	—	—	—	

NOTES:
1994—Colorado was in third place in N.L. West at time of season-ending strike (August 12).
1995—Lost to Atlanta in N.L. divisional playoff.

PERSONAL: Born August 27, 1951, in Pittsburgh. ... 6-3/200. ... Batted right, threw right. ... Full name: David Gus Bell. ... Father of David Bell, second baseman, St. Louis Cardinals; father of Mike Bell, third baseman, Arizona Diamondbacks; and son of Gus Bell, major league outfielder with four teams (1950-64).

HIGH SCHOOL: Moeller (Cincinnati).

COLLEGE: Xavier, then Miami of Ohio.

TRANSACTIONS/CAREER NOTES: Selected by Cleveland Indians organization in 16th round of free-agent draft (June 5, 1969). ... On disabled list (May 27-June 17 and August 8-September 1, 1974). ... Traded by Indians to Texas Rangers for 3B Toby Harrah (December 8, 1978). ... On disabled list (June 9-24, 1980). ... Traded by Rangers to Cincinnati Reds for OF Duane Walker and a player to be named later (July 19, 1985); Rangers organization acquired P Jeff Russell to complete deal (July 23, 1985). ... On Cincinnati disabled list (March 26-April 10 and April 14-May 11, 1988). ... Traded by Reds to Houston Astros for a player to be named later (June 19, 1988); Reds organization acquired P Carl Grovom to complete deal (October 20, 1988). ... On Houston disabled list (August 4-19, 1988). ... Released by Astros (December 21, 1988). ... Signed by Rangers (January 9, 1989). ... On disabled list (April 8-28, 1989). ... Announced retirement (June 24, 1989).

HONORS: Won A.L. Gold Glove at third base (1979-84). ... Named third baseman on THE SPORTING NEWS A.L. All-Star team (1981 and 1984). ... Named third baseman on THE SPORTING NEWS A.L. Silver Slugger team (1984).

STATISTICAL NOTES: Led Gulf Coast League second basemen with 26 double plays in 1969. ... Led A.L. third basemen with 144 putouts and 44 double plays in 1973. ... Led A.L. third basemen with 495 total chances in 1978, 361 in 1981, 540 in 1982 and 523 in 1983. ... Tied for A.L. lead in double plays by third basemen with 30 in 1978. ... Had 21-game hitting streak (June 24-July 17, 1980). ... Led A.L. third basemen with 364 assists in 1979 and 281 in 1981. ... Led A.L. third basemen with .981 fielding percentage in 1980 and .976 in 1982. ... Led A.L. with 10 sacrifice flies in 1981. ... Career major league grand slams: 8.

							BATTING									FIELDING		
Year Team (League)	Pos.	G	AB	R	H	2B	3B	HR	RBI	Avg.	BB	SO	SB	PO	A	E	Avg.
1969— Sarasota (GCL)..........	2B	51	170	18	39	4	•3	3	24	.229	17	15	3	119	108	7	*.970
1970— Western Carolinas......	3B-2B-SS	121	442	81	117	19	3	12	75	.265	44	43	9	116	189	27	.919
1971— Wichita (A.A.)..............	3-2-S-O	129	470	65	136	23	1	11	59	.289	42	51	7	*139	203	16	.955
1972— Cleveland (A.L.)..........	OF-3B	132	466	49	119	21	1	9	36	.255	34	29	5	284	23	3	.990
1973— Cleveland (A.L.)..........	3B-OF	156	631	86	169	23	7	14	59	.268	49	47	7	†146	363	22	.959
1974— Cleveland (A.L.)..........	3B	116	423	51	111	15	1	7	46	.262	35	29	1	112	274	15	.963
1975— Cleveland (A.L.)..........	3B	153	553	66	150	20	4	10	59	.271	51	72	6	*146	330	25	.950
1976— Cleveland (A.L.)..........	3B-1B	159	604	75	170	26	2	7	60	.281	44	49	3	109	331	20	.957
1977— Cleveland (A.L.)..........	3B-OF	129	479	64	140	23	4	11	64	.292	45	63	1	134	253	16	.960
1978— Cleveland (A.L.)..........	3B	142	556	71	157	27	8	6	62	.282	39	43	1	125	*355	15	.970
1979— Texas (A.L.)■..............	3B-SS	•162	*670	89	200	42	3	18	101	.299	30	45	3	147	†429	17	.971
1980— Texas (A.L.)..............	3B-SS	129	490	76	161	24	4	17	83	.329	40	39	3	125	282	8	†.981
1981— Texas (A.L.)..............	3B-SS	97	360	44	106	16	1	10	64	.294	42	30	3	67	†284	14	.962
1982— Texas (A.L.)..............	3B-SS	148	537	62	159	27	2	13	67	.296	70	50	5	*131	397	13	†.976
1983— Texas (A.L.)..............	3B	156	618	75	171	35	3	14	66	.277	50	48	3	123	*383	17	.967
1984— Texas (A.L.)..............	3B	148	553	88	174	36	5	11	83	.315	63	54	2	129	323	•20	.958
1985— Texas (A.L.)..............	3B	84	313	33	74	13	3	4	32	.236	33	21	3	70	192	16	.942
— Cincinnati (N.L.)■......	3B	67	247	28	54	15	2	6	36	.219	34	27	0	54	105	9	.946
1986— Cincinnati (N.L.)	3B-2B	155	568	89	158	29	3	20	75	.278	73	49	2	105	291	10	.975
1987— Cincinnati (N.L.)	3B	143	522	74	148	19	2	17	70	.284	71	39	4	93	241	7	*.979
1988— Cincinnati (N.L.)	3B-1B	21	54	3	10	0	0	0	3	.185	7	3	0	14	26	2	.952
— Houston (N.L.)■........	3B-1B	74	269	24	68	10	1	7	37	.253	19	29	1	74	114	13	.935
1989— Texas (A.L.)..............	3B-1B	34	82	4	15	4	0	0	3	.183	7	10	0	10	13	0	1.000
American League totals (15 years)		1945	7335	933	2076	352	48	151	885	.283	632	629	48	1858	4232	221	.965
National League totals (4 years)		460	1660	218	438	73	8	50	221	.264	204	147	7	340	777	41	.965
Major league totals (18 years)		2405	8995	1151	2514	425	56	201	1106	.279	836	776	55	2198	5009	262	.965

ALL-STAR GAME RECORD

					BATTING								FIELDING		
Year League	Pos.	AB	R	H	2B	3B	HR	RBI	Avg.	BB	SO	SB	PO	A	E	Avg.
1973— American..................	PH	1	0	1	0	1	0	0	1.000	0	0	0	0	0	0	...
1980— American..................	3B	2	0	0	0	0	0	0	.000	0	1	0	2	0	1.000
1981— American..................	3B	1	0	0	0	0	0	1	.000	0	0	0	1	2	0	1.000
1982— American..................	PH-3B	3	0	0	0	0	0	0	.000	0	2	0	0	1	1	.500
1984— American..................	3B	1	0	0	0	0	0	0	.000	0	0	0	0	1	0	1.000
All-Star Game totals (5 years)		8	0	1	0	1	0	1	.125	0	3	0	1	6	1	.875

RECORD AS MANAGER

BACKGROUND: Minor league hitting instructor, Cleveland Indians organization (1990). ... Director of minor league instruction, Chicago White Sox organization (1991-93). ... Coach, Indians (1994-95).

		REGULAR SEASON				POSTSEASON						
						Playoff		Champ. Series		World Series		All-Star Game
Year Team (League)	W	L	Pct.	Pos.	W	L	W	L	W	L	W	L
1996— Detroit (A.L.).................................	53	109	.327	5th (E)	—	—	—	—	—	—	—	—
1997— Detroit (A.L.).................................	79	83	.488	3rd (E)	—	—	—	—	—	—	—	—
Major league totals (2 years)...................	132	192	.407		—	—	—	—	—	—	—	—

BOCHY, BRUCE
PADRES

PERSONAL: Born April 16, 1955, in Landes de Boussac, France. ... 6-4/225. ... Batted right, threw right. ... Full name: Bruce Douglas Bochy. ... Brother of Joe Bochy, catcher, Minnesota Twins organization (1969-72). ... Name pronounced BO-chee.

HIGH SCHOOL: Melbourne (Fla.).

JUNIOR COLLEGE: Brevard Community College (Fla.).

COLLEGE: Florida State.

TRANSACTIONS/CAREER NOTES: Selected by Chicago White Sox organization in eighth round of free-agent draft (January 9, 1975); did not sign. ... Selected by Houston Astros organization in secondary phase of free-agent draft (June 4, 1975). ... Traded by Astros to New York Mets organization for two players to be named later (February 11, 1981); Astros acquired IF Randy Rodgers and C Stan Hough to complete deal (April 3, 1981). ... Released by Mets (January 21, 1983). ... Signed by Las Vegas, San Diego Padres organization (February 23, 1983). ... On disabled list (April 13-May 6, 1987). ... Granted free agency (November 9, 1987).

STATISTICAL NOTES: Tied for Florida State League lead with 12 passed balls in 1977.

							BATTING							FIELDING		
Year Team (League)	Pos.	G	AB	R	H	2B	3B	HR	RBI	Avg.	BB	SO	SB	PO	A	E	Avg.
1975— Covington (Appal.)	C	37	145	31	49	9	0	4	34	.338	11	18	0	231	36	4	.985
1976— Columbus (Sou.)	C	69	230	9	53	6	0	0	16	.230	14	30	0	266	45	6	.981
— Dubuque (Midwest)....	C-1B	30	103	9	25	4	0	1	8	.243	12	11	1	165	25	5	.974
1977— Cocoa (Fla. St.)	C	128	430	40	109	18	2	3	35	.253	35	50	0	*492	67	12	.979
1978— Columbus (Sou.)	C	79	261	25	70	10	2	7	34	.268	13	30	0	419	49	7	.985
— Houston (N.L.)	C	54	154	8	41	8	0	3	15	.266	11	35	0	268	35	8	.974
1979— Houston (N.L.)	C	56	129	11	28	4	0	1	6	.217	17	25	0	198	29	7	.970
1980— Houston (N.L.)	C-1B	22	22	0	4	1	0	0	0	.182	0	0	0	19	1	0	1.000
1981— Tidewater (Int'l)■.....	C	85	269	23	61	11	2	8	38	.227	22	47	0	253	35	3	.990
1982— Tidewater (Int'l)	C	81	251	32	57	11	0	15	52	.227	19	47	2	427	57	5	.990
— New York (N.L.).........	C-1B	17	49	4	15	4	0	2	8	.306	4	6	0	92	8	4	.962
1983— Las Vegas (PCL)■	C	42	145	28	44	8	1	11	33	.303	15	25	3	157	21	3	.983
— San Diego (N.L.)	C	23	42	2	9	1	1	0	3	.214	0	9	0	51	5	0	1.000
1984— Las Vegas (PCL)	C	34	121	18	32	7	0	7	22	.264	17	13	0	189	17	2	.990
— San Diego (N.L.)	C	37	92	10	21	5	1	4	15	.228	3	21	0	147	12	2	.988
1985— San Diego (N.L.)	C	48	112	16	30	2	0	6	13	.268	6	30	0	148	11	2	.988
1986— San Diego (N.L.)	C	63	127	16	32	9	0	8	22	.252	14	23	1	202	22	2	.991
1987— San Diego (N.L.)	C	38	75	8	12	3	0	2	11	.160	11	21	0	95	7	4	.962
1988— Las Vegas (PCL)	C	53	147	17	34	5	0	5	13	.231	17	28	0	207	19	3	.987
Major league totals (9 years)		358	802	75	192	37	2	26	93	.239	66	170	1	1220	130	29	.979

CHAMPIONSHIP SERIES RECORD

							BATTING							FIELDING		
Year Team (League)	Pos.	G	AB	R	H	2B	3B	HR	RBI	Avg.	BB	SO	SB	PO	A	E	Avg.
1980— Houston (N.L.)	C	1	1	0	0	0	0	0	0	.000	0	0	0	5	1	0	1.000

WORLD SERIES RECORD

							BATTING							FIELDING		
Year Team (League)	Pos.	G	AB	R	H	2B	3B	HR	RBI	Avg.	BB	SO	SB	PO	A	E	Avg.
1984— San Diego (N.L.)	PH	1	1	0	1	0	0	0	0	1.000	0	0	0	...	...	...	...

RECORD AS MANAGER

BACKGROUND: Player/coach, Las Vegas, San Diego Padres organization (1988). ... Coach, Padres (1993-94).

HONORS: Named N.L. Manager of the Year by THE SPORTING NEWS (1996). ... Named N.L. Manager of the Year by the Baseball Writers' Association of America (1996). ... Coach, N.L. All-Star team (1997)

	REGULAR SEASON				POSTSEASON							
					Playoff		Champ. Series		World Series		All-Star Game	
Year Team (League)	W	L	Pct.	Pos.	W	L	W	L	W	L	W	L
1989— Spokane (Northwest)	41	34	.547	1st (N)	2	1	—	—	—	—	—	—
1990— Riverside (California)	35	36	.493	4th (S)	—	—	—	—	—	—	—	—
— (Second half)	29	42	.408	5th (S)	—	—	—	—	—	—	—	—
1991— High Desert (California)	31	37	.456	3rd (S)	—	—	—	—	—	—	—	—
— (Second half)	42	26	.618	1st (S)	6	2	—	—	—	—	—	—
1992— Wichita (Texas)	39	29	.574	1st (W)	—	—	—	—	—	—	—	—
— (Second half)	31	37	.456	4th (W)	6	1	—	—	—	—	—	—
1995— San Diego (N.L.)	70	74	.486	3rd (W)	—	—	—	—	—	—	—	—
1996— San Diego (N.L.)	91	71	.562	1st (W)	—	—	0	3	—	—	—	—
1997— San Diego (N.L.)	76	86	.469	4th (W)	—	—	—	—	—	—	—	—
Major league totals (3 years)............................	237	231	.506				0	3	—	—	—	—

NOTES:

1989—Defeated Southern Oregon in league championship.

1991—Defeated Bakersfield, three games to none, in semifinals; defeated Stockton, three games to two, in league championship.

1992—Defeated El Paso, two games to one, in semifinals; defeated Shreveport, four games to none, in league championship.

1996—Lost to St. Louis in N.L. divisional playoff.

COLLINS, TERRY   ANGELS

PERSONAL: Born May 27, 1949, in Midland, Mich. ... 5-8/160. ... Batted left, threw right. ... Full name: Terry Lee Collins.

HIGH SCHOOL: Midland (Mich.).

COLLEGE: Eastern Michigan (bachelor of science degree).

TRANSACTIONS/CAREER NOTES: Selected by Pittsburgh Pirates organization in 19th round of free-agent draft (June 8, 1971). ... Released by Pirates organization (January 7, 1974). ... Signed by Los Angeles Dodgers organization (January 14, 1974). ... On disabled list (July 2-August 6, 1976). ... Released by Dodgers organization (February 28, 1978). ... Signed by Dodgers organization as player (May 14, 1978). ... On disabled list (June 26-July 6, 1978). ... Signed as player/coach for Albuquerque Dukes for 1979. ... On temporarily inactive list (entire 1979 season). ... Released by Dodgers organization (December 7, 1979). ... Re-signed by Dodgers organization as coach (January 30, 1980); became player/coach for Dodgers organization (May 18, 1980). ... On disabled list (May 29-July 1 and July 12-August 17, 1980). ... Released by Dodgers organization (September 18, 1980). ... Re-signed by Dodgers organization as player/manager (August 17, 1984). ... Released as player by Dodgers organization (September 28, 1984).

STATISTICAL NOTES: Led New York-Pennsylvania League shortstops with 310 total chances and 37 double plays in 1971.

							BATTING							FIELDING		
Year Team (League)	Pos.	G	AB	R	H	2B	3B	HR	RBI	Avg.	BB	SO	SB	PO	A	E	Avg.
1971— Niagara Falls (NYP)	SS	70	265	51	81	12	3	1	26	.306	36	35	12	*112	*179	19	*.939
1972— Salem (Carolina)	2B	126	459	77	116	17	7	1	41	.253	70	75	8	*254	333	*25	.959

Year—Team (League)	Pos.	G	AB	R	H	2B	3B	HR	RBI	Avg.	BB	SO	SB	PO	A	E	Avg.
					BATTING										FIELDING		
1973—Sherbrooke (East.)	2-O-3-P-S	114	324	52	76	9	0	0	20	.235	59	54	7	177	206	12	.970
1974—Waterbury (Eastern)■	2B-SS	86	230	28	46	3	2	1	23	.200	46	42	2	144	243	11	.972
1975—Waterbury (Eastern)	SS	4	9	2	1	0	0	0	1	.111	3	2	0	3	9	2	.857
—Albuquerque (PCL)	2B-SS-3B	64	153	24	48	5	4	0	10	.314	18	19	2	87	53	11	.927
1976—Albuquerque (PCL)	3B-OF-SS	67	174	23	42	4	5	2	24	.241	19	21	6	46	64	3	.973
1977—Albuquerque (PCL)	2-3-S-P	54	158	27	39	6	3	0	15	.247	32	21	2	64	113	9	.952
1978—Albuquerque (PCL)	2-3-S-P-O-1	72	217	29	60	9	4	1	22	.276	21	20	4	115	162	12	.958
1979—								Did not play.									
1980—Albuquerque (PCL)	DH	11	14	1	2	0	0	0	1	.143	3	4	1	...	...	...	...
1981—								Did not play.									
1982—								Did not play.									
1983—								Did not play.									
1984—Albuquerque (PCL)	SS-2B	3	6	1	1	0	0	0	0	.167	0	0	0	5	3	0	1.000

RECORD AS PITCHER

Year—Team (League)	W	L	Pct.	ERA	G	GS	CG	ShO	Sv.	IP	H	R	ER	BB	SO
1973—Sherbrooke (Eastern)	0	0	...	2.25	3	0	0	0	2	4	3	1	1	3	0
1977—Albuquerque (PCL)	0	0	...	0.00	1	0	0	0	0	2	2	0	0	0	1
1978—Albuquerque (PCL)	0	0	...	0.00	2	0	0	0	1	3	1	0	0	1	1

RECORD AS MANAGER

BACKGROUND: Player/coach, Waterbury, Dodgers organization (1975). ... Player/coach, Albuquerque, Dodgers organization (1977-80). ... Coach, Pittsburgh Pirates (November 26, 1991-November 17, 1993).

HONORS: Named Minor League Manager of the Year by THE SPORTING NEWS (1987). ... Named Pacific Coast League Manager of the Year (1988). ... Coach, N.L. All-Star team (1995).

| Year—Team (League) | REGULAR SEASON | | | | POSTSEASON | | | | | | | | |
| | | | | | Playoff | | Champ. Series | | World Series | | All-Star Game | | |
	W	L	Pct.	Pos.	W	L	W	L	W	L	W	L
1981—Lodi (California)	30	40	.429	7th	—	—	—	—	—	—	—	—
—(Second half)	43	27	.614	T2nd	5	2	—	—	—	—	—	—
1982—Vero Beach (Florida State)	38	31	.551	2nd (S)	—	—	—	—	—	—	—	—
—(Second half)	42	22	.656	1st (S)	1	2	—	—	—	—	—	—
1983—San Antonio (Texas)	33	34	.493	3rd (W)	—	—	—	—	—	—	—	—
—(Second half)	3	4	.429		—	—	—	—	—	—	—	—
—Albuquerque (PCL), second half	42	26	.618	1st (S)	3	5	—	—	—	—	—	—
1984—Albuquerque (Pacific Coast)	36	36	.500	5th (S)	—	—	—	—	—	—	—	—
—(Second half)	26	45	.366	5th (S)	—	—	—	—	—	—	—	—
1985—Albuquerque (Pacific Coast)	36	35	.507	4th (S)	—	—	—	—	—	—	—	—
—(Second half)	31	41	.431	4th (S)	—	—	—	—	—	—	—	—
1986—Albuquerque (Pacific Coast)	28	43	.394	5th (S)	—	—	—	—	—	—	—	—
—(Second half)	26	45	.366	5th (S)	—	—	—	—	—	—	—	—
1987—Albuquerque (Pacific Coast)	43	27	.614	1ot (S)	—	—	—	—	—	—	—	—
—(Second half)	34	38	.472	4th (S)	6	1	—	—	—	—	—	—
1988—Albuquerque (Pacific Coast)	38	33	.535	2nd (S)	—	—	—	—	—	—	—	—
—(Second half)	48	23	.676	1st (S)	0	3	—	—	—	—	—	—
1989—Buffalo (American Association)	80	62	.563	2nd (E)	—	—	—	—	—	—	—	—
1990—Buffalo (American Association)	85	62	.578	2nd (E)	—	—	—	—	—	—	—	—
1991—Buffalo (American Association)	81	62	.566	1st (E)	2	3	—	—	—	—	—	—
1994—Houston (N.L.)	66	49	.574		—	—	—	—	—	—	—	—
1995—Houston (N.L.)	76	68	.528	2nd (C)	—	—	—	—	—	—	—	—
1996—Houston (N.L.)	82	80	.506	2nd (C)	—	—	—	—	—	—	—	—
1997—Anaheim (A.L.)	84	78	.519	2nd (W)	—	—	—	—	—	—	—	—
American League totals (1 year)	84	78	.519		—	—	—	—	—	—	—	—
National League totals (3 years)	224	197	.532		—	—	—	—	—	—	—	—
Major league totals (4 years)	308	275	.528		—	—	—	—	—	—	—	—

NOTES:
1981—Defeated Reno, two games to one, in semifinals; defeated Visalia, three games to two, in league championship.
1982—Lost to Fort Lauderdale in playoffs.
1983—Replaced Albuquerque manager Del Crandall (June 29). Defeated Las Vegas, three games to two, in playoffs; lost to Portland, three games to none, in league championship.
1987—Defeated Las Vegas, three games to none, in playoffs; defeated Calgary, three games to one, in league championship.
1988—Lost to Las Vegas in playoffs.
1991—Lost to Denver in league championship.
1994—Houston was in second place in N.L. Central at time of season-ending strike (August 12).

COX, BOBBY — BRAVES

PERSONAL: Born May 21, 1941, in Tulsa, Okla. ... 6-0/185. ... Batted right, threw right. ... Full name: Robert Joe Cox.
HIGH SCHOOL: Selma (Calif.).
JUNIOR COLLEGE: Reedley Junior College (Calif.).
TRANSACTIONS/CAREER NOTES: Signed by Los Angeles Dodgers organization (1959). ... Selected by Chicago Cubs organization from Dodgers organization in Rule 5 minor league draft (November 30, 1964). ... Acquired by Atlanta Braves organization (1966). ... On Austin disabled list (May 8-18 and May 30-June 9, 1966). ... On disabled list (May 1-June 12, 1967). ... Traded by Braves to New York Yankees for C Bob Tillman and P Dale Roberts (December 7, 1967); Roberts later was transferred to Richmond. ... On disabled list (May 28-June 18, 1970). ... Released by Yankees organization (September 22, 1970). ... Signed by Fort Lauderdale, Yankees organization (July 17, 1971). ... Released as player by Fort Lauderdale (August 28, 1971).
STATISTICAL NOTES: Led Alabama-Florida League shortstops with 71 double plays in 1961. ... Led Pacific Coast League third basemen with .954 fielding percentage in 1965.

Year	Team (League)	Pos.	G	AB	R	H	2B	3B	HR	RBI	Avg.	BB	SO	SB	PO	A	E	Avg.
1960—	Reno (California)	2B	125	440	99	112	20	5	13	75	.255	95	129	28	282	*385	*39	.945
1961—	Salem (Northwest)	2B	14	44	3	9	2	0	0	2	.205	0	14	0	25	25	2	.962
	—Panama City (Al.-Fla.)	2B	92	335	66	102	27	4	17	73	.304	48	72	17	220	247	8	*.983
1962—	Salem (Northwest)	3B-2B	*141	514	83	143	26	7	16	82	.278	63	119	7	174	296	28	.944
1963—	Albuquerque (Texas) ..	3B	17	53	5	15	2	0	2	5	.283	3	12	1	8	27	1	.972
	—Great Falls (Pio.)	3B	109	407	103	137	*31	4	19	85	.337	73	84	7	82	211	21	*.933
1964—	Albuquerque (Texas) ..	2B	138	523	98	152	29	13	16	91	.291	52	84	8	*322	*415	*28	.963
1965—	Salt Lake (PCL)■	3B-2B	136	473	58	125	32	1	12	55	.264	35	96	1	133	337	22	†.955
1966—	Tacoma (PCL)	3B-2B	10	34	2	4	1	0	0	4	.118	6	9	0	23	15	0	1.000
	—Austin (Texas)■	2B-3B	92	339	35	77	11	1	7	30	.227	25	55	7	140	216	12	.967
1967—	Richmond (Int'l)	3B-1B	99	350	52	104	17	4	14	51	.297	34	73	3	84	136	8	.965
1968—	New York (A.L.)■	3B	135	437	33	100	15	1	7	41	.229	41	85	3	98	279	17	.957
1969—	New York (A.L.)	3B	85	191	17	41	7	1	2	17	.215	34	41	0	50	147	11	.947
1970—	Syracuse (Int'l)	3B-SS-2B	90	251	34	55	15	0	9	30	.219	49	40	0	86	163	13	.950
1971—	Fort Lauder. (FSL)	2B-P	4	9	1	1	0	0	0	0	.111	1	0	0	4	5	0	1.000
Major league totals (2 years)			220	628	50	141	22	2	9	58	.225	75	126	3	148	426	28	.953

RECORD AS PITCHER

Year	Team (League)	W	L	Pct.	ERA	G	GS	CG	ShO	Sv.	IP	H	R	ER	BB	SO
1971—	Fort Lauderdale (FSL)	0	1	.000	5.40	3	0	0	0	0	10	15	9	6	5	4

RECORD AS MANAGER

BACKGROUND: Minor league instructor, New York Yankees (October 28, 1970-March 24, 1971). ... Player/manager, Fort Lauderdale, Yankees organization (1971). ... Coach, Yankees (1977).

HONORS: Coach, A.L. All-Star team (1985). ... Named Major League Manager of the Year by THE SPORTING NEWS (1985). ... Named A.L. Manager of the Year by the Baseball Writers' Association of America (1985). ... Named N.L. Manager of the Year by THE SPORTING NEWS (1991 and 1993). ... Named N.L. Manager of the Year by the Baseball Writers' Association of America (1991).

						REGULAR SEASON			POSTSEASON						
							Playoff		Champ. Series		World Series		All-Star Game		
Year	Team (League)	W	L	Pct.	Pos.		W	L	W	L	W	L	W	L	
1971—	Fort Lauderdale (Florida State)	71	70	.504	4th (E)		—	—	—	—	—	—	—	—	
1972—	West Haven (Eastern)	84	56	.600	1st (A)		3	0	—	—	—	—	—	—	
1973—	Syracuse (International)...........................	76	70	.521	3rd (A)		—	—	—	—	—	—	—	—	
1974—	Syracuse (International)...........................	74	70	.514	2nd (N)		—	—	—	—	—	—	—	—	
1975—	Syracuse (International)...........................	72	64	.529	3rd		—	—	—	—	—	—	—	—	
1976—	Syracuse (International)...........................	82	57	.590	2nd		6	1	—	—	—	—	—	—	
1978—	Atlanta (N.L.)	69	93	.426	6th (W)		—	—	—	—	—	—	—	—	
1979—	Atlanta (N.L.)	66	94	.413	6th (W)		—	—	—	—	—	—	—	—	
1980—	Atlanta (N.L.)	81	80	.503	4th (W)		—	—	—	—	—	—	—	—	
1981—	Atlanta (N.L.)	25	29	.463	4th (W)		—	—	—	—	—	—	—	—	
	—(Second half)	25	27	.481	5th (W)		—	—	—	—	—	—	—	—	
1982—	Toronto (A.L.)	78	84	.481	T6th (E)		—	—	—	—	—	—	—	—	
1983—	Toronto (A.L.)	89	73	.549	4th (E)		—	—	—	—	—	—	—	—	
1984—	Toronto (A.L.)	89	73	.549	2nd (E)		—	—	—	—	—	—	—	—	
1985—	Toronto (A.L.)	99	62	.615	1st (E)		—	—	3	4	—	—	—	—	
1990—	Atlanta (N.L.)	40	57	.412	6th (W)		—	—	—	—	—	—	—	—	
1991—	Atlanta (N.L.)	94	68	.580	1st (W)		—	—	4	3	3	4	—	—	
1992—	Atlanta (N.L.)	98	64	.605	1st (W)		—	—	4	3	2	4	0	1	
1993—	Atlanta (N.L.)	104	59	.642	1st (W)		—	—	2	4	—	—	0	1	
1994—	Atlanta (N.L.)	68	46	.596			—	—	—	—	—	—	—	—	
1995—	Atlanta (N.L.)	90	54	.625	1st (E)		3	1	4	0	4	2	—	—	
1996—	Atlanta (N.L.)	96	66	.593	1st (E)		3	0	4	3	2	4	1	0	
1997—	Atlanta (N.L.)	101	61	.623	1st (E)		3	0	2	4	—	—	0	1	
American League totals (4 years)		355	292	.549			—	—	3	4	—	—	—	—	
National League totals (12 years)		957	797	.546			9	1	20	17	11	14	1	3	
Major league totals (16 years)		1312	1089	.546			9	1	23	21	11	14	1	3	

NOTES:
1972—Defeated Three Rivers in playoff.
1976—Defeated Memphis, three games to none, in playoffs; defeated Richmond, three games to one, in league championship.
1985—Lost to Kansas City in A.L. Championship Series.
1990—Replaced Atlanta manager Russ Nixon with club in sixth place and record of 25-40 (June 22).
1991—Defeated Pittsburgh in N.L. Championship Series; lost to Minnesota in World Series.
1992—Defeated Pittsburgh in N.L. Championship Series; lost to Toronto in World Series.
1993—Lost to Philadelphia in N.L. Championship Series.
1994—Atlanta was in second place in N.L. East at time of season-ending strike (August 12).
1995—Defeated Colorado in N.L. divisional playoff; defeated Cincinnati in N.L. Championship Series; defeated Cleveland in World Series.
1996—Defeated Los Angeles in N.L. divisional playoff; defeated St. Louis in N.L. Championship Series; lost to New York Yankees in World Series.
1997—Defeated Houston in N.L. divisional playoff; lost to Florida in N.L. Championship Series.

DIERKER, LARRY   ASTROS

PERSONAL: Born September 22, 1946, in Hollywood, Calif. ... 6-4/205. ... Threw right, batted right. ... Full name: Lawrence Edward Dierker. ... Brother of Richard Dierker, pitcher, Baltimore Orioles organization (1972-75). ... Name pronounced DUR-ker..

COLLEGE: UC Santa Barbara, then Houston.

TRANSACTIONS/CAREER NOTES: Signed as free agent by Houston Astros organization (1964). ... Served in military (June 25, 1967-remainder of season). ... On disabled list (March 21-May 22 and June 16-July 12, 1973). ... Traded by Astros with IF Jerry DaVanon to St. Louis Cardinals for C/OF Joe Ferguson and OF Bobby Detherage (November 23, 1976). ... On disabled list (March 23-May 19 and July 23, 1977-remainder of season). ... Released by Cardinals (March 28, 1978).

STATISTICAL NOTES: Led N.L. with 20 wild pitches in 1968. ... Pitched 6-0 no-hit victory against Montreal (July 9, 1976).

MISCELLANEOUS: Holds Houston Astros franchise all-time records for most innings pitched (2,296) and most shutouts (25). ... Television and radio color analyst, Astros (1979-1996).

Year	Team (League)	W	L	Pct.	ERA	G	GS	CG	ShO	Sv.	IP	H	R	ER	BB	SO
1964—Cocoa (Cocoa Rookie)........		2	3	.400	3.23	9	9	0			39	21	19	14	18	61
—Houston (N.L.)		0	1	.000	2.00	.3	1	0	0	0	9	7	4	2	3	5
1965—Houston (N.L.)		7	8	.467	3.49	26	19	1	0	0	147	135	69	57	37	109
1966—Houston (N.L.)		10	8	.556	3.18	29	28	8	2	0	187	173	73	66	45	108
1967—Houston (N.L.)		6	5	.545	3.36	15	15	4	0	0	99	95	44	37	25	68
1968—Houston (N.L.)		12	15	.444	3.31	32	32	10	1	0	234	206	95	86	89	161
1969—Houston (N.L.)		20	13	.606	2.33	39	37	20	4	0	305	240	97	79	72	232
1970—Houston (N.L.)		16	12	.571	3.87	37	36	17	2	1	270	263	124	116	82	191
1971—Houston (N.L.)		12	6	.667	2.72	24	23	6	2	0	159	150	50	48	33	91
1972—Houston (N.L.)		15	8	.652	3.39	31	31	12	5	0	215	209	87	81	51	115
1973—Houston (N.L.)		1	1	.500	4.33	14	3	0	0	0	27	27	14	13	13	18
1974—Houston (N.L.)		11	10	.524	2.89	33	33	7	3	0	224	189	76	72	82	150
1975—Houston (N.L.)		14	16	.467	4.00	34	34	14	2	0	232	225	109	103	91	127
1976—Houston (N.L.)		13	14	.481	3.69	28	28	7	4	0	188	171	85	77	72	112
1977—St. Louis (N.L.)■		2	6	.250	4.62	11	9	0	0	0	39	40	21	20	16	6
Major league totals (14 years)....		**139**	**123**	**.531**	**3.30**	**356**	**329**	**106**	**25**	**1**	**2335**	**2130**	**948**	**857**	**711**	**1493**

ALL-STAR GAME RECORD

Year	League	W	L	Pct.	ERA	GS	CG	ShO	Sv.	IP	H	R	ER	BB	SO
1969— National		0	0	. . .	0.00	0	0	0	0	1/3	1	0	0	0	0
1971— National................................				Selected, did not play—injured.											

RECORD AS MANAGER

			REGULAR SEASON					POSTSEASON					
							Playoff		Champ. Series		World Series		All-Star Game
Year	Team (League)	W	L	Pct.	Pos.	W	L	W	L	W	L	W	L
1997—Houston (N.L.)..		84	78	.519	1st (C)	0	3	—	—	—	—	—	—

NOTES:
1997—Lost to Atlanta in N.L. divisional playoff.

FRANCONA, TERRY   PHILLIES

PERSONAL: Born April 22, 1959, in New Brighton, Pa. ... 6-1/175. ... Batted left, threw left. ... Full name: Terry Jon Francona. ... Son of Tito Francona, major league outfielder/first baseman with nine teams (1956-70).

HIGH SCHOOL: New Brighton (Pa.).

COLLEGE: Arizona.

TRANSACTIONS/CAREER NOTES: Selected by Chicago Cubs organization in second round of free-agent draft (June 7, 1977); did not sign. ... Selected by Montreal Expos organization in first round (22nd pick overall) of free-agent draft (June 3, 1980); pick received as compensation for New York Yankees signing free-agent P Rudy May. ... On disabled list (June 17-September 27, 1982 and June 15-September 5, 1984). ... Released by Expos (April 1, 1986). ... Signed by Chicago Cubs organization (May 2, 1986). ... Granted free agency (October 18, 1986). ... Signed by Cincinnati Reds (March 23, 1987). ... Granted free agency (November 12, 1987). ... Signed by Colorado Springs, Cleveland Indians organization (February 28, 1988). ... Granted free agency (November 4, 1988). ... Signed by Milwaukee Brewers (March 30, 1989). ... Granted free agency (November 13, 1989). ... Re-signed by Brewers (December 12, 1989). ... Released by Brewers (April 27, 1990). ... Signed by Louisville, St. Louis Cardinals organization (May 5, 1990). ... Released by Louisville (April 2, 1991).

HONORS: Named Golden Spikes Award winner by USA Baseball (1980). ... Named College Player of the Year by The Sporting News (1980). ... Named outfielder on The Sporting News college All-America team (1980).

							BATTING								FIELDING		
Year	Team (League)	Pos.	G	AB	R	H	2B	3B	HR	RBI	Avg.	BB	SO	SB	PO	A	E	Avg.
1980—Memphis (Southern)..		OF	60	210	20	63	13	2	1	23	.300	10	20	1	59	4	4	.940
1981—Memphis (Southern)..		OF-1B	41	161	20	56	8	1	0	18	.348	7	18	0	102	7	5	.956
—Denver (A.A.)............		OF	93	355	53	125	17	*9	1	58	.352	16	22	7	158	7	3	.982
—Montreal (N.L.)..........		OF-1B	34	95	11	26	0	1	1	8	.274	5	6	1	41	5	0	1.000
1982—Montreal (N.L.)..........		OF-1B	46	131	14	42	3	0	0	9	.321	8	11	2	65	0	3	.956
1983—Montreal (N.L.)..........		OF-1B	120	230	21	59	11	1	3	22	.257	6	20	0	172	10	3	.984
1984—Montreal (N.L.)..........		1B-OF	58	214	18	74	19	2	1	18	.346	5	12	0	431	50	3	.994
1985—Montreal (N.L.)..........		1B-3-OF	107	281	19	75	15	1	2	31	.267	12	12	5	431	40	6	.987
1986—Chicago (N.L.)■..........		OF-1B	86	124	13	31	3	0	2	8	.250	6	8	0	123	7	0	1.000
—Iowa (Am. Assoc.)......		1B-OF	17	60	7	15	3	2	0	8	.250	4	5	1	82	3	1	.988
1987—Cincinnati (N.L.)■......		1B-OF	102	207	16	47	5	0	3	12	.227	10	12	2	377	45	2	.995
1988—Colo. Spr. (PCL)■........		OF-1B	68	235	29	76	15	5	0	32	.323	13	18	0	115	11	3	.977
—Cleveland (A.L.)..........		DH-1B-OF	62	212	24	66	8	0	1	12	.311	5	18	0	47	5	1	.981
1989—Milwaukee (A.L.)■......		1-DH-O-P	90	233	26	54	10	1	3	23	.232	8	20	2	339	26	4	.989
1990—Milwaukee (A.L.)..........		1B	3	4	1	0	0	0	0	0	.000	0	0	0	6	0	0	1.000
—Louisville (A.A.)■.......		OF-1B-P	86	285	29	75	9	3	6	30	.263	12	23	1	126	7	3	.985
American League totals (3 years)			**155**	**449**	**51**	**120**	**18**	**1**	**4**	**35**	**.267**	**13**	**38**	**2**	**392**	**31**	**5**	**.988**
National League totals (7 years)			**553**	**1282**	**112**	**354**	**56**	**5**	**12**	**108**	**.276**	**52**	**81**	**10**	**1640**	**157**	**17**	**.991**
Major league totals (10 years)			**708**	**1731**	**163**	**474**	**74**	**6**	**16**	**143**	**.274**	**65**	**119**	**12**	**2032**	**188**	**22**	**.990**

DIVISION SERIES RECORD

							BATTING								FIELDING		
Year	Team (League)	Pos.	G	AB	R	H	2B	3B	HR	RBI	Avg.	BB	SO	SB	PO	A	E	Avg.
1981—Montreal (N.L.)...........		OF	5	12	0	4	0	0	0	0	.333	2	2	2	8	0	0	1.000

CHAMPIONSHIP SERIES RECORD

							BATTING								FIELDING		
Year	Team (League)	Pos.	G	AB	R	H	2B	3B	HR	RBI	Avg.	BB	SO	SB	PO	A	E	Avg.
1981—Montreal (N.L.)...........		PH-OF	2	1	0	0	0	0	0	0	.000	0	1	0	0	0	0	. . .

RECORD AS PITCHER

Year	Team (League)	W	L	Pct.	ERA	G	GS	CG	ShO	Sv.	IP	H	R	ER	BB	SO
1989— Milwaukee (A.L.)		0	0	...	0.00	1	0	0	0	0	1	0	0	0	0	1
1990— Louisville (A.A.)		0	0	...	1.17	5	0	0	0	0	7 2/3	4	1	1	2	6
Major league totals (1 year)		0	0	...	0.00	1	0	0	0	0	1	0	0	0	0	1

RECORD AS MANAGER

BACKGROUND: Manager, Scottsdale Scorpions, Arizona Fall League (1994, record: 26-25, second place/Northern Division). ... Coach, Detroit Tigers (1996).

HONORS: Named Southern League Manager of the Year (1993).

		REGULAR SEASON					POSTSEASON						
						Playoff		Champ. Series		World Series		All-Star Game	
Year	Team (League)	W	L	Pct.	Pos.	W	L	W	L	W	L	W	L
1992— South Bend (Midwest)	35	33	.515	3rd (N)	—	—	—	—	—	—	—	—
— (Second half)	38	31	.551	2nd (N)	—	—	—	—	—	—	—	—
1993— Birmingham (Southern)	35	36	.493	2nd (W)	—	—	—	—	—	—	—	—
— (Second half)	43	28	.606	1st (W)	6	1	—	—	—	—	—	—
1994— Birmingham (Southern)	31	38	.449	4th (W)	—	—	—	—	—	—	—	—
— (Second half)	34	36	.486	5th (W)	—	—	—	—	—	—	—	—
1995— Birmingham (Southern)	33	39	.458	4th (W)	—	—	—	—	—	—	—	—
— (Second half)	47	25	.653	2nd (W)	—	—	—	—	—	—	—	—
1997— Philadelphia (N.L.)	68	94	.420	5th (E)	—	—	—	—	—	—	—	—

NOTES:

1992—South Bend tied one game in first half of season.

1993—Defeated Nashville, three games to none, in first round; defeated Knoxville, three games to one, in league championship.

GARNER, PHIL   BREWERS

PERSONAL: Born April 30, 1949, in Jefferson City, Tenn. ... 5-10/177. ... Batted right, threw right. ... Full name: Philip Mason Garner.

HIGH SCHOOL: Beardon (Knoxville, Tenn.).

COLLEGE: Tennessee (degree in general business, 1973).

TRANSACTIONS/CAREER NOTES: Selected by Montreal Expos organization in eighth round of free-agent draft (June 4, 1970); did not sign. ... Selected by Oakland Athletics organization in secondary phase of free-agent draft (January 13, 1971). ... Traded by A's with IF Tommy Helms and P Chris Batton to Pittsburgh Pirates for P Doc Medich, P Dave Giusti, P Rick Langford, P Doug Bair, OF Mitchell Page and OF Tony Armas (March 15, 1977). ... On Pittsburgh disabled list (April 2-23, 1981). ... Traded by Pirates to Houston Astros for 2B Johnny Ray and two players to be named later (August 31, 1981); Pirates organization acquired OF Kevin Houston and P Randy Niemann to complete deal (September 9, 1981). ... Granted free agency (November 12, 1986). ... Re-signed by Astros (January 6, 1987). ... Traded by Astros to Los Angeles Dodgers for a player to be named later (June 19, 1987); Astros organization acquired P Jeff Edwards to complete deal (June 26, 1987). ... Granted free agency (November 9, 1987). ... Signed by San Francisco Giants (January 28, 1988). ... On San Francisco disabled list (April 13-September 2, 1988); included rehabilitation assignment to Phoenix (August 5-24). ... Granted free agency (November 3, 1988).

RECORDS: Shares major league record for most grand slams in two consecutive games—2 (September 14 and 15, 1978).

STATISTICAL NOTES: Led Pacific Coast League third basemen with 104 putouts, 261 assists, 35 errors, 400 total chances and 23 double plays in 1973. ... Led A.L. second basemen with 26 errors in 1975. ... Led A.L. second basemen with 865 total chances in 1976. ... Led N.L. second basemen with 499 assists, 21 errors, 869 total chances and 116 double plays in 1980. ... Career major league grand slams: 3.

							BATTING							FIELDING			
Year	Team (League)	Pos.	G	AB	R	H	2B	3B	HR	RBI	Avg.	BB	SO	SB	PO	A	E	Avg.
1971— Burlington (Midw.)	3B	116	439	73	122	22	4	11	70	.278	49	73	8	*122	203	29	.918
1972— Biringham. (Sou.)	3B	71	264	45	74	10	6	12	40	.280	27	43	3	74	116	13	.936
— Iowa (Am. Assoc.)	3B	70	247	33	60	18	4	9	22	.243	30	73	7	50	140	10	.950
1973— Tucson (PCL)	3B-SS	138	516	87	149	23	12	14	73	.289	72	90	3	†107	†270	†35	.915
— Oakland (A.L.)	3B	9	5	0	0	0	0	0	0	.000	0	3	0	2	3	0	1.000
1974— Tucson (PCL)	3B-SS	96	388	78	128	29	10	11	51	.330	53	58	4	92	182	15	.948
— Oakland (A.L.)	3B-SS-2B	30	28	4	5	1	0	0	1	.179	1	5	1	11	24	1	.972
1975— Oakland (A.L.)	2B-SS	•160	488	46	120	21	5	6	54	.246	30	65	4	355	427	†26	.968
1976— Oakland (A.L.)	2B	159	555	54	145	29	12	8	74	.261	36	71	35	378	*465	22	.975
1977— Pittsburgh (N.L.)■	3B-2B-SS	153	585	99	152	35	10	17	77	.260	55	65	32	223	351	17	.971
1978— Pittsburgh (N.L.)	3B-2B-SS	154	528	66	138	25	9	10	66	.261	66	71	27	258	389	28	.959
1979— Pittsburgh (N.L.)	3B-2B-SS	150	549	76	161	32	8	11	59	.293	55	74	17	234	396	22	.966
1980— Pittsburgh (N.L.)	2B-SS	151	548	62	142	27	6	5	58	.259	46	53	32	349	†500	†21	.976
1981— Pittsburgh (N.L.)	2B	56	181	22	46	6	2	1	20	.254	21	21	4	121	148	9	.968
— Houston (N.L.)■	2B	31	113	13	27	3	1	0	6	.239	15	11	6	62	102	3	.982
1982— Houston (N.L.)	2B-3B	155	588	65	161	33	8	13	83	.274	40	92	24	285	464	17	.978
1983— Houston (N.L.)	3B	154	567	76	135	24	2	14	79	.238	63	84	18	100	311	24	.945
1984— Houston (N.L.)	3B-2B	128	374	60	104	17	6	4	45	.278	43	63	3	136	251	12	.970
1985— Houston (N.L.)	3B-2B	135	463	65	124	23	10	6	51	.268	34	72	4	101	229	21	.940
1986— Houston (N.L.)	3B-2B	107	313	43	83	14	3	9	41	.265	30	45	12	66	152	23	.905
1987— Houston (N.L.)	SS-2B	43	112	15	25	5	0	3	15	.223	8	20	1	28	55	2	.976
— Los Angeles (N.L.)■	3B-2B-SS	70	126	14	24	4	0	2	8	.190	20	24	5	37	89	11	.920
1988— San Fran. (N.L.)■	3B	15	13	0	2	0	0	0	1	.154	1	3	0	0	0	0	...
— Phoenix (PCL)	2B-3B	17	45	5	12	2	1	1	5	.267	4	4	0	12	22	0	1.000
American League totals (4 years)		358	1076	104	270	51	17	14	129	.251	67	144	40	746	919	49	.971
National League totals (12 years)		1502	5060	676	1324	248	65	95	609	.262	497	698	185	2000	3437	210	.963
Major league totals (16 years)		1860	6136	780	1594	299	82	109	738	.260	564	842	225	2746	4356	259	.965

DIVISION SERIES RECORD

							BATTING							FIELDING		
Year	Team (League)	Pos.	G	AB	R	H	2B	3B	HR	RBI	Avg.	BB	SO	SB	PO	A	E	Avg.
1981— Houston (N.L.)	2B	5	18	1	2	0	0	0	0	.111	3	3	0	6	8	1	.933

CHAMPIONSHIP SERIES RECORD

							BATTING								FIELDING		
Year	Team (League)	Pos.	G	AB	R	H	2B	3B	HR	RBI	Avg.	BB	SO	SB	PO	A	E	Avg.
1975—	Oakland (A.L.)	2B	3	5	0	0	0	0	0	0	.000	0	1	0	7	4	1	.917
1979—	Pittsburgh (N.L.)	2B-SS	3	12	4	5	0	1	1	1	.417	1	0	0	8	9	0	1.000
1986—	Houston (N.L.)	3B	3	9	1	2	1	0	0	2	.222	1	2	0	1	9	0	1.000
Championship series totals (3 years)			9	26	5	7	1	1	1	3	.269	2	3	0	16	22	1	.974

WORLD SERIES RECORD

RECORDS: Shares single-series record for collecting one or more hits in each game (1979).
NOTES: Member of World Series championship team (1979).

							BATTING								FIELDING		
Year	Team (League)	Pos.	G	AB	R	H	2B	3B	HR	RBI	Avg.	BB	SO	SB	PO	A	E	Avg.
1979—	Pittsburgh (N.L.)	2B	7	24	4	12	4	0	0	5	.500	3	1	0	21	23	2	.957

ALL-STAR GAME RECORD

					BATTING								FIELDING		
Year	League	Pos.	AB	R	H	2B	3B	HR	RBI	Avg.	BB	SO	SB	PO	A	E	Avg.
1976—	American	2B	1	0	0	0	0	0	0	.000	0	1	0	1	1	0	1.000
1980—	National	2B	2	1	1	0	0	0	0	.500	1	1	1	1	3	0	1.000
1981—	National	2B	0	0	0	0	0	0	0	...	0	0	0	0	0	0	...
All-Star Game totals (3 years)			3	1	1	0	0	0	0	.333	1	2	1	2	4	0	1.000

RECORD AS MANAGER

BACKGROUND: Coach, Houston Astros (1989-91).
HONORS: Coach, A.L. All-Star team (1995).

		REGULAR SEASON				POSTSEASON								
						Playoff		Champ. Series		World Series		All-Star Game	
Year	Team (League)	W	L	Pct.	Pos.	W	L	W	L	W	L	W	L
1992—	Milwaukee (A.L.)	92	70	.568	2nd (E)	—	—	—	—	—	—	—	—
1993—	Milwaukee (A.L.)	69	93	.426	7th (E)	—	—	—	—	—	—	—	—
1994—	Milwaukee (A.L.)	53	62	.461		—	—	—	—	—	—	—	—
1995—	Milwaukee (A.L.)	65	79	.451	4th (C)	—	—	—	—	—	—	—	—
1996—	Milwaukee (A.L.)	80	82	.494	3rd (C)	—	—	—	—	—	—	—	—
1997—	Milwaukee (A.L.)	78	83	.484	3rd (C)	—	—	—	—	—	—	—	—
Major league totals (6 years)		437	469	.482		—	—	—	—	—	—	—	—

NOTES:
1993—On suspended list (September 24-27).
1994—Milwaukee was in fifth place in A.L. Central at time of season-ending strike (August 12).
1995—On suspended list (July 27-31).

HARGROVE, MIKE   INDIANS

PERSONAL: Born October 26, 1949, in Perryton, Texas. ... 6-0/195. ... Batted left, threw left. ... Full name: Dudley Michael Hargrove.
HIGH SCHOOL: Perryton (Texas).
COLLEGE: Northwestern State, Okla. (degree in physical education and social sciences).
TRANSACTIONS/CAREER NOTES: Selected by Texas Rangers organization in 25th round of free-agent draft (June 6, 1972). ... Traded by Rangers with 3B Kurt Bevacqua and C Bill Fahey to San Diego Padres for OF Oscar Gamble, C Dave Roberts and cash (October 25, 1978). ... Traded by Padres to Cleveland Indians for OF Paul Dade (June 14, 1979). ... Granted free agency (November 12, 1985).
HONORS: Named Texas League Player of the Year (1973). ... Named A.L. Rookie Player of the Year by THE SPORTING NEWS (1974). ... Named A.L. Rookie of the Year by Baseball Writers' Association of America (1974).
STATISTICAL NOTES: Led New York-Pennsylvania League first basemen with 58 double plays in 1972. ... Led Western Carolinas League with 247 total bases in 1973. ... Led Western Carolinas League first basemen with 118 double plays in 1973. ... Had 23-game hitting streak (April 16-May 15, 1980). ... Led A.L. first basemen with 1,489 total chances in 1980. ... Led A.L. with .432 on-base percentage in 1981. ... Career major league grand slams: 1.

							BATTING								FIELDING		
Year	Team (League)	Pos.	G	AB	R	H	2B	3B	HR	RBI	Avg.	BB	SO	SB	PO	A	E	Avg.
1972—	Geneva (NY-Penn)	1B	•70	243	38	65	8	0	4	37	.267	52	44	3	*537	•40	10	*.983
1973—	Gastonia (W. Car.)	1B	•130	456	88	*160	*35	8	12	82	*.351	68	47	10	*1121	•77	14	*.988
1974—	Texas (A.L.)	1B-DH-OF	131	415	57	134	18	6	4	66	.323	49	42	0	638	72	9	.987
1975—	Texas (A.L.)	OF-1B-DH	145	519	82	157	22	2	11	62	.303	79	66	4	513	45	13	.977
1976—	Texas (A.L.)	1B	151	541	80	155	30	1	7	58	.287	*97	64	2	1222	110	*21	.984
1977—	Texas (A.L.)	1B	153	525	98	160	28	4	18	69	.305	103	59	2	1393	100	11	.993
1978—	Texas (A.L.)	1B-DH	146	494	63	124	24	1	7	40	.251	*107	47	2	1221	*116	*17	.987
1979—	San Diego (N.L.)■	1B	52	125	15	24	5	0	0	8	.192	25	15	0	323	17	5	.986
	Cleveland (A.L.)■......	OF-1B-DH	100	338	60	110	21	4	10	56	.325	63	40	2	356	16	2	.995
1980—	Cleveland (A.L.)	1B	160	589	86	179	22	2	11	85	.304	111	36	4	*1391	88	10	.993
1981—	Cleveland (A.L.)	1B-DH	94	322	43	102	21	0	2	49	.317	60	16	5	766	76	•9	.989
1982—	Cleveland (A.L.)	1B-DH	160	591	67	160	26	1	4	65	.271	101	58	2	1293	*123	5	.996
1983—	Cleveland (A.L.)	1B-DH	134	469	57	134	21	4	3	57	.286	78	40	0	1098	115	7	.994
1984—	Cleveland (A.L.)	1B	133	352	44	94	14	2	2	44	.267	53	38	0	790	83	8	.991
1985—	Cleveland (A.L.)	1B-DH-OF	107	284	31	81	14	1	1	27	.285	39	29	1	599	66	6	.991
American League totals (12 years)			1614	5439	768	1590	261	28	80	678	.292	940	535	24	11280	1010	118	.990
National League totals (1 year)			52	125	15	24	5	0	0	8	.192	25	15	0	323	17	5	.986
Major league totals (12 years)			1666	5564	783	1614	266	28	80	686	.290	965	550	24	11603	1027	123	.990

ALL-STAR GAME RECORD

					BATTING								FIELDING		
Year	League	Pos.	AB	R	H	2B	3B	HR	RBI	Avg.	BB	SO	SB	PO	A	E	Avg.
1975—	American	PH	1	0	0	0	0	0	0	.000	0	0	0	...	...	...	...

RECORD AS MANAGER

BACKGROUND: Minor league coach, Cleveland Indians organization (1986). ... Coach, Indians (1990-July 6, 1991).

HONORS: Named Carolina League Manager of the Year (1987). ... Named Pacific Coast League Manager of the Year (1989). ... Coach, A.L. All-Star team (1994 and 1997). ... Named A.L. Manager of the Year by THE SPORTING NEWS (1995).

| | | | | | ——— REGULAR SEASON ——— | | | | ——— POSTSEASON ——— | | | | |
| | | | | | | | Playoff | | Champ. Series | | World Series | | All-Star Game | |
Year	Team (League)	W	L	Pct.	Pos.	W	L	W	L	W	L	W	L
1987—	Kinston (Carolina)	33	37	.471	T3rd (S)	—	—	—	—	—	—	—	—
	— (Second half)	42	28	.600	1st (S)	3	3	—	—	—	—	—	—
1988—	Williamsport (Eastern)	66	73	.475	6th	—	—	—	—	—	—	—	—
1989—	Colorado Springs (Pacific Coast)	44	26	.629	1st (S)	—	—	—	—	—	—	—	—
	— (Second half)	34	38	.472	3rd (S)	2	3	—	—	—	—	—	—
1991—	Cleveland (A.L.)	32	53	.376	7th (E)	—	—	—	—	—	—	—	—
1992—	Cleveland (A.L.)	76	86	.469	T4th (E)	—	—	—	—	—	—	—	—
1993—	Cleveland (A.L.)	76	86	.469	6th (E)	—	—	—	—	—	—	—	—
1994—	Cleveland (A.L.)	66	47	.584		—	—	—	—	—	—	—	—
1995—	Cleveland (A.L.)	100	44	.694	1st (C)	3	0	4	2	2	4	—	—
1996—	Cleveland (A.L.)	99	62	.615	1st (C)	1	3	—	—	—	—	0	1
1997—	Cleveland (A.L.)	86	75	.534	1st (C)	3	2	4	2	3	4	—	—
	Major league totals (7 years)	535	453	.541		7	5	8	4	5	8	0	1

NOTES:

1987—Defeated Winston-Salem, two games to none, in playoffs; lost to Salem, three games to one, in league championship.

1989—Lost to Albuquerque in playoffs.

1991—Replaced Cleveland manager John McNamara with club in seventh place and record of 25-52 (July 6).

1994—Cleveland was in second place in A.L. Central at time of season-ending strike (August 12).

1995—Defeated Boston in A.L. divisional playoff; defeated Seattle in A.L. Championship Series; lost to Atlanta in World Series.

1996—Lost to Baltimore in A.L. divisional playoff.

1997—Defeated New York in A.L. divisional playoff; defeated Baltimore in A.L. Championship Series; lost to Florida in World Series.

HOWE, ART   ATHLETICS

PERSONAL: Born December 15, 1946, in Pittsburgh. ... 6-1/185. ... Batted right, threw right. ... Full name: Arthur Henry Howe Jr.

HIGH SCHOOL: Shaler (Glenshaw, Pa.).

COLLEGE: Wyoming (bachelor of science degree in business administration, 1969).

TRANSACTIONS/CAREER NOTES: Signed as free agent by Pittsburgh Pirates organization (June, 1971). ... On disabled list (August 17-September 2, 1972 and April 13-May 6, 1973). ... Traded by Pirates to Houston Astros (January 6, 1976), completing deal in which Astros traded 2B Tommy Helms to Pirates for a player to be named later (December 12, 1975). ... On disabled list (May 12-June 19, 1982 and March 27, 1983-entire season). ... Granted free agency (November 7, 1983). ... Signed by St. Louis Cardinals (March 21, 1984). ... Released by Cardinals (April 22, 1985).

STATISTICAL NOTES: Tied for Carolina League lead in putouts by third baseman with 95 in 1971. ... Led International League third basemen with 22 errors and 24 double plays in 1972. ... Had 23-game hitting streak (May 1-24, 1981). ... Career major league grand slams: 1.

| | | | | | | | | ——— BATTING ——— | | | | | | | ——— FIELDING ——— | | | |
Year	Team (League)	Pos.	G	AB	R	H	2B	3B	HR	RBI	Avg.	BB	SO	SB	PO	A	E	Avg.
1971—	Salem (Carolina)	3B-SS	114	382	77	133	27	7	12	79	*.348	82	74	11	‡110	221	21	.940
1972—	Char., W.Va. (Int'l)	3B-2B-SS	109	365	68	99	21	3	14	53	.271	63	69	8	105	248	†24	.936
1973—	Char., W.Va. (Int'l)	3B-2B-SS	119	372	50	85	20	1	8	44	.228	54	70	6	141	229	21	.946
1974—	Char., W.Va. (Int'l)	3B	60	207	26	70	17	4	8	36	.338	31	27	4	35	90	9	.933
	— Pittsburgh (N.L.)	3B-SS	29	74	10	18	4	1	1	5	.243	9	13	0	11	49	4	.938
1975—	Char., W.Va. (Int'l)	3B-2B	11	42	4	15	1	3	0	3	.357	2	4	0	15	23	1	.974
	— Pittsburgh (N.L.)	3B-SS	63	146	13	25	9	0	1	10	.171	15	15	1	19	89	7	.939
1976—	Memphis (Int'l)■	3B-1B	74	259	50	92	21	3	12	59	.355	34	31	1	93	120	14	.938
	— Houston (N.L.)	3B-2B	21	29	0	4	1	0	0	0	.138	6	6	0	17	16	1	.971
1977—	Houston (N.L.)	2B-3B-SS	125	413	44	109	23	7	8	58	.264	41	60	0	213	333	8	.986
1978—	Houston (N.L.)	2B-3B-1B	119	420	46	123	33	3	7	55	.293	34	41	2	240	302	13	.977
1979—	Houston (N.L.)	2B-3B-1B	118	355	32	88	15	2	6	33	.248	36	37	3	188	261	7	.985
1980—	Houston (N.L.)	1-3-2-S	110	321	34	91	12	5	10	46	.283	34	29	1	598	86	10	.986
1981—	Houston (N.L.)	3B-1B	103	361	43	107	22	4	3	46	.296	41	23	1	67	206	9	.968
1982—	Houston (N.L.)	3B-1B	110	365	29	87	15	1	5	38	.238	41	45	2	344	174	7	.987
1983—								Did not play.											
1984—	St. Louis (N.L.)■	3-1-2-S	89	139	17	30	5	0	2	12	.216	18	18	0	71	80	3	.981
1985—	St. Louis (N.L.)	1B-3B	4	3	0	0	0	0	0	0	.000	0	0	0	5	1	0	1.000
	Major league totals (11 years)		891	2626	268	682	139	23	43	293	.260	275	287	10	1773	1597	69	.980

DIVISION SERIES RECORD

| | | | | | | | ——— BATTING ——— | | | | | | | ——— FIELDING ——— | | | |
Year	Team (League)	Pos.	G	AB	R	H	2B	3B	HR	RBI	Avg.	BB	SO	SB	PO	A	E	Avg.
1981—	Houston (N.L.)	3B	5	17	1	4	0	0	1	1	.235	2	1	0	6	9	0	1.000

CHAMPIONSHIP SERIES RECORD

| | | | | | | | ——— BATTING ——— | | | | | | | ——— FIELDING ——— | | | |
Year	Team (League)	Pos.	G	AB	R	H	2B	3B	HR	RBI	Avg.	BB	SO	SB	PO	A	E	Avg.
1974—	Pittsburgh (N.L.)	PH	1	1	0	0	0	0	0	0	.000	0	0	0	...	...	...	...
1980—	Houston (N.L.)	1B-PH	5	15	0	3	1	1	0	2	.200	2	2	0	29	3	0	1.000
	Championship series totals (2 years)		6	16	0	3	1	1	0	2	.188	2	2	0	29	3	0	1.000

RECORD AS MANAGER

BACKGROUND: Coach, Texas Rangers (May 21, 1985-88). ... Scout, Los Angeles Dodgers organization (1994). ... Coach, Colorado Rockies (1995).

HONORS: Coach, N.L. All-Star team (1991).

		REGULAR SEASON				POSTSEASON							
						Playoff		Champ. Series		World Series		All-Star Game	
Year	Team (League)	W	L	Pct.	Pos.	W	L	W	L	W	L	W	L
1989— Houston (N.L.)		86	76	.531	3rd (W)	—	—	—	—	—	—	—	—
1990— Houston (N.L.)		75	87	.463	T4th (W)	—	—	—	—	—	—	—	—
1991— Houston (N.L.)		65	97	.401	6th (W)	—	—	—	—	—	—	—	—
1992— Houston (N.L.)		81	81	.500	4th (W)	—	—	—	—	—	—	—	—
1993— Houston (N.L.)		85	77	.525	3rd (W)	—	—	—	—	—	—	—	—
1996— Oakland (A.L.)		78	84	.481	3rd (W)	—	—	—	—	—	—	—	—
1997— Oakland (A.L.)		65	97	.401	4th (W)	—	—	—	—	—	—	—	—
National League totals (5 years)		392	418	.484		—	—	—	—	—	—	—	—
American League totals (2 years)		143	181	.441		—	—	—	—	—	—	—	—
Major league totals (7 years)		535	599	.472		—	—	—	—	—	—	—	—

JOHNSON, TIM   BLUE JAYS

PERSONAL: Born July 22, 1949, in Grand Forks, N.D. ... 6-3/185. ... Batted left, threw right. ... Full name: Timothy Evald Johnson. ... Brother of Sandy Johnson, special assistant to Arizona Diamondbacks general manager and former minor league player and manager.

HIGH SCHOOL: Montebello (Calif.).

TRANSACTIONS/CAREER NOTES: Signed as non-drafted free agent by Los Angeles Dodgers organization (August 10, 1967). ... Traded by Dodgers to Milwaukee Brewers for SS Rick Auerbach (April 24, 1973). ... On disabled list (June 24-July 11 and July 28-September 26, 1975). ... On disabled list (July 11-August 2 and August 19-September 15, 1977). ... Traded by Brewers to Toronto Blue Jays for IF Tim Nordbrook (April 28, 1978). ... Released by Blue Jays (November 1, 1979).

STATISTICAL NOTES: Led California League shortstops with 69 double plays and tied for lead in putouts with 231 in 1968.

					BATTING										FIELDING		
Year	Team (League)	Pos.	G	AB	R	H	2B	3B	HR	RBI	Avg.	BB	SO	SB	PO	A	E	Avg.
1968— Bakersfield (Calif.)	SS-OF-2B	134	494	57	111	22	2	2	40	.225	37	140	9	‡232	344	41	.934
1969— Albuquerque (Tex.)	SS	92	328	33	81	8	2	1	24	.247	16	73	8	148	287	32	.931
1970— Albuquerque (Tex.)	SS	102	361	45	95	17	8	6	40	.263	24	58	5	177	315	11	*.978
1971— Spokane (PCL)	SS-2B-3B	98	305	38	75	10	1	2	20	.246	39	61	3	141	247	27	.935
1972— El Paso (Texas)	SS	112	409	46	99	11	3	6	35	.242	23	109	6	144	294	35	.926
1973— Albuquerque (PCL)	SS	8	27	2	7	0	0	0	4	.259	3	3	0	9	33	0	1.000
— Milwaukee (A.L.)■	SS	136	465	39	99	10	2	0	32	.213	29	93	6	*253	381	25	.962
1974— Milwaukee (A.L.)	S-2-0-3	93	245	25	60	7	7	0	25	.245	11	48	4	139	230	9	.976
1975— Milwaukee (A.L.)	2-3-S-1	38	85	6	12	1	0	0	2	.141	6	17	3	38	63	5	.953
1976— Milwaukee (A.L.)	2-3-S-1	105	273	25	75	4	3	0	14	.275	19	32	4	167	238	8	.981
1977— Milwaukee (A.L.)	2-S-3-0	30	33	5	2	1	0	0	2	.061	5	10	1	17	19	1	.973
1978— Milwaukee (A.L.)	SS	3	3	1	0	0	0	0	0	.000	2	0	1	1	0	0	1.000
— Toronto (A.L.)■■	SS-2B	68	79	9	19	2	0	0	3	.241	8	16	0	37	92	2	.985
1979— Toronto (A.L.)	2B-3B-1B	43	86	6	16	2	1	0	6	.186	8	15	0	91	70	7	.958
Major league totals (7 years)		516	1269	116	283	27	13	0	84	.223	88	231	18	743	1093	57	.970

RECORD AS MANAGER

BACKGROUND: Scout, Major League Scouting Bureau (1980-82). ... Scout, Los Angeles Dodgers (1983-86). ... Scout, Montreal Expos (1991-92). ... Coach, Expos (1993-94). ... Coach, Boston Red Sox (1995-96).

HONORS: Named Pioneer League Manager of the Year (1987 and 1988).

		REGULAR SEASON				POSTSEASON							
						Playoff		Champ. Series		World Series		All-Star Game	
Year	Team (League)	W	L	Pct.	Pos.	W	L	W	L	W	L	W	L
1987— Great Falls (Pioneer)		35	34	.507	3rd (N)	—	—	—	—	—	—	—	—
1988— Great Falls (Pioneer)		52	17	.754	1st (N)	3	2	—	—	—	—	—	—
1989— Bakersfield (California)		41	30	.577	1st (S)	—	—	—	—	—	—	—	—
— (Second half)		41	30	.577	T2nd (S)	6	1	—	—	—	—	—	—
1990— Indianapolis (American Association)		61	85	.418	4th (E)	—	—	—	—	—	—	—	—
1997— Iowa (American Association)		74	69	.517	1st (W)	3	3	—	—	—	—	—	—

NOTES:
1988—Defeated Butte in league championship
1989—Defeated San Bernardino, three games to one, in playoffs; defeated Stockton, three games to none, in league championship.
1997—Defeated New Orleans, three games to none; lost to Buffalo, three games to none, in league championship.

KELLY, TOM   TWINS

PERSONAL: Born August 15, 1950, in Graceville, Minn. ... 5-11/185. ... Batted left, threw left. ... Full name: Jay Thomas Kelly.

HIGH SCHOOL: St. Mary's (South Amboy, N.J.).

JUNIOR COLLEGE: Mesa (Ariz.) Community College.

COLLEGE: Monmouth College (N.J.).

TRANSACTIONS/CAREER NOTES: Selected by Seattle Pilots organization in eighth round of free-agent draft (June 7, 1968). ... Seattle franchise moved to Milwaukee and renamed Brewers (1970). ... On temporarily inactive list (April 16-20, April 25-30 and August 21, 1970-remainder of season). ... On military list (August 27, 1970-February 3, 1971). ... Released by Jacksonville (April 6, 1971). ... Signed by Charlotte, Minnesota Twins organization (April 28, 1971). ... Loaned by Twins organization to Rochester, Baltimore Orioles organization (April 5-September 22, 1976). ... On temporarily inactive list (April 15-19, 1977). ... On disabled list (July 25-August 4, 1977). ... Released by Toledo (December 18, 1978). ... Signed by Visalia, Twins organization (January 2, 1979). ... Released by Visalia (December 2, 1980).

STATISTICAL NOTES: Led Pacific Coast League outfielders with six double plays in 1972.

Year Team (League)	Pos.	G	AB	R	H	2B	3B	HR	RBI	Avg.	BB	SO	SB	PO	A	E	Avg.
1968—Newark (NY-Penn)......	OF	65	218	50	69	11	4	2	10	.317	43	31	*16	*144	*9	3	.981
1969—Clinton (Midwest).......	OF	100	269	47	60	10	2	6	35	.223	82	31	10	158	15	4	.977
1970—Jacksonville (Sou.)......	OF-1B	93	266	33	64	10	1	8	38	.241	41	37	2	204	19	4	.982
1971—Charlotte (Sou.)■.......	1B-OF	100	303	50	89	17	0	6	41	.294	59	52	2	508	38	9	.984
1972—Tacoma (PCL)	OF-1B	132	407	76	114	19	2	10	52	.280	70	95	4	282	19	10	.968
1973—Tacoma (PCL)	OF-1B	114	337	67	87	10	2	17	49	.258	89	64	4	200	20	6	.973
1974—Tacoma (PCL)	OF-1B	115	357	68	110	16	0	18	69	.308	78	41	4	514	41	3	.995
1975—Tacoma (PCL)	OF-1B	62	202	38	51	5	0	9	29	.252	47	36	6	185	12	6	.970
—Minnesota (A.L.)	1B-DH-OF	49	127	11	23	5	0	1	11	.181	15	22	0	360	28	6	.985
1976—Rochester (Int'l)■......	OF-1B	127	405	71	117	19	3	18	70	.289	85	71	2	323	28	4	.989
1977—Tacoma (PCL)■	1B-OF-P	113	363	80	99	12	1	12	64	.273	78	61	11	251	15	6	.978
1978—Toledo (Int'l)..........	1B-OF	119	325	47	74	13	0	10	49	.228	*91	61	2	556	46	5	.992
1979—Visalia (California)■...	1B-P	2	0	0	0	0	0	0	0	...	1	0	0	3	4	0	1.000
Major league totals (1 year)		49	127	11	23	5	0	1	11	.181	15	22	0	360	28	6	.985

RECORD AS PITCHER

Year Team (League)	W	L	Pct.	ERA	G	GS	CG	ShO	Sv.	IP	H	R	ER	BB	SO
1977—Tacoma (PCL)	0	0	...	6.00	1	0	0	0	0	3	2	2	2	3	0
1979—Visalia (California)	1	0	1.000	2.25	1	1	0	0	0	8	5	3	2	7	2
1980—Visalia (California)	0	0	...	0.69	2	1	0	0	0	13	12	1	1	6	2

RECORD AS MANAGER

BACKGROUND: Player/manager, Tacoma, Minnesota Twins organization (June 1977-remainder of season). ... Player/coach, Toledo, Twins organization (1978). ... Coach, Twins (1983-September 11, 1986).

HONORS: Named California League Manager of the Year (1979). ... Named California League co-Manager of the Year (1980). ... Named Southern League Manager of the Year (1981). ... Coach, A.L. All-Star team (1991). ... Named A.L. Manager of the Year by THE SPORTING NEWS (1991). ... Named A.L. Manager of the Year by the Baseball Writers' Association of America (1991).

			REGULAR SEASON			POSTSEASON						
						Playoff		Champ. Series		World Series		All-Star Game
Year Team (League)	W	L	Pct.	Pos.	W	L	W	L	W	L	W	L
1977—Tacoma (Pacific Coast)	28	26	.519	3rd (W)	—	—	—	—	—	—	—	—
1979—Visalia (California)	44	26	.629	1st (S)	—	—	—	—	—	—	—	—
—(Second half)	42	28	.600	2nd (S)	1	2	—	—	—	—	—	—
1980—Visalia (California)	27	43	.386	4th (S)	—	—	—	—	—	—	—	—
—(Second half)	44	26	.629	1st (S)	2	4	—	—	—	—	—	—
1981—Orlando (Southern)	42	27	.609	1st (E)	—	—	—	—	—	—	—	—
—(Second half)	37	36	.507	3rd (E)	6	2	—	—	—	—	—	—
1982—Orlando (Southern)	31	38	.449	5th (E)	—	—	—	—	—	—	—	—
—(Second half)	43	32	.573	2nd (E)	—	—	—	—	—	—	—	—
1986—Minnesota (A.L.)	12	11	.522	6th (W)	—	—	—	—	—	—	—	—
1987—Minnesota (A.L.)	85	77	.525	1st (W)	—	—	4	1	4	3	—	—
1988—Minnesota (A.L.)	91	71	.562	2nd (W)	—	—	—	—	—	—	1	0
1989—Minnesota (A.L.)	80	82	.494	5th (W)	—	—	—	—	—	—	—	—
1990—Minnesota (A.L.)	74	88	.457	7th (W)	—	—	—	—	—	—	—	—
1991—Minnesota (A.L.)	95	67	.586	1st (W)	—	—	4	1	4	3	—	—
1992—Minnesota (A.L.)	90	72	.556	2nd (W)	—	—	—	—	—	—	1	0
1993—Minnesota (A.L.)	71	91	.438	T5th (W)	—	—	—	—	—	—	—	—
1994—Minnesota (A.L.)	53	60	.469		—	—	—	—	—	—	—	—
1995—Minnesota (A.L.)	56	88	.389	5th (C)	—	—	—	—	—	—	—	—
1996—Minnesota (A.L.)	78	84	.481	4th (C)	—	—	—	—	—	—	—	—
1997—Minnesota (A.L.)	68	94	.420	4th (C)	—	—	—	—	—	—	—	—
Major league totals (12 years)	853	885	.491		—	—	8	2	8	6	2	0

NOTES:
1977—Replaced Tacoma manager Del Wilber with record of 40-49 and became player/manager (June).
1979—Lost to San Jose in semifinals.
1980—Defeated Fresno, two games to one, in semifinals; lost to Stockton, three games to none, in league championship.
1981—Defeated Savannah, three games to one, in semifinals; defeated Nashville, three games to one, in league championship.
1986—Replaced Minnesota manager Ray Miller with club in seventh place and record of 59-80 (September 12).
1987—Defeated Detroit in A.L. Championship Series; defeated St. Louis in World Series.
1991—Defeated Toronto in A.L. Championship Series; defeated Atlanta in World Series.
1994—Minnesota was in fourth place in A.L. Central at time of season-ending strike (August 12).

LA RUSSA, TONY — CARDINALS

PERSONAL: Born October 4, 1944, in Tampa. ... 6-0/185. ... Batted right, threw right. ... Full name: Anthony La Russa Jr.
HIGH SCHOOL: Jefferson (Tampa).
COLLEGE: University of Tampa (Fla.), then South Florida (degree in industrial management), then Florida State (law degree, 1980).
TRANSACTIONS/CAREER NOTES: Signed by Kansas City Athletics organization (June 6, 1962). ... On disabled list (May 9-September 8, 1964; June 3-July 15, 1965; and April 12-May 6 and July 3-September 5, 1967). ... A's franchise moved from Kansas City to Oakland (October 1967). ... Contract sold by A's to Atlanta Braves (August 14, 1971). ... Traded by Braves to Chicago Cubs for P Tom Phoebus (October 20, 1972). ... Contract sold by Cubs to Pittsburgh Pirates organization (March 23, 1974). ... Released by Pirates organization (April 4, 1975). ... Signed by Chicago White Sox organization (April 7, 1975). ... On disabled list (August 8-18, 1976). ... Contract sold by White Sox to St. Louis Cardinals organization (December 13, 1976). ... Released by Cardinals organization (September 29, 1977).
STATISTICAL NOTES: Led International League in being hit by pitch with 11 in 1972.

Year Team (League)	Pos.	G	AB	R	H	2B	3B	HR	RBI	Avg.	BB	SO	SB	PO	A	E	Avg.
1962—Daytona Beach (FSL)..	SS	64	225	37	58	7	0	1	32	.258	42	47	11	135	173	38	.890
—Binghamton (Eastern)	SS-2B	12	43	3	8	0	0	0	4	.186	5	9	2	20	27	8	.855
1963—Kansas City (A.L.)	SS-2B	34	44	4	11	1	1	0	1	.250	7	12	0	29	25	2	.964

Year	Team (League)	Pos.	G	AB	R	H	2B	3B	HR	RBI	Avg.	BB	SO	SB	PO	A	E	Avg.
					BATTING											FIELDING		
1964— Lewiston (N'west)	2B-SS	90	329	50	77	22	1	1	25	.234	53	56	10	188	218	18	.958	
1965— Birmingham (Sou.).....	2B	75	259	24	50	11	2	1	18	.193	26	37	5	202	161	21	.945	
1966— Modesto (California) ..	2B	81	316	67	92	20	1	7	54	.291	44	37	18	201	212	20	.954	
— Mobile (Southern) ...	2B	51	170	20	50	9	4	4	26	.294	23	24	4	117	133	10	.962	
1967— Birmingham (Sou.).....	2B	41	139	12	32	6	1	5	22	.230	10	11	3	88	120	5	.977	
1968— Oakland (A.L.)	PH	5	3	0	1	0	0	0	0	.333	0	0	0	...	...	...	...	
— Vancouver (PCL)	2B	122	455	55	109	16	8	5	29	.240	52	58	4	249	321	14	*.976	
1969— Iowa (Am. Assoc.)......	2B	67	235	37	72	11	1	4	27	.306	0	1	5	177	222	15	.964	
— Oakland (A.L.)	PH	8	8	0	0	0	0	0	0	.000	42	30	0	...	...	...	...	
1970— Iowa (Am. Assoc.)........	2B	22	88	13	22	5	0	2	5	.250	9	14	0	52	59	3	.974	
— Oakland (A.L.)	2B	52	106	6	21	4	1	0	6	.198	15	19	0	67	89	5	.969	
1971— Iowa (Am. Assoc.)......	2-3-S-O	28	107	21	31	5	1	2	11	.290	10	11	0	70	85	2	.987	
— Oakland (A.L.)	2B-SS-3B	23	8	3	0	0	0	0	0	.000	0	4	0	8	7	2	.882	
— Atlanta (N.L.)■..........	2B	9	7	1	2	0	0	0	0	.286	1	1	0	8	6	1	.933	
1972— Richmond (Int'l)......	2B	122	389	68	120	13	2	10	42	.308	72	41	0	305	289	20	.967	
1973— Wichita (A.A.)■.......	2B-1B-3B	106	392	82	123	16	0	5	75	.314	60	46	10	423	213	26	.961	
— Chicago (N.L.)	PR	1	0	1	0	0	0	0	0	...	0	0	0	...	...	...	...	
1974— Char., W.Va. (Int'l)■..	2B	139	457	50	119	17	1	8	35	.260	51	50	4	262	*378	17	.974	
1975— Denver (A.A.)■	3-0-S-2	118	354	87	99	23	2	7	46	.280	70	46	13	95	91	10	.949	
1976— Iowa (Am. Assoc.)......3-2-S-1-O-P		107	332	53	86	11	0	4	34	.259	40	43	10	132	160	22	.930	
1977— New Orleans (A.A.)■..	2B-3B	50	128	17	24	2	2	3	6	.188	20	21	0	66	87	7	.956	
American League totals (5 years)		122	169	13	33	5	2	0	7	.195	64	65	0	104	121	9	.962	
National League totals (2 years)		10	7	2	2	0	0	0	0	.286	1	1	0	8	6	1	.933	
Major league totals (6 years)		132	176	15	35	5	2	0	7	.199	65	66	0	112	127	10	.960	

RECORD AS PITCHER

Year	Team (League)	W	L	Pct.	ERA	G	GS	CG	ShO	Sv.	IP	H	R	ER	BB	SO
1976— Iowa (Am. Assoc.).............		0	0	...	3.00	3	0	0	0	0	3	3	1	1	0	0

RECORD AS MANAGER

BACKGROUND: Coach, St. Louis Cardinals organization (June 20-September 29, 1977). ... Coach, Chicago White Sox (July 3, 1978-remainder of season).

RECORDS: Shares major league single-season record for most clubs managed—2 (1986).

HONORS: Named Major League Manager of the Year by THE SPORTING NEWS (1983). ... Named A.L. Manager of the Year by the Baseball Writers' Association of America (1983, 1988 and 1992). ... Coach, A.L. All-Star team (1984 and 1987). ... Named A.L. Manager of the Year by THE SPORTING NEWS (1988 and 1992).

Year	Team (League)	W	L	Pct.	Pos.	Playoff W	L	Champ. Series W	L	World Series W	L	All-Star Game W	L
								REGULAR SEASON / POSTSEASON					
1978— Knoxville (Southern)	49	21	.700	1st (W)	—	—	—	—	—	—	—	—	
— (Second half)	4	4	.500		—	—	—	—	—	—	—	—	
1979— Iowa (American Association)	54	52	.509		—	—	—	—	—	—	—	—	
— Chicago (A.L.)	27	27	.500	5th (W)	—	—	—	—	—	—	—	—	
1980— Chicago (A.L.)	70	90	.438	5th (W)	—	—	—	—	—	—	—	—	
1981— Chicago (A.L.)	31	22	.585	3rd (W)	—	—	—	—	—	—	—	—	
— (Second half)	23	30	.434	6th (W)	—	—	—	—	—	—	—	—	
1982— Chicago (A.L.)	87	75	.537	3rd (W)	—	—	—	—	—	—	—	—	
1983— Chicago (A.L.)	99	63	.611	1st (W)	—	—	1	3	—	—	—	—	
1984— Chicago (A.L.)	74	88	.457	T5th (W)	—	—	—	—	—	—	—	—	
1985— Chicago (A.L.)	85	77	.525	3rd (W)	—	—	—	—	—	—	—	—	
1986— Chicago (A.L.)	26	38	.406		—	—	—	—	—	—	—	—	
— Oakland (A.L.)	45	34	.570	T3rd (W)	—	—	—	—	—	—	—	—	
1987— Oakland (A.L.)	81	81	.500	3rd (W)	—	—	—	—	—	—	—	—	
1988— Oakland (A.L.)	104	58	.642	1st (W)	—	—	4	0	1	4	—	—	
1989— Oakland (A.L.)	99	63	.611	1st (W)	—	—	4	1	4	0	1	0	
1990— Oakland (A.L.)	103	59	.636	1st (W)	—	—	4	0	0	4	1	0	
1991— Oakland (A.L.)	84	78	.519	4th (W)	—	—	—	—	—	—	1	0	
1992— Oakland (A.L.)	96	66	.593	1st (W)	—	—	2	4	—	—	—	—	
1993— Oakland (A.L.)	68	94	.420	7th (W)	—	—	—	—	—	—	—	—	
1994— Oakland (A.L.)	51	63	.447		—	—	—	—	—	—	—	—	
1995— Oakland (A.L.)	67	77	.465	4th (W)	—	—	—	—	—	—	—	—	
1996— St. Louis (N.L.)	88	74	.543	1st (C)	3	0	3	4	—	—	—	—	
1997— St. Louis (N.L.)	73	89	.451	4th (C)	—	—	—	—	—	—	—	—	
American League totals (17 years)	1320	1183	.527		—	—	15	8	5	8	3	0	
National League totals (2 years)	161	163	.497		3	0	3	4	—	—	—	—	
Major League totals (19 years)	1481	1346	.524		3	0	18	12	5	8	3	0	

NOTES:

1978—Became Chicago White Sox coach and replaced as Knoxville manager by Joe Jones, with club in third place (July 3).

1979—Replaced as Iowa manager by Joe Sparks, with club in second place (August 3); replaced Chicago manager Don Kessinger with club in fifth place and record of 46-60 (August 3).

1983—Lost to Baltimore in A.L. Championship Series.

1986—Replaced as White Sox manager by interim manager Doug Rader, with club in sixth place (June 20); replaced Oakland manager Jackie Moore (record of 29-44) and interim manager Jeff Newman (record of 2-8) with club in seventh place and record of 31-52 (July 7).

1988—Defeated Boston in A.L. Championship Series; lost to Los Angeles in World Series.

1989—Defeated Toronto in A.L. Championship Series; defeated San Francisco in World Series.

1990—Defeated Boston in A.L. Championship Series; lost to Cincinnati in World Series.

1992—Lost to Toronto in A.L. Championship Series.

1993—On suspended list (October 1-remainder of season).

1994—Oakland was in second place in A.L. West at time of season-ending strike (August 12).

1996—Defeated San Diego in N.L. divisional playoff; lost to Atlanta in N.L. Championship Series.

MAJOR LEAGUE MANAGERS

PERSONAL: Born December 25, 1946, in Rockford, Ill. ... 6-1/190. ... Batted both, threw right. ... Full name: Gene William Lamont.
HIGH SCHOOL: Hiawatha (Kirkland, Ill).
COLLEGE: Northern Illinois, then Western Illinois.
TRANSACTIONS/CAREER NOTES: Selected by Detroit Tigers organization in first round (13th pick overall) of free-agent draft (June 29, 1965). ... On disabled list (May 18-28, 1966). ... On temporarily inactive list (May 20-25, 1967). ... On military list (May 25, 1967-remainder of season). ... On temporarily inactive list (July 15-31, 1972). ... Traded by Tigers to Atlanta Braves organization for C Bob Didier (May 14, 1973). ... Selected by Tigers from Braves organization in Rule 5 major league draft (December 3, 1973). ... Released by Evansville, Tigers organization (December 20, 1977).
STATISTICAL NOTES: Led Southern League catchers with nine errors in 1969. ... Led Southern League catchers with 730 putouts, 72 assists, 814 total chances, 9 double plays and 15 passed balls in 1972. ... Led American Association catchers with eight double plays in 1976.

							BATTING								FIELDING		
Year	Team (League)	Pos.	G	AB	R	H	2B	3B	HR	RBI	Avg.	BB	SO	SB	PO	A	E	Avg.
1965—	Syracuse (Int'l)..........	C	5	9	1	1	0	0	1	1	.111	0	6	0	...	...	...	...
	—Daytona Beach (FSL)..	C	38	104	9	24	5	1	1	16	.231	13	33	1	222	19	3	.988
1966—	States. (W. Caro.).......	C	45	137	14	27	4	2	3	19	.197	21	49	1	283	28	8	.975
	—Rocky Mt. (Caro.).......	C	36	102	9	26	4	1	2	9	.255	16	23	0	213	19	5	.979
1967—	Rocky Mt. (Caro.).......	C	19	56	4	8	2	0	1	5	.143	8	8	0	107	16	1	.992
1968—	Rocky Mt. (Caro.).......	C-OF-3B	101	304	36	76	10	0	4	39	.250	24	60	1	498	72	7	.988
1969—	Montgomery (Sou.)....	C-3B	86	268	24	63	15	1	3	29	.235	32	37	0	410	92	†16	.969
1970—	Toledo (Int'l).............	C-3B-OF	74	230	27	61	9	1	4	32	.265	19	46	1	313	59	5	.987
	—Detroit (A.L.).............	C	15	44	3	13	3	1	1	4	.295	2	9	0	87	8	0	1.000
1971—	Toledo (Int'l).............	C	63	180	17	41	8	1	5	19	.228	19	29	0	321	43	9	.976
	—Detroit (A.L.).............	C	7	15	2	1	0	0	0	1	.067	0	5	0	38	2	2	.952
1972—	Montgomery (Sou.)....	C-OF	119	385	47	105	19	1	6	51	.273	64	72	1	†731	†72	12	.985
	—Detroit (A.L.).............	C	1	0	0	0	0	0	0	0	...	0	0	0	1	0	0	1.000
1973—	Richmond (Int'l)■.......	C-1B	101	275	29	69	11	1	2	25	.251	41	64	0	411	34	3	.993
1974—	Detroit (A.L.)■.............	C	60	92	9	20	4	1	3	8	.217	7	19	0	204	21	6	.974
1975—	Detroit (A.L.).............	C	4	8	1	3	1	0	0	1	.375	0	2	1	14	3	1	.944
	—Evansville (A.A.).........	C	49	130	15	40	9	0	3	20	.308	20	20	1	211	23	4	.983
1976—	Evansville (A.A.).........	C	96	269	23	63	13	0	5	25	.234	36	47	2	467	47	7	.987
1977—	Evansville (A.A.).........	C	3	5	0	2	1	0	0	0	.400	1	1	0	4	1	0	1.000
Major league totals (5 years)			87	159	15	37	8	1	4	14	.233	9	35	1	344	34	9	.977

RECORD AS MANAGER

BACKGROUND: Coach, Pittsburgh Pirates (1986-91). ... Scout and adviser to the general manager (July 7, 1995-remainder of season). ... Coach, Pirates (1996).
HONORS: Named Southern League Manager of the Year (1982). ... Named A.L. Manager of the Year by the Baseball Writers' Association of America (1993). ... Coach, A.L. All-Star team (1994).

		REGULAR SEASON				POSTSEASON							
						Playoff		Champ. Series		World Series		All-Star Game	
Year	Team (League)	W	L	Pct.	Pos.	W	L	W	L	W	L	W	L
1978—	Fort Myers (Florida State)........................	38	30	.559	1st (S)	—	—	—	—	—	—	—	—
	—(Second half)	33	36	.478	5th (S)	0	1	—	—	—	—	—	—
1979—	Fort Myers (Florida State)........................	38	32	.543	3rd (S)	—	—	—	—	—	—	—	—
	—(Second half)	31	37	.456	4th (S)	—	—	—	—	—	—	—	—
1980—	Jacksonville (Southern)	31	40	.437	4th (E)	—	—	—	—	—	—	—	—
	—(Second half)	32	41	.438	5th (E)	—	—	—	—	—	—	—	—
1981—	Jacksonville (Southern)	34	36	.486	4th (E)	—	—	—	—	—	—	—	—
	—(Second half)	31	41	.431	4th (E)	—	—	—	—	—	—	—	—
1982—	Jacksonville (Southern)	41	31	.569	1st (E)	—	—	—	—	—	—	—	—
	—(Second half)	42	30	.583	1st (E)	4	4	—	—	—	—	—	—
1983—	Jacksonville (Southern)	36	36	.500	2nd (E)	—	—	—	—	—	—	—	—
	—(Second half)	41	32	.562	1st (E)	4	4	—	—	—	—	—	—
1984—	Omaha (American Association)	68	86	.442	8th	—	—	—	—	—	—	—	—
1985—	Omaha (American Association)	73	69	.514	3rd (W)	—	—	—	—	—	—	—	—
1992—	Chicago (A.L.)................	86	76	.531	3rd (W)	—	—	—	—	—	—	—	—
1993—	Chicago (A.L.)................	94	68	.580	1st (W)	—	—	2	4	—	—	—	—
1994—	Chicago (A.L.)................	67	46	.593		—	—	—	—	—	—	—	—
1995—	Chicago (A.L.)................	11	20	.355		—	—	—	—	—	—	—	—
1997—	Pittsburgh (N.L.)................	79	83	.488	2nd (C)	—	—	—	—	—	—	—	—
American League totals (4 years)		258	210	.551		—	—	2	4	—	—	—	—
National League totals (1 year)		79	83	.488		—	—	—	—	—	—	—	—
Major league totals (5 years)		337	293	.535		—	—	2	4	—	—	—	—

NOTES:
1978—Lost to Miami in Southern Division championship.
1981—Jacksonville tied one game.
1982—Defeated Columbus, three games to one, in Eastern Division championship; lost to Nashville, three games to one, in league championship.
1983—Defeated Savannah, three games to one, in Eastern Division championship; lost to Birmingham, three games to one, in league championship.
1993—Lost to Toronto in A.L. Championship Series.
1994—Chicago was in first place in A.L. Central at time of season-ending strike (August 12).
1995—Replaced as White Sox manager by Terry Bevington, with club in fourth place (June 2).

LEYLAND, JIM | MARLINS

PERSONAL: Born December 15, 1944, in Toledo, Ohio. ... 5-11/170. ... Batted right, threw right. ... Full name: James Richard Leyland. ... Name pronounced LEE-lund.

HIGH SCHOOL: Perrysburg (Ohio).
TRANSACTIONS/CAREER NOTES: Signed as free agent by Detroit Tigers organization (September 21, 1963). ... On disabled list (June 15-27, 1964). ... Released by Rocky Mount, Tigers organization (March 27, 1971).

							BATTING								FIELDING			
Year	Team (League)	Pos.	G	AB	R	H	2B	3B	HR	RBI	Avg.	BB	SO	SB	PO	A	E	Avg.
1964—	Lakeland (Fla. St.)	C	52	129	8	25	0	1	0	8	.194	18	33	1	268	17	6	.979
	—Cocoa Tigers (CRL)	C	24	52	2	12	1	1	0	4	.231	13	7	1	122	15	3	.979
1965—	Jamestown (NYP)	C-3B-P	82	211	18	50	7	2	1	21	.237	37	44	2	318	36	6	.983
1966—	Rocky Mt. (Caro.)	C	67	173	24	42	6	0	0	16	.243	32	35	0	369	23	1	.997
1967—	Montgomery (Sou.)	C	62	171	11	40	3	0	1	16	.234	16	27	0	350	25	6	.984
1968—	Montgomery (Sou.)	C-3B-SS	81	264	19	51	3	0	1	20	.193	14	54	2	511	43	7	.988
1969—	Montgomery (Sou.)	C	16	39	1	8	0	0	0	1	.205	4	7	0	64	6	3	.959
	—Lakeland (Fla. St.)	C-P	60	179	20	43	8	0	1	16	.240	31	17	0	321	28	4	.989
1970—	Montgomery (Sou.)	C	2	3	0	0	0	0	0	0	.000	0	0	0	6	0	1	.857

RECORD AS PITCHER

Year	Team (League)	W	L	Pct.	ERA	G	GS	CG	ShO	Sv.	IP	H	R	ER	BB	SO
1965—	Jamestown (NYP)	0	0	...	0.00	1	0	0	0	...	2	2	0	0	0	1
1969—	Lakeland (Fla. St.)	0	0	...	9.00	1	0	0	0	0	2	4	2	2	0	1

RECORD AS MANAGER

BACKGROUND: Coach, Detroit Tigers organization (1970-June 5, 1971); served as player/coach (1970). ... Coach, Chicago White Sox (1982-85).
HONORS: Named Florida State League Manager of the Year (1977-78). ... Named American Association Manager of the Year (1979). ... Named N.L. co-Manager of the Year by THE SPORTING NEWS (1988). ... Coach, N.L. All-Star team (1990-91 and 1994). ... Named N.L. Manager of the Year by THE SPORTING NEWS (1990 and 1992). ... Named N.L. Manager of the Year by the Baseball Writers' Association of America (1990 and 1992).

		REGULAR SEASON				POSTSEASON						
						Playoff		Champ. Series		World Series		All-Star Game
Year	Team (League)	W	L	Pct.	Pos.	W	L	W	L	W	L	W	L
1971—	Bristol (Appalachian)	31	35	.470	3rd (S)	—	—	—	—	—	—	—	—
1972—	Clinton (Midwest)	22	41	.349	5th (N)	—	—	—	—	—	—	—	—
	—(Second half)	27	36	.429	4th (N)	—	—	—	—	—	—	—	—
1973—	Clinton (Midwest)	36	26	.581	2nd (N)	—	—	—	—	—	—	—	—
	—(Second half)	37	25	.597	1st (N)	0	2	—	—	—	—	—	—
1974—	Montgomery (Southern)	61	76	.445	3rd (W)	—	—	—	—	—	—	—	—
1975—	Clinton (Midwest)	29	31	.483	4th (S)	—	—	—	—	—	—	—	—
	—(Second half)	38	30	.559	2nd (S)	—	—	—	—	—	—	—	—
1976—	Lakeland (Florida State)	74	64	.536	2nd (N)	4	0	—	—	—	—	—	—
1977—	Lakeland (Florida State)	85	53	.616	1st (N)	5	1	—	—	—	—	—	—
1978—	Lakeland (Florida State)	31	38	.449	4th (N)	—	—	—	—	—	—	—	—
	—(Second half)	47	22	.681	1st (N)	2	2	—	—	—	—	—	—
1979—	Evansville (American Association)	78	58	.574	1st (E)	4	2	—	—	—	—	—	—
1980—	Evansville (American Association)	61	74	.452	2nd (E)	—	—	—	—	—	—	—	—
1981—	Evansville (American Association)	73	63	.537	1st (E)	1	3	—	—	—	—	—	—
1986—	Pittsburgh (N.L.)	64	98	.395	6th (E)	—	—	—	—	—	—	—	—
1987—	Pittsburgh (N.L.)	80	82	.494	T4th (E)	—	—	—	—	—	—	—	—
1988—	Pittsburgh (N.L.)	85	75	.525	2nd (E)	—	—	—	—	—	—	—	—
1989—	Pittsburgh (N.L.)	74	88	.457	5th (E)	—	—	—	—	—	—	—	—
1990—	Pittsburgh (N.L.)	95	67	.586	1st (E)	—	—	2	4	—	—	—	—
1991—	Pittsburgh (N.L.)	98	64	.605	1st (E)	—	—	3	4	—	—	—	—
1992—	Pittsburgh (N.L.)	96	66	.593	1st (E)	—	—	3	4	—	—	—	—
1993—	Pittsburgh (N.L.)	75	87	.463	5th (E)	—	—	—	—	—	—	—	—
1994—	Pittsburgh (N.L.)	53	61	.465		—	—	—	—	—	—	—	—
1995—	Pittsburgh (N.L.)	58	86	.403	5th (C)	—	—	—	—	—	—	—	—
1996—	Pittsburgh (N.L.)	73	89	.451	5th (C)	—	—	—	—	—	—	—	—
1997—	Florida (N.L.)	92	70	.568	2nd (E)	3	0	4	2	4	3	—	—
Major league totals (12 years)		943	933	.503		3	0	12	14	4	3	—	—

NOTES:
1973—Lost to Wisconsin Rapids in playoff.
1976—Defeated Miami, two games to none, in semifinals; defeated Tampa, two games to none, in league championship.
1977—Defeated Miami, two games to none, in semifinals; defeated St. Petersburg, three games to one, in league championship.
1978—Defeated St. Petersburg, one game to none, in Northern Division championship; lost to Miami, two games to one, in league championship.
1979—Defeated Oklahoma City in league championship.
1981—Lost to Denver in semifinals.
1985—Served as acting manager of Chicago White Sox (record of 1-1), with club in fourth place, while manager Tony La Russa served a suspension (August 10 and 11).
1990—Lost to Cincinnati in N.L. Championship Series.
1991—Lost to Atlanta in N.L. Championship Series.
1992—Lost to Atlanta in N.L. Championship Series.
1993—On suspended list (August 27-September 1).
1994—Pittsburgh was tied for third place in N.L. Central at time of season-ending baseball strike (August 12).
1997—Defeated San Francisco in N.L. divisional playoff; defeated Atlanta in N.L. Championship Series; defeated Cleveland in World Series.

MANUEL, JERRY   WHITE SOX

PERSONAL: Born December 23, 1953, in Hahira, Ga. ... 5-11/180. ... Batted right, threw right.
HIGH SCHOOL: Cordova (Rancho Cordova, Calif.).
TRANSACTIONS/CAREER NOTES: Selected by Detroit Tigers organization in first round (20th pick overall) of free-agent draft (June 6, 1972). ... On disabled list (August 18-September 1, 1978). ... Traded by Tigers to Montreal Expos organization for C Duffy Dyer (March 14, 1980). ... On disabled list (May 2-July 31, and August 15-September 1, 1981). ... Traded by Expos to San Diego Padres organization for P Kim Seaman (May 22, 1982). ... Traded by Padres to Expos organization for a player to be named later (June 8, 1982); Padres acquired P Mike

Griffin to complete deal (August 30, 1982). ... Traded by Expos to Chicago Cubs organization for C Butch Benton (February 4, 1983). ... Granted free agency following 1983 season. ... Signed by Chicago White Sox organization (April 8, 1984). ... Granted free agency following 1985 season. ... Signed by Expos organization for 1986 season. ... On disabled list (June 23-July 17 and July 25-August 4, 1986).

STATISTICAL NOTES: Led Appalachian League shortstops with 303 total chances and 29 double plays in 1972. ... Led American Association second basemen with 688 total chances and 81 double plays in 1974. ... Led American Association second basemen with 758 total chances and 108 double plays in 1975. ... Led American Association second basemen with 234 putouts, 363 assists and 611 total chances in 1979. ... Led American Association shortstops with 612 total chances in 1980.

Year Team (League)	Pos.	G	AB	R	H	2B	3B	HR	RBI	Avg.	BB	SO	SB	PO	A	E	Avg.
1972— Bristol (Appal.)	SS	67	233	31	56	8	8	4	29	.240	19	61	11	*112	*176	15	*.950
1973— Lakeland (Fla. St.)	SS	117	433	66	109	17	4	2	28	.252	52	98	20	167	349	29	.947
— Toledo (Int'l)	SS	27	72	8	20	0	0	0	2	.278	3	16	2	44	90	4	.971
1974— Evansville (A.A.)	2B	127	384	44	81	5	5	1	24	.211	35	74	3	*315	356	17	.975
1975— Evansville (A.A.)	2B	*137	501	63	115	10	4	4	43	.230	44	101	5	*348	*394	16	.979
— Detroit (A.L.)	2B	6	18	0	1	0	0	0	0	.056	0	4	0	11	23	2	.944
1976— Detroit (A.L.)	2B-SS	54	43	4	6	1	0	0	2	.140	3	9	1	40	64	8	.929
— Evansville (A.A.)	2B	11	44	6	8	1	0	1	3	.182	2	9	0	25	29	1	.982
1977— Evansville (A.A.)	2B-SS	110	375	52	102	19	7	1	38	.272	45	55	12	198	304	17	.967
1978— Evansville (A.A.)	2B-SS	114	430	65	113	18	5	7	50	.263	50	83	8	264	321	20	.967
1979— Evansville (A.A.)	2B-SS	130	460	71	116	26	3	9	75	.252	67	67	8	†265	†434	22	.969
1980— Denver (A.A.)■	SS	128	491	105	136	23	2	6	61	.277	81	62	11	†233	*357	22	.964
— Montreal (N.L.)	SS	7	6	0	0	0	0	0	0	.000	0	2	0	5	11	1	.941
1981— Montreal (N.L.)	2B-SS	27	55	10	11	5	0	3	10	.200	6	11	0	37	41	1	.987
1982— Wichita (A.A.)■	S-3-2-O	71	263	31	67	22	0	3	37	.255	15	34	2	99	152	11	.958
— San Diego (N.L.)	2B-3B-SS	2	5	0	1	0	1	0	1	.200	1	0	0	1	1	0	1.000
— Hawaii (PCL)	SS	26	92	8	18	3	1	0	7	.196	11	12	2	41	73	1	.991
1983— Iowa (Am. Assoc.)■ ..	2-O-S-3	85	279	37	74	14	3	3	33	.265	22	46	6	129	143	9	.968
1984— Denver (A.A.)■	SS-2B-OF	109	335	43	98	14	3	4	40	.293	37	32	7	184	262	18	.961
1985—								Did not play.									
1986— Indianapolis (A.A.)■ ..	3B-2B	22	41	4	16	2	0	1	9	.390	2	5	0	5	7	1	.923
American League totals (2 years)		60	61	4	7	1	0	0	2	.115	3	13	1	51	87	10	.932
National League totals (3 years)		36	66	10	12	5	1	3	11	.182	7	13	0	43	53	2	.980
Major league totals (5 years)		96	127	14	19	6	1	3	13	.150	10	26	1	94	140	12	.951

DIVISION SERIES RECORD

Year Team (League)	Pos.	G	AB	R	H	2B	3B	HR	RBI	Avg.	BB	SO	SB	PO	A	E	Avg.
1981— Montreal (N.L.)	2B	5	14	0	1	0	0	0	0	.071	2	5	0	13	19	3	.914

CHAMPIONSHIP SERIES RECORD

Year Team (League)	Pos.	G	AB	R	H	2B	3B	HR	RBI	Avg.	BB	SO	SB	PO	A	E	Avg.
1981— Montreal (N.L.)	PR	1	1	0	0	0	0	0	0	.000	0	0	0	...	...	...	...

RECORD AS MANAGER

BACKGROUND: Scout, Chicago White Sox (1985). ... Player/coach, Indianapolis, American Association (1986). ... Roving infield instructor, Montreal Expos organization (1987). ... Minor league field coordinator, Expos (1988-89). ... Coach, Expos (June 3, 1991-1996). ... Coach, Florida Marlins (1997).

HONORS: Named Southern League co-Manager of the Year (1990).

Year Team (League)	REGULAR SEASON				POSTSEASON						
					Playoff		Champ. Series		World Series		All-Star Game
	W	L	Pct.	Pos.	W	L	W	L	W	L	W	L
1990— Jacksonville (Southern)	38	33	.535	2nd (E)	—	—	—	—	—	—	—	—
— (Second half)	46	27	.630	1st (E)	1	3	—	—	—	—	—	—
1991— Indianapolis (A.A.)	28	22	.560	—	—	—	—	—	—	—	—	—

NOTES:
1990—Lost to Orlando in playoffs.
1991—Replaced as Indianapolis manager by Pat Kelly (June 2).

McKEON, JACK — REDS

PERSONAL: Born November 23, 1930, in South Amboy, N.J. ... 5-8/205. ... Batted right, threw right. ... Full name: John Aloysius McKeon. ... Brother of Bill McKeon, minor league catcher (1952-54 and 1956-57); scout, Kansas City Royals (1969-70); scout, San Diego Padres (1981-87); and father-in-law of Greg Booker, pitcher, San Diego Padres and Minnesota Twins (1983-89).

HIGH SCHOOL: St. Mary's (South Amboy, N.J.).

COLLEGE: Holy Cross, then Seton Hall, then Elon (N.C.) College (degree in physical education and science).

TRANSACTIONS/CAREER NOTES: Released by Pittsburgh Pirates organization (September 28, 1954). ... Played 10 games with Fayetteville, five games with Greensboro and was player/manager with Fayetteville for 44 games during 1955 season. ... Player/manager, Missoula, Pioneer League (1956-58).

STATISTICAL NOTES: Led Carolina catchers with 17 double plays in 1953. ... Led Alabama State League catchers with nine double plays in 1949.

Year Team (League)	Pos.	G	AB	R	H	2B	3B	HR	RBI	Avg.	BB	SO	SB	PO	A	E	Avg.
1949— Greenville (Alabama St.)	C	116	390	54	98	12	1	1	49	.251	41	34	8	*806	65	13	*.985
1950— York (International)	C	1	3	...	1	...	...	...	...	.333	...	...	...	...	...	...	...
— Gloverton (Can.-Amer.)	C	72	209	18	45	5	0	0	14	.215	19	28	2	281	30	15	.954
1951—								In military service.									
1952— Hutchinson (W. Assn.).	C	116	358	42	78	10	1	4	40	.218	69	54	0	756	68	11	.987
1953— Burlington (Caro.)	C	140	474	46	86	19	2	6	52	.181	60	110	3	*836	*82	21	.978
1954— Burlington (Caro.)	C	17	30	1	4	0	0	0	2	.133	1	5	0	60	9	0	1.000
— Hutchinson (W. Assn.).	C	46	140	18	29	5	0	1	13	.207	27	31	1	273	33	4	.987
1955— Fay.-Greens. (Caro.) ..	C	59	172	20	29	3	0	1	17	.169	29	28	1	292	20	6	.981

Year	Team (League)	Pos.	G	AB	R	H	2B	3B	HR	RBI	Avg.	BB	SO	SB	PO	A	E	Avg.
								BATTING									FIELDING	
1956— Missoula (Pioneer).....		C-P	113	370	44	63	8	0	0	29	.170	53	62	3	630	78	9	.987
1957— Missoula (Pioneer).....		C-P	102	299	37	65	7	0	4	40	.217	60	44	6	645	55	10	.986
1958— Missoula (Pioneer).....		C-P	108	354	49	93	16	0	8	51	.263	51	55	2	739	64	12	.985
1959— Fox Cities (Three-I)		C	11	20	1	2	0	0	0	1	.100	8	3	0	...	...	...	...

RECORD AS PITCHER

Year	Team (League)	W	L	Pct.	ERA	G	GS	CG	ShO	Sv.	IP	H	R	ER	BB	SO
1956— Missoula (Pioneer)............		0	0	...	0.00	8	...	...	...	...	...	...	...	...	...	...
1957— Missoula (Pioneer)............		0	0	...	0.00	6	...	...	...	...	...	...	...	...	...	...
1958— Missoula (Pioneer)............		0	0	...	0.00	2	...	...	...	...	...	...	...	...	...	...

RECORD AS MANAGER

BACKGROUND: Scout, Minnesota Twins (1965-67). ... Coach, Oakland Athletics (April 7-May 22, 1978). ... Scout/assistant to general manager, San Diego Padres (1980). ... Vice-president of baseball operations, Padres (1981-90). ... Senior adviser/player personnel, Cincinnati Reds (Janury 6, 1993-July 25, 1997).
HONORS: Coach, N.L. All-Star team (1989).

		REGULAR SEASON				POSTSEASON							
						Playoff		Champ. Series		World Series		All-Star Game	
Year	Team (League)	W	L	Pct.	Pos.	W	L	W	L	W	L	W	L
1955— Fayetteville (Carolina).............................		70	67	.511	3rd	—	—	—	—	—	—	—	—
1956— Missoula (Pioneer).................................		61	71	.462	7th	—	—	—	—	—	—	—	—
1957— Missoula (Pioneer).................................		26	35	.426	6th	—	—	—	—	—	—	—	—
— (Second half)		36	29	.554	3rd	—	—	—	—	—	—	—	—
1958— Missoula (Pioneer).................................		34	29	.540	4th	—	—	—	—	—	—	—	—
— (Second half)		36	30	.545	3rd	—	—	—	—	—	—	—	—
1959— Fox Cities (Three-I)		26	39	.400	7th	—	—	—	—	—	—	—	—
— (Second half)		33	28	.541	4th	—	—	—	—	—	—	—	—
1960— Wilson (Carolina).................................		36	34	.514	3rd	—	—	—	—	—	—	—	—
— (Second half)		37	31	.544	2nd	—	—	—	—	—	—	—	—
1961— Wilson (Carolina).................................		41	28	.594	1st	—	—	—	—	—	—	—	—
— (Second half)		42	28	.600	1st	—	—	—	—	—	—	—	—
1962— Vancouver (Pacific Coast.).........................		72	79	.477	7th	—	—	—	—	—	—	—	—
1963— Dallas-Fort Worth (Pacific Coast)		79	79	.500	3rd (S)	—	—	—	—	—	—	—	—
1964— Atlanta (International).................................		19	42	.311		—	—	—	—	—	—	—	—
1968— High Point-Thomasville (Carolina)		69	71	.493	2nd (W)	5	1	—	—	—	—	—	—
1969— Omaha (American Association)		85	55	.607	1st	—	—	—	—	—	—	—	—
1970— Omaha (American Association)		73	65	.529	1st (E)	5	5	—	—	—	—	—	—
1971— Omaha (American Association)		69	70	.496	3rd (E)	—	—	—	—	—	—	—	—
1972— Omaha (American Association)		71	69	.507	2nd (E)	—	—	—	—	—	—	—	—
1973— Kansas City (A.L.).................................		88	74	.543	2nd (W)	—	—	—	—	—	—	—	—
1974— Kansas City (A.L.).................................		77	85	.475	5th (W)	—	—	—	—	—	—	—	—
1975— Kansas City (A.L.).................................		50	46	.521		—	—	—	—	—	—	—	—
1976— Richmond (International)		69	71	.493	4th	—	—	—	—	—	—	—	—
1977— Oakland (A.L.).................................		26	27	.491		—	—	—	—	—	—	—	—
1978— Oakland (A.L.).................................		45	78	.366	4th (W)	—	—	—	—	—	—	—	—
1980— Denver (American Association)		62	73	.459	3rd	—	—	—	—	—	—	—	—
1988— San Diego (N.L.).................................		67	48	.583	3rd (W)	—	—	—	—	—	—	—	—
1989— San Diego (N.L.).................................		89	73	.549	2nd (W)	—	—	—	—	—	—	—	—
1990— San Diego (N.L.).................................		37	43	.436		—	—	—	—	—	—	—	—
1997— Cincinnati (N.L.).................................		33	30	.524	3rd (C)	—	—	—	—	—	—	—	—
American League totals (5 years)............		**286**	**310**	**.480**		—	—	—	—	—	—	—	—
National League totals (4 years)................		**226**	**194**	**.538**		—	—	—	—	—	—	—	—
Major league totals (9 years)................		**512**	**504**	**.504**		—	—	—	—	—	—	—	—

NOTES:
1955—Replaced Fayetteville manager Aaron Robinson (June 11). Replaced as Fayetteville manager by John Sanford (August 6) because of hand injury with team tied for first place (record is for full season).
1964—Replaced as Atlanta manager by Peter Appleton with club in eighth place (June 21).
1968—Defeated Greensboro, one game to none, in quarterfinals; defeated Lynchburg, two games to none in semifinals; defeated Raleigh-Durham, two games to one, in championship.
1970—Defeated Denver, four games to one, in championship; lost to Syracuse, four games to one, in Junior World Series.
1975—Replaced as Kansas City manager by Whitey Herzog, with club in second place (July 24).
1977—Replaced as Oakland manager by Bobby Winkles, with club tied for fifth place (June 10).
1978—Replaced Oakland manager Bobby Winkles, with club in first place and record of 24-15 (May 23).
1988—Replaced San Diego manager Larry Bowa, with club in fifth place and record of 16-30 (May 28).
1990—Replaced as San Diego manager by Greg Riddoch, with club in fourth place (July 11).
1997—Replaced Cincinnati manager Ray Knight, with club in fourth place and record of 43-56 (July 25).

MILLER, RAY — ORIOLES

PERSONAL: Born April 30, 1945, in Takoma Park, Md. ... 6-3/215. ... Threw right, batted right. ... Full name: Raymond Roger Miller.
HIGH SCHOOL: Suitland (Md.).
TRANSACTIONS/CAREER NOTES: Signed as free agent by San Francisco Giants organization (August 15, 1963). ... Drafted by Cleveland Indians from Giants organization in first-year draft (November 30, 1964). ... On disabled list (June 24-July 8, 1965). ... On disabled list (June 28-July 24, 1966). ... On temporarily inactive list (June 17-July 4, 1967). ... On temporarily inactive list (June 13-July 1, 1968). ... On temporarily inactive list (May 15-18, 1970). ... Traded by Indians organization with C Larry Wallin to Baltimore Orioles organization for P Dale Spier and P Rick Thoms (May 12, 1971).
STATISTICAL NOTES: Pitched eighth-inning 0-0 no-hitter (tie, rain) vs. Statesville (August 3, 1964). ... Led Midwest League with 16 hit batsmen in 1965. ... Led California League with 12 hit batsmen in 1966 and 13 in 1968.
MISCELLANEOUS: Appeared in one game as outfielder (1968).

Year Team (League)	W	L	Pct.	ERA	G	GS	CG	ShO	Sv.	IP	H	R	ER	BB	SO
1964—Lexington (West. Carolinas)	9	•11	.450	1.87	36	18	7	*5	...	159	97	64	33	*109	195
1965—Salinas (Calif.)■	0	1	.000	6.00	3	1	0	0	...	6	3	4	4	8	5
—Dubuque (Midw.)	7	9	.438	3.76	30	15	7	1	...	122	97	66	51	78	147
1966—Pawtucket (East.)	0	0	...	9.00	1	0	0	0	...	2	3	2	2	1	2
—Reno (California)	5	7	.417	6.39	24	11	3	0	...	93	87	75	66	55	94
1967—Reno (California)	1	3	.250	4.95	34	1	0	0	...	60	50	40	33	41	49
1968—Reno (California)	16	8	.667	3.22	29	25	16	3	...	193	170	86	69	81	206
1969—Portland (PCL)	11	5	.688	3.38	45	7	2	0	5	112	107	51	42	56	73
1970—Wichita (Am. Assoc.)	6	6	.500	3.67	•56	1	0	0	7	98	94	49	40	46	87
1971—Wichita (Am. Assoc.)	0	1	.000	2.45	8	0	0	0	1	11	12	3	3	5	10
—Rochester (Int'l)■	3	2	.600	3.16	44	0	0	0	11	57	49	26	20	28	48
1972—Rochester (Int'l)	7	5	.583	3.21	47	0	0	0	7	73	66	31	26	38	61
1973—Rochester (Int'l)	1	1	.500	1.38	14	0	0	0	1	26	13	8	4	15	15

RECORD AS MANAGER

BACKGROUND: Player/coach, Rochester, Baltimore Orioles organizationn (1973). ... Minor league pitching instructor, Orioles organization (1974-77). ... Pitching coach, Texas Rangers (November 21, 1977-1978). ... Pitching coach, Orioles (1978-June 20, 1985). ... Pitching coach, Pittsburgh Pirates (1987-1996). ... Pitching coach (1997).

| | REGULAR SEASON | | | | | POSTSEASON | | | | | | |
| | | | | | | Playoff | | Champ. Series | | World Series | | All-Star Game | |
Year Team (League)	W	L	Pct.	Pos.		W	L	W	L	W	L	W	L
1985—Minnesota (A.L.)	50	50	.500	4th (W)		—	—	—	—	—	—	—	—
1986—Minnesota (A.L.)	59	80	.424			—	—	—	—	—	—	—	—
Major league totals (2 years)	109	130	.456			—	—	—	—	—	—	—	—

NOTES:

1985—Replaced Minnesota manager Billy Gardner, with club in sixth place and record of 27-35 (June 21).

1986—Replaced as Twins manager by Tom Kelly, with club in seventh place (September 12).

MUSER, TONY — ROYALS

PERSONAL: Born August 1, 1947, in Los Angeles. ... 6-2/190. ... Batted left, threw left. ... Full name: Anthony Joseph Muser.

HIGH SCHOOL: Lakewood (Calif.).

JUNIOR COLLEGE: San Diego Mesa.

TRANSACTIONS/CAREER NOTES: Signed as non-drafted free agent by Boston Red Sox organization (1967). ... On military list (beginning of 1968 season-July 15, 1968). ... Traded by Red Sox with P Vicente Romo to Chicago White Sox for P Danny Murphy and C Duane Josephson (March 30, 1971). ... Traded by White Sox to Baltimore Orioles for P Jesse Jefferson (June 15, 1975). ... Released by Orioles (February 21, 1978). ... Signed by Milwaukee Brewers organization (March 20, 1978). ... Released by Brewers (February 12, 1979).

| | | | | | | | BATTING | | | | | | | | FIELDING | | |
Year Team (League)	Pos.	G	AB	R	H	2B	3B	HR	RBI	Avg.	BB	SO	SB	PO	A	E	Avg.
1967—Waterloo (Midw.)	1B	68	251	40	71	15	1	6	42	.283	38	42	3	674	28	11	.985
1968—Greenv. (W. Car.)	1B-OF	33	114	13	31	7	0	2	12	.272	18	17	1	223	23	2	.992
—Win.-Salem (Car.)	OF-1B	7	21	1	8	0	0	0	2	.381	1	3	1	13	1	0	1.000
1969—Louisville (Int'l)	1B	120	457	57	129	14	4	7	62	.282	43	53	7	1029	63	15	.986
—Boston (A.L.)	1B	2	9	0	1	0	0	0	1	.111	1	1	0	17	3	0	1.000
1970—Louisville (Int'l)	1B	114	462	66	130	25	7	5	45	.281	38	49	1	1013	45	9	*.992
1971—Indianapolis (A.A.)■	1B	85	310	36	91	10	3	3	31	.294	35	27	0	720	42	6	.992
—Chicago (A.L.)	1B	11	16	2	5	0	1	0	0	.313	1	1	0	23	3	1	.963
1972—Tucson (PCL)	1B	83	318	41	86	17	0	3	40	.270	29	28	3	680	49	12	.984
—Chicago (A.L.)	1B-OF	44	61	6	17	2	2	1	9	.279	2	6	1	135	7	2	.986
1973—Chicago (A.L.)	1B-OF	109	309	38	88	14	3	4	30	.285	33	36	8	681	38	6	.992
1974—Chicago (A.L.)	1B	103	206	16	60	5	1	1	18	.291	6	22	1	419	13	1	.998
1975—Chicago (A.L.)	1B	43	111	11	27	3	0	0	6	.243	7	8	2	263	22	2	.993
—Baltimore (A.L.)■	1B	80	82	11	26	3	0	0	11	.317	8	9	0	213	15	1	.996
1976—Baltimore (A.L.)	1B-OF	136	326	25	74	7	1	1	30	.227	21	34	1	693	63	7	.991
1977—Baltimore (A.L.)	1B-OF	120	118	14	27	6	0	0	7	.229	13	16	1	232	20	3	.988
1978—Spokane (PCL)■	1B-OF	78	283	48	83	13	0	6	38	.293	33	25	2	572	50	4	.994
—Milwaukee (A.L.)	1B	15	30	0	4	1	1	0	5	.133	3	5	0	79	5	1	.988
1979—Seibu (Jp. Pac.)■	...	65	168	...	33	...	...	2	10	.196	...	...	...	...	...	...	...
Major league totals (9 years)		663	1268	123	329	41	9	7	117	.259	95	138	14	2755	189	24	.992

RECORD AS MANAGER

BACKGROUND: Coach, Milwaukee Brewers (1985-89). ... Scout, Brewers (1990). ... Coach, Chicago Cubs (1993-July 8, 1997).

| | REGULAR SEASON | | | | | POSTSEASON | | | | | | |
| | | | | | | Playoff | | Champ. Series | | World Series | | All-Star Game | |
Year Team (League)	W	L	Pct.	Pos.		W	L	W	L	W	L	W	L
1980—Stockton (California)	49	21	.700	1st (N)		—	—	—	—	—	—	—	—
—(Second half)	41	30	.577	1st (N)		3	0	—	—	—	—	—	—
1981—El Paso (Texas)	37	31	.544	2nd (W)		—	—	—	—	—	—	—	—
—(Second half)	28	38	.424	4th (W)		—	—	—	—	—	—	—	—
1982—El Paso (Texas)	42	23	.646	1st (W)		—	—	—	—	—	—	—	—
—(Second half)	34	37	.479	2nd (W)		2	3	—	—	—	—	—	—
1983—El Paso (Texas)	35	33	.515	2nd (W)		—	—	—	—	—	—	—	—
—Vancouver(Pacific Coast)	29	41	.414	4th (N)		—	—	—	—	—	—	—	—
1984—Vancouver (Pacific Coast)	32	40	.444	3rd (N)		—	—	—	—	—	—	—	—
—(Second half)	39	31	.557	3rd (N)		—	—	—	—	—	—	—	—

Year Team (League)	W	L	Pct.	Pos.	Playoff W	L	Champ. Series W	L	World Series W	L	All-Star Game W	L
1991—Denver (American Association)	79	65	.549	1st (W)	7	3	—	—	—	—	—	—
1992—Denver (American Association)	73	71	.507	2nd (W)	—	—	—	—	—	—	—	—
1997—Kansas City (A.L.)	31	48	.392	4th (C)	—	—	—	—	—	—	—	—
Major league totals (1 year)	31	48	.392	5th (C)	—	—	—	—	—	—	—	—

NOTES:
1980—Defeated Visalia in league championship.
1982—Defeated Midland, two games to one, in playoffs; lost to Tulsa, three games to none, in league championship.
1983—Replaced Vancouver manager Dick Phillips (June 22).
1991—Defeated Buffalo, three games to two, in league championship; defeated Columbus (International League), four games to one, in Class AAA Alliance championship.
1997—Replaced Kansas City manager Bob Boone with club in fourth place and record of 36-46 (July 9).

OATES, JOHNNY — RANGERS

PERSONAL: Born January 21, 1946, in Sylva, N.C. ... 5-11/185. ... Batted left, threw right. ... Full name: Johnny Lane Oates.
HIGH SCHOOL: Prince George (Va.).
COLLEGE: Virginia Tech (received bachelor of science degree in health and physical education).
TRANSACTIONS/CAREER NOTES: Selected by Chicago White Sox organization in second round of free-agent draft (June 1966); did not sign. ... Selected by Baltimore Orioles organization in secondary phase of free-agent draft (January 28, 1967). ... On military list (April 21-August 22, 1970). ... Traded by Orioles with P Pat Dobson, P Roric Harrison and 2B Dave Johnson to Atlanta Braves for C Earl Williams and IF Taylor Duncan (November 30, 1972). ... On disabled list (July 17-September 2, 1973). ... Traded by Braves with 1B Dick Allen to Philadelphia Phillies for C Jim Essian, OF Barry Bonnell and cash (May 7, 1975). ... On disabled list (April 14-June 1, 1976). ... Traded by Phillies with P Quency Hill to Los Angeles Dodgers for IF Ted Sizemore (December 20, 1976). ... Released by Dodgers (March 27, 1980). ... Signed by New York Yankees (April 4, 1980). ... Granted free agency (November 13, 1980). ... Re-signed by Yankees organization (January 23, 1981). ... On Columbus disabled list (August 3-25, 1981). ... Released by Yankees organization (October 27, 1981).
STATISTICAL NOTES: Led International League catchers with 727 total chances in 1971. ... Led N.L. with 15 passed balls in 1974. ... Tied for N.L. lead in double plays by catcher with 10 in 1975.

Year Team (League)	Pos.	G	AB	R	H	2B	3B	HR	RBI	Avg.	BB	SO	SB	PO	A	E	Avg.
1967—Bluefield (Appal.)	C	5	12	5	5	1	0	1	4	.417	2	0	0	23	5	0	1.000
—Miami (Fla. St.)	C-OF	48	156	22	45	5	2	3	19	.288	24	13	2	271	37	8	.975
1968—Miami (Fla. St.)	C-OF	70	194	24	51	9	3	0	23	.263	33	14	2	384	42	3	.993
1969—Dall./Fort W. (Tex.)	C	66	191	24	55	12	2	1	18	.288	20	9	0	253	42	4	.987
1970—Rochester (Int'l)	C	9	16	1	6	1	0	0	4	.375	4	2	0	24	2	0	1.000
—Baltimore (A.L.)	C	5	18	2	5	0	1	0	2	.278	2	0	0	30	1	2	.939
1971—Rochester (Int'l)	C	114	346	49	96	16	3	7	44	.277	49	31	10	*648	*73	6	.992
1972—Baltimore (A.L.)	C	85	253	20	66	12	1	4	21	.261	28	31	5	391	31	2	*.995
1973—Atlanta (N.L.)■	C	93	322	27	80	6	0	4	27	.248	22	31	1	409	57	9	.981
1974—Atlanta (N.L.)	C	100	291	22	65	10	0	1	21	.223	23	24	2	434	55	4	.992
1975—Atlanta (N.L.)	C	8	18	0	4	1	0	0	0	.222	1	4	0	21	1	0	1.000
—Philadelphia (N.L.)■	C	90	269	28	77	14	0	1	25	.286	33	29	1	429	44	5	.990
1976—Philadelphia (N.L.)	C	37	99	10	25	2	0	0	8	.253	8	12	0	155	15	1	.994
1977—Los Angeles (N.L.)■	C	60	156	18	42	4	0	3	11	.269	11	11	1	258	37	4	.987
1978—Los Angeles (N.L.)	C	40	75	5	23	1	0	0	6	.307	5	3	0	77	10	4	.956
1979—Los Angeles (N.L.)	C	26	46	4	6	2	0	0	2	.130	4	1	0	64	13	2	.975
1980—New York (A.L.)■	C	39	64	6	12	3	0	1	3	.188	2	3	1	99	10	1	.991
1981—New York (A.L.)	C	10	26	4	5	1	0	0	0	.192	2	0	0	49	3	2	.963
American League totals (4 years)		139	361	32	88	16	2	5	26	.244	34	34	6	569	45	7	.989
National League totals (7 years)		454	1276	114	322	40	0	9	100	.252	107	115	5	1847	232	29	.986
Major league totals (11 years)		593	1637	146	410	56	2	14	126	.250	141	149	11	2416	277	36	.987

CHAMPIONSHIP SERIES RECORD

Year Team (League)	Pos.	G	AB	R	H	2B	3B	HR	RBI	Avg.	BB	SO	SB	PO	A	E	Avg.
1976—Philadelphia (N.L.)	C	1	1	0	0	0	0	0	0	.000	0	0	0	1	0	0	1.000

WORLD SERIES RECORD

Year Team (League)	Pos.	G	AB	R	H	2B	3B	HR	RBI	Avg.	BB	SO	SB	PO	A	E	Avg.
1977—Los Angeles (N.L.)	C	1	1	0	0	0	0	0	0	.000	0	0	0	1	0	0	1.000
1978—Los Angeles (N.L.)	C	1	1	0	1	0	0	0	0	1.000	1	0	0	3	1	0	1.000
World Series totals (2 years)		2	2	0	1	0	0	0	0	.500	1	0	0	4	1	0	1.000

RECORD AS MANAGER

BACKGROUND: Player/coach, Columbus, New York Yankees organization (July 30, 1981-remainder of season). ... Coach, Chicago Cubs (1984-87). ... Coach, Baltimore Orioles (1989-May 23, 1991).
HONORS: Named International League Manager of the Year (1988). ... Coach, A.L. All-Star team (1993, 1995 and 1997). ... Named A.L. Manager of the Year by THE SPORTING NEWS (1993 and 1996). ... Named co-A.L. Manager of the Year by Baseball Writers' Association of America (1996).

Year Team (League)	W	L	Pct.	Pos.	Playoff W	L	Champ. Series W	L	World Series W	L	All-Star Game W	L
1982—Nashville (Southern)	32	38	.457	4th (W)	—	—	—	—	—	—	—	—
—(Second half)	45	29	.608	1st (W)	6	2	—	—	—	—	—	—
1983—Columbus (International)	83	57	.593	1st	2	3	—	—	—	—	—	—
1988—Rochester (International)	77	64	.546	1st (W)	5	5	—	—	—	—	—	—

		REGULAR SEASON			POSTSEASON							
					Playoff		Champ. Series		World Series		All-Star Game	
Year Team (League)	W	L	Pct.	Pos.	W	L	W	L	W	L	W	L
1991— Baltimore (A.L.)	54	71	.432	6th (E)	—	—	—	—	—	—	—	—
1992— Baltimore (A.L.)	89	73	.549	3rd (E)	—	—	—	—	—	—	—	—
1993— Baltimore (A.L.)	85	77	.525	T3rd (E)	—	—	—	—	—	—	—	—
1994— Baltimore (A.L.)	63	49	.563		—	—	—	—	—	—	—	—
1995— Texas (A.L.)	74	70	.514	3rd (W)	—	—	—	—	—	—	—	—
1996— Texas (A.L.)	90	72	.556	1st (W)	1	3	—	—	—	—	—	—
1997— Texas (A.L.)	77	85	.475	3rd (W)	—	—	—	—	—	—	—	—
Major league totals (7 years)	532	497	.517		1	3	—	—	—	—	—	—

NOTES:

1982—Defeated Knoxville, three games to one, in playoffs; defeated Jacksonville, three games to one, in league championship.

1983—Lost to Tidewater in playoffs.

1988—Defeated Tidewater, three games to one, in league championship; lost to Indianapolis (American Association), four games to two, in Class AAA-Alliance championship.

1991—Replaced Baltimore manager Frank Robinson with club in seventh place and record of 13-24 (May 23).

1994—Baltimore was in second place in A.L. East at time of season ending strike (August 12).

1996—Lost to New York in A.L. divisional playoff.

PINIELLA, LOU — MARINERS

PERSONAL: Born August 28, 1943, in Tampa. ... 6-2/199. ... Batted right, threw right. ... Full name: Louis Victor Piniella. ... Cousin of Dave Magadan, first baseman/third baseman, Oakland Athletics. ... Name pronounced pin-ELL-uh.

HIGH SCHOOL: Jesuit (Tampa).

COLLEGE: Tampa.

TRANSACTIONS/CAREER NOTES: Signed as free agent by Cleveland Indians organization (June 9, 1962). ... Selected by Washington Senators organization from Jacksonville, Indians organization, in Rule 5 major league draft (November 26, 1962). ... On military list (March 9-July 20, 1964). ... Traded by Senators organization to Baltimore Orioles organization (August 4, 1964), completing deal in which Orioles traded P Lester (Buster) Narum to Senators for cash and a player to be named later (March 31, 1964). ... On suspended list (June 27-29, 1965). ... Traded by Orioles organization to Indians organization for C Camilo Carreon (March 10, 1966). ... On temporarily inactive list (May 19-22, 1967). ... On disabled list (May 22-June 6, 1968). ... On temporarily inactive list (June 6-25, 1968). ... Selected by Seattle Pilots in expansion draft (October 15, 1968). ... Traded by Pilots to Kansas City Royals for OF Steve Whitaker and P John Gelnar (April 1, 1969). ... On military list (August 7-22, 1969). ... On disabled list (May 5-June 8, 1971). ... Traded by Royals with P Ken Wright to New York Yankees for P Lindy McDaniel (December 7, 1973). ... On disabled list (June 17-July 6, 1975; August 23-September 7, 1981; and March 30-April 22, 1983). ... Placed on voluntarily retired list (June 17, 1984).

RECORDS: Shares major league record for most assists by outfielder in one inning—2 (May 27, 1974, third inning).

HONORS: Named A.L. Rookie of the Year by Baseball Writers' Association of America (1969).

STATISTICAL NOTES: Led A.L. in grounding into double plays with 25 in 1972. ... Career major league grand slams: 1.

							BATTING								FIELDING		
Year Team (League)	Pos.	G	AB	R	H	2B	3B	HR	RBI	Avg.	BB	SO	SB	PO	A	E	Avg.
1962— Selma (Ala.-Fla.)	OF	70	278	40	75	10	5	8	44	.270	10	57	4	94	6	9	.917
1963— Peninsula (Caro.)■	OF	143	548	71	170	29	4	16	77	.310	34	70	8	271	*23	8	.974
1964— Aberdeen (North.)	OF	20	74	8	20	8	3	0	12	.270	6	9	1	37	1	1	.974
— Baltimore (A.L.)■	PH	4	1	0	0	0	0	0	0	.000	0	0	0	...	...	...	...
1965— Elmira (Eastern)	OF	126	490	64	122	29	6	11	64	.249	22	57	5	176	5	7	.963
1966— Portland (PCL)■	OF	133	457	47	132	22	3	7	52	.289	20	52	6	177	11	11	.945
1967— Portland (PCL)	OF	113	396	46	122	20	1	8	56	.308	23	47	2	199	7	6	.972
1968— Portland (PCL)	OF	88	331	49	105	15	3	13	62	.317	19	31	0	167	6	7	.961
— Cleveland (A.L.)	OF	6	5	1	0	0	0	0	1	.000	0	0	1	1	0	0	1.000
1969— Kansas City (A.L.)■	OF	135	493	43	139	21	6	11	68	.282	33	56	2	278	13	7	.977
1970— Kansas City (A.L.)	OF-1B	144	542	54	163	24	5	11	88	.301	35	42	3	250	6	4	.985
1971— Kansas City (A.L.)	OF	126	448	43	125	21	5	3	51	.279	21	43	5	201	6	3	.986
1972— Kansas City (A.L.)	OF	151	574	65	179	*33	4	11	72	.312	34	59	7	275	8	7	.976
1973— Kansas City (A.L.)	OF-DH	144	513	53	128	28	1	9	69	.250	30	65	5	196	9	3	.986
1974— New York (A.L.)■	OF-DH-1B	140	518	71	158	26	0	9	70	.305	32	58	1	270	16	3	.990
1975— New York (A.L.)	OF-DH	74	199	7	39	4	1	0	22	.196	16	22	0	65	5	1	.986
1976— New York (A.L.)	OF-DH	100	327	36	92	16	6	3	38	.281	18	34	0	199	10	4	.981
1977— New York (A.L.)	OF-DH-1B	103	339	47	112	19	3	12	45	.330	20	31	2	86	3	2	.978
1978— New York (A.L.)	OF-DH	130	472	67	148	34	5	6	69	.314	34	36	3	213	4	7	.969
1979— New York (A.L.)	OF-DH	130	461	49	137	22	2	11	69	.297	17	31	3	204	13	4	.982
1980— New York (A.L.)	OF-DH	116	321	39	92	18	0	2	27	.287	29	20	0	157	8	5	.971
1981— New York (A.L.)	OF-DH	60	159	16	44	9	0	5	18	.277	13	9	0	69	2	1	.986
1982— New York (A.L.)	DH-OF	102	261	33	80	17	1	6	37	.307	18	18	0	68	2	0	1.000
1983— New York (A.L.)	OF-DH	53	148	19	43	9	1	2	16	.291	11	12	1	67	4	3	.959
1984— New York (A.L.)	OF-DH	29	86	8	26	4	1	1	6	.302	7	5	0	40	3	0	1.000
Major league totals (18 years)		1747	5867	651	1705	305	41	102	766	.291	368	541	33	2639	112	54	.981

DIVISION SERIES RECORD

							BATTING								FIELDING		
Year Team (League)	Pos.	G	AB	R	H	2B	3B	HR	RBI	Avg.	BB	SO	SB	PO	A	E	Avg.
1981— New York (A.L.)	DH-PH	4	10	1	2	1	0	1	3	.200	0	0	0	...	...	...	...

CHAMPIONSHIP SERIES RECORD

							BATTING								FIELDING		
Year Team (League)	Pos.	G	AB	R	H	2B	3B	HR	RBI	Avg.	BB	SO	SB	PO	A	E	Avg.
1976— New York (A.L.)	DH-PH	4	11	1	3	1	0	0	0	.273	0	1	0	...	...	...	...
1977— New York (A.L.)	OF-DH	5	21	1	7	3	0	0	2	.333	0	1	0	9	1	0	1.000
1978— New York (A.L.)	OF	4	17	2	4	0	0	0	0	.235	0	3	0	13	0	0	1.000
1980— New York (A.L.)	OF	2	5	1	1	0	0	1	1	.200	2	1	0	5	0	0	1.000
1981— New York (A.L.)	PH-DH-OF	3	5	2	3	0	0	1	3	.600	0	0	0	0	0	0	...
Championship series totals (5 years)		18	59	7	18	4	0	2	6	.305	2	6	0	27	1	0	1.000

WORLD SERIES RECORD

RECORDS: Shares single-series record for collecting one or more hits in each game (1978).
NOTES: Member of World Series championship teams (1977 and 1978).

Year	Team (League)	Pos.	G	AB	R	H	2B	3B	HR	RBI	Avg.	BB	SO	SB	PO	A	E	Avg.
1976—New York (A.L.)	DH-OF-PH	4	9	1	3	1	0	0	0	.333	0	0	0	1	0	0	1.000
1977—New York (A.L.)	OF	6	22	1	6	0	0	0	3	.273	0	3	0	16	1	1	.944
1978—New York (A.L.)	OF	6	25	3	7	0	0	0	4	.280	0	0	1	14	1	0	1.000
1981—New York (A.L.)	OF-PH	6	16	2	7	1	0	0	3	.438	0	1	1	7	0	0	1.000
World Series totals (4 years)		22	72	7	23	2	0	0	10	.319	0	4	2	38	2	1	.976

ALL-STAR GAME RECORD

Year	League	Pos.	AB	R	H	2B	3B	HR	RBI	Avg.	BB	SO	SB	PO	A	E	Avg.
1972—American	PH	1	0	0	0	0	0	0	0	.000	0	0	0	...	...	...	...

RECORD AS MANAGER

BACKGROUND: Coach, New York Yankees (June 25, 1984-85). ... Vice-president/general manager, Yankees (beginning of 1988 season-June 22, 1988). ... Special adviser, Yankees (1989).
HONORS: Named A.L. Manager of the Year by Baseball Writers' Association of America (1995).

			REGULAR SEASON			Playoff		Champ. Series		World Series		All-Star Game	
Year	Team (League)	W	L	Pct.	Pos.	W	L	W	L	W	L	W	L
1986—New York (A.L.)	90	72	.556	2nd (E)	—	—	—	—	—	—	—	—
1987—New York (A.L.)	89	73	.549	4th (E)	—	—	—	—	—	—	—	—
1988—New York (A.L.)	45	48	.484	5th (E)	—	—	—	—	—	—	—	—
1990—Cincinnati (N.L.)	91	71	.562	1st (W)	—	—	4	2	4	0	—	—
1991—Cincinnati (N.L.)	74	88	.457	5th (W)	—	—	—	—	—	—	0	1
1992—Cincinnati (N.L.)	90	72	.556	2nd (W)	—	—	—	—	—	—	—	—
1993—Seattle (A.L.)	82	80	.506	4th (W)	—	—	—	—	—	—	—	—
1994—Seattle (A.L.)	49	63	.438		—	—	—	—	—	—	—	—
1995—Seattle (A.L.)	79	66	.545	1st (W)	3	2	2	4	—	—	—	—
1996—Seattle (A.L.)	85	76	.528	2nd (W)	—	—	—	—	—	—	—	—
1997—Seattle (A.L.)	90	72	.556	1st (W)	1	3	—	—	—	—	—	—
American League totals (8 years)	609	550	.525		4	5	2	4	—	—	—	—
National League totals (3 years)	255	231	.525		—	—	4	2	4	0	0	1
Major league totals (11 years)	864	781	.525		4	5	6	6	4	0	0	1

NOTES:
1988—Replaced New York manager Billy Martin with club in second place and record of 40-28 (June 23).
1990—Defeated Pittsburgh in N.L. Championship Series; defeated Oakland in World Series.
1994—Seattle was in third place in A.L. West at time of season-ending strike (August 12).
1995—Defeated New York in A.L. divisional playoff; lost to Cleveland in A.L. Championship Series.
1997—Lost to Baltimore in A.L. divisional playoff.

RIGGLEMAN, JIM   CUBS

PERSONAL: Born December 9, 1952, in Fort Dix, N.J. ... 5-11/175. ... Batted right, threw right. ... Full name: James David Riggleman.
HIGH SCHOOL: Richard Montgomery (Rockville, Md.).
COLLEGE: Frostburg (Md.) State (degree in physical education).
TRANSACTIONS/CAREER NOTES: Selected by Los Angeles Dodgers organization in fourth round of free-agent draft (June 5, 1974). ... Traded by Dodgers organization to St. Louis Cardinals organization for C Sergio Robles (July 19, 1976). ... On Springfield disabled list (April 14-July 3, 1978). ... Released by Arkansas to become coach (May 25, 1981).
STATISTICAL NOTES: Led Eastern League third basemen with 30 double plays in 1975.

							BATTING								FIELDING		
Year	Team (League)	Pos.	G	AB	R	H	2B	3B	HR	RBI	Avg.	BB	SO	SB	PO	A	E	Avg.
1974—Waterbury (Eastern)	2B-3B	80	252	29	67	13	1	8	41	.266	25	56	1	159	175	20	.944
1975—Waterbury (Eastern)	3B	129	439	61	113	14	7	11	57	.257	54	86	14	109	267	53	.876
1976—Waterbury (Eastern)	OF-3B	84	287	38	75	14	2	6	39	.261	31	47	4	99	29	18	.877
—Arkansas (Texas)■	3B-OF-1B	47	154	29	46	9	1	5	25	.299	19	13	1	38	73	10	.917
1977—Arkansas (Texas)	3B	27	93	10	26	7	2	0	11	.280	16	9	6	25	48	5	.936
—New Orleans (A.A.)	3B-OF-SS	103	346	52	83	16	0	17	52	.240	34	65	10	88	149	24	.908
1978—Arkansas (Texas)	3B-OF	59	174	34	51	8	1	4	34	.293	43	39	2	29	60	14	.864
1979—Arkansas (Texas)	3B-OF-1B	46	110	17	30	9	0	1	23	.273	13	23	5	34	22	4	.933
—Springfield (A.A.)	3B-OF-1B	35	93	9	22	4	0	2	9	.237	5	26	3	47	4	6	.895
1980—Arkansas (Texas)	3B-OF	127	431	84	127	29	7	21	90	.295	60	67	28	123	243	26	.934
1981—Arkansas (Texas)	OF-3B	37	133	17	32	7	1	1	15	.241	16	29	3	56	22	5	.940

RECORD AS MANAGER

BACKGROUND: Coach, Arkansas, St. Louis Cardinals organization, (May 25, 1981-remainder of season). ... Coach, Louisville, Cardinals organization (April 13-May 31, 1982). ... Director of player development, Cardinals (June 21, 1988-remainder of season). ... Coach, Cardinals (1989-90).
HONORS: Coach, N.L. All-Star team (1995).

			REGULAR SEASON			Playoff		Champ. Series		World Series		All-Star Game	
Year	Team (League)	W	L	Pct.	Pos.	W	L	W	L	W	L	W	L
1982—St. Petersburg (Florida State)	8	4	.667	2nd	—	—	—	—	—	—	—	—
—(Second half)	35	30	.538	2nd	—	—	—	—	—	—	—	—
1983—St. Petersburg (Florida State)	33	35	.485	T3rd	—	—	—	—	—	—	—	—
—(Second half)	37	29	.561	2nd	—	—	—	—	—	—	—	—

Year Team (League)	W	L	Pct.	Pos.	Playoff W	L	Champ. Series W	L	World Series W	L	All-Star Game W	L
1984— St. Petersburg (Florida State)	39	38	.506	3rd	—	—	—	—	—	—	—	—
— (Second half)	32	35	.478	3rd	—	—	—	—	—	—	—	—
1985— Arkansas (Texas)	33	30	.524	1st (E)	—	—	—	—	—	—	—	—
— (Second half)	31	40	.437	4th (E)	0	2	—	—	—	—	—	—
1986— Arkansas (Texas)	35	28	.556	3rd (E)	—	—	—	—	—	—	—	—
— (Second half)	32	39	.451	3rd (E)	—	—	—	—	—	—	—	—
1987— Arkansas (Texas)	36	29	.554	2nd (E)	—	—	—	—	—	—	—	—
— (Second half)	36	34	.514	3rd (E)	—	—	—	—	—	—	—	—
1988— Arkansas (Texas)	30	37	.448	3rd (E)	—	—	—	—	—	—	—	—
— (Second half)	2	1	.667		—	—	—	—	—	—	—	—
1991— Las Vegas (Pacific Coast)	36	34	.514	4th (S)	—	—	—	—	—	—	—	—
— (Second half)	29	41	.414	5th (S)	—	—	—	—	—	—	—	—
1992— Las Vegas (Pacific Coast)	41	31	.569	1st (S)	—	—	—	—	—	—	—	—
— (Second half)	33	39	.458	3rd (S)	2	3	—	—	—	—	—	—
— San Diego (N.L.)	4	8	.333	3rd (W)	—	—	—	—	—	—	—	—
1993— San Diego (N.L.)	61	101	.377	7th (W)	—	—	—	—	—	—	—	—
1994— San Diego (N.L.)	47	70	.402		—	—	—	—	—	—	—	—
1995— Chicago (N.L.)	73	71	.507	3rd (C)	—	—	—	—	—	—	—	—
1996— Chicago (N.L.)	76	86	.469	4th (C)	—	—	—	—	—	—	—	—
1997— Chicago (N.L.)	68	94	.420	5th (C)	—	—	—	—	—	—	—	—
Major league totals (6 years)	329	430	.433		—	—	—	—	—	—	—	—

NOTES:

1982—Replaced St. Petersburg manager Nick Leyva with club in fourth place and record of 26-30 (June 4).
1985—Lost to Jackson in semifinals.
1988—Replaced as Arkansas manager by Darold Knowles (June 21).
1992—Lost to Colorado Springs in semifinals. Replaced San Diego manager Greg Riddoch with club in third place and record of 78-72 (September 23).
1994—San Diego was in fourth place in N.L. West at time of season-ending baseball strike (August 12).

ROTHSCHILD, LARRY — P — DEVIL RAYS

PERSONAL: Born March 12, 1954, in Chicago. ... 6-2/185. ... Threw right, batted right. ... Full name: Lawrence Lee Rothschild.
HIGH SCHOOL: Homewood-Flossmoor (Flossmoor, Ill.).
COLLEGE: Bradley, then Florida State.
TRANSACTIONS/CAREER NOTES: Signed as non-drafted free agent by Cincinnati Reds organization (June 10, 1975). ... Loaned to San Diego Padres organization (May 11, 1978). ... Returned to Reds organization (July 18, 1978). ... Selected by Detroit Tigers from Reds organization in major league draft (December 8, 1980). ... Sold to Las Vegas, Pacific Coast League (February 25, 1983). ... On disabled list (April 10-May 4, 1983). ... Sold to Denver, American Association (December 18, 1983). ... Sold to Iowa, American Association (October 15, 1984).

Year Team (League)	W	L	Pct.	ERA	G	GS	CG	ShO	Sv.	IP	H	R	ER	BB	SO
1975—Billings (Pioneer)	0	2	.000	7.88	6	0	0	0	1	8	14	11	7	7	12
—Eugene (Northwest)	3	0	1.000	2.73	21	0	0	0	•6	33	17	11	10	21	36
1976—Three Rivers (East.)	11	3	*.786	2.05	30	12	10	5	5	123	96	33	28	29	75
1977—Indianapolis (A.A.)	4	4	.500	4.21	29	14	2	1	1	92	93	51	43	34	43
1978—Nashville (Southern)	0	0	. . .	4.50	5	0	0	0	1	12	14	7	6	4	9
—Amarillo (Texas)■	5	5	.500	4.17	12	12	5	1	0	82	83	42	38	21	57
—Indianapolis (A.A.)■	4	0	1.000	2.20	8	6	2	0	0	45	31	15	11	19	38
1979—Indianapolis (A.A.)	1	6	.143	5.27	33	10	0	0	6	82	85	52	48	56	68
1980—Indianapolis (A.A.)	8	7	.533	4.22	33	14	1	0	1	113	111	60	53	44	74
1981—Evansville (A.A.)■	8	5	.615	3.27	56	0	0	0	15	77	62	32	28	29	81
—Detroit (A.L.)	0	0	. . .	1.50	5	0	0	0	0	6	4	1	1	6	1
1982—Evansville (A.A.)	6	4	.600	3.65	45	0	0	0	10	69	73	34	28	30	45
—Detroit (A.L.)	0	0	. . .	13.50	2	0	0	0	0	2⅔	4	4	4	2	0
1983—Las Vegas (PCL)■	9	2	.818	5.09	38	0	0	0	2	74½	88	43	42	34	39
1984—Denver (Am. Assoc.)■	6	3	.667	4.02	31	9	1	1	2	109⅔	109	58	49	51	71
1985—Iowa (Am. Assoc.)■	1	5	.167	5.32	40	3	0	0	0	89⅔	101	58	53	34	58
Major league totals (2 years)	0	0	. . .	5.19	7	0	0	0	0	8⅔	8	5	5	8	1

RECORD AS MANAGER

BACKGROUND: Coach, Cincinnati Reds organization (1986-89). ... Coach, Reds (1990-May 24, 1993). ... Coach, Atlanta Braves organization (1994). ... Coach, Florida Marlins (1995-97).

RUSSELL, BILL — DODGERS

PERSONAL: Born October 21, 1948, in Pittsburg, Kan. ... 6-0/175. ... Batted right, threw right. ... Full name: William Ellis Russell.
TRANSACTIONS/CAREER NOTES: Selected by Los Angeles Dodgers organization in 37th round of free-agent draft (June 12, 1966). ... On military list (August 1-19, 1969; July 3-19, 1970; June 19-July 3, 1971; and July 7-22, 1972). ... On disabled list (April 13-May 6 and May 11-June 30, 1975 and May 14-June 4 and August 12-27, 1984). ... On voluntarily retired list (October 24-November 12, 1986). ... Released by Dodgers (November 12, 1986).
RECORDS: Shares major league single-game record (nine innings) for most strikeouts—5 (June 9, 1971).
HONORS: Named shortstop on THE SPORTING NEWS N.L. All-Star team (1973).
STATISTICAL NOTES: Tied for California League lead in double plays by outfielder with four in 1968. ... Led N.L. in intentional bases on balls received with 25 in 1974. ... Led N.L. shortstops in double plays with 102 in 1977. ... Led N.L. shortstops in total chances with 834 in 1973.

Year Team (League)	Pos.	G	AB	R	H	2B	3B	HR	RBI	Avg.	BB	SO	SB	PO	A	E	Avg.
1966— Ogden (Pioneer)	OF	39	97	19	31	5	1	3	21	.320	7	19	4	25	3	2	.933
1967— Dubuque (Midw.)	OF	67	263	29	58	11	1	5	21	.221	18	58	6	98	11	10	.916

Year	Team (League)	Pos.	G	AB	R	H	2B	3B	HR	RBI	Avg.	BB	SO	SB	PO	A	E	Avg.
1968—Bakersfield (Calif.)......		OF	115	439	76	123	16	3	17	55	.280	34	106	23	255	*22	7	.975
1969—Los Angeles (N.L.).....		OF	98	212	35	48	6	2	5	15	.226	22	45	4	132	4	3	.978
1970—Spokane (PCL)	OF-3B-SS	55	237	48	86	13	5	3	30	.363	11	26	12	112	39	6	.962
—Los Angeles (N.L.)....	OF-SS	81	278	30	72	11	9	0	28	.259	16	28	9	167	10	3	.983
1971—Los Angeles (N.L.)....	2B-OF-SS	91	211	29	48	7	4	2	15	.227	11	39	6	131	124	8	.970
1972—Los Angeles (N.L.)....	SS-OF	129	434	47	118	19	5	4	34	.272	34	64	14	209	439	*34	.950
1973—Los Angeles (N.L.)....	SS	•162	615	55	163	26	3	4	56	.265	34	63	15	243	*560	31	.963
1974—Los Angeles (N.L.)....	SS-OF	160	553	61	149	17	6	5	65	.269	53	53	14	194	491	*39	.946
1975—Los Angeles (N.L.)....	SS	84	252	24	52	9	2	0	14	.206	23	28	5	94	230	11	.967
1976—Los Angeles (N.L.)....	SS	149	554	53	152	17	3	5	65	.274	21	46	15	251	476	28	.963
1977—Los Angeles (N.L.)....	SS	153	634	84	176	28	6	4	51	.278	24	43	16	234	523	29	.963
1978—Los Angeles (N.L.)....	SS	155	625	72	179	32	4	3	46	.286	30	34	10	245	533	31	.962
1979—Los Angeles (N.L.)....	SS	153	627	72	170	26	4	7	56	.271	24	43	6	218	452	30	.957
1980—Los Angeles (N.L.)....	SS	130	466	38	123	23	2	3	34	.264	18	44	13	179	387	19	.968
1981—Los Angeles (N.L.)....	SS	82	262	20	61	9	2	0	22	.233	19	20	2	128	261	14	.965
1982—Los Angeles (N.L.)....	SS	153	497	64	136	20	2	3	46	.274	63	30	10	216	502	29	.961
1983—Los Angeles (N.L.)....	SS	131	451	47	111	13	1	1	30	.246	33	31	13	192	392	22	.964
1984—Los Angeles (N.L.)....	SS-OF-2B	89	262	25	70	12	1	0	19	.267	25	24	4	115	173	9	.970
1985—Los Angeles (N.L.)....	S-O-2-3	76	169	19	44	6	1	0	13	.260	18	9	4	60	82	10	.934
1986—Los Angeles (N.L.)....	O-S-2-3	105	216	21	54	11	0	0	18	.250	15	23	7	103	84	5	.974
Major league totals (18 years)			2181	7318	796	1926	292	57	46	627	.263	483	667	167	3111	5723	355	.961

DIVISION SERIES RECORD

Year	Team (League)	Pos.	G	AB	R	H	2B	3B	HR	RBI	Avg.	BB	SO	SB	PO	A	E	Avg.
1981—Los Angeles (N.L.)	SS	5	16	1	4	1	0	0	2	.250	3	1	0	10	15	2	.926

CHAMPIONSHIP SERIES RECORD

Year	Team (League)	Pos.	G	AB	R	H	2B	3B	HR	RBI	Avg.	BB	SO	SB	PO	A	E	Avg.
1974—Los Angeles (N.L.)	SS	4	18	1	7	0	0	0	3	.389	1	0	0	13	16	0	1.000
1977—Los Angeles (N.L.)	SS	4	18	3	5	1	0	0	2	.278	0	0	0	11	12	2	.920
1978—Los Angeles (N.L.)	SS	4	17	1	7	1	0	0	2	.412	1	1	0	14	10	0	1.000
1981—Los Angeles (N.L.)	SS	5	16	2	5	0	1	0	1	.313	1	1	0	10	13	0	1.000
1983—Los Angeles (N.L.)	SS	4	14	1	4	0	0	0	0	.286	2	4	1	4	10	1	.933
Championship series totals (5 years)		21	83	8	28	2	1	0	8	.337	5	6	1	42	65	3	.973

WORLD SERIES RECORD

NOTES: Member of World Series championship team (1981).

Year	Team (League)	Pos.	G	AB	R	H	2B	3B	HR	RBI	Avg.	BB	SO	SB	PO	A	E	Avg.
1974—Los Angeles (N.L.)	SS	5	18	0	4	0	1	0	2	.222	0	2	0	4	11	1	.938
1977—Los Angeles (N.L.)	SS	6	26	3	4	0	1	0	2	.154	1	3	0	9	21	0	1.000
1978—Los Angeles (N.L.)	SS	6	26	1	11	2	0	0	2	.423	2	2	1	11	20	3	.912
1981—Los Angeles (N.L.)	SS	6	25	1	6	0	0	0	2	.240	0	1	1	4	26	1	.968
World Series totals (4 years)		23	95	5	25	2	2	0	8	.263	3	8	2	28	78	5	.955

ALL-STAR GAME RECORD

Year	League	Pos.	AB	R	H	2B	3B	HR	RBI	Avg.	BB	SO	SB	PO	A	E	Avg.
1973—National	SS	2	0	0	0	0	0	0	.000	0	0	0	0	2	0	1.000
1976—National	SS	1	0	0	0	0	0	0	.000	0	0	0	1	2	0	1.000
1980—National	SS	2	0	0	0	0	0	0	.000	0	0	0	0	2	0	1.000
All-Star Game totals (3 years)		5	0	0	0	0	0	0	.000	0	0	0	1	6	0	1.000

RECORD AS MANAGER

BACKGROUND: Coach, Los Angeles Dodgers (1987-91 and 1994-96).
HONORS: Coach, N.L. All-Star team (1989).

			REGULAR SEASON				POSTSEASON					
							Playoff		Champ. Series		World Series		All-Star Game
Year	Team (League)	W	L	Pct.	Pos.	W	L	W	L	W	L	W	L
1992—Albuquerque (PCL)	65	78	.455	8th	—	—	—	—	—	—	—	—
1993—Albuquerque (PCL)	71	72	.497	5th	—	—	—	—	—	—	—	—
1996—Los Angeles (N.L.)	49	37	.570	2nd (W)	0	3	—	—	—	—	—	—
1997—Los Angeles (N.L.)	88	74	.543	2nd (W)	—	—	—	—	—	—	—	—
Major league totals (2 years)	137	111	.552		0	3	—	—	—	—	—	—

NOTES:
1996—Replaced Los Angeles manager Tom Lasorda with club in first place and record of 41-35; was 14-16 as interim manager and 35-21 after being named manager. Lost to Atlanta in N.L. divisional playoff.

SHOWALTER, BUCK · DIAMONDBACKS

PERSONAL: Born May 23, 1956, in DeFuniak Springs, Fla. ... 5-9/195. ... Batted left, threw left. ... Full name: William Nathaniel Showalter III.
JUNIOR COLLEGE: Chipola Junior College (Fla.).
COLLEGE: Mississippi State.
TRANSACTIONS/CAREER NOTES: Selected by New York Yankees organization in fifth round of free-agent draft (June 7, 1977). ... On disabled list (July 1-11 and July 19-August 4, 1981).
STATISTICAL NOTES: Led Southern League first basemen with 1,281 putouts in 1982.

Year	Team (League)	Pos.	G	AB	R	H	2B	3B	HR	RBI	Avg.	BB	SO	SB	PO	A	E	Avg.
1977—	Fort Lauderdale (FSL)	OF	56	196	32	71	8	1	1	25	.362	36	13	4	96	2	2	.980
1978—	West Haven (East.).....	OF	123	429	52	124	13	2	3	46	.289	55	34	19	192	•15	7	.967
1979—	West Haven (East.).....	1B-OF	129	469	71	131	7	3	6	51	.279	36	30	8	575	52	7	.989
1980—	Nashville (Southern) ..	OF-1B	142	550	84	*178	19	3	1	82	.324	53	23	6	71	2	1	.986
1981—	Columbus (Int'l)	OF	14	37	6	7	1	0	1	3	.189	3	0	0	11	0	1	.917
	—Nashville (Southern) ..	OF-1B	90	307	46	81	17	6	0	38	.264	46	16	3	201	14	7	.968
1982—	Nashville (Southern) ..	1B-OF	132	517	66	*152	29	3	3	46	.294	61	42	2 †1282	51	13	.990
1983—	Nashville (Southern) ..	1B-OF-P	89	297	35	82	13	4	1	37	.276	39	22	1	127	6	2	.985
	—Columbus (Int'l)	1B-P	18	63	9	15	3	0	1	8	.238	7	3	1	139	14	1	.994

RECORD AS PITCHER

Year	Team (League)	W	L	Pct.	ERA	G	GS	CG	ShO	Sv.	IP	H	R	ER	BB	SO
1983—	Nashville (Southern)	0	0	...	9.00	1	0	0	0	0	1	2	1	1	0	1
	—Columbus (Int'l)	0	0	...	0.00	1	0	0	0	0	2	0	0	0	0	2

RECORD AS MANAGER

BACKGROUND: Minor league coach, New York Yankees organization (1984). ... Coach, Yankees (1990-91).

HONORS: Named New York-Pennsylvania League Manager of the Year (1985). ... Named Eastern League Manager of the Year (1989). ... Coach, A.L. All-Star team (1992). ... Named A.L. Manager of the Year by THE SPORTING NEWS (1994). ... Named A.L. Manager of the Year by Baseball Writers' Association of America (1994).

| | | REGULAR SEASON | | | | POSTSEASON | | | | | | | |
| | | | | | | Playoff | | Champ. Series | | World Series | | All-Star Game | |
Year	Team (League)	W	L	Pct.	Pos.	W	L	W	L	W	L	W	L
1985—	Oneonta (New York-Pennsylvania)............	55	23	.705	1st (N)	3	0	—	—	—	—	—	—
1986—	Oneonta (New York-Pennsylvania)............	59	18	.766	1st (Y)	0	1	—	—	—	—	—	—
1987—	Fort Lauderdale (Florida State)	85	53	.616	1st (S)	5	1	—	—	—	—	—	—
1988—	Fort Lauderdale (Florida State)	39	29	.574	3rd (E)	—	—	—	—	—	—	—	—
	—(Second half)	30	36	.455	T3rd (E)	—	—	—	—	—	—	—	—
1989—	Albany/Colonie (Eastern)	92	48	.657	1st	6	2	—	—	—	—	—	—
1992—	New York (A.L.)	76	86	.469	T4th (E)	—	—	—	—	—	—	—	—
1993—	New York (A.L.)	88	74	.543	2nd (E)	—	—	—	—	—	—	—	—
1994—	New York (A.L.)	70	43	.619	6th (E)	—	—	—	—	—	—	—	—
1995—	New York (A.L.)	79	65	.549	2nd (E)	2	3	—	—	—	—	—	—
Major league totals (4 years)		**313**	**268**	**.539**		**2**	**3**	**—**	**—**	**—**	**—**	**—**	**—**

NOTES:
1985—Defeated Geneva in one-game semifinal playoff; defeated Auburn, two games to none, in league championship.
1986—Lost to Newark in playoffs.
1987—Defeated Lakeland, two games to none, in playoffs; defeated Osceola, three games to one, in league championship.
1989—Defeated Reading, three games to one, in playoffs; defeated Harrisburg, three games to one, in league championship.
1994—New York was in first place in A.L. East at time of season-ending strike (August 12).
1995—Lost to Seattle in A.L. divisional playoff. Named Arizona Diamondbacks manager (November 15).

TORRE, JOE — YANKEES

PERSONAL: Born July 18, 1940, in Brooklyn, N.Y. ... 6-1/210. ... Batted right, threw right. ... Full name: Joseph Paul Torre. ... Brother of Frank Torre, first baseman, Milwaukee Braves and Philadelphia Phillies (1956-60, 1962-63). ... Name pronounced TORE-ee.

HIGH SCHOOL: St. Francis Prep (Brooklyn, N.Y.).

TRANSACTIONS/CAREER NOTES: Signed by Jacksonville, Milwaukee Braves organization (August 24, 1959). ... On military list (September 30, 1962-March 26, 1963). ... Braves franchise moved from Milwaukee to Atlanta (1966). ... On disabled list (April 18-May 9, 1968). ... Traded by Braves to St. Louis Cardinals for 1B Orlando Cepeda (March 17, 1969). ... Traded by Cardinals to New York Mets for P Tommy Moore and P Ray Sadecki (October 13, 1974). ... Released as player by Mets (June 18, 1977).

RECORDS: Shares major league single-game record for most times grounded into double play—4 (July 21, 1975).

HONORS: Named catcher on THE SPORTING NEWS N.L. All-Star team (1964-66). ... Won N.L. Gold Glove at catcher (1965). ... Named Major League Player of the Year by THE SPORTING NEWS (1971). ... Named N.L. Player of the Year by THE SPORTING NEWS (1971). ... Named third baseman on THE SPORTING NEWS N.L. All-Star team (1971). ... Named N.L. Most Valuable Player by Baseball Writers' Association of America (1971).

STATISTICAL NOTES: Led N.L. catchers with .995 fielding percentage in 1964 and .996 in 1968. ... Led N.L. in grounding into double plays with 26 in 1964, 21 in 1965, 22 in 1967 and 21 in 1968. ... Led N.L. catchers with 12 double plays in 1967. ... Led N.L. with 352 total bases in 1971. ... Hit for the cycle (June 27, 1973). ... Led N.L. first basemen with 102 assists and 144 double plays in 1974. ... Career major league grand slams: 3.

Year	Team (League)	Pos.	G	AB	R	H	2B	3B	HR	RBI	Avg.	BB	SO	SB	PO	A	E	Avg.
1960—	Eau Claire (North.)	C	117	369	63	127	23	3	16	74	*.344	70	45	7	636	64	9	.987
	—Milwaukee (N.L.)........	PH	2	2	0	1	0	0	0	0	.500	0	1	0	...	...	...	...
1961—	Louisville (A.A.).........	C	27	111	18	38	8	2	3	24	.342	6	9	0	185	14	2	.990
	—Milwaukee (N.L.).........	C	113	406	40	113	21	4	10	42	.278	28	60	3	494	50	10	.982
1962—	Milwaukee (N.L.).........	C	80	220	23	62	8	1	5	26	.282	24	24	1	325	39	5	.986
1963—	Milwaukee (N.L.).........	C-1B-OF	142	501	57	147	19	4	14	71	.293	42	79	1	919	76	6	.994
1964—	Milwaukee (N.L.).........	C-1B	154	601	87	193	36	5	20	109	.321	36	67	4	1081	94	7	†.994
1965—	Milwaukee (N.L.).........	C-1B	148	523	68	152	21	1	27	80	.291	61	79	0	1022	73	8	.993
1966—	Atlanta (N.L.).............	C-1B	148	546	83	172	20	3	36	101	.315	60	61	0	874	87	12	.988
1967—	Atlanta (N.L.).............	C-1B	135	477	67	132	18	1	20	68	.277	75	49	2	785	81	8	.991
1968—	Atlanta (N.L.).............	C-1B	115	424	45	115	11	2	10	55	.271	34	72	1	733	48	2	†.997
1969—	St. Louis (N.L.)■.........	1B-C	159	602	72	174	29	6	18	101	.289	66	85	0	1360	91	7	.995
1970—	St. Louis (N.L.)..........	C-3B-1B	•161	624	89	203	27	9	21	100	.325	70	91	2	651	162	13	.984
1971—	St. Louis (N.L.)..........	3B	161	634	97	*230	34	8	24	*137	*.363	63	70	4	*136	271	•21	.951
1972—	St. Louis (N.L.)..........	3B-1B	149	544	71	157	26	6	11	81	.289	54	74	3	336	198	15	.973
1973—	St. Louis (N.L.)..........	1B-3B	141	519	67	149	17	2	13	69	.287	65	78	2	881	128	12	.988
1974—	St. Louis (N.L.)..........	1B-3B	147	529	59	149	28	1	11	70	.282	69	68	1	1173	†121	14	.989

Year	Team (League)	Pos.	G	AB	R	H	2B	3B	HR	RBI	Avg.	BB	SO	SB	PO	A	E	Avg.
							BATTING									**FIELDING**		
1975— New York (N.L.)■		3B-1B	114	361	33	89	16	3	6	35	.247	35	55	0	172	157	15	.956
1976— New York (N.L.)		1B-3B	114	310	36	95	10	3	5	31	.306	21	35	1	593	52	7	.989
1977— New York (N.L.)		1B-3B	26	51	2	9	3	0	1	9	.176	2	10	0	83	3	1	.989
Major league totals (18 years)			2209	7874	996	2342	344	59	252	1185	.297	805	1058	25	11618	1731	163	.988

ALL-STAR GAME RECORD

Year	League	Pos.	AB	R	H	2B	3B	HR	RBI	Avg.	BB	SO	SB	PO	A	E	Avg.
							BATTING								**FIELDING**		
1963— National								Did not play.										
1964— National		C	2	0	0	0	0	0	0	.000	0	0	0	5	0	0	1.000
1965— National		C	4	1	1	0	0	1	2	.250	0	0	0	5	1	0	1.000
1966— National		C	3	0	0	0	0	0	0	.000	0	1	0	5	0	0	1.000
1967— National		C	2	0	0	0	0	0	0	.000	0	0	0	4	1	0	1.000
1970— National		PH	1	0	0	0	0	0	0	.000	0	0	0	...	...	...	...
1971— National		3B	3	0	0	0	0	0	0	.000	0	1	0	1	0	0	1.000
1972— National		3B	3	0	0	0	0	0	0	.000	0	1	0	1	2	0	1.000
1973— National		1B-3B	3	0	0	0	0	0	0	.000	0	0	0	5	0	0	1.000
All-Star Game totals (8 years)			21	1	1	0	0	1	2	.048	0	3	0	26	4	0	1.000

RECORD AS MANAGER

BACKGROUND: Player/manager, New York Mets (May 31-June 18, 1977).

HONORS: Coach, N.L. All-Star team (1983 and 1992). ... Named Sportsman of the Year by THE SPORTING NEWS (1996). ... Named co-A.L. Manager of the Year by Baseball Writers' Association of America (1996).

Year	Team (League)	W	L	Pct.	Pos.	Playoff W	Playoff L	Champ. Series W	Champ. Series L	World Series W	World Series L	All-Star Game W	All-Star Game L
						POSTSEASON							
1977— New York (N.L.)		49	68	.419	6th (E)	—	—	—	—	—	—	—	—
1978— New York (N.L.)		66	96	.407	6th (E)	—	—	—	—	—	—	—	—
1979— New York (N.L.)		63	99	.389	6th (E)	—	—	—	—	—	—	—	—
1980— New York (N.L.)		67	95	.414	5th (E)	—	—	—	—	—	—	—	—
1981— New York (N.L.)		17	34	.333	5th (E)	—	—	—	—	—	—	—	—
— (Second half)		24	28	.462	4th (E)	—	—	—	—	—	—	—	—
1982— Atlanta (N.L.)		89	73	.549	1st (W)	—	—	0	3	—	—	—	—
1983— Atlanta (N.L.)		88	74	.543	2nd (W)	—	—	—	—	—	—	—	—
1984— Atlanta (N.L.)		80	82	.494	T2nd (W)	—	—	—	—	—	—	—	—
1990— St. Louis (N.L.)		24	34	.414	6th (E)	—	—	—	—	—	—	—	—
1991— St. Louis (N.L.)		84	78	.519	2nd (E)	—	—	—	—	—	—	—	—
1992— St. Louis (N.L.)		83	79	.512	3rd (E)	—	—	—	—	—	—	—	—
1993— St. Louis (N.L.)		87	75	.537	3rd (E)	—	—	—	—	—	—	—	—
1994— St. Louis (N.L.)		53	61	.465		—	—	—	—	—	—	—	—
1995— St. Louis (N.L.)		20	27	.426	4th (C)	—	—	—	—	—	—	—	—
1996— New York (A.L.)		92	70	.568	1st (E)	3	1	4	1	4	2	—	—
1997— New York (A.L.)		96	66	.593	2nd (E)	2	3	—	—	—	—	1	0
American League totals (2 years)		188	136	.580		5	4	4	1	4	2	1	0
National League totals (14 years)		894	1003	.471		—	—	0	3	—	—	—	—
Major league totals (16 years)		1082	1139	.487		5	4	4	4	4	2	1	0

NOTES:

1977—Replaced New York manager Joe Frazier with club in sixth place and record of 15-30 (May 31); served as player/manager (May 31-June 18, when released as player).

1982—Lost to St. Louis in N.L. Championship Series.

1990—Replaced St. Louis manager Whitey Herzog (33-47) and interim manager Red Schoendienst (13-11) with club in sixth place and record of 46-58 (August 1).

1994—St. Louis was tied for third place in N.L. Central at time of season-ending strike (August 12).

1995—Replaced as Cardinals manager by interim manager Mike Jorgensen, with club in fourth place (June 16).

1996—Defeated Texas in A.L. divisional playoff; defeated Baltimore in A.L. Championship Series; defeated Atlanta in World Series.

1997—Lost to Cleveland in A.L. divisional playoff.

VALENTINE, BOBBY — METS

PERSONAL: Born May 13, 1950, in Stamford, Conn. ... 5-10/185. ... Batted right, threw right. ... Full name: Robert John Valentine. ... Son-in-law of Ralph Branca, pitcher, Brooklyn Dodgers, Detroit Tigers, New York Yankees (1944-54 and 1956).

HIGH SCHOOL: Rippowan (Stamford, Conn.).

COLLEGE: Arizona State, then Southern California.

TRANSACTIONS/CAREER NOTES: Selected by Los Angeles Dodgers organization in first round (fifth pick overall) of free-agent draft (June 7, 1968). ... Traded by Dodgers with IF Billy Grabarkewitz, OF Frank Robinson, P Bill Singer and P Mike Strahler to California Angels for P Andy Messersmith and 3B Ken McMullen (November 28, 1972). ... On disabled list (May 17, 1973-remainder of season and May 29-June 13, 1974). ... Loaned by Angels to Charleston, Pittsburgh Pirates organization (April 4-June 20, 1975). ... Traded by Angels with a player to be named later to San Diego Padres for P Gary Ross (September 17, 1975); Padres acquired IF Rudy Meoli to complete deal (November 4, 1975). ... Traded by Padres with P Paul Siebert to New York Mets for IF/OF Dave Kingman (June 15, 1977). ... Released by Mets (March 26, 1979). ... Signed by Seattle Mariners (April 10, 1979). ... Granted free agency (November 1, 1979).

HONORS: Named Pacific Coast League Player of the Year (1970).

STATISTICAL NOTES: Led Pioneer League outfielders with 107 putouts and tied for lead with eight assists in 1968. ... Led Pacific Coast League shortstops with 38 errors in 1969. ... Led Pacific Coast League with 324 total bases, with 10 sacrifice flies and in double plays by shortstop with 106 in 1970. ... Led Pacific Coast League shortstops with 217 putouts and 54 errors in 1970.

Year	Team (League)	Pos.	G	AB	R	H	2B	3B	HR	RBI	Avg.	BB	SO	SB	PO	A	E	Avg.
							BATTING								**FIELDING**		
1968— Ogden (Pioneer)		OF-SS	62	224	*62	63	14	4	6	26	.281	39	27	*20	†111	‡10	6	.953
1969— Spokane (PCL)		SS-OF	111	402	61	104	19	5	3	35	.259	32	57	34	166	254	†38	.917

Year	Team (League)	Pos.	G	AB	R	H	2B	3B	HR	RBI	Avg.	BB	SO	SB	PO	A	E	Avg.
	—Los Angeles (N.L.)	PR	5	0	3	0	0	0	0	0	...	0	0	0	...	...	...	...
1970—	Spokane (PCL)	SS-2B	•146	*621	*122	*211	*39	*16	14	80	*.340	47	51	29	†217	474	†54	.928
1971—	Spokane (PCL)	SS	7	30	7	10	2	0	1	2	.333	3	6	3	13	18	3	.912
	—Los Angeles (N.L.)	S-3-2-O	101	281	32	70	10	2	1	25	.249	15	20	5	123	176	16	.949
1972—	Los Angeles (N.L.)	2-3-0-S	119	391	42	107	11	2	3	32	.274	27	33	5	178	245	23	.948
1973—	California (A.L.)■.....	SS-OF	32	126	12	38	5	2	1	13	.302	5	9	6	63	75	6	.958
1974—	California (A.L.)	O-S-3-DH	117	371	39	97	10	3	3	39	.261	25	25	8	160	116	17	.942
1975—	Char., W.Va. (Int'l)■...	3B	56	175	27	41	4	0	1	17	.234	30	16	8	44	74	6	.952
	—Salt Lake (PCL)■.....	1-0-3-2	46	147	29	45	6	1	0	17	.306	31	15	13	92	14	3	.972
	—California (A.L.)	DH-1-3-O	26	57	5	16	2	0	0	5	.281	4	3	0	27	1	2	.933
	—San Diego (N.L.)	OF	7	15	1	2	0	0	1	1	.133	4	0	1	4	0	0	1.000
1976—	Hawaii (PCL)	1-0-3-S	120	395	67	120	23	2	13	89	.304	47	32	9	578	47	4	.994
	—San Diego (N.L.)■.....	OF-1B	15	49	3	18	4	0	0	4	.367	6	2	0	55	6	0	1.000
1977—	San Diego (N.L.)	...	44	67	5	12	3	0	1	10	.179	7	10	0	...	...	...	...
	—New York (N.L.)■.....	...	42	83	8	11	1	0	1	3	.133	6	9	0	...	...	...	...
1978—	New York (N.L.)	2B-3B	69	160	17	43	7	0	1	18	.269	19	18	1	78	109	6	.969
1979—	Seattle (A.L.)■ S-O-2-3-C-DH	62	98	9	27	6	0	0	7	.276	22	5	1	32	38	2	.972
American League totals (4 years)			237	652	65	178	23	5	4	64	.273	56	42	15	282	230	27	.950
National League totals (7 years)			488	1196	124	286	40	4	10	106	.239	97	111	12	...	...	...	...
Major league totals (10 years)			725	1848	189	464	63	9	14	170	.251	153	153	27	...	...	...	...

RECORD AS MANAGER

BACKGROUND: Scout and minor league instructor, San Diego Padres (1981). ... Minor league instructor, New York Mets (1982). ... Coach, Mets (1983-May 15, 1985). ... Coach, Cincinnati Reds (1993).
HONORS: Coach, A.L. All-Star team (1988).

						Playoff		Champ. Series		World Series		All-Star Game	
Year	Team (League)	W	L	Pct.	Pos.	W	L	W	L	W	L	W	L
1985—	Texas (A.L.)..	53	76	.411	7th (W)	—	—	—	—	—	—	—	—
1986—	Texas (A.L.)..	87	75	.537	2nd (W)	—	—	—	—	—	—	—	—
1987—	Texas (A.L.)..	75	87	.463	T6th (W)	—	—	—	—	—	—	—	—
1988—	Texas (A.L.)..	70	91	.435	6th (W)	—	—	—	—	—	—	—	—
1989—	Texas (A.L.)..	83	79	.512	4th (W)	—	—	—	—	—	—	—	—
1990—	Texas (A.L.)..	83	79	.512	3rd (W)	—	—	—	—	—	—	—	—
1991—	Texas (A.L.)..	85	77	.525	3rd (W)	—	—	—	—	—	—	—	—
1992—	Texas (A.L.)..	45	41	.523		—	—	—	—	—	—	—	—
1994—	Norfolk (Int'l)..	67	75	.472	4th (W)	—	—	—	—	—	—	—	—
1995—	Chiba Lotte (Jp. Cnt.)............................	69	58	.543	2nd (P)	—	—	—	—	—	—	—	—
1996—	Norfolk (Int'l)..	76	57	.571		—	—	—	—	—	—	—	—
	—New York (N.L.)............................	12	19	.387	4th (E)	—	—	—	—	—	—	—	—
1997—	New York (N.L.)............................	88	74	.543	3rd (E)	—	—	—	—	—	—	—	—
American League totals (8 years)		581	605	.490		—	—	—	—	—	—	—	—
National League totals (2 years)		100	93	.518		—	—	—	—	—	—	—	—
Major league totals (10 years)		681	698	.494		—	—	—	—	—	—	—	—

NOTES:
1985—Replaced Texas manager Doug Rader with club in seventh place and record of 9-23 (May 16).
1992—Replaced as Texas manager by Toby Harrah with club in third place (July 9).
1995—Chiba Lotte tied three games.
1996—Replaced New York manager Dallas Green with club in fourth place and record of 59-72 (August 26).

WILLIAMS, JIMY   RED SOX

PERSONAL: Born October 4, 1943, in Santa Maria, Calif. ... 5-11/170. ... Batted right, threw right. ... Full name: James Francis Williams.
COLLEGE: Fresno State College (received bachelor of science degree in agribusiness).
TRANSACTIONS/CAREER NOTES: Selected by St. Louis Cardinals organization from Toronto, Boston Red Sox organization (November 29, 1965). ... In military service (July 24, 1966-remainder of season). ... Traded by Cardinals with C Pat Corrales to Cincinnati Reds for C John Edwards (February 8, 1968). ... Selected by Montreal Expos in expansion draft (October 14, 1968). ... On disabled list (May 13-30 and June 24-September 2, 1969). ... On suspended list (June 7-16, 1971). ... Sold to New York Mets organization (June 16, 1971). ... On temporary inactive list (August 12-16, 1971). ... On disabled list (May 15-July 17 and July 29-August 20, 1975).

Year	Team (League)	Pos.	G	AB	R	H	2B	3B	HR	RBI	Avg.	BB	SO	SB	PO	A	E	Avg.
1965—	Waterloo (Midwest)....	SS	115	435	64	125	19	3	2	31	.287	41	74	10	173	*312	26	*.949
1966—	St. Louis (N.L.)..........	SS-2B	13	11	1	3	0	0	0	1	.273	1	5	0	2	5	0	1.000
1967—	Arkansas (Texas)........	SS	28	101	8	21	1	1	0	8	.208	9	14	0	49	80	2	.985
	—Tulsa (PCL)	SS	61	164	18	37	2	0	1	21	.226	18	33	4	87	156	26	.903
	—St. Louis (N.L.)	SS	1	2	0	0	0	0	0	0	.000	0	1	0	6	1	0	1.000
1968—	Indianapolis (PCL)■..	SS-2B	120	403	38	91	19	5	2	34	.226	20	59	5	198	323	27	.951
1969—	Vancouver (PCL)■....	3B-OF-SS	35	66	7	17	1	1	0	9	.258	4	8	1	17	23	2	.952
1970—	Winnipeg (Int'l)	SS-2B-3B	109	361	49	83	15	0	3	18	.230	34	48	5	178	244	30	.934
1971—	Winn.-Tide. (Int'l)■..	SS-3B-2B	105	327	40	84	7	4	5	31	.257	38	46	7	120	219	22	.939
1972—	....				Did not play.													
1973—	....				Did not play.													
1974—	....				Did not play.													
1975—	El Paso (Texas)..........	DH	6	17	3	2	0	0	0	2	.118	2	2	0	...	...	...	...
Major league totals (2 years)			14	13	1	3	0	0	0	1	.231	0	0	0	8	6	0	1.000

RECORD AS MANAGER

BACKGROUND: Coach, Toronto Blue Jays (1980-85). ... Minor league instructor, Atlanta Braves (October 4, 1989-June 25, 1990). ... Coach, Braves (1990-96).

HONORS: Named Pacific Coast League Manager of the Year (1976 and 1979).

| | | REGULAR SEASON | | | | POSTSEASON | | | | | | | | |
| | | | | | | Playoff | | Champ. Series | | World Series | | All-Star Game | |
Year Team (League)	W	L	Pct.	Pos.		W	L	W	L	W	L	W	L
1974—Quad Cities (Midwest)	33	26	.559	1st (S)		—	—	—	—	—	—	—	—
—(Second half)	32	32	.500	3rd (S)		1	2	—	—	—	—	—	—
1975—El Paso (Texas)	62	71	.466	3rd (W)		—	—	—	—	—	—	—	—
1976—Salt Lake City (Pacific Coast)	90	54	.625	1st (E)		2	3	—	—	—	—	—	—
1977—Salt Lake City (Pacific Coast)	74	65	.532	2nd (E)		—	—	—	—	—	—	—	—
1978—Springfield (American Association)	70	66	.515	3rd (E)		—	—	—	—	—	—	—	—
1979—Salt Lake City (Pacific Coast)	34	40	.447	4th (S)		—	—	—	—	—	—	—	—
—(Second half)	46	28	.622	1st (S)		5	0	—	—	—	—	—	—
1986—Toronto (A.L.)	86	76	.531	4th (E)		—	—	—	—	—	—	—	—
1987—Toronto (A.L.)	96	66	.593	2nd (E)		—	—	—	—	—	—	—	—
1988—Toronto (A.L.)	87	75	.537	T3rd (E)		—	—	—	—	—	—	—	—
1989—Toronto (A.L.)	12	24	.333			—	—	—	—	—	—	—	—
1997—Boston (A.L.)	78	84	.481	4th (E)		—	—	—	—	—	—	—	—
Major league totals (5 years)	**359**	**325**	**.525**			—	—	—	—	—	—	—	—

NOTES:
1974—Lost to Danville in playoffs.
1976—Lost to Hawaii in championship playoff.
1979—Defeated Albuquerque, two games to none, in playoff; defeated Hawaii, three games to none, in championship playoff.
1989—Replaced as Toronto manager by Cito Gaston, with club tied for sixth place (May 15).

Hall of Fame Inductee
Don Sutton

324 Wins

4-time All-Star

178 Complete Games

58 Shutouts

4 World Series appearances

PERSONAL: Born April 2, 1945, in Clio, Alabama. ... 6-1/185. ... Threw right, batted right. ... Full name: Donald Howard Sutton.

HIGH SCHOOL: Tate (Pensacola, Fla.).

JUNIOR COLLEGE: Gulf Coast Community College (Fla.).

COLLEGE: Mississippi College, then Southern California, then Whittier College (Calif.).

TRANSACTIONS/CAREER NOTES: Signed as free agent by Los Angeles Dodgers organization (September 11, 1964). ... Granted free agency (October 23, 1980). ... Signed by Houston Astros (December 4, 1980). ... Traded by Astros to Milwaukee Brewers for three players to be named later (August 30, 1982); Astros acquired P Frank DiPino, P Mike Madden and OF Kevin Bass to complete deal (September 3, 1982). ... Traded by Brewers to Oakland A's for P Ray Burris, P Eric Barry and a player to be named later (December 7, 1984); Brewers acquired P Ed Myers to complete deal (March 25, 1985). ... Traded by A's to California Angels for two players to be named later (September 10, 1985); A's acquired P Robert Sharpnack and OF Jerome Nelson to complete deal (September 25, 1985). ... Granted free agency (November 12, 1985). ... Re-signed by Angels (December 5, 1985). ... Released by Angels (October 30, 1987). ... Signed by Dodgers (January 5, 1988). ... On disabled list (June 29-August 9, 1988); included rehabilitation assignment to Bakersfield (July 23-August 9). ... Released by Dodgers (August 10, 1988).

RECORDS: Holds record for most consecutive games lost to one club, lifetime—13 (April 23, 1966 through July 24, 1969 (vs. Chicago). ... Shares N.L. record for most consecutive home runs allowed in one inning (third), May 27, 1980 (third inning). ... Shares modern N.L. career record for most one-hit games lifetime—5.

HONORS: Named Texas League Player of the Year (1965). ... Named N.L. Rookie of the Year by THE SPORTING NEWS (1966.). ... Named righthanded pitcher on THE SPORTING NEWS N.L. All-Star Team (1976).

STATISTICAL NOTES: Tied for National League lead with three balks in 1968.

MISCELLANEOUS: Holds Los Angeles Dodgers all-time records for most wins (233), most strikeouts (2,696), most innings pitched (3,814), most games played by pitcher (550) and most shutouts (52).

Year	Team (League)	W	L	Pct.	ERA	G	GS	CG	ShO	Sv.	IP	H	R	ER	BB	SO
1965—	Santa Barbara (Calif.)	8	1	.889	1.50	10	10	8	1	0	84	59	18	14	15	101
—	Albuquerque (Tex.)	15	6	.714	2.78	21	21	16	2	0	165	151	60	51	30	138
1966—	Los Angeles (N.L.)	12	12	.500	2.99	37	35	6	2	0	225 2/3	192	82	75	52	209
1967—	Los Angeles (N.L.)	11	15	.423	3.95	37	34	11	3	1	232 2/3	192	106	102	57	169
1968—	Spokane (PCL)	1	1	.500	1.13	2	2	0	0	0	16	11	2	2	5	19
—	Los Angeles (N.L.)	11	15	.423	2.60	35	27	7	2	1	207 2/3	179	64	60	59	162
1969—	Los Angeles (N.L.)	17	18	.486	3.47	41	41	11	4	0	293 1/3	269	123	113	91	217
1970—	Los Angeles (N.L.)	15	13	.536	4.08	38	38	10	4	0	260 1/3	251	127	118	78	201
1971—	Los Angeles (N.L.)	17	12	.586	2.54	38	37	12	4	1	265 1/3	231	85	75	55	194
1972—	Los Angeles (N.L.)	19	9	.679	2.08	33	33	18	*9	0	272 2/3	186	78	63	63	207

Year	Team (League)	W	L	Pct.	ERA	G	GS	CG	ShO	Sv.	IP	H	R	ER	BB	SO
1973—	Los Angeles (N.L.)	18	10	.643	2.42	33	33	14	3	0	256 1/3	196	78	69	56	200
1974—	Los Angeles (N.L.)	19	9	.679	3.23	40	*40	10	5	0	276	241	111	99	80	179
1975—	Los Angeles (N.L.)	16	13	.552	2.87	35	35	11	4	0	254 1/3	202	87	81	62	175
1976—	Los Angeles (N.L.)	21	10	.677	3.06	35	34	15	4	0	267 2/3	231	98	91	82	161
1977—	Los Angeles (N.L.)	14	8	.636	3.18	33	33	9	3	0	240 1/3	207	93	85	69	150
1978—	Los Angeles (N.L.)	15	11	.577	3.55	34	34	12	2	0	238 1/3	228	109	94	54	154
1979—	Los Angeles (N.L.)	12	15	.444	3.82	33	32	6	1	1	226	201	109	96	61	146
1980—	Los Angeles (N.L.)	13	5	.722	*2.20	32	31	4	2	1	212 1/3	163	56	52	47	128
1981—	Houston (N.L.)■	11	9	.550	2.61	23	23	6	3	0	158 2/3	132	51	46	29	104
1982—	Houston (N.L.)	13	8	.619	3.00	27	27	4	0	0	195	169	75	65	46	139
—	Milwaukee (A.L.)■	4	1	.800	3.29	7	7	2	1	0	54 2/3	55	21	20	18	36
1983—	Milwaukee (A.L.)	8	13	.381	4.08	31	31	4	0	0	220 1/3	209	109	100	54	134
1984—	Milwaukee (A.L.)	14	12	.538	3.77	33	33	1	0	0	212 2/3	224	103	89	51	143
1985—	Oakland (A.L.)■	13	8	.619	3.89	29	29	1	1	0	194 1/3	194	88	84	51	91
—	California (A.L.)■	2	2	.500	3.69	5	5	0	0	0	31 2/3	27	13	13	8	16
1986—	California (A.L.)	15	11	.577	3.74	34	34	3	1	0	207	192	93	86	49	116
1987—	California (A.L.)	11	11	.500	4.70	35	34	1	0	0	191 2/3	199	101	100	41	99
1988—	Los Angeles (N.L.)■	3	6	.333	3.92	16	16	0	0	0	87 1/3	91	44	38	30	44
A.L. totals (6 years)		67	58	.536	3.98	174	173	12	3	0	1112 1/3	1100	528	492	272	635
N.L. totals (18 years)		257	198	.565	3.07	600	583	166	55	5	4170	3561	1576	1422	1071	2939
Major league totals (23 years)		324	256	.559	3.26	774	756	178	58	5	5282 1/3	4661	2104	1914	1343	3574

CHAMPIONSHIP SERIES RECORD

RECORDS: Holds record for most innings pitched in four-game series—17 (1974). ... Shares single-series record for most games won—2 (1974). ... Shares N.L. record for most strikeouts, four-game series—13 (1974).

Year	Team (League)	W	L	Pct.	ERA	G	GS	CG	ShO	Sv.	IP	H	R	ER	BB	SO
1974—	Los Angeles (N.L.)	2	0	1.000	0.53	2	2	1	1	0	17	7	1	1	2	13
1977—	Los Angeles (N.L.)	1	0	1.000	1.00	1	1	1	0	0	9	9	1	1	0	4
1978—	Los Angeles (N.L.)	0	1	.000	6.35	1	1	0	0	00	5 2/3	7	7	4	2	0
1982—	Milwaukee (A.L.)	1	0	1.000	3.52	1	1	0	0	0	7 2/3	8	3	3	2	9
1986—	California (A.L.)	0	0	. . .	1.86	2	1	0	0	0	9 2/3	6	2	2	1	4
Champ. series totals (5 years)		4	1	.800	2.02	7	6	2	1	0	49	37	14	11	7	30

The Dodgers' 1966 rotation featured Hall of Famers—Sutton (left), Don Drysdale and Sandy Koufax.

Sutton, who was named the N.L. Rookie of the Year by THE SPORTING NEWS in 1966, finished his career as the Dodgers all-time leader in victories with 233.

WORLD SERIES RECORD

RECORDS: Shares records for most consecutive home runs allowed in one inning—2 (October 16, 1977, eighth inning); most runs allowed in six-game series—10 (1978).

Year Team (League)	W	L	Pct.	ERA	G	GS	CG	ShO	Sv.	IP	H	R	ER	BB	SO
1974—Los Angeles (N.L.)	1	0	1.000	2.77	2	2	0	0	0	13	9	4	4	3	12
1977—Los Angeles (N.L.)	1	0	1.000	3.94	2	2	1	0	0	16	17	7	7	1	6
1978—Los Angeles (N.L.)	0	2	.000	7.50	2	2	0	0	0	12	17	10	10	4	8
1982—Milwaukee (A.L.)	0	1	.000	7.84	2	2	0	0	0	10 1/3	12	11	9	1	5
World Series totals (4 years)	2	3	.400	5.26	8	8	1	0	0	51 1/3	38	32	30	9	31

ALL-STAR GAME RECORD

NOTES: Named Most Valuable Player (1977).

Year League	W	L	Pct.	ERA	GS	CG	ShO	Sv.	IP	H	R	ER	BB	SO
1972—National	0	0	. . .	0.00	0	0	0	0	2	1	0	0	0	2
1973—National	0	0	. . .	0.00	0	0	0	0	1	0	0	0	0	0
1975—National	0	0	. . .	0.00	0	0	0	0	2	3	0	0	0	1
1977—National	1	0	1.000	0.00	1	0	0	0	3	1	0	0	1	4
All-Star totals (4 years)	1	0	1.000	0.00	1	0	0	0	8	5	0	0	1	7

1997 A.L. Statistical Leaders

BATTING

BATTING AVERAGE
.347 Frank Thomas, Chi.
.330 Edgar Martinez, Sea.
.329 David Justice, Cle.
.328 Bernie Williams, N.Y.
.328 Manny Ramirez, Cle.

GAMES
162 Brian Hunter, Det.
162 Cal Ripken Jr., Bal.
161 Albert Belle, Chi.
159 Tony Clark, Det.
159 Derek Jeter, N.Y.

AT-BATS
684 Nomar Garciaparra, Bos.
658 Brian Hunter, Det.
654 Derek Jeter, N.Y.
634 Albert Belle, Chi.
634 Ray Durham, Chi.

RUNS SCORED
125 Ken Griffey Jr., Sea.
122 Nomar Garciaparra, Bos.
117 Chuck Knoblauch, Min.
116 Derek Jeter, N.Y.
112 Rusty Greer, Tex.
112 Brian Hunter, Det.

HITS
209 Nomar Garciaparra, Bos.
193 Rusty Greer, Tex.
190 Derek Jeter, N.Y.
189 Garret Anderson, Ana.
187 Ivan Rodriguez, Tex.

RUNS BATTED IN
147 Ken Griffey Jr., Sea.
141 Tino Martinez, N.Y.
131 Juan Gonzalez, Tex.
129 Tim Salmon, Ana.
125 Frank Thomas, Chi.

TOTAL BASES
393 Ken Griffey Jr., Sea.
365 Nomar Garciaparra, Bos.
343 Tino Martinez, N.Y.
324 Frank Thomas, Chi.
319 Rusty Greer, Tex.

DOUBLES
47 John Valentin, Bos.
46 Jeff Cirillo, Mil.
45 Albert Belle, Chi.
44 Nomar Garciaparra, Bos.
42 Carlos Delgado, Tor.
42 Rusty Greer, Tex.
42 Paul O'Neill, N.Y.

TRIPLES
11 Nomar Garciaparra, Bos.
10 Chuck Knoblauch, Min.
8 Jeromy Burnitz, Mil.
8 Johnny Damon, K.C.
7 Luis Alicea, Ana.
7 Brady Anderson, Bal.
7 Brian Hunter, Det.
7 Derek Jeter, N.Y.
7 Shannon Stewart, Tor.

HOME RUNS
56 Ken Griffey Jr., Sea.
44 Tino Martinez, N.Y.
42 Juan Gonzalez, Tex.
40 Jay Buhner, Sea.
40 Jim Thome, Cle.

WALKS
120 Jim Thome, Cle.
119 Jay Buhner, Sea.
119 Edgar Martinez, Sea.
109 Frank Thomas, Chi.
102 Tony Phillips, Chi.-Ana.

ON-BASE PERCENTAGE
.456 Frank Thomas, Chi.
.456 Edgar Martinez, Sea.
.423 Jim Thome, Cle.
.420 Mo Vaughn, Bos.
.418 David Justice, Cle.

SLUGGING PERCENTAGE
.646 Ken Griffey Jr., Sea.
.611 Frank Thomas, Chi.
.596 David Justice, Cle.
.589 Juan Gonzalez, Tex.
.579 Jim Thome, Cle.

STOLEN BASES
74 Brian Hunter, Det.
62 Chuck Knoblauch, Min.
50 Tom Goodwin, K.C.-Tex.
47 Otis Nixon, Tor.
43 Omar Vizquel, Cle.

CAUGHT STEALING
18 Brian Hunter, Det.
16 Ray Durham, Chi.
16 Tom Goodwin, K.C.-Tex.
13 Jeromy Burnitz, Mil.
13 Damion Easley, Det.
13 Marquis Grissom, Cle.

SACRIFICE BUNTS
16 Omar Vizquel, Cle.
14 Deivi Cruz, Det.
12 Mike Bordick, Bal.
11 Alex Gonzalez, Tor.
11 Tom Goodwin, K.C.-Tex.
11 Ozzie Guillen, Chi.
11 Jeff Reboulet, Bal.

SACRIFICE FLIES
13 Tino Martinez, N.Y.
12 Ken Griffey Jr., Sea.
12 Jeff King, K.C.
12 Paul Molitor, Min.
11 Travis Fryman, Det.
11 Tim Salmon, Ana.

STRIKEOUTS
175 Jay Buhner, Sea.
157 Melvin Nieves, Det.
154 Mo Vaughn, Bos.
146 Jim Thome, Cle.
144 Tony Clark, Det.

INTENTIONAL WALKS
23 Ken Griffey Jr., Sea.
17 Mo Vaughn, Bos.
16 Chili Davis, K.C.
14 Tino Martinez, N.Y.
14 B.J. Surhoff, Bal.

PITCHING

EARNED-RUN AVERAGE

2.05	Roger Clemens, Tor.
2.28	Randy Johnson, Sea.
2.82	David Cone, N.Y.
2.88	Andy Pettitte, N.Y.
3.02	Thompson, Justin, Det.

WINS

21	Roger Clemens, Tor.
20	Randy Johnson, Sea.
20	Brad Radke, Min.
18	Andy Pettitte, N.Y.
17	Jamie Moyer, Sea.

LOSSES

15	James Baldwin, Chi.
15	Cal Eldred, Mil.
15	Tim Wakefield, Bos.
14	Jaime Navarro, Chi.
14	Scott Sanders, Sea.-Det.
14	Woody Williams, Tor.

GAMES

88	Mike Myers, Det.
78	Buddy Groom, Oak.
77	Jeff Nelson, N.Y.
77	Paul Quantrill, Tor.
76	Heathcliff Slocumb, Bos.-Sea.

GAMES STARTED

35	Jeff Fassero, Sea.
35	Pat Hentgen, Tor.
35	Andy Pettitte, N.Y.
35	Brad Radke, Min.
34	Six players tied

GAMES FINISHED

73	Doug Jones, Mil.
61	Heathcliff Slocumb, Bos.-Sea.
58	John Wetteland, Tex.
57	Rick Aguilera, Min.
57	Randy Myers, Bal.

COMPLETE GAMES

9	Roger Clemens, Tor.
9	Pat Hentgen, Tor.
5	Randy Johnson, Sea.
5	Bob Tewksbury, Min.
5	David Wells, N.Y.

INNINGS PITCHED

264	Roger Clemens, Tor.
264	Pat Hentgen, Tor.
240⅓	Andy Pettitte, N.Y.
239⅔	Brad Radke, Min.
235⅔	Kevin Appier, K.C.

SHUTOUTS

3	Roger Clemens, Tor.
3	Pat Hentgen, Tor.
2	Scott Erickson, Bal.
2	Randy Johnson, Sea.
2	Omar Olivares, Det.-Sea.
2	Bob Tewksbury, Min.
2	Tim Wakefield, Bos.
2	David Wells, N.Y.

HITS ALLOWED

267	Jaime Navarro, Chi.
253	Pat Hentgen, Tor.
253	Charles Nagy, Cle.
245	Bobby Witt, Tex.
242	Tim Belcher, K.C.

HOME RUNS ALLOWED

37	Allen Watson, Ana.
33	Bobby Witt, Tex.
32	Jason Dickson, Ana.
32	Dennis Springer, Ana.
31	Tim Belcher, K.C.
31	Cal Eldred, Mil.
31	Pat Hentgen, Tor.
31	Woody Williams, Tor.

RUNS ALLOWED

155	Jaime Navarro, Chi.
128	James Baldwin, Chi.
128	Tim Belcher, K.C.
121	Allen Watson, Ana.
118	Cal Eldred, Mil.
118	Dennis Springer, Ana.
118	Bobby Witt, Tex.

EARNED RUNS ALLOWED

135	Jaime Navarro, Chi.
119	Tim Belcher, K.C.
117	James Baldwin, Chi.
112	Cal Eldred, Mil.
112	Dennis Springer, Ana.
112	Bobby Witt, Tex.

BATTING AVERAGE YIELDED

.194	Randy Johnson, Sea.
.213	Roger Clemens, Tor.
.218	David Cone, N.Y.
.226	Tom Gordon, Bos.
.233	Justin Thompson, Det.

WALKS

95	Ken Hill, Tex.-Ana.
89	Cal Eldred, Mil.
87	Tim Wakefield, Bos.
86	David Cone, N.Y.
84	Jeff Fassero, Sea.

STRIKEOUTS

292	Roger Clemens, Tor.
291	Randy Johnson, Sea.
222	David Cone, N.Y.
218	Mike Mussina, Bal.
196	Kevin Appier, K.C.

HIT BATSMEN

16	Tim Wakefield, Bos.
15	Aaron Sele, Bos.
13	Omar Olivares, Det.-Sea.
12	Roger Clemens, Tor.
11	Orel Hershiser, Cle.
11	Darren Oliver, Tex.

WILD PITCHES

14	Kevin Appier, K.C.
14	James Baldwin, Chi.
14	David Cone, N.Y.
14	Jaime Navarro, Chi.
13	Jeff Fassero, Sea.

SAVES

45	Randy Myers, Bal.
43	Mariano Rivera, N.Y.
36	Doug Jones, Mil.
31	Todd Jones, Det.
31	John Wetteland, Tex.

STATISTICAL LEADERS

1997 N.L. Statistical Leaders

BATTING

BATTING AVERAGE
.372	Tony Gwynn, S.D.
.366	Larry Walker, Col.
.362	Mike Piazza, L.A.
.333	Kenny Lofton, Atl.
.327	Wally Joyner, S.D.

GAMES
162	Jeff Bagwell, Hou.
162	Craig Biggio, Hou.
162	Eric Karros, L.A.
162	Sammy Sosa, Chi.
160	Todd Zeile, L.A.

AT-BATS
649	Mark Grudzielanek, Mtl.
642	Sammy Sosa, Chi.
641	Tony Womack, Pit.
628	Eric Karros, L.A.
622	Eric Young, Col.-L.A.

RUNS SCORED
146	Craig Biggio, Hou.
143	Larry Walker, Col.
123	Barry Bonds, S.F.
120	Andres Galarraga, Col.
109	Jeff Bagwell, Hou.

HITS
220	Tony Gwynn, S.D.
208	Larry Walker, Col.
201	Mike Piazza, L.A.
191	Craig Biggio, Hou.
191	Andres Galarraga, Col.
191	Raul Mondesi, L.A.

RUNS BATTED IN
140	Andres Galarraga, Col.
135	Jeff Bagwell, Hou.
130	Larry Walker, Col.
124	Mike Piazza, L.A.
121	Jeff Kent, S.F.

TOTAL BASES
409	Larry Walker, Col.
355	Mike Piazza, L.A.
351	Andres Galarraga, Col.
335	Jeff Bagwell, Hou.
335	Vinny Castilla, Col.

DOUBLES
54	Mark Grudzielanek, Mtl.
49	Tony Gwynn, S.D.
46	Larry Walker, Col.
45	Mike Lansing, Mtl.
42	Raul Mondesi, L.A.

TRIPLES
14	Delino DeShields, St.L
10	Neifi Perez, Col.
9	Wilton Guerrero, L.A.
9	Joe Randa, Pit.
9	Tony Womack, Pit.

HOME RUNS
49	Larry Walker, Col.
43	Jeff Bagwell, Hou.
41	Andres Galarraga, Col.
40	Barry Bonds, S.F.
40	Vinny Castilla, Col.
40	Mike Piazza, L.A.

WALKS
145	Barry Bonds, S.F.
127	Jeff Bagwell, Hou.
121	Gary Sheffield, Fla.
96	J.T. Snow, S.F.
95	Ray Lankford, St.L

ON-BASE PERCENTAGE
.452	Larry Walker, Col.
.446	Barry Bonds, S.F.
.431	Mike Piazza, L.A.
.425	Jeff Bagwell, Hou.
.424	Gary Sheffield, Fla.

SLUGGING PERCENTAGE
.720	Larry Walker, Col.
.638	Mike Piazza, L.A.
.592	Jeff Bagwell, Hou.
.585	Andres Galarraga, Col.
.585	Ray Lankford, St.L
.585	Barry Bonds, S.F.

STOLEN BASES
60	Tony Womack, Pit.
56	Deion Sanders, Cin.
55	Delino DeShields, St.L
47	Craig Biggio, Hou.
45	Eric Young, Col.-L.A.

CAUGHT STEALING
20	Kenny Lofton, Atl.
15	Raul Mondesi, L.A.
15	Edgar Renteria, Fla.
14	Eric Young, L.A.
14	Delino DeShields, St.L

SACRIFICE BUNTS
19	Edgar Renteria, Fla.
17	Tom Glavine, Atl.
15	Brett Butler, L.A.
14	Rey Ordonez, N.Y.
13	Jose Vizcaino, S.F.
13	Wilton Guerrero, L.A.

SACRIFICE FLIES
12	Bernard Gilkey, N.Y.
12	Tony Gwynn, S.D.
10	Jeff Kent, S.F.
10	Wally Joyner, S.D.
9	Eric Karros, L.A.
9	Jeff Blauser, Atl.
9	Darren Daulton, Phi.-Fla.

STRIKEOUTS
174	Sammy Sosa, Chi.
162	Ron Gant, St.L
149	Henry Rodriguez, Mtl.
141	Andres Galarraga, Col.
138	Scott Rolen, Phi.

INTENTIONAL WALKS
34	Barry Bonds, S.F.
27	Jeff Bagwell, Hou.
16	Todd Hundley, N.Y.
14	Larry Walker, Col.
13	J.T. Snow, S.F.

EARNED-RUN AVERAGE

1.90 Pedro J. Martinez, Mtl.
2.20 Greg Maddux, Atl.
2.57 Darryl Kile, Hou.
2.65 Ismael Valdes, L.A.
2.69 Kevin Brown, Fla.

WINS

20 Denny Neagle, Atl.
19 Greg Maddux, Atl.
19 Shawn Estes, S.F.
19 Darryl Kile, Hou.
17 Pedro Martinez, Mtl.
17 Curt Schilling, Phi.
17 Alex Fernandez, Fla.

LOSSES

17 Mark Leiter, Phi.
15 Steve Cooke, Pit.
14 Jon Lieber, Pit.
13 Terry Mulholland, Chi.-S.F.
13 Carlos Perez, Mtl.

GAMES

89 Julian Tavarez, S.F.
84 Stan Belinda, Cin.
78 Jeff Shaw, Cin.
77 Mel Rojas, Chi.-N.Y.
76 Bob Patterson, Chi.
76 Jerry Spradlin, Phi.

GAMES STARTED

35 Curt Schilling, Phi.
35 John Smoltz, Atl.
34 Mike Hampton, Hou.
34 Darryl Kile, Hou.
34 Denny Neagle, Atl.
34 Steve Trachsel, Chi.

GAMES FINISHED

66 Rod Beck, S.F.
65 Robb Nen, Fla.
62 Jeff Shaw, Cin.
61 Ricky Bottalico, Phi.
59 Trevor Hoffman, S.D.

COMPLETE GAMES

13 Pedro Martinez, Mtl.
8 Carlos Perez, Mtl.

7 Mike Hampton, Hou.
7 Curt Schilling, Phi.
7 John Smoltz, Atl.

INNINGS PITCHED

256 John Smoltz, Atl.
255⅔ Darryl Kile, Hou.
254⅓ Curt Schilling, Phi.
241⅓ Pedro Martinez, Mtl.
240 Tom Glavine, Atl.

SHUTOUTS

5 Carlos Perez, Mtl.
4 Darryl Kile, Hou.
4 Pedro J. Martinez, Mtl.
4 Denny Neagle, Atl.
2 10 tied

HITS ALLOWED

234 John Smoltz, Atl.
225 Steve Trachsel, Chi.
220 Frank Castillo, Chi.-Col.
217 Mike Hampton, Hou.
216 Mark Leiter, Phi.

HOME RUNS ALLOWED

32 Steve Trachsel, Chi.
28 Mark Gardner, S.F.
27 Roger Bailey, Col.
27 Kevin Foster, Chi.
25 Matt Beech, Phi.
25 Alex Fernandez, Fla.
25 Frank Castillo, Chi.-Col.
25 Curt Schilling, Phi.
25 Mark Leiter, Phi.

RUNS ALLOWED

132 Mark Leiter, Phi.
121 Frank Castillo, Chi.-Col.
113 Jamey Wright, Col.
110 Steve Trachsel, Chi.
109 Carlos Perez, Mtl.

EARNED RUNS ALLOWED

115 Mark Leiter, Phi.
111 Frank Castillo, Chi.-Col.
104 Jamey Wright, Col.
101 Steve Trachsel, Chi.
98 Hideo Nomo, L.A.

BATTING AVERAGE YIELDED

.184 Pedro Martinez, Mtl.
.213 Chan Ho Park, L.A.
.223 Shawn Estes, S.F.
.224 Curt Schilling, Phi.
.225 Darryl Kile, Hou.

WALKS

100 Shawn Estes, S.F.
94 Darryl Kile, Hou.
92 Hideo Nomo, L.A.
91 Al Leiter, Fla.
79 Tom Glavine, Atl.

STRIKEOUTS

319 Curt Schilling, Phi.
305 Pedro Martinez, Mtl.
241 John Smoltz, Atl.
233 Hideo Nomo, L.A.
205 Kevin Brown, Fla.
205 Darryl Kile, Hou.

HIT BATSMEN

14 Kevin Brown, Fla.
13 Roger Bailey, Col.
12 Jim Bullinger, Mtl.
12 Todd Stottlemyere, St.L
12 Al Leiter, Fla.
12 Joey Hamilton, S.D.
12 Esteban Loaiza, Pit.

WILD PITCHES

12 Mike Remlinger, Cin.
11 Mark Leiter, Phi.
10 Hideo Nomo, L.A.
10 John Smoltz, Atl.
10 Shawn Estes, S.F.

SAVES

42 Jeff Shaw, Cin.
37 Rod Beck, S.F.
37 Trevor Hoffman, S.D.
36 Dennis Eckersley, St.L
36 John Franco, N.Y.
35 Robb Nen, Fla.
35 Todd Worrell, L.A.

STATISTICAL LEADERS

1998 COMPLETE BASEBALL RECORD BOOK

The most accurate, comprehensive baseball record book ever compiled Records for the regular season, World Series, league championships and All-Star Games, plus team-by-team record and yearly stat leaders.

#594 Regularly $15.95
YOUR LOW PRICE $12.95

1998 BASEBALL GUIDE

The best information source on every Major League and minor league team. Features complete 1997 stats and standings, Major League rosters, calendar-style schedules and directories. A baseball fan's best friend.

#591 Regularly $15.95
YOUR LOW PRICE $12.95

1998 OFFICIAL BASEBALL RULES

The current official, updated rules book used by Major League professionals and amateur baseball organizations. An essential reference book for fans, coaches, umpires and players at every level of play.

#595 Regularly $6.95
YOUR LOW PRICE $5.95

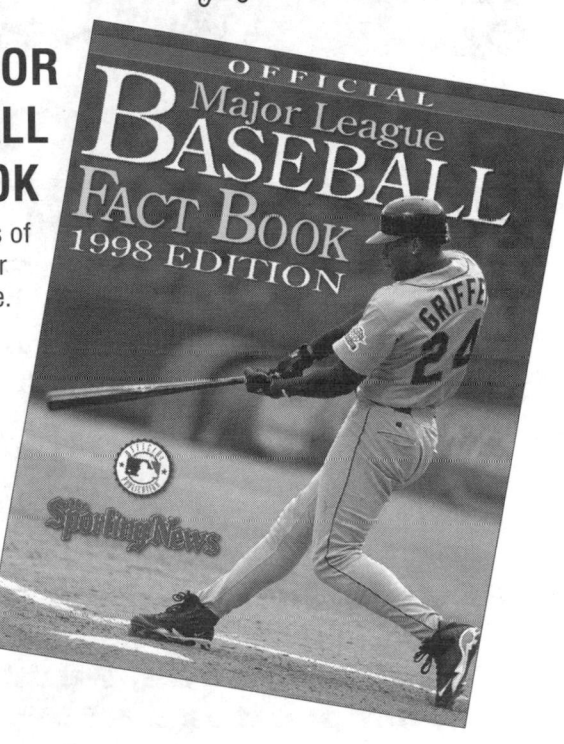